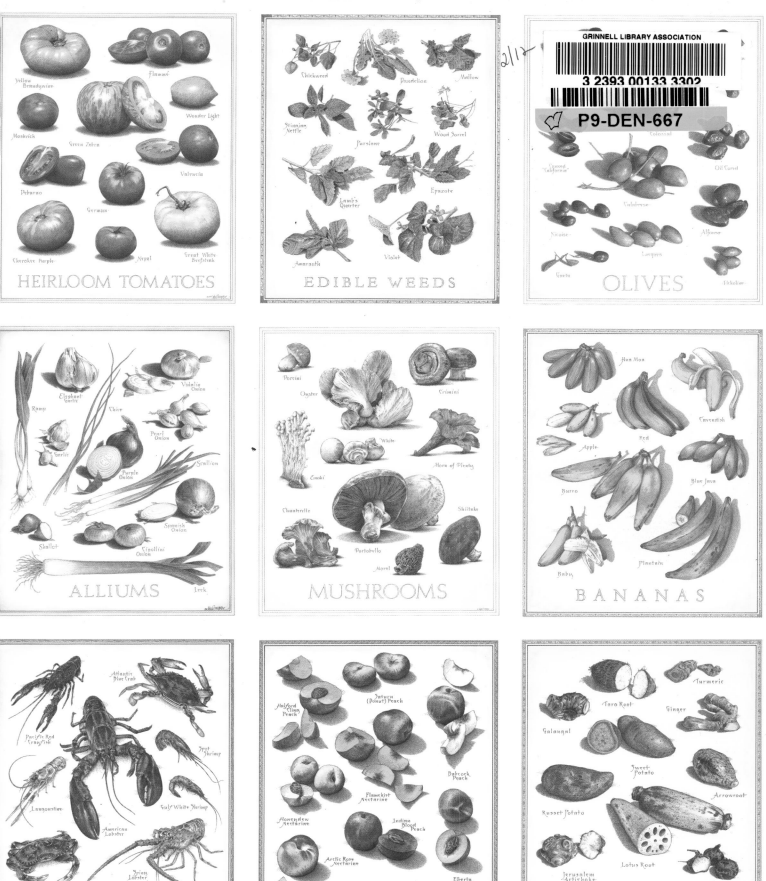

HEIRLOOM TOMATOES

Yellow Brandywine · Flammé · Wonder Light · Moskvich · Green Zebra · Valencia · Debarao · German · Cherokee Purple · Nepal · Great White Beefsteak

EDIBLE WEEDS

Chickweed · Dandelion · Mallow · Stinging Nettle · Purslane · Wood Sorrel · Lamb's Quarter · Epazote · Amaranth · Violet

OLIVES

Canned "California" · Colossal · Oil Cured · Calabrese · Alfonso · Niçoise · Gaeta · Luques · Picholine

ALLIUMS

Ramp · Elephant Garlic · Vidalia Onion · Chive · Pearl Onion · Garlic · Purple Onion · Scallion · Shallot · Spanish Onion · Cipollini Onion · Leek

MUSHROOMS

Porcini · Oyster · Crimini · White · Horn of Plenty · Emoki · Chanterelle · Shiitake · Portobello · Morel

BANANAS

Hua Moa · Cavendish · Apple · Red · Burro · Blue Java · Baby · Plantain

CRUSTACEANS

Atlantic Blue Crab · Pacific Red Crayfish · Spot Shrimp · Langoustine · Gulf White Shrimp · American Lobster · Spiny Lobster · Dungeness Crab

PEACHES AND NECTARINES

Halford Cling Peach · Saturn (Donut) Peach · Babcock Peach · Flamekist Nectarine · Honeydew Nectarine · Indian Blood Peach · Arctic Rose Nectarine · Elberta Peach

TUBERS AND RHIZOMES

Turmeric · Taro Root · Ginger · Galangal · Sweet Potato · Arrowroot · Russet Potato · Lotus Root · Jerusalem Artichoke · Water Chestnut

THE COOK'S ILLUSTRATED COOKBOOK

THE COOK'S ILLUSTRATED ≫ COOKBOOK ≪

2,000 Recipes from 20 Years of America's
Most Trusted Food Magazine

THE EDITORS AT AMERICA'S TEST KITCHEN

ILLUSTRATIONS BY JOHN BURGOYNE

America's
TEST KITCHEN

BROOKLINE, MASSACHUSETTS

America's Test Kitchen
17 Station Street, Brookline, MA 02445

Library of Congress Cataloging-in-Publication Data

The cook's illustrated cookbook : 2,000 recipes from 20 years of America's most trusted food magazine/ by the editors at America's Test Kitchen ; illustrations by John Burgoyne. -- 1st ed.
    p. cm.
Includes index.
ISBN 978-1-933615-89-9
1. Cooking, American. 2. Cookbooks. I. America's Test Kitchen (Firm)
TX715.C78545 2011
641.5973--dc23

                              2011025965

Hardcover: $40 US

Manufactured in the United States of America
10 9 8 7 6 5 4 3

Distributed by America's Test Kitchen
17 Station Street, Brookline, MA 02445

EDITORIAL DIRECTOR: Jack Bishop

EXECUTIVE EDITOR: Elizabeth Carduff

SENIOR EDITOR: Lori Galvin

CONTRIBUTING EDITORS: Keith Dresser, Louise Emerick, Elizabeth Emery, Kate Hartke, Rachel Toomey Kelsey, Dawn Yanagihara, and Dan Zuccarello

EDITORIAL ASSISTANT: Alyssa King

DESIGN DIRECTOR: Amy Klee

ART DIRECTOR: Greg Galvan

DESIGNERS: Beverly Hsu, Tiffani Beckwith, and Sarah Horwitch Dailey

FRONT COVER AND TITLE PAGE ARTWORK: Robert Papp

ILLUSTRATOR: John Burgoyne

PRODUCTION DIRECTOR: Guy Rochford

SENIOR PRODUCTION MANAGER: Jessica Quirk

SENIOR PROJECT MANAGER: Alice Carpenter

PRODUCTION AND TRAFFIC COORDINATOR: Kate Hux

ASSET AND WORKFLOW MANAGER: Andrew Mannone

PRODUCTION AND IMAGING SPECIALISTS: Judy Blomquist, Heather Dube, and Lauren Pettapiece

COPYEDITOR: Cheryl Redmond

PROOFREADER: Debra Hudak

INDEXER: Elizabeth Parson

CONTENTS

WELCOME TO AMERICA'S TEST KITCHEN

This book has been tested, written, and edited by the folks at America's Test Kitchen, a very real 2,500-square-foot kitchen located just outside of Boston. It is the home of *Cook's Illustrated* magazine and *Cook's Country* magazine and is the Monday-through-Friday destination for more than three dozen test cooks, editors, food scientists, tasters, and cookware specialists. Our mission is to test recipes over and over again until we understand how and why they work and until we arrive at the "best" version.

We start the process of testing a recipe with a complete lack of conviction, which means that we accept no claim, no theory, no technique, and no recipe at face value. We simply assemble as many variations as possible, test a half-dozen of the most promising, and taste the results blind. We then construct our own hybrid recipe and continue to test it, varying ingredients, techniques, and cooking times until we reach a consensus. The result, we hope, is the best version of a particular recipe, but we realize that only you can be the final judge of our success (or failure). As we like to say in the test kitchen, "We make the mistakes, so you don't have to."

All of this would not be possible without a belief that good cooking, much like good music, is indeed based on a foundation of objective technique. Some people like spicy foods and others don't, but there is a right way to sauté, there is a best way to cook a pot roast, and there are measurable scientific principles involved in producing perfectly beaten, stable egg whites. This is our ultimate goal: to investigate the fundamental principles of cooking so that you become a better cook. It is as simple as that.

You can watch us work (in our actual test kitchen) by tuning in to *America's Test Kitchen* (www.americastestkitchen.com) or *Cook's Country from America's Test Kitchen* (www.cookscountrytv.com) on public television, or by subscribing to *Cook's Illustrated* magazine (www.cooksillustrated.com) or *Cook's Country* magazine (www.cookscountry.com), which are each published every other month. We welcome you into our kitchen, where you can stand by our side as we test our way to the best recipes in America.

I started *Cook's Illustrated* magazine in 1992. The reason? My cooking teachers were unable to answer basic questions about why they scalded milk before making a béchamel, why they recommended whisking egg whites in a copper bowl (hey, this was a long time ago!), or when to use baking soda instead of baking powder. I also noticed that many of the recipes being offered (coulibiac of salmon comes to mind) were hopelessly outdated. And the other food magazines of the era, *Gourmet, Food & Wine, Cuisine,* and *Bon Appétit,* were celebrating the dining, not the cooking. Who was going to give me straight answers?

I finally realized that I was going to have to answer my own questions by starting a cooking magazine and building my own test kitchen. At first, we struggled, but today, we have a 2,500-square-foot test kitchen just outside of Boston with 45 test cooks who test everything from Crisp Roast Chicken and Vegetable Lasagna to Triple-Chocolate Mousse Cake and Blueberry Pies.

Many of you know that I grew up in Vermont although I am a flatlander by birth. I worked summers on a small mountain farm, learned to milk cows and pitch hay, shoveled my share of manure (both in the barn and in writing), and learned to cook under the watchful eye of Marie Briggs, the town baker who lived in a small yellow farmhouse next to the town line. This experience has given me the gift of independence of thought, a trait crucial to the ongoing mission of *Cook's Illustrated,* which is to take an unbiased, no-nonsense approach to the culinary arts in an effort to discover what works and what doesn't in America's home kitchens.

This reminds me, of course, of a story about the old-timer from Vermont's Northeast Kingdom who sat down one night to fill out his taxes. Now, like any thrifty farmer, he hardly found this a pleasant task, and staring him in the face at the head of a box in the top right-hand corner of the printed form were these words in bold type: DO NOT WRITE HERE.

Before going any further, the old gentleman took a firm grip on his pen and wrote in the box, in equally bold letters: I WRITE WHERE I GODDAMN PLEASE.

I guess that pretty much sums up how we go about recipe testing. If you tell us to scald the milk before making a béchamel, we'll try it cold, right out of the refrigerator. (It works just fine.) Or tell us to use natural cocoa and we'll test Dutch-processed. Or make a point of insisting on the use of bread flour and we'll try all-purpose. It's not just that we are contrary (we are), it's that we have spent too much time listening to culinary experts pontificate on the rules and regulations of cooking only to find that they hadn't fully tested their propositions; they were simply passing on conventional wisdom.

We often talk about the "best" way of making a recipe and many folks argue that there is no such thing. Fair enough. But there are lots of wrong ways to cook a recipe and we consider it our job to ferret out those mistakes before you do. And for the last 20 years we have been eager to share our discoveries with you, our friends and readers.

The Cook's Illustrated Cookbook is the fruit of that labor. It contains 2,000 recipes, representing almost our entire repertoire. (Older versions of a recipe were sometimes discarded in favor of better, newer approaches.) Looking back over this work as we edited this volume, we were reminded of some of our greatest hits, such as Foolproof Pie Dough (we add vodka for an

easy-to-roll-out but flaky crust), innumerable recipes based on brining and salting meats (our brined Thanksgiving turkey in 1993 launched a nationwide trend), Pan-Seared Thick-Cut Strip Steaks (we warm steaks in a low oven to promote enzymatic activity before finishing them in a sauté pan), Poached Salmon (a very shallow poaching liquid steams the fish instead of simmering it in water and robbing it of flavor), and Ultimate Chocolate Chip Cookies (we brown the butter for better flavor).

Now, you may not like change. You may prefer to follow your grandmother's recipes or, perhaps, those from a dog-eared community cookbook published in the 1930s. You would be much like the Vermonter who was asked by the city visitor, "I imagine you've seen a lot of great changes in your lifetime."

"Yes," replied the old-timer, "sure have. And I've been against every damn one of 'em!"

So, please take our findings with an independent spirit; use what you like, and ignore what you don't. You will find, however, that these pages are filled with two decades of first-hand testing, with the spirit of adventure and discovery, and with a heartfelt interest in making your cooking experience as foolproof and rewarding as possible. Recipes that you can count on, the first time and every time, is, indeed, a bold promise, but we stand by our work and are all ears. If you have a better suggestion or a new technique, send it in. We'll test it and let you know the results.

Cordially,
Christopher Kimball
Founder and Editor
America's Test Kitchen

ACKNOWLEDGMENTS

Since we started work on the first issue of *Cook's Illustrated* magazine in 1992, the editorial process has remained the same: Put people who know food and cooking around a table to hammer out ideas and then move into the kitchen to see how things really work. One person leads the development process for each recipe, but we all taste and critique each other's cooking. Every recipe, every article, and every review has been shaped by the ideas, opinions, and tastes of the entire staff working in our test kitchen at the time. *Cook's Illustrated* is truly a collaborative effort.

The launch team for *Cook's Illustrated* first worked together in the 1980s at *Cook's* magazine. Christopher Kimball, Pam Anderson, Mark Bittman, Stephanie Lyness, John Willoughby, and I created the editorial framework we still use today. Eva Katz ran our first test kitchen, Adam Ried was our first equipment guru, and Dawn Yanagihara developed many landmark recipes in those early years. Bridget Lancaster, Julia Collin Davison, and Rebecca Hays joined the magazine staff soon after and went on to become the faces of our test kitchen on television. Erin McMurrer transformed the small kitchen in which we developed our first recipes into the 2,500-square-foot facility we use today. Erin has worked with Keith Dresser to guide the recipe development process at the magazine for many years. Lisa McManus leads our team of product reviewers, and Guy Crosby guides us in matters of food science. Amanda Agee has edited the magazine for the past four years and manages our editorial team.

After nearly a decade away in New York, John Willoughby returned last year to lead all our magazine publishing efforts.

Choosing the recipes for this book reminded me of the many talented cooks who have worked in the test kitchen (or who are working in it now): Shannon Blaisdell, Liz Bomze, Erika Bruce, Matthew Card, Garth Clingingsmith, Hannah Crowley, Maryellen Driscoll, Keri Fisher, Andrea Geary, Elizabeth Germain, Amy Graves, Jolyon Helterman, Matt Heron, Charles Kelsey, Rachel Toomey Kelsey, Andrew Janjigian, Sean Lawler, Susan Light, Susan Logozzo, J. Kenji Lopez-Alt, John Olson, David Pazmiño, Raquel Pelzel, Kay Rentschler, Francisco J. Robert, Bryan Roof, Yvonne Ruperti, Sally Sampson, Taizeth Sierra, Dan Souza, Meg Suzuki, Anne Tuomey, Diane Unger, Sarah Wilson, Marcus Walser, Nina West, Sandra Wu, Anne Yamanaka, and Mark Zanger. In the early years of the magazine, we also relied on recipes from Katherine Alford, Melanie Barnard, Douglas Bellow, Stephana Bottom, Phillis M. Carey, Joe Castro, Elaine Corn, A. Cort Sinnes, Julia Della Croce, Brooke Dojny, Ann Flanigan, Sarah Fritschner, Sam Gugino, Gabrielle Hamilton, Melissa Hamilton, Cynthia Hizer, Dana Jacobi, Steve Johnson, Dan Macey, Jeanne Maguire, Nick Malgieri, Alice Medrich, Judy Monroe, Jamie Morris, Pamela Parseghian, Susan G. Purdy, Chris Schlesinger, Stephen Schmidt, Regina Schrambling, Michele Scicolone, Diana Shaw, Karen Tack, Lisa Weiss, Ann Marie Weiss-Armush, Eric Wolff, Rebecca Wood, and Stephanie D. Zonis.

Art has been an important part of *Cook's Illustrated* from the outset. Meg Birnbaum designed the first issues of the magazine and her ideas still inform our work today. Amy Klee has led the design team for 14 years and created a magazine where form perfectly matches function. Illustrator John Burgoyne, photographers Carl Tremblay and Daniel van Ackere, and stylists Marie Piraino and Mary Jane Sawyer create the artwork that brings our test kitchen's work to life. Julie Bozzo has skillfully led the art team since 2008.

David Mack has run the business side of the magazine for the past 15 years and is responsible for getting our magazine into millions of kitchens. Sharyn Chabot has managed the company's finances and guided our expansion over the last decade.

Lori Galvin turned 20 years of the magazine recipes into a single book, and Cheryl Redmond updated 2,000 recipes into a single style. Greg Galvan and Beverly Hsu created the handsome design, and Guy Rochford and Jessica Quirk delivered the perfect physical package. Elizabeth Carduff led the book team's efforts, as she has done with every book we have published in the last eight years.

Finally, the entire staff would like to thank our loyal readers. *Cook's Illustrated* has never taken advertising and your support has been essential to our success. It has been a pleasure to work for you these past 20 years.

Jack Bishop
Editorial Director
America's Test Kitchen

20 YEARS OF RECIPES THAT WORK

⇒ CONTENTS ⇐

Appetizers

Soups

Chilis, Stews, and Braises

Curries, Stir-Fries, and Asian Noodle Dishes

Pasta

Rice, Grains, and Beans

Vegetables

Poultry

Meat

Fish and Shellfish

Grilling

POULTRY

Eggs and Breakfast

Cookies, Brownies, and Bars

Cakes

Fruit Desserts

CHAPTER 1 Appetizers

SWEET AND SAVORY SPICED NUTS

☑ WHY THIS RECIPE WORKS

Most spiced nuts are made with a heavily sugared syrup that causes the nuts to clump awkwardly and leaves your hands in a sticky mess. We wanted to develop a recipe that was both tasty and neat. We eliminated two popular methods—boiling the nuts in syrup and tossing them in butter—straight off. The former made the nuts sticky and the latter dulled their flavor. What finally worked was a light glaze made from very small amounts of liquid, sugar, and butter, which left the nuts just tacky enough to pick up a coating of dry spices.

WARM-SPICED PECANS WITH RUM GLAZE
MAKES ABOUT 2 CUPS

We like the crunch and clean flavor of kosher salt in this recipe, but table salt can be substituted—just reduce the amount specified by half.

NUTS
2 cups pecans (8 ounces)

SPICE MIX
2 tablespoons sugar
¾ teaspoon kosher salt
½ teaspoon ground cinnamon
⅛ teaspoon ground cloves
⅛ teaspoon ground allspice

GLAZE
1 tablespoon rum, preferably dark
1 tablespoon unsalted butter
2 teaspoons vanilla extract
1 teaspoon brown sugar

1. FOR THE NUTS: Adjust oven rack to middle position and heat oven to 350 degrees. Line rimmed baking sheet with parchment paper and spread pecans in even layer; toast 4 minutes, rotate baking sheet, and continue to toast until fragrant and color deepens slightly, about 4 minutes longer. Transfer baking sheet to wire rack.

2. FOR THE SPICE MIX: While nuts are toasting, stir together sugar, salt, cinnamon, cloves, and allspice in medium bowl; set aside.

3. FOR THE GLAZE: Bring rum, butter, vanilla, and brown sugar to boil in medium saucepan over medium-high heat, whisking constantly. Stir in toasted pecans and cook, stirring constantly with wooden spoon, until nuts are shiny and almost all liquid has evaporated, about 1½ minutes.

4. Transfer glazed nuts to bowl with spice mix; toss well to coat. Return nuts to parchment-lined baking sheet to cool before serving. (Nuts can be stored at room temperature for up to 5 days.)

INDIAN-SPICED CASHEWS, PISTACHIOS, AND CURRANTS
MAKES ABOUT 2 CUPS

If substituting table salt for kosher, reduce the amount specified by half.

NUTS
1¼ cups raw cashews (6¼ ounces)
½   cup shelled pistachios (2 ounces)
2   tablespoons dried currants

SPICE MIX
1   tablespoon sugar
1   teaspoon kosher salt
1   teaspoon curry powder
¼   teaspoon ground cumin
¼   teaspoon ground coriander

GLAZE
2   tablespoons water
1   tablespoon unsalted butter
1   teaspoon brown sugar

1. FOR THE NUTS: Adjust oven rack to middle position and heat oven to 350 degrees. Line rimmed baking sheet with parchment paper and spread cashews in even layer; toast 4 minutes, rotate baking sheet, and toast 4 minutes longer. Add pistachios, spreading in even layer; continue to toast until fragrant and color deepens slightly, about 2 minutes longer. Transfer baking sheet to wire rack and add currants.

2. FOR THE SPICE MIX: While nuts are toasting, stir together sugar, salt, curry powder, cumin, and coriander in medium bowl; set aside.

3. FOR THE GLAZE: Bring water, butter, and brown sugar to boil in medium saucepan over medium-high heat, whisking constantly. Stir in toasted nut mix and cook, stirring constantly with wooden spoon, until nuts are shiny and almost all liquid has evaporated, about 1½ minutes.

4. Transfer glazed nuts and currants to bowl with spice mix; toss well to coat. Return nuts to parchment-lined baking sheet to cool before serving. (Nuts can be stored at room temperature for up to 5 days.)

MEXICAN-SPICED ALMONDS, PEANUTS, AND PUMPKIN SEEDS
MAKES ABOUT 2 CUPS

Pumpkin seeds, or pepitas, are available at most supermarkets and natural foods stores. If substituting table salt for kosher, reduce the amount specified by half.

NUTS
1¼ cups sliced almonds (4⅜ ounces)
⅔   cup dry-roasted peanuts (3⅓ ounces)
¼   cup raw pumpkin seeds (1 ounce)

SPICE MIX
1   tablespoon sugar
1   teaspoon kosher salt
¼   teaspoon ground cinnamon
¼   teaspoon ground cumin
¼   teaspoon ground coriander

⅛ teaspoon cayenne pepper
⅛ teaspoon garlic powder

GLAZE
2 tablespoons water
I tablespoon unsalted butter
I teaspoon brown sugar

I. FOR THE NUTS: Adjust oven rack to middle position and heat oven to 350 degrees. Line rimmed baking sheet with parchment paper and spread almonds in even layer. Toast 4 minutes, rotate baking sheet; add peanuts and pumpkin seeds, spreading in even layer. Continue to toast until fragrant and color deepens slightly, about 4 minutes longer. Transfer baking sheet to wire rack.

2. FOR THE SPICE MIX: While nuts and seeds are toasting, stir together sugar, salt, cinnamon, cumin, coriander, cayenne, and garlic powder in medium bowl; set aside.

3. FOR THE GLAZE: Bring water, butter, and brown sugar to boil in medium saucepan over medium-high heat, whisking constantly. Stir in toasted nuts and seeds and cook, stirring constantly with wooden spoon, until nuts are shiny and almost all liquid has evaporated, about 1½ minutes.

4. Transfer glazed nuts to bowl with spice mix; toss well to coat. Return nuts to parchment-lined baking sheet to cool before serving. (Nuts can be stored at room temperature for up to 5 days.)

QUICK AND EASY CHEESE ANTIPASTI

✔ WHY THIS RECIPE WORKS
Too often, appetizers require more work than they're worth. And while a cheese tray is an easy option, it does get tiresome and lacks the creative oomph we often want to display on an appetizer spread. We set out to create a few cheese-oriented appetizers that went beyond the usual but were still simple to prepare. We found that stuffing pitted dates with a small piece of nutty Parmesan made for an elegant bite perfect for enjoying with a glass of wine. Another great complement to cocktails is the Italian favorite frico, which is simply grated cheese pan-fried into crispy wafers.

DATES STUFFED WITH PARMESAN
SERVES 8

Use high-quality dates (such as Medjools) and only the finest Parmigiano-Reggiano in this antipasto.

16 whole dates
4 ounces Parmigiano-Reggiano cheese, room temperature

Slit dates lengthwise and remove pits. With paring knife, cut or break cheese into thin pieces roughly same length as dates. Place piece of cheese in each date, close date around cheese, and serve.

CRISPY CHEESE WAFERS (FRICO)
MAKES ABOUT 8

Traditionally, Montasio, an Italian cheese that has a delicate, mildly fruity and nutty flavor, is used, but we found Asiago also works well and is easier to find. Serve frico with drinks and a bowl of marinated olives or marinated sun-dried tomatoes. Frico is also good crumbled into salad, crouton-style.

I pound Montasio or aged Asiago cheese, grated fine (8 cups)

I. Sprinkle 2 ounces (about 1 cup) grated cheese over bottom of 10-inch non-stick skillet set over medium-high heat. Use heat-resistant rubber spatula or wooden spoon to tidy lacy outer edges of cheese. Cook, shaking pan occasionally to ensure even distribution of cheese over pan bottom, until edges are lacy and toasted, about 4 minutes. Remove pan from heat and allow cheese to set for about 30 seconds.

2. Using fork on top and heatproof spatula underneath, carefully flip cheese wafer and return pan to medium heat. Cook until second side is golden brown, about 2 minutes. Slide cheese wafer out of pan and transfer to plate. Repeat with remaining cheese. Serve within 1 hour.

MARINATED MUSHROOMS

✔ WHY THIS RECIPE WORKS
Today, most marinated mushrooms have morphed into little more than white button mushrooms soaked in bottled Italian dressing for days on end. The result is slimy, rubbery, brown orbs—hardly the life of the party. As a classic Italian antipasto, foraged wild mushrooms have an earthy flavor that, when blended with the right combination of bright acidity, heady herbs, and fine olive oil, will pack a punch in one small bite. We found that cremini and white mushrooms won points for flavor and availability. Crowding

---

TEST KITCHEN TIP NO. I **A GOOD WAY TO STORE CHEESE**

Whether you've got leftovers from your party cheese platter or a single wedge of Parmesan that you want to make last, the issues are the same—storage. Storing cheese presents a conundrum: as it sits, it releases moisture. If this moisture evaporates too quickly, the cheese dries out. But if the moisture stays on the cheese's surface, it encourages mold. Specialty cheese paper avoids this problem with a two-ply construction that lets cheese breathe without drying out, but usually requires mail-ordering. To find a simpler method, we tried wrapping cheddar, Brie, and fresh goat cheese in various materials, refrigerated the cheeses for six weeks, and monitored them for mold and dryness. Cheeses wrapped in plastic—whether cling wrap or zipper-lock bags—were the first to show mold. Cheeses in waxed or parchment paper alone lost too much moisture and dried out. The best method: waxed or parchment paper loosely wrapped with aluminum foil. The paper wicks moisture away, while the foil cover traps enough water to keep the cheese from drying out. Wrapped this way, even highly perishable goat cheese kept for about a week, and the Brie and cheddar were almost like new more than a month later.

the mushrooms in a 12-inch skillet generated, at first, an alarming amount of liquid; cranking up the heat, however, reduced that liquid down to a potent glaze with concentrated mushroom flavor. Best of all, the seven or so minutes that it took to reduce the liquid produced a tender yet al dente mushroom, with no slime in sight.

MARINATED MUSHROOMS
MAKES ABOUT 3½ CUPS

Cooking the mushrooms over relatively high heat encourages them to quickly release liquid, which can then be reduced to a concentrated, flavorful glaze.

- ¼ cup extra-virgin olive oil
- ⅛ teaspoon red pepper flakes
  Salt and pepper
- 1 pound cremini or white mushrooms, trimmed, left whole if small, halved if medium, quartered if large
- 3 tablespoons lemon juice
- 1 garlic clove, sliced very thin
- 1 large shallot, minced
- ¼ small red bell pepper, chopped fine
- 1 teaspoon minced fresh thyme or 1 tablespoon chopped fresh parsley or basil

1. Heat 3 tablespoons oil, pepper flakes, and ½ teaspoon salt in 12-inch skillet over medium-high heat until shimmering. Add mushrooms and 2 tablespoons lemon juice. Cook, stirring frequently, until mushrooms release moisture, moisture evaporates, and mushrooms have browned around edges, about 10 minutes. Spread mushrooms in single layer on large plate or rimmed baking sheet; cool to room temperature, about 20 minutes.

2. When cooled, transfer mushrooms to medium bowl, leaving behind any juices. Stir garlic, shallot, and bell pepper into mushrooms, cover with plastic wrap, and refrigerate at least 6 or up to 24 hours.

3. Allow mushrooms to stand at room temperature about 1 hour. Stir in remaining 1 tablespoon olive oil, 1 tablespoon lemon juice, and thyme and season with salt and pepper to taste before serving.

CLASSIC DEVILED EGGS

✓ WHY THIS RECIPE WORKS
Deviled eggs often fall to the extremes, with fillings that are either smooth, pasty, and monotonous or reminiscent of chunky egg salad. We had in mind the deviled eggs of our childhood: perfectly cooked nests of egg whites cradling a creamy filling made with simple ingredients and quickly whipped together. Naturally, it was key to start with perfectly hard-cooked eggs. We combined the yolks with mayonnaise, country-style mustard, cider vinegar, and Worcestershire sauce, which gave us a full-flavored, but balanced, filling. We like to use a pastry bag for filling the eggs, but a zipper-lock bag with the corner snipped off also works well.

CLASSIC DEVILED EGGS
MAKES 1 DOZEN

During testing we found it usual for a couple of the cooked whites to rip at least slightly, which worked out well because it meant the remaining whites were very well stuffed. If all of your egg white halves are in perfect shape, discard two. If you have a pastry bag, use it to fill the eggs with a large open-star tip or a large plain tip. Alternatively, a plastic bag can be used to fill the eggs—see the illustration on page 5. Fill the eggs as close to serving as possible for fresh, bright flavor.

- 7 large eggs (cold)
- 3 tablespoons mayonnaise
- 1½ teaspoons cider vinegar (or vinegar of your choice)
- ¾ teaspoon whole grain mustard
- ¼ teaspoon Worcestershire sauce
  Salt and pepper

1. Place eggs in medium saucepan, cover with 1 inch of water, and bring to boil over high heat. Remove pan from heat, cover, and let stand 10 minutes. Meanwhile, fill medium bowl with 1 quart cold water and about 14 ice cubes (1 tray). Transfer eggs to ice water with slotted spoon; let sit 5 minutes.

2. Peel eggs and slice each in half lengthwise with paring knife. Remove yolks to small bowl. Arrange whites on serving platter, discarding 2 worst-looking halves. Mash yolks with fork until no large lumps remain. Add mayonnaise, vinegar, mustard, Worcestershire, and salt and pepper to taste. Mix with rubber spatula, mashing mixture against side of bowl until smooth.

3. Fit pastry bag with large open-star tip. Fill bag with yolk mixture, twisting top

---

TEST KITCHEN TIP NO. 2 KEEPING MUSHROOMS FRESH

Mushrooms are a common ingredient in the test kitchen because we love the complex meatiness they contribute to soups, sauces, meats, and stuffings, or simply stuffed or marinated on their own. But due to their high moisture content, mushrooms are very perishable; most mushrooms can be kept fresh only a few days. Over the years we've tested numerous storage methods to find the best approach. Commonly suggested techniques of wrapping mushrooms in a paper bag or covering them with a damp paper towel only speed up their deterioration. We recommend storing loose mushrooms in a partially open zipper-lock bag, which maximizes air circulation without letting the mushrooms dry out. Packaged mushrooms should be stored in their original containers, which are designed to maximize the life of the mushrooms. When it comes to cleaning, you can ignore the advice against washing mushrooms, which exaggerates their ability to absorb water. As long as you wash them before they are cut, we found that 6 ounces of mushrooms only gained about a quarter ounce of water. If you plan to serve the mushrooms raw, however, you're better off brushing them off with a dry toothbrush, as rinsing can cause discoloration.

FILLING DEVILED EGGS

Spoon egg yolk mixture into plastic bag. Force mixture into one corner of bag and twist bag to keep filling in corner. Using scissors, snip off about ½ inch off corner of bag. Squeeze bag to pipe filling through hole into egg whites.

of pastry bag to help push mixture toward tip of bag. Pipe yolk mixture into egg white halves, mounding filling about ½ inch above flat surface of whites. Serve at room temperature.

TO MAKE AHEAD: You can make the deviled eggs up to 2 days ahead. Wrap the peeled egg-white halves tightly with a double layer of plastic wrap and place the filling in a zipper-lock plastic bag (squeezing out all the air). Refrigerate until ready to fill and serve.

CLASSIC DEVILED EGGS WITH ANCHOVY AND BASIL

Rinse, dry, and finely chop 8 anchovy fillets. Mince 2 tablespoons basil. Mix anchovy fillets and 2 teaspoons minced basil into mashed yolks along with mayonnaise, vinegar, mustard, Worcestershire, and salt and pepper. Sprinkle filled eggs with remaining 4 teaspoons shredded basil.

CLASSIC DEVILED EGGS WITH TUNA, CAPERS, AND CHIVES

Drain and finely chop 2 ounces canned tuna (you should have about ½ cup). Rinse and drain 1 tablespoon capers; chop 1 tablespoon chives. Mix tuna, capers, and 2 teaspoons chives into mashed yolks along with mayonnaise, vinegar, mustard, and salt and pepper. Omit Worcestershire. Sprinkle filled eggs with remaining 1 teaspoon chives.

HERB-POACHED SHRIMP WITH COCKTAIL SAUCE

✔ **WHY THIS RECIPE WORKS**
Shrimp cocktail should boast tender, sweet shrimp and a lively, well-seasoned cocktail sauce. To infuse the shrimp with as much flavor as possible, we cooked the shrimp in a stock made from the shells, wine, lemon juice, herbs, and spices. Shrimp cook very quickly, so there's little time to add flavor to them in the pan, but by bringing the stock to a boil, adding the shrimp, and then taking the pot off the heat, the shrimp could then be left to "steep" for almost 10 minutes. For the sauce, we wanted to keep the identity of the classic but give it a boost. Starting with ketchup that we seasoned ourselves was hands down a better route than beginning with preseasoned, store-bought chili sauce. Including a variety of heat sources gave our cocktail sauce nice complexity and balance.

HERB-POACHED SHRIMP WITH COCKTAIL SAUCE
SERVES 4

When using larger or smaller shrimp, increase or decrease cooking times for shrimp by one to two minutes, respectively.

- 1 pound jumbo shrimp (16 to 20 per pound), peeled and deveined, shells reserved
- 1 teaspoon salt
- 1 cup dry white wine
- 5 sprigs fresh parsley
- 1 sprig fresh tarragon
- 1 teaspoon lemon juice
- 5 coriander seeds
- 4 whole peppercorns
- ½ bay leaf

COCKTAIL SAUCE
- 1 cup ketchup
- 1 tablespoon lemon juice
- 2½ teaspoons prepared horseradish
- 1 teaspoon ancho chili powder (or other mild chili powder)
- ¼ teaspoon salt
- ¼ teaspoon pepper
  Pinch cayenne pepper

1. FOR THE SHRIMP: Bring reserved shells, 3 cups water, and salt to boil in medium saucepan over medium-high heat; reduce heat to low, cover, and simmer until fragrant, about 20 minutes. Strain stock through sieve, pressing on shells to extract all liquid.

2. Bring stock, wine, parsley, tarragon, lemon juice, coriander seeds, peppercorns, and bay leaf to boil in large saucepan over high heat; boil 2 minutes. Turn off heat and stir in shrimp; cover and let stand until firm and pink, 8 to 10 minutes. Drain shrimp, reserving stock for another use. Plunge shrimp into ice water to stop cooking, then drain again. Transfer to bowl, cover with plastic wrap, and refrigerate until chilled, about 1 hour.

3. FOR THE COCKTAIL SAUCE: Stir all ingredients together in small bowl. Season with salt and pepper to taste. Serve with shrimp.

SPANISH-STYLE GARLIC SHRIMP

✔ **WHY THIS RECIPE WORKS**
Gambas al ajillo—*a Spanish* tapa (read: small portion) *of little shrimp sizzling in a pool of olive and garlic—is a popular choice to enjoy alongside other tapas offerings when dining out. But scaling up this dish at home to take center stage at cocktail hour results in shrimp drowning in oil and too much garlic. Traditional recipes call for submerging the shrimp in oil, which allows them to heat evenly and gently at a low temperature.*

But submerging a full pound of shrimp requires 2 cups of oil. We wanted to use a more reasonable ½ cup. Using a 12-inch skillet ensured the shrimp could fit in a single layer, with oil reaching halfway up the side of each shrimp. After a brief period, we turned the shrimp to cook the other side. But using only a thin layer of oil meant the shrimp couldn't absorb much garlic flavor. So we added garlic in three ways: we added raw minced garlic to a marinade, we browned smashed cloves in the oil in which the shrimp would be cooked, and we cooked slices of garlic along with the shrimp.

SPANISH-STYLE GARLIC SHRIMP
SERVES 6

Serve shrimp with crusty bread for dipping in the richly flavored olive oil. The dish can be served directly from the skillet (make sure to use a trivet) or, for a sizzling effect, transferred to an 8-inch cast-iron skillet that's been heated for 2 minutes over medium-high heat. We prefer the slightly sweet flavor of dried chiles in this recipe, but ¼ teaspoon sweet paprika can be substituted. If sherry vinegar is unavailable, use 2 teaspoons dry sherry and 1 teaspoon white vinegar.

    14   garlic cloves, peeled
     1   pound large shrimp (31 to 40 per
         pound), peeled, deveined, and
         tails removed
    ½   cup olive oil
    ½   teaspoon salt
     1   bay leaf
     1   (2-inch) piece mild dried chile, such
         as New Mexican, roughly broken,
         seeds included
   1½ teaspoons sherry vinegar
     1   tablespoon chopped fresh parsley

1. Mince 2 garlic cloves and toss with shrimp, 2 tablespoons olive oil, and salt in medium bowl. Let shrimp marinate at room temperature for 30 minutes.

2. Meanwhile, using flat side of chef's knife, smash 4 garlic cloves. Heat smashed garlic with remaining 6 tablespoons olive oil in 12-inch skillet over medium-low heat, stirring occasionally, until garlic is light golden brown, 4 to 7 minutes. Remove pan from heat and allow oil to cool to room temperature. Using slotted spoon, remove smashed garlic from skillet and discard.

3. Thinly slice remaining 8 garlic cloves. Return skillet to low heat and add sliced garlic, bay leaf, and chile. Cook, stirring occasionally, until garlic is tender but not browned, 4 to 7 minutes. (If garlic has not begun to sizzle after 3 minutes, increase heat to medium-low.) Increase heat to medium-low; add shrimp with marinade to pan in single layer. Cook shrimp, undisturbed, until oil starts to gently bubble, about 2 minutes. Using tongs, flip shrimp and continue to cook until almost cooked through, about 2 minutes longer. Increase heat to high and add sherry vinegar and parsley. Cook, stirring constantly, until shrimp are cooked through and oil is bubbling vigorously, 15 to 20 seconds. Serve immediately.

SHRIMP TEMPURA

✔ WHY THIS RECIPE WORKS
Undermix tempura batter by a hair and it will be too thin and won't provide enough of a barrier for the shrimp against the hot oil. Overmix and you wind up with a coating so thick it would be more at home on a corn dog. We wanted a foolproof recipe that landed us between the extremes. Using the largest shrimp available helped us avoid overcooking, and keeping the frying oil at 400 degrees helped limit grease absorption. For the batter, we had to slow down gluten development, which occurs when water and flour are combined. First, we replaced a bit of the flour with cornstarch to lighten the structure and we swapped ice water for seltzer since the acidity in the latter would help delay gluten development (as a bonus, the carbonation helped make the coating airy). But the batter still turned thicker as it sat. While water (the seltzer) contributes to gluten, alcohol does not, so we replaced half the seltzer with vodka. These shrimp emerged from the hot oil light and crisp, batch after batch.

SHRIMP TEMPURA
SERVES 4

Do not omit the vodka; it is critical for a crisp coating. You will need a Dutch oven with a capacity of at least 7 quarts. Be sure to begin mixing the batter when the oil reaches 385 degrees (the final temperature should be 400 degrees). It is important to maintain a high oil temperature throughout cooking. Jumbo (16 to 20) or extra-large (21 to 25) shrimp may be substituted. Fry smaller shrimp in three batches, reducing the cooking time to 1½ to 2 minutes per batch. When cooking shrimp for tempura, the underside tends to shrink more than the top, causing the shrimp to curl tightly and the batter to clump. To prevent this, we make two shallow cuts on the shrimp's underside (see the illustration on page 7).

    12   cups vegetable oil
   1½ pounds colossal shrimp (8 to 12 per
         pound), peeled and deveined, tails
         left on
   1½ cups all-purpose flour
    ½   cup cornstarch
     1   cup vodka
     1   large egg
     1   cup seltzer water
         Kosher salt
     1   recipe dipping sauce
         (recipes follow)

1. Adjust oven rack to upper-middle position and heat oven to 200 degrees. In

Dutch oven, heat oil over medium-low to 385 degrees, 18 to 22 minutes.

2. While oil heats, make 2 shallow cuts about ¼ inch deep and 1 inch apart on underside of each shrimp, following illustration. Whisk flour and cornstarch together in large bowl. Whisk vodka and egg together in second large bowl. Whisk seltzer water into egg mixture.

3. When oil reaches 385 degrees, pour liquid mixture into bowl with flour mixture and whisk gently until just combined (it is OK if small lumps remain). Submerge half of shrimp in batter. Using tongs, remove shrimp from batter 1 at a time, allowing excess batter to drip off, and carefully place in oil (temperature should now be at 400 degrees). Fry, stirring with chopstick or wooden skewer to prevent sticking, until light brown, 2 to 3 minutes. Using slotted spoon, transfer shrimp to paper towel–lined plate and sprinkle with salt. Once paper towels absorb excess oil, place shrimp on wire rack set in rimmed baking sheet and place in oven.

4. Return oil to 400 degrees, about 4 minutes, and repeat with remaining shrimp. Serve immediately with dipping sauce.

STRAIGHTENING OUT SHRIMP

When cooking shrimp for tempura, the underside tends to shrink more than the top, causing the shrimp to curl tightly and the batter to clump up and cook unevenly inside the curl. Here's a way to alleviate that problem.

After peeling and deveining shrimp, hold it on its back on cutting board. Use tip of paring knife to make two ¼-inch-deep incisions on underside about 1 inch apart.

GINGER-SOY DIPPING SAUCE
MAKES ABOUT ¾ CUP

- ¼ cup soy sauce
- 3 tablespoons mirin
- 1 teaspoon sugar
- 1 teaspoon toasted sesame oil
- 1 scallion, sliced thin
- 2 teaspoons grated fresh ginger
- 1 garlic clove, minced

Whisk all ingredients together in medium bowl.

CHILE AÏOLI DIPPING SAUCE
MAKES ABOUT ¾ CUP

Sriracha, an Asian chili sauce made with garlic and chiles, adds both heat and flavor to this sauce.

- ½ cup mayonnaise
- 2 tablespoons sriracha sauce
- 2 tablespoons lime juice
- 1 tablespoon grated fresh ginger
- ¼ teaspoon soy sauce

Whisk all ingredients together in medium bowl.

TEPPANYAKI MUSTARD DIPPING SAUCE
MAKES ABOUT ¾ CUP

This dipping sauce gets its zesty bite from mustard, ginger, and horseradish.

- 3 tablespoons mayonnaise
- 2 tablespoons Dijon mustard
- 2 teaspoons lime juice
- 2 teaspoons prepared horseradish
- 2 teaspoons soy sauce
- 1 teaspoon grated fresh ginger

Whisk all ingredients together in medium bowl.

GRAVLAX

✓ WHY THIS RECIPE WORKS

Gravlax, served with thin slices of toasted rye and a few condiments, is a terrific choice when you're looking for a satisfyingly rich appetizer to serve a group. Gravlax is simply salt- and sugar-cured salmon. The salt draws liquid from the fish and cures it, while the sugar serves to counter the harshness of the salt. But because a traditional cure has little or no liquid, the fish can develop oversalted areas that are too dry and even a bit tough. For an easy method for making gravlax that was evenly moist, tender, and consistently salted, we opted for a wet brine in red onion juice. The procedure was simple enough: We skinned the salmon and placed the fillet and curing ingredients in a zipper-lock bag, thereby maximizing brine penetration and eliminating the need to flip the fillet. All the fish needed was to be weighted down and refrigerated for 12 to 18 hours (depending on thickness). The gravlax was ready when the fish was no longer translucent and its flesh was firm, with no give.

GRAVLAX
SERVES 10 TO 12

Don't buy a larger side of salmon; it won't fit well in the bag. Serve sliced gravlax with lightly toasted rye bread.

- 3 red onions, peeled and quartered
- 1 cup kosher salt
- ¾ cup sugar
- 2 cups coarsely chopped fresh dill (both stems and leaves) plus 1 cup minced fresh dill
- 1 teaspoon pepper
- 1 (3- to 4-pound) whole side of salmon, skinned, excess fat and brown flesh removed, and pinbones removed
- 1 recipe Onion Relish and/or Cilantro Cream (recipes follow)

1. Process onions in food processor until liquefied, about 4 minutes. Strain mixture through fine-mesh strainer to extract 2 cups of liquid, then stir in salt and sugar until dissolved. Stir in coarsely chopped dill and pepper.

2. Place salmon diagonally in 2-gallon zipper-lock bag and add onion mixture. Seal bag, removing any excess air, and lay fish skin side up on rimmed baking sheet. Place second baking sheet on top and set about 7 pounds of weight (such as heavy cans or bricks) on top. Refrigerate weighted fish until very firm, 12 to 18 hours.

3. Remove salmon from bag and pat dry with paper towels, removing any dill stems. Before serving, sprinkle minced dill over top and sides of salmon and slice very thin on bias. Serve with Onion Relish and/or Cilantro Cream. (Salmon can be wrapped in parchment paper, then plastic wrap, and refrigerated for up to 1 week.)

ONION RELISH
MAKES 2 CUPS

The onions are cooked slowly to bring out their sweetness while the sugar and vinegar temper the heat of the chiles, but this relish is still potent, so use sparingly.

2   tablespoons olive oil
2   white onions (about 1 pound), peeled and chopped fine
2   serrano or jalapeño chiles, seeded and minced
1   red bell pepper, stemmed, seeded, and chopped fine
¼   cup sugar
¼   cup white wine vinegar

Heat oil in large sauté pan. Add onions; cook over medium heat until soft but not colored, 7 to 9 minutes. Stir in chiles and bell pepper; continue to cook until all vegetables have softened, about 5 minutes longer. Stir in sugar and vinegar and cook until pan is almost dry, about 5 minutes.

PREPARING A SALMON FILLET FOR GRAVLAX

1. After removing skin by running a long, flexible knife from tail to head-end, between flesh and skin, check for any pinbones. Run your fingers over surface to feel for pinbones, then remove them with tweezers or needle-nosed pliers.

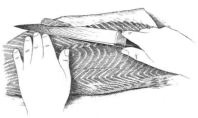

2. Hold sharp chef's knife at slight downward angle to flesh and cut off and discard whitish, fatty portion of belly.

Transfer mixture to airtight container and refrigerate until flavors meld, at least 1 hour. Bring to room temperature before serving. (Relish can be refrigerated for up to 1 week.)

CILANTRO CREAM
MAKES ABOUT 1 CUP

1   cup crème fraîche or sour cream
4   teaspoons minced fresh cilantro

Combine all ingredients in small bowl. Cover and refrigerate until ready to serve. (Cilantro Cream can be refrigerated for up to 1 day.)

RESTAURANT-STYLE HUMMUS

✔ WHY THIS RECIPE WORKS
We wanted hummus with a light, silky-smooth texture and balanced flavor profile. We quickly settled on using convenient canned beans (we would also develop an "ultimate" hummus variation using dried beans). In theory, the best way to guarantee a creamy texture is to remove the chickpeas' tough skins, but we couldn't find an approach that wasn't tedious or futile. The food processor, while it couldn't remove all the graininess when we pureed the chickpeas alone, did produce the desired texture when we used it to make an emulsion (much like mayonnaise). We started by grinding just the chickpeas and then slowly added a small amount of water and lemon juice. Then we whisked the olive oil and a generous amount of tahini together and drizzled the mixture into the puree while processing; this created a lush, light, and flavorful puree. Earthy cumin, a pinch of cayenne, lemon juice, and garlic kept the flavors balanced.

RESTAURANT-STYLE HUMMUS
MAKES ABOUT 2 CUPS

We recommend Joyva or Krinos tahini and Pastene chickpeas.

¼   cup water
3   tablespoons lemon juice
6   tablespoons tahini
2   tablespoons extra-virgin olive oil, plus extra for drizzling
1   (15-ounce) can chickpeas, rinsed
1   small garlic clove, minced
½   teaspoon salt
¼   teaspoon ground cumin
     Pinch cayenne pepper
1   tablespoon minced fresh cilantro or parsley

1. Combine water and lemon juice in small bowl or measuring cup. Whisk

together tahini and 2 tablespoons oil in second small bowl. Set aside 2 tablespoons chickpeas for garnish.

2. Process remaining chickpeas, garlic, salt, cumin, and cayenne in food processor until almost fully ground, about 15 seconds. Scrape down bowl with rubber spatula. With machine running, add lemon juice mixture in steady stream. Scrape down bowl and continue to process for 1 minute. With machine running, add tahini mixture in steady stream; continue to process until hummus is smooth and creamy, about 15 seconds, scraping down bowl as needed.

3. Transfer hummus to serving bowl, sprinkle reserved chickpeas and cilantro over surface, cover with plastic wrap, and let stand until flavors meld, at least 30 minutes. Drizzle with olive oil and serve. (Hummus can be refrigerated for up to 5 days; refrigerate garnishes separately. When ready to serve, stir in approximately 1 tablespoon of warm water if texture is too thick.)

ARTICHOKE-LEMON HUMMUS

Rinse and pat dry 1 cup drained canned artichoke hearts. Chop ¼ cup artichoke hearts and set aside for garnish. Increase lemon juice to 4 tablespoons (2 lemons) and omit cumin. Process entire can of chickpeas (do not reserve 2 tablespoons) along with remaining ¾ cup artichokes and ¼ teaspoon grated lemon zest in

step 2. Garnish hummus with reserved artichokes, 2 teaspoons chopped fresh parsley or mint, and olive oil.

HUMMUS WITH SMOKED PAPRIKA

Process entire can of chickpeas (do not reserve 2 tablespoons) in step 2 and substitute 1 teaspoon smoked paprika for cumin. Omit cilantro. Garnish hummus with 1 tablespoon thinly sliced scallion greens, 2 tablespoons toasted pine nuts, and olive oil.

ROASTED GARLIC HUMMUS

Remove outer papery skins from 2 heads garlic; cut top quarters off heads and discard. Wrap garlic in aluminum foil and roast in 350-degree oven until browned and very tender, about 1 hour. Meanwhile, heat 2 tablespoons olive oil and 2 thinly sliced garlic cloves in 8-inch skillet over medium-low heat. Cook, stirring occasionally, until golden brown, about 15 minutes. Using slotted spoon, transfer garlic slices to paper towel–lined plate and set aside; reserve oil. Once roasted garlic is cool, squeeze cloves from their skins (you should have about ¼ cup). Substitute garlic cooking oil for olive oil in step 1 and omit cumin. Process entire can of chickpeas (do not reserve 2 tablespoons) along with roasted garlic puree in step 2. Garnish hummus with toasted garlic slices, 2 teaspoons chopped fresh parsley, and olive oil.

ROASTED RED PEPPER HUMMUS

Omit water and cumin. Process entire can of chickpeas (do not reserve 2 tablespoons) along with ¼ cup jarred roasted red peppers that have been rinsed and dried thoroughly with paper towels in step 2. Garnish hummus with 2 tablespoons toasted sliced almonds, 2 teaspoons chopped fresh parsley, and olive oil.

ULTIMATE HUMMUS

Pick through and rinse ½ cup dried chickpeas. Place beans in large bowl, cover with 1 quart water, and soak overnight. Drain. Bring beans, ⅛ teaspoon baking soda, and 1 quart water to boil in large saucepan over high heat. Reduce heat to low and simmer gently, stirring occasionally, until beans are tender, about 1 hour. Drain, reserving ¼ cup bean cooking water, and cool. Continue with recipe, replacing tap water with cooking water.

BABA GHANOUSH

✓ WHY THIS RECIPE WORKS
For a baba ghanoush that fulfills its potential—redolent with smoky eggplant flavor and brightened with garlic and lemon juice—we found we got the best results by following tradition and grilling the eggplant over a hot charcoal fire. The smokiness of the fire induced other ingredients to relate to one another in a more interesting way than if cooked using other methods. Nevertheless, we found we could get perfectly acceptable results by oven-roasting if grilling wasn't convenient. No matter the method, it was critical to work with fresh eggplants and cook them until the flesh was almost sloshy; undercooked eggplant, while misleadingly soft to the touch, tasted spongy-green and remained unmoved by additional seasonings. To avoid a watery texture, we drained the eggplant of

---

excess fluid. A few tests more tests proved that less is more with flavorings—we stuck with tahini, garlic, and lemon juice.

GRILLED BABA GHANOUSH
MAKES 2 CUPS

When buying eggplants, select those with shiny, taut, and unbruised skins and an even shape (eggplants with a bulbous shape won't cook evenly). Grill until the eggplant walls have collapsed and the insides feel sloshy when pressed with tongs. We prefer to serve baba ghanoush only lightly chilled; if cold, let it stand at room temperature for about 20 minutes before serving. Baba ghanoush does not keep well, so plan to make it the day you want to serve it. Serve with pita bread, black olives, tomato wedges, or cucumber slices.

2 pounds eggplant (about 2 large globe eggplants, 5 medium Italian eggplants, or 12 medium Japanese eggplants), pricked all over with fork
2 tablespoons tahini
1 tablespoon lemon juice
1 tablespoon extra-virgin olive oil, plus extra for serving
1 small garlic clove, minced
   Salt and pepper
2 teaspoons chopped fresh parsley

1A. FOR A CHARCOAL GRILL: Open bottom vent completely. Light large chimney starter filled with charcoal briquettes (6 quarts). When top coals are partially covered with ash, pour evenly over grill. Set cooking grate in place, cover, and open lid vent completely. Heat grill until hot, about 5 minutes.

1B. FOR A GAS GRILL: Turn all burners to high, cover, and heat grill until hot, about 15 minutes. Turn all burners to medium. (Adjust burners as needed to maintain grill temperature around 350 degrees.)

2. Clean and oil cooking grate. Set eggplants on cooking grate and cook until skins darken and wrinkle on all sides and eggplants are uniformly soft when pressed with tongs, about 25 minutes for large globe eggplants, 20 minutes for Italian eggplants, and 15 minutes for Japanese eggplants, turning every 5 minutes and reversing direction of eggplants on grill with each turn. Transfer eggplants to rimmed baking sheet and cool 5 minutes.

3. Set small colander over bowl. Trim top and bottom off each eggplant. Slit eggplants lengthwise and use spoon to scoop hot pulp from skins and place pulp in colander (you should have about 2 cups packed pulp); discard skins. Let pulp drain 3 minutes.

4. Transfer pulp to food processor. Add tahini, lemon juice, oil, garlic, ¼ teaspoon salt, and ¼ teaspoon pepper. Process until mixture has coarse, choppy texture, about 8 pulses. Season with salt and pepper to taste. Transfer to serving bowl, cover with plastic wrap flush with surface of dip, and refrigerate 45 to 60 minutes. Make trough in center of dip using large spoon and spoon olive oil into it. Sprinkle with parsley and serve.

OVEN-ROASTED BABA GHANOUSH

Adjust oven rack to middle position and heat oven to 500 degrees. Line rimmed baking sheet with aluminum foil, set eggplants on baking sheet and roast, turning every 15 minutes, until eggplants are uniformly soft when pressed with tongs, about 60 minutes for large globe eggplants, 50 minutes for Italian eggplants, and 40 minutes for Japanese eggplants. Cool eggplants on baking sheet 5 minutes, then follow recipe from step 3.

BABA GHANOUSH WITH SAUTÉED ONION

Sautéed onion gives the baba ghanoush a sweet, rich flavor.

Heat 1 tablespoon extra-virgin olive oil in 8-inch skillet over low heat until shimmering; add 1 small onion, chopped fine, and cook, stirring occasionally, until edges are golden brown, about 10 minutes. Stir onion into dip after processing.

ISRAELI-STYLE BABA GHANOUSH

Replacing the tahini with mayonnaise makes this baba ghanoush pleasantly light and brings out the smoky flavor of charcoal-grilled eggplant.

Substitute 2 tablespoons mayonnaise for tahini.

CREAMY PARTY DIPS

✔ WHY THIS RECIPE WORKS
For dips that would draw a crowd, we needed to develop a well-balanced, creamy base and choose a few fresh and assertive flavorings. For our creamy base, we tested mayonnaise, sour cream, yogurt, buttermilk, heavy cream, cottage cheese, and cream cheese. Two combinations made it across the finish line: mayonnaise with sour cream and mayonnaise with yogurt. Mayonnaise contributes the body, richness, and velvety texture sought after in a creamy dip, while both sour cream and yogurt heighten flavor. Yogurt had one problem, however. Right out of the container it was too slack and required draining to thicken it. We found that an overnight stay in the refrigerator in a fine-mesh sieve firmed up the yogurt perfectly. Add flavor-charged ingredients—the fewer the better—for maximum flavor that will stand up to the richness of the dairy products.

"CAESAR" DIP WITH PARMESAN AND ANCHOVIES
MAKES 1½ CUPS

Serve with crudités.

- 1 cup mayonnaise
- ½ cup sour cream
- ¼ cup grated Parmesan cheese
- 1 tablespoon lemon juice
- 1 tablespoon minced fresh parsley
- 2 garlic cloves, minced
- 2 anchovy fillets, rinsed and minced
- ⅛ teaspoon pepper

Combine all ingredients in medium bowl until smooth and creamy. Transfer dip to serving bowl, cover with plastic wrap, and refrigerate until flavors are blended, at least 1 hour. Serve. (Dip can be refrigerated for up to 2 days.)

CHIPOTLE-LIME DIP WITH SCALLIONS
MAKES 1½ CUPS

Serve with crudités.

- 1 cup mayonnaise
- ½ cup sour cream
- 3 scallions, sliced thin
- 2 garlic cloves, minced
- 1 tablespoon minced canned chipotle chile in adobo sauce plus ½ teaspoon adobo sauce
- 1 teaspoon grated lime zest plus 1 tablespoon juice

Combine all ingredients in medium bowl until smooth and creamy. Transfer dip to serving bowl, cover with plastic wrap, and refrigerate until flavors are blended, at least 1 hour. (Dip can be refrigerated for up to 2 days.)

CREAMY HORSERADISH DIP
MAKES 1½ CUPS

Serve with crudités.

- ¾ cup mayonnaise
- ¾ cup sour cream
- 2 scallions, sliced thin
- ¼ cup prepared horseradish, squeezed of excess liquid
- 1 tablespoon minced fresh parsley
- ⅛ teaspoon pepper

Combine all ingredients in medium bowl until smooth and creamy. Transfer dip to serving bowl, cover with plastic wrap, and refrigerate until flavors are blended, at least 1 hour. Serve. (Dip can be refrigerated for up to 2 days.)

FETA-MINT DIP WITH YOGURT
MAKES ABOUT 1¼ CUPS

Serve with crudités.

- 1 cup plain whole-milk yogurt
- ½ cup mayonnaise
- 3 ounces feta cheese, crumbled (⅔ cup)
- ¼ cup chopped fresh mint
- 2 scallions, sliced
- 2 teaspoons lemon juice

1. Place yogurt in fine-mesh strainer or cheesecloth-lined colander set over bowl. Cover with plastic wrap and refrigerate 8 to 24 hours; discard liquid in bowl.

2. Process all ingredients in food processor until smooth and creamy, about 30 seconds. Transfer dip to serving bowl, cover with plastic wrap, and refrigerate until flavors are blended, at least 1 hour. Serve. (Dip can be refrigerated for up to 2 days.)

GREEN GODDESS DIP
MAKES 1½ CUPS

Serve with crudités.

- ¾ cup mayonnaise
- ¾ cup sour cream
- ¼ cup minced fresh parsley
- ¼ cup minced fresh chives
- 2 tablespoons minced fresh tarragon
- 1 tablespoon lemon juice
- 2 garlic cloves, minced
- ⅛ teaspoon salt
- ⅛ teaspoon pepper

Combine all ingredients in medium bowl until smooth and creamy. Transfer dip to serving bowl, cover with plastic wrap, and refrigerate until flavors are blended, at least 1 hour. Serve. (Dip can be refrigerated for up to 3 days.)

CLAM DIP WITH BACON AND SCALLIONS
MAKES ABOUT 2 CUPS

Serve with chips or crackers.

- 4 slices bacon, cut into ¼-inch pieces
- ¾ cup sour cream
- ¾ cup mayonnaise
- 1 teaspoon lemon juice
- 1 teaspoon Worcestershire sauce
- 2 (6½-ounce) cans minced clams, drained
- 2 scallions, sliced thin
  Salt and pepper
  Cayenne pepper

1. Cook bacon in 8-inch skillet over medium heat until crisp, 5 to 7 minutes. Transfer bacon to paper towel–lined plate.

2. Whisk together sour cream, mayonnaise, lemon juice, and Worcestershire in medium bowl. Stir in minced clams, scallions, and bacon. Season with salt, pepper, and cayenne to taste. Transfer dip to serving bowl, cover with plastic wrap, and refrigerate until flavors are blended, at least 1 hour. Serve. (Dip can be refrigerated for up to 2 days.)

SMOKED SALMON DIP WITH DILL AND HORSERADISH

MAKES ABOUT 2 CUPS

Serve with chips or crackers.

¾	cup sour cream
¾	cup mayonnaise
3	ounces smoked salmon
2	teaspoons lemon juice
1	teaspoon prepared horseradish
2	tablespoons minced fresh dill
	Salt and pepper

Process sour cream, mayonnaise, salmon, lemon juice, and horseradish in food processor until smooth and creamy. Transfer mixture to serving bowl, stir in dill, and season with salt and pepper to taste. Cover with plastic wrap and refrigerate until flavors are blended, at least 1 hour. Serve. (Dip can be refrigerated for up to 3 days.)

SPINACH DIP

✔ WHY THIS RECIPE WORKS
Spinach dip with sour cream and soup mixes are flat, overly salty, and stale-tasting, and nothing near fresh. This lackluster 1950s relic was long overdue for a face-lift, and the solution turned out to be surprisingly easy. We found that dips made with fresh spinach tasted meek and lacked the more intense, vibrant flavor of those made with frozen. A combination of mayonnaise and sour cream created a smooth and creamy base, while dill, parsley, garlic, and hot sauce were smart replacements for soup mix as the flavoring components. Using partially thawed

spinach cooled the dip and avoided the 2-hour chilling time required for dip made with completely thawed spinach.

CREAMY HERBED SPINACH DIP

MAKES ABOUT 1½ CUPS

Partial thawing of the spinach produces a cold dip that can be served without further chilling. The garlic must be minced before going into the food processor; otherwise, the dip will contain large chunks of garlic.

10	ounces frozen chopped spinach
½	cup sour cream
½	cup mayonnaise
½	cup packed flat-leaf parsley
3	scallions, white parts only, sliced thin
1	tablespoon chopped fresh dill
1	small garlic clove, minced
¼	teaspoon hot sauce
½	teaspoon salt
¼	teaspoon pepper
½	red bell pepper, chopped fine

1. Thaw spinach in microwave for 3 minutes on medium power (spinach should be soft enough to be broken apart into icy chunks). Squeeze partially frozen spinach to remove excess water.

2. Process spinach, sour cream, mayonnaise, parsley, scallions, dill, garlic, hot sauce, salt, and pepper until smooth and creamy, about 30 seconds. Transfer mixture to medium bowl and stir in bell pepper. Serve. (Dip can be refrigerated for up to 2 days.)

SPINACH DIP WITH BLUE CHEESE AND BACON

If making this dip in advance, hold off on sprinkling the bacon over it until just before serving.

Cook 3 slices bacon, cut into ¼-inch pieces, in 8-inch skillet over medium-high heat until crisp, about 5 minutes. Transfer to paper towel–lined plate and set aside.

Omit dill, hot sauce, salt, and red bell pepper. Process 1½ ounces crumbled blue cheese (⅓ cup) along with spinach. Season with salt to taste and sprinkle bacon over dip.

SPINACH DIP WITH FETA, LEMON, AND OREGANO

Omit hot sauce, salt, and red bell pepper. Process ½ cup crumbled feta cheese, 2 tablespoons fresh oregano, and 1 teaspoon grated lemon zest plus 1 tablespoon lemon juice along with spinach. Season with salt to taste.

CILANTRO-LIME SPINACH DIP WITH CHIPOTLE CHILE

This dip pairs well with tortilla chips.

Omit hot sauce and red bell pepper. Process ¼ cup packed cilantro leaves, 1 tablespoon minced canned chipotle chile in adobo sauce, ½ teaspoon grated lime zest plus 1 tablespoon lime juice, ½ teaspoon light brown sugar, and ⅛ teaspoon ground cumin along with spinach.

BACON, SCALLION, AND CARAMELIZED ONION DIP

✔ WHY THIS RECIPE WORKS
Onion dip is an old favorite, but we wanted a recipe that went beyond stirring powdered onion soup mix into sour cream and mayonnaise. For a more modern, grown-up take, we started with caramelized onions, which lent our dip a sweet, more complex flavor. We discovered several keys to making caramelized onions that weren't burnt, gummy, bland, or greasy. First, we sautéed the onions in a nonstick pan in butter and oil over high heat to quickly release the moisture, then we turned down the heat to medium until they were cooked through. This ensured clear onion flavor and a yielding yet firm texture. Adding light brown sugar to the pan helped bring out their

sweetness and complemented their caramel-like flavor. Then we incorporated complementary flavors to give the dip more heft. Bacon added a smokiness that perfectly balanced the sweet onions, while fresh minced scallions reinforced the onion flavor and added a touch of color.

BACON, SCALLION, AND CARAMELIZED ONION DIP

MAKES ABOUT 1½ CUPS

This recipe uses half a recipe of Caramelized Onions. Leftover onions can be used in a number of dishes, including omelets, frittatas, sandwiches, or pizza.

- 3 slices bacon, cut into ¼-inch pieces
- ¾ cup sour cream
- ½ cup Caramelized Onions (recipe follows)
- 2 scallions, minced
- ½ teaspoon cider vinegar
  Salt and pepper

1. Cook bacon in 8-inch skillet over medium heat until crisp, 5 to 7 minutes. Transfer to paper towel–lined plate and set aside.

2. Combine sour cream, caramelized onions, scallions, vinegar, and bacon in medium bowl. Season with salt and pepper to taste and serve. (Dip can be refrigerated for up to 3 days.)

SLICING ONIONS POLE TO POLE

When slicing onions for caramelizing, be sure to slice them with the grain, from pole to pole. When sliced the opposite way, against the grain, the onions will have a stringy texture.

CARAMELIZED ONIONS

MAKES 1 CUP

If the onions are sizzling or scorching in step 2, reduce the heat. If the onions are not browning after 15 to 20 minutes, raise the heat.

- 1 tablespoon unsalted butter
- 1 tablespoon vegetable oil
- 1 teaspoon light brown sugar
- ½ teaspoon salt
- 2 pounds onions, halved and sliced pole to pole into ¼-inch-thick pieces
- 1 tablespoon water
  Pepper

1. Heat butter and oil in 12-inch non-stick skillet over high heat and stir in sugar and salt. Add onions and stir to coat. Cook, stirring occasionally, until onions begin to soften and release some moisture, about 5 minutes.

2. Reduce heat to medium and cook, stirring frequently, until onions are deeply browned and slightly sticky, about 40 minutes longer.

3. Off heat, stir in water. Season with pepper to taste. (Onions can be refrigerated for up to 1 week.)

SWEET AND SPICY ROASTED RED PEPPER DIP

✓ WHY THIS RECIPE WORKS
Sweet red bell peppers take on a whole new layer of complex, smoky flavor when roasted. We wanted a method for roasting them that was more efficient than the common technique of roasting each pepper over a gas burner, letting it steam in a covered bowl, then laboriously removing the skin bit by bit. We also hoped to transform our perfectly roasted peppers into a full-flavored dip. For the roasting method, we discovered the broiler offered an easy, consistent, and more hands-off option than the burner (roasting in either a hot or

low oven yielded soggy, overcooked peppers). To get around the issue of whole peppers hitting the broiler element, we cut the peppers into pieces that lay flat on a sheet pan. After 10 minutes, the peppers were done and we could easily peel off the blistered skin. For our dip, we adapted a recipe for a sweet and spicy Middle Eastern–style dip by combining our roasted peppers with jalapeño and tangy pomegranate molasses.

SWEET AND SPICY ROASTED RED PEPPER DIP

MAKES ABOUT 2 CUPS

For more information on preparing the bell peppers for roasting, see page 273. Look for pomegranate molasses in Middle Eastern markets or the international foods aisle of supermarkets. If you cannot find it, 2 tablespoons of molasses combined with 2 tablespoons of lime juice can be substituted for the pomegranate molasses. Serve with grilled or toasted pita bread.

- 3 red bell peppers, stemmed, seeded, ribs removed, and cut to lie flat
- 6 tablespoons olive oil
- 1 small onion, chopped coarse
- ½ jalapeño chile or other hot red or green fresh chile, minced
- 1 tablespoon ground cumin
- 1 small garlic clove, minced
- ¼ cup chopped fresh parsley
- ¼ cup pomegranate molasses
  Salt and pepper

1. Adjust oven rack 2½ to 3½ inches from broiler element and heat broiler. If necessary, set upside-down rimmed baking sheet on oven rack to elevate pan.

2. Spread peppers out over aluminum foil–lined baking sheet and broil until skin is charred and puffed but flesh is still firm, 8 to 10 minutes, rotating sheet halfway through cooking.

3. Transfer peppers to medium bowl, cover with foil, and let steam until skin peels off easily, 10 to 15 minutes. Peel and discard skin; set peppers aside.

4. Heat oil in 10-inch skillet over medium-high heat. Add onion and sauté until softened, about 5 minutes. Add chile, cumin, and garlic; sauté until garlic softens, about 1 minute longer.

5. Transfer mixture to food processor. Add peppers, parsley, and pomegranate molasses; process until very smooth. Season with salt and pepper to taste. Transfer to bowl and serve. (Dip can be refrigerated for up to 1 week.)

FRESH TOMATO SALSA

✔ **WHY THIS RECIPE WORKS**

Even at the peak of tomato season, fresh tomato salsas can be inconsistent and less than stellar. Complicating matters, salsa's popularity has opened the door to versions employing extravagant and extraneous ingredients. We wanted a fresh, chunky salsa cruda that would emphasize the tomatoes. To solve the problem of watery salsa, we drained diced tomatoes in a colander. This put all tomatoes, regardless of origin, ripeness, or juiciness, on a level—and dry—playing field. Red onions were preferred over other varieties for color and flavor. Jalapeño chiles beat out the alternatives because of their wide availability, slight vegetal flavor, and moderate heat. Lime juice tasted more authentic (and better) than red wine vinegar, rice vinegar, or lemon juice. We investigated the best way to combine the ingredients and rejected all but the simplest technique: We layered each ingredient (chopped) on top of the tomatoes while they drained in the colander. Once the tomatoes were ready, it all just needed a few stirs before being finished with the lime juice, sugar, and salt.

FRESH TOMATO SALSA
MAKES ABOUT 3 CUPS

For more heat, include the jalapeño seeds and ribs when mincing. The amount of sugar and lime juice to use depends on the ripeness of the tomatoes. The salsa can be made 2 to 3 hours in advance, but hold off adding the lime juice, salt, and sugar until just before serving. This salsa is perfect for tortilla chips, but it's also a nice accompaniment to grilled steaks, chicken, and fish.

1½	pounds tomatoes, cut into ½-inch dice
½	cup finely chopped red onion
¼	cup chopped fresh cilantro
1	large jalapeño chile, stemmed, seeded, and minced
1	small garlic clove, minced
2–6	teaspoons lime juice (1 to 2 limes)
½	teaspoon salt
	Pinch pepper
	Sugar

1. Set large colander in large bowl. Place tomatoes in colander and let drain 30 minutes. As tomatoes drain, layer onion, cilantro, jalapeño, and garlic on top.

2. Shake colander to drain off excess tomato juice. Discard juice; wipe out bowl.

3. Transfer tomato mixture to bowl. Add 2 teaspoons lime juice, salt, and pepper and toss to combine. Add sugar to taste and additional lime juice to taste before serving.

ONE-MINUTE SALSA

✔ **WHY THIS RECIPE WORKS**

When we're considering a quick snack of chips and salsa or a topping for our ultimate nachos, we don't want to settle for the watery, overprocessed jarred stuff, especially when we can make a far better option from scratch in a few minutes. For a salsa that avoids the hassle of chopping multiple vegetables and herbs, we turned to the food processor. After a few tests, we happily discovered this salsa tastes just fine, and still beats out the commercial varieties, when made with canned diced tomatoes.

ONE-MINUTE SALSA
MAKES ABOUT 1 CUP

This quick salsa can be made with either fresh or canned tomatoes, but if you're using fresh, make sure they are sweet, ripe, in-season tomatoes. If they aren't, canned tomatoes are a better choice.

½	small jalapeño chile or ¾ teaspoon minced canned chipotle chile in adobo sauce
¼	small red onion
2	tablespoons fresh cilantro leaves
2	teaspoons lime juice
1	small garlic clove, minced
¼	teaspoon salt
	Pinch pepper
2	small tomatoes (12 ounces), cored and cut into eighths, or 1 (14.5-ounce) can diced tomatoes, drained

---

TEST KITCHEN TIP NO. 4 TOMATOES—SKIP THE FRIDGE, PLEASE

We never store tomatoes in the refrigerator. Cold damages tomatoes in two ways: It destroys an enzyme that produces flavorful compounds, and it makes water in the tomato expand, rupturing cells and turning the flesh mealy. But what about storing a partially used tomato? We cut a dozen ripe tomatoes in two, stored half of each in the fridge, and kept the other half at room temperature (both were wrapped tightly in plastic wrap). After a few days, the halves at room temperature had begun to soften, while the refrigerated halves were still as firm as the day they were cut. Upon tasting, however, we found the refrigerated halves were bland and mealy compared with the never-refrigerated halves. Our advice? Keep cut tomatoes tightly wrapped at room temperature and consume them within a few days. The shelf life gained by refrigeration doesn't make up for the loss in flavor and texture.

Pulse all ingredients except tomatoes in food processor until minced, about 5 pulses, scraping sides of bowl as necessary. Add tomatoes and pulse until roughly chopped, about 2 pulses. Serve.

CHUNKY GUACAMOLE

✓ WHY THIS RECIPE WORKS

Most guacamole recipes sacrifice the extraordinary character of the avocados by adding too many other flavorings, and the texture of these dips is usually reduced to an utterly smooth, listless puree. We wanted to highlight the buttery texture and nutty flavor of the avocado; any additions needed to provide bright counterpoints to the avocado without overwhelming it. Neither pureeing in a food processor nor mashing all the avocados at once—two commonly used methods—gave us guacamole with the right texture. Instead, mashing one of the avocados lightly with a fork and mixing it with most of the other ingredients, then gently mixing in the remaining avocados, broke down the cubes just enough to make an appealingly chunky yet cohesive dip. Restraint when incorporating additional ingredients was key. We added just enough onion, garlic, cumin, and jalapeño to lend balance and depth to our dip without overwhelming the starring ingredient. Acidity, in the form of lime juice, was a necessity, not only for flavor but also to help preserve the mixture's green color.

CHUNKY GUACAMOLE
MAKES 2½ TO 3 CUPS

To minimize the risk of discoloration, prepare the minced ingredients first so they are ready to mix with the avocados as soon as they are cut. Ripe avocados are essential here. To test for ripeness, try to flick the small stem off the end of the avocado. If it comes off easily and you can see green underneath it, the avocado is ripe. If it does not come off or if you see brown

underneath after prying it off, the avocado is not ripe. If you like, garnish the guacamole with diced tomatoes and chopped cilantro just before serving.

3	avocados
¼	cup minced fresh cilantro
2	tablespoons finely chopped onion
I	small jalapeño chile, stemmed, seeded, and minced
I	garlic clove, minced
½	teaspoon ground cumin (optional)
	Salt
2	tablespoons lime juice

1. Halve 1 avocado, remove pit, and scoop flesh into medium bowl. Mash flesh lightly with cilantro, onion, jalapeño, garlic, cumin, if using, and ¼ teaspoon salt with fork until just combined.

2. Halve, pit, and cube remaining 2 avocados. Add cubes to bowl with mashed avocado mixture.

3. Sprinkle lime juice over cubed avocado and mix lightly with fork until combined but still chunky. Season with salt to taste and serve. (Guacamole can be covered with plastic wrap, pressed directly onto surface, and refrigerated for up to 1 day. Return to room temperature, removing plastic wrap at the last moment, before serving.)

TEST KITCHEN TIP NO. 5 AVOCADOS—FROM ROCK-HARD TO RIPE

Avocados have a notoriously small window for ripeness. You'll almost never find perfectly ripe avocados from the supermarket on the day you want to use them, so it pays to think—and shop—ahead. We've tested various ways to ripen avocados, but in the end, we've found that the only thing that matters is the temperature at which the avocados are stored. In our tests, rock-hard avocados at room temperature ripened within two days, but many of them ended up ripening unevenly, developing soft spots and air pockets on one side just as the other side was ripening. After completely ripening, they lasted two days on average if kept at room temperature (stored in the fridge after ripening, they lasted five days). Avocados ripened in the refrigerator, whether in a bag or out in the open, took around four days to soften, but did so evenly. Stored in the fridge, they lasted a full five days before starting to show signs of overripening. The bottom line: If you need your avocados to ripen sooner rather than later, keep them on the counter. Otherwise, for better quality, you're better off putting them in the fridge and allowing them to ripen slowly. In either case, store the ripened fruit in the fridge to extend shelf life.

CHEESY NACHOS

✓ WHY THIS RECIPE WORKS

With the help of prepackaged shredded cheese, jarred salsa, and the microwave, nachos have turned into bland, subpar snack food. We set a few standards for our revamped recipe. First, the chips should be crisp and hot, not lukewarm, soggy, or charred. Ten minutes in a 400-degree oven produced warm, toasted chips and perfectly melted cheese (cooler ovens dried out the chips; hotter ovens and the broiler burnt them). Second, there should be no shortage of cheese; a chip without cheese is not a nacho. We settled on using a full pound of cheddar. To ensure that all of the chips got good coverage, we found it was best to layer the chips and cheese; tossing them together broke the chips and sent much of the cheese to the bottom of the dish. Layering the jalapeños along with the cheese ensured good heat in every bite. Third, minimalism has no place in a great plate of nachos. In addition to abundant cheese, we topped our recipe with ample amounts of salsa and guacamole. Using fresh, homemade versions of these garnishes made all the difference.

CHEESY NACHOS WITH GUACAMOLE AND SALSA

SERVES 4 TO 6

Do not substitute store-bought guacamole or salsa; using homemade guacamole and salsa is key to making this recipe above average.

8	ounces tortilla chips
1	pound cheddar cheese, shredded (4 cups)
2	large jalapeño chiles, stemmed and sliced thin crosswise
2	scallions, sliced thin
1½	cups Chunky Guacamole (page 15)
1	recipe One-Minute Salsa (page 14)
½	cup sour cream
	Lime wedges

1. Adjust oven rack to middle position and heat oven to 400 degrees. Spread half of chips in even layer in 13 by 9-inch baking dish or similar ovensafe platter; sprinkle evenly with 2 cups cheese and half of jalapeño slices. Repeat with remaining chips, cheese, and jalapeños.

2. Bake until cheese is melted, 7 to 10 minutes. Remove nachos from oven, cool 2 minutes, then sprinkle with scallions. Drop scoops of guacamole, salsa, and sour cream around edges of nachos. Serve immediately, passing lime wedges separately.

CHEESY NACHOS WITH REFRIED BEANS

We far prefer making our own refried beans (page 240) to using store-bought, but if you are short on time you can substitute your favorite store-bought variety.

Drop ¾ cup refried beans in small spoonfuls on each chip layer before sprinkling with cheese.

CHEESY NACHOS WITH SPICY BEEF

This variation makes for a heartier option.

2	teaspoons corn or vegetable oil
1	small onion, chopped fine
1	large garlic clove, minced
1	tablespoon chili powder
½	teaspoon ground cumin
½	teaspoon ground coriander
¼	teaspoon cayenne pepper
¼	teaspoon dried oregano
⅛	teaspoon salt
8	ounces 90 percent lean ground beef

1. Heat oil in 10-inch skillet over medium heat until shimmering, about 2 minutes. Add onion and cook, stirring occasionally, until softened, about 4 minutes. Add garlic, chili powder, cumin, coriander, cayenne, oregano, and salt and cook, stirring constantly, until fragrant, about 1 minute. Add ground beef and cook, breaking up meat with wooden spoon, until beef is no longer pink, about 5 minutes.

2. Follow recipe for Cheesy Nachos with Guacamole and Salsa, sprinkling half of beef mixture on each chip layer before sprinkling with cheese.

QUESADILLAS

✔ WHY THIS RECIPE WORKS

Quesadillas have evolved into a version of bad Mexican pizza, becoming stale and soggy supermarket tortillas topped with almost everything under the sun. We wanted to make quesadillas that were authentic in spirit (if not quite in substance) yet also quick enough to make a satisfying snack. We kept the tortillas crisp by lightly toasting them in a dry skillet. We then filled them with cheese, lightly coated them with oil, and returned them to the skillet until they were well browned and the cheese was fully melted. Not yet satisfied that our recipe was speedy enough, we made the process even more convenient by switching to small 8-inch tortillas and folding them in half around the filling. This allowed us to cook two at one time in the same skillet, and the fold also kept our cheesy filling from oozing out.

QUESADILLAS

MAKES 2 FOLDED 8-INCH QUESADILLAS

Cooling the quesadillas before cutting and serving is important; straight from the skillet, the cheese is molten and will ooze out. This recipe is easy to double or triple to serve a crowd. Finished quesadillas can be held on a baking sheet in a 200-degree oven for up to 20 minutes.

2	(8-inch) flour tortillas
2⅔	ounces Monterey Jack or cheddar cheese, shredded (⅔ cup)
1	tablespoon minced jarred jalapeños (optional)
	Vegetable oil for brushing tortillas
	Kosher salt

1. Heat 10-inch nonstick skillet over medium heat until hot, about 2 minutes. Place 1 tortilla in skillet and toast until soft and puffed slightly at edges, about 2 minutes. Flip tortilla and toast until puffed and slightly browned, 1 to 2 minutes longer. Slip tortilla onto cutting board. Repeat to toast second tortilla while assembling first quesadilla.

2. Sprinkle ⅓ cup cheese and half of jalapeños, if using, over half of tortilla, leaving ½-inch border around edge. Fold tortilla in half over filling and press to flatten. Brush top generously with oil, sprinkle lightly with salt, and set aside. Repeat to form second quesadilla.

3. Place quesadillas in skillet, oiled sides down. Cook over medium heat until crisp and well browned, 1 to 2 minutes. Brush tops with oil and sprinkle lightly with salt. Flip quesadillas and cook until second sides are crisp, 1 to 2 minutes. Transfer quesadillas to cutting board. Cool about 3 minutes, halve each quesadilla, and serve.

CHEDDAR, BACON, AND SCALLION QUESADILLAS

For more bacon flavor, substitute the rendered bacon fat for the oil and omit the salt.

Cook 2 slices bacon, cut into ½-inch pieces, in 10-inch nonstick skillet over medium heat until crisp, 5 to 7 minutes. Transfer bacon to paper towel–lined plate and wipe out skillet with paper towels. Use cheddar cheese and sprinkle half of bacon and 1 tablespoon thinly sliced scallions over cheese in each quesadilla.

CORN AND BLACK BEAN QUESADILLAS WITH PEPPER JACK CHEESE

Cook ⅓ cup thawed frozen corn in 10-inch nonstick skillet over medium-high heat, stirring occasionally, until kernels begin to brown and pop, 3 to 5 minutes; transfer to bowl. Heat 2 teaspoons vegetable oil in skillet over medium heat until shimmering. Add ⅓ cup minced red onion and cook until softened, about 3 minutes. Add 1 teaspoon minced garlic and ½ teaspoon chili powder and cook until fragrant, about 1 minute; stir in ⅓ cup canned black beans and cook until heated through, about 1 minute. Return corn to skillet and gently press mixture with spatula to lightly crush beans. Transfer mixture to bowl, stir in 2 teaspoons lime juice, and season with salt. Substitute pepper Jack cheese for Monterey Jack and divide corn-and-bean filling between quesadillas.

QUESADILLAS WITH QUESO FRESCO AND ROASTED PEPPERS

Use a light hand when seasoning with kosher salt, as the cheese is rather salty.

Substitute ⅔ cup crumbled queso fresco for the Monterey Jack and add 1 tablespoon chopped roasted red pepper, patted dry, and ¼ teaspoon chopped fresh cilantro to the filling in each quesadilla.

CUBANO QUESADILLAS

Use a light hand when seasoning with salt, as the cheese is rather salty.

Omit the Monterey Jack and jarred jalapeños. In step 2, spread 2 teaspoons yellow mustard over half of each toasted tortilla, then top with 2 slices deli ham, ⅓ cup shredded Gruyère cheese, and 1 tablespoon each finely chopped onion and pickles. Fold tortillas in half over filling and proceed with recipe as directed.

BRUSCHETTA

✔ WHY THIS RECIPE WORKS
The ingredients in modern bruschetta—toasted bread, tomatoes, and basil—may seem like an appealing combination but in reality, the tomatoes usually lack flavor, excess liquid results in soggy bread, and precariously stacked toppings often end up on your shirt. We wanted to establish a solid recipe for classic bruschetta and then go on to develop several more bruschetta recipes featuring smart flavor combinations that didn't require a bib; we were after a mix of recipes that gave us both lighter and heartier topping options. Along with fresh ingredients like mushrooms, we found that pantry ingredients, such as marinated peppers paired with sharp feta cheese or dried figs teamed up with goat cheese and salty prosciutto, fit the bill when summer tomatoes weren't an option. Creating a "glue" by pulsing ingredients in the food processor helped us anchor lighter toppings to the bread for several recipes.

TOASTED BREAD FOR BRUSCHETTA
SERVES 8 TO 10

Toast the bread as close as possible to the time at which you plan to assemble the bruschetta.

1	loaf country bread with thick crust (about 10 by 5 inches), ends discarded, sliced crosswise into ¾-inch-thick pieces
½	garlic clove, peeled Extra-virgin olive oil Salt

Adjust oven rack 4 inches from broiler element and heat broiler. Place bread on aluminum foil–lined baking sheet. Broil until bread is deep golden, 1 to 2 minutes. Flip and repeat on second side. Lightly rub 1 side of each bread slice with garlic and brush with oil. Season with salt to taste.

TEST KITCHEN TIP NO. 6 KEEPING A SHARP EDGE

With three dozen test cooks, editors, and cookware specialists working side by side in the test kitchen, we take knife care very seriously. Simply put, a dull knife is a dangerous knife. Here's why: The duller the blade, the more work it takes to do the job—and the easier it is for the blade to slip and miss the mark (slippery ingredients like onions are the worst offenders), quickly sending the knife toward your hand. With a sharp knife, the blade does the work—and the razorlike edge is far less likely to slip.

To determine if your knife is sharp, put it to a simple test. Hold a folded, but not creased, sheet of newspaper by one end. Lay the blade against the top edge at an angle and slice outward. If the knife fails to slice cleanly, try running the blade over a sharpening steel. A sharpening steel is a tune-up device, not a knife sharpener. Just a few minutes of cutting can knock the edge of a knife out of alignment and running the blade over the sharpening steel can reset the edge. That said, if your knife still fails to slice cleanly after using a steel, it means the edge is worn down and needs proper sharpening.

To sharpen your knife, you have three choices. You can send it out to a professional for sharpening, you can use a whetstone (tricky for anyone but a professional), or—the most convenient option—you can use an electric or manual sharpener.

BRUSCHETTA WITH TOMATOES AND BASIL

SERVES 8 TO 10

This is the classic bruschetta, although you can substitute other herbs. Decrease the quantity of stronger herbs, such as thyme or oregano. Toast the bread as close as possible to the time at which you plan to assemble the bruschetta.

- 1 recipe Toasted Bread for Bruschetta (page 17)
- 3 tablespoons extra-virgin olive oil
- 1½ pounds tomatoes, cored and cut into ½-inch dice
- ⅓ cup shredded fresh basil
  Salt and pepper

Brush toasts with oil. Combine tomatoes and basil in medium bowl and season with salt and pepper to taste. Divide tomato mixture evenly among toasts. Serve immediately.

BRUSCHETTA WITH BLACK OLIVE PESTO, RICOTTA, AND BASIL

SERVES 8 TO 10

Use only a high-quality whole-milk ricotta for this recipe. Toast the bread as close as possible to the time at which you plan to assemble the bruschetta.

- 1 recipe Toasted Bread for Bruschetta (page 17)
- 6 tablespoons extra-virgin olive oil, plus extra for serving
- ½ cup pitted kalamata olives
- 1 small shallot, minced
- 1½ teaspoons lemon juice
- 1 garlic clove, minced
- 1½ cups whole-milk ricotta cheese
  Salt and pepper
- 2 tablespoons shredded fresh basil

Brush toasts with ¼ cup oil. Process olives, remaining 2 tablespoons oil, shallot, lemon juice, and garlic in food processor until uniform paste forms, about 10 seconds, scraping down bowl once during processing. Combine ricotta with salt and pepper to taste in small bowl. Divide olive pesto evenly among toasts and spread to edges. Top with ricotta and carefully spread over pesto. Drizzle with olive oil to taste, sprinkle with basil, and serve.

BRUSCHETTA WITH RED ONIONS, MINT, AND PARMESAN

SERVES 8 TO 10

Fresh mint gives the onion and cheese topping a refreshing finish, but parsley can be substituted. Toast the bread as close as possible to the time at which you plan to assemble the bruschetta.

- 1 recipe Toasted Bread for Bruschetta (page 17)
- 6 tablespoons extra-virgin olive oil
- 4 red onions, halved and sliced thin
- 4 teaspoons sugar
- 2 tablespoons balsamic vinegar
- 1½ tablespoons minced fresh mint
  Salt and pepper
- 3 tablespoons grated Parmesan cheese

1. Brush toasts with 2½ tablespoons oil. Heat remaining 3½ tablespoons oil in 12-inch skillet over medium-high heat. Add onions and sugar and cook, stirring often, until onions are softened, 7 to 8 minutes. Reduce heat to medium-low and continue to cook, stirring often, until onions are sweet and tender, 7 to 8 minutes longer. Stir in vinegar and mint and season with salt and pepper to taste.

2. Divide onion mixture evenly among toasts, then sprinkle with cheese.

3. Broil until cheese just melts. Transfer bruschetta to large platter and serve immediately. (Onion mixture can be covered and refrigerated for 1 week.)

BRUSCHETTA WITH WHIPPED FETA AND ROASTED RED PEPPERS

SERVES 8 TO 10

Toast the bread as close as possible to the time at which you plan to assemble the bruschetta.

- 1 recipe Toasted Bread for Bruschetta (page 17)
- 6 tablespoons extra-virgin olive oil, plus extra for serving
- 1½ cups jarred roasted red peppers, rinsed, patted dry, and cut into ½-inch dice
- 2 tablespoons red wine vinegar
- 2 tablespoons sugar
- 1 medium garlic clove, minced

TEST KITCHEN TIP NO. 7 OLIVES—WHAT'S THE DIFFERENCE?

Jarred olives come in three basic types at the supermarket: brine-cured green, brine-cured black, and salt-cured black (often erroneously labeled "oil-cured"). Brine-cured olives are soaked in a salt solution; salt-cured olives are packed in salt until nearly all their liquid has been extracted, then covered in oil to be re-plumped. Both processes traditionally take weeks or even months. Generally we find that brine-cured black or green olives can be used interchangeably in any recipe based on personal preference. Often labeled "Spanish" olives, green olives are picked before fully ripened and their mild flavor adds a bright, acidic dimension to food. Picked when mature, black olives lend a more robust, fruity taste. Among our test cooks, only a few olive aficionados favored the concentrated, bitter taste of salt-cured olives—we don't recommend cooking with them unless a recipe specifically calls for them. And as for canned olives? We avoid them entirely, finding them almost tasteless, with a firm yet oddly slippery texture.

¼ teaspoon red pepper flakes
  Salt and pepper
8 ounces feta cheese, crumbled
  (2 cups)
2 teaspoons lemon juice

Brush toasts with ¼ cup oil. Combine roasted peppers, vinegar, sugar, garlic, pepper flakes, and ¼ teaspoon salt in medium bowl; set aside. Process feta, lemon juice, remaining 2 tablespoons olive oil, and ¼ teaspoon black pepper in food processor until smooth, about 10 seconds, scraping down bowl with rubber spatula once during processing. Divide feta mixture evenly among toasts and spread to edges. Using fork, lift peppers from vinegar mixture and place on toasts. Drizzle with olive oil to taste and serve.

BRUSCHETTA WITH GRILLED PORTOBELLO MUSHROOMS

SERVES 8 TO 10

The mushrooms are grilled with the gill-covered undersides facing up to prevent loss of juices. For serving, the mushrooms are flipped onto the bread so their juices seep down into the toast. Toast the bread as close as possible to the time at which you plan to assemble the bruschetta.

1 recipe Toasted Bread for
  Bruschetta (page 17)
6 tablespoons extra-virgin olive oil
4 portobello mushrooms, stemmed
1 tablespoon minced fresh rosemary

1A. FOR A CHARCOAL GRILL: Open bottom vent completely. Light large chimney starter filled with charcoal briquettes (6 quarts). When top coals are partially covered with ash, pour evenly over grill. Set cooking grate in place, cover, and open lid vent completely. Heat grill until hot, about 5 minutes.

1B. FOR A GAS GRILL: Turn all burners to high, cover, and heat grill until hot, about 15 minutes. Turn all burners to medium. (Adjust burners as needed to maintain grill temperature around 350 degrees.)

2. While grill heats, brush toasts with 2½ tablespoons oil. Place mushroom caps on large baking sheet. Mix remaining 3½ tablespoons oil, rosemary, and salt and pepper to taste in small bowl. Brush oil mixture over both sides of mushrooms.

3. Clean and oil cooking grate. Grill mushrooms, gill side up, until caps are cooked through and grill-marked, 8 to 10 minutes.

4. Halve grilled mushrooms. Place 1 half, gill side down, on each toast. Serve immediately.

BRUSCHETTA WITH PORT-CARAMELIZED ONIONS, BLUE CHEESE, AND WALNUTS

SERVES 8 TO 10

Toast the bread as close as possible to the time at which you plan to assemble the bruschetta.

1 recipe Toasted Bread for
  Bruschetta (page 17)
¼ cup extra-virgin olive oil, plus
  extra for serving
1½ teaspoons unsalted butter
1½ teaspoons vegetable oil
1 pound onions, sliced ¼ inch thick
½ teaspoon light brown sugar
¼ teaspoon salt
1 cup port, preferably ruby
8 ounces mild blue cheese, crumbled
  (2 cups)
3 tablespoons milk
⅛ teaspoon cayenne pepper
  Pepper
¼ cup walnuts, toasted and
  chopped fine

1. Brush toasts with ¼ cup oil. Heat butter and vegetable oil in 10-inch non-stick skillet over high heat; add onions, sugar, and ¼ teaspoon salt and stir to coat. Cook, stirring occasionally, until onions soften and begin to release some moisture, about 5 minutes. Reduce heat to medium; cook, stirring frequently, until onions are deeply browned and sticky, about 35 minutes (if onions are sizzling or scorching, reduce heat; if onions are not browning after 15 minutes, increase heat). Stir in port and continue to cook until port reduces to glaze consistency, 4 to 6 minutes.

2. Using fork, mash blue cheese and milk together in medium bowl until smooth, spreadable consistency is formed. Stir in cayenne, ¼ teaspoon black pepper, and walnuts. Divide blue cheese mixture evenly among toasts and spread to edges. Top with onions and distribute evenly over surface of cheese. Sprinkle with black pepper to taste, drizzle with olive oil to taste, and serve.

BRUSCHETTA WITH SAUTÉED SWEET PEPPERS

SERVES 8 TO 10

Toast the bread as close as possible to the time at which you plan to assemble the bruschetta.

1 recipe Toasted Bread for
  Bruschetta (page 17)
6 tablespoons plus 1 teaspoon
  extra-virgin olive oil
4 large red bell peppers, stemmed,
  seeded, and cut into 3-by
  ¼-inch strips
2 onions, halved and sliced thin
¾ teaspoon salt
3 garlic cloves, minced
¼ teaspoon red pepper flakes
1 (14.5-ounce) can diced
  tomatoes, drained with ¼ cup
  juice reserved
1½ teaspoons minced fresh thyme
4 teaspoons sherry vinegar
2 ounces Parmesan cheese, shaved
  into strips with vegetable peeler

Brush both sides of toasts with 3 tablespoons oil. Heat 3 tablespoons more oil, bell peppers, onions, and ½ teaspoon salt in 12-inch skillet over medium-high heat; cook, stirring occasionally, until vegetables are softened and browned at the edges, 10 to 12 minutes. Reduce heat to medium, push vegetables to sides of skillet, and add remaining 1 teaspoon oil, garlic, and red pepper flakes to center of skillet. Cook, mashing garlic with wooden spoon, until fragrant, about 30 seconds, then stir into vegetables. Reduce heat to low and stir in tomatoes, reserved juice, and thyme. Cover and cook, stirring occasionally, until moisture has evaporated, 15 to 18 minutes. Off heat, stir in vinegar and remaining ¼ teaspoon salt. Divide pepper mixture evenly among toasts, top with shaved Parmesan, and serve.

BRUSCHETTA WITH SUMMER SQUASH, BACON, AND BLUE CHEESE
SERVES 8 TO 10

Toast the bread as close as possible to the time at which you plan to assemble the bruschetta.

-   1   recipe Toasted Bread for Bruschetta (page 17)
-   5   tablespoons extra-virgin olive oil
-   4   slices bacon, minced
-   4   summer squash and/or zucchini, halved lengthwise, seeded and cut into matchsticks
-   1   tablespoon red wine vinegar
-   ½   teaspoon salt
-   ¼   teaspoon pepper
-   4   ounces blue cheese, crumbled (1 cup)
-   ¼   cup chopped fresh basil

1. Brush toasts with 3 tablespoons oil. Position oven rack 4 inches from broiler element and heat broiler. Cook bacon in 8-inch skillet over medium-high heat until crisp, about 5 minutes. Transfer to paper towel–lined plate.

2. Combine squash, vinegar, remaining 2 tablespoons oil, salt, and pepper in medium bowl. Let stand 5 minutes, then fold in bacon, cheese, and basil.

3. Divide mixture evenly among toasts. Broil bruschetta until cheese begins to melt, about 1½ minutes. Serve immediately.

BRUSCHETTA WITH ARTICHOKE HEARTS AND PARMESAN
SERVES 8 TO 10

Use artichoke hearts packed in water. Toast the bread as close as possible to the time at which you plan to assemble the bruschetta.

-   1   recipe Toasted Bread for Bruschetta (page 17)
-   6   tablespoons extra-virgin olive oil, plus extra for serving
-   1   (14-ounce) can artichoke hearts, rinsed and patted dry
-   2   tablespoons chopped fresh basil
-   2   teaspoons lemon juice
-   1   garlic clove, minced
-   ¼   teaspoon salt
        Pepper
-   2   ounces Parmesan cheese, 1 ounce grated fine (½ cup), 1 ounce shaved into strips with vegetable peeler

Brush toasts with ¼ cup oil. Pulse artichoke hearts, remaining 2 tablespoons oil, basil, lemon juice, garlic, salt, and ¼ teaspoon pepper in food processor until coarsely pureed, about 6 pulses, scraping down bowl once during processing. Add grated Parmesan and pulse to combine, about 2 pulses. Divide artichoke mixture evenly among toasts and spread to edges. Top with shaved Parmesan. Sprinkle with pepper to taste, drizzle with olive oil to taste, and serve.

BRUSCHETTA WITH ARUGULA, RED ONIONS, AND ROSEMARY–WHITE BEAN SPREAD
SERVES 8 TO 10

Toast the bread as close as possible to the time at which you plan to assemble the bruschetta.

-   1   recipe Toasted Bread for Bruschetta (page 17)
-   6   tablespoons extra-virgin olive oil
-   1   (15-ounce) can cannellini beans, rinsed
-   2   tablespoons water
-   1   tablespoon lemon juice
-   1   small garlic clove, crushed
-   ¾   teaspoon salt
-   ¼   teaspoon pepper
-   ¼   teaspoon chopped fresh rosemary
-   1   tablespoon balsamic vinegar
-   ¼   red onion, sliced thin
-   2   ounces arugula (2 cups), cut into ½-inch strips

1. Brush toasts with 3 tablespoons oil. In food processor, process two-thirds of beans, 2 tablespoons oil, water, lemon juice, garlic, ½ teaspoon salt, and ⅛ teaspoon pepper until smooth, about 10 seconds. Add remaining beans and rosemary; pulse until incorporated but not smooth, about 5 pulses.

2. Whisk remaining 1 tablespoon oil, vinegar, remaining ¼ teaspoon salt, and remaining ⅛ teaspoon pepper in medium bowl; add onion and toss.

3. Divide bean spread evenly among toasts. Toss arugula with onion until coated, then top toasts with portion of onion and arugula. Serve immediately.

BRUSCHETTA WITH GOAT CHEESE, FIGS, AND PROSCIUTTO
SERVES 8 TO 10

A soft, mild goat cheese works best here. Toast the bread as close as possible to the time at which you plan to assemble the bruschetta.

1 recipe Toasted Bread for
 Bruschetta (page 17)
¼ cup extra-virgin olive oil, plus
 extra for serving
5 ounces dried Calimyrna or Turkish
 figs, chopped coarse (about 1 cup)
¾ cup water
¼ cup balsamic vinegar
 Salt
8 ounces goat cheese, room
 temperature
4 ounces thinly sliced prosciutto,
 torn into bite-size pieces

1. Brush toasts with ¼ cup oil. Bring figs, water, and vinegar to boil in small saucepan over high heat. Reduce heat to low, cover, and simmer, stirring occasionally, until mixture is almost dry and figs have softened, about 20 minutes (if after 20 minutes mixture is still moist, remove lid and continue to cook until almost dry). Process fig mixture in food processor until uniform paste forms, about 10 seconds, scraping down bowl once during processing.

2. Divide goat cheese evenly among toasts and spread to edges. Top with fig mixture and carefully spread over cheese. Top each slice with pieces of prosciutto, drizzle with olive oil to taste, and serve.

TOMATO AND MOZZARELLA TART

✔ WHY THIS RECIPE WORKS
Falling somewhere in between pizza and quiche, a tomato and mozzarella tart shares the flavors of both but features problems unique unto itself. For starters, some sort of pastry crust is required. Second, the moisture in the tomatoes almost guarantees a soggy crust. Third, tomato tarts are often short on flavor. We set out to develop a recipe that could easily be made at home with a solid bottom crust and great vine-ripened flavor. The best results came from using a two-step baking method—we parbaked the

unfilled crust until golden, then baked it again once the topping had been added, which gave us a flaky yet rigid crust. "Waterproofing" the crust with egg wash and using two kinds of cheese in layers prevented sogginess. We also salted the sliced tomatoes for 30 minutes, then gently pressed them with paper towels to remove excess juice.

TOMATO AND MOZZARELLA TART
SERVES 6 TO 8

Thawing the frozen puff pastry in the refrigerator overnight will help prevent cracking while unfolding it. Be sure to use low-moisture supermarket mozzarella sold in block form, not fresh water-packed mozzarella.

1 box frozen puff pastry, thawed in
 box in refrigerator overnight
1 large egg, beaten

2 ounces Parmesan cheese, grated
 (1 cup)
1 pound plum tomatoes, cored and
 cut crosswise into ¼-inch-thick slices
 Salt and pepper
2 garlic cloves, minced
2 tablespoons extra-virgin olive oil
8 ounces whole-milk mozzarella
 cheese, shredded (2 cups)
2 tablespoons chopped fresh basil

1. Adjust oven rack to lower-middle position and heat oven to 425 degrees. Dust counter with flour and unfold both pieces puff pastry onto counter. Following illustrations, form 1 large sheet, then make border, using beaten egg as directed. Sprinkle Parmesan evenly over shell. Using fork, uniformly poke holes in shell all over. Bake 13 to 15 minutes, then reduce oven temperature to 350 degrees.

FORMING THE TART SHELL

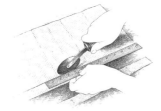

1. Brush egg along 1 short edge of 1 sheet of puff pastry. Overlap with second sheet of dough by 1 inch and press to seal pieces together.

2. With rolling pin, smooth out seam. Dough should measure about 18 by 9 inches. Use pizza wheel or knife to trim edges straight, if necessary.

3. With pizza wheel or knife, cut 1-inch strip from 1 long side of dough. Cut another 1-inch strip from same side.

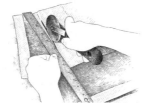

4. Cut 1-inch strip from 1 short side of dough. Cut another 1-inch strip from same side. Transfer pieces of dough to parchment-lined baking sheet and brush with egg.

5. Gently press 1 long strip of dough onto each long edge of dough and brush with egg. Gently press 1 short strip of dough onto each short edge and brush with egg.

6. With pizza wheel or knife, trim excess dough from corners.

Continue to bake until golden brown and crisp, 13 to 15 minutes longer. Transfer to wire rack; increase oven temperature to 425 degrees.

2. While shell bakes, place tomato slices in single layer on double layer of paper towels and sprinkle evenly with ½ teaspoon salt; let stand 30 minutes. Place another double layer of paper towels on top of tomatoes and press firmly to dry tomatoes. Combine garlic, olive oil, and pinch each salt and pepper in small bowl; set aside.

3. Sprinkle mozzarella evenly over baked shell. Shingle tomato slices width-wise on top of cheese (about 4 slices per row); brush tomatoes with garlic oil. Bake until shell is deep golden brown and cheese is melted, 15 to 17 minutes. Cool on wire rack 5 minutes. Sprinkle with basil, slide onto cutting board or serving platter, cut into pieces, and serve.

TO MAKE AHEAD: Tart shell can be prebaked through step 1, cooled to room temperature, wrapped in plastic wrap, and kept at room temperature for up to 2 days before being topped and baked with mozzarella and tomatoes.

CHERRY TOMATO AND
MOZZARELLA TART

Omit salted and drained plum tomatoes and substitute the following mixture: In medium bowl, gently toss 1½ pounds (2 pints) halved cherry tomatoes with ¼ cup olive oil, 1 tablespoon balsamic vinegar, 3 thinly sliced large garlic cloves, 1½ teaspoons sugar, ½ teaspoon salt, ¼ teaspoon red pepper flakes, and ¼ teaspoon pepper. Spread mixture in even layer on rimmed baking sheet and, after removing tart shell from oven, roast tomatoes until skins are slightly shriveled (tomatoes should retain their shape) about 30 minutes. (Do not stir tomatoes during roasting.) Prepare garlic oil and sprinkle mozzarella over baked shell as

directed, then use slotted spoon to scatter roasted cherry tomato mixture on top of cheese. Brush with garlic oil and proceed as directed.

SUN-DRIED TOMATO AND
MOZZARELLA TART

Replacing the plum tomatoes with sun-dried tomatoes turns this into an appetizer you can make any time of year.

Substitute ½ cup oil-packed sun-dried tomatoes, drained, rinsed, and chopped fine, for plum tomatoes.

TOMATO AND SMOKED
MOZZARELLA TART

Substitute 6 ounces smoked mozzarella for whole-milk mozzarella.

TOMATO AND MOZZARELLA TART
WITH PROSCIUTTO

Place 2 ounces thinly sliced prosciutto in single layer on top of mozzarella before arranging tomato slices.

FRESH SPRING ROLLS

✔ **WHY THIS RECIPE WORKS**
Fresh spring rolls should offer a textural symphony (soft wrapper, firm noodles, and crunchy vegetables) as well as appealing contrasts in flavor (mint, basil, cilantro, chiles, peanuts, and fish sauce). But too often, spring rolls are disappointing combinations of gummy noodles, bland vegetables, and mushy rice paper. We set out to develop a recipe for easy-to-make spring rolls packed with fresh, bright flavors and accompanied by a spicy, not-too-sweet peanut sauce for dipping. First, we soaked the spring roll wrappers in water for just 10 seconds, just long enough to make them pliable. Second, marinating the noodle-vegetable filling ingredients ensured superior flavor. Third, we eliminated the

typical glut of sugar from the dipping sauce to put the peanut flavor at the forefront.

FRESH SPRING ROLLS
MAKES 8 SPRING ROLLS

If you can't find Thai basil, do not substitute regular basil; its flavor is too gentle to stand up to the other, more assertive flavors in the filling. Mint makes a better substitute. Be sure to only make one spring roll at a time to keep the wrappers moist and pliable.

2½	tablespoons lime juice (2 limes)
1½	tablespoons fish sauce
1	teaspoon sugar
3	ounces rice vermicelli
1	teaspoon salt
1	large carrot, peeled and shredded
⅓	cup chopped dry-roasted peanuts
1	jalapeño chile or 2 Thai chiles, stemmed, seeded, and minced, or ½ teaspoon red pepper flakes
1	large cucumber, peeled, halved, seeded, and cut into matchsticks
4	leaves red leaf lettuce or Boston lettuce, halved lengthwise
8	(8-inch) round rice paper wrappers
½	cup loosely packed fresh Thai basil or mint, small leaves left whole, medium and large leaves torn into ½-inch pieces
½	cup loosely packed fresh cilantro leaves
1	recipe Peanut Dipping Sauce (recipe follows)

1. Combine lime juice, fish sauce, and sugar in small bowl.

2. Bring 4 quarts water to boil in large pot. Remove from heat, stir in rice vermicelli and salt and let sit, stirring occasionally, until noodles are tender but not mushy, about 10 minutes. Drain noodles, transfer to medium bowl, and toss with 2 tablespoons fish sauce mixture.

3. Combine carrot, peanuts, and jalapeño in small bowl. Add 1 tablespoon

fish sauce mixture; toss to combine. Toss cucumber in remaining 1 tablespoon fish sauce mixture.

4. Place lettuce on platter. Spread clean, damp kitchen towel on counter. Fill 9-inch pie plate with 1 inch room-temperature water. Immerse each wrapper in water until just pliable, about 2 minutes; lay softened wrapper on towel. Scatter about 6 Thai basil leaves and 6 cilantro leaves over wrapper. Following illustrations, arrange 5 cucumber sticks horizontally on wrapper, top with 1 tablespoon carrot mixture, then arrange about 2½ tablespoons noodles on top of carrot mixture. Wrap spring roll and set on 1 lettuce piece on platter. Cover with second damp kitchen towel. Repeat with remaining wrappers and filling. Serve with peanut dipping sauce, wrapping lettuce around exterior of each roll. (Spring rolls are best eaten immediately, but they can be held for up to 4 hours in the refrigerator, covered with a clean, damp kitchen towel.)

PEANUT DIPPING SAUCE
MAKES ABOUT ¾ CUP

- ¼ cup creamy peanut butter
- ¼ cup hoisin sauce
- ¼ cup water
- 2 tablespoons tomato paste
- 1 teaspoon Asian chili-garlic sauce (optional)

ASSEMBLING SPRING ROLLS

1. After layering herbs, cucumber, carrot mixture, and noodles on wrapper, fold up bottom 2-inch border of wrapper over filling.

2. Fold left, then right edge of wrapper over filling.

3. Roll filling to top edge of wrapper to form tight cylinder.

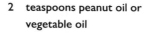

- 2 teaspoons peanut oil or vegetable oil
- 2 garlic cloves, minced
- 1 teaspoon red pepper flakes

Whisk peanut butter, hoisin sauce, water, tomato paste, and chili-garlic sauce, if using, in small bowl. Heat oil, garlic, and pepper flakes in small saucepan over medium heat until fragrant, 1 to 2 minutes. Stir in peanut butter mixture; bring to simmer, then reduce heat to medium-low and cook, stirring occasionally, until flavors blend, about 3 minutes. (Sauce should have ketchuplike consistency; if too thick, add water, 1 teaspoon at a time, until proper consistency is reached.) Transfer to bowl; cool to room temperature. (Sauce can be refrigerated for up to 3 days. Bring to room temperature before serving.)

FRESH SPRING ROLLS WITH SHRIMP

Peel and remove tails from 8 ounces medium shrimp (41 to 50 per pound). Add shrimp to boiling water along with salt in step 2; cook until shrimp are opaque, about 3 minutes. Using slotted spoon, transfer shrimp to small bowl; use water to cook rice vermicelli as in step 2. When cool enough to handle, coarsely chop shrimp. When assembling spring rolls, place about 2 tablespoons chopped shrimp on top of noodles.

SCALLION PANCAKES

✓ WHY THIS RECIPE WORKS
Scallion pancakes should boast multiple paper-thin layers laced with scallions and just a hint of sesame flavor. The exterior should be brown and crisp while the interior retains a soft chew. We found 2 tablespoons of scallions per pancake was just right for bold allium flavor. Cilantro lent a great herbal flavor. Brushing a thin layer of sesame oil onto the pancakes before sprinkling on the scallions and cilantro added the right sesame flavor. As for forming the pancakes, we got the best results from rolling the dough into a pancake, sprinkling the flavorings over, rolling it into a log, then coiling it around itself like a snake and rolling it out into a pancake again. This was easier to do than expected and the result was a pancake with tender layers and evenly incorporated scallions.

SCALLION PANCAKES
SERVES 4 TO 6

We like these pancakes with the dipping sauce, but if preferred, you can omit the sauce and simply sprinkle with salt to taste before serving.

- 1½ cups all-purpose flour
- 1 teaspoon salt
- ½ cup room-temperature water, plus extra if needed
- ¼ cup vegetable oil, plus extra for brushing
- 2 teaspoons toasted sesame oil
- 6 scallions, minced (½ cup)
- 2 tablespoons minced fresh cilantro
- 1 recipe Scallion Dipping Sauce (page 26)

1. Whisk flour and salt together in medium bowl. Add water and mix with dinner fork until combined. (If there are any floury bits left in bottom of bowl, add additional water, 1 teaspoon at a time, until dough comes together.) Turn dough out onto lightly floured counter and knead until smooth and satiny, about 5 minutes,

adding extra flour to counter or your hands as needed to prevent sticking. Transfer dough to clean bowl, brush with thin layer of vegetable oil, and let rest at room temperature for 30 minutes.

2. Divide dough into 4 equal pieces and cover to keep dough from drying out. Working with 1 piece of dough at a time, roll into 7-inch circle about ⅛ inch thick on lightly floured counter. Brush dough round lightly with sesame oil, then sprinkle with 2 tablespoons scallions and 1½ teaspoons cilantro.

3. Following illustrations, roll dough into cylinder, then coil cylinder into round, tucking tail end underneath. Roll into 5-inch pancake about ¼ inch thick. Set aside and cover while repeating with remaining dough pieces.

4. Heat 1 tablespoon vegetable oil in 12-inch nonstick skillet over medium heat until shimmering. Swirl oil to coat skillet, then add 1 dough round and cook until golden brown on both sides, 1½ to 2 minutes per side. Transfer pancake to cutting board, tent with aluminum foil, and repeat 3 more times with remaining 3 tablespoons oil and remaining 3 dough rounds. Slice cooked pancakes into wedges and serve with Scallion Dipping Sauce.

STEAMED CHINESE DUMPLINGS

✓ WHY THIS RECIPE WORKS

The open-faced dumplings known as shu mai are ubiquitous on Cantonese menus, but home-made versions often disappoint us with their one-dimensional, mealy meatball flavor. For moist, tender, deeply flavored dumplings, we ground the pork ourselves from country-style pork ribs, since preground pork from the supermarket tends to cook up with unpredictable, inconsistent results. Grinding the meat to two textures ensured our filling held together but still had some texture, while adding a little gelatin and cornstarch kept the filling moist and supple. We tested a variety of wrappers and settled on delicate, easy-to-find egg roll wrappers.

STEAMED CHINESE DUMPLINGS (SHU MAI)

MAKES ABOUT 40 DUMPLINGS, SERVES 6 TO 8

Do not trim the excess fat from the ribs; it contributes flavor and moisture. Use any size shrimp except popcorn shrimp; there's no need to halve shrimp smaller than 26 to 30 per pound before processing.

2	tablespoons soy sauce
½	teaspoon unflavored gelatin
1	pound boneless country-style pork ribs, cut into 1-inch pieces
8	ounces shrimp, peeled, tails removed and halved lengthwise
¼	cup water chestnuts, chopped
4	dried shiitake mushroom caps (about ¾ ounce), soaked in hot water 30 minutes, squeezed dry, and chopped fine
2	tablespoons cornstarch
2	tablespoons minced fresh cilantro
1	tablespoon toasted sesame oil
1	tablespoon Chinese rice cooking wine or dry sherry
1	tablespoon rice vinegar
2	teaspoons sugar
2	teaspoons grated fresh ginger
½	teaspoon salt
½	teaspoon pepper
1	(1-pound) package 5½-inch square egg roll wrappers
¼	cup finely grated carrot (optional)
1	recipe Chili Oil, for serving (recipe follows)

1. Combine soy sauce and gelatin in small bowl. Set aside to allow gelatin to soften, about 5 minutes.

ROLLING AND FORMING SCALLION PANCAKES

1. Divide dough into 4 equal pieces and cover. Working with 1 piece of dough at a time, roll dough into 7-inch circle about ⅛ inch thick on lightly floured counter. Brush round lightly with sesame oil, then sprinkle with 2 tablespoons scallions and 1½ teaspoons cilantro.

2. Roll round into tight cylinder, brushing away any clumps of flour that have stuck to bottom of dough.

3. Coil cylinder into tight round, tucking end underneath.

4. Roll round into 5-inch pancake about ¼ inch thick, adding additional flour to counter as needed to prevent sticking.

2. Meanwhile, place half of pork in food processor and pulse until coarsely ground into approximate ⅛-inch pieces, about 10 pulses; transfer to large bowl. Add shrimp and remaining pork to food processor and pulse until coarsely chopped into approximate ¼-inch pieces, about 5 pulses. Transfer to bowl with more finely ground pork. Stir in soy sauce mixture, water chestnuts, mushrooms, cornstarch, cilantro, sesame oil, wine, vinegar, sugar, ginger, salt, and pepper.

3. Divide egg roll wrappers into 3 stacks (6 to 7 per stack). Using 3-inch biscuit cutter, cut two 3-inch rounds from each stack of egg roll wrappers (you should have 40 to 42 rounds). Cover rounds with moist paper towels to prevent drying.

4. Working with 6 rounds at a time, brush edges of each round lightly with water. Place heaping tablespoon of filling into center of each round. Following illustrations, form dumplings, crimping wrapper around sides of filling and leaving top exposed. Transfer to parchment paper–lined baking sheet, cover with clean, damp kitchen towel, and repeat with remaining wrappers and filling. Top center of each dumpling with pinch of grated carrot, if using.

5. Cut piece of parchment slightly smaller than diameter of steamer basket and place in basket. Poke about 20 small holes in parchment and lightly coat with vegetable oil spray. Place batches of dumplings on parchment liner, making sure they are not touching. Set steamer over simmering water and cook, covered, until no longer pink, 8 to 10 minutes. Serve immediately with chili oil. (Dumplings may be frozen for up to 3 months; cook straight from the freezer for about an extra 5 minutes.)

CHILI OIL
MAKES ABOUT ½ CUP

1	tablespoon soy sauce
2	teaspoons sugar
½	teaspoon salt
½	cup peanut oil
¼	cup red pepper flakes
2	garlic cloves, peeled

Combine soy sauce, sugar, and salt in small bowl; set aside. Heat oil in small saucepan over medium heat until it is just shimmering and registers 300 degrees. Remove pan from heat and stir in pepper flakes, garlic, and soy sauce mixture. Let cool to room temperature, stirring occasionally, about 1 hour. Discard garlic before serving.

PORK AND CABBAGE POTSTICKERS

✓ WHY THIS RECIPE WORKS

Too often, potstickers are dense, flavorless meatballs wrapped in a doughy blanket. We wanted tender, well-seasoned dumplings. To lighten the filling, we increased the amount of cabbage (after first salting and draining it to get rid of excess moisture) and then added lightly beaten egg whites. Turning to the wrappers, we found that store-bought gyoza-style wrappers and wonton wrappers both made terrific potstickers, although tasters preferred the slightly chewy texture of the gyoza-style. To keep the filling in place and the wrapper from puffing up and away from the meat during cooking, we found it best to fold each meat-filled wrapper into a half-moon, pinch the middle closed, then carefully press out any air while sealing the edges. Our final challenge was the cooking procedure. A sequence of browning, steaming, then cranking up the heat produced potstickers with a pleasing balance of soft and crisp textures.

PORK AND CABBAGE POTSTICKERS
MAKES 24 DUMPLINGS, SERVES 6

These dumplings are best served hot from the skillet; we recommend that you serve the first batch immediately, then cook the second batch.

ASSEMBLING SHU MAI

1. Brush wrapper edges lightly with water. Place heaping tablespoon of filling in center.

2. Pinch opposite sides of wrapper. Rotate 90 degrees and repeat. Continue until you have 8 equidistant folds.

3. Gather sides of shu mai and squeeze gently at top to create "waist."

4. Hold shu mai in your hand and gently but firmly pack down filling with butter knife.

FILLING

½ head napa cabbage, chopped fine
¾ teaspoon salt
12 ounces ground pork
4 scallions, minced
1 large egg, lightly beaten
4 teaspoons soy sauce
1½ teaspoons grated fresh ginger
1 garlic clove, minced
⅛ teaspoon pepper

DUMPLINGS

24 round gyoza wrappers
4 teaspoons vegetable oil
1 cup water, plus extra for brushing
1 recipe Scallion Dipping Sauce
   (recipe follows)

1. FOR FILLING: Toss cabbage with salt in colander set over bowl and let stand until cabbage begins to wilt, about 20 minutes. Press cabbage gently with rubber spatula to squeeze out any excess moisture, then transfer to medium bowl. Add pork, scallions, egg, soy sauce, ginger, garlic, and pepper and mix thoroughly to combine. Cover with plastic wrap and refrigerate until mixture is cold, at least 30 minutes or up to 24 hours.

2. FOR DUMPLINGS: Working with 4 wrappers at a time (keep remaining wrappers covered with plastic wrap), follow illustrations to fill, seal, and shape dumplings using generous 1 tablespoon of chilled filling per dumpling. Transfer dumplings to baking sheet and repeat with remaining wrappers and filling; you should have about 24 dumplings.

3. Line large plate with double layer of paper towels. Brush 2 teaspoons oil over bottom of 12-inch nonstick skillet and arrange half of dumplings in skillet, flat side down (overlapping just slightly if necessary). Place skillet over medium-high heat and cook dumplings, without moving, until golden brown on bottom, about 5 minutes.

4. Reduce the heat to low, add ½ cup water, and cover immediately. Continue to cook, covered, until most of water is absorbed and wrappers are slightly translucent, about 10 minutes. Uncover skillet, increase heat to medium-high, and continue to cook, without stirring, until dumpling bottoms are well browned and crisp, 3 to 4 minutes more. Slide dumplings onto paper towel–lined plate, browned side facing down, and let drain briefly. Transfer dumplings to serving platter and serve with scallion dipping sauce. Let skillet cool until just warm, then wipe out with paper towels and repeat step 3 with remaining dumplings, oil, and water. (Uncooked dumplings can be placed on plate, wrapped tightly with plastic wrap, and refrigerated for 1 day, or frozen for 1 month. Once frozen, dumplings can be transferred to zipper-lock bag to save space in freezer; do not thaw before cooking.)

SHRIMP POTSTICKERS

Substitute 12 ounces peeled, deveined shrimp (any size), tails removed, pulsed 10 times in food processor, for pork.

SCALLION DIPPING SAUCE
MAKES ¾ CUP

The sauce can be refrigerated overnight.

¼ cup soy sauce
2 tablespoons rice vinegar
2 tablespoons mirin
2 tablespoons water
1 teaspoon chili oil (optional)
½ teaspoon toasted sesame oil
1 scallion, minced

Combine all ingredients in bowl and serve.

WRAPPING POTSTICKERS

1. Place rounded tablespoon of filling in center of wrapper.

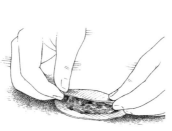

2. After moistening edge of wrapper, fold it in half to make half-moon shape.

3. With forefinger and thumb, pinch dumpling closed, pressing out any air pockets.

4. Place dumpling on its side and press gently to flatten bottom.

CHAPTER 2 Salads

FOOLPROOF VINAIGRETTES

WHY THIS RECIPE WORKS

Vinaigrettes often seem a little slipshod—harsh and bristling in one bite, dull and oily in the next—plus they tend to separate soon after being prepared. We found that top-notch ingredients are crucial for best, balanced flavor. Fruity extra-virgin olive oil is preferred as an all-purpose option, while walnut oil is best for nuttier vinaigrettes. Wine vinegar (red or white) is a better match for mild greens and balsamic vinegar is pungent enough to stand up to assertive greens. For a well-balanced vinaigrette that wouldn't separate, we whisked the oil and vinegar together with a little mayonnaise, which acts as an emulsifier.

FOOLPROOF VINAIGRETTE

MAKES ABOUT ¼ CUP

This vinaigrette works with nearly any type of greens. For a hint of garlic flavor, rub the inside of the salad bowl with a clove of garlic before adding the lettuce. You can use red wine, white wine, or champagne vinegar here; however, it is important to use high-quality ingredients. Use about 2 tablespoons of this dressing per 4 cups greens, serving two.

I	tablespoon wine vinegar
I ½	teaspoons minced shallot
½	teaspoon regular or light mayonnaise
½	teaspoon Dijon mustard
⅛	teaspoon salt
	Pepper
3	tablespoons extra-virgin olive oil

1. Combine vinegar, shallot, mayonnaise, mustard, salt, and pepper to taste in small bowl. Whisk until mixture is milky in appearance and no lumps of mayonnaise remain.

2. Place oil in small measuring cup so that it is easy to pour. Whisking constantly, very slowly drizzle oil into vinegar mixture. If pools of oil gather on surface as you whisk, stop addition of oil and whisk mixture well to combine, then resume whisking in oil in slow stream. Vinaigrette should be glossy and lightly thickened, with no pools of oil on its surface. (Vinaigrette can be refrigerated for up to 2 weeks.)

LEMON VINAIGRETTE

This is best for dressing mild greens.

Substitute fresh lemon juice for vinegar, omit shallot, and add ¼ teaspoon finely grated lemon zest and pinch of sugar along with salt and pepper.

BALSAMIC-MUSTARD VINAIGRETTE

This is best for dressing assertive greens.

Substitute balsamic vinegar for wine vinegar, increase mustard to 2 teaspoons, and add ½ teaspoon chopped fresh thyme along with salt and pepper.

WALNUT VINAIGRETTE

Substitute 1½ tablespoons roasted walnut oil and 1½ tablespoons regular olive oil for extra-virgin olive oil.

HERB VINAIGRETTE

Add 1 tablespoon minced fresh parsley or chives and ½ teaspoon minced fresh thyme, tarragon, marjoram, or oregano to vinaigrette just before use.

BOLD SALAD DRESSINGS

WHY THIS RECIPE WORKS

To develop salad dressings with bold flavor, we relied on ingredients not usually used in dressings, such as apples, raisins, carrot juice, and ruby port. We balanced these ingredients with fats such as cream, buttermilk, mayonnaise, nut oils, and yogurt and punctuated the mixture with condiments such as chili paste and orange marmalade. To give our dressings intense flavor, we reduced the wine and juices and toasted the spices.

CREAMY AVOCADO RANCH DRESSING

MAKES 1½ CUPS

Crisp lettuces like iceberg and romaine are a perfect match for this creamy dressing. Shaved red onion, grape tomatoes, and crumbled bacon make excellent garnishes for greens tossed with this dressing. Use 1 to 2 tablespoons of this dressing per 4 cups greens, serving two.

I	avocado, halved and pitted
I	tablespoon lime juice
½	teaspoon hot sauce
½	cup buttermilk
¼	cup mayonnaise
I	tablespoon minced red onion
I	tablespoon minced fresh cilantro
I	garlic clove, minced
½	teaspoon sugar
¾	teaspoon salt
¼	teaspoon pepper

TEST KITCHEN TIP NO. 8 VINAIGRETTES 1–2–3

After making and testing hundreds of vinaigrettes both straight and on salads, we've arrived at a few conclusions. To start, ratios: For most green salads, a ratio of 4 parts oil to 1 part vinegar works best. We might alter this ratio when the vinegar is unusually mild (like rice wine vinegar), when citrus juices are used, or when the dressing is heavily flavored by another ingredient that needs a good kick (such as tomatoes). And salads like Chef's Salad (page 37) benefit from an acidic dressing that cuts through the richness of the meat and cheese. Second, extra-virgin olive oil is our top choice for most vinaigrettes, except those that have strong Asian flavors. Third, we've found that simply shaking all the vinaigrette ingredients together in a jar with a sealed lid in the easiest method of making the dressing; there is no extra bowl or whisk to wash and you can store what is left over in the same jar. Most vinaigrettes last about a week in the refrigerator. Just bring the dressing to room temperature and shake vigorously to recombine before serving.

Puree avocado, lime juice, and hot sauce in food processor until avocado is broken down, about 30 seconds. Add remaining ingredients and process until dressing is completely smooth. (Dressing can be refrigerated for up to 1 week.)

FRESH APPLE AND PARSLEY DRESSING
MAKES 1½ CUPS

If using a tart apple, add up to 1 tablespoon brown sugar. This dressing is nice on spicy greens like arugula and watercress with garnishes such as shaved Parmesan, toasted nuts, and thin slices of apple or fennel. Use about 2 tablespoons of this dressing per 4 cups greens, serving two.

1	apple, cored, quartered, and cut into 1-inch cubes
¼	cup fresh parsley leaves
1	scallion, sliced
2	tablespoons cider vinegar
1	teaspoon hot sauce
¾	teaspoon salt
⅛	teaspoon pepper
2–3	tablespoons water
½	cup vegetable oil

Combine apple, parsley, scallion, vinegar, hot sauce, salt, and pepper in blender; pulse, scraping down blender jar and adding water as needed, until very finely chopped. With blender running, gradually add oil, scraping down blender jar as needed. (Dressing can be refrigerated for up to 1 week.)

MOROCCAN-SPICED VINAIGRETTE
MAKES ABOUT 1 CUP

Mellow salad greens, as well as spinach, pair nicely with this vinaigrette. Olives, shredded carrots, and golden raisins are good garnish options. Use about 2 tablespoons of this dressing per 4 cups greens, serving two.

2	tablespoons golden raisins
¼	teaspoon ground coriander
⅛	teaspoon ground cumin
½	cup carrot juice
2	tablespoons red wine vinegar
4	sprigs fresh cilantro
1	tablespoon plain yogurt
1	teaspoon honey
½	teaspoon red pepper flakes
½	teaspoon salt
½	cup extra-virgin olive oil

1. Place raisins in small bowl. Toast coriander and cumin in 8-inch skillet over medium heat until fragrant, 2 to 3 minutes. Transfer spices to bowl with raisins. Wipe out skillet; add carrot juice to skillet and simmer over medium heat until reduced to ¼ cup, about 6 minutes. Pour carrot juice over raisins; let cool to room temperature.

2. Process carrot juice–raisin mixture, vinegar, cilantro, yogurt, honey, pepper flakes, and salt in blender until thoroughly combined. With blender running, gradually add oil, scraping down blender jar as needed. (Dressing can be refrigerated for up to 1 week.)

ORANGE-PORT DRESSING WITH WALNUT OIL
MAKES ABOUT 1 CUP

Use this sweet, smooth dressing on assertive bitter greens such as escarole, radicchio, and endive. Appropriate salad garnishes include toasted nuts and crumbled blue cheese. For two servings, start with 1 tablespoon of this dressing per 4 cups greens, adding more as desired.

1½	cups ruby port
½	cup orange juice
2	tablespoons red wine vinegar
2	tablespoons heavy cream, room temperature
2	tablespoons orange marmalade
½	teaspoon minced fresh thyme
¼	teaspoon salt
⅛	teaspoon pepper
¼	cup vegetable oil
2	tablespoons walnut oil

1. Simmer port and orange juice in small saucepan over medium heat until reduced to ½ cup, 25 to 30 minutes. Transfer to medium bowl; let cool to room temperature.

2. Whisk vinegar, cream, marmalade, thyme, salt, and pepper into cooled port reduction. Whisk in vegetable oil and walnut oil until incorporated. (Dressing can be refrigerated for up to 1 week)

SWEET SESAME-SOY VINAIGRETTE
MAKES 1½ CUPS

We like this vinaigrette on soft, tender greens such as Boston or Bibb lettuce, mâche, or a mixture of baby greens. Complementary salad garnishes include thinly sliced radishes or cucumbers, bean sprouts, slivers of red bell pepper, and scallions. Use about 2 tablespoons of this dressing per 4 cups greens, serving two.

⅓	cup rice vinegar
¼	cup packed light brown sugar
2½	tablespoons soy sauce
2	teaspoons Asian chili-garlic sauce
½	teaspoon grated fresh ginger
½	cup vegetable oil
1	tablespoon toasted sesame oil
2	teaspoons sesame seeds, toasted

Whisk vinegar, sugar, soy sauce, chili-garlic paste, and ginger in medium bowl until sugar dissolves. Gradually whisk in vegetable oil and sesame oil; whisk in sesame seeds. (Dressing can be refrigerated for up to 2 weeks.)

BLUE CHEESE DRESSING

✔ WHY THIS RECIPE WORKS

We found that the secret to good blue cheese dressing lay in the creamy components, which we narrowed down to three: mayonnaise to give the dressing body, sour cream to supply tang, and buttermilk both to thin out the dressing and to support the sour cream. We also added a little white wine vinegar for zing and just a bit of sugar to take off any harsh edge. As for the main ingredient—the cheese—we ruled out really pungent blue cheeses as too overpowering; a mild blue cheese works best. For the right chunky consistency, we mixed the crumbled blue cheese with the buttermilk before adding any other ingredients.

RICH AND CREAMY
BLUE CHEESE DRESSING
MAKES ¾ CUP

In a pinch, whole milk may be used in place of buttermilk. The dressing will be a bit lighter and milder in flavor, but will still taste good. We dressed a variety of different salad greens and found that delicate ones, such as mesclun and butterhead lettuce, became soggy under the weight of the dressing. Sturdy romaine and curly leaf lettuce were our two favorites. Remember that aggressive seasoning with salt and pepper is necessary because the dressing will be dispersed over the greens. Use 1 to 2 tablespoons of this dressing per 4 cups greens, serving two.

2½ ounces blue cheese, crumbled
    (½ cup)
3   tablespoons buttermilk
3   tablespoons sour cream
2   tablespoons mayonnaise
2   teaspoons white wine vinegar
¼   teaspoon sugar
⅛   teaspoon garlic powder
    Salt and pepper

Mash blue cheese and buttermilk in small bowl with fork until mixture resembles cottage cheese with small curds. Stir in sour cream, mayonnaise, vinegar, sugar, and garlic powder. Season with salt and pepper to taste. (Dressing can be refrigerated for up to 1 week.)

MAYONNAISE

✔ WHY THIS RECIPE WORKS

Mayonnaise acts as a creamy binder and adds richness to any salad. Whisking transforms three thin liquids—vegetable oil, lemon juice, and egg yolk—into a thick, creamy sauce. But sometimes mayonnaise can "break" as the ingredients revert back to their original form. To keep mayonnaise from breaking, we whisked the egg yolk and lemon juice thoroughly and added the oil slowly to the mixture. We preferred the flavor of corn oil in our mayonnaise. Canola oil made a lighter-tasting mayonnaise and extra-virgin olive oil made a mayonnaise that was harsh and bitter.

MAYONNAISE
MAKES ABOUT ¾ CUP

Each time you add oil, make sure to whisk until it is thoroughly incorporated. It's fine to stop for a rest or to measure the next addition of oil. If the mayonnaise appears grainy or beaded after the last addition of oil, continue to whisk until smooth.

1   large egg yolk
1½   teaspoons lemon juice
1   teaspoon white wine vinegar
¼   teaspoon Dijon mustard
¼   teaspoon salt
¾   cup corn oil

1. Whisk egg yolk vigorously in medium bowl for 15 seconds. Add lemon juice, vinegar, mustard, and salt and whisk until yolk thickens and color brightens, about 30 seconds.

2. Add ¼ cup oil in slow, steady stream, continuing to whisk vigorously until oil is incorporated completely and mixture thickens, about 1 minute. Add ¼ cup oil, whisking until completely incorporated, about 30 seconds more. Add remaining ¼ cup oil all at once and whisk until completely incorporated, about 30 seconds more. (Mayonnaise can be refrigerated for up to 3 days.)

LEMON MAYONNAISE

Add 1½ teaspoons grated lemon zest along with lemon juice.

DIJON MAYONNAISE

Whisk 2 tablespoons more Dijon mustard into finished mayonnaise.

TARRAGON MAYONNAISE

Stir 1 tablespoon minced fresh tarragon into finished mayonnaise.

FOOD PROCESSOR MAYONNAISE
MAKES ABOUT 1½ CUPS

Use 1 whole large egg and double quantities of the other ingredients in Mayonnaise. Pulse all ingredients except oil in food processor 3 or 4 times to combine. With food processor running, add oil through feed tube in thin, steady stream until completely incorporated.

AÏOLI

✔ WHY THIS RECIPE WORKS

Aïoli is a quick emulsion sauce that by tradition is the centerpiece of a simple supper served with cooked vegetables and potatoes and steamed fish. When it's made badly, the overwhelming impression is one of garlic: bitter, sharp, and long-lasting. We found that fine, evenly minced garlic maintained the smooth texture of the sauce and prevented oversize garlic bombs that exploded in the mouth. A garlic press or rasp-style grater helped us achieve an acceptably fine mince. We also scaled back the quantity of garlic—a single clove provided a pleasant, not shocking, heat. Finally, we balanced the sour lemon juice with a little sugar and used mild regular olive oil instead of the traditional extra-virgin choice. Armed with a food processor, we whipped our aïoli together in just 30 seconds.

AïOLI
MAKES ABOUT ¾ CUP

Use this sauce as a condiment for meats, fish, and vegetables, or spread it on sandwiches. If necessary, remove the green germ (or stem) in the garlic before pressing or grating it; the germ will give the aïoli a bitter, hot flavor. If you do not have regular olive oil, use a blend of equal parts extra-virgin olive oil and vegetable oil. Ground white pepper is preferred because it's not as visible in the finished aïoli as black pepper, but either can be used.

1	garlic clove, peeled
2	large egg yolks
4	teaspoons lemon juice
⅛	teaspoon sugar
	Salt
	Ground white pepper (or black, if white is unavailable)
¾	cup olive oil

1. Press garlic through garlic press or grate very fine on rasp-style grater. Measure out 1 teaspoon garlic; discard remaining garlic.

2. Process garlic, egg yolks, lemon juice, sugar, ¼ teaspoon salt, and pepper to taste in food processor until combined, about 10 seconds. With food processor running, gradually add oil in slow steady stream (process should take about 30 seconds); scrape down sides of bowl with rubber spatula and process 5 seconds longer. Season with salt and pepper to taste and serve. (Aïoli can be refrigerated for up to 3 days.)

ROSEMARY-THYME AïOLI

Serve this robust aïoli with roasted and grilled meats or grilled vegetables.

Add 1 teaspoon chopped fresh rosemary and 1 teaspoon chopped fresh thyme to food processor with garlic.

SAFFRON AïOLI

Saffron aïoli is a nice accompaniment to fish and shellfish.

Combine ⅛ teaspoon saffron threads, crumbled, and 1 teaspoon boiling water in small bowl; let steep 10 minutes. Add saffron to food processor with garlic; transfer finished aïoli to bowl, cover with plastic wrap, and refrigerate at least 2 hours to allow saffron flavor to bloom. Stir before serving.

BASIL OR DILL AïOLI

This mellow herb-flavored aïoli pairs nicely with seafood or vegetables.

Stir 2 tablespoons minced fresh basil or 1 tablespoon minced fresh dill into aïoli just before serving.

ARUGULA SALAD

✔ WHY THIS RECIPE WORKS
Arugula has a lively, peppery bite and so for salad, it's important to choose accompaniments that can stand up to its assertive character. We found that the sweet and salty notes of fruits and cheeses work well as supporting players to arugula, and crunchy elements like nuts also provided a nice counterpoint. As for the dressing, a vinaigrette made with mustard alone turned out to be too spicy, but a surprise solution—a spoonful of jam—added fruity sweetness, pulling the flavors of the salad right in line.

ARUGULA SALAD WITH FIGS, PROSCIUTTO, WALNUTS, AND PARMESAN
SERVES 6

Although frying the prosciutto adds crisp texture to the salad, if you prefer, you can simply cut it into ribbons and use it as a garnish. Honey can be substituted for the raspberry jam.

¼	cup extra-virgin olive oil
2	ounces thinly sliced prosciutto, cut into ¼-inch-wide ribbons
3	tablespoons balsamic vinegar
1	tablespoon raspberry jam
½	cup dried figs, stemmed and chopped into ¼-inch pieces
1	small shallot, minced
	Salt and pepper
5	ounces (5 cups) baby arugula
½	cup walnuts, toasted and chopped
2	ounces Parmesan cheese, shaved into thin strips with vegetable peeler (1 cup)

1. Heat 1 tablespoon oil in 10-inch nonstick skillet over medium heat; add prosciutto and fry until crisp, stirring frequently, about 7 minutes. Using slotted spoon, transfer to paper towel–lined plate and set aside to let cool.

2. Whisk vinegar and jam in medium microwave-safe bowl; stir in figs. Cover with plastic wrap, cut several steam vents in plastic, and microwave on high until figs are plump, 30 seconds to 1 minute. Whisk in remaining 3 tablespoons oil, shallot, ¼ teaspoon salt, and ⅛ teaspoon pepper; toss to combine. Let cool to room temperature.

3. Toss arugula and vinaigrette in large bowl; season with salt and pepper to taste. Divide salad among individual plates; top each with portion of prosciutto, walnuts, and Parmesan. Serve immediately.

ARUGULA SALAD WITH GRAPES, FENNEL, GORGONZOLA, AND PECANS

SERVES 6

Honey can be substituted for the apricot jam.

- 3 tablespoons white wine vinegar
- 3 tablespoons extra-virgin olive oil
- 1 small shallot, minced
- 4 teaspoons apricot jam
  Salt and pepper
- ½ small fennel bulb, fronds chopped (¼ cup), stalks discarded, bulb sliced very thin (1 cup)
- 5 ounces (5 cups) baby arugula
- 6 ounces red seedless grapes, halved lengthwise (1 cup)
- 3 ounces Gorgonzola cheese, crumbled (¾ cup)
- ½ cup pecans, toasted and chopped

Whisk vinegar, oil, shallot, jam, ¼ teaspoon salt, and ¼ teaspoon pepper in large bowl. Toss fennel bulb with vinaigrette; let stand 15 minutes. Add arugula, fennel fronds, and grapes; toss and season with salt and pepper to taste. Divide salad among individual plates; top each with portion of Gorgonzola and pecans. Serve immediately.

ARUGULA SALAD WITH ORANGES, FETA, AND SUGARED PISTACHIOS

SERVES 6

The sugared pistachios can be made ahead and stored in an airtight container at room temperature. You can substitute an equal amount of roughly chopped toasted pistachios. Honey can be substituted for the marmalade.

SUGARED PISTACHIOS
- ½ cup shelled pistachios
- 1 large egg white, lightly beaten
- ⅓ cup sugar

SALAD
- 2 large oranges
- 3 tablespoons extra-virgin olive oil
- 2 tablespoons plus 2 teaspoons lemon juice
- 5 teaspoons orange marmalade
- 1 small shallot, minced
- 1 tablespoon minced fresh mint
  Salt and pepper
- 5 ounces (5 cups) baby arugula
- 3 ounces feta cheese, crumbled (¾ cup)

1. FOR THE SUGARED PISTACHIOS: Line 8-inch square baking pan with parchment paper. Adjust oven rack to middle position and heat oven to 325 degrees. Toss pistachios with egg white in small bowl. Using slotted spoon, transfer nuts to prepared baking pan; discard excess egg white. Add sugar and stir until nuts are completely coated. Bake, stirring mixture every 5 to 10 minutes, until coating turns nutty brown, 25 to 30 minutes. Transfer nuts to plate in single layer and let cool.

2. FOR THE SALAD: Peel oranges, cut them into segments, then halve segments and drain to remove excess juice. Whisk oil, lemon juice, marmalade, shallot, mint, ¼ teaspoon salt, and ⅛ teaspoon pepper in large bowl. Add arugula and oranges; toss and season with salt and pepper to taste. Divide salad among individual plates; top each with portion of feta and sugared pistachios. Serve immediately.

ARUGULA SALAD WITH PEAR, ALMONDS, GOAT CHEESE, AND APRICOTS

SERVES 6

Honey can be substituted for the apricot jam.

- 3 tablespoons white wine vinegar
- 1 tablespoon apricot jam
- ½ cup dried apricots, chopped into ¼-inch pieces
- 3 tablespoons extra-virgin olive oil
- 1 small shallot, minced
- ¼ small red onion, sliced very thin
  Salt and pepper
- 5 ounces (5 cups) baby arugula
- 1 pear, halved, cored, and sliced into ¼-inch-thick slices
- ⅓ cup sliced almonds, toasted
- 3 ounces goat cheese, crumbled (¾ cup)

1. Whisk vinegar and jam in medium microwave-safe bowl; stir in apricots. Cover with plastic wrap, cut several steam vents in plastic, and microwave on high until apricots are plump, 30 seconds to 1 minute. Whisk in oil, shallot, onion, ¼ teaspoon salt, and ⅛ teaspoon pepper; toss to combine. Let cool to room temperature.

2. Toss arugula, pear, and vinaigrette in large bowl; season with salt and pepper to taste. Divide salad among individual plates; top each with portion of almonds and goat cheese. Serve immediately.

TEST KITCHEN TIP NO. 9 **CLEANING SALAD GREENS**

The first step in making any salad is cleaning the greens. Nothing ruins a salad faster than gritty leaves. Our favorite way to wash small amounts of lettuce is in the bowl of a salad spinner; larger amounts require a sink. Make sure there is ample room to swish the leaves around with your hands to rid them of dirt and sand. The dirt will loosen and sink to the bottom. Exceptionally dirty leaves (spinach and arugula often fall into this category) may take at least two changes of water. Do not run water directly from the faucet onto the greens, as the force of the water can bruise them. When you are satisfied that the leaves are grit-free, spin them dry in a salad spinner. Placing your salad spinner in the corner of the sink and pushing it down and against the walls increases your leverage by stabilizing the spinner. Greens must be quite dry; otherwise, the vinaigrette will slide off and taste diluted.

ROQUEFORT SALAD

✓ **WHY THIS RECIPE WORKS**

The intensity, complexity, and sophistication of blue cheese can overwhelm the flavors of an otherwise mild and subdued salad. We found that the blue cheese really shined in this salad when partnered with sweet, tart, bitter, and crunchy ingredients. As for the base of the salad, greens like bitter radicchio and peppery arugula mixed with milder lettuces provided the perfect contrast to the rich, sharp cheese. A good shot of vinegar gave necessary tartness to the dressing, and a spoonful of honey performed double duty, tempering the acidity of the vinegar and highlighting the saltiness of the cheese.

SALAD WITH APPLE, CELERY, HAZELNUTS, AND ROQUEFORT

SERVES 6

This salad features rich, creamy Roquefort. If you prefer to use a very mild and mellow blue cheese, we recommend Danish blue; if you prefer a sharp and piquant one, try Stilton. To remove the skins from the hazelnuts, rub the hot toasted nuts in a clean kitchen towel. Blanched slivered almonds can be substituted for the hazelnuts.

- 3 tablespoons cider vinegar
- 3 tablespoons extra-virgin olive oil
- 1 tablespoon honey
  Salt and pepper
- 1 Braeburn or Fuji apple, cored, halved, and sliced very thin
- 2 celery ribs, sliced very thin on bias
- 1 head red or green leaf lettuce (12 ounces), torn into bite-size pieces
- ¼ cup chopped parsley
- ½ cup hazelnuts, toasted, skinned, and chopped fine
- 6 ounces Roquefort cheese, crumbled (1½ cups)

1. Whisk vinegar, oil, honey, ¼ teaspoon salt, and ⅛ teaspoon pepper in small bowl until combined. In medium bowl, toss apple and celery with 2 tablespoons vinaigrette; let stand 5 minutes.

2. Toss lettuce, parsley, and remaining vinaigrette in large bowl; season with salt and pepper to taste. Divide greens among individual plates; top each with portion of apple mixture, nuts, and Roquefort. Serve immediately.

SALAD WITH FENNEL, DRIED CHERRIES, WALNUTS, AND ROQUEFORT

SERVES 6

This salad features rich, creamy Roquefort. If you prefer to use a very mild and mellow blue cheese, we recommend Danish blue; if you prefer a sharp and piquant one, try Stilton.

- 3 tablespoons red wine vinegar
- 2 teaspoons honey
- ½ cup dried sweet cherries or cranberries
- 3 tablespoons extra-virgin olive oil
  Salt and pepper
- 1 small fennel bulb, fronds chopped (¼ cup), stalks discarded, bulb sliced very thin (1 cup)
- 1 small head red or green leaf lettuce (8 ounces), torn into bite-size pieces
- 1 small head radicchio (6 ounces), quartered, cored, and cut crosswise into ⅛-inch-wide strips
- ½ cup walnuts, toasted and chopped
- 6 ounces Roquefort cheese, crumbled (1½ cups)

1. Whisk vinegar and honey in medium microwave-safe bowl; stir in cherries. Cover with plastic wrap, cut several steam vents in plastic, and microwave on high until cherries are plump, about 1 minute. Whisk in oil, ¼ teaspoon salt, and ⅛ teaspoon pepper; while mixture is still warm, add sliced fennel bulb and toss to combine. Let cool to room temperature.

2. Toss lettuce, radicchio, fennel fronds, and dried cherry mixture in large bowl; season to taste with salt and pepper. Divide salad among individual plates; top each with portion of nuts and Roquefort. Serve immediately.

SALAD WITH ROASTED BEETS, FRIED SHALLOTS, AND ROQUEFORT

SERVES 6

This salad features rich, creamy Roquefort. If you prefer to use a very mild and mellow blue cheese, we recommend Danish blue; if you prefer a sharp and piquant one, try Stilton. Use paper towels to rub the skins from the cooked and cooled beets.

- 12 ounces beets, trimmed
- 3 shallots, sliced thin and separated into rings (1 cup)
- 2 tablespoons all-purpose flour
  Salt and pepper
- 6 tablespoons extra-virgin olive oil
- 2 tablespoons sherry vinegar
- 2 teaspoons honey
- 6 ounces (6 cups) baby arugula
- 1 head Boston or Bibb lettuce (8 ounces), torn into bite-size pieces
- 6 ounces Roquefort cheese, crumbled (1½ cups)

1. Adjust oven rack to lower-middle position; heat oven to 400 degrees. Wrap each beet in aluminum foil and roast until paring knife can be inserted and removed with little resistance, 50 to 60 minutes. Unwrap beets; when cool enough to handle, peel and cut beets into ¼-inch-thick wedges and place in medium bowl.

2. While beets are roasting, toss shallots with flour, ¼ teaspoon salt, and ⅛ teaspoon pepper in medium bowl. Heat 3 tablespoons oil in 12-inch nonstick skillet over medium-high heat until just smoking; add shallots and cook, stirring frequently, until golden and crisped, about 5 minutes.

Using slotted spoon, transfer shallots to paper towel–lined plate.

3. Whisk remaining 3 tablespoons oil, vinegar, honey, ¼ teaspoon salt, and ⅛ teaspoon pepper in small bowl until combined. Add 1 tablespoon vinaigrette to beets, season beets with salt and pepper to taste, and toss to combine.

4. Toss arugula, lettuce, and remaining vinaigrette in large bowl; season with salt and pepper to taste. Divide greens among individual plates; top each with portion of beets, fried shallots, and Roquefort. Serve immediately.

SALAD WITH AVOCADO, TOMATOES, BACON, AND ROQUEFORT

SERVES 6

This salad features rich, creamy Roquefort. If you prefer to use a very mild and mellow blue cheese, we recommend Danish blue; if you prefer a sharp and piquant one, try Stilton.

5   slices bacon, cut into ½-inch pieces
3   tablespoons red wine vinegar
3   tablespoons extra-virgin olive oil
    Salt and pepper
6   ounces cherry tomatoes, halved
1   avocado, halved, pitted, and cut into ¼-inch pieces
6   ounces (6 cups) baby arugula
1   head Boston or Bibb lettuce (8 ounces), torn into bite-size pieces
3   scallions, green parts only, sliced thin
6   ounces Roquefort cheese, crumbled (1½ cups)

1. Cook bacon in 10-inch skillet over medium heat until browned and crisped, 5 to 7 minutes; transfer with slotted spoon to paper towel–lined plate and set aside.

2. Whisk vinegar, oil, ¼ teaspoon salt, and ⅛ teaspoon pepper in small bowl until combined.

3. In medium bowl, toss tomatoes and avocado with 1 tablespoon vinaigrette; let sit 5 minutes.

4. Toss arugula, lettuce, and remaining vinaigrette in large bowl; season with salt and pepper to taste. Divide greens among individual plates; top each with portion of tomato mixture, then sprinkle with portion of bacon, scallions, and Roquefort. Serve immediately.

TEST KITCHEN TIP NO. 10 STORING SALAD GREENS

It's not unusual for the test kitchen fridge to be packed with salad greens. And although we try to work with the greens the day they arrive, it's not always a possibility. As a result, we've come up with a couple of storage tips for greens. First, remove any rubber band or tie from the greens. Constriction only encourages rotting. Gently wash the greens and spin them dry in a salad spinner. Then, depending on the type of greens, store them one of two ways:

For delicate greens, line an empty salad spinner with paper towels. Layer the dried greens in the bowl, covering each layer with additional towels, and refrigerate. Greens stored in this manner should keep for at least two days.

For sturdier greens, loosely roll the leaves in paper towels, then seal in a zipper-lock bag and refrigerate. Greens stored this way should keep for up to one week.

We applied our storage techniques to basil too, because recipes often call for just a few leaves. First, we found that it's essential not to wash the basil before storage. In our tests, washing basil before storage decreased its storage life by half. Instead, gently wrap unwashed basil in a damp paper towel. It should keep for up to one week.

CLASSIC CAESAR SALAD

✓ WHY THIS RECIPE WORKS

For our Caesar salad, we wanted crisp-tender romaine lettuce napped in a creamy, garlicky dressing boasting a pleasing salty undertone, with crunchy, savory croutons strewn throughout. To start, we cut the extra-virgin olive oil in the dressing with canola oil, which made for a less harsh flavor, and we used egg yolks instead of a whole egg to add richness. For a robust, though not aggressive, garlic flavor we grated the garlic into a pulp and then steeped it in lemon juice. Incorporating a portion of the Parmesan into the dressing while saving some to serve over the salad provided a double layer of cheese flavor. We preferred chewy, crisp ciabatta bread for our croutons and tossed them with a little water before frying them in a skillet until crisp. The water ensured the interiors stay moist and chewy while the exterior crisped. For a flavor boost, we tossed the croutons with a mixture of garlic, olive oil, and Parmesan. Tossed with slices of crisp romaine, our Caesar is better than ever.

CLASSIC CAESAR SALAD

SERVES 4 TO 6

If you can't find ciabatta, a similar crusty, rustic loaf of bread can be substituted. A quarter cup of Egg Beaters may be substituted for the egg yolks. Since anchovy fillets vary in size, more than 6 fillets may be necessary to yield 1 tablespoon of minced anchovies. The easiest way to turn garlic cloves into a paste is to grate them on a rasp-style grater.

CROUTONS

2   garlic cloves, peeled
5   tablespoons extra-virgin olive oil
½–¾   loaf ciabatta, cut into ¾-inch cubes (about 5 cups)
¼   cup water
¼   teaspoon salt
2   tablespoons finely grated Parmesan

SALAD

2–3 tablespoons lemon juice
2 large egg yolks
6 anchovy fillets, rinsed, patted dry,
minced, and mashed to paste
with fork (1 tablespoon)
½ teaspoon Worcestershire sauce
5 tablespoons canola oil
5 teaspoons extra-virgin olive oil
1½ ounces Parmesan, grated fine
(¾ cup)
Pepper
2–3 romaine lettuce hearts (12 to
18 ounces), cut into ¾-inch pieces,
rinsed, and dried

1. FOR THE CROUTONS: Press garlic through garlic press or grate very fine on rasp-style grater. Measure out ½ teaspoon garlic paste for croutons and ¾ teaspoon garlic paste for dressing (discard remaining garlic). Combine 1 tablespoon oil and ½ teaspoon garlic paste in small bowl; set aside. Place bread cubes in large bowl. Sprinkle with water and salt. Toss, squeezing gently so bread absorbs water. Place remaining 4 tablespoons oil and soaked bread cubes in 12-inch nonstick skillet. Cook over medium-high heat, stirring frequently, until browned and crisp, 7 to 10 minutes.

2. Remove skillet from heat, push croutons to sides of skillet to clear center; add garlic mixture to clearing and cook with residual heat of pan, 10 seconds. Sprinkle with Parmesan; toss until garlic and Parmesan are evenly distributed. Transfer croutons to bowl; set aside.

3. FOR THE SALAD: Whisk 2 tablespoons lemon juice and reserved ¾ teaspoon garlic paste together in large bowl. Let stand 10 minutes.

4. Whisk egg yolks, anchovies, and Worcestershire into garlic mixture. While whisking constantly, drizzle canola oil and olive oil into bowl in slow, steady stream until fully emulsified. Add ½ cup Parmesan and pepper to taste; whisk until incorporated.

5. Add romaine to dressing and toss to coat. Add croutons and mix gently until evenly distributed. Taste and season with up to additional 1 tablespoon lemon juice. Serve immediately, passing remaining ¼ cup Parmesan separately.

THAI BEEF SALAD

✓ WHY THIS RECIPE WORKS
This traditional Thai salad features slices of deeply charred steak tossed with thinly sliced shallots and handfuls of torn mint and cilantro in a bright, bracing dressing. We started on developing our own version at the grill, choosing flank steak for its generous marbling, beefy flavor, and moderate price. Grilling the steak over a modified two-level fire and flipping it just when moisture beaded on the surface yielded perfectly charred, juicy meat. Adding a fresh Thai chile and a mix of toasted cayenne and paprika gave the dressing a fruity, fiery heat. Toasted rice powder, a traditional tableside condiment that gives the dressing fuller body and a subtle crunch, is not widely available, but we found it easy enough to make our own.

GRILLED THAI BEEF SALAD
SERVES 4 TO 6

Serve with rice, if desired. If fresh Thai chiles are unavailable, substitute ½ serrano chile. Don't skip the toasted rice; it's integral to the texture and flavor of the dish. Any variety of white rice can be used. Toasted rice powder (kao kua) can also be found in many Asian markets; substitute 1 tablespoon rice powder for the white rice.

1 teaspoon paprika
1 teaspoon cayenne pepper
1 tablespoon white rice
3 tablespoons lime juice (2 limes)
2 tablespoons fish sauce
2 tablespoons water
½ teaspoon sugar
1 (1½-pound) flank steak, trimmed

Salt and coarsely ground white
pepper
4 shallots, sliced thin
1½ cups fresh mint leaves, torn
1½ cups fresh cilantro leaves
1 Thai chile, stemmed, seeded, and
sliced thin into rounds
1 seedless English cucumber,
sliced ¼ inch thick on bias

1. Heat paprika and cayenne in 8-inch skillet over medium heat; cook, shaking pan, until fragrant, about 1 minute. Transfer to small bowl. Return skillet to medium-high heat, add rice and toast, stirring constantly, until deep golden brown, about 5 minutes. Transfer to small bowl and let cool 5 minutes. Grind rice with spice grinder, mini food processor, or mortar and pestle until it resembles fine meal, 10 to 30 seconds (you should have about 1 tablespoon rice powder).

2. Whisk lime juice, fish sauce, water, sugar, and ¼ teaspoon toasted paprika mixture in large bowl and set aside.

3A. FOR A CHARCOAL GRILL: Open bottom vent completely. Light large chimney starter filled with charcoal briquettes (6 quarts). When top coals are partially covered with ash, pour in even layer over half of grill. Set cooking grate in place, cover, and open lid vent completely. Heat grill until hot, about 5 minutes.

3B. FOR A GAS GRILL: Turn all burners to high, cover, and heat grill until hot, about 15 minutes. Leave primary burner on high and turn off other burner(s).

4. Clean and oil grate. Season steak with salt and pepper. Place steak on grate over hot part of grill and cook until beginning to char and beads of moisture appear on outer edges of meat, 5 to 6 minutes. Flip steak, continue to cook on second side until meat registers 125 degrees, about 5 minutes longer. Transfer to carving board, tent loosely with aluminum foil, and rest for 10 minutes (or allow to cool to room temperature, about 1 hour).

5. Line large platter with cucumber slices. Slice meat, against grain, on bias, into ¼-inch thick slices. Transfer sliced steak to bowl with fish sauce mixture, add shallots, mint, cilantro, chile, and half of rice powder, and toss to combine. Arrange steak over cucumber-lined platter. Serve, passing remaining rice powder and toasted paprika mixture separately.

GREEK SALAD

✔ **WHY THIS RECIPE WORKS**
Most versions of Greek salad consist of iceberg lettuce, chunks of green pepper, and a few pale wedges of tomato, sparsely dotted with cubes of feta and garnished with one forlorn olive of questionable heritage. For our Greek salad, we aimed a little higher: we wanted a salad with crisp ingredients and bold flavors, highlighted by briny olives and tangy feta, all blended together with a bright-tasting dressing infused with fresh herbs. For a dressing with balanced flavor, we used a combination of lemon juice and red wine vinegar and added fresh oregano, olive oil, and a small amount of garlic. We poured the dressing over fresh vegetables, including romaine lettuce, tomatoes, onions, and cucumbers, as well as other ingredients, including fresh mint and parsley, roasted peppers, and a generous sprinkling of feta cheese and olives. Marinating the onion and cucumber in the vinaigrette tones down the onion's harshness and flavors the cucumber.

GREEK SALAD
SERVES 6 TO 8

For the sake of efficiency, prepare the other salad ingredients while the onion and cucumber marinate.

VINAIGRETTE
- 6 tablespoons olive oil
- 3 tablespoons red wine vinegar
- 2 teaspoons minced fresh oregano
- 1½ teaspoons lemon juice
- 1 garlic clove, minced
- ½ teaspoon salt
- ⅛ teaspoon pepper

SALAD
- ½ red onion, sliced thin
- 1 cucumber, peeled, halved lengthwise, seeded, and cut into ⅛-inch-thick slices
- 2 romaine lettuce hearts (12 ounces), torn into 1½-inch pieces
- 2 large tomatoes, cored, seeded, and cut into 12 wedges
- ¼ cup chopped fresh parsley
- ¼ cup torn fresh mint
- 1 cup jarred roasted red peppers, rinsed, patted dry, and cut into 2 by ½-inch strips
- ½ cup large pitted kalamata olives, quartered lengthwise
- 5 ounces feta cheese, crumbled (1¼ cup)

1. FOR THE VINAIGRETTE: Whisk all ingredients in large bowl until combined. Add onion and cucumber to vinaigrette and toss; let stand 20 minutes.

2. FOR THE SALAD: Add romaine, tomatoes, parsley, mint, and peppers to bowl with onions and cucumbers; toss to coat with dressing.

3. Transfer salad to wide, shallow serving bowl or platter; sprinkle olives and feta over salad. Serve immediately.

COUNTRY-STYLE GREEK SALAD

This salad made without lettuce is known as "country" or "peasant" salad and is served throughout Greece. It's excellent with garden-ripe summer tomatoes.

Reduce red wine vinegar to 1½ tablespoons and lemon juice to 1 teaspoon in vinaigrette. Use 2 cucumbers, peeled, halved lengthwise, seeded, and cut into ⅛-inch-thick slices and 6 large tomatoes, cored, seeded, and cut into 12 wedges; omit romaine.

SALAD NIÇOISE

✔ **WHY THIS RECIPE WORKS**
The ideal salad niçoise should have well-dressed, well-seasoned components that complement rather than crowd one another. We paired fruity extra-virgin olive oil and lemon juice to create the base of the vinaigrette, then added fresh thyme, basil, and oregano, shallot, and Dijon mustard to deepen the flavor. We used only the finest tuna, vine-ripened tomatoes, butterhead lettuce, fresh green beans, freshly cooked eggs, and Red Bliss potatoes—and seasoned and dressed each component of the salad individually for great flavor in every forkful. Niçoise olives are a hallmark of salad niçoise. If they're not available, substitute another small, black, brined olive (do not use canned olives). Anchovies are another classic garnish, but they met with mixed reviews from our tasters, so they are optional. If you cannot find tuna packed in olive oil, substitute water-packed solid white tuna, not tuna packed in vegetable oil. Or use fresh tuna. For a grilled variation on our salad, we marinated tuna steaks in olive oil and then seasoned the tuna with salt and pepper before grilling them until they were medium-rare.

SALAD NIÇOISE
SERVES 6

Prepare all the vegetables before you begin cooking the potatoes and this salad will come together very easily. Try to buy potatoes that are about 2 inches in diameter. Compose the salad on your largest, widest, flattest serving platter. Do not blanket the bed of lettuce with the other ingredients; leave some space between the mounds of potatoes, tomatoes and onions, and beans so that leaves of lettuce peek through.

VINAIGRETTE
- ¾ cup extra-virgin olive oil
- ½ cup lemon juice (2 to 3 lemons)
- 1 shallot, minced
- 2 tablespoons minced fresh basil
- 1 tablespoon minced fresh thyme

2   teaspoons minced fresh oregano
1   teaspoon Dijon mustard
    Salt and pepper

    SALAD
1¼ pounds small new red potatoes,
    quartered
    Salt and pepper
2   tablespoons dry vermouth
2   heads Boston lettuce or Bibb
    lettuce (1 pound), torn into
    bite-size pieces
2   (6-ounce) cans olive oil–packed
    tuna, drained
3   small tomatoes, cored and
    cut into eighths
1   small red onion, sliced very thin
8   ounces green beans, trimmed and
    halved crosswise
4   Foolproof Hard-Cooked Eggs
    (page 534), peeled and quartered
¼   cup niçoise olives, pitted
10–12 anchovy fillets, rinsed (optional)
2   tablespoons capers, rinsed
    (optional)

1. FOR THE VINAIGRETTE: Whisk oil, lemon juice, shallot, basil, thyme, oregano, and mustard in medium bowl; season with salt and pepper to taste and set aside.

2. FOR THE SALAD: Bring potatoes and 4 quarts cold water to boil in large Dutch oven or stockpot over high heat. Add 1 tablespoon salt and cook until potatoes are tender when poked with paring knife, 5 to 8 minutes. With slotted spoon, gently transfer potatoes to medium bowl (do not discard boiling water). Toss warm potatoes with vermouth and salt and pepper to taste; let stand 1 minute. Toss in ¼ cup vinaigrette; set aside.

3. While potatoes cook, toss lettuce with ¼ cup vinaigrette in large bowl until coated. Arrange bed of lettuce on very large, flat serving platter. Place tuna in now-empty bowl and break up with fork. Add ½ cup vinaigrette and stir to combine; mound tuna in center of lettuce. Toss

tomatoes, onion, 3 tablespoons vinaigrette, and salt and pepper to taste in now-empty bowl; arrange tomato-onion mixture in mound at edge of lettuce bed. Arrange reserved potatoes in separate mound at edge of lettuce bed.

4. Return water to boil; add 1 tablespoon salt and green beans. Cook until tender but crisp, 3 to 5 minutes. Meanwhile, fill medium bowl with 1 quart water and 1 tray ice cubes. Drain beans, transfer to ice water, and let stand until just cool, about 30 seconds; dry beans well on triple layer of paper towels. Toss beans, 3 tablespoons vinaigrette, and salt and pepper to taste in now-empty bowl; arrange in separate mound at edge of lettuce bed.

5. Arrange eggs, olives, and anchovies, if using, in separate mounds at edge of lettuce bed. Drizzle eggs with remaining 2 tablespoons dressing, sprinkle entire salad with capers, if using, and serve immediately.

SALAD NIÇOISE WITH GRILLED FRESH TUNA

1. Combine two 8-ounce tuna steaks, each about ¾ inch thick, with 2 tablespoons olive oil in gallon-size zipper-lock bag; seal bag, place in refrigerator, and marinate, turning several times, for at least 1 hour or overnight. Remove tuna from bag, sprinkle with salt and pepper, and set aside.

2A. FOR A CHARCOAL GRILL: Open bottom vent completely. Light large chimney starter filled with charcoal briquettes (6 quarts). When top coals are partially covered with ash, pour evenly over half of grill. Set cooking grate in place, cover grill, and heat grill until hot, about 5 minutes.

2B. FOR A GAS GRILL: Turn all burners to high, cover, and heat grill until hot, about 15 minutes.

3. Clean grate. Lightly dip wad of paper towels in oil; holding wad with tongs, wipe grate. Continue to wipe grate with oiled paper towels, redipping towels in oil

between applications, until grate is black and glossy, 5 to 10 times. Grill fish (with lid down for gas grill) without moving until grill marks form and bottom surface is opaque, about 1½ minutes. Carefully flip, cooking until grill marks form on second side, about 1½ minutes longer for rare (opaque at perimeter and translucent red at center when checked with tip of paring knife) or 3 minutes for medium-rare (opaque at perimeter and reddish pink at center). Cut into ½-inch-thick slices. Substitute grilled tuna for canned tuna.

CHEF'S SALAD

✔ WHY THIS RECIPE WORKS
Ingredients for chef's salads are often haphazard and vague, resulting in bland, muddled flavors, while the procedures are often fussy, time-consuming, and ultimately self-defeating. We wanted a hearty green salad topped with boiled eggs, tomatoes, cold meats, and cheese bound together with a brightly flavored vinaigrette. For our ideal salad, we chose sturdy but mild greens like Bibb, romaine, and red- and green-leaf lettuces, which held their shape under the weight of the other components and stood up to the strong flavors of the meat and cheese. We also included a small amount of spicy greens, such as watercress or arugula, to add bite. We found that thick slices of meat and cheese nicely complemented the greens and that an acidic vinaigrette held its own among the rich components of the salad.

CHEF'S SALAD
SERVES 6 TO 8

At the deli counter, be sure to have the meats and cheeses sliced ¼ inch thick.

    VINAIGRETTE
6   tablespoons extra-virgin olive oil
3   tablespoons red wine vinegar
2   teaspoons minced shallot

1   garlic clove, minced
1   teaspoon minced fresh thyme
¼   teaspoon salt
⅛   teaspoon pepper

SALAD

1   cucumber, peeled, halved
    lengthwise, seeded, and sliced
    crosswise ¼ inch thick
2   heads leaf lettuce, washed, dried,
    and torn into bite-size pieces
    (about 3 quarts)
8   ounces (8 cups) baby arugula
6   ounces radishes, trimmed, halved,
    and sliced thin
12 ounces cherry tomatoes, halved or
    quartered if large
3   Foolproof Hard-Cooked Eggs
    (page 534), peeled and quartered
8   ounces deli ham, sliced ¼ inch thick
    and cut into 2-inch-long matchsticks
8   ounces deli turkey, sliced ¼ inch
    thick and cut into 2-inch-long
    matchsticks
8   ounces sharp cheddar cheese,
    sliced ¼ inch thick and cut into
    2-inch-long matchsticks
1½ cups Garlic Croutons (page 79)

1. FOR THE VINAIGRETTE: Whisk all ingredients in medium bowl until combined. Add cucumber to vinaigrette and toss; let stand 20 minutes.

2. FOR THE SALAD: Toss lettuce, arugula, and radishes in large, wide serving bowl. Add cucumbers and all but 1 tablespoon dressing and toss to combine. Season with salt and pepper to taste. Toss tomatoes in remaining dressing in bowl; arrange tomatoes around perimeter of greens. Arrange egg wedges in ring inside tomatoes and drizzle with any dressing in bowl. Arrange ham, turkey, and cheese over center of greens; sprinkle with croutons and serve immediately.

CHEF'S SALAD WITH FENNEL, ASIAGO, AND SALAMI

SERVES 6 TO 8

If you can't find water-packed artichoke hearts, use marinated artichoke hearts, but rinse and drain them before use. For this salad, opt for a mild, soft Asiago cheese that crumbles easily; avoid aged Asiago that has a hard, dry texture.

VINAIGRETTE

6   tablespoons extra-virgin olive oil
3   tablespoons balsamic vinegar
1   teaspoon minced garlic
¼   teaspoon salt
⅛   teaspoon pepper

SALAD

2   heads romaine lettuce
    (1½ pounds), torn into bite-size
    pieces
4   ounces (4 cups) watercress, torn
    into 2-inch pieces
1   small fennel bulb, stalks discarded,
    halved, cored, and sliced thin
½   cup chopped fresh parsley
1   cup jarred roasted red peppers,
    rinsed, patted dry, and cut
    crosswise into ½-inch-wide strips
1   (14-ounce) can artichoke hearts,
    drained and halved
8   ounces hard salami, sliced ¼ inch
    thick and cut into 2-inch-long
    matchsticks
8   ounces deli turkey, sliced ¼ inch
    thick and cut into 2-inch-long
    matchsticks
8   ounces Asiago cheese, crumbled
    (2 cups)
1½ cups Garlic Croutons (page 79)
½   cup pitted kalamata olives,
    chopped

1. FOR THE VINAIGRETTE: Whisk all ingredients in medium bowl until combined.

---

2. FOR THE SALAD: Toss romaine, watercress, fennel, and parsley in large serving bowl. Add all but 1 tablespoon dressing and toss to combine. Season with salt and pepper to taste. Toss peppers and artichokes in remaining dressing, then arrange around perimeter of greens. Arrange salami, turkey, and cheese over center of greens; top with croutons and olives. Serve immediately.

CHEF'S SALAD WITH SPINACH, CHICKEN, AND GOUDA

SERVES 6 TO 8

VINAIGRETTE

6   tablespoons extra-virgin olive oil
3   tablespoons sherry vinegar
2   teaspoons Dijon mustard
1   garlic clove, minced
¼   teaspoon salt
⅛   teaspoon pepper

SALAD

6   slices thick-cut bacon, cut into
    ¼-inch pieces
14 ounces (14 cups) flat-leaf spinach
1   small head radicchio (6 ounces),
    leaves separated and cut into
    ½-inch strips
1   Belgian endive (4 ounces), halved,
    cored, and cut crosswise into
    ½-inch strips (about 1 cup)
½   cup fresh basil leaves, torn into
    bite-size pieces
½   red onion, sliced very thin
2   avocados, halved, pitted, and cut
    into ½-inch pieces
8   ounces deli chicken breast,
    sliced ¼ inch thick and cut into
    2-inch-long matchsticks
8   ounces Gouda cheese (regular or
    smoked), sliced ¼ inch thick and
    cut into 2-inch-long matchsticks
1½ cups Garlic Croutons (page 79)

1. FOR THE VINAIGRETTE: Whisk all ingredients in medium bowl until combined.

2. FOR THE SALAD: Cook bacon in 10-inch skillet over medium heat, stirring occasionally, until crisp, 5 to 7 minutes. Transfer to paper towel–lined plate. Combine spinach, radicchio, endive, and basil in large serving bowl. Add onion and all but 1 tablespoon dressing and toss to combine. Season with salt and pepper to taste. Toss avocados in remaining dressing in bowl; arrange avocados around perimeter of greens. Arrange chicken and cheese over center of greens; sprinkle with bacon and croutons and serve immediately.

CHOPPED SALAD

✔ **WHY THIS RECIPE WORKS**

Chopped salads should be lively, thoughtfully chosen compositions of lettuce, vegetables, and perhaps fruit, cut into bite-size pieces, with supporting players like nuts and cheese contributing hearty flavors and textures. Too often, though, the salad is a bland mix of watery vegetables. To prevent the cut-up produce from exuding moisture, we turned to techniques like seeding cucumbers and quartering grape tomatoes before salting them to expose more surface area to the salt. An assertive combination of equal parts oil and vinegar delivered the bright acidic flavor we were looking for in our dressing. Briefly marinating the other ingredients in the dressing delivered an additional flavor boost.

FENNEL AND APPLE CHOPPED SALAD

SERVES 4

Pecans can be substituted for the walnuts. Good apple choices include Braeburn, Jonagold, and Red Delicious.

1 cucumber, peeled, halved lengthwise, seeded, and cut into ½-inch dice
 Salt and pepper
3 tablespoons extra-virgin olive oil
3 tablespoons white wine vinegar
1 fennel bulb, stalks discarded, halved, cored, and cut into ¼-inch dice
2 apples, cored and cut into ¼-inch dice
½ small red onion, chopped fine
¼ cup chopped fresh tarragon
1 romaine lettuce heart (6 ounces), cut into ½-inch pieces
½ cup walnuts, toasted and chopped
4 ounces goat cheese, crumbled (1 cup)

1. Combine cucumber and ½ teaspoon salt in colander set over bowl and let stand 15 minutes.

2. Whisk oil and vinegar together in large bowl. Add drained cucumber, fennel, apples, onion, and tarragon; toss and let stand at room temperature to blend flavors, 5 minutes.

3. Add romaine and walnuts; toss to combine. Season with salt and pepper to taste. Divide salad among plates; top each with some goat cheese and serve.

MEDITERRANEAN CHOPPED SALAD

SERVES 4

In-season cherry tomatoes can be substituted for the grape tomatoes.

1 cucumber, peeled, halved lengthwise, seeded, and cut into ½-inch dice
10 ounces grape tomatoes, quartered
 Salt and pepper
3 tablespoons extra-virgin olive oil
3 tablespoons red wine vinegar
1 garlic clove, minced
1 (15-ounce) can chickpeas, rinsed
½ cup pitted kalamata olives, chopped
½ small red onion, chopped fine
½ cup chopped fresh parsley
1 romaine lettuce heart (6 ounces), cut into ½-inch pieces
4 ounces feta cheese, crumbled (1 cup)

1. Combine cucumber, tomatoes, and 1 teaspoon salt in colander set over bowl and let stand 15 minutes.

2. Whisk oil, vinegar, and garlic together in large bowl. Add drained cucumber and tomatoes, chickpeas, olives, onion, and parsley; toss and let stand at room temperature to blend flavors, 5 minutes.

3. Add romaine and feta; toss to combine. Season with salt and pepper to taste and serve.

PEAR AND CRANBERRY CHOPPED SALAD

SERVES 4

If you prefer to use a very mild and mellow blue cheese, we recommend Danish blue; if you prefer a sharp and piquant one, try Stilton.

1 cucumber, peeled, halved lengthwise, seeded, and cut into ½-inch dice
 Salt and pepper
3 tablespoons extra-virgin olive oil
3 tablespoons sherry vinegar
1 red bell pepper, stemmed, seeded, and cut into ¼-inch pieces
1 ripe but firm pear cut into ¼-inch pieces
½ small red onion, chopped fine
½ cup dried cranberries
1 romaine lettuce heart (6 ounces), cut into ½-inch pieces
4 ounces blue cheese, crumbled (1 cup)
½ cup shelled pistachios, toasted and chopped

1. Combine cucumber and ½ teaspoon salt in colander set over bowl and let stand 15 minutes.

2. Whisk oil and vinegar together in large bowl. Add drained cucumber, bell pepper, pear, onion, and cranberries; toss and let stand at room temperature to blend flavors, 5 minutes.

3. Add romaine, blue cheese, and pistachios; toss to combine. Season with salt and pepper to taste and serve.

RADISH AND ORANGE CHOPPED SALAD
SERVES 4

Pepitas, or pumpkin seeds, are available at most supermarkets and natural foods stores. For more information on preparing the oranges, see page 50.

- 1 cucumber, peeled, halved lengthwise, seeded, and cut into ½-inch dice
  Salt and pepper
- 3 tablespoons extra-virgin olive oil
- 3 tablespoons lime juice (2 limes)
- 1 garlic clove, minced
- 2 oranges
- 10 radishes, halved and sliced thin
- 1 avocado, halved, pitted, and cut into ½-inch pieces
- ½ small red onion, chopped fine
- ½ cup fresh cilantro, chopped
- 1 romaine lettuce heart (6 ounces), cut into ½-inch pieces
- 3 ounces Manchego cheese, shredded (¾ cup)
- ½ cup unsalted pepitas, toasted

1. Combine cucumber and ½ teaspoon salt in colander set over bowl and let stand 15 minutes. Whisk oil, lime juice, and garlic together in large bowl.

2. Peel oranges, making sure to remove all pith, and cut into ½-inch pieces. Add oranges, drained cucumber, radishes, avocado, onion, and cilantro; toss and let stand at room temperature to blend flavors, 5 minutes.

3. Add lettuce, cheese, and pepitas; toss to combine. Season with salt and pepper to taste and serve.

COBB SALAD

✔ WHY THIS RECIPE WORKS
Cobb salad's classic vinaigrette dressing is both the tie that binds the dish together and its biggest problem. More often than not, the flavors are dull and muted, with the salad components either drowned in inch-deep puddles of liquid or sitting high and unhappily dry. We found that using Dijon mustard instead of dry powder and extra-virgin olive oil instead of the more common vegetable oil and water addition made a rich, well-seasoned dressing. Romaine lettuce gave our salad the best crunch and watercress added flavor. For greatest ease, we broiled the chicken breasts, used grape tomatoes instead of tasteless beefsteak tomatoes, and plenty of avocado and blue cheese. Finally, we dressed each ingredient separately before arranging them on a platter to ensure that each is perfectly seasoned.

CLASSIC COBB SALAD
SERVES 6 TO 8

You'll need a large platter or shallow wide pasta bowl to accommodate this substantial salad. Though watercress is traditional, feel free to substitute an equal amount of arugula, chicory, curly endive, or a mixture of assertive lettuce greens. Grape tomatoes are preferred, but cherry tomatoes can be used.

VINAIGRETTE
- ½ cup extra-virgin olive oil
- 2 tablespoons red wine vinegar
- 2 teaspoons lemon juice
- 1 teaspoon Worcestershire sauce
- 1 teaspoon Dijon mustard
- 1 garlic clove, minced
- ½ teaspoon salt
- ¼ teaspoon sugar
- ⅛ teaspoon pepper

SALAD
- 3 (6-ounce) boneless, skinless chicken breasts, trimmed
  Salt and pepper
- 1 large head romaine lettuce (14 ounces), torn into bite-size pieces
- 4 ounces (4 ounces) watercress, torn into bite-size pieces
- 10 ounces grape tomatoes, halved
- 3 Foolproof Hard-Cooked Eggs (page 534), peeled and cut into ½-inch cubes
- 2 avocados, halved, pitted, and cut into ½-inch pieces
- 8 slices bacon, cut into ¼-inch pieces, cooked in 10-inch skillet over medium heat until crisp, 5 to 7 minutes, and drained
- 2 ounces blue cheese, crumbled (½ cup)
- 3 tablespoons minced fresh chives

1. FOR THE VINAIGRETTE: Whisk all ingredients in medium bowl until well combined; set aside.

2. FOR THE SALAD: Season chicken with salt and pepper. Adjust oven rack to 6 inches from broiler element; heat

---

TEST KITCHEN TIP NO. 11 **TOASTING NUTS**

For nuts and seeds to contribute the most flavor, they need to be toasted. To toast a small amount (under 1 cup), put the nuts or seeds in a dry small skillet over medium heat. Shake the skillet occasionally to prevent scorching and toast until they are lightly browned and fragrant, 3 to 8 minutes. Watch closely since they can go from golden to burned very quickly.

broiler. Spray broiler-pan top with vegetable oil spray; place chicken breasts on top and broil chicken until lightly browned, 4 to 8 minutes. Using tongs, flip chicken over and continue to broil until thickest part is no longer pink when cut into and registers about 160 degrees, 6 to 8 minutes. When cool enough to handle, cut chicken into ½-inch cubes and set aside.

3. Toss romaine and watercress with 5 tablespoons vinaigrette in large bowl until coated; arrange on very large, flat serving platter. Place chicken in now-empty bowl, add ¼ cup vinaigrette and toss to coat; arrange in row along one edge of greens. Place tomatoes in now-empty bowl, add 1 tablespoon vinaigrette and toss gently to combine; arrange on opposite edge of greens. Arrange eggs and avocado in separate rows near center of greens and drizzle with remaining vinaigrette. Sprinkle bacon, cheese, and chives evenly over salad and serve immediately.

HERBED BAKED GOAT CHEESE SALAD

✔ WHY THIS RECIPE WORKS

Warm goat cheese salad, a French classic, can often misfire, being nothing more than flavorless warm cheese melted onto limp greens. We wanted creamy cheese infused with the flavor of fresh herbs and surrounded by crisp, golden breading, all cradled in lightly dressed greens. For cheese rounds with an exceptionally crisp crust, we found that white Melba toast crumbs beat out other contenders like fresh bread crumbs and other cracker crumbs. Freezing the breaded goat cheese rounds for 30 minutes before baking them in a hot oven ensured a crunchy coating and a smooth, but not melted, interior. Just like in the finest French bistros, we served our warm, breaded goat cheese on hearty greens, lightly dressed with a classic vinaigrette.

HERBED BAKED GOAT CHEESE
MAKES 12 ROUNDS

The baked goat cheese should be served warm.

3	ounces white Melba toasts (2 cups)
1	teaspoon pepper
3	large eggs
2	tablespoons Dijon mustard
1	tablespoon minced fresh thyme
1	tablespoon minced fresh chives
12	ounces goat cheese, firm
	Extra-virgin olive oil

1. Process Melba toasts in a food processor to fine even crumbs, about 1½ minutes; transfer crumbs to medium bowl and stir in pepper. Whisk eggs and mustard in medium bowl until combined. Combine thyme and chives in small bowl.

2. Using kitchen twine or dental floss, divide cheese into 12 evenly sized pieces. Roll each piece into a ball; roll each ball in herbs to coat lightly. Transfer 6 pieces to egg mixture, turn each piece to coat; transfer to Melba crumbs and turn each piece to coat, pressing crumbs into cheese. Flatten each ball into disk about 1½ inches wide and 1 inch thick and set on baking sheet. Repeat process with remaining 6 pieces cheese. Freeze cheese until firm, about 30 minutes. (Cheese may be wrapped tightly in plastic wrap and frozen for 1 week.) Adjust oven rack to top position; heat oven to 475 degrees.

3. Remove cheese from freezer and brush tops and sides evenly with olive oil. Bake until crumbs are golden brown and cheese is slightly soft, 7 to 9 minutes (or 9 to 12 minutes if cheese is completely frozen). Using thin metal spatula, transfer cheese to paper towel–lined plate and let cool 3 minutes before serving on top of greens.

SALAD WITH HERBED BAKED GOAT CHEESE AND VINAIGRETTE
SERVES 6

Prepare the salad components while the cheese is in the freezer, then toss the greens and vinaigrette while the cheese cools a bit after baking. Hearty salad greens, such as a mix of arugula and frisée, work best here.

2	tablespoons red wine vinegar
1	tablespoon Dijon mustard
1	teaspoon minced shallot
¼	teaspoon salt
6	tablespoons extra-virgin olive oil
	Pepper
14	ounces (14 cups) mixed hearty salad greens
1	recipe Herbed Baked Goat Cheese

1. Combine vinegar, mustard, shallot, and salt in small bowl. Whisking constantly, drizzle in oil; season with pepper to taste.

2. Place greens in large bowl, drizzle vinaigrette over, and toss to coat. Divide greens among individual plates; place 2 rounds warm goat cheese on each salad. Serve immediately.

SALAD WITH APPLES, WALNUTS, DRIED CHERRIES, AND HERBED BAKED GOAT CHEESE
SERVES 6

Prepare the salad components while the cheese is in the freezer, then toss the greens and vinaigrette while the cheese cools a bit after baking. Hearty salad greens, such as a mix of arugula and frisée, work best here.

1	cup dried cherries
2	tablespoons cider vinegar
1	tablespoon Dijon mustard
1	teaspoon minced shallot
¼	teaspoon salt
¼	teaspoon sugar

6   tablespoons extra-virgin olive oil
     Pepper
14   ounces (14 cups) mixed hearty
     salad greens
2   Granny Smith apples, cored,
     quartered, and cut into ⅛-inch-
     thick slices
½   cup walnuts, toasted and chopped
1   recipe Herbed Baked Goat Cheese
     (page 41)

1. Plump cherries in ½ cup hot water in small bowl, about 10 minutes; drain.

2. Combine vinegar, mustard, shallot, salt, and sugar in small bowl. Whisking constantly, drizzle in oil; season with pepper to taste. Place greens in large bowl, drizzle vinaigrette over, and toss to coat. Divide greens among individual plates; divide cherries, apples, and walnuts among plates; and place 2 rounds goat cheese on each salad. Serve immediately.

SALAD WITH GRAPES, PINE NUTS, PROSCIUTTO, AND HERBED BAKED GOAT CHEESE

SERVES 6

Prepare the salad components while the cheese is in the freezer, then toss the greens and vinaigrette while the cheese cools a bit after baking. Hearty salad greens, such as a mix of arugula and frisée, work best here.

2   tablespoons balsamic vinegar
1   tablespoon Dijon mustard
1   teaspoon minced shallot
¼   teaspoon salt
6   tablespoons extra-virgin olive oil
     Pepper
14   ounces (14 cups) mixed hearty
     salad greens
1¼   cups red seedless grapes, halved
½   cup pine nuts, toasted
6   ounces thinly sliced prosciutto
1   recipe Herbed Baked Goat Cheese
     (page 41)

Combine vinegar, mustard, shallot, and salt in small bowl. Whisking constantly, drizzle in oil; season with pepper to taste. Place greens in large bowl, drizzle vinaigrette over, and toss to coat. Divide greens among individual plates; divide grapes and pine nuts among plates; and arrange 2 slices prosciutto and 2 rounds goat cheese on each salad. Serve immediately.

FRESH SPINACH SALAD

✔ WHY THIS RECIPE WORKS

With such smooth and flat leaves, baby spinach tends to stick together in salad. We knew that we needed a sturdier element to break up the leaves, but we wanted one that wouldn't overwhelm the spinach. The first step was rethinking our knife work. Thinly slicing the vegetables (or at least tearing them into pieces) allowed us to use harder, more crisp produce, such as carrots. In addition to fluffing up the spinach, carrots worked in welcome crunch and sweetness. We also reasoned that fresh fruit would add bright, clean flavors and textural appeal. For the dressing, we altered the oil-to-acid ratio of our Foolproof Vinaigrette (page 28) until it was tangy enough to bring out the fruit's natural acidity.

FRESH SPINACH SALAD WITH CARROT, ORANGE, AND SESAME

SERVES 6

---

6   ounces (6 cups) baby spinach
2   carrots, peeled and shaved with
     vegetable peeler lengthwise into
     ribbons
2   oranges, ½ teaspoon finely grated
     zest from one, both peeled and
     segmented
2   scallions, sliced thin
7   teaspoons rice vinegar
1   small shallot, minced
1   teaspoon Dijon mustard

¾   teaspoon mayonnaise
¼   teaspoon salt
3   tablespoons vegetable oil
1½   tablespoons toasted sesame oil
1   tablespoon sesame seeds, toasted

1. Place spinach, carrots, orange segments, and scallions in large bowl.

2. Combine orange zest, vinegar, shallot, mustard, mayonnaise, and salt in small bowl. Whisk until mixture appears milky and no lumps remain. Place vegetable oil and sesame oil in liquid measuring cup. Whisking constantly, very slowly drizzle oils into mixture. If pools of oil gather on surface, stop addition of oils and whisk mixture well to combine, then resume whisking in oils in slow stream. Vinaigrette should be glossy and lightly thickened.

3. Pour dressing over spinach mixture and toss to coat; sprinkle with sesame seeds and serve immediately.

FRESH SPINACH SALAD WITH FENNEL AND APPLES

SERVES 6

Fuji apples are also good in place of Golden Delicious in this salad.

6   ounces (6 cups) baby spinach
1   fennel bulb, fronds minced and
     ¼ cup reserved, stalks discarded,
     bulb halved, cored, and sliced thin
2   Golden Delicious apples, cored and
     cut into 1-inch-long matchsticks
1½   teaspoons finely grated lemon zest
     plus 7 teaspoons juice
1   small shallot, minced
1   tablespoon whole grain mustard
¾   teaspoon mayonnaise
¼   teaspoon salt
4½   tablespoons extra-virgin olive oil

1. Place spinach, fennel, fennel fronds, and apples in large bowl.

2. Combine lemon zest and juice,

shallot, mustard, mayonnaise, and salt in small bowl. Whisk until mixture appears milky and no lumps remain. Place oil in liquid measuring cup. Whisking constantly, very slowly drizzle oil into mixture. If pools of oil gather on surface, stop addition of oil and whisk mixture well to combine, then resume whisking in oil in slow stream. Vinaigrette should be glossy and lightly thickened.

3. Pour dressing over spinach mixture and toss to coat. Serve immediately.

FRESH SPINACH SALAD WITH FRISÉE AND STRAWBERRIES

SERVES 6

This salad is best when made with in-season strawberries.

6	ounces (6 cups) baby spinach
1	head frisée (6 ounces) torn into 2-inch pieces
10	ounces strawberries, hulled and quartered (2 cups)
2	tablespoons chopped fresh basil
7	teaspoons balsamic vinegar
1	small shallot, minced
1	teaspoon Dijon mustard
¾	teaspoon mayonnaise
¼	teaspoon salt
½	teaspoon pepper
4½	tablespoons extra-virgin olive oil

1. Place spinach, frisée, strawberries, and basil in large bowl.

2. Combine vinegar, shallot, mustard, mayonnaise, salt, and pepper in small bowl. Whisk until mixture appears milky and no lumps remain. Place oil in liquid measuring cup. Whisking constantly, very slowly drizzle oil into mixture. If pools of oil gather on surface, stop addition of oil and whisk mixture well to combine, then resume whisking in oil in slow stream. Vinaigrette should be glossy and lightly thickened.

3. Pour dressing over spinach mixture and toss to coat. Serve immediately.

FRESH SPINACH SALAD WITH RADICCHIO AND MANGO

SERVES 6

This salad is especially good paired with grilled foods.

6	ounces (6 cups) baby spinach
1	small head radicchio (6 ounces), halved, cored, and sliced very thin
1	mango, peeled and cut into ½-inch pieces
¼	cup chopped fresh cilantro
1	teaspoon finely grated lime zest plus 7 teaspoons juice
1	tablespoon honey
1	small shallot, minced
1	teaspoon Dijon mustard
¾	teaspoon mayonnaise
¼	teaspoon salt
4½	tablespoons extra-virgin olive oil

1. Place spinach, radicchio, mango, and cilantro in large bowl.

2. Combine lime zest and juice, honey, shallot, mustard, mayonnaise, and salt in small bowl. Whisk until mixture appears milky and no lumps remain. Place oil in liquid measuring cup so it is easy to pour. Whisking constantly, very slowly drizzle oil into mixture. If pools of oil gather on surface, stop addition of oil and whisk mixture well to combine, then resume whisking in oil in slow stream. Vinaigrette should be glossy and lightly thickened.

3. Pour dressing over spinach mixture and toss to coat. Serve immediately.

WILTED SPINACH SALAD

✔ WHY THIS RECIPE WORKS

For a wilted spinach salad with bright flavors and a tender texture, we started with baby spinach. Thickly cut bacon added presence to our salad, and hard-cooked eggs, cut into wedges, formed a natural partnership with the bacon and added a hearty element. Dressing made with bacon drippings had a rich flavor, and a combination of 3 tablespoons each of bacon fat and vinegar was perfect. The warm dressing is often used to wilt the spinach, but a heavy hand can lead to a swampy salad. We were able to cut back on the dressing by adding sautéed onions to the salad—they not only added another layer of sweet/savory flavor but also enough volume and heat to wilt the spinach without ruining its texture.

WILTED SPINACH SALAD WITH WARM BACON DRESSING

SERVES 4 TO 6

This salad comes together quickly, so have the ingredients ready before you begin cooking. When adding the vinegar mixture to the skillet, step back from the stovetop—the aroma is quite potent.

6	ounces (6 cups) baby spinach
3	tablespoons cider vinegar
½	teaspoon sugar
¼	teaspoon pepper
	Pinch salt
8	slices thick-cut bacon, cut into ½-inch pieces
½	red onion, chopped medium
1	small garlic clove, minced
3	Foolproof Hard-Cooked Eggs (page 534), peeled and quartered

---

TEST KITCHEN TIP NO. 12 **STORING LEFTOVER SPINACH**

We call for specific sizes of bags or packages of baby spinach when it works for a recipe, but sometimes you might not find that particular size. If you have leftover spinach, make sure to store it in its original bag and fold the opened end over and tape it shut. These specially designed breathable bags keep the spinach fresh as long as possible; if you transfer the spinach to a sealed airtight bag, it will spoil prematurely.

1. Place spinach in large bowl. Stir vinegar, sugar, pepper, and salt together in small bowl until sugar dissolves; set aside.

2. Cook bacon in 10-inch skillet over medium-high heat, stirring occasionally, until crisp, about 5 minutes. Using slotted spoon, transfer bacon to paper towel–lined plate. Pour fat into heatproof bowl, then return 3 tablespoons fat to skillet. Add onion to skillet and cook over medium heat, stirring frequently, until slightly softened, about 3 minutes; stir in garlic until fragrant, about 15 seconds. Add vinegar mixture, then remove skillet from heat; working quickly, scrape bottom of skillet with wooden spoon to loosen browned bits. Pour hot dressing over spinach, add bacon, and toss gently with tongs until spinach is slightly wilted. Divide among individual plates, arrange egg quarters over each, and serve.

CUCUMBER SALAD

WHY THIS RECIPE WORKS
Cucumbers can make a cool, crisp salad, but often they turn soggy from their own moisture. For a cucumber salad with good crunch, we found that weighting salted cucumbers forced more water from them than salting alone. After many tests, we determined that 1 to 3 hours worked best: Even at 12 hours, the cucumbers gave up no more water than they had after 3 hours. For a bit of zip, we like pairing cucumbers with onion—and found that salting and draining the onion along with the cucumbers removes its sharp sting. Whether we dressed them with a lively vinaigrette or rich, creamy dressing, our cucumbers retained maximum crunch.

CREAMY DILL CUCUMBER SALAD
SERVES 4

Fresh dill is essential to the flavor of this salad; do not substitute dried.

3	cucumbers (2 pounds), peeled, halved lengthwise, seeded, and sliced ¼ inch thick
1	small red onion, sliced very thin
1	tablespoon salt
1	cup sour cream
3	tablespoons cider vinegar
1	teaspoon sugar
¼	cup minced fresh dill

1. Toss cucumber and onion with salt in colander set over large bowl. Weight cucumbers with gallon-size zipper-lock bag filled with water; drain for 1 to 3 hours. Rinse and pat dry.

2. Whisk remaining ingredients together in medium bowl. Add cucumbers and onion; toss to coat. Serve chilled.

YOGURT-MINT CUCUMBER SALAD
SERVES 4

3	cucumbers (2 pounds), peeled, halved lengthwise, seeded, and sliced ¼ inch thick
1	small red onion, sliced very thin
	Salt and pepper
1	cup plain low-fat yogurt
2	tablespoons extra-virgin olive oil
¼	cup minced fresh mint
1	garlic clove, minced
½	teaspoon ground cumin

1. Toss cucumber and onion with 1 tablespoon salt in colander set over large bowl. Weight cucumbers with gallon-size zipper-lock bag filled with water; drain for 1 to 3 hours. Rinse and pat dry.

2. Whisk yogurt, oil, mint, garlic, cumin, and salt and pepper to taste in medium bowl. Add cucumbers and onion; toss to coat. Serve chilled.

SESAME LEMON CUCUMBER SALAD
SERVES 4

3	cucumbers (2 pounds), peeled, halved lengthwise, seeded, and sliced ¼ inch thick
1	tablespoon salt
¼	cup rice vinegar
1	tablespoon lemon juice
2	tablespoons toasted sesame oil
2	teaspoons sugar
⅛	teaspoon red pepper flakes, plus more to taste
1	tablespoon sesame seeds, toasted

1. Toss cucumber with salt in colander set over large bowl. Weight cucumbers with gallon-size zipper-lock bag filled with water; drain for 1 to 3 hours. Rinse and pat dry.

2. Whisk remaining ingredients together in medium bowl. Add cucumbers; toss to coat. Serve chilled or at room temperature.

SWEET-AND-TART CUCUMBER SALAD
SERVES 4

Based on a common Thai relish served with sautés, this salad is also great with grilled salmon or grilled chicken breasts.

3	cucumbers (2 pounds), peeled, halved lengthwise, seeded, and sliced ¼ inch thick
½	red onion, sliced very thin
1	tablespoon salt
½	cup rice vinegar
2½	tablespoons sugar
2	small jalapeño chiles, seeded and minced (or more, to taste)

1. Toss cucumber and onion with salt in colander set over large bowl. Weight cucumbers with gallon-size zipper-lock bag filled with water; drain for 1 to 3 hours. Rinse and pat dry.

2. Bring ⅔ cup water and vinegar to boil in small nonreactive saucepan over medium heat. Stir in sugar to dissolve; reduce heat and simmer 15 minutes. Let cool to room temperature.

3. Meanwhile, mix cucumbers, onion, and jalapeños in medium bowl. Pour dressing over cucumber mixture; toss to coat. Serve chilled.

CHERRY TOMATO SALAD

✔ WHY THIS RECIPE WORKS
Cherry tomatoes can make a great salad but they often exude lots of liquid when cut, quickly turning a salad into soup. To get rid of some of the tomato juice without throwing away flavor, we quartered, salted, and drained the tomatoes before whirling them in a salad spinner to separate the seeds and jelly from the flesh. After we strained and discarded the seeds, we reduced the jelly to a flavorful concentrate (adding garlic, oregano, shallot, olive oil, and vinegar) and reunited it with the tomatoes. Cheese adds richness and another layer of flavor to this great all-season salad.

GREEK CHERRY TOMATO SALAD

SERVES 4 TO 6

If in-season cherry tomatoes are unavailable, substitute vine-ripened cherry tomatoes or grape tomatoes. Cut grape tomatoes in half along the equator (rather than quartering them). If you don't have a salad spinner, after the salted tomatoes have stood for 30 minutes, wrap the bowl tightly with plastic wrap and gently shake to remove seeds and excess liquid. Strain the liquid and proceed with the recipe as directed. The amount of liquid given off by the tomatoes will depend on their ripeness. If you have less

than ½ cup of juice after spinning, proceed with the recipe using the entire amount of juice and reduce it to 3 tablespoons as directed (the cooking time will be shorter).

1½	pounds cherry tomatoes, quartered
	Salt and pepper
½	teaspoon sugar
2	garlic cloves, minced
½	teaspoon dried oregano
1	shallot, minced
1	tablespoon red wine vinegar
2	tablespoons extra-virgin olive oil
1	small cucumber, peeled, halved lengthwise, seeded, and cut into ½-inch dice
½	cup chopped pitted kalamata olives
4	ounces feta cheese, crumbled (1 cup)
3	tablespoons chopped fresh parsley

1. Toss tomatoes, ¼ teaspoon salt, and sugar in medium bowl; let stand for 30 minutes. Transfer tomatoes to salad spinner and spin until seeds and excess liquid have been removed, 45 to 60 seconds, stirring to redistribute tomatoes several times during spinning. Return tomatoes to bowl and set aside. Strain tomato liquid through fine-mesh strainer into liquid measuring cup, pressing on solids to extract as much liquid as possible.

2. Bring ½ cup tomato liquid (discard any extra), garlic, oregano, shallot, and vinegar to simmer in small saucepan over medium heat. Simmer until reduced to 3 tablespoons, 6 to 8 minutes. Transfer mixture to small bowl and let cool to

room temperature, about 5 minutes. Whisk in oil and pepper to taste until combined. Taste and season with up to ⅛ teaspoon salt.

3. Add cucumber, olives, feta, dressing, and parsley to bowl with tomatoes; toss gently and serve.

CHERRY TOMATO SALAD WITH BASIL AND FRESH MOZZARELLA

Substitute balsamic vinegar for red wine vinegar and omit garlic and oregano in step 2. Substitute 1½ cups fresh basil leaves, roughly torn, and 8 ounces fresh mozzarella, cut into ½-inch cubes and patted dry with paper towels, for cucumber, olives, feta, and parsley in step 3.

CHERRY TOMATO SALAD WITH TARRAGON AND BLUE CHEESE

Substitute cider vinegar for red wine vinegar, omit garlic and oregano, and add 2 teaspoons Dijon mustard and 4 teaspoons honey to tomato liquid in step 2. Substitute ½ cup roughly chopped toasted pecans, 2 ounces crumbled blue cheese, and 1½ tablespoons chopped fresh tarragon leaves for cucumber, olives, feta, and parsley in step 3.

CHERRY TOMATO SALAD WITH WATERMELON AND FETA CHEESE

Substitute white wine vinegar for red wine vinegar, omit garlic and oregano, and substitute vegetable oil for olive oil in step 2.

TEST KITCHEN TIP NO. 13　FETA CHEESE

Within the European Union, only cheese made in Greece from a mixture of sheep's and goat's milk can be legally called feta, but most of the feta in American supermarkets is made from pasteurized cow's milk that has been curdled, shaped into blocks, sliced (feta is Greek for "slice"), and steeped in a brine. Feta can range from soft to semihard and has a tangy, salty flavor. Feta dries out quickly when removed from its brine, so always store feta in the brine in which it is packed, and never buy the blocks sold shrinkwrapped on the Styrofoam tray packaged without brine. It's a good idea to rinse feta packed in brine just before serving to remove excess salt.

Substitute 1 cup watermelon, cut into ½-inch cubes, and 3 tablespoons chopped fresh mint for cucumber, olives, and parsley in step 3.

CHERRY TOMATO SALAD WITH MANGO AND LIME CURRY VINAIGRETTE

Substitute 4 teaspoons fresh lime juice and ¼ teaspoon curry powder for garlic and oregano in step 2. Substitute 1 mango, peeled, pitted, and cut into ½-inch dice, ½ cup toasted slivered almonds, and 3 tablespoons chopped fresh cilantro for cucumber, olives, and parsley in step 3.

PITA BREAD SALAD

✔ **WHY THIS RECIPE WORKS**
Traditionally, Mediterranean bread salads like fattoush consist of small bites of days-old pita bread mixed with cucumbers and tomatoes and dressed with lemon juice and fruity olive oil. The dry bread should hold up to the dressing and vegetables without becoming soggy. To prevent the bread from turning soggy under the vinaigrette, we crisped the already dried bread in the oven. We also salted and drained the cucumbers to rid them of liquid and ensure they stayed crisp and flavorful. A lemony vinaigrette with a generous amount of mint and cilantro kept the flavors in the salad fresh and bright.

PITA BREAD SALAD WITH CUCUMBERS, CHERRY TOMATOES, AND FRESH HERBS

SERVES 6

This simple version of fattoush is dressed with the juice of fresh lemons instead of vinegar, which gives the salad a lovely, refreshing tartness. While draining the cucumbers is an extra step, it keeps the salad from becoming soggy.

1	cucumber, peeled, halved lengthwise, seeded, and cut into ¼-inch dice
	Salt and pepper
4	(6-inch) pita breads, several days old, torn into ½-inch pieces
12	ounces cherry tomatoes, halved
6	scallions, whites and 2 inches of greens, sliced thin
¼	cup minced fresh mint
¼	cup minced fresh cilantro or parsley
½	cup extra-virgin olive oil
6	tablespoons lemon juice (2 lemons)

1. Heat oven to 375 degrees. Put cucumber in colander; sprinkle with ¼ teaspoon salt. Weight cucumbers with gallon-size zipper-lock bag filled with water; drain to release most of liquid, about 30 minutes. Rinse and pat dry.

2. Put bread pieces on baking sheet; bake until crisp but not browned, 5 to 7 minutes. Transfer to large bowl; add cucumber, tomatoes, scallions, and herbs, and toss well. In small bowl, combine oil and lemon juice and salt and pepper to taste. Add to large bowl, toss again, and serve immediately.

ITALIAN BREAD SALAD

✔ **WHY THIS RECIPE WORKS**
When the rustic Italian bread salad, panzanella, is done well, the sweet juice of the tomatoes mixes with a bright-tasting vinaigrette, moistening chunks of thick-crusted bread until they're soft and just a little chewy—but the line between lightly moistened and unpleasantly soggy is very thin. Toasting fresh bread in the oven, rather than using the traditional day-old bread, was a good start. The bread lost enough moisture in the oven to absorb the dressing without getting waterlogged. A 10-minute soak in the flavorful dressing yielded perfectly

moistened, nutty-tasting bread ready to be tossed with the tomatoes, which we salted to intensify their flavor. A thinly sliced cucumber and shallot for crunch and bite plus a handful of chopped fresh basil perfected our salad.

ITALIAN BREAD SALAD (PANZANELLA)

SERVES 4

The success of this recipe depends on high-quality ingredients, including ripe, in-season tomatoes and fruity olive oil. Fresh basil is also a must. Your bread may vary in density, so you may not need the entire loaf for this recipe.

1	(1-pound) loaf rustic Italian or French bread, cut or torn into 1-inch pieces (about 6 cups)
½	cup extra-virgin olive oil
	Salt and pepper
1½	pounds tomatoes, cored, seeded, and cut into 1-inch pieces
3	tablespoons red wine vinegar
1	cucumber, peeled, halved lengthwise, seeded, and sliced thin
1	shallot, sliced thin
¼	cup chopped fresh basil

1. Adjust oven rack to middle position and heat oven to 400 degrees. Toss bread pieces with 2 tablespoons oil and ¼ teaspoon salt; arrange bread in single layer on rimmed baking sheet. Toast bread pieces until just starting to turn light golden, 15 to 20 minutes, stirring halfway through baking. Set aside and let cool to room temperature.

2. Gently toss tomatoes and ½ teaspoon salt in large bowl. Transfer to colander set over bowl; set aside to drain for 15 minutes, tossing occasionally.

3. Whisk remaining 6 tablespoons oil, vinegar, and ¼ teaspoon pepper into tomato juices. Add bread pieces, toss to coat, and let stand for 10 minutes, tossing occasionally.

4. Add tomatoes, cucumber, shallot, and basil to bowl with bread pieces and toss to coat. Season with salt and pepper to taste and serve immediately.

ITALIAN BREAD SALAD WITH PEPPERS AND ARUGULA

Substitute 1 thinly sliced red pepper for cucumber and 1 cup coarsely chopped baby arugula for basil.

ITALIAN BREAD SALAD WITH OLIVES AND FETA

Add ⅓ cup coarsely chopped kalamata olives and ½ cup crumbled feta cheese to salad in step 4.

ITALIAN BREAD SALAD WITH GARLIC AND CAPERS

Add 1 minced garlic clove, 2 minced anchovy fillets, and 2 tablespoons rinsed capers to dressing in step 3.

ROASTED VEGETABLE SALAD

✔ WHY THIS RECIPE WORKS

Roasting can give new life to tired produce, but it can also make for a limp, soggy salad. We wanted a simple, flavorful salad built on a base of roasting vegetables with compatible flavors and colors. We chose combinations of vegetables (like beets and carrots) that kept their structure when cut into same-size pieces and cooked to a firm yet tender consistency. Tossing the roasted vegetables with a vinaigrette while they were still hot allowed for better flavor absorption. To make our roasted vegetable salad a true salad, we added crisp and raw ingredients to the mix.

ROASTED BEET AND CARROT SALAD WITH WATERCRESS

SERVES 4

To prevent the beets from staining your cutting board, lightly spray the board first with vegetable oil spray. A thin coating adds no discernible slickness and will allow you to quickly wipe the board clean with a paper towel.

1	pound beets, peeled and cut into ½-inch thick wedges, wedges cut in half crosswise if beets are large
1	pound carrots, peeled and cut on bias into ¼-inch-thick slices
3	tablespoons extra-virgin olive oil
	Salt and pepper
¼	teaspoon sugar
2	tablespoons white wine vinegar
1	teaspoon honey
1	shallot, minced
6	ounces (6 cups) watercress, torn into bite-size pieces

1. Adjust oven rack to lowest position, place large rimmed baking sheet on rack, and heat oven to 500 degrees. Toss beets and carrots with 2 tablespoons oil, ½ teaspoon salt, ¼ teaspoon pepper, and sugar in large bowl. Remove baking sheet from oven and, working quickly, carefully transfer beets and carrots to hot baking sheet and spread in even layer. (Do not wash bowl.) Roast until vegetables are tender and well browned on one side, 20 to 25 minutes (do not stir during roasting).

2. Meanwhile, whisk remaining tablespoon oil, vinegar, honey, shallot, ¼ teaspoon salt, and ⅛ teaspoon pepper in now-empty bowl.

3. Toss hot vegetables with vinaigrette and let cool to room temperature, about 30 minutes. Stir in watercress, transfer to serving platter, and serve.

ROASTED FENNEL AND MUSHROOM SALAD WITH RADISHES

SERVES 4

If fennel fronds (the delicate greenery attached to the fennel stems) are unavailable, substitute 1 to 2 tablespoons chopped fresh tarragon.

2	fennel bulbs, fronds chopped and ⅓ cup reserved, stalks discarded, bulbs quartered, cored, and cut crosswise into ½-inch-thick slices
1¼	pounds cremini mushrooms, trimmed and quartered if large or halved if medium
3	tablespoons extra-virgin olive oil
	Salt and pepper
¼	teaspoon sugar
2	tablespoons lemon juice
1	teaspoon Dijon mustard
4–6	radishes, cut in half and sliced thin (¾ cup)

1. Adjust oven rack to lowest position, place large rimmed baking sheet on rack, and heat oven to 500 degrees. Toss fennel and mushrooms with 2 tablespoons oil, ½ teaspoon salt, ¼ teaspoon pepper, and sugar in large bowl. Remove baking sheet from oven and, working quickly, carefully transfer fennel and mushrooms to hot baking sheet and spread in even layer. (Do not wash bowl.) Roast until vegetables are tender and well-browned on one side, 20 to 25 minutes (do not stir during roasting).

2. Meanwhile, whisk remaining tablespoon oil, lemon juice, mustard, ¼ teaspoon salt, and ⅛ teaspoon pepper in now-empty bowl.

3. Toss hot vegetables with vinaigrette and let cool to room temperature, about 30 minutes. Stir in radishes and reserved fennel fronds, transfer to serving platter, and serve.

ROASTED GREEN BEAN AND POTATO SALAD WITH RADICCHIO

SERVES 4

Avoid very thin beans as they'll overcook and shrivel under the high heat of the oven.

- 1 pound green beans, trimmed and cut into 1½-inch pieces
- 1 pound red potatoes, cut into ½-inch pieces
- 3 tablespoons extra-virgin olive oil
  Salt and pepper
- ¼ teaspoon sugar
- 2 tablespoons red wine vinegar
- 1 small garlic clove, minced
- 1 small head radicchio, (6 ounces), washed and cut into 2-inch by ¼-inch slices (4 cups)

1. Adjust oven rack to lowest position, place large rimmed baking sheet on rack, and heat oven to 500 degrees. Toss beans and potatoes with 2 tablespoons oil, ½ teaspoon salt, ¼ teaspoon pepper, and sugar in large bowl. Remove baking sheet from oven and, working quickly, carefully transfer beans and potatoes to hot baking sheet and spread in even layer. (Do not wash bowl.) Roast until vegetables are tender and well-browned on one side, 20 to 25 minutes (do not stir during roasting).

2. Meanwhile, whisk remaining 1 tablespoon oil, vinegar, garlic, ¼ teaspoon salt, and ⅛ teaspoon pepper in now-empty bowl.

3. Toss hot vegetables with vinaigrette and let cool to room temperature, about 30 minutes. Stir in radicchio, transfer to serving platter, and serve.

ASPARAGUS SALAD

✔ WHY THIS RECIPE WORKS

For a bright, fresh-flavored asparagus salad, cooking method is paramount. Steaming produced bland, sometimes mushy spears, while sautéing the asparagus over high heat delivered deep flavor and tender texture. A zesty dressing lent the asparagus bold flavor and the addition of nuts, beans, cheese, or hard-cooked eggs made our salad more substantial as well as flavorful.

ASPARAGUS, RED PEPPER, SPINACH SALAD WITH SHERRY VINEGAR AND GOAT CHEESE

SERVES 4 TO 6

Substitute feta for the goat cheese, if you like.

- 6 tablespoons extra-virgin olive oil
- 1 red bell pepper, stemmed, seeded, and cut into 1- by ¼-inch strips
- 1 pound asparagus, trimmed and cut on bias into 1-inch lengths
  Salt and pepper
- 1 shallot, sliced thin
- 1 tablespoon plus 1 teaspoon sherry vinegar
- 1 garlic clove, minced
- 6 ounces (6 cups) baby spinach
- 4 ounces goat cheese, cut into small chunks

1. Heat 2 tablespoons oil in 12-inch nonstick skillet over high heat until beginning to smoke; add red pepper and cook until lightly browned, about 2 minutes, stirring only once after 1 minute. Add asparagus, ¼ teaspoon salt, and ⅛ teaspoon pepper; cook until asparagus is browned and almost tender, about 2 minutes, stirring only once after 1 minute. Stir in shallot and cook until softened and asparagus is crisp-tender, about 1 minute, stirring occasionally. Transfer to large plate and let cool 5 minutes.

2. Meanwhile, whisk remaining 4 tablespoons oil, vinegar, garlic, ¼ teaspoon salt, and ⅛-teaspoon pepper in medium bowl until combined. In large bowl, toss spinach with 2 tablespoons dressing and divide among salad plates. Toss asparagus mixture with remaining dressing and place a portion over spinach; divide goat cheese among salads and serve.

ASPARAGUS AND MESCLUN SALAD WITH CAPERS, CORNICHONS, AND HARD-COOKED EGGS

SERVES 4 TO 6

Mesclun is typically a mixture of such specialty greens as arugula, Belgian endive, and radicchio.

- 5 tablespoons extra-virgin olive oil
- 1 pound asparagus, trimmed and cut on bias into 1-inch lengths
  Salt and pepper
- 2 tablespoons white wine vinegar
- 1 small shallot, minced
- 2 tablespoons minced cornichons
- 1 teaspoon chopped capers
- 2 teaspoons chopped fresh tarragon
- 6 ounces (6 cups) mesclun
- 3 Foolproof Hard-Cooked Eggs (page 534), peeled and chopped medium

1. Heat 1 tablespoon oil in 12-inch nonstick skillet over high heat until beginning to smoke. Add asparagus, ¼ teaspoon salt, and ¼ teaspoon pepper; cook until browned and crisp-tender, about 4 minutes, stirring once every minute. Transfer to large plate and let cool 5 minutes.

2. Meanwhile, whisk remaining

4 tablespoons oil, vinegar, shallot, cornichons, capers, tarragon, and ¼ teaspoon pepper in medium bowl until combined. In large bowl, toss mesclun with 2 tablespoons dressing and divide among salad plates. Toss asparagus with remaining dressing and place a portion over mesclun; divide chopped eggs among salads and serve.

ASPARAGUS, WATERCRESS, AND CARROT SALAD WITH THAI FLAVORS

SERVES 4 TO 6

The asparagus in this salad tastes best chilled. Five minutes in the freezer makes quick work of cooling down the just-cooked asparagus.

2	tablespoons lime juice
2	tablespoons fish sauce
2	tablespoons water
2	teaspoons sugar
1	small garlic clove, minced
1	small jalapeño chile, minced
2	carrots, peeled and cut into 2-inch-long matchsticks
1	tablespoon peanut oil or vegetable oil
1	pound asparagus, trimmed and cut on bias into 1-inch lengths
6	ounces (6 cups) watercress
¼	cup chopped fresh mint
⅓	cup chopped unsalted roasted peanuts

1. Whisk lime juice, fish sauce, water, sugar, garlic, and jalapeño in medium bowl until sugar dissolves. Reserve 1 tablespoon in large bowl; toss carrots with remaining dressing and set aside.

2. Heat oil in 12-inch nonstick skillet over high heat until beginning to smoke; add asparagus and cook until browned and crisp-tender, about 4 minutes, stirring once

every minute. Transfer to large plate and place in freezer 5 minutes.

3. Toss watercress with reserved 1 tablespoon dressing and divide among salad plates. Toss asparagus and mint with carrot mixture and place a portion over watercress; sprinkle salads with peanuts and serve.

ASPARAGUS AND ARUGULA SALAD WITH CANNELLINI BEANS AND BALSAMIC VINEGAR

SERVES 4 TO 6

Rinsing the canned beans eliminates any slimy texture.

5	tablespoons extra-virgin olive oil
½	red onion, sliced ⅛ inch thick
1	pound asparagus, trimmed and cut on bias into 1-inch lengths Salt and pepper
1	(15-ounce) can cannellini beans, rinsed
2	tablespoons plus 2 teaspoons balsamic vinegar
6	ounces (6 cups) baby arugula

1. Heat 2 tablespoons oil in 12-inch nonstick skillet over high heat until beginning to smoke; stir in onion and cook until beginning to brown, about 1 minute. Add asparagus, ¼ teaspoon salt, and ¼ teaspoon pepper; cook until asparagus is browned and crisp-tender, about 4 minutes, stirring once every minute. Off heat, stir in beans; transfer to large plate and let cool 5 minutes.

2. Meanwhile, whisk remaining 3 tablespoons oil, vinegar, ¼ teaspoon salt, and ⅛ teaspoon pepper in medium bowl until combined. In large bowl, toss arugula with 2 tablespoons dressing and divide among salad plates. Toss asparagus mixture with remaining dressing, place a portion over arugula, and serve.

ORANGE SALAD

✔ WHY THIS RECIPE WORKS
Oranges often fall apart once tossed in salad and contribute too-sweet flavor. For a better orange salad, we came up with these rules: for bold flavor, include lime juice in the dressing; allow the oranges to drain before tossing them with the other ingredients to eliminate excess juice; use just a small amount of greens (or none at all); and toss the salad very gently to prevent the orange pieces from falling apart.

ORANGE AND RADISH SALAD WITH ARUGULA

SERVES 4

For more information on preparing the oranges, see page 50.

3	oranges
5	teaspoons lime juice
¼	teaspoon Dijon mustard
½	teaspoon ground coriander, toasted in small dry skillet until fragrant, about 30 seconds
⅛	teaspoon salt Pepper
3	tablespoons vegetable oil
4	ounces (4 cups) baby arugula
5	radishes, quartered lengthwise and cut crosswise into ⅛-inch-thick slices

1. Peel oranges, making sure to remove all pith, and cut into ¼-inch pieces. Place orange pieces in mesh strainer set over bowl; let stand to drain excess juice. Meanwhile, whisk lime juice, mustard, coriander, salt, and pepper to taste in large bowl until combined. Whisking constantly, gradually add oil.

2. Add oranges, arugula, and radishes to bowl and toss gently to combine. Divide salad among individual plates and

drizzle with any dressing in bowl; serve immediately.

ORANGE, AVOCADO, AND WATERCRESS SALAD WITH GINGER-LIME VINAIGRETTE

SERVES 4

Do not use an overly ripe avocado here or it will turn the salad gluey.

3	oranges
1	tablespoon lime juice
1	tablespoon minced fresh mint
1	teaspoon grated fresh ginger
¼	teaspoon Dijon mustard
	Pinch cayenne pepper
	Salt
3	tablespoons vegetable oil
¼	small red onion, sliced very thin
1	avocado
2½	ounces (2½ cups) watercress, torn into 2-inch pieces

1. Peel oranges, making sure to remove all pith, and cut into ¼-inch pieces. Place orange pieces in mesh strainer set over bowl; let stand to drain excess juice. Meanwhile, whisk lime juice, mint, ginger, mustard, cayenne, and ⅛ teaspoon salt in large bowl until combined. Whisking constantly, gradually add oil. Toss onion in dressing and set aside.

2. Halve and pit avocado; cut each half lengthwise to form quarters. Using paring knife, slice flesh of each quarter (do not cut through skin) lengthwise into fifths. Using soupspoon, carefully scoop flesh out of skin and fan slices from each quarter onto individual plates; season avocado lightly with salt.

3. Add oranges to bowl with onion; toss to coat. Add watercress and toss gently. Divide watercress among individual plates, mounding it in center; place portion of orange pieces and onion on top of watercress. Drizzle any dressing in bowl over salad; serve immediately.

ORANGE-JÍCAMA SALAD WITH SWEET AND SPICY PEPPERS

SERVES 4

If you're not a fan of cilantro, substitute fresh parsley.

3	oranges
3	tablespoons lime juice (2 limes)
¼	teaspoon Dijon mustard
½	teaspoon ground cumin, toasted in small dry skillet until fragrant, about 30 seconds
	Salt
¼	cup vegetable oil
1	jícama (1 pound), peeled and cut into 2-inch-long matchsticks

1	red bell pepper, stemmed, seeded and cut into ⅛-inch-wide strips
2	jalapeño chiles, stemmed, seeded, quartered lengthwise, then cut crosswise into ⅛-inch-thick slices
½	cup fresh cilantro, chopped
3	scallions, green parts only, sliced thin on bias

1. Peel oranges, making sure to remove all pith, and cut into ¼-inch pieces. Place orange pieces in mesh strainer set over bowl; let stand to drain excess juice. Meanwhile, whisk lime juice, mustard, cumin, and ¼ teaspoon salt in large bowl until combined. Whisking constantly, gradually add oil.

2. Toss jícama and red bell pepper with ⅛ teaspoon salt in medium bowl until combined. Add jícama mixture, oranges, jalapeños, cilantro, and scallions to bowl with dressing and toss well to combine. Divide among individual plates, drizzle with any dressing in bowl, and serve immediately.

PAN-ROASTED PEAR SALAD

✓ WHY THIS RECIPE WORKS
For our pear salad recipe, we wanted a simple technique for caramelizing pears that wouldn't overcook the fruit. We cooked the quartered pears on top of the stove, which prevented the interiors from softening too much, and tossed them with sugar before cooking to encourage better browning. Since we were already using balsamic vinegar in the vinaigrette (its fruity flavor accentuates the pear flavor), we tried adding a couple of extra tablespoons of balsamic vinegar to the hot pan while roasting the pears. The result gave us our best pear salad recipe: the extra vinegar instantly reduced to form a glazy coating on the pears, perfectly matching the flavor of the salad.

CUTTING ORANGES

1. Cut thin slice from top and bottom, stand on end, and slice away rind and white pith.

2. Cut in half from end to end, remove stringy pith, cut each half into 3 wedges, and cut crosswise into pieces as directed in recipe.

PAN-ROASTED PEAR SALAD WITH WATERCRESS, PARMESAN, AND PECANS

SERVES 4 TO 6

The test kitchen prefers Bartlett pears for this recipe, but Bosc pears can also be used. With either variety, the pears should be ripe but firm; the flesh at the neck of the pear should give slightly when pressed gently with a finger. If using Bartletts, look for pears that are starting to turn from green to yellow. Romaine lettuce may be substituted for green leaf.

3	(8-ounce) pears, quartered and cored
2½	teaspoons sugar
	Salt and pepper
2	tablespoons plus 2 teaspoons olive oil
¼	cup balsamic vinegar
1	small shallot, minced
½	head green leaf lettuce (6 ounces), torn into 1-inch pieces
4	ounces (4 cups) watercress
4	ounces Parmesan cheese, shaved into strips with vegetable peeler
¾	cup pecans, toasted and chopped

1. Toss pears, 2 teaspoons sugar, ¼ teaspoon salt, and ⅛ teaspoon pepper in medium bowl. Heat 2 teaspoons oil in 12-inch skillet over medium-high heat until just smoking. Add pears cut side down in single layer and cook until golden brown, 2 to 4 minutes. Using small spatula or fork, tip each pear onto second cut side; continue to cook until second side is light brown, 2 to 4 minutes longer. Turn off heat, leave skillet on burner, and add 2 tablespoons vinegar; gently stir until vinegar becomes glazy and coats pears, about 30 seconds. Transfer pears to large plate and let cool to room temperature, about 45 minutes. Cut each pear quarter crosswise into ½-inch pieces.

2. Whisk remaining 2 tablespoons oil, remaining 2 tablespoons vinegar, remaining ½ teaspoon sugar, and shallot together in large bowl; season with salt and pepper to taste. Add lettuce, watercress, and cooled pears to bowl; toss and season with salt and pepper to taste. Divide salad among individual plates; top each with portions of cheese and nuts. Serve immediately.

PAN-ROASTED PEAR SALAD WITH RADICCHIO, BLUE CHEESE, AND WALNUTS

Substitute 1 large head radicchio, quartered, cored, and cut crosswise into ½-inch pieces (4 cups) for watercress, 4 ounces crumbled Gorgonzola or Stilton cheese (1 cup) for Parmesan, and ¾ cup toasted and chopped walnuts for pecans.

PAN-ROASTED PEAR SALAD WITH FRISÉE, GOAT CHEESE, AND ALMONDS

Substitute 1 head frisée torn into 1-inch pieces (4 cups) for watercress, 4 ounces crumbled goat cheese (1 cup) for Parmesan, and ¾ cup toasted sliced almonds for pecans.

THREE-BEAN SALAD

✓ WHY THIS RECIPE WORKS

Recipes for that familiar picnic standby, canned green, yellow, and kidney beans tossed in a sweet, vinegary dressing, have changed little since the salad's heyday in the 1950s. We wanted an updated, fresher-tasting three-bean salad recipe so we used a combination of canned kidney beans and fresh yellow and green beans. For the dressing, we relied on canola oil for mildness and red wine vinegar for tang. Heating the oil and vinegar with sugar, garlic, salt, and pepper intensified the vinaigrette flavor and sweetness. Refrigerating the salad overnight allows the flavors to meld.

CLASSIC THREE-BEAN SALAD

SERVES 8 TO 10

Allowing the beans to marinate in the dressing improves their flavor so prepare the salad 1 day before you plan to serve it.

1	cup red wine vinegar
¾	cup sugar
½	cup canola oil
2	garlic cloves, minced
	Salt and pepper
8	ounces green beans, trimmed and cut into 1-inch lengths
8	ounces yellow wax beans, trimmed and cut into 1-inch lengths
1	(15-ounce) can red kidney beans, rinsed
½	red onion, chopped medium
¼	cup minced fresh parsley

1. Heat vinegar, sugar, oil, garlic, 1 teaspoon salt, and pepper to taste in small saucepan over medium heat, stirring occasionally, until sugar dissolves, about 5 minutes. Transfer to a large bowl and let cool to room temperature.

2. Bring 3 quarts water to boil in large saucepan over high heat. Add 1 tablespoon salt and green and yellow beans; cook until crisp-tender, about 5 minutes. Meanwhile, fill medium bowl with ice water. When beans are done, drain and immediately plunge into ice water to stop cooking process; let sit until chilled, about 2 minutes. Drain well.

3. Add green and yellow beans, kidney beans, onion, and parsley to vinegar mixture; toss well to coat. Cover and refrigerate overnight to let flavors meld. Let stand at room temperature 30 minutes before serving. (Salad can be refrigerated for up to 4 days.)

Separate 2 oranges into segments, remove membrane from sides of each segment, then cut each segment into half lengthwise. Set aside. Substitute ¼ cup lime juice for ¼ cup red wine vinegar, and heat 1 teaspoon ground cumin with vinegar mixture. Substitute minced fresh cilantro for parsley and add halved orange segments to vinegar mixture along with beans.

TABBOULEH

✔ WHY THIS RECIPE WORKS

In the Middle East, tabbouleh is basically a parsley salad with bulgur rather than the bulgur salad with parsley that is frequently found in the U.S. Perfect tabbouleh should be tossed in a penetrating, minty lemon dressing with bits of ripe tomato. For the parsley, we found that either type—flat-leaf "Italian" or curly leaf—made an acceptable salad. As for processing the bulgur, the all-out winning method simply involved rinsing and then mixing it with fresh lemon juice. The mixture is then set aside to allow the juice to be absorbed. When treated in this way, bulgur acquires a fresh and intense flavor, but without the heaviness that the added olive oil produces. Finally, we liked a ratio of 5 parts parsley to 3 or 4 parts grain. When we tried increasing the parsley, the wholesome goodness of the wheat was lost.

TABBOULEH
SERVES 4 TO 6

Middle Eastern cooks frequently serve this salad with the crisp inner leaves of romaine lettuce, using them as spoons to scoop the salad from the serving dish.

½	cup bulgur, fine or medium grain, rinsed under running water and drained
⅓	cup lemon juice (2 lemons)
⅓	cup olive oil
	Salt
⅛	teaspoon cayenne pepper (optional)
2	cups minced fresh parsley
2	tomatoes, cored, halved, seeded, and cut into very small dice
4	scallions, minced
2	tablespoons minced fresh mint or 1 teaspoon dried

1. Mix bulgur with ¼ cup of the lemon juice in medium bowl; set aside until grains are tender and fluffy, 20 to 40 minutes, depending on age and type of bulgur.

2. Mix remaining lemon juice, olive oil, salt to taste and cayenne, if desired. Mix bulgur, parsley, tomatoes, scallions, and mint; add dressing and toss to combine. Cover and refrigerate to let flavors blend, 1 to 2 hours. Serve.

PASTA SALAD WITH PESTO

✔ WHY THIS RECIPE WORKS

At its best, pesto is fresh, green, and full of herbal flavor, but when incorporated into an American-style pasta salad, it can turn dull and muddy. We found that adding another green element—fresh baby spinach—provided the pesto with long-lasting color without interfering with the basil flavor. Adding mayonnaise to the pesto created the perfect binder, keeping the salad creamy and luscious and preventing it from clumping up and drying out.

PASTA SALAD WITH PESTO
SERVES 8 TO 10

This salad is best served the day it is made; if it's been refrigerated, bring it to room temperature before serving. Garnish with additional shaved or grated Parmesan.

¾	cup pine nuts
2	garlic cloves, unpeeled
	Salt
1	pound farfalle
5	tablespoons extra-virgin olive oil
3	cups fresh basil leaves
1	ounce (1 cup) baby spinach
½	teaspoon pepper
2	tablespoons lemon juice
1½	ounces Parmesan cheese, grated fine (¾ cup), plus extra for serving
6	tablespoons mayonnaise
12	ounces cherry tomatoes, quartered, or grape tomatoes, halved (optional)

1. Bring 4 quarts water to boil in large pot over high heat. Toast pine nuts in small dry skillet over medium heat, shaking pan occasionally, until just golden and fragrant, 4 to 5 minutes.

2. When water is boiling, add garlic and let cook 1 minute. Remove garlic with slotted spoon and rinse under cold water to stop cooking; set aside and let cool. Add 1 tablespoon salt and pasta to water, stir to separate, and cook until tender (just past al dente). Reserve ¼ cup cooking water, drain pasta, toss with 1 tablespoon oil, spread in single layer on rimmed baking sheet, and let cool to room temperature, about 30 minutes.

3. When garlic is cool, peel and mince or press through garlic press. Place ¼ cup nuts, garlic, basil, spinach, pepper, lemon juice, remaining ¼ cup oil, and 1 teaspoon salt in bowl of food processor and process until smooth, scraping sides of bowl as necessary. Add cheese and mayonnaise and process until thoroughly combined. Transfer mixture to large serving bowl. Cover and refrigerate until ready to assemble salad.

4. When pasta is cool, toss with pesto, adding reserved pasta water, 1 tablespoon at a time, until pesto evenly coats pasta. Fold in remaining ½ cup nuts and tomatoes, if using; serve with extra Parmesan.

PASTA SALAD WITH BROCCOLI AND OLIVES

✓ **WHY THIS RECIPE WORKS**

Developing the best pasta salad recipe was tricky: While some acidity was clearly needed to brighten the flavor of the salad, too much caused the pasta to soften and dulled the vegetables, both in flavor and appearance. We liked lemon juice for contributing a nice bright flavor that was neither puckery nor sour. When we turned our attention to the vegetables, we discovered that, as we suspected, grilling and roasting added more flavor to most vegetables (broccoli and cauliflower being the exceptions) than blanching.

PASTA SALAD WITH BROCCOLI AND OLIVES

SERVES 6 TO 8

If you prefer a spicier salad, increase the red pepper flakes.

- 3 pounds broccoli (2 medium bunches), florets cut into bite-size pieces (7 cups)
- ½ teaspoon grated lemon zest plus ¼ cup juice (2 lemons)
  Salt
- 1 garlic clove, minced
- ½ teaspoon red pepper flakes
- ½ cup extra-virgin olive oil
- 1 pound bite-size pasta such as fusilli, farfalle, or orecchiette
- ½ cup kalamata olives or other brine-cured variety, pitted and chopped
- ½ cup chopped fresh basil

1. Bring 4 quarts water to boil in large pot over high heat. In separate pot blanch broccoli in boiling salted water until crisp-tender, about 2 minutes; drain and let cool to room temperature.

2. Meanwhile, whisk lemon juice and zest, ¾ teaspoon salt, garlic, and pepper flakes in large bowl; whisk in oil in slow, steady stream until smooth.

3. Add pasta and 1 tablespoon salt to boiling water. Cook until pasta is al dente and drain. Whisk dressing again to blend; add hot pasta, cooled broccoli, olives, and basil; toss to mix thoroughly. Let cool to room temperature, adjust seasonings, and serve. (Pasta salad can be refrigerated for up to 1 day; return to room temperature before serving.)

PASTA SALAD WITH EGGPLANT, TOMATOES, AND BASIL

SERVES 6 TO 8

The eggplants can be broiled until golden brown if you prefer not to grill them.

- 1 pound eggplant, cut into ½-inch-thick rounds
- ½ cup extra-virgin olive oil, plus extra for brushing on eggplant
  Salt and pepper
- ½ teaspoon grated lemon zest plus ¼ cup juice and (2 lemons)
- 1 garlic clove, minced
- ½ teaspoon red pepper flakes
- 1 pound bite-size pasta, such as fusilli, farfalle, or orecchiette
- 2 large tomatoes, cored, seeded, and cut into ½-inch dice
- ½ cup chopped fresh basil

1A. FOR A CHARCOAL GRILL: Open bottom vent completely. Light large chimney starter filled with charcoal briquettes (6 quarts). When top coals are partially covered with ash, pour evenly over grill. Set cooking grate in place, cover, and open lid vent completely. Heat grill until hot, about 5 minutes.

1B. FOR A GAS GRILL: Turn all burners to high, cover, and heat grill until hot, about 15 minutes. Leave all burners on high. (Adjust burners as needed to maintain grill temperature around 350 degrees.)

2. Clean and oil cooking grate. Lightly brush eggplant with oil and sprinkle with salt and pepper to taste. Grill, turning once, until marked with dark stripes, about 10 minutes. Let cool and cut into bite-size pieces.

3. Meanwhile, bring 4 quarts water to boil in large pot over high heat. Whisk lemon juice and zest, garlic, ¾ teaspoon salt, and pepper flakes in large bowl; whisk in ½ cup oil in slow, steady stream until smooth.

4. Add pasta and 1 tablespoon salt to boiling water. Cook until pasta is al dente and drain. Whisk dressing again to blend; add hot pasta, cooled eggplant, tomatoes, and basil; toss to mix thoroughly. Let cool to room temperature, adjust seasonings, and serve. (Pasta salad can be refrigerated for up to 1 day; return to room temperature before serving.)

PASTA SALAD WITH ARUGULA AND SUN-DRIED TOMATO VINAIGRETTE

SERVES 6

We like the assertive flavor of red wine vinegar in this recipe.

- Salt
- 1 pound fusilli
- 1 tablespoon extra-virgin olive oil
- ½ cup oil-packed sun-dried tomatoes
- 2 tablespoons red wine vinegar
- 1 garlic clove, minced
- ¼ teaspoon salt
- ⅛ teaspoon pepper
- 4 ounces (4 cups) baby arugula
- ½ cup green olives, pitted and sliced
- 6 ounces fresh mozzarella cheese, cut into ½-inch cubes

1. Bring 4 quarts water to boil in large pot over high heat. Add pasta and 1 tablespoon salt to boiling water. Cook until pasta is al dente and drain. Rinse pasta under cold running water. Drain pasta well, transfer it to large mixing bowl, and toss it with olive oil. Set aside.

2. Drain tomatoes, reserving oil. (You

should have ⅓ cup reserved oil. If necessary, make up difference with extra-virgin olive oil.) Coarsely chop tomatoes. Whisk reserved oil with vinegar, garlic, salt, and pepper in small bowl.

3. Add arugula, olives, mozzarella, and chopped tomatoes to bowl with pasta. Pour tomato vinaigrette over pasta, toss gently, and serve immediately.

PASTA SALAD WITH FENNEL, RED ONIONS, AND SUN-DRIED TOMATOES
SERVES 6 TO 8

When roasted, fennel mellows and turns slightly sweet.

- 2 fennel bulbs, stalks discarded, halved, cored, and cut into ½-inch wedges
- 2 red onions, sliced into ½-inch-thick rings
- ½ cup plus 2 tablespoons extra-virgin olive oil
  Salt and pepper
- ½ teaspoon grated lemon zest plus ¼ cup juice (2 lemons)
- 1 garlic clove, minced
- 1 pound bite-size pasta such as fusilli, farfalle, or orecchiette
- ½ cup oil-packed sun-dried tomatoes, patted dry and sliced thin
- ½ cup chopped fresh basil

1. Adjust oven rack to middle position and heat oven to 425 degrees. Toss fennel and onions with 2 tablespoons oil and salt and pepper to taste and transfer to large baking sheet. Roast until tender and lightly browned, 15 to 17 minutes. Let cool to room temperature.

2. Meanwhile, whisk lemon juice and zest, garlic, ¾ teaspoon salt, and pepper to taste in large bowl; whisk in remaining ½ cup oil in slow, steady stream until smooth.

3. Bring 4 quarts water to boil in large pot over high heat. Add pasta and 1 tablespoon salt to boiling water. Cook until pasta is al dente and drain. Whisk dressing again to blend; add hot pasta, cooled fennel and onions, sun-dried tomatoes, and basil; toss to mix thoroughly. Let cool to room temperature, season with salt and pepper to taste, and serve. (Pasta salad can be refrigerated for up to 1 day; return to room temperature before serving.)

PASTA SALAD WITH ASPARAGUS AND RED PEPPERS
SERVES 6 TO 8

Chives work particularly well with the asparagus and peppers, but you can substitute fresh mint, parsley, or basil.

- 1½ pounds asparagus, trimmed and cut into 2-inch pieces
- 3 large red bell peppers, stemmed, seeded, and cut into 1½-inch pieces
- ½ cup plus 2 tablespoons extra-virgin olive oil
  Salt and pepper
- ½ teaspoon grated lemon zest plus ¼ cup juice (2 lemons)
- 1 garlic clove, minced
- 1 pound bite-size pasta such as fusilli, farfalle, or orecchiette
- 3 tablespoons chopped fresh chives
- ⅓ cup grated Parmesan cheese

1. Adjust oven rack to middle position and heat oven to 425 degrees. Toss asparagus and peppers with 2 tablespoons oil, salt and pepper to taste, and transfer to large baking sheet. Roast until tender and lightly browned, 15 to 17 minutes; let cool to room temperature.

2. Meanwhile, whisk lemon juice and zest, ¾ teaspoon salt, garlic, and pepper to taste in large bowl; whisk in remaining ¾ cup oil in slow, steady stream until smooth.

3. Bring 4 quarts water to boil in large pot over high heat. Add pasta and 1 tablespoon salt to boiling water. Cook until pasta is al dente and drain. Whisk dressing again to blend; add hot pasta, cooled asparagus and peppers, chives, and grated Parmesan; toss to mix thoroughly. Let cool to room temperature, season with salt and pepper to taste, and serve. (Pasta salad can be refrigerated for up to 1 day; return to room temperature before serving.)

CABBAGE SALAD

✔ WHY THIS RECIPE WORKS
Cabbage salads are a nice change of pace from the same old slaw. But cabbage tends to become watery and bland once dressed and allowed to sit, because the cabbage itself exudes water. We solved this problem by salting the cabbage to draw out the liquid. A lively vinaigrette and fresh, crisp supporting players like fruits and vegetables rounded out the salad's flavor and texture.

SWEET AND SOUR CABBAGE SALAD WITH APPLE AND FENNEL
SERVES 6 TO 8

This salad pairs especially well with chicken or pork.

- ½ head green cabbage (1 pound), cored and shredded (6 cups)
  Salt and pepper
- ½ small red onion, chopped fine
- 1 tablespoon honey
- 2 tablespoons rice vinegar
- 2 tablespoons extra-virgin olive oil
- 1 teaspoon Dijon mustard
- 2 teaspoons minced fresh tarragon
- 1 large Granny Smith apple, peeled, cored, and cut into ¼-inch pieces
- 1 fennel bulb, stalks discarded, halved, cored, and sliced thin

1. Toss shredded cabbage and 1 teaspoon salt in colander or large-mesh strainer set over medium bowl. Let stand until cabbage wilts, at least 1 hour or up to 4 hours. Rinse cabbage under cold running water (or in large bowl of ice water if serving immediately). Press, but do not squeeze, to drain; pat dry with paper towels. (Cabbage can be stored in zipper-lock bag and refrigerated overnight.)

2. Stir together onion, honey, vinegar, oil, mustard, and tarragon in medium bowl. Immediately toss cabbage, apple, and fennel in dressing. Season with salt and pepper to taste; cover and refrigerate until ready to serve. (Salad can be refrigerated for up to 1 day.)

TWO WAYS TO SHRED CABBAGE

1. After quartering and coring cabbage, separate cabbage quarters into stacks of leaves that flatten when pressed lightly.

BY HAND

2A. Use chef's knife to cut each stack of cabbage diagonally into thin shreds. To chop cabbage, turn pile of shredded cabbage crosswise, then cut shreds into fine dice.

IN A FOOD PROCESSOR

2B. Roll leaves crosswise and place them in feed tube. Using slicing disk and pressing lightly on pusher, shred cabbage. Repeat with other stacks.

CABBAGE AND RED PEPPER SALAD WITH LIME-CUMIN VINAIGRETTE

SERVES 6 TO 8

Serve this Southwestern-flavored slaw with grilled meat, poultry, or fish.

- ½ head green cabbage (1 pound), cored and shredded fine (6 cups) Salt
- 1 teaspoon grated lime zest plus 2 tablespoons juice
- 2 tablespoons olive oil
- 1 tablespoon rice vinegar or sherry vinegar
- 1 tablespoon honey
- 1 teaspoon ground cumin Pinch cayenne pepper
- 1 red bell pepper, stemmed, seeded, and cut into thin strips

1. Toss shredded cabbage and 1 teaspoon salt in colander or large-mesh strainer set over medium bowl. Let stand until cabbage wilts, at least 1 hour or up to 4 hours. Rinse cabbage under cold running water (or in large bowl of ice water if serving immediately). Press, but do not squeeze, to drain; pat dry with paper towels. (Cabbage can be stored in zipper-lock bag and refrigerated overnight.)

2. Stir together lime juice and zest, oil, vinegar, honey, cumin, and cayenne in medium bowl. Toss cabbage and red pepper in dressing. Season with salt to taste; cover and refrigerate until ready to serve. (Salad can be refrigerated for up to 1 day.)

CONFETTI CABBAGE SALAD WITH SPICY PEANUT DRESSING

SERVES 6 TO 8

Grate the carrot on the large holes of a box grater or with the cabbage on the shredding disk of a food processor.

- ½ head green cabbage (1 pound), cored and shredded (6 cups)
- 1 large carrot, peeled and grated Salt
- 2 tablespoons smooth peanut butter
- 2 tablespoons peanut oil
- 2 tablespoons rice vinegar
- 1 tablespoon soy sauce
- 1 teaspoon honey
- 2 garlic cloves, chopped coarse
- 1 (1½-inch) piece ginger, peeled
- ½ jalapeño chile, stemmed, halved, and seeded
- 4 radishes, halved lengthwise and sliced thin
- 4 scallions, sliced thin

1. Toss shredded cabbage, carrot, and 1 teaspoon salt in colander or large-mesh strainer set over medium bowl. Let stand until cabbage wilts, at least 1 hour or up to 4 hours. Rinse cabbage and carrot under cold running water (or in large bowl of ice water if serving immediately). Press, but do not squeeze, to drain; pat dry with paper towels. (Vegetables can be stored in zipper-lock bag and refrigerated overnight.)

2. Puree peanut butter, oil, vinegar, soy sauce, honey, garlic, ginger, and jalapeño in food processor until smooth paste is formed, about 30 seconds. Toss cabbage and carrot, radishes, scallions, and dressing together in medium bowl. Season with salt to taste; cover and refrigerate until ready to serve. (Salad can be refrigerated for up to 1 day.)

CREAMY BUTTERMILK COLESLAW

✔ WHY THIS RECIPE WORKS

We wanted a recipe for buttermilk coleslaw that would produce a salad with crisp, evenly cut pieces of cabbage lightly coated with a flavorful buttermilk dressing that would cling to the cabbage instead of collecting in the bottom of the bowl. We found that salting and draining the cabbage removed excess water and wilted it to a pickle-crisp texture. For a dressing that was both hefty and tangy, we combined buttermilk, mayonnaise, and sour cream.

CREAMY BUTTERMILK COLESLAW
SERVES 4

If you are planning to serve the coleslaw immediately, rinse the salted cabbage in a large bowl of ice water, drain it in a colander, pick out any ice cubes, then pat the cabbage dry before dressing. For information on shredding cabbage, see page 55.

- ½ head red or green cabbage (1 pound), cored and shredded (6 cups)
  Salt
- 1 carrot, peeled and shredded
- ½ cup buttermilk
- 2 tablespoons mayonnaise
- 2 tablespoons sour cream
- 1 small shallot, minced
- 2 tablespoons minced fresh parsley
- ½ teaspoon cider vinegar
- ½ teaspoon sugar
- ¼ teaspoon Dijon mustard
- ⅛ teaspoon pepper

1. Toss shredded cabbage and 1 teaspoon salt in colander or large-mesh strainer set over medium bowl. Let stand until cabbage wilts, at least 1 hour or up to 4 hours. Rinse cabbage under cold running water. Press, but do not squeeze, to drain; pat dry with paper towels. Place wilted cabbage and carrot in large bowl.

2. Stir buttermilk, mayonnaise, sour cream, shallot, parsley, vinegar, sugar, mustard, ¼ teaspoon salt, and pepper together in small bowl. Pour dressing over cabbage and toss to combine; refrigerate until chilled, about 30 minutes. (Coleslaw can be refrigerated for up to 3 days.)

BUTTERMILK COLESLAW WITH GREEN ONIONS AND CILANTRO

Omit mustard, substitute 1 tablespoon minced cilantro for parsley and 1 teaspoon lime juice for cider vinegar, and add 2 thinly sliced scallions to dressing.

LEMONY BUTTERMILK COLESLAW

Substitute 1 teaspoon lemon juice for vinegar and add 1 teaspoon minced fresh thyme and 1 tablespoon minced fresh chives to dressing.

DELI-STYLE COLESLAW

✔ WHY THIS RECIPE WORKS

For a deli-style slaw with crisp cabbage and a piquant dressing that wasn't too sharp, we salted the cabbage. Salting helps the cabbage exude its liquid, leaving the cabbage pickle-crisp. After a number of failed experiments with dressings, we decided to give low-acidity rice vinegar a try. We drizzled a bit over the mayonnaise-tossed cabbage and found its mild acidity perfect.

DELI-STYLE COLESLAW
SERVES 4

If you like caraway or celery seeds in your coleslaw, you can add one-quarter teaspoon of either with the mayonnaise and vinegar. You can shred, salt, rinse, and pat the cabbage dry a day ahead, but dress it close to serving time. For information on shredding cabbage, see page 55.

- ½ head red or green cabbage (1 pound), cored and shredded or chopped (6 cups)
- 1 large carrot, peeled and shredded
- 1 teaspoon salt
- ½ small onion, minced
- ½ cup mayonnaise
- 2 tablespoons rice vinegar
  Pepper

1. Toss cabbage and carrots with salt in colander set over medium bowl. Let stand until cabbage wilts, at least 1 hour or up to 4 hours.

2. Pour draining liquid from bowl; rinse bowl and dry. Dump wilted cabbage and carrots into bowl. Rinse thoroughly in cold water (ice water if serving slaw immediately). Pour vegetables back into colander. Pat dry with paper towels. (Vegetables can be stored in zipper-lock bag and refrigerated overnight.)

3. Pour cabbage and carrots back again into bowl. Add onion, mayonnaise, and vinegar; toss to coat. Season with pepper to taste. Cover and refrigerate until ready to serve. (Coleslaw can be refrigerated for up to 1 day.)

CURRIED COLESLAW WITH APPLES AND RAISINS
SERVES 6

Since rice wine vinegar tends to mellow, you may want to use cider vinegar if making the slaw a day ahead. The presence of the sugar in this recipe keeps you from having to rinse off salt from the cabbage, as is ordinarily the case. For information on shredding cabbage, see page 55.

- ½ head red or green cabbage (1 pound), cored and shredded or chopped (6 cups)
- 1 large carrot, peeled and grated
- ½ cup sugar
- 1 teaspoon salt
- ¼ teaspoon celery seeds

6 tablespoons vegetable oil
¼ cup rice vinegar
1 teaspoon curry powder
1 medium tart apple, peeled and
  cut into small dice
¼ cup raisins (optional)
  Pepper

1. Toss cabbage and carrots with sugar, salt, and celery seeds in colander set over medium bowl. Let stand until cabbage wilts, at least 1 hour or up to 4 hours.

2. Pour draining liquid from bowl; rinse bowl and dry. Dump wilted cabbage and carrots from colander into bowl. Rinse thoroughly under cold running water (ice water if serving slaw immediately).

3. Add oil, vinegar, curry powder, apple, and raisins, if using; toss to coat. Season with pepper to taste. Cover and refrigerate until ready to serve. (Coleslaw can be refrigerated for up to 1 day.)

SWEET AND TANGY COLESLAW

✓ WHY THIS RECIPE WORKS

For a bright, refreshing coleslaw, we started by ditching the mayonnaise in favor of a light dressing of oil, cider vinegar, and sugar. To keep the moisture of the cabbage from diluting the dressing, we salted the cabbage and put it in the microwave, which pulled out ½ cup of excess water in just 2 minutes. Chilling the dressing compensated for the warm cabbage, and a brief chill in the fridge allowed the flavors to meld. Replacing the usual domineering onion with grated carrot and chopped parsley and adding ¼ teaspoon of celery seeds for a little zip gave us a refreshing slaw that would go with almost anything.

SWEET AND TANGY COLESLAW
SERVES 4

When it comes to the sweetness level of coleslaw, tastes vary. For this reason, prepare the coleslaw as directed and then season to taste with up to 2 teaspoons of sugar or up to 2 teaspoons of vinegar, adding 1 teaspoon at a time. For information on shredding cabbage, see page 55.

¼ cup apple cider vinegar, plus
  extra for seasoning
2 tablespoons vegetable oil
¼ teaspoon celery seeds
¼ teaspoon pepper
½ head green cabbage (1 pound),
  cored and shredded (6 cups)
¼ cup sugar, plus extra for seasoning
  Salt
1 large carrot, peeled and grated
2 tablespoons chopped fresh parsley

1. Combine vinegar, oil, celery seeds, and pepper in medium bowl. Place bowl in freezer until vinegar mixture is well chilled, at least 15 or up to 30 minutes.

2. While mixture chills, toss cabbage with sugar and 1 teaspoon salt in large bowl. Cover and microwave for 1 minute. Stir briefly, re-cover, and continue to microwave until cabbage is partially wilted and has reduced in volume by one-third, 30 to 60 seconds longer.

3. Transfer cabbage to salad spinner and spin cabbage until excess water is removed, 10 to 20 seconds. Remove bowl from freezer, add cabbage, carrots, and parsley to cold vinegar mixture, and toss to combine. Adjust flavor with sugar or vinegar and season with salt to taste. Refrigerate until chilled, about 15 minutes. Toss again before serving.

SWEET AND TANGY COLESLAW WITH RED PEPPER AND JALAPEÑO

Substitute 2 tablespoons lime juice for celery seeds, ½ thinly sliced red bell pepper and 1 or 2 seeded and minced jalapeños for carrot, and 1 thinly sliced scallion for parsley.

SWEET AND TANGY COLESLAW WITH FENNEL AND ORANGE

Increase cider vinegar to ⅓ cup. Substitute 1 teaspoon grated orange zest and 3 tablespoons orange juice for celery seeds, ½ thinly sliced fennel bulb and ¼ cup golden raisins for carrot, and 1 tablespoon minced fennel fronds for parsley.

SWEET AND TANGY COLESLAW WITH APPLE AND TARRAGON

Reduce cider vinegar to 3 tablespoons. Substitute ½ teaspoon Dijon mustard for celery seeds, 1 Granny Smith apple cut into matchsticks for carrot, and 2 teaspoons minced fresh tarragon for parsley.

CELERY ROOT SALAD

✓ WHY THIS RECIPE WORKS

Unlike cooked purees or gratins, a celery root salad should maintain the vegetable's pristine white appearance, its crunchy, coleslawlike texture, and (most important) its refreshing herbal flavor. For easy peeling, we removed the top and bottom from the celery root and then used a paring knife to remove the outer layer of flesh from top to bottom. For thin pieces of celery root that would still retain their crunch, we used the coarse side of a box grater or a food processor. We dressed the celery root with a vinaigrette finished with sour cream, which lent the salad creamy, tangy richness.

CELERY ROOT SALAD WITH APPLE AND PARSLEY

SERVES 4 TO 6

Add a teaspoon or so more oil to the dressed salad if it seems a bit dry.

DRESSING
2   tablespoons lemon juice
1½ tablespoons Dijon mustard
1   teaspoon honey
½   teaspoon salt
3   tablespoons vegetable or canola oil
3   tablespoons sour cream

SALAD
1   head celery root (14 ounces), peeled
½   Granny Smith apple, peeled and cored
2   scallions, sliced thin
2   teaspoons minced fresh parsley
2   teaspoons minced fresh tarragon (optional)
    Salt and pepper

1. FOR THE DRESSING: In medium bowl, whisk together lemon juice, mustard, honey, and salt. Whisk in oil in slow, steady stream. Add sour cream; whisk to combine. Set aside.

2. FOR THE SALAD: If using food processor, cut celery root and apple into 1½-inch pieces and grate with shredding disc. (Alternatively, grate on large holes of box grater.) You should have about 3 cups total. Add immediately to prepared dressing; toss to coat. Stir in scallions, parsley, and tarragon, if using. Season with salt and pepper to taste. Refrigerate until chilled, about 30 minutes. Serve. (Salad can be refrigerated for up to 1 day.)

CELERY ROOT SALAD WITH APPLE, CARAWAY, AND HORSERADISH

Add ½ teaspoon caraway seeds and 1½ teaspoons prepared horseradish along with herbs.

CELERY ROOT SALAD WITH PEAR AND HAZELNUTS

To remove the skins from the hazelnuts, rub the hot toasted nuts in a clean kitchen towel.

Substitute ½ firm pear, grated, for apple and add ¼ cup hazelnuts, toasted, skinned, and chopped along with herbs.

CELERY ROOT SALAD WITH RED ONION, MINT, ORANGE, AND FENNEL SEEDS

Substitute 2 tablespoons finely chopped red onion for scallion and add 2 teaspoons minced fresh mint, ½ teaspoon grated orange zest, and 1 teaspoon fennel seeds along with parsley.

ALL-AMERICAN POTATO SALAD

✓ WHY THIS RECIPE WORKS

Classic potato salad is too often blanketed in a mayonnaise-rich dressing that results in bland flavor. We were looking for flavorful, tender potatoes punctuated by crunchy bits of onion and celery. We found that seasoning the potatoes while they're hot maximizes flavor, so we tossed hot russet potatoes with white vinegar. A conservative hand with the mayonnaise made for a creamy, but not soupy, salad. In the crunch department, celery is a must, and one rib fit the bill. Among scallions, shallots, and red, yellow, white, and Vidalia onions, red onion was the winner for its bright color and taste. For a pickled flavor, we decided on pickle relish, which requires no preparation and gives the potato salad a subtle sweetness. We tested celery seeds, a seasoning that has fallen out of favor; celery seeds didn't merely add strong celery flavor but also provided an underlying complexity and depth.

ALL-AMERICAN POTATO SALAD

SERVES 4 TO 6

Note that this recipe calls for celery seeds, not celery salt; if only celery salt is available, use the same amount but omit the addition of salt in the dressing. When testing the potatoes for doneness, simply taste a piece; do not overcook the potatoes or they will become mealy and will break apart. The potatoes must be just warm, or even fully cooled, when you add the dressing. If the potato salad seems a little dry, add up to 2 tablespoons more mayonnaise.

2   pounds russet potatoes, peeled and cut into ¾-inch cubes
    Salt
2   tablespoons distilled white vinegar
1   celery rib, chopped fine
½   cup mayonnaise
3   tablespoons sweet pickle relish
2   tablespoons minced red onion
2   tablespoons minced fresh parsley
¾   teaspoon dry mustard
¾   teaspoon celery seeds
¼   teaspoon pepper
2   large Hard-Cooked Eggs (page 534), peeled and cut into ¼-inch cubes (optional)

1. Place potatoes in large saucepan and add water to cover by 1 inch. Bring to boil over medium-high heat; add 1 tablespoon salt, reduce heat to medium, and simmer, stirring once or twice, until potatoes are tender, about 8 minutes.

2. Drain potatoes and transfer to large bowl. Add vinegar and, using rubber spatula, toss gently to combine. Let stand until potatoes are just warm, about 20 minutes.

3. Meanwhile, in small bowl, stir together celery, mayonnaise, relish, onion, parsley, mustard, celery seeds, pepper, and ½ teaspoon salt. Using rubber spatula, gently fold dressing and eggs, if using, into potatoes. Cover with plastic wrap and refrigerate until chilled, about 1 hour; serve. (Potato salad can be refrigerated for up to 1 day.)

GARLICKY POTATO SALAD WITH TOMATOES AND BASIL

SERVES 4 TO 6

When testing the potatoes for doneness, simply taste a piece; do not overcook the potatoes or they will become mealy and will break apart. The potatoes must be just warm, or even fully cooled, when you add the dressing. If the potato salad seems a little dry, add up to 2 tablespoons more mayonnaise.

2   pounds russet potatoes, peeled and cut into ¾-inch cubes
    Salt
2   tablespoons distilled white vinegar
1   celery rib, chopped fine
½   cup mayonnaise
2   tablespoons minced red onion
2   tablespoons minced fresh parsley
1   garlic clove, minced
¼   teaspoon pepper
2   Foolproof Hard-Cooked Eggs (page 534), peeled and cut into ¼-inch cubes (optional)
½   cup chopped fresh basil
6   ounces cherry tomatoes, halved

1. Place potatoes in large saucepan and add water to cover by 1 inch. Bring to boil over medium-high heat; add 1 tablespoon salt, reduce heat to medium, and simmer, stirring once or twice, until potatoes are tender, about 8 minutes.

2. Drain potatoes and transfer to large bowl. Add vinegar and, using rubber spatula, toss gently to combine. Let stand until potatoes are just warm, about 20 minutes.

3. Meanwhile, in small bowl, stir together celery, mayonnaise, onion, parsley, garlic, pepper, and ½ teaspoon salt. Using rubber spatula, gently fold dressing and eggs, if using, into potatoes. Cover with plastic wrap and refrigerate until chilled, about 1 hour. Just before serving, add basil and tomatoes; serve. (Potato salad can be refrigerated for up to 1 day.)

FRENCH POTATO SALAD

✓ WHY THIS RECIPE WORKS

French potato salad should be pleasing not only to the eye but also to the palate. The potatoes (small red potatoes are traditional) should be tender but not mushy, and the flavor of the vinaigrette should penetrate the relatively bland potatoes. To eliminate torn skins and broken slices, a common pitfall in boiling skin-on red potatoes, we sliced the potatoes before boiling them. Then to evenly infuse the potatoes with the garlicky mustard vinaigrette, we spread the warm potatoes out on a sheet pan and poured the vinaigrette over the top. Gently folding in fresh herbs just before serving helped keep the potatoes intact.

FRENCH POTATO SALAD WITH DIJON MUSTARD AND FINES HERBES

SERVES 6

If fresh chervil isn't available, substitute an additional ½ tablespoon of minced parsley and an additional ½ teaspoon of tarragon. For best flavor, serve the salad warm.

2   pounds small red potatoes, cut into ¼-inch-thick slices
2   tablespoons salt
1   garlic clove, peeled and threaded on skewer
1½ tablespoons champagne vinegar or white wine vinegar
2   teaspoons Dijon mustard
¼   cup olive oil
½   teaspoon pepper
1   small shallot, minced
1   tablespoon minced fresh chervil
1   tablespoon minced fresh parsley
1   tablespoon minced fresh chives
1   teaspoon minced fresh tarragon

1. Place potatoes and salt in large saucepan and add water to cover by 1 inch; bring to boil over high heat, then reduce heat to medium. Lower skewered garlic into simmering water and partially blanch, about 45 seconds. Immediately run garlic under cold running water to stop cooking; remove garlic from skewer and set aside. Continue to simmer potatoes, uncovered, until tender but still firm (thin-bladed paring knife can be slipped into and out of center of potato slice with no resistance), about 5 minutes. Drain potatoes, reserving ¼ cup cooking water. Arrange hot potatoes close together in single layer on rimmed baking sheet.

2. Press garlic through garlic press or mince by hand. Whisk garlic, reserved potato cooking water, vinegar, mustard, oil, and pepper in small bowl until combined. Drizzle dressing evenly over warm potatoes; let stand 10 minutes.

3. Toss shallot and herbs in small bowl. Transfer potatoes to large serving bowl; add shallot-herb mixture and mix gently with rubber spatula to combine. Serve immediately.

TO MAKE AHEAD: Follow recipe through step 2, cover with plastic wrap, and refrigerate. Before serving, bring salad to room temperature, then add shallots and herbs.

FRENCH POTATO SALAD WITH ARUGULA, ROQUEFORT, AND WALNUTS

Omit herbs and toss dressed potatoes with ½ cup walnuts, toasted and coarsely chopped, 4 ounces Roquefort cheese, crumbled, and 3 ounces baby arugula, torn into bite-size pieces (3 cups) along with the shallots in step 3.

FRENCH POTATO SALAD WITH FENNEL, TOMATO, AND OLIVES

When chopping the fennel fronds for this variation, use only the delicate wispy leaves, not the tough, fibrous stems to which they are attached.

Trim stalks and fronds from 1 small

fennel bulb; roughly chop and reserve ¼ cup fronds. Halve bulb lengthwise; using paring knife, core 1 half of bulb, reserving second half for another use. Cut half crosswise into very thin slices. Omit chervil, chives, and tarragon, and increase parsley to 3 tablespoons. Toss dressed potatoes with fennel, 1 tomato, peeled, seeded, and diced medium, and ¼ cup oil-cured black olives, pitted and quartered, along with shallots and parsley in step 3.

FRENCH POTATO SALAD WITH RADISHES, CORNICHONS, AND CAPERS

Omit herbs and substitute 2 tablespoons minced red onion for shallot. Toss dressed potatoes with 2 thinly sliced red radishes, ¼ cup capers, rinsed and drained, and ¼ cup cornichons, thinly sliced, along with red onion in step 3.

GERMAN POTATO SALAD

✔ **WHY THIS RECIPE WORKS**
German potato salad is best served warm and offers a balance of big flavors from bacon and vinegar. To avoid the common problems of disintegrating potatoes and a flavorless vinaigrette, we used low-starch potatoes (e.g., small red potatoes) cut in half and cooked in heavily salted water. For flavor, we fried up plenty of bacon, then used just part of the rendered fat in the vinaigrette, along with white vinegar, whole grain mustard, sugar, and some of the potato cooking water, which added body to the dressing.

GERMAN POTATO SALAD
SERVES 6 TO 8

We prefer to use medium red potatoes, measuring 1 to 2 inches in diameter, in this recipe. A traditional skillet, unlike a nonstick skillet, will allow the bacon to form caramelized bits on the skillet bottom. This will result in a richer-tasting dressing and a more flavorful salad.

2   pounds red potatoes, halved if smaller or quartered if larger
     Salt
8   slices bacon, cut into ½-inch pieces
1   onion, chopped fine
½   teaspoon sugar
½   cup white vinegar
1   tablespoon whole grain mustard
¼   teaspoon pepper
¼   cup chopped fresh parsley

1. Place potatoes, 1 tablespoon salt, and water to cover in large saucepan or Dutch oven, bring to boil over high heat, then reduce heat to medium and simmer until potatoes are tender (thin-bladed paring knife can be slipped into and out of potatoes with little resistance), about 10 minutes. Reserve ½ cup potato cooking water, then drain potatoes; return potatoes to pot and cover to keep warm.

2. While potatoes are simmering, cook bacon in 12-inch skillet over medium heat, stirring occasionally, until brown and crisp, 5 to 7 minutes. With slotted spoon, transfer bacon to paper towel–lined plate; pour off all but ¼ cup bacon grease. Add onion to skillet and cook, stirring occasionally over medium heat until softened and beginning to brown, about 4 minutes. Stir in sugar until dissolved, about 30 seconds. Add vinegar and reserved potato cooking water; bring to simmer and cook until mixture is reduced to about 1 cup, about 3 minutes. Off heat, whisk in mustard and pepper. Add potatoes, parsley, and bacon to skillet and toss to combine; adjust seasoning with salt. Transfer to serving bowl and serve. (Potato salad can be refrigerated for up to 1 day.)

AUSTRIAN-STYLE POTATO SALAD

✔ **WHY THIS RECIPE WORKS**
For a creamy and light potato salad, we did as the Austrians do: ditch the mayo and look to the soup pot. Simmering the potatoes in a shallow pan with chicken stock, water, sugar, and salt yielded deeply flavored potatoes. Yukon Golds had just enough starch to contribute creaminess without breaking apart. For the dressing, a little mashed potato thickened it perfectly every time.

TEST KITCHEN TIP NO. 14   KEEPING POTATO SALAD SAFE

Mayonnaise has gotten a bad reputation, being blamed for spoiled potato salads and upset stomachs after many summer picnics and barbecues. You may think that switching from a mayonnaise-based dressing to a vinaigrette will protect your potato salad (and your family) from food poisoning. Think again.

The main ingredients in mayonnaise are raw eggs, vegetable oil, and an acid (usually vinegar or lemon juice). The eggs used in commercially made mayonnaise have been pasteurized to kill salmonella and other bacteria. Its high acidity is another safeguard; because bacteria do not fare well in acidic environments, the lemon juice or vinegar inhibits bacterial growth. Mayonnaise, even when homemade, is rarely a problem unless it contains very little acid. It's the potatoes that are more likely to go bad.

The bacteria usually responsible for spoiled potato salad are Bacillus cereus and Staphylococcus aureus (commonly known as staph). Both are found in soil and dust, and they thrive on starchy, low-acid foods like rice, pasta, and potatoes. If they find their way into your potato salad via an unwashed cutting board or contaminated hands, they can wreak havoc on your digestive system.

Most foodborne bacteria grow well at temperatures between 40 and 140 degrees Fahrenheit. This is known as the temperature danger zone and if contaminated food remains in this zone for too long, the bacteria can produce enough toxins to make you sick. The U.S. Food and Drug Administration recommends refrigerating food within two hours of its preparation, or one hour if the room temperature is above 90 degrees. Heat from the sun is often what causes the trouble at summer picnics.

To ensure that good memories are the only thing people pick up at your party, play it safe; don't leave potato salad out for more than two hours and promptly refrigerate any leftovers.

AUSTRIAN-STYLE POTATO SALAD
SERVES 4 TO 6

The finished salad should be creamy and loose, with chunks of potato that keep their shape but are very tender. If you can't find cornichons, chopped kosher dill pickles can be substituted. For best results, don't refrigerate the salad; it should be served within 4 hours of preparation.

    2   pounds Yukon Gold potatoes,
        peeled, quartered lengthwise, and
        cut into ½-inch-thick slices
    1   cup low-sodium chicken broth
    1   cup water
        Salt and pepper
    1   tablespoon sugar
    2   tablespoons white wine vinegar
    1   tablespoon Dijon mustard
    ¼   cup vegetable oil
    1   small red onion, chopped fine
    6   cornichons, minced
        (2 tablespoons)
    2   tablespoons minced fresh chives

1. Bring potatoes, broth, water, 1 teaspoon salt, sugar, and 1 tablespoon vinegar to boil in 12-inch skillet over high heat. Reduce heat to medium-low, cover, and cook until potatoes offer no resistance when pierced with paring knife, 15 to 17 minutes. Remove cover, increase heat to high (so cooking liquid will reduce), and cook 2 minutes.

2. Drain potatoes in colander set over large bowl, reserving cooking liquid. Set drained potatoes aside. Pour off and discard all but ½ cup cooking liquid (if ½ cup liquid does not remain, add water to make ½ cup). Whisk remaining tablespoon vinegar, mustard, and oil into cooking liquid.

3. Add ½ cup cooked potatoes to bowl with cooking liquid mixture and mash with potato masher or fork until thick sauce forms (mixture will be slightly chunky). Add remaining potatoes, onion,

cornichons, and chives, folding gently with rubber spatula to combine. Season with salt and pepper to taste. Serve warm or at room temperature.

CHICKEN SALAD

✔ WHY THIS RECIPE WORKS
To create a creamy chicken salad that tasted moist and flavorful, not bland or waterlogged, we tried wet cooking methods, including poaching and steaming, roasting in foil (which is similar to steaming), and, in a method new to us, dropping the chicken into simmering aromatic water and then removing the pot from the heat and letting the chicken and water cool to room temperature. Unfortunately, all four methods produced a bland, unmistakably boiled flavor. Roasting chicken breasts was another matter. Even after the flavorful skin and bones were removed, the meat tasted roasted, and the resulting chicken salad was superb. A mayonnaise-based dressing brightened with lemon juice and accented with celery, scallions, and parsley bound together our moist chicken for a chicken salad that was anything but boring.

CLASSIC CREAMY CHICKEN SALAD
SERVES 6

In addition to the parsley, you can flavor the salad with 2 tablespoons of minced fresh tarragon or basil. Use the higher amount of mayonnaise for a creamier chicken salad and likewise, use the higher amount of lemon juice for a tangier flavor.

    CHICKEN
    2   (1½-pound) whole bone-in
        chicken breasts
    1   tablespoon vegetable oil
        Salt

    SALAD
    2   celery ribs, cut into small dice
    2   scallions, minced
    ¾–1 cup mayonnaise
    1½–2 tablespoons lemon juice
    2   tablespoons minced fresh parsley

1. Adjust oven rack to middle position and heat oven to 400 degrees. Set breasts on small, aluminum foil–lined rimmed baking sheet. Brush with oil and sprinkle generously with salt. Roast until chicken registers 160 degrees, 35 to 40 minutes. Let cool to room temperature, remove skin and bones, and shred meat into bite-size pieces (about 5 cups).

2. Using the lesser amounts of mayonnaise and lemon juice, mix all salad ingredients (including chicken) together in large bowl. Adjust flavor and consistency with additional mayonnaise and lemon juice and salt and pepper to taste. Serve. (Chicken salad can be refrigerated overnight.)

CURRIED CHICKEN SALAD WITH RAISINS AND HONEY

Add 6 tablespoons golden raisins, 1 tablespoon honey, and 2 teaspoons curry powder. Substitute cilantro for parsley.

WALDORF CHICKEN SALAD

Add 1 large crisp apple, cored and cut into medium dice, and 6 tablespoons chopped toasted walnuts.

CHICKEN SALAD WITH HOISIN DRESSING

Try serving this Asian-style salad on a bed of baby spinach leaves with sliced cucumber and radishes or rolled in a flour tortilla with shredded iceberg lettuce or watercress.

Omit mayonnaise and lemon juice. In small bowl, whisk together ⅓ cup rice vinegar, 3 tablespoons hoisin sauce, 1½ tablespoons soy sauce, and 1 tablespoon minced or grated fresh ginger. Whisk in

3 tablespoons vegetable oil and 1 tablespoon toasted sesame oil until combined. Substitute cilantro for parsley.

DINNER-STYLE CHICKEN SALAD

✔ WHY THIS RECIPE WORKS

While we love traditional, creamy chicken salad, sometimes we crave a dinner-style chicken salad. Trading in vinaigrette dressing for the usual mayonnaise was our first step. Adding an emulsifier such as pureed roasted red pepper or peanut butter, not only provided stability but also contributed bold flavor. Using a blender to mix the dressings provided insurance against separation. We preferred a mix of white and dark meat so we opted to roast a whole chicken. With bright, creamy dressing at the ready, we just stirred in handfuls of fresh vegetables, herbs, and toasted nuts along with the chicken for a fresh, flavorful take on classic chicken salad.

CHICKEN SALAD WITH ASPARAGUS AND SUN-DRIED TOMATO DRESSING

SERVES 6

This recipe is best served over salad greens.

½ cup extra-virgin olive oil plus 1 additional tablespoon
¼ cup red wine vinegar
½ cup oil-packed sun-dried tomatoes, rinsed and minced
1 small garlic clove, minced
   Salt and pepper
½ pound asparagus, trimmed and cut on bias into 1-inch lengths
1 cup chopped fresh basil
1 recipe Classic Roast Chicken (page 336), cooled, meat removed and shredded into 2-inch pieces
3 ounces goat cheese, crumbled (¾ cup) (optional)
½ cup pine nuts, toasted

1. Puree ½ cup oil, vinegar, sun-dried tomatoes, garlic, ¼ teaspoon salt, and ½ teaspoon pepper in blender until smooth. Transfer to large bowl. (Dressing may be made ahead of time, covered, and refrigerated overnight. Whisk to recombine before using.)

2. Heat remaining tablespoon oil in 10-inch nonstick skillet over high heat until beginning to smoke; add asparagus, ¼ teaspoon salt, and ¼ teaspoon pepper; cook until asparagus is browned and almost tender, about 3 minutes, stirring occasionally. Transfer to plate and let cool.

3. Add cooled asparagus and basil to vinaigrette; stir to combine. Add chicken and toss gently to combine; let stand at room temperature 15 minutes. Season with salt and pepper to taste and sprinkle with goat cheese, if using, and pine nuts. Serve immediately.

THAI-STYLE CHICKEN SALAD WITH SPICY PEANUT DRESSING

SERVES 6

This recipe is best served over salad greens.

½ cup canola oil
3 tablespoons smooth peanut butter
½ cup lime juice (3 to 4 limes)
2 tablespoons water
   Salt and pepper
3 small garlic cloves, minced
2 teaspoons grated fresh ginger
2 tablespoons light brown sugar
1½ teaspoons red pepper flakes
½ cucumber, peeled, halved lengthwise, seeded, and cut into 1-inch-long matchsticks
1 carrot, peeled and shredded
4 scallions, sliced thin
3 tablespoons minced fresh cilantro
1 recipe Classic Roasted Chicken (page 336), cooled, meat removed and shredded into 2-inch pieces
½ cup unsalted peanuts, toasted and chopped

1. Puree oil, peanut butter, lime juice, water, ¼ teaspoon salt, garlic, ginger, brown sugar, and pepper flakes in blender until combined. Transfer to large bowl. (Dressing may be made ahead of time, covered, and refrigerated overnight. Whisk to recombine before using.)

2. Add cucumber, carrot, scallions, and cilantro to vinaigrette; toss to combine. Add chicken and toss gently to combine; let stand at room temperature 15 minutes. Season with salt and pepper to taste and sprinkle with peanuts. Serve immediately.

SPANISH-STYLE CHICKEN SALAD WITH ROASTED RED PEPPER DRESSING

SERVES 6

This recipe is best served over salad greens.

1⅓ cups chopped jarred roasted red peppers
½ cup extra-virgin olive oil
3 tablespoons sherry vinegar or balsamic vinegar
1 small garlic clove, minced
   Salt and pepper
2 celery ribs, sliced very thin
½ cup chopped pitted green olives
3 tablespoons minced fresh parsley
1 small shallot, minced
1 recipe Classic Roasted Chicken (page 336), cooled, meat removed and shredded into 2-inch pieces
½ cup sliced almonds, toasted

1. Puree ⅔ cup roasted red peppers, oil, vinegar, garlic, ¼ teaspoon salt, and ½ teaspoon pepper in blender until smooth. Transfer to bowl.

2. Add celery, olives, parsley, shallot, and remaining ⅔ cup red peppers to vinaigrette; stir to combine. Add chicken and toss gently to combine; let stand at room temperature 15 minutes. Season with salt and pepper to taste and sprinkle with almonds. Serve immediately.

CLASSIC TUNA SALAD

✔ WHY THIS RECIPE WORKS

For tuna salad that is evenly textured, moist, and well seasoned every time, we used high-quality solid white water-packed tuna. For best texture, we broke down the chunks of tuna with our fingers and seasoned the tuna before adding mayonnaise. Celery, red onion, pickles, garlic, and parsley are musts for classic tuna salad. Other flavor combinations like balsamic vinegar and grapes or lime and horseradish offer lively interpretations of the sandwich classic.

CLASSIC TUNA SALAD

MAKES ABOUT 2 CUPS,
ENOUGH FOR 4 SANDWICHES

2	(6-ounce) cans solid white tuna in water
2	tablespoons lemon juice
	Salt and pepper
1	small celery rib, minced
2	tablespoons minced red onion
2	tablespoons chopped pickles (sweet or dill)
½	small garlic clove, minced
2	tablespoons minced fresh parsley
½	cup mayonnaise
¼	teaspoon Dijon mustard

Drain tuna in colander and shred with fingers until no clumps remain and texture is fine and even. Transfer tuna to medium bowl and mix in lemon juice, ½ teaspoon salt, ¼ teaspoon pepper, celery, onion, pickles, garlic, and parsley until evenly blended. Fold in mayonnaise and mustard until tuna is evenly moistened. (Tuna salad can be refrigerated for up to 3 days.)

TUNA SALAD WITH BALSAMIC VINEGAR AND GRAPES

Omit lemon juice, pickles, garlic, and parsley and add 2 tablespoons balsamic vinegar, 6 ounces halved red seedless grapes (1 cup), ¼ cup lightly toasted slivered almonds, and 2 teaspoons minced fresh thyme to tuna along with salt and pepper.

CURRIED TUNA SALAD WITH APPLES AND CURRANTS

Omit pickles, garlic, and parsley and add 1 firm apple, cut into ¼-inch dice (1 cup), ¼ cup currants, and 2 tablespoons minced fresh basil to tuna along with lemon juice, salt, and pepper. Mix 1 tablespoon curry powder into mayonnaise before folding into tuna.

TUNA SALAD WITH LIME AND HORSERADISH

Omit lemon juice, pickles, and garlic and add ½ teaspoon grated lime zest and 2 tablespoons lime juice and 3 tablespoons prepared horseradish to tuna along with salt and pepper.

TUNA SALAD WITH CAULIFLOWER, JALAPEÑO, AND CILANTRO

Omit pickles, garlic, and parsley and add 4 ounces cauliflower florets cut into ½-inch pieces (1 cup), 1 minced jalapeño chile, 2 minced scallions, and 2 tablespoons minced fresh cilantro to tuna along with lemon juice, salt, and pepper.

SHRIMP SALAD

✔ WHY THIS RECIPE WORKS

Great shrimp salad should possess firm and tender shrimp and a perfect deli-style dressing that complements, but does not mask, the flavor of the shrimp or drown out the other ingredients. We started by cooking the shrimp in cold court bouillon, then heated the shrimp and liquid to just a near simmer. We kept the traditional mayonnaise in our shrimp salad recipe, but limited the amount to ¼ cup per pound of shrimp.

We prefer milder minced shallot over onion and minced celery for its subtle flavor and crunch.

SHRIMP SALAD

SERVES 4

This recipe can also be prepared with large shrimp (31 to 40 per pound); the cooking time will be 1 to 2 minutes less. The shrimp can be cooked up to 24 hours in advance, but hold off on dressing the salad until ready to serve. The recipe can be easily doubled; cook the shrimp in a 7-quart Dutch oven and increase the cooking time to 12 to 14 minutes. Serve the salad over greens or on buttered and grilled buns.

1	pound extra-large shrimp (21 to 25 per pound), peeled, deveined, and tails removed
5	tablespoons lemon juice (2 lemons), spent halves reserved
5	sprigs fresh parsley plus 1 teaspoon minced
3	sprigs fresh tarragon plus 1 teaspoon minced
1	teaspoon whole black peppercorns
1	tablespoon sugar
	Salt and pepper
¼	cup mayonnaise
1	small shallot, minced
1	small celery rib, minced

1. Combine shrimp, ¼ cup lemon juice, reserved lemon halves, parsley sprigs, tarragon sprigs, whole peppercorns, sugar, and 1 teaspoon salt with 2 cups cold water in medium saucepan. Place saucepan over medium heat and cook shrimp, stirring several times, until pink, firm to touch, and centers are no longer translucent, 8 to 10 minutes (water should be just bubbling around edge of pan and register 165 degrees). Remove pan from heat, cover, and let shrimp sit in broth for 2 minutes.

2. Meanwhile, fill medium bowl with ice water. Drain shrimp into colander, discard lemon halves, herbs, and spices.

Immediately transfer shrimp to ice water to stop cooking and chill thoroughly, about 3 minutes. Remove shrimp from ice water and pat dry with paper towels.

3. Whisk together mayonnaise, shallot, celery, remaining 1 tablespoon lemon juice, minced parsley, and minced tarragon in medium bowl. Cut shrimp in half lengthwise and then cut each half into thirds; add shrimp to mayonnaise mixture and toss to combine. Season with salt and pepper to taste and serve. (Shrimp salad can be refrigerated overnight.)

SHRIMP SALAD WITH ROASTED RED PEPPER AND BASIL

Omit tarragon sprigs from cooking liquid. Replace celery, minced parsley, and minced tarragon with 1/3 cup thinly sliced jarred roasted red peppers, 2 teaspoons rinsed capers, and 3 tablespoons chopped fresh basil.

SHRIMP SALAD WITH AVOCADO AND ORANGE

Omit tarragon sprigs from cooking liquid. Replace celery, minced parsley, and minced tarragon with 4 halved and thinly sliced radishes; 1 large orange, peeled and cut into 1/2-inch pieces; 1/2 avocado, halved, pitted, and cut into 1/2-inch pieces; and 2 teaspoons minced fresh mint.

SPICY SHRIMP SALAD WITH CORN AND CHIPOTLE

Substitute lime juice (3 to 4 limes; save spent halves) for lemon juice and omit tarragon sprigs from cooking liquid. Replace celery, minced parsley, and minced tarragon with 1/2 cup cooked corn kernels, 2 tablespoons minced canned chipotle chile in adobo sauce, and 1 tablespoon minced fresh cilantro.

SHRIMP SALAD WITH WASABI AND PICKLED GINGER

Omit tarragon sprigs from cooking liquid. Replace shallot, minced parsley, and minced tarragon with 2 thinly sliced scallions, 2 tablespoons chopped pickled ginger, 1 tablespoon toasted sesame seeds, and 2 teaspoons wasabi powder.

CLASSIC EGG SALAD

✔ WHY THIS RECIPE WORKS

For creamy, flavorful egg salad with perfectly cooked eggs and just the right amount of crunch, we followed a few simple steps. First, we relied on our recipe for Hard-Cooked Eggs (page 534), which yielded eggs with perfectly creamy yolks, tender whites, and no green ring. We diced the eggs to keep the salad from turning pasty. Then we combined them with mayonnaise (our tasters dismissed ingredients such as cottage cheese, sour cream, and cream cheese as extraneous), lemon juice, mustard, red onion, celery, and parsley.

CLASSIC EGG SALAD

MAKES 2½ CUPS, ENOUGH FOR
4 SANDWICHES

Be sure to use red onion; yellow onion is too harsh.

- 6 Foolproof Hard-Cooked Eggs (page 534), peeled and diced medium
- ¼ cup mayonnaise
- 2 tablespoons minced red onion
- 1 tablespoon minced fresh parsley
- ½ celery rib, minced
- 2 teaspoons Dijon mustard
- 2 teaspoons lemon juice
- ¼ teaspoon salt
  Pepper

Mix all ingredients together in medium bowl, including pepper to taste. Serve. (Egg salad can be refrigerated in an airtight container for 1 day.)

EGG SALAD WITH RADISH, SCALLIONS, AND DILL

Substitute 1 tablespoon minced fresh dill for parsley, 1 thinly sliced scallion for red onion, and add 3 minced radishes.

CURRIED EGG SALAD

Substitute 1 tablespoon minced fresh cilantro for parsley and add 1½ teaspoons curry powder. Omit salt.

CREAMY EGG SALAD WITH CAPERS AND ANCHOVIES

Add 1 minced small garlic clove, 2 tablespoons chopped capers, and 1 minced anchovy fillet. Omit salt.

CREAMY EGG SALAD WITH BACON, SHALLOTS, AND WATERCRESS

In 10-inch skillet over medium heat, cook 4 slices bacon, cut into ¼-inch pieces, until brown and crisp, 5 to 7 minutes. Transfer bacon with slotted spoon to paper towel–lined plate; pour off all but 1 tablespoon of fat from pan. Add 2 large shallots, chopped medium, and sauté until softened and browned, about 5 minutes. Omit celery and salt, substitute sautéed shallots for red onion, and add the bacon and ¼ cup watercress leaves, chopped coarse.

CHAPTER 3 Soups

QUICK CHICKEN STOCK

✔ **WHY THIS RECIPE WORKS**

Many recipes for homemade chicken stock simmer a whole chicken in water; we found that cutting the chicken parts into small pieces released the chicken flavor in a shorter amount of time since more surface area of the meat is exposed. This also exposed more bone marrow, key for both flavor and a thicker consistency. After testing a variety of vegetables, we found only onion was crucial. Sweating the chicken pieces for 20 minutes before adding the water further sped along the release of flavor, keeping our cooking time short. Make sure to use 6-quart or larger stockpot or Dutch oven for this recipe.

QUICK CHICKEN STOCK

MAKES ABOUT 8 CUPS

To defat hot stock, we recommend using a ladle or fat separator. Alternatively, after the stock has been refrigerated, the fat hardens on the surface and is very easy to remove with a spoon.

1	tablespoon vegetable oil
1	onion, chopped
4	pounds whole chicken legs or backs and wingtips, cut into 2-inch pieces
8	cups boiling water
½	teaspoon salt
2	bay leaves

1. Heat oil in stockpot or Dutch oven over medium-high heat until shimmering. Add half of chicken pieces and cook until lightly browned, about 5 minutes per side. Transfer cooked chicken to bowl and repeat with remaining chicken pieces; transfer to bowl with first batch. Add onion and cook, stirring frequently, until onion is translucent, 3 to 5 minutes.

2. Return onion and chicken to pot. Reduce heat to low, cover, and sweat until chicken releases its juices, about 20 minutes. Increase heat to high and add boiling water, salt, and bay leaves. Bring to boil, then reduce heat to low, cover, and simmer slowly until stock is rich and flavorful, about 20 minutes, skimming foam off surface if desired.

3. Strain stock through fine-mesh strainer; discard solids. Before using, defat stock. (Stock can be refrigerated for up to 4 days or frozen for up to 6 months.)

RICH BEEF STOCK

✔ **WHY THIS RECIPE WORKS**

To develop a rich beef stock, we made six stocks with six different cuts of beef, adding marrowbones to the boneless cuts to establish an equal meat-to-bone ratio in each pot. Tasters liked the stock made from shanks best, though beef chuck also worked well. In addition to using the right cut, we found the best stock is made with lots of beef. Most recipes skimp, but we found a full 6 pounds of shanks was required to make 8 cups of rich-tasting stock. To extract maximum flavor and body from the meat and bones, we discovered beef stock must be simmered much longer than chicken stock. Red wine, used to deglaze the pan after browning the beef, added an extra layer of flavor.

RICH BEEF STOCK

MAKES 8 CUPS

To defat hot stock, we recommend using a ladle or fat separator. Alternatively, after the stock has been refrigerated, the fat hardens on the surface and is very easy to remove with a spoon. Make sure to use 6-quart or larger stockpot or Dutch oven for this recipe.

2	tablespoons vegetable oil
1	large onion, chopped
6	pounds beef shanks, meat cut from bone in large chunks, or 4 pounds beef chuck, cut into 3-inch chunks, and 2 pounds small marrowbones
½	cup dry red wine
8	cups boiling water
½	teaspoon salt
2	bay leaves

1. Heat 1 tablespoon oil in stockpot or Dutch oven over medium-high heat until shimmering. Add onion and cook, stirring occasionally, until slightly softened, 2 to 3 minutes. Transfer to large bowl.

2. Brown meat and bones on all sides in 3 or 4 batches, about 5 minutes per batch, adding remaining oil to pot as necessary; do not overcrowd. Transfer to bowl with onion. Add wine to pot and cook, scraping up browned bits with wooden spoon, until wine is reduced to about 3 tablespoons, about 2 minutes. Return browned beef and onion to pot, reduce heat to low, cover, and sweat until meat releases juices, about 20 minutes. Increase heat to high, add boiling water, salt, and bay leaves. Bring to boil, then reduce heat to low, cover, and simmer slowly until meat is tender and stock is flavorful, 1½ to 2 hours, skimming foam off surface. Strain and discard bones and onion; reserve meat for another use, if desired.

3. Before using, defat stock. (Stock can be refrigerated for up to 4 days or frozen for up to 6 months.)

FISH STOCK

✔ **WHY THIS RECIPE WORKS**

Unlike long-simmering chicken or beef stews, fish stews (and soups) typically cook for a short period, so using a full-flavored homemade fish stock can make a big difference. Fish bones are key for flavoring stock as well as adding viscosity, and we tested a wide variety of fish to see which worked and which didn't. Bones from mild white fish worked best, while those from oily fish had an overpowering flavor. We found that sweating the vegetables tended to cloud the stock's flavors, so we simply brought all the ingredients to a simmer and added wine for some acidity. For those times when we didn't want to fuss with making old-fashioned fish stock, we found that doctoring clam juice was a good stand-in and took just half an hour to prepare.

CLASSIC FISH STOCK
MAKES ABOUT 8 CUPS

You can often buy fish frames (skeletons) cheaply at your local fish market, or ask for them at the fish counter of your local supermarket. We like frames from mild white fish the most. Note that the type of fish bones you use can make a big difference in the flavor of the stock; see below for more information. Make sure to use 6-quart or larger stockpot or Dutch oven for this recipe.

2	tablespoons unsalted butter
3	pounds fish frames, cleaned
2	onions, chopped
1	large celery rib, chopped coarse
5	ounces white mushrooms, trimmed and quartered
½	ounce dried porcini mushrooms, rinsed (optional)
5	garlic cloves, peeled and smashed
1¾	cups dry white wine
8	cups water
6	sprigs fresh parsley
5	sprigs fresh thyme
2	teaspoons salt
8	whole black peppercorns
2	bay leaves

1. Melt butter in stockpot or Dutch oven over high heat. Add fish frames, onions, celery, white mushrooms, porcini mushrooms, if using, and garlic, cover, and cook, stirring occasionally, until fish frames have begun to release some liquid, 6 to 8 minutes.

2. Reduce heat to medium and continue to cook, covered, stirring often with wooden spoon to break apart fish frames, until vegetables and bones are soft and aromatic, 6 to 8 minutes longer.

3. Add wine, cover, and simmer gently for 10 minutes. Add water, parsley, thyme, salt, peppercorns, and bay leaves. Return to gentle simmer and cook, uncovered, skimming as needed, until stock tastes rich and flavorful, about 30 minutes longer.

4. Strain stock through fine-mesh strainer, then defat stock. (Stock can be refrigerated for up to 4 days or frozen for up to 1 month.)

CHEATER'S FISH STOCK
MAKES ABOUT 4 CUPS

Clam juice is very salty so don't add salt to this stock until after you add the clam juice and taste it.

1	small onion, chopped
1	carrot, chopped
1	celery rib, chopped
8	sprigs fresh parsley
1	cup dry white wine
6	(8-ounce) bottles clam juice
2	bay leaves
8	whole black peppercorns
½	teaspoon dried thyme
	Salt

Bring all ingredients to boil in medium saucepan and simmer to blend flavors, about 30 minutes. Strain stock through cheesecloth, pressing on solids with back of spoon to extract as much liquid as possible. Season with salt to taste. Use immediately.

ULTIMATE VEGETABLE STOCK

✔ WHY THIS RECIPE WORKS
We wanted a nicely balanced, robust stock that vegetarians and nonvegetarians alike would consider making. Caramelizing plenty of onion, shallot, and garlic was a great start to ensuring depth and a sweetness that wasn't one-dimensional. Then we tossed in a few nontraditional ingredients—cauliflower, collard greens, lemon grass, and scallions—to add complexity. Finally, finishing with a splash of rice vinegar produced a full-flavored stock that could stand on its own.

ULTIMATE VEGETABLE STOCK
MAKES ABOUT 4 CUPS

It is important to use a heavy-bottomed Dutch oven or stockpot so that the vegetables caramelize properly without burning. Lemon grass is available in some grocery stores and most Asian markets. You can omit lemon grass if you cannot find it; the flavor of the stock will still be very good.

2	onions, peeled and chopped
1	head garlic (10 to 12 cloves), cloves peeled and smashed
8	ounces shallots, sliced thin
1	celery rib, chopped
1	small carrot, peeled and chopped
	Vegetable oil spray
2	pounds leeks, white and light green parts only, halved lengthwise, chopped, and washed thoroughly
8½	cups boiling water
	Stems from 1 bunch fresh parsley
2	bay leaves

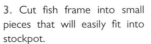

1. Lift gill cover and detach gills with kitchen shears.

2. Remove and discard gills. Rinse fish frame under cool running water.

3. Cut fish frame into small pieces that will easily fit into stockpot.

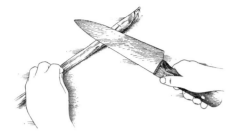

To bruise lemon grass, smack stalk with back of large chef's knife.

1½	teaspoons salt
1	teaspoon black peppercorns, coarsely cracked
1	pound collard greens, sliced crosswise into 2-inch strips
12	ounces cauliflower, chopped fine
8–10	sprigs fresh thyme
1	lemon grass stalk, trimmed to bottom 6 inches and bruised
4	scallions, sliced into 2-inch pieces
2	teaspoons rice vinegar

1. Combine onions, garlic, shallots, celery, and carrot in 8-quart stockpot or Dutch oven; spray vegetables lightly with vegetable oil spray and toss to coat. Cover and cook over low heat, stirring frequently, until pan bottom shows light brown glaze, 20 to 30 minutes. Add leeks and increase heat to medium; cook, covered, until leeks soften, about 10 minutes. Add 1½ cups boiling water and cook, partially covered, until water has evaporated to a glaze and vegetables are very soft, 25 to 35 minutes.

2. Add parsley stems, bay leaves, salt, peppercorns, and remaining 7 cups boiling water. Increase heat to medium-high and bring to simmer; reduce heat to medium-low and simmer gently, covered, to blend flavors, about 15 minutes.

3. Add collard greens, cauliflower, thyme, lemon grass, and scallions. Increase heat to medium-high and bring to simmer; reduce heat to low and simmer gently, covered, to blend flavors, about 15 minutes longer. Strain stock through large strainer into large bowl or container, allowing stock to drip through to drain thoroughly (do not press on solids). Stir vinegar into stock. (Stock can be refrigerated for up to 4 days or frozen for up to 2 months.)

CLASSIC CHICKEN NOODLE SOUP

✔ WHY THIS RECIPE WORKS
For a full-flavored chicken soup recipe that we could make without taking all day, we began by browning a cut-up chicken to set the foundation for a flavorful base. Sweating most of the browned pieces (we reserved the breast meat for shredding into the soup) with an onion allowed the meat to release its flavorful juices quickly. Then we added water and simmered just 20 minutes longer. We cooked the breast meat in the broth to infuse both with flavor and keep the meat moist. Egg noodles (also cooked right in the broth), celery, carrot, onion, thyme, and parsley rounded out our classic recipe.

CLASSIC CHICKEN NOODLE SOUP
SERVES 6 TO 8

Make sure to reserve the chicken breast pieces until step 2; they should not be browned. If you use a cleaver, you will be able to cut up the chicken parts quickly. A chef's knife or kitchen shears will also work. Be sure to reserve 2 tablespoons of chicken fat for sautéing the aromatics in step 4; however, if you prefer not to use chicken fat, vegetable oil can be substituted. Make sure to use a 6-quart or larger Dutch oven for this recipe.

STOCK

1	tablespoon vegetable oil
1	(4-pound) whole chicken, breast removed, split, and reserved; remaining chicken cut into 2-inch pieces
1	onion, chopped
8	cups boiling water
2	teaspoons salt
2	bay leaves

SOUP

2	tablespoons chicken fat, reserved from making stock, or vegetable oil
1	onion, chopped
1	large carrot, peeled and sliced ¼ inch thick
1	celery rib, sliced ¼ inch thick
½	teaspoon dried thyme
3	ounces egg noodles
¼	cup minced fresh parsley
	Salt and pepper

1. FOR THE STOCK: Heat oil in Dutch oven over medium-high heat until shimmering. Add half of chicken pieces and cook until lightly browned, about 5 minutes per side. Transfer cooked chicken to bowl and repeat with remaining chicken pieces; transfer to bowl with first batch. Add onion and cook, stirring frequently, until onion is translucent, 3 to 5 minutes. Return chicken pieces to pot. Reduce heat to low, cover, and cook until chicken releases its juices, about 20 minutes.

2. Increase heat to high; add boiling water, reserved chicken breast pieces, salt, and bay leaves. Reduce heat to medium-low and simmer until flavors have blended, about 20 minutes.

3. Remove breast pieces from pot. When cool enough to handle, remove skin from breasts, then remove meat from bones and shred into bite-size pieces; discard

skin and bones. Strain stock through fine-mesh strainer; discard solids. Allow liquid to settle, about 5 minutes, then skim off fat; reserve 2 tablespoons, if desired (see note).

4. FOR THE SOUP: Heat reserved chicken fat in Dutch oven over medium-high heat. Add onion, carrot, and celery and cook until softened, about 5 minutes. Add thyme and reserved stock and simmer until the vegetables are tender, 10 to 15 minutes.

5. Add noodles and reserved shredded chicken and cook until just tender, 5 to 8 minutes. Stir in parsley, season with salt and pepper to taste, and serve. (After skimming broth in step 3, shredded chicken, strained stock, and fat can be refrigerated in separate containers for up to 2 days.)

CLASSIC CHICKEN SOUP WITH ORZO AND SPRING VEGETABLES

Substitute 1 leek, quartered lengthwise, sliced thin crosswise, and washed thoroughly, for onion and ½ cup orzo for egg noodles. Along with orzo, add 4 ounces trimmed asparagus, cut into 1-inch lengths, and ¼ cup fresh or frozen peas. Substitute 2 tablespoons minced fresh tarragon for parsley.

CLASSIC CHICKEN SOUP WITH SHELLS, TOMATOES, AND ZUCCHINI

Add 1 zucchini, diced medium, to pot with onions, carrot, and celery in step 4, increasing cooking time to 7 minutes. Add 1 tomato, cored, seeded, and chopped, to pot along with broth in step 4. Substitute 1 cup small shells or macaroni for egg noodles and simmer until noodles are just tender. Substitute ¼ cup minced fresh basil for parsley and serve with grated Parmesan, if desired.

CLASSIC CHICKEN SOUP WITH LEEKS, WILD RICE, AND MUSHROOMS
SERVES 6 TO 8

STOCK
- 1 tablespoon vegetable oil
- 1 (4-pound) whole chicken, breast removed, split, and reserved; remaining chicken cut into 2-inch pieces
- 1 onion, chopped
- 8 cups boiling water
  Salt
- 2 bay leaves
- ½ ounce dried shiitake mushrooms or other dried wild mushrooms

SOUP
- 2 tablespoons chicken fat, reserved from making stock, or vegetable oil
- 1 large carrot, peeled and sliced ¼ inch thick
- 1 leek, white and light green parts only, quartered lengthwise, sliced thin, and washed thoroughly
- 4 ounces cremini or white mushrooms, trimmed and sliced thin
- ½ teaspoon dried thyme
- ½ cup cooked wild rice
- ¼ cup minced fresh parsley
  Pepper

1. FOR THE STOCK: Heat oil in Dutch oven over medium-high heat until shimmering. Add half of chicken pieces and cook until lightly browned, about 5 minutes per side. Transfer cooked chicken to bowl and repeat with remaining chicken pieces; transfer to bowl with first batch. Add onion and cook, stirring frequently, until onion is translucent, 3 to 5 minutes. Return chicken pieces to pot. Reduce heat to low, cover, and cook until chicken releases its juices, about 20 minutes.

2. Increase heat to high; add boiling water, reserved chicken breast pieces, salt, and bay leaves. Reduce heat to medium-low and simmer until flavors have blended, about 20 minutes. Remove 1 cup of stock and pour over dried mushrooms and let sit for 30 minutes to rehydrate.

3. Remove breast pieces from pot. When cool enough to handle, remove skin from breasts, then remove meat from bones and shred into bite-size pieces; discard skin and bones. Strain stock through

TEST KITCHEN TIP NO. 15 STORING AND REHEATING SOUP

Soups, stews, and chilis make a generous number of servings, but it's easy enough to stock your freezer with last night's leftovers so you can reheat them whenever you like. First you'll need to cool the soup, but as tempting as it might seem, avoid transferring hot soup straight to the refrigerator. You may speed up the cooling process, but you'll also increase the fridge's internal temperature to unsafe levels, which is dangerous for all the other food stored in the fridge. We find that letting the soup cool on the countertop for an hour helps the temperature drop to about 85 degrees; then the soup can be transferred to the fridge. If you don't have an hour to cool your soup or stew at room temperature, you can divide it into a number of storage containers to allow the heat to dissipate more quickly, or you can cool the soup rapidly by using a frozen bottle of water to stir the contents of the pot. To freeze soups and stews in handy single servings, fill paper cups for hot beverages with a portion of cooled soup or stew, wrap well in plastic wrap, and freeze. To reheat soups and stews, we prefer to gently simmer them on the stovetop in a sturdy, heavy-bottomed pot, but a spin in the microwave works too. Just be sure to cover the dish to prevent a mess. And note that while most soups store just fine, those that contain dairy or pasta do not.

For soups that contain dairy or pasta, the dairy curdles as it freezes and the pasta turns bloated and mushy. Instead, make and freeze the soup without the dairy or pasta component included. After you have thawed the soup and it has been heated through, either stir in the uncooked pasta and simmer until just tender or stir in the dairy and continue to heat gently until hot (do not boil).

fine-mesh strainer; discard solids. Allow liquid to settle, about 5 minutes, then skim off fat; reserve 2 tablespoons, if desired (see note).

4. FOR THE SOUP: Heat reserved chicken fat in Dutch oven over medium-high heat. Add carrot and leek and cook until softened, about 5 minutes. Add fresh mushrooms to pot with carrot and leek and cook until softened, about 5 minutes. Drain and chop rehydrated dried mushrooms, reserving soaking liquid. Strain soaking liquid through fine-mesh strainer lined with coffee filter. Add thyme, reserved stock, chopped mushrooms, and strained mushroom soaking liquid and simmer until vegetables are tender, 10 to 15 minutes.

5. Add rice and reserved shredded chicken and cook until just tender, about 5 minutes. Stir in parsley, season with salt and pepper to taste, and serve. (After skimming broth in step 3, shredded chicken, strained stock, and fat can be refrigerated in separate containers for up to 2 days.)

HEARTY CHICKEN NOODLE SOUP

✔ **WHY THIS RECIPE WORKS**

For a soup that was chock-full of chicken, noodles, and vegetables and didn't rely on a whole chicken or a lot of work for success, we bolstered the flavor of our soup base (a simple combination of water and chicken broth) by sautéing store-bought ground chicken in the pot before adding the liquid. With all of its surface area, the ground chicken was ideal for giving up plenty of flavor quickly. Cornstarch helped give our stock the body and texture it needed. We then poached chicken breasts in the broth, shredded the meat and added it back to the pot. With egg noodles, celery, potato, carrots, onion, and chard also in the mix, this soup lived up to its name.

HEARTY CHICKEN NOODLE SOUP
SERVES 4 TO 6

When skimming the fat off the stock, we prefer to leave a little bit on the surface to enhance the soup's flavor.

STOCK
- 1 tablespoon vegetable oil
- 1 pound ground chicken
- 1 small onion, chopped
- 1 carrot, peeled and chopped
- 1 celery rib, chopped
- 8 cups low-sodium chicken broth
- 4 cups water
- 2 (12-ounce) bone-in split chicken breasts, trimmed and cut in half crosswise
- 2 bay leaves
- 2 teaspoons salt

SOUP
- 3 tablespoons cornstarch
- ¼ cup cold water
- 1 small onion, halved and sliced thin
- 2 carrots, peeled, halved lengthwise, and cut crosswise into ¾-inch pieces
- 1 celery rib, halved lengthwise and cut crosswise into ½-inch pieces
- 1 russet potato (6 ounces), peeled and cut into ¾-inch cubes
- 4 ounces egg noodles
- 2 ounces Swiss chard, stemmed and leaves torn into 1-inch pieces (optional)
- 1 tablespoon minced fresh parsley
  Salt and pepper

1. FOR THE STOCK: Heat oil in Dutch oven over medium-high heat until shimmering. Add ground chicken, onion, carrot, and celery. Cook, stirring frequently, until chicken is no longer pink, 5 to 10 minutes (do not brown chicken).

2. Reduce heat to medium-low. Add broth, water, chicken breasts, bay leaves, and salt; cover and cook for 30 minutes. Remove lid, increase heat to high, and bring to boil. (If liquid is already boiling when lid is removed, remove chicken breasts immediately and continue with recipe.) Transfer chicken breasts to large plate and set aside. Continue to cook stock for 20 minutes, adjusting heat to maintain gentle boil. Strain stock through fine-mesh strainer into large pot or container, pressing on solids to extract as much liquid as possible. Allow liquid to settle, about 5 minutes, and skim off fat.

3. FOR THE SOUP: Return stock to Dutch oven set over medium-high heat. In small bowl, combine cornstarch and water until smooth slurry forms; stir into stock and bring to gentle boil. Add onion, carrots, celery, and potato and cook until potato pieces are almost tender, 10 to 15 minutes, adjusting heat as necessary to maintain gentle boil. Add egg noodles and continue to cook until all vegetables and noodles are tender, about 5 minutes longer.

4. Meanwhile, remove skin from reserved cooked chicken, then remove meat from bones and shred into bite-size pieces; discard skin and bones. Add shredded chicken, Swiss chard, if using, and parsley to soup and cook until heated through, about 2 minutes. Season with salt and pepper to taste and serve. (After skimming broth in step 2, stock and chicken breasts can be refrigerated separately for up to 2 days.)

GREEK EGG-LEMON SOUP

✔ **WHY THIS RECIPE WORKS**

For this classic Greek recipe, we simmered the stock with lemon zest for bold citrus flavor. Using room-temperature eggs (the key ingredient for thickening the soup to the right silky consistency) yielded a slightly smoother soup, and tempering them slowly with hot stock before adding them to the soup ensured they didn't curdle. Whole eggs produced soup with better body but yolks lent more flavor, so we settled on a combination of the two. The starch in the rice helped further thicken our stock and gave the soup some heft.

GREEK EGG-LEMON SOUP
SERVES 6 TO 8

Homemade chicken stock gives this soup the best flavor and body, but in a pinch you can use low-sodium store-bought chicken broth. Make sure to zest the lemons before juicing them. The longer the final soup cooks after the eggs have been added, the thicker it becomes. About 5 minutes of heating produces a soft, velvety texture; any longer and the soup begins to turn pasty. Scallions and fresh mint, individually or together, make simple and flavorful garnishes. Serve the soup immediately; it thickens to a gravylike consistency when reheated.

8	cups Quick Chicken Stock (page 66)
½	cup long-grain white rice
1	bay leaf
4	green cardamom pods, crushed, or 2 whole cloves
12	(4-inch) strips lemon zest plus ¼ cup juice (2 lemons)
1½	teaspoons salt
2	large eggs plus 2 large yolks, room temperature
1	scallion, sliced thin and/or 3 tablespoons chopped fresh mint

1. Bring chicken stock to boil in medium saucepan over high heat. Add rice, bay leaf, cardamom, lemon zest, and salt. Reduce heat to medium and simmer until rice is tender and stock is aromatic from lemon zest, 16 to 20 minutes.

2. Remove and discard bay leaf, cardamom, and zest strips. Increase heat to high and return stock to boil, then reduce heat to low.

3. Gently whisk whole eggs, egg yolks, and lemon juice in medium bowl until combined. Whisking constantly, slowly ladle about 2 cups hot stock into egg mixture and whisk until combined. Pour egg mixture back into saucepan and cook over low heat, stirring constantly, until soup is slightly thickened and wisps of steam appear, 4 to 5 minutes (do not simmer or boil). Divide soup among serving bowls, sprinkle with scallion and/or mint, and serve immediately.

EGG-LEMON SOUP WITH CINNAMON AND CAYENNE

This variation is based on a Tunisian-style egg-lemon soup.

Substitute one 2-inch stick cinnamon and pinch cayenne for cardamom.

EGG-LEMON SOUP WITH SAFFRON

Add ¼ teaspoon saffron threads, crumbled, to stock along with rice, bay leaf, cardamom, zest, and salt.

EGG-LEMON SOUP WITH CHICKEN

Add two 6-ounce boneless, skinless chicken breasts, cut into ½-inch cubes, to stock along with rice, seasonings, and zest.

TORTILLA SOUP

✔ WHY THIS RECIPE WORKS
We wanted a recipe that gave us soup with authentic flavor but used easy-to-find ingredients and could be made on a weeknight. After breaking the classic recipe down to its three main components—the flavor base (tomatoes, garlic, onion, and chiles), the chicken stock, and the garnishes (including fried tortilla chips)—we came up with substitute ingredients and a manageable approach to each. Typically, the vegetables are charred on a comal (griddle), then pureed and fried. To simplify, we made a puree from smoky chipotle chiles plus tomatoes, onion, garlic, and jalapeño, then fried the puree over high heat in oil. We poached chicken in store-bought broth infused with onion, garlic, cilantro, and oregano (which we substituted for the pungent Mexican herb epazote), which gave our base plenty of flavor without having to make a from-scratch stock. And turning to the garnish, we oven-toasted tortilla strips instead of frying them and substituted sour cream when we couldn't find Mexican crema (a cultured cream), and Monterey Jack for traditional Cotija cheese.

TORTILLA SOUP
SERVES 8

Despite its somewhat lengthy ingredient list, this recipe is very easy to prepare. If you desire a soup with mild spiciness, trim the ribs and seeds from the jalapeño (or omit the jalapeño altogether) and use 1 teaspoon chipotle chile pureed with tomatoes in step 3. If you want a spicier soup, add up to 1 tablespoon more adobo sauce in step 4 before you add the shredded chicken.

TORTILLA STRIPS

8	(6-inch) corn tortillas, cut into ½-inch-wide strips
1	tablespoon vegetable oil
	Salt

SOUP

2	(12-ounce) bone-in split chicken breasts or 4 (5-ounce) bone-in chicken thighs, skin removed and trimmed
8	cups low-sodium chicken broth
1	large white onion, trimmed of root end, quartered, and peeled
4	garlic cloves, peeled
8–10	sprigs fresh cilantro plus 1 sprig fresh oregano or 2 sprigs fresh epazote
	Salt
2	tomatoes, cored and quartered
½	jalapeño chile
1	tablespoon minced canned chipotle chile in adobo sauce
1	tablespoon vegetable oil

Canned chipotle chiles are jalapeños that have been ripened until red and then smoked and dried. They are sold as is or packed in a tomato-based sauce. We prefer the latter since they are already reconstituted by the sauce, making them easier to use. Most recipes don't use an entire can, but these chiles can keep for two weeks in the refrigerator or they can be frozen. To freeze, puree the chiles and quick-freeze teaspoonfuls on a plastic wrap–covered plate. Once these "chipotle chips" are hard, peel them off the plastic and transfer them to a zipper-lock freezer bag. Then thaw what you need before use. They can be stored this way for up to two months.

GARNISHES

- 1 avocado, halved, pitted, and diced fine
- 8 ounces Cotija cheese, crumbled, or Monterey Jack cheese, diced fine
  Lime wedges
  Fresh cilantro
  Minced jalapeño chile
  Mexican crema or sour cream

1. FOR THE TORTILLA STRIPS: Adjust oven rack to middle position; heat oven to 425 degrees. Spread tortilla strips on rimmed baking sheet; drizzle with oil and toss until evenly coated. Bake until strips are deep golden brown and crisped, about 14 minutes, rotating baking sheet and shaking strips (to redistribute) halfway through baking. Season strips lightly with salt and transfer to paper towel–lined plate.

2. FOR THE SOUP: While tortilla strips bake, bring chicken, broth, 2 onion quarters, 2 garlic cloves, cilantro and oregano, and ½ teaspoon salt to boil over medium-high heat in large saucepan. Reduce heat to low, cover, and simmer until chicken is just cooked through, about 20 minutes. Using tongs, transfer chicken to large plate. Pour broth through fine-mesh strainer and discard solids. When cool enough to handle, shred chicken into bite-size pieces, discarding bones.

3. Puree tomatoes, remaining 2 onion quarters, remaining 2 garlic cloves, jalapeño, and chipotle in food processor until smooth. Heat oil in Dutch oven over high heat until shimmering. Add tomato-onion puree and ⅛ teaspoon salt and cook, stirring frequently, until mixture has darkened in color, about 10 minutes.

4. Stir strained broth into tomato mixture, bring to boil, then reduce heat to low and simmer to blend flavors, about 15 minutes. Add shredded chicken and simmer until heated through, about 5 minutes. Place portions of tortilla strips in bowls and ladle soup over. Serve, passing garnishes separately.

TO MAKE AHEAD: Soup can be prepared up to adding shredded chicken to soup at end of step 4; let cool and refrigerate for up to 4 days. Return soup to simmer over medium-high heat before proceeding. Tortilla strips and garnishes are best prepared day of serving.

THAI-STYLE CHICKEN SOUP

✔ WHY THIS RECIPE WORKS
For an authentic-tasting Thai coconut soup without all the exotic ingredients, we began by making a rich base with chicken broth and coconut milk. Thai curry paste from the supermarket was an easy substitution for the assortment of obscure ingredients like kaffir lime leaves, galangal, and bird's eye chiles used in from-scratch recipes. Pungent fish sauce and tart lime juice contributed the salty and sour flavors.

THAI-STYLE CHICKEN SOUP
SERVES 6 TO 8

For a lighter soup, substitute light coconut milk for one or both cans of regular coconut milk. The fresh lemon grass can be omitted, but the soup will lack some complexity; don't be tempted to use jarred or dried lemon grass, as their flavor is characterless. If you want a spicier soup, add more red curry paste to taste. For a more substantial meal, serve the soup over 2 to 3 cups of cooked jasmine rice.

SOUP

- 1 teaspoon vegetable oil
- 3 lemon grass stalks, trimmed to bottom 6 inches, halved lengthwise and sliced thin crosswise
- 3 large shallots, chopped
- 8 sprigs fresh cilantro, chopped coarse
- 3 tablespoons fish sauce
- 4 cups low-sodium chicken broth
- 2 (14-ounce) cans coconut milk
- 1 tablespoon sugar
- 8 ounces white mushrooms, trimmed and sliced ¼ inch thick
- 1 pound boneless, skinless chicken breasts (about 3 breasts), trimmed, halved lengthwise, and sliced on bias into ⅛-inch-thick pieces
- 3 tablespoons lime juice (2 limes)
- 2 teaspoons Thai red curry paste

GARNISHES

- ½ cup fresh cilantro leaves
- 2 serrano chiles, stemmed, seeded, and sliced thin
- 2 scallions, sliced thin on bias
  Lime wedges

1. FOR THE SOUP: Heat oil in large saucepan over medium heat until just shimmering. Add lemon grass, shallots, cilantro, and 1 tablespoon fish sauce and cook, stirring frequently, until lemon grass and shallots are just softened but not browned, 2 to 5 minutes.

2. Stir in chicken broth and 1 can coconut milk and bring to simmer over high heat. Cover, reduce heat to low, and simmer until flavors have blended, about 10 minutes. Pour broth through fine-mesh strainer and discard solids. Rinse saucepan and return broth mixture to pan.

3. Stir remaining can coconut milk and sugar into broth mixture and bring to simmer over medium-high heat. Reduce heat to medium, add mushrooms, and cook until just tender, 2 to 3 minutes. Add chicken and cook, stirring constantly, until no longer pink, 1 to 3 minutes. Remove soup from heat. Combine lime juice, curry paste, and remaining 2 tablespoons fish sauce in small bowl and stir into soup.

4. FOR THE GARNISH: Ladle soup into bowls and garnish with cilantro, chiles, and scallions. Serve immediately with lime wedges.

TO MAKE AHEAD: Soup can be prepared through step 1 and refrigerated for up to 1 day. Complete steps 2 through 4 immediately before serving, as the chicken and mushrooms can easily overcook.

HOT AND SOUR SOUP

✔ WHY THIS RECIPE WORKS
Authentic versions of this soup call for ingredients like mustard pickle, pig's-foot tendon, and dried sea cucumber. To get an authentically spicy, rich, and complex version that would use only ingredients from our local supermarket, we created a "hot" side for our soup using two heat sources—a full teaspoon of distinctive, penetrating white pepper and a little chili oil. To create the "sour" side, we preferred Chinese black vinegar but found a combination of balsamic and red wine vinegar to be an acceptable substitute. Cornstarch pulled triple duty, going into our slurry to thicken the soup, into the marinade to keep the meat tender, and getting beaten with the egg to keep the egg light, wispy, and cohesive. We settled on fresh shiitakes in lieu of wood ear mushrooms and canned bamboo shoots instead of lily buds.

HOT AND SOUR SOUP
SERVES 6 TO 8

To make slicing the pork chop easier, freeze it for 15 minutes. We prefer the distinctive flavor of Chinese black vinegar; look for it in Asian supermarkets. If you can't find it, a combination of red wine vinegar and balsamic vinegar approximates its flavor. This soup is very spicy. For a less spicy soup, omit the chili oil altogether or add only 1 teaspoon. You can make your own chili oil (page 25) or use store-bought.

7	ounces extra-firm tofu, drained
¼	cup soy sauce
1	teaspoon toasted sesame oil
3	tablespoons plus 1½ teaspoons cornstarch
1	(6-ounce) boneless center-cut pork loin chop, ½ inch thick, trimmed and cut into 1 by ⅛-inch matchsticks
3	tablespoons plus 1 teaspoon cold water
1	large egg
6	cups low-sodium chicken broth
1	(5-ounce) can bamboo shoots, sliced lengthwise into ⅛-inch-thick strips
4	ounces shiitake mushrooms, stemmed and sliced ¼ inch thick
5	tablespoons black Chinese vinegar or 1 tablespoon red wine vinegar plus 1 tablespoon balsamic vinegar
2	teaspoons chili oil
1	teaspoon ground white pepper
3	scallions, sliced thin

1. Place tofu in paper towel–lined pie plate, top with heavy plate, and weight with 2 heavy cans. Let tofu drain until it has released about ½ cup liquid, about 15 minutes.

2. Whisk 1 tablespoon soy sauce, sesame oil, and 1 teaspoon cornstarch in medium bowl. Add pork to bowl, toss to coat, and let marinate for at least 10 minutes or up to 30 minutes.

3. Combine 3 tablespoons cornstarch with 3 tablespoons water in small bowl. Mix remaining ½ teaspoon cornstarch with remaining 1 teaspoon water in second small bowl. Add egg and beat with fork until combined.

4. Bring broth to boil in large saucepan over medium-high heat. Reduce heat to medium-low, add bamboo shoots and mushrooms, and simmer until mushrooms are just tender, about 5 minutes. While broth simmers, cut tofu into ½-inch cubes. Add tofu and pork with its marinade, to pan, stirring to separate any pieces of pork that stick together. Continue to simmer until pork is no longer pink, about 2 minutes.

5. Stir cornstarch mixture to recombine, then add to soup and increase heat to medium-high. Cook, stirring occasionally,

until soup thickens and turns translucent, about 1 minute. Stir in vinegar, chili oil, pepper, and remaining 3 tablespoons soy sauce and turn off heat.

6. Without stirring soup, use soupspoon to slowly drizzle very thin streams of egg mixture into pot in circular motion. Let soup sit 1 minute, then return saucepan to medium-high heat. Bring soup to gentle boil, then immediately remove from heat. Gently stir soup once to evenly distribute egg. Ladle soup into bowls, top with scallions, and serve.

QUICK BEEF AND VEGETABLE SOUP

✔ WHY THIS RECIPE WORKS
For a beef and vegetable soup that we could make in just an hour, we turned to quick-cooking, richly flavored sirloin tip steaks and doctored store-bought broth with a few of the test kitchen's favorite ingredients for accentuating meatiness: mushrooms, tomato paste, soy sauce, and red wine. To give our quick version the rich texture of a long-simmered soup, we added a tablespoon of gelatin softened in cold water, which provided the body typically lent by gelatin released from the beef bones in a traditional recipe.

QUICK BEEF AND VEGETABLE SOUP
SERVES 6

Choose whole sirloin tip steaks over ones that have been cut into small pieces, often labeled for stir-fries. If sirloin tip steaks are unavailable, substitute blade or flank steak, removing any hard gristle or excess fat. White mushrooms can be used in place of the cremini. Feel free to add 1 cup of frozen peas, frozen corn, or frozen cut green beans during the last 5 minutes of cooking. For a heartier soup, add 10 ounces of red potatoes, cut into ½-inch pieces (2 cups), during the last 15 minutes of cooking.

1   pound sirloin tip steaks, trimmed and cut into ½-inch pieces
2   tablespoons soy sauce
1   teaspoon vegetable oil
1   pound cremini mushrooms, trimmed and quartered
1   large onion, chopped
2   tablespoons tomato paste
1   garlic clove, minced
½   cup red wine
4   cups beef broth
1¾   cups low-sodium chicken broth
4   carrots, peeled and cut into ½-inch pieces
2   celery ribs, cut into ½-inch pieces
1   bay leaf
1   tablespoon unflavored gelatin
½   cup cold water
2   tablespoons minced fresh parsley
     Salt and pepper

1. Combine beef and soy sauce in medium bowl. Let sit for 15 minutes.

2. Heat oil in Dutch oven over medium-high heat until just smoking. Add mushrooms and onion and cook, stirring frequently, until onion is browned, 8 to 12 minutes. Transfer vegetables to bowl.

3. Add beef and cook, stirring occasionally, until liquid evaporates and meat starts to brown, 6 to 10 minutes. Add tomato paste and garlic to pot and cook, stirring constantly, until aromatic, about 30 seconds. Stir in wine, scraping bottom of pot with wooden spoon to loosen browned bits, and cook until liquid reduces and becomes syrupy, 1 to 2 minutes.

4. Add beef broth, chicken broth, carrots, celery, bay leaf, and browned mushrooms and onion to pot and bring to boil. Reduce heat to low, cover, and simmer until vegetables and meat are tender, 25 to 30 minutes. Remove from heat and remove and discard bay leaf.

5. Meanwhile, sprinkle gelatin over cold water and allow to soften 5 minutes.

Add gelatin mixture to pot with soup and stir until completely dissolved. Stir in parsley, season with salt and pepper to taste, and serve.

VIETNAMESE-STYLE SOUPS

✔ WHY THIS RECIPE WORKS
Vietnamese noodle soups are based on a homemade broth, enhanced with exotic flavorings, and then filled with rice noodles and paper-thin slices of beef, along with a variety of vegetables and herbs. We wanted to create a flavorful yet simple base for a couple of quick Asian-style soups using canned chicken broth and easily accessible ingredients. We combined strong flavorings like ginger, star anise, garlic, and fish sauce with the broth, simmered the mixture for 20 minutes, and then added meat (or chicken), vegetables, and herbs. The result: fast, aromatic, and flavorful Vietnamese-style soups.

VIETNAMESE-STYLE BEEF NOODLE SOUP
SERVES 4

This recipe moves quickly; be sure to have all the vegetables and herbs prepped when you begin cooking.

NOODLES
8   ounces wide rice noodles

BROTH
5   cups low-sodium chicken broth
4   garlic cloves, peeled and smashed
1   (2-inch) piece fresh ginger, peeled, cut into ⅛-inch rounds, and smashed
2   (3-inch-long) cinnamon sticks
2   star anise pods
2   tablespoons fish sauce
1   tablespoon soy sauce
1   tablespoon sugar

MEAT AND VEGETABLES

- 1 (12-ounce) shell sirloin steak, trimmed and sliced crosswise into ¼-inch strips
  Salt and pepper
- 1 tablespoon vegetable oil
- 5 ounces bean sprouts (2½ cups)
- 1 jalapeño chile, stemmed, seeded, and sliced thin crosswise
- 2 scallions, sliced thin on bias
- ⅓ cup fresh basil, large leaves torn in half
- ½ cup fresh mint, large leaves torn in half
- ½ cup fresh cilantro leaves
- 2 tablespoons chopped unsalted roasted peanuts
  Lime wedges

1. FOR THE NOODLES: Bring 4 quarts water to boil in large pot. Off heat, add noodles and let sit until tender but not mushy, 10 to 15 minutes. Drain and distribute among 4 bowls.

2. FOR THE BROTH: Bring all ingredients to boil in medium saucepan over medium-high heat. Reduce heat to low and simmer, partially covered, 20 minutes. Remove solids from pan with slotted spoon and discard. Cover broth and keep hot over low heat until ready to serve.

SMASHING GINGER

To release the flavorful oils from fresh ginger, thinly slice a knob and then use the end of a chef's knife to smash each piece.

3. FOR THE MEAT AND VEGETABLES: Season steak with salt and pepper. Heat oil in 10-inch skillet over medium-high heat until shimmering. Add half of steak slices in single layer and sear until well-browned, 1 to 2 minutes on each side; set aside. Repeat with remaining slices.

4. Divide sprouts among bowls with noodles, add steak, then ladle in broth. Sprinkle each serving with jalapeño, scallions, basil, mint, cilantro, and peanuts and serve, passing lime wedges separately.

VIETNAMESE-STYLE CHICKEN NOODLE SOUP

SERVES 4

NOODLES

- 8 ounces wide rice noodles

BROTH AND CHICKEN

- 5 cups low-sodium chicken broth
- 12 ounces boneless, skinless chicken thighs (about 3 thighs), trimmed
- 4 garlic cloves, peeled and smashed
- 1 (2-inch) piece fresh ginger, peeled, cut into ⅛-inch rounds, and smashed
- 2 star anise pods
- 3 tablespoons fish sauce
- 1 tablespoon soy sauce
- 2 teaspoons sugar
  Salt

VEGETABLES

- 4 cups shredded napa cabbage
- 2 scallions, sliced thin on bias
- ½ cup fresh mint, large leaves torn in half
- ½ cup fresh cilantro leaves
- 2 tablespoons chopped unsalted roasted peanuts
  Lime wedges

1. FOR THE NOODLES: Bring 4 quarts water to boil in large pot. Off heat, add noodles and let sit until tender but not mushy, 10 to 15 minutes. Drain and distribute among 4 bowls.

2. FOR THE BROTH AND CHICKEN: Bring all ingredients except salt to boil in medium saucepan over medium-high heat. Reduce heat to low and simmer, partially covered, to blend flavors, 10 to 15 minutes, until chicken is cooked through, about 10 minutes.

3. Remove chicken with slotted spoon and continue to simmer broth, about 10 minutes. When chicken is cool enough to handle, slice thin. Strain broth through fine-mesh strainer and return to pot. Season with salt to taste. Cover broth and keep hot over low heat until ready to serve.

4. FOR THE VEGETABLES: Divide cabbage and chicken among bowls with noodles, then ladle in broth. Sprinkle each serving with scallions, mint, cilantro, and peanuts and serve, passing lime wedges separately.

BEST FRENCH ONION SOUP

✔ WHY THIS RECIPE WORKS

We found that the secret to a rich onion soup was caramelizing the onions a full 2½ hours in the oven and then deglazing the pot several times with a combination of water, chicken broth, and beef broth. For the classic crouton topping, we toasted the bread before floating it in the soup to ward off sogginess, and we sprinkled the toasts with just a modest amount of nutty Gruyère to keep its flavor from overwhelming the soup.

BEST FRENCH ONION SOUP

SERVES 6

Use a Dutch oven with at least a 7-quart capacity for this recipe. Sweet onions, such as Vidalia or Walla Walla, will make this recipe overly sweet. Note that the entire process for caramelizing the onions takes 45 to 60 minutes. Use broiler-safe crocks and keep the rim of the bowls 4 to 5 inches from the heating element to obtain a proper gratinée of melted, bubbly cheese. If using ordinary soup bowls, sprinkle the toasted bread slices with Gruyère and return them to the broiler until the cheese melts, then float them on top of the soup.

SOUP

- 4 pounds onions, halved and sliced through the root end into ¼-inch-thick pieces
- 3 tablespoons unsalted butter, cut into 3 pieces
- Salt and pepper
- 2 cups water, plus extra for deglazing
- ½ cup dry sherry
- 4 cups low-sodium chicken broth
- 2 cups beef broth
- 6 sprigs fresh thyme, tied with kitchen twine
- I bay leaf

CHEESE CROUTONS

- I small baguette, cut into ½-inch slices
- 8 ounces shredded Gruyère cheese (2 cups)

I. FOR THE SOUP: Adjust oven rack to lower-middle position and heat oven to 400 degrees. Generously spray inside of Dutch oven with vegetable oil spray. Add onions, butter, and 1 teaspoon salt. Cook, covered, for 1 hour (onions will be moist and slightly reduced in volume). Remove pot from oven and stir onions, scraping bottom and sides of pot. Return pot to oven with lid slightly ajar and continue to cook until onions are very soft and golden brown, 1½ to 1¾ hours longer, stirring onions and scraping bottom and sides of pot after 1 hour.

2. Carefully remove pot from oven (leave oven on) and place over medium-high heat. Cook onions, stirring frequently and scraping bottom and sides of pot, until liquid evaporates and onions brown, 15 to 20 minutes (reduce heat to medium if onions brown too quickly). Continue to cook, stirring frequently, until bottom of pot is coated with dark crust, 6 to 8 minutes, adjusting heat as necessary. (Scrape any browned bits that collect on spoon back into onions.) Stir in ¼ cup water, scraping

pot bottom to loosen crust, and cook until water evaporates and pot bottom has formed another dark crust, 6 to 8 minutes. Repeat process of deglazing 2 or 3 more times, until onions are very dark brown. Stir in sherry and cook, stirring frequently, until sherry evaporates, about 5 minutes.

3. Stir in 2 cups water, chicken broth, beef broth, thyme, bay leaf, and ½ teaspoon salt, scraping up any final bits of browned crust on bottom and sides of pot. Increase heat to high and bring to simmer. Reduce heat to low, cover, and simmer 30 minutes. Remove and discard herbs and season with salt and pepper to taste.

4. FOR THE CHEESE CROUTONS: While soup simmers, arrange baguette slices in single layer on rimmed baking sheet and bake until bread is dry, crisp, and golden at edges, about 10 minutes. Set aside.

5. TO SERVE: Adjust oven rack 7 to 8 inches from broiler element and heat broiler. Set 6 broiler-safe crocks on rimmed baking sheet and fill each with about 1¾ cups soup. Top each bowl with 1 or 2 baguette slices (do not overlap slices) and sprinkle evenly with Gruyère. Broil until cheese is melted and bubbly around edges, 3 to 5 minutes. Let cool 5 minutes before serving.

TO MAKE AHEAD: Onions can be prepared through step 1, cooled in pot, and refrigerated for up to 3 days before proceeding with recipe. Soup can be prepared through step 3 and refrigerated for up to 2 days.

QUICKER FRENCH ONION SOUP

This variation uses a microwave for the initial cooking of the onions, which dramatically reduces the cooking time. The soup's flavor, however, will not be quite as deep as with the stovetop method. If you don't have a

---

TEST KITCHEN TIP NO. 18   CHOPPING ONIONS WITHOUT TEARS

We can't tell you how many onions we've chopped over the years in the test kitchen. Let's just say a lot. Streams of flowing tears caused us to wonder why cut onions are so pesky? It turns out that when an onion is cut, the cells that are damaged in the process release sulfuric compounds as well as various enzymes, notably one called sulfoxide lyase. Those compounds and enzymes, which are separated when the onion's cell structure is intact, activate and mix to form the real culprit behind crying, a volatile new compound called thiopropanal sulfoxide. When thiopropanal sulfoxide evaporates in the air, it irritates the eyes, causing redness and tears.

Over time, we've collected dozens of ideas from readers, books, and conversations with colleagues for combating tears while cutting onions. We finally decided to put those ideas to the test. They ranged from common sense (work underneath an exhaust fan or freeze onions for 30 minutes before slicing) to comical (wear ski goggles or hold a toothpick in your teeth). Overall, the methods that worked best were to protect our eyes by covering them with goggles or contact lenses or to introduce a flame near the cut onions. The flame, which can be produced by either a candle or a gas burner, changes the activity of the thiopropanal sulfoxide (the volatile compound that causes tearing) by completing its oxidization. Contact lenses and goggles form a physical barrier that the vapors cannot penetrate. So if you want to keep tears at bay when handling onions, light a candle or gas burner—or put on some ski goggles, even if it does look a bit silly.

microwave-safe bowl large enough to accommodate all of the onions, microwave in a smaller bowl in 2 batches.

Combine onions and 1 teaspoon salt in large bowl and cover with large plate (plate should completely cover bowl and not rest on onions). Microwave for 20 to 25 minutes until onions are soft and wilted, stirring halfway through cooking. (Use oven mitts to remove bowl from microwave and remove plate away from you to avoid steam.) Drain onions (about ½ cup liquid should drain off) and proceed with step 2, melting butter in Dutch oven before adding wilted onions.

CREAM OF TOMATO SOUP

✓ WHY THIS RECIPE WORKS
We wanted a recipe that didn't depend on a bounty of fresh, in-season tomatoes. We got the most robust tomato flavor by caramelizing whole canned tomatoes; sprinkling the tomatoes with brown sugar before roasting them helped induce caramelization. Blending the liquid and tomatoes lightened the color of our soup by aerating it, but blending just the solids maintained its deep red hue. This soup was also quick to make; because the rest of the soup could be prepared while the tomatoes roasted, we were able to keep stovetop time to 20 minutes.

CLASSIC CREAM OF
TOMATO SOUP
SERVES 4

Make sure to use canned whole tomatoes that are not packed in puree; you will need some of the juice to make the soup.

2 (28-ounce) cans whole tomatoes, drained, tomatoes seeded, and 3 cups juice reserved
1½ tablespoons dark brown sugar
4 tablespoons unsalted butter

4 large shallots, minced
1 tablespoon tomato paste
Pinch ground allspice
2 tablespoons all-purpose flour
1¾ cups low-sodium chicken broth
½ cup heavy cream
2 tablespoons brandy or dry sherry
Salt
Cayenne pepper

1. Adjust oven rack to upper-middle position and heat oven to 450 degrees. Spread tomatoes in single layer over aluminum foil–lined rimmed baking sheet and sprinkle evenly with brown sugar. Bake until all liquid has evaporated and tomatoes begin to color, about 30 minutes. Let tomatoes cool slightly, then peel them off foil and transfer to small bowl.

2. Melt butter in medium saucepan over medium heat. Add shallots, tomato paste, and allspice. Reduce heat to low, cover, and cook, stirring occasionally, until shallots are softened, 7 to 10 minutes. Add flour and cook, stirring constantly, until thoroughly combined, about 30 seconds. Whisking constantly, gradually add chicken broth. Stir in reserved tomato juice and roasted tomatoes. Cover, increase heat to medium, and bring to boil, then reduce heat to low and simmer, stirring occasionally, to blend flavors, about 10 minutes.

3. Strain mixture into medium bowl and rinse out saucepan. Transfer tomatoes and solids in strainer to blender. Add 1 cup strained liquid to blender and puree until smooth. Add remaining strained liquid.

4. Return the pureed mixture to the saucepan, stir in cream, and heat over low heat until hot, about 3 minutes. Off heat, stir in brandy. Season with salt and cayenne to taste. Serve immediately.

MAKE-AHEAD: Soup can be prepared through step 3 and refrigerated for up to 3 days or frozen for up to 2 months. Reheat over low heat before proceeding with step 3.

CREAMLESS CREAMY
TOMATO SOUP

✓ WHY THIS RECIPE WORKS
We wanted a creamy tomato soup recipe that would have velvety smoothness and a bright tomato taste—without added cream. We started with canned tomatoes for their convenience, year-round availability, and consistent quality. For sautéing onion and garlic, we found that butter muted the tomato flavor so we opted for olive oil. A little brown sugar toned down acidity, and a surprise ingredient—slices of white bread torn into pieces—helped give our tomato soup recipe body without added cream.

CREAMLESS CREAMY
TOMATO SOUP
SERVES 6 TO 8

Make sure to purchase canned whole tomatoes in juice, not puree. If half of the soup fills your blender by more than two-thirds, process the soup in three batches. You can also use an immersion blender to process the soup directly in the pot. For an even smoother soup, pass the pureed mixture through a fine-mesh strainer before stirring in the chicken broth in step 2.

¼ cup extra-virgin olive oil, plus extra for drizzling
1 onion, chopped
3 garlic cloves, minced
Pinch red pepper flakes (optional)
1 bay leaf
2 (28-ounce) cans whole tomatoes
3 slices hearty white sandwich bread, crusts removed, torn into 1-inch pieces
1 tablespoon brown sugar
2 cups low-sodium chicken broth
2 tablespoons brandy (optional)
Salt and pepper
¼ cup chopped fresh chives
1 recipe Butter Croutons (recipe follows)

1. Heat 2 tablespoons oil in Dutch oven over medium-high heat until shimmering. Add onion, garlic, pepper flakes, if using, and bay leaf. Cook, stirring frequently, until onion is translucent, 3 to 5 minutes. Stir in tomatoes and their juice. Using potato masher, mash until no pieces bigger than 2 inches remain. Stir in bread and sugar. Bring soup to boil. Reduce heat to medium and cook, stirring occasionally, until bread is completely saturated and starts to break down, about 5 minutes. Remove and discard bay leaf.

2. Transfer half of soup to blender. Add 1 tablespoon oil and process until soup is smooth and creamy, 2 to 3 minutes. Transfer to large bowl and repeat with remaining soup and oil. Rinse out Dutch oven and return soup to pot. Stir in chicken broth and brandy, if using. Return soup to boil and season with salt and pepper to taste. Ladle soup into bowls, sprinkle with chives, and drizzle with olive oil. Serve.

BUTTER CROUTONS
MAKES ABOUT 3 CUPS

Either fresh or stale bread can be used in this recipe, although stale bread is easier to cut and crisps more quickly in the oven. If using stale bread, reduce the baking time by about 2 minutes. Croutons made from stale bread will be more crisp than those made from fresh. Be sure to use regular or thick-sliced bread (do not use thin-sliced bread).

6 slices hearty white sandwich bread, crusts removed, cut into ½-inch cubes (about 3 cups)
Salt and pepper
3 tablespoons unsalted butter

1. Adjust oven rack to upper-middle position and heat oven to 350 degrees.

Combine bread cubes and salt and pepper to taste in medium bowl. Drizzle with butter and toss well with rubber spatula to combine.

2. Spread bread cubes in single layer on rimmed baking sheet or in shallow baking dish. Bake croutons until golden brown and crisp, 8 to 10 minutes, stirring halfway through baking time. Let cool on baking sheet to room temperature. (Croutons can be stored in airtight container for up to 3 days.)

CLASSIC GAZPACHO

✔ WHY THIS RECIPE WORKS
For gazpacho with clearly flavored, distinct vegetables in a bright tomato broth, we started by chopping the vegetables by hand, which ensured they retained their color and firm texture. Tossing them in a sherry vinegar marinade and letting them sit briefly guaranteed well-seasoned vegetables, while a combination of tomato juice and ice cubes (which helped chill the soup) provided the right amount of liquid. Chilling our soup for a minimum of 4 hours proved critical to allowing the flavors to develop and meld.

CLASSIC GAZPACHO
SERVES 8 TO 10

Use a Vidalia, Maui, or Walla Walla onion here. This recipe makes a large quantity because the leftovers are so good, but it can be halved if you prefer. Traditionally, diners garnish their gazpacho with more of the same diced vegetables that are in the soup, so cut some extra vegetables when you prepare those called for in the recipe. In addition to the Garlic Croutons, chopped pitted black olives, chopped hard-cooked eggs, and finely diced avocados all make appealing garnishes. For a finishing touch, serve in chilled bowls.

1½ pounds tomatoes, cored and cut into ¼-inch cubes
2 red bell peppers, stemmed, seeded, and cut into ¼-inch dice
2 small cucumbers, one cucumber peeled, both sliced lengthwise, seeded, and cut into ¼-inch dice
½ small sweet onion or 2 large shallots, minced (about ½ cup)
⅓ cup sherry vinegar
2 garlic cloves, minced
Salt and pepper
5 cups tomato juice
1 teaspoon hot sauce (optional)
8 ice cubes
8–10 teaspoons extra-virgin olive oil, for serving
1 recipe Garlic Croutons (recipe follows)

1. Combine tomatoes, bell peppers, cucumbers, onion, vinegar, garlic, and 2 teaspoons salt in large (at least 4-quart) bowl and season with pepper to taste. Let stand until vegetables just begin to release their juices, about 5 minutes. Stir in tomato juice, hot sauce, if using, and ice cubes. Cover tightly and refrigerate to blend flavors, at least 4 hours or up to 2 days.

2. Remove and discard unmelted ice cubes and season with salt and pepper to taste. Serve cold, drizzling each portion with 1 teaspoon oil and topping with desired garnishes.

QUICK FOOD PROCESSOR GAZPACHO

Core and quarter tomatoes and process in food processor until broken down into ¼- to ¾-inch pieces, about 12 pulses, then transfer to large bowl. Cut stemmed and seeded peppers and seeded cucumbers into rough 1-inch pieces and process separately until broken down into ¼- to ¾-inch pieces, about 12 pulses, and add to bowl with tomatoes. Mince onion and garlic by hand, then add to bowl with vegetables along with vinegar, salt, and pepper to taste; continue with recipe.

SPICY GAZPACHO WITH CHIPOTLE CHILES AND LIME

Omit hot sauce and stir in 2½ tablespoons minced canned chipotle chile in adobo sauce, ¼ cup minced fresh cilantro, 6 tablespoons juice from 3 limes, and 2 teaspoons grated lemon zest with tomato juice and ice cubes in step 1.

GARLIC CROUTONS
MAKES ABOUT 3 CUPS

- 3 tablespoons extra-virgin olive oil
- 3 garlic cloves, minced
- ¼ teaspoon salt
- 6 slices hearty white sandwich bread, crusts removed, cut into ½-inch cubes (about 3 cups)

1. Adjust oven rack to middle position and heat oven to 350 degrees. Combine oil, garlic, and salt in small bowl. Let stand 20 minutes, then pour through fine-mesh strainer into medium bowl. Discard garlic. Add bread cubes to bowl with oil and toss to coat.

2. Spread bread cubes in single layer on rimmed baking sheet and bake, stirring occasionally, until golden, about 15 minutes. Let cool on baking sheet to room temperature. (Croutons can be stored in airtight container or zipper-lock bag for up to 1 day.)

CREAMY GAZPACHO ANDALUZ

✔ WHY THIS RECIPE WORKS

The gazpacho popular in Andalusia, the southern region of Spain, is creamy and complex, with the bright, fresh flavor of naturally ripened vegetables. The key to fresh tomato flavor was salting the tomatoes and letting them sit to release more flavor. We then followed the same process with the other vegetables—cucumber, bell pepper, and onion—and soaked the bread, which we used to thicken the soup, in the exuded vegetable juices. A final dash of olive oil and sherry vinegar further brightened the flavor of our gazpacho, and a diced-vegetable garnish lent a fresh finish.

CREAMY GAZPACHO ANDALUZ
SERVES 4 TO 6

For ideal flavor, allow the gazpacho to sit in the refrigerator overnight before serving. Red wine vinegar can be substituted for the sherry vinegar. Although we prefer to use kosher salt in this soup, half the amount of table salt can be used. Serve the soup with additional extra-virgin olive oil, sherry vinegar, ground black pepper, and diced vegetables for diners to season and garnish their own bowls as desired.

- 3 pounds tomatoes, cored
- 1 small cucumber, peeled, halved lengthwise, and seeded
- 1 green bell pepper, stemmed, halved, and seeded
- 1 small red onion, peeled and halved
- 2 garlic cloves, peeled and quartered
- 1 small serrano chile, stemmed and halved lengthwise
  Kosher salt and pepper
- 1 slice hearty white sandwich bread, crust removed, torn into 1-inch pieces

- ½ cup extra-virgin olive oil, plus extra for serving
- 2 tablespoons sherry vinegar, plus extra for serving
- 2 tablespoons minced parsley, chives, or basil

1. Coarsely chop 2 pounds tomatoes, half of cucumber, half of bell pepper, and half of onion and place in large bowl. Add garlic, chile, and 1½ teaspoons salt and toss to combine.

2. Cut remaining tomatoes, cucumber, and bell pepper into ¼-inch dice and place in medium bowl. Mince remaining onion and add to diced vegetables. Toss with ½ teaspoon salt and transfer to fine-mesh strainer set over medium bowl. Drain for 1 hour. Transfer drained diced vegetables to medium bowl and set aside, reserving exuded liquid (there should be about ¼ cup; discard extra liquid).

3. Add bread pieces to exuded liquid and soak 1 minute. Add soaked bread and any remaining liquid to roughly chopped vegetables and toss thoroughly to combine.

4. Transfer half of vegetable-bread mixture to blender and process 30 seconds. With blender running, slowly drizzle in ¼ cup oil and continue to blend until completely smooth, about 2 minutes. Strain soup through fine-mesh strainer into large bowl, using back of ladle or rubber spatula to press soup through strainer. Repeat with remaining vegetable-bread mixture and ¼ cup oil.

5. Stir vinegar, parsley, and half of diced vegetables into soup and season with salt and pepper to taste. Cover and refrigerate overnight or for at least 2 hours to chill completely and develop flavors. Serve, passing remaining diced vegetables, oil, vinegar, and pepper separately.

CREAMY GREEN PEA SOUP

✔ WHY THIS RECIPE WORKS

Sweet pea soup typically calls for stewing fresh blanched peas, leeks, and lettuce in butter, moistening with veal stock, and then passing through a fine sieve. The soup was then finished with cream. To cut back on the fuss, we pureed frozen peas in the food processor and combined them with just butter, lettuce, and shallots or leeks, so as not to overwhelm the delicate flavor of the peas. And adding flour to the vegetables helped thicken the soup to a silken texture.

CREAMY GREEN PEA SOUP

SERVES 4 TO 6

Remove the peas from the freezer just before starting the soup so that when you are ready to process them, as the stock simmers, they will be only partially thawed. To preserve its delicate flavor and color, this soup is best served immediately.

- 4 tablespoons unsalted butter
- 5 shallots, minced, or 1 leek, white and light green parts only, halved lengthwise, chopped fine, and rinsed thoroughly
- 2 tablespoons all-purpose flour
- 3½ cups low-sodium chicken broth
- 1½ pounds frozen peas (about 4½ cups), partially thawed at room temperature for 10 minutes
- 12 leaves Boston lettuce from 1 small head
- ½ cup heavy cream
- 1 recipe Butter Croutons (page 78)
  Salt and pepper

1. Melt butter in large saucepan over low heat. Add shallots, and cook, covered, until softened, 8 to 10 minutes, stirring occasionally. Add flour and cook, stirring constantly, until thoroughly combined, about 30 seconds. Stirring constantly, gradually add chicken broth. Increase heat to high and bring to boil, then reduce heat to medium-low and simmer 3 to 5 minutes.

2. Meanwhile, process partially thawed peas in food processor until coarsely chopped, about 20 seconds. Add peas and lettuce to simmering broth. Increase heat to medium-high, cover and return to simmer; simmer 3 minutes. Uncover, reduce heat to medium-low, and continue to simmer 2 minutes longer.

3. Working in 2 batches, puree soup in blender until smooth, then strain into large bowl. Clean saucepan and return pureed mixture to pan. Stir in cream and heat mixture over low heat until hot, about 3 minutes. Season with salt and pepper to taste. Serve immediately.

COUNTRY-STYLE POTATO-LEEK SOUP

✔ WHY THIS RECIPE WORKS

For a country-style potato-leek soup with the best flavor, we found low-starch red potatoes were best, as they held their shape and didn't become waterlogged during cooking. Sautéing plenty of leeks in butter helped pump up the flavor, and leaving our soup full of chunks of potato and some pieces of leek kept up the rustic theme. We removed the pot from the heat toward the end to allow the potatoes to finish cooking in the hot broth without becoming overcooked or mushy.

COUNTRY-STYLE POTATO-LEEK SOUP

SERVES 6 TO 8

Leeks can vary in size. If yours have large white and light green sections, use fewer leeks.

- 6 tablespoons unsalted butter
- 4–5 pounds leeks, white and light green parts only, halved lengthwise, sliced into 1-inch pieces, and washed thoroughly (11 cups)
- 1 tablespoon all-purpose flour
- 5¼ cups low-sodium chicken broth
- 1 bay leaf
- 1¾ pounds red potatoes, peeled and cut into ¾-inch chunks
  Salt and pepper

1. Melt butter in Dutch oven over medium-low heat. Stir in leeks, increase heat to medium, cover, and cook, stirring occasionally, until leeks are tender but not mushy, 15 to 20 minutes (do not brown). Sprinkle flour over leeks, stir to coat, and cook until flour dissolves, about 2 minutes.

2. Increase heat to high and, whisking constantly, gradually add broth. Add bay leaf and potatoes, cover, and bring to boil. Reduce heat to medium-low and simmer, covered, until potatoes are almost tender, 5 to 7 minutes. Remove from heat and let stand until potatoes are tender and flavors meld, 10 to 15 minutes. Discard bay leaf and season with salt and pepper to taste. Serve immediately.

TEST KITCHEN TIP NO. 19   BUYING LEEKS

We try to buy leeks with the longest white stems, the most tender and usable part of a leek; the white parts can vary from 4 up to 8 inches, so it pays to be discriminating when selecting them. But don't be fooled by supermarkets that sell leeks that are already trimmed down to the lighter base part. This may seem like a good deal because you aren't paying for the upper leaves, which are discarded anyway, but the truth is that the actual purpose of this procedure is to trim away aging leaves and make tough, old leeks look fresher to the unwary consumer. The bottom line: Hand-select your leeks, and try to find a store that sells them untrimmed.

COUNTRY-STYLE POTATO-LEEK SOUP WITH KIELBASA

Eight ounces of cooked ham, cut into ½-inch dice, can be substituted for the sausage, if desired. Whichever you choose, season the soup with care, since both ham and kielbasa are fully seasoned.

Before removing pot from heat, stir 8 ounces kielbasa sausage, cut into ½-inch slices, into soup.

COUNTRY-STYLE POTATO-LEEK SOUP WITH WHITE BEANS

Reduce potatoes to ¾ pound. Before removing pot from heat, stir 1 cup hot water and 1 cup canned cannellini beans, rinsed, into soup.

CREAMY LEEK-POTATO SOUP

✔ WHY THIS RECIPE WORKS
Most versions of this soup are gluey and drown the potato and leek flavor in an overabundance of cream. We learned that overwhipping the potatoes in the blender causes them to leach too much starch and turn gluey. By using fewer potatoes than you'd find in most recipes (we opted for russets since they broke down well), we lessened the amount of starch and thus the risk of glueyness. And instead of tossing out the leeks' dark green parts, we simmered them in the broth to give our soup potent leek flavor. We added a slice of bread to the blender when pureeing our soup to help thicken it without masking the flavor as cream would.

CREAMY LEEK-POTATO SOUP
SERVES 4 TO 6

Don't fill the blender by more than two-thirds with hot soup; if necessary, process in three batches. You can also use an immersion blender to process the soup directly in the pot. Use the lowest setting on your toaster to dry out the bread without overbrowning it. A garnish is essential to add texture and flavor to this soup. In addition to the Fried Leeks, we also like to serve this soup with crisp bacon bits, a dollop of sour cream, freshly chopped chives, and Garlic Chips (page 82) or Garlic Croutons (page 79).

4   medium leeks, white and light green parts halved lengthwise, sliced thin (4 cups), and washed thoroughly; dark green parts halved, cut into 2-inch pieces, and washed thoroughly
2   cups low-sodium chicken broth
2   cups water
4   tablespoons unsalted butter
1   onion, chopped
    Salt and pepper
1   small russet potato (about 6 ounces), peeled, halved lengthwise, and cut into ¼-inch slices
1   bay leaf
1   sprig fresh thyme or tarragon
1   slice hearty white sandwich bread, lightly toasted and torn into ½-inch pieces
1   recipe Fried Leeks (recipe follows)

1. Bring dark green leek pieces, broth, and water to boil in large saucepan over high heat. Reduce heat to low, cover, and simmer 20 minutes. Strain broth through fine-mesh strainer into medium bowl, pressing on solids to extract as much liquid as possible; set aside. Discard solids in strainer and rinse out saucepan.

2. Melt butter in now-empty saucepan over medium-low heat. Stir in sliced leeks, onion, and 1 teaspoon salt, reduce heat to low, and cook, stirring frequently, until vegetables are softened, about 10 minutes.

3. Increase heat to high, stir in reserved broth, potato, bay leaf, and thyme and bring to boil. Reduce heat to low and simmer until potato is tender, about 10 minutes. Add toasted bread and simmer until bread is completely saturated and starts to break down, about 5 minutes.

4. Remove and discard bay leaf and thyme. Transfer half of soup to blender and process until smooth and creamy, 2 to 3 minutes. Transfer to large bowl and repeat with remaining soup. Return soup to saucepan and bring to simmer. Season with salt and pepper to taste and serve with Fried Leeks.

FRIED LEEKS
MAKES ABOUT ½ CUP

1   medium leek, white and light green parts only, halved lengthwise, sliced into very thin 2-inch strips, washed thoroughly, and dried
2   tablespoons all-purpose flour
    Salt and pepper
½   cup olive oil

Toss leeks, flour, and pinch each salt and pepper in medium bowl. Heat oil in 12-inch skillet until shimmering. Add half of leeks and fry, stirring often, until golden brown, about 6 minutes. Using slotted spoon, transfer leeks to paper towel–lined plate, then sprinkle with salt and pepper to taste. Repeat with remaining leeks.

GARLIC-POTATO SOUP

✔ WHY THIS RECIPE WORKS
Choosing the right potato was the first step in developing our garlic-potato soup. We liked peeled russets for the way they broke down and thickened the broth, but we found adding red potatoes to the mix ramped up the potato flavor. The key to getting the garlic right proved to be not quantity but cooking technique. We settled on incorporating garlic in two ways: We sautéed three cloves in the pot before adding the broth (the base of our soup), and we poached two whole heads of garlic in the broth, then

squeezed out the softened pods, mashed them, and added them back to the soup. Topping the soup with crisp garlic chips cooked quickly in a skillet made just the right garnish.

GARLIC-POTATO SOUP
SERVES 6

A garnish is essential to add texture to this soup. We like Garlic Chips, but crisp bacon bits, Fried Leeks (page 81), or Garlic Croutons (page 79) are good options, too. A potato masher can be used instead of an immersion blender to mash some of the potatoes right in the pot, though the consistency will not be as creamy. If leeks are not available, substitute an equal amount of yellow onion. The test kitchen prefers the soup made with chicken broth, but vegetable broth can be substituted.

3	tablespoons unsalted butter
1	leek, white and light green parts only, halved lengthwise, chopped small, and washed thoroughly
3	garlic cloves, minced, plus 2 whole heads garlic, outer papery skins removed, and top third of heads cut off and discarded
6–7	cups low-sodium chicken broth
2	bay leaves
	Salt and pepper
1½	pounds russet potatoes, peeled and cut into ½-inch cubes
1	pound red potatoes (unpeeled), cut into ½-inch cubes
½	cup heavy cream
1½	teaspoons minced fresh thyme
¼	cup minced fresh chives
1	recipe Garlic Chips (recipe follows)

1. Melt butter in Dutch oven over medium heat. Add leeks and cook until soft (do not brown), 5 to 8 minutes. Stir in minced garlic and cook until fragrant, about 1 minute. Add garlic heads, 6 cups broth, bay leaves, and ¾ teaspoon salt. Partially cover pot and bring to simmer over medium-high heat. Reduce heat and simmer until garlic is very tender when pierced with tip of knife, 30 to 40 minutes. Add russet potatoes and red potatoes and continue to simmer, partially covered, until potatoes are tender, 15 to 20 minutes.

2. Discard bay leaves. Remove garlic heads from pot and, using tongs or paper towels, squeeze at root end until cloves slip out of their skins into bowl. Using fork, mash garlic to smooth paste.

3. Stir cream, thyme, and half of mashed garlic into soup. Heat soup until hot, about 2 minutes. Taste soup and add remaining garlic paste if desired.

4. Using immersion blender, process soup until creamy, with some potato chunks remaining. Alternatively, transfer 1½ cups potatoes and 1 cup broth to blender or food processor and process until smooth. (Process more potatoes for thicker consistency.) Return puree to pot and stir to combine, adjusting consistency with up to 1 cup more broth if necessary. Season with salt and pepper to taste, sprinkle with chives and Garlic Chips, and serve.

GARLIC CHIPS
MAKES ABOUT ¼ CUP

3	tablespoons olive oil
6	garlic cloves, sliced thin lengthwise
	Salt

Heat oil and garlic in 10-inch skillet over medium-high heat. Cook, turning frequently, until light golden brown, about 3 minutes. Using slotted spoon, transfer garlic to paper towel–lined plate. Season with salt to taste.

BROCCOLI-CHEESE SOUP

✔ WHY THIS RECIPE WORKS
We were after a soup with pure broccoli flavor that wasn't hiding behind the cream or the cheese. Overcooked broccoli has a sulfurous flavor, but we discovered when we cooked our broccoli beyond the point of just overcooked—for a full hour—those sulfur-containing compounds broke down, leaving behind intense, nutty broccoli. Its texture was fairly soft, but that was perfect for use in a soup. Adding baking soda to the pot sped up the process, shortening the broccoli's cooking time to a mere 20 minutes. A little spinach lent bright green color to the soup without taking over the flavor. After adding cheddar and Parmesan, we had a soup so full of flavor and richness that it didn't even need the cream.

BROCCOLI-CHEESE SOUP
SERVES 6 TO 8

To make a vegetarian version of this soup, substitute vegetable broth for the chicken broth.

2	tablespoons unsalted butter
2	pounds broccoli, florets chopped into 1-inch pieces, stalks peeled and sliced ¼ inch thick
1	onion, chopped coarse
2	garlic cloves, minced
1½	teaspoons dry mustard
	Pinch cayenne pepper
	Salt and pepper
3–4	cups water
¼	teaspoon baking soda
2	cups low-sodium chicken broth
2	ounces baby spinach (2 cups)
3	ounces sharp cheddar cheese, shredded (¾ cup)
1½	ounces Parmesan cheese, grated fine (¾ cup), plus extra for serving
1	recipe Butter Croutons (page 78)

1. Melt butter in Dutch oven over medium-high heat. Add broccoli, onion, garlic, mustard, cayenne, and 1 teaspoon salt and cook, stirring frequently, until fragrant, about 6 minutes. Add 1 cup water and baking soda. Bring to simmer, cover, and cook until broccoli is very soft, about 20 minutes, stirring once during cooking.

2. Add broth and 2 cups water and increase heat to medium-high. When mixture begins to simmer, stir in spinach and cook until wilted, about 1 minute. Transfer half of soup to blender, add cheddar and Parmesan, and process until smooth, about 1 minute. Transfer soup to medium bowl and repeat with remaining soup. Return soup to Dutch oven, place over medium heat and bring to simmer. Adjust consistency of soup with up to 1 cup water. Season with salt and pepper to taste. Serve, passing extra Parmesan.

SILKY BUTTERNUT SQUASH SOUP

✔ WHY THIS RECIPE WORKS

For soup with intense squash flavor, we sautéed shallots and butter with the squash seeds and fibers, simmered the mixture in water, and then used the liquid to steam the unpeeled squash. We scooped the squash flesh from the skin once cooled, then pureed it with the reserved steaming liquid for a perfectly smooth texture with big butternut squash flavor.

BUTTERNUT SQUASH SOUP
SERVES 4 TO 6

Lightly toasted pumpkin seeds, a drizzle of balsamic vinegar, or a dusting of paprika make appealing accompaniments to this soup in addition to the croutons.

4   tablespoons unsalted butter
1   large shallot, minced
3   pounds butternut squash, cut in half lengthwise, each half cut in half widthwise; seeds and fibers scraped out and reserved
6   cups water
    Salt
½   cup heavy cream
1   teaspoon dark brown sugar
    Pinch ground nutmeg
    Buttered Cinnamon-Sugar Croutons (recipe follows)

1. Melt butter in Dutch oven over medium-low heat. Add shallot and cook, stirring frequently, until translucent, about 3 minutes. Add seeds and fibers from squash and cook, stirring occasionally, until butter turns saffron color, about 4 minutes.

2. Add water and 1 teaspoon salt to pot and bring to boil over high heat. Reduce heat to medium-low, place squash, cut side down, in steamer basket, and lower basket into pot. Cover and steam until squash is completely tender, about 30 minutes. Take pot off heat and use tongs to transfer squash to rimmed baking sheet. When cool enough to handle, use large spoon to scrape flesh from skin. Reserve squash flesh in bowl and discard skin.

3. Strain steaming liquid through fine-mesh strainer into second bowl; discard solids in strainer. (You should have 2½ to 3 cups liquid.) Rinse and dry pot.

4. Working in batches and filling blender jar only halfway for each batch, puree squash, adding enough reserved steaming liquid to obtain smooth consistency. Transfer puree to clean pot and stir in remaining steaming liquid, cream, and brown sugar. Warm soup over medium-low heat until hot, about 3 minutes. Stir in nutmeg, season with salt to taste, and serve. (Soup can be refrigerated for up to 2 days.)

BUTTERED CINNAMON-SUGAR CROUTONS
MAKES ABOUT 1 CUP

---

2   slices hearty white sandwich bread, crusts removed, cut into ½-inch cubes (about 1 cup)
1   tablespoon unsalted butter, melted
2   teaspoons sugar
½   teaspoon ground cinnamon

1. Adjust oven rack to middle position and heat oven to 350 degrees. Combine bread cubes and melted butter in medium bowl and toss to coat. Combine sugar and cinnamon in small bowl, then add to bowl with bread cubes and toss to coat.

2. Spread bread cubes in single layer on parchment paper–lined rimmed baking sheet and bake, stirring occasionally, until crisp, 8 to 10 minutes. Let cool on baking sheet to room temperature. (Croutons can be stored for up to 3 days.)

CURRIED BUTTERNUT SQUASH SOUP WITH CILANTRO YOGURT

Sprinkle lightly toasted pumpkin seeds over each bowl of soup for a nice textural contrast.

Follow recipe for Silky Butternut Squash Soup. While squash is steaming, stir together ¼ cup plain whole-milk yogurt, 2 tablespoons minced fresh cilantro, 1 teaspoon lime juice, and ⅛ teaspoon salt in small bowl. Add 1½ teaspoons curry powder to squash while pureeing in blender. Continue with recipe, garnishing each bowl of soup with dollop of cilantro yogurt.

CREAMY MUSHROOM SOUP

✔ WHY THIS RECIPE WORKS

For a substantial mushroom soup with a distinctive, deep mushroom flavor and a rich texture that was neither too thick nor thin, we cooked readily available white mushrooms low and slow with butter and shallots before pureeing them. Finishing the soup with a splash of Madeira (a classic match for mushrooms), cream, and lemon juice brightened the soup and added complexity. A garnish of sautéed wild mushrooms added a hit of earthiness and flavor to our soup. To make sure that the soup has a fine, velvety texture, puree it hot off the stove, but do not fill the blender jar more than halfway, as the hot liquid may cause the lid to pop off.

CREAMY MUSHROOM SOUP
SERVES 6 TO 8

The mushroom garnish adds visual appeal and texture to this creamy soup.

- 6 tablespoons unsalted butter
- 6 large shallots, minced
- 1 garlic clove, minced
- ½ teaspoon ground nutmeg
- 2 pounds white mushrooms, trimmed and sliced ¼ inch thick
- 3½ cups low-sodium chicken broth
- 4 cups hot water
- ½ ounce dried porcini mushrooms, rinsed
- ⅓ cup Madeira or dry sherry
- 1 cup heavy cream
- 2 teaspoons lemon juice
  Salt and pepper
- 1 recipe Sautéed Wild Mushroom Garnish (recipe follows)

1. Melt butter in Dutch oven over medium-low heat. Add shallots and sauté, stirring frequently, until softened, about 4 minutes. Stir in garlic and nutmeg; cook until fragrant, about 1 minute longer. Increase heat to medium; add white mushrooms and stir to coat with butter. Cook, stirring occasionally, until mushrooms release liquid, about 7 minutes. Reduce heat to medium-low, cover pot, and cook, stirring occasionally, until softened and mushrooms have released all liquid, about 20 minutes.

2. Add broth, water, and porcini mushrooms to pot. Cover and bring to simmer, then reduce heat to low and simmer until mushrooms are fully tender, about 20 minutes.

3. Puree soup in batches in blender until smooth, filling blender jar only halfway for each batch. Rinse and dry pot and return soup to pot. Stir in Madeira and cream and bring to simmer over low heat. Add lemon juice, season with salt and pepper to taste, and serve with Sautéed Wild Mushroom Garnish. (Soup, minus garnish, can be refrigerated for up to 2 days.)

SAUTÉED WILD MUSHROOM GARNISH
MAKES ENOUGH TO GARNISH 6 TO 8 SERVINGS OF SOUP

- 2 tablespoons unsalted butter
- 8 ounces shiitake, chanterelle, oyster, or cremini mushrooms, stemmed and sliced thin
  Salt and pepper

1. Melt butter in 10-inch skillet over low heat. Add mushrooms and season with salt and pepper to taste. Cover and cook, stirring occasionally, until mushrooms release their liquid, about 10 minutes for shiitakes and chanterelles, about 5 minutes for oysters, and about 9 minutes for cremini.

2. Uncover and continue to cook, stirring occasionally, until liquid released by mushrooms has evaporated and mushrooms are browned, about 2 minutes for shiitakes, about 3 minutes for chanterelles, and about 2 minutes for oysters and cremini. Serve immediately as garnish for soup.

HEARTY VEGETABLE SOUP

✔ WHY THIS RECIPE WORKS

For a vegetable soup that satisfies, we started by roasting a combination of carrot, celery, onion, portobellos (key for meaty flavor), and a head of garlic, then simmered the roasted vegetables in broth along with leek greens, plenty of herbs, and flavor-packed dried porcini mushrooms for a deep, rich soup base. Tossing the vegetables in tomato paste before roasting enriched their flavor even more. We squeezed the roasted garlic out of its skin and into the fortified broth to both thicken and flavor it. Potatoes, carrots, celery root, and lima beans gave our soup heft, and mashing some of the potatoes helped to further thicken it. Finishing with escarole gave it fresh flavor. For a textural contrast, we topped the soup with garlicky crostini slices.

HEARTY VEGETABLE SOUP
SERVES 4 TO 6

If you can get "petite cut" canned diced tomatoes, they can be used after draining, without any additional chopping. Serve with toasted slices of baguette rubbed with the cut side of a garlic clove and brushed with extra-virgin olive oil.

STOCK

- 1 large carrot, peeled and chopped
- 1 celery rib, chopped
- 1 onion, chopped
- 3 portobello mushrooms, chopped coarse
- 1 head garlic, outer papery skins removed and top third of head cut off and discarded
- 3 tablespoons olive oil
- 4 teaspoons tomato paste
- 9 cups low-sodium chicken broth or vegetable broth
- 2 medium leeks, halved lengthwise, green parts chopped and washed thoroughly, white parts sliced thin, washed thoroughly, and reserved for soup
- 10 sprigs fresh parsley

4 sprigs fresh thyme

2 bay leaves

½ ounce dried porcini mushrooms, rinsed

SOUP

1 (14.5-ounce) can diced tomatoes, drained, tomato pieces chopped coarse

12 ounces russet potatoes, peeled and cut into ½-inch pieces

2 carrots, peeled and cut into ½-inch pieces

½ head celery root (14 ounces), peeled and cut into ½-inch pieces

1 small head escarole (12 ounces), stemmed and leaves cut into 1-inch pieces (4 cups)

1 cup frozen baby lima beans, thawed (optional)

2 tablespoons minced fresh parsley
Salt and pepper

1. FOR THE STOCK: Adjust oven rack to middle position and heat oven to 450 degrees. Place carrot, celery, onion, portobellos, and garlic head on rimmed baking sheet. Drizzle with oil and toss to coat. Add tomato paste and toss again to coat. Spread vegetables in even layer, set garlic head cut side up, and roast until vegetables are well browned, 25 to 30 minutes.

2. Combine roasted vegetables, broth, leek greens, parsley, thyme, bay leaves, and porcini in Dutch oven. Cover and bring to simmer over medium-high heat, then reduce heat to medium-low and simmer, partially covered, 30 minutes.

3. Remove garlic head from pot and, using tongs or paper towels, squeeze at root end until cloves slip out of their skins into small bowl. Using fork, mash garlic to smooth paste and set aside. Strain stock through large fine-mesh strainer, pressing on solids to extract as much liquid as possible. Discard solids in strainer.

4. FOR THE SOUP: Rinse and wipe out Dutch oven. Add tomatoes, potatoes, carrots, celery root, reserved whites of leeks, strained broth, and garlic paste to pot and bring to simmer over medium-high heat, then reduce heat to medium-low and simmer, partially covered, until vegetables are tender when poked with skewer or paring knife, about 25 minutes. With back of wooden spoon, mash some potatoes against side of pot to thicken soup. Stir in escarole and lima beans, if using, and cook until escarole is wilted and lima beans are heated through, about 5 minutes. Stir in parsley and season with salt and pepper to taste. Serve immediately. (Fortified broth can be refrigerated for up to 3 days or frozen for up to 2 months.)

HEARTY MINESTRONE

✔ WHY THIS RECIPE WORKS

We wanted a minestrone with fresh, bright flavors that didn't have to rely on market-fresh vegetables like the best Italian versions. First, we needed a manageable list of supermarket vegetables for our base, and we settled on onions, celery, and carrots, along with cabbage, zucchini, and tomato. Slowly layering flavors to create complexity was key. We started by sautéing pancetta, then browned the vegetables in the rendered fat. Salt-soaking dried beans (chosen over canned for superior texture) seasoned them throughout, and simmering them vigorously in the soup base helped them release starch and thicken the soup. A diced supermarket tomato did nothing for the taste of our soup, so we turned to V8 juice, which ensured consistent tomato flavor. Adding a Parmesan rind to the soup infused it with cheesy flavor. And finally, we took a cue from the minestrone of northern Italy and finished the soup with a deconstructed pesto, adding chopped basil, a swirl of fruity olive oil, and freshly grated Parmesan.

HEARTY MINESTRONE
SERVES 6 TO 8

If you are pressed for time you can "quick salt soak" your beans. In step 1, combine the salt, water, and beans in a Dutch oven and bring to a boil over high heat. Remove the pot from the heat, cover, and let stand 1 hour. Drain and rinse the beans and proceed with the recipe. We prefer cannellini beans, but navy or great Northern beans can be used. We prefer pancetta, but bacon can be used. To make this soup vegetarian, substitute vegetable broth for chicken broth and 2 teaspoons olive oil for the pancetta. Parmesan rind is added for flavor, but can be replaced with a 2-inch chunk of the cheese. In order for the starch from the beans to thicken the soup, it is important to maintain a vigorous simmer in step 3.

Salt and pepper

½ pound dried cannellini beans (1 cup), picked over and rinsed

3 ounces pancetta, cut into ¼-inch pieces

1 tablespoon extra-virgin olive oil, plus extra for serving

2 celery ribs, cut into ½-inch pieces

1 carrot, peeled and cut into ½-inch pieces

2 small onions, cut into ½-inch pieces

1 zucchini, cut into ½-inch pieces (1 cup)

2 garlic cloves, minced

½ small head green cabbage, halved, cored, and cut into ½-inch pieces (2 cups)

⅛–¼ teaspoon red pepper flakes

8 cups water

2 cups low-sodium chicken broth

1 Parmesan cheese rind

1 bay leaf

1½ cups V8 juice

½ cup chopped fresh basil
Grated Parmesan cheese

1. Dissolve 1½ tablespoons salt in 2 quarts cold water in large bowl or container. Add beans and soak for at least 8 hours and up to 24 hours. Drain beans and rinse well.

2. Heat pancetta and oil in Dutch oven over medium-high heat. Cook, stirring occasionally, until pancetta is lightly browned and fat has rendered, 3 to 5 minutes. Add celery, carrot, onions, and zucchini and cook, stirring frequently, until vegetables are softened and lightly browned, 5 to 9 minutes. Stir in garlic, cabbage, ½ teaspoon salt, and pepper flakes and continue to cook until cabbage starts to wilt, 1 to 2 minutes longer. Transfer vegetables to rimmed baking sheet and set aside.

3. Add soaked beans, water, broth, Parmesan rind, and bay leaf to Dutch oven and bring to boil over high heat. Reduce heat and simmer vigorously, stirring occasionally, until beans are fully tender and liquid begins to thicken, 45 to 60 minutes.

4. Add reserved vegetables and V8 juice to pot and cook until vegetables are soft, about 15 minutes. Discard bay leaf and Parmesan rind, stir in chopped basil, and season with salt and pepper to taste. Serve with oil and grated Parmesan. (Soup can be refrigerated for up to 2 days. Reheat it gently and add basil just before serving.)

SPLIT PEA AND HAM SOUP

✔ **WHY THIS RECIPE WORKS**
We wanted a spoon-coating, richly flavorful broth studded with tender shreds of sweet-smoky meat, all without requiring the old-fashioned ham bone traditionally used to infuse the soup with flavor. Substituting ham hock made the soup greasy and was skimpy on the meat. Ham steak, however, was plenty meaty and infused the soup with a fuller pork flavor. Without the bone, our soup needed richness and smokiness, and adding a few strips of raw bacon to the pot

did the job. Unsoaked peas broke down just as well as soaked and were better at absorbing the flavor of the soup.

SPLIT PEA AND HAM SOUP
SERVES 6 TO 8

Four ounces of regular sliced bacon can be used, but the thinner slices are a little harder to remove from the soup. Depending on the age and brand of split peas, the consistency of the soup may vary slightly. If the soup is too thin at the end of step 3, increase the heat and simmer, uncovered, until the desired consistency is reached. If it is too thick, thin it with a little water. In addition to sprinkling the soup with the Butter Croutons, we also like to garnish it with fresh peas, chopped mint, and a drizzle of aged balsamic vinegar.

2	tablespoons unsalted butter
1	large onion, chopped fine
	Salt and pepper
2	garlic cloves, minced
7	cups water
1	ham steak (about 1 pound), skin removed, cut into quarters
3	slices thick-cut bacon
1	pound green split peas (2 cups), picked over and rinsed
2	sprigs fresh thyme
2	bay leaves
2	carrots, peeled and cut into ½-inch pieces
1	celery rib, cut into ½-inch pieces
1	recipe Butter Croutons (page 78)

1. Heat butter in Dutch oven over medium-high heat. Add onion and ½ teaspoon salt and cook, stirring frequently, until onion is softened, about 3 to 4 minutes. Add garlic and cook until fragrant, about 30 seconds. Add water, ham steak, bacon, peas, thyme, and bay leaves. Increase heat to high and bring to simmer, stirring frequently to keep peas from sticking to bottom. Reduce heat to low, cover, and simmer until peas are tender but not falling apart, about 45 minutes.

2. Remove ham steak, cover with aluminum foil or plastic wrap to prevent drying out, and set aside. Stir in carrots and celery and continue to simmer, covered, until vegetables are tender and peas have almost completely broken down, about 30 minutes longer.

3. When cool enough to handle, shred ham into small bite-size pieces. Remove and discard thyme, bay leaves, and bacon slices. Stir ham back into soup and return to simmer. Season with salt and pepper to taste and serve. (Soup can be refrigerated for up to 3 days. If necessary, thin it with water when reheating.)

HEARTY LENTIL SOUP

✔ **WHY THIS RECIPE WORKS**
We wanted a lentil soup that would give us a brightly colored and flavored soup that was hearty but not too thick, with a subtle, smoky depth from meat. We sweated the lentils in a covered pan with aromatics and bacon before adding the liquid, which helped them hold their shape and boosted their flavor. Pureeing only some of the soup ensured the final result had appealing texture that was not overly smooth. Finishing with a splash of balsamic vinegar brightened the dish.

HEARTY LENTIL SOUP
SERVES 4 TO 6

Lentilles du Puy, sometimes called French green lentils, are our first choice for this recipe, but brown, black, or regular green lentils are fine, too. Note that cooking times will vary depending on the type of lentils used. Lentils lose flavor with age, and because most packaged lentils do not have expiration dates, try to buy them from a store that specializes in natural foods and grains. Before use, rinse and then carefully sort through the lentils to remove small stones and pebbles.

3 slices bacon, cut into ¼-inch pieces
1 large onion, chopped fine
2 carrots, peeled and chopped
3 garlic cloves, minced
1 (14.5-ounce) can diced tomatoes, drained
1 bay leaf
1 teaspoon minced fresh thyme
7 ounces lentils (1 cup), picked over and rinsed
1 teaspoon salt
 Pepper
½ cup dry white wine
4½ cups low-sodium chicken broth
1½ cups water
1½ teaspoons balsamic vinegar
3 tablespoons minced fresh parsley

1. Cook bacon in Dutch oven over medium-high heat, stirring occasionally, until bacon is crisp, about 5 minutes. Add onion and carrots and cook, stirring occasionally, until vegetables begin to soften, about 2 minutes. Add garlic and cook until fragrant, about 30 seconds. Stir in tomatoes, bay leaf, and thyme and cook until fragrant, about 30 seconds. Stir in lentils and salt and season with pepper to taste. Cover, reduce heat to medium-low, and cook until vegetables are softened and lentils have darkened, 8 to 10 minutes.

2. Uncover, increase heat to high, add wine, and bring to simmer. Add chicken broth and water, bring to boil, cover partially, and reduce heat to low. Simmer until lentils are tender but still hold their shape, 30 to 35 minutes.

3. Remove bay leaf from pot and discard. Puree 3 cups soup in blender until smooth, then return to pot. Stir in vinegar and heat soup over medium-low heat until hot, about 5 minutes. Stir in 2 tablespoons parsley and serve, garnishing each bowl with remaining parsley.

MAKE-AHEAD: After adding vinegar in step 3, refrigerate soup in airtight container for up to 2 days. To serve, heat it over medium-low heat until hot, then stir in the parsley.

HEARTY LENTIL SOUP WITH SPINACH

Replace parsley with 5 ounces baby spinach and continue to heat soup in step 3, stirring frequently, until spinach is wilted, about 3 minutes.

HEARTY LENTIL SOUP WITH FRAGRANT SPICES

Add 1 teaspoon ground cumin, 1 teaspoon ground coriander, 1 teaspoon ground cinnamon, and ¼ teaspoon cayenne along with garlic. Substitute lemon juice for balsamic vinegar and minced cilantro for parsley.

PASTA E FAGIOLI

✓ WHY THIS RECIPE WORKS
To develop a pasta and bean soup recipe with great flavor and proper texture in less than an hour, we started by cooking some pancetta (bacon worked well, too) in a Dutch oven, then cooked our vegetables in the rendered fat. Adding the tomatoes and beans together allowed them to absorb flavor from each other, and a 3:2 ratio of chicken broth to water added richness without turning our pasta and bean soup into chicken soup. We knew from experience that adding a Parmesan rind to the pot would give our soup depth and infuse a slight cheese flavor throughout. Finally, parsley and minced anchovies lent the necessary bright notes to our soup.

PASTA E FAGIOLI
SERVES 8 TO 10

Parmesan rind is added for flavor, but can be replaced with a 2-inch chunk of the cheese. You can substitute another small pasta for the orzo, such as ditalini, tubettini, or conchigliette.

1 tablespoon extra-virgin olive oil, plus extra for drizzling
3 ounces pancetta or 3 slices bacon, chopped fine
1 onion, chopped fine
1 celery rib, chopped fine
4 garlic cloves, minced
1 teaspoon dried oregano
¼ teaspoon red pepper flakes
3 anchovy fillets, rinsed and minced
1 (28-ounce) can diced tomatoes
1 Parmesan cheese rind
2 (15-ounce) cans cannellini beans, rinsed
3½ cups low-sodium chicken broth
2½ cups water
 Salt and pepper
1 cup orzo
¼ cup chopped fresh parsley
2 ounces Parmesan cheese, grated (1 cup)

1. Heat oil in Dutch oven over medium-high heat until shimmering. Add pancetta and cook, stirring occasionally, until beginning to brown, 3 to 5 minutes. Add onion and celery and cook, stirring occasionally, until vegetables are softened, 5 to 7 minutes. Add garlic, oregano, pepper flakes, and anchovies and cook, stirring constantly, until fragrant, about 1 minute. Stir in tomatoes, scraping up any browned bits from bottom of pan. Add Parmesan rind and beans and bring to boil, then reduce heat to low and simmer to blend flavors, 10 minutes.

2. Add chicken broth, water, and 1 teaspoon salt to pot. Increase heat to high and bring to boil. Add pasta and cook until al dente, about 10 minutes.

3. Remove and discard Parmesan rind. Off heat, stir in 3 tablespoons parsley and season with salt and pepper to taste. Ladle soup into bowls, drizzle with olive oil and sprinkle with remaining parsley. Serve immediately, passing grated Parmesan separately.

TO MAKE AHEAD: Soup can be prepared through step 1 and refrigerated for up to 3 days. When ready to serve, discard Parmesan rind, add liquid, bring soup to a boil, and proceed with recipe.

ITALIAN PASTA AND BEAN SOUP WITH ORANGE AND FENNEL

Ditalini and orzo are especially good pasta shapes for this variation.

Trim stalks from 1 fennel bulb (12 ounces), then halve and core. Slice bulb lengthwise into ¼-inch-thick strips, then chop fine. Cook fennel along with onion and celery and add 2 teaspoons grated orange zest and ½ teaspoon fennel seeds along with garlic, oregano, pepper flakes, and anchovies in step 1.

TUSCAN WHITE BEAN SOUP

✔ **WHY THIS RECIPE WORKS**
Tuscan white bean soup should be a testament to restraint, comprising only two components: tender, creamy beans, and a broth perfumed with the fragrance of garlic and rosemary. We tossed out all the rules about how to prepare dried beans for this recipe. First, we skipped the presoak (soaked beans exploded once cooked), instead simmering them right in what would become the broth for our soup. We cooked them until just barely done, then let residual heat

gently cook them through to ensure even cooking. We also added salt to the pot, something typically thought to cause the beans' exteriors to toughen. We felt the salt actually helped keep the beans from bursting, and it also seasoned them nicely. Adding onion, garlic, bay leaf, and pancetta to our cooking broth gave the beans a welcome sweet and sour flavor. And since cooking rosemary with the beans gave the soup a bitter, medicinal flavor, we steeped the herb in the broth off the heat.

TUSCAN WHITE BEAN SOUP
SERVES 6 TO 8

For a more authentic soup, place a small slice of lightly toasted Italian bread in the bottom of each bowl and ladle the soup over. To make this a vegetarian soup, omit the pancetta and add a piece of Parmesan rind to the pot along with the halved onion and unpeeled garlic in step 1.

- 6 ounces pancetta, cut into 1-inch cubes
- 12 cups water, plus extra as needed
- 1 pound dried cannellini beans (2 cups), picked over and rinsed
- 1 large onion, unpeeled and halved, plus 1 small onion, chopped
- 4 garlic cloves, unpeeled, plus 3 garlic cloves, minced
- 1 bay leaf
  Salt and pepper
- ¼ cup extra-virgin olive oil, plus extra for serving
- 1 sprig fresh rosemary
  Balsamic vinegar, for serving

1. Cook pancetta in Dutch oven over medium heat until just golden, 8 to 10 minutes. Add water, beans, halved onion, unpeeled garlic cloves, bay leaf, and 1 teaspoon salt and bring to boil over medium-high heat. Cover pot partially, reduce heat to low, and simmer, stirring occasionally, until beans are almost

tender, 1 to 1¼ hours. Remove beans from heat, cover, and let stand until beans are tender, about 30 minutes.

2. Drain beans, reserving cooking liquid (you should have about 5 cups; if not, add enough water to reach 5 cups). Discard pancetta, onion, unpeeled garlic cloves, and bay leaf. Spread beans in even layer on rimmed baking sheet and let cool.

3. While beans are cooling, heat oil in pot over medium heat until shimmering. Add chopped onion and cook, stirring occasionally, until softened, 5 to 6 minutes. Stir in minced garlic and cook until fragrant, about 30 seconds. Add cooled beans and reserved cooking liquid. Increase heat to medium-high and bring to simmer. Submerge rosemary in liquid, cover, and let stand off heat 15 to 20 minutes. Discard rosemary and season with salt and pepper to taste. Ladle soup into bowls, drizzle with olive oil, and serve, passing balsamic vinegar separately.

WHITE BEAN SOUP WITH WINTER VEGETABLES
SERVES 10 TO 12

For a more authentic soup, place a small slice of lightly toasted Italian bread in the bottom of each bowl and ladle the soup over. To make this a vegetarian soup, omit the pancetta and add a piece of Parmesan rind to the pot along with the halved onion and unpeeled garlic in step 1.

- 6 ounces pancetta, cut into 1-inch cubes
- 12 cups water, plus extra as needed
- 1 pound dried cannellini beans (2 cups), picked over and rinsed
- 1 large onion, unpeeled and halved, plus 1 small onion, chopped
- 4 garlic cloves, unpeeled, plus 3 garlic cloves, minced
- 1 bay leaf
  Salt and pepper

¼ cup extra-virgin olive oil, plus extra for serving

2 small carrots, diced medium

2 celery ribs, diced medium

2 small leeks, white and light green parts only, halved lengthwise, sliced crosswise into ½-inch pieces, and rinsed thoroughly

4 ounces kale, stemmed and leaves cut into ½-inch strips

4 ounces escarole, stemmed and leaves cut into ½-inch strips

6 ounces red potatoes, diced medium

1 (14.5-ounce) can diced tomatoes, drained

1 sprig fresh rosemary

1. Cook pancetta in Dutch oven over medium heat until just golden, 8 to 10 minutes. Add water, beans, halved onion, unpeeled garlic cloves, bay leaf, and 1 teaspoon salt and bring to boil over medium-high heat. Cover pot partially, reduce heat to low, and simmer, stirring occasionally, until beans are almost tender, 1 to 1¼ hours. Remove beans from heat, cover, and let stand until beans are tender, about 30 minutes.

2. Drain beans, reserving cooking liquid. Discard pancetta, onion, unpeeled garlic cloves, and bay leaf. Spread beans in even layer on rimmed baking sheet and let cool.

3. While beans are cooling, heat oil in pot over medium heat until shimmering. Add carrots, celery, leeks, and chopped onion and cook, stirring occasionally, until softened but not browned, about 7 minutes. Stir in minced garlic and cook until fragrant, about 30 seconds. Add enough water to reserved bean cooking liquid to equal 9 cups and add to pot with kale and escarole. Increase heat to medium-high and bring to boil, cover, reduce heat to low, and simmer 30 minutes. Add potatoes

and tomatoes, cover, and cook until potatoes are tender, about 20 minutes.

4. Add cooled beans to pot, increase heat to medium-high, and bring to simmer. Submerge rosemary in liquid, cover, and let stand off heat 15 to 20 minutes. Discard rosemary and season with salt and pepper to taste. Ladle soup into bowls, drizzle with olive oil, and serve.

QUICK TUSCAN WHITE BEAN SOUP

SERVES 6

This quick variation uses canned beans and can be on the table in just 40 minutes.

6 ounces pancetta, cut into 1-inch cubes

2 tablespoons extra-virgin olive oil, plus extra for serving

1 small onion, chopped

3 garlic cloves, minced
Salt and pepper

3½ cups water

4 (15-ounce) cans cannellini beans, rinsed

1 sprig fresh rosemary
Balsamic vinegar, for serving

1. Cook pancetta in Dutch oven over medium heat until just golden, 8 to 10 minutes. Discard pancetta and add oil to pot with rendered pancetta fat. Add onion and cook, stirring occasionally, until softened, 5 to 6 minutes. Stir in garlic and cook until fragrant, about 30 seconds.

2. Add beans, ½ teaspoon salt, and 3½ cups water. Increase heat to medium-high and bring to simmer. Submerge rosemary in liquid; cover and let stand off heat 15 to 20 minutes. Discard rosemary and season with salt and pepper to taste. Ladle soup into bowls, drizzle with olive oil, and serve, passing balsamic vinegar separately.

BLACK BEAN SOUP

✓ WHY THIS RECIPE WORKS

For a black bean soup recipe full of sweet, spicy, smoky flavors, we went with dried beans, which release flavor into the broth as they cook, unlike canned beans. Furthermore, they proved to be a timesaver: We discovered that it was unnecessary to soak them overnight or to use the "quick-soak method" to make them tender. We also found that we didn't need from-scratch stock; we maximized flavor by using a mixture of water and store-bought chicken broth enhanced with ham and seasonings.

BLACK BEAN SOUP

SERVES 6

Dried beans tend to cook unevenly, so be sure to taste several beans to determine their doneness in step 1. For efficiency, you can prepare the soup ingredients while the beans simmer and the garnishes while the soup simmers. Though you do not need to offer all of the garnishes listed below, do choose at least a couple; garnishes are essential for this soup as they add not only flavor but texture and color as well.

BEANS

5 cups water, plus extra as needed

1 pound dried black beans (2 cups), picked over and rinsed

4 ounces ham steak, trimmed

2 bay leaves

⅛ teaspoon baking soda

1 teaspoon salt

SOUP

3 tablespoons olive oil

2 large onions, chopped fine

1 large carrot, chopped fine

3 celery ribs, chopped fine

½ teaspoon salt

5–6 garlic cloves, minced

½ teaspoon red pepper flakes

1½ tablespoons ground cumin
6 cups low-sodium chicken broth
2 tablespoons cornstarch
2 tablespoons water
2 tablespoons lime juice

GARNISHES
Lime wedges
Minced fresh cilantro
Red onion, diced fine
Avocado, halved, pitted, and diced
Sour cream

1. FOR THE BEANS: Place water, beans, ham, bay leaves, and baking soda in large saucepan with tight-fitting lid. Bring to boil over medium-high heat. Using large spoon, skim foam from surface as needed. Stir in salt, reduce heat to low, cover, and simmer briskly until beans are tender, 1¼ to 1½ hours (if after 1½ hours the beans are not tender, add 1 cup more water and continue to simmer until tender); do not drain beans. Discard bay leaves. Remove ham steak, cut into ¼-inch cubes, and set aside.

2. FOR THE SOUP: Heat oil in Dutch oven over medium-high heat until shimmering. Add onions, carrot, celery, and salt and cook, stirring occasionally, until vegetables are soft and lightly browned, 12 to 15 minutes. Reduce heat to medium-low, add garlic, pepper flakes, and cumin and cook, stirring constantly, until fragrant, about 3 minutes. Stir in beans, bean cooking liquid, and chicken broth. Increase heat to medium-high and bring to boil, then reduce heat to low and simmer, uncovered, stirring occasionally, to blend flavors, about 30 minutes.

3. Ladle 1½ cups beans and 2 cups liquid into food processor or blender, process until smooth, and return to pot. Stir together cornstarch and water in small bowl until combined, then gradually stir half of cornstarch mixture into soup. Bring to boil over medium-high heat, stirring occasionally, to fully thicken. If soup is still thinner than desired once boiling, stir remaining cornstarch mixture to recombine and gradually stir mixture into soup; return to boil to fully thicken. Off heat, stir in lime juice and reserved ham; ladle soup into bowls and serve immediately, passing garnishes separately. (Soup can be refrigerated for up to 4 days. If necessary, thin it with additional chicken broth when reheating.)

BLACK BEAN SOUP WITH CHIPOTLE CHILES

The addition of chipotle chiles in adobo—smoked jalapeños packed in a seasoned tomato-vinegar sauce—makes this a spicier, smokier variation on Black Bean Soup.

Omit pepper flakes and add 1 tablespoon minced canned chipotle chile in adobo sauce plus 2 teaspoons adobo sauce along with chicken broth in step 2.

CLASSIC CORN CHOWDER

✔ WHY THIS RECIPE WORKS
To create a classic corn chowder, we started by browning salt pork in our Dutch oven, and we used the rendered fat (along with a little butter) to sauté onions and create a richly flavored base. To pump up the corn flavor, we added grated corn and corn milk, which comes from scraping the cobs with the back of a knife early on, then stirred in more whole kernels toward the end. With whole milk as our primary dairy component (tasters rejected all heavy cream as too rich), we added a few tablespoons of flour, which not only thickened our soup nicely but also helped stabilize the dairy and kept it from curdling.

CLASSIC CORN CHOWDER
SERVES 6

Be sure to use salt pork, not fatback, for the chowder. Streaks of lean meat distinguish salt pork from fatback; fatback is pure fat. We prefer Spanish onions for their sweet, mild flavor, but all-purpose yellow onions will work fine, too.

10 ears corn, husks and silk removed
3 ounces salt pork, rind removed, cut into two 1-inch cubes
1 tablespoon unsalted butter

TEST KITCHEN TIP NO. 20 WHY SOUPS TASTE BETTER THE NEXT DAY

We often find when making soups or stews that they actually taste better reheated than straight off the stovetop. Curious as to why, our science editor explained that even after cooking ceases, many chemical reactions continue to take place in food. In the case of a soup or stew containing milk or cream, the lactose breaks down into sweeter-tasting glucose. Similarly, the carbohydrates in onions develop into sugars such as fructose and glucose. Proteins in meat turn into individual amino acids that act as flavor enhancers. Finally, starches in potatoes and flour break down into flavorful compounds.

We tested this theory with batches of French onion soup, beef chili, cream of tomato soup, and black bean soup, cooking one batch and refrigerating it for two days, then serving it, reheated, alongside a fresh batch. The two-day-old soups were unanimously preferred for being sweeter, more robust, and well-rounded. The chili divided tasters; some preferred the sharper-tasting fresh sample while others like the sweetness of the reheated chili. If you like vibrant chili flavor, it's best to serve chili the same day you make it, but for sweet, well-rounded flavors in soups and stews, make them a day or two ahead of time.

1 large onion, preferably Spanish, chopped fine
2 garlic cloves, minced
3 tablespoons all-purpose flour
3 cups low-sodium chicken broth
12 ounces red potatoes, cut into ¼-inch cubes
2 cups whole milk
1 teaspoon minced fresh thyme or ¼ teaspoon dried
1 bay leaf
1 cup heavy cream
2 tablespoons minced fresh parsley
  Salt and pepper

1. Using paring knife, cut kernels from 4 ears corn (you should have about 3 cups). Grate kernels from remaining 6 ears on large holes of box grater into bowl, then firmly scrape any pulp remaining on cobs with back of butter knife or vegetable peeler (you should have 2 generous cups grated kernels and pulp).

2. Sauté salt pork in Dutch oven over medium-high heat, turning with tongs and pressing down on pieces to render fat, until cubes are crisp and golden brown, about 10 minutes. Reduce heat to low, stir in butter and onion, cover, and cook until onion is softened, about 12 minutes. Remove salt pork and reserve. Add garlic and sauté until fragrant, about 1 minute. Whisk in flour and cook, stirring constantly, about 2 minutes. Whisking constantly, gradually add broth. Add grated corn and pulp, potatoes, milk, thyme, bay leaf, and reserved salt pork and bring to boil. Reduce heat to medium-low and simmer until potatoes are almost tender, 8 to 10 minutes. Add reserved corn kernels and heavy cream and return to simmer. Simmer until corn kernels are tender yet still slightly crunchy, about 5 minutes. Discard bay leaf and salt pork. Stir in parsley, season with salt and pepper to taste, and serve immediately.

MODERN CORN CHOWDER

✓ WHY THIS RECIPE WORKS

For this version of corn chowder, we were looking for a recipe that would pack lots of corn flavor in every spoonful while still maintaining a satisfying, yet not too thick, chowder texture. Inspired by a recipe we found that juiced corn kernels, a trick that delivered pronounced corn flavor, we strained the scrapings and pulp from several cobs through a kitchen towel to get unadulterated corn juice (when we added the unstrained pulp to the pot, the soup curdled). This delivered the intense corn flavor we were after. We lightened things up by using water as our primary liquid, which allowed the pure corn flavor to shine through, then added just 1 cup of half-and-half to give our chowder the right richness. A sprinkling of basil before serving lent a fresh finish.

MODERN CORN CHOWDER
SERVES 6

When removing the kernels from the cob make sure to remove only the part of the kernel sticking out of the cob. Cutting deeper will result in too much fibrous material coming off the corn. Yukon Gold potatoes can be substituted for the red potatoes. Minced chives can be used in place of the basil.

8 ears corn, husks and silk removed
3 tablespoons unsalted butter
1 onion, chopped fine
4 slices bacon, halved lengthwise, then cut crosswise into ¼-inch pieces
2 teaspoons minced fresh thyme
  Salt and pepper
¼ cup all-purpose flour
5 cups water
12 ounces red potatoes, cut into ½-inch cubes
1 cup half-and-half
  Sugar
3 tablespoons chopped fresh basil

1. Using paring knife, cut kernels from corn (you should have 5 to 6 cups). Holding cobs over second bowl, use back of butter knife or vegetable peeler to firmly scrape any pulp remaining on cobs into bowl (you should have 2 to 2½ cups of pulp). Transfer pulp to center of clean kitchen towel set in medium bowl. Wrap towel tightly around pulp and squeeze tightly until dry. Discard pulp in towel and set corn juice aside (you should have about ⅔ cup of juice).

2. Melt butter in Dutch oven over medium heat. Add onion, bacon, thyme, 2 teaspoons salt, and 1 teaspoon pepper and cook, stirring frequently, until onion is softened and beginning to brown, 8 to 10 minutes. Stir in flour and cook, stirring constantly, for 2 minutes. Whisking constantly, gradually add water and then bring to boil. Add corn kernels and potatoes. Return to simmer, reduce heat to medium-low, and cook until potatoes have softened, 15 to 18 minutes.

3. Transfer 2 cups chowder to blender and process until smooth, 1 to 2 minutes. Return puree to pot, stir in half-and-half, and return to simmer. Remove pot from heat and stir in reserved corn juice. Season with salt, pepper, and up to 1 tablespoon sugar to taste. Sprinkle with basil and serve.

CUTTING CORN KERNELS
FROM THE COB

To cut kernels off an ear of corn without having them fly all over the kitchen counter, hold ear on its end inside large, wide bowl and use paring knife to cut off kernels.

NEW ENGLAND CLAM CHOWDER

✓ WHY THIS RECIPE WORKS

For the ultimate clam chowder recipe, we started with the clams. We found that medium-size, hard-shell clams guaranteed the most clam flavor. And rather than deal with the pain of shucking them raw, we simply steamed them open, pulling them out when they just started to open to guard against overcooking. We then used the steaming liquid as our broth. Yukon Gold potatoes, with their moderate levels of starch and moisture, worked best, releasing starch into the soup while also maintaining their shape. In lieu of the traditional salt pork, bacon gave our chowder the right subtle smokiness, and just 1 cup of heavy cream lent richness without diluting the flavor.

NEW ENGLAND CLAM CHOWDER
SERVES 6

Be sure to use fresh clams. This chowder uses a combination of the clam steaming liquid and bottled clam juice; a chowder made entirely from the clam steaming liquid will taste unpalatably salty. Serve with oyster crackers.

- 3   cups water
- 6   pounds medium hard-shell clams, such as cherrystones, scrubbed
- 2   slices bacon, chopped fine
- 2   onions, chopped fine
- 2   celery ribs, chopped fine
- 1   teaspoon minced fresh thyme leaves or ¼ teaspoon dried
- ⅓   cup all-purpose flour
- 3   (8-ounce) bottles clam juice
- 1½ pounds Yukon Gold potatoes, peeled and cut into ½-inch pieces
- 1   bay leaf
- 1   cup heavy cream
- 2   tablespoons minced fresh parsley
     Salt and pepper

1. Bring water to boil in Dutch oven. Add clams, cover, and cook for 5 minutes. Stir clams thoroughly, cover, and continue to cook until they just begin to open, 2 to 5 minutes. As clams open, transfer them to large bowl and let cool slightly. Discard any unopened clams.

2. Measure out and reserve 2 cups clam steaming liquid, avoiding any gritty sediment that has settled on bottom of pot. Use paring knife to remove clam meat from shells and chop coarse.

3. In clean Dutch oven, cook bacon over medium heat until crisp, 5 to 7 minutes. Stir in onions and celery and cook until vegetables are softened, 5 to 7 minutes. Stir in thyme and cook until fragrant, about 30 seconds. Stir in flour and cook for 1 minute.

4. Gradually whisk in bottled clam juice and reserved clam steaming liquid, scraping up any browned bits and smoothing out any lumps. Stir in potatoes and bay leaf and bring to boil. Reduce to gentle simmer and cook until potatoes are tender, 20 to 25 minutes.

5. Stir in cream and return to brief simmer. Off heat, remove bay leaf, stir in parsley, and season with salt and pepper to taste. Stir in chopped clams, cover, and let stand until clams are warmed through, about 1 minute. Serve.

RICH AND VELVETY SHRIMP BISQUE

✓ WHY THIS RECIPE WORKS

Shrimp bisque recipes are usually tediously long and complicated, and are rarely worth the effort it takes to prepare them. We wanted a simple, rich, faultlessly smooth recipe, full of sweet shrimp flavor. Because shrimp shells are loaded with flavor, we sautéed both shells and meat, then pureed them together in a food processor and simmered this mixture in our soup base before straining out the solids. We found that flambéing the shrimp-shell mixture in brandy prior to processing extracted even more shrimp flavor. With the additions of cream, sherry, wine, and some tomatoes to cut through the richness, our bisque achieved a complex yet

---

PREPARING CLAMS FOR CHOWDER

1. Before cooking, use soft brush (sometimes sold as vegetable brush) to scrub away any bits of sand trapped in shells.

2. Steam clams until they just open, as seen on left, rather than completely open, as shown on right.

3. Carefully use paring knife to open steamed clams.

4. Once open, discard top shell and use knife to cut clam from bottom shell.

balanced flavor where the shrimp took center stage. Stirring in half a pound of shrimp at the end and poaching them until just cooked through lent texture and boosted the shrimp flavor to the next level.

RICH AND VELVETY SHRIMP BISQUE

SERVES 4 TO 6

Shrimp shells contribute a lot of flavor to the bisque, so be sure to purchase shell-on shrimp. Before flambéing, be sure to roll up long shirtsleeves, tie back long hair, and turn off the exhaust fan and any lit burners.

2	pounds extra-large shell-on shrimp (21 to 25 per pound)
3	tablespoons olive oil
⅓	cup brandy or cognac, warmed
2	tablespoons unsalted butter
1	small carrot, chopped fine
1	small celery rib, chopped fine
1	small onion, chopped fine
1	garlic clove, minced
½	cup all-purpose flour
4	(8-ounce) bottles clam juice
1½	cups dry white wine
1	(14.5-ounce) can diced tomatoes, drained
1	cup heavy cream
1	tablespoon lemon juice
1	sprig fresh tarragon
	Pinch cayenne pepper
2	tablespoons dry sherry or Madeira
	Salt and pepper

1. Peel ½ pound shrimp, reserving shells, and cut each peeled shrimp into thirds and set aside. Pat dry reserved shells and remaining unpeeled shrimp with paper towels.

2. Heat 12-inch skillet over high heat until very hot, about 3 minutes. Add 1½ tablespoons oil and swirl to coat bottom of pan. Add half of shell-on shrimp and half of reserved shells and cook until shrimp are deep pink and shells are lightly browned, about 2 minutes. Transfer shrimp to medium bowl and repeat with remaining 1½ tablespoons oil, shell-on shrimp, and shells. Return first batch of shrimp to skillet. Off heat, pour brandy over shrimp and let warm through, about 5 seconds. Wave lit match over pan until brandy ignites, then shake pan to distribute flames. When flames subside, transfer shrimp and shells to food processor and process until mixture resembles fine meal, about 10 seconds.

3. Heat butter in Dutch oven over medium heat. Add carrot, celery, onion, garlic, and ground shrimp and shells. Cover and cook, stirring frequently, until vegetables are slightly softened and mixture is fragrant, about 5 minutes. Add flour and cook, stirring constantly, until thoroughly combined, about 1 minute. Stir in clam juice, wine, and tomatoes, scraping pan bottom with wooden spoon to loosen any browned bits. Cover, increase heat to medium-high, and bring to boil. Reduce heat to low and simmer, stirring frequently, until soup is thickened and flavors meld, about 20 minutes.

4. Strain bisque through fine-mesh strainer into medium bowl, pressing on solids to extract as much liquid as possible. Wash and dry Dutch oven, return strained bisque to pot, and stir in cream, lemon juice, tarragon, and cayenne. Bring to simmer over medium-high heat. Add reserved peeled and cut shrimp and simmer until shrimp are firm but tender, about 1½ minutes. Discard tarragon, stir in sherry, season with salt and pepper to taste, and serve.

CREOLE-STYLE SHRIMP AND SAUSAGE GUMBO

✔ WHY THIS RECIPE WORKS

With shrimp, sausage, and vegetables in a deeply flavored, rich brown sauce with a touch of heat, gumbo is a unique one-pot meal. We wanted a foolproof, streamlined technique for gumbo that featured a thick, smooth sauce with lots of well-seasoned vegetables, meat, and shrimp. The basis of gumbo is the roux, which is flour cooked in fat. For a deep, dark roux in half the time, we heated the oil before adding the flour. We also added the roux to room-temperature shrimp stock (supplemented with clam juice) to prevent separating. Although tomatoes are traditional in gumbo, our tasters didn't think they were necessary—but garlic was, and lots of it. Some cayenne pepper added the requisite heat. We also added spicy andouille sausage and tossed in the shrimp only during the last few minutes of cooking.

CREOLE-STYLE SHRIMP AND SAUSAGE GUMBO

SERVES 6 TO 8

Making a dark roux can be dangerous, as the mixture reaches temperatures in excess of 400 degrees. Therefore, use a deep pot for cooking the roux and long-handled utensils for stirring it, and be careful not to splash it on yourself. One secret to smooth gumbo is adding shrimp stock that is neither too hot nor too cold to the roux. For a stock that is at the right temperature when the roux is done, start preparing it before you tend to the vegetables and other ingredients, strain it, and then give it a head start on cooling by immediately adding the ice water and clam juice. So that your constant stirring of the roux will not be interrupted, start the roux only after you've made the stock. Spicy andouille sausage is a Louisiana specialty that may not be available everywhere; kielbasa or any fully cooked smoked sausage makes a fine substitute. Gumbo is traditionally served over white rice.

1½	pounds small shrimp (51 to 60 per pound), peeled and deveined; shells reserved
3½	cups ice water
1	(8-ounce) bottle clam juice
½	cup vegetable oil
½	cup all-purpose flour
2	onions, chopped fine
1	red bell pepper, stemmed, seeded, and chopped fine
1	celery rib, chopped fine
6	garlic cloves, minced
1	teaspoon dried thyme
	Salt and pepper
	Cayenne pepper
2	bay leaves
1	pound smoked sausage, such as andouille or kielbasa, sliced ¼ inch thick
½	cup minced fresh parsley leaves
4	scallions, sliced thin

1. Bring reserved shrimp shells and 4½ cups water to boil in stockpot or large saucepan over medium-high heat. Reduce heat to medium-low and simmer for 20 minutes. Strain stock and add ice water and clam juice (you should have about 8 cups of tepid stock, 100 to 110 degrees); discard shells. Set stock aside.

2. Heat oil in Dutch oven or large saucepan over medium-high heat until it registers 200 degrees on instant-read thermometer, 1½ to 2 minutes. Reduce heat to medium and gradually stir in flour with wooden spatula or spoon, making sure to work out any lumps that may form. Continue stirring constantly, reaching into corners of pan, until mixture has toasty aroma and is deep reddish brown, about 20 minutes. (Roux will thin as it cooks; if it begins to smoke, remove pan from heat and stir roux constantly to cool slightly.)

3. Add onions, bell pepper, celery, garlic, thyme, 1 teaspoon salt, and ¼ teaspoon cayenne to roux and cook, stirring frequently, until vegetables soften, 8 to 10 minutes. Add 4 cups reserved stock in slow, steady stream while stirring vigorously. Stir in remaining 4 cups stock. Increase heat to high and bring to boil. Reduce heat to medium-low, skim foam from the surface with wide spoon, add bay leaves, and simmer, uncovered, about 30 minutes, skimming foam as it rises to surface. (Mixture can be covered and set aside for several hours or refrigerated up to 2 days. Reheat when ready to proceed.)

4. Stir in sausage and continue simmering to blend flavors, about 30 minutes. Stir in shrimp and simmer until cooked through, about 5 minutes. Off heat, stir in parsley and scallions and season with salt, pepper, and cayenne to taste. Discard bay leaves and serve immediately.

SHRIMP AND SAUSAGE GUMBO WITH OKRA

Fresh okra may be used in place of frozen, though it tends to be more slippery, a quality that diminishes with increased cooking. Substitute an equal amount of fresh okra for frozen; trim the caps, slice the pods ¼ inch thick, and increase the sautéing time with the onions, bell pepper, and celery to 10 to 15 minutes.

Add 10 ounces thawed frozen cut okra to roux along with onions, bell pepper, and celery.

SHRIMP AND SAUSAGE GUMBO WITH FILÉ

Add 1½ teaspoons filé powder along with parsley and scallions in step 4 after gumbo has been removed from heat. Let rest until slightly thickened, about 5 minutes. Adjust seasonings and serve.

CHAPTER 4 Chilis, Stews, and Braises

SIMPLE BEEF CHILI

✔ **WHY THIS RECIPE WORKS**

With the goal of developing a no-fuss chili that would taste far better than the sum of its parts, we discovered that adding the spices to the pan with the aromatics boosted their potency. Commercial chili powder, backed by cumin, coriander, cayenne, oregano, and red pepper flakes, provided plenty of spice notes and heat. For the meat, 85 percent lean ground beef gave us full, deep flavor. Using a one-two punch for the tomatoes—diced tomatoes and tomato puree—provided both chunks of tomato and a rich, thick sauce. Adding the beans with the tomatoes ensured that they cooked enough to absorb flavor but not so much that they fell apart. Finally, cooking the chili with the lid on for half the simmering time resulted in a rich, thick consistency.

SIMPLE BEEF CHILI WITH KIDNEY BEANS

SERVES 8 TO 10

Good choices for condiments include diced fresh tomatoes, diced avocado, sliced scallions, finely chopped red onion, minced fresh cilantro, sour cream, and/or shredded Monterey Jack or cheddar cheese. If you are a fan of spicy food, consider using a little more of the red pepper flakes or cayenne—or both. The flavor of the chili improves with age; if possible, make it the day before you plan to serve it.

2   tablespoons vegetable oil
2   onions, chopped fine
1   red bell pepper, stemmed, seeded, and cut into ½-inch pieces
6   garlic cloves, minced
¼   cup chili powder
1   tablespoon ground cumin
2   teaspoons ground coriander
1   teaspoon red pepper flakes
1   teaspoon dried oregano
½   teaspoon cayenne pepper
2   pounds 85 percent lean ground beef

2   (15-ounce) cans red kidney beans, rinsed
1   (28-ounce) can diced tomatoes, drained with juice reserved
1   (28-ounce) can tomato puree
     Salt
     Lime wedges

1. Heat oil in Dutch oven over medium heat until shimmering but not smoking. Add onions, bell pepper, garlic, chili powder, cumin, coriander, pepper flakes, oregano, and cayenne and cook, stirring occasionally, until vegetables are softened and beginning to brown, about 10 minutes. Increase heat to medium-high and add half of beef. Cook, breaking up pieces with spoon, until no longer pink and just beginning to brown, 3 to 4 minutes. Add remaining beef and cook, breaking up pieces with spoon, until no longer pink, 3 to 4 minutes.

2. Add beans, tomatoes, tomato puree, and ½ teaspoon salt; bring to boil, then reduce heat to low and simmer, covered, stirring occasionally, for 1 hour. Remove cover and continue to simmer 1 hour longer, stirring occasionally (if chili begins to stick to bottom of pot, stir in ½ cup water and continue to simmer), until beef is tender and chili is dark, rich, and slightly thickened. Season with salt to taste. Serve with lime wedges and condiments, if desired. (Chili can be refrigerated for up to 2 days.)

BEEF CHILI WITH BACON AND BLACK BEANS

Cook 8 slices bacon, cut into ½-inch pieces, in Dutch oven over medium heat, stirring frequently, until browned, about 8 minutes. Pour off all but 2 tablespoons fat, leaving bacon in pot. Substitute bacon fat in Dutch oven for vegetable oil and canned black beans for canned kidney beans.

CHILI CON CARNE

✔ **WHY THIS RECIPE WORKS**

True Texas-style chili is all meat—no beans and minimal additional adornment. For big beefy flavor, we started with a chuck roast, cut into sizable, hefty Texas-size chunks. For the boldest chili flavor, we toasted and ground ancho and New Mexican dried chiles (but store-bought chili powders of the same varieties pack plenty of heat, too). The flavor was also improved by adding bacon, which lent our chili sweetness and smokiness. From among the many recommended liquids to use in chili con carne, we chose water—everything else diluted or competed with the flavor of the chiles. To thicken the sauce to a velvety consistency that would cling to the big chunks of meat, we stirred in masa harina or cornstarch, which made for a smoother, more appealing sauce. Crushed tomatoes provided an underlying tomato flavor and sauciness, and lime juice finished off our chili con carne with a bit of brightness.

CHILI CON CARNE

SERVES 6

For best flavor, we like to make this chili 1 day ahead. Select dried chiles that are moist and pliant. Toast the cumin seeds in a dry skillet over medium heat until fragrant, about 4 minutes. For hotter chili, boost the heat with a pinch of cayenne or a dash of hot pepper sauce near the end of cooking. Serve the chili with any of the following: warm pinto or kidney beans, cornbread or chips, corn tortillas or tamales, rice, biscuits, or crackers. Top with chopped fresh cilantro, finely chopped onion, diced avocado, shredded cheddar or Monterey Jack cheese, and/or sour cream.

3   tablespoons ancho chili powder or 3 chiles (about ½ ounce), toasted and ground
3   tablespoons New Mexican chili powder or 3 medium chiles (about ¾ ounce), toasted and ground

2 tablespoons cumin seeds, toasted

2 teaspoons dried oregano, preferably Mexican

7½ cups plus ⅔ cup water

I (4-pound) chuck-eye roast, trimmed and cut into 1-inch pieces
Salt and pepper

8 slices bacon, cut into ¼-inch pieces

I onion, chopped fine

5 garlic cloves, minced

4–5 small jalapeño chiles, stemmed, seeded, and minced

I cup canned crushed tomatoes or plain tomato sauce

2 tablespoons lime juice

5 tablespoons masa harina or 3 tablespoons cornstarch

I. Combine chili powders, cumin, and oregano in small bowl and stir in ½ cup water to form thick paste; set aside. Season beef with 2 teaspoons salt; set aside.

2. Cook bacon in Dutch oven over medium-low heat until crisp, about 10 minutes. Using slotted spoon, transfer bacon to paper towel–lined plate. Pour all but 2 teaspoons fat into small bowl; set aside. Increase heat to medium-high and sauté meat in 4 batches until well browned on all sides, about 5 minutes per batch, adding additional 2 teaspoons bacon fat to pot as necessary. Reduce heat to medium and add 3 tablespoons bacon fat to now-empty pan. Add onion and cook until softened, 5 to 7 minutes. Add garlic and jalapeños and cook until fragrant, about 1 minute. Add chile paste and cook until fragrant, 2 to 3 minutes. Add reserved bacon and browned beef, crushed tomatoes, lime juice, and 7 cups water and bring to simmer. Continue to simmer until meat is tender and juices are dark, rich, and starting to thicken, about 2 hours.

3. Mix masa harina with remaining ⅔ cup water (or cornstarch with 3 tablespoons water) in small bowl to form smooth paste. Increase heat to medium,

stir in paste, and simmer until thickened, 5 to 10 minutes. Season with salt and pepper to taste and serve. (Chili can be refrigerated for up to 2 days.)

SMOKY CHIPOTLE CHILI CON CARNE

Make sure you start with a chuck-eye roast that is at least 3 inches thick. The grilling is meant to flavor the meat by searing the surface and smoking it lightly, not to cook it.

I. Do not cut meat into 1-inch pieces. Puree 4 garlic cloves with 2 teaspoons salt. Rub intact chuck roast with puree and sprinkle evenly with 2 tablespoons New Mexican chili powder. Using large piece of heavy-duty aluminum foil, wrap 1 cup soaked mesquite or hickory wood chips in foil packet and cut several vent holes in top.

2A. FOR A CHARCOAL GRILL: Open bottom vent halfway. Light large chimney starter filled with charcoal briquettes (6 quarts). When top coals are partially covered with ash, pour in even layer over half of grill. Place wood chip packet on coals. Set cooking grate in place, cover, and open lid vent halfway. Heat grill until hot and wood chips are smoking, about 5 minutes.

2B. FOR A GAS GRILL: Place wood chip packet over primary burner. Turn all burners to high, cover, and heat grill until hot and wood chips are smoking, about 15 minutes. Leave all burners on high.

3. Clean and oil cooking grate. Sear meat on all sides until well browned, about 12 minutes per side. Transfer roast to carving board, let cool, then cut into 1-inch cubes, discarding excess fat and reserving juices. Proceed with recipe from step 2 but do not brown beef. Substitute 2½ tablespoons minced canned chipotle chile in adobo sauce for jalapeños, add browned beef with juices to pot with crisped bacon and proceed as directed.

ULTIMATE BEEF CHILI

✓ WHY THIS RECIPE WORKS

Our goal in creating an "ultimate" beef chili was to determine which of the "secret ingredients" recommended by chili experts around the world were spot-on—and which were expendable. We started with the beef—most recipes call for ground beef, but we preferred meaty blade steaks, which don't require much trimming and stayed in big chunks in our finished chili. For complex chile flavor, we traded in the commercial chili powder in favor of ground dried ancho and de árbol chiles; for a grassy heat, we added fresh jalapeños. Dried beans, brined before cooking, stayed creamy for the duration of cooking. Beer and chicken broth outperformed red wine, coffee, and beef broth as the liquid component. To balance the sweetness of our pot, light molasses beat out other offbeat ingredients (including prunes and Coca-Cola). For the right level of thickness, flour and peanut butter didn't perform as promised; instead, a small amount of ordinary cornmeal sealed the deal, providing just the right consistency in our ultimate beef chili.

ULTIMATE BEEF CHILI
SERVES 6 TO 8

A 4-pound chuck-eye roast, well trimmed of fat, can be substituted for the steak. Because much of the chili flavor is held in the fat of this dish, refrain from skimming fat from the surface. Dried New Mexican or guajillo chiles make a good substitute for the anchos; each dried de árbol may be replaced with ⅛ teaspoon cayenne. If you prefer not to work with any whole dried chiles, the anchos and de árbols can be replaced with ½ cup commercial chili powder and ¼ to ½ teaspoon cayenne pepper, though the texture of the chili will be slightly compromised. Good choices for condiments include diced avocado, finely chopped red onion, chopped cilantro, lime wedges, sour cream, and shredded Monterey Jack or cheddar cheese.

Salt

8 ounces (1¼ cups) dried pinto beans, picked over and rinsed

6 dried ancho chiles, stemmed, seeded, and torn into 1-inch pieces

2–4 dried de árbol chiles, stemmed, seeded, and split in 2 pieces

3 tablespoons cornmeal

2 teaspoons dried oregano

2 teaspoons ground cumin

2 teaspoons cocoa

2½ cups low-sodium chicken broth

2 onions, cut into ¾-inch pieces

3 small jalapeño chiles, stemmed, seeded, and cut into ½-inch pieces

3 tablespoons vegetable oil

4 garlic cloves, minced

1 (14.5-ounce) can diced tomatoes

2 teaspoons molasses

3½ pounds blade steak, ¾ inch thick, trimmed and cut into ¾-inch pieces

1 (12-ounce) bottle mild lager, such as Budweiser

1. Combine 3 tablespoons salt, 4 quarts water, and beans in Dutch oven and bring to boil over high heat. Remove pot from heat, cover, and let stand 1 hour. Drain and rinse well.

2. Adjust oven rack to lower-middle position and heat oven to 300 degrees.

Place ancho chiles in 12-inch skillet set over medium-high heat; toast, stirring frequently, until flesh is fragrant, 4 to 6 minutes, reducing heat if chiles begin to smoke. Transfer to food processor and cool. Do not wash out skillet.

3. Add de árbol chiles, cornmeal, oregano, cumin, cocoa, and ½ teaspoon salt to food processor with toasted ancho chiles; process until finely ground, about 2 minutes. With processor running, slowly add ½ cup broth until smooth paste forms, about 45 seconds, scraping down sides of bowl as necessary. Transfer paste to small bowl. Place onions in now-empty processor and pulse until roughly chopped, about 4 pulses. Add jalapeños and pulse until consistency of chunky salsa, about 4 pulses, scraping down bowl as necessary.

4. Heat 1 tablespoon oil in Dutch oven over medium-high heat. Add onion mixture and cook, stirring occasionally, until moisture has evaporated and vegetables are softened, 7 to 9 minutes. Add garlic and cook until fragrant, about 1 minute. Add chile paste, tomatoes, and molasses; stir until chile paste is thoroughly combined. Add remaining 2 cups broth and drained beans; bring to boil, then reduce heat to simmer.

5. Meanwhile, heat 1 tablespoon oil in 12-inch skillet over medium-high heat until shimmering. Pat beef dry with paper towels and sprinkle with 1 teaspoon salt. Add half of beef and cook until browned on all sides, about 10 minutes. Transfer meat to Dutch oven. Add half of beer to skillet, scraping up browned bits from bottom of pan, and bring to simmer. Transfer beer to Dutch oven. Repeat with remaining 1 tablespoon oil, remaining steak, and remaining beer. Stir to combine and return mixture to simmer.

6. Cover pot and transfer to oven. Cook until meat and beans are fully tender, 1½ to 2 hours. Let chili stand, uncovered, for 10 minutes. Stir well, season with salt to taste, and serve. (Chili can be refrigerated up to 3 days.)

WHITE CHICKEN CHILI

✔ WHY THIS RECIPE WORKS

Chili made with chicken promises a lighter, fresher alternative to the red kind, but most of the time, the resulting chili is bland and watery and the chicken is dry, rather than moist and flavorful. We found not one but three solutions to boring chicken chili. To solve the problem of insufficient chile flavor, we used a trio of fresh chiles: jalapeño, poblano, and New Mexican. To fix the watery sauce, we pureed some of our sautéed aromatics (a mix of chiles, garlic, and onions) and broth with beans to thicken the base. And finally, to avoid floating bits of rubbery chicken, we browned, poached, and shredded bone-in, skin-on chicken breasts, which gave our chicken pieces a tender texture and full flavor.

WHITE CHICKEN CHILI
SERVES 6 TO 8

Adjust the heat in this dish by adding the minced ribs and seeds from the jalapeño as directed in step 6. If New Mexican chiles cannot be found, add an additional poblano and jalapeño to the chili. Serve this chili with sour cream, tortilla chips, and lime wedges.

3 pounds bone-in split chicken breasts or thighs, trimmed
Salt and pepper
1 tablespoon vegetable oil, plus extra as needed
3 jalapeño chiles
3 poblano chiles, stemmed, seeded, and cut into large pieces
3 New Mexican chile peppers, stemmed, seeded, and cut into large pieces
2 onions, cut into large pieces
6 garlic cloves, minced
1 tablespoon ground cumin
1½ teaspoons ground coriander
2 (15-ounce) cans cannellini beans, rinsed
3 cups low-sodium chicken broth
3 tablespoons lime juice (2 limes)
¼ cup minced fresh cilantro
4 scallions, sliced thin

1. Season chicken with 1 teaspoon salt and ¼ teaspoon pepper. Heat oil in Dutch oven over medium-high heat until just smoking. Add chicken, skin side down, and cook without moving until skin is golden brown, about 4 minutes. Using tongs, flip chicken and lightly brown on other side, about 2 minutes. Transfer chicken to plate; remove and discard skin.

2. While chicken is browning, remove and discard ribs and seeds from 2 jalapeños, then mince jalapeños and set aside. Process half of poblano chiles, New Mexican chiles, and onions in food processor until consistency of chunky salsa, 10 to 12 pulses, scraping down sides of bowl halfway through. Transfer mixture to medium bowl. Repeat with remaining poblano chiles, New Mexican chiles, and onions; combine with first batch (do not wash food processor).

3. Pour off all but 1 tablespoon fat from Dutch oven (adding additional vegetable oil if necessary) and reduce heat to medium. Add minced jalapeños, chile mixture, garlic, cumin, coriander, and ¼ teaspoon salt.

Cover and cook, stirring occasionally, until vegetables have softened, about 10 minutes. Remove pot from heat.

4. Transfer 1 cup cooked vegetable mixture to now-empty food processor. Add 1 cup beans and 1 cup broth and process until smooth, about 20 seconds. Add vegetable-bean mixture, remaining 2 cups broth, and chicken breasts to Dutch oven and bring to boil over medium-high heat. Reduce heat to medium-low and simmer, covered, stirring occasionally, until chicken registers 160 degrees (175 degrees if using thighs), 15 to 20 minutes (40 minutes if using thighs).

5. Transfer chicken to large plate. Stir in remaining beans and continue to simmer, uncovered, until beans are heated through and chili has thickened slightly, about 10 minutes.

6. Mince remaining jalapeño, reserving and mincing ribs and seeds, and set aside. When cool enough to handle, shred chicken into bite-size pieces, discarding bones. Stir shredded chicken, lime juice, cilantro, scallions, and remaining minced jalapeño (with seeds if desired) into chili and return to simmer. Season with salt and pepper to taste and serve.

WHITE TURKEY CHILI

Substitute 1 bone-in, skin-on split turkey breast (about 2½ pounds), trimmed, for chicken breast halves. In step 1, cook turkey, skin side down, until skin is golden brown, 6 to 8 minutes. Using tongs, flip turkey and lightly brown on other side, about 2 minutes. Transfer turkey to plate; remove and discard skin. In step 4, add turkey breast, bone side down, to Dutch oven, bring to boil over medium-high heat, reduce heat to medium-low and simmer, covered, stirring occasionally, until turkey registers 160 degrees, 30 to 35 minutes.

LIGHTER CHICKEN AND DUMPLINGS

✔ WHY THIS RECIPE WORKS

The best chicken and dumplings boast dumplings as airy as drop biscuits in a broth full of clean, concentrated chicken flavor. We found that browning chicken thighs and then adding store-bought chicken broth (which, unlike water, contributed a savory depth) produced the most flavorful stew base. To give our broth body, we added chicken wings to the pot—they readily gave up their collagen, giving the stew a velvety texture. For a light but sturdy dumpling recipe with good flavor, we came up with a formula that employed buttermilk for flavor and swapped in baking soda for baking powder. Wrapping the lid of the Dutch oven in a kitchen towel to prevent moisture from saturating our light-as-air dumplings was the final step in perfecting our chicken and dumplings.

LIGHTER CHICKEN AND DUMPLINGS

SERVES 6

We strongly recommend buttermilk for the dumplings, but it's acceptable to substitute ½ cup plain yogurt thinned with ¼ cup milk. If you want to include white meat (and don't mind losing a bit of flavor in the process), replace 2 chicken thighs with two 8-ounce boneless, skinless chicken breasts; brown the chicken breasts along with the thighs and remove them from the stew once they register 160 degrees, 20 to 30 minutes. The collagen in the wings helps thicken the stew; do not omit or substitute. Since the wings yield only about 1 cup of meat, using their meat is optional.

STEW
2½ pounds bone-in chicken thighs, trimmed
Salt and pepper
2 teaspoons vegetable oil
2 small onions, chopped fine
2 carrots, peeled and cut into ¾-inch pieces
1 celery rib, chopped fine

¼ cup dry sherry
6 cups low-sodium chicken broth
1 teaspoon minced fresh thyme
1 pound chicken wings
¼ cup chopped fresh parsley

DUMPLINGS
2 cups (10 ounces) all-purpose flour
1 teaspoon sugar
1 teaspoon salt
½ teaspoon baking soda
¾ cup buttermilk, chilled
4 tablespoons unsalted butter, melted and hot
1 large egg white

1. FOR THE STEW: Pat chicken thighs dry with paper towels and season with 1 teaspoon salt and ¼ teaspoon pepper. Heat oil in Dutch oven over medium-high heat until shimmering. Add chicken thighs, skin side down, and cook until skin is crisp and well browned, 5 to 7 minutes. Using tongs, flip chicken pieces and brown on second side, 5 to 7 minutes longer; transfer to large plate. Discard all but 1 teaspoon fat from pot.

2. Add onions, carrots, and celery to now-empty pot; cook, stirring occasionally, until caramelized, 7 to 9 minutes. Stir in sherry, scraping up any browned bits from bottom of pot. Stir in broth and thyme. Return chicken thighs, with any accumulated juices, to pot and add chicken wings. Bring to simmer, cover, and cook until thigh meat offers no resistance when poked with tip of paring knife but still clings to bones, 45 to 55 minutes.

3. Remove pot from heat and transfer chicken to cutting board. Allow broth to settle 5 minutes, then skim fat from surface. When cool enough to handle, remove and discard skin from chicken. Using fingers or fork, pull meat from chicken thighs (and wings, if desired) and cut into 1-inch pieces. Return meat to pot. (At this point, stew can be cooled to room temperature,

then refrigerated for up to 2 days. Bring to simmer over medium-low heat before proceeding.)

4. FOR THE DUMPLINGS: Whisk flour, sugar, salt, and baking soda in large bowl. Combine buttermilk and melted butter in medium bowl, stirring until butter forms small clumps; whisk in egg white. Add buttermilk mixture to dry ingredients and stir with rubber spatula until just incorporated and batter pulls away from sides of bowl.

5. Return stew to simmer, stir in parsley, and season with salt and pepper to taste. Using greased tablespoon measure (or #60 portion scoop), scoop level amount of batter and drop over top of stew, spacing about ¼ inch apart (you should have about 24 dumplings). Wrap lid of Dutch oven with clean kitchen towel (keeping towel away from heat source) and cover pot. Simmer gently until dumplings have doubled in size and toothpick inserted into center comes out clean, 13 to 16 minutes. Serve immediately.

QUICK CHICKEN FRICASSEE

✔ WHY THIS RECIPE WORKS
In search of a streamlined technique that would give this classic French braise weeknight potential and a brighter, more complex sauce, we replaced the bone-in chicken parts with the busy cook's favorite timesaver: boneless, skinless breasts and thighs. We found two ways to add back the richness that we'd lost when we opted for boneless, skinless chicken pieces: We browned the meat in a combination of butter and oil, and we browned the vegetables until they developed their own fond to serve as the base of the sauce. Increasing the amount of glutamate-rich mushrooms boosted the fricassee's meaty flavor. As a final step, we finished the sauce with sour cream, which added body and pleasant tang. Also, whisking an egg yolk into the sour cream thickened the sauce and made it incredibly silky.

QUICK CHICKEN FRICASSEE
SERVES 4 TO 6

Two tablespoons of chopped fresh parsley may be substituted for the tarragon in this recipe.

2 pounds boneless, skinless chicken breasts and/or thighs, trimmed
Salt and pepper
1 tablespoon unsalted butter
1 tablespoon olive oil
1 pound cremini mushrooms, trimmed and sliced ¼ inch thick
1 onion, chopped fine
¼ cup dry white wine
1 tablespoon all-purpose flour
1 garlic clove, minced
1½ cups low-sodium chicken broth
⅓ cup sour cream
1 large egg yolk
½ teaspoon freshly grated nutmeg
2 teaspoons lemon juice
2 teaspoons minced fresh tarragon

1. Pat chicken dry with paper towels and season with 1 teaspoon salt and ½ teaspoon pepper. Heat butter and oil in 12-inch skillet over medium-high heat until butter is melted. Place chicken in skillet and cook until browned, about 4 minutes. Using tongs, flip chicken and cook until browned on second side, about 4 minutes longer. Transfer chicken to large plate.

2. Add mushrooms, onion, and wine to now-empty skillet and cook, stirring occasionally, until liquid has evaporated and mushrooms are browned, 8 to 10 minutes. Add flour and garlic; cook, stirring constantly, 1 minute. Add broth and bring mixture to boil, scraping up browned bits from bottom of pan. Add chicken and any accumulated juices to skillet. Reduce heat to medium-low, cover, and simmer until breasts register 160 degrees and thighs register 175 degrees, 5 to 10 minutes.

3. Transfer chicken to clean platter and tent loosely with aluminum foil. Whisk sour cream and egg yolk together in medium bowl.

Whisking constantly, slowly stir ½ cup hot sauce into sour cream mixture to temper. Stirring constantly, slowly pour sour cream mixture into simmering sauce. Stir in nutmeg, lemon juice, and tarragon; return to simmer. Season with salt and pepper to taste, pour sauce over chicken, and serve.

COQ AU VIN

✔ **WHY THIS RECIPE WORKS**

Coq au vin was all the rage in the 1960s, when French cooking really began to take hold in American kitchens. Now, however, it seems a far less exotic dish, and the many recipes for it that have appeared over the years are often bland and boring. We wanted a tasty coq au vin, in which tender, juicy chicken is infused with the flavors of red wine, mushrooms, onions, and bacon. For maximum flavor and richness, we relied on chicken legs alone, rather than a combination of legs and breasts, and gave the sauce and wine enough time to fully reduce. Tomato paste was a fuss-free way to add extra depth and body to the sauce, and a hefty amount of aromatics, as well as the classic pearl onions and white mushrooms, amped up the traditional savory notes of the dish. Reserving the cooked bacon on the side until the end ensured it was still crispy in the finished dish, which we had thickened using a beurre manié (equal parts uncooked flour and butter).

COQ AU VIN
SERVES 4

Use any $10 bottle of fruity, medium-bodied red wine such as a Pinot Noir or Zinfandel.

4	chicken leg quarters (about 3 pounds), trimmed, thighs and drumsticks separated
	Salt and pepper
1	(750-ml) bottle medium-bodied red wine
2½	cups low-sodium chicken broth
1	teaspoon dried thyme
10	parsley stems plus 2 tablespoons minced fresh parsley
1	bay leaf
5	slices thick-cut bacon, cut into ¼-inch pieces
6–7	tablespoons unsalted butter, room temperature
1	large carrot, chopped coarse
1	large onion, chopped coarse
2	shallots, peeled and quartered
2	garlic cloves, skin on and smashed
1½	teaspoons tomato paste
¾	cup frozen pearl onions, thawed
8	ounces white mushrooms, trimmed and halved if medium or quartered if large
2–3	tablespoons all-purpose flour

1. Pat chicken dry with paper towels and season with salt and pepper; set aside. Bring red wine and chicken broth to boil in large saucepan; reduce heat to medium-high and simmer until reduced to about 4 cups, about 20 minutes. Assemble thyme, parsley, and bay leaf together in double layer of cheesecloth and tie securely with kitchen twine to form bouquet garni.

2. Meanwhile, cook bacon in Dutch oven over medium heat until fat has rendered and bacon is crisp, 5 to 7 minutes. Remove bacon with slotted spoon to paper towel–lined plate; set aside. Heat 1 tablespoon butter with rendered bacon fat; add carrot, onion, shallots, and garlic and sauté until lightly browned, 10 to 15 minutes. Press vegetables against side of pan with slotted spoon to squeeze out as much fat as possible; transfer vegetables to pan with reduced wine mixture (off heat) and discard all but 1 tablespoon fat from Dutch oven.

3. Add 1 tablespoon butter to Dutch oven and heat over medium-high heat. Add chicken (in batches if necessary to avoid overcrowding) and cook until well browned, 12 to 16 minutes. Transfer chicken to plate; set aside. Pour off fat from Dutch oven; return to heat and add wine-vegetable mixture. Bring to boil, scraping up browned bits from bottom of pan. Add browned chicken, bouquet garni, and tomato paste, bring to simmer, then reduce to low and simmer gently, partially covered, until chicken is tender, flipping once, 45 to 60 minutes.

4. While chicken and sauce are cooking, heat 2 tablespoons butter in medium skillet over medium-low heat. Add pearl onions and cook, stirring occasionally, until lightly browned and almost cooked through, 5 to 8 minutes. Add mushrooms, season with salt, cover, increase heat to medium, and cook until mushrooms release their liquid, about 5 minutes. Uncover, increase heat to high, and

boil until liquid evaporates and onions and mushrooms are golden brown, 2 to 3 minutes longer. Transfer onions and mushrooms to plate with bacon; set aside.

5. Transfer chicken to platter and tent loosely with aluminum foil. Strain sauce through fine-mesh strainer into large measuring cup, pressing on solids to release as much liquid as possible (you should have 2 to 3 cups liquid). Return sauce to pan and skim fat off surface. For each cup of sauce, mash 1 tablespoon each of butter and flour in small bowl or plate to make beurre manié (you should have 2 to 3 tablespoons each of butter and flour). Bring sauce to boil and whisk in beurre manié until smooth. Add reserved chicken, bacon, onions and mushrooms; season with salt and pepper to taste, reduce heat to medium-low, and simmer gently to warm through and blend flavors, about 5 minutes. Season with salt and pepper to taste and stir in minced parsley. Transfer chicken to serving platter, pour sauce over chicken, and serve immediately.

CHICKEN BOUILLABAISSE

✓ WHY THIS RECIPE WORKS
Like France's famous fish stew, chicken bouillabaisse should be boldly flavored with saffron, pastis (an anise-flavored liqueur), garlic, fennel, and orange. To adapt the traditional version to use chicken, we replaced the homemade fish stock with store-bought chicken broth. To give the broth extra body and depth, we added flour and tomato paste to our sautéed aromatics. So the alcoholic taste of the pastis could burn off, we added it at the start of the simmer. As for other ingredients, white wine added brightness, while diced canned tomatoes were the best way to ensure consistently good tomato flavor year-round. After lightly browning and simmering the chicken, it was tender and well flavored, but the

skin was flabby. Steam rising from the simmering liquid was soaking the chicken skin when we tried to cook it in the broth, so we made a switch from the stovetop to the oven, where the heat from above kept the moisture from condensing on the chicken. This change, plus a final blast under the intense heat of the broiler, kept the skin crisp.

CHICKEN BOUILLABAISSE
SERVES 4 TO 6

The rouille and croutons (steps 4 and 5) can be prepared either as the chicken cooks or up to 2 days in advance. Leftover rouille will keep refrigerated for up to 1 week and can be used in sandwiches or as a sauce for vegetables and fish.

BOUILLABAISSE

3	pounds bone-in chicken pieces (breasts, thighs, and drumsticks, with breasts cut in half), trimmed
	Salt and pepper
2	tablespoons olive oil
1	large leek, white and light green parts only, halved lengthwise, sliced thin, and washed thoroughly
1	small fennel bulb, stalks discarded, halved, cored, and sliced thin
4	garlic cloves, minced
1	tablespoon tomato paste
1	tablespoon all-purpose flour
¼	teaspoon saffron threads
¼	teaspoon cayenne pepper
3	cups low-sodium chicken broth
1	(14.5-ounce) can diced tomatoes, drained
12	ounces Yukon Gold potatoes, cut into ¾-inch pieces
½	cup dry white wine
¼	cup pastis or Pernod
1	(3-inch) strip orange zest
1	tablespoon chopped fresh tarragon or parsley

ROUILLE AND CROUTONS

3	tablespoons water
¼	teaspoon saffron threads
1	(12-inch) baguette
4	teaspoons lemon juice
1	large egg yolk
2	teaspoons Dijon mustard
2	small garlic cloves, minced
¼	teaspoon cayenne pepper
½	cup vegetable oil
½	cup plus 2 tablespoons extra-virgin olive oil
	Salt and pepper

1. FOR THE BOUILLABAISSE: Adjust oven racks to middle and lower positions and heat oven to 375 degrees. Pat chicken dry with paper towels and season with salt and pepper. Heat oil in Dutch oven over medium-high heat until just smoking. Add chicken pieces, skin side down, and cook without moving until well browned, 5 to 8 minutes. Using tongs, flip chicken and brown other side, about 3 minutes. Transfer chicken to large plate.

2. Add leek and fennel and cook, stirring often, until vegetables begin to soften and turn translucent, about 4 minutes. Add garlic, tomato paste, flour, saffron, and cayenne and cook until fragrant, about 30 seconds. Add broth, tomatoes, potatoes, wine, pastis, and orange zest; bring to simmer. Reduce heat to medium-low and simmer 10 minutes.

3. Nestle chicken thighs and drumsticks into simmering liquid with skin above surface of liquid; cook, uncovered, 5 minutes. Nestle breast pieces into simmering liquid, adjusting pieces as necessary to ensure skin stays above surface of liquid. Bake on middle rack, uncovered, until breasts register 145 degrees and thighs/drumsticks register 160 degrees 10 to 20 minutes.

4. FOR THE ROUILLE: While chicken cooks, microwave water and saffron in medium microwave-safe bowl until water

is steaming, 10 to 20 seconds. Let sit for 5 minutes. Cut 3-inch piece off baguette; remove and discard crust. Tear crustless bread into 1-inch chunks (you should have about 1 cup). Stir bread pieces and lemon juice into saffron-infused water; soak 5 minutes. Using whisk, mash soaked bread mixture until uniform paste forms, 1 to 2 minutes. Whisk in egg yolk, mustard, garlic, and cayenne until smooth, about 15 seconds. Whisking constantly, slowly drizzle in vegetable oil in steady stream until smooth mayonnaise-like consistency is reached, scraping down bowl as necessary. Slowly whisk in ½ cup olive oil in steady stream until smooth. Season with salt and pepper to taste.

5. FOR THE CROUTONS: Cut remaining baguette into ¾-inch-thick slices. Arrange slices in single layer on rimmed baking sheet. Drizzle with remaining 2 tablespoons olive oil and season with salt and pepper to taste. Bake on lower rack until light golden brown (can be toasted while bouillabaisse is in oven), 10 to 15 minutes.

6. Remove bouillabaisse and croutons from oven. Position oven rack 6 inches from broiler element and heat broiler. Return bouillabaisse to oven and cook until chicken skin is crisp and breast registers 160 degrees and drumsticks/thighs register 175 degrees, 5 to 10 minutes (smaller pieces may cook faster than larger pieces; remove individual pieces as they reach correct temperature).

7. Transfer chicken pieces to large plate. Skim excess fat from broth. Stir tarragon into broth and season with salt and pepper to taste. Transfer broth and potatoes to large shallow serving bowls and top with chicken pieces. Drizzle 1 tablespoon rouille over each portion and spread 1 teaspoon rouille on each crouton. Serve, floating 2 croutons in each bowl and passing remaining croutons and rouille separately.

CHICKEN CACCIATORE

✔ **WHY THIS RECIPE WORKS**

Chicken cacciatore should boast moist meat and a silken, robust sauce. Too often the chicken is dry and the sauce greasy and unbalanced. Using chicken thighs and removing the skin after rendering the fat solved the problems of dry meat, soggy skin, and greasy sauce. Cooking the chicken in a combination of red wine, chicken broth, and diced tomatoes, seasoned with fresh thyme, yielded moist, well-seasoned chicken. The addition of portobello mushrooms gave the braise a meatier flavor and fresh sage, to finish, highlighted our cacciatore's woodsy notes.

CHICKEN CACCIATORE WITH PORTOBELLO MUSHROOMS AND SAGE

SERVES 4

If your Dutch oven is large enough to hold all the chicken pieces in a single layer without crowding, brown all the pieces at once instead of in batches. The Parmesan cheese rind is optional, but we highly recommend it for the rich, savory flavor it adds to the dish. An equal amount of minced fresh rosemary can be substituted for the sage.

8	(5- to 7-ounce) bone-in chicken thighs, trimmed
	Salt and pepper
1	teaspoon olive oil
1	onion, chopped
3	medium portobello mushroom caps, cut into ¾-inch cubes
4	garlic cloves, minced
1½	tablespoons all-purpose flour
1½	cups dry red wine
½	cup low-sodium chicken broth
1	(14.5-ounce) can diced tomatoes, drained
2	teaspoons minced fresh thyme
1	Parmesan cheese rind (optional)
2	teaspoons minced fresh sage

1. Season chicken with salt and pepper. Heat oil in Dutch oven over medium-high heat until shimmering, about 2 minutes. Add 4 chicken thighs, skin side down, and cook without moving until skin is crisp and well browned, about 5 minutes. Using tongs, flip chicken and brown on second side, about 5 minutes longer. Transfer chicken to large plate; brown remaining 4 chicken thighs, transfer to plate, and set aside.

2. Drain off all but 1 tablespoon fat from pot. Add onion, mushrooms, and ½ teaspoon salt and cook over medium-high heat, stirring occasionally, until vegetables are beginning to brown, 6 to 8 minutes. When chicken is cool enough to handle, remove and discard skin. Add garlic to pot and cook until fragrant, about 30 seconds. Stir in flour and cook, stirring constantly, about 1 minute. Add wine, scraping browned bits from bottom of pot. Stir in broth, tomatoes, thyme, cheese rind, if using, ½ teaspoon salt (omit salt if using cheese rind), and pepper to taste. Submerge chicken pieces in liquid and bring to boil; cover, reduce heat to low, and simmer until chicken is tender and cooked through, about 45 minutes, turning chicken pieces halfway through cooking. Discard cheese rind, stir in sage, season with salt and pepper to taste, and serve.

CHICKEN CACCIATORE WITH WHITE WINE AND TARRAGON

Substitute 3 minced large shallots for onion, 10 ounces white mushrooms, quartered if large, halved if medium, for portobellos, dry white wine for red wine, and 2 teaspoons minced fresh tarragon for sage.

CHICKEN CHASSEUR

✔ **WHY THIS RECIPE WORKS**

Classic chicken chasseur was a preparation designed for freshly killed game birds, where white wine, wild mushrooms, and aromatic herbs helped mask musky, gamy flavors. Hours of gentle stewing transformed the tough flesh into fall-off-the-bone morsels, just as the stewing liquid eventually thickened into a hearty, flavorful sauce. We wanted a streamlined version that would work with chicken bagged at the supermarket—specifically, chicken breasts. We set aside the traditional braising method in favor of searing the chicken pieces in the pan and then roasting them in the oven while we finished the sauce in the skillet. This ensured the chicken was cooked through but not dried out, and the skin became crisp and evenly browned in the same amount of time the sauce needed to thicken. We stayed with the classic chasseur sauce flavors, adding mushrooms, an accent of tomatoes, and a finish of cold butter and fresh herbs, but we also added a hit of flambéed brandy to bring a sweet complexity and elegance to the finished dish.

CHICKEN CHASSEUR
SERVES 4

If fresh tarragon is unavailable, double the amount of fresh parsley; do not use dried tarragon. Before flambéing, be sure to roll up long shirtsleeves, tie back long hair, and turn off the exhaust fan and any lit burners. Buttered egg noodles or mashed potatoes make a good accompaniment.

- 4   (10- to 12-ounce) bone-in split chicken breasts, trimmed
  Salt and pepper
- 2   tablespoons vegetable oil
- 8   ounces white mushrooms, trimmed and sliced ⅛ inch thick
- 1   shallot, minced
- 3   tablespoons brandy or cognac
- ½   cup dry white wine
- 3½ cups low-sodium chicken broth
- ⅓   cup canned diced tomatoes, drained
- 3   tablespoons unsalted butter, cut into 4 pieces and chilled
- 1   tablespoon minced fresh parsley
- 1   tablespoon minced fresh tarragon

1. Adjust oven rack to middle position; heat oven to 400 degrees. Season chicken with salt and pepper. Heat oil in 12-inch skillet over medium-high heat until almost smoking. Add chicken, skin side down, and cook without moving until skin is crisp and well browned, 5 to 8 minutes. Using tongs, flip chicken and brown on second side, about 5 minutes longer. Place browned chicken, skin side up, on baking sheet and set aside.

2. Pour off all but 2 tablespoons fat from skillet. Add mushrooms and cook over medium-high heat until mushrooms start to brown, 6 to 8 minutes. Reduce heat to medium and add shallot; cook until softened, about 1 minute longer.

3. Off heat, add brandy and let warm through, about 5 seconds. Wave lit match over skillet to ignite, then shake pan to distribute flames. When flames subside, return skillet to medium-high heat, add wine, and scrape browned bits from bottom of pan. Simmer until reduced to glaze, about 3 minutes.

4. Add broth and tomatoes and simmer until liquid, mushrooms, and tomatoes measure 1½ cups, about 25 minutes.

5. While sauce simmers, place chicken in oven. Cook until chicken registers 160 degrees, 15 to 20 minutes. Transfer chicken pieces to serving platter and tent loosely with aluminum foil.

6. When sauce is properly reduced, whisk in butter, 1 piece at a time, until melted and incorporated. Add parsley and tarragon and season with salt and pepper to taste. Spoon sauce over chicken and serve immediately.

CHICKEN PROVENÇAL

✔ **WHY THIS RECIPE WORKS**

Chicken Provençal represents the best of rustic peasant food—bone-in chicken simmered all day in a tomatoey, garlicky herb broth that is flavorful enough to mop up with thick slices of crusty bread. To achieve our ideal, we started with bone-in, skin-on chicken thighs and browned them in olive oil to develop rich flavor and leave behind browned bits in the pan. To keep the sauce from becoming greasy, we spooned off the excess fat left behind, but left a tablespoon to sauté our garlic and onion. Diced tomatoes, white wine, and chicken broth also went into the sauce before we braised the browned chicken; minced anchovy made it taste richer and fuller. We seasoned the dish with fresh herbs in addition to the traditional herbes de Provence, as well as with grated lemon zest and pitted niçoise olives, for a chicken Provençal with authentic, long-simmered flavor.

CHICKEN PROVENÇAL
SERVES 4

This dish is often served with rice or slices of crusty bread, but soft polenta is also a good accompaniment. Be sure to use niçoise olives here; other olives are too potent.

- 8   (5- to 7-ounce) bone-in chicken thighs, trimmed
  Salt
- 1   tablespoon extra-virgin olive oil
- 1   small onion, chopped fine
- 6   garlic cloves, minced
- 1   anchovy fillet, rinsed and minced
- ⅛   teaspoon cayenne pepper
- 1   cup dry white wine
- 1   (14.5-ounce) can diced tomatoes, drained
- 1   cup low-sodium chicken broth
- 2½   tablespoons tomato paste
- 1½   tablespoons chopped fresh thyme
- 1   teaspoon chopped fresh oregano
- 1   teaspoon herbes de Provence (optional)

1 bay leaf
1½ teaspoons grated lemon zest
½ cup niçoise olives, pitted
1 tablespoon chopped fresh parsley

1. Adjust oven rack to lower-middle position; heat oven to 300 degrees. Season both sides of chicken with salt. Heat 1 teaspoon oil in Dutch oven over medium-high heat until shimmering. Add 4 chicken thighs, skin side down, and cook without moving until skin is crisp and well browned, about 5 minutes. Using tongs, flip chicken and brown on second side, about 5 minutes longer; transfer to large plate. Repeat with remaining 4 chicken thighs and transfer to plate; set aside. Discard all but 1 tablespoon fat from pot.

2. Add onion to fat in Dutch oven and cook, stirring occasionally, over medium heat until browned, about 4 minutes. Add garlic, anchovy, and cayenne; cook, stirring constantly, until fragrant, about 1 minute. Add wine and scrape up browned bits from bottom of pan. Stir in tomatoes, chicken broth, tomato paste, thyme, oregano, herbes de Provence, if using, and bay leaf. Remove and discard skin from chicken thighs, then submerge chicken in liquid and add accumulated chicken juices to pot. Increase heat to high, bring to simmer, cover, and transfer pot to oven; cook until chicken offers no resistance when poked with tip of paring knife but still clings to bones, about 1¼ hours.

3. Using slotted spoon, transfer chicken to serving platter and tent with aluminum foil. Discard bay leaf. Set Dutch oven over high heat, stir in 1 teaspoon lemon zest, bring to boil, and cook, stirring occasionally, until slightly thickened and reduced to 2 cups, about 5 minutes. Stir in olives and cook until heated through, about 1 minute. Meanwhile, mix remaining ½ teaspoon zest with parsley. Spoon sauce over chicken, drizzle chicken with remaining 2 teaspoons olive oil, sprinkle with parsley mixture, and serve.

CHICKEN PROVENÇAL WITH SAFFRON, ORANGE, AND BASIL

Add ⅛ teaspoon saffron threads with wine in step 2. Substitute orange zest for lemon zest and 2 tablespoons chopped fresh basil for parsley.

CHICKEN PAPRIKASH

✔ WHY THIS RECIPE WORKS

Chicken paprikash should be an easy-to-make braise with succulent chicken; a balance of heat, spice, and aromatics; and a rich, flavorful sauce with paprika at center stage. To get to this goal, we pared down the usual mile-long ingredient list. After browning chicken thighs, we ditched the skin so the sauce wouldn't become greasy. Sautéing a handful of aromatics and vegetables in the fond led to a rich base for our sauce, which we enhanced with paprika twice: once while sautéing the vegetables to let its flavor bloom, then once again after adding sour cream to finish the dish and instill it with spicy richness.

CHICKEN PAPRIKASH
SERVES 4

Rice, mashed potatoes, and buttered egg noodles all make good accompaniments.

8 (5- to 7-ounce) bone-in chicken thighs, trimmed
Salt and pepper
1 teaspoon vegetable oil
1 large onion, halved and sliced thin
1 large red bell pepper, stemmed, seeded, halved widthwise, and cut into ¼-inch strips
1 large green bell pepper, stemmed, seeded, halved widthwise, and cut into ¼-inch strips
3½ tablespoons paprika
1 tablespoon all-purpose flour
¼ teaspoon dried marjoram
½ cup dry white wine

1 (14.5-ounce) can diced tomatoes, drained
⅓ cup sour cream
2 tablespoons chopped fresh parsley

1. Adjust oven rack to lower-middle position; heat oven to 300 degrees. Season both sides of chicken with salt and pepper. Heat oil in Dutch oven over medium-high heat until shimmering. Add 4 chicken thighs, skin side down, and cook without moving until skin is crisp and well browned, about 5 minutes. Using tongs, flip chicken and brown on second side, about 5 minutes longer; transfer to large plate. Repeat with remaining 4 chicken thighs and transfer to plate; set aside. When chicken is cool enough to handle, remove and discard skin. Discard all but 1 tablespoon fat from pan.

2. Add onion to fat left in Dutch oven and cook, stirring occasionally, over medium heat until softened, 5 to 7 minutes. Add bell peppers and cook, stirring occasionally, until onions are browned and peppers are softened, about 3 minutes. Stir in 3 tablespoons paprika, flour, and marjoram and cook, stirring constantly, until fragrant, about 1 minute. Add wine, scraping up browned bits from bottom of pot; stir in tomatoes and 1 teaspoon salt. Add chicken and any accumulated juices, submerging them in vegetables; bring to a simmer, then cover and place pot in oven. Cook until chicken is no longer pink when cut into with paring knife, about 30 minutes. Remove pot from oven. (At this point, stew can be cooled to room temperature, then refrigerated for up to 3 days. Bring to simmer over medium-low heat before proceeding.)

3. Combine sour cream and remaining ½ tablespoon paprika in small bowl. Place chicken on individual plates. Stir a few tablespoons of hot sauce into sour cream to temper, then stir mixture back into sauce in pot. Spoon sauce and peppers over chicken, sprinkle with parsley, and serve immediately.

CHICKEN CANZANESE

✔ WHY THIS RECIPE WORKS

Chicken canzanese is a regional Italian braised chicken dish that transforms tough old birds into a moist and tender meal. For an interpretation that offered tender and juicy meat, we opted for chicken thighs, which contain more connective tissue than breasts. Sautéed prosciutto and garlic formed a rich flavor base, which we simmered in white wine and chicken broth to concentrate the flavors. We then returned the chicken to the pan and cooked it in the oven uncovered, which allowed our sauce to reduce and also preserved the chicken's crisp skin. To round out the sauce, we added a quick squeeze of lemon, a generous pat of butter, and a sprinkling of chopped rosemary.

CHICKEN CANZANESE
SERVES 4 TO 6

When seasoning the dish at the end, be mindful that the prosciutto adds a fair amount of salt. It is important to use a piece of thickly sliced prosciutto in this recipe; thin strips will become tough and stringy. Serve the chicken with boiled potatoes, noodles, or polenta to absorb the extra sauce.

1	tablespoon olive oil
2	ounces prosciutto (¼ inch thick), cut into ¼-inch pieces
4	garlic cloves, sliced thin
8	(5- to 7-ounce) bone-in chicken thighs, trimmed
	Salt and pepper
2	teaspoons all-purpose flour
2	cups dry white wine
1	cup low-sodium chicken broth
12	whole fresh sage leaves
1	sprig fresh rosemary, leaves removed and minced fine, stem reserved
4	whole cloves
2	bay leaves
¼–½	teaspoon red pepper flakes
2	tablespoons unsalted butter
1	tablespoon lemon juice

1. Adjust oven rack to lower-middle position and heat oven to 325 degrees. Heat 1 teaspoon oil in 12-inch ovensafe skillet over medium heat until shimmering. Add prosciutto and cook, stirring frequently, until just starting to brown, about 3 minutes. Add garlic slices and cook, stirring frequently, until garlic is golden brown, about 1½ minutes. Using slotted spoon, transfer garlic and prosciutto to small bowl and set aside. Do not rinse pan.

2. Increase heat to medium-high; add remaining 2 teaspoons oil and heat until just smoking. Pat chicken dry with paper towels and season with pepper. Add chicken, skin side down, and cook without moving until well browned, 5 to 8 minutes. Using tongs, flip chicken and brown on second side, about 5 minutes longer. Transfer chicken to large plate.

3. Remove all but 2 tablespoons fat from pan. Sprinkle flour over fat and cook, stirring constantly, for 1 minute. Slowly add wine and broth; bring to simmer, scraping up browned bits from bottom of pan. Cook until liquid is slightly reduced, 3 minutes. Stir in sage leaves, rosemary stem, cloves, bay leaves, pepper flakes, and reserved prosciutto and garlic. Nestle chicken into liquid, skin side up (skin should be above surface of liquid), and bake, uncovered, until fork slips easily in and out meat, but meat is not falling off bones, about 1¼ hours. (Check chicken after 15 minutes; broth should be barely bubbling. If bubbling vigorously, reduce oven temperature to 300 degrees.)

4. Transfer chicken to serving platter and tent with aluminum foil. Remove and discard sage leaves, rosemary stem, cloves, and bay leaves. Place skillet over high heat and bring sauce to boil. Cook until sauce is reduced to 1¼ cups, 2 to 5 minutes. Off heat, stir in minced rosemary, butter, and lemon juice. Season with salt and pepper to taste. Pour sauce around chicken and serve.

MOROCCAN CHICKEN WITH OLIVES AND LEMON

✔ WHY THIS RECIPE WORKS

Time-consuming techniques and esoteric ingredients make cooking authentic Moroccan chicken a daunting proposition. We wanted a recipe that was ready in an hour and relied on supermarket staples. For depth and flavor, we used a mix of white and dark chicken and browned the meat first. After removing the chicken from the pot, we sautéed onion, strips of lemon zest, garlic, and a spice blend in the leftover brown bits and some oil; this ensured that no flavor went to waste. A number of everyday spices were necessary to recreate the authentic notes in Moroccan chicken, including paprika, cumin, cayenne, ginger, coriander, and cinnamon; honey contributed a missing sweetness. Greek green olives provided the meatiness and piquant flavor of hard-to-find Moroccan olives. Chopped cilantro, stirred in right before serving, was the perfect finishing touch to our exotic dinner.

MOROCCAN CHICKEN WITH OLIVES AND LEMON
SERVES 4

Bone-in chicken parts can be substituted for the whole chicken. For best results, use four chicken thighs and two chicken breasts, each breast split in half; the dark meat contributes valuable flavor to the broth and should not be omitted. Use a vegetable peeler to remove wide strips of zest from the lemon before juicing it. Make sure to trim any white pith from the zest, as it can impart bitter flavor. If the olives are particularly salty, give them a rinse. Serve with couscous.

1¼	teaspoons paprika
½	teaspoon ground cumin
½	teaspoon ground ginger
¼	teaspoon cayenne pepper
¼	teaspoon ground coriander
¼	teaspoon ground cinnamon
3	(2-inch) strips lemon zest
5	garlic cloves, minced

1 (3½- to 4-pound) whole chicken, cut into 8 pieces (4 breast pieces, 2 thighs, 2 drumsticks), trimmed, wings discarded
   Salt and pepper
1 tablespoon olive oil
1 large onion, halved and sliced ¼ inch thick
1¾ cups low-sodium chicken broth
1 tablespoon honey
2 carrots, peeled and cut crosswise into ½-inch-thick rounds, very large pieces cut into half-moons
1 cup cracked green olives, pitted and halved
3 tablespoons lemon juice
2 tablespoons chopped fresh cilantro

1. Combine paprika, cumin, ginger, cayenne, coriander, and cinnamon in small bowl and set aside. Mince 1 strip lemon zest and combine with 1 teaspoon minced garlic and mince together until reduced to fine paste; set aside.

2. Season both sides of chicken pieces with salt and pepper. Heat oil in Dutch oven over medium-high heat until beginning to smoke. Add chicken pieces, skin side down, and cook without moving until skin is deep golden, about 5 minutes. Using tongs, flip chicken pieces and brown on second side, about 4 minutes longer. Transfer chicken to large plate; when cool enough to handle, remove and discard skin. Pour off and discard all but 1 tablespoon fat from pot.

3. Add onion and 2 remaining lemon zest strips to pot and cook, stirring occasionally, until onion slices have browned at edges but still retain their shape, 5 to 7 minutes (add 1 tablespoon water if pan gets too dark). Add remaining 4 teaspoons garlic and cook, stirring, until fragrant, about 30 seconds. Add spices and cook, stirring constantly, until darkened and very fragrant, 45 seconds to 1 minute. Stir in broth and honey, scraping up browned bits from bottom of pot. Add thighs and

drumsticks, reduce heat to medium, and simmer for 5 minutes.

4. Add carrots and breast pieces with any accumulated juices to pot, arranging breast pieces in single layer on top of carrots. Cover, reduce heat to medium-low, and simmer until breast pieces register 160 degrees, 10 to 15 minutes.

5. Transfer chicken to plate and tent with aluminum foil. Add olives to pot; increase heat to medium-high and simmer until liquid has thickened slightly and carrots are tender, 4 to 6 minutes. Return chicken to pot and stir in garlic mixture, lemon juice, and cilantro; season with salt and pepper to taste. Serve immediately.

MOROCCAN CHICKEN WITH CHICKPEAS AND APRICOTS

Replace 1 carrot with 1 cup dried apricots, halved, and replace olives with one 15-ounce can chickpeas, rinsed.

BOUILLABAISSE-STYLE FISH STEW

✔ WHY THIS RECIPE WORKS

This classic Provençal fisherman's stew is a tough one to translate for American home kitchens. Most recipes call for expensive, hard-to-find varieties of fish, a homemade fish stock, and a host of diverse ingredients, not to mention hours upon hours standing at the stove. We wanted to bring bouillabaisse stateside without sacrificing flavor or a paycheck. For our streamlined and economical stew, we simplified the homemade fish stock with fish frames from the fishmonger. Ditching the obscure kinds of seafood, we chose appropriate and available varieties; marinating our seafood mix in the easy-to-find ingredients of saffron, Pernod (an anise-flavored liqueur), and garlic instilled it with all the great flavors of Provence (but with minimal effort on our part). Finally, we topped off our fish stew with garlic-rubbed croutons and a dollop of heady rouille.

BOUILLABAISSE-STYLE FISH STEW
SERVES 8 TO 10

For the white wine, we prefer white Côtes de Provence. If you decide to make the fish stock ahead, it must be used within 2 days or frozen and defrosted. You will need a pot that holds at least 8 quarts for this recipe. We recommend buying "dry" scallops, those without chemical additives. Dry scallops will look ivory or pinkish and feel tacky; wet scallops look bright white and feel slippery. Use only the freshest fish. We prefer monkfish, sea bass, and ocean perch or red snapper. See page 198 for instructions on debearding mussels and see page 67 for instructions on cleaning fish frames. The chopped vegetables for the stock must be fairly small (no larger than 1 inch in diameter) and evenly cut.

FISH AND MARINADE
1½ pounds skinless fish fillets, cut into 1- to 1½-inch cubes
8 ounces medium shrimp (41 to 50 per pound) peeled and deveined, shells reserved
8 ounces large sea scallops, tendons removed and scallops halved
⅓ cup shredded fresh basil
¼ cup olive oil
3 tablespoons Pernod
3 garlic cloves, minced
2 teaspoons salt
½ teaspoon saffron threads
¼ teaspoon red pepper flakes

FISH STOCK
2 onions, chopped
1 fennel bulb, stalks discarded, halved, cored, and chopped
1 large carrot, chopped
¼ cup olive oil
3 garlic heads, outer papery skin removed, heads intact
1 (750-ml) bottle dry white wine
2 (28-ounce) cans diced tomatoes, drained with juice reserved
3 pounds fish frames, cleaned and cut into 6-inch pieces

4 cups water

2 large leeks, white and light green parts only, halved lengthwise, chopped, and washed thoroughly

I bunch fresh parsley, stems only

5 sprigs fresh thyme

2 bay leaves

2 teaspoons whole black peppercorns

2 teaspoons salt

8 (2-inch) strips orange zest (2 oranges)

½ teaspoon saffron threads

STEW

2 pounds mussels, scrubbed and debearded
Garlic Toasts (recipe follows)
Red Pepper Rouille (recipe follows)

I. FOR THE FISH AND MARINADE: Combine all ingredients (except shrimp shells) in large bowl. Toss well, cover flush with plastic wrap, and refrigerate 4 hours.

2. FOR THE FISH STOCK: Meanwhile, stir onions, fennel, carrot, and oil together in large stockpot or Dutch oven. Cover pot and set over medium-low heat; cook, stirring frequently, until vegetables are fragrant, about 15 minutes. Place garlic in large heavy-duty zipper-lock bag and seal. Smash garlic with rolling pin or meat pounder until flattened. Add smashed garlic to vegetables and continue to cook, stirring frequently, until vegetables are dry and just beginning to stick, about 15 minutes longer. (Take care not to let garlic burn.) Add wine and stir to scrape pot bottom, then add tomatoes with their juice, fish frames, shrimp shells, water, leeks, parsley stems, thyme, bay leaves, peppercorns, and salt. Bring to simmer over medium-high heat, reduce heat to medium-low, and simmer, pressing down on fish bones occasionally with spoon to submerge, until stock is rich and flavorful, about 1 hour.

3. Strain stock through large fine-mesh strainer into large bowl or container (you

should have about 9 cups); rinse and wipe out stockpot and return strained stock to pot. Bring stock to boil over high heat and simmer briskly until reduced to 8 cups, about 10 minutes. Off heat, add orange zest and saffron and let stand for 10 minutes to infuse flavors. Strain stock through fine-mesh strainer; set aside.

4. FOR THE STEW: Return fish broth to clean stockpot and bring to boil over high heat. Stir in marinated fish and shellfish and mussels, cover pot, and return to simmer; cook for 7 minutes, stirring occasionally. Off heat, cover and let stand until fish is cooked through and mussels have opened, about 2 minutes. Season with salt and pepper to taste, ladle into bowls, and float 1 garlic toast topped with dollop of rouille in each bowl. Serve immediately.

GARLIC TOASTS
MAKES 10

I pound country-style French bread, cut into ten ½-inch-thick slices (remainder reserved for rouille if using for bouillabaisse)

6 garlic cloves, peeled and halved

3 tablespoons olive oil

Position oven rack 6 inches from broiler element and heat broiler. Arrange bread slices in single layer on baking sheet; broil until lightly toasted, about 1½ minutes. Flip slices and rub second side of each slice with raw garlic, then brush with oil. Broil until light golden brown, about 1½ minutes longer.

RED PEPPER ROUILLE
MAKES ABOUT I CUP

See page 273 for instructions on roasting bell peppers.

I large red bell pepper, roasted, peeled, and cut into large pieces

2 ounces country-style French bread, crusts removed and cut into large cubes (about 2 cups)

2 garlic cloves, minced

⅛ teaspoon cayenne pepper

½ cup extra-virgin olive oil
Salt

Process roasted pepper, bread, garlic, and cayenne in food processor until smooth, about 20 seconds. With processor running, drizzle oil in; process until rouille has thick, mayonnaise-like consistency. Season with salt to taste.

HEARTY TUSCAN BEAN STEW

✔ WHY THIS RECIPE WORKS
We wanted to convert rustic Tuscan bean soup into a hearty stew. Determined to avoid tough, exploded beans in our stew, we soaked the beans overnight in salted water, which softened the skins. Then we experimented with cooking times and temperatures, discovering that gently cooking the beans in a 250-degree oven produced perfectly cooked beans that stayed intact. We added tomatoes toward the end of cooking, since their acid kept the beans from becoming too soft. To complete our stew, we chose other traditional Tuscan flavors, including pancetta, kale, lots of garlic, and a sprig of rosemary.

HEARTY TUSCAN BEAN STEW
SERVES 8

We prefer the creamier texture of beans soaked overnight for this recipe. If you're short on time, quick-soak them: Place the rinsed beans in a large heat-resistant bowl. Bring 8 cups water and 3 tablespoons salt to a boil. Pour the water over the beans and let them sit for 1 hour. Drain and rinse the beans well before proceeding with step 2. If pancetta is unavailable, substitute 4 slices of bacon.

Salt and pepper
1   pound dried cannellini beans
    (2 cups), picked over and rinsed
1   tablespoon extra-virgin olive oil,
    plus extra for drizzling
6   ounces pancetta, cut into ¼-inch
    pieces
1   large onion, chopped
2   carrots, peeled and cut into
    ½-inch pieces
2   celery ribs, cut into ½-inch pieces
8   garlic cloves, peeled and crushed
4   cups low-sodium chicken broth
3   cups water
2   bay leaves
1   pound kale or collard greens,
    stemmed and leaves chopped
    into 1-inch pieces
1   (14.5-ounce) can diced tomatoes,
    drained
1   sprig fresh rosemary
8   slices country white bread,
    1¼ inch thick, broiled until
    golden brown on both sides
    and rubbed with garlic clove
    (optional)

1. Dissolve 3 tablespoons salt in 4 quarts cold water in large bowl or container. Add beans and soak at room temperature for at least 8 hours or up to 24 hours. Drain and rinse well.

2. Adjust oven rack to lower-middle position and heat oven to 250 degrees. Heat oil and pancetta in Dutch oven over medium heat. Cook, stirring occasionally, until pancetta is lightly browned and fat has rendered, 6 to 10 minutes. Add onion, carrots, and celery and cook, stirring occasionally, until vegetables are softened and lightly browned, 10 to 16 minutes. Stir in garlic and cook until fragrant, about 1 minute. Stir in broth, water, bay leaves, and soaked beans. Increase heat to high and bring to simmer. Cover pot, transfer to oven, and cook until beans are almost tender (very center of beans will still be firm), 45 minutes to 1 hour.

3. Remove pot from oven and stir in kale and tomatoes. Return pot to oven and continue to cook until beans and greens are fully tender, 30 to 40 minutes longer.

4. Remove pot from oven and submerge rosemary in stew. Cover and let stand 15 minutes. Discard bay leaves and rosemary and season stew with salt and pepper to taste. If desired, use back of spoon to press some beans against side of pot to thicken stew. Serve over toasted bread, if desired, and drizzle with olive oil.

HEARTY TUSCAN BEAN STEW WITH SAUSAGE AND CABBAGE

This variation has much more meat and is made with crinkly savoy cabbage.

Substitute 1½ pounds sweet Italian sausage, casings removed, for pancetta; ½ head savoy cabbage, cut into 1-inch pieces, for kale; and 1 sprig fresh oregano for rosemary. Cook sausage in oil in step 2, breaking meat into small pieces with wooden spoon until it loses its raw color, about 8 minutes. Transfer sausage to paper towel–lined plate and place in refrigerator. Proceed with recipe as directed, stirring sausage and cabbage into stew along with tomatoes in step 3.

VEGETARIAN HEARTY TUSCAN BEAN STEW

Omit pancetta, substituting 3 cups vegetable broth for the chicken broth, and increase water to 4½ cups. Microwave ½ ounce dried porcini mushrooms with ½ cup water in covered bowl until steaming, about 1 minute. Let stand until the mushrooms soften, about 5 minutes. Drain mushrooms through fine-mesh strainer lined with coffee filter, reserve liquid, and mince mushrooms. Stir mushrooms and reserved liquid into broth in step 2.

QUICK HEARTY TUSCAN BEAN STEW

To speed up this recipe, we used canned beans and cooked the stew completely on the stovetop.

Replace dried cannellini beans with 4 (15-ounce) cans cannellini beans, drained and rinsed well. Skip step 1 and omit oven instructions from the recipe. Reduce amount of chicken broth to 3 cups and water amount to 2 cups.

FRENCH PORK AND WHITE BEAN CASSEROLE

☑ WHY THIS RECIPE WORKS
Cassoulet, though a homey, hearty classic French dish, requires ingredients that can be tough to find and demands hours of effort. We wanted to both streamline our cassoulet and use the even, constant heat of the oven for most of the cooking, so the cook would be off-duty. To replace the duck confit, which can be expensive to buy and time-consuming to make, we added salt pork, which provided the necessary richness. Pork shoulder fit the bill as the requisite stewing pork. Because we'd taken liberties with the ingredient list thus far, we opted to keep the fresh French garlic sausage. To prevent the tall sides of our pot from trapping moisture and prohibiting us from getting a crisp crust while the cassoulet baked covered, we used half of our bread crumbs to absorb the liquid. Then we uncovered the pot, added the remaining crumbs, and let the dish cook until they were crisp.

FRENCH PORK AND WHITE BEAN CASSEROLE (CASSOULET)
SERVES 8 TO 10

Instead of an overnight soak, you can "quick brine" the beans: In step 1, combine the salt, water, and beans in a Dutch oven and bring to a boil over high heat. Remove the pot from the heat, cover, and let stand 1 hour. Drain and rinse the beans and proceed with the recipe. If you can't find fresh French garlic sausage,

Irish bangers or bratwurst may be substituted. To make a more authentic version of the dish, see our related recipe for French Pork and White Bean Casserole with Homemade Duck Confit (recipe follows).

	Salt and pepper
I	pound dried cannellini beans (2 cups), picked over and rinsed
2	celery ribs
I	bay leaf
4	sprigs fresh thyme
I ½	pounds fresh French garlic sausage
4	ounces salt pork, rinsed
¼	cup vegetable oil
I	(1½-pound) pork shoulder, cut into 1-inch chunks
I	large onion, chopped fine
2	carrots, peeled and cut into ¼-inch pieces
4	garlic cloves, minced
I	tablespoon tomato paste
½	cup dry white wine
I	(14.5-ounce) can diced tomatoes
4	cups low-sodium chicken broth
4	slices hearty white sandwich bread, torn into rough pieces
½	cup chopped fresh parsley

I. Dissolve 2 tablespoons salt in 4 quarts cold water in large bowl or container. Add beans and soak at room temperature for at least 8 hours or up to 24 hours. Drain and rinse well.

2. Adjust oven rack to lower-middle position and heat oven to 300 degrees. Using kitchen twine, tie together celery, bay leaf, and thyme. Place sausage and salt pork in medium saucepan and add cold water to cover by 1 inch; bring to boil over high heat. Reduce heat to simmer and cook 5 minutes. Transfer sausage to cutting board, allow to cool slightly, then cut into 1-inch pieces. Remove salt pork from water; set aside.

3. Heat 2 tablespoons oil in Dutch oven over medium-high heat until beginning to smoke. Add sausage pieces and brown on all sides, 8 to 12 minutes total. Transfer to medium bowl. Add pork shoulder and brown on all sides, 8 to 12 minutes total. Add onion and carrots; cook, stirring constantly, until onion is translucent, about 2 minutes. Add garlic and tomato paste and cook, stirring constantly, until fragrant, 30 seconds. Return sausage to Dutch oven; add white wine, scraping browned bits from bottom of pan. Cook until slightly reduced, about 30 seconds. Stir in tomatoes, celery bundle, and reserved salt pork.

4. Stir in broth and beans, pressing beans into even layer, adding up to 1 cup water so beans are at least partially submerged (beans may still break surface of liquid). Increase heat to high and bring to simmer. Cover pot, transfer to oven, and cook until beans are tender, about 1½ hours. Remove celery bundle and salt pork and discard. (Alternatively, dice salt pork and return to casserole.) Using large spoon, skim fat from surface and discard. Season with salt and pepper to taste. Increase oven temperature to 350 degrees and bake, uncovered, 20 minutes.

5. Meanwhile, pulse bread and remaining 2 tablespoons oil in food processor until crumbs are no larger than ⅛ inch, 8 to 10 pulses. Transfer to medium bowl, add parsley, and toss to combine. Season with salt and pepper to taste.

6. Sprinkle ½ cup bread-crumb mixture evenly over casserole; bake, covered, 15 minutes. Remove lid and bake 15 minutes longer. Sprinkle remaining bread-crumb mixture over top of casserole and bake until topping is golden brown, about 30 minutes. Let rest 15 minutes before serving.

FRENCH PORK AND WHITE BEAN CASSEROLE WITH HOMEMADE DUCK CONFIT

The two components of this recipe, the confit and the stew, are cooked simultaneously. In order for the confit and stew to finish cooking at the same time (step 7), start cooking the confit (step 3) and then wait about 1½ hours before starting the stew (step 4). The cooked confit, covered with fat, will last up to 1 month. Three turkey drumsticks can be substituted for the duck legs. We prefer the duck confit prepared with duck fat, but canola oil can be substituted. We prefer the creamier texture of beans soaked overnight for this recipe. If you're short on time, quick-soak them: Place the rinsed beans in a large heat-resistant bowl. Bring 8 cups water and 3 tablespoons salt to a boil. Pour the water over the beans and let them sit for 1 hour. Drain and rinse the beans well before proceeding with step 3. If you can't find fresh French garlic sausage, Irish bangers or bratwurst may be substituted.

TEST KITCHEN TIP NO. 23   FRESH OR DRIED BAY LEAVES?

Dried bay leaves are so common that most cooks probably use them without a second thought, but fresh bay leaves have become available in many supermarkets. In the test kitchen, we generally use fresh herbs rather than dried—bay leaves being an exception. To decide whether we should switch, we cooked up two batches of a béchamel sauce, simmering dried bay leaves in one and fresh in the other. Surprisingly, they finished in a dead heat. Here's why: The aromatic molecules in most herbs are more volatile than water. When an herb is dried, most of the flavor evaporates along with the water. Herbs that grow in hot, arid environments—like bay leaves—are different. Their aromatic molecules are less volatile, retaining flavor even after water evaporates. Similarly, in long-cooked applications, we've found that dried rosemary, thyme, oregano, sage, and other herbs native to hot, arid environments do as well as their fresh counterparts. Because bay leaves are used only on long-cooked recipes and keep fresh for months in the freezer, we'll continue using dried bay leaves instead of springing for fresh, which cost twice as much.

DUCK CONFIT

1	large onion, cut into 1-inch pieces
¼	cup salt
6	garlic cloves
2	tablespoons whole black peppercorns
12	sprigs fresh parsley
2	bay leaves
6	duck legs
4	cups duck fat or canola oil

BEAN STEW

	Salt and pepper
1	pound dried cannellini beans (2 cups), picked over and rinsed
2	celery ribs
1	bay leaf
4	sprigs thyme
1	pound fresh French garlic sausage
4	ounces salt pork, rinsed
¼	cup vegetable oil
1	pound pork shoulder, cut into 1-inch chunks
1	large onion, chopped fine
2	carrots, peeled and cut into ¼-inch pieces
4	garlic cloves, minced
1	tablespoon tomato paste
½	cup dry white wine
1	(14.5-ounce) can diced tomatoes
4	cups low-sodium chicken broth
4	slices hearty white sandwich bread, torn into rough pieces
½	cup chopped fresh parsley

1. FOR THE CONFIT: Process onion, salt, garlic, peppercorns, parsley, and bay leaves in food processor until smooth paste with some small chunks forms, about 30 seconds, scraping down sides of bowl as necessary. Massage duck legs with salt mixture and place in gallon-sized zipper-lock bag. Press out air, seal bag, and place in refrigerator for 12 to 18 hours.

2. FOR THE STEW: Dissolve 2 tablespoons salt in 4 quarts cold water in large bowl or container. Add beans and soak at room temperature, for at least 8 hours or up to 24 hours. Drain and rinse well.

3. Adjust oven rack to lower-middle position and heat oven to 300 degrees. Rinse duck legs, rubbing off any salt mixture, and pat dry with paper towels. Heat duck fat in large saucepan over medium heat until completely transparent (if using canola oil, it should register about 135 degrees). Add duck legs, making sure they are completely submerged in fat. Transfer pot to oven and cook until fork slips easily in and out of meat, 3 to 4 hours.

4. Using kitchen twine, tie together celery, bay leaf, and thyme, and set aside. Place sausage and salt pork in medium saucepan and add cold water to cover by 1 inch; bring to boil over high heat. Reduce heat to simmer and cook 5 minutes. Transfer sausage to cutting board, allow to cool slightly, then cut into 1-inch pieces. Remove salt pork from water; set aside.

5. Heat 2 tablespoons oil in Dutch oven over medium-high heat until beginning to smoke. Add sausage pieces and brown on all sides, 8 to 12 minutes total. Transfer to medium bowl. Add pork shoulder and brown on all sides, 8 to 12 minutes. Add onion and carrots; cook, stirring constantly, until onion is translucent, about 2 minutes. Add garlic and tomato paste and cook, stirring constantly, until fragrant, 30 seconds. Return sausage to Dutch oven; add white wine, scraping up browned bits from bottom of pan. Cook until slightly reduced, about 30 seconds. Stir in tomatoes, celery bundle, and reserved salt pork.

6. Stir in broth and beans, pressing beans into even layer, adding up to 1 cup water to ensure beans are at least partially submerged (beans may still break surface of liquid). Increase heat to high and bring to simmer. Cover pot, transfer to oven, and cook until beans are tender, about 1½ hours.

7. Remove confit and stew from oven and increase temperature to 350 degrees. Using slotted spoon, transfer duck legs to large plate. When cool enough to handle, remove and discard skin. Remove meat from bones, leaving meat in large pieces; discard bones. Meanwhile, remove celery bundle and salt pork from bean stew and discard. (Alternatively, dice salt pork and return to stew.) Using large spoon or ladle, skim fat from surface of stew and discard. Season stew with salt and pepper to taste. Add duck meat and stir gently to combine. Bake, uncovered, for 20 minutes.

8. Meanwhile, pulse bread and remaining 2 tablespoons oil in food processor until crumbs are no larger than ⅛ inch, 8 to 10 pulses. Transfer to medium bowl, add parsley, and toss to combine. Season with salt and pepper to taste.

9. Sprinkle ½ cup bread-crumb mixture evenly over casserole; bake, covered, 15 minutes. Remove lid and bake 15 minutes longer. Sprinkle remaining bread-crumb mixture over top of casserole and bake until topping is golden brown and beans are bubbling around edges of pot, about 30 minutes. Let rest 15 minutes before serving.

OLD-FASHIONED BEEF STEW

✔ WHY THIS RECIPE WORKS

Few things are as soul-satisfying as a steaming bowl of old-fashioned beef stew. We wanted to create a simple yet classic beef stew with rich, deep flavor and tender bites of beef and vegetables. We chose chuck-eye roast for its great flavor and abundance of intramuscular fat and connective tissue, which makes it well-suited for long, slow, moist cooking. To thicken our stew, we followed the traditional path and stirred in some flour with the onions and garlic, right before we added red wine and chicken broth (which provided more complexity than beef broth). After the meat cooked awhile, we added the essential carrots and potatoes; frozen peas were added just before serving, as they needed only a few minutes to warm through. With minimal ease and fuss, we had created a simple but intensely flavored old-fashioned beef stew.

OLD-FASHIONED BEEF STEW
SERVES 6 TO 8

Try to find beef that is well marbled with white veins of fat. Meat that is too lean will come out slightly dry. For the red wine in this stew, we like Cabernet Sauvignon.

- 1 (3-pound) boneless beef chuck-eye roast, pulled apart at seams, trimmed, and cut into 1½-inch pieces
  Salt and pepper
- 3 tablespoons vegetable oil
- 2 onions, chopped coarse
- 3 garlic cloves, minced
- 3 tablespoons all-purpose flour
- 1 cup full-bodied red wine
- 2 cups low-sodium chicken broth
- 2 bay leaves
- 1 teaspoon dried thyme
- 1 pound small red potatoes, peeled and halved
- 4 large carrots, peeled and sliced ¼ inch thick
- 1 cup frozen peas, thawed
- ¼ cup minced fresh parsley

1. Heat oven to 300 degrees. Season beef with 1½ teaspoons salt and 1 teaspoon pepper; toss to coat. Heat 2 tablespoons oil over medium-high heat in Dutch oven. Brown meat on all sides in 2 batches, about 5 minutes per batch, adding remaining 1 tablespoon oil if necessary. Remove meat and set aside. Add onions to now-empty pot and cook until almost softened, 4 to 5 minutes. Reduce heat to medium and add garlic; cook until fragrant, about 30 seconds. Stir in flour; cook until lightly colored, 1 to 2 minutes. Add wine, scraping up browned bits on bottom of pot. Add broth, bay leaves, and thyme and bring to simmer. Add meat and return to simmer. Cover and place in oven and simmer 1 hour.

2. Remove pot from oven, add potatoes and carrots, cover, and return to oven. Simmer until meat is just tender, about 1 hour. Remove stew from oven. (At this point, stew can be cooled to room temperature, then refrigerated for up to 3 days. Bring to simmer, then remove from heat before proceeding.)

3. Stir in peas and let stand 5 minutes. Stir in parsley, season with salt and pepper to taste, and serve. (Stew can be refrigerated for up to 2 days.)

OLD-FASHIONED BEEF STEW WITH BACON, MUSHROOMS, AND PEARL ONIONS

Instead of the frozen pearl onions, you can use an equal amount of fresh pearl onions that have been blanched, peeled, and steamed.

Before preparing beef, cook 4 slices bacon, cut into small dice, in Dutch oven until browned and crisp. Transfer bacon to paper towel–lined plate, reserving fat. Substitute fat for oil when browning meat. Return bacon to Dutch oven with broth, bay leaves, and thyme. Omit potatoes, carrots, and peas. Heat 2 tablespoons of reserved fat in large skillet until hot and add 1 pound white mushrooms, quartered; cook over high heat until browned, 5 to 7 minutes. Add 1 cup frozen pearl onions, thawed, and cook until lightly browned, about 3 minutes. When meat is almost tender, 2 to 2½ hours, add mushrooms and pearl onions to stew. Cover and return to oven. Cook until meat and pearl onions are tender, 20 to 30 minutes longer. Stir in parsley, season with salt and pepper to taste, and serve.

OLD-FASHIONED BEEF STEW WITH TOMATOES, ORANGE ZEST, AND OLIVES

Substitute 1 cup canned diced tomatoes with their juice for 1 cup of broth. Add two 2-inch strips orange zest with broth. Substitute herbes de Provence for thyme. Omit potatoes, carrots, and peas. Stir in 1 cup pitted kalamata olives in step 3, cover stew, and let stand 5 minutes. Stir in parsley, season with salt and pepper to taste, and serve.

OLD-FASHIONED BEEF STEW WITH TOMATOES, CINNAMON, AND CLOVES

Add 1 tablespoon tomato paste after cooking flour. Substitute 1 cup canned diced tomatoes for 1 cup broth and add 1 teaspoon ground cinnamon and ⅛ teaspoon ground cloves with broth, bay leaves, and thyme. Omit potatoes, carrots, and peas. Heat 1 tablespoon oil in medium skillet; add 1 cup frozen pearl onions, thawed, and cook until lightly browned, about 3 minutes. When meat is almost tender, 2 to 2½ hours, add pearl onions and ⅓ cup currants to stew. Cover and return to oven. Cook until meat and pearl onions are tender, 20 to 30 minutes longer. Stir in parsley, season with salt and pepper to taste, and serve.

MODERN BEEF STEW

✔ WHY THIS RECIPE WORKS
We wanted a rich-tasting but approachable beef stew with tender meat, flavorful vegetables, and a rich brown gravy—and we planned to take a no-holds-barred attitude toward the ingredient list. To begin, we chose a tasty cut of beef, chuck, and browned it properly, taking care not to crowd the meat in the pan. Along with

traditional stew components like onion, carrots, garlic, red wine, and chicken broth, we added glutamate-rich ingredients like tomato paste, salt pork, and anchovies. Glutamates are compounds that give meat its savory taste and they contribute considerable flavor to the dish. To mimic the luxurious, mouth-coating texture of beef stews made with homemade stock (provided by the collagen in bones that is transformed into gelatin when simmered), we included powdered gelatin and flour. Potatoes, pearl onions, and peas rounded out our rich-tasting, yet updated, take on beef stew.

MODERN BEEF STEW
SERVES 6 TO 8

Use a good-quality, medium-bodied wine, such as a Côtes du Rhône or Pinot Noir, for this stew. Try to find beef that is well marbled with white veins of fat. Meat that is too lean will come out slightly dry. You can use 4 pounds of blade steaks, trimmed, instead of the chuck-eye roast. While the blade steak will yield slightly thinner pieces after trimming, it should still be cut into 1½-inch pieces. Look for salt pork that is roughly 75 percent lean.

- 2 garlic cloves, minced
- 4 anchovy fillets, rinsed and minced
- 1 tablespoon tomato paste
- 1 (4-pound) boneless beef chuck-eye roast, pulled apart at seams, trimmed, and cut into 1½-inch pieces
- 2 tablespoons vegetable oil
- 1 large onion, halved and sliced ⅛ inch thick
- 4 carrots, peeled and cut into 1-inch pieces
- ¼ cup all-purpose flour
- 2 cups red wine
- 2 cups low-sodium chicken broth
- 4 ounces salt pork, rinsed
- 2 bay leaves
- 4 sprigs fresh thyme
- 1 pound Yukon Gold potatoes, cut into 1-inch pieces
- 1½ cups frozen pearl onions, thawed
- 2 teaspoons unflavored gelatin
- ½ cup water
- 1 cup frozen peas, thawed
   Salt and pepper

1. Adjust oven rack to lower-middle position and heat oven to 300 degrees. Combine garlic and anchovies in small bowl; press with back of fork to form paste. Stir in tomato paste and set aside.

2. Pat meat dry with paper towels. Do not season. Heat 1 tablespoon oil in Dutch oven over high heat until just starting to smoke. Add half of beef and cook until well browned on all sides, about 8 minutes. Transfer beef to large plate. Repeat with remaining beef and remaining 1 tablespoon oil, leaving second batch of meat in pot after browning.

3. Reduce heat to medium and return first batch of beef to pot. Stir in onion and carrots and cook, scraping bottom of pan to loosen browned bits, until onion is softened, 1 to 2 minutes. Add garlic mixture and cook, stirring constantly, until fragrant, about 30 seconds. Add flour and cook, stirring constantly, until no dry flour remains, about 30 seconds.

4. Slowly add wine, scraping bottom of pan to loosen browned bits. Increase heat to high and simmer until wine is thickened and slightly reduced, about 2 minutes. Stir in broth, pork, bay leaves, and thyme. Bring to simmer, cover, transfer to oven, and cook for 1½ hours.

5. Remove pot from oven; remove and discard bay leaves and salt pork. Stir in potatoes, cover, return to oven, and cook until potatoes are almost tender, about 45 minutes.

6. Using large spoon, skim excess fat from surface of stew. Stir in pearl onions; cook over medium heat until potatoes and onions are cooked through and fork slips easily in and out of beef (meat should not be falling apart), about 15 minutes. Meanwhile, sprinkle gelatin over water in small bowl and allow to soften for 5 minutes.

7. Increase heat to high, stir in softened gelatin mixture and peas; simmer until gelatin is fully dissolved and stew is thickened, about 3 minutes. Season with salt and pepper to taste; serve. (Stew can be refrigerated for up to 2 days.)

TRIMMING A CHUCK-EYE ROAST

To ensure consistent texture and flavor, avoid packaged stew meat (which can include odd-size pieces from all over the cow) and start with a chuck roast.

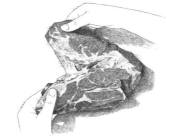

1. Pull roast apart at its major seams (marked by lines of fat and silver skin). Use knife as necessary.

2. With a sharp chef's knife or boning knife, trim off the thick layers of fat and silver skin.

DAUBE PROVENÇAL

✔ WHY THIS RECIPE WORKS

Daube Provençal, also known as daube niçoise, has all the elements of the best French fare: tender beef, a luxurious sauce, and complex flavors. But it usually ends up as beef stew with a few misplaced ingredients. We wanted to translate the flavors of Provence—olive oil, olives, garlic, wine, herbs, oranges, tomatoes, mushrooms, and anchovies—to an American home kitchen, with ingredients that married into a robust but unified dish. We started with our reliable set of techniques for turning tough but flavorful beef into a tender stew and then concentrated on refining the complex blend of ingredients. We chose briny niçoise olives, bright tomatoes, floral orange peel, and the regional flavors of thyme and bay. A few anchovies added complexity without a fishy taste, and salt pork contributed rich body. A whole bottle of wine added bold flavor and needed just a little cooking to tame its raw bite. Finally, to keep the meat from drying out during the long braising time, we cut it into relatively large 2-inch pieces.

DAUBE PROVENÇAL
SERVES 4 TO 6

Serve this French beef stew with buttered egg noodles or boiled potatoes. If niçoise olives are not available, kalamata olives, though not authentic, can be substituted. Cabernet Sauvignon is our favorite wine for this recipe, but Côtes du Rhône and Zinfandel also work. Our favorite cut of beef for this recipe is chuck-eye roast, but any boneless roast from the chuck will work. Because the tomatoes are added just before serving, it is preferable to use canned whole tomatoes and dice them yourself—uncooked, they are more tender than canned diced tomatoes. Once the salt pork, thyme, and bay leaves are removed in step 4, the daube can be cooled and refrigerated in an airtight container for up to 4 days. Before reheating, skim the hardened fat from the surface, then continue with the recipe.

¾ ounce dried porcini mushrooms, rinsed
2 cups water
1 (3½-pound) boneless beef chuck-eye roast, pulled apart at seams, trimmed, and cut into 2-inch pieces
1 teaspoon salt
1 teaspoon pepper
4 tablespoons olive oil
5 ounces salt pork, rind removed
4 carrots, peeled and cut into 1-inch rounds
2 onions, halved and sliced ⅛ inch thick
4 garlic cloves, sliced thin
2 tablespoons tomato paste
⅓ cup all-purpose flour
1 (750-ml) bottle red wine
1 cup low-sodium chicken broth
4 (2-inch) strips orange zest, cut lengthwise into thin strips
1 cup niçoise olives, pitted
3 anchovy fillets, rinsed and minced
5 sprigs fresh thyme, tied together with kitchen twine
2 bay leaves
1 (14.5-ounce) can whole tomatoes, drained and cut into ½-inch pieces
2 tablespoons minced fresh parsley

1. Microwave 1 cup water and mushrooms in covered bowl until steaming, about 1 minute. Lift mushrooms from liquid with fork and chop into ½-inch pieces (you should have about ¼ cup). Strain liquid through paper towel–lined fine-mesh strainer into medium bowl. Set mushrooms and liquid aside.

2. Adjust oven rack to lower-middle position; heat oven to 325 degrees. Pat beef dry and season with salt and pepper. Heat 2 tablespoons oil in Dutch oven over medium-high heat until shimmering. Add half of beef and cook without moving until well browned, about 2 minutes per side. Transfer meat to medium bowl. Repeat with remaining oil and remaining meat.

3. Reduce heat to medium and add salt pork, carrots, onions, garlic, and tomato paste to now-empty pot; cook, stirring occasionally, until light brown, about 2 minutes. Stir in flour and cook, stirring constantly, about 1 minute. Slowly add wine, scraping bottom of pan to loosen browned bits. Add broth, remaining 1 cup

---

MINCING ANCHOVIES

1. Using chef's knife, cut fillet lengthwise into ⅛-inch strips. Gather strips in bundle, turn it 90 degrees, and mince crosswise.

2. Using back of fork, press and smear the anchovies against surface of cutting board into uniform paste.

water, and beef with any accumulated juices. Increase heat to medium-high and bring to simmer. Stir in mushrooms and their liquid, orange zest, ½ cup olives, anchovies, thyme, and bay leaves, arranging beef so it is completely covered by liquid; partially cover pot and place in oven. Cook until fork slips easily in and out of beef (meat should not be falling apart), 2½ to 3 hours.

4. Discard salt pork, thyme, and bay leaves. Add tomatoes and remaining ½ cup olives and cook over medium-high heat until heated through, about 1 minute. Cover pot and let stew sit, about 5 minutes. Using large spoon, skim fat from surface of stew. Stir in parsley and serve.

HUNGARIAN BEEF STEW

✔ *Why this recipe works* The Americanized versions of Hungarian goulash served in the United States bear little resemblance to the traditional dish. Mushrooms, green peppers, and most herbs have no place in the pot and sour cream is not authentic to the dish. We wanted the real deal—a simple dish of tender braised beef packed with paprika flavor. To achieve the desired level of spicy intensity, we created our own version of paprika cream, a condiment common in Hungarian cooking but hard to find in the U.S. Pureeing the paprika with roasted red peppers and a little tomato paste and vinegar imparted vibrant paprika flavor without any offensive grittiness. Searing the meat first competed with the paprika's brightness, so we skipped the sear. We softened the onions in the pot first, added the paprika paste, carrots, and then meat before placing the covered pot in the oven; the onions and meat released enough liquid to stew the meat. A bit of broth added near the end of cooking thinned out the stewing liquid to just the right consistency.

HUNGARIAN BEEF STEW
SERVES 6

Do not substitute hot, half-sharp, or smoked Spanish paprika for the sweet paprika in the stew, as they will compromise the flavor of the dish. Since paprika is vital to this recipe, it is best to use a fresh container. We prefer chuck-eye roast, but any boneless roast from the chuck will work. Cook the stew in a Dutch oven with a tight-fitting lid. (Alternatively, to ensure a tight seal, place a sheet of aluminum foil over the pot before adding the lid.) Serve the stew over boiled potatoes or buttered egg noodles.

1	(3½- to 4-pound) boneless beef chuck-eye roast, pulled apart at seams, trimmed, and cut into 1½-inch pieces
	Salt and pepper
⅓	cup paprika
1	cup jarred roasted red peppers, rinsed and patted dry
2	tablespoons tomato paste
1	tablespoon white vinegar
2	tablespoons vegetable oil
4	large onions, chopped fine
4	large carrots, peeled and cut into 1-inch-thick rounds
1	bay leaf
1	cup beef broth, warmed
¼	cup sour cream (optional)

1. Adjust oven rack to lower-middle position and heat oven to 325 degrees. Season meat evenly with 1 teaspoon salt and let stand 15 minutes. Process paprika, roasted peppers, tomato paste, and 2 teaspoons vinegar in food processor until smooth, 1 to 2 minutes, scraping down sides as needed.

2. Combine oil, onions, and 1 teaspoon salt in Dutch oven; cover and set over medium heat. Cook, stirring occasionally, until onions soften but have not yet begun to brown, 8 to 10 minutes. (If onions begin to brown, reduce heat to medium-low and stir in 1 tablespoon water.)

3. Stir in paprika mixture; cook, stirring occasionally, until onions stick to bottom of pan, about 2 minutes. Add beef, carrots, and bay leaf; stir until beef is well coated. Using rubber spatula, scrape down sides of pot. Cover pot and transfer to oven. Cook until meat is almost tender and surface of liquid is ½ inch below top of meat, 2 to 2½ hours, stirring every 30 minutes. Remove pot from oven and add enough beef broth so that surface of liquid is ¼ inch from top of meat (beef should not be fully submerged). Return covered pot to oven and continue to cook until fork slips easily in and out of beef, about 30 minutes longer.

4. Using large spoon, skim fat from surface of stew; stir in remaining teaspoon vinegar and sour cream, if using. Remove bay leaf, season with salt and pepper to taste, and serve. (Stew, minus optional sour cream, can be refrigerated for up to 2 days. Stir sour cream into reheated stew just before serving.)

CARBONNADE À LA FLAMANDE

✔ WHY THIS RECIPE WORKS
In a good beef carbonnade, the heartiness of the beef should meld with the soft sweetness of sliced onions in a lightly thickened broth laced with the malty flavor of beer. Our tests revealed that the small, long, shoulder-cut blade steak was our best beef option, given its generous fat marbling, which provides flavor and a tender, buttery texture. Lots of thinly sliced yellow onions found their way into the pot next, and a spoonful of tomato paste and a couple of minced garlic cloves boosted the flavor. The key element of this Belgian stew, however, was the dark, potent ale, which bathed the chunks of

tender meat and the slivers of sweet onions. The beer, combined with equal portions of chicken and beef broth, gave us a beef stew with a strong, complex flavor.

CARBONNADE À LA FLAMANDE (BELGIAN BEEF, BEER, AND ONION STEW)

SERVES 6

Top blade steaks (also called blade or flat-iron steaks) are our first choice, but any boneless roast from the chuck will work. If you end up using a chuck roast, look for the chuck-eye roast, an especially flavorful cut that can easily be trimmed and cut into 1-inch pieces. Buttered egg noodles or mashed potatoes make excellent accompaniments to carbonnade. The traditional copper-colored Belgian ale works best in this stew. If you can't find one, choose another dark or amber-colored ale of your liking.

3½ pounds blade steaks, 1 inch thick, trimmed and cut into 1-inch pieces
Salt and pepper
3 tablespoons vegetable oil
2 pounds onions, halved and sliced ¼ inch thick
1 tablespoon tomato paste
2 garlic cloves, minced
3 tablespoons all-purpose flour
¾ cup low-sodium chicken broth
¾ cup beef broth
1½ cups beer
4 sprigs fresh thyme, tied with kitchen twine
2 bay leaves
1 tablespoon cider vinegar

1. Adjust oven rack to lower-middle position; heat oven to 300 degrees. Pat beef dry with paper towels and season with salt and pepper. Heat 2 teaspoons oil in Dutch oven over medium-high heat until beginning to smoke; add about one-third of beef to pot. Cook without moving until well browned, 2 to 3 minutes; using tongs, turn each piece and continue cooking until second side is well browned, about 5 minutes longer. Transfer browned beef to medium bowl. Repeat with 2 teaspoons oil and half of remaining beef. (If drippings in bottom of pot are very dark, add about ½ cup of chicken or beef broth and scrape pan bottom with wooden spoon to loosen browned bits; pour liquid into bowl with browned beef, then proceed.) Repeat once more with 2 teaspoons oil and remaining beef.

2. Add remaining 1 tablespoon oil to now-empty Dutch oven; reduce heat to medium-low. Add onions, ½ teaspoon salt, and tomato paste; cook, scraping bottom of pot to loosen browned bits, until onions have released some moisture, about 5 minutes. Increase heat to medium and continue to cook, stirring occasionally, until onions are lightly browned, 12 to 14 minutes. Stir in garlic and cook until fragrant, about 30 seconds. Add flour and stir until onions are evenly coated and flour is lightly browned, about 2 minutes. Stir in chicken and beef broths, scraping pan bottom to loosen browned bits; stir in beer, thyme, bay leaves, vinegar, browned beef with any accumulated juices, and salt and pepper to taste. Increase heat to medium-high and bring to simmer, stirring occasionally; cover partially, then place pot in oven. Cook until fork slips easily in and out of beef, about 2 hours.

3. Discard thyme and bay leaves. Season with salt and pepper to taste and serve. (Stew can be refrigerated for up to 2 days.)

BEEF BURGUNDY

✔ WHY THIS RECIPE WORKS

Classic beef Burgundy combines satisfyingly large chunks of tender meat with a velvety sauce brimming with the flavor of good Burgundy wine and studded with caramelized mushrooms and pearl onions. Unfortunately, we've seen too many versions of this rustic French dish end up with tough meat or a dull sauce. For the best beef Burgundy, we started by rendering salt pork until crisp, then browned large chunks of beef chuck roast in the rendered fat. For the braising liquid, a combination of chicken broth and water, enhanced with a small amount of dried porcini mushrooms and tomato paste, provided balanced, well-rounded flavor. Using anything less than a full bottle of red wine left the sauce lacking and unremarkable. We deglazed the pan twice, used a roux to thicken the sauce, and then added the wine. While the liquid reduced to a velvety sauce, we simmered pearl onions then sautéed them briefly with mushrooms to create the perfect garnish for our rich, tender beef.

TRIMMING BLADE STEAKS

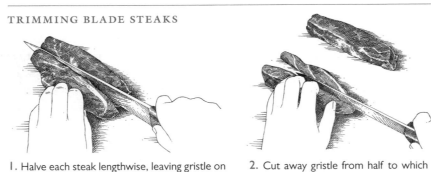

1. Halve each steak lengthwise, leaving gristle on one half.

2. Cut away gristle from half to which it is still attached, then cut trimmed meat into pieces.

BEEF BURGUNDY
SERVES 6

For the wine, we like to use a Burgundy or Pinot Noir. If you cannot find salt pork, thick-cut bacon can be substituted. Cut it crosswise into ¼-inch pieces and treat it just as you would salt pork, but note that you will have no rind to include in the vegetable and herb bouquet. Boiled potatoes are the traditional accompaniment, but mashed potatoes or buttered noodles are nice as well.

BEEF STEW

- 6 ounces salt pork, rind removed and reserved, salt pork cut into 1 by ¼ by ¼-inch pieces
- 2 onions, chopped coarse
- 2 carrots, chopped coarse
- 1 head garlic, cloves separated and crushed but unpeeled
- ½ ounce dried porcini mushrooms, rinsed (optional)
- 10 sprigs fresh parsley, torn into pieces
- 6 sprigs fresh thyme
- 2 bay leaves, crumbled
- ½ teaspoon whole black peppercorns
- 1 (4- to 4¼-pound) boneless beef chuck-eye roast, pulled apart at seams, trimmed, and cut into 1½- to 2-inch chunks
  Salt and pepper
- 2½ cups water
- 4 tablespoons unsalted butter, cut into 4 pieces
- ⅓ cup all-purpose flour
- 1¾ cups low-sodium chicken broth
- 1 (750-ml) bottle red wine
- 1 teaspoon tomato paste

ONION AND MUSHROOM GARNISH

- 1 cup frozen pearl onions, thawed
- 1 tablespoon unsalted butter
- 1 tablespoon sugar
  Salt and pepper
- ¾ cup water

- 10 ounces white mushrooms, trimmed, whole if small, halved if medium, quartered if large
- 2 tablespoons brandy
- 3 tablespoons minced fresh parsley

1. FOR THE STEW: Bring salt pork, reserved salt pork rind, and 3 cups water to boil in medium saucepan over high heat. Boil 2 minutes, then drain well.

2. Cut two 22-inch lengths cheesecloth and place on top of each other. Wrap onions, carrots, garlic, porcini mushrooms, parsley, thyme, bay leaves, peppercorns, and blanched salt pork rind in cheesecloth and set in Dutch oven. Adjust oven rack to lower-middle position and heat oven to 300 degrees.

3. Heat salt pork in large skillet over medium heat and cook until lightly browned and crisp, about 12 minutes. Using slotted spoon, transfer to pot; pour off all but 2 teaspoons fat and reserve. Season beef with salt and pepper. Increase heat to high and brown half of beef in single layer, turning once or twice, until deep brown, about 7 minutes; transfer browned

beef to pot. Pour ½ cup water into skillet and scrape pan to loosen browned bits; add liquid to pot.

4. Return skillet to high heat and add 2 teaspoons reserved pork fat; swirl to coat pan bottom. When fat begins to smoke, brown remaining beef in single layer, turning once or twice, until deep brown, about 7 minutes; transfer browned beef to pot. Pour ½ cup water into skillet and scrape pan to loosen browned bits; add liquid to pot.

5. Melt butter in now-empty skillet over medium heat. Whisk in flour until evenly moistened and cook, whisking constantly, until mixture has toasty aroma and resembles light-colored peanut butter, about 5 minutes. Gradually whisk in chicken broth and remaining 1½ cups water; increase heat to medium-high and bring to simmer, stirring frequently, until thickened. Pour mixture into pot. Add 3 cups wine, tomato paste, and salt and pepper to taste to pot and stir to combine. Set pot over high heat and bring to boil. Cover and transfer to oven; cook until meat is tender, 2½ to 3 hours.

6. Carefully remove pot from oven and,

TEST KITCHEN TIP NO. 24   HOW MUCH ALCOHOL IS COOKED OFF?

We are frequently asked how much alcohol is cooked off from wine, beer, and spirits used to flavor dishes. The common belief is that the alcohol (ethanol) completely burns off with time (or direct heat—see flambéing on page 757), but we've found out that it's not that simple.

When alcohol and water mix, they form a solution called an azeotrope—a mixture of two different liquids that behaves as if it were a single compound. Even though alcohol evaporates at a lower temperature than water, the vapors coming off of an alcohol-water azeotrope will contain both alcohol and water—they become inextricably mixed.

We measured the alcohol content of the stew liquid in our Beef Burgundy before it went into the oven. Every hour, we sampled the liquid to measure the alcohol concentration, and every time, it had dropped—but not as much as might be expected. After three hours of stewing, the alcohol concentration of the stew liquid had decreased by 60 percent. A major reason for the retention of alcohol in this dish is the use of a lid. If the surface of the liquid is not ventilated, alcohol vapor will accumulate, reducing further evaporation. Because most stews and braises are cooked in lidded pots, significant alcohol retention is the rule rather than the exception, even after hours of cooking.

Alcohol cooked in a skillet, say for a pan sauce, evaporates faster and more completely if allowed to reduce almost completely before liquids are added, though a certain percentage of alcohol will remain. Our conclusion? Though it is possible to remove the majority of alcohol in food through cooking, traces will always remain.

using tongs, transfer vegetable and herb bouquet to strainer set over pot. Press out liquid into pot and discard bouquet. With slotted spoon, remove beef to medium bowl; set aside. Allow braising liquid to settle for 15 minutes; with large spoon, skim fat from surface and discard.

7. Bring liquid in pot to boil over medium-high heat. Simmer briskly, stirring occasionally to ensure that bottom is not burning, until sauce is reduced to about 3 cups and thickened to consistency of heavy cream, 15 to 25 minutes.

8. FOR THE GARNISH: While sauce is reducing, bring pearl onions, butter, sugar, ¼ teaspoon salt, and ½ cup water to boil in medium skillet over high heat; cover and reduce heat to medium-low and simmer, shaking pan occasionally, until onions are tender, about 5 minutes. Uncover, increase heat to high, and simmer until all liquid evaporates, about 3 minutes. Add mushrooms and ¼ teaspoon salt; cook, stirring occasionally, until liquid released by mushrooms evaporates and vegetables are browned and glazed, about 5 minutes. Transfer vegetables to large plate and set aside. Add remaining ¼ cup water to skillet and stir to loosen browned bits. When pan bottom and sides are clean, add liquid to reducing sauce.

9. When sauce has reduced to about 3 cups and thickened to the consistency of heavy cream, reduce heat to medium-low; stir in beef, mushrooms and onions (and any accumulated juices), remaining wine from bottle, and brandy into pot. Cover pot and cook until just heated through, 5 to 8 minutes. Season with salt and pepper to taste and serve, sprinkling individual servings with minced parsley.

TO MAKE AHEAD: In step 6, use tongs to transfer vegetable and herb bouquet to mesh strainer set over pot. Press out liquid into pot and discard bouquet. Let beef cool to room temperature in liquid in pot, then cover and refrigerate for up to 2 days. With slotted spoon, skim fat from surface and

discard. Set pot over medium-high heat and bring to simmer; with slotted spoon remove beef to medium bowl and set aside. Simmer sauce briskly, stirring occasionally to ensure that bottom is not burning, until reduced to about 3 cups and thickened to consistency of heavy cream. Continue with recipe from step 8.

CLASSIC POT ROAST

✔ WHY THIS RECIPE WORKS

We started our pot roast by selecting a well-marbled chuck-eye roast. Splitting the roast along its natural seams meant we could trim off excess fat that would have made the finished dish greasy. Working with two smaller roasts instead of one large one also allowed us to cut back on cooking time. To beef up the gravy, we used a combination of water, beef broth, and red wine for the braising liquid. We also added a bit of glutamate-rich tomato paste. In the interest of streamlining, we determined that the initial sear called for in most pot roast recipes wasn't necessary—we found that the "dry" part of the meat that stays above the braising liquid eventually browns, even without searing. Blending the cooked vegetables with the defatted cooking liquid and extra beef broth gave us a full-bodied gravy, which we finished with a spoonful of balsamic vinegar and a bit more wine for brightness.

TYING MEAT FOR POT ROAST

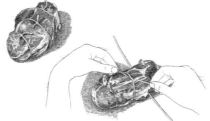

Tie 3 pieces of kitchen twine around each piece of meat so that the meat cooks evenly and doesn't fall apart.

CLASSIC POT ROAST
SERVES 6 TO 8

Chilling the whole cooked pot roast overnight improves its flavor and makes it moister and easier to slice.

- 1 (3½- to 4-pound) boneless beef chuck-eye roast, pulled apart at seams and trimmed
  Kosher salt and pepper
- 2 tablespoons unsalted butter
- 2 onions, halved and sliced thin
- 1 large carrot, peeled and chopped
- 1 celery rib, chopped
- 2 garlic cloves, minced
- 2–3 cups beef broth
- ¾ cup dry red wine
- 1 tablespoon tomato paste
- 1 bay leaf
- 1 sprig fresh thyme plus ¼ teaspoon chopped
- 1 tablespoon balsamic vinegar

1. Season pieces of meat with 1 tablespoon salt, place on wire rack set in rimmed baking sheet, and let stand at room temperature for 1 hour.

2. Adjust oven rack to lower-middle position and heat oven to 300 degrees. Melt butter in Dutch oven over medium heat. Add onions and cook, stirring occasionally, until softened and beginning to brown, 8 to 10 minutes. Add carrot and celery; continue to cook, stirring occasionally, about 5 minutes. Add garlic and cook until fragrant, about 30 seconds. Stir in 1 cup broth, ½ cup wine, tomato paste, bay leaf, and thyme sprig; bring to simmer.

3. Pat beef dry with paper towels and season with pepper. Tie 3 pieces of kitchen twine around each piece of meat into even shape.

4. Nestle meat on top of vegetables. Cover pot tightly with large piece of aluminum foil and cover with lid; transfer pot to oven. Cook beef until fully tender and fork slips easily in and out of meat, 3½ to

4 hours, turning meat halfway through cooking.

5. Transfer roasts to carving board and tent loosely with foil. Strain liquid through fine-mesh strainer into 4-cup liquid measuring cup. Discard bay leaf and thyme sprig. Transfer vegetables to blender. Let liquid settle for 5 minutes, then skim fat; add beef broth to bring liquid amount to 3 cups. Add liquid to blender and blend until smooth, about 2 minutes. Transfer sauce to medium saucepan and bring to simmer over medium heat.

6. Meanwhile, remove twine from roasts and slice against grain into ½-inch-thick slices. Transfer meat to serving platter. Stir remaining ¼ cup wine, chopped thyme, and vinegar into gravy and season with salt and pepper to taste. Spoon half of gravy over meat; pass remaining gravy separately.

TO MAKE AHEAD: Pot roast can be made up to 2 days ahead. Follow recipe through step 4, then transfer cooked roasts to large bowl. Strain and defat liquid and add beef broth to bring liquid amount to 3 cups; transfer liquid and vegetables to bowl with roasts, let cool for 1 hour, cover with plastic wrap, cut vents in plastic, and refrigerate overnight or up to 48 hours. One hour before serving, adjust oven rack to middle position and heat oven to 325 degrees. Slice roasts as directed, place in 13 by 9-inch baking dish, cover tightly with foil, and bake until heated through, about 45 minutes. Blend liquid and vegetables, bring gravy to simmer, and finish as directed.

CLASSIC POT ROAST WITH ROOT VEGETABLES

Add 1 pound carrots, peeled and cut into 2-inch pieces, 1 pound parsnips, peeled and cut into 2-inch pieces, and 1½ pounds russet potatoes, peeled and halved lengthwise, each half quartered, to pot after cooking beef for 3 hours. Continue to cook until beef is fully tender, 30 minutes to 1 hour longer. Transfer large pieces of carrot, parsnip, and potato to serving platter using slotted spoon, cover tightly with aluminum foil, and proceed with recipe as directed.

CLASSIC POT ROAST WITH MUSHROOM AND PRUNE GRAVY

Substitute ½ cup dark beer (porter or stout) for red wine. Add 1 ounce dried porcini mushrooms, rinsed, soaked for 1 hour, and drained, and ½ cup pitted prunes with broth and beer. While roast is resting, sauté 1 pound thinly sliced cremini mushrooms in 2 tablespoons butter until softened and lightly browned and add to finished gravy, along with ¼ cup dark beer instead of balsamic vinegar.

FRENCH-STYLE POT ROAST

✓ WHY THIS RECIPE WORKS
To update boeuf à la mode while maintaining its status as an elegant dish that takes the simple pot roast to a new level, we eliminated the fussy step of larding the beef, which involves inserting strips of fat into the meat. Instead we salted the meat and browned it in bacon drippings to add a little smoky flavor. Reducing the wine before adding it to the braising liquid maximized its complex fruit flavors and minimized sourness and astringency. This step also eliminated the need for a marinade. Since the braising liquid is used for the final sauce, we balanced the wine flavor by adding sautéed onion and garlic and large chunks of carrots. Our final challenge in updating the French-style pot roast was to achieve the proper consistency, which we managed to do not with pork trotters and split calves' feet, as is tradition, but by adding gelatin after the sauce had finished reducing.

FRENCH-STYLE POT ROAST
SERVES 6 TO 8

A medium-bodied, fruity red wine, such as a Côtes du Rhône or Pinot Noir, is best for this recipe. The gelatin lends richness and body to the finished sauce; don't omit it. Serve this dish with boiled potatoes, buttered noodles, or steamed rice.

1	(4- to 5-pound) boneless beef chuck-eye roast, pulled apart at seams and trimmed Kosher salt and pepper
1	(750-ml) bottle red wine
10	sprigs fresh parsley plus 2 tablespoons minced
2	sprigs fresh thyme
2	bay leaves
3	slices thick-cut bacon, cut into ¼-inch pieces
1	onion, chopped fine
3	garlic cloves, minced
1	tablespoon all-purpose flour
2	cups beef broth
4	carrots, peeled and cut on bias into 1½-inch pieces
2	cups frozen pearl onions, thawed
3	tablespoons unsalted butter
2	teaspoons sugar
¾	cup water
10	ounces white mushrooms, trimmed, halved if small and quartered if large
1	tablespoon unflavored gelatin

1. Season pieces of meat with 2 teaspoons salt, place on wire rack set in rimmed baking sheet, and let rest at room temperature for 1 hour.

2. Meanwhile, bring wine to simmer in large saucepan over medium-high heat. Cook until reduced to 2 cups, about 15 minutes. Using kitchen twine, tie parsley sprigs, thyme sprigs, and bay leaves into bundle.

3. Pat beef dry with paper towels and

season generously with pepper. Tie 3 pieces of kitchen twine around each piece of meat to keep it from falling apart.

4. Adjust oven rack to lower-middle position and heat oven to 300 degrees. Cook bacon in Dutch oven over medium-high heat, stirring occasionally, until crisp, 6 to 8 minutes. Using slotted spoon, transfer bacon to paper towel–lined plate and reserve. Pour off all but 2 tablespoons fat; return Dutch oven to medium-high heat and heat until fat begins to smoke. Add beef to pot and brown on all sides, 8 to 10 minutes total. Transfer beef to large plate and set aside.

5. Reduce heat to medium; add onion and cook, stirring occasionally, until beginning to soften, 2 to 4 minutes. Add garlic, flour, and reserved bacon; cook, stirring constantly, until fragrant, about 30 seconds. Add reduced wine, broth, and herb bundle, scraping bottom of pot to loosen browned bits. Return roast and any accumulated juices to pot; increase heat to high and bring liquid to simmer, then place large sheet of aluminum foil over pot and cover tightly with lid. Set pot in oven and cook, using tongs to turn beef every hour, until fork slips easily in and out of meat, 2½ to 3 hours, adding carrots to pot after 2 hours.

6. While meat cooks, bring pearl onions, butter, sugar, and ½ cup water to boil in large skillet over medium-high heat. Reduce heat to medium, cover, and cook until onions are tender, 5 to 8 minutes. Uncover, increase heat to medium-high, and cook until all liquid evaporates, 3 to 4 minutes. Add mushrooms and ¼ teaspoon salt; cook, stirring occasionally, until vegetables are browned and glazed, 8 to 12 minutes. Remove from heat and set aside. Place remaining ¼ cup cold water in small bowl and sprinkle gelatin on top.

7. Transfer beef to carving board; tent with foil to keep warm. Let braising liquid settle, about 5 minutes; using large spoon, skim fat from surface. Remove herb

bundle and stir in onion-mushroom mixture. Bring liquid to simmer over medium-high heat and cook until mixture is slightly thickened and reduced to 3¼ cups, 20 to 30 minutes. Season sauce with salt and pepper to taste. Add softened gelatin and stir until completely dissolved.

8. Remove twine from roasts and discard. Slice meat against grain into ½-inch-thick slices. Divide meat among warmed bowls or transfer to platter; arrange vegetables around meat, pour sauce over top, and sprinkle with minced parsley. Serve immediately.

TO MAKE AHEAD: Follow recipe through step 7, skipping step of softening and adding gelatin. Place meat back in pot, cool to room temperature, cover, and refrigerate for up to 2 days. To serve, slice beef and arrange in 13 by 9-inch baking dish. Bring sauce to simmer and stir in gelatin until completely dissolved. Pour warm sauce over meat, cover with foil, and bake in 350-degree oven until heated through, about 30 minutes.

BEEF BRAISED IN BAROLO

✔ WHY THIS RECIPE WORKS

This Italian spin on pot roast requires the famed Piedmontese wine Barolo—most bottles of which start at $30. For that kind of investment, we didn't want to risk tough and stringy meat in a weak, insipid sauce. We started with a chuck-eye roast, our favorite cut for pot roast recipes, split the roast in two, trimmed the fat, seasoned each half, and then tied the two pieces together. Using this process, we had not only a roast that wouldn't fall apart but one that was internally seasoned. Browning the roast in the fat rendered from pancetta added rich flavor. We had two breakthroughs when we turned our attention to the wine. First, we learned that we shouldn't reduce the wine because the flavor became too concentrated—just pouring the whole bottle into

the pot worked well. Second, we found that the Barolo is so bold-flavored that we needed something in the braising liquid to temper it, and that proved to be a can of diced tomatoes.

BEEF BRAISED IN BAROLO
SERVES 6

Purchase pancetta that is cut to order, about ¼ inch thick. If pancetta is not available, substitute an equal amount of meaty salt pork, cut it into ¼-inch cubes, and boil it in 3 cups of water for about 2 minutes to remove excess salt. After draining, use it as you would pancetta.

1	(3½-pound) boneless beef chuck-eye roast, pulled apart at seams and trimmed
4	ounces pancetta, cut into ¼-inch cubes
2	onions, chopped
2	carrots, chopped
2	celery ribs, chopped
1	tablespoon tomato paste
3	garlic cloves, minced
1	tablespoon all-purpose flour
½	teaspoon sugar
1	(750-ml) bottle Barolo wine
1	(14.5-ounce) can diced tomatoes, drained
10	sprigs fresh parsley
1	sprig fresh rosemary
1	sprig fresh thyme, plus 1 teaspoon minced

1. Adjust oven rack to middle position; heat oven to 300 degrees. Pat beef dry with paper towels, season with salt and pepper and tie both pieces together with kitchen twine. Place pancetta in 8-quart Dutch oven; cook over medium heat, stirring occasionally, until browned and crisp, about 8 minutes. Using slotted spoon, transfer pancetta to paper towel–lined plate and set aside. Pour off all but 2 tablespoons fat; set Dutch oven over medium-high heat and heat until beginning to smoke. Add

beef to pot and cook until well browned on all sides, about 8 minutes. Transfer beef to large plate and set aside.

2. Reduce heat to medium, add onions, carrots, celery, and tomato paste to pot and cook, stirring occasionally, until vegetables begin to soften and brown, about 6 minutes. Add garlic, flour, sugar, and reserved pancetta; cook, stirring constantly, until fragrant, about 30 seconds. Add wine and tomatoes, scraping bottom of pan to loosen browned bits; add parsley, rosemary, and thyme sprigs. Return roast and any accumulated juices to pot; increase heat to high and bring liquid to boil, then place large sheet of aluminum foil over pot and cover tightly with lid. Set pot in oven and cook, using tongs to turn beef every 45 minutes, until fork slips easily in and out of meat, about 3 hours.

3. Transfer beef to carving board; tent with foil to keep warm. Let braising liquid settle, about 5 minutes; using large spoon, skim fat from surface. Add minced thyme, bring liquid to boil over high heat, and cook, whisking vigorously to help vegetables break down, until mixture is thickened and reduced to about 3½ cups, about 18 minutes. Strain liquid through large fine-mesh strainer, pressing on solids to extract as much liquid as possible; you should have 1½ cups strained sauce (if necessary, return strained sauce to Dutch oven and reduce to 1½ cups). Discard solids in strainer. Season sauce with salt and pepper to taste.

4. Remove twine from roasts and discard. Slice meat against grain into ½-inch-thick slices. Divide meat among warmed bowls or plates; pour about ¼ cup sauce over top and serve immediately.

TO MAKE AHEAD: Follow recipe through step 2. Cool to room temperature, cover, and refrigerate for up to 2 days. To serve, skim fat from surface and gently warm until meat is heated through. Proceed with recipe from step 3.

BEEF STROGANOFF

✓ WHY THIS RECIPE WORKS

For a stroganoff with big beefy flavor, we substituted sirloin steak tips for the traditional, but expensive tenderloin. Marinating the meat in soy sauce made it just as tender as tenderloin. Pan-roasting the meat in larger pieces developed rich flavor and ensured against overcooked, dried-out beef, and letting it rest before cutting it into strips preserved its juiciness. While mushrooms aren't traditional, they're a popular addition. Microwaving the mushrooms released enough of their moisture so that they quickly browned along with the onions. As for the mustard, the traditional Russian choice, a sweet-hot blend, isn't widely available, so we replaced it with a paste made of dry mustard bloomed in hot water. We also found that the sauce benefited from the subtle depth provided by a small amount of tomato paste. Adding just a touch of sour cream to the sauce completed our ideal beef stroganoff by providing body and tang (which we enhanced with white wine) without overwhelming the other flavors.

BEEF STROGANOFF
SERVES 4

Steak tips, also known as flap meat, are sold as whole steak, cubes, and strips. To ensure uniform pieces that cook evenly, we prefer to purchase whole steak tips and cut them ourselves. One and a half pounds of blade steak can be substituted for the steak tips; if using, cut each steak in half lengthwise and remove the gristle that runs down the center before cooking. Since blade steak yields smaller strips of meat, reduce the cooking time in step 3 by several minutes. If the mushrooms are larger than 1 inch, cut them into 6 even wedges. Serve the stroganoff over buttered egg noodles.

1¼	pounds sirloin steak tips, trimmed and cut lengthwise with grain into 4 equal pieces
2	teaspoons soy sauce
1	pound white mushrooms, trimmed and quartered
1	tablespoon dry mustard
2	teaspoons hot water

TEST KITCHEN TIP NO. 25 WHEN SEASONINGS GO AWRY

It's happened to all of us: a dash that's more like a pinch, or a tablespoon when you meant to add a teaspoon. If you've added too much salt, sugar, or spice to a dish, the damage is done, but in mild cases, the overpowering ingredient can sometimes be masked by the addition of another from the opposite end of the flavor spectrum. The following chart offers ideas. To avoid future seasoning mishaps, remember to account for the reduction of liquids when seasoning a dish—a perfectly seasoned stew will likely taste too salty after several hours of simmering. Your best bet: season with a light hand during the cooking process, then adjust the seasoning just before serving.

IF YOUR FOOD IS...	ADD...	SUCH AS...
Too salty	An acid or sweetener	Vinegar, lemon or lime juice, unsalted canned tomatoes, sugar, honey, or maple syrup
Too sweet	An acid or seasonings	Vinegar, lemon or lime juice, chopped fresh herbs, a dash of cayenne, or, for sweet dishes, a bit of liqueur or instant espresso powder
Too spicy or acidic	A fat or sweetener	Butter, cream, sour cream, cheese, olive oil, sugar, honey, or maple syrup

1 teaspoon sugar
   Salt and pepper
1 tablespoon vegetable oil
1 onion, chopped fine
4 teaspoons all-purpose flour
2 teaspoons tomato paste
1½ cups beef broth
⅓ cup plus 1 tablespoon white wine
   or dry vermouth
½ cup sour cream
1 tablespoon chopped fresh parsley
   or dill

1. Using fork, poke each piece of steak 10 to 12 times. Place in baking dish; rub both sides evenly with soy sauce. Cover with plastic wrap and refrigerate at least 15 minutes or up to 1 hour.

2. While meat marinates, place mushrooms in medium bowl, cover, and microwave until mushrooms have decreased in volume by half, 4 to 5 minutes (there should be as much as ¼ cup liquid in bowl). Drain mushrooms and set aside; discard liquid. Combine mustard, water, sugar, and ½ teaspoon pepper in small bowl until smooth paste forms; set aside.

3. Pat steak pieces dry with paper towels and season with pepper. Heat oil in 12-inch skillet over medium-high heat until just smoking. Place steak pieces in skillet and cook until browned on all sides and meat registers 125 to 130 degrees, 6 to 9 minutes. Transfer meat to large plate and set aside while cooking sauce.

4. Add mushrooms, onion, and ½ teaspoon salt to skillet and cook until vegetables begin to brown and dark bits form on bottom of pan, 6 to 8 minutes. Add flour and tomato paste and cook, stirring constantly, until onions and mushrooms are coated, about 1 minute. Stir in beef broth, ⅓ cup wine, and mustard paste and bring to simmer, scraping bottom of pan to loosen browned bits. Reduce heat to medium and cook until sauce has reduced slightly and begun to thicken, 4 to 6 minutes.

5. While sauce is reducing, cut steak pieces across grain into ¼-inch-thick slices. Stir meat and any accumulated juices into thickened sauce and cook until beef has warmed through, 1 to 2 minutes. Remove pan from heat and let any bubbles subside. Stir in sour cream and remaining tablespoon wine; season with salt and pepper to taste. Sprinkle with parsley and serve.

POT-AU-FEU

✔ WHY THIS RECIPE WORKS
Pot-au-feu, literally translated as "pot on fire" (referring to the stovetop simmering method), is the French version of boiled dinner. But boiled dinners are notorious for their washed-out flavor and bland meat and vegetables. We wanted a pot-au-feu with a broth flavorful enough to serve as its own course with crusty bread, followed by the sliced, meltingly tender beef and an assortment of perfectly cooked vegetables, all presented family-style alongside traditional condiments such as horseradish, cornichons, and mustard. We used three cuts of beef—chuck-eye, short ribs, and beef shanks—and batch-cooked the vegetables separately in salted water so they were perfectly cooked. To cook the beef, we sautéed carrots, onions, and celery in a little oil until they begin to exude their juices and cut the amount of water for the richest possible broth.

POT-AU-FEU
SERVES 8 TO 10

A stockpot with at least a 12-quart capacity is necessary for this recipe. Cheesecloth is ideal for straining the broth, although a quadruple layer of paper towels will do in a pinch. Once the beef braise reaches a boil, reduce the heat to maintain a steady simmer; if left to boil, the resulting broth will be murky. We prefer to use small red potatoes, measuring 1 to 2 inches in diameter, in this recipe. For serving, arrange the meat and vegetables on a large warmed platter and give diners individual shallow soup bowls to serve themselves.

BEEF BRAISE
2 onions, chopped
2 carrots, chopped
1 celery rib, chopped
2 teaspoons vegetable oil
1 (3-pound) beef chuck-eye roast,
   trimmed and tied
3 pounds beef short ribs (about
   5 large ribs), trimmed and tied
2 pounds beef shanks, 1½ inches
   thick, trimmed and tied
20 cups water
3 bay leaves
1 teaspoon whole black peppercorns
5 whole cloves
1 large head garlic, outer papery skins
   removed and top third of head cut
   off and discarded
10 sprigs fresh parsley
8 sprigs fresh thyme
1 tablespoon salt

VEGETABLES
2 pounds small red potatoes, halved if
   larger than 1½ inches
2 tablespoons salt
1½ pounds carrots, peeled, halved
   crosswise, thicker half quartered
   lengthwise, thinner half halved
   lengthwise
1½ pounds parsnips, peeled, halved
   crosswise, thicker half quartered
   lengthwise, thinner half halved
   lengthwise
1 pound green beans, trimmed

GARNISHES AND CONDIMENTS
¼ cup chopped fresh parsley
1 baguette, sliced thick
   Dijon mustard or whole grain
   mustard
   Sea salt
   Cornichons
   Prepared horseradish

1. FOR THE BEEF BRAISE: Combine onions, carrots, celery, and oil in large stockpot; cook, covered, over low heat, stirring frequently, until vegetables are softened but not browned, 8 to 10 minutes. (If vegetables begin to brown before softening, add 1 tablespoon water and continue to cook.) Add roast, ribs, shanks, water, bay leaves, peppercorns, and cloves; increase heat to medium-high and bring to boil, using large spoon to skim any fat. Reduce heat to low and simmer, uncovered, for 2½ hours, skimming surface of fat every 30 minutes.

2. Add garlic, parsley stems, thyme, and salt. Simmer until tip of paring knife inserted into meats meets little resistance, 1 to 1½ hours.

3. Using tongs, transfer roast, ribs, shanks, and garlic to large carving board and tent with aluminum foil. Strain broth through mesh strainer lined with double layer cheesecloth into large container (you should have about 12 cups liquid). Let broth settle for at least 5 minutes; using large spoon, skim fat from surface.

4. FOR THE VEGETABLES: While broth settles, rinse out stockpot and add potatoes, salt, and 16 cups water; bring to boil over high heat and cook for 7 minutes. Add carrots and parsnips and cook for 3 minutes. Add green beans and cook for 4 minutes. Using slotted spoon, transfer vegetables to large serving platter and tent with foil.

5. Using tongs, squeeze garlic cloves out of skins and into small serving bowl. Remove twine from roast and separate roast at its seams; cut roast across grain into ½-inch-thick slices and transfer to platter with vegetables. Remove twine from shanks and ribs and arrange on platter. Ladle about 1 cup broth over meat and vegetables and sprinkle with parsley. Serve, ladling broth over individual servings and passing garlic, baguette, and condiments separately.

BRAISED BONELESS BEEF SHORT RIBS

✓ WHY THIS RECIPE WORKS

Short ribs have great flavor and luscious texture, but they can release a lot of fat during cooking, necessitating an overnight rest so the fat can solidify into an easy-to-remove layer. We wanted a more convenient (and less time-consuming) approach, so we decided to make the most of boneless short ribs, which traditionally render less fat. To restore the body that the bones' connective tissue would have added, we sprinkled a bit of gelatin into the sauce. To ramp up the richness of the sauce, we reduced wine with browned aromatics (onions, garlic, and carrots) before using the liquid to cook the meat. As for the excess fat, the level was low enough that we could strain and defat the liquid in a fat separator. Reducing the liquid concentrated the flavors and made for a rich, luxurious sauce for our fork-tender boneless short ribs.

BRAISED BONELESS BEEF SHORT RIBS

SERVES 6

Make sure that the ribs are at least 4 inches long and 1 inch thick. If boneless ribs are unavailable, substitute 7 pounds of bone-in beef short ribs at least 4 inches long with 1 inch of meat above the bone. To remove the meat from the bone, see the illustrations. We recommend a bold red wine such as a Cabernet Sauvignon. Serve with buttered egg noodles, mashed potatoes, or roasted potatoes.

3½ pounds boneless beef short ribs, trimmed
    Kosher salt and pepper
2   tablespoons vegetable oil
2   large onions, sliced thin
1   tablespoon tomato paste
6   garlic cloves, peeled
2   cups red wine
1   cup beef broth
4   large carrots, peeled and cut into 2-inch pieces
4   sprigs fresh thyme
1   bay leaf
¼   cup cold water
½   teaspoon unflavored gelatin

1. Adjust oven rack to lower-middle position and heat oven to 300 degrees. Pat beef dry with paper towels and season with 2 teaspoons salt and 1 teaspoon pepper. Heat 1 tablespoon oil in Dutch oven over medium-high heat until smoking. Add half of beef and cook, without moving, until well browned, 4 to 6 minutes. Turn beef and continue to cook on second side until well browned, 4 to 6 minutes longer, reducing heat if fat begins to smoke. Transfer beef to medium bowl. Repeat with remaining 1 tablespoon oil and meat.

2. Reduce heat to medium, add onions, and cook, stirring occasionally, until softened and beginning to brown, 12 to 15 minutes. (If onions begin to darken too quickly, add 1 to 2 tablespoons water to pan.) Add tomato paste and cook, stirring

BONING SHORT RIBS

1. With chef's knife as close as possible to bone, carefully remove meat.

2. Trim excess hard fat and silver skin from both sides of meat.

constantly, until it browns on sides and bottom of pan, about 2 minutes. Add garlic and cook until fragrant, about 30 seconds. Increase heat to medium-high, add wine and simmer, scraping bottom of pan to loosen browned bits, until reduced by half, 8 to 10 minutes. Add broth, carrots, thyme, and bay leaf. Add beef and any accumulated juices to pot; cover and bring to simmer. Transfer pot to oven and cook, turning meat twice during cooking, until fork slips easily in and out of meat, 2 to 2½ hours.

3. Place water in small bowl and sprinkle gelatin on top; let stand at least 5 minutes. Using tongs, transfer meat and carrots to serving platter and tent with aluminum foil. Strain cooking liquid through fine-mesh strainer into fat separator or bowl, pressing on solids to extract as much liquid as possible; discard solids. Let liquid settle for 5 minutes and strain off fat. Return cooking liquid to pot and cook over medium heat until reduced to 1 cup, 5 to 10 minutes. Remove from heat and stir in gelatin mixture; season with salt and pepper to taste. Pour sauce over meat and serve.

BRAISED BONELESS BEEF SHORT RIBS WITH GUINNESS AND PRUNES

Substitute 1 cup Guinness (or other full-flavored porter or stout) for red wine and omit wine reduction time in step 2. Add ⅓ cup pitted prunes to pot along with broth.

SHORT RIBS BRAISED IN RED WINE

✔ WHY THIS RECIPE WORKS

Bone-in braised short ribs are a terrific make-ahead option when cooking for company since it's best to rest them over night before serving. Most recipes call for a time-consuming stovetop browning strategy, but we wanted a simpler option. We opted to brown the short ribs all at once in the oven, which allowed the ribs to spend more time in the heat, maximizing the amount of fat rendered. To supplement the flavor lost from not browning our meat on the stovetop, we made sure lots of savory ingredients were added to the mix—a hefty amount of garlic, red wine, rosemary, thyme, and tomato paste made the cut. Plenty of fat still came out in the braise, so we let the braised ribs rest to allow the fat to separate out and solidify. Once solidified, the fat was easy to scoop off the top. Crisped bacon and sautéed pearl onions and parsnips added crunch and sweetness to our tender, succulent short ribs.

SHORT RIBS BRAISED IN RED WINE WITH BACON, PARSNIPS, AND PEARL ONIONS

SERVES 6

If braising and serving the ribs on the same day, bypass cooling the ribs in the braising liquid; instead, remove them from the pot straight out of the oven, strain the liquid, then let it settle so that the fat separates to the top. With a wide shallow spoon, skim off as much fat as possible and continue with the recipe. This recipe will work with either English-style short ribs or flanken-style short ribs. We recommend a full-bodied red wine, such as a Cabernet Sauvignon.

STEW

6 pounds bone-in English-style beef short ribs, trimmed, or bone-in flanken-style beef short ribs, trimmed
   Salt and Pepper
3 cups dry red wine

3   large onions, chopped
2   carrots, chopped
1   large celery rib, chopped
9   garlic cloves, chopped
¼   cup all-purpose flour
4   cups low-sodium chicken broth
1   (14.5-ounce) can diced tomatoes, drained
1½ tablespoons minced fresh rosemary
1   tablespoon minced fresh thyme
3   bay leaves
1   teaspoon tomato paste

BACON, PEARL ONION, AND PARSNIP GARNISH

6   slices bacon, cut into ¼-inch pieces
10 ounces parsnips, peeled and cut diagonally into ¾-inch pieces
1   cup frozen pearl onions, thawed
¼   teaspoon granulated sugar
¼   teaspoon salt
6   tablespoons chopped fresh parsley

1. FOR THE STEW: Adjust oven rack to lower-middle position and heat oven to 450 degrees. Arrange short ribs bone side down in single layer in large roasting pan; season with salt and pepper. Roast until meat begins to brown, about 45 minutes; drain off all liquid. Return pan to oven and continue to cook until meat is well browned, 15 to 20 minutes longer. (For flanken-style short ribs, continue to cook until browned, about 8 minutes; using tongs, flip each piece and cook until second side is browned, about 8 minutes longer.) Transfer ribs to large plate; set aside. Drain off and reserve fat. Reduce oven temperature to 300 degrees. Heat roasting pan on 2 stovetop burners over medium heat; add wine and bring to simmer, scraping up browned bits. Set pan with wine aside.

2. Heat 2 tablespoons reserved fat in Dutch oven over medium-high heat; add onions, carrots, and celery and cook, stirring occasionally, until vegetables soften,

about 12 minutes. Add garlic and cook until fragrant, about 30 seconds. Stir in flour until combined, about 45 seconds. Stir in wine from roasting pan, broth, tomatoes, rosemary, thyme, bay leaves, tomato paste, and salt and pepper to taste. Bring to boil and add ribs, completely submerging meat in liquid; return to boil, cover, transfer to oven, and simmer until ribs are tender, 2 to 2½ hours. Transfer pot to wire rack and cool, partially covered, until warm, about 2 hours.

3. Transfer ribs to large plate and discard loose bones. Strain braising liquid into medium bowl, pressing out liquid from solids; discard solids. Cover ribs and liquid separately and refrigerate overnight. (Ribs and liquid can be refrigerated up to 3 days.)

4. FOR THE GARNISH: In Dutch oven, cook bacon over medium heat until just crisp, 8 to 10 minutes; using slotted spoon, transfer to paper towel–lined plate. Add parsnips, pearl onions, sugar, and salt to pot and cook over high heat, stirring occasionally, until browned, about 5 minutes. Spoon off and discard solidified fat from reserved braising liquid. Add defatted liquid and bring to simmer, stirring occasionally; season with salt and pepper to taste. Submerge ribs in liquid, return to simmer. Reduce heat to medium and cook, partially covered, until ribs are heated through and vegetables are tender, about 5 minutes longer; gently stir in bacon. Divide ribs and sauce among individual bowls, sprinkle each with 1 tablespoon parsley, and serve.

PORTER-BRAISED SHORT RIBS WITH PRUNES, BRANDY, AND LEMON ESSENCE

Brandy-soaked prunes take the place of vegetables here, so this version is particularly suited to a mashed root vegetable or potato accompaniment.

Substitute 3 cups porter beer for red wine, omit rosemary, and substitute 2 tablespoons Dijon mustard and 2 teaspoons Worcestershire sauce for tomato paste. Continue with recipe through step 3. For garnish, bring ½ cup brandy to boil in small saucepan; off heat, add 8 ounces pitted prunes, halved, and let stand until plump and softened, about 15 minutes. Meanwhile, spoon off and discard fat from braising liquid. Bring liquid to boil in Dutch oven over medium-high heat, stirring occasionally. Add prunes, brandy, and 2 teaspoons brown sugar; season with salt and pepper to taste. Submerge ribs in liquid and return to simmer. Reduce heat to medium-low and cook until ribs are heated through, about 5 minutes longer; gently stir in 2 teaspoons grated lemon zest. Divide ribs and sauce among individual bowls, sprinkle each with 1 tablespoon parsley, and serve.

ONION-BRAISED BEEF BRISKET

✔ WHY THIS RECIPE WORKS

While brisket is naturally flavorful, it can be hard to keep it moist and tender because the fat is all on the surface; there's no marbling to keep the interior moist. We wondered if replacing some of the moisture after braising might help. We left the meat in the sauce after cooking it, and after about an hour there was a noticeable difference. Refrigerating the cooked meat and sauce overnight was even better. The meat reabsorbed some of the liquid, becoming more moist and easier to carve without shredding. The sauce—based on red wine, chicken broth, and lots of onions—had improved as well; the fat had risen to the surface and congealed, making it easier to remove. All we had to do was reheat the sliced meat in the sauce, and this hearty dish was ready.

ONION-BRAISED BEEF BRISKET
SERVES 6 TO 8

This recipe requires a few hours of unattended cooking as well as advance preparation. After cooking, the brisket must stand overnight in the braising liquid that later becomes the sauce; this helps to keep the brisket moist and flavorful. Defatting the sauce is essential. If you prefer a spicy sauce, increase the amount of cayenne pepper to ¼ teaspoon. You will need 18-inch-wide heavy-duty aluminum foil for this recipe. Good accompaniments to braised brisket include mashed potatoes and buttered egg noodles. Matzo meal or potato starch can be substituted for the flour.

1	(4- to 5- pound) beef brisket, flat cut preferred, trimmed
	Salt and pepper
	Vegetable oil
2½	pounds onions, halved and sliced ½ inch thick
1	tablespoon brown sugar
3	garlic cloves, minced
1	tablespoon tomato paste
1	tablespoon paprika
⅛	teaspoon cayenne pepper
2	tablespoons all-purpose flour
1	cup low-sodium chicken broth
1	cup dry red wine
3	bay leaves
3	sprigs fresh thyme
2	teaspoons cider vinegar

1. Adjust oven rack to lower-middle position and heat oven to 300 degrees. Line 13 by 9-inch baking dish with two 24-inch-long sheets of 18-inch-wide heavy-duty foil, positioning sheets perpendicular to each other and allowing excess foil to extend beyond edges of pan. Pat brisket dry with paper towels. Place brisket fat side up on cutting board; using dinner fork, poke holes in meat through fat layer about 1 inch apart. Season both sides of brisket with salt and pepper.

2. Heat 1 teaspoon oil in 12-inch skillet over medium-high heat until oil just begins to smoke. Place brisket, fat side up, in skillet (brisket may climb up sides of pan); weight brisket with heavy Dutch oven or cast-iron skillet and cook until well browned, about 7 minutes. Remove Dutch oven; using tongs, flip brisket and cook on second side without weight until well browned, about 7 minutes longer. Transfer brisket to platter.

3. Pour off all but 1 tablespoon fat from pan (or, if brisket was lean, add enough oil to fat in skillet to equal 1 tablespoon); stir in onions, sugar, and ¼ teaspoon salt and cook over medium-high heat, stirring occasionally, until onions are softened, 10 to 12 minutes. Add garlic and cook, stirring frequently, until fragrant, about 1 minute; add tomato paste and cook, stirring to combine, until paste darkens, about 2 minutes. Add paprika and cayenne and cook, stirring constantly, until fragrant, about 1 minute. Add flour and cook, stirring constantly, until well combined, about 2 minutes. Add broth, wine, bay leaves, and thyme, stirring to scrape up browned bits from pan; bring to simmer and simmer for 5 minutes to fully thicken.

4. Pour sauce and onions into foil-lined baking dish. Nestle brisket, fat side up, in sauce and onions. Fold foil extensions over and seal (do not tightly crimp foil because foil must later be opened to test for doneness). Place in oven and cook until fork slips easily in and out of meat, 3½ to 4 hours (when testing for doneness, open foil with caution as contents will be steaming). Carefully open foil and let brisket cool at room temperature, 20 to 30 minutes.

5. Transfer brisket to large bowl; set fine-mesh strainer over bowl and strain sauce over brisket. Discard bay leaves and thyme from onions and transfer onions to small bowl. Cover both bowls with plastic wrap, cut vents in plastic, and refrigerate overnight.

6. About 45 minutes before serving, adjust oven rack to lower-middle position; heat oven to 350 degrees. While oven heats, transfer cold brisket to carving board. Scrape off and discard any fat from surface of sauce, then heat sauce in medium saucepan over medium heat until warm, skimming any fat on surface with wide shallow spoon (you should have about 2 cups sauce without onions; if necessary, simmer sauce over medium-high heat until reduced to 2 cups). Slice brisket against grain into ¼-inch-thick slices and place slices in 13 by 9-inch baking dish. Stir reserved onions and vinegar into warmed sauce and season with salt and pepper to taste. Pour sauce over brisket slices, cover baking dish with foil, and bake until heated through, 25 to 30 minutes. Serve immediately.

SAME-DAY ONION-BRAISED BEEF BRISKET

After removing brisket from oven in step 4, reseal foil and let brisket sit at room temperature for 1 hour. Transfer brisket to carving board and continue with straining, defatting, and reheating sauce and slicing meat; omit step of returning brisket to oven once reheated sauce is poured over it.

CORNED BEEF AND CABBAGE

✔ WHY THIS RECIPE WORKS
We wanted a corned beef and cabbage dish with a full-flavored medley of meaty, tender, well-seasoned beef; subtle spice; and sweet, earthy, vegetables, each distinct in flavor and texture. For our home-corned beef recipe, we selected point-cut brisket, which is thicker and fattier than the flat-cut brisket. Staggering the addition of the vegetables, based on their cooking times, ensured that nothing overcooked and became washed out. Finally, we brought everything together at the end for the perfect combination of flavors and textures.

NEW ENGLAND–STYLE CORNED BEEF AND CABBAGE
SERVES 8 TO 10

If you prefer a leaner piece of meat, feel free to use the flat cut. Leave a bit of fat attached for better texture and flavor. The meat is cooked fully when it is tender, the muscle fibers have loosened visibly, and a skewer slides in with minimal resistance. Serve with horseradish, either plain or mixed with sour cream, or with grainy mustard.

½	cup kosher salt
1	tablespoon black peppercorns, cracked
1	tablespoon dried thyme
2¼	teaspoons ground allspice
1½	teaspoons paprika
2	bay leaves, crumbled
1	(4- to 6- pound) beef brisket, preferably point cut, trimmed, rinsed, and patted dry
7–8	pounds vegetables, chosen from categories below

SLOWER-COOKING VEGETABLES
Carrots, peeled and halved crosswise, thin end halved lengthwise, thick end quartered lengthwise
Rutabagas (small), peeled and halved crosswise; each half cut into 6 chunks
Turnips, peeled and quartered
Red potatoes (small), scrubbed and left whole
Boiling onions (small), peeled and left whole

FASTER-COOKING VEGETABLES
Green cabbage (1 small head),
uncored and cut into 6 to 8 wedges
Parsnips, peeled and halved
crosswise, thin end halved
lengthwise, thick end quartered
lengthwise
Brussels sprouts, trimmed

1. Combine salt, peppercorns, thyme, allspice, paprika, and bay leaves in small bowl. Poke brisket about 30 times per side with fork or metal skewer. Rub each side evenly with salt mixture; place in 2-gallon zipper-lock bag, forcing out as much air as possible. Place in pan large enough to hold it, cover with second, similar-size pan, and weight with 2 bricks or heavy cans. Refrigerate 5 to 7 days, turning once a day.

2. Rinse brisket and pat it dry. Place brisket in large stockpot, add water to cover, and bring to boil, skimming the surface. Cover and simmer until skewer inserted in thickest part of brisket slides out easily, 2 to 3 hours.

3. Heat oven to 200 degrees. Transfer meat to large platter and ladle about 1 cup cooking liquid over top to keep it moist. Cover with aluminum foil and set in oven.

4. Add vegetables from category 1 to pot and bring to boil; cover and simmer until vegetables begin to soften, about 10 minutes. Add vegetables from category 2 and bring to boil; cover and simmer until all vegetables are tender, 10 to 15 minutes longer.

5. Meanwhile, remove meat from oven and slice across grain into ¼-inch slices. Transfer vegetables to platter, drizzle with broth, and serve.

BRAISED LAMB SHOULDER CHOPS WITH TOMATOES AND RED WINE

✓ WHY THIS RECIPE WORKS
When buying lamb, many people turn to the tried, true, and expensive rib or loin chop. The oddly shaped, much less expensive shoulder chop rarely gets a second look, which is unfortunate because it is less exacting to cook and a few chops make for a speedy weeknight supper. Because they aren't a tough cut of meat, lamb shoulder chops don't need to cook for a long time for the sake of tenderness—we found a much shorter braise worked well. After just 15 to 20 minutes, the lamb was tender, and the much-anticipated sauce we made with the deglazing liquid, using onion, garlic, red wine, and tomatoes, was delicious.

BRAISED LAMB SHOULDER CHOPS WITH TOMATOES AND RED WINE
SERVES 4

Because they are generally leaner, round bone chops, also called arm chops, are preferable for this braise. If available, however, lean blade chops also braise nicely.

4	lamb shoulder chops, about ¾ inch thick, trimmed
	Salt and pepper
2	tablespoons olive oil
1	small onion, chopped fine
2	small garlic cloves, minced
⅓	cup dry red wine
1	cup canned whole peeled tomatoes, chopped
2	tablespoons minced fresh parsley

1. Season chops with salt and pepper. Heat 1 tablespoon oil in 12-inch skillet over medium-high heat. Brown chops, in batches if necessary, on both sides, 4 to 5 minutes. Set aside.

2. Pour off fat from pan. Add remaining 1 tablespoon oil and heat over medium heat. Add onion and cook until softened, about 4 minutes. Add garlic and cook until fragrant, about 30 seconds longer. Add wine and simmer until reduced by half, scraping to loosen browned bits from bottom of pan, 2 to 3 minutes. Stir in tomatoes, then return chops to pan. Reduce heat to low and cover and simmer until chops are cooked through and tender, 15 to 20 minutes.

3. Transfer chops to individual plates. Stir parsley into sauce and simmer until sauce thickens, 2 to 3 minutes. Season with salt and pepper to taste, spoon sauce over each chop, and serve.

BRAISED LAMB SHOULDER CHOPS WITH TOMATOES, ROSEMARY, AND OLIVES

Add 1 tablespoon minced fresh rosemary with garlic and stir in ⅓ cup pitted and sliced kalamata olives with tomatoes.

BRAISED LAMB SHOULDER CHOPS WITH CAPERS, BALSAMIC VINEGAR, AND RED PEPPER

Add 1 diced red bell pepper with onion and stir in 2 tablespoons rinsed capers and 2 tablespoons balsamic vinegar with parsley.

BRAISED LAMB SHOULDER CHOPS WITH FIGS AND NORTH AFRICAN SPICES

Soak ⅓ cup dried figs in ⅓ cup warm water for 30 minutes. Drain and reserve liquid and cut figs into quarters. Add 1 teaspoon ground coriander, ½ teaspoon ground cumin, ½ teaspoon cinnamon, and ⅛ teaspoon cayenne pepper with garlic. Omit red wine and replace with ⅓ cup soaking water from figs. Add 2 tablespoons honey with tomatoes. Stir figs in with parsley.

LAMB SHANKS BRAISED IN RED WINE WITH HERBES DE PROVENCE

✔ WHY THIS RECIPE WORKS

Lamb shanks are flavorful cuts of meat, but they're full of connective tissue that needs to be properly cooked down to guarantee tender, juicy (not tough) meat. For our lamb shanks, we found that we preferred to braise them in the oven rather than on the stovetop, as the oven provided more even, gentle heat. Browning the shanks over high heat in a skillet first added intense flavor. Braising the shanks in chicken broth (which complemented, rather than overpowered, the lamb, as beef or veal stock might have), white wine, and herbs flavored the shanks throughout.

LAMB SHANKS BRAISED IN RED WINE WITH HERBES DE PROVENCE
SERVES 6

If you're using smaller shanks than the ones called for in this recipe, reduce the braising time by up to 30 minutes. Serve with polenta or mashed potatoes. Côtes du Rhône works particularly well here.

- 6 (12- to 16-ounce) lamb shanks, trimmed
  Salt and pepper
- 2 tablespoons vegetable oil
- 3 carrots, peeled and cut into 2-inch pieces
- 2 onions, sliced thick
- 2 celery ribs, cut into 2-inch pieces
- 4 garlic cloves, minced
- 2 tablespoons tomato paste
- 1 tablespoon herbes de Provence
- 2 cups dry red wine
- 3 cups low-sodium chicken broth

1. Adjust oven rack to middle position and heat oven to 350 degrees. Pat lamb shanks dry and season with salt. Heat oil in Dutch oven over medium-high heat until just smoking. Brown half of shanks on all sides, 7 to 10 minutes. Transfer shanks to large plate and repeat with remaining tablespoon oil and remaining lamb shanks.

2. Drain all but 2 tablespoons fat off pan. Add carrots, onions, celery, garlic, tomato paste, herbes de Provence, and pinch salt and cook until vegetables are just starting to soften, 3 to 4 minutes. Stir in wine, then broth, scraping up browned bits on bottom of pan, and bring to simmer. Nestle shanks, along with any accumulated juices, into pot.

3. Bring to simmer, cover pot, transfer to oven, and cook for 1½ hours. Uncover and continue to cook until tops of shanks are browned, about 30 minutes. Flip shanks and continue to cook until remaining sides are browned and fork slips easily in and out of shanks, 15 to 30 minutes longer.

4. Remove pot from oven and let rest for 15 minutes. Using tongs, transfer shanks and vegetables to large plate and tent with aluminum foil. Skim fat from braising liquid and season with salt and pepper to taste. Return shanks to braising liquid to warm through before serving.

LAMB SHANKS BRAISED WITH WHITE BEANS, SWISS CHARD, AND MARJORAM

Substitute 2 teaspoons minced fresh marjoram or 1 teaspoon dried for herbes de Provence and dry white wine for red wine. After skimming excess fat from braising liquid, add 1 recipe Simple Cannellini Beans (page 240), 3 ounces stemmed, chopped Swiss chard, and 1 teaspoon more minced fresh marjoram. Cook over medium heat until greens wilt and flavors meld, about 5 minutes. Spoon over each shank; serve.

LAMB SHANKS BRAISED WITH LEMON AND MINT

Add 1 quartered lemon to braising liquid. Substitute 1 tablespoon minced fresh mint for herbes de Provence and substitute dry white wine for red wine. After skimming fat from braising liquid, stir in 1 tablespoon grated lemon zest and 1 tablespoon more minced fresh mint.

LAMB SHANKS BRAISED WITH NORTH AFRICAN SPICES

Serve with couscous and one or more of the following: sautéed onion, lemon zest, parsley, mint, toasted almonds, or ras al hanout (recipe follows).

Substitute 2 tablespoons ras al hanout for herbes de Provence. Add 2 minced ancho chile peppers (or 2 or 3 jalapeños) to onions, carrots, and celery.

RAS AL HANOUT
MAKES ABOUT ½ CUP

- 8 allspice berries
- 8 cardamom pods
- 15 whole black peppercorns
- 1 (½-inch) cinnamon stick
- 1 tablespoon ground ginger
- 1 teaspoon fennel seeds
- 1 teaspoon coriander seeds
- 1 teaspoon ground nutmeg
- ½ teaspoon anise seeds
- ½ teaspoon cumin seeds
- ⅛ teaspoon red pepper flakes
- ⅛ teaspoon mace

Combine all ingredients and, using spice grinder, grind to fine powder. Transfer to small bowl.

TEST KITCHEN TIP NO. 26 HERBES DE PROVENCE

Herbes de Provence is a mixture representative of those herbs used most frequently in the south of France. Usually a combination of basil, fennel seed, lavender, marjoram, rosemary, sage, summer savory, and thyme, herbes de Provence can be found in most large grocery stores or ordered online.

CHAPTER 5 Curries, Stir-Fries, and
Asian Noodle Dishes

CHICKEN TIKKA MASALA

✔ WHY THIS RECIPE WORKS

Though arguably the most popular Indian restaurant dish, chicken tikka masala is not actually authentic—it was invented in a London curry house. Recipes we found produced dry chicken and sauces that were unbearably rich and/or overspiced. We wanted an approachable method for producing moist, tender chunks of chicken in a rich, lightly spiced tomato sauce. To season the chicken, we rubbed it with salt, coriander, cumin, and cayenne and refrigerated it. Then we dipped it in yogurt mixed with oil, garlic, and ginger and broiled it. Since large pieces don't dry out as quickly as smaller ones under the broiler, we cooked the chicken breasts whole, cutting them into pieces only after cooking. While the chicken was cooking, we made the masala sauce. The ingredients in a masala sauce depend on the whim of the cook, although tomatoes and cream are always present. We added onion, ginger, garlic, chile, and a readily available commercial garam masala spice mixture. A little tomato paste and sugar gave our sauce color and sweetness.

CHICKEN TIKKA MASALA
SERVES 4 TO 6

This dish is best when prepared with whole-milk yogurt, but low-fat yogurt can be substituted. For a spicier dish, do not remove the ribs and seeds from the chile. If you prefer, substitute 2 teaspoons ground coriander, ¼ teaspoon ground cardamom, ¼ teaspoon ground cinnamon, and ½ teaspoon ground black pepper for the garam masala. Serve with Basmati Rice Pilaf (page 223).

CHICKEN
I	teaspoon salt
½	teaspoon ground cumin
½	teaspoon ground coriander
¼	teaspoon cayenne pepper

2	pounds boneless, skinless chicken breasts, trimmed
I	cup plain whole-milk yogurt
2	tablespoons vegetable oil
I	tablespoon grated fresh ginger
2	garlic cloves, minced

SAUCE
3	tablespoons vegetable oil
I	onion, chopped fine
2	garlic cloves, minced
2	teaspoons grated fresh ginger
I	fresh serrano chile, ribs and seeds removed, flesh minced
I	tablespoon tomato paste
I	tablespoon garam masala
I	(28-ounce) can crushed tomatoes
2	teaspoons sugar
	Salt
⅔	cup heavy cream
¼	cup chopped fresh cilantro

I. FOR THE CHICKEN: Combine salt, cumin, coriander, and cayenne in small bowl. Sprinkle both sides of chicken with spice mixture, pressing gently so mixture adheres. Place chicken on plate, cover with plastic wrap, and refrigerate for 30 to 60 minutes. Meanwhile, whisk yogurt, oil, ginger, and garlic together in large bowl and set aside.

2. FOR THE SAUCE: Heat oil in large Dutch oven over medium heat until shimmering. Add onion and cook, stirring frequently, until light golden, 8 to 10 minutes. Add garlic, ginger, serrano, tomato paste, and garam masala and cook, stirring frequently, until fragrant, about 3 minutes. Add crushed tomatoes, sugar, and ½ teaspoon salt and bring to boil. Reduce heat to medium-low, cover, and simmer for 15 minutes, stirring occasionally. Stir in cream and return to simmer. Remove pan from heat and cover to keep warm.

3. TO COOK THE CHICKEN: While sauce simmers, position oven rack 6 inches from heating element and heat broiler. Using tongs, dip chicken into yogurt mixture (chicken should be coated with thick layer of yogurt) and arrange on wire rack set in aluminum foil–lined rimmed baking sheet or broiler pan. Discard excess yogurt mixture. Broil chicken until thickest part registers 160 degrees and exterior is lightly charred in spots, 10 to 18 minutes, flipping chicken halfway through cooking.

4. Let chicken rest 5 minutes, then cut into 1-inch chunks and stir into warm sauce (do not simmer chicken in sauce). Stir in cilantro, season with salt to taste, and serve. (Sauce can be made ahead, refrigerated for up to 4 days and gently reheated before adding hot chicken.)

INDIAN CURRIES

✔ WHY THIS RECIPE WORKS

We wanted a complex but not heavy-flavored Indian curry that wouldn't take all day to prepare. Toasting a combination of whole spices in oil before adding aromatics, jalapeño, and ground spices provided the authentic, intense flavor we were after. Instead of browning the meat, we simply stirred it into the pot along with crushed tomatoes and cooked the mixture until the liquid evaporated and the oil separated. This is a classic Indian technique that allows the spices to further release and develop their flavors in the oil, which is then absorbed by the meat. We then added water and simmered the mixture until the meat was tender. Adding potatoes lent heartiness and appealing contrasting texture, and a little cilantro provided a fresh finish. We found we could create several variations using chicken, shrimp, or beef, and various vegetables including spinach and peas, as well as yellow split peas. In some cases we swapped the tomatoes for yogurt for a creamier, richer curry.

INDIAN LAMB CURRY WITH WHOLE SPICES

SERVES 4 TO 6

Gather and prepare all of your ingredients before you begin. Garlic and ginger may be pureed by hand or in a minichop food processor. If using a minichopper, process the garlic and ginger with 1 to 2 tablespoons of water until pureed. You may substitute a scant ½ teaspoon of cayenne pepper for the jalapeño, adding it to the skillet with the other ground dried spices. Feel free to increase the aromatics (garlic, ginger, jalapeños, and onions) or dry spice quantities. For a creamier curry, use the yogurt rather than the crushed tomatoes. Serve with Basmati Rice Pilaf (page 223).

WHOLE SPICE BLEND
- 1½ (3-inch-long) cinnamon sticks
- 4 whole cloves
- 4 green cardamom pods
- 8 black peppercorns
- 1 bay leaf

CURRY
- ¼ cup vegetable oil
- 1 onion, sliced thin
- 1½ pounds boneless leg of lamb, trimmed and cut into ¾-inch cubes
- ⅔ cup crushed tomatoes
- 4 large garlic cloves, minced
- 1 tablespoon grated fresh ginger
- 2 teaspoons ground cumin
- 2 teaspoons ground coriander
- 1 teaspoon ground turmeric
  Salt
- 2 cups water
- 1 jalapeño chile, cut in half lengthwise, stemmed and seeded
- 4 medium boiling potatoes, peeled and cut into ¾-inch cubes
- 4 tablespoons chopped fresh cilantro

1. FOR THE SPICE BLEND: Combine ingredients in small bowl.

2. FOR THE CURRY: Heat oil in large Dutch oven over medium-high heat until shimmering. Add spice blend and cook, stirring with wooden spoon until cinnamon stick unfurls and cloves pop, about 5 seconds. Add onions and cook until softened, 3 to 4 minutes.

3. Stir in lamb, tomatoes, garlic, ginger, cumin, coriander, turmeric, and ½ teaspoon salt and cook, stirring frequently, until liquid evaporates, oil separates and turns orange, and spices begin to fry, 5 to 7 minutes. Continue to cook, stirring constantly, until spices are very fragrant, about 30 seconds longer.

4. Add water and jalapeño Bring to simmer, then reduce heat, cover, and simmer until meat is tender, 30 to 40 minutes.

5. Add potatoes and cook until tender, about 15 minutes. Stir in cilantro, simmer 3 minutes, season with salt to taste, and serve.

LAMB CURRY WITH FIGS AND FENUGREEK

Omit whole spice blend and potatoes. Add ½ teaspoon fenugreek along with cumin, coriander, and turmeric in step 3 and ¼ cup dried figs, chopped coarse, along with water in step 4.

INDIAN CHICKEN CURRY WITH YOGURT, CILANTRO, AND ZUCCHINI

In step 2, saute onions until golden brown, 5 to 7 minutes. Substitute 6 skinless chicken thighs for lamb and ½ cup plain whole-milk yogurt for tomatoes. In step 4, add 1 cup chopped cilantro before adding water and cook until chicken is cooked through, 20 to 30 minutes. Substitute 4 zucchini, cut into ½-inch cubes, for potatoes. Reduce cilantro stirred into curry in step 5 to 2 tablespoons.

INDIAN CHICKEN CURRY WITH SPINACH AND FENUGREEK

In this variation, the spinach becomes the sauce.

Omit whole spice blend. Add ½ teaspoon fenugreek along with cumin, coriander, and turmeric in step 3 and substitute 6 skinless chicken thighs for lamb. Add 1½ pounds spinach, stemmed and chopped coarse, to pot before adding water in step 4. Once chicken is tender, 20 to 30 minutes, remove and keep warm and continue to cook sauce over high heat until thickened, about 10 minutes.

INDIAN SHRIMP CURRY WITH YOGURT AND PEAS

Omit whole spice blend, lamb, and potatoes and sauté onions in step 2 until golden brown, 5 to 7 minutes. Substitute ½ cup plain whole-milk cup for tomatoes. Add 1 cup chopped cilantro before adding water in step 4 and stir in 1½ pounds extra-large shrimp (21 to 25 per pound), peeled and deveined, and 1 cup frozen peas, thawed, with cilantro in step 5, reducing cilantro to 2 tablespoons.

BEEF CURRY WITH CRUSHED SPICES AND CHANNA DAL

Channa dal is the name for yellow Indian split peas, available at Indian specialty food shops. Four red potatoes, peeled and cut into ¾-inch pieces, or regular green split peas may be substituted for the channa dal. Gather and prepare all of your ingredients before you begin. You may substitute a scant ½ teaspoon of cayenne pepper for the jalapeño, adding it to the skillet with the other ground dried spices. Feel free to increase the aromatics (garlic, ginger, jalapeños, and onions) or dry spice quantities. Serve the curry with Basmati Rice Pilaf (page 223) .

¼	cup vegetable oil
1	teaspoon cumin seeds
2	teaspoons coriander seeds
1	onion, sliced thin
4	large garlic cloves, minced
1	tablespoon grated fresh ginger
1½	pounds top sirloin, trimmed and cut into ¾-inch cubes
⅔	cup crushed tomatoes
1	teaspoon ground turmeric
	Salt
2	cups water
1	jalapeño chile, cut in half lengthwise, stemmed, and seeded
½	cup channa dal (Indian split peas)
2–4	tablespoons chopped fresh cilantro

1. Heat oil in Dutch oven over medium-high heat until shimmering. Crush cumin and coriander seeds in mortar and pestle and add to skillet. Add onion to skillet and cook until softened, 3 to 4 minutes.

2. Crush garlic and ginger along with pinch salt in mortar and pestle. Stir crushed garlic-ginger mixture, beef, tomatoes, turmeric, and ½ teaspoon salt into pot and cook, stirring frequently, until liquid evaporates, oil separates and turns orange, and spices begin to fry, 5 to 7 minutes. Continue to cook, stirring constantly, until spices are very fragrant, about 30 seconds longer.

3. Add water and jalapeño. Bring to simmer, then reduce heat, cover, and simmer until meat is tender, 30 to 40 minutes.

4. Add channa dal and cook until tender, about 15 minutes. Stir in cilantro, simmer 3 minutes, season with salt to taste, and serve.

INDIAN-STYLE VEGETABLE CURRY

✔ WHY THIS RECIPE WORKS
Vegetable curries can be complicated affairs, with lengthy ingredient lists and fussy techniques meant to compensate for the lack of meat. We wanted a curry we could make on a weeknight in less than an hour—without sacrificing flavor or overloading the dish with spices. Toasting store-bought curry powder in a skillet turned it into a flavor powerhouse and adding a few pinches of garam masala added even more spice flavor. To build the rest of our flavor base we started with a generous amount of sautéed onion, vegetable oil, garlic, ginger, fresh chile, and tomato paste for sweetness. When we chose our vegetables (chickpeas and potatoes for heartiness and cauliflower and peas for texture and color), we found that sautéing the spices and main ingredients together enhanced and melded the flavors. Finally, we rounded out our sauce with a combination of water, pureed canned tomatoes, and a splash of cream or coconut milk.

INDIAN CURRY WITH POTATOES, CAULIFLOWER, PEAS, AND CHICKPEAS

SERVES 4 TO 6

This curry is moderately spicy when made with one chile. For more heat, use an additional half chile. For a mild curry, remove the chile's ribs and seeds before mincing. The onions can be pulsed in a food processor. You can substitute 2 teaspoons ground coriander, ½ teaspoon ground black pepper, ¼ teaspoon ground cardamom, and ¼ teaspoon ground cinnamon for the garam masala. In addition to the suggested condiments, serve with Basmati Rice Pilaf (page 223) and plain whole-milk yogurt.

2	tablespoons sweet or mild curry powder
1½	teaspoons garam masala
1	(14.5-ounce) can diced tomatoes
¼	cup vegetable oil
2	onions, chopped fine
12	ounces red potatoes, cut into ½-inch pieces)
3	garlic cloves, minced
1	tablespoon grated fresh ginger
1–1½	serrano chiles, minced
1	tablespoon tomato paste
½	head cauliflower (1 pound), cored and cut into 1-inch florets
1	(15-ounce) can chickpeas, rinsed
1¼	cups water
	Salt
1½	cups frozen peas
¼	cup heavy cream or coconut milk

CONDIMENTS
Onion Relish (recipe follows)
Cilantro-Mint Chutney (recipe follows)

1. Toast curry powder and garam masala in small skillet over medium-high heat, stirring constantly, until spices darken slightly and become fragrant, about 1 minute. Transfer to small bowl and set aside. Pulse tomatoes in food processor until coarsely chopped, 3 to 4 pulses.

2. Heat 3 tablespoons oil in large Dutch oven over medium-high heat until shimmering. Add onions and potatoes and cook, stirring occasionally, until onions are caramelized and potatoes are golden brown on edges, about 10 minutes. (Reduce heat to medium if onions darken too quickly.)

3. Reduce heat to medium. Clear center of pot and add remaining 1 tablespoon oil, garlic, ginger, serrano, and tomato paste and cook, stirring constantly, until fragrant, about 30 seconds. Add reserved toasted spices and cook, stirring constantly, about 1 minute. Add cauliflower and cook, stirring constantly, until spices coat florets, about 2 minutes longer.

4. Add tomatoes, chickpeas, water, and 1 teaspoon salt. Increase heat to medium-high and bring mixture to boil, scraping bottom of pot with wooden spoon to loosen browned bits. Cover and reduce heat to medium. Simmer briskly, stirring occasionally, until vegetables are tender, 10 to 15 minutes.

5. Stir in peas and cream and continue to cook until heated through, about 2 minutes. Season with salt to taste and serve immediately, passing condiments separately.

INDIAN-STYLE CURRY WITH SWEET POTATOES, EGGPLANT, GREEN BEANS, AND CHICKPEAS

Substitute 12 ounces sweet potatoes, peeled and cut into ½-inch dice, for red potatoes. Substitute 1½ cups green beans, trimmed and cut into 1-inch pieces, and 1 eggplant, cut into ½-inch pieces (3 cups), for cauliflower. Omit peas.

ONION RELISH
MAKES ABOUT 1 CUP

If using a regular yellow onion, increase the sugar to 1 teaspoon.

- 1 Vidalia onion, diced fine
- ½ teaspoon paprika
- 1 tablespoon lime juice
- ½ teaspoon sugar
- ⅛ teaspoon salt
  Pinch cayenne pepper

Combine all ingredients in medium bowl. (Relish can be refrigerated for up to 1 day.)

CILANTRO-MINT CHUTNEY
MAKES ABOUT 1 CUP

- 2 cups fresh cilantro leaves
- 1 cup fresh mint leaves
- ⅓ cup plain whole-milk yogurt
- ¼ cup finely chopped onion
- 1 tablespoon lime juice
- 1½ teaspoons sugar
- ½ teaspoon ground cumin
- ¼ teaspoon salt

Process all ingredients in food processor until smooth, about 20 seconds, scraping down sides of bowl halfway through. (Chutney can be refrigerated for up to 1 day.)

STIR-FRIED SICHUAN GREEN BEANS

✔ WHY THIS RECIPE WORKS
The appeal of Sichuan green beans lies in their crinkled, chewy texture and intriguing spicy tang, but it's a result traditionally achieved by deep-frying. For the same dish without the mess, we stir-fried our beans longer than usual so that they became charred in places. This gave them the deep, caramelized flavor we wanted. For our

sauce, we combined dry mustard, dry sherry, a little sugar, ground white pepper, chopped scallions, and a drizzle of sesame oil, then added ground pork, which worked fine as a replacement for the shredded bits of Chinese barbecued pork often added at restaurants.

STIR-FRIED SICHUAN GREEN BEANS
SERVES 4

To make this dish vegetarian, substitute 4 ounces shiitake mushrooms, stemmed and minced, for the pork, adding 1 teaspoon oil to the pan in step 3 before adding the mushrooms. The cooking of this dish goes very quickly, so be sure to have all of the ingredients prepped before you start. Serve with Simple White Rice (page 222).

- 2 tablespoons soy sauce
- 2 tablespoons water
- 1 tablespoon dry sherry
- 1 teaspoon sugar
- ½ teaspoon cornstarch
- ¼ teaspoon ground white pepper
- ¼ teaspoon red pepper flakes
- ¼ teaspoon dry mustard
- 2 tablespoons vegetable oil
- 1 pound green beans, trimmed and cut into 2-inch pieces
- ¼ pound ground pork
- 3 garlic cloves, minced
- 1 tablespoon grated fresh ginger
- 3 scallions, white and light green parts only, sliced thin
- 1 teaspoon toasted sesame oil

1. Stir together soy sauce, water, sherry, sugar, cornstarch, white pepper, pepper flakes, and dry mustard in small bowl until sugar dissolves.

2. Heat oil in 12-inch nonstick skillet over high heat until just smoking. Add beans and cook, stirring frequently, until crisp-tender and skins are shriveled and blackened in spots, 5 to 8 minutes (reduce heat to medium-high if beans darken too quickly). Transfer beans to large plate.

3. Reduce heat to medium-high and add pork to skillet. Cook, breaking pork into small pieces, until no pink remains, about 2 minutes. Add garlic and ginger and cook, mashing mixture into pan, until fragrant, 15 to 20 seconds. Stir sauce to recombine and return beans to skillet with sauce. Toss and cook until sauce is thickened, 5 to 10 seconds. Remove from heat and stir in scallions and sesame oil. Serve immediately.

THAI-STYLE STIR-FRIED VEGETABLES

✔ WHY THIS RECIPE WORKS
Thai cooking is known for its unique balance of salty, sweet, sour, and spicy flavors, but traditional recipes often call for a laundry list of ingredients to meet that goal. For our Thai-style stir-fried vegetables, we found a way to give our dish authentic Thai flavor without using a lot of hard-to-find ingredients. A simple sauce base of fish sauce, lime juice and zest, brown sugar, and red pepper flakes gave our veggies the complex flavor we were looking for.

STIR-FRIED EGGPLANT WITH GARLIC AND BASIL SAUCE
SERVES 4 TO 6

Serve with Simple White Rice (page 222).

SAUCE
3   tablespoons fish sauce
1   teaspoon grated lime zest plus
     1 tablespoon juice
1   tablespoon light brown sugar
⅛   teaspoon red pepper flakes

VEGETABLES
1   tablespoon plus 1 teaspoon
     vegetable oil
1   eggplant, cut into ¾-inch cubes
6   garlic cloves, minced

1   tablespoon grated fresh ginger
2   scallions, sliced thin
½   cup fresh basil leaves, torn into
     rough ½-inch pieces

1. FOR THE SAUCE: Stir together all ingredients in small bowl until sugar is dissolved.

2. FOR THE VEGETABLES: Heat 1 tablespoon oil in 12-inch nonstick skillet over high heat until shimmering, 2 to 3 minutes. Add eggplant and cook, stirring every 10 to 15 seconds, until browned and tender, 4 to 5 minutes.

3. Clear center of skillet; add remaining 1 teaspoon oil, garlic, and ginger and cook, mashing mixture into pan, until fragrant, 15 to 20 seconds. Stir mixture into eggplant. Add sauce and cook until thickened, 5 to 10 seconds. Off heat, stir in scallions and basil and serve immediately.

STIR-FRIED BROCCOLI AND RED PEPPERS WITH PEANUT SAUCE
SERVES 4 TO 6

Serve with Simple White Rice (page 222).

SAUCE
¾   cup coconut milk
¼   cup water
3   tablespoons smooth peanut butter
3   tablespoons fish sauce
1   teaspoon grated lime zest plus
     1 tablespoon juice
1   tablespoon light brown sugar
⅛   teaspoon red pepper flakes

VEGETABLES
1   tablespoon plus 1 teaspoon
     vegetable oil
1   large red bell pepper, stemmed,
     seeded, and cut into ½-inch strips
10   ounces broccoli florets, cut into
     1-inch pieces
2   garlic cloves, minced
1   teaspoon grated fresh ginger

1. FOR THE SAUCE: Whisk all ingredients together in small bowl until smooth.

2. FOR THE VEGETABLES: Heat 1 tablespoon oil in 12-inch nonstick skillet over high heat until shimmering, 2 to 3 minutes. Add red pepper and broccoli and cook, stirring every 10 to 15 seconds, until just barely tender, about 2 minutes. Clear center of skillet; add remaining 1 teaspoon oil, garlic, and ginger and cook, mashing mixture into pan, until fragrant, 15 to 20 seconds. Stir mixture into vegetables. Reduce heat to medium-low and stir in sauce mixture. Simmer to heat through and blend flavors, about 1 minute. Serve immediately.

STIR-FRIED CAULIFLOWER WITH THAI RED CURRY SAUCE
SERVES 4 TO 6

Serve with Simple White Rice (page 222).

SAUCE
1   cup coconut milk
3   tablespoons fish sauce
1   teaspoon grated lime zest plus
     1 tablespoon juice
1   tablespoon light brown sugar
2   teaspoons red curry paste
⅛   teaspoon red pepper flakes

CAULIFLOWER
1   tablespoon plus 1 teaspoon
     vegetable oil
1   large head cauliflower (3 pounds),
     cored and cut into ¾-inch florets
2   garlic cloves, minced
1   teaspoon grated fresh ginger
6   ounces snow peas, strings removed
2   tablespoons minced fresh basil

1. FOR THE SAUCE: Whisk all ingredients together in small bowl until smooth.

2. FOR THE CAULIFLOWER: Heat 1 tablespoon oil in 12-inch nonstick skillet over high heat until shimmering, 2 to

3 minutes. Add cauliflower and cook, stirring occasionally, until just barely tender, about 3 minutes. Clear center of skillet; add remaining 1 teaspoon oil, garlic, and ginger and cook, mashing mixture into pan, until fragrant, 15 to 20 seconds. Stir mixture into cauliflower. Reduce heat to medium-high and stir in sauce mixture. Simmer, stirring occasionally, until cauliflower is just tender, about 2 minutes. Add snow peas and continue to simmer until cauliflower is fully tender, about 3 minutes longer. Sprinkle with basil. Serve immediately.

STIR-FRIED BROCCOLI

✔ WHY THIS RECIPE WORKS
For stir-fried broccoli with tender yet still crisp broccoli and a flavorful Asian-inspired sauce that wouldn't drown our perfectly cooked vegetables, we prepared the stalks and florets separately since they cook at different rates. Because a blazing hot flame consistently resulted in mushy, torched broccoli, we instead stir-fried the vegetables over medium-high heat. Tossing the broccoli with a sprinkling of sugar before adding the sauce deepened the caramelization. We also developed a variety of flavorful sauces, and thickened each slightly with cornstarch to prevent it from inundating the florets and turning them soggy.

STIR-FRIED BROCCOLI WITH CHILI-GARLIC SAUCE
SERVES 4

There are several Asian chili sauces available; we like chili-garlic sauce here because it offers heat with a little complexity.

¼	cup low-sodium chicken broth
1	tablespoon dry sherry
2	teaspoons soy sauce
2	teaspoons Asian chili-garlic sauce
1	teaspoon toasted sesame oil
1	teaspoon cornstarch
2	garlic cloves, minced
⅛	teaspoon red pepper flakes
1	teaspoon plus 1 tablespoon vegetable oil
1½	pounds broccoli, florets cut into ¾-inch pieces, stalks peeled and cut on bias into ¼-inch-thick slices
¼	teaspoon sugar

1. Whisk broth, sherry, soy sauce, chili-garlic sauce, sesame oil, and cornstarch together in small bowl. Combine garlic, pepper flakes, and 1 teaspoon vegetable oil in second small bowl.

2. Heat remaining 1 tablespoon vegetable oil in 12-inch nonstick skillet over medium-high heat until just beginning to smoke. Add broccoli and sprinkle with sugar. Cook, stirring frequently, until broccoli is well browned, 8 to 10 minutes.

3. Clear center of skillet, add oil-garlic mixture and cook, mashing mixture into pan, until fragrant, 15 to 20 seconds. Stir mixture into broccoli. Add chicken broth mixture and cook, stirring constantly, until florets are cooked through, stalks are crisp-tender, and sauce is thickened, 30 to 45 seconds. Serve.

STIR-FRIED BROCCOLI WITH OYSTER SAUCE

Reduce chicken broth to 3 tablespoons and substitute 3 tablespoons oyster sauce for soy sauce and 1 teaspoon brown sugar for chili-garlic sauce. Reduce amount of garlic to 1 clove and proceed with recipe as directed from step 2.

STIR-FRIED BROCCOLI WITH HOISIN AND FIVE-SPICE POWDER

Substitute 3 tablespoons hoisin sauce for sherry, ⅛ teaspoon five-spice powder for chili-garlic sauce, and increase soy sauce to 1 tablespoon. Reduce amount of garlic to 1 clove and proceed with recipe as directed from step 2.

STIR-FRIED BROCCOLI WITH ORANGE AND GINGER

Substitute ¼ cup fresh orange juice for sherry and omit toasted sesame oil and chili-garlic sauce. Reduce amount of garlic to 1 clove, increase amount of red pepper flakes to ½ teaspoon, and add 1 tablespoon minced or grated fresh ginger to garlic-oil mixture in step 1. Proceed with recipe as directed from step 2.

TEST KITCHEN TIP NO. 28 STIR-FRYING? THROW OUT YOUR WOK!

We love the theatrics of the kitchen, and few pans seem as fun to use as a wok. So imagine our disappointment when we realized woks simply don't perform as well as we thought. A wok's shape is the culprit. The conical bottom is designed for a pit-style stove; the flames lick and engulf the pan, making most of the surface area hot even when food is added. But when you set a wok over a conventional stovetop, the heat becomes concentrated in the pan's bottom and the larger surface area of the sides simply doesn't heat as well. And when food is added to the wok, the pan's temperature drops. The results? Meat that steams instead of searing and vegetables that turn soggy, rather than crisp-tender. So what does work on a conventional stovetop? A large nonstick skillet. Its flat-bottom design allows more of the surface area to come in direct contact with the flat burner and enables it to remain hot even after food is added. This higher heat translates to better browning and more flavor. The bottom line? Don't invest in a wok; use what you probably already have—a skillet.

STIR-FRIED SNOW PEAS

✓ **WHY THIS RECIPE WORKS**

We wanted to take snow peas from their typical second-fiddle position in stir-fries to starring role. Our goal was bring out their sweet, grassy flavor while preserving their crisp bite. Cooking them with a little sugar over intense heat, without stirring, allowed for browning, thus caramelizing their natural sugars and bumping up their flavor. Adding bright and savory ingredients like shallot, herbs, and lemon zest and juice and lemon grass and basil complemented the snow peas and turned them into a standout side dish.

STIR-FRIED SNOW PEAS WITH LEMON AND PARSLEY

SERVES 4

Chives or tarragon can be used in place of the parsley.

I	small shallot, minced
I	tablespoon vegetable oil
I	teaspoon grated lemon zest plus 1 teaspoon juice
	Salt and pepper
⅛	teaspoon sugar
12	ounces snow peas, strings removed
I	tablespoon minced fresh parsley

1. Combine shallot, 1 teaspoon oil, and lemon zest in small bowl. Combine ¼ teaspoon salt, ⅛ teaspoon pepper, and sugar in second small bowl.

2. Heat remaining 2 teaspoons oil in 12-inch nonstick skillet over high heat until just smoking. Add snow peas, sprinkle with salt mixture, and cook, without stirring, 30 seconds. Stir and continue to cook, without stirring, 30 seconds longer. Continue to cook, stirring constantly, until peas are crisp-tender, 1 to 2 minutes longer.

3. Clear center of skillet, add shallot mixture, and cook, mashing mixture into pan, until fragrant, about 20 seconds. Stir mixture into vegetables. Transfer peas to bowl and stir in lemon juice and parsley. Season with salt and pepper to taste and serve.

STIR-FRIED SNOW PEAS WITH GINGER, GARLIC, AND SCALLION

Substitute 2 minced garlic cloves, 2 teaspoons minced or grated fresh ginger, and 2 minced scallion whites for shallot and lemon zest and red pepper flakes for black pepper. In step 3, substitute rice vinegar for lemon juice and 2 sliced scallion greens for parsley.

STIR-FRIED SNOW PEAS WITH GARLIC, CUMIN, AND CILANTRO

Substitute 2 minced garlic cloves and ½ teaspoon toasted and lightly crushed cumin seed for shallot and ½ teaspoon lime zest for lemon zest. In step 3, substitute lime juice for lemon juice and cilantro for parsley.

STIR-FRIED SNOW PEAS WITH SHALLOT, LEMON GRASS, AND BASIL

Substitute 2 teaspoons minced fresh lemon grass for lemon zest. In step 3, substitute lime juice for lemon juice and basil for parsley.

VEGETABLE STIR-FRIES

✓ **WHY THIS RECIPE WORKS**

When designing a satisfying vegetable stir-fry recipe, we focused on hefty portobellos or eggplant to stand in for meat, then settled on a selection of other complementary vegetables to round out the meal. The key was infusing this stir-fry with flavor and ensuring each vegetable was properly cooked. Cooking the mushrooms in batches guaranteed even cooking and, in addition to the sauce, we found that adding a glaze—a concentrated version of the sauce—really boosted the mushrooms' flavor (we found this trick also worked well with tofu and eggplant). As for the other vegetables, we stir-fried in stages, first steam-sautéing long-cooking vegetables, then cooking the quicker-cooking vegetables.

STIR-FRIED PORTOBELLOS WITH GINGER-OYSTER SAUCE

SERVES 3 TO 4

This stir-fry cooks quickly, so have everything chopped and ready before you begin cooking. Serve with Simple White Rice (page 222).

GLAZE

¼	cup low-sodium chicken broth or vegetable broth
2	tablespoons soy sauce
2	tablespoons sugar

SAUCE

I	cup low-sodium chicken broth or vegetable broth
3	tablespoons oyster sauce
I	tablespoon soy sauce
I	tablespoon cornstarch
2	teaspoons toasted sesame oil

VEGETABLES

4	teaspoons grated fresh ginger
2	garlic cloves, minced
¼	cup vegetable oil
I ½	pounds portobello mushroom caps, gills removed, cut into 2-inch wedges
3	carrots, peeled and sliced ¼ inch thick on bias
½	cup low-sodium chicken broth or vegetable broth
2	ounces snow peas, strings removed
I	pound bok choy or napa cabbage, stalks or cores cut on bias into ¼-inch pieces and greens cut into ¾-inch strips
I	tablespoon sesame seeds, toasted (optional)

1. **FOR THE GLAZE:** Whisk all ingredients together in small bowl.

2. **FOR THE SAUCE:** Whisk all ingredients together in second small bowl.

3. **FOR THE VEGETABLES:** Combine ginger, garlic, and 1 teaspoon oil in third small bowl and set aside. Heat 3 tablespoons vegetable oil in 12-inch nonstick skillet over medium-high heat until shimmering. Add mushrooms and cook, without stirring, until browned on one side, 2 to 3 minutes. (Skillet will be crowded at first; arrange mushrooms in single layer as they shrink.) Flip mushrooms over, reduce heat to medium, and cook until second side is browned and mushrooms are tender, about 5 minutes. Increase heat to medium-high, add glaze mixture, and cook, stirring constantly, until glaze is thickened and mushrooms are coated, 1 to 2 minutes. Transfer mushrooms to plate. Rinse skillet clean and dry with paper towels.

4. Heat 1 teaspoon oil in skillet over medium-high heat until just smoking. Add carrots and cook, stirring occasionally, until beginning to brown, 1 to 2 minutes. Add 1 broth, cover, and cook until carrots are just tender, 2 to 3 minutes. Uncover and cook until liquid evaporates, about 30 seconds. Transfer carrots to plate with mushrooms.

5. Heat remaining 1 teaspoon vegetable oil in skillet over medium-high heat until just smoking. Add snow peas and bok choy stalks and cook, stirring occasionally, until beginning to brown and soften, 1 to 2 minutes. Add greens and cook, stirring frequently, until wilted, about 1 minute.

6. Clear center of skillet, add ginger mixture, and cook, mashing mixture into pan, until fragrant, 15 to 20 seconds. Stir mixture into greens.

7. Return vegetables to skillet, add sauce, and cook, stirring constantly, until sauce is thickened and vegetables are coated, 2 to 3 minutes. Transfer to platter, top with sesame seeds if using, and serve immediately.

STIR-FRIED PORTOBELLOS WITH SOY-MAPLE SAUCE

SERVES 3 TO 4

For a spicier dish, increase the red pepper flakes to ½ teaspoon. Serve with Simple White Rice (page 222).

GLAZE

3	tablespoons maple syrup
2	tablespoons soy sauce
2	tablespoons mirin

SAUCE

¾	cup low-sodium chicken broth or vegetable broth
3	tablespoons soy sauce
2	tablespoons mirin
1	tablespoon rice vinegar
1	tablespoon cornstarch
2	teaspoons toasted sesame oil

VEGETABLES

2	garlic cloves, minced
2	teaspoons grated fresh ginger
¼	teaspoon red pepper flakes
¼	cup vegetable oil
1½	pounds portobello mushroom caps, gills removed, cut into 2-inch wedges
8	ounces green beans, trimmed
½	cup low-sodium chicken broth or vegetable broth
1	red bell pepper, stemmed, seeded, and cut into ¾-inch pieces
1	pound bok choy or napa cabbage, stalks or cores cut into ¼-inch pieces on bias and greens cut into ¾-inch strips
¼	cup roasted cashews (optional)

1. **FOR THE GLAZE:** Whisk all ingredients together in small bowl.

2. **FOR THE SAUCE:** Whisk all ingredients together in second small bowl.

3. **FOR THE VEGETABLES:** Combine garlic, ginger, pepper flakes, and 1 teaspoon oil in third small bowl and set aside. Heat 3 tablespoons vegetable oil in 12-inch nonstick skillet over medium-high heat until shimmering. Add mushrooms and cook, without stirring, until browned on one side, 2 to 3 minutes. (Skillet will be crowded at first; arrange mushrooms in single layer as they shrink). Flip mushrooms over, reduce heat to medium, and cook until second side is browned and mushrooms are tender, about 5 minutes. Increase heat to medium-high, add glaze mixture, and cook, stirring, until glaze is thickened and mushrooms are coated, 1 to 2 minutes. Transfer mushrooms to plate. Rinse skillet clean and dry with paper towels.

4. Heat 1 teaspoon oil over medium-high heat until just smoking. Add green beans and cook, stirring occasionally, until beginning to brown, 1 to 2 minutes. Add broth, cover, and cook until beans are just tender, 2 to 3 minutes. Uncover and cook until liquid evaporates, about 30 seconds. Transfer beans to plate with mushrooms.

5. Heat remaining 1 teaspoon oil over medium-high heat until just smoking. Add bell pepper and bok choy stems and cook, stirring occasionally, until beginning to brown and soften, 1 to 2 minutes. Add

---

TEST KITCHEN TIP NO. 29 **SESAME OIL**

Not all sesame oils are created alike. Raw sesame oil, which is very mild in flavor and light in color, is used mostly for cooking, while toasted sesame oil, which has a deep amber color, is primarily used for seasoning because of its intense, nutty flavor. For the biggest hit of sesame oil, we prefer to use toasted sesame oil. Just a little of this oil will give dishes a deep, nutty flavor—but too much will be overpowering.

greens and cook, stirring frequently, until wilted, about 1 minute.

6. Clear center of skillet, add garlic mixture, and cook, mashing mixture into pan, until fragrant, 15 to 20 seconds. Stir mixture into greens.

7. Return vegetables to skillet, add sauce, and cook, stirring, until sauce is thickened and vegetables are coated, about 1 minute. Transfer to platter, top with cashews, if using, and serve immediately.

STIR-FRIED PORTOBELLOS WITH SWEET CHILI-GARLIC SAUCE

Serve with Simple White Rice (page 222).

Replace sugar in glaze with 2 tablespoons honey. For sauce, increase soy sauce to 3 tablespoons, reduce broth to ¾ cup, and replace oyster sauce and sesame oil with 2 tablespoons honey, 1 tablespoon rice vinegar, and 1 teaspoon Asian chili-garlic sauce. Increase garlic to 4 cloves.

STIR-FRIED TOFU WITH GINGER-OYSTER SAUCE

When coated with cornstarch and stir-fried, tofu develops an appealingly crisp exterior and creamy interior. To cut tofu for this stir-fry, hold a chef's knife parallel to the cutting board and cut the block in half horizontally to form 2 rectangular planks. Cut each plank into 6 squares, then cut each square diagonally into 2 triangles. Serve with Simple White Rice (page 222).

Follow recipe for Stir-Fried Portobellos with Ginger-Oyster Sauce (page 136) through step 2. Cut 1 (14-ounce) block extra-firm tofu into 24 triangles (see note). Spread ⅓ cup cornstarch evenly in baking dish and dredge tofu in cornstarch to evenly coat. Heat 3 tablespoons vegetable oil in 12-inch nonstick skillet until shimmering, add tofu in single layer, and cook until golden brown, 4 to 6 minutes. Flip tofu over gently and cook until second side is browned, 4 to 6 minutes. Add glaze mixture to skillet and cook, stirring, until glaze is thick and tofu is coated, 1 to 2 minutes. Transfer tofu to plate. Rinse skillet clean and dry with paper towels. Proceed with step 3 as directed.

STIR-FRIED EGGPLANT WITH SWEET CHILI-GARLIC SAUCE

SERVES 3 TO 4

Eggplant can cook unevenly because the stem end is denser than the part containing most of the seeds. If some of the pieces seem cooked through in less than the allotted time, transfer these pieces to a plate and continue cooking the others until done. Return all the pieces to the pan before adding the glaze mixture. If you like a spicier stir-fry, increase the chili-garlic sauce to 2 teaspoons. Serve with Simple White Rice (page 222).

GLAZE
¼   cup low-sodium chicken broth or vegetable broth
2   tablespoons soy sauce
2   tablespoons honey

SAUCE
¾   cup low-sodium chicken broth or vegetable broth
3   tablespoons soy sauce
2   tablespoons honey
1   tablespoon rice vinegar
1   tablespoon cornstarch
1   teaspoon Asian chili-garlic sauce

VEGETABLES
4   garlic cloves, minced
2   teaspoons grated fresh ginger
¼   cup plus 1 tablespoon vegetable oil
1   large egg, lightly beaten
½   teaspoon salt
1½ pounds eggplant, peeled and cut crosswise into 1¼-inch-thick rounds, each round cut into pie-shaped wedges
⅓   cup cornstarch
5½ ounces broccoli florets
¾   cup low-sodium chicken broth or vegetable broth
1   red bell pepper, stemmed, seeded, and cut into ¼-inch pieces
1   pound bok choy or napa cabbage, stalks or cores cut into ¼-inch pieces on bias and greens cut into ¾-inch strips
2   tablespoons pine nuts, toasted and coarsely chopped (optional)

1. **FOR THE GLAZE:** Whisk all ingredients together in small bowl.

2. **FOR THE SAUCE:** Whisk all ingredients together in second small bowl.

3. **FOR THE VEGETABLES:** Combine garlic, ginger, and 1 teaspoon oil in third small bowl and set aside.

4. Whisk egg and salt together in large bowl. Add eggplant, toss to coat, then transfer to clean bowl, allowing any excess egg to drip off. Sprinkle cornstarch over eggplant and, using rubber spatula, toss to coat. Heat ¼ cup oil in 12-inch nonstick skillet over medium-high heat until shimmering. Add eggplant in single layer and cook, without moving, until golden brown on one side, 2 to 3 minutes. Reduce heat to medium, flip eggplant over gently, and continue to cook, shaking skillet occasionally, until pieces are golden brown and softened, about 10 minutes. (Some pieces may take longer than others; see note.) Increase heat to medium-high, add glaze mixture, and cook, stirring, until glaze is thickened and eggplant is coated, 1 to 2 minutes. Transfer eggplant to large plate. Rinse skillet clean and dry with paper towels.

5. Heat 1 teaspoon oil over medium-high heat until just smoking. Add broccoli and cook, stirring occasionally, until beginning to brown, 1 to 2 minutes. Add broth, cover, and cook until broccoli is just tender, 2 to 3 minutes. Uncover and cook until liquid evaporates, about 30 seconds. Transfer broccoli to plate with eggplant.

6. Heat 1 teaspoon oil over medium-high heat until just smoking. Add bell pepper and bok choy stems and cook, stirring occasionally, until beginning to brown and soften, 1 to 2 minutes. Add greens and cook, stirring frequently, until wilted, about 1 minute. Clear center of skillet, add garlic mixture, and cook, mashing mixture into pan, until fragrant, 15 to 20 seconds. Stir mixture into greens.

7. Return vegetables to skillet, add sauce, and cook, stirring, until sauce is thickened and vegetables are coated, about 1 minute. Transfer to platter, top with pine nuts, if using, and serve immediately.

THAI-STYLE CHICKEN WITH BASIL

✔ WHY THIS RECIPE WORKS

Capturing the flavors of this classic Thai ground-chicken dish required not only gathering the right ingredients but also learning a whole new way to stir-fry. Stir-frying at a low temperature (contrary to classic Chinese-style stir-frying) allowed us to cook the aromatics and a full cup of basil from the beginning so they could infuse the cooking oil with their flavors. Grinding the chicken in a food processor, along with some fish sauce, gave us coarse-textured meat that retained moisture during cooking. A combination of oyster sauce and white vinegar added rich but bright flavor. Stirring in another cup of basil at the end and cooking just until the leaves wilted added a fresh finish and boosted the basil flavor to the right level for this dish.

THAI-STYLE CHICKEN WITH BASIL
SERVES 4

Since tolerance for spiciness can vary, we've kept our recipe relatively mild. Sweetness without sufficient heat can become cloying, so we also cut back the sugar. For a very mild version of the dish, remove the seeds and ribs from the chiles. If fresh Thai chiles are unavailable, substitute 2 serranos or 1 medium jalapeño. In Thailand, crushed red pepper and sugar are passed at the table, along with extra fish sauce and white vinegar, so the dish can be adjusted to suit individual tastes. Serve with steamed rice and vegetables, if desired.

- 2 cups fresh basil leaves
- 3 garlic cloves, peeled
- 6 green or red Thai chiles, stemmed
- 2 tablespoons fish sauce, plus extra for serving
- 1 tablespoon oyster sauce
- 1 tablespoon sugar, plus extra for serving
- 1 teaspoon white vinegar, plus extra for serving
- 1 pound boneless, skinless chicken breasts, cut into 2-inch pieces
- 3 medium shallots, sliced thin
- 2 tablespoons vegetable oil
  Red pepper flakes, for serving

1. Pulse 1 cup basil, garlic, and chiles in food processor until finely chopped, 6 to 10 pulses, scraping down bowl once during processing. Transfer 1 tablespoon basil mixture to small bowl and stir in 1 tablespoon fish sauce, oyster sauce, sugar, and vinegar; set aside. Transfer remaining basil mixture to 12-inch nonstick skillet. Do not wash workbowl.

2. Pulse chicken and 1 tablespoon fish sauce in food processor until meat is chopped into approximate ¼-inch pieces, 6 to 8 pulses. Transfer to medium bowl and refrigerate 15 minutes.

3. Stir shallots and oil into basil mixture in skillet. Heat over medium-low heat (mixture should start to sizzle after about 1½ minutes; if it doesn't, adjust heat accordingly), stirring constantly, until garlic and shallots are golden brown, 5 to 8 minutes.

4. Add chicken, increase heat to medium, and cook, stirring and breaking up chicken with potato masher or rubber spatula, until only traces of pink remain, 2 to 4 minutes. Add reserved basil–fish sauce mixture and continue to cook, stirring constantly, until chicken is no longer pink, about 1 minute. Stir in remaining 1 cup basil and cook, stirring constantly, until basil is wilted, 30 to 60 seconds. Serve immediately, passing extra fish sauce, sugar, pepper flakes, and vinegar separately.

CHICKEN STIR-FRIES

✔ WHY THIS RECIPE WORKS

Tired of dry, stringy meat in our chicken stir-fry recipes, we came up with a solution: We soaked the chicken in a combination brine-marinade to add flavor and moisture, then dipped the marinated pieces of chicken in a cornstarch-oil mixture. The cornstarch coating, a modified version of the Chinese technique called velveting, helped the chicken stay moist even with a high-heat cooking method.

GINGERY STIR-FRIED CHICKEN AND BOK CHOY
SERVES 4

To make slicing the chicken easier, freeze it for 15 minutes. Serve with Simple White Rice (page 222).

SAUCE
¼	cup low-sodium chicken broth
2	tablespoons dry sherry
1	tablespoon soy sauce
1	tablespoon oyster sauce
2	teaspoons grated fresh ginger
½	teaspoon toasted sesame oil
1	teaspoon cornstarch
1	teaspoon sugar
¼	teaspoon red pepper flakes

CHICKEN STIR-FRY
2	teaspoons grated fresh ginger
1	garlic clove, minced
2	tablespoons plus 2 teaspoons vegetable oil
1	cup water
¼	cup soy sauce
¼	cup dry sherry
1	pound boneless, skinless chicken breasts, trimmed and sliced thin
2	tablespoons toasted sesame oil
1	tablespoon cornstarch
1	tablespoon all-purpose flour
1	pound bok choy, stalks cut on bias into ¼-inch slices and greens cut into ½-inch strips
1	small red bell pepper, stemmed, seeded, and cut into ¼-inch strips

1. FOR THE SAUCE: Whisk all ingredients together in small bowl and set aside.

2. FOR THE STIR-FRY: Combine ginger, garlic, and 1 teaspoon vegetable oil in small bowl and set aside. Combine water, soy sauce, and sherry in medium bowl. Add chicken and stir to break up clumps. Cover with plastic wrap and refrigerate for at least 20 minutes or up to 1 hour. Pour off excess liquid from chicken.

3. Mix sesame oil, cornstarch, and flour in medium bowl until smooth. Toss chicken in cornstarch mixture until evenly coated.

4. Heat 2 teaspoons vegetable oil in 12-inch nonstick skillet over high heat until smoking. Add half of chicken to skillet in single layer and cook, without stirring, until golden brown on first side, about 1 minute. Flip chicken pieces over and cook until lightly browned on second side, about 30 seconds. Transfer chicken to clean bowl. Repeat with 2 teaspoons vegetable oil and remaining chicken.

5. Add remaining 1 tablespoon vegetable oil to skillet and heat over high heat until just smoking. Add bok choy stalks and bell pepper and cook, stirring, until beginning to brown, about 1 minute. Clear center of skillet, add ginger mixture, and cook, mashing mixture into pan, until fragrant, 15 to 20 seconds. Stir mixture into vegetables and continue to cook until stalks are crisp-tender, about 30 seconds longer. Stir in bok choy greens and cook until beginning to wilt, about 30 seconds.

6. Return chicken to skillet. Whisk sauce to recombine, add to skillet, reduce heat to medium, and cook, stirring constantly, until sauce is thickened and chicken is cooked through, about 30 seconds. Transfer to platter and serve immediately.

SPICY STIR-FRIED SESAME CHICKEN WITH GREEN BEANS AND SHIITAKE MUSHROOMS
SERVES 4

To make slicing the chicken easier, freeze it for 15 minutes. Serve with Simple White Rice (page 222).

SAUCE
½	cup low-sodium chicken broth
3	tablespoons soy sauce
2	tablespoons dry sherry
1	tablespoon plus 1 teaspoon Asian chili-garlic sauce
1	tablespoon plus 1 teaspoon sugar
2	teaspoons sesame seeds, toasted
1	teaspoon toasted sesame oil
1	teaspoon cornstarch
1	garlic clove, minced

CHICKEN STIR-FRY
2	garlic cloves, minced
1	teaspoon grated fresh ginger
2	tablespoons plus 2 teaspoons vegetable oil

¼ cup soy sauce

¼ cup dry sherry

1 cup water

1 pound boneless, skinless chicken breasts, trimmed and sliced thin

2 tablespoons plus 1 teaspoon toasted sesame oil

1 tablespoon cornstarch

1 tablespoon all-purpose flour

1 pound green beans, trimmed and cut on bias into 1-inch pieces

8 ounces shiitake mushrooms, stemmed and sliced ⅛ inch thick

1 teaspoon sesame seeds, toasted

PREPARING CHICKEN BREASTS FOR STIR-FRIES

1. To produce uniform pieces of chicken, separate tenderloins from partially frozen boneless, skinless breasts.

2. Slice breasts across grain into ½-inch-wide strips that are 1½ to 2 inches long. Cut center pieces in half so they are approximately same length as end pieces.

3. Cut tenderloins on diagonal to produce pieces about same size as strips of breast meat.

1. FOR THE SAUCE: Whisk all ingredients together in small bowl.

2. FOR THE STIR-FRY: Combine garlic, ginger, and 1 teaspoon vegetable oil in small bowl and set aside. Combine soy sauce, sherry, and water in medium bowl. Add chicken and stir to break up clumps. Cover with plastic wrap and refrigerate for at least 20 minutes or up to 1 hour. Pour off excess liquid from chicken.

3. Mix 2 tablespoons sesame oil, cornstarch, and flour in medium bowl until smooth. Toss chicken in cornstarch mixture until evenly coated.

4. Heat 2 teaspoons vegetable oil in 12-inch nonstick skillet over high heat until smoking. Add half of chicken to skillet in even layer and cook, without stirring, until golden brown on first side, about 1 minute. Flip chicken pieces over and cook until lightly browned on second side, about 30 seconds. Transfer chicken to clean bowl. Repeat with 2 teaspoons vegetable oil and remaining chicken.

5. Add 1 tablespoon vegetable oil to skillet and heat until just smoking. Add green beans and cook, stirring occasionally, 1 minute. Add mushrooms and cook until mushrooms are lightly browned, about 3 minutes. Clear center of skillet, add garlic mixture, and cook, mashing mixture

into pan, until fragrant, 15 to 20 seconds. Stir mixture into beans and mushrooms and continue to cook until beans are crisp-tender, about 30 seconds.

6. Return chicken to skillet. Whisk sauce to recombine, add to skillet, reduce heat to medium, and cook, stirring constantly, until sauce is thickened and chicken is cooked through, about 30 seconds. Transfer to platter, drizzle with remaining 1 teaspoon sesame oil, and sprinkle with sesame seeds. Serve immediately.

SWEET, SOUR, AND SPICY ORANGE CHICKEN AND BROCCOLI WITH CASHEWS

SERVES 4

To make slicing the chicken easier, freeze it for 15 minutes. Serve with Simple White Rice (page 222).

SAUCE

¼ cup low-sodium chicken broth

¼ cup orange juice

¼ cup white vinegar

2 teaspoons soy sauce

2 teaspoons hoisin sauce

1 teaspoon cornstarch

1 tablespoon sugar

½ teaspoon red pepper flakes

CHICKEN STIR-FRY

2 garlic cloves, minced

1 teaspoon grated fresh ginger

3 tablespoons plus 1 teaspoon vegetable oil

1¼ cups water

¼ cup soy sauce

¼ cup dry sherry

1 pound boneless, skinless chicken breasts, trimmed and sliced thin

2 tablespoons toasted sesame oil

1 tablespoon cornstarch

1 tablespoon all-purpose flour

1 cup unsalted cashews, toasted

1½ pounds broccoli, florets cut into 1-inch pieces, stalks peeled and sliced on bias ¼ inch thick

4 medium scallions, sliced ¼-inch thick on bias

1. FOR THE SAUCE: Whisk ingredients together in small bowl and set aside.

2. FOR THE STIR-FRY: Combine garlic, ginger, and 1 tablespoon vegetable oil in small bowl and set aside. Combine 1 cup water, soy sauce, and sherry in medium bowl. Add chicken and stir to break up clumps. Cover with plastic wrap and refrigerate for at least 20 minutes or up to 1 hour. Pour off excess liquid from chicken.

3. Mix sesame oil, cornstarch, and flour in medium bowl until smooth. Toss chicken in cornstarch mixture until evenly coated.

4. Heat 2 teaspoons vegetable oil in 12-inch nonstick skillet over high heat until smoking. Add half of chicken in even layer and cook, without stirring, until golden brown on first side, about 1 minute. Flip chicken pieces over and cook until lightly browned on second side, about 30 seconds. Transfer chicken to clean bowl. Repeat with 2 teaspoons vegetable oil and remaining chicken.

5. Add remaining 1 tablespoon vegetable oil to skillet and heat until just smoking. Add broccoli and cook 30 seconds. Add remaining 1/4 cup water, cover, and lower heat to medium-low. Cook broccoli until crisp-tender, about 3 minutes, then transfer to paper towel–lined plate. Add garlic mixture to skillet, increase heat to medium-high, and cook, mashing mixture into pan, until fragrant and golden brown, 15 to 20 seconds.

6. Return chicken to skillet and toss to combine. Whisk sauce to recombine, add to skillet, and cook, stirring constantly, until sauce is thickened and evenly distributed, about 1 minute. Off heat, add broccoli and cashews and stir to combine. Transfer to platter, sprinkle with scallions, and serve.

CHICKEN STIR-FRY WITH CRISPY NOODLE CAKE

✔ WHY THIS RECIPE WORKS
While a stir-fry served on top of rice is great, a pan-fried noodle cake—crisp and crunchy on the outside and tender and chewy in the middle—offers a welcome change of pace. For the noodle cake, we had the most success with fresh Chinese egg noodles—they made for a cohesive cake with a crunchy exterior. A non-stick skillet was crucial because it kept the cake from sticking and falling apart and allowed us to use less oil so the cake wasn't greasy. We kept the stir-fry itself simple; chicken and bok choy are a classic combination. A quick marinade gave our chicken welcome flavor, and a modified version of the Chinese technique called velveting prevented the chicken from drying out over high heat.

STIR-FRIED CHICKEN WITH BOK CHOY AND CRISPY NOODLE CAKE
SERVES 4

To make slicing the chicken easier, freeze it for 15 minutes. Fresh Chinese noodles are often kept in the produce section of the grocery store. If you can't find them, substitute an equal amount of fresh spaghetti.

SAUCE
1/4	cup low-sodium chicken broth
2	tablespoons soy sauce
1	tablespoon dry sherry
1	tablespoon oyster sauce
1	teaspoon sugar
1	teaspoon cornstarch
1/4	teaspoon red pepper flakes

NOODLE CAKE
1	(9-ounce) package fresh Chinese noodles
1	teaspoon salt
2	scallions, sliced thin
1/4	cup vegetable oil

CHICKEN STIR-FRY
1	pound boneless, skinless chicken breasts, trimmed and sliced thin
1	tablespoon soy sauce
1	tablespoon dry sherry
2	tablespoons toasted sesame oil
1	tablespoon cornstarch
1	tablespoon all-purpose flour
2	tablespoons plus 2 teaspoons vegetable oil
1	tablespoon grated fresh ginger
1	medium garlic clove, minced
1	pound bok choy, stalks cut on bias into 1/4-inch pieces and greens cut into 1/2-inch strips
1	small red bell pepper, stemmed, seeded, and cut into 1/4-inch strips

1. FOR THE SAUCE: Combine all ingredients in small bowl.

2. FOR THE NOODLE CAKE: Bring 6 quarts water to boil in large pot. Add noodles and salt and cook, stirring often, until almost tender, 2 to 3 minutes. Drain noodles, then toss with scallions.

3. Heat 2 tablespoons oil in 12-inch nonstick skillet over medium heat until shimmering. Spread noodles evenly across bottom of skillet and press with spatula to flatten into cake. Cook until crisp and golden brown, 5 to 8 minutes.

4. Slide noodle cake onto large plate. Add remaining 2 tablespoons oil to skillet and swirl to coat. Invert noodle cake onto second plate and slide it, browned side up, back into skillet. Cook until golden brown on second side, 5 to 8 minutes.

5. Slide noodle cake onto cutting board and let sit for at least 5 minutes before slicing into wedges and serving. (Noodle cake can be transferred to wire rack set over baking sheet and kept warm in 200-degree oven for up to 20 minutes.) Wipe out skillet with wad of paper towels.

6. FOR THE STIR-FRY: While noodles boil, toss chicken with soy sauce and sherry in medium bowl and let marinate for at least 10 minutes or up to 1 hour. Whisk sesame oil, cornstarch, and flour together in large bowl. Combine 1 teaspoon vegetable oil, ginger, and garlic in small bowl.

7. Stir marinated chicken into cornstarch mixture. Heat 2 teaspoons vegetable oil in skillet over high heat until just smoking. Add half of chicken, break up any clumps, and cook without stirring until meat is browned at edges, about 1 minute. Stir chicken and continue to cook until

cooked through, about 1 minute longer. Transfer chicken to clean bowl and cover with aluminum foil to keep warm. Repeat with 2 teaspoons vegetable oil and remaining chicken.

8. Add remaining 1 tablespoon vegetable oil to skillet and return to high heat until just smoking. Add bok choy stalks and bell pepper and cook until lightly browned, 2 to 3 minutes.

9. Clear center of skillet, add ginger mixture, and cook, mashing mixture into pan, until fragrant, 15 to 20 seconds. Stir ginger mixture into vegetables, then stir in bok choy greens and cook until beginning to wilt, about 30 seconds.

10. Stir in chicken with any accumulated juices. Whisk sauce to recombine, then add to skillet and cook, tossing constantly, until sauce is thickened, about 30 seconds. Transfer to platter and serve with noodle cake.

BEEF AND VEGETABLE STIR-FRIES

✔ WHY THIS RECIPE WORKS
We made a few other discoveries while developing our perfect beef stir-fry: First and foremost, start with the right cut. Flank steak is affordable, has great beefy flavor, and is tender when sliced thin (freezing the meat made slicing it thin easier). A quick marinade added flavor and the soy sauce in our marinade acted like a brine, keeping the meat juicy. Cooking meat and vegetables in batches ensured they were all perfectly cooked, and adding the aromatics to the pan toward the end of cooking meant they didn't burn. An easy-to-make stir-fry sauce made with a modicum of cornstarch ensured that it clung to the beef and vegetables but didn't become overly thick.

TERIYAKI STIR-FRIED BEEF WITH GREEN BEANS AND SHIITAKES
SERVES 4

To make slicing the flank steak easier, freeze it for 15 minutes. You can substitute 1 tablespoon white wine or sake mixed with 1 teaspoon sugar for the mirin. Serve with Simple White Rice (page 222).

    SAUCE
½   cup low-sodium chicken broth
2   tablespoons soy sauce
2   tablespoons sugar
1   tablespoon mirin
1   teaspoon cornstarch
¼   teaspoon red pepper flakes

    BEEF STIR-FRY
2   tablespoons soy sauce
1   teaspoon sugar
1   (12-ounce) flank steak, trimmed and sliced thin across grain on slight bias
3   garlic cloves, minced
1   tablespoon grated fresh ginger
2   tablespoons vegetable oil
8   ounces shiitake mushrooms, stemmed and cut into 1-inch pieces
12   ounces green beans, trimmed and halved
¼   cup water
3   scallions, cut into 1½-inch pieces, white and light green pieces quartered lengthwise

1. FOR THE SAUCE: Whisk all ingredients together in small bowl and set aside.

2. FOR THE STIR-FRY: Combine soy sauce and sugar in medium bowl. Add beef, toss well, and marinate for at least 10 minutes or up to 1 hour, stirring once. Meanwhile, combine garlic, ginger, and 1 teaspoon oil in small bowl.

3. Drain beef and discard liquid. Heat 1 teaspoon oil in 12-inch nonstick skillet over high heat until just smoking. Add half

of beef in single layer, break up any clumps, and cook, without stirring, for 1 minute. Stir beef and continue to cook until browned, 1 to 2 minutes. Transfer beef to clean bowl. Repeat with 1 teaspoon oil and remaining beef. Rinse skillet clean and dry with paper towels.

4. Add remaining 1 tablespoon oil to skillet and heat until just smoking. Add mushrooms and cook until beginning to brown, about 2 minutes. Add green beans and cook, stirring frequently, until spotty brown, 3 to 4 minutes. Add water, cover, and continue to cook until green beans are crisp-tender, 2 to 3 minutes longer. Uncover, clear center of skillet, and add garlic mixture. Cook, mashing mixture into pan, until fragrant, 15 to 20 seconds. Stir mixture into vegetables. Return beef and any accumulated juices to skillet, add scallions, and stir to combine. Whisk sauce to recombine, add to skillet, and cook, stirring constantly, until thickened, about 30 seconds. Serve.

STIR-FRIED BEEF WITH SNAP PEAS AND RED PEPPERS
SERVES 4

To make slicing the flank steak easier, freeze it for 15 minutes. Serve with Simple White Rice (page 222).

    SAUCE
½   cup low-sodium chicken broth
¼   cup oyster sauce
2   tablespoons dry sherry
1   tablespoon sugar
1   teaspoon cornstarch

    BEEF STIR-FRY
2   tablespoons soy sauce
1   teaspoon sugar
1   (12-ounce) flank steak, trimmed and sliced thin across grain on slight bias
3   garlic cloves, minced

1 tablespoon grated fresh ginger

2 tablespoons vegetable oil

12 ounces sugar snap peas, stems and
strings removed

1 red bell pepper, stemmed, seeded,
and cut into ¼-inch slices

2 tablespoons water

1. FOR THE SAUCE: Whisk all ingredients together in small bowl and set aside.

2. FOR THE STIR-FRY: Combine soy sauce and sugar in medium bowl. Add beef, toss well, and marinate for at least 10 minutes or up to 1 hour, stirring once. Meanwhile, combine garlic, ginger, and 1 teaspoon oil in small bowl.

3. Drain beef and discard liquid. Heat 1 teaspoon oil in 12-inch nonstick skillet over high heat until just smoking. Add half of beef in single layer, break up any clumps, and cook, without stirring, for 1 minute. Stir beef and continue to cook until browned, 1 to 2 minutes. Transfer beef to clean bowl. Repeat with 1 teaspoon oil and remaining beef. Rinse skillet clean and dry with paper towels.

4. Add remaining 1 tablespoon oil to skillet and heat until just smoking. Add snap peas and bell pepper and cook, stirring frequently, until vegetables begin to brown, 3 to 5 minutes. Add water and continue to cook until vegetables are crisp-tender, 1 to 2 minutes longer. Clear center of skillet, add garlic-ginger mixture and cook, mashing mixture into pan, until

fragrant, 15 to 20 seconds. Stir mixture into vegetables. Return beef and any accumulated juices to skillet and stir to combine. Whisk sauce to recombine, add to skillet, and cook, stirring constantly, until thickened, about 30 seconds. Serve.

TANGERINE STIR-FRIED BEEF WITH ONIONS AND SNOW PEAS

SERVES 4

To make slicing the flank steak easier, freeze it for 15 minutes. Make sure to zest the tangerine for the beef and vegetables before juicing them for the sauce (you should need to zest only one of the tangerines). Two to three oranges can be substituted for the tangerines. If available, substitute 1 teaspoon toasted and ground Sichuan peppercorns for the red pepper flakes. Serve with Simple White Rice (page 222).

SAUCE

¾ cup tangerine juice (3 to
4 tangerines)

2 tablespoons soy sauce

1 tablespoon light brown sugar

1 teaspoon toasted sesame oil

1 teaspoon cornstarch

BEEF STIR-FRY

2 tablespoons soy sauce

1 teaspoon light brown sugar

1 (12-ounce) flank steak, trimmed
and sliced thin across grain on
slight bias

3 garlic cloves, minced

1 tablespoon grated fresh ginger

1 tablespoon black bean sauce

1 teaspoon grated tangerine zest

¼–½ teaspoon red pepper flakes

2 tablespoons vegetable oil

1 large onion, halved and cut into
½-inch wedges

10 ounces snow peas, stems and
strings removed

2 tablespoons water

1. FOR THE SAUCE: Whisk all ingredients together in small bowl and set aside.

2. FOR THE STIR-FRY: Combine soy sauce and sugar in medium bowl. Add beef, toss well, and marinate for at least 10 minutes or up to 1 hour, stirring once. Meanwhile, combine garlic, ginger, black bean sauce, tangerine zest, pepper flakes, and 1 teaspoon vegetable oil in small bowl.

3. Drain beef and discard liquid. Heat 1 teaspoon vegetable oil in 12-inch non-stick skillet over high heat until just smoking. Add half of beef in single layer, break up any clumps, and cook, without stirring, for 1 minute. Stir beef and continue to cook until browned, 1 to 2 minutes. Transfer beef to clean bowl. Repeat with 1 teaspoon vegetable oil and remaining beef. Rinse skillet clean and dry with paper towels.

4. Add remaining 1 tablespoon vegetable oil to skillet and heat until just smoking. Add onion and cook, stirring frequently, until beginning to brown, 3 to 5 minutes. Add snow peas and continue to cook until spotty brown, about 2 minutes longer. Add water and cook until vegetables are crisp-tender, about 1 minute. Clear center of skillet, add garlic mixture, and cook, mashing mixture into pan, until fragrant, 15 to 20 seconds. Stir mixture into vegetables. Return beef and any accumulated juices to skillet and stir to combine. Whisk sauce to recombine, add to skillet, and cook, stirring constantly, until thickened, about 30 seconds. Serve.

SLICING FLANK STEAK FOR STIR-FRIES

1. Using sharp chef's knife, slice partially frozen steak with grain into 2-inch-wide pieces.

2. Cut each 2-inch piece of flank steak across grain on slight bias into very thin slices.

KOREAN STIR-FRIED BEEF WITH KIMCHI

SERVES 4

To make slicing the flank steak easier, freeze it for 15 minutes. You can find kimchi, a spicy Korean pickled vegetable condiment, in the refrigerated section of Asian markets and some well-stocked supermarkets. Cut large pieces of kimchi into bite-size pieces before stir-frying. If the kimchi is made from green cabbage rather than napa cabbage, extend the cooking time by 1 to 2 minutes. Serve with Simple White Rice (page 222).

SAUCE
½ cup low-sodium chicken broth
2 tablespoons soy sauce
1 tablespoon sugar
1 teaspoon toasted sesame oil
1 teaspoon cornstarch

BEEF STIR-FRY
2 tablespoons soy sauce
1 teaspoon sugar
1 (12-ounce) flank steak, trimmed and sliced thin across grain on slight bias
3 garlic cloves, minced
1 tablespoon grated fresh ginger
2 tablespoons vegetable oil
1 cup kimchi, chopped into 1-inch pieces
4 ounces bean sprouts (2 cups)
5 scallions, cut into 1½-inch pieces, white and light green pieces quartered lengthwise

1. FOR THE SAUCE: Whisk all ingredients together in small bowl and set aside.

2. FOR THE STIR-FRY: Combine soy sauce and sugar in medium bowl. Add beef, toss well, and marinate for at least 10 minutes or up to 1 hour, stirring once. Meanwhile, combine garlic, ginger, and 1 teaspoon vegetable oil in small bowl.

3. Drain beef and discard liquid. Heat 1 teaspoon vegetable oil in 12-inch nonstick skillet over high heat until just smoking. Add half of beef in single layer, break up any clumps, and cook, without stirring, for 1 minute. Stir beef and continue to cook until browned, 1 to 2 minutes. Transfer beef to clean bowl. Repeat with 1 teaspoon vegetable oil and remaining beef. Rinse skillet clean and dry with paper towels.

4. Add remaining 1 tablespoon oil to skillet and heat until just smoking. Add kimchi and cook, stirring frequently, until aromatic, 1 to 2 minutes. Add bean sprouts and stir to combine. Clear center of skillet, add garlic mixture, and cook, mashing mixture into pan, until fragrant, 15 to 20 seconds. Stir mixture into vegetables. Return beef and any accumulated juices to skillet, add scallions, and stir to combine. Whisk sauce to recombine, add to skillet, and cook, stirring constantly, until thickened, about 30 seconds. Serve.

STIR-FRIED RED CURRY BEEF WITH EGGPLANT

SERVES 4

To make slicing the flank steak easier, freeze it for 15 minutes. Serve with Simple White Rice (page 222).

SAUCE
½ cup low-sodium chicken broth
3 tablespoons coconut milk
2 tablespoons light brown sugar
1 tablespoon lime juice
1 tablespoon fish sauce
1 teaspoon cornstarch

BEEF STIR-FRY
2 tablespoons soy sauce
1 teaspoon light brown sugar
1 (12-ounce) flank steak, trimmed and sliced thin across grain on slight bias
3 garlic cloves, minced
1½ teaspoons red curry paste
2 tablespoons vegetable oil
1 medium eggplant (about 1 pound), peeled and cut into ¾-inch cubes
2 cups fresh basil leaves
   Lime wedges

1. FOR THE SAUCE: Whisk all ingredients together in small bowl and set aside.

2. FOR THE STIR-FRY: Combine soy sauce and sugar in medium bowl. Add beef, toss well, and marinate for at least 10 minutes or up to 1 hour, stirring once. Meanwhile, combine garlic, curry paste, and 1 teaspoon oil in small bowl.

3. Drain beef and discard liquid. Heat 1 teaspoon oil in 12-inch nonstick skillet over high heat until just smoking. Add half of beef in single layer, break up any clumps, and cook, without stirring, for 1 minute. Stir beef and continue to cook until browned, 1 to 2 minutes. Transfer beef to clean bowl. Repeat with 1 teaspoon oil and remaining beef. Rinse skillet clean and dry with paper towels.

4. Add remaining 1 tablespoon oil to skillet and heat until just smoking. Add eggplant and cook, stirring frequently, until browned and no longer spongy, 5 to 7 minutes. Clear center of skillet, add garlic-curry mixture, and cook, mashing mixture into pan, until fragrant, 15 to 20 seconds. Stir mixture into eggplant. Return beef and any accumulated juices to skillet and stir to combine. Whisk sauce to recombine, add to skillet along with basil, and cook, stirring constantly, until thickened, about 30 seconds. Serve, passing lime wedges separately.

STIR-FRIED BEEF AND BROCCOLI WITH OYSTER SAUCE

WHY THIS RECIPE WORKS
Order beef and broccoli in most Chinese restaurants, and you are served a pile of tough meat with overcooked army-issue broccoli all drenched in a thick-as-pudding brown sauce. We set out to rescue beef and broccoli. For the meat, we found that flank steak offered the biggest beefy taste and slicing it thin made it tender. We cooked the beef in two batches over high heat to make sure it browned and didn't steam. Then we cooked the broccoli until crisp-tender using a combination of methods—sautéing and steaming—and added some red bell pepper for sweetness and color. For the sauce, oyster sauce, chicken broth, dry sherry, brown sugar, and sesame oil, lightly thickened with cornstarch made a sauce that clung to the beef and vegetables without being gloppy.

STIR-FRIED BEEF AND BROCCOLI WITH OYSTER SAUCE

SERVES 4

To make slicing the flank steak easier, freeze it for 15 minutes. Serve with Simple White Rice (page 222).

SAUCE
- 5 tablespoons oyster sauce
- 2 tablespoons low-sodium chicken broth
- 1 tablespoon dry sherry
- 1 tablespoon light brown sugar
- 1 teaspoon toasted sesame oil
- 1 teaspoon cornstarch

BEEF STIR-FRY
- 1 (1-pound) flank steak, trimmed and sliced thin across grain on slight bias (see illustrations on page 144)
- 3 tablespoons soy sauce
- 6 garlic cloves, minced
- 1 tablespoon grated fresh ginger
- 3 tablespoons vegetable oil

- 1¼ pounds broccoli, florets cut into bite-size pieces, stalks peeled and cut on bias into ⅛-inch-thick slices
- ⅓ cup water
- 1 small red bell pepper, stemmed, seeded, and cut into ¼-inch pieces
- 3 medium scallions, sliced ½-inch thick on bias

1. **FOR THE SAUCE:** Whisk all ingredients together in small bowl and set aside.

2. **FOR THE STIR-FRY:** Combine beef and soy sauce in medium bowl, toss to coat, and let marinate at least 10 minutes or up to 1 hour, stirring once. Meanwhile, combine garlic, ginger, and 1½ teaspoons vegetable oil in small bowl.

3. Drain beef and discard liquid. Heat 1½ teaspoons vegetable oil in 12-inch nonstick skillet over high heat until just smoking. Add half of beef in single layer, break up clumps, and cook, without stirring, for 1 minute. Stir beef and continue to cook until beef is browned, about 30 seconds. Transfer beef to medium bowl. Repeat with 1½ teaspoons vegetable oil and remaining beef.

4. Add 1 tablespoon vegetable oil to skillet and heat until just smoking. Add broccoli and cook for 30 seconds. Add water to pan, cover, and lower heat to medium. Steam broccoli until crisp-tender, about 2 minutes, then transfer to paper towel–lined plate. Add remaining 1½ teaspoons vegetable oil to skillet, increase heat to high and heat until just smoking. Add bell pepper and cook, stirring frequently, until spotty brown, about 1½ minutes. Clear center of skillet, add garlic mixture, and cook, mashing mixture into pan, until fragrant, 15 to 20 seconds, then stir mixture into peppers.

5. Return beef and broccoli to skillet and toss to combine. Whisk sauce to recombine, then add to skillet and cook, stirring constantly, until sauce is thickened and evenly distributed, about 30 seconds. Transfer to platter, sprinkle with scallions, and serve.

STIR-FRIED THAI BEEF

WHY THIS RECIPE WORKS
Traditional Thai-style beef relies on obscure ingredients like galangal, palm sugar, and dried prawns and requires hours of prep plus deep-frying. We wanted to use easily available ingredients and require minimal cooking time. We settled on inexpensive blade steak, which offers beefy flavor and tenderness when fully cooked. With a marinade made of fish sauce, white pepper, coriander, and a little light brown sugar, the beef needed to marinate for only 15 minutes to develop full flavor. To add heat, we introduced an easily controlled heat source—Asian chili-garlic sauce—that also added toasty garlicky flavors.

STIR-FRIED THAI-STYLE BEEF WITH CHILES AND SHALLOTS

SERVES 4

If you cannot find blade steaks, use flank steak. Because flank steak requires less trimming, you will need only about 1¾ pounds. To prepare the flank steak, first cut the steak with the grain into 1½-inch-wide strips, then cut the strips against the grain into ¼-inch-thick slices. To make slicing the steak easier, freeze it for 15 minutes. White pepper lends this stir-fry a unique flavor; black pepper is not a good substitute. Serve with steamed jasmine rice.

BEEF STIR-FRY
- 1 tablespoon fish sauce
- 1 teaspoon light brown sugar
- ¾ teaspoon ground coriander
- ⅛ teaspoon ground white pepper
- 2 pounds blade steak, trimmed (see illustrations on page 116) and cut crosswise into ¼-inch-thick strips

SAUCE AND GARNISH
- 2 tablespoons fish sauce
- 2 tablespoons rice vinegar
- 2 tablespoons water
- 1 tablespoon light brown sugar
- 1 tablespoon Asian chili-garlic sauce
- 3 garlic cloves, minced

3 tablespoons vegetable oil

3 serrano or jalapeño chiles, stemmed, seeded, and sliced thin

3 shallots, peeled, quartered, and layers separated

½ cup fresh mint leaves, large leaves torn into bite-size pieces

½ cup fresh cilantro leaves

⅓ cup dry-roasted peanuts, chopped Lime wedges

1. FOR THE STIR-FRY: Combine fish sauce, sugar, coriander, and white pepper in large bowl. Add beef, toss well to combine; marinate 15 minutes.

2. FOR THE SAUCE AND GARNISH: Stir together fish sauce, vinegar, water, sugar, and chili-garlic sauce in small bowl until sugar dissolves and set aside. In second small bowl, mix garlic and 1 teaspoon oil and set aside.

3. To prepare stir-fry, heat 2 teaspoons oil in 12-inch nonstick skillet over high heat until just smoking. Add one-third of beef to skillet in even layer. Cook, without stirring, until well browned, about 2 minutes, then stir and continue cooking until beef is browned around edges and no longer pink in center, about 30 seconds. Transfer beef to medium bowl. Repeat with 2 teaspoons oil more and remaining meat in 2 more batches.

4. Reduce heat to medium, add remaining 2 teaspoons oil to skillet and swirl to coat. Add chiles and shallots and cook, stirring frequently, until beginning to soften, 3 to 4 minutes. Clear center of skillet, add garlic-oil, and cook, mashing mixture into pan, until fragrant, 15 to 20 seconds. Stir garlic into chile mixture. Add fish sauce mixture to skillet, increase heat to high, and cook until slightly reduced and thickened, about 30 seconds.

5. Return beef and any accumulated juices to skillet and toss well to combine and coat with sauce. Stir in half of mint and cilantro. Serve immediately, sprinkling each serving with peanuts and remaining herbs, and passing lime wedges separately.

PORK AND VEGETABLE STIR-FRIES

✔ WHY THIS RECIPE WORKS

Marinating pork tenderloin in a soy-sherry mixture and cooking it quickly in batches over high heat ensured the meat was flavorful, juicy, and perfectly cooked. Because different vegetables cook at different rates, we batch-cooked the vegetables and added aromatics (like ginger and garlic) at the end so they cooked long enough to develop their flavors without burning. Chicken broth gave the sauce some backbone, and cornstarch helped the sauce lightly coated the meat and vegetables.

SPICY STIR-FRIED PORK, ASPARAGUS AND ONIONS WITH LEMON GRASS

SERVES 4

To make slicing the pork easier, freeze it for 15 minutes. Serve with Simple White Rice (page 222).

SAUCE

⅓ cup low-sodium chicken broth

2 tablespoons fish sauce

1 tablespoon light brown sugar

2 teaspoons lime juice

1 teaspoon cornstarch

PORK STIR-FRY

1 (12-ounce) pork tenderloin, trimmed and cut into thin strips

1 teaspoon fish sauce

1 teaspoon soy sauce

2 lemon grass stalks, trimmed to bottom 6 inches and minced

2 garlic cloves, minced

¾ teaspoon red pepper flakes

3½ tablespoons vegetable oil

1 pound asparagus, trimmed and cut on bias into 2-inch lengths

1 large onion, cut into ¼-inch wedges

¼ cup chopped fresh basil

1. FOR THE SAUCE: Whisk all ingredients together in small bowl and set aside.

2. FOR THE STIR-FRY: Combine pork, fish sauce, and soy sauce in small bowl. Cover with plastic wrap and refrigerate for at least 20 minutes or up to 1 hour. Meanwhile, combine lemon grass, garlic, pepper flakes, and 1 tablespoon oil in small bowl.

3. Heat 1½ teaspoons oil in 12-inch nonstick skillet over high heat until just smoking. Add half of pork to skillet, break up any clumps, and cook, stirring occasionally, until well browned, about 2 minutes. Transfer pork to medium bowl. Repeat with 1½ teaspoons oil and remaining pork.

4. Add 1 tablespoon oil to skillet, add asparagus, and cook, stirring every 30 seconds, until browned and almost tender, 4 to 5 minutes. Transfer to bowl with pork. Add remaining 1½ teaspoons oil to skillet, add onion, and cook, stirring occasionally, until beginning to brown and soften, about 2 minutes. Clear center of skillet,

SLICING PORK TENDERLOIN FOR STIR-FRIES

1. Using sharp chef's knife, slice partially frozen pork crosswise into ¼-inch-thick medallions.

2. Slice each medallion into ½-inch-wide strips.

add lemon grass mixture, and cook, mashing mixture into pan, until fragrant, about 1 minute. Stir mixture into onion.

5. Return pork and asparagus to skillet and toss to combine. Stir sauce to recombine, add to skillet, and cook, stirring constantly, until sauce is thickened and evenly distributed, about 30 seconds. Transfer to platter, sprinkle with basil, and serve.

STIR-FRIED PORK, GREEN BEANS, AND RED BELL PEPPER WITH GINGERY OYSTER SAUCE

SERVES 4

To make slicing the pork easier, freeze it for 15 minutes. Serve with Simple White Rice (page 222).

SAUCE
⅓ cup low-sodium chicken broth
2½ tablespoons oyster sauce
1 tablespoon dry sherry
2 teaspoons toasted sesame oil
1 teaspoon rice vinegar
1 teaspoon cornstarch
¼ teaspoon ground white pepper

PORK STIR-FRY
1 (12-ounce) pork tenderloin, trimmed and cut into thin strips
2 teaspoons soy sauce
2 teaspoons dry sherry
2 tablespoons grated fresh ginger
2 garlic cloves, minced
3 tablespoons vegetable oil
12 ounces green beans, trimmed and cut on bias into 2-inch lengths
1 large red bell pepper, stemmed, seeded, and cut into ¾-inch squares
3 scallions, sliced thin on bias

1. FOR THE SAUCE: Whisk all ingredients together in small bowl and set aside.

2. FOR THE STIR-FRY: Combine pork, soy sauce, and sherry in small bowl. Cover with plastic wrap and refrigerate for at least 20 minutes or up to 1 hour. Meanwhile, combine ginger, garlic, and 1½ teaspoons oil in small bowl.

3. Heat 1½ teaspoons vegetable oil in 12-inch nonstick skillet over high heat until smoking. Add half of pork, break up any clumps, and cook, stirring occasionally, until well-browned, about 2 minutes. Transfer pork to medium bowl. Repeat with 1½ teaspoons vegetable oil and remaining pork.

4. Add 1 tablespoon vegetable oil to skillet. Add green beans and cook, stirring occasionally, until spotty brown and crisp-tender, about 5 minutes. Transfer to bowl with pork. Add remaining 1½ teaspoons oil to skillet, add bell pepper, and cook, stirring frequently, until spotty brown, about 2 minutes.

5. Clear center of skillet, add ginger mixture, and cook, mashing mixture into pan, until fragrant, 15 to 20 seconds. Stir mixture into pepper.

6. Return pork and green beans to skillet and toss to combine. Whisk sauce to recombine, add to skillet, and cook, stirring constantly, until sauce is thickened and evenly distributed, about 30 seconds. Transfer to platter, sprinkle with scallions, and serve.

STIR-FRIED PORK, EGGPLANT, AND ONION WITH GARLIC AND BLACK PEPPER

SERVES 4

This take on classic Thai stir-fry is not for those with timid palates. To make slicing the pork easier, freeze it for 15 minutes. Serve with Simple White Rice (page 222).

SAUCE
2½ tablespoons fish sauce
2 tablespoons plus 1½ teaspoons soy sauce
2½ tablespoons light brown sugar
2 tablespoons low-sodium chicken broth
2 teaspoons lime juice
1 teaspoon cornstarch

PORK STIR-FRY
1 (12-ounce) pork tenderloin, trimmed and cut into thin strips
1 teaspoon fish sauce
1 teaspoon soy sauce
12 garlic cloves, minced
2 teaspoons pepper
3½ tablespoons vegetable oil
1 medium eggplant (1 pound), cut into ¾-inch cubes
1 large onion, cut into ¼- to ⅜-inch wedges
¼ cup coarsely chopped fresh cilantro

1. FOR THE SAUCE: Whisk all ingredients together in small bowl and set aside.

2. FOR THE STIR-FRY: Combine pork, fish sauce, and soy sauce in small bowl. Cover with plastic wrap and refrigerate for at least 20 minutes or up to 1 hour. Meanwhile, combine garlic, pepper, and 1 tablespoon oil in second small bowl and set aside.

3. Heat 1½ teaspoons oil in 12-inch nonstick skillet over high heat until just smoking. Add half of pork, break up any clumps, and cook, stirring occasionally, until well-browned, about 2 minutes. Transfer pork to medium bowl. Repeat with 1½ teaspoons oil and remaining pork.

4. Add 1 tablespoon oil to skillet. Add eggplant and cook, stirring every 30 seconds, until browned and no longer spongy, about 5 minutes. Transfer to bowl with pork. Add remaining 1½ teaspoons oil to skillet, add onion, and cook, stirring occasionally, until beginning to brown and soften, about 2 minutes.

5. Clear center of skillet, add garlic-pepper mixture, and cook, mashing mixture into pan, until fragrant and beginning to brown, about 1½ minutes. Stir mixture into onions.

6. Return pork and eggplant to skillet and toss to combine. Whisk sauce to recombine, add to skillet, and cook, stirring constantly, until sauce is thickened

and evenly distributed, about 30 seconds. Transfer to platter, sprinkle with cilantro, and serve.

THAI PORK LETTUCE WRAPS

✔ WHY THIS RECIPE WORKS

The classic Thai salad called larb *is made by tossing finely chopped meat and nutty rice powder with fresh herbs and a light dressing that embodies the cuisine's signature balance of sweet, sour, hot, and salty flavors. We aimed to develop a home-cook-friendly recipe. Grinding our own pork tenderloin in the food processor gave us more consistent results than preground pork from the supermarket. Marinating the meat in fish sauce lent flavor and moisture. We found we could replace the traditional rice powder with rice we toasted in a skillet and then ground in a mini food processor or mortar and pestle. The pungency of sliced shallots and the bright flavor of chopped mint and cilantro yielded a very flavorful salad without a trip to a specialty store.*

THAI PORK LETTUCE WRAPS

SERVES 6 AS AN APPETIZER OR
4 AS A MAIN COURSE

We prefer natural pork in this recipe. If using enhanced pork, skip the marinating in step 2 and reduce the amount of fish sauce to 2 tablespoons, adding it all in step 5. Don't skip the toasted rice; it's integral to the texture and flavor of the dish. Any style of white rice can be used. Toasted rice powder (kao kua) can also be found in many Asian markets; substitute 1 tablespoon rice powder for the white rice. This dish can be served with sticky rice and steamed vegetables as an entrée. To save time, prepare the other ingredients while the pork is in the freezer.

- 1 (1-pound) pork tenderloin, trimmed and cut into 1-inch chunks
- 2½ tablespoons fish sauce
- 1 tablespoon white rice
- ¼ cup low-sodium chicken broth
- 2 shallots, peeled and sliced into thin rings
- 3 tablespoons lime juice (2 limes)
- 3 tablespoons roughly chopped fresh mint
- 3 tablespoons roughly chopped fresh cilantro
- 2 teaspoons sugar
- ¼ teaspoon red pepper flakes
- 1 head Bibb lettuce (8 ounces), leaves separated

1. Place pork on large plate in single layer. Freeze meat until firm and starting to harden around edges but still pliable, 15 to 20 minutes.

2. Place half of meat in food processor and pulse until coarsely chopped, 5 to 6 pulses. Transfer ground meat to medium bowl and repeat with remaining chunks. Stir 1 tablespoon fish sauce into ground meat, cover with plastic wrap, and refrigerate for 15 minutes.

3. Toast rice in small skillet over medium-high heat, stirring constantly, until deep golden brown, about 5 minutes. Transfer to small bowl and cool 5 minutes. Grind rice with spice grinder, mini food processor, or mortar and pestle until it resembles fine meal, 10 to 30 seconds (you should have about 1 tablespoon rice powder).

4. Bring broth to simmer in 12-inch nonstick skillet over medium-high heat. Add pork and cook, stirring frequently, until about half of pork is no longer pink, about 2 minutes. Sprinkle 1 teaspoon rice powder over pork and continue to cook, stirring constantly, until remaining pork is no longer pink, 1 to 1½ minutes longer. Transfer pork to large bowl and let cool 10 minutes.

5. Add remaining 1½ tablespoons fish sauce, remaining 2 teaspoons rice powder, shallots, lime juice, mint, cilantro, sugar, and pepper flakes to pork and toss to combine. Serve with lettuce leaves, spooning meat into leaves at table.

STIR-FRIED SHRIMP

✔ WHY THIS RECIPE WORKS

Our typical high-heat stir-fry technique, which works well with chicken, beef and pork, doesn't fly with quick-cooking shrimp. We would need to modify it if we wanted to produce plump, juicy, well-seasoned shrimp in a balanced, flavorful sauce. We started out cooking the vegetables over high heat, then removed them and turned the heat down before adding the aromatics and shrimp (which we marinated in oil, salt, and garlic for better flavor and texture). Once the shrimp were cooked through in the sauce, we returned the vegetables to the pan. For our sauce, the heavily soy-based brews we turn to for meat stir-fries were a poor match with the shrimp. Sweeter or spicier sauces flavored with garlic and chiles were better suited, and they reduced to a consistency that tightly adhered to the shellfish.

STIR-FRIED SHRIMP WITH SNOW PEAS AND RED BELL PEPPER IN HOT AND SOUR SAUCE

SERVES 4

Serve with Simple White Rice (page 222).

SAUCE
- 3 tablespoons sugar
- 3 tablespoons white vinegar
- 1 tablespoon Asian chili-garlic sauce
- 1 tablespoon dry sherry or Chinese rice cooking wine
- 1 tablespoon ketchup
- 2 teaspoons toasted sesame oil
- 2 teaspoons cornstarch
- 1 teaspoon soy sauce

SHRIMP STIR-FRY
- 1 pound extra-large shrimp (21 to 25 per pound), peeled, deveined, and tails removed
- 3 tablespoons vegetable oil
- 1 tablespoon grated fresh ginger
- 2 garlic cloves, 1 minced, 1 sliced thin
- ½ teaspoon salt
- 1 large shallot, sliced thin

8 ounces snow peas or sugar snap peas, stems and strings removed

1 red bell pepper, stemmed, seeded, and cut into ¾-inch pieces

1. FOR THE SAUCE: Whisk all ingredients together in small bowl and set aside.

2. FOR THE STIR-FRY: Combine shrimp with 1 tablespoon vegetable oil, ginger, minced garlic, and salt in medium bowl. Let shrimp marinate at room temperature 30 minutes.

3. Combine sliced garlic with shallot in small bowl. Heat 1 tablespoon vegetable oil in 12-inch nonstick skillet over high heat until just smoking. Add snow peas and bell pepper and cook, stirring frequently, until vegetables begin to brown, 1½ to 2 minutes. Transfer vegetables to medium bowl.

4. Heat remaining 1 tablespoon vegetable oil over high heat until just smoking. Add shallot mixture and cook, stirring frequently, until just beginning to brown, about 30 seconds. Add shrimp, reduce heat to medium-low, and cook, stirring frequently, until shrimp are light pink on both sides, 1 to 1½ minutes. Stir sauce to recombine and add to skillet; return to high heat and cook, stirring constantly, until sauce is thickened and shrimp are cooked through, 1 to 2 minutes. Return vegetables to skillet, toss to combine, and serve.

STIR-FRIED SICHUAN-STYLE SHRIMP WITH ZUCCHINI, RED BELL PEPPER, AND PEANUTS

SERVES 4

Note that this recipe is spicy and not for the timid. If you can find a Chinese long pepper, use it in place of the jalapeño. Broad bean chili paste is also referred to as chili bean sauce or horse bean chili paste. If you can't find it, increase the amount of Asian chili-garlic sauce by 1 teaspoon. Sichuan peppercorns, available at Asian markets and some supermarkets, have purplish-red husks and shiny black seeds; it is preferable to buy them

with the seeds removed, as it's the husk that provides the aromatic, gently floral fragrance (and the notable numbing effect on the tongue). Serve with Simple White Rice (page 222).

SAUCE

2 tablespoons dry sherry or Chinese rice cooking wine

1 tablespoon broad bean chili paste

1 tablespoon Asian chili-garlic sauce

1 tablespoon white vinegar or Chinese black vinegar

2 teaspoons soy sauce

2 teaspoons chili oil or toasted sesame oil

1 teaspoon sugar

1 teaspoon cornstarch

½ teaspoon Sichuan peppercorns, toasted and ground (optional)

SHRIMP STIR-FRY

1 pound extra-large shrimp (21 to 25 per pound), peeled, deveined, and tails removed

3 tablespoons vegetable oil

2 garlic cloves, 1 minced, 1 sliced thin

½ teaspoon salt

½ cup dry-roasted peanuts

1 jalapeño chile, stemmed, halved, seeded, and sliced thin on bias

1 small zucchini, cut into ¾-inch dice

1 red bell pepper, stemmed, seeded, and cut into ¾-inch dice

½ cup fresh cilantro leaves

1. FOR THE SAUCE: Whisk all ingredients together in small bowl and set aside.

2. FOR THE STIR-FRY: Combine shrimp with 1 tablespoon vegetable oil, minced garlic, and salt in medium bowl. Let shrimp marinate at room temperature 30 minutes.

3. Combine sliced garlic, peanuts, and jalapeño in small bowl. Heat 1 tablespoon oil in 12-inch nonstick skillet over high heat until just smoking. Add zucchini and bell pepper and cook, stirring frequently, until zucchini is tender and well browned,

2 to 4 minutes. Transfer vegetables to medium bowl.

4. Add remaining 1 tablespoon oil to skillet and heat until just smoking. Add peanut mixture and cook, stirring frequently, until just beginning to brown, about 30 seconds. Add shrimp, reduce heat to medium-low, and cook, stirring frequently, until shrimp are light pink on both sides, 1 to 1½ minutes. Stir sauce to recombine and add to skillet. Return to high heat and cook, stirring constantly, until sauce is thickened and shrimp are cooked through, 1 to 2 minutes. Return vegetables to skillet, add cilantro, toss to combine, and serve.

STIR-FRIED SHRIMP WITH GARLICKY EGGPLANT, SCALLIONS, AND CASHEWS

SERVES 4

Serve with Simple White Rice (page 222).

SAUCE

2 tablespoons soy sauce

2 tablespoons oyster sauce

2 tablespoons dry sherry or Chinese rice cooking wine

2 tablespoons sugar

1 tablespoon toasted sesame oil

1 tablespoon white vinegar

2 teaspoons cornstarch

⅛ teaspoon red pepper flakes

SHRIMP STIR-FRY

1 pound extra-large shrimp (21 to 25 per pound), peeled, deveined, and tails removed

3 tablespoons vegetable oil

6 garlic cloves, 1 minced, 5 sliced thin

½ teaspoon salt

6 large scallions, whites sliced thin and greens cut into 1-inch pieces

½ cup cashews

12 ounces eggplant, cut into ¾-inch pieces

1. FOR THE SAUCE: Whisk all ingredients together in small bowl and set aside.

2. FOR THE STIR-FRY: Combine shrimp with 1 tablespoon vegetable oil, minced garlic, and salt in medium bowl. Let shrimp marinate at room temperature 30 minutes.

3. Combine sliced garlic with scallion whites and cashews in small bowl. Heat 1 tablespoon oil in 12-inch nonstick skillet over high heat until just smoking. Add eggplant and cook, stirring frequently, until lightly browned, 3 to 6 minutes. Add scallion greens and continue to cook until scallion greens begin to brown and eggplant is fully tender, 1 to 2 minutes longer. Transfer vegetables to medium bowl.

4. Add remaining 1 tablespoon oil to skillet and heat until just smoking. Add scallion whites mixture and cook, stirring frequently, until just beginning to brown, about 30 seconds. Add shrimp, reduce heat to medium-low, and cook, stirring frequently, until shrimp are light pink on both sides, 1 to 1½ minutes. Stir sauce to recombine and add to skillet. Return to high heat and cook, stirring constantly, until sauce is thickened and shrimp are cooked through, 1 to 2 minutes. Return vegetables to skillet, toss to combine, and serve.

KUNG PAO SHRIMP

✔ **WHY THIS RECIPE WORKS**
Kung pao is meant to have a fiery personality, but many restaurant versions are dismal, featuring tiny, tough shrimp drenched in a quart of pale, greasy, bland sauce. For a classic Sichuan stir-fry of large, tender shrimp, peanuts that were an ingredient not just a garnish, and an assertive, well-balanced brown sauce, we stir-fried marinated shrimp for just a few seconds, then added the peanuts and small whole red chiles. The chiles gave our dish some fire, and toasting the peanuts deepened their flavor. Finding other vegetables to be superfluous, we added only diced red pepper for sweetness and scallions for a little bite. For a potently flavored sauce, we used a mixture of chicken broth, black rice vinegar (it lent a fruity, salty complexity), sesame oil, oyster sauce, and hoisin sauce. Adding a little cornstarch thickened the sauce to just the right syrupy consistency.

TEST KITCHEN TIP NO. 32 **STORING FRESH GINGER**

We include fresh ginger in many of our recipes, but we generally use modest amounts. Although this is not an expensive ingredient, we hate to just pitch the remaining unused portion. To determine the best way to store fresh ginger, we cut several knobs and stored them in different ways: unwrapped in a dark pantry, on the counter exposed to sunlight, and in the refrigerator or freezer in a variety of unwrapped or aluminum foil– or plastic-wrapped permutations.

After two weeks, all of the samples had dried out, with the frozen ginger faring the worst—after a brief thaw, it was porous and mushy. The room-temperature ginger had shriveled and started to sprout. The wrapped, refrigerated ginger was moldy where condensation had been trapped in the wrapper. The one ray of light was the unwrapped, refrigerated ginger, which had a relatively fresh appearance, with no mold. So the next time you have a leftover knob of ginger, ditch the plastic wrap and foil, and just toss it into the refrigerator unwrapped.

KUNG PAO SHRIMP
SERVES 4

You can substitute plain rice vinegar for the black vinegar, but we prefer the latter for its more complex flavor. Tasters had difficulty detecting differences between various types of peppers in this recipe; de árbol work well and are readily available and pequín make a good second option. You can substitute 1 teaspoon dried red pepper flakes or 3 coarsely crumbled chiles for the whole chiles. Do not eat the whole chiles in the finished dish. You can substitute roasted unsalted cashews for the peanuts if preferred.

SAUCE

¾	cup low-sodium chicken broth
1	tablespoon oyster sauce
1	tablespoon hoisin sauce
2	teaspoons Chinese black vinegar or plain rice vinegar
2	teaspoons toasted sesame oil
1½	teaspoons cornstarch

SHRIMP

1	pound extra-large shrimp (21 to 25 per pound), peeled and deveined
1	tablespoon dry sherry or Chinese rice cooking wine
2	teaspoons soy sauce
3	garlic cloves, minced
2	teaspoons grated fresh ginger
3	tablespoons vegetable oil
½	cup dry-roasted peanuts
6	small whole dried red chiles (each about 2 inches long)
1	red bell pepper, stemmed, seeded, and cut into ½-inch pieces
3	scallions, sliced thin

1. FOR THE SAUCE: Whisk all ingredients together in small bowl and set aside.

2. FOR THE SHRIMP: Toss shrimp with sherry and soy sauce in medium bowl and let marinate 10 minutes. Meanwhile, mix garlic, ginger, and 1 tablespoon oil in small bowl. Combine peanuts and chiles in second small bowl and set aside.

3. Heat 1 tablespoon oil in 12-inch skillet over high heat until just smoking. Add shrimp and cook, stirring about every 10 seconds, until barely opaque, 30 to 40 seconds. Add peanuts and chiles and continue to cook until shrimp are almost completely opaque and peanuts have darkened slightly, 30 to 40 seconds longer. Transfer mixture to bowl and set aside.

4. Add remaining 1 tablespoon oil to skillet and return to high heat until just smoking. Add bell pepper and cook, stirring occasionally, until slightly softened, about 45 seconds. Clear center of skillet, add garlic mixture, and cook, mashing into pan, until fragrant, 10 to 15 seconds. Stir mixture into peppers until combined.

5. Stir sauce to recombine, then add to skillet along with reserved shrimp, peanuts, and chiles. Cook, stirring and scraping up any browned bits, until sauce has thickened to syrupy consistency, about 45 seconds. Stir in scallions and serve immediately.

KUNG PAO CHICKEN
SERVES 4

While we prefer this dish made with chicken thighs rather than breasts because the dark meat has richer flavor and is less prone to drying out, if you prefer, you can replace the thighs with breasts. You can substitute plain rice vinegar for the black vinegar, but we prefer the latter for its more complex flavor. Tasters had difficulty detecting differences between various types of peppers in this recipe; de árbol work well and are readily available and pequín make a good second option. You can substitute 1 teaspoon dried red pepper flakes or 3 coarsely crumbled chiles for the whole chiles. Do not eat the whole chiles in the finished dish. You can substitute roasted unsalted cashews for the peanuts if preferred.

SAUCE
- ¾ cup low-sodium chicken broth
- 1 tablespoon oyster sauce
- 1 tablespoon hoisin sauce
- 2 teaspoons Chinese black vinegar or plain rice vinegar
- 2 teaspoons toasted sesame oil
- 1½ teaspoons cornstarch

CHICKEN
- 1 pound boneless, skinless chicken thighs, trimmed and cut into 1-inch pieces

- 1 tablespoon dry sherry or Chinese rice cooking wine
- 2 teaspoons soy sauce
- 3 garlic cloves, minced
- 2 teaspoons grated fresh ginger
- 3 tablespoons vegetable oil
- ½ cup dry-roasted peanuts
- 6 small whole dried red chiles (each about 2 inches long)
- 1 red bell pepper, stemmed, seeded, and cut into ½-inch pieces
- 3 scallions, sliced thin

1. FOR THE SAUCE: Whisk all ingredients together in small bowl and set aside.

2. FOR THE CHICKEN: Toss chicken with sherry and soy sauce in medium bowl and let marinate 10 minutes. Meanwhile, mix garlic, ginger, and 1 tablespoon oil in small bowl; set aside. Combine peanuts and chiles in second small bowl and set aside.

3. Heat 1 tablespoon oil in 12-inch skillet over high heat until just smoking. Add chicken and cook, without stirring, for 2 minutes, allowing chicken to brown on the first side. Stir and cook until no longer pink, 1½ to 2 minutes. Stir peanuts and chiles into chicken and continue cooking until peanuts have darkened slightly, 30 to 40 seconds longer. Transfer mixture to bowl and set aside.

4. Add remaining 1 tablespoon oil to skillet and return to high heat until just smoking. Add bell pepper and cook, stirring occasionally, until slightly softened, about 45 seconds. Clear center of skillet, add garlic mixture, and cook, mashing mixture into pan, until fragrant, 10 to 15 seconds. Stir mixture into peppers until combined.

5. Stir sauce to recombine, then add to skillet along with reserved chicken, peanuts, and chiles. Cook, stirring and scraping up any browned bits, until sauce has thickened to syrupy consistency, about 45 seconds. Stir in scallions and serve immediately.

FRIED RICE

✓ WHY THIS RECIPE WORKS
Fried rice is often a greasy, soggy mess. We wanted a quick supper dish with firm, separate rice grains and light, clean flavors. We found that the best fried rice recipe began with cold, dry rice—leftover rice was, in fact, the best choice. Instead of soy sauce alone, we used flavorful oyster sauce that yielded well seasoned but not soggy rice. For fresh-tasting fried rice that wasn't greasy, we batch-cooked the components in just 3 tablespoons of oil.

FRIED RICE WITH PEAS AND BEAN SPROUTS
SERVES 4 TO 6

We prefer baby peas in this recipe.

- ¼ cup oyster sauce
- 1 tablespoon soy sauce
- 3 tablespoons peanut oil or vegetable oil
- 2 large eggs, lightly beaten
- 1 cup frozen peas, thawed
- 2 garlic cloves, minced
- 6 cups cold cooked white rice, large clumps broken up with fingers
- 2 ounces (1 cup) bean sprouts
- 5 scallions, sliced thin

1. Combine oyster sauce and soy sauce in small bowl and set aside.

2. Heat 1½ teaspoons oil in 12-inch nonstick skillet over medium heat until shimmering. Add eggs and cook, without stirring, until they just begin to set, about 20 seconds. Scramble and break into small pieces with wooden spoon; continue to cook, stirring constantly, until eggs are cooked through but not browned, about 1 minute longer. Transfer eggs to small bowl and set aside.

3. Add remaining 2½ tablespoons oil to skillet and heat over medium heat until shimmering. Add peas and cook, stirring constantly, about 30 seconds. Stir in garlic and cook until fragrant, about 30 seconds. Add rice and oyster sauce mixture and cook, stirring constantly and breaking up rice clumps, until mixture is heated through, about 3 minutes. Add eggs, bean sprouts, and scallions and cook, stirring constantly, until heated through, about 1 minute. Serve immediately.

FRIED RICE WITH SHRIMP, HAM, AND SHIITAKES

SERVES 4 TO 6

We prefer baby peas in this recipe.

- ½ ounce dried shiitake mushrooms
- ¼ cup oyster sauce
- 1 tablespoon soy sauce
- 3½ tablespoons peanut oil or vegetable oil
- 2 large eggs, lightly beaten
- 8 ounces small shrimp (51 to 60 per pound), peeled and deveined
- 1 cup frozen peas, thawed
- 8 ounces sliced smoked ham, cut into ½-inch pieces
- 2 garlic cloves, minced
- 5 cups cold cooked white rice, large clumps broken up with fingers
- 5 scallions, sliced thin

1. Cover dried shiitakes with 1 cup hot tap water in small bowl. Microwave mushrooms, covered, for 30 seconds. Let sit until softened, about 5 minutes. Lift mushrooms from liquid with fork; discard liquid. Trim stems, slice into ¼-inch strips, and set aside.

2. Combine oyster sauce and soy sauce in small bowl and set aside.

3. Heat 1½ teaspoons oil in 12-inch nonstick skillet over medium heat until shimmering. Add eggs and cook, without stirring, until they just begin to set, about 20 seconds. Scramble and break into small pieces with wooden spoon; continue to cook, stirring constantly, until eggs are cooked through but not browned, about 1 minute longer. Transfer eggs to small bowl and set aside.

4. Add 1½ teaspoons oil to skillet and heat over medium heat until shimmering. Add shrimp and cook, stirring constantly, until opaque and just cooked through, about 30 seconds. Transfer shrimp to bowl with eggs and set aside.

5. Add remaining 2½ tablespoons oil to skillet and heat over medium heat until shimmering. Add mushrooms, peas, and ham and cook, stirring constantly, for 1 minute. Stir in garlic and cook until fragrant, about 30 seconds. Add rice and oyster sauce mixture and cook, stirring constantly and breaking up rice clumps, until mixture is heated through, about 3 minutes. Add eggs, shrimp, and scallions and cook, stirring constantly, until heated through, about 1 minute. Serve immediately.

THAI-STYLE CURRIED CHICKEN FRIED RICE

SERVES 4 TO 6

If you can't find Thai green chiles, 3 jalapeño chiles can be substituted.

- 3 tablespoons fish sauce
- 1 tablespoon soy sauce
- 1 tablespoon dark brown sugar
- 1 pound boneless, skinless chicken breasts, trimmed and cut into 1-inch pieces
  Salt
- 3½ tablespoons peanut oil or vegetable oil
- 2 large eggs, lightly beaten
- 1 tablespoon plus 1 teaspoon curry powder
- 1 large onion, sliced thin
- 5 Thai green chiles, stemmed, seeded, and minced (about 2 tablespoons)
- 2 garlic cloves, minced
- 6 cups cold cooked white rice, large clumps broken up with fingers
- 5 scallions, sliced thin
- 2 tablespoons minced fresh cilantro
  Lime wedges

1. Combine fish sauce, soy sauce, and sugar in small bowl and stir to dissolve sugar. Set aside. Season chicken with ½ teaspoon salt; set aside.

2. Heat 1½ teaspoons oil in 12-inch nonstick skillet over medium heat until shimmering. Add eggs and cook, without stirring, until they just begin to set, about 20 seconds. Scramble and break into small pieces with wooden spoon; continue to cook, stirring constantly, until eggs are cooked through but not browned, about 1 minute longer. Transfer eggs to small bowl and set aside.

3. Add 1½ teaspoons oil to skillet and heat over medium heat until shimmering. Add 1 teaspoon curry powder and cook until fragrant, about 30 seconds. Add chicken and cook, stirring constantly, until cooked through, about 2 minutes. Transfer to bowl with eggs and set aside.

4. Add remaining 2½ tablespoons oil to skillet and heat over medium heat until shimmering. Add onion and remaining 1 tablespoon curry powder and cook, stirring constantly, until onion is softened, about 3 minutes. Stir in chiles and garlic and cook until fragrant, about 30 seconds. Add rice and fish sauce mixture and cook, stirring constantly and breaking up rice clumps, until mixture is heated through, about 3 minutes. Add eggs, chicken, scallions, and cilantro and cook, stirring constantly, until heated through, about 1 minute. Serve immediately with lime wedges.

INDONESIAN-STYLE FRIED RICE

✔ WHY THIS RECIPE WORKS

With well-seasoned grains of rice, crunchy fried shallots, and egg, Indonesian-style fried rice offers plenty of complexity in terms of both texture and flavor. Chile paste, a combination of shallots, garlic, and fresh Thai chiles, which gives the dish heady flavor, was easy to make in the food processor. Fish sauce plus shrimp, which we sautéed with the chile paste, worked well in lieu of shrimp paste, and adding dark brown sugar and molasses to regular soy sauce stood in for the specialty soy sauce typically used. Stir-frying freshly cooked rice results in mushy clumps, but we didn't want to mess with cooking rice a day ahead. Cooking rinsed rice in less water than our standard 3:2 ratio of water to rice, then chilling it for 20 minutes, got us very close to our goal, and coating the grains with oil before adding the water to the pan further guarded against mushy results. Scallions, lime, and slices of egg, which we cooked omelet-style was all we needed to finish the dish.

INDONESIAN-STYLE FRIED RICE
SERVES 4 TO 6

If fresh Thai chiles are unavailable, substitute 2 serranos or 1 medium jalapeño. Adjust the spiciness of this dish by removing the ribs and seeds from the chiles. This dish progresses very quickly beginning with step 5; it's imperative that your ingredients are in place and ready to go. This dish is traditionally served with sliced cucumbers and tomato wedges.

- 2 tablespoons plus ½ cup vegetable oil
- 2 cups jasmine or long-grain white rice, rinsed
- 2⅔ cups water
- 5 green or red Thai chiles, stemmed
- 7 large shallots, peeled
- 4 large garlic cloves, peeled
- 2 tablespoons dark brown sugar
- 2 tablespoons light or mild molasses
- 2 tablespoons soy sauce
- 2 tablespoons fish sauce
   Salt
- 4 large eggs
- 12 ounces extra-large shrimp (21 to 25 per pound), peeled, deveined, tails removed, and cut crosswise into thirds
- 4 large scallions, sliced thin
   Lime wedges

1. Heat 2 tablespoons oil in large saucepan over medium heat until shimmering. Add rice and stir to coat grains with oil, about 30 seconds. Add water, increase heat to high, and bring to boil. Reduce heat to low, cover, and simmer until all liquid is absorbed, about 18 minutes. Off heat, remove lid and place clean kitchen towel folded in half over saucepan; replace lid. Let stand until rice is just tender, about 8 minutes. Spread cooked rice onto rimmed baking sheet, set on wire rack, and cool for 10 minutes. Transfer to refrigerator and chill for 20 minutes.

2. While rice is chilling, pulse chiles, 4 shallots, and garlic in food processor until coarse paste is formed, about 15 pulses, scraping down sides of bowl as necessary. Transfer mixture to small bowl and set aside. In second small bowl, stir together brown sugar, molasses, soy sauce, fish sauce, and 1¼ teaspoons salt. Whisk eggs and ¼ teaspoon salt together in medium bowl.

3. Thinly slice remaining 3 shallots (you should have about 1 cup sliced shallots) and place in 12-inch nonstick skillet with remaining ½ cup oil. Heat over medium heat, stirring constantly, until shallots are golden and crisp, 6 to 10 minutes. Using slotted spoon, transfer shallots to paper towel–lined plate and season with salt to taste. Pour off oil and reserve. Wipe out skillet with paper towels

4. Heat 1 teaspoon reserved oil in now-empty skillet over medium heat until shimmering. Add half of eggs to skillet, gently tilting pan to evenly coat bottom. Cover and cook until bottom of omelet is spotty golden brown and top is just set, about 1½ minutes. Slide omelet onto cutting board and gently roll up into tight log. Using sharp knife, cut log crosswise into 1-inch segments (leaving segments rolled). Repeat with 1 teaspoon reserved oil and remaining eggs.

5. Remove rice from refrigerator and break up any large clumps with fingers. Heat 3 tablespoons reserved oil in now-empty skillet over medium heat until just shimmering. Add chile mixture and cook until mixture turns golden, 3 to 5 minutes. Add shrimp, increase heat to medium-high, and cook, stirring constantly, until exterior of shrimp is just opaque, about 2 minutes. Push shrimp to sides of skillet to clear center; stir molasses mixture to recombine and pour into center of skillet. When molasses mixture bubbles, add rice and cook, stirring and folding constantly, until shrimp is cooked, rice is heated through, and mixture is evenly coated, about 3 minutes. Stir in scallions, remove from heat, and transfer to serving platter. Garnish with egg segments, fried shallots, and lime wedges; serve immediately.

SESAME NOODLES WITH SHREDDED CHICKEN

✔ WHY THIS RECIPE WORKS

To avoid the pitfalls of most sesame noodle recipes—gummy noodles and bland, pasty sauce—we rinsed the cooked noodles to rid them of excess starch. Chunky peanut butter processed with toasted sesame seeds worked surprisingly well for the sauce's base. Garlic, ginger, soy sauce, rice vinegar, hot sauce, and brown sugar rounded out the flavors, and thinning the sauce with water achieved the best texture to coat the noodles without being gloppy. All that was needed was moist shreds of chicken, which we cooked quickly in the broiler.

SESAME NOODLES WITH SHREDDED CHICKEN

SERVES 4 TO 6

We prefer the flavor and texture of chunky peanut butter in the sauce. We like conventional chunky peanut butter here; it tends to be sweeter than natural or old-fashioned versions.

SAUCE

¼ cup sesame seeds, toasted
¼ cup chunky peanut butter
5 tablespoons soy sauce
2 tablespoons rice vinegar
2 tablespoons light brown sugar
1 tablespoon grated fresh ginger
2 garlic cloves, minced
1 teaspoon hot sauce
5 tablespoons hot water

CHICKEN AND NOODLES

1½ pounds boneless, skinless chicken breasts, trimmed
1 pound fresh Chinese noodles or 12 ounces dried spaghetti
1 tablespoon salt
2 tablespoons toasted sesame oil
4 scallions, sliced thin on bias
1 carrot, grated

1. FOR THE SAUCE: Puree 3 tablespoons sesame seeds, peanut butter, soy sauce, vinegar, sugar, ginger, garlic, and hot sauce in blender or food processor, about 30 seconds. With machine running, add hot water, 1 tablespoon at a time, until sauce has consistency of heavy cream.

2. FOR THE CHICKEN AND NOODLES: Bring 6 quarts water to boil in large pot. Position oven rack 6 inches from broiler element and heat broiler. Spray broiler pan top with vegetable oil spray, place chicken breasts on top, and broil until lightly browned, 4 to 8 minutes. Flip chicken over and continue to broil until meat

registers 160 to 165 degrees, 6 to 8 minutes. Transfer to cutting board and let rest 5 minutes. Shred chicken into bite-size pieces and set aside.

3. Add noodles and salt to boiling water and cook, stirring occasionally, until tender, about 4 minutes for fresh or 10 minutes for dried. Drain, then rinse under cold water until cool. Drain again, transfer to large bowl, add sesame oil, and toss to coat. Add shredded chicken, scallions, carrot, and sauce and toss to combine. Divide among bowls, sprinkle with remaining 1 tablespoon sesame seeds, and serve.

SESAME NOODLES WITH SWEET PEPPERS AND CUCUMBERS

Omit chicken. Add 1 red bell pepper, stemmed, seeded, and sliced into ¼ inch-thick strips and 1 cucumber, peeled, halved lengthwise, seeded, and cut crosswise into ⅛-inch-thick slices, to noodles with sauce. Sprinkle servings with 1 tablespoon chopped fresh cilantro along with sesame seeds.

SPICY SICHUAN NOODLES

✔ WHY THIS RECIPE WORKS

This popular Chinese street food (known as dan dan mian) tops noodles with a rich, savory sauce of ground pork, ginger, garlic, soy sauce, and Asian sesame paste, and, of course, spicy chiles. An authentic-tasting sauce was simple to put together using pantry staples. We used peanut butter in lieu of the sesame paste, though we recommend using the Asian sesame paste if you can find it, as it lends an unusual smoky, earthy flavor to the sauce. Red pepper flakes lend the heat of chiles. While dried or fresh Chinese noodles work best here, linguine are fine in a pinch.

SPICY SICHUAN NOODLES

SERVES 4

If you cannot find Asian noodles, linguine may be substituted. If you are using natural peanut butter or Asian sesame paste that has a pourable rather than spreadable consistency, use only 1 cup of chicken broth. Also note that the amount of sauce will coat 1 pound of fresh noodles but only 12 ounces of dried noodles, which bulk up during boiling.

8 ounces ground pork
3 tablespoons soy sauce
2 tablespoons Chinese rice cooking wine or dry sherry
 Ground white pepper
2 tablespoons oyster sauce
¼ cup peanut butter or Asian sesame paste
1 tablespoon rice vinegar
1–1¼ cups low-sodium chicken broth
1 tablespoon vegetable oil
6 garlic cloves, minced
1 tablespoon grated fresh ginger
¾ teaspoon red pepper flakes
1 tablespoon toasted sesame oil
12 ounces dried Asian noodles or 1 pound fresh Asian noodles (width between linguine and fettuccine) or 12 ounces linguine
3 medium scallions, sliced thin
4 ounces bean sprouts (2 cups) (optional)
1 tablespoon Sichuan peppercorns, toasted and ground (optional)

1. Combine pork, 1 tablespoon soy sauce, wine, and pinch white pepper in small bowl. Stir well and set aside. Whisk together oyster sauce, remaining 2 tablespoons soy sauce, peanut butter, vinegar, and pinch white pepper in medium bowl. Whisk in chicken broth and set aside.

2. Bring 4 quarts water to boil in

large pot over high heat. Meanwhile, heat 12-inch skillet over high heat, add vegetable oil and swirl to coat. Add pork and cook, breaking meat into small pieces, until well browned, about 5 minutes. Stir in garlic, ginger, and pepper flakes and cook until fragrant, about 1 minute. Add peanut butter mixture and bring to boil, whisking to combine, then reduce heat to medium-low and simmer to blend flavors, stirring occasionally, about 3 minutes. Stir in sesame oil.

3. While sauce simmers, add noodles to boiling water and cook until tender. Drain noodles and divide among bowls. Ladle sauce over noodles, sprinkle with scallions and bean sprouts and ground Sichuan peppercorns, if using. Serve immediately.

SPICY SICHUAN NOODLES WITH SHIITAKE MUSHROOMS

Soak 8 small dried shiitake mushrooms in 1 cup boiling water until softened, 15 to 20 minutes, then drain, reserving ½ cup soaking liquid. Trim and discard stems, cut mushrooms into ¼-inch slices, and set aside. Substitute reserved mushroom liquid for equal amount of chicken stock and stir sliced mushrooms into sauce along with sesame oil.

PAD THAI

✔ WHY THIS RECIPE WORKS
For pad thai with tender but not sticky noodles, we soaked rice sticks in hot tap water for 20 minutes before stir-frying them just briefly. To create the salty, sweet, sour, and spicy flavor profile of pad thai, we combined a few easily found ingredients: fish sauce, sugar, cayenne pepper, and vinegar. Tamarind paste, which we soaked then ran through a strainer to make a smooth puree, lent the fresh, bright, fruity taste that is essential to the dish.

PAD THAI
SERVES 4

Although pad thai cooks very quickly, the ingredient list is long, and everything must be prepared and within easy reach at the stovetop when you begin cooking. For maximum efficiency, use the time during which the tamarind and noodles soak to prepare the other ingredients. If tamarind paste is unavailable, substitute ⅓ cup lime juice and ⅓ cup water and use light brown sugar instead of granulated. To accurately measure boiling water, bring the water to a boil, then measure it. Look for rice stick noodles that are about the width of linguine. Tofu is a good and common addition to pad thai; if you like, add 4 ounces of extra-firm tofu or pressed tofu (available in Asian markets), cut into ½-inch cubes, to the noodles along with the bean sprouts.

2 tablespoons tamarind paste
¾ cup boiling water
3 tablespoons fish sauce
3 tablespoons sugar
1 tablespoon rice vinegar
¾ teaspoon cayenne pepper
¼ cup vegetable oil
8 ounces dried rice stick noodles, about ⅛ inch wide
2 large eggs
¼ teaspoon salt
12 ounces medium shrimp (41 to 50 per pound), peeled and deveined
3 garlic cloves, minced
1 shallot, minced
2 tablespoons dried shrimp, chopped fine (optional)
2 tablespoons Thai salted preserved radish (optional)
6 tablespoons dry-roasted peanuts, chopped
6 ounces bean sprouts (3 cups)
5 scallions, green parts only, sliced thin on bias
¼ cup fresh cilantro leaves (optional)
Lime wedges

1. Soak tamarind paste in boiling water for about 10 minutes, then push it through mesh strainer to remove seeds and fibers and extract as much pulp as possible. Stir fish sauce, sugar, rice vinegar, cayenne, and 2 tablespoons oil into tamarind liquid and set aside.

2. Cover rice sticks with hot tap water in large bowl; soak until softened, pliable, and limp but not fully tender, about 10 minutes. Drain noodles and set aside. Beat eggs and ⅛ teaspoon salt in small bowl; set aside.

3. Heat 1 tablespoon oil in 12-inch nonstick skillet over high heat until just smoking. Add shrimp, sprinkle with remaining ⅛ teaspoon salt, and cook, tossing occasionally, until shrimp are opaque and browned around the edges, about 3 minutes. Transfer shrimp to plate and set aside.

4. Off heat, add remaining 1 tablespoon oil and swirl to coat. Add garlic and shallot, return to medium heat, and cook, stirring constantly, until light golden brown, about 1½ minutes. Add eggs and stir vigorously until scrambled and barely moist, about 20 seconds.

5. Add noodles, along with dried shrimp and salted radish, if using, to skillet and toss to combine. Pour fish sauce mixture over noodles, increase heat to high, and cook, tossing constantly, until noodles are evenly coated.

6. Scatter ¼ cup peanuts, bean sprouts, all but ¼ cup scallions, and cooked shrimp over noodles. Continue to cook, tossing constantly, until noodles are tender, about 2½ minutes (if not yet tender, add 2 tablespoons water to skillet and continue to cook until tender). Transfer noodles to serving platter, sprinkle with remaining scallions, remaining 2 tablespoons peanuts, and cilantro. Serve immediately, passing lime wedges separately.

PORK LO MEIN

✔ WHY THIS RECIPE WORKS

For lo mein with chewy noodles tossed in a salty-sweet sauce and accented with bits of smoky pork and still-crisp cabbage, we seared strips of meat from naturally tender country-style pork ribs over high heat. Adding liquid smoke lent a flavor reminiscent of Chinese barbecued pork, or char siu, which is traditional in this dish. We used our meat marinade as a sauce base, along with a little chicken broth and a teaspoon of cornstarch for added body. In the absence of lo mein noodles from an Asian market, we found that dried linguine worked well. A little Asian chili-garlic sauce added at the end lent a nice finishing kick.

PORK LO MEIN
SERVES 4

Use a cast-iron skillet for this recipe if you have one, as it will help create the best sear on the pork. Look for Chinese rice wine that is amber in color; if not available, sherry wine may be used as a substitute. If boneless pork ribs are unavailable, substitute 1½ pounds of bone-in country-style ribs, followed by the next best option, pork tenderloin. It is important that the noodles are cooked at the last minute to avoid clumping.

- 3 tablespoons soy sauce
- 2 tablespoons oyster sauce
- 2 tablespoons hoisin sauce
- 1 tablespoon toasted sesame oil
- ¼ teaspoon five-spice powder
- ¼ teaspoon liquid smoke (optional)
- 1 pound boneless country-style pork ribs, trimmed and sliced crosswise into ⅛-inch pieces
- ½ cup low-sodium chicken broth
- 1 teaspoon cornstarch
- 2 garlic cloves, minced
- 2 teaspoons grated fresh ginger
- 4½ teaspoons vegetable oil
- ¼ cup Chinese rice cooking wine or dry sherry
- 8 ounces shiitake mushrooms, stemmed and sliced ¼ inch thick
- 2 bunches scallions, whites thinly sliced and greens cut into 1-inch pieces
- 1 small head napa or Chinese cabbage (1 pound), halved, cored, and sliced crosswise into ½-inch strips
- 12 ounces fresh Chinese egg noodles or 8 ounces dried linguine
- 1 tablespoon Asian chili-garlic sauce

1. Whisk soy sauce, oyster sauce, hoisin sauce, sesame oil, and five-spice powder together in medium bowl. Place 3 tablespoons soy sauce mixture and liquid smoke, if using, in large zipper-lock bag. Add pork, press out as much air as possible, and seal bag, making sure that all pieces are coated with marinade. Refrigerate at least 15 minutes or up to 1 hour. Meanwhile, whisk broth and cornstarch into remaining soy sauce mixture in medium bowl and set aside. In small bowl, combine garlic, ginger, and ½ teaspoon vegetable oil and set aside.

2. Bring 4 quarts water to boil in Dutch oven or large pot over high heat. Heat 1 teaspoon vegetable oil in 12-inch cast-iron or nonstick skillet over high heat until just smoking. Add half of pork in single layer, break up any clumps, and cook, without stirring, 1 minute. Continue to cook, stirring occasionally, until browned, 2 to 3 minutes. Add 2 tablespoons wine to skillet and cook, stirring constantly, until liquid is reduced and pork is well coated, 30 to 60 seconds. Transfer pork to medium bowl and repeat with 1 teaspoon vegetable oil, remaining pork, and remaining 2 tablespoons wine. Wipe skillet clean with paper towels.

3. Heat 1 teaspoon vegetable oil over high heat until just smoking. Add mushrooms and cook, stirring occasionally, until light golden brown, 4 to 6 minutes. Add scallions and continue to cook, stirring occasionally, until scallions are wilted, 2 to

3 minutes longer. Transfer vegetables to bowl with pork.

4. Add remaining 1 teaspoon vegetable oil and cabbage to skillet and cook, stirring occasionally, until spotty brown, 3 to 5 minutes. Clear center of skillet, add garlic mixture, and cook, mashing mixture into pan, until fragrant, 15 to 20 seconds. Stir garlic mixture into cabbage.

5. Return pork and vegetables to skillet. Add broth mixture and simmer until thickened and ingredients are well incorporated, 1 to 2 minutes. Remove skillet from heat.

6. Stir noodles into boiling water and cook, stirring occasionally, until noodles are tender, 3 to 4 minutes for fresh Chinese noodles or 10 minutes for dried linguine. Drain noodles and return to Dutch oven. Add cooked stir-fry mixture and chili-garlic sauce to pot with noodles and toss until sauce coats noodles. Serve immediately.

ASIAN NOODLES WITH WINTER GREENS

✔ WHY THIS RECIPE WORKS

Noodles and greens are a common pairing in Asia, so we set out to develop a few recipes with character. By cooking the noodles and greens together, we saved time as well as the trouble of washing another pot. Because fresh noodles cook so quickly, we made sure to add the greens to the pot before the noodles. For our first recipe, we started with meaty shiitake mushrooms and opted for a complementary sweet-savory sauce of sesame oil, chicken broth, mirin, and soy sauce. Chili-garlic sauce, ginger, and garlic gave it the right punch. For our second recipe, a combination of cinnamon, anise, cloves, and ginger infused the sauce with warmth, while Asian chili-garlic sauce added the heat we were after. Simmering slices of beef in this sauce infused both meat and sauce with flavor and kept things moving since the sauce reduced as the meat cooked through.

MUSTARD GREENS AND UDON NOODLES WITH SHIITAKE-GINGER SAUCE

SERVES 4

Shiitake mushrooms contain a tough stem that should be removed—if you use white mushrooms, the stem does not need to be removed. Fresh Japanese udon noodles can be found in the produce section of large supermarkets. If they are not available, you can substitute dried or frozen udon or dried fettuccine in step 2, add the dried or frozen noodles to the boiling water and cook, stirring occasionally, until they begin to soften, 5 to 6 minutes, then add the greens and cook 3 to 4 minutes, until the noodles are al dente and the greens are wilted. You can substitute vegetable broth for the chicken broth to make this a vegetarian recipe.

SAUCE

- 1½ cups low-sodium chicken broth
- 8 ounces shiitake mushrooms, stemmed, trimmed, and sliced thin or a combination of white and shiitake mushrooms
- ¼ cup rice vinegar
- ¼ cup mirin
- 2 tablespoons soy sauce
- 2 garlic cloves, crushed with side of chef's knife
- 1 (1-inch) piece ginger, halved and smashed with side of chef's knife
- 1 teaspoon toasted sesame oil
- ½ teaspoon Asian chili-garlic sauce
  Salt and pepper

GREENS AND NOODLES

- 1½ pounds mustard greens, stemmed and leaves chopped into 2-inch pieces
  Salt and pepper
- 14 ounces fresh udon noodles

1. FOR THE SAUCE: Combine all ingredients in large saucepan or skillet and simmer until liquid thickens and reduces by half, 8 to 10 minutes. Remove from heat, remove garlic and ginger, and season with salt and pepper to taste. Cover to keep warm.

2. FOR THE GREENS AND NOODLES: While sauce simmers, bring 5 quarts water to boil in large pot. Add greens and 1 tablespoon salt and cook until greens are almost tender, 4 to 5 minutes. Add noodles and cook until greens and noodles are tender, about 2 minutes longer. Reserve ⅓ cup cooking water, drain noodles and greens, and return to pot. Add sauce and reserved cooking water and cook over medium-low heat, stirring to meld flavors, about 1 minute. Season with salt and pepper to taste and serve immediately.

BOK CHOY, BEEF, AND CHINESE EGG NOODLES WITH SPICY SAUCE

SERVES 4

Dried linguine can be substituted for the fresh Chinese egg noodles; in step 3, add the linguine to the boiling water and cook, stirring occasionally, until it begins to soften, 5 to 6 minutes, then add the bok choy and cook 3 to 4 minutes, until the noodles are al dente and the bok choy is wilted.

SAUCE

- 1½ tablespoons vegetable oil
- 2 (3-inch-long) cinnamon sticks, broken in half
- 2 whole cloves
- 1 teaspoon anise seeds
- 4 garlic cloves, sliced thin
- 1 (1-inch) piece ginger, peeled and sliced into thin matchsticks
- 1 cup low-sodium chicken broth
- 1½ teaspoons Asian chili-garlic sauce

- 8 ounces beef sirloin or rib-eye steak, trimmed, halved crosswise, and sliced thin across the grain
  Salt and pepper

GREENS AND NOODLES

- 1½ pounds bok choy, bottom 2 inches of base discarded, remainder cut crosswise into ¾-inch pieces
  Salt and pepper
- 12 ounces fresh Chinese egg noodles

1. FOR THE SAUCE: Heat oil in a large sauté pan over medium-high heat until shimmering. Add cinnamon sticks, cloves, and anise seeds and stir until cinnamon sticks unfurl and cloves pop, about 1 minute. Add garlic and ginger and cook until beginning to soften, about 2 minutes. Add chicken stock and chili-garlic sauce, reduce heat to medium-low, and simmer until liquid reduces by half, about 4 minutes.

2. Remove cinnamon sticks and cloves. Add beef and simmer until meat is gray around edges and still slightly pink in center, about 1 minute. Remove from heat, season with salt and pepper to taste, and cover to keep warm.

3. FOR THE GREENS AND NOODLES: Meanwhile, bring 5 quarts water to boil in large pot. Add bok choy and 1 tablespoon salt and cook until bok choy is almost tender, 4 to 5 minutes. Add noodles and cook until bok choy and noodles are tender, about 2 minutes longer. Reserve ⅓ cup cooking water, drain noodles and bok choy, and return to pot. Add sauce and reserved cooking water and cook over medium-low heat, stirring to meld flavors, about 1 minute. Season with salt and pepper to taste and serve immediately.

CHAPTER 6 Pasta

PASTA WITH GARLIC AND OLIVE OIL

✔ WHY THIS RECIPE WORKS

Nothing sounds easier than pasta with olive oil and garlic, but too often this Italian pantry classic, aglio e olio, turns out oily or rife with burnt garlic. For deep, mellow garlic flavor, we cooked most of the garlic over low heat; a modest amount of raw garlic added at the end brought in some potent fresh garlic flavor. Extra-virgin olive oil and reserved pasta cooking water helped to keep our pasta saucy. A splash of lemon juice and a sprinkling of red pepper flakes added some brightness and heat to this simple, yet complex-flavored dish.

PASTA WITH GARLIC AND OLIVE OIL
SERVES 4

It pays to use high-quality extra-virgin olive oil in this dish.

1	pound spaghetti
	Salt
6	tablespoons extra-virgin olive oil
12	garlic cloves, minced
¾	teaspoon red pepper flakes
3	tablespoons chopped fresh parsley
2	teaspoons lemon juice
1	ounce Parmesan cheese, grated (½ cup)

1. Bring 4 quarts water to boil in large pot. Add pasta and 1 tablespoon salt and cook, stirring often, until al dente. Reserve ⅓ cup cooking water, then drain pasta.

2. Meanwhile, heat 3 tablespoons oil, two-thirds of garlic, and ½ teaspoon salt in 10-inch nonstick skillet over low heat. Cook, stirring constantly, until garlic foams and is sticky and straw-colored, about 10 minutes. Off heat, add remaining garlic, pepper flakes, parsley, lemon juice, and 2 tablespoons reserved cooking water.

3. Transfer drained pasta to warm serving bowl. Add garlic mixture, remaining 3 tablespoons oil, and remaining reserved cooking water to pasta and toss to combine. Season with salt to taste and serve immediately, passing Parmesan separately.

PASTA WITH SIMPLE OLIVE OIL SAUCES

✔ WHY THIS RECIPE WORKS

We love pasta with garlic and olive oil, but sometimes a fresh take on this classic is in order. We wanted to boost the flavor in this dish with easy-to-find pantry ingredients. Just a few garlic cloves delivered plenty of flavor. Fried capers are an simple way to give pasta loads of flavor, especially when combined with small amounts of minced anchovy or tomato paste for depth and balance; a few chopped sun-dried tomatoes added concentrated sweetness to contrast with olives in another variation.

SPAGHETTI WITH FRIED CAPERS AND ANCHOVIES
SERVES 4

To keep the capers from splattering during frying, pat them dry thoroughly with paper towels before adding them to the skillet.

⅓	cup extra-virgin olive oil
½	cup capers, rinsed and patted dry
4	anchovy fillets, rinsed and minced
4	garlic cloves, minced
	Salt and pepper
1	pound spaghetti or linguine
¼	cup chopped fresh parsley (optional)

1. Heat oil in 10-inch skillet over medium-high heat until shimmering. Add capers and cook, stirring occasionally, until capers darken, become crisp, and pop open, about 4 minutes. Remove capers with slotted spoon and transfer to paper towel–lined plate. Let skillet cool slightly, about 3 minutes.

2. Add anchovies, garlic, and ½ teaspoon salt to now-empty skillet and cook over medium-low heat, stirring constantly, until garlic turns golden but not brown, about 3 minutes; remove from heat.

3. Meanwhile, bring 4 quarts water to boil in large pot. Add pasta and 1 tablespoon salt and cook, stirring often, until al dente. Reserve ¼ cup cooking water, then drain pasta and return it to pot. Add crisp capers, garlic mixture, parsley, if using, and reserved cooking water to pasta and toss to combine. Season with salt and pepper to taste and serve immediately.

PASTA WITH OLIVES, GARLIC, AND HERBS
SERVES 4

For a milder olive flavor, use manzanilla olives in place of kalamata. Be sure to rinse the pitted olives before chopping them to remove excess

---

TEST KITCHEN TIP NO. 33   A FRESH CRUSH IS BEST

We're always looking for ways to make our kitchen work more efficient and will often prep ingredients in advance if we know we've got a lot of recipes to get through on a given day. But noticing that garlic can develop a particularly strong odor if minced too far in advance, we decided to run a quick test. We used garlic in three different applications: lightly cooked in Pasta with Garlic and Oil, stirred raw into mayonnaise, and whisked raw into vinaigrette. For each recipe, we used freshly minced garlic, garlic that had been minced six hours in advance, and garlic that had been minced the day before. Both the six-hour and one-day-old minced garlic were so powerful they overwhelmed the other flavors in the dish.

It turns out, the garlic flavor is not formed until after the garlic's cells are ruptured. As soon as you cut into garlic, the flavor will start to build and build until it becomes overwhelmingly strong. So if you're going to prep a recipe in advance, make sure to leave the garlic cloves whole until the last minute.

You've probably noticed that your neighborhood grocer has two different varieties of this recognizable herb available (though there are actually more than 30 varieties out there): curly-leaf and flat-leaf (also called Italian). Curly-leaf parsley is more popular, but in the test kitchen flat-leaf is by far the favorite. We find flat-leaf to have a sweet, bright flavor that's much preferable to the bitter, grassy tones of curly-leaf. Flat-leaf parsley is also much more fragrant than its curly cousin. While curly parsley might look nice alongside your steak, don't count on it to improve flavor if you use it in cooking.

salt. Use the smaller amount of red pepper flakes for a milder sauce. In addition to mezzi rigatoni or farfalle, any short, tubular, or molded pasta will work well.

1 cup pitted kalamata olives, rinsed and chopped coarse
¼ cup oil-packed sun-dried tomatoes, rinsed, patted dry, and cut into ¼-inch-wide strips
5 tablespoons extra-virgin olive oil
6 garlic cloves, minced
5 anchovy fillets, rinsed and minced
1 tablespoon tomato paste
¼–½ teaspoon red pepper flakes
2 slices hearty white sandwich bread, torn into quarters
Salt and pepper
1 pound mezzi rigatoni or farfalle
1½ cups chopped fresh basil
1 ounce Parmesan cheese, grated fine (½ cup), plus extra for serving
3 tablespoons chopped fresh parsley
Lemon wedges

1. Combine olives, sun-dried tomatoes, 3 tablespoons oil, half of garlic, anchovies, tomato paste, and pepper flakes; set aside.

2. Pulse bread in food processor to coarse crumbs, about 10 pulses. Heat remaining 2 tablespoons oil in 12-inch skillet over medium heat until shimmering. Add bread crumbs and cook, stirring often, until beginning to brown, 4 to 6 minutes. Stir in remaining garlic and ¼ teaspoon salt and continue to cook, stirring often, until garlic is fragrant and bread crumbs are dark golden brown, 1 to

2 minutes longer. Transfer crumb mixture to bowl and wipe skillet clean with paper towels.

3. Bring 4 quarts water to boil in large pot. Add pasta and 1 tablespoon salt and cook, stirring often, until just shy of al dente. While pasta is cooking, add olive mixture to now-empty skillet and cook over medium heat until aromatic and oil has turned rusty red, 4 to 6 minutes. Remove ¾ cup pasta cooking water from pot and add to skillet. Bring to simmer and cook for 2 minutes; set aside while pasta finishes cooking.

4. When pasta is just shy of al dente, reserve ½ cup cooking water, then drain pasta and return it to pot. Add olive mixture to pasta and cook over medium heat, tossing to combine, until pasta absorbs most of liquid, about 2 minutes.

5. Off heat, stir in basil, Parmesan, and parsley. Add reserved cooking water as needed to adjust consistency. Season with pepper to taste and serve, passing bread crumbs, lemon wedges, and Parmesan separately.

BASIL PESTO

WHY THIS RECIPE WORKS

Our goal in developing our pesto was to heighten the basil and subdue the garlic flavors so that each major element balanced the other. We started with plenty of fresh basil and pounded to bruise it and release flavorful oils. To tame the raw garlic edge, we toasted it, toasting the nuts as well to give them more intense flavor. And, we used a food processor to combine the ingredients in our pesto quickly and easily.

CLASSIC BASIL PESTO
MAKES ENOUGH FOR 1 POUND OF PASTA

Basil usually darkens in homemade pesto, but you can boost the green color a little by adding the optional parsley. For sharper flavor, use Pecorino Romano cheese in place of the Parmesan. When adding pesto to cooked pasta it is important to include 3 or 4 tablespoons of the pasta cooking water for proper consistency and even distribution.

3 garlic cloves, unpeeled
¼ cup pine nuts
2 cups fresh basil leaves
2 tablespoons fresh parsley leaves (optional)
7 tablespoons extra-virgin olive oil
Salt and pepper
¼ cup finely grated Parmesan cheese or Pecorino Romano cheese

1. Toast garlic in 8-inch skillet over medium heat, shaking pan occasionally, until softened and spotty brown, about 8 minutes; when cool enough to handle, remove and discard skins. While garlic cools, toast nuts in now-empty skillet over medium heat, stirring often, until golden and fragrant, 4 to 5 minutes.

2. Place basil and parsley, if using, in gallon-size zipper-lock bag. Pound bag with flat side of meat pounder or rolling pin until all leaves are bruised.

3. Process garlic, nuts, herbs, oil, and ½ teaspoon salt in food processor until smooth, about 1 minute, scraping down bowl as needed. Transfer mixture to small bowl, stir in Parmesan, and season with salt and pepper to taste. (Pesto can be refrigerated for up to 3 days in bowl with plastic wrap or thin layer of oil covering surface.)

TOMATO AND ALMOND PESTO

✔ WHY THIS RECIPE WORKS

Not all pesto is based on basil, pine nuts, and Parmesan. In Sicily, tomatoes and almonds take center stage. For our clean, bright version, we used toasted ground almonds, which provided body and crunch to offset the tomatoes' pulpiness, and a modest amount of olive oil to make the sauce creamy without too much richness. The result was a tomato pesto with fruity, vibrant sweetness.

TOMATO AND ALMOND PESTO (PESTO ALLA TRAPANESE)

MAKES ENOUGH FOR 1 POUND OF PASTA

You may substitute ½ teaspoon red wine vinegar and ¼ teaspoon of red pepper flakes for the pepperoncini. When adding pesto to cooked pasta it is important to include 3 or 4 tablespoons of the pasta cooking water for proper consistency and even distribution. Serve the pesto-coated pasta with grated Parmesan cheese.

12	ounces cherry or grape tomatoes
½	cup fresh basil leaves
¼	cup slivered almonds, toasted
1	small jarred pepperoncini, stemmed, seeded, and minced
1	garlic clove, minced
1	teaspoon salt
	Pinch red pepper flakes (optional)
⅓	cup extra-virgin olive oil

Process tomatoes, basil, almonds, pepperoncini, garlic, salt, and pepper flakes, if using, in food processor until smooth, about 1 minute, scraping down sides of bowl as needed. With machine running, slowly drizzle in oil, about 30 seconds. (Pesto can be refrigerated for up to 3 days in bowl with plastic wrap or thin layer of oil covering surface.)

TOMATO, PINE NUT, AND ARUGULA PESTO

Substitute ¼ cup pine nuts for almonds and ¾ cup baby arugula for basil. Add 1¼ teaspoons grated lemon zest and 1 teaspoon lemon juice to food processor with other ingredients. (Pesto can be refrigerated for up to 3 days in bowl with plastic wrap or thin layer of oil covering surface.)

WINTERTIME PESTO

✔ WHY THIS RECIPE WORKS

For a pesto that can be prepared in colder months when basil is hard to come by, we turned to arugula, parsley, and thyme in place of basil and added flavor with nuts, mushrooms, and roasted red peppers. For easy preparation, we use the food processor to puree the sauce.

ARUGULA AND RICOTTA PESTO

MAKES ENOUGH FOR 1 POUND OF PASTA

When adding pesto to cooked pasta it is important to include 3 or 4 tablespoons of the pasta cooking water for proper consistency and even distribution.

3	garlic cloves, unpeeled
¼	cup pine nuts
1	cup baby arugula
1	cup fresh parsley leaves
7	tablespoons extra-virgin olive oil
⅓	cup whole-milk ricotta cheese
2	tablespoons grated Parmesan cheese
	Salt and pepper

1. Toast garlic in 8-inch skillet over medium heat, shaking pan occasionally, until softened and spotty brown, about 8 minutes; when cool enough to handle, remove and discard skins. While garlic cools, toast nuts in now-empty skillet over medium heat, stirring often, until golden and fragrant, 4 to 5 minutes.

2. Place arugula and parsley in gallon-size zipper-lock bag. Pound bag with flat side of meat pounder or rolling pin until all leaves are bruised.

3. Process garlic, nuts, arugula, parsley, and oil in food processor until smooth, about 1 minute, scraping down bowl as needed. Transfer mixture to small bowl, stir in ricotta and Parmesan, and season with salt and pepper to taste. (Pesto can be refrigerated for up to 3 days in bowl with plastic wrap or thin layer of oil covering surface.)

MUSHROOM PESTO WITH PARSLEY AND THYME

MAKES ENOUGH FOR 1 POUND OF PASTA

When adding pesto to cooked pasta it is important to include 3 or 4 tablespoons of the pasta cooking water for proper consistency and even distribution.

½	cup water
½	ounce dried porcini mushrooms, rinsed
10	ounces white mushrooms, trimmed and sliced ¼ inch thick
9	tablespoons extra-virgin olive oil
	Salt and pepper
3	garlic cloves, unpeeled
¼	cup fresh parsley leaves
1	small shallot, chopped coarse
1	tablespoon minced fresh thyme
¼	cup grated Parmesan cheese

1. Microwave water and porcini in covered bowl until steaming, about 1 minute. Let stand until softened, about 5 minutes. Drain mushrooms through fine-mesh strainer lined with coffee filter, reserving liquid.

2. Adjust oven rack to lowest position and heat oven to 450 degrees. Toss white mushrooms with 2 tablespoons oil, ¼ teaspoon salt, and ¼ teaspoon pepper in bowl

and spread evenly over aluminum foil–lined rimmed baking sheet. Roast, stirring occasionally, until browned, about 25 minutes.

3. Meanwhile, toast garlic in 8-inch skillet over medium heat, shaking pan occasionally, until softened and spotty brown, about 8 minutes; when cool enough to handle, remove and discard skins.

4. Process roasted mushrooms, garlic, porcini, reserved porcini soaking liquid, parsley, shallot, thyme, and remaining 7 tablespoons oil in food processor until smooth, about 1 minute, scraping down bowl as needed. Transfer mixture to small bowl, stir in Parmesan, and season with salt and pepper to taste. (Pesto can be refrigerated for up to 3 days in bowl with plastic wrap or thin layer of oil covering surface.)

ROASTED RED PEPPER PESTO

MAKES ENOUGH FOR 1 POUND OF PASTA

When adding pesto to cooked pasta it is important to include 3 or 4 tablespoons of the pasta cooking water for proper consistency and even distribution.

2	red bell peppers, prepared following illustrations 1 and 2 on page 273
3	garlic cloves, unpeeled
7	tablespoons extra-virgin olive oil
¼	cup fresh parsley leaves
1	small shallot, chopped coarse
1	tablespoon minced fresh thyme
¼	cup grated Parmesan cheese
	Salt and pepper

1. Adjust oven rack 2½ to 3½ inches from broiler element and heat broiler. If necessary, set upside down rimmed baking sheet on oven rack to elevate pan (see illustration 4 on page 273).

2. Spread peppers out over aluminum foil–lined baking sheet and broil until skin is charred and puffed but flesh is still firm, 8 to 10 minutes, rotating sheet halfway through cooking.

3. Transfer peppers to medium bowl, cover with foil, and let steam until skin peels off easily, 10 to 15 minutes. Peel and discard skin; set peppers aside. While peppers steam, toast garlic in 8-inch skillet over medium heat, shaking pan occasionally, until softened and spotty brown, about 8 minutes; when cool enough to handle, remove and discard skins.

4. Process roasted peppers, garlic, oil, parsley, shallot, and thyme in food processor until smooth, about 1 minute, scraping down bowl as needed. Transfer mixture to small bowl, stir in Parmesan, and season with salt and pepper to taste. (Pesto can be refrigerated for up to 3 days in bowl with plastic wrap or thin layer of oil covering surface.)

TOASTED NUT AND PARSLEY PESTO

MAKES ENOUGH FOR 1 POUND OF PASTA

When adding pesto to cooked pasta it is important to include 3 or 4 tablespoons of the pasta cooking water for proper consistency and even distribution.

3	garlic cloves, unpeeled
1	cup pecans
7	tablespoons extra-virgin olive oil
¼	cup fresh parsley leaves
¼	cup grated Parmesan cheese

1. Toast garlic in 8-inch skillet over medium heat, shaking pan occasionally, until softened and spotty brown, about 8 minutes; when cool enough to handle, remove and discard skins. While garlic cools, toast nuts in now-empty skillet over medium heat, stirring often, until golden and fragrant, 4 to 5 minutes.

2. Process garlic, nuts, oil, and parsley in food processor until smooth, about 1 minute, scraping down bowl as needed. Transfer mixture to small bowl, stir in Parmesan, and season with salt and pepper to taste. (Pesto can be refrigerated for up to 3 days in bowl with plastic wrap or thin layer of oil covering surface.)

TEST KITCHEN TIP NO. 35 KEY TIPS TO PERFECT PASTA

We love pasta in the test kitchen. As a result, we're pretty opinionated about the best way to cook it. Here's what you need to know: When cooking pasta, make sure you have all the necessary ingredients and utensils assembled before you begin. You'll need 4 quarts of water to cook 1 pound of dried pasta. Any less and the noodles may stick. Use a pot large enough to accommodate the water and pasta without boil-overs—we like an 8-quart pot. It's crucial to properly season the cooking water—about 1 tablespoon table salt per 4 quarts water. Bring the water to a rolling boil before adding the salt and pasta and give it an immediate stir after adding the pasta to prevent sticking. And don't add oil to the pot—oil will prevent sauce from sticking to the pasta.

When serving pasta, if a sauce is too thick, we thin it with a little reserved pasta cooking water. The trouble is, it's easy to forget to save some water. As a reminder, we place a measuring cup in the colander. As for draining pasta, just give it a shake or two. You don't want the pasta bone dry. The little bit of hot cooking water clinging to the pasta will help the sauce coat it. And if you're using a large serving bowl for the pasta, place it underneath the colander while draining the pasta. The hot water heats up the bowl, which keeps the pasta warm longer.

SPAGHETTI AL LIMONE

✔ WHY THIS RECIPE WORKS

Unaccustomed to the spotlight, lemon can turn temperamental in this quick-hit Italian classic— unless you provide it with the perfect costars. We wanted a dish bursting with bright, bracing lemon flavor, moistened with just enough fruity olive oil to coat each delicate strand. Starting with lemon flavor, we found the window for the right amount of juice per pound of pasta was extremely small, and if we leaned more to either side, the lemon flavor became either too tart or barely noticeable. To boost the lemon's power without extra acidity, we added some grated zest to the sauce. As for the base of the sauce, we relied on an olive oil–cream sauce—the cream neutralized some of the acids in the juice while augmenting the oils responsible for the fruity, floral notes.

SPAGHETTI AL LIMONE

SERVES 4

Let the dish rest briefly before serving so the flavors develop and the sauce thickens.

I	pound spaghetti
	Salt and pepper
¼	cup extra-virgin olive oil, plus extra for drizzling
I	shallot, minced
¼	cup heavy cream
I	ounce Parmesan cheese, grated fine (½ cup), plus extra for serving
2	teaspoons grated lemon zest plus ¼ cup juice (2 lemons)
2	tablespoons chopped fresh basil

1. Bring 4 quarts water to boil in large pot. Add pasta and 1 tablespoon salt and cook, stirring often, until al dente. Reserve 1¾ cups cooking water, then drain pasta.

2. Heat 1 tablespoon oil in now-empty pot over medium heat until shimmering. Add shallot and ½ teaspoon salt and cook until softened, about 2 minutes. Stir in 1½ cups reserved cooking water and cream, bring to simmer, and cook for 2 minutes. Off heat, add drained pasta, remaining 3 tablespoons oil, Parmesan, lemon zest, lemon juice, and ½ teaspoon pepper and toss to combine.

3. Cover and let pasta rest for 2 minutes, tossing frequently and adding remaining cooking water as needed to adjust consistency. Stir in basil and season with salt and pepper to taste. Drizzle individual portions with oil and serve, passing Parmesan separately.

SPAGHETTI WITH PECORINO ROMANO AND BLACK PEPPER

✔ **WHY THIS RECIPE WORKS**

With just three main ingredients (cheese, pepper, and pasta), this Roman dish makes a delicious and quick pantry supper. But in versions we tried, the creamy sauce quickly turned into clumps of solidified cheese. For a smooth, intensely cheesy sauce that wouldn't separate once tossed with the pasta, we whisked together some of the pasta cooking water with the grated Romano—we chose real Pecorino Romano for the best flavor. Swapping out butter for cream further ensured a smooth sauce. Even after sitting on the table a full five minutes, there wasn't a clump in sight.

SPAGHETTI WITH PECORINO ROMANO AND BLACK PEPPER (CACIO E PEPE)

SERVES 4 TO 6

High-quality ingredients are essential in this dish, most importantly, imported Pecorino Romano. For a slightly less rich dish, substitute half-and-half for the heavy cream. Do not adjust the amount of water for cooking the pasta; the amount used is critical to the success of the recipe. Make sure to stir the pasta frequently while cooking so that it doesn't stick to the pot. Draining the pasta water into the serving bowl warms the bowl and helps keeps the dish hot until it is served. Letting the dish rest briefly before serving allows the flavors to develop and the sauce to thicken.

6	ounces Pecorino Romano cheese, 4 ounces grated fine (2 cups) and 2 ounces grated coarse (1 cup)
I	pound spaghetti
	Salt
2	tablespoons heavy cream
2	teaspoons extra-virgin olive oil
I½	teaspoons pepper

1. Place finely grated Pecorino in medium bowl. Set colander in large bowl.

2. Bring 2 quarts water to boil in large pot. Add pasta and 1½ teaspoons salt and cook, stirring often, until al dente. Drain pasta into prepared colander, reserving cooking water. Pour 1½ cups cooking water into liquid measuring cup and discard remainder. Return drained pasta to now-empty bowl.

3. Slowly whisk 1 cup reserved cooking water into finely grated Pecorino until smooth, then whisk in heavy cream, oil, and pepper. Gradually pour cheese mixture over pasta and toss to combine. Let pasta rest for 1 to 2 minutes, tossing frequently and adding remaining cooking water as needed to adjust consistency. Serve, passing coarsely grated Pecorino separately.

LINGUINE WITH GARLIC CREAM SAUCE

✔ **WHY THIS RECIPE WORKS**

Roasting gives garlic a smooth, nutty character, a flavor that partners perfectly with pasta. Many roasted garlic recipes recommend drizzling garlic with olive oil, wrapping it in aluminum foil, and tossing it in the oven, but we found this method to be unreliable and it also sometimes gave the garlic a bitter taste. One reason garlic can be tricky to roast is that it is relatively dry. To add some moisture to the garlic in our roasted garlic recipe, we first poached it in milk—producing a final product that was beautifully golden in color and perfectly tender. Once the garlic was roasted, the rest of the dish was a cinch. We mashed the garlic and whisked it into a mixture of milk, cream, and Parmesan. Tossed with pasta, the sauce delivered rich, creamy garlic flavor in every bite.

LINGUINE WITH GARLIC CREAM SAUCE
SERVES 4 TO 6

Use the smaller amount of red pepper flakes for a milder sauce.

1	garlic head
1	cup whole milk
½	teaspoon olive oil
½	cup heavy cream
1½	teaspoons minced fresh oregano or ½ teaspoon dried
¼–½	teaspoon red pepper flakes
¼	cup grated Parmesan cheese, plus extra for serving
	Salt and pepper
1	pound linguine

1. Adjust oven rack to middle position and heat oven to 350 degrees. Remove outer papery skins from garlic, then cut top quarter off head and discard. Place garlic, cut side down, in small saucepan. Add milk, bring to gentle simmer, and cook until garlic is softened slightly, about 10 minutes. Drain garlic, reserving milk, and rinse to remove milk residue.

2. Place softened garlic head in center of 8-inch square of aluminum foil. Drizzle garlic with oil, wrap securely, and place on rimmed baking sheet. Roast until cloves are very soft, about 1 hour.

3. Transfer packet to cutting board, cool for 10 minutes, then unwrap garlic and gently squeeze to remove cloves from skin. Transfer cloves to bowl and mash with fork until smooth.

4. Bring reserved milk, cream, oregano, and pepper flakes to simmer in medium saucepan and cook, whisking constantly, until mixture is reduced by half, about 30 minutes. Reduce heat to low, whisk in garlic paste, and continue to cook, whisking constantly, until sauce emulsifies slightly, 2 to 3 minutes. Slowly whisk in Parmesan until melted and season with salt and pepper to taste.

5. Meanwhile, bring 4 quarts water to boil in large pot. Add pasta and 1 tablespoon salt and cook, stirring often, until al dente. Reserve ½ cup cooking water, then drain pasta and return it to pot. Add sauce to pasta and toss to combine. Add reserved cooking water as needed to adjust consistency. Serve, passing Parmesan and pepper separately.

FETTUCCINE ALFREDO

✔ WHY THIS RECIPE WORKS

We discovered that fresh pasta was essential as a base for the best fettuccine Alfredo; dried noodles didn't hold on to the sauce. Turning our attention to the sauce, we found that a light hand was called for when adding two of the richer ingredients; just ¾ cup Parmigiano-Reggiano and 2 tablespoons butter were sufficient to add distinctive flavor without being overwhelming. Our real challenge was managing the heavy cream, which is usually reduced by half, making the sauce unpalatably thick. We reduced only a cup of the called-for cream, saving ½ cup and adding it, uncooked, at the end.

FETTUCCINE ALFREDO
SERVES 4 TO 6

Fresh pasta is the best choice for this dish. When boiling the pasta, undercook it slightly (even shy of al dente) because the pasta cooks an additional minute or two in the sauce. Note that this dish must be served immediately; it does not hold or reheat well.

1½	cups heavy cream
2	tablespoons unsalted butter
	Salt
½	teaspoon pepper
1	(9-ounce) package fresh fettuccine
1½	ounces Parmesan cheese, grated (¾ cup)
⅛	teaspoon ground nutmeg

1. Bring 1 cup heavy cream and butter to simmer in large saucepan. Reduce heat to low and simmer gently until mixture measures ⅔ cup, 12 to 15 minutes. Off heat, stir in remaining ½ cup cream, ½ teaspoon salt, and pepper.

2. While cream reduces, bring 4 quarts water to boil in large pot. Add pasta and 1 tablespoon salt and cook, stirring often, until just shy of al dente. Reserve ¼ cup cooking water, then drain pasta.

TEST KITCHEN TIP NO. 36 PREGRATE YOUR OWN PARMESAN?

We've never been tempted by the tasteless powdered Parmesan that comes in a green can—and in tests, we've found that the higher-quality grated cheese in the refrigerator section of the supermarket is uneven in quality. But what about pregrating or grinding your own Parmesan to always have at the ready? Do you sacrifice any flavor for convenience? To find out, we divided a block of Parmigiano-Reggiano in two, reducing one half to a powder in a food processor and leaving the other whole. We stored both the solid and grated cheese in the refrigerator for two weeks, then compared them side by side mixed into polenta, added to breading for chicken Milanese, and on their own. After two weeks of storage, tasters were hard-pressed to detect a difference between the cheeses, even in the side-by-side tasting. But after a full month of storage, tasters found a noticeable drop-off in flavor.

The bottom line: Pregrating is fine, as long as you don't store the cheese longer than two to three weeks. To grind Parmesan, cut a block into 1-inch chunks. Place the chunks in a food processor (no more than 1 pound at a time) and process until ground into coarse particles, about 20 seconds. Refrigerate in an airtight container until ready to use.

3. Meanwhile, return cream mixture to simmer. Reduce heat to low and add drained pasta, Parmesan, and nutmeg to cream mixture. Cook pasta over low heat, tossing to combine, until cheese is melted, sauce coats pasta, and pasta is just al dente, 1 to 2 minutes. Add reserved cooking water as needed to adjust consistency; sauce may look thin but will gradually thicken as pasta is served. Serve immediately.

SPAGHETTI ALLA CARBONARA

✔ WHY THIS RECIPE WORKS
Standard carbonara is often a lackluster spaghetti dish—either covered in a leaden sauce or riddled with dry bits of cheese. To add to the problems, if the dish gets to the table a few minutes too late, the sauce congeals and the pasta turns rubbery. We wanted a method for producing al dente spaghetti with a velvet sauce punctuated by bits of bacon and a trace of garlic. We determined that three whole eggs gave our carbonara superior texture and richness. Combining Pecorino Romano and Parmesan cheese gave us creaminess with a little bit of bite. Domestic bacon contributed the perfect crunch and smoky flavor. Combining the hot pasta with the sauce in a warm serving bowl produces a silky, not clumpy, sauce.

SPAGHETTI ALLA CARBONARA
SERVES 4 TO 6

Although we call for spaghetti in this recipe, you can substitute linguine or fettuccine.

¼ cup extra-virgin olive oil
8 slices bacon, halved lengthwise and cut into ¼-inch pieces
½ cup dry white wine
3 large eggs
1½ ounces Parmesan cheese, grated (¾ cup)

¼ cup finely grated Pecorino Romano cheese
2 garlic cloves, minced
1 pound spaghetti
   Salt and pepper

1. Adjust oven rack to lower-middle position, set large heatproof serving bowl on rack, and heat oven to 200 degrees.

2. Heat oil in 12-inch skillet over medium heat until shimmering. Add bacon and cook until crisp, about 8 minutes. Stir in wine, bring to simmer, and cook until alcohol aroma has cooked off and wine is slightly reduced, 6 to 8 minutes. Remove from heat and cover to keep warm. Beat eggs, Parmesan, Pecorino, and garlic together with fork in bowl; set aside.

3. Meanwhile, bring 4 quarts water to boil in large pot. Add pasta and 1 tablespoon salt and cook, stirring often, until al dente. Reserve ⅓ cup cooking water, then drain pasta and transfer it to warmed serving bowl. Immediately pour bacon and egg mixture over hot pasta and toss to combine. Add reserved cooking water as needed to adjust consistency. Season with salt and pepper to taste and serve immediately.

PASTA CAPRESE

✔ WHY THIS RECIPE WORKS
This summer dish combines ripe tomatoes, fresh mozzarella, and fragrant basil with hot pasta. The problem is that the cheese clumps into an intractable softball-size wad in the bottom of the pasta bowl. We found the solution in the freezer. Dicing the cheese and placing it in the freezer for a few minutes before combining it with the hot pasta allowed the cheese to soften but kept it from fully melting (and turning chewy) during cooking. Basil and lemon juice, added just before serving, gave the pasta a fresh, bright finish.

PASTA CAPRESE
SERVES 4

This dish will be very warm, not hot. The success of this recipe depends on high-quality ingredients, including ripe, in-season tomatoes and a fruity olive oil. Don't skip the step of freezing the mozzarella, as freezing prevents it from turning chewy when it comes in contact with the hot pasta. If handmade buffalo- or cow's-milk mozzarella is available (it's commonly found in gourmet and cheese shops packed in water), we highly recommend using it, but do not freeze it.

¼ cup extra-virgin olive oil
2 teaspoons lemon juice, plus extra as needed
1 small shallot, minced
1 small garlic clove, minced
   Salt and pepper
1½ pounds tomatoes, cored, seeded, and cut into ½-inch pieces
12 ounces fresh mozzarella cheese, cut into ½-inch pieces and patted dry with paper towels
1 pound penne, fusilli, or other short, tubular pasta
¼ cup chopped fresh basil
   Sugar

1. Whisk oil, lemon juice, shallot, garlic, ½ teaspoon salt, and ¼ teaspoon pepper together in large bowl. Add tomatoes and gently toss to combine; set aside. Do not marinate tomatoes for longer than 45 minutes.

2. While tomatoes are marinating, place mozzarella on plate and freeze until slightly firm, about 10 minutes. Bring 4 quarts water to boil in large pot. Add pasta and 1 tablespoon salt and cook, stirring often, until al dente. Drain pasta well

3. Add pasta and mozzarella to tomato mixture and gently toss to combine. Let sit for 5 minutes. Stir in basil, season with additional lemon juice, salt, pepper, and sugar to taste, and serve immediately.

PASTA AND SIMPLE TOMATO SAUCE

✔ WHY THIS RECIPE WORKS

An easy-to-make tomato sauce with few ingredients can still boast complex flavor. For our simple sauce, we chose canned tomatoes over fresh for consistent flavor year-round. After conducting a number of tests, we determined that garlic, fresh basil, olive oil, salt, and sugar are crucial ingredients to a well-balanced tomato sauce. We also found that cooking the garlic in oil until golden, but not brown, gave our sauce mellow, nutty garlic flavor throughout. The sauce can be easily varied with potent additions like anchovies, olives, and bacon.

PASTA AND CHUNKY TOMATO SAUCE

SERVES 4

While we prefer spaghetti, any pasta shape will work well here.

3	tablespoons extra-virgin olive oil
2	garlic cloves, minced
1	(28-ounce) can diced tomatoes
2	tablespoons coarsely chopped fresh basil
	Salt
¼	teaspoon sugar
1	pound spaghetti

1. Heat 2 tablespoons oil and garlic in 10-inch skillet over medium heat. Cook, stirring often, until garlic turns golden but not brown, about 3 minutes. Stir in tomatoes, bring to simmer, and cook until slightly thickened, about 10 minutes. Off heat, stir in basil, 1½ teaspoons salt, and sugar.

2. Meanwhile, bring 4 quarts water to boil in large pot. Add pasta and 1 tablespoon salt and cook, stirring often, until al dente. Reserve ½ cup cooking water, then drain pasta and return it to pot. Add sauce, remaining 1 tablespoon oil, and ¼ cup reserved cooking water to pasta and cook over medium heat, tossing to combine, until heated through, about 1 minute. Add remaining cooking water as needed to adjust consistency. Serve immediately.

PASTA AND CHUNKY TOMATO SAUCE WITH ANCHOVIES AND OLIVES

Increase garlic to 3 cloves and cook 3 rinsed and minced anchovy fillets and ½ teaspoon red pepper flakes with oil and garlic. Substitute ¼ cup minced fresh parsley for basil and add ¼ cup pitted kalamata olives, sliced, and 2 tablespoons rinsed capers to sauce along with parsley.

PASTA AND CHUNKY TOMATO SAUCE WITH BACON AND PARSLEY

Cook 4 slices bacon, cut into ½-inch pieces, in 10-inch skillet over medium-high heat until crisp, about 5 minutes. Remove bacon with slotted spoon and transfer to paper towel–lined plate. Pour off all but 2 tablespoons fat from skillet. Cool skillet slightly, about 3 minutes. Omit olive oil from sauce and cook garlic and ½ teaspoon red pepper flakes in fat left in skillet. Substitute 2 tablespoons chopped fresh parsley for basil and add crisp bacon to sauce along with parsley.

QUICK TOMATO SAUCE

✔ WHY THIS RECIPE WORKS

With pasta on hand, dinner can be just a few minutes away. Rather than reaching for a jar of sauce, we developed a quick tomato sauce that can be tossed with spaghetti, ziti, ravioli and more. To cook this brightly flavored, complex sauce in the time it takes to boil pasta, we chose minimally processed crushed tomatoes, which have a fresh taste but are already pureed. Minced onion sautéed in butter (rather than olive oil) greatly enhanced the flavor of the tomatoes. And adding sugar, garlic, and oregano to the cooked onions further boosted our sauce's flavor, as did adding chopped basil and olive oil just before serving.

QUICK TOMATO SAUCE

MAKES ENOUGH FOR 1 POUND OF PASTA

High-quality canned tomatoes will make a big difference in this sauce. Grate the onion on the large holes of a box grater.

2	tablespoons unsalted butter
¼	cup grated onion
1	teaspoon minced fresh oregano or ¼ teaspoon dried
	Salt and pepper
2	garlic cloves, minced
1	(28-ounce) can crushed tomatoes
¼	teaspoon sugar
2	tablespoons chopped fresh basil
1	tablespoon extra-virgin olive oil

TEST KITCHEN TIP NO. 37 MATCHING PASTA SHAPES WITH SAUCE

In Italy there is a fine art to matching pasta shapes and sauces, but in the test kitchen, we are a bit freer with the pairing and endorse just one general rule: you should be able to eat the pasta and sauce easily in each mouthful. This means that the texture and consistency of the sauce should work with the pasta shape. And no matter what the shape of the pasta or type of sauce, we adamantly believe that the pasta, not the sauce, should be the focal point.

Long strands are best with smooth sauces or pestos or light sauces, such as oil and garlic. In general, wider long noodles, such as fettuccine, can more easily support slightly chunkier sauces than can very thin noodles like spaghetti. Wide pastas like fettuccine or tagliatelle are also well suited to creamy sauces like Alfredo. Short tubular or molded pasta shapes do an excellent job of trapping chunkier sauces. Sauces with very large chunks are best with shells, rigatoni, or other large tubes. Sauces with small to medium chunks pair well with fusilli or penne.

Melt butter in medium saucepan over medium heat. Add onion, oregano, and ½ teaspoon salt and cook, stirring occasionally, until onion is softened and lightly browned, 5 to 7 minutes. Stir in garlic and cook until fragrant, about 30 seconds. Stir in tomatoes and sugar, bring to simmer, and cook until slightly thickened, about 10 minutes. Off heat, stir in basil and oil and season with salt and pepper to taste.

MARINARA SAUCE

✔ WHY THIS RECIPE WORKS

For a multidimensional marinara sauce that would take less than an hour to prepare, we chose canned whole tomatoes for their flavor and texture, hand-crushing them and removing the hard core and stray bits of skin at the same time. A minced onion lent our sauce sweet flavor. We boosted tomato flavor by sautéing the tomatoes until they glazed the bottom of the pan, after which we added their liquid. We also shortened the simmering time by using a skillet instead of a saucepan (the greater surface area of a skillet encourages faster evaporation and flavor concentration). Red wine added depth and complexity and uncooked tomatoes, basil, and olive oil added just before serving, gave our sauce a bright, fresh finish.

MARINARA SAUCE
MAKES ENOUGH FOR 1 POUND OF PASTA

Chianti or Merlot work well for the dry red wine. We like a smoother marinara, but if you prefer a chunkier sauce, give it just three or four pulses in the food processor in step 4.

2 (28-ounce) cans whole tomatoes
3 tablespoons extra-virgin olive oil
1 onion, chopped fine
2 garlic cloves, minced
2 teaspoons minced fresh oregano or ½ teaspoon dried
⅓ cup dry red wine
3 tablespoons chopped fresh basil
   Salt and pepper
   Sugar

1. Pour tomatoes and juice into strainer set over large bowl. Open tomatoes with hands and remove and discard seeds and fibrous cores; let tomatoes drain excess liquid, about 5 minutes. Remove ¾ cup tomatoes from strainer and set aside. Reserve 2½ cups tomato juice and discard remainder.

2. Heat 2 tablespoons oil in 12-inch skillet over medium heat until shimmering. Add onion and cook until softened and lightly browned, 5 to 7 minutes. Stir in garlic and oregano and cook until fragrant, about 30 seconds.

3. Stir in strained tomatoes and increase heat to medium-high. Cook, stirring often, until liquid has evaporated, tomatoes begin to stick to bottom of pan, and brown fond forms around pan edges, 10 to 12 minutes. Stir in wine and cook until thick and syrupy, about 1 minute. Stir in reserved tomato juice, scraping up any browned bits. Bring to simmer and cook, stirring occasionally, until sauce is thick, 8 to 10 minutes.

4. Transfer sauce and reserved tomatoes to food processor and pulse until slightly chunky, about 8 pulses. Return sauce to now-empty skillet, stir in basil and remaining 1 tablespoon oil, and season with salt, pepper, and sugar to taste.

PASTA WITH CREAMY TOMATO SAUCE

✔ WHY THIS RECIPE WORKS

Tomatoes and cream are seemingly incompatible—an imbalance of the tomatoes' acidity and the cream's richness can produce a sauce that's too sharp, too sweet, or lacking in tomato flavor. We wanted a smooth, full-flavored sauce in which the tomatoes and cream complemented each other. And we wanted to be able to make it year-round. We found that canned crushed tomatoes were the best product to use—they're readily available, bright in flavor, and easy to puree in the food processor. Cooking a little tomato paste with some onion and garlic deepened the flavor of the sauce, as did adding sun-dried tomatoes. A pinch of red pepper flakes, a splash of wine, and a little minced prosciutto lent depth—as did adding a bit of raw crushed tomatoes and another splash of wine at the last minute. As for adding the cream, the simplest approach was best—the sauce tasted most balanced when we stirred the cream into the finished tomato mixture and brought it up to temperature before tossing it with the pasta.

TEST KITCHEN TIP NO. 38 WHEN COOKWARE TURNS FOOD TINNY

When acidic ingredients are cooked in "reactive" pans, such as those made of aluminum or unseasoned cast iron, trace amounts of metal can loosen and leach into the food. Although these minute amounts are not harmful to consume, they may impart unwanted metallic flavors.

To see for ourselves, we simmered tomato sauce in an aluminum Dutch oven and in seasoned and unseasoned cast-iron Dutch ovens. As a control, we also cooked tomato sauce in a stainless steel pot. Tasters noticed a strong taste of iron in the sauce cooked in the unseasoned cast-iron pot and a more subtle metallic taste in the sauce cooked in the aluminum pot. The sauces cooked in seasoned cast iron (which has layers of oil compounds protecting the surface of the pan) and stainless steel tasted just fine. We then sent samples of each sauce to an independent lab to test for the presence of iron and aluminum and found that unseasoned cast iron did indeed release the most molecules of metal. The sauce from this pot contained nearly 10 times more iron (108 mg/kg) than the sauce from the seasoned cast-iron pot, which contained only a few more milligrams of iron than the sauce from the stainless steel pot. The sauce from the aluminum pot showed the presence of 14.3 mg/kg of aluminum, compared to less than 1 mg/kg in the sauce from the stainless steel pot. The verdict? Avoid reactive cookware when cooking acidic foods, since it can compromise flavor.

PASTA WITH CREAMY TOMATO SAUCE

SERVES 4

High-quality canned tomatoes will make a big difference in this sauce.

3	tablespoons unsalted butter
1	small onion, chopped fine
1	ounce thinly sliced prosciutto, minced
1	bay leaf
	Salt and pepper
	Pinch red pepper flakes
3	garlic cloves, minced
¼	cup oil-packed sun-dried tomatoes, rinsed, patted dry, and chopped coarse
2	tablespoons tomato paste
¼	cup plus 2 tablespoons dry white wine
2	cups plus 2 tablespoons crushed tomatoes (from one 28-ounce can)
1	pound penne, fusilli, or other short, tubular pasta
½	cup heavy cream
¼	cup chopped fresh basil
	Grated Parmesan cheese

1. Melt butter in medium saucepan over medium heat. Add onion, prosciutto, bay leaf, ¼ teaspoon salt, and pepper flakes and cook, stirring occasionally, until onion is softened and lightly browned, 5 to 7 minutes. Stir in garlic, increase heat to medium-high, and cook until fragrant, about 30 seconds. Add sun-dried tomatoes and tomato paste and cook, stirring constantly, until slightly darkened, 1 to 2 minutes. Add ¼ cup wine and cook, stirring often, until liquid has evaporated, 1 to 2 minutes.

2. Stir in 2 cups crushed tomatoes and bring to simmer. Reduce heat to low, partially cover, and simmer gently, stirring occasionally, until sauce is thickened, 25 to 30 minutes. Discard bay leaf.

3. Meanwhile, bring 4 quarts water to boil in large pot. Add pasta and 1 tablespoon salt and cook, stirring often, until al dente. Reserve ½ cup cooking water, then drain pasta and return it to pot.

4. Stir cream, remaining 2 tablespoons wine, and remaining 2 tablespoons crushed tomatoes into sauce and season with salt and pepper to taste. Add sauce and basil to pasta and toss to combine. Add reserved cooking water as needed to adjust consistency. Serve immediately, passing Parmesan separately.

PASTA WITH NO-COOK FRESH TOMATO SAUCES

✓ WHY THIS RECIPE WORKS

When summer tomatoes are at their peak, a no-cook tomato sauce can taste extraordinary. The problem is that summer tomatoes can contain excess liquid, which can result in a watery, bland pasta sauce. To remedy this problem, we seeded the tomatoes. For rich flavor, we used extra-virgin olive oil, which also worked to coat the pasta and bind it to the sauce. We then added ingredients like garlic, black olives, and Parmesan to bring the acidity and sweetness of the tomatoes into an ideal balance.

FARFALLE WITH TOMATOES, OLIVES, AND FETA

SERVES 4

The success of this dish depends on using ripe, flavorful tomatoes. Add the feta after the tomatoes have been tossed with the pasta to prevent the cheese from melting.

1	pound farfalle
	Salt and pepper
1½	pounds tomatoes, cored, seeded, and cut into ½-inch pieces
½	cup pitted kalamata olives, chopped coarse
¼	cup extra-virgin olive oil
1	tablespoon minced fresh mint
6	ounces feta cheese, crumbled (1½ cups)

1. Bring 4 quarts water to boil in large pot. Add pasta and 1 tablespoon salt and cook, stirring often, until al dente. Drain pasta and return it to pot.

2. Meanwhile, combine tomatoes, olives, oil, mint, ½ teaspoon salt, and ¼ teaspoon pepper. Add tomato mixture to pasta and toss to combine. Add feta and toss again. Season with salt and pepper to taste and serve immediately.

FUSILLI WITH TOMATOES AND FRESH MOZZARELLA

SERVES 4

The success of this dish depends on using ripe, flavorful tomatoes. For maximum creaminess, use fresh mozzarella packed in water rather than the shrink-wrapped cheese sold at supermarkets.

1	pound fusilli
	Salt and pepper
1½	pounds tomatoes cored, seeded, and cut into ½-inch pieces
¼	cup extra-virgin olive oil
3	scallions, sliced thin
1	garlic clove, minced

8 ounces fresh mozzarella cheese, cut into ½-inch pieces and patted dry with paper towels

1. Bring 4 quarts water to boil in large pot. Add pasta and 1 tablespoon salt and cook, stirring often, until al dente. Drain pasta and return it to pot.

2. Meanwhile, combine tomatoes, oil, scallions, garlic, ½ teaspoon salt, and ¼ teaspoon pepper. Add tomato mixture and mozzarella to pasta and toss to combine. Season with salt and pepper to taste and serve immediately.

ORECCHIETTE WITH TOMATOES, FENNEL, AND PARMESAN
SERVES 4

The success of this dish depends on using ripe, flavorful tomatoes.

- 1 pound orecchiette
  Salt and pepper
- 1½ pounds tomatoes cored, seeded, and cut into ½-inch pieces
- 1 small fennel bulb, stalks discarded, halved, cored, and sliced thin
- ¼ cup extra-virgin olive oil
- ¼ cup chopped fresh basil
- 2 ounces Parmesan cheese, shaved thin with vegetable peeler (1 cup)

1. Bring 4 quarts water to boil in large pot. Add pasta and 1 tablespoon salt and cook, stirring often, until al dente. Drain pasta and return it to pot.

2. Meanwhile, combine tomatoes, fennel, oil, basil, ½ teaspoon salt, and ¼ teaspoon pepper. Add tomato mixture to pasta and toss to combine. Season with salt and pepper to taste and serve immediately, passing Parmesan separately.

PASTA WITH CLASSIC FRESH TOMATO SAUCES

✔ WHY THIS RECIPE WORKS
To preserve the fresh tomato flavor in our tomato sauces while ensuring their meaty texture, we cooked the tomatoes in extra-virgin olive oil and garlic after peeling and seeding them. Cooking them in a wide pan promoted quick evaporation, and thinning out the sauce with a small amount of pasta water brought it to just the right consistency to cling to the pasta.

PASTA AND FRESH TOMATO SAUCE WITH GARLIC AND BASIL
SERVES 4

The success of this dish depends on using ripe, flavorful tomatoes. To peel tomatoes, dunk the cored tomatoes in a pot of boiling water until the skins split and begin to curl around the cored area, 15 to 30 seconds; transfer the tomatoes to a bowl of ice water, then peel off the skins with your fingers. This chunky sauce works best with tubular pasta, such as penne. To serve with spaghetti or linguine, puree the sauce in a blender or food processor before adding the basil.

- 3 tablespoons extra-virgin olive oil
- 2 garlic cloves, minced
- 2 pounds tomatoes, cored, peeled, seeded, and cut into ½-inch pieces
- 2 tablespoons chopped fresh basil
  Salt
- 1 pound penne, fusilli, or other short, tubular pasta

1. Heat 2 tablespoons oil and garlic in 12-inch skillet over medium heat. Cook, stirring often, until garlic turns golden but not brown, about 3 minutes. Stir in tomatoes, increase heat to medium-high, and cook until tomato pieces lose their shape and form chunky sauce, about 10 minutes. Stir in basil and season with salt to taste.

2. Meanwhile, bring 4 quarts water to boil in large pot. Add pasta and 1 tablespoon salt and cook, stirring often, until al dente. Reserve ½ cup cooking water, then drain pasta and return it to pot.

3. Add sauce, remaining 1 tablespoon oil, and ¼ cup reserved cooking water to pasta and toss to combine. Add remaining cooking water as needed to adjust consistency. Serve immediately.

PASTA AND FRESH TOMATO SAUCE WITH CHILE PEPPER AND BASIL

Heat ¾ teaspoon red pepper flakes along with oil and garlic.

PASTA AND FRESH TOMATO SAUCE WITH ANCHOVIES, OLIVES, AND CAPERS

Heat 3 rinsed and minced anchovy fillets with oil and garlic. Add ½ cup kalamata olives, pitted and chopped, and 1 tablespoon rinsed capers to sauce with basil.

PASTA AND FRESH TOMATO SAUCE WITH ONION AND BACON

Pancetta can be substituted for the bacon. Because it is leaner, cook it in 2 tablespoons of olive oil with the onion.

Heat 1 tablespoon olive oil in 12-inch skillet over medium heat until shimmering. Add 1 finely chopped onion and 4 slices chopped bacon and cook until onion begins to brown and bacon begins to crisp, about 6 minutes. Omit olive oil and garlic in sauce and cook tomatoes in skillet with onion and bacon mixture. Substitute 2 tablespoons minced fresh parsley for basil.

PASTA AND FRESH TOMATO CREAM SAUCE WITH ONION AND BUTTER

This rich sauce is best served with fresh fettuccine or cheese ravioli.

Substitute melted butter for olive oil in sauce and 1 finely chopped onion for garlic; cook onion until softened and lightly browned, 5 to 7 minutes. Add ½ cup heavy cream to tomatoes after chunky sauce has formed, then continue to cook until sauce thickens slightly, 2 to 3 minutes longer. Omit additional oil.

PASTA WITH ROBUST TOMATO SAUCES

✔ WHY THIS RECIPE WORKS

To capitalize on the full, lively flavor of great seasonal tomatoes, we found that any type of tomato tasted fine when skinned, seeded, chopped, and simmered in a skillet with garlic and olive oil—as long as it was ripe. But for suitable additions to finish our fresh tomato sauces, we needed to look beyond the usual suspects like parsley and ricotta and find forceful flavors—potent herbs and spices (piney rosemary), cured meats (smoky bacon), and assertive cheeses (pungent feta), using them judiciously to keep the sauce in balance.

PASTA AND FRESH TOMATO SAUCE WITH ROSEMARY AND BACON

SERVES 4

The success of this dish depends on using ripe, flavorful tomatoes. To peel the tomatoes, dunk the cored tomatoes in a pot of boiling water until the skins split and begin to curl around the cored area, about 15 to 30 seconds; transfer the tomatoes to a bowl of ice water, then peel off the skins with your fingers. Pancetta can be substituted for the bacon. Use the smaller amount of red pepper flakes for a milder sauce.

6	slices bacon, cut crosswise into ½-inch-wide pieces
2	tablespoons extra-virgin olive oil
2	garlic cloves, minced
½	teaspoon minced fresh rosemary
½–¾	teaspoon red pepper flakes
3	pounds tomatoes, cored, peeled, seeded, and cut into ½-inch pieces
1	pound penne, fusilli, or other short, tubular pasta
	Salt
1	tablespoon chopped fresh parsley
⅛	teaspoon pepper
	Sugar
2	ounces Parmesan cheese, shaved thin with vegetable peeler (1 cup)

1. Cook bacon in 12-inch skillet over medium heat until crisp, 5 to 7 minutes. Using slotted spoon, transfer bacon to paper towel–lined plate. Pour off all fat from skillet.

2. Heat oil in now-empty skillet over medium-high heat until shimmering. Add garlic, rosemary, and pepper flakes and cook, stirring constantly, until fragrant, about 30 seconds. Stir in tomatoes and cook until tomato pieces lose their shape and form chunky sauce, about 10 minutes.

3. Meanwhile, bring 4 quarts water to boil in large pot. Add pasta and 1 tablespoon salt and cook, stirring often, until al dente. Reserve ½ cup cooking water, then drain pasta and return it to pot.

4. Stir parsley, ¼ teaspoon salt, and pepper into sauce and season with sugar to taste. Add sauce to pasta and toss to combine. Add reserved cooking water as needed to adjust consistency. Serve, passing crisp bacon and Parmesan separately.

PASTA AND FRESH TOMATO SAUCE WITH FENNEL AND ORANGE

SERVES 4

The success of this dish depends on using ripe, flavorful tomatoes. To peel the tomatoes, dunk the cored tomatoes in a pot of boiling water until the skins split and begin to curl around the cored area, about 15 to 30 seconds; transfer the tomatoes to a bowl of ice water, then peel off the skins with your fingers.

¼	cup extra-virgin olive oil
1	fennel bulb, stalks discarded, halved, cored, and cut into ¼-inch pieces
2	garlic cloves, minced
2	(3-inch) strips orange zest plus 3 tablespoons juice
½	teaspoon fennel seeds, crushed
⅛	teaspoon red pepper flakes
	Pinch saffron, crumbled (optional)
3	pounds tomatoes, cored, peeled, seeded, and cut into ½-inch pieces
1	pound penne, fusilli, or other short, tubular pasta
	Salt
3	tablespoons chopped fresh basil
⅛	teaspoon pepper
	Sugar

1. Heat 2 tablespoons oil in 12-inch skillet over medium-high heat until shimmering. Add fennel and cook until softened and lightly browned, 5 to 7 minutes. Stir in garlic, orange zest, fennel seeds, pepper flakes, and saffron, if using, and cook until fragrant, about 30 seconds. Stir in tomatoes and cook until tomato pieces lose their shape and form chunky sauce, about 10 minutes. Discard orange zest.

2. Meanwhile, bring 4 quarts water to boil in large pot. Add pasta and 1 tablespoon salt and cook, stirring often, until al dente. Reserve ½ cup cooking water, then drain pasta and return it to pot.

3. Stir orange juice, basil, ¼ teaspoon salt, and pepper into sauce and season with sugar to taste. Add sauce and remaining 2 tablespoons oil to pasta and toss to combine. Add reserved cooking water as needed to adjust consistency. Serve.

PASTA AND FRESH TOMATO SAUCE WITH SALAMI, PEPPERONCINI, AND MOZZARELLA

SERVES 4

The success of this dish depends on using ripe, flavorful tomatoes. To peel the tomatoes, dunk the cored tomatoes in a pot of boiling water until the skins split and begin to curl around the cored area, 15 to 30 seconds; transfer the tomatoes to a bowl of ice water, then peel off the skins with your fingers. We prefer using spicy (not mild) pepperoncini to balance the richness of the sauce.

    3   tablespoons extra-virgin olive oil
    2   garlic cloves, minced
    3   pounds tomatoes, cored, peeled,
        seeded, and cut into ½-inch pieces
    4   ounces thickly sliced salami, slices
        cut half, then into ¼-inch-wide strips
    I   pound farfalle
        Salt
    ⅓   cup jarred pepperoncini rings,
        rinsed
    I   tablespoon chopped fresh oregano
    ⅛   teaspoon pepper
        Sugar
    12 ounces fresh mozzarella cheese,
        cut into ½-inch pieces and patted
        dry with paper towels

1. Heat 2 tablespoons oil and garlic in 12-inch skillet over medium-high heat. Cook, stirring often, until garlic turns golden but not brown, about 3 minutes. Stir in tomatoes and cook until tomato pieces lose their shape, about 8 minutes. Stir in salami and continue to cook until

salami is heated through and tomatoes have formed chunky sauce, about 2 minutes longer.

2. Meanwhile, bring 4 quarts water to boil in large pot. Add pasta and 1 tablespoon salt and cook, stirring often, until al dente. Reserve ½ cup cooking water, then drain pasta and return it to pot.

3. Stir pepperoncini, oregano, ¼ teaspoon salt, and pepper into sauce and season with sugar to taste. Add sauce, mozzarella, and remaining 1 tablespoon oil to pasta and toss to combine. Add reserved cooking water as needed to adjust consistency. Serve.

PASTA AND FRESH TOMATO SAUCE WITH MINT, FETA, AND SPINACH

SERVES 4

The success of this dish depends on using ripe, flavorful tomatoes. To peel the tomatoes, dunk the cored tomatoes in a pot of boiling water until the skins split and begin to curl around the cored area, 15 to 30 seconds; transfer the tomatoes to a bowl of ice water, then peel off the skins with your fingers. You can substitute 1 tablespoon chopped fresh oregano for the mint.

    3   tablespoons extra-virgin olive oil
    2   garlic cloves, minced
    3   pounds tomatoes, cored, peeled,
        seeded, and cut into ½-inch pieces
    5   ounces baby spinach (5 cups)
    I   pound fusilli
        Salt
    2   tablespoons chopped fresh mint
    2   tablespoons lemon juice
    ⅛   teaspoon pepper
        Sugar
    4   ounces feta cheese, crumbled
        (about I cup)

1. Heat 2 tablespoons oil and garlic in 12-inch skillet over medium-high heat. Cook, stirring often, until garlic turns golden but not brown, about 3 minutes. Stir in tomatoes and cook until tomato

pieces begin to lose their shape, about 8 minutes. Stir in spinach, 1 handful at a time, and continue to cook until spinach is wilted and tomatoes have formed chunky sauce, about 2 minutes longer.

2. Meanwhile, bring 4 quarts water to boil in large pot. Add pasta and 1 tablespoon salt and cook, stirring often, until al dente. Reserve ½ cup cooking water, then drain pasta and return it to pot.

3. Stir mint, lemon juice, ¼ teaspoon salt, and pepper into sauce and season with sugar to taste. Add sauce and remaining 1 tablespoon oil to pasta and toss to combine. Add reserved cooking water as needed to adjust consistency. Serve, passing feta separately.

PASTA AND FRESH TOMATO SAUCE WITH ROASTED RED PEPPERS, TOASTED GARLIC, AND PAPRIKA

SERVES 4

The success of this dish depends on using ripe, flavorful tomatoes. To peel the tomatoes, dunk the cored tomatoes in a pot of boiling water until the skins split and begin to curl around the cored area, 15 to 30 seconds; transfer the tomatoes to a bowl of ice water, then peel off the skins with your fingers. Parmesan or Asiago cheese can be substituted for the Manchego.

    3   tablespoons extra-virgin olive oil
    4   garlic cloves, sliced thin
    2   teaspoons paprika
    2   teaspoons minced fresh thyme or
        ½ teaspoon dried
    3   pounds tomatoes, cored, peeled,
        seeded, and cut into ½-inch pieces
    ½   cup jarred roasted red peppers,
        rinsed, patted dry, and chopped
        coarse
    I   pound orecchiette or campanelle
        Salt
    ⅛   teaspoon pepper
        Sugar
    2   ounces Manchego cheese, grated
        (I cup)

1. Heat 2 tablespoons oil and garlic in 12-inch skillet over medium-high heat. Cook, stirring often, until garlic turns golden but not brown, about 3 minutes. Stir in paprika and thyme and cook until fragrant, about 30 seconds. Stir in tomatoes and cook for 5 minutes. Stir in red peppers and continue to cook until tomato pieces lose their shape and form chunky sauce, about 5 minutes longer.

2. Meanwhile, bring 4 quarts water to boil in large pot. Add pasta and 1 tablespoon salt and cook, stirring often, until al dente. Reserve ½ cup cooking water, then drain pasta and return it to pot.

3. Stir ¼ teaspoon salt and pepper into sauce and season with sugar to taste. Add sauce and remaining 1 tablespoon oil to pasta and toss to combine. Add reserved cooking water as needed to adjust consistency. Serve, passing Manchego separately.

ROASTED TOMATO SAUCES

✔ WHY THIS RECIPE WORKS
For a great fresh tomato sauce with out-of-season fresh tomatoes, we turned to roasting, which caramelized natural sugars in the tomatoes, intensified flavor, and added a light touch of smokiness to our sauce. Keeping the seeds in the roasted tomatoes added needed moisture to our sauce, and tossing them with tomato paste gave our sauce a deep red color and another layer of tomato flavor.

ROASTED TOMATO SAUCE
MAKES ENOUGH FOR 1 POUND OF PASTA

This sauce is best served with short pasta shapes, such as ziti, penne, or fusilli. It can also be served over chicken Parmesan or grilled fish.

- 2 tablespoons tomato paste
- 2 tablespoons extra-virgin olive oil
- 2 teaspoons minced fresh thyme
  Salt and pepper

- ⅛ teaspoon red pepper flakes
- 3 pounds tomatoes, cored and halved
- 1 small onion, sliced into ½-inch-thick rounds
- 6 garlic cloves, peeled
- 1 teaspoon red wine vinegar
  Sugar
- 2 tablespoons chopped fresh basil

1. Adjust oven rack to middle position and heat oven to 475 degrees. Combine tomato paste, 1 tablespoon oil, thyme, ¾ teaspoon salt, ¼ teaspoon pepper, and pepper flakes in large bowl. Add tomatoes, onion, and garlic and toss until evenly coated. Place 4-inch square of aluminum foil in center of wire rack set in foil-lined rimmed baking sheet. Place garlic cloves and onion rounds on foil and arrange tomatoes, cut side down, around garlic and onion. Roast until vegetables are soft and tomato skins are well charred, 45 to 55 minutes.

2. Remove baking sheet from oven and cool for 5 minutes. Transfer garlic and onion to food processor and pulse until finely chopped, about 5 pulses. Add tomatoes, vinegar, and remaining 1 tablespoon oil to food processor and pulse until tomatoes are broken down but still chunky, about 5 pulses, scraping down bowl as needed. Season mixture with salt, pepper, and sugar to taste and pulse until sauce is slightly chunky, about 5 pulses. Transfer mixture to bowl and stir in basil.

ROASTED TOMATO SAUCE WITH FENNEL

Add ½ teaspoon fennel seeds to tomato paste mixture. Replace onion with 1 small fennel bulb, sliced ½ inch thick.

ROASTED TOMATO SAUCE WITH ROSEMARY AND GOAT CHEESE

Substitute 1 teaspoon minced fresh rosemary for thyme. Omit basil. After tossing sauce with pasta, sprinkle with 2 ounces crumbled fresh goat cheese.

PORCINI MUSHROOM SAUCES

✔ WHY THIS RECIPE WORKS
Dried porcini mushrooms boast concentrated mushroom flavor and can make a robust pasta sauce. To start, because dried mushrooms often contain grit, we rinsed the mushrooms before soaking. We soaked the porcini in water in the microwave to soften them and then we drained the porcini and reserved the flavorful soaking liquid to add to the sauce later. Onion, butter, and cream were all that was required to enrich the porcini's flavor in one creamy sauce and for another sauce, we used white mushrooms, fragrant rosemary, and garlic to complement the porcini.

PORCINI MUSHROOM SAUCE WITH CREAM
MAKES ENOUGH FOR 1 POUND OF PASTA

Serve with fettuccine.

- 2 cups water
- 2 ounces dried porcini mushrooms, rinsed
- 3 tablespoons unsalted butter
- 1 onion, chopped fine
- 6 tablespoons heavy cream
- 3 tablespoons minced fresh parsley
  Salt and pepper

1. Microwave water and mushrooms in covered bowl until steaming, about 1 minute. Let stand until softened, about 5 minutes. Drain mushrooms through fine-mesh strainer lined with coffee filter, reserving liquid, then chop mushrooms coarse.

2. Melt butter in 12-inch skillet over medium heat. Add onion and cook until softened and lightly browned, 5 to 7 minutes. Stir in mushrooms and cook until fragrant, 1 to 2 minutes. Stir in reserved porcini soaking liquid, scraping up any browned bits. Bring to simmer and cook until reduced by half, about 10 minutes.

Stir in cream and continue to cook until sauce begins to thicken, about 2 minutes longer. Stir in parsley and season with salt and pepper to taste.

PORCINI MUSHROOM SAUCE WITH ROSEMARY
MAKES ENOUGH FOR I POUND OF PASTA

This sauce is best served with orecchiette or small shells. So that the pasta better absorbs the sauce, simmer the cooked pasta and 1/3 cup of grated Parmesan cheese with the sauce for a minute or two, then serve.

- I cup water
- I ounce dried porcini mushrooms, rinsed
- 2 tablespoons unsalted butter
- I tablespoon olive oil
- I pound white mushrooms, trimmed and sliced thin
- I onion, chopped fine
- 2 garlic cloves, minced
- I teaspoon minced fresh rosemary
- 2 tablespoons minced fresh parsley
  Salt and pepper

I. Microwave water and mushrooms in covered bowl until steaming, about 1 minute. Let stand until softened, about 5 minutes. Drain mushrooms through fine-mesh strainer lined with coffee filter, reserving liquid, then chop mushrooms coarse.

2. Heat butter and oil in 12-inch skillet over medium heat until butter is melted. Add white mushrooms and onion and cook until softened and lightly browned, 8 to 10 minutes. Stir in porcini, garlic, and rosemary and cook until fragrant, 1 to 2 minutes. Stir in reserved porcini soaking liquid and bring to simmer. Stir in parsley and season with salt and pepper to taste.

TOMATO SAUCE WITH PORCINI MUSHROOMS

✔ WHY THIS RECIPE WORKS
Dried porcini mushrooms with their rich, earthy character, can pave the way for a deeply flavorful tomato sauce in almost no time. To start, we chose aromatics like onion, celery, and carrot for a sweet, vegetal backbone. Canned whole tomatoes gave our sauce consistent flavor year-round and seeding the tomatoes lent our sauce a refined character. Porcini require careful preparation—the mushrooms should be rinsed to rid them of grit and after rinsing them the mushrooms should be softened with water in the microwave. We don't discard the leftover soaking liquid—instead we strained it to give our sauce more mushroom flavor.

TOMATO SAUCE WITH PORCINI MUSHROOMS
MAKES ENOUGH FOR I POUND OF PASTA

This sauce is best served with spaghetti or fusilli and grated Parmesan cheese.

- I cup water
- I ounce dried porcini mushrooms, rinsed
- 3 tablespoons olive oil
- I onion, chopped fine
- I celery rib, minced
- I small carrot, peeled and minced
  Salt and pepper
- I (28-ounce) can whole tomatoes, drained and chopped coarse
- 3 tablespoons minced fresh parsley

I. Microwave water and mushrooms in covered bowl until steaming, about 1 minute. Let stand until softened, about 5 minutes. Drain mushrooms through fine-mesh strainer lined with coffee filter, reserving liquid, then chop mushrooms coarse.

2. Heat oil in 12-inch skillet over medium heat until shimmering. Add onion, celery, and carrot and cook until vegetables are softened, 8 to 10 minutes.

Stir in porcini and 1 teaspoon salt and cook until fragrant, 1 to 2 minutes. Stir in tomatoes and reserved porcini soaking liquid, bring to simmer, and cook until sauce thickens, about 15 minutes. Stir in parsley and season with salt and pepper to taste.

QUICK MUSHROOM RAGU

✔ WHY THIS RECIPE WORKS
Based on a Tuscan dish known as spaghetti alla boscaiola, or "woodsman's pasta," this dish swaps in hearty mushrooms for the long-simmered meat typically found in traditional ragus. We used portobellos for their meaty texture and added dried porcini to infuse the sauce with an ultraconcentrated smoky mushroom flavor. Pancetta imparted backbone to the sauce. For the tomatoes, we chose crushed whole tomatoes and we used fresh rosemary to brighten this quick-cooking ragu.

SPAGHETTI WITH MUSHROOM AND TOMATO SAUCE
SERVES 4

Use a spoon to scrape the dark brown gills from the portobellos.

- I cup low-sodium chicken broth
- I ounce dried porcini mushrooms, rinsed
- 4 ounces pancetta, cut into 1/2-inch pieces
- 8 ounces portobello mushrooms, stemmed, gills removed, and cut into 1/2-inch pieces
- 3 tablespoons extra-virgin olive oil
- 4 garlic cloves, sliced thin
- I tablespoon tomato paste
- 2 teaspoons minced fresh rosemary
- I (14.5-ounce) can whole tomatoes, drained with juice reserved, tomatoes coarsely crushed
  Salt and pepper
- I pound spaghetti
  Grated Pecorino Romano cheese

1. Microwave broth and porcini in covered bowl until steaming, about 1 minute. Let stand until softened, about 10 minutes. Drain mushrooms through fine-mesh strainer lined with coffee filter, reserving broth and finely chopping mushrooms.

2. Cook pancetta in 12-inch skillet over medium heat, stirring occasionally, until crisp, 7 to 10 minutes. Add chopped porcini, portobellos, oil, garlic, tomato paste, and rosemary and cook, stirring occasionally, until all liquid has evaporated and tomato paste starts to brown, 5 to 7 minutes. Add reserved broth, crushed tomatoes, and tomato juice, increase heat to high, and bring to simmer. Reduce heat to medium-low and cook until thickened, 15 to 20 minutes.

3. Meanwhile, bring 4 quarts water to boil in large pot. Add pasta and 1 tablespoon salt and cook, stirring often, until al dente. Reserve ½ cup cooking water, then drain pasta and return it to pot. Add sauce to pasta and toss to combine. Add reserved cooking water as needed to adjust consistency. Season with salt and pepper to taste and serve, passing Pecorino separately.

SPAGHETTI PUTTANESCA

✔ WHY THIS RECIPE WORKS
Many recipes for puttanesca produce a dish that is too fishy, too garlicky, too briny, or just plain too salty and acidic. Others are timidly flavored and dull. We wanted to bring out as much flavor as we could from each of the ingredients in our version, while not letting any one preside over the others. We bloomed the garlic, anchovies, ana red pepper flakes in hot olive oil to develop and blend their flavors. Then we added tomatoes and simmered for only eight minutes to preserve their sweetness and meaty texture. A drizzle of olive oil over individual portions adds moisture and richness.

SPAGHETTI PUTTANESCA
SERVES 4

The pasta and sauce cook in just about the same amount of time, so begin the sauce just after you add the pasta to the boiling water in step 1.

- 1   pound spaghetti
  Salt
- 1   (28-ounce) can diced tomatoes, drained with ½ cup juice reserved
- 2   tablespoons olive oil, plus extra for drizzling
- 8   anchovy fillets, rinsed and minced
- 4   garlic cloves, minced
- 1   teaspoon red pepper flakes
- ½   cup pitted kalamata olives, chopped coarse
- ¼   cup minced fresh parsley
- 3   tablespoons capers, rinsed

1. Bring 4 quarts water to boil in large pot. Add pasta and 1 tablespoon salt and cook, stirring often, until al dente. Reserve ½ cup cooking water, then drain pasta and return it to pot. Add ¼ cup reserved tomato juice and toss to combine.

2. Meanwhile, heat oil, anchovies, garlic, and pepper flakes in 12-inch skillet over medium heat. Cook, stirring often, until garlic turns golden but not brown, about 3 minutes. Stir in tomatoes and cook until slightly thickened, about 8 minutes.

3. Stir olives, parsley, and capers into sauce. Add sauce to pasta and toss to combine. Add remaining reserved tomato juice or reserved cooking water as needed to adjust consistency. Season with salt to taste. Drizzle additional olive oil over individual portions and serve immediately.

PENNE ALLA VODKA

✔ WHY THIS RECIPE WORKS
Splashes of vodka and cream can turn run-of-the-mill tomato sauce into luxurious restaurant fare or a boozy mistake. To achieve a sauce with the right balance of sweet, tangy, spicy, and creamy, we pureed half the tomatoes (which helped the sauce cling nicely to the pasta) and cut the rest into chunks. For sweetness, we added sautéed onion. We found that we needed a liberal amount of vodka to cut through the richness and add zing to the sauce, but we had to add it to the tomatoes early on to allow the alcohol to mostly (but not completely) cook off and prevent a harsh alcohol flavor. Adding a little heavy cream to the sauce gave it a nice consistency, and we finished cooking the penne in the sauce to encourage cohesiveness.

PENNE ALLA VODKA
SERVES 4 TO 6

So that the sauce and pasta finish cooking at the same time, drop the pasta into boiling water just after adding the vodka to the sauce. Use the smaller amount of red pepper flakes for a milder sauce.

TEST KITCHEN TIP NO. 40   IMPROVING CHEAP VODKA FOR COOKING

When cooking with vodka (such as in our Penne alla Vodka), we've always recommended buying a premium bottle. Vodka is made by fermenting and then distilling starch (usually potatoes). It is then passed through a charcoal filtration system to remove impurities before being diluted with water. Generally, the better the vodka, the more highly filtered it is and the more neutral its flavor. If the key to good vodka's clean flavor is charcoal filtration, we wondered: Could we improve cheap vodka by passing it through a home water filtration system? To find out, we held a blind tasting of three bottles of vodka: Grey Goose, Ruble (the cheapest vodka we could find), and "doctored" Ruble passed four times through a Brita water filter. We still preferred Grey Goose straight up, but in mixed drinks and penne alla vodka, Grey Goose and filtered Ruble both had supporters. So while straight-vodka connoisseurs may prefer to spring for a premium bottle, home-filtered cheap vodka is fine for cooking and cocktails.

1 (28-ounce) can whole tomatoes, drained with juice reserved
2 tablespoons olive oil
¼ cup finely chopped onion
1 tablespoon tomato paste
2 garlic cloves, minced
¼–½ teaspoon red pepper flakes
Salt
⅓ cup vodka
½ cup heavy cream
1 pound penne
2 tablespoons minced fresh basil
Grated Parmesan cheese

1. Pulse half of tomatoes in food processor until smooth, about 12 pulses. Cut remaining tomatoes into ½-inch pieces, discarding cores. Combine pureed and diced tomatoes in liquid measuring cup (you should have about 1⅔ cups). Add reserved juice to equal 2 cups; discard remaining juice.

2. Heat oil in large saucepan over medium heat until shimmering. Add onion and tomato paste and cook, stirring occasionally, until onion is softened and lightly browned, 5 to 7 minutes. Add garlic and pepper flakes and cook until fragrant, about 30 seconds.

3. Stir in tomato mixture and ½ teaspoon salt. Remove saucepan from heat and add vodka. Return saucepan to medium-high heat and simmer briskly, stirring often, until alcohol flavor is cooked off, 8 to 10 minutes, reducing heat if simmering becomes too vigorous. Stir in cream and cook until hot, about 1 minute.

4. Meanwhile, bring 4 quarts water to boil in large pot. Add pasta and 1 tablespoon salt and cook, stirring often, until al dente. Reserve ¼ cup cooking water, then drain pasta and return it to pot. Add sauce to pasta and cook over medium heat, tossing to combine, until pasta absorbs some of sauce, 1 to 2 minutes. Add reserved cooking water as needed to adjust consistency. Stir in basil and season with salt to taste. Serve immediately, passing Parmesan separately.

PENNE ALLA VODKA WITH PANCETTA

Heat 1 tablespoon olive oil in large saucepan over medium-high heat. Add 3 ounces thinly sliced pancetta, cut into ½-inch pieces, and cook until crisp, about 5 minutes. Remove pancetta with slotted spoon and transfer to bowl. Pour off all but 2 tablespoons fat from saucepan. Omit olive oil and cook onion and tomato paste in fat left in saucepan. Reduce salt to pinch in step 3 and add crisp pancetta to pasta with basil.

PASTA WITH TOMATO, BACON, AND ONION

✔ WHY THIS RECIPE WORKS

Like most Roman cooking, pasta alla Amatriciana is bold and brash. We wanted to create a recipe that would do this classic sauce justice, using ingredients found locally. To start, we used pancetta, if available (and substituted bacon if not). Diced tomatoes, onion, and red pepper flakes gave our sauce lively flavor. And adding the cooked pancetta at the end kept it crisp.

PASTA WITH TOMATO, BACON, AND ONION (PASTA ALLA AMATRICIANA)

SERVES 4

This dish is traditionally made with bucatini, also called perciatelli, which appear to be thick, round strands but are actually thin, extra-long tubes. Linguine works fine, too. When buying pancetta, ask the butcher to slice it ¼ inch thick; if using bacon, buy slab bacon and cut it into ¼-inch-thick slices yourself. If the pancetta that you're using is very lean, it's unlikely that you will need to drain off any fat before adding the onion.

2 tablespoons extra-virgin olive oil
6 ounces pancetta or bacon, sliced ¼ inch thick and cut into strips about 1 inch long and ¼ inch wide

1 onion, chopped fine
½ teaspoon red pepper flakes, or to taste
1 (28-ounce) can diced tomatoes
1 pound bucatini, perciatelli, or linguine
Salt
1½ ounces Pecorino Romano cheese, grated (¾ cup)

1. Heat oil in 12-inch skillet over medium heat until shimmering. Add pancetta and cook, stirring occasionally, until crisp, 5 to 7 minutes. Remove pancetta with slotted spoon and transfer to paper towel–lined plate. Pour off all but 2 tablespoons fat from skillet, add onion, and cook over medium heat until softened, about 5 minutes. Stir in pepper flakes and cook until fragrant, about 30 seconds. Stir in tomatoes, bring to simmer, and cook until slightly thickened, about 10 minutes.

2. Meanwhile, bring 4 quarts water to boil in large pot. Add pasta and 1 tablespoon salt and cook, stirring often, until al dente. Reserve ½ cup cooking water, then drain pasta and return it to pot.

3. Stir crisp pancetta into sauce and season with salt to taste. Add sauce and Pecorino to pasta and toss to combine. Add reserved cooking water as needed to adjust consistency. Serve.

PASTA WITH CHERRY TOMATO SAUCES

✔ WHY THIS RECIPE WORKS

For a wintertime fresh tomato sauce recipe with summertime flavor, we started with cherry tomatoes and then added more flavor by tossing them with a little sugar as well as salt, pepper, red pepper flakes, vinegar, and slivered garlic. We then roasted them in a single layer, which cooked off excess liquid and produced sweet and concentrated results in just

35 minutes. With our final touches of basil and cheese, we had produced a fresh tomato sauce recipe in late winter that we wouldn't mind eating during the summer.

FARFALLE WITH CHERRY TOMATOES, ARUGULA, AND GOAT CHEESE

SERVES 4

Grape tomatoes can be substituted, but because they tend to be sweeter, you will want to reduce or even omit the sugar. Do likewise if your cherry tomatoes are very sweet, but this is less likely when using winter cherry tomatoes.

1	shallot, sliced thin
¼	cup olive oil
2	pounds cherry tomatoes, halved
3	large garlic cloves, sliced thin
1	tablespoon sherry vinegar or red wine vinegar
1½	teaspoons sugar, or to taste
	Salt
¼	teaspoon red pepper flakes
¼	teaspoon pepper
1	pound farfalle
4	ounces baby arugula (4 cups)
4	ounces goat cheese, crumbled (1 cup)

1. Adjust oven rack to middle position and heat oven to 350 degrees. Toss shallot with 1 teaspoon oil in bowl. In separate bowl, gently toss tomatoes with remaining oil, garlic, vinegar, sugar, ½ teaspoon salt, pepper flakes, and pepper. Spread tomato mixture in even layer on rimmed baking sheet, scatter shallot over tomatoes, and roast until edges of shallot begin to brown and tomato skins are slightly shriveled, 35 to 40 minutes. (Do not stir tomatoes during roasting.) Cool for 5 to 10 minutes. 2. Meanwhile, bring 4 quarts water to boil in large pot. Add pasta and 1 tablespoon salt and cook, stirring often, until al dente. Reserve ½ cup cooking water, then drain pasta and return it to pot. Add arugula to pasta and toss until wilted. Using rubber spatula, scrape tomato mixture into pot on top of pasta and toss to combine. Add reserved cooking water as needed to adjust consistency. Serve immediately, passing goat cheese separately.

PENNE WITH CHERRY TOMATOES, GARLIC, AND BASIL

SERVES 4

Grape tomatoes can be substituted, but because they tend to be sweeter, you will want to reduce or even omit the sugar. Do likewise if your cherry tomatoes are very sweet, but this is less likely when using winter cherry tomatoes.

1	shallot, sliced thin
¼	cup olive oil
2	pounds cherry tomatoes, halved
3	large garlic cloves, sliced thin
1	tablespoon balsamic vinegar
1½	teaspoons sugar, or to taste
	Salt
¼	teaspoon red pepper flakes
¼	teaspoon pepper
1	pound penne
¼	cup coarsely chopped fresh basil
2	ounces Parmesan cheese, grated (1 cup)

1. Adjust oven rack to middle position and heat oven to 350 degrees. Toss shallot with 1 teaspoon oil in bowl. In separate bowl, gently toss tomatoes with remaining oil, garlic, vinegar, sugar, ½ teaspoon salt, pepper flakes, and pepper. Spread tomato mixture in even layer on rimmed baking sheet, scatter shallot over tomatoes, and roast until edges of shallot begin to brown and tomato skins are slightly shriveled, 35 to 40 minutes. (Do not stir tomatoes during roasting.) Cool for 5 to 10 minutes.

2. Meanwhile, bring 4 quarts water to boil in large pot. Add pasta and 1 tablespoon salt and cook, stirring often, until al dente. Reserve ½ cup cooking water, then drain pasta and return it to pot. Using rubber spatula, scrape tomato mixture into pot on top of pasta. Add basil and toss to combine. Add reserved cooking water as needed to adjust consistency. Serve immediately, passing Parmesan separately.

SPAGHETTI WITH CHERRY TOMATOES, OLIVES, CAPERS, AND PINE NUTS

SERVES 4

Grape tomatoes can be substituted, but because they tend to be sweeter, you will want to reduce or even omit the sugar. Do likewise if your cherry tomatoes are very sweet, but this is less likely when using winter cherry tomatoes.

2	pounds cherry tomatoes, halved
¼	cup olive oil
¼	cup capers, rinsed
3	large garlic cloves, sliced thin
1½	teaspoons sugar, or to taste
	Salt
½	teaspoon red pepper flakes
¼	teaspoon pepper
1	pound spaghetti
½	cup kalamata olives, pitted and chopped
3	tablespoons chopped fresh oregano
¼	cup pine nuts, toasted
2	ounces Pecorino Romano cheese, grated (1 cup)

1. Adjust oven rack to middle position and heat oven to 350 degrees. Gently toss tomatoes with oil, capers, garlic, sugar, ½ teaspoon salt, pepper flakes, and pepper in bowl. Spread tomato mixture in even layer on rimmed baking sheet and roast until tomato skins are slightly shriveled, 35 to 40 minutes. (Do not stir tomatoes during roasting.) Cool for 5 to 10 minutes.

2. Meanwhile, bring 4 quarts water to boil in large pot. Add pasta and 1 tablespoon salt and cook, stirring often, until al dente. Reserve ½ cup cooking water, then drain pasta and return it to pot. Using rubber spatula, scrape tomato

mixture into pot on top of pasta. Add olives and oregano and toss to combine. Add reserved cooking water as needed to adjust consistency. Serve immediately, sprinkling nuts over individual bowls and passing Pecorino separately.

SPRING VEGETABLE PASTA

✅ **WHY THIS RECIPE WORKS:**
In pasta primavera, the vegetables and pasta are tossed together in a heavy cream sauce. We love this classic, but sometimes we want a lighter, brighter version—one with a creamy sauce, but without the cream. As for the vegetables, we wanted true spring vegetables. To start, we chose asparagus and green peas, adding chives for bite and garlic and leeks for depth and sweetness. For a deeply flavored sauce that would unify the pasta and vegetables, we borrowed a technique from risotto, lightly toasting the pasta in olive oil before cooking it in broth and white wine. The sauce flavored the pasta as it cooked while the pasta added starch to the sauce, thickening it without the need for heavy cream. This nontraditional approach gave us a light but creamy sauce with sweet, grassy flavors that paired perfectly with the vegetables for a dish that truly tasted like spring.

SPRING VEGETABLE PASTA
SERVES 4 TO 6

Campanelle is our pasta of choice in this dish, but farfalle and penne are acceptable substitutes.

- 1½ pounds leeks, white and light green parts halved lengthwise, sliced ½ inch thick, and washed thoroughly; 3 cups coarsely chopped dark green parts, washed thoroughly
- 1 pound asparagus, tough ends trimmed, chopped coarse, and reserved; spears cut on bias into ½-inch lengths

- 2 cups frozen peas, thawed
- 4 garlic cloves, minced
- 4 cups vegetable broth
- 1 cup water
- 2 tablespoons minced fresh mint
- 2 tablespoons minced fresh chives
- ½ teaspoon grated lemon zest plus 2 tablespoons juice
- 6 tablespoons extra-virgin olive oil Salt and pepper
- ¼ teaspoon red pepper flakes
- 1 pound campanelle
- 1 cup dry white wine
- 1 ounce Parmesan cheese, grated (½ cup), plus extra for serving

1. Bring leek greens, asparagus trimmings, 1 cup peas, half of garlic, broth, and water to simmer in large saucepan. Reduce heat to medium-low and simmer gently for 10 minutes. While broth simmers, combine mint, chives, and lemon zest in bowl; set aside.

2. Strain broth through fine-mesh strainer into large liquid measuring cup, pressing on solids to extract as much liquid as possible (you should have 5 cups broth; add water as needed to measure 5 cups). Discard solids and return broth to saucepan. Cover and keep warm.

3. Heat 2 tablespoons oil in Dutch oven over medium heat until shimmering. Add leeks and pinch salt and cook, covered, stirring occasionally, until leeks begin to brown, about 5 minutes. Add asparagus and cook until asparagus is crisp-tender, 4 to 6 minutes. Add remaining garlic and pepper flakes and cook until fragrant, about 30 seconds. Add remaining 1 cup peas and continue to cook 1 minute longer. Transfer vegetables to plate and set aside. Wipe out pot.

4. Heat remaining ¼ cup oil in now-empty pot over medium heat until shimmering. Add pasta and cook, stirring often, until just beginning to brown, about 5 minutes. Add wine and cook, stirring constantly, until absorbed, about 2 minutes.

5. When wine is fully absorbed, add warm broth and bring to boil. Cook, stirring frequently, until most of liquid is absorbed and pasta is al dente, 8 to 10 minutes. Off heat, stir in half of herb mixture, vegetables, lemon juice, and Parmesan. Season with salt and pepper to taste and serve immediately, passing additional Parmesan and remaining herb mixture separately.

PASTA PRIMAVERA

✅ **WHY THIS RECIPE WORKS**
When developing our pasta primavera, we wanted to simplify the cooking process while keeping the vegetable flavors fresh. We found that it was actually fine to blanch the vegetables together rather than separately as is traditional, as long as they were put into the pot at different times to make sure each cooked properly. We also realized that we could reuse that same pot (without washing) to cook the tomatoes and mushrooms. Another staple of primavera, its cream sauce, is usually cooked separately from the mushroom and tomato sauce. Again, we found that we could simplify things and eliminate yet another cooking pan by adding the cream to the mushrooms and tomatoes.

CLASSIC PASTA PRIMAVERA
SERVES 4 TO 6

To peel the tomatoes, dunk the cored tomatoes in a pot of boiling water until the skins split and begin to curl around the cored area, about 15 to 30 seconds; transfer the tomatoes to a bowl of ice water, then peel off the skins with your fingers.

- Salt
- 6 ounces green beans, trimmed and cut into ¾-inch lengths
- 1 pound asparagus, trimmed and cut on bias into ¾-inch lengths
- 1 zucchini, cut into ½-inch pieces
- 1 cup frozen peas

6 tablespoons unsalted butter

8 ounces white mushrooms, trimmed and sliced thin

1 pound plum tomatoes, cored, peeled, and chopped

¼ teaspoon red pepper flakes (optional)

½ cup heavy cream

1 pound fettuccine

2 garlic cloves, minced

¼ cup chopped fresh basil

4½ teaspoons lemon juice
Grated Parmesan cheese

1. Bring 4 quarts water to boil in large pot for pasta. Bring 3 quarts water to boil in large saucepan for vegetables; add 1 tablespoon salt. Fill large bowl with ice water; set aside. Add green beans to boiling water in saucepan and cook for 1½ minutes. Add asparagus and cook for 30 seconds. Add zucchini and cook for 30 seconds. Add peas and cook for 30 seconds. Drain vegetables and immediately plunge them into prepared ice water bath to stop cooking. Let vegetables sit until chilled, about 3 minutes. Drain well and set aside.

2. Melt 3 tablespoons butter in now-empty saucepan over medium heat. Add mushrooms and cook until softened and lightly browned, 8 to 10 minutes. Stir in tomatoes and pepper flakes, if using, and cook until tomatoes begin to lose their shape, about 7 minutes. Stir in heavy cream, bring to simmer, and cook until sauce is slightly thickened, about 4 minutes; cover to keep warm and set aside.

3. Add pasta and 1 tablespoon salt to pot and cook, stirring often, until al dente. While pasta is cooking, melt remaining 3 tablespoons butter in 12-inch skillet over medium heat. Add garlic and cook until fragrant, about 30 seconds. Add blanched vegetables and cook until heated through and infused with garlic flavor, about 2 minutes. Season with salt to taste. Meanwhile,

bring tomato sauce back to simmer over medium heat.

4. Drain pasta and return it to pot. Add tomato sauce, vegetables, basil, and lemon juice to pasta and toss to combine. Season with salt to taste and serve immediately, passing Parmesan separately.

PASTA WITH ASPARAGUS

✓ WHY THIS RECIPE WORKS

Well aware that most vegetarian pasta recipes feature a flavorless, boring pile of starch, randomly studded with bland vegetables and topped with a mound of low-quality grated cheese, we set out to develop vegetarian pasta recipes with big and intense flavors that would also be easy to make. For our primary vegetable, we turned to fast-cooking, flavorful asparagus. We sautéed the asparagus to intensify its flavor and we used restraint in seasoning. A good balance of sweet, sour, and peppery ingredients allowed the asparagus flavor to shine. And rich ingredients like cheese and nuts prevented our pasta from tasting too lean—a downfall of many pasta and vegetable dishes.

CAMPANELLE WITH ASPARAGUS, BASIL, AND BALSAMIC GLAZE

SERVES 4 TO 6

Campanelle is a frilly trumpet-shaped pasta. If you cannot find it, fusilli works well. Be sure not to reduce the vinegar too much, or it will become bitter.

¾ cup balsamic vinegar

5 tablespoons extra-virgin olive oil

1 pound asparagus, trimmed and cut into 1-inch lengths

1 red onion, halved and sliced thin
Salt

½ teaspoon pepper

¼ teaspoon red pepper flakes

1 pound campanelle

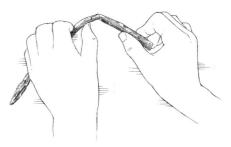

Bend spear about 1 inch up from bottom until it snaps.

---

1 cup chopped fresh basil

2 ounces Pecorino Romano cheese, shaved thin with vegetable peeler (1 cup)

1 tablespoon lemon juice

1. Bring vinegar to simmer in 8-inch skillet over medium heat and cook until syrupy and measures ¼ cup, 15 to 20 minutes.

2. Heat 2 tablespoons oil in 12-inch nonstick skillet over high heat until just smoking. Add asparagus, onion, ½ teaspoon salt, pepper, and pepper flakes and cook, without stirring, until asparagus begins to brown, about 1 minute. Stir and continue to cook, stirring occasionally, until asparagus is crisp-tender, about 4 minutes longer.

3. Meanwhile, bring 4 quarts water to boil in large pot. Add pasta and 1 tablespoon salt and cook, stirring often, until al dente. Reserve ½ cup cooking water, then drain pasta and return it to pot. Add asparagus mixture, basil, ½ cup Pecorino, lemon juice, and remaining 3 tablespoons oil to pasta and toss to combine. Add reserved cooking water as needed to adjust consistency. Serve immediately, drizzling 1 to 2 teaspoons balsamic glaze over individual portions and passing remaining ½ cup Pecorino separately.

CAVATAPPI WITH ASPARAGUS, ARUGULA, WALNUTS, AND BLUE CHEESE

SERVES 4 TO 6

Cavatappi is a short, tubular, corkscrew-shaped pasta. Penne is a fine substitute. The grated apple, added just before serving, balances the other flavors in this dish.

- 5 tablespoons extra-virgin olive oil
- 1 pound asparagus, trimmed and cut into 1-inch lengths
  Salt
- ½ teaspoon pepper
- 1 cup walnuts, chopped
- 4 ounces baby arugula (4 cups)
- 1 pound cavatappi
- 6 ounces strong blue cheese, such as Roquefort, crumbled (1½ cups)
- 2 tablespoons cider vinegar
- 1 Granny Smith apple, peeled

1. Heat 2 tablespoons oil in 12-inch nonstick skillet over high heat until just smoking. Add asparagus, ½ teaspoon salt, and pepper and cook, without stirring, until asparagus begins to brown, about 1 minute. Add walnuts and continue to cook, stirring occasionally, until asparagus is crisp-tender and nuts are toasted, about 4 minutes longer. Stir in arugula, 1 handful at a time, until wilted.

2. Meanwhile, bring 4 quarts water to boil in large pot. Add pasta and 1 tablespoon salt and cook, stirring often, until al dente. Reserve ½ cup cooking water, then drain pasta and return it to pot. Add asparagus mixture, blue cheese, vinegar, and remaining 3 tablespoons oil to pasta and toss to combine. Add reserved cooking water as needed to adjust consistency. Serve immediately, grating apple over individual portions.

FARFALLE WITH ASPARAGUS, TOASTED ALMONDS, AND BROWNED BUTTER

SERVES 4 TO 6

Campanelle can be substituted for the farfalle.

- 2 tablespoons vegetable oil
- 1 pound asparagus, trimmed and cut into 1-inch lengths
- 2 shallots, sliced into thin rings
- 3 large garlic cloves, sliced thin
  Salt
- ½ teaspoon pepper
- 6 tablespoons unsalted butter
- 1 cup sliced almonds
- ¼ cup sherry vinegar
- 1 teaspoon minced fresh thyme
- 1 pound farfalle
- 2 ounces Parmesan cheese, grated (1 cup)

1. Heat oil in 12-inch nonstick skillet over high heat until just smoking. Add asparagus and cook, without stirring, until beginning to brown, about 1 minute. Stir in shallots, garlic, ½ teaspoon salt, and pepper and continue to cook, stirring often, until asparagus is crisp-tender, about 4 minutes; transfer asparagus mixture to large plate.

2. Melt butter in now-empty skillet over medium-high heat. Add almonds and cook, stirring constantly, until toasted and browned and butter is nutty and fragrant, 1 to 2 minutes. Off heat, stir in asparagus mixture, vinegar, and thyme.

3. Meanwhile, bring 4 quarts water to boil in large pot. Add pasta and 1 tablespoon salt and cook, stirring often, until al dente. Reserve ½ cup cooking water, then drain pasta and return it to pot. Add asparagus mixture and ½ cup Parmesan to pasta and toss to combine. Add reserved cooking water as needed to adjust consistency. Serve immediately, passing remaining ½ cup Parmesan separately.

PASTA ALLA NORMA

✔ WHY THIS RECIPE WORKS

To create a bold, complex pasta alla norma without a lot of work, we came up with a few strategies. First, we microwaved cubes of salted eggplant to quickly draw the moisture from it. We then added a secret ingredient, anchovies, to our tomato sauce to give it a deep, savory flavor without any fishiness. We also found that the eggplant should be combined with the sauce at the last minute to prevent it from soaking up too much moisture and becoming soggy. Finally, before serving, we sprinkled ricotta salata, a salted, slightly aged ricotta that is traditional in pasta alla Norma, over the dish.

PASTA ALLA NORMA
SERVES 4

Ricotta salata is traditional, but French feta, Pecorino Romano, and Cotija (a firm, crumbly Mexican cheese) are acceptable substitutes. We prefer kosher salt because it clings best to the eggplant. If using table salt, reduce salt amounts by half. Use the smaller amount of red pepper flakes for a milder sauce.

- 1½ pounds eggplant, cut into ½-inch pieces
  Kosher salt
- ¼ cup extra-virgin olive oil
- 4 garlic cloves, minced
- 2 anchovy fillets, rinsed and minced
- ¼–½ teaspoon red pepper flakes
- 1 (28-ounce) can crushed tomatoes
- 6 tablespoons chopped fresh basil
- 1 pound ziti, rigatoni, or penne
- 3 ounces ricotta salata, shredded (1½ cups)

1. Toss eggplant with 1 teaspoon salt in large bowl. Line surface of large plate with double layer of coffee filters and lightly spray with vegetable oil spray. Spread eggplant in even layer over coffee filters; wipe out and reserve bowl.

Microwave eggplant, uncovered, until dry to touch and slightly shriveled, about 10 minutes, tossing halfway through cooking. Cool slightly.

2. Transfer eggplant to now-empty bowl, drizzle with 1 tablespoon oil, and toss gently to coat; discard coffee filters and reserve plate. Heat 1 tablespoon oil in 12-inch nonstick skillet over medium-high heat until shimmering. Add eggplant and cook, stirring every 1½ to 2 minutes (more frequent stirring may cause eggplant pieces to break apart), until well browned and fully tender, about 10 minutes. Transfer eggplant to now-empty plate and set aside. Cool skillet slightly, about 3 minutes.

3. Heat 1 tablespoon oil, garlic, anchovies, and pepper flakes in now-empty skillet over medium heat. Cook, stirring often, until garlic turns golden but not brown, about 3 minutes. Stir in tomatoes, bring to simmer, and cook, stirring occasionally, until slightly thickened, 8 to 10 minutes. Add eggplant and continue to cook, stirring occasionally, until eggplant is heated through and flavors meld, 3 to 5 minutes longer. Stir in basil and remaining 1 tablespoon oil and season with salt to taste.

4. Meanwhile, bring 4 quarts water to boil in large pot. Add pasta and 2 tablespoons salt and cook, stirring often, until al dente. Reserve ½ cup cooking water, then drain pasta and return it to pot. Add sauce to pasta and toss to combine. Add reserved cooking water as needed to adjust consistency. Serve immediately, passing ricotta salata separately.

PASTA ALLA NORMA WITH OLIVES AND CAPERS

Substitute 6 tablespoons chopped fresh parsley for basil and add ½ cup pitted and sliced kalamata olives and 2 tablespoons rinsed capers with parsley.

PASTA AND SUMMER SQUASH

♥ WHY THIS RECIPE WORKS

For a pasta and squash recipe that would marry the two ingredients in a light, flavorful way while avoiding blandness, we kept the skin on the squash to keep the pieces intact, then salted the squash to release excess liquid and concentrate the vegetable's flavor. We finished the sauce with an acid, such as balsamic vinegar, lemon juice, or red wine vinegar, to give it a kick and paired the sauce with farfalle to best trap the bits of flavor-packed ingredients.

PASTA AND SUMMER SQUASH WITH TOMATOES, BASIL, AND PINE NUTS

SERVES 4 TO 6

A combination of zucchini and summer squash makes for a nice mix of colors, but either may be used exclusively if desired. We prefer kosher salt because residual grains are easily wiped away from the squash. If using table salt, reduce salt amounts by half.

- 2 pounds zucchini and/or summer squash, halved lengthwise and sliced ½ inch thick
  Kosher salt and pepper
- 5 tablespoons extra-virgin olive oil
- 3 garlic cloves, minced
- ½ teaspoon red pepper flakes
- 1 pound farfalle
- 12 ounces grape tomatoes, halved
- ½ cup chopped fresh basil
- ¼ cup pine nuts, toasted
- 2 tablespoons balsamic vinegar
  Grated Parmesan cheese

1. Toss squash with 1 tablespoon salt, transfer to large colander set over bowl, and let stand 30 minutes. Spread squash evenly over double layer of paper towels. Pat squash dry with additional paper towels and wipe off residual salt.

2. Heat 1 tablespoon oil in 12-inch nonstick skillet over high heat until just smoking. Add half of squash and cook, stirring occasionally, until golden brown and slightly charred, 5 to 7 minutes, reducing heat if skillet begins to scorch. Transfer squash to large plate. Repeat with 1 tablespoon oil and remaining squash; transfer to plate.

3. Heat 1 tablespoon oil in now-empty skillet over medium heat until shimmering. Add garlic and pepper flakes and cook until fragrant, about 30 seconds. Stir in squash and cook until heated through, about 30 seconds.

4. Meanwhile, bring 4 quarts water to boil in large pot. Add pasta and 2 tablespoons salt and cook, stirring often, until al dente. Reserve ½ cup cooking water, then drain pasta and return it to pot. Add squash mixture, tomatoes, basil, pine nuts, vinegar, and remaining 2 tablespoons oil to pasta and toss to combine. Add reserved cooking water as needed to adjust consistency. Season with salt and pepper to taste and serve, passing Parmesan separately.

PASTA AND SUMMER SQUASH WITH TOMATOES, OLIVES, AND FETA

SERVES 4 TO 6

A combination of zucchini and summer squash makes for a nice mix of colors, but either may be used exclusively if desired. We prefer kosher salt because residual grains are easily wiped away from the squash. If using table salt, reduce salt amounts by half.

- 2 pounds zucchini and/or summer squash, halved lengthwise and sliced ½ inch thick
  Kosher salt and pepper
- 5 tablespoons extra-virgin olive oil
- 1 red onion, chopped fine
- 3 garlic cloves, minced
- 1 teaspoon grated lemon zest plus 1 tablespoon juice

1 pound farfalle

12 ounces grape tomatoes, halved

½ cup pitted kalamata olives, quartered

¼ cup minced fresh mint

2 teaspoons red wine vinegar

4 ounces feta cheese, crumbled (1 cup)

1. Toss squash with 1 tablespoon salt, transfer to large colander set over bowl, and let stand 30 minutes. Spread squash evenly over double layer of paper towels. Pat squash dry with additional paper towels and wipe off residual salt.

2. Heat 1 tablespoon oil in 12-inch nonstick skillet over high heat until just smoking. Add half of squash and cook, stirring occasionally, until golden brown and slightly charred, 5 to 7 minutes, reducing heat if skillet begins to scorch. Transfer squash to large plate. Repeat with 1 tablespoon oil and remaining squash; transfer to plate.

3. Heat 1 tablespoon oil in now-empty skillet over medium heat until shimmering. Add onion and cook until softened and lightly browned, 5 to 7 minutes. Stir in garlic, lemon zest, and ½ teaspoon pepper and cook until fragrant, about 30 seconds. Stir in squash and cook until heated through, about 30 seconds.

4. Meanwhile, bring 4 quarts water to boil in large pot. Add pasta and 2 tablespoons salt and cook, stirring often, until al dente. Reserve ½ cup cooking water, then drain pasta and return it to pot. Add squash mixture, lemon juice, tomatoes, olives, mint, vinegar, and remaining 2 tablespoons oil to pasta and toss to combine. Add reserved cooking water as needed to adjust consistency. Season with salt and pepper to taste and serve, passing feta separately.

PASTA AND SUMMER SQUASH WITH PARSLEY, SHALLOTS, LEMON, CAPERS, AND GOAT CHEESE

SERVES 4 TO 6

A combination of zucchini and summer squash makes for a nice mix of colors, but either may be used exclusively if desired. We prefer kosher salt because residual grains are easily wiped away from the squash. If using table salt, reduce salt amounts by half.

2 pounds zucchini and/or summer squash, halved lengthwise and sliced ½ inch thick

Kosher salt

5 tablespoons extra-virgin olive oil

3 large shallots, chopped fine

¼ cup capers, rinsed and chopped

2 teaspoons grated lemon zest plus 2 tablespoons juice

½ teaspoon pepper

1 pound farfalle

12 ounces grape tomatoes, halved

¼ cup chopped fresh parsley

4 ounces goat cheese, crumbled (1 cup)

1. Toss squash with 1 tablespoon salt, transfer to large colander set over bowl, and let stand 30 minutes. Spread squash evenly over double layer of paper towels. Pat squash dry with additional paper towels and wipe off residual salt.

2. Heat 1 tablespoon oil in 12-inch nonstick skillet over high heat until just smoking. Add half of squash and cook, stirring occasionally, until golden brown and slightly charred, 5 to 7 minutes, reducing heat if skillet begins to scorch. Transfer squash to large plate. Repeat with 1 tablespoon oil and remaining squash; transfer to plate.

3. Heat 1 tablespoon oil in now-empty skillet over medium heat until shimmering. Add shallots and cook until softened and lightly browned, 2 to 4 minutes. Stir in capers, lemon zest, pepper, and squash and cook until flavors meld, about 30 seconds.

4. Meanwhile, bring 4 quarts water to boil in large pot. Add pasta and 2 tablespoons salt and cook, stirring often, until al dente. Reserve ½ cup cooking water, then drain pasta and return it to pot. Add squash mixture, lemon juice, tomatoes, parsley, and remaining 2 tablespoons oil to pasta and toss to combine. Add reserved cooking water as needed to adjust consistency. Serve immediately, passing goat cheese separately.

PASTA WITH BROCCOLI

✓ WHY THIS RECIPE WORKS

Though the norm for pasta and broccoli is over-cooked broccoli with underseasoned pasta, we set out to create a version with crisp, sweet, tender vegetables that married well with the mild wheaty tones and tender texture of pasta. To cook the broccoli perfectly, we sautéed the florets and stalks in a frying pan with oil, then added water to the pan. The hot steam and moisture quickly turned the broccoli bright green and tender. As for flavorings, we found that broccoli has an affinity for garlic and anchovies, but also works well with heartier combinations, such as sausage and peppers or olives and feta.

FARFALLE WITH BROCCOLI, OLIVES, AND FETA

SERVES 4 TO 6

Begin cooking the broccoli immediately after adding the pasta to the boiling water.

1 pound farfalle

Salt

¼ cup extra-virgin olive oil

9 garlic cloves, minced

1 tablespoon grated lemon zest plus 2 tablespoons juice

½ teaspoon pepper

2 pounds broccoli, florets cut into
1-inch pieces, stalks peeled, halved
lengthwise, and sliced ¼ inch thick

½ cup pitted kalamata olives,
quartered

½ cup chopped fresh parsley

4 ounces feta cheese, crumbled
(1 cup)

1. Bring 4 quarts water to boil in large pot. Add pasta and 1 tablespoon salt and cook, stirring often, until al dente. Reserve ½ cup cooking water, then drain pasta and return it to pot.

2. Meanwhile, heat 2 tablespoons oil, garlic, lemon zest, ½ teaspoon salt, and pepper in 12-inch nonstick skillet over medium heat. Cook, stirring often, until garlic turns golden but not brown, about 3 minutes. Add broccoli and ½ cup water, increase heat to high, then cover and cook until broccoli begins to turn bright green, 1 to 2 minutes. Uncover and continue to cook, stirring often, until water has evaporated and broccoli is tender, 3 to 5 minutes longer. Off heat, stir in olives and parsley.

3. Add broccoli mixture, lemon juice, and remaining 2 tablespoons oil to pasta and toss to combine. Add reserved cooking water as needed to adjust consistency. Serve immediately, passing feta separately.

ORECCHIETTE WITH BROCCOLI, SAUSAGE, AND ROASTED PEPPERS

SERVES 4 TO 6

Begin cooking the broccoli immediately after adding the pasta to the boiling water.

1 pound orecchiette
  Salt
4 ounces sweet Italian sausage,
  casings removed
9 garlic cloves, minced
1 cup jarred roasted red peppers,
  cut into ½-inch pieces

½ teaspoon pepper

2 pounds broccoli, florets cut into
1-inch pieces, stalks peeled, halved
lengthwise, and sliced ¼ inch thick

1 tablespoon extra-virgin olive oil

2 ounces Pecorino Romano cheese,
grated (1 cup)

1. Bring 4 quarts water to boil in large pot. Add pasta and 1 tablespoon salt and cook, stirring often, until al dente. Reserve ½ cup cooking water, then drain pasta and return it to pot.

2. Meanwhile, brown sausage well in 12-inch nonstick skillet over medium-high heat, breaking up any large pieces with wooden spoon, about 5 minutes. Stir in garlic, roasted peppers, ½ teaspoon salt, and pepper and cook, stirring constantly, until fragrant, 1 to 2 minutes. Add broccoli and ½ cup water, increase heat to high, then cover and cook until broccoli begins to turn bright green, 1 to 2 minutes. Uncover and continue to cook, stirring often, until water has evaporated and broccoli is tender, 3 to 5 minutes longer.

3. Add broccoli mixture, oil, and Pecorino to pasta and toss to combine. Add reserved cooking water as needed to adjust consistency. Serve immediately.

SPAGHETTI WITH BROCCOLI, GARLIC, AND ANCHOVIES

SERVES 4 TO 6

Begin cooking the broccoli immediately after adding the pasta to the boiling water.

1 pound spaghetti
  Salt
¼ cup extra-virgin olive oil
5 anchovy fillets, rinsed and minced
9 garlic cloves, minced
½ teaspoon red pepper flakes
2 pounds broccoli, florets cut into
1-inch pieces, stalks peeled, halved
lengthwise, and sliced ¼ inch thick

2 ounces Parmesan cheese, grated
(1 cup)

3 tablespoons chopped fresh parsley

1. Bring 4 quarts water to boil in large pot. Add pasta and 1 tablespoon salt and cook, stirring often, until al dente. Reserve ½ cup cooking water, then drain pasta and return it to pot.

2. Meanwhile, heat 2 tablespoons oil, anchovies, garlic, pepper flakes, and ½ teaspoon salt in 12-inch nonstick skillet over medium heat. Cook, stirring often, until garlic turns golden but not brown, about 3 minutes. Add broccoli and ½ cup water, increase heat to high, then cover and cook until broccoli begins to turn bright green, 1 to 2 minutes. Uncover and continue to cook, stirring often, until water has evaporated and broccoli is tender, 3 to 5 minutes longer.

3. Add broccoli mixture, Parmesan, parsley, and remaining 2 tablespoons oil to pasta and toss to combine. Add reserved cooking water as needed to adjust consistency. Serve immediately.

PASTA WITH SUMMER VEGETABLES

✔ WHY THIS RECIPE WORKS

Bell peppers and zucchini are just a few late summer vegetables that pair well with pasta. We wanted to develop two simple pasta dishes that put the spotlight on each. For our red pepper sauce, we roasted the peppers, which transformed their character from sweet and crunchy to sweet, smoky, and silky. Minced garlic added a potent counterpoint and olive oil bound the flavors together. For our second sauce, we united red peppers with zucchini—sautéing them with fresh tomatoes and garlic to make a ratatouille-like sauce. Fresh thyme and mint infused the sauce with bright herbal flavor.

PASTA WITH ROASTED RED AND YELLOW PEPPER SAUCE WITH GARLIC

MAKES ENOUGH FOR I POUND OF PASTA

This sauce is best served with any string or ribbon-type pasta except angel hair.

- 2 yellow bell peppers, prepared following illustrations 1 and 2 on page 273
- 2 red bell peppers, prepared following illustrations 1 and 2 on page 273
- 6 tablespoons olive oil
- 2 garlic cloves, minced
  Salt and pepper
- 1 pound pasta

1. Adjust oven rack 2½ to 3½ inches from broiler element and heat broiler. If necessary, set upside-down rimmed baking sheet on oven rack to elevate pan.

2. Spread bell peppers out over aluminum foil–lined baking sheet and broil until skin is charred and puffed but flesh is still firm, 8 to 10 minutes, rotating sheet halfway through cooking.

3. Transfer bell peppers to medium bowl, cover with foil, and let steam until skin peels off easily, 10 to 15 minutes. Peel and discard skin and chop peppers fine.

4. Combine peppers with oil and garlic in bowl and season with salt and pepper to taste. Cover and set aside to let flavors meld, at least 30 minutes.

5. Meanwhile, bring 4 quarts water to boil in large pot. Add pasta and 1 tablespoon salt and cook, stirring often, until al dente. Reserve ½ cup cooking water, then drain pasta and return it to pot. Add sauce to pasta and toss to combine. Add reserved cooking water as needed to adjust consistency. Season with salt and pepper to taste and serve.

PASTA WITH ZUCCHINI, RED PEPPER, AND TOMATO SAUCE

SERVES 4

To peel the tomatoes, dunk the cored tomatoes in a pot of boiling water until the skins split and begin to curl around the cored area, about 15 to 30 seconds; transfer the tomatoes to a bowl of ice water, then peel off the skins with your fingers. This ratatouille-like sauce is best served with hearty wheat pasta or egg noodles

- 5 tablespoons olive oil
- 1 red bell pepper, stemmed, seeded, and cut into ¼-inch pieces
- 2 large shallots, minced
- 2 tablespoons minced fresh mint
- 2 tablespoons minced fresh thyme or 1 teaspoon dried
- 2 large garlic cloves, minced
- 2 teaspoons green peppercorns, cracked
- 2 zucchini, quartered lengthwise and sliced ¼ inch thick
- 2 tomatoes, cored, peeled, seeded, and sliced thin
- 1 pound pasta
  Salt and pepper

1. Heat 2 tablespoons oil in 12-inch skillet over medium heat until shimmering. Add bell pepper and shallots and cook until vegetables are softened, about 5 minutes. Stir in mint, thyme, garlic, and peppercorns and cook until fragrant, about 30 seconds. Stir in zucchini and tomatoes and cook until zucchini are softened and tomatoes release their juices and thicken slightly, 2 to 3 minutes. Off heat, stir in remaining 3 tablespoons oil.

2. Meanwhile, bring 4 quarts water to boil in large pot. Add pasta and 1 tablespoon salt and cook, stirring often, until al dente. Reserve ½ cup cooking water, then drain pasta and return it to pot. Add sauce to pasta and toss to combine. Add reserved cooking water as needed to adjust consistency. Season with salt and pepper to taste and serve.

PASTA WITH ROASTED VEGETABLES

✔ **WHY THIS RECIPE WORKS**
For roasted vegetable pasta with sweet and complex flavor, we chose vegetables that could stand up to the high heat of the oven—cauliflower, broccoli, and mushrooms. We sliced the vegetables to maximize the surface area available for browning and tossed them with oil, salt, pepper, and a little sugar to jump-start caramelization. We roasted the vegetables on a preheated baking sheet to cut cooking time and boost browning. For a sauce that would unite the components of our dish, we liked the earthy sweetness of a roasted garlic vinaigrette.

PASTA WITH ROASTED CAULIFLOWER, GARLIC, AND WALNUTS

SERVES 4 TO 6

Prepare the cauliflower for roasting after you put the garlic in the oven; this way, both should finish roasting at about the same time.

- 2 garlic heads
- 6 tablespoons plus 1 teaspoon extra-virgin olive oil
- 1 head cauliflower (2 pounds)
  Salt and pepper
- ¼ teaspoon sugar
- 1 pound fusilli, campanelle, or orecchiette
- ¼ teaspoon red pepper flakes
- 2 tablespoons lemon juice, plus extra as needed
- 2 ounces Parmesan cheese, grated (1 cup)
- 1 tablespoon chopped fresh parsley
- ¼ cup walnuts, toasted and chopped coarse

1. Adjust oven rack to middle position, place large rimmed baking sheet on rack, and heat oven to 500 degrees.

2. Remove outer papery skins from garlic, then cut top quarter off heads and

discard. Place garlic heads, cut side up, in center of 12-inch square of aluminum foil. Drizzle ½ teaspoon oil over each head and wrap securely. Place packet on oven rack and roast until garlic is very tender, about 40 minutes. Transfer packet to cutting board and cool for 10 minutes, then unwrap garlic and gently squeeze to remove cloves from skin. Transfer cloves to small bowl and mash with fork until smooth.

3. While garlic is roasting, trim outer leaves of cauliflower and cut stem flush with bottom. Cut head from pole to pole into 8 equal wedges. Place cauliflower in large bowl and toss with 2 tablespoons oil, 1 teaspoon salt, ¼ teaspoon pepper, and sugar.

4. Remove baking sheet from oven. Carefully transfer cauliflower to baking sheet and spread into even layer, placing cut sides down. Return baking sheet to oven and roast until cauliflower is well browned and tender, 20 to 25 minutes. Transfer cauliflower to cutting board, cool slightly, then cut into ½-inch pieces.

5. Meanwhile, bring 4 quarts water to boil in large pot. Add pasta and 1 tablespoon salt and cook, stirring often, until al dente. Reserve 1 cup cooking water, then drain pasta and return it to pot. Stir pepper flakes and lemon juice into mashed garlic, then slowly whisk in remaining ¼ cup oil.

6. Add chopped cauliflower, garlic sauce, ½ cup Parmesan, parsley, and ¼ cup cooking water and toss to combine. Add remaining cooking water as needed to adjust consistency. Season with salt, pepper, and additional lemon juice to taste. Serve immediately, sprinkling individual portions with walnuts and passing remaining ½ cup Parmesan separately.

PASTA WITH ROASTED BROCCOLI, GARLIC, AND ALMONDS

Cut 1½ pounds broccoli at juncture of crowns and stalks; remove outer peel from stalks. Cut stalks into 2- to 3-inch lengths and each length into ½-inch-thick pieces. Cut crowns into 4 wedges if 3 to 4 inches in diameter or 6 wedges if 4 to 5 inches in diameter. Substitute prepared broccoli for cauliflower and reduce roasting time in step 4 to 10 to 15 minutes. Substitute ¼ cup chopped fresh basil for parsley, grated Manchego cheese for Parmesan, and toasted slivered almonds for walnuts.

PASTA WITH ROASTED MUSHROOMS, GARLIC, AND PINE NUTS

Remove and discard stems and gills of 8 large portobello mushrooms and slice caps ¾ inch thick. Substitute prepared mushrooms for cauliflower and flip mushrooms halfway through cooking in step 4. Substitute 1 tablespoon chopped fresh rosemary for parsley, grated Pecorino Romano cheese for Parmesan, and toasted pine nuts for walnuts.

PASTA WITH BUTTERNUT SQUASH AND SAGE

✔ WHY THIS RECIPE WORKS

Butternut squash usually gets camouflaged inside ravioli, but we wanted to bump up its flavor and bring it out of hiding. To amplify butternut squash's mild flavor enough so that it could be tossed with pasta, we cooked sage in bacon fat, then sautéed the squash in the fat, infusing it with flavor while caramelizing it. Adding a bit of chicken broth and braising the squash for a few minutes transformed it into a sauce that was not only flavorful but also clung well to the pasta. Lemon juice added brightness to the sauce, Parmesan cheese gave it a layer of salty richness, and toasted sliced almonds provided some welcome crunch.

PASTA WITH BUTTERNUT SQUASH AND SAGE

SERVES 4 TO 6

Don't be tempted to use dried sage in this recipe.

- 4   slices bacon, halved lengthwise and cut into ¼-inch pieces
- 8   large fresh sage leaves, plus 1 tablespoon minced
       Olive oil
- 2   pounds butternut squash, peeled, seeded, and cut into ½-inch pieces (5½ cups)
- 1   tablespoon unsalted butter
- 6   scallions, sliced thin
- 1   teaspoon sugar
- ¾   teaspoon pepper
      Salt
- ¼   teaspoon ground nutmeg
- 2   cups low-sodium chicken broth
- 1   pound penne or other short, tubular pasta
- 2   tablespoons grated Parmesan cheese, plus extra for serving
- 4   teaspoons lemon juice
- ⅓   cup sliced almonds, toasted

1. Cook bacon in 12-inch skillet over medium heat until crisp, 5 to 7 minutes. Add whole sage leaves and cook until fragrant, about 1 minute. Strain mixture through fine-mesh strainer into small bowl, reserving fat and bacon mixture separately.

2. Heat 2 tablespoons reserved fat (adding olive oil if necessary) in now-empty skillet over high heat until shimmering. Add squash and cook, without stirring, until beginning to caramelize, 4 to 5 minutes. Continue cooking, stirring occasionally, until spotty brown, 3 to 4 minutes longer. Add butter and allow to melt, about 30 seconds. Add scallions, sugar, pepper, ½ teaspoon salt, nutmeg, and minced sage and cook, stirring occasionally, until scallions are softened, about 3 minutes. Add broth, bring to simmer, and cook until squash is tender, 1 to 3 minutes.

3. Meanwhile, bring 4 quarts water to boil in large pot. Add pasta and 1 tablespoon salt and cook, stirring often, until al dente. Reserve ½ cup cooking water, then drain pasta and return it to pot.

4. Add squash mixture, Parmesan, lemon juice, and reserved bacon mixture to pasta and toss to combine. Add reserved cooking water as needed to adjust consistency. Serve, passing almonds and Parmesan separately.

PASTA WITH SAUTÉED MUSHROOMS AND THYME

✔ WHY THIS RECIPE WORKS

For a weeknight pasta and mushrooms dish with a woodsy, full flavor, we used a combination of mushrooms: cremini for their rich, meaty nature and shiitakes for their hearty flavor and chewy texture. Cooking the mushrooms with salt released their juices and enhanced browning. We finished by adding garlic, shallots, and thyme to round out the flavors in a simple sauce of chicken broth, heavy cream, and lemon juice. We boiled the pasta just after adding the cremini to the skillet so both were ready simultaneously.

PASTA WITH SAUTÉED MUSHROOMS AND THYME

SERVES 4

For a vegetarian dish, substitute vegetable broth for the chicken broth.

- 2 tablespoons unsalted butter
- 2 tablespoons extra-virgin olive oil
- 4 large shallots, chopped fine
- 10 ounces shiitake mushrooms, stemmed and sliced ¼ inch thick
- 10 ounces cremini mushrooms, trimmed and sliced ¼ inch thick
  Salt and pepper
- 5 teaspoons minced fresh thyme
- 3 garlic cloves, minced
- 1¼ cups low-sodium chicken broth

- ½ cup heavy cream
- 1 tablespoon lemon juice
- 1 pound farfalle or campanelle
- 2 ounces Parmesan cheese, grated (1 cup)
- 2 tablespoons minced fresh parsley

1. Heat butter and oil in 12-inch skillet over medium-high heat until butter is melted. Add shallots and cook until softened, about 4 minutes. Add shiitake mushrooms and cook for 2 minutes. Add cremini mushrooms and ½ teaspoon salt and continue to cook, stirring occasionally, until mushrooms are lightly browned, about 8 minutes. Stir in thyme and garlic and cook until fragrant, about 30 seconds. Transfer mushrooms to bowl. Add broth to now-empty skillet and bring to boil, scraping up any browned bits. Off heat, stir in cream and lemon juice and season with salt and pepper to taste.

2. Meanwhile, bring 4 quarts water to boil in large pot. Add pasta and 1 tablespoon salt and cook, stirring often, until al dente. Reserve ½ cup cooking water, then drain pasta and return it to pot.

3. Add mushrooms, broth mixture, Parmesan, and parsley to pasta and cook over medium-low heat, tossing to combine, until pasta absorbs most of liquid, about 2 minutes. Add reserved cooking water as needed to adjust consistency. Serve immediately.

PASTA WITH SAUTÉED MUSHROOMS, PANCETTA, AND SAGE

Heat 2 tablespoons olive oil in 12-inch skillet over medium heat. Add 4 ounces pancetta, cut into ¼-inch cubes, and cook until lightly browned, about 6 minutes. Remove pancetta with slotted spoon and transfer to paper towel–lined plate. Substitute fat in skillet for butter and olive oil and 5 teaspoons minced fresh sage for thyme. Add pancetta to pasta along with sautéed mushrooms.

PASTA WITH SAUTÉED MUSHROOMS, PEAS, AND CAMEMBERT

Omit thyme and add 1 cup frozen peas to skillet along with broth. Substitute 6 ounces Camembert, cut into ½-inch cubes (do not remove rind) for Parmesan and 2 tablespoons minced chives for parsley.

PASTA WITH ESCAROLE AND WHITE BEANS

✔ WHY THIS RECIPE WORKS

For a quick and satisfying pantry supper, we paired fresh escarole with canned cannellini beans. To give the dish assertive flavor, we sautéed a generous amount of garlic in olive oil. We sautéed the escarole briefly in the garlic to wilt it, then steamed it with some water in the covered pan. Finally we uncovered the pan and steamed it again until it was tender. The creamy beans, stirred in at the end, added protein without any fuss.

ORECCHIETTE WITH ESCAROLE AND WHITE BEANS

SERVES 4

Because of the hearty cannellini beans, you only need 8 ounces of pasta for this dish.

- 6 tablespoons olive oil
- 6 garlic cloves, minced
- 2 teaspoons minced fresh oregano or ½ teaspoon dried
- 1 head escarole (1 pound), trimmed and sliced ½ inch thick
- ¾ cup water
- 1 (15-ounce) can cannellini beans, rinsed
  Salt and pepper
- 8 ounces orecchiette (2¼ cups)

1. Heat oil in 12-inch skillet over medium heat until shimmering. Add garlic and oregano and cook until fragrant, about

30 seconds. Add escarole, 1 handful at a time, and cook until completely wilted, 4 to 5 minutes. Stir in water and bring to gentle simmer. Cover, reduce heat to medium-low, and simmer gently for 5 minutes. Stir in beans, cover, and continue to simmer gently until flavors meld, 3 to 4 minutes longer. Season with salt and pepper to taste.

2. Meanwhile, bring 4 quarts water to boil in large pot. Add pasta and 1 tablespoon salt and cook, stirring often, until al dente. Reserve ½ cup cooking water, then drain pasta and return it to pot. Add sauce to pasta and toss to combine. Add reserved cooking water as needed to adjust consistency. Serve.

PASTA WITH SUN-DRIED TOMATOES

✓ WHY THIS RECIPE WORKS

Sun-dried tomatoes can either be parched and leathery or oily and overpowering, but their meaty, intense flavor partners perfectly with pasta. We wanted to get the most out of these tomatoes, while overcoming their shortcomings. We started with oil-packed tomatoes and drained them and patted them dry to rid them of their oily marinade. Then, to tame their presence, we cut the tomatoes into small pieces. Paired with equally strong ingredients like olives, garlic, anchovies, arugula, and capers, sun-dried tomatoes make a lively base to a full-flavored pasta sauce.

PASTA WITH ARUGULA, GOAT CHEESE, AND SUN-DRIED TOMATO PESTO

SERVES 4

Make sure to rinse the herbs and seasonings from the sun-dried tomatoes. Farfalle can be substituted for the campanelle.

- I   cup oil-packed sun-dried tomatoes, rinsed, patted dry, and chopped coarse

- I   ounce Parmesan cheese, grated (½ cup)
- 6   tablespoons extra-virgin olive oil
- ¼   cup walnuts, toasted
- I   small garlic clove, minced
     Salt
- ⅛   teaspoon pepper
- I   pound campanelle
- 10 ounces baby arugula (10 cups)
- 3   ounces goat cheese, crumbled (¾ cup)

1. Process tomatoes, Parmesan, oil, walnuts, garlic, ½ teaspoon salt, and pepper in food processor until smooth, about 1 minute, scraping down bowl as needed.

2. Meanwhile, bring 4 quarts water to boil in large pot. Add pasta and 1 tablespoon salt and cook, stirring often, until al dente. Reserve ¾ cup cooking water, then drain pasta and return it to pot; immediately stir in arugula, 1 handful at a time, until wilted. Add pesto and ½ cup reserved cooking water to pasta and toss to combine. Add remaining cooking water as needed to adjust consistency. Serve immediately, passing goat cheese separately.

PASTA WITH GREEN OLIVE– SUN-DRIED TOMATO SAUCE AND BREAD CRUMBS

SERVES 4

Make sure to rinse the herbs and seasonings from the sun-dried tomatoes.

- 2   slices hearty white sandwich bread, crusts removed and bread torn into quarters
- 2   tablespoons plus 1 teaspoon extra-virgin olive oil
- 3   garlic cloves, minced
- 3   anchovy fillets, rinsed and minced
- ¼   teaspoon red pepper flakes
- I   (14.5-ounce) can diced tomatoes, drained with ½ cup juice reserved, tomato pieces chopped fine
- 1½ cups pitted green olives, chopped

- I   cup oil-packed sun-dried tomatoes, rinsed, patted dry, and chopped fine
- I   pound spaghetti
- I   tablespoon salt
- I   tablespoon chopped fresh parsley

1. Pulse bread in food processor to coarse crumbs, about 10 pulses. Heat 1 teaspoon oil in 12-inch nonstick over medium heat until shimmering. Add bread crumbs and cook, stirring often, until crisp and golden brown, about 6 minutes; transfer to bowl. Wipe skillet clean with paper towels.

2. Heat remaining 2 tablespoons oil, garlic, anchovies, and pepper flakes in now-empty skillet over medium heat. Cook, stirring often, until garlic turns golden but not brown, about 3 minutes. Stir in diced tomatoes and cook until thickened slightly and dry, about 5 minutes. Stir in olives, sun-dried tomatoes, and reserved tomato juice and cook until heated through, about 1 minute.

3. Meanwhile, bring 4 quarts water to boil in large pot. Add pasta and salt and cook, stirring often, until al dente. Reserve ½ cup cooking water, then drain pasta and return it to pot. Add sauce and parsley to pasta and toss to combine. Add reserved cooking water as needed to adjust consistency. Serve immediately, passing bread crumbs separately.

PASTA WITH SUN-DRIED TOMATOES, RICOTTA, AND PEAS

SERVES 4

Make sure to rinse the herbs and seasonings from the sun-dried tomatoes.

- 2   tablespoons olive oil
- 2   garlic cloves, minced
- ¼   teaspoon red pepper flakes
- 12 ounces whole-milk ricotta (1½ cups)
- I   cup oil-packed sun-dried tomatoes, rinsed, patted dry, and chopped coarse

¼ cup grated Parmesan cheese,
   plus extra for serving
2 teaspoons minced fresh mint
   Salt
¼ teaspoon pepper
1 pound medium shells
1 cup frozen peas

1. Heat oil, garlic, and pepper flakes in 10-inch skillet over medium heat. Cook, stirring often, until garlic turns golden but not brown, about 3 minutes. Transfer mixture to large bowl, cool slightly, then stir in ricotta, tomatoes, Parmesan, mint, ½ teaspoon salt, and pepper.

2. Meanwhile, bring 4 quarts water to boil in large pot. Add pasta and 1 tablespoon salt and cook, stirring often, until al dente. Reserve ¾ cup cooking water, then drain pasta and return it to pot. Add ricotta mixture and ½ cup cooking water to pasta and toss to combine. Add remaining cooking water as needed to adjust consistency. Serve immediately, passing Parmesan separately.

PASTA WITH SUN-DRIED TOMATOES, CAULIFLOWER, AND THYME-INFUSED CREAM

SERVES 4 TO 6

To ensure that the sauce and pasta are done at the same time, start cooking the cauliflower before the pasta goes into the boiling water. Make sure to rinse the herbs and seasonings from the sun-dried tomatoes.

1 pound tagliatelle
   Salt
2 tablespoons unsalted butter
1 tablespoon vegetable oil
1 head cauliflower (2 pounds), cored and cut into ¾-inch florets

⅛ teaspoon pepper
1 small red onion, chopped fine
¾ cup dry white wine
2 cups heavy cream
1 cup oil-packed sun-dried tomatoes, rinsed, patted dry, and cut into ¼-inch-thick strips
1 tablespoon minced fresh thyme
1 ounce Parmesan cheese, grated (½ cup), plus extra for serving
¼ cup chopped fresh parsley
1½ teaspoons balsamic vinegar
¼ cup pine nuts, toasted

1. Bring 4 quarts water to boil in large pot. Add pasta and 1 tablespoon salt and cook, stirring often, until al dente. Reserve ½ cup cooking water, then drain pasta and return it to pot.

2. Meanwhile, heat 1 tablespoon butter and oil in 12-inch skillet over high heat until butter is melted. Add cauliflower, ⅓ cup water, ¼ teaspoon salt, and pepper, cover, and cook until cauliflower is crisp-tender, about 3 minutes. Uncover and continue to cook, stirring often, until water has evaporated and cauliflower is golden, about 3 minutes longer; transfer to plate.

3. Melt remaining 1 tablespoon butter in now-empty skillet over medium heat. Add onion and cook until softened, about 5 minutes. Stir in wine, increase heat to medium-high, and cook until reduced and mixture measures ½ cup, about 4 minutes. Stir in cream, tomatoes, and thyme and bring to simmer. Off heat, remove any foam from surface with large spoon, then stir in cauliflower and ½ teaspoon salt.

4. Add cauliflower mixture, Parmesan, parsley, and vinegar to pasta and toss to combine. Serve immediately, sprinkling individual portions with nuts and passing Parmesan separately.

WHOLE WHEAT SPAGHETTI SAUCES

✔ WHY THIS RECIPE WORKS

Whole wheat pasta has a distinctive, rustic, and nutty flavor that sets it apart from traditional white pasta. As a result, it lacks a blank-slate quality and can be difficult to pair with sauce. We wanted a handful of sauces that would provide just the right complement to the hearty flavor and firm texture of whole wheat pasta. Acidic tomato sauces, pestos, and rich cream-based sauces are not ideal for whole wheat pastas, so we opted for aglio e olio, a bold sauce of garlic and red pepper flakes in olive oil. With that as our inspiration, we began sautéing lots of chunky vegetables that would soak up flavor and provide a nice counterpoint to whole wheat pasta's hearty texture. We chose asparagus, fennel, and zucchini because they didn't need to be parcooked and neither competed with nor overpowered the earthy spaghetti. In each variation of this recipe, we worked in glutamate-rich ingredients that contributed savory flavor and enhanced the nuttiness of the spaghetti. Salty pancetta was a natural partner for the asparagus, anise-accented Italian sausage paired perfectly with the fennel, and the sweet, concentrated flavor of sun-dried tomatoes complemented the mild zucchini. A sprinkle of freshly grated Pecorino Romano (also packed with glutamates) over each serving provided a rich, salty tang that tasters preferred over Parmesan.

WHOLE WHEAT SPAGHETTI WITH ITALIAN SAUSAGE AND FENNEL

SERVES 4

Chop the basil at the last possible moment to prevent it from discoloring.

8 ounces sweet Italian sausage, casings removed
¼ cup extra-virgin olive oil
6 garlic cloves, minced

½ teaspoon red pepper flakes
   Salt
1 fennel bulb, stalks discarded, halved, cored, and sliced thin
½ cup pine nuts, toasted and chopped
½ cup coarsely chopped fresh basil
2 tablespoons lemon juice
1 pound whole wheat spaghetti
1 ounce Pecorino Romano cheese, grated (½ cup)

1. Brown sausage well in 12-inch non-stick skillet over medium-high heat, breaking up any large pieces with wooden spoon, about 5 minutes. Remove sausage with slotted spoon and transfer to paper towel–lined plate.

2. Combine oil, garlic, pepper flakes, and ½ teaspoon salt in bowl. Add fennel and ¼ teaspoon salt to fat left in skillet and cook over medium heat until softened, about 5 minutes. Clear center of skillet, add oil mixture, and cook until fragrant, about 30 seconds. Stir mixture into fennel and cook for 1 minute. Off heat, stir in browned sausage, nuts, basil, and lemon juice.

3. Meanwhile, bring 4 quarts water to boil in large pot. Add pasta and 1 tablespoon salt and cook, stirring often, until al dente. Reserve ¾ cup cooking water, then drain pasta and return it to pot. Add sausage mixture and reserved cooking water to pasta and toss to combine. Season with salt to taste. Serve, passing Pecorino separately.

WHOLE WHEAT SPAGHETTI WITH ZUCCHINI AND SUN-DRIED TOMATOES

Omit sausage. Substitute 2 zucchini, quartered lengthwise and sliced ½ inch thick, for fennel; heat 1 tablespoon extra-virgin olive oil in skillet over medium heat until shimmering before adding zucchini. Substitute ½ cup oil-packed sun-dried tomatoes, patted dry and chopped coarse, for lemon juice.

WHOLE WHEAT SPAGHETTI WITH ASPARAGUS AND PANCETTA

Omit sausage. Heat 1 tablespoon extra-virgin olive oil in skillet over medium heat until shimmering. Add 4 ounces pancetta, cut into ¼-inch pieces, and cook until crisp, 5 to 7 minutes; transfer to plate. Add 2 tablespoons rinsed and chopped capers to garlic mixture. Substitute 1 pound asparagus, trimmed and cut on bias into 1-inch lengths, and ½ cup thinly sliced red onion for fennel. Substitute 2 coarsely chopped hard-cooked eggs for basil.

WHOLE WHEAT SPAGHETTI WITH CAULIFLOWER AND RAISINS

Omit sausage. Add 6 rinsed and minced anchovy fillets to garlic mixture. Substitute ½ head cauliflower, cored and cut into 1-inch florets, for fennel; heat 2 tablespoons extra-virgin olive oil in skillet over medium-high heat until shimmering before adding cauliflower and cook until softened and well browned, 10 to 12 minutes. Substitute 3 tablespoons coarsely chopped fresh parsley for basil and add ½ cup chopped golden raisins along with nuts, parsley, and lemon juice.

WHOLE WHEAT PASTA WITH HEARTY GREENS

☑ WHY THIS RECIPE WORKS

Pasta, hearty greens, and beans can be a sublime dish, but these humble ingredients traditionally take time to make the transition to a full-flavored entrée. We wanted to retain the complex flavor of this classic Italian dish but make it an easy, quick, and satisfying midweek meal. To start, we restricted our choice of greens to kale and collard greens, which only require a quick braise, allowing us to cook the greens in a single batch while adding the flavors of aromatic onions, garlic, spicy red pepper flakes, and chicken broth at the same time. The greens, beans, and sauce had to simmer with the pasta for just a few minutes to create a gutsy, harmonious flavor. To compensate for the mild flavor of the canned beans we used heavy-hitting flavors: hearty pancetta, acidic tomatoes, briny olives, and earthy fontina and Parmesan cheese.

WHOLE WHEAT PASTA WITH GREENS, BEANS, PANCETTA, AND GARLIC BREAD CRUMBS

SERVES 4 TO 6

Prosciutto can be substituted for the pancetta.

2 slices hearty white sandwich bread, torn into quarters
3 tablespoons olive oil
6 garlic cloves, minced
   Salt and pepper
3 ounces pancetta, cut into ½-inch pieces
1 onion, chopped fine
¼ teaspoon red pepper flakes
1½ pounds kale or collard greens, stemmed and leaves cut into 1-inch pieces
1½ cups low-sodium chicken broth
1 (15-ounce) can cannellini beans, rinsed
1 pound whole wheat spaghetti
4 ounces fontina cheese, shredded (1 cup)

1. Pulse bread in food processor to coarse crumbs, about 10 pulses. Heat 2 tablespoons oil in 12-inch straight-sided sauté pan over medium heat until shimmering. Add bread crumbs and cook, stirring often, until beginning to brown, 4 to 6 minutes. Stir in half of garlic and ¼ teaspoon salt and continue to cook, stirring often, until garlic is fragrant and bread crumbs are dark golden brown, 1 to

2 minutes longer; transfer to bowl. Wipe pan clean with paper towels.

2. Heat remaining 1 tablespoon oil in now-empty pan over medium heat until shimmering. Add pancetta and cook until crisp, 5 to 7 minutes. Remove pancetta with slotted spoon and transfer to paper towel–lined plate.

3. Add onion to fat left in pan and cook over medium heat until softened and lightly browned, 5 to 7 minutes. Stir in remaining garlic and pepper flakes and cook until fragrant, about 30 seconds. Add half of greens and cook, tossing occasionally, until starting to wilt, about 2 minutes. Add remaining greens, broth, and ¾ teaspoon salt and bring to simmer. Reduce heat to medium, cover (pan will be very full), and cook, tossing occasionally, until greens are tender, about 15 minutes (mixture will be somewhat soupy). Stir in beans and crisp pancetta.

4. Meanwhile, bring 4 quarts water to boil in large pot. Add pasta and 1 tablespoon salt and cook, stirring often, until just shy of al dente. Reserve ½ cup cooking water, then drain pasta and return it to pot. Add greens mixture to pasta and cook over medium heat, tossing to combine, until pasta absorbs most of liquid, about 2 minutes.

5. Off heat, stir in fontina. Add reserved cooking water as needed to adjust consistency. Season with salt and pepper to taste and serve immediately, passing bread crumbs separately.

WHOLE WHEAT PASTA WITH GREENS, BEANS, TOMATOES, AND GARLIC CHIPS

SERVES 4 TO 6

For a vegetarian dish, substitute vegetable broth for the chicken broth.

- 3 tablespoons olive oil, plus extra for drizzling
- 8 garlic cloves, peeled, 5 cloves sliced thin lengthwise and 3 cloves minced
- Salt and pepper
- 1 onion, chopped fine
- ½ teaspoon red pepper flakes
- 1¼ pounds curly-leaf spinach, stemmed and leaves cut into 1-inch pieces
- ¾ cup low-sodium chicken broth
- 1 (14.5-ounce) can diced tomatoes, drained
- 1 (15-ounce) can cannellini beans, rinsed
- ¾ cup pitted kalamata olives, chopped coarse
- 1 pound whole wheat spaghetti
- 2 ounces Parmesan cheese, grated fine (1 cup), plus extra for serving

1. Heat oil and sliced garlic in 12-inch straight-sided sauté pan over medium heat. Cook, stirring often, until garlic turns golden but not brown, about 3 minutes. Remove garlic with slotted spoon and transfer to paper towel–lined plate. Sprinkle garlic lightly with salt.

2. Add onion to oil left in pan and cook over medium heat until softened and lightly browned, 5 to 7 minutes. Stir in minced garlic and pepper flakes and cook until fragrant, about 30 seconds. Add half of spinach and cook, tossing occasionally, until starting to wilt, about 2 minutes. Add remaining spinach, broth, tomatoes, and ¾ teaspoon salt and bring to simmer. Reduce heat to medium, cover (pan will be very full), and cook, tossing occasionally, until spinach is completely wilted, about 10 minutes (mixture will be somewhat soupy). Stir in beans and olives.

3. Meanwhile, bring 4 quarts water to boil in large pot. Add pasta and 1 tablespoon salt and cook, stirring often, until just shy of al dente. Reserve ½ cup cooking water, then drain pasta and return it to pot. Add greens mixture to pasta and cook over medium heat, tossing to combine, until pasta absorbs most of liquid, about 2 minutes.

4. Off heat, stir in Parmesan. Add reserved cooking water as needed to adjust consistency. Season with salt and pepper to taste and serve immediately, drizzling individual portions with oil and passing garlic chips and Parmesan separately.

SIMPLE ITALIAN-STYLE MEAT SAUCE

✔ WHY THIS RECIPE WORKS

For a quick meat sauce that tasted as if it had simmered all day, we discovered a few tricks: Instead of browning the meat, we browned mushrooms to give the sauce browned flavor without drying it out. We blended a panade (a mixture of bread and milk) into the meat before cooking, to keep it tender. Finally, for good tomato flavor, we added tomato paste to the browned vegetables and deglazed the pan with a tomato juice before adding canned tomatoes.

PASTA WITH SIMPLE ITALIAN-STYLE MEAT SAUCE

SERVES 8 TO 10

High-quality canned tomatoes will make a big difference in this sauce. If using dried oregano, add the entire amount with the canned tomato liquid in step 2.

- 4 ounces white mushrooms, trimmed and halved if small or quartered if large
- 1 slice hearty white sandwich bread, torn into quarters
- 2 tablespoons whole milk
- Salt and pepper
- 1 pound 85 percent lean ground beef
- 1 tablespoon olive oil
- 1 large onion, chopped fine
- 6 garlic cloves, minced
- ¼ teaspoon red pepper flakes
- 1 tablespoon tomato paste
- 1 (14.5-ounce) can diced tomatoes, drained with ¼ cup juice reserved

- 1 tablespoon minced fresh oregano or 1 teaspoon dried
- 1 (28-ounce) can crushed tomatoes
- ¼ cup grated Parmesan cheese, plus extra for serving
- 2 pounds spaghetti or linguine

1. Pulse mushrooms in food processor until finely chopped, about 8 pulses, scraping down sides as needed; transfer to bowl. Add bread, milk, ½ teaspoon salt, and ½ teaspoon pepper to now-empty food processor and pulse until paste forms, about 8 pulses. Add ground beef and pulse until mixture is well combined, about 6 pulses.

2. Heat oil in large saucepan over medium-high heat until just smoking. Add onion and mushrooms and cook until vegetables are softened and well browned, 6 to 12 minutes. Stir in garlic, pepper flakes, and tomato paste and cook until fragrant and tomato paste starts to brown, about 1 minute. Stir in reserved tomato juice and 2 teaspoons fresh oregano, scraping up any browned bits. Stir in meat mixture and cook, breaking up any large pieces with wooden spoon, until no longer pink, about 3 minutes, making sure that meat does not brown.

3. Stir in diced tomatoes and crushed tomatoes, bring to gentle simmer, and cook until sauce has thickened and flavors meld, about 30 minutes. Stir in Parmesan and remaining 1 teaspoon fresh oregano and season with salt and pepper to taste.

4. Meanwhile, bring 8 quarts water to boil in 12-quart pot. Add pasta and 2 tablespoons salt and cook, stirring often, until al dente. Reserve ½ cup cooking water, then drain pasta and return it to pot. Add 1 cup sauce and reserved cooking water to pasta and toss to combine. Serve, topping individual portions with more sauce, and passing Parmesan separately. (Sauce can be refrigerated for up to 2 days or frozen for up to 1 month.)

HEARTY ITALIAN MEAT SAUCE

✔ WHY THIS RECIPE WORKS
This ultra-hearty Italian-American tomato sauce typically calls for six cuts of meat and half a day at the stove. We wanted a full-flavored meal on the table in less than four hours, with no more than an hour of hands-on cooking. To start, we limited ourselves to pork sausage and baby back ribs, and replaced time-consuming braciole with standout meatballs. By combining our sauce components and then cooking them in the oven rather than on top of the stove (which requires constant monitoring), we could leave our sauce unattended for most of the cooking time.

PASTA WITH HEARTY ITALIAN MEAT SAUCE (SUNDAY GRAVY)
SERVES 8 TO 10

We prefer meatloaf mix (a combination of ground beef, pork, and veal) for the meatballs in this recipe. Ground beef may be substituted, but the meatballs won't be as flavorful. If you don't have buttermilk, you can substitute 6 tablespoons of plain yogurt thinned with 2 tablespoons of milk.

SAUCE
- 2 tablespoons olive oil
- 2¼ pounds baby back ribs, cut into 2-rib sections
- Salt and pepper
- 1 pound hot Italian sausage
- 2 onions, chopped fine
- 1¼ teaspoons dried oregano
- 3 tablespoons tomato paste
- 4 garlic cloves, minced
- 2 (28-ounce) cans crushed tomatoes
- ⅔ cup beef broth
- ¼ cup chopped fresh basil

MEATBALLS AND PASTA
- 2 slices hearty white sandwich bread, crusts removed and bread torn into small pieces
- ½ cup buttermilk
- 1 pound meatloaf mix
- 2 ounces thinly sliced prosciutto, chopped fine
- 1 ounce Pecorino Romano cheese, grated (½ cup)
- ¼ cup chopped fresh parsley
- 2 garlic cloves, minced
- 1 large egg yolk
- Salt
- ¼ teaspoon red pepper flakes
- ½ cup olive oil
- 1½ pounds spaghetti or linguine
- Grated Parmesan cheese

1. FOR THE SAUCE: Adjust oven rack to lower-middle position and heat oven to 325 degrees. Heat oil in Dutch oven over medium-high heat until just smoking. Pat ribs dry with paper towels and season with salt and pepper. Brown half of ribs well on both sides, 5 to 7 minutes. Transfer ribs to large plate and repeat with remaining ribs. After transferring second batch of ribs to plate, brown sausage well on all sides, 5 to 7 minutes; transfer to plate.

2. Add onions and oregano to fat left in pot and cook over medium heat, stirring occasionally, until onions are softened

---

TEST KITCHEN TIP № 41 FREEZING PASTA SAUCE

One of the greatest things about making a large batch of pasta sauce is that you can freeze it, for up to 1 month, in smaller batches for easy last-minute dinners. (The exception are dairy-based pasta sauces such as Alfredo, which do not freeze well.) We've found that the best way to freeze pasta sauce is to spoon it into zipper-lock freezer bags, then lay the bags flat in the freezer to save space. To reheat the sauce, simply cut away the bag, place the frozen block of sauce in a large pot with several tablespoons of water, and reheat gently over medium-low heat, stirring occasionally, until hot. Before serving, stir in any additional fresh herbs if desired, and season with salt and pepper.

and lightly browned, 5 to 7 minutes. Add tomato paste and cook, stirring constantly, until very dark, about 3 minutes. Stir in garlic and cook until fragrant, about 30 seconds. Stir in crushed tomatoes and broth, scraping up any browned bits. Nestle browned ribs and sausage into pot. Bring to simmer, cover, and transfer to oven. Cook until ribs are tender, about 2½ hours.

3. FOR THE MEATBALLS: While sauce cooks, mash bread and buttermilk in large bowl using fork. Let stand 10 minutes. Mix in meatloaf mix, prosciutto, Pecorino, parsley, garlic, egg yolk, ½ teaspoon salt, and pepper flakes using hands. Pinch off and roll mixture into 12 meatballs. Transfer meatballs to plate, cover with plastic wrap, and refrigerate until ready to use.

4. When sauce is 30 minutes from being done, heat oil in large nonstick skillet over medium-high heat until shimmering. Brown meatballs well on all sides, 5 to 7 minutes; transfer to paper towel–lined plate. Remove sauce from oven and remove fat from surface using large spoon. Gently nestle browned meatballs into sauce. Cover, return pot to oven, and continue to cook until meatballs are just cooked through, about 15 minutes.

5. Meanwhile, bring 6 quarts water to boil in large pot. Add pasta and 2 tablespoons salt and cook, stirring often, until al dente. Reserve ½ cup cooking water, then drain pasta and return it to pot.

6. Using tongs, transfer meatballs, ribs, and sausage to serving platter and cut each sausage in half. Stir basil into sauce and season with salt and pepper to taste. Add 1 cup sauce and reserved cooking water to pasta and toss to combine. Serve, passing remaining sauce, meat platter, and Parmesan separately. (Sauce and meatballs can be cooled and refrigerated for up to 2 days.)

PASTA WITH RUSTIC SLOW-SIMMERED MEAT SAUCE

✓ WHY THIS RECIPE WORKS

Many Italian meat sauces rely on pork for rich flavor. But we wondered if today's lean pork would give enough fat and flavor to the sauce. We tried pork chops, but they turned dry and leathery in our sauce during the long cooking time, so instead we used a fattier cut—country-style pork ribs. Country-style ribs turned meltingly tender and gave the tomato sauce a truly meaty, rich flavor. Beef short ribs can also be used, but since they tend to be thicker than pork ribs, it's important to remember to let them cook a little longer.

PASTA WITH RUSTIC SLOW-SIMMERED MEAT SAUCE

SERVES 4 TO 6

This sauce can be made with either beef or pork ribs. To prevent the sauce from becoming greasy, trim all external fat from the ribs.

1	tablespoon olive oil
1½	pounds beef short ribs, pork spareribs, or country-style pork ribs, trimmed
	Salt and pepper
1	onion, chopped fine
½	cup dry red wine
1	(28-ounce) can whole tomatoes, drained with juice reserved, tomatoes chopped fine
1	pound penne, ziti, or other short, tubular pasta
	Grated Parmesan cheese

1. Heat oil in 12-inch skillet over medium-high heat until just smoking. Pat ribs dry with paper towels and season with salt and pepper. Brown ribs well on all sides, 8 to 10 minutes; transfer to plate. Pour off all but 1 teaspoon fat from skillet, add onion, and cook over medium heat until softened, about 5 minutes. Stir in wine, scraping up any browned bits. Bring

to simmer and cook until wine reduces to glaze, about 2 minutes.

2. Stir in tomatoes and reserved tomato juice. Nestle browned ribs into sauce, along with any accumulated juices, and bring to gentle simmer. Reduce heat to low, cover, and simmer gently, turning ribs occasionally, until meat is very tender and falling off bones, 1½ hours (for pork spareribs or country-style ribs) to 2 hours (for beef short ribs).

3. Transfer ribs to clean plate, cool slightly, then shred meat into bite-size pieces, discarding fat and bones. Return shredded meat to sauce, bring to simmer, and cook until heated through and thickened slightly, about 5 minutes. Season with salt and pepper to taste. (Sauce can be refrigerated for up to 2 days or frozen for up to 1 month.)

4. Meanwhile, bring 4 quarts water to boil in large pot. Add pasta and 1 tablespoon salt and cook, stirring often, until al dente. Reserve ½ cup cooking water, then drain pasta and return it to pot. Add sauce to pasta and toss to combine. Add reserved cooking water as needed to adjust consistency. Serve immediately, passing Parmesan separately.

PASTA WITH TOMATO-BEEF SAUCE WITH CINNAMON, CLOVES, AND PARSLEY

Use only beef short ribs for this recipe.

Add 2 tablespoons minced fresh parsley, ½ teaspoon ground cinnamon, and pinch ground cloves to softened onion and cook until fragrant, about 30 seconds.

PASTA WITH TOMATO-PORK SAUCE WITH ROSEMARY AND GARLIC

Use only pork spareribs or country-style ribs for this recipe.

Substitute 3 minced garlic cloves and 2 teaspoons minced fresh rosemary for onion and cook until fragrant, about 30 seconds.

PASTA WITH CLASSIC BOLOGNESE SAUCE

✔ **WHY THIS RECIPE WORKS**

A good Bolognese sauce should be thick and smooth with rich, complex flavor. The meat should be first and foremost, but there should be sweet, salty, and acidic flavors in the background. To get this complexity, we built our Bolognese in layers, starting with just onions, carrots, and celery, sautéed in butter. Then we added meatloaf mix (a combination of ground beef, veal, and pork). For dairy, we used milk, which complemented the meat flavor without adding too much richness. Once the milk was reduced, we added white wine to the pot for a more robust sauce, followed by chopped whole canned tomatoes. A long, slow simmer produced a luxuriously rich sauce with layers of flavor and tender meat.

PASTA WITH CLASSIC BOLOGNESE SAUCE

SERVES 4 TO 6

Don't drain the pasta of its cooking water too meticulously when using this sauce; a little water left clinging to the noodles will help distribute the very thick sauce evenly into the noodles. If you would like to double this recipe, increase the simmering times for the milk and the wine to 30 minutes each, and the simmering time once the tomatoes are added to 4 hours. You can substitute equal amounts of 80 percent lean ground beef, ground veal, and ground pork for the meatloaf mix (the total amount of meat should be 12 ounces). Just about any pasta shape complements this meaty sauce, but spaghetti and linguine are the test kitchen favorites.

5	tablespoons unsalted butter
2	tablespoons finely chopped onion
2	tablespoons minced carrot
2	tablespoons minced celery
12	ounces meatloaf mix
	Salt
1	cup whole milk
1	cup dry white wine
1	(28-ounce) can whole tomatoes, drained with juice reserved, tomatoes chopped fine
1	pound linguine or fettuccine
	Grated Parmesan cheese

1. Melt 3 tablespoons butter in Dutch oven over medium heat. Add onion, carrot, and celery and cook until softened, 5 to 7 minutes. Stir in meatloaf mix and ½ teaspoon salt and cook, breaking up any large pieces with wooden spoon, until no longer pink, about 3 minutes.

2. Stir in milk, bring to simmer, and cook until milk evaporates and only rendered fat remains, 10 to 15 minutes. Stir in wine, bring to simmer and cook until wine evaporates, 10 to 15 minutes. Stir in tomatoes and reserved tomato juice and bring to simmer. Reduce heat to low so that sauce continues to simmer just barely, with occasional bubble or two at surface, until liquid has evaporated, about 3 hours. Season with salt to taste. (Sauce can be refrigerated for up to 2 days or frozen for up to 1 month.)

3. Meanwhile, bring 4 quarts water to boil in large pot. Add pasta and 1 tablespoon salt and cook, stirring often, until al dente. Reserve ½ cup cooking water, then drain pasta and return it to pot. Add sauce and remaining 2 tablespoons butter to pasta and toss to combine. Add reserved cooking water as needed to adjust consistency. Serve, passing Parmesan separately.

BEEF BOLOGNESE SAUCE

Substitute 12 ounces 85 percent lean ground beef for meatloaf mix.

WEEKNIGHT PASTA BOLOGNESE

✔ **WHY THIS RECIPE WORKS**

Bolognese gets its big flavor from the braising of ground meat and softened vegetables in slowly reducing liquids—most often milk and wine— and then, finally, tomatoes. To streamline this typically hours-long project recipe into a weeknight dinner—one that tasted like it had simmered all day—we used the food processor to chop most of the ingredients, substituted sweet white wine to offset the acidity of the sauce, added dried porcini mushrooms and pancetta to amplify the sauce's meaty flavor, and cooked the meat in milk, which helped break it down and soften it to give it that long-cooked flavor and texture.

TEST KITCHEN TIP NO. 42 BOILING WATER—WHAT'S THE RUSH?

With many home cooks now counting meal preparation time in terms of minutes rather than hours, waiting for a pot of water to boil can seem like an eternity. (A full boil makes the water as hot as possible—212 degrees at sea level, with many large bubbles constantly breaking the surface.) To speed up the process, many of us in the test kitchen start with water that is hot from the tap, but a few still insist on cold tap water, claiming that it makes a difference to the flavor of foods like pasta. To see if this is really the case, we set up a test.

We brought 4 quarts each of hot and cold tap water to a boil and then added 1 tablespoon salt and 1 pound pasta to each. When the pasta was done, it was drained and tasted plain (no oil, no sauce). Tasters could not discern any difference in flavor. In fact, the only difference was in the time it took the pots to reach a boil—13½ minutes for the hot tap water and 15 minutes for the cold.

Before you reach for the hot tap, though, you might want to consider what the U.S. Environmental Protection Agency (EPA) has to say about cooking with hot tap water. According to the EPA, water hot from the tap can contain much higher levels of lead than cold tap water. They say that even cold tap water should be run for a while (until the water is as cold as it can get) to ensure that any lead deposits are "flushed" out of the system. That extra minute and a half doesn't seem quite so long, does it?

WEEKNIGHT PASTA BOLOGNESE
SERVES 4 TO 6

You can substitute equal amounts of 80 percent lean ground beef, ground veal, and ground pork for the meatloaf mix (the total amount of meat should be 1¼ pounds). If using pancetta that is sliced thinner than 1 inch, reduce the processing time in step 3 from 30 seconds to about 5 seconds. To obtain the best texture, be careful not to break up the meat too much when cooking it with the milk in step 4. With additional cooking and stirring, it will continue to break up. Just about any pasta shape complements this meaty sauce, but spaghetti and linguine are the test kitchen favorites.

½	cup water
½	ounce dried porcini mushrooms, rinsed
1¼	cups sweet white wine
1	small carrot, peeled and cut into ½-inch pieces
⅓	cup finely chopped onion
3	ounces pancetta, sliced 1 inch thick and cut into 1-inch pieces
1	(28-ounce) can whole tomatoes
2	tablespoons unsalted butter
1	teaspoon sugar
1	small garlic clove, minced
1¼	pounds meatloaf mix
1½	cups whole milk
2	tablespoons tomato paste
	Salt
⅛	teaspoon pepper
1	pound spaghetti or linguine
	Grated Parmesan cheese

1. Microwave water and mushrooms in covered bowl until steaming, about 1 minute. Let stand until softened, about 5 minutes. Drain mushrooms through fine-mesh strainer lined with coffee filter, reserving liquid.

2. Bring wine to simmer in 10-inch nonstick skillet and cook until reduced and measures 2 tablespoons, about 20 minutes; set aside.

3. Meanwhile, pulse carrot in food processor until broken down into rough ¼-inch pieces, about 10 pulses. Add onion and pulse until vegetables are broken down to ⅛-inch pieces, about 10 pulses; transfer vegetables to small bowl. Process softened porcini until well ground, about 15 seconds, scraping down bowl as needed; transfer to bowl with onion and carrot. Process pancetta until pieces are no larger than ¼ inch, 30 to 35 seconds, scraping down bowl as needed; transfer to separate bowl. Pulse tomatoes with their juice until finely chopped, 6 to 8 pulses.

4. Melt butter in 12-inch skillet over medium-high heat. Add pancetta and cook, stirring often, until well browned, about 2 minutes. Stir in chopped vegetable mixture and cook until vegetables are softened, about 5 minutes. Stir in sugar and garlic and cook until fragrant, about 30 seconds. Stir in meatloaf mix and cook, breaking meat into 1-inch pieces with wooden spoon, for 1 minute. Stir in milk and bring to simmer, breaking meat into ½-inch pieces. Continue to cook, stirring often, to break up meat into small pieces, until most of liquid has evaporated and meat begins to sizzle, 18 to 20 minutes longer. Stir in tomato paste and cook until combined, about 1 minute. Stir in chopped tomatoes, reserved porcini soaking liquid, ¼ teaspoon salt, and pepper, bring to simmer, and cook until sauce is thickened but still moist, 12 to 15 minutes. Stir in reduced wine and simmer until flavors meld, about 5 minutes. (Sauce can be refrigerated for up to 2 days or frozen for up to 1 month.)

5. Meanwhile, bring 4 quarts water to boil in large pot. Add pasta and 1 tablespoon salt and cook, stirring often, until al dente. Reserve ¼ cup cooking water, then drain pasta and return it to pot. Add 2 cups sauce and 2 tablespoons pasta water to pasta and toss to combine. Add remaining cooking water as needed to adjust consistency. Serve, passing remaining sauce and Parmesan separately.

OLD-FASHIONED SPAGHETTI AND MEATBALLS

✔ WHY THIS RECIPE WORKS
One of the problems with meatballs is that they're thought of as smaller, rounder versions of hamburgers. This would be fine if meatballs were generally cooked to rare or medium-rare, as most hamburgers are, but meatballs are often cooked through until well-done. This can leave them flavorless, dry, and dense. Consequently, they need some help to lighten their texture. What we were after was nothing short of great meatballs: crusty and dark brown on the outside, soft and moist on the inside. Buttermilk mixed to a paste with fresh bread crumbs helped lighten our meatballs and added great flavor. An egg was also important for texture and flavor; its fats and emulsifiers added moistness and richness to our meatballs. An egg yolk alone worked best; the white just made the mixture sticky and hard to handle, with no benefits. A mix of ground beef and ground pork yielded meatballs with rich, meaty flavor. As for boosting the flavor further, Parmesan and garlic did the trick. After browning our meatballs in a skillet, we used the flavorful fond left behind as a base to an easy, but flavorful tomato sauce. Simmering the meatballs in the sauce also further boosted flavor— to both the sauce and meatballs.

OLD-FASHIONED SPAGHETTI AND MEATBALLS
SERVES 4 TO 6

If you don't have buttermilk, you can substitute 6 tablespoons plain yogurt thinned with 2 tablespoons milk. When forming the meatballs, use a light touch; if you compact the meatballs too much, they can become dense and hard.

MEATBALLS

2	slices hearty white sandwich bread, crusts removed, bread torn into small pieces
½	cup buttermilk
12	ounces 85 percent lean ground beef
4	ounces ground pork

¼ cup grated Parmesan cheese
2 tablespoons minced fresh parsley
1 large egg yolk
1 garlic clove, minced
¾ teaspoon salt
⅛ teaspoon pepper
Vegetable oil

TOMATO SAUCE
2 tablespoons extra-virgin olive oil
1 garlic clove, minced
1 (28-ounce) can crushed tomatoes
1 tablespoon minced fresh basil
Salt and pepper

1 pound spaghetti
1 tablespoon salt
Grated Parmesan cheese

1. FOR THE MEATBALLS: Mash bread and buttermilk in large bowl using fork. Let stand 10 minutes. Mix in ground beef, ground pork, Parmesan, parsley, egg yolk, garlic, salt and pepper using hands. Pinch off and roll mixture into 1½-inch meatballs (about 14 meatballs total).

2. Add oil to 12-inch skillet until it measures ¼ inch deep. Heat oil over medium-high heat until shimmering. Carefully add meatballs in single layer and cook until well browned on all sides, about 10 minutes. Remove meatballs with slotted spoon and transfer to paper towel–lined plate. Discard remaining oil.

3. FOR THE SAUCE: Heat oil and garlic in now-empty skillet over medium heat. Cook, stirring often and scraping up any browned bits, until garlic turns golden but not brown, about 3 minutes. Stir in tomatoes, bring to simmer, and cook until sauce thickens, about 10 minutes. Stir in basil and season with salt and pepper to taste. Gently nestle meatballs into sauce, bring to simmer, and cook, turning meatballs occasionally, until heated through, about 5 minutes. (Sauce and meatballs can be cooled and refrigerated for up to 2 days.)

4. Meanwhile, bring 4 quarts water to

boil in large pot. Add pasta and salt and cook, stirring often, until al dente. Reserve ½ cup cooking water, then drain pasta and return it to pot. Add 1 cup sauce (without meatballs) to pasta and toss to combine. Add reserved cooking water as needed to adjust consistency. Serve, topping individual portions with more tomato sauce and several meatballs and passing Parmesan separately.

CLASSIC SPAGHETTI AND MEATBALLS FOR A CROWD

✓ WHY THIS RECIPE WORKS
Making spaghetti and meatballs to serve a crowd can try the patience of even the toughest Italian grandmother. We sought an easier way. We found that roasting our meatballs on a wire rack, rather than frying them in batches, made our recipe faster and cleaner. Adding some powdered gelatin to a mix of ground chuck and ground pork served to plump the meatballs and lent them a soft richness. Prosciutto gave the meatballs extra meatiness and a panade, which we made with panko, kept the meat moist and prevented it from getting tough. To create a rich, flavorful sauce, we braised the meatballs in marinara sauce for about an hour. And to make sure the sauce didn't overreduce, we swapped almost half of the crushed tomatoes in our marinara recipe for an equal portion of tomato juice.

CLASSIC SPAGHETTI AND MEATBALLS FOR A CROWD
SERVES 12

If you don't have buttermilk, you can substitute 1 cup plain yogurt thinned with ½ cup milk. Grate the onion on the large holes of a box grater. You can cook the pasta in two separate pots if you do not have a large enough pot to cook all of the pasta together. The ingredients in this recipe can be reduced by two-thirds to serve 4.

MEATBALLS
2¼ cups panko bread crumbs
1½ cups buttermilk
1½ teaspoons unflavored gelatin
3 tablespoons water
2 pounds 85 percent lean ground beef
1 pound ground pork
6 ounces thinly sliced prosciutto, chopped fine
3 large eggs
3 ounces Parmesan cheese, grated (1½ cups)
6 tablespoons minced fresh parsley
3 garlic cloves, minced
1½ teaspoons salt
½ teaspoon pepper

SAUCE
3 tablespoons extra-virgin olive oil
1 large onion, grated
6 garlic cloves, minced
1 teaspoon dried oregano
½ teaspoon red pepper flakes
3 (28-ounce) cans crushed tomatoes
6 cups tomato juice
6 tablespoons dry white wine
Salt and pepper
½ cup minced fresh basil
3 tablespoons minced fresh parsley
Sugar

3 pounds spaghetti
2 tablespoons salt
Grated Parmesan cheese

1. FOR THE MEATBALLS: Adjust oven racks to lower-middle and upper-middle positions and heat oven to 450 degrees. Set wire racks in 2 aluminum foil–lined rimmed baking sheets and spray racks with vegetable oil spray.

2. Combine bread crumbs and buttermilk in large bowl and let sit, mashing occasionally with fork, until smooth paste forms, about 10 minutes. Meanwhile, sprinkle gelatin over water in small bowl and allow to soften for 5 minutes.

3. Mix ground beef, ground pork, prosciutto, eggs, Parmesan, parsley, garlic, salt, pepper, and gelatin mixture into bread-crumb mixture using hands. Pinch off and roll mixture into 2-inch meatballs (about 40 meatballs total) and arrange on prepared baking sheets. Bake until well browned, about 30 minutes, switching and rotating baking sheets halfway through baking.

4. FOR THE SAUCE: While meatballs bake, heat oil in Dutch oven over medium heat until shimmering. Add onion and cook until softened and lightly browned, 5 to 7 minutes. Stir in garlic, oregano, and pepper flakes and cook until fragrant, about 30 seconds. Stir in crushed tomatoes, tomato juice, wine, 1½ teaspoons salt, and ¼ teaspoon pepper, bring to simmer, and cook until thickened slightly, about 15 minutes.

5. Remove meatballs from oven and reduce oven temperature to 300 degrees. Gently nestle meatballs into sauce. Cover, transfer to oven, and cook until meatballs are firm and sauce has thickened, about 1 hour. (Sauce and meatballs can be cooled and refrigerated for up to 2 days. To reheat, drizzle ½ cup of water over sauce, without stirring, and reheat on lower-middle rack of 325-degree oven for 1 hour.)

6. Meanwhile, bring 10 quarts water to boil in 12-quart pot. Add pasta and salt and cook, stirring often, until al dente. Reserve ½ cup cooking water, then drain pasta and return it to pot.

7. Gently stir basil and parsley into sauce and season with sugar, salt, and pepper to taste. Add 2 cups sauce (without meatballs) to pasta and toss to combine. Add reserved cooking water as needed to adjust consistency. Serve, topping individual portions with more tomato sauce and several meatballs and passing Parmesan separately.

PASTA WITH CHICKEN, BROCCOLI, AND SUN-DRIED TOMATOES

✔ WHY THIS RECIPE WORKS

Popular versions of this recipe too often produce bland chicken and dreary broccoli, both drowning in a fatty cream sauce whose only flavor is that of old chopped garlic. We needed a clean, fresh sauce that would enhance the flavors of fresh, crisp broccoli and tender chicken, all tossed with pasta that still had a bit of a bite. Lightly browning chicken breast strips in butter started building flavor. We kept the chicken tender and added more flavor by letting the chicken finish cooking in the sauce, and we kept the broccoli fresh and crisp by blanching it in the boiling pasta water and then putting it aside until the dish was assembled. But our real breakthrough in developing this dish was to replace the cream sauce typically used with a broth-based sauce, which we rounded out with a few tablespoons of butter, a handful of Asiago cheese, and some sun-dried tomatoes.

PASTA WITH CHICKEN, BROCCOLI, AND SUN-DRIED TOMATOES

SERVES 4 TO 6

Be sure to use low-sodium chicken broth in this recipe; regular chicken broth will make the dish extremely salty. The broccoli is blanched in the same water that is later used to cook the pasta. Remove the broccoli when it is tender at the edges but still crisp at the core—it will continue to cook with residual heat.

4	tablespoons unsalted butter
1	pound boneless, skinless chicken breasts, trimmed and sliced crosswise ¼ inch thick
1	small onion, chopped fine
	Salt and pepper
6	garlic cloves, minced
2	teaspoons minced fresh thyme
2	teaspoons all-purpose flour
¼	teaspoon red pepper flakes
2	cups low-sodium chicken broth
1	cup dry white wine
2	ounces Asiago or Parmesan cheese, grated (1 cup), plus extra for serving
1	cup oil-packed sun-dried tomatoes, patted dry and cut into ¼-inch strips
1	tablespoon minced fresh parsley
1½	pounds broccoli, florets cut into 1-inch pieces, stalks discarded
8	ounces penne, ziti, or campanelle (2½ cups)
	Lemon wedges (optional)

1. Melt 1 tablespoon butter in 12-inch nonstick skillet over medium-high heat. Add chicken, break up any clumps, and cook, without stirring, until meat is browned at edges, about 1 minute. Stir chicken and continue to cook until almost all of pink color has disappeared, about 2 minutes longer. Transfer chicken to bowl; set aside.

2. Melt 1 tablespoon butter in now-empty skillet over medium heat. Add onion and ¼ teaspoon salt and cook until softened and lightly browned, 5 to 7 minutes. Stir in garlic, thyme, flour, and pepper flakes and cook until fragrant, about 30 seconds. Slowly whisk in chicken broth and wine, bring to simmer, and cook, stirring occasionally, until sauce has thickened slightly and measures 1¼ cups, about 15 minutes. Stir in cooked chicken, Asiago, tomatoes, parsley, and remaining 2 tablespoons butter and cook until chicken is hot and cooked through, about 1 minute. Season with pepper to taste.

3. Meanwhile, bring 4 quarts water to boil in large pot. Add broccoli and 1 tablespoon salt and cook until broccoli is crisp-tender, about 2 minutes. Remove broccoli using slotted spoon and transfer to paper towel–lined plate. Return water to boil, then add pasta and cook, stirring often, until al dente. Reserve ½ cup cooking water, then drain pasta and return it to pot.

4. Add sauce and broccoli to pasta and toss to combine. Add reserved cooking water as needed to adjust consistency. Serve immediately, passing Asiago and lemon wedges, if using, separately.

GARLICKY SHRIMP PASTA

✔ WHY THIS RECIPE WORKS

In theory, garlic shrimp pasta has all the makings of an ideal weeknight meal—just toss a few quick-cooking ingredients with boiled dried pasta. In reality, however, delicate shrimp cooks fast, which translates to overcooked in a matter of seconds. Meanwhile, volatile garlic can become overbearing or bitter (or simply disappear), depending on how it's treated. To get everything we wanted—al dente pasta and moist shrimp bound by a supple sauce infused with a deep garlic flavor—we cut the shrimp in thirds before marinating them with minced garlic. Then we cooked whole garlic cloves in our cooking oil, infusing it with garlic flavor, before adding the shrimp to the pan. To deglaze the pan, we liked the clean flavor of vermouth; bottled clam juice added complexity to the sauce. To get the sauce for our shrimp and pasta recipe to cling to the pasta, we simply stirred flour into the oil as a thickener just before adding the liquid and tossed in some cold butter to finish.

GARLICKY SHRIMP PASTA
SERVES 4

Marinate the shrimp while you prepare the remaining ingredients. Use the smaller amount of red pepper flakes for a milder sauce.

- 1 pound large shrimp (31 to 40 per pound), peeled, deveined, and each shrimp cut into 3 pieces
- 3 tablespoons olive oil
- 9 garlic cloves, peeled, 5 cloves minced and 4 cloves smashed
  Salt and pepper

- 1 pound penne, ziti, or other short, tubular pasta
- ¼–½ teaspoon red pepper flakes
- 2 teaspoons all-purpose flour
- ½ cup dry vermouth or white wine
- ¾ cup bottled clam juice
- ½ cup chopped fresh parsley
- 3 tablespoons unsalted butter
- 1 teaspoon lemon juice plus lemon wedges

1. Combine shrimp, 1 tablespoon oil, one-third of minced garlic, and ¼ teaspoon salt in bowl. Let shrimp marinate at room temperature for 20 minutes.

2. Heat smashed garlic and remaining 2 tablespoons oil in 12-inch skillet over medium-low heat, stirring often, until garlic turns golden but not brown, 4 to 7 minutes. Off heat, remove garlic with slotted spoon and discard. Set skillet with oil aside.

3. Bring 4 quarts water to boil in large pot. Add pasta and 1 tablespoon salt and cook, stirring often, until al dente. Reserve ½ cup cooking water, then drain pasta and return it to pot.

4. While pasta cooks, return skillet to medium heat. Add shrimp along with marinade, spread into even layer, and cook, without stirring, until oil starts to bubble gently, 1 to 2 minutes. Stir shrimp and continue to cook until almost cooked through, about 1 minute longer. Remove shrimp with slotted spoon and transfer to clean bowl. Add remaining minced garlic and pepper flakes to skillet and cook over medium heat until fragrant, about 30 seconds. Add flour and cook, stirring constantly, for 1 minute. Slowly whisk in vermouth and cook for 1 minute. Stir in clam juice and parsley and cook until mixture starts to thicken, 1 to 2 minutes. Off heat, whisk in butter until melted, then stir in lemon juice.

5. Add shrimp and sauce to pasta and toss to combine. Add reserved cooking water as needed to adjust consistency. Season with pepper to taste. Serve immediately, passing lemon wedges separately.

PASTA WITH FRESH CLAM SAUCE

✔ WHY THIS RECIPE WORKS

Pasta with clam sauce is an easy enough dish made of simple enough ingredients. To be at its best, though, it must be made with fresh ingredients, especially the clams—we like littlenecks or cherrystones. As for the method, we cooked the littlenecks first, just until they gave up their juices, then removed them from the pan (when overcooked, clams get tough). We then recombined the clams with the sauce at the end of cooking just enough to reheat them. For flavor, white wine, as well as just a couple of diced tomatoes (which also helped to color the dish), complemented the clams perfectly.

PASTA WITH FRESH CLAM SAUCE
SERVES 4

Any small clams, such as littlenecks or cherrystones, work well in this recipe.

- 4 pounds littleneck or cherrystone clams, scrubbed
- ½ cup dry white wine
  Pinch cayenne pepper
- ¼ cup extra-virgin olive oil
- 2 garlic cloves, minced
- 2 plum tomatoes, peeled, seeded, and minced
  Salt and pepper
- 1 pound spaghetti or linguine
- ¾ cup chopped fresh parsley

1. Bring clams, wine, and cayenne to boil in 12-inch straight-sided sauté pan, cover, and cook, shaking pan occasionally, for 5 minutes. Stir clams thoroughly, cover, and continue to cook until they just begin to open, 2 to 5 minutes longer. As clams open, remove them with slotted spoon and transfer to bowl. Discard any unopened clams.

2. Drain steaming liquid through fine-mesh strainer lined with coffee filter, avoiding any gritty sediment that has settled on bottom of pan. Measure out and reserve

1 cup of liquid; set aside. (If necessary, add water to make 1 cup.) Wipe out skillet with paper towels.

3. Heat oil and garlic in now-empty pan over medium heat. Cook, stirring often, until garlic turns golden but not brown, about 3 minutes. Stir in tomatoes, increase heat to medium-high, and cook until tomatoes soften, about 2 minutes. Stir in littlenecks, cover, and cook until all clams are completely opened, about 2 minutes.

4. Meanwhile, bring 4 quarts water to boil in large pot. Add pasta and 1 tablespoon salt and cook, stirring often, until al dente. Drain pasta and return it to pot. Add sauce and reserved clam steaming liquid to pasta and cook over medium heat, tossing to combine, until flavors meld, about 30 seconds. Stir in parsley and season with salt and pepper to taste. Serve immediately.

PASTA WITH MUSSELS

✔ **WHY THIS RECIPE WORKS**
When quick-cooking mussels are paired with pasta, a meal can be on the table in under 30 minutes. To start, we steamed the mussels in white wine for maximum flavor. We reserved the cooking liquid, making sure to discard the gritty sediment that had settled to the bottom of the pan. Sautéed garlic added another layer of flavor to our mussels, while red pepper flakes gave it bite, and lemon imparted a bright lift. Tossed with hot spaghetti or linguine, this meal is both fast and full of flavor.

PASTA WITH MUSSELS, LEMON, AND WHITE WINE
SERVES 4

Serve this dish with crusty bread to help soak up the flavorful sauce.

- 1   pound mussels, scrubbed and debearded
- ½   cup dry white wine
- 1   tablespoon olive oil
- 2   garlic cloves, minced
- ½   teaspoon red pepper flakes
- 1   teaspoon grated lemon zest plus 2 tablespoons juice
- 1   pound spaghetti or linguine
     Salt
- 2   tablespoons minced fresh parsley

1. Bring mussels and wine to boil in 12-inch straight-sided sauté pan, cover, and cook, shaking pan occasionally, until mussels open, about 5 minutes. As mussels open, remove them with slotted spoon and transfer to bowl. Discard any unopened mussels. (If desired, remove mussels from shells.) Drain steaming liquid through fine-mesh strainer lined with coffee filter, avoiding any gritty sediment that has settled on bottom of pan. Reserve liquid and set aside. Wipe out skillet with paper towels.

2. Heat oil, garlic, and pepper flakes in now-empty pan over medium heat. Cook, stirring often, until garlic turns golden but not brown, about 3 minutes. Stir in reserved mussel steaming liquid, lemon zest, and lemon juice, bring to simmer, and cook until flavors meld, 3 to 4 minutes. Stir in mussels, cover, and cook until heated through, about 2 minutes.

DEBEARDING MUSSELS

Mussels often contain a weedy beard protruding from the crack between the two shells. It's fairly small and can be difficult to tug out of place. To remove it easily, trap the beard between the side of a small knife and your thumb and pull to remove it. The flat surface of a paring knife gives you some leverage to remove the beard.

---

3. Meanwhile, bring 4 quarts water to boil in large pot. Add pasta and 1 tablespoon salt and cook, stirring often, until al dente. Reserve ½ cup cooking water, then drain pasta and return it to pot. Add sauce to pasta and toss to combine. Add reserved cooking water as needed to adjust consistency. Stir in parsley and season with salt to taste. Serve immediately.

TOMATO SAUCE WITH TUNA AND GREEN OLIVES

✔ **WHY THIS RECIPE WORKS**
Tomato sauce takes on a whole new dimension when you add tuna and olives to the mix. While tuna packed in water made a decent sauce, we found that tuna packed in olive oil gave us a sauce with richer flavor. Green olives trumped black with their bright flavor and meaty texture. As for the pasta, farfalle or fusilli perfectly captured the chunky sauce for flavor in every forkful.

TOMATO SAUCE WITH TUNA AND GREEN OLIVES
SERVES 4

High-quality ingredients are essential in this dish, most importantly, canned tomatoes, green olives, and Italian-style canned tuna packed in olive oil.

- 3   tablespoons olive oil
- 2   garlic cloves, minced
- 1   (28-ounce) can whole tomatoes, drained with ¾ cup juice reserved, tomatoes chopped coarse
- 1   (6-ounce) can tuna in olive oil, drained and shredded
- ⅔   cup pitted green olives, chopped coarse
- 2   tablespoons minced fresh parsley
     Salt and pepper
     1 pound farfalle or fusilli

1. Heat oil and garlic in large saucepan over medium heat. Cook, stirring often, until garlic turns golden but not brown, about 3 minutes. Stir in tomatoes and reserved tomato juice, bring to simmer, and cook until tomatoes soften and sauce thickens slightly, about 15 minutes. Stir tuna and olives into sauce and continue to simmer until flavors meld, about 5 minutes longer. Stir in parsley and season with salt and pepper to taste.

2. Meanwhile, bring 4 quarts water to boil in large pot. Add pasta and 1 tablespoon salt and cook, stirring often, until al dente. Reserve ½ cup cooking water, then drain pasta and return it to pot. Add sauce to pasta and toss to combine. Add reserved cooking water as needed to adjust consistency. Serve immediately.

PANTRY PASTA SAUCES WITH TUNA

✔ **WHY THIS RECIPE WORKS**
While oil-packed tuna works best as a supporting player in tomato-based pasta sauce, we prefer the type packed in water when tuna is the star of the show. For a well-balanced sauce we shredded the tuna to a fine, even texture and carefully chose ingredients to complement its flavor. Capers, garlic, lemon, red peppers, and olives all made the cut. As for the type of pasta, spaghetti and linguine failed to hold onto the sauce, but short, tubular shapes held onto it well.

PASTA AND GARLIC-LEMON TUNA SAUCE WITH CAPERS AND PARSLEY

SERVES 4

In addition to penne or fusilli, any short, tubular, or molded pasta will work well.

3 tablespoons olive oil
3 tablespoons capers, rinsed
6 garlic cloves, minced
½ teaspoon red pepper flakes
½ cup dry white wine
2 (6-ounce) cans solid white tuna in water, drained and shredded
   Salt and pepper
1 pound penne or fusilli
¼ cup chopped fresh parsley
1 teaspoon grated lemon zest
3 tablespoons unsalted butter, cut into 6 pieces

1. Heat oil, capers, half of garlic, and pepper flakes in 12-inch skillet over medium heat. Cook, stirring often, until garlic turns golden but not brown, about 3 minutes. Stir in wine, bring to simmer, and cook until alcohol aroma has cooked off, about 1 minute. Stir in tuna and 2 teaspoons salt and cook, stirring often, until tuna is heated through, about 1 minute.

2. Meanwhile, bring 4 quarts water to boil in large pot. Add pasta and 1 tablespoon salt and cook, stirring often, until al dente. Reserve ¼ cup cooking water, then drain pasta and return it to pot. Add sauce, parsley, lemon zest, butter, and remaining garlic to pasta and toss to combine. Add reserved cooking water as needed to adjust consistency. Season with salt and pepper to taste and serve immediately.

PASTA AND RED PEPPER TUNA SAUCE WITH ANCHOVIES, GARLIC, AND BASIL

Omit capers, lemon zest, and butter. Add 2 rinsed and minced anchovy fillets and 1 cup jarred roasted red peppers, cut into ½-inch pieces, to cooked garlic mixture and cook for 30 seconds before adding wine. Substitute 2 tablespoons chopped fresh basil for parsley and add 3 tablespoons olive oil and 1 tablespoon lemon juice to pasta with sauce.

PASTA AND SICILIAN-STYLE TUNA SAUCE WITH RAISINS, GREEN OLIVES, AND BASIL

Omit capers and lemon zest. Add ½ cup pitted green olives, sliced, and ½ cup raisins to cooked garlic mixture and cook for 30 seconds before continuing with recipe. Substitute ¼ cup dry red wine for white wine and add ¼ cup balsamic vinegar and 2 tablespoons sugar along with wine. Substitute 2 tablespoons chopped fresh basil for parsley and add 1 tablespoon balsamic vinegar to pasta with sauce.

PASTA AND TOMATO TUNA SAUCE WITH GARLIC AND MINT

Omit capers, lemon zest, and butter. Reduce olive oil to 2 tablespoons in step 1. Add one 28-ounce can diced tomatoes, drained, to cooked garlic mixture and cook for 30 seconds before continuing with recipe. Substitute ½ cup dry red wine for white wine. Substitute 2 tablespoons minced fresh mint for parsley and add 3 tablespoons olive oil and 1 tablespoon balsamic vinegar to pasta along with sauce.

SHRIMP FRA DIAVOLO WITH LINGUINE

✔ **WHY THIS RECIPE WORKS**
Most recipes for shrimp fra diavolo ("brother devil" in Italian) lack depth of flavor, with the star ingredients, shrimp and garlic, contributing little to an acrid, unbalanced tomato sauce. We wanted a seriously garlicky, spicy, winey tomato sauce studded with sweet, firm shrimp. To get there, we seared and flambéed the shrimp with cognac to caramelize them and enrich their sweetness. Then we sautéed the garlic slowly for a mellow, nutty flavor and reserved a tablespoon of raw garlic for a last-minute punch of heat and spice. Simmering diced canned tomatoes with a splash of white wine (balanced by a bit of sugar) completed our perfect fra diavolo recipe in less than 30 minutes.

SHRIMP FRA DIAVOLO WITH LINGUINE

SERVES 4

One teaspoon of red pepper flakes will give the sauce a little kick, but you may want to add more depending on your taste. Before flambé-ing, be sure to roll up long shirtsleeves, tie back long hair, and turn off the exhaust fan and any lit burners.

- 1   pound linguine or spaghetti
      Salt
- 1   pound large shrimp (31 to 40 per pound), peeled and deveined
- 6   tablespoons extra-virgin olive oil
- 1   teaspoon red pepper flakes, or to taste
- ¼   cup cognac or brandy
- 12 garlic cloves, minced
- 1   (28-ounce) can diced tomatoes, drained
- 1   cup dry white wine
- ½   teaspoon sugar
- ¼   cup minced fresh parsley

1. Bring 4 quarts water to boil in large pot. Add pasta and 1 tablespoon salt and cook, stirring often, until al dente. Reserve ½ cup cooking water, then drain pasta and return it to pot.

2. Meanwhile, toss shrimp with 2 table-spoons oil, ½ teaspoon red pepper flakes, and ¾ teaspoon salt. Heat 12-inch skillet over high heat. Add shrimp, spread into even layer, and cook, without stirring, until bottoms of shrimp turn spotty brown, about 30 seconds. Off heat, flip shrimp, then add cognac and let warm through, about 5 seconds. Wave lit match over pan until cognac ignites, then shake pan to dis-tribute flames. When flames subside, trans-fer shrimp to bowl and set aside. Cool skillet slightly, about 3 minutes.

3. Heat 3 tablespoons oil and three-quarters of garlic in now-empty skillet over low heat. Cook, stirring constantly, until garlic foams and is sticky and straw-colored, about 10 minutes. Stir in toma-toes, wine, sugar, ¾ teaspoon salt, and remaining ½ teaspoon pepper flakes, increase heat to medium-high, and simmer until thickened, about 8 minutes.

4. Stir shrimp along with any accumu-lated juices, parsley, and remaining gar-lic into sauce. Simmer until shrimp have heated through, about 1 minute. Off heat, stir in remaining 1 tablespoon oil. Add ½ cup sauce (without shrimp) to pasta and toss to combine. Add reserved cook-ing water as needed to adjust consistency. Serve immediately, topping individual bowls with shrimp and more sauce.

SCALLOPS FRA DIAVOLO WITH LINGUINE

The scallops leave more flavorful drippings in the skillet than the shrimp, and these drippings can make the garlic appear straw-colored before it is done cooking. Make sure that it is fragrant, looks sticky, and has cooked for the full 10 minutes.

Substitute 1 pound sea scallops, ten-dons removed, for shrimp.

FRESH EGG PASTA

✔ WHY THIS RECIPE WORKS

Some sauces, such as Alfredo sauce, are best paired with fresh pasta, and some filled pasta like ravioli also require fresh pasta. While fresh pasta can be found in many supermarkets and specialty shops—if you're lucky enough to live near one—we wanted a foolproof recipe for fresh pasta and we wanted it to be easy to knead. We found that the food processor effec-tively kneaded our simple dough, made with just flour and eggs, almost to perfection. Kneading the dough by hand for an additional minute or two made our pasta dough silky and smooth. Running the dough, in pieces, through a manual pasta machine until it was translucent gave us the delicate pasta we were after.

FRESH EGG PASTA

MAKES ABOUT 1 POUND FRESH PASTA

Although the food processor does most of the work, finish kneading this dough by hand. This pasta dough can be used for ravioli, tortellini, or fettuccine.

- 2   cups all-purpose flour, plus extra as needed
- 3   large eggs, beaten
      Water

1. Pulse flour in food processor to aer-ate. Add eggs and process until dough forms rough ball, about 30 seconds. (If dough resembles small pebbles, add water, ½ teaspoon at a time; if dough sticks to side of bowl, add flour, 1 tablespoon at a time, and process until dough forms rough ball.)

2. Turn out dough ball and any small bits onto counter and knead by hand until dough is smooth, 1 to 2 minutes. Cover with plastic wrap and set aside to relax for at least 15 minutes or up to 2 hours.

3. Cut dough into 5 even pieces and, using manual pasta machine, roll out dough into sheets. (Leave pasta in sheets for filled and hand-shaped pastas or cut into long strands to make fettuccine.)

FRESH HERB PASTA

Add ⅓ cup minced fresh herbs (parsley, basil, mint, or any combination) to flour along with eggs.

SPINACH PASTA

Decrease eggs to 2. Add 3 ounces frozen chopped spinach, thawed and squeezed very dry, with eggs.

CLASSIC FILLED PASTA

✓ WHY THIS RECIPE WORKS

Commercial filled pastas like ravioli and tortellini can be tough and doughy, not supple and tender like homemade versions. We set out to develop an approachable method for making ravioli and tortellini at home. Starting with our Fresh Egg Pasta (page 200), we rolled the sheets thin to ensure that the edges, where the pasta is sealed, wouldn't turn out too chewy. To prevent the pasta from bursting open while boiling, we were especially careful to use just-rolled pasta sheets that were still moist and pliable (sheets rolled even 20 minutes ahead of time were too brittle to manipulate). Brushing the edges with water made the best seal (egg yolk was too sticky).

A modest amount of filling proved best for pillowy ravioli and tortellini that stayed contained during cooking.

MEAT AND RICOTTA RAVIOLI OR TORTELLINI

SERVES 6 TO 8

This recipe produces 2-inch square ravioli or large tortellini.

GARDEN TOMATO SAUCE

- 3 tablespoons unsalted butter
- I small onion, chopped fine
- I carrot, peeled and minced
- I (28-ounce) can crushed tomatoes
   Salt and pepper

MEAT AND RICOTTA FILLING

- I tablespoon olive oil
- 2 garlic cloves, minced
- 8 ounces 85 percent lean ground beef, ground pork, or ground veal
- 8 ounces (1 cup) whole-milk ricotta cheese
- ¼ cup grated Parmesan cheese
- ¼ cup minced fresh basil
- I large egg yolk
- ¼ teaspoon pepper

- All-purpose flour, for dusting
- I recipe Fresh Egg Pasta (page 200)
- I tablespoon salt
   Grated Parmesan cheese

I. FOR THE SAUCE: Melt butter in medium saucepan over medium heat. Add onion and carrot and cook until vegetables are softened, about 5 minutes. Stir in tomatoes and ½ teaspoon salt, bring to simmer, and cook until sauce thickens, about 1 hour. Season with salt and pepper to taste. Cover and set aside to keep warm. (Sauce can be refrigerated for up to 2 days. Bring back to simmer before cooking ravioli.)

2. FOR THE FILLING: Heat oil and garlic in 10-inch skillet over medium heat. Cook, stirring often, until garlic turns golden but not brown, about 3 minutes. Stir in ground beef and cook, breaking up any large pieces with wooden spoon, until fat is rendered and meat is browned, about 5 minutes. Remove browned meat with slotted spoon, transfer to large bowl, and let cool slightly. Stir in ricotta, Parmesan, basil, egg yolk, and pepper until well combined. Cover and refrigerate mixture until cool, about 30 minutes. (Filling can be refrigerated for up to 2 days.)

3A. TO FORM RAVIOLI: Dust 2 rimmed baking sheets and counter with flour. Working with 1 pasta sheet at a time, cut pasta into long rectangles measuring 4 inches across with pizza wheel or sharp knife. Place rounded 1-teaspoon dollops of

ROLLING OUT PASTA DOUGH

I. Run disk of pasta through rollers set to widest position.

2. Bring ends of dough toward middle and press down to seal.

3. Feed open side of pasta through rollers. Repeat steps I and 2.

4. Without folding again, run pasta through widest setting twice or until dough is smooth. If dough is at all sticky, lightly dust it with flour. Begin to roll pasta thinner by putting it through the machine repeatedly, narrowing setting each time.

5. Roll until dough is thin and satiny, dusting with flour if sticky. You should be able to see outline of your hand through pasta. Lay pasta on clean kitchen towel and cover it with damp cloth. Repeat with other pieces of dough.

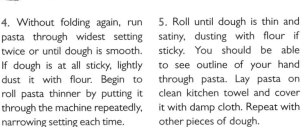

6. To make fettuccine, run each sheet through wide cutter on pasta machine. Each noodle will measure ⅛ to ¼ inch across.

filling 1 inch from bottom edge of dough and spaced about 1¼ inches apart. (If edges of dough seem dry, dab with water.) Fold top of pasta over filling and press layers of dough together securely around each mound of filling to seal. Using fluted pastry wheel, cut ravioli apart and trim edges. Transfer finished ravioli to prepared sheets and cover with damp kitchen towels. Repeat with remaining pasta and filling. (Towel-covered sheets of ravioli can be wrapped with plastic wrap and refrigerated for up to 4 hours, or frozen; when completely frozen, ravioli can be transferred to zipper-lock bag and stored in freezer for up to 1 month. Do not thaw ravioli before boiling.)

3B. TO FORM TORTELLINI: Dust 2 rimmed baking sheets and counter with flour. Working with 1 pasta sheet at a time, cut pasta into 2½-inch squares with pizza wheel or sharp knife. Place ½-teaspoon dollops of filling in center of each square. (If edges of dough seem dry, dab with water.) Fold 1 corner of square diagonally over filling, leaving thin border of bottom dough layer exposed. Press layers of dough

together securely around filling to seal. Lift each filled triangle and wrap back of triangle around top of index finger. Squeeze bottom corners of triangle together. Slide filled pasta off finger, transfer to prepared sheets, and cover with damp kitchen towels. Repeat with remaining pasta and filling. (Towel-covered sheets of tortellini can be wrapped with plastic wrap and refrigerated for up to 4 hours, or frozen; when completely frozen, tortellini can be transferred to zipper-lock bag and stored in freezer for up to 1 month. Do not thaw tortellini before boiling.)

4. Bring 4 quarts water to simmer in large pot. Add half of pasta and 1 tablespoon salt and cook, stirring often, until pasta is tender, about 2 minutes (3 to 4 minutes if frozen), adjusting heat as needed to maintain simmer. Remove pasta with slotted spoon and transfer to warm serving bowl. Add some of warm sauce to pasta, toss gently to combine, and cover to keep warm. Repeat with remaining pasta and transfer to serving bowl. Add remaining sauce to pasta, toss gently to combine, and serve immediately, passing Parmesan separately.

SPINACH AND RICOTTA RAVIOLI OR TORTELLINI

SERVES 6 TO 8

This recipe produces 2-inch square ravioli or large tortellini.

- 12 ounces curly-leaf spinach, stemmed and leaves cut into 1-inch pieces
- 2 tablespoons unsalted butter
- ¼ cup finely chopped onion
- 8 ounces (1 cup) whole-milk ricotta cheese
- 1½ ounces Parmesan cheese, grated (¾ cup)
- 1 large egg yolk
- ¼ teaspoon pepper
  All-purpose flour, for dusting
- 1 recipe Fresh Egg Pasta (page 200)
- 1 tablespoon salt
- 1 recipe Garden Tomato Sauce (page 201), warmed
  Grated Parmesan cheese

1. Microwave spinach and ¼ cup water in large covered bowl until wilted, about

MAKING RAVIOLI

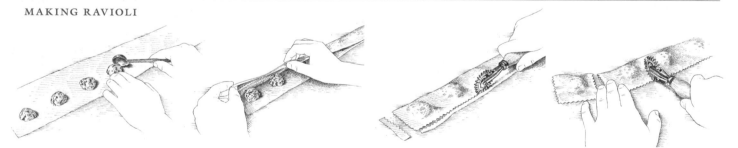

1. Use pizza wheel or sharp knife to cut 1 fresh pasta sheet at a time into long rectangles measuring 4 inches across. Place filling (about 1 rounded teaspoon each) in line 1 inch from bottom of pasta sheet. Leave 1¼ inches between balls of filling.

2. Fold top of pasta over filling and line it up with bottom edge. Press layers of dough together securely around each mound of filling, sealing bottom and 2 open sides with your finger.

3. Use fluted pastry wheel to cut along 2 sides and bottom of sealed pasta sheet.

4. Run pastry wheel between mounds of filling to cut out ravioli.

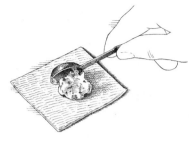

1. Use pizza wheel or sharp knife to cut 1 fresh pasta sheet at a time into 2½-inch squares. Place small balls of filling (about ½ teaspoon each) in center of each square.

2. Fold 1 corner of square diagonally over filling to form triangle, leaving thin border of bottom triangle exposed. Press layers of dough together securely around filling to seal.

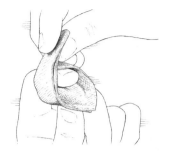

3. Lift each filled triangle and wrap long side of triangle around top of index finger.

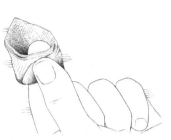

4. Squeeze bottom corners of triangle together.

4 minutes. Drain spinach in colander, pressing on spinach with spatula to release any excess liquid. Let spinach cool slightly, then chop fine.

2. Melt butter in 12-inch skillet over medium heat. Add onion and cook until softened, about 5 minutes. Stir in chopped spinach and cook until heated through, about 1 minute. Transfer spinach mixture to large bowl, cool slightly, then stir in ricotta, Parmesan, egg yolk, and pepper. Cover and refrigerate mixture until cool, about 30 minutes. (Filling can be refrigerated for up to 2 days.)

3A. TO FORM RAVIOLI: Dust 2 rimmed baking sheets and counter with flour. Working with 1 pasta sheet at a time, cut pasta into long rectangles measuring 4 inches across with pizza wheel or sharp knife. Place rounded 1-teaspoon dollops of filling 1 inch from bottom edge of dough and spaced about 1¼ inches apart. (If edges of dough seem dry, dab with water.) Fold top of pasta over filling and press layers of dough together securely around each mound of filling to seal. Using fluted pastry wheel, cut ravioli apart and trim edges. Transfer finished ravioli to prepared sheets and cover with damp kitchen towels. Repeat with remaining pasta and filling. (Towel-covered sheets of ravioli can be

wrapped with plastic wrap and refrigerated for up to 4 hours, or frozen; when completely frozen, ravioli can be transferred to zipper-lock bag and stored in freezer for up to 1 month. Do not thaw ravioli before boiling.)

3B. TO FORM TORTELLINI: Dust 2 rimmed baking sheets and counter with flour. Working with 1 pasta sheet at a time, cut pasta into 2½-inch squares with pizza wheel or sharp knife. Place ½-teaspoon dollops of filling in center of each square. (If edges of dough seem dry, dab with water.) Fold 1 corner of square diagonally over filling, leaving thin border of bottom dough layer exposed. Press layers of dough together securely around filling to seal. Lift each filled triangle and wrap back of triangle around top of index finger. Squeeze bottom corners of triangle together. Slide filled pasta off finger, transfer to prepared sheets, and cover with damp kitchen towels. Repeat with remaining pasta and filling. (Towel-covered sheets of tortellini can be wrapped with plastic wrap and refrigerated for up to 4 hours, or frozen; when completely frozen, tortellini can be transferred to zipper-lock bag and stored in freezer for up to 1 month. Do not thaw tortellini before boiling.)

4. Bring 4 quarts water to simmer in large pot. Add half of pasta and 1 tablespoon salt and cook, stirring often, until pasta is tender, about 2 minutes (3 to 4 minutes if frozen), adjusting heat as needed to maintain simmer. Remove pasta with slotted spoon and transfer to warm serving bowl. Add some of warm sauce to pasta, toss gently to combine, and cover to keep warm. Repeat with remaining pasta and transfer to serving bowl. Add remaining sauce to pasta, toss gently to combine, and serve immediately, passing Parmesan separately.

SQUASH AND PROSCIUTTO RAVIOLI OR TORTELLINI

SERVES 6 TO 8

This recipe produces 2-inch square ravioli or large tortellini.

SQUASH AND PROSCIUTTO FILLING

- 1   acorn squash (1½ pounds), halved pole to pole and seeded
- 4   ounces thinly sliced prosciutto, chopped fine
- 2   ounces Parmesan cheese, grated (1 cup)
- 1   large egg yolk

1 tablespoon minced fresh sage
⅛ teaspoon ground nutmeg
All-purpose flour, for dusting
1 recipe Fresh Egg Pasta (page 200)
1 tablespoon salt
Grated Parmesan cheese

BROWN BUTTER SAUCE
½ cup pine nuts
4 tablespoons unsalted butter
¼ cup minced fresh parsley

1. FOR THE FILLING: Adjust oven rack to middle position and heat oven to 400 degrees. Place squash, cut sides down, on rimmed baking sheet and bake until tender, about 35 minutes.

2. Let squash cool slightly, then scoop out flesh and transfer to food processor. Process until squash is smooth, about 20 seconds, scraping down bowl as needed. Transfer squash to large bowl and stir in prosciutto, Parmesan, egg yolk, sage, and nutmeg. Cover and refrigerate mixture until cool, about 30 minutes. (Filling can be refrigerated for up to 2 days.)

3A. TO FORM RAVIOLI: Dust 2 rimmed baking sheets and counter with flour. Working with 1 pasta sheet at a time, cut pasta into long rectangles measuring 4 inches across with pizza wheel or sharp knife. Place rounded 1-teaspoon dollops of filling 1 inch from bottom edge of dough and spaced about 1¼ inches apart. (If edges of dough seem dry, dab with water.) Fold top of pasta over filling and press layers of dough together securely around each mound of filling to seal. Using fluted pastry wheel, cut ravioli apart and trim edges. Transfer finished ravioli to prepared sheets and cover with damp kitchen towels. Repeat with remaining pasta and filling. (Towel-covered sheets of ravioli can be wrapped with plastic wrap and refrigerated for up to 4 hours, or frozen; when completely frozen, ravioli can be transferred to zipper-lock bag and stored in freezer

for up to 1 month. Do not thaw ravioli before boiling.)

3B. TO FORM TORTELLINI: Dust 2 rimmed baking sheets and counter with flour. Working with 1 pasta sheet at a time, cut pasta into 2½-inch squares with pizza wheel or sharp knife. Place ½-teaspoon dollops of filling in center of each square. (If edges of dough seem dry, dab with water.) Fold 1 corner of square diagonally over filling, leaving thin border of bottom dough layer exposed. Press layers of dough together securely around filling to seal. Lift each filled triangle and wrap back of triangle around top of index finger. Squeeze bottom corners of triangle together. Slide filled pasta off finger, transfer to prepared sheets, and cover with damp kitchen towels. Repeat with remaining pasta and filling. (Towel-covered sheets of tortellini can be wrapped with plastic wrap and refrigerated for up to 4 hours, or frozen; when completely frozen, tortellini can be transferred to zipper-lock bag and stored in freezer for up to 1 month. Do not thaw tortellini before boiling.)

4. FOR THE SAUCE: Heat pine nuts and butter in 10-inch skillet over medium-high heat and cook, swirling occasionally, until butter is melted and browned and releases nutty aroma, about 3 minutes. Off heat, stir in parsley and cover to keep warm.

5. Bring 4 quarts water to simmer in large pot. Add half of pasta and 1 tablespoon salt and cook, stirring often, until pasta is tender, about 2 minutes (3 to 4 minutes if frozen), adjusting heat as needed to maintain simmer. Remove pasta with slotted spoon and transfer to warm serving bowl. Add some of warm sauce to pasta, toss gently to combine, and cover to keep warm. Repeat with remaining pasta and transfer to serving bowl. Swirl 2 tablespoons of cooking water into remaining sauce, then add to pasta and toss gently to combine. Serve immediately, passing Parmesan separately.

WILD MUSHROOM RAVIOLI OR TORTELLINI

SERVES 6 TO 8

This recipe produces 2-inch square ravioli or large tortellini.

1 ounce dried porcini mushrooms, rinsed
2 tablespoons olive oil
2 garlic cloves, minced
10 ounces white or cremini mushrooms, trimmed and chopped fine
¼ cup minced fresh parsley
Salt and pepper
8 ounces (1 cup) whole-milk ricotta cheese
⅓ cup grated Parmesan cheese
1 large egg yolk
All-purpose flour, for dusting
1 recipe Fresh Egg Pasta (page 200)
1 tablespoon salt
1 recipe Brown Butter Sauce, warmed
Grated Parmesan cheese

1. Microwave 1 cup water and porcini in covered bowl until steaming, about 1 minute. Let stand until softened, about 5 minutes. Drain mushrooms through fine-mesh strainer lined with coffee filter, reserving liquid for another use and finely chopping porcini.

2. Heat oil and garlic in 10-inch skillet over medium heat. Cook, stirring often, until garlic turns golden but not brown, about 3 minutes. Add mushrooms and cook until softened, about 5 minutes. Stir in porcini and parsley and cook until mushrooms are lightly browned, about 2 minutes longer. Season with salt and pepper to taste. Transfer mushroom mixture to large bowl, cool slightly, then stir in ricotta, Parmesan, and egg yolk. Cover and refrigerate mixture until cool, about 30 minutes. (Filling can be refrigerated for up to 2 days.)

3A. TO FORM RAVIOLI: Dust 2 rimmed baking sheets and counter with flour. Working with 1 pasta sheet at a time, cut pasta into long rectangles measuring 4 inches across with pizza wheel or sharp knife. Place rounded 1-teaspoon dollops of filling 1 inch from bottom edge of dough and spaced about 1¼ inches apart. (If edges of dough seem dry, dab with water.) Fold top of pasta over filling and press layers of dough together securely around each mound of filling to seal. Using fluted pastry wheel, cut ravioli apart and trim edges. Transfer finished ravioli to prepared sheets and cover with damp kitchen towels. Repeat with remaining pasta and filling. (Towel-covered sheets of ravioli can be wrapped with plastic wrap and refrigerated for up to 4 hours, or frozen; when completely frozen, ravioli can be transferred to zipper-lock bag and stored in freezer for up to 1 month. Do not thaw ravioli before boiling.)

3B. TO FORM TORTELLINI: Dust 2 rimmed baking sheets and counter with flour. Working with 1 pasta sheet at a time, cut pasta into 2½-inch squares with pizza wheel or sharp knife. Place ½-teaspoon dollops of filling in center of each square. (If edges of dough seem dry, dab with water.) Fold 1 corner of square diagonally over filling, leaving thin border of bottom dough layer exposed. Press layers of dough together securely around filling to seal. Lift each filled triangle and wrap back of triangle around top of index finger. Squeeze bottom corners of triangle together. Slide filled pasta off finger, transfer to prepared sheets, and cover with damp kitchen towels. Repeat with remaining pasta and filling. (Towel-covered sheets of tortellini can be wrapped with plastic wrap and refrigerated for up to 4 hours, or frozen; when completely frozen, tortellini can be transferred to zipper-lock bag and stored in freezer for up to 1 month. Do not thaw tortellini before boiling.)

4. Bring 4 quarts water to simmer in large pot. Add half of pasta and 1 tablespoon salt and cook, stirring often, until pasta is tender, about 2 minutes (3 to 4 minutes if frozen), adjusting heat as needed to maintain simmer. Remove pasta with slotted spoon and transfer to warm serving bowl. Add some of warm sauce to pasta, toss gently to combine, and cover to keep warm. Repeat with remaining pasta and transfer to serving bowl. Swirl 2 tablespoons of cooking water into remaining sauce, then add to pasta and toss gently to combine. Serve immediately, passing Parmesan separately.

POTATO GNOCCHI

✔ WHY THIS RECIPE WORKS

Good potato gnocchi are something of a culinary paradox, light, airy pillows created from dense, starchy ingredients. The method is simple: knead the mashed potatoes into a dough with a minimum of flour; shape; and boil for a minute. And yet the potential pitfalls are numerous (lumpy mashed potatoes, too much or too little flour, a heavy hand when kneading, and bland flavor). We wanted a foolproof recipe for impossibly light gnocchi with unmistakable potato flavor. Baking russets (streamlined by parcooking the potatoes in the microwave) produced intensely flavored potatoes—an excellent start to our gnocchi base. To avoid lumps, which can cause gnocchi to break apart during cooking, we turned to a ricer for a smooth, supple mash. While many recipes offer a range of flour, which ups the chances of overworking the dough (and producing leaden gnocchi), we used an exact amount based on the ratio of potato to flour so that our gnocchi dough was mixed as little as possible. And we found that an egg, while not traditional, tenderized our gnocchi further, delivering delicate pillowlike dumplings.

POTATO GNOCCHI WITH BROWNED BUTTER AND SAGE SAUCE

SERVES 4

Gnocchi, like many baking recipes, require accurate measurement in order to achieve the proper texture; it's best to weigh the potatoes and flour. After processing, you may have slightly more than the 3 cups (16 ounces) of potatoes required for this recipe; do not be tempted to use more than 3 cups. Eat or discard any extra. If you prefer, replace the browned butter sauce with Gorgonzola-Cream Sauce, Porcini Mushroom Broth, or Parmesan Sauce with Pancetta and Walnuts (page 206).

POTATO GNOCCHI

2 pounds russet potatoes
1 large egg, lightly beaten
¾ cup plus 1 tablespoon (4 ounces) all-purpose flour, plus extra for counter
Salt

BROWN BUTTER AND SAGE SAUCE

4 tablespoons unsalted butter, cut into 4 pieces
1 small shallot, minced
1 teaspoon minced fresh sage
1½ teaspoons lemon juice
¼ teaspoon salt

1. FOR THE GNOCCHI: Adjust oven rack to middle position and heat oven to 450 degrees. Poke each potato 8 times with paring knife over entire surface. Place potatoes on plate and microwave until slightly softened at ends, about 10 minutes, flipping potatoes halfway through cooking. Transfer potatoes directly to oven rack and bake until skewer glides easily through flesh and potatoes yield to gentle pressure, 18 to 20 minutes.

2. Hold potato with pot holder or kitchen towel and peel with paring knife.

Process potato through ricer or food mill onto rimmed baking sheet. Repeat with remaining potatoes. Gently spread potatoes into even layer and cool for 5 minutes.

3. Transfer 3 cups (16 ounces) warm potatoes to large bowl. Using fork, gently stir in egg until just combined. Sprinkle flour and 1 teaspoon salt over potato mixture. Using fork, gently combine until no pockets of dry flour remain. Press mixture into rough dough, transfer to lightly floured counter, and gently knead until smooth but slightly sticky, about 1 minute, lightly dusting counter with flour as needed to prevent sticking.

4. Line 2 rimmed baking sheets with parchment paper and dust liberally with flour. Cut dough into 8 pieces. Lightly dust counter with flour. Gently roll piece of dough into ½-inch-thick rope, dusting with flour to prevent sticking. Cut rope into ¾-inch lengths. Hold fork, with tines facing down, in 1 hand and press side of each piece of dough against ridged surface with thumb to make indentation in center; roll dough down and off tines to form ridges. Transfer formed gnocchi to prepared sheets and repeat with remaining dough.

5. FOR THE SAUCE: Melt butter in 12-inch skillet over medium-high heat, swirling occasionally, until butter is browned and releases nutty aroma, about 1½ minutes. Off heat, add shallot and sage, stirring until shallot is fragrant, about 1 minute. Stir in lemon juice and salt and cover to keep warm.

6. Bring 4 quarts water to boil in large pot. Add 1 tablespoon salt. Using parchment paper as sling, add half of gnocchi and cook until firm and just cooked through, about 90 seconds (gnocchi should float to surface after about 1 minute). Remove gnocchi with slotted spoon, transfer to skillet with sauce, and cover to keep warm. Repeat with remaining gnocchi and transfer to skillet. Gently toss gnocchi with sauce to combine and serve.

GORGONZOLA-CREAM SAUCE
MAKES ABOUT 1 CUP

Adjust the consistency of the sauce with up to 2 tablespoons cooking water before adding it to the gnocchi.

- ¾ cup heavy cream
- ¼ cup dry white wine
- 4 ounces Gorgonzola cheese, crumbled (1 cup)
- 2 tablespoons minced fresh chives
  Salt and pepper

Bring cream and wine to simmer in 12-inch skillet over medium-high heat. Gradually add Gorgonzola while whisking constantly and cook until melted and sauce is thickened, 2 to 3 minutes. Stir in chives and season with salt and pepper to taste. Remove from heat and cover to keep warm.

PORCINI MUSHROOM BROTH
MAKES ABOUT 1¼ CUPS

Serve with grated Parmesan cheese.

- 1¾ cups low-sodium chicken broth
- ½ ounce dried porcini mushrooms, rinsed
- 3 tablespoons extra-virgin olive oil
- 1 small shallot, minced
- 2 garlic cloves, sliced thin
- ⅓ cup dry white wine
- 2 tablespoons minced fresh parsley
  Salt and pepper

1. Microwave broth and mushrooms in covered bowl until steaming, about 1 minute. Let stand until softened, about 5 minutes. Drain mushrooms through fine-mesh strainer lined with coffee filter, reserving liquid and chopping porcini.

2. Heat 1 tablespoon oil in 12-inch skillet over medium heat until shimmering. Add chopped mushrooms, shallot, and garlic and cook until lightly browned, 2 to 4 minutes. Stir in reserved porcini soaking liquid, wine, and remaining 2 tablespoons oil, scraping up any browned bits. Bring mixture to boil and cook, whisking occasionally, until reduced and measures 1¼ cups, 6 to 9 minutes. Stir in parsley and season with salt and pepper to taste. Remove from heat and cover to keep warm.

PARMESAN SAUCE WITH PANCETTA AND WALNUTS
MAKES ABOUT 1 CUP

Serve with extra grated Parmesan cheese on the side.

- ½ cup low-sodium chicken broth
- 1 ounce Parmesan cheese, grated (½ cup)
- ¼ cup heavy cream
- 2 large egg yolks
- ⅛ teaspoon pepper
- 2 teaspoons olive oil
- 3 ounces pancetta, chopped fine
- ½ cup walnuts, chopped coarse
  Salt

Whisk broth, Parmesan, cream, egg yolks, and pepper together in bowl until smooth. Heat oil in 12-inch skillet over medium heat until shimmering. Add pancetta and cook until crisp, 5 to 7 minutes. Stir in walnuts and cook until golden and fragrant, about 1 minute. Off heat, gradually add broth mixture, whisking constantly. Return skillet to medium heat and cook, stirring often, until sauce is thickened slightly, 2 to 4 minutes. Season with salt to taste. Remove from heat and cover to keep warm.

RICOTTA GNOCCHI

✓ WHY THIS RECIPE WORKS

Ricotta gnocchi is the lighter cousin of potato gnocchi. But achieving the right texture requires more than a simple ricotta-for-potato swap. We wanted an easy-to-make but delicate ricotta gnocchi that cooked up light and tender, not heavy and dull. To keep the dough light and workable, we drained the ricotta, replaced much of the flour with dried bread crumbs, and refrigerated it for 15 minutes before rolling it out and slicing it into small pillow-shaped pieces. A short simmer was all the cooking required for our perfected ricotta gnocchi.

RICOTTA GNOCCHI WITH BROWNED BUTTER AND SAGE SAUCE

SERVES 4

When rolling the gnocchi, use just enough flour to keep the dough from sticking to your hands and work surface. If you prefer, replace the browned butter sauce with Porcini Mushroom Sauce with Cream (page 173) or Classic Basil Pesto (page 161).

- 1 pound (2 cups) whole-milk ricotta cheese
- 2 slices hearty white sandwich bread, crusts removed and bread torn into quarters
- 1 ounce Parmesan cheese, grated (½ cup)
- 6 tablespoons all-purpose flour, plus extra as needed
- 1 large egg
- 2 tablespoons minced fresh basil
- 2 tablespoons minced fresh parsley
  Salt
- ¼ teaspoon pepper
- 1 recipe Brown Butter and Sage Sauce, warm (page 205)

1. Set fine-mesh strainer over bowl and line with 3 coffee filters. Place ricotta in prepared strainer, cover, and refrigerate for 1 hour. Adjust oven rack to middle position and heat oven to 300 degrees.

2. Meanwhile, pulse bread in food processor to fine crumbs, about 15 pulses. Spread crumbs on rimmed baking sheet and bake, stirring occasionally, until dry and just beginning to turn golden brown, about 10 minutes. Transfer to bowl, cool to room temperature, then stir in Parmesan and flour.

3. Transfer drained ricotta to now-empty food processor and pulse until curds break down into fine, grainy consistency, about 8 pulses. Transfer ricotta to large bowl and stir in egg, basil, parsley, ½ teaspoon salt, and pepper. Stir in bread-crumb mixture until well combined. Refrigerate dough until slightly tacky and few crumbs stick to fingers when touched, about 15 minutes. (If dough is too wet and several crumbs stick to fingers, stir in flour, 1 tablespoon at a time, until dough is slightly tacky.)

4. Line 2 rimmed baking sheets with parchment paper and dust lightly with flour. Cut dough into 8 pieces. Lightly dust counter with flour. Gently roll piece of dough into ¾-inch-thick rope, dusting with flour to prevent sticking. Cut rope into ¾-inch lengths and transfer to prepared sheets. Repeat with remaining dough.

5. Bring 4 quarts water to simmer in large pot. Add 1 tablespoon salt. Using parchment paper as sling, add half of gnocchi and cook until firm and just cooked through, about 3 minutes, adjusting heat as needed to maintain simmer (gnocchi should float to surface after about 1 minute). Remove gnocchi with slotted spoon, transfer to skillet with sauce, and cover to keep warm. Repeat with remaining gnocchi and transfer to skillet. Gently toss gnocchi with sauce to combine and serve.

TO MAKE AHEAD: Sheets of gnocchi can be wrapped with plastic wrap and refrigerated for up to 24 hours or frozen; when completely frozen, gnocchi can be transferred to zipper-lock bag and stored in freezer for up to 1 month. Spread frozen gnocchi on baking sheet and thaw overnight in refrigerator or at room temperature for 1 hour before cooking.

BAKED MANICOTTI

✓ WHY THIS RECIPE WORKS

Despite being composed of a straightforward collection of ingredients (pasta, cheese, and tomato sauce), manicotti is surprisingly fussy to prepare. Blanching, shocking, draining, and stuffing slippery pasta requires a lot of patience and time. We wanted an easy-to-prepare recipe that still produced great-tasting manicotti. Our biggest challenge was filling the slippery manicotti tubes. We solved the problem by discarding the tubes completely and spreading the filling onto lasagna noodles, which we then rolled up. For the lasagna noodles, we found that the no-boil variety were ideal. We soaked the noodles in boiling water for five minutes until pliable, then used the tip of a knife to separate them and prevent sticking. For the cheese filling, we needed only to taste-test several ricottas (part-skim proved to have an ideal level of richness). Eggs, Parmesan, and an ample amount of mozzarella added richness, flavor, and structure to the ricotta filling. For a quick but brightly flavored tomato sauce, we pureed canned diced tomatoes and simmered them until slightly thickened with sautéed garlic and red pepper flakes, then finished the sauce with fresh basil.

BAKED MANICOTTI
SERVES 6 TO 8

Note that some pasta brands contain only 12 no-boil noodles per package; this recipe requires 16 noodles. If your baking dish is not broiler-safe, brown the manicotti at 500 degrees for about 10 minutes.

TOMATO SAUCE

2   (28-ounce) cans diced tomatoes
2   tablespoons extra-virgin olive oil
3   garlic cloves, minced
½   teaspoon red pepper flakes (optional)
    Salt
2   tablespoons chopped fresh basil

CHEESE FILLING

24 ounces (3 cups) part-skim ricotta cheese
8   ounces mozzarella cheese, shredded (2 cups)
4   ounces Parmesan cheese, grated (2 cups)
2   large eggs
2   tablespoons chopped fresh parsley
2   tablespoons chopped fresh basil
¾   teaspoon salt
½   teaspoon pepper

16 no-boil lasagna noodles

1. FOR THE SAUCE: Pulse 1 can tomatoes with their juice in food processor until coarsely chopped, 3 or 4 pulses; transfer to bowl. Repeat with remaining can tomatoes; transfer to bowl.

2. Heat oil, garlic, and pepper flakes, if using, in large saucepan over medium heat. Cook, stirring often, until garlic turns golden but not brown, about 3 minutes. Stir in chopped tomatoes and ½ teaspoon salt, bring to simmer, and cook until thickened slightly, about 15 minutes. Stir in basil and season with salt to taste.

3. FOR THE CHEESE FILLING: Combine ricotta, mozzarella, 1 cup Parmesan, eggs, parsley, basil, salt, and pepper in bowl.

4. Adjust oven rack to middle position and heat oven to 375 degrees. Pour 2 inches boiling water into 13 by 9-inch broiler-safe baking dish. Slip noodles into water, 1 at a time, and soak until pliable, about 5 minutes, separating noodles with tip of sharp knife to prevent sticking. Remove noodles from water and place in single layer on clean kitchen towels; discard water and dry dish.

5. Spread 1½ cups sauce evenly over bottom of dish. Using spoon, spread ¼ cup cheese mixture evenly onto bottom three-quarters of each noodle (with short side facing you), leaving top quarter of noodle exposed. Roll into tube shape and arrange in dish seam side down. Top evenly with remaining sauce, making certain that pasta is completely covered. (Assembled manicotti can be covered with sheet of parchment paper, wrapped in aluminum foil, and refrigerated for up to 3 days or frozen for up to 1 month. If frozen, thaw manicotti in refrigerator for 1 to 2 days. To bake, remove parchment, replace foil, and increase baking time to 1 to 1¼ hours.)

6. Cover dish tightly with foil and bake until bubbling, about 40 minutes, rotating dish halfway through baking. Remove dish from oven and remove foil. Adjust oven rack 6 inches from broiler element and heat broiler. Sprinkle manicotti evenly with remaining 1 cup Parmesan. Broil until cheese is spotty brown, 4 to 6 minutes. Cool manicotti for 15 minutes before serving.

BAKED MANICOTTI WITH SAUSAGE

Cook 1 pound hot or sweet Italian sausage, casings removed, in 2 tablespoons olive oil in large saucepan over medium-high heat, breaking sausage into ½-inch pieces with wooden spoon, until no longer pink, about 6 minutes. Omit olive oil in sauce and cook remaining sauce ingredients in saucepan with sausage.

BAKED MANICOTTI WITH PROSCIUTTO

Reduce salt in cheese filling to ½ teaspoon and arrange 1 thin slice prosciutto on each noodle before topping with cheese mixture.

TEST KITCHEN TIP NO. 43 FREEZING RICOTTA

Ricotta is a fresh cheese that contains a lot of water, so when we considered freezing it, our suspicion was that freezing would cause the extra water to leach out when thawed, giving the cheese a gritty texture. To find out for sure, we froze a few previously opened containers of ricotta for two months, then defrosted them and used them to make manicotti, ricotta cheesecake, and Pasta with Sun-Dried Tomatoes, Ricotta, and Peas (page 187). We also made each of these recipes with fresh ricotta, and we tasted both ricottas plain.

When sampled plain, tasters preferred the never-frozen cheese for its smooth, clean taste. The frozen ricotta was more granular, looser in texture, and slightly watery. Few tasters could detect any differences when the ricotta was baked in the manicotti, and while the cheesecake made with frozen ricotta was slightly firmer and not quite as moist, the difference was negligible. But the frozen ricotta tossed with pasta was objectionable. In this recipe, the ricotta does not get cooked, and its texture was noticeably granular. So if you have trouble using ricotta up before it spoils, go ahead and freeze the extra—just make sure to use it in a recipe where it will be cooked.

Cook 3 rinsed and minced anchovy fillets with oil, garlic, and pepper flakes. Add ¼ cup pitted kalamata olives, quartered, and 2 tablespoons rinsed capers to cheese filling.

Add one 10-ounce package frozen chopped spinach, thawed, squeezed dry, and chopped fine, and pinch ground nutmeg to cheese filling. Increase salt in filling to 1 teaspoon.

FOUR-CHEESE LASAGNA

✔ WHY THIS RECIPE WORKS

Cheese lasagna offers an elegant alternative to meat-laden, red-sauce lasagna. But some cheese lasagna is just heavy and bland, due to the use of plain-tasting cheeses. And even those with good cheese flavor can have soupy, dry, or greasy textures. We wanted a robust cheese lasagna with great structure, creamy texture, and maximum flavor. For the best cheese flavor, we settled on a combination of fontina, Parmesan, Gorgonzola, and Gruyère cheeses. We found that making the white sauce (a béchamel) with a high ratio of flour to butter created a thick binder that provided enough heft to keep the lasagna layers together. And replacing some of the milk with chicken broth was the key to balancing the richness of the sauce and bringing the cheese flavor forward. But the real secret of a great four-cheese lasagna proved to be a fifth cheese. While ricotta didn't add much flavor, it gave the lasagna body without making the dish heavy and starchy. Our final challenge was to keep the baking time short enough to avoid harming this delicate pasta dish. Both presoaking the no-boil noodles and using a low-heat/high-heat baking method—baking at a moderate temperature and then briefly broiling to brown the top—kept the lasagna from overbaking.

FOUR-CHEESE LASAGNA
SERVES 10

Note that some pasta brands contain only 12 no-boil noodles per package; this recipe requires 15 noodles. Whole milk is best in the sauce, but skim and low-fat milk also work. Supermarket-brand cheeses work fine in this recipe. The Gorgonzola may be omitted, but the flavor of the lasagna won't be as complex. It's important to not overbake the lasagna. Once the sauce starts bubbling around the edges, uncover the lasagna and turn the oven to broil. If your lasagna dish is not broiler-safe, brown the lasagna at 500 degrees for about 10 minutes. This lasagna is very rich; serve small portions with a green salad.

- 6 ounces Gruyère cheese, shredded (1½ cups)
- 2 ounces Parmesan cheese, grated fine (1 cup)
- 12 ounces (1½ cups) part-skim ricotta cheese
- 1 large egg
- ¼ teaspoon pepper
- 2 tablespoons plus 2 teaspoons minced fresh parsley
- 3 tablespoons unsalted butter
- 1 shallot, minced
- 1 garlic clove, minced
- ⅓ cup all-purpose flour
- 2½ cups whole milk
- 1½ cups low-sodium chicken broth
- ½ teaspoon salt
- 1 bay leaf
  Pinch cayenne pepper
- 15 no-boil lasagna noodles
- 8 ounces fontina cheese, shredded (2 cups)
- 3 ounces Gorgonzola cheese, finely crumbled (¾ cup)

1. Place Gruyère and ½ cup Parmesan in large heatproof bowl. Combine ricotta, egg, black pepper, and 2 tablespoons parsley in medium bowl. Set both bowls aside.

2. Melt butter in medium saucepan over medium heat. Add shallot and garlic and cook, stirring often, until shallot is softened, about 2 minutes. Add flour and cook, stirring constantly, until thoroughly combined, about 1½ minutes; mixture should not brown. Gradually whisk in milk and broth; increase heat to medium-high and bring to boil, whisking often. Stir in salt, bay leaf, and cayenne, reduce heat to medium-low, and simmer until sauce thickens and measures 4 cups, about 10 minutes, stirring occasionally and making sure to scrape bottom and corners of pan.

3. Discard bay leaf. Gradually whisk ¼ cup sauce into ricotta mixture. Pour remaining sauce over Gruyère mixture and stir until smooth.

4. Adjust oven rack to upper-middle position and heat oven to 350 degrees. Pour 2 inches boiling water into 13 by 9-inch broiler-safe baking dish. Slip noodles into water, 1 at a time, and soak until pliable, about 5 minutes, separating noodles with tip of sharp knife to prevent sticking. Remove noodles from water and place in single layer on clean kitchen towels; discard water. Dry dish and spray lightly with vegetable oil spray.

5. Spread ½ cup sauce evenly over bottom of dish. Arrange 3 noodles in single layer on top of sauce. Spread ½ cup ricotta mixture evenly over noodles and sprinkle with ½ cup fontina and 3 tablespoons Gorgonzola. Spoon ½ cup sauce over top. Repeat layering of noodles, ricotta mixture, fontina, Gorgonzola, and sauce 3 more times. For final layer, arrange remaining 3 noodles on top and cover completely with remaining sauce. Sprinkle with remaining ½ cup Parmesan.

6. Cover dish tightly with aluminum foil that has been sprayed with oil spray and bake until edges are just bubbling, 25 to 30 minutes, rotating dish halfway through baking. Remove foil and turn oven to broil. Broil lasagna until surface is spotty brown, 3 to 5 minutes. Cool lasagna for 15 minutes, then sprinkle with remaining 2 teaspoons parsley and serve.

FOUR-CHEESE LASAGNA WITH ARTICHOKES AND PROSCIUTTO

Adjust oven rack to upper-middle position and heat oven to 450 degrees. Line rimmed baking sheet with aluminum foil. Toss 18 ounces frozen artichoke hearts, thawed and patted dry, with 1 teaspoon olive oil, ½ teaspoon salt, and ¼ teaspoon, then spread over prepared sheet. Roast artichokes until browned at edges, 20 to 25 minutes, rotating baking sheet halfway through roasting. Let artichokes cool slightly, then chop coarse. Sprinkle each of first 4 lasagna layers with ⅓ cup roasted artichokes and 2 tablespoons thinly sliced prosciutto along with fontina and Gorgonzola.

SIMPLE VEGETABLE LASAGNA

✔ WHY THIS RECIPE WORKS

We wanted a vegetable lasagna with tender, flavorful vegetables, great cheese flavor, and a light tomato sauce. To start, we zeroed in on our choice of vegetables and settled on eggplant and zucchini. Roasting the vegetables intensified their flavor and rid them of excess moisture. We skipped the usual ricotta and instead turned to mozzarella which melted into gooey layers—Parmesan added another layer of flavor. And a quick tomato sauce bound together the layers with a minimum of fuss.

VEGETABLE LASAGNA WITH ROASTED ZUCCHINI AND EGGPLANT

SERVES 8 TO 10

Note that some pasta brands contain only 12 no-boil noodles per package; this recipe requires 15 noodles. Smoked mozzarella, Gruyère, or fontina can be substituted for the mozzarella and Pecorino Romano for the Parmesan.

1	pound zucchini, cut into ½-inch pieces
1	pound eggplant, cut into ½-inch pieces
5	tablespoons olive oil
6	garlic cloves, minced
	Salt and pepper
1	(28-ounce) can crushed tomatoes
2	tablespoons chopped fresh basil or parsley
	Water
15	no-boil lasagna noodles
1	pound mozzarella cheese, shredded (4 cups)
2½	ounces Parmesan cheese, grated (1¼ cups)

1. Adjust oven rack to upper-middle and lower-middle positions and heat oven to 400 degrees. Grease two rimmed baking sheets. Toss zucchini and eggplant with 3 tablespoons oil, two-thirds of garlic, ¼ teaspoon salt, and ¼ teaspoon pepper and spread onto prepared sheets. Roast until vegetables are golden brown, about 35 minutes, stirring halfway through roasting; set aside to cool.

2. While vegetables roast, heat remaining 2 tablespoons oil and remaining garlic in 10-inch skillet over medium heat. Cook, stirring often, until garlic turns golden but not brown, about 3 minutes. Stir in tomatoes, bring to simmer, and cook until thickened slightly, about 10 minutes. Stir in basil and season with salt and pepper to taste. Transfer sauce to large measuring cup and add enough water to make 3½ cups.

3. Adjust oven rack to middle position and reduce oven temperature to 375 degrees. Pour 2 inches boiling water into 13 by 9-inch baking dish. Slip noodles into water, 1 at a time, and soak until pliable, about 5 minutes, separating noodles with tip of sharp knife to prevent sticking. Remove noodles from water and place in single layer on clean kitchen towels; discard water. Dry dish and spray with vegetable oil spray.

4. Spread ½ cup sauce evenly over bottom of prepared dish. Arrange 3 noodles in single layer on top of sauce. Spread ¾ cup roasted vegetables evenly over noodles. Spoon ½ cup sauce over vegetables and sprinkle with ¾ cup mozzarella and 2 tablespoons Parmesan. Repeat layering of noodles, vegetables, sauce, mozzarella, and Parmesan 3 more times. For final layer, arrange remaining 3 noodles on top and cover completely with remaining sauce. Sprinkle with remaining 1 cup mozzarella and remaining ¼ cup Parmesan.

5. Cover dish tightly with aluminum foil that has been sprayed with oil spray and bake until edges are just bubbling, 25 to 30 minutes, rotating dish halfway

---

TEST KITCHEN TIP NO. 44 PARMESAN VS. PECORINO ROMANO

While Parmesan is a cow's milk cheese, Pecorino is made from sheep's milk but the two do have a similar texture and flavor and often you'll see one as an alternative to the other in recipes. We have found that Parmesan and Pecorino Romano can generally be used interchangeably, especially when the amount called for is moderate. However, when Parmesan is called for in larger quantities as it is in some recipes, it is best to stick with the Parmesan, as Pecorino Romano can be fairly pungent.

through baking. Remove foil and continue to bake until top turns spotty brown, about 15 minutes longer. Cool lasagna for 15 minutes before serving.

HEARTY VEGETABLE LASAGNA

♦ WHY THIS RECIPE WORKS
For a complex vegetable lasagna with bold flavor, we started with a summery mix of zucchini, yellow squash, and eggplant, salting and microwaving the eggplant and sautéing the vegetables to cut down on excess moisture and deepen their flavor. Garlic and spinach and olives added textural contrast and flavor without much work. We dialed up the usual cheese filling by switching mild-mannered ricotta for tangy cottage cheese mixed with heavy cream for richness and Parmesan and garlic for added flavor. Our creamy, quick no-cook tomato sauce brought enough moisture to our lasagna that we found that we could skip the usual step of soaking the no-boil noodles before assembling the dish.

HEARTY VEGETABLE LASAGNA
SERVES 8 TO 10

Part-skim mozzarella can also be used in this recipe, but avoid preshredded cheese, as it does not melt well. We prefer kosher salt because it clings best to the eggplant. If using table salt, reduce salt amounts by half. To make assembly easier, the roasted vegetable filling can be made and stored in the refrigerator for up to a day.

TOMATO SAUCE
- 1   (28-ounce) can crushed tomatoes
- ¼   cup minced fresh basil
- 2   tablespoons extra-virgin olive oil
- 2   garlic cloves, minced
- 1   teaspoon kosher salt
- ¼   teaspoon red pepper flakes

CREAM SAUCE
- 8   ounces (1 cup) whole-milk cottage cheese
- 1   cup heavy cream
- 4   ounces Parmesan, grated (2 cups)
- 2   garlic cloves, minced
- 1   teaspoon cornstarch
- ½   teaspoon kosher salt
- ½   teaspoon pepper

VEGETABLE FILLING
- 1½ pounds eggplant, peeled and cut into ½-inch pieces
     Kosher salt and pepper
- 1   pound zucchini, cut into ½-inch pieces
- 1   pound yellow squash, cut into ½-inch pieces
- 5   tablespoons plus 1 teaspoon extra-virgin olive oil
- 4   garlic cloves, minced
- 1   tablespoon minced fresh thyme
- 12 ounces baby spinach (12 cups)
- ½   cup pitted kalamata olives, minced
- 12 ounces whole-milk mozzarella cheese, shredded (3 cups)

- 12 no-boil lasagna noodles
- 2   tablespoons chopped fresh basil

1. FOR THE TOMATO SAUCE: Whisk all ingredients together in bowl; set aside.

2. FOR THE CREAM SAUCE: Whisk all ingredients together in separate bowl; set aside.

3. FOR THE FILLING: Adjust oven rack to middle position and heat oven to 375 degrees. Toss eggplant with 1 teaspoon salt in large bowl. Line surface of large plate with double layer of coffee filters and lightly spray with vegetable oil spray. Spread eggplant in even layer over coffee filters; wipe out and reserve bowl. Microwave eggplant, uncovered, until dry to touch and slightly shriveled, about 10 minutes, tossing halfway through

cooking. Cool slightly. Return eggplant to bowl and toss with zucchini and summer squash.

4. Combine 1 tablespoon oil, garlic, and thyme in small bowl. Heat 2 tablespoons oil in 12-inch nonstick skillet over medium-high heat until shimmering. Add half of eggplant mixture, ¼ teaspoon salt, and ¼ teaspoon pepper and cook, stirring occasionally, until vegetables are lightly browned, about 7 minutes. Clear center of skillet, add half of garlic mixture, and cook, mashing with spatula, until fragrant, about 30 seconds. Stir garlic mixture into vegetables and transfer to medium bowl. Repeat with remaining eggplant mixture, 2 tablespoons oil, and remaining garlic mixture; transfer to bowl.

5. Heat remaining 1 teaspoon oil in now-empty skillet over medium-high heat until shimmering. Add spinach and cook, stirring frequently, until wilted, about 3 minutes. Transfer spinach to paper towel–lined plate and drain for 2 minutes. Stir into eggplant mixture.

6. Grease 13 by 9-inch baking dish. Spread 1 cup tomato sauce evenly over bottom of dish. Arrange 4 noodles on top of sauce (noodles will overlap). Spread half of vegetable mixture over noodles, followed by half of olives. Spoon half of cream sauce over top and sprinkle with 1 cup mozzarella. Repeat layering with 4 noodles, 1 cup tomato sauce, remaining vegetables, remaining olives, remaining cream sauce and 1 cup more mozzarella. For final layer, arrange remaining 4 noodles on top and cover completely with remaining tomato sauce. Sprinkle with remaining 1 cup mozzarella.

7. Cover dish tightly with aluminum foil that has been sprayed with oil spray and bake until edges are just bubbling, about 35 minutes, rotating dish halfway through baking. Cool lasagna for 25 minutes, then sprinkle with basil and serve.

SPINACH LASAGNA

✔ WHY THIS RECIPE WORKS

We preferred cottage cheese to ricotta in our spinach lasagna recipe, for the extra tang and creaminess it lent to the dish. We found other components useful as well: no-boil noodles that we soaked in hot tap water for five minutes to soften and blanched spinach from which we wrung out all excess water. Our resulting spinach lasagna recipe was a simple success: fresh, green spinach highlighted by a delicate, savory sauce; tender noodles; and mild, creamy cheese.

SPINACH LASAGNA
SERVES 8 TO 10

Italian fontina works best in this dish. If it is not available, substitute whole-milk mozzarella. If your lasagna dish is not broiler-safe, brown the lasagna at 500 degrees for about 10 minutes.

SAUCE
Salt
1¼ pounds curly-leaf spinach, stemmed
5 tablespoons unsalted butter
4 large shallots, minced
4 garlic cloves, minced
¼ cup all-purpose flour
3½ cups whole milk
2 bay leaves
¾ teaspoon ground nutmeg
¼ teaspoon pepper
1 ounce Parmesan cheese, grated
  (½ cup)

CHEESE FILLING
8 ounces (1 cup) whole-milk cottage cheese
1 large egg
¼ teaspoon salt
2 ounces Parmesan cheese, grated (1 cup)
8 ounces Italian fontina cheese, shredded (2 cups)
12 no-boil lasagna noodles

1. FOR THE SAUCE: Bring 4 quarts water to boil in large pot. Fill large bowl with ice water. Add spinach and 1 tablespoon salt to boiling water and cook, stirring often until spinach is just wilted, about 5 seconds. Remove spinach with slotted spoon, transfer to ice water, and soak until completely cool, about 1 minute; drain spinach and transfer to clean kitchen towel. Wrap towel tightly around spinach to form ball and wring until dry. Chop spinach and set aside.

2. Melt butter in medium saucepan over medium heat. Add shallots and garlic and cook, stirring often, until shallots are softened, about 4 minutes. Add flour and cook, stirring constantly, until thoroughly combined, about 1½ minutes; mixture should not brown. Gradually whisk in milk; increase heat to medium high and bring to boil, whisking often. Stir in bay leaves, nutmeg, ½ teaspoon salt, and pepper, reduce heat to low, and simmer, whisking occasionally, for 10 minutes. Discard bay leaves, then whisk in Parmesan until completely melted. Measure out and reserve ½ cup sauce in small bowl; press plastic wrap directly against surface, and set aside. Transfer remaining sauce to separate bowl and stir in chopped spinach, mixing well to break up any clumps; press plastic directly against surface, and set aside.

3. FOR THE CHEESE FILLING: Process cottage cheese, egg, and salt in food processor until very smooth, about 30 seconds.

4. Adjust oven rack to middle position and heat oven to 425 degrees. Pour 2 inches boiling water into 13 by 9-inch broiler-safe baking dish. Slip noodles into water, 1 at a time, and soak until pliable, about 5 minutes, separating noodles with tip of sharp knife to prevent sticking. Remove noodles from water and place in single layer on clean kitchen towels; discard water. Dry and grease dish.

5. Spread reserved ½ cup sauce evenly over bottom of prepared dish. Arrange 3 noodles in single layer on top of sauce. Spread 1 cup spinach mixture evenly over noodles, sprinkle with Parmesan, and top with 3 more noodles. Spread 1 cup more spinach mixture evenly over top, sprinkle with 1 cup fontina, and top with 3 more noodles. Spread 1 cup spinach mixture evenly over top, followed by cottage cheese mixture. For final layer, arrange remaining 3 noodles on top and cover with remaining spinach mixture. Sprinkle with remaining 1 cup fontina.

6. Cover dish tightly with aluminum foil that has been sprayed with vegetable oil spray and bake until edges are just bubbling, about 20 minutes, rotating dish halfway through baking. Remove dish from oven and remove foil. Adjust oven rack 6 inches from broiler element and heat broiler. Broil lasagna until cheese is spotty brown, 4 to 6 minutes. Cool lasagna for 15 minutes before serving.

SPINACH LASAGNA WITH PROSCIUTTO

Melt 2 tablespoons butter in sauce in medium saucepan over medium heat. Add 2 ounces thinly sliced prosciutto, chopped, and cook until crisp, 5 to 7 minutes. Remove prosciutto with slotted spoon and transfer to paper towel–lined plate; set aside. Add remaining 3 tablespoons butter to fat left in saucepan and melt over medium heat before adding shallots and garlic in step 2. Sprinkle crisp prosciutto over cottage cheese mixture while assembling lasagna.

SPINACH LASAGNA WITH MUSHROOMS

Melt 2 tablespoons unsalted butter in medium saucepan over medium heat. Add 8 ounces trimmed and thinly sliced white mushrooms and cook until softened and lightly browned, 8 to 10 minutes; transfer to bowl. Sprinkle softened mushrooms over cottage cheese mixture while assembling lasagna.

MUSHROOM LASAGNA

✓ WHY THIS RECIPE WORKS

American-style mushroom lasagnas lose the mushrooms in a sea of tomato sauce and mozzarella. Italian-style recipes put the emphasis on the mushrooms, but many call for esoteric or expensive wild mushrooms as well as a lot of preparation time. We wanted to make Italian-style mushroom lasagna approachable, which meant using widely available mushrooms and no-boil noodles. For the primary mushrooms, we found that roasting portobellos concentrated their flavor. The texture of the sauce was a problem (our no-boil noodles sucked up all the moisture), but a very loose béchamel sauce had the right consistency, and attained substantial mushroom flavor when we replaced conventional chicken broth with the water used to rehydrate dried porcini. We ultimately maximized the mushroom flavor by mixing in duxelles (sautéed, finely chopped white mushrooms) flavored with garlic and vermouth. Parmesan and fontina cheese added a complementary buttery nuttiness. Finally, we added a gremolata-like topping of minced parsley, basil, lemon zest, and garlic for complexity and freshness.

MUSHROOM LASAGNA
SERVES 8 TO 10

Italian fontina works best in this dish. If it is not available, substitute whole-milk mozzarella. Whole milk is best in the sauce, but skim or low-fat milk also work.

TEST KITCHEN TIP NO. 45 MUSHROOM PREP

Culinary wisdom holds that raw mushrooms must never touch water, lest they soak up the liquid and become soggy. Many sources call for cleaning mushrooms with a brush or a damp cloth. These fussy techniques may be worth the effort if you plan to eat the mushrooms raw, but we wondered whether mushrooms destined for the sauté pan could be simply rinsed and patted dry. To test this, we submerged white mushrooms in water for 5 minutes. We drained and weighed the mushrooms and found that they had soaked up only ¼ ounce (about 1½ teaspoons) of water, not nearly enough to affect their texture. So when we plan to cook mushrooms we now simply place the mushrooms in a salad spinner, rinse the dirt and grit away with cold water, and spin to remove excess moisture.

1	cup water
½	ounce dried porcini mushrooms, rinsed
2	pounds portobello mushroom caps, gills removed and caps halved and sliced crosswise ¼ inch thick
¼	cup olive oil
	Salt and pepper
4	red onions, chopped
8	ounces white mushrooms, trimmed and halved if small or quartered if large
4	garlic cloves, minced
½	cup dry vermouth
3	tablespoons unsalted butter
3	tablespoons all-purpose flour
3½	cups whole milk
¼	teaspoon ground nutmeg
¼	cup plus 2 tablespoons minced fresh basil
¼	cup minced fresh parsley
12	no-boil lasagna noodles
8	ounces Italian fontina cheese, shredded (2 cups)
1½	ounces Parmesan cheese, grated (¾ cup)
½	teaspoon grated lemon zest

1. Microwave water and porcini mushrooms in covered bowl until steaming, about 1 minute. Let stand until softened, about 5 minutes. Drain mushrooms through fine-mesh strainer lined with coffee filter, reserving liquid and coarsely chopping mushrooms.

2. Adjust oven rack to middle position and heat oven to 425 degrees. Toss portobello mushrooms with 2 tablespoons oil, ½ teaspoon salt, and ½ teaspoon pepper and spread onto rimmed baking sheet. Roast mushrooms until shriveled and all liquid released from mushrooms has evaporated, about 30 minutes, stirring halfway through roasting. Transfer mushrooms to large bowl and set aside to cool.

3. While portobello mushrooms roast, heat 1 tablespoon more oil in 12-inch nonstick skillet over medium heat until shimmering. Add onions, ¼ teaspoon salt, and ¼ teaspoon pepper and cook, stirring occasionally, until softened and lightly browned, 8 to 10 minutes. Transfer onions to bowl with mushrooms.

4. Meanwhile, pulse white mushrooms in food processor until coarsely chopped, about 6 pulses, scraping down bowl as needed. Heat remaining 1 tablespoon oil in now-empty skillet over medium-high heat until shimmering. Add chopped mushrooms and cook, stirring occasionally, until browned and all moisture has evaporated, 6 to 8 minutes. Stir in porcini mushrooms, 1 tablespoon garlic, 1 teaspoon salt, and 1 teaspoon pepper, reduce heat to medium, and cook, stirring often, until garlic is fragrant, about 30 seconds. Stir in vermouth and cook, stirring occasionally, until liquid has evaporated, 2 to 3 minutes.

5. Stir in butter and cook until melted. Add flour and cook, stirring constantly, for 1 minute. Slowly stir in reserved porcini soaking liquid, scraping up any browned bits. Stir in milk and nutmeg, bring to simmer, and cook until sauce has thickened and measures 4 cups, 10 to 15 minutes. Off heat, stir in ¼ cup basil and 2 tablespoons parsley.

6. Pour 2 inches boiling water into 13 by 9-inch baking dish. Slip noodles into water, 1 at a time, and soak until pliable, about 5 minutes, separating noodles with tip of sharp knife to prevent sticking. Remove noodles from water and place in

single layer on clean kitchen towels; discard water. Dry and grease dish.

7. Combine fontina and Parmesan in bowl. Spread 1 cup mushroom sauce evenly over bottom of prepared dish. Arrange 3 noodles in single layer on top of sauce. Spread ¾ cup sauce evenly over noodles, then sprinkle with 2 cups mushroom mixture and ¾ cup cheese mixture. Repeat layering of noodles, sauce, mushroom mixture, and cheese mixture 2 more times. For final layer, arrange remaining 3 noodles on top and cover completely with remaining sauce. Sprinkle with remaining cheese.

8. Cover dish tightly with aluminum foil that has been sprayed with vegetable oil spray and bake until edges are just bubbling, about 20 minutes, rotating dish halfway through baking. While lasagna is baking, combine remaining 1 teaspoon garlic, remaining 2 tablespoons parsley, remaining 2 tablespoons basil, and lemon zest in bowl. Remove foil, increase oven temperature to 500 degrees, and continue to bake until cheese on top becomes spotty brown, 6 to 8 minutes longer. Sprinkle lasagna with herb mixture and cool for 15 minutes before serving.

MUSHROOM LASAGNA WITH GOAT CHEESE, BROCCOLI RABE, AND SUN-DRIED TOMATOES

Bring 3 quarts water to boil in large saucepan. Add 8 ounces broccoli rabe, trimmed and cut into 1-inch pieces, and ½ teaspoon salt and cook until crisp-tender, about 2 minutes. Drain broccoli rabe, rinse under cold water to stop cooking, then squeeze dry and transfer to paper towel–lined plate. Combine blanched broccoli rabe and 1 cup oil-packed sun-dried tomatoes, patted dry and chopped coarse, in bowl with roasted portobellos and softened onions. Substitute 1 tablespoon minced fresh thyme for basil in sauce. Reduce fontina to 6 ounces and add 4 ounces crumbled goat cheese to fontina and Parmesan mixture.

MUSHROOM LASAGNA WITH PANCETTA AND SAGE

Add 8 ounces chopped pancetta to shimmering oil in step 3 and cook until crisp, 5 to 7 minutes. Remove pancetta with slotted spoon and transfer to bowl with roasted portobellos. Pour off all but 1 tablespoon fat from skillet, then cook onions in fat left in skillet. Substitute 1 tablespoon minced fresh sage for basil in sauce.

WILD MUSHROOM LASAGNA

Combine 1 pound oyster mushrooms, trimmed and cut into 1-inch pieces, 12 ounces chanterelle mushrooms, trimmed and cut into 1-inch pieces, and 10 ounces shiitake mushrooms, stemmed and sliced ¼ inch thick, in bowl. Melt 2 tablespoons unsalted butter in 12-inch nonstick skillet over medium-high heat. Add half of mushrooms, ¼ teaspoon salt, and ¼ teaspoon pepper and cook until tender and most of liquid has evaporated, about 5 minutes. Transfer mushrooms to large bowl. Repeat with 2 more tablespoons butter, remaining mushrooms, ¼ teaspoon salt, and ¼ teaspoon pepper. Substitute cooked wild mushroom mixture for roasted portobellos in step 2. Substitute 8 ounces cremini mushrooms for white mushrooms. Adjust oven rack to middle position and heat oven to 425 degrees before assembling lasagna.

SIMPLIFIED LASAGNA BOLOGNESE

✔ WHY THIS RECIPE WORKS

In authentic lasagna Bolognese, meat is the main idea. Three kinds of meat, in fact: beef, pork, and veal simmered until tender and delicately sweet in a slowly reducing sauce of milk, wine, and tomatoes. This rich sauce is bound between thin sheets of pasta with a creamy béchamel sauce and Parmesan cheese. In simplifying this Italian classic, there was no denying the appeal of no-boil noodles. After several tests, we found that a five-minute soak proved most effective for getting sturdy, al dente noodles that bound together the layers of ragu and béchamel without soaking up all the moisture. Stumbling through multiple rounds of meat sauce testing gave us the idea of combining the ragu and béchamel when both were lukewarm. The resulting sauce was thickened but easy to spread, with enough moisture for cooking the noodles.

SIMPLIFIED LASAGNA BOLOGNESE
SERVES 10

Note that some pasta brands contain only 12 no-boil noodles per package; this recipe requires 15 noodles. For assembly, both the meat sauce and the béchamel should be just warm to the touch, not piping hot.

MEAT SAUCE

1	carrot, peeled and chopped coarse
1	celery rib, chopped coarse
½	cup coarsely chopped onion
1	(28-ounce) can whole tomatoes
2	tablespoons unsalted butter
8	ounces 90 percent lean ground beef
8	ounces ground pork
8	ounces ground veal

1½	cups whole milk
1½	cups dry white wine
2	tablespoons tomato paste
1	teaspoon salt
¼	teaspoon pepper

BÉCHAMEL

4	tablespoons unsalted butter
¼	cup all-purpose flour
4	cups whole milk
¾	teaspoon salt

| 15 | no-boil lasagna noodles |
| 4 | ounces Parmesan cheese, grated (2 cups) |

1. FOR THE MEAT SAUCE: Pulse carrot, celery, and onion in food processor until finely chopped, about 10 pulses, scraping down bowl as needed; transfer to bowl. Pulse tomatoes with their juice in now-empty food processor until finely chopped, 6 to 8 pulses.

2. Melt butter in Dutch oven over medium heat. Add chopped vegetable mixture and cook, stirring occasionally, until softened, about 5 minutes. Stir in ground beef, ground pork, and ground veal and cook, breaking meat into 1-inch pieces with wooden spoon, for 1 minute. Stir in milk and bring to simmer, breaking meat into ½-inch pieces. Continue to cook, stirring often to break up meat into small pieces, until most of liquid has evaporated, 18 to 20 minutes. Add wine, bring to simmer, and cook, stirring occasionally, until liquid has evaporated, 20 to 30 minutes. Stir in tomato paste and cook until combined, about 1 minute. Stir in chopped tomatoes, salt, and pepper, bring to simmer, and cook until sauce is thickened slightly and measures 6 cups, about

15 minutes. Transfer meat sauce to bowl and set aside to cool, about 30 minutes. (Meat sauce can be cooled and refrigerated for up to 2 days; gently reheat before assembling lasagna.)

3. FOR THE BÉCHAMEL: While meat sauce simmers, melt butter in medium saucepan over medium heat. Add flour and cook, stirring constantly, until thoroughly combined, about 1½ minutes; mixture should not brown. Gradually whisk in milk; increase heat to medium-high and bring to boil, whisking frequently. Add salt, reduce heat to medium-low, and simmer until sauce thickens and measures 3½ cups, about 10 minutes, stirring occasionally and making sure to scrape bottom and corners of saucepan. Transfer béchamel to separate bowl and set aside to cool, about 30 minutes. (Béchamel can be cooled and refrigerated for up to 2 days; gently reheat before assembling lasagna.)

4. Adjust oven rack to middle position and heat oven to 425 degrees. Pour 2 inches boiling water into 13 by 9-inch baking dish. Slip noodles into water, 1 at a time, and soak until pliable, about 5 minutes, separating noodles with tip of sharp knife to prevent sticking. Remove noodles from water and place in single layer on clean kitchen towels; discard water. Dry dish and spray lightly with vegetable oil spray.

5. Stir warm béchamel to recombine, then stir ¾ cup béchamel into warm meat sauce until thoroughly combined. Spread 1 cup béchamel-enriched meat sauce evenly over bottom of prepared dish. Arrange 3 noodles in single layer on top of sauce. Spoon 1¼ cups béchamel-enriched meat sauce over noodles, spreading sauce to edge of noodles but not to

edge of dish. Drizzle ⅓ cup béchamel evenly over meat sauce and sprinkle with ⅓ cup Parmesan. Repeat layering of noodles, béchamel-enriched meat sauce, béchamel, and Parmesan 3 more times. For final layer, arrange remaining 3 noodles on top and cover completely with remaining béchamel. Sprinkle with remaining ⅔ cup Parmesan.

6. Cover dish tightly with aluminum foil that has been sprayed with oil spray and bake until edges are just bubbling, about 30 minutes, rotating dish halfway through baking. Remove foil, increase oven temperature to 450 degrees, and continue to bake until cheese on top becomes spotty brown, about 15 minutes. Cool lasagna for 15 minutes before serving.

SIMPLE LASAGNA WITH HEARTY TOMATO-MEAT SAUCE

✓ WHY THIS RECIPE WORKS
Determined to formulate a really good 90-minute meat lasagna recipe, we came up with several shortcuts: We made a 12-minute tomato meat sauce by cooking onions, garlic, and meatloaf mixture (ground beef, pork, and veal) and then adding cream and tomatoes. We chose no-boil lasagna noodles to eliminate the process of boiling and draining. We created a classic cheese layer quickly with ricotta, mozzarella, Parmesan, fresh basil, and an egg to help thicken and bind the mixture. Covering the lasagna with aluminum foil before baking helped soften the noodles; removing the foil during the last 25 minutes of baking allowed the cheeses to brown properly.

SIMPLE LASAGNA WITH HEARTY TOMATO-MEAT SAUCE

SERVES 8 TO 10

You can substitute equal amounts of 85 percent lean ground beef, ground veal, and ground pork for the meatloaf mix (the total amount of meat should be 1 pound).

TOMATO-MEAT SAUCE

1	tablespoon olive oil
1	onion, chopped fine
6	garlic cloves, minced
1	pound meatloaf mix
½	teaspoon salt
½	teaspoon pepper
¼	cup heavy cream
1	(28-ounce) can tomato puree
1	(28-ounce) can diced tomatoes, drained

CHEESE FILLING

14	ounces (1¾ cups) whole-milk or part-skim ricotta cheese
2½	ounces Parmesan cheese, grated (1¼ cups)
½	cup chopped fresh basil
1	large egg
½	teaspoon salt
½	teaspoon pepper
16	ounces whole-milk mozzarella, shredded (4 cups)
12	no-boil lasagna noodles

1. FOR THE SAUCE: Heat oil in Dutch oven over medium heat until shimmering. Add onion and cook, stirring occasionally, until softened, about 5 minutes. Stir in garlic and cook until fragrant, about 30 seconds. Stir in meatloaf mix, salt, and pepper, increase heat to medium-high, and cook, breaking up any large pieces with wooden spoon, until no longer pink, about 3 minutes. Add cream, bring to simmer, and cook, stirring occasionally, until liquid evaporates and only rendered fat remains, about 4 minutes. Stir in tomato puree and diced tomatoes, bring to simmer, and cook until flavors meld, about 3 minutes. Set aside. (Sauce can be cooled and refrigerated for up to 2 days; reheat before assembling lasagna.)

2. FOR THE CHEESE FILLING: Adjust oven rack to middle position and heat oven to 375 degrees. Combine ricotta, 1 cup Parmesan, basil, egg, salt, and pepper in bowl.

3. Spread ¼ cup meat sauce evenly over bottom of 13 by 9-inch baking dish (avoiding large chunks of meat). Arrange 3 noodles in single layer on top of sauce. Spread each noodle evenly with 3 tablespoons of ricotta mixture and sprinkle entire layer with 1 cup mozzarella. Spoon 1½ cups meat sauce over top. Repeat layering of noodles, ricotta, mozzarella, and sauce 2 more times. For final layer, arrange remaining 3 noodles on top and cover completely with remaining sauce. Sprinkle with remaining 1 cup mozzarella, then sprinkle with remaining ¼ cup Parmesan.

4. Cover dish tightly with aluminum foil that has been sprayed with vegetable oil spray. Bake for 15 minutes, then remove foil, and continue to bake until cheese is spotty brown and edges are just bubbling, about 25 minutes longer. Cool lasagna for 15 minutes before serving.

LASAGNA WITH MEATBALLS

✓ WHY THIS RECIPE WORKS

The Neapolitan lasagna traditionally made during the festival of Carnivale boasts small, tender meatballs, distinct layers, and a moderate amount of deeply flavored sauce, but it requires a host of ingredients and takes an entire day to prepare. In search of a recipe that would replicate those classic tastes without all the labor, we started with the cheese. Creamy whole-milk mozzarella was favored over ricotta, as mozzarella melted into gooey layers that bound the noodles together nicely. A little Parmesan or Pecorino-Romano provided a pleasant contrast to the mozzarella's mild taste. Baking the meatballs in the oven (rather than frying them in oil) made this step a snap. A simple tomato sauce proved best here and we made one by simmering crushed tomatoes with garlic for just 10 minutes and finished it with fresh basil. When layered with the meatballs, cheeses, and noodles, it gave us a lasagna just as satisfying as the traditional Neapolitan version.

LASAGNA WITH MEATBALLS

SERVES 8

The size of the noodles will depend on the brand; if the noodles are short (such as DeCecco) you will need to layer them crosswise in the dish, but if they are long (such as Barilla and Ronzoni) layer them lengthwise in the dish. Regardless of which brand of noodle you are using, there should be 3 noodles per layer.

MEATBALLS AND SAUCE

1	pound 85 percent lean ground beef
2	ounces Parmesan or Pecorino Romano cheese, grated (1 cup)
½	cup plain dried bread crumbs
2	large eggs, lightly beaten
½	cup minced fresh basil or parsley
	Salt and pepper
3	tablespoons olive oil
2	garlic cloves, minced
1	(28-ounce) can crushed tomatoes

NOODLES AND CHEESE

12	dried lasagna noodles
1	tablespoon salt
1	pound whole-milk mozzarella cheese, shredded (4 cups)
4	ounces Parmesan or Pecorino Romano cheese, grated (2 cups)

1. FOR THE MEATBALLS AND SAUCE: Adjust oven rack to middle position and heat oven to 450 degrees. Spray rimmed baking sheet with vegetable oil spray; set aside. Mix beef, Parmesan, bread crumbs, eggs, 5 tablespoons basil, 1 teaspoon salt, and ½ teaspoon pepper together until uniform. Pinch off scant 1 teaspoon–size pieces of mixture, roll into small balls, and arrange on prepared baking sheet. Bake meatballs until just cooked through and lightly browned, 8 to 10 minutes. Transfer meatballs to paper towel–lined platter and set aside. Reduce heat to 400 degrees.

2. Heat oil and garlic in medium saucepan over medium heat until garlic starts to sizzle, about 30 seconds. Stir in tomatoes, bring to simmer, and cook until sauce thickens slightly, 10 to 15 minutes. Off heat, stir in remaining 3 tablespoons basil and season with salt and pepper to taste. Stir meatballs into sauce and cover to keep warm until needed.

3. FOR THE NOODLES AND CHEESE: Meanwhile, bring 4 quarts water to boil in large pot. Stir in noodles and salt and cook, stirring often, until pasta is al dente. Drain noodles and rinse them under cold water until cool. Spread noodles out in single layer over clean kitchen towels. (Do not use paper towels; they will stick to pasta.)

4. Spray 13 by 9-inch baking dish with oil spray. Smear 3 tablespoons tomato sauce (without any meatballs) over bottom of pan. Arrange 3 noodles in single layer on top of sauce, making sure that noodles touch but do not overlap. Spread 1½ cups tomato sauce with meatballs evenly over pasta. Sprinkle evenly with 1 cup mozzarella and ½ cup Parmesan. Repeat layering pasta, tomato sauce with meatballs, and cheeses 2 more times. For final layer, arrange remaining 3 noodles on top, cover with remaining 1 cup mozzarella, and sprinkle with remaining ½ cup Parmesan.

5. Bake until cheese on top turns golden brown in spots and sauce is bubbling, 20 to 25 minutes. Let lasagna cool for 5 to 10 minutes before serving.

BAKED ZITI

✔ WHY THIS RECIPE WORKS

Most versions of baked ziti are forgettable: overcooked ziti in a dull, grainy sauce topped with a rubbery mass of mozzarella. We wanted to rescue baked ziti so we could have perfectly al dente pasta, a rich and flavorful sauce, and melted cheese in every bite. For a sauce that's big on flavor and light on prep, we cooked sautéed garlic with canned diced tomatoes and tomato sauce. Fresh basil and dried oregano added aromatic flavor. Rather than using traditional ricotta, we turned to cottage cheese— its curds have a texture similar to ricotta, but are creamier and tangier. For more flavor, we combined the cottage cheese with eggs, Parmesan, and heavy cream thickened with cornstarch. Adding this milky, tangy mixture to the tomato sauce produced a sauce that was bright, rich, and creamy. When it came to the pasta, we undercooked it and then baked it with a generous amount of sauce for perfectly al dente pasta and plenty of sauce left to keep our baked ziti moist. As for the mozzarella, we cut it into small cubes instead of shredding it, which dotted the finished casserole with gooey bits of cheese.

BAKED ZITI
SERVES 8 TO 10

We prefer baked ziti made with heavy cream, but whole milk can be substituted by increasing the amount of cornstarch to 2 teaspoons and increasing the cooking time in step 3 by 1 to 2 minutes. Part-skim mozzarella can also be used.

1	pound ziti, penne, or other short, tubular pasta
	Salt and pepper
1	pound (2 cups) whole-milk or 1-percent cottage cheese
2	large eggs
3	ounces Parmesan cheese, grated (1½ cups)

2	tablespoons extra-virgin olive oil
5	garlic cloves, minced
1	(28-ounce) can tomato sauce
1	(14.5-ounce) can diced tomatoes
1	teaspoon dried oregano
½	cup plus 2 tablespoons chopped fresh basil
1	teaspoon sugar
¾	teaspoon cornstarch
1	cup heavy cream
8	ounces whole-milk mozzarella cheese, cut into ¼-inch pieces (1½ cups)

1. Adjust oven rack to middle position and heat oven to 350 degrees. Bring 4 quarts water to boil in large pot. Add pasta and 1 tablespoon salt and cook, stirring often, until pasta begins to soften but is not yet cooked through, 5 to 7 minutes. Drain pasta and leave in colander (do not wash pot).

2. Meanwhile, whisk cottage cheese, eggs, and 1 cup Parmesan together in medium bowl; set aside. Heat oil and garlic in 12-inch skillet over medium heat. Cook, stirring often, until garlic turns golden but not brown, about 3 minutes. Stir in tomato sauce, diced tomatoes, and oregano, bring to simmer, and cook until thickened, about 10 minutes. Off heat, stir in ½ cup basil and sugar and season with salt and pepper to taste.

3. Stir cornstarch and heavy cream together in small bowl; transfer mixture to now-empty pot set over medium heat. Bring to simmer and cook until thickened, 3 to 4 minutes. Off heat, stir in cottage cheese mixture, 1 cup of tomato sauce, and ¾ cup of mozzarella. Add pasta to sauce and toss to combine.

4. Transfer pasta to 13 by 9-inch baking dish and spread remaining tomato sauce evenly over top. Sprinkle with remaining ¾ cup mozzarella and remaining ½ cup Parmesan. Cover dish tightly with aluminum foil that has been sprayed with vegetable oil spray. Bake for 30 minutes, then remove foil and continue to bake until cheese is bubbling and beginning to brown, about 30 minutes longer. Cool casserole for 20 minutes, then sprinkle with remaining 2 tablespoons basil and serve.

CREAMY BAKED FOUR-CHEESE PASTA

✓ WHY THIS RECIPE WORKS
Pasta ai quattro formaggi, *the classic Italian pasta dish made with four cheeses and heavy cream, often turns into an inedible mess. We wanted to deliver a pasta dinner that is silky smooth and rich but not heavy—a grown-up, sophisticated version of macaroni and cheese with Italian flavors.*

The cheese was first up for consideration; for the best flavor and texture, we used Italian fontina, Gorgonzola, Pecorino Romano, and Parmesan cheeses. Heating the cheese and cream together made a greasy, curdled mess, so instead we built a basic white sauce (a béchamel) by cooking butter with flour and then adding cream. Combining the hot sauce and pasta with the cheese—and not cooking the cheese in the sauce—preserved the fresh flavor of the different cheeses. Knowing the pasta would spend some time in the oven, we drained it before it was al dente so it wouldn't turn to mush when baked. Topped with bread crumbs and more Parmesan, and baked briefly in a very hot oven, our pasta dinner was just what we wanted: creamy, rich, and undeniably flavorful.

CREAMY BAKED FOUR-CHEESE PASTA
SERVES 4 TO 6

To streamline the process, prepare the breadcrumb topping and shred, crumble, and grate the cheeses while you wait for the pasta water to boil.

- 3 slices hearty white sandwich bread, torn into quarters
- 1 ounce Parmesan cheese, grated (½ cup)
  Salt and pepper
- 4 ounces fontina cheese, shredded (1 cup)
- 3 ounces Gorgonzola cheese, crumbled (¾ cup)
- 1 ounce Pecorino Romano cheese, grated (½ cup)
- 1 pound penne pasta
- 1 tablespoon unsalted butter
- 2 teaspoons all-purpose flour
- 1½ cups heavy cream

1. Pulse bread in food processor to coarse crumbs, about 10 pulses. Transfer bread crumbs to small bowl and stir in ¼ cup Parmesan, ¼ teaspoon salt, and ⅛ teaspoon pepper; set aside. Combine fontina, Gorgonzola, Pecorino, and remaining ¼ cup Parmesan in large bowl; set aside.

2. Adjust oven rack to middle position and heat oven to 500 degrees. Bring 4 quarts water to boil in large pot. Add pasta and 1 tablespoon salt and cook, stirring often, until just shy of al dente. Drain pasta, leaving it slightly wet.

3. While pasta is cooking, melt butter in small saucepan over medium heat. Whisk in flour until no lumps remain, about 30 seconds. Slowly whisk in cream and bring to boil, stirring occasionally. Reduce heat to medium-low and simmer for 1 minute. Stir in ¼ teaspoon salt and ¼ teaspoon pepper.

4. Add pasta to bowl with cheeses; immediately pour cream mixture over top, then cover bowl and let stand 3 minutes. Uncover bowl and stir with rubber spatula, scraping bottom of bowl, until cheeses are melted and mixture is thoroughly combined.

5. Transfer pasta to 13 by 9-inch baking dish, then sprinkle evenly with breadcrumb mixture, pressing down lightly. Bake until topping is golden brown, about 7 minutes. Serve immediately.

CREAMY BAKED FOUR-CHEESE PASTA WITH TOMATOES AND BASIL

Add one 14.5-ounce can diced tomatoes, drained, to pasta along with cream mixture and stir in ¼ cup coarsely chopped basil just before transferring pasta to baking dish.

CREAMY BAKED FOUR-CHEESE PASTA WITH PROSCIUTTO AND PEAS

Omit salt from cream mixture and add 4 ounces prosciutto, chopped, and 1 cup frozen peas to pasta along with cream mixture.

STOVETOP MACARONI AND CHEESE

✓ WHY THIS RECIPE WORKS
Just about the only thing boxed macaroni and cheese has going for it is its fast prep—and the fact that kids will almost always gobble it up. We wanted a quick stovetop macaroni and cheese with an ultra-creamy texture and authentic cheese flavor—so good that it would satisfy everyone at the table. We cooked the macaroni to just shy of al dente, then drained and combined it with butter and an egg custard mixture that included evaporated milk, eggs, hot sauce, and dry mustard. For the cheese we

chose cheddar, American, or Monterey Jack—and plenty of it. We stirred the cheese into the macaroni mixture until thick and creamy and then topped the mixture with toasted homemade bread crumbs—the final touch to this easy-to-prepare family favorite.

STOVETOP MACARONI AND CHEESE
SERVES 4

If you're in a hurry or prefer to sprinkle the dish with crumbled crackers (saltines aren't bad), you can skip the bread-crumb step.

BREAD CRUMBS
3   slices hearty white sandwich bread, torn into quarters
2   tablespoons unsalted butter, melted
    Salt

MACARONI AND CHEESE
2   large eggs
1   (12-ounce) can evaporated milk
1   teaspoon dry mustard, dissolved in 1 teaspoon water
    Salt
¼   teaspoon pepper
¼   teaspoon hot sauce
8   ounces elbow macaroni (2 cups)
4   tablespoons unsalted butter
12   ounces sharp cheddar, American, or Monterey Jack cheese, shredded (3 cups)

1. FOR THE BREAD CRUMBS: Pulse bread in food processor to coarse crumbs, about 10 pulses. Melt butter in 12-inch skillet over medium heat. Add bread crumbs and cook, stirring often, until beginning to brown, 4 to 6 minutes. Season with salt to taste; set aside.

2. FOR THE MACARONI AND CHEESE: Mix eggs, 1 cup of evaporated milk, mustard mixture, ½ teaspoon salt, pepper, and hot sauce in bowl.

3. Meanwhile, bring 2 quarts water to boil in Dutch oven. Add pasta and 1½ teaspoons salt and cook, stirring often, until al dente. Drain pasta and return to pot over low heat. Add butter and toss to melt.

4. Add egg mixture and three-quarters of cheese mixture to pasta and toss until thoroughly combined and cheese starts to melt. Gradually add remaining evaporated milk and remaining cheese mixture, stirring constantly, until mixture is hot and creamy, about 5 minutes. Serve immediately, sprinkling individual portions with toasted bread crumbs.

"BAKED" MACARONI AND CHEESE

Add ¼ cup grated Parmesan cheese to toasted bread crumbs. Adjust oven rack 6 inches from broiler element and heat broiler. Transfer macaroni and cheese mixture to 13 by 9-inch broiler-safe baking dish and sprinkle with bread-crumb mixture. Broil until topping turns deep golden brown, 1 to 2 minutes. Cool casserole for 5 minutes before serving.

CLASSIC MACARONI AND CHEESE

✔ WHY THIS RECIPE WORKS
Old-fashioned macaroni and cheese takes no shortcuts. This family favorite should boast tender pasta in a smooth, creamy sauce with great cheese flavor. Too often, the dish, which is baked in the oven, dries out or curdles. We aimed to create a foolproof version. We cooked the pasta until just past al dente and then combined it with a béchamel-based cheese sauce. For best flavor and a creamy texture, we used a combination of sharp cheddar and Monterey Jack. We combined the cooked pasta with the sauce and heated it through on the stovetop, rather than in the oven. This step helped ensure the dish didn't dry out,

but remained smooth and creamy. And to give the dish a browned topping, we sprinkled it with bread crumbs and ran it briefly under the broiler.

CLASSIC MACARONI AND CHEESE
SERVES 6 TO 8

It's crucial to cook the pasta until tender—that is, just past the al dente stage. Whole, low-fat, and skim milk all work well in this recipe. The recipe may be halved and baked in an 8-inch square broiler-safe baking pan. If desired, offer celery salt or hot sauce for sprinkling at the table.

6   slices hearty white sandwich bread, torn into quarters
8   tablespoons unsalted butter, 3 tablespoons cut into 6 pieces and chilled
1   pound elbow macaroni
    Salt
6   tablespoons all-purpose flour
1½   teaspoons dry mustard
¼   teaspoon cayenne pepper (optional)
5   cups milk
8   ounces Monterey Jack cheese, shredded (2 cups)
8   ounces sharp cheddar cheese, shredded (2 cups)

1. Pulse bread and 3 tablespoons chilled butter in food processor to coarse crumbs, about 10 pulses; set aside.

2. Adjust oven rack to lower-middle position and heat broiler. Bring 4 quarts water to boil in large pot. Add pasta and 1 tablespoon salt and cook, stirring often, until tender; drain pasta.

3. Melt remaining 5 tablespoons butter in now-empty pot over medium-high heat. Add flour, mustard, 1 teaspoon salt, and cayenne, if using, and cook, whisking constantly, until mixture becomes fragrant and deepens in color, about 1 minute. Gradually whisk in milk; bring mixture to boil, whisking constantly. Reduce heat to medium and simmer, whisking occasionally, until thickened, about 5 minutes. Off heat, slowly whisk in cheeses until completely melted. Add pasta to sauce and cook over medium-low heat, stirring constantly, until mixture is steaming and heated through, about 6 minutes.

4. Transfer mixture to 13 by 9-inch broiler-safe baking dish and sprinkle with bread-crumb mixture. Broil until topping is deep golden brown, 3 to 5 minutes. Cool casserole for 5 minutes before serving.

CLASSIC MACARONI AND CHEESE WITH HAM AND PEAS

Add 8 ounces deli ham, sliced ¼ inch thick, and cut into 1-inch pieces, and 1 cup frozen peas to cheese sauce along with pasta.

CLASSIC MACARONI AND CHEESE WITH KIELBASA AND MUSTARD

Add 1 finely chopped onion to melted butter in step 3 and cook until softened and lightly browned, 5 to 7 minutes. Add flour to onion and continue with recipe, reducing salt in sauce to ½ teaspoon. Add 8 ounces kielbasa, quartered lengthwise and sliced ½ inch thick, and 4 teaspoons whole grain Dijon mustard to cheese sauce along with pasta.

TURKEY TETRAZZINI

✔ WHY THIS RECIPE WORKS
Overcooking is the inevitable fate of many casseroles, as the contents are usually cooked twice: once on their own and once again when joined with the other casserole ingredients. We wanted a casserole with a silky sauce, a generous portion of turkey meat, and noodles cooked just till done. We found we could cut the second cooking time down to just 15 minutes by baking the recipe in a shallow dish that would allow it to heat through quickly. Most recipes for turkey Tetrazzini call for a béchamel sauce, in which milk is added to a roux (a paste made from fat and flour that is then cooked on the stovetop). In switching to a velouté, which is based on chicken broth rather than milk, we brightened up the texture and the flavor. We also used less sauce than most recipes call for, giving the other ingredients a chance to express themselves. Still looking for brighter flavor, we spruced things up with a shot of sherry and a little lemon juice and nutmeg. Parmesan cheese provided tang and bite, and a full 2 teaspoons of fresh thyme helped to freshen the overall impression of the dish.

TURKEY TETRAZZINI
SERVES 8

Don't skimp on the salt and pepper; this dish needs aggressive seasoning.

BREAD-CRUMB TOPPING
- 6 slices hearty white sandwich bread, torn into quarters
- 4 tablespoons unsalted butter, melted Pinch salt
- ¼ cup grated Parmesan cheese

FILLING
- 8 tablespoons unsalted butter
- 8 ounces white mushrooms, trimmed and sliced thin
- 2 onions, chopped fine Salt and pepper
- 6 tablespoons all-purpose flour
- 3 cups low-sodium chicken broth
- 1½ ounces Parmesan cheese, grated (¾ cup)
- ¼ cup dry sherry
- 1 tablespoon lemon juice
- 2 teaspoons minced fresh thyme
- ¼ teaspoon ground nutmeg
- 12 ounces spaghetti or other long-strand pasta, broken in half
- 2 cups frozen peas
- 4 cups cooked turkey or chicken, cut into ¼-inch pieces

1. FOR THE TOPPING: Adjust oven rack to middle position and heat oven to 350 degrees. Pulse bread in food processor to coarse crumbs, about 10 pulses. Combine bread crumbs, butter, and salt, spread onto rimmed baking sheet, and bake, stirring occasionally, until golden brown and crisp, 15 to 20 minutes. Transfer crumbs to medium bowl, cool slightly, then stir in Parmesan; set aside.

2. FOR THE FILLING: Increase oven temperature to 450 degrees. Grease 13 by 9-inch baking dish. Melt 2 tablespoons butter in 12-inch skillet over medium heat. Add mushrooms and onions and cook, stirring often, until liquid from mushrooms evaporates, 12 to 15 minutes. Season with salt and pepper to taste, then transfer to medium bowl and set aside. Wipe out skillet with paper towels.

3. Melt remaining 6 tablespoons butter in now-empty skillet over medium heat. Add flour and cook, whisking constantly, until flour turns golden, 1 to 2 minutes. Slowly whisk chicken broth, bring to simmer, and cook until thickened, 3 to 4 minutes. Off heat, whisk in Parmesan, sherry, lemon juice, thyme, nutmeg, and ½ teaspoon salt.

4. Meanwhile, bring 4 quarts water to boil in large pot. Add pasta and 1 tablespoon salt and cook until al dente. Reserve ½ cup cooking water, then drain pasta and return it to pot. Add sauce, mushroom mixture, peas, turkey, and reserved cooking water to pasta and toss to combine. Season with salt and pepper to taste.

5. Transfer mixture to prepared dish and sprinkle with bread crumbs. Bake until topping is golden brown and mixture is bubbling around edges, 13 to 15 minutes. Serve immediately.

CHAPTER 7 Rice, Grains, and Beans

SIMPLE WHITE RICE

✔ WHY THIS RECIPE WORKS

White rice seems like an easy enough dish to make, but it can be deceptively temperamental, quickly dissolving into unpleasant, gummy grains. For really great long-grain rice with distinct, separate grains that didn't clump together, we rinsed the rice of excess starch first. Then, to add a rich dimension, we sautéed the grains in butter, before covering them with boiling water. After simmering the rice until all of the liquid was absorbed, we placed a kitchen towel between the lid and pot to absorb excess moisture and ensure dry, fluffy grains.

SIMPLE WHITE RICE
SERVES 6

You will need a saucepan with a tight-fitting lid for this recipe.

    2   cups long-grain white rice
    1   tablespoon unsalted butter or
        vegetable oil
    3   cups water
    1   teaspoon salt

1. Place rice in colander or fine-mesh strainer and rinse under cold running water until water runs clear. Place strainer over bowl and set aside.

2. Melt butter in large saucepan over medium heat. Add rice and cook, stirring constantly, until grains become chalky and opaque, 1 to 3 minutes. Add water and salt, increase heat to high, and bring to boil, swirling pot to blend ingredients. Reduce heat to low, cover, and simmer until all liquid is absorbed, 18 to 20 minutes. Off heat, remove lid and place kitchen towel folded in half over saucepan; replace lid. Let stand for 10 to 15 minutes. Fluff rice with fork and serve.

RICE PILAF

✔ WHY THIS RECIPE WORKS

Rice pilaf should be fragrant and fluffy, perfectly steamed, and tender. While recipes for rice pilaf abound, none seem to agree on the best method for guaranteeing these results; many espouse rinsing the rice and soaking it overnight, but we wondered if this was really necessary for a simple rice dish. For the best pilaf, we started with long-grain white rice. Instead of the traditional 1:2 ratio for rice and water, we preferred a little less water for each cup of rice. We found that while an overnight soak wasn't necessary, rinsing the rice before cooking gave us beautifully separated grains. Sautéing the rice in butter for just a minute gave our pilaf great flavor.

RICE PILAF
SERVES 4

Olive oil can be substituted for the butter. While it's not necessary, soaking the rice overnight in water results in more tender, separate grains. To soak the rice, add enough water to cover the rice by 1 inch after rinsing in step 1, then cover the bowl with plastic wrap and let it sit at room temperature for 8 to 24 hours; reduce the amount of water to cook the rice to 2 cups. You will need a saucepan with a tight-fitting lid for this recipe.

    1½ cups long-grain white rice
    2¼ cups water
    1½ teaspoons salt
        Pinch pepper
    3   tablespoons unsalted butter
    1   small onion, chopped fine

1. Place rice in bowl and add enough water to cover by 2 inches; using hands, gently swish grains to release excess starch. Carefully pour off water, leaving rice in bowl. Repeat 4 to 5 times, until water runs almost clear. Drain rice in fine-mesh strainer, place over bowl, and set aside.

2. Bring water to boil, covered, in small saucepan over medium-high heat. Add salt and pepper and cover to keep hot. Meanwhile, melt butter in large saucepan over medium heat. Add onion and cook until softened but not browned, about 4 minutes. Add rice and stir to coat grains with butter; cook until edges of grains begin to turn translucent, about 3 minutes. Stir hot seasoned water into rice. Return to boil, then reduce heat to low, cover, and simmer until all liquid has been absorbed, 16 to 18 minutes. Off heat, remove lid and place kitchen towel folded in half over saucepan; replace lid. Let stand for 10 minutes. Fluff rice with fork and serve.

RICE PILAF WITH CURRANTS AND PINE NUTS

Add 2 minced garlic cloves, ½ teaspoon turmeric, and ¼ teaspoon ground cinnamon to softened onion and cook until fragrant, about 30 seconds. When rice is off heat, before covering saucepan with towel, sprinkle ¼ cup currants over top of rice (do not mix in). When fluffing rice with fork, toss in ¼ cup toasted pine nuts.

RICE PILAF WITH VERMICELLI

If you're using soaked rice, use 3 cups of water.

Increase water to 3¼ cups. Melt 1½ tablespoons butter in saucepan over medium heat; add 4 ounces vermicelli, broken into 1-inch pieces (about 1 cup), and cook, stirring occasionally, until browned, about 3 minutes. Transfer to small bowl and set aside. Melt remaining 1½ tablespoons butter and cook onion. Add 2 minced garlic cloves, ½ teaspoon ground cumin, ½ teaspoon ground coriander, and pinch allspice to softened onion; cook until fragrant, about 30 seconds. Add vermicelli along with rice.

BASMATI RICE PILAF

✓ **WHY THIS RECIPE WORKS**

We wanted a simple, speedy rice pilaf that made the most of the aroma and flavor of basmati rice—no rinsing or soaking necessary. For rice with warm spice notes, we thoughtfully selected a number of whole spices (cinnamon, cardamom, and cloves) and toasted them before adding the rice to the pot. Thinly sliced onion provided an aromatic background, and simmering until all the water was absorbed gave us tender, evenly cooked grains of rice.

BASMATI RICE PILAF
SERVES 4

You will need a saucepan with a tight-fitting lid for this recipe.

- 1   tablespoon vegetable oil
- 1   (3-inch) cinnamon stick, halved
- 2   green cardamom pods
- 2   whole cloves
- ¼   cup thinly sliced onion
- 1   cup basmati rice
- 1½ cups water
- 1   teaspoon salt

1. Heat oil in medium saucepan over high heat until almost smoking. Add cinnamon stick, cardamom, and cloves and cook, stirring, until they pop. Add onion and cook, stirring until translucent, about 2 minutes. Stir in rice and cook, stirring until fragrant, about 1 minute.

2. Add water and salt; bring to boil. Reduce heat, cover tightly, and simmer until all water has been absorbed, about 17 minutes. Let stand, covered, for 10 minutes. Fluff rice with fork and serve.

MEXICAN RICE

✓ **WHY THIS RECIPE WORKS**

Rice cooked the Mexican way is a flavorful pilaf-style dish, but we've had our share of soupy or greasy versions. We wanted tender rice infused with well-balanced fresh flavor. To keep the rice grains distinct, we rinsed the rice of excess starch before cooking it. Sautéing the rice in vegetable oil before adding the cooking liquid produced superior grains. We found that equal portions of chicken broth and fresh tomatoes (combined in a 2:1 ratio with the rice) were ideal for a flavorful liquid base. To further guarantee the right flavor, color, and texture, we added a little tomato paste and stirred the rice midway through cooking to reincorporate the tomato mixture. Baking the rice in the oven (rather than on the stovetop) ensured even cooking. More than a garnish, fresh cilantro, minced jalapeño, and a squirt of fresh lime juice complemented the richer tones of the cooked tomatoes, garlic, and onions.

MEXICAN RICE
SERVES 6 TO 8

Because the spiciness of jalapeños varies from chile to chile, we try to control the heat by removing the ribs and seeds (the source of most of the heat) from those chiles that are cooked in the rice. It is important to use an ovensafe pot about 12 inches in diameter so that the rice cooks evenly and in the time indicated. The pot's depth is less important than its diameter; we've successfully used both a straight-sided sauté pan and a Dutch oven. Whichever type of pot you use, it should have a tight-fitting, ovensafe lid. Vegetable broth can be substituted for the chicken broth.

- 2   tomatoes, cored and quartered
- 1   white onion, peeled and quartered
- 3   jalapeño chiles
- 2   cups long-grain white rice
- ⅓   cup vegetable oil
- 4   garlic cloves, minced
- 2   cups low-sodium chicken broth
- 1   tablespoon tomato paste
- 1½ teaspoons salt
- ½   cup minced fresh cilantro
        Lime wedges

1. Adjust oven rack to middle position and heat oven to 350 degrees. Process tomatoes and onion in food processor until smooth, about 15 seconds, scraping down bowl if necessary. Transfer mixture to liquid measuring cup; you should have 2 cups (if necessary, spoon off excess so that volume equals 2 cups). Remove ribs and seeds from 2 jalapeños and discard; mince flesh and set aside. Mince remaining jalapeño, including ribs and seeds; set aside.

2. Place rice in large fine-mesh strainer and rinse under cold running water until water runs clear, about 1½ minutes. Shake rice vigorously in strainer to remove excess water.

3. Heat oil in ovensafe 12-inch straight-sided sauté pan or Dutch oven over medium-high heat for 1 to 2 minutes. Drop 3 or 4 grains rice in oil; if grains sizzle, oil is ready. Add rice and cook, stirring frequently, until rice is light golden and translucent, 6 to 8 minutes. Reduce heat to medium, add garlic and seeded minced jalapeños, and cook, stirring constantly, until fragrant, about 1½ minutes. Stir in pureed tomatoes and onions, chicken broth, tomato paste, and salt, increase heat to medium-high, and bring to boil. Cover pan and transfer to oven; bake until liquid is absorbed and rice is tender, 30 to 35 minutes, stirring well halfway through cooking.

4. Stir in cilantro and reserved minced jalapeño with seeds to taste. Serve immediately, passing lime wedges separately.

MEXICAN RICE WITH CHARRED TOMATOES, CHILES, AND ONION

SERVES 6 TO 8

The vegetables are charred in a cast-iron skillet, which gives the finished dish a deeper color and a slightly toasty, smoky flavor. A cast-iron skillet works best for toasting the vegetables; a traditional or even a nonstick skillet will be left with burnt spots that are difficult to remove, even with vigorous scrubbing. Vegetable broth can be substituted for the chicken broth. Include the ribs and seeds when mincing the third jalapeño.

2	tomatoes, cored
I	white onion, peeled and halved crosswise, thin end halved lengthwise, thick end quartered lengthwise
6	garlic cloves, unpeeled
3	jalapeño chiles, 2 stemmed, halved, and seeded, I stemmed and minced
2	cups long-grain white rice
⅓	cup vegetable oil
2	cups low-sodium chicken broth
I	tablespoon tomato paste
I½	teaspoons salt
½	cup minced fresh cilantro
	Lime wedges

I. Heat 12-inch cast-iron skillet over medium-high heat for about 2 minutes. Add tomatoes, onion, garlic, and halved jalapeños and toast, using tongs to turn them frequently, until vegetables are softened and almost completely blackened, about 10 minutes for tomatoes and 15 to 20 minutes for other vegetables. When cool enough to handle, trim root ends from onion and halve each piece. Remove skins from garlic and mince. Mince jalapeños.

2. Adjust oven rack to middle position and heat oven to 350 degrees. Process toasted tomatoes and onion in food processor until smooth, about 15 seconds, scraping down bowl if necessary. Transfer mixture to liquid measuring cup; you should have 2 cups (if necessary, spoon off any excess so that volume equals 2 cups).

3. Place rice in large fine-mesh strainer and rinse under cold running water until water runs clear, about 1½ minutes. Shake rice vigorously in strainer to remove excess water.

4. Heat oil in ovensafe 12-inch straight-sided sauté pan or Dutch oven over medium-high heat, 1 to 2 minutes. Drop 3 or 4 grains rice in oil; if grains sizzle, oil is ready. Add rice and cook, stirring frequently, until rice is light golden and translucent, 6 to 8 minutes. Reduce heat to medium, add toasted minced garlic and toasted minced jalapeños, and cook, stirring constantly, until fragrant, about 1½ minutes. Stir in pureed tomatoes and onions, chicken broth, tomato paste, and salt, increase heat to medium-high, and bring to boil. Cover pan and transfer to oven; bake until liquid is absorbed and rice is tender, 30 to 35 minutes, stirring well halfway through cooking.

5. Stir in cilantro and reserved minced jalapeño with seeds to taste. Serve immediately, passing lime wedges separately.

FOOLPROOF BAKED BROWN RICE

✔ WHY THIS RECIPE WORKS
Brown rice should be ultimately satisfying, with a nutty, gutsy flavor and more textural personality—slightly sticky and just a bit chewy—than white rice. To achieve this ideal, we stayed close to the water-to-rice ratio established in our Simple White Rice (page 222), settling on 2⅓ cups water to 1½ cups rice. But unlike our white rice method, we cooked the rice in the oven to approximate the controlled, indirect heat of a rice cooker. A couple of teaspoons of butter or oil added to the cooking water added mild flavor while allowing the earthy, nutty flavor of the rice to take center stage.

FOOLPROOF BAKED BROWN RICE

SERVES 4 TO 6

To minimize any loss of water through evaporation, cover the saucepan and use the water as soon as it reaches a boil. An 8-inch ceramic baking dish with a lid may be used instead of the baking dish and aluminum foil. To double the recipe, use a 13 by 9-inch baking dish; the baking time does not to be increased.

TEST KITCHEN TIP NO. 46   RICE—NO SOAKING REQUIRED

The question of whether rice should be soaked prior to cooking is often up for debate in our test kitchen. During the testing of our brown rice recipe, we decided to put this one to rest. Some recipes call for soaking brown rice for three hours, so that's just what we did. We pitted the soaked rice against rice that was not soaked, using both to make our recipe, slightly reducing the water in the recipe for the soaked batch. What did we find? To be frank, soaking was a waste of time. The rice was overcooked, and the grains tended to "blow out."

This result led us to test the wisdom of soaking other types of rice. And when we cooked up batches of long-grain white rice and basmati rice that had been soaked, we produced nearly identical results: bloated, mushy rice.

Does that mean that there's no place for water in the world of rice preparation? Not necessarily. We found that the extra step of rinsing long-grain white in several changes of water was indispensable for a pilaf with distinct, separate grains. Rinsing washes away starches on these grains and doesn't cause the problems associated with soaking. What about rinsing brown rice? Our tests showed no benefit (or harm). Because the bran is still intact, brown rice doesn't have starch on its exterior. So rinsing doesn't accomplish anything—except for wasting time and water.

1½ cups long-grain, medium-grain, or short-grain brown rice
2⅓ cups water
2 teaspoons unsalted butter or vegetable oil
½ teaspoon salt

1. Adjust oven rack to middle position and heat oven to 375 degrees. Spread rice in 8-inch square baking dish.

2. Bring water and butter to boil, covered, in medium saucepan. Once boiling, immediately stir in salt and pour water over rice in baking dish. Cover baking dish tightly with 2 layers of aluminum foil. Transfer baking dish to oven and bake rice until tender, about 1 hour.

3. Remove baking dish from oven and uncover. Fluff rice with fork, then cover dish with kitchen towel and let rice stand for 5 minutes. Uncover and let rice stand 5 minutes longer. Serve immediately.

BAKED BROWN RICE WITH PARMESAN, LEMON, AND HERBS

Increase amount of butter to 2 tablespoons and melt in 10-inch nonstick skillet over medium heat. Add 1 minced small onion and cook until translucent, about 3 minutes; set aside. Substitute low-sodium chicken broth for water and reduce salt to ⅛ teaspoon. Stir onion mixture into rice after adding broth. Cover and bake rice as directed. After removing foil, stir in ½ cup grated Parmesan, ¼ cup minced fresh parsley, ¼ cup chopped fresh basil, 1 teaspoon grated lemon zest, ½ teaspoon lemon juice, and ⅛ teaspoon pepper. Cover dish with kitchen towel and proceed as directed.

CURRIED BAKED BROWN RICE WITH TOMATOES AND PEAS

Increase amount of butter to 2 tablespoons and melt in 10-inch nonstick skillet over medium heat. Add 1 minced small onion and cook until translucent, about 3 minutes. Add 1 minced garlic clove, 1 tablespoon grated fresh ginger, 1½ teaspoons curry powder, and ¼ teaspoon salt and cook until fragrant, about 1 minute. Add one 14.5-ounce can drained diced tomatoes and cook until heated through, about 2 minutes. Set aside. Substitute vegetable broth for water and reduce amount of salt to ⅛ teaspoon. After pouring broth over rice, stir tomato mixture into rice and spread rice and tomato mixture into even layer. Bake as directed, increasing baking time to 70 minutes. Before covering baking dish with kitchen towel, stir in ½ cup thawed frozen peas.

BAKED BROWN RICE WITH SAUTÉED MUSHROOMS AND LEEKS

Substitute low-sodium chicken broth for water and reduce amount of salt to ⅛ teaspoon; bake as directed. When rice has about 10 minutes baking time remaining, melt 1 tablespoon unsalted butter with 1 tablespoon olive oil in 12-inch nonstick skillet over medium-high heat. Add 1 leek, white part only, sliced into ¼-inch-thick rings, and cook, stirring occasionally, until wilted, about 2 minutes. Add 6 ounces cremini mushrooms, trimmed and sliced ¼ inch thick, and ¼ teaspoon salt and cook, stirring occasionally, until moisture has evaporated and mushrooms are browned, about 8 minutes. Stir in 1½ teaspoons minced fresh thyme and ⅛ teaspoon pepper. After removing kitchen towel, stir in mushroom-leek mixture and 1½ teaspoons sherry vinegar; serve immediately.

HEARTY BAKED BROWN RICE

✔ WHY THIS RECIPE WORKS

For our Foolproof Baked Brown Rice (page 224), we tackled how to create perfect, evenly cooked rice by baking it in the oven where the consistent, indirect heat simulates the environment of a rice cooker. But for a heartier dish, with aromatics and vegetables added to complement the flavor and texture of the rice, we found that we needed to tinker with the liquid-to-rice ratio. Increasing the amount of liquid ensured that the rice cooked through perfectly every time. Fresh herbs, citrus, and cheese, added just before serving, brightened the dish and balanced the earthiness of the rice.

HEARTY BAKED BROWN RICE WITH ONIONS AND ROASTED RED PEPPERS

SERVES 4 TO 6

Short-grain brown rice can also be used.

4 teaspoons olive oil
2 onions, chopped fine
2¼ cups water
1 cup low-sodium chicken broth
1½ cups long-grain brown rice
1 teaspoon salt
¾ cup chopped jarred roasted red peppers
½ cup minced fresh parsley
¼ teaspoon pepper
1 ounce Parmesan cheese, grated (½ cup)
Lemon wedges

1. Adjust oven rack to middle position and heat oven to 375 degrees. Heat oil in ovensafe Dutch oven over medium heat until shimmering. Add onions and cook, stirring occasionally, until well browned, 12 to 14 minutes.

2. Add water and broth, cover, and bring to boil. Off heat, stir in rice and salt. Cover, transfer pot to oven, and bake rice until tender, 65 to 70 minutes.

3. Remove pot from oven and uncover. Fluff rice with fork, stir in roasted red peppers, and replace lid; let stand 5 minutes. Stir in parsley and pepper. Serve, passing Parmesan and lemon wedges separately.

HEARTY BAKED BROWN RICE WITH BLACK BEANS AND CILANTRO

Substitute 1 finely chopped green bell pepper for 1 onion. Once vegetables are well browned in step 1, stir in 3 minced garlic cloves and cook until fragrant, about 30 seconds. Substitute one 15-ounce can black beans for roasted red peppers and ¼ cup minced fresh cilantro for parsley. Omit Parmesan and substitute lime wedges for lemon wedges.

HEARTY BAKED BROWN RICE WITH PEAS, FETA, AND MINT

Reduce amount of olive oil to 1 tablespoon and omit 1 onion. Substitute 1 cup thawed frozen peas for roasted red peppers, ¼ cup minced fresh mint for parsley, ½ teaspoon grated lemon zest for pepper, and 2 ounces crumbled feta (½ cup) for Parmesan.

HEARTY BAKED BROWN RICE WITH ANDOUILLE, CORN, AND RED PEPPERS

If you cannot find andouille sausage, substitute chorizo, linguiça, or kielbasa.

Omit 1 onion. Reduce amount of olive oil to 1 tablespoon. Heat olive oil in Dutch oven over medium heat until shimmering. Add 6 ounces andouille sausage, cut into ½-inch pieces, to pot and cook until lightly browned, 4 to 6 minutes. Using slotted spoon, transfer sausage to paper towel–lined plate; set aside. Add onion and 1 finely chopped red bell pepper to

fat left in pot and cook, stirring occasionally, until well browned, 12 to 14 minutes; add 3 minced garlic cloves and cook until fragrant, about 30 seconds, before adding water and broth. Substitute ½ cup thawed frozen corn for roasted red peppers; add reserved sausage with corn. Substitute ¼ cup chopped fresh basil for parsley and omit Parmesan.

WILD RICE PILAF WITH PECANS AND DRIED CRANBERRIES

✔ WHY THIS RECIPE WORKS
Sometimes wild rice turns out undercooked and difficult to chew, other times the rice is overcooked and gluey. We wanted to figure out how to turn out properly cooked wild rice every time. Through trial and error, we learned to simmer the rice slowly in plenty of liquid, checking it for doneness every couple of minutes past the 35-minute mark. For the simmering liquid, we combined water and chicken broth—the broth's mild yet rich profile tempered the rice's muddy flavor to a pleasant earthiness and affirmed its subdued nuttiness. To further tame the strong flavor of the wild rice, we added some white rice to the mixture, then added onions, carrots, dried cranberries, and toasted pecans for a winning pilaf.

WILD RICE PILAF WITH PECANS AND DRIED CRANBERRIES

SERVES 6 TO 8

Wild rice goes quickly from tough to pasty, so begin testing the rice at the 35-minute mark and drain the rice as soon as it is tender.

1¾	cups low-sodium chicken broth
2½	cups water
2	bay leaves
8	sprigs fresh thyme, divided into 2 bundles, each tied together with kitchen twine
1	cup wild rice, picked over and rinsed
1½	cups long-grain white rice
3	tablespoons unsalted butter
1	onion, chopped fine
1	large carrot, peeled and chopped fine
	Salt and pepper
¾	cup dried cranberries
¾	cup pecans, toasted and chopped coarse
4½	teaspoons minced fresh parsley

1. Bring broth, ¼ cup water, bay leaves, and 1 bundle thyme to boil in medium saucepan over medium-high heat. Add wild rice, cover, and reduce heat to low; simmer until rice is plump and tender and has absorbed most of liquid, 35 to

---

45 minutes. Drain rice in fine-mesh strainer to remove excess liquid. Remove bay leaves and thyme. Return rice to now-empty saucepan, cover, and set aside.

2. While wild rice is cooking, place white rice in medium bowl and add enough water to cover by 2 inches; using hands, gently swish grains to release excess starch. Carefully pour off water, leaving rice in bowl. Repeat 4 to 5 times, until water runs almost clear. Drain rice in fine-mesh strainer.

3. Melt butter in medium saucepan over medium-high heat. Add onion, carrot, and 1 teaspoon salt and cook, stirring frequently, until vegetables are softened but not browned, about 4 minutes. Add rinsed white rice and stir to coat grains with butter; cook, stirring frequently, until grains begin to turn translucent, about 3 minutes. Meanwhile, bring remaining 2¼ cups water to boil in small saucepan or in microwave. Add boiling water and second thyme bundle to rice and return to boil. Reduce heat to low, sprinkle cranberries evenly over rice, and cover. Simmer until all liquid is absorbed, 16 to 18 minutes. Off heat, remove thyme, fluff rice with fork.

4. Combine wild rice, white rice mixture, pecans, and parsley in large bowl and toss with rubber spatula. Season with salt and pepper to taste; serve immediately.

NO-FUSS RISOTTO

✔ WHY THIS RECIPE WORKS
Classic risotto can demand half an hour of stovetop tedium for the best creamy results. Our goal was 5 minutes of stirring, tops. First, we swapped out the saucepan for a Dutch oven, which has a thick, heavy bottom, deep sides, and tight-fitting lid—perfect for trapping and distributing heat as evenly as possible. Typical recipes dictate adding the broth in small increments after the wine has been absorbed (and stirring constantly after each addition), but we added most of the broth at once and covered the pan, allowing the rice to simmer until almost all the broth had been absorbed (stirring just twice). After adding the second and final addition of broth, we stirred the pot to ensure the bottom didn't cook more quickly than the top and turned off the heat. Without sitting over a direct flame, the sauce turned out perfectly creamy and the rice was thickened, velvety, and just barely chewy. To finish, we simply stirred in butter, herbs, and a squeeze of lemon juice to brighten the flavors.

NO-FUSS RISOTTO WITH PARMESAN AND HERBS
SERVES 6

This more hands-off method requires precise timing, so we strongly recommend using a timer.

5	cups low-sodium chicken broth
1½	cups water
4	tablespoons unsalted butter
1	large onion, chopped fine
	Salt and pepper
1	garlic clove, minced
2	cups Arborio rice
1	cup dry white wine
2	ounces Parmesan cheese, grated (1 cup)
2	tablespoons chopped fresh parsley
2	tablespoons chopped fresh chives
1	teaspoon lemon juice

1. Bring broth and water to boil in large saucepan over high heat. Reduce heat to medium-low to maintain gentle simmer.

2. Melt 2 tablespoons butter in Dutch oven over medium heat. Add onion and ¾ teaspoon salt and cook, stirring frequently, until onion is softened, 5 to 7 minutes. Add garlic and stir until fragrant, about 30 seconds. Add rice and cook, stirring frequently, until grains are translucent around edges, about 3 minutes.

3. Add wine and cook, stirring constantly, until fully absorbed, 2 to 3 minutes. Stir 5 cups hot broth mixture into rice; reduce heat to medium-low, cover, and simmer until almost all liquid has been absorbed and rice is just al dente, 16 to 19 minutes, stirring twice during cooking.

4. Add ¾ cup hot broth mixture and stir gently and constantly until risotto becomes creamy, about 3 minutes. Stir in Parmesan. Remove pot from heat, cover, and let stand for 5 minutes. Stir in remaining 2 tablespoons butter, parsley, chives, and lemon juice. To loosen texture of risotto, add remaining broth mixture to taste. Season with salt and pepper to taste and serve immediately.

NO-FUSS RISOTTO WITH CHICKEN AND HERBS
SERVES 6

This more hands-off method requires precise timing, so we strongly recommend using a timer. Be aware that the thinner ends of the chicken breasts may be fully cooked by the time the broth is added to the rice, with the thicker ends finishing about 5 minutes later.

5	cups low-sodium chicken broth
2	cups water
1	tablespoon olive oil
2	(12-ounce) bone-in split chicken breasts, trimmed and cut in half crosswise
4	tablespoons unsalted butter
1	large onion, chopped fine
	Salt and pepper
1	garlic clove, minced
2	cups Arborio rice
1	cup dry white wine
2	ounces Parmesan cheese, grated (1 cup)
2	tablespoons chopped fresh parsley
2	tablespoons chopped fresh chives
1	teaspoon lemon juice

1. Bring broth and water to boil in large saucepan over high heat. Reduce heat to medium-low to maintain gentle simmer.

2. Heat oil in Dutch oven over medium heat until just starting to smoke. Add

chicken, skin side down, and cook without moving until golden brown, 4 to 6 minutes. Flip chicken and cook second side until lightly browned, about 2 minutes. Transfer chicken to saucepan of simmering broth and cook until chicken registers 160 degrees, 10 to 15 minutes. Transfer to large plate.

3. Melt 2 tablespoons butter in now-empty Dutch oven over medium heat. Add onion and ¾ teaspoon salt and cook, stirring frequently, until onion is softened, 5 to 7 minutes. Add garlic and stir until fragrant, about 30 seconds. Add rice and cook, stirring frequently, until grains are translucent around edges, about 3 minutes.

4. Add wine and cook, stirring constantly, until fully absorbed, 2 to 3 minutes.

Stir 5 cups hot broth mixture into rice; reduce heat to medium-low, cover, and simmer until almost all liquid has been absorbed and rice is just al dente, 16 to 18 minutes, stirring twice during cooking.

5. Add ¾ cup hot broth mixture to risotto and stir gently and constantly until risotto becomes creamy, about 3 minutes. Stir in Parmesan. Remove pot from heat, cover, and let stand for 5 minutes.

6. Meanwhile, remove and discard skin and bones from chicken and shred meat into bite-size pieces. Gently stir shredded chicken, remaining 2 tablespoons butter, parsley, chives, and lemon juice into risotto. To loosen texture of risotto, add remaining broth mixture to taste. Season with salt and pepper to taste and serve immediately.

TEST KITCHEN TIP NO. 48 ARBORIO RICE SWAP

The stubby, milky grains of Arborio rice, once grown exclusively in Italy, are valued for their high starch content and the subsequent creaminess they bring to risotto, but can a different type of rice be used to make risotto?

Varieties of rice are roughly grouped as long grain, medium grain, or short grain according to their cooked length and width. Long-grain rice is about four times as long as it is wide, medium grain is twice as long, and short grain is almost round. The manner in which they cook is largely defined by the ratio of two starches that (in part) constitute rice: amylose and amylopectin. The former does not break down (gelatinize) when heated; the latter does. Rice with a high percentage of amylose, then, is long, firm, and discrete when cooked; rice with a lower percentage (and thus more amylopectin) is shorter and starchy, or "sticky." For comparison's sake, long-grain rice contains between 23 and 26 percent amylose, and medium-grain rice contains between 18 and 26 percent amylose. Arborio rice, the classic choice for risotto, contains roughly 19 to 21 percent amylose. However, that is not the only difference. The desirable "bite" in risotto is due to a defect in Arborio rice called chalk. During maturation, the starch structures at the grain's core deform, making for a firm, toothy center when cooked.

What if you can't find Arborio rice? To see how other rices stacked up, we made our Parmesan risotto with four types of rice: standard long grain, converted parcooked long grain, regular medium grain, and short grain (sushi-style rice). The two long-grain varieties bombed, turning mushy and lacking the creaminess essential to risotto. The parboiled rice also had the jarring, unmistakable flavor of precooked rice. Medium- and short-grain rice fared much better, earning passing grades from most tasters, who agreed that these batches possessed all the creaminess of risotto made with Arborio, though not its al dente bite.

So the long and short of it? If you're in a pinch and can't find Arborio, look for medium- or short-grain rice for an acceptable—but not perfect—batch of risotto. But for the best risotto, choose Arborio rice.

NO-FUSS RISOTTO WITH CHICKEN, LEEK, AND GARLIC
SERVES 6

This more hands-off method requires precise timing, so we strongly recommend using a timer.

5	cups low-sodium chicken broth
2	cups water
1	tablespoon olive oil
2	(12-ounce) bone-in split chicken breasts, trimmed and cut in half crosswise
4	tablespoons unsalted butter
1	leek, white and light green parts only, halved lengthwise, chopped fine, and washed thoroughly
	Salt and pepper
3	large garlic cloves, minced
2	cups Arborio rice
1	cup dry white wine
10	ounces frozen chopped spinach, thawed and squeezed dry
2	ounces Parmesan cheese, grated (1 cup)
2	tablespoons chopped fresh parsley
2	tablespoons chopped fresh chives
1	teaspoon lemon juice

1. Bring broth and water to boil in large saucepan over high heat. Reduce heat to medium-low to maintain gentle simmer.

2. Heat oil in Dutch oven over medium heat until just starting to smoke. Add chicken, skin side down, and cook without moving until golden brown, 4 to 6 minutes. Flip chicken and cook second side until lightly browned, about 2 minutes. Transfer chicken to saucepan of simmering broth and cook until chicken registers 160 degrees, 10 to 15 minutes. Transfer to large plate.

3. Melt 2 tablespoons butter in

now-empty Dutch oven over medium heat. Add leek and ¾ teaspoon salt and cook, stirring frequently, until leek is softened, 5 to 7 minutes. Add garlic and stir until fragrant, about 30 seconds. Add rice and cook, stirring frequently, until grains are translucent around edges, about 3 minutes.

4. Add wine and cook, stirring constantly, until fully absorbed, 2 to 3 minutes. Stir 5 cups hot broth mixture into rice; reduce heat to medium-low, cover, and simmer until almost all liquid has been absorbed and rice is just al dente, 16 to 18 minutes, stirring twice during cooking.

5. Add ¾ cup hot broth mixture to risotto and stir gently and constantly until risotto becomes creamy, about 3 minutes. Stir in spinach and Parmesan. Remove pot from heat, cover, and let stand for 5 minutes.

6. Meanwhile, remove and discard skin and bones from chicken and shred meat into bite-size pieces. Gently stir shredded chicken, remaining 2 tablespoons butter, parsley, chives, and lemon juice into risotto. To loosen texture of risotto, add remaining broth mixture to taste. Season with salt and pepper to taste and serve immediately.

NO-FUSS LEMON RISOTTO WITH CHICKEN, FENNEL, AND GREEN OLIVES

SERVES 6

This more hands-off method requires precise timing, so we strongly recommend using a timer.

5   cups low-sodium chicken broth
2   cups water
1   tablespoon olive oil
2   (12-ounce) bone-in split chicken breasts, trimmed and cut in half crosswise
4   tablespoons unsalted butter
1   large onion, chopped fine
1   fennel bulb, fronds minced, stalks discarded, bulb halved, cored, and chopped fine
     Salt and pepper
1   garlic clove, minced
2   cups Arborio rice
1   cup dry white wine
2   ounces Parmesan cheese, grated (1 cup)
⅓   cup chopped green olives
2   tablespoons chopped fresh parsley
2   tablespoons chopped fresh chives
1   teaspoon grated lemon zest plus 1 teaspoon juice

1. Bring broth and water to boil in large saucepan over high heat. Reduce heat to medium-low to maintain gentle simmer.

2. Heat oil in Dutch oven over medium heat until just starting to smoke. Add chicken, skin side down, and cook without moving until golden brown, 4 to 6 minutes. Flip chicken and cook second side until lightly browned, about 2 minutes. Transfer chicken to saucepan of simmering broth and cook until chicken registers 160 degrees, 10 to 15 minutes. Transfer to large plate.

3. Melt 2 tablespoons butter in now-empty Dutch oven set over medium heat. Add onion, fennel, and ¾ teaspoon salt and cook, stirring frequently, until onion is softened, 5 to 7 minutes. Add garlic and stir until fragrant, about 30 seconds. Add rice and cook, stirring frequently, until grains are translucent around edges, about 3 minutes.

4. Add wine and cook, stirring constantly, until fully absorbed, 2 to 3 minutes. Stir 5 cups hot broth mixture into rice; reduce heat to medium-low, cover, and simmer until almost all liquid has been absorbed and rice is just al dente, 16 to 18 minutes, stirring twice during cooking.

5. Add ¾ cup hot broth mixture to risotto and stir gently and constantly until risotto becomes creamy, about 3 minutes. Stir in Parmesan and olives. Remove pot from heat, cover, and let stand for 5 minutes.

6. Meanwhile, remove and discard skin and bones from chicken and shred meat into bite-size pieces. Gently stir shredded chicken, remaining 2 tablespoons butter, parsley, chives, lemon zest and juice, and 2 tablespoons fennel fronds into risotto. To loosen texture of risotto, add remaining broth mixture to taste. Season with salt and pepper to taste and serve immediately.

NO-FUSS SAFFRON RISOTTO WITH CHICKEN AND PEAS

SERVES 6 AS A SIDE DISH

This more hands-off method requires precise timing, so we strongly recommend using a timer.

5   cups low-sodium chicken broth
2   cups water
1   tablespoon olive oil
2   (12-ounce) bone-in split chicken breasts, trimmed and cut in half crosswise
4   tablespoons unsalted butter
1   large onion, chopped fine
     Salt and pepper
1   large garlic clove, minced
2   cups Arborio rice
1   cup dry white wine
¼   teaspoon saffron threads
2   ounces Parmesan cheese, grated (1 cup)
¾   cup frozen peas
2   tablespoons chopped fresh parsley
2   tablespoons chopped fresh chives
1   teaspoon lemon juice

1. Bring broth and water to boil in large saucepan over high heat. Reduce heat to medium-low to maintain gentle simmer.

2. Heat oil in Dutch oven over medium heat until just starting to smoke. Add chicken, skin side down, and cook without moving until golden brown, 4 to 6 minutes. Flip chicken and cook second side until lightly browned, about 2 minutes. Transfer chicken to saucepan of simmering broth and cook until chicken registers 160 degrees, 10 to 15 minutes. Transfer to large plate.

3. Melt 2 tablespoons butter in now-empty Dutch oven over medium heat. Add onion and ¾ teaspoon salt and cook, stirring frequently, until onion is softened, 5 to 7 minutes. Add garlic and stir until fragrant, about 30 seconds. Add rice and cook, stirring frequently, until grains are translucent around edges, about 3 minutes.

4. Add wine and cook, stirring constantly, until fully absorbed, 2 to 3 minutes. Stir 5 cups hot broth mixture and saffron into rice; reduce heat to medium-low, cover, and simmer until almost all liquid has been absorbed and rice is just al dente, 16 to 18 minutes, stirring twice during cooking.

5. Add ¾ cup hot broth mixture to risotto and stir gently and constantly until risotto becomes creamy, about 3 minutes. Stir in Parmesan and peas. Remove pot from heat, cover, and let stand for 5 minutes.

6. Meanwhile, remove and discard skin and bones from chicken and shred meat into bite-size pieces. Gently stir shredded chicken, remaining 2 tablespoons butter, parsley, chives, and lemon juice into risotto. To loosen texture of risotto, add remaining broth mixture to taste. Season with salt and pepper to taste and serve immediately.

SPRING VEGETABLE RISOTTO

☑ WHY THIS RECIPE WORKS
Bland flavor and mushy vegetables can ruin this Italian classic. We wanted a risotto primavera with fresh yet complex flavors and vegetables that retained some bite. We started with the classic combination of asparagus and leeks. The leeks melted down beautifully as their delicate flavor infused the rice. The asparagus had to be handled separately; sautéing the trimmed spears and stirring them into the rice right before serving kept them from turning into mush. For a third vegetable, we added frozen peas. For a stronger backbone of flavor, we simmered the leek greens

and tough stems of the asparagus in the chicken broth we used for cooking the rice. To round out and brighten the dish, we topped it with a gremolata of parsley, mint, and lemon zest.

SPRING VEGETABLE RISOTTO
SERVES 4

To make this dish vegetarian, replace the chicken broth with vegetable broth. Onions can be substituted for the leeks. If substituting onions, use 1 roughly chopped onion in the broth and 2 finely chopped onions in the risotto.

GREMOLATA
2 tablespoons minced fresh parsley, stems reserved
2 tablespoons minced fresh mint, stems reserved
½ teaspoon grated lemon zest

RISOTTO
1 pound asparagus, trimmed, tough ends reserved and chopped coarse, spears cut on bias into ½-inch lengths
2 leeks, white and light green parts halved lengthwise, sliced thin, and washed thoroughly; dark green parts chopped coarse
4 cups low-sodium chicken broth
3 cups water
5 tablespoons unsalted butter
Salt and pepper
½ cup frozen peas
2 garlic cloves, minced
1½ cups Arborio rice
1 cup dry white wine
1½ ounces Parmesan cheese grated (¾ cup), plus extra for serving
2 teaspoons lemon juice

1. FOR THE GREMOLATA: Combine all ingredients in small bowl and set aside.

2. FOR THE RISOTTO: Bring chopped asparagus ends, chopped dark green leek parts, reserved parsley and mint stems, broth, and water to boil in large saucepan

over high heat. Reduce heat to medium-low, partially cover, and simmer 20 minutes. Strain broth through fine-mesh strainer into medium bowl, pressing on solids to extract as much liquid as possible. Return strained broth to saucepan, cover, and set over low heat to keep broth warm.

3. Melt 1 tablespoon butter in Dutch oven over medium heat. Add asparagus spears, pinch salt, and pinch pepper. Cook, stirring occasionally, until asparagus is crisp-tender, 4 to 6 minutes. Add peas and continue to cook for 1 minute. Transfer vegetables to plate and set aside.

4. Melt 3 tablespoons butter in now-empty Dutch oven over medium heat. Add white and light green leek parts, garlic, ½ teaspoon salt, and ½ teaspoon pepper. Cook, stirring occasionally, until leeks are softened, 5 to 7 minutes. Add rice and cook, stirring frequently, until grains are translucent around edges, about 3 minutes. Add wine and cook, stirring frequently, until fully absorbed, 2 to 3 minutes.

5. Add 3 cups hot broth mixture to rice. Simmer, stirring every 3 to 4 minutes, until liquid is absorbed and bottom of pan is almost dry, about 12 minutes.

6. Stir in about ½ cup hot broth mixture and cook, stirring constantly, until absorbed, about 3 minutes; repeat with additional broth mixture 3 or 4 times until rice is al dente. Off heat, stir in remaining 1 tablespoon butter, Parmesan, and lemon juice. Gently fold in asparagus and peas. To loosen texture of risotto, add remaining broth mixture to taste. Serve immediately, sprinkling each serving with gremolata and passing Parmesan separately.

SPRING VEGETABLE RISOTTO WITH CARROTS AND WATERCRESS

Substitute 3 carrots, peeled and cut into ½-inch pieces, peels and trimmings chopped coarse, for asparagus; boil chopped carrot peels and trimmings with dark green leek parts. Cook carrots in step 3 until crisp-tender, 8 to 10 minutes; transfer to plate and set aside. Substitute 4 ounces watercress (4 cups) for peas; once rice is al dente in step 6, stir in watercress, cover pot, and let stand for 1 minute. After stirring in butter, Parmesan, and lemon juice, gently fold in carrots.

SPRING VEGETABLE RISOTTO WITH FENNEL AND SPINACH

Substitute 1 large bulb fennel, trimmed of stalks, bulb halved, cored, and cut into ½-inch pieces, stalks and core chopped coarse, for asparagus; boil chopped fennel stalks and core with dark green leek parts. Cook fennel in step 3 until crisp-tender, 8 to 10 minutes; transfer to plate and set aside. Substitute 6 ounces baby spinach (6 cups) for peas; once rice is al dente in step 6, stir in spinach, cover pot, and let stand for 1 minute. After stirring in butter, Parmesan, and lemon juice, gently fold in fennel.

FARRO RISOTTO

WHY THIS RECIPE WORKS
Italians prepare farro, the whole grain form of wheat, much like how they cook Arborio rice for risotto, by cooking the farro slowly into a creamy dish called farotto. *We set out to come up with our own version, one that took half an hour or less, yet still produced a dish that was creamy and rich, while highlighting farro's nutty flavor and chewy texture. To do so, we adapted the method we developed for No-Fuss Risotto (page 227), which adds the bulk of the liquid at the beginning of cooking, keeps the pot covered, and requires less stirring throughout. A few modifications were in order, however. Farro, it turns out, does require frequent stirring to ensure that the grains cook evenly. And instead of keeping the lid on, we removed it—after all, it made sense if we were stirring. We also found that we didn't need to warm the liquid before adding it to the pot—the farro cooked through just fine. As for flavorings, onion was a good start and garlic, thyme, and sweet, earthy carrots made our farro even better. In early tests, we followed risotto-making tradition by finishing the farro with butter and Parmesan, but these additions masked the nutty grain. Instead, we opted for a fresher finish, substituting fresh chopped parsley and lemon juice, which delivered a light, bright version of this rich and creamy grain dish.*

FARRO RISOTTO
SERVES 4 TO 6

Look for farro in well-stocked supermarkets near the rice and other grains or in the bulk foods section.

1	tablespoon olive oil
1	onion, chopped fine
1	carrot, peeled and chopped fine
	Salt and pepper
3	garlic cloves, minced
1	teaspoon minced fresh thyme
1½	cups farro
2	cups low-sodium chicken broth
1½	cups water
2	tablespoons chopped fresh parsley
1	teaspoon lemon juice

1. Combine oil, onion, carrot, and ¼ teaspoon salt in large saucepan. Cover and cook over medium-low heat, stirring occasionally, until vegetables are softened, 8 to 10 minutes. Stir in garlic and thyme and cook until fragrant, about 30 seconds.

2. Stir in farro and cook until lightly toasted, about 2 minutes. Stir in broth and water and bring to simmer. Reduce heat to low and continue to simmer, stirring often, until farro is tender, 20 to 25 minutes.

3. Stir in parsley and lemon juice. Season with salt and pepper to taste and serve.

BUTTERNUT SQUASH RISOTTO

✔ **WHY THIS RECIPE WORKS**

Butternut squash and risotto should make a perfect culinary couple, but too often the squash and rice never become properly intertwined. The squash is reduced to overly sweet orange blobs or the whole dish becomes a gluey squash paste. We wanted a creamy, orange-tinted rice fully infused with deep (but not overly sweet) squash flavor. To perfect our risotto, we concentrated on developing the flavor of the squash and keeping it tender. First, we sautéed the squash to intensify its flavor. Next, we found that adding the squash in two stages, half with the toasted rice and half just before serving, gave us great squash flavor and preserved its delicate texture. Finally, we sautéed the squash seeds and fibers, then steeped them in the chicken broth before straining the liquid and using it to cook the rice—this step infused the dish with sweet, earthy butternut squash flavor. Parmesan cheese added richness and fresh sage and nutmeg lent our risotto woodsy, warm notes.

BUTTERNUT SQUASH RISOTTO
SERVES 4

We found that a 2-pound squash consistently yields a cup or so more than the 3½ cups needed in step 1; the extra squash can be added to the skillet along with the squash fibers and seeds in step 2. To make this dish vegetarian, vegetable broth can be used instead of chicken broth, but the resulting risotto will have a more pronounced sweetness.

2 tablespoons olive oil
2 pounds butternut squash, peeled, seeded with fibers and seeds reserved, and cut into ½-inch cubes
  Salt and pepper
4 cups low-sodium chicken broth
1 cup water
4 tablespoons unsalted butter
2 small onions, chopped fine
2 garlic cloves, minced
2 cups Arborio rice
1½ cups dry white wine
1½ ounces Parmesan cheese, grated (¾ cup)
2 tablespoons minced fresh sage
¼ teaspoon ground nutmeg

1. Heat oil in 12-inch nonstick skillet over medium-high heat until shimmering. Add 3½ cups squash, spread in even layer, and cook without stirring until golden brown, 4 to 5 minutes. Stir in ¼ teaspoon salt and ¼ teaspoon pepper. Continue to cook, stirring occasionally, until squash is tender and browned, about 5 minutes. Transfer squash to bowl and set aside.

2. Return skillet to medium heat; add reserved squash fibers and seeds and any leftover squash cubes. Cook, stirring frequently to break up fibers, until lightly browned, about 4 minutes. Transfer to large saucepan and add broth and water. Cover saucepan and bring mixture to simmer over high heat, then reduce heat to medium-low to maintain bare simmer.

3. Melt 3 tablespoons butter in now-empty skillet over medium heat. Add onions, garlic, ½ teaspoon salt, and ½ teaspoon pepper and cook, stirring occasionally, until onions are softened, 5 to 7 minutes. Add rice to skillet and cook, stirring frequently, until grains are translucent around edges, about 3 minutes. Add wine and cook, stirring frequently, until fully absorbed, 4 to 5 minutes.

4. Meanwhile, strain hot broth mixture through fine-mesh strainer into medium bowl, pressing on solids to extract as much liquid as possible. Return strained broth to saucepan and discard solids; cover saucepan and set over low heat.

5. Add 3 cups hot broth mixture and half of reserved squash to rice. Simmer, stirring every 3 to 4 minutes, until liquid is absorbed and bottom of pan is almost dry, about 12 minutes.

6. Stir in ½ cup hot broth mixture and cook, stirring constantly, until absorbed, about 3 minutes; repeat with additional broth 2 or 3 times until rice is al dente. Off heat, stir in remaining 1 tablespoon butter, Parmesan, sage, and nutmeg; gently fold in remaining cooked squash. Serve immediately.

BUTTERNUT SQUASH RISOTTO WITH SPINACH AND TOASTED PINE NUTS

In step 2, after transferring sautéed squash seeds and fibers to saucepan, heat 1 teaspoon olive oil in now-empty skillet until shimmering. Add 4 ounces baby spinach (4 cups) and cook, covered, over medium heat, until leaves begin to wilt, about 2 minutes. Uncover and cook, stirring constantly, until fully wilted, about 30 seconds. Transfer spinach to fine-mesh strainer. Drain excess liquid from spinach and stir into risotto along with remaining squash in step 6. Top individual servings with ¼ cup toasted pine nuts.

MUSHROOM RISOTTO

✔ **WHY THIS RECIPE WORKS**

Mushroom risotto should be earthy-tasting, creamy, and rich—not bland and gummy with watery, flavorless mushrooms. For meaty, complex flavor, we used a combination of dried porcini and fresh mushrooms. To retain the textural bite of the fresh mushrooms, we cooked them separately with onions and garlic for flavor and added them to the finished risotto. A full cup of white wine contributed brightness and a decidedly un-Italian ingredient, soy sauce, helped to intensify the earthiness of the mushrooms and round out the flavors.

MUSHROOM RISOTTO
SERVES 6

White mushrooms, although less flavorful, make a fine substitution for the cremini mushrooms.

2	bay leaves
6	sprigs fresh thyme
4	sprigs fresh parsley plus 2 tablespoons minced parsley
1	ounce dried porcini mushrooms, rinsed
3¾	cups water
3½	cups low-sodium chicken broth
2	teaspoons soy sauce
6	tablespoons unsalted butter
1¼	pounds cremini mushrooms, trimmed and cut into quarters if small or sixths if medium or large
2	onions, chopped fine
	Salt and pepper
3	garlic cloves, minced
2	cups plus 2 tablespoons Arborio rice
1	cup dry white wine or dry vermouth
2	ounces Parmesan cheese, grated fine (1 cup)

1. Tie bay leaves, thyme sprigs, and parsley sprigs together with kitchen twine. Bring bundled herbs, porcini mushrooms, 3½ cups water, broth, and soy sauce to boil in medium saucepan over medium-high heat; reduce heat to medium-low and simmer until dried mushrooms are softened and fully hydrated, about 15 minutes. Remove and discard herb bundle and strain broth through fine-mesh strainer set over medium bowl; return liquid to saucepan and keep warm over low heat. Finely mince porcini and set aside.

2. Adjust oven rack to middle position and heat oven to 200 degrees. Melt 2 tablespoons butter in 12-inch non-stick skillet over medium-high heat. Add cremini mushrooms, half of onions, and ½ teaspoon salt and cook, stirring occasionally, until moisture released by mushrooms evaporates and mushrooms are well browned, about 7 minutes. Add garlic and cook until fragrant, about 30 seconds, then transfer mushrooms to bowl and keep warm in oven. Off heat, add remaining ¼ cup water to now-empty skillet and scrape with wooden spoon to loosen any browned bits; pour liquid from skillet into saucepan with broth.

3. Melt 3 tablespoons butter in large saucepan over medium heat. Add remaining onions and ¼ teaspoon salt and cook, stirring occasionally, until onions are softened, 5 to 7 minutes. Add rice and cook, stirring frequently, until grains are translucent around edges, about 3 minutes. Add wine and cook, stirring frequently, until fully absorbed, 2 to 3 minutes. Add minced porcini and 3½ cups hot broth mixture and cook, stirring every 2 to 3 minutes, until liquid is absorbed, 9 to 11 minutes. Stir in additional ½ cup broth every 2 to 3 minutes until rice is cooked through but grains are still somewhat firm at center, 10 to 12 minutes. Stir in remaining 1 tablespoon butter, then stir in mushrooms and any accumulated juices, Parmesan, and minced parsley. Season with salt and pepper to taste and serve immediately.

MUSHROOM RISOTTO WITH PANCETTA AND SAGE

Omit thyme. In step 3, omit 3 tablespoons butter. Cook 2 ounces finely chopped pancetta and 1 tablespoon butter in large saucepan over medium heat, stirring frequently, until pancetta has rendered some fat, about 5 minutes. Add remaining onions and cook until softened, 5 to 7 minutes. Proceed as directed, adding 1 tablespoon minced fresh sage along with Parmesan and parsley.

SOUTHERN SPOONBREAD

✓ WHY THIS RECIPE WORKS
Ideally, spoonbread should be as light as air, with a tender, rich crumb, but this can be difficult to achieve. Most recipes call for whisking cornmeal into simmering liquid before stirring in eggs and butter and baking. But if the whisking isn't done properly, the meal can separate from the liquid and turn into a bunch of lumps rather than a smooth mush. We found that the key to great spoonbread is nonstop whisking until the mixture has properly thickened and is lump-free. Both yellow and white cornmeal work well, but using the right grind is crucial: the cornmeal must be finely ground for the smoothest texture possible. Separating the eggs and beating the whites to stiff peaks before folding them in ensures a sky-high spoonbread.

SOUTHERN SPOONBREAD
SERVES 6 TO 8

If you can't find finely ground cornmeal, you can approximate it by processing medium-grind cornmeal in a food processor or blender. Processing will take several minutes, but eventually you will have little clouds of powder-fine meal in the bottom of the bowl. An 8-inch soufflé dish works beautifully, but any heavy straight-sided pan will work, even a cast-iron skillet. Because the spoonbread soon falls from its spectacular height, serve it as quickly as possible; even in its deflated state, though, spoonbread still tastes delicious. Serve leftovers with maple or cane syrup.

3	cups half-and-half
1	teaspoon salt
1	cup fine-ground cornmeal
2	tablespoons unsalted butter
3	large eggs, room temperature, separated

1. Heat oven to 350 degrees. Grease 6-cup soufflé dish.

2. Bring half-and-half and salt to

simmer in large saucepan. Reduce heat to low and slowly whisk in cornmeal. Continue whisking until cornmeal thickens and develops satin sheen, 2 to 4 minutes. Off heat, stir in butter; set aside.

3. Whisk egg yolks and 1 to 2 teaspoons water together in small bowl until lemon-colored and very frothy. Stir into cooled cornmeal mixture, a little at a time to keep egg yolks from cooking. Using stand mixer fitted with whisk, whip egg whites on medium-low speed until foamy, about 1 minute. Increase speed to medium-high and whip until stiff peaks form, 3 to 4 minutes; gently fold into cornmeal mixture.

4. Pour mixture into prepared dish. Bake until golden brown and risen above rim, about 45 minutes. Serve immediately.

SOUTHERN SPOONBREAD WITH CHEDDAR CHEESE

Stir in 1 cup shredded sharp cheddar cheese (4 ounces) along with butter.

CREAMY PARMESAN POLENTA

✔ WHY THIS RECIPE WORKS

If you don't stir polenta almost constantly, it forms intractable lumps. Is there a way to get creamy, smooth polenta with rich corn flavor, but without the fussy process? From the outset, we knew that the right type of cornmeal was essential. Coarse-ground degerminated cornmeal gave us the soft but hearty texture and nutty flavor we were looking for. Taking a clue from dried bean recipes, which use baking soda to help break down the tough bean skins and accelerate cooking, we added a pinch to our polenta. The baking soda helped soften the cornmeal's endosperm, which cut the cooking time in half and eliminated the need for stirring. Parmesan cheese and butter, stirred in at the last minute, ensured a satisfying, rich dish.

CREAMY PARMESAN POLENTA
SERVES 4

Coarse-ground degerminated cornmeal such as yellow grits (with grains the size of couscous) works best in this recipe. Avoid instant and quick-cooking products, as well as whole grain, stone-ground, and regular cornmeal. Do not omit the baking soda—it reduces the cooking time and makes for a creamier polenta. If the polenta bubbles or sputters even slightly after the first 10 minutes, the heat is too high and you may need a flame tamer. For a main course, serve the polenta with a topping (recipes follow) or with a wedge of rich cheese (like gorgonzola) or a meat sauce.

7½ cups water
1½ teaspoons salt
Pinch baking soda
1½ cups coarse-ground cornmeal
4 ounces Parmesan cheese, grated (2 cups), plus extra for serving
2 tablespoons unsalted butter
Pepper

1. Bring water to boil in large saucepan over medium-high heat. Stir in salt and baking soda. Slowly pour cornmeal into water in steady stream, while stirring back and forth with wooden spoon or rubber spatula. Bring mixture to boil, stirring constantly, about 1 minute. Reduce heat to lowest possible setting and cover.

2. After 5 minutes, whisk polenta to smooth out any lumps that may have formed, about 15 seconds. (Make sure to scrape down sides and bottom of pan.) Cover and continue to cook, without stirring, until grains of polenta are tender but slightly al dente, about 25 minutes longer. (Polenta should be loose and barely hold its shape but will continue to thicken as it cools.)

3. Remove from heat, stir in Parmesan and butter, and season with pepper to taste. Let stand, covered, for 5 minutes. Serve, passing extra Parmesan separately.

SAUTÉED CHERRY TOMATO AND FRESH MOZZARELLA TOPPING
MAKES ENOUGH FOR 4 SERVINGS

Don't stir the cheese into the sautéed tomatoes or it will melt prematurely and turn rubbery.

3 tablespoons extra-virgin olive oil
2 garlic cloves, peeled and sliced thin
Pinch red pepper flakes
Pinch sugar
1½ pounds cherry tomatoes, halved
Salt and pepper
6 ounces fresh mozzarella cheese, cut into ½-inch cubes (1 cup)
2 tablespoons shredded fresh basil

Heat oil, garlic, pepper flakes, and sugar in 12-inch nonstick skillet over medium-high heat until fragrant and sizzling, about 1 minute. Stir in tomatoes and cook until they just begin to soften, about 1 minute. Season with salt and pepper to taste and remove from heat. Spoon tomato mixture over individual portions of polenta, top with mozzarella, sprinkle with basil, and serve.

WILD MUSHROOM AND ROSEMARY TOPPING
MAKES ENOUGH FOR 4 SERVINGS

If you use shiitake mushrooms, they should be stemmed.

2 tablespoons unsalted butter
2 tablespoons olive oil
1 small onion, chopped fine
2 garlic cloves, minced
2 teaspoons minced fresh rosemary
1 pound wild mushrooms (such as cremini, shiitake, or oyster), trimmed and sliced
⅓ cup low-sodium chicken broth

1. Heat butter and oil in 12-inch non-stick skillet over medium-high heat until shimmering. Add onion and cook, stirring

frequently, until onion softens and begins to brown, 5 to 7 minutes. Stir in garlic and rosemary and cook until fragrant, about 30 seconds longer.

2. Add mushrooms and cook, stirring occasionally, until juices release, about 6 minutes. Add broth, and salt and pepper to taste; simmer briskly until sauce thickens, about 8 minutes. Spoon mushroom mixture over individual portions of polenta and serve.

BROCCOLI RABE, SUN-DRIED TOMATO, AND PINE NUT TOPPING

MAKES ENOUGH FOR 4 SERVINGS

½ cup oil-packed sun-dried tomatoes, chopped coarse
3 tablespoons extra-virgin olive oil
6 garlic cloves, minced
½ teaspoon red pepper flakes
Salt
1 pound broccoli rabe, trimmed and cut into 1½-inch pieces
¼ cup low-sodium chicken broth
3 tablespoons pine nuts, toasted

Heat sun-dried tomatoes, oil, garlic, pepper flakes, and ½ teaspoon salt in 12-inch nonstick skillet over medium-high heat, stirring frequently, until garlic is fragrant and slightly toasted, about 1½ minutes.

Add broccoli rabe and broth, cover, and cook until rabe turns bright green, about 2 minutes. Uncover and cook, stirring frequently, until most of broth has evaporated and rabe is just tender, 2 to 3 minutes. Season with salt to taste. Spoon broccoli rabe mixture over individual portions of polenta, sprinkle with pine nuts, and serve.

SWEET AND SOUR ONION RELISH TOPPING

MAKES ENOUGH FOR 4 SERVINGS

2 tablespoons extra-virgin olive oil
2 red onions, sliced thin
4 sprigs fresh thyme
Salt and pepper
2 tablespoons balsamic vinegar
2 tablespoons water
1 tablespoon light brown sugar
6 ounces extra-sharp cheddar cheese, shredded (1½ cups)
½ cup toasted walnuts, chopped coarse

Heat oil in 12-inch nonstick skillet over medium-high heat until shimmering. Add onions, thyme, and ½ teaspoon salt and cook, stirring frequently, until onions soften and begin to brown, 5 to 7 minutes. Reduce heat to low, stir in vinegar,

water, and sugar and simmer until liquid has evaporated and onions are glossy, 5 to 7 minutes. Discard thyme and season with salt and pepper to taste. Serve over polenta, sprinkling individual portions with cheese and walnuts.

COUSCOUS

✔ WHY THIS RECIPE WORKS

Couscous, granules of semolina, traditionally serves as a sauce absorber under stews and braises, but it can also be a quick and flavorful side dish for a variety of foods. We wanted to develop a classic version for saucy dishes as well as a handful of flavor-packed versions, as convenient as the box kind, but much fresher-tasting. Toasting the couscous grains in butter deepened their flavor and helped them cook up fluffy and separate. And to bump up the flavor even further, we replaced half of the cooking liquid with chicken broth. For our enriched variations, dried fruit, nuts, and citrus juice added textural interest and sweet, bright notes.

CLASSIC COUSCOUS

SERVES 4 TO 6

2 tablespoons unsalted butter
2 cups couscous
1 cup water
1 cup low-sodium chicken broth
1 teaspoon salt
Pepper

Melt butter in medium saucepan over medium-high heat. Add couscous and cook, stirring frequently, until grains are just beginning to brown, about 5 minutes. Add water, broth, and salt and stir briefly to combine. Cover and remove pan from heat. Let stand until grains are tender, about 7 minutes. Uncover and fluff grains with fork. Season with pepper to taste and serve.

TEST KITCHEN TIP NO. 50 CORNMEAL VARIETIES

In the supermarket, cornmeal can be labeled anything from yellow grits to corn semolina. Forget the names. When shopping for the right product to make polenta, there are three things to consider: "instant" or "quick-cooking" versus the traditional style, degerminated or full-grain meal, and grind size. Instant and quick-cooking cornmeals are parcooked and comparatively bland—leave them on the shelf. Though we loved the full-corn flavor of whole grain cornmeal, it remains slightly gritty no matter how long you cook it. We prefer degerminated cornmeal, in which the hard hull and germ are removed from each kernel (check the back label or ingredient list to see if your cornmeal is degerminated; if it's not explicitly labeled as such, you can assume it's whole grain).

As for grind, we found coarser grains brought the most desirable and pillowy texture to our Creamy Parmesan Polenta (page 234). However, grind coarseness can vary dramatically from brand to brand since there are no standards to ensure consistency: One manufacturer's "coarse" may be another's "fine." To identify coarse polenta as really coarse, the grains should be about the size of couscous.

COUSCOUS WITH DATES AND PISTACHIOS

Increase butter to 3 tablespoons and add ½ cup chopped dates, 1 tablespoon grated fresh ginger, and ½ teaspoon ground cardamom to saucepan with couscous. Increase amount of water to 1¼ cups. Stir ¾ cup coarsely chopped toasted pistachios, 3 tablespoons minced fresh cilantro, and 2 teaspoons lemon juice into couscous before serving.

COUSCOUS WITH DRIED CHERRIES AND PECANS

Increase butter to 3 tablespoons and add ½ cup coarsely chopped dried cherries, 2 minced garlic cloves, ¾ teaspoon garam masala, and ⅛ teaspoon cayenne pepper to saucepan with couscous. Increase amount of water to 1¼ cups. Stir ¾ cup coarsely chopped toasted pecans, 2 thinly sliced scallions, and 2 teaspoons lemon juice into couscous before serving.

COUSCOUS WITH CARROTS, RAISINS, AND PINE NUTS

Increase butter to 3 tablespoons and add 2 grated carrots and ½ teaspoon ground cinnamon; cook, stirring frequently, until carrot softens, about 2 minutes. Add ½ cup raisins to saucepan with couscous and increase water to 1¼ cups. Stir ¾ cup toasted pine nuts, 3 tablespoons minced fresh cilantro, ½ teaspoon grated orange zest, and 1 tablespoon orange juice into couscous before serving.

COUSCOUS WITH SHALLOTS, GARLIC, AND ALMONDS

Increase butter to 3 tablespoons and add 3 thinly sliced shallots; cook, stirring frequently, until softened and lightly browned, about 5 minutes. Add 1 minced garlic clove and cook until fragrant, about 30 seconds. Stir ¾ cup toasted sliced almonds, ¾ cup minced fresh parsley, ½ teaspoon grated lemon zest, and 2 teaspoons lemon juice into couscous before serving.

TOASTED ORZO

✔ WHY THIS RECIPE WORKS
Most versions of orzo pilaf are bland at best, little more than a generic starch used to bulk up a meal. We wanted a flavorful orzo pilaf that would hold its own when paired with any main dish. Toasting the orzo until golden brown before cooking it was the key to an outstanding pilaf. After toasting the orzo with butter and onion, we added a combination of white wine and chicken broth and cooked the orzo over moderate heat. A generous amount of peas made our pilaf more substantial and added some color. Finely grated Parmesan gave the pilaf a creamy texture, while a pinch of nutmeg added warmth.

TOASTED ORZO WITH PEAS AND PARMESAN

SERVES 6 TO 8

2	tablespoons unsalted butter
1	onion, chopped fine
	Salt and pepper
2	garlic cloves, minced
1	pound orzo
3½	cups low-sodium chicken broth
¾	cup dry white wine or dry vermouth
1¾	cups frozen peas
2	ounces Parmesan cheese, grated (1 cup)
	Pinch ground nutmeg

1. Melt butter in 12-inch nonstick skillet over medium-high heat. Add onion and ¾ teaspoon salt and cook, stirring frequently, until onion has softened and is beginning to brown, 5 to 7 minutes. Add garlic and cook until fragrant, about 30 seconds. Add orzo and cook, stirring frequently, until most of orzo is lightly browned and golden, 5 to 6 minutes. Off heat, add broth and wine. Bring to boil over medium-high heat; reduce heat to medium-low and simmer, stirring occasionally, until all liquid has been absorbed and orzo is tender, 10 to 15 minutes.

2. Stir in peas, Parmesan, nutmeg, and pepper to taste. Off heat, let stand until peas are heated through, about 2 minutes. Season with salt to taste and serve.

TOASTED ORZO WITH BACON, ROSEMARY, AND PEAS

Cook 4 slices bacon, cut into ¼-inch pieces, in 12-inch nonstick skillet over medium-high heat until crisp and brown, about 5 minutes. Using slotted spoon, transfer bacon to paper towel–lined plate; set aside. Substitute bacon fat for butter and reduce salt to ½ teaspoon. Add 1 rosemary sprig to pan with broth and wine. Stir reserved bacon in with Parmesan and nutmeg and discard rosemary.

TOASTED ORZO WITH FENNEL, ORANGE, AND OLIVES

Add 1 small fennel bulb, stalks discarded, halved, cored, and cut into ¼-inch dice, ¾ teaspoon fennel seeds, and pinch red pepper flakes along with onion. Add 1 teaspoon grated orange zest along with garlic and substitute ½ cup coarsely chopped olives for peas.

BLACK BEANS

✓ WHY THIS RECIPE WORKS

Black beans are more often than not dull, dry, and mealy. We wanted tender, creamy black beans that were boldly flavored. We started by cooking them with a ham hock for meaty, smoky flavor. We bypassed the usual salt-soaking step and instead added salt right at the start of cooking to help season the beans properly. For a flavorful background, we cooked our sofrito—the aromatic trio of onion, bell pepper, and garlic—in rendered bacon fat, then mashed a portion of the beans with the sofrito to ensure our dish had the creamy, thick consistency we were after. Finishing the black beans with balsamic vinegar and cilantro added bright, fresh notes.

BLACK BEANS WITH BACON AND BALSAMIC VINEGAR

SERVES 6

Garnish the dish with a spoonful of sour cream, a sprinkling of minced red onion, and a dash or two of hot sauce.

BEANS
12	cups water
1	pound dried black beans (2½ cups), picked over and rinsed
1	smoked ham hock, rinsed
1	green bell pepper, stemmed, seeded, and quartered
1	onion, chopped fine
6	garlic cloves, minced
2	bay leaves
1½	teaspoons salt

TEST KITCHEN TIP NO. 51 **STORING DRIED BEANS**

When shopping for beans, it is imperative to select "fresh" dried beans. Buy those that are uniform in size and have a smooth exterior. When dried beans are fully hydrated and cooked, they should be plump with a taut skin and have creamy insides; spent beans will have wrinkled skins and a dry, almost gritty texture. Uncooked beans should be stored in a cool, dry place in a sealed plastic or glass container. Though dried beans can be stored for up to one year, it is best to use them within a month or two of purchase.

SOFRITO
8	slices bacon, cut into ½-inch pieces
1	onion, chopped fine
1	red bell pepper, stemmed, seeded, and minced
8	garlic cloves, minced
2	teaspoons dried oregano
	Salt and pepper
1½	teaspoons ground cumin
2	teaspoons balsamic vinegar
½	cup minced fresh cilantro, minced

1	recipe Simple White Rice (page 222)

1. FOR THE BEANS: Bring all ingredients to boil over medium-high heat in Dutch oven, skimming foam as necessary. Reduce heat to low and simmer, partially covered, adding more water if cooking liquid reduces to level of beans, until tender but not splitting, about 2 hours. Remove ham hock. When cool enough to handle, remove ham from bone, discard bone and skin, and cut meat into bite-size pieces; set aside.

2. FOR THE SOFRITO: Meanwhile, cook bacon in 10-inch skillet over medium heat until crisp and brown, about 5 minutes. Using slotted spoon, transfer bacon to paper towel–lined plate; set aside. Add onion, bell pepper, garlic, oregano, and ¾ teaspoon salt to fat left in pan and cook until vegetables have softened, 8 to 10 minutes. Add cumin and cook until fragrant, about 1 minute.

3. Add 1 cup beans and 2 cups bean cooking liquid into pan with sofrito and mash beans with potato masher or fork until smooth. Simmer over medium heat until liquid is reduced and thickened, about 6 minutes. Transfer sofrito mixture and reserved ham and bacon to pot and simmer until beans are creamy and liquid thickens to sauce consistency, 15 to 20 minutes. Add vinegar and simmer for 1 minute. Stir in cilantro, season with salt and pepper to taste, and serve over rice.

BLACK BEANS WITH HAM HOCK AND DRY SHERRY

Omit bacon and substitute 2 tablespoons olive oil for bacon fat in step 2. Substitute 1 small green bell pepper for red bell pepper in sofrito. Add 1 teaspoon ground coriander to sofrito along with cumin, substitute 1 tablespoon dry sherry for balsamic vinegar, and omit cilantro.

CUBAN-STYLE BLACK BEANS AND RICE

✓ WHY THIS RECIPE WORKS

Beans and rice is a familiar combination the world over, but Cuban black beans and rice is unique in that the rice is cooked in the inky concentrated liquid left over from cooking the beans, which renders the grains just as flavorful. For our own superlative version, we reserved a portion of the sofrito (the traditional combination of garlic, bell pepper, and onion) and simmered it with our beans to infuse them with flavor. Instead of just draining off and throwing away the flavorful bean cooking liquid, we used it again to cook our rice and beans together. Lightly browning the remaining sofrito vegetables and spices with rendered salt pork added complex, meaty flavor, and baking the dish in the oven eliminated the crusty bottom that can form when the dish is cooked on the stove.

CUBAN-STYLE BLACK BEANS AND RICE

SERVES 6 TO 8

It is important to use lean—not fatty—salt pork. If you can't find it, substitute 6 slices of bacon. If using bacon, decrease the cooking time in step 4 to 8 minutes. You will need a Dutch oven with a tight-fitting lid for this recipe.

    Salt
1   cup dried black beans, picked over and rinsed
2   cups low-sodium chicken broth
2   cups water
2   large green bell peppers, stemmed, seeded, and halved
1   large onion, halved at equator and peeled, root end left intact
1   head garlic, 5 cloves minced, rest of head halved at equator with skin left intact
2   bay leaves
1½   cups long-grain white rice
2   tablespoons olive oil
6   ounces lean salt pork, cut into ¼-inch dice
4   teaspoons ground cumin
1   tablespoon minced fresh oregano
2   tablespoons red wine vinegar
2   scallions, sliced thin
    Lime wedges

1. Dissolve 1½ tablespoons salt in 2 quarts cold water in large bowl or container. Add beans and soak at room temperature for at least 8 hours or up to 24 hours. Drain and rinse well.

2. In Dutch oven, stir together drained beans, broth, water, 1 pepper half, 1 onion half (with root end), halved garlic head, bay leaves, and 1 teaspoon salt. Bring to simmer over medium-high heat, cover, and reduce heat to low. Cook until beans are just soft, 30 to 35 minutes. Using tongs, remove and discard pepper, onion, garlic,

and bay leaves. Drain beans in colander set over large bowl, reserving 2½ cups bean cooking liquid. (If you don't have enough bean cooking liquid, add water to equal 2½ cups.) Do not wash out Dutch oven.

3. Adjust oven rack to middle position and heat oven to 350 degrees. Place rice in large fine-mesh strainer and rinse under cold running water until water runs clear, about 1½ minutes. Shake strainer vigorously to remove all excess water; set rice aside. Cut remaining peppers and onion into 2-inch pieces and process in food processor until broken into rough ¼-inch pieces, about 8 pulses, scraping down bowl as necessary; set vegetables aside.

4. In now-empty Dutch oven, heat 1 tablespoon oil and salt pork over medium-low heat and cook, stirring frequently, until lightly browned and rendered, 15 to 20 minutes. Add remaining 1 tablespoon oil, chopped peppers and onion, cumin, and oregano. Increase heat to medium and continue to cook, stirring frequently, until vegetables are softened and beginning to brown, 10 to 15 minutes longer. Add minced garlic and cook, stirring constantly, until fragrant, about 1 minute. Add rice and stir to coat, about 30 seconds.

5. Stir in beans, reserved bean cooking liquid, vinegar, and ½ teaspoon salt. Increase heat to medium-high and bring to simmer. Cover and transfer to oven. Cook until liquid is absorbed and rice is tender, about 30 minutes. Fluff with fork and let rest, uncovered, 5 minutes. Serve, passing scallions and lime wedges separately.

VEGETARIAN CUBAN-STYLE BLACK BEANS AND RICE

Substitute water for chicken broth and omit salt pork. Add 1 tablespoon tomato paste with vegetables in step 4 and increase amount of salt in step 5 to 1½ teaspoons.

BOSTON BAKED BEANS

✔ WHY THIS RECIPE WORKS
To create a recipe for Boston baked beans packed with multiple levels of intense flavor, yet traditional enough to make a New Englander proud, we started with a combination of salt pork and bacon and browned them in a Dutch oven before adding dried white beans. Using the oven, not the stovetop, ensured the beans cooked through gently and evenly. Cider vinegar gave our sauce tanginess while mustard and molasses boosted its flavor. We removed the lid for the last hour of cooking to reduce the sauce to a syrupy, intensified state.

BOSTON BAKED BEANS

SERVES 4 TO 6

Be sure to use mild molasses; dark molasses will taste too strong.

4   ounces salt pork, rind removed, cut into ½-inch pieces
2   slices bacon, cut into ¼-inch pieces
1   onion, chopped fine
9   cups water
1   pound dried small white beans (2½ cups), picked over and rinsed
½   cup plus 1 tablespoon mild molasses
1½   tablespoons brown mustard
    Salt and pepper
1   teaspoon cider vinegar

1. Adjust oven rack to lower-middle position and heat oven to 300 degrees. Cook salt pork and bacon in Dutch oven over medium heat, stirring occasionally, until lightly browned and most of fat is rendered, about 7 minutes. Add onion and continue to cook, stirring occasionally, until onion is softened, 5 to 7 minutes. Add water, beans, ½ cup molasses, mustard, and 1¼ teaspoons salt, increase heat

Why does soaking dried beans in salted water make them cook up with softer skins? Calcium and magnesium, two minerals present in beans, strengthen the cell walls of the bean skins, making it difficult for water to penetrate the skins and soften the beans. These minerals are also commonly found in tap water. You could use distilled water to avoid reinforcing the toughening effect of the minerals, but a handier and more effective solution is to add salt to tap water. As the beans soak, the sodium ions in the salt replace some of the calcium and magnesium ions in the skins. Because sodium ions are weaker than mineral ions, they allow more water to penetrate into the skins, leading to a softer texture. During soaking, the sodium ions will only filter partway into the beans, so their greatest effect is on the cells in the outermost part of the beans.

to medium-high, and bring to boil. Cover pot and transfer to oven. Bake until beans are tender, about 4 hours, stirring halfway through cooking.

2. Carefully remove lid and continue to bake until liquid has thickened to syrupy consistency, 1 to 1½ hours longer. Remove beans from oven. Stir in remaining 1 tablespoon molasses and vinegar and season with salt and pepper to taste. Serve. (The baked beans can be cooled and refrigerated in an airtight container for up to 4 days.)

RED BEANS AND RICE

✔ WHY THIS RECIPE WORKS

Red beans and rice is a Monday night tradition in New Orleans, but some of its key ingredients are nearly impossible to find outside Louisiana. Plus, many recipes are plagued by blown-out beans, bland or pasty sauces, and flavors that never quite come together. We wanted a smoky, spicy, creamy stew that stayed true to its Cajun roots. To replicate this recipe using ingredients easily found in our neighborhood supermarket, we made some simple substitutions: small red beans for the traditional local dried red beans, bacon for hard-to-find tasso, and vinegar for pickled pork shoulder (not a direct substitution, but it provided ample tang). Soaking the beans overnight in a saltwater brine made their texture

even better and seasoned them all the way through. Fine-tuning the proportions of sautéed green peppers, onions, and celery gave the dish balance, and the right ratio of chicken broth to water added complexity without giving the dish an overpowering chicken flavor.

RED BEANS AND RICE
SERVES 6 TO 8

If you are pressed for time you can "quick-brine" your beans. In step 1, combine the salt, water, and beans in a large Dutch oven and bring to a boil over high heat. Remove the pot from the heat, cover, and let stand 1 hour. Drain and rinse the beans and proceed with the recipe. If you can't find andouille sausage, substitute kielbasa. Tasso can be difficult to find, but if you use it, omit the bacon and paprika in step 2 and cook 4 ounces finely chopped tasso in 2 teaspoons vegetable oil until lightly browned, 4 to 6 minutes, then proceed with the recipe. In order for the starch from the beans to thicken the cooking liquid, it is important to maintain a vigorous simmer in step 2. The beans can be cooled and refrigerated in an airtight container for up to 2 days. To reheat, add enough water to the beans to thin them slightly.

    Salt and pepper
1 pound small red beans (2½ cups), picked over and rinsed
4 slices bacon, chopped fine
1 onion, chopped fine

1 small green bell pepper, stemmed, seeded, and chopped fine
1 celery rib, minced
3 garlic cloves, minced
1 teaspoon fresh thyme
1 teaspoon sweet paprika
2 bay leaves
¼ teaspoon cayenne pepper
6 cups water
3 cups low-sodium chicken broth
8 ounces andouille sausage, halved lengthwise and sliced ¼ inch thick
1 teaspoon red wine vinegar, plus extra for seasoning
1 recipe Simple White Rice (page 222)
3 scallions, sliced thin
    Hot sauce (optional)

1. Dissolve 3 tablespoons salt in 4 quarts cold water in large bowl or container. Add beans and soak at room temperature for at least 8 hours or up to 24 hours. Drain and rinse well.

2. Heat bacon in Dutch oven over medium heat, stirring occasionally, until browned and fat is almost fully rendered, 5 to 8 minutes. Add onion, green pepper, and celery and cook, stirring frequently, until vegetables are softened, 6 to 7 minutes. Stir in garlic, thyme, paprika, bay leaves, cayenne, and ¼ teaspoon black pepper and cook until fragrant, about 30 seconds. Stir in beans, water, and broth and bring to boil over high heat. Reduce heat and vigorously simmer, stirring occasionally, until beans are just soft and liquid begins to thicken, 45 to 60 minutes.

3. Stir in sausage and 1 teaspoon vinegar and cook until liquid is thick and beans are fully tender and creamy, about 30 minutes. Season with salt, pepper, and additional vinegar to taste. Serve over rice, sprinkling with scallions and passing hot sauce separately, if desired.

REFRIED BEANS

✔ WHY THIS RECIPE WORKS

Refried beans are all too often mealy, dry, and flavorless. We wanted deeply flavored refried beans that boasted a rich, creamy texture. In traditional frijoles refritos, dried pinto beans are cooked in lard and mashed. To start, we found that dried beans aren't essential—rinsed canned pinto beans work just fine. For authentic flavor, we reached for salt pork, which we sautéed to render its fat. Using the fat to cook the onion and chiles deepened the flavor of the beans exponentially. Processing a portion of the beans with broth created the creamy texture we were after, while pulsing the remaining beans ensured some chunky bites. Onion, garlic, two types of chiles, and cumin gave the dish complexity, and cilantro and lime juice added at the end gave our refried beans brightness.

REFRIED BEANS
SERVES 4 TO 6

Refried beans are an essential component of our Huevos Rancheros (page 540).

- ½   cup low-sodium chicken broth
- 2   (15-ounce) cans pinto beans, rinsed
- 1   tablespoon vegetable oil
- 3   ounces salt pork, rind removed, chopped fine
- 1   small onion, chopped fine
- 1   jalapeño chile, stemmed, seeded, and minced
- 1   poblano chile, stemmed, seeded, and minced
- ¼   teaspoon salt
- 3   small garlic cloves, minced
- ½   teaspoon ground cumin
- 1   tablespoon minced fresh cilantro
- 2   teaspoons lime juice (optional)

1. Process broth and all but 1 cup beans in food processor until smooth, about 15 seconds, scraping down bowl if necessary. Add remaining beans and process until slightly chunky, about 10 pulses.

2. Heat oil in 12-inch nonstick skillet over medium heat until shimmering. Add salt pork and cook, stirring occasionally, until fat has rendered and pork is well browned, about 10 to 15 minutes. Using slotted spoon, transfer pork to small bowl and discard (you should have about 2 tablespoons of fat left in skillet).

3. Increase heat to medium-high and add onion, chiles, and salt and cook, stirring occasionally, until softened and beginning to brown, about 5 minutes. Add garlic and cumin and cook, stirring frequently, until fragrant, about 30 seconds. Add beans and stir until thoroughly combined. Reduce heat to medium and cook, stirring occasionally, until beans are thick and creamy, about 5 minutes. Stir in cilantro and lime juice, if using, and serve.

SIMPLE CANNELLINI BEANS

✔ WHY THIS RECIPE WORKS

For beans with a creamy texture and well-seasoned flavor, forget conventional wisdom, which warns against salting beans before they're cooked. Our testing revealed that adding salt to the overnight soaking liquid (2 teaspoons per quart of water)—in effect "brining" the beans—yields better-seasoned and more evenly cooked results. We also found that a bay leaf and garlic add complementary flavors.

SIMPLE CANNELLINI BEANS
SERVES 4 TO 6

These beans are especially good served with braised meats like braised lamb shanks (see page 128) in lieu of mashed potatoes or polenta. If you're serving them with less rich fare, drizzle the beans with extra-virgin olive oil and season them with salt and pepper.

-     Salt
- 8   ounces dried cannellini beans (1¼ cups), picked over and rinsed
- 4   garlic cloves, peeled
- 1   bay leaf

1. Dissolve 4 teaspoons salt in 2 quarts cold water in large bowl or container. Add beans and soak at room temperature for at least 8 hours or up to 24 hours. Drain and rinse well.

2. Bring beans, garlic cloves, bay leaf, and 7 cups water to simmer in large saucepan. Simmer, partially covered, until beans are just tender, 30 to 40 minutes. Off heat, stir in 1½ teaspoons salt, cover, and let stand until completely tender, about 15 minutes longer. Drain beans; discard garlic cloves and bay leaf. Serve.

TEST KITCHEN TIP NO. 53   RINSING CANNED BEANS

Canned beans are made by pressure-cooking dried beans directly in the can with water, salt, and preservatives. As the beans cook, starches and proteins leach into the liquid, thickening it. To find out if rinsing the beans is really necessary, we used canned beans in two recipes: chickpeas for Restaurant-Style Hummus (page 8) and red kidney beans for Simple Beef Chili with Kidney Beans (page 96). Tasters found no difference in the chili; there are so many bold flavors and contrasting textures in this dish that rinsing the beans didn't matter.

We detected notable differences in the hummus. Most tasters thought the version with rinsed beans was brighter in flavor and less pasty than the version with unrinsed beans. So while rinsing the beans may not be necessary for a robust dish like chili, a thick, salty bean liquid does have the potential to throw a simpler recipe, such as hummus (or Refried Beans), off-kilter. As rinsing beans only takes a few seconds, we recommend doing so.

CHAPTER 8   Vegetables

STEAMED ARTICHOKES

✔ WHY THIS RECIPE WORKS

There are several routes we could have taken for cooking fresh artichokes—roasting, braising, boiling, microwaving, or steaming—and we found steaming produced evenly cooked artichokes with an intense, rich flavor and was easy and quick. Some recipes call for snipping the tip of each sharp, pointy leaf, but we found we could skip this tedious step since the tips soften as they cook. We also found adding a lemon to the pot, as directed in a lot of recipes, didn't help preserve the color of vegetable—it turned a muddier green color no matter what—so we skipped that step. A steamer basket proved useful but not necessary when we steamed whole artichokes, as we could use the artichoke's trimmings as a rack. Our method worked well for hearts as well as whole artichokes and, complemented by a flavorful vinaigrette, they were a guaranteed success.

STEAMED ARTICHOKE HEARTS
SERVES 4

Toss the warm artichoke hearts with butter and lemon juice and serve as a vegetable or cool them to room temperature, drizzle with a vinaigrette (recipes follow), and serve as an antipasto or salad.

- 4 large artichokes (10–12 ounces each) or 12 baby artichokes (2–4 ounces each)
- ½ teaspoon salt

1. Trim, peel, and halve artichokes, then scrape out purple leaves and fuzzy choke. Fit large saucepan with steamer basket. Add water, keeping level below basket. Bring water to boil, add artichoke hearts, and sprinkle with salt. Cover and steam over medium-high heat until tender, about 20 minutes for large hearts (10 minutes if halved) or about 10 minutes for baby hearts.

2. Transfer artichoke hearts to serving bowl and serve. (Artichoke hearts can be refrigerated overnight; bring to room temperature before serving.)

STEAMED WHOLE ARTICHOKES
SERVES 4

The artichokes are steamed upside down but served right side up. The entire artichoke cannot be eaten. The cooked heart can be eaten with a knife and fork. The edible portion at the bottom of the leaves is best scraped off with your teeth. The artichokes can be served warm or at room temperature with melted butter or with a vinaigrette (recipes follow).

- 4 large artichokes (10–12 ounces each) or 12 baby artichokes (2–4 ounces each)
- ½ teaspoon salt

1. Using chef's knife, cut off stem so that artichoke sits upright, then trim off top quarter of artichoke.

2. Fit large saucepan with steamer basket. Add water, keeping level below basket, and bring water to boil. Place prepared artichokes, stem end up, in steamer basket. Sprinkle artichokes with salt, cover, and steam over medium-high heat until tender, about 40 minutes for large artichokes or 25 minutes for baby artichokes (outer leaves should pull away easily and stem end should be thoroughly tender).

3. Gently remove artichokes with tongs. Serve immediately or cool, stem end up, to room temperature. (Artichokes can be refrigerated overnight; bring to room temperature before serving.)

PREPARING ARTICHOKE HEARTS FOR STEAMING

1. Holding artichoke by stem, bend back and snap off thick outer leaves, leaving bottom portion of each leaf attached. Continue snapping off leaves until light yellow inner leaves are exposed.

2. Using paring knife, trim away dark skin where leaves were snapped off.

3. Cut dark, purplish tip off top of choke.

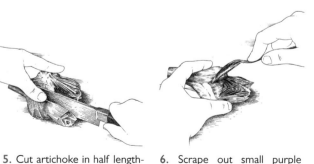

4. Using vegetable peeler, peel away dark, tough skin covering stem, then trim bottom ½ inch off stem.

5. Cut artichoke in half lengthwise.

6. Scrape out small purple leaves and the fuzzy choke in center with a melon baller or spoon.

BALSAMIC VINAIGRETTE

MAKES ENOUGH FOR 1 RECIPE
STEAMED ARTICHOKE HEARTS OR
STEAMED WHOLE ARTICHOKES

Using a good balsamic vinegar makes a difference here.

- ¼ cup balsamic vinegar
- 2 tablespoons sherry, red, or white wine vinegar
- ½ teaspoon salt
- ¼ teaspoon pepper
- ⅔ cup olive oil

Whisk balsamic vinegar, wine vinegar, salt, and pepper together in small bowl. Gradually whisk in oil so mixture emulsifies.

LEMON-CHIVE VINAIGRETTE

MAKES ENOUGH FOR 1 RECIPE
STEAMED ARTICHOKE HEARTS OR
STEAMED WHOLE ARTICHOKES

Fresh dill or parsley can be substituted for the chives.

- 4½ tablespoons fresh lemon juice
- ½ teaspoon salt
- ⅔ cup olive oil
- 2 tablespoons chopped fresh chives

Whisk lemon juice and ½ teaspoon salt in small bowl. Gradually whisk in oil so mixture emulsifies. Just before serving, stir in chives.

TEST KITCHEN TIP NO. 54 ARTICHOKES—DETERMINING FRESHNESS

The leaves of a fresh artichoke should look plump and not shriveled. When bent back, the leaves should snap, not tear. A small amount of brown discoloration at the stem and tips is fine, but avoid shriveled brown stems and leaves. Choose artichokes that feel heaviest.

SIMPLE BROILED ASPARAGUS

✔ WHY THIS RECIPE WORKS

Broiling asparagus concentrates its flavor and helps to lightly caramelize its exterior, and perhaps best of all, it can be done in just minutes. And while we enjoyed the spears as is—with a little oil, salt, and pepper—we also came up with a few complementary light vinaigrettes, which we could whisk together while the asparagus cooked. All we had to do was drizzle the dressing over the hot asparagus before serving and voilà, a perfect quick side dish worthy of a special-occasion meal.

SIMPLE BROILED ASPARAGUS
SERVES 6 TO 8

Serve with one of the vinaigrettes (recipes follow) if desired.

- 2 pounds thin asparagus, trimmed (see illustration on page 179)
- 1 tablespoon olive oil
  Salt and pepper

1. Adjust oven rack 4 inches from broiler element and heat broiler.

2. Toss asparagus with oil, season with salt and pepper to taste, then lay spears in single layer on rimmed baking sheet. Broil until asparagus is tender and lightly browned, 8 to 10 minutes, shaking pan halfway through cooking to turn spears. Cool asparagus 5 minutes and serve.

SOY-GINGER VINAIGRETTE

MAKES ENOUGH FOR 1 RECIPE
SIMPLE BROILED ASPARAGUS

Pair broiled asparagus with this vinaigrette when you're serving an Asian-inspired menu.

- ¼ cup lime juice (2 limes)
- 3 tablespoons toasted sesame oil
- 3 tablespoons soy sauce
- 1 tablespoon honey
- 2 scallions, minced
- 1 tablespoon grated fresh ginger
- 2 garlic cloves, minced

Whisk all ingredients together in small bowl.

LEMON-SHALLOT VINAIGRETTE

MAKES ENOUGH FOR 1 RECIPE
SIMPLE BROILED ASPARAGUS

Make sure to zest the lemon before you juice it.

- ⅓ cup extra-virgin olive oil
- 1 shallot, minced
- 1 tablespoon minced fresh thyme
- 1 teaspoon grated lemon zest plus 1 tablespoon juice
- ¼ teaspoon Dijon mustard
  Salt and pepper

Whisk all ingredients together in small bowl and season with salt and pepper to taste.

TOMATO-BASIL VINAIGRETTE

MAKES ENOUGH FOR 1 RECIPE
SIMPLE BROILED ASPARAGUS

Make this vinaigrette when tomatoes are at their peak of ripeness.

- 1 tomato, cored, seeded, and chopped fine (½ cup)
- 3 tablespoons extra-virgin olive oil

1 shallot, minced
1½ tablespoons lemon juice
1 tablespoon minced fresh basil
Salt and pepper

Whisk all ingredients together in small bowl and season with salt and pepper to taste.

BACON, RED ONION, AND BALSAMIC VINAIGRETTE

MAKES ENOUGH FOR 1 RECIPE
SIMPLE BROILED ASPARAGUS

Using a good balsamic vinegar makes a difference here.

6 slices bacon, cut into ¼-inch pieces
¼ cup extra-virgin olive oil
¼ cup balsamic vinegar
2 tablespoons minced red onion
1 tablespoon minced fresh parsley
Salt and pepper

Cook bacon in 10-inch skillet over medium heat until crisp, 5 to 7 minutes. Transfer bacon to paper towel–lined plate and set aside. Whisk oil, vinegar, onion, and parsley together in small bowl and season with salt and pepper to taste. Drizzle over asparagus, sprinkle with bacon, and serve immediately.

PAN-ROASTED ASPARAGUS

✔ WHY THIS RECIPE WORKS
Pan-roasting is a simple stovetop cooking method that delivers crisp, evenly browned spears without the fuss of having to rotate each spear individually. We started with thicker spears (thin ones overcooked before browning) and arranged them in the pan with half pointed in one direction and half in the other. To help the asparagus release moisture, which would encourage caramelization and better flavor, we parcooked it, covered, with butter and oil before browning it. The water evaporating from the butter helped to steam the asparagus, producing bright green, crisp-tender spears. At this point, we removed the lid and cranked up the heat until the spears were evenly browned on the bottom. We found there was no need to brown the asparagus all over; tasters preferred the flavor of spears browned on only one side and, as a bonus, the half-browned spears never had a chance to go limp. We then came up with a few variations that included accent ingredients like cherry tomatoes, olives, sautéed red peppers, and goat cheese. We simply cooked any garnish ingredients first, then set them aside while we prepared the asparagus.

PAN-ROASTED ASPARAGUS

SERVES 4 TO 6

This recipe works best with asparagus that is at least ½ inch thick near the base. If using thinner spears, reduce the covered cooking time to 3 minutes and the uncovered cooking time to 5 minutes. Do not use pencil-thin asparagus; it cannot withstand the heat and overcooks too easily.

1 tablespoon olive oil
1 tablespoon unsalted butter
2 pounds thick asparagus (see note), trimmed
Salt and pepper
½ lemon (optional)

1. Heat oil and butter in 12-inch skillet over medium-high heat. When butter has melted, add half of asparagus to skillet with tips pointed in one direction; add remaining spears with tips pointed in opposite direction. Using tongs, distribute spears evenly (spears will not quite fit into single layer); cover and cook until asparagus is bright green and still crisp, about 5 minutes.

2. Uncover and increase heat to high; season asparagus with salt and pepper to taste. Cook until spears are tender and well browned along one side, 5 to 7 minutes, using tongs to occasionally move spears from center of pan to edge of pan to ensure all are browned. Transfer asparagus to serving dish, adjust seasonings with salt and pepper, and, if desired, squeeze lemon half over spears. Serve immediately.

PAN-ROASTED ASPARAGUS WITH TOASTED GARLIC AND PARMESAN

Heat 2 tablespoons olive oil and 3 garlic cloves, sliced thin, in 12-inch skillet over medium heat. Cook, stirring occasionally, until garlic is crisp and golden but not dark brown, about 5 minutes. Using slotted spoon, transfer garlic to paper towel–lined plate. Follow recipe for Pan-Roasted Asparagus, adding butter to oil already in skillet. After transferring asparagus to serving dish, sprinkle with 2 tablespoons grated Parmesan and toasted garlic. Season with lemon juice, salt, and pepper to taste and serve immediately.

PAN-ROASTED ASPARAGUS WITH WARM ORANGE-ALMOND VINAIGRETTE

Heat 2 tablespoons olive oil in 12-inch skillet over medium heat until shimmering. Add ¼ cup slivered almonds and cook, stirring frequently, until golden, about 5 minutes. Add ½ cup orange juice and 1 teaspoon chopped fresh thyme, increase heat to medium-high, and simmer until thickened, about 4 minutes. Off heat, stir in 2 tablespoons minced shallot, 2 tablespoons sherry vinegar, and season with salt and pepper to taste. Transfer vinaigrette to small bowl. Wipe out skillet and follow recipe for Pan-Roasted Asparagus. After transferring asparagus to serving dish, pour vinaigrette over and toss to combine. Seasoning with salt and pepper to taste and serve immediately.

PAN-ROASTED ASPARAGUS WITH CHERRY TOMATOES AND BLACK OLIVES

Kalamata olives are a good choice for this recipe.

Add 1 tablespoon olive oil and 2 garlic cloves, sliced thin, to 12-inch skillet and cook over medium heat, stirring occasionally, until garlic turns golden around edges but does not darken, 2 to 3 minutes. Add 1 pint halved cherry tomatoes and ⅓ cup brine-cured olives, pitted and chopped. Cook until tomatoes begin to break down and release liquid, 1 to 2 minutes. Transfer mixture to bowl, season with salt and pepper to taste and cover to keep warm. Follow recipe for Pan-Roasted Asparagus, topping asparagus with tomato mixture, 4 tablespoons chopped fresh basil, and 1 ounce grated Parmesan cheese before serving.

PAN-ROASTED ASPARAGUS WITH RED ONION AND BACON

Cook 4 slices bacon, cut into ¼-inch pieces, in 12-inch skillet over medium heat until crisp, 5 to 7 minutes. Using slotted spoon, transfer bacon to paper towel–lined plate; set aside. Pour off all but 1 tablespoon fat from pan. Return skillet to medium-high heat and add 1 large red onion, halved and sliced thin. Cook, stirring occasionally, until edges darken and onion begins to soften, about 3 minutes. Add 2 tablespoons balsamic vinegar and 1 tablespoon maple syrup to skillet and cook until liquids reduce and cling to onions, about 2 minutes. Transfer onions to bowl, season with salt and pepper to taste, and cover to keep warm. Follow recipe for Pan-Roasted Asparagus, topping asparagus with onion mixture and bacon before serving.

TEST KITCHEN TIP NO. 55 STORING ASPARAGUS

To determine how to best maintain asparagus's bright color and crisp texture, we tested refrigerating spears in the plastic bag we'd bought them in, enclosed in a paper bag, wrapped in a damp paper towel, and with the stalk ends trimmed and standing up in a small amount of water. After three days the results were clear. Those left in the plastic bag had become slimy, while the paper bag and towel bunches had shriveled tips and limp stalks. However, the bunch stored in water looked as good as fresh and retained its firm texture. To store asparagus this way, trim the bottom ½ inch of the stalks and stand the spears upright in a glass. Add enough water to cover the bottom of the stalks by 1 inch and place the glass in the refrigerator. Asparagus stored this way should remain relatively fresh for about four days; you may need to add a little more water every few days. Re-trim the very bottom of the stalks before using.

PAN-ROASTED ASPARAGUS WITH RED PEPPERS AND GOAT CHEESE

Heat 1 tablespoon olive oil in 12-inch skillet over medium-high heat until shimmering. Add 2 red bell peppers, stemmed, seeded, and cut into ¼-inch-wide strips, and cook, stirring occasionally, until skins begin to blister, 4 to 5 minutes. Transfer peppers to bowl, season with salt and pepper to taste, and cover to keep warm. Follow recipe for Pan-Roasted Asparagus, topping asparagus with peppers, 2 tablespoons chopped fresh mint, 4 ounces crumbled goat cheese, and ¼ cup toasted pine nuts before serving.

MAKE-AHEAD GREEN BEANS

✔ WHY THIS RECIPE WORKS
Green beans are a classic side for any holiday meal but we wanted a recipe that would alleviate some of the typical last-minute cooking frenzy. For green beans that could be cooked ahead of time and given a quick finishing touch before serving, we found blanching to be the best method, as it guaranteed evenly cooked, well-seasoned beans with a crisp texture. Once the beans were blanched and cooled, we refrigerated them for up to three days. On the day of serving, we simply tossed them in a hot skillet with a little water to warm them through quickly. To dress up the green beans, we came up with a few simple butter sauces.

BLANCHED GREEN BEANS
SERVES 4

To serve the beans right away, increase the blanching time to 5 to 6 minutes and don't bother shocking them in ice water.

1 pound green beans, trimmed
1 teaspoon salt

Bring 2½ quarts water to boil in large saucepan over high heat. Add green beans and salt, return to boil, and cook until beans are bright green and crisp-tender, 3 to 4 minutes. Meanwhile, fill large bowl with ice water. Drain beans, then transfer immediately to ice water bath. When beans no longer feel warm to touch, drain beans again, then dry thoroughly with paper towels. Transfer beans to large zipper-lock bag and refrigerate until ready to use, up to 3 days.

GREEN BEANS WITH SAUTÉED SHALLOTS AND VERMOUTH
SERVES 4

The amount of shallots in this recipe may seem like a lot, but they cook down.

4 tablespoons unsalted butter
5 ounces shallots, sliced thin
1 recipe Blanched Green Beans
   Salt and pepper
2 tablespoons dry vermouth

1. Melt 2 tablespoons butter in 8-inch skillet over medium heat. Add shallots and cook, stirring frequently, until golden brown, fragrant, and just crisp around the edges, about 10 minutes. Set aside.

2. Heat beans and ¼ cup water in 12-inch skillet over high heat and cook, tossing frequently with tongs, until beans are warmed through, 1 to 2 minutes. Season with salt and pepper to taste and transfer to serving platter.

3. Return shallots to high heat, stir in vermouth, and bring to simmer. Whisk in remaining 2 tablespoons butter, 1 tablespoon at a time; season with salt and pepper to taste. Top beans with shallots and sauce and serve immediately.

GREEN BEANS WITH BUTTERED BREAD CRUMBS AND ALMONDS

SERVES 4

An equal amount of chopped walnuts or pecans can be substituted for the almonds.

I	slice hearty white sandwich bread, crust removed and bread torn into I ½-inch pieces
2	tablespoons sliced almonds, crumbled by hand into ¼-inch pieces
2	garlic cloves, minced
2	teaspoons chopped fresh parsley
I	recipe Blanched Green Beans (page 245)
	Salt and pepper
4	tablespoons unsalted butter

I. Process bread in food processor to fine crumbs, 20 to 30 seconds (you should have about ¼ cup bread crumbs). Transfer bread crumbs to 10-inch nonstick skillet, add almonds, and toast over medium-high heat, stirring constantly, until golden brown, about 5 minutes. Off heat, add garlic and parsley and toss with hot crumbs. Season with salt and pepper to taste, transfer to small bowl, and set aside. (Do not wash skillet.)

2. Heat beans and ¼ cup water in 12-inch skillet over high heat and cook, tossing frequently with tongs, until beans are warmed through, about 1 to 2 minutes. Season with salt and pepper to taste and transfer to platter.

3. Melt butter in now-empty 12-inch skillet over medium-high heat, add bread-crumb mixture and cook, stirring frequently, until fragrant, about 1 to 2 minutes. Top beans with buttered crumb-almond mixture and serve immediately.

GREEN BEANS WITH TOASTED HAZELNUTS AND BROWNED BUTTER

SERVES 4

To skin toasted hazelnuts, rub the warm nuts in a clean kitchen towel—the skins should rub right off.

4	tablespoons unsalted butter
½	cup hazelnuts, toasted, skinned, and chopped fine
	Salt and pepper
I	recipe Blanched Green Beans (page 245)

I. Heat butter in small saucepan over medium heat and cook, swirling frequently, until butter turns deep chocolate brown and becomes fragrant, 4 to 5 minutes. Add hazelnuts and cook, stirring constantly, until fragrant and combined, about 1 minute. Season with salt and pepper to taste.

2. Heat beans and ¼ cup water in 12-inch skillet over high heat and cook, tossing frequently, until beans are warmed through, about 1 to 2 minutes. Season with salt and pepper to taste and transfer to platter. Top beans with toasted hazelnuts and brown butter and serve immediately.

SAUTÉED GREEN BEANS

✓ WHY THIS RECIPE WORKS

For tender, lightly browned, fresh-tasting beans using just one pan, we turned to sautéing. But simply sautéing raw beans in oil resulted in blackened exteriors and undercooked interiors. Cooking the beans in water in a covered pan, then removing the lid to evaporate the liquid and brown the beans was better, but not foolproof. For the best results, we sautéed the beans until spotty brown, then added water to the pan and covered it so the beans could cook through. Once the beans were soft, we lifted the lid to vaporize whatever water remained in the pan and promote additional browning. A little softened butter (or olive oil, in the case of a few variations) added to the pan at this stage lent richness and promoted even more browning. A few additional ingredients, such as garlic and herbs, added flavor without overcomplicating our recipe.

SAUTÉED GREEN BEANS WITH GARLIC AND HERBS

SERVES 4

This recipe yields crisp-tender beans. If you prefer a slightly more tender texture (or you are using large, tough beans), increase the water by I tablespoon and increase the covered cooking time by I minute.

I	tablespoon unsalted butter, softened
3	garlic cloves, minced
I	teaspoon chopped fresh thyme
I	teaspoon olive oil
I	pound green beans, trimmed and cut into 2-inch lengths
	Salt and pepper
I	tablespoon chopped fresh parsley
2	teaspoons lemon juice

I. Combine butter, garlic, and thyme in small bowl; set aside. Heat oil in 12-inch nonstick skillet over medium heat until just smoking. Add beans, ¼ teaspoon salt, and ⅛ teaspoon pepper; cook, stirring occasionally, until spotty brown, 4 to 6 minutes. Add ¼ cup water, cover, and cook until beans are bright green and still crisp, about 2 minutes. Uncover, increase heat to high, and cook until water evaporates, 30 to 60 seconds.

2. Add butter mixture to skillet and continue to cook, stirring frequently, until beans are crisp-tender, lightly browned, and beginning to wrinkle, 1 to 3 minutes longer. Transfer beans to serving bowl and toss with parsley and lemon juice. Season with salt and pepper to taste and serve immediately.

SAUTÉED GREEN BEANS WITH SMOKED PAPRIKA AND ALMONDS

Do not use more than the specified amount of smoked paprika or it will overpower the beans.

Omit thyme and parsley. Stir ¼ teaspoon smoked paprika into softened butter with garlic. Sprinkle cooked beans with ¼ cup toasted slivered almonds before serving.

SAUTÉED GREEN BEANS WITH TARRAGON AND LIME

Substitute 2 scallions, sliced thin, and ½ teaspoon grated lime zest for the garlic and thyme. Toss beans with 1½ teaspoons lime juice and 2 teaspoons chopped fresh tarragon before serving.

SAUTÉED SPICY GREEN BEANS WITH GINGER AND SESAME

Combine 1 teaspoon toasted sesame oil, 1 teaspoon grated fresh ginger, and 1 tablespoon Asian chili-garlic sauce in small bowl. Substitute vegetable oil for olive oil, increasing amount to 2 teaspoons. Cook green beans as directed, replacing butter mixture with sesame oil mixture and omitting lemon juice and parsley. Sprinkle cooked beans with 2 teaspoons toasted sesame seeds before serving.

SAUTÉED GREEN BEANS WITH ROASTED RED PEPPERS AND BASIL

Combine 2 teaspoons olive oil, 1 minced shallot, and ⅛ teaspoon red pepper flakes in small bowl. Replace butter mixture with oil-shallot mixture. Add ⅓ cup jarred roasted red peppers, rinsed, patted dry, and cut into ½-inch pieces, to skillet with oil-shallot mixture. Substitute 1 teaspoon red wine vinegar for lemon juice and 2 tablespoons chopped fresh basil for parsley.

BRAISED GREEN BEANS

✓ WHY THIS RECIPE WORKS

Braising green beans is a slower method than sautéing or steaming them, but the upside is that you can simultaneously cook and flavor the beans, and it is a great method for cooking older, tougher beans. We used tomatoes or cream as the braising liquid for our green beans. The beans lost some color no matter what we tried, but they picked up wonderful flavors from the braising medium. We found that the beans needed 15 to 20 minutes in the liquid to pick up enough flavor to make the method worthwhile; any longer and the color and texture of the beans suffered.

GREEN BEANS AND MUSHROOMS BRAISED IN CREAM

SERVES 4 TO 6

This recipe takes the flavors of the tired green bean casserole and gives them a new lift.

2	tablespoons unsalted butter
1	tablespoon vegetable oil
4	ounces shallots, sliced thin
1	pound green beans, trimmed
8	ounces white mushrooms, trimmed and quartered
⅔	cup heavy cream
2	teaspoons lemon juice
1½	teaspoons fresh thyme, minced
	Salt and pepper

1. Heat butter and oil in 12-inch skillet over medium-high heat. Add shallots and cook until golden brown and crisp, about 7 minutes. Transfer with slotted spoon to paper towel–lined plate; set aside.

2. Combine green beans, mushrooms, cream, lemon juice, and thyme in now-empty pan and bring to simmer. Reduce heat to low, cover, and simmer, stirring occasionally, until beans are crisp-tender, 15 to 20 minutes.

3. Uncover and, if sauce is too thin, simmer briskly to thicken cream. Season

with salt and pepper to taste. Transfer to serving bowl, garnish with fried shallots, and serve immediately.

GREEN BEANS BRAISED IN TOMATOES

SERVES 4 TO 6

This recipe uses a simple tomato sauce flavored with onions and garlic as the braising medium. You can substitute basil for the parsley if desired.

2	tablespoons olive oil
1	small onion, diced
1	garlic clove, minced
1	cup canned diced tomatoes
1	pound green beans, trimmed
	Salt and pepper
2	tablespoons minced fresh parsley

1. Heat oil in 12-inch skillet over medium heat. Add onion and cook until softened, about 5 minutes. Add garlic and cook 1 minute. Add tomatoes and simmer until juices thicken slightly, about 5 minutes.

2. Add green beans and ¼ teaspoon salt, stir well, cover, and cook, stirring occasionally, until beans are crisp-tender, about 20 minutes. Stir in parsley, season with salt and pepper to taste, and serve immediately.

SKILLET GREEN BEANS

✓ WHY THIS RECIPE WORKS

For no-fuss green beans packed with flavor, we built a sauce with aromatics and flour for thickening power, then we added the beans, and finally chicken broth. We covered the skillet and cooked the beans until almost tender, then removed the lid to finish them through and thicken the sauce to the perfect consistency. In variations, we gussied the beans up further with glazed nuts or seasoned bread crumbs.

GREEN BEANS WITH ORANGE ESSENCE AND TOASTED MAPLE PECANS

SERVES 8

These green beans will add pizzazz to Thanksgiving dinner.

¾ cup pecans, chopped coarse
3 tablespoons unsalted butter
2 tablespoons maple syrup
   Salt and pepper
2 shallots, minced
½ teaspoon grated orange zest plus ⅓ cup juice
   Pinch cayenne pepper
2 teaspoons all-purpose flour 1½ pounds green beans, trimmed
⅔ cup low-sodium chicken broth
1 teaspoon minced fresh sage

1. Toast pecans in 12-inch nonstick skillet over medium-high heat, stirring occasionally, until fragrant, about 3 minutes. Off heat, stir in 1 tablespoon butter, maple syrup, and ⅛ teaspoon salt. Return skillet to medium heat and cook, stirring constantly, until nuts are dry and glossy, about 45 seconds; transfer to plate and set aside.

2. Wipe out skillet. Melt remaining 2 tablespoons butter in skillet over medium heat. Add shallots, orange zest, and cayenne and cook, stirring occasionally, until shallots are softened, about 2 minutes. Stir in flour until combined, then add green beans. Add chicken broth, orange juice, and sage. Increase heat to medium-high, cover, and cook until beans are crisp-tender, about 4 minutes. Uncover and cook, stirring occasionally, until beans are tender and sauce has thickened slightly, about 4 minutes. Off heat, season with salt and pepper to taste. Transfer to serving dish, sprinkle with pecans, and serve.

GARLIC-LEMON GREEN BEANS WITH TOASTED BREAD CRUMBS

SERVES 8

You can reduce the amount of garlic if you prefer more subtle flavoring.

2 slices hearty white sandwich bread, torn into quarters
3 tablespoons unsalted butter
2 tablespoons grated Parmesan cheese
   Salt and pepper
6 garlic cloves, minced
2 teaspoons all-purpose flour
1 teaspoon minced fresh thyme
⅛ teaspoon red pepper flakes
1½ pounds green beans, trimmed
1 cup low-sodium chicken broth
1 tablespoon lemon juice

1. Pulse bread in food processor to fine, even crumbs, about 10 pulses. Melt 1 tablespoon butter in 12-inch nonstick skillet over medium-high heat. Add bread crumbs and cook, stirring frequently, until golden brown, 3 to 5 minutes. Transfer to medium bowl and stir in Parmesan, ¼ teaspoon salt, and ⅛ teaspoon pepper; set aside.

2. Wipe out skillet. Add remaining 2 tablespoons butter, garlic, and ¼ teaspoon salt. Cook over medium heat, stirring constantly, until garlic is golden, 3 to 5 minutes. Stir in flour, thyme, and pepper flakes, then add green beans. Add chicken broth, increase heat to medium-high, cover, and cook until beans are crisp-tender, about 4 minutes. Uncover and cook, stirring occasionally, until beans are tender and sauce has thickened slightly, about 4 minutes. Off heat, stir in lemon juice and season with salt and pepper to taste. Transfer to serving dish, sprinkle with bread crumbs, and serve.

SKILLET GREEN BEAN CASSEROLE

SERVES 8

This recipe turns the holiday favorite into an easy weeknight recipe.

3 large shallots, sliced thin
3 tablespoons all-purpose flour
   Salt and pepper
5 tablespoons vegetable oil
10 ounces cremini mushrooms, trimmed and sliced ¼ inch thick
2 tablespoons unsalted butter
1 onion, minced
2 garlic cloves, minced
1½ pounds green beans, trimmed
3 sprigs fresh thyme
2 bay leaves
¾ cup heavy cream
¾ cup low-sodium chicken broth

1. Line baking sheet with triple layer of paper towels. Toss shallots with 2 tablespoons flour, ¼ teaspoon salt, and ⅛ teaspoon pepper in small bowl. Heat 3 tablespoons oil in 12-inch nonstick skillet over medium-high heat until just smoking; add shallots and cook, stirring frequently, until golden and crisp, about 5 minutes. Transfer shallots with oil to prepared baking sheet and set aside.

2. Wipe out skillet and return to medium-high heat. Add remaining 2 tablespoons oil, mushrooms, and ¼ teaspoon salt; cook, stirring occasionally, until browned, about 8 minutes. Transfer to plate and set aside.

3. Wipe out skillet. Melt butter in skillet over medium heat, add onion, and cook, stirring occasionally, until edges begin to brown, about 2 minutes. Stir in garlic and remaining 1 tablespoon flour; toss in green beans, thyme, and bay leaves. Add cream and broth, increase heat to medium-high, cover, and cook until beans are partly tender but still crisp at center, about 4 minutes. Add mushrooms and continue to cook, uncovered, until green

beans are tender and sauce has thickened slightly, about 4 minutes. Off heat, discard bay leaves and thyme; adjust seasonings with salt and pepper. Transfer to serving dish, sprinkle evenly with shallots, and serve.

ROASTED GREEN BEANS

✓ WHY THIS RECIPE WORKS
Mature supermarket green beans are often tough and dull, needing special treatment to become tender and flavorful. We wanted out-of-season green beans that would not only taste great on their own but that could also accommodate some interesting flavor variations. We discovered that roasting them in a 450-degree oven for 20 minutes with only oil, salt, and pepper transformed aged specimens into deeply caramelized, full-flavored beans. A little oil encouraged browning without making the beans greasy, and incorporating ingredients like garlic and ginger halfway through cooking prevented them from scorching. Adding honey or maple syrup helped liquid seasoning (such as vinegar or sesame oil) cling to the beans and helped with caramelization. Finishing with fresh herbs or nuts added the right complexity and texture.

ROASTED GREEN BEANS
SERVES 4

An aluminum foil liner prevents burning on dark nonstick baking sheets. When using baking sheets with a light finish, foil is not required, but we recommend it for easy cleanup.

1 pound green beans, trimmed
1 tablespoon olive oil
   Salt and pepper

1. Adjust oven rack to middle position and heat oven to 450 degrees. Line rimmed baking sheet with aluminum foil and spread beans on baking sheet. Drizzle with oil and, using hands, toss to coat.

Sprinkle with ½ teaspoon salt, toss to coat, and distribute in even layer. Transfer to oven and roast 10 minutes.

2. Remove baking sheet from oven. Using tongs, redistribute beans. Continue roasting until beans are dark golden brown in spots and have started to shrivel, 10 to 12 minutes. Season with salt and pepper to taste and serve.

ROASTED GREEN BEANS WITH SUN-DRIED TOMATOES, GOAT CHEESE, AND OLIVES
SERVES 4

The assertive flavors in these green beans are a great match for steak.

1   teaspoon extra-virgin olive oil
1   tablespoon lemon juice
½   cup oil-packed sun-dried tomatoes, rinsed, patted dry, and chopped coarse
½   cup pitted kalamata olives, chopped
2   teaspoons minced fresh oregano
1   recipe Roasted Green Beans
    Salt and pepper
2   ounces crumbled goat cheese (½ cup)

Combine oil, lemon juice, sun-dried tomatoes, olives, and oregano in medium bowl. Add beans and toss well to combine. Season with salt and pepper to taste, transfer to serving dish, top with goat cheese, and serve.

ROASTED GREEN BEANS WITH RED ONION AND WALNUTS
SERVES 4

The walnuts add nice texture to this recipe.

1   tablespoon balsamic vinegar
1   teaspoon honey
1   teaspoon minced fresh thyme
2   garlic cloves, sliced thin
1   pound green beans, trimmed

½   red onion, cut into ½-inch-thick wedges
1   tablespoon olive oil
⅓   cup chopped walnuts, toasted

1. Adjust oven rack to middle position and heat oven to 450 degrees. Combine vinegar, honey, thyme, and garlic in small bowl; set aside.

2. Line rimmed baking sheet with aluminum foil and spread beans and onion wedges on baking sheet. Drizzle onions and beans with oil and, using hands, toss to coat. Sprinkle with ½ teaspoon salt, toss again to coat, and distribute in even layer. Transfer to oven and roast for 10 minutes.

3. Remove baking sheet from oven. Pour vinegar-honey mixture over beans and, using tongs, toss to coat. Redistribute beans and onions in even layer and continue to roast until onions and beans are dark golden brown in spots and beans have started to shrivel, 10 to 12 minutes.

4. Season with salt and pepper to taste, transfer to serving dish, sprinkle with walnuts, and serve.

ROASTED SESAME GREEN BEANS
SERVES 4

The Asian-inspired flavors of these beans pair well with salmon.

½   teaspoon toasted sesame oil
2   teaspoons honey
¼   teaspoon red pepper flakes
3   garlic cloves, minced
1   teaspoon grated fresh ginger   1 pound green beans, trimmed
1   tablespoon olive oil
    Salt
4   teaspoons sesame seeds, toasted

1. Adjust oven rack to middle position and heat oven to 450 degrees. Combine oil, honey, pepper flakes, garlic, and ginger in small bowl; set aside.

2. Line rimmed baking sheet with aluminum foil and spread beans on baking sheet. Drizzle with oil and, using hands, toss to coat. Sprinkle with ½ teaspoon salt, toss to coat, and distribute in even layer. Transfer to oven and roast for 10 minutes.

3. Remove baking sheet from oven. Pour garlic-ginger mixture over beans and, using tongs, toss to coat. Redistribute in even layer and continue to roast until beans are dark golden brown in spots and starting to shrivel, 10 to 12 minutes.

4. Season with salt to taste, transfer to serving dish, sprinkle with sesame seeds, and serve.

ROASTED MAPLE-MUSTARD GREEN BEANS

SERVES 4

These beans are a great match for pork.

- 1 tablespoon maple syrup
- 1 tablespoon Dijon mustard
- 1 tablespoon whole grain mustard
  Pinch cayenne pepper
- 1 pound green beans, trimmed
- 2 carrots, peeled and cut into 2-inch-long matchsticks
- 1 tablespoon vegetable oil
  Salt
- 1 tablespoon minced fresh parsley

1. Adjust oven rack to middle position and heat oven to 450 degrees. Combine maple syrup, Dijon mustard, whole grain mustard, and cayenne in small bowl.

2. Line rimmed baking sheet with aluminum foil and spread beans and carrots on baking sheet. Drizzle with oil and, using hands, toss to coat. Sprinkle with ½ teaspoon salt, toss to coat, and distribute in even layer. Transfer to oven and roast for 10 minutes.

3. Remove baking sheet from oven. Pour maple mixture over beans and, using tongs, toss to coat. Redistribute in even

layer and continue to roast until carrots and beans are dark golden brown in spots and beans are starting to shrivel, 10 to 12 minutes.

4. Season with salt to taste, transfer to serving dish, sprinkle with parsley, and serve.

GREEN BEAN CASSEROLE

✓ WHY THIS RECIPE WORKS

Green bean casserole is a classic, but we wanted a fresher spin that skipped frozen green beans, condensed soup, and canned onions. Using fresh green beans was an obvious place to start, and in place of canned soup, we made a mushroom variation of the classic French velouté sauce (traditionally made by thickening white stock with a roux). Ultimately, we found that the canned onions couldn't be replaced in our version without sacrificing the level of convenience we thought appropriate to the dish, but we masked their commercial flavor by combining them with freshly made buttered bread crumbs.

ULTIMATE GREEN BEAN CASSEROLE

SERVES 10 TO 12

This recipe can be halved and baked in a 2-quart (or 8-inch square) baking dish. If making a half batch, decrease the cooking time of the sauce in step 3 to about 6 minutes (reducing it to 1¾ cups) and the baking time in step 4 to 10 minutes.

TOPPING

- 4 slices hearty white sandwich bread, torn into quarters
- 2 tablespoons unsalted butter, softened
- ¼ teaspoon salt
- ⅛ teaspoon pepper
- 3 cups canned fried onions (about 6 ounces)

BEANS AND SAUCE

- 2 pounds green beans, trimmed and halved crosswise
  Salt and pepper
- 3 tablespoons unsalted butter
- 1 pound white mushrooms, trimmed and broken into ½-inch pieces
- 3 garlic cloves, minced
- 3 tablespoons all-purpose flour
- 1½ cups low-sodium chicken broth
- 1½ cups heavy cream

1. FOR THE TOPPING: Pulse bread, butter, salt, and pepper in food processor until mixture resembles coarse crumbs, about 10 pulses. Transfer to large bowl and toss with onions; set aside.

2. FOR THE BEANS AND SAUCE: Adjust oven rack to middle position and heat oven to 425 degrees. Fill large bowl with ice water. Line baking sheet with paper towels. Bring 4 quarts water to boil in Dutch oven. Add beans and 2 tablespoons salt. Cook beans until bright green and crisp-tender, about 6 minutes. Drain beans in colander, then plunge immediately into ice water to stop cooking. Spread beans on prepared baking sheet to drain.

3. Melt butter in now-empty Dutch oven over medium-high heat. Add mushrooms, garlic, ¾ teaspoon salt, and ⅛ teaspoon pepper and cook until mushrooms release moisture and liquid evaporates, about 6 minutes. Add flour and cook for 1 minute, stirring constantly. Stir in broth and bring to simmer, stirring constantly. Add cream, reduce heat to medium, and simmer until sauce is thickened and reduced to 3½ cups, about 12 minutes. Season with salt and pepper to taste.

4. Add green beans to sauce and stir until evenly coated. Arrange in even layer in 3-quart (or 13 by 9-inch) baking dish. Sprinkle with topping and bake until top is golden brown and sauce is bubbling around edges, about 15 minutes. Serve immediately.

TO MAKE AHEAD: Store the breadcrumb topping in refrigerator for up to 2 days and combine with onions just before cooking. Combine beans and cooled sauce in baking dish, cover with plastic wrap, and refrigerate for up to 24 hours. To serve, remove plastic wrap and heat casserole in 425-degree oven for 10 minutes, then add topping and bake as directed.

BEETS

✓ WHY THIS RECIPE WORKS
In our search for the best way to cook beets, we paid special attention to minimizing "bleeding"—many cooks avoid beets due to the mess they can cause both in the kitchen and on the plate. Boiling was eliminated quickly since it created a mess. But steaming produced beets with a minimum of mess and they were lusciously moist—especially when we combined them with orange slices, rosemary, and warm spices to make pickled beets. We also found success with roasting beets. Foil-wrapped roasted beets were more moist than unwrapped roasted beets, but the latter had more flavor. Whatever the cooking method, we minimized bleeding by not peeling the skin and by not slicing off the tops of the beets prior to cooking.

STEAMED BEETS
SERVES 8

Don't let the pan run out of water during this long steaming process.

2   pounds beets, greens removed, stems trimmed to 1 inch

Fit large saucepan with steamer basket. Add water, keeping level below basket. Place beets in basket, bring water to boil, cover, and steam beets over high heat until they can be easily poked with paring knife, 30 to 45 minutes. Remove beets using tongs, cool slightly, and remove skins. Serve.

PICKLED BEETS WITH ORANGE AND ROSEMARY
MAKES ABOUT 2 QUARTS

Use small beets, about the size of a golf ball, if available. Bigger beets should be quartered or sliced after steaming.

4   pounds beets, trimmed
⅔   cup red wine
½   cup sweet vermouth
¼   cup cider vinegar
¼   cup honey or brown sugar
1   teaspoon whole cloves
1   (3-inch) stick ground cinnamon
1   sprig fresh rosemary
2   orange slices, seeds removed
     Salt and pepper

1. Fit large saucepan with steamer basket. Add water, keeping level below basket. Place beets in basket, bring water to boil, cover, and steam beets over high heat until they can be easily poked with paring knife, 30 to 45 minutes. Remove beets using tongs, cool slightly, and remove skins. Place beets in medium bowl.

2. In a medium saucepan, bring wine, vermouth, vinegar, honey, cloves, cinnamon, rosemary, and orange slices to boil, then reduce heat and simmer to blend flavors, about 3 minutes. Season with salt and pepper to taste, then pour mixture over beets. Cool to room temperature, cover, and refrigerate until ready to serve. (Pickled beets can be refrigerated for up to 1 month.)

ROASTED BEETS
SERVES 8

Roasted beets bleed very little when cut, so they can also be used in recipes. Just remember that the dish will take on a sweet and very distinct roasted flavor.

2   pounds beets, trimmed
1   tablespoon olive oil (if roasting without aluminum foil)

Adjust oven rack to middle position and heat oven to 350 degrees. Wrap beets in foil or brush with olive oil and place in small roasting pan. Roast until beets can be easily poked with paring knife, about 1 hour. Cool slightly, remove skins, and serve.

STEAMED BROCCOLI

✓ WHY THIS RECIPE WORKS
Boiling broccoli can result in army-green mush. But another moist-heat method, steaming, works well with broccoli because it keeps the florets tender but also cooks the stalks thoroughly. We found the delicate florets were best cooked above water by steaming, and peeling the stems and cutting them into small pieces ensured they cooked through at the same rate as the florets. For instant flavor without fuss, we tossed the steamed broccoli with one of several simple dressings. Bolder vinaigrettes paired best with the broccoli's somewhat strong flavor.

TEST KITCHEN TIP NO. 56 **BEATING BEET STAINS**

When cut, beets can bleed onto your cutting board, making it easy to discolor other foods you might be chopping next. Instead of stopping to wash the board between uses, we had a better idea: giving its surface a light coat of nonstick cooking spray before chopping. This thin coating added no discernible slickness under our knife and allowed us to quickly wipe the board clean with a paper towel before proceeding with our next task.

STEAMED BROCCOLI
SERVES 4

Cutting the florets and peeled stalks into equal-size pieces ensures that they will all cook at the same rate. The sweet flavor of the steamed broccoli pairs well with bold, bright flavors. Serve it with best-quality olive oil, your favorite vinaigrette, or one of the vinaigrette recipes that follow. For maximum absorption, toss steamed broccoli with the oil or dressing when hot.

1½	pounds broccoli, florets cut into 1-inch pieces, stalks peeled, cut in half lengthwise, then sliced crosswise ¼ inch thick
2	tablespoons extra-virgin olive oil
	Salt and pepper

Fit large saucepan with steamer basket. Add water, keeping level below basket. Bring water to boil, add broccoli, cover, and steam until broccoli is just tender, 4½ to 5 minutes. Transfer broccoli to serving bowl and toss with oil and salt and pepper to taste. Serve hot or at room temperature.

SESAME VINAIGRETTE
MAKES ENOUGH FOR
1 RECIPE STEAMED BROCCOLI

If using this vinaigrette, prepare the broccoli without the oil, salt, and pepper.

6	tablespoons vegetable oil
¼	cup sesame seeds, toasted
1½	tablespoons rice vinegar
1	tablespoon soy sauce
1	tablespoon sugar
1	teaspoon toasted sesame oil

Process all ingredients in food processor until sesame seeds are ground and vinaigrette is well blended, about 15 seconds.

BALSAMIC-BASIL VINAIGRETTE
MAKES ENOUGH FOR
1 RECIPE STEAMED BROCCOLI

Use a high-quality, aged balsamic vinegar to reduce harshness. If using this vinaigrette, prepare the broccoli without the oil, salt, and pepper.

6	tablespoons extra-virgin olive oil
2	tablespoons balsamic vinegar
1	shallot, minced
1	tablespoon minced fresh basil
1	garlic clove, minced
	Salt and pepper

Mix all ingredients in medium bowl until well blended and add salt and pepper to taste.

LIME-CUMIN DRESSING
MAKES ENOUGH FOR
1 RECIPE STEAMED BROCCOLI

This recipe takes its cue from Caribbean cooking. The dressing is quite potent, so a little goes a long way. If using this vinaigrette, prepare the broccoli without the oil, salt, and pepper.

3	tablespoons extra-virgin olive oil
1	teaspoon grated lime zest plus 1 tablespoon juice
½	teaspoon ground cumin
½	teaspoon salt
	Hot sauce
¼	cup minced red onion

Mix oil, lime zest and juice, cumin, and salt together in medium bowl until well blended. Season with hot sauce to taste. Stir in onion.

SPANISH GREEN HERB SAUCE
MAKES ENOUGH FOR
1 RECIPE STEAMED BROCCOLI

Make sure to scrape down the sides of the food processor bowl to incorporate all the ingredients into the sauce. If using this vinaigrette, prepare the broccoli without the oil, salt, and pepper.

½	cup fresh parsley leaves
½	cup fresh cilantro leaves
3	tablespoons extra-virgin olive oil
1	tablespoon lemon juice
2	garlic cloves, peeled
½	teaspoon salt

Process all ingredients in food processor until smooth, about 30 seconds.

PAN-ROASTED BROCCOLI

✓ WHY THIS RECIPE WORKS
For pan-roasted broccoli with bright green florets and toasty-brown stalks, we trimmed the florets into small pieces and the stalks into oblong coins for maximum browning. For broccoli that was nicely browned but also cooked through properly, we layered the stalks evenly in a hot, lightly oiled skillet. Once they began to brown we added the florets along with water and allowed the mixture to steam until nearly tender. Stirring the seasoning right into the steaming water kept things simple and allowed us to infuse the broccoli with flavor.

PAN-ROASTED BROCCOLI
SERVES 4

Avoid buying broccoli with stalks that are cracked or bend easily or with florets that are yellow or brown. If your broccoli stalks are especially thick, split them in half lengthwise before slicing. Serve as is or with a sauce (recipes follow).

3	tablespoons water
¼	teaspoon salt
⅛	teaspoon pepper
2	tablespoons vegetable oil
1¾	pounds broccoli, florets cut into 1½-inch pieces, stalks peeled and cut on bias into ¼-inch-thick slices

1. Stir water, salt, and pepper together in small bowl until salt dissolves; set aside. Heat oil in 12-inch nonstick skillet over medium-high heat until just smoking. Add broccoli stalks in even layer and cook, without stirring, until browned on bottoms, about 2 minutes. Add florets to skillet and toss to combine; cook, without stirring, until bottoms of florets just begin to brown, 1 to 2 minutes longer.

2. Add water mixture and cover skillet; cook until broccoli is bright green but still crisp, about 2 minutes. Uncover and continue to cook until water has evaporated, broccoli stalks are tender, and florets are crisp-tender, about 2 minutes. Serve.

PAN-ROASTED BROCCOLI WITH CREAMY GRUYÈRE SAUCE

SERVES 4

Make sure to cook the broccoli before preparing the sauce.

- 1 tablespoon unsalted butter
- 1 shallot, sliced thin
- ½ cup heavy cream
- ½ teaspoon Dijon mustard
- ½ teaspoon dry sherry
    Pinch cayenne pepper
- ⅛ teaspoon salt
- 4–5 tablespoons very finely grated Gruyère cheese
- 1 teaspoon lemon juice
- 1 recipe Pan-Roasted Broccoli (page 252)

Melt butter in 12-inch nonstick skillet over medium heat. Add shallot and cook, stirring frequently, until golden and softened, about 2 minutes. Stir in cream, mustard, sherry, cayenne, and salt. Increase heat to medium-high and cook until mixture bubbles and thickens, about 1 minute. Off heat, add 3 tablespoons Gruyère and lemon juice and stir until cheese is melted.

Add broccoli and stir to reheat and coat. Transfer to serving dish, sprinkle with remaining 1 to 2 tablespoons Gruyère, and serve immediately.

PAN-ROASTED BROCCOLI WITH LEMON BROWNED BUTTER

SERVES 4

Watch the butter carefully as it cooks, as it can go from brown to black in a matter of seconds.

- 4 tablespoons unsalted butter
- 1 small shallot, minced
- 2 garlic cloves, minced
- ¼ teaspoon salt
- ⅛ teaspoon pepper
- 1½ teaspoons lemon juice
- ½ teaspoon minced fresh thyme
- 1 recipe Pan-Roasted Broccoli (page 252)

Melt butter in 12-inch nonstick skillet over medium-high heat and continue to cook, swirling occasionally, until butter is browned and releases nutty aroma, about 1½ minutes. Off heat, add shallot, garlic, salt, and pepper and stir until garlic and shallot are fragrant, about 1 minute. Stir in lemon juice and thyme. Add broccoli to skillet, toss to coat with browned butter, and serve immediately.

PAN-ROASTED BROCCOLI WITH SPICY SOUTHEAST ASIAN FLAVORS

SERVES 4

The peanuts add a nice textural contrast here.

SAUCE

- 1 tablespoon creamy peanut butter
- 1 tablespoon hoisin sauce
- 2 teaspoons lime juice
- 2 garlic cloves, minced
- 1 teaspoon packed brown sugar
- ¾ teaspoon Asian chili-garlic sauce

BROCCOLI

- 3 tablespoons water
- ¼ teaspoon salt
- ⅛ teaspoon pepper
- 2 tablespoons vegetable oil
- 1¾ pounds broccoli, florets cut into 1½-inch pieces, stalks peeled, and cut on bias into ¼-inch-thick slices about 1½ inches long

- ¼ cup coarsely chopped fresh basil
- 2 tablespoons chopped unsalted roasted peanuts

1. FOR THE SAUCE: Combine all ingredients in medium bowl and set aside.

2. FOR THE BROCCOLI: Stir water,

PREPARING BROCCOLI

1. Place head of broccoli upside down on cutting board and trim off florets very close to their heads with large knife. Cut florets into 1-inch pieces.

2. Stand each stalk up on cutting board and square it off with knife to remove tough outer ⅛ inch. Cut stalk in half lengthwise, then into 1-inch pieces.

salt, and pepper together in small bowl until salt dissolves; set aside. Heat oil in 12-inch nonstick skillet over medium-high heat until just smoking. Add broccoli stalks in even layer and cook, without stirring, until browned on bottoms, about 2 minutes. Add florets to skillet and toss to combine; cook, without stirring, until bottoms of florets just begin to brown, 1 to 2 minutes longer.

3. Add water mixture and cover skillet; cook until broccoli is bright green but still crisp, about 2 minutes. Uncover and continue to cook until water has almost evaporated, broccoli stalks are tender, and florets are crisp-tender, about 1 minute more. Add basil and cook, stirring, until leaves wilt, about 30 seconds. Add sauce and toss until broccoli is evenly coated and heated through, about 30 seconds. Transfer to serving dish, top with chopped peanuts, and serve immediately.

ROASTED BROCCOLI

✔ WHY THIS RECIPE WORKS
Roasting is a great way to deepen the flavor of vegetables, but broccoli can be tricky to roast given its awkward shape, dense, woody stalks, and shrubby florets. We wanted a roasted broccoli recipe that would give us evenly cooked broccoli—stalks and florets—and add concentrated flavor and dappled browning. The way we prepared the broccoli was the key. We sliced the crown in half, then cut each half into uniform wedges. We cut the stalks into rectangular pieces slightly smaller than the more delicate wedges. This promoted even cooking and great browning by maximizing the vegetable's contact with the baking sheet. Tossing a scant ½ teaspoon of sugar over the broccoli along with salt, pepper, and a splash of olive oil gave us blistered, bubbled, and browned stalks that were sweet and full-flavored, along with crisp-tipped florets.

ROASTED BROCCOLI
SERVES 4

Make sure to trim away the outer peel from the broccoli stalks as directed; otherwise, it will turn tough when cooked.

1¾	pounds broccoli
3	tablespoons extra-virgin olive oil
½	teaspoon salt
½	teaspoon sugar
	Pepper
	Lemon wedges

1. Adjust oven rack to lowest position, place large rimmed baking sheet on rack, and heat oven to 500 degrees. Cut broccoli at juncture of florets and stalks; remove outer peel from stalk. Cut stalk into 2- to 3-inch lengths and each length into ½-inch-thick pieces. Cut crowns into 4 wedges if 3 to 4 inches in diameter or 6 wedges if 4 to 5 inches in diameter. Place broccoli in large bowl; drizzle with oil and toss well until evenly coated. Sprinkle with salt, sugar, and pepper to taste and toss to combine.

2. Working quickly, remove baking sheet from oven. Carefully transfer broccoli to baking sheet and spread into even layer, placing flat sides of broccoli pieces down. Return baking sheet to oven and roast until stalks are well browned and tender and florets are lightly browned, 9 to 11 minutes. Transfer to platter and serve immediately with lemon wedges.

ROASTED BROCCOLI WITH SHALLOTS, FENNEL SEEDS, AND PARMESAN

While broccoli roasts, heat 1 tablespoon extra-virgin oil in 8-inch skillet over medium heat until shimmering. Add 3 thinly sliced shallots and cook, stirring frequently, until soft and beginning to turn light golden brown, 5 to 6 minutes. Add 1 teaspoon coarsely chopped fennel seeds and continue to cook until shallots are golden brown, 1 to 2 minutes longer. Off heat, toss roasted broccoli with shallots, sprinkle with 1 ounce shaved Parmesan, and serve immediately.

ROASTED BROCCOLI WITH GARLIC

Stir 3 cloves minced garlic into olive oil before drizzling it over prepared broccoli in step 1.

ROASTED BROCCOLI WITH OLIVES, GARLIC, OREGANO, AND LEMON

Omit pepper when seasoning broccoli in step 1. While broccoli roasts, heat 2 tablespoons extra-virgin olive oil, 5 garlic cloves, sliced thin, and ½ teaspoon red pepper flakes in 8-inch skillet over medium-low heat. Cook, stirring frequently, until garlic is soft and beginning to turn light golden brown, 5 to 7 minutes. Remove from heat and stir in 2 tablespoons finely chopped pitted black olives, 1 teaspoon oregano, and 2 teaspoons lemon juice. Toss roasted broccoli with olive mixture and serve immediately.

ROASTED BROCCOLI WITH GARLIC AND ANCHOVIES

Make sure to trim away the outer peel from the broccoli stalks; otherwise, it will turn tough when cooked.

While broccoli roasts, melt 2 tablespoons unsalted butter in 8-inch skillet over low heat. Add 4 minced garlic cloves and 4 anchovy fillets, rinsed, patted dry, and minced. Cover and cook, stirring occasionally, until anchovies have largely melted and garlic is softened, 8 to 10 minutes. Off heat, stir in 1 teaspoon minced fresh thyme. Toss roasted broccoli with garlic mixture and serve immediately.

BROCCOLI RABE

✓ WHY THIS RECIPE WORKS

Some people prefer to eat broccoli rabe in its naturally bitter state, but for others, that bitterness is overwhelming. We wanted to develop a quick and dependable method of cooking this aggressive vegetable that would deliver less bitterness and a rounder, more balanced flavor. We found that blanching the rabe in a large amount of salted water tamed its bitterness. We sautéed the blanched rabe with ingredients that complemented its strong flavor, such as garlic, red pepper flakes, and sun-dried tomatoes.

BROCCOLI RABE WITH GARLIC AND RED PEPPER FLAKES

SERVES 4

Using a salad spinner makes easy work of drying the cooled blanched broccoli rabe. You can reduce the amount of red pepper flakes if you prefer to make this dish less spicy.

14 ounces broccoli rabe, trimmed and cut into 1-inch pieces
    Salt
2   tablespoons extra-virgin olive oil
3   garlic cloves, minced
¼   teaspoon red pepper flakes

1. Fill large bowl with ice water and set aside. Bring 3 quarts water to boil in large saucepan. Stir in broccoli rabe and 2 teaspoons salt and cook until rabe is wilted and tender, about 2½ minutes. Drain rabe, then transfer to bowl of ice water. Drain again; squeeze well to dry.

2. Heat oil, garlic, and pepper flakes in 10-inch skillet over medium heat until garlic begins to sizzle, about 3 to 4 minutes. Increase heat to medium high, add broccoli rabe, and cook, stirring to coat with oil, until heated through, about 1 minute. Season with salt to taste and serve immediately.

BROCCOLI RABE WITH SUN-DRIED TOMATOES AND PINE NUTS

Add ¼ cup oil-packed sun-dried tomatoes, cut into thin strips, along with garlic and red pepper flakes. Add 3 tablespoons toasted pine nuts to skillet along with broccoli rabe.

BRUSSELS SPROUTS

✓ WHY THIS RECIPE WORKS

In our search for a fuss-free cooking method that would produce tender, not-too-bitter Brussels sprouts that retained an attractive green hue, braising won out. Our initial test was performed using water and since it was so successful, we tried braising in other liquids as well. In the end, the tastiest results came from braising the Brussels sprouts in heavy cream, a classic French technique for cooking vegetables.

BRAISED BRUSSELS SPROUTS

SERVES 2 TO 4

When buying Brussels sprouts, choose those with small, tight heads, no more than 1½ inches in diameter. Larger sprouts can often be trimmed of loose leaves along the stem and still be quite good, but they cook best when cut in half. Serve these tender Brussels sprouts seasoned simply with ground black pepper and butter.

1   pound Brussels sprouts, trimmed
½   teaspoon salt

Bring sprouts, ½ cup water, and salt to boil in 2-quart saucepan over medium-high heat. Lower heat, cover, and simmer, shaking pan once or twice to redistribute sprouts, until knife tip inserted in center of sprout meets no resistance, 8 to 10 minutes. Drain well and serve.

BRUSSELS SPROUTS BRAISED IN CREAM

SERVES 4

This rich dish is perfect for the holidays. Don't drain the sprouts after braising; the cream reduces to form a sauce.

1   pound Brussels sprouts, trimmed
1   cup heavy cream
½   teaspoon salt
    Pinch fresh ground nutmeg
    Pepper

Bring sprouts, cream, and salt to boil in 2-quart saucepan over medium-high heat. Lower heat, cover, and simmer, shaking pan once or twice to redistribute sprouts, until knife tip inserted in center of sprout meets no resistance, 10 to 12 minutes. Season with nutmeg and pepper to taste and serve.

GLAZED BRUSSELS SPROUTS WITH CHESTNUTS

SERVES 4 TO 6

If chestnuts are unavailable, substitute ½ cup toasted chopped hazelnuts.

1   pound Brussels sprouts, trimmed
    Salt and pepper
3   tablespoons unsalted butter
1   tablespoon sugar
1   (16-ounce) can peeled chestnuts in water, drained

1. Bring sprouts, ½ cup water, and ½ teaspoon salt to boil in 2-quart saucepan over medium-high heat. Lower heat, cover, and simmer, shaking pan once or twice to redistribute sprouts, until knife tip inserted in center of sprout meets no resistance, 8 to 10 minutes. Drain well, cut into quarters, and set aside.

2. Heat 2 tablespoons butter and sugar

in 10-inch skillet over medium-high heat until butter melts and sugar dissolves. Stir in chestnuts, turn heat to low, and cook, stirring occasionally, until chestnuts are glazed, about 3 minutes.

3. Add remaining 1 tablespoon butter and sprouts and cook, stirring occasionally, until heated through, about 5 minutes. Season with salt and pepper to taste and serve.

SAUTÉED BRUSSELS SPROUTS WITH GARLIC AND PINE NUTS
SERVES 4

Garlic pairs especially well with Brussels sprouts.

- 1   **pound Brussels sprouts, trimmed**
  Salt and pepper
- 2   **tablespoons olive oil**
- ¼   **cup pine nuts**
- 3   **garlic cloves, minced**

1. Bring sprouts, ½ cup water, and ½ teaspoon salt to boil in 2-quart saucepan over medium-high heat. Lower heat, cover, and simmer, shaking pan once or twice to redistribute sprouts, until knife tip inserted in center of sprout meets no resistance, 8 to 10 minutes. Drain well and set aside.

2. Heat oil in 12-inch skillet over medium heat. Add pine nuts and cook, stirring frequently, until nuts begin to brown, about 2 minutes. Add garlic and cook until softened, about 1 minute. Stir in sprouts and cook, stirring constantly, until heated through, 2 to 3 minutes. Season with salt and pepper to taste and serve.

GLAZED CARROTS

✓ **WHY THIS RECIPE WORKS**

For well-seasoned carrots with a glossy, clingy, yet modest glaze, we started by slicing the carrots on the bias, which lent visual appeal without requiring much work. Most glazed carrot recipes start by steaming, parboiling, or blanching the carrots prior to glazing. To make glazed carrots a one-pot operation, we steamed them directly in the skillet, and we used chicken broth rather than water (along with some salt and sugar) for fuller flavor. When the carrots were almost tender, we removed the lid and turned up the heat to reduce the cooking liquid. Then we added butter and a bit more sugar, and finally finished with a sprinkling of fresh lemon juice and a bit of black pepper to give the dish sparkle.

GLAZED CARROTS
SERVES 4

Glazed carrots are a good accompaniment to roasts of any kind—beef, pork, lamb, or poultry. A nonstick skillet is easier to clean, but this recipe can be prepared in any 12-inch skillet with a cover.

- 1   **pound carrots, peeled and sliced ¼ inch thick on bias**
- ½   **cup low-sodium chicken broth**
- 3   **tablespoons sugar**
- ½   **teaspoon salt**
- 1   **tablespoon unsalted butter, cut into 4 pieces**
- 2   **teaspoons lemon juice**
  Pepper

1. Bring carrots, broth, 1 tablespoon sugar, and salt to boil, covered, in 12-inch nonstick skillet over medium-high heat. Reduce heat to medium and simmer, stirring occasionally, until carrots are almost tender when poked with paring knife, about 5 minutes. Uncover, increase heat to high, and simmer rapidly, stirring occasionally, until liquid is reduced to about 2 tablespoons, 1 to 2 minutes.

2. Add butter and remaining 2 tablespoons sugar to skillet, toss carrots to coat, and cook, stirring frequently, until carrots are completely tender and glaze is light gold, about 3 minutes. Off heat, add lemon juice and toss to coat. Transfer carrots to serving dish, scraping glaze from pan. Season with pepper to taste and serve immediately.

GLAZED CARROTS WITH GINGER AND ROSEMARY

Add one 1-inch piece ginger, peeled and sliced into ¼-inch-thick rounds, to skillet along with carrots and 1 teaspoon minced fresh rosemary along with butter. Discard ginger pieces before serving.

GLAZED CURRIED CARROTS WITH CURRANTS AND ALMONDS

Lightly toasting curry powder in a warm, dry skillet brings forth its full flavor.

Toast ¼ cup sliced almonds in 12-inch nonstick skillet over medium heat until fragrant and lightly browned, about 5 minutes; transfer to small bowl and set aside. Off heat, sprinkle 1½ teaspoons curry powder in skillet; stir until fragrant, about 2 seconds. Add carrots, broth, 1 tablespoon sugar, and salt, to skillet along with curry powder. Add ¼ cup currants along with butter and remaining 2 tablespoons sugar; add toasted almonds along with lemon juice.

HONEY-GLAZED CARROTS WITH LEMON AND THYME

Substitute equal 3 tablespoons honey for sugar and add ½ teaspoon minced fresh thyme and ½ teaspoon grated lemon zest along with butter.

GLAZED TURNIPS AND CARROTS

✔ WHY THIS RECIPE WORKS

Winter root vegetables are usually cooked in a way that masks their naturally bitter, earthy, and sweet flavors. We wanted to create turnips and carrots with nicely browned exteriors and tender, creamy interiors, all accented with a lightly sweetened glaze. We started by cutting the vegetables into large pieces of equal size for even cooking. Then, by caramelizing the vegetables in butter and simmering them in a combination of broth, seasonings, and a small amount of brown sugar, we created tender, but not mushy, vegetables with great flavor and browning. A little lemon zest added a nice complementary brightness, and from there it was easy to create a glaze by quickly reducing the remaining liquid.

GLAZED TURNIPS AND CARROTS WITH LEMON AND THYME

SERVES 4

When selecting turnips, choose the smallest available (about the size of plums), as they tend to be less fibrous and less bitter than their larger counterparts. Do not substitute yellow turnips for the white turnips called for in this recipe.

1½	tablespoons unsalted butter
1	pound white turnips, peeled and cut into ¾-inch cubes
3	carrots, peeled, tapered ends sliced ½ inch thick on bias, large upper portions halved lengthwise, then sliced ½ inch thick on bias
⅔	cup low-sodium chicken broth or vegetable broth
1½	tablespoons packed brown sugar
1	teaspoon fresh thyme
1	teaspoon grated lemon zest plus 1 teaspoon juice
½	teaspoon salt
⅛	teaspoon pepper

1. Melt butter in 12-inch nonstick skillet over medium-high heat. Add turnips and carrots in even layer and cook, without stirring, until browned, about 4 minutes. Stir and continue to cook, stirring occasionally, until well browned on all sides, about 4 minutes longer. Add broth, sugar, thyme, lemon zest, salt, and pepper. Cover skillet, reduce heat to medium-low, and simmer until vegetables are just tender (vegetables will give only slight resistance when poked with paring knife), about 8 minutes.

2. Uncover, increase heat to high, and cook, stirring frequently, until liquid in skillet reduces to glaze, about 1 minute. Stir in lemon juice and serve immediately.

ROASTED CARROTS

✔ WHY THIS RECIPE WORKS

Roasting carrots draws out their natural sugars and intensifies their flavor—if you can prevent them from coming out dry, shriveled, and jerky-like. Cutting the carrots into large batons about ½ inch thick gave us evenly cooked results with the best browning, and precooking the carrots before roasting kept their moisture in and minimized withering. We avoided dirtying a second pan by precooking the carrots (which we'd buttered and seasoned) right on the baking sheet, covered with foil. Then when the carrots were tender, we uncovered the baking sheet and returned it to the oven, where we roasted the carrots until their surface moisture evaporated and they took on nut-brown caramelized streaks.

ROASTED CARROTS

SERVES 4 TO 6

While cutting the carrots into uniformly sized pieces is key for even cooking, it's the large size of the pieces that makes the recipe work so make sure not to cut them too small.

1½	pounds carrots, peeled
2	tablespoons unsalted butter, melted
	Salt and pepper

1. Adjust oven rack to middle position and heat oven to 425 degrees. Cut the carrots in half crosswise, then into halves or quarters lengthwise if necessary to create uniformly sized pieces. In large bowl, combine carrots with butter, ½ teaspoon salt, and ¼ teaspoon pepper and toss to coat. Transfer carrots to foil- or parchment-lined rimmed baking sheet and spread in single layer.

2. Cover baking sheet tightly with foil and cook for 15 minutes. Remove foil and continue to cook, stirring twice, until carrots are well browned and tender, 30 to

---

TEST KITCHEN TIP NO. 57 STORING STRATEGY FOR CARROTS

In tests, we've found carrots with green tops still attached have better flavor than those sold already trimmed. But what's the best way to store them? Since the vegetable will continue to feed the leafy tops in storage, should you remove the tops when you get home from the market? We purchased several bunches of carrots, left the tops intact on half, and removed the tops from the other half. We then stored the carrots in our refrigerator's crisper drawer for two weeks. When we examined the samples, those stored with their tops attached were extremely limp, indicating moisture loss. But to our surprise, the trimmed carrots fared only slightly better.

Clearly, we needed to reevaluate our storage method. We repeated the test, this time placing both trimmed and untrimmed batches in open zipper-lock bags—a setup that trapped most of their moisture but allowed some to escape. After two weeks, the carrots with their tops on had still softened significantly, while the trimmed ones were just as firm and sweet-tasting as they had been two weeks prior.

35 minutes. Transfer to serving platter, season with salt and pepper to taste, and serve.

ROASTED CARROTS AND FENNEL WITH TOASTED ALMONDS AND LEMON

Reduce amount of carrots to 1 pound. Add 1 small fennel bulb, stalks discarded, halved, cored, and sliced ½ inch thick, to bowl with carrots and roast as directed. Toss vegetables with ¼ cup toasted sliced almonds, 2 teaspoons chopped fresh parsley, and 1 teaspoon lemon juice before serving.

ROASTED CARROTS AND PARSNIPS WITH ROSEMARY

Reduce amount of carrots to 1 pound. Add 8 ounces peeled parsnips and 1 teaspoon chopped fresh rosemary to bowl with carrots and roast as directed. Toss vegetables with 2 teaspoons chopped fresh parsley before serving.

ROASTED CARROTS AND SHALLOTS WITH LEMON AND THYME

Reduce amount of carrots to 1 pound. Add 6 shallots, peeled and halved lengthwise, and 1 teaspoon chopped fresh thyme to bowl with carrots and roast as directed. Toss vegetables with 1 teaspoon lemon juice before serving.

STEAMED AND BRAISED CAULIFLOWER

✔ WHY THIS RECIPE WORKS
We wanted a quick method for properly cooking this often-overcooked vegetable, and we also wanted to come up with a few imaginative, easy ways to flavor it. We started by nailing down a "cook first, flavor later" option. Boiling caused the cauliflower to taste watery, but steaming proved an easy method for bringing

out the vegetable's fresh, sweet taste. Seven to eight minutes yielded evenly cooked florets with clean, bright flavor, and once the cauliflower was steamed, it was easy to add the flavorings. For a "flavor while cooking" technique, we settled on a combination of sautéing and braising, since braising alone took too long and resulted in soggy cauliflower. Sautéing concentrated its flavor, then we added liquid and flavorings to the pan and cooked the cauliflower, covered, just until it was done.

STEAMED CAULIFLOWER
SERVES 4

Steamed cauliflower is best complemented by mild seasonings or the simple flavors of the recipes that follow.

  1 head cauliflower (2 pounds), cored and cut into 1-inch florets

Fit large saucepan with steamer basket. Add water, keeping level below basket. Bring water to boil, add cauliflower florets, reduce heat to medium, and cover. Steam until florets are tender but still offer some resistance when poked with paring knife, 7 to 8 minutes. Remove cauliflower from basket and serve.

STEAMED CAULIFLOWER WITH BREAD CRUMBS, CAPERS, AND CHOPPED EGGS
SERVES 4

Crumble the hard-cooked egg by pressing it through a sieve.

  2 tablespoons unsalted butter
  3 tablespoons dry bread crumbs
  1 recipe Steamed Cauliflower
  1 Foolproof Hard-Cooked Egg (page 534), crumbled fine
  2 tablespoons minced fresh parsley
  2 tablespoons capers, rinsed
  1½ tablespoons lemon juice
     Salt and pepper

Melt butter in 12-inch skillet over medium heat, add bread crumbs, and cook, stirring occasionally, until lightly browned, about 5 minutes. Add cauliflower and cook until heated through, about 1 minute. Add egg, parsley, capers, and lemon juice, and toss lightly to distribute. Season with salt and pepper to taste and serve immediately.

STEAMED CAULIFLOWER WITH DILL-WALNUT VINAIGRETTE
SERVES 4

Mustard adds a great bright punch to this dressing.

  2 tablespoons minced fresh dill
  ½ shallot, minced
  2 tablespoons olive oil
  1 tablespoon red wine vinegar
  1 tablespoon lemon juice
  1 teaspoon Dijon mustard
  ½ cup walnuts, toasted and chopped
  1 recipe Steamed Cauliflower
     Salt and pepper

Whisk dill, shallot, oil, vinegar, lemon juice, and mustard together in small bowl. Toss dressing immediately with walnuts and warm cauliflower. Season with salt and pepper to taste and serve.

BROWNED AND BRAISED CAULIFLOWER WITH GARLIC, GINGER, AND SOY
SERVES 4

The stronger flavor of browned cauliflower stands up well to bolder, more complex flavor combinations, such as these Asian flavorings.

  1½ tablespoons vegetable oil
  1 head cauliflower (2 pounds), cored and cut into 1-inch florets
  2 tablespoons grated fresh ginger
  2 garlic cloves, minced
  1 teaspoon toasted sesame oil
  ¼ cup water

2 tablespoons soy sauce
2 tablespoons rice vinegar
1 tablespoon dry sherry
2 scallions, minced
  Pepper

1. Heat vegetable oil in 12-inch skillet over medium-high heat until just smoking. Add cauliflower and cook, stirring occasionally, until beginning to brown, 6 to 7 minutes.

2. Clear center of skillet and add ginger, garlic, and sesame oil. Cook, mashing mixture into pan, until fragrant, about 1 minute. Stir ginger mixture into cauliflower and cook 30 seconds more. Reduce heat to low and add water, soy sauce, vinegar, and sherry. Cover and cook until florets are tender but still offer some resistance when poked with paring knife, 4 to 5 minutes. Add scallions and toss lightly to distribute. Season with pepper to taste and serve immediately.

BROWNED AND BRAISED CAULIFLOWER WITH INDIAN SPICES

SERVES 4

Cooking the spices for a minute or two removes their raw edge and allows their flavors to deepen.

1½ tablespoons canola oil
1 head cauliflower (2 pounds), cored and cut into 1-inch florets
½ onion, sliced thin
1 teaspoon ground cumin
1 teaspoon ground coriander
1 teaspoon ground turmeric
¼ teaspoon red pepper flakes
¼ cup plain yogurt
¼ cup water
1 tablespoon lime juice
½ cup frozen green peas, thawed (optional)
¼ cup chopped fresh cilantro
  Salt and pepper

1. Heat oil in 12-inch skillet over medium-high heat until just smoking. Add cauliflower and cook, stirring occasionally, until beginning to soften, 2 to 3 minutes. Add onion and continue cooking until florets begin to brown and onion softens, about 4 minutes longer.

2. Stir in cumin, coriander, turmeric, and pepper flakes and cook until spices begin to toast and are fragrant, about 1 to 2 minutes. Reduce heat to low and add yogurt, water, and lime juice. Cover and cook until flavors meld, about 4 minutes. Add peas, if using, and cilantro and toss to distribute. Cover and cook until florets are fully tender but offer some resistance when poked with paring knife, about 2 minutes more. Season with salt and pepper to taste and serve immediately.

ROASTED CAULIFLOWER

✔ WHY THIS RECIPE WORKS

We wanted to add flavor to cauliflower without drowning it in a heavy blanket of cheese sauce, so we developed a roasted cauliflower recipe that gave us cauliflower with a golden, nutty exterior and sweet interior. We discovered that steaming (in a covered sheet pan) followed by roasting produced nicely caramelized cauliflower with a creamy texture. Though the cauliflower is excellent on its own, we also developed some simple sauces to dress it up.

ROASTED CAULIFLOWER

SERVES 4 TO 6

This dish stands well on its own, drizzled with extra-virgin olive oil, but it can also be prepared with a sauce (recipes follow).

1 head cauliflower (2 pounds)
¼ cup extra-virgin olive oil
  Salt and pepper

CUTTING CAULIFLOWER FOR ROASTING

Cut the head of cauliflower into 8 large wedges through the center core. The core will help the wedges of cauliflower hold together and make them easy to flip over during cooking.

1. Adjust oven rack to lowest position and heat oven to 475 degrees. Trim outer leaves off cauliflower and cut stem flush with bottom. Cut head into 8 equal wedges. Place wedges cut side down on foil- or parchment-lined rimmed baking sheet. Drizzle with 2 tablespoons oil and season with salt and pepper to taste. Gently rub seasonings and oil into cauliflower. Gently flip cauliflower and repeat on second cut side with remaining 2 tablespoons oil, salt, and pepper.

2. Cover baking sheet tightly with foil and cook for 10 minutes. Remove foil and continue to roast until bottoms of cauliflower pieces are golden, 8 to 12 minutes. Remove baking sheet from oven, and, using spatula, carefully flip wedges. Return baking sheet to oven and continue to roast until cauliflower is golden all over, 8 to 12 minutes longer. Season with salt and pepper to taste and serve immediately.

SPICY ROASTED CAULIFLOWER

Stir 2 teaspoons curry powder or chili powder into the oil before seasoning the cauliflower in step 1.

CURRY-YOGURT SAUCE WITH CILANTRO

MAKES ENOUGH FOR
1 RECIPE ROASTED CAULIFLOWER

If using this sauce, use vegetable oil to roast the cauliflower instead of olive oil.

1   tablespoon vegetable oil
1   shallot, minced
2   teaspoons curry powder
¼   teaspoon red pepper flakes
⅓   cup water
¼   cup plain whole-milk yogurt
2   tablespoons minced fresh cilantro
1   teaspoon lime juice
    Salt and pepper

Heat oil in small skillet over medium-high heat until shimmering. Add shallot and cook until softened, about 2 minutes. Stir in curry powder and pepper flakes; cook until fragrant, about 1 minute. Remove from heat and whisk in water, yogurt, cilantro, lime juice, and salt and pepper to taste. Drizzle sauce over roasted cauliflower before serving.

SOY-GINGER SAUCE WITH SCALLION

MAKES ENOUGH FOR
1 RECIPE ROASTED CAULIFLOWER

If using this sauce, use vegetable oil to roast the cauliflower instead of olive oil.

2   teaspoons vegetable oil
1   tablespoon grated fresh ginger
2   garlic cloves, minced
¼   cup water
2   tablespoons soy sauce
2   tablespoons mirin
1   tablespoon rice vinegar
1   teaspoon toasted sesame oil
1   scallion, sliced thin

Heat oil in 8-inch skillet over medium-high heat until shimmering. Add ginger

and garlic and cook until fragrant, about 1 minute. Reduce heat to medium-low and add water, soy sauce, mirin, and vinegar. Simmer until slightly syrupy, 4 to 6 minutes. Drizzle sauce and sesame oil over roasted cauliflower and garnish with scallion before serving.

SHERRY VINEGAR–HONEY SAUCE WITH ALMONDS

MAKES ENOUGH FOR
1 RECIPE ROASTED CAULIFLOWER

Both regular and golden raisins work well here.

1   tablespoon extra-virgin olive oil
¼   cup raisins
2   large garlic cloves, minced
¼   cup water
3   tablespoons sherry vinegar
2   tablespoons honey
¼   cup sliced almonds, toasted
2   tablespoons minced fresh parsley
    Salt and pepper
1   tablespoon chopped fresh chives

Heat oil in 8-inch skillet over medium-high heat until shimmering. Add raisins and garlic and cook, stirring constantly, until garlic is fragrant, about 1 minute. Reduce heat to medium and add water, vinegar, and honey. Simmer until lightly syrupy, 4 to 6 minutes. Stir in almonds, parsley, and salt and pepper to taste. Drizzle sauce over roasted cauliflower and garnish with chives before serving.

CAULIFLOWER GRATIN

✔ WHY THIS RECIPE WORKS

Cauliflower gratin often falls short, with the cauliflower either undercooked or overcooked and the sauce a gluey mass that manages to swamp the bread-crumb topping. We wanted tender cauliflower florets, a lightly thickened sauce, and buttery, crisp crumbs. We parcooked the florets before adding them to the gratin to ensure they were perfectly cooked through. Then we made a Mornay sauce with shallots, garlic, nutmeg, cayenne, and Parmesan cheese. Using heavy cream instead of the usual milk gave us a cleaner flavor because it required less roux to thicken up to the right consistency. Freshly baked bread crumbs gave our gratin a perfectly toasted crust. From there, we decided to come up with a broccoli variation. The broccoli required less blanching time and a lighter sauce made with chicken broth and heavy cream. We also strongly preferred cheddar to Parmesan in this version.

CAULIFLOWER GRATIN
SERVES 6

Gruyère or cheddar can be used in place of the Parmesan.

TOPPING
4   slices hearty white sandwich bread, torn into quarters
2   tablespoons unsalted butter, softened
¼   teaspoon salt
⅛   teaspoon pepper

FILLING

- 1 large head cauliflower (3 pounds), cored and cut into ¾-inch florets
- 1 tablespoon plus ¼ teaspoon salt
- 2 tablespoons unsalted butter
- 1 shallot, minced
- 1 garlic clove, minced
- 1 tablespoon all-purpose flour
- 1½ cups heavy cream
- 1 ounce Parmesan cheese, grated (½ cup), plus 2 tablespoons
- 1 teaspoon minced fresh thyme
- ⅛ teaspoon pepper
  Pinch ground nutmeg
  Pinch cayenne pepper

1. FOR THE TOPPING: Pulse bread, butter, salt, and pepper in food processor until mixture resembles coarse crumbs, about 10 pulses; set aside.

2. FOR THE FILLING: Adjust oven rack to middle position and heat oven to 450 degrees. Bring 4 quarts water to boil in Dutch oven over high heat. Add cauliflower and 1 tablespoon salt and cook until just tender, 3 to 4 minutes. Drain cauliflower in colander and rinse under cold water until no longer hot. Leave cauliflower in colander to drain while preparing sauce.

3. Melt butter in 12-inch skillet over medium heat, add shallot, and cook until softened, about 2 minutes. Add garlic and cook until fragrant, about 30 seconds. Stir in flour until combined, about 1 minute. Whisk in cream and bring to boil. Stir in ½ cup Parmesan, thyme, remaining ¼ teaspoon salt, pepper, nutmeg, and cayenne until incorporated. Off heat, gently stir in cauliflower until evenly combined. Transfer mixture to 11 by 7-inch (2-quart) gratin dish. Sprinkle remaining 2 tablespoons Parmesan evenly over surface, then sprinkle evenly with bread-crumb topping. Bake until golden brown and sauce is bubbling around edges, 10 to 12 minutes. Serve immediately.

TO MAKE AHEAD: Topping and cauliflower can be prepared and stored at room temperature for up to 2 hours. Don't prepare sauce or bake gratin until just before serving.

CAULIFLOWER GRATIN WITH LEEKS AND GRUYÈRE

Add 1 pound leeks, white and light green parts only, halved lengthwise, sliced ¼-inch thick, and washed thoroughly, to skillet with shallot in step 3 and increase cooking time to about 4 minutes, until leeks are softened. Substitute 2 ounces Gruyère cheese, grated (½ cup), plus 2 tablespoons, for the Parmesan.

CAULIFLOWER GRATIN WITH HAM AND CHEDDAR CHEESE

Add 6 ounces ham steak, cut into ½-inch cubes, to skillet with shallot in step 3. Substitute 2 ounces cheddar cheese, grated (½ cup), plus 2 tablespoons, for the Parmesan.

BROCCOLI AND CHEDDAR GRATIN
SERVES 6

This spin on our cauliflower gratin brings together the classic pair of broccoli and cheddar in a rich, satisfying casserole.

TOPPING

- 4 slices hearty white sandwich bread, torn into quarters
- 2 tablespoons unsalted butter, softened
- ¼ teaspoon salt
- ⅛ teaspoon pepper

FILLING

- 2 pounds broccoli, florets cut into 1-inch pieces, stalks peeled and chopped
- 1 tablespoon plus ¼ teaspoon salt
- 2 tablespoons unsalted butter
- 1 shallot, minced
- 1 garlic clove, minced
- 1 tablespoon all-purpose flour
- ¾ cup heavy cream
- ¾ cup low-sodium chicken broth
- 4 ounces sharp cheddar cheese, grated (1 cup)
- 1 teaspoon minced fresh thyme
- ⅛ teaspoon pepper
  Pinch ground nutmeg
  Pinch cayenne pepper

1. FOR THE TOPPING: Pulse bread, butter, salt, and pepper in food processor until mixture resembles coarse crumbs, about 10 pulses; set aside.

2. FOR THE FILLING: Adjust oven rack to middle position and heat oven to 450 degrees. Bring 4 quarts water to boil in Dutch oven over high heat. Add broccoli and 1 tablespoon salt and cook until just tender, about 3 minutes. Drain broccoli in colander; leave in colander to drain while preparing sauce.

3. Melt butter in large skillet over medium heat, add shallot, and cook until softened, about 2 minutes. Add garlic and cook until fragrant, about 30 seconds; stir in flour until combined, about 1 minute. Whisk in cream and broth and bring to boil. Stir in ⅔ cup cheddar, thyme, remaining ¼ teaspoon salt, pepper, nutmeg, and cayenne until incorporated. Off heat, gently stir in broccoli until evenly combined. Transfer mixture to 11 by 7-inch (2-quart) gratin dish. Sprinkle remaining ⅓ cup cheese evenly over surface, then sprinkle evenly with bread-crumb topping. Bake until golden brown and sauce is bubbling around edges, 10 to 12 minutes. Serve immediately.

TO MAKE AHEAD: Topping and broccoli can be prepared and stored at room temperature for up to 2 hours. Don't prepare sauce or bake gratin until just before serving.

CORN ON THE COB

✔ WHY THIS RECIPE WORKS

Although boiling corn on the cob is pretty straight-forward, there are some variables to consider. We found that corn boiled in salted water was predictably tougher than corn boiled in unsalted water. Sugar-seasoned water, however, brought out the natural sweetness of the corn in the same way that salted water enhances the flavors of other vegetables, assuming the corn is not of the supersweet variety (which is what you'll typi-cally find in supermarkets during the off-season because of its long shelf life). We tried cooking the corn in milk but this only masked the corn's flavor, so we stuck with water.

BOILED CORN ON THE COB
SERVES 8

If you want to serve more corn, bring a second pot of water to a boil at the same time or cook the corn in batches in just one pot. If you know that you have supersweet corn, omit the sugar.

- 4 teaspoons sugar (optional)
- 8 ears corn, husks and silk removed
  Salt and pepper
- I recipe flavored butter (recipes follow), or plain butter (optional)

Bring 4 quarts water and sugar, if using, to boil in large pot. Add corn, return to boil, and cook until tender, 5 to 7 minutes. Drain corn, season with salt and pepper to taste, and serve immediately with butter, if using.

STEAMED CORN ON THE COB
SERVES 8

Make sure your pot is big enough to accommo-date all 8 ears of corn.

- 8 ears corn, husks and silk removed
  Salt and pepper
- I recipe flavored butter (recipes follow), or plain butter (optional)

Fit large stockpot with steamer basket. Add water, keeping level below basket. Bring water to boil over high heat, then carefully place corn in basket. Cover and steam corn until tender, 7 to 10 minutes. Using tongs, remove corn from basket, season with salt and pepper to taste, and serve immediately with butter, if using.

LIME-CILANTRO BUTTER
MAKES ENOUGH FOR I RECIPE BOILED CORN ON THE COB OR STEAMED CORN ON THE COB

This brightly flavored butter is perfect when pair-ing the corn with a Mexican or Spanish meal.

- 6 tablespoons unsalted butter, softened
- I½ teaspoons grated lime zest
- I tablespoon minced fresh cilantro
  Pinch cayenne pepper

Using fork, beat butter in small bowl until light and fluffy. Beat in lime zest, cilantro, and cayenne until thoroughly combined.

ROASTED GARLIC AND HERB BUTTER
MAKES ENOUGH FOR I RECIPE BOILED CORN ON THE COB OR STEAMED CORN ON THE COB

Dry-toasting garlic is a good option when you want to mellow the punch of raw garlic but don't have time to roast a whole head of garlic in the oven.

- 10 garlic cloves, skins left on
- 6 tablespoons unsalted butter, softened
- I tablespoon minced fresh parsley
- I tablespoon minced fresh basil
- ⅛ teaspoon pepper

I. Toast garlic in 10-inch skillet over medium heat, shaking pan occasionally, until softened and spotty brown, about 8 minutes. When cool, skin and mince cloves.

2. Using fork, beat butter in small bowl until light and fluffy. Beat in garlic, pars-ley, basil, and pepper until thoroughly combined.

CREAMY CORN PUDDING

✔ WHY THIS RECIPE WORKS

We wanted a corn pudding with a tender, creamy custard (one that didn't curdle or weep) and lots of corn flavor. We used a combina-tion of whole and grated kernels, as well as the "milk" from the cobs (which we collected by scraping the cleaned cobs with the back of a butter knife) to achieve big corn flavor and an appealing texture. Cooking the pudding in a water bath helped ensure a creamy tex-ture. To remedy the weeping problem, we first cooked the corn in butter until most of the liq-uid had evaporated, then simmered it in heavy cream (which, unlike milk or light cream, won't curdle when boiled). Cayenne added a good finishing kick.

CREAMY CORN PUDDING
SERVES 6

This recipe should be served hot and cannot be reheated, so plan ahead accordingly.

- 6 ears corn, husks and silk removed
- 3 tablespoons unsalted butter plus extra for baking dish
- ⅔ cup heavy cream
- I½ teaspoons salt
- I teaspoon sugar
- ¼ teaspoon cayenne pepper
- I⅓ cups whole milk
- 4 large eggs, lightly beaten
- I tablespoon cornstarch

I. Cut kernels from 5 ears corn into medium bowl, then scrape cobs with back of butter knife over bowl to collect milk

GRATING AND MILKING CORN

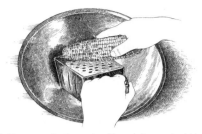

1. To grate the kernels off ear of corn, hold box grater over large, wide bowl and grate each ear over large holes of grater.

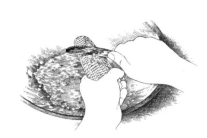

2. Firmly scrape each cob with back of butter knife to remove milk and pulp.

(you should have about 2½ cups kernels and milk). Grate remaining 1 ear corn on coarse side of box grater (you should have about ½ cup grated kernels). Add grated kernels to bowl with cut kernels.

2. Adjust oven rack to lower-middle position, place roasting pan or large baking dish on rack, and heat oven to 350 degrees. Generously butter 8-inch square baking dish. Bring 2 quarts water to boil in kettle or saucepan.

3. Melt butter in 12-inch skillet over medium heat. Add corn and cook, stirring occasionally, until corn is bright yellow and liquid has almost evaporated, about 5 minutes. Add cream, salt, sugar, and cayenne and cook, stirring occasionally, until thickened and spoon leaves trail when pan bottom is scraped, about 5 minutes. Transfer mixture to medium bowl. Stir milk into mixture, then whisk in eggs and cornstarch. Pour mixture into buttered baking dish.

4. Set filled dish in roasting pan or large baking dish already in oven. Fill outer pan with boiling water to reach halfway up inner dish. Bake until center jiggles slightly when shaken and pudding has browned lightly in spots, 20 to 25 minutes. Remove baking dish from water bath, cool for 10 minutes, and serve.

SAUTÉED EGGPLANT

✔ WHY THIS RECIPE WORKS

Cooking eggplant can be challenging because it's such a porous, watery vegetable. For eggplant with rich, meaty flavor, we turned to salting and pressing strips of eggplant. We let the salted eggplant sit in a colander for at least 1½ hours, and preferably 2 to 3, to allow the salt to do its job. Next, we firmly pressed the drained eggplant between sheets of paper towels to extrude more juice and compact the flesh. We found the vegetable always came out firmer, browner, and sweeter when cooked slowly rather than quickly.

SAUTÉED EGGPLANT
SERVES 4 TO 6

You can substitute finely shredded basil for the parsley if desired.

2	pounds eggplant, cut crosswise into ¾-inch-thick rounds, then cut into ¾-inch strips
	Kosher salt and pepper
3	tablespoons extra-virgin olive oil
3	garlic cloves, minced
2–4	tablespoons minced fresh parsley

1. Line baking sheet with triple layer of paper towels and set aside. Toss eggplant with 1 tablespoon salt in large bowl, transfer to colander, and let sit for at

least 1½ hours, or up to 3 hours, stirring periodically.

2. Wipe excess salt from eggplant. Lay eggplant strips about 1 inch apart on prepared baking sheet, then cover with another triple layer of paper towels. Using your palms, press each eggplant strip very firmly until it looks green and translucent and feels firm and leathery when pressed between fingertips. (Repeat pressing process on fresh towels if eggplant has not yet reached this stage.)

3. Heat oil in 12-inch skillet until it shimmers and becomes fragrant. Add eggplant strips and cook until they begin to brown, about 3 minutes. Reduce heat to medium-low and cook, stirring occasionally, until eggplant is fully tender and lightly browned, 15 to 20 minutes. Stir in garlic and cook for 2 minutes. Off heat, stir in parsley, season with salt and pepper to taste, and serve.

TO MAKE AHEAD: Eggplant can be prepared through step 2 and refrigerated for up to 3 hours.

SAUTÉED EGGPLANT WITH CRISPED BREAD CRUMBS

Pulse 1 slice hearty white sandwich bread, torn into quarters, in food processor to coarse crumbs, about 10 pulses. Add bread crumbs with garlic in step 3 and toss lightly to coat strips. Turn heat to high and cook until crumbs begin to brown, about 1 minute. Toss and continue to cook until crumbs are fully browned, about 1 minute longer. Substitute finely shredded basil for parsley.

SAUTÉED EGGPLANT IN SPICY GARLIC SAUCE

Any type of vinegar works in this recipe.

Combine 2 tablespoons dry sherry, 2 tablespoons soy sauce, 2 tablespoons vinegar, and 1 teaspoon sugar in small bowl; set aside. Substitute 2 tablespoons toasted sesame oil and 1 tablespoon peanut or vegetable oil for olive oil. Increase garlic to 6 cloves and add 2 teaspoons grated fresh ginger and ¼ teaspoon crushed red pepper flakes with garlic in step 3. Cook 1 minute, add sherry mixture, and simmer until eggplant absorbs liquid, about 1 minute. Substitute 2 tablespoons minced cilantro plus 2 tablespoons thinly sliced scallions for parsley.

SAUTÉED EGGPLANT IN TOMATO SAUCE WITH BASIL

Stir in 1¼ cups crushed tomatoes after garlic has cooked for 1 minute. Simmer until tomatoes thicken slightly, 2 to 3 minutes. Substitute ⅓ cup finely shredded fresh basil for parsley.

CAPONATA

✔ WHY THIS RECIPE WORKS

This classic Sicilian dish, featuring a mix of sautéed vegetables (primarily tomatoes and eggplant) and accented with anchovies, capers, and pine nuts, can turn out greasy thanks to the spongy nature of eggplants, which causes them to soak up oil.. For a balanced and boldly flavored caponata with eggplant that didn't turn to oil-soaked mush, we found that salting and microwaving the eggplant, rather than just salting and draining, was critical for drying it out sufficiently. Adding V8 juice, in addition to the tomatoes, gave our caponata a bright, fresh flavor, while brown sugar and red wine vinegar gave it the sweet and sour finish that distinguishes caponata from other vegetable dishes like ratatouille.

CAPONATA
MAKES 3 CUPS

Serve caponata spooned over slices of toasted baguette or alongside grilled meat or fish. Adjust the vinegar as necessary, depending on the acidity of your tomatoes and what you are serving with the caponata. To allow the steam released by the eggplant to escape, remove the plate from the microwave immediately. Although the test kitchen prefers the complex flavor of V8 vegetable juice, tomato juice can be substituted. Caponata is best made a day in advance to allow the flavors to meld.

1½	pounds eggplant, cut into ½-inch pieces
¾	teaspoon kosher salt
¾	cup V8 juice
¼	cup red wine vinegar, plus extra for seasoning
¼	cup minced fresh parsley
2	tablespoons light brown sugar
3	anchovy fillets, rinsed and minced
8	ounces tomatoes, cored, seeded, and cut into ½-inch pieces
¼	cup raisins
2	tablespoons minced black olives
1	tablespoon plus 2 teaspoons extra-virgin olive oil, plus extra 1 teaspoon if needed
1	celery rib, cut into ¼-inch pieces
1	small red bell pepper, stemmed, seeded and cut into ¼-inch pieces
1	small onion, chopped fine
¼	cup pine nuts, toasted

1. Toss eggplant and salt together in bowl. Line surface of large plate with double layer of coffee filters and lightly spray with vegetable oil spray. Spread eggplant in even layer over coffee filters. Microwave until eggplant is dry and shriveled to one-third its size but is not brown, 8 to 15 minutes. (If microwave has no turntable, rotate plate after 5 minutes.) Remove eggplant from microwave and immediately transfer to paper towel–lined plate.

2. Meanwhile, whisk V8 juice, vinegar, parsley, brown sugar, and anchovies together in medium bowl. Stir in tomatoes, raisins, and olives.

3. Heat 1 tablespoon oil in 12-inch nonstick skillet over medium-high heat until shimmering. Add eggplant and cook, stirring occasionally, until edges are browned, 4 to 8 minutes, adding up to 1 teaspoon oil if pan appears dry. Transfer to bowl and set aside.

4. Add remaining 2 teaspoons oil to now-empty skillet and heat until shimmering. Add celery and red pepper and cook, stirring occasionally, until softened and edges are spotty brown, 2 to 4 minutes. Add onion and continue to cook until vegetables are browned, about 4 minutes longer.

5. Reduce heat to medium-low and stir in eggplant and V8 juice mixture. Bring to simmer and cook until vegetable juice is thickened and coats vegetables, 4 to 7 minutes. Transfer to serving bowl and cool to room temperature. Taste and season with up to 1 teaspoon additional vinegar, if necessary. Sprinkle with pine nuts before serving. (Caponata can be refrigerated for up to 1 week.)

RATATOUILLE

✔ WHY THIS RECIPE WORKS

All too often, ratatouille can turn out flavorless, oily, and mushy. We were after a ratatouille that would bring together firm eggplant, zucchini, caramelized onions, garlic, herbs, and sweet, juicy tomatoes into a stewlike dish with maximum flavor and texture. To get the best out of each component, we handled each one carefully, salting and pressing the eggplant cubes to keep them from soaking up lots of oil, then roasting them in the oven with zucchini, which caramelized the flavors and allowed both vegetables to retain their shape. The garlic, onion, and tomatoes were at their best when sautéed together on the stovetop, and we waited to add the tomatoes until close to the end of cooking to ensure they didn't turn to mush. Then we tossed the roasted vegetables and stirred in the chopped herbs at the very end to maintain their freshness.

RATATOUILLE
SERVES 4 TO 6

For the best-flavored ratatouille, we recommend very ripe beefsteak tomatoes.

2½ pounds eggplant, cut into 1-inch cubes
    Kosher salt and pepper
3   zucchini, cut into 1-inch cubes
¼   cup olive oil
1   large onion, chopped
2   garlic cloves, minced
1   pound tomatoes, cored, peeled, and cut into 2-inch cubes
2   tablespoons chopped fresh parsley
2   tablespoons chopped fresh basil
1   tablespoon minced fresh thyme

1. Line baking sheet with triple layer of paper towels and set aside. Toss eggplant and 1 tablespoon salt together in bowl, then transfer to colander. Let eggplant sit at least 1 hour or up to 3 hours. Wipe excess salt from eggplant, then arrange on prepared baking sheet. Cover with another triple layer of paper towels, then press firmly on eggplant until eggplant is dry and feels firm.

2. Adjust oven racks to upper-middle and lower-middle positions and heat oven to 500 degrees. Line 2 rimmed baking sheets with aluminum foil.

3. Toss eggplant, zucchini, and 2 tablespoons oil together in large bowl, then divide evenly between prepared baking sheets, spreading in single layer on each. Season with salt to taste and roast, stirring every 10 minutes, until well-browned and tender, 30 to 40 minutes, rotating baking sheets from top to bottom halfway through roasting time. Set aside.

4. Heat remaining 2 tablespoons oil in Dutch oven over medium heat until shimmering. Add onion, reduce heat to medium-low, and cook, stirring frequently, until softened and golden brown, 15 to 20 minutes. Stir in garlic and cook until fragrant, about 30 seconds. Add tomatoes and cook until they release their juices and begin to break down, about 5 minutes. Add roasted eggplant and zucchini, stirring gently but thoroughly to combine, and cook until just heated through, about 5 minutes. Stir in parsley, basil, and thyme. Season with salt and pepper to taste and serve. (Ratatouille can be refrigerated for up to 3 days.)

PEELING TOMATOES

1. Place cored tomatoes in pot of boiling water. Boil until skins split and begin to curl around core area, 15 seconds for very ripe tomatoes or up to 30 seconds for underripe ones. Remove tomatoes from water with slotted spoon and place in bowl of ice water.

2. Let tomatoes cool for 1 minute. Using paring knife, peel skins from the flesh starting at curled edges at core.

BRAISED WINTER GREENS

✔ WHY THIS RECIPE WORKS
We wanted a one-pot approach to turning winter greens like kale and collards tender, without spending hours or leaving them awash in liquid. We sautéed half of the greens before adding the rest with a little bit of liquid and covered the pot. When the greens almost had the tender-firm texture we wanted, we removed the lid to allow the liquid to cook off. With the texture right where we wanted it, all we had to do was come up with a few flavorful ingredients to add to the pot.

BRAISED WINTER GREENS
SERVES 4

For the best results, be sure the greens are fully cooked and tender in step 1 before moving on to step 2.

3   tablespoons olive oil
1   onion, chopped fine
5   garlic cloves, minced
⅛   teaspoon red pepper flakes
2   pounds kale or collard greens, stemmed and leaves chopped into 3-inch pieces
1   cup low-sodium chicken broth
1   cup water
    Salt and pepper
2–3 teaspoons lemon juice

1. Heat 2 tablespoons oil in Dutch oven over medium heat until shimmering. Add onion and cook, stirring frequently, until softened and beginning to brown, 4 to 5 minutes. Add garlic and pepper flakes and cook until garlic is fragrant, about 1 minute. Add half of greens and stir until beginning to wilt, about 1 minute. Add remaining greens, broth, water, and ¼ teaspoon salt. Quickly cover pot and reduce heat to medium-low. Cook, stirring occasionally, until greens are tender, 25 to 35 minutes for kale and 35 to 45 minutes for collards.

When prepping hearty greens like collards or kale for our Braised Winter Greens, cutting out the central rib from each leaf individually can be tedious and time-consuming. Here's a way to speed up the process.

1. Stack 3 or 4 leaves on top of each other, large to small, aligning their central ribs.

2. Fold stack of greens in half along the central rib.

3. Trim central rib using one knife stroke. Repeat with remaining leaves.

4. Chop leaves crosswise into 3-inch pieces.

2. Remove lid and increase heat to medium-high. Cook, stirring occasionally, until most of liquid has evaporated (bottom of pot will be almost dry and greens will begin to sizzle), 8 to 12 minutes. Off heat, stir in 2 teaspoons lemon juice and remaining 1 tablespoon oil. Season with salt, pepper, and lemon juice to taste and serve.

BRAISED WINTER GREENS WITH BACON AND ONION

Cook 6 slices bacon, cut into ¼-inch pieces, over medium heat until crisp, 5 to 7 minutes. Transfer bacon to paper towel–lined plate and pour off all but 2 tablespoons fat. Use rendered fat in place of 2 tablespoons olive oil, substitute 1 red onion, halved and cut into ¼-inch slices, for minced onion, and 3 to 4 teaspoons cider vinegar for lemon juice. Stir reserved bacon into greens before serving.

BRAISED WINTER GREENS WITH COCONUT AND CURRY

Substitute 2 teaspoons grated fresh ginger and 1 teaspoon curry powder for red pepper flakes and one 14-ounce can coconut milk for water. Substitute 2 to 3 teaspoons

lime juice for lemon juice and sprinkle greens with ⅓ cup toasted cashews before serving.

BRAISED WINTER GREENS WITH CHORIZO

Heat oil as directed in step 1, then add 8 ounces Spanish chorizo sausage, cut into ¼-inch-thick half-moons, and cook until lightly browned, 4 to 6 minutes. Transfer chorizo to paper towel–lined plate. Proceed with recipe, cooking onion and garlic in remaining oil and substituting 1½ teaspoons ground cumin for red pepper flakes. Stir in reserved chorizo before serving.

SAUTÉED BABY SPINACH

✔ WHY THIS RECIPE WORKS

Baby spinach is convenient—no stems to remove or grit to rinse out—but cooking often turns the tender greens into a watery, mushy mess. We were determined to find a method for cooking baby spinach that would give us a worthwhile side dish. Parcooking the spinach in the microwave turned out to be the best way to help the vegetable release plenty of liquid. We pressed the microwaved spinach against a colander to eliminate more water, coarsely

chopped it, and pressed it again. Then all we had to do was quickly sauté it. We then combined the spinach with a few complementary flavors and appealing textures to finish the dish.

SAUTÉED BABY SPINACH WITH ALMONDS AND GOLDEN RAISINS

SERVES 4

If you don't have a bowl large enough to accommodate the entire amount of spinach, cook it in a smaller bowl in two batches. Reduce the water to 2 tablespoons per batch and cook the spinach for about 1½ minutes.

18	ounces baby spinach
¼	cup water
2	tablespoons plus 2 teaspoons extra-virgin olive oil
4	garlic cloves, sliced thin crosswise
¼	teaspoon red pepper flakes
½	cup golden raisins
	Salt
2	teaspoons sherry vinegar
⅓	cup slivered almonds, toasted

1. Place spinach and water in large bowl. Cover bowl with large dinner plate (plate should completely cover bowl and not rest on spinach). Microwave until spinach is wilted and decreased in volume by half, 3 to 4 minutes. Remove bowl from microwave and keep covered for 1 minute. Carefully remove plate and transfer spinach to colander. Using back of rubber spatula, gently press spinach against colander to release excess liquid. Transfer spinach to cutting board and chop coarse. Return spinach to colander and press again.

2. Heat 2 tablespoons oil, garlic, pepper flakes, and raisins in 10-inch skillet over medium-high heat. Cook, stirring constantly, until garlic is light golden brown and beginning to sizzle, 3 to 6 minutes. Add spinach to skillet, using tongs to stir and coat with oil. Sprinkle with ¼ teaspoon salt and continue stirring with tongs until spinach is uniformly wilted and glossy green, about 2 minutes. Sprinkle with vinegar and almonds; stir to combine. Drizzle with remaining 2 teaspoons oil and season with salt to taste. Serve immediately.

SAUTÉED BABY SPINACH WITH PECANS AND FETA

SERVES 4

If you don't have a bowl large enough to accommodate the entire amount of spinach, cook it in a smaller bowl in two batches. Reduce the water to 2 tablespoons per batch and cook the spinach for about 1½ minutes.

- 18 ounces baby spinach
- ¼ cup water
- 2 tablespoons plus 2 teaspoons extra-virgin olive oil
- 4 shallots, sliced thin
  Salt
- ⅓ cup pecans, toasted and chopped
- 2 teaspoons red wine vinegar
- 1½ ounces feta cheese, crumbled (⅓ cup)

1. Place spinach and water in large bowl. Cover bowl with large dinner plate (plate should completely cover bowl and not rest on spinach). Microwave until

spinach is wilted and decreased in volume by half, 3 to 4 minutes. Remove bowl from microwave and keep covered for 1 minute. Carefully remove plate and transfer spinach to colander. Using back of rubber spatula, gently press spinach against colander to release excess liquid. Transfer spinach to cutting board and chop coarse. Return spinach to colander and press again.

2. Heat 2 tablespoons oil and shallots in 10-inch skillet over medium-high heat. Cook, stirring constantly, until shallots are golden brown, 3 to 5 minutes. Add spinach to skillet, using tongs to stir and coat with oil. Sprinkle with ¼ teaspoon salt and continue stirring with tongs until spinach is uniformly wilted and glossy green, about 2 minutes. Sprinkle with pecans and vinegar and stir to combine. Drizzle with remaining 2 teaspoons oil and sprinkle with feta. Season with salt to taste and serve immediately.

SAUTÉED BABY SPINACH WITH CHICKPEAS AND SUN-DRIED TOMATOES

SERVES 4

If you don't have a bowl large enough to accommodate the entire amount of spinach, cook it in a smaller bowl in two batches. Reduce the water to 2 tablespoons per batch and cook the spinach for about 1½ minutes.

- 18 ounces baby spinach
- ¼ cup plus 2 tablespoons water
- 2 tablespoons plus 2 teaspoons extra-virgin olive oil
- 4 garlic cloves, sliced thin crosswise
- ¾ cup canned chickpeas, rinsed
- ½ cup oil-packed sun-dried tomatoes, drained and sliced thin
  Salt
- 1 ounce Parmesan cheese, grated (½ cup)

1. Place spinach and ¼ cup water in large bowl. Cover bowl with large dinner

plate (plate should completely cover bowl and not rest on spinach). Microwave until spinach is wilted and decreased in volume by half, 3 to 4 minutes. Remove bowl from microwave and keep covered for 1 minute. Carefully remove plate and transfer spinach to colander. Using back of rubber spatula, gently press spinach against colander to release excess liquid. Transfer spinach to cutting board and chop coarse. Return spinach to colander and press again.

2. Heat 2 tablespoons oil and garlic in 10-inch skillet over medium-high heat. Cook, stirring constantly, until garlic is light golden brown and beginning to sizzle, 3 to 6 minutes. Add chickpeas, tomatoes, and remaining 2 tablespoons water and cook, stirring occasionally, until water evaporates and tomatoes are softened, 1 to 2 minutes. Add spinach to skillet, using tongs to stir and coat with oil. Sprinkle with ¼ teaspoon salt and continue stirring with tongs until spinach is uniformly wilted and glossy green, about 2 minutes. Sprinkle with 2 tablespoons Parmesan and stir to combine. Drizzle with remaining 2 teaspoons oil and sprinkle with remaining 6 tablespoons Parmesan. Season with salt to taste and serve immediately.

SAUTÉED BABY SPINACH WITH LEEKS AND HAZELNUTS

SERVES 4

If you don't have a bowl large enough to accommodate the entire amount of spinach, cook it in a smaller bowl in two batches. Reduce the water to 2 tablespoons per batch and cook the spinach for about 1½ minutes.

- 18 ounces baby spinach
- ¼ cup water, plus extra if needed
- 2 tablespoons unsalted butter
- 2 leeks, white and light green parts only, halved lengthwise, sliced thin, and washed thoroughly
- ½ teaspoon grated lemon zest plus 1 tablespoon juice

Salt

⅛ teaspoon ground nutmeg

2 tablespoons heavy cream

⅓ cup hazelnuts, toasted, skinned, and chopped

1. Place spinach and ¼ cup water in large bowl. Cover bowl with large dinner plate (plate should completely cover bowl and not rest on spinach). Microwave until spinach is wilted and decreased in volume by half, 3 to 4 minutes. Remove bowl from microwave and keep covered for 1 minute. Carefully remove plate and transfer spinach to colander. Using back of rubber spatula, gently press spinach against colander to release excess liquid. Transfer spinach to cutting board and chop coarse. Return spinach to colander and press again.

2. Melt butter in 10-inch skillet over medium heat. Add leeks and cook, stirring occasionally, until softened, 10 to 15 minutes, adding 1 teaspoon water to skillet if leeks begin to color. Add spinach to skillet, using tongs to stir and coat with butter. Sprinkle with lemon zest, ¼ teaspoon salt, and nutmeg and continue stirring with tongs until spinach is uniformly wilted and glossy green, about 2 minutes. Drizzle with lemon juice and cream and stir to combine. Sprinkle with hazelnuts and season with salt to taste. Serve immediately.

SAUTÉED SPINACH WITH GARLIC AND LEMON

✔ WHY THIS RECIPE WORKS
Overcooked spinach, burnt garlic, and pallid lemon flavor are all too often the hallmarks of this side dish. We were after tender sautéed spinach seasoned with a perfect balance of garlic and lemon. We started with bunched flat-leaf spinach and cooked it in fruity extra-virgin olive oil with slivered garlic (lightly browned in the pan

before the spinach was added). Squeezing the spinach in a colander got rid of excess moisture. A combination of lemon juice and zest gave it the right lemony flavor, and red pepper flakes lent some good heat.

SAUTÉED SPINACH WITH GARLIC AND LEMON
SERVES 4

The amount of spinach may seem excessive, but the spinach wilts considerably with cooking. We like to use a salad spinner to wash and dry the spinach. If you have kosher or coarsely ground sea salt on hand, use it for the final sprinkling just before serving. This spinach dish makes an excellent accompaniment to almost any main course, from chicken and fish to steak and pork.

2 tablespoons plus 1 teaspoon extra-virgin olive oil

4 garlic cloves, sliced very thin

30 ounces curly-leaf spinach, stemmed

½ teaspoon grated lemon zest plus 2 teaspoons juice

Salt

Pinch red pepper flakes

1. Heat 2 tablespoons oil and garlic in Dutch oven over medium-high heat and cook until garlic is light golden brown, shaking pan back and forth when garlic begins to sizzle, about 3 minutes (stirring with a spoon will cause the garlic to clump). Add spinach by the handful, using tongs to stir and coat spinach with oil.

2. Once all spinach is added, sprinkle with lemon zest, ¼ teaspoon salt, and pepper flakes and continue stirring with tongs until spinach is uniformly wilted and glossy green, about 2 minutes. Using tongs, transfer spinach to colander and gently squeeze with tongs to release excess liquid. Return spinach to Dutch oven, sprinkle with lemon juice, and stir to coat. Drizzle with remaining 1 teaspoon oil and season with additional salt to taste. Serve immediately.

FENNEL

✔ WHY THIS RECIPE WORKS
While fennel is excellent served raw in salads or antipasti, its crisp anise flavor turns mild and sweet once cooked. We found that fennel generally responds best to dry-heat cooking methods because they promote caramelization, which intensifies its sweet character (braising is the exception, as this method allows the fennel to absorb flavors from the cooking liquid). The problem with cooking fennel lies in trying to achieve uniformly tender pieces. A combination of proper vegetable prep and cooking technique turned out to be the key to evenly cooked fennel. Fan-shaped wedges proved good for braising, while smaller pieces were necessary for sautéing and roasting. In all cases, it was important to cook the fennel slowly to deliver uniformly tender but not mushy results.

BRAISED FENNEL WITH WHITE WINE AND PARMESAN
SERVES 4

This rich side dish works well with beef or veal.

3 tablespoons butter

2 fennel bulbs, stalks discarded, bulbs halved, cored, and cut crosswise into ½-inch-thick slices

Salt and pepper

⅓ cup dry white wine

¼ cup grated Parmesan cheese

1. Melt butter over medium heat in 12-inch skillet. Add fennel and sprinkle with salt and pepper to taste. Add wine, cover, and simmer for 15 minutes. Turn slices over and continue to simmer, covered, until fennel is quite tender, has absorbed most of pan liquid, and starts to turn golden, about 10 minutes longer. Turn fennel again and continue cooking until fennel begins to turn golden on other side, about 4 minutes longer.

2. Sprinkle fennel with cheese and serve immediately.

ROASTED FENNEL WITH RED ONIONS AND CARROTS

SERVES 4

Drizzling balsamic vinegar over the vegetables during the last minutes of roasting highlights their sweetness. Serve this as a side dish with chicken or veal.

- 2 fennel bulbs, stalks discarded, bulbs halved, cored, and cut crosswise into ½-inch-thick slices
- 1 red onion, cut into 8 wedges
- 2 carrots, peeled, halved lengthwise, and cut crosswise into 2-inch lengths
- 2 tablespoons olive oil
   Salt
- 1 tablespoon balsamic vinegar

1. Adjust oven rack to middle position and heat oven to 425 degrees. Toss fennel, onion, and carrots in large roasting pan with oil. Season with salt to taste. Roast 30 minutes, turning vegetables once after 20 minutes.

2. Drizzle vinegar over vegetables and toss gently. Continue roasting until vegetables are richly colored and tender, about 5 minutes longer. Season with salt to taste. Serve hot or warm.

SAUTÉED FENNEL WITH GARLIC AND PARSLEY

SERVES 4

Sautéing causes the anise flavor of fennel to fade but concentrates the natural sugars in the vegetable. This side dish particularly complements seafood or poultry.

- 3 tablespoons olive oil
- 4 garlic cloves, minced
- 2 fennel bulbs, fronds minced, stalks discarded, bulbs halved, cored, and cut crosswise into ½-inch-thick slices
- 2 tablespoons minced fresh parsley

1. Heat oil in 12-inch skillet over medium heat. Add garlic and cook until lightly colored, about 1 minute. Add fennel strips and toss to coat with oil. Cook, stirring often, until fennel has softened considerably but still offers some resistance when poked with paring knife, about 15 minutes.

2. Season with salt and pepper to taste. Stir in 1 tablespoon minced fronds and parsley. Serve immediately.

TWO WAYS TO PREPARE FENNEL

FOR FANS

Slice trimmed bulb lengthwise through base into ½-inch-thick pieces that resemble fans.

FOR STRIPS

1. Cut trimmed bulb in half through base. Using small, sharp knife, remove pyramid-shaped core.

2. Lay cored fennel half on work surface cut side down. With knife parallel to work surface, cut in half crosswise. Then cut lengthwise into ½-inch-thick strips.

BRAISED BELGIAN ENDIVES

✓ WHY THIS RECIPE WORKS

The right cooking method transforms sharp, bitter endives into a side dish of uncommonly complex flavor—at once mellow, sweet, and rich, yet still faintly bitter. Our challenge was to develop the deep flavor, richness, and gentle sweetness necessary to balance the endives' natural bite. We browned the endives in butter and sugar for maximum richness and sweetness, then braised them quickly in white wine and chicken broth for a deep yet brightly flavored vegetable side dish.

BRAISED BELGIAN ENDIVES

SERVES 4

To avoid discoloration, do not cut the endives far in advance of cooking. Delicate endives can fall apart easily if not handled gently. Move the halved endives in the pan by grasping the curved sides gingerly with tongs and supporting the cut sides with a spatula while lifting and turning.

- 3 tablespoons unsalted butter
- ½ teaspoon sugar
   Salt and pepper
- 4 heads Belgian endive (4 ounces each), halved lengthwise
- ¼ cup dry white wine
- ¼ cup low-sodium chicken broth
- ½ teaspoon minced fresh thyme
- 1 tablespoon minced fresh parsley
- 1 teaspoon lemon juice

1. Melt 2 tablespoons butter in 12-inch heavy-bottomed skillet over medium-high heat. Sprinkle sugar and ¼ teaspoon salt evenly in skillet and set endives, cut sides down, in single layer. Cook, shaking skillet occasionally to prevent sticking, until golden brown, about 5 minutes (reduce heat if endives brown too quickly). Turn endives over and cook until curved sides are golden brown, about 3 minutes longer. Carefully turn endives cut sides down. Add wine, broth, and thyme and reduce heat to low, cover, and simmer, checking

occasionally, until leaves open up slightly and endives are tender throughout when poked with paring knife, 13 to 15 minutes (add 2 tablespoons water during cooking if pan appears dry). Transfer endives to warmed serving platter and set aside.

2. Increase heat to medium-high and bring liquid in skillet to boil; reduce heat and simmer until reduced to syrupy consistency, 1 to 2 minutes. Off heat, whisk in remaining 1 tablespoon butter, parsley, and lemon juice. Season with salt and pepper to taste, spoon sauce over endives, and serve immediately.

BRAISED BELGIAN ENDIVES WITH BACON AND CREAM

Cook 3 slices bacon, cut into ¼-inch pieces, in 12-inch skillet over medium heat until crisp, 5 to 7 minutes. Transfer bacon to paper towel–lined plate and set aside. Pour off all but 2 tablespoons fat from skillet. Substitute rendered fat for butter when browning endives in step 1, and substitute 2 tablespoons heavy cream for butter in step 2. Omit lemon juice. Sprinkle sauced endives with reserved bacon and serve.

CIDER-BRAISED BELGIAN ENDIVES WITH APPLES

Because the apples absorb some of the braising liquid, more cider is added to the pan before the sauce is reduced.

Add 1 Granny Smith apple, peeled, cored, and cut into ¼-inch-thick wedges, to skillet with endives. Substitute ½ cup apple cider for chicken broth and wine. Remove apples from skillet along with endives at end of step 1, then add 2 tablespoons more cider to skillet and continue with recipe from step 2, omitting lemon juice.

SAUTÉED MUSHROOMS

✔ WHY THIS RECIPE WORKS
Supermarket mushrooms shrink and shrivel when sautéed. We wanted to develop a quick sauté method that delivered enough white mushrooms to make a delicious, ample side dish. To get more flavor and less shriveling, we discovered that overloading the skillet and extending the cooking time allowed the mushrooms to give up just enough liquid to eventually fit in a single layer without shrinking to nothing. They browned nicely after we added a little oil or butter, and from there it was easy to enhance our sautéed mushroom recipe with additions like garlic, herbs, wine, soy sauce, and bread crumbs.

SAUTÉED MUSHROOMS WITH GARLIC, PARMESAN, AND BREAD CRUMBS

SERVES 4

Make sure to toss the cooked mushrooms with the Parmesan soon after you transfer them to the bowl so that the cheese melts properly.

- 2 slices hearty white sandwich bread, torn into quarters
- 3 tablespoons unsalted butter
- 1 tablespoon vegetable oil
- 1½ pounds white mushrooms, trimmed and halved if small or quartered if large
- 2 garlic cloves, minced
  Salt and pepper
- 1 ounce Parmesan cheese, grated (½ cup)
- 2 tablespoons minced fresh parsley

1. Pulse bread in food processor to coarse crumbs, about 10 pulses. Melt 2 tablespoons butter in 12-inch skillet over medium-high heat. Add bread crumbs and cook, stirring frequently, until dark brown, about 3 minutes. Transfer crumbs to bowl and set aside.

2. Heat oil in now-empty skillet over medium-high heat until shimmering. Add mushrooms and cook, stirring occasionally, until mushrooms release liquid, about 5 minutes. Increase heat to high and cook, stirring occasionally, until liquid has completely evaporated, about 8 minutes longer. Add remaining 1 tablespoon butter, reduce heat to medium, and continue to cook, stirring once every minute, until mushrooms are dark brown, about 8 minutes longer.

3. Add garlic and cook, stirring constantly, until fragrant, about 30 seconds. Season with salt and pepper to taste and transfer to bowl. Toss hot mushrooms with Parmesan until cheese melts. Toss with bread crumbs and parsley and serve.

SAUTÉED MUSHROOMS WITH SESAME AND GINGER

SERVES 4

We like to use a rasp-style grater for grating ginger quickly, though the small holes of a box grater also work well.

- 2 tablespoons peanut oil
- 1½ pounds white mushrooms, trimmed and halved if small or quartered if large
- 1 tablespoon sesame seeds, toasted
- 1 tablespoon grated fresh ginger
- 2 tablespoons mirin
- 2 tablespoons soy sauce
- 1 teaspoon toasted sesame oil
- 2 scallions, sliced thin on bias

1. Heat 1 tablespoon peanut oil in 12-inch skillet over medium-high heat until shimmering. Add mushrooms and cook, stirring occasionally, until mushrooms release liquid, about 5 minutes. Increase heat to high and cook, stirring occasionally, until liquid has completely evaporated, about 8 minutes longer. Add remaining

1 tablespoon peanut oil, reduce heat to medium, and continue to cook, stirring once every minute, until mushrooms are dark brown, about 8 minutes longer.

2. Add sesame seeds and ginger and cook, stirring constantly, until ginger is fragrant, about 30 seconds. Add mirin and soy sauce and cook, stirring constantly, until liquid has evaporated, about 30 seconds. Remove from heat and stir in sesame oil. Transfer to serving dish, sprinkle with scallions, and serve.

SAUTÉED MUSHROOMS WITH SHALLOTS AND THYME

SERVES 4

Marsala is a classic choice for complementing the earthy flavor of mushrooms.

I	tablespoon vegetable oil
I½	pounds white mushrooms, trimmed and halved if small or quartered if large
I	tablespoon unsalted butter
I	shallot, minced
I	tablespoon minced fresh thyme
¼	cup dry Marsala
	Salt and pepper

I. Heat oil in 12-inch skillet over medium-high heat until shimmering. Add mushrooms and cook, stirring occasionally, until mushrooms release liquid, about 5 minutes. Increase heat to high and cook, stirring occasionally, until liquid has completely evaporated, about 8 minutes longer. Add butter, reduce heat to medium, and continue to cook, stirring once every minute, until mushrooms are dark brown, about 8 minutes longer.

2. Add shallot and thyme and cook until softened, about 3 minutes. Add Marsala and cook until liquid has evaporated, about 2 minutes. Season with salt and pepper to taste and serve.

SAUTÉED MUSHROOMS WITH BACON AND PEARL ONIONS

SERVES 4

Do not thaw the pearl onions here; they should be added to the skillet still frozen.

4	slices bacon, cut into ½-inch pieces
I	cup frozen pearl onions
I	teaspoon sugar
½	cup ruby port
I½	pounds white mushrooms, trimmed and halved if small or quartered if large
I	tablespoon unsalted butter
I	tablespoon minced fresh parsley
	Salt and pepper
2	ounces blue cheese, crumbled (½ cup) (optional)

I. Cook bacon in 12-inch skillet over medium-high heat until beginning to render fat, about 1 minute. Add onions and sugar and cook, stirring occasionally, until bacon is crisp and onions are light brown, about 8 minutes. Using slotted spoon, transfer onions and bacon to medium bowl. Reserve 1 tablespoon bacon fat in small bowl; discard remaining fat. Add ¼ cup port to now-empty skillet, return to medium-high heat, and simmer about 30 seconds, scraping up any browned bits with wooden spoon. Pour port into bowl with bacon and onions; wipe out skillet with paper towels.

2. Heat reserved fat in now-empty skillet over medium-high heat until shimmering. Add mushrooms and cook, stirring occasionally, until mushrooms release liquid, about 5 minutes. Increase heat to high and cook, stirring occasionally, until liquid has completely evaporated and mushrooms start to brown, about 8 minutes longer. Add butter, reduce heat to medium, and continue to cook, stirring once every minute, until mushrooms are dark brown,

about 8 minutes longer. Add bacon mixture and remaining ¼ cup port and cook, stirring frequently, until liquid has evaporated and mushrooms are glazed, about 2 minutes. Stir in parsley and season with salt and pepper to taste. Transfer to serving dish, sprinkle with blue cheese, if using, and serve.

STUFFED PORTOBELLO MUSHROOMS

✓ WHY THIS RECIPE WORKS

We wanted the ultimate stuffed mushroom side dish, showcasing meaty, earthy, intense mushrooms with a filling that contributed complementary flavors and textures. Choosing portobello caps for their large size, rich flavor, and wide availability, we removed excess moisture by cutting slits in the caps before precooking them in the oven (salting only made them slimy). Then we developed a few rules for the perfect filling: chopped stems made a convenient and good base, cheese (rather than bread crumbs or béchamel sauce) worked best for a binder, and some cream added richness. Fresh bread crumbs toasted with butter gave our stuffed mushroom recipe a final flourish and contrasting texture.

STUFFED PORTOBELLO MUSHROOMS WITH SPINACH AND GOAT CHEESE

SERVES 4 AS A MAIN COURSE OR 8 AS A SIDE DISH

When shopping, choose dense mushrooms with a cupped shape. Blue cheese can be substituted for the goat cheese. This recipe can easily be halved. Make sure to buy whole portobello mushrooms for this recipe, not just prepackaged caps.

10 portobello mushrooms (4 to 5 inches in diameter), stems removed and reserved

¼ cup olive oil
    Salt and pepper

12 ounces baby spinach (12 cups)

2 tablespoons water

2 slices hearty white sandwich bread, torn into quarters

2 tablespoons unsalted butter

2 onions, chopped fine

4 garlic cloves, minced

½ cup dry sherry

4 ounces goat cheese, crumbled (1 cup)

1 cup walnuts, toasted and chopped coarse

¼ cup heavy cream

2 tablespoons chopped fresh thyme

2 teaspoons lemon juice

1. Adjust oven rack to upper-middle position, place rimmed baking sheet on rack, and heat oven to 400 degrees. Using sharp knife, cut ¼-inch-deep slits, spaced ½ inch apart, in crosshatch pattern on smooth surface (non-gill side) of 8 mushrooms. Dice remaining 2 mushroom caps and reserved stems into ½-inch pieces; set aside (you should have about 3 cups).

2. Brush both sides of whole caps with 2 tablespoons oil and sprinkle evenly with 1 teaspoon salt. Carefully place caps, gill side up, on preheated baking sheet. Roast until mushrooms have released some of their juices and are beginning to brown around edges, 8 to 12 minutes. Flip caps over and continue to roast until liquid has completely evaporated and caps are golden brown, 8 to 12 minutes longer. Remove mushrooms from oven and heat broiler.

3. While mushrooms roast, place spinach and water in large bowl. Cover bowl with large dinner plate (plate should completely cover bowl and not rest on spinach).

Microwave until spinach is wilted and decreased in volume by half, 3 to 4 minutes. Remove bowl from microwave and keep covered for 1 minute. Carefully remove plate and transfer spinach to colander. Using back of rubber spatula, gently press spinach against colander to release excess liquid. Transfer spinach to cutting board and chop coarse. Return spinach to colander and press again. Set aside.

4. Pulse bread in food processor to coarse crumbs, about 10 pulses (you should have about 1½ cups). Heat 1 tablespoon oil and 1 tablespoon butter in 12-inch skillet over medium heat until butter is melted. Add bread crumbs and ¼ teaspoon salt and cook, stirring frequently, until light golden brown, 5 to 8 minutes. Transfer crumbs to small bowl and wipe out skillet with paper towels.

5. Return now-empty skillet to medium-high heat, add remaining 1 tablespoon oil, and heat until smoking. Add chopped mushrooms and cook, without stirring, for 2 minutes. Continue cooking, stirring occasionally, until lightly browned, 4 to 6 minutes longer. Transfer to medium bowl.

6. Add remaining 1 tablespoon butter and onions to skillet and cook, stirring occasionally, until onions are light brown, 5 to 6 minutes. Add garlic and cook until fragrant, about 30 seconds. Stir in sherry and cook until almost no liquid remains, 1 to 2 minutes. Reduce heat to low and stir in reserved cooked mushrooms, spinach, goat cheese, walnuts, cream, and thyme. Continue cooking until cheese is melted and vegetables are well coated, 1 to 2 minutes. Remove pan from heat, stir in lemon juice, and season with salt and pepper to taste.

7. Flip caps gill side up and distribute filling evenly among mushroom caps. Top each stuffed cap with 2 tablespoons bread-crumb mixture. Broil mushrooms until

crumbs are golden brown, 1 to 3 minutes. Serve immediately.

TO MAKE AHEAD: Filling can be made up to 2 days ahead and refrigerated. Rewarm before stuffing mushrooms. Do not roast mushrooms in advance, as they become leathery once rewarmed.

STUFFED PORTOBELLO MUSHROOMS WITH CHEDDAR AND PROSCIUTTO

SERVES 4 AS A MAIN COURSE OR 8 AS A SIDE DISH

For time efficiency, place mushrooms in the oven after you begin to sauté the diced mushrooms. When shopping, choose dense mushrooms with a cupped shape. This recipe can easily be halved.

12 portobello mushrooms (4 to 5 inches in diameter), stems removed and reserved

5 tablespoons olive oil
    Salt and pepper

2 slices hearty white sandwich bread, torn into quarters

2 tablespoons unsalted butter

3 ounces prosciutto, chopped

2 onions, chopped fine

4 garlic cloves, minced

½ cup dry sherry

4 ounces cheddar cheese, shredded (1 cup)

¼ cup heavy cream

2 tablespoons chopped fresh thyme

2 tablespoons roughly chopped fresh parsley

2 teaspoons lemon juice

1. Adjust oven rack to upper-middle position, place rimmed baking sheet on rack, and heat oven to 400 degrees. Using sharp knife, cut ¼-inch-deep slits, spaced ½ inch apart, in crosshatch pattern on smooth surface (non-gill side) of

8 mushrooms. Dice remaining 4 mushroom caps and reserved stems into ½-inch pieces; set aside (you should have about 6 cups).

2. Brush both sides of whole caps with 2 tablespoons oil and sprinkle evenly with 1 teaspoon salt. Carefully place caps, gill side up, on preheated baking sheet. Roast until mushrooms have released some of their juices and are beginning to brown around edges, 8 to 12 minutes. Flip caps over and continue to roast until liquid has completely evaporated and caps are golden brown, 8 to 12 minutes longer. Remove mushrooms from oven and heat broiler.

3. Pulse bread in food processor to coarse crumbs, about 10 pulses (you should have about 1½ cups). Heat 1 tablespoon oil and 1 tablespoon butter in 12-inch skillet over medium heat until butter is melted. Add bread crumbs and ¼ teaspoon salt and cook, stirring frequently, until light golden brown, 5 to 8 minutes. Transfer crumbs to small bowl and wipe out skillet with paper towels.

4. Return now-empty skillet to medium-high heat, add 1 tablespoon oil, and heat until smoking. Add half of chopped mushrooms and cook, without stirring, for 2 minutes. Continue cooking, stirring occasionally, until lightly browned, 4 to 6 minutes longer. Transfer to medium bowl and repeat with remaining 1 tablespoon oil and remaining mushrooms.

5. Add remaining 1 tablespoon butter, prosciutto, and onions to skillet and cook, stirring occasionally, until onions are light brown, 5 to 6 minutes. Add garlic and cook until fragrant, about 30 seconds. Stir in sherry and cook until almost no liquid remains, 1 to 2 minutes. Reduce heat to low and stir in reserved cooked mushrooms, cheddar, cream, thyme, and parsley. Continue cooking until cheddar is melted and vegetables are well coated, 1 to 2 minutes. Remove pan from heat, stir in lemon juice, and season with salt and pepper to taste.

6. Flip caps gill side up and distribute filling evenly among mushroom caps. Top each stuffed cap with 2 tablespoons breadcrumb mixture. Broil mushrooms until crumbs are golden brown, 1 to 3 minutes. Serve immediately.

TO MAKE AHEAD: Filling can be made up to 2 days ahead and refrigerated. Rewarm before stuffing mushrooms. Do not roast mushrooms in advance, as they become leathery once rewarmed.

ROASTED RED BELL PEPPERS

✓ WHY THIS RECIPE WORKS

Sweet red bell peppers take on a whole new layer of complex, smoky flavor when roasted. We wanted a method for roasting them that was more efficient than the common technique of roasting each pepper over a gas burner, letting it steam in a covered bowl, then laboriously removing the skin bit by bit. We discovered the broiler offered an easy, consistent, and more hands-off option than the burner (roasting in either a hot or low oven yielded soggy, overcooked peppers). To get around the issue of whole peppers hitting the broiler element, we cut the peppers into pieces that lay flat on a sheet pan. After 10 minutes, the peppers were done and we could easily peel off the blistered skin.

ROASTED RED BELL PEPPERS
MAKES 4 ROASTED PEPPERS

Cooking times vary, depending on the broiler, so watch the peppers carefully as they roast. You can substitute yellow or orange peppers here, but note that they roast faster than red ones, so decrease their cooking time by 2 to 4 minutes.

4   red bell peppers, stemmed, seeded, ribs removed, and cut to lie flat

---

PREPARING BELL PEPPERS FOR ROASTING

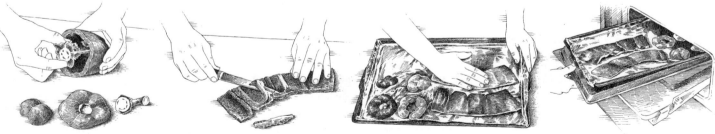

1. Slice ¼ inch from top and bottom of bell pepper, then gently remove stem from top slice. Pull core out of pepper.

2. Make slit down 1 side of pepper, then lay it flat, skin side down, in 1 long strip. Slide sharp knife along inside of pepper and remove all ribs and seeds.

3. Arrange strips of peppers and tops and bottoms skin side up on foil-lined baking sheet. Flatten the strips with palm of your hand.

4. Adjust oven rack to top position. If rack is more than 3 inches from heating element, set rimmed baking sheet, bottom up, on rack under baking sheet.

1. Adjust oven rack 2½ to 3½ inches from broiler element and heat broiler. If necessary, set upside down rimmed baking sheet on oven rack to elevate pan (see illustration 4 on page 273). Line baking sheet with aluminum foil.

2. Spread peppers out over prepared baking sheet and broil until skin is charred and puffed but flesh is still firm, 8 to 10 minutes, rotating baking sheet halfway through cooking.

3. Transfer peppers to medium bowl, cover with foil, and let steam until skin peels off easily, 10 to 15 minutes. Peel and discard skin.

BLANCHED SUGAR SNAP PEAS

✔ WHY THIS RECIPE WORKS

We wanted to determine a cooking method that would highlight the crisp texture and sweet flavor of sugar snap peas. We found that salt was a must. Blanching them in salted water produced peas with excellent flavor and texture. The only problem was that blanched peas tend to shrivel or pucker a bit as they cool. We solved this problem by plunging the cooked peas in ice water as soon as they were drained. This also helped to set their bright color and prevent further softening from residual heat.

BLANCHED SUGAR SNAP PEAS
SERVES 6

See following recipes for seasoning ideas.

    1   teaspoon salt
    1   pound sugar snap peas, strings
        removed

1. Fill a large bowl with ice water and set aside. Bring 6 cups water to boil in large saucepan. Add salt and peas and cook until peas are crisp-tender, 1½ to 2 minutes.

2. Drain peas, transfer to bowl with ice water, drain again, and pat dry. (Peas can be set aside for up to 1 hour.)

SUGAR SNAP PEAS WITH LEMON, GARLIC, AND BASIL
SERVES 6

Keep a close eye on the garlic, as it can go from soft to brown quickly during cooking.

    2   tablespoons olive oil
    1½   teaspoons grated lemon zest plus
         1 tablespoon juice
    1   garlic clove, minced
    1   recipe Blanched Sugar Snap Peas
    2   tablespoons chopped fresh basil
         Salt and pepper

Heat oil over medium heat in 10-inch skillet until shimmering. Add zest and garlic and cook until garlic is soft but not browned, about 2 minutes. Add peas, lemon juice, and basil and toss to combine. Cook until just heated through, 1 to 1½ minutes. Season with salt and pepper to taste and serve immediately.

SUGAR SNAP PEAS WITH HAM AND MINT
SERVES 6

Do not use sliced deli ham for this recipe.

    1   tablespoon unsalted butter
    3   ounces country ham or smoked
        ham, cut into ¼-inch pieces
    1   recipe Blanched Sugar Snap Peas
    2   tablespoons chopped fresh mint
        Salt and pepper

Melt butter over medium heat in 10-inch skillet. Add ham and cook 1 minute. Add peas and mint and toss to combine. Cook until just heated through, 1 to 1½ minutes. Season with salt and pepper to taste and serve immediately.

SUGAR SNAP PEAS WITH ASIAN DRESSING
SERVES 6

To mingle the flavors, you can let the peas and dressing stand for up to 10 minutes; longer than that and the peas start to lose their bright green color.

    2   tablespoons orange juice
    2   tablespoons rice vinegar
    1   teaspoon honey
    ½   teaspoon soy sauce
    1   scallion, sliced thin
    ½   teaspoon grated fresh ginger
    2   tablespoons peanut oil
    1   teaspoon toasted sesame oil
    2   teaspoons sesame seeds, toasted
         Salt and pepper
    1   recipe Blanched Sugar Snap Peas

Combine orange juice, vinegar, honey, soy sauce, scallion, and ginger in small bowl. Whisk in peanut oil and sesame oil. Stir in sesame seeds and season with salt and pepper to taste. (Dressing can be set aside for several hours.) Toss dressing with peas and serve.

SUGAR SNAP PEAS WITH HAZELNUT BUTTER AND SAGE
SERVES 6

Because you must judge the color of the butter as it cooks, avoid dark-colored pans like nonstick.

    2   tablespoons unsalted butter
    1   recipe Blanched Sugar Snap Peas
    2   tablespoons chopped fresh sage
    2   tablespoons toasted, skinned, and
         chopped hazelnuts
         Salt and pepper

Melt butter over medium heat in 10-inch skillet and continue to cook until it browns to color of brown sugar and smells nutty, about 5 minutes. Add peas, sage, and nuts and toss to combine. Cook until just heated through, 1 to 1½ minutes. Season with salt and pepper to taste and serve immediately.

SAUTÉED PEAS

✔ WHY THIS RECIPE WORKS

Frozen peas have already been blanched, so the keys to making a good and easy-to-prepare side dish from them are to avoid overcooking and to pair the peas with ingredients that don't require much preparation. We found that five minutes of simmering was all that was needed to produce bright, tender green peas. Switching from a saucepan to a skillet allowed the peas to heat more quickly and evenly over the larger surface. Butter stirred in after the peas finished simmering contributed body without drowning them in fat, while a generous dose of chopped fresh mint provided a nice aromatic complement. A healthy squirt of lemon juice stirred into the peas just before serving rounded out the flavors, and a smidge of sugar added to the broth brought everything into balance. From there, it was easy to come up with several flavorful variations.

SAUTÉED PEAS WITH SHALLOTS AND MINT

SERVES 4

Do not thaw the peas before cooking. Regular frozen peas can be used in place of baby peas; increase the cooking time in step 2 by 1 to 2 minutes. Add the lemon juice right before serving; otherwise, the peas will turn brown.

- 2 teaspoons olive oil
- 1 small shallot, minced
- 1 garlic clove, minced
- 3 cups frozen baby peas
- ¼ cup low-sodium chicken broth
- ¼ teaspoon sugar
- ¼ cup minced fresh mint
- 1 tablespoon unsalted butter
- 2 teaspoons lemon juice
  Salt and pepper

1. Heat oil in 12-inch skillet over medium-high heat until shimmering. Add shallot and cook, stirring frequently, until softened, about 2 minutes. Add garlic and cook, stirring frequently, until fragrant, about 30 seconds.

2. Stir in peas, broth, and sugar. Cover and cook until peas are bright green and just heated through, 3 to 5 minutes. Add mint and butter and toss to combine. Off heat, stir in lemon juice. Season with salt and pepper to taste and serve immediately.

SAUTÉED PEAS WITH LEEKS AND TARRAGON

Substitute 1 small leek, white and light green parts only, halved lengthwise, cut into ¼-inch pieces, and washed thoroughly, for shallot and increase cooking time in step 1 to 3 to 5 minutes (leek should be softened). Substitute heavy cream for broth, 2 tablespoons minced tarragon for mint, and white wine vinegar for lemon juice.

SAUTÉED PEAS WITH MUSHROOMS AND THYME

Substitute 6 ounces trimmed and quartered cremini mushrooms for shallot, and increase cooking time in step 1 to 3 to 5 minutes (mushrooms should be light golden brown). Substitute 2 tablespoons minced fresh thyme for mint.

SAUTÉED PEAS WITH HAM AND CHIVES

Substitute 3 ounces deli ham, cut into ¼-inch cubes (about ½ cup), for shallot and decrease cooking time in step 1 to 1 minute. Substitute 2 tablespoons minced fresh chives for mint.

SAUTÉED PEAS WITH FENNEL

Substitute ½ small fennel bulb, fronds minced, stalks discarded, bulb halved, cored, and cut into ¼-inch pieces, for shallot and increase cooking time in step 1 to 3 to 5 minutes (fennel should be softened). Substitute 2 tablespoons minced fennel fronds for mint.

SAUTÉED PEAS WITH COCONUT MILK AND CILANTRO

Substitute 2 tablespoons grated fresh ginger for shallot and decrease cooking time in step 1 to 1 minute. Substitute ¼ cup coconut milk for broth, ¼ cup minced cilantro for mint, and 2 teaspoons lime juice for lemon.

SKILLET-ROASTED POTATOES

✔ WHY THIS RECIPE WORKS

Greasy potatoes, burnt crusts, and uneven cooking were just three of the problems we had to solve to resurrect this classic method of roasting spuds on the stovetop. We wanted to find a way to make skillet-roasted potatoes that were as good as oven-roasted. This would be our go-to recipe when we craved roasted potatoes but there was no room in the oven for the conventional kind. The key turned out to be choosing the right potatoes and cutting them uniformly: red potatoes, halved or quartered depending on their size, offered a great crust and a moist interior. The winning cooking technique for our stovetop-roasted potatoes was to first brown the potatoes over high heat, then cover them and finish the cooking over low heat, which allowed the insides to cook through while the outsides stayed crisp.

SKILLET-ROASTED POTATOES
SERVES 3 TO 4

Small and medium potatoes will both work in this recipe. Small potatoes (1½ to 2 inches in diameter) should be cut in half; medium potatoes (2 to 3 inches in diameter) should be cut into quarters to make ¾- to 1-inch chunks. Large potatoes should not be used because the cut pieces will be uneven and won't cook at the same rate. For even cooking and proper browning, the potatoes must be cooked in a single layer and should not be crowded in the pan. A nonstick skillet simplifies cleanup but is not essential.

1½	pounds small red potatoes
2	tablespoons olive oil
½	teaspoon salt
¼	teaspoon pepper

1. Rinse potatoes in cold water and drain well; spread on clean kitchen towel and thoroughly pat dry.

2. Heat oil in 12-inch nonstick skillet over medium-high heat until shimmering. Add potatoes, cut side down, in single layer and cook, without stirring, until golden brown (oil should sizzle but not smoke), 5 to 7 minutes. Using tongs, turn potatoes skin side down if using halved small potatoes or second cut side down if using quartered medium potatoes. Cook, without stirring, until deep golden brown, 5 to 6 minutes longer. Stir potatoes, then redistribute in single layer. Reduce heat to medium-low, cover, and cook until potatoes are tender (paring knife can be inserted into potatoes with no resistance), 6 to 9 minutes.

3. When potatoes are tender, sprinkle with salt and pepper and toss or stir gently to combine; serve immediately.

SKILLET-ROASTED POTATOES WITH GARLIC AND ROSEMARY

Combine 3 small minced garlic cloves and 2 teaspoons minced fresh rosemary in small bowl. After seasoning potatoes with salt and pepper in step 3, clear center of skillet and add garlic and rosemary mixture. Cook over medium-low heat, mashing with heatproof spatula, until fragrant, about 45 seconds, then stir mixture into potatoes.

SPICY SKILLET-ROASTED POTATOES WITH CHILI AND CUMIN

Stir 1 teaspoon chili powder, 1 teaspoon sweet paprika, ½ teaspoon ground cumin, and ¼ teaspoon cayenne together in small bowl. Substitute chili mixture for pepper, adding to the pan in step 3 and cooking until spices are fragrant, about 30 seconds.

TEST KITCHEN TIP NO. 60 CHOOSE THE RIGHT POTATO

Although all vegetables vary by size and freshness, most markets carry only a single variety. Broccoli is broccoli, carrots are carrots. With potatoes, this is not the case. Make french fries with red potatoes and the fries will be greasy and heavy. Use russets in salad or corn chowder and they will fall apart in a soggy mess. We find that potato varieties can be divided into three major categories based on texture:

DRY, FLOURY POTATOES (Russet, Russet Burbank, Idaho): Also known as "baking" potatoes, this group contains more total starch (20 percent to 22 percent) and amylose than other categories, giving these varieties a dry, mealy texture. These potatoes are the best choice when baking and frying. They are also great potatoes for mashing, because they can drink up butter and cream. They are good when you want to thicken a stew or soup but not if you want distinct chunks of potatoes.

IN-BETWEEN POTATOES (Yukon Gold, Yellow Finn, Purple Peruvian, Kennebec, Katahdin): These potatoes contain less total starch (18 percent to 20 percent) and amylose than dry, floury potatoes but more total starch and amylose than firm, waxy potatoes. Although they are "in-between" potatoes, their texture is more mealy than firm, putting them closer to dry, floury potatoes. They can be mashed or baked and they can be used in salads and soups but won't be quite as firm as waxy potatoes.

FIRM, WAXY POTATOES (Red Bliss, French Fingerling, Red Creamer, White Rose): Also known as "boiling" potatoes, these potatoes contain a relatively low amount of total starch (16 percent to 18 percent) and very little amylose, which means they have a firm, smooth, waxy texture. Freshly dug potatoes, which are often called "new" potatoes, fall into this group. These potatoes are perfect when you want the potatoes to hold their shape, as with potato salad; they're also a good choice when roasting or boiling.

SMASHED POTATOES

✔ WHY THIS RECIPE WORKS

Bold flavors and a rustic, chunky texture make smashed potatoes a satisfying side dish that pairs well with a range of entrées. We were after a good contrast of textures, with chunks of potato bound by a rich, creamy puree. Low-starch, high-moisture red potatoes were the best choice for smashing since their compact structure held up well under pressure, maintaining its integrity, and their red skins provided nice contrasting color. For the best chunky texture, we smashed the potatoes, which we had cooked whole in salted water with a bay leaf, with a rubber spatula or back of a wooden spoon. Giving the potatoes a few minutes to dry ensured the skins weren't too slippery, making the job even easier. A combination of cream cheese, melted butter, and a little reserved potato cooking water gave our potatoes a unified creamy consistency.

SMASHED POTATOES

SERVES 4 TO 6

White potatoes can be used instead of red, but the dish won't be as colorful. We prefer to use small potatoes, 2 inches in diameter, in this recipe. Try to get potatoes of equal size; if that's not possible, test the larger potatoes for doneness. If only larger potatoes are available, increase the cooking time by about 10 minutes.

- 2 pounds small red potatoes
  Salt and pepper
- 1 bay leaf
- 4 ounces cream cheese, room temperature
- 4 tablespoons unsalted butter, melted
- 3 tablespoons chopped fresh chives (optional)

1. Place potatoes in large saucepan and cover with 1 inch cold water. Add 1 teaspoon salt and bay leaf. Bring to boil over high heat, then reduce heat to medium-low

and simmer gently until paring knife can be inserted into potatoes with no resistance, 35 to 45 minutes. Reserve ½ cup cooking water, then drain potatoes. Return potatoes to pot, discard bay leaf, and let potatoes sit in pot, uncovered, until surfaces are dry, about 5 minutes.

2. While potatoes dry, whisk softened cream cheese and melted butter in medium bowl until smooth and fully incorporated. Add ¼ cup of reserved cooking water, ½ teaspoon pepper, chives, if using, and ½ teaspoon salt. Using rubber spatula or back of wooden spoon, smash potatoes just enough to break skins. Fold in cream cheese mixture until most of liquid has been absorbed and chunks of potatoes remain. Add more cooking water as needed, 1 tablespoon at a time, until potatoes are slightly looser than desired (potatoes will thicken slightly with sitting). Season with salt and pepper to taste; serve immediately.

GARLIC-ROSEMARY SMASHED POTATOES

Add 2 peeled garlic cloves to potatoes in saucepan along with salt and bay leaf in step 1. Melt 4 tablespoons butter in 8-inch skillet over medium heat. Add ½ teaspoon chopped fresh rosemary and 1 minced garlic clove and cook until just fragrant, about 30 seconds; substitute butter-garlic mixture for melted butter, adding cooked garlic cloves to cream cheese along with butter-garlic mixture. Omit chives.

SMASHED POTATOES WITH BACON AND PARSLEY

Cook 6 slices bacon, cut lengthwise then into ¼-inch pieces, in 10-inch skillet over medium heat until crisp, 5 to 7 minutes. Using slotted spoon, transfer bacon to paper towel–lined plate; reserve 1 tablespoon fat. Substitute bacon fat for 1 tablespoon melted unsalted butter,

2 tablespoons chopped fresh parsley for chives, and reduce salt added to cream cheese mixture to ¼ teaspoon. Sprinkle potatoes with cooked bacon before serving.

ROASTED SMASHED POTATOES

✔ WHY THIS RECIPE WORKS

We were after a new potato side dish with mashed-potato creaminess and crackly-crisp crusts without deep frying. Using red potatoes for their moist texture and thin skin, we parcooked the potatoes on a baking sheet covered in aluminum foil on the oven's bottom rack with a splash of water in the pan. This drier-heat method gave us potatoes with creamy flesh that tasted sweet, deep, and earthy. After a short rest (very hot potatoes crumbled apart when smashed), we drizzled the potatoes with olive oil and pressed them into patties on the baking sheet. To do this, we simply placed another baking sheet on top of them and then pushed down evenly and firmly. In one fell swoop, we had perfect cracked patties. With a little more seasoning and another stint in the oven on the top rack, we had browned, crisped potatoes.

ROASTED SMASHED POTATOES

SERVES 4 TO 6

This recipe is designed to work with potatoes 1½ to 2 inches in diameter; do not use potatoes any larger. It is important to thoroughly cook the potatoes so that they will smash easily. Remove the potatoes from the baking sheet as soon as they are done browning—they will toughen if left too long. A potato masher can also be used to "smash" the potatoes.

- 2 pounds small red potatoes
- 6 tablespoons extra-virgin olive oil
- 1 teaspoon chopped fresh thyme
  Salt and pepper

1. Adjust oven racks to top and bottom positions and heat oven to 500 degrees. Arrange potatoes on rimmed baking sheet, pour ¾ cup water into baking sheet, and wrap tightly with aluminum foil. Cook on bottom rack until paring knife or skewer slips in and out of potatoes easily (poke through foil to test), 25 to 30 minutes. Remove foil and cool 10 minutes. If any water remains on baking sheet, blot dry with paper towel.

2. Drizzle 3 tablespoons oil over potatoes and roll to coat. Space potatoes evenly on baking sheet and place second baking sheet on top; press down firmly on baking sheet, flattening potatoes until ⅓ to ½ inch thick. Sprinkle with thyme, season with salt and pepper to taste, and drizzle evenly with remaining 3 tablespoons oil. Roast potatoes on top rack for 15 minutes, then transfer potatoes to bottom rack and continue to roast until well browned, 20 to 30 minutes longer. Serve immediately.

CRISP ROASTED POTATOES

WHY THIS RECIPE WORKS

For roasted potatoes with the crispiest exterior and creamiest interior, we had to find the right spud, the right shape, and the right cooking method. Parcooking proved key, as gently simmering our potatoes drew starch and sugar to the surface and washed away the excess quickly. In the oven, the starch and sugar hardened into a crisp shell. Slicing the potatoes into ½-inch-thick rounds before parcooking them allowed for perfectly even cooking and browning, and vigorously tossing the parcooked rounds with olive oil and salt created a roughed-up surface, which in turn sped up evaporation during roasting, making the exterior crusts even crispier. After testing several varieties, we settled on Yukon Golds, which crisped up perfectly yet had enough moisture to give us the creamy interior we were after.

CRISP ROASTED POTATOES
SERVES 4 TO 6

The steps of parcooking the potatoes before roasting and tossing the potatoes with salt and oil until they are coated with starch are the keys to developing a crisp exterior and creamy interior. The potatoes should be just undercooked when they are removed from the boiling water.

- 2½ pounds Yukon Gold potatoes, cut into ½-inch-thick slices
  Salt and pepper
- 5 tablespoons olive oil

1. Adjust oven rack to lowest position, place rimmed baking sheet on rack, and heat oven to 450 degrees. Place potatoes and 1 tablespoon salt in Dutch oven, then cover with 1 inch cold water. Bring to boil over high heat, then reduce heat and gently simmer until exteriors of potatoes have softened but centers offer resistance when poked with paring knife, about 5 minutes. Drain potatoes well and transfer to large bowl.

2. Drizzle potatoes with 2 tablespoons oil and sprinkle with ½ teaspoon salt; using rubber spatula, toss to combine. Repeat with 2 tablespoons oil and ½ teaspoon salt and continue to toss until exteriors of potato slices are coated with starchy paste, 1 to 2 minutes.

3. Working quickly, remove baking sheet from oven and drizzle remaining 1 tablespoon oil over surface. Carefully transfer potatoes to baking sheet and spread into even layer (place end pieces skin side up). Bake until bottoms of potatoes are golden brown and crisp, 15 to 25 minutes, rotating baking sheet after 10 minutes.

4. Remove baking sheet from oven and, using metal spatula and tongs, loosen potatoes from pan and carefully flip each slice. Continue to roast until second side is golden and crisp, 10 to 20 minutes longer, rotating baking sheet as needed to ensure potatoes brown evenly. Season with salt and pepper to taste and serve immediately.

GREEK-STYLE GARLIC-LEMON POTATOES

WHY THIS RECIPE WORKS

When well prepared, Greek-style garlic and lemon potatoes are nicely browned and crisped on the outside, fluffy on the inside, and accented by a full (but not overpowering) lemon flavor and plenty of garlic bite. We chose Yukon Golds and browned them in a nonstick skillet in butter and vegetable oil for deep flavor and color, then covered the pan to allow the potatoes to finish cooking through. A combination of juice and zest gave them a full lemon flavor and four cloves hit the right level of garlic. A sprinkling of salt, oregano, and parsley finished this side dish perfectly.

GREEK-STYLE GARLIC-LEMON POTATOES
SERVES 4

We prefer to use medium potatoes, 7 to 8 ounces each, for this recipe. If your potatoes are larger, you may have to increase the covered cooking time by up to 4 minutes. Though a nonstick pan makes cleanup easier, it is not essential.

- 1 tablespoon vegetable oil
- 1 tablespoon unsalted butter
- 2 pounds Yukon Gold potatoes, peeled, each potato cut lengthwise into 8 wedges
- 2 tablespoons minced fresh oregano
- 4 garlic cloves, minced
- 1 tablespoon extra-virgin olive oil
- 1 tablespoon grated lemon zest plus 2 tablespoons juice
- 1 teaspoon salt
- ½ teaspoon pepper
- 2 tablespoons minced fresh parsley

1. Heat vegetable oil and butter in 12-inch nonstick skillet over medium-high heat until butter melts. Add potatoes in single layer and cook until golden brown on first cut side (pan should sizzle but not smoke), about 6 minutes. Using tongs, flip

potatoes onto second cut side and cook until deep golden brown, about 5 minutes longer. Reduce heat to medium-low, cover tightly, and cook until potatoes are tender when poked with paring knife, about 5 minutes.

2. While potatoes cook, combine oregano, garlic, olive oil, and lemon zest and juice in small bowl. When potatoes are tender, add garlic mixture, salt, and pepper to skillet, stirring carefully (so as not to break potato wedges) to distribute. Cook, uncovered, until seasoning mixture is heated through and fragrant, 1 to 2 minutes. Sprinkle potatoes with parsley, stir gently to distribute, and serve immediately.

GREEK-STYLE GARLIC-LEMON POTATOES WITH OLIVES AND FETA

We like kalamata olives here, but any brine-cured black olive will work.

Stir 3 ounces crumbled feta cheese and ¼ cup sliced pitted kalamata olives into skillet along with parsley in step 2.

GREEK-STYLE GARLIC-LEMON POTATOES WITH SPINACH AND ANCHOVIES

You can make this recipe without the anchovies if preferred.

Stir 1 teaspoon minced anchovies along with garlic mixture into skillet in step 2, then add 2½ ounces baby spinach (2½ cups) and gently stir to distribute. Omit parsley.

SPICY GREEK-STYLE GARLIC-LEMON POTATOES

Note that the seeds and membranes of the jalapeños are left intact in this recipe; this variation is for those who like spicy food.

Add 2 small jalapeño chiles, cut crosswise into ¼-inch-thick slices, to skillet just before covering skillet in step 1.

GREEK-STYLE GARLIC-LEMON POTATOES WITH SUN-DRIED TOMATOES AND SCALLIONS

Add ¼ cup chopped oil-packed sun-dried tomatoes and 2 thinly sliced scallions along with garlic mixture to skillet in step 2.

CLASSIC MASHED POTATOES

✔ WHY THIS RECIPE WORKS

Many people would never consider consulting a recipe when making mashed potatoes, instead adding chunks of butter and spurts of cream until their conscience tells them to stop. Little wonder then that mashed potatoes made this way are consistent only in their mediocrity. We wanted mashed potatoes that were perfectly smooth and creamy, with great potato flavor and plenty of buttery richness every time. We began by selecting russet potatoes for their high starch content. Boiling them whole and unpeeled yielded mashed potatoes that were rich, earthy, and sweet. We used a food mill or ricer for the smoothest texture (a potato masher can be used if you prefer your potatoes a little chunky). For smooth, velvety potatoes, we added melted butter first and then half-and-half. Melting, rather than merely softening, the butter enabled it to coat the starch molecules quickly and easily, so the potatoes turned out creamy and light. From there, it was easy to come up with a number of flavorful variations.

CLASSIC MASHED POTATOES
SERVES 4

Russet potatoes make fluffier mashed potatoes, but Yukon Golds have an appealing buttery flavor and can be used.

    2   pounds russet potatoes
    8   tablespoons unsalted butter, melted
    1   cup half-and-half, warmed
  1½   teaspoons salt
         Pepper

1. Place potatoes in large saucepan and cover with 1 inch cold water. Bring to boil over high heat, reduce heat to medium-low, and simmer until potatoes are just tender (paring knife can be slipped in and out of potatoes with little resistance), 20 to 30 minutes. Drain.

2. Set ricer or food mill over now-empty saucepan. Using potholder (to hold potatoes) and paring knife, peel skins from potatoes. Working in batches, cut peeled potatoes into large chunks and press or mill into saucepan.

3. Stir in butter until incorporated. Gently whisk in half-and-half, add salt, and season with pepper to taste. Serve.

GARLIC MASHED POTATOES

Avoid using unusually large garlic cloves, which will not soften adequately during toasting. For chunky mashed potatoes, use a potato masher,

---

TEST KITCHEN TIP NO. 61   GREEN POTATOES CAN MAKE YOU GREEN

When potatoes are left on the counter for more than a few days, they sometimes turn slightly green under the skin. It turns out that when potatoes are exposed to light for prolonged periods of time, they begin to produce chlorophyll in the form of a green ring under the skin. While the chlorophyll itself is tasteless and harmless, it does mark the potential presence of solanine, a toxin that can cause gastrointestinal distress. Since solanine develops on the skin of the potato (or just below), discarding the peel greatly reduces the risk of becoming ill from a slightly green spud. We've found that potatoes stored in a well-ventilated, dark, dry, cool place will stay solanine-free for up to a month, while potatoes left on the counter will begin to exhibit signs of solanine in as little as a week.

decrease the half-and-half to ¾ cup, and mash the garlic to a paste with a fork before you add it to the potatoes.

Toast 22 unpeeled garlic cloves (about 3 ounces, or ⅔ cup), covered, in 8-inch skillet over low heat, shaking pan frequently, until cloves are dark spotty brown and slightly softened, about 22 minutes. Off heat, let sit, covered, until fully softened, 15 to 20 minutes. Peel cloves and, with paring knife, cut off woody root end; set aside. Press or mill garlic along with potatoes in step 2.

GARLIC MASHED POTATOES WITH SMOKED GOUDA AND CHIVES

Reduce salt in Garlic Mashed Potatoes to 1¼ teaspoons and stir in 4 ounces grated smoked Gouda cheese (1 cup) along with half-and-half; set pot over low heat and stir until cheese is melted and incorporated. Stir in 3 tablespoons chopped fresh chives.

MASHED POTATOES WITH SCALLIONS AND HORSERADISH

You can substitute 2 tablespoons prepared horseradish for the grated fresh horseradish.

After stirring butter into potatoes in step 3, season with 1½ teaspoons salt and ½ teaspoon pepper. Whisk 2 tablespoons prepared horseradish, ¼ cup grated fresh horseradish, and 3 minced scallions, green parts only, into warm half-and-half. Add mixture to potatoes and stir until just combined. Serve immediately.

MASHED POTATOES WITH SMOKED CHEDDAR AND GRAINY MUSTARD

After stirring butter into potatoes in step 3, season with 1¼ teaspoons salt and ½ teaspoon pepper. Add 2 tablespoons whole grain mustard and 3 ounces grated smoked cheddar cheese (¾ cup) with half-and-half, and stir until just combined. Serve immediately.

MASHED POTATOES WITH SMOKED PAPRIKA AND TOASTED GARLIC

Don't be deterred by the extra steps in these mashed potatoes—they are worth the trouble.

While potatoes are simmering, toast 1 teaspoon smoked paprika in 8-inch skillet over medium heat, stirring frequently, until fragrant, about 2 minutes. Transfer to small bowl; set aside. Melt 8 tablespoons butter in small saucepan over medium-low heat. Add 3 minced garlic cloves, reduce heat to low, and cook, stirring frequently, until garlic begins to brown, 12 to 14 minutes. Remove saucepan from heat immediately and set aside for 5 minutes (garlic will continue to brown). Pour butter-garlic mixture through mesh strainer; reserve butter and set toasted garlic aside. Rice or mill potatoes as directed, then stir butter into potatoes until just incorporated. Season potatoes with toasted paprika, 1½ teaspoons salt, and ½ teaspoon pepper. Add warm half-and-half and stir until just combined. Serve immediately, sprinkling with reserved toasted garlic.

MASHED POTATOES WITH BLUE CHEESE AND PORT-CARAMELIZED ONIONS

SERVES 4

The port adds a sweet depth to the onions that perfectly complements the blue cheese.

ONIONS
1½ teaspoons unsalted butter
1½ teaspoons vegetable oil
½ teaspoon light brown sugar
¼ teaspoon salt
1 pound onions, halved and sliced ¼ inch thick
1 cup ruby port

POTATOES
¾ cup half-and-half
1 teaspoon chopped fresh thyme
2 pounds russet potatoes
6 tablespoons unsalted butter, melted
1¼ teaspoons salt
½ teaspoon pepper
4 ounces blue cheese, crumbled (1 cup)

1. FOR THE ONIONS: Heat butter and oil in 8-inch nonstick skillet over high heat until butter melts, then stir in sugar and

---

TEST KITCHEN TIP NO. 62 CAN YOU SLICE ONIONS AHEAD?

Old wives' tales claim that storing slices of chopped onions in water will help keep their pungency from intensifying, but we found the exact opposite to be the case. We stored sliced onions for two days submerged in water as well as placed directly in zipper-lock bags, and then compared their odor and flavor to freshly sliced onions. The onions submerged in water were unanimously deemed to be the most odorous with the sharpest flavor. It turns out that over time, water facilitates the distribution of enzymes across the cut surfaces of the onion, which in turn leads to an increase in the creation of the thiosulfinates that produce an onion's strong odor and flavor. Your best bet to tame onion flavor is to simply slice or chop onions as you need them, but if you find yourself with an excess, store them in the fridge in a zipper-lock bag and give them a quick rinse right before using to remove any thiosulfinates on the surface. One trick that does work? Slicing the onion with the grain, from pole to pole, ruptures fewer cells and releases fewer enzymes that cutting against the grain, giving you less pungent onions.

salt. Add onions, stir to coat, and cook, stirring occasionally, until onions begin to soften and release some moisture, about 5 minutes. Reduce heat to medium and cook, stirring frequently, until onions are deeply browned and sticky, about 35 minutes longer (if onions are sizzling or scorching, reduce heat; if onions are not browning after 15 minutes, increase heat). Stir in port and continue to cook until port reduces to glaze, 4 to 6 minutes.

2. FOR THE POTATOES: While onions are cooking, bring half-and-half and thyme to boil in small saucepan; cover to keep warm.

3. Place potatoes in large saucepan and cover with 1 inch cold water. Bring to boil over high heat, reduce heat to medium-low, and simmer until potatoes are just tender (paring knife can be slipped in and out of potatoes with very little resistance), 20 to 30 minutes. Drain.

4. Set ricer or food mill over now-empty saucepan. Using potholder (to hold potatoes) and paring knife, peel skins from potatoes. Working in batches, cut peeled potatoes into large chunks and press or mill into saucepan.

5. Stir in butter until just incorporated. Add salt and pepper, then gently stir in half-and-half and blue cheese until just combined. Serve immediately topped with onions.

BUTTERMILK MASHED POTATOES

✔ WHY THIS RECIPE WORKS
Merely replacing butter and cream with buttermilk to create tangy, creamy buttermilk mashed potatoes doesn't work—the finished potatoes are curdled, crumbly, chalky, and dry. We wanted easy mashed potatoes with buttermilk's trademark distinctive tang, but we didn't want to sacrifice texture to get them. Many recipes for buttermilk mashed potatoes remove so

much butter that the potatoes taste lean and lack creaminess. We started by restoring some of the butter, then we tackled the curdling problem. By adding the butter, melted, to room-temperature buttermilk, we coated the proteins in the buttermilk and protected them from the heat shock that causes curdling. We also simplified the recipe by choosing peeled and cut Yukon Gold potatoes rather than using unpeeled russets (our usual choice for mashed potatoes). Because Yukon Golds have less starch and are less absorbent than russets, they don't become soggy and thinned out when simmered without their skins.

BUTTERMILK MASHED POTATOES
SERVES 4

To achieve the proper texture, it is important to cook the potatoes thoroughly; they are done if they break apart when a knife is inserted and gently wiggled. Buttermilk substitutes such as clabbered milk do not produce sufficiently tangy potatoes. To reduce the chance of curdling, the buttermilk must be at room temperature when mixed with the cooled melted butter.

- 2 **pounds Yukon Gold potatoes, peeled and cut into 1-inch chunks**
  Salt and pepper
- 6 **tablespoons unsalted butter, melted and cooled**
- ⅔ **cup buttermilk, room temperature**

1. Place potatoes in large saucepan and cover with 1 inch cold water. Add 1 tablespoon salt, bring to boil over high heat, then reduce heat to medium and simmer until potatoes break apart when paring knife is inserted, about 18 minutes. Drain potatoes and return to saucepan set on still-hot burner.

2. Using potato masher, mash potatoes until few small lumps remain. Gently mix melted butter and buttermilk in small bowl until combined. Add buttermilk mixture to potatoes and, using rubber spatula, fold gently until just incorporated. Season with salt and pepper to taste; serve immediately.

BUTTERMILK RANCH MASHED POTATOES

Add 1 minced garlic clove, 3 scallions, sliced very thin, 2 tablespoons minced fresh parsley, and ⅓ cup sour cream along with buttermilk mixture in step 2.

BUTTERMILK MASHED POTATOES WITH LEEK AND CHIVES

Add 1 bay leaf to saucepan with potatoes in step 1. While potatoes are cooking, melt 1 tablespoon unsalted butter in 8-inch nonstick skillet over medium heat. Add 1 leek, white and light green parts only, halved lengthwise, sliced ¼ inch thick, and washed thoroughly. Cook, stirring occasionally, until lightly browned and wilted, about 8 minutes. Add leek and 3 tablespoons minced fresh chives to potatoes with buttermilk mixture in step 2.

FLUFFY MASHED POTATOES

✔ WHY THIS RECIPE WORKS
For our Classic Mashed Potatoes (page 279), we boiled potatoes in their jackets for earthy potato flavor (and peeled them while still hot). We don't mind this somewhat inconvenient method when we've got time to spare, but thought an easier alternative was in order. Cooking potatoes in their skins keeps the starch granules from absorbing too much water, thereby preventing gluey mashed potatoes. To give peeled potatoes the same protection, we made two alterations. Steaming rather than boiling the potatoes exposed the potato pieces to less water, reducing the chance of the granules swelling to the point of bursting. When they were cooked partway, we rinsed them under cold water to rid them of free amylose, the substance that results in gluey mashed potatoes, and returned them to the steamer to finish cooking. Because potatoes cooked this way are so full of rich potato flavor, we were able to use less butter and substitute whole milk for cream.

This recipe works best with either a metal colander that sits easily in a Dutch oven or a large pasta pot with a steamer insert. To prevent excess evaporation, it is important for the lid to fit as snugly as possible over the colander or steamer. A steamer basket will work, but you will have to transfer the hot potatoes out of the basket to rinse them off halfway through cooking. For the lightest, fluffiest texture, use a ricer. A food mill is the next best alternative. Russets and white potatoes will work in this recipe, but avoid red potatoes.

2 pounds Yukon Gold potatoes, peeled, cut into 1-inch chunks, rinsed well, and drained
4 tablespoons unsalted butter, melted
Salt and pepper
⅔ cup whole milk, warm

1. Fit large pot or Dutch oven with metal colander or steamer basket. Add water, keeping level below colander, and bring water to boil. Put potatoes in colander, cover, and cook potatoes over medium-high heat for 10 minutes. Transfer colander to sink and rinse potatoes under cold water until no longer hot, 1 to 2 minutes. Return colander and potatoes to pot, cover, and continue to cook until potatoes are soft and paring knife inserted in potato meets no resistance, 10 to 15 minutes longer. Pour off water from Dutch oven.

2. Set ricer or food mill over now-empty pot. Working in batches, press or mill into pot, removing any potatoes stuck to bottom. Using rubber spatula, stir in melted butter and ½ teaspoon salt until incorporated. Stir in warm milk until incorporated. Season to taste with salt and pepper; serve immediately.

FRENCH-STYLE MASHED POTATOES WITH CHEESE AND GARLIC

✔ **WHY THIS RECIPE WORKS**

Aligot is French cookery's intensely rich, cheesy take on mashed potatoes. These potatoes get their elastic, satiny texture through prolonged, vigorous stirring—which can easily go awry and lead to a gluey, sticky mess. After making aligot with different potatoes, we found medium-starch Yukon Golds to be the clear winner. We boiled the potatoes, then used a food processor to "mash" them. Traditional aligot uses butter and crème fraîche to add flavor and creaminess and loosen the texture before mixing in the cheese. But crème fraîche isn't always easy to find, so we substituted whole milk, which provided depth without going overboard. For the cheese, a combination of mild mozzarella and nutty Gruyère proved just right. As for the stirring, we needed to monitor the consistency closely: too much stirring and the aligot turned rubbery, too little and the cheese didn't marry with the potatoes for that essential elasticity.

FRENCH-STYLE MASHED POTATOES WITH CHEESE AND GARLIC (ALIGOT)

SERVES 6

The finished potatoes should have a smooth and slightly elastic texture. White cheddar can be substituted for the Gruyère.

2 pounds Yukon Gold potatoes, peeled, cut into ½-inch-thick slices, rinsed well, and drained
Salt and pepper
6 tablespoons unsalted butter
2 garlic cloves, minced
1–1½ cups whole milk
4 ounces mozzarella cheese, shredded (1 cup)
4 ounces Gruyère cheese, shredded (1 cup)

1. Place potatoes in large saucepan, cover with 1 inch cold water, and add 1 tablespoon salt. Partially cover saucepan and bring potatoes to boil over high heat. Reduce heat to medium-low and simmer until potatoes are tender and just break apart when poked with fork, 12 to 17 minutes. Drain potatoes and dry saucepan.

2. Transfer potatoes to food processor. Add butter, garlic, and 1½ teaspoons salt and pulse until butter is melted and incorporated into potatoes, about 10 pulses. Add 1 cup milk and continue to process until potatoes are smooth and creamy, about 20 seconds, scraping down sides halfway through.

3. Transfer potato mixture to saucepan and set over medium heat. Stir in cheeses, 1 cup at a time, until incorporated. Continue to cook potatoes, stirring vigorously, until cheese is fully melted and mixture is smooth and elastic, 3 to 5 minutes.

TEST KITCHEN TIP NO. 63 · BE PICKY ABOUT PICKING GARLIC

Heads of garlic vary in quality and age throughout the year, and it can be hard to pick a flavorful head. Here's the test kitchen's advice: go for the loose garlic, not the heads sold packaged in little cellophane-wrapped boxes that don't allow for close inspection. Look for heads with no spots of mold or signs of sprouting. Take a whiff; the garlic should not smell unusually fragrant or fermented—signs of spoilage, to be sure. Finally, squeeze the head in your hand. If you feel hollow skins where cloves used to reside or if the head feels at all spongy or rubbery, pass it up—a head of garlic should feel firm and solid.

If mixture is difficult to stir and seems thick, stir in 2 tablespoons milk at a time (up to ½ cup) until potatoes are loose and creamy. Season with salt and pepper to taste. Serve immediately.

GARLIC AND OLIVE OIL MASHED POTATOES

✓ WHY THIS RECIPE WORKS

The Mediterranean approach of flavoring mashed potatoes with olive oil and garlic is an appealing one, but it's not as simple as replacing the dairy with oil: olive oil can turn the texture pasty and garlic can be harsh and overpowering. We wanted to translate these bold flavors into a light and creamy mashed potato side dish that would partner well with simple grilled meats or fish. We first simmered the potatoes (we preferred russets) and then put the drained, peeled, still-hot potatoes through a ricer or food mill for a smooth texture. We created a mild flavor base by slowly cooking minced garlic in oil, then heightened the garlic flavor a bit by adding just a little raw garlic, mashed to a paste. Fruity extra-virgin olive oil and a splash of fresh lemon juice brightened the final dish.

GARLIC AND OLIVE OIL MASHED POTATOES

SERVES 6

As this dish is denser and more intensely flavored than traditional mashed potatoes, our suggested serving size is smaller than you might expect. These potatoes make a fine accompaniment to simply seasoned grilled meats, fish, and poultry.

- 2 pounds russet potatoes
- 5 garlic cloves, peeled
- 1¼ teaspoons salt

- ½ cup plus 2 tablespoons extra-virgin olive oil
- ½ teaspoon pepper
- 2 teaspoons lemon juice

1. Place potatoes in large saucepan and cover with 1 inch cold water. Bring to boil over high heat, then reduce heat to medium-low and simmer until just tender (paring knife can be slipped in and out of potatoes with very little resistance), 40 to 45 minutes.

2. While potatoes are simmering, mince 1 garlic clove, then place on cutting board and sprinkle with ⅛ teaspoon salt. Using flat side of chef's knife, drag garlic and salt back and forth across cutting board in small circular motions until garlic is ground into smooth paste. Transfer to medium bowl and set aside.

3. Mince remaining 4 garlic cloves. Place in small saucepan with ¼ cup oil and cook over low heat, stirring constantly, until garlic foams and is soft, fragrant, and golden, 5 minutes. Transfer oil and garlic to bowl with raw garlic paste.

4. Set ricer or food mill over now-empty saucepan. Using potholder (to hold potatoes) and paring knife, peel skins from potatoes. Working in batches, cut peeled potatoes into large chunks and press or mill into saucepan.

5. Add remaining 1⅛ teaspoons salt, pepper, lemon juice, and remaining 6 tablespoons oil to bowl with garlic and cooked oil and whisk to combine. Fold mixture into potatoes and serve.

MASHED POTATOES AND ROOT VEGETABLES

✓ WHY THIS RECIPE WORKS

Root vegetables like carrots, parsnips, turnips, and celery root can add an earthy, intriguing flavor to mashed potatoes, but because root vegetables and potatoes have different starch levels and water content, treating them the same way creates a bad mash. We wanted a potato and root vegetable mash with a creamy consistency and a balanced flavor. We found that a 1:3 ratio of root vegetables to potatoes provided an optimal consistency, and caramelizing the root vegetables first in a little butter helped bring out their natural earthy sweetness and boosted the overall flavor of the dish. To use just one pot, we first sautéed the root vegetables in butter until caramelized and then added the potatoes with a little chicken broth. To avoid a gluey texture, we rinsed the peeled, sliced potatoes in several changes of water before cooking them.

MASHED POTATOES AND ROOT VEGETABLES

SERVES 4

Russet potatoes will yield a slightly fluffier, less creamy mash, but they can be used in place of the Yukon Gold potatoes if desired. Rinsing the potatoes in water reduces starch and prevents the mashed potatoes from becoming gluey. It is important to cut the potatoes and root vegetables into evenly sized pieces so they cook at the same rate. This recipe can be doubled and cooked in a large Dutch oven. If doubling, increase the cooking time in step 2 to 40 minutes.

4 tablespoons unsalted butter

8 ounces carrots, parsnips, turnips, or celery root, peeled; carrots or parsnips cut into ¼-inch-thick half-moons; turnips or celery root cut into ½-inch dice (about 1½ cups)

1½ pounds Yukon Gold potatoes, peeled, quartered lengthwise, and cut crosswise into ¼-inch-thick slices; rinsed well in 3 or 4 changes of cold water and drained well

⅓ cup low-sodium chicken broth
Salt and pepper

¾ cup half-and-half, warmed

3 tablespoons minced fresh chives

1. Melt butter in large saucepan over medium heat. Add root vegetables and cook, stirring occasionally, until butter is browned and vegetables are dark brown and caramelized, 10 to 12 minutes. (If after 4 minutes vegetables have not started to brown, increase heat to medium-high.)

2. Add potatoes, broth, and ¾ teaspoon salt and stir to combine. Cook, covered, over low heat (broth should simmer gently; do not boil), stirring occasionally, until potatoes fall apart easily when poked with fork and all liquid has been absorbed, 25 to 30 minutes. (If liquid does not gently simmer after a few minutes, increase heat to medium-low.) Remove pan from heat, remove lid, and allow steam to escape for 2 minutes.

3. Gently mash potatoes and root vegetables in saucepan with potato masher (do not mash vigorously). Gently fold in warm half-and-half and chives. Season with salt and pepper to taste; serve immediately.

MASHED POTATOES AND ROOT VEGETABLES WITH BACON AND THYME

Cook 4 slices bacon, cut into ½-inch pieces, in large saucepan over medium heat until crisp, 5 to 7 minutes. Using slotted spoon, transfer bacon to paper towel–lined plate; set aside. Pour off all but 2 tablespoons fat from pan. Add 2 tablespoons butter to pan and continue with step 1, cooking root vegetables in bacon fat mixture instead of butter. Substitute 1 teaspoon minced fresh thyme for chives and fold reserved bacon into potatoes along with thyme.

MASHED POTATOES AND ROOT VEGETABLES WITH PAPRIKA AND PARSLEY

This variation is particularly nice with carrots.

Toast 1½ teaspoons smoked or sweet paprika in 8-inch skillet over medium heat until fragrant, about 30 seconds. Substitute parsley for chives and fold toasted paprika into potatoes along with parsley.

BEST BAKED POTATOES

✔ WHY THIS RECIPE WORKS
In the world of June Cleaver, potatoes were baked at 350 degrees because they were put into the oven along with the roast, which cooked at 350 degrees. We wanted to determine if there was a faster—or even just a better—route to baked potatoes.

After a lot of experimentation, we discovered that June had it right: Traditional slow baking is best. This is mainly because of the effect it has on the skin; the skin of a potato baked at 350 degrees for an hour and 15 minutes simply had no peer. We found the most important step to a fluffy potato was opening it wide when it was hot to let the steam escape, rather than getting trapped in the potato and making it soggy.

BEST BAKED POTATOES
SERVES 4

The most important step to a fluffy potato is opening it wide when it's hot and letting the steam escape to the air rather than being trapped in the potato.

4 russet potatoes (8 ounces each), rubbed lightly with vegetable oil

Adjust oven rack to middle position and heat oven to 350 degrees. Place potatoes directly on rack and bake 1¼ hours. Remove from oven and pierce with fork several times to create dotted X. Press in at ends of potato to push flesh up and out. Serve.

MICROWAVE-BAKED POTATOES
SERVES 4

Note that the skin on a microwaved potato doesn't crisp like it will on a traditional oven-baked potato. This method is a good option, however, if you are pressed for time and plan on stuffing the potatoes (see recipes on pages 286–287).

4 russet potatoes (8 ounces each)

Place potatoes in shallow baking dish. Microwave potatoes until skewer or paring knife can be inserted into and removed from potatoes with little resistance, 9 to 12 minutes, turning potatoes every 3 minutes. Remove baking dish from microwave. Serve.

TWICE-BAKED POTATOES

✔ WHY THIS RECIPE WORKS
Twice-baked potatoes are not difficult to make, but the process can be time-consuming, and too many versions of this dish feature rubbery skins filled with pasty, bland fillings. We wanted to perfect the process to achieve twice-baked potatoes with slightly crisp skins and a rich, creamy filling. We oiled the potatoes before baking for a crisp skin, and we let the baked potatoes cool slightly before slicing them open and removing the flesh. We found that we could prevent the hollowed-out shells from turning soggy by keeping them in the oven while making the filling. And

for the filling, we found it best to combine the potato with tangy dairy ingredients—sour cream and buttermilk were ideal—a small amount of butter, and sharp cheddar cheese for its bold flavor. For a perfect finish, we placed the filled potatoes under the broiler for a brown, crisp topping.

TWICE-BAKED POTATOES
SERVES 6 TO 8

To vary the flavor a bit, try substituting other types of cheese, such as Gruyère, fontina, or feta, for the cheddar. Yukon Gold potatoes, though slightly more moist than our ideal, can be substituted for the russets.

- 4 russet potatoes (7 to 8 ounces each), rubbed lightly with vegetable oil
- 4 ounces sharp cheddar cheese, shredded (1 cup)
- ½ cup sour cream
- ½ cup buttermilk
- 2 tablespoons unsalted butter, room temperature
- 3 scallions, sliced thin
- ½ teaspoon salt
  Pepper

1. Adjust oven rack to upper-middle position and heat oven to 400 degrees. Bake potatoes on aluminum foil–lined baking sheet until skin is crisp and deep brown and paring knife easily pierces flesh, about 1 hour. Transfer potatoes to wire rack and let sit until cool enough to handle, about 10 minutes; set baking sheet aside.

2. Using oven mitt or folded kitchen towel to handle hot potatoes, cut each potato in half lengthwise. Using soup-spoon, scoop flesh from each half into medium bowl, leaving ⅛- to ¼-inch thickness of flesh in each shell. Return potato shells, cut side up, to foil-lined baking sheet and return to oven until dry and slightly crisped, about 10 minutes.

Meanwhile, mash potato flesh with fork until smooth. Stir in cheese, sour cream, buttermilk, butter, scallions, salt, and pepper to taste until well combined.

3. Remove shells from oven and heat broiler. Holding shells steady on pan with oven mitt or towel-protected hand, spoon mashed potato mixture into crisped shells, mounding slightly at the center. Return potatoes to oven and broil until spotty brown and crisp on top, 10 to 15 minutes. Cool for 10 minutes. Serve warm.

TWICE-BAKED POTATOES WITH INDIAN SPICES AND PEAS

Melt 2 tablespoons butter in 10-inch skillet over medium heat. Add 1 finely chopped onion and cook until soft, 3 to 4 minutes. Add 3 minced garlic cloves, 1 teaspoon grated fresh ginger, 1 teaspoon ground cumin, 1 teaspoon ground coriander, ¼ teaspoon ground cinnamon, ¼ teaspoon ground turmeric, and ¼ teaspoon ground cloves. Cook until fragrant, about 30 seconds, being careful not to brown garlic or ginger. Off heat, stir in 1 cup thawed frozen peas; set aside. Omit cheese and butter and stir reserved spiced peas into filling mixture in step 2.

TWICE-BAKED POTATOES WITH CHIPOTLE CHILE AND ONION

For a slightly smoky aftertaste with just a hint of heat, limit the chipotle pepper to 1 tablespoon. For a little bit of upfront heat, increase the chipotle to 1½ tablespoons.

Melt 2 tablespoons butter in 10-inch skillet over medium heat. Add 1 finely chopped onion and cook until soft, 3 to 4 minutes. Omit butter and add 1 to 1½ tablespoons minced chipotle chile in adobo sauce, reserved sautéed onion, and 2 tablespoons chopped fresh cilantro to filling mixture in step 2.

TWICE-BAKED POTATOES WITH PEPPER JACK CHEESE AND BACON

Cook 8 slices bacon, cut into ¼-inch pieces, in 10-inch skillet over medium heat until crisp, 5 to 7 minutes. Transfer bacon to paper towel–lined plate; set aside. Substitute pepper Jack cheese for cheddar and add reserved bacon to filling mixture in step 2.

TWICE-BAKED POTATOES WITH MONTEREY JACK AND PESTO

Substitute Monterey Jack cheese for cheddar, reduce buttermilk to ¼ cup, omit butter, and add ¼ cup prepared or homemade basil pesto to filling mixture in step 2.

TWICE-BAKED POTATOES WITH SMOKED SALMON AND CHIVES

This variation makes a great brunch dish.

Omit cheese and scallions. Stir 4 ounces smoked salmon, cut into ½-inch pieces, and 3 tablespoons minced fresh chives into filling mixture in step 2. Sprinkle potatoes with additional chopped chives as garnish just before serving.

HEARTY STUFFED BAKED POTATOES

✓ WHY THIS RECIPE WORKS
While twice-baked potatoes incorporate additions like cheese, herbs, or other flavorings, the amounts of these additions is restrained so that the emphasis is still largely on the potato. We wanted a potato side dish that wasn't just twice-baked, but was also really stuffed—with cheese, vegetables, or other add-ins—that would turn the potato into a full-flavored, hearty side or one-dish meal. For a crisp potato shell, we

scooped out the flesh (after baking or microwaving the potatoes) and dried the emptied skins in the oven. When it came to the fillings, we found raw vegetables exuded too much liquid. Broccoli, cabbage, and ham all worked well if we precooked them, and we crisped bacon in a skillet first to help rid it of fat before it went into the potato. Butter, sour cream, and half-and-half gave our fillings a luxurious texture. We maximized the cheese by mixing it into the filling and sprinkling it on top. Broiling the potatoes made for a grand, golden finale.

STUFFED BAKED POTATOES WITH BROCCOLI, CHEDDAR, AND SCALLIONS

SERVES 4 AS A MAIN COURSE OR 8 AS A SIDE DISH

To be time-efficient, cook the broccoli while the potatoes are in the oven.

- 1 recipe Best Baked Potatoes (page 284), cooled for 10 minutes
- 2 tablespoons unsalted butter, plus 2 tablespoons melted
- 1 pound broccoli florets, cut into ½- to 1-inch pieces
  Salt
- 1 teaspoon lemon juice
- 6 ounces sharp cheddar cheese, shredded (1½ cups)
- 3 scallions, sliced thin
- ½ cup sour cream
- ¼ cup half-and-half
- ¼ teaspoon dry mustard
  Pepper

1. Melt 2 tablespoons butter in 12-inch skillet over medium-high heat. Add broccoli and ½ teaspoon salt and cook, stirring occasionally, until lightly browned, about 2 minutes. Add 2 tablespoons water, cover, and cook until crisp-tender, about 1 minute. Uncover and continue to cook until water evaporates, about 1 minute. Transfer

to bowl and stir in lemon juice.

2. Halve each potato lengthwise. Using soupspoon, scoop flesh from each half into bowl, leaving about ⅛- to ¼-inch thickness of flesh in each shell. Place shells, cut side up, on aluminum foil–lined baking sheet and return to oven until dry and slightly crisp, about 10 minutes.

3. Meanwhile, mash potato flesh with fork until smooth. Stir in melted 2 tablespoons butter, ¾ teaspoon salt, 1 cup cheese, scallions, sour cream, half-and-half, mustard, and pepper to taste until well combined, then stir in broccoli.

4. Remove shells from oven and heat broiler. Mound filling into shells, sprinkle with remaining ½ cup cheese, and broil until spotty brown, 6 to 10 minutes. Cool for 5 minutes and serve.

STUFFED BAKED POTATOES WITH BACON, CABBAGE, AND CHEDDAR

SERVES 4 AS A MAIN COURSE OR 8 AS A SIDE DISH

Tender savoy cabbage is our first choice for this recipe, but the soft outer leaves from a head of regular green cabbage can also be used. To be time-efficient, cook the bacon while the potatoes are in the oven.

- 1 recipe Best Baked Potatoes (page 284), cooled for 10 minutes
- 8 slices bacon, cut into ½-inch pieces
- 1 tablespoon unsalted butter, plus 2 tablespoons melted
- 6 cups savoy cabbage, cored and sliced into ½ by 1-inch pieces
  Salt and pepper
- ½ cup water
- 2 teaspoons red wine vinegar
- 6 ounces sharp cheddar cheese, shredded (1½ cups)
- 3 scallions, sliced thin
- ½ cup sour cream
- ¼ cup half-and-half

1. Cook bacon in 12-inch skillet over medium heat until crisp, 5 to 7 minutes. Using slotted spoon, transfer bacon to paper towel–lined plate. Pour off all but 1 tablespoon fat. Add 1 tablespoon butter to skillet with fat and heat over medium-high until butter is melted. Add cabbage and ½ teaspoon salt and cook, stirring occasionally, until cabbage begins to wilt and is lightly browned, about 2 minutes. Add ½ cup water, cover, and cook until crisp-tender, 5 to 7 minutes. Uncover and continue to cook until water evaporates, about 30 seconds. Transfer to bowl and stir in vinegar.

2. Halve each potato lengthwise. Using soupspoon, scoop flesh from each half into bowl, leaving ⅛- to ¼-inch thickness of flesh in each shell. Place shells, cut side up, on aluminum foil–lined baking sheet and return to oven until dry and slightly crisp, about 10 minutes.

3. Meanwhile, mash potato flesh with fork until smooth. Stir in melted 2 tablespoons butter, cabbage, ½ teaspoon salt, ¼ cup bacon, 1 cup cheese, scallions, sour cream, half-and-half, and pepper to taste.

4. Remove shells from oven and heat broiler. Mound filling into shells, then sprinkle with remaining ½ cup cheese and bacon and broil until spotty brown, 6 to 10 minutes. Cool for 5 minutes; serve.

SHREDDING SEMISOFT CHEESE NEATLY

To prevent cheese from clogging the holes of your box grater and to make cleanup a breeze, lightly coat the coarse side with vegetable oil spray and then shred the cheese as usual.

TWICE-BAKED STUFFED POTATOES WITH HAM, PEAS, AND GRUYÈRE

SERVES 4 AS A MAIN COURSE OR
8 AS A SIDE DISH

To be time-efficient, cook the ham while the potatoes are in the oven.

- 1 recipe Best Baked Potatoes (page 284), cooled for 10 minutes
- 1 tablespoon unsalted butter, plus 2 tablespoons melted
- 12 ounces deli-style baked ham, sliced ¼ inch thick and cut into ¼-inch cubes
- 1 cup frozen peas
- 6 ounces Gruyère cheese, shredded (1½ cups)
- ½ cup sour cream
- ¼ cup half-and-half
- 2 tablespoons whole grain mustard Salt and pepper

1. Melt 1 tablespoon butter in 12-inch skillet over medium-high heat. Add ham in even layer and cook, without stirring, until lightly browned, about 2 minutes. Stir and cook 30 seconds longer. Off heat, stir in peas; transfer mixture to large plate.

2. Halve each potato lengthwise. Using soupspoon, scoop flesh from each half into bowl, leaving ⅛- to ¼-inch thickness of flesh in each shell. Place shells, cut side up, on aluminum foil–lined baking sheet and return to oven until dry and slightly crisp, about 10 minutes.

3. Meanwhile, mash potato flesh with fork until smooth. Stir in melted 2 tablespoons butter, ham mixture, 1 cup cheese, sour cream, half-and-half, mustard, and salt and pepper to taste.

4. Remove shells from oven and heat broiler. Mound filling into shells, then sprinkle with remaining ½ cup cheese and broil until spotty brown, 6 to 10 minutes. Cool for 5 minutes; serve.

CLASSIC FRENCH FRIES

✔ WHY THIS RECIPE WORKS

We wanted to find a recipe and method for making french fries that would rival restaurant versions. For us, the ideal fry would be long and crisp, with right-angle sides, a nice crunch on the outside, and an earthy potato taste. Waxy potatoes were too watery and fried up with hollow cavities that simply filled with oil. Russet potatoes turned out to be the best choice, but because they are starchy, we found it was important to rinse the starch off the surface after cutting the potatoes. Refrigerating the potatoes in a bowl of ice water for at least 30 minutes meant that when the potatoes first entered the hot oil, they were nearly frozen, which allowed a slow, thorough cooking of the inner potato pulp. (Without this step, the fries started to brown well before the insides were fully cooked.) We liked our fries best cooked in peanut oil but vegetable oil was a good second choice. We fried the potatoes twice: The first fry was at a relatively low temperature to secure a soft and rich-tasting interior; the quick second fry was at a higher temperature to crisp and color the exterior.

CLASSIC FRENCH FRIES
SERVES 4

Flavoring the oil with a few tablespoons of bacon fat gives the fries a mild, meaty flavor, but omitting it will not affect the final texture of the fries. The oil will bubble up when you add the fries, so be sure you leave at least 3 inches of room between the oil and the top of your pot. We prefer peanut oil for frying, but vegetable oil can be substituted. You will need at least a 6-quart Dutch oven for this recipe.

- 4 large russet potatoes (10 to 12 ounces each), peeled and cut lengthwise into ¼-inch-thick fries
- 2 quarts peanut oil
- 4 tablespoons bacon fat, strained (optional) Salt and pepper

1. Rinse cut potatoes in large bowl under cold running water until water turns from milky to clear. Cover with at least 1 inch of water, then cover with ice. Refrigerate at least 30 minutes, or up to 3 days.

2. Heat oil in Dutch oven over medium-low heat until 325 degrees. While oil heats, add bacon fat, if using. Set wire rack in rimmed baking sheet, line rack with triple layer of paper towels, and set aside.

3. Pour off ice and water, quickly wrap potatoes in clean kitchen towel, and thoroughly pat dry. Increase heat to medium-high and add potatoes, a handful at a time, to hot oil. Fry, stirring with wire skimmer or slotted spoon, until potatoes are limp and soft and start to turn from white to blond, 6 to 8 minutes. (Oil temperature will drop 50 to 60 degrees during this frying.) Using skimmer or slotted spoon, transfer fries to prepared wire rack and let drain for at least 10 minutes.

4. When ready to serve fries, reheat oil to 350 degrees. Using paper towels as funnel, pour potatoes into hot oil. Discard paper towels and line wire rack with another triple layer of paper towels. Fry potatoes, stirring frequently, until golden brown and puffed, about 1 minute. Transfer to prepared rack and drain. Season with salt and pepper to taste. Serve immediately.

TO MAKE AHEAD: Potatoes can be prepared through step 3 and sit at room temperature for up to 2 hours, or they can be wrapped in paper towels, sealed in zipper-lock bag, and frozen for up to 1 month, before proceeding with step 4.

EASIER FRENCH FRIES

✔ WHY THIS RECIPE WORKS

When we wanted to make french fries with half the oil and no double frying (we didn't even want to have to pull out a thermometer), we submerged the potatoes in room-temperature oil before frying them over high heat until browned. This gave the potatoes' interiors an opportunity to soften and cook through before the exteriors started to crisp. Starchy russets turned leathery with the longer cooking time. With lower-starch Yukon Golds, however, the result was a crisp exterior and a creamy interior. And because of their thin skin, we didn't even have to peel them. They stuck to the bottom of the pot at first, but letting the potatoes cook in the oil for 20 minutes before stirring allowed enough time for them to form a crust that would protect them. Thinner fries were also less likely to stick.

EASIER FRENCH FRIES
SERVES 3 TO 4

Flavoring the oil with a few tablespoons bacon fat gives the fries a mild, meaty flavor, but omitting it will not affect the final texture of the fries. We prefer peanut oil for frying, but vegetable oil can be substituted. This recipe will not work with sweet potatoes or russets. Serve with ketchup or a dipping sauce (recipes follow), if desired. You will need at least a 6-quart Dutch oven for this recipe.

2½	pounds Yukon Gold potatoes, dried, sides squared off, and cut lengthwise into ¼-inch-thick fries
6	cups peanut oil
4	tablespoons bacon fat, strained (optional)
	Kosher salt

1. Set wire rack in rimmed baking sheet, line rack with triple layer of paper towels, and set aside. Combine potatoes, oil, and bacon fat, if using, in Dutch oven. Cook over high heat until oil has reached rolling boil, about 5 minutes. Continue to cook, without stirring, until potatoes are limp but exteriors are beginning to firm, about 15 minutes.

2. Using tongs, stir potatoes, gently scraping up any that stick, and continue to cook, stirring occasionally, until golden and crisp, 5 to 10 minutes longer. Using skimmer or slotted spoon, transfer fries to prepared wire rack. Season with salt and serve immediately.

BELGIAN-STYLE DIPPING SAUCE
MAKES ABOUT ½ CUP

In Belgium, mayonnaise-based dipping sauces for fries are standard. Hot sauce gives this dipping sauce a bit of a kick.

5	tablespoons mayonnaise
3	tablespoons ketchup
1	garlic clove, minced
½–¾	teaspoon hot sauce
¼	teaspoon salt

Whisk all ingredients together in small bowl.

CHIVE AND BLACK PEPPER DIPPING SAUCE
MAKES ABOUT ½ CUP

5	tablespoons mayonnaise
3	tablespoons sour cream
2	tablespoons chopped fresh chives
1½	teaspoons lemon juice
¼	teaspoon salt
¼	teaspoon pepper

Whisk all ingredients together in small bowl.

OVEN FRIES

✔ WHY THIS RECIPE WORKS

The ease and neatness of oven-frying—as opposed to deep-frying in a pot of hot oil—is such an engaging proposition that we decided to try to make oven fries worth eating on their own terms. We were after fries with a golden, crisp crust and a richly creamy interior. We soaked peeled russet potatoes, cut into wedges, in hot water for 10 minutes to remove excess starch, and to prevent the potatoes from sticking, we poured oil, salt, and pepper on the baking sheet, instead of on the potatoes, which elevated them just enough off of the pan. To get the combination of creamy interior and crisp crust, we covered the potatoes with aluminum foil to steam them for the first five minutes of cooking and then uncovered them and continued to bake until they were golden and crisp.

OVEN FRIES
SERVES 3 TO 4

Take care to cut the potatoes into evenly sized wedges so that all of the pieces will cook at about the same rate. Although it isn't required, a nonstick baking sheet works particularly well for this recipe. It not only keeps the fries from sticking to the pan but, because of its dark color, it also encourages deep and even browning. Whether you choose a nonstick baking sheet or a regular baking sheet, make sure that it is heavy duty. The intense heat of the oven may cause lighter pans to warp. You can substitute vegetable oil for the peanut oil if desired.

2¼	pounds russet potatoes, peeled and cut lengthwise into 10 to 12 even wedges
5	tablespoons peanut oil
	Salt and pepper

1. Adjust oven rack to lowest position and heat oven to 475 degrees. Place

potatoes in large bowl, cover with hot tap water, and soak for 10 minutes. Meanwhile, coat 18 by 12-inch heavy-duty rimmed baking sheet with 4 tablespoons oil and sprinkle evenly with ¾ teaspoon salt and ¼ teaspoon pepper; set aside. Line second baking sheet with triple layer of paper towels and set aside.

2. Drain potatoes. Spread potatoes out on paper towel–lined baking sheet, then thoroughly pat dry with additional paper towels. Rinse and wipe out now-empty bowl. Return potatoes to bowl and toss with remaining 1 tablespoon oil. Arrange potatoes in single layer on oiled baking sheet, cover tightly with aluminum foil, and bake 5 minutes. Remove foil and continue to bake until bottoms of potatoes are spotty golden brown, 15 to 20 minutes, rotating baking sheet after 10 minutes. Using metal spatula and tongs, scrape to loosen potatoes from pan, then flip each wedge, keeping potatoes in single layer. Continue baking until fries are golden and crisp, 5 to 15 minutes longer, rotating pan as needed if fries are browning unevenly.

3. While fries bake, line baking sheet with triple layer of paper towels. Transfer baked fries to prepared baking sheet to drain. Season with additional salt and pepper to taste and serve.

POTATOES LYONNAISE

✔ WHY THIS RECIPE WORKS

The French bistro classic, potatoes lyonnaise, uses only four ingredients—butter, onion, potatoes, and parsley. But despite its apparent simplicity, we found that most recipes produced sodden, greasy, heavy potatoes accompanied by waterlogged onions. For perfectly browned slices of tender potato tossed with soft, sweet strands of onion, our first step was zeroing in on the right potato. Yukon Golds beat out crumbly, high-starch russets and rubbery, low-starch red potatoes. We parcooked the potatoes in the microwave so that once they were added to the skillet they would cook through in the time they took to brown (without the microwave, the potatoes charred on the outside before cooking through). While the potatoes were in the microwave, we cooked the onion just long enough to release moisture and cook in its own juices. Finally, we united the onion and potatoes in a brief sauté for the perfect melding of flavors.

POTATOES LYONNAISE
SERVES 3 TO 4

Toss the potatoes halfway through the microwaving time to prevent uneven cooking. If using a lightweight skillet, you will need to stir the potatoes more frequently to prevent burning.

3	tablespoons unsalted butter
1	large onion, halved and sliced ¼ inch thick
½	teaspoon salt
2	tablespoons water
1½	pounds Yukon Gold potatoes, peeled and sliced crosswise into ¼-inch-thick rounds
¼	teaspoon pepper
1	tablespoon minced fresh parsley

1. Melt 1 tablespoon butter in 12-inch nonstick skillet over medium-high heat, add onion and ¼ teaspoon salt, and stir to coat. Cook, stirring occasionally, until onion begins to soften, about 3 minutes. Reduce heat to medium and cook, covered, stirring occasionally, until onion is light brown and soft, about 12 minutes longer, deglazing with water when pan gets dry, about halfway through cooking time. Transfer to bowl and cover. (Do not wash skillet.)

2. While onion cooks, microwave 1 tablespoon butter in large bowl until melted, about 20 seconds. Add potatoes and toss to coat with melted butter. Microwave until potatoes just start to turn tender (potatoes will offer some resistance when poked with paring knife), about 6 minutes, tossing halfway through cooking. Toss potatoes again and set aside.

3. Melt remaining 1 tablespoon butter in now-empty skillet over medium-high heat. Add potatoes and shake skillet to distribute evenly. Cook, without stirring, until browned on bottom, about 3 minutes. Using spatula, stir potatoes carefully and continue to cook, stirring every 2 to 3 minutes, until potatoes are well browned and tender when poked with paring knife, 8 to 10 minutes more. Sprinkle with remaining ¼ teaspoon salt and pepper.

4. Return onion to skillet and stir to combine. Cook until onion is heated through and flavors have melded, 1 to 2 minutes. Transfer to large plate, sprinkle with parsley, and serve.

SCALLOPED POTATOES

✔ WHY THIS RECIPE WORKS

Rich and creamy scalloped potatoes are a holiday favorite and typically require holiday-style (read: labor-intensive) preparation. We wanted a lighter, quicker version of scalloped potatoes that we could make for weeknight dinners. We used traditional russet potatoes to form tight, cohesive layers, and equal parts canned chicken broth and heavy cream to offset the typical heaviness of the dish. We parboiled the sliced potatoes in the broth-cream mixture on top of the stove, then poured the whole mixture into a casserole dish and finished it in the oven.

SCALLOPED POTATOES
SERVES 4 TO 6

The quickest way to slice the potatoes is in a food processor fitted with an ⅛-inch slicing blade. If the potatoes are too long to fit into the feed tube, halve them crosswise and put them in the feed tube cut side down so that they sit on a flat surface. If the potato slices discolor as they sit, put them in a bowl and cover with the cream and chicken broth. You can substitute Parmesan for the cheddar if desired.

2	tablespoons unsalted butter
I	onion, minced
I	tablespoon chopped fresh thyme
2	garlic cloves, minced
I¼	teaspoons salt
¼	teaspoon pepper
2½	pounds russet potatoes, peeled and sliced ⅛ inch thick
I	cup low-sodium chicken broth
I	cup heavy cream
2	bay leaves
4	ounces cheddar cheese, shredded (1 cup)

1. Adjust oven rack to middle position and heat oven to 425 degrees.

2. Melt butter in Dutch oven over medium-high heat. Add onion and cook, stirring occasionally, until soft and lightly browned, about 4 minutes. Add thyme, garlic, salt, and pepper and cook until fragrant, about 30 seconds. Add potatoes, chicken broth, cream, and bay leaves and bring to simmer. Cover, reduce heat to medium-low, and simmer until potatoes are almost tender (paring knife can be slipped in and out of potato slice with some resistance), about 10 minutes. Remove and discard bay leaves.

3. Transfer mixture to 8-inch square baking dish (or other 1½-quart gratin dish), press into an even layer, and sprinkle evenly with cheese. Bake until cream is bubbling around edges and top is golden brown, about 15 minutes. Cool 10 minutes before serving.

TO MAKE AHEAD: Once potatoes have been pressed into an even layer in step 3, refrigerate for up to 1 day. When ready to bake, add cheese, cover with aluminum foil, and bake in 400-degree oven until mixture is hot and bubbling, about 45 minutes. Remove foil and cook until cheese begins to brown, about 30 minutes longer. Cool for 10 minutes before serving.

SCALLOPED POTATOES WITH CHIPOTLE CHILE AND SMOKED CHEDDAR CHEESE

Add 2 teaspoons minced canned chipotle chile in adobo sauce along with thyme, garlic, salt, and pepper in step 2, and substitute smoked cheddar cheese for cheddar.

SCALLOPED POTATOES WITH WILD MUSHROOMS

Add 8 ounces cremini mushrooms, trimmed and sliced ¼ inch thick, and 4 ounces shiitake mushrooms, stemmed and sliced ¼ inch thick, to butter along with onion in step 2; cook until moisture released by mushrooms has evaporated, about 5 minutes. Proceed with recipe as directed.

MAKING SIMPLIFIED
POTATO GALETTE

Dumping, instead of meticulously layering, most of the potatoes over a single neatly arranged layer cuts out much of the usual galette-making fuss.

SIMPLIFIED POTATO GALETTE

✓ WHY THIS RECIPE WORKS

Pommes Anna, the classic French potato cake (or galette) in which thinly sliced potatoes are tossed with clarified butter, tightly shingled in a skillet, and cooked slowly on the stovetop, delivers showstopping results, but it requires so much labor and time that we're willing to make it only once a year. We wanted a potato galette with a crisp, deeply bronzed crust encasing a creamy center that tastes of earthy potatoes and sweet butter—and we wanted one we could make on a weeknight. We started by neatly arranging just the first layer of potatoes in the skillet, and casually packed the rest of the potatoes into the pan; once the galette was inverted onto the plate, only the tidy layer was visible. We swapped the traditional cast-iron skillet for a nonstick pan and achieved superior browning by starting the galette on the stovetop, then transferring it to the bottom rack of the oven. Regular melted butter was just as good as clarified and less work, and for a galette that held together but wasn't gluey, we rinsed the potatoes to rid them of excess starch, then incorporated a little cornstarch for just the right amount of adhesion. And in lieu of occasionally tamping down on the galette during cooking as in traditional recipes, we simply filled a cake pan with pie weights and set it on the galette for a portion of the baking time.

SIMPLIFIED POTATO GALETTE
SERVES 6 TO 8

In order for the potato cake to hold together, it is important to slice the potatoes no more than ⅛ inch thick and to make sure the slices are thoroughly dried before assembling the cake. Use a mandoline slicer or the slicing attachment of a food processor to slice the potatoes uniformly thin. A pound of dried beans, rice, or coins can be substituted for the pie weights. You will need a 10-inch ovensafe nonstick skillet for this recipe.

2½   pounds Yukon Gold potatoes, sliced ⅛ inch thick

5   tablespoons unsalted butter, melted

1   tablespoon cornstarch

1½   teaspoons chopped fresh rosemary (optional)

1   teaspoon salt

½   teaspoon pepper

1. Adjust oven rack to lowest position and heat oven to 450 degrees. Place potatoes in large bowl and fill with cold water. Using hands, swirl to remove excess starch, drain, then spread potatoes onto kitchen towels and dry thoroughly.

2. Whisk 4 tablespoons butter, cornstarch, rosemary, if using, salt, and pepper together in large bowl. Add dried potatoes and toss to thoroughly coat. Place remaining 1 tablespoon butter in 10-inch oven-safe nonstick skillet and swirl to coat. Place 1 potato slice in center of skillet, then overlap slices in circle around center slice, followed by outer circle of overlapping slices. Gently place remaining sliced potatoes on top of first layer, arranging so they form even thickness.

3. Place skillet over medium-high heat and cook until sizzling and potatoes around edge of skillet start to turn translucent, about 5 minutes. Spray 12-inch square of aluminum foil with vegetable oil spray. Place foil, sprayed side down, on top of potatoes. Place 9-inch cake pan on top of foil and fill with 2 cups pie weights. Firmly press down on cake pan to compress potatoes. Transfer skillet to oven and bake 20 minutes.

4. Remove cake pan and foil from skillet. Continue to bake until potatoes are tender when paring knife is inserted in center, 20 to 25 minutes. Return skillet to stovetop and cook over medium heat, gently shaking pan, until galette releases from sides of pan, 2 to 3 minutes.

5. Off heat, place cutting board over skillet. Using oven mitts or potholders, hold cutting board in place with one hand and with other hand on skillet handle, carefully invert skillet and cutting board together. Lift skillet off galette. Using serrated knife, gently cut into wedges and serve immediately.

POTATO ROESTI

✔ WHY THIS RECIPE WORKS

Roesti—a broad, golden brown cake of simply seasoned grated potatoes fried in butter—is hugely popular in Switzerland. We set out to master a stateside recipe with a crunchy, crisp exterior encasing a tender, creamy interior; one with good potato flavor, rich with butter. Producing a golden-brown crust for our roesti recipe wasn't much of a problem, but the inside always came out gluey and half-cooked. For a better roesti, inside and out, we eliminated moisture by wringing the raw grated potatoes in a kitchen towel. Covering the potatoes to start, then uncovering them to finish cooking created surprisingly light potatoes. Our final breakthrough came when we removed excess starch with a rinse in cold water before squeezing, then tossed the potatoes with a teaspoon of cornstarch to provide just enough starch to hold the cake together.

POTATO ROESTI
SERVES 4

The test kitchen prefers a roesti prepared with potatoes that have been cut through the large shredding disk of a food processor. It is possible to use a box grater to cut the potatoes, but they should be cut lengthwise, so you are left with long shreds. It is imperative to squeeze the potatoes as dry as possible. A well-seasoned cast-iron skillet can be used in place of the nonstick skillet. With the addition of fried eggs, ham, bacon, cheese, cooked onions, and/or tomatoes, roesti can be turned into a light meal.

1½   pounds Yukon Gold potatoes, peeled and shredded

1   teaspoon cornstarch

½   teaspoon salt
      Pepper

4   tablespoons unsalted butter

1. Place potatoes in large bowl and fill with cold water. Using hands, swirl to remove excess starch, then drain.

2. Wipe bowl dry. Place half of potatoes in center of kitchen towel. Gather ends together and twist as tightly as possible to expel maximum moisture. Transfer potatoes to bowl and repeat process with remaining potatoes.

MAKING POTATO ROESTI

1. Shake skillet to loosen roesti, then slide it onto large plate.

2. Cover roesti with second plate, then invert roesti so that browned side is facing up.

3. Melt remaining butter in skillet and slide roesti, browned side up, back into skillet and continue to cook on second side.

3. Sprinkle cornstarch, salt, and pepper to taste over potatoes. Using hands or fork, toss ingredients together until well blended.

4. Melt 2 tablespoons butter in 10-inch nonstick skillet over medium heat. Add potato mixture and spread into even layer. Cover and cook 6 minutes. Remove cover and, using spatula, gently press potatoes down to form round cake. Cook, occasionally pressing on potatoes to shape into uniform round cake, until bottom is deep golden brown, 4 to 6 minutes longer.

5. Shake skillet to loosen roesti and slide onto large plate. Add remaining 2 tablespoons butter to skillet and swirl to coat pan. Invert roesti onto second plate and slide it, browned side up, back into skillet. Cook, occasionally pressing down on cake, until bottom is well browned, 7 to 9 minutes. Remove pan from heat and allow cake to cool in pan for 5 minutes. Transfer roesti to cutting board, cut into 4 pieces, and serve immediately.

POTATO ROESTI WITH TOMATO AND FONTINA

SERVES 2 AS A MAIN COURSE

Line plate with triple layer of paper towels, place 1 large tomato, sliced thin, on plate, sprinkle with ⅛ teaspoon salt, and let drain for 30 minutes; pat tomatoes dry. Follow recipe as directed, sprinkling roesti with ½ to ¾ cup shredded fontina cheese, then shingling drained tomato slices in single layer over cheese in step 5 about 3 minutes before fully cooked on second side.

POTATO ROESTI WITH FRIED EGGS AND PARMESAN

SERVES 2 AS A MAIN COURSE

Slide 2 Fried Eggs (page 537) onto finished roesti, sprinkle with ½ cup grated Parmesan cheese, and season with salt to taste.

POTATO ROESTI WITH BACON, ONION, AND SHERRY VINEGAR

SERVES 2 AS A MAIN COURSE

Cook 3 chopped slices bacon in 10-inch skillet over medium-high heat until crisp, 5 to 7 minutes. Transfer bacon to paper–towel lined plate and pour off all but 1 tablespoon fat from skillet. Add 1 large onion, sliced thin, to skillet, season with salt and pepper to taste, and cook until onion is softened, about 5 to 7 minutes, topping finished roesti with bacon and onion and sprinkling with sherry vinegar to taste before serving.

CHEESY POTATO ROESTI

SERVES 2 AS A MAIN COURSE

While not traditional, sharp cheddar, Manchego, Italian fontina, and Havarti cheeses are each a good match to this potato dish.

Sprinkle ½ cup shredded Gruyère or Swiss cheese over roesti in step 5 about 3 minutes before fully cooked on second side.

POTATO ROESTI WITH PROSCIUTTO

SERVES 2 AS A MAIN COURSE

Drape 4 slices prosciutto over roesti in step 5 about 3 minutes before fully cooked on second side. Sprinkle with ½ teaspoon minced fresh thyme or rosemary, season with coarsely ground black pepper, and serve with whole grain mustard.

FAMILY-SIZE POTATO ROESTI

SERVES 6

Increase amount of potatoes to 2½ pounds. Squeeze potatoes in 3 batches and increase salt to ¾ teaspoon and cornstarch to 1½ teaspoons. Cook roesti in 12-inch nonstick skillet, adding additional

1½ teaspoons butter per side (5 tablespoons total). Increase uncovered cooking time in step 4 to 8 to 10 minutes and cooking time in step 5 to 8 to 10 minutes.

POTATO LATKES

✔ WHY THIS RECIPE WORKS

Often served as a side dish during holidays such as Hanukkah, potato latkes are usually made from grated potatoes mixed with eggs, onions, matzo meal, and seasonings and then fried. Ideally, latkes should be somewhat thick, golden, very crisp on the outside, and very creamy in the center. Medium-starch Yukon Golds produced pancakes with an attractive yellow-gold color, a sweet and mild flavor, and a creamy—but neither gluey nor sticky—texture. The food processor was key to quickly producing large shreds of potato. After shredding, we removed about half of the potatoes, added chunks of onion to the potatoes left in the workbowl, and processed the mixture until coarsely chopped. The large shreds of potato cooked up nice and crisp along the outside of the pancake, while the processed mixture provided the makings of a creamy interior.

THICK AND CREAMY POTATO LATKES

MAKES APPROXIMATELY 14 (3-INCH) PANCAKES

We prefer Yukon Gold potatoes here but russet potatoes will also work. Matzo meal is a traditional binder, though we found that the texture of the pancakes does not suffer without it. Applesauce and sour cream are classic accompaniments for potato latkes.

2 pounds Yukon Gold or russet potatoes, peeled
1 onion, cut into 8 wedges
1 large egg
4 scallions, minced

3   tablespoons minced fresh parsley
2   tablespoons matzo meal (optional)
    Salt and pepper
I   cup vegetable oil

1. Grate potatoes in food processor fitted with coarse shredding blade. Place half of grated potatoes in fine-mesh strainer set over bowl and reserve. Fit food processor with steel blade, add onions, and pulse with remaining potatoes until coarsely chopped, 5 to 6 pulses. Mix with reserved potato shreds and press against sieve to drain as much liquid as possible into bowl below. Let potato liquid sit until starch settles to bottom, about 1 minute. Pour off liquid, leaving starch in bowl. Beat egg, then potato mixture, scallions, parsley, matzo meal, if using, and salt and pepper to taste, into starch.

2. Set wire rack in rimmed baking sheet and line with triple layer of paper towels; set aside. Pour oil into 12-inch skillet to depth of ¼ inch and heat over medium-high heat until shimmering. Gently squeeze ¼ cup potato mixture to remove excess liquid, shape into ½-inch-thick disk, and place in oil. Press gently with nonstick spatula to compact latke; repeat until 5 latkes are in skillet.

3. Maintaining heat so fat bubbles around latke edges, fry until golden brown on bottom and edges, about 3 minutes. Using spatula, flip latkes and continue frying until golden brown all over, about 3 minutes more. Transfer to prepared wire rack to drain. Repeat with remaining potato mixture, returning oil to medium-high heat between each batch and replacing oil after every second batch. Season with salt and pepper to taste and serve immediately.

TO MAKE AHEAD: Finished latkes can be cooled, covered loosely, and held at room temperature for 4 hours. When ready to serve, transfer to baking sheet and reheat in 375-degree oven until crisp and hot, about 5 minutes per side.

ROASTED SWEET POTATOES

✔ WHY THIS RECIPE WORKS
Too often, roasted sweet potatoes turn out starchy and wan. We wanted a method that gave us potatoes with a nicely caramelized exterior, a smooth, creamy interior, and an earthy sweetness. Cutting them into ¾-inch-thick rounds and laying them flat on a baking sheet ensured even cooking. A few experiments proved a lower roasting temperature resulted in a sweeter potato, so we started the sliced potatoes in a cold (versus preheated) oven and covered them with aluminum foil, which allowed plenty of time for their starches to convert to sugars. We removed the foil after 30 minutes and continued to roast the potatoes until crisp.

ROASTED SWEET POTATOES
SERVES 4 TO 6

Note that this recipe calls for starting the potatoes in a cold oven. Choose potatoes that are as even in width as possible; trimming the small ends prevents them from burning. If you prefer not to peel the potatoes, just scrub them well before cutting.

3   pounds sweet potatoes, ends trimmed, peeled, rinsed, and cut into ¾-inch-thick rounds
2   tablespoons vegetable oil
I   teaspoon salt
    Pepper

1. Toss potatoes in large bowl with oil, salt, and pepper to taste until evenly coated. Line rimmed baking sheet with aluminum foil and coat with vegetable oil spray. Arrange potatoes in single layer on baking sheet and cover tightly with foil. Adjust oven rack to middle position and place potatoes in cold oven. Turn oven to 425 degrees and bake potatoes for 30 minutes.

2. Remove baking sheet from oven and carefully remove top piece of foil. Return potatoes to oven and cook, uncovered, until bottom edges of potatoes are golden brown, 15 to 25 minutes.

3. Remove baking sheet from oven and, using thin metal spatula, flip potato slices over. Continue to roast until bottom edges of potatoes are golden brown, 18 to 22 minutes longer. Remove from oven, cool for 5 to 10 minutes, and serve.

ROASTED SWEET POTATOES WITH MAPLE-THYME GLAZE

Whisk ¼ cup maple syrup, 2 tablespoons melted unsalted butter, and 2 teaspoons minced fresh thyme together in small bowl. Follow recipe as directed through step 2. After removing baking sheet from oven in step 3, brush potatoes with half of maple syrup glaze, flip slices over with thin metal spatula, and brush with remaining glaze. Return potatoes to oven and proceed as directed.

ROASTED SWEET POTATOES WITH SPICED BROWN SUGAR GLAZE

Heat ¼ cup packed light brown sugar, 2 tablespoons apple juice, 2 tablespoons unsalted butter, ¼ teaspoon ground cinnamon, ¼ teaspoon ground ginger, and ⅛ teaspoon ground nutmeg in small saucepan over medium heat. Cook, stirring constantly, until butter has melted and sugar is dissolved, 2 to 4 minutes. Follow recipe as directed through step 2. After removing baking sheet from oven in step 3, brush potatoes with half of spice glaze, flip slices over with thin metal spatula, and brush with remaining glaze. Return potatoes to oven and proceed as directed.

MASHED SWEET POTATOES

✔ WHY THIS RECIPE WORKS

We wanted a method for making mashed sweet potatoes that would push their deep, earthy sweetness to the fore and produce a silky puree with enough body to hold its shape on a fork. We braised sliced sweet potatoes in a mixture of butter and heavy cream to impart a smooth richness. Adding salt brought out the potatoes' delicate flavor, and just a teaspoon of sugar bolstered their sweetness. Once the potatoes were tender, we mashed them in the saucepan with a potato masher. We skipped the typical pumpkin pie seasoning and instead let the simple sweet potato flavor shine through.

MASHED SWEET POTATOES
SERVES 4

Cutting the sweet potatoes into slices of even thickness is important in getting them to cook at the same rate. A potato masher will yield slightly lumpy sweet potatoes; a food mill will make a perfectly smooth puree.

- 2   pounds sweet potatoes, peeled, quartered lengthwise, and cut crosswise into ¼-inch-thick slices
- 4   tablespoons unsalted butter, cut into 4 pieces
- 2   tablespoons heavy cream
- I   teaspoon sugar
- ½   teaspoon salt
      Pinch pepper

1. Combine sweet potatoes, butter, cream, sugar, and salt in large saucepan and cook, covered, over low heat, stirring occasionally, until potatoes fall apart when poked with fork, 35 to 45 minutes.

2. Off heat, mash sweet potatoes in saucepan with potato masher (Alternatively, you can you use ricer or food mill to press or mill potatoes into warmed serving bowl.) Stir in pepper; serve immediately.

MAPLE-ORANGE MASHED SWEET POTATOES

Stir in 2 tablespoons maple syrup and ½ teaspoon grated orange zest along with pepper just before serving.

INDIAN-SPICED MASHED SWEET POTATOES WITH RAISINS AND CASHEWS

Substitute dark brown sugar for granulated sugar and add ¾ teaspoon garam masala to saucepan along with sweet potatoes in step 1. Stir ¼ cup golden raisins and ¼ cup roasted unsalted cashews, chopped coarse, into mashed sweet potatoes along with pepper just before serving.

GARLIC MASHED SWEET POTATOES WITH COCONUT

Substitute ½ cup coconut milk for butter and cream and add ¼ teaspoon red pepper flakes and 1 small minced garlic clove to saucepan along with sweet potatoes in step 1. Stir in 1 tablespoon minced fresh cilantro along with pepper just before serving.

SWEET POTATO CASSEROLE

✔ WHY THIS RECIPE WORKS

More dessert than side dish, the typical version of this holiday favorite swamps this casserole in sugar, fat, and spices. We wanted to bring the sweet potatoes to the forefront. We rejected a number of topping options we found in other versions—nuts, canned pineapple, maraschino cherries, corn flakes, Rice Krispies, bread crumbs—and settled on a streusel made with dark brown sugar and slightly bitter pecans, which kept the sweetness to a minimum while adding texture. And we cut back on the traditionally excessive amounts of sugar and cream in the filling and boosted the sweet potato flavor by roasting the potatoes. A food processor created a silky smooth base, to which we added some reserved
potato chunks for textural interest. We were stingy with the spices; nutmeg, black pepper, vanilla, and a splash of lemon juice added brightness without making the casserole taste like pie.

SWEET POTATO CASSEROLE
SERVES 10 TO 12

Because natural sugar levels in sweet potatoes vary greatly depending on variety, size, and season, it's important to taste the filling before adding sugar. If the filling is bland, add up to 4 tablespoons sugar; if the potatoes are naturally sweet, you may opt to omit the sugar altogether. When sweetening the filling, keep in mind that the streusel topping is quite sweet. If you can find them, Beauregard, Garnet, or Jewel sweet potatoes have the best texture for this recipe. For even cooking, buy potatoes that are uniform in size. Avoid potatoes larger than 1½ pounds; they require a longer roasting time and tend to cook unevenly. The potatoes can be baked up to 2 days ahead. Scrape the flesh from the skins and refrigerate in an airtight container. To serve 4 to 6, halve all the ingredients and bake the casserole in an 8-inch square baking dish for 35 to 40 minutes.

POTATOES
- 7   pounds sweet potatoes

STREUSEL
- 5   tablespoons unsalted butter, cut into 5 pieces and softened, plus extra for pan
- ½   cup (2½ ounces) all-purpose flour
- ½   cup packed (3½ ounces) dark brown sugar
- ¼   teaspoon salt
- I   cup pecans

FILLING
- 5   tablespoons unsalted butter, melted
- I   tablespoon vanilla extract
- 4   teaspoons lemon juice
- 2   teaspoons salt
- ½   teaspoon ground nutmeg

½ teaspoon pepper
    Granulated sugar
4 large egg yolks
1½ cups half-and-half

1. FOR THE POTATOES: Adjust oven rack to lower-middle position and heat oven to 400 degrees. Poke sweet potatoes several times with paring knife and space evenly on aluminum foil–lined rimmed baking sheet. Bake potatoes, turning once, until they are very tender and can be squeezed easily with tongs, 1 to 1½ hours (or 45 minutes for small sweet potatoes). Remove potatoes from oven and cut in half lengthwise to let steam escape; cool at least 10 minutes. Reduce oven temperature to 375 degrees.

2. FOR THE STREUSEL: While potatoes are baking, butter 13 by 9-inch baking dish. Pulse flour, brown sugar, and salt in food processor until blended, about 4 pulses. Sprinkle butter pieces over flour mixture and pulse until crumbly mass forms, 6 to 8 pulses. Sprinkle nuts over mixture and pulse until combined but some large nut pieces remain, 4 to 6 pulses. Transfer streusel to medium bowl and return now-empty workbowl to processor.

3. Once potatoes have cooled slightly, use soupspoon to scoop flesh into large bowl (you should have about 8 cups). Transfer half of potato flesh to food processor. Using rubber spatula, break remaining potato flesh in bowl into coarse 1-inch chunks.

4. FOR THE FILLING: Add melted butter, vanilla, lemon juice, salt, nutmeg, and pepper to potatoes in food processor and process until smooth, about 20 seconds. Taste for sweetness, then add up to 4 tablespoons granulated sugar, if necessary. Add egg yolks. With processor running, pour in half-and-half and process until blended, about 20 seconds. Transfer mixture to bowl with potato pieces and stir gently until combined.

5. TO ASSEMBLE AND BAKE CASSEROLE: Pour filling into prepared baking dish and spread into even layer with spatula. Sprinkle with streusel, breaking up any large pieces with fingers. Bake until topping is well browned and filling is slightly puffy around edges, 40 to 45 minutes. Cool at least 10 minutes before serving.

ACORN SQUASH WITH BROWN SUGAR

✔ WHY THIS RECIPE WORKS

After what seems like eons in the oven, acorn squash often lands on the table with little flavor and a dry, grainy texture. We wanted perfectly cooked squash with a sweet, nutty flavor and moist flesh—without taking hours. Microwaving turned out to be the winning cooking method, resulting in squash that was tender and silky, with nary a trace of dryness or stringiness. We found it was best to halve and seed the squash

before cooking; whole pierced squash cooked unevenly. Equal portions of butter and dark brown sugar gave the squash ample but not excessive sweetness. Briefly broiling the squash gave it a welcome roasted texture and a perfectly glazed surface.

ACORN SQUASH WITH BROWN SUGAR

SERVES 4

Squash smaller than 1½ pounds will likely cook faster, so begin checking for doneness a few minutes early. Conversely, larger squash will take slightly longer. However, keep in mind that the cooking time is largely dependent on the microwave. If microwaving the squash in Pyrex, the manufacturer recommends adding water to the dish (or bowl) prior to cooking. If you are cooking the squash in a bowl, you will need one that holds about 4 quarts.

2 acorn squash (1½ pounds each), halved pole to pole and seeded
    Salt
3 tablespoons unsalted butter
3 tablespoons dark brown sugar

1. Sprinkle squash halves with salt and place, cut sides down, in 13 by 9-inch baking dish or arrange halves in large bowl so that cut sides face out. If using Pyrex, add ¼ cup water to dish or bowl. Cover and microwave until squash is very tender and offers no resistance when poked with paring knife, 15 to 25 minutes. Remove baking dish or bowl from microwave and set on clean, dry surface (avoid damp or cold surfaces).

2. While squash is cooking, adjust oven rack 6 inches from broiler element and heat broiler. Melt butter, brown sugar, and ⅛ teaspoon salt in small saucepan over low heat, whisking occasionally, until combined.

3. Using tongs, transfer cooked squash, cut side up, to rimmed baking

sheet. Spoon portion of butter mixture onto each squash half. Broil until brown and caramelized, 5 to 8 minutes, rotating baking sheet as necessary and removing squash halves as they are done. Serve immediately.

ACORN SQUASH WITH ROSEMARY-DRIED FIG COMPOTE

While squash is cooking, combine 1 cup orange juice, 4 chopped dried black figs, 1 tablespoon dark brown sugar, ½ teaspoon minced fresh rosemary, ¼ teaspoon pepper, and ⅛ teaspoon salt in small saucepan. Simmer over medium-high heat, stirring occasionally, until syrupy and liquid is reduced to about 3 tablespoons, 15 to 20 minutes. Stir in 1 tablespoon unsalted butter. Substitute fig compote for butter mixture.

SAUTÉED ZUCCHINI

✔ WHY THIS RECIPE WORKS
Because zucchini is so watery, it often cooks up soggy and bland. We wanted to find a way to make sautéed zucchini with concentrated flavor and appealing texture. We found that the secret was to remove water using two methods: salting and draining as well as shredding and squeezing. We grated the zucchini using a box grater, tossed the shreds with salt, drained them in a colander, and wrung them out in a kitchen towel. We tossed the dry shreds with a little olive oil and added them to a hot skillet, where they became tender and lightly browned with minimal stirring. A little garlic and lemon lent bright flavor.

SAUTÉED SHREDDED ZUCCHINI WITH GARLIC AND LEMON
SERVES 4

The bread-crumb topping adds a nice textural contrast to this recipe, but you may omit it if you prefer.

TOPPING
2   slices hearty white sandwich bread, torn into quarters
2   tablespoons unsalted butter

ZUCCHINI
5   zucchini, halved lengthwise, seeded, and shredded
    Salt and pepper
I   tablespoon plus I teaspoon extra-virgin olive oil, plus extra for drizzling
I   small garlic clove, minced
I–2 teaspoons lemon juice

I. FOR THE TOPPING: Pulse bread in food processor to coarse crumbs, about 10 pulses. Melt butter in 12-inch nonstick skillet over medium-high heat. Add bread crumbs and cook, stirring frequently, until golden brown, about 3 minutes. Transfer to small bowl; set aside.

2. FOR THE ZUCCHINI: Toss zucchini with 1½ teaspoons salt in large bowl. Transfer to colander and let drain for 5 to 10 minutes. Place zucchini in center of kitchen towel and wring out excess moisture, in batches if necessary.

3. Place zucchini in medium bowl and separate any large clumps. Combine 2 teaspoons oil with garlic in small bowl. Add to zucchini and toss to combine.

4. Heat remaining 2 teaspoons oil in 12-inch nonstick skillet over high heat until just smoking. Add zucchini in even layer and cook, without stirring, until bottom layer browns, about 2 minutes. Stir well, breaking up any clumps with tongs, then cook until bottom layer browns, about 2 minutes more. Off heat, season with

lemon juice and salt and pepper to taste. Sprinkle with topping, drizzle with olive oil, and serve immediately.

SAUTÉED SHREDDED ZUCCHINI WITH TOMATOES AND BASIL

Omit bread-crumb topping. Combine 3 cored, seeded, and diced plum tomatoes, 2 tablespoons chopped fresh basil, 2 teaspoons extra-virgin olive oil, 1 teaspoon balsamic vinegar, 1 minced garlic clove, and ¼ teaspoon salt in small bowl and set aside. Omit garlic in step 3 and replace lemon juice with tomato mixture in step 4. Transfer to serving platter, sprinkle with ¼ cup grated Parmesan, and serve immediately, drizzling with additional olive oil if desired.

SAUTÉED SHREDDED ZUCCHINI WITH SPICED CARROTS AND ALMONDS

Omit bread-crumb topping. Follow steps 2 and 3 as directed, omitting garlic, then heat 1 tablespoon extra-virgin olive oil in 12-inch nonstick skillet over medium heat until shimmering. Add 2 peeled and grated carrots and cook, stirring occasionally, until tender, about 5 minutes. Add ½ teaspoon ground coriander and ¼ teaspoon red pepper flakes and cook, stirring constantly, until fragrant, about 30 seconds. Add grated zucchini and ½ cup golden raisins to skillet, spread into even layer, and cook as directed. Add ½ cup sliced toasted almonds and toss to combine before seasoning with lemon juice, salt, and pepper.

SAUTÉED SHREDDED ZUCCHINI WITH PEAS AND HERBS

Omit bread-crumb topping and lemon juice. Follow steps 2 and 3 as directed, omitting garlic, then heat 2 teaspoons oil in 12-inch nonstick skillet over medium heat until shimmering. Add finely chopped whites from 1 bunch scallions and cook, stirring, until softened and beginning to brown, about 3 minutes. Increase heat to high, add zucchini and cook as directed. Once browned, add 1 cup thawed frozen peas and ½ cup heavy cream and cook, stirring, until cream is mostly reduced, about 2 minutes. Off heat, stir in 2 tablespoons chopped fresh dill or mint and thinly sliced scallion greens and season with salt and pepper to taste. Serve with lemon wedges.

STUFFED ZUCCHINI

✔ WHY THIS RECIPE WORKS

We wanted stuffed zucchini worth eating—hearty and full-flavored enough for a side or main course. To avoid soggy and flavorless results, after scooping out the seeds we briefly roasted the zucchini, cut side down before stuffing and baking them. This step added flavor and speeded up the cooking process. For a hearty filling, we started with potatoes and found ingredients like black beans, tomatoes, fresh corn, lamb, and mango worked well. Cheese helped bind some of our fillings, while yogurt added a creamy, bright counterpoint to our Indian-style lamb mixture. Precooking the filling separately meant every component was cooked through perfectly. All we had to do was stuff the zucchini and return them to the hot oven for a quick blast of heat.

STUFFED ZUCCHINI WITH CORN, BLACK BEANS, AND CHIPOTLE CHILES

SERVES 4 AS A MAIN COURSE OR 8 AS A SIDE DISH

Buy firm zucchini with tiny prickly hairs around the stem ends; the hairs are a sign of freshness.

- 4 zucchini (8 ounces each), halved lengthwise
  Salt and pepper
- 4 tablespoons olive oil
- 1 red potato (6 ounces), cut into ½-inch cubes
- 1 onion, chopped fine
- 2 ears corn, husks and silk removed, kernels cut from cobs
- 5 garlic cloves, minced
- 2 teaspoons minced canned chipotle chiles in adobo sauce
- 2 tomatoes, cored, seeded, and chopped
- 1 (15-ounce) can black beans, rinsed
- ⅓ cup chopped fresh cilantro
- 6 ounces Monterey Jack cheese, shredded (1½ cups)

1. Adjust oven racks to upper-middle and lowest positions, place rimmed baking sheet on each rack, and heat oven to 400 degrees.

2. With small spoon, scoop out seeds and most of flesh from zucchini halves, leaving ¼-inch thickness of flesh in each shell. Season cut sides of zucchini with salt and pepper to taste and brush with 2 tablespoons oil. Toss potato with 1 tablespoon oil in small bowl and season with salt and pepper to taste.

3. Place zucchini, cut side down, on preheated baking sheet on lower rack and spread potato pieces in single layer on preheated baking sheet on upper rack. Roast zucchini until slightly softened and skins are wrinkled, about 10 minutes; roast potato until tender and lightly browned, 10 to 12 minutes. Using tongs, flip zucchini halves over on baking sheet and set aside.

4. Heat remaining 1 tablespoon oil in 12-inch skillet over medium heat until shimmering. Add onion and cook, stirring occasionally, until softened and beginning to brown, about 10 minutes. Increase heat to medium-high, stir in corn, and cook until almost tender, about 3 minutes. Add garlic and chipotle and cook until fragrant, about 30 seconds. Stir in tomatoes, black beans, and roasted potatoes. Cook, stirring occasionally, until heated through, about 3 minutes. Off heat, stir in cilantro and ½ cup cheese. Season with salt and pepper to taste.

5. Divide filling evenly among zucchini halves on baking sheet and pack lightly. Sprinkle with remaining 1 cup cheese and return zucchini to oven to upper-middle rack. Bake until heated through and cheese is spotty brown, about 6 minutes. Serve immediately.

STUFFED ZUCCHINI WITH CURRIED LAMB, MANGO, AND CURRANTS

SERVES 4 AS A MAIN COURSE OR 8 AS A SIDE DISH

Buy firm zucchini with tiny prickly hairs around the stem end; the hairs are a sign of freshness.

- 4 zucchini (8 ounces each), halved lengthwise
  Salt and pepper
- 4 tablespoons olive oil
- 1 red potato (6 ounces), cut into ½-inch cubes
- 1 onion, chopped fine
- 5 garlic cloves, minced
- 2 tablespoons curry powder
  Pinch cayenne pepper
- 8 ounces ground lamb
- ½ cup dried currants
- 1½ cups plain yogurt
- 2 tomatoes, cored, seeded, and chopped
- ½ mango, peeled, pitted, and cut into ¼-inch pieces
- ⅓ cup chopped fresh parsley

1. Adjust oven racks to upper-middle and lowest positions, place rimmed baking sheet on each rack, and heat oven to 400 degrees.

2. With small spoon, scoop out seeds and most of flesh from zucchini halves, leaving ¼-inch thickness of flesh in each shell. Season cut sides of zucchini with salt and pepper to taste and brush with 2 tablespoons oil. Toss potato with 1 tablespoon olive oil in small bowl and season with salt and pepper to taste.

3. Place zucchini, cut side down, on preheated baking sheet on lower rack and spread potato pieces in single layer on preheated baking sheet on upper rack. Roast zucchini until slightly softened and skins are wrinkled, about 10 minutes; roast potato until tender and lightly browned, 10 to 12 minutes. Using tongs, flip zucchini halves over on baking sheet and set aside.

4. Heat remaining 1 tablespoon oil in 12-inch skillet over medium heat until shimmering. Add onion and cook, stirring occasionally, until softened and beginning to brown, about 10 minutes. Increase heat to medium-high, stir in garlic, curry powder, and cayenne and cook until fragrant, about 30 seconds. Add lamb and currants, breaking lamb into bite-size pieces with wooden spoon, and cook, stirring occasionally, until lamb begins to brown, about 3 minutes. Stir in yogurt, 2 tablespoons at a time, allowing it to sizzle and most of moisture to cook off with each addition (this process should take about 5 minutes). After last addition, simmer mixture until almost all liquid has evaporated, about 5 minutes. Stir in tomatoes, mango, and roasted potatoes. Cook, stirring occasionally, until heated through, about 3 minutes. Off heat, stir in parsley and season with salt and pepper to taste.

5. Divide filling evenly among zucchini halves on baking sheet and pack lightly. Return zucchini to oven to upper-middle rack. Bake until heated through, about 6 minutes. Serve immediately.

STUFFED ZUCCHINI WITH TOMATOES AND JACK CHEESE
SERVES 4 AS A MAIN COURSE OR 8 AS A SIDE DISH

Buy firm zucchini with tiny prickly hairs around the stem end; the hairs are a sign of freshness.

- 4 zucchini (8 ounces each), halved lengthwise
  Salt and pepper
- 4 tablespoons olive oil
- 1 pound red potatoes, cut into ½-inch cubes
- 1 onion, chopped fine
- 5 garlic cloves, minced
- 3 tomatoes, cored, seeded, and chopped
- ⅓ cup shredded fresh basil
- 6 ounces Monterey Jack cheese, shredded (1½ cups)

1. Adjust oven racks to upper-middle and lowest positions, place rimmed baking sheet on each rack, and heat oven to 400 degrees.

2. With small spoon, scoop out seeds and most of flesh from zucchini halves, leaving ¼-inch thickness of flesh in each shell. Season cut sides of zucchini with salt and pepper to taste and brush with 2 tablespoons oil. Toss potatoes with 1 tablespoon olive oil in small bowl and season with salt and pepper to taste.

3. Place zucchini, cut side down, on preheated baking sheet on lower rack and spread potatoes in single layer on preheated baking sheet on upper rack. Roast zucchini until slightly softened and skins are wrinkled, about 10 minutes; roast potatoes until tender and lightly browned, 10 to 12 minutes. Using tongs, flip zucchini halves over on baking sheet and set aside.

4. Heat remaining 1 tablespoon oil in 12-inch skillet over medium heat until shimmering. Add onion and cook, stirring occasionally, until softened and beginning to brown, about 10 minutes. Increase heat to medium-high, stir in garlic, and cook until fragrant, about 30 seconds. Add tomatoes and roasted potatoes and cook, stirring occasionally, until heated through, about 3 minutes. Off heat, stir in basil and ½ cup cheese and season with salt and pepper to taste.

5. Divide filling evenly among zucchini halves on baking sheet and pack lightly. Sprinkle with remaining 1 cup cheese.

Return zucchini to oven to upper-middle rack. Bake until heated through and cheese is spotty brown, about 6 minutes. Serve immediately.

SUMMER VEGETABLE GRATIN

✔ WHY THIS RECIPE WORKS

Layering summer's best vegetables into a gratin can lead to a memorable side dish—or a soggy mess. We wanted a simple Provençal-style vegetable gratin, where a golden brown, cheesy topping provides a rich contrast to the fresh, bright flavor of the vegetables. The typical combination of tomatoes, zucchini, and summer squash made the cut (eggplant was too mushy and bell peppers took on a steamed flavor). To eliminate excess moisture, we baked the casserole uncovered after salting the vegetables. Salting worked like a charm to both season and dry out the zucchini and summer squash, but proved insufficient to deal with all the tomato juice. So we moved the tomatoes to the top gratin layer, which allowed them to roast and caramelize. Drizzled with an aromatic garlic and thyme oil, the tomatoes had great flavor. For more complexity, we added a layer of caramelized onions between the squash and tomato layers, and we sprinkled the dish with Parmesan bread crumbs before baking.

SUMMER VEGETABLE GRATIN
SERVES 6 TO 8

The success of this recipe depends on good-quality produce. Buy zucchini and summer squash of roughly the same diameter. While we like the visual contrast zucchini and summer squash bring to the dish, you can also use just one or the other. A similarly sized broiler-safe gratin dish can be substituted for the 13 by 9-inch baking dish. Serve the gratin alongside grilled fish or meat and accompanied by bread to soak up any flavorful juices.

6 tablespoons extra-virgin olive oil
1 pound zucchini, ends trimmed and sliced ¼ inch thick
1 pound yellow summer squash, ends trimmed and sliced ¼ inch thick
2 teaspoons salt
1½ pounds tomatoes, cored and sliced ¼ inch thick
2 onions, halved and sliced thin
¾ teaspoon pepper
2 garlic cloves, minced
1 tablespoon minced fresh thyme
1 slice hearty white sandwich bread, torn into quarters
2 ounces Parmesan cheese, grated (1 cup)
2 shallots, minced
¼ cup chopped fresh basil

1. Adjust oven rack to upper-middle position and heat oven to 400 degrees. Brush 13 by 9-inch baking dish with 1 tablespoon oil and set aside. Line 2 baking sheets with triple layer of paper towels and set aside.

2. Toss zucchini and summer squash slices with 1 teaspoon salt in large bowl; transfer to colander. Let sit until zucchini and squash release at least 3 tablespoons of liquid, about 45 minutes. Arrange slices on 1 prepared baking sheet and cover with another triple layer of paper towels. Firmly press each slice to remove as much liquid as possible.

3. Place tomato slices in single layer on second prepared baking sheet, sprinkle evenly with ½ teaspoon salt, and let sit 30 minutes. Cover with double layer of paper towels and press firmly to dry tomatoes.

4. Meanwhile, heat 1 tablespoon oil in 12-inch nonstick skillet over medium heat until shimmering. Add onions, remaining ½ teaspoon salt, and ¼ teaspoon pepper. Cook, stirring occasionally, until onions are softened and dark golden brown, 20 to 25 minutes. Set onions aside.

5. Combine garlic, 3 tablespoons oil, remaining ½ teaspoon pepper, and thyme in small bowl. In large bowl, toss zucchini and summer squash in half of oil mixture, then arrange in prepared baking dish. Arrange caramelized onions in even layer over squash. Slightly overlap tomato slices in single layer on top of onions. Spoon remaining garlic-oil mixture evenly over tomatoes. Bake until vegetables are tender and tomatoes are starting to brown on edges, 40 to 45 minutes.

6. Meanwhile, process bread in food processor until finely ground, about 10 seconds. (You should have about 1 cup crumbs.) Combine bread crumbs, remaining 1 tablespoon oil, Parmesan, and shallots in medium bowl. Remove baking dish from oven and increase heat to 450 degrees. Sprinkle bread-crumb mixture evenly on top of tomatoes. Bake gratin until bubbling and cheese is lightly browned, 5 to 10 minutes. Sprinkle with basil and let sit for 10 minutes before serving.

SUMMER VEGETABLE GRATIN
WITH ROASTED PEPPERS AND
SMOKED MOZZARELLA

You can use store-bought roasted red peppers or make your own (see recipe on page 273). If using store-bought, rinse and pat the peppers dry before using.

Substitute 4 ounces shredded smoked mozzarella (1 cup) for Parmesan and 3 roasted red peppers, cut into 1-inch pieces, for summer squash (do not salt roasted peppers).

ASSEMBLING VEGETABLE GRATIN

1. Toss salted zucchini and squash in half of garlic-oil mixture, then arrange in prepared greased baking dish.

2. Spread caramelized onions in even layer on top of zucchini and squash.

3. Slightly overlap salted tomatoes in single layer on top of onions, then top with remaining garlic-oil mixture.

4. When vegetables are tender, sprinkle gratin with bread-crumb mixture, then continue to bake until golden brown.

EGGPLANT PARMESAN

✓ *Why this recipe works Frying the eggplant for this classic Italian dish is not only time-consuming but can also make the dish heavy and dull. In the hope of eliminating the grease as well as some of the prep time, we opted to cook the breaded eggplant in the oven after salting and draining the slices (which removed bitterness and improved texture). Baking the eggplant on preheated and oiled baking sheets resulted in crisp, golden brown slices, and a traditional bound breading of flour, egg, and fresh bread crumbs worked best for giving the eggplant a crisp coating. While the eggplant was in the oven, we made a quick tomato sauce using garlic, red pepper flakes, basil, and canned diced tomatoes. We layered the sauce, baked breaded eggplant slices, and mozzarella in a baking dish and left the top layer of eggplant mostly unsauced, which ensured it would crisp up nicely in the oven.*

EGGPLANT PARMESAN
SERVES 6 TO 8

Use kosher salt when salting the eggplant. The coarse grains don't dissolve as readily as the fine grains of regular table salt, so any excess can be easily wiped away. To be time-efficient, use the 30 to 45 minutes during which the salted eggplant sits to prepare the breading, cheeses, and sauce.

EGGPLANT

2	pounds eggplant, sliced into ¼-inch-thick rounds
	Kosher salt and pepper
8	slices hearty white sandwich bread, torn into quarters
2	ounces Parmesan cheese, grated (1 cup)
1	cup all-purpose flour
4	large eggs
6	tablespoons vegetable oil

SAUCE

3	(14.5-ounce) cans diced tomatoes
2	tablespoons extra-virgin olive oil
4	garlic cloves, minced
¼	teaspoon red pepper flakes
¼	cup chopped fresh basil
	Kosher salt and pepper
8	ounces whole-milk or part-skim mozzarella, shredded (2 cups)
1	ounce Parmesan cheese, grated (½ cup)
10	fresh basil leaves, roughly torn

1. FOR THE EGGPLANT: Line baking sheet with triple layer of paper towels and set aside. Toss eggplant and 1½ teaspoons salt together in bowl, then transfer to colander. Let sit until eggplant releases about 2 tablespoons liquid, 30 to 45 minutes. Wipe excess salt from eggplant, then arrange on prepared baking sheet. Cover with another triple layer of paper towels and firmly press each slice to remove as much liquid as possible.

2. While eggplant is draining, adjust oven racks to upper-middle and lower-middle positions, place rimmed baking sheet on each rack, and heat oven to 425 degrees. Pulse bread in food processor to fine, even crumbs, about 15 pulses (you should have about 4 cups). Transfer crumbs to pie plate or shallow dish and stir in Parmesan, and ½ teaspoon pepper; set aside. Wipe out food processor bowl (do not wash) and set aside.

3. Combine flour and 1 teaspoon pepper in large zipper-lock bag and shake to combine. Beat eggs in second pie plate or shallow dish. Place 8 to 10 eggplant slices in bag with flour, seal bag, and shake to coat eggplant. Remove eggplant slices, shaking off excess flour, then dip in eggs, letting excess egg run off. Then coat

evenly with bread-crumb mixture. Set breaded slices on wire rack set in rimmed baking sheet. Repeat with remaining eggplant.

4. Remove preheated baking sheets from oven. Add 3 tablespoons oil to each sheet, tilting to coat evenly with oil. Place half of breaded eggplant on each baking sheet in single layer; bake until eggplant is well browned and crisp, about 30 minutes, switching and rotating baking sheets after 10 minutes, and flipping eggplant slices with wide spatula after 20 minutes. (Do not turn off oven.)

5. FOR THE SAUCE: While eggplant bakes, process 2 cans diced tomatoes in food processor until almost smooth, about 5 seconds. Heat olive oil, garlic, and pepper flakes in large saucepan over medium-high heat, stirring occasionally, until fragrant and garlic is light golden, about 3 minutes. Stir in processed tomatoes and remaining can diced tomatoes. Bring sauce to boil, then reduce heat to medium-low and simmer, stirring occasionally, until slightly thickened and reduced, about 15 minutes (you should have about 4 cups). Stir in basil and season with salt and pepper to taste.

6. TO ASSEMBLE: Spread 1 cup tomato sauce over bottom of 13 by 9-inch baking dish. Layer in half of eggplant slices, overlapping slices to fit. Distribute 1 cup sauce over eggplant, then sprinkle with 1 cup mozzarella. Layer in remaining eggplant, then dot with 1 cup sauce, leaving majority of eggplant exposed so it will remain crisp. Sprinkle with Parmesan and remaining 1 cup mozzarella. Bake until bubbling and cheese is browned, 13 to 15 minutes. Cool 10 minutes, scatter basil over top, and serve, passing remaining tomato sauce separately.

STUFFED TOMATOES

✔ **WHY THIS RECIPE WORKS**

Most stuffed tomatoes are mealy and bland, with a stuffing of waterlogged tasteless bread. We were after ripe, sun-drenched summer tomatoes filled with garden-fresh herbs, garlicky bread crumbs, and sharp cheese. To combat sogginess, we salted and drained the tomatoes prior to stuffing. We used homemade bread crumbs as a base for a stuffing that also included olive oil, cheese, garlic, and fresh basil. We generously filled the tomatoes and baked for just 20 minutes for tender tomatoes topped with a crisp, golden crust.

STUFFED TOMATOES WITH PARMESAN, GARLIC, AND BASIL
SERVES 6

Make sure not to use tomatoes that are too ripe, as they will not hold their shape.

- 6 firm, ripe large tomatoes (8 ounces each), ⅛ inch sliced off stem end, cored, and seeded
- 1 teaspoon kosher salt
- 1 slice hearty white sandwich bread, torn into quarters
- 3 tablespoons plus 1 teaspoon olive oil
- 1½ ounces Parmesan cheese, grated (¾ cup)
- ⅓ cup shredded fresh basil
- 2 garlic cloves, minced
  Pepper

1. Line baking sheet with double layer of paper towels. Sprinkle inside of each tomato with salt and place upside down on baking sheet. Let sit to remove excess moisture, about 30 minutes.

2. Meanwhile, adjust oven rack to upper-middle position and heat oven to 375 degrees. Line bottom of 13 by 9-inch baking dish with aluminum foil;

set aside. Pulse bread in food processor to coarse crumbs, about 10 pulses. Toss with 1 tablespoon olive oil, Parmesan, basil, and garlic in small bowl; season with pepper to taste.

3. Pat inside of each tomato dry with paper towels. Arrange tomatoes in single layer in prepared baking dish. Brush top cut edges of tomatoes with 1 teaspoon oil. Mound stuffing into tomatoes (about ¼ cup per tomato) and drizzle with remaining 2 tablespoons oil. Bake until tops are golden brown and crisp, about 20 minutes. Serve immediately.

STUFFED TOMATOES WITH GOAT CHEESE, OLIVES, AND OREGANO

Substitute 3 ounces crumbled goat cheese (¾ cup) for Parmesan, omit basil, and add 3 tablespoons minced fresh parsley, 1½ teaspoons minced fresh oregano, and 3 tablespoons chopped black olives to bread-crumb mixture in step 2.

STUFFED BELL PEPPERS

✔ **WHY THIS RECIPE WORKS**

All too often, stuffed peppers aren't worth eating. They turn out either too mushy or too firm and are full of uninteresting, greasy fillings. We wanted stuffed peppers that would yield a tender bite yet retain enough structure to stand up proudly on the plate, with a simple yet gratifying filling, neither humdrum nor packed with odd ingredients. We found that blanching the peppers for three minutes and allowing them to finish cooking with residual heat gave us the sturdiness we needed. For the filling, we updated the classic 1950s filling of rice and ground beef with sautéed onions, garlic, and cheese, then came up with several flavorful variations. Cooking the rice in the same water

we used to blanch the peppers kept things moving. A little cheese helped bind the filling, while drained diced tomatoes added the right amount of moisture.

CLASSIC STUFFED BELL PEPPERS
SERVES 4

This recipe works well for four people as either a light main course or as side dish.

- 4 red, yellow, or orange bell peppers (6 ounces each), ½ inch trimmed off tops, stemmed, and seeded
  Salt and pepper
- ½ cup long-grain white rice
- 1½ tablespoons olive oil
- 1 onion, chopped fine
- 12 ounces 85 percent lean ground beef
- 3 garlic cloves, minced
- 1 (14.5-ounce) can diced tomatoes, drained, with ¼ cup juice reserved
- 5 ounces Monterey Jack cheese, shredded (1¼ cups)
- 2 tablespoons chopped fresh parsley
- ¼ cup ketchup

1. Bring 4 quarts water to boil in Dutch oven over high heat. Add bell peppers and 1 tablespoon salt. Cook until peppers just begin to soften, about 3 minutes. Using slotted spoon, remove peppers from pot, drain off excess water, and place peppers, cut side up, on large paper towel–lined plate. Return water to boil, add rice, and boil until tender, about 13 minutes. Drain rice, then transfer to large bowl; set aside.

2. Adjust oven rack to middle position and heat oven to 350 degrees.

3. Meanwhile, heat oil in 12-inch skillet over medium-high heat until shimmering. Add onion and cook, stirring occasionally, until softened and beginning to brown, about 5 minutes. Add ground beef and cook, breaking beef into small pieces with spoon, until no longer pink, about

4 minutes. Stir in garlic and cook until fragrant, about 30 seconds. Transfer mixture to bowl with rice, stir in tomatoes, 1 cup cheese, and parsley and season with salt and pepper to taste.

4. Combine ketchup and reserved tomato juice in small bowl. Place peppers, cut side up, in 9-inch square baking dish. Using soupspoon, divide filling evenly among peppers. Spoon 2 tablespoons ketchup mixture over each filled pepper and sprinkle each with 1 tablespoon cheese. Bake until cheese is browned and filling is heated through, 25 to 30 minutes. Serve immediately.

STUFFED BELL PEPPERS WITH CHICKEN, SMOKED MOZZARELLA, AND BASIL

Substitute 12 ounces ground chicken for beef, cooking until opaque in step 3, about 4 minutes. Substitute 4 ounces smoked shredded mozzarella cheese (about 1 cup) for the Monterey Jack, adding all 4 ounces to rice mixture in step 3, and substitute 2 tablespoons chopped fresh basil for parsley. Do not reserve any juice when draining diced tomatoes and omit ketchup. Instead, pulse 1 slice hearty white sandwich bread, crust removed, and bread torn into quarters, in food processor to coarse crumbs, about 10 pulses. Sprinkle stuffed peppers with bread crumbs before baking.

STUFFED BELL PEPPERS WITH SPICED LAMB, CURRANTS, AND FETA CHEESE

Substitute 12 ounces ground lamb for beef and add 1 tablespoon ground cumin, 1 teaspoon ground cardamom, ½ teaspoon ground cinnamon, and ½ teaspoon red pepper flakes to pan with lamb, cooking until no longer pink, about 4 minutes. Stir in ¼ cup currants and 1 tablespoon grated fresh ginger with garlic in step 3. Substitute 4 ounces crumbled feta (1 cup) for Monterey Jack, adding all 4 ounces to rice mixture in step 3, and substitute 2 tablespoons chopped fresh cilantro for parsley. Do not reserve any juice when draining diced tomatoes and omit ketchup. Instead, spoon ⅓ cup chopped, toasted salted cashews over filled peppers before baking.

KEEPING STUFFED PEPPERS UPRIGHT

Your peppers should fit snugly inside of the baking dish and remain upright, but here are some alternatives if you don't have the right size bakeware.

A. Place stuffed peppers in a tube pan, where they will snuggly fit.

B. Place stuffed peppers in a muffin tin—the cups of the tin will hold the peppers firmly.

C. Place each stuffed pepper in an individual ovensafe ramekin. This is also a great system if you want to cook just a few at a time.

ULTIMATE VEGGIE BURGERS

WHY THIS RECIPE WORKS
Store-bought veggie burgers border on inedible, but most homemade renditions are a lot of work. We wanted a recipe that delivered results worth the effort. We didn't want them to taste like hamburgers, but we did want them to act like hamburgers, having a modicum of chew, a harmonious blend of savory ingredients, and the ability to go from grill to bun without falling apart. We found veggie burgers made with soy-based products bland, sour, or gummy, so we turned to lentils and bulgur, which, when combined, gave us just the texture we were after. For meaty flavor, we turned to food rich in umami—specifically, cremini mushrooms and cashews. Panko bread crumbs were the perfect binder.

ULTIMATE VEGGIE BURGERS
MAKES 12 BURGERS

Canned lentils can be used, though some flavor will be sacrificed. Use a 15-ounce can, drain the lentils in a fine-mesh strainer, and thoroughly rinse under cold running water before spreading them on paper towels and drying them, as directed in step 1 below. If you cannot find panko, use 1 cup of plain bread crumbs. If you plan to freeze the patties, note that you will need to increase the amount of bread crumbs since the patties increase in moisture content with freezing and thawing (see make-ahead directions below).

- ¾ cup dried brown lentils, picked over and rinsed
- 2½ teaspoons salt
- ¾ cup bulgur
- ¼ cup vegetable oil
- 2 onions, chopped fine
- 1 celery rib, chopped fine
- 1 small leek, white and light green parts only, halved lengthwise, chopped fine, and washed thoroughly

2   garlic cloves, minced
I   pound cremini or white
     mushrooms, trimmed and sliced
     ¼ inch thick
I   cup raw cashews
⅓   cup mayonnaise
2   cups panko bread crumbs
     Pepper
12   hamburger rolls

1. Bring 3 cups water, lentils, and 1 teaspoon salt to boil in medium saucepan over high heat. Reduce heat to medium-low and simmer, uncovered, stirring occasionally, until lentils are just beginning to fall apart, about 25 minutes. Drain in fine-mesh strainer. Line baking sheet with triple layer of paper towels and spread drained lentils over paper towels. Gently pat lentils dry with additional paper towels. Cool lentils to room temperature.

2. While lentils simmer, bring 2 cups water and ½ teaspoon salt to boil in small saucepan. Stir bulgur into boiling water and cover immediately; let sit off heat until water is absorbed, 15 to 20 minutes. Drain in fine-mesh strainer, then use rubber spatula to press out excess moisture. Transfer bulgur to medium bowl and set aside.

3. Heat 1 tablespoon oil in 12-inch nonstick skillet over medium-high heat until shimmering. Add onions, celery, leek, and garlic and cook, stirring occasionally, until vegetables begin to brown, about 10 minutes. Spread vegetable mixture onto second baking sheet to cool; set aside. Heat 1 tablespoon oil in now-empty skillet over high heat until shimmering. Add mushrooms and cook, stirring occasionally, until golden brown, about 12 minutes. Spread mushrooms on baking sheet with vegetable mixture; cool to room temperature, about 20 minutes.

4. Process cashews in food processor until finely chopped, about 15 pulses (do not wash workbowl). Stir cashews into bowl with bulgur, then stir in cooled lentils, vegetable-mushroom mixture, and mayonnaise. Transfer half of mixture to now-empty food processor and pulse until coarsely chopped, 15 to 20 pulses (mixture should be cohesive but roughly textured). Transfer processed mixture to large bowl and repeat with remaining unprocessed mixture; combine with first batch.

5. Stir in panko and remaining 1 teaspoon salt and season with pepper to taste. Line baking sheet with paper towels. Divide mixture into 12 portions, about ½ cup each, shaping each into tightly packed patty about 4 inches in diameter and ½ inch thick. Place patties on prepared baking sheet (paper towels will absorb excess moisture).

6A. FOR THE STOVETOP: Heat remaining 2 tablespoons vegetable oil in 12-inch nonstick skillet over medium-high heat until shimmering. Cook burgers, 4 at a time, until well browned, about 4 minutes per side (if browning too quickly, lower heat to medium). Repeat with additional oil and burgers. Serve. (Cooked burgers can be kept warm in 250-degree oven for up to 30 minutes.)

6B. FOR THE GRILL: For charcoal grill, open bottom vent halfway. Light large chimney starter filled with charcoal briquettes (6 quarts). When top coals are partially covered with ash, pour evenly over grill. Set cooking grate in place, cover, and open lid vent halfway. Heat grill until hot, about 5 minutes. For gas grill, turn all burners to high, cover, and heat grill until hot, about 15 minutes. Clean and oil cooking grate. Grill burgers, without moving them, until well browned, about 5 minutes; flip burgers and continue cooking until well browned on second side, about 5 minutes. Serve.

TO MAKE AHEAD: Patties can be prepared through step 5 and refrigerated for up to 3 days. Alternatively, you can freeze patties. For each burger to be frozen, add 1 teaspoon panko bread crumbs or ½ teaspoon plain bread crumbs to mixture before shaping. Thaw frozen patties overnight in refrigerator on triple layer of paper towels, covered loosely. Before cooking, pat patties dry with paper towels and reshape to make sure they are tightly packed and cohesive.

SPANAKOPITA

✔ WHY THIS RECIPE WORKS
The roots of this savory spinach and feta pie, with its trademark layers of flaky, crisp phyllo, run deep in Greek culture, yet most stateside versions are nothing more than soggy layers of phyllo with a sparse, bland filling. We wanted a casserole-style pie with a perfect balance of zesty spinach filling and shatteringly crisp phyllo crust—and we didn't want to spend all day in the kitchen. Using store-bought phyllo was an easy timesaver. Among the various spinach options (baby, frozen, mature curly-leaf), tasters favored the bold flavor of fresh curly-leaf spinach that had been microwaved, coarsely chopped, then squeezed of excess moisture. Crumbling the feta into fine pieces ensured a salty tang in every bite, while the addition of Greek yogurt buffered the assertiveness of the feta. We found that Pecorino Romano (a good stand-in for a traditional Greek hard sheep's-milk cheese) added complexity to the filling and, when sprinkled between the sheets of phyllo, helped the flaky layers hold together. Using a baking sheet rather than a baking dish allowed excess moisture to easily evaporate, ensuring a crisp crust.

WEEKNIGHT SPANAKOPITA

SERVES 6 TO 8 AS A MAIN COURSE
OR 10 TO 12 AS AN APPETIZER

It is important to rinse the feta; this step removes some of its salty brine, which would overwhelm the spinach. Full-fat sour cream can be substituted for whole-milk Greek yogurt. Phyllo dough is also available in larger 14 by 18-inch sheets; if using, cut them in half to make 14 by 9-inch sheets. Don't thaw the phyllo in the microwave; let it sit in the refrigerator overnight or on the counter for 4 to 5 hours.

FILLING

- 1¼ pounds curly-leaf spinach, stemmed
- ¼ cup water
- 12 ounces feta cheese, rinsed, patted dry, and crumbled into fine pieces (3 cups)
- ¾ cup whole-milk Greek yogurt
- 4 scallions, sliced thin
- 2 large eggs, beaten
- ¼ cup minced fresh mint
- 2 tablespoons minced fresh dill
- 3 garlic cloves, minced
- 1 teaspoon grated lemon zest plus 1 tablespoon juice
- 1 teaspoon ground nutmeg
- ½ teaspoon pepper
- ¼ teaspoon salt
- ⅛ teaspoon cayenne pepper

PHYLLO LAYERS

- 7 tablespoons unsalted butter, melted
- 8 ounces (14 by 9-inch) phyllo, thawed
- 1½ ounces Pecorino Romano cheese, grated (¾ cup)
- 2 teaspoons sesame seeds (optional)

1. FOR THE FILLING: Place spinach and water in large bowl. Cover bowl with large dinner plate (plate should completely cover bowl and not rest on spinach). Microwave until spinach is wilted and decreased in volume by half, about 5 minutes. Remove bowl from microwave and keep covered for 1 minute. Carefully remove plate and transfer spinach to colander. Using back of rubber spatula, gently press spinach against colander to release excess liquid. Transfer spinach to cutting board and chop coarse. Transfer spinach to clean kitchen towel and squeeze to remove excess water. Place drained spinach in large bowl. Add remaining filling ingredients and mix until thoroughly combined.

2. FOR THE PHYLLO LAYERS: Adjust oven rack to lower-middle position and heat oven to 425 degrees. Line rimmed baking sheet with parchment paper. Using pastry brush, lightly brush 14 by 9-inch rectangle in center of parchment with melted butter to cover area same size as phyllo. Lay 1 phyllo sheet on buttered parchment and brush thoroughly with melted butter. Repeat with 9 more phyllo sheets, brushing each with butter (you should have total of 10 layers of phyllo).

3. Spread spinach mixture evenly over phyllo, leaving ¼-inch border on all sides. Cover spinach with 6 more phyllo sheets, brushing each with butter and sprinkling each with about 2 tablespoons Pecorino cheese. Lay 2 more phyllo sheets on top, brushing each with butter (do not sprinkle these layers with Pecorino).

4. Working from center outward, use palms of your hands to compress layers and press out any air pockets. Using sharp knife, score spanakopita through top 3 layers of phyllo into 24 equal pieces. Sprinkle with sesame seeds, if using. Bake until phyllo is golden and crisp, 20 to 25 minutes. Cool on baking sheet 10 minutes, or up to 2 hours. Slide spanakopita, still on parchment, onto cutting board. Cut into squares and serve.

TO MAKE AHEAD: Filling can be made up to 24 hours in advance and refrigerated. Freeze assembled, unbaked spanakopita on baking sheet, wrapped well in plastic wrap, or cut spanakopita in half crosswise and freeze smaller sections on plate. Bake spanakopita frozen, increasing baking time by 5 to 10 minutes.

TIPS FOR TAMING PHYLLO

Frozen packaged phyllo dough functions as light, flaky pastry in traditional Greek dishes such as baklava and spanakopita and as a ready-made tart crust or wrapper for both sweet and savory fillings. But the tendency of these paper-thin sheets to tear, dry out quickly, or stick together can be maddening. Here are some tips for mastering this delicate dough.

1. To help prevent cracking, phyllo must be kept moist until you're ready to work with it. The usual approach is to cover the stack with a damp kitchen towel. But it's all too easy to overmoisten the towel and turn the dough sticky. We prefer to cover the stack with plastic wrap to protect the phyllo and then a damp towel.

2. Because phyllo is so fragile, some sheets crack and even tear while still in the box. Don't worry about rips, just make sure to adjust the orientation of the sheets as you stack them so that cracks in different sheets don't line up.

3. When phyllo sheets emerge from the box fused at their edges, don't try to separate the sheets. Instead, trim the fused portion and discard.

VEGETABLE TORTA

✔ WHY THIS RECIPE WORKS

Vegetable tortas can be eye-catching showstoppers that often turn out to be piles of soggy, bland vegetables. For a four-star, make-ahead vegetable torta showcasing flavorful late-summer vegetables, we knew we would have to figure out the best approach for removing as much moisture as possible from the vegetables. We began by salting and pressing the eggplant, zucchini, and tomatoes. Extensive testing proved that each vegetable would require a unique step to complete the job. The eggplant and zucchini required precooking—we roasted the eggplant in a 450-degree oven until browned and dry and microwaved the more delicate zucchini between paper towels weighted with a plate. The salted and drained tomatoes, however, didn't require precooking—they continued to dry out while being baked right on top of the torta. A simple egg custard bound the vegetables together and a bread-crumb crust protected the edges from sticking and burning.

VEGETABLE TORTA WITH ASIAGO AND HERBS

SERVES 6 TO 8 AS A MAIN COURSE OR 8 TO 10 AS A SIDE DISH

To prevent sticking, the eggplant slices are roasted on wire racks set in rimmed baking sheets. Alternatively, they can be roasted directly on well-oiled baking sheets; after roasting, use a thin spatula to carefully remove the slices. Hard Italian Asiago is too mild for this recipe—use a domestic Asiago (available in supermarkets) that yields to pressure when pressed. The torta is best served warm or at room temperature.

VEGETABLES

- 3 pounds eggplant, peeled, halved crosswise, and cut lengthwise into ½-inch-thick slices
  Kosher salt
- 3 tablespoons olive oil, plus extra for brushing wire racks
- 1 garlic head, outer papery skin removed and top third of head cut off and discarded
  Pepper
- 2 red bell peppers
- 2 large tomatoes, cored and cut into ¼-inch-thick slices
- 4 zucchini, cut ¼ inch thick on steep bias

CRUST

- 4 slices hearty white sandwich bread, torn into quarters
- 3 tablespoons unsalted butter, melted
- 2 ounces Asiago cheese, grated fine (1 cup)

CUSTARD AND GARNISH

- 3 large eggs
- ¼ cup heavy cream
- 2 teaspoons minced fresh thyme
- 2 tablespoons fresh lemon juice
- 3 ounces Asiago cheese, grated fine (1½ cups)
- 2 tablespoons shredded fresh basil

1. FOR THE VEGETABLES: Line baking sheet with triple layer of paper towels and set aside. Toss eggplant slices with 1 tablespoon salt in large bowl. Transfer to colander and let drain until eggplant releases about 2 tablespoons liquid, about 30 minutes. Wipe excess salt from eggplant. Arrange eggplant slices in single layer on prepared baking sheet, then cover with another triple layer of paper towels. Firmly press each slice to flatten and remove as much liquid as possible.

2. While eggplant drains, adjust oven racks to upper-middle and lower-middle positions and heat oven to 450 degrees. Set 2 wire racks in 2 rimmed baking sheets and brush both racks with oil. Place garlic, cut side up, on sheet of aluminum foil and drizzle with 1½ teaspoons oil. Wrap foil tightly around garlic and set aside. 3. Arrange salted and pressed eggplant slices on oiled racks. Brush slices on both sides with 2 tablespoons oil and season with pepper to taste.

4. Brush peppers with remaining 1½ teaspoons oil and place 1 pepper on each baking sheet with eggplant. Transfer eggplant and peppers to oven, placing foil-wrapped garlic on lower oven rack alongside baking sheet. Roast vegetables until eggplant slices are soft, well browned, and collapsed, and peppers are blistered and beginning to brown, 30 to 35 minutes, rotating baking sheets and turning peppers over halfway through baking time. Transfer peppers to medium bowl, cover with plastic wrap, and set aside; allow eggplant to cool on wire racks. Continue to roast garlic until cloves are very soft and golden brown, 10 to 15 minutes longer. Set garlic aside to cool. Reduce oven to 375 degrees.

5. While vegetables roast, line baking sheet with double layer of paper towels, arrange tomato slices on baking sheet, and sprinkle with 1 teaspoon salt. Let sit 30 minutes, then cover with another double layer of paper towels and gently press to dry tomatoes.

6. While tomatoes drain, toss zucchini slices with 1 tablespoon salt in large bowl. Transfer to colander and let drain until zucchini releases about ⅓ cup liquid, about 30 minutes. Line large plate with triple layer of paper towels, arrange one-third of zucchini slices on plate, then cover with another triple layer of paper towels and press to dry. Repeat, arranging remaining zucchini in 2 additional layers separated by triple layer of paper towels, and placing triple layer of paper towels on top of final zucchini layer. Place a second plate on top of zucchini and press down firmly to compress. Microwave until zucchini is steaming, about 10 minutes. Using potholders, carefully remove from microwave and let sit 5 minutes; remove top plate.

7. When peppers are cool, remove skins. Slit peppers pole to pole, discard stem and

seeds, and cut each pepper lengthwise into 3 pieces. (Eggplant, garlic, and peppers can be roasted, cooled, and refrigerated separately for up to 1 day before assembly.)

8. FOR THE CRUST: Pulse bread in food processor to coarse crumbs, about 10 pulses. With processor running, pour in butter and process until combined, about 4 seconds. Add ⅔ cup cheese and pulse to combine, about 3 pulses. Transfer mixture to bowl. (Do not wash workbowl.)

9. Thoroughly grease 9-inch springform pan. Sprinkle 1 cup bread-crumb mixture over bottom of pan and, using flat bottom of measuring cup, press crumbs into even layer. Holding pan upright, press additional 1¼ cups bread-crumb mixture into sides of pan, forming thick, even layer that stops about ¼ inch from top of pan. Set remaining bread-crumb mixture aside.

10. FOR THE CUSTARD: Squeeze garlic head at root end to remove cloves from skins. In small bowl, mash cloves with fork, then transfer to food processor. Add eggs, cream, thyme, and lemon juice. Process until thoroughly combined, about 30 seconds.

11. TO ASSEMBLE AND BAKE: Arrange single layer of eggplant on top of bread-crumb crust, tearing pieces as needed to cover entire bottom surface. Sprinkle evenly with 2 tablespoons cheese. Arrange single layer of zucchini and sprinkle with 2 tablespoons cheese. Repeat with another layer of eggplant and cheese. Layer in all red pepper pieces and sprinkle with 2 tablespoons cheese. Pour half of custard over vegetables, tilting pan and shake gently from side to side to distribute evenly over vegetables and down sides. Repeat layering of eggplant and zucchini, sprinkling each layer with 2 tablespoons cheese (about 4 more layers). Pour remaining custard over vegetables, then tilt and gently shake pan to distribute. Arrange tomato slices starting around perimeter of pan, overlapping to fit, then fill in center with remaining slices. Press down on tomatoes gently with hands. Sprinkle torta with 3 tablespoons reserved bread-crumb mixture (discard any remaining bread crumbs).

12. Set torta on baking sheet and bake on lower-middle rack until tomatoes are dry, bread-crumb topping is lightly browned, center of torta looks firm and level (not soft or wet), and torta registers 175 degrees, 75 to 90 minutes. Cool torta for 10 minutes on wire rack. Run thin, sharp knife around inside of pan to loosen, then remove springform pan ring. (Baked torta can be refrigerated overnight. Allow the torta to sit at room temperature for about 1 hour before serving.)

13. TO SERVE: Slide thin metal spatula between crust and pan bottom to loosen. Let sit 20 minutes longer (to serve warm) or cool to room temperature, sprinkle with basil, and cut into wedges.

ASSEMBLING VEGETABLE TORTA

1. Press bread-crumb mixture into bottom of pan, then tilt pan upright over bowl and press crumbs against sides of pan.

2. Layer eggplant into pan without overlapping. Tear slices as needed to fill in gaps.

3. After adding custard, tilt pan from side to side and shake gently back and forth to ensure even distribution.

4. Arrange tomatoes in circular pattern on top of torta, partially overlapping.

CHAPTER 9 Poultry

SAUTÉED CHICKEN CUTLETS WITH LIGHTER PAN SAUCES

✔ WHY THIS RECIPE WORKS

Sautéed chicken cutlets topped with a flavorful pan sauce are quick and easy to prepare. But while the chicken is lean, the sauces themselves are not—classic French pan sauces typically call for a generous amount of butter. We wanted a lighter, less rich sauce for our chicken that would still take advantage of the fond left in the skillet for serious flavor. We followed the usual steps for preparing a pan sauce—sautéing aromatics in the empty skillet, adding liquid and scraping up the browned bits from the bottom of the pan, simmering to concentrate flavors, and finally finishing the sauce with cold butter. But adding just a teaspoon of flour to the aromatics as a thickener was a simple step that allowed us to cut back substantially on the butter (to just 1 tablespoon). Cutting back on the butter had the added benefit of allowing the other flavors (in this case, lemon, capers, and parsley) to take center stage.

SAUTÉED CHICKEN CUTLETS WITH LEMON-CAPER PAN SAUCE
SERVES 4

To make slicing the chicken easier, freeze it for 15 minutes. More pan sauce recipes follow.

CHICKEN
4   (6- to 8-ounce) boneless, skinless chicken breasts, tenderloins removed, trimmed
    Salt and pepper
2   tablespoons vegetable oil

LEMON-CAPER PAN SAUCE
2   teaspoons vegetable oil
1   shallot, minced
1   teaspoon all-purpose flour
¾   cup low-sodium chicken broth
1   tablespoon capers, rinsed and chopped

1   tablespoon chopped fresh parsley
1   tablespoon unsalted butter, chilled
2   teaspoons lemon juice
    Salt and pepper

1. FOR THE CHICKEN: Adjust oven rack to middle position and heat oven to 200 degrees. Halve chicken horizontally, then cover chicken halves with plastic wrap and pound to even ¼-inch thickness with meat pounder. Pat chicken dry with paper towels and season with salt and pepper.

2. Heat 1 tablespoon oil in 12-inch skillet over medium-high heat until just smoking. Place 4 cutlets in skillet and cook until browned on first side, about 2 minutes. Flip cutlets and continue to cook until second side is opaque, 15 to 20 seconds; transfer to large ovensafe platter. Repeat with remaining 1 tablespoon oil and remaining 4 cutlets; transfer to platter. Tent loosely with aluminum foil and transfer to oven to keep warm while preparing sauce.

3. FOR THE PAN SAUCE: Heat oil in now-empty skillet over low heat until shimmering. Add shallot and cook, stirring often, until softened, about 2 minutes. Add flour and cook, stirring constantly, for 30 seconds. Slowly whisk in broth, scraping up any browned bits. Bring to simmer and

cook until reduced to ½ cup, 2 to 3 minutes. Stir in any accumulated chicken juices; return to simmer and cook for 30 seconds. Off heat, whisk in capers, parsley, butter, and lemon juice. Season with salt and pepper to taste. Pour sauce over chicken and serve immediately.

VERMOUTH, LEEK, AND TARRAGON PAN SAUCE

MAKES ENOUGH FOR 1 RECIPE
SAUTÉED CHICKEN CUTLETS

2   teaspoons vegetable oil
1   leek, white and light green parts only, halved lengthwise, sliced ¼ inch thick, and washed thoroughly
1   teaspoon all-purpose flour
¾   cup low-sodium chicken broth
½   cup dry vermouth or dry white wine
1   tablespoon unsalted butter, chilled
2   teaspoons chopped fresh tarragon
1   teaspoon whole grain mustard
    Salt and pepper

Heat oil in now-empty skillet over medium heat until shimmering. Add leek and cook,

---

SLICING CHICKEN BREASTS INTO CUTLETS

Cutlets are about half the thickness of boneless, skinless breasts and are called for in many recipes. Rather than buy them already cut, we prefer to make them ourselves—store-bought cutlets are often ragged and they vary widely in size and thickness.

1. Lay chicken breast flat on cutting board, smooth side facing up. Rest 1 hand on top of chicken and, using sharp chef's knife, carefully slice chicken in half horizontally.

2. This will yield 2 thin cutlets between ¼ and ½ inch thick.

stirring often, until softened and lightly browned, about 5 minutes. Add flour and cook, stirring constantly, for 30 seconds. Slowly whisk in broth and vermouth, scraping up any browned bits. Bring to simmer and cook until reduced to ¾ cup, 3 to 5 minutes. Stir in any accumulated chicken juices; return to simmer and cook for 30 seconds. Off heat, whisk in butter, tarragon, and mustard. Season with salt and pepper to taste. Pour sauce over chicken and serve immediately.

SHERRY, RED PEPPER, AND TOASTED GARLIC PAN SAUCE

MAKES ENOUGH FOR 1 RECIPE
SAUTÉED CHICKEN CUTLETS

2	teaspoons vegetable oil
3	garlic cloves, minced
1	teaspoon all-purpose flour
¼	teaspoon paprika
¾	cup low-sodium chicken broth
½	cup plus 1 teaspoon dry sherry
¼	cup jarred roasted red peppers, patted dry and cut into ¼-inch pieces
1	tablespoon unsalted butter, chilled
½	teaspoon chopped fresh thyme
	Salt and pepper

Heat oil and garlic in now-empty skillet over low heat. Cook, stirring often, until garlic turns golden but not brown, about 1 minute. Add flour and paprika and cook, stirring constantly, for 30 seconds. Slowly whisk in broth and ½ cup sherry, scraping up any browned bits. Bring to simmer and cook until reduced to ¾ cup, 3 to 5 minutes. Stir in any accumulated chicken juices; return to simmer and cook for 30 seconds. Off heat, whisk in peppers, butter, thyme, and remaining 1 teaspoon sherry. Season with salt and pepper to taste. Pour sauce over chicken and serve immediately.

BRANDY, CREAM, AND CHIVE PAN SAUCE

MAKES ENOUGH FOR 1 RECIPE
SAUTÉED CHICKEN CUTLETS

Be sure to add the broth to the skillet before adding the brandy.

2	teaspoons vegetable oil
1	shallot, minced
1	teaspoon all-purpose flour
¾	cup low-sodium chicken broth
¼	cup plus 1 tablespoon brandy
2	tablespoons heavy cream
2	tablespoons chopped fresh chives
2	teaspoons lemon juice
1	teaspoon Dijon mustard
	Salt and pepper

Heat oil in now-empty skillet over low heat until shimmering. Add shallot and cook, stirring often, until softened, about 2 minutes. Add flour and cook, stirring constantly, for 30 seconds. Slowly whisk in broth, then ¼ cup brandy, scraping up any browned bits. Bring to simmer and cook until reduced to ½ cup, 2 to 3 minutes. Stir in cream and any accumulated chicken juices; return to simmer and cook until thickened, about 1 minute. Off heat, whisk in chives, lemon juice, mustard, and remaining 1 tablespoon brandy. Season with salt and pepper to taste. Pour sauce over chicken and serve immediately.

SAUTÉED CHICKEN CUTLETS WITH PORCINI SAUCE

✓ **WHY THIS RECIPE WORKS**
Chicken braised in a wine and mushroom sauce is a classic Northern Italian dish. It's rich and flavorful—and takes hours to prepare. We wanted to keep the flavor but cut the cooking time by distilling the essence of this braise into a quick-cooking but complex-tasting pan sauce. We started by coating eight thinly pounded cutlets in flour (which aided in browning and also helped the sauce adhere) and sautéing them in two speedy batches. For the sauce, we found that substituting vermouth for wine (and adding a bit of sugar) helped replicate the flavor of a long-simmered wine sauce, while adding a dash of soy sauce to our dried porcini enhanced their meaty flavor. Some thyme and fresh lemon juice were the finishing touches to our quick yet flavorful pan sauce.

TEST KITCHEN TIP NO. 66 WHY WE'RE FOND OF FOND

Ever wonder how restaurants make rich sauces to accompany sautéed cutlets and steaks? Chances are it's a pan sauce, made with the delicious caramelized browned bits (called fond) that sit on the bottom of the pan after the meat has been sautéed or pan-seared.

Pan sauces are usually made by adding liquid (broth, wine, or juice) to the pan once the cooked cutlets or steaks have been transferred to a plate to rest. The liquid dissolves the fond (a process known as deglazing) and incorporates it into the sauce.

So what makes those browned bits so flavorful and so valuable? When meat or chicken browns, a process called the Maillard reaction occurs. This process is named after the French chemist who first described this reaction about 100 years ago. When the amino acids (or protein components) and natural sugars in meat are subjected to intense heat, like that found in a skillet, they begin to combine and form new compounds. These compounds in turn break down and form yet more new flavor compounds, and so on and so on, like rabbits multiplying. The browned bits left in the pan once the meat has been cooked are packed with complex flavors, which are carried over to the pan sauce once the fond has been dissolved. And fond isn't useful only for pan sauces—we also rely on fond to flavor braises, as well as other dishes where meat is browned, such as soups and stews.

SAUTÉED CHICKEN CUTLETS
WITH PORCINI SAUCE

SERVES 4

Look for dried mushrooms that are smooth and have small pores; shriveled porcini with large holes will retain dirt and grit even after rinsing. To make slicing the chicken easier, freeze it for 15 minutes. For even more intense mushroom flavor, grind an additional ½ ounce of dried porcini mushrooms in a spice grinder until reduced to a fine dust. Sift the dust through a fine-mesh strainer and then stir it into the flour before dredging the chicken.

1	cup low-sodium chicken broth
½	ounce dried porcini mushrooms, rinsed
4	(6- to 8-ounce) boneless, skinless chicken breasts, tenderloins removed, trimmed
¼	cup plus 1 teaspoon all-purpose flour
	Salt and pepper
2	tablespoons plus 1 teaspoon vegetable oil
1	small shallot, minced
¼	cup dry vermouth
1	teaspoon tomato paste
1	teaspoon soy sauce
½	teaspoon sugar
2	tablespoons unsalted butter, cut into 2 pieces and chilled
½	teaspoon minced fresh thyme
½	teaspoon lemon juice

1. Microwave chicken broth and porcini in covered bowl until steaming, about 1 minute. Let stand until softened, about 5 minutes. Drain mushrooms through fine-mesh strainer lined with coffee filter, reserve liquid, and chop mushrooms into ¾-inch pieces.

2. Halve chicken horizontally, then cover chicken halves with plastic wrap and pound to even ¼-inch thickness with meat pounder. Combine ¼ cup flour, 1 teaspoon salt, and ½ teaspoon pepper in shallow dish or pie plate. Pat chicken dry with paper towels. Working with 1 cutlet at a time, dredge in flour mixture, shaking off excess, and transfer to large plate.

3. Heat 1 tablespoon oil in 12-inch skillet over medium-high heat until shimmering. Place 4 cutlets in skillet and cook until golden brown on first side, about 3 minutes. Flip cutlets, reduce heat to medium, and continue to cook until no longer pink and lightly browned on second side, about 2 minutes longer; transfer to large platter. Wipe out skillet with paper towels. Repeat with 1 tablespoon more oil and remaining 4 cutlets; transfer to plate. Tent loosely with aluminum foil and set aside while preparing sauce.

4. Heat remaining 1 teaspoon oil in now-empty skillet over low heat until shimmering. Add shallot and cook, stirring often, until softened, about 2 minutes. Add remaining 1 teaspoon flour and cook, stirring constantly, for 30 seconds. Slowly whisk in vermouth, scraping up any browned bits. Stir in tomato paste, soy sauce, sugar, soaked porcini, and reserved porcini soaking liquid. Bring to simmer and cook until reduced to 1 cup, 3 to 5 minutes.

5. Return cutlets and any accumulated juices to skillet. Bring to simmer, cover, and cook until cutlets are heated through, about 1 minute; transfer to platter. Off heat, whisk butter, 1 piece at a time, thyme, and lemon juice into sauce and season with salt and pepper to taste. Pour sauce over chicken and serve immediately.

CRISP BREADED
CHICKEN CUTLETS

✔ WHY THIS RECIPE WORKS
Most chicken cutlets offer a thin, uneven, pale crust; we wanted a thick, crisp, flavorful coating that wouldn't fall off. Starting with the chicken, we found that pounding the chicken ensured the cutlets would cook evenly. Homemade bread crumbs were a must, providing a subtly sweet flavor and light, crisp texture, while adding a little oil to our egg wash allowed the crust to brown more deeply. Finally, pan-frying the cutlets two at a time (rather than four) reduced the amount of steam in the skillet, allowing the breading to crisp and brown evenly.

CRISP BREADED
CHICKEN CUTLETS

SERVES 4

If you'd rather not prepare fresh bread crumbs, use panko, the extra-crisp Japanese bread crumbs. The chicken is cooked in batches of two because the crust is noticeably more crisp if the pan is not overcrowded.

4	(6- to 8-ounce) boneless, skinless chicken breasts, tenderloins removed, trimmed
	Salt and pepper
3	slices hearty white sandwich bread, torn into quarters
¾	cup all-purpose flour
2	large eggs
1	tablespoon plus ¾ cup vegetable oil
	Lemon wedges

1. Cover chicken breasts with plastic wrap and pound to even ½-inch thickness with meat pounder. Pat chicken dry with paper towels and season chicken with salt and pepper.

2. Adjust oven rack to middle position and heat oven to 200 degrees. Set wire rack in rimmed baking sheet. Pulse bread in food processor to coarse crumbs, about 10 pulses; transfer to shallow dish or pie plate. Place flour in second dish. Lightly beat eggs and 1 tablespoon oil together in third dish.

3. Working with 1 cutlet at a time, dredge in flour, shaking off excess, then coat with egg mixture, allowing excess to drip off. Coat all sides of cutlet with bread crumbs, pressing gently so that crumbs adhere; transfer to prepared wire rack and let sit for 5 minutes.

4. Heat 6 tablespoons oil in 12-inch nonstick skillet over medium-high heat until shimmering. Place 4 cutlets in skillet and cook until deep golden brown and crisp on first side, about 3 minutes. Flip cutlets, reduce heat to medium, and continue to cook until deep golden brown and crisp on second side and meat feels firm when pressed gently, about 3 minutes longer. Drain cutlets briefly on paper towel–lined plate, then transfer to clean wire rack set in baking sheet and keep warm in oven. Pour off all oil left in skillet and wipe out with paper towels. Repeat with remaining 6 tablespoons oil and remaining 4 cutlets. Serve with lemon wedges.

DEVILED CRISP BREADED CHICKEN CUTLETS

Rub each breast with generous pinch cayenne before dredging in flour. Lightly beat 3 tablespoons Dijon mustard, 1 tablespoon Worcestershire sauce, and 2 teaspoons minced fresh thyme into eggs along with oil.

CRISP BREADED CHICKEN CUTLETS WITH GARLIC AND OREGANO

Lightly beat 3 tablespoons minced fresh oregano and 8 garlic cloves, minced to paste, into eggs along with oil.

CRISP BREADED CHICKEN CUTLETS WITH PARMESAN (CHICKEN MILANESE)

Though Parmesan is the traditional cheese to use in this dish, feel free to substitute Pecorino Romano cheese if you prefer a stronger, more tangy flavor. The cheese is quite susceptible to burning, so be sure to keep a very close eye on the cutlets as they cook.

Substitute ¼ cup finely grated Parmesan cheese for an equal amount of bread crumbs.

PARMESAN-CRUSTED CHICKEN CUTLETS

✓ WHY THIS RECIPE WORKS

Unlike classic Italian-style chicken cutlets, where the coating primarily consists of bread crumbs, Parmesan-crusted chicken breasts offer a thin, crispy-yet-chewy, waferlike sheath of Parmesan cheese. But this dish can be hard to get right: baked versions are pale and gummy while pan-fried recipes produce patchy, bitter-tasting crusts. We started by coating the cutlets with flour, then egg, and finally grated Parmesan instead of the usual bread crumbs. Eliminating the yolks prevented the crust from having a souffléed texture, and adding some grated Parmesan to the flour layer provided a serious flavor boost. For the outermost layer, shredding the cheese on the large holes of a box grater gave us a sturdier, more even crust, and a little flour added to this cheese helped the coating turn crisp. Pan-frying in a nonstick skillet over medium heat prevented sticking and browned the cheese without making it bitter.

PARMESAN-CRUSTED CHICKEN CUTLETS
SERVES 4

We like the flavor that authentic Parmigiano-Reggiano lends to this recipe. To make slicing the chicken easier, freeze it for 15 minutes. Although the portion size (1 cutlet per person) might seem small, these cutlets are rather rich due to the cheese content. Do not be tempted to cook all four cutlets at once; this will cause excessive sticking between cutlets and make flipping them difficult. To make 8 cutlets, double the ingredients and cook the chicken in four batches, transferring the cooked cutlets to the warm oven and wiping out the skillet after each batch. Serve this chicken with a simple salad.

TEST KITCHEN TIP NO. 68 CHICKEN—ONE SIZE DOESN'T FIT ALL

Every good chicken dish starts with high-quality fresh chicken. But there are an overwhelming number of choices at the supermarket—so how do you recognize superior poultry? Here are a few tips the test kitchen has learned over time: If you're buying boneless, skinless chicken breasts, you should be aware that breasts of different sizes are often packaged together, and it's usually impossible to tell what you've bought until you've opened the package. If possible, buy chicken breasts individually. If that isn't an option, pound the thicker ends of the larger pieces of chicken to match those of the smaller pieces. Some breasts will still be larger than others, but pounding will help make their thickness the same and ensure even cooking. As for chicken parts—say for making a dish such as fried chicken or stew— we prefer to butcher our own birds rather than buy packaged parts. Not only is this a less expensive option, but the parts will be consistently sized. (We also use this approach with stew meat—there's no guarantee that packaged stew meat is going to be cut into even-size pieces or be from the same cut or even the same cow!)

- 2 (8-ounce) boneless, skinless chicken breasts, tenderloins removed, trimmed
- ¼ cup plus I tablespoon all-purpose flour
- 6½ ounces Parmesan cheese, ½ ounce grated fine (¼ cup) and 6 ounces grated coarse (2 cups)
- 3 large egg whites
- 2 tablespoons minced fresh chives (optional)
  Salt and pepper
- 4 teaspoons olive oil
  Lemon wedges

1. Adjust oven rack to middle position and heat oven to 200 degrees. Set wire rack in rimmed baking sheet. Halve chicken horizontally, then cover chicken halves with plastic wrap and pound to even ¼-inch thickness with meat pounder.

2. Combine ¼ cup flour and finely grated Parmesan in shallow dish or pie plate. Lightly beat egg whites and chives, if using, together until slightly foamy in second dish. Combine 2 cups coarsely grated Parmesan and remaining 1 tablespoon flour in third dish.

3. Pat chicken dry with paper towels and season with salt and pepper. Working with 1 cutlet at a time, dredge in flour mixture, shaking off excess, then coat with egg white mixture, allowing excess to drip off. Coat all sides of cutlet with coarsely grated Parmesan mixture, pressing gently so that cheese adheres; transfer to prepared wire rack.

4. Heat 2 teaspoons oil in 12-inch nonstick skillet over medium-high heat until shimmering. Place 2 cutlets in skillet and cook until golden brown on first side, about 3 minutes. While chicken is cooking, use thin nonstick spatula to gently separate any cheesy edges that have melted together. Flip cutlets, reduce heat to medium, and continue to cook until lightly browned on second side, about 2 minutes longer. Transfer cutlets to clean wire rack set in baking sheet and keep warm in oven. Wipe out skillet with paper towels. Repeat with remaining 2 teaspoons oil and remaining 2 cutlets. Serve immediately with lemon wedges.

UPDATED CHICKEN PARMESAN

✔ WHY THIS RECIPE WORKS

Chicken Parmesan is a surefire crowd pleaser, but its multiple components can make it a time-consuming affair. We wanted to streamline chicken Parmesan and make it a dish we could get on the table in just 30 minutes. Pounding the cutlets thin ensured that they cooked evenly and quickly. After dipping the cutlets in an egg wash we rolled them in the crumb coating, made with ultra-crisp panko bread crumbs. The coating also stayed crisp underneath the layers of tangy tomato sauce and gooey cheese. Pan-frying the cutlets in olive oil added another layer of flavor and produced an even, beautifully browned crust.

TEST KITCHEN TIP NO. 69 HIGH SEASONING

Ever notice that some chefs season food by sprinkling it from a good foot above the counter? Is this just kitchen theatrics, or is there a reason behind this practice? To find out, we sprinkled chicken breasts with ground black pepper from different heights—4 inches, 8 inches, and 12 inches—and found the higher the starting point, the more evenly the seasoning was distributed. At 4 inches, the pepper was clumped in the middle of the breast, but at 12 inches, it was lightly and evenly spread over the whole surface. And the more evenly the seasoning is distributed, the better food tastes. So go ahead and add a little flourish the next time you season.

UPDATED CHICKEN PARMESAN
SERVES 4

To make slicing the chicken easier, freeze it for 15 minutes. To ensure that the chicken and pasta are done at the same time, start cooking the pasta immediately after placing the chicken in the skillet.

TOMATO SAUCE
- ¼ cup extra-virgin olive oil
- 2 garlic cloves, minced
- I (28-ounce) can crushed tomatoes
- ½ teaspoon dried basil
- ¼ teaspoon dried oregano
- ¼ teaspoon sugar
  Salt and pepper

CHICKEN AND PASTA
- 2 (8-ounce) boneless, skinless chicken breasts, tenderloins removed, trimmed
- I large egg
  Salt and pepper
- I cup panko bread crumbs
- ¼ cup extra-virgin olive oil
- 3 ounces part-skim mozzarella cheese, shredded (¾ cup)
- I ounce Parmesan cheese, grated (½ cup), plus extra for serving
- 8 ounces spaghetti or linguine

I. FOR THE TOMATO SAUCE: Heat oil and garlic in large saucepan over medium heat. Cook, stirring often, until garlic turns golden but not brown, about 3 minutes. Stir in tomatoes, basil, oregano, sugar, ¼ teaspoon pepper, and pinch salt, bring to simmer, and cook until sauce thickens and flavors meld, 10 to 12 minutes. Off heat, season with salt to taste and cover to keep warm.

2. FOR THE CHICKEN AND PASTA: Adjust oven rack 6 inches from broiler element and heat broiler. Set wire rack in rimmed baking sheet. Halve chicken horizontally, then cover chicken halves with

plastic wrap and pound to even ¼-inch thickness with meat pounder.

3. Lightly beat egg and ¼ teaspoon salt together in shallow dish or pie plate. Combine bread crumbs, ¼ teaspoon salt, and ¼ teaspoon pepper in second dish. Pat chicken dry with paper towels and season with salt and pepper. Working with 1 cutlet at a time, coat with egg mixture, allowing excess to drip off. Coat all sides of cutlet with bread-crumb mixture, pressing gently so that crumbs adhere. Transfer breaded cutlets to prepared wire rack.

4. Heat oil in 12-inch skillet over medium-high heat until shimmering. Place cutlets in skillet and cook until deep golden brown and crisp on first side, about 3 minutes. Flip cutlets, reduce heat to medium, and continue to cook until deep golden brown and crisp on second side, about 2 minutes longer. Transfer cutlets to clean wire rack set in baking sheet and sprinkle evenly with mozzarella and Parmesan. Broil cutlets until cheese is melted and spotty brown, about 3 minutes.

5. Meanwhile, bring 4 quarts water to boil in large pot. Add pasta and 1 tablespoon salt and cook, stirring often, until al dente. Drain pasta. Serve chicken with pasta, spooning sauce over individual portions and passing Parmesan separately.

CHICKEN FRANCESE

✔ WHY THIS RECIPE WORKS

Chicken francese is a simple yet refined dish consisting of pan-fried cutlets with a light but substantial eggy coating and a bright lemony sauce. But a rubbery coating and puckery lemon sauce are all-too-common problems. Dredging the cutlets in flour, then dipping them in egg, and finally dredging them again in flour produced a delicate, soft coating that stayed put. Adding just a couple tablespoons of milk to the egg ensured a tender coating. To prevent a bitter sauce, we skipped whole lemon slices in favor of fresh lemon juice,

which we augmented with wine and chicken broth. Thickening our sauce with a roux (a combination of flour and butter) ensured it would cling to our coating. We wanted more sauce, but the extra time required for it to reduce caused the chicken to dry out while waiting in the oven. Reversing the typical order of things, our solution was to make the sauce first, then cook the chicken and finish the sauce.

CHICKEN FRANCESE
SERVES 4

To make slicing the chicken easier, freeze it for 15 minutes. The sauce is very lemony—for less tartness, reduce the amount of lemon juice by 1 tablespoon.

SAUCE

3 tablespoons unsalted butter, cut into 3 pieces and chilled
⅓ cup finely chopped onion
1 tablespoon all-purpose flour
2¼ cups low-sodium chicken broth
½ cup dry white wine or dry vermouth
⅓ cup lemon juice (2 lemons)
Salt and pepper

CHICKEN

4 (6- to 8-ounce) boneless, skinless chicken breasts, tenderloins removed, trimmed
1 cup all-purpose flour
Salt and pepper
2 large eggs
2 tablespoons milk
2 tablespoons olive oil
2 tablespoons unsalted butter
2 tablespoons minced fresh parsley

TEST KITCHEN TIP NO. 70 FREEZING AND THAWING CHICKEN

Chicken can be frozen in its original packaging or after repackaging. If you are freezing it for longer than two months, rewrap (or wrap over packaging) with foil or plastic wrap, or place inside a zipper-lock freezer bag. You can keep it frozen for several months, but after two months the texture and flavor will suffer. Don't thaw frozen chicken on the counter; this puts it at risk of growing bacteria. Thaw it in the refrigerator overnight or in a large bowl in the sink under cold running water.

---

1. FOR THE SAUCE: Melt 1 tablespoon butter in medium saucepan over medium heat. Add onion and cook, stirring occasionally, until softened, about 5 minutes. Add flour and cook, stirring constantly, until light golden brown, about 1 minute. Slowly whisk in broth, wine, and lemon juice, bring to simmer, and cook until sauce thickens and measures 1½ cups, 10 to 15 minutes. Strain sauce through fine-mesh strainer; set aside, discarding solids.

2. FOR THE CHICKEN: Adjust oven rack to middle position and heat oven to 200 degrees. Set wire rack in rimmed baking sheet. Halve chicken horizontally, then cover chicken halves with plastic wrap and pound to even ¼-inch thickness with meat pounder.

3. Combine flour, 1 teaspoon salt, and ¼ teaspoon pepper in shallow dish or pie plate. Lightly beat eggs and milk together in second dish. Pat chicken dry with paper towels and season with salt and pepper. Working with 1 cutlet at a time, dredge in flour mixture, shaking off excess, then coat with egg mixture, allowing excess to drip off. Dredge cutlets in flour mixture again and shake off excess. Transfer cutlets to prepared wire rack.

4. Heat 1 tablespoon oil and 1 tablespoon butter in 12-inch nonstick skillet over medium-high heat until butter is melted. Place 4 cutlets in skillet and cook until golden brown on first side, about 3 minutes. Flip cutlets, reduce heat to medium, and continue to cook until lightly browned on second side, about 2 minutes longer. Transfer cutlets to clean wire rack set in baking sheet. Wipe out skillet with paper towels. Repeat with remaining 1 tablespoon oil, remaining 1 tablespoon butter, and remaining 4 cutlets; transfer to wire rack. Tent loosely with aluminum foil and transfer to oven to keep warm while finishing sauce. Wipe out skillet with paper towels.

5. Transfer sauce to now-empty skillet and cook over low heat until heated through, about 1 minute. Whisk in remaining 2 tablespoons butter, 1 piece at a time, and season with salt and pepper to taste. Return 4 cutlets to skillet, turn to coat with sauce, then transfer each portion (2 cutlets) to individual plates. Repeat with remaining cutlets. Spoon 2 tablespoons of sauce over each portion and sprinkle with parsley. Serve immediately, passing remaining sauce separately.

CHICKEN FRANCESE WITH TOMATO AND TARRAGON

Add 1 sprig fresh parsley and 1 sprig fresh tarragon to sauce along with broth, wine, and lemon juice. Add 1 tomato, cored, seeded, and cut into ¼-inch pieces, to sauce before spooning additional sauce over each portion in step 5. Substitute 1 tablespoon minced fresh tarragon for parsley.

CHICKEN SALTIMBOCCA

✔ WHY THIS RECIPE WORKS

Chicken saltimbocca is a new spin on an old Italian classic, veal saltimbocca. It sounds promising, but adaptations typically take this dish too far from its roots. We wanted to avoid overcomplicating this dish and give each of its three main elements—chicken, prosciutto, and sage— their due. Flouring the chicken before adding the prosciutto and sage allowed the chicken to brown evenly and prevented gummy, uncooked spots. Using thinly sliced prosciutto prevented its flavor from overwhelming the dish. A single sage leaf is the usual garnish, but we wanted

more sage flavor, so, in addition to a whole leaf garnish, we also sprinkled some chopped fresh sage over the floured chicken before adding the prosciutto.

CHICKEN SALTIMBOCCA
SERVES 4

Make sure to buy prosciutto that is thinly sliced, not shaved; also avoid slices that are too thick, as they won't stick to the chicken. The prosciutto slices should be large enough to fully cover one side of each cutlet. To make slicing the chicken easier, freeze it for 15 minutes. Although whole sage leaves make a beautiful presentation, they are optional and can be left out of step 3.

4	(6- to 8-ounce) boneless, skinless chicken breasts, tenderloins removed, trimmed
½	cup all-purpose flour
	Salt and pepper
1	tablespoon minced fresh sage plus 8 large fresh leaves (optional)
8	thin slices prosciutto (3 ounces)
¼	cup olive oil
1¼	cups dry vermouth or dry white wine
2	teaspoons lemon juice
4	tablespoons unsalted butter, cut into 4 pieces and chilled
1	tablespoon minced fresh parsley

1. Halve chicken horizontally, then cover chicken halves with plastic wrap and pound to even ¼-inch thickness with meat pounder. Combine flour and 1 teaspoon pepper in shallow dish or pie plate.

2. Pat chicken dry with paper towels. Working with 1 cutlet at a time, dredge in flour mixture, shaking off excess, and transfer to work surface. Sprinkle cutlets evenly with minced sage. Place 1 prosciutto slice on top of each cutlet, covering sage, and press lightly to help it adhere.

3. Heat 2 tablespoons oil in 12-inch skillet over medium-high heat until shimmering. Add sage leaves, if using, and cook until leaves begin to change color and are fragrant, about 15 to 20 seconds. Remove sage with slotted spoon and transfer to paper towel–lined plate; set aside.

4. Place 4 cutlets in now-empty skillet, prosciutto side down, and cook over medium-high heat until golden brown on first side, about 3 minutes. Flip cutlets, reduce heat to medium, and continue to cook until no longer pink and lightly browned on second side, about 2 minutes longer. Transfer cutlets to large platter. Wipe out skillet with paper towels. Repeat with remaining 2 tablespoons oil and remaining 4 cutlets; transfer to platter. Tent loosely with aluminum foil and set aside while preparing sauce.

SIMPLIFIED SALTIMBOCCA

1. There's no need to flour the prosciutto before sautéing, just the chicken.

2. Sprinkling the floured cutlets evenly with minced sage then adding prosciutto distributes flavor evenly.

3. We skip the typical toothpick and start the cutlets prosciutto side down, which helps the ham stick.

5. Pour off all fat left in skillet. Add vermouth, scraping up any browned bits. Bring to simmer and cook until reduced to ⅓ cup, 5 to 7 minutes. Stir in lemon juice. Reduce heat to low and whisk in butter, 1 tablespoon at a time. Off heat, stir in parsley and season with salt and pepper to taste. Pour sauce over chicken, place sage leaf on top of each cutlet, if using, and serve immediately.

CHICKEN MARSALA

✔ **WHY THIS RECIPE WORKS**

Chicken Marsala is an Italian restaurant staple that sounds promising, but often disappoints, with watery sauce, dry chicken, and overcooked, slimy mushrooms. To rescue this dish, we began by determining the best way to cook it. Not surprisingly, the classic method of sautéing the meat, then using the browned bits left behind as a flavor base for the sauce, was the way to go. Adding some pancetta to the skillet after cooking the chicken gave our dish a flavor boost, and also provided rendered fat in which to cook the mushrooms; this allowed them to brown and crisp. For the sauce, we found that using sweet Marsala—and no chicken broth—was best; reducing it concentrated its flavor, while a little lemon juice tempered the Marsala's sweetness. We finished our sauce with butter for a silky richness.

CHICKEN MARSALA
SERVES 4

Our wine of choice for this dish is Sweet Marsala Fine, an imported wine that gives the sauce body, soft edges, and a smooth finish. To make slicing the chicken easier, freeze it for 15 minutes.

- 4 (6- to 8-ounce) boneless, skinless chicken breasts, tenderloins removed, trimmed
- 1 cup all-purpose flour
  Salt and pepper
- ¼ cup vegetable oil

- 2½ ounces pancetta, cut into pieces 1 inch long and ⅛ inch wide
- 8 ounces white mushrooms, trimmed and sliced thin
- 1 garlic clove, minced
- 1 teaspoon tomato paste
- 1½ cups sweet Marsala wine
- 4½ teaspoons lemon juice
- 4 tablespoons unsalted butter, cut into 4 pieces and chilled
- 2 tablespoons chopped fresh parsley

1. Adjust oven rack to middle position and heat oven to 200 degrees. Halve chicken horizontally, then cover chicken halves with plastic wrap and pound to even ¼-inch thickness with meat pounder. Place flour in shallow dish or pie plate.

2. Pat chicken dry with paper towels and season with salt and pepper. Working with 1 cutlet at a time, dredge in flour mixture, shaking off excess, and transfer to large plate.

3. Heat 2 tablespoons oil in 12-inch skillet over medium-high heat until shimmering. Place 4 cutlets in skillet and cook until golden brown on first side, about 3 minutes. Flip cutlets, reduce heat to medium, and cook until no longer pink and lightly browned on second side, about 2 minutes longer; transfer to large oven-safe platter. Wipe out skillet. Repeat with remaining 2 tablespoons oil and remaining 4 cutlets; transfer to platter. Tent loosely with aluminum foil and transfer to oven to keep warm while making sauce.

4. Cook pancetta in now-empty skillet over low heat, stirring occasionally and scraping up any browned bits, until crisp, about 5 minutes. Remove pancetta with slotted spoon and transfer to paper towel–lined plate. Add mushrooms to now-empty skillet, increase heat to medium-high, and cook, stirring occasionally, until softened and lightly browned, about 8 minutes. Stir in garlic, tomato paste, and crisp pancetta and cook until tomato paste begins to brown, about 1 minute. Off heat stir in Marsala, scraping up any browned bits. Return to high heat, bring to vigorous simmer, and cook, stirring occasionally, until sauce is thickened and measures 1¼ cups, about 5 minutes. Off heat, stir in lemon juice and any accumulated chicken juices. Whisk in butter, 1 piece at a time. Stir in parsley and season with salt and pepper to taste. Pour sauce over chicken and serve immediately.

NUT-CRUSTED CHICKEN BREASTS

✔ WHY THIS RECIPE WORKS

Adding chopped nuts to a coating is a great way to add robust flavor to otherwise lean and mild boneless, skinless chicken breasts. But nut coatings are often dense and leaden, and the rich flavor of the nuts rarely comes through. Using a combination of chopped almonds and panko bread crumbs—rather than all nuts—kept the coating light and crunchy, and the bread crumbs helped the coating adhere. Instead of frying the breaded cutlets, we found that baking them in the oven was not only easier, but also helped the meat stay juicy and ensured an even golden crust. But it wasn't until we cooked the coating in browned butter prior to breading the chicken that we finally achieved the deep nutty flavor we sought.

NUT-CRUSTED CHICKEN BREASTS WITH LEMON AND THYME
SERVES 4

This recipe is best with almonds, but works well with any type of nut. We prefer kosher salt in this recipe. If using table salt, reduce salt amounts by half.

- 4 (6- to 8-ounce) boneless, skinless chicken breasts, tenderloins removed, trimmed
  Kosher salt
- 1 cup almonds, chopped coarse
- 4 tablespoons unsalted butter
- 1 shallot, minced
- 1 cup panko bread crumbs
- 2 teaspoons finely grated lemon zest, zested lemon cut into wedges
- 1 teaspoon minced fresh thyme
- ⅛ teaspoon cayenne pepper
- 1 cup all-purpose flour
- 3 large eggs
- 2 teaspoons Dijon mustard
- ¼ teaspoon pepper

1. Adjust oven rack to lower-middle position and heat oven to 350 degrees. Set wire rack in rimmed baking sheet. Pat chicken dry with paper towels. Using fork, poke thickest half of breasts 5 to 6 times and sprinkle with ½ teaspoon salt. Transfer breasts to prepared wire rack and refrigerate, uncovered, while preparing coating.

2. Pulse almonds in food processor until they resemble coarse meal, about 20 pulses. Melt butter in 12-inch skillet over medium heat, swirling occasionally, until butter is browned and releases nutty aroma, 4 to 5 minutes. Add shallot and ½ teaspoon salt and cook, stirring constantly, until just beginning to brown, about 3 minutes. Reduce heat to medium-low, add bread crumbs and ground almonds and cook, stirring often, until golden brown, 10 to 12 minutes. Transfer panko mixture to shallow dish or pie plate and stir in lemon

zest, thyme, and cayenne. Place flour in second dish. Lightly beat eggs, mustard, and pepper together in third dish.

3. Pat chicken dry with paper towels. Working with 1 breast at a time, dredge in flour, shaking off excess, then coat with egg mixture, allowing excess to drip off. Coat all sides of breast with panko mixture, pressing gently so that crumbs adhere. Return breaded breasts to wire rack.

4. Bake until chicken registers 160 degrees, 20 to 25 minutes. Let chicken rest for 5 minutes before serving with lemon wedges.

NUT-CRUSTED CHICKEN BREASTS WITH ORANGE AND OREGANO

This version works particularly well with pistachios or hazelnuts.

Substitute 1 teaspoon grated orange zest for lemon zest (cutting zested orange into wedges) and 1 teaspoon minced fresh oregano for thyme.

NUT-CRUSTED CHICKEN BREASTS WITH LIME AND CHIPOTLE

This version works particularly well with peanuts.

Substitute 1 teaspoon grated lime zest for lemon zest (cutting zested lime into wedges). Omit thyme and add 1 teaspoon chipotle chile powder, ½ teaspoon ground cumin, and ½ teaspoon ground coriander to toasted panko along with lime zest.

PECAN-CRUSTED CHICKEN BREASTS WITH BACON

Substitute 1 cup pecans, coarsely chopped, for almonds. Cook 2 finely chopped slices bacon in 12-inch skillet over medium heat until crisp, 5 to 7 minutes. Remove bacon from skillet with slotted spoon and transfer to paper towel–lined plate. Pour off all but 2 tablespoons fat left in skillet. Reduce butter to 2 tablespoons and melt in fat left

in skillet over medium heat before adding shallot. Increase shallots to 2. Omit lemon zest and lemon wedges and substitute 1 tablespoon minced fresh parsley for thyme. Add crisp bacon to toasted panko along with parsley.

CHICKEN PICCATA

✔ WHY THIS RECIPE WORKS

Chicken piccata is a simple dish that should be easy to get right. But many recipes miss the mark with extraneous ingredients or paltry amounts of lemon juice and capers. We wanted to cook the chicken properly and make a streamlined sauce that would allow the star ingredients to make their presence known. To ensure evenly sized pieces of chicken, we found it best to buy breasts and slice them in half horizontally into thin cutlets. Dredging the cutlets in flour aided in browning. For the sauce, we deglazed the pan with chicken broth and added a shallot (garlic also worked well). For a strong lemon flavor that wasn't harsh or overly acidic, we simmered thin slices of lemon in the broth and added a full ¼ cup of lemon juice at the end of cooking to keep it tasting fresh. We also used plenty of capers—2 tablespoons— adding them when the sauce was nearly done so they retained their flavor and structural integrity.

CHICKEN PICCATA
SERVES 4

To make slicing the chicken easier, freeze it for 15 minutes. Because this sauce is so light, we find that each person should be served 3 cutlets.

- 2 lemons
- 6 (6- to 8-ounce) boneless, skinless chicken breasts, tenderloins removed, trimmed
- ½ cup all-purpose flour
  Salt and pepper
- 2 tablespoons plus ¼ cup vegetable oil

- 1 small shallot, minced, or 1 garlic clove, minced
- 1 cup low-sodium chicken broth
- 2 tablespoons capers, rinsed
- 3 tablespoons unsalted butter, cut into 3 pieces and chilled
- 2 tablespoons minced fresh parsley

1. Halve 1 lemon lengthwise. Trim ends from 1 half and slice crosswise ⅛ to ¼ inch thick; set aside. Juice remaining half and whole lemon to obtain ¼ cup juice; set aside.

2. Adjust oven rack to middle position and heat oven to 200 degrees. Halve chicken horizontally, then cover chicken halves with plastic wrap and pound to even ¼-inch thickness with meat pounder. Place flour in shallow dish or pie plate.

3. Pat chicken dry with paper towels and season with salt and pepper. Working with 1 cutlet at a time, dredge in flour mixture, shaking off excess, and transfer to large plate.

4. Heat 2 tablespoons oil in 12-inch skillet over medium-high heat until shimmering. Place 4 chicken cutlets in skillet and cook until golden brown on first side, about 3 minutes. Flip cutlets, reduce heat to medium, and cook until no longer pink and lightly browned on second side, about 2 minutes longer; transfer to large oven-safe platter. Repeat with remaining ¼ cup oil and remaining cutlets, working in 2 batches; transfer to platter. Tent loosely with aluminum foil and transfer to oven to keep warm while making sauce.

5. Add shallot to now-empty skillet and cook over medium heat until fragrant, about 30 seconds. Stir in broth and lemon slices, scraping up any browned bits. Bring to simmer and cook until reduced to ⅓ cup, about 4 minutes. Stir in lemon juice and capers, bring to simmer, and cook until reduced to ⅓ cup, about 1 minute. Off heat, whisk in butter, 1 piece at a time. Stir in parsley. Pour sauce over chicken and serve immediately.

PEPPERY CHICKEN PICCATA

Add ½ teaspoon coarsely ground pepper to sauce along with lemon juice and capers.

CHICKEN PICCATA WITH PROSCIUTTO

Add 2 ounces thinly sliced prosciutto, cut into pieces 1 inch long and ¼ wide, to skillet along with shallot and cook until prosciutto is lightly crisped, about 45 seconds.

CHICKEN PICCATA WITH BLACK OLIVES

Add ¼ cup pitted and chopped black olives to sauce along with lemon juice and capers.

PAN-SEARED CHICKEN BREASTS

✔ WHY THIS RECIPE WORKS

Exposing boneless, skinless chicken breasts to the intensity of a hot pan usually yields dry, leathery meat. We wanted pan-seared boneless, skinless breasts every bit as flavorful, moist, and tender as their skin-on counterparts. After much trial and error, we landed on a novel solution: First we salted the breasts (and poked them with a fork to help the salt penetrate the meat) and cooked them, covered, in a low oven. We then seared the breasts in a hot skillet on the stovetop. Salting the chicken breasts helped keep them moist, as did finishing them covered in the oven. Coating the chicken with a mixture of butter, flour, and cornstarch before searing gave our breasts a crisp, even crust.

PAN-SEARED CHICKEN BREASTS WITH LEMON AND CHIVE PAN SAUCE

SERVES 4

For the best results, buy similarly sized chicken breasts. If the breasts have the tenderloin attached, leave it in place and follow the upper range of baking time in step 1. For optimal texture, sear the chicken immediately after removing it from the oven. We prefer kosher salt in this recipe. If using table salt, reduce salt amounts by half. The chicken can be prepared without the pan sauce; if not making pan sauce, let the chicken rest for 5 minutes before serving in step 2. More pan sauce recipes follow.

CHICKEN
- 4 (6- to 8-ounce) boneless, skinless chicken breasts, trimmed
- 2 teaspoons kosher salt
- 1 tablespoon vegetable oil
- 2 tablespoons unsalted butter, melted
- 1 tablespoon all-purpose flour
- 1 teaspoon cornstarch
- ½ teaspoon pepper

PAN SAUCE
- 1 shallot, minced
- 1 teaspoon all-purpose flour
- 1 cup low-sodium chicken broth
- 1 tablespoon lemon juice
- 1 tablespoon minced fresh chives
- 1 tablespoon unsalted butter, chilled
  Salt and pepper

1. FOR THE CHICKEN: Adjust oven rack to lower-middle position and heat oven to 275 degrees. Using fork, poke thickest half of breasts 5 to 6 times and sprinkle with ½ teaspoon salt. Transfer breasts, skinned side down, to 13 by 9-inch baking dish and cover tightly with aluminum foil. Bake until breasts register 145 to 150 degrees, 30 to 40 minutes.

2. Remove chicken from oven and transfer, skinned side up, to paper towel–lined plate and pat dry with paper towels. Heat oil in 12-inch skillet over medium-high heat until just smoking. While skillet is heating, whisk butter, flour, cornstarch, and pepper together in bowl. Lightly brush top of chicken with half of butter mixture. Place chicken in skillet, coated side down, and cook until browned,

about 4 minutes. While chicken browns, brush with remaining butter mixture. Flip chicken, reduce heat to medium, and cook until second side is browned and chicken registers 160 degrees, 3 to 4 minutes. Transfer chicken to large plate and let rest while preparing sauce (if not making pan sauce, let chicken rest for 5 minutes before serving).

3. FOR THE PAN SAUCE: Add shallot to now-empty skillet and cook over medium heat until softened, about 2 minutes. Add flour and cook, stirring constantly, for 30 seconds. Slowly whisk in broth, scraping up any browned bits. Bring to vigorous simmer and cook until reduced to ¾ cup, 3 to 5 minutes. Stir in any accumulated chicken juices; return to simmer and cook for 30 seconds. Off heat, whisk in lemon juice, chives, and butter. Season with salt and pepper to taste. Pour sauce over chicken and serve immediately.

BOURBON AND CRANBERRY PAN SAUCE

MAKES ABOUT ¾ CUP, ENOUGH FOR
I RECIPE PAN-SEARED CHICKEN BREASTS

Be sure to add broth to skillet before adding bourbon.

- I   shallot, minced
- I   teaspoon all-purpose flour
- ¾   cup low-sodium chicken broth
- ½   cup bourbon
- ⅓   cup dried cranberries
- ½   teaspoon minced fresh thyme
- I   tablespoon unsalted butter, chilled
- I   teaspoon red wine vinegar
     Salt and pepper

Add shallot to now-empty skillet and cook over medium heat until softened, about 2 minutes. Add flour and cook, stirring constantly, for 30 seconds. Slowly whisk in broth, then bourbon, cranberries, and thyme, scraping up any browned bits. Bring to vigorous simmer and cook until reduced to ¾ cup, 3 to 5 minutes. Stir in any accumulated chicken juices; return to simmer and cook for 30 seconds. Off heat, whisk in butter and vinegar. Season with salt and pepper to taste. Pour sauce over chicken and serve immediately.

FENNEL AND MUSTARD PAN SAUCE

MAKES ABOUT ¾ CUP, ENOUGH FOR
I RECIPE PAN-SEARED CHICKEN BREASTS

We prefer whole grain mustard, but Dijon mustard can be substituted.

- I   shallot, minced
- I   teaspoon fennel seeds
- I   teaspoon all-purpose flour
- ¾   cup low-sodium chicken broth
- ½   cup dry vermouth or dry white wine
- 2   tablespoons whole grain mustard
- I   tablespoon unsalted butter, chilled
- I   teaspoon chopped fresh tarragon
     Salt and pepper

Add shallot and fennel seeds to now-empty skillet and cook over medium heat, stirring often, until shallot is softened and lightly browned, about 3 minutes. Add flour and cook, stirring constantly, for 30 seconds. Slowly whisk in broth and vermouth, scraping up any browned bits. Bring to vigorous simmer and cook until reduced and measures ¾ cup, 3 to 5 minutes. Stir in any accumulated chicken juices; return to simmer and cook for 30 seconds. Off heat, whisk in mustard, butter, and tarragon. Season with salt and pepper to taste. Pour sauce over chicken and serve immediately.

OVEN-BARBECUED CHICKEN

✔ WHY THIS RECIPE WORKS

The idea of oven-barbecued chicken is an appealing one; combine the ease of a week-night chicken dish with the sweet, tangy, spicy flavors of a rich tomatoey sauce—without firing up the grill. But tough, dry chicken slathered in greasy, stale-tasting sauce is usually the result. For juicy, tender, and evenly cooked chicken, we found that mild-tasting boneless, skinless chicken breasts made the perfect backdrop for a Kansas City–style sauce. We lightly seared the breasts in a skillet, removed them from the pan, and then made a simple barbecue sauce right in the same pan. To finish, we returned the chicken to the pan, placed it in the oven to finish cooking, and then turned on the broiler to lightly caramelize the sauce.

SWEET AND TANGY OVEN-BARBECUED CHICKEN

SERVES 4

For the best results, buy similarly sized chicken breasts. Real maple syrup is preferable to imitation syrup, and "mild" or "original" molasses is preferable to darker, more bitter types. Use a rasp-style grater or the fine holes of a box grater to grate the onion. Broiling times may differ from one oven to another, so we recommend checking the chicken after 3 minutes of broiling.

- I   cup ketchup
- 3   tablespoons molasses
- 3   tablespoons cider vinegar
- 2   tablespoons finely grated onion
- 2   tablespoons Worcestershire sauce
- 2   tablespoons Dijon mustard
- 2   tablespoons maple syrup
- I   teaspoon chili powder
- ¼   teaspoon cayenne pepper
- 4   (6- to 8-ounce) boneless, skinless chicken breasts, trimmed
     Salt and pepper
- I   tablespoon vegetable oil

1. Adjust oven rack to upper-middle position and heat oven to 325 degrees. Whisk ketchup, molasses, vinegar, onion, Worcestershire, mustard, maple syrup, chili powder, and cayenne together in bowl. Pat chicken dry with paper towels and season with salt and pepper.

2. Heat oil in 12-inch ovensafe skillet over medium-high heat until just smoking. Lightly brown chicken on both sides, about 2 minutes per side; transfer to plate.

3. Pour off all oil left in skillet and add barbecue sauce, scraping up any browned bits. Bring to simmer over medium heat and cook, stirring often, until sauce is thick and glossy, and spatula leaves clear trail in sauce, about 4 minutes.

4. Off heat, return chicken to skillet and coat well with sauce. Turn chicken breasts skinned side up and spoon extra sauce over each piece to create thick coating. Transfer skillet to oven and bake until breasts register 130 degrees, 10 to 14 minutes.

5. Using potholders (skillet handle will be hot) remove skillet from oven. Adjust oven rack 5 inches from broiler element and heat broiler. Broil chicken until breasts register 160 degrees, 5 to 10 minutes. Transfer chicken to platter and let rest for 5 minutes. Meanwhile, being careful of hot skillet handle, stir sauce left in skillet to combine and transfer to bowl. Serve chicken, passing sauce separately.

CHICKEN SCARPARIELLO

✔ WHY THIS RECIPE WORKS

Chicken scarpariello, chicken with sausage, peppers, and onions, is an Italian-American dish that holds the promise of an easy weeknight meal you can make all in one skillet. But most recipes don't address the problems of greasy sauce, flabby skin, and an overwhelming spiciness. Using sweet Italian sausage rather than hot tamed the spiciness of this dish and since

sausage is plenty rich, we decided to streamline our recipe and use only white meat. Split bone-in, skin-on chicken breasts could easily be cut into halves or thirds to speed up cooking time. We wiped the skillet clean after sautéing the sausage and chicken to avoid a greasy sauce. After adding the chicken—skin side up—back to the vegetables, we slid the skillet into the oven; this kept the skin nice and crisp. Finally, to temper the heat of the hot cherry peppers, we removed the seeds.

CHICKEN SCARPARIELLO
SERVES 4 TO 6

To manage the heat, adjust the amount of cherry peppers as desired. If your skillet is not ovensafe, add the cornstarch mixture to the skillet in step 3 (instead of step 5) along with the vinegar and simmer until slightly thickened, 3 to 4 minutes. Stir in the sausage and transfer mixture to a 13 by 9-inch baking dish. Arrange the chicken over the mixture and bake as directed. If using large chicken breasts (about 1 pound each), cut each breast into 3 pieces. If using smaller breasts (10 to 12 ounces each), cut each breast into 2 pieces. To make this dish with chicken thighs, increase the cooking time in the oven to about 25 minutes, or until the thighs register 175 degrees. See page 330 for information on trimming split chicken breasts.

- 1 tablespoon vegetable oil
- 8 ounces sweet Italian sausage, casings removed
- 2 pounds bone-in split chicken breasts, trimmed of rib sections and cut crosswise into 2 or 3 pieces
     Salt and pepper
- 1 onion, halved and sliced ¼ inch thick
- 1 large red bell pepper, stemmed, seeded, and cut into ¼-inch strips
- 3–5 jarred pickled hot cherry peppers, stemmed, seeded, and cut into ¼-inch strips
- 3 garlic cloves, minced

- ¾ cup plus 1 tablespoon low-sodium chicken broth
- ⅓ cup white wine vinegar, plus extra as needed
- 2 teaspoons sugar
- 1 teaspoon cornstarch
- 1 teaspoon minced fresh thyme
- 1 tablespoon minced fresh parsley

1. Adjust oven rack to middle position and heat oven to 350 degrees. Heat 1 teaspoon oil in 12-inch ovensafe skillet over medium-high heat until shimmering. Add sausage and cook, breaking it up into ½-inch pieces with wooden spoon, until browned, about 3 minutes. Remove sausage with slotted spoon and transfer to paper towel–lined plate. Pour off all fat left in skillet into bowl and reserve; wipe out skillet with paper towels.

2. Pat chicken dry with paper towels and season with salt and pepper. Heat remaining 2 teaspoons oil in now-empty skillet over medium-high heat until just smoking. Place chicken skin side down in skillet and cook until well browned, 6 to 8 minutes, reducing heat if pan begins to scorch. Flip chicken skin side up and continue to cook until lightly brown on second side, about 3 minutes. Transfer chicken to large plate. Pour off all fat left in skillet into bowl with sausage fat; wipe out skillet with paper towels.

3. Heat 1 tablespoon reserved fat in now-empty skillet over medium-high heat until shimmering. Add onion and cook until beginning to soften, about 2 minutes. Add bell pepper and cherry peppers and cook, stirring occasionally, until bell pepper begins to soften, about 4 minutes. Stir in garlic and cook until fragrant, about 30 seconds. Stir in ¾ cup broth, vinegar, and sugar, scraping up any browned bits, and bring to simmer.

4. Return sausage and chicken, along with any accumulated juices to skillet, arranging chicken pieces in single layer,

skin side up, on top of peppers and onion. Transfer skillet to oven and roast chicken until breast pieces register 160 degrees, 18 to 22 minutes. Meanwhile, combine cornstarch, thyme, and remaining 1 tablespoon broth in bowl.

5. Using potholders (skillet handle will be hot) remove skillet from oven. Transfer chicken to platter and let rest while finishing sauce. Being careful of hot skillet handle, stir cornstarch mixture into sauce. Bring to simmer over medium-high heat and cook until slightly thickened, 2 to 3 minutes. Off heat, season with salt, pepper, and vinegar to taste. Spoon sauce around chicken, being careful not to pour it directly over chicken. Sprinkle with parsley and serve immediately.

CHICKEN VESUVIO

✔ WHY THIS RECIPE WORKS

Chicken Vesuvio is a dish indigenous to Chicago's Italian restaurants—with crispy-skinned chicken, bronzed potatoes, and a fiery garlic, herb, and wine sauce, it's a welcome diversion from the ordinary baked chicken dinner. To start, chicken and potato wedges are browned on the stovetop, then transferred to the oven to finish cooking with the sauce. The problem is that the chicken skin becomes soggy from sitting in the sauce. We browned the chicken skin side down, then layered the chicken and potatoes, starting the

chicken on the bottom (to soak up the flavors of the sauce), then switching the chicken to the top (to allow the skin to crisp).

CHICKEN VESUVIO
SERVES 4

An equal weight of bone-in, skin-on chicken thighs, legs (separated into thigh and drumstick pieces), or split breasts (each breast halved lengthwise) may be substituted for the whole chicken. If you don't care for chicken skin, simply remove it after pan-frying and before baking. A large, 8-quart Dutch oven with a diameter of 12 inches serves this dish well. If using a Le Creuset Dutch oven, heat the oil for an extra minute. See page 333 for information on cutting up a whole chicken.

1	(3- to 4-pound) whole chicken, cut into 8 pieces (4 breast pieces, 2 drumsticks, 2 thighs), wings discarded
	Salt and pepper
2	tablespoons olive oil
1½	pounds Yukon Gold potatoes, peeled and cut lengthwise into 8 wedges about ¾ inch thick
8	garlic cloves, minced
1	cup dry white wine
2	sprigs fresh oregano
2	sprigs fresh thyme
1	sprig fresh rosemary
2	tablespoons lemon juice
2	tablespoons minced fresh parsley

1. Adjust oven rack to lower-middle position and heat oven to 400 degrees. Pat chicken dry with paper towels and season with salt and pepper.

2. Heat 1 tablespoon oil in Dutch oven over medium-high heat until just smoking. Place chicken skin side down in skillet and cook until well browned, 6 to 8 minutes, reducing heat if pan begins to scorch. Flip chicken skin side up and continue to cook until well browned on second side, 6 to 8 minutes longer. Transfer chicken to plate.

3. Heat remaining 1 tablespoon oil in now-empty pot over medium heat until shimmering. Add potatoes, arranging them in single layer with 1 flat side of each wedge against bottom of pot, and cook until golden brown, 6 to 8 minutes. Reduce heat to medium-low, turn potatoes, and continue to cook until golden brown on all sides, 8 to 10 minutes longer. Transfer potatoes to separate plate. Let pot cool slightly, about 2 minutes.

4. Add all but 1 teaspoon garlic to now-empty pot and cook, using pot's residual heat, until fragrant, about 30 seconds. Stir in wine, oregano, thyme, rosemary, ¼ teaspoon salt, and ¼ teaspoon pepper, scraping up any browned bits. Return chicken pieces skin side up to pot, then arrange potatoes on top.

5. Bake, uncovered, for 10 minutes. Using tongs, arrange chicken on top of potatoes and facing skin side up. Bake until breasts register 160 degrees, 8 to 10 minutes longer. Transfer breast pieces to serving dish and tent loosely with aluminum foil. Continue to cook thighs, drumsticks, and potatoes until thighs and drumsticks register 175 degrees, 5 to 10 minutes longer. Transfer thighs, drumsticks, and potatoes to serving dish.

6. Discard herb sprigs. Stir remaining 1 teaspoon garlic and lemon juice into sauce. Pour sauce over chicken and potatoes, sprinkle with parsley, and serve.

TEST KITCHEN TIP NO. 72 WHITE WINE FOR COOKING

When a recipe calls for dry white wine, it's tempting to grab whatever open bottle is in the fridge. Chardonnay and Pinot Grigio may taste different straight from the glass, but how much do those distinctive flavor profiles really come through in a cooked dish? To find out, we tried four varietals and a supermarket "cooking wine" in five different recipes. Only Sauvignon Blanc consistently boiled down to a "clean" yet sufficiently acidic flavor that played nicely with the rest of the ingredients. Vermouth can be an acceptable substitute in certain recipes, but because its flavor is stronger, we don't recommend using vermouth unless it is listed as an option in the recipe. Never buy supermarket "cooking wine," which has a significant amount of added sodium and an unappealing vinegary flavor.

SIMPLE BROILED CHICKEN

✔ WHY THIS RECIPE WORKS

Broiled chicken can be a quick and easy dinner, but that doesn't mean it has to be ordinary. When done right, the result is moist, well-seasoned meat encased in a crisp, caramelized exterior. For chicken parts of similar size (that would cook at the same rate), we found it best to buy a whole chicken and cut it up ourselves. Brining the chicken was a must for moist, well-seasoned meat and caramelized skin (owing to the sugar in the brine). We broiled the chicken on the lowest rack to prevent the skin from charring, but moved it up closer to the heating element for the last couple minutes of cooking for better browning. Finally, slashing the skin and starting the chicken skin side down ensured that plenty of fat rendered from the skin, resulting in a crisp exterior.

SIMPLE BROILED CHICKEN
SERVES 4

If using kosher chicken, do not brine in step 1, and season with salt as well as pepper. See page 333 for information on cutting up a whole chicken.

- ½ cup salt
- ½ cup sugar
- 1 (3- to 4-pound) whole chicken, cut into 8 pieces (4 breast pieces, 2 drumsticks, 2 thighs), wings discarded
- Pepper

1. Dissolve salt and sugar in 2 quarts cold water in large container. Submerge chicken in brine, cover, and refrigerate for 30 to 60 minutes. Remove chicken from brine and pat dry with paper towels. Using sharp knife, make 2 or 3 short slashes into skin of each piece of chicken, taking care not to cut into meat; season with pepper.

2. Meanwhile, adjust 1 oven rack to lowest position and second rack 5 inches from broiler element; heat broiler. Set wire rack in aluminum foil–lined rimmed baking sheet. Place chicken pieces skin side down on prepared wire rack.

3. Broil chicken on lower rack until just beginning to brown, 12 to 16 minutes. Flip chicken pieces skin side up and continue to broil on lower rack until skin is slightly crisp and breasts register 160 degrees, about 10 minutes longer (if some chicken parts are browning too quickly, cover only those pieces with small pieces of foil). Transfer breast pieces to large plate and tent loosely with foil. Continue to broil thighs and drumsticks on lower rack until they register 175 degrees, 5 to 10 minutes longer.

4. Return breast pieces skin side up to wire rack and broil on upper rack until chicken is spotty brown and skin is thin and crisp, about 1 minute. Serve immediately.

SIMPLE BROILED CHICKEN BREASTS

If using kosher chicken, do not brine in step 1, and season with salt and pepper. If you're making Garlic, Lemon, and Rosemary Rub or Spicy Jamaican Jerk Dipping Sauce (recipes follow), prepare them while the chicken brines. See page 330 for information on trimming split chicken breasts.

Substitute four 12-ounce bone-in split chicken breasts, trimmed of rib sections, for whole chicken. Move chicken to upper rack once breasts register 160 degrees and broil until spotty brown and skin is thin and crisp, about 1 minute.

SIMPLE BROILED CHICKEN THIGHS

If using kosher chicken, do not brine in step 1, and season with salt and pepper. If you're making Garlic, Lemon, and Rosemary Rub or Spicy Jamaican Jerk Dipping Sauce (recipes follow), prepare them while the chicken brines.

Substitute eight 6-ounce bone-in chicken thighs for whole chicken. Broil chicken on bottom rack until just beginning to brown, 12 to 16 minutes. Flip chicken skin side up and continue to broil on lower rack until thighs register 175 degrees, 15 to 20 minutes longer, before broiling on upper rack.

GARLIC, LEMON, AND ROSEMARY RUB FOR BROILED CHICKEN

MAKES ENOUGH FOR 3 TO 4 POUNDS OF CHICKEN

Prepare the rub while the chicken brines.

- 5 garlic cloves, minced
- 2 teaspoons grated lemon zest plus ¼ cup juice (2 lemons)

We have been brining meat in the test kitchen for years and were interested in finding out how much sodium penetrates the meat during the process. To answer this question, we brined boneless, skinless chicken breasts and natural pork chops in standard quick-brine solutions of ½ cup table salt dissolved in 2 quarts of cold water. After 30 minutes, we removed the chicken and pork, patted them dry, and cooked them in different skillets. We also cooked a kosher chicken breast that had been salted during processing and an "enhanced" pork chop (injected with a saltwater solution).

We sent the samples to a food lab to measure sodium content. The brined pork chops had a sodium content of 245 milligrams per 100 grams of meat (just under ⅛ teaspoon per serving); the enhanced pork had a bit more, with 268 milligrams. The kosher chicken breast weighed in at 252 milligrams of sodium. The brined chicken came in with the most sodium of all, at 353 milligrams (just over ⅛ teaspoon per serving). Why did the chicken absorb more salt during brining than the pork? The loose white muscle fibers in chicken absorb salt water more quickly than the tighter muscle fibers in pork. The U.S. Department of Agriculture recommends limiting your daily sodium intake to 2,300 milligrams, about 1 teaspoon.

1 tablespoon minced fresh rosemary
¼ teaspoon pepper
3 tablespoons extra-virgin olive oil

Combine garlic, lemon zest, rosemary, and pepper in bowl. Combine lemon juice and oil in separate bowl. Follow recipe for Simple Broiled Chicken, Simple Broiled Chicken Breasts, or Simple Broiled Chicken Thighs, spreading portion of garlic rub under skin of chicken pieces before slashing skin. Brush chicken pieces with lemon juice mixture before broiling on upper rack.

SPICY JAMAICAN JERK DIPPING SAUCE FOR BROILED CHICKEN

MAKES ENOUGH FOR 3 TO 4 POUNDS OF CHICKEN

Prepare the dipping sauce while the chicken brines.

1 garlic clove, unpeeled
1 habanero chile
¼ cup lime juice (2 limes)
¼ cup packed brown sugar
½ cup finely chopped onion
2 scallions, minced
1 (1½-inch) piece ginger, peeled and minced
½ teaspoon dried thyme
Pinch ground allspice

1. Toast garlic and habanero in 8-inch skillet over medium heat, shaking pan occasionally, until softened and spotty brown, about 8 minutes; when cool enough to handle, peel and mince garlic and stem, seed, and mince habanero.

2. Whisk lime juice and sugar together in bowl until sugar is completely dissolved. Combine minced garlic, minced habanero, onion, scallions, ginger, thyme, and allspice in small bowl. Stir in 2 tablespoons of lime juice mixture; set aside as dipping sauce for cooked chicken. Follow recipe for Simple Broiled Chicken, Simple Broiled Chicken Breasts, or Simple Broiled Chicken Thighs, brushing chicken pieces with remaining lime juice mixture before broiling on upper rack. Serve chicken, passing dipping sauce separately.

SPICE-RUBBED PICNIC CHICKEN

✔ WHY THIS RECIPE WORKS

Cold barbecued chicken is a picnic classic with a host of problems; namely, sticky sauce, flabby skin, and dry meat. We wanted the flavor and appeal of great barbecued chicken—without turning on the grill. To start, we immediately replaced the sauce with a dry rub; by rubbing the spice mixture all over the chicken, even under the skin, we achieved the robust barbecue flavor we sought, and the skin was noticeably less soggy. To further improve the skin, we trimmed the pieces of excess fat and cut slits in the skin to allow even more fat to render. But our biggest discovery came when we opted to salt the chicken instead of brine it; by adding the salt to our spice rub and refrigerating the chicken pieces overnight, we allowed both the salt and spices to penetrate the meat for even deeper flavor. We roasted the chicken at 425 degrees before cranking up the heat to 500 to crisp the skin.

SPICE-RUBBED PICNIC CHICKEN

SERVES 8

If you plan to serve the chicken later on the same day that you cook it, refrigerate it immediately after it has cooled, then let it come back to room temperature before serving. If using large chicken breasts (about 1 pound each), cut each breast into 3 pieces. On the breast pieces, we use toothpicks to secure the skin, which otherwise shrinks considerably in the oven, leaving the meat exposed and prone to drying out. We think the extra effort is justified, but you can omit this step.

3 tablespoons brown sugar
2 tablespoons chili powder
2 tablespoons paprika
1 tablespoon salt
2 teaspoons pepper
¼–½ teaspoon cayenne pepper
5 pounds bone-in chicken pieces (split breasts cut in half, drumsticks, and/or thighs), trimmed

TEST KITCHEN TIP NO. 74   *SWEET AND HOT PAPRIKA*

"Paprika" is a generic term for a spice made from ground dried red peppers. Sweet paprika (or "Hungarian paprika," or simply "paprika") is the most common form, with a brilliant red color and subtle flavor. Hot paprika, most often used in chilis, curries, or stews, can range from slightly spicy to punishingly assertive. Both sweet and hot paprika come from the dried pods of *Capsicum annuum L.*, which includes a large swath of pepper varieties ranging from sweet red bell peppers to hot chile peppers. The type of pepper used will influence the flavor, spiciness, and intensity of the paprika. Sweet paprika is made from only the middle layer of the pepper's outer wall (the mesocarp), while hot paprika also contains some of the white veins (the placenta) and seeds, where most of the heat resides.

We compared sweet and hot paprika in three applications—Chicken Paprikash (page 105), barbecue sauce, and a dry rub in Spice-Rubbed Picnic Chicken. Most tasters found the sweet paprika, with its "bright," "well-balanced," and "smoky" flavors, to be a better choice in the chicken paprikash; the hot paprika was less flavorful, aside from its pronounced heat. The differences were even more apparent in the spice-rubbed chicken breasts, where the hot paprika took on an unpleasant bitter edge. In the barbecue sauce, however, tasters found both varieties perfectly acceptable, and some preferred the sauce made with the hot paprika. Here, its spiciness seemed less aggressive and was actually a virtue. If yours is going to be a one-paprika household, we recommend stocking the more versatile sweet, as a pinch or two of cayenne pepper can be added to replicate the flavor of the hot stuff.

1. Set wire rack in rimmed baking sheet. Combine sugar, chili powder, paprika, salt, pepper, and cayenne in bowl.

2. Using sharp knife, make 2 or 3 short slashes into skin of each piece of chicken, taking care not to cut into meat. Coat chicken with spice mixture, gently lifting skin to distribute spice mixture underneath but leaving it attached to chicken. Transfer chicken skin side up to prepared wire rack (if desired, secure skin of each breast piece with 2 or 3 toothpicks placed near edges of skin). Tent chicken loosely with aluminum foil and refrigerate for at least 6 hours or up to 24 hours.

3. Adjust oven rack to middle position and heat oven to 425 degrees. Roast chicken until smallest piece registers 140 degrees, 15 to 20 minutes. Increase oven temperature to 500 degrees and continue roasting until chicken is browned and crisp and breast pieces register 160 degrees, 5 to 8 minutes longer. (Smaller pieces may cook faster than larger pieces. Remove pieces from oven as they reach correct temperature.) Continue to roast thighs and/or drumsticks until they register 170 degrees, about 5 minutes longer. Transfer chicken to wire rack and let cool completely before refrigerating or serving.

TANDOORI CHICKEN

✔ WHY THIS RECIPE WORKS
Tandoori chicken is a dish that calls for a 24-hour marinade and a 900-degree oven. We wanted to turn this Indian classic into an easy weeknight dinner we could make indoors. We skipped the long marinade in favor of a two-step approach to flavoring the chicken. First we rubbed a salt-spice mixture into the chicken pieces and left them to sit for half an hour; we then dipped the pieces in a spice-flavored yogurt mixture. After several tests, we realized that attempting to mimic the extreme heat of

a tandoor oven simply wouldn't work in a home kitchen—cranking up the oven temperature only resulted in dry, charred meat. Instead, we started the chicken in a moderate 325-degree oven, then finished it under the broiler to crisp the exterior.

TANDOORI CHICKEN
SERVES 4

We prefer this dish with whole-milk yogurt, but low-fat yogurt can be substituted. Serve with basmati rice and a few chutneys or relishes. If using large chicken breasts (about 1 pound each), cut each breast into 3 pieces. If using smaller breasts (10 to 12 ounces each), cut each breast into 2 pieces.

  2   tablespoons vegetable oil
  6   garlic cloves, minced
  2   tablespoons grated fresh ginger
  1   tablespoon garam masala
  2   teaspoons ground cumin
  2   teaspoons chili powder
  1   cup plain whole-milk yogurt
  ¼   cup lime juice (2 limes), plus 1 lime, cut into wedges
  2   teaspoons salt
  3   pounds bone-in chicken pieces (split breasts cut in half, drumsticks, and/or thighs), trimmed

1. Heat oil in 10-inch skillet over medium heat until shimmering. Add garlic and ginger and cook until fragrant, about 30 seconds. Stir in garam masala, cumin, and chili powder and continue to cook until fragrant, 30 seconds longer. Transfer half of garlic mixture to medium bowl, stir in yogurt and 2 tablespoons lime juice, and set aside. In large bowl, combine remaining garlic mixture, remaining 2 tablespoons lime juice, and salt.

2. Using sharp knife, make 2 or 3 short slashes into skin of each piece of chicken, taking care not to cut into meat. Transfer chicken to large bowl and gently rub

with salt-spice mixture until all pieces are evenly coated. Let sit at room temperature for 30 minutes.

3. Adjust oven rack to upper-middle position and heat oven to 325 degrees. Set wire rack in aluminum foil–lined rimmed baking sheet. Pour yogurt mixture over chicken and toss until chicken is evenly coated with thick layer. Arrange chicken pieces, scored side down, on prepared wire rack. Discard excess yogurt mixture. Roast chicken until breast pieces register 125 degrees and thighs and/or drumsticks register 130 degrees, 15 to 25 minutes. (Smaller pieces may cook faster than larger pieces. Remove pieces from oven as they reach correct temperature.)

4. Adjust oven rack 6 inches from broiler element and heat broiler. Return chicken to prepared wire rack, scored side up, and broil until chicken is lightly charred in spots and breast pieces register 160 degrees and thighs and/or drumsticks register 175 degrees, 8 to 15 minutes. Transfer chicken to serving plate, tent loosely with foil, and let rest for 5 minutes. Serve with lime wedges.

RAITA
MAKES ABOUT 1 CUP

The raita is best made with whole-milk yogurt, although low-fat yogurt can be used. Do not use nonfat yogurt; the sauce will taste hollow and bland.

  1   cup plain whole-milk yogurt
  2   tablespoons minced fresh cilantro
  1   garlic clove, minced
      Salt
      Cayenne pepper

Mix all ingredients together and season with salt and cayenne to taste. Cover and refrigerate until needed.

CHICKEN TERIYAKI

✔ WHY THIS RECIPE WORKS

Americanized adaptations of chicken teriyaki are lackluster at best, with soggy skin shellacked in a corn-syrupy sauce. We found that the deep, meaty flavor of chicken thighs stands up best to the salty profile of teriyaki sauce. We kept the skin on as it created a protective barrier against the heat of the oven, keeping the meat moist; however, we opted to remove the bones, which allowed the meat to cook faster and made it easy to slice the chicken into thin strips. Broiling the chicken on the middle rack allowed for the most consistent level of browning. And instead of marinating the thighs in the sauce (which resulted in soggy skin), we decided to spoon the sauce over the chicken just before serving. A traditional combination of soy sauce, sugar, and mirin was a good start, but the additions of ginger and garlic provided depth, while a little cornstarch gave our sauce the ideal glazy consistency.

CHICKEN TERIYAKI
SERVES 4

There is a fair amount of soy sauce in this dish, so there is no need to season with salt before serving.

8   (5-ounce) bone-in chicken thighs, trimmed and boned
      Salt and pepper
½   cup soy sauce
½   cup sugar
2   tablespoons mirin
1   garlic clove, minced
½   teaspoon grated fresh ginger
½   teaspoon cornstarch

1. Adjust oven rack 8 inches from broiler element and heat broiler. Set wire rack in aluminum foil–lined rimmed baking sheet.

2. Using sharp knife, make 2 or 3 short slashes into skin of each piece of chicken, taking care not to cut into meat. Season chicken with salt and pepper and arrange skin side up on prepared wire rack, tucking exposed meat under skin and lightly flattening thighs to be of relatively even thickness. Broil until skin is crisp and golden brown and thighs register 175 degrees, 8 to 14 minutes, rotating baking sheet halfway through broiling.

3. Meanwhile, whisk soy sauce, sugar, mirin, garlic, ginger, and cornstarch together in small saucepan. Bring mixture to simmer over medium-high heat and cook, stirring occasionally, until sauce is syrupy and measures ¾ cup, about 4 minutes. Remove from heat and cover to keep warm.

4. Transfer chicken to cutting board and let rest for 5 minutes. Cut meat crosswise into ½-inch-wide strips and transfer to serving platter. Stir teriyaki sauce to recombine, then drizzle half of sauce over chicken. Serve immediately, passing remaining sauce separately.

ORANGE-FLAVORED CHICKEN

✔ WHY THIS RECIPE WORKS

Orange-flavored chicken continues to be a Chinese restaurant favorite, despite its frequent disappointing performance—the fried chicken is often too heavily breaded and the sauce is overly sticky and unbearably sweet. For a coating that would be moderately crunchy and maintain its texture beneath a blanket of well-balanced sauce, we dipped the chicken first in egg white and then in cornstarch. A little cayenne added some zip and some baking soda helped the coating develop a golden brown hue. Chicken thighs retained moisture better than delicate white meat when deep-fried. For extra flavor and to

---

BONING CHICKEN THIGHS FOR TERIYAKI

1. After trimming excess skin and fat (leaving enough skin to cover meat), cut slit along white line of fat from one joint to other joint to expose bone.

2. Using tip of sharp knife, cut and scrape meat from bone at both joints.

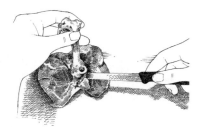

3. Slip knife under bone to separate meat completely from bone.

4. Discard bone. Trim any remaining cartilage from thigh.

---

help the chicken retain its juiciness, we marinated the chicken in a soy sauce–based mixture, reserving some marinade to become the base for the final sauce. A healthy dose of orange juice and zest, ginger, garlic, and cayenne gave us the balanced sauce we sought, with sweet, sour, and spicy background notes.

ORANGE-FLAVORED CHICKEN
SERVES 4

We prefer the flavor and texture of thigh meat for this recipe, though an equal amount of boneless, skinless chicken breasts can be used. You will need at least a 6-quart Dutch oven for this recipe. Unless you have a taste for the incendiary, do not eat the whole chiles in the finished dish.

MARINADE AND SAUCE
¾ cup low-sodium chicken broth
8 (2-inch) strips orange zest plus 1½ teaspoons grated zest and ¾ cup juice (2 oranges)
6 tablespoons white vinegar
¼ cup soy sauce
½ cup packed dark brown sugar
3 garlic cloves, minced
1 tablespoon grated fresh ginger
¼ teaspoon cayenne pepper
1½ pounds boneless, skinless chicken thighs, trimmed and cut in 1½-inch pieces
2 tablespoons cold water
1 tablespoon plus 2 teaspoons cornstarch
8 small whole dried red chiles (optional)

COATING AND FRYING OIL
3 large egg whites
1 cup cornstarch
¼ teaspoon cayenne pepper
½ teaspoon baking soda
3 cups peanut oil

1. FOR THE MARINADE AND SAUCE: Whisk broth, grated orange zest, orange juice, vinegar, soy sauce, sugar, garlic, ginger, and cayenne together in large saucepan. Transfer ¾ cup mixture to medium bowl and add chicken. Let marinate for at least 10 minutes or up to 1 hour.

2. Whisk water and cornstarch together in bowl. Bring broth mixture in saucepan to simmer over high heat. Whisk in cornstarch mixture, bring to simmer, and cook stirring occasionally, until thick and translucent and measures 1½ cups, about 1 minute. Off heat, stir in orange peel and chiles, if using; set aside.

3. FOR THE COATING: Set wire rack in rimmed baking sheet. Lightly beat egg whites in shallow dish or pie plate until frothy. Combine cornstarch, cayenne, and baking soda in second dish. Drain chicken and pat dry with paper towels. Place half of chicken pieces in egg whites and turn to coat; transfer pieces to cornstarch mixture and coat thoroughly. Place dredged chicken pieces on prepared wire rack; repeat with remaining chicken.

4. TO FRY THE CHICKEN: Heat oil in Dutch oven over high heat until it registers 350 degrees. Carefully place half of chicken in oil, 1 piece at a time, and fry until golden brown, about 5 minutes, turning each piece with tongs halfway through frying and adjusting heat as necessary to maintain oil at 350 degrees. Transfer chicken to large paper towel–lined plate. Return oil to 350 degrees (if necessary) over high heat and repeat with remaining chicken.

5. TO SERVE: Reheat sauce over medium heat until simmering, about 2 minutes. Add chicken and gently toss until evenly coated and heated through. Serve immediately.

OLD-FASHIONED FRIED CHICKEN

✔ WHY THIS RECIPE WORKS
For fried chicken to be worth the effort, it should be crisp and crackling with flavor and sport a deep mahogany exterior without any evidence of greasiness. Brining was a must for juicy, well-seasoned meat, while soaking the chicken in buttermilk tenderized the meat and added further flavor. Combining the two steps to create a buttermilk brine streamlined the process. Flour beat out all other coatings for the light crust it produced, while a double breading of flour, then egg, then more flour was better still, providing a superior base coat. Air-drying the brined chicken before breading and adding a little baking soda, baking powder, and buttermilk to the egg wash gave us a bronzed crust that remained crisp even as it cooled. Rather than submerge the chicken pieces entirely in oil, we found that pan-frying (where only half of each piece is submerged) in a large Dutch oven was much easier.

ULTIMATE CRISPY FRIED CHICKEN
SERVES 4 TO 6

Avoid using kosher chicken in this recipe or it will be too salty. You will need at least a 6-quart Dutch oven for this recipe. Maintaining an even oil temperature is key. If using large chicken breasts (about 1 pound each), cut each breast into 3 pieces. If using smaller breasts (10 to 12 ounces each), cut each breast into 2 pieces.

8 cups buttermilk
½ cup plus 2 tablespoons salt
¼ cup sugar
2 tablespoons paprika
3 garlic heads, cloves separated, peeled, and smashed
3 bay leaves, crumbled
3½ pounds bone-in chicken pieces (split breasts cut in half, drumsticks, and/or thighs), trimmed

3–4   cups peanut oil or vegetable
       shortening
4   cups all-purpose flour
1   large egg
1   teaspoon baking powder
½   teaspoon baking soda

1. Whisk 7 cups buttermilk, salt, sugar, paprika, garlic, and bay leaves together in large container. Add chicken and turn to coat. Cover and refrigerate for 2 to 3 hours.

2. Set wire rack in rimmed baking sheet. Rinse chicken well, place in single layer on prepared wire rack, and refrigerate, uncovered, for 2 hours. (At this point, chicken can be wrapped in plastic wrap and refrigerated for up to 6 more hours.)

3. Adjust oven rack to middle position and heat oven to 200 degrees. Add oil to Dutch oven until it measures 2 inches deep. Heat oil over medium-high heat until it registers 375 degrees.

4. Meanwhile, place flour in shallow dish or pie plate. Lightly beat egg, baking powder, and baking soda together in medium bowl, then whisk in remaining 1 cup buttermilk (mixture will bubble and foam). Working with 1 chicken piece at a time, dredge in flour, shaking off excess, then coat with egg mixture, allowing excess to drip off. Dredge chicken in flour again, shake off excess, and return to wire rack.

5. When oil is hot, carefully place half of chicken in pot, skin side down, cover, and fry until deep golden brown, 7 to 11 minutes, adjusting heat as necessary to maintain oil at 325 degrees. (After 4 minutes, check chicken pieces for even browning and rearrange if some pieces are browning faster than others.) Turn chicken pieces over and continue to cook until breast pieces register 160 degrees and thighs and/or drumsticks register 175 degrees, 6 to 8 minutes. (Smaller pieces may cook faster than larger pieces. Remove pieces from pot as they reach correct temperature.) Drain chicken briefly on paper towel–lined plate, then transfer to clean wire rack set over rimmed baking sheet and keep warm in oven.

6. Return oil to 375 degrees (if necessary) over medium-high heat and repeat with remaining chicken. Serve.

EASIER FRIED CHICKEN

✓ WHY THIS RECIPE WORKS

Is it possible to achieve fried chicken with a crisp crust without resorting to a quart of oil? To find an easier way to fry chicken, we started with a standard procedure of soaking the chicken in a salt and buttermilk brine and then dredging it in seasoned flour (along with a little baking powder which keeps the crust light and crisp due to the carbon dioxide released by the powder during frying). And finally, we mixed buttermilk into the dry ingredients before dredging the chicken. This created small clumps of batter that became super-crisp as they fried. After much trial and error, we discovered that a hybrid cooking method delivered an easier fried chicken with deep-fried flavor. We started by frying the chicken on the stovetop in minimal amounts of oil until it formed a light brown crust, then finished it in a hot oven to cook it through and deepen its color.

EASIER FRIED CHICKEN
SERVES 4

A whole 4-pound chicken, cut into 8 pieces, can be used instead of the chicken parts. Skinless chicken pieces are also an acceptable substitute, but the meat will come out slightly drier. If using large chicken breasts (about 1 pound each), cut each breast into 3 pieces. If using smaller breasts (10 to 12 ounces each), cut each breast into 2 pieces. A Dutch oven with an 11-inch diameter can be used in place of the straight-sided sauté pan.

1¼   cups buttermilk
      Salt and pepper
1   teaspoon garlic powder

1   teaspoon paprika
¼   teaspoon cayenne pepper
       Dash hot sauce
3½   pounds bone-in chicken pieces (split
       breasts cut in half, drumsticks, and/
       or thighs), trimmed
2   cups all-purpose flour
2   teaspoons baking powder
1¾   cups vegetable oil

1. Whisk 1 cup buttermilk, 1 tablespoon salt, 1 teaspoon pepper, ¼ teaspoon garlic powder, ¼ teaspoon paprika, pinch cayenne, and hot sauce together in large bowl. Add chicken and turn to coat. Cover and refrigerate at least 1 hour or up to overnight.

2. Adjust oven rack to middle position and heat oven to 400 degrees. Set wire rack in rimmed baking sheet. Whisk flour, baking powder, 1 teaspoon salt, 2 teaspoons pepper, remaining ¾ teaspoon garlic powder, remaining ¾ teaspoon paprika, and remaining cayenne together in large bowl. Add remaining ¼ cup buttermilk to flour mixture and mix with fingers until combined and small clumps form. Working with 1 chicken piece at a time, dredge in flour mixture, pressing mixture onto pieces to form thick, even coating. Place dredged chicken on large plate, skin side up.

3. Heat oil in 11-inch straight-sided sauté pan over medium-high heat until it registers 375 degrees. Carefully place chicken in pan, skin side down, and fry until golden brown, 3 to 5 minutes. (Adjust heat as necessary to maintain oil at 375 degrees.) Carefully flip and continue to fry until golden brown on second side, 2 to 4 minutes longer. Transfer chicken to prepared wire rack and bake until breast pieces register 160 degrees and/or thighs and drumsticks register 175 degrees, 15 to 20 minutes. (Smaller pieces may cook faster than larger pieces. Remove pieces from oven as they reach correct temperature.) Let chicken rest for 5 minutes before serving.

OVEN-FRIED CHICKEN

✔ **WHY THIS RECIPE WORKS**

Oven-fried chicken offers the promise of a quick weeknight alternative to the real thing. But most recipes leave us wondering if it really is possible to achieve real crunch and satisfying flavor in the oven. Since we knew the coatings—both the moist one that helps the crumbs adhere and the dry one that provides texture and crunch—would be the most important components, we started there. A combination of egg and Dijon mustard gave the meat a wonderfully subtle flavor and held on to a uniform layer of crumbs. Melba toast was the surprising winner for the crumb coating, providing a crunchy, flavorful, and beautifully browned exterior. Thighs and drumsticks were less prone to drying out in the oven, and we found it best to remove the skin, which doesn't render and crisp in the oven.

CRUNCHY OVEN-FRIED CHICKEN
SERVES 4

Avoid using kosher chicken in this recipe or it will be too salty. If you don't want to buy whole chicken legs and cut them into drumsticks and thighs, simply buy 4 drumsticks and 4 thighs. To make Melba toast crumbs, place the toasts in a 1-gallon zipper-lock bag, seal, and pound with a meat pounder or other heavy blunt object. Leave some crumbs in the mixture the size of pebbles, but most should resemble coarse sand.

- 1 (5-ounce) box plain Melba toast, crushed
- ¼ cup vegetable oil
- 2 large eggs
- 1 tablespoon Dijon mustard
- 1 teaspoon dried thyme
- ¾ teaspoon salt
- ½ teaspoon pepper
- ½ teaspoon dried oregano
- ¼ teaspoon garlic powder
- ¼ teaspoon cayenne pepper (optional)

- 4 whole chicken legs, separated into drumsticks and thighs and skin removed

1. Adjust oven rack to upper-middle position and heat oven to 400 degrees. Set wire rack in rimmed baking sheet.

2. Thoroughly combine crushed Melba toast and oil in shallow dish or pie plate. Lightly beat eggs, mustard, thyme, salt, pepper, oregano, garlic powder, and cayenne, if using, together in second dish.

3. Working with 1 chicken piece at a time, coat with egg mixture, allowing excess to drip off. Coat all sides of chicken with crumb mixture, pressing gently so that crumbs adhere. Transfer breaded chicken to prepared wire rack.

4. Bake until chicken is deep nutty brown and registers 175 degrees, about 40 minutes. Serve.

STUFFED CHICKEN BREASTS

✔ **WHY THIS RECIPE WORKS**

To transform chicken breasts into a four-star affair, French chefs use a forcemeat filling (made from the chicken itself) to stuff the breasts. We wanted a less fussy, but still elegant, version of this dish. We decided to use just boneless, skinless breasts (rather than a whole chicken) for ease of preparation. Trimming a little bit of meat from each chicken breast, pureeing it, and then adding it to a mushroom-leek mixture worked great, with the pureed chicken serving as a cohesive binder for the stuffing. We spread the mixture onto pounded chicken breasts and rolled them up to form roulades; this allowed the chicken and stuffing to be uniformly distributed. Trimming the breasts after pounding was even better, as we were able to form the breasts into even rectangles that were easy to roll. Finally, we browned the chicken before adding some broth to the skillet to allow the chicken to gently finish cooking.

STUFFED CHICKEN BREASTS
SERVES 4

To make butterflying the chicken easier, freeze it for 15 minutes. If the chicken breasts come with the tenderloin attached, pull them off and reserve them to make the puree in step 2. Because the stuffing contains raw chicken, it is important to check its temperature in step 6.

CHICKEN
- 4 (8-ounce) boneless, skinless chicken breasts, tenderloins removed, trimmed
- 3 tablespoons vegetable oil
- 10 ounces white mushrooms, trimmed and sliced thin
- 1 small leek, white part only, halved lengthwise, sliced thin, and washed thoroughly
- 2 garlic cloves, minced
- ½ teaspoon chopped fresh thyme
- 1 tablespoon lemon juice
- ½ cup dry white wine
- 1 tablespoon chopped fresh parsley
   Salt and pepper
- 1 cup low-sodium chicken broth

SAUCE
- 1 teaspoon Dijon mustard
- 2 tablespoons unsalted butter, cut into 2 pieces

1. FOR THE CHICKEN: Slice each chicken breast horizontally, stopping ½ inch from edges so halves remain attached. Pound between 2 sheets of plastic wrap to even ¼-inch thickness (each cutlet should measure about 8 by 6 inches) with meat pounder. Trim about ½ inch from long sides of cutlets (about 1½ to 2 ounces of meat per cutlet, or total of ½ cup from all 4 cutlets) to form rectangles that measure about 8 by 5 inches. Transfer chicken cutlets to plate, cover, and refrigerate while making stuffing.

2. Process all trimmings in food

processor until smooth, about 20 seconds. Transfer puree to medium bowl and set aside. (Do not wash food processor bowl.)

3. Heat 1 tablespoon oil in 12-inch skillet over medium-high heat until shimmering. Add mushrooms and cook, stirring occasionally, until softened and lightly browned, 8 to 10 minutes. Stir in 1 tablespoon oil and leek and cook, stirring often, until leek is softened, 2 to 4 minutes. Stir in garlic and thyme and cook until fragrant, about 30 seconds. Stir in 1½ teaspoons lemon juice and cook until all moisture has evaporated, about 30 seconds. Transfer mixture to food processor. Add wine to now-empty skillet, scraping up any browned bits. Transfer wine to small bowl and set aside. Rinse and dry skillet.

4. Pulse mushroom mixture in food processor until roughly chopped, about 5 pulses. Transfer mushroom mixture to bowl with pureed chicken. Add 1½ teaspoons parsley, ¾ teaspoon salt, and ½ teaspoon pepper. Using rubber spatula, fold together stuffing ingredients until well combined (you should have about 1½ cups stuffing).

5. TO ASSEMBLE AND COOK: With thinnest ends of cutlets pointing away from you, spread one-quarter of stuffing evenly over each cutlet with rubber spatula, leaving ¾-inch border along short sides of cutlet and ¼-inch border along long sides. Roll each breast up as tightly as possible without squeezing out filling and place on plate seam side down. Evenly space 3 pieces of kitchen twine (each about 12 inches long) beneath each breast and tie, trimming any excess.

6. Season chicken with salt and pepper. Heat remaining 1 tablespoon oil in skillet over medium-high heat until just smoking. Add chicken bundles and brown on all sides, about 8 minutes per side. Add broth and reserved wine to skillet and bring to boil. Reduce heat to low, cover, and cook until chicken bundles register 160 degrees, 12 to 18 minutes. Transfer chicken to carving board and tent loosely with aluminum foil.

7. FOR THE SAUCE AND TO SERVE: While chicken rests, whisk mustard into cooking liquid, scraping up any browned bits. Bring to simmer over high heat and cook until dark brown and measures ½ cup, 7 to 10 minutes. Off heat, whisk in butter, 1 piece at a time, remaining 1½ teaspoons lemon juice, and remaining 1½ teaspoons parsley. Season with salt and pepper to taste. Remove twine and cut each chicken bundle on bias into 6 medallions. Spoon sauce over chicken and serve.

CHICKEN KIEV

✔ WHY THIS RECIPE WORKS
Chicken Kiev has developed a reputation as bad banquet fare. We wanted to bring this dish back to its roots as an elegant dish of crisply breaded chicken packed with a flavorful herb butter. We butterflied the cutlets and pounded them thin (even thinner at the edges) so that we could roll the chicken up snugly and completely encase the butter, which prevented it from leaking out. Chilling the rolled cutlets for an hour in the refrigerator further sealed the seams. Toasting the bread crumbs prior to coating the chicken allowed us to skip the step of pan-frying so we could cook the chicken entirely in the oven.

CHICKEN KIEV
SERVES 4

To make butterflying the chicken easier, freeze it for 15 minutes.

HERB BUTTER
8	tablespoons unsalted butter, softened
1	tablespoon lemon juice
1	tablespoon minced shallot
1	tablespoon minced fresh parsley
½	teaspoon minced fresh tarragon

STUFFING CHICKEN BREASTS

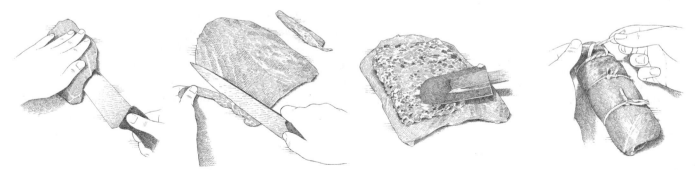

1. Slice each breast horizontally, stopping ½ inch from edges so halves remain attached.

2. After pounding each butterflied chicken breast to uniform ¼-inch thickness, trim about ½ inch from long sides of each cutlet to form 8 by 5-inch rectangle.

3. Spread stuffing evenly over each cutlet, leaving ¾-inch border along short sides and ¼-inch border along long sides.

4. With short side facing you, roll up each cutlet and secure it snugly with kitchen twine.

⅜ teaspoon salt

⅛ teaspoon pepper

CHICKEN

4 slices hearty white sandwich bread, torn into quarters

2 tablespoons vegetable oil

Salt and pepper

4 (8-ounce) boneless, skinless chicken breasts, tenderloins removed, trimmed

1 cup all-purpose flour

3 large eggs

1 teaspoon Dijon mustard

1. FOR THE HERB BUTTER: Mix all ingredients in medium bowl with rubber spatula until thoroughly combined. Form into 3-inch square on sheet of plastic wrap; wrap tightly and refrigerate until firm, about 1 hour.

2. FOR THE CHICKEN: Adjust oven rack to the lower-middle position and heat oven to 300 degrees. Pulse bread in food processor to coarse crumbs, about 10 pulses; transfer to large bowl. Transfer crumbs to large bowl, add oil, ⅛ teaspoon salt, and ⅛ teaspoon pepper and toss until crumbs are evenly coated. Spread crumbs on rimmed baking sheet and bake until golden brown and dry, about 25 minutes, stirring twice during baking. Let cool to room temperature.

3. Slice each chicken breast horizontally, stopping ½ inch from edges so halves remain attached. Pound between 2 sheets of plastic wrap to even ¼-inch thickness with meat pounder. Pound outer perimeter to ⅛ inch. Unwrap herb butter and cut it into 4 rectangular pieces. Pat chicken dry with paper towels, place on counter, and season with salt and pepper. Position breasts cut side up and place 1 piece of butter in center of bottom half of each breast. Roll bottom edge of chicken over butter, then fold in sides and

ASSEMBLING CHICKEN KIEV

1. Place butter piece near tapered end of cutlet and roll up end to cover completely. Fold in sides and continue rolling to form cylinder, pressing on seam to seal. Refrigerate.

2. After dredging chilled, rolled chicken bundles in flour, shake off excess, then roll in egg mixture, letting excess drip off.

3. Roll chicken bundles in bread crumbs, pressing to adhere crumbs to chicken.

continue rolling to form a neat, tight bundle, pressing on seam to seal. Repeat with remaining butter and chicken. Refrigerate chicken, uncovered, to allow edges to seal, about 1 hour.

4. Adjust oven rack to middle position and heat oven to 350 degrees. Set wire rack in rimmed baking sheet. Combine flour, ¼ teaspoon salt, and ⅛ teaspoon pepper in shallow dish or pie plate. Lightly beat eggs and mustard together in second dish. Place bread crumbs in third dish. Working with 1 chicken bundle at a time, dredge in flour, shaking off the excess, then coat with egg mixture, allowing excess to drip off. Coat all sides of chicken bundle with bread crumbs, pressing gently so that crumbs adhere. Place on prepared wire rack.

5. Bake chicken until center of bundles register 160 degrees, 40 to 45 minutes. Let rest for 5 minutes before serving.

TO MAKE AHEAD: Unbaked, breaded chicken Kiev can be refrigerated overnight and baked the next day or frozen for up to 1 month. To cook frozen chicken Kiev, increase the baking time to 50 to 55 minutes (do not thaw the chicken).

GLAZED CHICKEN BREASTS

✔ WHY THIS RECIPE WORKS

Glazed chicken has a reputation for being humdrum at best, overly sweet at worst. To elevate this dish to an elegant weeknight dinner, we knew the chicken needed to have perfectly rendered skin and moist meat sufficiently coated with a complexly flavored glaze. We started by browning the chicken on the stovetop, setting it aside to prepare the sauce in the same pan, and then finished cooking it in the oven. We found that a combination of orange juice, corn syrup, and honey gave us a thick and not-too-sweet glaze (corn syrup has half as much sugar as other sweeteners) and it also helped the meat seem juicier. Some minced shallot, vinegar, mustard, and red pepper flakes added complexity. Flouring the chicken prior to cooking helped the glaze cling to the chicken.

ORANGE-HONEY GLAZED CHICKEN BREASTS

SERVES 4

We prefer to split whole chicken breasts ourselves because store-bought split chicken breasts are often sloppily butchered. However, if you prefer to purchase split chicken breasts, try to choose 10- to 12-ounce pieces with skin intact. If the glaze looks dry during baking, add up to 2 tablespoons more orange juice to the pan.

1½ cups plus 2 tablespoons orange juice (4 oranges), plus extra as needed
⅓   cup light corn syrup
3   tablespoons honey
1   tablespoon Dijon mustard
1   tablespoon white vinegar
⅛   teaspoon red pepper flakes
    Salt and pepper
½   cup all-purpose flour
2   (1½-pound) whole bone-in chicken breasts, split through breastbone and trimmed
2   tablespoons vegetable oil
1   shallot, minced

1. Adjust oven rack to middle position and heat oven to 375 degrees. Whisk 1½ cups orange juice, corn syrup, honey, mustard, vinegar, pepper flakes, ⅛ teaspoon salt, and ⅛ teaspoon pepper together in bowl. Place flour in shallow dish or pie plate.

2. Pat chicken dry with paper towels and season with salt and pepper. Working with 1 breast at a time, dredge in flour mixture, shaking off excess, and transfer to large plate.

TRIMMING SPLIT CHICKEN BREASTS

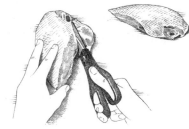

Using kitchen shears, trim off rib sections from each breast, following vertical line of fat from tapered end of breast up to socket where wing was attached.

3. Heat oil in 12-inch ovensafe skillet over medium heat until shimmering. Place chicken breasts skin side down in skillet and cook until well browned, 8 to 14 minutes, reducing heat if pan begins to scorch. Flip chicken skin side up and continue to cook until lightly browned on second side, about 5 minutes. Transfer chicken to clean plate.

4. Pour off all but 1 teaspoon fat from skillet. Add shallot and cook over medium heat until softened, about 2 minutes. Add orange juice mixture, bring to simmer, and cook, stirring occasionally, until syrupy and measures 1 cup, 6 to 10 minutes. Remove skillet from heat and tilt to one side so glaze pools in corner of pan. Using tongs, roll each chicken breast in pooled glaze to coat evenly and place, skin side down, in skillet.

5. Transfer skillet to oven and bake until chicken registers 160 degrees, 25 to 30 minutes, flipping chicken skin side up halfway through baking.

6. Using potholders (skillet handle will be hot) remove skillet from oven. Transfer chicken to serving platter and let rest while making sauce. Meanwhile, being careful of hot skillet handle, return skillet to high heat and cook glaze, stirring constantly, until thick and syrupy, about 1 minute. Off heat, whisk in remaining 2 tablespoons orange juice. Spoon 1 teaspoon glaze over each breast and serve, passing remaining glaze separately.

APPLE-MAPLE GLAZED CHICKEN BREASTS

Substitute apple cider for orange juice and 2 tablespoons maple syrup for honey.

PINEAPPLE–BROWN SUGAR GLAZED CHICKEN BREASTS

Substitute pineapple juice for orange juice and 2 tablespoons brown sugar for honey.

PAN-ROASTED CHICKEN BREASTS

✔ WHY THIS RECIPE WORKS

Bone-in, skin-on chicken breasts offer more flavor than their boneless, skinless counterparts, but getting the skin to crisp without overcooking the delicate breast meat can be a challenge. For the best results, we turned to pan-roasting, a restaurant technique in which food is browned in a skillet on the stovetop and then slid, skillet and all, into a hot oven to finish cooking. Brining the chicken ensured the meat stayed moist and flavorful. We then browned the chicken on all sides on the stovetop before placing the skillet in the oven. Cooking the chicken at 450 degrees allowed the skin to crisp while the meat cooked through relatively quickly. Finally, we used the caramelized drippings, or fond, left in the pan to make a quick and flavorful sauce.

PAN-ROASTED CHICKEN BREASTS WITH SAGE-VERMOUTH SAUCE

SERVES 4

We prefer to split whole chicken breasts ourselves because store-bought split chicken breasts are often sloppily butchered. However, if you prefer to purchase split chicken breasts, try to choose 10- to 12-ounce pieces with skin intact. If using kosher chicken, do not brine in step 1, and season with salt as well as pepper. The chicken can be prepared without the pan sauce; if not making a pan sauce, let the chicken rest for 5 minutes before serving in step 4.

CHICKEN
½   cup salt
2   (1½-pound) whole bone-in chicken breasts, split through breastbone and trimmed
    Pepper
1   tablespoon vegetable oil

SAUCE

I large shallot, minced
¾ cup low-sodium chicken broth
½ cup dry vermouth
4 fresh sage leaves, each leaf torn in half
3 tablespoons unsalted butter, cut into 3 pieces and chilled
Salt and pepper

I. FOR THE CHICKEN: Dissolve salt in 2 quarts cold water in large container. Submerge chicken in brine, cover, and refrigerate for 30 to 60 minutes. Remove chicken from brine and pat dry with paper towels. Season chicken with pepper.

2. Adjust oven rack to lowest position and heat oven to 450 degrees. Heat oil in 12-inch ovensafe skillet over medium-high heat until just smoking. Place chicken breasts skin side down in skillet and cook until well browned, 6 to 8 minutes, reducing heat if pan begins to scorch. Flip chicken skin side up and continue to cook until lightly browned on second side, about 3 minutes.

3. Flip chicken skin side down and transfer skillet to oven. Roast until chicken registers 160 degrees, 15 to 18 minutes.

4. Using potholders (skillet handle will be hot) remove skillet from oven. Transfer chicken to serving platter and let rest while making sauce (if not making sauce, let chicken rest 5 minutes before serving).

5. FOR THE SAUCE: Being careful of hot skillet handle, pour off all but 1 teaspoon fat left in skillet, add shallot, and cook over medium-high heat until softened, about 2 minutes. Stir in chicken broth, vermouth, and sage leaves, scraping up any browned bits. Bring to simmer and cook until thickened and measures ¾ cup, about 5 minutes. Stir in any accumulated chicken juices; return to simmer and cook for 30 seconds.

6. Off heat, discard sage leaves and whisk in butter 1 piece at a time. Season with salt and pepper to taste. Pour sauce over chicken and serve immediately.

PAN-ROASTED CHICKEN BREASTS WITH GARLIC-SHERRY SAUCE

Substitute 7 sliced garlic cloves for shallot and cook, stirring often, until garlic turns golden but not brown, about 1½ minutes. Substitute dry sherry for dry vermouth and 2 sprigs fresh thyme for sage leaves. Stir ½ teaspoon lemon juice into sauce before seasoning with salt and pepper.

PAN-ROASTED CHICKEN BREASTS WITH ONION AND ALE SAUCE

Brown ale gives this sauce a nutty, toasty, bittersweet flavor. Newcastle Brown Ale and Samuel Smith Nut Brown Ale are good choices.

Substitute ½ onion, sliced very thin, for shallot and cook until onion is softened, about 5 minutes. Substitute ½ cup brown ale for dry vermouth and 1 sprig fresh thyme for sage. Stir 1 bay leaf and 1 tablespoon brown sugar into skillet along with chicken broth. Stir ½ teaspoon cider vinegar into sauce before seasoning with salt and pepper.

PAN-ROASTED CHICKEN BREASTS WITH SWEET-TART RED WINE SAUCE

This sauce is a variation on the Italian sweet-sour flavor combination called agrodolce.

Substitute ¼ cup red wine and ¼ cup red wine vinegar for dry vermouth and 1 bay leaf for sage leaves. Stir 1 tablespoon sugar and ¼ teaspoon pepper into skillet with chicken broth.

ROASTED CHICKEN BREASTS

✔ WHY THIS RECIPE WORKS

Recipes for roasted chicken breasts often produce bland, dry meat and flabby skin. Attempts to cover up such disappointment with potent ingredients only make matters worse for this simple dish. We discovered that cooking whole (rather than split) breasts helped the meat retain more moisture. Before serving, we simply carved the meat off the bone into thin slices for an attractive presentation. Elevating the meat was also key: we not only perched the chicken on the slotted top of a broiler pan, but also created a natural rack by pulling out the rib cage on each side of the whole breast so that it could stand up on its own, allowing the heat to circulate evenly around the meat. Gently separating the skin from the meat and rubbing butter and salt underneath the skin and oil on top further guaranteed ultra-crisp skin and well-seasoned meat.

ROASTED CHICKEN BREASTS
SERVES 4

To make sure that the breasts cook at the same rate, purchase 2 similarly sized whole breasts (not split breasts) with skins fully intact. Whole chicken breasts weighing about 1½ pounds work best because they require a cooking time long enough to ensure that the skin will brown and crisp nicely.

2 tablespoons unsalted butter, softened
Salt and pepper
2 (1½-pound) whole bone-in chicken breasts, trimmed
I tablespoon vegetable oil

I. Adjust oven rack to middle position and heat oven to 450 degrees. Set wire rack in aluminum foil–lined rimmed baking sheet.

2. Combine butter and ¼ teaspoon salt in bowl. Pat chicken dry with paper towels. Using your hands or handle of wooden spoon, gently loosen center portions of skin covering each breast. Place butter (about 1½ teaspoons per breast) under skin, directly on meat in center of each breast. Gently press on skin to distribute butter evenly over meat. Rub skin with oil and season with pepper. Set chicken breasts on prepared wire rack, propping up breasts on rib bones.

3. Roast until chicken registers 160 degrees, 35 to 40 minutes. Transfer chicken to carving board and let rest for 5 minutes. Carve chicken and serve.

ROASTED CHICKEN BREASTS WITH HERBS AND PORCINI MUSHROOMS

Microwave ¼ cup water and 2 tablespoons dried porcini mushrooms in covered bowl until steaming, about 1 minute. Let stand until softened, about 5 minutes. Drain mushrooms through fine-mesh strainer lined with coffee filter, discarding liquid and finely chopping mushrooms.

Mix chopped mushrooms, 1 teaspoon minced fresh thyme, and 1 teaspoon minced fresh rosemary into softened butter along with salt.

ROASTED CHICKEN BREASTS WITH GARLIC, ROSEMARY, AND LEMON

Mix 2 minced garlic cloves, 2 teaspoons minced fresh rosemary, and 1 teaspoon grated lemon zest into softened butter along with salt.

ROASTED CHICKEN BREASTS WITH CHIPOTLE, CUMIN, AND CILANTRO

Mix 2 teaspoons minced canned chipotle chile in adobo, 1 teaspoon ground cumin, and 2 teaspoons chopped fresh cilantro into softened butter along with salt.

ROASTED CHICKEN BREASTS WITH OLIVES, PARSLEY, AND LEMON

Mix 1 tablespoon chopped pitted kalamata olives, 1 teaspoon grated lemon zest, and 2 teaspoons chopped fresh parsley into softened butter along with salt.

PREPARING CHICKEN BREASTS FOR ROASTING

1. Gently lift skin at bottom of breast to create small pocket for butter.

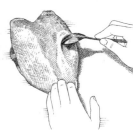

2. Using your fingers or small spoon, place one-quarter of butter in center of each breast. Gently press on skin to spread butter over meat.

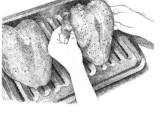

3. Carefully pull out rib cage from each side of breast to create stable base.

PAN-ROASTED CHICKEN

✔ WHY THIS RECIPE WORKS

Roasting a whole chicken requires some planning, and even then it can be a challenge to cook. We wanted to shorten the preparation and cooking time without sacrificing crisp skin. To do so, we turned to pan-roasting. We cut up a whole chicken into eight pieces, which fit comfortably in a 12-inch skillet. Brining took just 30 minutes and added welcome flavor and moisture. Before roasting the chicken pieces, we browned them on both sides in oil on the stovetop, turned the chicken skin side down, then slid the pan into a 450-degree oven to finish cooking. The whole process took only 20 minutes. Once the chicken was removed from the skillet, the fond was crusty and plentiful, so we needed only a handful of ingredients—some minced shallot, chicken broth, vermouth, thyme, and butter—to turn it into a flavorful sauce.

PAN-ROASTED CHICKEN WITH SHALLOT AND VERMOUTH SAUCE
SERVES 4

If using kosher chicken, do not brine in step 1, and season with salt as well as pepper. The chicken can be prepared without the pan sauce; if not making the pan sauce, let the chicken rest for 5 minutes before serving in step 4.

CHICKEN
½   cup salt
1   (3½- to 4-pound) whole chicken, cut into 8 pieces (4 breast pieces, 2 drumsticks, 2 thighs), wings discarded
    Pepper
1   tablespoon vegetable oil

SAUCE
1   large shallot, minced
¾   cup low-sodium chicken broth
½   cup dry vermouth

2 sprigs fresh thyme

3 tablespoons unsalted butter, cut
   into 3 pieces and chilled
   Salt and pepper

1. FOR THE CHICKEN: Dissolve salt in 2 quarts cold water in large container. Submerge chicken in brine, cover, and refrigerate for 30 to 60 minutes. Remove chicken from brine and pat dry with paper towels. Season chicken with pepper.

2. Adjust oven rack to lowest position and heat oven to 450 degrees. Heat oil in 12-inch ovensafe skillet over medium-high heat until just smoking. Place chicken skin side down in skillet and cook until well browned, 6 to 8 minutes, reducing heat if pan begins to scorch. Flip chicken skin side up and continue to cook until lightly browned on second side, about 3 minutes.

3. Flip chicken skin side down and transfer skillet to oven. Roast chicken until breasts register 160 degrees and thighs and drumsticks register 175 degrees, about 10 minutes longer.

4. Using potholders (skillet handle will be hot) remove skillet from oven. Transfer chicken to serving platter and let rest while making sauce (if not making sauce, let chicken rest 5 minutes before serving).

5. FOR THE SAUCE: Being careful of hot skillet handle, pour off all but 1 teaspoon fat left in skillet, add shallot, and cook over medium-high heat until softened, about 2 minutes. Stir in chicken broth, vermouth, and thyme sprigs, scraping up any browned bits. Bring to simmer and cook until thickened and measures ⅔ cup, about 6 minutes Stir in any accumulated chicken juices; return to simmer and cook for 30 seconds. Off heat, discard thyme sprigs and whisk in butter, 1 piece at a time. Season with salt and pepper to taste. Pour sauce over chicken and serve immediately.

PAN-ROASTED CHICKEN WITH SHERRY-ROSEMARY SAUCE

Substitute ½ cup dry sherry for dry vermouth and 2 sprigs fresh rosemary for thyme sprigs.

PAN-ROASTED CHICKEN WITH COGNAC-MUSTARD SAUCE

Be sure to add the broth to the skillet before adding the cognac.

Substitute ¼ cup white wine and ¼ cup cognac or brandy for dry vermouth and 1 tablespoon Dijon mustard for 1 tablespoon of butter.

CHICKEN WITH 40 CLOVES OF GARLIC

WHY THIS RECIPE WORKS

Chicken with 40 cloves of garlic is a classic French braise, but too often this dish falls short, with chalky chicken, flabby skin, and washed-out garlic flavor. We wanted full-flavored chicken with crisp brown skin, spreadable garlic with a sweet, nutty flavor, and a savory sauce to unite the two. We replaced a long-cooking whole bird with a cut-up chicken that would braise faster and more evenly. First, we roasted the garlic cloves, then we added the braising liquid (chicken broth and dry vermouth) to the chicken. To achieve moist meat and browned skin, we

CUTTING UP A WHOLE CHICKEN

1. With sharp chef's knife, cut through skin around leg where it attaches to breast.

2. Using both hands, pop leg out of its socket. With chef's knife, cut through flesh and skin to detach leg from body.

3. A line of fat separates thigh and drumstick. Cut through joint at this point with chef's knife. Repeat steps 1 through 3 with other leg.

4. Bend wing out from breast and use boning knife to cut through joint. Repeat with other wing.

5. Using kitchen shears, cut along ribs to completely separate back from breast. Discard backbone.

6. Place chef's knife directly on breastbone, then apply pressure to cut through and separate breast into halves. If necessary, cut each breast in half crosswise into 2 pieces.

browned the chicken on top of the stove before transferring it to the oven to finish cooking and broiled it briefly to crisp the skin.

CHICKEN WITH 40 CLOVES OF GARLIC

SERVES 4

If using kosher chicken, do not brine in step 1, and season with salt as well as pepper. Try not to purchase heads of garlic that contain enormous cloves; if unavoidable, increase the foil-covered baking time to 40 to 45 minutes so that the largest cloves soften fully. A Dutch oven can be used in place of a skillet, if you prefer. Broiling the chicken for a few minutes at the end of cooking crisps the skin, but this step is optional. Serve the dish with slices of crusty baguette for dipping into the sauce and spreading with the roasted garlic cloves. See page 333 for information on cutting up a whole chicken.

   Salt and pepper
1 (3½- to 4-pound) whole chicken, cut into 8 pieces (4 breast pieces, 2 drumsticks, 2 thighs), wings discarded
3 large garlic heads, cloves separated and unpeeled
2 shallots, peeled and quartered lengthwise
5 teaspoons olive oil
2 sprigs fresh thyme
1 sprig fresh rosemary
1 bay leaf
¾ cup dry vermouth or dry white wine
¾ cup low-sodium chicken broth
2 tablespoons unsalted butter, cut into 2 pieces and chilled

1. Dissolve ½ cup salt in 2 quarts cold water in large container. Submerge chicken in brine, cover, and refrigerate for 30 to 60 minutes. Remove chicken from brine and pat dry with paper towels. Season chicken with pepper.

2. Meanwhile, adjust oven rack to middle position and heat oven to 400 degrees. Toss garlic and shallots with 2 teaspoons oil, ¼ teaspoon salt, and ¼ teaspoon pepper in shallow dish or pie plate; cover tightly with aluminum foil and roast until softened and beginning to brown, about 30 minutes, shaking dish once to toss contents after 15 minutes (foil can be left on during tossing). Uncover, stir, and continue to roast, uncovered, until garlic is browned and fully tender, 10 minutes longer, stirring halfway through cooking. Remove from oven and increase oven temperature to 450 degrees.

3. Using kitchen twine, tie together thyme sprigs, rosemary sprig, and bay leaf; set aside. Heat remaining 1 tablespoon oil in 12-inch ovensafe skillet over medium-high heat until just smoking. Place chicken skin side down in skillet and cook until well browned, 6 to 8 minutes, reducing heat if pan begins to scorch. Flip chicken skin side up and continue to cook until lightly browned on second side, about 3 minutes. Transfer chicken to large plate and pour off all fat left in skillet. Off heat, add vermouth, chicken broth, and herb bundle to now-empty skillet, scraping up any browned bits. Set skillet over medium heat, add garlic mixture, then nestle chicken pieces, skin side up, on top of and between garlic cloves.

4. Transfer skillet to oven and roast chicken until breast pieces register 160 degrees and thighs and drumsticks register 175 degrees, 10 to 12 minutes. If desired, heat broiler and broil chicken to crisp skin, 3 to 5 minutes.

5. Using potholders (skillet handle will be hot), remove skillet from oven. Transfer chicken to serving platter. Remove 10 to 12 garlic cloves with slotted spoon and reserve. Remove remaining garlic cloves and shallots with slotted spoon and transfer to platter with chicken. Discard herb bundle. Place reserved garlic cloves in fine-mesh strainer. With rubber spatula, push garlic cloves through strainer into bowl; discard skins. Add garlic paste to sauce in skillet and bring to simmer, whisking occasionally to incorporate garlic. Season with salt and pepper to taste. Off heat, whisk in butter. Serve chicken, passing sauce separately.

QUICKER STOVETOP ROAST CHICKEN

✔ WHY THIS RECIPE WORKS
Roasting chicken in the oven is the usual route to crisp skin, but sometimes your oven is crowded with side dishes or dessert. We wanted to cook chicken entirely on the stovetop—and we wanted crisp, golden skin, evenly cooked meat, and a flavorful pan sauce. In addition, we wanted this recipe to be relatively quick, so we opted not to brine. We tried simply browning the chicken and then turning down the heat to cook it through; we also tried browning the chicken and then adding some liquid to the pan, but neither approach worked. Nor did reversing the order of the steps—steaming the chicken and then searing. After trying every possible approach, we realized a multistep process of searing the chicken, steaming it, and then searing it again gave us the results we wanted. With a flavorful fond left in the skillet, we made a quick pan sauce with shallot, lemon juice, herbs, and butter.

STOVETOP ROAST CHICKEN WITH LEMON-HERB SAUCE

SERVES 4

A whole 4-pound chicken, cut into 8 pieces, can be used instead of the chicken parts. If using large chicken breasts (about 1 pound each), cut each breast into 3 pieces. If using smaller breasts (10 to 12 ounces each), cut each breast into 2 pieces.

   CHICKEN
3½ pounds bone-in chicken pieces (split breasts cut in half, drumsticks, and/or thighs), trimmed
   Salt and pepper

1   tablespoon vegetable oil
¾–1¼   cups low-sodium chicken broth

SAUCE
1   teaspoon vegetable oil
1   shallot, minced
1   teaspoon all-purpose flour
1½   tablespoons minced fresh parsley
1½   tablespoons minced fresh chives
1   tablespoon lemon juice
1   tablespoon unsalted butter, chilled
   Salt and pepper

1. FOR THE CHICKEN: Pat chicken dry with paper towels and season with salt and pepper. Heat 2 teaspoons oil in 12-inch nonstick skillet over medium-high heat until just smoking. Place chicken skin side down in skillet and cook until well browned, 6 to 8 minutes, reducing heat if pan begins to scorch. Flip chicken skin side up. Reduce heat to medium-low, add ¾ cup of broth to skillet, cover, and cook until breast pieces register 155 degrees and thighs and/or drumsticks register 170 degrees, 10 to 16 minutes. Transfer chicken to plate, skin side up.

2. Pour off all liquid from skillet into liquid measuring cup and reserve. Wipe out skillet with paper towels. Heat remaining 1 teaspoon oil in now-empty skillet over medium-high heat until shimmering. Return chicken, skin side down, to skillet and cook undisturbed until skin is deep golden brown and crisp, breast pieces register 160 degrees, and thighs and/or drumsticks register 175 degrees, 4 to 7 minutes. (Smaller pieces may cook faster than larger pieces. Remove pieces from skillet as they reach correct temperature.) Transfer chicken to serving platter and tent loosely with aluminum foil. Using spoon, skim any fat from reserved cooking liquid and add enough broth to measure ¾ cup.

3. FOR THE SAUCE: Heat oil in now-empty skillet over low heat. Add shallot and cook, stirring often, until softened, about 2 minutes. Add flour and cook, stirring

constantly, for 30 seconds. Increase heat to medium-high and slowly whisk in reserved cooking liquid, scraping up any browned bits. Bring to rapid simmer and cook until reduced to ½ cup, 2 to 3 minutes. Stir in any accumulated chicken juices; return to simmer, and cook for 30 seconds. Off heat, whisk in parsley, chives, lemon juice, and butter. Season with salt and pepper to taste. Pour sauce around chicken and serve immediately.

STOVETOP ROAST CHICKEN WITH SPICY THAI SAUCE

Omit sauce ingredients. Add ¼ cup sugar, 2 tablespoons lime juice, 1 tablespoon fish sauce, 2 minced garlic cloves, and 1 teaspoon Thai red curry paste to now-empty skillet in step 3. Cook over medium-high heat, scraping up any browned bits, until sauce is thickened and spoon leaves wide trail when dragged through sauce, about 2 minutes. Stir in reserved cooking liquid, return to simmer, and cook until reduced to ½ cup, 2 to 3 minutes. Stir in any accumulated chicken juices; return to simmer, and cook for 30 seconds. Off heat, stir in 2 tablespoons chopped fresh cilantro and 1 tablespoon lime juice. Pour sauce around chicken and serve immediately.

STOVETOP ROAST CHICKEN WITH GRAPEFRUIT-TARRAGON SAUCE

Omit sauce ingredients. Cut away rind and pith from 1 grapefruit. Cut segments into ½-inch pieces and reserve ½ cup juice. Heat 1 teaspoon vegetable oil in now-empty skillet over medium-high heat in step 3. Add 1 minced shallot and cook, stirring often, until softened, about 2 minutes. Stir in reserved cooking liquid and reserved grapefruit juice, scraping up any browned bits. Bring to rapid simmer and cook until reduced to ¼ cup, 4 to 6 minutes. Stir in grapefruit segments, 1 tablespoon honey, and any accumulated chicken juices; return

to simmer and cook for 30 seconds. Off heat, stir in 1 tablespoon chopped fresh tarragon and 1 tablespoon chilled butter. Season with salt and pepper to taste. Pour sauce around chicken and serve immediately.

STOVETOP ROAST CHICKEN WITH SAKE GLAZE

Omit sauce ingredients. Whisk 3 tablespoons sugar, 3 tablespoons soy sauce, and 1 teaspoon cornstarch together in bowl. Add ¾ cup sake, reserved cooking liquid, and soy sauce mixture to now-empty skillet in step 3. Cook over medium-high heat, scraping up any browned bits, until reduced to ½ cup, about 6 minutes. Stir in any accumulated chicken juices; return to simmer, and cook for 30 seconds. Off heat, whisk in 2 tablespoons chilled butter and 2 tablespoons thinly sliced scallion. Pour sauce around chicken and serve immediately.

CLASSIC ROAST CHICKEN

✔ WHY THIS RECIPE WORKS
Roasting chicken should be a simple affair, but getting the white and dark meat to cook at the same rate while also developing crisp, golden skin is often a challenge. After testing almost every variable we could think of—oven temperature, turning the bird halfway through cooking, basting, and trussing—we found that roasting a chicken is actually quite easy as long as you use the proper technique. Roasting the chicken at 400 degrees for the duration of cooking (rather than adjusting the temperature partway) worked best. Continuous basting didn't improve our roast chicken; we found that applying butter under the skin and rubbing the bird with olive oil before it went into the oven gave it great color and a crisp texture. Trussing also proved unnecessary; the dark meat cooked more quickly when left untrussed. The only extra step we found truly important was turning the bird twice for evenly cooked meat and crisp, browned skin.

CLASSIC ROAST CHICKEN
SERVES 2 TO 3

If using kosher chicken, do not brine in step 1, and season with salt as well as pepper in step 3. We recommend using a V-rack to roast the chicken. If you don't have a V-rack, set the bird on a regular roasting rack and use balls of aluminum foil to keep the roasting chicken propped up on its side.

½	cup salt
½	cup sugar
1	(3-pound) whole chicken, giblets discarded
2	tablespoons unsalted butter, softened
1	tablespoon olive oil
	Pepper

1. Dissolve salt and sugar in 2 quarts cold water in large container. Submerge chicken in brine, cover, and refrigerate for 1 hour. Remove chicken from brine and pat dry with paper towels.

2. Adjust oven rack to lower-middle position, place roasting pan on rack, and heat oven to 400 degrees. Coat V-rack with vegetable oil spray and set aside.

3. Use your fingers to gently loosen center portion of skin covering each breast; place butter under skin, directly on meat in center of each breast. Gently press on skin

APPLYING BUTTER UNDER SKIN

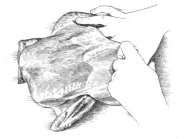

Loosen skin on breasts and thighs of chicken by sliding your fingers between skin and meat.

1. Cut chicken where leg meets breast.

2. Pull leg quarter away from carcass. Separate joint by gently pressing leg out to side and pushing up on joint.

3. Carefully cut through joint to remove leg quarter.

4. Cut through joint that connects drumstick to thigh. Repeat on second side to remove other leg.

5. Cut down along one side of breastbone, pulling breast meat away from you as you cut.

6. Remove wing from breast by cutting through wing joint. Slice breast into attractive slices.

to distribute butter over meat. Tuck wings behind back. Rub skin with oil, season with pepper, and place chicken, wing side up, on prepared V-rack. Place V-rack in preheated roasting pan and roast for 15 minutes.

4. Remove roasting pan from oven and, using 2 large wads of paper towels, rotate chicken so that opposite wing side is facing up. Return roasting pan to oven and roast for another 15 minutes.

5. Using 2 large wads of paper towels, rotate chicken again so that breast side is facing up and continue to roast until breast registers 160 degrees and thighs register 175 degrees, about 20 to 25 minutes longer. Transfer chicken to carving board and let rest for 10 minutes. Carve and serve immediately.

CRISP ROAST CHICKEN

✔ WHY THIS RECIPE WORKS

Most roast chicken recipes put juiciness and evenly cooked meat first and simply make do with so-so skin. Our goal was to create a roast chicken with super-crisp skin that would crackle with every bite. First we rubbed the chicken with a mixture of salt and baking powder, then let the chicken air-dry in the refrigerator overnight—this combination of steps dehydrated the skin, leading to a crunchier texture. But for the ultimate crisp skin, we need to provide an escape route for the rendered fat. Making a few incisions along the back of the bird, separating the skin from the meat, and poking holes in the skin of the breast and thighs allowed multiple channels for excess fat and juices to escape. Finally, we roasted the chicken at high heat until the skin was a perfect golden brown.

CRISP ROAST CHICKEN
SERVES 3 TO 4

Do not brine the bird; it will prohibit the skin from becoming crisp. The sheet of foil between the roasting pan and V-rack will keep drippings from burning and smoking.

- 1 (3½- to 4-pound) whole chicken, giblets discarded
- 1½ teaspoons salt
- 1 teaspoon baking powder
- ½ teaspoon pepper

1. Place chicken breast side down on cutting board. Insert tip of sharp knife to make four 1-inch incisions along back of chicken. Using your fingers, gently loosen skin covering breast and thighs. Using metal skewer, poke 15 to 20 holes in fat deposits on top of breast and thighs. Tuck wings behind back.

2. Combine salt, baking powder, and pepper in bowl. Pat chicken dry with paper towels and sprinkle evenly all over with salt mixture. Rub in mixture with hands, coating entire surface evenly. Set chicken breast side up in V-rack set on rimmed baking sheet and refrigerate, uncovered, for 12 to 24 hours.

3. Adjust oven rack to lowest position and heat oven to 450 degrees. Using paring knife, poke 20 holes about 1½ inches apart in 16 by 12-inch piece of aluminum foil. Place foil loosely in roasting pan. Flip chicken breast side down and set V-rack in prepared pan on top of foil. Roast chicken for 25 minutes.

4. Remove pan from oven. Using 2 large wads of paper towels, rotate chicken breast side up. Continue to roast until breast registers 135 degrees, 15 to 25 minutes.

5. Increase oven temperature to 500 degrees. Continue to roast chicken until skin is golden brown and crisp, breast registers 160 degrees, and thighs register 175 degrees, 10 to 20 minutes. Transfer chicken to carving board and let rest for 20 minutes. Carve and serve immediately.

ROAST LEMON CHICKEN

✔ **WHY THIS RECIPE WORKS**
For really great roast lemon chicken, we needed to bring out the full potential of the two main ingredients. We wanted evenly roasted, moist chicken with crisp skin and bright, pure lemon flavor—without a trace of bitterness. We brined the chicken for extra juiciness and then filled its cavity with a quartered lemon and garlic cloves before roasting. Once it was cooked, we cut the chicken into four pieces and broiled them to get evenly crisped skin. After trying to introduce more lemon flavor by adding strips of peel to the pan drippings, we discovered they were the source of the bitter flavor. Instead, we finished our roast chicken by adding some fresh lemon juice to a simple pan sauce of chicken broth, butter, and fresh herbs for the ultimate lemon flavor.

ROAST LEMON CHICKEN
SERVES 3 TO 4

If using kosher chicken, do not brine in step 1, and season with salt as well as pepper in step 3. Broiling the fully roasted and quartered chicken skin side up as it sits in a shallow pool of sauce crisps and browns the skin while keeping the meat succulent. If you decide to skip the broiling step, go directly from quartering the chicken to finishing the sauce with lemon juice, butter, and herbs.

- Salt and pepper
- 1 (3½- to 4-pound) whole chicken, giblets discarded
- 2 lemons
- 6 garlic cloves, lightly crushed and peeled
- 4 tablespoons unsalted butter, 2 tablespoons melted and 2 tablespoons cut into 2 pieces and chilled
- 1¾ cups low-sodium chicken broth
- 1 tablespoon minced fresh parsley
- 1 teaspoon minced fresh thyme

PREPARING CRISP ROAST CHICKEN

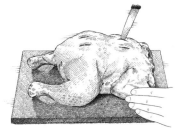

1. Cut incisions in skin along chicken's back to create openings for fat to escape.

2. Loosen skin from breast and thighs to allow rendering fat to trickle out.

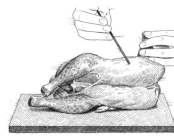

3. Poke holes in skin of breast and thighs to create additional channels for fat and juices to escape.

4. Apply rub; air-dry in refrigerator before roasting.

1. Dissolve ½ cup salt in 2 quarts cold water in large container. Submerge chicken in brine, cover, and refrigerate for 1 hour. Remove chicken from brine and pat dry with paper towels.

2. Adjust oven rack to lower-middle position and heat oven to 375 degrees. Set V-rack in flameproof roasting pan and lightly spray with vegetable oil spray.

3. Cut 1 lemon lengthwise into quarters. Place lemon quarters and garlic in cavity of chicken. Brush breast side of chicken with 1 tablespoon melted butter and season with pepper. Place chicken breast side down in V-rack, then brush back of chicken with remaining 1 tablespoon melted butter and season with pepper.

4. Roast chicken for 40 minutes. Remove pan from oven; increase oven temperature to 450 degrees. Using 2 large wads of paper towels, rotate chicken breast side up; add 1 cup chicken broth to pan. Return pan to oven and continue roasting until breast registers 160 degrees and thighs register 175 degrees, 35 to 40 minutes longer. Remove pan from oven; tip V-rack to let juices from chicken cavity run into roasting pan. Transfer chicken to carving board and let rest while making sauce. Remove V-rack from pan.

5. Adjust oven rack to upper-middle position and heat broiler. Remove fat from surface of drippings in pan using large spoon and stir in remaining ¾ cup chicken broth, scraping up any browned bits. Place pan over 2 burners, bring sauce to simmer, and cook until reduced to ½ cup, about 4 minutes. Remove from heat.

6. Discard lemons and garlic from chicken cavity. Cut chicken into quarters, adding any accumulated juices to pan. Place chicken quarters skin side up in sauce in pan; broil chicken until skin is crisp and deep golden brown, 3 to 5 minutes. Transfer chicken to serving platter.

7. Halve remaining lemon lengthwise; squeeze juice of 1 half into pan; cut remaining half into 4 wedges and set aside. Whisk chilled butter into sauce until combined; stir in parsley and thyme. Season with salt and pepper to taste. Serve chicken with sauce and lemon wedges.

ROAST CHICKEN WITH ROOT VEGETABLES

✔ WHY THIS RECIPE WORKS

Roasting some vegetables alongside a chicken should make for an easy one-dish meal. But getting both components to cook just right is a challenge, and most recipes focus on the chicken at the expense of the vegetables, which wind up greasy, with a mushy consistency. To our surprise, the best way to infuse the vegetables with great chicken flavor was to cook them separately. We added some broth to the pan partway through roasting the chicken (to prevent the fond from burning), then while the chicken was resting we prepared the vegetables. We simply tossed them with oil, salt, and pepper and placed them in the oven to roast. We then drizzled some of the reserved broth over the vegetables to infuse them with chicken flavor and put them under the broiler to allow the liquid to reduce to a glaze that coated the vegetables.

ROAST CHICKEN WITH ROOT VEGETABLES

SERVES 4 TO 6

If using kosher chicken, do not brine in step 1, and season with salt as well as pepper in step 2. If using a nonstick roasting pan, refrain from turning up the oven to broil when cooking the vegetables and stir them every 5 to 7 minutes to ensure they don't become too dark. If your broiler does not accommodate a roasting pan, continue to cook the vegetables at 500 degrees until done. We prefer to use small red potatoes in this recipe. Use potatoes that are 1½ to 2-inches in diameter; larger potatoes should be cut into halves or quarters. You can substitute the following seasonal vegetables for any of those in the recipe: beets, celery root, fennel, rutabagas, and turnips; peel these vegetables (except for the fennel) and cut them into 2- to 3-inch pieces.

CHICKEN

½ cup salt
½ cup sugar
2 garlic heads, cloves separated and lightly crushed
6 bay leaves, crumbled
1 (6- to 7-pound) whole chicken, giblets discarded
  Pepper
1 cup low-sodium chicken broth, plus extra as needed

VEGETABLES

1 pound small red potatoes
1 pound carrots, peeled and cut into 2- to 3-inch lengths, tapered ends left whole, large upper portions halved lengthwise
8 ounces parsnips, peeled and cut into 2- to 3-inch lengths, tapered ends left whole, large upper portions halved lengthwise
3 small onions, peeled, root end left intact, and quartered
3 tablespoons vegetable oil
½ teaspoon salt
⅛ teaspoon pepper

1. FOR THE CHICKEN: Dissolve salt and sugar in 2 quarts cold water in large container; stir in garlic and bay leaves. Submerge chicken in brine, cover, and refrigerate for 1 hour. Remove chicken from brine and pat dry with paper towels.

2. Adjust oven rack to middle position and heat oven to 400 degrees. Set V-rack in roasting pan and lightly spray with vegetable oil spray. Tuck chicken wings behind back and season chicken with pepper. Place chicken wing side up on prepared V-rack and roast for 30 minutes. Remove pan from oven and, using 2 large wads of paper towels, rotate chicken so that other wing side faces up; continue to roast for 30 minutes.

3. Remove pan from oven and, using 2 large wads of paper towels, turn chicken breast side up. Add broth to pan and continue to roast until chicken is golden brown, breast registers 160 degrees, and thighs register 175 degrees, about 40 minutes. (If pan begins to smoke and sizzle, add additional ½ cup broth to pan.) Transfer chicken to carving board and let rest while roasting vegetables. Remove V-rack from pan.

4. FOR THE VEGETABLES: While chicken is resting, adjust oven rack to middle position and increase oven temperature to 500 degrees. Using wooden spoon, scrape browned bits in pan and pour drippings into fat separator. Return now-empty pan to oven and heat until oven reaches 500 degrees, about 5 minutes.

5. Toss potatoes, carrots, parsnips, and onions with oil, salt, and pepper and scatter in single layer in pan, arranging potatoes and onions cut side down. Roast, without stirring, for 25 minutes.

6. While vegetables are roasting, measure out and reserve ½ cup liquid from fat separator; discard remaining liquid and fat (if necessary, add additional broth to make ½ cup). Remove pan from oven and heat broiler. Drizzle liquid over vegetables and broil, without stirring, for 5 minutes. Stir vegetables, coating well with juices, and continue to broil until tender and deep golden brown, about 5 minutes. Transfer vegetables to serving platter. While vegetables are broiling, carve chicken. Transfer to platter with vegetables and serve.

TWO ROAST CHICKENS WITH ROOT VEGETABLES

Substitute two 3- to 4-pound chickens for one 6- to 7-pound chicken. Reduce wing-side-up roasting time to 20 minutes per side in step 2. Continue to roast chicken as directed, reducing breast-side-up roasting time to 30 to 40 minutes.

GARLIC-ROSEMARY ROAST CHICKEN WITH JUS

WHY THIS RECIPE WORKS

Roast chicken infused with garlic and rosemary is a Tuscan classic, but the flavors can be overly aggressive. We wanted to harness the flavors of garlic and rosemary and unite them with a perfectly roasted chicken. Adding crushed garlic and rosemary to our brine was the first step toward subtly infusing the chicken with flavor. Rubbing a paste of olive oil, rosemary, and raw minced garlic under the skin of the breast and thighs was next for a pleasantly punchy bite. Finally, we created a sauce, using the pan drippings as the flavor base and adding wine, broth, rosemary, and mashed roasted garlic for a sweet, nutty finish.

GARLIC-ROSEMARY ROAST CHICKEN WITH JUS

SERVES 3 TO 4

If using kosher chicken, do not brine in step 1.

CHICKEN
Salt and pepper
12 garlic cloves, peeled, 10 cloves lightly crushed and 2 cloves minced
3 sprigs fresh rosemary plus 2 teaspoons minced
1 (3½- to 4-pound) whole chicken, giblets discarded
2 tablespoons extra-virgin olive oil

JUS
10 large garlic cloves, unpeeled
½ teaspoon extra-virgin olive oil
1¾ cups low-sodium chicken broth, plus extra as needed
½ cup water, plus extra as needed
¼ cup dry white wine or dry vermouth
1 sprig fresh rosemary
Salt and pepper

1. FOR THE CHICKEN: Dissolve ½ cup salt in 2 cups hot water in large container; stir in crushed garlic and rosemary sprigs and let sit for 10 minutes. Stir in 1½ quarts cold water. Submerge chicken in brine, cover, and refrigerate for 1 hour.

2. Adjust oven rack to lower-middle position and heat oven to 450 degrees. Set V-rack in roasting pan and lightly spray with vegetable oil spray. Combine 1 tablespoon oil, minced garlic, minced rosemary, ¼ teaspoon pepper, and ⅛ teaspoon salt in bowl.

3. Remove chicken from brine and pat dry with paper towels. Rub generous 1½ teaspoons garlic paste in cavity of chicken. Use your fingers to gently loosen center portion of skin covering each side of breast; place half of remaining paste under skin, directly on meat in center of each side of breast. Gently press on skin to distribute paste over meat. Tie ends of drumsticks together with kitchen twine and tuck wings behind back. Rub skin with 2 teaspoons oil and season with pepper. Set chicken breast side down on prepared V-rack and roast 15 minutes.

4. FOR THE JUS: While chicken is roasting, toss garlic with oil; after chicken has roasted for 15 minutes, scatter cloves in pan and continue to roast for 15 minutes longer.

5. Remove pan from oven; decrease oven temperature to 375 degrees. Using 2 large wads of paper towels, rotate chicken breast side up; brush breast with remaining 1 teaspoon oil. Place 1 cup broth and water in bottom of pan and continue to roast until chicken is light golden brown, breast registers 160 degrees, and thighs register 175 degrees, 20 to 25 minutes. (If pan begins to smoke and sizzle, add additional ½ cup broth to pan.) Remove pan from oven; tip V-rack to let juices from chicken cavity run into pan. Transfer chicken to carving board and let rest while making jus. Remove V-rack from pan.

6. Remove garlic cloves from pan with slotted spoon and transfer to cutting board. Using wooden spoon, scrape up browned bits in pan and pour drippings into 2-cup liquid measuring cup. Allow drippings to settle; meanwhile, peel garlic

and mash to paste with fork. Remove fat from surface of drippings using spoon (you should have about ⅔ cup skimmed liquid; if not, add additional water). Transfer liquid to small saucepan and stir in wine, rosemary sprig, remaining ¾ cup broth, and garlic paste. Bring to simmer and cook until reduced to 1 cup, about 8 minutes. Discard rosemary sprig. Season with salt and pepper to taste. Carve chicken, adding any accumulated juices to jus. Serve, passing jus separately

---

GARLIC-ROSEMARY ROAST CHICKEN WITH POTATOES

We prefer to use medium red potatoes, measuring about 2 inches in diameter, in this recipe.

Omit all jus ingredients except garlic. During first 15 minutes of roasting, toss 1½ pounds medium red potatoes, quartered, and garlic with 4½ teaspoons extra-virgin olive oil, ¼ teaspoon salt, and ¼ teaspoon pepper in bowl. After chicken has roasted for 15 minutes, scatter potatoes and garlic in single layer in pan; roast for another 15 minutes. Continue with recipe from step 5 as directed, omitting the addition of liquid to pan and stirring potatoes after rotating the chicken; when chicken is done, do not tip V-rack with roast chicken to allow juices to run into pan. While chicken rests, transfer potatoes and garlic to large paper towel–lined plate and pat with additional paper towels. Carve chicken and serve with potatoes and garlic.

GLAZED ROAST CHICKEN

✔ WHY THIS RECIPE WORKS
Glazed roast chicken sounds simple but actually presents a host of troubles, as the problems inherent in roasting chicken (dry breast meat, flabby skin, big deposits of fat under the skin) are compounded by the glaze (won't stick to the meat, burns in patches, introduces moisture

to already flabby skin). For our roast chicken, we wanted an evenly glazed chicken with crisp skin and moist meat. To dehydrate the skin and make it crisp, we separated it from the meat and poked holes in the fat deposits to allow rendered fat to escape, then rubbed the skin with salt and baking powder before vertically roasting the chicken—a technique usually associated with the grill. We found that resting the roasted bird before blasting it with higher heat resulted in the kind of burnished skin we were looking for, especially after we thickened the glaze with cornstarch to help it adhere to the bird.

GLAZED ROAST CHICKEN
SERVES 4 TO 6

For best results, use a 16-ounce can of beer. A larger can will work, but avoid using a 12-ounce can, as it will not support the weight of the chicken. A vertical poultry roaster can be used in place of the beer can, but we recommend only using a model that can be placed in a roasting pan. Taste your marmalade before using it; if it is overly sweet, reduce the amount of maple syrup in the glaze by 2 tablespoons.

CHICKEN
- 1 (6- to 7-pound) whole chicken, giblets discarded
- 2½ teaspoons salt
- 1 teaspoon baking powder
- 1 teaspoon pepper
- 1 (16-ounce) can beer

GLAZE
- 1 teaspoon cornstarch
- 1 tablespoon water, plus extra as needed
- ½ cup maple syrup
- ½ cup orange marmalade
- ¼ cup cider vinegar
- 2 tablespoons unsalted butter
- 2 tablespoons Dijon mustard
- 1 teaspoon pepper

1. FOR THE CHICKEN: Place chicken breast side down on cutting board. Use

tip of sharp knife to make four 1-inch incisions along back of chicken. Using your fingers, gently loosen skin covering breast and thighs. Using metal skewer, poke 15 to 20 holes in fat deposits on top of breast and thighs. Tuck wings behind back.

2. Combine salt, baking powder, and pepper in bowl. Pat chicken dry with paper towels and sprinkle evenly all over with salt mixture. Rub in mixture with hands, coating entire surface evenly. Set chicken, breast side up, on wire rack set in rimmed baking sheet and refrigerate, uncovered, for 30 to 60 minutes. Meanwhile, adjust oven rack to lowest position and heat oven to 325 degrees.

3. Open beer can and pour out (or drink) about half of liquid. Place can in middle of roasting pan and spray lightly with vegetable oil spray. Slide chicken over can so drumsticks reach down to bottom of can, chicken stands upright, and breast is perpendicular to bottom of pan. Roast chicken until skin starts to turn golden and breast registers 140 degrees, 1¼ to 1½ hours. Carefully remove chicken and pan from oven and increase oven temperature to 500 degrees.

4. FOR THE GLAZE: While chicken cooks, stir cornstarch and water together in bowl until no lumps remain. Bring remaining glaze ingredients to simmer in medium saucepan over medium-low heat and cook, stirring occasionally, until reduced to ¾ cup, 6 to 8 minutes. Slowly whisk in cornstarch mixture; return to simmer and cook for 1 minute. Remove pan from heat.

5. When oven has come to temperature, place 1½ cups water in bottom of roasting pan and return to oven. Roast until entire chicken skin is browned and crisp, breast registers 160 degrees, and thighs register 175 degrees, 24 to 30 minutes. Check chicken halfway through roasting; if top is becoming too dark, place 7-inch square piece of aluminum foil over neck and wingtips of chicken and continue to

roast. (If pan begins to smoke and sizzle, add additional ½ cup water to pan.)

6. Brush chicken with ¼ cup glaze and continue to roast until browned and sticky, about 5 minutes. (If glaze has become stiff, return to low heat to soften.) Carefully remove chicken from oven, transfer chicken, still on can, to carving board, and brush with ¼ cup glaze. Let rest for 20 minutes.

7. While chicken rests, strain juices from pan through fine-mesh strainer into fat separator; allow liquid to settle for 5 minutes. Whisk ½ cup juices into remaining ¼ cup glaze in saucepan and set over low heat. Using 2 large wads of paper towels, carefully lift chicken off can and onto carving board. Carve chicken, adding any accumulated juices to sauce. Serve, passing sauce separately.

PERUVIAN ROAST CHICKEN WITH GARLIC AND LIME

✔ WHY THIS RECIPE WORKS
Authentic versions of Peruvian garlic-lime chicken require a wood-fired oven and hard-to-find ingredients. We wanted to replicate this robustly flavored dish using an oven and supermarket staples. A paste of salt, garlic, oil, lime zest, and cumin rubbed underneath and on top of the skin produced well-seasoned meat and a heady flavor. To this basic paste we added fresh mint (replacing the black mint paste called for in authentic recipes), oregano, pepper, and minced habanero chile for tangy spice, while a little smoked paprika subtly mimicked the smokiness we were missing from the rotisserie. Roasting the chicken vertically allowed it to cook evenly, while using two different oven temperatures helped us achieve both moist meat and well-browned skin.

PERUVIAN ROAST CHICKEN WITH GARLIC AND LIME
SERVES 3 TO 4

If habanero chiles are unavailable, 1 tablespoon of minced serrano chile can be substituted. Wear gloves when working with hot chiles. This recipe calls for a vertical poultry roaster. If you don't have one, substitute a 12-ounce can of beer. Open the beer and pour out (or drink) about half of the liquid. Spray the can lightly with vegetable oil spray and proceed with the recipe. Serve with Spicy Mayonnaise (recipe follows).

¼	cup fresh mint leaves
6	garlic cloves, chopped coarse
3	tablespoons extra-virgin olive oil
1	tablespoon salt
1	tablespoon pepper
1	tablespoon ground cumin
1	tablespoon sugar
2	teaspoons smoked paprika
2	teaspoons dried oregano
2	teaspoons finely grated lime zest plus ¼ cup juice (2 limes)
1	teaspoon minced habanero chile
1	(3½- to 4-pound) whole chicken, giblets discarded

1. Process all ingredients except chicken in blender until smooth paste forms, 10 to 20 seconds. Use your fingers to gently loosen skin covering breast and thighs; place half of paste under skin, directly on meat of breast and thighs. Gently press on skin to distribute paste over meat. Spread entire exterior surface of chicken with remaining paste. Tuck wings behind back. Place chicken in 1-gallon zipper-lock bag and refrigerate at least 6 hours or up to 24 hours.

2. Adjust oven rack to lowest position and heat oven to 325 degrees. Place vertical roaster on rimmed baking sheet. Slide chicken onto vertical roaster so drumsticks reach down to bottom of roaster, chicken stands upright, and breast is perpendicular to bottom of pan. Roast chicken until skin just begins to turn golden and breast registers

140 degrees, 45 to 55 minutes. Carefully remove chicken and pan from oven and increase oven temperature to 500 degrees.

3. Once oven has come to temperature, place 1 cup water in bottom of baking sheet and continue to roast until entire chicken skin is browned and crisp, breast registers 160 degrees, and thighs register 175 degrees, about 20 minutes, rotating baking sheet halfway through roasting. Check chicken halfway through roasting; if top is becoming too dark, place 7-inch square piece of aluminum foil over neck and wingtips of chicken and continue to roast. (If pan begins to smoke and sizzle, add additional water to pan.)

4. Carefully remove chicken from oven and let rest, still on vertical roaster, for 20 minutes. Using 2 large wads of paper towels, carefully lift chicken off vertical roaster and onto carving board. Carve chicken and serve, passing Spicy Mayonnaise separately.

SPICY MAYONNAISE
MAKES ABOUT 1 CUP

If you have concerns about consuming raw eggs, ¼ cup of an egg substitute can be used in place of the egg.

1	large egg
2	tablespoons water
1	tablespoon minced onion
1	tablespoon lime juice
1	tablespoon minced fresh cilantro
1	tablespoon minced jarred jalapeños
1	garlic clove, minced
1	teaspoon yellow mustard
¼	teaspoon salt
1	cup vegetable oil

Process all ingredients except oil in food processor until combined, about 5 seconds. With machine running, slowly drizzle in oil in steady stream until mayonnaise-like consistency is reached, scraping down bowl as necessary.

HERBED ROAST CHICKEN

❦ WHY THIS RECIPE WORKS

For a roast chicken recipe that gets the entire bird—not just the breast—seasoned throughout, we butterflied the chicken and made shallow cuts in the dark meat. A thick herb paste not only adhered to the now-flat chicken but also penetrated the pockets created by the cuts, giving us the flavorful and aromatic chicken recipe we were looking for.

HERBED ROAST CHICKEN
SERVES 4

If using kosher chicken, do not brine in step 1. If you like, substitute an equal amount of basil for the tarragon and replace the thyme with rosemary, oregano, or sage. Do not use dried herbs, which lose potency during cooking and turn the dish gritty. The chicken should not exceed 5 pounds or it won't fit in the skillet. The chicken may slightly overhang the skillet at first, but once browned it will fit.

CHICKEN
- 1 (5-pound) whole chicken, giblets discarded
- ½ cup plus ¼ teaspoon salt
- 6 scallions, green parts only, sliced thin
- ¼ cup fresh tarragon leaves
- 1 tablespoon fresh thyme leaves
- 1 garlic clove, minced Pepper
- 6 tablespoons unsalted butter, softened
- 1 tablespoon vegetable oil

SAUCE
- 1–1½ cups low-sodium chicken broth
- 2 teaspoons all-purpose flour
- 1 teaspoon lemon juice Salt and pepper

1. FOR THE CHICKEN: Using kitchen shears, cut along both sides of backbone to remove it. Flatten breastbone and tuck wings underneath. Using sharp knife, lightly score skin of thighs and legs, making 2 slashes on each part about ⅛ inch into meat and about ¾ inch apart. Dissolve ½ cup salt in 2 quarts cold water in large container. Submerge chicken in brine, cover, and refrigerate for 1 hour.

2. Meanwhile, adjust oven rack to middle position and heat oven to 450 degrees. Place scallions, tarragon, thyme, garlic, ¼ teaspoon pepper, and remaining ¼ teaspoon salt on cutting board; mince to fine paste. Transfer herb paste to medium bowl, add butter, and mix until combined. Transfer 2 tablespoons herb butter to separate bowl and refrigerate; set aside remainder at room temperature.

3. Remove chicken from brine and pat dry with paper towels. Using your fingers, gently loosen center portion of skin covering each side of breast; place 1 tablespoon softened herb butter under skin, directly on meat in center of each side of breast. Gently press on skin to distribute butter over meat. Season with pepper.

4. Heat oil in 12-inch ovensafe skillet over medium-high heat until just smoking. Place chicken skin side down in skillet and reduce heat to medium. Cook until lightly browned, 8 to 10 minutes. Transfer skillet to oven and roast chicken for 25 minutes. Using 2 large wads of paper towels, flip chicken skin side up. Using spoon or spatula, evenly coat skin with remaining softened herb butter and return to oven. Roast chicken until skin is golden brown, breast registers 160 degrees, and thighs register 175 degrees, 15 to 20 minutes. Transfer chicken to carving board and let rest for 20 minutes.

5. FOR THE SAUCE: While chicken rests, pour pan juices into fat separator; allow liquid to settle for 5 minutes. Pour juices into 2-cup liquid measuring cup and add enough chicken broth to measure 1½ cups. Heat 2 teaspoons fat from fat separator in now-empty skillet over medium heat until shimmering. Add flour and cook, stirring constantly, until golden, about 1 minute. Slowly whisk in broth, scraping up any browned bits. Bring to rapid simmer and cook until reduced to 1 cup, 5 to 7 minutes. Stir in any accumulated chicken juices; return to simmer and cook for 30 seconds. Off heat, whisk in cold herb butter and lemon juice and season with salt and pepper to taste. Carve chicken and serve, passing sauce separately.

BUTTERFLYING A CHICKEN OR TURKEY

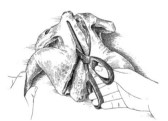  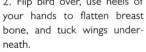 

1. Using kitchen shears, cut along both sides of backbone to remove it.

2. Flip bird over, use heels of your hands to flatten breast bone, and tuck wings underneath.

3. Using your fingers, gently loosen center portion of skin covering each side of breast (and thighs if necessary).

CRISP-SKIN, HIGH-ROAST BUTTERFLIED CHICKEN WITH POTATOES

✓ WHY THIS RECIPE WORKS

The technique of high-roasting a chicken (cooking it at temperatures in excess of 450 degrees) promises crisp, golden skin and a short cooking time—but also dry meat and billows of smoke. To ensure the chicken stayed moist, we butterflied it—this allowed the thighs greater exposure to the heat so that they would cook at about the same rate as the delicate breast meat. Since 500 degrees was the optimal temperature for the crisp, browned skin we were looking for, we needed to find a solution to the smoking problem. We found our answer in potatoes—placing them in a broiler pan with a slotted top protected them from the high heat of the oven, and they absorbed the dripping fat (and flavor) of the chicken, preventing smoke and making for a flavorful side dish all at once.

CRISP-SKIN HIGH-ROAST BUTTERFLIED CHICKEN WITH POTATOES

SERVES 3 TO 4

If using kosher chicken, do not brine in step 1, and season with salt as well as pepper in step 3. Because you'll be cooking the chicken under high heat, it's important that you rinse it thoroughly before proceeding—otherwise, the sugar remaining on the skin from the brine will caramelize and ultimately burn. For this cooking technique, russet potatoes offer the best potato flavor, but Yukon Golds develop a beautiful color and retain their shape better after cooking. Either works well in this recipe. A food processor makes quick and easy work of slicing the potatoes.

- 1 (3½- to 4-pound) whole chicken, giblets discarded
  Salt and pepper
- ½ cup sugar
- 2½ pounds russet or Yukon Gold potatoes, peeled and sliced ⅛ to ¼ inch thick
- 2 tablespoons olive oil
- 2 tablespoons unsalted butter or flavored butter (recipes follow), softened

1. Using kitchen shears, cut along both sides of backbone to remove it. Flatten breastbone and tuck wings behind back. Dissolve ½ cup salt and sugar in 2 quarts cold water in large container. Submerge chicken in brine, cover, and refrigerate for 1 hour.

2. Adjust oven rack to lower-middle position and heat oven to 500 degrees. Line broiler-pan bottom with aluminum foil. Toss potatoes with 1 tablespoon oil, ½ teaspoon salt, and ¼ teaspoon pepper in bowl. Spread potatoes in even layer in prepared broiler-pan bottom and cover with broiler-pan top.

3. Remove chicken from brine, rinse thoroughly, and pat dry with paper towels. Using your fingers, gently loosen center portion of skin covering breast and thighs. Place butter under skin, directly on meat in center of each side of breast and on thighs. Gently press on skin to distribute butter over meat. Rub skin with remaining 1 tablespoon oil and season with pepper. Place chicken on broiler-pan top and push each leg up to rest between thigh and breast.

4. Roast chicken until skin has crisped and turned deep brown, breast registers 160 degrees, and thighs register 175 degrees, 40 to 45 minutes, rotating pan halfway through roasting. Transfer chicken to carving board and let rest for 10 minutes.

5. While chicken rests, remove broiler-pan top and, using paper towels, soak up excess grease from potatoes. Transfer potatoes to serving platter. Carve chicken, transfer to platter with potatoes, and serve.

CHIPOTLE BUTTER WITH LIME AND HONEY

MAKES ABOUT 3 TABLESPOONS

- 2 tablespoons unsalted butter, softened
- 2 teaspoons minced canned chipotle chile in adobo sauce
- 1 garlic clove, minced
- 1 teaspoon honey
- 1 teaspoon grated lime zest

Mash all ingredients together in bowl.

MUSTARD-GARLIC BUTTER WITH THYME

MAKES ABOUT 3 TABLESPOONS

- 2 tablespoons unsalted butter, softened
- 1 tablespoon Dijon mustard
- 1 teaspoon minced fresh thyme
- 1 garlic clove, minced
- ¼ teaspoon pepper

Mash all ingredients together in bowl.

FRENCH CHICKEN IN A POT

✓ WHY THIS RECIPE WORKS

The basic method for poulet en cocotte, *or French chicken in a pot, is simple: Place a seasoned chicken in a pot, scatter in some vegetables, cover, and bake. When done right, this dish forgoes crisp skin for unbelievably tender, succulent meat and rich, concentrated flavor. The key is a dry cooking environment; unlike braising, little to no liquid is added. Our main challenge was to prevent the humidity in the pot from diluting the flavor of the meat as it cooked. By removing the chunks of vegetables we had been adding—the liquid they released made the pot too steamy—and cooking the* chicken by itself in a tightly sealed pot, we got the rich, concentrated flavor we sought. Cooking the bird at a low 250 degrees ensured the breast meat didn't dry out. Finally, we found that we could add a small amount of potently flavored aromatics if they were lightly browned with the chicken to remove most of their moisture.

FRENCH CHICKEN IN A POT
SERVES 4

You will need at least a 6-quart Dutch oven with a tight-fitting lid for this recipe. If you choose not to serve the skin with the chicken, simply remove it before carving. The amount of jus will vary depending on the size of the chicken; season it with about ¼ teaspoon lemon juice for every ¼ cup.

1	(4½- to 5-pound) whole chicken, giblets discarded
	Salt and pepper
1	tablespoon olive oil
1	small onion, chopped medium
1	small celery rib, chopped medium
6	garlic cloves, peeled
1	bay leaf
1	sprig fresh rosemary (optional)
½–1	teaspoon lemon juice

1. Adjust oven rack to lowest position and heat oven to 250 degrees. Pat chicken dry with paper towels, tuck wings behind back, and season with salt and pepper. Heat oil in Dutch oven over medium heat until just smoking. Add chicken breast side down; scatter onion, celery, garlic, bay leaf, and rosemary sprig, if using, around chicken. Cook until breast is lightly browned, about 5 minutes. Using wooden spoon inserted into cavity of bird, flip chicken breast side up and cook until chicken and vegetables are well browned, 6 to 8 minutes.

2. Off heat, place large sheet of aluminum foil over pot and cover tightly with lid. Transfer pot to oven and cook chicken until breast registers 160 degrees and thighs register 175 degrees, 1 hour 20 minutes to 1 hour 50 minutes.

3. Transfer chicken to carving board, tent with foil, and let rest for 20 minutes. Meanwhile, strain chicken juices from pot through fine-mesh strainer into fat separator, pressing on solids to extract liquid; discard solids. Let juices settle for 5 minutes, then pour into saucepan and set over low heat. Carve chicken, adding any accumulated juices to saucepan. Season with lemon juice, salt, and pepper to taste. Serve chicken, passing sauce separately.

CHICKEN AND RICE

✓ WHY THIS RECIPE WORKS
Chicken and rice is a dish with obvious appeal: It's a one-dish supper, it's easy, and it's eminently variable. The solution to overcooked breast meat was simple; we just added it to the pot about 15 minutes after the legs went in. Avoiding heavy, greasy rice was a little more challenging. We finally found the answer in reducing the amount of liquid (a combination of white wine, water, chopped canned tomatoes, and tomato liquid) that we added to the rice. Decreasing the amount of liquid helped, as long as we stirred the rice once to prevent the top layer from drying out. Although we tried (and liked) several varieties of rice, we settled on basic long-grain rice for this all-purpose dish.

CHICKEN AND RICE WITH TOMATOES, WHITE WINE, AND PARSLEY
SERVES 4

Though we rarely suggest stirring rice while it cooks, in this dish it is necessary, or the top layer might dry out or be undercooked. If you prefer, substitute 2 pounds of breast meat or boneless thighs for the pieces of a whole chicken. See page 333 for information on cutting up a whole chicken.

1	(3½- to 4-pound) whole chicken, cut into 8 pieces (4 breast pieces, 2 drumsticks, 2 thighs), wings discarded
	Salt and pepper
2	tablespoons olive oil
1	onion, chopped fine
3	garlic cloves, minced
1½	cups long-grain white rice
2	cups water
1	(14.5-ounce) can diced tomatoes, drained with ½ cup juice reserved
½	cup dry white wine
⅓	cup chopped fresh parsley

1. Pat chicken dry with paper towels and season with salt and pepper. Heat oil in Dutch oven over medium-high heat until just smoking. Place chicken skin side down in pot and cook until well browned, 6 to 8 minutes, reducing heat if pan begins to scorch. Flip chicken skin side up and continue to cook until lightly browned on second side, about 3 minutes; transfer to plate.

2. Pour off all but 2 tablespoons fat from pot, add onion, and cook over medium heat, stirring often, until softened, about 5 minutes. Stir in garlic and cook until fragrant, about 30 seconds. Add rice and cook, stirring frequently, until coated and glistening, about 1 minute. Stir in water, tomatoes with reserved juice, wine, and 1 teaspoon salt, scraping up any browned bits. Nestle chicken thighs and legs into pot and bring to boil. Reduce heat to low, cover, and simmer gently for 15 minutes. Nestle chicken breast pieces into pot and stir ingredients gently until rice is thoroughly mixed; cover and simmer until both rice and chicken are tender, 10 to 15 minutes longer. Stir in parsley, cover, and let dish sit for 5 minutes; serve immediately.

CHICKEN AND RICE WITH SAFFRON, PEAS, AND PAPRIKA

Add 1 green bell pepper, cut into ¼-inch pieces, to pot along with onion. Stir

4 teaspoons paprika and ¼ teaspoon saffron into pot along with garlic. Stir 1 cup thawed frozen peas into pot along with parsley.

CHICKEN AND RICE WITH CHILES, CILANTRO, AND LIME

Add 2 minced jalapeño chiles to pot along with onion. Stir 2 teaspoons ground cumin, 2 teaspoons ground coriander, and 1 teaspoon chili powder into pot along with garlic. Substitute ¼ cup chopped fresh cilantro and 3 tablespoons lime juice (2 limes) for parsley.

CHICKEN AND RICE WITH INDIAN SPICES

Omit parsley. Add 1 cinnamon stick to pot in step 2 and cook, stirring often, until it unfurls, about 15 seconds, before adding onion and 2 green bell peppers, cut into ¼-inch pieces. Stir 1 teaspoon ground turmeric, 1 teaspoon ground coriander, and 1 teaspoon ground cumin into pot with garlic.

CHICKEN AND RICE WITH ANCHOVIES, OLIVES, AND LEMON

Add 5 rinsed and minced anchovy fillets to pot along with onion. Stir ½ cup pitted Italian black olives, halved, 1 tablespoon lemon juice, and 2 teaspoons grated lemon zest into pot along with parsley.

LATIN-STYLE CHICKEN AND RICE

✔ WHY THIS RECIPE WORKS
When done right, arroz con pollo (literally, "rice with chicken") is satisfying Latino comfort food—tender chicken nestled in rice rich with peppers, onions, and herbs. But the traditional method for making it takes all day; we wanted to turn this one-dish dinner into a fast but flavorful weeknight meal. Using just thighs

(rather than a combination of white and dark meat) ensured that all the chicken would cook through at the same rate, while removing the skin and bones after cooking made our dish less greasy and easier to eat. Poaching the thighs in chicken broth gave our dish even more chicken flavor for minimal effort. A quick 15-minute marinade before cooking, and a quick toss with marinade after cooking, contributed bold flavor to our chicken. To cut even more time off our efforts, we added the rice to the pot before the chicken finished cooking—a few quick stirs guaranteed each component cooked quickly and evenly.

LATIN-STYLE CHICKEN AND RICE (ARROZ CON POLLO)

SERVES 4 TO 6

To keep the dish from becoming greasy, it is important to remove excess fat from the chicken thighs and most of the skin, leaving just enough to protect the meat. To use long-grain rice instead of medium grain, increase the amount of water added in step 3 from ¼ cup to ¾ cup and add the additional ¼ cup water in step 4 as needed. When removing the chicken from the bones in step 5, we found it better to use two spoons rather than two forks; forks tend to shred the meat, while spoons pull it apart in chunks.

6	garlic cloves, minced
5	teaspoons white vinegar
	Salt and pepper
½	teaspoon dried oregano
4	pounds bone-in chicken thighs, trimmed
2	tablespoons olive oil
1	onion, chopped fine
1	small green bell pepper, stemmed, seeded, and chopped fine
¼	teaspoon red pepper flakes
¼	cup minced fresh cilantro
1¾	cups low-sodium chicken broth
1	(8-ounce) can tomato sauce
¼	cup water, plus extra as needed
3	cups medium-grain white rice
½	cup green Manzanilla olives, pitted and halved
1	tablespoon capers, rinsed
½	cup jarred whole pimentos, cut into 2 by ¼-inch strips
	Lemon wedges

1. Adjust oven rack to middle position and heat oven to 350 degrees. Combine garlic, 1 tablespoon vinegar, 1 teaspoon salt, ½ teaspoon pepper, and oregano in large bowl. Add chicken, coat evenly with marinade, and set aside for 15 minutes.

2. Heat 1 tablespoon oil in Dutch oven over medium heat until shimmering. Add onion, bell pepper, and pepper flakes and cook, stirring occasionally, until vegetables begin to soften, about 5 minutes. Stir in 2 tablespoons cilantro.

3. Clear center of pot and increase heat to medium-high. Add chicken to center of pot, skin side down, and cook until outer layer of meat becomes opaque, 2 to 4 minutes per side, reducing heat if chicken begins to brown. Stir in broth, tomato sauce, and water. Bring to simmer, cover, reduce heat to medium-low, and simmer for 20 minutes.

4. Stir in rice, olives, capers, and ¾ teaspoon salt and bring to simmer. Cover, transfer to oven, and cook, stirring every 10 minutes, until thighs register 175 degrees, about 30 minutes. If, after 20 minutes of cooking, rice appears dry and bottom of pot begins to scorch, stir in additional ¼ cup water.

5. Transfer chicken to plate and set pot aside, covered. Pull chicken into large chunks using 2 spoons, discarding skin and bones. Place chicken in large bowl, toss with remaining 2 teaspoons vinegar, remaining 1 tablespoon oil, remaining 2 tablespoons cilantro, and pimentos and season with salt and pepper to taste. Place chicken on top of rice, cover, and let stand until warmed through, about 5 minutes. Serve with lemon wedges.

Bacon adds a welcome layer of richness and red peppers bring subtle sweet flavor and color to this variation. To use long-grain rice, increase the amount of water to ¾ cup in step 3 and the salt added in step 4 to 1 teaspoon.

1. Substitute 2 teaspoons paprika for oregano and sherry vinegar for white vinegar.

2. Cook 4 slices bacon, cut into ½-inch pieces, in Dutch oven over medium heat until crisp, 5 to 7 minutes. Remove bacon with slotted spoon and transfer to paper towel–lined plate; pour off all but 1 tablespoon bacon fat from pot. Continue with step 2, substituting 1 small red bell pepper, stemmed, seeded, and chopped fine, and 1 carrot, peeled and chopped fine, for green bell pepper and cooking vegetables in fat left in pot.

3. Continue with recipe, substituting ¼ cup minced fresh parsley for cilantro, omitting olives and capers, and substituting ½ cup roasted red peppers, cut into 2 by ¼-inch strips, for pimentos. Garnish chicken and rice with reserved crisp bacon before serving.

Ham gives this variation further richness and orange zest and juice provide a bright accent. To use long-grain rice, increase the amount of water to ¾ cup in step 3 and the salt added in step 4 to 1 teaspoon.

1. Substitute 1 tablespoon ground cumin for oregano.

2. Continue with step 2, adding 8 ounces ham steak or Canadian bacon, cut into ½-inch pieces, with onion, bell pepper, and pepper flakes.

3. Continue with step 3, adding three 3-inch strips orange zest with rice, olives,

capers, and salt. Add 1 cup frozen peas to pot with ¼ cup water, if necessary, after stirring contents of pot for second time.

4. In step 5, toss chicken with 3 tablespoons orange juice along with vinegar, olive oil, cilantro, and pimentos and proceed with recipe.

CHICKEN BIRYANI

✔ **WHY THIS RECIPE WORKS**
Traditional recipes for the Indian classic chicken biryani are long in both ingredients and labor. We wanted to streamline this dish without losing its rich flavor and complexity. Right off the bat we made three timesaving discoveries—we could skip the step of marinating the chicken, we could prepare the entire dish on the stovetop (rather than transferring it to the oven), and we could cook the onions and chicken in the same pan. Rich, meaty chicken thighs gave our dish a lot of flavor without much work, and wrapping the spices in a bundle of cheesecloth allowed us to infuse the rice cooking water with the bold flavors of biryani without having to tediously remove the spices from the finished dish. Garlic, jalapeño, currants, cilantro, and mint finished our biryani with a blend of heat, sweetness, and fresh herb flavor.

CHICKEN BIRYANI
SERVES 4

You will need a 3½- to 4-quart saucepan about 8 inches in diameter for this recipe. Do not use a wide Dutch oven, as it will adversely affect both the layering of the dish and the final cooking times. For more heat, add the jalapeño seeds and ribs when mincing.

YOGURT SAUCE
1 **cup plain whole-milk or low-fat yogurt**
1 **garlic clove, minced**
2 **tablespoons minced fresh cilantro**

2 **tablespoons minced fresh mint**
  Salt and pepper

CHICKEN AND RICE
10 **cardamom pods, preferably green, smashed**
1 **cinnamon stick**
1 **(2-inch) piece ginger, peeled, sliced into ½-inch-thick rounds, and smashed**
½ **teaspoon cumin seeds**
12 **cups water**
  Salt and pepper
4 **(5- to 7-ounce) bone-in chicken thighs, trimmed**
3 **tablespoons unsalted butter**
2 **onions, halved and sliced thin**
2 **jalapeño chiles, stemmed, seeded, and minced**
4 **garlic cloves, minced**
1¼ **cups basmati rice**
½ **teaspoon saffron threads, crumbled**
¼ **cup dried currants or raisins**
2 **tablespoons chopped fresh cilantro**
2 **tablespoons chopped fresh mint**

1. FOR THE YOGURT SAUCE: Combine yogurt, garlic, cilantro, and mint in bowl; season with salt and pepper to taste and set aside. (Sauce can be covered and refrigerated for up to 2 days.)

2. FOR THE CHICKEN AND RICE: Wrap cardamom pods, cinnamon stick, ginger, and cumin seeds in small piece of cheesecloth and secure with kitchen twine. Bring water, spice bundle, and 1½ teaspoons salt to boil in medium saucepan. Reduce heat to medium, partially cover, and simmer until spices have infused water, at least 15 minutes (but no longer than 30 minutes).

3. Meanwhile, pat chicken dry with paper towels and season with salt and pepper. Melt butter in 12-inch nonstick skillet over medium-high heat. Add onions and cook, stirring often, until soft and dark brown around edges, 10 to 12 minutes. Stir in jalapeños and garlic and cook, stirring often, until fragrant, about 2 minutes. Transfer onion mixture to bowl, season with salt to taste, and set aside. Wipe out skillet with paper towels.

4. Brown chicken thighs, skin side down, in now-empty skillet over medium-high heat until well browned, 6 to 8 minutes, reducing heat if pan begins to scorch. Flip chicken skin side up and continue to cook until lightly browned on second side, about 3 minutes. Transfer chicken to plate and remove and discard skin. Tent loosely with aluminum foil.

5. If necessary, return spice-infused water to boil; add rice and cook for 5 minutes, stirring occasionally. Drain rice through fine-mesh strainer, reserving ¾ cup cooking liquid; discard spice bundle. Transfer rice to medium bowl and stir in saffron and currants (rice will turn splotchy yellow).

6. Spread half of rice evenly in bottom of now-empty saucepan using rubber spatula. Scatter half of onion mixture over rice, then place chicken thighs, skinned side up, on top of onions; add any accumulated chicken juices. Sprinkle evenly with cilantro and mint, scatter remaining onion mixture over herbs, then cover with remaining rice. Pour reserved cooking liquid evenly over rice.

7. Cover saucepan and cook over medium-low heat until rice is tender and chicken is cooked through, about 30 minutes (if large amount of steam is escaping from pot, reduce heat to low).

8. Run heatproof rubber spatula around inside rim of saucepan to loosen any affixed rice. Using large serving spoon, spoon biryani into individual bowls, scooping from bottom of pot. Serve, passing yogurt sauce separately.

CHICKEN AND SHRIMP JAMBALAYA

✔ WHY THIS RECIPE WORKS

Done right, jambalaya is a one-pot meal with a standout combination of sweetness, spice, and smoke, but when poorly executed, it's a thin-flavored imposter with gummy rice, overcooked shrimp, and tough, dry chicken. To keep the chicken moist, we skipped the white meat and used just chicken thighs. We stuck with classic andouille sausage, which contributed spice and smoke. A food processor made short work of chopping the bell pepper, onion, celery and garlic, and the small, even pieces sautéed more quickly than when hand-chopped. Simmering the rice in a combination of chicken broth, clam juice, and tomato juice boosted its flavor, and reducing the amount of liquid kept it from being gummy and heavy. Adding the raw shrimp to the pot just five minutes before the rice was finished left them perfectly tender. Our finished jambalaya was smoky and sweet, spicy and savory, with each element perfectly cooked.

CHICKEN AND SHRIMP JAMBALAYA
SERVES 4 TO 6

If you cannot find andouille sausage, either chorizo or linguiça can be substituted. For a spicier jambalaya, you can add ¼ teaspoon of cayenne pepper along with the vegetables, and/or serve it with hot sauce.

1½	pounds bone-in chicken thighs, trimmed
	Salt and pepper
1	tablespoon vegetable oil
8	ounces andouille sausage, halved lengthwise and sliced ¼ inch thick
1	onion, chopped fine
1	red bell pepper, stemmed, seeded, and chopped fine
1	celery rib, minced
5	garlic cloves, peeled
1½	cups long-grain white rice
½	teaspoon minced fresh thyme
¼	teaspoon cayenne pepper
1	(14.5-ounce) can diced tomatoes, drained with ¼ cup juice reserved
1½	cups low-sodium chicken broth
1	(8-ounce) bottle clam juice
2	bay leaves
1	pound large shrimp (31 to 40 per pound), peeled and deveined
2	tablespoons minced fresh parsley

1. Pat chicken dry with paper towels and season with salt and pepper. Heat oil in Dutch oven over medium-high heat until just smoking. Place chicken thighs skin side down in pot and cook until well browned, 6 to 8 minutes, reducing heat if pan begins to scorch. Flip chicken skin side up and continue to cook until lightly browned on second side, about 3 minutes. Transfer chicken to plate and remove and discard skin. Tent loosely with aluminum foil.

2. Pour off all but 1 tablespoon fat from pot, add sausage, and cook over medium heat, stirring often, until browned, about 3 minutes. Remove sausage with slotted spoon and transfer to paper towel–lined plate.

3. Heat fat left in pot over medium-low heat until shimmering. Add onion, bell pepper, and celery and cook, stirring occasionally and scraping up any browned bits, until vegetables have softened, about 5 minutes. Add rice, 1 teaspoon salt, thyme, and cayenne and cook, stirring often, until rice is coated with fat, about 1 minute. Stir in tomatoes with reserved juice, chicken broth, clam juice, bay leaves, and browned sausage.

4. Place chicken, skinned side down, on rice and bring to boil. Reduce heat to low, cover, and simmer for 15 minutes. Stir once, keeping chicken on top with skinned side down. Cover and continue to simmer until chicken is tender and cooked through, about 10 minutes longer; transfer

chicken to clean plate and set aside. Scatter shrimp over rice, cover, and continue to cook until rice is fully tender and shrimp are opaque and cooked through, about 5 minutes.

5. While shrimp are cooking, use 2 forks to shred chicken into bite-size pieces. When shrimp are cooked, discard bay leaves. Off heat, stir in parsley and shredded chicken and serve immediately.

OLD-FASHIONED CHICKEN POT PIE

✔ WHY THIS RECIPE WORKS

We wanted a chicken pot pie with moist meat, flavorful vegetables, great gravy, and a crisp crust. To get there, we poached chicken breasts (or thighs) in chicken broth for added flavor and then shredded the meat before adding it to the pie. We then used the reserved chicken broth as the base of our sauce—we enriched the sauce with milk, thickened it with flour, and added sherry for complexity. Sautéing the vegetables before baking them in the pie helped them retain their color and flavor. We skipped the double crust and instead opted to roll a simple pie dough over the top of the pie, where it baked up crisp and buttery.

OLD-FASHIONED CHICKEN POT PIE
SERVES 6

Mushrooms can be sautéed along with the celery and carrots, and blanched pearl onions can stand in for the onion.

POT PIE DOUGH
1½	cups (7½ ounces) all-purpose flour
½	teaspoon salt
4	tablespoons vegetable shortening, cut into ¼-inch pieces and chilled
8	tablespoons unsalted butter, cut into ¼-inch pieces and chilled
3–4	tablespoons ice water

ARRANGING DOUGH ON A POT PIE

1. After rolling out crust, loosely roll it around rolling pin, then gently unroll it over filled baking dish.

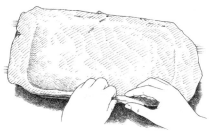

2. Using scissors, trim all but ½ inch of dough overhanging edge of baking dish. Tuck edges of dough underneath, then crimp using tines of fork.

FILLING
1½	pounds boneless, skinless chicken breasts or boneless, skinless chicken thighs, trimmed
2	cups low-sodium chicken broth
4½	teaspoons vegetable oil
1	large onion, chopped fine
3	carrots, peeled and sliced ¼ inch thick
2	small celery ribs, sliced ¼ inch thick Salt and pepper
4	tablespoons unsalted butter
½	cup all-purpose flour
1½	cups whole milk
½	teaspoon dried thyme
¾	cup frozen peas, thawed
3	tablespoons dry sherry
3	tablespoons minced fresh parsley

1. FOR THE PIE DOUGH: Process flour and salt in food processor until combined. Scatter shortening over top and pulse until mixture resembles coarse cornmeal, about 10 pulses. Scatter butter pieces over top and pulse mixture until it resembles coarse crumbs, about 10 pulses; transfer to large bowl.

2. Sprinkle 3 tablespoons ice water over flour mixture. Stir and press dough together, using stiff rubber spatula, until dough sticks together. If dough does not come together, stir in remaining 1 tablespoon water.

3. Turn dough onto sheet of plastic wrap and flatten into 4-inch disk. Wrap dough tightly in plastic and refrigerate for at least 1 hour. Before rolling out dough, let it sit on counter to soften slightly, about 10 minutes.

4. FOR THE FILLING: Bring chicken and broth to simmer in covered Dutch oven and cook until chicken is tender and cooked through, 8 to 10 minutes. Transfer chicken to large bowl. Pour broth through fine-mesh strainer into liquid measuring cup and reserve. Do not wash pot. Meanwhile, adjust oven rack to lower-middle position and heat oven to 400 degrees.

5. Heat oil in now-empty pot over medium heat until shimmering. Add onion, carrots, celery, ¼ teaspoon salt, and ¼ teaspoon pepper and cook until softened, about 5 minutes. While vegetables are cooking, use 2 forks to shred chicken into bite-size pieces. Transfer vegetables to bowl with chicken; set aside.

6. Melt butter in again-empty pot over medium heat. Add flour and cook, stirring constantly, for 1 minute. Slowly whisk in reserved chicken broth, milk, any accumulated chicken juices, and thyme. Bring to simmer and cook until sauce thickens, about 1 minute. Off heat, stir in chicken-vegetable mixture, peas, sherry, and parsley and season with salt and pepper to taste.

7. Pour chicken mixture into 13 by 9-inch baking dish. Roll dough out to 15 by 11-inch rectangle, about ⅛ inch thick, on lightly floured counter. Loosely roll dough around rolling pin and gently unroll it over filling. Trim, fold, and crimp edges, and cut 4 vent holes in top.

8. Place pot pie on aluminum foil–lined rimmed baking sheet and bake until filling is bubbling on sides and crust is golden brown, about 30 minutes. Let cool for 10 minutes before serving.

TO MAKE AHEAD: Dough can be wrapped and refrigerated for up to 2 days or frozen for up to 1 month. If frozen, let dough thaw completely in refrigerator before rolling out. Chicken filling can be cooled and refrigerated overnight. Reheat filling before transferring to baking dish and proceeding with recipe.

CHICKEN POT PIE WITH SAVORY CRUMBLE TOPPING

✔ **WHY THIS RECIPE WORKS**

For a streamlined chicken pot pie recipe, we poached boneless, skinless breasts and thighs in chicken broth, which we then used as the foundation of a full-bodied sauce. We opted for the traditional vegetable combination of onions, carrots, and celery and sautéed them separately to preserve their texture. To add chicken flavor to our chicken pot pie's sauce, we stirred a butter-and-flour roux into milk and the poaching liquid and used sautéed mushrooms, soy sauce, and tomato paste to enhance its savory character. Sweet, bright green frozen peas required no precooking—just a stir into the filling. Every chicken pot pie recipe—even a speedy one—needs a crisp, buttery top, so we settled on a "crumble" crust. It was a snap to prepare, and a quick stay in the oven before topping the pot pie with it made sure the savory crumble crust cooked through and crisped up once baked on top of the pot pie.

CHICKEN POT PIE WITH SAVORY CRUMBLE TOPPING

SERVES 6

This recipe relies on two unusual ingredients: soy sauce and tomato paste. Do not omit them. They don't convey their distinctive tastes but greatly deepen the savory flavor of the filling. When making the topping, do not substitute milk or half-and-half for the heavy cream.

FILLING

1½	pounds boneless, skinless chicken breasts and/or thighs, trimmed
3	cups low-sodium chicken broth
2	tablespoons vegetable oil
1	onion, chopped fine
3	carrots, peeled and sliced ¼ inch thick
2	small celery ribs, minced
	Salt and pepper
10	ounces cremini mushrooms, trimmed and sliced thin
1	teaspoon soy sauce
1	teaspoon tomato paste
4	tablespoons unsalted butter
½	cup all-purpose flour
1	cup whole milk
2	teaspoons lemon juice
3	tablespoons minced fresh parsley
¾	cup frozen peas

CRUMBLE TOPPING

2	cups (10 ounces) all-purpose flour
2	teaspoons baking powder
¾	teaspoon salt
½	teaspoon pepper
⅛	teaspoon cayenne pepper
6	tablespoons unsalted butter, cut into ½-inch pieces and chilled
1	ounce Parmesan cheese, grated fine (½ cup)
¾	cup plus 2 tablespoons heavy cream

1. FOR THE FILLING: Bring chicken and broth to simmer in covered Dutch oven and cook until chicken is tender and cooked through, 8 to 10 minutes. Transfer chicken to large bowl. Pour broth through fine-mesh strainer into liquid measuring cup and reserve. Do not wash pot. Meanwhile, adjust oven rack to upper-middle position and heat oven to 450 degrees.

2. FOR THE TOPPING: Combine flour, baking powder, salt, pepper, and cayenne in large bowl. Sprinkle butter pieces over top of flour. Using fingers, rub butter into flour mixture until it resembles coarse cornmeal. Stir in Parmesan. Add cream and stir until just combined. Crumble mixture into irregularly shaped pieces ranging from ½ to ¾ inch each onto parchment paper–lined rimmed baking sheet. Bake until fragrant and starting to brown, 10 to 13 minutes. Set aside.

3. Heat 1 tablespoon oil in now-empty pot over medium heat until shimmering. Add onion, carrots, celery, ¼ teaspoon salt, and ¼ teaspoon pepper; cover and cook, stirring occasionally, until just tender, 5 to 7 minutes. While vegetables are cooking, use 2 forks to shred chicken into bite-size pieces. Transfer vegetables to bowl with chicken; set aside.

4. Heat remaining 1 tablespoon oil in again-empty pot over medium heat until shimmering. Add mushrooms; cover and cook, stirring occasionally, until mushrooms have released their liquid, about 5 minutes. Remove cover and stir in soy sauce and tomato paste. Increase heat to medium-high and cook, stirring often, until liquid has evaporated, mushrooms are well browned, and dark fond begins to form on surface of pan, about 5 minutes. Transfer mushrooms to bowl with chicken and vegetables. Set aside.

5. Melt butter in again-empty pot over medium heat. Add flour and cook, stirring constantly, for 1 minute. Slowly whisk in reserved chicken broth and milk. Bring to simmer, scraping up any browned bits, and cook until sauce thickens, about 1 minute. Off heat, stir in lemon juice and

2 tablespoons parsley, then stir chicken mixture and peas into sauce. Season with salt and pepper to taste.

6. Pour chicken mixture into 13 by 9-inch baking dish. Scatter crumble topping evenly over filling. Place pot pie on aluminum foil–lined rimmed baking sheet and bake until filling is bubbling and topping is well browned, 12 to 15 minutes. Sprinkle with remaining 1 tablespoon parsley and serve.

CHICKEN ENCHILADAS WITH RED CHILI SAUCE

✔ WHY THIS RECIPE WORKS

Chicken enchiladas are a labor of love—the multistep process and traditional cooking methods require an entire day in the kitchen. We wanted to make enchiladas in 90 minutes from start to finish. We first saved time preparing the tortillas by spraying them with vegetable oil (rather than dipping them in hot oil) and warming them on a baking sheet in the oven. For the sauce, we ditched the dried chiles, instead using a blend of chili powder, cumin, and coriander, and sautéed the spices with the aromatics for fuller flavor. To save even more time, we cooked boneless, skinless thighs right in the sauce. Pickled jalapeño and fresh cilantro added complexity to our filling without much work.

CHICKEN ENCHILADAS WITH RED CHILI SAUCE

SERVES 4 TO 5

If you prefer, Monterey Jack can be used instead of cheddar or, for a mellower flavor and creamier texture, try substituting an equal amount of farmer's cheese. Be sure to cool the chicken filling before filling the tortillas; otherwise, the hot filling will make the enchiladas soggy.

SAUCE AND FILLING
1½   tablespoons vegetable oil
1   onion, chopped fine
3   garlic cloves, minced
3   tablespoons chili powder
2   teaspoons ground coriander
2   teaspoons ground cumin
½   teaspoon salt
2   teaspoons sugar
12   ounces boneless, skinless chicken thighs, trimmed and cut into ¼-inch-wide strips
2   (8-ounce) cans tomato sauce
¾   cup water
½   cup chopped fresh cilantro
¼   cup jarred jalapeños, chopped
8   ounces sharp cheddar cheese, shredded (2 cups)

TORTILLAS AND TOPPINGS
10   (6-inch) corn tortillas
   Vegetable oil spray
3   ounces sharp cheddar cheese, shredded (¾ cup)
¾   cup sour cream
1   avocado, pitted and cut into ½-inch pieces
5   romaine lettuce leaves, shredded
   Lime wedges

1. FOR THE SAUCE AND FILLING: Heat oil in medium saucepan over medium-high heat until shimmering. Add onion and cook, stirring occasionally, until softened and lightly browned, 5 to 7 minutes. Stir in garlic, chili powder, coriander, cumin, salt, and sugar and cook, stirring constantly, until fragrant, about 30 seconds. Add chicken and cook, stirring constantly, until coated with spices, about 30 seconds. Add tomato sauce and water, bring to simmer, and cook, stirring occasionally, until chicken is cooked through and flavors have melded, about 8 minutes. Strain mixture through fine-mesh strainer into bowl, pressing on chicken and onion to extract as much sauce as possible; set sauce aside. Transfer chicken mixture to plate; place in refrigerator for 20 minutes to cool, then combine with cilantro, jalapeños, and cheddar in bowl and set aside.

2. Adjust oven racks to upper-middle and lower-middle positions and heat oven to 350 degrees.

3. TO ASSEMBLE: Spread ¾ cup chili sauce evenly over bottom of 13 by 9-inch baking dish. Place tortillas in single layer on 2 baking sheets. Spray both sides of tortillas lightly with vegetable oil spray. Bake until tortillas are soft and pliable, 2 to 4 minutes. Increase oven temperature to 400 degrees. Place warm tortillas on counter and spread ⅓ cup chicken filling down center of each tortilla. Roll each tortilla tightly and place in baking dish, seam side down. Pour remaining chili sauce over top of enchiladas and spread into even layer so that it coats top of each tortilla. Sprinkle cheddar down center of enchiladas and cover tightly with aluminum foil.

4. Bake enchiladas on lower rack until heated through and cheese is melted, 20 to 25 minutes. Uncover and serve immediately, passing sour cream, avocado, lettuce, and lime wedges separately.

ENCHILADAS VERDES

✔ WHY THIS RECIPE WORKS

Enchiladas verdes feature tender pieces of chicken wrapped in soft corn tortillas topped with melted cheese and a bright-tasting sauce made from fresh green chiles and tangy tomatillos. But this restaurant favorite can be hard to re-create at home. Broiling poblano chiles and tomatillos concentrated their flavor and promoted charring, thus closely replicating the results achieved from using a comal (a traditional cast-iron vessel that imparts smokiness and concentrates flavor). A few pulses in the food processor kept our sauce pleasantly chunky, while a little chicken broth thinned it just enough. To keep our recipe streamlined, we poached quick-cooking chicken breasts and shredded the meat, to which we added pepper Jack cheese and chopped cilantro to round out the filling. Spraying the tortillas with vegetable oil before baking kept them pliable and easy to use.

ENCHILADAS VERDES
SERVES 4 TO 6

You can substitute three 11-ounce cans tomatillos, drained and rinsed, for the fresh ones in this recipe. Halve large tomatillos (more than 2 inches in diameter) and place them skin side up for broiling in step 2 to ensure even cooking and charring. If you can't find poblanos, substitute 4 large jalapeño chiles (with seeds and ribs removed). To increase the spiciness of the sauce, reserve some of the chiles' ribs and seeds and add them to the food processor in step 4. Be sure to cool the chicken filling before filling the tortillas; the hot filling will make the enchiladas soggy.

- 4   teaspoons vegetable oil
- 1   onion, chopped medium
- ½   teaspoon ground cumin
- 3   garlic cloves, minced
- 1½   cups low-sodium chicken broth
- 1   pound boneless, skinless chicken breasts, trimmed
- 1½   pounds tomatillos (16 to 20 medium), husks and stems removed, rinsed well and dried
- 3   poblano chiles, halved lengthwise, stemmed, and seeded
- 1–2½   teaspoons sugar
-    Salt and pepper
- ½   cup chopped fresh cilantro
- 8   ounces pepper Jack or Monterey Jack cheese, shredded (2 cups)
- 12   (6-inch) corn tortillas
-    Vegetable oil spray

   GARNISHES
- 2   scallions, sliced thin
-    Thinly sliced radishes
-    Sour cream

1. Adjust 1 oven rack to middle position and another rack 6 inches from broiler element and heat broiler. Heat 2 teaspoons oil in medium saucepan over medium heat until shimmering. Add onion and cook, stirring often, until softened and lightly browned, 5 to 7 minutes. Stir in cumin and two-thirds of garlic and cook, stirring often, until fragrant, about 30 seconds. Decrease heat to low and stir in broth. Add chicken, cover, and simmer until it registers 160 degrees, 15 to 20 minutes, flipping chicken halfway through cooking. Transfer chicken to large bowl; place in refrigerator to cool, about 20 minutes. Measure out and reserve ¼ cup broth and set aside; discard remaining liquid.

2. Meanwhile, toss tomatillos and poblanos with remaining 2 teaspoons oil. Arrange tomatillos cut side down and poblanos skin side up on aluminum foil–lined rimmed baking sheet. Broil on top rack until vegetables blacken and start to soften, 5 to 10 minutes, rotating baking sheet halfway through broiling.

3. Remove tomatillos and poblanos from oven, let cool slightly, then remove skins from poblanos (leave tomatillo skins intact). Decrease oven temperature to 350 degrees. Discard foil from baking sheet and set baking sheet aside for warming tortillas.

4. Transfer vegetables, along with any accumulated juices, to food processor. Add 1 teaspoon sugar, 1 teaspoon salt, remaining garlic, and reserved cooking liquid to food processor and process until sauce is somewhat chunky, about 8 pulses. Season with salt and pepper to taste and adjust tartness by stirring in remaining sugar, ½ teaspoon at a time; set aside.

5. When chicken is cool, use 2 forks to shred into bite-size pieces. Combine chicken with cilantro and 1½ cups pepper Jack; season with salt to taste.

6. Spread ¾ cup tomatillo sauce evenly over bottom of 13 by 9-inch baking dish. Place tortillas in single layer on 2 baking sheets. Spray both sides of tortillas lightly with vegetable oil spray. Bake until tortillas are soft and pliable, 2 to 4 minutes. Increase oven temperature to 450 degrees. Place warm tortillas on counter and spread ⅓ cup chicken filling down center of each tortilla. Roll each tortilla tightly and place in baking dish, seam side down. Pour remaining tomatillo sauce over top of enchiladas and spread into even layer so that it coats top of each tortilla. Sprinkle with remaining ½ cup pepper Jack and cover tightly with foil.

7. Bake enchiladas on lower rack until heated through and cheese is melted, 15 to 20 minutes. Uncover, sprinkle with scallions, and serve immediately, passing radishes and sour cream separately.

SAUTÉED TURKEY CUTLETS

✓ WHY THIS RECIPE WORKS
Turkey cutlets offer a quick and satisfying option for a weeknight dinner, but sautéing them just right requires something of a balancing act. Choosing cutlets of even thickness was the first step in ensuring that they cooked uniformly from end to end. We found it wasn't necessary to flour the cutlets as long as the pan was hot enough, and olive oil was the best medium for sautéing the cutlets, providing pleasant flavor and a relatively high smoke point. Heating the pan properly was essential to a well-browned crust. Finally, we determined it was best to brown the cutlets on one side only; they are simply too thin to brown well on both sides without overcooking.

SAUTÉED TURKEY CUTLETS WITH HONEY-MUSTARD PAN SAUCE
SERVES 4

One cutlet per person makes a skimpy serving, so we call for a total of six to serve four people. If you prefer, replace the Honey-Mustard Pan Sauce with Warm-Spiced Pan Sauce with Currants and Almonds (recipe follows). The turkey can be prepared without the pan sauce; if not making a pan sauce, let the turkey rest for 5 minutes before serving in step 2.

   TURKEY
- 6   (4-ounce) turkey cutlets, trimmed
- 2   tablespoons olive oil

HONEY-MUSTARD PAN SAUCE

- 1   shallot, minced
- 1   cup dry white wine
- ½   cup low-sodium chicken broth
- 2   teaspoons honey
- 3   tablespoons unsalted butter, cut into 3 pieces and chilled
- 1   tablespoon Dijon mustard
- 1   tablespoon chopped fresh tarragon
  Salt and pepper

1. FOR THE TURKEY: Adjust oven rack to middle position and heat oven to 200 degrees. Pat turkey dry with paper towels and season with salt and pepper.

2. Heat 1 tablespoon oil in 12-inch skillet over medium-high heat. Place half of cutlets in skillet and cook until light golden brown on first side, 2 to 2½ minutes. Flip cutlets and continue to cook until second side is opaque, about 1 minute; transfer to large ovensafe platter. Repeat with remaining 1 tablespoon oil and remaining cutlets; transfer to platter. Tent loosely with aluminum foil and transfer to oven to keep warm while preparing sauce.

3. FOR THE PAN SAUCE: Add shallot to oil left in skillet and cook over medium-low heat, stirring constantly, until softened, about 1 minute. Stir in wine, broth, and honey, scraping up any browned bits. Bring to boil and cook until liquid is reduced to ⅓ cup, about 10 minutes, adding any accumulated turkey juices after about 8 minutes. Off heat, whisk in butter and mustard until butter is melted and sauce is slightly thickened. Stir in tarragon and season with salt and pepper to taste. Spoon sauce over turkey and serve immediately.

WARM-SPICED PAN SAUCE WITH CURRANTS AND ALMONDS

MAKES ABOUT ⅔ CUP, ENOUGH FOR 6 CUTLETS

We prefer a fruity red wine, such as Zinfandel, in this recipe.

- 2   teaspoons brown sugar
- ⅛   teaspoon cayenne pepper
  Pinch ground cloves
  Pinch ground allspice
- 1   tablespoon olive oil
- 2   cinnamon sticks
- 1   shallot, minced
- 2   garlic cloves, minced
- 2   teaspoons grated fresh ginger
- 1   cup red wine
- ½   cup low-sodium chicken broth
- 3   tablespoons dried currants
- 3   tablespoons unsalted butter, cut into 3 pieces and chilled
- 2   tablespoons chopped fresh parsley
  Salt and pepper
- ¼   cup sliced almonds, toasted

Mix brown sugar, cayenne, cloves, and allspice in bowl; set aside. Add oil, spice mixture, and cinnamon sticks to now-empty skillet and cook, stirring constantly, until fragrant, about 1 minute. Add shallot and cook, stirring frequently, until softened, about 1 minute. Add garlic and ginger and cook, stirring constantly, until fragrant, about 30 seconds. Stir in wine, broth, and currants, scraping up any browned bits. Bring to boil and cook until liquid is reduced to ⅓ cup, about 10 minutes, adding any accumulated turkey juices after about 8 minutes. Off heat, discard cinnamon sticks, then whisk in butter until melted and sauce is slightly thickened. Stir in parsley and season with salt and pepper to taste. Spoon sauce over turkey, sprinkle with almonds, and serve immediately.

ROAST TURKEY BREAST

✔ WHY THIS RECIPE WORKS

Achieving crisp skin without drying out the delicate white meat is easier said than done when roasting a whole turkey breast. Brining was a good first step, flavoring the mild breast meat and helping it hold moisture. Loosening the skin and rubbing the meat underneath with softened butter promoted even browning and crispier skin. But the real challenge was determining the best roasting technique. After testing a range of oven temperatures, we determined that a dual-temperature approach was necessary: starting the turkey breast in a 425-degree oven jump-started the browning process, while reducing the heat to 325 degrees for the remainder of the time allowed the meat to gently finish cooking.

PREPARING A TURKEY BREAST FOR ROASTING

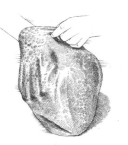

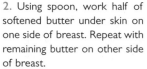

1. Using your fingers, separate skin from meat, taking care to not tear membrane around perimeter of breast; release skin on either side of breastbone.

2. Using spoon, work half of softened butter under skin on one side of breast. Repeat with remaining butter on other side of breast.

3. Using your hands, gently rub turkey skin to evenly distribute butter over the entire breast.

EASY ROAST TURKEY BREAST

SERVES 8 TO 10

Many supermarkets are now selling "hotel-style" turkey breasts. Try to avoid these if you can, as they still have the wings and rib cage attached. If this is the only type of breast you can find, you will need to remove the wings and cut away the rib cage with kitchen shears before proceeding with the recipe. If using a self-basting turkey or kosher turkey, do not brine in step 1.

½   cup salt
1   (6- to 7-pound) whole bone-in turkey breast, trimmed
4   tablespoons unsalted butter, softened
¼   teaspoon pepper

1. Dissolve salt in 1 gallon cold water in large container. Submerge turkey in brine, cover, and refrigerate for 3 to 6 hours.

2. Adjust oven rack to middle position and heat oven to 425 degrees. Set V-rack inside roasting pan and spray with vegetable oil spray. Combine butter and pepper in bowl.

3. Remove turkey from brine and pat dry with paper towels. Using your fingers, gently loosen center portion of skin covering each side of breast; place butter mixture under skin, directly on meat in center of each side of breast. Gently press on skin to distribute butter mixture over meat. Place turkey skin side up on prepared V-rack and add 1 cup water to pan.

4. Roast turkey for 30 minutes. Reduce oven temperature to 325 degrees and continue to roast until turkey registers 160 degrees, about 1 hour longer. Transfer turkey to carving board and let rest for 20 minutes. Carve turkey and serve.

EASY ROAST TURKEY BREAST WITH LEMON AND THYME

Add 3 minced garlic cloves, 2 tablespoons minced fresh thyme, and 1 teaspoon grated lemon zest to butter mixture.

EASY ROAST TURKEY BREAST WITH ORANGE AND ROSEMARY

Add 3 minced garlic cloves, 1 tablespoon minced fresh rosemary, 1 teaspoon grated orange zest, and ¼ teaspoon red pepper flakes to butter mixture.

EASY ROAST TURKEY BREAST WITH SOUTHWESTERN FLAVORS

Add 3 minced garlic cloves, 1 tablespoon minced fresh oregano, 2 teaspoons ground cumin, 2 teaspoons chili powder, ¾ teaspoon cocoa, and ½ teaspoon cayenne pepper to butter mixture.

ROAST BRINED TURKEY

✔ WHY THIS RECIPE WORKS

Cooking the holiday turkey can strike fear into the most seasoned cook, so we set out to determine what makes a difference (and what doesn't) once you bring home the bird. First, we found that a standard brine solution works with most any size bird, but timing is key—at least six hours is required to get the full benefits of brining. We chose to skip stuffing the turkey, since cooking the stuffing to a safe internal temperature almost always resulted in an overcooked bird. A V-rack proved essential, not only to hold the turkey in place but also to elevate the meat above the roasting pan, which promoted more even browning and cooking. Turning the bird once during roasting protected the delicate breast meat from overcooking and brushing the turkey with butter at the outset contributed to browning. Finally, letting the turkey rest after roasting allowed for the redistribution and reabsorption of the juices in the meat.

TEST KITCHEN TIP NO. 75   HOW BRINING SAVED THANKSGIVING

Once upon a time, the only thing the Thanksgiving turkey had going for it was tradition, which often involved bringing a dry, tasteless bird to the table (with extra helpings of gravy). But things started to look up when nearly two decades ago, the test kitchen came upon an obscure technique called brining. Brining turkey involves soaking the turkey in a saltwater solution (which sometimes includes sugar) before cooking—this protects it from the ravages of heat and guarantees tender, flavorful meat from the surface all the way to the bone. (Brining does the same for other delicate white meat like chicken and pork.) How does brining work? Simply put, the brining solution flows into the meat, distributing moisture and seasoning. In our testing, we found that while a turkey roasted straight out of its package will retain about 82 percent of its total weight after cooking, a brined turkey will retain about 93 percent of its total weight after cooking—and thus be moister and more flavorful.

What equipment do you need for brining? A clean container that's large enough to accommodate the meat and brine. For large containers (such as a washtub or cooler) that won't fit in a refrigerator, you need ice packs to keep the temperature at 40 degrees F. For a whole chicken, the test kitchen likes to use a large, clear bucket marked with level graduations—these make handy containers for rising bread dough, too. (Look for these containers at restaurant supply stores or online.)

After pulling your turkey out of the brine, pat it dry to prevent soggy skin. You can also place the turkey on a wire rack set on a baking sheet and allow it to dry overnight in the refrigerator—this will further encourage crisp skin during roasting. As for the salt, the test kitchen prefers table salt. Kosher salt works fine, but the size of the grains varies between the two major brands, which can make recipe testing (and writing) difficult. The ratio of salt to water varies a bit from recipe to recipe, but generally the test kitchen uses 1 cup table salt to 2 gallons of water (this is enough brine for a 12- to 14-pound turkey).

Once a little-known technique, brining has now become mainstream—and Thanksgiving dinners everywhere are all the better for it.

ROAST BRINED TURKEY
SERVES 10 TO 12

If using a self-basting turkey or kosher turkey, do not brine in step 1, and season with salt after brushing with melted butter in step 5. Resist the temptation to tent the roasted turkey with foil while it rests on the carving board. Covering the bird will make the skin soggy.

- 1   cup salt
- 1   (12- to 14-pound) turkey, trimmed, neck, giblets, and tailpiece removed and reserved for gravy (recipe follows)
- 6   sprigs fresh thyme
- 2   onions, chopped coarse
- 2   carrots, peeled and chopped coarse
- 2   celery ribs, chopped coarse
- 3   tablespoons unsalted butter, melted
- 1   cup water, plus extra as needed
- 1   recipe Giblet Pan Gravy (recipe follows)

1. Dissolve salt in 2 gallons cold water in large container. Submerge turkey in brine, cover, and refrigerate or store in very cool spot (40 degrees or less) for 6 to 12 hours.

2. Set wire rack in rimmed baking sheet. Remove turkey from brine and pat dry, inside and out, with paper towels. Place turkey on prepared wire rack. Refrigerate, uncovered, for at least 8 hours or overnight.

3. Adjust oven rack to lowest position and heat oven to 400 degrees. Line V-rack with heavy-duty aluminum foil and poke several holes in foil. Set V-rack in roasting pan and spray foil with vegetable oil spray.

4. Toss thyme and half of vegetables with 1 tablespoon melted butter in bowl and place inside turkey. Tie legs together with kitchen twine and tuck wings behind back. Scatter remaining vegetables in pan.

5. Pour water over vegetable mixture in pan. Brush turkey breast with 1 tablespoon melted butter, then place turkey breast side down on V-rack. Brush with remaining 1 tablespoon butter.

6. Roast turkey for 45 minutes. Remove pan from oven. Using 2 large wads of paper towels, turn turkey breast side up. If liquid in pan has totally evaporated, add another ½ cup water. Return turkey to oven and roast until breast registers 160 degrees and thighs register 175 degrees, 50 to 60 minutes.

7. Remove turkey from oven. Gently tip turkey so that any accumulated juices in cavity run into pan. Transfer turkey to carving board and let rest, uncovered, for 30 minutes. Carve turkey and serve with gravy.

GIBLET PAN GRAVY
MAKES ABOUT 6 CUPS

Complete step 1 up to a day ahead, if desired. Begin step 3 once the bird has been removed from the oven and is resting on a carving board.

- 1   tablespoon vegetable oil
      Reserved turkey neck, giblets, and tailpiece
- 1   onion, chopped
- 4   cups low-sodium chicken broth
- 2   cups water
- 2   sprigs fresh thyme
- 8   sprigs fresh parsley
- 3   tablespoons unsalted butter
- ¼   cup all-purpose flour
- 1   cup dry white wine
      Salt and pepper

1. Heat oil in Dutch oven over medium heat until shimmering. Add neck, giblets, and tailpiece and cook until golden and fragrant, about 5 minutes. Stir in onion and cook until softened, about 5 minutes.

Reduce heat to low, cover, and cook until turkey parts and onion release their juices, about 15 minutes. Stir in broth, water, thyme, and parsley, bring to boil, and adjust heat to low. Simmer, uncovered, skimming any impurities that may rise to surface, until broth is rich and flavorful, about 30 minutes longer. Strain broth into large container and reserve giblets. When cool enough to handle, chop giblets. Refrigerate giblets and broth until ready to use. (Broth can be stored in refrigerator for up to 1 day.)

2. While turkey is roasting, return reserved turkey broth to simmer in saucepan. Melt butter in separate large saucepan over medium-low heat. Add flour and cook, whisking constantly (mixture will froth and then thin out again), until nutty brown and fragrant, 10 to 15 minutes. Vigorously whisk all but 1 cup of hot broth into flour mixture. Bring to boil, then continue to simmer, stirring occasionally, until gravy is lightly thickened and very flavorful, about 30 minutes longer. Set aside until turkey is done.

3. When turkey has been transferred to carving board to rest, spoon out and discard as much fat as possible from pan, leaving caramelized herbs and vegetables. Place pan over 2 burners set on medium-high heat. Return gravy to simmer. Add wine to pan of caramelized vegetables, scraping up any browned bits. Bring to boil and cook until reduced by half, about 5 minutes. Add remaining 1 cup turkey broth, bring to simmer, and cook for 15 minutes; strain pan juices into gravy, pressing as much juice as possible out of vegetables. Stir reserved giblets into gravy and return to boil. Season with salt and pepper to taste and serve.

TURKEY FOR A CROWD

☑ **WHY THIS RECIPE WORKS**

When you're expecting a crowd for Thanksgiving dinner, but have just one oven to dedicate to roasting the turkey, only a really large bird will do. But a 20-pound-plus turkey presents some problems: Finding a container big enough to brine it and turning the bird halfway through cooking were two concerns. Buying an already brined or kosher turkey was the first step in eliminating one of these hurdles. Initial high heat gave our turkey crisp skin, while lowering the heat for the remainder of the cooking time prevented the meat from drying out. Though we did turn the bird once for even cooking, we decided to make this step optional since it is so cumbersome. We brushed the turkey just once with butter before going into the oven, which saved us the step of continuous basting. Finally, trussing was another step we could happily skip—the thigh meat cooked faster when left untrussed.*

TURKEY FOR A CROWD
SERVES ABOUT 20

Rotating the bird helps produce moist, evenly cooked meat, but for the sake of ease, you may opt not to rotate it. In that case, skip the step of lining the V-rack with foil and roast the bird breast side up for the entire cooking time. Because we do not brine the bird, we had the best results with a frozen Butterball turkey (injected with salt and water) or a kosher bird (soaked in salt water during processing). Follow illustrations for how to carve the turkey.

- 3 onions, chopped coarse
- 3 carrots, peeled and chopped coarse
- 3 celery ribs, chopped coarse
- 1 lemon, quartered
- 6 sprigs fresh thyme
- 5 tablespoons unsalted butter, melted
- 1 (18- to 22-pound) frozen Butterball or kosher turkey, trimmed, neck, giblets, and tailpiece removed and reserved for gravy (recipe follows)
- 1 cup water, plus extra as needed
  Salt and pepper
- 1 recipe Giblet Pan Gravy for a Crowd (recipe follows)

1. Adjust oven rack to lowest position. Heat oven to 425 degrees. Line V-rack with heavy-duty aluminum foil and poke several holes in foil. Set V-rack in flame-proof roasting pan and spray foil with vegetable oil spray.

2. Toss half of vegetables, half of lemon, and thyme with 1 tablespoon of melted butter in bowl and place inside turkey. Tie legs together with kitchen twine and tuck wings behind back. Scatter remaining vegetables into pan.

3. Pour water over vegetable mixture in pan. Brush turkey breast with 2 tablespoons melted butter, then sprinkle with ½ teaspoon salt and ½ teaspoon pepper. Place turkey, breast side down, on prepared V-rack. Brush with remaining 2 tablespoons melted butter and sprinkle with ½ teaspoon salt and ½ teaspoon pepper.

4. Roast turkey for 1 hour. Baste turkey with juices from pan. Using 2 large wads of paper towels, turn turkey breast side up. If liquid in pan has totally evaporated, add another ½ cup water. Lower oven temperature to 325 degrees. Continue to roast until breast registers 160 degrees and thighs register 175 degrees on, about 2 hours longer.

CARVING A WHOLE ROASTED TURKEY

1. Remove any twine used to truss turkey. Start by slicing turkey where leg meets breast.

2. Pull leg quarter away from carcass. Separate joint by gently pressing leg out to side and pushing up on joint, then carefully cut through joint to remove leg quarter.

3. Cut through joint that connects drumstick to thigh. Repeat on second side to remove other leg. Slice meat off of leg and thigh pieces, leaving a bit of skin attached to each slice.

4. Pull wing away from carcass and carefully cut through joint between wing and breast to remove wing. Cut wing in half for easier eating.

5. Cut down along 1 side of breastbone, pulling breast meat away from you as you cut.

6. Cut breast into attractive slices.

5. Remove turkey from oven. Gently tip turkey up so that any accumulated juices in cavity run into pan. Transfer turkey to carving board. Let rest, uncovered, for 35 to 40 minutes. Carve turkey and serve with gravy.

GIBLET PAN GRAVY FOR A CROWD
MAKES ABOUT 8 CUPS

Complete step 1 up to a day ahead, if desired. Begin step 3 once the bird has been removed from the oven and is resting on a carving board.

- 1   tablespoon vegetable oil
      Reserved turkey neck, giblets, and tailpiece
- 1   onion, unpeeled and chopped
- 6   cups low-sodium chicken broth
- 3   cups water
- 2   sprigs fresh thyme
- 8   sprigs fresh parsley
- 5   tablespoons unsalted butter
- ¼   cup plus 2 tablespoons all-purpose flour
- 1½   cups dry white wine
      Salt and pepper

1. Heat oil in Dutch oven over medium heat until shimmering. Add neck, giblets, and tailpiece and cook until golden and fragrant, about 5 minutes. Stir in onion and cook until softened, about 5 minutes. Reduce heat to low, cover, and cook until turkey parts and onion release their juices, about 15 minutes. Stir in broth, water, and herbs, bring to boil, and adjust heat to low. Simmer, uncovered, skimming any impurities that may rise to surface, until broth is rich and flavorful, about 30 minutes longer. Strain broth into large container and reserve giblets. When cool enough to handle, chop giblets. Refrigerate giblets and broth until ready to use. (Broth can be stored in refrigerator for up to 1 day.)

2. While turkey is roasting, return reserved turkey broth to simmer in medium saucepan. Melt butter in large saucepan over medium-low heat. Add flour and cook, whisking constantly (the mixture will froth and then thin out again), until nutty brown and fragrant, 10 to 15 minutes. Vigorously whisk all but 2 cups of hot broth into flour mixture. Bring to boil, then continue to simmer, stirring occasionally, until gravy is lightly thickened and very flavorful, about 35 minutes longer. Set aside until turkey is done.

3. When turkey has been transferred to carving board to rest, spoon out and discard as much fat as possible from roasting pan, leaving caramelized herbs and vegetables. Place pan over 2 burners set on medium-high heat. Return gravy to simmer. Add wine to pan of caramelized vegetables, scraping up any browned bits. Bring to boil and cook until reduced by half, about 7 minutes. Add remaining 2 cups turkey broth, bring to simmer, and cook for 15 minutes; strain pan juices into gravy, pressing as much juice as possible out of vegetables. Stir reserved giblets into gravy and return to boil. Season with salt and pepper to taste and serve.

ROAST SALTED TURKEY

✔ WHY THIS RECIPE WORKS
Brining is our go-to technique when we want moist, well-seasoned turkey. But with refrigerator space at a premium around the holidays, we looked to salting as a space-saving alternative. We carefully separated the skin from the meat and rubbed the meat thoroughly with kosher salt. We discovered that salting the turkey (which is actually a kind of dry brine) and refrigerating it for 24 to 48 hours resulted in a turkey that was well seasoned throughout, though it wasn't quite as moist as a traditionally brined turkey. Since the dryness was concentrated in the breast, we iced the breast before the turkey went into the oven—because the breast meat started at a lower temperature than the dark meat, we were able to remove the turkey when the dark meat was thoroughly cooked but the breast wasn't overdone.

ROAST SALTED TURKEY
SERVES 10 TO 12

If using a self-basting turkey or kosher turkey, do not salt in step 1, and season with salt after brushing with melted butter in step 5. This recipe was developed and tested using Diamond Crystal kosher salt. If you have Morton's kosher salt, which is denser than Diamond Crystal, use

---

TEST KITCHEN TIP NO. 76   **TURKEY—PRETTY IN PINK?**

Having prepared thousands of turkeys in the test kitchen, we have experienced the occasional slice of pink turkey meat. First off, always rely on an instant-read thermometer to ascertain doneness when roasting poultry. In the case of turkey, look for 160 degrees in the thickest portion of the breast and 175 degrees in the thickest part of the thigh.

   So what about the unsettling color? Just because a slice of turkey has a pinkish tint doesn't necessarily mean it is underdone. In general, the red or pink color in meat is due to the red protein pigment called myoglobin in the muscle cells that store oxygen. Because the areas that tend to get the most exercise—the legs and thighs—require more oxygen, they contain more myoglobin (and are therefore darker in color) than the breasts. When oxygen is attached to myoglobin in the cells, it is bright red. As turkey (or chicken) roasts in the oven, the oxygen attached to the myoglobin is released, and the meat becomes lighter and browner in color. However, if there are trace amounts of other gases formed in a hot oven or grill, they may react to the myoglobin to produce a pink color, even if the turkey is fully cooked.

   When cooking turkey or other poultry, don't be afraid if you see a little bit of pink. As long as you've let your thermometer be your guide, the meat is perfectly safe to eat.

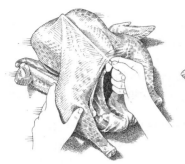

1. Use your fingers or thin wooden spoon handle to separate skin from meat over breast, legs, thighs, and back.

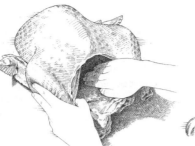

2. Rub salt inside main cavity.

3. Lift skin and apply salt over each side of breast, placing half of salt on each end of each side of breast, then massaging salt evenly over meat.

4. Apply salt over top and bottom of each leg.

only 4½ teaspoons of salt in the cavity, 2¼ teaspoons of salt for each half of the breast, and 1 teaspoon of salt per leg. Table salt is too fine and is not recommended for this recipe. If serving with Giblet Pan Gravy (page 354), note that you can complete step 1 of the gravy recipe up to a day ahead, if desired. Begin step 3 once the bird has been removed from the oven and is resting on a carving board. For information no carving the turkey, see page 355.

- 1 (12- to 14-pound) turkey, trimmed, neck, giblets, and tailpiece removed and reserved for gravy
- 4 tablespoons kosher salt
- 1 (5-pound) bag ice cubes
- 4 tablespoons unsalted butter, melted
- 3 onions, chopped coarse
- 2 carrots, peeled and chopped coarse
- 2 celery ribs, chopped coarse
- 6 sprigs fresh thyme
- 1 cup water
- 1 recipe Giblet Pan Gravy (page 354)

1. Use your fingers or thin wooden spoon handle to gently loosen skin covering breast, thighs, drumsticks, and back of turkey; avoid breaking skin. Rub 1 tablespoon salt evenly inside cavity of turkey, 1 tablespoon salt under skin of each side of breast, and 1½ teaspoons salt under skin of each leg. Wrap turkey tightly with plastic wrap and refrigerate for at least 24 hours or up to 48 hours.

2. Remove turkey from refrigerator. Rinse off any excess salt between meat and skin and in cavity, then pat dry, inside and out, with paper towels. Add ice to two 1-gallon zipper-lock bags until each is half full. Place bags in roasting pan and lay turkey breast side down on top of ice. Add ice to two 1-quart zipper-lock bags until each is one-third full; place 1 bag of ice in large cavity of turkey and other bag in neck cavity. (Make sure that ice touches breast only, not thighs or legs.) Keep turkey on ice for 1 hour (pan should remain on counter).

3. Meanwhile, adjust oven rack to lowest position and heat oven to 425 degrees. Line V-rack with heavy-duty aluminum foil, poke several holes in foil, and spray foil with vegetable oil spray.

4. Remove turkey from ice and pat dry with paper towels (discard ice). Tuck tips of drumsticks into skin at tail to secure and tuck wings behind back. Brush turkey breast with 2 tablespoons melted butter.

5. Set V-rack in pan, then scatter vegetables and thyme into pan and pour water over vegetable mixture. Place turkey, breast side down, on V-rack. Brush turkey with remaining 2 tablespoons melted butter.

6. Roast turkey for 45 minutes. Remove pan from oven and reduce oven temperature to 325 degrees. Using 2 large wads of paper towels, rotate turkey breast side up; continue to roast until breast registers 160 degrees and thighs register 175 degrees, 1 to 1½ hours longer. Transfer turkey to carving board and let rest, uncovered, for 30 minutes. Carve turkey and serve with gravy.

ROAST SALTED TURKEY FOR A CROWD
SERVES 14 TO 16

Serve with Giblet Pan Gravy for a Crowd (page 356), if desired.

Substitute 15- to 18-pound turkey for 12- to 14-pound turkey, increasing salt rubbed into cavity to 2 tablespoons and into each side of breast to 1½ tablespoons. Increase initial roasting time to 1 hour in step 6; reduce oven temperature to 325 degrees, flip turkey, and continue roasting until it reaches proper internal temperature, 1½ to 2 hours longer.

HERBED ROAST TURKEY

✔️ **WHY THIS RECIPE WORKS**

Herbed roast turkey is a welcome alternative to the annual plain roasted bird, but getting great herb flavor in every bite is a challenge. After attempting to add herb flavor a variety of ways—through brining, injecting, and butterflying—we realized the answer was relatively simple. We made a vertical slit in the breast meat with a paring knife and then swept the blade back and forth. This created a pocket into which we could rub a small amount of herb paste (a combination of parsley, thyme, sage, rosemary, shallot, garlic, lemon zest, mustard, and oil). We used the same paste in three other applications—underneath the skin, inside the cavity, and over the skin—to give the turkey fragrant herb flavor throughout.

HERBED ROAST TURKEY
SERVES 10 TO 12

If using a self-basting turkey or kosher turkey, do not brine in step 1. If you have the time and the refrigerator space, air-drying produces extremely crisp skin and is worth the effort. After brining and patting the turkey dry, place the turkey breast side up on a wire rack set in a rimmed baking sheet and refrigerate, uncovered, for 8 to 24 hours. Proceed with the recipe.

TURKEY AND BRINE

- 1 cup salt
- 1 (12- to 14-pound) turkey, trimmed, neck, giblets, and tailpiece removed and discarded
- 1 recipe All-Purpose Gravy (page 359)

HERB PASTE

- 1¼ cups chopped fresh parsley
- 4 teaspoons minced fresh thyme
- 2 teaspoons chopped fresh sage
- 1½ teaspoons minced fresh rosemary
- 1 shallot, minced
- 2 garlic cloves, minced
- ¾ teaspoon grated lemon zest
- ¾ teaspoon salt
- 1 teaspoon pepper
- ¼ cup olive oil
- 1 teaspoon Dijon mustard

1. FOR THE TURKEY AND BRINE: Dissolve salt in 2 gallons cold water in large container. Submerge turkey in brine, cover, and refrigerate or store in very cool spot (40 degrees or less) for 6 to 12 hours.

2. Remove turkey from brine and pat dry, inside and out, with paper towels. Place turkey, breast side up, on wire rack set in rimmed baking sheet or roasting pan and refrigerate, uncovered, for 30 minutes.

3. FOR THE HERB PASTE: Pulse parsley, thyme, sage, rosemary, shallot, garlic, lemon zest, salt, and pepper together in food processor until coarse paste is formed, 10 pulses. Add oil and mustard; continue to pulse until mixture forms smooth paste, 10 to 12 two-second pulses; scrape bowl with rubber spatula after 5 pulses. Transfer mixture to bowl.

4. TO PREPARE THE TURKEY: Adjust oven rack to lowest position and heat oven to 400 degrees. Line V-rack with heavy-duty aluminum foil and poke several holes in foil. Set V-rack in roasting pan and spray foil with vegetable oil spray. Remove turkey from refrigerator and wipe away any water collected in baking sheet; set turkey breast side up on baking sheet.

5. Using your fingers, gently loosen

ACHIEVING HERB FLAVOR

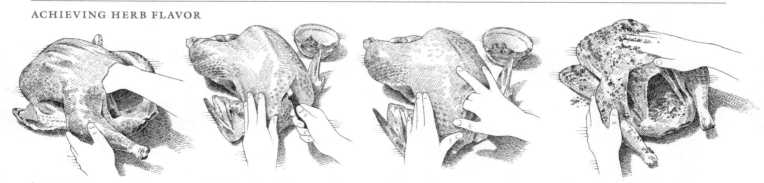

1. Carefully separate skin from meat on breast, thigh, and drumstick areas. Rub herb paste under skin and directly onto flesh, distributing it evenly.

2. Make 1½-inch slit in each breast. Swing knife tip through breast to create large pocket.

3. Place thin layer of paste inside each pocket, then rub over meat.

4. Rub remaining paste inside turkey and on skin.

CARVING AN HERBED ROAST TURKEY

The wings and legs on our Herbed Roast Turkey (page 358) can be carved just as they would be on any other turkey (see illustrations 1, 2, and 3 on page 355), but the breast, which is stuffed with herb paste, needs some special attention. Here's how to ensure that every slice has a nice swirl of herbs.

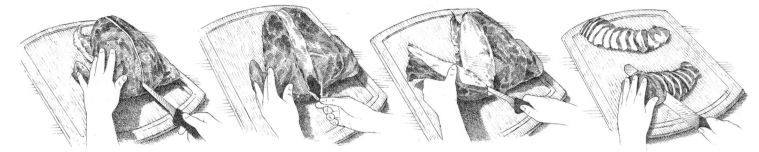

1. With wings facing toward you, cut along both sides of breastbone, slicing from tip of breastbone to carving board.

2. Gently pull each breast half away to expose wishbone. Then pull and remove wishbone.

3. Using knife tip, cut along rib cage to remove breast completely.

4. Place entire breast half on carving board and cut on bias into thin slices. Repeat step 3 on other side.

skin covering breast, thighs, and drumsticks. Place 1½ tablespoons paste under breast skin on each side of turkey. Gently press on skin to distribute paste over breast, thigh, and drumstick meat.

6. Using sharp paring knife, cut 1½-inch vertical slit into thickest part of each side of breast. Starting from top of incision, swing knife tip down to create 4- to 5-inch pocket within flesh. Place 1 tablespoon paste in pocket of each side of breast; using your fingers, rub paste in thin, even layer.

7. Rub 1 tablespoon paste inside turkey cavity. Rotate turkey breast side down; apply half of remaining herb paste to turkey skin; flip turkey breast side up and apply remaining herb paste to skin, pressing and patting to make paste adhere; reapply herb paste that falls onto baking sheet. Tuck tips of drumsticks into skin at tail to secure, and tuck wings behind back.

8. TO ROAST THE TURKEY: Place turkey breast side down on prepared V-rack. Roast turkey for 45 minutes.

9. Remove pan from oven. Using 2 large wads of paper towels, rotate turkey breast side up. Continue to roast until breast registers 160 degrees and thighs register 175 degrees, 50 to 60 minutes longer. Transfer turkey to carving board and let rest, uncovered, for 30 minutes. Carve turkey and serve with gravy.

ALL-PURPOSE GRAVY

✔ WHY THIS RECIPE WORKS

Gravy is an ideal accompaniment to a variety of dishes, not just holiday roasts. We wanted a top-notch all-purpose gravy without having to rely on the juices and pan drippings from a roast. For the liquid component, equal amounts of chicken broth and beef broth struck just the right balance. To develop a pleasant roasted flavor without roasted meat, we found that if we extended the cooking time of our mirepoix (a combination of carrots, onions, and celery), the vegetables would brown and develop a rich fond on the bottom of the pan. After sautéing the vegetables in butter, we added flour to form a roux and cooked it for a long time until it was the color of milk chocolate; this toasted roux provided an unexpectedly rich, roasted flavor.

ALL-PURPOSE GRAVY
MAKES 2 CUPS

This gravy can be served with almost any type of poultry or meat or with mashed potatoes. If you would like to double the recipe, use a Dutch oven to give the vegetables ample space for browning and increase the cooking times by roughly 50 percent.

1	small carrot, peeled and chopped
1	small celery rib, chopped
1	small onion, chopped
3	tablespoons unsalted butter
¼	cup all-purpose flour
2	cups low-sodium chicken broth
2	cups beef broth
1	bay leaf
¼	teaspoon dried thyme
5	whole black peppercorns
	Salt and pepper

1. Pulse carrot in food processor until broken into rough ¼-inch pieces, about 5 pulses. Add celery and onion; pulse until all vegetables are broken into ⅛-inch pieces, about 5 pulses.

2. Melt butter in large saucepan over medium-high heat. Add vegetables and cook, stirring often, until softened and well browned, about 7 minutes. Reduce heat to medium; add flour and cook, stirring constantly, until thoroughly browned and fragrant, about 5 minutes. Slowly whisk in chicken broth and beef broth; bring to boil, skimming off any foam that forms on surface. Add bay leaf, thyme, and peppercorns, reduce to simmer, and cook, stirring occasionally, until thickened and measures 3 cups, 20 to 25 minutes.

3. Strain gravy into clean saucepan, pressing on solids to extract as much liquid as possible; discard solids. Season with salt and pepper to taste and serve.

TO MAKE AHEAD: Finished gravy can be frozen for up to 1 month. To thaw either single or double recipe, place gravy and 1 tablespoon water in saucepan over low heat and bring slowly to simmer. Gravy may appear broken or curdled as it thaws, but vigorous whisking will recombine it.

SPICE-RUBBED ROAST TURKEY

✔ WHY THIS RECIPE WORKS
Spices can give a holiday bird a serious flavor boost, provided they don't fall off or turn into a soggy mess. We wanted a spice-rubbed turkey featuring succulent meat perfumed with spices and covered with crisp, flavor-packed, mahogany-colored skin. Determining when to apply the spice rub was key, and we discovered it was best to add it after brining. We brined and then air-dried the turkey for maximum skin crispness and then applied the rub not only to the skin but also to the meat underneath and inside the cavity. Lifting the skin had the added advantage of creating pockets of air between the skin and flesh that made it easier for the fat to render. For best flavor, we ground our own spices (coriander, cumin, allspice, and mustard seeds), then mixed them with paprika, ground ginger, thyme, cayenne, and ground cinnamon.

SPICE-RUBBED ROAST TURKEY
SERVES 10 TO 12

If using a self-basting turkey or kosher turkey, do not brine in step 1, and season with salt after rubbing the turkey with the spice mixture in step 4. Serve this turkey with chutney or a cranberry sauce (page 367) rather than gravy. See page 355 for information on carving the turkey.

1	cup salt
1	(12- to 14-pound) turkey, trimmed, neck, giblets, and tailpiece removed and discarded
1½	tablespoons coriander seeds
1	tablespoon cumin seeds
1	tablespoon allspice berries
2	teaspoons mustard seeds
3	tablespoons paprika
2	tablespoons ground ginger
1	tablespoon dried thyme
1	teaspoon cayenne pepper
1	teaspoon ground cinnamon
1½	teaspoons vegetable oil

1. Dissolve salt in 2 gallons cold water in large container. Submerge turkey in brine, cover, and refrigerate or store in very cool spot (40 degrees or less) for 6 to 12 hours.

2. Meanwhile, toast coriander, cumin, allspice, and mustard in small skillet over medium heat, shaking pan occasionally, until fragrant and wisps of smoke appear, 3 to 5 minutes. Cool mixture to room temperature, then grind to fine powder in spice grinder. Transfer mixture to small bowl and stir in paprika, ginger, thyme, cayenne, and cinnamon; cover and set aside.

3. Remove turkey from brine and pat dry, inside and out, with paper towels. Place turkey, breast side up, on wire rack set in rimmed baking sheet or roasting pan and refrigerate, uncovered, for 30 minutes. Meanwhile, mix 1 tablespoon spice rub with vegetable oil in separate bowl and set aside.

4. TO PREPARE THE TURKEY: Remove turkey from refrigerator and wipe away any water collected in baking sheet; set turkey on baking sheet. Using your fingers, gently loosen skin covering each side of breast; place oil–spice rub mixture under skin, directly on meat in center of each breast. Gently press on skin to distribute mixture over meat. Rub 3 tablespoons spice rub inside turkey cavity. Rotate turkey breast side down; apply half of remaining spice rub to turkey skin; flip turkey breast side up and apply remaining spice rub, pressing and patting to make spices adhere; reapply any spice rub that falls onto baking sheet. Tuck wings behind back and tie ends of drumsticks together with kitchen twine. Place turkey breast side up on wire rack, set wire rack on baking sheet, and refrigerate, uncovered, 6 to 24 hours.

5. TO ROAST THE TURKEY: Adjust oven rack to lowest position and heat oven to 400 degrees. Line V-rack with heavy-duty aluminum foil and poke several holes in foil. Set V-rack in roasting pan and spray foil with vegetable oil spray. Place turkey breast side down on prepared V-rack. Reapply any spice rub that has fallen off. Roast for 45 minutes.

6. Remove pan from oven. Using 2 large wads of paper towels, turn turkey wing side up. Return turkey to oven and

continue to roast for 15 minutes. Remove turkey from oven and turn other wing side up; roast for another 15 minutes. Remove turkey from oven and turn it breast side up; roast until breast registers 160 degrees and thighs register 175 degrees, 30 to 45 minutes.

7. Transfer turkey to carving board and let rest, uncovered, for 30 minutes. Carve turkey and serve.

OLD-FASHIONED STUFFED TURKEY

✓ WHY THIS RECIPE WORKS
Stuffing a turkey generally complicates the matter of properly cooking the bird; still, we couldn't help but wonder if there was a way to have it all—juicy meat, burnished skin, richly flavored stuffing, and drippings suitable for gravy. Focused first on crisp skin, we opted to salt the bird rather than brine it; using a minimal amount of salt ensured the gravy wouldn't be too salty. We also rubbed the skin with a mixture of baking powder and salt and poked holes in the skin to help render the fat. Starting the turkey in a low oven and then cranking up the heat yielded breast meat that was moist and tender. To solve the stuffing dilemma, we removed the stuffing from the turkey when the meat had reached a safe temperature. Because it was saturated with turkey juices, we were able to mix it with the remaining stuffing (the portion that didn't fit in the bird) so that every bite of stuffing was infused with turkey flavor. Finally, we draped salt pork over the turkey during the first part of cooking for an intense flavor boost.

OLD-FASHIONED STUFFED TURKEY
SERVES 10 TO 12

If using a self-basting turkey or kosher turkey, do not salt in step 1. Table salt is not recommended for this recipe because it is too fine. Look for salt pork that is roughly equal parts fat and lean meat. If serving with Giblet Pan Gravy (page 354), note that you can complete step 1 of the gravy recipe up to a day ahead, if desired. Begin step 3 once the bird has been removed from the oven and is resting on a carving board. The bread can be toasted up to 1 day in advance. See page 362 for more stuffing recipes and see page 355 for information on carving the turkey.

TURKEY
- 1 (12- to 14-pound) turkey, trimmed, neck, giblets, and tailpiece removed and reserved for gravy
- 3 tablespoons plus 2 teaspoons kosher salt
- 2 teaspoons baking powder
- 1 (36-inch) square cheesecloth, folded in quarters

CLASSIC HERB STUFFING
- 1½ pounds hearty white sandwich bread, cut into ½-inch cubes (12 cups)
- 4 tablespoons unsalted butter
- 1 onion, chopped fine
- 2 celery ribs, minced
- 1 teaspoon table salt
- 1 teaspoon pepper
- 2 tablespoons minced fresh thyme
- 1 tablespoon minced fresh marjoram
- 1 tablespoon minced fresh sage
- 1½ cups low-sodium chicken broth
- 2 large eggs

- 12 ounces salt pork, cut into ¼-inch-thick slices and rinsed
- 1 recipe Giblet Pan Gravy (page 354)

1. FOR THE TURKEY: Use your fingers or thin wooden spoon handle to gently loosen skin covering breast, thighs, drumsticks, and back; avoid breaking skin. Rub 1 tablespoon salt evenly inside cavity of turkey, 1½ teaspoons salt under skin of each side of breast, and 1½ teaspoons salt under skin of each leg. Wrap turkey tightly with plastic wrap and refrigerate for at least 24 hours or up to 48 hours.

2. FOR THE STUFFING: Adjust oven rack to lowest position and heat oven to 250 degrees. Spread bread cubes in single layer on rimmed baking sheet; bake until edges have dried but centers are slightly moist (cubes should yield to pressure), about 45 minutes, stirring several times during baking. (Bread can be toasted up to 1 day in advance.) Transfer dried bread to large bowl.

3. While bread dries, melt butter in 12-inch skillet over medium-high heat. Add onion, celery, salt, and pepper and cook, stirring occasionally, until vegetables are softened and lightly browned, 5 to 7 minutes. Stir in thyme, marjoram, and sage and cook until fragrant, about 1 minute. Add vegetable mixture to bowl with dried bread; add 1 cup broth and toss until evenly moistened (you should have about 12 cups stuffing).

4. Remove turkey from refrigerator and pat dry, inside and out, with paper towels. Using metal skewer, poke 15 to 20 holes in fat deposits on top of breast halves and thighs, 4 to 5 holes in each deposit. Tuck wings behind back.

5. Increase oven temperature to 325 degrees. Combine remaining 2 teaspoons salt and baking powder in bowl. Sprinkle surface of turkey with salt mixture and rub in mixture with hands, coating entire surface evenly. Line turkey cavity with cheesecloth, pack with 4 to 5 cups stuffing, and tie ends of cheesecloth together. Cover remaining stuffing with plastic wrap and refrigerate. Using kitchen twine, loosely tie turkey legs together. Place turkey breast side down in V-rack set in roasting pan and drape salt pork slices over back.

6. Roast turkey until breast registers 130 degrees, 2 to 2½ hours. Remove pan

from oven (close oven door to retain oven heat) and increase oven temperature to 450 degrees. Transfer turkey in V-rack to rimmed baking sheet. Remove and discard salt pork. Using 2 large wads of paper towels, rotate turkey breast side up. Cut twine binding legs and remove stuffing bag; empty into reserved stuffing in bowl. Pour drippings from roasting pan into fat separator and reserve for gravy, if making.

7. Once oven has come to temperature, return turkey in V-rack to roasting pan and roast until skin is golden brown and crisp, breast registers 160 degrees, and thighs register 175 degrees, about 45 minutes, rotating pan halfway through roasting. Transfer turkey to carving board and let rest, uncovered, for 30 minutes.

8. While turkey rests, reduce oven temperature to 400 degrees. Whisk eggs and remaining ½ cup broth from stuffing recipe together in bowl. Pour egg mixture over stuffing and toss to combine, breaking up any large chunks; spread stuffing into buttered 13 by 9-inch baking dish. Bake until stuffing registers 165 degrees and top is golden brown, about 15 minutes. Carve turkey and serve with stuffing and gravy.

DRIED FRUIT AND NUT STUFFING
MAKES ABOUT 12 CUPS

Dried cranberries can be substituted for the raisins.

- 1½ pounds hearty white sandwich bread, cut into ½-inch cubes (12 cups)
- 4 tablespoons unsalted butter
- 1 onion, chopped fine
- 2 celery ribs, minced
- 1 teaspoon salt
- 1 teaspoon pepper
- 2 tablespoons minced fresh thyme
- 1 tablespoon minced fresh marjoram
- 1 tablespoon minced fresh sage
- 1 cup raisins
- 1 cup dried apples, chopped fine
- 1 cup walnuts, chopped coarse
- 1½ cups low-sodium chicken broth
- 3 large eggs

1. Adjust oven rack to lowest position and heat oven to 250 degrees. Spread bread cubes in single layer on rimmed baking sheet; bake until edges have dried but centers are slightly moist (cubes should yield to pressure), about 45 minutes, stirring several times during baking. (Bread can be toasted up to 1 day in advance.) Transfer dried bread to large bowl and increase oven temperature to 325 degrees.

2. While bread dries, melt butter in 12-inch skillet over medium-high heat. Add onion, celery, salt, and pepper and cook, stirring occasionally, until vegetables are softened and lightly browned, 5 to 7 minutes. Stir in thyme, marjoram, and sage and cook until fragrant, about 1 minute. Add vegetable mixture, raisins, dried apples, and walnuts to bowl with dried bread; add 1 cup broth and toss until evenly moistened (you should have about 12 cups stuffing).

3. Use stuffing as directed in Old-Fashioned Stuffed Turkey (page 361), adding eggs and remaining ½ cup broth in step 6.

SAUSAGE AND FENNEL STUFFING
MAKES ABOUT 12 CUPS

See page 269 for information on preparing the fennel.

- 1½ pounds hearty white sandwich bread, cut into ½-inch cubes (12 cups)
- 1 teaspoon vegetable oil
- 8 ounces bulk pork sausage
- 4 tablespoons unsalted butter
- 1 onion, chopped fine
- 1 fennel bulb, stalks discarded, bulb halved, cored, and chopped fine
- 1 teaspoon salt
- 1 teaspoon pepper
- 2 tablespoons minced fresh sage
- 1 tablespoon minced fresh thyme
- 1 tablespoon minced fresh marjoram
- 1½ cups low-sodium chicken broth
- 3 large eggs

1. Adjust oven rack to lowest position and heat oven to 250 degrees. Spread bread cubes in single layer on rimmed baking sheet; bake until edges have dried but centers are slightly moist (cubes should yield to pressure), about 45 minutes, stirring several times during baking. (Bread can be toasted up to 1 day in advance.) Transfer dried bread to large bowl and increase oven temperature to 325 degrees.

2. While bread dries, heat oil in 12-inch nonstick skillet over medium-high heat until shimmering. Add sausage and cook, breaking it up into small pieces with wooden spoon, until browned, 5 to 7 minutes. Remove sausage with slotted spoon and transfer to paper towel–lined plate.

3. Melt butter in fat left in skillet over medium-high heat. Add onion, fennel, salt, and pepper and cook, stirring occasionally, until vegetables are softened and lightly browned, 5 to 7 minutes. Stir in sage, marjoram, and thyme and cook until fragrant, about 1 minute. Add vegetable mixture and sausage to bowl with dried bread; add 1 cup broth and toss until evenly moistened (you should have about 12 cups stuffing).

4. Use stuffing as directed in Old-Fashioned Stuffed Turkey (page 361), adding eggs and remaining ½ cup broth in step 6.

GLAZED BUTTERFLIED TURKEY

✔ WHY THIS RECIPE WORKS

A glossy, tangy-sweet glaze is the perfect complement to a beautifully bronzed turkey, but it often pools at the bottom of the roasting pan and prevents the skin from crisping. The solution to avoiding soggy skin was a simple matter of timing: adding the glaze at the outset of cooking led to predictably flabby skin, but brushing it on toward the very end of cooking—when we cranked up the heat to brown the skin—worked great. Molasses served as the sticky base of our glaze, but it needed to be thinned out to be spreadable, so we added some apple cider and apple cider vinegar. Now our glaze was too thin and was running off the bird into the pan. Thickening it with some cranberries (which contain pectin) partially solved the problem; butterflying the turkey—so it would lay flat and cook evenly—got us the rest of the way there.

BUTTERFLIED TURKEY WITH CRANBERRY-MOLASSES GLAZE

SERVES 10 TO 12

If using a self-basting turkey or kosher turkey, do not salt in step 1. Table salt is not recommended for this recipe because it is too fine. If you have a V-rack that, when inverted, still fits into your roasting pan, place the turkey on that rather than on the onions. See page 342 for information on how to butterfly a turkey.

TURKEY

- 1 (12- to 14-pound) turkey, trimmed, neck, giblets, and tailpiece removed and discarded
   Kosher salt and pepper
- 2 teaspoons baking powder
- 2 large onions, halved

GLAZE

- 3 cups apple cider
- 1 cup frozen or fresh cranberries
- ½ cup molasses
- ½ cup apple cider vinegar
- 1 tablespoon Dijon mustard
- 1 tablespoon grated fresh ginger
- 2 tablespoons unsalted butter, cut into 2 pieces and chilled

1. FOR THE TURKEY: Using kitchen shears, cut along both sides of backbone to remove it. Flatten breastbone and tuck wings underneath. Using your fingers, gently loosen skin covering breast and thighs. Using metal skewer, poke 15 to 20 holes in fat deposits on top of breast and thighs, 4 to 5 holes in each deposit. Rub bone side of turkey evenly with 2 teaspoons salt and 1 teaspoon pepper. Flip turkey skin side up and rub 1 tablespoon salt evenly under skin. Tuck wings under turkey. Push legs up to rest on lower portion of breast and tie legs together with kitchen twine.

2. Combine 1 tablespoon salt, 1 teaspoon pepper, and baking powder in bowl. Pat skin side of turkey dry with paper towels. Sprinkle surface of turkey with salt mixture and rub in mixture with hands, coating entire surface evenly. Transfer turkey to roasting pan, skin side up. Place 1 onion half under each breast and thigh to elevate turkey off bottom of roasting pan. Allow turkey to stand at room temperature for 1 hour.

3. Adjust oven rack to lower-middle position and heat oven to 275 degrees. Roast turkey until breast registers 160 degrees and thighs register 175 degrees, 2½ to 3 hours. Remove pan from oven and allow turkey to rest in pan for at least 30 minutes or up to 1½ hours.

Thirty minutes before returning turkey to oven, increase oven temperature to 450 degrees.

4. FOR THE GLAZE: While turkey rests, bring cider, cranberries, molasses, vinegar, mustard, and ginger to boil in medium saucepan. Cook, stirring occasionally, until reduced to 1½ cups, about 30 minutes. Strain mixture through fine-mesh strainer into 2-cup liquid measuring cup, pressing on solids to extract as much liquid as possible. Discard solids (you should have about 1¼ cups glaze). Transfer ½ cup glaze to small saucepan and set aside.

5. Brush turkey with one-third of glaze in measuring cup, transfer to oven, and roast for 7 minutes. Brush on half of remaining glaze in measuring cup and roast additional 7 minutes. Brush on remaining glaze in measuring cup and roast until skin is evenly browned and crisp, 7 to 10 minutes. Transfer turkey to carving board and let rest for 20 minutes.

6. While turkey rests, remove onions from pan and discard. Strain liquid from pan into fat separator (you should have about 2 cups liquid). Allow liquid to settle for 5 minutes, then pour into saucepan with reserved glaze, discarding any remaining fat. Bring mixture to boil and cook until slightly syrupy, about 10 minutes. Remove pan from heat and whisk in butter. Carve turkey and serve, passing sauce separately.

BUTTERFLIED TURKEY WITH APPLE-MAPLE GLAZE

Substitute ½ cup dried apples for cranberries and ½ cup maple syrup for molasses.

SLOW-ROASTED TURKEY WITH GRAVY

✔ WHY THIS RECIPE WORKS

We wanted no less than the perfect turkey recipe—an approach that would get our fowl from supermarket to table in just a few hours. We required meat as moist as prime rib, crisp, crackling skin, and it all needed to be accompanied by rich gravy. For a greater challenge, we wanted to do it without salting the turkey or brining it, both of which take the better part of a day. Forgoing the impressive presentation of a whole bird, we opted for turkey parts. Without the insulating effect of the turkey's backbone and breast meat, the thighs and drumsticks reached their proper temperature by the time the breast meat was done. We roasted a breast and two leg quarters (thighs and drumsticks) on a rack over a baking sheet to promote air circulation. The results? Tender, juicy meat. To achieve super-crisp skin without overcooking the meat, we let the turkey rest before returning it for a final blast of heat in a 500-degree oven.

SLOW-ROASTED TURKEY WITH GRAVY

SERVES 10 TO 12

Instead of drumsticks and thighs, you may use 2 (1½- to 2-pound) whole leg quarters. The recipe will also work with a turkey breast alone; in step 2, reduce the butter to 1½ tablespoons, the salt to 1½ teaspoons, and the pepper to 1 teaspoon. Many supermarkets carry "hotel-style" turkey breasts. Try to avoid these if you can, as they still have the wings and rib cage attached. If this is the only type of breast you can find, you will need to remove the wings and cut away the rib cage with kitchen shears before proceeding with the recipe.

TURKEY

- 3 onions, chopped
- 3 celery ribs, chopped
- 2 carrots, peeled and chopped
- 5 sprigs fresh thyme
- 5 garlic cloves, peeled and halved
- 1 cup low-sodium chicken broth
- 1 (5- to 7-pound) whole bone-in turkey breast, trimmed
- 4 pounds turkey drumsticks and thighs, trimmed
- 3 tablespoons unsalted butter, melted
- 1 tablespoon salt
- 2 teaspoons pepper

GRAVY

- 2 cups low-sodium chicken broth
- 3 tablespoons unsalted butter
- 3 tablespoons all-purpose flour
- 2 bay leaves
  Salt and pepper

1. FOR THE TURKEY: Adjust oven rack to lower-middle position and heat oven to 275 degrees. Arrange onions, celery, carrots, thyme, and garlic in even layer on rimmed baking sheet. Pour broth into baking sheet. Place wire rack on top of vegetables.

2. Pat turkey pieces dry with paper towels. Brush turkey pieces on all sides with melted butter and season with salt and pepper. Place breast skin side down and drumsticks and thighs skin side up on rack on vegetable-filled baking sheet, leaving at least ¼ inch between pieces.

3. Roast turkey pieces for 1 hour. Using 2 large wads of paper towels, turn turkey breast skin side up. Continue roasting until breast registers 160 degrees and thighs register 175 degrees, 1 to 2 hours longer. Remove baking sheet from oven and transfer rack with turkey to second baking sheet. Allow pieces to rest for at least 30 minutes or up to 1½ hours.

4. FOR THE GRAVY: Strain vegetables and liquid from baking sheet through fine-mesh strainer set in 4-cup liquid measuring cup, pressing on solids to extract as much liquid as possible; discard solids. Add chicken broth to measuring cup (you should have about 3 cups liquid).

5. Melt butter in medium saucepan over medium-high heat. Add flour and cook, stirring constantly, until flour is dark golden brown and fragrant, about 5 minutes. Slowly whisk in broth mixture and bay leaves and gradually bring to boil. Reduce to simmer and cook, stirring occasionally, until gravy is thick and measures 2 cups, 15 to 20 minutes. Discard bay leaves. Off heat, season gravy with salt and pepper to taste. Cover to keep warm.

6. TO SERVE: Heat oven to 500 degrees. Place baking sheet with turkey in oven. Roast until skin is golden brown and crisp, about 15 minutes. Transfer turkey to carving board and let rest, uncovered, for 20 minutes. Carve and serve with gravy.

BAKED BREAD STUFFING

✔ WHY THIS RECIPE WORKS

Stuffing baked in a dish definitely has appeal—you can make as much as you want and you don't have to time its doneness to coincide with the doneness of the meat—but it lacks the rich flavor from the bird's flavorful juices. As the base for our stuffing we chose ordinary sandwich bread, which we "staled" in a low oven; this allowed it to soak up plenty of liquid. To infuse the stuffing with meaty turkey flavor, we browned turkey wings on the stovetop, then used the same pan to sauté the aromatics. When we placed the stuffing in a baking dish, we arranged the seared wings on top—as they cooked, their rendered fat infused the stuffing with rich flavor. Covering the baking dish with foil prevented the top of the stuffing from drying out, while placing a baking sheet underneath the dish protected the bottom layer from the oven's heat.

BAKED BREAD STUFFING WITH SAUSAGE, DRIED CHERRIES, AND PECANS

SERVES 10 TO 12

Two pounds of chicken wings can be substituted for the turkey wings. If using chicken wings, separate them into 2 sections (it's not necessary to separate the tips) and poke each segment 4 or 5 times. Also, increase the amount of broth to 3 cups, reduce the amount of butter to 2 tablespoons, and cook the stuffing for only 60 minutes (the wings should register over 175 degrees at the end of cooking). Use the meat from the cooked wings to make salad or soup.

2	pounds hearty white sandwich bread, cut into ½-inch cubes (16 cups)
3	pounds turkey wings, divided at joints
2	teaspoons vegetable oil
1	pound bulk pork sausage
4	tablespoons unsalted butter
1	large onion, chopped fine
3	celery ribs, minced
	Salt
2	tablespoons minced fresh thyme
2	tablespoons minced fresh sage
1	teaspoon pepper
2½	cups low-sodium chicken broth
3	large eggs
1	cup dried cherries
1	cup pecan halves, toasted and chopped fine

1. Adjust oven racks to upper-middle and lower-middle positions and heat oven to 250 degrees. Spread bread cubes in even layer on 2 rimmed baking sheets; bake until edges have dried but centers are slightly moist (cubes should yield to pressure), 45 to 60 minutes, stirring several times during baking. (Bread can be toasted up to 1 day in advance.) Transfer dried bread to large bowl and increase oven temperature to 375 degrees.

2. While bread dries, use paring knife to poke 10 to 15 holes in each wing segment. Heat oil in 12-inch skillet over medium-high heat until shimmering. Add wings in single layer and cook until golden brown on both sides, 8 to 12 minutes. Transfer wings to separate bowl and set aside.

3. Return now-empty skillet to medium-high heat, add sausage, and cook, breaking it up into ½-inch pieces with wooden spoon, until browned, 5 to 7 minutes. Remove sausage with slotted spoon and transfer to paper towel–lined plate.

4. Melt butter in fat left in skillet over medium heat. Add onion, celery, and ½ teaspoon salt and cook, stirring occasionally, until vegetables are softened, 7 to 9 minutes. Stir in thyme, sage, and pepper and cook until fragrant, about 30 seconds. Stir in 1 cup broth, scraping up any browned bits, and bring to simmer. Add vegetable mixture to bowl with dried bread and toss to combine.

5. Grease 13 by 9-inch baking dish. Whisk eggs, remaining 1½ cups broth, 1½ teaspoons salt, and any accumulated juices from wings together in bowl. Add egg mixture, cherries, pecans, and sausage to bread mixture and toss to combine; transfer to prepared baking dish. Arrange wings on top of stuffing, cover tightly with aluminum foil, and place baking dish on rimmed baking sheet.

6. Bake on lower rack until wings register 175 degrees, 60 to 75 minutes. Remove foil and transfer wings to dinner plate to reserve for another use. Using fork, gently fluff stuffing. Let rest for 5 minutes before serving.

BAKED BREAD STUFFING WITH LEEKS, BACON, AND APPLE

Omit pecans. Substitute 12 ounces bacon, cut into ½-inch pieces, for sausage. In step 3, cook bacon in skillet until crisp, about 5 minutes. Remove bacon with slotted spoon and transfer to paper towel–lined plate; pour off all but 2 tablespoons fat from skillet. Proceed with recipe from step 4, substituting 2 leeks, white and light green parts, sliced thin, for onion, and 3 Granny Smith apples, cut into ¼-inch pieces, for dried cherries.

BAKED BREAD STUFFING WITH FRESH HERBS

Omit sausage. After browned turkey wings have been removed in step 2, increase butter to 6 tablespoons and melt in skillet over medium heat. Proceed with recipe from step 4, substituting 3 tablespoons chopped fresh parsley for dried cherries and pecans.

PREPARING TURKEY WINGS

Cut through joint with sharp knife. If turkey wing comes with tip, cut through this joint as well.

CORNBREAD STUFFING

✓ WHY THIS RECIPE WORKS

Most cornbread stuffings are either dry and crumbly or wet and soggy. We wanted a cornbread stuffing with a toasted top, moist interior, and satisfyingly rich interior. Tearing the cornbread into bite-size pieces created enough crumbs to release the cornbread flavor, but enough bigger pieces remained for substance. Cornbread that had been staled had the best texture. Eggs made our stuffing cohesive, chicken broth added the necessary moisture, and half-and-half gave our stuffing a full, rich flavor. Soaking the bread in the liquid mixture for just one hour took our stuffing to the next level. To finish, we added some sautéed herbs and aromatics along with sausage for a meaty punch.

CORNBREAD STUFFING WITH SAUSAGE
SERVES 10 TO 12

To make the stuffing a day in advance, increase both the chicken broth and half-and-half by ¼ cup each and refrigerate the unbaked stuffing 12 to 24 hours; before transferring it to the baking dish, let the stuffing stand at room temperature for about 30 minutes so that it loses its chill.

12	cups cornbread (recipe follows) broken into 1-inch pieces (include crumbs)
1¾	cups low-sodium chicken broth
1	cup half-and-half
2	large eggs
12	ounces bulk pork sausage, broken into 1-inch pieces
3	onions, chopped fine
3	celery ribs, minced
2	tablespoons unsalted butter
2	tablespoons minced fresh thyme
2	tablespoons minced fresh sage
3	garlic cloves, minced
1½	teaspoons salt
2	teaspoons pepper

1. Adjust oven racks to upper-middle and lower-middle positions and heat oven to 250 degrees. Spread cornbread pieces in even layer on 2 rimmed baking sheets and dry in oven 50 to 60 minutes. Transfer dried cornbread to large bowl and increase oven temperature to 375 degrees.

2. Whisk broth, half-and-half, and eggs together in medium bowl. Add broth mixture to cornbread and toss very gently to coat so that bread does not break into smaller pieces. Set aside.

3. Cook sausage in 12-inch skillet over medium-high heat until browned, 5 to 7 minutes. Remove sausage with slotted spoon and transfer to paper towel–lined plate. Add half of onions and celery to fat left in skillet and cook, stirring occasionally, over medium-high heat until softened, about 5 minutes. Transfer onion mixture to bowl with sausage. Melt butter in now-empty skillet over medium-high heat. Add remaining onions and celery and cook, stirring occasionally, until softened, about 5 minutes. Stir in thyme, sage, garlic, salt, and pepper and cook until fragrant, about 30 seconds. Add vegetable mixture and sausage mixture to bowl with cornbread and stir gently to combine (try not to break bread into smaller pieces). Cover bowl with plastic wrap and refrigerate to blend flavors, at least 1 hour or up to 4 hours.

4. Adjust oven rack to lower-middle position and heat oven to 400 degrees. Grease 15 by 10-inch baking dish (or two 9-inch square or 11 by 7-inch baking dishes).

Transfer stuffing to prepared baking dish; pour any liquid accumulated in bottom of bowl over stuffing and, if necessary, gently press stuffing with rubber spatula to fit into baking dish. Bake until golden brown, 35 to 40 minutes.

SPICY CORNBREAD STUFFING WITH RED PEPPER, CHIPOTLE CHILES, AND ANDOUILLE SAUSAGE

Andouille is a spicy smoked Cajun sausage. If you cannot find any, chorizo can be substituted.

Omit sausage and increase butter to 4 tablespoons. Melt 2 tablespoons butter in 12-inch skillet over medium-high heat. Add 2 red bell peppers, stemmed, seeded, and cut into ¼-inch pieces, along with one-third of onions and celery and cook until softened, about 5 minutes; transfer to bowl. Melt remaining 2 tablespoons butter in now-empty skillet over medium-high heat. Add remaining onions and celery and cook, stirring occasionally, until softened, about 5 minutes. Stir in 4 tablespoons minced chipotle chile in adobo sauce along with thyme, sage, and garlic. Add bell pepper mixture, along with softened onion mixture and 1½ pounds andouille sausage, cut into ½-inch pieces, to bowl with cornbread.

GOLDEN CORNBREAD
MAKES ABOUT 16 CUPS CRUMBLED CORNBREAD

You need about three-quarters of this recipe for the stuffing; the rest is for nibbling.

2	cups cornmeal (10 ounces)
2	cups (10 ounces) all-purpose flour
2	tablespoons sugar

4	teaspoons baking powder
1	teaspoon baking soda
1	teaspoon salt
1⅓	cups buttermilk
1⅓	cups whole milk
4	large eggs
4	tablespoons unsalted butter, melted

1. Adjust oven rack to middle position and heat oven to 375 degrees. Grease 13 by 9-inch baking dish.

2. Whisk cornmeal, flour, sugar, baking powder, baking soda, and salt together in large bowl. Push dry ingredients up sides of bowl to make well. Whisk buttermilk, milk, and eggs together in separate bowl, then pour into well and stir with whisk until just combined; stir in melted butter.

3. Pour batter into prepared baking dish. Bake until top is golden brown and the edges have pulled away from sides of pan, 30 to 40 minutes. Remove cornbread from oven and let cool to room temperature on wire rack before using, about 1 hour.

SIMPLE CRANBERRY SAUCE

✔ WHY THIS RECIPE WORKS

Cranberry sauce should have enough sweetness to temper the assertively tart fruit (but no so much that it is cloying) and its texture should be that of a soft gel, neither too liquid-y nor too stiff. Because it has only three basic ingredients—cranberries, sweetener, and liquid—we simply had to find the right proportions. We started with a 12-ounce bag of cranberries, since that is what is commonly available in the supermarket. One cup of granulated sugar balanced the

tartness of the berries with a direct sweetness, without adding a strong flavor profile of its own. We found that no other liquid offered a single advantage over plain water, and ¾ cup was just right. We also discovered that adding just a pinch of salt brought out an unexpected sweetness in the berries, heightening the flavor of the sauce overall.

SIMPLE CRANBERRY SAUCE
MAKES 2¼ CUPS

If you've got frozen cranberries, do not defrost them before use; just pick through them and add about 2 minutes to the simmering time.

1	cup sugar
¾	cup water
¼	teaspoon salt
1	(12-ounce) bag cranberries, picked through

Bring sugar, water, and salt to boil in medium saucepan, stirring occasionally to dissolve sugar. Stir in cranberries; return to boil, then reduce to simmer and cook until saucy and slightly thickened, and about two-thirds of berries have popped open, about 5 minutes. Transfer to bowl, let cool to room temperature, and serve. (Cranberry sauce can be refrigerated for up to 1 week.)

SIMPLE CRANBERRY-ORANGE SAUCE

Orange juice adds little flavor, but we found that zest and liqueur pack the orange kick we were looking for in this sauce.

Heat 1 tablespoon grated orange zest (2 oranges) with sugar mixture. Off heat, stir in 2 tablespoons orange liqueur (such as triple sec or Grand Marnier).

SIMPLE CRANBERRY SAUCE WITH PEARS AND FRESH GINGER

Peel, core, and cut 2 firm, ripe Bosc pears into ½-inch pieces; set aside. Heat 1 tablespoon grated fresh ginger and ¼ teaspoon ground cinnamon with sugar mixture and stir pears into liquid along with cranberries.

SIMPLE CRANBERRY SAUCE WITH CHAMPAGNE AND CURRANTS

Substitute champagne for water and add 3 tablespoons dried currants to liquid along with cranberries.

ROAST STUFFED CORNISH GAME HENS

✔ WHY THIS RECIPE WORKS

Though Cornish hens are small, they still present many challenges—the breast meat easily overcooks; it can be difficult to get the birds to brown with such a short stay in the oven; stuffing them is never easy; and they are in need of a serious flavor boost. To prevent steaming, we lifted the birds up and out of the roasting pan and onto a wire rack. Turning the birds once proved to be crucial for moist and juicy breast meat. The ideal roasting temperature was 400 degrees, though we cranked up the oven to 450 degrees at the end of cooking to promote browning. For even more color, we opted to glaze the birds with balsamic vinegar; this gave them a pleasant, spotty brown barbecued look. Heating the stuffing before placing it inside the birds let it come up to the proper temperature more quickly during cooking, thereby keeping the breast meat from overcooking. We also created a simpler approach (without stuffing) where we butterfly the hen so it roasts quickly and evenly and is seasoned with an herb butter for an extra boost of flavor.

ROAST STUFFED CORNISH GAME HENS
SERVES 6

If your game hens are frozen, be sure to thaw them in the refrigerator for 24 to 36 hours before brining. Pouring a little broth into the baking sheet at the 25-minute mark, once the hens have been turned, both prevents them from smoking during cooking and makes instant jus, eliminating the need to deglaze the pan.

   Salt and pepper
6 (1¼- to 1½-pound) Cornish game hens, trimmed, giblets removed and discarded
6 tablespoons balsamic vinegar
3 tablespoons olive oil
1 recipe prepared stuffing (recipes follow)
1 cup low-sodium chicken broth
¼ cup dry vermouth or dry white wine

1. Dissolve ½ cup salt in 4 quarts cold water in large container. Submerge hens in brine, cover, and refrigerate for 30 minutes to 1 hour.

2. Adjust oven rack to middle position and heat oven to 400 degrees. Set wire rack in aluminum foil–lined rimmed baking sheet. Remove hens from brine and pat dry with paper towels. Season with pepper and tuck wings behind back.

3. Whisk vinegar and oil together in small bowl and set aside. Microwave stuffing in covered bowl until very hot, about 2 minutes. Spoon ½ cup of hot stuffing into cavity of each hen, then tie each hen's legs together with kitchen twine. Arrange

hens, breast side down and with wings facing out, on prepared wire rack.

4. Roast hens until backs are golden brown, about 25 minutes. Remove pan from oven and brush each hen with vinegar glaze. Rotate hens breast side up and with wings facing out, and brush with glaze. Add ½ cup broth to pan and continue to roast until stuffed cavity registers 150 degrees, 15 to 20 minutes longer.

5. Remove baking sheet from oven and increase oven temperature to 450 degrees. Brush each hen with glaze, add remaining ½ cup broth to baking sheet, and continue to roast until hens are spotty brown and cavity registers 160 degrees, 5 to 10 minutes longer. Remove hens from oven, transfer to carving board, and let rest for 10 minutes. Remove twine used to truss hens.

6. Meanwhile, pour cooking juices from pan into small saucepan and let settle for 5 minutes. Remove any fat from surface with large spoon. Add vermouth, bring to simmer, and cook until sauce thickens slightly and flavors meld, 3 to 5 minutes. Season with salt and pepper to taste. Serve hens, passing sauce separately.

COUSCOUS STUFFING WITH CURRANTS, APRICOTS, AND PISTACHIOS

MAKES ABOUT 3 CUPS, ENOUGH FOR 6 CORNISH HENS

Toasted slivered almonds can be substituted for the pistachio nuts.

2 tablespoons unsalted butter
1 small onion, chopped fine
2 garlic cloves, minced
¼ teaspoon ground cinnamon
⅛ teaspoon ground ginger
⅛ teaspoon ground turmeric
1 cup couscous
1⅓ cups low-sodium chicken broth
¼ cup shelled pistachios, toasted and chopped coarse
¼ cup dried apricots, chopped fine
3 tablespoons dried currants
2 tablespoons minced fresh parsley
1 teaspoon lemon juice
   Salt and pepper

1. Melt butter in medium saucepan over medium heat. Add onion and cook, stirring occasionally, until softened, about

PREPARING STUFFED CORNISH GAME HENS

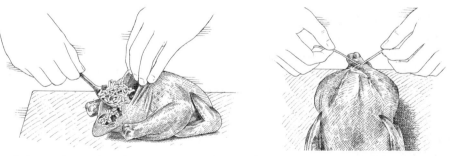

1. Spoon ½ cup of hot filling into cavity of each hen.

2. Tie legs of each hen together with kitchen twine.

5 minutes. Stir in garlic, cinnamon, ginger, and turmeric and cook until fragrant, about 30 seconds. Stir in couscous and cook until well coated, 1 to 2 minutes.

2. Stir in broth and bring to simmer. Remove saucepan from heat, cover, and let stand for 5 minutes. Fluff couscous with fork and transfer to medium bowl. Stir in pistachios, apricots, currants, parsley, and lemon juice. Season with salt and pepper to taste. (Stuffing can be refrigerated for up to 24 hours.)

WILD RICE STUFFING WITH CARROTS, MUSHROOMS, AND THYME

MAKES ABOUT 3 CUPS, ENOUGH FOR 6 CORNISH HENS

The wild rice blend in this stuffing holds together when pressed with a fork. You can use wild rice, but the cooked grains will remain separate.

- 2 cups low-sodium chicken broth
- 1 cup wild rice blend
- 2 tablespoons unsalted butter
- 1 small onion, chopped fine
- 1 carrot, peeled and chopped fine
- ½ celery rib, minced
- 1 ounce dried porcini mushrooms, rinsed and minced
- 4 ounces shiitake mushrooms, stemmed and sliced thin
- 2 tablespoons minced fresh parsley
- 2 teaspoons minced fresh thyme
  Salt and pepper

1. Bring broth to boil in medium saucepan. Add rice and return to boil. Reduce heat to low, cover, and simmer until rice is fully cooked, 40 to 50 minutes. Transfer rice to medium bowl and fluff with fork.

2. Meanwhile, melt butter in 10-inch skillet over medium heat. Add onion, carrot, celery, and porcini and cook, stirring occasionally, until softened, about 5 minutes. Add shiitakes and cook until tender and liquid evaporates, 8 to 10 minutes. Stir mushroom mixture into rice, along with parsley and thyme. Season with salt and pepper to taste. (Stuffing can be refrigerated for up to 24 hours.)

WILD RICE STUFFING WITH CRANBERRIES AND TOASTED PECANS

MAKES ABOUT 3 CUPS, ENOUGH FOR 6 CORNISH HENS

The wild rice blend in this stuffing holds together when pressed with a fork. You can use wild rice, but the cooked grains will remain separate.

- 2 cups low-sodium chicken broth
- 1 cup wild rice blend
- 2 tablespoons unsalted butter
- 1 onion, chopped fine
- ½ celery rib, minced
- ¼ cup pecans, toasted and chopped coarse
- ¼ cup dried cranberries
- 2 tablespoons minced fresh parsley
- 2 teaspoons minced fresh thyme
  Salt and pepper

1. Bring broth to boil in medium saucepan. Add rice and return to boil. Reduce heat to low, cover, and simmer until rice is fully cooked, 40 to 50 minutes. Transfer rice to medium bowl and fluff with fork.

2. Meanwhile, melt butter in 10-inch skillet over medium heat. Add onion and celery and cook, stirring occasionally, until softened, about 5 minutes. Stir onion mixture into rice, along with pecans, cranberries, parsley, and thyme. Season with salt and pepper to taste. (Stuffing can be refrigerated for up to 24 hours.)

SIMPLE ROAST BUTTERFLIED CORNISH GAME HENS

SERVES 4

In this variation, we skip the stuffing. Butterflying a Cornish game hen is similar to butterflying a chicken or turkey (see page 342). Use kitchen shears to cut out and remove the backbone, then make a ¼-inch cut in the breastbone to separate the breast halves and lightly press down to flatten the bird. Finally, with the skin facing up, fold the wingtips behind the bird to secure them.

- ½ teaspoon salt
- ½ teaspoon pepper
- ½ teaspoon dried thyme, basil, or tarragon
- 4 (1¼- to 1½-pound) Cornish game hens, trimmed, giblets removed and discarded
- 2 teaspoons butter, softened

1. Adjust oven rack to lower-middle position and heat oven to 400 degrees. Set wire rack in aluminum foil–lined rimmed baking sheet. Combine salt, pepper, and thyme in bowl.

2. Butterfly hens, flatten breastbone, and tuck wings underneath. Pat hens dry with paper towels, then use your fingers to gently loosen skin covering breast and thighs. Rub one-quarter of salt mixture under skin of each hen. Using metal skewer, poke 4 or 5 holes in skin of each hen, then rub skin with ½ teaspoon butter. Place hens skin side up on prepared rack.

3. Roast hens until lightly browned and thighs register 160 degrees, 20 to 25 minutes.

4. Remove baking sheet from oven and heat broiler. Broil hens until golden brown, breasts register 160 degrees and thighs register 175 degrees, about 5 minutes. Transfer hens to carving board and let rest for 10 minutes. Drizzle any accumulated pan juices over each hen and serve.

CRISP ROAST DUCK

✔ WHY THIS RECIPE WORKS

Duck has one main problem—it is extremely fatty. We wanted knockout duck with crisp skin and moist, flavorful meat, minus a lot of the fat. We found that it was important to get rid of much of the fat from the outset so that the skin could crisp properly. Loose skin, including most of the flap that covers the neck cavity, also had to be cut away. Taking a cue from Asian roast duck recipes, we first steamed the duck to render additional fat. Then, because the legs were still too fatty, we cut the duck into pieces before roasting. Once the legs were no longer protected from the heat, they rendered much more fat during their stay in the oven. And because we roasted the parts skin side down and finished them skin side up, the skin was beautifully browned and crisp.

PREPARING ROAST DUCK

Trim away skin that is not directly over meat or bone. Pull back skin in neck cavity and cut away pieces of fat to expose wing joints.

CRISP ROAST DUCK WITH PORT WINE GLAZE

SERVES 4 TO 6

Port comes in many styles, but we prefer to use an inexpensive Tawny port here. For duck with very moist, tender meat and slightly crisp skin once roasted, steam the duck for about 40 minutes in step 2. Steam 10 minutes longer for somewhat denser meat and very crisp skin after roasting.

- 1¼ cups port
- 2 garlic cloves, sliced thin
- 4 sprigs fresh thyme
- 1 (4½- to 5-pound) whole duck, trimmed, neck and giblets discarded
  Salt and pepper

1. Bring port, garlic, and thyme to simmer in small saucepan and cook until thickened and measures ¼ cup, 25 to 30 minutes. Discard garlic and thyme sprigs; set glaze aside until ready to use.

2. Meanwhile, set V-rack in flameproof roasting pan and place duck breast side up on rack. Add water to just below bottom of duck, place pan over 2 burners, and bring to boil. Reduce heat to medium, cover pan tightly with aluminum foil, and steam, until skin has pulled away from at least 1 leg, about 40 minutes (add more hot water to maintain water level if necessary). Transfer duck to carving board, let cool slightly, then carve into 6 pieces (2 boneless breasts, 2 legs, 2 wings). Remove rack and discard steaming liquid. Wipe out pan with paper towels.

3. Adjust oven rack to lowest position and heat oven to 425 degrees. Lightly spray now-empty pan with vegetable oil spray. Season duck pieces with salt and pepper and place skin side down in prepared pan. Roast duck, carefully removing fat if more than 2 tablespoons accumulate in pan, until skin on breast pieces is rich golden brown and crisp, about 25 minutes. Transfer breast pieces to plate and cover with foil to keep warm.

4. Again, carefully remove excess fat from pan, turn leg and wing pieces skin side up, and continue roasting until skin is deep golden brown and crisp, 15 to 20 minutes longer. Again, carefully remove excess fat from pan. Return breast pieces to pan and brush both sides of each piece with glaze; position pieces skin side up once glazed. Roast until glaze is hot and richly colored on duck pieces, 3 to 4 minutes. Serve immediately.

CRISP ROAST DUCK WITH ORANGE GLAZE

The lime juice keeps this thick, syrupy glaze from being too sweet.

Substitute 1 cup orange juice (2 oranges), 2 tablespoons lime juice, and 2 tablespoons honey for port and omit garlic and thyme.

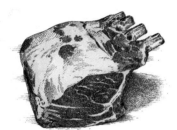

CHAPTER 10   Meat

SIMPLE PAN-SEARED STEAKS

✔ WHY THIS RECIPE WORKS

For the best pan-seared steak, we used smaller, more expensive cuts like rib eye, boneless strip, and sirloin, which browned evenly and had a full, rich flavor. As for our pan-searing technique, we started with a very hot pan that would sear the steak upon contact. We found it best to heat the oil in the pan over medium-high heat and then retain this heat level throughout cooking. The oil also helped to brown the steak and keep it from sticking to the pan.

SIMPLE PAN-SEARED STEAKS
SERVES 4

Serve the steaks as is or with a flavored butter or sauce (recipes follow).

I	tablespoon vegetable oil
4	(8- to 10-ounce) boneless strip steaks or rib-eye steaks, I to I¼ inches thick
	Salt and pepper
I	recipe butter or pan sauce (optional) (recipes follow)

1. Heat oil in 12-inch skillet over medium-high heat until just smoking. Meanwhile, pat steaks dry with paper towels and season both sides with salt and pepper.

2. Lay steaks in pan, leaving ¼ inch between them. Cook, without moving steaks, until well browned, about 4 minutes. Using tongs, flip steaks and continue to cook until meat registers 115 to 120 degrees (for rare) or 120 to 125 degrees (for medium-rare), 3 to 7 minutes. Transfer steaks to serving platter and tent loosely with aluminum foil to rest or while preparing butter or pan sauce, if using, then serve.

ROQUEFORT BUTTER
MAKES ABOUT ¼ CUP, ENOUGH FOR I RECIPE SIMPLE PAN-SEARED STEAKS

Mash together 2 tablespoons room-temperature butter, ¼ cup crumbled Roquefort cheese, and ½ teaspoon brandy. Season with salt and pepper to taste. Top each cooked steak with portion of flavored butter and serve.

HORSERADISH–SOUR CREAM SAUCE
MAKES ABOUT ½ CUP, ENOUGH FOR I RECIPE SIMPLE PAN-SEARED STEAKS

Stir together ¼ cup each sour cream and prepared horseradish. Season with salt and pepper to taste and serve alongside each cooked steak.

MUSTARD SAUCE
MAKES ABOUT I CUP, ENOUGH FOR I RECIPE SIMPLE PAN-SEARED STEAKS

Wipe fat from skillet; add 1½ cups chicken broth, then boil until reduced by one-half. Stir in 3 tablespoons Dijon mustard, 2 tablespoons butter, and salt and pepper to taste; spoon portion of sauce over each cooked steak.

RESTAURANT-STYLE STEAK SAUCES

✔ WHY THIS RECIPE WORKS

We love the ultra-rich flavor and glossy consistency that a classic French demi-glace (a savory, full-bodied reduction traditionally made from veal bones and stock) adds to a sauce, but making it is a time-consuming process usually left to the expertise of professional cooks. We wanted to find a shortcut for making demi-glace at home, so that we could use it as the base of a sauce for crusty, pan-seared steaks. Chopping up vegetables (to increase their surface area, thus providing more opportunity for flavorful browning) as well as adding mushrooms, tomato paste, and seasonings to red wine and beef broth was a good start, but it wasn't enough. To replicate the meaty flavor and unctuous gelatin given up by roasted bones, we sautéed ground beef with the tomato paste and stirred powdered gelatin into the final reduction.

TEST KITCHEN TIP NO. 77 **A MORE AFFORDABLE DRY-AGED STEAK**

In commercial dry-aging, butchers hold large primal cuts of beef (typically the rib or short loin sections) for up to 30 days in humid refrigerators ranging between 32 and 40 degrees. The humidity is necessary to prevent the meat's exterior from drying out too much. As moisture evaporates, the fat becomes more concentrated, increasing meaty flavor. The dehydration process also triggers the breakdown of muscle proteins, resulting in a dense, more tender texture. At the same time, the breakdown of muscle encourages the formation of amino acids and peptides, which impart a meatier, smokier taste.

To try replicating these results at home, we bought rib-eye and strip steaks (each $10.99 per pound) and stored them in the back of the refrigerator, where the temperature is coldest. Since home refrigerators are less humid than commercial dry-aging units, we wrapped the steaks in cheesecloth to allow air to pass through while preventing excess dehydration. We checked them after four days (the longest length of time we felt comfortable storing raw beef in a home fridge).

Next, we pan-seared the home-aged steaks and tasted them alongside a batch of the same commercially dry-aged cuts costing $19.99 per pound. Sure enough, our "home" dry-aged steaks boasted a comparably smoky flavor and dense, tender texture. So, save yourself a few bucks, but remember to wrap the meat in plenty of cheesecloth, place it on a wire rack for air circulation, and store it in the coldest part of the fridge.

PAN-SEARED STEAKS WITH RESTAURANT-STYLE SAUCE
SERVES 4

We like this sauce with strip or rib-eye steaks, but it will work with any type of pan-seared steak.

I	recipe Simple Pan-Seared Steaks (page 372)
I	small shallot, minced
½	cup white wine
¼	cup Sauce Base (½ recipe; recipe follows)
¼	teaspoon white wine vinegar
I ½	teaspoons minced fresh chives
I ½	teaspoons minced fresh parsley
I	teaspoon minced fresh tarragon
I	tablespoon unsalted butter
	Salt and pepper

After transferring steaks to platter to rest, return now-empty skillet to medium-low heat; add shallot and cook, stirring constantly, until lightly browned, about 2 minutes. Add wine and bring to simmer, scraping bottom of skillet with wooden spoon to loosen any browned bits. Add Sauce Base, vinegar, and any accumulated juices from steak; return to simmer and cook until slightly reduced, about 1 minute. Off heat, whisk in chives, parsley, tarragon, and butter; season with salt and pepper to taste. Spoon sauce over steaks and serve.

PAN-SEARED STEAKS WITH BRANDY AND GREEN PEPPERCORN SAUCE

Substitute brandy for white wine and red wine vinegar for white wine vinegar. Omit chives, parsley, tarragon, and butter. Add ¼ cup heavy cream, 2 tablespoons rinsed whole green peppercorns, and ¼ teaspoon chopped fresh thyme to skillet along with Sauce Base and vinegar.

TEST KITCHEN TIP NO. 78 REDUCTION DEDUCTION

We've all seen recipe instructions such as "Reduce sauce to ½ cup" or "Simmer until broth is reduced to 2 cups." Those directions are clear, but when you look into a pan of sauce, can you really discern volume? Unless you have wizardlike abilities, the answer is probably "No."

Here in the test kitchen, we know that getting the right amount of sauce can make or break a dish, and to be sure of success we keep a heatproof liquid measuring cup next to the stove. As the sauce appears to be getting near the targeted amount, we pour it into the cup to get an exact measure. If it needs more time on the stove, back into the pan it goes until it's reduced to just the right amount. No guessing, no problem.

PAN-SEARED STEAKS WITH PORT WINE SAUCE

Substitute ruby port for white wine and balsamic vinegar for white wine vinegar. Substitute ¼ teaspoon chopped fresh thyme for chives, parsley, and tarragon.

SAUCE BASE
MAKES ½ CUP

The sauce base recipe yields more than called for in the steak recipe; leftovers can be refrigerated for up to 3 days or frozen for up to 1 month.

I	small onion, peeled and cut into rough ½-inch pieces
I	small carrot, peeled and cut into rough ½-inch pieces
8	ounces cremini mushrooms, trimmed and halved
2	garlic cloves, peeled
I	tablespoon vegetable oil
8	ounces 85 percent lean ground beef
I	tablespoon tomato paste
2	cups dry red wine
4	cups beef broth
4	sprigs fresh thyme
2	bay leaves
2	teaspoons whole black peppercorns
5	teaspoons unflavored gelatin

1. Pulse onion, carrot, mushrooms, and garlic in food processor into ⅛-inch pieces, 10 to 12 pulses, scraping down bowl as needed.

2. Heat oil in Dutch oven over medium-high heat until shimmering; add beef and tomato paste and cook, stirring frequently, until beef is well browned, 8 to 10 minutes. Add vegetable mixture and cook, stirring occasionally, until any exuded moisture has evaporated, about 8 minutes. Add wine and bring to simmer, scraping bottom of pot with wooden spoon to loosen any browned bits. Add broth, thyme, bay leaves, and peppercorns; bring to boil. Reduce heat and gently boil, occasionally scraping bottom and sides of pot and skimming fat from surface, until reduced to 2 cups, 20 to 25 minutes.

3. Strain mixture through fine-mesh strainer set over small saucepan, pressing on solids with rubber spatula to extract as much liquid as possible (you should have about 1 cup stock). Sprinkle gelatin over sauce base and stir to dissolve. Place saucepan over medium-high heat and bring sauce base to boil. Gently boil, stirring occasionally, until reduced to ½ cup, 5 to 7 minutes. Remove from heat and cover to keep warm.

PAN-SEARED INEXPENSIVE STEAKS

✔ WHY THIS RECIPE WORKS

Looking for an alternative to pricey cuts of meat, we wanted to find the best inexpensive (under $6.99 per pound) steaks for pan-searing that would still deliver solid beefy flavor and tender texture. We tested 12 different cuts using a pan-searing technique of heating oil in a skillet until smoking, cooking the steaks over medium-high heat on one side, then reducing the heat when we flipped the steaks. This approach ensured a nice sear on both sides without overcooking or allowing the fond to burn. We tried a variety of preparation methods—salting, aging, tenderizing, marinating—but none really improved flavor and texture. In the end, only two cuts earned favored status: boneless shell sirloin steak (aka top butt) and flap meat steak (aka sirloin tips).

PAN-SEARED INEXPENSIVE STEAKS
SERVES 4

A pan sauce can be made while the steaks rest after cooking (recipes follow); if you plan to make a sauce, be sure to prepare all of the sauce ingredients before cooking the steaks. You can substitute a 2-pound whole flap meat steak for the shell sirloin steaks. To serve two instead of four, use a 10-inch skillet to cook a 1-pound steak and halve the sauce ingredients. Keep in mind that even those tasters who usually prefer rare beef preferred these steaks cooked medium-rare or medium because the texture is firmer and not quite so chewy.

- 2 tablespoons vegetable oil
  Salt and pepper
- 2 (1-pound) boneless shell sirloin steaks (top butt), 1¼ inches thick
- 1 recipe pan sauce (optional) (recipes follow)

1. Heat oil in 12-inch skillet over medium-high heat until just smoking. Meanwhile, pat steaks dry with paper towels and season both sides with salt and pepper. Place steaks in skillet; cook, without moving, until well browned, about 2 minutes. Using tongs, flip steaks; reduce heat to medium. Cook until well browned on second side and meat registers 120 to 125 degrees (for medium-rare) or 130 to 135 degrees (for medium), 5 to 6 minutes.

2. Transfer steaks to large plate and tent loosely with aluminum foil; let rest 12 to 15 minutes. Meanwhile, prepare pan sauce, if making.

3. Using sharp knife, slice steak about ¼ inch thick against grain on bias, arrange on platter or on individual plates, and spoon sauce, if using, over steak; serve.

MUSTARD-CREAM PAN SAUCE
MAKES ¾ CUP, ENOUGH FOR
1 RECIPE PAN-SEARED INEXPENSIVE STEAKS

- 1 shallot, minced
- 2 tablespoons dry white wine
- ½ cup low-sodium chicken broth
- 6 tablespoons heavy cream
- 3 tablespoons whole grain Dijon mustard
  Salt and pepper

After transferring steaks to large plate, pour off all but 1 tablespoon fat from now-empty skillet. Return skillet to low heat and add shallot; cook, stirring frequently, until beginning to brown, 2 to 3 minutes. Add wine and increase heat to medium-high; simmer rapidly, scraping bottom of skillet with wooden spoon to loosen any browned bits, until liquid is reduced to glaze, about 30 seconds; add broth and simmer until reduced to ¼ cup, about 3 minutes. Add cream and any meat juices; cook until heated through, about 1 minute. Stir in mustard; season with salt and pepper to taste. Spoon sauce over sliced steak and serve.

TOMATO-CAPER PAN SAUCE
MAKES ¾ CUP, ENOUGH FOR
1 RECIPE PAN-SEARED INEXPENSIVE STEAKS

If ripe fresh tomatoes are not available, substitute 2 to 3 canned whole tomatoes.

- 1 shallot, minced
- 1 teaspoon all-purpose flour
- 2 tablespoons dry white wine
- 1 cup low-sodium chicken broth
- 2 tablespoons capers, rinsed
- 1 ripe tomato, cored, seeded and cut into ¼-inch dice
- ¼ cup minced fresh parsley
  Salt and pepper

After transferring steaks to large plate, pour off all but 1 tablespoon fat from now-empty skillet. Return skillet to low heat and add shallot; cook, stirring frequently, until beginning to brown, 2 to 3 minutes. Sprinkle flour over shallot; cook, stirring constantly, until combined, about 1 minute. Add wine and increase heat to medium-high; simmer rapidly, scraping bottom of skillet with wooden spoon to loosen any browned bits, until liquid is reduced to glaze, about 30 seconds; add broth and simmer until reduced to ⅔ cup,

When shopping, it's best to avoid shallots packaged in cardboard or cellophane boxes, which prevent you from checking out each shallot. Instead, go for loose shallots or ones packaged in plastic netting. They should feel firm and heavy and have no soft spots. Since most of our recipes call for less than 3 tablespoons of minced shallots, in the test kitchen we use primarily medium shallots (which yield about 3 tablespoons minced) or small shallots (which yield 2 tablespoons or less). A medium shallot should be about 1½ to 2 inches wide.

about 4 minutes. Reduce heat to medium; add capers, tomato, and any meat juices and cook until flavors are blended, about 1 minute. Stir in parsley and season with salt and pepper to taste; spoon sauce over sliced steak and serve.

PAN-SEARED THICK-CUT STRIP STEAKS

✔ WHY THIS RECIPE WORKS

Pan-searing thick-cut steaks poses one main problem—by the time a good crust has developed and the very center is a rosy medium-rare, the rest of the meat is dry and gray. To solve this problem, we needed to find a way to quickly sear the exterior while slowly cooking the interior to allow for more even heat distribution. We tried flipping the steaks every 15 seconds and also pan-roasting them (searing them on the stovetop then moving the skillet to a hot oven), but neither of these approaches was practical or worked very well. The key turned out to be starting the steaks in a cool oven and then quickly searing them to keep the meat directly under the crust from turning gray. Cooked this way, the steaks developed a beautiful brown crust, while the rest of the meat stayed pink, juicy, and tender.

PAN-SEARED THICK-CUT STRIP STEAKS

SERVES 4

Rib eye or filet mignon of similar thickness can be substituted for the strip steaks. If using filet mignon, buying a 2-pound center-cut tenderloin roast and portioning it into four 8-ounce steaks yourself will produce more consistent results than individual store-cut steaks. If using filet mignon, increase the oven time by about 5 minutes. When cooking lean strip steaks (without an external fat cap) or filet mignon, add an extra tablespoon of oil to the pan. If desired, serve with a pan sauce, relish, or butter (recipes follow).

2 (1-pound) boneless strip steaks, 1½ to 1¾ inches thick
   Salt and pepper
1 tablespoon vegetable oil
1 recipe pan sauce, relish, or butter (optional) (recipes follow)

1. Adjust oven rack to middle position and heat oven to 275 degrees. Pat steaks dry with paper towels. Cut each steak in half vertically to create four 8-ounce steaks. Season steaks with salt and pepper; gently press sides of steaks until uniform 1½ inches thick. Place steaks on wire rack set in rimmed baking sheet. Cook until meat registers 90 to 95 degrees (for rare to medium-rare), 20 to 25 minutes, or 100 to 105 degrees (for medium), 25 to 30 minutes.

2. Heat oil in 12-inch skillet over high heat until just smoking. Place steaks in skillet and sear until well browned and crusty, about 1½ to 2 minutes, lifting once halfway through cooking to redistribute fat underneath each steak. (Reduce heat if fond begins to burn.) Using tongs, turn steaks and cook until well browned on second side, 2 to 2½ minutes. Transfer all steaks to clean wire rack and reduce heat under pan to medium. Use tongs to stand 2 steaks on their sides. Holding steaks together, return to skillet and sear on all sides until browned, about 1½ minutes. Repeat with remaining 2 steaks.

3. Transfer steaks to wire rack and let rest, tented loosely with aluminum foil, for 10 minutes while preparing pan sauce, if using. Arrange steaks on individual plates and spoon sauce over steaks; serve.

RED WINE–MUSHROOM PAN SAUCE

MAKES ABOUT 1 CUP, ENOUGH FOR 1 RECIPE PAN-SEARED THICK-CUT STRIP STEAKS

Prepare all ingredients for the pan sauce while the steaks are in the oven.

1   tablespoon vegetable oil
8   ounces white mushrooms, trimmed and sliced thin
1   small shallot, minced
1   cup dry red wine
½   cup low-sodium chicken broth
1   tablespoon balsamic vinegar
1   teaspoon Dijon mustard
2   tablespoons unsalted butter, cut into 4 pieces and chilled
1   teaspoon minced fresh thyme
    Salt and pepper

After transferring steaks to wire rack, pour off fat from now-empty skillet. Heat oil over medium-high heat until just smoking. Add mushrooms and cook, stirring occasionally, until beginning to brown and liquid has evaporated, about 5 minutes. Add shallot and cook, stirring frequently,

---

TEST KITCHEN TIP NO. 80   **THE SEARING TRUTH**

Thinner steaks can be cooked through over relatively high heat, while thicker steaks usually cook in two stages: a quick sear in a hot skillet to brown the surface, along with a gentler cooking to bring the interior up to (or close to) its final temperature. Many people believe that searing a raw steak somehow "seals in" juices, resulting in a juicier finished product than meat browned at the end of cooking. Yet we've all seen well-seared steaks exude moisture as they rest, so we decided to put this theory to the test. We weighed steaks before and after cooking, searing one half before cooking them through in the oven, and cooking the other half through before searing. We found the steaks all lost an equal amount of liquid: about 22 percent of their original weight. Searing the steaks first did nothing to seal in liquid. In the end, this theory just doesn't hold water.

until beginning to soften, about 1 minute. Increase heat to high; add red wine and broth, scraping bottom of skillet with wooden spoon to loosen any browned bits. Simmer rapidly until liquid and mushrooms are reduced to 1 cup, about 6 minutes. Add vinegar, mustard, and any juices from resting steaks; cook until thickened, about 1 minute. Off heat, whisk in butter and thyme; season with salt and pepper to taste. Spoon sauce over steaks and serve.

SUN-DRIED TOMATO RELISH

MAKES ½ CUP, ENOUGH FOR I RECIPE
PAN-SEARED THICK-CUT STRIP STEAKS

This relish also pairs well with grilled chicken.

- ½ cup low-sodium chicken broth
  Pinch red pepper flakes
- 2 tablespoons oil-packed sun-dried tomatoes, rinsed and chopped
- 1 tablespoon capers, rinsed and chopped
- 1 tablespoon extra-virgin olive oil
- 2 teaspoons lemon juice
- 1 teaspoon honey
- 2 tablespoons chopped fresh parsley
- 1 tablespoon minced fresh mint
  Salt and pepper

After transferring steaks to wire rack, pour off fat from now-empty skillet and return to high heat. Add broth and scrape bottom of pan with wooden spoon to loosen any browned bits. Add pepper flakes and boil until liquid is reduced to 2 tablespoons, about 5 minutes. Add any meat juices to pan. Add tomatoes, capers, oil, lemon juice, and honey to pan and swirl vigorously to emulsify. Off heat, add parsley and mint. Season with salt and pepper to taste. Spoon sauce over steaks and serve.

TEQUILA-POBLANO PAN SAUCE

MAKES ⅔ CUP, ENOUGH FOR I RECIPE
PAN-SEARED THICK-CUT STRIP STEAKS

Before flambéing, be sure to roll up long shirtsleeves, tie back long hair, and turn off the exhaust fan and any lit burners.

- 1 small shallot, minced
- 1 poblano chile, stemmed, seeded, and chopped fine
- ½ teaspoon ground cumin
- ½ cup white tequila
- ½ cup low-sodium chicken broth
- 1 tablespoon lime juice
- 3 tablespoons cold unsalted butter, cut into 3 pieces and chilled
- 1 tablespoon chopped fresh cilantro
  Salt and pepper

After transferring steaks to wire rack, pour off all but 1 tablespoon fat from now-empty skillet. Return pan to high heat and add shallot and poblano; cook, stirring frequently, until lightly browned and fragrant, 1 to 2 minutes. Add cumin and continue to cook 30 seconds. Transfer pan contents to bowl. Off heat, add tequila, reserving 2 teaspoons, and let warm through, about 5 seconds. Wave lit match over pan until tequila ignites, then shake pan to distribute flames. When flames subside, add broth and 2 teaspoons lime juice. Reduce to ⅓ cup, about 6 minutes. Add remaining 2 teaspoons tequila, remaining 1 teaspoon lime juice, and any meat juices to pan. Remove from heat and whisk in cold butter, cilantro, and poblano and shallot; season with salt and pepper to taste. Spoon sauce over steaks and serve.

THAI CHILI BUTTER

MAKES ½ CUP, ENOUGH FOR I RECIPE
PAN-SEARED THICK-CUT STRIP STEAKS

If red curry paste isn't available, increase the chili-garlic sauce to 2½ teaspoons.

- 4 tablespoons unsalted butter, softened
- 1 tablespoon chopped fresh cilantro
- 2 teaspoons Asian chili-garlic sauce
- 1½ teaspoons thinly sliced scallion, green part only
- ½ teaspoon red curry paste
- 1 small garlic clove, minced
- 2 teaspoons lime juice
  Salt

Beat butter vigorously with spoon until soft and fluffy. Add cilantro, chili-garlic sauce, scallion, red curry paste, and garlic; beat to incorporate. Add lime juice a little at a time, beating vigorously between each addition until fully incorporated. Season with salt to taste. Top each cooked steak with portion of flavored butter and serve.

PAN-SEARED FILETS MIGNONS

✔ WHY THIS RECIPE WORKS

Our goal in developing a recipe for filet mignon was simple—to replicate the best restaurant filet at home, with a rich, brown crust and a tender interior, topped with a richly flavored pan sauce. To cook our filets perfectly, inside and out, we pan-seared evenly cut, well-dried filets in a 10-inch skillet, then transferred the meat to a hot oven. Finishing the steak in the oven prevented the fond (the richly flavored brown bits in the bottom of the pan) from burning and gave us time to start the sauce, which we made in minutes with Madeira, Dijon mustard, and anchovies (which added complexity without fishy flavor) while the steaks were in the oven.

PAN-SEARED FILETS MIGNONS
SERVES 4

If you choose to serve the steaks with the Madeira sauce (recipe follows), have all the sauce ingredients ready before searing the steaks. Begin the sauce while the steaks are in the oven. To cook six steaks instead of four, switch to a 12-inch pan and use 8 teaspoons of olive oil.

- 4 (7- to 8-ounce) center-cut filets mignons, 1½ inches thick
- 6 teaspoons olive oil
-    Salt and pepper
- 1 recipe Madeira Pan Sauce with Mustard and Anchovies (optional) (recipe follows)

1. Adjust oven rack to lower-middle position, place rimmed baking sheet on oven rack, and heat oven to 450 degrees. When oven reaches 450 degrees, heat 2 teaspoons oil in 10-inch skillet over high heat until just smoking.

2. Meanwhile, rub each side of steaks with ½ teaspoon oil and season with salt and pepper. Place steaks in skillet and cook, without moving them, until well browned, about 3 minutes. Turn steaks with tongs

---

GAUGING STEAK DONENESS

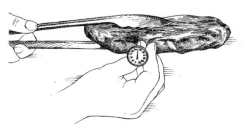

To accurately determine whether your steak is cooked to your liking, hold the meat with tongs and insert an instant-read thermometer through the side of the steak and avoid any bones. Use this tip for gauging the temperature of other thinner cuts of meat, such as pork chops and chicken breasts.

---

and cook until well browned on second side, about 3 minutes longer. Off heat, use tongs to transfer steaks to hot baking sheet in oven.

3. Roast until meat registers 115 to 120 degrees (for rare), 120 to 125 degrees (for medium-rare), or 130 to 135 degrees (for medium), 2 to 10 minutes. Meanwhile, prepare pan sauce, if using. Transfer steaks to large plate, tent loosely with aluminum foil, and let rest about 5 minutes before serving.

BACON-WRAPPED PAN-SEARED FILETS MIGNONS

Wrap 1 slice bacon around circumference of each filet, overlapping ends and securing to meat with toothpick. Hold filets two or three at a time on their sides briefly with tongs in skillet to crisp bacon slightly before transferring to oven.

MADEIRA PAN SAUCE WITH MUSTARD AND ANCHOVIES
MAKES ⅔ CUP, ENOUGH FOR 1 RECIPE PAN-SEARED FILETS MIGNONS

- 1 shallot, minced
- 1 cup Madeira or sherry
- 1 tablespoon chopped fresh parsley
- 1 tablespoon chopped fresh thyme
- 1 tablespoon Dijon mustard
- 1 tablespoon lemon juice
- 2 anchovy fillets, rinsed and minced to paste (about 1 teaspoon)
- 3 tablespoons unsalted butter, softened
-    Salt and pepper

After transferring steaks to oven, set now-empty skillet over medium-low heat; add shallot and cook, stirring constantly, until softened, about 1 minute. Add Madeira, increase heat to high, and scrape bottom of skillet with wooden spoon to loosen any browned bits. Simmer until liquid is

---

reduced to about ⅓ cup, 6 to 8 minutes. (If steaks are not yet out of oven, set skillet off heat and wait for steaks to come out of oven and rest for 2 minutes before proceeding.) Add accumulated meat juices from baking sheet and reduce liquid 1 minute longer. Off heat, whisk in parsley, thyme, mustard, lemon juice, and anchovies, then whisk in butter until butter has melted and sauce is slightly thickened. Season with salt and pepper to taste, spoon sauce over steaks, and serve.

PEPPER-CRUSTED FILETS MIGNONS

✔ WHY THIS RECIPE WORKS
Black peppercorns can give mild-tasting filet mignon a welcome flavor boost. But they can also create a punishing blast of heat. For a pepper-crusted filet mignon with a crust that wouldn't overwhelm the meat, we mellowed the peppercorns' heat by gently simmering them in olive oil. We then used a two-step process to create a well-browned and attractive pepper crust: First, we rubbed the raw steaks with a paste of the cooked cracked peppercorns, oil, and salt; then we pressed the paste into each steak using a sheet of plastic wrap to ensure it stayed put. The paste not only added flavor to the meat but also drew out the meat's own beefy flavor.

PEPPER-CRUSTED FILETS MIGNONS
SERVES 4

To crush the peppercorns, spread half of them on a cutting board, place a skillet on top, and, pressing down firmly with both hands, use a rocking motion to crush the peppercorns beneath the "heel" of the skillet. Repeat with the remaining peppercorns. While heating the peppercorns in oil tempers much of their pungent heat, this recipe is still pretty spicy. If you prefer a very mild pepper flavor, drain the cooled peppercorns in a fine-mesh strainer in step 1, toss them with 5 tablespoons of fresh oil, add the salt, and proceed. Serve with either Blue Cheese–Chive Butter or Port Cherry Reduction (recipes follow).

5 tablespoons black peppercorns, crushed
5 tablespoons plus 2 teaspoons olive oil
1 tablespoon kosher salt
4 (7- to 8-ounce) center-cut filets mignons, 1½ to 2 inches thick

1. Heat peppercorns and 5 tablespoons oil in small saucepan over low heat until faint bubbles appear. Continue to cook at bare simmer, swirling pan occasionally, until pepper is fragrant, 7 to 10 minutes. Remove from heat and set aside to cool. When mixture is room temperature, add salt and stir to combine. Rub steaks with oil and pepper mixture, thoroughly coating top and bottom of each steak with peppercorns. Cover steaks with plastic wrap and press gently to make sure peppercorns adhere; let stand at room temperature for 1 hour.

2. Meanwhile, adjust oven rack to middle position, place baking sheet on oven rack, and heat oven to 450 degrees. When oven reaches 450 degrees, heat remaining 2 teaspoons oil in 12-inch skillet over medium-high heat until just smoking. Place steaks in skillet and cook, without moving, until dark brown crust has formed, 3 to 4 minutes. Using tongs, turn steaks and cook until well browned on second side, about 3 minutes. Off heat, transfer steaks to hot baking sheet in oven. Roast until meat registers 115 to 120 degrees (for rare), 120 to 125 degrees (for medium-rare), or 130 to 135 degrees (for medium), 3 to 7 minutes. Transfer steaks to wire rack and let rest, tented loosely with aluminum foil, for 5 minutes before serving.

BLUE CHEESE–CHIVE BUTTER

MAKES ABOUT ½ CUP, ENOUGH FOR
1 RECIPE PEPPER-CRUSTED FILETS MIGNONS

1½ ounces mild blue cheese, room temperature
3 tablespoons unsalted butter, softened
⅛ teaspoon salt
2 tablespoons minced fresh chives

Combine blue cheese, butter, and salt in medium bowl and mix with stiff rubber spatula until smooth. Fold in chives. While steaks are resting, spoon 1 to 2 tablespoons butter onto each one.

PORT-CHERRY REDUCTION

MAKES ABOUT 1 CUP, ENOUGH FOR
1 RECIPE PEPPER-CRUSTED FILETS MIGNONS

1½ cups port
½ cup balsamic vinegar
½ cup dried tart cherries
1 shallot, minced
2 sprigs fresh thyme
1 tablespoon unsalted butter
Salt

1. Combine port, vinegar, cherries, shallot, and thyme in medium saucepan; simmer over medium-low heat until liquid has reduced to about ⅓ cup, about 30 minutes. Set aside, covered.

2. While steaks are resting, reheat sauce. Off heat, remove thyme, then whisk in butter until melted. Season with salt to taste; spoon over steak and serve.

STEAK AU POIVRE

✔ WHY THIS RECIPE WORKS

Steak au poivre is a simple dish, but that doesn't mean it's easy to execute well. All too often the peppercorns fall off the steak, revealing an underbrowned crust, while the peppercorn coating prevents the steak from forming drippings in the skillet that are the foundation of a rich sauce. We peppered only one side of the steak, which allowed the unpeppered side a chance to brown and create a fond in the skillet. Cooking the steaks for less time on the peppered side also prevented the peppercorns from scorching. For the sauce, we reduced a combination of chicken broth and beef broth, then used this reduction to deglaze the skillet. Brandy, cream, and butter were the finishing touches to our rich, flavorful pan sauce.

TEST KITCHEN TIP NO. 81 BEEF—GETTING A GOOD GRADE

The U.S. Department of Agriculture (USDA) assigns different quality grades to beef, but most of the meat available to consumers is confined to just three: prime, choice, and select. Grading is strictly voluntary on the part of the meat packer. If meat is graded, the meat should bear a USDA stamp indicating the grade, though it may not be visible to the consumer. To grade meat, inspectors evaluate color, grain, surface texture, and fat content and distribution. Prime meat (often available only at butcher shops) has a deep maroon color, fine-grained muscle tissue, and a smooth surface that is silky to the touch. It also contains fat that is evenly distributed and creamy white instead of yellow, which indicates an older animal that may have tougher meat. Choice beef has less marbling than prime, and select beef is leaner still.

Our blind tasting of all three grades of rib-eye steaks produced predictable results: Prime ranked first for its tender, buttery texture and rich, beefy flavor. Next came choice, with good meaty flavor and a little more chew. The tough and stringy select steak followed, with flavor that was barely acceptable. Our advice: When you're willing to splurge, go for prime steak (which in our sampling cost $3 per pound more than the choice meat), but a choice steak that exhibits a moderate amount of marbling is a fine, affordable option. Just steer clear of select-grade steak.

STEAK AU POIVRE WITH BRANDIED CREAM SAUCE
SERVES 4

To save time, crush the peppercorns and trim the steaks while the broth mixture simmers. To crush the peppercorns, spread half of them on a cutting board, place a skillet on top, and, pressing down firmly with both hands, use a rocking motion to crush the peppercorns beneath the "heel" of the skillet. Repeat with the remaining peppercorns.

SAUCE

4	tablespoons unsalted butter
1	shallot, minced
1	cup beef broth
¾	cup low-sodium chicken broth
¼	cup heavy cream
¼	cup plus 1 tablespoon brandy
1	teaspoon lemon juice or champagne vinegar
	Salt

STEAKS

4	(8- to 10-ounce) boneless strip steaks, ¾ to 1 inch thick and no larger than 3 inches at widest points, trimmed
	Salt
4	teaspoons black peppercorns, crushed
1	tablespoon vegetable oil

1. FOR THE SAUCE: Melt 1 tablespoon butter in 12-inch skillet over medium heat; add shallot and cook, stirring occasionally, until softened, about 2 minutes. Add beef and chicken broths, increase heat to high, and boil until reduced to about ½ cup, about 8 minutes. Set reduced broth mixture aside. Rinse and wipe out skillet.

2. FOR THE STEAKS: Meanwhile, pat steaks dry with paper towels and season both sides of steaks with salt; rub 1 side of each steak with 1 teaspoon crushed peppercorns, and, using fingers, press peppercorns into steaks to make them adhere.

3. Heat oil in now-empty skillet over medium heat until hot, about 4 minutes. Lay steaks, unpeppered side down, in skillet, increase heat to medium-high, firmly press down on steaks with bottom of cake pan, and cook steaks without moving them until well browned, about 6 minutes. Using tongs, flip steaks, firmly press down on steaks with bottom of cake pan, and cook on peppered side, until meat registers 115 to 120 degrees (for rare), 120 to 125 degrees (for medium-rare), or 130 to 135 degrees (for medium), 3 to 5 minutes longer. Transfer steaks to large plate and tent loosely with aluminum foil.

4. While meat is resting, pour reduced broth, cream, and ¼ cup brandy into now-empty skillet; increase heat to high and bring to boil, scraping bottom of skillet with wooden spoon to loosen any browned bits. Simmer until deep golden brown and thick enough to heavily coat back of metal tablespoon or soupspoon, about 5 minutes. Off heat, whisk in remaining 3 tablespoons butter, remaining 1 tablespoon brandy, lemon juice, and any accumulated meat juices. Season with salt to taste.

5. Arrange steaks on platter or individual plates, spoon sauce over steaks, and serve.

STEAK FRITES

✔ WHY THIS RECIPE WORKS

Steak frites is a Parisian bistro classic; when done right, the steak is cooked to perfection and the fries are fluffy on the inside and crisp on the outside—even when bathed in the juices from the meat. We wanted to re-create this restaurant favorite in our own kitchen, and we started with the fries. We determined that the fries needed to be cooked in two batches, a procedure that minimizes the drop in oil temperature that naturally occurs when potatoes (high-starch russets were the best choice) are added to frying oil. Our real breakthrough in our steak frites recipe, however, occurred when we coated the fries with a layer of cornstarch, which added a protective sheath around each fry. For the steaks, we found that thick rib eyes gave us plenty of time to get a good sear on the outside without overcooking the interior.

STEAK FRITES
SERVES 4

In order to have four steaks that fit in a skillet at the same time, it is necessary to buy two 1-pound steaks and cut them in half according to their thickness. If your steaks are 1¼ to 1¾ inches thick, cut them in half vertically into small, thick steaks. If your steaks are thicker than 1¾ inches, cut them in half horizontally into two thinner steaks. Make sure to dry the potatoes well before tossing them with the cornstarch. For safety, use a Dutch oven with a capacity of at least 7 quarts. Use refined peanut oil (such as Planters) to fry the potatoes, not toasted peanut oil. A 12-inch skillet is essential for cooking four steaks at once. The ingredients can be halved to serve two—keep the oil amount the same and forgo blanching and frying the potatoes in batches.

2½	pounds russet potatoes, scrubbed, sides squared off and cut lengthwise into ¼-inch by ¼-inch fries
2	tablespoons cornstarch
3	quarts peanut oil
1	tablespoon vegetable oil
2	(1-pound) boneless strip or rib-eye steaks, cut in half Kosher salt and pepper
1	recipe Herb Butter (recipe follows)

1. Rinse cut potatoes in bowl under cold running water until water turns clear. Cover with cold water and refrigerate for 30 minutes or up to 12 hours.

2. Pour off water, spread potatoes onto kitchen towels, and dry thoroughly. Transfer potatoes to bowl and toss with cornstarch until evenly coated. Transfer

potatoes to wire rack set in rimmed baking sheet and let rest until fine white coating forms, about 20 minutes.

3. Meanwhile, heat peanut oil in Dutch oven over medium heat to 325 degrees. Line baking sheet with brown paper bag or triple layer of paper towels.

4. Add half of potatoes, a handful at a time, to hot oil and increase heat to high. Fry, stirring with wire skimmer or slotted spoon, until potatoes start to turn from white to blond, 4 to 5 minutes. (Oil temperature will drop about 75 degrees during this frying.) Transfer fries to prepared baking sheet. Return oil to 325 degrees and repeat with remaining potatoes. Reduce heat to medium and let fries cool while cooking steaks, at least 10 minutes. (Recipe can be prepared through step 4 up to 2 hours in advance; turn off heat under oil, turning heat back to medium when you start step 6.)

5. Heat vegetable oil in 12-inch skillet over medium-high heat until just smoking. Meanwhile, pat steaks dry with paper towels and season with salt and pepper. Lay steaks in pan, leaving ¼ inch between them. Cook, without moving steaks, until well browned, about 4 minutes. Using tongs, flip steaks and continue to cook until meat registers 115 to 120 degrees (for rare) or 120 to 125 degrees (for medium-rare), 3 to 7 minutes. Transfer steaks to large plate, top with herb butter, and tent loosely with aluminum foil; let rest while finishing fries.

6. Increase heat under Dutch oven to high and heat oil to 375 degrees. Add half of fries, a handful at a time, and fry until golden brown and puffed, 2 to 3 minutes. Transfer to clean brown paper bag or paper towels. Return oil to 375 degrees and repeat with remaining fries. Season fries with salt and serve with steaks.

HERB BUTTER

MAKES ¼ CUP, ENOUGH FOR
I RECIPE STEAK FRITES

---

4 tablespoons unsalted butter, softened
½ shallot, minced
I tablespoon minced fresh parsley
I tablespoon minced fresh chives
I garlic clove, minced
¼ teaspoon salt
¼ teaspoon pepper

Combine all ingredients in bowl.

STEAK DIANE

✔ **WHY THIS RECIPE WORKS**
Steak Diane is a restaurant classic. But with its hallmark rich sauce based on an all-day veal stock reduction, we knew this dish was in need of some streamlining. We chose flavorful strip steaks and pounded them to a ½-inch thickness for even cooking. We made a faux veal stock by using tomato paste, vegetables, red wine, and a mix of chicken and beef broth and we made the sauce right in the pan in which we cooked the steak, adding cognac and butter. With these modifications, we were able to get steak Diane on the table in less than an hour.

STEAK DIANE

SERVES 4 TO 6

If desired, drizzle Steak Diane with white truffle oil just before serving. Before flambéing, be sure to roll up long shirtsleeves, tie back long hair, and turn off the exhaust fan and any lit burners. If you do not wish to flambé, simmer the cognac in step 4 for 10 to 15 seconds for a slightly less sweet flavor profile.

SAUCE BASE
2 tablespoons vegetable oil
4 teaspoons tomato paste
I onion, chopped
I carrot, chopped
4 garlic cloves, peeled
¼ cup water
4 teaspoons all-purpose flour
I½ cups dry red wine
3½ cups beef broth
I¾ cups low-sodium chicken broth
2 teaspoons black peppercorns
8 sprigs fresh thyme
2 bay leaves

STEAKS
2 tablespoons vegetable oil
4 (12-ounce) boneless strip steaks, trimmed and pounded to even ½-inch thickness
Salt and pepper

SAUCE
I tablespoon vegetable oil
I small shallot, minced
¼ cup cognac
2 teaspoons Dijon mustard
2 tablespoons unsalted butter, chilled
I teaspoon Worcestershire sauce
2 tablespoons minced fresh chives
Salt and pepper

I. FOR THE SAUCE BASE: Heat oil and tomato paste in Dutch oven over medium-high heat; cook, stirring constantly, until paste begins to brown, about 3 minutes. Add onion, carrot, and garlic; cook, stirring frequently, until mixture is reddish brown, about 2 minutes. Add 2 tablespoons water and continue to cook, stirring constantly, until mixture is well browned, about 3 minutes, adding remaining water as needed to prevent scorching. Add flour and cook, stirring constantly, 1 minute. Add wine and scrape bottom and sides of pot with wooden spoon to loosen any browned bits; bring to boil, stirring occasionally (mixture will thicken slightly). Add beef and chicken broths, peppercorns, thyme, and bay leaves; bring to boil and cook, uncovered, occasionally scraping bottom and sides of pot with spatula, until reduced to 2½ cups, 35 to 40 minutes.

2. Strain mixture through fine-mesh strainer, pressing on solids to extract as much liquid as possible; you should have about 1¼ cups.

3. FOR THE STEAKS: Heat 1 tablespoon oil in 12-inch skillet over medium-high heat until just smoking. Meanwhile, pat steaks dry with paper towels and season with salt and pepper. Place 2 steaks in skillet and cook without moving them until well browned, about 1½ minutes. Flip steaks and weight with heavy-bottomed pan; continue to cook until well browned on second side, about 1½ minutes longer. Transfer steaks to large platter and tent with aluminum foil. Add 1 tablespoon oil to now-empty skillet and repeat with remaining steaks; transfer second batch of steaks to platter.

4. FOR THE SAUCE: Off heat, add oil and shallot to now-empty skillet; using skillet's residual heat, cook, stirring frequently, until shallots are slightly softened and browned, about 45 seconds. Add cognac; let stand until cognac warms slightly, about 10 seconds, then set skillet over high heat. Wave lit match over pan until cognac ignites, then shake pan to distribute flames. When flames subside, simmer cognac until reduced to about 1 tablespoon, about 10 seconds. Add sauce base and mustard; simmer until slightly thickened and reduced to 1 cup, 2 to 3 minutes. Whisk in butter; off heat, add Worcestershire, any accumulated juices from steaks, and 1 tablespoon chives. Season with salt and pepper to taste.

5. Transfer steaks to individual plates, spoon 2 tablespoons sauce over each steak, sprinkle with remaining 1 tablespoon chives, and serve, passing remaining sauce separately.

STEAK TIPS WITH MUSHROOM-ONION GRAVY

✔ WHY THIS RECIPE WORKS
Steaks tips smothered in mushroom and onion gravy is a classic combination, but the resulting dish is often disappointing—chewy, overcooked beef swimming in a thick sludge of bland gravy. We wanted a much better rendition, one that could also be streamlined and made all in one skillet. Relatively inexpensive sirloin tips, with plentiful internal marbling for tenderness, proved ideal. We added dried porcini for extra mushroom flavor and used the moisture from deeply browned mushrooms and onions to make a rich, flavorful sauce. A sprinkling of flour thickened our gravy and minced garlic and woodsy thyme finished the sauce. We were happy to find that preparing it all in one skillet was as simple as searing the beef and setting it aside, building the gravy, and then adding the meat back to the gravy to cook through.

STEAK TIPS WITH MUSHROOM-ONION GRAVY
SERVES 4 TO 6

Steak tips, also known as flap meat, are sold as whole steaks, cubes, and strips. To ensure evenly sized chunks, we prefer to purchase whole steak tips and cut them ourselves. If you can only find cubes or strips, reduce the cooking time slightly to avoid overcooking any smaller or thinner pieces. Cremini mushrooms can be used in place of the white mushrooms. Serve over rice or egg noodles.

1	tablespoon soy sauce
1	teaspoon sugar
1½	pounds sirloin steak tips, trimmed and cut into 1½-inch chunks
1¾	cups beef broth
¼	ounce dried porcini mushrooms, rinsed
	Salt and pepper
2	tablespoons vegetable oil
1	pound white mushrooms, trimmed and cut into ¼-inch slices
1	large onion, halved and sliced thin
4	teaspoons all-purpose flour
1	garlic clove, minced
½	teaspoon minced fresh thyme
1	tablespoon chopped fresh parsley

TEST KITCHEN TIP NO. 82 THAWING MEAT

In the test kitchen, we've noticed that meat seems to thaw more quickly when left on a metal surface rather than a wood or plastic one. To confirm our observation, we froze inch-thick steaks, pork chops, and ground beef overnight and defrosted them the next day on plastic and wood cutting boards; heavy stainless steel, cast-iron, and nonstick skillets; and lightweight aluminum baking trays. After one hour, the meat on the cutting boards was still frozen solid, the meat on the aluminum trays had made slightly more progress, and the meat on the heavy pans was almost completely thawed. What was going on?

Unlike plastic and wood, which contain atoms bound together in a relatively rigid matrix, metal contains lots of moving atoms that allow it to transfer ambient heat much more quickly. We found heavy steel and cast-iron skillets worked best—which makes sense, given that the heavier and thicker the metal, the more efficient the transference of heat. To thaw frozen wrapped steaks, chops, or ground meat (flattened to 1 inch thick before freezing), place them in a skillet in a single layer (keep the wrapping on). Flip the meat every half hour until it's thawed. Irregularly shaped meats such as poultry or whole roasts that can't make good contact with the skillet will not benefit from this method.

1. Combine soy sauce and sugar in medium bowl. Add beef, toss well, and marinate at least 30 minutes or up to 1 hour, tossing once.

2. Meanwhile, microwave ¼ cup broth and porcini mushrooms in covered bowl until steaming, about 1 minute. Let stand until softened, about 5 minutes. Drain mushrooms through fine-mesh strainer lined with coffee filter, reserve liquid, and mince mushrooms. Set mushrooms and liquid aside.

3. Pat meat dry with paper towels and sprinkle with ½ teaspoon pepper. Heat 1 tablespoon oil in 12-inch skillet over medium-high heat until just smoking. Add meat and cook until well browned on all sides, 6 to 8 minutes. Transfer to large plate and set aside.

4. Return skillet to medium-high heat and add remaining 1 tablespoon oil, white mushrooms, minced porcini mushrooms, and ¼ teaspoon salt; cook, stirring frequently, until all liquid has evaporated and mushrooms start to brown, 7 to 9 minutes. Scrape bottom of pan with wooden spoon to loosen any browned bits. Add onion and ¼ teaspoon salt; continue to cook, stirring frequently, until onion begins to brown and dark bits form on pan bottom, 6 to 8 minutes longer. Add flour, garlic, and thyme; cook, stirring constantly, until vegetables are coated with flour, about 1 minute. Stir in remaining 1½ cups beef broth and porcini soaking liquid, scraping bottom of skillet with wooden spoon to loosen any browned bits, and bring to boil.

5. Nestle steak pieces into mushroom and onion mixture and add any accumulated juices to skillet. Reduce heat to medium-low and simmer until steak registers 130 degrees, 3 to 5 minutes, turning beef over several times. Season with salt and pepper to taste, sprinkle with parsley, and serve.

VEAL SCALOPPINI

✔ WHY THIS RECIPE WORKS

Supermarket veal cutlets are a far cry from the delicate fare served in restaurants—bland flavor, tough meat, and a slimy exterior are just some of their problems. We wanted veal cutlets with tender meat and delicate flavor, a perfect backdrop for a boldly flavored sauce. We discovered that a decidedly unglamorous product, Adolph's Tenderizer, turned reasonably priced supermarket cutlets into cutlets every bit as tender as those found in restaurants. But cooking them was still a challenge—we wanted nicely browned cutlets, but flouring and browning both sides overcooked the meat. The answer? We floured and browned just one side of the cutlet and cooked the second, unfloured side only briefly. Making the pan sauce before cooking the cutlets—then finishing it in the skillet to take advantage of the fond left behind from the cutlets—ensured our quick-cooking veal cutlets were warm upon serving.

VEAL SCALOPPINI
SERVES 4

Cook the veal in batches to avoid overcrowding the skillet; because the size of packaged cutlets varies, each batch may contain as few as three cutlets or as many as six. Start preparing the sauce before cooking the cutlets, then finish in the skillet used to brown the cutlets. Because meat tenderizer contains sodium, it is unnecessary to salt the cutlets.

1½	pounds veal cutlets, about ¼ inch thick
¾	teaspoon meat tenderizer
⅛	teaspoon pepper
½	cup all-purpose flour
3	tablespoons vegetable oil
1	recipe sauce (recipes follow)

1. If cutlets are thicker than ¼ inch, place between 2 sheets of plastic wrap or waxed paper and pound to even ¼-inch thickness with skillet or meat pounder. If some cutlets are thinner than ¼ inch, pound to even ⅛-inch thickness then fold in half. Pat cutlets dry with paper towels. Sprinkle tenderizer and pepper evenly over both sides of cutlets.

2. Place flour in rimmed baking sheet and spread to thin, even layer. Heat 1 tablespoon oil in 12-inch nonstick skillet over high heat until just smoking. Dredge first batch of cutlets in flour on 1 side only, shake off excess, and place in skillet, floured side down, making sure cutlets do not overlap. Cook, without moving cutlets, until well browned, 1 to 1½ minutes. Flip with tongs and cook until second sides are no longer pink and cutlets feel firm when pressed, about 30 seconds. Transfer cutlets to platter and tent loosely with aluminum foil. Repeat to cook remaining cutlets in 2 batches, using additional 1 tablespoon oil for each batch. (If skillet becomes too dark after cooking second batch, rinse before continuing.) Return pan to medium heat, finish pan sauce, pour over cutlets, and serve.

LEMON-PARSLEY SAUCE
MAKES ABOUT ¾ CUP, ENOUGH FOR 1 RECIPE VEAL SCALOPPINI

2	teaspoons vegetable oil
2	shallots, minced
1½	cups low-sodium chicken broth
2	tablespoons minced fresh parsley
2	tablespoons unsalted butter, cut into 4 pieces
	Salt and pepper
1–2	tablespoons lemon juice

1. Heat oil in medium saucepan over medium-high heat until shimmering. Add shallots and cook until beginning to soften, about 1 minute. Add broth and increase heat to high; simmer rapidly until liquid is reduced to ¾ cup, about 8 minutes. Set aside.

2. After transferring last batch of cutlets to platter, pour sauce into now-empty skillet and bring to simmer, scraping bottom of pan with wooden spoon to loosen any browned bits. Off heat, whisk in parsley and butter and season with salt, pepper, and lemon juice to taste. Pour sauce over cutlets and serve.

PORCINI-MARSALA PAN SAUCE

MAKES ABOUT 1 CUP, ENOUGH FOR
1 RECIPE VEAL SCALOPPINI

½ cup hot water
⅓ ounce dried porcini mushrooms, rinsed
2 teaspoons vegetable oil
2 shallots, minced
1 cup dry Marsala
1½ cups low-sodium chicken broth
2 tablespoons unsalted butter, cut into 4 pieces
1 tablespoon minced fresh chives
Salt and pepper

1. Microwave water and porcini mushrooms in covered bowl until steaming, about 1 minute. Let stand until softened, about 5 minutes. Drain mushrooms through fine-mesh strainer lined with coffee filter, reserve liquid, and chop mushrooms into ¼-inch pieces. Set mushrooms and liquid aside.

2. Heat oil in medium saucepan over medium-high heat until shimmering. Add shallots and cook until beginning to soften, about 1 minute. Off heat, add Marsala. Return pan to high heat; simmer rapidly until liquid is reduced to ½ cup, about 4 minutes. Add mushrooms and strained soaking liquid and simmer until liquid in pan is again reduced to ½ cup, about 4 minutes. Add broth and simmer until liquid is reduced to 1 cup, about 8 minutes. Set aside.

3. After transferring last batch of cutlets to platter, pour sauce into empty pan and bring to simmer, scraping bottom of pan with wooden spoon to loosen any browned bits. Off heat, whisk in butter and chives and season with salt and pepper to taste. Pour sauce over cutlets and serve.

TARRAGON-SHERRY CREAM SAUCE

MAKES ¾ CUP, ENOUGH FOR
1 RECIPE VEAL SCALOPPINI

---

2 teaspoons vegetable oil
2 shallots, minced
¾ cup dry sherry
½ cup low-sodium chicken broth
¾ cup heavy cream
2 tablespoons minced fresh tarragon
½ teaspoon lemon juice
Salt and pepper

1. Heat oil in 10-inch skillet over medium-high heat until shimmering. Add shallots and cook until beginning to soften, about 1 minute. Add sherry and increase heat to high; simmer rapidly until liquid is reduced to ½ cup, about 2 minutes. Add broth and simmer until liquid is again reduced to ½ cup, about 4 minutes. Add cream and set aside until last batch of cutlets is cooked.

2. After transferring last batch of cutlets to platter, return pan to medium heat. Pour sauce into pan and bring to simmer, scraping bottom of pan with wooden spoon to loosen any browned bits. Pour sauce through fine-mesh strainer into bowl, pressing on any solids in strainer with spatula to extract liquid. Wipe pan clean with paper towels; add strained sauce and set pan over medium-high heat. Simmer until sauce is reduced to ¾ cup, about 5 minutes. Stir in tarragon and lemon juice and season with salt and pepper to taste. Pour sauce over cutlets and serve.

PERFECT PRIME RIB

✓ WHY THIS RECIPE WORKS

Prime rib is typically cooked at the standard 350 degrees, resulting in a roast that's overcooked around the exterior. Cooking the roast at a surprisingly low 200 degrees was the simple solution. Unlike roasts that cooked at higher temperatures, the prime rib cooked at 200 degrees was rosy pink from the surface to the center and was the juiciest and most tender of all the roasts we cooked. The only issue we had with this slow-roasted prime rib was its raw-looking, unrendered fatty exterior. By searing the meat on the stovetop before slow-roasting it, though, we easily solved this problem.

PERFECT PRIME RIB

SERVES 6 TO 8

With two pieces of kitchen twine running parallel to the bone, tie the roast at both ends to prevent the outer layer of meat from pulling away from the rib-eye muscle and overcooking. Serve with Individual Yorkshire Puddings (recipe follows), if desired.

1 (7-pound) first-cut beef rib roast, 3 ribs, set at room temperature for 3 hours, trimmed and tied
1 tablespoon vegetable oil
Salt and pepper

1. Adjust oven rack to lowest position and heat oven to 200 degrees. Pat roast dry with paper towels. Heat oil in large roasting pan over 2 burners set at medium-high heat. Place roast in pan and cook on all sides until nicely browned and about ½ cup fat has been rendered, 6 to 8 minutes.

2. Remove roast from pan. Spoon off fat from roasting pan, reserving 3 tablespoons for Yorkshire puddings, if making. Set wire rack in pan, then set roast on rack. Season with salt and pepper.

3. Place roast in oven and roast until

1. Use carving fork to hold roast in place and cut along rib bones to sever meat from bones.

2. Set roast cut side down and carve meat across grain into ¾-inch-thick slices

meat registers 125 degrees (for medium-rare), about 3½ hours (or about 30 minutes per pound). Let rest for 20 minutes.

4. Transfer to carving board and carve; serve.

INDIVIDUAL YORKSHIRE PUDDINGS
MAKES 12

Prepare the Yorkshire pudding batter after the beef has roasted for 1 hour, then, while the roast rests, add the beef fat to the batter and get the puddings into the oven. An accurate oven temperature is key for properly risen puddings, so check your oven with an oven thermometer before making this recipe. Work quickly to fill the muffin tin with batter and do not open the oven door during baking.

3	large eggs, room temperature
1½	cups whole milk, room temperature
1½	cups (7½ ounces) all-purpose flour
¾	teaspoon salt
3	tablespoons beef fat

1. Whisk eggs and milk in large bowl until well combined, about 20 seconds. Whisk flour and salt in bowl and add to egg mixture; whisk quickly until flour is just incorporated and mixture is smooth, about 30 seconds. Cover batter with plastic wrap and let stand at room temperature for at least 1 hour or up to 3 hours.

2. After removing roast from oven, whisk 1 tablespoon beef fat into batter until bubbly and smooth, about 30 seconds. Transfer batter to 1-quart liquid measuring cup or other pitcher.

3. Measure ½ teaspoon beef fat into each cup of standard muffin pan. When roast is out of oven, increase temperature to 450 degrees and place pan in oven to heat for 3 minutes (fat will smoke). Working quickly, remove pan from oven, close oven door, and divide batter evenly among 12 muffin cups, filling each about two-thirds full. Immediately return pan to oven. Bake, without opening oven door, for 20 minutes; reduce oven temperature to 350 degrees and bake until deep golden brown, about 10 minutes longer. Remove pan from oven and pierce each pudding with skewer to release steam and prevent collapse. Using hands or dinner knife, lift each pudding out of tin and serve immediately.

ROAST BEEF TENDERLOIN

✔ WHY THIS RECIPE WORKS
Most roast beef tenderloins have one of two problems—either the meat is evenly cooked but it lacks a dark, caramelized crust, or the beef has optimal flavor and an appealing crust, but is marred by a thick, gray band of overdone meat. We wanted a technique that would produce perfectly cooked and deeply flavored meat—ideally without too much fuss. We decided to use a Châteaubriand; this center-cut roast has an even shape and smaller size, making it easier to cook evenly. We reversed the usual cooking process for tenderloin, roasting first and then searing, to eliminate the ring of overdone meat just below the crust and give the roast a ruby coloring from edge to edge. Salting the meat and rubbing it with softened butter helped it hold on to its juices and gave it richness.

ROAST BEEF TENDERLOIN
SERVES 4 TO 6

Ask your butcher to prepare a trimmed center-cut Châteaubriand from the whole tenderloin, as this cut is not usually available without special ordering. If you are cooking for a crowd, this recipe can be doubled to make two roasts. Sear the roasts one after the other, wiping out the pan and adding new oil after searing the first roast. Both pieces of meat can be roasted on the same rack.

1	(2-pound) beef tenderloin center-cut Châteaubriand, trimmed
2	teaspoons kosher salt
1	teaspoon coarsely ground black pepper
2	tablespoons unsalted butter, softened
1	tablespoon vegetable oil
1	recipe flavored butter (recipes follow)

1. Using 12-inch lengths of kitchen twine, tie roast crosswise at 1½-inch intervals. Sprinkle roast evenly with salt, cover loosely with plastic wrap, and let stand at room temperature for 1 hour. Meanwhile, adjust oven rack to middle position and heat oven to 300 degrees.

2. Pat roast dry with paper towels. Sprinkle roast evenly with pepper and spread unsalted butter evenly over surface. Transfer roast to wire rack set in rimmed baking sheet. Roast until meat registers 125 degrees (for medium-rare), 40 to 55 minutes, or 135 degrees (for medium), 55 to 70 minutes, flipping roast halfway through cooking.

3. Heat oil in 12-inch skillet over medium-high heat until just smoking. Place roast in skillet and sear until well browned on all sides, 4 to 8 minutes. Transfer roast to carving board and spread 2 tablespoons flavored butter evenly over top of roast; let rest 15 minutes. Remove twine and cut meat crosswise into ½-inch-thick slices. Serve, passing remaining flavored butter separately.

SHALLOT AND PARSLEY BUTTER

MAKES ABOUT ½ CUP, ENOUGH FOR
1 RECIPE ROAST BEEF TENDERLOIN

4   tablespoons unsalted butter, softened
½   shallot, minced
1   tablespoon minced fresh parsley
1   garlic clove, minced
¼   teaspoon salt
¼   teaspoon pepper

Combine all ingredients in bowl.

CHIPOTLE AND GARLIC BUTTER WITH LIME AND CILANTRO

MAKES ABOUT ½ CUP, ENOUGH FOR
1 RECIPE ROAST BEEF TENDERLOIN

5   tablespoons unsalted butter, softened
1   tablespoon minced canned chipotle chile in adobo sauce, with 1 teaspoon adobo sauce
1   tablespoon minced fresh cilantro
1   garlic clove, minced
1   teaspoon honey
1   teaspoon grated lime zest
½   teaspoon salt

Combine all ingredients in bowl.

STUFFED ROAST BEEF TENDERLOIN

✔ WHY THIS RECIPE WORKS
Stuffed beef tenderloin could be the ultimate main course, if only it weren't so hard to get right. A tenderloin's thick, tapered shape makes it difficult to cook evenly, while a stuffing that's too bulky or absorbent makes an unappealing mess. For stuffed beef tenderloin with a deeply charred crust, a tender, rosy-pink interior, and an intensely flavored stuffing that stayed neatly rolled in the meat, we chose the almost perfectly cylindrical Châteaubriand and used a "double-butterfly" procedure—making two cuts so the roast opened up into three parts. In this way, the roast accommodated 50 percent more filling than a conventionally butterflied roast. We tried a "deluxe" filing of lobster and chanterelles, but the mix was so chunky that the stuffing fell out of the meat once sliced. Instead we turned to earthy cremini and caramelized onions. The caramelized onions contributed sweetness and bound the mushrooms into a thick, slightly sticky, jamlike stuffing that stayed in place during carving. Garlic, a splash of Madeira, and a layer of baby spinach rounded out the flavors. We created a suitable crust for our tenderloin in a shortened cooking time by coating the exterior of the roast with kosher salt an hour before searing, which allowed the salt to begin to break down the protein fibers in the outermost layer of meat, so that it browned quickly.

TEST KITCHEN TIP NO. 83   THE IMPORTANCE OF RESTING MEAT

You'll never see anyone in the test kitchen cut into a roast, or any meat, straight from the oven. We always let it rest before slicing. Exposed to heat during cooking, proteins, which resemble coiled springs, undergo a radical transformation in which they uncoil and then reconnect to each other in haphazard structures. This process, called coagulation, is the reason that proteins become firm and lose moisture during the cooking process. The longer that proteins are exposed to heat, the tighter they coagulate and the more liquid they drive toward both the surface and the center of the meat, much like wringing a wet kitchen towel.

If you were to cut the meat immediately after removing it from the heat source, the liquid suspended between the interior proteins is driven toward the surface and would simply pool (or what many chefs call bleed) on the carving board or plate because the proteins have not had time to relax. The best way to prevent this pooling of juices and a dry hunk of meat is to rest the roast. Although the process of coagulation is not reversible, allowing the protein molecules to relax after cooking slows the rate which they continue to squeeze the liquid between their tight coils and increases their capacity to retain moisture. A short rest on the carving board will decrease the amount of liquid lost during carving by about 40 percent. There's another good reason to have some patience and let your meat rest—it allows you some time to finish the other components of dinner, which is especially useful around the holidays when there are typically loads of sides to get to the table too.

ROAST BEEF TENDERLOIN WITH CARAMELIZED ONION AND MUSHROOM STUFFING

SERVES 6 TO 8

This recipe can be doubled to make two roasts. Sear the roasts one after the other, wiping out the pan and adding new oil after searing the first roast. Both pieces of meat can be roasted on the same rack.

STUFFING

8	ounces cremini mushrooms, trimmed and broken into rough pieces
½	tablespoon unsalted butter
1½	teaspoons olive oil
1	onion, halved and sliced ¼ inch thick
¼	teaspoon salt
⅛	teaspoon pepper
1	garlic clove, minced
½	cup Madeira or sweet Marsala wine

BEEF ROAST

1	(2- to 3-pound) beef tenderloin center-cut Châteaubriand, trimmed Kosher salt and pepper
½	cup baby spinach
3	tablespoons olive oil

HERB BUTTER

4	tablespoons unsalted butter, softened
1	tablespoon whole grain mustard
1	tablespoon chopped fresh parsley
1	garlic clove, minced
¾	teaspoon chopped fresh thyme
⅛	teaspoon salt
⅛	teaspoon pepper

1. FOR THE STUFFING: Process mushrooms in food processor until coarsely chopped, about 6 pulses. Heat butter and oil in 12-inch nonstick skillet over medium-high heat. Add onion, salt, and pepper; cook, stirring occasionally, until onion begins to soften, about 5 minutes. Add mushrooms and cook, stirring occasionally, until all moisture has evaporated, 5 to 7 minutes. Reduce heat to medium and continue to cook, stirring frequently, until vegetables are deeply browned and sticky, about 10 minutes. Stir in garlic and cook until fragrant, 30 seconds. Slowly stir in Madeira and cook, scraping bottom of skillet with wooden spoon to loosen any browned bits, until liquid has evaporated, 2 to 3 minutes. Transfer mushroom mixture to plate and cool to room temperature.

2. FOR THE ROAST: To butterfly roast, insert chef's knife about 1 inch from bottom of roast and cut horizontally, stopping just before edge. Open meat like a book. Make another cut diagonally into thicker portion of roast. Open up this flap, smoothing out butterflied rectangle of meat. Season cut side of roast with kosher salt and pepper. Spread cooled stuffing mixture over interior of roast, leaving ½-inch border on all sides; lay spinach on top of stuffing. Roll roast lengthwise and tie with 8 pieces kitchen twine evenly spaced.

3. Stir 1 tablespoon oil, 1½ teaspoons kosher salt, and 1½ teaspoons pepper together in small bowl. Rub roast with oil mixture and let stand at room temperature for 1 hour.

4. Adjust oven rack to middle position and heat oven to 450 degrees. Heat remaining 2 tablespoons oil in 12-inch skillet over medium-high heat until just smoking. Add beef and cook until well browned on all sides, 8 to 10 minutes total. Transfer beef to wire rack set in rimmed baking sheet and place in oven. Roast until thickest part of roast registers 120 degrees (for rare), 16 to 18 minutes, or 125 degrees (for medium-rare), 20 to 22 minutes.

5. FOR THE HERB BUTTER: While meat roasts, combine butter ingredients in bowl. Transfer tenderloin to carving board; spread half of butter evenly over top of roast. Loosely tent roast with aluminum foil; let rest for 15 minutes.

Cut roast between pieces of twine into thick slices. Remove twine and serve with remaining butter.

ROAST BEEF TENDERLOIN WITH DRIED FRUIT AND NUT STUFFING

SERVES 6 TO 8

This recipe can be doubled to make two roasts. Sear the roasts one after the other, wiping out the pan and adding new oil after searing the first roast. Both pieces of meat can be roasted on the same rack.

STUFFING

2	teaspoons olive oil
1	shallot, minced
⅔	cup ruby port
¼	cup chopped prunes
¼	cup dried chopped apricots
½	teaspoon minced fresh thyme
¼	teaspoon salt
⅛	teaspoon pepper
2	tablespoons balsamic vinegar

BEEF ROAST

1	(2- to 3-pound) beef tenderloin center-cut Châteaubriand, trimmed Kosher salt and pepper
2	tablespoons toasted pecans, chopped
3	tablespoons olive oil

STILTON BUTTER

1	ounce Stilton cheese, crumbled
3	tablespoons unsalted butter, softened
1	tablespoon chopped fresh parsley
⅛	teaspoon salt

1. FOR THE STUFFING: Heat oil in medium saucepan over medium heat until shimmering. Add shallot and cook, stirring occasionally, until softened and golden brown, 2 to 3 minutes. Meanwhile, combine port, prunes, and apricots in bowl; cover and microwave until simmering, about 2 minutes.

2. When shallot is softened, add fruit mixture, thyme, salt, and pepper; continue to cook, stirring occasionally, until mixture is thick, 1 to 2 minutes. Off heat, stir in balsamic vinegar. Transfer fruit mixture to plate. Set aside and cool to room temperature.

3. FOR THE ROAST: To butterfly roast, insert chef's knife about 1 inch from bottom of roast and cut horizontally, stopping just before edge. Open meat like a book. Make another cut diagonally into thicker portion of roast. Open up this flap, smoothing out butterflied rectangle of meat. Season cut side of roast with kosher salt and pepper. Spread cooled stuffing mixture over interior of roast, leaving ½-inch border on all sides; distribute pecans on top of stuffing. Roll roast lengthwise and tie with 8 pieces kitchen twine evenly spaced.

4. Stir 1 tablespoon oil, 1½ teaspoons kosher salt, and 1½ teaspoons pepper together in small bowl. Rub roast with oil mixture and let stand at room temperature for 1 hour.

5. Adjust oven rack to middle position and heat oven to 450 degrees. Heat remaining 2 tablespoons oil in 12-inch skillet over medium-high heat until just smoking. Add beef and cook until well browned on all sides, 8 to 10 minutes total. Transfer beef to wire rack set in rimmed baking sheet and place in oven. Roast until thickest part of roast registers 120 degrees (for rare), 16 to 18 minutes, or 125 degrees (for medium-rare), 20 to 22 minutes.

6. FOR THE STILTON BUTTER: While meat roasts, combine butter ingredients in bowl. Transfer tenderloin to carving board; spread half of butter evenly over top of roast. Loosely tent roast with aluminum foil; let rest for 15 minutes. Cut roast between pieces of twine into thick slices. Remove twine and serve with remaining butter.

HORSERADISH-CRUSTED BEEF TENDERLOIN WITH CREAM SAUCE

✔ WHY THIS RECIPE WORKS
We love the buttery-smooth texture of beef tenderloin, but this mild-tasting cut is usually in need of a flavor boost. We wanted to combine the bracing flavor of horseradish with a crisp, golden crust that would also add textural contrast to perfectly cooked, rosy, medium-rare meat. So we chose Châteaubriand, a center-cut roast with a uniform shape that cooks evenly; we used homemade fried potato shreds and panko instead of regular bread crumbs to counter the moisture of the horseradish coating; and we left the bottom of the roast uncoated so that meat juices had a place to escape without ruining the crust. The result was the best horseradish-crusted beef tenderloin we've ever had.

HORSERADISH-CRUSTED BEEF TENDERLOIN WITH CREAM SAUCE
SERVES 6

Add the gelatin to the horseradish paste at the last moment, or the mixture will become unspreadable. If desired, serve the roast with Horseradish Cream Sauce (page 389; you will need 2 jars of prepared horseradish for both the roast and sauce). If you choose to salt the tenderloin in advance, remove it from the refrigerator 1 hour before cooking.

1   (2-pound) beef tenderloin center-cut Châteaubriand, trimmed
    Kosher salt and pepper
3   tablespoons panko bread crumbs
2   teaspoons plus 1 cup vegetable oil
¼   cup well-drained prepared horseradish
2   tablespoons minced fresh parsley
1   small shallot, minced
2   garlic cloves, minced
½   teaspoon minced fresh thyme

BUTTERFLYING, STUFFING, AND TYING A TENDERLOIN

1. Insert chef's knife about 1 inch from bottom of roast and slowly cut horizontally, stopping just before edge. Open meat like a book.

2. Make another cut diagonally into thicker portion of roast. Open up this flap, smoothing out butterflied rectangle of meat. Butterflying the roast gives you a wide, even surface to spread the stuffing.

3. Spread filling evenly over surface, leaving ½-inch border on all sides. Press spinach leaves or pecans evenly on top of filling. Using both hands, gently but firmly roll up stuffed tenderloin.

4. Evenly space 8 pieces kitchen twine (each about 14 inches) beneath roast. Tie each strand tightly around roast, starting with ends.

1   small russet potato (6 ounces), peeled and grated on large holes of box grater
1½   teaspoons mayonnaise
1½   teaspoons Dijon mustard
½   teaspoon unflavored gelatin

1. Sprinkle roast with 1 tablespoon salt, cover with plastic wrap, and let stand at room temperature for 1 hour or refrigerate for up to 24 hours. Adjust oven rack to middle position and heat oven to 400 degrees.

2. Toss panko with 2 teaspoons oil, ¼ teaspoon salt, and ¼ teaspoon pepper in 10-inch nonstick skillet. Cook over medium heat, stirring frequently, until deep golden brown, 3 to 5 minutes. Transfer to rimmed baking sheet and cool to room temperature (wipe out skillet). Once cool, toss bread crumbs with 2 tablespoons horseradish, parsley, shallot, garlic, and thyme.

3. Rinse grated potato under cold water, then squeeze dry in kitchen towel. Transfer potato and remaining 1 cup oil to 10-inch nonstick skillet. Cook over high heat, stirring frequently, until potato is golden brown and crisp, 6 to 8 minutes. Using slotted spoon, transfer potato to paper towel–lined plate and season with salt to taste; cool for 5 minutes. Reserve 1 tablespoon oil from skillet and discard remainder. Once potato is cool, transfer to 1-quart zipper-lock bag and crush until coarsely ground. Transfer potato to baking sheet with bread-crumb mixture and toss to combine.

4. Pat tenderloin dry with paper towels and sprinkle evenly with 1 teaspoon pepper. Heat reserved 1 tablespoon oil in 12-inch nonstick skillet over medium-high heat until just smoking. Sear tenderloin until well browned on all sides, 5 to 7 minutes. Transfer to wire rack set in rimmed baking sheet and let rest for 10 minutes.

5. Combine remaining 2 tablespoons horseradish, mayonnaise, and mustard in small bowl. Just before coating tenderloin, add gelatin and stir to combine. Spread horseradish paste on top and sides of meat, leaving bottom and ends bare. Roll coated sides of tenderloin in bread-crumb mixture, pressing gently so crumbs adhere in even layer that just covers horseradish paste; pat off any excess.

6. Return tenderloin to wire rack. Roast until meat registers 120 to 125 degrees (for medium-rare), 25 to 30 minutes.

7. Transfer roast to carving board and let rest for 20 minutes. Carefully cut meat into ½-inch-thick slices and serve.

TO MAKE AHEAD: To make recipe 1 day in advance, prepare through step 3, but in step 2 do not toss bread crumbs with other ingredients until ready to sear meat.

TOP LOIN ROAST

WHY THIS RECIPE WORKS

Looking beyond prime rib and beef tenderloin, we wanted to find a top-quality boneless roast that was tender, flavorful, and easy to carve. After testing different cuts—sirloin tip roast, top sirloin roast, and top loin roast—we found just what we were looking for in the top loin roast. It was tender, perfectly marbled, and full-flavored. We aged the meat for one to three days for a mellow, buttery, and nutty flavor. Finally, an unconventional method for cooking a roast yielded the best results. We started cooking the roast in a skillet on the stove and then finished it in the oven for a beautiful mahogany-brown crust and a juicy pink interior.

TOP LOIN ROAST
SERVES 8 TO 10

If you do not own an ovensafe skillet, sear the roast in any skillet, then transfer it to a roasting pan for oven cooking. We prefer the flavor and texture of this roast when cooked rare. If medium-rare is more to your liking, cook the roast until it registers 120 to 125 degrees.

Serve with Garlic-Herb Butter if desired (recipe follows).

1   (5- to 5½-pound) boneless top loin roast
3   tablespoons olive oil
4   teaspoons kosher salt
1   tablespoon pepper

1. Line rimmed baking sheet with paper towels and set wire rack in baking sheet. Pat roast dry with additional paper towels, then set roast on wire rack. Refrigerate, uncovered, on lowest shelf for 1 to 3 days.

2. Adjust oven rack to lower-middle position and heat oven to 250 degrees. Remove roast from refrigerator; using sharp paring knife, trim fat and silver skin from roast and shave off hard, dried exterior surfaces. Rub roast with 2 tablespoons oil; let roast stand at room temperature for 1 hour.

3. Combine salt and pepper in small bowl; season all surfaces of roast with salt-pepper mixture, pressing so salt and pepper adhere. Heat remaining 1 tablespoon oil in 12-inch ovensafe skillet over medium-high heat until just smoking; set roast in skillet, fat-trimmed side down, and cook until well browned, about 3 minutes. Using tongs to turn roast, brown on all sides, 2 to 3 minutes on each side. Turn roast fat-trimmed side up, transfer skillet to oven, and roast until center registers 115 to 120 degrees, 40 to 50 minutes. Using potholders to handle skillet, transfer roast to carving board, loosely tent roast with aluminum foil, and let rest for 20 minutes. Cut meat into ¼-inch-thick slices and serve.

GARLIC-HERB BUTTER
MAKES ⅓ CUP, ENOUGH FOR
1 RECIPE TOP LOIN ROAST

---

4   tablespoons unsalted butter, softened

1½ tablespoons chopped fresh thyme
1 tablespoon chopped fresh sage
1 tablespoon chopped fresh parsley
1 small garlic clove, minced
Salt and pepper

While meat roasts, stir together butter, herbs, and garlic, and season with salt and pepper to taste; set aside until needed. After roast has rested, spread butter evenly over surface of roast.

SLOW-ROASTED BEEF

✔ WHY THIS RECIPE WORKS

Roasting inexpensive beef usually yields tough meat best suited for sandwiches. We wanted to transform a bargain cut into a tender, juicy roast that could stand on its own at dinner. The eye-round roast has good flavor and relative tenderness, and it also has a uniform shape that guarantees even cooking. Searing the meat before roasting as well as salting it a full 24 hours before roasting vastly improved flavor. But the big surprise was the method that produced remarkably tender and juicy beef—roasting the meat at a very low 225 degrees and then turning off the oven toward the end of cooking. This approach allowed the meat's enzymes to act as natural tenderizers, breaking down its tough connective tissue.

SLOW-ROASTED BEEF
SERVES 6 TO 8

We don't recommend cooking this roast past medium. Open the oven door as little as possible and remove the roast from the oven while taking its temperature. If the roast has not reached the desired temperature in the time specified in step 3, heat the oven to 225 degrees for 5 minutes, shut it off, and continue to cook the roast to the desired temperature. For a smaller (2½- to 3½-pound) roast, reduce the amount of salt to 1 tablespoon and pepper to 1½ teaspoons. For a 4½- to 6-pound roast, cut in half crosswise before cooking to create 2 smaller roasts. Slice the roast as thin as possible and serve with Horseradish Cream Sauce (recipe follows), if desired.

1 (3½- to 4½-pound) boneless eye-round roast
4 teaspoons kosher salt
2 teaspoons plus 1 tablespoon vegetable oil
2 teaspoons pepper

1. Season all sides of roast evenly with salt. Wrap with plastic wrap and refrigerate 18 to 24 hours.

2. Adjust oven rack to middle position and heat oven to 225 degrees. Pat roast dry with paper towels; rub with 2 teaspoons oil and season all sides evenly with

---

pepper. Heat remaining 1 tablespoon oil in 12-inch skillet over medium-high heat until just smoking. Sear roast until browned on all sides, about 12 minutes. Transfer roast to wire rack set in rimmed baking sheet. Roast until meat registers 115 degrees (for medium-rare), 1¼ to 1¾ hours, or 125 degrees (for medium), 1¾ to 2¼ hours.

3. Turn oven off; leave roast in oven, without opening door, until meat registers 130 degrees (for medium-rare) or 140 degrees (for medium), 30 to 50 minutes longer. Transfer roast to carving board and let rest for 15 minutes. Slice meat as thin as possible and serve.

HORSERADISH CREAM SAUCE
MAKES ABOUT 1 CUP, ENOUGH FOR 1 RECIPE SLOW-ROASTED BEEF

½ cup heavy cream
½ cup prepared horseradish
1 teaspoon salt
⅛ teaspoon pepper

Whisk cream in bowl until thickened but not yet holding soft peaks, 1 to 2 minutes. Gently fold in horseradish, salt, and pepper. Transfer to serving bowl and refrigerate at least 30 minutes or up to 1 hour before serving.

OLD-FASHIONED GLAZED MEATLOAF

✔ WHY THIS RECIPE WORKS

While some could argue all day about what should (or shouldn't) go into meatloaf, we wanted to focus on more basic issues—what meat or mix of meats delivers the best flavor, what fillers make the loaf sliceable and moist, and whether it should be cooked free-form or in a loaf pan. We found that a trio of beef, pork,

---

TEST KITCHEN TIP NO. 84 **SALTING—THE SECRET TO JUICY ROASTS**

We're big advocates of brining in the test kitchen (see pages 321 and 353). But brining works best for lean types of meat like poultry and pork. Is there an alternative to brining for fattier meats like beef? There is—salting. Salting is a kind of "dry brine" in which meat is rubbed with salt and then refrigerated for several hours. How does salting do its work? Initially, the salt draws out moisture from the meat, and this moisture mixes with the salt to form a shallow brine. Over time, the salt migrates from the shallow brine into the meat, just as it does in our usual brining technique. Once inside the meat, the salt changes the structure of the muscle fibers, allowing the meat to hold on to more water, so that it turns out juicy and well-seasoned.

We tried salting in developing our Slow-Roasted Beef and found that salting for 24 hours worked best—the results were remarkable. In addition to the slow-cooking technique we use in this recipe, salting helped transform our bargain eye round into a tender, juicy roast that rivals beef tenderloin. Smaller cuts of meat, like steaks, do not need to be salted nearly as long—about 40 minutes is sufficient.

and veal, with a higher proportion of ground chuck, was best. Loaves made without filler were too hamburger-like. Those made with binders, on the other hand, had a characteristic meatloaf texture. Cracker crumbs, quick-cooking oatmeal, and fresh bread crumbs all worked to improve the texture of our meatloaf without adding a distracting flavor. Finally, we found that the high-sided standard loaf pan causes the meat to stew rather than bake. Baking the meatloaf free-form in a shallow baking pan gave us the results we wanted.

BACON-WRAPPED MEATLOAF WITH BROWN SUGAR–KETCHUP GLAZE

SERVES 6 TO 8

If you like, you can omit the bacon topping from the loaf. In this case, brush on half the glaze before baking and the other half during the last 15 minutes of baking. If available at your supermarket in the meat case or by special order, you can use 2 pounds meatloaf mix in place of the ground beef, pork, and veal.

BROWN SUGAR–KETCHUP GLAZE

½ cup ketchup or chili sauce
¼ cup packed brown sugar
4 teaspoons cider vinegar or white vinegar

MEATLOAF

2 teaspoons vegetable oil
1 onion, chopped
2 garlic cloves, minced
½ cup whole-milk or plain yogurt
2 large eggs
2 teaspoons Dijon mustard
2 teaspoons Worcestershire sauce
1 teaspoon salt
½ teaspoon pepper
½ teaspoon dried thyme
¼ teaspoon hot sauce
1 pound ground beef chuck
½ pound ground pork
½ pound ground veal

⅔ cup crushed saltines (about 16) or ⅔ cup quick oats or 1⅓ cups fresh bread crumbs
⅓ cup minced fresh parsley
8–12 slices bacon

1. FOR THE GLAZE: Combine all ingredients in small saucepan; set aside.

2. FOR THE MEATLOAF: Line 13 by 9-inch baking pan with aluminum foil; set aside. Heat oven to 350 degrees. Heat oil in 10-inch skillet over medium heat. Add onion and garlic; cook until softened, about 5 minutes. Set aside to cool while preparing remaining ingredients.

3. In large bowl, combine milk, eggs, mustard, Worcestershire, salt, pepper, thyme, and hot sauce. Add meat, saltines, parsley, and sautéed onion mixture; mix with fork until evenly blended and meat mixture does not stick to bowl. (If mixture sticks, add additional milk, 2 tablespoons at a time, until mixture no longer sticks.)

4. Turn meat mixture onto work surface. With wet hands, pat mixture into approximately 9 by 5-inch loaf shape. Place in prepared baking pan. Brush with half of glaze, then arrange bacon slices, crosswise, over loaf, overlapping slightly and tucking only bacon tip ends under loaf.

5. Bake loaf until bacon is crisp and loaf registers 160 degrees, about 1 hour. Cool at least 20 minutes. Simmer remaining glaze over medium heat until thickened slightly. Slice meatloaf and serve with extra glaze.

LOAF-PAN MEATLOAF

Omit bacon. Turn meat mixture into meatloaf pan with perforated bottom, fitted with drip pan. Use fork to pull mixture from pan sides to prevent glaze from dripping into oven. Brush with one-quarter of glaze. Bake until glaze is set, about 45 minutes. Top with another one-quarter of glaze; continue to bake until second coat has set and loaf registers 160 degrees,

about 15 minutes longer. Cool at least 20 minutes. Simmer remaining glaze over medium heat until thickened slightly. Slice meatloaf and serve with extra glaze.

GLAZED ALL-BEEF MEATLOAF

✔ WHY THIS RECIPE WORKS

For a tender, moist, and light meatloaf, using a combination of ground beef, pork, and veal (known as meatloaf mix) is usually the way to go. But sometimes we can't find meatloaf mix or don't have it on hand for a quick, last-minute dinner. For an all-beef loaf that's just as good as one made with meatloaf mix, we used equal parts ground chuck and sirloin, which provided just the right balance of juicy, tender meat and assertive beefy flavor. Chicken broth was a surprisingly successful add-in; it transformed the loaf from liver-y to savory. To replace the gelatin that was lost with the ground veal in the meatloaf mix, we used a mere half teaspoon of powdered gelatin to give the texture of our glazed meatloaf a luxurious smoothness.

GLAZED ALL-BEEF MEATLOAF

SERVES 6 TO 8

If you can't find chuck and/or sirloin, substitute any 85 percent lean ground beef. Handle the meat gently; it should be thoroughly combined but not pastelike. To avoid using the broiler, glaze the loaf in a 500-degree oven; increase cooking time for each interval by 2 to 3 minutes.

MEATLOAF

3 ounces Monterey Jack cheese, shredded (¾ cup)
1 tablespoon unsalted butter
1 onion, chopped fine
1 celery rib, chopped fine
2 teaspoons minced fresh thyme
1 garlic clove, minced
1 teaspoon paprika
¼ cup tomato juice

½ cup low-sodium chicken broth
2 large eggs
½ teaspoon unflavored gelatin
⅔ cup crushed saltines (about 16)
2 tablespoons minced fresh parsley
1 tablespoon soy sauce
1 teaspoon Dijon mustard
¾ teaspoon salt
½ teaspoon pepper
1 pound ground sirloin
1 pound ground beef chuck

GLAZE
½ cup ketchup
1 teaspoon hot sauce
½ teaspoon ground coriander
¼ cup cider vinegar
3 tablespoons packed light brown sugar

1. FOR THE MEATLOAF: Adjust oven rack to middle position; heat oven to 375 degrees. Spread cheese on plate and place in freezer until ready to use. Fold piece of heavy-duty aluminum foil to form 10 by 6-inch rectangle. Center foil on wire rack and place rack in rimmed baking sheet. Poke holes in foil with skewer about half inch apart. Spray foil with vegetable oil spray and set aside.

2. Melt butter in 10-inch skillet over medium-high heat; add onion and celery and cook, stirring occasionally, until beginning to brown, 6 to 8 minutes. Add thyme, garlic, and paprika and cook, stirring constantly, until fragrant, about 1 minute. Reduce heat to low and add tomato juice. Cook, scraping bottom of skillet with wooden spoon to loosen any browned bits, until thickened, about 1 minute. Transfer mixture to bowl and set aside to cool.

3. Whisk broth and eggs in large bowl until combined. Sprinkle gelatin over liquid and let stand for 5 minutes. Stir in saltines, parsley, soy sauce, mustard, salt, pepper, and onion mixture. Crumble frozen cheese into coarse powder and sprinkle over mixture. Add ground beef; mix gently with

hands until thoroughly combined, about 1 minute. Transfer meat to aluminum foil rectangle and shape into 10 by 6-inch oval about 2 inches high. Smooth top and edges of meatloaf with moistened spatula. Bake until meatloaf registers 135 to 140 degrees, 55 to 65 minutes. Remove meatloaf from oven and turn on broiler.

4. FOR THE GLAZE: While meatloaf cooks, combine glaze ingredients in small saucepan; bring to simmer over medium heat and cook, stirring, until thick and syrupy, about 5 minutes. Spread half of glaze evenly over cooked meatloaf with rubber spatula; place under broiler and cook until glaze bubbles and begins to brown at edges, about 5 minutes. Remove meatloaf from oven and spread evenly with remaining glaze; place back under broiler and cook until glaze is again bubbling and beginning to brown, about 5 minutes more. Cool meatloaf about 20 minutes before slicing.

PAN-SEARED BURGERS

✓ **WHY THIS RECIPE WORKS**
Making an exceptional hamburger isn't hard or time-consuming; you just need the right beef—and to know how to season, form, and cook it properly. After a side-by-side taste test of various cuts of beef all ground to order with 20 percent fat, we quickly concluded that most cuts are pleasant but bland when compared with robust, beefy flavored ground chuck. Because ground beef labels at some retailers do not indicate the cut from which the meat has been ground, you might want to buy a chuck roast and have your butcher grind it for you (or you can grind it yourself in a food processor). We also found that when making a dish as simple as a hamburger, the little things matter. Seasoning the meat before shaping is key, as is using a light hand when shaping the patties.

You can use a 12-inch cast-iron or nonstick skillet or a stovetop grill pan for this recipe.

1¼ pounds 100 percent ground chuck
¾ teaspoon salt
¼ teaspoon pepper
1 tablespoon vegetable oil
4 hamburger rolls

1. Break up beef to increase surface area for seasoning. Add salt and pepper; toss lightly with hands to distribute seasoning. Divide meat into 4 equal portions (5 ounces each); with cupped hands, toss 1 portion of meat back and forth to form a loose ball. Pat lightly to flatten into 1-inch-thick burger, about 4 inches across, using fingertips to create pocked, textured surface. Repeat with remaining portions of meat.

2. Heat oil over medium-high heat until just smoking. Add patties and cook, turning once, until meat registers 120 to 125 degrees (for medium-rare). Serve with buns and desired toppings.

OLD-FASHIONED BURGERS

✓ **WHY THIS RECIPE WORKS**
Classic drive-in burgers used to mean freshly ground high-quality beef, but today fast-food burgers are nothing more than tasteless, mass-produced patties. We wanted to bring back the original—an ultra-crisp, ultra-browned, ultra-beefy burger perfect for catching dripping juices, melted cheese, and tangy sauce. We learned that freshly ground beef was essential and a combination of sirloin steak tips and boneless beef short ribs was best. We also found that the meat must be very loosely packed to prevent rubbery, tough patties. Topped with a sweet and tangy sauce, cheese, and a few thin slices of onion, this burger recaptures the flavor and texture that started a nationwide craze.

BEST OLD-FASHIONED BURGERS
SERVES 4

Sirloin steak tips are also sold as flap meat. Flank steak can be used in its place. This recipe yields juicy medium to medium-well burgers. It's important to use very soft buns. If doubling the recipe, process the meat in three batches in step 2. Because the cooked burgers do not hold well, fry four burgers and serve them immediately before frying more, or cook them in two pans. Extra patties can be frozen for up to 2 weeks. Stack the patties, separated by parchment, and wrap them in three layers of plastic wrap. Thaw burgers in a single layer on a baking sheet at room temperature for 30 minutes before cooking.

- 10 ounces sirloin steak tips, trimmed and cut into 1-inch chunks
- 6 ounces boneless beef short ribs, trimmed and cut into 1-inch chunks Salt and pepper
- 1 tablespoon unsalted butter
- 4 hamburger rolls
- ½ teaspoon vegetable oil
- 4 slices American cheese Thinly sliced onion
- 1 recipe Classic Burger Sauce (recipe follows)

1. Place beef chunks on baking sheet in single layer, leaving ½ inch of space around each chunk. Freeze meat until very firm and starting to harden around edges but still pliable, 15 to 25 minutes.

2. Pulse half of meat in food processor until coarsely ground, 10 to 15 pulses, stopping and redistributing meat around bowl as necessary to ensure beef is evenly ground. Transfer meat to baking sheet, overturning workbowl and without directly touching meat. Repeat grinding with remaining meat. Spread meat over sheet and inspect carefully, discarding any long strands of gristle or large chunks of hard meat or fat.

3. Gently separate ground meat into 4 equal mounds. Without picking meat up, use fingers to gently shape each mound into loose patty ½ inch thick and 4 inches in diameter, leaving edges and surface ragged. Season top of each patty with salt and pepper. Using spatula, flip patties and season other side. Refrigerate while toasting buns.

4. Melt ½ tablespoon butter in 12-inch skillet over medium heat. Add bun tops, cut side down, and toast until light golden brown, about 2 minutes. Repeat with remaining butter and bun bottoms. Set buns aside and wipe out skillet with paper towels.

5. Return skillet to high heat; add oil and heat until just smoking. Using spatula, transfer burgers to skillet and cook without moving for 3 minutes. Using spatula, flip burgers over and cook for 1 minute. Top each patty with slice of cheese and continue to cook until cheese is melted, about 1 minute longer.

6. Transfer patties to bun bottoms and top with onion. Spread about 1 tablespoon of burger sauce on each bun top. Cover burgers and serve immediately.

CLASSIC BURGER SAUCE
MAKES ABOUT ¼ CUP, ENOUGH FOR 1 RECIPE BEST OLD-FASHIONED BURGERS

- 2 tablespoons mayonnaise
- 1 tablespoon ketchup
- ½ teaspoon sweet pickle relish
- ½ teaspoon sugar
- ½ teaspoon white vinegar
- ¼ teaspoon pepper

Whisk all ingredients together in bowl.

JUICY PUB-STYLE BURGERS

✔ WHY THIS RECIPE WORKS

Few things are as satisfying as a thick, juicy pub-style burger. But avoiding the usual gray band of overcooked meat is a challenge. We wanted a patty that was well-seared, juicy, and evenly rosy from center to edge. Grinding our own meat in the food processor was a must, and sirloin steak tips were the right cut for the job. Cutting the meat into small ½-inch chunks before grinding and lightly packing the meat to form patties gave the burgers just enough structure to hold their shape in the skillet. A little melted butter improved their flavor and juiciness, but our biggest discovery came when we transferred the burgers from the stovetop to the oven to finish cooking—the stovetop provided intense heat for searing, while the oven's gentle ambient heat allowed for even cooking, thus eliminating the overcooked gray zone.

JUICY PUB-STYLE BURGERS
SERVES 4

Sirloin steak tips are also sold as flap meat. When stirring the butter and pepper into the ground meat and shaping the patties, take care not to overwork the meat or the burgers will become dense. For the best flavor, season the burgers aggressively just before cooking. The burgers can be topped as desired or with one of the test kitchen's favorite combinations (recipes follow).

- 2 pounds sirloin steak tips or boneless beef short ribs, trimmed and cut into ½-inch chunks
- 4 tablespoons unsalted butter, melted and cooled slightly Salt and pepper
- 1 teaspoon vegetable oil
- 4 large hamburger rolls, toasted and buttered

1. Place beef chunks on baking sheet in single layer. Freeze meat until very firm and starting to harden around edges but still pliable, 15 to 25 minutes.

2. Place one-quarter of meat in food processor and pulse until finely ground into $\frac{1}{16}$-inch pieces, about 35 pulses, stopping and redistributing meat around bowl as necessary to ensure beef is evenly ground. Transfer meat to baking sheet, overturning workbowl and without directly touching meat. Repeat grinding with remaining 3 batches of meat. Spread meat over baking sheet and inspect carefully, discarding any long strands of gristle or large chunks of hard meat or fat.

3. Adjust oven rack to middle position and heat oven to 300 degrees. Drizzle melted butter over ground meat and add 1 teaspoon pepper. Gently toss with fork to combine. Divide meat into 4 lightly packed balls. Gently flatten into patties $\frac{3}{4}$ inch thick and about $4\frac{1}{2}$ inches in diameter. Refrigerate patties until ready to cook. (Patties can be refrigerated for up to 1 day.)

4. Season 1 side of patties with salt and pepper. Using spatula, flip patties and season other side. Heat oil in 12-inch skillet over high heat until just smoking. Using spatula, transfer burgers to skillet and cook without moving for 2 minutes. Using spatula, flip burgers over and cook for 2 minutes longer. Transfer patties to rimmed baking sheet and bake until burgers register 125 degrees (for medium-rare), 3 to 5 minutes.

5. Transfer burgers to plate and let rest for 5 minutes. Transfer to buns, add desired toppings, and serve.

PUB-STYLE BURGER SAUCE

MAKES ABOUT 1 CUP, ENOUGH FOR
1 RECIPE JUICY PUB-STYLE BURGERS

- ¾ cup mayonnaise
- 2 tablespoons soy sauce
- 1 tablespoon packed dark brown sugar
- 1 tablespoon Worcestershire sauce
- 1 tablespoon minced chives
- 1 garlic clove, minced
- ¾ teaspoon pepper

Whisk all ingredients together in bowl.

JUICY PUB-STYLE BURGERS WITH CRISPY SHALLOTS AND BLUE CHEESE

Heat ½ cup vegetable oil and 3 thinly sliced shallots in medium saucepan over high heat; cook, stirring frequently, until shallots are golden, about 8 minutes. Using slotted spoon, transfer shallots to paper towel–lined plate, season with salt, and let drain until crisp, about 5 minutes. (Cooled shallots can be stored at room temperature for up to 3 days.) Top each burger with 1 ounce crumbled blue cheese before transferring to oven. Top with crispy shallots just before serving.

JUICY PUB-STYLE BURGERS WITH SAUTÉED ONIONS AND SMOKED CHEDDAR

Heat 2 tablespoons vegetable oil in 12-inch skillet over medium-high heat until just smoking. Add 1 thinly sliced onion and ¼ teaspoon salt; cook, stirring frequently, until softened and lightly browned, 5 to 7 minutes. Top each burger with 1 ounce grated smoked cheddar cheese before transferring to oven. Top with onions just before serving.

JUICY PUB-STYLE BURGERS WITH PEPPERED BACON AND AGED CHEDDAR

Adjust oven rack to middle position and heat oven to 375 degrees. Arrange 6 bacon slices on rimmed baking sheet and sprinkle with 2 teaspoons coarsely ground pepper. Place second rimmed baking sheet on top of bacon and bake until bacon is crisp, 15 to 20 minutes. Transfer bacon to paper towel–lined plate and cool. Cut bacon in half crosswise. Top each burger with 1 ounce grated aged cheddar cheese before transferring to oven. Top with bacon just before serving.

JUICY PUB-STYLE BURGERS WITH PAN-ROASTED MUSHROOMS AND GRUYÈRE

Heat 2 tablespoons vegetable oil in 12-inch skillet over medium-high heat until just smoking. Add 10 ounces trimmed and thinly sliced cremini mushrooms, ¼ teaspoon salt, and ¼ teaspoon pepper; cook, stirring frequently, until browned, 5 to 7 minutes. Add 1 minced shallot and 2 teaspoons minced thyme and cook until fragrant. Remove skillet from heat and stir in 2 tablespoons dry sherry. Top each burger with 1 ounce grated Gruyère cheese before transferring to oven. Top with mushrooms just before serving.

STEAK TACOS

⊘ WHY THIS RECIPE WORKS
Steak tacos are great on the grill, but we wanted to bring steak tacos indoors for those times when grilling outside isn't an option. Cutting the beef (flank steak) into smaller pieces and pan-searing all four sides gave us the browned exterior and crisp, brittle edges characteristic

of grilled meat. A paste of oil, cilantro, scallions, garlic, and jalapeño applied to the meat and scraped off just before cooking gave our steak taco recipe a flavor boost without sacrificing browning.

STEAK TACOS
SERVES 4 TO 6

For a more spicy dish, add the seeds from the chiles. In addition to the toppings suggested below, try serving the tacos with Sweet and Spicy Pickled Onions (recipe follows), thinly sliced radishes or cucumber, or salsa.

HERB PASTE
- ½   cup packed fresh cilantro leaves
- 3   garlic cloves, chopped coarse
- 3   scallions, chopped coarse
- 1   jalapeño chile, stemmed, seeds reserved, and chopped coarse
- ½   teaspoon ground cumin
- ¼   cup vegetable oil
- 1   tablespoon lime juice

STEAK
- 1   (1½- to 1¾-pound) flank steak, trimmed and cut lengthwise (with grain) into 4 equal pieces
- 1   tablespoon kosher salt
- ½   teaspoon sugar
- ½   teaspoon pepper
- 2   tablespoons vegetable oil

TACOS
- 12 (6-inch) corn tortillas, warmed
  Fresh cilantro
  Minced white or red onion
  Lime wedges

1. FOR THE HERB PASTE: Pulse cilantro, garlic, scallions, jalapeño, and cumin in food processor until finely chopped, 10 to 12 pulses, scraping down sides of bowl as necessary. Add oil and process until mixture is smooth and resembles pesto, about 15 seconds, scraping down sides of bowl as necessary. Transfer 2 tablespoons herb paste to medium bowl; whisk in lime juice and set aside.

2. FOR THE STEAK: Using dinner fork, poke each piece of steak 10 to 12 times on each side. Place in large baking dish; rub all sides of steak pieces evenly with salt and then coat with remaining herb paste. Cover with plastic wrap and refrigerate at least 30 minutes or up to 1 hour.

3. Scrape herb paste off steak and sprinkle all sides of pieces evenly with sugar and pepper. Heat oil in 12-inch nonstick skillet over medium-high heat until just smoking. Place steak in skillet and cook until well browned, about 3 minutes. Flip steak and sear until second side is well browned, 2 to 3 minutes. Using tongs, stand each piece on a cut side and cook, turning as necessary, until all cut sides are well browned and meat registers 125 to 130 degrees, 2 to 7 minutes. Transfer steak to carving board and let rest for 5 minutes.

4. FOR THE TACOS: Slice steak pieces across grain into thin pieces. Transfer sliced steak to bowl with herb paste–lime juice mixture and toss to coat. Season with salt to taste. Spoon small amount of sliced steak into center of each warm tortilla and serve, passing toppings separately.

SLICING FLANK STEAK

With its pronounced longitudinal grain, flank steak can be tough and chewy if sliced the wrong way. Make sure to cut the meat into thin slices on the bias, across the grain. This cuts through the connective tissue in the meat and make it more tender.

SWEET AND SPICY PICKLED ONIONS
MAKES ABOUT 2 CUPS

To make this dish spicier, add the reserved chile seeds with the vinegar.

- 1   red onion, sliced thin (1½ cups)
- 1   cup red wine vinegar
- ⅓   cup sugar
- 2   jalapeño chiles, stemmed, seeds reserved, and cut into thin rings
- ¼   teaspoon salt

Place onion in medium heatproof bowl. Bring vinegar, sugar, jalapeños, and salt to simmer in small saucepan over medium-high heat, stirring occasionally, until sugar dissolves. Pour vinegar mixture over onion, cover loosely, and cool to room temperature, about 30 minutes. Once cool, drain and discard liquid. (Pickled onions can be refrigerated in airtight container for up to 1 week.)

BEEF TACOS

✔ WHY THIS RECIPE WORKS
Most everyone in the test kitchen has fond memories of enjoying ground beef tacos growing up, but in reality the stale-tasting fillings (made with supermarket seasoning packets) and greasy store-bought shells leave a lot to be desired. We set out to develop a ground beef taco recipe with a boldly spiced beef mixture and fresh toppings. We fried corn tortillas to make superior homemade taco shells. For the filling, we sautéed onions and garlic, then sautéed the spices to bring out their flavor. Using very lean ground beef prevented greasiness, and adding tomato sauce, chicken broth, brown sugar, and vinegar created roundness and depth.

GROUND BEEF TACOS

MAKES 8 TACOS, SERVING 4

Tomato sauce is sold in cans in the same aisle that carries canned whole tomatoes. Do not use jarred pasta sauce in its place. There's no need to prepare all of the toppings listed below, but cheese, lettuce, and tomatoes are, in our opinion, essential.

BEEF FILLING

- 2 teaspoons vegetable oil or corn oil
- 1 small onion, chopped fine
- 3 garlic cloves, minced
- 2 tablespoons chili powder
- 1 teaspoon ground cumin
- 1 teaspoon ground coriander
- ½ teaspoon dried oregano
- ¼ teaspoon cayenne pepper
  Salt and pepper
- 1 pound 90 percent lean ground beef
- ½ cup tomato sauce
- ½ cup low-sodium chicken broth
- 2 teaspoons vinegar (preferably cider)
- 1 teaspoon packed brown sugar

SHELLS AND TOPPINGS

- 8 Home-Fried Taco Shells (recipe follows)
- 4 ounces cheddar or Monterey Jack cheese, shredded (1 cup)
- 2 cups shredded iceberg lettuce
- 2 small tomatoes, cored and chopped fine
- ½ cup sour cream
- 1 avocado, pitted and chopped fine
- 1 small onion, chopped fine
- 2 tablespoons minced fresh cilantro
  Hot sauce

1. FOR THE FILLING: Heat oil in 12-inch skillet over medium heat until shimmering, about 2 minutes; add onion and cook, stirring occasionally, until softened, about 4 minutes. Add garlic, chili powder, cumin, coriander, oregano, cayenne, and ½ teaspoon salt; cook, stirring constantly, until fragrant, about 1 minute. Add ground beef and cook, breaking meat up with wooden spoon and scraping pan bottom to prevent scorching, until beef is no longer pink, about 5 minutes. Add tomato sauce, broth, vinegar, and brown sugar; bring to simmer. Reduce heat to medium-low and simmer, uncovered, stirring frequently and breaking meat up so that no chunks remain, until liquid has reduced and thickened (mixture should not be completely dry), about 10 minutes. Season with salt and pepper to taste.

2. TO SERVE: Using wide, shallow spoon, divide filling evenly among taco shells; place 2 tacos on individual plates. Serve, passing toppings separately.

HOME-FRIED TACO SHELLS

MAKES 8 TACO SHELLS, ENOUGH FOR
1 RECIPE BEEF TACOS

Be sure to use a heavy-bottomed skillet for this recipe. Taco shells can be fried before you make filling and rewarmed in 200-degree oven for about 10 minutes before serving.

- ¾ cup vegetable oil
- 8 (6-inch) corn tortillas

1. Heat oil in 8-inch skillet over medium heat to 350 degrees, about 5 minutes (oil should bubble when small piece of tortilla is dropped in; tortilla piece should rise to surface in 2 seconds and be light golden brown in about 1½ minutes). Meanwhile, line rimmed baking sheet with double layer of paper towels.

2. Using tongs to hold tortilla, slip half of tortilla into hot oil. With metal spatula in other hand, keep half of tortilla submerged in oil. Fry until just set, but not brown, about 30 seconds.

3. Flip tortilla; hold tortilla open about 2 inches while keeping bottom submerged in oil. Fry until golden brown, about 1½ minutes. Flip again and fry other side until golden brown, about 30 seconds.

4. Transfer shell upside down to prepared baking sheet to drain. Repeat with remaining tortillas, adjusting heat as necessary to keep oil between 350 and 375 degrees.

BEEF EMPANADAS

✔ WHY THIS RECIPE WORKS

As all-in-one meals go, empanadas—the South American equivalent of Britain's pasties, or meat turnovers—are hard to beat: a moist, savory filling encased in a tender yet sturdy crust. But most recipes for empanadas are enormously time-consuming and fussy. We wanted a streamlined recipe that would be hearty enough to stand as a centerpiece on our dinner table. The first step was to enhance ground chuck with aromatics, spices, and a mixture of chicken broth and bread, which kept the beef tender as it cooked. For the crust, we made a few Latin-inspired changes to our Foolproof Pie Dough (page 708). We traded some of the flour for masa harina, the cornmeal used in Mexican cooking, omitted the shortening, and switched to all butter for better flavor. Finally, we finished our empanadas by brushing the tops with oil for a shiny, crunchy crust. Placing them on a preheated oiled baking sheet ensured that the underside of the empanadas got as crisp as the top.

BEEF EMPANADAS

MAKES 12 EMPANADAS, SERVING 4 TO 6

The alcohol in the dough is essential to the texture of the crust and imparts no flavor—do not substitute. Masa harina can be found in the international foods aisle with other Latin American foods or in the baking aisle with the flour. If you cannot find masa harina, replace it with additional all-purpose flour (for a total of 4 cups).

FILLING

- 1 slice hearty white sandwich bread, torn into quarters
- 2 tablespoons plus ½ cup low-sodium chicken broth
- 1 pound 85 percent lean ground beef
  Salt and pepper
- 1 tablespoon olive oil
- 2 onions, chopped fine
- 4 garlic cloves, minced
- 1 teaspoon ground cumin
- ¼ teaspoon cayenne pepper
- ⅛ teaspoon ground cloves
- ½ cup packed cilantro leaves, chopped coarse
- 2 hard-cooked eggs, chopped coarse
- ⅓ cup raisins, chopped coarse
- ¼ cup green olives, pitted and chopped coarse
- 4 teaspoons cider vinegar

DOUGH

- 3 cups (15 ounces) all-purpose flour
- 1 cup (5 ounces) masa harina
- 1 tablespoon sugar
- 2 teaspoons salt
- 12 tablespoons unsalted butter, cut into ½-inch pieces and chilled
- ½ cup cold vodka or tequila
- ½ cup cold water
- 5 tablespoons olive oil

1. FOR THE FILLING: Process bread and 2 tablespoons broth in food processor until paste forms, about 5 seconds, scraping down sides of bowl as necessary. Add beef, ¾ teaspoon salt, and ½ teaspoon pepper and pulse until mixture is well combined, 6 to 8 pulses.

2. Heat oil in 12-inch nonstick skillet over medium-high heat until shimmering. Add onions and cook, stirring frequently, until beginning to brown, about 5 minutes. Stir in garlic, cumin, cayenne, and cloves; cook until fragrant, about 1 minute. Add beef mixture and cook, breaking meat into 1-inch pieces with wooden spoon, until browned, about 7 minutes.

Add remaining ½ cup broth and simmer until mixture is moist but not wet, 3 to 5 minutes. Transfer mixture to bowl and cool for 10 minutes. Stir in cilantro, eggs, raisins, olives, and vinegar. Season with salt and pepper to taste and refrigerate until cool, about 1 hour. (Filling can be refrigerated for up to 2 days.)

3. FOR THE DOUGH: Process 1 cup flour, masa harina, sugar, and salt in food processor until combined, about 2 pulses. Add butter and process until homogeneous and dough resembles wet sand, about 10 seconds. Add remaining 2 cups flour and pulse until mixture is evenly distributed around bowl, 4 to 6 quick pulses. Empty mixture into large bowl.

4. Sprinkle vodka and water over mixture. Using hands, mix dough until it forms tacky mass that sticks together. Divide dough in half, then divide each half into 6 equal pieces. Transfer dough pieces to plate, cover with plastic wrap, and refrigerate until firm, about 45 minutes or up to 2 days.

5. TO ASSEMBLE: Adjust oven racks to upper-middle and lower-middle positions, place 1 rimmed baking sheet on each rack, and heat oven to 425 degrees. While baking sheets are preheating, remove dough from refrigerator. Roll out each dough piece out on lightly floured counter into 6-inch circle about ⅛ inch thick, covering each dough round with plastic wrap while rolling remaining dough. Place about ⅓ cup filling in center of each dough round. Brush edges of dough with water and fold dough over filling. Trim any ragged edges. Press edges to seal. Crimp edges of empanadas using fork. (Empanadas can be made through step 5, covered tightly with plastic wrap, and refrigerated for up to 2 days.)

6. TO BAKE: Drizzle 2 tablespoons oil over surface of each hot baking sheet, then return to oven for 2 minutes. Brush empanadas with remaining 1 tablespoon oil. Carefully place 6 empanadas on each baking sheet and cook until well browned and crisp, 25 to 30 minutes, switching and

rotating baking sheets halfway through baking. Cool empanadas on wire rack for 10 minutes and serve.

BEEF EMPANADAS WITH CORN AND BLACK BEAN FILLING

Omit raisins and cook ½ cup frozen corn kernels and ½ cup rinsed canned black beans along with onions in step 2.

BEEF EMPANADAS WITH SPICY CHORIZO FILLING

MAKES 12 EMPANADAS, SERVING 4 TO 6

Portuguese linguiça can be substituted for the chorizo. Use Spanish chorizo sausage, which is fully cooked, in this recipe.

FILLING

- 1 slice hearty white sandwich bread, torn into quarters
- 2 tablespoons low-sodium chicken broth
- 1 pound 85 percent lean ground chuck
  Salt and pepper
- 6 tablespoons olive oil
- 6 ounces Spanish chorizo sausage, cut into ¼-inch dice
- 2 onions, chopped fine
- 4 garlic cloves minced
- 1 tablespoon ground chipotle powder
- 1 teaspoon ground cumin
- 1 (14.5-ounce) can tomato sauce
- ½ cup chopped fresh cilantro
- ⅓ cup raisins, chopped coarse
- 4 teaspoons cider vinegar

DOUGH

- 3 cups (15 ounces) all-purpose flour
- 1 cup (5 ounces) masa harina
- 1 tablespoon sugar
- 2 teaspoons salt
- 12 tablespoons unsalted butter, cut into ½-inch pieces and chilled
- ½ cup cold vodka or tequila
- ½ cup cold water
- 5 tablespoons olive oil

1. **FOR THE FILLING:** Process bread and broth in food processor until paste forms, about 5 seconds, scraping down sides of bowl as necessary. Add beef, ¾ teaspoon salt, and ½ teaspoon pepper and pulse until mixture is well combined, 6 to 8 pulses.

2. Heat oil in 12-inch nonstick skillet over medium-high heat until shimmering. Add chorizo and cook until crisp, about 5 minutes. Transfer chorizo to bowl using slotted spoon, leaving rendered fat in skillet. Add onions to skillet and cook, stirring frequently, until beginning to brown, about 5 minutes. Stir in garlic, chipotle, and cumin; cook until fragrant, about 1 minute. Add beef mixture and cook, breaking meat into 1-inch pieces with wooden spoon, until browned, about 7 minutes. Add tomato sauce and reserved chorizo and simmer until mixture is moist but not wet, 3 to 5 minutes. Transfer mixture to bowl and cool for 10 minutes. Stir in cilantro, raisins, and vinegar. Season with salt and pepper to taste and refrigerate until cool, about 1 hour. (Filling can be refrigerated for up to 2 days.)

3. **FOR THE DOUGH:** Process 1 cup flour, masa harina, sugar, and salt in food processor until combined, about 2 pulses. Add butter and process until homogeneous and dough resembles wet sand, about 10 seconds. Add remaining 2 cups flour and pulse until mixture is evenly distributed around bowl, 4 to 6 quick pulses. Empty mixture into large bowl.

4. Sprinkle vodka and water over mixture. Using hands, mix dough until it forms tacky mass that sticks together. Divide dough in half, then divide each half into 6 equal pieces. Transfer dough pieces to plate, cover with plastic wrap, and refrigerate until firm, about 45 minutes or up to 2 days.

5. **TO ASSEMBLE AND BAKE:** Adjust oven racks to upper-middle and lower-middle positions, place 1 rimmed baking sheet on each rack, and heat oven to 425 degrees. While baking sheets are preheating, remove dough from refrigerator. Roll each dough piece out on lightly floured counter into 6-inch circle about ⅛ inch thick, covering each dough round with plastic wrap while rolling remaining dough. Place about ⅓ cup filling in center of each dough round. Brush edges of dough with water and fold dough over filling. Trim any ragged edges. Press edges to seal. Crimp edges of empanadas using fork. (Empanadas can be made through step 5, covered tightly with plastic wrap, and refrigerated for up to 2 days.)

6. **TO BAKE:** Drizzle 2 tablespoons oil over surface of each hot baking sheet, then return to oven for 2 minutes. Brush empanadas with remaining 1 tablespoon oil. Carefully place 6 empanadas on each baking sheet and cook until well browned and crisp, 25 to 30 minutes, switching and rotating baking sheets halfway through baking. Cool empanadas on wire rack for 10 minutes and serve.

SWEDISH MEATBALLS

✔ WHY THIS RECIPE WORKS

Most of us know Swedish meatballs as lumps of flavorless ground beef or pork covered in heavy gravy that congeals as it sits. But when done right these main-course meatballs are melt-in-your-mouth tender, substantial yet delicate. To achieve the right texture, we combined beef, pork, a panade (a mixture of bread, egg, and cream), and a surprise ingredient, baking powder, which kept the meatballs delicate and juicy. Whipping the pork in a mixer with the dry ingredients before folding in the panade and beef gave our meatballs just the right amount of springiness. For the gravy, we wanted a light cream sauce instead of heavy brown one. To get this, we added a bit of cream to our stock to lighten it up and a splash of lemon juice for bright flavor.

SWEDISH MEATBALLS
SERVES 4 TO 6

The traditional accompaniments for Swedish meatballs are lingonberry preserves and Swedish Pickled Cucumbers (recipe follows). If you can't find lingonberry preserves, cranberry preserves may be used. For a slightly less sweet dish, omit the brown sugar in the meatballs and reduce the brown sugar in the sauce to 2 teaspoons. A 12-inch slope-sided skillet can be used in place of the sauté pan—use 1½ cups of oil to fry instead of 1¼ cups. Serve the meatballs with mashed potatoes, boiled red potatoes, or egg noodles.

MEATBALLS
1	large egg
¼	cup heavy cream
1	slice hearty white sandwich bread, crusts removed and bread torn into 1-inch pieces
8	ounces ground pork
¼	cup grated onion
1½	teaspoons salt
1	teaspoon packed brown sugar
1	teaspoon baking powder
⅛	teaspoon ground nutmeg
⅛	teaspoon ground allspice
⅛	teaspoon pepper
8	ounces 85 percent lean ground beef
1¼	cups vegetable oil

SAUCE
1	tablespoon unsalted butter
1	tablespoon all-purpose flour
1½	cups low-sodium chicken broth
1	tablespoon packed brown sugar
½	cup heavy cream
2	teaspoons lemon juice
	Salt and pepper

1. **FOR MEATBALLS:** Whisk egg and cream together in bowl. Stir in bread and set aside. Meanwhile, using stand mixer fitted with paddle attachment, beat pork, onion, salt, sugar, baking powder, nutmeg, allspice, and pepper on high speed until smooth

and pale, about 2 minutes, scraping down bowl as necessary. Using fork, mash bread mixture until no large dry bread chunks remain; add mixture to mixer bowl and beat on high speed until smooth and homogeneous, about 1 minute, scraping down bowl as necessary. Add beef and mix on medium-low speed until just incorporated, about 30 seconds, scraping down bowl as necessary. Using moistened hands, form generous tablespoon of meat mixture into 1-inch round meatball; repeat with remaining mixture to form 25 to 30 meatballs.

2. Heat oil in 10-inch straight-sided sauté pan over medium-high heat until edge of meatball dipped in oil sizzles (oil should register 350 degrees on instant-read thermometer), 3 to 5 minutes. Add meatballs in single layer and fry, flipping once halfway through cooking, until lightly browned all over and cooked through, 7 to 10 minutes. (Adjust heat as needed to keep oil sizzling but not smoking.) Using slotted spoon, transfer browned meatballs to paper towel–lined plate.

3. FOR SAUCE: Pour off and discard oil in pan, leaving any browned bits behind. Return pan to medium-high heat and melt butter. Add flour and cook, whisking constantly, until flour is light brown, about 30 seconds. Slowly whisk in broth, scraping bottom of pan with wooden spoon to loosen any browned bits. Add sugar and bring to simmer. Reduce heat to medium and cook until sauce is reduced to about 1 cup, about 5 minutes. Stir in cream and return to simmer.

4. Add meatballs to sauce and simmer, turning occasionally, until heated through, about 5 minutes. Stir in lemon juice, season with salt and pepper to taste, and serve.

TO MAKE AHEAD: Meatballs can be fried and then frozen for up to 2 weeks. To continue with recipe, thaw meatballs in refrigerator overnight and proceed from step 3, using clean pan.

SWEDISH PICKLED CUCUMBERS

MAKES 3 CUPS, ENOUGH FOR
1 RECIPE SWEDISH MEATBALLS

Kirby cucumbers are also called pickling cucumbers. If these small cucumbers are unavailable, substitute 1 large American cucumber. Serve the pickles chilled or at room temperature.

- 3   small Kirby cucumbers (1 pound), sliced into 1/8- to 1/4-inch-thick rounds
- 1 1/2 cups white vinegar
- 1 1/2 cups sugar
- 1   teaspoon salt
- 12   whole allspice berries

Place cucumber slices in medium heatproof bowl. Bring vinegar, sugar, salt, and allspice to simmer in small saucepan over high heat, stirring occasionally to dissolve sugar. Pour vinegar mixture over cucumbers and stir to separate slices. Cover bowl with plastic wrap and let sit for 15 minutes. Uncover and cool to room temperature, about 15 minutes.

TO MAKE AHEAD: Pickles can be refrigerated in their liquid in airtight container for up to 2 weeks.

EASY PORK CHOPS

✔ WHY THIS RECIPE WORKS
Pork chops are relatively quick-cooking, making them ideal for a simple weeknight dinner. But all too often, one bite reveals dry, tough meat. We wanted to find a simple way to guarantee the elusive juicy pork chop. We passed over hefty chops in favor of 1/2-inch-thick, bone-in rib chops. We placed the chops in a cold pan over medium heat, then covered them. Although starting meat in a cold pan sounds odd, we found that this unconventional method was the key to tender, *juicy chops. The only drawback was that starting the chops in a cold pan meant they didn't have a chance to brown; adding a little sugar to the seasoning easily solved this problem.*

EASY PORK CHOPS
SERVES 4

We prefer natural to "enhanced pork" (pork that has been injected with a salt solution to increase moistness and flavor) for this recipe. Electric burners are slower to heat than gas burners, so, if using one, begin heating the burner before seasoning the chops. Serve these simple pork chops with chutney or applesauce, or try one of the variations.

- 4   (6- to 8-ounce) bone-in pork rib or center-cut chops, 1/2 to 3/4 inch thick, trimmed
- 1   teaspoon vegetable oil
     Salt and pepper
- 1/2 teaspoon sugar

1. Pat chops dry with paper towels. Cut 2 slits, about 2 inches apart, through outer layer of fat and silver skin on each chop. If using electric stove, turn burner to medium heat. Rub both sides of each chop with 1/8 teaspoon oil and season with salt and pepper. Sprinkle 1 side of each chop evenly with 1/8 teaspoon sugar, avoiding bone.

2. Place chops, sugared side down, in 12-inch nonstick skillet. Using hands, press meat of each chop into pan. Set skillet over medium heat; cook until lightly browned, 4 to 9 minutes (chops should be sizzling after 2 minutes). Using tongs, flip chops, positioning them in same manner. Cover skillet, reduce heat to low, and cook until each chop registers 145 degrees, 3 to 6 minutes (begin checking temperature after 2 minutes); chops will barely brown on second side. Transfer chops to platter, tent loosely with aluminum foil, and let

rest for 5 minutes; do not discard liquid in skillet.

3. Add any accumulated meat juices to skillet. Set skillet over high heat and simmer vigorously until reduced to about 3 tablespoons, 30 to 90 seconds; season with salt and pepper to taste. Off heat, return pork chops to skillet, turning chops to coat with reduced juices. Serve chops, browned side up, pouring any remaining juices over.

EASY PORK CHOPS WITH MUSTARD-SAGE SAUCE

After transferring chops to platter, pour liquid in skillet into bowl. While chops are resting, add 1 teaspoon vegetable oil and 1 minced garlic clove to now-empty skillet; set skillet over medium heat and cook until fragrant, about 30 seconds. Add ¼ cup low-sodium chicken broth; increase heat to high and simmer until reduced to about 2 tablespoons, about 3 minutes. Add pork chop juices to skillet. Off heat, whisk in 3 tablespoons unsalted butter and 1 tablespoon Dijon mustard until combined. Stir in 1 tablespoon minced fresh sage and season with salt and pepper to taste; spoon sauce over chops and serve.

NO-CURL PORK CHOPS

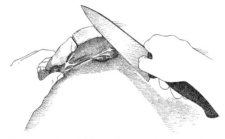

To prevent pork chops from curling in a hot pan, cut two slits, about 2 inches apart, into the fat and silver skin of each chop (this method works for both bone-in and boneless chops). A flat chop will develop a better crust, cook evenly, and taste better.

EASY PORK CHOPS WITH BRANDY AND PRUNES

Cover ⅓ cup chopped pitted prunes with ¼ cup brandy and let stand. After transferring chops to platter, pour liquid in skillet into bowl. While chops are resting, add 1 teaspoon vegetable oil and 1 minced shallot to now-empty skillet; set skillet over medium heat and cook, stirring occasionally, until shallot is softened, about 2 minutes. Off heat, add brandy and prunes; set skillet over medium-high heat and cook until brandy is reduced to about 2 tablespoons, about 3 minutes. Add pork chop juices to skillet. Off heat, whisk in 2 tablespoons minced fresh thyme and 3 tablespoons butter until combined. Season with salt and pepper to taste; spoon sauce over chops and serve.

PAN-SEARED THICK-CUT PORK CHOPS

✔ WHY THIS RECIPE WORKS

Thick pork chops typically boast a juicy interior or a nicely caramelized exterior—but rarely both. We wanted it all, in one recipe. To start, we turned the conventional cooking method upside down, first cooking salted chops in a low oven, then searing them in a super hot pan. Slowly cooking the meat allowed enzymes to break down protein, tenderizing the chops. The salted surface gently dried out in the oven and became beautifully caramelized in the pan. The result was pan-seared pork chops that were perfect inside and out.

PAN-SEARED THICK-CUT PORK CHOPS

SERVES 4

Buy chops of similar thickness so that they cook at the same rate. If the pork is enhanced (injected with a salt solution), do not salt in
step 1, but season with salt in step 2. Serve the chops with a pan sauce (recipes follow) or with applesauce.

4	(12-ounce) bone-in pork rib chops, 1½ inches thick, trimmed Kosher salt and pepper
1–2	tablespoons vegetable oil
1	recipe pan sauce (recipes follow)

1. Adjust oven rack to middle position and heat oven to 275 degrees. Pat chops dry with paper towels. Cut 2 slits, about 2 inches apart, through outer layer of fat and silver skin on each chop. Sprinkle each chop with 1 teaspoon salt. Place chops on wire rack set in rimmed baking sheet and let stand at room temperature for 45 minutes.

2. Season chops with pepper; transfer baking sheet to oven. Cook until chops register 120 to 125 degrees, 30 to 45 minutes.

3. Heat 1 tablespoon oil in 12-inch skillet over high heat until just smoking. Place 2 chops in skillet and sear until well browned and crusty, 1½ to 3 minutes, lifting once halfway through to redistribute fat underneath each chop. (Reduce heat if browned bits in pan start to burn.) Using tongs, turn chops and cook until well browned on second side, 2 to 3 minutes. Transfer chops to plate and repeat with remaining 2 chops, adding extra 1 tablespoon oil if pan is dry.

4. Reduce heat to medium. Use tongs to stand 2 pork chops on their sides. Holding chops together with tongs, return to skillet and sear sides of chops (with exception of bone side) until browned and chops register 145 degrees, about 1½ minutes. Repeat with remaining 2 chops. Let chops rest, tented loosely with aluminum foil, for 10 minutes while preparing sauce.

CILANTRO AND COCONUT PAN SAUCE

MAKES ½ CUP, ENOUGH FOR 1 RECIPE
PAN-SEARED THICK-CUT PORK CHOPS

1	large shallot, minced
1	tablespoon grated fresh ginger
2	garlic cloves, minced
¾	cup coconut milk
¼	cup low-sodium chicken broth
1	teaspoon sugar
¼	cup chopped fresh cilantro
2	teaspoons lime juice
1	tablespoon unsalted butter

Pour off all but 1 teaspoon oil from pan used to cook chops and return pan to medium heat. Add shallot, ginger, and garlic and cook, stirring constantly, until softened, about 1 minute. Add coconut milk, broth, and sugar, scraping bottom of pan with wooden spoon to loosen any browned bits. Simmer until reduced to ½ cup, 6 to 7 minutes. Off heat, stir in cilantro and lime juice, then whisk in butter. Season with salt and pepper to taste and serve with chops.

GARLIC AND THYME PAN SAUCE

MAKES ½ CUP, ENOUGH FOR 1 RECIPE
PAN-SEARED THICK-CUT PORK CHOPS

1	large shallot, minced
2	garlic cloves, minced
¾	cup low-sodium chicken broth
½	cup dry white wine
1	teaspoon minced fresh thyme
¼	teaspoon white wine vinegar
3	tablespoons unsalted butter, cut into 3 pieces and chilled

Pour off all but 1 teaspoon oil from pan used to cook chops and return pan to medium heat. Add shallot and garlic and cook, stirring constantly, until softened, about 1 minute. Add broth and wine, scraping bottom of pan with wooden spoon to loosen any browned bits. Simmer until reduced to ½ cup, 6 to 7 minutes. Off heat, stir in thyme and vinegar, then whisk in butter, 1 tablespoon at a time. Season with salt and pepper to taste and serve with chops.

PORK CHOPS WITH VINEGAR AND SWEET PEPPERS

✓ WHY THIS RECIPE WORKS

Pork chops cooked with sweet peppers and tart vinegar is an Italian dish full of big flavors, at least in theory. But pairing the lean supermarket pork found in this country with the traditional braising method results in chalky chops. We found that brining tender rib chops added much-needed flavor and moisture, and sautéing them created a good crust. And instead of using jarred peppers—which tend to be bitter and dull—we decided to make our own vinegar peppers. We chose white wine vinegar for its clean, sweet taste. Sautéing the peppers briefly, just enough to eliminate their raw crunch, then adding vinegar to the pan and simmering the lot was much easier than roasting the peppers and gave us the perfect accompaniment to our tender chops.

PORK CHOPS WITH VINEGAR AND SWEET PEPPERS
SERVES 4

For this recipe, we prefer rib chops, but center-cut chops, which contain a portion of tenderloin, can be used instead. If the pork is enhanced (injected with a salt solution), do not brine in step 1, and season with salt in step 1. To keep the chops from overcooking and becoming tough and dry, they are removed from the oven when they are just shy of fully cooked; as they sit in the hot skillet, they continue to cook with residual heat. The vinegar stirred into the sauce at the end adds a bright, fresh flavor. However, taste the sauce before you add the vinegar—you may prefer to omit it.

	Salt
3	tablespoons sugar
4	(8- to 10-ounce) bone-in pork rib chops, ¾ to 1 inch thick, trimmed
	Pepper
2	tablespoons olive oil
1	large onion, chopped fine
1	large red bell pepper, stemmed, seeded, and cut into ¼-inch-wide strips
1	large yellow bell pepper, stemmed, seeded, and cut into ¼-inch-wide strips
2	anchovy fillets, rinsed and minced
1	sprig fresh rosemary
2	garlic cloves, minced
¾	cup water
½	cup plus 2 tablespoons white wine vinegar
2	tablespoons unsalted butter, chilled
2	tablespoons chopped fresh parsley

1. Dissolve 3 tablespoons salt and sugar in 1½ quarts cold water in large container. Submerge chops in brine, cover, and refrigerate for 30 minutes to 1 hour. Remove chops from brine; thoroughly pat dry with paper towels, season with ¾ teaspoon pepper, and set aside.

2. Adjust oven rack to middle position; heat oven to 400 degrees. Heat oil in 12-inch ovensafe skillet over medium-high heat until just smoking; swirl skillet to coat with oil. Place chops in skillet; cook until well browned, 3 to 4 minutes, using spoon or spatula to press down on center of chops to aid in browning. Using tongs, flip chops and brown lightly on second side, about 1 minute. Transfer chops to large plate; set aside.

3. Set skillet over medium-high heat. Add onion and cook, stirring occasionally, until just beginning to soften, about 2 minutes. Add peppers, anchovies, and rosemary; cook, stirring frequently, until peppers just begin to soften, about 4 minutes. Add garlic and cook, stirring constantly, until fragrant, about 30 seconds.

Add water and ½ cup vinegar and bring to boil, scraping bottom of pan with wooden spoon to loosen any browned bits. Reduce heat to medium; simmer until liquid is reduced to about ⅓ cup, 6 to 8 minutes. Off heat, discard rosemary.

4. Return pork chops, browned side up, to skillet; nestle chops in peppers, but do not cover chops with peppers. Add any accumulated juices to skillet; set skillet in oven and cook until chops registers 145 degrees, 8 to 12 minutes (begin checking temperature after 6 minutes). Using potholders, carefully remove skillet from oven (handle will be very hot) and cover skillet with lid or aluminum foil; let rest for 5 to 7 minutes. Transfer chops to platter or individual plates. Swirl butter into sauce and peppers in skillet; stir in 2 tablespoons vinegar (if using) and parsley. Season with salt and pepper to taste, then pour or spoon sauce and peppers over chops. Serve.

PORK CHOPS WITH BALSAMIC VINEGAR AND SWEET PEPPERS

Substitute balsamic vinegar for white wine vinegar and add 1 tablespoon chopped fresh thyme along with parsley in step 4.

SMOTHERED PORK CHOPS

✓ WHY THIS RECIPE WORKS

Smothered pork chops is a homey dish of chops braised in deeply flavored onion gravy—that is, if dry pork and near-tasteless, gelatinous gravy don't ruin it. We determined that bone-in pork rib chops were the most juicy and flavorful. Further, we found that thin, ½-inch chops picked up more flavor than thick chops and didn't overwhelm the gravy. The best cooking method was to sear the chops in bacon fat, then braise them in an onion gravy thickened with a bacon fat and flour roux; the sweet, salty, smoky flavor of the roux underscored and deepened all of the other flavors.

SMOTHERED PORK CHOPS
SERVES 4

Serve these smothered chops with a starch to soak up the rich gravy. Simple egg noodles are our favorite, but rice or mashed potatoes also taste great.

- 3 slices bacon, cut into ¼-inch pieces
- 2 tablespoons all-purpose flour
- 1¾ cups low-sodium chicken broth
- 2 tablespoons vegetable oil, plus extra as needed
- 4 (6- to 8-ounce) bone-in pork rib chops, ½ to ¾ inch thick, trimmed
  Salt and pepper
- 2 onions, halved and sliced thin
- 2 tablespoons water
- 2 garlic cloves, minced
- 1 teaspoon minced fresh thyme
- 2 bay leaves
- 1 tablespoon minced fresh parsley

1. Fry bacon in small saucepan over medium heat, stirring occasionally, until lightly browned, 8 to 10 minutes. Using slotted spoon, transfer bacon to paper towel–lined plate, leaving fat in saucepan (you should have 2 tablespoons bacon fat; if not, supplement with vegetable oil). Reduce heat to medium-low and gradually whisk flour into fat until smooth. Cook, whisking frequently, until mixture is light brown, about the color of peanut butter, about 5 minutes. Whisk in chicken broth in slow, steady stream; increase heat to medium-high and bring to boil, stirring occasionally; cover and set aside off heat.

2. Pat pork chops dry with paper towels and season with ½ teaspoon pepper. Heat 1 tablespoon oil in 12-inch skillet over high heat until just smoking. Brown chops in single layer until deep golden brown on first side, about 3 minutes. Flip chops and cook until browned on second side, about 3 minutes longer. Transfer chops to large plate and set aside.

3. Reduce heat to medium and add 1 tablespoon oil, onions, ¼ teaspoon salt, and water to now-empty skillet. Scrape bottom of skillet with wooden spoon to loosen any browned bits and cook, stirring frequently, until onions are softened and browned around the edges, about 5 minutes. Stir in garlic and thyme and cook until fragrant, about 30 seconds. Return chops to skillet in single layer, covering chops with onions. Pour in warm sauce and any accumulated juices from pork; add bay leaves. Cover, reduce heat to low, and simmer until pork is tender and paring knife inserted in chops meets very little resistance, about 30 minutes.

4. Transfer chops to warmed serving platter and tent loosely with aluminum foil. Increase heat to medium-high and simmer sauce rapidly, stirring frequently, until thickened to gravylike consistency, about 5 minutes. Discard bay leaves, stir in parsley, and season with salt and pepper to taste. Spoon sauce over chops, sprinkle with reserved bacon, and serve.

SMOTHERED PORK CHOPS WITH CIDER AND APPLES

Substitute apple cider for chicken broth and 1 large Granny Smith apple, peeled, cored, and cut into ⅜-inch wedges, for one of the onions, and increase salt added to onions to ½ teaspoon.

SMOTHERED PORK CHOPS WITH SPICY COLLARD GREENS

Increase oil in step 3 to 2 tablespoons, omit 1 onion, and increase garlic to 4 cloves. Just before returning browned chops to pan in step 3, add 4 cups stemmed and thinly sliced collard greens and ½ teaspoon red pepper flakes.

CRISPY PAN-FRIED PORK CHOPS

✔ WHY THIS RECIPE WORKS

A breaded coating can be just the thing to give lean, bland pork chops a flavor boost— but not when it turns gummy and flakes off the meat. Using boneless chops was fast and easy. Cornstarch formed an ultra-crisp sheath. Buttermilk brought a lighter texture and tangy flavor to the breading, and minced garlic and mustard perked up the breading's flavor. Crushed cornflakes added a craggy texture to the pork chops, especially once we added cornstarch to them before dredging the meat. Finally, to ensure our breading adhered to the meat, we lightly scored the chops before coating them, and then gave the breaded chops a short rest before adding them to the pan.

CRISPY PAN-FRIED PORK CHOPS
SERVES 4

We prefer natural to enhanced pork (pork that has been injected with a salt solution to increase moistness and flavor) for this recipe. Don't let the chops drain on the paper towels for longer than 30 seconds, or the heat will steam the crust and make it soggy. You can substitute ¾ cup store-bought cornflake crumbs for the whole cornflakes. If using crumbs, omit the processing step and mix the crumbs with the cornstarch, salt, and pepper.

- ⅔ cup cornstarch
- 1 cup buttermilk
- 2 tablespoons Dijon mustard
- 1 garlic clove, minced
- 3 cups cornflakes
  Salt and black pepper
- 8 (3- to 4-ounce) boneless pork chops, ½ to ¾ inch thick, trimmed
- ⅔ cup vegetable oil
  Lemon wedges

1. Place ⅓ cup cornstarch in shallow dish or pie plate. In second shallow dish, whisk buttermilk, mustard, and garlic until combined. Process cornflakes, ½ teaspoon salt, ½ teaspoon pepper, and remaining ⅓ cup cornstarch in food processor until cornflakes are finely ground, about 10 seconds. Transfer cornflake mixture to third shallow dish.

2. Adjust oven rack to middle position and heat oven to 200 degrees. Cut 1/16-inch-deep slits on both sides of chops, spaced ½ inch apart, in crosshatch pattern. Season chops with salt and pepper. Dredge 1 chop in cornstarch; shake off excess. Using tongs, coat with buttermilk mixture; let excess drip off. Coat with cornflake mixture; gently pat off excess. Transfer coated chop to wire rack set in rimmed baking sheet and repeat with remaining chops. Let coated chops stand for 10 minutes.

3. Heat ⅓ cup oil in 12-inch nonstick skillet over medium-high heat until shimmering. Place 4 chops in skillet and cook until golden brown and crisp, 2 to 5 minutes. Carefully flip chops and continue to cook until second side is golden brown, crisp, and chops register 145 degrees, 2 to 5 minutes longer. Transfer chops to paper towel–lined plate and let drain 30 seconds on each side. Transfer to clean wire rack set in rimmed baking sheet, then transfer to oven to keep warm. Discard oil in skillet and wipe clean with paper towels. Repeat process with remaining oil and pork chops. Serve with lemon wedges.

CRISPY PAN-FRIED PORK CHOPS
WITH LATIN SPICE RUB

Combine 1½ teaspoons ground cumin, 1½ teaspoons chili powder, ¾ teaspoon ground coriander, ⅛ teaspoon ground cinnamon, and ⅛ teaspoon red pepper flakes in bowl. Omit black pepper; coat chops with spice rub after seasoning with salt in step 2.

CRISPY PAN-FRIED PORK CHOPS
WITH THREE-PEPPER RUB

Combine 1½ teaspoons black pepper, 1½ teaspoons white pepper, ¾ teaspoon coriander, ¾ teaspoon ground cumin, ¼ teaspoon red pepper flakes, and ¼ teaspoon ground cinnamon in bowl. Omit black pepper and coat chops with spice rub after seasoning with salt in step 2.

GLAZED PORK CHOPS

✔ WHY THIS RECIPE WORKS

Thin boneless chops often cook up dry and bland, but their convenience is enticing. For moist chops with a pronounced sear and moist, juicy interior, we determined that pan-searing was the best method. For flavor, we decided to add a glaze. To prevent the chops from drying out, we seared them on just one side until they were well browned, added the glaze mixture, then gently "poached" the chops in the glaze. This approach helped the chops retain moisture and reduced the glaze to the right consistency.

GLAZED PORK CHOPS
SERVES 4

If your chops are on the thinner side, check their internal temperature after the initial sear. If they are already at the 145-degree mark, remove them from the skillet and allow them to rest, tented loosely with aluminum foil, for 5 minutes, then add the pork juices and glaze ingredients to the skillet and proceed with step 3. If your chops are closer to 1 inch thick, you may need to increase the simmering time in step 2.

- ½ cup distilled white vinegar or cider vinegar
- ⅓ cup packed light brown sugar
- ⅓ cup apple cider or apple juice
- 2 tablespoons Dijon mustard

- 1 tablespoon soy sauce
  Pinch cayenne pepper
- 4 (5- to 7-ounce) boneless pork chops, ½ to ¾ inch thick, trimmed
  Salt and pepper
- 1 tablespoon vegetable oil

1. Combine vinegar, sugar, cider, mustard, soy sauce, and cayenne in bowl; mix thoroughly and set aside. Pat chops dry with paper towels. Cut 2 slits, about 2 inches apart, through outer layer of fat and silver skin. Season chops with salt and pepper.

2. Heat oil in 12-inch skillet over medium-high heat until just smoking. Add chops to skillet and cook until well browned, 4 to 6 minutes. Turn chops and cook 1 minute longer; transfer chops to plate and pour off any oil in skillet. Return chops to skillet, browned side up, and add glaze mixture; cook over medium heat until chops register 145 degrees, 5 to 8 minutes. Off heat, transfer chops to clean platter, tent loosely with foil, and let rest for 5 minutes.

3. When chops have rested, add any accumulated juices to skillet and set over medium heat. Simmer, whisking constantly, until glaze is thick and color of dark caramel (heatproof spatula should leave wide trail when dragged through glaze), 2 to 6 minutes. Return chops to skillet; turn to coat both sides with glaze. Transfer chops back to platter, browned-side up, and spread remaining glaze over chops. Serve.

GLAZED PORK CHOPS WITH ASIAN FLAVORS

Toast 1 teaspoon sesame seeds in small dry skillet over medium heat, stirring frequently, until lightly browned and fragrant, 3 to 5 minutes; set aside in bowl. Substitute ½ cup rice vinegar for white vinegar, omit cider, and add 3 tablespoons each orange juice and mirin and 1 teaspoon grated fresh ginger to glaze ingredients. In step 3, stir another 2 teaspoons rice vinegar into glaze before returning chops to skillet. Before serving, garnish chops with reserved sesame seeds and 1 teaspoon toasted sesame oil.

GLAZED PORK CHOPS WITH GERMAN FLAVORS

Toast ¾ teaspoon caraway seeds in small dry skillet over medium heat, stirring frequently, until fragrant, 3 to 5 minutes. Chop seeds coarse and set aside. Substitute ⅓ cup beer for cider, reduce soy sauce to 2 teaspoons, and add 3 tablespoons whole grain mustard (along with Dijon mustard), 1 tablespoon minced fresh thyme, and reserved caraway seeds to glaze ingredients. Omit cayenne.

STUFFED THICK-CUT PORK CHOPS

✔ WHY THIS RECIPE WORKS
Stuffed pork chops are rarely well executed, typically crammed full of a soggy bread stuffing. What we were after was our favorite pork chop—thick and juicy, seared crusty brown on the outside—enhanced by a flavorful stuffing. First, we had to find the right chop. The perfect choice turned out to be the rib chop, which has an unbroken eye of meat into which a wide pocket can be cut with a sharp paring knife. We then developed stuffing mixtures that incorporated enough moisture, fat, and assertive flavors to enhance the lean, mild pork. As for cooking them, we got the best results when we seared the brined, stuffed chops in a hot skillet and transferred them to a preheated baking sheet to finish cooking in the oven.

STUFFED THICK-CUT PORK CHOPS
SERVES 4

If the pork is enhanced (injected with a salt solution), do not brine in step 1, and season with salt in step 2. Prepare the stuffing while the chops brine. (The stuffing can also be made a day in advance, but it must be microwaved just to room temperature before being packed into the chops.) One stuffed chop makes for a very generous serving. If desired, remove the meat from the bone and cut it into ½-inch slices to serve 6.

- 4 (12- to 14-ounce) bone-in pork rib chops, 1½ inches thick, trimmed
- 3 tablespoons salt
- 3 tablespoons packed light brown sugar
- 1 recipe stuffing (recipes follow)
  Pepper
- 2 teaspoons vegetable oil

1. Using sharp paring knife, cut 1-inch opening into side of each chop, then cut pocket for stuffing by swinging blade through middle of chop. Dissolve salt and sugar in 1½ quarts cold water in large container. Submerge chops in brine, cover, and refrigerate for 1 hour.

2. Adjust oven rack to lower-middle position, place rimmed baking sheet on rack, and heat oven to 450 degrees. Remove chops from brine and thoroughly pat dry with paper towels. Place one-quarter of stuffing in pocket of each chop—enlarge pocket opening to 1-inch, if necessary. Trim reserved orange (or lemon) wedges from stuffing recipe to 2-inch lengths; insert one orange (or lemon) wedge into each pocket to contain stuffing. Season chops with pepper. (Chops can be stuffed and refrigerated up to 1 day ahead.)

3. Heat oil in 12-inch skillet over medium-high heat until just smoking. Arrange chops in skillet and cook without

moving chops until well browned, about 3 minutes. Using tongs, flip chops and cook until well browned on second side, 2 to 3 minutes longer.

4. Using tongs, transfer chops to preheated baking sheet in oven; cook until stuffing registers 140 degrees, 15 to 20 minutes, flipping chops halfway through cooking time. Transfer chops to platter, tent loosely with aluminum foil, and let rest for 10 minutes. Serve.

RED ONION JAM STUFFING WITH PORT, PECANS, AND DRIED FRUIT

MAKES ENOUGH FOR 1 RECIPE
STUFFED THICK-CUT PORK CHOPS

1	tablespoon olive oil
1	large red onion, halved and sliced ⅛ inch thick (about 4 cups)
1	tablespoon sugar
⅓	cups chopped dates
⅓	cup dried tart cherries
¾	cup ruby port
1	orange, cut into 4 wedges
3	tablespoons white wine vinegar
2	teaspoons minced fresh thyme
¼	teaspoon salt
	Pepper
⅓	cup pecans, toasted

1. Heat oil in medium saucepan over medium heat until shimmering; add onion and sugar and cook, stirring occasionally, until beginning to color, 20 to 25 minutes. Meanwhile, combine dates, cherries, and port in bowl; cover and microwave until simmering, about 1 minute. Set aside until needed. Squeeze juice from orange wedges into small bowl; reserve juiced wedges for sealing stuffing pockets in chops.

2. When onions are soft, add dried fruit mixture, ¼ cup orange juice, 2 tablespoons vinegar, thyme, salt, and pepper to taste; continue to cook, stirring occasionally, until mixture is jamlike, 10 to 12 minutes. Stir in remaining 1 tablespoon vinegar and pecans; transfer to bowl and cool until just warm, about 15 minutes.

SPINACH AND FONTINA STUFFING WITH PINE NUTS

MAKES ENOUGH FOR 1 RECIPE
STUFFED THICK-CUT PORK CHOPS

Either whole-milk or part-skim ricotta work in this recipe.

1	slice hearty white sandwich bread, torn into quarters
¼	cup pine nuts, toasted
1	tablespoon olive oil
2	garlic cloves, minced
6	ounces baby spinach (6 cups),
2	ounces Italian fontina cheese, shredded (½ cup)
¼	cup ricotta cheese
1	ounce Parmesan cheese, grated (½ cup)
1	lemon, cut into 4 wedges
¼	teaspoon salt
	Pinch ground nutmeg
	Pepper

1. Pulse bread and pine nuts in food processor until evenly ground, about 10 pulses.

2. Heat oil in 12-inch skillet over medium-high heat until shimmering; add garlic and cook, stirring constantly, until fragrant, about 30 seconds. Add spinach; using tongs, turn spinach to coat with oil. Cook, stirring with tongs, until spinach is wilted, about 2 minutes. Transfer spinach to colander set in sink and gently squeeze to release excess moisture; cool spinach until just warm.

3. Combine fontina, ricotta, and Parmesan in bowl. Add spinach and breadcrumb mixture; using spatula, mix well to break up clumps. Squeeze juice from lemon wedges into bowl; reserve juiced wedges for sealing stuffing pockets in chops. Stir 1 tablespoon lemon juice, salt, nutmeg, and pepper to taste into stuffing.

CUTTING A PORK CHOP POCKET

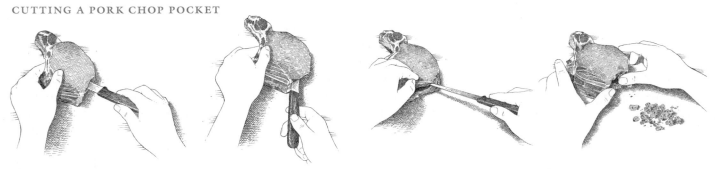

1. With knife positioned as shown, insert blade through center of side of chop until tip touches bone.

2. Holding chop firmly, carefully swing tip of blade through middle of chop to create pocket.

3. Remove knife from chop and, if necessary, enlarge pocket opening to measure 1 inch.

4. With your fingers, gently press stuffing mixture into pocket, without enlarging opening.

CRUNCHY BAKED PORK CHOPS

✔ WHY THIS RECIPE WORKS

When done right, baked breaded pork chops are the ultimate comfort food—tender cutlets surrounded by a crunchy coating that crackles apart with each bite. But use a packaged supermarket breading and you get a thin, sandy crust. Make your own breading and you have different problems: a soggy, patchy crust that won't stick to the meat. For breaded pork chops with a thick coating that wouldn't fall off in the oven, we made a quick, batterlike egg wash by whisking enough flour into an egg white and mustard mixture to give it the consistency of mayonnaise. Once the chops were coated in this powerful glue, they held on to our flavorful mixture of toasted bread crumbs, garlic, Parmesan, and herbs. Chops that were between ¾ and 1 inch thick gave us just the right ratio of meat to crust, and baking the chops in the oven (rather than frying) eliminated the need for excess oil.

CRUNCHY BAKED PORK CHOPS
SERVES 4

If the pork is enhanced (injected with a salt solution), do not brine in step 1, and season with salt in step 4.

Salt and pepper
4   (6- to 8-ounce) boneless pork chops, ¾ to 1 inch thick, trimmed
4   slices hearty white sandwich bread, torn into 1-inch pieces
2   tablespoons vegetable oil
1   small shallot, minced
3   garlic cloves, minced
2   tablespoons grated Parmesan cheese
2   tablespoons minced fresh parsley
½   teaspoon minced fresh thyme
¼   cup plus 6 tablespoons all-purpose flour
3   large egg whites
3   tablespoons Dijon mustard
Lemon wedges

1. Adjust oven rack to middle position and heat oven to 350 degrees. Dissolve 3 tablespoons salt in 1½ quarts cold water in large container. Submerge chops in brine, cover, and refrigerate for 30 minutes to 1 hour. Remove chops from brine and thoroughly pat dry with paper towels.

2. Meanwhile, pulse bread in food processor until coarsely ground, about 8 pulses (you should have about 3½ cups crumbs). Transfer crumbs to rimmed baking sheet and add oil, shallot, garlic, ¼ teaspoon salt, and ¼ teaspoon pepper. Toss until crumbs are evenly coated with oil. Bake until deep golden brown and dry, about 15 minutes, stirring twice during baking time. (Do not turn off oven.) Cool to room temperature. Add crumbs to Parmesan, parsley, and thyme. (Bread-crumb mixture can be prepared up to 3 days in advance.)

3. Place ¼ cup flour in pie plate. In second pie plate, whisk egg whites and mustard until combined; add remaining 6 tablespoons flour and whisk until almost smooth, with pea-size lumps remaining.

4. Increase oven temperature to 425 degrees. Spray wire rack with vegetable oil spray and set in rimmed baking sheet. Season chops with pepper. Dredge 1 pork chop in flour; shake off excess. Using tongs, coat with egg mixture; let excess drip off. Coat all sides of chop with bread-crumb mixture, pressing gently so that thick layer of crumbs adheres to chop. Transfer breaded chop to wire rack. Repeat with remaining 3 chops.

5. Bake until chops register 145 degrees, 17 to 25 minutes. Let rest on rack 5 minutes before serving with lemon wedges.

TO MAKE AHEAD: Breaded chops can be frozen for up to 1 week. Do not thaw before baking; simply increase cooking time in step 5 to 35 to 40 minutes.

CRUNCHY BAKED PORK CHOPS WITH PROSCIUTTO AND ASIAGO CHEESE

Omit salt added to bread-crumb mixture in step 2. Before breading, place ⅛-inch-thick slice Asiago cheese (about ½ ounce) on top of each chop. Wrap each chop with thin slice prosciutto, pressing on prosciutto so that cheese and meat adhere to one another. Proceed with recipe from step 4, being careful when handling chops so that cheese and meat do not come apart during breading.

TEST KITCHEN TIP NO. 85   WHY IS THAT PORK STILL PINK?

In the test kitchen, we steer clear of dishes like Parchingly Dry Pork Chops and No-Pink Pork Loin. But there's a reason that older recipes recommend cooking pork to startlingly high internal temperatures. Years ago, when pork quality was inconsistent and trichinosis concerns ran high, pink pork was considered a safety risk, thus most recipes recommended cooking pork to 190 degrees. Today, however, the risk of trichinosis is nearly nonexistent in the United States. What's more, even when the trichinosis parasite is present, it is killed when the temperature of the meat rises to 137 degrees.

Both the U.S. Department of Agriculture and the National Pork Board recommend cooking pork to a final internal temperature of 160 degrees. If you are concerned about contamination with salmonella (which is possible in any type of meat), you must cook the pork to 160 degrees to be certain that all potential pathogens are eliminated. Unfortunately, given the leanness of today's pork, these recommendations result in dry, tough meat. (In fact, today's pork has 50 percent less fat than it did 50 years ago, which explains why older recipes that called for cooking pork to 190 degrees weren't a total disaster—all that fat kept even overcooked pork moist.)

In the test kitchen, we have found cooking modern pork beyond 150 degrees to be a waste of time and money (unless it is a fatty cut such as pork shoulder or ribs). We cook most pork to an internal temperature of 145 degrees—the meat will still be slightly rosy in the center and juicy. As the meat rests, the internal temperature will continue to climb to the final serving temperature of 150. Of course, if safety is your top concern, cook all meat (including pork) until it is well-done.

SAUTÉED PORK CUTLETS

✔ WHY THIS RECIPE WORKS

Packaged pork cutlets seem like an easy short-cut to a quick dinner, but they are usually poorly butchered, resulting in dry, stringy meat once cooked. We wanted better sautéed pork cutlets, and knew the first step would be revisiting the butcher case. Instead of using supermarket pork cutlets, we opted for boneless country-style spare ribs—these meaty ribs are full of flavor and require little work to be fashioned into cutlets. We added sugar to our brine to help the cutlets retain moisture and to encourage browning, then sautéed the pork in a combination of olive oil and butter, which promoted browning even further. For the pan sauce, we reduced a flour-thickened mixture of cider, broth, and seasonings and swirled in whole grain mustard and butter for a rich, glossy sauce that perfectly coated our tender, browned cutlets.

SAUTÉED PORK CUTLETS WITH MUSTARD-CIDER SAUCE

SERVES 4

If the pork is enhanced (injected with a salt solution), do not brine in step 1, and season with salt in step 3. Look for ribs that are about 3 to 5 inches long. Cut ribs over 5 inches in half crosswise before slicing them lengthwise to make pounding more manageable.

PORK

1½	pounds boneless country-style pork spare ribs, trimmed
3	tablespoons salt
3	tablespoons sugar
	Pepper
1	tablespoon olive oil
½	tablespoon unsalted butter, cut into 2 pieces

MUSTARD-CIDER SAUCE

1	tablespoon unsalted butter
1	small shallot, minced
1	teaspoon all-purpose flour
1	teaspoon dry mustard

½	cup beef broth or low-sodium chicken broth
¼	cup apple cider
½	teaspoon minced fresh sage
2	teaspoons whole grain mustard
	Salt and pepper

1. FOR THE PORK: Cut each rib lengthwise to create 2 or 3 cutlets about ⅜ inch wide. Place cutlets between 2 layers of plastic wrap and gently pound to ¼-inch thickness. Dissolve salt and sugar in 1½ quarts cold water in large container. Submerge pork in brine, cover, and refrigerate for 30 minutes to 1 hour.

2. FOR THE SAUCE: While pork brines, melt ½ tablespoon butter in small saucepan over medium heat; add shallot and cook, stirring frequently, until softened, about 1½ minutes. Add flour and dry mustard; cook, stirring constantly, about 30 seconds. Slowly add broth, whisking constantly to avoid forming lumps. Add cider and sage and bring to boil. Reduce heat to low and simmer 5 minutes. Off heat, cover and set aside. Adjust oven rack to middle position and heat oven to 200 degrees.

3. TO COOK PORK: Remove pork from brine, thoroughly pat dry with paper towels, and season with pepper. Heat oil in 12-inch skillet over medium-high heat until just smoking. Add 1 piece butter, allow to melt, and quickly add half of pork cutlets. Cook cutlets until browned, about 1 to 2 minutes. Using tongs, flip cutlets and continue to cook until browned on second side, 1 to 2 minutes longer. Transfer cutlets to large plate and transfer plate to warm oven. Repeat with remaining cutlets and remaining butter.

4. After second batch of cutlets is cooked, reduce skillet heat to medium, add reserved sauce, and bring to simmer. Cook, scraping bottom of skillet with wooden spoon to loosen any browned bits, until slightly thickened and reduced to about ½ cup, about 2 minutes. Stir in any pork juices; return to simmer and cook

30 seconds. Off heat, whisk in whole grain mustard and remaining ½ tablespoon butter; season with salt and pepper to taste. Spoon sauce over pork and serve.

SAUTÉED PORK CUTLETS WITH LEMON-CAPER SAUCE

Substitute white wine for cider and 2 teaspoons lemon juice for sage in step 2. Substitute 1 teaspoon minced fresh parsley leaves, 1 teaspoon grated lemon zest, and 2 tablespoons rinsed capers for mustard in step 4.

PORK SCHNITZEL

✔ WHY THIS RECIPE WORKS

Pork schnitzel is often a soggy, greasy affair. But when done right, it features an irresistible combination of light, puffy bread-crumb coating and tender juicy meat. For remarkably tender texture and mild flavor, we used pounded medallions of pork tenderloin. It was no surprise that homemade bread crumbs were superior to store-bought crumbs—and a quick spin in the microwave produced dry crumbs that cooked up extra-crisp. And to achieve the wrinkled, puffy exterior that is schnitzel's signature, we found it essential to use an ample amount of oil and to shake the pan, gently and continuously, while the cutlets cooked.

CUTTING PORK TENDERLOIN FOR CUTLETS

Cut tenderloin in half at about 20-degree angle. Using same angle, cut each half in half again, cutting tapered tail pieces slightly thicker than middle medallions.

PORK SCHNITZEL
SERVES 4

The 2 cups of oil called for in this recipe may seem like a lot, but this amount is necessary to achieve a wrinkled texture on the finished cutlets. When properly cooked, the cutlets absorb very little oil. To ensure ample cooking space, a large Dutch oven is essential. In lieu of an instant-read thermometer to gauge the oil's temperature, place a fresh (not dry) bread cube in the oil and start heating; when the bread is deep golden brown, the oil is ready.

PORK

7   slices hearty white sandwich bread, crusts removed, bread cut into ¾-inch cubes

½   cup all-purpose flour

2   large eggs

1   tablespoon plus 2 cups vegetable oil

1   (1¼-pound) pork tenderloin, trimmed and cut on angle into 4 equal pieces
  Salt and pepper

GARNISHES
  Lemon wedges

2   tablespoons chopped fresh parsley

2   tablespoons capers, rinsed

1   large hard-cooked egg, yolk and white separated and passed separately through fine-mesh strainer (optional)

1. Place bread cubes on large plate. Microwave on high power for 4 minutes, stirring well halfway through cooking. Microwave on medium power until bread is dry and few pieces start to lightly brown, 3 to 5 minutes longer, stirring every minute. Process dry bread in food processor to very fine crumbs, about 45 seconds. Transfer bread crumbs to shallow dish (you should have about 1¼ cups crumbs). Spread flour in second shallow dish. Beat eggs with 1 tablespoon oil in third shallow dish.

2. Working with 1 piece at a time, place pork, with 1 cut side down, between 2 sheets of parchment paper or plastic wrap and pound to even thickness between ⅛ and ¼ inch. Pat cutlets dry with paper towels and season with salt and pepper. Working with 1 cutlet at a time, dredge cutlets thoroughly in flour, shaking off excess, then coat with egg mixture, allowing excess to drip back into dish to ensure very thin coating, and coat evenly with bread crumbs, pressing on crumbs to adhere. Place breaded cutlets in single layer on wire rack set over baking sheet; let coating dry for 5 minutes.

3. Heat remaining 2 cups oil in large Dutch oven over medium-high heat until it registers 375 degrees. Lay 2 cutlets, without overlapping, in pan and cook, shaking pan continuously and gently, until cutlets are wrinkled and light golden brown on both sides, 1 to 2 minutes per side. Transfer cutlets to paper towel–lined plate and flip cutlets several times to blot excess oil. Repeat with remaining cutlets. Serve with garnishes.

CRISP BREADED PORK CUTLETS

✔ **WHY THIS RECIPE WORKS**

Breaded pork cutlets can make a flavorful, satisfying meal—as long as they're not tough disks of meat shrouded in a greasy, pale crust. We wanted tender, well-seasoned pork cutlets with a crisp, golden, substantial breading. We made our cutlets from pork tenderloin and pounded them ½ inch thick, substantial enough to offer some chew and provide a cushion against overcooking. A coating of fresh bread crumbs was light, crisp, and flavorful. Finally, we found that using plenty of oil, allowing enough time for it to heat, and not crowding the pan were all essential steps for an ultra-crisp, golden brown coating.

CRISP BREADED PORK CUTLETS
SERVES 3

If you have two skillets, you can use both at once to cut the time it takes to fry. Our favorite accompaniments for breaded pork cutlets are applesauce, mashed potatoes, or coleslaw.

6   slices hearty white sandwich bread, crusts removed, bread torn into rough 1½-inch pieces

½   cup all-purpose flour

2   large eggs

1   tablespoon plus 1 cup vegetable oil

1   (1-pound) pork tenderloin, trimmed and cut on angle into 6 equal pieces
  Salt and pepper

1. Process bread in food processor until evenly fine-textured, 10 to 15 seconds (you should have about 3 cups fresh bread crumbs); transfer crumbs to pie plate or shallow baking dish.

2. Adjust oven rack to lower-middle position, set large ovensafe plate on rack, and heat oven to 200 degrees. Spread flour in second pie plate. Beat eggs with 1 tablespoon oil in third pie plate.

3. Working with 1 piece at a time, place pork, with 1 cut side down, between 2 sheets of parchment paper or plastic wrap and pound to even ½-inch thickness. Pat cutlets dry with paper towels and season with salt and pepper. Working with 1 cutlet at a time, dredge cutlets thoroughly in flour, shaking off excess. Using tongs, dip both sides of cutlets in egg mixture, allowing excess to drip back into pie plate to ensure very thin coating. Dip both sides of cutlets in bread crumbs, pressing crumbs with fingers to form even, cohesive coat. Place breaded cutlets in single layer on wire rack set over baking sheet and allow coating to dry about 5 minutes.

4. Meanwhile, heat ½ cup oil in 12-inch nonstick skillet over medium-high heat until shimmering, about 2½ minutes.

Lay 3 cutlets in skillet; fry until deep golden brown and crisp on first side, gently pressing down on cutlets with wide metal spatula to help ensure even browning and checking browning partway through, about 2½ minutes (smaller cutlets from tail end of tenderloin may cook faster). Using tongs, flip cutlets, reduce heat to medium, and continue to cook until meat feels firm when pressed gently and second side is deep golden brown and crisp, again checking browning partway through, about 2½ minutes longer. Line warmed plate with double layer of paper towels and set cutlets on top; return plate to oven.

5. Discard oil in skillet and wipe skillet clean. Repeat step 4 using remaining ½ cup oil and preheating oil just 2 minutes to cook remaining 3 cutlets.

JAPANESE-STYLE CRISP BREADED PORK CUTLETS

Substitute 6 (3- to 4-ounce) boneless pork chops, trimmed, for pork tenderloin and pound to between ½ and ¼ inch thick; substitute equal amount cornstarch for flour and panko for fresh bread crumbs. To serve, slice cutlets into ¾-inch wide strips and drizzle with Tonkatsu Sauce (recipe follows).

TONKATSU SAUCE
MAKES ¾ CUP

1	teaspoon water
½	teaspoon dry mustard
½	cup ketchup
2	tablespoons Worcestershire sauce
2	teaspoons soy sauce

Mix water and mustard in medium bowl until smooth. Add ketchup, Worcestershire, and soy sauce and mix thoroughly.

MAPLE-GLAZED PORK TENDERLOIN

✓ WHY THIS RECIPE WORKS
A glaze is the perfect way to enhance mild pork tenderloin—if you can get it to stick. We wanted lean yet tender meat coated with subtle spice and inviting sweetness. First, we settled on a stovetop-to-oven method that gave us a good crust and a moist, tender interior. For a balanced and substantial maple glaze that would adhere to the meat, we mixed the syrup with molasses and mustard, primed the tenderloin with cornstarch so the glaze would bond to it, and applied a second coat of the glaze when the meat was nearly done.

MAPLE-GLAZED PORK TENDERLOINS
SERVES 6

If the pork is enhanced (injected with a salt solution), do not add salt to the cornstarch mixture in step 1. If your tenderloins are smaller than 1¼ pounds, reduce the cooking time in step 3. If the tenderloins don't fit in the skillet initially, let their ends curve toward each other; the meat will eventually shrink as it cooks. Make sure to cook the tenderloins until they turn deep golden brown in step 2 or they will appear pale after glazing. We prefer grade B maple syrup in this recipe. (Don't be tempted to substitute imitation maple syrup—it will be too sweet.) Be sure to pat off the cornstarch mixture thoroughly in step 1, as any excess will leave gummy spots on the tenderloins.

¾	cup maple syrup
¼	cup light or mild molasses
2	tablespoons bourbon or brandy
⅛	teaspoon ground cinnamon
	Pinch ground cloves
	Pinch cayenne pepper
¼	cup cornstarch
2	tablespoons sugar

1	tablespoon salt
2	teaspoons pepper
2	(1¼- to 1½-pound) pork tenderloins, trimmed
2	tablespoons vegetable oil
1	tablespoon whole grain mustard

1. Adjust oven rack to middle position and heat oven to 375 degrees. Stir ½ cup maple syrup, molasses, bourbon, cinnamon, cloves, and cayenne together in 2-cup liquid measure; set aside. Whisk cornstarch, sugar, salt, and pepper in small bowl until combined. Transfer cornstarch mixture to rimmed baking sheet. Pat tenderloins dry with paper towels, then roll in cornstarch mixture until evenly coated on all sides. Thoroughly pat off excess cornstarch mixture.

2. Heat oil in 12-inch nonstick skillet over medium-high heat until just smoking. Reduce heat to medium and place both tenderloins in skillet, leaving at least 1 inch in between. Cook until well browned on all sides, 8 to 12 minutes. Transfer tenderloins to wire rack set in rimmed baking sheet.

3. Pour off excess fat from skillet and return to medium heat. Add syrup mixture to skillet, scraping bottom of skillet with wooden spoon to loosen any browned bits, and cook until reduced to ½ cup, about 2 minutes. Transfer 2 tablespoons glaze to small bowl and set aside. Using remaining glaze, brush each tenderloin with approximately 1 tablespoon glaze. Roast until thickest part of tenderloins registers 130 degrees, 12 to 20 minutes. Brush each tenderloin with 1 tablespoon glaze and continue to roast until thickest part of tenderloins registers 145 degrees, 2 to 4 minutes longer. Remove tenderloins from oven and brush each with remaining glaze; let rest, uncovered, 10 minutes.

4. While tenderloins rest, stir remaining ¼ cup maple syrup and mustard into reserved 2 tablespoons glaze. Brush each tenderloin with 1 tablespoon mustard glaze. Transfer meat to carving board and slice into ¼-inch-thick pieces. Serve, passing extra mustard glaze separately.

MAPLE-GLAZED PORK TENDERLOINS WITH SMOKED PAPRIKA AND GINGER

Substitute dry sherry for bourbon and ¼ teaspoon smoked paprika and 1 teaspoon grated fresh ginger for cinnamon, cloves, and cayenne pepper. Omit mustard in step 4.

MAPLE-GLAZED PORK TENDERLOINS WITH ORANGE AND CHIPOTLE

Substitute 2 tablespoons frozen orange juice concentrate for 2 tablespoons molasses. Omit cinnamon, cloves, and cayenne pepper and add 2 small finely minced canned chipotle chiles plus 2 teaspoons adobo sauce to maple syrup mixture in step 1. Omit mustard in step 4.

THICK-CUT PORK TENDERLOIN MEDALLIONS

✔ WHY THIS RECIPE WORKS

We wanted a simple, straightforward approach to cooking pork tenderloin without drying it out, and we also wanted a couple of boldly flavored sauces that could accompany our tenderloin for a quick weeknight meal. Cutting the tenderloins into 1½-inch-thick medallions and tying them allowed us to create a beautiful sear on all sides in the time it took for the pork to cook through. The searing process had the extra benefit of producing enough fond to create an easy, flavorful pan sauce while the pork rested.

THICK-CUT PORK TENDERLOIN MEDALLIONS

SERVES 4 TO 6

We prefer natural to enhanced pork (pork that has been injected with a salt solution to increase moistness and flavor) for this recipe, though either will work. Begin checking the doneness of smaller medallions 1 or 2 minutes early; they may need to be taken out of the pan a little sooner.

2   (1- to 1¼-pound) pork tenderloins, trimmed, cut crosswise into 1½-inch pieces, and tied; thinner end pieces tied together
    Salt and pepper
2   tablespoons vegetable oil
1   recipe pan sauce (recipes follow)

Pat pork dry with paper towels and season with salt and pepper. Heat oil in 12-inch skillet over medium-high heat until shimmering. Add pork cut side down and cook, without moving pieces, until well browned, 3 to 5 minutes. Flip pork and brown on second side, 3 to 5 minutes more. Reduce heat to medium. Using tongs, stand each piece on its side and cook, turning pieces as necessary, until sides are well browned and pork registers 145 degrees, 8 to 12 minutes. Transfer pork to serving platter and tent loosely with aluminum foil; let rest while making pan sauce, then serve.

BACON-WRAPPED THICK-CUT PORK TENDERLOIN MEDALLIONS

The number of bacon slices you use will depend on how many medallions you have cut.

Place 12 to 14 bacon slices, slightly overlapping, in pie plate and cover. Cook in microwave until slices shrink and release about ½ cup fat but are neither browned nor crisp, 1 to 3 minutes. Transfer bacon to paper towels until cool, 2 to 3 minutes. Wrap each piece of pork with 1 slice bacon and secure with 2 toothpicks where ends of bacon strip overlap, inserting toothpicks on angle and gently pushing them through to other side. Season pork with pepper (do not salt) and proceed with browning (time for searing sides may be slightly longer).

TURNING THE TENDERLOIN END PIECE INTO A MEDALLION

After cutting the tenderloins into symmetrical 1½-inch medallions, you will inevitably have a few irregularly shaped pieces left over. The tapered end pieces of the tenderloin can be scored, folded, and tied into medallions (as shown here).

1. Score tenderloin's tapered end piece.

2. Fold in half at incision.

3. Tie medallion with kitchen twine, making sure top and bottom surfaces are flat.

APPLE CIDER SAUCE

MAKES 1⅓ CUPS, ENOUGH FOR 1 RECIPE
THICK-CUT PORK TENDERLOIN MEDALLIONS

1½ cups apple cider
1   cup low-sodium chicken broth
2   teaspoons cider vinegar
1   cinnamon stick
4   tablespoons unsalted butter, cut into 4 pieces
2   large shallots, minced
1   Granny Smith apple, peeled, cored, and diced small
¼   cup Calvados or apple-flavored brandy
1   teaspoon minced fresh thyme
    Salt and pepper

1. Combine cider, broth, vinegar, and cinnamon stick in medium saucepan; simmer over medium-high heat until liquid is reduced to 1 cup, 10 to 12 minutes. Remove cinnamon stick and discard. Set sauce aside until pork is cooked.

2. Pour off any fat from skillet in which pork was cooked. Add 1 tablespoon butter and melt over medium heat. Add shallots and apple and cook, stirring occasionally, until softened and beginning to brown, 1 to 2 minutes. Remove skillet from heat and add Calvados. Return skillet to heat and cook about 1 minute, scraping bottom of skillet with wooden spoon to loosen any browned bits. Add reduced cider mixture, any accumulated pork juices, and thyme; increase heat to medium-high and simmer until thickened and reduced to 1¼ cups, 3 to 4 minutes. Off heat, whisk in remaining 3 tablespoons butter and season with salt and pepper to taste. Pour sauce over pork and serve.

MAPLE-MUSTARD SAUCE

MAKES 1 CUP, ENOUGH FOR 1 RECIPE
THICK-CUT PORK TENDERLOIN MEDALLIONS

2   teaspoons vegetable oil
1   onion, halved and sliced thin
1   cup low-sodium chicken broth
⅓   cup maple syrup
3   tablespoons balsamic vinegar
3   tablespoons whole grain mustard
    Salt and pepper

Pour off any fat from skillet in which pork was cooked. Add oil and heat skillet over medium heat until shimmering. Add onion and cook, stirring occasionally, until softened and beginning to brown, 3 to 4 minutes. Increase heat to medium-high and add broth; bring to simmer, scraping bottom of skillet with wooden spoon to loosen any browned bits. Simmer until liquid is reduced to ⅓ cup, 3 to 4 minutes. Add syrup, vinegar, mustard, and any accumulated pork juices and cook until thickened and reduced to 1 cup, 3 to 4 minutes longer. Season with salt and pepper to taste, pour sauce over pork, and serve.

HOISIN-SESAME SAUCE

MAKES ¾ CUP, ENOUGH FOR 1 RECIPE
THICK-CUT PORK TENDERLOIN MEDALLIONS

1   teaspoon vegetable oil
2   teaspoons grated fresh ginger
¼   cup hoisin sauce
½   cup fresh orange juice
½   cup low-sodium chicken broth
1   teaspoon toasted sesame oil
2   scallions, white and green parts sliced ⅛ inch thick on bias
    Salt and pepper

Pour off any fat from skillet in which pork was cooked. Add oil and heat skillet over medium heat until shimmering. Add ginger and cook, stirring constantly, until fragrant, about 15 seconds. Add hoisin sauce, orange juice, broth, and any accumulated pork juices and bring to simmer, scraping bottom of skillet with wooden spoon to loosen any browned bits. Simmer until liquid is reduced to 1 cup, 2 to 3 minutes. Stir in sesame oil and scallions. Season with salt and pepper to taste, pour sauce over pork, and serve.

TYING PORK MEDALLIONS

Thick medallions allow for more browning, but they can flop over in the pan. To prevent this, tie each piece with twine or a strip of parcooked bacon secured with two toothpicks.

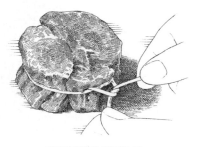

KITCHEN TWINE

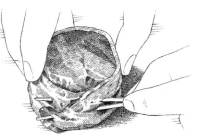

BACON "TWINE"

PAN-SEARED OVEN-ROASTED PORK TENDERLOINS

🗸 WHY THIS RECIPE WORKS

Pork tenderloin has a lot going for it—it's supremely tender with a buttery, fine-grained texture; it's easy to prepare; it cooks quickly; and its mild flavor is the perfect backdrop for a variety of sauces. But because it's so lean, it's usually served dry and overcooked. We wanted a recipe that would produce flavorful and juicy pork tenderloin every time. After attempting to cook the tenderloin in the oven at a wide range of temperatures, we discovered that the best approach was to start it on the stovetop (for a good sear) and then finish it in the oven (for gentle, even cooking). A pan sauce was a natural way to add flavor. While the meat was in the oven, we had plenty of time to deglaze the skillet and prepare the sauce.

PAN-SEARED OVEN-ROASTED PORK TENDERLOINS

SERVES 4

We prefer natural to enhanced pork (pork that has been injected with a salt solution to increase moistness and flavor) for this recipe. Because two are cooked at once, tenderloins larger than 1 pound apiece will not fit comfortably in a 12-inch skillet. If time allows, season the tenderloins up to 30 minutes before cooking; the seasonings will better penetrate the meat. The recipe will work in a nonstick or a traditional skillet. A pan sauce can be made while the tenderloins roast (recipes follow); if you intend to make a sauce, make sure to prepare all of the sauce ingredients before cooking the pork.

- 2 (12- to 16-ounce) pork tenderloins, trimmed
- 1¼ teaspoons kosher salt
- ¾ teaspoon pepper
- 2 teaspoons vegetable oil
- 1 recipe pan sauce or chutney (optional) (recipes follow)

1. Adjust oven rack to middle position; heat oven to 400 degrees. Sprinkle tenderloins evenly with salt and pepper; rub seasoning into meat. Heat oil in 12-inch ovensafe skillet over medium-high heat until just smoking. Place both tenderloins in skillet; cook until well browned, 3 minutes. Using tongs, rotate tenderloins ¼ turn; cook until well browned, 1 to 2 minutes. Repeat until all sides are browned. Transfer tenderloins to rimmed baking sheet and place in oven (reserve skillet if making pan sauce); roast until tenderloins register 145 degrees, 10 to 16 minutes. (Begin pan sauce, if making, while meat roasts.)

2. Transfer tenderloins to carving board and tent loosely with aluminum foil (continue with pan sauce, if making); let rest 10 minutes. Cut tenderloins crosswise into ½-inch-thick slices, arrange on serving platter or individual plates, and spoon sauce, if using, over; serve.

DRIED CHERRY–PORT SAUCE WITH ONION AND MARMALADE

MAKES 1½ CUPS, ENOUGH FOR
1 RECIPE PAN-SEARED OVEN-ROASTED
PORK TENDERLOINS

- 1 teaspoon vegetable oil
- 1 large onion, halved and sliced ½ inch thick
- ¾ cup port
- ¾ cup dried cherries
- 2 tablespoons orange marmalade
- 3 tablespoons unsalted butter, cut into 3 pieces
  Salt and pepper

1. Immediately after placing pork in oven, add oil to still-hot skillet, swirl to coat, and set skillet over medium-high heat; add onion and cook, stirring frequently, until softened and browned around edges, 5 to 7 minutes (if drippings are browning too quickly, add 2 tablespoons water and scrape up browned bits with wooden spoon). Set skillet aside off heat.

2. While pork is resting, set skillet over medium-high heat and add port and cherries; simmer, scraping bottom of pan with wooden spoon to loosen any browned bits, until mixture is slightly thickened, 4 to 6 minutes. Add any accumulated pork juices and continue to simmer until thickened, about 2 minutes longer. Off heat, whisk in orange marmalade and butter, 1 piece at a time. Season with salt and pepper to taste.

GARLICKY LIME SAUCE WITH CILANTRO

MAKES ½ CUP, ENOUGH FOR 1 RECIPE PAN-SEARED OVEN-ROASTED PORK TENDERLOINS

A rasp-style grater is the best way to break down the garlic to a fine paste. Another option is to put the garlic through a press and then finish mincing it to a paste with a knife. If your garlic cloves contain green sprouts or shoots, remove the sprouts before grating—their flavor is bitter and hot. The initial cooking of the garlic off heat will prevent scorching.

- 10 garlic cloves, peeled and grated to fine paste on rasp-style grater (2 tablespoons)
- 2 tablespoons water
- 1 tablespoon vegetable oil
- ¼ teaspoon red pepper flakes
- 2 teaspoons packed light brown sugar
- 3 tablespoons lime juice (2 limes)
- ¼ cup chopped fresh cilantro
- 1 tablespoon chopped fresh chives
- 4 tablespoons unsalted butter, cut into 4 pieces
  Salt and pepper

1. Immediately after placing pork in oven, mix garlic paste with water in small bowl. Add oil to still-hot skillet and swirl to coat; add garlic paste and cook with

skillet's residual heat, scraping bottom of skillet with wooden spoon to loosen any browned bits, until sizzling subsides, about 2 minutes. Set skillet over low heat and continue cooking, stirring frequently, until garlic is sticky, 8 to 10 minutes; set skillet aside off heat.

2. While pork is resting, set skillet over medium heat; add pepper flakes and sugar to skillet and cook until sticky and sugar is dissolved, about 1 minute. Add lime juice, cilantro, and chives; simmer to blend flavors, 1 to 2 minutes. Add any accumulated pork juices and simmer 1 minute longer. Off heat, whisk in butter, 1 piece at a time. Season with salt and pepper to taste.

SHALLOT-BALSAMIC SAUCE WITH ROSEMARY AND MUSTARD

MAKES ½ CUP, ENOUGH FOR 1 RECIPE PAN-SEARED OVEN-ROASTED PORK TENDERLOINS

4	tablespoons unsalted butter, cut into 4 pieces
2	shallots, sliced thin
2	tablespoons water
1	teaspoon packed light brown sugar
¾	cup balsamic vinegar
2	teaspoons chopped fresh rosemary
1	tablespoon Dijon mustard
	Salt and pepper

1. Immediately after placing pork in oven, add 1 tablespoon butter to still-hot skillet; when melted, stir in shallots, water, and sugar. Cook over medium-low heat, stirring frequently, until shallots are browned and caramelized, 7 to 10 minutes; set skillet aside off heat.

2. While pork is resting, set skillet over medium-low heat and add vinegar; simmer, scraping bottom of skillet with wooden spoon to loosen any browned bits, until mixture is slightly thickened, 5 to 7 minutes. Add rosemary and any accumulated pork juices; continue to simmer until

syrupy and reduced to about ⅓ cup, about 2 minutes longer. Off heat, whisk in mustard and remaining 3 tablespoons butter, 1 piece at a time. Season with salt and pepper to taste.

BANANA-DATE CHUTNEY

MAKES 1 ½ CUPS, ENOUGH FOR 1 RECIPE PAN-SEARED OVEN-ROASTED PORK TENDERLOINS

10	dates, chopped into ½-inch pieces
¼	cup malt vinegar or apple cider vinegar
1	tablespoon unsalted butter
1	small onion, chopped fine
2	tablespoons water
1	tablespoon grated fresh ginger
1	garlic clove, minced
1	teaspoon curry powder
1	large ripe banana (10 ounces), peeled and cut crosswise into ½-inch pieces
½	small jalapeño chile, stemmed, seeded, and minced
1	tablespoon packed light brown sugar
	Salt and pepper
3	tablespoons chopped fresh mint

1. Immediately after placing pork in oven, combine dates and vinegar in bowl and set aside. Add butter to still-hot skillet and set skillet over medium heat; when melted, stir in onion and water and cook, stirring occasionally, until softened and lightly browned, about 4 minutes. Stir in ginger, garlic, and curry powder and cook until fragrant, about 1 minute; set aside off heat.

2. While pork is resting, set skillet over medium heat; add date mixture, banana, jalapeño, and sugar to skillet and cook, stirring occasionally, until dates are tender and banana begins to break down, 5 to 8 minutes. Season with salt and pepper to taste and stir in mint.

MAPLE-GLAZED PORK ROAST

✔ WHY THIS RECIPE WORKS

Sweet maple syrup, with its delicate flavor notes of smoke, caramel, and vanilla, makes an ideal foil for pork, and maple-glazed pork roast is a New England classic. But this dish often fall short of its savory-sweet promise; dry pork is a problem, yes, but the real issue is the glaze, which is usually either too thin or overly sweet. We found that searing the roast (tasters preferred a blade-end loin roast) first on the stovetop ensured a crisp, caramelized crust before reducing the maple syrup in the skillet used to sear the pork. Roasting the pork in that same skillet was the best way to get a beautifully glazed roast. The smaller surface area of the skillet prevented the glaze from spreading out and burning, and allowed the roast to sit right in the glaze for the entire roasting time.

MAPLE-GLAZED PORK ROAST

SERVES 4 TO 6

Note that you should not trim the pork of its thin layer of fat. The flavor of grade B maple syrup (sometimes called "cooking maple") is stronger and richer than grade A, but grade A syrup will work well, too. This dish is unapologetically sweet, so we recommend side dishes that take well to the sweetness. Garlicky sautéed greens, braised cabbage, and soft polenta are good choices.

½	cup maple syrup
⅛	teaspoon ground cinnamon
	Pinch ground cloves
	Pinch cayenne pepper
1	(2½-pound) boneless blade-end pork loin roast, tied at even intervals along length with 5 pieces kitchen twine
¾	teaspoon salt
½	teaspoon pepper
2	teaspoons vegetable oil

1. Adjust oven rack to middle position and heat oven to 325 degrees. Stir maple syrup, cinnamon, cloves, and cayenne together in measuring cup or bowl; set aside. Pat roast dry with paper towels, then season with salt and pepper.

2. Heat oil in 10-inch ovensafe nonstick skillet over medium-high heat until just smoking, about 3 minutes. Place roast fat side down in skillet and cook until well browned, about 3 minutes. Using tongs, rotate roast one-quarter turn and cook until well browned, about 2½ minutes; repeat until roast is well browned on all sides. Transfer roast to large plate. Reduce heat to medium and pour off fat from skillet; add maple syrup mixture and cook until fragrant, about 30 seconds (syrup will bubble immediately). Off heat, return roast to skillet; using tongs, roll to coat roast with glaze on all sides. Place skillet in oven and roast until meat registers 140 degrees, 35 to 45 minutes, using tongs to roll and spin roast to coat with glaze twice during roasting time (skillet handle will be hot). Transfer roast to carving board; set skillet aside to cool slightly to thicken glaze, about 5 minutes. Pour glaze over roast and let rest 15 minutes longer. Snip twine off roast, cut into ¼-inch-thick slices, and serve.

MAPLE-GLAZED PORK ROAST WITH ROSEMARY

Substitute 2 teaspoons minced fresh rosemary for cinnamon, cloves, and cayenne.

MAPLE-GLAZED PORK ROAST WITH ORANGE ESSENCE

Add 1 tablespoon grated orange zest to maple syrup along with spices.

MAPLE-GLAZED PORK ROAST WITH STAR ANISE

Add 4 star anise pods to maple syrup along with spices.

MAPLE-GLAZED PORK ROAST WITH SMOKED PAPRIKA

Add 2 teaspoons smoked hot paprika to maple syrup along with spices.

ROAST STUFFED PORK LOIN

✓ WHY THIS RECIPE WORKS

Roast stuffed pork loin could be an impressive centerpiece to a holiday meal, if only it didn't suffer time and again from the same problems: meat that is tough and dry by the time the stuffing is done; stuffing with a dull flavor and poor texture; and a sloppy appearance, with stuffing oozing out the ends of the roast. To ensure that our pork loin would have moist meat and a flavorful stuffing in one cohesive package, we first brined the boneless pork roast for improved flavor and texture and then butterflied and pounded it to an even thickness, increasing the meat's surface area to maximize the amount of stuffing we could use. For the stuffing, we used fresh bread as a base and flavored it with dried fruit, nuts, and herbs, adding eggs as a binder. Prebaking the stuffing before stuffing the roast raised the stuffing's temperature so that we didn't have to roast the pork until it was dry and overcooked.

ROAST PORK LOIN WITH APRICOT, FIG, AND PISTACHIO STUFFING

SERVES 8 TO 10

If the pork is enhanced (injected with a salt solution), do not brine in step 2. Timing is important; coordinate brining and stuffing so that the pork is out of the brine and ready to be stuffed when the precooked stuffing comes out of the oven. To achieve this, begin preparing the stuffing ingredients immediately after setting the pork in the brine. Bamboo skewers, available in supermarkets, are our favorite way to fasten the roast around the stuffing. Alternatively, use poultry lacers.

PORK AND BRINE

- 1   (4½-pound) boneless blade-end pork loin roast, trimmed
- ¾   cup sugar
- 6   tablespoons salt
- 10   garlic cloves, lightly crushed and peeled
- 3   bay leaves, crumbled
- 1   tablespoon allspice berries, lightly crushed
- 1   tablespoon whole black peppercorns, lightly crushed

STUFFING AND GLAZE

- 7–8 ounces baguette (not sourdough), torn into rough 1-inch pieces (5 cups)
- ½   cup dried apricots
- 1   garlic clove, peeled
-      Pinch ground cumin
-      Pinch ground coriander
-      Pinch ground cinnamon
-      Pinch cayenne pepper
- 2   tablespoons grated onion
- ½   cup dried figs, halved lengthwise
- ½   cup shelled pistachios, toasted and chopped coarse
- 2   tablespoons minced fresh parsley
- 2   teaspoons minced fresh thyme
- 1   teaspoon salt
-      Pepper
- 2   large eggs
- ½   cup heavy cream
- ½   cup apricot preserves

1. FOR THE PORK AND BRINE: Using sharp knife, slice pork open down middle, from end to end, cutting about two-thirds of way through meat. Open pork loin like

book. Carefully slice along initial cut just until pork lays flat, being careful not to cut all the way through. Pound pork loin to even 1-inch thickness.

2. Dissolve sugar and salt in 2 quarts cold water in large container. Add garlic, bay leaves, allspice, and peppercorns; stir to combine. Submerge pork in brine, cover, and refrigerate for 1½ to 2 hours. Remove pork from brine, pick spices off meat, and thoroughly pat pork dry with paper towels.

3. FOR THE STUFFING AND GLAZE: Once pork is in brine, adjust oven rack to lower-middle position and heat oven to 325 degrees. Process half of bread pieces in food processor to crumbs with few pieces no larger than about ¼ inch, about 45 seconds; transfer to large bowl and set aside. Repeat process with remaining bread pieces (you should have about 4 cups crumbs total).

4. In now-empty food processor, process apricots, garlic, cumin, coriander, cinnamon, and cayenne until finely ground, about 30 seconds; add mixture to reserved bread crumbs. Add onion, figs, pistachios, parsley, thyme, salt, and pepper to taste to bread-crumb and apricot mixture; toss

until well distributed, breaking up any apricot clumps as necessary. Beat eggs and cream in bowl; pour over bread-crumb and apricot mixture and toss with hands until evenly moistened and portion of mixture holds together when pressed.

5. On parchment paper–lined baking sheet or inverted rimmed baking sheet, form stuffing into log shape equal in length to butterflied pork. Cover stuffing with aluminum foil and bake until firm and cooked through and butterflied pork has been removed from brine and prepared for stuffing, about 45 minutes. Remove stuffing from oven; increase oven temperature to 450 degrees.

6. While stuffing bakes, heat apricot preserves in small saucepan over medium-low heat, stirring occasionally, until melted but not liquefied, 5 to 7 minutes. Strain through small strainer into bowl (you should have about ⅓ cup) and set aside; discard solids in strainer.

7. TO STUFF AND GLAZE THE ROAST: Set wire rack in rimmed baking sheet (or shallow roasting pan) lined with foil and set aside. Spoon stuffing onto center of pork. Bring sides of roast together to encase stuffing and tie with twine at 1-inch

intervals. Place stuffed roast on rack, brush half of apricot glaze evenly over exposed surface of meat, and roast for 20 minutes. Remove roast from oven and, with tongs, rotate roast so that bottom side faces up. Brush exposed surface with remaining apricot glaze; return roast to oven and roast 25 minutes longer (glaze should be medium golden brown and internal temperature of both meat and stuffing should register 140 degrees). Transfer roast to carving board, tent loosely with foil, and let rest for 5 minutes. Cut off twine, slice, and serve.

ROAST PORK LOIN WITH APRICOT, CHERRY, AND PECAN STUFFING

Substitute ½ cup dried tart cherries for figs and ½ cup coarsely chopped toasted pecans for pistachios in stuffing mixture.

ROAST PORK LOIN WITH APRICOT, PRUNE, AND PINE NUT STUFFING

Substitute ½ cup pitted prunes, halved lengthwise, for figs and ½ cup coarsely chopped toasted pine nuts for pistachios in stuffing mixture.

STUFFING A BONELESS PORK LOIN

1. Slice pork open down middle, from end to end, cutting about two-thirds of way through meat. Open pork loin like book.

2. Carefully slice along initial cut, being careful not to cut all the way through, and press pork flat.

3. Pound roast to even 1-inch thickness. Then, mound filling evenly down center of roast.

4. Wrap sides of pork around filling, then tie roast closed with kitchen twine at 1-inch intervals. Don't tie roast too tight or you may squeeze out filling.

TUSCAN-STYLE GARLIC-ROSEMARY ROAST PORK LOIN

✓ **WHY THIS RECIPE WORKS**

It's easy to fall in love with Tuscan-style pork roast. Flavored with garlic and rosemary and served in thick slices, its juicy meat and crisp crust are part of its allure—that is, when it's not dry, tough, or bitter. To start, we chose a bone-in, center-cut pork rib roast. Its protective cap of fat and muscle made it the tastiest of all the cuts we sampled, and its rack of bones helped to protect the meat during roasting. Brining the meat in a mixture of water, salt, brown sugar, garlic, and rosemary ensured juiciness and imparted flavor. To add even more flavor, we butterflied the pork loin, then rubbed the meat with a garlic, rosemary, and olive oil paste.

TUSCAN-STYLE GARLIC-ROSEMARY ROAST PORK LOIN

SERVES 6 TO 8

If the pork is enhanced (injected with a salt solution), do not brine in step 1, and season with salt in step 4. The roasting time is determined in part by the shape of the roast; a long, thin roast will cook faster than a roast with a large circumference. Though not traditionally served, the ribs are rich with flavor. If you'd like to serve them, increase the oven temperature to 375 degrees, untie the roast and remove the loin as directed, then scrape off the excess garlic-rosemary paste from the ribs, set them on a rimmed baking sheet, and return them to the oven for about 20 minutes, until they are brown and crisp. Slice in between bones and serve.

PORK AND BRINE

- 1   (4-pound) bone-in center-cut pork rib roast, trimmed
- 2⅓ cups packed dark brown sugar
- 1   cup salt
- 10 large garlic cloves, lightly crushed and peeled
- 5   sprigs fresh rosemary
- 1   tablespoon olive oil
- 1   cup dry white wine
- 1   teaspoon pepper

GARLIC-ROSEMARY PASTE

- 8   garlic cloves, minced
- 1½ tablespoons minced fresh rosemary
- 1   tablespoon extra-virgin olive oil
- 1   teaspoon pepper
  Pinch salt

JUS

- 1   shallot, minced
- 1½ teaspoons minced fresh rosemary
- 1¾ cups low-sodium chicken broth
- 2   tablespoons unsalted butter, cut into 4 pieces and softened

1. FOR THE PORK AND BRINE: Using boning knife, carefully cut meat away from rack of bones. Dissolve sugar and salt in 2 quarts cold water in large container. Stir in garlic and rosemary. Submerge pork and bones in brine, cover, and refrigerate for 1½ to 2 hours.

2. FOR THE GARLIC-ROSEMARY PASTE: While pork brines, mix garlic, rosemary, olive oil, pepper, and salt together in bowl to form paste; set aside.

3. Remove meat and ribs from brine and thoroughly pat dry with paper towels. Adjust oven rack to middle position and heat oven to 325 degrees. Heat oil in 12-inch skillet over medium heat until just smoking, about 4 minutes. Place roast fat side down in skillet and cook until well browned, about 8 minutes. Transfer roast browned side up to carving board and set aside to cool. Pour off fat from skillet and add wine; increase heat to high and bring to boil, scraping bottom of skillet with wooden spoon to loosen any browned bits. Set skillet off heat.

4. Make lengthwise incision in pork loin and spread meat flat. Rub with one-third of garlic-rosemary paste, rub remaining paste on cut side of ribs, and tie meat back to ribs. Season browned side of roast with pepper and set roast rib side down in flameproof roasting pan. Pour reserved wine and browned bits from skillet into roasting pan. Roast, basting loin with pan drippings every 20 minutes, until meat registers 140 degrees, 65 to 80 minutes. (If wine evaporates, add about ½ cup water to roasting pan to prevent scorching.) Transfer roast to clean carving board and tent loosely with aluminum foil; let rest about 15 minutes.

5. FOR THE JUS: While roast rests, spoon off most of fat from roasting pan and place over 2 burners at high heat. Add shallot and rosemary; scrape bottom of pan with wooden spoon to loosen any browned bits and boil until liquid is reduced by half and shallot has softened, about 2 minutes.

BONING A PORK LOIN

1. Position roast so bones are perpendicular to cutting board. Starting from far end and working toward you, make series of small, easy strokes with boning knife between meat and bones.

2. Gradually cut along curved rib bones down to backbone until meat is free from bones.

1. With fat side of roast down, slice through center of entire length of meat, stopping 1 inch shy of edge. Spread meat flat.

2. Rub one-third of garlic-rosemary paste mixture in even layer on one side of cut, leaving ½ inch on each end bare.

3. Spread remaining garlic-rosemary paste mixture evenly along bones from where meat was cut, leaving ½ inch on each end bare.

4. Fold meat back together and tie meat on bones exactly from where it was cut with 7 individual lengths of kitchen twine.

Add broth and continue to cook, stirring occasionally, until reduced by half, about 8 minutes. Add any accumulated pork juices and cook 1 minute longer. Off heat, whisk in butter; strain jus into serving bowl.

6. Snip twine off roast and remove meat from bones. Set meat browned side up on carving board and cut into ¼-inch-thick slices. Serve, passing jus separately.

GARLIC-ROSEMARY ROAST PORK LOIN WITH ROASTED POTATOES

Reduce wine to ¾ cup and omit shallot, rosemary, chicken broth, and butter. When pork has roasted 15 minutes, quarter 2 pounds red potatoes; toss with 2 tablespoons olive oil in bowl and season with salt and pepper to taste. After pork has roasted 30 minutes, add potatoes to roasting pan; stir to coat potatoes with pan juices. After transferring roast to carving board, turn potato pieces with wide metal spatula and spread them in even layer. Increase oven temperature to 400 degrees and return potatoes to oven; continue to roast until tender and browned, 5 to 15 minutes longer. Serve potatoes with roast.

GARLIC-ROSEMARY ROAST PORK LOIN WITH FENNEL

Trim 2 fennel bulbs of stalks and fronds; finely chop 2 teaspoons fronds. Halve, core, and cut each bulb lengthwise into eighths. Toss fennel with 1 tablespoon olive oil in medium bowl and season with salt and pepper to taste. Add 1 teaspoon finely chopped fennel seeds and chopped fennel fronds to garlic-rosemary paste. Reduce wine to ¾ cup and omit shallot, rosemary, chicken broth, and butter. Add fennel to roasting pan along with wine. After transferring roast to carving board, return fennel to oven; continue to roast until tender, 5 to 15 minutes. Serve fennel with roast.

HERB-CRUSTED PORK ROAST

✔ WHY THIS RECIPE WORKS

A fresh herb crust is a great way to enliven a boneless pork roast; we just needed a way to keep the crust from falling off. Starting with the roast itself, we knew that both brining it and browning it would be crucial for the best flavor. For maximum herb flavor, we cut a single horizontal pocket across the middle of the roast that could hold a good quantity of herb paste. With the pork's internal herb flavor guaranteed, we went to work on the crust, using the same herb paste we had used to fill the pocket (along with bread crumbs, Parmesan, and some minced shallot); to keep it attached to the outside of the roast, we found we needed to score a crosshatch pattern into the fat cap, giving our herb crust something to grip.

HERB-CRUSTED PORK ROAST
SERVES 4 TO 6

If the pork is enhanced (injected with a salt solution), do not brine in step 1, and season with salt in step 4. Note that you should not trim the pork of its layer of fat. Do not substitute dried thyme for fresh or the herb crust will be dry and dusty tasting. The roasting time will vary widely depending on the thickness of the meat.

1	(2½- to 3-pound) boneless center-cut pork loin roast
	Salt and pepper
¼	cup sugar
1	slice hearty white sandwich bread, torn into pieces
1	ounce Parmesan or Pecorino Romano cheese, grated (½ cup)
1	shallot, minced
¼	cup plus 2 teaspoons olive oil

⅓ cup packed fresh parsley or basil

2 tablespoons minced fresh thyme

1 teaspoon minced fresh rosemary or ½ teaspoon dried

1 large garlic clove, minced

1. Lightly score fat cap on pork, making ¼-inch crosshatch pattern. Create pocket by inserting knife ½ inch from end of roast and cutting along side of pork stopping ½ inch shorter of other end. Pull open roast and use gentle strokes to cut deeper pocket. Dissolve ¼ cup salt and sugar in 2 quarts cold water in large container. Submerge pork in brine, cover, and refrigerate for 1½ to 2 hours. Remove roast from brine and thoroughly pat dry with paper towels.

2. Meanwhile, adjust oven rack to lower-middle position and heat oven to 325 degrees. Pulse bread in food processor until coarsely ground, about 16 pulses (you should have 1 cup crumbs). Transfer crumbs to medium bowl (do not wash food processor bowl) and add 2 tablespoons Parmesan, shallot, 1 tablespoon oil, ⅛ teaspoon salt, and ⅛ teaspoon pepper. Using fork, toss mixture until crumbs are evenly coated with oil.

3. Add parsley, thyme, rosemary, garlic, remaining 6 tablespoons Parmesan, 3 tablespoons oil, ⅛ teaspoon salt, and ⅛ teaspoon pepper to now-empty food processor and process until smooth, about 12 pulses. Transfer herb paste to bowl.

4. Spread ¼ cup herb paste inside roast and tie. Season roast with pepper.

5. Heat remaining 2 teaspoons oil in 12-inch skillet over medium-high heat until just smoking. Add roast, fat side down, and brown on all sides, 8 to 10 minutes, lowering heat if fat begins to smoke. Transfer roast to wire rack set in aluminum foil–lined rimmed baking sheet.

6. Snip and remove twine from roast; discard twine. Spread remaining herb paste over roast and top with bread-crumb mixture. Transfer baking sheet with roast to oven and cook until thickest part of roast registers 145 degrees, 50 to 75 minutes. Remove roast from oven and let rest for 10 minutes. Using spatula and meat fork, transfer roast to carving board, taking care not to squeeze juices out of pocket in roast. Cut roast into ½-inch-thick slices and serve.

TO MAKE AHEAD: Roast can be brined, stuffed, and tied 1 day ahead, but don't prepare bread-crumb topping until you are ready to cook.

HERB-CRUSTED PORK ROAST WITH MUSTARD AND CARAWAY

Substitute 1 tablespoon minced garlic for shallot in bread-crumb mixture, replace rosemary with 4 teaspoons whole grain mustard and 1 tablespoon toasted caraway seeds, and reduce oil in step 3 to 2 tablespoons.

SLOW-ROASTED PORK SHOULDER

✓ WHY THIS RECIPE WORKS

When we think of a pork roast, the first thing that comes to mind these days is pork loin. It may be lean, but it typically needs a serious flavor boost. We wanted to explore the glories of old-fashioned, more flavorful (read: less lean) pork. One such cut is the shoulder roast. It may take longer to cook, but it's also inexpensive, loaded with flavorful intramuscular fat, and boasts a thick fat cap that renders to a bronze, bacon-like crust. We started by rubbing the roast's exterior with brown sugar and salt, then left it to rest overnight. The sugar dried out the exterior and boosted browning. Elevating the pork shoulder on a V-rack and pouring water in the roasting

---

PREPARING HERB-CRUSTED PORK ROAST

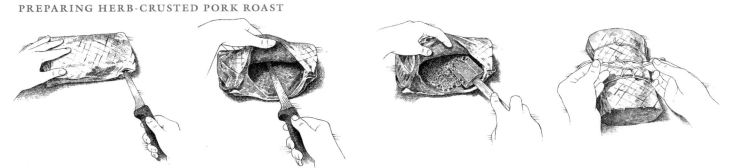

1. Starting ½ inch from end of roast, insert knife into middle of roast, with blade parallel to counter.

2. Cut along side of pork, stopping ½ inch short of other end. Pull open roast and use gentle strokes to cut deeper pocket.

3. Spread ¼ cup herb paste evenly into pocket, using spatula and fingers to make sure paste reaches corners of pocket.

4. Return roast to original shape and tie at even intervals along its length with 3 pieces of kitchen twine.

pan kept the pork's drippings from burning as it roasted. It also created a significant jus with no burning. Finally, a fruity sauce with sweet and sour elements cut the pork shoulder's richness.

SLOW-ROASTED PORK SHOULDER WITH PEACH SAUCE

SERVES 8 TO 12

Add more water to the roasting pan as necessary during the last hours of cooking to prevent the fond from burning. Serve the pork with the accompanying peach sauce or with cherry sauce or a sweet-tart chutney (recipes follow).

PORK ROAST

1	(6- to 8-pound) bone-in pork butt roast
⅓	cup kosher salt
⅓	cup packed light brown sugar
	Pepper

PEACH SAUCE

10	ounces frozen peaches, cut into 1-inch chunks, or 2 fresh peaches, peeled, pitted, and cut into ½-inch wedges
2	cups dry white wine
½	cup granulated sugar
¼	cup plus 1 tablespoon unseasoned rice vinegar
2	sprigs fresh thyme
1	tablespoon whole grain mustard

1. FOR THE PORK ROAST: Using sharp knife, cut slits 1 inch apart in crosshatch pattern in fat cap of roast, being careful not to cut into meat. Combine salt and brown sugar in bowl. Rub salt mixture over entire pork shoulder and into slits. Wrap roast tightly in double layer of plastic wrap, place on rimmed baking sheet, and refrigerate for 12 to 24 hours.

2. Adjust oven rack to lowest position and heat oven to 325 degrees. Unwrap roast and brush any excess salt mixture from surface. Season roast with pepper.

Set V-rack in large roasting pan, spray with vegetable oil spray, and place roast on rack. Add 1 quart water to roasting pan.

3. Cook roast, basting twice during cooking, until meat is extremely tender and roast near (but not touching) bone registers 190 degrees, 5 to 6 hours. Transfer roast to carving board and let rest, tented loosely with aluminum foil, for 1 hour. Transfer liquid in roasting pan to fat separator and let stand for 5 minutes. Pour off ¼ cup jus and set aside; discard fat and reserve remaining jus for another use.

4. FOR THE SAUCE: Bring peaches, wine, sugar, ¼ cup vinegar, ¼ cup defatted jus, and thyme sprigs to simmer in small saucepan; cook, stirring occasionally, until reduced to 2 cups, about 30 minutes. Stir in remaining 1 tablespoon vinegar and mustard. Remove thyme sprigs, cover, and keep warm.

5. Using sharp paring knife, cut around inverted T-shaped bone until it can be pulled free from roast (use clean kitchen towel to grasp bone). Using serrated knife, slice roast. Serve, passing sauce separately.

SLOW-ROASTED PORK SHOULDER WITH CHERRY SAUCE

Substitute 10 ounces fresh or frozen pitted cherries for peaches, red wine for white wine, and red wine vinegar for rice vinegar, and add ¼ cup ruby port along with defatted jus. Increase granulated sugar to ¾ cup, omit thyme sprigs and mustard, and reduce mixture to 1½ cups.

FENNEL-APPLE CHUTNEY

MAKES ABOUT 2 CUPS, ENOUGH FOR 1 RECIPE SLOW-ROASTED PORK SHOULDER

1	tablespoon olive oil
1	large fennel bulb, stalks discarded, halved, cored, and cut into ¼-inch pieces
1	onion, chopped fine
2	Granny Smith apples peeled, cored, and cut in ½-inch pieces
1	cup rice vinegar
¾	cup sugar
2	teaspoons grated lemon zest
1	teaspoon salt
½	teaspoon red pepper flakes

Heat oil in medium saucepan over medium heat until shimmering. Add fennel and onion and cook until softened, about 10 minutes. Add apples, vinegar, sugar, zest, salt, and pepper flakes. Bring to simmer and cook until thickened, about 20 minutes. Cool to room temperature, about 2 hours or refrigerate overnight. Serve with pork.

RED BELL PEPPER CHUTNEY

MAKES ABOUT 2 CUPS, ENOUGH FOR 1 RECIPE SLOW-ROASTED PORK SHOULDER

1	tablespoon olive oil
1	red onion, chopped fine
4	red bell peppers, stemmed, seeded, and cut into ½-inch pieces
1	cup white wine vinegar
½	cup plus 2 tablespoons sugar
2	garlic cloves, peeled and smashed
1	(1-inch) piece ginger, peeled, sliced into thin coins, and smashed
1	teaspoon yellow mustard seeds
1	teaspoon salt
½	teaspoon red pepper flakes

Heat oil in medium saucepan over medium heat until shimmering. Add onion and cook until softened, about 7 minutes. Add peppers, vinegar, sugar, garlic, ginger, mustard seeds, salt, and pepper flakes. Bring to simmer and cook until thickened, about 40 minutes. Cool to room temperature, about 2 hours or refrigerate overnight. Serve with pork.

GREEN TOMATO CHUTNEY

MAKES ABOUT 2 CUPS, ENOUGH FOR 1 RECIPE SLOW-ROASTED PORK SHOULDER

2 pounds green tomatoes, cored and cut into 1-inch pieces
¾ cup sugar
¾ cup distilled white vinegar
1 teaspoon coriander seeds
1 teaspoon salt
½ teaspoon red pepper flakes
2 teaspoons lemon juice

Bring tomatoes, sugar, vinegar, coriander seeds, salt, and pepper flakes to simmer in medium saucepan. Cook until thickened, about 40 minutes. Cool to room temperature, about 2 hours or refrigerate overnight. Stir in lemon juice just before serving with pork.

INDOOR PULLED PORK

✔ WHY THIS RECIPE WORKS

When we have a hankering for pulled pork, we typically head outside to the grill to create smoky-tasting barbecue. But here in New England, the long winter months are no time to be outdoors tending a grill. We wanted to bring pulled pork indoors—without sacrificing tender, shreddable meat, deep smoke flavor, and a dark, richly seasoned crust. We found that cooking pulled pork indoors requires a dual cooking method to keep the meat moist inside while developing a flavorful outer crust. Cooking the meat covered for part of the time kept it moist, while uncovering it for the remainder of the time allowed a substantial crust to form. For smoky barbecue flavor, we found that liquid smoke, which we used both in the brine and rubbed on the meat, did the trick. And of course pulled pork wouldn't be complete without a sauce—we developed three authentically regional ones, all of which add moisture and flavor to the meat.

INDOOR PULLED PORK WITH SWEET AND TANGY BARBECUE SAUCE

SERVES 6 TO 8

Boneless pork butt roast is often labeled Boston butt in the supermarket. If the pork is enhanced (injected with a salt solution), do not brine in step 1. Sweet paprika may be substituted for the smoked paprika. Covering the pork with parchment and then foil prevents the acidic mustard from eating holes in the foil. Serve the pork on hamburger rolls with pickle chips and thinly sliced onion. Lexington Vinegar Barbecue Sauce or South Carolina Mustard Barbecue Sauce (recipes follow) can be substituted for the Sweet and Tangy Barbecue Sauce. Alternatively, use 2 cups of your favorite barbecue sauce thinned with ½ cup of the defatted pork cooking liquid in step 5.

PORK
Salt and pepper
6 tablespoons sugar
3 tablespoons plus 2 teaspoons liquid smoke
1 (5-pound) boneless pork butt roast, cut in half horizontally
¼ cup yellow mustard
2 tablespoons smoked paprika
1 teaspoon cayenne pepper

SWEET AND TANGY BARBECUE SAUCE
1½ cups ketchup
¼ cup light or mild molasses
2 tablespoons Worcestershire sauce
1 tablespoon hot sauce
½ teaspoon salt
½ teaspoon pepper

1. FOR THE PORK: Dissolve ¼ cup salt, ¼ cup sugar, and 3 tablespoons liquid smoke in 2 quarts cold water in large container. Submerge pork in brine, cover, and refrigerate for 1½ to 2 hours.

2. While pork brines, combine mustard and remaining 2 teaspoons liquid smoke in

bowl; set aside. Combine 2 teaspoons salt, 2 tablespoons pepper, remaining 2 tablespoons sugar, paprika, and cayenne in second bowl; set aside. Adjust oven rack to lower-middle position and heat oven to 325 degrees.

3. Remove pork from brine and thoroughly pat dry with paper towels. Rub mustard mixture over entire surface of each piece of pork. Sprinkle entire surface of each piece with spice mixture. Place pork on wire rack set in aluminum foil–lined rimmed baking sheet. Place piece of parchment paper over pork, then cover with sheet of aluminum foil, sealing edges to prevent moisture from escaping. Roast pork for 3 hours.

4. Remove pork from oven; remove and discard foil and parchment. Carefully pour off liquid in bottom of baking sheet into fat separator and reserve for sauce. Return pork to oven and cook, uncovered, until well browned and tender and internal temperature registers 200 degrees, about 1½ hours. Transfer pork to serving dish, tent loosely with foil, and let rest for 20 minutes.

5. FOR THE SAUCE: While pork rests, pour ½ cup defatted cooking liquid from fat separator into medium bowl; whisk in sauce ingredients.

6. TO SERVE: Using 2 forks, shred pork into bite-size pieces. (Shredded and sauced pork can be cooled, tightly covered, and refrigerated for up to 2 days. Reheat gently before serving.) Toss with 1 cup sauce and season with salt and pepper to taste. Serve, passing remaining sauce separately.

LEXINGTON VINEGAR BARBECUE SAUCE

MAKES ABOUT 2½ CUPS, ENOUGH FOR 1 RECIPE INDOOR PULLED PORK

1 cup cider vinegar
½ cup ketchup
½ cup water

1 tablespoon sugar
¾ teaspoon salt
¾ teaspoon red pepper flakes
½ teaspoon pepper

Combine all ingredients in medium bowl with ½ cup defatted cooking liquid, reserved from step 5, and whisk to combine.

SOUTH CAROLINA MUSTARD BARBECUE SAUCE

MAKES ABOUT 2½ CUPS, ENOUGH FOR
1 RECIPE INDOOR PULLED PORK

1 cup yellow mustard
½ cup white vinegar
¼ cup packed light brown sugar
¼ cup Worcestershire sauce
2 tablespoons hot sauce
1 teaspoon salt
1 teaspoon pepper

Combine all ingredients in medium bowl with ½ cup defatted cooking liquid, reserved from step 5, and whisk to combine.

MEXICAN PULLED PORK

✓ WHY THIS RECIPE WORKS
Like the best barbecue, carnitas—Mexico's version of pulled pork—offers fall-apart hunks of crisp meat. In carnitas, the flavor of the pork, subtly accented by earthy oregano and sour orange, takes center stage. Another appealing aspect of this dish is that it is cooked indoors, so it can be made any time of year. Rather than frying chunks of meat in gallons of lard, we were able to replicate deep-fried taste and texture by braising the pork in small amount of liquid, then reducing the liquid to a syrupy consistency and incorporating it back into the dish. Broiling the glazed meat on a rack not only crisped the exterior, but also allowed the excess fat to drip off,
preventing a greasy final dish. Refining our cooking liquid's flavors with a mixture of lime and orange juices, bay leaves, and oregano was the finishing touch.

MEXICAN PULLED PORK (CARNITAS)

SERVES 6

We like serving carnitas spooned into small corn tortillas, taco-style, but you can also use it as a filling for tamales, enchiladas, and burritos. Boneless pork butt roast is often labeled Boston butt in the supermarket.

PORK
1 (3½- to 4-pound) boneless pork butt roast, fat cap trimmed to ⅛ inch thick and cut into 2-inch chunks
2 cups water
1 onion, peeled and halved
2 tablespoons lime juice
1 teaspoon dried oregano
1 teaspoon ground cumin
2 bay leaves
  Salt and pepper
1 orange, halved

TORTILLAS AND GARNISHES
18 (6-inch) corn tortillas, warmed
  Lime wedges
  Minced white or red onion
  Fresh cilantro
  Thinly sliced radishes
  Sour cream

1. Adjust oven rack to lower-middle position and heat oven to 300 degrees. Combine pork, water, onion, lime juice, oregano, cumin, bay leaves, 1 teaspoon salt, and ½ teaspoon pepper in Dutch oven (liquid should just barely cover meat). Juice orange into bowl and remove any seeds (you should have about ⅓ cup juice). Add juice and spent orange halves to pot. Bring mixture to simmer over medium-high heat, stirring occasionally. Cover pot
and transfer to oven; cook until meat is soft and falls apart when prodded with fork, about 2 hours, flipping pieces of meat once during cooking.

2. Remove pot from oven and turn oven to broil. Using slotted spoon, transfer pork to bowl; remove orange halves, onion, and bay leaves from cooking liquid and discard (do not skim fat from liquid). Place pot over high heat (use caution, as handles will be very hot) and simmer liquid, stirring frequently, until thick and syrupy (heat-resistant spatula should leave wide trail when dragged through glaze), 8 to 12 minutes. You should have about 1 cup reduced liquid.

3. Using 2 forks, pull each piece of pork in half. Fold in reduced liquid; season with salt and pepper to taste. Spread pork in even layer on wire rack set in rimmed baking sheet or on broiler pan (meat should cover almost entire surface of rack or broiler pan). Place baking sheet on lower-middle rack and broil until top of meat is well browned (but not charred) and edges are slightly crisp, 5 to 8 minutes. Using wide metal spatula, flip pieces of meat and continue to broil until top is well browned and edges are slightly crisp, 5 to 8 minutes longer. Serve with warm tortillas and garnishes.

SPICY MEXICAN SHREDDED PORK TOSTADAS

✓ WHY THIS RECIPE WORKS
Tinga is a spicy Mexican dish of shredded pork possessing an intense, meaty sweetness. The pork is sautéed after braising until it acquires deeply browned edges, then briefly simmered in sauce before being served atop crunchy tostada shells. To get smoky, fork-tender pork on the stovetop, we simmered cubed Boston butt in water flavored with garlic, onion, and thyme, then shredded the pork and sautéed it in a hot frying pan to crisp it. (Shredding the meat

before sautéing maximizes the surface area available for browning.) Finally, we used canned tomato sauce and chipotle chile powder to build a deep and complex sauce for our shredded pork tostadas.

SPICY MEXICAN SHREDDED PORK (TINGA) TOSTADAS
SERVES 4 TO 6

Boneless pork butt roast is often labeled Boston butt in the supermarket. The trimmed pork should weigh about 1½ pounds. Tinga is traditionally served on tostadas (crisp fried corn tortillas), but you can also use the meat in tacos and burritos or simply served over rice. Make sure to buy tortillas made only with corn, lime, and salt—preservatives will compromise quality. We prefer the complex flavor of chipotle powder, but two minced canned chipotle chiles can be used in its place.

TINGA
- 2 pounds boneless pork butt roast, trimmed and cut into 1-inch pieces
- 2 onions, 1 quartered and 1 chopped fine
- 5 garlic cloves, 3 peeled and smashed and 2 minced
- 4 sprigs fresh thyme
  Salt
- 2 tablespoons olive oil
- ½ teaspoon dried oregano
- 1 (14.5-ounce) can tomato sauce
- 1 tablespoon ground chipotle powder
- 2 bay leaves

TOSTADAS
- ¾ cup vegetable oil
- 12 (6-inch) corn tortillas
  Salt

GARNISHES
Queso fresco or feta cheese
Fresh cilantro
Sour cream

Diced avocado
Lime wedges

1. **FOR THE TINGA:** Bring pork, quartered onion, smashed garlic, thyme sprigs, 1 teaspoon salt, and 6 cups water to simmer in large saucepan over medium-high heat, skimming off any foam that rises to surface. Reduce heat to medium-low, partially cover, and cook until pork is tender, 1¼ to 1½ hours. Drain pork, reserving 1 cup cooking liquid. Discard onion, garlic, and thyme sprigs. Return pork to saucepan and, using potato masher, mash until shredded into rough ½-inch pieces; set aside. (Pork can be prepared through step 1 and refrigerated for 2 days.)

2. Heat oil in 12-inch nonstick skillet over medium-high heat until shimmering. Add shredded pork, chopped onion, and oregano; cook, stirring often, until pork is well browned and crisp, 7 to 10 minutes. Add minced garlic and cook until fragrant, about 30 seconds.

3. Stir in tomato sauce, reserved pork cooking liquid, chipotle powder, and bay leaves; simmer until almost all liquid has evaporated, 5 to 7 minutes. Remove and discard bay leaves and season with salt to taste.

4. **FOR THE TOSTADAS:** Heat oil in 8-inch skillet over medium heat to 350 degrees. Using fork, poke center of each tortilla 3 or 4 times. Fry one at a time, holding metal potato masher in upright position on top of tortilla to keep it submerged, until crisp and lightly browned, 45 to 60 seconds (no flipping is necessary). Drain on paper towel–lined plate and season with salt to taste. Repeat with remaining tortillas. (Tostadas can be made up to 1 day in advance and stored in airtight container.)

5. **TO SERVE:** Spoon small amount of shredded pork onto center of each tostada and serve, passing garnishes separately.

SPICY MEXICAN SHREDDED PORK TOSTADAS WITH HOMEMADE CHORIZO
SERVES 6 TO 8

Increase amount of pork to 3 pounds (2½ pounds after trimming). Using two-thirds of pork (1½ pounds), follow recipe as directed in step 1. To make chorizo, place remaining pork pieces on large plate in single layer and freeze until firm but still pliable, about 15 minutes. Once firm, toss pork with 1 tablespoon red wine vinegar, 1¼ teaspoons chili powder, 1 small minced garlic clove, 1 teaspoon salt, ¾ teaspoon hot paprika, ¾ teaspoon ground chipotle powder, ¾ teaspoon dried oregano, ¼ teaspoon pepper, and ⅛ teaspoon ground cumin in medium bowl. Pulse half of chorizo mixture in food processor until meat is finely chopped, 8 to 10 pulses. Transfer to bowl and repeat with remaining chorizo mixture. In step 2, heat oil as directed and add chorizo mixture; cook, stirring occasionally, until slightly crisp and no longer pink, 3 to 5 minutes. Transfer meat to paper towel–lined plate, leaving rendered fat in skillet. Proceed with recipe as directed, using rendered fat to cook shredded pork and returning chorizo mixture to skillet along with tomato sauce in step 3.

OVEN-BARBECUED SPARERIBS

✔ WHY THIS RECIPE WORKS
When the craving for crisp-crusted, smoky spareribs strikes in midwinter, we usually have two options: head to a local barbecue joint or attempt them in the oven. But most oven recipes slather on smoke-flavored sauce only to cover up the disappointingly tough meat beneath. We wanted to replicate the deep, rich flavor and fork-tender texture of barbecued ribs indoors.

First off, we rejected stovetop smokers in favor the oven, which better contained the smoke and was able to accommodate the ribs in one batch. To replace the wood chips of a stovetop smoker, we sprinkled the smoldering, strong-tasting tea, Lapsang Souchong, underneath the ribs, which added rich smokiness to the meat. Finally, to prevent the meat from drying out (roasting the tea leaves requires high heat), we found it necessary to freeze the ribs before they went into the oven.

OVEN-BARBECUED SPARERIBS
SERVES 4

To make this recipe, you will need a baking stone. It's fine if the ribs overlap slightly on the wire rack. Removing the surface fat keeps the ribs from being too greasy and removing the membrane from the ribs allows the smoke to penetrate both sides of the racks and also makes the ribs easier to eat. Note that the ribs must be coated with the rub and refrigerated at least 8 hours or up to 24 hours ahead of cooking. Be careful when opening the crimped foil to add the juice, as hot steam and smoke will billow out. Serve ribs with barbecue sauce, if desired.

- 6 tablespoons yellow mustard
- 2 tablespoons ketchup
- 3 garlic cloves, minced
- 3 tablespoons packed brown sugar
- 1½ tablespoons kosher salt
- 1 tablespoon sweet paprika
- 1 tablespoon chili powder
- 2 teaspoons pepper
- ½ teaspoon cayenne pepper
- 2 (2½- to 3-pound) racks St. Louis–style spareribs, trimmed, membrane removed, and each rack cut in half
- ¼ cup finely ground Lapsang Souchong tea leaves (from about 10 tea bags, or ½ cup loose tea leaves ground to a powder in a spice grinder)
- ½ cup apple juice

1. Combine mustard, ketchup, and garlic in bowl; combine sugar, salt, paprika, chili powder, pepper, and cayenne in separate bowl. Spread mustard mixture in thin, even layer over both sides of ribs; coat both sides with spice mixture, then wrap ribs in plastic and refrigerate for 8 to 24 hours.

2. Transfer ribs from refrigerator to freezer for 45 minutes. Adjust oven racks to lowest and upper-middle positions (at least 5 inches below broiler). Place baking stone on lower rack; heat oven to 500 degrees. Sprinkle ground tea evenly over bottom of rimmed baking sheet; set wire rack in baking sheet. Place ribs meat side up on rack and cover with heavy-duty aluminum foil, crimping edges tightly to seal. Place baking sheet on stone and roast ribs for 30 minutes, then reduce oven temperature to 250 degrees, leaving oven door open for 1 minute to cool. While oven is

open, carefully open 1 corner of foil and pour apple juice into bottom of baking sheet; reseal foil. Continue to roast until meat is very tender and begins to pull away from bones, about 1½ hours. (Begin to check ribs after 1 hour; leave loosely covered with foil for remaining cooking time.)

3. Remove foil and carefully flip racks bone side up; place baking sheet on upper-middle rack. Turn on broiler; cook ribs until well browned and crispy in spots, 5 to 10 minutes. Flip ribs meat side up and cook until second side is well browned and crispy, 5 to 7 minutes more. Cool for at least 10 minutes before cutting into individual ribs. Serve with barbecue sauce, if desired.

CHINESE BARBECUED PORK

✔ WHY THIS RECIPE WORKS

Chinese barbecued pork features a ruby-red color, deeply browned and crusty edges, and an irresistibly sticky exterior. The meat is actually "barbecued" in the oven, making it an ideal candidate for home cooking—at least in theory. But traditional recipes call for cutting the meat into thin strips and hanging them on metal rods that go in refrigerator-size ovens. We wanted to develop a recipe suited for a home oven. We started by slicing a boneless pork butt into strips. Our marinade of soy sauce, sherry, hoisin sauce, five-spice powder, sesame oil, ginger, and garlic introduced traditional Asian flavors, and pricking the meat with a fork enhanced the marinade's penetration. For optimal browning and intense flavor, we needed a two-heat process—first cooking the meat, covered, at a low temperature to render fat and then cranking up the heat to develop a burnished crust. The classic lacquered appearance was achieved by applying a ketchup-honey glaze right before broiling, which also gave our Chinese barbecued pork its traditional red color.

REMOVING THE MEMBRANE FROM THE RIB RACK

For Oven-Barbecued Spareribs, we recommend removing the thin membrane that lines the concave side of the rib rack. The ribs are easier to manipulate (and eat), and the smoke penetrates both sides of the rack directly.

1. Insert spoon handle between membrane and ribs to loosen slightly.

2. Using paper towel, grasp loosened membrane and pull away gently to remove.

CHINESE BARBECUED PORK
SERVES 6

Boneless pork butt roast is often labeled Boston butt in the supermarket. The pork will release liquid and fat during the cooking process, so be careful when removing the pan from the oven. If you don't have a wire rack that fits in a rimmed baking sheet, substitute a broiler pan, although the meat may not darken as much. Pay close attention to the meat when broiling—you are looking for it to darken and caramelize, not blacken. Do not use a drawer broiler—the heat source will be too close to the meat. Instead, increase the oven temperature in step 5 to 500 degrees and cook for 8 to 12 minutes before glazing and 6 to 8 minutes once the glaze has been applied; flip meat and repeat on second side. This recipe can be made with boneless country-style ribs, but the meat will be slightly drier and less flavorful. To use ribs, reduce the uncovered cooking time in step 4 to 20 minutes and increase the broiling and glazing times in step 5 by 2 to 3 minutes per side. This dish is best served with rice and a vegetable side dish. Leftover pork makes an excellent addition to fried rice or an Asian noodle soup.

4	pounds boneless pork butt roast, halved lengthwise, each half turned on its side, cut into 8 strips, and trimmed
½	cup sugar
½	cup soy sauce
6	tablespoons hoisin sauce
¼	cup dry sherry
2	tablespoons grated fresh ginger
1	tablespoon toasted sesame oil
2	garlic cloves, minced
1	teaspoon five-spice powder
¼	teaspoon ground white pepper
⅓	cup honey
¼	cup ketchup

1. Using fork, prick pork 10 to 12 times on each side. Place pork in 2-gallon plastic zipper-lock bag. Combine sugar, soy sauce, hoisin, sherry, ginger, oil, garlic, five-spice powder, and pepper in medium bowl. Measure out ½ cup marinade and set aside. Pour remaining marinade into bag with pork. Press out as much air as possible; seal bag. Refrigerate for at least 30 minutes or up to 4 hours.

2. While meat marinates, combine honey and ketchup with reserved marinade in small saucepan. Cook glaze over medium heat until syrupy and reduced to 1 cup, 4 to 6 minutes.

3. Adjust oven rack to middle position and heat oven to 300 degrees. Set wire rack in aluminum foil–lined rimmed baking sheet and spray with vegetable oil spray.

4. Remove pork from marinade, letting any excess drip off, and place on wire rack. Pour ¼ cup water into bottom of pan. Cover pan with heavy-duty foil, crimping edges tightly to seal. Cook pork for 20 minutes. Remove foil and continue to cook until edges of pork begin to brown, 40 to 45 minutes.

5. Turn on broiler. Broil pork until evenly caramelized, 7 to 9 minutes. Remove pan from oven and brush pork with half of glaze; broil until deep mahogany color, 3 to 5 minutes. Using tongs, flip meat and broil until other side caramelizes, 7 to 9 minutes. Brush meat with remaining glaze and continue to broil until second side is deep mahogany, 3 to 5 minutes. Cool for at least 10 minutes, then cut into thin strips and serve.

SORGHUM-GLAZED COUNTRY HAM

✌ WHY THIS RECIPE WORKS

We figured cooking a country ham would be pretty straightforward, but a little research proved that there are many different approaches. First we focused on the soaking and cooking method. Soaking a cured ham causes the salty meat to absorb water, thereby softening the ham and preventing excessive dryness. Soaking time depends on how long the ham has aged. Hams aged for fewer than six months don't need to be soaked; hams aged for six months to a year should be soaked for 36 hours; and hams aged for more than a year should be soaked for three days, with the water being changed every day. As for cooking, we liked simmering, which adds a touch of moisture and makes it easier to remove the ham bone for more convenient serving.

SORGHUM-GLAZED COUNTRY HAM
SERVES 30

If using an older ham, scrub mold off with a food-grade scrub brush (such as a vegetable brush), under running water. Not removing the hock from the ham makes for a nicer presentation, but if desired, use a hack saw to remove

---

BUTCHERING PORK BUTT

Pork butts are usually about 4 inches thick. If using a pork butt that is thinner than 4 inches, cut into 6 strips instead of 8.

1. Cut roast in half lengthwise.

2. Turn each half on cut side and slice lengthwise into 4 equal pieces.

3. Trim excess hard, waxy fat, leaving some fat to render while cooking.

the hock so that the ham fits more easily into the pot (this can also be done by your butcher). To soak a hock-on ham, we found a large clean cooler to be an ideal soaking vessel.

- 1 (14- to 15-pound) country ham
- 3 carrots, cut into large chunks
- 3 celery ribs, cut into large chunks
- 2 onions, cut into large chunks
- 6 sprigs fresh thyme or fresh rosemary
- ½ cup sorghum or packed brown sugar

1. Place ham in stockpot and cover with water. Soak ham, changing water at least daily, to release salt and rehydrate ham, about 36 hours for hams aged 6 to 12 months and 3 days for hams aged over a year.

2. Bring large kettle of water to boil. Adjust oven rack to lowest position and heat oven to 325 degrees. Drain ham; discard soaking water. Cover bottom of roasting pan with large piece of aluminum foil (foil should be long enough to form tent over ham). Arrange carrots and celery in even layer over foil, tucking onion chunks and thyme in between. Set ham over vegetable bed, fat side up. Place pan in oven. Pour boiling water halfway up pan sides; pull foil around ham, forming loose tent. Bake until thickest part of ham registers 125 to 130 degrees, 2½ to 3 hours.

3. Remove pan from oven (cool ham slightly, if necessary). Carefully remove skin with knife, leaving ¼-inch layer of fat. Score diamond pattern into fat, if desired, then brush with sorghum. Remove vegetables and cooking liquid from roasting pan, return ham to pan; bake until temperature registers 145 to 150 degrees (depending on desired crispness), 30 minutes to 1 hour longer. Transfer to a carving board. Cool slightly; carve into thin slices and serve.

ROAST FRESH HAM

✔ WHY THIS RECIPE WORKS
We wanted to develop a recipe for fresh ham worthy of a holiday table, one with moist meat and crackling crisp skin. Since a whole leg is too large for most occasions, we settled on using the shank end (from the bottom of the leg) and scored the fat. Then we brined the ham in a solution flavored with brown sugar, garlic, bay leaves, and black peppercorns. Starting the ham at high heat and finishing at low heat gave us a crisp, flavorful skin and tender meat. We finished our fresh ham with a sweet—but not cloying—glaze.

ROAST FRESH HAM
SERVES 8 TO 10

If you don't have room in your refrigerator, you can brine the ham in a large insulated cooler or a small plastic garbage can; add five or six freezer packs to the brine to keep it well cooled.

HAM AND BRINE
- 1 (6- to 8-pound) bone-in, skin-on ham, preferably shank end, rinsed
- 3 cups packed brown sugar
- 2 cups salt
- 2 garlic heads, cloves separated, lightly crushed and peeled
- ½ cup whole black peppercorns, crushed
- 10 bay leaves

GARLIC AND HERB RUB
- 1 cup fresh sage, lightly packed
- ½ cup fresh parsley
- ¼ cup olive oil
- 8 garlic cloves, peeled
- 1½ teaspoons salt
- 1½ teaspoons pepper

GLAZE
- 1 recipe glaze (recipes follow)

1. FOR THE HAM AND BRINE: Carefully slice through skin and fat with serrated knife, making 1-inch diamond pattern. Be careful not to cut into meat.

2. Dissolve sugar and salt in 2 gallons cold water in large container; stir in garlic, peppercorns, and bay leaves. Submerge ham in brine, cover, and refrigerate for 8 to 24 hours.

3. Set large disposable roasting pan on baking sheet for extra support; place flat

---

CARVING TWO CUTS OF HAM

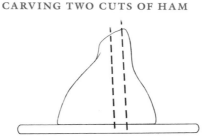

SHANK END

1. Transfer ham to carving board and carve lengthwise alongside bone, following 2 dotted lines in illustration above.
2. Lay large boneless pieces you have just carved flat on carving board and slice into ½-inch pieces.

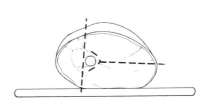

SIRLOIN END

1. Transfer ham to carving board and carve into 3 pieces around bone along dotted lines in illustration above.
2. Lay large boneless pieces you have just carved flat on carving board and slice into ½-inch pieces.

---

wire rack in roasting pan. Remove ham from brine and thoroughly pat dry with paper towels. Place ham, wide cut side down, on rack. (If using sirloin end, place ham skin side up.) Let ham stand, uncovered, at room temperature for 1 hour.

4. FOR THE RUB: Meanwhile, adjust oven rack to lowest position and heat oven to 500 degrees. Process all rub ingredients in food processor until mixture forms smooth paste, about 30 seconds. Rub all sides of ham with paste.

5. Roast ham at 500 degrees for 20 minutes. Reduce oven temperature to 350 degrees and continue to roast, brushing ham with glaze every 45 minutes, until ham registers 145 to 150 degrees, about 2½ hours longer. Transfer to carving board, tent loosely with aluminum foil, and let rest for 30 to 40 minutes. Carve and serve.

COLA-BRINED ROAST FRESH HAM

Substitute 6 liters cola for water in brine, omitting sugar and reducing salt to 1½ cups.

APPLE CIDER AND BROWN SUGAR GLAZE

MAKES 1½ CUPS, ENOUGH FOR 1 RECIPE ROAST FRESH HAM

2 cups packed brown sugar
1 cup apple cider
5 whole cloves

Bring sugar, cider, and cloves to boil in small saucepan over high heat; reduce heat to medium-low and simmer until syrupy and reduced to about 1⅓ cups, 5 to 7 minutes. (Glaze will thicken as it cools between bastings; cook over medium heat about 1 minute, stirring once or twice, before using.)

ORANGE, CINNAMON, AND STAR ANISE GLAZE

MAKES ABOUT 1½ CUPS, ENOUGH FOR 1 RECIPE ROAST FRESH HAM

2 cups packed brown sugar
1 tablespoon grated orange zest plus 1 cup juice (2 oranges)
4 star anise pods
1 (3-inch) cinnamon stick

Bring sugar, orange zest and juice, star anise, and cinnamon to boil in small saucepan over high heat; reduce heat to medium-low and simmer until syrupy and reduced to about 1⅓ cups, 5 to 7 minutes. (Glaze will thicken as it cools between bastings; cook over medium heat about 1 minute, stirring once or twice, before using.)

SPICY PINEAPPLE-GINGER GLAZE

MAKES 1½ CUPS, ENOUGH FOR 1 RECIPE ROAST FRESH HAM

2 cups packed brown sugar
1 cup pineapple juice
1 tablespoon grated fresh ginger
1 tablespoon red pepper flakes

Bring sugar, pineapple juice, ginger, and pepper flakes to boil in small saucepan over high heat; reduce heat to medium-low and simmer until syrupy and reduced to about 1⅓ cups, 5 to 7 minutes. (Glaze will thicken as it cools between bastings; cook over medium heat about 1 minute, stirring once or twice, before using.)

GLAZED SPIRAL-SLICED HAM

✔ WHY THIS RECIPE WORKS

Glazed ham is appealingly simple but often comes out dry and jerkylike. We wanted a top-notch glazed ham that is always moist and tender, with a glaze that complements, but doesn't overwhelm the meat. Bone-in hams that have been spiral-sliced offered the best flavor with the least amount of carving necessary. We found it important to avoid labels that read "ham with water added" as these hams simply didn't taste as good. Heating the ham to an internal temperature of no higher than 120 degrees was enough to take the chill off without drying it out. Soaking the ham in warm water before heating it and placing it in an oven bag kept it moist and also reduced cooking time. Finally, we determined that it was best to apply the glaze toward the end of cooking and then again once it came out of the oven.

GLAZED SPIRAL-SLICED HAM
SERVES 12 TO 14, WITH LEFTOVERS

You can bypass the 90-minute soaking time, but the heating time will increase to 18 to 20 minutes per pound for a cold ham. If there is a tear or hole in the ham's inner covering, wrap it in several layers of plastic wrap before soaking it in hot water. Instead of using the plastic oven bag, the ham may be placed cut side down in the roasting pan and covered tightly with foil, but you will need to add 3 to 4 minutes per pound to the heating time. If using an oven bag, be sure to cut slits in the bag so it does not burst. We've included two optional glazes.

1 (7- to 10-pound) spiral-sliced bone-in half ham
1 large plastic oven bag
1 recipe glaze (recipes follow)

1. Leaving ham's inner plastic or foil covering intact, place ham in large container and cover with hot tap water; set aside for 45 minutes. Drain and cover again with hot tap water; set aside for another 45 minutes.

2. Adjust oven rack to lowest position and heat oven to 250 degrees. Unwrap ham; remove and discard plastic disk covering bone. Place ham in oven bag. Gather top of bag tightly so bag fits snugly around ham, tie bag, and trim excess plastic. Set ham cut side down in large roasting pan and cut 4 slits in top of bag with paring knife.

3. Bake ham until center registers 100 degrees, 1 to 1½ hours (about 10 minutes per pound).

4. Remove ham from oven and increase oven temperature to 350 degrees. Cut open oven bag and roll back sides to expose ham. Brush ham with one-third of glaze and return to oven until glaze becomes sticky, about 10 minutes (if glaze is too thick to brush, return to heat to loosen).

5. Remove ham from oven, transfer to carving board, and brush entire ham with one-third of glaze. Let ham rest, tented loosely with aluminum foil, for 15 minutes. While ham rests, heat remaining one-third of glaze with 4 to 6 tablespoons of ham juices until it forms thick but fluid sauce. Carve and serve ham, passing sauce at table.

CHERRY-PORT GLAZE

MAKES I CUP, ENOUGH FOR I RECIPE
SPIRAL-SLICED HAM

½ cup ruby port
I cup packed dark brown sugar
½ cup cherry preserves
I teaspoon pepper

Simmer port in small saucepan over medium heat until reduced to 2 tablespoons, about 5 minutes. Add remaining

BROWNING RACKS OF LAMB

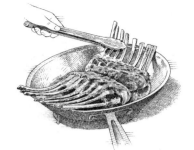

I. Place racks in hot pan with meat in center and ribs facing outward.

2. After meat is browned, stand racks up in pan and lean them against each other to brown bottoms.

---

ingredients and cook, stirring occasionally, until sugar dissolves and mixture is thick, syrupy, and reduced to 1 cup, 5 to 10 minutes; set aside.

MAPLE-ORANGE GLAZE

MAKES I CUP, ENOUGH FOR I RECIPE
SPIRAL-SLICED HAM

¾ cup maple syrup
½ cup orange marmalade
2 tablespoons unsalted butter
I tablespoon Dijon mustard
I teaspoon pepper
¼ teaspoon ground cinnamon

Combine all ingredients in small saucepan. Cook over medium heat, stirring occasionally, until mixture is thick, syrupy, and reduced to 1 cup, 5 to 10 minutes; set aside.

APPLE-GINGER GLAZE

MAKES I½ CUPS, ENOUGH FOR I RECIPE
SPIRAL-SLICED HAM

I cup packed dark brown sugar
¾ cup apple jelly
3 tablespoons apple butter
I tablespoon grated fresh ginger
Pinch ground cloves

Combine all ingredients in small saucepan. Cook over medium heat, stirring occasionally, until sugar dissolves and mixture is thick, syrupy, and reduced to 1½ cups, 5 to 10 minutes; set aside.

SIMPLE ROASTED RACK OF LAMB

✔ WHY THIS RECIPE WORKS
If you're going to spend the money on rack of lamb, you want to be sure you cook it right— as with other simple dishes, there's no disguising imperfection. We wanted to develop a foolproof recipe for roasted rack of lamb, with perfectly pink and juicy meat encased in an intensely brown, crisp shell. To prepare the racks, we frenched them (cleaned the rib bones of meat and fat), and also discovered that we needed to remove a second layer of internal fat (along with a thin strip of meat) to avoid a greasy finished dish. After testing various oven temperatures, we decided that searing the racks first on the stovetop and then finishing them in a 425-degree oven was best. As a bonus, we were able to use the resulting pan drippings to make a simple yet flavorful pan sauce.

SIMPLE ROASTED RACK OF LAMB
SERVES 4 TO 6

Have your butcher french the racks for you; inevitably, the ribs will need some cleaning up, but at least the bulk of the work will be done. Should you choose to make an accompanying pan sauce (recipes follow), have all the ingredients ready before browning the lamb and begin the sauce just as the lamb goes into the oven. This way, the sauce will be ready with the meat.

- 2 (1¼- to 1½-pound) racks of lamb (each 8 to 9 ribs), frenched and trimmed
  Salt and pepper
- 2 tablespoons vegetable oil
- 1 recipe pan sauce (optional) (recipes follow)

1. Adjust oven rack to lower-middle position, place rimmed baking sheet on oven rack, and heat oven to 425 degrees.

2. Season lamb with salt and pepper. Heat oil in 12-inch skillet over high heat until shimmering. Place racks of lamb in skillet, meat side down in the center of the pan, with ribs facing outwards; cook until well browned and nice crust has formed on surface, about 4 minutes. Using tongs, stand racks up in skillet, leaning them against each other to brown bottoms; cook until bottom sides have browned, about 2 minutes longer.

3. Transfer lamb to preheated baking sheet. (Begin pan sauce, if making.) Roast until center of each rack registers about 130 to 135 degrees (for medium), 12 to 15 minutes. Tent loosely with aluminum foil and let rest about 10 minutes. Carve, slicing between each rib into individual chops, and season with salt and pepper to taste or serve with an accompanying sauce.

RED WINE PAN SAUCE WITH ROSEMARY

MAKES ABOUT ¾ CUP, ENOUGH FOR 1 RECIPE SIMPLE ROASTED RACK OF LAMB

- 2 shallots, minced
- 1 cup dry red wine
- 2½ teaspoons minced fresh rosemary
- 1 cup low-sodium chicken broth
- 2 tablespoons unsalted butter, softened
  Salt and pepper

Pour off all but 1½ tablespoons fat from skillet used to brown lamb; place skillet over medium heat. Add shallots and cook until softened, about 1 minute. Add red wine and rosemary, scrape bottom of pan with wooden spoon to loosen any browned bits, and increase heat to medium-high and simmer until dark and syrupy, about 7 minutes. Add broth; simmer until reduced to about ¾ cup, about 5 minutes longer. Off heat, swirl in butter, season with salt and pepper to taste, and serve with lamb.

ORANGE PAN SAUCE WITH MIDDLE EASTERN SPICES

MAKES ABOUT ¾ CUP, ENOUGH FOR 1 RECIPE SIMPLE ROASTED RACK OF LAMB

- 2 shallots, minced
- 2 teaspoons sugar
- 1 teaspoon ground cumin
- ¼ teaspoon pepper
- ¼ teaspoon ground cinnamon
- ¼ teaspoon ground cardamom
- ⅛ teaspoon cayenne pepper
- 3 tablespoons red wine vinegar
- ¼ cup orange juice
- 1½ cups low-sodium chicken broth
- 1 tablespoon minced fresh cilantro
  Salt

TRIMMING AND FRENCHING RACKS OF LAMB

1. If the rack has a fat cap, peel back thick outer layer of fat from racks, along with thin flap of meat underneath it. Use boning knife to cut any tissue connecting fat cap to rack.

2. Using sharp boning or paring knife, trim remaining thin layer of fat that covers loin, leaving strip of fat that separates the loin and small eye of meat directly above it.

3. Make straight cut along top side of bones, an inch up from small eye of meat.

4. Remove any fat above this line and scrape any remaining meat or fat from exposed bones.

Pour off all but 1½ tablespoons fat from skillet used to brown lamb; place skillet over medium heat. Add shallots and cook until softened, about 1 minute. Stir in sugar, cumin, pepper, cinnamon, cardamom, and cayenne; cook until fragrant, about 1 minute. Stir in vinegar, scraping bottom of pan with wooden spoon to loosen any browned bits. Add orange juice, increase heat to medium-high, and simmer until very thick and syrupy, about 2 minutes. Add broth and simmer until slightly thickened and reduced to about ¾ cup, 8 to 10 minutes. Off heat, stir in cilantro, season with salt to taste, and serve with lamb.

SWEET AND SOUR MINT SAUCE

MAKES ABOUT ½ CUP, ENOUGH FOR
1 RECIPE SIMPLE ROASTED RACK OF LAMB

The sauce should be made before you begin cooking the lamb so the sugar has time to dissolve while the lamb cooks.

- ¼ cup chopped fresh mint
- ¼ cup red wine vinegar
- 1 tablespoon sugar
  Salt

Stir mint, vinegar, and sugar together in bowl. Let stand about 20 minutes to allow sugar to dissolve. Season with salt to taste and serve with lamb.

TEST KITCHEN TIP NO. 86 BUYING LAMB

When you're buying lamb, the biggest determinant of flavor is origin. Domestic lamb is distinguished by its larger size and milder flavor, and lamb imported from Australia and New Zealand features a far gamier taste. The reason for this difference in taste boils down to diet—and the chemistry of lamb fat. Imported lamb has been pasture-fed on mixed grasses, whereas lambs raised in the United States begin on a diet of grass but finish with grain. This change of diet has a direct impact on the composition of the animal's fat, reducing the concentration of certain fats that give the lamb its characteristic "lamb-y" flavor—and ultimately leading to sweeter-tasting meat.

GARLIC-ROASTED LEG OF LAMB

✓ WHY THIS RECIPE WORKS

Few roasts make as grand an entrance as roasted leg of lamb, but its charm quickly fades upon carving—copious amounts of sinew and fat make serving this roast a challenge, while lamb fat is the key source of the musky flavor that even adventurous eaters can find off-putting. We wanted a roasted leg of lamb without the gristle or gaminess. We started with a meaty, boneless shank-end roast for best flavor and easy carving. We then separated the meaty lobes to create three tidy mini-roasts from which we could easily trim away all visible fat and gristle, thus eliminating gamy flavor. Next, we introduced garlic and herb flavors to our lamb with a seasoned brine. Finally, we added even more garlic flavor by rubbing a roasted garlic paste onto one side of the lamb.

GARLIC-ROASTED LEG OF LAMB

SERVES 8 TO 10

Look for rolled, boneless leg of lamb wrapped in netting, not butterflied and wrapped on a tray. The desirable cut is the "shank end," which is the whole boneless leg without the sirloin muscle attached. If only bone-in or semiboneless leg is available, ask your butcher to remove the bones for you. Plan on spending about 30 minutes trimming the lamb of fat and silver skin. This advance work is well worth the effort; your roasts will present elegantly and have a much cleaner flavor. (That said, even 10 minutes of trimming will improve the taste dramatically). If you opt for the 30-minute trim, you will have enough meat scraps left over to make the Roasted Garlic Jus (recipe follows).

LAMB AND BRINE

- ¼ cup sugar
- 2 tablespoons salt
- 12 garlic cloves, crushed
- 1 (5- to 7-pound) boneless leg of domestic lamb with sirloin muscle removed, separated into 3 smaller roasts, trimmed, and scored

GARLIC-PARSLEY PASTE

- 2 garlic heads, outer papery skins removed and top third of head cut off and discarded
- 1 tablespoon olive oil
- 2 tablespoons minced fresh parsley
  Salt and pepper
- 3 tablespoons vegetable oil

1. FOR THE LAMB AND BRINE: Dissolve sugar and salt in 2 quarts water in large container; stir in crushed garlic. Submerge lamb in brine, cover, and refrigerate for 2 hours.

2. FOR THE PASTE: While lamb brines, adjust oven rack to middle position and heat oven to 400 degrees. Place garlic heads cut side up on sheet of aluminum foil and drizzle with olive oil. Wrap foil tightly around garlic; place on baking sheet and roast until cloves are very soft and golden brown, 40 to 45 minutes. When cool enough to handle, squeeze garlic head to remove cloves from skins. Mash cloves into paste with side of chef's knife. Combine 2 tablespoons garlic paste and parsley in small bowl. (Reserve remaining paste for Roasted Garlic Jus, if making; recipe follows.)

PREPARING THE LAMB

This method takes about 30 minutes. Instead, you can simply separate the lamb into 3 roasts (illustration 1) and spend just 10 minutes trimming, concentrating on the exterior fat and gristle, then cut a deep, lengthwise pocket into each roast, rub the paste on the interior surface, and tie the roasts.

1. Following natural seams (delineated by lines of fat), separate into 3 smaller roasts, using sharp boning knife as needed.

2. Trim visible fat and gristle from exterior of each roast. Penetrate deeper to remove interior pockets of gristle, fat, and silver skin. (Roasts will open up and flatten slightly.)

3. As you trim meat, remove any large, meaty scraps that come loose from larger pieces. Reserve these for making Roasted Garlic Jus (see related recipe), if desired.

4. Lightly score inside of each roast, making ¼-inch-deep cuts spaced 1 inch apart in cross-hatch pattern.

5. Rub scored surface of brined lamb with garlic-parsley paste, working paste into grooves.

6. Roll into compact roast, tucking in flaps, to form log shape. Tie with kitchen twine at 1-inch intervals.

---

3. Remove lamb from brine and thoroughly pat dry with paper towels. Rub surface of lamb with garlic paste, roll, and tie with kitchen twine at 1-inch intervals. Season each roast with salt and pepper.

4. Heat vegetable oil in 12-inch oven-safe skillet over medium-high heat until shimmering. Place lamb roasts in skillet and cook until well browned on all sides, about 12 minutes total. Place skillet in oven and roast until each roast registers 120 to 125 degrees (for medium-rare) or 130 to 135 degrees (for medium). (Roasting time will range from 8 to 25 minutes depending on size of roasts; begin checking after 7 minutes and transfer each roast to platter as it reaches desired temperature.) Let lamb rest, tented loosely with foil, about 15 minutes. Snip off twine, cut into ¼-inch slices, and serve.

TO MAKE AHEAD: Lamb can be trimmed, brined, rubbed with paste, and tied, then stored overnight in refrigerator (do not season meat). Allow lamb to stand at room temperature for 30 minutes before proceeding with recipe.

ROASTED GARLIC JUS
MAKES ABOUT 2 CUPS

Trimming the lamb into three roasts will yield a few large, meaty scraps, which we recommend using to make an accompanying jus. (Discard smaller pieces of fat and silver skin.) Start the jus while the lamb is in the oven, and finish simmering it while the lamb rests. Keep it warm in a small saucepan and return to a simmer just before serving.

1   tablespoon vegetable oil
1–1½   cups meaty lamb scraps, trimmed of fat and cut into 1-inch pieces
1   onion, chopped
½   cup dry white wine
4   cups low-sodium chicken broth
2   tablespoons garlic paste (reserved from Garlic-Roasted Leg of Lamb)
1   teaspoon red wine vinegar

Heat oil in Dutch oven over medium-high heat until shimmering; add lamb and onion and cook, stirring occasionally, until lamb is well browned and onion is soft and golden, about 8 minutes (reduce heat to medium if pan becomes very dark). Add wine and simmer until reduced by half, about 1 minute, scraping bottom of pot with wooden spoon to loosen any browned bits. Add broth and garlic paste; simmer until reduced by half, 15 to 20 minutes. Add any accumulated lamb juices from platter. Strain jus through fine-mesh strainer into small saucepan; add vinegar and serve with sliced lamb, or keep warm until needed.

ROAST BONELESS LEG OF LAMB

✔ WHY THIS RECIPE WORKS

Boneless leg of lamb would seem to be an easy supper. But it's not just as easy as seasoning the lamb, throwing it in the oven, and then checking it occasionally. We wanted a foolproof method for achieving a crisp crust and perfectly cooked interior every time. We first settled on a half leg as the right amount to serve four to six people. Next we found that pan-searing the roast and then finishing it in the oven produced a great crust and perfectly cooked interior. We applied a simple rub of aromatics to enhance but not overpower the flavor of the lamb. For crunch and even more flavor, we added a savory crumb crust.

1. Cover lamb with plastic wrap and pound to uniform ¾-inch thickness. Season meat with salt and pepper.

2. Spread herb mixture over meat, leaving 1-inch border around edge. Roll meat lengthwise, around filling, into a roast.

3. Tie roast with kitchen twine to secure.

4. To brown ends of roast, hold roast upright with tongs.

5. When lamb is almost midway through cooking, remove it from oven and carefully remove twine.

6. Coat lamb with mustard and herb and bread-crumb mixture, pressing it on well to ensure that it sticks.

3. Place wire rack in rimmed baking sheet. Heat remaining 1 tablespoon oil in 12-inch skillet over medium-high heat until just smoking, about 3 minutes. Sear lamb until well browned on all sides, about 8 minutes; then, using tongs, stand roast on each end to sear, about 30 seconds per end. Transfer to rack and roast until meat registers 120 degrees, 30 to 35 minutes. Transfer lamb to carving board; remove and discard twine. Brush lamb exterior with mustard, then carefully press bread-crumb mixture onto top and sides of roast with hands, pressing firmly to form a solid, even coating that adheres to the meat. Return coated roast to rack; roast until meat registers 130 to 135 degrees (for medium), 15 to 25 minutes longer. Transfer meat to carving board, tent loosely with aluminum foil, and let rest for 10 to 15 minutes. Cut into ½-inch-thick slices and serve.

ROAST BONELESS LEG OF LAMB WITH GARLIC, HERB, AND BREAD-CRUMB CRUST

SERVES 4 TO 6

We prefer the sirloin end rather than the shank end for this recipe, though either will work well.

1	slice hearty white sandwich bread
¼	cup olive oil
¼	cup minced fresh parsley
3	tablespoons minced fresh rosemary
2	tablespoons minced fresh thyme
3	garlic cloves, peeled
1	ounce Parmesan cheese, grated (½ cup)
1	(3½- to 4-pound) boneless half leg of lamb, untied, trimmed, and pounded to even ¾-inch thickness, room temperature
	Salt and pepper
1	tablespoon Dijon mustard

1. Adjust oven rack to lower-middle position and heat oven to 375 degrees. Meanwhile, pulse bread in food processor until coarsely ground, about 10 pulses (you should have about 1 cup crumbs). Transfer to bowl and set aside. In now-empty food processor, process 1 teaspoon oil, parsley, rosemary, thyme, and garlic until minced, scraping down bowl with rubber spatula as necessary, about 1 minute. Transfer 1½ tablespoons herb mixture to bowl and reserve. Scrape remaining mixture into bowl of bread crumbs; stir in Parmesan and 1 tablespoon oil and set aside.

2. Lay lamb with rough interior side (which was against bone) facing up; rub with 2 teaspoons oil and season with salt and pepper. Spread reserved 1½ tablespoons herb mixture evenly over meat, leaving 1-inch border around edge. Roll and tie roast. Season roast with salt and pepper, then rub with 1 tablespoon oil.

INDIAN-SPICED ROAST BONELESS LEG OF LAMB WITH HERBED ALMOND-RAISIN CRUST

SERVES 4 TO 6

Garam masala is an Indian spice blend.

¼	cup fresh mint leaves
¼	cup fresh cilantro leaves
3	tablespoons olive oil
1	(1-inch) piece fresh ginger, peeled and quartered
3	garlic cloves, peeled
1	teaspoon garam masala
¼	teaspoon ground coriander
¼	teaspoon ground cumin
¼	cup slivered almonds
¼	cup raisins
1	tablespoon plain yogurt
1	(3½- to 4-pound) boneless half leg of lamb, untied, trimmed, and pounded to even ¾-inch thickness, room temperature
	Salt and pepper

1. Adjust oven rack to lower-middle position and heat oven to 375 degrees. Process mint, cilantro, 1 teaspoon oil, ginger, garlic, ½ teaspoon garam masala, ⅛ teaspoon coriander, and ⅛ teaspoon cumin in food processor until herbs are minced, scraping down sides of bowl with rubber spatula as necessary, about 1 minute. Transfer 1½ tablespoons herb mixture to bowl and reserve. Add almonds and raisins to food processor; continue processing until finely ground, about 45 seconds, and transfer to another bowl. Combine yogurt with remaining ½ teaspoon garam masala, ⅛ teaspoon coriander, and ⅛ teaspoon cumin; set aside.

2. Lay lamb with rough interior side (which was against bone) facing up; rub with 2 teaspoons oil and season with salt and pepper. Spread reserved 1½ tablespoons herb mixture evenly over meat, leaving 1-inch border around edge. Roll and tie roast. Season roast with salt and pepper, then rub with 1 tablespoon oil.

3. Place wire rack on rimmed baking sheet. Heat remaining 1 tablespoon oil in 12-inch skillet over medium-high heat until just smoking, about 3 minutes. Sear lamb until well browned on all sides, about 8 minutes; then, using tongs, stand roast on each end to sear, about 30 seconds per end. Transfer to rack and roast until meat registers 120 degrees, 30 to 35 minutes. Transfer lamb to carving board; remove and discard twine. Brush lamb exterior with yogurt mixture, then carefully press almond-raisin mixture onto top and sides of roast with hands, pressing firmly to form a solid, even coating that adheres to the meat. Return coated roast to rack; roast until meat registers 130 to 135 degrees (for medium), 15 to 25 minutes longer. Transfer meat to carving board, tent loosely with aluminum foil, and let rest for 10 to 15 minutes. Cut into ½-inch-thick slices and serve.

GREEK-STYLE LAMB PITA SANDWICHES

✔ WHY THIS RECIPE WORKS

When we crave Greek gyros—sandwiches of seasoned, marinated lamb, tomato, lettuce, and cucumber-yogurt sauce stuffed inside a soft pita—we usually head for the nearest Greek restaurant. We wanted gyros we could make at home that would have the same flavors and textures as restaurant gyros, even if they didn't have the traditional appearance. Rather than the traditional shaved slices of meat from a vertical rotisserie, we pan-fried ground lamb patties flavored with oregano, onion, and minced garlic. To make the patties juicier, we added a panade (a paste of fresh bread crumbs and lemon juice), using pita for the bread. Cooking the patties in a hot oiled skillet ensured a crisp outside and moist inside. Topped with lettuce, tomato, yogurt sauce, and a sprinkling of feta, these home-style gyros are a satisfying alternative to the real deal.

GREEK-STYLE LAMB PITA SANDWICHES

SERVES 4

Since the yogurt and cucumbers in the Tzatziki Sauce (recipe follows) need to drain for 30 minutes, start making the sauce before the patties. For the patties, we prefer the flavor of fresh oregano, but 1 teaspoon of dried can be substituted. The skillet may appear crowded when you begin cooking the patties, but they will shrink slightly as they cook. If using pocketless pitas, heat them in a single layer on a baking sheet in a 350-degree oven for 5 minutes. Do not cut top quarters off pocketless pitas; instead, use a portion of a fifth pita to create crumbs in step 1. When cooking the patties, use a splatter screen to keep the mess to a minimum.

LAMB PATTIES
- 4   (8-inch) pita breads
- ½   onion, chopped coarse
- 1   tablespoon minced fresh oregano
- 4   teaspoons lemon juice
- 2   garlic cloves, minced
- ½   teaspoon salt
- ¼   teaspoon pepper
- 1   pound ground lamb
- 2   teaspoons vegetable oil

ACCOMPANIMENTS
- 1   recipe Tzatziki Sauce (recipe follows)
- 1   large tomato, cored and sliced thin
- 2   cups shredded iceberg lettuce
- 2   ounces feta cheese, crumbled (½ cup)

1. FOR THE LAMB PATTIES: Adjust oven rack to middle position and heat oven to 350 degrees. Cut top quarter off each pita bread. Tear quarters into 1-inch pieces. (You should have ¾ cup pita pieces.) Stack pitas and tightly wrap with aluminum foil. Process pita bread pieces, onion, oregano, lemon juice, garlic, salt, and pepper in food processor until smooth paste forms, about 30 seconds. Transfer bread mixture to large bowl; add lamb and gently mix with hands

---

TEST KITCHEN TIP NO. 87 FLIP TRACKER

When cooking the patties for our Greek-Style Lamb Pita Sandwiches, we found that with 12 small patties all frying at once in a large pan, it was hard to keep track of when each patty needed to be flipped or removed. Laying the meat down in an organized spiral—working clockwise from the handle and toward the center of the pan—made it a simple matter of flipping the meat in the same order that it went into the pan.

This same technique can be applied any time you need to keep track of a large number of items in a pan, from searing scallops to frying meatballs. It's also helpful when managing a grill full of meat or vegetables (for rectangular grills, work in even rows, from left to right and back to front).

until thoroughly combined. Divide mixture into 12 equal pieces and roll into balls. Gently flatten balls into round disks about ½ inch thick and 2½ inches in diameter. (Patties can be prepared through step 1 and refrigerated for up to 1 day or frozen before cooking as directed in step 2. Frozen patties should be thawed in refrigerator prior to cooking.)

2. Place foil-wrapped pitas directly on oven rack and heat for 10 minutes. Meanwhile, heat oil in 12-inch nonstick skillet over medium-high heat until just smoking. Add patties and cook until well browned and crust forms, 3 to 4 minutes. Flip patties, reduce heat to medium, and cook until well browned and crust forms on second side, about 5 minutes longer. Transfer patties to paper towel–lined plate.

3. Using soupspoon, spread ¼ cup Tzatziki Sauce inside each pita. Divide patties evenly among pitas; fill each sandwich with tomato slices, ½ cup shredded lettuce, and 2 tablespoons feta. Serve immediately.

GREEK-STYLE LAMB PITA SANDWICHES WITH BEEF

Decrease lemon juice to 1 tablespoon, increase oregano to 2 tablespoons, increase garlic to 3 cloves, and increase oil to 1 tablespoon. Substitute 1 pound 80 percent lean ground chuck for lamb.

GRILLED GREEK-STYLE LAMB PITA SANDWICHES

The grill imparts a smoky flavor to the meat and pitas in this variation.

1A. FOR A CHARCOAL GRILL: Open bottom vent completely. Light large chimney starter filled three-quarters full with charcoal (4½ quarts). When top coals are partially covered with ash, pour evenly over half of grill. Set cooking grate in place and cover. Heat grill until hot, about 5 minutes.

1B. FOR A GAS GRILL: Turn all burners to high, cover, and heat grill until hot, about 15 minutes. Leave primary burner on high and reduce other burner(s) to medium-high.

2. Clean and oil cooking grate. Place patties on hotter side of grill, cover (if using gas), and cook, turning once, until well browned and crust forms on each side, 8 to 12 minutes. Transfer patties to plate. Place pitas in single layer on hotter side of grill. Cook, turning once, until each pita is thoroughly warmed and faint grill marks appear, 30 to 40 seconds. Remove pitas from grill and wrap tightly with aluminum foil until ready to assemble sandwiches.

TZATZIKI SAUCE

MAKES ABOUT ⅔ CUP, ENOUGH FOR 1 RECIPE GREEK-STYLE LAMB PITA SANDWICHES

Although we prefer the richness of plain whole-milk yogurt, low-fat yogurt can be substituted. Greek yogurt can also be substituted, but use ½ cup and skip the step of draining. While we didn't like the flavor of dried mint, ½ teaspoon dried dill may be used in place of fresh dill.

1	cup plain whole-milk yogurt
½	cucumber, peeled, halved lengthwise, seeded, and chopped fine
1	tablespoon lemon juice
⅜	teaspoon salt
1	tablespoon finely chopped fresh mint or dill
1	small garlic clove, minced

1. Line fine-mesh strainer set over deep container or bowl with 1 paper coffee filter. Spoon yogurt into lined strainer, cover, and refrigerate for 1 hour.

2. Meanwhile, combine cucumber, lemon juice, and ⅛ teaspoon salt in colander set over bowl and let stand 30 minutes.

3. Discard drained liquid from yogurt. Combine thickened yogurt, drained cucumber, remaining ¼ teaspoon salt, mint, and garlic in clean bowl.

CHAPTER 11   Fish and Shellfish

PAN-ROASTED FISH FILLETS

✔ WHY THIS RECIPE WORKS

Pan-roasted fish seems like a simple dish, but in reality it is usually only well executed by practiced chefs. Attempts made by home cooks often result in dry, overbaked fillets. We set out to develop a foolproof recipe for producing succulent, well-browned fillets. We quickly learned we needed thick fillets; skinnier pieces overcooked by the time they achieved a serious sear. We then turned to a common restaurant method to cook the fish: we seared the fillets in a hot pan, flipped them, then transferred the pan to a hot oven to finish cooking. Sprinkling the fillets with sugar accelerated browning on the stovetop, shortening the cooking time and thus ensuring the fish didn't dry out. After a short stay in the oven to finish cooking through, the fish emerged well browned, tender and moist, and best of all, not one taster detected any out-of-place sweetness.

PAN-ROASTED FISH FILLETS

SERVES 4

Thick white fish fillets with a meaty texture, like halibut, cod, sea bass, or red snapper, work best in this recipe. Because most fish fillets differ in thickness, some pieces may finish cooking before others—be sure to immediately remove any fillet that reaches 135 degrees. You will need a 12-inch ovensafe nonstick skillet for this recipe.

- 4   (6- to 8-ounce) skinless white fish fillets, 1 to 1½ inches thick
      Salt and pepper
- ½   teaspoon sugar
- 1   tablespoon vegetable oil
      Lemon wedges or relish (recipes follow)

Adjust oven rack to middle position and heat oven to 425 degrees. Pat fish dry with paper towels and season with salt and pepper. Sprinkle very light dusting of sugar (about ⅛ teaspoon) evenly over 1 side of each fillet. Heat oil in 12-inch ovensafe nonstick skillet over high heat until just smoking. Place fillets in skillet, sugar side down, and press down lightly to ensure even contact with pan. Cook until browned, 1 to 1½ minutes. Using 2 spatulas, flip fillets, then transfer skillet to oven. Roast fillets until centers are just opaque and register 135 degrees, 7 to 10 minutes. Immediately transfer to serving plates and serve with lemon wedges or relish spooned over each fillet.

GREEN OLIVE, ALMOND, AND ORANGE RELISH

MAKES ABOUT 1½ CUPS

If the olives are marinated, rinse and drain them before chopping.

- ½   cup slivered almonds, toasted
- ½   cup green olives, pitted and chopped coarse
- 1   garlic clove, minced
- 1   teaspoon grated orange zest plus ¼ cup juice
- ¼   cup extra-virgin olive oil
- ¼   cup minced fresh mint
- 2   teaspoons white wine vinegar
      Salt and cayenne pepper

Pulse almonds, olives, garlic, and orange zest in food processor until nuts and olives are finely chopped, 10 to 12 pulses. Transfer to bowl and stir in orange juice, oil, mint, and vinegar. Season with salt and cayenne to taste.

ROASTED RED PEPPER, HAZELNUT, AND THYME RELISH

MAKES ABOUT 1½ CUPS

Rubbing the toasted hazelnuts in a kitchen towel is an easy way to remove their skins.

- ½   cup hazelnuts, toasted and skinned
- ½   cup jarred roasted red peppers, rinsed, patted dry, and chopped coarse
- 1   garlic clove, minced
- ½   teaspoon grated lemon zest plus 4 teaspoons juice
- ¼   cup extra-virgin olive oil
- 2   tablespoons chopped fresh parsley
- 1   teaspoon chopped fresh thyme
- ¼   teaspoon smoked paprika
      Salt and pepper

Pulse hazelnuts, roasted peppers, garlic, and lemon zest in food processor until finely chopped, 10 to 12 pulses. Transfer to bowl and stir in lemon juice, oil, parsley, thyme, and paprika. Season with salt and pepper to taste.

REMOVING SKIN FROM FISH FILLETS

If you happen to buy skin-on fillets, some quick knife work can remove it.

1. With sharp knife, separate corner of skin from fish.

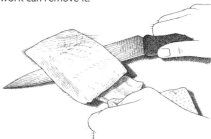

2. Using paper towel to hold skin, slide knife between fish and skin to separate them.

SAUTÉED WHITE FISH FILLETS

✔ WHY THIS RECIPE WORKS

To have the fish and sauce in our sautéed fish fillet recipe ready to serve at the same time, we used fillets of uniform size, between ¼ and I inch thick, small enough so that four fillets could fit in a skillet. We reversed the cooking process specified in most sautéed fish fillet recipes, making the sauce first and keeping it warm in a separate saucepan while cooking the fish.

SAUTÉED WHITE FISH FILLETS
SERVES 4

When it comes to the size of a fish fillet, there are two general categories: thick and thin. Thickness determines in part how long the fillet must be cooked. Do not use fillets thinner than ¼ inch, as they will overcook very quickly. These fillets are good served simply with lemon wedges, or you can prepare them with a sauce (recipes follow).

- ½ cup all-purpose flour
- 4 (6-ounce) boneless, skinless fish fillets, ½ to 1 inch thick, or 8 (3-ounce) boneless, skinless fish fillets, ¼ to ½ inch thick
  Salt and pepper
- 2 tablespoons vegetable oil
  Lemon wedges

I. Place flour in baking dish or pie plate. Pat fish dry with paper towels. Season both sides of each fillet with salt and pepper; let stand until fillets are glistening with moisture, about 5 minutes. If using any tail-end fillets, score and tuck tail under. Coat both sides of fillets with flour, shake off excess, and place in single layer on baking sheet.

2. Heat 1 tablespoon oil in 12-inch nonstick skillet over high heat until shimmering. Place half of fillets in skillet in single layer and immediately reduce heat to medium-high. For thick fillets: Cook,

without moving fish, until edges of fillets are opaque and bottoms are golden brown, 3 to 4 minutes. For thin fillets: Cook, without moving fish, until edges of fillets are opaque and bottoms are lightly browned, 2 to 3 minutes.

3. Using 2 spatulas, gently flip fillets. For thick fillets: Cook on second side until thickest part of fillets is firm to touch and fish flakes easily, 2 to 3 minutes. For thin fillets: Cook on second side until thickest part of fillets is firm to touch and fish flakes easily, 30 to 60 seconds.

4. Transfer fillets to serving platter and tent with aluminum foil. Repeat steps 2 and 3 with remaining 1 tablespoon oil and remaining fillets.

5. Place second batch of fillets on platter with first batch; tilt platter to discard any accumulated liquid. Serve fish immediately with lemon wedges.

SAUTÉED WHITE FISH FILLETS WITH COCONUT–RED CURRY SAUCE
SERVES 4

For those who like assertive flavors, the amount of red curry paste can be doubled; in this case, be conservative when seasoning with salt and pepper. Make sure to prepare the sauce through step I before cooking the fish.

- 2 teaspoons vegetable oil
- 2 teaspoons minced fresh ginger
- 2 teaspoons red curry paste
- 1 small garlic clove, minced
- ½ teaspoon brown sugar
- 1 cup coconut milk
- 3 tablespoons water
- 1½ tablespoons lime juice
- 2 teaspoons fish sauce
- 1 tablespoon chopped fresh cilantro
  Salt and pepper
- 1 recipe Sautéed White Fish Fillets
  Lime wedges

I. Heat oil in medium saucepan over medium heat until shimmering. Off heat, add ginger, curry paste, garlic, and sugar and cook, stirring constantly, until fragrant, about 30 seconds. Add coconut milk, water, lime juice, and fish sauce. Increase heat to high, bring sauce to boil, and boil until sauce is reduced to about 1 cup, about 3 minutes. Off heat, stir in cilantro and season with salt and pepper to taste. Cover to keep warm and set aside, stirring once after about 1 minute, while preparing fish.

2. Stir sauce to recombine and spoon ½ cup over cooked fish fillets. Serve immediately with lime wedges, passing remaining sauce separately.

TUCKING THE FILLET TAIL

I. With sharp knife, cut halfway through flesh crosswise, 2 to 3 inches from tail end. This will create seam to fold tail under.

2. Fold tail end under to create fillet of relatively even thickness.

SAUTÉED WHITE FISH FILLETS WITH GRAPEFRUIT-LIME VINAIGRETTE WITH MINT AND CHIVES

SERVES 4

Remove all white pith and membranes from grapefruit sections destined for garnishing the fish. Make sure to prepare the sauce through step 1 before cooking the fish.

- 2 tablespoons grapefruit juice plus 1 grapefruit half, cut into sections
- 2 tablespoons lime juice
- 1 shallot, minced
- 1 teaspoon honey
- 6 tablespoons extra-virgin olive oil
- 1 tablespoon chopped fresh mint
- 1 tablespoon chopped fresh chives
  Salt and pepper
- 1 recipe Sautéed White Fish Fillets (page 435)

1. Combine grapefruit juice, lime juice, shallot, and honey in bowl. Whisking constantly, gradually add oil. Add mint and chives and season with salt and pepper to taste. Set aside while preparing fish.

2. To serve, whisk vinaigrette to recombine. Drizzle vinaigrette over cooked fish fillets and serve immediately with grapefruit sections.

SAUTÉED WHITE FISH FILLETS WITH ORANGE-TARRAGON CREAM SAUCE

SERVES 4

We like the delicate, fruit flavor of champagne vinegar in this sauce, but white wine vinegar can also be used. Make sure to prepare the sauce through step 1 before cooking the fish.

- 2 teaspoons vegetable oil
- 1 shallot, minced
- 1 cup orange juice
- 3 tablespoons champagne vinegar
- ¼ cup heavy cream
- 2 tablespoons unsalted butter, chilled
- 1 tablespoon minced fresh tarragon
  Salt and pepper
- 1 recipe Sautéed White Fish Fillets (page 435)
  Orange wedges

1. Heat oil in medium saucepan over medium heat until shimmering; add shallot and cook, stirring frequently, until softened and beginning to color, about 1½ minutes. Add orange juice and vinegar, increase heat to high, and bring to boil; boil until reduced to ¾ cup, 4 to 6 minutes. Add heavy cream and continue to cook until slightly reduced, about 1 minute. Off heat, whisk in butter and tarragon, and season with salt and pepper to taste. Cover to keep warm and set aside, stirring once after about 1 minute, while preparing fish.

2. To serve, stir sauce to recombine and spoon ½ cup over cooked fish fillets. Serve immediately with orange wedges, passing remaining sauce separately.

SAUTÉED WHITE FISH FILLETS WITH WHITE WINE–SHALLOT SAUCE

SERVES 4

One tablespoon of lemon juice is cooked into the sauce; an additional tablespoon can be added later, if desired, for a bright, tart flavor. Make sure to prepare the sauce through step 1 before cooking the fish.

- 2 teaspoons vegetable oil
- 2 large shallots, minced
- ½ cup dry white wine
- 1–2 tablespoons lemon juice plus lemon wedges
- 4 tablespoons unsalted butter, chilled
- 1 tablespoon capers, rinsed
- 1 tablespoon chopped fresh parsley
  Salt and pepper
- 1 recipe Sautéed White Fish Fillets (page 435)

1. Heat oil in medium saucepan over medium heat until shimmering. Add shallots and cook, stirring frequently, until softened and beginning to color, about 1½ minutes. Add wine and 1 tablespoon lemon juice, increase heat to high, and bring to boil. Boil until reduced to ¾ cup, 3 to 5 minutes. Off heat, whisk in butter, capers, parsley, and, if desired, remaining 1 tablespoon lemon juice until combined; season with salt and pepper to taste. Cover to keep warm and set aside, stirring once after about 1 minute, while preparing fish.

2. To serve, stir sauce to recombine and spoon ½ cup over cooked fish fillets. Serve immediately with lemon wedges, passing remaining sauce separately.

TEST KITCHEN TIP NO. 88 SHIMMER AND SMOKE

Pan-searing and sautéing both require you to heat the oil in the skillet to a certain heat level. But how do you know when the pan is hot enough? We find visual cues helpful and offer them in our recipes, as follows: When searing thick fish fillets or thick cuts of meat like a roast, steak, bone-in chop, you want the pan very hot. Searing over high heat will give your food a well-browned crust. Look for wisps of smoke rising from the oil—this means the pan is ripping hot and ready. By contrast, when sautéing thin fish fillets, thin, delicate cuts of meat like cutlets, or vegetables such as onions, you want the oil to be just moderately hot. You'll know the pan is ready when the oil shimmers. Why does it make a difference? If you put a thin fillet into a smoking hot pan, the food will do more than sear—it will cook through before you've had time to flip it.

FISH MEUNIÈRE

WHY THIS RECIPE WORKS

The best versions of fish meunière feature perfectly cooked fillets that are delicately crisp and golden brown on the outside and moist and flavorful on the inside, napped with a buttery yet light sauce. Whole Dover sole is the most authentic choice, but it's also prohibitively expensive; either sole or flounder fillets proved to be good stand-ins. To prevent the likelihood of overcooking the fish, the fillets needed to be no less than ⅜ inch thick. For the perfect coating, there was no need to use eggs or bread crumbs. We simply dried the fillets, seasoned them with salt and pepper, and allowed them to sit for five minutes, in which time beads of moisture appeared on the fillets' surface. Then we simply dredged the fillets in flour. A nonstick skillet coated with a mixture of oil and butter prevented sticking. For the sauce, we browned the butter in a traditional skillet (so the changing color was easy to monitor), and brightened it with lemon juice, then poured the mixture over the fish.

FISH MEUNIÈRE WITH BROWNED BUTTER AND LEMON

SERVES 4 TO 6

Try to purchase fillets that are of similar size, and avoid those that weigh less than 5 ounces because they will cook too quickly. A nonstick skillet ensures that the fillets will release from the pan, but for the sauce a traditional skillet is preferable because its light-colored surface will allow you to monitor the color of the butter as it browns.

FISH
- ½ cup all-purpose flour
- 4 (5- to 6-ounce) boneless, skinless sole or flounder fillets, ⅜ inch thick
  Salt and pepper
- 2 tablespoons vegetable oil
- 2 tablespoons unsalted butter, cut into 2 pieces

TEST KITCHEN TIP NO. 89 **SAUTÉING DELICATE FISH FILLETS**

Sautéing delicate fish fillets such as sole or flounder can be tricky because the tender fish is apt to stick to the pan and break apart. Some recipe coat the fillets with egg and flour, which does create a barrier against sticking, but its thick texture and rich flavor overwhelm the fish. Other recipes dredge the fish in flour, but the flour tends to stick in some places and not others, resulting in "bald" spots and uneven browning. The solution we've found is simple: Sprinkle the fillets with salt and pepper and let them stand for 5 minutes. The salt draws out moisture in the fish, creating a thin, wet sheen—just enough for the flour to evenly adhere to. This method produces a crust thin enough to protect the fish without overwhelming the fillets' texture or flavor.

BROWNED BUTTER
- 4 tablespoons unsalted butter, cut into 4 pieces
- 1 tablespoon chopped fresh parsley
- 1½ tablespoons lemon juice
  Salt
  Lemon wedges

1. FOR THE FISH: Adjust oven rack to lower-middle position, set 4 heatproof dinner plates on rack, and heat oven to 200 degrees. Place flour in baking dish or pie plate. Pat fish dry with paper towels, season both sides generously with salt and pepper, and let stand until fillets are glistening with moisture, about 5 minutes. Coat both sides of fillets with flour, shake off excess, and place in single layer on baking sheet.

2. Heat 1 tablespoon oil in 12-inch nonstick skillet over high heat until shimmering, then add 1 tablespoon butter and swirl to coat pan bottom. Carefully place 2 fillets, skinned side up, in skillet. Immediately reduce heat to medium-high and cook, without moving fish, until edges of fillets are opaque and bottom is golden brown, about 3 minutes. Using 2 spatulas, gently flip fillets and cook on second side until thickest part of fillet easily separates into flakes when toothpick is inserted, about 2 minutes longer. Transfer fillets, one to each heated dinner plate, keeping skinned side down, and return plates to oven. Wipe out skillet and repeat with remaining 1 tablespoon oil, remaining 1 tablespoon butter, and remaining fish fillets.

3. FOR THE BROWNED BUTTER: Heat butter in 10-inch skillet over medium-high heat until butter melts, 1 to 1½ minutes. Continue to cook, swirling pan constantly, until butter is golden brown and has nutty aroma, 1 to 1½ minutes. Remove skillet from heat.

4. Remove plates from oven and sprinkle fillets with parsley. Add lemon juice to browned butter and season with salt to taste. Spoon sauce over fish and serve immediately with lemon wedges.

FISH MEUNIÈRE WITH CAPERS

Add 2 tablespoons rinsed capers along with lemon juice in step 3.

FISH MEUNIÈRE WITH TOASTED SLIVERED ALMONDS

Add ¼ cup slivered almonds to skillet when butter has melted in step 2.

COD BAKED IN FOIL

✓ WHY THIS RECIPE WORKS

Cooking mild fish like cod en papillote—in a tightly sealed, artfully folded parchment package so it can steam in its own juices—is an easy, mess-free way to enhance its delicate flavor. If you throw in vegetables, it should add up to a light but satisfying meal. However, without the right blend of flavorings, the fish can taste lean and bland, and not all vegetables pair well with cod. We found that foil was easier to work with than parchment. Placing the packets on the oven's lower-middle rack concentrated the exuded liquid and deepened the flavor. Leeks, carrots, fennel, and zucchini all worked well as the vegetable component. And a tomato and olive oil "salsa" or a compound butter contributed to a full-flavored sauce.

COD BAKED IN FOIL WITH LEEKS AND CARROTS

SERVES 4

Haddock, red snapper, halibut, and sea bass also work well in this recipe as long as the fillets are 1 to 1¼ inches thick. The packets may be assembled several hours ahead of time and refrigerated until ready to cook. If the packets have been refrigerated for more than 30 minutes, increase the cooking time by 2 minutes. Open each packet promptly after baking to prevent overcooking and make sure to open packets away from you to avoid steam burns.

- 4 tablespoons unsalted butter, softened
- 2 garlic cloves, minced
- 1¼ teaspoons finely grated lemon zest, plus lemon wedges
- 1 teaspoon minced fresh thyme
  Salt and pepper
- 2 tablespoons minced fresh parsley
- 2 carrots, peeled and cut into matchsticks
- 2 leeks, white and light green parts only, halved lengthwise, washed thoroughly, and cut into 1-inch-long matchsticks
- ¼ cup dry vermouth or dry white wine
- 4 (6-ounce) skinless cod fillets, 1 to 1¼ inches thick

1. Combine butter, 1 teaspoon garlic, ¼ teaspoon lemon zest, thyme, ¼ teaspoon salt, and ⅛ teaspoon pepper in small bowl. Combine parsley, remaining lemon zest, and remaining garlic in another small bowl and set aside. Place carrots and leeks in medium bowl, season with salt and pepper to taste, and toss to combine.

2. Adjust oven rack to lower-middle position and heat oven to 450 degrees. Cut eight 12-inch-long sheets of aluminum foil; arrange 4 pieces flat on counter. Divide carrot-leek mixture among arranged foil sheets, mounding vegetables in center of each piece. Pour 1 tablespoon vermouth over each mound of vegetables. Pat fish dry with paper towels, season with salt and pepper, and place 1 fillet on top of each vegetable mound. Divide butter mixture among fillets, spreading over top of each piece. Place second square of foil on top of fish, crimp edges together in ½-inch fold, then fold over 3 more times to create a packet about 7 inches square. Place packets on rimmed baking sheet, overlapping slightly if necessary.

3. Bake packets 15 minutes, then carefully open foil, allowing steam to escape away from you. Using thin metal spatula, gently slide fish and vegetables onto plate, along with any accumulated juices, and sprinkle with parsley mixture. Serve immediately, passing lemon wedges separately.

HOW TO CUT CARROTS AND LEEKS INTO MATCHSTICKS

FOR THE CARROTS

1. Peel, then cut carrot into 2-inch segments. Cut thin slice from each segment to create flat base.

2. Using knuckles of non-knife hand to steady carrot, cut each segment into ⅛-inch-thick planks.

3. Working with 3 planks at a time, stack planks and cut into ⅛-inch-thick matchsticks.

FOR THE LEEKS

1. Trim dark green top and bottom ¼ inch of root end from leek, then cut into 2-inch segments.

2. Halve each segment lengthwise and rinse under cold water to remove sediment.

3. Working with 3 to 4 layers at a time, stack layers, then fold in half crosswise and cut into ⅛-inch-thick matchsticks.

COD BAKED IN FOIL WITH FENNEL AND SHALLOTS

SERVES 4

Haddock, red snapper, halibut, and sea bass also work well in this recipe as long as the fillets are 1 to 1¼ inches thick. The packets may be assembled several hours ahead of time and refrigerated until ready to cook. If the packets have been refrigerated for more than 30 minutes, increase the cooking time by 2 minutes. Open each packet promptly after baking to prevent overcooking and make sure to open packets away from you to avoid steam burns.

1	large fennel bulb, stalks discarded, halved, cored, and sliced into ¼-inch strips
2	large shallots, sliced thin
4	tablespoons unsalted butter, softened
2	teaspoons minced fresh tarragon
1	garlic clove, minced
¼	teaspoon grated orange zest plus 2 oranges peeled, quartered, and cut crosswise into ¼-inch-thick pieces
	Salt and pepper
¼	cup dry vermouth or dry white wine
4	(6-ounce) skinless cod fillets, 1 to 1¼ inches thick

1. Combine fennel and shallots in large bowl, cover tightly, and microwave until fennel has started to wilt, 3 to 4 minutes, stirring once halfway through cooking. Combine butter, 1 teaspoon tarragon, garlic, orange zest, ¼ teaspoon salt, and ⅛ teaspoon pepper in small bowl. Combine orange pieces and remaining 1 teaspoon tarragon in second small bowl and set aside.

2. Adjust oven rack to lower-middle position and heat oven to 450 degrees. Cut eight 12-inch-long sheets of aluminum foil; arrange 4 pieces flat on counter. Divide fennel-shallot mixture among arranged foil sheets, mounding vegetables in center of each piece. Pour 1 tablespoon

1. Arrange vegetables on foil first so they will be closest to heat source, then drizzle with vermouth to deepen flavor.

2. Top vegetables with fish and spread compound butter or topping over for increased richness.

3. Top with second piece of foil and crimp edges together in ½-inch fold, then fold over 3 more times to create airtight packet.

vermouth over each mound of vegetables. Pat fish dry with paper towels, season with salt and pepper, and place 1 fillet on top of each vegetable mound. Divide butter mixture among fillets, spreading over top of each piece. Place second square of foil on top of fish, crimp edges together in ½-inch fold, then fold over 3 more times to create a packet about 7 inches square. Place packets on rimmed baking sheet, overlapping slightly if necessary.

3. Bake packets 15 minutes, then carefully open foil, allowing steam to escape away from you. Using thin metal spatula, gently slide fish and vegetables onto plate, along with any accumulated juices. Spoon orange and tarragon mixture over fish and serve immediately.

COD BAKED IN FOIL WITH ZUCCHINI AND TOMATOES

SERVES 4

Haddock, red snapper, halibut, and sea bass also work well in this recipe as long as the fillets are 1 to 1¼ inches thick. The packets may be assembled several hours ahead of time and refrigerated until ready to cook. If the packets have been refrigerated for more than 30 minutes, increase the cooking time by 2 minutes. Open each packet promptly after baking to prevent overcooking and make sure to open packets away from you to avoid steam burns.

2	zucchini, sliced ¼ inch thick
	Salt and pepper
2	plum tomatoes, cored, seeded, and cut into ½-inch pieces
2	tablespoons extra virgin olive oil
2	garlic cloves, minced
1	teaspoon minced fresh oregano
⅛	teaspoon red pepper flakes
¼	cup dry vermouth or dry white wine
4	(6-ounce) skinless cod fillets, 1 to 1¼ inches thick
¼	cup minced fresh basil
	Lemon wedges

1. Toss zucchini with ½ teaspoon salt in large bowl, transfer to colander, and let sit until zucchini releases 1 to 2 tablespoons liquid, about 30 minutes. Line baking sheet with triple layer of paper towels, arrange zucchini on top, cover with another triple layer of paper towels, and firmly press each slice to remove as much liquid as possible. Meanwhile, combine tomatoes, oil, garlic, oregano, pepper flakes, ¼ teaspoon salt, and ⅛ teaspoon pepper in medium bowl.

2. Adjust oven rack to lower-middle position and heat oven to 450 degrees. Cut eight 12-inch-long sheets of aluminum foil; arrange 4 pieces flat on counter. Distribute salted zucchini among arranged foil sheets, mounding vegetables in center of each piece. Pour 1 tablespoon vermouth

over each mound of vegetables. Pat fish dry with paper towels, season with salt and pepper, and place 1 fillet on top of each vegetable mound. Divide tomato mixture among fillets. Place second square of foil on top of fish, crimp edges together in ½-inch fold, then fold over 3 more times to create a packet about 7 inches square. Place packets on rimmed baking sheet, overlapping slightly if necessary.

3. Bake packets 15 minutes, then carefully open foil, allowing steam to escape away from you. Using thin metal spatula, gently slide fish and vegetables onto plate, along with any accumulated juices, and sprinkle with basil. Serve immediately, passing lemon wedges separately.

FISH AND CHIPS

✓ WHY THIS RECIPE WORKS

The fish and chips served at most American pubs is mediocre at best. We wanted to develop a batter that would not only protect the fish as it cooked but would also provide the flesh with a nice, crisp contrast. A wet batter proved to be the most effective way to coat and protect the fish, and we liked beer, the traditional choice, as the liquid component. To keep the coating crisp, we found a 3:1 ratio of flour to cornstarch, along

with a teaspoon of baking powder for airy lightness, was the key. A final layer of flour over the battered fish kept the coating in place as the fish fried.

FISH AND CHIPS
SERVES 4

Any other similarly thick white fish, such as hake or haddock, would work here. For safety, use a Dutch oven with at least a 7-quart capacity. Any beer (even nonalcoholic beer), with the exception of dark stouts and ales, will work in this recipe. Serve with malt vinegar or tartar sauce.

3	pounds russet potatoes, peeled, dried, sides squared off, and cut lengthwise into ½-inch-thick fries
3	quarts plus ¼ cup peanut oil or canola oil
1½	cups all-purpose flour
½	cup cornstarch
	Salt
½	teaspoon cayenne pepper
½	teaspoon paprika
⅛	teaspoon pepper
1	teaspoon baking powder
1½	pounds boneless cod fillets, 1 inch thick, cut into 8 (3-ounce) pieces
1½	cups beer, chilled

1. Place potatoes in large bowl and toss with ¼ cup oil. Cover and microwave until potatoes are partially translucent and pliable but still offer some resistance when pierced with paring knife, 6 to 8 minutes, tossing halfway through cooking time. Carefully uncover, then transfer to fine-mesh strainer set in sink. Rinse potatoes well under cold running water, then spread onto kitchen towels and pat dry. Let rest until room temperature, at least 10 minutes or up to 1 hour.

2. While potatoes cool, whisk flour, cornstarch, 2 teaspoons salt, cayenne, paprika, and pepper in large bowl. Transfer ¾ cup flour mixture to rimmed baking sheet and set aside. Add baking powder to bowl with remaining flour mixture and whisk to combine.

3. Heat 2 quarts oil in Dutch oven over medium heat until 350 degrees. Line baking sheet with triple layer of paper towels. Add fries to hot oil and increase heat to high. Fry, stirring with skimmer or slotted spoon, until potatoes turn light golden and just begin to brown at corners, 6 to 8 minutes. Transfer fries to prepared baking sheet and let drain.

4. Reduce heat to medium-high, add remaining 1 quart oil, and heat oil to 375 degrees. Line baking sheet with triple layer of paper towels. Meanwhile, thoroughly dry fish with paper towels, then dredge in flour mixture on baking sheet, shaking off excess. Transfer coated pieces to wire rack. Add 1¼ cups beer to flour mixture in mixing bowl and stir until mixture is just combined (batter will be lumpy). Add remaining beer as needed, 1 tablespoon at a time, whisking after each addition, until batter falls from whisk in thin, steady stream and leaves faint trail across surface of batter.

5. Using tongs, dip 1 piece fish in batter and, shaking gently, let excess run off. Place battered fish back onto baking sheet with flour mixture and turn to coat both

PREPARING POTATOES FOR FISH AND CHIPS

1. Trim each end. Carefully cut thin slice from 1 side. Rotate the potato, and repeat with remaining sides.

2. Cut each potato lengthwise into ½-inch-thick slices.

3. Cut each potato slice into ½-inch batons.

sides. Repeat with remaining fish, keeping pieces in single layer on baking sheet.

6. When oil reaches 375 degrees, increase heat to high and, using tongs, gently shake excess flour from fish fillets and add fish to oil. Fry, stirring occasionally, until golden brown, 7 to 8 minutes. Transfer fish to prepared baking sheet and let drain. Allow oil to return to 375 degrees.

7. Line baking sheet with triple layer of paper towels. Add all fries back to oil and fry until golden brown and crisp, 3 to 5 minutes. Transfer to paper towels to drain. Season fries with salt to taste and serve immediately with fish.

CRUNCHY OVEN-FRIED FISH

✔ WHY THIS RECIPE WORKS
Batter-fried is the gold standard for fish with a flavorful coating, but frying can be a messy operation, and sometimes we want a healthier alternative. We wanted a recipe for moist, flavorful oven-baked fillets coated in a crunchy crust that would not merely play second fiddle to batter-fried fish, but stand as a worthy dish on its own. Meaty, dense varieties of fish, like swordfish and tuna, didn't provide contrast between crust and interior, and thin fillets overcooked before the coating browned. Cod and haddock proved the best bet. Fresh bread crumbs created the best coating. To avoid soft, undercooked crumbs, we started by adding melted butter while processing the bread crumbs, and then crisped the crumbs in the oven to a deep golden-brown. We dipped the fillets first in flour and then in a thick wash made from eggs and mayonnaise before applying the browned crumbs. Placing the coated fish on a wire rack while baking allowed air to circulate, crisping all sides. We also boosted flavor by adding shallots and parsley to the breading and horseradish, cayenne, and paprika to the egg wash. As a final touch, we made a quick tartar sauce.

CRUNCHY OVEN-FRIED FISH
SERVES 4

To prevent overcooking, buy fish fillets at least 1 inch thick. The bread crumbs can be made up to 3 days in advance, cooled, and stored at room temperature in an airtight container. Serve with Sweet and Tangy Tartar Sauce (recipe follows).

4	hearty slices white sandwich bread, torn into quarters
2	tablespoons unsalted butter, melted
	Salt and pepper
2	tablespoons minced fresh parsley
1	shallot, minced
½	cup plus 1 tablespoon all-purpose flour
2	large eggs
3	tablespoons mayonnaise
2	teaspoons prepared horseradish (optional)
½	teaspoon paprika
¼	teaspoon cayenne pepper (optional)
1¼	pounds skinless cod, haddock, or other thick white fish fillets, 1 to 1½ inches thick, cut into 4 pieces
	Lemon wedges

1. Adjust oven rack to middle position and heat oven to 350 degrees. Pulse bread, melted butter, ¼ teaspoon salt, and ¼ teaspoon pepper in food processor to coarse crumbs, about 10 pulses (you should have about 3½ cups crumbs). Transfer to rimmed baking sheet and bake until deep golden brown and dry, about 15 minutes, stirring twice during baking time. Cool crumbs to room temperature, about 10 minutes. Transfer crumbs to pie plate and toss with parsley and shallot. Increase oven temperature to 425 degrees.

2. Place ¼ cup flour in second pie plate. In third pie plate, whisk eggs, mayonnaise, horseradish (if using), paprika, cayenne (if using), and ¼ teaspoon pepper until combined. Whisk in remaining ¼ cup plus 1 tablespoon flour until smooth.

3. Spray wire rack with vegetable oil spray and place in rimmed baking sheet. Dry fish thoroughly with paper towels and season with salt and pepper. Dredge 1 fillet in flour and shake off excess. Using tongs, coat fillet with egg mixture, then coat with bread-crumb mixture, pressing gently so that thick layer of crumbs adheres to fish. Transfer breaded fish to prepared wire rack. Repeat with remaining 3 fillets.

4. Bake fish until fillets register 140 degrees, 18 to 25 minutes. Using thin spatula, transfer fillets to plates and serve immediately with lemon wedges.

SWEET AND TANGY TARTAR SAUCE
MAKES ABOUT 1 CUP

Making this classic seafood sauce at home is easy and the results are far better than store-bought options.

¾	cup mayonnaise
½	shallot, minced
2	tablespoons capers, rinsed and minced
2	tablespoons sweet pickle relish
1½	teaspoons white vinegar
½	teaspoon Worcestershire sauce
½	teaspoon pepper

TEST KITCHEN TIP NO. 90 THAWING FROZEN FISH

Frozen fish should be fully thawed before cooking, ideally defrosted overnight in the refrigerator. Remove the fish from its packaging, lay it in a single layer on a rimmed plate (to catch any released water), and cover it with plastic wrap. Thoroughly dry fish before cooking. Alternatively, defrost fish under cold running water in its original packaging.

Mix all ingredients together in small bowl. Cover and let sit to blend flavors, about 15 minutes. Stir again before serving. (Sauce can be refrigerated for up to 1 week.)

BAKED SOLE FILLETS WITH HERBS AND BREAD CRUMBS

☑ WHY THIS RECIPE WORKS

We wanted a fuss-free, foolproof sole preparation that was suitable for a weeknight dinner yet impressive and elegant enough to serve to company. We found that rolling the fillets into compact bundles eased the transport from baking dish to plate and covering the baking dish with foil protected the delicate fish from the drying heat of the oven. To ramp up the fillets' mild flavor, we brushed them with Dijon mustard; seasoned them with salt, pepper, fresh herbs, and lemon zest; and drizzled them with melted butter and garlic. Then we rolled them up, drizzled them with more butter, and baked them. For texture, we added a mixture of herbs, butter, and panko bread crumbs to the sole at two intervals. We removed the foil before the fish was done cooking, basted the fillets with pan juices, topped them with most of the bread-crumb mixture, and then returned them to the oven uncovered. Just before serving, we sprinkled the remaining crumbs over the fillets.

BAKED SOLE FILLETS WITH HERBS AND BREAD CRUMBS

SERVES 6

Try to purchase fillets of similar size. If using smaller fillets (about 3 ounces each), serve 2 fillets per person and reduce the baking time in step 3 to 20 minutes. We strongly advise against using frozen fish in this recipe. Freezing can undermine the texture of the fish, making it hard to roll. Fresh basil or dill can be used in place of the tarragon.

3	tablespoons minced fresh parsley
3	tablespoons minced fresh chives
1	tablespoon minced fresh tarragon
1	teaspoon grated lemon zest
5	tablespoons unsalted butter, cut into 5 pieces
2	garlic cloves, minced
6	(6-ounce) boneless, skinless sole or flounder fillets
	Salt and pepper
1	tablespoon Dijon mustard
⅔	cup panko bread crumbs
	Lemon wedges

1. Adjust oven rack to middle position and heat oven to 325 degrees. Combine parsley, chives, and tarragon in small bowl. Reserve 1 tablespoon herb mixture; stir lemon zest into remaining herb mixture.

2. Heat 4 tablespoons butter in 8-inch skillet over medium heat until just melted. Add half of garlic and cook, stirring frequently, until fragrant, 1 to 2 minutes. Remove from heat and set aside.

3. Pat fillets dry with paper towels and season both sides with salt and pepper. Arrange fillets, skinned side up, with tail end pointing away from you. Spread ½ teaspoon mustard on each fillet, sprinkle each evenly with about 1 tablespoon herb–lemon zest mixture, and drizzle each with about 1½ teaspoons garlic butter. Tightly roll fillets from thick end to form cylinders. Set fillets, seam side down, in 13 by 9-inch baking dish. Drizzle remaining garlic butter over fillets, cover baking dish with aluminum foil, and bake 25 minutes. Wipe out skillet with paper towels but do not wash.

4. While fillets are baking, melt remaining 1 tablespoon butter in now-empty skillet over medium heat. Add panko and cook, stirring frequently, until crumbs are deep golden brown, 5 to 8 minutes. Reduce heat to low, add remaining garlic, and cook, stirring constantly, until garlic is fragrant and evenly distributed in crumbs, about 1 minute. Transfer to small bowl, stir in ¼ teaspoon salt, and season with pepper to taste. Let cool, then stir in reserved 1 tablespoon herb mixture.

5. After fillets have baked 25 minutes, remove baking dish from oven. Baste fillets with melted garlic butter from baking dish, sprinkle with all but 3 tablespoons bread crumbs, and continue to bake, uncovered, until fillets register 135 degrees, 6 to 10 minutes longer. Using thin metal spatula, transfer fillets to plates, sprinkle with remaining bread crumbs, and serve with lemon wedges.

TEST KITCHEN TIP NO. 91 FISH: BUYING AND STORING BASICS

When buying fish, whether it's at a specialty seafood shop or a neighborhood supermarket, make sure the source is one with a high volume. High volume means high turnover, which ensures freshness. The store should smell like the sea, not fishy or sour. The fish should be stored on ice (but not sitting in water) or well refrigerated. The flesh should appear moist and shiny, not dull, and with even coloring. It should feel firm, not mushy. Try to have the fish monger slice steaks and fillets to order; it's best to avoid precut. Remember to chill the fish immediately upon getting it home. Fish stored at 32 degrees will keep twice as long as fish stored at the typical home refrigerator temperature of 40 degrees. To create the optimum storage conditions, place fish in a zipper-lock bag on ice (or cover it with ice packs) and store it at the back of the fridge where it's coldest.

SIMPLE PAN-SEARED SALMON

✓ WHY THIS RECIPE WORKS

We wanted to find an effortless method for cooking skin-on salmon that would exploit the fish's high oil content and natural moistness while creating a crisp, even, deeply golden crust; pan-searing was the answer. We preheated the pan over high heat, added a scant teaspoon of oil (butter was too rich and tended to burn), then turned down the heat soon after adding the salmon to the skillet to avoid scorching. We found that removing the salmon just before it was done prevented overcooking; the residual heat finished cooking the fish.

SIMPLE PAN-SEARED SALMON
SERVES 4

To ensure uniform pieces of fish that cook at the same rate, buy a whole center-cut fillet and cut it into 4 pieces. With the addition of the fish fillets, the pan temperature drops; compensate for the heat loss by keeping the heat on medium-high for 30 seconds after adding them. A splatter screen helps reduce the mess of pan-searing. Serve salmon with a sweet and sour chutney (recipe follows), a fresh salsa, an herb-spiked vinaigrette, or a squirt of lemon or lime.

- 1   (1½-pound) skin-on salmon fillet, about 1½ inches thick
      Salt and pepper
- 1   teaspoon canola oil or vegetable oil
      Lime or lemon wedges

1. Use sharp knife to remove any whitish fat from belly of salmon and cut fillet into 4 equal pieces. Pat fillets dry with paper towels and season with salt and pepper. Heat oil in 12-inch nonstick skillet until shimmering, add fillets, skin side down, and cook, without moving, 30 seconds. Reduce heat to medium-high and continue to cook until skin side is well browned and bottom half of fillets turns opaque, 4½ minutes.

BUTTERFLYING SALMON

1. Slice down middle of each fillet, cutting down to but not through skin.

2. Fold halves away from each other so each side lies flat. Skin should act as a hinge.

3. Butterflied salmon should look like salmon steak.

---

2. Turn fillets and cook second side, without moving, until fillets are no longer translucent on exterior and are firm, but not hard, when pressed, 3 minutes for medium-rare (125 degrees). Transfer fillets to serving platter and let sit 1 minute. Pat with paper towels to absorb excess fat on surface, if desired. Serve immediately with lime wedges.

SWEET AND SOUR CHUTNEY WITH ONIONS AND WARM SPICES
MAKES ABOUT ⅓ CUP

Since it takes several minutes to make this chutney, prepare it before cooking the salmon. A little of this intensely flavored condiment goes a long way.

- 1   teaspoon fennel seeds
- ½   teaspoon ground cumin
- ½   teaspoon ground coriander
- ¼   teaspoon ground cardamom
- ¼   teaspoon paprika
- ¼   teaspoon salt
- 2   teaspoons olive oil
- ½   onion, chopped fine
- ¼   cup red wine vinegar
- 1   tablespoon sugar
- 2   tablespoons water
- 1   tablespoon minced fresh parsley

Mix fennel seeds, cumin, coriander, cardamom, paprika, and salt in small bowl; set aside. Heat oil in 10-inch skillet over medium heat. Add onion and cook until soft, 3 to 4 minutes. Add reserved spice mixture and cook until fragrant, about 1 minute. Increase heat to medium-high and add vinegar, sugar, and water; cook until mixture reduces by about one-third and reaches syrupy consistency, about 1½ minutes. Stir in parsley.

PAN-SEARED BUTTERFLIED SALMON

Butterflied salmon should look similar to a salmon steak. The advantage of this method is that both sides of the flesh get a good sear, so there is twice as much of the brown, flavorful crust. We don't recommend it for skin lovers, because the skin never crisps since it is never exposed to the heat.

To butterfly salmon, slice down middle of each fillet, cutting down to but not through skin. Fold halves away from each other so each side lies flat; skin should act as a hinge. Cook butterflied fillets for just 2 to 3 minutes on first side.

PAN-SEARED SALMON WITH SESAME SEED CRUST

For heightened sesame flavor, rub the fish fillets with toasted sesame oil instead of canola or vegetable oil. If you pair this variation with the butterflied fillets variation, double the quantity of sesame seeds and coat both sides of each fillet.

Spread ¼ cup sesame seeds in pie plate.

Rub fillets with 2 teaspoons canola or vegetable oil before seasoning with salt and pepper, then press flesh sides of fillets in sesame seeds to coat. Cook fillets as directed.

GLAZED SALMON

✓ WHY THIS RECIPE WORKS

The traditional method for glazed salmon calls for broiling, but reaching into a broiling-hot oven every minute to baste the fish is a hassle and, even worse, the fillets often burn if your timing isn't spot-on. We wanted a foolproof method for glazed salmon that was succulent and pink throughout while keeping the slightly crusty, flavorful browned exterior commonly associated with broiling. Reducing the temperature and gently baking the fish cooked the salmon perfectly. To rapidly caramelize the fillets before their exteriors had a chance to toughen, we sprinkled the fillets with sugar and quickly pan-seared each side before transferring them to the oven. To ensure the glaze stayed put, we rubbed the fish with a mixture of cornstarch, brown sugar, and salt before searing.

GLAZED SALMON
SERVES 4

To ensure uniform pieces of fish that cook at the same rate, buy a whole center-cut fillet and cut it into 4 pieces. Prepare the glaze before you cook the salmon. You will need a 12-inch ovensafe nonstick skillet for this recipe. If your nonstick skillet isn't ovensafe, sear the salmon as directed in step 2, then transfer it to a rimmed baking sheet, glaze it, and bake as directed in step 3.

- 1 teaspoon packed light brown sugar
- ½ teaspoon kosher salt
- ¼ teaspoon cornstarch
- 1 (1½- to 2-pound) skin-on salmon fillet, about 1½ inches thick
  Pepper
- 1 teaspoon vegetable oil
- 1 recipe glaze (recipes follow)

1. Adjust oven rack to middle position and heat oven to 300 degrees. Combine brown sugar, salt, and cornstarch in small bowl. Use sharp knife to remove any whitish fat from belly of salmon and cut fillet into 4 equal pieces. Pat fillets dry with paper towels and season with pepper. Sprinkle brown sugar mixture evenly over top of flesh side of salmon, rubbing to distribute.

2. Heat oil in 12-inch ovensafe nonstick skillet over medium-high heat until just smoking. Place salmon, flesh side down, in skillet and cook until well browned, about 1 minute. Using tongs, carefully flip salmon and cook on skin side for 1 minute.

3. Remove skillet from heat and spoon glaze evenly over salmon fillets. Transfer skillet to oven and cook until fillets register 125 degrees (for medium-rare) and are still translucent when cut into with paring knife, 7 to 10 minutes. Transfer fillets to serving platter or individual plates and serve.

ASIAN BARBECUE GLAZE
MAKES ABOUT ½ CUP

Toasted sesame oil gives this teriyaki-like glaze rich flavor.

- 2 tablespoons ketchup
- 2 tablespoons hoisin sauce
- 2 tablespoons rice vinegar
- 2 tablespoons packed light brown sugar
- 1 tablespoon soy sauce
- 1 tablespoon toasted sesame oil
- 2 teaspoons Asian chili-garlic sauce
- 1 teaspoon grated fresh ginger

Whisk ingredients together in small saucepan. Bring to boil over medium-high heat; simmer until thickened, about 3 minutes. Remove from heat and cover to keep warm.

POMEGRANATE-BALSAMIC GLAZE
MAKES ABOUT ½ CUP

This fruity, tangy glaze is a perfect match for rich salmon.

- 3 tablespoons light brown sugar
- 3 tablespoons pomegranate juice
- 2 tablespoons balsamic vinegar
- 1 tablespoon whole grain mustard
- 1 teaspoon cornstarch
  Pinch cayenne pepper

Whisk ingredients together in small saucepan. Bring to boil over medium-high heat; simmer until thickened, about 1 minute. Remove from heat and cover to keep warm.

ORANGE-MISO GLAZE
MAKES ABOUT ½ CUP

Miso is a fermented soy bean paste that adds deep flavor to foods. We prefer milder, white miso here, rather than the strong-flavored red miso.

- 1 teaspoon grated orange zest plus ¼ cup juice
- 2 tablespoons white miso
- 1 tablespoon packed light brown sugar
- 1 tablespoon rice vinegar
- 1 tablespoon whole grain mustard
- ¾ teaspoon cornstarch
  Pinch cayenne pepper

TEST KITCHEN TIP NO. 92 JUDGING DONENESS OF FISH

An instant-read thermometer is a useful tool to check doneness in thick fish fillets, but with thin fillets you have to resort to a more primitive test—nicking the fish with a paring knife and then peeking into the interior to judge color and flakiness. White fish, such as cod, should be cooked to medium (about 140 degrees)—that is, the flesh should be opaque but still moist and just beginning to flake; salmon is best cooked to medium-rare (about 125 degrees), with the center still translucent; and tuna is best when rare (about 110 degrees), with only the outer layer opaque and the rest of the fish translucent.

Whisk ingredients together in small saucepan. Bring to boil over medium-high heat; simmer until thickened, about 1 minute. Remove from heat and cover to keep warm.

OVEN-ROASTED SALMON

✓ WHY THIS RECIPE WORKS
Roasting a salmon fillet can create a brown exterior, but often the price is a dry, overcooked interior. For a nicely browned exterior and a silky, moist interior, we developed a hybrid roasting method, preheating the oven to 500 degrees but then turning down the heat to 275 just before placing the fish in the oven. The initial blast of high heat firmed the exterior and rendered some excess fat. Then the fish gently cooked through and at the same time stayed moist as the temperature slowly dropped, while some of the remaining fat was eliminated through several slits made in the skin. Adding an easy relish lent acidity and flavors that balanced the richness of the fish.

OVEN-ROASTED SALMON
SERVES 4

To ensure uniform pieces of fish that cook at the same rate, buy a whole center-cut fillet and cut it into 4 pieces. If your knife is not sharp enough to easily cut through the skin, try a serrated knife. It is important to keep the skin on during cooking to protect the flesh; remove it afterward if you choose not to serve it.

1   (1¾- to 2-pound) skin-on salmon
    fillet, about 1½ inches thick
2   teaspoons olive oil
    Salt and pepper
1   recipe relish (recipes follow)

1. Adjust oven rack to lowest position, place rimmed baking sheet on rack, and heat oven to 500 degrees. Use sharp knife to remove any whitish fat from belly of salmon and cut fillet into 4 equal pieces.

Make 4 or 5 shallow slashes about an inch apart along skin side of each piece of salmon, being careful not to cut into flesh.

2. Pat salmon dry with paper towels. Rub fillets evenly with oil and season with salt and pepper. Reduce oven temperature to 275 degrees and remove baking sheet. Carefully place salmon, skin side down, on baking sheet. Roast until centers of thickest part of fillets are still translucent when cut into with paring knife and thickest part of fillets registers 125 degrees, 9 to 13 minutes. Transfer fillets to serving platter or individual plates, top with relish, and serve.

FRESH TOMATO RELISH
MAKES ABOUT 1½ CUPS

Use fine summer tomatoes for this relish.

12   ounces tomatoes, cored, seeded,
     and cut into ¼-inch dice
½   small shallot, minced
1   small garlic clove, minced
1   tablespoon extra-virgin olive oil
1   teaspoon red wine vinegar
2   tablespoons chopped fresh basil
     Salt and pepper

Combine all ingredients in medium bowl. Season with salt and pepper to taste.

SPICY CUCUMBER RELISH
MAKES ABOUT 2 CUPS

Parsley can be substituted for the mint.

1   cucumber, peeled, halved
      lengthwise, seeded, and cut into
      ¼-inch dice
1   serrano chile, stemmed, seeded,
      and minced
2   tablespoons chopped fresh mint
½   small shallot, minced
1–2   tablespoons lime juice
      Salt

Combine cucumber, chile, mint, shallot, 1 tablespoon lime juice, and ¼ teaspoon salt in medium bowl. Let stand at room temperature to blend flavors, 15 minutes. Adjust seasoning with additional lime juice and salt to taste.

TANGERINE AND GINGER RELISH
MAKES ABOUT 1¼ CUPS

Oranges can be substituted for the tangerines.

4   tangerines
1   scallion, sliced thin
1½   teaspoons grated fresh ginger
2   teaspoons lemon juice
2   teaspoons extra-virgin olive oil
      Salt and pepper

1. Peel tangerines, making sure to remove all pith, and cut into ½-inch pieces. Place pieces in fine-mesh strainer set over medium bowl and drain for 15 minutes.

2. Pour off all but 1 tablespoon tangerine juice from bowl; whisk in scallion, ginger, lemon juice, and oil. Stir in tangerine pieces and season with salt and pepper to taste.

GRAPEFRUIT AND BASIL RELISH
MAKES ABOUT 1 CUP

Regular grapefruits can be substituted for the red grapefruits.

2   red grapefruits
2   tablespoons chopped fresh basil
½   small shallot, minced
2   teaspoons lemon juice
2   teaspoons extra-virgin olive oil
      Salt and pepper

1. Peel grapefruits, making sure to remove all pith, and cut into ½-inch pieces. Place pieces in fine-mesh strainer set over medium bowl and drain for 15 minutes.

2. Pour off all but 1 tablespoon grapefruit juice from bowl; whisk in basil, shallot,

lemon juice, and oil. Stir in grapefruit pieces and season with salt and pepper to taste.

ORANGE AND MINT RELISH
MAKES ABOUT 1 CUP

Orange and mint make a refreshing contrast to the rich salmon. For more information on peeling and cutting oranges, see page 50.

- 3 oranges
- 2 tablespoons chopped fresh mint
- ½ small shallot, minced
- 2 teaspoons lemon juice
- 2 teaspoons extra-virgin olive oil
  Salt and pepper

1. Peel oranges, making sure to remove all pith, and cut into ½-inch pieces. Place pieces in fine-mesh strainer set over medium bowl and drain for 15 minutes.

2. Pour off all but 1 tablespoon orange juice from bowl; whisk in mint, shallot, lemon juice, and oil. Stir in orange pieces and season with salt and pepper to taste.

BROILED SALMON

✔ WHY THIS RECIPE WORKS
We wanted to pull off a crowd-pleasing side of salmon that was moist and firm, with a golden brown crumb crust for a textural contrast. A plain bread-crumb topping seemed bland, but when we toasted the crumbs and mixed in crushed potato chips and chopped dill, the result was a crisp and flavorful coating. A thin layer of mustard boosted flavor and helped the crumb mixture adhere to the fish. One problem: the crust burned by the time the fish was cooked through. We switched gears and broiled the fish almost unadorned until it was nearly done, then spread on the mustard and crumbs for a second run under the broiler to crisp the crust.

BROILED SALMON WITH MUSTARD AND CRISP DILLED CRUST
SERVES 8 TO 10

Heavy-duty aluminum foil measuring 18 inches wide is essential for creating a sling that aids in transferring the cooked fillet to a carving board. Use a large baking sheet so that the salmon will lie flat. If you can't get the fish to lie flat, even when positioning it diagonally on the baking sheet, trim the tail end. If you prefer to cook a smaller 2-pound fillet, ask to have it cut from the thick center of the fillet, not the thin tail end, and begin checking doneness a minute earlier. We prefer thick-cut and kettle-cooked potato chips in this recipe; ridged chips would work in a pinch.

- 3 slices hearty white sandwich bread, crusts removed
- 4 ounces plain high-quality potato chips, crushed into rough ⅛-inch pieces (about 1 cup)
- 6 tablespoons chopped fresh dill
- 1 (3½-pound) skin-on side of salmon, pinbones removed
- 1 teaspoon olive oil
- ¾ teaspoon salt
  Pepper
- 3 tablespoons Dijon mustard

1. Adjust 1 oven rack to upper-middle position and other rack 3 inches from broiler element; heat oven to 400 degrees.

2. Pulse bread in food processor to fairly even ¼-inch pieces, about 10 pulses. Spread crumbs evenly on rimmed baking sheet; toast on lower rack, shaking pan once or twice, until golden brown and crisp, 4 to 5 minutes. Toss bread crumbs, crushed potato chips, and dill together in small bowl and set aside.

3. Change oven setting to heat broiler. Use sharp knife to remove any whitish fat from belly of salmon. Cut piece of heavy-duty foil to be 6 inches longer than fillet. Fold foil lengthwise in thirds and place

lengthwise on rimmed baking sheet; position salmon lengthwise on foil, allowing excess foil to overhang baking sheet. Rub fillet evenly with oil and season with salt and pepper. Broil salmon on upper rack until surface is spotty brown and outer ½ inch of thick end is opaque when gently flaked with paring knife, 9 to 11 minutes. Remove fish from oven, spread evenly with mustard, and press bread-crumb mixture onto fish. Return to lower rack and continue broiling until crust is deep golden brown, about 1 minute longer.

4. Transfer salmon and foil sling to carving board, slide salmon off sling onto carving board and serve.

BROILED SALMON WITH SPICY CITRUS-CILANTRO PASTE AND CRISP CRUST

Process one 1-inch piece peeled fresh ginger, 3 garlic cloves, 3 shallots, 2 stemmed and seeded jalapeño chiles, 2 teaspoons grated lime zest plus 3 tablespoons juice (2 limes), 2 tablespoons honey, and 2 cups cilantro leaves in food processor until smooth, about 30 seconds, scraping down bowl as necessary. Omit dill and substitute ½ cup citrus-cilantro paste for Dijon mustard.

REMOVING PINBONES FROM SALMON

Run your fingers over the surface to feel for pinbones, then remove them with tweezers or needle-nose pliers.

BROILED SALMON WITH CHUTNEY AND CRISP SPICED CRUST

Use a smooth mango chutney for this recipe. If you can find only chunky mango chutney, puree it in a food processor until smooth before using.

Melt 2 tablespoons unsalted butter in 8-inch skillet over medium heat. Off heat, add 1 minced garlic clove, ½ teaspoon ground cumin, ½ teaspoon paprika, ¼ teaspoon ground cinnamon, ¼ teaspoon cayenne, and ¼ teaspoon salt. Set aside. Substitute 3 tablespoons chopped fresh parsley for dill, toss butter-spice mixture into bread crumbs along with potato chips, and substitute 3 tablespoons smooth mango chutney for Dijon mustard.

POACHED SALMON

✔ WHY THIS RECIPE WORKS

When salmon is poached incorrectly, not only is it dry, but the flavor is so washed out that not even the richest sauce can redeem it. We wanted irresistibly supple salmon accented by the delicate flavor of the poaching liquid, accompanied by a simple pan sauce—all in under half an hour. Poaching the salmon in just enough liquid to come half an inch up the side of the fillets meant all we needed was a couple of shallots, a few herbs, and some wine to boost the flavor of the liquid. However, the part of the salmon that wasn't submerged in liquid needed to be steamed for thorough cooking, and the low cooking temperature required to poach the salmon evenly didn't create enough steam. The solution was to increase the ratio of wine to water. The additional alcohol lowered the liquid's boiling point, producing more vapor even at the lower temperature. To keep the bottom of the fillets from overcooking due to direct contact with the pan, we placed them on top of lemon slices for insulation. After removing the salmon, we reduced the liquid and added a few tablespoons of olive oil to create an easy vinaigrette-style sauce.

POACHED SALMON WITH HERB AND CAPER VINAIGRETTE
SERVES 4

To ensure uniform pieces of fish that cook at the same rate, buy a whole center-cut fillet and cut it into 4 pieces. If a skinless whole fillet is unavailable, remove the skin yourself or follow the recipe as directed with a skin-on fillet, adding 3 to 4 minutes to the cooking time in step 2. This recipe will yield salmon fillets cooked to medium-rare.

- 2   lemons
- 2   tablespoons chopped fresh parsley, stems reserved
- 2   tablespoons chopped fresh tarragon, stems reserved
- 1   large shallot, minced
- ½   cup dry white wine
- ½   cup water
- 1   (1¾- to 2-pound) skinless salmon fillet, about 1½ inches thick
- 2   tablespoons capers, rinsed and chopped
- 2   tablespoons extra-virgin olive oil
- 1   tablespoon honey
       Salt and pepper

1. Line plate with paper towels. Cut top and bottom off 1 lemon, then cut into eight to ten ¼-inch-thick slices. Cut remaining lemon into 8 wedges and set aside. Arrange lemon slices in single layer across bottom of 12-inch skillet. Scatter herb stems and 2 tablespoons minced shallot evenly over lemon slices. Add wine and water to skillet.

2. Use sharp knife to remove any whitish fat from belly of salmon and cut fillet into 4 equal pieces. Place salmon fillets in skillet, skinned side down, on top of lemon slices. Set pan over high heat and bring liquid to simmer. Reduce heat to low, cover, and cook until sides are opaque but center of thickest part of fillet is still translucent when cut into with paring knife, or until fillet registers 125 degrees (for medium-rare),

11 to 16 minutes. Remove pan from heat and, using spatula, carefully transfer salmon and lemon slices to prepared plate and tent loosely with aluminum foil.

3. Return pan to high heat and simmer cooking liquid until slightly thickened and reduced to 2 tablespoons, 4 to 5 minutes. Meanwhile, combine chopped parsley and tarragon, remaining minced shallot, capers, oil, and honey in medium bowl. Strain reduced cooking liquid through fine-mesh strainer into bowl with herb mixture, pressing on solids to extract as much liquid as possible. Whisk to combine and season with salt and pepper to taste.

4. Season salmon with salt and pepper. Using spatula, carefully lift and tilt salmon fillets to remove lemon slices. Place salmon on serving platter or individual plates and spoon vinaigrette over top. Serve, passing lemon wedges separately.

POACHED SALMON WITH DILL AND SOUR CREAM SAUCE
SERVES 4

To ensure uniform pieces of fish that cook at the same rate, buy a whole center-cut fillet and cut it into 4 pieces. If a skinless whole fillet is unavailable, remove the skin yourself or follow the recipe as directed with a skin-on fillet, adding 3 to 4 minutes to the cooking time in step 2. This recipe will yield salmon fillets that are cooked to medium-rare.

- 2   lemons
- 2   tablespoons minced fresh dill fronds plus 8–12 dill stems
- 1   large shallot, minced
- ½   cup dry white wine
- ½   cup water
- 1   (1¾- to 2-pound) skinless salmon fillet, about 1½ inches thick
- 1   tablespoon Dijon mustard
- 2   tablespoons sour cream
- 2   tablespoons unsalted butter

1. Line plate with paper towels. Cut top and bottom off 1 lemon, then cut into eight to ten ¼-inch-thick slices. Cut remaining lemon into 8 wedges and set aside. Arrange lemon slices in single layer across bottom of 12-inch skillet. Scatter dill stems and 2 tablespoons minced shallots evenly over lemon slices. Add wine and water to skillet.

2. Use sharp knife to remove any whitish fat from belly of salmon and cut fillet into 4 equal pieces. Place salmon fillets in skillet, skinned side down, on top of lemon slices. Set pan over high heat and bring liquid to simmer. Reduce heat to low, cover, and cook until sides are opaque but center of thickest part of fillet is still translucent when cut into with paring knife or until fillet registers 125 degrees (for medium-rare), 11 to 16 minutes. Remove pan from heat and, using spatula, carefully transfer salmon and lemon slices to prepared plate and tent loosely with aluminum foil.

3. Return pan to high heat and simmer cooking liquid until slightly thickened and reduced to 2 tablespoons, 4 to 5 minutes. Strain cooking liquid through fine-mesh strainer into medium bowl; discard solids. Return strained liquid to skillet; whisk in Dijon mustard and remaining 2 tablespoons shallot. Simmer over high heat until slightly thickened and reduced to 2 tablespoons, 4 to 5 minutes. Whisk in sour cream and juice from 1 reserved lemon wedge; simmer 1 minute. Remove from heat; whisk in butter and 2 tablespoons minced dill fronds. Season with salt and pepper to taste.

4. Season salmon lightly with salt and pepper. Using spatula, carefully lift and tilt salmon fillets to remove lemon slices. Place salmon on serving platter or individual plates and spoon sauce over top. Serve, passing lemon wedges separately.

POACHED SALMON WITH BOURBON AND MAPLE
SERVES 4

To ensure uniform pieces of fish that cook at the same rate, buy a whole center-cut fillet and cut it into 4 pieces. If a skinless whole fillet is unavailable, remove the skin yourself or follow the recipe as directed with a skin-on fillet, adding 3 to 4 minutes to the cooking time in step 2. This recipe will yield salmon fillets that are cooked to medium-rare.

1	lemon
3	tablespoons maple syrup
2	tablespoons bourbon or brandy
2	tablespoons whole grain mustard
1	tablespoon cider vinegar
1	shallot, sliced thin
¾	cup water
1	(1¾- to 2-pound) skinless salmon fillet, about 1½ inches thick
1	tablespoon unsalted butter
1	tablespoon chopped chives
	Salt and pepper

1. Line plate with paper towels. Cut top and bottom off lemon, then cut into eight to ten ¼-inch-thick slices. Arrange lemon slices in single layer across bottom of 12-inch skillet. Whisk maple syrup, bourbon, mustard, vinegar, and shallot together in small bowl. Add syrup mixture and water to skillet.

2. Use sharp knife to remove any whitish fat from belly of salmon and cut fillet into 4 equal pieces. Place salmon fillets in skillet, skinned side down, on top of lemon slices. Set pan over high heat and bring liquid to simmer. Reduce heat to low, cover, and cook until sides are opaque but center of thickest part of fillet is still translucent when cut into with paring knife, or until fillet registers 125 degrees (for medium-rare), 11 to 16 minutes. Remove pan from heat and, using spatula, carefully transfer

salmon and lemon slices to prepared plate and tent loosely with aluminum foil.

3. Return pan to high heat and simmer cooking liquid until slightly thickened and reduced to 2 tablespoons, 4 to 5 minutes. Remove pan from heat and whisk in butter and chives. Season with salt and pepper to taste.

4. Season salmon with salt and pepper. Using spatula, carefully tilt salmon fillets to remove lemon slices. Place salmon on serving platter or individual plates, spoon sauce over top, and serve.

OVEN-POACHED SIDE OF SALMON

✔ WHY THIS RECIPE WORKS

Serving a side of salmon is an elegant choice when entertaining, but fish poachers are a costly investment and hardly seem worth it for use only a few times a year. We wanted a method for achieving a side of salmon cooked in a moist environment without the need for a poacher. To do this, we decided to get rid of the water altogether and steam the salmon in its own moisture. We wrapped the seasoned fish in heavy-duty aluminum foil and placed it directly on the oven rack, which offered more even cooking between top and bottom than using a baking sheet. Cooking it low and slow gave us the best results—moist, rich fish.

OVEN-POACHED SIDE OF SALMON
SERVES 8 TO 10

If serving a big crowd, you can oven-poach two individually wrapped sides of salmon in the same oven (on the upper-middle and lower-middle racks) without altering the cooking time. White wine vinegar can be substituted for the cider vinegar. The salmon is good on its own with just lemon wedges, or you can serve it with Horseradish Cream Sauce with Chives (recipe follows).

1. Cut 2 sheets of heavy-duty foil about 1 foot longer than fish. Fold up 1 long side of each piece of foil by 3 inches.

2. Lay sheets side by side, folded sides together; overlap edges and fold to create 1-inch seam, then press seam flat with fingers.

3. Lay third sheet of foil over seam and spray with vegetable oil spray.

4. Lay salmon down center of foil and fold edges up and over salmon, creating seam at top. Fold ends to secure seam, making sure not to crimp too tightly.

---

1   (4-pound) skin-on side of salmon, pinbones removed
    Salt
2   tablespoons cider vinegar
6   sprigs fresh tarragon or dill
2   lemons, sliced thin
2   tablespoons minced fresh tarragon or dill
    Lemon wedges

1. Adjust oven rack to middle position and heat oven to 250 degrees. Cut 2 sheets of heavy-duty aluminum foil about 1 foot longer than fish. Fold up 1 long side of each piece of foil by 3 inches. Lay sheets side by side, folded sides together; overlap edges and fold to create 1-inch seam, then press seam flat with your fingers. Lay third sheet of foil over seam and spray with vegetable oil spray.

2. Pat salmon dry with paper towels, then season with salt. Lay salmon, skin side down, on top of foil. Sprinkle with vinegar and lay herb sprigs on top. Arrange lemon slices on top of herbs. Crimp foil down over fish.

3. Lay foil-wrapped fish directly on baking rack (without baking sheet) and cook until flesh has turned from pink to orange and thickest part registers 135 to 140 degrees, 45 to 60 minutes.

4. Remove fish from oven and open foil. Let salmon cool at room temperature for 30 minutes.

5. Pour off any accumulated liquid. Reseal salmon in foil and refrigerate until cold, about 1 hour.

6. To serve, unwrap salmon. Brush away lemon, herbs, and any solidified poaching liquid. Transfer fish to serving platter. Sprinkle salmon with minced tarragon and serve with lemon wedges.

HORSERADISH CREAM SAUCE WITH CHIVES

MAKES ABOUT 2 CUPS

The cream in this sauce is meant to be thickened only, not fully whipped. If you like your sauce less spicy, feel free to use less horseradish.

1   cup heavy cream, chilled
¼   cup minced fresh chives
1   (2-inch) piece fresh horseradish root, grated, or 2 tablespoons prepared horseradish
2   teaspoons lemon juice

Beat cream in deep bowl with hand-held mixer at medium speed until thick but not yet able to hold soft peaks, about 1½ minutes. Whisk in chives, horseradish root, and lemon juice until just combined. (Sauce can be covered and refrigerated for up to 2 hours; whisk briefly just before serving).

CRISPY SALMON CAKES

✔ WHY THIS RECIPE WORKS

We wanted to give the classic New England fish cake, usually made with cod or haddock, a new spin by using salmon. We were after pure salmon flavor, combined with a few choice complementary ingredients and just enough binder to hold the cakes together. This recipe also needed to be easy enough to make for a midweek supper. Fresh salmon easily beat out canned, and we quickly ditched the typical fish cake's potato binder in favor of mayonnaise and bread crumbs. For cakes that held together but weren't pasty, we pulsed 1-inch pieces of fresh salmon in the food processor in batches. Coating the cakes in ultra-crisp panko bread crumbs ensured just the right crisped exterior. A few additions— Dijon mustard, scallion, shallot, lemon juice, and parsley—took our salmon cakes to the next level without adding much more work. After a few minutes in the skillet, our fresh salmon cakes were ready for the table.

CRISPY SALMON CAKES
SERVES 4

When processing the salmon it is okay to have some pieces that are larger than ¼ inch. It is important to avoid overprocessing the fish. If buying a skin-on salmon fillet, purchase 1⅓ pounds of fish; this will yield 1¼ pounds of fish after skinning.

- 3 tablespoons plus ¾ cup panko bread crumbs
- 1 scallion, sliced thin
- 1 shallot, minced
- 2 tablespoons minced fresh parsley
- 2 tablespoons mayonnaise
- 4 teaspoons lemon juice
- 1 teaspoon Dijon mustard
- ¾ teaspoon salt
- ¼ teaspoon pepper
  Pinch cayenne pepper
- 1 (1¼-pound) skinless salmon fillet, cut into 1-inch pieces
- ½ cup vegetable oil
  Lemon wedges, 1 recipe Sweet and Tangy Tartar Sauce (page 441), or 1 recipe Creamy Lemon-Herb Dipping Sauce (recipe follows)

1. Line plate with paper towels and set aside. Combine 3 tablespoons panko, scallion, shallot, parsley, mayonnaise, lemon juice, mustard, salt, pepper, and cayenne in bowl. Working in 3 batches, pulse salmon in food processor until coarsely chopped into ¼-inch pieces, about 2 pulses, transferring each batch to bowl with panko mixture. Gently mix until uniformly combined.

2. Place remaining ¾ cup panko in shallow baking dish or pie plate. Using ⅓-cup measure, scoop level amount of salmon mixture and transfer to baking sheet; repeat to make 8 cakes. Carefully coat each cake in bread crumbs, gently patting cake into disk measuring 2¾ inches in diameter and 1 inch high. Return coated cakes to baking sheet.

3. Heat oil in 12-inch skillet over medium-high heat until shimmering. Place cakes in skillet and cook, without moving, until golden brown, about 2 minutes. Carefully flip cakes and cook until second side is golden brown, 2 to 3 minutes. Transfer cakes to prepared plate to drain for 1 minute. Serve with lemon wedges or sauce.

CRISPY SALMON CAKES WITH LOX, DILL, AND CAPERS

You can substitute smoked salmon for the fresh salmon here if lox is unavailable.

Substitute 4 ounces chopped lox for 4 ounces of fresh salmon. Omit parsley and reduce salt to ½ teaspoon. Add 1 tablespoon chopped capers and 1 tablespoon chopped fresh dill to mixture in step 1.

CREAMY LEMON-HERB DIPPING SAUCE
MAKES ABOUT ½ CUP

- ½ cup mayonnaise
- 2 tablespoons plus 1½ teaspoons lemon juice
- 1 tablespoon minced fresh parsley
- 1 tablespoon minced fresh thyme
- 1 scallion, minced
- ½ teaspoon salt
  Pepper

Mix all ingredients in small bowl and season with pepper to taste. Cover and chill until flavors blend, at least 30 minutes.

CLASSIC PAN-FRIED CRAB CAKES

✔ WHY THIS RECIPE WORKS

We wanted cakes with a crisp brown exterior and creamy, well-seasoned filling that tasted of sweet crab, not filler. Fresh crabmeat provided the best taste and texture and was worth its high price tag. We found pasteurized crabmeat was a good second choice, but that canned crabmeat (sold near canned tuna) should be avoided at all costs. After experimenting with different binders, we settled on fine dry bread crumbs; their mild flavor kept the crabmeat front and center, they held the cakes together well, and they mixed easily with the crab. An egg and some mayonnaise bound the cakes together. Old Bay is the traditional seasoning for crab, and there was no reason to leave it out; some herbs and white pepper were the only other additions we found necessary. Carefully folding the ingredients together rather than stirring them kept the texture chunky rather than pasty, and a short stint in the refrigerator ensured that the cakes wouldn't fall apart during their cooking time in the skillet.

PAN-FRIED CRAB CAKES
SERVES 4

The amount of bread crumbs you add will depend on the crabmeat's juiciness. Start with the smallest amount, and add more after adding the egg only if the cakes won't hold together. If you can't find fresh jumbo lump crabmeat, pasteurized crabmeat, though not as good, is a decent substitute. Either a nonstick or a traditional skillet will work for this recipe, but a nonstick simplifies cleanup.

- 1 pound jumbo lump crabmeat, picked over to remove cartilage and shell fragments
- 4 scallions, green parts only, minced
- 1 tablespoon chopped fresh parsley, cilantro, dill, or basil
- ¼ cup mayonnaise
- 2–4 tablespoons plain dry bread crumbs
- 1½ teaspoons Old Bay seasoning
  Salt and ground white pepper
- 1 large egg, lightly beaten
- ¼ cup all-purpose flour
- ¼ cup vegetable oil
  Lemon wedges, 1 recipe Sweet and Tangy Tartar Sauce (page 441), or 1 recipe Creamy Chipotle Chile Sauce (recipe follows)

1. Line rimmed baking sheet with parchment paper. Gently mix crabmeat, scallions, parsley, mayonnaise, 2 tablespoons bread crumbs, and Old Bay in medium bowl, being careful not to break up crab lumps. Season with salt and white pepper to taste. Carefully fold in egg with rubber spatula until mixture just clings together. If cakes don't bind, add more bread crumbs, 1 tablespoon at a time, until they do.

2. Divide crab mixture into 4 portions and shape each portion into fat, round cake, about 3 inches in diameter and 1½ inches thick. Arrange on prepared baking sheet, cover, and refrigerate at least 30 minutes or up to 24 hours.

3. Place flour in shallow baking dish or pie plate. Lightly dredge cakes in flour. Heat oil in 12-inch nonstick skillet over medium-high heat until shimmering. Gently lay floured cakes in skillet and cook until exteriors are crisp and browned, 4 to 5 minutes per side. Serve immediately with lemon wedges or sauce.

CREAMY CHIPOTLE CHILE SAUCE
MAKES ABOUT ½ CUP

You can vary the spiciness of this sauce by adjusting the amount of chipotle to suit your taste.

- ¼ cup mayonnaise
- ¼ cup sour cream
- 2 teaspoons minced canned chipotle chile in adobo sauce
- 2 teaspoons minced fresh cilantro
- 1 small garlic clove, minced
- 1 teaspoon lime juice

Mix all ingredients in small bowl. Cover and refrigerate until flavors blend, about 30 minutes. (Sauce can be refrigerated for up to 4 days.)

PAN-ROASTED HALIBUT STEAKS

✔ WHY THIS RECIPE WORKS

Chefs often choose to braise halibut instead of pan-roasting or sautéing because this moist-heat cooking technique keeps the fish from drying out. The problem is that braising doesn't allow for browning, which adds great flavor to fish. We didn't want to make any compromises on either texture or flavor, so we set out to develop a technique for cooking halibut that would produce perfectly cooked, moist, and tender fish with good browning. A combination of pan-searing and oven-roasting proved best. To be sure the steaks wouldn't overcook, we seared them on one side in a piping-hot skillet, then turned them over before placing them in the oven to finish cooking through. When they were done, the steaks were browned but still moist inside. To complement the lean fish, we developed a few flavored butters and a bright vinaigrette.

PAN-ROASTED HALIBUT STEAKS
SERVES 4 TO 6

If you plan to serve the fish with a flavored butter or sauce (recipes follow), prepare it before cooking the fish. Even well-dried fish can cause the hot oil in the pan to splatter. You can minimize splattering by laying the halibut steaks in the pan gently and putting the edge closest to you in the pan first so the far edge falls away from you.

- 2 (1¼-pound) skin-on full halibut steaks, 1¼ inches thick and 10 to 12 inches long, trimmed of cartilage
- 2 tablespoons olive oil
  Salt and pepper
- 1 recipe flavored butter or vinaigrette (recipes follow)

1. Rinse halibut steaks, dry well with paper towels, and trim cartilage from both ends. Adjust oven rack to middle position and heat oven to 425 degrees. When oven reaches 425 degrees, heat oil in 12-inch skillet over high heat until just smoking.

2. Meanwhile, sprinkle both sides of steaks with salt and pepper. Reduce heat to medium-high and swirl oil in skillet to distribute. Carefully lay steaks in skillet and cook, without moving, until spotty brown, about 4 minutes (if steaks are thinner than 1¼ inches, check browning at 3½ minutes; steaks thicker than 1½ inches may require extra time, so check at 4½ minutes). Off heat, flip steaks using 2 thin-bladed metal spatulas.

3. Transfer skillet to oven and roast until steaks register 140 degrees, flakes loosen, and flesh is opaque when checked with paring knife, about 9 minutes (thicker steaks may take up to 10 minutes). Carefully remove hot skillet from oven and separate skin and bones from fish with spatula. Transfer fish to warm platter and serve immediately dolloped with flavored butter or drizzled with vinaigrette.

TRIMMING CARTILAGE
FROM HALIBUT

Cutting off the cartilage at the ends of the steaks ensures that they will fit neatly in the pan and diminishes the likelihood that the small bones located there will end up on your dinner plate.

ANCHOVY-GARLIC BUTTER WITH LEMON AND PARSLEY

MAKES ABOUT ¼ CUP

The anchovy adds great depth to this butter.

- 4 tablespoons unsalted butter, softened
- 2 tablespoons minced fresh parsley
- 1½ teaspoons lemon juice
- 1 garlic clove, minced
- 1 anchovy fillet, rinsed and minced
- ½ teaspoon salt

Beat butter with fork until light and fluffy. Stir in parsley, lemon juice, garlic, anchovy, and salt until thoroughly combined.

CHIPOTLE-GARLIC BUTTER WITH LIME AND CILANTRO

MAKES ABOUT ¼ CUP

This flavorful butter is great with halibut as well as swordfish and other meaty fish.

- 4 tablespoons unsalted butter, softened
- 2 teaspoons minced fresh cilantro
- 1½ teaspoons minced canned chipotle chile in adobo sauce plus 1 teaspoon adobo sauce
- 1 garlic clove, minced
- 1 teaspoon honey
- 1 teaspoon grated lime zest
- ½ teaspoon salt

Beat butter with fork until light and fluffy. Stir in cilantro, chipotle and adobo sauce, garlic, honey, lime zest, and salt until thoroughly combined.

CHUNKY CHERRY TOMATO–BASIL VINAIGRETTE

MAKES 1½ CUPS

Scallions can be substituted for the shallots.

- 6 ounces cherry or grape tomatoes, quartered
- ¼ teaspoon salt
- ¼ teaspoon pepper
- 6 tablespoons extra-virgin olive oil
- 3 tablespoons lemon juice
- 2 shallots, minced
- 2 tablespoons minced fresh basil

Combine tomatoes with salt and pepper in medium bowl and let stand until juicy and seasoned, about 10 minutes. Whisk oil, lemon juice, shallots, and basil in small bowl; add to tomatoes and toss to combine.

PAN-SEARED SESAME-CRUSTED TUNA STEAKS

✓ WHY THIS RECIPE WORKS
Moist and rare in the middle with a nice exterior crust, pan-seared tuna is a popular entrée in restaurants. To make this dish at home, we found starting with high-quality tuna—sushi grade if possible—was paramount. A thickness of at least 1 inch was necessary for the tuna to remain rare at the center and at the same time achieve a good sear on the exterior. Before searing the tuna in a nonstick skillet, we rubbed the steaks with oil and coated them with sesame seeds. The sesame seeds browned during cooking and formed a beautiful, nutty-tasting crust.

PAN-SEARED SESAME-CRUSTED TUNA STEAKS

SERVES 4

Most members of the test kitchen staff prefer their tuna steaks rare to medium-rare; the cooking times given in the recipe are for steaks cooked to these two degrees of doneness. For tuna steaks cooked medium, observe the timing for medium-rare, then tent the steaks with aluminum foil for 5 minutes before slicing. If you prefer tuna steaks cooked so rare that they are still cold in the center, try to purchase steaks that are 1½ inches thick and cook them according to the timing below for rare steaks. Bear in mind, though, that the cooking times below are estimates; check for doneness by nicking the fish with a paring knife. Serve with Ginger-Soy Sauce with Scallions or Avocado-Orange Salsa (recipes follow), if desired.

- ¾ cup sesame seeds
- 4 (8-ounce) tuna steaks, 1 inch thick
- 2 tablespoons vegetable oil
  Salt and pepper

1. Spread sesame seeds in shallow baking dish or pie plate. Pat tuna steaks dry with paper towels, rub steaks all over with 1 tablespoon oil, then season with salt and pepper. Press both sides of each steak in sesame seeds to coat.

2. Heat remaining 1 tablespoon oil in 12-inch nonstick skillet over high heat until just smoking. Add tuna steaks and cook 30 seconds without moving. Reduce heat to medium-high and continue to cook until seeds are golden brown, about 1½ minutes. Using tongs, carefully flip tuna steaks and cook, without moving, until golden brown on second side and centers register 110 degrees (for rare), about 1½ minutes (steaks will be opaque at perimeters and translucent red at center when checked with tip of paring knife), or 125 degrees (for medium-rare), about 3 minutes (steaks will be opaque at perimeters and reddish pink at center). Cut into ¼-inch-thick slices and serve.

SERVING HALIBUT STEAKS

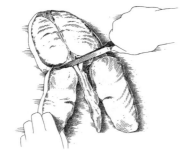

Remove skin from cooked steaks and separate each quadrant of meat from bones by slipping spatula or knife gently between them.

PAN-SEARED PEPPER-CRUSTED TUNA STEAKS

Omit sesame seeds and press ½ teaspoon cracked black or white peppercorns into each side of oiled tuna steaks.

GINGER-SOY SAUCE WITH SCALLIONS
MAKES I SCANT CUP

If available, serve pickled ginger and wasabi, passed separately, with the tuna and this sauce.

- ¼ cup soy sauce
- ¼ cup rice vinegar
- ¼ cup water
- 2½ teaspoons sugar
- 1 scallion, sliced thin
- 2 teaspoons grated fresh ginger
- 1½ teaspoons toasted sesame oil
- ½ teaspoon red pepper flakes

Combine all ingredients in a small bowl, stirring to dissolve sugar.

AVOCADO-ORANGE SALSA
MAKES ABOUT I CUP

To keep the avocado from discoloring, prepare this salsa just before you cook the main dish. See page 50 for information on segmenting oranges.

- 1 large orange
- 1 avocado, halved, pitted, and diced medium
- 2 tablespoons minced red onion
- 2 tablespoons minced fresh cilantro
- 1 small jalapeño chile, stemmed, seeded, and minced
- 4 teaspoons lime juice
- Salt

Peel orange, making sure to remove all pith, and cut into pieces. Combine all ingredients in small bowl and season with salt to taste.

PAN-SEARED SCALLOPS

✔ WHY THIS RECIPE WORKS

Producing crisp-crusted restaurant-style scallops means overcoming two obstacles: chemically treated scallops and weak stovetops. We wanted to achieve superior pan-seared scallops that had a perfectly brown crust and no hint of off-flavors. We decided to work with wet scallops (those that are chemically treated with STP, a solution of water and sodium tripolyphosphate, to increase shelf life and retain moisture) first. If we could develop a good recipe for finicky wet scallops, it would surely work with premium dry (untreated) scallops. We found that waiting to add the scallops to the skillet until the oil was beginning to smoke, cooking the scallops in two batches instead of one, and switching to a nonstick skillet were all steps in the right direction. But it wasn't until we tried a common restaurant technique—butter basting—that our scallops really improved. We seared the scallops in oil on one side and added butter to the skillet after flipping them. (Butter contains milk proteins and sugars that brown rapidly when heated.) We then used a large spoon to ladle the foaming butter over the scallops. Waiting to add the butter ensured that it had just enough time to work its browning magic on the scallops, but not enough time to burn. Next we addressed the lingering flavor of STP. Unable to rinse it away, we decided to mask it by soaking the scallops in a saltwater brine containing lemon juice. For dry scallops, we simply skipped the soaking step and proceeded with the recipe.

TEST KITCHEN TIP NO. 93 **BUYING SCALLOPS**

When buying sea scallops, look first at their color. Scallops are naturally ivory or pinkish tan; processing (dipping them into a phosphate and water mixture to extend shelf life) turns them bright white. Processed scallops are slippery and swollen and are usually sitting in a milky white liquid at the store. You should look for unprocessed scallops (also called dry scallops), which are sticky and flabby; they will taste fresher than processed scallops and will develop a nice crust when browned because they are not pumped full of water.

PAN-SEARED SCALLOPS
SERVES 4

We strongly recommend purchasing "dry" scallops (those without chemical additives). Dry scallops will look ivory or pinkish and feel tacky; wet scallops look bright white and feel slippery. If using wet scallops, soak them in a solution of I quart cold water, ¼ cup lemon juice, and 2 tablespoons salt for 30 minutes before proceeding with step I, and do not season with salt in step 2. To remove the tendons from the scallops, simply peel away the small, rough textured crescent-shaped tendon and discard.

- 1½ pounds large sea scallops, tendons removed
  Salt and pepper
- 2 tablespoons vegetable oil
- 2 tablespoons unsalted butter
  Lemon wedges or sauce (recipes follow)

1. Place scallops on rimmed baking sheet lined with clean kitchen towel. Place second clean kitchen towel on top of scallops and press gently on towel to blot liquid. Let scallops sit at room temperature 10 minutes while towels absorb moisture.

2. Sprinkle scallops on both sides with salt and pepper. Heat 1 tablespoon oil in 12-inch nonstick skillet over high heat until just smoking. Add half of scallops in single layer, flat side down, and cook, without moving, until well browned, 1½ to 2 minutes.

3. Add 1 tablespoon butter to skillet. Using tongs, flip scallops and continue to cook, using large spoon to baste scallops with melted butter (tilt skillet so butter runs to one side) until sides of scallops are firm and centers are opaque, 30 to 90 seconds longer (remove smaller scallops as they finish cooking). Transfer scallops to large plate and tent loosely with aluminum foil. Wipe out skillet with wad of paper towels and repeat cooking with remaining oil, scallops, and butter. Serve immediately with lemon wedges or sauce.

GINGER BUTTER SAUCE
MAKES ABOUT ¾ CUP

The richness of the cream and butter is balanced well by the bolder ingredients, like the cayenne and white wine vinegar, in this recipe.

½	cup dry white wine
2	tablespoons white wine vinegar
I	tablespoon grated fresh ginger
3	garlic cloves, minced
I	small shallot, minced
¼	cup heavy cream
12	tablespoons unsalted butter, cut into 12 pieces and chilled
½	teaspoon salt
	Pinch cayenne pepper

Combine wine, vinegar, ginger, garlic, and shallot in small saucepan and bring to boil over high heat. Lower heat to medium-high and simmer until mixture is reduced by half, about 5 minutes. Add cream and continue to simmer until mixture is reduced by half, 2 to 3 minutes longer. Strain mixture through fine-mesh strainer into small bowl; wipe out saucepan. Return mixture to saucepan set over medium heat. Whisk in 2 pieces of butter until melted. Continue adding butter, 2 pieces at a time, until all butter has been incorporated. Stir in salt and cayenne; cover and keep warm.

LEMON BROWNED BUTTER
MAKES ABOUT ¼ CUP

Watch the butter carefully, as it can go from brown to burnt quickly.

4	tablespoons unsalted butter, cut into 4 pieces
I	small shallot, minced
I	tablespoon minced fresh parsley
½	teaspoon minced fresh thyme
2	teaspoons lemon juice
	Salt and pepper

Heat butter in small saucepan over medium heat and cook, swirling pan constantly, until butter turns dark golden brown and has nutty aroma, 4 to 5 minutes. Add shallot and cook until fragrant, about 30 seconds. Remove pan from heat and stir in parsley, thyme, and lemon juice. Season with salt and pepper to taste. Cover to keep warm.

TOMATO-GINGER SAUCE
MAKES ABOUT ½ CUP

Watch the butter carefully, as it can go from brown to burnt quickly.

6	tablespoons unsalted butter
I	plum tomato, cored, seeded, and chopped
I	tablespoon grated fresh ginger
I	tablespoon lemon juice
¼	teaspoon red pepper flakes
	Salt

Heat butter in small saucepan over medium heat and cook, swirling pan constantly, until butter turns dark golden brown and has nutty aroma, 4 to 5 minutes. Add tomato, ginger, lemon juice, and pepper flakes and cook, stirring constantly, until fragrant, about 1 minute. Season with salt to taste. Cover to keep warm.

ORANGE-LIME VINAIGRETTE
MAKES ABOUT ½ CUP

We like the fruity, peppery flavor extra-virgin olive oil adds to this vinaigrette, but it is overpowering on its own so we use half vegetable oil, half extra-virgin olive oil here.

2	tablespoons orange juice
2	tablespoons lime juice
I	small shallot, minced
I	tablespoon minced fresh cilantro
⅛	teaspoon red pepper flakes
2	tablespoons vegetable oil
2	tablespoons extra-virgin olive oil
	Salt

Combine orange juice, lime juice, shallot, cilantro, and pepper flakes in medium bowl. Slowly whisk in vegetable and olive oils. Season with salt to taste.

PAN-SEARED SHRIMP

✔ WHY THIS RECIPE WORKS
A good recipe for pan-seared shrimp is hard to find. Of the handful of recipes we uncovered, the majority resulted in shrimp that were either dry and flavorless or pale, tough, and gummy. We wanted shrimp that were well caramelized but still moist, briny, and tender. Brining peeled shrimp inhibited browning so instead, we seasoned the shrimp with salt, pepper, and sugar, which brought out their natural sweetness and aided in browning. We cooked the shrimp in batches in a large, piping-hot skillet and then paired them with thick, glazelike sauces with assertive ingredients and plenty of acidity as a foil for the shrimp's richness.

PAN-SEARED SHRIMP
SERVES 4

Either a nonstick or a traditional skillet will work for this recipe, but a nonstick will simplify cleanup.

2 tablespoons vegetable oil

1½ pounds extra-large shrimp (21 to 25 per pound), peeled and deveined

¼ teaspoon salt

¼ teaspoon pepper

⅛ teaspoon sugar

Heat 1 tablespoon oil in 12-inch skillet over high heat until just smoking. Meanwhile, toss shrimp, salt, pepper, and sugar in medium bowl. Add half of shrimp to pan in single layer and cook until spotty brown and edges turn pink, about 1 minute. Off heat, flip each shrimp using tongs and allow shrimp to continue to cook in skillet until all but very center is opaque, about 30 seconds. Transfer shrimp to large plate. Repeat with remaining 1 tablespoon oil and remaining shrimp. After second batch has cooked off heat, return first batch to skillet and toss to combine. Cover skillet and let sit until shrimp are cooked through, 1 to 2 minutes. Serve immediately.

PAN-SEARED SHRIMP WITH GARLIC-LEMON BUTTER

Beat 3 tablespoons softened unsalted butter with fork in small bowl until light and fluffy. Stir in 2 tablespoons chopped fresh parsley, 1 tablespoon lemon juice, 1 minced garlic clove, and ⅛ teaspoon salt until combined. Add butter mixture to skillet when returning first batch of shrimp to skillet. Serve with lemon wedges if desired.

PAN-SEARED SHRIMP WITH GINGER-HOISIN GLAZE

Stir together 2 tablespoons hoisin sauce, 1 tablespoon rice vinegar, 2 teaspoons grated fresh ginger, 2 teaspoons water, 1½ teaspoons soy sauce, and 2 scallions, sliced thin, in small bowl. Substitute ¼ teaspoon red pepper flakes for pepper and add hoisin mixture to skillet when returning first batch of shrimp to skillet.

PAN-SEARED SHRIMP WITH CHIPOTLE-LIME GLAZE

Stir together 2 tablespoons lime juice, 2 tablespoons chopped fresh cilantro, 1½ teaspoons minced canned chipotle chile in adobo sauce and 2 teaspoons adobo sauce, and 4 teaspoons packed brown sugar in small bowl. Add chipotle mixture to skillet when returning first batch of shrimp to skillet.

SIMPLE SHRIMP SCAMPI

✓ WHY THIS RECIPE WORKS

Restaurant versions of shrimp scampi run the gamut from batter-dipped, deep-fried shrimp drenched in bad oil to boiled shrimp and tomato sauce on a bed of pasta. We wanted shrimp in a light sauce, smacking of garlic and lemon, garnished with parsley. Cooking the shrimp and garlic quickly was the key to avoiding overcooked, tough shrimp and bitter-tasting garlic. We first cooked the shrimp in a large skillet in batches and set them aside, then cooked the garlic in butter. Vermouth and lemon juice added the right punch. Adding the parsley at the end of cooking ensured it kept its fresh flavor.

SIMPLE SHRIMP SCAMPI
SERVES 4

Use the cayenne sparingly; you are after only the faintest hint of spiciness. Serve with bread to sop up the remaining juices from both plate and skillet.

2 tablespoons olive oil

2 pounds extra-large shrimp (21 to 25 per pound), peeled and deveined

3 tablespoons unsalted butter

4 garlic cloves, minced

2 tablespoons lemon juice

1 tablespoon dry vermouth or dry white wine

2 tablespoons minced fresh parsley
   Pinch cayenne pepper
   Salt and pepper

1. Heat 1 tablespoon oil in 12-inch skillet over high heat until just smoking. Add 1 pound shrimp and cook, stirring occasionally, until just opaque, about 1 minute; transfer to medium bowl. Repeat with remaining 1 tablespoon oil and remaining 1 pound shrimp, transferring shrimp to bowl with first batch.

The first step to ensuring perfectly cooked shrimp is buying the right size of shellfish called for in your recipe. How frustrating, then, that the names for the different shrimp sizes vary from vendor to vendor, so that one company's large is another company's extra-large. The best way to eliminate ambiguity is to disregard the name and select shrimp based on the actual count per pound, which is clearly labeled on the packaging. The latter U (for "under") means that there should be fewer than that number of shrimp in a pound; two numbers separated by a slash indicates the range of shrimp in a pound in that particular size. Most important: The smaller the number per pound, the bigger the shrimp.

TEST KITCHEN NAME	COUNT PER POUND
Extra-Small	61/70
Small	51/60
Medium	41/50
Medium-Large	31/40
Large	26/30
Extra-Large	21/25
Jumbo	16/20
Extra-Jumbo	U/15
Colossal	U/12

2. Melt 1 tablespoon butter in now-empty skillet over medium-low heat. Add garlic and cook, stirring constantly, until fragrant, about 30 seconds. Off heat, add lemon juice and vermouth. Whisk in remaining 2 tablespoons butter, add parsley and cayenne, and season with salt and pepper to taste. Return shrimp and accumulated juices to skillet. Toss to combine; serve immediately.

SIMPLE SHRIMP SCAMPI WITH ORANGE ZEST AND CILANTRO

Because it is spicy, this dish is best served with white rice.

Add 1 teaspoon grated orange zest and ¼ teaspoon red pepper flakes to skillet with garlic in step 2. Omit cayenne and substitute 2 tablespoons minced fresh cilantro for parsley.

SIMPLE SHRIMP SCAMPI WITH CUMIN, PAPRIKA, AND SHERRY VINEGAR

This variation is deeply flavorful but has slightly less heat than either of the other two versions.

Add 2 teaspoons paprika and 1 teaspoon ground cumin to skillet with garlic in step 2. Omit cayenne and substitute 2 tablespoons sherry vinegar for lemon juice.

GARLICKY SHRIMP WITH BUTTERED BREAD CRUMBS

✔ **WHY THIS RECIPE WORKS**
The generic recipes we found for casseroles of shrimp in a sherry-garlic sauce topped with bread crumbs all produced rubbery shrimp and gluey toppings. We were after all the potent flavors and contrasting textures that the name of this dish promises. Most recipes call for poaching the shrimp on the stovetop and then baking them in a casserole dish. Making the entire dish in a skillet on the stovetop was a good start

---

DEVEINING SHRIMP

Deveining usually creates a large, unsightly slit on the outer curve of shrimp. Try this technique for more attractive results.

 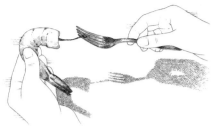

I. Insert one tine of a dinner fork into the shrimp, pass the tine beneath the vein, and hook it under.

2. Draw the vein out through the very small hole you've created, leaving the shrimp looking virtually untouched.

---

to avoiding overcooking. We tossed the shrimp with sugar, along with salt and pepper, to promote browning. After searing the shrimp on one side, we removed them to build the sauce; we would add the shrimp back at the end to heat through and finish cooking. For the sauce, we started with garlic. We balanced the boozy flavor of the sherry with clam juice. A pinch of flour and some butter thickened the sauce, and lemon juice brightened everything up. A baguette made the perfect buttery bread crumbs; sprinkled on at the last minute, they were sturdy enough to stay crisp on the saucy shrimp.

GARLICKY SHRIMP WITH BUTTERED BREAD CRUMBS

SERVES 4

Vermouth can be substituted for the sherry. If using vermouth, increase the amount to ½ cup and reduce the amount of clam juice to ½ cup. To prepare this recipe in a 10-inch skillet, brown the shrimp in three batches for about 2 minutes each, using 2 teaspoons oil per batch. Serve the shrimp with rice and either broccoli or asparagus.

1	(3-inch) piece baguette, cut into small pieces
5	tablespoons unsalted butter, cut into 5 pieces
1	small shallot, minced
	Salt and pepper

2	tablespoons minced fresh parsley
2	pounds extra-large shrimp (21 to 25 per pound), peeled and deveined
¼	teaspoon sugar
4	teaspoons vegetable oil
4	garlic cloves, minced
⅛	teaspoon red pepper flakes
2	teaspoons all-purpose flour
⅔	cup bottled clam juice
⅓	cup dry sherry
2	teaspoons lemon juice plus lemon wedges

I. Pulse bread in food processor until coarsely ground, about 8 pulses. Melt 1 tablespoon butter in 12-inch nonstick skillet over medium heat. Add crumbs, shallot, ⅛ teaspoon salt, and ⅛ teaspoon pepper. Cook, stirring occasionally, until golden brown, 7 to 10 minutes. Stir in 1 tablespoon parsley and transfer to plate to cool. Wipe out skillet with paper towels.

2. Pat shrimp dry with paper towels. Toss shrimp with sugar, ¼ teaspoon salt, and ¼ teaspoon pepper in bowl. Heat 2 teaspoons oil in now-empty skillet over high heat until shimmering. Add half of shrimp in single layer and cook until spotty brown and edges turn pink, about 3 minutes (do not flip shrimp). Remove pan from heat and transfer shrimp to large plate. Wipe out skillet with paper towels.

Repeat with remaining 2 teaspoons oil and remaining 1 pound shrimp; transfer shrimp to plate with first batch.

3. Melt 1 tablespoon butter in now-empty skillet over medium heat. Add garlic and pepper flakes and cook, stirring frequently, until garlic just begins to color, about 1 minute. Add flour and cook, stirring frequently, for 1 minute. Increase heat to medium-high and slowly whisk in clam juice and sherry. Bring to simmer and cook until mixture reduces to ¾ cup, 3 to 4 minutes. Whisk in remaining 3 tablespoons butter, 1 tablespoon at a time. Stir in lemon juice and remaining tablespoon parsley.

4. Reduce heat to medium-low, return shrimp to skillet with sauce, and toss to combine. Cook, covered, until shrimp are pink and cooked through, 2 to 3 minutes. Uncover and sprinkle with toasted bread crumbs. Serve with lemon wedges.

GREEK-STYLE SHRIMP WITH TOMATOES AND FETA

✔ WHY THIS RECIPE WORKS

In the traditional Greek dish shrimp saganaki, sweet, briny shrimp are covered with a garlic- and herb-accented tomato sauce and topped with crumbles of creamy, salty feta cheese. Restaurant versions, however, can be a gamble. The shrimp can be tough and rubbery, the tomato sauce can turn out dull or overwhelming, and the feta is often lackluster. We set out to develop a foolproof recipe for home cooks. Canned diced tomatoes along with sautéed onion and garlic provided our sauce's base. Dry white wine added acidity. Ouzo, the slightly sweet anise-flavored Greek liqueur, added welcome complexity. While the shrimp are typically layered with the tomato sauce and feta and baked, we were after a quick and easy dish. We opted to cook the shrimp right in

the sauce; adding the shrimp raw to the sauce helped infuse them with the sauce's bright flavor. And for even more flavor, we marinated the shrimp with olive oil, ouzo, garlic, and lemon zest first while we made the sauce. A generous sprinkling of feta and chopped fresh dill over the sauced shrimp finished our recipe.

GREEK-STYLE SHRIMP WITH TOMATOES AND FETA

SERVES 4 TO 6

This recipe works equally well with either jumbo shrimp (16 to 20 per pound) or extra-large shrimp (21 to 25 per pound), but the cooking times in step 3 will vary slightly depending on which you use. If you don't have ouzo, you can substitute an equal amount of Pernod or 1 tablespoon vodka plus ⅛ teaspoon anise seeds. Serve the shrimp with crusty bread or steamed white rice.

1½	pounds shrimp, peeled and deveined, tails left on if desired
¼	cup extra-virgin olive oil
3	tablespoons ouzo
5	garlic cloves, minced
1	teaspoon grated lemon zest
	Salt and pepper
1	small onion, chopped
½	red bell pepper, chopped
½	green bell pepper, chopped
½	teaspoon red pepper flakes
1	(28-ounce) can diced tomatoes, drained with ⅓ cup juice reserved
¼	cup dry white wine
2	tablespoons coarsely chopped fresh parsley
6	ounces feta cheese, crumbled (1½ cups)
2	tablespoons chopped fresh dill

1. Toss shrimp, 1 tablespoon oil, 1 tablespoon ouzo, 1 teaspoon garlic, lemon zest, ¼ teaspoon salt, and ⅛ teaspoon pepper in small bowl until well combined. Set aside while preparing sauce.

2. Heat 2 tablespoons oil in 12-inch skillet over medium heat until shimmering. Add onion, red bell pepper, green bell pepper, and ¼ teaspoon salt and stir to combine. Cover skillet and cook, stirring occasionally, until vegetables release their moisture, 3 to 5 minutes. Uncover and continue to cook, stirring occasionally, until moisture cooks off and vegetables have softened, about 5 minutes longer. Add remaining garlic and pepper flakes and cook until fragrant, about 1 minute. Add tomatoes and reserved juice, wine, and remaining 2 tablespoons ouzo, increase heat to medium-high, and bring to simmer. Reduce heat to medium and simmer, stirring occasionally, until flavors have melded and sauce is slightly thickened (sauce should not be completely dry), 5 to 8 minutes. Stir in parsley and season with salt and pepper to taste.

3. Reduce heat to medium-low and add shrimp along with any accumulated juices

---

TEST KITCHEN TIP NO. 95 FRESH OR FROZEN SHRIMP?

We're often asked whether it's better to cook with fresh or frozen shrimp. It's somewhat of a trick question—almost all shrimp are frozen after being harvested, so the "fresh" shrimp you see at the market have very likely been frozen and then thawed by your fishmonger. Since there's no way to know for certain when these "fresh" shrimp were defrosted, quality varies dramatically. In the test kitchen, we find that buying frozen shrimp and defrosting them at home yields superior results. Make sure to buy frozen shrimp with their shells on; shelled shrimp don't survive the freezing and thawing process very well and will surely be mushy (and the shrimp shells can be used to make a quick and flavorful shrimp stock). To defrost shrimp, place them in a colander until cold running water; they will be thawed and ready to cook in a few minutes (always thoroughly dry them first).

to pan; stir to coat and distribute evenly. Cover and cook, stirring occasionally, until shrimp are opaque throughout, 6 to 9 minutes for extra-large or 7 to 11 minutes for jumbo, adjusting heat as needed to maintain bare simmer. Remove pan from heat and sprinkle with feta. Drizzle remaining tablespoon oil over top and sprinkle with dill. Serve immediately.

PAELLA

✔ WHY THIS RECIPE WORKS

The key to our paella was finding equipment and ingredients that stayed true to the dish's heritage. First, we substituted a Dutch oven for the more obscure specialty vessel, the paella pan. Then we pared down our ingredient list, dismissing lobster (too much work), diced pork (sausage would be enough), fish (flakes too easily), and rabbit and snails (too unconventional). Chorizo, chicken, shrimp, and mussels (favored over scallops, clams, and calamari) were all in. Canned diced tomatoes replaced the typical fresh. And when we focused on the rice, we found we preferred short-grain varieties. Valencia was our favorite, with Italian Arborio a close second. Chicken broth, white wine, saffron and a bay leaf were the perfect choices for liquid and seasoning, adding the right amount of flavor without overcomplicating our recipe.

PAELLA
SERVES 6

This recipe is for making paella in a Dutch oven (the Dutch oven should be 11 to 12 inches in diameter with at least a 6-quart capacity). With minor modifications, it can also be made in a paella pan (see recipe that follows). Dry-cured Spanish chorizo is the sausage of choice for paella, but fresh chorizo or linguiça is an acceptable substitute. Socarrat, a layer of crusty browned rice that forms on the bottom of the pan, is a traditional part of paella. In our version, socarrat does not develop because most of the cooking is done in the oven. We have provided instructions to develop socarrat in step 5; if you prefer, skip this step and go directly from step 4 to 6. To debeard the mussels, simply pull off the weedy black fibers.

1 pound extra-large shrimp (21 to 25 per pound), peeled and deveined
Salt and pepper
2 tablespoons olive oil, plus extra as needed
8 garlic cloves, minced
1 pound boneless, skinless chicken thighs, trimmed and halved crosswise
1 red bell pepper, stemmed, seeded and cut into ½-inch-wide strips
8 ounces Spanish chorizo sausage, sliced ½ inch thick on bias
1 onion, chopped fine
1 (14.5-ounce) can diced tomatoes, drained, minced, and drained again
2 cups Valencia or Arborio rice
3 cups low-sodium chicken broth
⅓ cup dry white wine
½ teaspoon saffron threads, crumbled
1 bay leaf
12 mussels, scrubbed and debearded
½ cup frozen peas, thawed
2 teaspoons chopped fresh parsley
Lemon wedges

1. Adjust oven rack to lower-middle position and heat oven to 350 degrees. Toss shrimp, ¼ teaspoon salt, ¼ teaspoon pepper, 1 tablespoon oil, and 1 teaspoon garlic in medium bowl. Cover and refrigerate until needed. Season chicken thighs with salt and pepper and set aside.

2. Heat 2 teaspoons oil in Dutch oven over medium-high heat until shimmering. Add bell pepper and cook, stirring occasionally, until skin begins to blister and turn spotty black, 3 to 4 minutes. Transfer bell pepper to small plate and set aside.

3. Heat 1 teaspoon oil in now-empty pot until shimmering. Add chicken pieces in single layer and cook, without moving, until browned, about 3 minutes. Turn pieces and cook until browned on second side, about 3 minutes. Transfer chicken to medium bowl. Reduce heat to medium and add chorizo to pot. Cook, stirring frequently, until deeply browned and fat begins to render, 4 to 5 minutes. Transfer chorizo to bowl with chicken and set aside.

4. Add enough oil to fat in pot to equal 2 tablespoons and heat over medium heat until shimmering. Add onion and cook, stirring frequently, until softened, about 3 minutes. Stir in remaining garlic and cook until fragrant, about 1 minute. Stir in tomatoes and cook until mixture begins to darken and thicken slightly, about 3 minutes. Stir in rice and cook until grains are well coated with tomato mixture, 1 to 2 minutes. Stir in chicken broth, wine, saffron, bay leaf, and ½ teaspoon salt. Return chicken and chorizo to pot, increase heat to medium-high and bring to boil, stirring occasionally. Cover pot, transfer to oven, and cook until rice absorbs almost all liquid, about 15 minutes. Remove pot from oven. Uncover pot, scatter shrimp over rice, insert mussels, hinged side down, into rice (so they stand upright), arrange bell pepper strips in pinwheel pattern, and scatter peas over top. Cover, return to oven, and cook until shrimp are opaque and mussels have opened, 10 to 12 minutes.

5. FOR SOCARRAT: If socarrat is desired, set pot, uncovered, over medium-high heat for about 5 minutes, rotating pot 180 degrees after about 2 minutes for even browning.

6. Let paella stand, covered, for 5 minutes. Discard any mussels that have not opened and bay leaf, if it can be easily removed. Sprinkle with parsley and serve, passing lemon wedges separately.

PAELLA IN A PAELLA PAN

A paella pan makes for an attractive and impressive presentation. Use one that is 14 to 15 inches in diameter; the ingredients will not fit in a smaller pan.

Increase chicken broth to 3¼ cups and wine to ½ cup. Before placing pan in oven, cover it tightly with aluminum foil. For socarrat, cook paella, uncovered, over medium-high heat for about 3 minutes, rotating pan 180 degrees after about 1½ minutes for even browning.

MUSSELS STEAMED IN WHITE WINE

✔ WHY THIS RECIPE WORKS

Preparing mussels can be an all-day affair, what with scrubbing, debearding, and rinsing. Yet despite all that work, the broth is often gritty and the mussels sometimes taste funky. For steamed mussels that were quick to prepare, flavorful, and grit-free, we began with rope-cultured Great Eastern bottom mussels (a widely available variety), which we found to be the cleanest. Garlic in the broth balanced and enriched the flavor of the mollusks and simmering the cooking liquid with a few flavorful additions (like shallots, garlic, and parsley) for a few minutes before adding the mussels deepened the flavor. We found that larger mussels needed to cook a few minutes after they opened to firm up. It all evened out if we simply cooked them until all the mussels opened.

MUSSELS STEAMED IN WHITE WINE
SERVES 4

To debeard the mussels, simply pull off the weedy black fibers. Serve with crusty bread or rice to soak up the flavorful cooking liquid.

- 2   cups white wine
- ½   cup minced shallots
- 4   garlic cloves, minced
- ½   cup chopped fresh parsley
- 1   bay leaf
- 4   pounds mussels, scrubbed and debearded
- 4   tablespoons unsalted butter, cut into 4 pieces

1. Bring wine, shallots, garlic, parsley, and bay leaf to simmer in Dutch oven and simmer to blend flavors, about 3 minutes. Increase heat to high, add mussels, cover, and cook, stirring twice, until mussels open, 4 to 8 minutes. Discard any unopened mussels.

2. Remove mussels from liquid and transfer to serving bowl. Whisk in butter, 1 tablespoon at a time. Pour broth over mussels, season with salt and pepper to taste, and serve immediately.

STEAMED MUSSELS WITH ASIAN FLAVORS
SERVES 4

Serve with crusty bread or rice to soak up the flavorful cooking liquid.

- 1   cup low-sodium chicken broth
- 2   teaspoons rice vinegar
- ⅛   teaspoon cayenne pepper
- 2   tablespoons grated fresh ginger
- 2   garlic cloves, minced
- 4   scallions, minced
- 2   tablespoons grated lime zest (3 limes) (optional) plus lime wedges
- 4   pounds mussels, scrubbed and debearded
- 2   tablespoons minced fresh chives, cilantro, or scallions

1. Bring chicken broth, rice vinegar, cayenne, ginger, garlic, scallions, and lime zest (if using) to simmer in Dutch oven and simmer to blend flavors, about 3 minutes. Increase heat to high, add mussels, cover, and cook, stirring twice, until mussels open, 4 to 8 minutes.

2. Remove mussels from liquid and transfer to serving bowl. Pour broth over mussels, garnish with chives. Serve immediately with lime wedges.

STEAMED MUSSELS WITH TOMATO AND BASIL

Serve these tomato-bathed mussels over cappellini or angel hair pasta.

Decrease wine to 1 cup and substitute ½ cup chopped fresh basil for parsley. After removing mussels from broth in step 2, add 2 cups canned crushed tomatoes. Substitute ¼ cup olive oil for butter, simmering after adding to pot until reduced to sauce consistency, about 10 minutes. Season with salt and pepper to taste. Return mussels to pot with reduced sauce and gently stir to coat. Serve.

STEAMED MUSSELS WITH CURRY AND BASIL

Add 1 teaspoon Madras curry powder to wine mixture in step 1 and reduce parsley to 2 tablespoons. Right before swirling in butter, stir in 2 tablespoons chopped fresh cilantro and 2 tablespoons chopped fresh basil.

LOBSTER

✔ WHY THIS RECIPE WORKS

The secret to tender lobster is not so much in the preparation and cooking as in the selection of the creature itself. After some research into the life cycle of the lobster, we discovered that the variations in the texture of lobster meat depended a great deal on what part of the molting cycle a lobster is in. You will find both hard-shell and soft-shell lobsters available; lobsters are in their prime when their shells are fully hardened. Soft-shell lobsters have claw meat that is shriveled, scrawny, and spongy in texture and tail meat that is underdeveloped. Steaming is far tidier than boiling, as you avoid dealing with waterlogged crustaceans at the dinner table.

Neither beer no wine improved the flavor. As for dry heat cooking methods, we found the steady heat of the oven preferable to broiling. And to keep the tail from curling during roasting, we simply ran a skewer through it.

STEAMED WHOLE LOBSTERS
SERVES 4

While we prefer hard-shell lobsters to soft-shell lobsters, soft-shell lobsters are more available in the summer (late spring and early summer is the best time to find hard-shell lobsters). However, because hard-shell lobsters are more packed with meat than soft-shell ones, you may want to buy 1½- to 1¾-pound soft-shell lobsters per person.

PREPARING A LOBSTER FOR ROASTING

1. With chef's knife facing head, kill lobster by plunging knife into body where shell forms "T," then move blade straight through head.

2. Turn lobster over, and, holding upper body with one hand, cut through body toward tail, making sure not to cut all the way through shell.

3. Holding half of tail in each hand, crack, but do not break, back shell to butterfly lobster.

4. Using spoon, remove and discard stomach sac.

5. Using fingers, remove and discard intestinal tract, then remove and discard green tomalley.

6. Run skewer up 1 side of lobster tail to keep it from curling during cooking.

---

4 live lobsters
8 tablespoons butter, melted (optional)
  Lemon wedges

Fit stockpot or Dutch oven with steamer basket or pasta insert. Add water, keeping level below basket. Bring water to boil. Add lobsters, cover, and return water to boil. Reduce heat to medium-high and steam until lobsters are done, following cooking times in chart on page 461. Serve immediately with melted butter and lemon wedges.

OVEN-ROASTED LOBSTER WITH HERBED BREAD CRUMBS
SERVES 4

Panko, extra-crisp Japanese bread crumbs can be substituted for the dry bread crumbs. You will need four 12-inch metal skewers for this recipe.

4 live lobsters
4 tablespoons butter
½ cup plain dry bread crumbs
2 tablespoons minced fresh parsley or 1 tablespoon minced fresh tarragon or snipped chives
  Salt and ground white pepper
  Lemon wedges

1. Line 2 rimmed baking sheets with aluminum foil. Adjust oven rack to upper-middle position and heat oven to 450 degrees.

2. TO PREPARE LOBSTERS: With chef's knife facing head, kill each lobster by plunging knife into body where shell forms "T," then move blade straight through head. Turn lobster over, and cut through body toward tail, making sure not to cut all the way through shell. Holding half of tail in each hand, crack, but do not break, back shell to butterfly lobster. Remove and

REMOVING MEAT FROM STEAMED LOBSTERS

1. After cooked lobster has cooled slightly, twist tail and claw appendages to remove them from body. Discard body.

2. Twist tail flippers off tail, then use fork or your finger to push tail meat out through wide end of tail.

3. Use lobster crackers or mallet to break open claw and remove meat.

4. Crack open claw appendage's connecting joint and remove meat with cocktail fork.

---

discard stomach sac, intestinal tract, and green tomalley. Run skewer up 1 side of lobster tail.

3. Melt 1 tablespoon butter in 8-inch skillet over medium heat. Add bread crumbs and cook, stirring constantly, until toasted and golden brown, 3 to 4 minutes. Stir in herbs and set aside.

4. Arrange lobsters on prepared baking sheets, alternating tail and claw ends. Melt

remaining 3 tablespoons butter and brush over body and tail meat of each lobster and season with salt and white pepper to taste. Sprinkle bread-crumb mixture evenly over body and tail meat of lobsters.

5. Roast lobsters until tail meat is opaque and bread crumbs are crisp, 12 to 15 minutes. Serve immediately with lemon wedges.

PAN-FRIED SOFT-SHELL CRABS

✔ WHY THIS RECIPE WORKS

Restaurants are the usual venue for eating soft-shell crabs—blue crabs taken out of the water just after they have shed their shells and eaten whole. Restaurants usually deep-fry them; we wanted a way to get a truly crispy soft-shell crab at home without deep-frying. We found that pan-frying lightly floured crabs created that satisfyingly crisp result without the mess. Because juice pours out of a live crab when you clean it, we found that the crabs needed to be cooked immediately after cleaning for them to be plump and juicy when they reached the dinner table.

PAN-FRIED SOFT-SHELL CRABS WITH LEMON, CAPERS, AND HERBS
SERVES 4

For maximum crispness, cook the crabs in two pans, each covered with a splatter screen, so that you can serve the crabs as soon as they are cooked. If you are working with just one splatter screen and pan, cook 4 crabs in 4 tablespoons butter, transfer to a platter in a 300-degree oven, wipe out the pan, and repeat with the remaining crabs. The pan sauce is powerfully flavored; you only need about 1 tablespoon per serving.

1	cup all-purpose flour
8	(medium to large) soft-shell crabs
10	tablespoons unsalted butter
1	teaspoon lemon juice
1	teaspoon sherry vinegar
1½	tablespoons minced fresh parsley
1	scallion, minced
1	teaspoon minced fresh tarragon
1	teaspoon capers, rinsed and minced
	Pepper

1. TO CLEAN THE CRABS: Cut off crab's mouth with kitchen shears. Cut off eyes, if desired. Lift pointed sides of crab and cut out spongy off-white gills

APPROXIMATE STEAMING TIMES AND MEAT YIELDS FOR LOBSTER

LOBSTER SIZE	COOKING TIME	MEAT YIELD
1 lb.		
Soft-Shell	8 to 9 min.	about 3 oz.
Hard-Shell	10 to 11 min.	4 to 4½ oz.
1¼ lbs.		
Soft-Shell	11 to 12 min.	3½ to 4 oz.
Hard-Shell	13 to 14 min.	5½ to 6 oz.
1½ lbs.		
Soft-Shell	13 to 14 min.	5½ to 6 oz.
Hard-Shell	15 to 16 min.	7½ to 8 oz.
1¾ – 2 lbs.		
Soft-Shell	17 to 18 min.	6¼ to 6½ oz.
Hard-Shell	about 19 min.	8½ to 9 oz.

underneath. Cut off triangular "apron flap." Pat the crabs dry with paper towels.

2. Place flour in shallow baking dish or pie plate and line platter or 2 large plates with paper towels. Dredge crabs in flour, gently shaking off excess. Melt 4 tablespoons butter in each of two 12-inch skillets over medium-high heat, swirling skillets to keep butter from burning. Turn heat to high and add 4 crabs, shell side down, to each skillet. Cover each skillet with splatter screen and cook, adjusting heat as necessary to keep butter from burning, until crabs turn reddish brown, about 3 minutes. Turn crabs with spatula or tongs and cook until second side is browned, about 3 minutes. Transfer crabs to prepared platter or plates.

3. Set 1 skillet aside and pour off butter from remaining skillet. Off heat, add remaining 2 tablespoons butter, lemon juice, vinegar, parsley, scallion, tarragon, capers, and pepper to taste, swirling pan to melt butter. Arrange 2 crabs per person on 4 plates. Spoon about 1 tablespoon sauce over each serving and serve immediately.

PAN-FRIED SOFT-SHELL CRABS ON A BED OF SPINACH

SERVES 4

You can substitute mustard greens or collard greens for the spinach in this recipe—just make sure they are cooked in boiling salted water until tender, then drained, rinsed in cold water, and squeezed dry. Chop them coarse, then proceed with the recipe.

8	(medium to large) soft-shell crabs
2	pounds curly-leaf spinach, stemmed
I	cup all-purpose flour
10	tablespoons unsalted butter
4	garlic cloves, minced
½	teaspoon salt
2–3	tablespoons lemon juice
	Pepper

CLEANING A SOFT SHELL CRAB

I. Cut off crab's mouth with kitchen shears. Cut off eyes, if desired (eyes are edible; remove purely for aesthetic reasons).

2. Lift pointed sides of crab and cut out spongy off-white gills underneath.

3. Turn crab on its back and cut off triangular or T-shaped "apron flap."

I. **TO CLEAN THE CRABS:** Cut off crab's mouth with kitchen shears. Cut off eyes, if desired. Lift pointed sides of crab and cut out spongy off-white gills underneath. Cut off triangular "apron flap." Pat the crabs dry with paper towels.

2. Fit stockpot or Dutch oven with steamer basket or pasta insert. Bring 1 inch water to boil. Add spinach, cover and steam, stirring once, until just tender, about 4 minutes. Drain spinach, refresh under cold water, then squeeze out excess liquid. Chop spinach coarse and set aside.

3. Place flour in baking dish or pie plate and line large plate or platter with paper towels. Dredge crabs in flour, gently shaking off excess. Melt 4 tablespoons butter each in two 12-inch skillets over medium-high heat, swirling skillets to keep butter from burning. Turn heat to high and add 4 crabs, shell-side down, to each skillet. Cover each skillet with splatter screen and cook, adjusting heat as necessary to keep butter from burning, until crabs turn reddish brown, about 3 minutes. Turn crabs with spatula or tongs and cook until second side is browned, about 3 minutes. Transfer crabs to prepared platter or plates.

4. Set 1 skillet aside and pour off butter from remaining skillet. Melt remaining 2 tablespoons butter in skillet over medium-high heat, add half of garlic and cook until fragrant, about 30 seconds. Add spinach and salt and cook until heated through, 1 to 2 minutes. Add remaining garlic and cook for 30 seconds. Off heat, stir in lemon juice to taste and season with pepper to taste. Divide spinach among 4 plates and arrange 2 crabs on each bed of spinach. Serve immediately.

CHAPTER 12   Grilling

GRILLED BONELESS CHICKEN BREASTS

✔ WHY THIS RECIPE WORKS

Because they have no skin and little fat, plain boneless chicken breasts invariably turn out dry and leathery when grilled. A common solution—marinating them in bottled salad dressings, which are typically laden with sweeteners and stabilizers—often imparts off-flavors. We wanted grilled chicken breasts that would come off the grill juicy and flavorful and we wanted to look beyond bottled salad dressing to get there. To start, we made a simple homemade marinade with olive oil, lemon juice, garlic, parsley, sugar, and Dijon mustard—and we made a separate vinaigrette to serve with the grilled chicken for extra moisture and flavor. We slowly cooked the chicken breasts on the cool side of the grill until they were almost done. We then gave the breasts a quick sear on the hot side of the grill to finishing cooking and add grill flavor. With a drizzle of our simple vinaigrette, these chicken breasts were moist, tender, and full of flavor.

GRILLED LEMON-PARSLEY CHICKEN BREASTS

SERVES 4

The chicken should be marinated for no less than 30 minutes and no more than 1 hour. Serve with a simply prepared vegetable or use in a sandwich or salad.

6	tablespoons olive oil
2	tablespoons lemon juice
1	tablespoon minced fresh parsley
1¼	teaspoons sugar
1	teaspoon Dijon mustard
	Salt and pepper
2	tablespoons water
3	garlic cloves, minced
4	(6- to 8-ounce) boneless, skinless chicken breasts, trimmed

1. Whisk 3 tablespoons oil, 1 tablespoon lemon juice, parsley, ¼ teaspoon sugar, mustard, ¼ teaspoon salt, and ¼ teaspoon pepper together in bowl and set aside for serving.

2. Whisk remaining 3 tablespoons oil, remaining 1 tablespoon lemon juice, remaining 1 teaspoon sugar, 1½ teaspoons salt, ½ teaspoon pepper, water, and garlic together in bowl. Place marinade and chicken in 1-gallon zipper-lock bag and toss to coat; press out as much air as possible and seal bag. Refrigerate for at least 30 minutes or up to 1 hour, flipping bag every 15 minutes.

3A. FOR A CHARCOAL GRILL: Open bottom vent completely. Light large chimney starter filled with charcoal briquettes (6 quarts). When top coals are partially covered with ash, pour evenly over half of grill. Set cooking grate in place, cover, and open lid vent completely. Heat grill until hot, about 5 minutes.

3B. FOR A GAS GRILL: Turn all burners to high, cover, and heat grill until hot, about 15 minutes. Leave primary burner on high and turn off other burner(s).

4. Clean and oil cooking grate. Remove chicken from bag, allowing excess marinade to drip off. Place chicken on cooler side of grill, smooth side down, with thicker sides facing coals and flames. Cover and cook until bottom of chicken just begins to develop light grill marks and is no longer translucent, 6 to 9 minutes.

5. Flip chicken and rotate so that thinner sides face coals and flames. Cover and continue to cook until chicken is opaque and firm to touch and registers 140 degrees, 6 to 9 minutes longer.

6. Move chicken to hot side of grill and cook until dark grill marks appear on both sides and chicken registers 160 degrees, 2 to 6 minutes longer.

7. Transfer chicken to carving board, tent loosely with aluminum foil, and let rest for 5 to 10 minutes. Slice each breast on bias into ¼-inch-thick slices and transfer to individual plates. Drizzle with reserved sauce and serve.

GRILLED CHIPOTLE-LIME CHICKEN BREASTS

Substitute lime juice for lemon juice and use an extra teaspoon juice in reserved sauce. Substitute minced canned chipotle chile in adobo sauce for mustard and cilantro for parsley.

GRILLED ORANGE-TARRAGON CHICKEN BREASTS

Substitute orange juice for lemon juice and tarragon for parsley. Add ¼ teaspoon grated orange zest to reserved sauce.

TEST KITCHEN TIP NO. 96 LIGHT MY FIRE

Don't even think of using lighter fluid to light your charcoal. Sometimes we've found that we can taste the fluid residually on grilled food, especially delicate foods like chicken and fish—and who wants that? Electric starters are fine, but most people don't have an electrical outlet near their grill. Where does that leave you? A chimney starter. A chimney starter is a metal cylinder with a heatproof handle. Simply dump in the charcoal, light, and wait until the coals are partially covered with a layer of ash. At this point the hot coals can be poured into the grill and arranged as necessary. One thing to keep in mind when buying a chimney starter is the charcoal capacity. We like a large chimney that holds about 6 quarts of charcoal briquettes—just the right amount for grilling most foods in a large kettle grill.

GRILLED CHICKEN FAJITAS

✔ WHY THIS RECIPE WORKS

Too often, chicken fajitas need to be slathered with guacamole, sour cream, and salsa to mask the bland flavor of the soggy underlying ingredients. We wanted to go back to the basics, creating a simple combination of smoky grilled vegetables and strips of chicken wrapped up in warm flour tortillas. Marinating the chicken in a high-acid mixture created a bright, unadulterated tang. We created two levels of heat by covering two-thirds of the grill with the coals and leaving the remaining one-third empty, which allowed us to grill the chicken, peppers, and onions simultaneously. We set the chicken over high heat and the vegetables over medium-high heat so they would brown nicely and cook through without burning. We finished the chicken and vegetables with a final burst of fresh flavor by tossing the cooked ingredients in just a small amount of reserved marinade. Six-inch tortillas made the perfect wrappers, and we heated them briefly on the cooler side of the grill until they puffed up and lost their raw, gummy texture.

GRILLED CHICKEN FAJITAS

SERVES 4 TO 6

You can use red, yellow, orange, or green bell peppers in this recipe. The chicken tenderloins can be reserved for another use or marinated and grilled along with the breasts. When you head outside to grill, bring a clean kitchen towel in which to wrap the tortillas and keep them warm. The chicken and vegetables have enough flavor on their own, but accompaniments (guacamole, salsa, sour cream, shredded cheddar or Monterey Jack cheese, and lime wedges) can be offered at the table.

- 6   tablespoons vegetable oil
- ⅓   cup lime juice (3 limes)
- 1   jalapeño chile, stemmed, seeded, and minced
- 1½   tablespoons minced fresh cilantro
- 3   garlic cloves, minced
- 1   tablespoon Worcestershire sauce
- 1½   teaspoons brown sugar
       Salt and pepper
- 1½   pounds boneless, skinless chicken breasts, tenderloins removed, trimmed, pounded to ½-inch thickness
- 1   large red onion, peeled and cut into ½-inch-thick rounds (do not separate rings)
- 2   large bell peppers, quartered, stemmed, and seeded
- 8–12   (6-inch) flour tortillas

1. Whisk ¼ cup oil, lime juice, jalapeño, cilantro, garlic, Worcestershire, sugar, 1 teaspoon salt, and ¾ teaspoon pepper together in bowl. Reserve ¼ cup marinade and set aside. Add 1 teaspoon salt to remaining marinade. Place marinade and chicken in 1-gallon zipper-lock bag and toss to coat; press out as much air as possible and seal bag. Refrigerate for at least 15 minutes, flipping bag halfway through marinating. Brush both sides of onion rounds and peppers with remaining 2 tablespoons oil and season with salt and pepper to taste.

2A. FOR A CHARCOAL GRILL: Open bottom vent completely. Light large chimney starter filled with charcoal briquettes (6 quarts). When top coals are partially covered with ash, pour coals over two-thirds of grill, leaving remaining one-third empty. Set cooking grate in place, cover, and open lid vent completely. Heat grill until hot, about 5 minutes.

2B. FOR A GAS GRILL: Turn all burners to high, cover, and heat grill until hot, about 15 minutes. Leave primary burner on high and turn other burner(s) to medium.

3. Clean and oil cooking grate. Remove chicken from bag, allowing excess marinade to drip off. Place chicken on hotter side of grill, smooth side down. Cook (covered if using gas) until well browned on first side, 4 to 6 minutes. Flip and continue to cook until chicken registers 160 degrees, 4 to 6 minutes longer. Transfer chicken to carving board, tent loosely with aluminum foil, and let rest for 5 to 10 minutes.

4. While chicken cooks, place onion rounds and peppers (skin side down) on cooler side of grill and cook until tender and charred on both sides, 8 to 12 minutes, flipping every 3 minutes. Transfer onions and peppers to carving board with chicken.

5. Working in 2 or 3 batches, place tortillas in single layer on cooler side of grill. Cook until warm and lightly browned, about 20 seconds per side (do not grill too long or tortillas will become brittle). As tortillas are done, wrap in kitchen towel or large sheet of aluminum foil.

6. Separate onions into rings and place in medium bowl. Slice peppers into ¼-inch strips and place in bowl with onions. Add 2 tablespoons reserved marinade and toss to combine. Slice each breast on bias into ¼-inch-thick slices, place in second bowl, and toss with remaining 2 tablespoons reserved marinade.

7. Transfer chicken and vegetables to serving platter and serve with warmed tortillas.

INDOOR CHICKEN FAJITAS
SERVES 4 TO 6

You can use red, yellow, orange, or green bell peppers in this recipe. The chicken tenderloins can be reserved for another use or marinated and cooked along with the breasts. The chicken and vegetables have enough flavor on their own, but accompaniments (guacamole, salsa, sour cream, shredded cheddar or Monterey Jack cheese, and lime wedges) can be offered at the table.

6	tablespoons plus 2 teaspoons vegetable oil
⅓	cup lime juice (3 limes)
1	jalapeño chile, stemmed, seeded, and minced
4½	teaspoons minced fresh cilantro
3	garlic cloves, minced
1	tablespoon Worcestershire sauce
1½	teaspoons brown sugar Salt and pepper
1½	pounds boneless, skinless chicken breasts, tenderloins removed, trimmed, pounded to ½-inch thickness
1	large red onion, peeled and cut into ½-inch-thick rounds (do not separate rings)
2	large bell peppers, quartered, stemmed, and seeded
8–12	(6-inch) flour tortillas

1. Whisk ¼ cup oil, lime juice, jalapeño, cilantro, garlic, Worcestershire, sugar, 1 teaspoon salt, and ¾ teaspoon pepper together in bowl. Reserve ¼ cup marinade and set aside. Add 1 teaspoon salt to remaining marinade. Place marinade and chicken in 1-gallon zipper-lock bag and toss to coat; press out as much air as possible and seal bag. Refrigerate for at least 15 minutes, flipping bag halfway through marinating. Brush both sides of onion rounds and peppers with 2 tablespoons oil and season with salt and pepper.

2. Adjust 1 oven rack to upper middle position and second rack to lower-middle position and heat broiler.

3. Arrange onion rounds and peppers (skin sides up) in single layer on rimmed baking sheet. Wrap tortillas securely in aluminum foil in 2 packets, each containing half of tortillas.

4. Remove chicken from marinade and pat dry with paper towels. Heat remaining 2 teaspoons oil in 12-inch nonstick skillet over medium-high heat until just smoking. Place chicken in pan, smooth side down, and cook until well browned on both sides, 5 to 7 minutes, flipping halfway through cooking. Reduce heat to medium and continue to cook until chicken registers 160 degrees, 3 to 5 minutes longer. Transfer chicken to carving board, tent loosely with foil, and let rest for 5 to 10 minutes.

5. While chicken is cooking, place baking sheet with vegetables in oven on upper rack and place tortilla packets on lower rack. Broil vegetables until spottily charred and peppers are crisp-tender, 6 to 8 minutes. Using tongs, transfer peppers to carving board. Flip onion rounds and continue to broil until charred and tender, 2 to 4 minutes longer. Turn off broiler and remove vegetables, leaving tortillas in oven until needed.

6. Separate onions into rings and place in medium bowl. Slice peppers into ¼-inch strips and place in bowl with onions. Add 2 tablespoons reserved marinade and toss to combine. Slice each breast on bias into ¼-inch-thick slices, place in second bowl, and toss with remaining 2 tablespoons marinade.

7. Transfer chicken and vegetables to serving platter and serve with warmed tortillas.

BARBECUED CHICKEN KEBABS

✔ WHY THIS RECIPE WORKS
Skewered chicken can often turn dry and chalky on the grill. As for the flavor, that's usually sub par, too, because by the time the barbecue flavor develops, the meat has dried out. We wanted moist chunks of well-seasoned chicken with full-on barbecued flavor. To give us a head start on the flavor we "marinated" the chicken chunks in bacon paste (made by processing bacon in a food processor) instead of oil, aromatics, and herbs. Tasters liked the smoky flavor that the bacon added, but wanted more. Smoked paprika gave the chicken the flavor tasters were after. For more depth, we also coated the chicken with sweet paprika and turbinado sugar. To keep the skewers from drying

PREVENTING PROPANE TANK PANIC

There's nothing worse than running out of fuel halfway through grilling. If your grill doesn't have a gas gauge, use this technique to estimate how much gas is left in the tank.

1. Bring 1 cup water to boil. Pour water over side of tank.

2. Feel metal with your hand. Where water has succeeded in warming tank, it is empty; where tank remains cool to touch, there is still propane inside.

out, we turned them every two minutes. In the final minutes on the grill, we brushed the chicken with a simple barbecue sauce for a final layer of flavor.

BARBECUED CHICKEN KEBABS
SERVES 6

Use the large holes of a box grater to grate the onion for the sauce. We prefer flavorful dark thigh meat for these kebabs, but white meat can be used. Whichever you choose, don't mix white and dark meat on the same skewer, since they cook at different rates. If you have thin pieces of chicken, cut them larger than 1 inch and roll or fold them into approximate 1-inch cubes. Turbinado sugar is commonly sold as Sugar in the Raw. Demerara sugar can be substituted. You will need four 12-inch metal skewers for this recipe.

SAUCE
- ½ cup ketchup
- ¼ cup molasses
- 2 tablespoons grated onion
- 2 tablespoons Worcestershire sauce
- 2 tablespoons Dijon mustard
- 2 tablespoons cider vinegar
- 1 tablespoon packed light brown sugar

CHICKEN
- 2 tablespoons sweet paprika
- 4 teaspoons turbinado sugar
- 2 teaspoons kosher salt
- 2 teaspoons smoked paprika
- 2 slices bacon, cut into ½-inch pieces
- 2 pounds boneless, skinless chicken thighs or breasts, trimmed, cut into 1-inch chunks

1. FOR THE SAUCE: Bring all ingredients to simmer in small saucepan over medium heat and cook, stirring occasionally, until reduced to about 1 cup, 5 to 7 minutes. Transfer ½ cup sauce to small bowl and set remaining sauce aside for serving.

2. FOR THE CHICKEN: Combine sweet paprika, sugar, salt, and smoked paprika in large bowl. Process bacon in food processor

until smooth paste forms, 30 to 45 seconds, scraping down bowl as needed. Add bacon paste and chicken to spice mixture and mix with hands or rubber spatula until ingredients are thoroughly blended and chicken is completely coated. Cover with plastic wrap and refrigerate for 1 hour. Thread chicken tightly onto four 12-inch metal skewers.

3A. FOR A CHARCOAL GRILL: Open bottom vent completely. Light large chimney starter three-quarters filled with charcoal briquettes (4½ quarts). When top coals are partially covered with ash, pour evenly over half of grill. Set cooking grate in place, cover, and open lid vent completely. Heat grill until hot, about 5 minutes.

3B. FOR A GAS GRILL: Turn all burners to high, cover, and heat grill until hot, about 15 minutes. Turn all burners to medium-high.

4. Clean and oil cooking grate. Place skewers on hot part of grill (if using charcoal), and cook (covered if using gas), turning kebabs every 2 to 2½ minutes, until well browned and slightly charred, 8 to 10 minutes. Brush top surface of skewers with ¼ cup sauce, flip, and cook until sauce is sizzling and browning in spots, about 1 minute. Brush second side with remaining ¼ cup sauce, flip, and continue to cook until sizzling and browning in spots, about 1 minute longer.

5. Transfer skewers to serving platter, tent loosely with aluminum foil, and let rest for 5 to 10 minutes. Serve, passing reserved sauce separately.

GRILLED SPICE-RUBBED BONE-IN CHICKEN BREASTS

✔ WHY THIS RECIPE WORKS
We set out to create savory, robust spice rub recipes for grilled chicken that would give us deeply browned crusts filled with complex, concentrated flavors. For speed and ease, we chose preground spices (the dry heat of a grill toasts the spices right on the chicken, intensifying their flavors) and added only a modest amount of salt. We found that 1 tablespoon of spice rub was just the amount needed to coat each breast. We brined the chicken for best flavor and started the chicken over the hot side of the grill, finishing it over the cooler side for juicy, tender meat.

SPICE-RUBBED GRILLED BONE-IN CHICKEN BREASTS
SERVES 4

If using kosher chicken, do not brine in step 1. See page 330 for instructions on removing the rib sections from the breasts.

- ½ cup salt
- ½ cup sugar
- 4 (10- to 12-ounce) bone-in split chicken breasts, trimmed
- ¼ cup spice rub (recipes follow)

1. Dissolve salt and sugar in 2 quarts cold water in large container. Submerge chicken in brine, cover, and refrigerate for 30 minutes to 1 hour. Remove chicken

---

TEST KITCHEN TIP NO. 98 BETTER CHARCOAL GRILLING

1. Use enough charcoal. There's no sense spending $50 on steaks and then steaming them over an inadequate fire. Follow the recipe for charcoal amounts. In the end, you want a fire that is slightly larger than the space on the cooking grate occupied by the food.

2. Make sure the coals are covered with fine gray ash before you start to grill. Fine gray ash is a sign that the coals are fully lit and hot.

3. Once the coals are ready, set the cooking grate in place and let it heat up for five minutes. Once the grate is hot, scrape it clean with a grill brush.

from brine and pat dry with paper towels. Rub each breast evenly with 1 tablespoon spice rub.

2A. FOR A CHARCOAL GRILL: Open bottom vent completely. Light large chimney starter filled with charcoal briquettes (6 quarts). When top coals are partially covered with ash, pour evenly over half of grill. Set cooking grate in place, cover, and open lid vent completely. Heat grill until hot, about 5 minutes.

2B. FOR A GAS GRILL: Turn all burners to high, cover, and heat grill until hot, about 15 minutes. Leave primary burner on high and turn off other burner(s). (Adjust primary burner as needed during cooking to maintain grill temperature around 350 degrees.)

3. Clean and oil cooking grate. Place chicken on hot side of grill, skin side down. Cook (covered if using gas) until well browned on both sides, 6 to 8 minutes, flipping halfway through cooking. Move to cool side of grill, cover, and continue to cook until chicken registers 160 degrees, 20 to 30 minutes longer.

4. Transfer chicken to serving platter, tent loosely with aluminum foil, and let rest for 5 to 10 minutes before serving.

CAJUN SPICE RUB
MAKES ABOUT 1 CUP

Store leftover spice rub in an airtight container for up to 3 months. If brining the chicken, omit the salt from the spice rub.

½	cup paprika
2	tablespoons kosher salt
2	tablespoons garlic powder
1	tablespoon dried thyme
2	teaspoons ground celery seeds
2	teaspoons pepper
2	teaspoons cayenne pepper

Combine all ingredients in bowl.

CURRY-CUMIN SPICE RUB
MAKES ABOUT 1 CUP

Store leftover spice rub in an airtight container for up to 3 months. If brining the chicken, omit the salt from the spice rub.

¼	cup curry powder
¼	cup ground cumin
¼	cup chili powder
3	tablespoons pepper
3	tablespoons packed brown sugar
1	tablespoon kosher salt

Combine all ingredients in bowl.

JAMAICAN SPICE RUB
MAKES ABOUT 1 CUP

Store leftover spice rub in an airtight container for up to 3 months. If brining the chicken, omit the salt from the spice rub.

¼	cup packed brown sugar
3	tablespoons kosher salt
3	tablespoons ground coriander
2	tablespoons ground ginger
2	tablespoons garlic powder
1	tablespoon ground allspice
1	tablespoon pepper
2	teaspoons cayenne pepper
2	teaspoons ground nutmeg
1½	teaspoons ground cinnamon

Combine all ingredients in bowl.

TEX-MEX SPICE RUB
MAKES ABOUT 1 CUP

Store leftover spice rub in an airtight container for up to 3 months. If brining the chicken, omit the salt from the spice rub.

¼	cup ground cumin
2	tablespoons chili powder
2	tablespoons ground coriander
2	tablespoons dried oregano
2	tablespoons garlic powder
4	teaspoons kosher salt
2	teaspoons cocoa
1	teaspoon cayenne pepper

Combine all ingredients in bowl.

THAI-STYLE GRILLED CHICKEN

✔ **WHY THIS RECIPE WORKS**
Thai-style grilled chicken is coated in an herb and spice mixture and served with a sweet and spicy dipping sauce. The flavors are wonderfully aromatic and complex, a refreshing change from typical barbecue. We set out to develop our own version. We chose bone-in chicken breasts for our recipe. After testing numerous rub combinations, the simplest version won out, made only with cilantro, black pepper, lime juice, and garlic, accented with the earthy flavor of coriander and fresh ginger. To flavor the meat and skin, we placed a thick layer of the rub under the skin as well as on top of it. The true Thai flavors of this dish come through in the sauce, a classic combination of sweet and spicy. Most recipes suffered from the extremes, but we found balance in a blend of sugar, lime juice, white vinegar, hot red pepper flakes, fish sauce, and garlic.

THAI-STYLE GRILLED CHICKEN WITH SPICY SWEET AND SOUR DIPPING SAUCE
SERVES 4

If using kosher chicken, do not brine in step 1. Some of the rub is inevitably lost to the grill, but the chicken will still be flavorful.

CHICKEN

½	cup salt
½	cup sugar
4	(10- to 12-ounce) bone-in split chicken breasts, trimmed

SAUCE

1/3	cup sugar
1/4	cup distilled white vinegar
1/4	cup lime juice (2 limes)
2	tablespoons fish sauce
3	small garlic cloves, minced
1	teaspoon red pepper flakes

RUB

2/3	cup chopped fresh cilantro
1/4	cup lime juice (2 limes)
12	garlic cloves, minced
2	tablespoons minced fresh ginger
2	tablespoons pepper
2	tablespoons ground coriander
2	tablespoons vegetable oil

1. FOR THE CHICKEN: Dissolve salt and sugar in 2 quarts cold water in large container. Submerge chicken in brine, cover, and refrigerate for 30 minutes to 1 hour. Remove chicken from brine and pat dry with paper towels.

2. FOR THE SAUCE: Whisk all ingredients together in bowl until sugar dissolves; set aside.

3. FOR THE RUB: Combine all ingredients in bowl. Slide fingers between skin and meat to loosen skin, taking care not to detach skin. Rub about 2 tablespoons mixture under skin on each breast, then rub even layer of mixture over outside of each breast. Place chicken in bowl, cover with plastic wrap, and refrigerate while preparing grill.

4A. FOR A CHARCOAL GRILL: Open bottom vent completely. Light large chimney starter filled with charcoal briquettes (6 quarts). When top coals are partially covered with ash, pour evenly over half of grill. Set cooking grate in place, cover, and open lid vent completely. Heat grill until hot, about 5 minutes.

4B. FOR A GAS GRILL: Turn all burners to high, cover, and heat grill until hot, about 15 minutes. Leave primary burner on high and turn off other burner(s).

(Adjust primary burner as needed during cooking to maintain grill temperature around 350 degrees.)

5. Clean and oil cooking grate. Place chicken on hot side of grill, skin side down. Cook (covered if using gas) until well browned on both sides, 6 to 8 minutes, flipping halfway through cooking. Move to cool side of grill, cover, and continue to cook until chicken registers 160 degrees, 20 to 30 minutes longer.

6. Transfer chicken to serving platter, tent loosely with aluminum foil, and let rest for 5 to 10 minutes before serving with sauce.

GRILLED CHICKEN BREASTS WITH BARBECUE SAUCE

✔ **WHY THIS RECIPE WORKS**
The problem with most barbecued chicken is that the sauce is applied too early, so the sugars burn before the chicken has had a chance to cook through. To ensure moist barbecued chicken with great grilled flavor, we first seared the chicken breasts over high heat, then finished cooking them over cooler, indirect heat. During the last few minutes of grilling, we brushed the breasts with a sweet and tangy barbecue sauce made with onion, tomatoes, orange juice, molasses, and chili powder and served more sauce on the side at the table.

GRILLED BONE-IN CHICKEN BREASTS WITH BARBECUE SAUCE
SERVES 4

If using kosher chicken, do not brine in step 3, and season with salt as well as pepper. You will not need all of the barbecue sauce for the chicken. Refrigerate the remaining sauce in an airtight container for up to 2 weeks. See page 330 for instructions on removing the rib sections from the breasts.

SAUCE

2	tablespoons vegetable oil
1	onion, chopped fine
	Salt and pepper
1	(28-ounce) can whole tomatoes
1	(8-ounce) can tomato sauce
3/4	cup distilled white vinegar
1/4	cup packed dark brown sugar
1/4	cup orange juice
2	tablespoons molasses
1	tablespoon paprika
1	tablespoon chili powder

CHICKEN

1/2	cup salt
1/2	cup sugar
4	(10- to 12-ounce) bone-in split chicken breasts, trimmed
	Pepper

1. FOR THE SAUCE: Heat oil in large saucepan over medium heat until shimmering. Add onion and 1/2 teaspoon salt and

---

TEST KITCHEN TIP NO. 99   BETTER GAS GRILLING

1. Remove the warming rack before lighting the grill unless you know you are going to need it. On most grills, the rack is very close to the cooking surface, and it can be hard to reach foods on the back of the grill without burning your hands on the hot metal.

2. Heat the grill with all the burners turned to high (even if you plan on cooking over low heat) and keep the lid down for at least 15 minutes. Once the grill is hot, scrape the cooking grate clean with a grill brush and then adjust the burners as desired.

3. Whether cooking by direct or indirect heat, we often keep the lid down. Keeping the lid down concentrates the heat when searing and keeps the temperature steady when slow-cooking.

cook, stirring occasionally, until golden, 7 to 10 minutes. Stir in tomatoes, tomato sauce, vinegar, sugar, orange juice, molasses, paprika, and chili powder, bring to simmer, and cook over low heat until thickened, 2 to 2½ hours.

2. Process sauce in blender (or food processor) until smooth. Season with salt and pepper to taste. Measure out and reserve 1 cup sauce for brushing on chicken and set remaining sauce aside for serving.

3. FOR THE CHICKEN: While sauce simmers, dissolve salt and sugar in 2 quarts cold water in large container. Submerge chicken in brine, cover, and refrigerate for 30 minutes to 1 hour. Remove chicken from brine and pat dry with paper towels. Season chicken with pepper.

4A. FOR A CHARCOAL GRILL: Open bottom vent completely. Light large chimney starter filled with charcoal briquettes (6 quarts). When top coals are partially covered with ash, pour evenly over half of grill. Set cooking grate in place, cover, and open lid vent completely. Heat grill until hot, about 5 minutes.

4B. FOR A GAS GRILL: Turn all burners to high, cover, and heat grill until hot, about 15 minutes. Leave primary burner on high and turn off other burner(s). (Adjust primary burner as needed during cooking to maintain grill temperature around 350 degrees.)

5. Clean and oil cooking grate. Place chicken on hot side of grill, skin side down. Cook (covered if using gas) until well browned on both sides, 6 to 8 minutes, flipping halfway through cooking. Move to cool side of grill, still skin side up, cover, and continue to cook until chicken registers 150 degrees, 15 to 20 minutes longer. Brush chicken generously with ½ cup reserved sauce and cook for 5 to 10 minutes. Flip chicken, brush with ½ cup sauce and continue to

cook, uncovered, until chicken registers 160 degrees, 2 to 3 minutes longer.

6. Transfer chicken to serving platter, tent loosely with aluminum foil, and let rest for 5 to 10 minutes before serving, passing sauce for serving separately.

GRILLED CHICKEN BREASTS WITH ASIAN BARBECUE SAUCE

Add 6 tablespoons soy sauce, 6 tablespoons rice vinegar, 3 tablespoons sugar, 1½ tablespoons toasted sesame oil, and 1 tablespoon minced fresh ginger to sauce after pureeing.

GRILLED CHICKEN BREASTS WITH MEXICAN BARBECUE SAUCE

Add 6 tablespoons lime juice, 3 tablespoons chopped fresh cilantro, 1½ teaspoons ground cumin, and 1½ teaspoons chili powder to sauce after pureeing.

SPICY SAUCES FOR GRILLING CHICKEN OR PORK

✓ WHY THIS RECIPE WORKS
We like tomato-based barbecue sauces, but sometimes we crave a barbecue sauce with more exciting flavors. We started by brainstorming for alternatives to ketchup or tomato sauce that would lend viscosity, stickiness, and an ability to serve as a foundation for a variety of flavorful add-ins. An unconventional idea, caramel, fit the bill. Super-adhesive and plenty thick, it couldn't have been simpler to make. It took all of five minutes to caramelize the sugar and then we added a balance of sweet-tangy flavors such as hoisin sauce and pineapple juice, apple butter and whole grain mustard, orange marmalade and orange juice, and coconut milk and lime juice, along with spicy ingredients like red curry paste, chipotle chiles, and red pepper flakes.

APPLE-MUSTARD GRILLING SAUCE
MAKES ABOUT 1 CUP

Our grilling sauces work equally well on chicken or pork and yield enough to coat 6 to 8 pieces (3 to 4 pounds) of meat, plus extra for the table. Wait to apply until the last 5 minutes of grilling (the meat should be about 5 degrees below the desired final internal temperature). Brush one side of the meat with ¼ cup of the sauce reserved for cooking, then flip it and cook until browned, about 2 minutes. Brush the second side with another ¼ cup of sauce reserved for cooking, then flip it and cook until browned on the second side, 2 to 3 minutes. Serve, passing the remaining ½ cup sauce separately. We prefer to make this sauce in a heavy-bottomed saucepan because its insulation protects against scorching.

⅔ cup apple cider or apple juice
⅓ cup apple butter
3 tablespoons whole grain mustard
1 teaspoon dry mustard
2 tablespoons cider vinegar
½ teaspoon salt
⅛ teaspoon cayenne pepper
⅓ cup water
⅓ cup sugar

1. Whisk cider, apple butter, whole grain and dry mustards, vinegar, salt, and cayenne in medium bowl.

2. Place water in 2-quart saucepan; pour sugar in center of pan, taking care not to let sugar crystals adhere to sides of pan. Cover and bring mixture to boil over high heat; once boiling, uncover and continue to boil until syrup is thick and straw-colored, 3 to 4 minutes. Reduce heat to medium and continue to cook until syrup is golden amber, 1 to 2 minutes longer. Quickly remove saucepan from heat and whisk in cider mixture. Return to medium heat and cook, whisking constantly, until caramel has dissolved and sauce has thickened, about 2 minutes. Transfer ½ cup

sauce to medium bowl to use for grilling. Set aside remaining sauce for serving.

HOISIN GRILLING SAUCE

Whisk ½ cup hoisin sauce, 3 tablespoons rice vinegar, 3 tablespoons pineapple juice, 1 tablespoon soy sauce, 1 tablespoon minced fresh ginger, ¼ teaspoon red pepper flakes, and pinch five-spice powder in medium bowl and substitute for cider mixture in step 2.

ORANGE-CHIPOTLE GRILLING SAUCE

Whisk ½ cup orange marmalade, ½ teaspoon finely grated orange zest, ⅓ cup orange juice, ¼ cup white vinegar, 1 tablespoon minced canned chipotle chile in adobo sauce, and ½ teaspoon salt in medium bowl and substitute for cider mixture in step 2.

COCONUT–RED CURRY GRILLING SAUCE

Whisk 1¼ cups coconut milk, ½ teaspoon finely grated lime zest and ¼ cup lime juice (2 limes), 1 tablespoon red curry paste, and 1 tablespoon fish sauce in medium bowl and substitute for cider mixture in step 2, increasing final sauce thickening time to 6 to 7 minutes.

GRILLED STUFFED CHICKEN BREASTS

✔ **WHY THIS RECIPE WORKS**
The smokiness of grilled chicken requires a more flavorful stuffing than chicken cooked in the oven. Instead of the traditional deli ham and Swiss cheese, we opted for prosciutto and fontina, a moist melting cheese with moderate tang. We cut a pocket in each chicken breast to hold the filling. To keep the cheese from oozing out on the grill, we cut it into sticks, then wrapped the prosciutto around it and placed the whole bundle inside the chicken. For even more flavor and moisture, we spread softened butter flavored with shallot and tarragon inside the chicken before adding the prosciutto and cheese.

GRILLED STUFFED CHICKEN BREASTS WITH PROSCIUTTO AND FONTINA

SERVES 4

If using kosher chicken, do not brine in step 1. You can serve the chicken on the bone, but we prefer to carve it off and slice it before serving.

4   (10- to 12-ounce) bone-in split chicken breasts, trimmed
    Salt and pepper
4   tablespoons unsalted butter, softened

1   shallot, minced
4   teaspoons chopped fresh tarragon
2   ounces fontina cheese, rind removed, cut into four 3 by ½-inch sticks
4   thin slices prosciutto

1. Using sharp knife and starting on thick side of breast closest to breastbone, cut horizontal pocket in each breast, stopping ½ inch from edge so halves remain attached. Dissolve ¼ cup salt in 2 quarts cold water in large container. Submerge chicken breasts in brine, cover, and refrigerate for 30 minutes to 1 hour. Remove chicken from brine and pat dry with paper towels. Season chicken with pepper.

2A. FOR A CHARCOAL GRILL: Open bottom vent completely. Light large chimney starter filled with charcoal briquettes (6 quarts). When top coals are partially covered with ash, pour evenly over half of grill. Set cooking grate in place, cover, and open lid vent completely. Heat grill until hot, about 5 minutes.

2B. FOR A GAS GRILL: Turn all burners to high, cover, and heat grill until hot, about 15 minutes. Leave primary burner on high and turn off other burner(s). (Adjust primary burner as needed during cooking to maintain grill temperature around 350 degrees.)

ASSEMBLING STUFFED CHICKEN BREASTS FOR GRILLING

  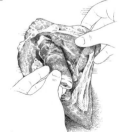 

1. Starting on thick side closest to breastbone, cut horizontal pocket in each breast, stopping ½ inch from edge.

2. Spread equal portion of flavored butter inside each breast.

3. Place one meat-wrapped piece of cheese inside each breast and fold breast over to enclose.

4. Tie each breast with three 12-inch pieces of kitchen twine at even intervals.

3. Meanwhile, combine butter, shallot, and tarragon in bowl. Roll each piece of fontina in 1 slice prosciutto. Spread equal amount of butter mixture inside each breast. Place 1 prosciutto-wrapped piece of fontina inside each breast and fold breast over to enclose. Evenly space 3 pieces kitchen twine (each about 12 inches long) beneath each breast and tie, trimming any excess.

4. Clean and oil cooking grate. Place chicken on hot side of grill, skin side down. Cook (covered if using gas) until well browned on first side, 4 to 6 minutes. Flip chicken and cook until second side is just opaque, about 2 minutes. Move chicken to cool side of grill, skin side up with thicker side of breasts facing coals and flames. Cover and continue to cook until chicken registers 160 degrees, 25 to 35 minutes longer.

5. Transfer chicken to carving board, tent loosely with aluminum foil, and let rest for 5 to 10 minutes. Remove twine, cut meat from bone, slice ½ inch thick, and serve.

GRILLED STUFFED CHICKEN BREASTS WITH BLACK FOREST HAM AND GRUYÈRE

Substitute 1 teaspoon minced fresh thyme for tarragon and add 1 tablespoon Dijon mustard to butter. Substitute Gruyère cheese for fontina and 4 slices Black Forest ham for prosciutto.

GRILLED STUFFED CHICKEN BREASTS WITH SALAMI AND MOZZARELLA

Substitute 3 minced garlic cloves for shallot, basil for tarragon, low-moisture mozzarella cheese for fontina, and 8 slices Genoa salami for prosciutto.

GRILLED GLAZED BONE-IN CHICKEN BREASTS

✓ WHY THIS RECIPE WORKS

We wanted glazed chicken breasts with tender meat and crisp, lacquered skin. Brining the chicken breasts before grilling helped ensure juicy, seasoned meat. For the glazes, we balanced sweet ingredients, like molasses and sugar, with bold flavors, like chipotle chiles, ginger, and curry powder. To keep the glazes from burning on the grill, we followed our method for Grilled Bone-In Chicken Breasts with Barbecue Sauce (page 469), first searing the breasts over high heat, then moving them to the cool side of the grill, where we brushed them with the glaze in the last few minutes. For extra flavor, we reserved half of the glaze for serving.

GRILLED GLAZED BONE-IN CHICKEN BREASTS

SERVES 4

If using kosher chicken, do not brine in step 1, and season with salt as well as pepper. Remember to reserve half of the glaze for serving.

- ½ cup salt
- 4 (10- to 12-ounce) bone-in split chicken breasts, trimmed
  Pepper
- 1 recipe glaze (recipes follow)

1. Dissolve salt in 2 quarts cold water in large container. Submerge chicken breasts in brine, cover, and refrigerate for 30 minutes to 1 hour. Remove chicken from brine and pat dry with paper towels. Season chicken with pepper.

2A. FOR A CHARCOAL GRILL: Open bottom vent completely. Light large chimney starter filled with charcoal briquettes (6 quarts). When top coals are partially covered with ash, pour evenly over half of grill. Set cooking grate in place, cover, and open lid vent completely. Heat grill until hot, about 5 minutes.

2B. FOR A GAS GRILL: Turn all burners to high, cover, and heat grill until hot, about 15 minutes. Leave primary burner on high and turn off other burner(s). (Adjust primary burner as needed during cooking to maintain grill temperature around 350 degrees.)

3. Clean and oil cooking grate. Place chicken on hot side of grill, skin side up, and cook (covered if using gas) until lightly browned on both sides, 6 to 8 minutes, flipping halfway through cooking. Move chicken, skin side down, to cool side of grill, with thicker end of breasts facing coals and flames. Cover and continue to cook until chicken registers 150 degrees, 15 to 20 minutes longer.

4. Brush bone side of chicken generously with half of glaze, move to hot side of grill, and cook until browned, 5 to 10 minutes. Brush skin side of chicken with remaining glaze, flip chicken, and continue to cook until chicken registers 160 degrees, 2 to 3 minutes longer.

5. Transfer chicken to serving platter, tent loosely with aluminum foil, and let rest for 5 to 10 minutes before serving, passing reserved glaze separately.

ORANGE-CHIPOTLE GLAZE

MAKES ABOUT ¾ CUP, ENOUGH FOR 1 RECIPE GRILLED GLAZED BONE-IN CHICKEN BREASTS

For a spicier glaze, use the greater amount of chipotle chiles.

- 1 teaspoon grated orange zest plus ⅔ cup juice (2 oranges)
- 1–2 tablespoons minced canned chipotle chile in adobo sauce
- 1 small shallot, minced
- 2 teaspoons minced fresh thyme
- 1 tablespoon molasses
- ¾ teaspoon cornstarch
  Salt

Combine orange zest and juice, chipotle, shallot, and thyme in small saucepan. Whisk in molasses and cornstarch, bring to simmer, and cook over medium heat until thickened, about 5 minutes. Season with salt to taste. Reserve half of glaze for serving and use remaining glaze to brush on chicken.

SOY-GINGER GLAZE

MAKES ABOUT ¾ CUP, ENOUGH FOR
1 RECIPE GRILLED GLAZED BONE-IN
CHICKEN BREASTS

Reduce the amount of salt in the brine to ¼ cup when using this glaze.

- ⅓ cup water
- ¼ cup soy sauce
- 2 tablespoons mirin
- 1 tablespoon grated fresh ginger
- 2 garlic cloves, minced
- 3 tablespoons sugar
- ¾ teaspoon cornstarch
- 2 scallions, minced

Combine water, soy sauce, mirin, ginger, and garlic in small saucepan, then whisk in sugar and cornstarch. Bring to simmer over medium heat and cook until thickened, about 5 minutes; stir in scallions. Reserve half of glaze for serving and use remaining glaze to brush on chicken.

CURRY-YOGURT GLAZE

MAKES ABOUT ¾ CUP, ENOUGH FOR
1 RECIPE GRILLED GLAZED BONE-IN
CHICKEN BREASTS

- ¾ cup plain whole-milk yogurt
- 2 garlic cloves, minced
- 2 teaspoons grated fresh ginger
- 2 teaspoons minced fresh cilantro
- ½ teaspoon grated lemon zest
- 1½ teaspoons curry powder
- ½ teaspoon sugar
  Salt and pepper

Whisk all ingredients together in bowl and season with salt and pepper to taste. Reserve half of glaze for serving and use remaining glaze to brush on chicken.

MAHOGANY GRILLED CHICKEN THIGHS OR LEGS

✔ WHY THIS RECIPE WORKS

For evenly cooked, moist, tender chicken legs and thighs with dark and crisp skin, we seared the chicken over a medium-hot fire and then moved it to a medium-low fire to finish cooking. Rubbing the chicken with a spice paste prior to grilling proved far more satisfactory than marinating. We also found that brining the chicken seasoned and slightly firmed up the texture of the meat in little time.

MAHOGANY GRILLED CHICKEN THIGHS OR LEGS

SERVES 4

Chicken leg quarters consist of drumsticks attached to thighs; often also attached are backbone sections that must be trimmed away. Brining improves the chicken's flavor, but if you're short on time, you can skip step 1 and simply flavor the chicken (see the paste recipes that follow).

- ½ cup sugar
- ½ cup salt
- 4 (14-ounce) chicken leg quarters or 8 (5- to 7 -ounce) bone-in chicken thighs, trimmed
  Pepper

1. Dissolve sugar and salt in 2 quarts cold water in large container. Submerge chicken leg quarters in brine, cover, and refrigerate for 30 minutes to 1 hour. Remove chicken from brine and pat dry with paper towels. Season chicken with pepper.

2A. FOR A CHARCOAL GRILL: Open bottom vent completely. Light large chimney starter filled with charcoal briquettes (6 quarts). When top coals are partially covered with ash, pour two-thirds evenly over grill, then pour remaining coals over half of grill. Set cooking grate in place, cover, and open lid vent completely. Heat grill until hot, about 5 minutes.

2B. FOR A GAS GRILL: Turn all burners to high, cover, and heat grill until hot, about 15 minutes. Turn all burners to medium-high.

3. Clean and oil cooking grate. Place chicken on grill (hotter side if using charcoal), skin side down. Cook (covered if using gas) until well browned on both sides, 4 to 6 minutes, flipping halfway through cooking. Move chicken to cooler

TRIMMING LEG QUARTERS

1. Carefully grasp leg and bend backbone section to pop joint.

2. Using sharp boning knife, cut backbone section from leg.

3. Trim away any large pockets of fat.

side of grill (if using charcoal) or turn burners to medium-low (if using gas). Cover and continue to cook, turning occasionally, until chicken is dark and registers 175 degrees, 16 to 20 minutes for whole legs and 12 to 16 minutes for thighs.

4. Transfer chicken to serving platter, tent loosely with aluminum foil, and let rest for 5 to 10 minutes before serving.

ASIAN SPICE PASTE
MAKES ABOUT ½ CUP, ENOUGH FOR
I RECIPE MAHOGANY GRILLED CHICKEN
THIGHS OR LEGS

2 tablespoons fresh cilantro leaves
2 tablespoons soy sauce
2 tablespoons peanut oil
I tablespoon minced jalapeño chile
I tablespoon minced fresh ginger
2 garlic cloves

Process all ingredients in food processor or blender until smooth, about 20 seconds. Rub paste generously under chicken skin and grill as directed.

CHILI SPICE PASTE WITH CITRUS AND CILANTRO
MAKES ABOUT ⅓ CUP, ENOUGH FOR
I RECIPE MAHOGANY GRILLED CHICKEN
THIGHS OR LEGS

2 tablespoons fresh cilantro leaves
I tablespoon orange juice
I tablespoon pineapple juice
I tablespoon lime juice
I tablespoon olive oil
I teaspoon ground cumin
I teaspoon chili powder
I teaspoon paprika
I teaspoon ground coriander
I small garlic clove
2 dashes hot sauce

Process all ingredients in food processor or blender until smooth, about 20 seconds. Rub paste generously under chicken skin and grill as directed.

MEDITERRANEAN SPICE PASTE
MAKES ABOUT ½ CUP, ENOUGH FOR
I RECIPE MAHOGANY GRILLED CHICKEN
THIGHS OR LEGS

4 garlic cloves
2 tablespoons grated lemon zest
   (2 lemons)
¼ cup fresh parsley
¼ cup olive oil
I tablespoon fresh thyme
I tablespoon fresh rosemary
I tablespoon fresh sage

Process all ingredients in food processor or blender until smooth, about 20 seconds. Rub paste generously under chicken skin and grill as directed.

SWEET AND SOUR CURRY SPICE PASTE
MAKES ABOUT ½ CUP, ENOUGH FOR
I RECIPE MAHOGANY GRILLED CHICKEN
THIGHS OR LEGS

¼ cup red wine vinegar
¼ cup distilled white vinegar
¼ cup peanut oil
I tablespoon ground cumin
I tablespoon curry powder
I tablespoon crushed coriander seeds
I tablespoon paprika
I tablespoon packed brown sugar
2 garlic cloves, minced

Combine all ingredients in bowl. Grill chicken as directed, brushing some spice mixture on both sides of chicken while chicken cooks on cooler side of grill.

BARBECUED PULLED CHICKEN

✔ WHY THIS RECIPE WORKS
Made-from-scratch barbecued pulled chicken sandwiches often consist of boneless chicken breasts and bottled barbecue sauce. The result is a sandwich with no smoke, tough meat, and artificial flavor. We wanted a recipe that gave us tender, smoky chicken meat in a tangy, sweet sauce. We chose whole chicken legs for great flavor, low cost, and resistance to overcooking. The legs cooked gently but thoroughly over indirect heat, absorbing plenty of smoke flavor along the way. Cooking the chicken to a higher-than-usual temperature also dissolved connective tissue and rendered more fat, making the meat tender and less greasy. Once the chicken finished cooking, we hand-shredded half and machine-processed the other half for a texture similar to pulled pork. The chicken then just had to be combined with a tangy barbecue sauce to become truly bun-worthy.

BARBECUED PULLED CHICKEN
SERVES 6 TO 8

Chicken leg quarters consist of drumsticks attached to thighs; often also attached are backbone sections that must be trimmed away. Two medium wood chunks, soaked in water for I hour, can be substituted for the wood chip packet on a charcoal grill. Serve the pulled chicken on hamburger rolls or sandwich bread, with pickles and coleslaw.

CHICKEN
2 cups wood chips, soaked in water
   for 15 minutes and drained
I (16 by 12-inch) disposable
   aluminum roasting pan (if using
   charcoal)
I tablespoon vegetable oil
8 (14-ounce) chicken leg quarters,
   trimmed
   Salt and pepper

SAUCE

1	large onion, peeled and quartered
¼	cup water
1½	cups ketchup
1½	cups apple cider
¼	cup molasses
¼	cup apple cider vinegar
3	tablespoons Worcestershire sauce
3	tablespoons Dijon mustard
½	teaspoon pepper
1	tablespoon vegetable oil
1½	tablespoons chili powder
2	garlic cloves, minced
½	teaspoon cayenne pepper
	Hot sauce

1. FOR THE CHICKEN: Using large piece of heavy-duty aluminum foil, wrap soaked chips in foil packet and cut several vent holes in top.

2A. FOR A CHARCOAL GRILL: Open bottom vent halfway and place roasting pan in center of grill. Light large chimney starter three-quarters filled with charcoal briquettes (4½ quarts). When top coals are partially covered with ash, pour into 2 even piles on either side of roasting pan. Place wood chip packet on 1 pile of coals. Set cooking grate in place, cover, and open lid vent halfway. Heat grill until hot and wood chips are smoking, about 5 minutes.

IMPROVISED GRILL BRUSH

Food that is being grilled is much less likely to stick to a clean grate. We recommend cleaning the hot grate with a grill brush. But if you don't have one handy, a brush can be improvised with a pair of tongs and a crumpled wad of aluminum foil.

2B. FOR A GAS GRILL: Place wood chip packet directly on primary burner. Turn all burners to high, cover, and heat grill until hot and wood chips are smoking, about 15 minutes. Turn all burners to medium. (Adjust burners as needed during cooking to maintain grill temperature between 250 and 300 degrees.)

3. Clean and oil cooking grate. Pat chicken dry with paper towels and season with salt and pepper. Place chicken in single layer on center of grill (over roasting pan if using charcoal), skin side up, or evenly over grill (if using gas). Cover (position lid vent over meat if using charcoal) and cook until chicken registers 185 degrees, 1 to 1½ hours, rotating the chicken pieces halfway through cooking. Transfer chicken to carving board, tent loosely with foil, and let rest until cool enough to handle.

4. FOR THE SAUCE: Meanwhile, process onion and water in food processor until mixture resembles slush, about 30 seconds. Pass through fine-mesh strainer into liquid measuring cup, pressing on solids with rubber spatula (you should have ¾ cup strained onion juice). Discard solids in strainer.

5. Whisk onion juice, ketchup, cider, molasses, 3 tablespoons vinegar, Worcestershire, mustard, and ½ teaspoon pepper together in bowl. Heat oil in large saucepan over medium heat until shimmering. Stir in chili powder, garlic, and cayenne and cook until fragrant, about 30 seconds. Stir in ketchup mixture, bring to simmer, and cook over medium-low heat until slightly thickened, about 15 minutes (you should have about 4 cups of sauce). Transfer 2 cups sauce to serving bowl; leave remaining sauce in saucepan.

6. TO SERVE: Remove and discard skin from chicken legs. Using your fingers, pull meat off bones, separating larger pieces (which should fall off bones easily) from smaller, drier pieces into 2 equal piles.

7. Pulse smaller chicken pieces in food processor until just coarsely chopped, 3 to 4 pulses, stirring chicken with rubber spatula

after each pulse. Add chopped chicken to sauce in saucepan. Using your fingers or 2 forks, pull larger chicken pieces into long shreds and add to saucepan. Stir in remaining 1 tablespoon cider vinegar, cover, and heat chicken over medium-low heat, stirring occasionally, until heated through, about 10 minutes. Add hot sauce to taste and serve, passing remaining sauce separately.

BARBECUED PULLED CHICKEN
FOR A CROWD

This recipe serves 10 to 12. This technique works well on a charcoal grill but not so well on a gas grill. If your gas grill is large and can accommodate more than 8 legs, follow the master recipe, adding as many legs as will comfortably fit in a single layer.

Increase amount of charcoal briquettes to 6 quarts. Use 12 chicken legs and slot them into V-shaped roasting rack set on top of cooking grate over disposable aluminum pan. Increase cooking time in step 3 to 1½ to 1¾ hours. In step 5, remove only 1 cup of sauce from saucepan. In step 7, pulse chicken in food processor in 2 batches.

SMOKED CHICKEN

✔ WHY THIS RECIPE WORKS

Smoked chicken needs to be cooked for a long time to be truly imbued with smoke flavor, but the breast meat dries out easily, and without high heat it's difficult to get the skin to crisp. We wanted a recipe for perfectly cooked meat with a pervasive smoky flavor and crisp mahogany skin. First, a salt and sugar brine guaranteed moist, well-seasoned meat. We found that chicken parts were easier and better than whole chickens; the breasts could cook evenly on the coolest part of the grill and more of the bird was exposed to the smoke and heat, adding flavor and rendering more fat from the skin. To keep the skin moist, we brushed it with oil and added a pan of water to the grill. One wood chip packet burned too quickly to permeate the meat, so we added a second, which produced the ideal amount of smoke for meat subtly flavored all the way through. In the end, we had wonderfully smoky, moist chicken with glossy skin after only 90 minutes on the grill.

SMOKED CHICKEN
SERVES 6 TO 8

If using kosher chicken, do not brine in step 1. Two medium wood chunks, soaked in water for 1 hour, can be substituted for the wood chip packet on a charcoal grill.

- 1 cup salt
- 1 cup sugar
- 6 pounds bone-in chicken parts (breasts, thighs, and/or drumsticks), trimmed
- 3 tablespoons vegetable oil
  Pepper
- 3 cups wood chips, 1½ cups soaked in water for 15 minutes and drained, plus 1½ cups wood chips unsoaked
- 1 (16 by 12-inch) disposable aluminum roasting pan (if using charcoal) or disposable aluminum pie plate (if using gas)

1. Dissolve salt and sugar in 4 quarts cold water in large container. Submerge chicken pieces in brine, cover, and refrigerate for 30 minutes to 1 hour. Remove chicken from brine and pat dry with paper towels. Brush chicken evenly with oil and season with pepper.

2. Using large piece of heavy-duty aluminum foil, wrap soaked chips in foil packet and cut several vent holes in top. Repeat with another sheet of foil and unsoaked wood chips.

3A. FOR A CHARCOAL GRILL: Open bottom vent halfway. Arrange 2 quarts unlit charcoal banked against 1 side of grill and disposable pan filled with 2 cups water on empty side of grill. Light large chimney starter half filled with charcoal briquettes (3 quarts). When top coals are partially covered with ash, pour on top of unlit charcoal, to cover one-third of grill with coals steeply banked against side of grill. Place wood chip packets on top of coals. Set cooking grate in place, cover, and open lid vent halfway. Heat grill until hot and wood chips begin to smoke, about 5 minutes.

3B. FOR A GAS GRILL: Place wood chip packets directly on primary burner. Place disposable pie plate filled with 2 cups water on other burner(s). Turn all burners to high, cover, and heat grill until hot and wood chips begin to smoke, about 15 minutes. Turn primary burner to medium-high and turn off other burner(s). (Adjust primary burner as needed to maintain grill temperature around 325 degrees.)

4. Clean and oil cooking grate. Place chicken on cool side of grill, skin side up, as far away from heat as possible with thighs closest to heat and breasts furthest away. Cover (positioning lid vents over chicken if using charcoal) and cook until breasts register 160 degrees and thighs/drumsticks register 175 degrees, 1¼ to 1½ hours.

5. Transfer chicken to serving platter, tent loosely with foil, and let rest for 5 to 10 minutes before serving.

GRILLED LEMON CHICKEN

✔ WHY THIS RECIPE WORKS
Most lemon chicken tastes sparsely of lemon (if at all) and the meat is often tough and dry. We wanted grilled chicken with bright lemon flavor that went straight to the bone—yet still came off the grill moist and juicy. To achieve our goal, we grilled the chicken until it was nearly done, pulling it off the grill to dip it in a lemon sauce flavored with extra-virgin olive oil, garlic, and thyme, returning it to the grill over low heat for about five more minutes, and then dipping it in reserved lemon sauce once more before serving.

GRILLED LEMON CHICKEN
SERVES 6 TO 8

If using kosher chicken, do not brine in step 1. If you have it, 1 tablespoon minced fresh rosemary makes a nice addition to the lemon sauce.

- ¾ cup salt
- 2 (3½- to 4-pound) whole chickens, each cut into 10 pieces (4 breast pieces, 2 drumsticks, 2 thighs, 2 wings)
  Pepper
- ¼ cup extra-virgin olive oil
- 6 garlic cloves, minced into paste
- 1 cup lemon juice (6 lemons)
- 1 tablespoon minced fresh thyme or 1½ teaspoons dried

1. Dissolve salt in 3 quarts cold water in large container. Submerge chicken in brine, cover, and refrigerate for 30 minutes to 1 hour. Remove chicken from brine and pat dry with paper towels. Season chicken with pepper.

2A. FOR A CHARCOAL GRILL: Open bottom vent completely. Light large chimney starter filled with charcoal briquettes (6 quarts). When top coals are partially covered with ash, pour two-thirds coals evenly over grill, then pour remaining coals over half of grill. Set cooking grate in place, cover, and open lid vent completely. Heat grill until hot, about 5 minutes.

2B. FOR A GAS GRILL: Turn all burners to high, cover, and heat grill until hot, about 15 minutes.

3. While grill heats, heat oil and garlic in small saucepan over low heat until garlic sizzles, 1 to 2 minutes. Stir in lemon juice. Transfer half of mixture to small bowl and set aside. Transfer remaining half of mixture to 13 by 9-inch baking dish.

4. Clean and oil cooking grate. Place chicken on grill (hotter side if using charcoal), skin side down. Cook (covered if using gas) until well browned on both sides, 15 to 20 minutes, flipping halfway through

cooking. Stir thyme into lemon juice mixture in baking dish, then place chicken pieces in baking dish and turn to coat.

5. Return chicken pieces to cooler side of grill (if using charcoal), skin side up, or turn burners to medium-low (if using gas). Continue to cook (covered if using gas) until breasts register 160 degrees and thighs/drumsticks register 175 degrees, about 5 minutes longer, brushing with reserved lemon mixture twice.

6. Transfer chicken to serving platter, tent loosely with aluminum foil, and let rest for 5 to 10 minutes before serving.

LIME CHICKEN WITH JALAPEÑO AND CORIANDER

An equal amount of toasted and crushed cumin seeds may be substituted for the coriander seeds.

Add 2 teaspoons minced jalapeño chiles and 2 teaspoons crushed coriander seeds with garlic. Substitute 1 cup lime juice (10 limes) for lemon juice and 2 tablespoons minced fresh cilantro for thyme.

GRILL-ROASTED WHOLE CHICKEN

✔ WHY THIS RECIPE WORKS
Many people avoid grilling whole chickens because the exterior of the bird chars before the interior cooks through. We wanted to find a way to grill a chicken that would produce tender, juicy meat with deeply smoky flavor and crisp mahogany skin. For well-seasoned meat that wouldn't dry out, we brined the chicken and then, for more flavor, we coated the chicken with an aromatic spice rub. We arranged the coals on either side of the grill with a roasting pan in the middle. We cooked the chicken in the middle of the grill over the roasting pan where it wouldn't burn, but would receive ample heat from both piles of coals. For a gas grill, a medium fire worked well. And for maximum smoky flavor, we used wood chips.

GRILL-ROASTED WHOLE CHICKEN
SERVES 4

If using kosher chicken, do not brine in step 1. When using a charcoal grill, we prefer wood chunks to wood chips whenever possible; substitute 4 medium wood chunks, soaked in water for 1 hour, for the wood chip packets.

- ½   cup salt
- 1   (3½- to 4-pound) whole chicken
- 3   tablespoons spice rub (recipes follow)
- 2   cups wood chips, soaked in water for 15 minutes and drained
- 1   (16 by 12-inch) disposable aluminum roasting pan (if using charcoal)

1. Dissolve salt in 2 quarts cold water in large container. Submerge chicken in brine, cover, and refrigerate for 1 hour. Remove chicken from brine and pat dry with paper towels. Rub chicken evenly, inside and out, with spice rub, lifting up skin over breast and rubbing spice rub directly onto meat.

2. Using large piece of heavy-duty aluminum foil, wrap soaked chips in foil packet and cut several vent holes in top.

3A. FOR A CHARCOAL GRILL: Open bottom vent halfway and place roasting pan in center of grill. Light large chimney starter filled with charcoal briquettes (6 quarts). When top coals are partially covered with ash, pour into 2 even piles on either side of roasting pan. Place 1 wood chip packet on each pile of coals. Set cooking grate in place, cover, and open lid vent halfway. Heat grill until hot and wood chips are smoking, about 5 minutes.

3B. FOR A GAS GRILL: Place wood chip packets directly on primary burner. Turn all burners to high, cover, and heat grill until hot and wood chips are smoking, about 15 minutes. Turn all burners to medium. (Adjust burners as needed to maintain grill temperature around 325 degrees.)

4. Clean and oil cooking grate. Place chicken on center of grill (over roasting pan if using charcoal), breast side down, cover (position lid vent over meat if using charcoal), and cook for 30 minutes.

5. Working quickly, remove lid and, using 2 large wads of paper towels, turn chicken breast side up. Cover and continue to cook until breast registers 160 degrees and thighs register 175 degrees, 25 to 35 minutes longer. Transfer chicken to carving board, tent loosely with foil, and let rest for 15 minutes before carving and serving.

FRAGRANT DRY SPICE RUB
MAKES ABOUT ½ CUP

Store leftover spice rub in an airtight container for up to 3 months.

- 2   tablespoons ground cumin
- 2   tablespoons curry powder
- 2   tablespoons chili powder
- 1   tablespoon ground allspice
- 1   tablespoon pepper
- 1   teaspoon ground cinnamon

Combine all ingredients in bowl.

CITRUS-CILANTRO WET SPICE RUB
MAKES ABOUT 3 TABLESPOONS, ENOUGH FOR 1 RECIPE GRILL-ROASTED WHOLE CHICKEN

For more heat, add up to ½ teaspoon cayenne pepper.

- 1   tablespoon minced fresh cilantro
- 1   tablespoon orange juice
- 1½   teaspoons lime juice
- 1½   teaspoons extra-virgin olive oil
- 1   small garlic clove, minced
- ½   teaspoon ground cumin
- ½   teaspoon chili powder
- ½   teaspoon paprika
- ½   teaspoon ground coriander

Combine all ingredients in bowl. Use immediately.

GRILL-ROASTED WHOLE CHICKEN WITH SWEET AND TANGY BARBECUE SAUCE

If you like, barbecue sauce can be used along with the spice rub. Wait until the bird is almost done to brush on the barbecue sauce, so that it does not scorch. See our Sweet and Tangy Barbecue Sauce (recipe follows) or use your favorite.

After rotating chicken breast side up in step 5, cook until thighs register 160 degrees, about 15 minutes. Working quickly, remove lid and brush outside and inside of chicken with ½ cup barbecue sauce. Cover and continue to cook until breast registers 160 degrees and thighs register 175 degrees, 10 to 15 minutes longer. Serve, passing additional barbecue sauce separately.

SWEET AND TANGY BARBECUE SAUCE

MAKES ABOUT 1½ CUPS

Leftover sauce can be refrigerated in an airtight container for up to 1 week.

1	onion, peeled and quartered
¼	cup water
1	cup ketchup
5	tablespoons molasses
2	tablespoons cider vinegar
2	tablespoons Worcestershire sauce
2	tablespoons Dijon mustard
1½	teaspoons liquid smoke (optional)
1	teaspoon hot sauce
¼	teaspoon pepper
2	tablespoons vegetable oil
1	garlic clove, minced
1	teaspoon chili powder
¼	teaspoon cayenne pepper

1. Process onion and water in food processor until mixture resembles slush, about 30 seconds. Pass through fine-mesh strainer into liquid measuring cup, pressing on solids with rubber spatula (you should have ½ cup strained onion juice). Discard solids in strainer.

2. Whisk onion juice, ketchup, molasses, vinegar, Worcestershire, mustard, liquid smoke, if using, hot sauce, and pepper together in bowl.

3. Heat oil in large saucepan over medium heat until shimmering. Stir in garlic, chili powder, and cayenne and cook until fragrant, about 30 seconds. Stir in ketchup mixture, bring to simmer, and cook over medium-low heat until slightly thickened, 10 to 15 minutes. Cool sauce to room temperature before using.

GRILL-ROASTED BEER CAN CHICKEN

✓ WHY THIS RECIPE WORKS
Beer can chicken on the grill is spectacular. The beer in the open can simmers and turns to steam as the chicken roasts, which makes the meat remarkably juicy and rich similar to braised chicken. As an added bonus, the dry heat of the grill crisps the skin and renders the fat away. To perfect the technique, we added woods chips to the fire for smoky flavor. As for our Grill-Roasted Whole Chicken (page 477), the best grilling setup (for a charcoal grill) proved to be banking the lit coals on either side of the grill and propping the chicken up on an open can of beer on the grill in the center, using the bird's drumsticks to form a tripod. For the gas grill, a medium fire did the trick. Finally, we found we didn't have to spend money on an expensive beer—the beer flavor wasn't really detectable in the chicken, so a cheap brew worked just fine (so did lemonade, which proved an acceptable substitute for the beer).

GRILL-ROASTED BEER CAN CHICKEN

SERVES 4

Two medium wood chunks, soaked in water for 1 hour, can be substituted for the wood chip packet on a charcoal grill. If you prefer, use lemonade instead of beer; fill an empty 12-ounce soda or beer can with 10 ounces (1¼ cups) of lemonade and proceed as directed.

1	(12-ounce) can beer
2	bay leaves
1	(3½- to 4-pound) whole chicken
3	tablespoons spice rub (recipe follows)
2	cups wood chips, soaked in water for 15 minutes and drained
1	(13 by 9-inch) disposable aluminum roasting pan (if using charcoal)

1. Open beer can and pour out (or drink) about ¼ cup. With church key can opener, punch 2 more large holes in the top of can (for total of 3 holes). Crumble bay leaves into beer.

2. Pat chicken dry with paper towels. Rub chicken evenly, inside and out, with spice rub, lifting up skin over breast and rubbing spice rub directly onto meat. Using skewer, poke skin all over. Slide chicken over beer can so that drumsticks reach down to bottom of can and chicken stands upright; set aside at room temperature.

3. Using large piece of heavy-duty aluminum foil, wrap soaked chips in foil packet and cut several vent holes in top.

4A. FOR A CHARCOAL GRILL: Open bottom vent halfway and place roasting pan in center of grill. Light large chimney starter two-thirds filled with charcoal briquettes (4 quarts). When top coals are partially covered with ash, pour into 2 even piles on either side of roasting pan. Place wood chip packet on 1 pile of coals.

Set cooking grate in place, cover, and open lid vent halfway. Heat grill until hot and wood chips are smoking, about 5 minutes.

4B. FOR A GAS GRILL: Place wood chip packet directly on primary burner. Turn all burners to high, cover, and heat grill until hot and wood chips are smoking, about 15 minutes. Turn all burners to medium. (Adjust burners as needed to maintain grill temperature around 325 degrees.)

5. Clean and oil cooking grate. Place chicken (with can) in center of grill (over roasting pan if using charcoal), using drumsticks to help steady bird. Cover (position lid vent over chicken if using charcoal) and cook until breast registers 160 degrees and thighs register 175 degrees, 1 to 1½ hours.

6. Using large wad of paper towels, carefully transfer chicken (with can) to tray, making sure to keep can upright. Tent loosely with foil and let rest for 15 minutes. Carefully lift chicken off can and onto carving board. Discard remaining beer and can. Carve chicken and serve.

SETTING UP BEER CAN CHICKEN

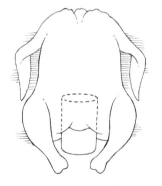

With legs pointing down, slide chicken over open beer can. Two legs and beer can form tripod that steadies chicken on grill.

SPICE RUB
MAKES 1 CUP

Store leftover spice rub in an airtight container for up to 3 months.

½   cup paprika
2   tablespoons kosher salt
2   tablespoons garlic powder
1   tablespoon dried thyme
2   teaspoons ground celery seeds
2   teaspoons pepper
2   teaspoons cayenne pepper

Combine all ingredients in bowl.

ITALIAN-STYLE GRILLED CHICKEN

✓ **WHY THIS RECIPE WORKS**
We wanted an Italian-style grilled chicken with evenly cooked, juicy meat, crackly skin, and bold Mediterranean flavor. We started by butterflying the bird, which helped it cook through evenly. Next, we salted it so it would retain its juices, which had the added advantage of loosening the chicken's skin from the meat, increasing crispness. We briefly sautéed Mediterranean seasonings in olive oil, strained the mixture and then spread the resulting paste under the skin in our grilled chicken, to infuse the meat with flavor without making the skin soggy. Preheated bricks provided heat from above as we cooked the butterflied chicken on both sides.

ITALIAN-STYLE GRILLED CHICKEN
SERVES 4

Use an oven mitt or kitchen towel to safely grip and maneuver the hot bricks. You will need two standard-size bricks for this recipe. Placing the bricks on the chicken while it cooks ensures that the skin will be evenly browned and well

rendered. A cast-iron skillet or other heavy pan can be used in place of the bricks.

⅓   cup extra-virgin olive oil
8   garlic cloves, minced
1   teaspoon grated lemon zest plus 2 tablespoons juice
     Pinch red pepper flakes
4   teaspoons minced fresh thyme
1   tablespoon minced fresh rosemary
     Salt and pepper
1   (3½- to 4-pound) whole chicken

1. Heat oil, garlic, lemon zest, and pepper flakes in small saucepan over medium-low heat until sizzling, about 3 minutes. Stir in 1 tablespoon thyme and 2 teaspoons rosemary and continue to cook for 30 seconds longer. Strain mixture through fine-mesh strainer set over small bowl, pushing on solids to extract oil. Transfer solids to bowl and cool; set oil and solids aside.

2. TO BUTTERFLY CHICKEN: Use kitchen shears to cut along both sides of backbone to remove it. Flatten breastbone and tuck wings behind back. Use hands or handle of wooden spoon to loosen skin over breast and thighs and remove any excess fat.

3. Combine 1½ teaspoons salt and 1 teaspoon pepper in bowl. Mix 2 teaspoons salt mixture with cooled garlic solids. Spread salt-garlic mixture evenly under skin over chicken breast and thighs. Sprinkle remaining ½ teaspoon salt mixture on exposed meat of bone side. Place chicken skin side up on wire rack set in rimmed baking sheet and refrigerate for 1 to 2 hours.

4A. FOR A CHARCOAL GRILL: Open bottom vent halfway. Light large chimney starter three-quarters filled with charcoal briquettes (4½ quarts). When top coals are partially covered with ash, pour evenly over half of grill. Set cooking grate in place, wrap 2 bricks tightly in aluminum foil, and place on cooking grate. Cover and open lid vent halfway. Heat grill until hot, about 5 minutes.

4B. FOR A GAS GRILL: Wrap 2 bricks tightly in aluminum foil and place on cooking grate Turn all burners to high, cover, and heat grill until hot, about 15 minutes. Leave primary burner on high and turn off other burner(s). (Adjust primary burner as needed during cooking to maintain grill temperature around 350 degrees.)

5. Clean and oil cooking grate. Place chicken on cooler side of grill, skin side down, with legs facing coals and flames. Place hot bricks lengthwise over each breast half, cover, and cook until skin is lightly browned and faint grill marks appear, 22 to 25 minutes. Remove bricks from chicken. Using tongs, grip legs and flip chicken (chicken should release freely from grill; use thin metal spatula to loosen if stuck), then transfer to hot side of grill, skin side up. Place bricks over breast, cover, and cook until chicken is well browned, 12 to 15 minutes.

6. Remove bricks, flip chicken skin side down, and continue to cook until skin is well browned and breast registers 160 degrees and thighs register 175 degrees, 5 to 10 minutes longer. Transfer chicken to carving board, tent loosely with foil, and let rest for 15 minutes.

7. Whisk lemon juice, remaining 1 teaspoon thyme, and remaining 1 teaspoon rosemary into reserved oil and season with salt and pepper to taste. Carve chicken and serve, passing sauce separately.

GRILL-ROASTED CORNISH GAME HENS

✔ WHY THIS RECIPE WORKS

Cornish game hens provide crisp skin and delicate meat and are an elegant alternative to chicken, especially when grilling. We found that by butterflying the game hens we could keep all of the skin on one side, which meant it crisped more quickly when placed facing the coals and flames. Butterflying also produced a uniformly thick bird, which promoted even cooking. We needed to secure the legs to the body to keep the skin from tearing, so we developed a special skewering procedure that stabilized the legs, which also made it easier to fit the birds on the cooking grate. A spice rub gave the hens a sweet and savory complexity and helped crisp the skin even further. Our glaze of ketchup, brown sugar, and soy sauce provided the crowning touch.

BUTTERFLYING AND SKEWERING GAME HENS

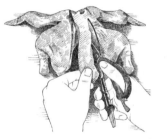

1. Use kitchen shears to cut through bones on either side of backbone.

2. With skin side down, make ¼-inch cut into bone separating breast halves.

3. Lightly press on ribs with fingers to flatten game hen.

4. With skin facing up, fold wing tips behind bird to secure them. Brine birds.

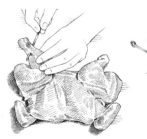

5. Insert flat metal skewer ½ inch from end of drumstick through skin and meat and out other side.

6. Turn leg so that end of drumstick faces wing, then insert tip of skewer into meaty section of thigh under bone.

7. Press skewer all the way through breast and second thigh. Fold end of drumstick toward wing and insert skewer ½ inch from end.

8. Press skewer so that blunt end rests against bird and stretch skin tight over legs, thighs, and breast halves.

GRILL-ROASTED CORNISH GAME HENS

SERVES 4

To add smoke flavor to the hens, use the optional wood chips; however, when using a charcoal grill, we prefer wood chunks to wood chips whenever possible; substitute 4 medium wood chunks, soaked in water for 1 hour, for the wood chip packets. You will need four 8- to 10-inch flat metal skewers for this recipe.

½ cup salt
4 (1¼- to 1½-pound) whole Cornish game hens
2 tablespoons packed brown sugar
1 tablespoon paprika
2 teaspoons garlic powder
2 teaspoons chili powder
1 teaspoon ground black pepper
1 teaspoon ground coriander
⅛ teaspoon cayenne pepper
4 cups wood chips, soaked in water for 15 minutes and drained (optional)
1 (16 by 12-inch) disposable aluminum roasting pan
1 recipe glaze (recipes follow)

1. TO BUTTERFLY GAME HENS: Use kitchen shears to cut along both sides of backbone to remove it. With skin side down, make ¼-inch cut into bone separating breast halves. Lightly press on ribs to flatten hen. Fold wing tips behind bird to secure them.

2. Dissolve salt in 4 quarts cold water in large container. Submerge hens in brine, cover, and refrigerate for 30 minutes to 1 hour.

3. Combine sugar, paprika, garlic powder, chili powder, pepper, coriander, and cayenne in bowl. Remove hens from brine and pat dry with paper towels.

4. TO SKEWER HENS: Insert flat metal skewer ½ inch from end of drumstick through skin and meat and out other side. Turn leg so that end of drumstick faces wing, then insert tip of skewer into meaty section of thigh under bone. Press skewer all the way through breast and second thigh. Fold end of drumstick toward wing and insert skewer ½ inch from end. Press skewer so that blunt end rests against bird and stretch skin tight over legs, thighs, and breast halves. Rub hens evenly with spice mixture and refrigerate while preparing grill.

5. Using 2 large pieces of heavy-duty aluminum foil, wrap soaked chips, if using, in 2 foil packets and cut several vent holes in tops.

6A. FOR A CHARCOAL GRILL: Open bottom vent completely and place roasting pan in center of grill. Light large chimney starter filled with charcoal briquettes (6 quarts). When top coals are partially covered with ash, pour into 2 even piles on either side of roasting pan. Place 1 wood chip packet, if using, on each pile of coals. Set cooking grate in place, cover, and open lid vent completely. Heat grill until hot and wood chips are smoking, about 5 minutes.

6B. FOR A GAS GRILL: Place wood chip packets, if using, directly on primary burner. Turn all burners to high, cover, and heat grill until hot and wood chips are smoking, about 15 minutes. Turn all burners to medium. (Adjust burners as needed during cooking to maintain grill temperature around 325 degrees.)

7. Clean and oil cooking grate. Place hens in center of grill (over roasting pan if using charcoal), skin side down. Cover (position lid vent over birds if using charcoal) and cook until thighs register 160 degrees, 20 to 30 minutes.

8. Using tongs, move the birds to the hot sides of the grill (if using charcoal; 2 hens per side), keeping them skin side down, or turn all burners to high (if using gas). Cover and continue to cook until browned, about 5 minutes. Brush the birds with half of glaze, flip, and cook for 2 minutes. Brush remaining glaze over hens, flip, and continue to cook until breasts register 160 degrees and thighs register 175 degrees, 1 to 3 minutes longer.

9. Transfer hens to carving board, tent loosely with foil, and let rest for 5 to 10 minutes. Cut hens in half through the breastbone and serve.

BARBECUE GLAZE

MAKES ABOUT ½ CUP, ENOUGH FOR 1 RECIPE GRILL-ROASTED CORNISH GAME HENS

½ cup ketchup
2 tablespoons brown sugar
1 tablespoon soy sauce
1 tablespoon distilled white vinegar
1 tablespoon yellow mustard
1 garlic clove, minced

Combine all ingredients in small saucepan, bring to simmer, and cook, stirring occasionally, until thickened, about 5 minutes.

ASIAN BARBECUE GLAZE

MAKES ABOUT ½ CUP, ENOUGH FOR 1 RECIPE GRILL-ROASTED CORNISH GAME HENS

¼ cup ketchup
¼ cup hoisin sauce
2 tablespoons rice vinegar
1 tablespoon soy sauce
1 tablespoon toasted sesame oil
1 tablespoon grated fresh ginger

Combine all ingredients in small saucepan, bring to simmer, and cook, stirring occasionally, until thickened, about 5 minutes.

GRILL-ROASTED TURKEY

✔ WHY THIS RECIPE WORKS

For grill-roasted whole turkey with crisp skin and moist meat wonderfully perfumed with smoke, we determined that a small (less than 14-pound) bird was best; the skin on larger birds will burn before the meat is done. Brining the turkey in a mixture of water and salt before cooking helped to keep the meat from drying out. To protect the skin and promote slow cooking, we placed the turkey on a V-rack and cooked the turkey over indirect heat. Turning the turkey three times ensured that all four sides got equal exposure to the hot side of the grill.

GRILL-ROASTED TURKEY
SERVES 10 TO 12

If using a self-basting turkey or kosher turkey, do not brine in step 1, and season with salt after brushing with melted butter in step 2. When using a charcoal grill, we prefer wood chunks to wood chips whenever possible; substitute 6 medium wood chunks, soaked in water for 1 hour, for the wood chip packets. The total cooking time is 2 to 2½ hours, depending on the size of the bird, the ambient conditions (the bird will require more time on a cool, windy day), and the intensity of the fire.

1 cup salt
1 (12- to 14-pound) turkey, trimmed, neck, giblets, and tailpiece removed, and wings tucked behind back
2 tablespoons unsalted butter, melted
6 cups wood chips, soaked in water for 15 minutes and drained

1. Dissolve salt in 2 gallons cold water in large container. Submerge turkey in brine, cover, and refrigerate or store in very cool spot (40 degrees or less) for 6 to 12 hours.

2. Lightly spray V-rack with vegetable oil spray. Remove turkey from brine and pat dry, inside and out, with paper towels. Brush both sides of turkey with melted butter and place breast side down in prepared V-rack.

3. Using 3 large pieces of heavy-duty aluminum foil, wrap soaked chips in 3 foil packets and cut several vent holes in top.

4A. FOR A CHARCOAL GRILL: Open bottom vent halfway. Light large chimney mounded with charcoal briquettes (7 quarts). When top coals are partially covered with ash, pour into steeply banked pile against side of grill. Place 1 wood chip packet on pile of coals. Set cooking grate in place, cover, and open lid vent halfway. Heat grill until hot and wood chips are smoking, about 5 minutes.

4B. FOR A GAS GRILL: Place 1 wood chip packet directly on primary burner. Turn all burners to high, cover, and heat grill until hot and wood chips are smoking, about 15 minutes. Turn primary burner to medium-high and turn off other burner(s). (Adjust primary burner as needed during cooking to maintain grill temperature around 325 degrees.)

5. Clean and oil cooking grate. Place V-rack with turkey on cool side of grill with leg and wing facing coal, cover (position lid vent over turkey if using charcoal), and cook for 1 hour.

6. Using potholders, transfer V-rack with turkey to rimmed baking sheet or roasting pan. If using charcoal, remove cooking grate and add 12 new briquettes and second wood chip packet to pile of coals; set cooking grate in place. If using gas, place remaining wood chip packets directly on primary burner. With wad of paper towels in each hand, flip turkey breast side up in rack and return V-rack with turkey to cool side of grill, with other leg and wing facing heat. Cover (position

---

TURNING BONE-IN TURKEY BREAST INTO BONELESS TURKEY ROAST

1. Starting at 1 side of breast and using fingers to separate skin from meat, peel skin off breast meat and reserve.

2. Using boning knife, cut along breastbone to separate breast halves.

3. Arrange 1 breast half cut side up; top with second breast half, cut side down, thick end over tapered end. Drape skin over breast halves and tuck ends under.

4. Tie one 36-inch piece of kitchen twine lengthwise around roast. Then tie 5 to 7 pieces of twine at 1-inch intervals crosswise along roast.

lid vent over turkey if using charcoal) and cook for 45 minutes.

7. Using potholders, carefully rotate V-rack with turkey (breast remains up) 180 degrees. Cover and continue to cook until breast registers 160 degrees and thighs register 175 degrees, 15 to 45 minutes longer. Transfer turkey to carving board, tent loosely with foil, and let rest for 20 to 30 minutes. Carve and serve.

GRILL-ROASTED BONELESS TURKEY BREAST

✔ WHY THIS RECIPE WORKS

Turkey, especially breast meat, is temperamental. Cooked just a few moments too long, it will dry out and toughen—there's simply not enough fat in the meat to keep it moist. We wanted a deeply bronzed, crisp-skinned turkey breast with smoky, moist meat. To achieve our goal, we started with a skin-on bone-in breast and took it off the bone, but kept the skin for extra flavor and moisture. We sprinkled the meat with salt and tied it to make a roast with an even thickness. We then brushed the outside of the roast with oil to protect the exterior from the heat of the grill and cooked the breast slowly over steady, moderate heat. A quick sear over high heat took care of the skin, giving our grill-roasted boneless turkey breast its finishing touch.

GRILL-ROASTED BONELESS TURKEY BREAST

SERVES 6 TO 8

We prefer either a natural (unbrined) or kosher turkey breast for this recipe. Using a kosher turkey breast (rubbed with salt and rinsed during processing) or self-basting turkey breast (injected with salt and water) eliminates the need for salting in step 2. If the breast has a pop-up timer, remove it before cooking. When using a charcoal grill, we prefer wood chunks to wood chips whenever possible; substitute 1 small wood chunk, soaked in water for 1 hour, for the wood chip packet.

½   cup wood chips, soaked in water for 15 minutes and drained (optional)
1   (5- to 7-pound) whole bone-in turkey breast, trimmed
2   teaspoons salt
1   teaspoon vegetable oil
      Pepper

1. Using large piece of heavy-duty aluminum foil, wrap soaked chips, if using, in foil packet and cut several vent holes in top.

2. Remove skin from breast meat and then cut along rib cage to remove breast halves (discard bones or save for stock). Pat turkey breast halves dry with paper towels and season with salt. Stack breast halves on top of one another with cut sides facing, and alternating thick and tapered ends. Stretch skin over exposed meat and tuck in ends. Tie kitchen twine lengthwise around roast. Then tie 5 to 7 pieces of twine at 1-inch intervals crosswise along roast. Transfer roast to wire rack set in rimmed baking sheet and refrigerate for 1 hour.

3A. FOR A CHARCOAL GRILL: Open bottom vent halfway. Light large chimney starter filled with charcoal briquettes (6 quarts). When top coals are partially covered with ash, pour evenly over half of grill. Place wood chip packet, if using, on coals. Set cooking grate in place, cover, and open lid vent halfway. Heat grill until hot and wood chips are smoking, about 5 minutes.

3B. FOR A GAS GRILL: Place wood chip packet, if using, directly on primary burner. Turn all burners to high, cover, and heat grill until hot and wood chips are smoking, about 15 minutes. Turn all burners to medium-low. (Adjust burner(s) as needed during cooking to maintain grill temperature around 300 degrees.)

4. Clean and oil cooking grate. Rub surface of roast with oil and season with pepper. Place roast on grill (cool side if using charcoal). Cover (position lid vents over meat if using charcoal) and cook until roast registers 150 degrees, 40 minutes to 1 hour, turning 180 degrees halfway through cooking.

5. Slide roast to hot side of grill (if using charcoal) or turn all burners to medium-high (if using gas). Cook until roast is browned and skin is crisp on all sides, 8 to 10 minutes, rotating every 2 minutes.

6. Transfer roast to carving board, tent loosely with foil, and let rest for 15 minutes. Cut into ½-inch-thick slices, removing twine as you cut. Serve.

GRILL-ROASTED BONELESS TURKEY BREAST WITH HERB BUTTER

Mince ¼ cup tarragon leaves, 1 tablespoon thyme leaves, 2 minced garlic cloves, and ¼ teaspoon pepper to fine paste. Combine herb paste and 4 tablespoons softened unsalted butter. Spread butter evenly over cut side of each turkey breast half before assembling roast.

GRILL-ROASTED BONELESS TURKEY BREAST WITH OLIVES AND SUN-DRIED TOMATOES

Combine ¼ cup finely chopped kalamata olives, 3 tablespoons finely chopped sun-dried tomatoes, 1 minced garlic clove, 1 teaspoon minced fresh thyme, ½ teaspoon anchovy paste, and ½ teaspoon red pepper flakes in bowl. Spread olive mixture evenly over cut side of each turkey breast half before assembling roast.

TURKEY BURGERS

✔ WHY THIS RECIPE WORKS

A lean, fully cooked turkey burger, simply seasoned with salt and pepper, is a poor stand-in for an all-beef burger. Simply put, it's dry, tasteless, and colorless. Add a grill to the equation and things only get worse. We wanted a turkey burger that grilled up juicy and full of flavor— one that would rival a beef burger. After trying all kinds of supermarket ground turkey, we discovered that the best-tasting burger was made from boned and skinless turkey thighs that we ground in the food processor ourselves. A little Worcestershire sauce and Dijon mustard seasoned the burgers, which cooked up quickly on a hot grill. For quicker turkey burgers, supermarket ground turkey can be used but we found that the moisture and richness of ricotta cheese improved both the flavor and texture of the meat.

GREAT GRILLED TURKEY BURGERS
SERVES 4

We found that the extra step of grinding fresh turkey thighs ourselves made the most flavorful, best-textured burgers.

- 1 (2-pound) bone-in turkey thigh, skinned and boned, cut into 1-inch chunks
- 2 teaspoons Worcestershire sauce
- 2 teaspoons Dijon mustard
- ½ teaspoon salt
- ½ teaspoon pepper
- 1 tablespoon vegetable oil
- 4 hamburger rolls, toasted

1. Arrange turkey chunks on baking sheet and freeze until semifirm, about 30 minutes.

2. Working in 3 batches, pulse semifrozen turkey chunks in food processor until largest pieces are no bigger than ⅛ inch, 12 to 14 pulses. Transfer ground turkey to bowl and stir in Worcestershire, mustard, salt, and pepper. Divide meat into 4 portions and lightly toss 1 portion from hand to hand to form ball, then lightly flatten ball with fingertips into 1-inch-thick patty. Press center of patty down with fingertips until it is about ½ inch thick, creating a slight depression. Repeat with remaining portions.

3A. FOR A CHARCOAL GRILL: Open bottom vent completely. Light large chimney starter three-quarters filled with charcoal briquettes (4½ quarts). When top coals are partially covered with ash, pour two-thirds evenly over grill, then pour remaining coals over half of grill. Set cooking grate in place, cover, and open lid vent completely. Heat grill until hot, about 5 minutes.

3B. FOR A GAS GRILL: Turn all burners to high, cover, and heat grill until hot, about 15 minutes.

4. Clean and oil cooking grate. Place burgers on grill (hot side if using charcoal) and cook, without pressing on them, until well browned on both sides, 5 to 7 minutes, flipping halfway through cooking.

5. Move burgers to cooler side of grill (if using charcoal), or turn all burners to medium (if using gas). Cover and continue to cook until burgers are cooked through, 5 to 7 minutes longer, flipping halfway through cooking.

6. Transfer burgers to serving platter, tent loosely with aluminum foil, and let rest for 5 to 10 minutes before serving on rolls.

QUICKER TURKEY BURGERS

This recipe will enrich store-bought ground lean turkey so that it makes excellent burgers. Ricotta cheese can burn easily, so keep a close watch on the burgers as they cook.

Substitute 1¼ pounds 93 percent lean ground turkey for turkey thighs and add ½ cup whole-milk ricotta cheese to turkey with seasonings.

MISO TURKEY BURGERS

Japanese miso, a paste made from fermenting rice, barley, or soybeans, gives the turkey burgers a particularly savory, beefy flavor.

Stir 2 teaspoons white miso together with 2 teaspoons water. Omit Worcestershire sauce and mustard and add miso mixture with seasonings.

INDOOR TURKEY BURGERS

Pan-frying develops an especially nice crust on the burgers when grilling isn't an option.

Heat 2 teaspoons vegetable oil in 12-inch skillet over medium heat until just smoking. Add burgers to pan and cook over medium heat without moving burgers until bottom side of each is dark brown and crusted, 3 to 4 minutes. Flip burgers and continue to cook until bottom side is light brown but not yet crusted, 3 to 4 minutes longer. Reduce heat to low, position skillet lid slightly ajar on pan to allow steam to escape, and continue to cook 8 to 10 minutes longer, flipping burgers if necessary to promote deep browning, until burgers register 160 degrees. Serve immediately.

SIMPLE GRILLED HAMBURGERS

✔ WHY THIS RECIPE WORKS

Burgers often come off the grill tough, dry, and bulging in the middle. We wanted a moist and juicy burger, with a texture that was tender and cohesive, not dense and heavy. Just as important, we wanted a flavorful, deeply caramelized reddish brown crust that would stick to the meat, and we wanted a nice flat surface capable of holding as many condiments as we could pile on. For juicy, robustly flavored meat, we opted for chuck, ground to order with a ratio of

20 percent fat to 80 percent lean. We formed the meat into 6-ounce patties that were fairly thick, with a depression in the middle. Rounds of testing taught us that indenting the center of each burger ensured that the patties would come off the grill with an even thickness instead of puffed up like a tennis ball. For our cheeseburgers, we took an unconventional approach and mixed the cheese in with the meat for an even distribution of cheese flavor.

GRILLED HAMBURGERS
SERVES 4

Weighing the meat on a kitchen scale is the most accurate way to portion it. If you don't own a scale, do your best to divide the meat evenly into quarters. Eighty percent lean ground chuck is our favorite for flavor, but 85 percent lean works, too.

- 1½ pounds 80 percent lean ground chuck
- 1 teaspoon salt
- ½ teaspoon pepper
- 4 hamburger rolls, toasted

1. Using hands, gently break up meat, season with salt and pepper, and toss lightly to incorporate. Divide meat into 4 portions and lightly toss 1 portion from hand to hand to form ball, then lightly flatten ball with fingertips into ¾-inch-thick patty. Press center of patty down with fingertips until it is about ½ inch thick, creating slight depression. Repeat with remaining portions.

2A. FOR A CHARCOAL GRILL: Open bottom vent completely. Light large chimney starter filled with charcoal briquettes (6 quarts). When top coals are partially covered with ash, pour evenly over grill. Set cooking grate in place, cover, and open lid vent completely. Heat grill until hot, about 5 minutes.

2B. FOR A GAS GRILL: Turn all burners to high, cover, and heat grill until hot, about 15 minutes.

3. Clean and oil cooking grate. Place burgers on grill and cook, without pressing on them, until well browned on first side, 2 to 3 minutes. Flip burgers and continue to grill, 2 to 3 minutes for rare, 2½ to 3½ minutes for medium-rare, and 3 to 4 minutes for medium.

4. Transfer burgers to serving platter, tent loosely with aluminum foil, and let rest for 5 to 10 minutes before serving on rolls.

GRILLED CHEESEBURGERS

Since the cheese is evenly distributed in these burgers, just a little goes a long way.

Mix ¾ cup shredded cheddar, Swiss, or Monterey Jack cheese or ¾ cup crumbled blue cheese into meat with salt and pepper.

GRILLED HAMBURGERS WITH GARLIC, CHIPOTLES, AND SCALLIONS

Toast 3 unpeeled garlic cloves in small skillet over medium heat until fragrant, about 8 minutes. When cool enough to handle, peel and mince. Mix garlic, 2 tablespoons minced scallion, and 1 tablespoon minced chipotle chile in adobo sauce into meat with salt and pepper.

GRILLED HAMBURGERS WITH PORCINI MUSHROOMS AND THYME

Mix ½ ounce dried porcini mushrooms, rinsed and minced, and 1 tablespoon minced fresh thyme into meat with salt and pepper.

GRILLED HAMBURGERS WITH COGNAC, MUSTARD, AND CHIVES

Mix 1½ tablespoons cognac, 1 tablespoon minced fresh chives, and 2 teaspoons Dijon mustard in bowl. Mix cognac mixture into meat with salt and pepper.

GRILLED WELL-DONE HAMBURGERS

✔ WHY THIS RECIPE WORKS

These days, many backyard cooks prefer grilling burgers to medium-well and beyond. The problem is that the meat comes off the grill dry and tough. We wanted a well-done burger that was tender and moist-as-can-be. Taste tests proved that well-done burgers made with 80 percent lean chuck were noticeably moister than burgers made from leaner beef, but they still weren't juicy enough. Because we couldn't force the meat to retain moisture, we opted to pack the patties with a panade, a paste made from bread and milk that's often used to keep meatloaf and

---

TEST KITCHEN TIP NO. 100 PREVENTING PUFFY BURGERS

To prevent hamburgers from puffing up during cooking, many sources (including the test kitchen) recommend making a slight depression in the center of the raw patty before placing it on the heat. But we find the need for a dimple depends entirely on how the burger is cooked. Meat inflates upon cooking when its connective tissue, or collagen, shrinks at temperatures higher than 140 degrees. If burgers are cooked on a grill or under a broiler, a dimple is in order. Cooked with these methods, the meat is exposed to direct heat not only from below or above but also on its sides; as a result, the edges of the patty shrink, cinching the hamburger like a belt, compressing its interior up and out. But when the patty is cooked in a skillet, as in our recipe for Juicy Pub-Style Burgers (page 392), only the part of the patty in direct contact with the pan gets hot enough to shrink the collagen. Because the edges of the burger never directly touch the heat, the collagen it contains doesn't shrink much at all, and the burger doesn't puff.

meatballs moist. To punch up the flavor, we also added minced garlic and tangy steak sauce.

GRILLED WELL-DONE HAMBURGERS
SERVES 4

Adding bread and milk to the beef creates burgers that are juicy and tender even when well-done. For cheeseburgers, follow the optional instructions below.

1	slice hearty white sandwich bread, crust removed, bread cut into ¼-inch pieces
2	tablespoons whole milk
2	teaspoons steak sauce
1	garlic clove, minced
¾	teaspoon salt
¾	teaspoon pepper
1½	pounds 80 percent lean ground chuck
6	ounces sliced cheese (optional)
4	hamburger rolls, toasted

1. Mash bread and milk in large bowl with fork until homogeneous. Stir in steak sauce, garlic, salt, and pepper. Using hands, gently break up meat over bread mixture and toss lightly to distribute. Divide meat into 4 portions and lightly toss 1 portion from hand to hand to form ball, then lightly flatten ball with fingertips into ¾-inch-thick patty. Press center of patty down with fingertips until it is about ½ inch thick, creating slight depression. Repeat with remaining portions.

2A. FOR A CHARCOAL GRILL: Open bottom vent completely. Light large chimney starter filled with charcoal briquettes (6 quarts). When top coals are partially covered with ash, pour evenly over grill. Set cooking grate in place, cover, and open lid vent completely. Heat grill until hot, about 5 minutes.

2B. FOR A GAS GRILL: Turn all burners to high, cover, and heat grill until hot, about 15 minutes.

3. Clean and oil cooking grate. Place burgers on grill (on hot side if using charcoal) and cook, without pressing on them, until well browned on first side, 2 to 4 minutes. Flip burgers and cook 3 to 4 minutes for medium-well or 4 to 5 minutes for well-done, adding cheese, if using, about 2 minutes before reaching desired doneness and covering grill to melt cheese.

4. Transfer burgers to serving platter, tent loosely with aluminum foil, and let rest for 5 to 10 minutes before serving on rolls.

WELL-DONE BACON-CHEESEBURGERS

Most bacon burgers simply top the burgers with bacon. We also add bacon fat to the ground beef, which adds juiciness and unmistakable bacon flavor throughout the burger.

Cook 8 slices bacon in skillet over medium heat until crisp, 7 to 9 minutes. Transfer bacon to paper towel–lined plate and set aside. Reserve 2 tablespoons fat and refrigerate until just warm. Follow recipe for Grilled Well-Done Hamburgers, including optional cheese and adding reserved bacon fat to beef mixture. Top each burger with 2 slices bacon before serving.

GRILLED BEEF TERIYAKI

✔ WHY THIS RECIPE WORKS
This Japanese-American standard is synonymous with chewy, flavorless meat shellacked with saccharine-sweet sauce. We wanted great teriyaki: juicy, charred steak embellished by a well-balanced glaze that would be robust enough to stand up to the beef. For the meat, we decided to use inexpensive steak tips, which became very tender when marinated in a soy sauce–based marinade flavored with scallions, ginger, garlic, and a bit of orange zest. We also found that a few teaspoons of oil in the marinade prevented the meat from sticking to the grill. Slicing the meat into "cutlets" across the grain shortened the muscle fibers so the texture was more tender. For a well-balanced sweet and savory glaze that came together quickly, we added cornstarch to sake, mirin, soy sauce, fresh ginger, and sugar. It took only 15 minutes of cooking to give the sauce a nice syrupy texture.

GRILLED BEEF TERIYAKI
SERVES 4

If you can't find sirloin steak tips, sometimes labeled "flap meat," flank steak is a good alternative. Mirin, a sweet Japanese rice wine, is a key component of teriyaki; it can be found in Asian markets and the international section of most supermarkets. Alternatively, substitute ¼ cup vermouth or sake and 2 teaspoons sugar for every ¼ cup mirin. Serve with Simple White Rice (page 222).

STEAK

2	pounds sirloin steak tips, trimmed
⅓	cup soy sauce
¼	cup mirin
2	tablespoons vegetable oil
3	garlic cloves, minced
1	tablespoon grated fresh ginger
1	tablespoon sugar
1	teaspoon grated orange zest
2	scallions, whites minced and greens sliced thin on bias, separated

SAUCE

½	cup sugar
½	cup sake or vermouth
½	cup mirin
⅓	cup soy sauce
1	teaspoon grated fresh ginger
1	teaspoon cornstarch

1. **FOR THE STEAK:** Cut each steak with grain into 2 to 3 even pieces. Holding knife at 45-degree angle to meat, slice each piece against grain into 4 to 5 slices about ½ inch thick.

2. Combine soy sauce, mirin, oil, garlic, ginger, sugar, orange zest, and scallion whites in bowl. Place marinade and beef in 1-gallon zipper-lock bag and toss to coat; press out as much air as possible and seal bag. Refrigerate for at least 30 minutes to 1 hour, flipping bag every 15 minutes.

3A. **FOR A CHARCOAL GRILL:** Open bottom vent completely. Light large chimney starter filled with charcoal briquettes (6 quarts). When top coals are partially covered with ash, pour evenly over half of grill. Set cooking grate in place, cover, and open lid vent completely. Heat grill until hot, about 5 minutes.

3B. **FOR A GAS GRILL:** Turn all burners to high, cover, and heat grill until hot, about 15 minutes.

4. **FOR THE SAUCE:** Meanwhile, whisk all ingredients together in small saucepan, bring to simmer, and cook over medium-low heat until syrupy and reduced to 1 cup, 12 to 15 minutes. Reserve ¾ cup sauce for serving.

5. **TO COOK:** Clean and oil cooking grate. Remove beef from bag and pat dry with paper towels. Place beef on grill (on hot side if using charcoal) and cook (covered if using gas) until dark brown on both sides, 6 to 8 minutes, flipping halfway through cooking. Brush with 2 tablespoons sauce, flip, and cook for 30 seconds. Brush with remaining 2 tablespoons sauce, flip, and continue to cook for 30 seconds longer.

6. Transfer meat to serving platter, tent loosely with aluminum foil, and let rest for 5 to 10 minutes. Sprinkle with scallion greens and serve, passing reserved sauce separately.

GRILLED BEEF KEBABS

✓ WHY THIS RECIPE WORKS

Most beef kebabs are disappointing, with overcooked meat and vegetables that are either raw or mushy. We wanted to develop a foolproof approach to creating meaty kebabs that looked and tasted like the real thing: chunks of beef with a thick, caramelized char on the outside and a juicy, pink interior, all thoroughly seasoned by a marinade and paired with nicely browned, tender-firm vegetables. For the meat, we chose well-marbled steak tips, with their beefy flavor and tender texture. For the marinade, we included salt for moisture, oil for flavor, and sugar for browning. For even more depth, we used tomato paste, a host of seasonings and herbs, and beef broth. We chose three grill favorites for the vegetables: peppers, onions, and zucchini. Grilling the beef kebabs and vegetables on separate skewers over a two-level fire, which has hotter and cooler areas, allowed us to cook the vegetables over a lower temperature while the beef seared over the hotter area.

GRILLED BEEF KEBABS WITH LEMON AND ROSEMARY MARINADE

SERVES 4 TO 6

If you can't find sirloin steak tips, sometimes labeled "flap meat," substitute 2½ pounds blade steak; if using, cut each steak in half to remove the gristle. You will need four 12-inch metal skewers for this recipe. If you have long, thin pieces of meat, roll or fold them into approximate 2-inch cubes before skewering.

MARINADE
- 1   onion, chopped
- ⅓   cup beef broth
- ⅓   cup vegetable oil
- 3   tablespoons tomato paste
- 6   garlic cloves, chopped
- 2   tablespoons chopped fresh rosemary
- 2   teaspoons grated lemon zest
- 2   teaspoons salt
- 1½   teaspoons sugar
- ¾   teaspoon pepper

BEEF AND VEGETABLES
- 2   pounds sirloin steak tips, trimmed and cut into 2-inch chunks
- 1   large zucchini or summer squash, halved lengthwise and sliced 1 inch thick
- 1   large red or green bell pepper, stemmed, seeded, and cut into 1½-inch pieces
- 1   large red or sweet onion, peeled, halved lengthwise, each half cut into 4 wedges and each wedge cut crosswise into thirds

CUTTING SIRLOIN STEAK TIPS

1. Cut steak with grain into 2 or 3 even pieces.

2. Hold knife at 45-degree angle to meat and cut ½-inch-thick slices.

3. Each piece of steak should yield 4 to 5 slices.

1. FOR THE MARINADE: Process all ingredients in blender until smooth, about 45 seconds. Transfer ¾ cup marinade to large bowl and set aside.

2. FOR THE BEEF AND VEGETABLES: Place remaining marinade and beef in 1-gallon zipper-lock bag and toss to coat; press out as much air as possible and seal bag. Refrigerate for at least 1 to 2 hours, flipping bag every 30 minutes.

3. Add zucchini, bell pepper, and onion to bowl with reserved marinade and toss to coat. Cover and let sit at room temperature for at least 30 minutes.

4. Remove beef from bag and pat dry with paper towels. Thread beef tightly onto two 12-inch metal skewers. Thread vegetables onto two 12-inch metal skewers, in alternating pattern of zucchini, bell pepper, and onion.

5A. FOR A CHARCOAL GRILL: Open bottom vent completely. Light large chimney starter mounded with charcoal briquettes (7 quarts). When top coals are partially covered with ash, pour evenly over center of grill, leaving 2-inch gap between grill wall and charcoal. Set cooking grate in place, cover, and open lid vent completely. Heat grill until hot, about 5 minutes.

5B. FOR A GAS GRILL: Turn all burners to high, cover, and heat grill until hot, about 15 minutes. Leave primary burner on high and turn other burner(s) to medium-low.

6. Clean and oil cooking grate. Place beef skewers on grill (directly over coals if using charcoal or over hotter side of grill if using gas). Place vegetable skewers on grill (near edge of coals but still over coals if using charcoal or over cooler side of grill if using gas). Cook (covered if using gas), turning skewers every 3 to 4 minutes, until beef skewers are well browned and register 120 to 125 degrees (for medium-rare) or 130 to 135 degrees

(for medium), 12 to 16 minutes. Transfer beef skewers to platter and tent loosely with foil. Continue cooking vegetable skewers until tender and lightly charred, about 5 minutes longer; serve with beef skewers.

GRILLED BEEF KEBABS WITH NORTH AFRICAN MARINADE

Substitute 20 cilantro sprigs, 2 teaspoons sweet paprika, 1½ teaspoons ground cumin, and ½ teaspoon cayenne pepper for lemon zest and rosemary.

GRILLED BEEF KEBABS WITH RED CURRY MARINADE

Substitute ½ cup packed fresh basil leaves, 3 tablespoons red curry paste, 2 teaspoons lime zest, and 2 teaspoons grated fresh ginger for lemon zest and rosemary.

GRILLED STEAK TIPS

✔ WHY THIS RECIPE WORKS
Steak tips have long been the darling of all-you-can-eat restaurant chains where quantity takes precedence over quality. Sometimes they are mushy, but usually they're tough and dry. We wanted steak tips with deep flavor and tender texture. For the meat, we chose sirloin steak tips, also known as flap meat, an affordable cut of meat that stayed tender and moist during a brief stint on the grill. To further tenderize and flavor the meat, we use a soy sauce–based marinade. Grilling the tips over a two-level fire, which has hotter and cooler areas, helped us cook this often unevenly shaped cut evenly. Letting the steak tips rest for five to ten minutes after grilling also helped to ensure juicy meat.

GRILLED STEAK TIPS
SERVES 4 TO 6

Sirloin steak tips are sometimes labeled "flap meat." A two-level fire allows you to brown the steak over the hot side of the grill, then move it to the cooler side if it is not yet cooked through. If your steak is thin, however, you may not need to use the cooler side of the grill. Serve lime wedges with the Southwestern-marinated tips, orange wedges with the tips marinated in garlic, ginger, and soy sauce, and lemon wedges with the garlic-herb marinade.

1 recipe marinade (recipes follow)
2 pounds sirloin steak tips, trimmed
   Lime, orange, or lemon wedges

1. Combine marinade and beef in 1-gallon zipper-lock bag and toss to coat; press out as much air as possible and seal bag. Refrigerate for 1 hour, flipping bag halfway through marinating.

2A. FOR A CHARCOAL GRILL: Open bottom vent completely. Light large chimney starter filled with charcoal briquettes (6 quarts). When top coals are partially covered with ash, pour two-thirds evenly over grill, then pour remaining coals over half of grill. Set cooking grate in place, cover, and open lid vent completely. Heat grill until hot, about 5 minutes.

2B. FOR A GAS GRILL: Turn all burners to high, cover, and heat grill until hot, about 15 minutes.

3. Clean and oil cooking grate. Remove beef from bag and pat dry with paper towels. Place steak tips on grill (on hotter side if using charcoal) and cook (covered if using gas) until well browned on first side, about 4 minutes. Flip steak tips and continue to cook (covered if using gas) until meat registers 120 to 125 degrees (for medium-rare) or 130 to 135 degrees (for medium), 6 to 10 minutes longer. If exterior of meat is browned but steak is not yet

cooked through, move to cooler side of grill (if using charcoal) or turn down burners to medium (if using gas) and continue to cook to desired doneness.

4. Transfer steak tips to carving board, tent loosely with aluminum foil, and let rest for 5 to 10 minutes. Slice steak tips very thin on bias and serve with lime, orange, or lemon wedges.

SOUTHWESTERN MARINADE

MAKES ABOUT ¾ CUP, ENOUGH FOR
1 RECIPE GRILLED STEAK TIPS

- ⅓ cup soy sauce
- ⅓ cup vegetable oil
- 3 garlic cloves, minced
- 1 tablespoon packed dark brown sugar
- 1 tablespoon tomato paste
- 1 tablespoon chili powder
- 2 teaspoons ground cumin
- ¼ teaspoon cayenne pepper

Combine all ingredients in bowl.

GARLIC, GINGER, AND SOY MARINADE

MAKES ABOUT ⅔ CUP, ENOUGH FOR
1 RECIPE GRILLED STEAK TIPS

- ⅓ cup soy sauce
- 3 tablespoons vegetable oil
- 3 tablespoons toasted sesame oil
- 2 tablespoons packed dark brown sugar
- 1 tablespoon grated fresh ginger
- 2 teaspoons grated orange zest
- 1 scallion, sliced thin
- 3 garlic cloves, minced
- ½ teaspoon red pepper flakes

Combine all ingredients in bowl.

GARLIC AND HERB MARINADE

MAKES ABOUT ¾ CUP, ENOUGH FOR
1 RECIPE GRILLED STEAK TIPS

- ⅓ cup soy sauce
- ⅓ cup olive oil
- 3 garlic cloves, minced
- 1 tablespoon minced fresh rosemary
- 1 tablespoon minced fresh thyme
- 1 tablespoon packed dark brown sugar
- 1 tablespoon tomato paste
- 1 teaspoon pepper

Combine all ingredients in bowl.

GRILLED STRIP OR RIB-EYE STEAKS

✔ WHY THIS RECIPE WORKS

Like filet mignon, grilled strip or rib-eye steaks are premium steaks. These cuts boast big, beefy flavor and require little adornment beyond salt and pepper, although a spice rub or marinade offers further flavor. To ensure that these steaks came off the grill with a charred exterior and perfectly tender interior, we built a fire with two heat zones, starting the steaks over the hot side and moving them to the cooler side to finish cooking through. Resting the steaks before serving is key—if sliced into right off the grill, the meat will exude its flavorful juices and be dry.

GRILLED STRIP OR RIB-EYE STEAKS

SERVES 6

Try to buy steaks of even thickness so they cook at the same rate.

- 4 (12- to 16-ounce) strip or rib-eye steaks, with or without bone, 1¼ to 1½ inches thick
  Salt and pepper

1A. FOR A CHARCOAL GRILL: Open lid vent completely. Light large chimney starter filled with charcoal briquettes (6 quarts). When top coals are partially covered with ash, pour two-thirds evenly over grill, then pour remaining coals over half of grill. Set cooking grate in place, cover, and heat grill until hot, about 5 minutes.

1B. FOR A GAS GRILL: Turn all burners to high, cover, and heat grill until hot, about 15 minutes. Leave one burner on high and turn other burner(s) to medium.

2. Clean and oil cooking grate. Pat steaks dry with paper towels and season with salt and pepper. Place steaks on grill (hotter side if using charcoal) and cook, uncovered, until well browned on both sides, 4 to 6 minutes, flipping steaks halfway through cooking. Move steaks to cooler side of grill (if using charcoal) or turn all burners to medium (if using gas) and continue to cook until meat registers 115 to 120 degrees (for rare) or 120 to

---

TEST KITCHEN TIP NO. 101 THE MAGIC OF BRINERATING

Successful marinating is all about getting as much of the soaking liquid flavors into (and on) the meat as possible. Brining in a saltwater solution is a way to create more juiciness. To pump up flavor as well as juiciness, our marinades combine both approaches, with soaking liquids that not only contain lots of seasonings and flavorings but so much salt (often in the form of soy sauce), you might even call them "brinerades." As in a brine, salt in a marinade affects meat in two ways. Through osmotic pressure it pulls moisture from a place of higher water concentration (the marinade) into a place with a lower one (the meat). In addition, it restructures the protein molecules in the meat, creating gaps that fill with water to further increase juiciness. It also seasons the meat, enhancing its inherent flavors.

125 degrees (for medium-rare) 5 to 8 minutes longer.

3. Transfer steaks to serving platter, tent loosely with aluminum foil, and let rest for 10 minutes before serving.

MARINADES FOR GRILLED STEAK

✓ WHY THIS RECIPE WORKS

Marinades are supposed to make steaks more flavorful and tender, but most do neither. We wanted our marinades to accomplish both these tasks, without having to marinate the meat overnight. We started with soy sauce. The salt in soy sauce acted much like a brine, helping the meat retain moisture during cooking and making it more tender. For depth of flavor, we added more strong seasonings. We found some of them in the international section of the supermarket, with ingredients as diverse as red curry paste, Dijon mustard, and chipotle chiles. We divided up the marinade's tasks to meet our time limit. After setting aside some of the marinade, we marinated the meat to tenderize it. Then, before we allowed the cooked steak to rest, we dipped it in the reserved marinade to absorb flavor.

CLASSIC STEAK MARINADE

MAKES ABOUT I CUP, ENOUGH TO
MARINATE 4 TO 6 INDIVIDUAL STEAKS
OR ONE 2-POUND STEAK

Use with less expensive steaks such as flap meat, boneless shell sirloin, or skirt steak. This marinade is similar in flavor to the bottled variety but much fresher tasting.

½ cup soy sauce
⅓ cup vegetable oil
¼ cup Worcestershire sauce
2 tablespoons packed dark brown sugar
2 tablespoons minced chives

AVOIDING CROSS-CONTAMINATION

Grilled meat, poultry, and fish should not be returned to the same platter that was used to carry the raw food to the grill. Instead of last-minute fumbling for a clean platter, this method uses a single platter for both jobs and saves on cleanup time.

1. Cover platter with aluminum foil before placing raw food on it.

2. While food is grilling, remove foil so that you can use same platter when food comes off grill.

---

4 garlic cloves, minced
I ½ teaspoons pepper
2 teaspoons balsamic vinegar

1. Combine soy sauce, oil, Worcestershire, sugar, chives, garlic, and pepper in bowl. Transfer ¼ cup marinade to bowl and stir in vinegar; set aside.

2. Place remaining marinade and steaks in 1-gallon zipper-lock bag; press out as much air as possible and seal bag. Refrigerate for 1 hour, flipping bag after 30 minutes to ensure that steaks marinate evenly.

3. Remove steaks from marinade, letting any excess marinade drip back into bag. Discard bag and marinade. Grill steaks as desired.

4. Transfer steaks to shallow pan and pour reserved marinade over top. Tent loosely with aluminum foil and let rest for 10 minutes, turning meat halfway through resting. Slice steaks or serve whole, passing reserved marinade if desired.

MOLE MARINADE

MAKES ABOUT I CUP, ENOUGH TO
MARINATE 4 TO 6 INDIVIDUAL STEAKS
OR ONE 2-POUND STEAK

Use with less expensive steaks such as flap meat, boneless shell sirloin, or skirt steak. Use less chipotle chile if you prefer a milder marinade.

½ cup soy sauce
⅓ cup vegetable oil
2 tablespoons packed dark brown sugar
2 tablespoons minced canned chipotle chile in adobo sauce
4 teaspoons cocoa
4 garlic cloves, minced
I ½ teaspoons dried oregano
I teaspoon pepper
2 tablespoons lime juice

1. Combine soy sauce, oil, sugar, chipotle, cocoa, garlic, oregano, and pepper in bowl. Transfer ¼ cup marinade to bowl and stir in lime juice; set aside.

2. Place remaining marinade and steaks in 1-gallon zipper-lock bag; press out as much air as possible and seal bag. Refrigerate for 1 hour, flipping bag after 30 minutes to ensure that steaks marinate evenly.

3. Remove steaks from marinade, letting any excess marinade drip back into bag. Discard bag and marinade. Grill steaks as desired.

4. Transfer steaks to shallow pan and pour reserved marinade over top. Tent loosely with aluminum foil and let rest for 10 minutes, turning meat halfway through resting. Slice steaks or serve whole, passing reserved marinade if desired.

HONEY-MUSTARD MARINADE

MAKES ABOUT 1 CUP, ENOUGH TO
MARINATE 4 TO 6 INDIVIDUAL STEAKS
OR ONE 2-POUND STEAK

Use with less expensive steaks such as flap meat, boneless shell sirloin, or skirt steak. This marinade also works well with pork.

- ½ cup soy sauce
- ⅓ cup vegetable oil
- 3 tablespoons Dijon mustard
- 2 tablespoons chopped fresh tarragon
- 4 teaspoons honey
- 4 garlic cloves, minced
- 1½ teaspoons ground black pepper
- 1 teaspoon cider vinegar

1. Combine soy sauce, oil, mustard, tarragon, honey, garlic, and pepper in bowl. Transfer ¼ cup marinade to bowl and stir in vinegar; set aside.

2. Place remaining marinade and steaks in 1-gallon zipper-lock bag; press out as much air as possible and seal bag. Refrigerate for 1 hour, flipping bag after 30 minutes to ensure that steaks marinate evenly.

3. Remove steaks from marinade, letting any excess marinade drip back into bag. Discard bag and marinade. Grill steaks as desired.

4. Transfer steaks to shallow pan and pour reserved marinade over top. Tent loosely with aluminum foil and let rest for 10 minutes, turning meat halfway through resting. Slice steaks or serve whole, passing reserved marinade if desired.

MOJO STEAK MARINADE

MAKES ABOUT 1¼ CUP, ENOUGH TO
MARINATE 4 TO 6 INDIVIDUAL STEAKS
OR ONE 2-POUND STEAK

Use with less expensive steaks such as flap meat, boneless shell sirloin, or skirt steak. Fresh parsley can be substituted for the cilantro.

- ½ cup soy sauce
- ⅓ cup vegetable oil
- 6 garlic cloves, minced
- 2 tablespoons chopped fresh cilantro
- 2 tablespoons packed dark brown sugar
- 1 teaspoon grated orange zest plus 2 tablespoons juice
- 1 teaspoon pepper
- ½ teaspoon ground cumin
- ½ teaspoon dried oregano
- 2 teaspoons distilled white vinegar

1. Combine soy sauce, oil, garlic, cilantro, sugar, orange zest, pepper, cumin, and oregano in bowl. Transfer ¼ cup marinade to bowl and stir in orange juice and vinegar; set aside.

2. Place remaining marinade and steaks in 1-gallon zipper-lock bag; press out as much air as possible and seal bag. Refrigerate for 1 hour, flipping bag after 30 minutes to ensure that steaks marinate evenly.

3. Remove steaks from marinade, letting any excess marinade drip back into bag. Discard bag and marinade. Grill steaks as desired.

4. Transfer steaks to shallow pan and pour reserved marinade over top. Tent loosely with aluminum foil and let rest for 10 minutes, turning meat halfway through resting. Slice steaks or serve whole, passing reserved marinade if desired.

SOUTHEAST ASIAN MARINADE

MAKES ABOUT 1 CUP, ENOUGH TO
MARINATE 4 TO 6 INDIVIDUAL STEAKS
OR ONE 2-POUND STEAK

Use with less expensive steaks such as flap meat, boneless shell sirloin, or skirt steak. Red curry paste and fish sauce are commonly found in the Asian foods section at most supermarkets.

- ⅓ cup soy sauce
- ⅓ cup vegetable oil
- 2 tablespoons fish sauce
- 2 tablespoons packed dark brown sugar
- 2 tablespoons red curry paste
- 2 tablespoons grated fresh ginger
- 4 garlic cloves, minced
- 2 tablespoons lime juice

1. Combine soy sauce, oil, fish sauce, sugar, curry paste, ginger, and garlic in bowl. Transfer ¼ cup marinade to bowl and stir in lime juice; set aside.

2. Place remaining marinade and steaks in 1-gallon zipper-lock bag; press out as much air as possible and seal bag. Refrigerate for 1 hour, flipping bag after 30 minutes to ensure that steaks marinate evenly.

3. Remove steaks from marinade, letting any excess marinade drip back into bag. Discard bag and marinade. Grill steaks as desired.

4. Transfer steaks to shallow pan and pour reserved marinade over top. Tent loosely with aluminum foil and let rest for 10 minutes, turning meat halfway through resting. Slice steaks or serve whole, passing reserved marinade if desired.

SPICE RUBS FOR GRILLED STEAK

✓ WHY THIS RECIPE WORKS

As we set out to find a simple spice rub to dress up steaks, we wondered how many spices we'd need for the best rub. We found that because relatively few spices taste better when heated, a five-ingredient spice rub (made with carefully chosen ingredients) was preferable to a pantry-emptying rub. Many proponents of spice rubs swear by the benefits of toasting whole versions of all spices and grinding them fresh. To our great surprise, the flavor of steaks rubbed with freshly toasted and ground spices was indistinguishable from that of steaks rubbed with pre-ground, untoasted spices.

TARRAGON–MUSTARD SEED RUB

MAKES ABOUT ⅓ CUP; ENOUGH FOR
4 TO 6 INDIVIDUAL STEAKS OR ONE
2-POUND STEAK

This recipe can be doubled or tripled. Unused rub can be stored in an airtight container for up to 1 month.

3	tablespoons dried tarragon
2	tablespoons yellow mustard seeds
1	tablespoon salt
2¼	teaspoons black peppercorns

Grind all ingredients in spice grinder until no whole peppercorns remain. Pat steaks with rub, pressing to adhere, no more than 2 hours before grilling.

PEPPERY CORIANDER AND DILL RUB

MAKES ABOUT ⅓ CUP, ENOUGH FOR
4 TO 6 INDIVIDUAL STEAKS OR ONE
2-POUND STEAK

This recipe can be doubled or tripled. Unused rub can be stored in an airtight container for up to 1 month.

2	tablespoons black peppercorns
2	tablespoons coriander seeds
1	tablespoon dill seeds
2½	teaspoons salt
1½	teaspoons red pepper flakes

Grind all ingredients in spice grinder until no whole peppercorns remain. Pat steaks with rub, pressing to adhere, no more than 2 hours before grilling.

COCOA-CUMIN ALLSPICE RUB

MAKES ABOUT ⅓ CUP, ENOUGH FOR
4 TO 6 INDIVIDUAL STEAKS OR ONE
2-POUND STEAK

This recipe can be doubled or tripled. Unused rub can be stored in an airtight container for up to 1 month.

4	teaspoons black peppercorns
4	teaspoons ground cumin
1	tablespoon cocoa
2	teaspoons salt
2	teaspoons ground allspice

Grind all ingredients in spice grinder until no whole peppercorns remain. Pat steaks with rub, pressing to adhere, no more than 2 hours before grilling.

STAR ANISE AND COFFEE BEAN RUB

MAKES ABOUT ⅓ CUP, ENOUGH FOR
4 TO 6 INDIVIDUAL STEAKS OR ONE
2-POUND STEAK

This recipe can be doubled or tripled. Unused rub can be stored in an airtight container for up to 1 month.

6	star anise pods
2	tablespoons whole coffee beans
1	tablespoon black peppercorns
2	teaspoons salt
1	teaspoon sugar

Grind all ingredients in spice grinder until no whole peppercorns remain. Pat steaks with rub, pressing to adhere, no more than 2 hours before grilling.

CHILE-CUMIN SPICE RUB

MAKES ABOUT ⅓ CUP, ENOUGH FOR
4 TO 6 INDIVIDUAL STEAKS OR ONE
2-POUND STEAK

This recipe can be doubled or tripled. Unused rub can be stored in an airtight container for up to 1 month.

3	dried chipotle chiles, stemmed, seeded, and cut into rough pieces
2	dried ancho chiles, stemmed, seeded, and cut into rough pieces
1	tablespoon ground cumin

1	tablespoon salt
2	teaspoons sugar

Grind chiles in spice grinder until powdery. Whisk ground chiles, cumin, salt, and sugar together in bowl. Pat steaks with rub, pressing to adhere, no more than 2 hours before grilling.

GRILLED TUSCAN STEAK WITH OLIVE OIL AND LEMON

✓ WHY THIS RECIPE WORKS

Grilled Tuscan-style steaks can be raw on the inside even when the outer crust is perfectly seared, and the flavor of the olive oil and lemon juice just doesn't come through. We wanted perfectly grilled steak accented by olive oil to complement the flavor of the meat and lemon juice, to sharpen the flavors of the dish and cut its richness. For our version, we seared the steaks on the hotter side of a two-level fire, then moved them to the cooler side of the grill to finish cooking, as we do with our grilled porterhouse and T-bone recipe. To bring out the full, fresh flavor of the olive oil and lemon juice, we drizzled them over the steak after cooking rather than before, as many recipes recommend.

GRILLED TUSCAN STEAK WITH OLIVE OIL AND LEMON (BISTECCA ALLA FIORENTINA)

SERVES 4 TO 6

Be sure to buy steaks that are at least 1 inch thick.

2	(1¾-pound) porterhouse or T-bone steaks, 1 to 1½ inches thick, trimmed
	Salt and pepper
3	tablespoons extra-virgin olive oil
	Lemon wedges

IA. FOR A CHARCOAL GRILL: Open bottom vent completely. Light large chimney starter three-quarters filled with charcoal briquettes (4½ quarts). When top coals are partially covered with ash, pour evenly over half of grill. Set cooking grate in place, cover, and open lid vent completely. Heat grill until hot, about 5 minutes.

IB. FOR A GAS GRILL: Turn all burners to high, cover, and heat grill until hot, about 15 minutes. Leave primary burner on high and turn other burner(s) to low.

2. Clean and oil cooking grate. Pat steaks dry with paper towels and season with salt and pepper. Place steaks on hot side of grill with tenderloin sides (smaller side of T-bone) facing cool side of grill. Cook (covered if using gas) until dark crust forms, 6 to 8 minutes. (If steaks start to flame, move them to cooler side of fire and/or extinguish flames with squirt bottle.) Flip steaks and turn so that tenderloin sides are facing cool side of grill. Continue to cook (covered if using gas) until dark brown crust forms on second side, 6 to 8 minutes longer.

3. Transfer steaks to cool side of grill with bone side facing hot side of grill. Cover grill and continue to cook until meat registers 115 to 120 degrees (for rare) or 120 to 125 degrees (for medium-rare), 2 to 4 minutes longer, flipping halfway through cooking.

4. Transfer steaks to carving board, tent loosely with aluminum foil, and let rest for 10 minutes. Cut strip and tenderloin pieces off bones, then cut each piece crosswise into ¼-inch slices. Transfer to serving platter, drizzle with oil, and serve with lemon wedges.

GRILLED TUSCAN STEAK WITH GARLIC ESSENCE

Rub halved garlic cloves over bone and meat on each side of steaks before seasoning with salt and pepper.

GRILLED PORTERHOUSE OR T-BONE STEAKS

✔ WHY THIS RECIPE WORKS

For a grilled steak that sported a dark (but not blackened) crust, smoky aroma, and deep grilled flavor, we first seared the meat directly over a hot fire, then gently finished cooking it over indirect heat. Since a T-bone is really two steaks—a tender New York strip steak on one side of the bone and a buttery, quicker-cooking tenderloin on the other, we positioned the meat so that the tenderloin always faced the cooler side of the grill, which prevented that portion from becoming overcooked and dry. Salting the meat for one hour before grilling boosted flavor from crust to bone.

GRILLED PORTERHOUSE OR T-BONE STEAKS

SERVES 4 TO 6

Be sure to buy steaks that are at least 1 inch thick.

- 2 (1¾-pound) porterhouse or T-bone steaks, 1 to 1½ inches thick, trimmed
- 2 teaspoons salt
- 2 teaspoons pepper
- 1 recipe Chive Butter (page 494; optional)

I. Season entire surface of each steak with 1 teaspoon salt and let sit at room temperature for 1 hour. Pat steaks dry with paper towels and season each with 1 teaspoon pepper.

2A. FOR A CHARCOAL GRILL: Open bottom vent completely. Light large chimney starter three-quarters filled with charcoal briquettes (4½ quarts). When top coals are partially covered with ash, pour evenly over half of grill. Set cooking grate in place, cover, and open lid vent completely. Heat grill until hot, about 5 minutes.

2B. FOR A GAS GRILL: Turn all burners to high, cover, and heat grill until hot, about 15 minutes. Leave primary burner on high and turn other burner(s) to low.

3. Clean and oil cooking grate. Place steaks on hot side of grill with tenderloin sides (smaller side of T-bone) facing cool side of grill. Cook (covered if using gas) until dark crust forms, 6 to 8 minutes. (If steaks start to flame, move them to cooler side of fire and/or extinguish flames with squirt bottle.) Flip steaks and turn so that tenderloin sides are facing cool side of grill. Continue to cook (covered if using gas) until dark brown crust forms on second side, 6 to 8 minutes longer.

SLICING T-BONE AND PORTERHOUSE STEAKS

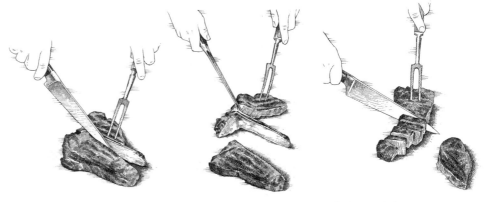

I. Cut along bone to remove large top loin, or strip, section.

2. Cut smaller tenderloin section off bone.

3. Cut each large piece crosswise into ¼-inch-thick slices for serving.

4. Brush with butter, if using, and transfer steaks to cool side of grill with bone side facing hot side of grill. Cover grill and continue to cook until meat registers 115 to 120 degrees (for rare) or 120 to 125 degrees (for medium-rare), 2 to 4 minutes longer, flipping halfway through cooking.

5. Transfer steaks to carving board, tent loosely with aluminum foil, and let rest for 10 minutes. Cut strip and tenderloin pieces off bones, then cut each piece crosswise into ¼-inch slices. Serve.

CHIVE BUTTER

MAKES ABOUT 6 TABLESPOONS, ENOUGH
FOR I RECIPE GRILLED PORTERHOUSE
OR T-BONE STEAKS

---

4   tablespoons unsalted butter, melted
2   tablespoons minced shallot
I   garlic clove, minced
I   tablespoon minced fresh chives
    Salt and pepper

Combine all ingredients in bowl and season with salt and pepper to taste.

GRILLED ARGENTINE STEAKS

✔ WHY THIS RECIPE WORKS
We wanted an Argentine-style grilled steak with a mahogany-hued char that snapped with each bite and tasted the way a roaring fireplace smells: woody (not smoky). We chose well-marbled strip steak for its beefy flavor and moist meat. To give our steaks authentic Argentine wood-smoke flavor, we added wood chip packets to the grill. For the steaks' requisite deep-brown char, we needed to get the exterior bone-dry. To do this, we sprinkled the steaks with salt and cornstarch (which helped

dry out the exterior) and then left them uncovered in the freezer. Finally, all we needed was the traditional steak condiment, chimichurri sauce, which we made with parsley, cilantro, oregano, garlic, red wine vinegar, red pepper flakes, and salt—all emulsified with extra-virgin olive oil.

GRILLED ARGENTINE STEAKS WITH CHIMICHURRI SAUCE

SERVES 6 TO 8

Our preferred steak for this recipe is strip steak, also known as New York strip. A less expensive alternative is a boneless shell sirloin steak (or top sirloin steak). Four medium wood chunks, unsoaked, can be substituted for the wood chip packets on a charcoal grill.

SAUCE
¼   cup hot water
2   teaspoons dried oregano
I   teaspoon salt
I⅓ cups parsley leaves
⅔   cup cilantro leaves
6   garlic cloves, minced
½   teaspoon red pepper flakes
¼   cup red wine vinegar
½   cup extra-virgin olive oil

STEAKS
I   tablespoon cornstarch
I½ teaspoons salt
4   (1-pound) boneless strip steaks,
    I½ inches thick, trimmed
4   cups wood chips, soaked in water
    for 15 minutes and drained
    Pepper

I. FOR THE SAUCE: Combine water, oregano, and salt in small bowl and let sit until oregano is softened, about 15 minutes. Pulse parsley, cilantro, garlic, and pepper flakes in food processor until coarsely chopped, about 10 pulses. Add water mixture and vinegar and pulse to combine.

Transfer mixture to bowl and slowly whisk in oil until emulsified. Cover with plastic wrap and let sit at room temperature for 1 hour.

2. FOR THE STEAKS: Combine cornstarch and salt in bowl. Pat steaks dry with paper towels and place on wire rack set in rimmed baking sheet. Rub entire surface of steaks with cornstarch mixture and place steaks, uncovered, in freezer until very firm, about 30 minutes.

3. Using 2 large pieces of heavy-duty aluminum foil, wrap soaked chips in 2 foil packets and cut several vent holes in tops.

4A. FOR A CHARCOAL GRILL: Open bottom vent halfway. Light large chimney starter filled with charcoal briquettes (6 quarts). When top coals are partially covered with ash, pour evenly over grill. Place wood chip packets on coals. Set cooking grate in place, cover, and open lid vent halfway. Heat grill until hot and wood chips are smoking, about 5 minutes.

4B. FOR A GAS GRILL: Place wood chip packets on cooking grate. Turn all burners to high, cover, and heat grill until hot, about 15 minutes. Leave all burners on high.

5. Clean and oil cooking grate. Season steaks with pepper. Place steaks on grill, cover, and cook until beginning to brown on both sides, 4 to 6 minutes, flipping halfway through cooking.

6. Flip steaks and cook until well browned on first side, 2 to 4 minutes. Flip steaks and continue to cook until meat registers 115 to 120 degrees (for rare) or 120 to 125 degrees (for medium-rare), 2 to 6 minutes longer.

7. Transfer steaks to carving board, tent loosely with foil, and let rest for 10 minutes. Cut each steak crosswise into ¼-inch slices. Transfer to serving platter and serve, passing sauce separately.

GRILLED FILETS MIGNONS

✔ WHY THIS RECIPE WORKS

To get grilled filets mignons with a great crust and juicy interior, a very hot fire was essential, but the thick steaks cooked over consistently high heat burned. Instead, we turned to a two-level fire (by building two heat zones on the grill). We seared the steaks first over high heat, then finished cooking them through on the cooler side. Rubbing the steaks with olive oil before grilling improved browning and added flavor. To add a little richness to the steaks, we made two compound butters, one with smoked paprika and roasted red peppers, the other with lemon, parsley, and garlic—perfect for melting down the sides of the still-warm steaks.

GRILLED FILETS MIGNONS
SERVES 4

We suggest serving the steaks with one of our flavored butters (recipes follow).

- 4 (7- to 8-ounce) center-cut filets mignons, 1½ to 2 inches thick, trimmed
- 4 teaspoons olive oil
  Salt and pepper

1A. FOR A CHARCOAL GRILL: Open bottom vent completely. Light large chimney starter filled with charcoal briquettes (6 quarts). When top coals are partially covered with ash, pour two-thirds evenly over grill, then pour remaining coals over half of grill. Set cooking grate in place, cover, and open lid vent completely. Heat grill until hot, about 5 minutes.

1B. FOR A GAS GRILL: Turn all burners to high, cover, and heat grill until hot, about 15 minutes. Leave all burners on high.

2. Meanwhile, pat steaks dry with paper towels and lightly rub with oil. Season steaks with salt and pepper.

3. Clean and oil cooking grate. Place steaks on grill (hotter side if using charcoal) and cook (covered if using gas) until well browned on both sides, 4 to 6 minutes, flipping halfway through cooking. Move steaks to cooler side of grill (if using charcoal) or turn all burners to medium (if using gas) and continue to cook (covered if using gas), until meat registers 115 to 120 degrees (for rare) or 120 to 125 degrees (for medium-rare), 5 to 9 minutes longer.

4. Transfer steaks to serving platter, tent loosely with aluminum foil, and let rest for 10 minutes before serving.

ROASTED RED PEPPER AND SMOKED PAPRIKA BUTTER

MAKES ¼ CUP, ENOUGH FOR 1 RECIPE GRILLED FILETS MIGNONS

- 4 tablespoons unsalted butter, softened
- 2 tablespoons finely chopped jarred roasted red peppers
- 1 tablespoon minced fresh thyme
- ¾ teaspoon smoked paprika
- ½ teaspoon salt
  Pinch pepper

Combine all ingredients in bowl and mix until smooth. While steaks are resting, spoon 1 tablespoon of butter on each one.

LEMON, GARLIC, AND PARSLEY BUTTER

MAKES ¼ CUP, ENOUGH FOR 1 RECIPE GRILLED FILETS MIGNONS

- 4 tablespoons unsalted butter, softened
- 1 tablespoon minced fresh parsley
- 1 garlic clove, minced
- ½ teaspoon grated lemon zest
- ½ teaspoon salt
  Pinch pepper

Combine all ingredients in bowl and mix until smooth. While steaks are resting, spoon 1 tablespoon of butter on each one.

GRILLED FILET MIGNONS WITH OLIVE OIL AND LEMON

A peppery extra-virgin olive oil is ideal here.

Just before serving, drizzle each steak with 2 teaspoons extra-virgin olive oil. Serve with lemon wedges.

GRILLED LONDON BROIL

✔ WHY THIS RECIPE WORKS

Inexpensive steaks are often labeled "London broil," a generic term butchers use to sell large, cheap steaks that might be otherwise be ignored—they can be tough and liver-y. When developing our recipe, we gave the steaks a salt rubdown, which brought out the beefy flavors and masked the liver-y ones. We then wrapped the beef tightly in plastic wrap and submerged it in warm water for the last hour of salting, which raised the temperature of the meat and so shortened the cooking time, giving the fatty acids in the meat less time to break down into off-tasting compounds. Slicing the meat diagonally into ultra-thin slices dramatically diminished chewiness for a tender grilled steak with a charred crust and beefy flavor.

GRILLED LONDON BROIL
SERVES 4 TO 6

While top round can be substituted for the bottom round in this recipe, it is harder to get an even sear on its less uniform surface. If desired, serve with Sweet and Smoky Grilled Tomato Salsa (recipe follows) or Chimichurri Sauce (page 494). We do not recommend cooking London broil beyond medium-rare.

1 teaspoon salt
1 (2- to 2½-pound) bottom round steak, 1½ inches thick, trimmed
1 tablespoon vegetable oil
½ teaspoon pepper

1. Sprinkle both sides of steak evenly with salt; wrap tightly with plastic wrap, and refrigerate for at least 3 hours or up to 24 hours.

2. Fill large pot or bucket with 1 gallon warm water (about 100 degrees). Place wrapped steak in zipper-lock plastic bag, squeeze out excess air, and seal bag tightly. Place steak in water, covering with plate or bowl to keep bag submerged. Set aside for 1 hour.

3A. FOR A CHARCOAL GRILL: Open bottom vent completely. Light large chimney starter filled with charcoal briquettes (6 quarts). When top coals are partially covered with ash, pour evenly over half of grill. Set cooking grate in place, cover, and open lid vent completely. Heat grill until hot, about 5 minutes.

3B. FOR A GAS GRILL: Turn all burners to high, cover, and heat grill until hot, about 15 minutes. Leave all burners on high.

4. Clean and oil cooking grate. Remove steak from water and unwrap. Brush both sides with oil (salt will have dissolved) and season with pepper.

5. Place steak on grill (on hot side if using charcoal) and cook, flipping steak every minute, until dark brown crust forms on both sides, 8 to 12 minutes. Move steak to cooler side of grill (if using charcoal) or turn all burners to medium (if using gas). Cover and continue to cook until meat registers 115 to 120 degrees (for rare) or 120 to 125 degrees (for medium-rare), 6 to 12 minutes longer, flipping steak halfway through cooking.

6. Transfer steak to carving board, tent loosely with aluminum foil, and let rest for 10 minutes. Holding knife at 45-degree angle to meat, slice very thin, then serve.

SWEET AND SMOKY GRILLED TOMATO SALSA

MAKES ABOUT 3 CUPS

Sugar and lime juice should be added at the end to taste, depending on the ripeness of the tomatoes. To make this salsa spicier, add the chile seeds. The salsa can be refrigerated in an airtight container for up to 2 days; bring back to room temperature before serving. Wood chunks are not recommended for this recipe.

1 cup wood chips, soaked in water for 15 minutes and drained
2 pounds plum tomatoes, cored and halved lengthwise
2 large jalapeño chiles
2 teaspoons vegetable oil
3 tablespoons minced red onion
2 tablespoons chopped fresh cilantro
2 tablespoons extra virgin olive oil
  Salt and pepper
1–2 tablespoons lime juice
½–1 teaspoon sugar

1. Using large piece of heavy-duty aluminum foil, wrap soaked chips in foil packet and cut several vent holes in top.

2A. FOR A CHARCOAL GRILL: Open bottom vent halfway. Light large chimney starter filled with charcoal briquettes (6 quarts). When top coals are partially covered with ash, pour evenly over half of grill. Set cooking grate in place, cover, and open lid vent halfway. Heat grill until hot, about 5 minutes.

2B. FOR A GAS GRILL: Turn all burners to high, cover, and heat grill until hot, about 15 minutes.

3. Toss tomatoes, jalapeños, and vegetable oil together in bowl. Place tomatoes cut side down on grill (hot side if using charcoal), cover, and cook until evenly charred on both sides and juices bubble, 8 to 12 minutes, flipping halfway through cooking.

4. Meanwhile, cook jalapeños (hot side if using charcoal) until skins are blackened on all sides, 8 to 10 minutes, turning as needed.

5. Transfer tomatoes and jalapeños to baking dish. If using charcoal, remove cooking grate and place wood chip packet on coals; set cooking grate in place. If using gas, place wood chip packet over primary burner; leave primary burner on high and turn other burner(s) to medium-low.

6. Place tomatoes and jalapeños on cool side of grill, cover (position lid vent over tomatoes if using charcoal), and cook for 2 minutes. Transfer tomatoes and jalapeños to cutting board and let sit until cool enough to handle.

7. Stem, peel, seed, and finely chop jalapeños. Pulse tomatoes in food processor until broken down but still chunky, about 6 pulses. Transfer tomatoes to bowl and stir in jalapeños, onion, cilantro, olive oil, 1 teaspoon salt, and ¼ teaspoon pepper. Season with lime juice, sugar, salt, and pepper to taste. Let sit for 10 minutes before serving.

CLASSIC BEEF FAJITAS

✔ WHY THIS RECIPE WORKS

While skirt steak is the traditional choice for the meat component of fajitas, it isn't readily available, so we chose widely available and reasonably priced flank steak for our recipe. For flavor, we tried a variety of marinades and rubs, but simplicity won out. A little salt, pepper, and a sprinkle of fresh lime juice gave the meat the best flavor. Perfecting our grilled beef fajitas was also a matter of timing: While the steak rested, we had ample time to grill the onions and peppers—after cutting them large enough so they couldn't fall through the grate. To complete the dish, we toasted the tortillas over the dying fire.

CLASSIC BEEF FAJITAS
SERVES 4 TO 6

You can use red, yellow, orange, or green bell peppers in this recipe. When you head outside to grill, bring a clean kitchen towel in which to wrap the tortillas and keep them warm. Chunky Guacamole (page 15) and Fresh Tomato Salsa (page 14) make good accompaniments.

1	(2- to 2½-pound) flank steak, trimmed
¼	cup lime juice
	Salt and pepper
1	large red onion, peeled and cut into ½-inch-thick rounds (do not separate rings)
2	large bell peppers, quartered, stemmed, and seeded
8–12	(6-inch) flour tortillas

1A. FOR A CHARCOAL GRILL: Open bottom vent completely. Light large chimney starter mounded with charcoal briquettes (7 quarts). When top coals are partially covered with ash, pour evenly over half of grill. Set cooking grate in place, cover, and open lid vent completely. Heat grill until hot, about 5 minutes.

1B. FOR A GAS GRILL: Turn all burners to high, cover, and heat grill until hot, about 15 minutes.

2. Clean and oil cooking grate. Pat steak dry with paper towels and sprinkle with lime juice, salt, and pepper. Place steak on grill (hot side if using charcoal) and cook (covered if using gas) until well browned on first side, 4 to 7 minutes. Flip steak and continue to cook until meat registers 120 to 125 degrees (for medium-rare) or 130 to 135 degrees (for medium), 3 to 8 minutes. Transfer steak to carving board, tent loosely with aluminum foil, and let rest for 10 minutes.

3. While steak rests, place onion rounds and peppers (skin side down) on hot side of grill (if using charcoal) or turn all burners to medium (if using gas). Cook until tender and charred on both sides, 8 to 12 minutes, flipping every 3 minutes. Transfer onions and peppers to carving board with beef.

4. Place tortillas in single layer on hot side of grill (if using charcoal) or turn all burners to low (if using gas). Cook until warm and lightly browned, about 20 seconds per side (do not grill too long or tortillas will become brittle). As tortillas are done, wrap in clean kitchen towel or large sheet of foil.

5. Separate onions into rings and slice peppers into ¼-inch strips. Slice steak, against grain, ¼-inch-thick. Transfer beef and vegetables to serving platter and serve with warmed tortillas.

GRILLED STUFFED FLANK STEAK

✔ WHY THIS RECIPE WORKS
While this Italian-American dish may look nice and tidy raw, the meat buckles when cooked, forcing the filling to escape. We wanted a filling that stayed put and delivered a complement to the rich, smoky beef in each bite. To start, we butterflied and pounded the steak, for the flattest and widest surface possible. As for the filling, we eliminated bread crumbs from consideration—after grilling, they contributed a taste of burnt toast. The classic Italian-American combo of prosciutto and provolone won raves for its salty savor and the way the dry cheese melted inside the pinwheel yet turned crisp where exposed to the grill. To prevent the meat from shrinking on the grill and squeezing the centers of the pinwheels, we rolled up our flank steak, tied it with kitchen twine, and skewered it at 1-inch intervals before slicing and grilling it. The twine kept the steak from unraveling, while the skewers prevented the meat from shrinking.

GRILLED STUFFED FLANK STEAK
SERVES 4 TO 6

Look for a flank steak measuring approximately 8 by 6 inches, with the grain running the long way. Depending on the steak's size, you may have more or less than 8 slices of meat at the end of step 2. You will need both wooden skewers and kitchen twine for this recipe.

2	tablespoons olive oil
2	tablespoons minced fresh parsley
1	small shallot, minced
2	garlic cloves, minced
1	teaspoon minced fresh sage
1	(2- to 2½-pound) flank steak, trimmed
4	ounces thinly sliced prosciutto
4	ounces thinly sliced provolone cheese
	Salt and pepper

1. Combine oil, parsley, shallot, garlic, and sage in bowl.

2. Soak 8 to 12 wooden skewers in warm water to cover (you will need 1 skewer per inch of rolled steak length) for 30 minutes. Drain, dry, and set aside.

3. Lay steak on cutting board with grain running parallel to counter edge. Cut horizontally through meat, leaving ½-inch "hinge" along top edge. Open up steak and pound flat into rough rectangle, trimming any ragged edges. Rub herb mixture evenly over opened side of steak. Lay prosciutto evenly over steak, leaving 2-inch border along top edge. Cover prosciutto with even layer of cheese, leaving 2-inch border along top edge. Starting from short edge, roll beef into tight log and place on cutting board seam side down.

HOW TO BUTTERFLY AND STUFF FLANK STEAK

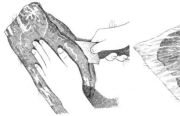

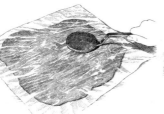

1. Butterfly meat by cutting through steak horizontally, leaving ½-inch "hinge" along top edge.

2. Open up steak and pound flat into rough rectangle, trimming any ragged edges.

3. Rub with herb mixture; layer with prosciutto and cheese, leaving 2-inch border at top, Roll into tight log.

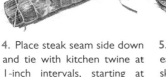

4. Place steak seam side down and tie with kitchen twine at 1-inch intervals, starting at center.

5. Skewer steak directly through each piece of twine, allowing skewer to extend ½ inch on opposite side.

6. Slice steak between pieces of twine into 1-inch-thick pinwheels.

4. Starting ½ inch from end of rolled steak, evenly space eight to twelve 14-inch pieces of kitchen twine at 1-inch intervals underneath steak. Tie middle piece first, then, working from outer pieces toward center, tightly tie roll and turn tied steak 90 degrees so seam is facing you.

5. Skewer beef directly through outer flap of steak near seam through each piece of twine, allowing skewers to extend ½ inch on other side. Using chef's knife, slice roll between each piece of twine into 1-inch-thick pinwheels. Season pinwheels with salt and pepper.

6A. FOR A CHARCOAL GRILL: Open bottom vent completely. Light large chimney starter three-quarters filled with charcoal briquettes (4½ quarts). When top coals are partially covered with ash, pour evenly over half of grill. Set cooking grate in place, cover, and open lid vent

completely. Heat grill until hot, about 5 minutes.

6B. FOR A GAS GRILL: Turn all burners to high, cover, and heat grill until hot, about 15 minutes.

7. Clean and oil cooking grate. Place pinwheels on grill (hot side if using charcoal) and cook (covered if using gas) until well browned on both sides, 6 to 12 minutes, flipping halfway through cooking. Move pinwheels to cool side of grill (if using charcoal) or turn all burners to medium (if using gas). Cover and cook until meat registers 125 to 130 degrees (for medium-rare) or 130 to 135 degrees (for medium), 1 to 5 minutes.

8. Transfer pinwheels to serving platter, tent loosely with aluminum foil, and let rest for 5 to 10 minutes. Remove and discard skewers and twine and serve.

GRILLED STUFFED FLANK STEAK WITH SPINACH AND PINE NUTS

Microwave 4 ounces chopped spinach, 1 tablespoon water, ½ teaspoon pepper, and ½ teaspoon salt in bowl until spinach is wilted and decreased in volume by half, 3 to 4 minutes. Cool completely, then stir in ¼ cup toasted pine nuts. Replace prosciutto with spinach mixture.

GRILLED STUFFED FLANK STEAK WITH SUN-DRIED TOMATOES AND CAPERS

Combine ½ cup drained and chopped sun-dried tomatoes, ½ cup shredded Asiago cheese, and ¼ cup rinsed and chopped capers in bowl. Replace prosciutto with sun-dried tomato mixture.

GRILLED MARINATED FLANK STEAK

✔ WHY THIS RECIPE WORKS

A common way to prepare flank steak is to marinate it in a bottle of Italian-style salad dressing. Unfortunately, the acid in the vinegar can ruin the texture, making the exterior mushy and gray. We wanted to develop a fresh, Mediterranean-style marinade without acid—a marinade that would really boost flavor without overtenderizing the meat. Because fat carries flavor so well, we knew oil would be a key ingredient—the challenge was to infuse Mediterranean flavors (garlic, shallots, and rosemary) into the oil and then into the steak. We developed two key steps. First, we minced the aromatics and combined them with the oil in a blender to create a marinade paste. Next, we invented a novel "marinating" technique—prick the steak all over with a fork, rub it first with salt and then with the marinade paste, then let it sit for up to 24 hours. After marinating, the paste is wiped off to prevent burning, and the steak is ready for the grill.

Our technique was so successful, we were free to create two more marinades—one with Asian flavors, and the other with a smoky-spicy kick.

GRILLED MARINATED FLANK STEAK

SERVES 4 TO 6

Other thin steaks with a loose grain, such as skirt steak or steak tips, can be substituted for the flank steak.

- I   (2- to 2½-pound) flank steak, trimmed
- I   teaspoon salt
- I   recipe wet paste marinade (recipes follow)
       Pepper

1. Pat steak dry with paper towels and place in large baking dish. Using dinner fork, prick steak about 20 times on each side. Rub both sides of steak evenly with salt, then with paste. Cover with plastic wrap and refrigerate for at least 1 hour or up to 24 hours.

2A. FOR A CHARCOAL GRILL: Open bottom vent completely. Light large chimney starter filled with charcoal briquettes (6 quarts). When top coals are partially covered with ash, pour two-thirds evenly over grill, then pour remaining coals over half of grill. Set cooking grate in place, cover, and open lid vent completely. Heat grill until hot, about 5 minutes.

2B. FOR A GAS GRILL: Turn all burners to high, cover, and heat grill until hot, about 15 minutes.

3. Clean and oil cooking grate. Using paper towels, wipe paste off steak and season with pepper. Place steak on grill (hot side if using charcoal) and cook (covered if using gas) until well browned on first side, 4 to 6 minutes. Flip steak and cook (covered if using gas) until meat registers 120 to 125 degrees (for medium-rare) or 130 to 135 degrees (for medium), 3 to 6 minutes. If exterior of meat is browned but steak is not yet cooked through, move to cooler side of grill (if using charcoal) or turn down burners (if using gas) and continue to cook to desired doneness.

4. Transfer steak to carving board, tent loosely with aluminum foil, and let rest for 10 minutes. Slice steak ¼ inch thick against grain on bias and serve.

GARLIC-SHALLOT-ROSEMARY WET PASTE MARINADE

MAKES ABOUT ⅔ CUP; ENOUGH FOR I RECIPE GRILLED MARINATED FLANK STEAK

- 6   tablespoons olive oil
- I   shallot, minced
- 6   garlic cloves, minced
- 2   tablespoons minced fresh rosemary

Process all ingredients in blender until smooth, about 30 seconds, scraping down bowl as needed.

GARLIC-CHILE WET PASTE MARINADE

MAKES ABOUT ⅔ CUP; ENOUGH FOR I RECIPE GRILLED MARINATED FLANK STEAK

- 6   tablespoons vegetable oil
- 6   garlic cloves, minced
- 2   scallions, minced
- I   tablespoon minced canned chipotle chile in adobo sauce
- I   jalapeño chile, stemmed, seeded, and minced

Process all ingredients in blender until smooth, about 30 seconds, scraping down bowl as needed.

GARLIC-GINGER-SESAME WET PASTE MARINADE

MAKES ABOUT ⅔ CUP; ENOUGH FOR I RECIPE GRILLED MARINATED FLANK STEAK

- ¼   cup toasted sesame oil
- 3   tablespoons grated fresh ginger
- 2   tablespoons vegetable oil
- 2   scallions, minced
- 3   garlic cloves, minced

Process all ingredients in blender until smooth, about 30 seconds, scraping down bowl as needed.

ROASTED BEEF WITH GARLIC AND ROSEMARY

✔ WHY THIS RECIPE WORKS

To capture perfectly juicy, tender, and inexpensive beef on the grill, we started with the meat. Top sirloin won out over other inexpensive contenders. To keep our grill-roasted beef tender, we seared it on the hot side of the grill, then transferred the roast inside a disposable pan (in which we poked holes to preserve the sear) and continued cooking it on the cool side of the grill. We also found that cutting the roast into thin slices made the meat taste even more tender.

INEXPENSIVE GRILL-ROASTED BEEF WITH GARLIC AND ROSEMARY

SERVES 6 TO 8

A pair of kitchen shears works well for punching the holes in the aluminum pan. We prefer a top sirloin roast, but you can substitute a top round or bottom round roast. Start this recipe the day before you plan to grill so the salt rub has time to flavor and tenderize the meat.

6   garlic cloves, minced
2   tablespoons minced fresh rosemary
4   teaspoons kosher salt
1   tablespoon pepper
1   (3- to 4-pound) top sirloin roast
1   (13 by 9-inch) disposable aluminum
    roasting pan

1. Combine garlic, rosemary, salt, and pepper in bowl. Sprinkle all sides of roast evenly with salt mixture, wrap with plastic wrap, and refrigerate for 18 to 24 hours.

2A. FOR A CHARCOAL GRILL: Open bottom vent halfway. Light large chimney starter half filled with charcoal briquettes (3 quarts). When top coals are partially covered with ash, pour evenly over one-third of grill. Set cooking grate in place, cover, and open lid vent halfway. Heat grill until hot, about 5 minutes.

2B. FOR A GAS GRILL: Turn all burners to high, cover, and heat grill until hot, about 15 minutes.

3. Clean and oil cooking grate. Place roast on grill (hot side if using charcoal) and cook (covered if using gas) until well browned on all sides, 10 to 12 minutes, turning as needed. (If flare-ups occur, move roast to cooler side of grill until flames die down.)

4. Meanwhile, punch fifteen ¼-inch holes in center of disposable pan in area roughly same size as roast. Once browned, place beef in pan over holes and set pan over cool side of grill (if using charcoal) or turn all burners to medium (if using gas). (Adjust burners as needed during cooking to maintain grill temperature between 250 and 300 degrees.) Cover and cook until meat registers 120 to 125 degrees (for medium-rare) or 130 to 135 degrees (for medium), 40 minutes to 1 hour, rotating pan halfway through cooking.

5. Transfer meat to wire rack set in rimmed baking sheet, tent loosely with aluminum foil, and let rest for 20 minutes.

Transfer meat to carving board, slice thin against grain, and serve.

INEXPENSIVE GRILL-ROASTED BEEF WITH SHALLOT AND TARRAGON

Substitute 1 minced shallot for garlic and 2 tablespoons minced fresh tarragon for rosemary.

GRILL-ROASTED PRIME RIB

✔ WHY THIS RECIPE WORKS

While you can achieve a well-charred crust by searing the prime rib on all sides quickly in a hot skillet, this approach often produces sputtering grease and billowing smoke. We wanted a great crust without the mess and without setting off the smoke detectors, so we took our roast to the grill. We built a fire on one side of the grill and placed a roasting pan on the other side to create two cooking zones—one hot and one cool. We seared the fat-covered side of the roast over the hot side of the grill, then we moved the roast to the cooler side of the grill. To get a flavorful, crisp crust, we applied a dry salt rub to the roast three hours before grilling. This drew out moisture from just below the surface, allowing for faster browning once we began searing. To achieve more depth, we added 2 cups wood chips to the fire—just enough for the smoke flavor to lightly permeate the meat.

CHARCOAL GRILL–ROASTED PRIME RIB

SERVES 6 TO 8

Your butcher can remove the bones and trim excess fat from the roast; just make sure that the bones are packed up along with the meat, as you need them to protect the meat from overbrowning. Two medium wood chunks, soaked in water for 1 hour, can be substituted for the wood chip packet on a charcoal grill.

Serve the roast with Horseradish Cream Sauce (page 389), if desired.

1   (7-pound) first-cut (3- or 4-rib) beef
    standing rib roast, meat removed
    from bones, bones reserved,
    exterior fat trimmed to ⅛ inch
1   tablespoon vegetable oil
    Pepper
¼   cup kosher salt
2   cups wood chips, soaked in water
    for 15 minutes and drained
1   (16 by 12-inch) disposable aluminum
    roasting pan (if using charcoal)

1. Pat roast dry with paper towels, rub with oil, and season with pepper. Spread salt on rimmed baking sheet and press roast into salt to coat evenly on all sides. Tie meat back onto bones exactly from where it was cut, passing 2 lengths of kitchen twine between each set of bones and knotting securely. Refrigerate roast, uncovered, for 1 hour, then let sit at room temperature for 2 hours.

2. Using large piece of heavy-duty aluminum foil, wrap soaked chips in foil packet and cut several vent holes in top.

3A. FOR A CHARCOAL GRILL: Open bottom vent halfway and place roasting pan on one side of grill. Light large chimney starter two-thirds filled with charcoal briquettes (4 quarts). When top coals are partially covered with ash, pour evenly over half of grill (opposite roasting pan). Place wood chip packet on coals. Set cooking grate in place, cover, and open lid vent halfway. Heat grill until hot and wood chips are smoking, about 5 minutes.

3B. FOR A GAS GRILL: Turn all burners to high, cover, and heat grill until hot and wood chips are smoking, about 15 minutes. Turn primary burner to medium and turn off other burner(s). (Adjust primary burner as needed during cooking to maintain grill temperature around 325 degrees.)

4. Clean and oil cooking grate. Place roast on hot side of grill and cook (covered if using gas) until well browned on all sides, 10 to 15 minutes, turning as needed. (If flare-ups occur, move roast to cooler side of grill until flames die down.)

5. Transfer roast to rimmed baking sheet. If using charcoal, remove cooking grate and place wood chip packet on pile of coals; set cooking grate in place. If using gas, place wood chip packet directly on primary burner. Place roast on cool side of grill, bone side down, with tips of bones pointed away from fire. Cover (position lid vent over meat if using charcoal) and cook until meat registers 115 to 120 degrees (for rare) or 120 to 125 degrees (for medium-rare), 2 to 2½ hours.

6. Transfer roast to carving board, tent loosely with foil, and let rest for 20 minutes. Remove twine and bones, cut into ½-inch-thick slices, and serve.

GRILL-ROASTED PRIME RIB WITH GARLIC-ROSEMARY CRUST

Combine ½ cup extra-virgin olive oil, 12 minced garlic cloves (¼ cup), and ¼ cup minced fresh rosemary in bowl. Brush paste onto roast after browning.

GRILL-ROASTED WHOLE PRIME RIB

A whole prime rib roast can weigh as much as 20 pounds and easily serves a crowd (16 to 20 people). Because the whole rib tapers slightly, expect the smaller end to be slightly more cooked than the thicker end.

Substitute 1 whole beef standing rib roast for first-cut roast and increase salt to ½ cup. If using charcoal, after roast cooks on cool side of grill for 1¼ hours, transfer roast to rimmed baking sheet; light additional large chimney starter three-quarters filled with charcoal briquettes (4½ quarts). When top coals are partially covered with ash, pour evenly over half of grill (opposite roasting pan). Set cooking grate in

place and return roast to cool side of grill. Cover and continue to cook for 2½ to 3 hours longer.

GRILL-ROASTED BEEF TENDERLOIN

✔ WHY THIS RECIPE WORKS
Grilled tenderloin sounds appealing, but with a whole tenderloin going for as much as $100, uneven cooking, bland flavor, and a tough outer crust just don't cut it. To flavor the meat, we salted it, wrapped it in plastic, and let it rest on the counter before hitting the hot grill. Tucking the narrow tip end of the tenderloin under and tying it securely gave the tenderloin a more consistent thickness that allowed it to cook through more evenly on the grill. Direct heat was too hot for the roast to endure throughout the entire cooking time, so after briefly searing the meat over the coals and flames, we moved it away from the heat for grill-roasting via indirect heat. We also tried using wood chips to gently boost the meat's smoky flavor and made this an option.

GRILL-ROASTED BEEF TENDERLOIN
SERVES 10 TO 12

Beef tenderloins purchased from wholesale clubs require a good amount of trimming before cooking. At the grocery store, however, you may have the option of having the butcher trim it for you. Once trimmed, and with the butt tenderloin still attached (the butt tenderloin is the lobe attached to the large end of the roast), the roast should weigh 4½ to 5 pounds. If you purchase an already-trimmed tenderloin without the butt tenderloin attached, begin checking for doneness about 5 minutes early. When using a charcoal grill, we prefer wood chunks to wood chips whenever possible; substitute 2 medium wood chunks, soaked in water for 1 hour, for the wood chip packet (if using). Serve with Cilantro-Parsley Sauce with Pickled Jalapeños, Romesco Sauce, or Salsa Verde (recipes follow), if desired.

1   (6-pound) beef tenderloin, trimmed of fat and silver skin, tail end tucked and tied with kitchen twine at 2-inch intervals

1½ tablespoons kosher salt

2   cups wood chips, soaked in water for 15 minutes and drained (optional)

2   tablespoons olive oil

1   tablespoon pepper

1. Pat tenderloin dry with paper towels and rub with salt. Cover loosely with plastic wrap and let sit at room temperature for 1 hour.

2. Using large piece of heavy-duty aluminum foil, wrap soaked wood chips, if using, in foil packet and cut several vent holes in top.

3A. FOR A CHARCOAL GRILL: Open bottom vent halfway. Light large chimney starter filled with charcoal briquettes (6 quarts). When top coals are partially covered with ash, pour evenly over half of grill. Place wood chip packet, if using, on coals. Set cooking grate in place, cover, and open lid vent halfway. Heat grill until hot and wood chips are smoking, about 5 minutes.

3B. FOR A GAS GRILL: Place wood chip packet, if using, opposite primary burner. Turn all burners to high, cover, and heat grill until hot and wood chips are smoking, about 15 minutes.

4. Clean and oil cooking grate. Rub tenderloin with oil and season with pepper. Place roast on hot side of grill if using charcoal or opposite primary burner if using gas and cook (covered if using gas) until well browned on all sides, 8 to 10 minutes, turning as needed.

5. For gas grill, leave primary burner on, turning off other burner(s). (Adjust primary burner as needed during cooking to maintain grill temperature around 350 degrees.) Move roast to cool side of grill, cover (position lid vent over meat if using charcoal), and cook until meat registers 115 to 120 degrees (for rare) or 120 to 125 degrees (for medium-rare), 15 to 30 minutes.

6. Transfer roast to carving board, tent loosely with foil, and let rest for 10 to 15 minutes. Remove twine, cut into ½-inch-thick slices, and serve.

CILANTRO-PARSLEY SAUCE WITH PICKLED JALAPEÑOS
MAKES ABOUT 1½ CUPS

This sauce will discolor if left to sit for too long; it's best served within 4 hours of making it.

2–3   slices hearty white sandwich bread, crusts removed, bread lightly toasted and cut into ½-inch pieces (1 cup)
1   cup extra-virgin olive oil
¼   cup lemon juice (2 lemons)
2   cups fresh cilantro leaves
2   cups fresh parsley leaves
3   tablespoons chopped pickled jalapeño slices
1   garlic clove, minced
    Salt

Process bread, oil, and lemon juice in food processor until smooth, 10 to 15 seconds. Add cilantro, parsley, jalapeños, garlic, and ¼ teaspoon salt and pulse until finely chopped (mixture should not be smooth), about 10 pulses. Season with salt to taste and transfer to serving bowl.

ROMESCO SAUCE
MAKES ABOUT 2 CUPS

In addition to being an excellent accompaniment to beef, fish, and poultry, this sauce is also terrific spread on toasted bread or used as a dip for crudités.

1–2   slices hearty white sandwich bread, crusts removed, bread lightly toasted, and cut into ½-inch pieces (½ cup)
3   tablespoons slivered almonds, toasted
1¾   cups jarred roasted red peppers
1   small ripe tomato, cored, seeded, and chopped
2   tablespoons extra-virgin olive oil
1½   tablespoons sherry vinegar
1   large garlic clove, minced
¼   teaspoon cayenne pepper
    Salt

Process bread and almonds in food processor until nuts are finely ground, 10 to 15 seconds. Add red peppers, tomato, oil, vinegar, garlic, cayenne, and ½ teaspoon salt. Process until mixture has texture similar to mayonnaise, 20 to 30 seconds. Season with salt to taste and transfer to serving bowl. (Sauce can be refrigerated for up to 2 days.)

SALSA VERDE

✔ WHY THIS RECIPE WORKS
Despite its innate simplicity, salsa verde can easily go wrong. In fact, many of the recipes we tested were overly potent and harsh, leaving tasters with puckered lips and raging garlic breath. The texture was problematic, too; all of those first salsas separated into pools of oil and clumps of parsley. Processing chunks of toasted bread with oil and lemon juice—not vinegar—in a food processor created a smooth base. We then added the remaining ingredients: anchovies for a touch of complexity, capers for brininess, a little garlic for bite, and parsley to make the sauce "verde." In one variation, we replaced the parsley with fragrant basil and in another, we swapped in peppery arugula.

TRIMMING A BEEF TENDERLOIN

Although wholesale clubs offer whole beef tenderloins at an affordable price, most come "unpeeled," with the fat and silver skin (a tough membrane) intact. Here's how to trim a tenderloin for the grill. Expect to lose between 1 and 1½ pounds during the trimming process. A boning knife is the best tool for this task.

1. Pull away outer layer of fat to expose fatty chain of meat.

2. Pull chain of fat away from roast, cut it off, and discard chain.

3. Scrape silver skin at creases in thick end to expose lobes.

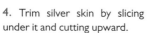

4. Trim silver skin by slicing under it and cutting upward.

5. Remove remaining silver skin in creases at thick end.

6. Turn tenderloin over and remove fat from underside.

SALSA VERDE

MAKES 1½ CUPS

Salsa verde is excellent with grilled or roasted meats, fish, or poultry; poached fish; boiled or steamed potatoes; or sliced tomatoes. It is also good on sandwiches.

2–3 slices hearty white sandwich bread, lightly toasted and cut into ½-inch pieces (about 1½ cups)
1 cup extra-virgin olive oil
¼ cup lemon juice (2 lemons)
4 cups parsley leaves
¼ cup capers, rinsed
4 anchovy fillets, rinsed
1 garlic clove, minced
¼ teaspoon salt

Process bread, oil, and lemon juice in food processor until smooth, about 10 seconds. Add parsley, capers, anchovies, garlic, and salt and pulse until finely chopped (mixture should not be smooth), about 5 pulses. Transfer to serving bowl. (Salsa verde can be refrigerated for up to 2 days.)

LEMON-BASIL SALSA VERDE

Replace 2 cups parsley with 2 cups fresh basil leaves, increase garlic to 2 cloves, and add 1 teaspoon grated lemon zest.

SALSA VERDE WITH ARUGULA

Arugula gives this variation a peppery kick that's a nice match for grilled foods.

Replace 2 cups parsley with 2 cups chopped arugula and increase garlic to 2 cloves.

TEXAS-STYLE BARBECUED BEEF RIBS

✔ WHY THIS RECIPE WORKS

In Texas, good beef ribs are all about intense meat flavor—not just smoke and spice. We found that the juiciest meat with the most flavor was accomplished by the leaving the fat and membrane on the back of the ribs in place. The fat not only bastes the ribs as they cook but also renders to a crisp, baconlike texture. A simple mixture of salt, pepper, cayenne, and chili powder rubbed into each rack was all that it took to bring out the flavor of the meat. To turn our grill into a backyard smoker, we made a slow, even fire with a temperature in the range of 250 to 300 degrees. A couple hours of slow cooking were enough to render some of the fat and make the ribs juicy, tender, and slightly toothy. For real Texas-style barbecue sauce to pair with our ribs, we pulled together the usual ingredients—vinegar, onion, and molasses, to name a few—with dry mustard and chipotle chiles for spiciness. Savory Worcestershire sauce added depth while tomato juice (in place of ketchup) provided tangy flavor and helped thin the sauce out.

TEXAS-STYLE BARBECUED BEEF RIBS

SERVES 4

It is important to use beef ribs with a decent amount of meat, not bony scraps; otherwise, the rewards of making this recipe are few. Two medium wood chunks, soaked in water for 1 hour, can be substituted for the wood chip packet on a charcoal grill.

4 teaspoons chili powder
2 teaspoons salt
1½ teaspoons pepper
½ teaspoon cayenne pepper
4 (1¼-pound) beef rib slabs, trimmed
2 cups wood chips, soaked in water for 15 minutes and drained
1 recipe Barbecue Sauce for Texas-Style Beef Ribs (recipe follows)

1. Combine chili powder, salt, pepper, and cayenne in bowl. Pat ribs dry with paper towels, rub evenly with spice mixture, and let sit at room temperature for 1 hour.

2. Using large piece of heavy-duty aluminum foil, wrap soaked chips in foil packet and cut several vent holes in top.

3A. FOR A CHARCOAL GRILL: Open bottom vent halfway. Light large chimney starter one-third filled with charcoal briquettes (2 quarts). When top coals are partially covered with ash, pour into a steeply banked pile against 1 side of grill. Place wood chip packet on coals. Set cooking grate in place, cover, and open lid vent halfway. Heat grill until hot and wood chips are smoking, about 5 minutes.

3B. FOR A GAS GRILL: Place wood chip packet directly on primary burner. Turn all burners to high, cover, and heat grill until hot and wood chips are smoking, about 15 minutes. Turn primary burner to medium and turn off other burner(s). (Adjust primary burner as needed during cooking to maintain grill temperature between 250 and 300 degrees.)

4. Clean and oil cooking grate. Place ribs meat side down on cool side of grill (the ribs may overlap slightly).

TEST KITCHEN TIP NO. 102 **GOOD WOOD**

You can use any hardwood as fuel for grilling or smoking (softwoods like pine contain too much resin and give foods an unpleasant flavor), but most stores carry only hickory and mesquite. In the test kitchen, we've found that mesquite is too assertively flavored for smoking applications, but it can give good, musky flavor to meats that don't spend too much time on the grill. Our favorite all-purpose wood for grilling and smoking is hickory, which gives food a subtle, slightly sweet flavor.

Cover (position lid vent over meat if using charcoal) and cook for 1 hour.

5. If using charcoal, remove cooking grate and add 20 new briquettes; set cooking grate in place. Flip ribs meat side up and rotate racks. Cover (position lid vent over meat if using charcoal) and continue to cook until meat begins to pull away from bone, 1¼ to 1¾ hours longer.

6. Transfer ribs to carving board, tent loosely with aluminum foil, and let rest for 5 to 10 minutes. Cut ribs between bones and serve, passing sauce separately.

BARBECUE SAUCE FOR TEXAS-STYLE BEEF RIBS
MAKES ABOUT 1¾ CUPS

This is a simple, vinegary dipping sauce quite unlike the sweet, thick barbecue sauces found in the supermarket. The sauce can be refrigerated in an airtight container for up to 4 days; bring to room temperature before serving.

2	tablespoons unsalted butter
¼	cup finely chopped onion
1½	teaspoons chili powder
1	garlic clove, minced
2	cups tomato juice
¾	cup distilled white vinegar
2	tablespoons Worcestershire sauce
2	tablespoons molasses
1	teaspoon minced canned chipotle chile in adobo sauce
½	teaspoon dry mustard mixed with 1 tablespoon water
	Salt and pepper

1. Melt butter in small saucepan over medium heat. Add onion and cook, stirring occasionally, until softened, 2 to 3 minutes. Stir in chili powder and garlic and cook until fragrant, about 30 seconds. Add tomato juice, ½ cup vinegar, Worcestershire, molasses, chipotle, mustard mixture, ½ teaspoon salt, and ¼ teaspoon pepper. Bring to simmer and cook over medium heat,

stirring occasionally, until slightly thickened and reduced to 1½ cups, 30 to 40 minutes.

2. Off heat, stir in remaining ¼ cup vinegar and season with salt and pepper to taste. Cool to room temperature before serving.

KOREAN GRILLED SHORT RIBS

✔ WHY THIS RECIPE WORKS

Korean barbecue should be a quick process, but when we quickly grilled short ribs the meat was barely chewable and overly fatty. We wanted crusty, browned meat that had a barbecued char but was nonetheless tender—all accomplished in minutes. Butchering the short ribs properly proved to be the most important step to reaching our goal. Using English-style short ribs (the cut most widely available in markets), we made four slices from each rib, evening them out (and tenderizing them) with a quick pounding. The right marinade was also critical—pear puree turned out to be a key ingredient. The pear balanced the acidity of the rice vinegar, adding sweetness and a fruit flavor. For a crusty exterior, we cooked the meat over a hot fire and flipped it every couple minutes.

KOREAN GRILLED SHORT RIBS (KALBI)
SERVES 4 TO 6

Make sure to buy English-style ribs that have at least 1 inch of meat on top of the bone, avoiding ones that have little meat and large bones. Two pounds of boneless short ribs at least 4 inches long and 1 inch thick can be used instead of bone-in ribs. Alternatively, 2½ pounds of thinly sliced Korean-style ribs can be used (no butchering is required), but if using charcoal, reduce to 3 quarts. Serve with steamed rice, kimchi (spicy pickled vegetables), and, if available, a spicy bean paste called gochujang. Traditionally, all these ingredients are wrapped in a lettuce leaf with the meat and eaten like a taco.

1	ripe pear, peeled, cored, and chopped coarse
½	cup soy sauce
6	tablespoons sugar
2	tablespoons toasted sesame oil
6	garlic cloves, peeled
4	teaspoons minced fresh ginger
1	tablespoon rice vinegar
3	scallions, sliced thin
½	teaspoon red pepper flakes (optional)
5	pounds bone-in English-style short ribs, meat removed from bone, trimmed, sliced widthwise at angle into ½- to ¾-inch-thick pieces, and pounded ¼ inch thick

1. Process pear, soy sauce, sugar, oil, garlic, ginger, and vinegar in food processor until smooth, 20 to 30 seconds. Transfer to medium bowl and stir in scallions and pepper flakes, if using.

2. Spread one-third of marinade in 13 by 9-inch pan. Place half of meat in single layer over marinade. Pour half of remaining marinade over meat, followed by remaining meat and marinade. Cover tightly with plastic wrap and refrigerate for at least 4 hours or up to 12 hours, turning meat once or twice.

3A. FOR A CHARCOAL GRILL: Open bottom vent completely. Light large chimney starter two-thirds filled with charcoal briquettes (4 quarts). When top coals are partially covered with ash, pour into even layer over half of grill. Set cooking grate in place, cover, and open lid vent completely. Heat grill until hot, about 5 minutes.

3B. FOR A GAS GRILL: Turn all burners to high, cover, and heat grill until hot, about 15 minutes. Leave primary burner on high and turn off other burner(s).

4. Clean and oil cooking grate. Place half of meat on hot side of grill and cook (covered if using gas), turning every 2 to

If using boneless ribs, skip to step 2.

1. Remove meat from bone, positioning chef's knife as close as possible to bone.

2. Trim excess hard fat and silver skin from both sides of meat.

3. Slice meat at angle into 4 to 5 pieces ranging from ½ to ¾ inch thick.

4. Place plastic wrap over meat and pound into even ¼-inch-thick pieces.

---

3 minutes, until well browned on both sides, 8 to 13 minutes. Move first batch of meat to cool side of grill and repeat browning with second batch.

5. Transfer second batch of meat to serving platter. Return first batch of meat to hot side of grill and warm for 30 seconds; transfer to serving platter and serve.

BARBECUED BEEF BRISKET

✔ WHY THIS RECIPE WORKS
In researching recipes for barbecued brisket, we found cooks could agree on one thing: cooking low and slow (for up to 12 hours) for the purpose of tenderizing. That seemed like a lot of time. We wanted to figure out a way to make cooking this potentially delicious cut of meat less daunting and less time-consuming and we wanted to trade in a specialized smoker for a backyard grill. Brining the brisket seasoned it throughout and allowed the meat to remain juicy even after hours on the grill. To get a good crust, we added a little sugar to the salt and pepper rub. Our "aha!" moment came when we realized that fire can burn down as well as up. We layered unlit briquettes on the bottom of our grill and added 4 quarts of hot coals on top. The result? A fire that burned consistently in the optimal 300-degree range for about three hours. We then transferred the brisket to the oven to finish cooking.

BARBECUED BEEF BRISKET
SERVES 8 TO 10

If your brisket is smaller than 5 pounds or the fat cap has been removed, or if you are using a small charcoal grill, it may be necessary to build an aluminum foil shield in order to keep the brisket from becoming too dark. If using the fattier point cut, omit the step of brining. Two medium wood chunks, soaked in water for 1 hour, can be substituted for the wood chip packet on a charcoal grill. Some of the traditional accompaniments to barbecued brisket include barbecue sauce (see Barbecue Sauce for Texas-Style Beef Ribs on page 504), sliced white bread or saltines, pickle chips, and thinly sliced onion.

1	(5- to 6-pound) beef brisket, flat cut
⅔	cup table salt
½	cup plus 2 tablespoons sugar
2	cups wood chips, soaked in water for 15 minutes and drained
3	tablespoons kosher salt
2	tablespoons pepper
1	(13 by 9-inch) disposable aluminum roasting pan (if using charcoal) or 1 disposable aluminum pie plate (if using gas)

1. Using sharp knife, cut slits in fat cap, spaced 1 inch apart, in crosshatch pattern, being careful to not cut into meat. Dissolve table salt and ½ cup sugar in 4 quarts cold water in large container. Submerge brisket in brine, cover, and refrigerate for 2 hours.

2. Using large piece of heavy-duty aluminum foil, wrap soaked chips in foil packet and cut several vent holes in top.

3. Combine remaining 2 tablespoons sugar, kosher salt, and pepper in bowl. Remove brisket from brine and pat dry with paper towels. Transfer to rimmed baking sheet and rub salt mixture over entire brisket and into slits.

4A. FOR A CHARCOAL GRILL: Open bottom vent halfway. Arrange 3 quarts unlit charcoal banked against 1 side of grill and disposable pan filled with 2 cups water on empty side of grill. Light large chimney starter two-thirds filled with charcoal (4 quarts). When top coals are partially covered with ash, pour on top of unlit charcoal, to cover one-third of grill with coals steeply banked against side of grill. Place wood chip packet on top of coals. Set cooking grate in place, cover, and open lid vent halfway. Heat grill until hot and wood chips begin to smoke, about 5 minutes.

4B. FOR A GAS GRILL: Place wood chip packet directly on primary burner. Place disposable aluminum pie plate filled with 2 cups water on other burner(s). Turn all burners to high, cover, and heat grill until hot and wood chips begin to smoke, about 15 minutes. Turn primary burner to medium and turn off other burner(s).

(Adjust primary burner as needed during cooking to maintain grill temperature between 250 and 300 degrees.)

5. Line rimmed baking sheet with foil and set wire rack inside. Clean and oil cooking grate. Place brisket on cool side of grill, fat side down, as far away from coals and flames as possible with thickest side facing coals and flames. Loosely tent meat with foil. Cover (position lid vent over meat if using charcoal) and cook for 3 hours. Transfer brisket to prepared baking sheet.

6. Adjust oven rack to middle position and heat oven to 325 degrees. Roast brisket until tender and meat registers 195 degrees, about 2 hours.

7. Transfer brisket to carving board, tent loosely with foil, and let rest for 30 minutes. Cut brisket across grain into long, thin slices and serve.

GRILLED SAUSAGES WITH ONIONS

✔ WHY THIS RECIPE WORKS
This classic pairing sounds tailor-made for the grill. But the reality is usually onions that are both crunchy and charred and sausages that dry out or—worse—catch fire. We wanted a foolproof method for grilling sausages and vegetables simultaneously that would produce nicely browned links with juicy interiors and tender vegetables. We adapted a ballpark technique, first cooking the meat with the onions away from direct heat and then finishing them directly over the flames. Early in our testing, we found the onions needed a jump start, so we microwaved them with thyme, salt, and pepper. We then layered the raw sausages over the hot onions in the roasting pan (wrapped tightly in foil) and placed the pan on the grill. Once the onions were softened and the sausages were almost cooked through, we removed the sausages to the cooking grate to brown and then finished the dish by allowing the liquid to evaporate from the onions in the pan so they caramelized.

GRILLED SAUSAGES WITH ONIONS
SERVES 4

This recipe will work with any raw, uncooked sausage. Serve sausages as is or in toasted rolls.

- 2 large onions, sliced thin
- 1 teaspoon fresh thyme leaves
- ½ teaspoon salt
- ¼ teaspoon pepper
- 1 (13 by 9-inch) disposable aluminum roasting pan
- 2 pounds sweet or hot Italian sausage (8 to 12 links)

1A. FOR A CHARCOAL GRILL: Open bottom vent completely. Light large chimney starter filled with charcoal briquettes (6 quarts). When top coals are partially covered with ash, pour evenly over grill. Set cooking grate in place, cover, and open lid vent completely. Heat grill until hot, about 5 minutes.

1B. FOR A GAS GRILL: Turn all burners to high, cover, and heat grill until hot, about 15 minutes. Turn all burners to medium-high.

2. Meanwhile, microwave onions, thyme, salt, and pepper in medium bowl, covered, until onions begin to soften and tips turn slightly translucent, 4 to 6 minutes, stirring once halfway through cooking (be careful of steam). Transfer onions to disposable pan. Place sausages in single layer over onions and wrap roasting pan tightly with aluminum foil.

3. Clean and oil cooking grate. Place roasting pan in center of grill, cover grill, and cook for 15 minutes. Move pan to one side of grill and carefully remove foil. Using tongs, place sausages on grate and cook (covered if using gas) until golden brown on all sides, 5 to 7 minutes, turning as needed.

4. Transfer sausages to serving platter and tent loosely with foil. Cover grill and continue to cook onions, stirring occasionally, until liquid evaporates and onions begin to brown, 5 to 10 minutes longer. Serve sausages, passing onions separately.

GRILLED SAUSAGES WITH PEPPERS AND ONIONS

Omit thyme and add 3 seeded and quartered red bell peppers to roasting pan with sausages. Transfer pepper pieces to cooking grate with sausages and cook until charred patches form, 5 to 7 minutes, flipping halfway through cooking.

GRILLED SAUSAGE WITH FENNEL

Substitute 2 cored and thinly sliced fennel bulbs for 1 onion and 2 tablespoons minced fennel fronds for thyme.

GRILLED BRATWURST WITH SAUERKRAUT AND APPLES

Combine 3 peeled and coarsely shredded Granny Smith apples, 2 cups drained sauerkraut, and ½ teaspoon minced fresh sage in disposable roasting pan (do not microwave before adding to pan). Substitute apple mixture for onions and thyme and bratwurst for Italian sausages.

GRILLED PORK CHOPS

✔ WHY THIS RECIPE WORKS
Too many grilled pork chops are burnt on the outside and raw on the inside. And even if they are cooked evenly, they can still be tough and bland. We wanted great-looking and great-tasting chops with a crisp, perfectly grilled crust and juicy, flavorful meat. What's more, we wanted our chops plump and meaty, not thin and tough.

We started with the right chops—tender and flavorful bone-in rib loin or center-cut loin chops worked best—and brined them to pump up their flavor and lock in moisture. To brown the pork chops, only a really hot fire would do. But keeping them over high heat long enough to cook through dried them out. So we grilled the chops over a two-level fire, with one side of the grill intensely hot to sear the chops, and the other only moderately hot to allow the chops to cook through without burning the exterior. A spice rub, made with potent spices and applied before grilling, added big flavor and gave our chops a nice crust.

GRILLED PORK CHOPS
SERVES 4

Rib loin chops are our top choice for their big flavor and juiciness. The spice rub adds a lot of flavor for very little effort, but the chops can also be seasoned with pepper alone just before grilling. If the pork is enhanced (see page 509), do not brine and add 2 teaspoons salt to spice rub or pepper.

- 3 tablespoons salt
- 3 tablespoons sugar
- 4 (12-ounce) bone-in pork rib or center-cut chops, 1½ inches thick, trimmed
- 1 recipe Basic Spice Rub for Pork Chops (recipe follows) or 2 teaspoons pepper

1. Dissolve salt and sugar in 1½ quarts cold water in large container. Submerge chops in brine, cover, and refrigerate for 30 minutes to 1 hour. Remove chops from brine and pat dry with paper towels. Rub chops with spice rub.

2A. FOR A CHARCOAL GRILL: Open bottom vent completely. Light large chimney starter filled with charcoal briquettes (6 quarts). When top coals are partially covered with ash, pour two-thirds evenly over grill, then pour remaining coals over half of grill. Set cooking grate in place, cover, and open lid vent completely. Heat grill until hot, about 5 minutes.

2B. FOR A GAS GRILL: Turn all burners to high, cover, and heat grill until hot, about 15 minutes. Leave primary burner on high and turn off other burner(s).

3. Clean and oil cooking grate. Place chops on hotter side of grill and cook (covered if using gas) until browned on both sides, 4 to 8 minutes. Move chops to cool side of grill, cover, and continue to cook, turning once, until meat registers 145 degrees, 7 to 9 minutes longer. Transfer chops to serving platter, tent loosely with aluminum foil, and let rest for 5 to 10 minutes. Serve.

BASIC SPICE RUB FOR PORK CHOPS
MAKES ¼ CUP, ENOUGH FOR 1 RECIPE GRILLED PORK CHOPS

- 1 tablespoon ground cumin
- 1 tablespoon chili powder
- 1 tablespoon curry powder
- 2 teaspoons packed brown sugar
- 1 teaspoon pepper

Combine all ingredients in bowl.

GRILL-SMOKED PORK CHOPS

WHY THIS RECIPE WORKS
For great grill-smoked pork chops with rosy-pink, ultra-moist meat and true smoke flavor throughout, we built a fire on two sides of the grill, leaving the center empty, except for a disposable aluminum roasting pan. We started the chops low and slow on the grill over the roasting pan. Then we applied a few coats of sauce and achieved a beautiful crust by searing them over the hot sides of the grill. We determined that bone-in chops were our best bet. The bones add flavor to the meat as it cooks and contain connective tissues and fat that break down to

lend suppleness. *What's more, the hollow structure of a bone acts as an insulator, slowing down heat penetration. We used this to our advantage by resting each chop on its bone instead of laying it flat. To keep them from toppling over, we speared them together with skewers, making sure to leave a good inch between each one to allow smoke to circulate, then stood them upright in the center of the grill with bone, not meat, touching the grill.*

GRILL-SMOKED PORK CHOPS
SERVES 4

Buy chops of the same thickness so they will cook uniformly. Use the large holes on a box grater to grate the onion for the sauce. Two medium wood chunks, soaked in water for 1 hour, can be substituted for the wood chip packet on a charcoal grill. You will need two 10-inch metal skewers for this recipe.

SAUCE
- ½ cup ketchup
- ¼ cup molasses
- 2 tablespoons grated onion
- 2 tablespoons Worcestershire sauce
- 2 tablespoons Dijon mustard
- 2 tablespoons cider vinegar
- 1 tablespoon packed light brown sugar

CHOPS
- 2 cups wood chips, soaked in water for 15 minutes and drained
- 4 (12-ounce) bone-in pork rib chops, 1½ inches thick, trimmed
- 2 teaspoons salt
- 2 teaspoons pepper
- 1 (13 by 9-inch) disposable aluminum roasting pan (if using charcoal)

1. **FOR THE SAUCE:** Bring all ingredients to simmer in small saucepan over medium heat and cook, stirring occasionally, until reduced to about 1 cup, 5 to 7 minutes. Transfer ½ cup sauce to

Pass 2 skewers through loin muscle of each chop to provide stability when standing on grill.

small bowl and set aside remaining sauce for serving.

2. FOR THE CHOPS: Using large piece of heavy-duty aluminum foil, wrap soaked chips in foil packet and cut several vent holes in top. Pat pork chops dry with paper towels. Use sharp knife to cut 2 slits about 1 inch apart through outer layer of fat and connective tissue. Season each chop with ½ teaspoon salt and ½ teaspoon pepper. Place chops side by side, facing in same direction, on cutting board with curved rib bone facing down. Pass 2 skewers through loin muscle of each chop, close to bone, about 1 inch from each end, then pull apart to create 1-inch space between each.

3A. FOR A CHARCOAL GRILL: Open bottom vent halfway and place roasting pan in center of grill. Light large chimney starter filled with charcoal briquettes (6 quarts). When top coals are partially covered with ash, pour into 2 even piles on either side of roasting pan. Place wood chip packet on 1 pile of coals. Set cooking grate in place, cover, and open lid vent halfway. Heat grill until hot and wood chips are smoking, about 5 minutes.

3B. FOR A GAS GRILL: Place wood chip packet over primary burner. Turn all burners to high, cover, and heat grill until hot and wood chips are smoking, about 15 minutes. Turn all burners to medium-high. (Adjust burners as needed during cooking to maintain grill temperature between 300 and 325 degrees.)

4. Clean and oil cooking grate. Place skewered chops bone side down on grill (over pan if using charcoal). Cover and cook until meat registers 120 degrees, 28 to 32 minutes.

5. Remove skewers from chops, tip chops onto flat side and brush surface of each with 1 tablespoon sauce. Transfer chops, sauce side down, to hotter parts of grill (if using charcoal) or turn all burners to high (if using gas) and cook until browned on first side, 2 to 6 minutes. Brush top of each chop with 1 tablespoon sauce, flip, and continue to cook until browned on second side and meat registers 140 degrees, 2 to 6 minutes longer.

6. Transfer chops to serving platter, tent loosely with aluminum foil, and let rest for 5 to 10 minutes. Serve, passing reserved sauce separately.

GRILLED PORK TENDERLOIN

✔ **WHY THIS RECIPE WORKS**

The problem when grilling pork tenderloin is how to achieve a good crust without destroying the delicate texture of the meat. For tender, juicy, flavorful meat, we brined the tenderloins for one hour, then added a rub (wet and dry rubs worked equally well), and grilled them over a fire with one hot side and one cooler side. As we often do when grilling tender cuts of meat, we first seared the tenderloins over high heat, then finished them on the cooler part of the grill so they could cook through without charring.

GRILLED PORK TENDERLOIN
SERVES 6 TO 8

If the pork is enhanced (injected with a salt solution), do not brine. Pork tenderloins are often sold two to a package, each piece usually weighing 12 to 16 ounces. The cooking times below are for two average 12-ounce tenderloins; if necessary, adjust the times to suit the size of the cuts you are cooking. If you opt not to brine, bypass step 1 in the recipe and season the tenderloins generously with salt before grilling.

- ¼ cup salt
- ¼ cup sugar
- 2 (12- to 16-ounce) pork tenderloins, trimmed
- 1 recipe spice rub (recipes follow)

1. Dissolve salt and sugar in 2 quarts cold water in large container. Submerge pork tenderloins in brine, cover, and refrigerate for 1 hour. Remove pork from brine and pat dry with paper towels. Coat tenderloins with spice rub.

2A. FOR A CHARCOAL GRILL: Open bottom vent completely. Light large chimney starter filled with charcoal briquettes (6 quarts). When top coals are partially covered with ash, pour evenly over half of grill. Set cooking grate in place, cover, and open lid vent completely. Heat grill until hot, about 5 minutes.

2B. FOR A GAS GRILL: Turn all burners to high, cover, and heat grill until hot, about 15 minutes.

3. Clean and oil cooking grate. Place tenderloins on grill (hot side if using charcoal) and cook (covered if using gas) until well browned on all sides, 10 to 12 minutes, turning as needed. Move tenderloins to cool part of grill (if using charcoal) or turn all burners to medium-low (if using gas), cover, and continue to cook until meat registers 140 degrees, 2 to 3 minutes longer.

4. Transfer tenderloins to carving board, tent loosely with aluminum foil, and let rest for 5 to 10 minutes. Slice crosswise into 1-inch-thick pieces and serve.

FRAGRANT DRY SPICE RUB

MAKES ABOUT ¼ CUP; ENOUGH FOR
1 RECIPE GRILLED PORK TENDERLOIN

If using this spice rub, coat the tenderloins with 2 tablespoons vegetable oil to help the spices adhere.

I	tablespoon fennel seeds
I	tablespoon cumin seeds
I	tablespoon coriander seeds
I ½	teaspoons dry mustard
I ½	teaspoons packed light brown sugar
¾	teaspoon ground cinnamon
¼	teaspoon pepper

Toast fennel, cumin, and coriander seeds in small skillet over medium heat, shaking pan occasionally, until fragrant, 3 to 5 minutes. Transfer to bowl, let cool to room temperature, and grind to powder in spice grinder. Stir in mustard, sugar, cinnamon, and pepper.

TEST KITCHEN TIP NO. 103   KOSHER? YES. ENHANCED? NO.

In the test kitchen we often brine chicken and pork to ensure moist, well-seasoned meat. But there are options at the store that allow you to skip this step. For chicken, that means buying a kosher bird. Koshering is a process similar to brining; it involves coating the chicken with salt to draw out any impurities. Kosher birds are also all-natural and contain no hormones or antibiotics, which makes them a good option.

Some people are surprised that pork is lean and prone to drying out. In fact, today's pork is 50 percent leaner than its 1950s counterpart, and less fat means less flavor and moisture. The industry has addressed this issue by introducing enhanced pork, which is meat injected with a solution of water, salt, and sodium phosphate. The idea is to both season the pork and prevent it from drying out. We've conducted countless tests comparing enhanced pork to natural pork and unequivocally prefer the latter. Natural pork has a better flavor and, if it's cooked correctly, moisture isn't an issue. We also strongly recommend brining most cuts of pork, which lends both moisture and seasoning to the meat. Manufacturers don't use the terms "enhanced" or "natural" on package labels, but if the pork has been enhanced it will have an ingredient list. Natural pork contains just pork and won't have an ingredient list. While natural pork benefits from brining, enhanced pork should not be brined because it's already pretty salty.

ORANGE-GARLIC WET RUB

MAKES ABOUT ½ CUP; ENOUGH FOR
1 RECIPE GRILLED PORK TENDERLOIN

Honey can be substituted for the marmalade.

I	tablespoon grated orange zest
3	garlic cloves, minced
I	tablespoon chopped fresh sage
I	tablespoon extra-virgin olive oil
I	tablespoon orange marmalade
½	teaspoon pepper
¼	teaspoon salt

Combine all ingredients in bowl.

ASIAN BARBECUE WET RUB

MAKES ABOUT ⅓ CUP; ENOUGH FOR
1 RECIPE GRILLED PORK TENDERLOIN

If you don't have sambal oelek chili paste, substitute ½ teaspoon dried red pepper flakes.

2	tablespoons grated fresh ginger
2	scallions, minced
2	tablespoons packed light brown sugar
3	garlic cloves, minced
I	tablespoon hoisin sauce
I	tablespoon toasted sesame oil
I	teaspoon sambal oelek
¼	teaspoon five-spice powder
¼	teaspoon salt

Combine all ingredients in bowl.

GRILLED STUFFED PORK TENDERLOIN

✔ WHY THIS RECIPE WORKS

Though pork tenderloin is sublimely tender, it is also lean and often lacking flavor. We wanted a grilled tenderloin packed with flavor—in a stuffing—so we started with potent ingredients like olives, anchovies, Manchego cheese, and smoked paprika. To fit plenty of flavor inside this skinny cut, we pounded the tenderloin thin and rolled it around the filling, opting for a thick paste topped with baby spinach leaves. Indirect heat on the grill allowed the stuffing to heat through before the exterior of the pork overcooked, and a brown sugar rub caramelized nicely, giving the pork a deep amber hue.

GRILLED STUFFED PORK TENDERLOIN

SERVES 6 TO 8

We prefer natural to enhanced pork (pork that has been injected with a salt solution to increase moistness and flavor) for this recipe.

4	teaspoons packed dark brown sugar
	Salt and pepper
2	(1¼- to 1½-pound) pork tenderloins, trimmed
I	recipe stuffing (recipes follow)
I	cup baby spinach
2	tablespoons olive oil

1. Combine sugar, 1 teaspoon salt, and 1 teaspoon pepper in bowl. Cut each tenderloin in half horizontally, stopping ½ inch from edge so halves remain attached. Open up tenderloins, cover with plastic wrap, and pound to ¼-inch thickness. Trim any ragged edges to create rough rectangle about 10 inches by 6 inches. Season interior of pork with salt and pepper.

2. With long side of pork facing you, spread half of stuffing mixture over bottom half of pork followed by ½ cup of spinach. Roll away from you into tight cylinder, taking care not to squeeze stuffing out ends. Position tenderloin seam side down, evenly space 5 pieces kitchen twine underneath, and tie. Repeat with remaining tenderloin, stuffing, and spinach.

3A. FOR A CHARCOAL GRILL: Open bottom vent completely. Light large chimney starter filled with charcoal briquettes (6 quarts). When top coals are partially covered with ash, pour evenly over half of grill. Set cooking grate in place, cover, and open lid vent completely. Heat grill until hot, about 5 minutes.

3B. FOR A GAS GRILL: Turn all burners to high, cover, and heat grill until hot, about 15 minutes. Leave primary burner on high and turn off other burner(s). (Adjust primary burner as needed during cooking to maintain grill temperature between 325 and 350 degrees.)

4. Clean and oil cooking grate. Coat pork with oil, then rub entire surface with brown sugar mixture. Place pork on cool side of grill, cover, and cook until meat registers 140 degrees, 25 to 30 minutes, rotating pork halfway through cooking.

5. Transfer pork to carving board, tent loosely with aluminum foil, and let rest for 20 minutes. Remove twine, slice pork into ½-inch-thick slices, and serve.

PEPPER AND MANCHEGO STUFFING

MAKES ABOUT 1 CUP; ENOUGH FOR 1 RECIPE GRILLED STUFFED PORK TENDERLOIN

Roasted red peppers may be substituted for the piquillo peppers.

- 1 slice hearty white sandwich bread, torn into ½-inch pieces
- ¾ cup jarred piquillo peppers, rinsed and patted dry
- 2 ounces Manchego cheese, shredded (½ cup)
- ¼ cup pine nuts, toasted
- 2 garlic cloves, minced
- 1 teaspoon minced fresh thyme
- ½ teaspoon smoked paprika
  Salt and pepper

Pulse all ingredients except salt and pepper in food processor until coarsely chopped, 5 to 10 pulses; season with salt and pepper to taste.

OLIVE AND SUN-DRIED TOMATO STUFFING

MAKES ABOUT 1 CUP; ENOUGH FOR 1 RECIPE GRILLED STUFFED PORK TENDERLOIN

- ½ cup pitted kalamata olives
- ½ cup oil-packed sun-dried tomatoes, rinsed and chopped coarse
- 4 anchovy fillets, rinsed
- 2 garlic cloves, minced
- 1 teaspoon minced fresh thyme
- 1 teaspoon grated lemon zest
  Salt and pepper

Pulse all ingredients except salt and pepper in food processor until coarsely chopped, 5 to 10 pulses; season with salt and pepper to taste.

PORCINI AND ARTICHOKE STUFFING

MAKES ABOUT 1 CUP; ENOUGH FOR 1 RECIPE GRILLED STUFFED PORK TENDERLOIN

Avoid jarred or canned artichokes; frozen artichokes have a much fresher flavor.

- ½ ounce dried porcini mushrooms, rinsed and minced
- 3 ounces frozen artichoke hearts, thawed and patted dry (¾ cup)
- 1 ounce Parmesan cheese, grated (½ cup)
- ¼ cup oil-packed sun-dried tomatoes, rinsed and chopped coarse
- ¼ cup fresh parsley leaves
- 2 tablespoons pine nuts, toasted
- 2 garlic cloves, minced
- 1 teaspoon grated lemon zest plus 2 teaspoons juice
  Salt and pepper

Pulse all ingredients except salt and pepper in food processor until coarsely chopped, 5 to 10 pulses; season with salt and pepper to taste.

GRILL-ROASTED BONE-IN PORK RIB ROAST

✔ WHY THIS RECIPE WORKS
Grilling a bulky cut of meat like a pork rib roast may sound difficult, but it's not. We found that a tender, quick-cooking center-cut rib roast and a simple salt rub were all that we needed for a juicy grilled roast with a thick mahogany crust. We grilled it over indirect heat (on the cooler side of the grill) so it could cook through slowly, adding a single soaked wood chunk for a subtle tinge of smoke flavor. After little more than an hour on the grill, our roast was tender and juicy, with plenty of rich, deep flavor. A fresh orange salsa is the perfect counterpoint to the roast's richness.

GRILL-ROASTED BONE-IN PORK RIB ROAST

SERVES 6 TO 8

If you buy a blade-end roast (sometimes called a "rib-end roast"), tie it into a uniform shape with kitchen twine at 1-inch intervals; this step is unnecessary with a center-cut roast. For easier carving, ask the butcher to remove the tip of the chine bone and to cut the remainder of the chine bone between each rib. One medium wood chunk, soaked in water for 1 hour, can be substituted for the wood chip packet on a charcoal grill.

1	(4- to 5-pound) center-cut rib or blade-end bone-in pork roast, tip of chine bone removed, fat trimmed to ¼-inch thickness
4	teaspoons kosher salt
1	cup wood chips, soaked in water for 15 minutes and drained
1½	teaspoons pepper
1	recipe Orange Salsa with Cuban Flavors (optional; recipe follows)

1. Pat roast dry with paper towels. Using sharp knife, cut slits in surface fat layer, spaced 1 inch apart, in crosshatch pattern, being careful not to cut into meat. Season roast with salt. Wrap with plastic wrap and refrigerate for at least 6 hours or up to 24 hours.

2. Using large piece of heavy-duty aluminum foil, wrap soaked chips in foil packet and cut several vent holes in top.

3A. FOR A CHARCOAL GRILL: Open bottom vent halfway. Light large chimney starter filled with charcoal briquettes (6 quarts). When top coals are partially covered with ash, pour into steeply banked pile against side of grill. Place wood chip packet on coals. Set cooking grate in place, cover, and open lid vent halfway. Heat grill until hot and wood chips are smoking, about 5 minutes.

3B. FOR A GAS GRILL: Place wood chip packet over primary burner. Turn all burners to high, cover, and heat grill until hot and wood chips are smoking, about 15 minutes. Turn primary burner to medium-high and turn off other burner(s). (Adjust primary burner as needed during cooking to maintain grill temperature around 325 degrees.)

4. Clean and oil cooking grate. Unwrap roast and season with pepper. Place roast on grate with meat near, but not over, coals and flames and bones facing away from coals and flames. Cover (position lid vent over meat if using charcoal) and cook until meat registers 140 degrees, 1¼ to 1½ hours.

5. Transfer roast to carving board, tent loosely with aluminum foil, and let rest for 30 minutes. Carve into thick slices by cutting between ribs. Serve, passing salsa, if using, separately.

ORANGE SALSA WITH CUBAN FLAVORS

MAKES ABOUT 2½ CUPS

To make this salsa spicier, add the reserved chile seeds.

½	teaspoon grated orange zest plus 5 oranges peeled and segmented; each segment quartered crosswise
½	cup minced red onion
1	jalapeño chile, stemmed, seeds reserved, and minced
2	tablespoons lime juice
2	tablespoons minced fresh parsley
1	tablespoon extra-virgin olive oil
2	teaspoons packed brown sugar
1½	teaspoons distilled white vinegar
1½	teaspoons minced fresh oregano
1	garlic clove, minced
½	teaspoon ground cumin
½	teaspoon salt
½	teaspoon pepper

Combine all ingredients in medium bowl.

GRILL-ROASTED PORK LOIN

WHY THIS RECIPE WORKS

A juicy, crisp-crusted pork loin is a great way to dress up an outdoor dinner, but it can be a challenge to keep the lean roast from drying out on the grill. First, we chose the best cut. Our top choice—the blade-end roast—was moist and flavorful and was the hands-down winner over center-cut and sirloin roasts. Brining the meat before grilling ensured that our finished roast met with rave reviews from testers and stayed juicy and moist, and a generous coating of black pepper—or our own spicy rub—provided ample flavoring. As we did with our pork tenderloin recipe (page 508), we seared the roast for a nice crust and finished it over indirect heat.

GRILL-ROASTED PORK LOIN

SERVES 4 TO 6

If the pork is enhanced (injected with a salt solution; see page 509), do not brine and add 1 tablespoon salt to the pepper or spice rub. Two medium wood chunks, soaked in water for 1 hour, can be substituted for the wood chip packet on a charcoal grill.

¼	cup salt
1	(2½- to 3-pound) boneless blade-end pork loin roast, trimmed and tied with kitchen twine at 1½-inch intervals
2	tablespoons olive oil
1	tablespoon pepper or 1 recipe spice rub (recipes follow)
2	cups wood chips, soaked in water for 15 minutes and drained

1. Dissolve salt in 2 quarts cold water in large container. Submerge pork loin in brine, cover, and refrigerate for 1 to 1½ hours. Remove pork from brine and pat dry with paper towels. Rub pork loin with oil and coat with pepper. Let sit at room temperature for 1 hour.

2. Using large piece of heavy-duty aluminum foil, wrap soaked chips in foil packet and cut several vent holes in top.

3A. FOR A CHARCOAL GRILL: Open bottom vent halfway (and place roasting pan on 1 side of grill). Light large chimney starter three-quarters filled with charcoal briquettes (4½ quarts). When top coals are partially covered with ash, pour evenly over half of grill. Place wood chip packet on coals. Set cooking grate in place, cover, and open lid vent halfway. Heat grill until hot and wood chips are smoking, about 5 minutes.

3B. FOR A GAS GRILL: Place wood chip packet directly on primary burner. Turn all burners to high, cover, and heat grill until hot and wood chips are smoking, about 15 minutes. Leave primary burner on high and turn off other burner(s). (Adjust primary burner as needed during cooking to maintain grill temperature between 300 and 325 degrees.)

4. Clean and oil cooking grate. Place pork loin on hot side of grill, fat side up, and cook (covered if using gas) until well browned on all sides, 10 to 12 minutes, turning as needed. Move to cool side of grill, positioning roast parallel with and as close as possible to heat. Cover (position lid vent over roast if using charcoal) and cook for 20 minutes.

5. Rotate roast 180 degrees, cover, and continue to cook until meat registers 145 degrees, 10 to 30 minutes longer, depending on thickness of roast.

6. Transfer roast to carving board, tent loosely with aluminum foil, and let rest for 15 minutes. Remove twine, cut roast into ½-inch-thick slices, and serve.

SWEET AND SAVORY SPICE RUB
MAKES ABOUT 2 TABLESPOONS, ENOUGH FOR 1 RECIPE GRILL-ROASTED PORK LOIN

The warm spices in this rub are a perfect match with pork.

1	tablespoon cumin seeds
1½	teaspoons coriander seeds
1	teaspoon fennel seeds
½	teaspoon ground cinnamon
¼	teaspoon ground allspice

Toast cumin, coriander, and fennel seeds in small skillet over medium heat, shaking pan occasionally, until fragrant, about 2 minutes. Transfer to bowl, let cool to room temperature, and grind to powder in spice grinder. Stir in cinnamon and allspice.

CHILI-MUSTARD SPICE RUB
MAKES ABOUT 2 TABLESPOONS, ENOUGH FOR 1 RECIPE GRILL-ROASTED PORK LOIN

This rub packs some heat, so use the lesser amount of cayenne if you want a milder rub.

2	teaspoons chili powder
2	teaspoons dry mustard
1	teaspoon ground cumin
½–1	teaspoon cayenne pepper

Combine all ingredients in bowl.

GRILLED STUFFED PORK LOIN

✓ WHY THIS RECIPE WORKS
Center-cut pork loin is an especially lean cut, making it difficult to cook without drying out. We wanted to add moisture to this cut using an approach other than traditional brines or sauces so we decided to stuff it. We bought a short and wide roast, more square than cylindrical. This shape only required four straight, short cuts to open to a long, flat sheet that was easy to fill and roll up. We needed a thick and flavorful stuffing to stay put in the roast and stand up to the meat. Poaching apples and cranberries in a blend of apple cider, apple cider vinegar, and spices developed a filling with the dense, chewy consistency we wanted. And this process had an added bonus—we had ample poaching liquid left, which could be reduced to a glaze.

GRILLED PORK LOIN WITH APPLE-CRANBERRY FILLING
SERVES 6

This recipe is best prepared with a loin that is 7 to 8-inches long and 4 to 5 inches wide and not enhanced (injected with a salt solution). To make cutting the pork easier, freeze it for 30 minutes. If mustard seeds are unavailable, stir an equal amount of whole grain mustard into the filling after the apples have been processed. Use more or less cayenne, depending on how spicy you'd like the stuffing. The pork loin can be stuffed and tied a day ahead of time, but don't season the exterior until you are ready to grill. Two medium wood chunks, soaked in water for 1 hour, can be substituted for the wood chip packet on a charcoal grill.

FILLING

1½	cups packed dried apples
1	cup apple cider
¾	cup packed light brown sugar
½	cup cider vinegar
½	cup packed dried cranberries
1	large shallot, halved lengthwise and sliced thin crosswise
1	tablespoon grated fresh ginger
1	tablespoon yellow mustard seeds
½	teaspoon ground allspice
⅛–¼	teaspoon cayenne pepper

PORK

2	cups wood chips, soaked in water for 15 minutes and drained
1	(2½-pound) boneless center-cut pork loin roast, trimmed
	Salt and pepper

1. **FOR THE FILLING:** Bring all ingredients to simmer in medium saucepan over medium-high heat. Cover, reduce heat to low, and cook until apples are very soft, about 20 minutes. Pour mixture through fine-mesh strainer set over bowl, pressing with back of spoon to extract as much liquid as possible. Return liquid to saucepan and simmer over medium-high heat until reduced to ⅓ cup, about 5 minutes; reserve for glazing. Pulse apple mixture in food processor until coarsely chopped, about 15 pulses. Transfer filling to bowl and refrigerate until needed.

2. **FOR THE PORK:** Position roast fat side up. Insert knife ½ inch from bottom of roast and cut horizontally, stopping ½ inch before edge. Open up this flap. Cut through thicker half of roast about ½ inch from bottom, stopping about ½ inch before edge. Open up this flap. Repeat until pork loin is even ½ inch thickness throughout. If uneven, cover with plastic wrap and use meat pounder to even. Season interior with salt pepper and spread filling in even layer, leaving ½-inch border. Roll tightly and tie with kitchen twine at 1-inch intervals. Season with salt and pepper.

3. Using large piece of heavy-duty aluminum foil, wrap soaked chips in foil packet and cut several vent holes in top.

4A. FOR A CHARCOAL GRILL: Open bottom vent halfway (and place roasting pan on 1 side of grill). Light large chimney starter three-quarters filled with charcoal briquettes (4½ quarts). When top coals are partially covered with ash, pour evenly over half of grill. Place wood chip packet on coals. Set cooking grate in place, cover, and open lid vent halfway. Heat grill until hot and wood chips are smoking, about 5 minutes.

4B. FOR A GAS GRILL: Place wood chip packet directly on primary burner. Turn all burners to high, cover, and heat grill until hot and wood chips are smoking, about 15 minutes. Leave primary burner on medium-high and turn off other burner(s). (Adjust primary burner as needed during cooking to maintain grill temperature between 300 and 325 degrees.)

5. Clean and oil cooking grate. Place pork loin, fat side up, on cool side of grill, cover (position lid vent over roast if using charcoal), and cook until meat registers 130 to 135 degrees, 55 minutes to 1 hour 10 minutes, flipping halfway through cooking.

6. Brush roast evenly with reserved glaze. (You may need to reheat glaze briefly to make it spreadable.) Continue to cook until glaze is thick and glossy and meat registers 145 degrees, 5 to 10 minutes longer.

7. Transfer roast to carving board, tent loosely with aluminum foil, and let rest for 15 minutes. Remove twine, cut roast into ½-inch-thick slices, and serve.

GRILLED PORK LOIN WITH APPLE-CHERRY FILLING WITH CARAWAY

Substitute dried cherries for cranberries and 1 teaspoon caraway seeds for ginger, mustard seeds, and allspice. After processing filling in food processor, transfer to bowl and stir in 2 teaspoons minced fresh thyme.

HOW TO STUFF A PORK LOIN

1. Position roast fat side up. Insert knife ½ inch from bottom of roast and cut horizontally, stopping ½ inch before edge. Open up this flap.

2. Cut through thicker half of roast about ½ inch from bottom, stopping about ½ inch before edge. Open up this flap.

3. Repeat until pork loin is even ½ inch thickness throughout. If uneven, cover with plastic wrap and use meat pounder to even out.

4. With long side of meat facing you, season meat and spread filling, leaving ½-inch border on all sides.

5. Starting from short side, roll pork loin tightly.

6. Tie roast with twine at 1-inch intervals.

CUBAN-STYLE GRILL-ROASTED PORK

✔ WHY THIS RECIPE WORKS

We wanted a boldly flavored Cuban-style roast pork with crackling-crisp skin and tender meat infused with flavor. To speed up cooking, we abandoned cooking the pork completely on the grill (which required constant refueling and rotating over several hours) in favor of a combination cooking method: cooking the pork on the grill until our initial supply of coals died down and then finishing it in the oven. To give the pork added flavor, we again combined methods, first marinating the pork in a powerful solution that included two heads of garlic and 4 cups of orange juice, then rubbing a similarly flavored paste into slits cut all over the pork.

CUBAN-STYLE GRILL-ROASTED PORK

SERVES 8 TO 10

Let the meat rest for a full hour before serving it or it will not be as tender. This roast has a crisp skin that should be served along with the meat. Top the meat with Mojo Sauce (recipe follows). Traditional accompaniments include black beans, rice, and fried plantains.

PORK AND BRINE
- 1 (7- to 8- pound) bone-in, skin-on pork picnic shoulder
- 3 cups sugar
- 2 cups salt
- 2 garlic heads, unpeeled cloves separated and crushed
- 4 cups orange juice

PASTE
- 12 garlic cloves, chopped coarse
- 2 tablespoons ground cumin
- 2 tablespoons dried oregano
- 1 tablespoon salt
- 1½ teaspoons pepper
- 6 tablespoons orange juice
- 2 tablespoons distilled white vinegar
- 2 tablespoons olive oil

1. FOR THE PORK AND BRINE: Cut 1-inch-deep slits (about 1 inch long) all over roast, spaced about 2 inches apart. Dissolve sugar and salt in 6 quarts cold water in large container. Stir in garlic and orange juice. Submerge pork in brine, cover, and refrigerate for 18 to 24 hours. Remove pork from brine and pat dry with paper towels.

2. FOR THE PASTE: Pulse garlic, cumin, oregano, salt, and pepper in food processor to coarse paste, about 10 pulses. With processor running, add orange juice, vinegar, and oil and process until smooth, about 20 seconds. Rub paste all over pork and into slits. Wrap meat in plastic wrap and let sit at room temperature for 1 hour.

3A. FOR A CHARCOAL GRILL: Open bottom vent halfway. Light large chimney starter two-thirds filled with charcoal briquettes (4 quarts). When top coals are partially covered with ash, pour into steeply banked pile against side of grill. Set cooking grate in place, cover, and open lid vent halfway. Heat grill until hot, about 5 minutes.

3B. FOR A GAS GRILL: Turn all burners to high, cover, and heat grill until hot, about 15 minutes. Turn primary burner to medium-high and turn off other burner(s). (Adjust primary burner as needed during cooking to maintain grill temperature of 300 to 325 degrees.)

4. Clean and oil cooking grate. Place roast skin side up on cool side of grill. Cover (position lid vent over meat if using charcoal) and cook for 2 hours. During final 20 minutes of cooking, adjust oven rack to lower-middle position and heat oven to 325 degrees.

5. Transfer pork to wire rack set in rimmed baking sheet and cook in oven until skin is browned and crisp and meat registers 190 degrees, 3 to 4 hours.

6. Transfer roast to carving board and let rest for 1 hour. Remove skin in 1 large piece. Scrape off and discard top layer of fat, then cut meat away from bone in 3 or 4 large pieces. Cut pieces of meat against grain into ¼-inch-thick slices. Scrape excess fat from underside of skin and cut into strips. Serve.

CUBAN-STYLE OVEN-ROASTED PORK

Adjust oven rack to lower-middle position and heat oven to 325 degrees. Place paste-rubbed pork, skin side down, on wire rack set in rimmed baking sheet and cook for 3 hours. Flip roast skin side up and continue to cook until meat registers 190 degrees, about 3 hours longer, lightly tenting roast with aluminum foil if skin begins to get too dark.

MOJO SAUCE

MAKES ABOUT 1 CUP; ENOUGH FOR 1 RECIPE CUBAN-STYLE GRILL-ROASTED PORK

This sauce can be refrigerated in an airtight container for up to 1 day; bring to room temperature before serving.

- 4 garlic cloves, minced
- 2 teaspoons kosher salt
- ½ cup olive oil
- ½ teaspoon ground cumin
- ¼ cup distilled white vinegar
- ¼ cup orange juice
- ¼ teaspoon dried oregano
- ⅛ teaspoon pepper

1. Place minced garlic on cutting board and sprinkle with salt. Using flat side of chef's knife, drag garlic and salt back and forth across cutting board in small circular motions until garlic is ground into smooth paste.

2. Heat oil in medium saucepan over medium heat until shimmering. Add garlic paste and cumin and cook, stirring, until fragrant, about 30 seconds. Off heat, whisk in vinegar, orange juice, oregano, and pepper. Transfer to bowl and let cool to room temperature. Whisk sauce to recombine before serving.

BARBECUED PULLED PORK

✔ WHY THIS RECIPE WORKS
Slow-cooked pulled pork is a summertime favorite; however, many barbecue procedures demand the regular attention of the cook for eight hours or more. We wanted to find a way to make moist, fork-tender pulled pork without the marathon cooking time and constant attention to the grill. For the meat, we determined that a shoulder roast (also called Boston butt), which has significant fat, retained the most moisture and flavor during a long, slow cook.

We massaged a spicy chili rub into the meat, then wrapped the roast in plastic and refrigerated it for at least three hours to "marinate." We cooked the roast first on the grill to absorb smoky flavor (from wood chips—no smoker required), then finished it in the oven, as we did with our Cuban-Style Grill-Roasted Pork (page 514). Finally, we let the pork rest in a paper bag so the meat would steam and any remaining collagen would break down, allowing the flavorful juices to be reabsorbed.

BARBECUED PULLED PORK
SERVES 8

Pulled pork can be made with a fresh ham or picnic roast, although our preference is for Boston butt. If using a fresh ham or picnic roast, remove the skin by cutting through it with the tip of a chef's knife; slide the blade just under the skin and work around to loosen it while pulling it off with your other hand. Four medium wood chunks, soaked in water for 1 hour, can be substituted for the wood chip packets on a charcoal grill. Serve on plain white bread or warmed rolls with dill pickle chips and coleslaw.

- 1 (6- to 8-pound) bone-in Boston butt roast
- ¾ cup Dry Rub for Barbecue (recipe follows)
- 4 cups wood chips, soaked in water for 15 minutes and drained
- 1 (13 by 9-inch) disposable aluminum roasting pan
- 2 cups barbecue sauce (recipes follow)

1. Pat pork dry with paper towels, then massage dry rub into meat. Wrap meat in plastic wrap and refrigerate for at least 3 hours or up to 3 days.

2. At least 1 hour prior to cooking, remove roast from refrigerator, unwrap, and let sit at room temperature. Using 2 large pieces of heavy-duty aluminum foil, wrap soaked chips in 2 foil packets and cut several vent holes in tops.

3A. FOR A CHARCOAL GRILL: Open bottom vent halfway. Light large chimney starter three-quarters filled with charcoal briquettes (4½ quarts). When top coals are partially covered with ash, pour evenly over half of grill. Place wood chip packets on coals. Set cooking grate in place, cover, and open lid vent halfway. Heat grill until hot and wood chips are smoking, about 5 minutes.

3B. FOR A GAS GRILL: Place wood chip packets directly on primary burner. Turn all burners to high, cover, and heat grill until hot and wood chips are smoking, about 15 minutes. Turn primary burner to medium-high and turn off other burner(s). (Adjust primary burner as needed to maintain grill temperature around 325 degrees.)

4. Clean and oil cooking grate. Set roast in disposable pan, place on cool side of grill, and cook for 3 hours. During final 20 minutes of cooking, adjust oven rack to lower-middle position and heat oven to 325 degrees.

5. Wrap disposable pan with heavy-duty foil and cook in oven until meat is fork-tender, about 2 hours.

6. Carefully slide foil-wrapped pan with roast into brown paper bag. Crimp end shut and let rest for 1 hour.

7. Transfer roast to carving board and unwrap. Separate roast into muscle sections, removing fat, if desired, and tearing meat into shreds with your fingers. Place shredded meat in large bowl and toss with 1 cup barbecue sauce. Serve, passing remaining sauce separately.

DRY RUB FOR BARBECUE
MAKES ABOUT 1 CUP

You can adjust the proportions of spices in this all-purpose rub or add or subtract a spice, as you wish.

- ¼ cup paprika
- 2 tablespoons chili powder
- 2 tablespoons ground cumin
- 2 tablespoons packed dark brown sugar
- 2 tablespoons salt
- 1 tablespoon dried oregano
- 1 tablespoon granulated sugar
- 1 tablespoon black pepper
- 1 tablespoon white pepper
- 1–2 teaspoons cayenne pepper

Combine all ingredients in small bowl.

EASTERN NORTH CAROLINA BARBECUE SAUCE
MAKES ABOUT 2 CUPS

This sauce can be refrigerated in an airtight container for up to 4 days.

- 1 cup distilled white vinegar
- 1 cup cider vinegar
- 1 tablespoon sugar
- 1 tablespoon red pepper flakes
- 1 tablespoon hot sauce
- Salt and pepper

Mix all ingredients except salt and pepper together in bowl and season with salt and pepper to taste.

WESTERN SOUTH CAROLINA BARBECUE SAUCE
MAKES 2 CUPS

This sauce can be refrigerated in an airtight container for up to 4 days.

- 1 tablespoon vegetable oil
- ½ cup finely chopped onion
- 2 garlic cloves, minced
- ½ cup cider vinegar
- ½ cup Worcestershire sauce
- 1 tablespoon dry mustard
- 1 tablespoon packed dark brown sugar
- 1 tablespoon paprika
- 1 teaspoon salt
- 1 teaspoon cayenne pepper
- 1 cup ketchup

Heat oil in small saucepan over medium heat. Add onion and cook, stirring occasionally, until softened, 5 to 7 minutes. Stir in garlic and cook until fragrant, about 30 seconds. Stir in vinegar, Worcestershire, mustard, sugar, paprika, salt, and cayenne, bring to simmer, and stir in ketchup. Cook over low heat until thickened, about 15 minutes.

MID-SOUTH CAROLINA MUSTARD SAUCE
MAKES ABOUT 2½ CUPS

This sauce can be refrigerated in an airtight container for up to 4 days.

- 1 cup cider vinegar
- 1 cup vegetable oil
- 6 tablespoons Dijon mustard
- 2 tablespoons maple syrup or honey
- 4 teaspoons Worcestershire sauce
- 1 teaspoon hot sauce
  Salt and pepper

Mix all ingredients except salt and pepper together in bowl and season with salt and pepper to taste.

AUTHENTIC BARBECUED PORK RIBS

✔ WHY THIS RECIPE WORKS
Authentic ribs, like Barbecued Pulled Pork (page 515), can take a full day in the barbecue pit to develop deep, smoky flavor. For our ribs, we applied a spice rub and let the ribs sit at room temperature for 1 hour so the spices could penetrate. Then, as with our pulled pork, we cooked the ribs on the grill to absorb smoky flavor (from wood chips—no smoker required), then transferred them to the oven and continued to cook them until they were tender. Barbecued ribs need barbecue sauce, which we applied to the ribs before they went into the oven, reserving a portion to serve alongside the ribs.

BARBECUED PORK SPARERIBS
SERVES 4 TO 6

Two medium wood chunks, soaked in water for 1 hour, can be substituted for the wood chip packet on a charcoal grill. To remove the membrane (the thin white sheath that lines the concave side of the rack), insert a spoon handle between the membrane and the ribs of one rack to loosen slightly. Using a paper towel, grasp the loosened membrane and pull away gently to remove.

- 2 (2½- to 3-pound) racks pork spareribs, preferably St. Louis cut, trimmed and membrane removed
- ¾ cup Dry Rub (recipe follows)
- 1 recipe barbecue sauce (recipes follow)
- 2 cups woods chips, soaked in water for 15 minutes and drained

1. Rub 3 tablespoons dry rub on each side of racks of ribs. Let ribs sit at room temperature for 1 hour.

2. Using large piece of heavy-duty aluminum foil, wrap soaked chips in foil packet and cut several vent holes in top.

3A. FOR A CHARCOAL GRILL: Open bottom vent halfway. Light large chimney starter two-thirds filled with charcoal briquettes (4 quarts). When top coals are partially covered with ash, pour evenly over half of grill. Place wood chip packet on coals. Set cooking grate in place, cover, and open lid vent halfway. Heat grill until hot and wood chips are smoking, about 5 minutes.

3B. FOR A GAS GRILL: Place wood chip packet directly on primary burner. Turn all burners to high, cover, and heat grill until hot and wood chips are smoking, about 15 minutes. Turn primary burner to medium-high and turn off other burner(s). (Adjust primary burner as needed during cooking to maintain grill temperature between 300 and 325 degrees.)

4. Clean and oil cooking grate. Place ribs meat side down on cool side of grill. Cover (position lid vent over meat if using charcoal) and cook until ribs are deep red and smoky, about 2 hours, flipping and rotating racks halfway through cooking. During final 20 minutes of cooking, adjust oven rack to lower-middle position and heat oven to 325 degrees.

5. Transfer ribs to wire rack set in rimmed baking sheet and brush evenly with ½ cup sauce. Cover tightly with foil and cook in oven until tender, 1 to 2 hours.

6. Remove ribs from oven and let rest, still covered, for 30 minutes. Unwrap ribs, slice between bones, and serve, passing remaining sauce separately.

DRY RUB
MAKES ABOUT 1⅓ CUPS

Store leftover spice rub in an airtight container for up to 3 months.

- ¼ cup paprika
- 3 tablespoons celery salt
- 3 tablespoons garlic powder
- 2 tablespoons salt
- 2 tablespoons chili powder

TEST KITCHEN TIP NO. 104 FIGHTING FLARE-UPS

Flare-ups from the grill are a not-so-rare occurrence, caused primarily by fats melting into the fire. They are much more problematic with charcoal grills since the burners on gas grills often have covers to protect them. Regardless, sometimes there's just no avoiding them, so it's important to make sure a little flare-up doesn't turn into an out-of-control grease fire that ruins your meal. We recommend keeping a squirt bottle filled with water near the grill. At the first sign of flames, pull foods to a cool part of the grill and douse the flames with water.

2 tablespoons ground cumin

2 tablespoons packed dark brown
sugar

1 tablespoon granulated sugar

1 tablespoon dried oregano

1 tablespoon white pepper

1 tablespoon black pepper

2 teaspoons cayenne pepper
(optional)

Combine all ingredients in bowl.

BARBECUE SAUCE
MAKES ABOUT 1 CUP

This sauce can be refrigerated for up to 4 days.

4 tablespoons unsalted butter

1 small onion, chopped fine

2 garlic cloves, minced

2 tablespoons lemon juice

1 tablespoon pepper

1 teaspoon paprika

1 teaspoon dry mustard

½ teaspoon hot sauce

½ teaspoon salt

1 (15-ounce) can tomato sauce

¼ cup cider vinegar

Heat butter in medium saucepan over medium heat. Add onion and cook, stirring occasionally, until softened, 5 to 7 minutes. Stir in garlic and cook until fragrant, about 30 seconds. Stir in lemon juice, pepper, paprika, mustard, hot sauce, and salt, bring to simmer, and cook for 5 minutes. Add tomato sauce and vinegar and continue to simmer until thickened, about 15 minutes longer.

KENTUCKY SMOKED BARBECUE SAUCE

Increase lemon juice to ¼ cup (2 lemons) and paprika to 2 teaspoons. Add ½ teaspoon liquid smoke and 2 tablespoons packed brown sugar with lemon juice.

LOUISIANA SWEET BARBECUE SAUCE

Increase vinegar to 6 tablespoons. Add ¼ cup molasses, 2 tablespoons sweet sherry, and 1 tablespoon packed brown sugar with tomato sauce.

SPICY RIO GRANDE BARBECUE SAUCE

For an even hotter sauce, add ⅛ to ¼ teaspoon cayenne pepper.

Increase garlic to 4 cloves, lemon juice to ¼ cup (2 lemons), and hot sauce to 1 teaspoon. Add one 7-ounce can diced mild green chiles with lemon juice.

MEMPHIS-STYLE BARBECUED SPARERIBS

✔ WHY THIS RECIPE WORKS

In Memphis, ribs get flavor from spice rub and a thin, vinegary liquid—called a mop—that is basted on the ribs throughout cooking. As with our Barbecued Pork Spareribs (page 516), we applied a spice rub to the ribs and let them sit for one hour before grilling. To keep the meat moist on the grill, we stowed a pan of water underneath the cooking grate on the cooler side of the grill, where it would absorb heat and work to keep the temperature stable. For the mop, we combined apple cider and apple cider vinegar and brushed it on the ribs while they cooked on the grill. Last, as with our other barbecue recipes, we transferred the ribs to the oven to cook through until tender.

MEMPHIS-STYLE BARBECUED SPARERIBS
SERVES 4 TO 6

Don't remove the membrane that runs along the bone side of the ribs; it prevents some of the fat from rendering out and is authentic to this style of ribs. Two medium wood chunks, soaked in water for 1 hour, can be substituted for the wood chip packet on a charcoal grill.

2 (2½- to 3-pound) racks pork spareribs, preferably St. Louis cut, trimmed

1 recipe Spice Rub (recipe follows)

2 cup wood chips, soaked in water for 15 minutes and drained

½ cup apple juice

3 tablespoons apple cider vinegar

1 (13 by 9-inch) disposable aluminum roasting pan

1. Rub 2 tablespoons dry rub on each side of racks of ribs. Let ribs sit at room temperature for 1 hour.

2. Using large piece of heavy-duty aluminum foil, wrap soaked chips in foil packet and cut several vent holes in top. Combine apple juice and vinegar in small bowl and set aside.

3A. FOR A CHARCOAL GRILL: Open bottom vent halfway and place roasting pan filled with 2 cups water on 1 side of grill. Light large chimney starter three-quarters filled with charcoal briquettes (4½ quarts). When top coals are partially covered with ash, pour evenly over half of grill opposite roasting pan. Place wood chip packet on coals. Set cooking grate in place, cover, and open lid vent halfway. Heat grill until hot and wood chips are smoking, about 5 minutes.

3B. FOR A GAS GRILL: Place wood chip packet directly on primary burner. Place roasting pan filled with 2 cups water on other burner(s). Turn all burners to high, cover, and heat grill until hot and wood chips are smoking, about 15 minutes. Turn primary burner to medium-high and turn off other burner(s). (Adjust primary burner as needed during cooking to maintain grill temperature between 300 and 325 degrees.)

4. Clean and oil cooking grate. Place ribs meat side down on cool side of grill over water-filled pan. Cover (position lid vent over meat if using charcoal) and cook until ribs are deep red and smoky, about 2 hours, brushing with apple cider mixture and

flipping and rotating racks halfway through cooking. During final 20 minutes of cooking, adjust oven rack to lower-middle position and heat oven to 325 degrees.

5. Set wire rack in rimmed baking sheet and add enough water to cover pan bottom. Transfer ribs to prepared rack and brush with apple cider mixture. Cover tightly with foil and cook in oven until tender, 1 to 2 hours.

6. Remove ribs from oven, loosen foil to release steam, and let rest for 30 minutes. Slice ribs between bones and serve.

SPICE RUB

MAKES ABOUT ½ CUP, ENOUGH
FOR I RECIPE MEMPHIS-STYLE
BARBECUED SPARERIBS

For less spiciness, reduce the cayenne to ½ teaspoon.

- 2 tablespoons paprika
- 2 tablespoons packed light brown sugar
- I tablespoon salt
- 2 teaspoons chili powder
- I½ teaspoons black pepper
- I½ teaspoons garlic powder
- I½ teaspoons onion powder
- I½ teaspoons cayenne pepper
- ½ teaspoon dried thyme

Combine all ingredients in bowl.

TEST KITCHEN TIP NO. 105 LOW-TECH GRILL CHAMP

With the proliferation of grilling tools and gadgets on the market, you might be surprised to hear what grilling "tool" we find indispensable—a simple disposable aluminum pan. Whether large enough to hold a 20-pound turkey or small enough to cover a single sausage link, disposable aluminum pans are a grill-cook's best friend. We routinely use these inexpensive trays to cover meats (and retain heat) on windy days, to hold our grilling tools, and to transfer food from kitchen to grill and back. When preparing many of our recipes, we like to place a disposable aluminum roasting pan in the center of the grill before adding the lit charcoal. Once the charcoal in the starter is lit and covered with light gray ash, we pour the coals into equal piles on either side of the pan. The pan ensures that the coals stay in place for even heating and makes cleanup a cinch—all of the rendered fat collects in the disposable pan, not on the bottom of the grill. This setup isn't necessary for gas grills, but when smoking on a gas grill, you can also use a smaller disposable pan to hold the wood chips.

BARBECUED BABY BACK RIBS

✓ WHY THIS RECIPE WORKS

More often than not, baby back ribs taste like dry shoe leather on a bone. We wanted ribs that were juicy, tender, and fully seasoned, with an intense smokiness. Meaty ribs—racks between 1½ and 2 pounds if possible—provided substantial, satisfying portions. For ribs that are so good and moist they don't even need barbecue sauce, they must be brined first and then rubbed with a spice mix before barbecuing. Chili powder, cayenne pepper, cumin, and dark brown sugar formed a nice, crisp crust on the ribs and provided the best balance of sweet and spicy.

BARBECUED BABY BACK RIBS
SERVES 4

Two medium wood chunks, soaked in water for 1 hour, can be substituted for the wood chip packet on a charcoal grill. For information on removing the membrane from the ribs, see page 422.

- ½ cup sugar
- ½ cup salt
- 2 (1½- to 2-pound) racks baby back or loin back ribs, trimmed, membrane removed
- I recipe Spice Rub (recipe follows)
- 2 cups wood chips, soaked in water for 15 minutes and drained

1. Dissolve sugar and salt in 4 quarts cold water in large container. Submerge racks in brine, cover, and refrigerate for 1 hour. Remove pork from brine and pat dry with paper towels. Rub 1 tablespoon dry rub on each side of racks of ribs. Let ribs sit at room temperature for 1 hour.

2. Using large piece of heavy-duty aluminum foil, wrap soaked chips in foil packet and cut several vent holes in top. Combine apple juice and vinegar in small bowl and set aside.

3A. FOR A CHARCOAL GRILL: Open bottom vent halfway. Light large chimney starter three-quarters filled with charcoal briquettes (4½ quarts). When top coals are partially covered with ash, pour evenly over half of grill. Place wood chip packet on coals. Set cooking grate in place, cover, and open lid vent halfway. Heat grill until hot and wood chips are smoking, about 5 minutes.

3B. FOR A GAS GRILL: Place wood chip packet directly on primary burner. Turn all burners to high, cover, and heat grill until hot and wood chips are smoking, about 15 minutes. Turn primary burner to medium-high and turn off other burner(s). (Adjust primary burner as needed during cooking to maintain grill temperature of 300 to 325 degrees.)

4. Clean and oil cooking grate. Place ribs meat side down on cool side of grill. Cover (position lid vent over meat if using charcoal) and cook until ribs are deep red and smoky, about 2 hours, flipping and rotating racks halfway through cooking. During final 20 minutes of cooking, adjust oven rack to lower-middle position and heat oven to 325 degrees.

5. Transfer ribs to wire rack set in rimmed baking sheet. Cover tightly with foil and cook in oven until tender, 1 to 2 hours.

6. Remove ribs from oven, loosen foil to release steam, and let rest for 30 minutes. Slice ribs between bones and serve.

4	teaspoons paprika
1¾	teaspoons ground cumin
1½	teaspoons chili powder
1½	teaspoons packed dark brown sugar
1	teaspoon white pepper
¾	teaspoon dried oregano
¾	teaspoon black pepper
½	teaspoon cayenne pepper

Combine all ingredients in bowl.

GRILLED RACK OF LAMB

✔ **WHY THIS RECIPE WORKS**

Lamb and the grill have great chemistry. The intense heat of the coals produces a great crust and melts away the meat's abundance of fat, distributing flavor throughout, while imparting a smokiness that's the perfect complement to lamb's rich, gamy flavor. But the rendering fat can cause flare-ups that scorch the meat and impart sooty flavors, ruining this pricey cut. To solve this problem, we trimmed the excess fat from the racks of lamb and stacked the coals to the sides of the grill, creating a cooler center where the fat could safely render before we moved the lamb over direct heat to brown the exterior. A simple wet rub of robust herbs and a little oil enhanced the meat's flavor without overwhelming it. Our method gave us a rack of lamb that was pink and juicy, with a well-browned crust that contrasted nicely with the lush, ultra-tender exterior.

GRILLED RACK OF LAMB
SERVES 4 TO 6

We prefer the milder taste and bigger size of domestic lamb, but you may substitute lamb from New Zealand or Australia. Since imported racks are generally smaller, follow the shorter cooking times given in the recipe. While most lamb is sold frenched (meaning part of each rib bone is exposed), chances are there will still be some extra fat between the bones. Remove the majority of this fat, leaving an inch at the top of the small eye of meat. For more information on frenching the rib bones, see page 427. Also, make sure that the chine bone (along the bottom of the rack) has been removed to ensure that it will be easy to cut between the ribs after cooking. Ask the butcher to do it; it's very hard to cut off at home.

1	(12 by 8-inch) disposable aluminum pan (if using charcoal)
4	teaspoons olive oil
4	teaspoons chopped fresh rosemary
2	teaspoons chopped fresh thyme
2	garlic cloves, minced
2	(1½- to 1¾-pound) racks of lamb (8 ribs each), frenched and trimmed
	Salt and pepper

1A. FOR A CHARCOAL GRILL: Open bottom vent completely and place pan in center of grill. Light large chimney starter filled with charcoal briquettes (6 quarts). When top coals are partially covered with ash, pour into two even piles on either side of pan. Set cooking grate in place, cover, and open lid vent completely. Heat grill until hot, about 5 minutes.

1B. FOR A GAS GRILL: Turn all burners to high, cover, and heat grill until hot, about 15 minutes. Leave primary burner on high, turning off other burners.

2. Combine 1 tablespoon oil, rosemary, thyme, and garlic in bowl. Pat lamb dry with paper towels, rub with remaining teaspoon oil, and season with salt and pepper. Place racks bone side up on cooler part of grill with meaty side of racks very close to, but not quite over, hot coals or lit burner. Cover and cook until meat is lightly browned, faint grill marks appear, and fat has begun to render, 8 to 10 minutes.

3. Flip racks over, bone side down, and move to hotter parts of grill. Cook until well browned, 3 to 4 minutes. Brush racks with herb mixture. Flip racks bone side up and continue to cook until well browned, 3 to 4 minutes longer. Stand racks up and lean them against each other; continue to cook (over hotter side of grill if using charcoal) until bottom is well browned and meat registers 120 to 125 degrees (for medium-rare) or 130 to 135 degrees (for medium), 3 to 8 minutes longer.

4. Transfer lamb to carving board, tent loosely with aluminum foil, and let rest for 15 minutes. Cut between ribs to separate chops and serve.

GRILLED RACK OF LAMB WITH SWEET MUSTARD GLAZE

Omit rosemary and add 3 tablespoons Dijon mustard, 2 tablespoons honey, and ½ teaspoon grated lemon zest to oil, thyme, and garlic. Reserve 2 tablespoons glaze, then brush racks as directed in step 3 and brush with reserved glaze after meat rests.

GRILLED LAMB KEBABS

✔ WHY THIS RECIPE WORKS

We wanted lamb shish kebabs with tender, juicy meat and evenly cooked vegetables. To avoid the raw lamb and charred vegetables that cooking on skewers often delivers, we cut the meat (boneless leg of lamb, trimmed of fat and silver skin) into 1-inch cubes and narrowed the vegetable field. Onions and peppers were the vegetable combination most preferred by tasters; they aren't incredibly watery like tomatoes, which were out from the beginning, and they cooked at the same rate as the meat. Marinating the meat for two hours added extra flavor; for the marinades, we used fruity, sweet, and spicy ingredients that stood up well to the hearty lamb.

GRILLED LAMB KEBABS
SERVES 6

You can use red, yellow, orange, or green bell peppers in this recipe. You will need four 12-inch metal skewers for this recipe. If you have long, thin pieces of meat, roll or fold them into approximate 1-inch cubes before skewering.

- 1 recipe marinade (recipes follow)
- 1 (2¼-pound) shank end boneless leg of lamb, trimmed and cut into 1-inch chunks
- 1 large bell pepper, stemmed, seeded, and cut into 1-inch pieces
- 1 large red or sweet onion, peeled, halved lengthwise, each half cut into 4 wedges and each wedge cut crosswise into thirds
- Lemon or lime wedges (optional)

1. Place marinade and lamb in 1-gallon zipper-lock bag and toss to coat; press out as much air as possible and seal bag. Refrigerate for at least 2 hours or up to 24 hours, flipping bag every hour.

2. Remove lamb from bag and pat dry with paper towels. Starting and ending with meat, thread 4 pieces of meat, 3 pieces of onion (three 3-layer stacks), and 6 pieces of pepper in mixed order on four 12-inch metal skewers.

3A. FOR A CHARCOAL GRILL: Open bottom vent completely. Light large chimney starter mounded with charcoal briquettes (7 quarts). When top coals are partially covered with ash, pour evenly over grill. Set cooking grate in place, cover, and open lid vent completely. Heat grill until hot, about 5 minutes.

3B. FOR A GAS GRILL: Turn all burners to high, cover, and heat grill until hot, about 15 minutes.

4. Clean and oil cooking grate. Place skewers on grill and cook (covered if using gas), turning skewers every 3 to 4 minutes, until well browned and lamb registers

120 to 125 degrees (for medium-rare) or 130 to 135 degrees (for medium), 7 to 12 minutes.

5. Transfer skewers to serving platter, tent loosely with aluminum foil, and let rest for 5 to 10 minutes before serving with lemon wedges, if using.

WARM-SPICED PARSLEY MARINADE WITH GINGER

MAKES ABOUT 1 CUP, ENOUGH FOR 1 RECIPE GRILLED LAMB KEBABS

- ½ cup olive oil
- ½ cup packed fresh parsley leaves
- 1 jalapeño chile, stemmed, seeded, and chopped coarse
- 2 tablespoons grated fresh ginger
- 3 garlic cloves, peeled
- 1 teaspoon ground cumin
- 1 teaspoon ground cardamom
- 1 teaspoon ground cinnamon
- 1 teaspoon salt
- ⅛ teaspoon pepper

Process all ingredients in food processor until smooth, about 1 minute.

SWEET CURRY MARINADE WITH BUTTERMILK

MAKES ABOUT 1 CUP, ENOUGH FOR 1 RECIPE GRILLED LAMB KEBABS

- ¾ cup buttermilk
- 1 tablespoon lemon juice
- 3 garlic cloves, minced
- 1 tablespoon packed brown sugar
- 1 tablespoon curry powder
- 1 teaspoon red pepper flakes
- 1 teaspoon ground coriander
- 1 teaspoon chili powder
- 1 teaspoon salt
- ⅛ teaspoon pepper

Combine all ingredients in 1-gallon zipper-lock bag in which meat will marinate.

GARLIC AND CILANTRO MARINADE WITH GARAM MASALA

MAKES ABOUT ¾ CUP, ENOUGH FOR 1 RECIPE GRILLED LAMB KEBABS

- ½ cup olive oil
- ½ cup fresh cilantro
- ¼ cup raisins
- 1½ tablespoons lemon juice
- 3 garlic cloves, peeled
- 1 teaspoon salt
- ½ teaspoon garam masala
- ⅛ teaspoon pepper

Process all ingredients in food processor until smooth, about 1 minute.

ROSEMARY-MINT MARINADE WITH GARLIC AND LEMON

MAKES ABOUT ¾ CUP, ENOUGH FOR 1 RECIPE GRILLED LAMB KEBABS

- ½ cup olive oil
- 10 fresh mint leaves
- 1½ teaspoons chopped fresh rosemary
- 1½ teaspoons grated lemon zest plus 2 tablespoons juice
- 3 garlic cloves, peeled
- 1 teaspoon salt
- ⅛ teaspoon pepper

Process all ingredients in food processor until smooth, about 1 minute.

GRILLED SALMON FILLETS

✔ WHY THIS RECIPE WORKS
We wanted grilled salmon with a tender interior and crisp skin, and we wanted each fillet to hold together on the grill. We chose thicker salmon fillets, which could stand the heat of the grill for a little while longer before the first turn. To prevent the fish from sticking and falling apart, we dried the fish's exterior by wrapping it in clean kitchen

towels and "seasoned" our cooking grate by brushing it over and over with multiple layers of oil until it developed a dark, shiny coating. After laying the fillets on the grate, we easily flipped each fillet without even the tiniest bit of sticking. For moist, tender fish we cooked the salmon to a perfect medium-rare—any longer and the fish began to dry out.

GRILLED SALMON FILLETS
SERVES 4

This recipe can be used with any thick, firm-fleshed white fish, including red snapper, grouper, halibut, and sea bass (cook white fish to 140 degrees, up to 2 minutes longer per side). If you are using skinless fillets, treat the skinned side of each as if it were the skin side. If desired, serve with Olive Vinaigrette or Almond Vinaigrette (recipes follow).

- 1 (1½- to 2-pound) skin-on salmon fillet, 1½ inches thick
   Vegetable oil
   Salt and pepper
   Lemon wedges

1. Use sharp knife to remove any whitish fat from belly of salmon and cut fillet into 4 equal pieces. Place fillets skin side up on large plate lined with clean kitchen towel. Place second clean kitchen towel on top of fillets and press down to blot liquid. Refrigerate fish, wrapped in towels, while preparing grill, at least 20 minutes.

2A. FOR A CHARCOAL GRILL: Open bottom vent completely. Light large chimney starter two-thirds filled with charcoal briquettes (4 quarts). When top coals are partially covered with ash, pour evenly over half of grill. Set cooking grate in place, cover, and open lid vent completely. Heat grill until hot, about 5 minutes.

2B. FOR A GAS GRILL: Turn all burners to high, cover, and heat grill until hot, about 15 minutes.

3. Clean cooking grate, then repeatedly brush grate with well-oiled paper towels until grate is black and glossy, 5 to 10 times. Lightly brush both sides of fish with oil and season with salt and pepper. Place fish skin side down on hot side of grill (if using charcoal) or turn all burners to medium (if using gas) with fillets diagonal to grate. Cover and cook until skin is well browned and crisp, 3 to 5 minutes. (Try lifting fish gently with spatula after 3 minutes; if it doesn't cleanly lift off grill, continue to cook, checking at 30-second intervals, until it releases.)

4. Flip fish and continue to cook, covered, until center is still translucent when checked with tip of paring knife and registers 125 degrees (for medium-rare) and is still translucent when cut into with paring knife, 2 to 6 minutes longer. Serve immediately with lemon wedges.

ALMOND VINAIGRETTE
MAKES ABOUT ½ CUP; ENOUGH FOR 1 RECIPE GRILLED SALMON FILLETS

- ⅓ cup whole almonds, toasted
- 1 small shallot, minced
- 4 teaspoons white wine vinegar
- 2 teaspoons honey
- 1 teaspoon Dijon mustard
- ⅓ cup extra-virgin olive oil
- 1 tablespoon cold water
- 1 tablespoon chopped fresh tarragon
   Salt and pepper

Place almonds in zipper-lock bag and, using rolling pin or bottom of skillet, pound until pieces no larger than ½ inch remain. Combine pounded almonds, shallot, vinegar, honey, and mustard in medium bowl. Whisking constantly, slowly drizzle in oil until smooth emulsion forms. Add water and tarragon and whisk to combine, then season with salt and pepper to taste. Whisk to recombine before serving.

OLIVE VINAIGRETTE
MAKES ABOUT ½ CUP; ENOUGH FOR 1 RECIPE GRILLED SALMON FILLETS

- ½ cup green or kalamata olives, pitted and chopped coarse
- ¼ cup extra-virgin olive oil
- 2 tablespoons chopped fresh parsley
- 1 small shallot, minced
- 2 teaspoons lemon juice
   Salt and pepper

Combine all ingredients except salt and pepper in bowl and season with salt and pepper to taste. Whisk to recombine before serving.

GRILLED GLAZED SALMON

✓ WHY THIS RECIPE WORKS

We wanted glazed grilled salmon that would allow the glaze not only to form a glossy, deeply caramelized crust, but also to permeate the flesh, making the last bite every bit as good as the first. Marinating the fish in soy sauce seasoned it through and through, but we needed to add a viscous sweetener, either honey or maple syrup, to help the marinade cling to the fish. Oiling the cooking grate multiple times prevented sticking, a particular problem when grilling fish. Searing the salmon over high heat, then brushing it with some of the glaze, and finally pulling it to the cooler side of the grill to cook through gave us the best grilled glazed salmon we had ever tried.

GRILLED GLAZED SALMON
SERVES 4

Scraping the cooking grate clean and oiling the grate will help prevent the fish from sticking.

- 1   recipe glaze (recipes follow)
- ⅓   cup soy sauce
- ⅓   cup maple syrup
- 1   (1½- to 2-pound) skin-on salmon fillet, 1½ inches thick
-       Pepper
-       Lemon wedges

1. Measure 2 tablespoons glaze into bowl for serving and set aside.

2. Whisk soy sauce and maple syrup together in 13 by 9-inch baking dish. Use sharp knife to remove any whitish fat from belly of salmon and cut fillet into 4 equal pieces. Place fillets skin side up in baking dish (do not coat salmon skin with marinade) and refrigerate fish while preparing grill, at least 20 minutes.

3A. FOR A CHARCOAL GRILL: Open bottom vent completely. Light large chimney starter filled with charcoal briquettes

(6 quarts). When top coals are partially covered with ash, pour two-thirds evenly over grill, then pour remaining coals over half of grill. Set cooking grate in place, cover, and open lid vent completely. Heat grill until hot, about 5 minutes.

3B. FOR A GAS GRILL: Turn all burners to high, cover, and heat grill until hot, about 15 minutes.

4. Clean cooking grate, then repeatedly brush grate with well-oiled paper towels until black and glossy, 5 to 10 times. Remove salmon from marinade and season with pepper. Place fish flesh side down on grill (hot side if using charcoal) with fillets diagonal to grate. Cook (covered if using gas) until grill marks form, 1 to 3 minutes. Flip fish, brush with glaze, and cook until salmon is opaque about halfway up thickness of fillets, 3 to 5 minutes.

5. Brush fillets again with glaze, then flip and move to cool side of grill (if using charcoal) or turn all burners down to medium-low (if using gas). Cook until center is still translucent when checked with tip of paring knife and registers 125 degrees (for medium-rare), 1 to 3 minutes longer.

6. Transfer fillets to serving platter, brush with reserved 2 tablespoons glaze, and serve with lemon wedges.

MAPLE-SOY GLAZE

Bring ¼ cup maple syrup and 2 tablespoons soy sauce to simmer in small saucepan over medium-high heat and cook until thickened slightly, 3 to 4 minutes.

HONEY-MUSTARD GLAZE

Bring ¼ cup honey and 2 tablespoons soy sauce to simmer in small saucepan over medium-high heat and cook until thickened slightly, 3 to 4 minutes. Off heat, whisk in 3 tablespoons Dijon mustard.

MAPLE-CHIPOTLE GLAZE

Offer lime wedges instead of lemon wedges when serving.

Bring ¼ cup maple syrup, 2 tablespoons soy sauce, and 1 teaspoon minced canned chipotle chile in adobo to simmer in small saucepan over medium-high heat and cook until thickened slightly, 3 to 4 minutes. Off heat, whisk in 2 tablespoons lime juice.

GRILLED BLACKENED RED SNAPPER

✓ WHY THIS RECIPE WORKS

Blackened fish is usually prepared in a cast-iron skillet, but it can lead to a relentlessly smoky kitchen. We thought we'd solve this issue by throwing our fish on the grill, but this introduced a host of new challenges—curled fillets that stuck to the grill and spices that tasted raw and harsh. To prevent curling fillets, we simply needed to score the skin. We solved the sticking problem by oiling the grate with a heavy hand. Finally, to give the fish its flavorful "blackened but not burned" coating, we bloomed our spice mixture in melted butter, allowed it to cool, and then applied the coating to the fish. Once on the grill, the spice crust acquired the proper depth and richness while the fish cooked through.

GRILLED BLACKENED RED SNAPPER
SERVES 4

Striped bass, halibut, or grouper can be substituted for the snapper; if the fillets are thicker or thinner, they will have slightly different cooking times. For a gas grill, we super-heat the cooking grate by pressing aluminum foil directly onto the surface before cooking; be sure to use heavy-duty foil (thin foil will melt), and skip this step if your grill has ceramic cooking grates (it may damage the ceramic). Serve the fish with lemon wedges, *Rémoulade*, or *Pineapple and Cucumber Salsa with Mint* (recipes follow).

2 tablespoons paprika
2 teaspoons onion powder
2 teaspoons garlic powder
¾ teaspoon ground coriander
¾ teaspoon salt
¼ teaspoon cayenne pepper
¼ teaspoon black pepper
¼ teaspoon white pepper
3 tablespoons unsalted butter
4 (6- to 8-ounce) red snapper fillets, ¾ inch thick

1. Combine paprika, onion powder, garlic powder, coriander, salt, cayenne, black pepper, and white pepper in bowl. Melt butter in 10-inch skillet over medium heat. Stir in spice mixture and cook, stirring frequently, until fragrant and spices turn dark rust color, 2 to 3 minutes. Transfer mixture to pie plate and let cool to room temperature. Use a fork to break up any large clumps.

2A. FOR A CHARCOAL GRILL: Open bottom vent completely. Light large chimney starter two-thirds filled with charcoal briquettes (4 quarts). When top coals are partially covered with ash, pour evenly over half of grill. Set cooking grate in place, cover, and open lid vent completely. Heat grill until hot, about 5 minutes.

2B. FOR A GAS GRILL: Turn all burners to high, cover, and heat grill until hot, about 15 minutes.

3. Clean cooking grate, then repeatedly brush grate with well-oiled paper towels until black and glossy, 5 to 10 times.

4. Meanwhile, pat fillets dry with paper towels. Using sharp knife, make shallow diagonal slashes every inch along skin side of fish, being careful not to cut into flesh. Place fillets skin side up on large plate. Using your fingers, rub spice mixture in thin, even layer on top and sides of fish. Flip fillets over and repeat on other side (you should use all of spice mixture).

5. Place fish skin side down on grill (hot side if using charcoal) with fillets diagonal to grate. Cook until skin is very dark brown and crisp, 3 to 5 minutes. Carefully flip fish and continue to cook until dark brown and beginning to flake and center is opaque but still moist, about 5 minutes longer. Serve.

PINEAPPLE AND CUCUMBER SALSA WITH MINT

MAKES ABOUT 3 CUPS, ENOUGH FOR 1 RECIPE GRILLED BLACKENED RED SNAPPER

To make this dish spicier, add the reserved chile seeds.

½ large pineapple, peeled, cored, and cut into ¼-inch pieces
½ cucumber, peeled, halved lengthwise, seeded, and cut into ¼-inch pieces
1 small shallot, minced
1 serrano chile, stemmed, seeds reserved, and minced
2 tablespoons chopped fresh mint
1–2 tablespoons lime juice
½ teaspoon grated fresh ginger
Salt
Sugar

Combine pineapple, cucumber, shallot, chile, mint, 1 tablespoon lime juice, ginger, and ½ teaspoon salt in bowl and let sit at room temperature for 15 to 30 minutes. Season with lime juice, salt, and sugar to taste. Transfer to serving bowl.

RÉMOULADE

MAKES ABOUT ½ CUP, ENOUGH FOR 1 RECIPE GRILLED BLACKENED RED SNAPPER

The rémoulade can be refrigerated for up to 3 days.

½ cup mayonnaise
1½ teaspoons sweet pickle relish
1 teaspoon hot sauce
1 teaspoon lemon juice
1 teaspoon minced fresh parsley
½ teaspoon capers, rinsed
½ teaspoon Dijon mustard
1 small garlic clove, minced
Salt and pepper

Pulse all ingredients in food processor until well combined but not smooth, about 10 pulses. Season with salt and pepper to taste. Transfer to serving bowl.

GRILLED TUNA STEAKS WITH VINAIGRETTE

✔ WHY THIS RECIPE WORKS
Ideally, grilled tuna should combine a hot, smoky, charred exterior with a cool, rare, sashimi-like center. Grilling tuna to this degree of perfection might be old hat for a practiced chef, but for the home cook, who grills tuna as a once-in-awhile treat during the summer, the ideal can be elusive. For grilled tuna steaks with an intense smoky char and a tender interior, we started with a hot grill. We moistened the tuna steaks' flesh with a vinaigrette to promote browning and allow the oil to penetrate the meat of the tuna steaks. And instead of using sugar in our vinaigrette, we used honey. Both promote browning, but honey does it faster.

GRILLED TUNA STEAKS
WITH VINAIGRETTE
SERVES 6

We prefer our tuna served rare or medium-rare. If you like your fish cooked medium, observe the timing for medium-rare, then tent the steaks loosely with foil for 5 minutes before serving.

- 3 tablespoons plus 1 teaspoon red wine vinegar
- 2 tablespoons chopped fresh thyme or rosemary
- 2 tablespoons Dijon mustard
- 2 teaspoons honey
  Salt and pepper
- ¾ cup olive oil
- 6 (8-ounce) tuna steaks, 1 inch thick

1A. FOR A CHARCOAL GRILL: Open bottom vent completely. Light large chimney starter filled with charcoal briquettes (6 quarts). When top coals are partially covered with ash, pour evenly over half of grill. Set cooking grate in place, cover, and open lid vent completely. Heat grill until hot, about 5 minutes.

1B. FOR A GAS GRILL: Turn all burners to high, cover, and heat grill until hot, about 15 minutes. (Adjust burners as needed to maintain hot fire.)

2. Clean cooking grate, then repeatedly brush grate with well-oiled paper towels until grate is black and glossy, 5 to 10 times.

3. Meanwhile, whisk vinegar, thyme, mustard, honey, ½ teaspoon salt, and pinch pepper together in large bowl. Whisking constantly, slowly drizzle oil into vinegar mixture until lightly thickened and emulsified. Measure out ¾ cup vinaigrette and set aside for cooking fish. Reserve remaining vinaigrette for serving.

4. Pat fish dry with paper towels. Generously brush both sides of fish with vinaigrette and season with salt and pepper. Place fish on grill (hot side if using charcoal) and cook (covered if using gas) until grill marks form and bottom surface is opaque, 1 to 3 minutes.

5. Flip fish and cook until opaque at perimeter and translucent red at center when checked with tip of paring knife and registers 110 degrees (rare), about 1½ minutes, or until opaque at perimeter and reddish pink at center when checked with tip of paring knife and registers 125 degrees (medium-rare), about 3 minutes. Serve, passing reserved vinaigrette.

GRILLED TUNA STEAKS WITH PROVENÇAL VINAIGRETTE

Substitute 1 tablespoon minced fresh oregano for thyme and add ¼ cup chopped pitted oil-cured black olives, 2 tablespoons minced fresh parsley, 2 minced anchovies, and 1 minced garlic clove to vinaigrette.

GRILLED TUNA STEAKS WITH CHARMOULA VINAIGRETTE

Substitute 2 tablespoons minced fresh parsley for thyme and add ¼ cup minced fresh cilantro, 4 minced garlic cloves, 1 teaspoon paprika, 1 teaspoon ground cumin, and ½ teaspoon ground coriander to vinaigrette.

GRILLED TUNA STEAKS WITH SOY-GINGER VINAIGRETTE

Substitute rice vinegar for red wine vinegar and 2 thinly sliced scallions for thyme. Omit salt and add 3 tablespoons soy sauce, 1 tablespoon toasted sesame oil, 2 teaspoons grated fresh ginger, and ½ teaspoon red pepper flakes to vinaigrette.

GRILLED SEA SCALLOPS

✔ WHY THIS RECIPE WORKS

In theory, the blazing-hot fire of a grill is perfect for cooking scallops with an extra-crisp crust and moist interior, but in practice they're usually rubbery and overcooked by the time they develop a good sear, and they inevitably stick to the grate. For great grilled scallops, we needed to figure out how to build the biggest fire possible. The solution was a disposable aluminum pan—it allowed us to corral the coals in just the center of the grill for a tall, even, super-hot fire that gave us scallops with impressive char and juicy centers. Drying the scallops with clean kitchen towels before cooking helped ensure browning, and threading them on double metal skewers made them easy to flip all at once. To combat the problem of sticking, we lightly coated the scallops in a mixture of flour, cornstarch, oil, and sugar. With this simple coating, our scallops were crisp-crusted, moist and tender within, and released without hesitation.

GRILLED SEA SCALLOPS
SERVES 4

We recommend buying "dry" scallops, those without chemical additives. Dry scallops will look ivory or pinkish and feel tacky; wet scallops look bright white and feel slippery. If using wet scallops, soak them in a solution of 1 quart water, ¼ cup lemon juice, and 2 tablespoons salt for 30 minutes before step 1, and do not season with salt in step 3. Double-skewering the scallops makes flipping easier. To skewer, thread 4 to 6 scallops onto one skewer and then place a second skewer through the scallops parallel to and about ¼ inch from the first. You will need eight to twelve 12-inch metal skewers for this recipe. You will also need a deep (at least 2¾ inches) disposable 13 by 9-inch aluminum roasting pan.

1½ pounds large dry sea scallops, tendons removed
1 (13 by 9-inch) disposable aluminum roasting pan
2 tablespoons vegetable oil
1 tablespoon all-purpose flour
1 teaspoon cornstarch
1 teaspoon sugar
Salt and pepper
Lemon wedges
1 recipe vinaigrette (optional; recipes follow)

1. Place scallops on rimmed baking sheet lined with clean kitchen towel. Place second clean kitchen towel on top of scallops and press gently on towel to blot liquid. Let scallops sit at room temperature, covered with towel, for 10 minutes. With scallops on work surface, thread onto doubled skewers so that flat sides will directly touch cooking grate, 4 to 6 scallops per doubled skewer. Return skewered scallops to towel-lined baking sheet; refrigerate, covered with second towel, while preparing grill.

2A. FOR A CHARCOAL GRILL: Loosely cover cooking grate with large piece of heavy-duty aluminum foil. Light large chimney starter mounded with charcoal (7 quarts) and allow to burn until coals are fully ignited and partially covered with thin layer of ash, about 25 minutes. Remove and discard foil. Meanwhile, poke twelve ½-inch holes in bottom of disposable aluminum roasting pan and place in center of grill. Empty coals into pan.

2B. FOR A GAS GRILL: Turn all burners to high, cover, and heat grill until hot, about 15 minutes.

3. While grill is heating, whisk oil, flour, cornstarch, and sugar together in small bowl. Remove towels from scallops. Brush both sides of skewered scallops with oil mixture and season with salt and pepper.

4. Clean cooking grate, then repeatedly brush grate with well-oiled paper towels until grate is black and glossy, 5 to 10 times.

5. Place skewered scallops directly over hot coals. Cook, covered if using gas, without moving scallops until lightly browned, 2½ to 4 minutes. Carefully flip skewers and continue to cook until second side is browned, sides of scallops are firm, and centers are opaque, 2 to 4 minutes longer. Serve immediately with lemon wedges and vinaigrette, if using.

CHILE-LIME VINAIGRETTE

MAKES ABOUT 1 CUP, ENOUGH FOR 1 RECIPE GRILLED SEA SCALLOPS

1 teaspoon grated lime zest plus 3 tablespoons juice (2 limes)
1 tablespoon sriracha sauce
2 tablespoons honey
2 teaspoons fish sauce
½ cup vegetable oil

Whisk lime zest and juice, sriracha sauce, honey, and fish sauce until combined. Whisking constantly, slowly drizzle in oil until emulsified.

BARBECUE SAUCE VINAIGRETTE

MAKES ABOUT 1 CUP, ENOUGH FOR 1 RECIPE GRILLED SEA SCALLOPS

3 tablespoons barbecue sauce
1 tablespoon ketchup
2 tablespoons cider vinegar
2 teaspoons sugar
½ teaspoon salt
½ cup vegetable oil

Whisk barbecue sauce, ketchup, vinegar, sugar, and salt together in medium bowl until combined. Whisking constantly, slowly drizzle in oil until emulsified.

BASIL VINAIGRETTE

MAKES ABOUT 1 CUP, ENOUGH FOR 1 RECIPE GRILLED SEA SCALLOPS

2 tablespoons champagne vinegar
1 cup packed fresh basil
3 tablespoons minced fresh chives
2 garlic cloves, minced
2 teaspoons sugar
1 teaspoon salt
½ teaspoon pepper
⅔ cup vegetable oil

Pulse vinegar, basil, chives, garlic, sugar, salt, and pepper in blender until roughly chopped, 5 to 7 pulses. With blender running, slowly drizzle in oil until emulsified, about 1 minute, scraping down sides of jar as necessary.

BACON AND BROWNED BUTTER VINAIGRETTE

MAKES ABOUT 1 CUP, ENOUGH FOR 1 RECIPE GRILLED SEA SCALLOPS

8 tablespoons unsalted butter
1 slice bacon, diced
3 tablespoons sherry vinegar
3 tablespoons vegetable oil
1 medium shallot, minced
1 tablespoon maple syrup
2 teaspoons Dijon mustard

1. Heat 6 tablespoons butter in 10-inch skillet over medium-high heat until melted. Continue to cook, swirling pan constantly until butter is dark golden brown and has

nutty aroma, 1 to 3 minutes. Remove skillet from heat and transfer browned butter to large heatproof bowl. Stir remaining 2 tablespoons butter into hot butter to melt. Wipe skillet clean with paper towel.

2. Cook bacon in now-empty skillet over medium heat, stirring occasionally, until crisp, 5 to 7 minutes. Using slotted spoon, transfer bacon to paper towel–lined plate. Pour off any bacon fat into browned butter. Add vinegar, oil, shallot, maple syrup, and mustard to browned butter mixture; whisk until emulsified. Stir in reserved bacon.

GRILLED SHRIMP SKEWERS

✔ WHY THIS RECIPE WORKS
Shrimp can turn from moist and juicy to rubbery and dry in the blink of an eye—especially when grilled. While grilling shrimp in their shells can shield them from the coals' scorching heat, any seasonings are stripped off along with the shells when it's time to eat. For tender, juicy, boldly seasoned grilled shrimp we decided to go with peeled shrimp and find a way to prevent them from drying out. We seasoned the shrimp with salt, pepper, and sugar (to help browning) and set them over a very hot fire. This worked well with jumbo shrimp, but smaller shrimp overcooked before charring. Because jumbo shrimp cost as much as $25 per pound, we wanted a less expensive solution. We created faux jumbo shrimp by cramming a skewer with several normal-sized shrimp pressed tightly together. Our final step was to take the shrimp off the fire before they were completely cooked (but after they had picked up attractive grill marks). We finished cooking them in a heated sauce waiting on the cool side of the grill; this final simmer infused them with bold flavor.

GRILLED SHRIMP SKEWERS
SERVES 4

The shrimp and sauce (recipes follow) finish cooking together on the grill, so prepare the sauce ingredients while the grill is heating. To fit all of the shrimp on the cooking grate at once, you will need three 14-inch metal skewers. Serve with grilled bread.

1½	pounds extra-large shrimp (21 to 25 per pound), peeled and deveined
2–3	tablespoons olive oil
	Salt and pepper
¼	teaspoon sugar
1	recipe sauce (recipes follow)
	Lemon wedges

1. Pat shrimp dry with paper towels. Thread the shrimp onto 3 skewers, alternating direction of heads and tails. Brush both sides of shrimp with oil and season with salt and pepper. Sprinkle 1 side of each skewer evenly with sugar.

2A. FOR A CHARCOAL GRILL: Open bottom vent completely. Light large chimney starter filled with charcoal briquettes (6 quarts). When top coals are partially covered with ash, pour evenly over half of

SKEWERING SHRIMP

Pass skewer through center of each shrimp. As you add shrimp to skewer, alternate direction of heads and tails for compact arrangement of about 12 shrimp. Shrimp should be crowded and touching each other.

grill. Set cooking grate in place, cover, and open lid vent completely. Heat grill until hot, about 5 minutes.

2B. FOR A GAS GRILL: Turn all burners to high, cover, and heat grill until hot, about 15 minutes. Leave primary burner on high and turn other burner(s) to medium-low.

3. Clean cooking grate, then repeatedly brush grate with well-oiled paper towels until grate is black and glossy, 5 to 10 times. Place disposable pan with sauce ingredients on hot side of grill and cook, stirring occasionally, until hot, 1 to 3 minutes. Move pan to cool side of grill.

4. Place shrimp skewers sugared side down on hot side of grill and use tongs to push shrimp together on skewers if they have separated. Cook shrimp until lightly charred, 4 to 5 minutes. Using tongs, flip and continue to cook until second side is pink and slightly translucent, 1 to 2 minutes longer.

5. Using potholder, carefully lift each skewer from grill and use tongs to slide shrimp off skewers into pan with sauce. Toss shrimp and sauce to combine. Place pan on hot side of grill and cook, stirring, until shrimp are opaque throughout, about 30 seconds. Remove from the grill, add remaining sauce ingredients, and toss to combine. Transfer to serving platter and serve with lemon wedges.

SPICY LEMON-GARLIC SAUCE
MAKES ABOUT ½ CUP, ENOUGH FOR 1 RECIPE GRILLED SHRIMP SKEWERS

You will need a 10-inch disposable aluminum pie pan for this recipe.

4	tablespoons unsalted butter, cut into 4 pieces
¼	cup lemon juice (2 lemons)

Over the years, we've learned a lot about which skewers were the best and worst for grilling. Though wooden skewers are necessary in some cases (as in Grilled Potatoes on page 531), when the skewers go in the microwave, they are generally our least preferred since they can burn and break once over the high heat of the grill. Turning to metal skewers, we were frustrated by how food (especially shrimp) flopped around on round metal skewers. Our favorite are flat metal skewers, which never burn, last forever, and hold food in place.

3	garlic cloves, minced
½	teaspoon red pepper flakes
⅛	teaspoon salt
1	(10-inch) disposable aluminum pie pan
⅓	cup minced fresh parsley

Combine butter, lemon juice, garlic, pepper flakes, and salt in aluminum pan. Cook over hot side of grill, stirring occasionally, until butter melts, about 1½ minutes. Move to cool side of grill and proceed to grill shrimp, adding parsley just before serving.

CHARMOULA SAUCE

MAKES ABOUT ½ CUP; ENOUGH FOR
1 RECIPE GRILLED SHRIMP SKEWERS

You will need a 10-inch disposable aluminum pan or pie pan for this recipe.

¼	cup extra-virgin olive oil
1	small red bell pepper, stemmed, seeded, and finely chopped
⅓	cup finely chopped red onion
3	garlic cloves, minced
1	teaspoon paprika
½	teaspoon ground cumin
¼	teaspoon cayenne pepper
⅛	teaspoon salt
⅓	cup minced fresh cilantro
2	tablespoons fresh lemon juice

Combine oil, bell pepper, onion, garlic, paprika, cumin, cayenne, and salt in aluminum pan. Cook over hot side of grill, stirring occasionally, until vegetables soften, 5 to 7 minutes. Move to cool side of grill and proceed to grill shrimp, adding cilantro and lemon juice just before serving.

FRESH TOMATO SAUCE WITH FETA AND OLIVES

MAKES ABOUT ½ CUP, ENOUGH FOR
1 RECIPE GRILLED SHRIMP SKEWERS

You will need a 10-inch disposable aluminum pie pan for this recipe.

¼	cup extra-virgin olive oil
1	large tomato, cored, seeded, and minced
1	tablespoon minced fresh oregano
⅛	teaspoon salt
4	ounces feta cheese, crumbled (about 1 cup)
⅓	cup kalamata olives, pitted and chopped fine
2	tablespoons lemon juice
3	scallions, sliced thin

Combine oil, tomato, oregano, and salt in aluminum pan. Cook over hot side of grill, stirring occasionally, until hot, about 1½ minutes. Move to cool side of grill and proceed to grill shrimp, adding feta, olives, lemon juice, and scallions just before serving.

GRILLED ASPARAGUS

✔ WHY THIS RECIPE WORKS

For great grilled asparagus, we opted for thicker spears, which combined maximum char with a meaty, crisp-tender texture. A simple medium-hot fire worked best—the spears were on and off the grill in less than 10 minutes. We tried adding flavor with zesty marinades but because asparagus has a naturally tough outer skin, most of the flavor was left in the bowl or on the basting brush. The answer was as simple as brushing the asparagus with butter, rather than oil, before placing it on the grill. The spears tasted nuttier and more flavorful, and were crispier and browner than spears brushed with oil. Our final step was to create some flavored butters. Garlic was an obvious choice, as were the fresh, tangy flavors of lime and orange zests—especially when combined with pungent spices or fresh herbs.

GRILLED ASPARAGUS WITH GARLIC BUTTER

SERVES 4 TO 6

Use asparagus that is at least ½ inch thick near the base. Do not use pencil-thin asparagus; it cannot withstand the heat and will overcook. Age affects the flavor of asparagus enormously. For the sweetest taste, look for spears that are bright green and firm, with tightly closed tips.

3	tablespoons unsalted butter, melted
3	small garlic cloves, minced
1½	pounds thick asparagus spears, trimmed
	Salt and pepper

1A. FOR A CHARCOAL GRILL: Open bottom vent completely. Light large chimney starter three-quarters filled with charcoal briquettes (4½ quarts). When top coals are partially covered with ash, pour evenly over grill. Set cooking grate in place, cover, and open lid vent completely. Heat grill until hot, about 5 minutes.

1B. FOR A GAS GRILL: Turn all burners to high, cover, and heat grill until hot, about 15 minutes. Turn all burners to medium-high.

2. Combine butter and garlic in bowl. Brush asparagus with butter mixture and season with salt and pepper to taste.

3. Clean and oil cooking grate. Place asparagus in even layer on grill and cook until just tender and browned, 4 to 10 minutes, turning halfway through cooking. Transfer asparagus to serving platter and serve.

GRILLED ASPARAGUS WITH CHILI-LIME BUTTER

Substitute 1 teaspoon grated lime zest, ½ teaspoon chili powder, ¼ teaspoon cayenne pepper, and ⅛ teaspoon red pepper flakes for garlic.

GRILLED ASPARAGUS WITH ORANGE-THYME BUTTER

Substitute 1 teaspoon grated orange zest and 1 teaspoon minced fresh thyme for garlic.

GRILLED ASPARAGUS WITH CUMIN BUTTER

Reduce garlic to 2 cloves and add 1 teaspoon grated lemon zest, ½ teaspoon ground cumin, and ½ teaspoon ground coriander to butter.

GRILLED SWEET CORN

✔ **WHY THIS RECIPE WORKS**
Grilled corn on the cob is one thing. Grilled corn on the cob that's as juicy as boiled corn is another. We wanted to find a way to caramelize the outer corn kernels and infuse them throughout with that delicious smoky flavor without drying or charring them to death. We found that grilling the corn with only the innermost layer of husk still on keeps the corn from burning while at the same time allowing the smoky grilled flavor to come through. In short, we had stumbled across a perfect hybrid: the steamed-grilled ear of corn.

GRILLED SWEET CORN
SERVES 8

If you are certain that you have a supersweet variety of corn, remove the husks entirely, then follow instructions below, grilling until kernels are light caramel brown, 5 to 7 minutes.

8 ears corn, husks on
  Unsalted butter
  Salt and pepper

1A. FOR A CHARCOAL GRILL: Open bottom vent completely. Light large chimney starter three-quarters filled with charcoal briquettes (4½ quarts). When top coals are partially covered with ash, pour evenly over grill. Set cooking grate in place, cover, and open lid vent completely. Heat grill until hot, about 5 minutes.

1B. FOR A GAS GRILL: Turn all burners to high, cover, and heat grill until hot, about 15 minutes. Turn all burners to medium-high.

2. Meanwhile, remove all but innermost layer of husk from each ear of corn (kernels will be covered by, but visible through, last husk layer). Use scissors to snip off long silk ends at tips of ears.

3. Place corn on grill and cook until kernels have left dark outlines in husk

and husks are charred and beginning to peel away at tip to expose some kernels, 8 to 10 minutes, turning every 2 minutes. Transfer ears to serving platter and remove and discard charred husks and silk. Season corn with butter, salt, and pepper to taste and serve.

GRILLED CORN SALSA
MAKES ABOUT 2 CUPS

This salsa is a great way to use up leftover grilled corn. To make this salsa spicier, add the reserved chile seeds. Serve with grilled seafood or chicken, or even with tortilla chips.

2	ears grilled sweet corn, kernels cut from cobs (1 cup)
1	red bell pepper, stemmed, seeded, and chopped medium
1½	tablespoons vegetable oil
1½	tablespoons lime juice
½	jalapeño chile, stemmed, seeds reserved, and minced
1	tablespoon chopped fresh cilantro
1	scallion, sliced thin
1	teaspoon ground cumin
1	small garlic clove, minced
	Salt

Combine all ingredients in bowl and season with salt to taste. Serve.

MEXICAN-STYLE GRILLED CORN

✔ **WHY THIS RECIPE WORKS**
In Mexico, street vendors add kick to grilled corn by slathering it with a creamy, spicy, cheesy sauce. The corn takes on an irresistibly sweet, smoky, charred flavor, which is heightened by the lime juice and chili powder in the sauce. For our own rendition of this south-of-the-border street fare, we ditched the husks, coated the ears with oil to prevent sticking, and

grilled them directly on the grate over a hot fire so the corn could develop plenty of char. The traditional base for the sauce is crema, a thick, soured Mexican cream. But given its limited availability in supermarkets, we replaced the crema with a combination of mayonnaise (for richness) and sour cream (for tanginess). Most recipes call for queso fresco or Cotija, but these cheeses can be hard to find. Pecorino Romano made a good substitute.

MEXICAN-STYLE GRILLED CORN
SERVES 6

If you can find queso fresco or Cotija, use either in place of the Pecorino Romano. If you prefer the corn spicy, add the optional cayenne pepper.

1½	ounces Pecorino Romano cheese, grated (¾ cup)
¼	cup mayonnaise
3	tablespoons sour cream
3	tablespoons minced fresh cilantro
4	teaspoons lime juice
1	garlic clove, minced
¾	teaspoon chili powder
¼	teaspoon pepper
¼	teaspoon cayenne pepper (optional)
4	teaspoons vegetable oil
¼	teaspoon salt
6	ears corn, husks and silk removed

1A. FOR A CHARCOAL GRILL: Open bottom vent completely. Light large chimney starter filled with charcoal briquettes (6 quarts). When top coals are partially covered with ash, pour evenly over half of grill. Set cooking grate in place, cover, and open lid vent completely. Heat grill until hot, about 5 minutes.

1B. FOR A GAS GRILL: Turn all burners to high, cover, and heat grill until hot, about 15 minutes.

2. Meanwhile, combine Pecorino, mayonnaise, sour cream, cilantro, lime juice, garlic, ¼ teaspoon chili powder, pepper, and cayenne, if using, in large bowl and set aside. In second large bowl, combine oil, salt, and remaining ½ teaspoon chili powder. Add corn to oil mixture and toss to coat evenly.

3. Clean and oil cooking grate. Place corn on grill (hot side if using charcoal) and cook (covered if using gas) until lightly charred on all sides, 7 to 12 minutes, turning as needed. Place corn in bowl with cheese mixture, toss to coat evenly, and serve.

GRILLED ONIONS

✓ **WHY THIS RECIPE WORKS**
Onions are hard to manage on the grill. They slip through the grate, burn, or cook to a leathery texture on the outside while remaining raw on the inside. Because slicing onions into rounds exposes the greatest surface area, rounds were the logical shape for grilling, and slices cut ½ half inch thick were best. We found the onions too susceptible to burning over high heat; moderate heat, with the onions covered, was just right. We stopped the rounds from falling through the grate by skewering them. After developing our grilling technique, we conducted a taste test to choose the best variety. Spanish onions won; tasters loved their meaty texture and complex flavor profile.

SKEWERING ONIONS

Using long metal skewers, thread the onion rounds, from side to side, onto skewers.

GRILLED ONIONS
SERVES 4

A two-level fire in a charcoal grill allows you to cook an entrée over the hotter side while grilling the onions over the cooler side. Serve unadorned or use in one of the recipes that follow. You will need four 12-inch metal skewers for this recipe.

2	large Spanish onions, peeled and each cut crosswise into four ½-inch-thick rounds
3	tablespoons olive oil
	Salt and pepper

1. Thread onion rounds, from side to side, onto 4 metal skewers. Brush onions with oil and season with salt and pepper to taste.

2A. FOR A CHARCOAL GRILL: Open bottom vent completely. Light large chimney starter filled with charcoal briquettes (6 quarts). When top coals are partially covered with ash, pour two-thirds evenly over grill, then pour remaining coals over half of grill. Set cooking grate in place, cover, and open lid vent completely. Heat grill until hot, about 5 minutes.

2B. FOR A GAS GRILL: Turn all burners to high, cover, and heat grill until hot, about 15 minutes. Turn all burners to medium.

3. Place onions on grill (cooler side if using charcoal), cover, and cook until deep golden brown and just tender, 15 to 20 minutes, flipping and rotating skewers as needed. Transfer onions to platter and remove skewers; discard any charred outer rings. Serve hot, warm, or room temperature.

GRILLED ONION RELISH WITH ROQUEFORT AND WALNUTS

Serve this relish with grilled beef.

Cut cooled grilled onions into ½-inch pieces and toss with 6 ounces Roquefort cheese, crumbled (1½ cups), ¾ cup chopped toasted walnuts, ¼ cup chopped fresh chives, 1 tablespoon balsamic vinegar, and 1 tablespoon extra-virgin olive oil. Season with salt and pepper to taste.

SWEET AND SOUR GRILLED ONION RELISH WITH PARSLEY AND OLIVES

This relish makes a great accompaniment to grilled tuna.

Cut cooled grilled onions in ½-inch pieces and toss with 1 cup chopped pitted kalamata olives, ½ cup raisins, ½ cup chopped fresh parsley, 2 tablespoons red wine vinegar, 2 tablespoons extra-virgin olive oil, and 1 teaspoon sugar. Season with salt and pepper to taste.

GRILLED MIXED VEGETABLES

✔ WHY THIS RECIPE WORKS
Grilling vegetables can be tricky and, often, the big issue is flavor—there's just not enough of it. We first matched our vegetables in pairs to double up on flavor. Mindful of complementary cooking times, we paired zucchini with sweet red onion and eggplant with red peppers. For the grilling itself, we built a moderate, medium-heat fire and cooked the vegetables for about 20 minutes until they were perfectly tender and full of smoky flavor. To boost the taste further, we whisked up some quick vinaigrettes— lemon-basil and mint-cumin—to accompany the vegetables after they came off the grill. Drizzled with dressing while still warm, the vegetables had enough flavor to be the star attraction of a meal.

GRILLED ZUCCHINI AND RED ONION WITH LEMON-BASIL VINAIGRETTE

SERVES 4 TO 6

The vegetables can be served hot, warm, or at room temperature. After about 5 minutes, faint grill marks should begin to appear on the undersides of the vegetables; if necessary, adjust their position on the grill or adjust the heat level. You will need two 12-inch metal skewers for this recipe.

- 1   large red onion, peeled and cut crosswise into four ½-inch-thick rounds
- 3   zucchini, sliced lengthwise into ¾-inch-thick planks
- 6   tablespoons extra-virgin olive oil Salt and pepper
- 1   small garlic clove, minced
- 1   teaspoon grated lemon zest plus 1 tablespoon juice
- ¼   teaspoon Dijon mustard
- 1   tablespoon chopped fresh basil

1. Thread onion rounds, from side to side, onto 2 metal skewers. Brush onion and zucchini evenly with ¼ cup oil and season with 1 teaspoon salt and pepper to taste.

2. Whisk remaining 2 tablespoons oil, garlic, lemon zest and juice, mustard, and ¼ teaspoon salt together in bowl and set aside.

3A. FOR A CHARCOAL GRILL: Open bottom vent completely. Light large chimney starter three-quarters filled with charcoal briquettes (4½ quarts). When top coals are partially covered with ash, pour evenly over grill. Set cooking grate in place, cover, and open lid vent completely. Heat grill until hot, about 5 minutes.

3B. FOR A GAS GRILL: Turn all burners to high, cover, and heat grill until hot, about 15 minutes. Turn all burners to medium-high.

4. Clean and oil cooking grate. Place vegetables on grill and cook until tender and browned, 18 to 22 minutes, flipping halfway through cooking. Transfer vegetables to serving platter. Remove skewers from onion and discard any charred outer rings. Whisk vinaigrette to recombine and pour over vegetables. Sprinkle with basil and serve.

GRILLED EGGPLANT AND RED PEPPERS WITH MINT-CUMIN DRESSING

SERVES 4 TO 6

The vegetables can be served hot, warm, or at room temperature. After about 5 minutes, faint grill marks should begin to appear on the undersides of the vegetables; if necessary, adjust their position on the grill or adjust the heat level.

- 1   eggplant, cut crosswise into ½-inch-thick rounds
- 2   red bell peppers, stemmed, seeded, and cut into 2-inch strips
- 5   tablespoons extra-virgin olive oil Salt and pepper
- 2   tablespoons plain yogurt
- 1   tablespoon chopped fresh mint
- 1   tablespoon lemon juice
- 1   small garlic clove, minced
- ½   teaspoon ground coriander
- ½   teaspoon ground cumin

1. Brush eggplant and peppers evenly with ¼ cup oil and season with 1 teaspoon salt and pepper to taste.

2. Whisk remaining tablespoon oil, yogurt, mint, lemon juice, garlic, coriander, cumin, and ¼ teaspoon salt together in bowl and set aside.

3A. FOR A CHARCOAL GRILL: Open bottom vent completely. Light large chimney starter three-quarters filled with charcoal briquettes (4½ quarts). When top coals are partially covered with ash, pour evenly over grill. Set cooking grate in place, cover, and open lid vent completely. Heat grill until hot, about 5 minutes.

3B. FOR A GAS GRILL: Turn all burners to high, cover, and heat grill until hot, about 15 minutes. Turn all burners to medium-high.

4. Clean and oil cooking grate. Place vegetables on grill and cook until tender and browned, 16 to 18 minutes, flipping halfway through cooking. Transfer vegetables to serving platter. Whisk dressing to recombine, pour over vegetables, and serve.

GRILLED POTATOES

✓ **WHY THIS RECIPE WORKS**
Grilled potatoes are a summer classic, but we wanted to put a new spin on this dish by adding rosemary and garlic. Unfortunately, we found it was difficult to add garlic and rosemary flavors to plain grilled potatoes. Coating the potatoes with oil, garlic, and rosemary produced burnt, bitter garlic and charred rosemary. If we tossed the potatoes in garlic oil after cooking, the raw garlic was too harsh. It turned out that we needed to introduce the potatoes to the garlic-oil mixture not once, but three times. Before cooking, we pierced the potatoes, skewered

SKEWERING POTATOES FOR THE GRILL

Place potato half cut side down on counter and pierce center with skewer. Repeat, holding already-skewered potatoes for better leverage.

them, seasoned them with salt, brushed on a garlic-rosemary oil, and precooked them in the microwave. Then, before grilling, we brushed them again with the infused oil. After grilling, we tossed them with the garlic and rosemary oil yet again. We finally had it—tender grilled potatoes infused with the smoky flavor of the grill and enlivened with the bold flavors of garlic and rosemary.

GRILLED POTATOES WITH GARLIC AND ROSEMARY
SERVES 4

This recipe allows you to grill an entrée while the hot coals burn down in step 1. Once that item is done, start grilling the potatoes. This recipe works best with small potatoes that are about 1½ inches in diameter. If using medium potatoes, 2 to 3 inches in diameter, cut them into quarters. If the potatoes are larger than 3 inches in diameter, cut each potato into eighths. Since the potatoes are first cooked in the microwave, use wooden skewers.

¼	cup olive oil
9	garlic cloves, minced
1	teaspoon chopped fresh rosemary
	Salt and pepper
2	pounds small red potatoes, halved and skewered
2	tablespoons chopped fresh chives

1. Heat oil, garlic, rosemary, and ½ teaspoon salt in small skillet over medium heat until sizzling, about 3 minutes. Reduce heat to medium-low and continue to cook until garlic is light blond, about 3 minutes. Pour mixture through fine-mesh strainer into small bowl; press on solids. Measure 1 tablespoon of solids and 1 tablespoon of oil into large bowl and set aside. Discard remaining solids but reserve remaining oil.

2. Place skewered potatoes in single layer on large plate and poke each potato several times with skewer. Brush with

1 tablespoon of strained oil and season with salt. Microwave until the potatoes offer slight resistance when pierced with paring knife, about 8 minutes, turning halfway through cooking. Transfer potatoes to baking sheet coated with 1 tablespoon of strained oil. Brush with remaining 1 tablespoon strained oil and season with salt and pepper to taste.

3A. FOR A CHARCOAL GRILL: Open bottom vent completely. Light large chimney starter filled with charcoal briquettes (6 quarts). When top coals are partially covered with ash, pour two-thirds evenly over grill, then pour remaining coals over half of grill. Set cooking grate in place, cover, and open lid vent completely. Heat grill until hot, about 5 minutes.

3B. FOR A GAS GRILL: Turn all burners to high, cover, and heat grill until hot, about 15 minutes. Turn all burners down to medium-high.

4. Place potatoes on grill (hotter side if using charcoal) and cook (covered if using gas) until grill marks appear, 3 to 5 minutes, flipping halfway through cooking. Move potatoes to cooler side of grill (if using charcoal) or turn all burners to medium-low (if using gas). Cover and continue to cook until paring knife slips in and out of potatoes easily, 5 to 8 minutes longer.

5. Remove potatoes from skewers and transfer to bowl with reserved garlic-oil mixture. Add chives, season with salt and pepper to taste, and toss until thoroughly coated. Serve.

GRILLED POTATOES WITH OREGANO AND LEMON

Serve this variation with lemon wedges, if desired.

Reduce garlic to 3 cloves, substitute 2 tablespoons chopped fresh oregano for rosemary, and add 2 teaspoons grated lemon zest to oil in skillet. Substitute 2 teaspoons chopped fresh oregano for chives and add an additional 1 teaspoon grated lemon zest to potatoes when they come off grill.

GRILLED MARINATED PORTOBELLO MUSHROOMS

✔ WHY THIS RECIPE WORKS
When grilled, portobello mushrooms often turn limp and flaccid, burning on the outside before the interior fully cooks. We wanted perfect grilled portobello mushrooms: plump, juicy, and slightly charred with the smoky flavor from the grill. Cooking over direct heat charred the outside before the mushrooms had a chance to cook through. We tried cooking over indirect heat, away from the fire, and this solved the charring problem but not the cooking problem. We solved our problem by digging out an old tool of the campfire trade: aluminum foil. By wrapping each mushroom in a packet of foil, we were able to cook them through until done perfectly, in about 10 minutes. We then unwrapped each mushroom and set it directly over the fire for 30 to 60 seconds to sear in the grilled flavor.

GRILLED MARINATED PORTOBELLO MUSHROOMS
SERVES 4 TO 6

We prefer large 5- to 6-inch portobellos for grilling because they are sold loose— not prepackaged—and are typically fresher. However, if you cannot find large ones, use six 4- to 5-inch portobellos, which are usually sold three to a package; decrease their grilling time wrapped in foil to about 8 minutes.

½   cup olive oil
3   tablespoons lemon juice
6   garlic cloves, minced
¼   teaspoon salt
4   (5- to 6-inch) portobello mushrooms, stemmed

1. Combine oil, lemon juice, garlic, and salt in 1-gallon zipper-lock bag. Add mushrooms and toss to coat; press out as much air as possible and seal bag. Let sit at room temperature for 1 hour.

2. Meanwhile, cut four 12-inch-square pieces of aluminum foil (or six 9-inch-square pieces if using smaller mushrooms).

3A. FOR A CHARCOAL GRILL: Open bottom vent completely. Light large chimney starter three-quarters filled with charcoal briquettes (4½ quarts). When top coals are partially covered with ash, pour evenly over grill. Set cooking grate in place, cover, and open lid vent completely. Heat grill until hot, about 5 minutes.

3B. FOR A GAS GRILL: Turn all burners to high, cover, and heat grill until hot, about 15 minutes. Turn all burners to medium-high.

4. Clean and oil cooking grate. Remove mushrooms from marinade and place each on a foil square, gill side up. Fold foil around each mushroom and seal edges. Place foil packets on grill, sealed side up, and cook (covered if using gas) until juicy and tender, 9 to 12 minutes.

5. Using tongs, unwrap mushrooms, place gill side up on grill, and cook until grill-marked, 30 to 60 seconds. Transfer to serving platter and serve.

GRILLED MARINATED PORTOBELLOS WITH TARRAGON

Substitute 2 teaspoons rice vinegar for lemon juice, reduce garlic to 1 clove, and add 1 tablespoon chopped fresh tarragon to marinade.

CHAPTER 13 Eggs and Breakfast

POACHED EGGS

✅ **WHY THIS RECIPE WORKS**

A poached egg should be tender and evenly cooked, with a white like baked custard and a yolk that runs just a little. But a poached egg is very delicate; it can be hard to get it in and out of the water without breaking it, and the boiling water or the bottom of the pan can damage it as well. There's also the problem of those unappealing wandering strands of egg white. To address these difficulties, we traded in the usual saucepan for a shallow skillet, which gives the cook much easier access to the eggs. The addition of vinegar to the cooking water helped to set the eggs quickly, and salting the water seasoned the eggs nicely. Turning off the heat once the eggs were in the pan limited their exposure to rapidly boiling water, which can cause them to disintegrate. These simple tricks gave us perfectly cooked eggs with no feathering of whites.

POACHED EGGS
SERVES 2

To get 4 eggs into boiling water at the same time, crack each into a small cup with a handle. Holding two cups in each hand, lower the lip of each cup just into the water and then tip the eggs into the pan.

   Salt and pepper
2 **tablespoons white vinegar**
4 **large eggs, each cracked into small handled cup**

1. Fill 8- to 10-inch nonstick skillet nearly to rim with water, add 1 teaspoon salt and vinegar, and bring to boil over high heat.

2. Lower lip of each cup just into water at once; tip eggs into boiling water, cover, and remove from heat. Poach eggs for 4 minutes for medium-firm yolks, 4½ minutes for firmer yolks, or 3 minutes for looser yolks.

3. With slotted spoon, carefully lift and drain each egg over skillet. Season with salt and pepper to taste and serve immediately.

FOOLPROOF HARD-COOKED EGGS

✅ **WHY THIS RECIPE WORKS**

Hard-cooking an egg can be a crapshoot. There's no way to watch it cook inside its shell, and you certainly can't poke it with an instant-read thermometer. Let it sit in boiling water for too long and you'll get a rubbery white and chalky, green-tinged yolk; not long enough and you'll have eggs better suited for breakfast than egg salad. We finally got our foolproof recipe by tinkering with a technique recommended by the American Egg Board. We started the eggs in cold water, brought the water to a boil, then removed the pan from the heat and let the eggs steep for 10 minutes. This method consistently turned out perfect hard-cooked eggs with moist and creamy yolks, firm yet tender whites, and no trace of a green ring.

FOOLPROOF HARD-COOKED EGGS
MAKES 4

You can double or triple this recipe as long as you use a pot large enough to hold the eggs in a single layer, covered by an inch of water.

4 **large eggs**

Place eggs in medium saucepan, cover with 1 inch water, and bring to boil over high heat. Remove pan from heat, cover, and let sit 10 minutes. Meanwhile, fill medium bowl with 4 cups water and 1 tray of ice cubes. Transfer eggs to ice water bath with slotted spoon; let sit for 5 minutes. Peel eggs.

BEST SCRAMBLED EGGS

✅ **WHY THIS RECIPE WORKS**

Scrambled eggs often end up as either tough, dry slabs or pebbly, runny curds. We wanted foolproof scrambled eggs with fluffy, moist curds so creamy and light that they practically dissolved on the tongue. The first step was to add salt to the uncooked eggs; salt dissolves some of the egg proteins so they are unable to bond when cooked, creating more tender curds. Beating the eggs until just combined, using the gentler action of a fork rather than a whisk, ensured our scramble didn't turn tough. Half-and-half was preferred over milk, producing clean-tasting curds that were both fluffy and stable. To replicate the richer flavor of farm-fresh eggs, we added extra yolks. Finally, when it came to the

---

TEST KITCHEN TIP NO. 108   A SHELL GAME

We've always heard that fresh eggs are for frying and old eggs are for boiling, as the older an egg is, the easier it is to peel. But who keeps different boxes of eggs of different ages in their refrigerator? We wanted to find a way to make peeling even a fresh egg more foolproof. To this end, we hard-cooked 120 eggs and tested every egg-peeling myth, old wives' tale, and urban legend we could find. Ultimately, while we found that basics like peeling under running water and starting from the fat end (where the air pocket makes it easier to remove this first bit of shell) helped, only one trick nearly guaranteed perfectly peeled eggs: shocking the egg in ice water as soon as it is done cooking. Here's why: As an egg cooks, the layer of protein in the white that's closest to the outer shell will slowly bond with it. An egg left at room temperature or even under cold running water will cool relatively slowly, giving the hot proteins plenty of time to form a strong bond with the shell. Shocking the egg in ice water quickly halts this bonding process. In addition, the sudden cooling causes the cooked egg white to shrink and pull away from the shell, making it much easier to remove.

So, for best results, shock your hard-cooked eggs in ice water; roll them on the counter to crack their entire surface; and peel under cool running water, starting from the fat end. And if you like to keep hard-cooked eggs in the fridge, here's an easy way to distinguish them from raw eggs: Add a little balsamic vinegar to the water before you cook them; it will tint the shells, making them easy to tell apart.

cooking process, we started the eggs on medium-high heat to create puffy curds, then finished them over low heat to ensure that they wouldn't overcook.

BEST SCRAMBLED EGGS
SERVES 4

It's important to follow visual cues, as pan thickness will have an effect on cooking times. If you don't have half-and-half, you can substitute 8 teaspoons whole milk and 4 teaspoons heavy cream. To dress up the eggs, add 2 tablespoons minced fresh parsley, chives, basil, or cilantro or 1 tablespoon minced fresh dill or tarragon after reducing the heat to low.

8	large eggs plus 2 large yolks
¼	cup half-and-half
	Salt
¼	teaspoon pepper
1	tablespoon unsalted butter, chilled

1. Beat eggs, egg yolks, half-and-half, ¼ teaspoon salt, and ¼ teaspoon pepper with fork until thoroughly combined and mixture is pure yellow; do not overbeat.

2. Melt butter in 10-inch nonstick skillet over medium-high heat until foaming just subsides (butter should not brown), swirling to coat pan. Add egg mixture and, using heatproof rubber spatula, constantly and firmly scrape along bottom and sides of skillet until eggs begin to clump and spatula leaves trail on bottom of pan, 1½ to 2½ minutes. Reduce heat to low and gently but constantly fold eggs until clumped and just slightly wet, 30 to 60 seconds. Immediately transfer eggs to warmed plates and season with salt to taste. Serve immediately.

BEST SCRAMBLED EGGS FOR TWO

Reduce eggs to 4, egg yolks to 1, half-and-half to 2 tablespoons, salt and pepper to ⅛ teaspoon each, and butter to ½ tablespoon. Cook eggs in 8-inch skillet for 45 to 75 seconds over medium-high heat and then 30 to 60 seconds over low heat.

BEST SCRAMBLED EGGS FOR ONE

Reduce eggs to 2, egg yolks to 1, half-and-half to 1 tablespoon, salt and pepper to pinch each, and butter to ¼ tablespoon. Cook eggs in 8-inch skillet for 30 to 60 seconds over medium-high heat and then 30 to 60 seconds over low heat.

HEARTY SCRAMBLED EGGS

✔ WHY THIS RECIPE WORKS
Simply adding fillings to standard scrambled eggs results in a waterlogged mass of rubbery eggs instead of light, fluffy curds. To keep our scrambled eggs light while adding hearty ingredients like sausage and vegetables, we had to eliminate some of the added moisture. We sautéed the vegetables first, then wiped the skillet dry before adding the eggs. And we found that some ingredients worked better for this recipe than others. Drier leafy greens, crunchy vegetables, and breakfast meats all worked well, while tomatoes and mushrooms did not. Choosing the right ingredients gave us soft and fluffy scrambled eggs packed with hearty flavor for a satisfying meal morning, noon, or night.

SCRAMBLED EGGS WITH BACON, ONION, AND PEPPER JACK CHEESE
SERVES 4 TO 6

Either regular or thick-cut bacon can be used.

12	large eggs
6	tablespoons half-and-half
¾	teaspoon salt
¼	teaspoon pepper
4	slices bacon, cut into ½-inch pieces
1	onion, chopped medium
1	tablespoon unsalted butter
1½	ounces pepper Jack or Monterey Jack cheese, shredded (⅓ cup)
1	teaspoon minced fresh parsley (optional)

1. Beat eggs, half-and-half, salt, and pepper with fork in medium bowl until thoroughly combined.

2. Cook bacon in 12-inch nonstick skillet over medium heat, stirring occasionally, until crisp, 5 to 7 minutes. Using slotted spoon, transfer bacon to paper towel–lined plate; discard all but 2 teaspoons bacon fat. Add onion to skillet and cook, stirring occasionally, until lightly browned, 2 to 4 minutes; transfer onion to second plate.

3. Wipe out skillet with paper towels. Add butter to now-empty skillet and melt over medium heat, swirling to coat

pan. Pour in egg mixture. With heatproof rubber spatula, stir eggs constantly, slowly pushing them from side to side, scraping along bottom and sides of skillet, and lifting and folding eggs as they form curds (do not overscramble or curds formed will be too small). Cook until large curds form but eggs are still very moist, 2 to 3 minutes. Off heat, gently fold in onion, pepper Jack, and half of bacon until evenly distributed; if eggs are still underdone, return skillet to medium heat for no longer than 30 seconds. Divide eggs among individual plates, sprinkle with remaining bacon and parsley, if using, and serve immediately.

SCRAMBLED EGGS WITH ARUGULA, SUN-DRIED TOMATOES, AND GOAT CHEESE

SERVES 4 TO 6

Rinsing and patting the sun-dried tomatoes dry prevents them from making the eggs greasy.

12	large eggs
6	tablespoons half-and-half
¾	teaspoon salt
¼	teaspoon pepper
2	teaspoons olive oil
½	onion, chopped fine
⅛	teaspoon red pepper flakes
5	ounces baby arugula (5 cups), cut into ½-inch-wide strips
1	tablespoon unsalted butter
¼	cup oil-packed sun-dried tomatoes, rinsed, patted dry, and chopped fine
3	ounces goat cheese, crumbled (¾ cup)

1. Beat eggs, half-and-half, salt, and pepper with fork in medium bowl until thoroughly combined.

2. Heat oil in 12-inch nonstick skillet over medium heat until shimmering. Add onion and pepper flakes and cook until onion has softened, about 2 minutes. Add arugula and cook, stirring gently, until arugula begins to wilt, 30 to 60 seconds. Spread mixture in single layer on medium plate; set aside.

3. Wipe out skillet with paper towels. Add butter to now-empty skillet and melt over medium heat, swirling to coat pan. Pour in egg mixture. With heatproof rubber spatula, stir eggs constantly, slowly pushing them from side to side, scraping along bottom and sides of skillet, and lifting and folding eggs as they form curds (do not overscramble or curds formed will be too small). Cook until large curds form but eggs are still very moist, 2 to 3 minutes. Off heat, gently fold in arugula mixture and sun-dried tomatoes until evenly distributed; if eggs are still underdone, return skillet to medium heat for no longer than 30 seconds. Divide eggs among individual plates, sprinkle with goat cheese, and serve immediately.

SCRAMBLED EGGS WITH ASPARAGUS, PROSCIUTTO, AND PARMESAN

SERVES 4 TO 6

If your asparagus spears are very thick, after halving them lengthwise, cut them on the bias into ⅜-inch lengths, slightly smaller than indicated below.

12	large eggs
6	tablespoons half-and-half
¾	teaspoon salt
¼	teaspoon pepper
1	teaspoon vegetable oil
8	ounces asparagus, trimmed, halved lengthwise, and cut on bias into ½-inch lengths
1	tablespoon unsalted butter
3	ounces thinly sliced prosciutto, cut into ½-inch pieces
1	ounce Parmesan cheese, grated (½ cup)

1. Beat eggs, half-and-half, salt, and pepper with fork in medium bowl until thoroughly combined.

2. Heat oil in 12-inch nonstick skillet over medium heat until shimmering. Add asparagus and cook, stirring occasionally, until lightly browned and tender but still crisp, 3 to 4 minutes. Spread asparagus in single layer on medium plate; set aside.

3. Wipe out skillet with paper towels. Add butter to now-empty skillet and melt over medium heat, swirling to coat pan. Pour in egg mixture. With heatproof rubber spatula, stir eggs constantly, slowly pushing them from side to side, scraping along bottom and sides of skillet, and lifting and folding eggs as they form curds (do not over-scramble eggs or curds will be too small). Cook until large curds form but eggs are still very moist, 2 to 3 minutes. Off

TEST KITCHEN TIP NO. 110 **EGG SUBSTITUTIONS**

Eggs are widely available in four sizes, but here in the test kitchen, we develop and test all of our recipes using only large eggs. If you do not have large eggs on hand, substitutions are possible. See the chart for help in making accurate calculations. For half of an egg, whisk the yolk and white together, measure, and then divide in half.

LARGE		JUMBO	EXTRA-LARGE	MEDIUM
1	=	1	1	1
2	=	1½	2	2
3	=	2½	2½	3½
4	=	3	3½	4½
5	=	4	4	6
6	=	5	5	7

heat, gently fold in prosciutto, Parmesan, and asparagus until evenly distributed; if eggs are still underdone, return skillet to medium heat for no longer than 30 seconds. Divide eggs among individual plates and serve immediately.

SCRAMBLED EGGS WITH SAUSAGE, SWEET PEPPERS, AND CHEDDAR

SERVES 4 TO 6

We prefer sweet Italian sausage here, especially for breakfast, but you can substitute spicy sausage, if desired.

- 12 large eggs
- 6 tablespoons half-and-half
- ¾ teaspoon salt
- ¼ teaspoon pepper
- 1 teaspoon vegetable oil
- 8 ounces sweet Italian sausage, casings removed, sausage crumbled into ½-inch pieces
- 1 red bell pepper, stemmed, seeded, and cut into ½-inch pieces
- 3 scallions, white and green parts separated, both sliced thin on bias
- 1 tablespoon unsalted butter
- 1½ ounces sharp cheddar cheese, shredded (⅓ cup)

1. Beat eggs, half-and-half, salt, and pepper with fork in medium bowl until thoroughly combined.

2. Heat oil in 12-inch nonstick skillet over medium heat until shimmering. Add sausage and cook, breaking into ½-inch pieces until beginning to brown, about 2 minutes. Add bell pepper and scallion whites; continue to cook, stirring occasionally, until sausage is cooked through and pepper is beginning to brown, about 3 minutes. Spread mixture in single layer on medium plate; set aside.

3. Wipe out skillet with paper towels. Add butter to now-empty skillet and melt over medium heat, swirling to coat pan. Pour in egg mixture. With heatproof rubber spatula, stir eggs constantly, slowly pushing them from side to side, scraping along bottom and sides of skillet, and lifting and folding eggs as they form curds (do not overscramble or curds formed will be too small). Cook until large curds form but eggs are still very moist, 2 to 3 minutes. Off heat, gently fold in sausage mixture and cheddar until evenly distributed; if eggs are still underdone, return skillet to medium heat for no longer than 30 seconds. Divide eggs among individual plates, sprinkle with scallion greens, and serve immediately.

FRIED EGGS

✔ **WHY THIS RECIPE WORKS**
Anyone can make fried eggs, but few and far between are the cooks who can make them perfectly every time. Eggs can stick to the pan, yolks can break, and over- or undercooked eggs seem to be the norm. We decided to eliminate the guesswork and figure out the best and easiest way to fry the perfect egg every time. For us, this meant a firm white and a yolk that was thick yet still runny. We discovered that the first thing to do is to reach for a nonstick pan. The initial heat setting is also important. Preheating the pan over very low heat puts it at just the right temperature to receive the eggs, which should be added all at once. Cover the pan as soon as the eggs are added and cook just a couple of minutes for perfect fried eggs every time.

MAKING FRIED EGGS

To get all eggs into pan at once, crack eggs into 2 cups and slide eggs into hot skillet simultaneously.

FRIED EGGS

SERVES 4

Since burners vary, it may take an egg or two before you determine the ideal heat setting for frying eggs on your stovetop. It's important to follow visual cues, as pan thickness will have an effect on cooking times.

- 4 large eggs
- 1 tablespoon unsalted butter, chilled
  Salt and pepper

1. Heat 10-inch nonstick skillet over low heat for 5 minutes. Meanwhile, crack open 2 eggs into cup or small bowl; crack remaining 2 eggs into second cup or small bowl. Add butter to skillet, let melt, and swirl to coat pan.

2. Working quickly, pour 2 eggs into skillet on one side and remaining 2 eggs on opposite side. Season eggs with salt and pepper to taste, cover, and cook about 2½ minutes for runny yolks, 3 minutes for soft but set yolks, or 3½ minutes for firmly set yolks. Slide eggs onto plate; serve.

CLASSIC FILLED OMELET

✔ **WHY THIS RECIPE WORKS**
Omelets seem simple, but cooking the eggs properly in a hot pan can be a delicate matter. Add cheese, which must melt before the omelet turns brown and rubbery, and you've got a truly temperamental dish on your hands. We wanted a foolproof cooking method for a creamy, supple omelet with perfectly melted cheese that didn't leak all over the pan. We found a good-quality nonstick skillet and an easy-melting cheese were essential. A heatproof rubber spatula kept the eggs from tearing as we shaped the omelet with the sides of the pan. This technique gave us the omelet we had been looking for; moist and creamy with plenty of perfectly melted cheese.

CLASSIC FILLED OMELET
SERVES 1

You can substitute cheddar, Monterey Jack, or another semisoft cheese for the Gruyère.

3	large eggs
	Salt and pepper
½	tablespoon unsalted butter, plus melted butter for brushing omelet
3	tablespoons finely shredded Gruyère cheese
1	recipe filling (recipes follow)

1. Beat eggs and salt and pepper to taste with fork in small bowl until thoroughly combined.

2. Melt butter in 10-inch nonstick skillet over medium-high heat. Add eggs and cook until edges begin to set, 2 to 3 seconds. Using heatproof rubber spatula, stir in circular motion until slightly thickened, about 10 seconds. Use spatula to pull cooked edges in toward center, then tilt pan to one side so that uncooked eggs run to edge of pan. Repeat until omelet is just set but still moist on surface, 20 to 25 seconds. Sprinkle Gruyère and filling down center of omelet.

3. Remove skillet from burner. Using rubber spatula, fold lower third (portion nearest you) of omelet over filling; press gently with spatula to secure seams, maintaining fold.

4. Run spatula between outer edge of omelet and pan to loosen. Jerk pan sharply toward you a few times to slide omelet up far side of pan. Jerk pan again so that unfolded edge folds over itself, or use spatula to fold edge over. Invert omelet onto plate. Tidy edges with spatula, brush with melted butter, and serve.

MUSHROOM AND THYME FILLING
MAKES ½ CUP, ENOUGH TO FILL 2 OMELETS

This filling is particularly good paired with Gruyère.

Melt 1 tablespoon butter in 10-inch skillet over medium heat. Add 1 minced small shallot and cook until softened and just beginning to brown, about 2 minutes. Add 2 ounces white mushrooms, trimmed and sliced ¼ inch thick, and cook, stirring occasionally, until softened and lightly browned, about 3 minutes. Off heat, stir in 1 teaspoon minced fresh thyme and salt and pepper to taste; transfer mixture to small bowl and set aside, covered to keep warm, until ready to use.

BACON, ONION, AND SCALLION FILLING
MAKES ½ CUP, ENOUGH TO FILL 2 OMELETS

Smoked Gouda is a good match for this filling.

Cook 2 slices bacon, cut into ½-inch pieces, in 10-inch skillet over medium heat until crisp, 5 to 7 minutes. Transfer bacon to paper towel–lined plate using slotted spoon. Discard all but 1 tablespoon fat from skillet. Add ½ small onion, chopped fine, and cook over medium heat, stirring frequently, until golden brown, about 3 minutes. Off heat, stir in 1 thinly sliced scallion. Remove paper towel from underneath bacon and transfer onion mixture to plate with bacon; set aside, covered to keep warm, until ready to use.

RED BELL PEPPER, MUSHROOM, AND ONION FILLING
MAKES ½ CUP, ENOUGH TO FILL 2 OMELETS

Monterey Jack is our choice for this filling.

Melt 1 tablespoon butter in 10-inch skillet over medium heat. Add ½ small onion, chopped fine, and cook, stirring occasionally, until softened but not browned, about 2 minutes. Add 1 ounce white mushrooms, trimmed and sliced

---

MAKING A FILLED OMELET

1. Pull cooked eggs from edges of pan toward center, tilting pan so any uncooked eggs run to pan's edges.

2. Sprinkle filling down center of omelet. Remove skillet from burner. Fold lower third of eggs over filling. Press seam to secure.

3. Pull pan sharply toward you so omelet slides up far edge of pan.

4. Fold far edge of omelet toward center. Press to secure seam. Invert omelet onto plate.

¼ inch thick, and cook, stirring occasionally, until softened and beginning to brown, about 2 minutes. Add ¼ red bell pepper, cut into ½-inch pieces, and cook, stirring occasionally, until softened, about 2 minutes. Off heat, stir in 1 teaspoon minced fresh parsley. Transfer mixture to small bowl and season with salt and pepper to taste; set aside, covered to keep warm, until ready to use.

ASPARAGUS OMELET

✔ **WHY THIS RECIPE WORKS**

For a diner-style asparagus omelet that would be moist, tender, and sturdy enough to support the filling, we focused on how to manipulate the eggs in the pan and the temperature at which to cook them. We opted for the easy approach of lifting the setting omelet with a rubber spatula to allow the uncooked eggs to pool underneath and cook. We kept the heat at medium-low, finishing the omelet off the burner to keep it tender. This gave us a robust omelet that was moist, tender, and sturdy enough for plenty of asparagus and cheese.

ASPARAGUS OMELET
SERVES 2

When cooking the eggs, it is important to lift the edges of the omelet rather than push them toward the center.

2 tablespoons unsalted butter
8 ounces asparagus, trimmed and cut on bias into ¼-inch pieces
  Salt and pepper
1 shallot, halved and sliced thin
1 teaspoon lemon juice
5 large eggs
1½ ounces Gruyère cheese, shredded fine (⅓ cup)

1. Melt 1 tablespoon butter in 10-inch nonstick skillet over medium-high heat.

Omelets come together incredibly quickly, so you should be sure to have your filling at the ready. But equally important is to make sure your filling is hot, or at least warm. Once added to an omelet, the filling spends little time in the pan, so cold fillings will not have time to heat through.

Add asparagus, pinch salt, and pepper to taste and cook, stirring occasionally, for 2 minutes. Add shallot and cook, stirring occasionally, until asparagus is lightly browned and tender, 2 to 4 minutes longer. Add lemon juice and toss to coat; transfer to bowl. Meanwhile, beat eggs and salt and pepper to taste with fork in small bowl until combined.

2. Wipe skillet clean with paper towel. Melt remaining 1 tablespoon butter in now-empty skillet over medium-low heat. Add eggs and cook, without stirring, until eggs begin to set, 45 to 60 seconds. Using heatproof rubber spatula and working around edge of entire pan, lift edge of cooked egg, then tilt pan to one side so that uncooked eggs run underneath; gently scrape uncooked eggs toward rim of skillet, until top is just slightly wet, 1½ to 2 minutes. Let pan sit without moving for 30 seconds. Off heat, sprinkle asparagus mixture in even layer over omelet, then sprinkle cheese evenly over asparagus. Cover and let sit until eggs no longer appear wet, 4 to 5 minutes.

3. Return skillet to medium heat for 30 seconds. Using rubber spatula, loosen edges of omelet from skillet. Slide omelet halfway out of pan onto serving plate. Tilt pan so top of omelet folds over itself. Cut omelet in half and serve immediately.

ASPARAGUS OMELET WITH BLACK FOREST HAM AND MUSTARD

Add 2 teaspoons whole grain mustard to asparagus along with lemon juice in step 1. Add 3 ounces Black Forest ham, cut into ¼-inch pieces, along with asparagus mixture in step 2.

ASPARAGUS OMELET WITH ROASTED PEPPERS AND GARLIC

Before adding lemon juice in step 1, add 1 teaspoon minced fresh thyme, 1 minced garlic clove, and pinch cayenne pepper to skillet and cook until fragrant, about 30 seconds. Proceed as directed. Add ⅓ cup jarred roasted red peppers, rinsed, patted dry, and cut into ¼-inch pieces, to omelet along with asparagus. Substitute fontina for Gruyère.

PERFECT FRENCH OMELET

✔ **WHY THIS RECIPE WORKS**

In contrast to half-moon, diner-style omelets stuffed to the seams, the French omelet is a pristine, rolled affair. The temperature of the pan must be just right, the eggs beaten just so, and hand movements must be as swift as the ability to gauge the exact second the omelet is done. Even a few extra seconds can spell disaster. A French omelet should boast an ultra-creamy texture, rolled over minimal filling. We replaced the classic omelet pan and fork with a simple nonstick skillet and wooden skewers. We preheated the pan slowly over low heat to eliminate hot spots. Exact timing gives the omelet its creaminess, but we wanted to cheat with creamy ingredients; cold butter worked perfectly. Beating the eggs correctly is the key to lightness so we found the perfect number of strokes. We needed at least medium-high heat to puff up the eggs with steam, but the omelet cooked too quickly to judge when it was done. We turned off the heat when the eggs were still runny, letting residual heat do the rest of the cooking, giving us a flawless, creamy French omelet.

PERFECT FRENCH OMELETS
SERVES 2

Because making omelets is such a quick process, make sure to have all your ingredients and equipment at the ready. If you don't have skewers or chopsticks to stir the eggs in step 3, use the handle of a wooden spoon. Warm the plates in a 200-degree oven.

2	tablespoons unsalted butter, cut into 2 pieces
½	teaspoon vegetable oil
6	large eggs, chilled
⅛	teaspoon salt
	Pepper
2	tablespoons shredded Gruyère cheese
4	teaspoons minced fresh chives

1. Cut 1 tablespoon butter in half. Cut remaining 1 tablespoon butter into small pieces, transfer to small bowl, and place in freezer while preparing eggs and skillet, at least 10 minutes. Meanwhile, heat oil in 8-inch nonstick skillet over low heat for 10 minutes.

2. Crack 2 eggs into medium bowl and separate third egg; reserve egg white for another use and add egg yolk to bowl. Add salt and pinch pepper. Break egg yolks with fork, then beat eggs at moderate pace, about 80 strokes, until yolks and whites are well combined. Stir in half of frozen butter cubes.

3. When skillet is fully heated, use paper towels to wipe out oil, leaving thin film on bottom and sides of skillet. Add ½ tablespoon of reserved butter to skillet and heat until melted. Swirl butter to coat skillet, add egg mixture, and increase heat to medium-high. Use 2 chopsticks or wooden skewers to scramble eggs, using quick circular motion to move around skillet, scraping cooked egg from side of skillet as you go, until eggs are almost cooked but still slightly runny, 45 to 90 seconds. Turn off heat (remove skillet from heat if using electric burner) and smooth eggs into even layer using heatproof rubber spatula. Sprinkle omelet with 1 tablespoon Gruyère and 2 teaspoons chives. Cover skillet with tight-fitting lid and let sit for 1 minute for runnier omelet or 2 minutes for firmer omelet.

4. Heat skillet over low heat for 20 seconds, uncover, and, using rubber spatula, loosen edges of omelet from skillet. Place folded square of paper towel onto warmed plate and slide omelet out of skillet onto paper towel so that omelet lies flat on plate and hangs about 1 inch off paper towel. Roll omelet into neat cylinder and set aside. Return skillet to low heat and heat for 2 minutes before repeating instructions for second omelet starting with step 2. Serve.

HUEVOS RANCHEROS

✔ WHY THIS RECIPE WORKS

The huevos rancheros found on American brunch menus more often resemble heaping plates of nachos than the simple, satisfying Mexican meal of tortillas, eggs, and salsa they are meant to be. We wanted to use supermarket staples to produce the most authentic version possible. Starting at the top, with the salsa, we enhanced the flavor of the tomatoes, chiles, and onions by adding tomato paste and then roasting them. Garlic, cumin, cayenne pepper, lime juice, and cilantro gave the salsa a zesty, clean flavor. The fried eggs presented a true challenge: even if we didn't break the yolks when we placed the eggs on top of the tortilla, they ended up looking ragged. Poaching the eggs in the hot salsa left them looking perfect and gave them a boost of flavor. Finally, we brushed supermarket tortillas with oil, sprinkled a little salt on top, and toasted them so they'd be crisp and dry enough to provide a sturdy and flavorful base for the eggs and salsa.

MAKING A FRENCH OMELET

1. Add beaten egg mixture to skillet and stir with chopsticks to produce small curds, which result in silkier texture.

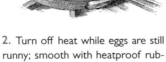

2. Turn off heat while eggs are still runny; smooth with heatproof rubber spatula into even layer.

3. After sprinkling with cheese and chives, cover so residual heat gently finishes cooking omelet.

4. Slide finished omelet onto paper towel–lined plate. Use paper towel to lift omelet and roll it up.

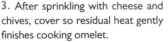

HUEVOS RANCHEROS
SERVES 2 TO 4

To save time in the morning, make the salsa the day before and store it overnight in the refrigerator. If you need to hold the tortillas for a short period of time, cover the baking sheet with aluminum foil. If you like, serve with Refried Beans (page 240).

SALSA
- 3 jalapeño chiles, stemmed, halved, and seeded
- 1½ pounds plum tomatoes, cored and halved
- ½ onion, cut into ½-inch wedges
- 2 garlic cloves, peeled
- 2 tablespoons vegetable oil
- 1 tablespoon tomato paste
  Salt and pepper
- ½ teaspoon ground cumin
- ⅛ teaspoon cayenne pepper
- 3 tablespoons minced fresh cilantro
- 1–2 tablespoons lime juice plus lime wedges

TORTILLAS AND EGGS
- 4 (6-inch) corn tortillas
- 1 tablespoon vegetable oil
  Salt and pepper
- 4 large eggs

1. FOR THE SALSA: Adjust oven rack to middle position and heat oven to 375 degrees. Mince 1 jalapeño; set aside. In medium bowl, combine tomatoes, remaining 2 jalapeños, onion, garlic, oil, tomato paste, 1 teaspoon salt, cumin, and cayenne; toss to mix thoroughly. Place vegetables cut side down on rimmed baking sheet. Roast until tomatoes are tender and skins begin to shrivel and brown, 35 to 45 minutes; let cool on baking sheet for 10 minutes. Increase oven temperature to 450 degrees. Transfer roasted onion, garlic, and jalapeños to food processor. Process until almost completely broken down, about 10 seconds, scraping down sides of bowl. Add tomatoes and process until salsa is slightly chunky, about 10 seconds. Add 2 tablespoons cilantro, reserved 1 minced jalapeño, and salt, pepper, and lime juice to taste.

2. FOR THE TORTILLAS AND EGGS: Brush both sides of each tortilla lightly with oil, sprinkle both sides with salt, and place on clean baking sheet. Bake until tops just begin to color, 5 to 7 minutes. Flip tortillas and continue to bake until golden brown, 2 to 3 minutes longer.

3. Meanwhile, bring salsa to gentle simmer in 12-inch nonstick skillet over medium heat. Remove from heat and make 4 shallow wells in salsa with back of large spoon. Break 1 egg into cup, then carefully pour egg into well in salsa; repeat with remaining eggs. Season each egg with salt and pepper to taste, then cover skillet and place over medium-low heat. Cook for 4 to 5 minutes for runny yolks or 6 to 7 minutes for set yolks.

4. TO SERVE: Place tortillas on serving plates; gently scoop 1 egg onto each tortilla. Spoon salsa around each egg, covering tortillas, but leaving portion of eggs exposed. Sprinkle with remaining 1 tablespoon cilantro and serve with lime wedges.

SPANISH TORTILLA

✔ WHY THIS RECIPE WORKS
This tapas bar favorite, boasting meltingly tender potatoes in a dense, creamy omelet, is immensely appealing. But the typical recipe calls for simmering the potatoes in up to 4 cups of extra-virgin olive oil. Using so much oil for a single, somewhat humble meal seemed excessive. We were able to cut the oil to a mere 6 tablespoons by substituting firmer, less starchy Yukon Gold potatoes for the standard russets. Traditional recipes call for flipping the tortilla with the help of a single plate, but when we tried this, the result was an egg-splattered floor. Sliding the omelet onto the plate and then using a second plate to flip it made a once-messy task foolproof. And while the tortillas were perfectly good plain, we prepared two versions with complementary ingredients (roasted red peppers and peas in one, and Spanish chorizo sausage in another) and served them with a batch of garlicky mayonnaise.

SPANISH TORTILLA WITH ROASTED RED PEPPERS AND PEAS
SERVES 4 TO 6

Spanish tortillas are often served warm or at room temperature with olives, pickles, and Garlic Mayonnaise (recipe follows) as an appetizer. They may also be served with a salad as a light entrée. For the most traditional tortilla, omit the roasted red peppers and peas.

- 6 tablespoons plus 1 teaspoon extra-virgin olive oil
- 1½ pounds Yukon Gold potatoes, peeled, quartered, and cut into ⅛-inch-thick slices
- 1 small onion, halved and sliced thin
- 1 teaspoon salt
- ¼ teaspoon pepper
- 8 large eggs
- ½ cup jarred roasted red peppers, rinsed, patted dry, and cut into ½-inch pieces
- ½ cup frozen peas, thawed
  Garlic Mayonnaise (page 542)

1. Toss 4 tablespoons oil, potatoes, onion, ½ teaspoon salt, and pepper in large bowl until potato slices are thoroughly separated and coated in oil. Heat 2 tablespoons more oil in 10-inch nonstick skillet over medium-high heat until shimmering. Reduce heat to medium-low, add potato mixture to skillet, and set bowl aside without washing. Cover and cook, stirring with heatproof rubber spatula every 5 minutes, until potatoes offer no resistance when poked with paring knife, 22 to 28 minutes (some potato slices may break into smaller pieces).

2. Meanwhile, whisk eggs and remaining ½ teaspoon salt in reserved bowl until just combined. Using rubber spatula, fold hot potato mixture, red peppers, and peas into eggs until combined, making sure to scrape all of potato mixture out of skillet. Return skillet to medium-high heat, add remaining 1 teaspoon oil, and heat until just beginning to smoke. Add egg-potato mixture and cook, shaking pan and folding mixture constantly for 15 seconds. Smooth top of mixture with rubber spatula. Reduce heat to medium, cover, and cook, gently shaking pan every 30 seconds until bottom is golden brown and top is lightly set, about 2 minutes.

3. Using rubber spatula, loosen tortilla from pan, shaking back and forth until tortilla slides around freely in pan. Slide tortilla onto large plate, invert onto second large plate, and slide, browned side up, back into skillet. Tuck edges of tortilla into skillet with rubber spatula. Return pan to medium heat and continue to cook, gently shaking pan every 30 seconds, until second side is golden brown, about 2 minutes longer. Slide tortilla onto cutting board or serving plate and let cool for at least 15 minutes. Cut tortilla into cubes or wedges and serve with Garlic Mayonnaise, if desired.

SPANISH TORTILLA WITH CHORIZO AND SCALLIONS

Use a cured, Spanish-style chorizo sausage for this recipe. Portuguese linguiça sausage is a suitable substitute.

Omit red peppers and peas. In step 1, heat 4 ounces Spanish-style chorizo with 1 tablespoon oil in 10-inch nonstick skillet over medium-high heat, stirring occasionally, until chorizo is browned and fat has rendered, about 5 minutes. Proceed with recipe as directed, adding potato mixture to skillet with chorizo and rendered fat and folding 4 thinly sliced scallions into eggs in step 2.

GARLIC MAYONNAISE
MAKES ABOUT 1¼ CUPS

2	large egg yolks
2	teaspoons Dijon mustard
2	teaspoons lemon juice
1	garlic clove, minced
¾	cup vegetable oil
1	tablespoon water
¼	cup extra-virgin olive oil
½	teaspoon salt
¼	teaspoon pepper

Process egg yolks, mustard, lemon juice, and garlic in food processor until combined, about 10 seconds. With processor running, slowly drizzle in vegetable oil, about 1 minute. Transfer mixture to medium bowl and whisk in water. Whisking constantly, slowly drizzle in olive oil, about 30 seconds. Whisk in salt and pepper. (Mayonnaise can be refrigerated for up to 4 days.)

CLASSIC FRITTATA

✔ WHY THIS RECIPE WORKS
Since few cookbooks agree on a method for making frittatas, we had to test a number of techniques to determine which would consistently yield the best frittata, an Italian version of the filled omelet. Whereas an omelet should be soft, delicate, and slightly runny, a frittata should be tender but firm. And whereas an omelet encases its filling, a frittata incorporates it evenly throughout. It should also be easy to make. Our testing found that starting the frittata on the stovetop and finishing it in the oven set it evenly so it didn't burn or dry out. Conventional skillets require so much oil to prevent sticking that frittatas cooked in them were likely to be greasy, so we used a nonstick pan (one with an ovenproof handle) for a clean release.

CLASSIC FRITTATA WITH CHEESE AND FRESH HERBS
SERVES 4

A 10-inch ovensafe nonstick skillet is a must for this recipe. Cheese and herbs are the simplest additions to a frittata. This recipe (as well as the variations) can be served for breakfast, brunch, or supper, along with a vegetable or salad.

1	tablespoon extra-virgin olive oil
½	small onion, chopped fine
2	tablespoons minced fresh parsley, basil, dill, tarragon, or mint
⅓	cup grated Parmesan cheese
¼	teaspoon salt
¼	teaspoon pepper
6	large eggs, lightly beaten

1. Adjust oven rack to upper-middle position and heat oven to 350 degrees.

2. Heat oil in 10-inch ovensafe nonstick skillet over medium heat until shimmering, swirling to coat pan. Add onion and cook until softened, about 4 minutes. Stir in parsley.

3. Meanwhile, stir Parmesan, salt, and pepper into eggs.

4. Pour egg mixture into skillet and stir lightly until eggs begin to set. Once bottom is set, use thin heatproof rubber spatula to lift frittata edge closest to you. Tilt skillet slightly toward you so uncooked eggs run underneath. Return skillet to level position and swirl gently to evenly distribute eggs. Continue to cook, about 40 seconds, then lift edge again, repeating process until top is no longer runny.

5. Transfer skillet to oven; bake until frittata top is set and dry to touch, 2 to 4 minutes, making sure to remove frittata immediately once top is just set. Run spatula around skillet edge to loosen and invert onto serving platter. Serve warm, at room temperature, or chilled.

CLASSIC FRITTATA WITH
LEEK AND POTATOES
SERVES 4

A 10-inch ovensafe nonstick skillet is a must for this recipe. We prefer to use medium red potatoes, measuring 2 to 3 inches in diameter, in this recipe.

8	ounces red potatoes, cut into ½-inch pieces
1¼	teaspoons salt
2	tablespoons extra-virgin olive oil
1	large leek, white part only, halved lengthwise, sliced thin, and washed thoroughly
2	tablespoons minced fresh parsley
1½	ounces Emmenthaler cheese, shredded (⅓ cup)
¼	teaspoon pepper
6	large eggs, lightly beaten

1. Bring potatoes, 2 cups water, and 1 teaspoon salt to boil in medium saucepan over high heat. Reduce heat and simmer until potatoes are just tender, about 6 minutes. Drain and set aside.

2. Adjust oven rack to upper-middle position and heat oven to 350 degrees.

3. Heat oil in 10-inch ovensafe nonstick skillet over medium heat until shimmering, swirling to coat pan. Add leek and cook until softened, 5 to 6 minutes. Add potatoes and parsley; toss to coat with oil. Spread into single layer.

4. Meanwhile, stir cheese, remaining ¼ teaspoon salt, and pepper into eggs.

5. Pour egg mixture into skillet; stir lightly until eggs begin to set. Once bottom is set, use thin heatproof rubber spatula to lift frittata edge closest to you. Tilt skillet slightly toward you so uncooked eggs run underneath. Return skillet to level position and swirl gently to evenly distribute eggs. Continue to cook, about 40 seconds, then lift edge again, repeating process until top is no longer runny.

6. Transfer skillet to oven; bake until frittata top is set and dry to touch, 2 to 4 minutes, making sure to remove frittata immediately once top is just set. Run spatula around skillet edge to loosen and invert onto serving platter. Serve warm, at room temperature, or chilled.

MAKING A CLASSIC FRITTATA

Once bottom of frittata is set, use thin heatproof rubber spatula to lift edge closest to you. Tilt skillet slightly toward you so uncooked eggs run underneath. Return skillet to level position and swirl gently to evenly distribute eggs.

CLASSIC FRITTATA WITH
ASPARAGUS, MINT, AND PARMESAN
SERVES 4

A 10-inch ovensafe nonstick skillet is a must for this recipe. Blanching the asparagus ensures it stays crisp and green in the frittata.

6	ounces asparagus, trimmed and cut into 1-inch lengths
1¼	teaspoons salt
2	tablespoons extra-virgin olive oil
1	shallot, minced
2	tablespoons minced fresh parsley
1	tablespoon minced fresh mint
5	tablespoons grated Parmesan cheese
¼	teaspoon pepper
6	large eggs, lightly beaten

1. Bring 1 quart water to boil in medium saucepan over high heat. Meanwhile, fill large bowl with ice water. Add asparagus and 1 teaspoon salt to boiling water and cook until crisp-tender, about 2 minutes. Drain asparagus and transfer immediately to ice water. Drain again and pat dry with paper towels.

2. Adjust oven rack to upper-middle position and heat oven to 350 degrees.

3. Heat oil in 10-inch ovensafe nonstick skillet over medium heat until shimmering, swirling to coat pan. Add shallot and cook until softened, about 4 minutes. Add parsley, mint, and asparagus; toss to coat with oil and spread into single layer.

4. Meanwhile, stir 3 tablespoons Parmesan, remaining ¼ teaspoon salt, and pepper into eggs.

5. Pour egg mixture into skillet; stir lightly until eggs begin to set. Once bottom is set, use thin heatproof rubber spatula to lift frittata edge closest to you. Tilt skillet slightly toward you so uncooked eggs run underneath. Return skillet to level position and swirl gently to evenly distribute eggs. Continue to cook, about 40 seconds, then lift edge again, repeating process until top is no longer runny.

6. Sprinkle remaining 2 tablespoons cheese over frittata and transfer skillet to oven. Bake until frittata top is set and dry to touch, 2 to 4 minutes, making sure to remove frittata immediately once top is just set. Run spatula around skillet edge to loosen and invert onto serving platter. Serve warm, at room temperature, or chilled.

CLASSIC FRITTATA WITH FETA,
OLIVES, AND SUN-DRIED TOMATOES
SERVES 4

A 10-inch ovensafe nonstick skillet is a must for this recipe.

1	tablespoon extra-virgin olive oil
1	small garlic clove, peeled and smashed
¼	cup oil-packed sun-dried tomatoes, rinsed, patted dry, and chopped coarse, oil reserved
¼	cup black olives or green olives, pitted and minced
1	tablespoon chopped fresh basil

1   tablespoon minced fresh oregano
1½ ounces feta cheese, crumbled
    (⅓ cup)
¼   teaspoon pepper
6   large eggs, lightly beaten

1. Adjust oven rack to upper-middle position and heat oven to 350 degrees.

2. Heat oil and garlic in 10-inch oven-safe nonstick skillet over medium heat. Remove garlic when it begins to color and discard. Swirl skillet to coat with oil. Stir in tomatoes, olives, basil, and oregano; toss to coat with oil and spread into single layer.

3. Meanwhile, stir cheese and pepper into eggs.

4. Pour egg mixture into skillet; stir lightly until eggs begin to set. Once bottom is set, use thin heatproof rubber spatula to lift frittata edge closest to you. Tilt skillet slightly toward you so uncooked eggs run underneath. Return skillet to level position and swirl gently to evenly distribute eggs. Continue to cook, about 40 seconds, then lift edge again, repeating process until top is no longer runny.

5. Transfer skillet to oven; bake until frittata top is set and dry to touch, 2 to 4 minutes, making sure to remove frittata immediately once top is just set. Run spatula around skillet edge to loosen; invert frittata onto serving platter. Serve warm, at room temperature, or chilled.

THICK AND HEARTY FRITTATA

✔ WHY THIS RECIPE WORKS
More challenging to cook properly than a classic frittata, a thick frittata loaded with meat and vegetables often ends up dry, overstuffed, and overcooked. We wanted a frittata big enough to make a substantial meal for six to eight people—with a pleasing balance of egg to filling, firm yet moist eggs, and a supportive browned crust. We needed to be a little fussy about the cheese—Gruyère, cheddar, goat cheese, and fontina worked well. We found that vegetables and meats must be cut into small pieces and pre-cooked to drive off excess moisture and fat. A little half-and-half added a touch of creaminess. Given the large number of eggs, we started the eggs on medium heat and stirred them so they could cook quickly yet evenly. Then we slid the skillet under the broiler until the top had puffed and browned, removing it just before the frittata was cooked through, allowing the residual heat to finish cooking the center.

HEARTY FRITTATA WITH ASPARAGUS, HAM, AND GRUYÈRE
SERVES 6 TO 8

A 12-inch ovensafe nonstick skillet is a must for this recipe. Because broilers vary so much in intensity, watch the frittata carefully as it cooks.

12 large eggs
3   tablespoons half-and-half
½   teaspoon salt
¼   teaspoon pepper
2   teaspoons olive oil
8   ounces asparagus, trimmed and
    cut on bias into ¼-inch pieces
4   ounces ¼-inch-thick deli ham,
    cut into ¼-inch cubes
1   shallot, minced
3   ounces Gruyère cheese, cut into
    ¼-inch cubes (¾ cup)

1. Adjust oven rack 5 inches from broiler element and heat broiler. Whisk eggs, half-and-half, salt, and pepper in medium bowl until well combined, about 30 seconds; set aside.

2. Heat oil in 12-inch ovensafe nonstick skillet over medium heat until shimmering; add asparagus and cook, stirring occasionally, until lightly browned and almost tender, about 3 minutes. Add ham and shallot; cook until shallot begins to soften, about 2 minutes. Stir Gruyère into eggs. Add egg

mixture to skillet and cook, using heatproof rubber spatula to stir and scrape bottom of skillet, until large curds form and spatula begins to leave wake but eggs are still very wet, about 2 minutes. Shake skillet to distribute eggs evenly; cook without stirring for 30 seconds to let bottom set.

3. Broil until frittata has risen and surface is puffed and spotty brown, 3 to 4 minutes; when cut into with paring knife, eggs should be slightly wet and runny. Remove skillet from oven and let sit for 5 minutes. Using spatula, loosen frittata from skillet and slide onto serving platter or cutting board. Cut into wedges and serve.

HEARTY FRITTATA WITH BACON, POTATO, AND CHEDDAR
SERVES 6 TO 8

A 12-inch ovensafe nonstick skillet is a must for this recipe. Because broilers vary so much in intensity, watch the frittata carefully as it cooks.

12 large eggs
3   tablespoons half-and-half
½   teaspoon salt
¼   teaspoon pepper
8   slices bacon, cut into ¼-inch pieces
1   pound Yukon Gold potatoes,
    peeled and cut into ½-inch cubes
4   ounces cheddar cheese, cut into
    ¼-inch cubes (¾ cup)
3   scallions, sliced thin on bias

1. Adjust oven rack 5 inches from broiler element and heat broiler. Whisk eggs, half-and-half, salt, and pepper in medium bowl until well combined, about 30 seconds; set aside.

2. Cook bacon in 12-inch ovensafe nonstick skillet over medium heat until crisp, 5 to 7 minutes. Using slotted spoon, transfer bacon to paper towel–lined plate; pour off all but 1 tablespoon bacon fat. Add potatoes to skillet and cook, stirring occasionally, until golden brown and

tender, 15 to 20 minutes. Stir cheddar, scallions, and bacon into eggs; add egg mixture to skillet and cook, using heat-proof rubber spatula to stir and scrape bottom of skillet, until large curds form and spatula begins to leave wake but eggs are still very wet, about 2 minutes. Shake skillet to distribute eggs evenly; cook without stirring for 30 seconds to let bottom set.

3. Broil until frittata has risen and surface is puffed and spotty brown, 3 to 4 minutes; when cut into with paring knife, eggs should be slightly wet and runny. Remove skillet from oven; let sit for 5 minutes. Using spatula, loosen frittata from skillet and slide onto serving platter or cutting board. Cut into wedges; serve.

HEARTY FRITTATA WITH BROCCOLI RABE, SUN-DRIED TOMATOES, AND FONTINA

SERVES 6 TO 8

A 12-inch ovensafe nonstick skillet is a must for this recipe. Because broilers vary so much in intensity, watch the frittata carefully as it cooks.

12	large eggs
3	tablespoons half-and-half
¾	teaspoon salt
¼	teaspoon pepper
2	teaspoons olive oil
8	ounces broccoli rabe, trimmed and cut into 1-inch pieces
1	garlic clove, minced
⅛	teaspoon red pepper flakes
3	ounces Italian fontina cheese, cut into ¼-inch cubes (¾ cup)
¼	cup oil-packed sun-dried tomatoes, rinsed, patted dry, and chopped coarse

1. Adjust oven rack 5 inches from broiler element and heat broiler. Whisk eggs, half-and-half, ½ teaspoon salt, and pepper in medium bowl until well combined, about 30 seconds; set aside.

2. Heat oil in 12-inch ovensafe nonstick skillet over medium heat until shimmering; add broccoli rabe and remaining ¼ teaspoon salt and cook until rabe is beginning to brown and soften, 6 to 8 minutes. Add garlic and pepper flakes and cook until fragrant, about 30 seconds. Stir fontina and sun-dried tomatoes into eggs; add egg mixture to skillet and cook, using heatproof rubber spatula to stir and scrape bottom of skillet, until large curds form and spatula begins to leave wake but eggs are still very wet, about 2 minutes. Shake skillet to distribute eggs evenly; cook without stirring for 30 seconds to let bottom set.

3. Broil until frittata has risen and surface is puffed and spotty brown, 3 to 4 minutes; when cut into with paring knife, eggs should be slightly wet and runny. Remove skillet from oven and let sit for 5 minutes. Using spatula, loosen frittata from skillet and slide onto serving platter or cutting board. Cut into wedges and serve.

HEARTY FRITTATA WITH LEEK, PROSCIUTTO, AND GOAT CHEESE

SERVES 6 TO 8

A 12-inch ovensafe nonstick skillet is a must for this recipe. Because broilers vary so much in intensity, watch the frittata carefully as it cooks.

12	large eggs
3	tablespoons half-and-half
¾	teaspoon salt
¼	teaspoon pepper
2	tablespoons unsalted butter
2	small leeks, white and light green parts only, halved lengthwise, sliced thin, and washed thoroughly
4	ounces goat cheese, crumbled (1 cup)
3	ounces thinly sliced prosciutto, cut into ½-inch strips
¼	cup chopped fresh basil

1. Adjust oven rack 5 inches from broiler element and heat broiler. Whisk eggs, half-and-half, ½ teaspoon salt, and pepper in medium bowl until well combined, about 30 seconds; set aside.

2. Melt butter in 12-inch ovensafe nonstick skillet over medium heat. Add leeks and remaining ¼ teaspoon salt; reduce heat to low and cook covered, stirring occasionally, until softened, 8 to 10 minutes. Stir half of goat cheese, then prosciutto, and basil into eggs; add egg mixture to skillet and cook, using heatproof rubber spatula to stir and scrape bottom of skillet, until large curds form and spatula begins to leave wake but eggs are still very wet, about 2 minutes. Shake skillet to distribute eggs evenly; cook without stirring for 30 seconds to let bottom set.

3. Sprinkle remaining goat cheese evenly over frittata. Broil until frittata has risen and surface is puffed and spotty brown, 3 to 4 minutes; when cut into with paring knife, eggs should be slightly wet and runny. Remove skillet from oven; let sit for 5 minutes. Using spatula, loosen frittata from skillet and slide onto serving platter or cutting board. Cut into wedges and serve.

CLASSIC QUICHE

✔ WHY THIS RECIPE WORKS
Our ideal quiche should have a tender, buttery pastry case embracing a velvety smooth custard that is neither too rich nor too lean. We tested numerous combinations of dairy and eggs to find the perfect combination for a medium-rich custard with a smooth texture. The baking temperature was equally important; 375 degrees was low enough to set the custard gently and hot enough to brown the top before the filling became dried out and rubbery. For the crust, we found that resting the dough in the refrigerator and then briefly chilling it in the freezer produced a flaky shell that kept its original shape and definition.

CLASSIC QUICHE LORRAINE
SERVES 8

You can use Foolproof, All-Butter, or Classic Single-Crust Pie Dough (pages 708–711) for this quiche. The center of the quiche will be surprisingly soft when it comes out of the oven, but the filling will continue to set (and sink somewhat) as it cools.

- 8 slices bacon, cut into ½-inch pieces
- 2 large eggs plus 2 large yolks
- 1 cup whole milk
- 1 cup heavy cream
- ½ teaspoon salt
- ½ teaspoon white pepper
  Pinch ground nutmeg
- 4 ounces Gruyère cheese, shredded (1 cup)
- 1 recipe Single-Crust Pie Dough, partially baked and warm

1. Adjust oven rack to middle position and heat oven to 375 degrees.

2. Cook bacon in 12-inch nonstick skillet over medium heat until crisp, 5 to 7 minutes. Using slotted spoon, transfer bacon to paper towel–lined plate. Whisk eggs, egg yolks, milk, cream, salt, white pepper, and nutmeg together in medium bowl.

3. Spread Gruyère and bacon evenly over bottom of warm pie shell and set shell on oven rack. Pour custard mixture into pie shell (it should come to about ½ inch below crust's rim). Bake until light golden brown and knife blade inserted about 1 inch from edge comes out clean and center feels set but still soft, 32 to 35 minutes. Transfer quiche to wire rack and let cool. Serve warm or at room temperature.

CRABMEAT QUICHE

Reduce milk and cream to ¾ cup each. Add 2 tablespoons dry sherry and pinch cayenne to custard mixture in step 2. Substitute 8 ounces (1 cup) cooked crabmeat tossed with 2 tablespoons minced fresh chives for bacon and cheese.

LEEK AND GOAT CHEESE QUICHE

Omit bacon. Melt 2 tablespoons unsalted butter in 12-inch nonstick skillet over medium heat. Add 2 leeks, white part only, halved lengthwise, cut into ½-inch pieces, and washed thoroughly, and cook until softened, 5 to 7 minutes. Reduce milk and cream to ¾ cup each. Substitute 4 ounces crumbled goat cheese for Gruyère; add leeks with cheese.

HAM AND ASPARAGUS QUICHE

Bring 1 quart water to boil in medium saucepan over high heat. Meanwhile, fill large bowl with ice water. Add 8 ounces asparagus, trimmed and cut on bias into ½-inch lengths, and 1 teaspoon salt to boiling water; cook until crisp-tender, about 2 minutes. Drain asparagus and transfer immediately to ice water. Drain again and pat dry with paper towels. Reduce milk and cream to ¾ cup each. Substitute asparagus and 4 ounces thinly sliced deli ham, cut into ¼-inch pieces, for bacon and cheese.

DEEP-DISH QUICHE LORRAINE

✔ WHY THIS RECIPE WORKS

There's nothing wrong with classic quiche, but sometimes we crave a thick-crusted quiche brimming with a luxuriously creamy custard with a healthy dose of perfectly suspended fillings. Rather than using a pie plate or tart pan, we turned to a cake pan, lined with a foil sling to help lift the pastry, to accommodate the extra filling. We draped a generous amount of dough up and over the sides of the pan to anchor the crust in place. A simple egg-white wash helped seal any would-be cracks. For a delicate custard with just the right ratio of eggs to liquid, we used whole eggs, plus the extra yolk from the egg wash, and equal amounts whole milk and heavy cream. To add the fillings without affecting our perfect custard, we whisked a little cornstarch into the dairy. This kept the custard glossy and rich from one edge of the pastry to the other, even when packed with the classic quiche Lorraine trio of bacon, onion, and shredded Gruyère.

DEEP-DISH QUICHE LORRAINE
SERVES 8 TO 10

To prevent the crust from sagging during blind baking, make sure it overhangs the pan's edge and use plenty of pie weights (3 to 4 cups). Be sure to use a cake pan with at least 2-inch-tall straight sides. To reheat the whole quiche, place it on a rimmed baking sheet on the middle rack of a 325-degree oven for 20 minutes; slices can be reheated in a 375-degree oven for 10 minutes. This recipe use a total of 9 eggs; one egg is separated and the white is used for the crust, while the yolk is used in the filling.

CRUST
- 1¾ cups (8¾ ounces) all-purpose flour
- ½ teaspoon salt
- 12 tablespoons unsalted butter, cut into ½-inch pieces and chilled
- 3 tablespoons sour cream
- ¼–⅓ cup ice water
- 1 large egg white, lightly beaten

CUSTARD FILLING
- 8 slices thick-cut bacon, cut into ¼-inch pieces
- 2 onions, chopped fine
- 1½ tablespoons cornstarch
- 1½ cups whole milk
- 8 large eggs plus 1 large yolk
- 1½ cups heavy cream
- ½ teaspoon salt

¼ teaspoon pepper

⅛ teaspoon ground nutmeg

⅛ teaspoon cayenne pepper

6 ounces Gruyère cheese, shredded (1½ cups)

1. FOR THE CRUST: Process flour and salt together in food processor until combined, about 3 seconds. Add butter and pulse until butter is size of large peas, about 10 pulses.

2. Combine sour cream and ¼ cup ice water in small bowl. Add half of sour cream mixture to flour mixture; pulse 3 times. Repeat with remaining sour cream mixture. Pinch dough with fingers; if dough is floury, dry, and does not hold together, add 1 to 2 tablespoons more ice water and pulse until dough forms large clumps and no dry flour remains, 3 to 5 pulses.

3. Turn dough out onto counter and flatten into 6-inch disk; wrap disk in plastic wrap and refrigerate until firm but not hard, 1 to 2 hours, before rolling. (Dough can be refrigerated for up to 1 day; let stand at room temperature for 15 minutes before rolling.)

4. Cut two 16-inch lengths of aluminum foil. Arrange foil pieces, perpendicular to each other, in 9-inch round cake pan, pushing them into corners and up sides of pan; press overhang against outside of pan. Spray foil lightly with vegetable oil spray.

5. Roll out dough on generously floured counter to 15-inch circle about ¼ inch thick. Roll dough loosely around rolling pin and unroll into prepared cake pan. Working around circumference, ease dough into pan by gently lifting edge of dough with 1 hand while pressing into pan bottom with other. Trim any dough that extends more than 1 inch over edge of pan. Patch any cracks or holes with dough scraps as needed. Refrigerate any remaining dough scraps. Refrigerate dough-lined pan until dough is firm, about 30 minutes, then freeze for 20 minutes.

6. Adjust oven rack to lower-middle

position and heat oven to 375 degrees. Line dough with foil or parchment paper and fill completely with pie weights, gently pressing weights into corners of shell. Bake on rimmed baking sheet until exposed edges of dough are beginning to brown but bottom is still light in color, 30 to 40 minutes. Carefully remove foil and pie weights. If any new holes or cracks have formed in dough, patch with reserved scraps. Return shell to oven and bake until bottom is golden brown, 15 to 20 minutes longer. Remove shell from oven and brush interior with egg white. Set aside while preparing filling. Reduce oven temperature to 350 degrees.

7. FOR THE CUSTARD FILLING: Cook bacon in 12-inch skillet over medium heat until crisp, 5 to 7 minutes. Transfer to paper towel–lined plate and discard all but 2 tablespoons bacon fat from skillet. Return to medium heat, add onions, and cook, stirring frequently, until softened and lightly browned, about 12 minutes. Set aside to cool slightly.

8. Whisk cornstarch and 3 tablespoons milk together in large bowl to dissolve cornstarch. Whisk in remaining milk, eggs, egg yolk, cream, salt, pepper, nutmeg, and cayenne until smooth.

9. Scatter onions, bacon, and cheese evenly over crust. Gently pour custard mixture over filling. Using fork, push filling ingredients down into custard and drag gently through custard to dislodge air bubbles. Gently tap pan on counter to dislodge any remaining air bubbles.

10. Bake until top of quiche is lightly browned, toothpick inserted in center comes out clean, and center registers 170 degrees, 1¼ to 1½ hours. Transfer to wire rack and let stand until cool to touch, about 2 hours.

11. When ready to serve, use sharp paring knife to remove any crust that extends beyond edge of pan. Lift foil overhang from sides of pan and remove quiche from pan; gently slide thin-bladed spatula between

quiche and foil to loosen, then slide quiche onto serving plate. Cut into wedges. Serve warm or at room temperature.

DEEP-DISH QUICHE WITH LEEKS AND BLUE CHEESE

Sweet leeks and tangy blue cheese make perfect partners in this variation.

Omit bacon and onions. Melt 1 tablespoon unsalted butter in 12-inch skillet over medium heat. Add 4 large leeks, white and light green parts only, halved lengthwise, sliced ¼ inch thick, and washed thoroughly; cook until softened, 10 to 12 minutes. Increase heat to medium-high; continue to cook, stirring constantly, until leeks are beginning to brown, about 5 minutes. Transfer leeks to plate lined with triple layer of paper towels; press with double layer of paper towels to remove excess moisture. Increase salt in filling to 1 teaspoon. Substitute 6 ounces crumbled blue cheese for Gruyère; scatter blue cheese and sautéed leeks evenly over crust before adding custard. Reduce baking time to 1 to 1¼ hours.

DEEP-DISH QUICHE WITH SAUSAGE, BROCCOLI RABE, AND MOZZARELLA

Be sure to use supermarket-style low-moisture mozzarella in this variation; fresh mozzarella will make for a too-wet filling.

Omit bacon and onions. Cook 8 ounces hot or sweet Italian sausage, casings removed, in 12-inch skillet over medium heat, breaking sausage into ½-inch pieces, until no longer pink, 5 to 7 minutes. Transfer to paper towel–lined plate and discard all but 2 tablespoons fat from skillet. Return skillet to medium heat, add 8 ounces broccoli rabe, trimmed and cut into ½-inch pieces, and cook until slightly softened, about 6 minutes. Transfer rabe to plate lined with triple layer of paper towels; press with double layer of paper towels to remove excess moisture. Increase salt in filling to

1 teaspoon. Substitute 6 ounces shredded low-moisture whole-milk mozzarella cheese for Gruyère; scatter mozzarella, cooked sausage, and broccoli rabe evenly over crust before adding custard. Reduce baking time to 1 to 1¼ hours.

FRENCH ONION AND BACON TART

✔ WHY THIS RECIPE WORKS

French onion tart is similar to quiche but delivers a more refined slice of pie, with more onions than custard. Trying to make an onion tart at home can produce a tough and crackerlike crust, hardly worth the long hours spent carefully cooking onions and making custard. We needed to simplify the crust and shorten the overall preparation time. We found that covering the onions throughout cooking worked best; they cooked in half the usual time and entirely in their own juices, thereby becoming tender, retaining their pure onion flavor, and cooking more evenly. We added bacon, which acted as a crisp foil to the creamy filling. We tried several classic crust recipes to find one with the butteriness of traditional tart dough but that could still be easily patted into a tart pan. Using a food processor to cut cold butter into the flour mixture required less ice water than a conventional crust, which kept the dough firm enough to press into the pan.

FRENCH ONION AND BACON TART
SERVES 6 TO 8

Either yellow or white onions work well in this recipe, but stay away from sweet onions, such as Vidalias, which will make the tart watery. Use a 9-inch tinned-steel tart pan. This tart can be served hot or at room temperature.

CRUST

1¼	cups (6¼ ounces) all-purpose flour
1	tablespoon sugar
½	teaspoon salt
8	tablespoons unsalted butter, cut into ½-inch cubes and chilled
2–3	tablespoons ice water

FILLING

4	slices bacon, cut into ¼-inch pieces
	Vegetable oil, if needed
1½	pounds onions, halved through root end and cut crosswise into ¼-inch slices
¾	teaspoon salt
1	sprig fresh thyme
2	large eggs
½	cup half-and-half
¼	teaspoon pepper

1. FOR THE CRUST: Spray 9-inch tart pan with vegetable oil spray. Pulse flour, sugar, and salt in food processor until combined, about 4 pulses. Scatter butter pieces over flour mixture; pulse until mixture resembles coarse sand, about 15 pulses. Add 2 tablespoons ice water and process until large clumps form and no powdery bits remain, about 5 seconds, adding up to 1 tablespoon more water if dough will not form clumps. Transfer dough to prepared tart pan; pat dough into pan. Lay plastic wrap over dough and smooth out any bumps or shallow areas. Place tart shell on plate and freeze for 30 minutes.

2. Adjust oven rack to middle position and heat oven to 375 degrees. Place frozen tart shell on baking sheet. Spray piece of extra-wide heavy-duty aluminum foil with vegetable oil spray and gently press against dough and over edges of tart pan. Fill with pie weights and bake until top edge just starts to color and surface of dough no longer looks wet, about 30 minutes. Remove from oven and remove foil and weights. Return baking sheet with tart shell to oven and bake until golden brown, 5 to 10 minutes. Set baking sheet with tart shell on wire rack. Do not turn off oven.

3. FOR THE FILLING: Meanwhile, cook bacon in 12-inch nonstick skillet over medium heat until crisp, 5 to 7 minutes. Using slotted spoon, transfer bacon to paper towel–lined plate. Pour off all but 2 tablespoons bacon fat from skillet (or add vegetable oil if needed to make this amount).

4. Add onions, salt, and thyme to skillet. Cover and cook until onions release liquid and start to wilt, about 10 minutes. Reduce heat to low and continue to cook, covered, until onions are very soft, about 20 minutes, stirring once or twice (if after 15 minutes onions look wet, remove lid and continue to cook another 5 minutes). Remove pan from heat and let onions cool for 5 minutes.

5. Whisk eggs, half-and-half, and pepper together in large bowl. Remove and discard thyme sprig from onions. Stir onions into egg mixture until just incorporated. Spread onion mixture over tart shell and sprinkle bacon evenly on top.

6. Bake tart on baking sheet until center of tart feels firm to touch, 20 to 25 minutes. Cool on wire rack at least 10 minutes. Remove tart pan ring; gently slide thin-bladed spatula between pan bottom and crust to loosen, then slide tart onto serving plate. Cut into wedges and serve.

BREAKFAST STRATA

✔ WHY THIS RECIPE WORKS

Many recipes for this savory bread pudding are soggy and laden with excessive custard and ingredients, rendering this simple casserole an overindulgence in both preparation and consumption. Looking for a savory breakfast casserole that was simple, with just enough richness to satisfy, we started with the bread. Whole dried bread slices had the best texture and appearance, and buttering them added richness. We carefully selected a few complementary ingredients for the filling, then sautéed them to remove excess moisture and prevent the casserole from becoming waterlogged. Weighing the strata down overnight improved its texture, and we could bake it the following morning for a perfect make-ahead breakfast.

BREAKFAST STRATA WITH POTATOES, ROSEMARY, AND FONTINA

SERVES 6

We prefer to use medium red potatoes, measuring 2 to 3 inches in diameter, in this recipe. To weigh down the assembled strata, use two 1-pound boxes of sugar. To double this recipe, use a 13 by 9-inch baking dish greased with 1½ tablespoons butter and increase the baking time to 1 hour and 20 minutes.

8–10   (½-inch-thick) slices French or
   Italian bread
5   tablespoons unsalted butter,
  softened
12   ounces red potatoes, cut into
   ½-inch cubes
   Salt and pepper
3   shallots, minced
2   garlic cloves, minced
1½   teaspoons minced fresh rosemary
½   cup medium-dry white wine, such
  as Sauvignon Blanc
6   ounces fontina cheese, shredded
  (1½ cups)
6   large eggs
2   tablespoons minced fresh parsley
1¾   cups half-and-half

1. Adjust oven rack to middle position and heat oven to 225 degrees. Arrange bread in single layer on baking sheet and bake until dry and crisp, about 40 minutes, turning slices over halfway through baking. (Alternatively, leave slices out overnight to dry.) When cooled, butter slices on one side with 2 tablespoons butter; set aside.

2. Bring 1 quart water to boil in medium saucepan over medium-high heat. Add potatoes and 1 teaspoon salt and boil potatoes until just tender when pierced with paring knife, about 4 minutes. Drain potatoes.

3. Melt 2 tablespoons butter in 10-inch nonstick skillet over medium heat. Add potatoes and cook until just beginning to brown, about 10 minutes. Add shallots and cook, stirring frequently, until softened and translucent, about 1 minute. Add garlic and rosemary and cook until fragrant, about 30 seconds. Transfer mixture to medium bowl; season with salt and pepper to taste and set aside. Add wine to skillet, increase heat to medium-high, and simmer until reduced to ¼ cup, 2 to 3 minutes. Set aside.

4. Grease 8-inch square baking dish with remaining 1 tablespoon butter and arrange half of bread slices, buttered side up, in single layer in dish. Sprinkle half of potato mixture, then ½ cup fontina evenly over bread slices. Arrange remaining bread slices in single layer over cheese; sprinkle remaining potato mixture and another ½ cup fontina evenly over bread. Whisk eggs and parsley together in medium bowl; add reduced wine, half-and-half, 1 teaspoon salt, and pepper to taste and whisk until combined. Pour egg mixture evenly over bread layers and cover strata tightly with plastic wrap, pressing wrap against surface of strata. Weigh strata down and refrigerate for at least 1 hour or up to 24 hours.

5. Remove strata from refrigerator and let sit at room temperature for 20 minutes. Meanwhile, adjust oven rack to middle position and heat oven to 325 degrees. Uncover strata and sprinkle remaining ½ cup fontina evenly over surface; bake until both edges and center are puffed and brown, about 10 minutes. Add shallots and cook, stirring frequently, until softened and translucent, about 1 minute. Add garlic and rosemary and cook until fragrant, about 30 seconds. Transfer mixture to medium bowl; season with salt and pepper to taste and set aside. Add wine to skillet, increase heat to medium-high, and simmer until reduced to ¼ cup, 2 to 3 minutes. Set aside. edges have pulled away slightly from sides of dish, 50 to 55 minutes. Cool on wire rack for 5 minutes; serve.

BREAKFAST STRATA WITH SAUSAGE, MUSHROOMS, AND MONTEREY JACK

To double this recipe, use a 13 by 9-inch baking dish greased with 1½ tablespoons butter and increase the baking time to 1 hour and 20 minutes.

8–10   (½-inch-thick) slices French or
   Italian bread
3   tablespoons unsalted butter,
  softened
8   ounces breakfast sausage, crumbled
3   shallots, minced
8   ounces white mushrooms, trimmed
  and quartered
  Salt and pepper
½   cup medium-dry white wine, such
  as Sauvignon Blanc
6   ounces Monterey Jack cheese,
  shredded (1½ cups)
6   large eggs
2   tablespoons minced fresh parsley
1¾   cups half-and-half

Follow recipe for Breakfast Strata with Potatoes, Rosemary, and Fontina through step 1. Cook sausage in 10-inch nonstick skillet over medium heat, breaking sausage apart with wooden spoon, until sausage has

---

ASSEMBLING BREAKFAST STRATA

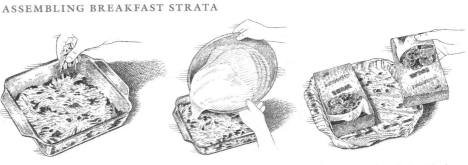

1. Layer bread and filling in 8-inch square baking dish.

2. Pour custard mixture evenly over assembled layers.

3. Cover surface flush with plastic wrap and weigh down strata.

lost raw color and begins to brown, about 4 minutes. Add shallots and cook, stirring frequently, until softened and translucent, about 1 minute. Add mushrooms and cook until mushrooms no longer release liquid, about 6 minutes; transfer mixture to medium bowl and season with salt and pepper to taste. Reduce wine as directed in step 3. Proceed as directed in step 4, substituting sausage mixture for potatoes and Monterey Jack for fontina.

BREAKFAST STRATA WITH SPINACH AND GRUYÈRE

To double this recipe, use a 13 by 9-inch baking dish greased with 1½ tablespoons butter and increase the baking time to 1 hour and 20 minutes.

8–10 (½-inch-thick) slices French or Italian bread
  5 tablespoons unsalted butter, softened
  4 shallots, minced
  10 ounces frozen chopped spinach, thawed and squeezed dry
    Salt and pepper
  ½ cup medium-dry white wine, such as Sauvignon Blanc
  6 ounces Gruyère cheese, shredded (1½ cups)
  6 large eggs
  1¾ cups half-and-half

Follow recipe for Breakfast Strata with Potatoes, Rosemary, and Fontina through step 1. Melt 2 tablespoons butter in 10-inch nonstick skillet over medium heat. Add shallots and cook until fragrant and translucent, about 3 minutes. Add spinach and salt and pepper to taste and cook, stirring occasionally, until spinach is warm, about 2 minutes. Transfer mixture to medium bowl. Reduce wine as directed in step 3. Proceed as directed in step 4, omitting parsley and substituting spinach mixture for potatoes and Gruyère for fontina.

FRENCH TOAST

WHY THIS RECIPE WORKS
French toast just isn't worth the trouble if the result is soggy, too eggy, or just plain bland. We first found out which type of bread fared best in a typical batter. Hearty white sandwich bread, dried in a low oven, produced French toast that was crisp on the outside and velvety on the inside, with no trace of sogginess. However, the toast still tasted more like scrambled eggs. Cutting the egg whites and adding melted butter to the soaking liquid made a huge difference, turning the toast rich and custardlike. For a final touch, we flavored the toast with cinnamon, vanilla, and brown sugar.

FRENCH TOAST
SERVES 4

To prevent the butter from clumping during mixing, warm the milk in a microwave or small saucepan until warm to the touch (about 80 degrees). The French toast can be cooked all at once on an electric griddle, but may take an extra 2 to 3 minutes per side. Set the griddle temperature to 350 degrees and use the entire amount of butter (4 tablespoons) for cooking. Serve with warm maple syrup.

  8 large slices hearty white sandwich bread or challah
  1½ cups whole milk, warmed
  3 large egg yolks
  3 tablespoons packed light brown sugar
  2 tablespoons unsalted butter plus 2 tablespoons melted
  1 tablespoon vanilla extract
  ½ teaspoon ground cinnamon
  ¼ teaspoon salt

1. Adjust oven rack to middle position and heat oven to 300 degrees. Place bread on wire rack set in rimmed baking sheet. Bake bread until almost dry throughout (center should remain slightly moist), about 16 minutes, flipping slices halfway

through baking. Remove bread from rack and let cool for 5 minutes. Return baking sheet with wire rack to oven and reduce temperature to 200 degrees.

2. Whisk milk, egg yolks, sugar, 2 tablespoons melted butter, vanilla, cinnamon, and salt in large bowl until well blended. Transfer mixture to 13 by 9-inch baking pan.

3. Soak bread in milk mixture until saturated but not falling apart, 20 seconds per side. Using firm slotted spatula, pick up 1 bread slice and allow excess milk mixture to drip off; repeat with remaining slices. Place soaked bread on another baking sheet or platter.

4. Melt ½ tablespoon butter in 12-inch skillet over medium-low heat. Using slotted spatula, transfer 2 slices soaked bread to skillet and cook until golden brown, 3 to 4 minutes. Flip and continue to cook until second side is golden brown, 3 to 4 minutes longer. (If toast is cooking too quickly, reduce temperature slightly.) Transfer to baking sheet in oven. Wipe out skillet with paper towels. Repeat cooking with remaining bread, 2 pieces at a time, adding ½ tablespoon of butter for each batch. Serve warm.

EXTRA-CRISP FRENCH TOAST

Process 1 slice hearty white sandwich bread or challah, torn into 1-inch pieces, 1 tablespoon packed light brown sugar, and ¼ teaspoon ground cinnamon in food processor until finely ground, 8 to 12 pulses (you should have about ½ cup). Sprinkle 1 tablespoon bread-crumb mixture over 1 side of each slice of soaked bread. Cook as directed in step 4, starting with crumb mixture side down.

ALMOND-CRUSTED FRENCH TOAST

Process ½ cup slivered almonds and 1 tablespoon packed light brown sugar in food processor until coarsely ground, 12 to 15 pulses (you should have about

½ cup). Add 1 tablespoon triple sec and 1 teaspoon grated orange zest to milk mixture in step 2. Sprinkle 1 tablespoon nut mixture over 1 side of each slice of soaked bread. Cook as directed in step 4, starting with nut mixture side down.

PECAN-RUM FRENCH TOAST

Substitute 8 large slices cinnamon-raisin bread for hearty white sandwich bread. Process ½ cup pecans, 1 tablespoon packed light brown sugar, and ¼ teaspoon ground cinnamon in food processor until coarsely ground, 12 to 15 pulses (you should have about ½ cup). Add 2 teaspoons dark rum to milk mixture in step 2. Sprinkle 1 tablespoon nut mixture over 1 side of each slice of soaked bread. Cook as directed in step 4, starting with nut mixture side down.

BEST BUTTERMILK PANCAKES

✔ WHY THIS RECIPE WORKS

Too often buttermilk pancakes lack true tang, and they rarely achieve the light and fluffy texture we desire. We wanted true buttermilk pancakes with a slightly crisp, golden crust surrounding a fluffy, tender center with just enough structure to withstand a good dousing of maple syrup. Since we wanted a tangy flavor and fluffy texture, we figured swapping out some of the regular milk for more buttermilk would do the trick. Wrong. We had better luck with an uncommon ingredient: sour cream. Since sour cream is cultured with the same bacteria as buttermilk, it has many of the same flavor compounds but in much higher concentration. But the pancakes still had a leavening problem; they were overinflating when they first cooked, then collapsing, becoming dense and wet on the plate. Reducing both the baking soda and baking powder produced pancakes that were light, fluffy, and full of their trademark tang.

BEST BUTTERMILK PANCAKES

MAKES SIXTEEN 4-INCH PANCAKES, SERVING 4 TO 6

The pancakes can be cooked on an electric griddle. Set the griddle temperature to 350 degrees and cook as directed. The test kitchen prefers a lower-protein all-purpose flour like Gold Medal or Pillsbury for this recipe. If you use an all-purpose flour with a higher protein content, like King Arthur, you will need to add an extra tablespoon or two of buttermilk. Serve with warm maple syrup.

2	cups (10 ounces) all-purpose flour
2	tablespoons sugar
I	teaspoon baking powder
½	teaspoon baking soda
½	teaspoon salt
2	cups buttermilk
¼	cup sour cream
2	large eggs
3	tablespoons unsalted butter, melted and cooled
I–2	teaspoons vegetable oil

1. Adjust oven rack to middle position and heat oven to 200 degrees. Spray wire rack set in rimmed baking sheet with vegetable oil spray; place in oven. Whisk flour, sugar, baking powder, baking soda, and salt together in medium bowl. In second medium bowl, whisk together buttermilk, sour cream, eggs, and melted butter. Make well in center of dry ingredients and pour in wet ingredients; gently stir until just combined (batter should remain lumpy, with few streaks of flour). Do not overmix. Let batter sit for 10 minutes before cooking.

2. Heat 1 teaspoon oil in 12-inch nonstick skillet over medium heat until shimmering. Using paper towels, carefully wipe out oil, leaving thin film of oil on bottom and sides of pan. Using ¼-cup measure, portion batter into pan in 4 places. Cook until edges are set, first side is golden brown, and bubbles on surface are just beginning to break, 2 to 3 minutes. Using thin, wide spatula, flip pancakes and continue to cook until second side is golden brown, 1 to 2 minutes longer. Serve pancakes immediately, or transfer to wire rack in preheated oven. Repeat with remaining batter, using remaining oil as necessary.

BLUEBERRY PANCAKES

✔ WHY THIS RECIPE WORKS

Blueberry pancakes are too often tough, rubbery, tasteless, and short on real berry flavor. We wanted light and fluffy pancakes, studded with juicy bursts of blueberry. We started with a perfect batter: We included both baking powder and soda for lift and color, just one egg, sugar, and plenty of melted butter. For dairy, we used soured milk (milk and lemon juice) as an always-ready buttermilk stand-in. Gently mixing small, fresh, wild blueberries (frozen can be substituted) kept the pancakes from ending up an unappetizing blue-gray. These pancakes were fluffy and flavorful, dotted with delicious berries.

BLUEBERRY PANCAKES

MAKES SIXTEEN 4-INCH PANCAKES, SERVING 4 TO 6

The pancakes can be cooked on an electric griddle. Set the griddle temperature to 350 degrees and cook as directed. To make sure frozen blueberries don't bleed, rinse them under cool water in a fine-mesh strainer until the water runs clear, then spread them on a paper towel–lined plate to dry. If you have buttermilk on hand, use 2 cups instead of the milk and lemon juice.

2	cups milk
I	tablespoon fresh lemon juice
2	cups (10 ounces) all-purpose flour
2	tablespoons sugar
2	teaspoons baking powder
½	teaspoon baking soda
½	teaspoon salt
I	large egg

3 tablespoons unsalted butter, melted and cooled
1–2 teaspoons vegetable oil
5 ounces (1 cup) fresh or frozen blueberries, rinsed and dried

1. Adjust oven rack to middle position and heat oven to 200 degrees. Spray wire rack set in rimmed baking sheet with vegetable oil spray; place in oven. Whisk milk and lemon juice together in large measuring cup; set aside to thicken while preparing other ingredients. Whisk flour, sugar, baking powder, baking soda, and salt together in medium bowl.

2. Add egg and melted butter to milk mixture and whisk until combined. Make well in center of dry ingredients; pour in milk mixture and whisk very gently until just combined (few lumps should remain). Do not overmix.

3. Heat 1 teaspoon oil in 12-inch nonstick skillet over medium heat until shimmering. Using paper towels, carefully wipe out oil, leaving thin film of oil on bottom and sides of pan. Using ¼-cup measure, portion batter into pan in 4 places. Sprinkle 1 tablespoon blueberries over each pancake. Cook pancakes until large bubbles begin to appear, 1½ to 2 minutes. Using thin, wide spatula, flip pancakes and cook until second side is golden brown, 1 to 1½ minutes longer. Serve pancakes immediately or transfer to wire rack in preheated oven. Repeat with remaining batter, using remaining oil as necessary.

LEMON-CORNMEAL BLUEBERRY PANCAKES

Add 2 teaspoons grated lemon zest to milk along with lemon juice and substitute 1½ cups stone-ground yellow cornmeal for 1 cup flour.

MULTIGRAIN PANCAKES

✔ WHY THIS RECIPE WORKS

Bland, dense, and gummy, most multigrain pancakes are more about appeasing your diet than pleasing your palate. We wanted flavorful, fluffy, and healthful flapjacks. After testing lots of grains, we found that muesli had all the ingredients and flavor we wanted in one convenient package—raw whole oats, wheat germ, rye, barley, toasted nuts, and dried fruit. But pancakes made with whole muesli were too chewy and gummy. We converted the muesli into a flour in the food processor and then found the perfect combination of muesli "flour," all-purpose flour, whole wheat flour, and leavening to achieve the lightness we wanted. The pancakes were perfect after we tweaked the flavor with a little butter, vanilla, and brown sugar and cut the acidity by replacing the buttermilk with a blend of milk and lemon juice.

MULTIGRAIN PANCAKES

MAKES SIXTEEN 4-INCH PANCAKES,
SERVING 4 TO 6

The pancakes can be cooked on an electric griddle. Set the griddle temperature to 350 degrees and cook as directed. Familia brand no-sugar-added muesli is the best choice for this recipe. If you can't find Familia, look for Alpen or any no-sugar-added muesli. (If you can't find muesli without sugar, muesli with sugar added will work; reduce the brown sugar in the recipe to 1 tablespoon.) Mix the batter first and then heat the pan. Letting the batter sit while the pan heats will give the dry ingredients time to absorb the wet ingredients; otherwise, the batter will be runny. Serve with maple syrup or Apple, Cranberry, and Pecan Topping (recipe follows).

2 cups whole milk
4 teaspoons fresh lemon juice
1¼ cups (6 ounces), plus 3 tablespoons no-sugar-added muesli
¾ cup (3¾ ounces) all-purpose flour

½ cup (2¾ ounces) whole wheat flour
2 tablespoons packed brown sugar
2¼ teaspoons baking powder
½ teaspoon baking soda
½ teaspoon salt
2 large eggs
3 tablespoons unsalted butter, melted and cooled
¾ teaspoon vanilla extract
1–2 teaspoons vegetable oil

1. Adjust oven rack to middle position and heat oven to 200 degrees. Spray wire rack set in rimmed baking sheet with vegetable oil spray; place in oven. Whisk milk and lemon juice together in large measuring cup; set aside to thicken while preparing other ingredients.

2. Process 1¼ cups muesli in food processor until finely ground, 2 to 2½ minutes; transfer to large bowl. Add remaining 3 tablespoons unground muesli, all-purpose flour, whole wheat flour, brown sugar, baking powder, baking soda, and salt; whisk to combine.

3. Add eggs, melted butter, and vanilla to milk mixture and whisk until combined. Make well in center of dry ingredients; pour in milk mixture and whisk very gently until just combined (batter should remain lumpy with few streaks of flour). Do not overmix. Allow batter to sit while pan heats.

4. Heat 1 teaspoon oil in 12-inch nonstick skillet over medium heat until shimmering. Using paper towels, carefully wipe out oil, leaving thin film of oil on bottom and sides of pan. Using ¼-cup measure, portion batter into pan in 4 places. Cook until small bubbles begin to appear evenly over surface, 2 to 3 minutes. Using thin, wide spatula, flip pancakes and cook until second side is golden brown, 1½ to 2 minutes longer. Serve pancakes immediately or transfer to wire rack in preheated oven. Repeat with remaining batter, using remaining oil as necessary.

APPLE, CRANBERRY, AND PECAN TOPPING

SERVES 4 TO 6

We prefer semifirm apples, such as Fuji, Gala, or Braeburn, for this topping. Avoid very tart apples, such as Granny Smith, and soft varieties like McIntosh.

3½ tablespoons unsalted butter, chilled
1¼ pounds apples, peeled, cored, and
  cut into ½-inch pieces
  Pinch salt
1 cup apple cider
½ cup dried cranberries
½ cup maple syrup
1 teaspoon lemon juice
½ teaspoon vanilla extract
¾ cup pecans, toasted and chopped
  coarse

Melt 1½ tablespoons butter in 12-inch skillet over medium-high heat. Add apples and salt; cook, stirring occasionally, until softened and browned, 7 to 9 minutes. Stir in cider and cranberries; cook until liquid has almost evaporated, 6 to 8 minutes. Stir in maple syrup and cook until thickened, 4 to 5 minutes. Add remaining 2 table-spoons butter, lemon juice, and vanilla; whisk until sauce is smooth. Serve with toasted nuts.

GERMAN APPLE PANCAKE

✓ WHY THIS RECIPE WORKS

German apple pancakes combine the best qualities of a popover and a pancake, but this old-world classic is prone to numerous pitfalls: insufficient rise, leaden texture, and eggy flavor. The perfect pancake should have crisp, lighter-than-air edges and a custardlike center, with buttery sautéed apples baked right into the bat-ter. To give the pancake a rich flavor without sacrificing the texture, we used half-and-half in the batter. Granny Smith apples provided a per-fect balance of sweetness and tartness. Cutting the apples into ½-inch-thick pieces kept them from turning mushy, and cooking them in brown sugar with cinnamon and lemon juice made them at once earthy and bright. Starting the pancake in a hot oven gave the batter the quick rise it needed; we then reduced the heat to a more moderate temperature, which cooked the pancake to perfection.

GERMAN APPLE PANCAKE

SERVES 4

A 10-inch ovensafe skillet is necessary for this recipe; we highly recommend using a nonstick skillet for the sake of easy cleanup, but a regular skillet will work as well. If you prefer tart apples, use Granny Smiths; if you prefer sweet ones, use Braeburns. For serving, dust the apple pancake with confectioners' sugar and pass warm maple syrup or Caramel Sauce (recipe follows) sepa-rately, if desired.

½ cup (2½ ounces) all-purpose flour
1 tablespoon granulated sugar
½ teaspoon salt
2 large eggs
⅔ cup half-and-half
1 teaspoon vanilla extract
2 tablespoons unsalted butter
1¼ pounds Granny Smith or Braeburn
  apples, peeled, cored, quartered,
  and cut into ½-inch-thick slices
¼ cup packed brown sugar
¼ teaspoon ground cinnamon
1 teaspoon lemon juice
  Confectioners' sugar

1. Adjust oven rack to upper-middle position and heat oven to 500 degrees.

2. Whisk flour, granulated sugar, and salt together in medium bowl. In second medium bowl, whisk eggs, half-and-half, and vanilla until combined. Add liquid ingredients to dry ingredients and whisk until no lumps remain, about 20 seconds; set aside.

3. Melt butter in 10-inch ovensafe non-stick skillet over medium-high heat. Add apples, brown sugar, and cinnamon; cook, stirring frequently, until apples are golden brown, about 10 minutes. Off heat, stir in lemon juice.

4. Working quickly, pour batter around and over apples. Place skillet in oven and immediately reduce oven temperature to 425 degrees. Bake until pancake edges are brown and puffy and have risen above edges of skillet, about 18 minutes.

5. Carefully remove skillet from oven and loosen pancake edges with heatproof rubber spatula; invert pancake onto serving platter. Dust with confectioners' sugar, cut into wedges, and serve.

MAKING GERMAN APPLE PANCAKE

1. Pour batter around edge of pan, then over apples.

2. Loosen edge of pancake with heatproof rubber spatula.

3. Invert pancake onto large plate or serving platter.

CARAMEL SAUCE

MAKES ABOUT 1½ CUPS

When the hot cream mixture is added in step 3, the hot sugar syrup will bubble vigorously (and dangerously), so don't use a smaller saucepan. If you make the caramel sauce ahead, reheat it in the microwave or a small saucepan over low heat until warm and fluid.

- ½ cup water
- 1 cup sugar
- 1 cup heavy cream
- ⅛ teaspoon salt
- ½ teaspoon vanilla extract
- ½ teaspoon lemon juice

1. Place water in 2-quart saucepan. Pour sugar in center of pan, taking care not to let sugar touch sides of pan. Cover and bring mixture to boil over high heat; once boiling, uncover and continue to boil until syrup is thick and straw-colored and registers 300 degrees, about 7 minutes. Reduce heat to medium and continue to cook until syrup is deep amber and registers 350 degrees, 1 to 2 minutes.

2. Meanwhile, bring cream and salt to simmer in small saucepan over high heat (if cream boils before sugar reaches deep amber color, remove cream from heat and cover to keep warm).

3. Remove sugar syrup from heat. Very carefully pour about one quarter of hot cream into syrup (mixture will bubble vigorously) and let bubbling subside. Add remaining cream, vanilla, and lemon juice; whisk until sauce is smooth. (Sauce can be refrigerated for up to 2 weeks.)

BUTTERMILK WAFFLES

✓ **WHY THIS RECIPE WORKS**
Most "waffle" recipes are merely repurposed pancake recipes that rely on butter and maple syrup to mask the mediocre results. Our waffles had to have a crisp, golden brown crust with a moist, fluffy interior. We started by trying to adapt our Best Buttermilk Pancakes recipe (page 551). The result: the terrific flavor we expected, but a gummy, wet interior and not much crust. We needed a drier batter with much more leavening oomph. In tempura batters, seltzer is often used because the tiny bubbles inflate the batter the same way as a chemical leavener. We tried replacing the buttermilk in our recipe with a mixture of seltzer and powdered buttermilk, plus baking soda for browning. The resulting waffles were light and perfectly browned, but after only a few moments off the heat, they lost their crispness. After some experimentation, we found that waffles made with oil stayed significantly crispier than those made with melted butter, which is partly water. And best of all, tasters didn't notice the swap, just the excellent flavor.

BUTTERMILK WAFFLES

MAKES ABOUT EIGHT 7-INCH
ROUND WAFFLES

While the waffles can be eaten as soon as they are removed from the waffle iron, they will have a crispier exterior if rested in a warm oven for 10 minutes. (This method also makes it possible to serve everyone at the same time.) Buttermilk powder is available in most supermarkets and is generally located near the dried-milk products or in the baking aisle. Leftover buttermilk powder can be kept in the refrigerator for up to a year. Seltzer or club soda gives these waffles a light texture that would otherwise be provided by whipped egg whites. (Avoid sparkling water such as Perrier—it's not bubbly enough.) Use a freshly opened container for maximum lift. Serve waffles with butter and warm maple syrup.

- 2 cups (10 ounces) all-purpose flour
- ½ cup dried buttermilk powder
- 1 tablespoon sugar
- ¾ teaspoon salt
- ½ teaspoon baking soda
- ½ cup sour cream
- 2 large eggs
- ¼ teaspoon vanilla extract
- ¼ cup vegetable oil
- 1¼ cups seltzer water

1. Adjust oven rack to middle position and heat oven to 200 degrees. Set wire rack in rimmed baking sheet; place in oven. Whisk flour, buttermilk powder, sugar, salt, and baking soda together in large bowl. Whisk sour cream, eggs, vanilla, and oil together in medium bowl to combine. Gently stir seltzer into wet ingredients. Make well in center of dry ingredients and pour in wet ingredients. Using a rubber spatula, gently stir until just combined (batter should remain lumpy with few streaks of flour).

2. Heat waffle iron and bake waffles according to manufacturer's instructions (use about ⅓ cup for 7-inch round iron). Transfer waffles to wire rack in preheated oven; repeat with remaining batter. Serve.

YEASTED WAFFLES

✓ **WHY THIS RECIPE WORKS**
Raised waffles are barely on the current culinary radar, and that's a shame. They sound old-fashioned and require an ounce of advance planning, but they are crisp, tasty, and easy to prepare We wanted to revive this breakfast treat with yeasted waffles that were creamy and airy, tangy and salty, refined and complex. We settled on all-purpose flour, found the right amount of yeast to provide a pleasant, tangy flavor, and added a full stick of melted butter for rich flavor. Refrigerating the batter overnight kept the growth of the yeast under control and produced waffles with superior flavor. Even better, now all we had to do in the morning was heat up the iron.

YEASTED WAFFLES

MAKES SEVEN 7-INCH ROUND OR
FOUR 9-INCH SQUARE WAFFLES

While the waffles can be eaten as soon as they are removed from the waffle iron, they will have a crispier exterior if rested in a warm oven for 10 minutes. (This method also makes it possible to serve everyone at the same time.) This batter must be made 12 to 24 hours in advance. We prefer the texture of the waffles made in a classic waffle iron, but a Belgian waffle iron will work, though it will make fewer waffles.

1¾	cups milk
8	tablespoons unsalted butter, cut into 8 pieces
2	cups (10 ounces) all-purpose flour
1	tablespoon sugar
1½	teaspoons instant or rapid-rise yeast
1	teaspoon salt
2	large eggs
1	teaspoon vanilla extract

1. Heat milk and butter in small saucepan over medium-low heat until butter is melted, 3 to 5 minutes. Let mixture cool until warm to touch.

2. Meanwhile, whisk flour, sugar, yeast, and salt together in large bowl. Gradually whisk warm milk mixture into flour mixture; continue to whisk until batter is smooth. Whisk eggs and vanilla together in small bowl until combined, then add egg mixture to batter and whisk until incorporated. Scrape down bowl with rubber spatula, cover bowl with plastic wrap, and refrigerate for at least 12 or up to 24 hours.

3. Adjust oven rack to middle position and heat oven to 200 degrees. Set wire rack in rimmed baking sheet; place in oven. Heat waffle iron according to manufacturer's instructions. Remove batter from refrigerator when waffle iron is hot (batter will be foamy and doubled in size). Whisk batter to recombine (batter will deflate). Bake waffles according to manufacturer's instructions (use about ½ cup for 7-inch round iron and about 1 cup for 9-inch square iron). Transfer waffles to wire rack in preheated oven; repeat with remaining batter. Serve.

BLUEBERRY YEASTED WAFFLES

We found that frozen wild blueberries—which are smaller—work best here. Larger blueberries release too much juice, which burns and becomes bitter when it comes in contact with the waffle iron.

After removing waffle batter from refrigerator in step 3, gently fold 1½ cups frozen blueberries into batter using rubber spatula. Bake waffles as directed.

PERFECT OATMEAL

✔ WHY THIS RECIPE WORKS
The Scottish and the Irish generally eschew rolled oats for the steel-cut variety, but steel-cut oats can be hard and chewy and take ages to cook. We set out to see which variety of oats, cooked in what way, would make the best bowl of oatmeal by our standards: flavorful and creamy without being mushy. After testing several types of oats, we found that steel-cut were worth the wait; the hot cereal they made was nutty and creamy. We toasted them with butter in a skillet to accent the nutty flavor. Steady simmering in a blend of milk and water over medium-low heat proved the best cooking technique. We also found that constant stirring was unnecessary; we only needed to stir during the last several minutes. Resting the oatmeal for a few minutes before serving helped it to thicken, giving up the creamy yet substantial oatmeal we were looking for.

PERFECT OATMEAL

SERVES 3 TO 4

To double the recipe, use a 12-inch skillet to toast the oats and increase the cooking time to 10 to 15 minutes once the salt has been added.

If desired, serve with maple syrup or brown sugar, or one of our toppings for oatmeal (recipes follow).

3	cups water
1	cup whole milk
1	tablespoon unsalted butter
1	cup steel-cut oats
¼	teaspoon salt

1. Bring water and milk to simmer in large saucepan over medium heat. Meanwhile, melt butter in 10-inch skillet over medium heat. Add oats and toast, stirring constantly, until golden and fragrant with butterscotch-like aroma, 1½ to 2 minutes.

2. Stir toasted oats into simmering liquid, reduce heat to medium-low, and simmer gently, until mixture thickens and resembles gravy, about 20 minutes. Add salt and stir lightly with spoon handle. Continue simmering, stirring occasionally with wooden spoon handle, until oats absorb almost all liquid and oatmeal is thick and creamy, with a pudding-like consistency, 7 to 10 minutes. Off heat, let sit uncovered for 5 minutes, then serve.

BANANA-RUM TOPPING WITH TOASTED PECANS

MAKES ABOUT 1 CUP, ENOUGH FOR
1 RECIPE PERFECT OATMEAL

1	tablespoon butter
1	tablespoon packed brown sugar
¼	cup dark rum
1	ripe banana, mashed
¼	cup pecans, toasted and chopped
	Pinch ground allspice

Heat butter and sugar in 8-inch skillet over medium-high heat until melted and bubbling, about 1 minute. Off heat, stir in rum; return skillet to heat and simmer mixture until reduced and syrupy, about 1 minute. Stir in banana, pecans, and allspice. Serve over individual bowls of hot oatmeal.

CRANBERRY-ORANGE TOPPING WITH CIDER AND BROWN SUGAR

MAKES ABOUT ¾ CUP, ENOUGH FOR
1 RECIPE PERFECT OATMEAL

Use more or less brown sugar to sweeten the oatmeal to your liking.

- ¾ cup dried cranberries
- ¾ cup apple cider
- ⅛ teaspoon grated orange zest
- 2–4 tablespoons packed brown sugar

Bring cranberries, cider, and orange zest to simmer in small saucepan over medium-high heat; cook until cranberries are softened and plumped, about 4 minutes. Sprinkle brown sugar over individual bowls of hot oatmeal, top with cranberry mixture, and serve.

HONEYED FIG TOPPING WITH VANILLA AND CINNAMON

MAKES ABOUT 1 CUP, ENOUGH FOR
1 RECIPE PERFECT OATMEAL

Both Turkish and Calimyrna figs work well here.

- 1 cup dried figs, stemmed and quartered
- 1½ tablespoons honey
- 1½ tablespoons water
- ⅛ teaspoon vanilla extract
- ⅛ teaspoon ground cinnamon

Bring all ingredients to simmer in small saucepan over medium-high heat; cook until liquid reduces to glaze, about 4 minutes. Serve over individual bowls of hot oatmeal.

CLASSIC GRANOLA

✔ WHY THIS RECIPE WORKS

For the best granola, we started with the grains. Thick rolled oats were chewy with a pleasant sweetness. The right proportion of nuts, seeds, and dried fruits—as much as or a little more than the amount of oats—gave us a combination of crunch, chewiness, and sweet and tart tastes in every mouthful. Sweetening with both honey and maple syrup, warmed to make coating the granola easier, made it slightly sweet, slightly clumpy, and perfectly moist. During baking, we made sure to stir every five minutes for even browning, and as soon as it was done we turned it out of the pan to cool, preventing over-browning and leaving us with perfectly chewy, crisp, and crumbly granola.

CLASSIC GRANOLA

MAKES ABOUT 7 CUPS

Do not substitute instant or quick oats in this recipe.

- 3 cups old-fashioned rolled oats
- 1 cup walnuts, chopped coarse
- ½ cup unsweetened shredded coconut
- ½ cup slivered almonds
- ¼ cup sesame seeds
- ¼ cup sunflower seeds
- ⅓ cup vegetable oil
- ¼ cup maple syrup
- ¼ cup honey
- 1 cup raisins

1. Adjust oven rack to middle position and heat oven to 325 degrees. Combine oats, walnuts, coconut, almonds, sesame seeds, and sunflower seeds in large bowl.

2. Heat oil, maple syrup, and honey in small saucepan, whisking occasionally, until warm. Pour mixture over dry ingredients. Using spatula, stir until mixture is thoroughly coated. Spread mixture into even layer on rimmed baking sheet.

3. Bake, stirring mixture and re-spreading into even layer every 5 minutes, until granola is light golden brown, about 15 minutes. Immediately transfer granola to second rimmed baking sheet. Stir in raisins, then spread granola into even layer. Set sheet on wire rack and let cool to room temperature. Loosen dried granola with spatula and transfer to airtight container. (Granola can be stored at room temperature for up to 1 week.)

TOAST AND ROAST GRANOLA

MAKES ABOUT 5 CUPS

For clumpy granola, right after you remove the mixture from the oven, press it into a ¾-inch layer with even edges, then press a single layer of paper towels onto the surface. When the granola is cool, remove the towels. Remove the cereal in sections and place in an airtight container. When ready to use, crumble the granola to the desired chunkiness. Do not substitute instant or quick oats in this recipe.

- ½ cup slivered almonds
- ½ cup cashews, chopped
- 2 cups old-fashioned rolled oats
- ⅔ cup unsweetened shredded coconut
- ¼ cup sunflower seeds
- 2 tablespoons sesame seeds
- ¼ cup honey
- ½ cup raisins

1. Adjust oven rack to middle position and heat oven to 325 degrees. Toast nuts in 12-inch skillet over medium heat, stirring often, until just beginning to color, about 3 minutes. Stir in oats and coconut; toast until oats color lightly, about 2 minutes. Add sunflower seeds and sesame seeds; toast, stirring constantly, until mixture turns an even beige, about 1 minute. Off heat, stir in honey until mixture is well coated.

2. Spread mixture into even layer on rimmed baking sheet. Bake, stirring mixture

and re-spreading into even layer, every 5 minutes, until granola is light golden brown, about 15 minutes. Immediately transfer granola to second rimmed baking sheet. Stir in raisins, then spread granola into even layer. Set sheet on wire rack and let cool to room temperature. Loosen dried granola with spatula and transfer to airtight container. (Granola can be stored at room temperature for up to 1 week.)

OVEN-FRIED BACON

✔ **WHY THIS RECIPE WORKS**

Most of us cook bacon by frying it in a pan, but controlling the temperature of a pan on the stovetop takes patience and constant attention, and even then it sometimes seems impossible to avoid getting raw and burnt spots. We'd heard that oven-fried bacon is just as good as fried bacon without the constant tending and the splattering fat, so we thought it was worth a try. The result? Cooking bacon in the oven was in fact just as good, and it even had a couple of advantages. The oven gives you a larger margin of error for perfectly cooked bacon than the frying pan. It also cooks the bacon strips more consistently, without raw or burnt spots. And the only tending needed is turning the pan halfway through cooking. Oven-frying does take a couple of minutes longer than pan-frying (10 to 12 minutes for 12 strips), but you get perfectly crisp, evenly cooked bacon with no hassle.

TEST KITCHEN TIP NO. 112 BACON BY THE SLICE

Bacon is most often sold by the pound or half-pound, but since recipes often call for just a few slices of bacon, you're bound to have some leftovers. And if you're not planning on cooking the rest soon, you may want to freeze it. But since some recipes only call for a slice or two for flavoring, how can you freeze bacon so that you can use each slice as needed? We have found that the best way to keep smaller amounts of bacon on hand is to simply roll one or two slices up tightly, put the rolled bacon in a zipper-lock bag, and freeze it. Then you can pull out the desired number of slices as you need them.

A large rimmed baking sheet is important here to contain the rendered bacon fat. If cooking more than one tray of bacon, switch their oven positions once about halfway through cooking. You can use thin- or thick-cut bacon here, though the cooking times will vary.

12   slices bacon

Adjust oven rack to middle position and heat oven to 400 degrees. Arrange bacon slices in rimmed baking sheet. Cook until fat begins to render, 5 to 6 minutes; rotate pan. Continue cooking until bacon is crisp and brown, 5 to 6 minutes for thin-cut bacon, 8 to 10 minutes for thick-cut bacon. Transfer bacon to paper towel–lined plate, drain, and serve.

DINER-STYLE HOME FRIES

✔ **WHY THIS RECIPE WORKS**

Home fries can be tough to get right—they can turn out greasy, bland, and too spicy. We wanted perfectly seasoned potatoes with a crisp, deep golden brown crust and a tender, moist interior. First, we determined that medium-starch Yukon Gold potatoes worked best. We cooked them briefly in water before sautéing them in a heavy skillet. To get them really brown and crisp, we

learned we needed to let them sit undisturbed in hot fat for a full four to five minutes before the first turn. Sautéed onion bumped up their flavor. A total of three or four more turns over another 10 to 15 minutes and seasoning with salt, pepper, and paprika gave us the delectable golden brown nuggets we wanted.

DINER-STYLE HOME FRIES

SERVES 2 TO 3

If doubling this recipe, instead of crowding the skillet, cook two batches of home fries separately. While making the second batch, keep the first batch hot and crisp by spreading the fries on a baking sheet placed in a 300-degree oven.

2½   tablespoons vegetable oil
1   onion, chopped fine
1   pound Yukon Gold potatoes, cut into ½-inch cubes
1¼   teaspoons salt
1   tablespoon unsalted butter
1   teaspoon paprika
    Pepper

1. Heat 1 tablespoon oil in 12-inch skillet over medium-high heat until shimmering. Add onion and cook, stirring frequently, until browned, 8 to 10 minutes. Transfer to small bowl; set aside.

2. Meanwhile, place potatoes and 1 teaspoon salt in large saucepan, cover with ½ inch water, and bring to boil over high heat. As soon as water begins to boil, drain potatoes thoroughly in colander.

3. Heat remaining 1½ tablespoons oil and butter in now-empty skillet over medium-high heat. Add potatoes and shake skillet to evenly distribute potatoes in single layer, making sure 1 side of each piece is touching skillet. Cook without stirring until potatoes are golden brown on bottom, about 4 to 5 minutes, then carefully

1. First, slice potato lengthwise into quarters.

2. Next, make 2 stacks and cut each stack lengthwise into quarters.

3. Finally, turn stacks 90 degrees and cut horizontally to complete dice.

turn potatoes, making sure potatoes remain in single layer. Repeat process until potatoes are tender and browned on most sides, turning 3 to 4 times, 10 to 15 minutes. Stir in onion, paprika, remaining ¼ teaspoon salt, and pepper to taste and serve.

CLASSIC HASH BROWNS

✔ WHY THIS RECIPE WORKS

A side of freshly made hash browns seems to be a rare breakfast treat these days. We wanted to bring these thin, crisply sautéed potato cakes back to the breakfast table with a great recipe. High-starch russet potatoes worked best; they adhered well, browned beautifully, and had the most pronounced potato flavor. And we found there was no need to precook the potatoes—raw grated potatoes (squeezed of their moisture) held together while cooking and had a more tender interior as well as more potato flavor and an attractive, deeply browned crust. Cooked in a sizzling hot pan with melted butter, these were the very best that hash browns have to offer.

CLASSIC HASH BROWNS
SERVES 4

We prefer hash browns prepared with potatoes that have been cut with the large shredding disk of a food processor, but a box grater can also be used. To prevent potatoes from turning brown, grate them just before cooking.

1   **pound russet potatoes, peeled and shredded**
¼   **teaspoon salt**
      Pepper
1   **tablespoon unsalted butter**

1. Wrap shredded potatoes in clean kitchen towel and squeeze thoroughly of excess moisture. Toss potatoes with ¼ teaspoon salt and pepper to taste.

2. Meanwhile, melt ½ tablespoon butter in 10-inch skillet over medium-high heat until it begins to brown, swirling to coat skillet. Scatter potatoes evenly over entire pan and press to flatten. Reduce heat to medium and cook until dark golden brown and crisp, 7 to 8 minutes.

3. Slide hash browns onto large plate. Add remaining ½ tablespoon butter to skillet and melt, swirling to coat pan. Invert hash browns onto second plate and slide, browned side up, back into skillet. Continue to cook over medium heat until bottom is dark golden brown and crisp, 5 to 6 minutes longer.

4. Fold hash brown cake in half; cook about 1 minute longer. Slide onto serving platter or cutting board, cut into wedges, and serve immediately.

HASH BROWN "OMELET" WITH CHEDDAR, TOMATO, AND BASIL

After melting butter in step 3 and sliding potatoes back into skillet, top hash browns with 1 diced tomato, 1 ounce shredded cheddar cheese, and 1 tablespoon chopped fresh basil. Proceed with recipe, folding potato cake in half and cooking until cheese melts.

OPEN-FACED HASH BROWN "OMELET" WITH HAM, TOMATO, AND SWISS CHEESE

After melting butter in step 2, divide potatoes into 4 equal portions and reduce cooking time to 5 minutes per side, turning them with spatula rather than inverting them using plate. Once potatoes are fully browned, top each with portion of 1 thin slice deli ham, quartered, 1 thinly sliced small tomato, and 1 ounce shredded Swiss cheese. Cover and continue to cook over medium heat until cheese melts, 1 to 2 minutes. Serve immediately.

MAKING HASH BROWNS

1. To release water from shredded potatoes, place them in clean kitchen towel and, using 2 hands, twist towel tightly.

2. Before serving, fold hash brown cake over, omelet style, using spatula. Transfer to cutting board and cut into wedges.

CHAPTER 14 Quick Breads and
Coffee Cakes

QUICK AND EASY CREAM BISCUITS

✓ WHY THIS RECIPE WORKS

We were after a biscuit recipe that would be simpler than the traditional versions that require cutting butter or shortening into flour, rolling out dough, and stamping biscuits. Cream biscuits, which rely on plain heavy cream in lieu of butter or shortening, were our answer to easy-to-make light and tender biscuits. While most biscuit dough should be handled lightly, we found this dough benefited from 30 seconds of kneading. Although it was easy enough to quickly shape the dough with our hands then stamp out rounds, alternatively we found we could shape the dough using an 8-inch cake pan, then turn the dough out onto the counter and cut it into wedges. Popping the shaped biscuits into the oven immediately kept them from spreading.

QUICK AND EASY CREAM BISCUITS
MAKES 8 BISCUITS

These biscuits come together in a flash and require no special equipment.

- 2   cups (10 ounces) all-purpose flour
- 2   teaspoons sugar
- 2   teaspoons baking powder
- ½   teaspoon salt
- 1½ cups heavy cream

1. Adjust oven rack to upper-middle position and heat oven to 450 degrees. Line baking sheet with parchment paper.

2. Whisk flour, sugar, baking powder, and salt together in medium bowl. Stir in cream with wooden spoon until dough forms, about 30 seconds. Turn dough out onto lightly floured counter and gather into ball. Knead dough briefly until smooth, about 30 seconds.

3. Shape dough into ¾-inch-thick circle. Cut dough into rounds with 2½-inch biscuit cutter or cut into wedges. Place rounds or wedges on prepared baking sheet. Bake until golden brown, about 15 minutes, rotating baking sheet halfway through baking. Serve.

CREAM BISCUITS WITH CHEDDAR CHEESE

Stir 2 ounces sharp cheddar cheese, cut into ¼-inch pieces, into flour along with sugar, baking powder, and salt. Increase baking time to 18 minutes.

CREAM BISCUITS WITH CRYSTALLIZED GINGER

Add 3 tablespoons minced crystallized ginger to flour along with sugar, baking powder, and salt. Before baking, brush tops of biscuits with 1 tablespoon heavy cream and sprinkle with 1 tablespoon sugar.

CREAM BISCUITS WITH FRESH HERBS

Any herb or combination of herbs will work here.

Whisk 2 tablespoons minced fresh herbs into flour along with sugar, baking powder, and salt.

EASY BUTTERMILK DROP BISCUITS

✓ WHY THIS RECIPE WORKS

We wanted a drop biscuit recipe that would offer a no-nonsense alternative to traditional rolled biscuits, with the same tenderness and buttery flavor. Too many drop biscuits are dense, gummy, and doughy or lean and dry; we wanted a biscuit that could be easily broken apart and eaten piece by buttery piece.

Identifying the best ingredients was the first task. While oil-based biscuits are easy to work with, they lack flavor, so butter was a must. Replacing the usual milk with buttermilk helped heighten the flavor; the biscuits now had a rich, buttery tang and were crisper on the exterior and fluffier on the interior. Choosing the right leavener was also important. We needed a substantial amount, but too much baking powder left a metallic taste. Since we'd added buttermilk, we could replace some of the baking powder with baking soda (buttermilk provides

---

SHAPING CREAM BISCUITS

FOR ROUNDS

1. Pat dough on lightly floured counter into ¾-inch-thick circle.

2. Punch out dough rounds with floured 2½-inch biscuit cutter. Repeat patting and punching dough rounds for a total of 8 biscuits.

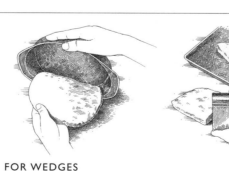

FOR WEDGES

1. Press dough into 8-inch cake pan, then turn dough out onto lightly floured counter.

2. Using bench scraper or sharp knife, cut dough into 8 wedges.

the acid that soda needs to act), which gave us the rise we needed without the metallic bitterness. Now we were left with only one problem. Properly combining the butter and buttermilk requires that both ingredients be at just the right temperature; if they aren't, the melted butter clumps in the buttermilk. Since this was supposed to be an easy recipe, we tried making a batch with the lumpy buttermilk. The result was a surprisingly better biscuit, slightly higher and with better texture. The water in the lumps of butter turned to steam in the oven, helping create additional height.

EASY BUTTERMILK DROP BISCUITS
MAKES 12 BISCUITS

A ¼ cup portion scoop can be used to portion the batter. To refresh day-old biscuits, heat them in a 300-degree oven for 10 minutes.

2	cups (10 ounces) all-purpose flour
2	teaspoons baking powder
½	teaspoon baking soda
1	teaspoon sugar
¾	teaspoon salt
1	cup buttermilk, chilled
8	tablespoons unsalted butter, melted and cooled slightly, plus 2 tablespoons melted

1. Adjust oven rack to middle position and heat oven to 475 degrees. Line rimmed baking sheet with parchment paper. Whisk flour, baking powder, baking soda, sugar, and salt in large bowl. Combine buttermilk and 8 tablespoons melted butter in medium bowl, stirring until butter forms small clumps.

2. Add buttermilk mixture to flour mixture and stir with rubber spatula until just incorporated and batter pulls away from sides of bowl. Using greased ¼-cup dry measure and working quickly, scoop level amount of batter and drop onto prepared baking sheet (biscuits should measure about 2¼ inches in diameter and 1¼ inches high). Repeat with remaining batter, spacing biscuits about 1½ inches apart. Bake until tops are golden brown and crisp, 12 to 14 minutes.

3. Brush biscuit tops with remaining 2 tablespoons melted butter. Transfer to wire rack and let cool for 5 minutes before serving.

FLAKY BUTTERMILK BISCUITS

✔ WHY THIS RECIPE WORKS
Truly flaky biscuits have become scarce, while their down-market imitators (think supermarket "tube" biscuits) are alarmingly common. We wanted to achieve a really flaky—not fluffy—biscuit, with a golden, crisp crust surrounding striated layers of tender, buttery dough. While ingredients (lard versus butter, buttermilk versus milk, and so on) influence texture and flavor, we discovered that the secret to the fluffy/flaky distinction is how the ingredients are handled: flaky butter equals flaky biscuits. To get "flaky" butter, we abandoned the food processor and worked thin slices into the flour by hand. Next, we rolled and folded the dough to flatten the butter into thin sheets sandwiched between equally thin layers of flour (as with puff pastry). In the oven, the butter melted and steam filled the thin spaces left behind, creating the flaky layers. Once we further tenderized the recipe by swapping a little shortening for some of the butter and softened the impact of the buttermilk with a little baking soda, we had an ultra-flaky biscuit with rich flavor.

FLAKY BUTTERMILK BISCUITS
MAKES 12 BISCUITS

The dough is a bit sticky when it comes together and during the first set of turns. Note that you will use up to 1 cup of flour for dusting the work surface, dough, and rolling pin to prevent sticking. Be careful not to incorporate large pockets of flour into the dough when folding it over. When cutting the biscuits, press down with firm, even pressure; do not twist the cutter.

2½	cups (12½ ounces) all-purpose flour
1	tablespoon baking powder
½	teaspoon baking soda
1	teaspoon salt
2	tablespoons vegetable shortening, cut into ½-inch chunks
8	tablespoons unsalted butter, chilled, lightly floured, and cut into ⅛-inch slices plus 2 tablespoons melted and cooled
1¼	cups buttermilk, chilled

1. Adjust oven rack to lower-middle position and heat oven to 450 degrees. Whisk flour, baking powder, baking soda, and salt in large bowl.

2. Add shortening to flour mixture; break up chunks with fingertips until only small, pea-size pieces remain. Working with a few butter slices at a time, drop butter slices into flour mixture and toss to coat. Pick up each slice of butter and press between well-floured fingertips into flat, nickel-size pieces. Repeat until all butter is incorporated, then toss to combine. Freeze mixture (in bowl) until chilled, about 15 minutes, or refrigerate for about 30 minutes.

TEST KITCHEN TIP NO. 113   **WHEN BAKING POWDER LOSES ITS PUNCH**

Over time, baking powder (which includes baking soda, acid, salt, and cornstarch), loses its ability to produce carbon dioxide and give baked goods their lift—sooner than many producers claim. We compared biscuits made with cans that had been opened and stored 1 month all the way up to a year. The rise of the biscuits began to decline to half the height of fresh at the 10-month mark. For best results, replace your baking powder (and soda) every 6 months.

3. Spray 24-inch-square area of counter with vegetable oil spray; spread spray evenly across surface with clean kitchen towel or paper towel. Sprinkle ⅓ cup flour across sprayed area, then gently spread flour across work surface with palm to form thin, even coating. Add 1 cup plus 2 tablespoons buttermilk to flour mixture. Stir briskly with fork until ball forms and no dry bits of flour are visible, adding remaining 2 tablespoons buttermilk as needed (dough will be sticky and shaggy but should clear sides of bowl). With rubber spatula, transfer dough onto center of prepared counter, dust surface lightly with flour, and, with floured hands, bring dough together into cohesive ball.

4. Pat dough into approximate 10-inch square, then roll into 18 by 14-inch rectangle about ¼ inch thick, dusting dough and rolling pin with flour as needed. Use bench scraper or thin metal spatula to fold dough into thirds, brushing any excess flour from surface of dough. Lift short end of dough and fold in thirds again to form approximate 6 by 4-inch rectangle. Rotate dough 90 degrees, dusting counter underneath with flour, then roll and fold dough again, dusting with flour as needed.

5. Roll dough into 10-inch square about ½ inch thick. Flip dough over and cut nine 3-inch rounds with floured 3-inch biscuit cutter, dipping cutter back into flour after each cut. Carefully invert and transfer rounds to ungreased baking sheet,

spacing them 1 inch apart. Gather dough scraps into ball and roll and fold once or twice until scraps form smooth dough. Roll dough into ½-inch-thick round and cut 3 more 3-inch rounds and transfer to baking sheet. Discard excess dough.

6. Brush biscuit tops with melted butter. Bake, without opening oven door, until tops are golden brown and crisp, 15 to 17 minutes. Let cool on baking sheet for 5 to 10 minutes before serving.

FLAKY BUTTERMILK BISCUITS WITH PARMESAN

Add ¼ cup finely grated Parmesan cheese, ¼ teaspoon pepper, and ⅛ teaspoon cayenne pepper to flour mixture in step 1. Sprinkle dough rounds with another ¼ cup finely grated Parmesan after brushing with melted butter in step 6.

BLUEBERRY SCONES

✓ WHY THIS RECIPE WORKS

More often berries weigh down scones and impart little flavor. Starting with traditional scone recipes, we increased the amounts of sugar and butter to add sweetness and richness; a combination of whole milk and sour cream lent more richness as well as tang. To lighten our scones, we borrowed a technique from puff

pastry, where the dough is turned, rolled, and folded multiple times to create layers that are forced apart by steam when baked. To ensure that the butter would stay as cold and solid as possible while baking, we froze it and grated it into the dry ingredients using a box grater. Adding the blueberries to the dry ingredients meant they got mashed when we mixed the dough, but when we added them to the already-mixed dough, we ruined our pockets of butter. The solution was pressing the berries into the dough, rolling the dough into a log, then pressing the log into a rectangle and cutting the scones.

BLUEBERRY SCONES
MAKES 8 SCONES

It is important to work the dough as little as possible—work quickly and knead and fold the dough only the number of times called for or else the scones will turn out tough, rather than tender. The butter should be frozen solid before grating. In hot or humid environments, chill the flour mixture and mixing bowls before use. While this recipe calls for 2 whole sticks of butter, only 10 tablespoons are actually used (see step 1). If fresh berries are unavailable, an equal amount of frozen berries, not thawed, can be substituted. An equal amount of raspberries, blackberries, or strawberries can be used in place of the blueberries. Cut larger berries into ¼- to ½-inch pieces before incorporating. Serve with Homemade Clotted Cream (recipe follows), if desired.

GIVING FLAKY BISCUITS THE LAYERED LOOK

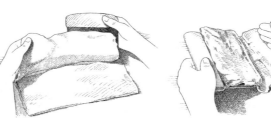

MAKING THIN PIECES OF BUTTER

1. After coating butter with flour to prevent sticking, cut butter into ⅛-inch-thick slices.

2. Pinch butter between floured fingertips into flat, nickel-size pieces.

FOLDING AND TURNING THE DOUGH

1. After mixing, patting, and rolling dough, use bench scraper to fold dough into thirds.

2. Fold dough into thirds again, rotate it 90 degrees, roll out and repeat folding and turning.

16 tablespoons unsalted butter (2 sticks), each stick frozen
7½ ounces (1½ cups) blueberries
½ cup whole milk
½ cup sour cream
2 cups (10 ounces) all-purpose flour
½ cup (3½ ounces) plus 1 tablespoon sugar
2 teaspoons baking powder
¼ teaspoon baking soda
½ teaspoon salt
1 teaspoon grated lemon zest

1. Adjust oven rack to middle position and heat oven to 425 degrees. Line baking sheet with parchment paper. Remove half of wrapper from each stick of frozen butter. Grate unwrapped ends (half of each stick) on large holes of box grater (you should grate total of 8 tablespoons). Place grated butter in freezer until needed. Melt 2 tablespoons of remaining ungrated butter and set aside. Save remaining 6 tablespoons butter for another use. Place blueberries in freezer until needed.

2. Whisk milk and sour cream together in medium bowl; refrigerate until needed. Whisk flour, ½ cup sugar, baking powder, baking soda, salt, and lemon zest in medium bowl. Add frozen grated butter to flour mixture and toss with fingers until butter is thoroughly coated.

3. Add milk mixture to flour mixture and fold with rubber spatula until just combined. Using spatula, transfer dough to liberally floured counter. Dust surface of dough with flour and with floured hands, knead dough 6 to 8 times, until it just holds together in ragged ball, adding flour as needed to prevent sticking.

4. Roll dough into approximate 12-inch square. Fold dough into thirds like a business letter, using bench scraper or metal spatula to release dough if it sticks to counter. Lift short ends of dough and fold into thirds again to form approximate 4-inch square. Transfer dough to plate

1. Fold dough into thirds (like business letter).

2. Fold in ends of dough to form 4-inch square, then chill dough in freezer for 5 minutes.

3. Reroll dough into 12-inch square, then press berries into dough.

4. Roll dough into jellyroll-like log to incorporate blueberries.

5. Arrange log seam side down and press into even 12 by 4-inch rectangle.

6. Cut dough crosswise into 4 rectangles, then diagonally to make 8 triangular pieces.

lightly dusted with flour and chill in freezer 5 minutes.

5. Transfer dough to floured counter and roll into approximate 12-inch square again. Sprinkle blueberries evenly over surface of dough, then press down so they are slightly embedded in dough. Using bench scraper or thin metal spatula, loosen dough from counter. Roll dough into cylinder, pressing to form tight log. Arrange log seam side down and press into 12 by 4-inch rectangle. Using sharp, floured knife, cut rectangle crosswise into 4 equal rectangles. Cut each rectangle diagonally to form 2 triangles and transfer to prepared baking sheet.

6. Brush tops with melted butter and sprinkle with remaining 1 tablespoon sugar. Bake until tops and bottoms are golden brown, 18 to 25 minutes. Transfer to wire rack and let cool for at least 10 minutes before serving.

TO MAKE AHEAD: After placing scones on baking sheet in step 5, either refrigerate them overnight or freeze for up to 1 month. When ready to bake, for refrigerated scones, heat oven to 425 degrees and follow directions in step 6. For frozen scones, do not thaw, heat oven to 375 degrees and follow directions in step 6, extending cooking time to 25 to 30 minutes.

HOMEMADE CLOTTED CREAM
MAKES 2 CUPS

Ultra-pasteurized heavy cream can be substituted but the resulting cream will be not as flavorful and tangy. This recipe can be halved or doubled as needed.

1½ cups pasteurized (not ultra-pasteurized) heavy cream
½ cup buttermilk

Combine cream and buttermilk in jar or measuring cup. Stir, cover, and let stand at room temperature until mixture has thickened to the consistency of softly whipped cream, 12 to 24 hours. Refrigerate; cream will continue to thicken as it chills. (Clotted cream can be refrigerated for up to 10 days.)

OATMEAL SCONES

✓ WHY THIS RECIPE WORKS

The oatmeal scones served in a typical coffee-house are so dry and leaden that they seem like a ploy to get people to buy more coffee to wash them down. We wanted rich toasted oat flavor in a tender, flaky, not-too-sweet scone. Whole rolled oats and quick oats performed better than instant and steel-cut oats, and toasting the oats brought out their nutty flavor. We used a minimal amount of sugar and baking powder, but plenty of cold butter. A mixture of milk and heavy cream added richness without making these scones too heavy. An egg proved to be the ultimate touch of richness. Cutting the cold butter into the flour, instead of using melted butter, resulted in a lighter texture. A very hot oven made the scones rise spectacularly, gave them a craggy appearance, and meant less time in the oven and therefore less time to dry out.

RICH AND TENDER OATMEAL SCONES

MAKES 8 SCONES

Rolled oats will give the scones a deeper oat flavor, but the quick-cooking oats will create a softer texture; either type will work here. Half-and-half is a suitable substitute for the milk and cream combination.

1½	cups (4½ ounces) old-fashioned rolled oats or quick oats
¼	cup whole milk
¼	cup heavy cream
1	large egg
1½	cups (7½ ounces) all-purpose flour
⅓	cup (2⅓ ounces) plus 1 tablespoon sugar
2	teaspoons baking powder
½	teaspoon salt
10	tablespoons unsalted butter, cut into ½-inch cubes and chilled

1. Adjust oven rack to middle position and heat oven to 375 degrees. Spread oats evenly on baking sheet and toast in oven until fragrant and lightly browned, 7 to 9 minutes; let cool on wire rack. Increase oven temperature to 450 degrees. When oats are cooled, measure out 2 tablespoons for dusting counter and set aside. Line second baking sheet with parchment paper.

2. Whisk milk, cream, and egg in large measuring cup until incorporated. Reserve 1 tablespoon in small bowl for glazing and set aside.

3. Pulse flour, ⅓ cup sugar, baking powder, and salt in food processor until combined, about 4 pulses. Scatter butter evenly over dry ingredients and pulse until mixture resembles coarse cornmeal, 12 to 14 pulses. Transfer mixture to medium bowl and stir in cooled oats. Using rubber spatula, fold in liquid ingredients until large clumps form. Mix dough by hand in bowl until dough forms cohesive mass.

4. Dust counter with 1 tablespoon reserved oats, turn dough out onto counter, and dust top with remaining 1 tablespoon reserved oats. Gently pat dough into 7-inch circle about 1 inch thick. Using bench scraper or chef's knife, cut dough into 8 wedges and place on prepared baking sheet, spacing wedges about 2 inches apart. Brush tops with reserved egg mixture and sprinkle with remaining 1 tablespoon sugar. Bake until golden brown, 12 to 14 minutes. Let scones cool on baking sheet on wire rack for 5 minutes, then transfer scones to wire rack and let cool to room temperature, about 30 minutes. Serve.

TO MAKE AHEAD: After placing scones on baking sheet in step 4, either refrigerate them overnight or freeze for up to 1 month. When ready to bake, bake as directed. For frozen scones, do not thaw, heat oven to 375 degrees, increasing baking time to 25 to 30 minutes.

CINNAMON-RAISIN OATMEAL SCONES

Add ¼ teaspoon cinnamon to food processor with flour and ½ cup raisins to flour-butter mixture with toasted oats.

APRICOT-ALMOND OATMEAL SCONES

Reduce oats to 1 cup and toast ½ cup slivered almonds with oats in step 1. Add ½ cup chopped dried apricots to flour-butter mixture with toasted oats and almonds.

GLAZED MAPLE-PECAN OATMEAL SCONES

Toast ½ cup chopped pecans with oats in step 1. Omit sugar and whisk ¼ cup maple syrup into milk mixture. When scones are cool, whisk 3 tablespoons maple syrup and ½ cup confectioners' sugar until combined, then drizzle over scones.

OATMEAL SCONES WITH DRIED CHERRIES AND HAZELNUTS

Reduce oats to 1¼ cups and toast ¼ cup chopped hazelnuts with oats in step 1. Stir ½ cup chopped dried tart cherries into flour-butter mixture with toasted oats.

TEST KITCHEN TIP NO. 114 STORING BISCUITS, QUICK BREADS, AND MUFFINS

Most leftover biscuits, scones, and muffins can be stored in a zipper-lock bag at room temperature for up to 3 days. If they include perishable flavorings like bacon, it is best to refrigerate them. When ready to serve, just refresh them by placing them on a baking sheet and warming them in a 300-degree oven for about 10 minutes before serving.

CREAM SCONES

✓ **WHY THIS RECIPE WORKS**

Traditional British scones are essentially fluffy biscuits. These scones should be sweet, but not too sweet, so that they can be enjoyed with jam and perhaps clotted cream. For a light, tender texture, we tried cake flour, but it made gummy scones. All-purpose flour, on the other hand, gave us light, feathery scones. A modest amount of sugar kept the sweetness level in check and there was no question we would rely on butter over shortening for best flavor. Heavy cream gave our scones a rich, not-too-dry character. A food processor made quick work of incorporating the butter into the flour; we stirred in the cream by hand and then lightly kneaded the dough before cutting it into wedges. We also found it was important to get the scones into the oven immediately after cutting them out for the best rise. While currants are traditional in British scones, we left them as optional.

SIMPLE CREAM SCONES
MAKES 8

Resist the urge to eat the scones hot out of the oven, as letting them cool for at least 10 minutes firms them up and improves their texture.

- 2 cups (10 ounces) all-purpose flour
- 3 tablespoons sugar
- 1 tablespoon baking powder
- ½ teaspoon salt
- 5 tablespoons unsalted butter, cut into ¼-inch pieces and chilled
- ½ cup dried currants (optional)
- 1 cup heavy cream

1. Adjust oven rack to middle position and heat oven to 450 degrees. Line baking sheet with parchment paper.

2. Pulse flour, sugar, baking powder, and salt together in food processor to combine, about 3 pulses. Scatter butter evenly over top and continue to pulse until mixture resembles coarse meal with some slightly larger pieces of butter, about 12 more pulses. Transfer mixture to large bowl and stir in currants, if using. Stir in cream until dough begins to form, about 30 seconds.

3. Turn dough and any floury bits out onto floured counter and knead until rough, slightly sticky ball forms, 5 to 10 seconds. Pat dough into 9-inch round and cut into 8 wedges.

4. Place wedges on prepared baking sheet. Bake until tops of scones are lightly golden brown, 12 to 15 minutes, rotating baking sheet halfway through baking. Transfer baking sheet to wire rack and let cool for at least 10 minutes. Serve warm or at room temperature.

SIMPLE GINGER CREAM SCONES

Substitute ½ cup coarsely chopped crystallized ginger for currants.

SIMPLE CRANBERRY-ORANGE CREAM SCONES

Add 1 teaspoon grated fresh orange zest with butter and substitute ¾ cup dried cranberries for currants.

BAKERY-STYLE MUFFINS

✓ **WHY THIS RECIPE WORKS**

We wanted jumbo bakery-size muffins with a rich full flavor and a thick, crisp crust protecting its fragile, tender crumb. We began by testing mixing techniques and chose creaming, which produced the most tender crumb. Increasing the butter and sugar made for a richly flavored muffin, perfect served on its own with jam or as a base for add-ins like dried fruit, citrus zest, nuts, and even chocolate chips. Liquids were up next, and we found that low-fat yogurt delivered the finest crumb and the most rounded and crusty top. And to ensure these muffins got that big rounded top we were after, we increased the amount of batter by one-third.

SIMPLE BAKERY-STYLE MUFFINS
MAKES 12 MUFFINS

If you are short on time, you can melt the butter, mix it with the eggs, and stir it into the dry ingredients. When thoroughly mixed, beat in the yogurt and proceed with the recipe. To cinnamon-coat muffin tops, dip warm muffins in melted butter, then in mixture of ½ cup granulated sugar and 2 teaspoons cinnamon. Serve these muffins warm with jam.

- 3 cups (15 ounces) all-purpose flour
- 1 tablespoon baking powder
- ½ teaspoon baking soda
- ½ teaspoon salt
- 10 tablespoons unsalted butter, softened
- 1¾ cups (12¼ ounces) plus 3 tablespoons sugar
- 2 large eggs
- 1½ cups plain low-fat yogurt

1. Adjust oven rack to lower-middle position and heat oven to 375 degrees. Spray 12-cup muffin tin with vegetable oil spray. Mix flour, baking powder, baking soda, and salt in medium bowl and set aside.

2. Using stand mixer fitted with paddle, beat butter and sugar on medium-high speed until pale and fluffy, about 3 minutes. Add eggs, one at a time, and beat until combined. Reduce speed to low and add dry ingredients in 2 additions, alternating with 3 additions of yogurt, scraping down bowl as needed. Give batter final stir by hand.

3. Using ice cream scoop or large spoon, divide batter evenly among prepared muffin cups. Bake until muffins are golden brown and toothpick inserted in center of muffin comes out with few crumbs attached, 25 to 30 minutes, rotating muffin tin halfway through baking. Invert muffins onto wire rack, stand muffins upright, and let cool 5 minutes. Serve.

MOCHA CHIP MUFFINS

Dissolve 3 tablespoons instant espresso powder in yogurt before adding to batter and fold 1 cup semisweet chocolate chips into finished batter.

APRICOT-ALMOND MUFFINS

Cream 1 ounce almond paste with butter and sugar and fold 1½ cups dried apricots, chopped fine, into finished batter. Sprinkle batter with ½ cup sliced almonds before baking.

RASPBERRY-ALMOND MUFFINS

We like raspberry jam here but any jam will work.

Cream 1 ounce almond paste with butter and sugar. In step 3, spoon half-portion batter into each muffin cup, then with small spoon make well in center of each portion of batter. Spoon about 1 teaspoon raspberry jam into each well. Fill cups with remaining batter and proceed as directed.

LEMON-BLUEBERRY MUFFINS

Add 1 teaspoon grated lemon zest to butter-sugar mixture and fold 7½ ounces blueberries into finished batter.

BANANA-WALNUT MUFFINS

Substitute 1 cup packed light brown sugar for granulated sugar. Add ½ teaspoon ground nutmeg to flour mixture in step 1, and fold 3 small bananas, chopped fine (about 1½ cups), and ¾ cup chopped walnuts into finished batter.

LEMON–POPPY SEED MUFFINS

Add 3 tablespoons poppy seeds to flour mixture and 1 tablespoon grated lemon zest to butter-sugar mixture. While muffins

are baking, heat ¼ cup sugar and ¼ cup lemon juice in small saucepan until sugar dissolves and mixture forms light syrup, 3 to 4 minutes. Brush warm syrup over warm muffins.

OLD-FASHIONED BLUEBERRY MUFFINS

✔ WHY THIS RECIPE WORKS

Blueberry muffins, for all of their simple, warm appeal, have a host of problems, as they emerge from the oven too sweet, too rough, too dense, or just plain bland, with little to no real blueberry flavor. We wanted smaller, more delicate muffins, with a balanced fresh blueberry flavor. For this more delicate texture, we decided to forget creaming the butter and sugar and instead whisked the sugar with melted butter. Then we added sour cream and gently folded in the dry ingredients. Using frozen wild blueberries meant we could enjoy these muffins year-round, and coating the muffin tops with a frosty sugar glaze ensured these muffins would disappear as quickly as we could make them.

OLD-FASHIONED BLUEBERRY MUFFINS
MAKES 12 MUFFINS

This recipe does not require a stand mixer, but when making the batter, be sure to whisk vigorously in step 2, then fold carefully in step 3. There should be no large pockets of flour in the finished batter, but small occasional spots may remain. Do not overmix the batter. These muffins are great unadorned, but for an extra flourish, dip warm muffins in melted butter, then in mixture of ½ cup granulated sugar and two teaspoons cinnamon.

- 2 cups (10 ounces) all-purpose flour
- 1 tablespoon baking powder
- ½ teaspoon salt
- 1 large egg

- 1 cup (7 ounces) sugar
- 4 tablespoons unsalted butter, melted and cooled
- 1¼ cups sour cream
- 6 ounces (1½ cups) frozen blueberries, preferably wild

1. Adjust oven rack to middle position and heat oven to 350 degrees. Spray 12-cup muffin tin with vegetable oil spray.

2. Whisk flour, baking powder, and salt in medium bowl until combined. Whisk egg in second medium bowl until well-combined and light-colored, about 20 seconds. Add sugar and whisk vigorously until thick and homogeneous, about 30 seconds. Add melted butter in 2 or 3 steps, whisking to combine after each addition. Add sour cream in 2 steps, whisking until just combined.

3. Add blueberries to dry ingredients and gently toss to combine. Add sour cream mixture and carefully fold with rubber spatula until batter comes together and berries are evenly distributed, 25 to 30 seconds (small spots of flour may remain and batter will be thick). Do not overmix.

4. Using ice cream scoop or large spoon, divide batter evenly among prepared muffin cups. Bake until muffins are golden brown and toothpick inserted in center of muffin comes out with few crumbs attached, 25 to 30 minutes, rotating muffing tin halfway through baking. Invert muffins onto wire rack, stand muffins upright, and let cool for 5 minutes. Serve.

LEMON-GLAZED OR GINGER-GLAZED BLUEBERRY MUFFINS

While muffins are baking, mix 1 teaspoon grated lemon zest or grated fresh ginger and ½ cup sugar in small bowl and set aside. Bring ¼ cup lemon juice and ¼ cup sugar to simmer in small saucepan over medium heat and simmer until mixture is thick and syrupy and reduced to about

4 tablespoons. After muffins have cooled for 5 minutes, brush tops with glaze, then, working one at a time, dip tops in lemon-sugar or ginger-sugar. Set muffins upright on wire rack and serve.

BLUEBERRY SWIRL MUFFINS

✔ WHY THIS RECIPE WORKS
Blueberry muffins should be packed with blueberry flavor and boast a moist crumb. But too often, the blueberry flavor is fleeting, thanks to the fact that the berries in the produce aisle have suffered from long-distance shipping. We wanted blueberry muffins that put the berry flavor at the forefront and would taste great with blueberries of any origin, even the watery supermarket kind. To achieve this goal, we tried combining blueberry jam with fresh supermarket blueberries. The muffins baked up with a pretty blue filling, but tasters thought the jam made them too sweet. To solve this, we made our own fresh, low-sugar berry jam by simmering fresh blueberries on the stovetop with a bit of sugar. Adding our cooled homemade jam to the batter along with fresh, uncooked berries gave us the best of both worlds: intense blueberry flavor and the liquid burst that only fresh berries could provide. As for the muffin base, we found that the quick-bread method—whisking together eggs and sugar before adding milk and melted butter, and then gently folding in the dry ingredients—produced a hearty, substantial crumb that could support a generous amount of fruit. We found that an equal amount of butter and oil gave us just the right combination of buttery flavor and moist, tender texture. To make the muffins even richer, we swapped the whole milk for buttermilk. Finally, for a nice crunch, we sprinkled lemon-scented sugar on top of the batter just before baking.

BLUEBERRY SWIRL MUFFINS
MAKES 12 MUFFINS

If buttermilk is unavailable, substitute ¾ cup plain whole-milk or low-fat yogurt thinned with ¼ cup milk.

LEMON-SUGAR TOPPING
⅓   cup (2⅓ ounces) sugar
1½   teaspoons grated lemon zest

MUFFINS
10   ounces (2 cups) blueberries
1⅛   cups (7¾ ounces) plus 1 teaspoon sugar
2½   cups (12½ ounces) all-purpose flour
2½   teaspoons baking powder
1   teaspoon salt
2   large eggs
4   tablespoons unsalted butter, melted and cooled
¼   cup vegetable oil
1   cup buttermilk
1½   teaspoons vanilla extract

1. FOR THE TOPPING: Stir together sugar and lemon zest in small bowl until combined and set aside.

2. FOR THE MUFFINS: Adjust oven rack to upper-middle position and heat oven to 425 degrees. Spray 12-cup muffin tin with vegetable oil spray. Bring 1 cup blueberries and 1 teaspoon sugar to simmer in small saucepan over medium heat. Cook, mashing berries with spoon several times and stirring frequently, until berries have broken down and mixture is thickened and reduced to ¼ cup, about 6 minutes. Transfer to small bowl and let cool to room temperature, 10 to 15 minutes.

3. Whisk flour, baking powder, and salt together in large bowl. Whisk remaining 1⅛ cups sugar and eggs together in medium bowl until thick and homogeneous, about 45 seconds. Slowly whisk in butter and oil until combined. Whisk in buttermilk and vanilla until combined. Using rubber spatula, fold egg mixture and remaining 1 cup blueberries into flour mixture until just moistened. (Batter will be very lumpy with few spots of dry flour; do not overmix.)

4. Using ice cream scoop or large spoon, divide batter evenly among prepared muffin cups (batter should completely fill cups and mound slightly). Spoon 1 teaspoon of cooked berry mixture into center of each mound of batter. Using chopstick or skewer, gently swirl berry filling into batter using figure-eight motion. Sprinkle lemon sugar evenly over muffins.

5. Bake until muffins are golden brown and toothpick inserted in center of muffin comes out with few crumbs attached, 17 to 19 minutes, rotating muffin tin halfway through baking. Let muffins cool in tin for 5 minutes, then transfer to wire rack and let cool for 5 minutes before serving.

BLUEBERRY SWIRL MUFFINS WITH FROZEN BLUEBERRIES

Substitute 8 ounces frozen blueberries for fresh blueberries. Cook 1 cup blueberries as directed in step 2. Rinse remaining berries under cold water and dry well. Proceed with recipe from step 3 as directed.

BLUEBERRY SWIRL MUFFINS WITH STREUSEL TOPPING

Omit Lemon-Sugar Topping. Instead combine 3 tablespoons granulated sugar, 3 tablespoons packed dark brown sugar, pinch salt, and ½ cup plus 3 tablespoons all-purpose flour in small bowl. Drizzle with 5 tablespoons warm, melted unsalted butter and toss with fork until evenly moistened and mixture forms large chunks with some pea-size pieces throughout. Proceed with recipe as directed, sprinkling streusel topping over muffins before baking.

BLUEBERRY SWIRL MUFFINS WITH ORANGE GLAZE

Turbinado sugar is often sold as Sugar in the Raw.

Omit Lemon-Sugar Topping. Add 2 teaspoons grated orange zest to egg mixture. Proceed with recipe as directed, sprinkling 4 teaspoons turbinado sugar over muffins before baking. While muffins cool, whisk together 1 cup confectioners' sugar and 1½ tablespoons orange juice until smooth. Drizzle each cooled muffin with 2 teaspoons glaze before serving.

BLUEBERRY SWIRL MUFFINS WITH ALMOND CRUNCH TOPPING

Turbinado sugar is often sold as Sugar in the Raw.

Omit Lemon-Sugar Topping. Instead combine ⅓ cup finely ground almonds and 4 teaspoons turbinado sugar in step 1 for topping and set aside. Add ⅓ cup finely ground almonds to flour mixture. Proceed with recipe as directed, adding 1 teaspoon almond extract to batter with vanilla extract and sprinkling almond topping over muffins before baking.

CRANBERRY-PECAN MUFFINS

✓ WHY THIS RECIPE WORKS

To tame the harsh bite of the cranberries found in most cranberry-nut muffins, we chopped the cranberries in a food processor and tossed them with confectioners' sugar and a little salt (which we often use to tame the bitterness in eggplant). As for the nuts, we took a cue from cakes made with nut flour and augmented some of the all-purpose flour with pecan flour (made by grinding pecans in a food processor). These muffins boasted a rich, hearty crumb. But because we were working with less flour, our muffins spread rather than baking up tall and self-contained. We fixed the problem by letting the batter rest for 30 minutes. This allowed what flour there

was to become more hydrated, resulting in a properly thickened batter that baked up perfectly domed. To replace the missing crunch of the nuts, we simply topped the muffins with a pecan streusel.

CRANBERRY-PECAN MUFFINS
MAKES 12 MUFFINS

If fresh cranberries aren't available, substitute frozen cranberries and microwave on high power until they are partially thawed, 30 to 45 seconds.

STREUSEL TOPPING

- ¼ cup (1¼ ounces) all-purpose flour
- 2 tablespoons packed light brown sugar
- 2 tablespoons granulated sugar
- 2 tablespoons unsalted butter, cut into ½-inch pieces, and softened
- ½ cup pecans

MUFFINS

- 1⅓ cups (6⅔ ounces) all-purpose flour
- 2 teaspoons baking powder
- 1 teaspoon salt
- 1¼ cups pecans, toasted and cooled
- 1 cup (7½ ounces) plus 1 tablespoon granulated sugar
- 2 large eggs
- 6 tablespoons unsalted butter, melted and cooled
- ½ cup whole milk
- 8 ounces (2 cups) fresh cranberries
- 1 tablespoon confectioners' sugar

1. Adjust oven rack to upper-middle position and heat oven to 425 degrees. Spray 12-cup muffin tin with vegetable oil spray.

2. FOR THE TOPPING: Process flour, brown sugar, granulated sugar, and butter in food processor until mixture resembles coarse sand, 4 to 5 pulses. Add pecans and process until mixture forms small clumps, 4 to 5 pulses. Transfer to small bowl; set aside.

3. FOR THE MUFFINS: Whisk flour, baking powder, ¾ teaspoon salt together in bowl; set aside.

4. Process toasted pecans and granulated sugar until mixture resembles coarse sand, 10 to 15 seconds. Transfer to large bowl and whisk in eggs, butter, and milk until combined. Whisk flour mixture into egg mixture until just moistened and no streaks of flour remain. Set batter aside for 30 minutes to thicken.

5. Pulse cranberries, remaining ¼ teaspoon salt, and confectioners' sugar in food processor until very coarsely chopped, 4 to 5 pulses. Using rubber spatula, fold cranberries into batter. Using ice cream scoop or large spoon, divide batter equally among prepared muffin cups (batter should completely fill cups and mound slightly). Evenly sprinkle streusel topping over muffins, gently pressing into batter to adhere.

6. Bake until muffin tops are golden and just firm, 17 to 18 minutes, rotating muffin tin halfway through baking. Let muffins cool in tin for 10 minutes, then transfer to wire rack and let cool for 10 minutes before serving.

BETTER BRAN MUFFINS

✓ WHY THIS RECIPE WORKS

Classic bran muffins rely on unprocessed wheat bran, but our supermarket survey showed that few stores carry this specialized ingredient. We wanted to make a moist, hearty muffin redolent of bran's rich, earthy flavor without tracking down unprocessed bran.

To start, we tested bran cereal from the supermarket and found that twig-style cereal worked better than flakes, but soaking the twigs in milk, as most recipes recommend, left our muffins dense and heavy. Instead, we stirred together the wet ingredients first and then added the cereal. Grinding half of the twigs in the food processor and leaving the rest whole gave us the rustic texture we wanted. Whole-milk yogurt, along with butter, added needed moisture to the batter. Molasses and brown sugar reinforced the earthy bran flavor. To address the texture of the muffins, we switched to baking soda instead of baking powder and used one egg plus a yolk—two eggs made the muffins too springy. To ensure that they would soften fully, we plumped the raisins in water in the microwave before adding them to the batter.

BETTER BRAN MUFFINS
MAKES 12 MUFFINS

We prefer Kellogg's All-Bran Original cereal in this recipe. Dried cranberries or dried cherries may be substituted for the raisins.

1	cup raisins
1	teaspoon water
2¼	cups (5 ounces) All-Bran Original cereal
1¼	cups (6¼ ounces) all-purpose flour
½	cup (2¾ ounces) whole wheat flour
2	teaspoons baking soda
½	teaspoon salt
1	large egg plus 1 large yolk
⅔	cup packed (4⅔ ounces) light brown sugar
3	tablespoons molasses
1	teaspoon vanilla extract
6	tablespoons unsalted butter, melted and cooled
1¾	cups plain whole-milk yogurt

1. Adjust oven rack to middle position and heat oven to 400 degrees. Spray 12-cup muffin tin with vegetable oil spray. Line plate with paper towel. Combine raisins and water in small bowl, cover, and microwave for 30 seconds. Let stand, covered, until raisins are softened and plump, about 5 minutes. Transfer raisins to prepared plate to cool.

2. Process 1 cup plus 2 tablespoons cereal in food processor until finely ground, about 1 minute. Whisk all-purpose flour, whole wheat flour, baking soda, and salt in large bowl until combined and set aside. Whisk egg and egg yolk together in medium bowl until well combined and light-colored, about 20 seconds. Add sugar, molasses, and vanilla to bowl with eggs and whisk until mixture is thick, about 30 seconds. Add melted butter and whisk to combine. Add yogurt and whisk to combine. Stir in processed cereal and remaining 1 cup plus 2 tablespoons unprocessed cereal. Let mixture sit until cereal is evenly moistened (there will still be some small lumps), about 5 minutes.

3. Add wet ingredients to dry ingredients and mix gently with rubber spatula until batter is just combined and evenly moistened (do not overmix.) Gently fold raisins into batter. Using ice cream scoop or large spoon, divide batter evenly among prepared muffin cups, dropping batter to form mounds (do not level or flatten batter).

4. Bake until muffins are dark golden and toothpick inserted in center of muffin comes out with few crumbs attached, 16 to 20 minutes, rotating muffin tin halfway through baking. Let muffins cool in tin for 5 minutes, then transfer to wire rack and let cool for 10 minutes before serving.

CORN MUFFINS

✓ WHY THIS RECIPE WORKS

A corn muffin shouldn't be as sweet and fluffy as a cupcake, nor should it be dense and "corny" like cornbread. It should taste like corn, but not overpoweringly, and should be moist with a tender crumb and a crunchy top. Our mission was to come up with a recipe that struck just the right balance in both texture and flavor. The cornmeal itself *proved to be an important factor, and degerminated meal just didn't have enough corn flavor. A fine-ground, whole grain meal provided better flavor and texture. Butter, sour cream, and milk provided the moisture, fat (for richness), and acidity (for its tenderizing effect) that we wanted. We tried mixing the ingredients with both the quick-bread and creaming methods; not only was the former the easier way to go, but it also resulted in less airy, cakey muffins. We got our crunchy top from a 400-degree oven. These muffins were subtly sweet, rich but not dense, and with a texture that was neither cake nor cornbread.*

CORN MUFFINS
MAKES 12 MUFFINS

We prefer stone-ground cornmeal because it has a fuller flavor but any kind of cornmeal will work.

2	cups (10 ounces) all-purpose flour
1	cup (5 ounces) stone-ground cornmeal
1½	teaspoons baking powder
1	teaspoon baking soda
½	teaspoon salt
2	large eggs
¾	cup (5¼ ounces) sugar
8	tablespoons unsalted butter, melted and cooled
¾	cup sour cream
½	cup whole milk

1. Adjust oven rack to middle position and heat oven to 400 degrees. Spray 12-cup muffin tin with vegetable oil spray.

2. Whisk flour, cornmeal, baking powder, baking soda, and salt together in medium bowl. Whisk eggs in second medium bowl until well combined and light-colored, about 20 seconds. Add sugar to eggs and whisk vigorously until thick and homogeneous, about 30 seconds. Add melted butter in 3 additions, whisking to combine after each addition.

Add 6 tablespoons sour cream and ¼ cup milk and whisk to combine, then whisk in remaining 6 tablespoons sour cream and remaining ¼ cup milk until combined.

3. Add wet ingredients to dry ingredients and mix gently with rubber spatula until batter is just combined and evenly moistened (do not overmix). Using ice cream scoop or large spoon, divide batter evenly among prepared muffin cups, dropping batter to form mounds (do not level or flatten batter).

4. Bake until muffins are light golden brown and toothpick inserted in center of muffin comes out clean, about 18 minutes, rotating muffin tin halfway through baking. Let muffins cool in muffin tin for 5 minutes, then transfer to wire rack, let cool 5 minutes longer, and serve warm.

BACON-SCALLION CORN MUFFINS WITH CHEDDAR CHEESE

Cook 3 slices bacon, cut into ½-inch pieces, in 10-inch skillet over medium heat until crisp, 5 to 7 minutes. Add 10 thinly sliced scallions, ¼ teaspoon salt, and ⅛ teaspoon pepper and cook to heat through, about 1 minute. Transfer mixture to plate to cool while making muffins. Follow recipe for Corn Muffins. Reduce sugar to ½ cup. Stir 1½ cups grated cheddar cheese and bacon mixture into wet ingredients, then add to dry ingredients and combine. Before baking, sprinkle ½ cup grated cheddar cheese over muffins.

CORN AND APRICOT MUFFINS WITH ORANGE ESSENCE

We prefer stone-ground cornmeal because it has a fuller flavor but any kind of cornmeal will work.

TOPPING
⅔ cup granulated sugar
1½ teaspoons grated orange zest

MUFFINS
1½ cups (8 ounces) dried apricots
½ teaspoon grated orange zest plus ⅔ cup juice (2 oranges)
2 cups (10 ounces) all-purpose flour
1 cup (5 ounces) stone-ground cornmeal
1½ teaspoons baking powder
1 teaspoon baking soda
½ teaspoon salt
2 large eggs
½ cup (3½ ounces) granulated sugar
¼ cup packed (1¾ ounces) dark brown sugar
8 tablespoons unsalted butter, melted and cooled
¾ cup sour cream
½ cup whole milk

1. Adjust oven rack to middle position and heat oven to 400 degrees. Spray 12-cup muffin tin with vegetable oil spray.

2. FOR THE TOPPING: In food processor, process sugar and orange zest until pale orange, about 10 seconds. Transfer to small bowl and set aside.

3. FOR THE MUFFINS: Pulse apricots in food processor until chopped fine, about 10 pulses. Transfer to medium bowl, add orange juice, cover, and microwave until simmering, about 1 minute. Let apricots stand, covered, until softened and plump, about 5 minutes. Strain apricots; discard juice.

4. Whisk flour, cornmeal, baking powder, baking soda, and salt together in medium bowl. Whisk eggs in second medium bowl until well combined and light-colored, about 20 seconds. Add granulated sugar and brown sugar to eggs and whisk vigorously until thick and homogeneous, about 30 seconds. Add melted butter in 3 additions, whisking to combine after each addition. Add 6 tablespoons sour cream and ¼ cup milk and whisk to combine, then whisk in remaining 6 tablespoons sour cream and remaining ¼ cup

milk until combined. Stir in orange zest and strained apricots.

5. Add wet ingredients to dry ingredients and mix gently with rubber spatula until batter is just combined and evenly moistened (do not overmix). Using ice cream scoop or large spoon, divide batter evenly among prepared muffin cups, dropping batter to form mounds (do not level or flatten batter). Sprinkle each muffin with orange-sugar topping.

6. Bake until muffins are light golden brown and toothpick inserted in center of muffin comes out clean, about 18 minutes, rotating muffing tin halfway through baking. Let muffins cool in tin for 10 minutes; serve warm.

POPOVERS

✔ WHY THIS RECIPE WORKS

Popovers, as their name suggests, should rise high over the lip of the popover pan. They should have crisp edges and an airy, moist, but not wet, eggy interior. We found that blending the batter (eggs, milk, flour, melted butter, and salt) together until smooth, then letting the batter rest, made the highest popovers. While some recipes dictate placing popovers into a cold oven, we found that preheating the popover pan actually helped set the batter best for the greatest rise.

POPOVERS
MAKES 6

High heat is crucial to the speedy, high rise of popovers. When it's time to fill the preheated popover pan with batter, get the pan out of and back into the oven as quickly as possible, making sure to close the oven door while you pour the batter into the pan. Popovers made in a muffin tin won't rise nearly as high as those made in a popover pan, but they still taste quite good (see the variation).

2 large eggs
1 cup whole milk
1 cup (5 ounces) all-purpose flour
1 tablespoon unsalted butter, melted and cooled
½ teaspoon salt
1 tablespoon vegetable oil

1. Process eggs and milk together in blender until smooth. Add flour, melted butter, and salt and continue to process on high speed until batter is bubbly and smooth, about 1 minute. Cover and let batter rest at room temperature for 30 minutes.

2. While batter is resting, measure ½ teaspoon oil into each cup of popover pan. Adjust oven rack to lowest position, place popover pan in oven, and heat oven to 450 degrees.

3. After batter has rested, pour it into 4-cup liquid measuring cup or another container with a spout (you should have about 2 cups batter). Working quickly, remove pan from oven and divide batter evenly among 6 cups in pan. Return pan to oven and bake for 20 minutes (do not open oven door).

4. Lower heat to 350 degrees and continue to bake until popovers are golden brown, 15 to 18 minutes longer. Gently flip popovers out onto wire rack and let cool slightly before serving.

MUFFIN TIN POPOVERS

Increase oil to 5 teaspoons. Use 12-cup muffin tin in place of popover pan and grease only 10 outer cups of tin. In step 3, divide batter evenly among outer 10 muffin cups.

BUTTERMILK DOUGHNUTS

✔ WHY THIS RECIPE WORKS

We wanted doughnuts that were crunchy on the outside, tender yet sturdy on the inside, laced delicately with the flavor of nutmeg, and as greaseless as fried doughnuts could be. For the frying oil, we tested all kinds of vegetable oil and had almost settled on peanut until we tried vegetable shortening. It won hands down, producing a much less greasy doughnut than the peanut oil. Temperature was important, too. At 350 degrees, the dough absorbed too much oil; at 385 degrees the outside started to burn before the inside could cook through. We got our best results by heating the oil to 375 degrees before adding the doughnuts; it fell back to 360 to 365 degrees once the doughnuts were dropped in. It was also important to bring the oil back up to 375 before adding each new batch of doughnuts. Although some recipes called for cooking times as long as 1½ minutes, we found that was too long; the longer the doughnuts cooked, the greasier they got. The shorter the frying time, the less chance the shortening had to penetrate the dough. We found just under a minute was ideal.

BUTTERMILK DOUGHNUTS
MAKES 15 TO 17 DOUGHNUTS

For a chewier doughnut with a less crisp exterior, add ¼ cup of flour. The dough can be made by hand, using a large bowl with a wooden spoon, or in a mixer as directed. Doughnuts rolled from scraps will be a little drier and less crisp than those cut from the first roll. You will need at least a 6-quart Dutch oven for this recipe. These doughnuts are best eaten very warm, as soon out of the pot as possible.

3½ cups (17½ ounces) all-purpose flour
1 cup sugar
½ teaspoon baking soda
2 teaspoons baking powder
1 teaspoon salt
1½ teaspoons ground nutmeg
¾ cup buttermilk
4 tablespoons unsalted butter, melted and cooled
2 large eggs plus 1 large yolk
6 cups vegetable shortening

1. Line baking sheet or wire rack with paper towels. Using stand mixer fitted with paddle, mix 1 cup flour, sugar, baking soda, baking powder, salt, and nutmeg on low speed to combine.

2. Mix buttermilk, butter, eggs, and egg yolk in liquid measuring cup. Add wet ingredients to dry ingredients and beat on medium speed until smooth, about 30 seconds. Decrease speed to low, gradually add remaining 2½ cups flour, and mix until just combined, about 30 seconds. Stir batter once or twice with wooden spoon or rubber spatula to ensure all liquid is incorporated. (Dough will be moist and tacky, a cross between cake batter and cookie dough.)

3. Heat shortening in Dutch oven over medium-high heat to 375 degrees. Meanwhile, turn dough out onto lightly floured counter. Roll out dough with heavily floured rolling pin to ½-inch thickness. Cut out dough rings with heavily floured doughnut cutter, reflouring between cuts. Transfer dough rounds to baking sheet or large wire rack. Gather scraps and gently press into disk; repeat rolling and stamping process until all dough is used. (Cut doughnuts can be covered and stored at room temperature for up to 2 hours.)

4. Carefully drop dough rings, 4 or 5 at a time, into hot fat. Turn doughnuts as they rise to surface with tongs, wire skimmer, or slotted spoon, frying doughnuts until golden brown, about 50 seconds per side. Drain on prepared baking sheet or wire rack. Repeat frying, returning fat to temperature between each batch. Serve.

Regular confectioners' sugar breaks down into a gummy glaze on the doughnuts, but Snow White Non-Melting Sugar makes a long-lasting coating.

Let fried doughnuts cool about 1 minute, then toss in 1 cup nonmelting sugar to coat.

CINNAMON-SUGARED BUTTERMILK DOUGHNUTS

Mix 1 cup sugar with 1½ tablespoons cinnamon in small bowl. Let fried doughnuts cool about 1 minute, then toss in cinnamon sugar to coat.

QUICK CINNAMON BUNS

✓ WHY THIS RECIPE WORKS

A tender, fluffy bun with a sweet cinnamon filling and rich glaze is a treat no one can turn down. Most recipes, though, require yeast, which makes cinnamon buns time-consuming to make. We went into the kitchen to find a shortcut to a good-tasting homemade version. Eliminating the yeast would reduce the prep time substantially, so we started with the assumption that our leavener would be baking powder. A cream biscuit recipe, which could be mixed all in one bowl, was our starting point; buttermilk rather than cream (plus baking soda to balance the acidity of the buttermilk) made the interior of the biscuits light and airy. A small amount of melted butter restored some of the richness we had lost by eliminating the cream, and a brief kneading ensured that the rolls would rise in the oven. We patted out the dough rather than rolling it and covered it with a filling of brown and granulated sugars, cinnamon, cloves, and salt; melted butter helped the mixture adhere to the dough. We rolled up the dough, cut the buns, and put them in a nonstick cake pan to bake. When they were done, we topped the buns with a quick glaze of confectioners' sugar, buttermilk, and cream cheese.

QUICK CINNAMON BUNS WITH BUTTERMILK ICING

MAKES 8 BUNS

Melted butter is used in both the filling and the dough and to grease the pan; it's easiest to melt the total amount (8 tablespoons) at once and measure it out as you need it. The finished buns are best eaten warm. For our yeasted cinnamon rolls, see page 590.

FILLING
- ¾ cup packed (5¼ ounces) dark brown sugar
- ¼ cup (1¾ ounces) granulated sugar
- 2 teaspoons ground cinnamon
- ⅛ teaspoon ground cloves
- ⅛ teaspoon salt
- 1 tablespoon unsalted butter, melted and cooled

DOUGH
- 2½ cups (12½ ounces) all-purpose flour
- 2 tablespoons granulated sugar
- 1¼ teaspoons baking powder
- ½ teaspoon baking soda
- ½ teaspoon salt
- 1¼ cups buttermilk
- 6 tablespoons unsalted butter, melted and cooled

ICING
- 2 tablespoons cream cheese, softened
- 2 tablespoons buttermilk
- 1 cup (4 ounces) confectioners' sugar

1. Adjust oven rack to upper-middle position and heat oven to 425 degrees. Pour 1 tablespoon melted butter in 9-inch nonstick cake pan; brush to coat pan. Spray wire rack with vegetable oil spray; set aside.

PREPARING QUICK CINNAMON BUNS

1. Pat dough into 12 by 9-inch rectangle and brush with melted butter. Sprinkle filling evenly over dough, leaving ½-inch border. Press filling firmly into dough.

2. Using bench scraper or metal spatula, loosen dough from counter. Starting at long side, roll dough, pressing lightly, to form tight cylinder. Pinch seam to seal.

3. Arrange cylinder seam side down and cut into 8 equal pieces. With hand, slightly flatten each piece of dough to seal open edges and keep filling in place.

4. Place 1 roll in center of prepared pan, then place remaining 7 rolls around perimeter.

---

2. FOR THE FILLING: Combine brown sugar, granulated sugar, cinnamon, cloves, and salt in small bowl. Add melted butter and stir with fork or fingers until mixture resembles wet sand; set aside.

3. FOR THE DOUGH: Whisk flour, sugar, baking powder, baking soda, and salt in large bowl. Whisk buttermilk and 2 tablespoons melted butter in measuring cup or small bowl. Add wet ingredients to dry ingredients and stir with wooden spoon until liquid is absorbed (dough will look very shaggy), about 30 seconds. Transfer dough to lightly floured counter and knead until just smooth and no longer shaggy.

4. Pat dough with hands into 12 by 9-inch rectangle. Brush dough with 2 tablespoons melted butter, then sprinkle evenly with filling, leaving ½-inch border around edges and press filling firmly into dough to adhere. Using bench scraper or metal spatula, loosen dough from counter. Starting at long side, roll dough, pressing lightly, to form tight cylinder. Pinch seam to seal. Arrange cylinder seam side down and cut into 8 equal pieces. With hand, slightly flatten each piece of dough to seal open edges and keep filling in place. Place 1 roll in center of prepared pan, then place remaining 7 rolls around perimeter of pan. Brush with remaining 2 tablespoons melted butter.

5. Bake until edges are golden brown, 23 to 25 minutes. Using offset metal spatula, loosen buns from pan; without separating, slide buns out of pan onto prepared wire rack. Let cool about 5 minutes before icing.

6. FOR THE ICING: While buns are cooling, line rimmed baking sheet with parchment paper and set rack with buns over baking sheet. Whisk cream cheese and buttermilk together in large bowl until thick and smooth (mixture will look like cottage cheese at first). Sift sugar over and whisk until smooth glaze forms, about 30 seconds. Spoon glaze evenly over buns; serve immediately.

NEW YORK–STYLE CRUMB CAKE

✔ WHY THIS RECIPE WORKS

The original crumb cake was brought to New York by German immigrants; sadly, the bakery-fresh versions have all but disappeared. Most modern recipes use butter cake rather than the traditional yeast dough, which made our job that much easier. The essence of this cake is the balance between the tender, buttery cake and the thick, lightly spiced crumb topping. Starting with our favorite yellow cake recipe, we realized we needed to reduce the amount of butter or the richness would be overwhelming. We compensated for the resulting dryness by substituting buttermilk for milk, which also helped make the cake sturdy enough to support the crumbs, and we left out an egg white so the cake wouldn't be rubbery. We wanted our crumb topping to be soft and cookielike, not a crunchy streusel, so we mixed granulated and brown sugars and melted the butter for a doughlike consistency, flavoring the mixture only with cinnamon. Broken into little pieces and sprinkled over the cake batter, our topping held together during baking and made a thick layer of moist crumbs with golden edges that didn't sink into the cake.

NEW YORK–STYLE CRUMB CAKE
SERVES 8 TO 10

Don't be tempted to substitute all-purpose flour for the cake flour, as doing so will make a dry, tough cake. If you can't find buttermilk, you can substitute an equal amount of plain low-fat yogurt. When topping the cake, take care to not push the crumbs into the batter. This recipe can be easily doubled and baked in a 13 by 9-inch baking dish. If doubling, increase the baking time to about 45 minutes.

CRUMB TOPPING
⅓ cup (2⅓ ounces) granulated sugar
⅓ cup packed (2⅓ ounces) dark brown sugar
¾ teaspoon ground cinnamon
⅛ teaspoon salt
8 tablespoons unsalted butter, melted and warm
1¾ cups (7 ounces) cake flour

CAKE
1¼ cups (5 ounces) cake flour
½ cup (3½ ounces) granulated sugar
¼ teaspoon baking soda
¼ teaspoon salt
6 tablespoons unsalted butter, cut into 6 pieces, softened but still cool
1 large egg plus 1 large yolk
1 teaspoon vanilla extract
⅓ cup buttermilk
Confectioners' sugar

1. Adjust oven rack to upper-middle position and heat oven to 325 degrees. Cut 16-inch length parchment paper or aluminum foil and fold lengthwise to 7-inch width. Spray 8-inch square baking dish with vegetable oil spray and fit parchment/foil into dish, pushing it into corners and up sides, allowing excess to hang over edges of dish.

2. FOR THE TOPPING: Whisk granulated sugar, brown sugar, cinnamon, salt, and butter together in medium bowl to combine. Add flour and stir with rubber spatula or wooden spoon until mixture resembles thick, cohesive dough; set aside to cool to room temperature, 10 to 15 minutes.

3. FOR THE CAKE: Using stand mixer fitted with paddle, mix flour, sugar, baking soda, and salt on low speed to combine. With mixer running, add butter 1 piece at a time. Continue beating until mixture resembles moist crumbs, with no visible butter chunks remaining, 1 to 2 minutes. Add whole egg, egg yolk, vanilla, and buttermilk and beat on medium-high speed until light and fluffy, about 1 minute, scraping down bowl as needed.

4. Transfer batter to prepared pan. Using rubber spatula, spread batter into even layer. Break apart crumb topping into large pea-size pieces and spread in even layer over batter, beginning with edges and then working toward center. Bake until crumbs are golden and toothpick inserted in center of cake comes out clean, 35 to 40 minutes. Let cool on wire rack at least 30 minutes. Remove cake from pan by lifting parchment overhang. Dust with confectioners' sugar just before serving.

CREAM CHEESE COFFEE CAKE

✔ **WHY THIS RECIPE WORKS**

This brunch staple is fraught with pitfalls, from dry, bland cake to lackluster fillings that sink to the bottom as they bake. We wanted a rich, moist cake with a texture that could support a tangy swirl of cream cheese filling. We settled on a straightforward creaming method for our batter: Beat softened butter with sugar, then add the eggs, milk, and dry ingredients. The resulting cake was full of flavor and capable of supporting our cheese filling, but it was also a bit dry. To add moisture, we replaced the milk with richer sour cream, added baking soda, and upped the amount of butter. For the filling, we settled on a mixture of softened cream cheese and sugar and added lemon juice to cut the richness and vanilla for depth. Incorporating some of the cake batter into the cheese mixture prevented graininess and helped the filling fuse seamlessly with the cake. A lemon-almond topping provided the crowning touch.*

CREAM CHEESE COFFEE CAKE
SERVES 12 TO 16

Leftovers should be stored in the refrigerator, covered tightly with plastic wrap. For the best texture, allow the cake to return to room temperature before serving.

TOPPING
¼	cup sugar
1½	teaspoons grated lemon zest
½	cup sliced almonds

CAKE
2¼	cups (11¼ ounces) all-purpose flour
1⅛	teaspoons baking powder
1⅛	teaspoons baking soda
1	teaspoon salt
10	tablespoons unsalted butter, softened but still cool
1⅛	cups (7¾ ounces) plus 5 tablespoons sugar
1	tablespoon grated lemon zest plus 4 teaspoons juice
4	large eggs
5	teaspoons vanilla extract
1¼	cups sour cream
8	ounces cream cheese, softened

1. FOR THE TOPPING: Adjust oven rack to middle position and heat oven to 350 degrees. Spray 10-inch tube pan with vegetable oil spray. Stir sugar and lemon zest in small bowl until combined and sugar is moistened. Stir in almonds; set aside.

2. FOR THE CAKE: Whisk flour, baking powder, baking soda, and salt together in medium bowl; set aside. Using stand mixer fitted with paddle, beat butter, 1 cup plus 2 tablespoons sugar, and lemon zest on medium-high speed until pale and fluffy, about 3 minutes. Add eggs, one at a time, and beat until combined. Add 4 teaspoons vanilla and mix to combine. Reduce speed to low and add flour mixture in 3 additions, alternating with 2 additions of sour cream, scraping down bowl as needed. Give batter final stir by hand.

3. Reserve 1¼ cups batter and set aside. Spoon remaining batter into prepared pan and smooth top. Return now-empty bowl to mixer and beat cream cheese, remaining 5 tablespoons sugar, lemon juice, and remaining 1 teaspoon vanilla on medium speed until smooth and slightly lightened, about 1 minute. Add ¼ cup reserved batter and mix until incorporated. Spoon cream cheese mixture evenly over batter, keeping filling about 1 inch from edges of pan; smooth top. Spread remaining 1 cup reserved batter over filling and smooth

---

ASSEMBLING CREAM CHEESE COFFEE CAKE

1. Reserve 1¼ cups batter, then fill pan with remaining batter; smooth top.

2. Beat ¼ cup reserved batter with filling ingredients; spoon filling evenly over batter.

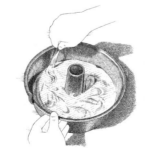

3. Top filling with remaining cup reserved batter; smooth top. Using figure-eight motion, swirl filling into batter. Tap pan on counter.

4. Sprinkle lemon sugar–almond topping onto batter, then gently press to adhere.

top. With butter knife or offset spatula, gently swirl filling into batter using figure-eight motion, being careful to not drag filling to bottom or edges of pan. Firmly tap pan on counter 2 or 3 times to dislodge any bubbles. Sprinkle sugar topping evenly over batter and gently press into batter to adhere.

4. Bake until top is golden and just firm, and skewer inserted in cake comes out clean (skewer will be wet if inserted in cream cheese filling), 45 to 50 minutes. Remove pan from oven and firmly tap on counter 2 or 3 times (top of cake may sink slightly). Let cake cool in pan on wire rack for 1 hour. Gently invert cake onto rimmed baking sheet (cake will be topping side down); remove tube pan, place wire rack on top of cake, and invert cake sugar side up. Let cool to room temperature, about 1½ hours, before serving.

SOUR CREAM COFFEE CAKE

✔ WHY THIS RECIPE WORKS

Sour cream coffee cakes should be buttery and rich, but not heavy and greasy like many versions tend to be. We wanted a pleasantly rich cake with lots of streusel on top and throughout. All-purpose flour gave us a better texture than the cake flour specified in many recipes. For richness, we used plenty of butter, sour cream, and eggs. A good dose of baking powder, along with baking soda, was necessary to make this hefty batter rise. Rather than creaming the butter and sugar, which made the cake too light and airy, we cut softened butter and some of the sour cream into the dry ingredients, then added the eggs and the rest of the sour cream; the result was a tighter crumb. In addition to the streusel in the middle of the cake, we wanted more on top, so we started with a mixture of brown and granulated

sugars and added a big hit of cinnamon and flour, which kept the streusel from congealing. We then divided the mixture, using some for the interior streusel layers (which we sweetened further with more brown sugar) and the rest for the topping. To the topping portion, we added pecans and butter for texture and richness.

SOUR CREAM COFFEE CAKE WITH BROWN SUGAR–PECAN STREUSEL

SERVES 12 TO 16

A fixed-bottom, 10-inch tube pan (with 10-cup capacity) is best for this recipe. Note that the streusel is divided into two parts—one for the inner swirls, one for the topping.

STREUSEL
- ¾ cup (3¾ ounces) all-purpose flour
- ¾ cup (5¼ ounces) granulated sugar
- ½ cup packed (3½ ounces) dark brown sugar
- 2 tablespoons ground cinnamon
- 2 tablespoons unsalted butter, cut into 2 pieces and chilled
- 1 cup pecans, chopped

CAKE
- 12 tablespoons unsalted butter, cut into ½-inch cubes and softened but still cool
- 4 large eggs
- 1½ cups sour cream
- 1 tablespoon vanilla extract
- 2¼ cups (11¼ ounces) all-purpose flour
- 1¼ cups (8¾ ounces) granulated sugar
- 1 tablespoon baking powder
- ¾ teaspoon baking soda
- ¾ teaspoon salt

1. FOR THE STREUSEL: Process flour, granulated sugar, ¼ cup brown sugar, and cinnamon in food processor until combined, about 15 seconds. Transfer 1¼ cups

of flour-sugar mixture to small bowl and stir in remaining ¼ cup brown sugar; set aside for streusel filling. Add butter and pecans to mixture in food processor and pulse until nuts and butter resemble small pebbly pieces, about 10 pulses. Set aside for streusel topping.

2. FOR THE CAKE: Adjust oven rack to lowest position and heat oven to 350 degrees. Grease and flour 10-inch tube pan softened butter. Whisk eggs, 1 cup sour cream, and vanilla in medium bowl until combined.

3. Using stand mixer fitted with paddle, mix flour, sugar, baking powder, baking soda, and salt on low speed for 30 seconds to combine. Add butter and remaining ½ cup sour cream and mix until dry ingredients are moistened and mixture resembles wet sand, with few large butter pieces remaining, about 1½ minutes. Increase speed to medium and beat until batter comes together, about 10 seconds; scrape down sides of bowl with rubber spatula. Lower speed to medium-low and gradually add egg mixture in 3 additions, beating for 20 seconds after each and scraping down sides of bowl. Increase speed to medium-high and beat until batter is light and fluffy, about 1 minute.

4. Using rubber spatula, spread 2 cups batter in bottom of prepared pan and smooth surface. Sprinkle evenly with ¾ cup streusel filling. Repeat with another 2 cups batter and remaining ¾ cup streusel filling. Spread remaining batter over filling, then sprinkle with streusel topping.

5. Bake until cake feels firm to touch and skewer inserted in center comes out clean (bits of sugar from streusel may cling to skewer), 50 to 60 minutes. Let cake cool in pan on wire rack for 30 minutes. Gently invert cake onto rimmed baking sheet (cake will be streusel side down); remove

tube pan, place wire rack on top of cake, and invert cake streusel side up. Let cool to room temperature, about 2 hours, before serving.

SOUR CREAM COFFEE CAKE WITH CHOCOLATE CHIPS

Sprinkle ½ cup chocolate chips over bottom layer of batter before sprinkling with streusel and another ½ cup chocolate chips over middle layer of batter before sprinkling with streusel.

LEMON-BLUEBERRY SOUR CREAM COFFEE CAKE

Toss 4 ounces frozen blueberries with 1 teaspoon grated lemon zest in small bowl. Sprinkle ½ cup blueberries over bottom layer of batter before sprinkling with streusel and remaining ½ cup blueberries over middle layer of batter before sprinkling with streusel.

APRICOT-ALMOND SOUR CREAM COFFEE CAKE

Substitute 1 cup slivered almonds for pecans in streusel and ½ teaspoon almond extract for vanilla extract in batter. Spoon six 2-teaspoon mounds apricot jam over bottom layer of batter before sprinkling with streusel and another six 2-teaspoon mounds jam over middle layer of batter before sprinkling with streusel.

ULTIMATE BANANA BREAD

✔ WHY THIS RECIPE WORKS
Our ideal banana bread is simple enough—a moist, tender loaf that really tastes like bananas. We discovered that doubling the dose of bananas in our favorite test recipe was both a blessing and a curse. The abundance of fruit made for intense banana flavor, but the weight

and moisture sank the loaf and gave it a cakelike structure. Looking to add banana flavor without moisture, we placed our bananas in a glass bowl and microwaved them for a few minutes, then transferred the fruit to a sieve to drain. We simmered the exuded banana liquid in a saucepan until it was reduced, then incorporated it into the batter. Brown sugar complemented the bananas better than granulated sugar, and vanilla worked well with the bananas' faintly boozy, rumlike flavor, as did swapping out the oil for the nutty richness of butter. Toasted walnuts lent a pleasing crunch. As a final embellishment, we sliced a sixth banana and shingled it on top of the loaf. A final sprinkle of sugar helped the slices caramelize and gave the loaf an enticingly crunchy top.

ULTIMATE BANANA BREAD
SERVES 10

Be sure to use very ripe, heavily speckled (or even black) bananas in this recipe. This recipe can be made using 5 thawed frozen bananas; since they release a lot of liquid naturally, they can bypass the microwaving in step 2 and go directly into the fine-mesh strainer. Do not use a thawed frozen banana in step 4; it will be too soft to slice. Instead, simply sprinkle the top of the loaf with sugar. We developed this recipe using a loaf pan that measures 8½ by 4½ inches; if you use a 9 by 5-inch loaf pan, start checking for doneness 5 minutes earlier than advised in the recipe. The texture is best when the loaf is eaten fresh, but it can be stored (let cool completely first), covered tightly with plastic wrap, for up to 3 days.

1¾ cups (8¾ ounces) all-purpose flour
1 teaspoon baking soda
½ teaspoon salt
6 large very ripe bananas (2¼ pounds), peeled
8 tablespoons unsalted butter, melted and cooled
2 large eggs
¾ cup packed (5¼ ounces) light brown sugar
1 teaspoon vanilla extract
½ cup walnuts, toasted and chopped coarse (optional)
2 teaspoons granulated sugar

1. Adjust oven rack to middle position and heat oven to 350 degrees. Spray 8½ by 4½-inch loaf pan with vegetable oil spray. Whisk flour, baking soda, and salt together in large bowl.

2. Place 5 bananas in separate bowl, cover, and microwave until bananas are soft and have released liquid, about 5 minutes. Transfer bananas to fine-mesh strainer over medium bowl and allow to drain, stirring occasionally, for 15 minutes (you should have ½ to ¾ cup liquid).

3. Transfer liquid to medium saucepan and cook over medium-high heat until reduced to ¼ cup, about 5 minutes. Remove pan from heat, stir reduced liquid into bananas, and mash with potato masher until mostly smooth. Whisk in butter, eggs, brown sugar, and vanilla.

4. Pour banana mixture into dry

TEST KITCHEN TIP NO. 115 BEST WAY TO RIPEN BANANAS

Strategies for speeding ripening in bananas abound, but as we worked our way through over eight cases of fruit while developing our Ultimate Banana Bread we found most of them ineffective. One theory, for example, holds that freezing or roasting underripe bananas in their skins will quickly render them sweet and soft enough for baking. While these methods do turn the bananas black—giving them the appearance of their super-sweet, overripe brethren—they actually do little to encourage the necessary conversion of starch to sugar.

The best way to ripen bananas is to enclose them in a paper bag for a few days. The bag will trap the ethylene gas produced by fruit that hastens ripening, while still allowing some moisture to escape. Since fully ripe fruit emits the most ethylene, placing a ripe banana or other ripe fruit in the bag will speed the process along by a day or two.

Layering thin banana slices on either side of the loaf adds even more banana flavor to our bread (and brings the total number of bananas in the recipe to six). To ensure an even rise, leave a 1½-inch-wide space down the center.

ingredients and stir until just combined, with some streaks of flour remaining. Gently fold in walnuts, if using. Scrape batter into prepared pan. Slice remaining banana diagonally into ¼-inch-thick slices. Shingle banana slices on top of loaf in 2 rows, leaving 1½-inch-wide space down center to ensure even rise. Sprinkle granulated sugar evenly over loaf.

5. Bake until toothpick inserted in center of loaf comes out clean, 55 to 75 minutes. Let loaf cool in pan for 10 minutes, then turn out onto wire rack and let cool for 1 hour before serving.

CRANBERRY NUT BREAD

✔ WHY THIS RECIPE WORKS

This simple bread is often subpar, too dense, or so overly sweetened that the contrast between the tart berries and what should be a slightly sweet cakelike bread is lost. We were looking for a crust that was golden brown and evenly thin all the way around and an interior texture that was somewhere between a dense breakfast bread and a light, airy cake. For the best texture, we used the quick-bread method of mixing, combining the liquid ingredients and dry ingredients separately, then stirring them together. Buttermilk lent a tangy flavor and moisture, while orange zest boosted flavor and added a hint of color.

CRANBERRY NUT BREAD
SERVES 10

Fresh or frozen cranberries (not thawed) will work here. We prefer sweet, mild pecans in this bread, but walnuts can be substituted. Resist the urge to cut into the bread while it is hot out of the oven; the texture improves as it cools, making it easier to slice. To toast pecans, heat griddle over medium heat. Add pecans, chopped coarse; toast, shaking pan frequently, until nuts are fragrant, 3 to 5 minutes. We developed this recipe using a loaf pan that measures 8½ by 4½ inches; if you use a 9 by 5-inch loaf pan, start checking for doneness 5 minutes earlier than advised in the recipe.

1	tablespoon grated orange zest plus ⅓ cup juice
⅔	cup buttermilk
6	tablespoons unsalted butter, melted and cooled
1	large egg, lightly beaten
2	cups (10 ounces) all-purpose flour
1	cup (7 ounces) sugar
1	teaspoon salt
1	teaspoon baking powder
¼	teaspoon baking soda
5¼	ounces (1½ cups) fresh or frozen cranberries, chopped coarse
½	cup pecans, toasted and chopped coarse

1. Adjust oven rack to middle position and heat oven to 350 degrees. Grease bottom of 8½ by 4½-inch loaf pan. Stir together orange zest, orange juice, buttermilk, butter, and egg in small bowl. Whisk together flour, sugar, salt, baking powder, and baking soda in second large bowl. Stir liquid ingredients into dry ingredients with rubber spatula until just moistened. Gently stir in cranberries and pecans (do not overmix).

2. Scrape batter into loaf pan and spread with rubber spatula into corners of pan. Bake until golden brown and toothpick inserted in center of loaf comes out clean, 55 to 75 minutes. Let loaf cool in pan for 10 minutes, then turn out onto wire rack and let cool at least 1 hour before serving.

DATE-NUT BREAD

✔ WHY THIS RECIPE WORKS

The dense texture and unmitigated sweetness of most date breads are overwhelming. We wanted to make a quick bread rich in date and nut flavor, with a moist, tender texture. We first decided on the best mixing method—the quick-bread method gave us the loaves with the best texture (compact but not too dense), and they were the easiest to prepare. For the best flavor and proper tenderness, we chose all-purpose flour and one egg. Butter won out over oil, as it added lushness and unparalleled flavor, while oil contributed only a greasy feel. Buttermilk brought a tanginess that balanced the sweetness of the dates. Hard chunks of dates marred the bread's texture; soaking them in hot water and baking soda softened the dates by breaking down their fibers. Adding the soaking liquid to the batter gave the bread even more flavor. Dark brown sugar complemented the flavor of the dates and gave our loaf an appealing color. Chopped toasted nuts added further flavor and some crunch.

DATE-NUT BREAD
SERVES 10

To make chopping the dates easier, coat the blade of your knife with a thin film of vegetable oil spray. Soaking the dates in boiling water and baking soda helps to soften their tough skins. For an accurate measurement of boiling water, bring a full kettle of water to a boil, then measure out the desired amount. The test kitchen's preferred loaf pan measures 8½ by 4½ inches; if you use a 9 by 5-inch loaf pan, start checking for doneness 5 minutes earlier than advised in the recipe.

10 ounces (1⅔ cups) pitted dates, chopped coarse
1 cup boiling water
1 teaspoon baking soda
2 cups (10 ounces) all-purpose flour
1 teaspoon baking powder
½ teaspoon salt
¾ cup packed (5¼ ounces) dark brown sugar
⅔ cup buttermilk
6 tablespoons unsalted butter, melted and cooled
1 large egg
1 cup pecans or walnuts, toasted and chopped coarse

1. Adjust oven rack to middle position and heat oven to 350 degrees. Grease 8½ by 4½-inch loaf pan.

2. Stir dates, water, and baking soda together in medium bowl. Cover and set aside until dates have softened, about 30 minutes.

3. Whisk flour, baking powder, and salt together in large bowl. In medium bowl, whisk brown sugar, buttermilk, melted butter, and egg together until smooth, then stir in date mixture until combined. Gently fold buttermilk mixture into flour mixture with rubber spatula until just combined (do not overmix). Gently fold in pecans.

4. Scrape batter into prepared pan and smooth top. Bake until golden brown and toothpick inserted in center of loaf comes out with few crumbs attached, 55 to 60 minutes, rotating loaf pan halfway through baking.

5. Let loaf cool in pan for 10 minutes, then turn out onto wire rack and let cool for 1 hour before serving.

ZUCCHINI BREAD

WHY THIS RECIPE WORKS

It can be difficult to muster enthusiasm for a slice of zucchini bread, especially if the bread is your typical bland loaf. We wanted a zucchini bread worth making and eating, one that boasted a moist, but not wet, crumb and was subtly spiced with great summery zucchini flavor. To start, we discovered the downfall of many zucchini breads—the excess moisture from the zucchini. Shredding the zucchini and then squeezing it in paper towels not only rid the zucchini of excess moisture for a drier loaf, but also intensified the zucchini flavor for a better-tasting bread. Many zucchini bread recipes use oil, but we found butter improved the flavor of the bread. Zucchini is subtle, so cinnamon and allspice, along with lemon juice, perked the flavor up further, as did the tang of yogurt, which we preferred over milk (too lean and bland) and sour cream (too rich). We tried sprinkling the loaves with nuts, but we preferred them the old-fashioned way, stirred into the batter for nutty flavor in every bite.

ZUCCHINI BREAD
SERVES 10

Small zucchini have smaller, drier seeds than large zucchini and are preferred in this recipe. If you are using a large zucchini, cut each zucchini in half lengthwise and use a spoon to scrape out and discard the seeds before shredding. The test kitchen's preferred loaf pan measures 8½ by 4½ inches; if you use a 9 by 5-inch loaf pan, start checking for doneness 5 minutes earlier than advised in the recipe.

2 small zucchini (1 pound), trimmed
2 cups (10 ounces) all-purpose flour
1 teaspoon baking soda
1 teaspoon baking powder
1 teaspoon ground cinnamon
1 teaspoon ground allspice
½ teaspoon salt
1½ cups (10½ ounces) sugar
6 tablespoons unsalted butter, melted and cooled
2 large eggs
¼ cup plain whole-milk or low-fat yogurt
1 tablespoon lemon juice
½ cup pecans or walnuts, toasted and chopped coarse

1. Adjust oven rack to middle position and heat oven to 350 degrees. Grease 8½ by 4½-inch loaf pan. Shred zucchini using large holes of box grater. Squeeze shredded zucchini between several layers of paper towels to absorb excess moisture.

2. Whisk flour, baking soda, baking powder, cinnamon, allspice, and salt together in large bowl. In medium bowl, whisk sugar, melted butter, eggs, yogurt, and lemon juice together until smooth. Gently fold shredded zucchini and yogurt mixture into flour mixture with rubber spatula until just combined (do not overmix). Gently fold in pecans.

3. Scrape batter into prepared pan and smooth top. Bake until golden brown and toothpick inserted in center of loaf comes out with few crumbs attached, about 1 hour, rotating loaf pan halfway through baking.

4. Let loaf cool in pan for 10 minutes, then turn out onto wire rack and let cool for 1 hour before serving.

ZUCCHINI BREAD WITH GOLDEN RAISINS OR DRIED CRANBERRIES

Fold ¾ cup golden raisins or dried cranberries into batter with pecans.

ALL-PURPOSE CORNBREAD

✓ WHY THIS RECIPE WORKS

Cornbread can be sweet and cakey (the Northern version) or savory and light (the Southern version). We wanted a combination of the two. And most important, we wanted our cornbread to be bursting with corn flavor. The secret was pretty simple: Use corn, not just cornmeal. While fresh corn was best, frozen was nearly as good and pureeing the kernels in a food processor made them easy to use while eliminating tough, chewy kernels. Buttermilk provided a tangy flavor, while light brown sugar enhanced the naturally sweet flavor of the corn. For a thick crust, we baked the bread at a higher than conventional temperature, producing a crunchy crust full of toasted corn flavor.

ALL-PURPOSE CORNBREAD
SERVES 6

Before preparing the baking dish or any of the other ingredients, measure out the frozen kernels and let them stand at room temperature until needed. When corn is in season, fresh cooked kernels can be substituted for the frozen corn. This recipe was developed with Quaker yellow cornmeal; a stone-ground whole grain cornmeal will work but will yield a drier and less tender cornbread. We prefer a Pyrex glass baking dish because it yields a nice golden brown crust, but a metal baking pan (nonstick or traditional) will also work. Serve with a flavored butter (recipes follow).

- 1½ cups (7½ ounces) all-purpose flour
- 1 cup (5 ounces) cornmeal
- 2 teaspoons baking powder
- ¼ teaspoon baking soda
- ¾ teaspoon salt
- ¼ cup packed (1¾ ounces) light brown sugar
- ¾ cup frozen corn, thawed
- 1 cup buttermilk
- 2 large eggs
- 8 tablespoons unsalted butter, melted and cooled

1. Adjust oven rack to middle position and heat oven to 400 degrees. Spray 8-inch square baking dish with vegetable oil spray. Whisk flour, cornmeal, baking powder, baking soda, and salt in medium bowl until combined; set aside.

2. In food processor or blender, process brown sugar, corn kernels, and buttermilk until combined, about 5 seconds. Add eggs and process until well combined (corn lumps will remain), about 5 seconds longer.

3. Using rubber spatula, make well in center of dry ingredients; pour wet ingredients into well. Begin folding dry ingredients into wet, giving mixture only a few turns to barely combine. Add melted butter and continue folding until dry ingredients are just moistened. Pour batter into prepared baking dish and smooth surface with rubber spatula.

4. Bake until cornbread is deep golden brown and toothpick inserted in center comes out clean, 25 to 35 minutes. Let cool on wire rack for 10 minutes, then invert onto wire rack, and turn right side up and let cool until warm, about 10 minutes longer, and serve. (Leftover cornbread can be wrapped in aluminum foil and reheated in a 350-degree oven for 10 to 15 minutes.)

SPICY JALAPEÑO-CHEDDAR CORNBREAD

Reduce salt to ½ teaspoon. Add ⅜ teaspoon cayenne pepper, 1 jalapeño chile, stemmed, seeded, and chopped fine, and 2 ounces shredded cheddar cheese to flour mixture and toss well to combine. Reduce brown sugar to 2 tablespoons and sprinkle 2 ounces shredded cheddar cheese over batter in dish just before baking.

BLUEBERRY BREAKFAST CORNBREAD

Reduce salt to ½ teaspoon. Reduce buttermilk to ¾ cup and add ¼ cup maple syrup to food processor along with buttermilk in step 2. Add 5 ounces fresh or 4 ounces (1 cup) frozen blueberries with melted butter in step 3. Sprinkle 2 tablespoons granulated sugar over batter in baking dish just before baking.

MOLASSES-PECAN BUTTER

- 8 tablespoons unsalted butter, softened
- ¼ cup pecans, toasted and chopped fine
- 4 teaspoons light molasses
- 2 teaspoons sugar
- ¼ teaspoon vanilla extract
  Pinch salt

Using stand mixer fitted with whisk, whip butter on medium speed until smooth, about 30 seconds. Add pecans, molasses, sugar, vanilla, and salt and whip until combined, about 15 seconds, then increase speed to high and whip until very light and fluffy, about 2 minutes, scraping down bowl as needed.

TEST KITCHEN TIP NO. 116 CORNMEAL—CHILL IT

Most people store cornmeal on a shelf in their pantry—just as they would sugar or flour. But cornmeal contains natural oils that will go rancid in as little as three months. (Whole wheat flour also contains natural oils that can go rancid quickly.) We prefer to transfer both cornmeal and whole wheat flour to zipper-lock bags and store them in the freezer. Stored this way, they should both keep up to one year.

SWEET ORANGE BUTTER

8 tablespoons unsalted butter, softened
2 teaspoons sugar
1 teaspoon grated orange zest
⅛ teaspoon vanilla extract
Pinch salt

Using stand mixer fitted with whisk, whip butter on medium speed until smooth, about 30 seconds. Add sugar, orange zest, vanilla, and salt and whip until combined, about 15 seconds, then increase speed to high and whip until very light and fluffy, about 2 minutes, scraping down bowl as needed.

WHIPPED HONEY BUTTER

8 tablespoons unsalted butter, room temperature
1 tablespoon honey
Pinch salt

Using stand mixer fitted with whisk, whip butter on medium speed until smooth, about 30 seconds. Add honey and salt and whip until combined, about 15 seconds, then increase speed to high and whip until very light and fluffy, about 2 minutes, scraping down bowl as needed.

TEST KITCHEN TIP NO. 117 REVIVING CRYSTALLIZED HONEY

If kept tightly capped in a moisture-tight container, processed (pasteurized) honey can be safely stored at room temperature for about two years. (In the test kitchen's experience, however, it can be stored for even longer without flavor degradation.) Honey might become cloudy or crystallized, but that doesn't mean it has gone bad, and there is an easy way to reverse its condition. Place the opened jar of honey in a saucepan filled with about an inch of water, place over very low heat, and stir often until the crystals melt. You can also heat the opened jar in the microwave in 10-second increments, stirring intermittently, until it has liquefied.

GOLDEN NORTHERN CORNBREAD

✔ WHY THIS RECIPE WORKS

While all cornbreads are quick to make and bake, there are two very distinct styles: Northern and Southern. We set out to make a classic Northern version. It needed to be slightly sweet, light in texture, and on the thicker side (compared to Southern versions which are often only about 1 inch thick). Traditionally, Northern cornbread recipes combine white flour and yellow cornmeal, and we found a 1:1 ratio was best for good corn flavor and light texture. We wanted our cornbread to be sweet but not like dessert; we tested recipes with honey, molasses, and light brown sugar, but in the end settled on granulated sugar. Just 4 teaspoons lent the right hint of sweetness. Equal amounts of milk and buttermilk lent rich flavor and slight but not overwhelming tang.

GOLDEN NORTHERN CORNBREAD
SERVES 9

Use stone-ground cornmeal for the best taste and texture.

1 cup (5 ounces) stone-ground cornmeal
1 cup (5 ounces) all-purpose flour
4 teaspoons sugar
2 teaspoons baking powder
½ teaspoon baking soda
½ teaspoon salt
2 large eggs
⅔ cup buttermilk
⅔ cup whole milk
2 tablespoons unsalted butter, melted and cooled

1. Adjust oven rack to center position and heat oven to 425 degrees. Grease 9-inch square baking pan. Stir cornmeal, flour, sugar, baking powder, baking soda, and salt in large bowl to combine. Make well in center of dry ingredients.

2. Crack eggs into well and stir gently with wooden spoon. Add buttermilk and milk, then quickly stir wet ingredients into dry ingredients, stirring until almost combined. Add butter and stir until ingredients are just combined.

3. Pour batter into prepared pan. Bake until top is golden brown and lightly cracked and edges have pulled away from sides of pan, about 25 minutes.

4. Transfer to wire rack to let cool slightly, 5 to 10 minutes, and serve.

GOLDEN NORTHERN CORNBREAD WITH CHEDDAR

You may use Monterey Jack instead of the cheddar.

Omit sugar. After adding butter to batter, quickly fold in 1 cup shredded cheddar cheese.

GOLDEN NORTHERN CORNBREAD WITH JALAPEÑOS

One jalapeño lends mild heat to the cornbread. For bolder heat, use up to 2 jalapeños, with seeds.

Omit sugar. After adding butter to batter, quickly fold in 1 small stemmed, seeded, and minced jalapeño chile.

GOLDEN NORTHERN CORNBREAD WITH BACON

Cook 8 slices bacon, chopped fine, over medium-high heat until crisp, about 5 minutes. Transfer to paper towel–lined plate and let cool. Omit sugar. After adding butter to batter, quickly fold in bacon.

SOUTHERN-STYLE CORNBREAD

✔ WHY THIS RECIPE WORKS

Classic Southern cornbread is made in a hot skillet greased with bacon fat, which causes it to develop a thin, crispy crust as the bread bakes. Traditionally, Southern-style corn bread is made from white cornmeal and has only trace amounts of sugar and flour. We wanted to perfect the proportions of ingredients and come up with our own crusty, savory Southern-style cornbread baked in a cast-iron skillet. Departing from tradition, we chose yellow cornmeal over white—cornbreads made with yellow cornmeal consistently had a more potent corn flavor than those made with white cornmeal. Combining part of the cornmeal with boiling water to create a cornmeal "mush" gave us a cornbread with great corn flavor, and it also produced a fine, moist crumb. Buttermilk lent good tang, and just a small amount of sugar enhanced the natural sweetness of the corn. Finally, we poured the batter into a hot, greased cast-iron skillet to bake until crusty and fragrant.

SOUTHERN-STYLE CORNBREAD
SERVES 8 TO 10

Cornmeal mush of just the right texture is essential to this bread. Make sure that the water is at a rapid boil when it is added to the cornmeal. And for an accurate measurement of boiling water, bring a kettle of water to a boil, then measure out the desired amount. Though we prefer to make cornbread in a preheated cast-iron skillet, a 9-inch round cake pan or 9-inch square baking pan, greased lightly with butter and not preheated, will also produce acceptable results if you double the recipe and bake the bread for 25 minutes.

- 4   teaspoons bacon drippings or 1 tablespoon melted unsalted butter plus 1 teaspoon vegetable oil
- 1   cup (5 ounces) stone-ground cornmeal
- 2   teaspoons granulated sugar
- 1   teaspoon baking powder
- ¼   teaspoon baking soda
- ½   teaspoon salt
- ⅓   cup boiling water
- ¾   cup buttermilk
- 1   large egg, lightly beaten

1. Adjust oven rack to lower middle position and heat oven to 450 degrees. Add bacon drippings to 8-inch cast-iron skillet and place skillet in preheating oven.

2. Place ⅓ cup cornmeal in medium bowl and set aside. Mix remaining ⅔ cup cornmeal, sugar, baking powder, baking soda, and salt in small bowl; set aside.

3. Pour boiling water over reserved ⅓ cup cornmeal and stir to make stiff mush. Gradually whisk in buttermilk, breaking up lumps until smooth. Whisk in egg. When

---

TEST KITCHEN TIP NO. 118 SEASONING CAST IRON

For years we've seasoned cast-iron cookware in the test kitchen by placing it over medium heat and wiping out the pan with coats of vegetable oil until its surface turns dark and shiny. When a pan starts to look patchy, we simply repeat the process. But when we heard about a new method that creates a slick surface so indestructible that touch-ups are almost never necessary, we were intrigued. Developed by blogger Sheryl Canter, the approach calls for treating the pan with multiple coats of flaxseed oil between hour-long stints in the oven.

We carried out Canter's approach on new, unseasoned cast-iron skillets and compared them with pans treated with vegetable oil—and the results amazed us. The flaxseed oil so effectively bonded to the skillets, forming a sheer, stick-resistant veneer, that even a run through our commercial dishwasher with a squirt of degreaser left them totally unscathed. But the vegetable oil–treated skillets showed rusty spots and patchiness when they emerged from the dishwasher, requiring reseasoning before use.

Why did the new treatment work so well? Flaxseed oil is the food-grade equivalent of linseed oil, used by artists to give their paintings a hard, polished finish, and it boasts six times the amount of omega-3 fatty acids as vegetable oil. Over prolonged exposure to high heat, these fatty acids combine to form a strong, solid matrix that polymerizes to the pan's surface.

Although lengthy, seasoning with flaxseed oil is a mainly hands-off undertaking. We highly recommend the treatment:

1. Warm an unseasoned pan (either new or stripped of seasoning*) for 15 minutes in a 200-degree oven to open its pores.

2. Remove the pan from the oven. Place 1 tablespoon flaxseed oil in the pan and, using tongs, rub the oil into the surface with paper towels. With fresh paper towels, thoroughly wipe out the pan to remove excess oil.

3. Place the oiled pan upside down in a cold oven, then set the oven to its maximum baking temperature. Once the oven reaches its maximum temperature, heat the pan for one hour. Turn off the oven; let the pan cool in the oven for at least two hours.

4. Repeat the process five more times, or until the pan develops a dark, semimatte surface.

* To strip a cast-iron pan of seasoning, spray it with oven cleaner, wait 30 minutes, wash with soapy water, and thoroughly wipe with paper towels.

oven is up to temperature and skillet very hot, stir dry ingredients into mush mixture until just moistened. Carefully remove skillet from oven. Pour hot bacon fat from skillet into batter and stir to incorporate, then quickly pour batter into heated skillet. Bake until golden brown, about 20 minutes. Remove from oven and immediately turn cornbread onto wire rack; let cool for 5 minutes, then serve.

SOUTHERN-STYLE CORN STICKS
MAKES ABOUT 12 CORN STICKS

Corn stick pans have anywhere from 7 to 12 molds. If your pan has fewer than 12 molds, you will need to bake the sticks in two batches.

Substitute heavy-gauge corn stick pan for cast-iron skillet; heat pan in oven as directed, omitting fat. Remove hot pan from oven, brush molds generously with bacon fat, then fill almost to rim with batter. Bake until cornbread is golden brown, 18 to 20 minutes. Turn sticks onto rack to cool. If making second batch, wipe crumbs from molds and reheat pan in oven for 5 minutes before brushing with additional fat and filling with remaining batter.

SOUTHERN-STYLE CORNBREAD FOR NORTHERN TASTES

The addition of extra sugar and cake flour moves this cornbread a small step away from its Southern roots. Though still very far removed from Northern-style cornbread, this version has a subtle sweetness and a very fine texture.

Increase sugar to 3 tablespoons and add ¼ cup cake flour to dry ingredients.

BOSTON BROWN BREAD

✔ WHY THIS RECIPE WORKS
Boston brown bread can be heavy and dense. We wanted a lighter loaf; moist, not dry, and flavored with molasses. To achieve our goals, we cut back on the amount of whole wheat flour that is typically called for and added some unbleached all-purpose flour in its place, dramatically improving the bread by lightening up its texture and flavor balance. We chose "robust," or dark, molasses for the deep color and bold, bittersweet flavor that it added to the loaves. To add moisture to our Boston brown bread, we opted for buttermilk rather than milk because its tanginess complemented the other flavors in the bread and its acidity reacted with the baking soda already in the batter to provide greater lift. Instead of the traditional but less-convenient coffee can, we used a loaf pan. After filling it with batter, we covered the pan tightly with foil, placed it in a Dutch oven with water reaching halfway up the sides of the pan, and cooked it on the stovetop, which worked perfectly to steam the loaf.

BOSTON BROWN BREAD
SERVES 10

Don't use blackstrap molasses here; if you can't find dark molasses, substitute light molasses. You can substitute a 1-pound coffee can (rinsed clean and liberally greased) for the loaf pan if desired; cover and steam as directed, making sure the water reaches halfway up the sides of the can. The test kitchen's preferred loaf pan measures 8½ by 4½ inches; if you use a 9 by 5-inch loaf pan, start checking for doneness 5 minutes earlier than advised in the recipe.

½	cup (2½ ounces) yellow cornmeal
½	cup (2⅔ ounces) rye flour
¼	cup (1⅓ ounces) whole wheat flour
¼	cup (1¼ ounces) all-purpose flour
1	teaspoon baking soda
½	teaspoon salt
1	cup buttermilk
⅓	cup dark molasses
½	cup raisins

1. Grease 8½ by 4½-inch loaf pan. Fold piece of heavy-duty aluminum foil into 12 by 8-inch rectangle, and grease one side.

2. Whisk cornmeal, rye flour, whole wheat flour, all-purpose flour, baking soda, and salt together in large bowl. Stir in buttermilk and molasses until combined and uniform. Stir in raisins. Scrape batter into prepared pan and smooth top. Wrap with prepared foil, greased side facing batter.

3. Set loaf pan in Dutch oven and fill pot with enough water to reach halfway up side of loaf pan. Bring to simmer over medium heat, then reduce heat to low, cover pot, and cook until toothpick inserted in center of loaf comes out clean, 50 minutes to 1 hour. (Check water level every 20 minutes to make sure water still reaches halfway up sides of loaf pan; add more water if necessary.)

4. Let loaf cool in pan for 10 minutes, then turn out onto wire rack and let cool for 1 hour before serving.

CLASSIC IRISH SODA BREAD

✔ WHY THIS RECIPE WORKS
American-style Irish soda bread adds eggs, butter, and sugar along with caraway seeds, raisins, and a multitude of other flavorings to the traditional Irish recipe. Meanwhile, authentic Irish soda bread is less sweet and more simple, often relying on only flour, baking soda, salt, and buttermilk. We wanted to see if we could come up with an appealing loaf that was closer to the traditional version. A loaf made with all-purpose flour produced a doughy, heavy bread with a thick crust. To soften the crumb, we added some cake flour (using just cake flour created a loaf that was too heavy). Our bread was lacking in flavor and still a little tough, so we turned to sugar and butter (very small amounts of both are sometimes added in traditional recipes). Two tablespoons sugar added flavor without making the bread sweet, and 3 tablespoons butter

softened the dough without making it overly rich. With its velvety crumb and rough-textured, crunchy crust, this bread is versatile enough to serve with butter and jam for breakfast, for sandwiches at lunch, and alongside the evening meal.

CLASSIC IRISH SODA BREAD
SERVES 8 TO 10

If you do not have a cast-iron skillet, the bread can be baked on a baking sheet, although the crust won't be quite as crunchy. Soda bread is best eaten on the day it is baked but does keep well covered and stored at room temperature for a couple of days, after which time it will become dry.

- 3 cups (15 ounces) all-purpose flour
- 1 cup (4 ounces) cake flour
- 2 tablespoons sugar
- 1½ teaspoons baking soda
- 1½ teaspoons cream of tartar
- 1½ teaspoons salt
- 2 tablespoons unsalted butter, softened, plus 1 tablespoon melted for brushing loaf
- 1¾ cups buttermilk

1. Adjust oven rack to middle position and heat oven to 400 degrees. Whisk all-purpose flour, cake flour, sugar, baking soda, cream of tartar, and salt together in large bowl. Add softened butter and use fingers to rub it into flour until completely incorporated. Make well in center of flour mixture and add 1½ cups buttermilk. Work buttermilk into flour mixture using fork until dough comes together in large clumps and there is no dry flour in bottom of bowl, adding up to ¼ cup more buttermilk, 1 tablespoon at a time, until all loose flour is just moistened. Turn dough onto lightly floured counter and pat together to form 6-inch round; dough will be scrappy and uneven.

2. Place dough in 12-inch cast-iron skillet. Score deep cross, about 5 inches long and ¾ inch deep, on top of loaf and place in oven. Bake until nicely browned and knife inserted in center of loaf comes out clean, 40 to 45 minutes. Remove from oven and brush with melted butter. Let cool at least 30 minutes before serving.

WHOLE WHEAT SODA BREAD

This variation is known as brown bread in Ireland. The dough will be sticky and you may need to add a small amount of flour as you mix it.

Reduce all-purpose flour to 1½ cups and cake flour to ½ cup and increase sugar to 3 tablespoons. Add 1½ cups whole wheat flour and ½ cup toasted wheat germ to dry ingredients.

QUICK CHEESE BREAD

✔ **WHY THIS RECIPE WORKS**
Run-of-the-mill cheese bread is at once dry and greasy, with almost no cheese flavor. We wanted a rich, moist loaf topped with a bold, cheesy crust. We started with all-purpose flour and added whole milk and sour cream for a clean, creamy flavor and rich, moist texture. Just a few tablespoons of butter added enough richness without greasiness, and using less fat made the texture heartier and less cakelike. A single egg gave rise and structure without an overly eggy flavor. As for the cheese, small chunks (rather than shreds) of cheddar mixed into the dough offered rich, cheesy pockets throughout the bread. For added cheesy flavor and a crisp, browned crust, we coated the pan and sprinkled the top of the loaf with shredded Parmesan.

QUICK CHEESE BREAD
SERVES 10

A mild Asiago, crumbled into ¼- to ½-inch pieces, can be used instead of the cheddar. Aged Asiago that is as firm as Parmesan is too sharp and piquant. If, when testing the bread for doneness, the toothpick comes out with what looks like uncooked batter clinging to it, try again in a different, but still central, spot; if the toothpick hits a pocket of cheese, it may give a false indication. The texture of the bread improves as it cools, so resist the urge to slice the loaf while it is piping hot. This cheese bread is best made with whole milk, but it will taste fine if you have only 2 percent milk on hand; do not use skim milk. We developed this recipe using a loaf pan that measures 8½ by 4½ inches; if you use a 9 by 5-inch loaf pan, start checking for doneness 5 minutes earlier than advised in the recipe.

- 3 ounces Parmesan cheese, shredded on large holes of box grater (1 cup)
- 2½ cups (12½ ounces) all-purpose flour
- 1 tablespoon baking powder
- 1 teaspoon salt
- ⅛ teaspoon cayenne pepper
- ⅛ teaspoon pepper
- 4 ounces extra-sharp cheddar cheese, cut into ½-inch cubes (1 cup)
- 1 cup whole milk
- ½ cup sour cream
- 3 tablespoons unsalted butter, melted and cooled
- 1 large egg, lightly beaten

1. Adjust oven rack to middle position and heat oven to 350 degrees. Spray 8½ by 4½-inch loaf pan with vegetable oil spray, then sprinkle ½ cup Parmesan evenly in bottom of pan.

2. In large bowl, whisk flour, baking powder, salt, cayenne, and pepper to combine. Using rubber spatula, mix in cheddar, breaking up clumps, until cheese is coated with flour. In medium bowl, whisk together milk, sour cream, butter, and egg. Using rubber spatula, gently fold wet ingredients into dry ingredients until just combined (batter will be heavy and thick; do not overmix). Scrape batter into prepared loaf pan; spread to sides of pan and level surface with rubber spatula. Sprinkle remaining ½ cup Parmesan evenly over surface.

3. Bake until loaf is deep golden brown and toothpick inserted in center of loaf comes out clean, 45 to 50 minutes. Let cool in pan on wire rack for 5 minutes, then invert loaf onto wire rack and turn right side up and continue to let cool until warm, about 45 minutes. Serve. (To freeze, wrap cooled loaf tightly with double layer of aluminum foil and freeze for up to 3 months. When ready to serve, adjust oven rack to middle position and heat oven to 375 degrees. Bake wrapped loaf until it yields under gentle pressure, 8 to 10 minutes. Remove foil and continue to bake until exterior is crisp, about 5 minutes longer. Let loaf cool on wire rack for 15 minutes before serving.)

QUICK CHEESE BREAD WITH BACON, ONION, AND GRUYÈRE

Cook 5 slices bacon, cut into ½-inch pieces, in 10-inch nonstick skillet over medium heat, stirring occasionally, until crisp, 5 to 7 minutes. Transfer the bacon to paper towel–lined plate and pour off all but 3 tablespoons fat from skillet. Add ½ cup minced onion to skillet and cook, stirring frequently, until softened, about 3 minutes; set skillet with onion aside. Substitute 4 ounces Gruyère, cut into ½-inch cubes, for cheddar and omit butter. Add bacon and onion to flour mixture with cheese in step 2.

QUICK CHEESE MUFFINS
MAKES 12 MUFFINS

Adjust oven rack to middle position and heat oven to 375 degrees. Reduce Parmesan cheese to 2 ounces and cut cheddar into ¼-inch cubes (or crumble mild

Asiago into ¼-inch pieces). Spray 12-cup muffin tin with vegetable oil spray, then sprinkle each muffin cup with about 1 teaspoon grated Parmesan cheese, tapping and shaking pan so that cheese evenly coats sides and bottom of each cup. Prepare batter as directed. Using ice cream scoop or large spoon, divide batter evenly among prepared muffin cups, dropping batter to form mounds (do not level or flatten batter). Sprinkle remaining Parmesan evenly over surface of batter. Reduce baking time to 20 to 25 minutes, rotating muffin tin halfway through baking. Let muffins cool in tin on wire rack for 5 minutes, then invert muffins onto wire rack, turn right side up, and continue to let cool until warm, about 30 minutes.

BEER BATTER BREAD

✔ WHY THIS RECIPE WORKS
Quick breads, like our Beer Batter Cheese Bread, can be on the table in less than an hour. The basic recipe is simple enough, yet our first attempts produced loaves that tasted sour, like stale beer, while others had negligible cheese flavor. And some loaves were so greasy that we had to pass out extra napkins. We wanted a lighter loaf of bread enhanced with the yeasty flavor of beer and a big hit of cheese—and it had to be quick and easy. We found that mild, domestic lagers gave our bread a clean, subtle flavor without any sourness at all. An assertive cheese like Gruyère allowed us to use less, so the bread was less greasy. Cutting back the butter from a full stick, as we found in most recipes, to half a stick made the loaf considerably lighter. And brushing butter on top of the loaf before baking made a super-crisp and flavorful crust.

BEER BATTER CHEESE BREAD
SERVES 10

Nonalcoholic beer works fine in this recipe. The test kitchen's preferred loaf pan measures 8½ by 4½ inches; if you use a 9 by 5-inch loaf pan, start checking for doneness 5 minutes earlier than advised in the recipe.

2½   cups (12½ ounces) all-purpose flour
4   ounces Gruyère cheese, shredded (1 cup)
3   tablespoons sugar
4   teaspoons baking powder
1   teaspoon salt
½   teaspoon pepper
1¼   cups light-bodied beer
5   tablespoons unsalted butter, melted and cooled

1. Adjust oven rack to middle position and heat oven to 375 degrees. Grease 8½ by 4½-inch loaf pan.

2. Stir flour, Gruyère, sugar, baking powder, salt, and pepper together in large bowl. Stir in beer and 4 tablespoons melted butter until just combined (do not overmix).

3. Scrape batter into prepared loaf pan, smooth top, and brush lightly with remaining 1 tablespoon melted butter. Bake until golden brown and toothpick inserted in center of loaf comes out with just a few crumbs attached, 40 to 45 minutes, rotating loaf pan halfway through baking.

4. Let loaf cool in pan for 10 minutes, then turn out onto wire rack and let cool for 1 hour before serving.

CHAPTER 15   Yeast Breads and Rolls

AMERICAN LOAF BREAD

✓ WHY THIS RECIPE WORKS

Many people who might enjoy making terrific sandwich bread at home don't even try it because they think it takes most of a day. We wanted a good, solid sandwich bread recipe that could be prepared in two hours, start to finish, including baking time. We found that sandwich bread improved markedly when kneaded with a stand mixer. This method helped us resist the temptation to add extra flour in an effort to tame the sticky bread dough, which tends to make the dough denser and less flavorful; it also makes it rise less. We were also surprised to find that we preferred rapid-rise yeast to active dry yeast for our sandwich bread recipe. Not only did it greatly reduce rising times, but it also made for better-tasting bread.

AMERICAN LOAF BREAD
MAKES ONE 9-INCH LOAF

All-purpose flour can be used if bread flour is unavailable. If you don't have a stand mixer, you can mix the dough by hand following the instructions. If you don't have a baking stone, bake the bread on an overturned and preheated rimmed baking sheet.

1	cup whole milk, heated to 110 degrees
⅓	cup water, heated to 110 degrees
3	tablespoons honey
2	tablespoons unsalted butter, melted
3½	cups (19¼ ounces) bread flour
2¼	teaspoons instant or rapid-rise yeast
2	teaspoons salt

1. Adjust oven rack to lowest position and heat oven to 200 degrees. Once oven temperature reaches 200 degrees, maintain heat for 10 minutes, then turn off oven.

2. Whisk milk, water, honey, and butter together in 4-cup liquid measuring cup. Using stand mixer fitted with dough hook, combine flour, yeast, and salt on low speed. Slowly add milk mixture and let dough come together, about 2 minutes. Increase speed to medium and knead until dough is smooth and satiny, about 10 minutes, scraping down dough from bowl and hook as needed. Transfer dough to lightly floured counter and knead by hand to form smooth, round ball, about 15 seconds. Place dough in large, lightly greased bowl; cover tightly with plastic wrap and let rise in warm oven until doubled in size, 40 to 50 minutes.

3. Grease 9 by 5-inch loaf pan. Transfer dough to lightly floured counter and press into rectangle about 1 inch thick and no longer than 9 inches, with long side facing you. Roll dough toward you into firm cylinder, keeping roll taut by tucking it under itself as you go. Turn loaf seam side up and pinch it closed. Place loaf seam side down in prepared pan, pressing gently into corners. Cover loaf loosely with greased plastic and let rise at room temperature until nearly doubled in size, 20 to 30 minutes. (Dough should barely spring back when poked with knuckle.)

4. One hour before baking, place baking stone on lowest rack, place empty loaf pan or other heatproof pan on baking stone, and heat oven to 350 degrees. Bring 2 cups water to boil on stovetop. Working quickly, pour boiling water into empty loaf pan in oven and set loaf in pan on baking stone. Bake until crust is golden brown and loaf registers 195 degrees, 40 to 50 minutes. Transfer pan to wire rack and let cool for 5 minutes. Remove loaf from pan, return to rack, and let cool to room temperature, about 2 hours, before slicing and serving. (Bread can be wrapped in double layer of plastic wrap and stored at room temperature for up to 3 days. Wrapped with additional layer of aluminum foil, bread can be frozen for up to 1 month.)

BUTTERMILK LOAF BREAD

Substitute ⅓ cup buttermilk, heated to 110 degrees, for whole milk. Increase first rise to 50 minutes to 1 hour.

OATMEAL LOAF BREAD

Do not substitute instant oats in this recipe. To turn this loaf into Oatmeal-Raisin Bread, knead ¾ cup raisins, tossed with 1 tablespoon all-purpose flour, into the dough after it comes out of the mixer.

Omit warm water from wet ingredients. Bring ¾ cup water to boil in small saucepan. Stir in ¾ cup old-fashioned rolled oats or quick oats and cook until softened slightly, about 90 seconds. Decrease flour to 2¾ cups and combine cooked oatmeal with flour and salt in mixer before adding milk mixture.

CORNMEAL LOAF BREAD

To turn this loaf into Anadama Bread, substitute 3 tablespoons molasses for honey.

Decrease milk to ¾ cup. Bring additional ½ cup water to boil in small saucepan. Slowly whisk in ¼ cup cornmeal and cook, stirring constantly, until mixture thickens, about 1 minute. Decrease flour to 3¼ cups and combine cornmeal mixture with flour and salt in mixer before incorporating milk mixture.

TEST KITCHEN TIP NO. 119   HAND-MIXING METHOD FOR DOUGH

We prefer to mix dough with a stand mixer because it's effortless and it produces great bread and pizza dough. However, you can also mix most doughs with your hands, following the instructions below. Note that there are two recipes in this book—Ciabatta (page 599) and Chicago-Style Deep-Dish Pizza (page 612)—for which a stand mixer must be used.

To mix the dough by hand: Stir wet and dry ingredients together along with the sponge (if using) with a stiff rubber spatula until the dough comes together and looks shaggy. Transfer the dough to a clean counter and knead by hand to form a smooth, round ball, 15 to 25 minutes, adding additional flour, if necessary, to prevent the dough from sticking to the counter. Proceed with recipe as directed.

WHOLE WHEAT SANDWICH BREAD

WHY THIS RECIPE WORKS

Most whole wheat bread recipes turn out either squat bricks or white bread in disguise. We wanted a nutty, hearty, light-textured sandwich loaf that really tasted like wheat. We started with a good white-flour recipe and worked our way backward to "unrefine" it. We made a series of white bread loaves, replacing different amounts of all-purpose flour with whole wheat to find the highest percentage of whole wheat flour that we could use before the texture suffered. To bump the amount of whole wheat up even more, we substituted protein-rich bread flour for the all-purpose flour. Next, we soaked the flour overnight in milk, with some wheat germ for added flavor. This softened the grain's fiber, kept the dough moist, and coaxed out sweet flavor. Finally, to give our bread well-developed flavor, we turned to a sponge, a mixture of flour, water, and yeast left to sit overnight to develop a full range of unique flavors. Adding honey for better flavor and complexity and swapping some butter for vegetable oil to cut the richness perfected our whole wheat sandwich bread.

WHOLE WHEAT SANDWICH BREAD

MAKES TWO 8-INCH LOAVES

If you don't have a stand mixer, you can mix the dough by hand following the instructions on page 586. If you don't have a baking stone, bake the bread on an overturned and preheated rimmed baking sheet.

SPONGE

- 2 cups (11 ounces) bread flour
- 1 cup water, heated to 110 degrees
- ½ teaspoon instant or rapid-rise yeast

SOAKER

- 3 cups (16½ ounces) whole wheat flour
- ½ cup wheat germ
- 2 cups whole milk

DOUGH

- 6 tablespoons unsalted butter, softened
- ¼ cup honey
- 2 tablespoons instant or rapid-rise yeast
- 2 tablespoons vegetable oil
- 4 teaspoons salt

1. FOR THE SPONGE: Combine flour, water, and yeast in large bowl and stir with wooden spoon until uniform mass forms and no dry flour remains, about 1 minute. Cover bowl tightly with plastic wrap and let sit at room temperature for at least 8 hours or up to 24 hours.

2. FOR THE SOAKER: Combine flour, wheat germ, and milk in separate large bowl and stir with wooden spoon until shaggy mass forms, about 1 minute. Transfer dough to lightly floured counter and knead by hand until smooth, 2 to 3 minutes. Return soaker to bowl, cover tightly with plastic, and refrigerate for at least 8 hours or up to 24 hours.

3. FOR THE DOUGH: Tear soaker apart into 1-inch pieces and place in bowl of stand mixer fitted with dough hook. Add sponge, butter, honey, yeast, oil, and salt and mix on low speed until cohesive mass starts to form, about 2 minutes. Increase speed to medium and knead until dough is smooth and elastic, 8 to 10 minutes. Transfer dough to lightly floured counter and knead by hand to form smooth, round ball, about 1 minute. Place dough in large, lightly greased bowl. Cover tightly with plastic and let rise at room temperature for 45 minutes.

4. Gently press down on center of dough to deflate. Spray rubber spatula or bowl scraper with vegetable oil spray; fold partially risen dough over itself by gently lifting and folding edge of dough toward middle. Turn bowl 90 degrees; fold again. Turn bowl and fold dough 6 more times (total of 8 folds). Cover tightly with plastic and allow to rise at room temperature until doubled in size, about 45 minutes.

5. Grease two 8½ by 4½-inch loaf pans. Transfer dough to well-floured counter and divide in half. Press 1 piece of dough into 17 by 8-inch rectangle, with short side facing you. Roll dough toward you into firm cylinder, keeping roll taut by tucking it under itself as you go. Turn loaf seam side up and pinch it closed. Place loaf seam side down in prepared pan, pressing gently into corners. Repeat with second piece of dough. Cover loaves loosely with greased plastic and let rise at room temperature until nearly doubled in size, 1 to 1½ hours (top of loaves should rise about 1 inch over lip of pan).

6. One hour before baking, adjust oven racks to middle and lowest positions, place baking stone on middle rack, place empty loaf pan or other heatproof pan on bottom rack, and heat oven to 400 degrees. Bring 2 cups water to boil on stovetop. Using

---

FOLDING BREAD DOUGH

Slide greased rubber spatula or bowl scraper under 1 side of dough; gently lift and fold edge of dough toward middle. Repeat folding as directed in recipe.

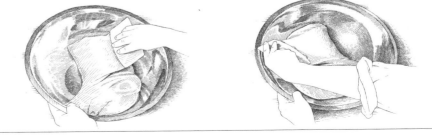

sharp serrated knife or single-edge razor blade, make one ¼-inch-deep slash lengthwise down center of each loaf. Working quickly, pour boiling water into empty loaf pan in oven and set loaves in pans on baking stone. Reduce oven temperature to 350 degrees. Bake until crust is dark brown and loaves register 200 degrees, 40 to 50 minutes, rotating loaves front to back and side to side halfway through baking. Transfer pans to wire rack and let cool for 5 minutes. Remove loaves from pans, return to rack, and let cool to room temperature, about 2 hours, before slicing and serving. (Bread can be wrapped in double layer of plastic wrap and stored at room temperature for up to 3 days. Wrapped with additional layer of aluminum foil, bread can be frozen for up to 1 month.)

MULTIGRAIN BREAD

✔ WHY THIS RECIPE WORKS
Often multigrain bread either has great flavor but is as dense and as heavy as a brick, or it has a nice, light sandwich-style texture but so little grain it might as well be white bread. We wanted a multigrain bread with both great flavor and balanced texture. Early tests showed that the whole grains impede the development of gluten, the protein that gives baked goods structure. Bread flour, with its high protein content, would seem the ideal candidate to combat this problem, but we found that it only made the bread chewier, not less dense. We switched to all-purpose flour and came up with a twofold solution: an autolyse, a resting period that gives the flour time to hydrate, followed by long kneading. The result was a loaf that baked up light yet chewy without being tough. For the whole grains, we hit upon a convenient, one-stop-shopping alternative: packaged seven-grain hot cereal. To soften the grains, we made a thick porridge with the cereal before adding it to the dough. A final step of rolling the shaped loaves in oats yielded a finished, professional look.

MULTIGRAIN BREAD
MAKES TWO 9-INCH LOAVES

If you don't have a stand mixer, you can mix the dough by hand following the instructions on page 586. Don't confuse seven-grain hot cereal mix with boxed cold breakfast cereals that may also be labeled "seven-grain." Our favorite brands of seven-grain mix are Bob's Red Mill and Arrowhead Mills. Do not substitute instant oats in this recipe. For an accurate measurement of boiling water, bring a full kettle of water to a boil, then measure out the desired amount.

1¼	cups (6¼ ounces) seven-grain hot cereal mix
2½	cups boiling water
3	cups (15 ounces) all-purpose flour, plus extra as needed
1½	cups (8¼ ounces) whole wheat flour
¼	cup honey
4	tablespoons unsalted butter, melted and cooled
2½	teaspoons instant or rapid-rise yeast
1	tablespoon salt
¾	cup unsalted pumpkin seeds or sunflower seeds
½	cup (1½ ounces) old-fashioned rolled oats or quick oats

1. Place cereal mix in bowl of stand mixer fitted with dough hook and pour boiling water over it; let stand, stirring occasionally, until mixture cools to 100 degrees and resembles thick porridge, about 1 hour. Whisk flours together in separate bowl.

2. Once grain mixture has cooled, add honey, butter, and yeast and mix on low speed until combined. Add flour mixture, ½ cup at a time, and knead until cohesive mass starts to form, 1½ to 2 minutes; cover bowl tightly with plastic wrap and let dough rest for 20 minutes. Add salt and knead on medium-low speed until dough clears sides of bowl, 3 to 4 minutes (if it does not clear sides, add 2 to 3 tablespoons additional all-purpose flour and knead until it does); continue to knead dough for 5 more minutes. Add seeds and knead for another 15 seconds. Transfer dough to lightly floured counter and knead by hand until seeds are dispersed evenly and dough forms smooth, round ball. Place dough in large, lightly greased bowl; cover tightly with plastic and let rise at room temperature until nearly doubled in size, 45 minutes to 1 hour.

3. Grease two 9 by 5-inch loaf pans. Transfer dough to lightly floured counter and divide in half. Press 1 piece of dough into 9 by 6-inch rectangle, with short side facing you. Roll dough toward you into firm cylinder, keeping roll taut by tucking it under itself as you go. Turn loaf seam side up and pinch it closed. Repeat with second piece of dough. Spray loaves lightly with water or vegetable oil spray. Roll each loaf in oats to coat evenly and place seam side down in prepared pans, pressing gently

---

SHAPING SANDWICH BREAD

This shaping method works well for Multigrain Bread as well as our other sandwich breads in this chapter.

1. Starting at farthest end, roll dough piece into log. Keep roll taut by tucking it under itself as you go.

2. To seal loaf, pinch seam gently with thumb and forefinger.

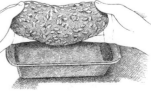

3. Place loaf seam side down in greased loaf pan, pressing gently into corners.

into corners. Cover loaves loosely with greased plastic and let rise at room temperature until nearly doubled in size, 30 to 40 minutes. (Dough should barely spring back when poked with knuckle.)

4. Thirty minutes before baking, adjust oven rack to middle position and heat oven to 375 degrees. Bake until loaves register 200 degrees, 35 to 40 minutes. Transfer pans to wire rack and let cool for 5 minutes. Remove loaves from pans, return to rack, and let cool to room temperature, about 2 hours, before slicing and serving. (Bread can be wrapped in double layer of plastic wrap and stored at room temperature for up to 3 days. Wrapped with additional layer of aluminum foil, bread can be frozen for up to 1 month.)

MULTIGRAIN DINNER ROLLS
MAKES 18 ROLLS

This recipe also works with a 13 by 9-inch baking dish.

1. After dough has nearly doubled in size in step 2, grease two 9-inch square baking dishes. Transfer dough to lightly floured counter and divide in half. Cut each half into thirds, then into thirds again, to make 18 equal pieces of dough. Loosely cup hand around each piece of dough (not directly over it) and, without applying pressure, move hand in small circular motions to form smooth, taut round, then roll 1 side of ball in oats. Arrange 9 rolls in each prepared baking dish, cover lightly with greased plastic wrap, and let rise until nearly doubled in size, 30 to 40 minutes. (Dough should barely spring back when poked with knuckle.)

2. Thirty minutes before baking, adjust oven rack to middle position and heat oven to 375 degrees. Bake until rolls register 200 degrees, 30 to 35 minutes. Transfer dishes to wire rack and let cool for 5 minutes. Remove rolls from dishes, return to rack, and let cool to room temperature, about 2 hours, before serving.

CINNAMON SWIRL BREAD

✔ WHY THIS RECIPE WORKS

Despite its forgiving nature, this bread can pose some problems. There are often gaps between the swirls of cinnamon filling and the bread, or the filling leaks out and burns in the pan. We wanted our bread to be moist and light but also firm enough to be sliced fresh. And while we were at it, we decided to develop a technique for ever-popular cinnamon rolls. To achieve the best texture and crust, we knew we needed to nail down the baking time and temperature as well as fine-tune the ingredients. For the dough, a compromise between rich brioche and lean sandwich bread yielded the best results. We found that brown sugar melted more readily and leaked through the dough, so we swapped it for white sugar. Pinching the loaf edges together tightly prevented the filling from leaking. Finally, we brushed the top of the loaf with an egg wash for a deep, shiny color before baking.

CINNAMON SWIRL BREAD
MAKES ONE 9-INCH LOAF

If you don't have a stand mixer, you can mix the dough by hand following the instructions on page 586. This recipe also doubles easily.

ENRICHED BREAD DOUGH

½	cup milk, heated to 110 degrees
½	cup water, heated to 110 degrees
2	large eggs
4	tablespoons unsalted butter, melted and cooled
3¼–3¾	cups (16¼ to 18¾ ounces) all-purpose flour
⅓	cup (2⅓ ounces) sugar
2¼	teaspoons instant or rapid-rise yeast
1½	teaspoons salt

FILLING AND GLAZE

¼	cup (1¾ ounces) sugar
5	teaspoons ground cinnamon
2	tablespoons milk
1	large egg, beaten with 2 teaspoons milk

1. FOR THE DOUGH: Whisk milk, water, eggs, and melted butter together in 2-cup liquid measuring cup. Using stand mixer fitted with dough hook, combine 3¼ cups flour, sugar, yeast, and salt on low speed. Slowly add milk mixture and let dough come together, about 2 minutes. Increase speed to medium and knead until dough is smooth and satiny, about 10 minutes. (If after 4 minutes dough seems very sticky, add remaining ½ cup flour, 2 tablespoons at a time, until dough clears sides of bowl but sticks to bottom.) Transfer dough to lightly floured counter and knead by hand to form smooth, round ball, about 15 seconds. Place dough in large, lightly greased bowl; cover tightly with plastic wrap and let rise at room temperature until doubled in size, 2 to 2½ hours.

2. FOR THE FILLING AND GLAZE: Grease 9 by 5-inch loaf pan. Mix sugar and cinnamon together in bowl. Transfer dough to lightly floured counter and press into 18 by 8-inch rectangle, with short side facing you. Brush dough liberally with milk, then sprinkle evenly with sugar mixture, leaving ½-inch border at bottom edge. Roll dough toward you into firm cylinder, keeping roll taut by tucking it under itself as you go. Turn loaf seam side up and pinch it closed. Place loaf seam side down in prepared pan, pressing gently into corners. Cover loaf loosely with greased plastic and let rise at room temperature until nearly doubled in size, about 90 minutes (top of loaf should rise about 1 inch over lip of pan).

3. Thirty minutes before baking, adjust oven rack to middle position and heat oven to 350 degrees. Brush egg mixture onto loaf. Bake until crust is golden brown and loaf registers 195 degrees, 30 to 35 minutes. Transfer pan to wire rack and let cool for 5 minutes. Remove loaf from pan, return to rack, and let cool to room temperature, about 2 hours, before slicing and serving. (Bread can be wrapped in double layer of plastic wrap and stored at room

temperature for up to 3 days. Wrapped with additional layer of aluminum foil, bread can be frozen for up to 1 month.)

TO MAKE AHEAD: Dough can be combined, refrigerated overnight, then shaped, proofed, and baked next day.

CINNAMON SWIRL ROLLS
MAKES 12 ROLLS

This variation turns the enriched bread dough from Cinnamon Swirl Bread into soft cinnamon rolls with sweet vanilla icing. If you don't have a baking stone, bake the rolls on an overturned and preheated rimmed baking sheet set on the lowest oven rack. For a quicker version of cinnamon rolls, see Quick Cinnamon Buns on page 572.

⅓   cup (2⅓ ounces) sugar
2   tablespoons ground cinnamon
1   recipe Enriched Bread Dough (page 589)
1   tablespoon milk
½   cup raisins (optional)
½   cup walnuts or pecans, chopped (optional)

ICING
1¼   cups (5 ounces) confectioners' sugar
2   tablespoons milk
½   teaspoon vanilla extract

1. Grease 13 by 9-inch baking pan. Mix sugar and cinnamon together in bowl.

2. Transfer dough to lightly floured counter and roll into 12 by 16-inch rectangle, with long side facing you. Brush dough liberally with milk, leaving ½-inch border along top edge. Sprinkle sugar mixture over dough, leaving ¾-inch border along top edge. Sprinkle raisins, if using, and/or walnuts, if using, over cinnamon mixture Starting at long side, roll dough, pressing lightly, to form tight cylinder. Pinch seam to seal. Very gently stretch to form cylinder of even diameter, pushing ends in to create even thickness. Using serrated knife

and gentle sawing motion, slice cylinder in half, then slice each half in half again to create evenly sized quarters. Slice each quarter evenly into thirds, yielding 12 buns (end pieces may be slightly smaller).

3. Arrange rolls cut side down in prepared baking pan, cover loosely with greased plastic wrap, and let rise at in warm, draft-free spot until rolls are puffy and pressed against one another, about 1½ hours. One hour before baking, adjust oven rack to lowest position, place baking stone on rack, and heat oven to 350 degrees.

4. Bake rolls until golden brown, 25 to 30 minutes. Let rolls cool in pan on wire rack for 10 minutes, then invert onto rack and let cool to room temperature, about 30 minutes.

5. **FOR THE ICING:** Whisk sugar, milk, and vanilla together in bowl until smooth. Re-invert rolls and place rack over piece of parchment paper. Drizzle icing over rolls with spoon. Pull apart or use serrated knife to cut apart buns and serve.

STICKY BUNS WITH PECANS

✔ WHY THIS RECIPE WORKS
Sticky buns are often too sweet, too big, too rich, and just too much. We wanted a bun that was neither dense nor bready, with a crumb that was tender and feathery and a gently gooey and chewy glaze. To keep the sticky bun glaze from hardening into a tooth-pulling, taffylike shell, we added cream, which kept the glaze supple. To the dough's basic mix of flour, yeast, and salt we added buttermilk, which gave the buns

a complex flavor and a little acidity that balanced the sweetness. Butter and eggs enriched the dough further. After the first rise, we spread the filling—brown sugar, cinnamon, cloves, and butter—over the dough, rolled it, cut the individual buns, and laid them in the pan with the caramel to rise once more before being baked. We found that setting the pan on a baking stone in the oven ensured that the bottoms of the buns (which would end up on top) baked completely. To preserve the crispness of the nuts, we created one more layer: toasted nuts in a lightly sweetened glaze to crown the rolls before serving.

STICKY BUNS WITH PECANS
MAKES 12 BUNS

Although the ingredient list may look long, note that many ingredients are repeated. If you don't have a baking stone, bake the rolls on an overturned and preheated rimmed baking sheet set on the lowest oven rack.

DOUGH
3   large eggs, room temperature
¾   cup buttermilk, room temperature
¼   cup (1¾ ounces) granulated sugar
2¼   teaspoons instant or rapid-rise yeast
1¼   teaspoons salt
4¼   cups (21¼ ounces) all-purpose flour
6   tablespoons unsalted butter, melted and cooled

GLAZE
6   tablespoons unsalted butter
¾   cup packed (5¼ ounces) light brown sugar
3   tablespoons corn syrup
2   tablespoons heavy cream
1   pinch salt

TEST KITCHEN TIP NO. 120   **ACHIEVING THE PROPER RISE**

A drafty or cold room can wreak havoc with rising times, slowing the yeast down to a snail's pace. We typically allow our bread to rise at room temperature (around 70 degrees); however, if your kitchen is particularly drafty or cold try the following: Create a warm rising spot by heating the oven at 200 degrees for 10 minutes and then turning it off. Make sure the oven is off before placing the dough inside.

FILLING

¾ cup packed (5¼ ounces) light brown sugar

2 teaspoons ground cinnamon

¼ teaspoon ground cloves

Pinch salt

1 tablespoon unsalted butter, melted and cooled

TOPPING

¼ cup packed (1¾ ounces) light brown sugar

3 tablespoons unsalted butter

3 tablespoons corn syrup

Pinch salt

1 teaspoon vanilla extract

¾ cup pecans, toasted and chopped coarse

1. FOR THE DOUGH: In bowl of standing mixer, whisk eggs to combine; add buttermilk and whisk to combine. Whisk in sugar, yeast, and salt. Add 2 cups flour and butter; stir with wooden spoon or rubber spatula until evenly moistened and combined. Add all but about ¼ cup remaining flour and knead with dough hook at low speed for 5 minutes. Check consistency of dough (dough should feel soft and moist but not wet and sticky; add more flour, if necessary); knead for 5 minutes longer (dough should clear sides of bowl but stick to bottom). Turn dough onto lightly floured counter; knead by hand for about 1 minute to ensure dough is uniform (dough should not stick to counter; if it does stick, knead in additional flour 1 tablespoon at a time).

2. Transfer dough to large, lightly greased bowl, spray dough lightly with vegetable oil spray, cover bowl, and set in warm, draft-free spot until doubled in volume, 2 to 2½ hours.

3. FOR THE GLAZE: Combine all ingredients in small saucepan and cook over medium heat, whisking occasionally, until butter is melted and mixture is thoroughly combined. Pour mixture into nonstick metal 13 by 9-inch baking pan. Using rubber spatula, spread mixture to cover surface of pan; set aside.

4. FOR THE FILLING: Combine sugar, cinnamon, cloves, and salt in small bowl and mix until thoroughly combined, using fingers to break up sugar lumps; set aside.

5. TO ASSEMBLE AND BAKE: Turn dough out onto lightly floured counter. Gently shape dough into rough rectangle with long side nearest you. Lightly flour dough and roll to 16 by 12-inch rectangle. Brush dough with melted butter, leaving ½-inch border along top edge; brush sides of baking dish with butter remaining on brush. Sprinkle filling mixture over dough, leaving ¾-inch border along top edge; smooth filling in even layer with hand, then gently press mixture into dough to adhere. Starting at long side, roll dough, pressing lightly, to form tight cylinder. Firmly pinch seam to seal. Arrange cylinder seam side down and cut into 8 equal pieces. Very gently stretch to form cylinder of even diameter and 18-inch length, pushing ends in to create even thickness. Using serrated knife and gentle sawing motion, slice cylinder in half, then slice each half in half again to create evenly sized quarters. Slice each quarter evenly into thirds, yielding 12 buns (end pieces may be slightly smaller).

6. Arrange buns cut side down in prepared baking pan, cover, and set in warm, draft-free spot until puffy and pressed against one another, about 1½ hours. Meanwhile, adjust oven rack to lowest position, place baking stone on rack, and heat oven to 350 degrees.

7. Place baking pan on baking stone and bake until rolls are golden brown, 25 to 30 minutes. Let cool on wire rack for 10 minutes; invert onto rimmed baking sheet, large rectangular platter, or cutting board. With rubber spatula, scrape any glaze remaining in baking pan onto buns; let cool while making pecan topping.

8. FOR THE TOPPING: Combine sugar, butter, corn syrup, and salt in

---

MAKING STICKY BUNS

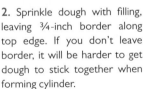

1. Spread hot glaze in baking pan.

2. Sprinkle dough with filling, leaving ¾-inch border along top edge. If you don't leave border, it will be harder to get dough to stick together when forming cylinder.

3. Roll dough into tight cylinder. Do this slowly and with great care since an uneven cylinder will yield, squat, misshapen rolls.

4. Firmly pinch seam to seal. A secure seam ensures the filling stays put.

5. Using a serrated knife and gentle sawing motion, cut cylinder into 12 buns.

6. Arrange buns in prepared pan over glaze.

small saucepan and bring to simmer over medium heat, whisking occasionally to thoroughly combine. Off heat, add vanilla and pecans and stir until pecans are evenly coated. Using soupspoon, spoon heaping 1 tablespoon nuts and topping over center of each sticky bun. Continue to let cool until sticky buns are warm, 15 to 20 minutes. Pull apart or use serrated knife to cut apart buns and serve.

OVERNIGHT STICKY BUNS WITH PECANS

Sticky buns can be prepared and shaped the night before and then refrigerated. Setting the baking dish in a warm-water bath the next morning speeds the dough's rise.

After forming and arranging buns in baking pan in step 5, cover pan and refrigerate for 10 to 14 hours. Place baking pan in warm-water bath (about 120 degrees) in kitchen sink or large roasting pan for 20 minutes. Remove from water bath and let stand at room temperature until buns look slightly puffy and are pressed against one another, about 1½ hours. About an hour before baking, adjust oven rack to lowest position, place baking stone on rack, and heat oven to 350 degrees. Proceed with step 6 as directed.

MAKE-AHEAD STICKY BUNS WITH PECANS

This make-ahead version makes sticky buns possible during hectic times, like the holidays.

After buns have risen 1½ hours, place baking pan, covered tightly with plastic wrap, in freezer and store for up to 1 month. To bake, adjust oven rack to middle position and heat oven to 350 degrees. Remove buns from freezer, remove plastic wrap, wrap dish tightly with aluminum foil, and set on baking sheet. Bake buns for 30 minutes, then remove foil and continue to bake until golden brown and center of dough registers about 180 degrees, about 20 minutes longer. Proceed with cooling buns and making topping as directed in step 7.

QUICK BRIOCHE LOAF

✔ **WHY THIS RECIPE WORKS**

Brioche is a particularly light and delicious pastry, but most home bakers avoid this flaky, buttery dough because preparing it with the traditional method—waiting for a sponge to rise, adding flour, rising the dough again, and chilling the dough—is very time-consuming. We wanted to shortcut and streamline the process to make a recipe that wouldn't scare off home cooks. The process can be shortened considerably by eliminating the sponge in favor of a one-step mixing method and by either shortening or eliminating the first rise. Only the final rise before baking is essential to the texture and flavor of the bread.

QUICK BRIOCHE LOAF
MAKES ONE 8-INCH LOAF

This bread also makes excellent toast.

½	cup whole milk, heated to 110 degrees
2¼	teaspoons instant or rapid-rise yeast
2¼	cups (11¼ ounces) all-purpose flour
6	tablespoons unsalted butter, cut into 6 pieces
3	tablespoons sugar
½	teaspoon salt
2	large eggs

1. Whisk milk and yeast together in medium bowl, then stir in 1 cup flour. Cover with plastic wrap and set aside.

2. Pulse butter, sugar, and salt in food processor until mixture is soft and smooth, about 5 pulses, scraping down bowl as needed. Add eggs, one at a time, and process after each addition until fully incorporated (mixture may look curdled). Add remaining 1¼ cups flour and yeast-flour mixture, pulse until mixture forms soft, smooth dough, then process continuously for 15 seconds (dough will be sticky at this point). Transfer dough to well-floured counter and knead by hand to form smooth and elastic ball. (Dough can be refrigerated for up to 24 hours.)

3. Grease 8½ by 4½-inch loaf pan, line bottom with parchment paper, then grease paper. Press dough into 8-inch square. Roll dough toward you into firm cylinder, keeping roll taut by tucking it under itself as you go. Turn loaf seam side up and pinch it closed. Place loaf seam side down in prepared pan, pressing gently into corners. Cover loaf loosely with greased plastic and let rise at room temperature until loaf rises about 1 inch over lip of pan, about 1 hour.

4. Thirty minutes before baking, adjust oven rack to middle position and heat oven to 350 degrees. Using sharp serrated knife or single-edge razor blade, make 1 slash lengthwise along top of loaf, starting and stopping about 1 inch from ends. Bake until loaf registers 195 degrees and crust is golden brown, about 40 minutes. Transfer pan to wire rack and let cool for 5 minutes. Remove loaf from pan, return to rack, and let cool to room temperature, about 2 hours, before slicing and serving.

DELI-STYLE RYE BREAD

✔ **WHY THIS RECIPE WORKS**

For a chewy, tangy, deli-style rye bread that won't go soggy or limp when piled with a stack of pastrami, we found the sponge method of preparing dough to be superior on several counts: Fermentation made for more flavor and a somewhat looser and less even texture (these being good things), and the bread made from a sponge also seemed to maintain more of its moistness during storage. While it's not easy to find more than one type of rye flour in the grocery store, after testing several, we found bran-free light or medium rye flour to be best. Because rye flour is low in gluten, it needed to be combined with protein-rich all-purpose flour. The kneading time for rye bread is low compared with what wheat bread requires: only about five minutes. To get a shiny, brittle crust, the hallmark of traditional Jewish rye bread, we brushed the top and sides of each loaf with a glaze made from egg whites and milk.

DELI-STYLE RYE BREAD

MAKES 1 LARGE LOAF OR 2 SMALLER LOAVES

If you don't have a stand mixer, you can mix the dough by hand following the instructions on page 586. The rye flakes add flavor to the bread, but if unavailable, they can be omitted from the recipe.

SPONGE

⅔	cup rye flakes (optional)
3	cups (15 ounces) all-purpose flour
2¾	cups water
2	tablespoons honey
1½	teaspoons instant or rapid-rise yeast

DOUGH

1½	cups (7½ ounces) all-purpose flour
3½	cups (12⅛ ounces) rye flour
2	tablespoons caraway seeds
2	tablespoons vegetable oil
1	tablespoon salt
	Cornmeal
1	large egg white, beaten with 1 tablespoon milk

1. FOR THE SPONGE: Adjust oven rack to lower middle position and heat oven to 350 degrees; toast rye flakes, if using, on rimmed baking sheet until fragrant and golden brown, 10 to 12 minutes. Let cool to room temperature. Using stand mixer fitted with dough hook, mix flour, water, honey, yeast, and rye flakes, if using, on low speed until mixture forms thick batter; cover bowl tightly with plastic wrap and let sit until bubbles form over entire surface, at least 2½ hours. (Sponge can stand at room temperature overnight.)

2. FOR THE DOUGH: Add all-purpose flour, 3¼ cups rye flour, caraway seeds, oil, and salt to sponge and knead on low speed until smooth yet sticky, about 5 minutes, adding remaining ¼ cup rye flour once dough becomes cohesive. With moistened hands, transfer dough to well-floured counter and knead by hand to form smooth, round ball. Place dough in large, lightly greased bowl; cover tightly with plastic and let rise at room temperature until doubled in size, 1¼ to 2 hours.

3. Generously sprinkle cornmeal on baking sheet. Transfer dough to lightly floured counter and press into 12 by 9-inch rectangle, with long side facing you. (For 2 smaller loaves, divide dough in half, then press each piece into 9 by 6½-inch rectangle.) Roll dough toward you into firm 12-inch (or 9-inch) cylinder, keeping roll taut by tucking it under itself as you go. Turn loaf seam side up and pinch it closed. Turn dough seam side down, and with fingertips, seal ends by tucking them into loaf. Place shaped loaf (or loaves) onto prepared baking sheet, cover loosely with greased plastic, and let rise at room temperature until dough looks bloated and dimply, and starts to spread out, 1 to 1¼ hours.

4. Thirty minutes before baking, heat oven to 425 degrees. Brush egg white mixture over sides and top of loaf (or loaves). Using sharp serrated knife or single-edge razor blade, make six or seven ½-inch-deep slashes on dough top(s). Bake for 15 minutes, then reduce oven temperature to 400 degrees and continue to bake until crust is golden brown and loaf registers 200 degrees, 15 to 20 minutes longer for small loaves and 25 to 30 minutes for larger loaf. Transfer loaf (or loaves) to wire rack and let cool to room temperature, about 2 hours, before slicing and serving. (Bread can be wrapped in double layer of plastic wrap and stored at room temperature for up to 3 days. Wrapped with additional layer of aluminum foil, bread can be frozen for up to 1 month. To recrisp crust, thaw bread at room temperature, if frozen, and place unwrapped bread in 450-degree oven for 6 to 8 minutes.)

ALMOST NO-KNEAD BREAD

✔ WHY THIS RECIPE WORKS

The no-knead method of bread making replaces kneading, the mechanical process that forms the gluten that gives bread structure, with a very high hydration level (85 percent—for every 10 ounces of flour, there are 8.5 ounces of water) and a 12-hour autolyse, or resting period, that allows the flour to hydrate and rest before the dough is briefly kneaded. It is baked in a preheated Dutch oven; the humid environment gives the loaf a dramatic open crumb structure and crisp crust. However, as we baked loaf after loaf, we found two big problems: the dough deflated when carried to the pot, causing misshapen loaves, and it lacked flavor. To give the dough more strength, we lowered the hydration and added the bare minimum of kneading time

---

TEST KITCHEN TIP NO. 121   WEIGHING IN ON WEIGHTS AND MEASURES

Variations in measurement can have a significant effect on baked goods. To prove this point, we asked 10 home cook volunteers to measure out 1 cup of flour and 3 tablespoons of water. The weights of the measured flour and water varied by as much as 20 percent! From these findings, we recommend three things to guarantee more consistent results from your baked goods:

WEIGH FLOUR: Don't rely on cup measurements alone. (One cup all-purpose flour weighs 5 ounces; 1 cup bread or whole wheat flour weighs 5½ ounces; and 1 cup cake flour weighs 4 ounces.)

USE THE RIGHT MEASURING CUP: Liquid measurements should be made in a liquid cup measure (not a dry cup measure). To measure accurately, place the cup on a level surface and bring your eyes down to the level of the measurement markings. Add liquid until the bottom of the curved top surface of the liquid (called the meniscus) is level with the measurement marking—not the edges of the surface, which can cling and ride up the walls of the measuring cup.

BE PRECISE: When measuring tablespoon or teaspoon amounts of liquid, make sure that the teaspoon is completely filled and that there is no excess liquid clinging to the bottom of the spoon after pouring.

(under a minute) to compensate. Using a parchment paper sling, we were able to transfer the dough without it deflating. For flavor, we introduced two elements that a starter adds to artisan breads: an acidic tang with vinegar and a shot of yeasty flavor with beer.

ALMOST NO-KNEAD BREAD
MAKES 1 LARGE ROUND LOAF

You will need at least a 6-quart Dutch oven for this recipe. An enameled cast-iron Dutch oven with a tight-fitting lid yields best results, but the recipe also works in a regular cast-iron Dutch oven or heavy stockpot. Take note of the knobs on your Dutch oven lid, as not all are ovensafe at 500 degrees; look for inexpensive replacement knobs from the manufacturer of your Dutch oven (or try using a metal drawer handle from a hardware store).

3	cups (15 ounces) all-purpose flour
1½	teaspoons salt
¼	teaspoon instant or rapid-rise yeast
¾	cup plus 2 tablespoons water, room temperature
6	tablespoons mild-flavored lager, room temperature
1	tablespoon white vinegar

1. Whisk flour, salt, and yeast together in large bowl. Add water, beer, and vinegar. Using rubber spatula, fold mixture, scraping up dry flour from bottom of bowl, until shaggy ball forms. Cover bowl with plastic wrap and let sit at room temperature for 8 to 18 hours.

2. Lay 18 by 12-inch sheet of parchment paper inside 10-inch skillet and spray with vegetable oil spray. Transfer dough to lightly floured counter and knead by hand 10 to 15 times. Shape dough into ball by pulling edges into middle. Transfer loaf, seam side down, to prepared skillet and spray surface of dough with oil spray. Cover loosely with plastic and let rise at room temperature until doubled in size, about 2 hours. (Dough should barely spring back when poked with knuckle.)

3. Thirty minutes before baking, adjust oven rack to lowest position, place Dutch oven (with lid) on rack, and heat oven to 500 degrees. Lightly flour top of dough and, using sharp serrated knife or single-edge razor blade, make one 6-inch-long, ½-inch-deep slash along top of dough. Carefully remove pot from oven and remove lid. Pick up loaf by lifting parchment overhang and lower into pot (let any excess parchment hang over pot edge). Cover pot and place in oven. Reduce oven temperature to 425 degrees and bake, covered, for 30 minutes. Remove lid and continue to bake until crust is deep golden brown and loaf registers 210 degrees, 20 to 30 minutes longer. Carefully remove loaf from pot; transfer to wire rack, discard parchment, and let cool to room temperature, about 2 hours, before slicing and serving. (Bread is best eaten on day it is baked but will keep wrapped in double layer of plastic wrap and stored at room temperature for up to 2 days. To recrisp crust, place unwrapped bread in 450-degree oven for 6 to 8 minutes.)

ALMOST NO-KNEAD BREAD WITH OLIVES, ROSEMARY, AND PARMESAN

If you prefer black olives, substitute them for the green olives, or try a mix of green and black olives.

Add 2 cups fine-grated Parmesan cheese and 1 tablespoon minced fresh rosemary to flour mixture in step 1. Add 1 cup green olives, pitted and chopped, with water.

ALMOST NO-KNEAD SEEDED RYE BREAD

Replace 1⅜ cups all-purpose flour with 1⅛ cups rye flour. Add 2 tablespoons caraway seeds to flour mixture in step 1.

ALMOST NO-KNEAD WHOLE WHEAT BREAD

Replace 1 cup all-purpose flour with 1 cup whole wheat flour. Stir 2 tablespoons honey into water before adding it to dry ingredients in step 1.

MAKING ALMOST NO-KNEAD BREAD

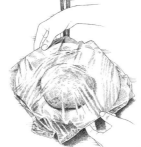
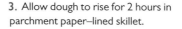

1. After mixing dough, leave dough to rest for 8 to 18 hours.

2. Knead dough 10 to 15 times and shape it into ball.

3. Allow dough to rise for 2 hours in parchment paper–lined skillet.

4. Place dough in preheated Dutch oven and bake it until it's deep brown.

This bread makes especially good toast.

Add ½ cup dried cranberries and ½ cup toasted pecans to flour mixture in step 1.

24-HOUR SOURDOUGH BREAD

✓ WHY THIS RECIPE WORKS

Most recipes for sourdough require weeks of preparation just to make the starter, plus several days to make the bread. We challenged ourselves to develop a faster sourdough bread recipe that would still deliver the taste and chew of real sourdough. We eliminated a homemade starter by buying a ready-made starter (easily available by mail order). We also found that the time for sponge development and fermentation for the dough could be reduced from two nights to just one day without sacrificing flavor. But we still needed to proof the shaped loaves overnight in the refrigerator to achieve the right deep, nutty sourness and wonderfully irregular crumb. We figured out a couple of reliable indicators that the right amount of proofing time had passed: the shaped dough should double in size, and when given a gentle poke, it should sluggishly recover. We baked the bread in a hot oven to promote crust development and a good rise.

24-HOUR SOURDOUGH BREAD
MAKES 2 LARGE ROUND LOAVES

If you don't have a stand mixer, you can mix the dough by hand following the instructions on page 586. If you don't have a baking stone, bake the bread on an overturned and preheated rimmed baking sheet set on the lowest oven rack. Once you have a healthy, refreshed starter (see page 596 for "Sourdough Starter Refreshment"), the bread will take about 24 hours (over the course of 2 days) before it is ready for baking. It is best to start the recipe in the morning, no

more than 12 hours after the last feeding of the starter. For the sponge, use the lower amount of water if you live in a humid climate, the higher amount in an arid climate. During kneading, this dough should not exceed a temperature of 80 degrees. If your kitchen is very warm or very cold, use water a few degrees cooler or warmer, respectively.

SPONGE

½	cup (4½ ounces) refreshed starter (recipe follows)
⅜–½	cup water, heated to 80 degrees
1	cup (5 ounces) all-purpose flour

DOUGH

1½	cups water, heated to 70 degrees
4¾	cups (23¾ ounces) all-purpose flour
2½	teaspoons salt

1. FOR THE SPONGE: Stir starter and water together in large bowl until fully combined. Stir in flour until combined (mixture should resemble thick pancake batter). Cover bowl tightly with plastic wrap and let rise at room temperature until doubled in size, 2 to 3 hours.

2. FOR THE DOUGH: Add water and sponge to bowl of stand mixer fitted with dough hook. With mixer on low speed, add flour, ½ cup at a time. Once all flour has been added, continue kneading until dough forms ball, about 1 minute longer; cover bowl tightly with plastic, and let dough rest for 20 minutes.

3. Using fingers, create pocket in rested dough, then add salt to pocket. Knead dough on low speed until soft, smooth, and moist (dough should not be sticky), about 5 minutes. Transfer dough to clean counter and knead by hand to form firm ball, about

30 seconds. Place dough in large, lightly greased bowl, and spray surface of dough lightly with vegetable oil spray. Take internal temperature of dough; then cover tightly with plastic. If temperature is below 78 degrees, set container at room temperature (about 70 degrees) in draft-free spot; if warmer than 78 degrees, set container at cool room temperature (about 65 degrees) in draft-free spot. Let rise until dough doubles in size, 3 to 5 hours.

4. Line 2 rimmed baking sheets with parchment paper. Transfer dough to clean counter. Gently stretch dough (to redistribute and refresh yeast) as far as possible without tearing, then fold it into thirds like business letter. Divide dough in half crosswise, then loosely shape each piece into ball, cover loosely with plastic, and let rest for 15 minutes. Cup hands stiffly around 1 piece of dough (keep other piece covered), and drag in short half-circular motions toward edge of counter, forming dough into round loaf with smooth, taut surface. Pinch bottom seam closed and set loaf seam side down on prepared baking sheet. Repeat with second piece of dough. Spray loaves lightly with oil spray, cover loosely with plastic, and refrigerate for at least 8 hours or up to 24 hours.

5. Slide parchment and covered loaves onto clean counter, spaced at least 6 inches apart. Loosen plastic to allow loaves to rise; let rise until nearly doubled in size, 3 to 4 hours. (Dough should barely spring back when poked with knuckle.)

6. One hour before baking, adjust oven rack to lower-middle position, place baking stone on rack, and heat oven to 500 degrees. Carefully slide parchment and rounds onto pizza peel. Using sharp

---

TEST KITCHEN TIP NO. 122 NO PIZZA PEEL? NO PROBLEM.

We like to transfer rustic breads and pizzas to the oven using a pizza peel. The long handle and thin board on the peel makes it easy to slide the parchment paper and dough onto the hot baking stone quickly. If you don't have a pizza peel, simply use an inverted rimmed baking sheet to help transfer your bread or pizza to the oven.

serrated knife or single-edge razor blade, held at 45-degree angle to work surface, slash surface of loaves ½ to ¾ inch deep. Working quickly, spray loaves with water, slide parchment with loaves onto baking stone, and immediately reduce oven temperature to 450 degrees. Bake, spraying loaves with water twice more during first 5 minutes of baking, until crust is deep golden brown and loaves register 210 degrees, about 30 minutes. Transfer loaves to wire rack, discard parchment, and let cool to room temperature, about 2 hours, before slicing and serving. (Bread can be wrapped in double layer of plastic wrap and stored at room temperature for up to 3 days. Wrapped with additional layer of aluminum foil, bread can be frozen for up to 1 month.)

SOURDOUGH STARTER REFRESHMENT

If you do not already have a starter, dried starter packets (sold by mail and in some natural foods stores) or fresh mail-order starters work well. Follow the package directions to get the starter going, then follow our directions for feeding once the starter is going strong. No matter where you get your starter and how carefully you maintain it, you should refresh it according to the instructions below before using it.

> 3 cups water, heated to 80 degrees
> 4½ cups (22½ ounces) all-purpose flour

1. Beginning in evening, 2 days before you intend to use starter, stir starter well to recombine. Measure out and reserve 1 cup (9 ounces) of starter; discard remaining starter (or give it to a friend). Stir reserved starter and 1 cup water together in large bowl until combined, then stir in 1½ cups flour until evenly moistened (mixture will be lumpy). Cover with plastic wrap and let mixture stand at room temperature for 8 hours to 12 hours.

2. In morning of following day, pour off all but 1 cup starter, stir in 1 cup water,

then stir in 1½ cups flour. Repeat with pouring off starter, stirring in remaining 1 cup water and remaining 1½ cups flour, letting it stand at room temperature for entire time. Starter will be fully refreshed and ready to use next morning, 8 to 12 hours after last feeding. (Starter can be kept alive over long period of nonuse in refrigerator. It's best to feed it weekly, according to instructions in step 1; let it stand at room temperature for 4 to 6 hours after feeding, then return it to refrigerator.)

FRENCH BAGUETTE

✔ WHY THIS RECIPE WORKS

Is it possible to make an outstanding baguette at home? We wanted ours to have a thin, golden brown crust, an airy texture, moist crumb, and fully developed flavor. Looking for the best way to rise the dough, we found that the sponge method (using a small amount of yeast to rise some of the dough for several hours) made loaves with superior flavor and texture. Our mixer tended to overheat the dough, so we stuck with hand-kneading. Kneading water into a relatively dry dough produced a more satiny texture than adding flour to a wet dough. We knew it was adequately kneaded when a small amount of dough could be stretched until almost translucent. Finally, cool fermentation (putting the shaped loaves in the refrigerator overnight) allowed the loaves to become better hydrated, develop more flavor, and achieve greater volume. Once baked, the flavor of these loaves was incomparable.

BAKERY-STYLE FRENCH BAGUETTES

MAKES TWO 15-INCH BAGUETTES

If you don't have a baking stone, bake the bread on an overturned and preheated rimmed baking sheet. This recipe will yield baguettes for breakfast; the variation uses altered rising

times so that the baguettes are baked in time for dinner. In either case, begin the recipe the day before you intend to serve the bread; the baguettes will emerge from the oven 20 to 24 hours after you start the sponge. Do not add flour while kneading or shaping the dough. The baguettes are best served within 2 hours after baking.

SPONGE

> 1 cup plus 3 tablespoons (6 ounces) all-purpose flour
> ¾ cup water, heated to 110 degrees
> ⅛ teaspoon instant or rapid-rise yeast

DOUGH

> ½ cup water, heated to 75 degrees, plus extra as needed
> ½ teaspoon instant or rapid-rise yeast
> 2 cups (10 ounces) all-purpose flour
> 1 teaspoon salt
> 1 large egg white, beaten with 1 tablespoon water

1. FOR THE SPONGE: Stir flour, water, and yeast together in medium bowl with wooden spoon to form thick batter. Scrape down bowl with rubber spatula. Cover with plastic wrap and punch holes in plastic with paring knife; let stand at room temperature. After 4 or 5 hours, sponge should be almost doubled in size and pitted with tiny bubbles. Let stand at room temperature until surface shows slight depression in center, indicating drop, 2 to 3 hours longer. Sponge now is ready to use.

2. FOR THE DOUGH: Measure out and reserve 2 tablespoons water. Add remaining water and yeast to sponge and stir briskly with wooden spoon until water is incorporated, about 30 seconds. Stir in flour and continue mixing with wooden spoon until shaggy ball forms. Transfer dough to clean counter and knead by hand, adding drops of water if necessary, until dry bits are absorbed into dough, about 2 minutes. (Dough will feel dry and tough.) Stretch

dough into rough 8 by 6-inch rectangle, make indentations in dough with fingertips, sprinkle with 1 tablespoon reserved water, fold edges of dough up toward center to encase water, and pinch edges to seal. Knead dough lightly by hand, about 30 seconds (dough will feel slippery as some water escapes but will become increasingly pliant as water is absorbed).

3. Begin "crashing" dough by flinging dough vigorously against counter. (This process helps dough absorb water more readily.) Knead and crash dough alternately until soft and supple and surface is almost powdery smooth, about 7 minutes. Stretch dough again into rough 8 by 6-inch rectangle and make indentations with fingertips; sprinkle dough with salt and remaining 1 tablespoon reserved water. Repeat folding and sealing edges and crashing and kneading until dough is once again soft and supple and surface is almost powdery smooth, about 7 minutes. If dough still feels tough and nonpliant, knead in 2 additional teaspoons water.

4. Determine if dough is adequately kneaded by stretching piece of dough until nearly translucent. If dough tears before stretching thin, knead 5 minutes longer and test again. Gather dough into ball, place in large, lightly greased bowl, and

cover with plastic. Let sit for 30 minutes, then remove dough from bowl and knead gently to deflate, about 10 seconds; gather into ball, return to bowl, and replace plastic. Let rise at room temperature until doubled in size, about 1½ hours.

5. Gently press down on center of dough to deflate. Transfer dough to counter, divide in half, and loosely cover with plastic. Cup hands stiffly around 1 piece of dough (keep other piece covered) and drag in short half-circular motions toward edge of counter, forming dough into rough torpedo shape with smooth, taut surface, about 6½ inches long. Repeat with second piece of dough. Cover dough with plastic and let rest for 15 to 20 minutes.

6. Top inverted rimmed baking sheet with parchment paper. Press indentation along length of 1 piece of dough with side of outstretched hand. Working along length of dough, press thumb against dough while folding and rolling upper edge of dough down with other hand to enclose thumb. Repeat folding and rolling 4 or 5 times until upper edge meets lower edge and creates seam; press seam to seal. (Dough will have formed cylinder about 12 inches long.) Roll dough cylinder seam side down; gently and evenly roll and stretch dough until it measures 15 inches

long by 2½ inches wide. Place seam side down on prepared baking sheet. Repeat with second piece of dough and place it about 6 inches from first piece on baking sheet. Drape clean kitchen towel over dough and slide baking sheet into large clean garbage bag; seal to close. Refrigerate until dough has risen moderately, at least 12 hours or up to 16 hours.

7. Remove baking sheet with baguettes from refrigerator and let baguettes stand covered at room temperature for 45 minutes; remove plastic bag and towel to let surface of dough dry, then let stand 15 minutes longer. (Baguettes should have nearly doubled in size and feel springy to touch.)

8. One hour before baking, adjust oven racks to lower-middle and lowest position, place baking stone on upper rack and second rimmed baking sheet on lower rack, and heat oven to 500 degrees. Bring 1 cup water to boil on stovetop. Using sharp serrated knife or single-edge razor blade, make five ¼-inch-deep diagonal slashes on each baguette. Brush baguettes with egg white mixture and mist with water. Working quickly, slide parchment with baguettes onto baking stone, then pour boiling water onto rimmed baking sheet on lower rack and quickly close oven door. Bake until crust is deep golden brown

SHAPING A BAGUETTE

1. Make indentation along length of dough with side of outstretched hand.

2. Working along length of dough, press thumb against dough while folding and rolling upper edge down with other hand. Repeat 5 times until upper edge meets lower edge.

3. Using fingertips, press seam to seal. At this point, dough will have formed cylinder about 12 inches long.

4. Roll dough cylinder seam side down; gently and evenly roll and stretch dough until it measures 15 inches long by 2½ inches wide.

and baguettes register 210 degrees, about 15 minutes, rotating baguettes front to back and side to side after first 10 minutes of baking. Transfer baguettes to wire rack and let cool slightly, about 30 minutes, before slicing and serving.

DINNER BAGUETTES

The altered rising times in this version help get the baguettes on the table at the same time as dinner.

Start sponge at about noon and use 75-degree water; let sponge rise 5 to 6 hours, then refrigerate overnight, 12 to 14 hours. In step 2, make dough using 110-degree water. Continue with recipe to knead, rise, and shape. Place shaped and covered dough in refrigerator until slightly risen, 7 to 10 hours before continuing with recipe in step 7.

RUSTIC ITALIAN BREAD

✓ WHY THIS RECIPE WORKS

We set out to turn four basic ingredients—flour, water, yeast, and salt—into a chewy, crusty bread that would put supermarket loaves to shame. Bread flour produced a hearty loaf with good height and a thick crust. Starting with a sponge (a pre-fermented dough made the day before) gave the bread wheaty, multidimensional flavors. Resting the dough for 20 minutes before the sponge was added allowed the flour to hydrate, giving us taller, better-shaped loaves with a cleaner flavor. To minimize handling, rather than kneading the dough, we turned it—delicately folding the dough over several times as it rose—and we shaped the loaf quickly and gently so as not to deflate air pockets. When baking, we started with a blast of high heat, then reduced the heat and spritzed the loaf with water to help form a crisp crust. These techniques gave us a rustic Italian bread that was chewy yet tender, crusty but not too tough, and easy enough to make at home.

RUSTIC ITALIAN BREAD
MAKES I LARGE LOAF

If you don't have a stand mixer, you can mix the dough by hand following the instructions on page 586. If you own two stand mixer bowls, in step 1 you can refrigerate the sponge in the bowl in which it was made. Use the second bowl to make the dough in step 2. If you don't have a baking stone, bake the bread on an overturned and preheated rimmed baking sheet set on the lowest oven rack. This recipe requires a bit of patience—the sponge, which gives the bread flavor, must be made 11 to 27 hours before the dough is made. We find it makes the most sense to prepare the sponge (which requires just 5 minutes of hands-on work) the day before you want to bake the bread. On the second day, remove the sponge from the refrigerator and begin step 2 at least 7 hours before you want to serve the bread.

SPONGE
2   cups (11 ounces) bread flour
¼   teaspoon instant or rapid-rise yeast
1   cup water, room temperature

DOUGH
3   cups (16½ ounces) bread flour
1   teaspoon instant or rapid-rise yeast
1⅓   cups water, room temperature
2   teaspoons salt

1. FOR THE SPONGE: Using stand mixer fitted with dough hook, mix flour, yeast, and water together on low speed until mixture forms shaggy dough, 2 to 3 minutes. Transfer sponge to medium bowl, cover tightly with plastic wrap, and let stand at room temperature until beginning to bubble and rise, about 3 hours. Refrigerate sponge for at least 8 hours or up to 24 hours.

2. FOR THE DOUGH: Remove sponge from refrigerator and let stand at room temperature while making dough. Using stand mixer fitted with dough hook, mix flour, yeast, and water together on low speed until rough dough is formed, about 3 minutes; cover bowl loosely with plastic and let dough rest for 20 minutes.

3. Add sponge and salt to dough and knead on low speed until ingredients are

---

SHAPING RUSTIC ITALIAN BREAD

1. After delicately pushing dough into 10-inch square, fold top right corner diagonally to middle.

2. Repeat step 1 with top left corner.

3. Begin to gently roll dough from top to bottom.

4. Continue rolling until dough forms rough log.

5. Roll dough onto its seam and, sliding your hands under each end, transfer dough to sheet of parchment paper.

6. Gently shape dough into 16-inch football shape by tucking bottom edges underneath.

We commonly advise checking the internal temperature of a loaf of bread before making the decision to pull it from the oven. A properly baked loaf should register a temperature between 190 and 210 degrees on an instant-read thermometer, depending upon the type of bread. But is internal temperature by itself sufficient proof that bread is fully baked?

We placed temperature probes in the center of two loaves of rustic Italian bread and monitored them as they baked. Halfway into the baking time, the internal temperature of the loaves had already passed 200 degrees, and they reached the optimal 210 degrees a full 15 minutes before the end of the recommended baking time. We pulled one loaf from the oven as soon as it neared 210 degrees and left the other in the oven for the recommended baking time. The temperature of the longer-baked loaf never rose above 210, because the moisture it contains, even when fully baked, prevents it from going past the boiling point of water, or 212 degrees. When we took the second loaf out of the oven, the differences between the two were dramatic: The loaf removed early had a pale, soft crust and a gummy interior, while the loaf that baked the full hour had a nicely browned, crisp crust and a perfectly baked crumb. So while it doesn't hurt to take the temperature of your bread, stick to the recommended baking time and wait for the crust to achieve the appropriate color before removing it from the oven.

incorporated and dough is formed (dough should clear sides of bowl but stick to very bottom), about 4 minutes. Increase mixer speed to medium-low and continue to knead until dough is smooth and elastic, about 1 minute. Transfer dough to large, lightly greased bowl; cover tightly with plastic and let rise at room temperature until doubled in size, about 1 hour.

4. Spray rubber spatula or bowl scraper with vegetable oil spray. Fold partially risen dough over itself by gently lifting and folding edge of dough toward middle. Turn bowl 180 degrees; fold again. Finally, fold dough in half, perpendicular to first folds. (Dough shape should be rough square.) Cover with plastic and let dough rise for 1 hour. Repeat folding, replace plastic, and let dough rise 1 hour longer.

5. Top pizza peel with parchment paper. Turn dough out onto well-floured counter (side of dough that was against bowl should now be facing up). Dust dough and hands liberally with flour and gently press dough into rough 10-inch square. Fold top corners of dough square into middle of dough, then gently roll and pinch dough into torpedo shape. Transfer loaf to prepared pizza peel, seam side down, and gently tuck dough into taut loaf. Spray loaf with oil spray, cover loosely with plastic, and let rise at room temperature until

nearly doubled in size, 1 to 1½ hours. (Dough should barely spring back when poked with knuckle.)

6. One hour before baking, adjust oven rack to lower-middle position, place baking stone on rack, and heat oven to 500 degrees. Using sharp serrated knife or single-edge razor blade, make one ½ inch deep slash lengthwise along top of loaf, starting and stopping about 1½ inches from ends. Spray loaf with water and slide parchment with loaf onto baking stone. Bake for 10 minutes, then reduce oven temperature to 400 degrees and quickly rotate loaf using edges of parchment; continue to bake until crust is deep golden brown and loaf registers 210 degrees, about 35 minutes longer. Transfer loaf to wire rack, discard parchment, and let cool to room temperature, about 2 hours, before slicing and serving. (Bread can be wrapped in double layer of plastic wrap and stored at room temperature for up to 3 days. Wrapped with additional layer of aluminum foil, bread can be frozen for up to 1 month.)

WHOLE WHEAT RUSTIC ITALIAN BREAD

Replace 1¼ cups bread flour with 1¼ cups whole wheat flour.

CIABATTA

✔ WHY THIS RECIPE WORKS

Whether they lack flavor or have holes so big there's hardly any bread, most loaves of ciabatta available just aren't any good. Uninterested in a lackluster loaf from the supermarket, we decided to make our own, aiming for a crisp, flavorful crust, a tangy flavor, and a chewy, open crumb. We started with the flour selection; all-purpose, with less protein than bread flour, produced loaves with a more open, springy texture. We built flavor through the sponge—as it ferments, the yeast produces lactic and acetic acids, which give the bread its characteristic sourness. Kneading on its own produced loaves that spread out instead of rising, so we turned to a combination of kneading, folding, and letting the dough rest. This process gave the dough structure but also oversized holes. Adding a small amount of milk slightly weakened the gluten strands and took down the size of those big bubbles. We baked the loaves at a cooler temperature than most recipes recommend and sprayed them with water in the first minutes of baking for a crispier crust and a bit more rise.

CIABATTA
MAKES 2 LOAVES

If you don't have a baking stone, bake the bread on an overturned and preheated rimmed baking sheet set on the lowest oven rack. As you make this bread, keep in mind that the dough is wet and very sticky. The key to manipulating it is working quickly and gently; rough handling will result in flat, tough loaves. When possible, use a large rubber spatula or bowl scraper to move the dough. If you have to use your hands, make sure they are well floured. Because the dough is so sticky, it must be prepared in a stand mixer.

SPONGE
1	cup (5 ounces) all-purpose flour
⅛	teaspoon instant or rapid-rise yeast
½	cup water, room temperature

DOUGH

2	cups (10 ounces) all-purpose flour
1½	teaspoons salt
½	teaspoon instant or rapid-rise yeast
¾	cup water, room temperature
¼	cup milk, room temperature

1. FOR THE SPONGE: Combine flour, yeast, and water in medium bowl and stir with wooden spoon until uniform mass forms, about 1 minute. Cover bowl tightly with plastic wrap and let stand at room temperature for at least 8 hours or up to 24 hours.

2. FOR THE DOUGH: Place sponge and dough ingredients in bowl of stand mixer fitted with paddle attachment. Mix on low speed until roughly combined and shaggy dough forms, about 1 minute, scraping down bowl and paddle as needed. Increase speed to medium-low and continue mixing until dough becomes uniform mass that collects on paddle and pulls away from sides of bowl, 4 to 6 minutes. Change to dough hook and knead bread on medium speed until smooth and shiny (dough will be very sticky), about 10 minutes, scraping down bowl and dough hook as needed. Transfer dough to large bowl, cover tightly with plastic, and let rise at room temperature until doubled in size, about 1 hour. (Dough should barely spring back when poked with knuckle.)

SHAPING CIABATTA

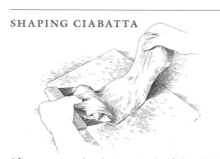

After pressing dough into rough 12 by 6-inch shape, grasp 1 end of dough with 1 hand and other end with bench scraper. Fold shorter sides of dough toward center, overlapping them like business letter to form 7 by 4-inch loaf.

---

3. Spray rubber spatula or bowl scraper with vegetable oil spray. Fold partially risen dough over itself by gently lifting and folding edge of dough toward middle. Turn bowl 90 degrees; fold again. Turn bowl and fold dough 6 more times (for total of 8 turns). Cover with plastic and let rise for 30 minutes. Repeat folding, replace plastic, and let rise until doubled in size, about 30 minutes longer.

4. One hour before baking, adjust oven rack to lower-middle position, place baking stone on rack, and heat oven to 450 degrees. Cut two 12 by 6-inch pieces of parchment paper and dust liberally with flour. Transfer dough to floured counter, being careful not to deflate it completely. Liberally flour top of dough and divide in half with bench scraper. Turn 1 piece of dough cut side up and dust with flour. With well-floured hands, press dough into rough 12 by 6-inch rectangle. Fold shorter sides of dough toward center, overlapping them like business letter to form 7 by 4-inch loaf. Repeat with second piece of dough. Gently transfer each loaf, seam side down, to parchment sheets, dust with flour, and cover with plastic. Let loaves sit at room temperature for 30 minutes (surface of loaves will develop small bubbles).

5. Slide parchment with loaves onto pizza peel. Using floured fingertips, evenly poke entire surface of each loaf to form 10 by 6-inch rectangle; spray loaves lightly with water. Slide parchment with loaves onto baking stone. Bake, spraying loaves with water twice more during first 5 minutes of baking time, until crust is deep golden brown and loaves register 210 degrees, 22 to 27 minutes. Transfer loaves to wire rack, discard parchment, and let cool to room temperature, about 1 hour, before slicing and serving. (Bread can be wrapped in double layer of plastic wrap and stored at room temperature for up to 3 days. Wrapped with additional layer of aluminum foil, bread can be frozen for up to 1 month. To recrisp crust, thaw bread at room temperature, if frozen, and place unwrapped bread in 450-degree oven for 6 to 8 minutes.)

OLIVE-ROSEMARY BREAD

✔ WHY THIS RECIPE WORKS

To make really good olive-rosemary bread, we needed a great homemade rustic bread—with a coarse crumb, chewy interior, and thick, burnished crust—and a way to add olives without ruining the bread. We started with our recipe for Rustic Italian Bread (page 598), but when we added olives, their moisture made the bread gummy, and the assertive olive flavor made it seem bland. To compensate, we added some whole wheat flour and reduced the hydration level (the weight of the water divided by the weight of the flour) from 68 to 63 percent. Honey added sweetness and brought out the olives' savory flavor. Rolling the olives up in the dough before the first rise gave us a nicely textured loaf with evenly dispersed olives. Just about any good brined or oil-cured olives worked well (after a quick rinse to control saltiness). Surprisingly, it took a whopping 2 tablespoons of rosemary to achieve the demure background flavor we wanted.

OLIVE-ROSEMARY BREAD
MAKES 2 LARGE LOAVES

If you don't have a stand mixer, you can mix the dough by hand following the instructions on page 586. If you don't have a baking stone, bake the bread on an overturned and preheated rimmed baking sheet set on the lowest oven rack. Almost any variety of brined or oil-cured olives works in this recipe, although we prefer a mix of both green and black olives.

1¾	cups water, room temperature
2	tablespoons honey
2	teaspoons instant or rapid-rise yeast
3½	cups (19¼ ounces) bread flour, plus extra as needed
½	cup (2¾ ounces) whole wheat flour

2 teaspoons salt
2 tablespoons chopped fresh rosemary
1½ cups olives, pitted, rinsed, and chopped coarse

1. Whisk water, honey, and yeast together in bowl of stand mixer fitted with dough hook. Add flours to bowl and mix on low speed until cohesive dough is formed, about 3 minutes; cover bowl tightly with plastic wrap and let sit at room temperature for 20 minutes.

2. Make well in center of dough and add salt and rosemary. Knead dough on low speed for 5 minutes, scraping down bowl and dough hook as needed. Increase speed to medium and continue to knead until dough is smooth and slightly tacky, about 1 minute. If dough is very sticky, add 1 to 2 tablespoons bread flour and continue mixing for 1 minute. Transfer dough to lightly floured counter and press into 12 by 6-inch rectangle, with long side facing you. Press olives evenly into dough, then roll dough toward you into firm cylinder, keeping roll taut by tucking it under itself as you go. Turn loaf seam side up and roll cylinder into coil. Transfer dough, spiral side up, to large, lightly greased bowl, cover tightly with plastic, and let rise at room temperature until it increases in size by 50 percent, about 1 hour.

3. Spray rubber spatula or bowl scraper with vegetable oil spray. Fold partially risen dough over itself by gently lifting and folding edge of dough toward middle. Turn bowl 90 degrees; fold again. Turn bowl again; fold once more. Cover with plastic and let rise for 30 minutes. Repeat folding, replace plastic, and let rise until doubled in size, about 30 minutes.

4. Transfer dough to lightly floured counter, being careful not to deflate. Divide dough in half, loosely shape each piece into ball, and let rest for 15 minutes. Flip each ball over and, starting from top, roll dough toward you into firm oval shape. Using palms, roll each oval (seam side down) from center outward until 12-inch loaf is formed. Poke any olives that fall off into bottom seam, then pinch seam closed. Transfer each loaf, seam side down, to 12 by 6-inch piece of parchment and cover with plastic. Let rise until doubled in size, 1 to 1½ hours. (Dough should barely spring back when poked with knuckle.)

5. One hour before baking, adjust oven rack to lower-middle position, place baking stone on rack, and heat oven to 450 degrees. Slide parchment with loaves onto pizza peel. Using sharp serrated knife or single-edge razor blade, make one 3½-inch-deep slash on diagonal along top of each fully risen loaf, starting and stopping about 1 inch from ends. Spray loaves with water and slide parchment with loaves onto baking stone. Bake for 15 minutes, spraying loaves with water twice more during first 5 minutes of baking time. Reduce oven temperature to 375 degrees and continue to bake until crust is deep golden brown and loaves register 210 degrees, 25 to 30 minutes. Transfer loaves to wire rack, discard parchment, and let cool to room temperature, about 2 hours, before slicing and serving. (Bread can be wrapped in double layer of plastic wrap and stored at room temperature for up to 3 days. Wrapped with additional layer of aluminum foil, bread can be frozen for up to 1 month. To recrisp the crust, thaw bread at room temperature, if frozen, and place unwrapped bread in 450-degree oven for 5 to 10 minutes.)

OLIVE-ROSEMARY ROLLS
MAKES 16 ROLLS

1. After final rise in step 3, transfer dough to lightly floured counter and gently stretch into 12 by 6-inch rectangle. Divide dough in half widthwise, then divide each half into 8 pieces (you should have 16 pieces). Loosely shape each piece into ball, cover with plastic wrap and let rest for 15 minutes. Loosely cup hand around each piece of dough (not directly over it) and, without applying pressure, move hand in small circular motions to form smooth, taut round. Arrange shaped rolls on 2 parchment paper–lined rimmed baking sheets and cover with plastic wrap. Let rise until doubled in size, about 1 hour. (Dough should barely spring back when poked with knuckle.)

2. Thirty minutes before baking, adjust oven racks to upper-middle and lower-middle positions, and heat oven to 500 degrees. Spray rolls lightly with water and place baking sheets in oven. Bake for 5 minutes, spraying rolls with water twice more. Reduce oven temperature to 400 degrees and continue to bake until rolls are deep golden brown, 15 to 20 minutes, switching and rotating baking sheets halfway through baking. Transfer rolls to wire rack and let cool to room temperature, about 1 hour, before serving.

RUSTIC DINNER ROLLS

✓ WHY THIS RECIPE WORKS
The remarkably crisp crust of European-style dinner rolls keeps them in the domain of professionals, who use steam-injected ovens to expose the developing crust to moisture. We wanted a reliable recipe for rustic dinner rolls with a crisp crust and chewy crumb as good as any from an artisanal bakery. But when we tasted our first batch, we found a dense, bland crumb beneath a leathery crust. The flavor was easy to improve—we added whole wheat flour for earthiness and honey for sweetness. A little extra yeast improved the crumb slightly, but making the dough wetter was the best fix; the water created steam bubbles during baking, producing an airier crumb. Next we came up with a two-step process to mimic a steam-injected oven: First, we misted the rolls with water before baking. We started baking them in a cake pan at a high temperature to help set their shape. Then we lowered the temperature, pulled the rolls apart, and returned them to the oven until we had golden rolls with a perfect crust and crumb.

RUSTIC DINNER ROLLS
MAKES 16 ROLLS

If you don't have a stand mixer, you can mix the dough by hand following the instructions on page 586. Because this dough is sticky, keep your hands well floured when handling it.

1½	cups plus 1 tablespoon water, room temperature
2	teaspoons honey
1½	teaspoons instant or rapid-rise yeast
3	cups plus 1 tablespoon (16½ ounces) bread flour, plus extra as needed
3	tablespoons whole wheat flour
1½	teaspoons salt

1. Whisk water, honey, and yeast together in bowl of stand mixer until well combined, making sure no honey sticks to bottom of bowl. Transfer bowl to stand mixer fitted with dough hook. Add flours and mix on low speed until cohesive dough is formed, about 3 minutes; cover bowl tightly with plastic wrap and let sit at room temperature for 30 minutes.

2. Sprinkle salt evenly over dough and knead on low speed for 5 minutes, scraping down bowl and dough hook as needed. Increase speed to medium and continue to knead until dough is smooth and slightly tacky, about 1 minute. If dough is very sticky, add 1 to 2 tablespoons flour and continue mixing for 1 minute. Transfer dough to large, lightly greased bowl; cover tightly with plastic and let rise at room temperature until doubled in size, about 1 hour.

3. Spray rubber spatula or bowl scraper with vegetable oil spray. Fold partially risen dough over itself by gently lifting and folding edge of dough toward middle. Turn bowl 90 degrees; fold again. Rotate the bowl again and fold once more. Cover with plastic and let rise for 30 minutes. Repeat folding, replace plastic, and let dough rise until doubled in size, about 30 minutes longer.

4. Grease two 9-inch round cake pans. Transfer dough to floured counter and sprinkle top with more flour. Using bench scraper, cut dough in half and gently stretch each half into 16-inch log. Cut each log into 16 equal pieces and dust top of each piece with more flour. With floured hands, gently pick up each piece and roll in palms to coat with flour, shaking off excess. Arrange rolls in prepared pans, placing one in center and seven spaced evenly around edges, with long side of each roll running from center of pan to edge and making sure cut side faces up. Loosely cover pans with lightly greased plastic and let rolls rise until doubled in size, about 30 minutes. (Dough should barely spring back when poked with knuckle.)

5. Thirty minutes before baking, adjust oven rack to middle position and heat oven to 500 degrees. Spray rolls lightly with water, bake until tops of rolls are brown, about 10 minutes, then remove them from oven. Reduce oven temperature to 400 degrees; using kitchen towels or oven mitts, invert rolls from both cake pans onto rimmed baking sheet. When rolls are cool enough to handle, turn them right side up, pull apart, and space evenly on baking sheet. Continue to bake until rolls develop deep golden brown crust and sound hollow when tapped on bottom, 10 to 15 minutes, rotating baking sheet halfway through baking. Transfer rolls to wire rack and let cool to room temperature, about 1 hour, before serving. (Rolls can be placed in zipper-lock bag and stored at room temperature for up to 3 days. Wrapped with aluminum foil before placing in bag, rolls can be frozen for up to 1 month. To recrisp the crust, thaw rolls at room temperature, if frozen, and place unwrapped rolls in 450-degree oven for 6 to 8 minutes.)

BEST AMERICAN DINNER ROLLS

✔ WHY THIS RECIPE WORKS
Quick recipes for dinner rolls produce rolls that aren't much better than what you buy at the supermarket because they don't allow enough time for the dough to develop much flavor. But homemade rolls—made right—are often too bothersome for an overextended home cook. We wanted to develop a largely make-ahead recipe that would deliver rich, soft, tender, airy, semisweet, pull-apart all-American dinner rolls. We started by getting the ingredients just right. Plenty of butter contributed richness; an additional egg gave the rolls more flavor and better texture; and scalded milk made the rolls soft, tender, and rich. For ideas about the best technique, we turned to the queen mother of rich breads: brioche. Traditionally, brioche undergoes several rises, including a slow, cool rise in the fridge that gives the flavors time to develop. The same magic worked on our rolls. This technique also had the advantage of allowing the bulk of the work to be completed a day (or even two days) in advance.

BEST AMERICAN DINNER ROLLS
MAKES 16 ROLLS

If you don't have a stand mixer, you can mix the dough by hand following the instructions on page 586. For this recipe, the dough is made and the rolls are shaped and refrigerated a day or two before being baked and served. Be sure to plan accordingly, as the refrigerated rolls require about 6 hours to rise before they're ready for baking. If your cake pans have a dark nonstick finish, bake the rolls in a 375-degree oven to moderate the browning. This dough should be moister than most; resist the urge to add more flour than is needed to keep the dough from sticking to your hands. Made on a humid day, the dough may require more flour than if made on a dry day.

¾	cup whole milk
8	tablespoons unsalted butter, melted
6	tablespoons sugar

SHAPING DINNER ROLLS

1. After patting dough into 12 by 10-inch rectangle, roll dough to form even cylinder, stretching to 18-inch length.

2. Using bench scraper or chef's knife, cut cylinder into 16 pieces.

3. Using circular motion, gently form dough pieces into rounds. (Tackiness of dough against counter and circular motion should work dough into smooth, even ball.)

4. Arrange rolls in pan, one in center, seven around edge.

1½ teaspoons salt
2   large eggs, room temperature
2¼ teaspoons instant or rapid-rise yeast
3   cups (15 ounces) all-purpose flour, plus extra as needed

1. Bring milk to boil in small saucepan over medium heat; let stand off heat until skin forms on surface, 3 to 5 minutes. Remove and discard skin from surface using spoon. Transfer milk to bowl of stand mixer and add 6 tablespoons melted butter, sugar, and salt; whisk to combine and let mixture cool. When mixture is just warm to touch (90 to 100 degrees), whisk in eggs and yeast until combined.

2. Place bowl on stand mixer fitted with dough hook, add flour, and mix on low speed until combined, 1 to 2 minutes. Increase speed to medium-low and knead about 3 minutes; when pressed with finger, dough should feel tacky and moist but should not stick to finger. (If dough is sticky, add another 1 to 3 tablespoons flour.) Continue to knead until cohesive, elastic dough has formed (it should clear sides of bowl but stick to bottom), 4 to 5 minutes longer. Transfer dough to lightly floured counter and knead by hand until very soft and moist but not overly sticky, 1 to 2 minutes. (If dough sticks excessively to hands and work surface, knead in flour 1 tablespoon at a time until dough is workable.) Place dough in large, lightly greased bowl; cover tightly with plastic wrap and let rise at room temperature until doubled in size, 2 to 3 hours.

3. Grease two 9-inch round cake pans. Transfer dough to lightly floured counter and press into rough 12 by 10-inch rectangle, with long side facing you. Roll dough toward you into firm cylinder, keeping roll taut by tucking it under itself as you go. Using palms, roll dough (seam side down) from center outward until cylinder measures 18 inches. Using bench scraper, cut cylinder into 16 equal pieces. Working with 1 piece of dough at a time, loosely cup hand around dough (not directly over it) and, without applying pressure, move hand in small circular motions to form smooth, taut round. Arrange shaped rolls in prepared pans (one in center and seven spaced evenly around edges); loosely cover cake pans with lightly greased plastic, then cover pans securely with foil. Refrigerate for at least 24 or up to 48 hours.

4. Remove foil (but not plastic) from cake pans; let rolls rise at cool room temperature until doubled in size (rolls should press against each other), 6 to 7 hours. Thirty minutes before baking, adjust oven rack to lower-middle position and heat oven to 400 degrees. Brush rolls with remaining 2 tablespoons melted butter and bake until deep golden brown, 14 to 18 minutes. Let rolls cool in pans on wire rack for about 3 minutes, then invert onto rack; re-invert rolls and let cool for 10 to 15 minutes longer. Break rolls apart and serve warm. (Rolls can be placed in zipper-lock bag and stored at room temperature for up to 3 days. Wrapped with aluminum foil before placing in bag, rolls can be frozen for up to 1 month.)

CRESCENT ROLLS

✔ WHY THIS RECIPE WORKS
Crescent rolls from the supermarket are artificial tasting and stale quickly, but making them at home is time-consuming. We were determined to come up with a recipe for rich, tender, flaky crescent rolls that could fit into an already-hectic holiday cooking schedule. We found that skim milk added flavor without density, and melted butter and extra eggs enriched the dough. An overnight chill made the finished rolls crisp and flaky, and the resilient dough could be shaped and refrigerated for 3 days (or parbaked and frozen for 1 month), then baked right before serving, for rich, buttery rolls without any fuss.

CRESCENT ROLLS
MAKES 16 ROLLS

We developed this recipe using lower-protein flour such as Gold Medal or Pillsbury. If using a higher-protein flour such as King Arthur, reduce the flour amount to 3½ cups (17½ ounces).

If you don't have a stand mixer, you can mix the dough by hand following the instructions on page 586.

¾ cup skim milk

16 tablespoons unsalted butter, cut into 16 pieces

¼ cup (1¾ ounces) sugar

3 large eggs

4 cups (20 ounces) all-purpose flour

1 teaspoon instant or rapid-rise yeast

1½ teaspoons salt

1 large egg white, beaten with 1 teaspoon water

SHAPING CRESCENT ROLLS

1. Roll dough into 20 by 13-inch rectangle. Using pizza wheel or sharp knife, cut dough in half lengthwise, then cut 16 triangles, trimming edges as needed to make uniform triangles.

2. Elongate each triangle of dough, stretching it an additional 2 to 3 inches in length.

3. Gently roll up each crescent, ending with pointed tip on bottom, and push ends toward each other to form crescent shape.

1. Microwave milk, butter, and sugar in 4-cup liquid measuring cup until butter is mostly melted and mixture is warm (110 degrees), about 1½ minutes. Whisk to dissolve butter and blend in sugar. Beat eggs lightly in medium bowl; add about one-third of warm milk mixture, whisking to combine. When bottom of bowl feels warm, add remaining milk mixture, whisking to combine.

2. Using stand mixer fitted with paddle, mix flour and yeast together on low speed until combined, about 15 seconds. Add egg mixture in steady stream and mix until loose, shiny dough forms (you may also see satiny webs as dough moves in bowl), about 1 minute. Increase speed to medium and beat for 1 minute; add salt slowly and continue beating until stronger webs form, about 3 minutes longer. (Dough will remain loose rather than forming neat, cohesive mass.) Transfer dough to large, lightly greased bowl; cover tightly with plastic wrap and let rise at room temperature until dough doubles in size and surface feels tacky, about 3 hours.

3. Line rimmed baking sheet with plastic. Sprinkle dough with flour (no more than 2 tablespoons) to prevent sticking, and press down gently to deflate. Transfer dough to floured counter and press into rough rectangle shape. Transfer rectangle to prepared baking sheet, cover with plastic, and refrigerate for 8 to 12 hours.

4. Transfer dough rectangle to lightly floured counter and line baking sheet with parchment paper. Roll dough into uniform 20 by 13-inch rectangle. Cut dough in half lengthwise, then cut each rectangle into 8 triangles, trimming edges as needed to make uniform triangles. Before rolling crescents, elongate each triangle of dough, stretching it an additional 2 to 3 inches in length. Starting at wide end, gently roll up dough, ending with pointed tip on bottom, and push ends toward each other to form crescent shape. Arrange crescents in 4 rows on prepared baking sheet; wrap baking sheet with plastic, and refrigerate for at least 2 hours or up to 3 days.

5. Remove baking sheet with chilled rolls from refrigerator, unwrap, and slide baking sheet into large clean garbage bag; seal to close. Let crescents rise until they feel slightly tacky and soft and have lost their chill, 45 minutes to 1 hour.

6. Thirty minutes before baking, adjust oven racks to lower-middle and lowest positions, place second rimmed baking sheet on lower rack, and heat oven to 425 degrees. Bring 1 cup water to boil on stovetop. Lightly brush risen crescent rolls with egg white mixture. Working quickly, place baking sheet with rolls on upper rack, then pour boiling water onto rimmed baking sheet on lower rack and quickly close oven door. Bake for 10 minutes, then reduce oven temperature to 350 degrees and continue baking until tops and bottoms of rolls are deep golden brown, 12 to 16 minutes longer. Transfer rolls to wire rack, let cool for 5 minutes, and serve warm. (Rolls can be placed in zipper-lock bag and stored at room temperature for up to 3 days. Wrapped with aluminum foil before placing in bag, rolls can be frozen for up to 1 month.)

TO MAKE AHEAD: Rolls can be partially baked and frozen until ready to serve. Begin baking rolls as instructed, but let them bake at 350 degrees for only 4 minutes, or until tops and bottoms brown slightly. Remove them from oven and let cool to room temperature. Place partially baked rolls in single layer inside zipper-lock bag and freeze. When ready to serve, defrost rolls at room temperature and place in preheated 350-degree oven for 12 to 16 minutes.

CHAPTER 16   Pizza, Calzones, and
Flatbreads

EASY HOMEMADE PIZZA

✔ WHY THIS RECIPE WORKS

While we all settle for convenience over quality on occasion, the difference between a takeout or frozen pizza and homemade is extreme. Homemade pizza really is superb, but the tomato sauce and dough are time-consuming. We set out to shortcut those steps for homemade pizza that could practically be made in the time it takes to heat the oven. For the crispiest crust, we liked using a pizza stone. We also found that a fast tomato sauce, enlivened with olive oil and garlic tasted just as good as a long-cooked tomato sauce. As for the toppings, we took a cue from high-end pizzerias and in addition to classic sausage and bell pepper, we combined mushrooms, fontina, and sage in one variation, and prosciutto and arugula in another.

CLASSIC PIZZA DOUGH

MAKES 2 POUNDS DOUGH, ENOUGH FOR
TWO 14-INCH PIZZAS

All-purpose flour can be substituted for the bread flour, but the resulting crust will be a little less chewy.

4–4¼	cups (22 to 23⅓ ounces) bread flour
2¼	teaspoons instant or rapid-rise yeast
1½	teaspoons salt
2	tablespoons olive oil
1½	cups water, heated to 110 degrees

1. Pulse 4 cups flour, yeast, and salt together in food processor (fitted with dough blade if possible) until combined, about 5 pulses. With food processor running, slowly add oil, then water; process until rough ball forms, 30 to 40 seconds. Let dough rest for 2 minutes, then process for 30 seconds longer. (If, after 30 seconds dough is sticky and clings to blade, add remaining ¼ cup flour 1 tablespoon at a time as needed.)

2. Transfer dough to lightly floured counter and knead by hand into smooth, round ball. Place dough in a large, lightly greased bowl; cover bowl tightly with greased plastic wrap and let rise at room temperature until doubled in size, 1 to 1½ hours, before using.

QUICK TOMATO SAUCE FOR PIZZA

MAKES ABOUT 3 CUPS

If you don't have time to cook this sauce, drain the tomatoes slightly, then mix the ingredients together and let them stand while you stretch the dough.

2	large garlic cloves, minced
2	tablespoons olive oil
1	(28-ounce) can crushed tomatoes
	Salt and pepper

Heat garlic with oil in saucepan over medium heat. When garlic starts to sizzle, add tomatoes, bring to simmer, and cook until sauce is thick enough to mound on spoon, about 15 minutes. Season with salt and pepper to taste. (Sauce can be stored in refrigerator for up to 1 week or frozen for up to 1 month.)

SAUSAGE AND BELL PEPPER PIZZA WITH BASIL AND MOZZARELLA

MAKES TWO 14-INCH PIZZAS,
SERVING 4 TO 6

If bulk sausage is not available, just buy cased sausage, remove the casing, and break the meat into bite-size chunks. If you don't have a baking stone, bake the pizzas on an overturned and preheated rimmed baking sheet set on the lowest oven rack. You can shape the second dough round while the first pizza bakes, but don't add the toppings until just before baking. For more information on shaping the pizza dough, see page 608.

1	tablespoon olive oil, plus extra as needed
4	ounces pork sausage, broken into bite-size pieces
1	red or yellow bell pepper, stemmed, seeded, and cut into thin strips

	Salt and pepper
1	recipe Classic Pizza Dough
1½	cups Quick Tomato Sauce for Pizza
¼	cup shredded fresh basil
4	ounces whole-milk mozzarella cheese, shredded (1 cup)

1. One hour before baking, adjust oven rack to lowest position, set baking stone on rack, and heat oven to 500 degrees.

2. Meanwhile, heat oil in 12-inch skillet over medium-high heat until shimmering. Add sausage and cook until browned, about 5 minutes. Remove sausage with slotted spoon and transfer to paper towel–lined plate. Pour off all but 1 tablespoon fat from skillet, add bell pepper, and cook over medium heat until softened, about 5 minutes. Season with salt and pepper to taste; set aside.

3. Transfer dough to lightly floured counter, divide in half, and cover with greased plastic wrap. Use fingertips to gently flatten 1 piece of dough into 8-inch disk (keep other piece covered). Using hands, gently stretch disk into 14-inch round, working along outer edge and giving disk quarter turns. Transfer dough to piece of parchment paper and reshape as needed.

4. Using back of spoon or ladle, spread ¾ cup tomato sauce over dough, leaving ½-inch border around edge. Sprinkle 2 tablespoons basil, half of sausage, and half of pepper over sauce. Slide parchment with pizza onto pizza peel, then slide onto baking stone. Bake until crust begins to brown, 7 to 8 minutes.

5. Remove pizza from oven by sliding parchment back onto pizza peel, close oven door, and top pizza evenly with ½ cup mozzarella. Return pizza to baking stone and continue baking until cheese is just melted, about 3 minutes longer. Transfer to cutting board and discard parchment; slice and serve immediately. Repeat steps 3 and 4 to shape, top, and bake second pizza.

MUSHROOM PIZZA WITH SAGE, FONTINA, AND PARMESAN

MAKES TWO 14-INCH PIZZAS,
SERVING 4 TO 6

If you don't have a baking stone, bake the pizzas on an overturned and preheated rimmed baking sheet set on the lowest oven rack. You can shape the second dough round while the first pizza bakes, but don't add the toppings until just before baking. For more information on shaping the pizza dough, see page 608.

2 tablespoons olive oil
2 large garlic cloves, minced
1 pound cremini or white mushrooms, trimmed and sliced thin
1 teaspoon minced fresh sage
   Salt and pepper
1 recipe Classic Pizza Dough (page 606)
1 cup Quick Tomato Sauce for Pizza (page 606)
4 ounces fontina cheese, shredded (1 cup)
¼ cup grated Parmesan cheese

1. One hour before baking, adjust oven rack to lowest position, set baking stone on rack, and heat oven to 500 degrees.

2. Meanwhile, heat oil and garlic in 12-inch skillet. When garlic begins to sizzle, add mushrooms and cook, stirring often, until mushrooms release their liquid and begin to brown, about 5 minutes. Stir in sage and season with salt and pepper to taste; set aside.

3. Transfer dough to lightly floured counter, divide in half, and cover with greased plastic wrap. Use fingertips to gently flatten 1 piece of dough into 8-inch disk (keep other piece covered). Using hands, gently stretch disk into 14-inch round, working along outer edge and giving disk quarter turns. Transfer dough to piece of parchment paper and reshape as needed.

4. Using back of spoon or ladle, spread ½ cup tomato sauce over dough, leaving ½-inch border around edge. Sprinkle half of mushrooms over sauce. Slide parchment with pizza onto pizza peel, then slide onto baking stone. Bake until crust begins to brown, 7 to 8 minutes.

5. Remove pizza from oven by sliding parchment back onto pizza peel, close oven door, and top pizza evenly with ½ cup fontina and 2 tablespoons Parmesan. Return pizza to baking stone and continue baking until cheese is just melted, about 3 minutes longer. Transfer to cutting board and discard parchment; slice and serve immediately. Repeat steps 3 and 4 to shape, top, and bake second pizza.

FRESH TOMATO PIZZA WITH ARUGULA AND PROSCIUTTO

MAKES TWO 14-INCH PIZZAS,
SERVING 4 TO 6

If you don't have a baking stone, bake the pizzas on an overturned and preheated rimmed baking sheet set on the lowest oven rack. You can shape the second dough round while the first pizza bakes, but don't add the toppings until just before baking. When tossing the arugula with oil, you may also sprinkle on a teaspoon or so of balsamic vinegar, if you like. For more information on shaping the pizza dough, see page 608.

1 recipe Classic Pizza Dough (page 606)
1 pound tomatoes, cored and sliced thin
   Salt and pepper
2 tablespoons olive oil
4 ounces thinly sliced prosciutto
4 ounces whole-milk mozzarella cheese, shredded (1 cup)
2 ounces (2 cups) baby arugula

1. One hour before baking, adjust oven rack to lowest position, set baking stone on rack, and heat oven to 500 degrees.

2. Transfer dough to lightly floured counter, divide in half, and cover with greased plastic wrap. Use fingertips to gently flatten 1 piece of dough into 8-inch disk (keep other piece covered). Using hands, gently stretch disk into 14-inch round, working along outer edge and giving disk quarter turns. Transfer dough to piece of parchment paper and reshape as needed.

3. Arrange half of tomatoes in concentric circles over dough and season with salt and pepper. Drizzle with 4 teaspoons oil. Slide parchment with pizza onto pizza peel, then slide onto baking stone. Bake until crust begins to brown, 7 to 8 minutes.

4. Remove pizza from oven by sliding parchment back onto pizza peel, close oven door, and top pizza evenly with half of prosciutto and ½ cup mozzarella. Return pizza to baking stone and continue baking until cheese is just melted, about 3 minutes longer. Meanwhile, toss arugula with remaining 2 teaspoons oil. Transfer pizza to cutting board and discard parchment. Sprinkle with half of arugula, slice, and serve immediately. Repeat steps 2 and 3 to shape, top, and bake second pizza.

TEST KITCHEN TIP NO. 124 THE BEAUTY OF BAKING STONES

Baking stones (also called pizza stones) were created for home ovens to simulate the steady, dry, intense heat of commercial tile-lined ovens. Both electric and gas home ovens are furnished with thermostats that switch on and off to maintain the oven's internal temperature. This change, coupled with the opening and closing of the oven door, causes the temperature to fluctuate, which can be damaging to baked goods that require extremely high heat like pizza or crusty artisanal bread. A stone prevents the fluctuation by absorbing and storing heat, thereby maintaining a constant temperature. Stones also wick the moisture away from pizza dough to guarantee a crisp crust. For the best results, they should be preheated for one hour to ensure that they are at the ideal temperature.

When purchasing a baking stone, be sure to look for the thickest and biggest possible stone (ensuring that it fits into your oven), which is indicative of a stone's ability to retain heat. Thick stones are also less likely to crack than their thinner, lighter counterparts.

PIZZA MARGHERITA

✔ WHY THIS RECIPE WORKS

Authentic recipes for this Neapolitan pizza call for an 800-degree oven and two days of proofing. We wanted real Margherita—a crisp crust with just a thin veil of tomato sauce, creamy mozzarella, and fresh basil—without the hassle. Our tests proved that a great pizza crust doesn't require much kneading; a food processor mixed our dough in just two minutes. We found we could shape the dough right out of the food processor, but the wet, sticky dough was tricky to roll as thin as we wanted. Our solution was using 1 part cake flour to roughly 2 parts all-purpose flour, which also helped make our pizza light and tender. For the topping, we pulsed canned diced tomatoes in a food processor, drained them to avoid a soggy crust, and added just a little sugar, salt, fresh basil, and garlic. Adding the fresh mozzarella halfway through baking preserved its fresh creamy texture and milky flavor.

PIZZA MARGHERITA

MAKES TWO 12-INCH PIZZAS,
SERVING 4 TO 6

If you don't have a baking stone, bake the pizzas on an overturned and preheated rimmed baking sheet set on the lowest oven rack. You can shape the second dough round while the first pizza bakes, but don't add the toppings until just before baking. If desired, you can slow down the dough's rising time by letting it rise in the refrigerator for 8 to 16 hours in step 2; let the refrigerated dough soften at room temperature for 30 minutes before using.

DOUGH

1¾	cups (8¾ ounces) all-purpose flour, plus extra as needed
1	cup (4 ounces) cake flour
2	teaspoons sugar
1½	teaspoons salt
1¼	teaspoons instant or rapid-rise yeast
1	cup water, heated to 110 degrees, plus extra as needed

SHAPING PIZZA DOUGH

1. Starting at center of dough and working outward, use fingertips to press dough into flattened disk.

2. Holding center in place, stretch dough, working along outer edge. Give disk quarter turn and stretch again. Repeat until dough reaches desired diameter.

TOPPING

1	(28-ounce) can diced tomatoes
½	teaspoon sugar
1	small garlic clove, minced (optional)
¼	cup chopped fresh basil
	Salt
8	ounces fresh mozzarella cheese, cut into 1-inch pieces and patted dry with paper towels
2	teaspoons extra-virgin olive oil

1. FOR THE DOUGH: Pulse flours, sugar, salt, and yeast in food processor (fitted with dough blade if possible) until combined, about 5 pulses. With food processor running, slowly add water; process until dough forms satiny, sticky ball that clears sides of bowl, 1½ to 2 minutes. (If after 1 minute dough is sticky and clings to blade, add 1 to 2 tablespoons all-purpose flour and continue processing. If dough appears dry and crumbly, add 1 to 2 tablespoons water and process until dough forms a ball.)

2. Transfer dough to lightly floured counter and knead by hand into smooth, round ball. Place dough in large, lightly oiled bowl; cover bowl tightly with greased plastic wrap and let rise at room temperature until doubled in size, about 1 hour.

3. FOR THE TOPPING: While dough rises, pulse tomatoes in clean bowl of food processor until coarsely ground, 2 or 3 pulses. Transfer tomatoes to fine-mesh strainer set over bowl and let drain at least 30 minutes, stirring occasionally

to release their liquid. Just before shaping pizza rounds, combine drained tomatoes, sugar, garlic, if using, 1 tablespoon basil, and ¼ teaspoon salt in bowl.

4. TO TOP AND BAKE THE PIZZA: Thirty minutes before baking, adjust oven rack to lowest position, set baking stone on rack, and heat oven to 500 degrees. Transfer dough to lightly floured counter, divide in half, and cover with greased plastic. Use fingertips to gently flatten 1 piece of dough into 8-inch disk (keep other piece covered). Using hands, gently stretch disk into 12-inch round, working along outer edge and giving disk quarter turns. Transfer dough to piece of parchment paper and reshape as needed. Using back of spoon or ladle, spread thin layer of tomato topping (about ½ cup) over dough, leaving ½-inch border around edge. Slide parchment with pizza onto pizza peel, then slide onto baking stone. Bake until crust begins to brown, about 5 minutes.

5. Remove pizza from oven by sliding parchment with pizza back onto pizza peel, close oven door, and top pizza evenly with half of mozzarella. Return pizza to baking stone and continue baking until cheese is just melted, 4 to 5 minutes more. Transfer to cutting board and discard parchment; sprinkle with half of remaining basil, 1 teaspoon olive oil, and pinch salt. Slice and serve immediately. Repeat steps 4 and 5 to shape, top, and bake second pizza.

WHOLE WHEAT PIZZA MARGHERITA

Use 1½ cups cake flour, ¾ cup whole wheat flour, and ½ cup all-purpose flour in dough.

NEW YORK–STYLE THIN-CRUST PIZZA

✔ WHY THIS RECIPE WORKS

With home ovens that reach only 500 degrees and dough that's impossible to stretch thin, even the savviest cooks can struggle to produce New York–style parlor-quality pizza. We were in pursuit of a New York–style pizza with a perfect crust—thin, crisp, and spottily charred on the exterior; tender yet chewy within. High-protein bread flour gave us a chewy, nicely tanned pizza crust and the right ratio of flour, water, and yeast gave us dough that would stretch and retain moisture as it baked. We kneaded the dough quickly in a food processor then let it proof in the refrigerator for a few hours to develop its flavors. After we shaped and topped the pizza, it went onto a blazing hot baking stone to cook. Placing the stone near the top of the oven was a surprising improvement, allowing the top of the pizza to brown as well as the bottom. In minutes we had a pizza with everything in sync: a thoroughly crisp, browned crust with a slightly chewy texture.

NEW YORK–STYLE THIN-CRUST PIZZA

MAKES TWO 13-INCH PIZZAS, SERVING 4 TO 6

If you don't have a baking stone, bake the pizzas on an overturned and preheated rimmed baking sheet. You can shape the second dough round while the first pizza bakes, but don't add the toppings until just before baking. You will need a pizza peel for this recipe. It is important to use ice water in the dough to prevent it from overheating in the food processor. Semolina flour is ideal for dusting the peel; use it in place of bread flour if you have it. The sauce will yield more than needed in the recipe; extra sauce can be refrigerated for up to 1 week or frozen for up to 1 month.

DOUGH

- 3 cups (16½ ounces) bread flour
- 2 teaspoons sugar
- ½ teaspoon instant or rapid-rise yeast
- 1⅓ cups ice water
- 1 tablespoon vegetable oil
- 1½ teaspoons salt

SAUCE

- 1 (28-ounce) can whole tomatoes, drained
- 1 tablespoon extra-virgin olive oil
- 1 teaspoon red wine vinegar
- 2 garlic cloves, minced

- 1 teaspoon salt
- 1 teaspoon dried oregano
- ¼ teaspoon pepper

CHEESE

- 1 ounce Parmesan cheese, grated fine (½ cup)
- 8 ounces whole-milk mozzarella, shredded (2 cups)

1. FOR THE DOUGH: Pulse flour, sugar, and yeast in food processor (fitted with dough blade if possible) until combined, about 5 pulses. With food processor running, slowly add water; process until dough is just combined and no dry flour remains, about 10 seconds. Let dough sit for 10 minutes.

2. Add oil and salt to dough and process until dough forms satiny, sticky ball that clears sides of bowl, 30 to 60 seconds. Transfer dough to lightly oiled counter and knead briefly by hand until smooth, about 1 minute. Shape dough into tight ball and place in large, lightly oiled bowl; cover bowl tightly with plastic wrap and refrigerate for at least 24 hours or up to 3 days.

3. FOR THE SAUCE: Process all ingredients in clean bowl of food processor until smooth, about 30 seconds. Transfer to bowl and refrigerate until ready to use.

4. TO TOP AND BAKE THE PIZZA: One hour before baking, adjust oven rack to upper-middle position (rack should be about 4 to 5 inches from broiler), set baking stone on rack, and heat oven to 500 degrees. Transfer dough to clean counter and divide in half. With cupped palms, form each half into smooth, tight ball. Place balls of dough on lightly greased baking sheet, spacing them at least 3 inches apart; cover loosely with greased plastic and let sit for 1 hour.

5. Coat 1 ball of dough generously with flour and place on well-floured counter (keep other ball covered). Use fingertips to gently flatten dough into 8-inch disk, leaving 1 inch of outer edge slightly

---

thicker than center. Using hands, gently stretch disk into 12-inch round, working along edges and giving disk quarter turns. Transfer dough to well-floured pizza peel and stretch into 13-inch round. Using back of spoon or ladle, spread ½ cup tomato sauce in thin layer over surface of dough, leaving ¼-inch border around edge. Sprinkle ¼ cup Parmesan evenly over sauce, followed by 1 cup mozzarella. Slide pizza carefully onto baking stone and bake until crust is well browned and cheese is bubbly and beginning to brown, 10 to 12 minutes, rotating pizza halfway through baking. Transfer pizza to wire rack and let cool for 5 minutes before slicing and serving. Repeat step 5 to shape, top, and bake second pizza.

NEW YORK–STYLE THIN-CRUST WHITE PIZZA

MAKES TWO 13-INCH PIZZAS, SERVING 4 TO 6

If you don't have a baking stone, bake the pizzas on an overturned and preheated rimmed baking sheet. You can shape the second dough round while the first pizza bakes, but don't add the toppings until just before baking. You will need a pizza peel for this recipe. It is important to use ice water in the dough to prevent overheating the dough while in the food processor. Semolina flour is ideal for dusting the peel; using it in place of bread flour if you have it. The sauce will yield more than needed in the recipe; extra sauce can be refrigerated for up to 1 week or frozen for up to 1 month.

DOUGH

- 3 cups (16½ ounces) bread flour
- 2 teaspoons sugar
- ½ teaspoon instant or rapid-rise yeast
- 1⅓ cups ice water
- 1 tablespoon vegetable oil
- 1½ teaspoons salt

WHITE SAUCE

- 1 cup whole-milk ricotta cheese
- ¼ cup extra-virgin olive oil
- ¼ cup heavy cream
- 1 large egg yolk
- 4 garlic cloves, minced
- 2 teaspoons minced fresh oregano
- 1 teaspoon minced fresh thyme
- ½ teaspoon salt
- ¼ teaspoon pepper
- ⅛ teaspoon cayenne pepper
- 2 scallions, sliced thin, dark green tops reserved for garnish

CHEESE

- 1 ounce Pecorino cheese, grated fine (½ cup)
- 8 ounces whole-milk mozzarella cheese, shredded (2 cups)
- ½ cup whole-milk ricotta cheese

1. FOR THE DOUGH: Pulse flour, sugar, and yeast in food processor (fitted with dough blade if possible) until combined, about 5 pulses. With food processor running, slowly add water; process until dough is just combined and no dry flour remains, about 10 seconds. Let dough sit for 10 minutes.

2. Add oil and salt to dough and process until dough forms satiny, sticky ball that clears sides of bowl, 30 to 60 seconds. Transfer dough to lightly oiled counter and knead briefly by hand until smooth, about 1 minute. Shape dough into tight ball and place in large, lightly oiled bowl; cover bowl tightly with plastic wrap and refrigerate for at least 24 hours and up to 3 days.

3. FOR THE SAUCE: Whisk all ingredients except scallion greens together in bowl; refrigerate until ready to use.

4. TO TOP AND BAKE THE PIZZA: One hour before baking, adjust oven rack to upper-middle position (rack should be about 4 to 5 inches from broiler), set baking stone on rack, and heat oven to 500 degrees. Transfer dough to clean counter and divide in half. With cupped palms, form each half into smooth, tight ball. Place balls of dough on lightly greased baking sheet, spacing them at least 3 inches apart; cover loosely with greased plastic and let sit for 1 hour.

5. Coat 1 ball of dough generously with flour and place on well-floured counter (keep other ball covered). Use fingertips to gently flatten dough into 8-inch disk, leaving 1 inch of outer edge slightly thicker than center. Using hands, gently stretch disk into 12-inch round, working along edges and giving disk quarter turns. Transfer dough to well-floured pizza peel and stretch into 13-inch round. Using back of spoon or ladle, spread ½ cup ricotta sauce in thin layer over surface of dough, leaving ¼-inch border around edge. Sprinkle ¼ cup Pecorino evenly over sauce, followed by 1 cup mozzarella. Dollop ¼ cup ricotta in teaspoon amounts evenly over pizza. Slide pizza carefully onto baking stone and bake until crust is well browned and cheese is bubbly and beginning to brown, 10 to 12 minutes, rotating pizza halfway through baking. Transfer pizza to wire rack and let cool for 5 minutes before slicing and serving. Repeat step 5 to shape, top, and bake second pizza.

TEST KITCHEN TIP NO. 126 **STICK-RESISTANT SEMOLINA FLOUR**

To prevent the pizza dough from sticking to the pizza peel, many recipes advise using cornmeal or bread crumbs. While both coatings work, they also leave a gritty or crunchy residue on the bottom of the pizza. We typically call for a generous dusting of flour, but even this isn't the perfect solution, as too much flour on the peel can lend a dusty, raw-flour taste to the crust, while too little will allow the dough to stick. The best approach is to spring for a bag of semolina flour. This coarsely ground wheat doesn't char as easily as all-purpose flour, so you can make two pies in succession without brushing off the stone. And almost any amount of semolina will allow pizza to release easily without leaving too gritty a residue.

GRILLED PIZZA

✔ WHY THIS RECIPE WORKS

Grilled pizzas often frustrate cooks with their charred crusts and sauce and cheese that drip onto the coals. We set out to find the secret to great grilled pizza. We found that for grilling, pizza dough has to be both thin (to cook through quickly) and sturdy (so that it doesn't fall apart when we turn it to grill the second side). We used high-protein bread flour to strengthen the dough, and a greater proportion of water made it easier to stretch. The crust also needed more flavor to stand up to the heat of the fire, so we added extra salt, a little whole wheat flour, and some olive oil, which also kept the crust from sticking. Using salted chopped tomatoes rather than sauce kept the crust from getting soggy, and a mixture of soft fontina and nutty Parmesan added more flavor than mozzarella. Spicy garlic oil and a scattering of fresh basil added complexity without heaviness.

GRILLED TOMATO AND CHEESE PIZZA

MAKES FOUR 9-INCH PIZZAS,
SERVING 4 TO 6

The pizzas cook very quickly on the grill, so before you begin, be sure to have all the equipment and ingredients you need at hand. Equipment includes a pizza peel (or baking sheet), a pair of tongs, a paring knife, a large cutting board, and a pastry brush. Ingredients includes all the toppings and a small bowl of flour for dusting. The pizzas are best served hot off the grill but can be kept warm for 20 to 30 minutes on a wire rack in a 200-degree oven.

DOUGH
- 1 cup water, room temperature
- 2 tablespoons olive oil
- 2 cups (11 ounces) bread flour
- 1 tablespoon whole wheat flour (optional)

- 2 teaspoons sugar
- 1¼ teaspoons salt
- 1 teaspoon instant or rapid-rise yeast

TOPPING
- 1½ pounds plum tomatoes, cored, seeded, and cut into ½-inch pieces
- ¾ teaspoon salt
- 6 ounces fontina cheese, shredded (1½ cups)
- 1½ ounces Parmesan cheese, grated fine (¾ cup)
- 1 recipe Spicy Garlic Oil (recipe follows)
- ½ cup chopped fresh basil
  Kosher salt

1. FOR THE DOUGH: Combine water and 2 tablespoons oil in liquid measuring cup. Pulse 1¾ cup bread flour, whole wheat flour, if using, sugar, salt, and yeast in food processor (fitted with dough blade if possible) until combined, about 5 pulses. With food processor running, slowly add water mixture; process until dough forms ball, about 1½ minutes. (If after 1½ minutes dough is sticky and clings to blade, add remaining ¼ cup flour 1 tablespoon at a time.) Transfer dough to large, lightly greased bowl; cover tightly with plastic wrap and let rise at room temperature until doubled in size, 1½ to 2 hours.

2. Gently press down on center of dough to deflate. Transfer dough to clean counter and divide into 4 equal pieces. With cupped palms, form each piece into smooth, tight ball. Set dough balls on well-floured counter. Press dough rounds by hand to flatten; cover loosely with plastic and let rest for 15 minutes.

3. FOR THE TOPPING: Meanwhile, toss tomatoes and salt in bowl; transfer to colander and drain for 30 minutes (wipe out and reserve bowl). Shake colander to drain off excess liquid; transfer tomatoes to now-empty bowl and set aside. Combine

fontina and Parmesan in second bowl and set aside.

4. Gently stretch 1 dough round (keep other rounds covered) into disk about ½ inch thick and 5 to 6 inches in diameter. Roll disk out to ⅛-inch thickness, 9 to 10 inches in diameter, on well-floured sheet of parchment paper, dusting with additional flour as needed to prevent sticking. (If dough shrinks when rolled out, cover with plastic and let rest until relaxed, 10 to 15 minutes.) Dust surface of rolled dough with flour and set aside. Repeat with remaining dough rounds, stacking sheets of rolled dough on top of each other (with parchment in between) and covering stack with plastic; set aside until grill is ready.

5A. FOR A CHARCOAL GRILL: Open bottom vent completely. Light large chimney starter filled with charcoal briquettes (6 quarts). When top coals are partially covered with ash, pour evenly over three-quarters of grill. Set cooking grate in place, cover, and open lid vent completely. Heat grill until hot, about 5 minutes.

5B. FOR A GAS GRILL: Turn all burners to high, cover, and heat grill until hot, about 15 minutes. Leave primary burner on high and turn off other burner(s).

6. Clean and oil cooking grate. Lightly flour pizza peel or baking sheet; invert 1 dough round onto peel, gently stretching it as needed to retain its shape (do not stretch dough too thin; thin spots will burn quickly). Peel off and discard parchment; carefully slide round onto hotter side of grill. Immediately repeat with another dough round. Cook (covered if using gas) until tops are covered with bubbles (pierce larger bubbles with paring knife) and bottoms are grill-marked and charred in spots, 1 to 4 minutes; while rounds cook, check undersides and slide to cooler area of grill if browning too quickly. Transfer crusts to cutting board, browned sides up. Repeat with 2 remaining dough rounds.

7. Brush 2 crusts generously with garlic oil; top each evenly with one-quarter of cheese mixture and one-quarter of tomatoes. Return pizzas to hotter side of grill and cover grill with lid; cook until bottoms are well browned and cheese is melted, 2 to 6 minutes, checking bottoms frequently to prevent burning. Transfer pizzas to cutting board; repeat with remaining 2 crusts. Sprinkle pizzas with basil and season with salt to taste; cut into wedges and serve.

SPICY GARLIC OIL
MAKES ABOUT ⅓ CUP; ENOUGH FOR 4 PIZZAS

⅓   cup extra-virgin olive oil
4   garlic cloves, minced
½–¾   teaspoon red pepper flakes

Cook all ingredients in small saucepan over medium heat, stirring occasionally, until garlic begins to sizzle, 2 to 3 minutes; transfer to small bowl.

CHICAGO-STYLE DEEP-DISH PIZZA

✔ WHY THIS RECIPE WORKS
We wanted a recipe to rival the best deep-dish pizza Chicago has to offer, with a thick, crisp crust; an airy, flaky interior; and a rich taste that could hold its own under any kind of topping. The recipes we came across in our research weren't bad, but they weren't as flaky as a Chicago-made crust. To increase the flakiness, we turned to laminating—layering butter and dough through a sequence of rolling and folding to create ultra-flaky pastries. Adding melted butter to the dough and spreading the rolled-out dough with softened butter before folding did the trick. Our only additional tweak was adding oil to the pan to crisp the edges. With our crust all set, we turned to the toppings. Following Chicago tradition, we covered the dough with freshly shredded mozzarella and then topped the cheese with our thick, quick-to-make tomato sauce. The cheese formed a barrier between the crust and sauce, which prevented our thick, flavorful crust from turning soggy.

CHICAGO-STYLE DEEP-DISH PIZZA
MAKES TWO 9-INCH PIZZAS, SERVING 6 TO 8

This dough must be prepared in a stand mixer. Place a damp kitchen towel under the mixer and watch it at all times during kneading to prevent it from wobbling off the counter. Handle the dough with slightly oiled hands to prevent sticking. Grate the onion on the large holes of a box grater.

DOUGH
3¼   cups (16¼ ounces) all-purpose flour
½   cup (2¾ ounces) yellow cornmeal
2¼   teaspoons instant or rapid-rise yeast
2   teaspoons sugar
1½   teaspoons salt
1¼   cups water, room temperature
3   tablespoons unsalted butter, melted, plus 4 tablespoons, softened
1   teaspoon plus 4 tablespoons olive oil

SAUCE
2   tablespoons unsalted butter
¼   cup grated onion

MAKING FLAKY CHICAGO-STYLE PIZZA CRUST

1. On dry counter, roll dough into 15 by 12-inch rectangle.

2. Spread softened butter over dough, leaving ½-inch border along edges.

3. Starting at short end closest to you, roll dough into tight cylinder.

4. Flatten cylinder into 18 by 4-inch rectangle. Halve crosswise.

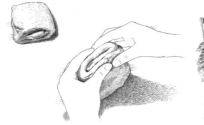

5. Fold each piece of dough into thirds; pinch seams to form balls.

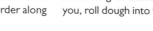

6. Let dough balls rise in refrigerator 40 to 50 minutes to chill butter.

7. Roll out each ball into 13-inch disk about ¼ inch thick.

8. Transfer disks to pans; press into corners and up sides.

¼ teaspoon dried oregano
Salt and pepper
2 garlic cloves, minced
1 (28-ounce) can crushed tomatoes
¼ teaspoon sugar
2 tablespoons chopped fresh basil
1 tablespoon extra-virgin olive oil

TOPPINGS
1 pound mozzarella, shredded (4 cups)
¼ cup grated Parmesan cheese

1. FOR THE DOUGH: Using stand mixer fitted with dough hook, mix together flour, cornmeal, yeast, sugar, and salt on low speed until combined, about 1 minute. Add water and melted butter and mix until fully combined, 1 to 2 minutes, scraping down bowl as needed. Increase speed to medium and knead until dough is glossy and smooth and pulls away from sides of bowl, 4 to 5 minutes. (Dough will only pull away from sides while mixer is on. When mixer is off, the dough will fall back to sides.)

2. Using fingers, coat large bowl with 1 teaspoon of olive oil, rubbing excess oil from fingers onto blade of rubber spatula. Using oiled spatula, transfer dough to prepared bowl, turning once to oil top. Cover bowl tightly with plastic wrap. Let dough rise at room temperature until nearly doubled in size, 45 minutes to 1 hour.

3. FOR THE SAUCE: While dough rises, melt butter in medium saucepan over medium heat. Add onion, oregano, and ½ teaspoon salt and cook, stirring occasionally, until onion is softened and lightly browned, about 5 minutes. Stir in garlic and cook until fragrant, about 30 seconds. Stir in tomatoes and sugar, bring to simmer, and cook until sauce has reduced to 2½ cups, 25 to 30 minutes. Off heat, stir in basil and oil, then season with salt and pepper to taste.

4. TO LAMINATE THE DOUGH: Adjust oven rack to lowest position and heat oven to 425 degrees. Using rubber spatula, turn dough out onto dry clean counter and roll into 15 by 12-inch rectangle with short side facing you. Spread softened butter over surface of dough using offset spatula, leaving ½-inch border along edges. Starting at short end, roll dough into tight cylinder. With seam side down, flatten cylinder into 18 by 4-inch rectangle. Cut rectangle in half crosswise. Working with 1 half at a time, fold dough into thirds like business letter, then pinch seams together to form ball. Return dough balls to oiled bowl, cover tightly with plastic, and let rise in refrigerator until nearly doubled in size, 40 to 50 minutes.

5. Coat two 9-inch round cake pans with 2 tablespoons olive oil each. Transfer 1 dough ball to clean counter and roll into 13-inch disk about ¼ inch thick. Transfer dough round to cake pan by rolling dough loosely around rolling pin, then unrolling dough into pan. Lightly press dough into pan, working it into corners and 1 inch up sides. If dough resists stretching, let it relax 5 minutes before trying again. Repeat with remaining dough ball.

6. TO TOP AND BAKE THE PIZZA: For each pizza, sprinkle 2 cups of mozzarella evenly over surface of dough. Spread 1¼ cups of tomato sauce over cheese and sprinkle 2 tablespoons of Parmesan over sauce for each pizza. Bake until crust is golden brown, 20 to 30 minutes. Remove pizzas from oven and let rest for 10 minutes before slicing and serving.

CHICAGO-STYLE DEEP-DISH PIZZA WITH SAUSAGE

Cook 1 pound hot Italian sausage, casings removed, in 12-inch nonstick skillet over medium-high heat, breaking it into ½-inch pieces with wooden spoon, until browned, about 5 minutes. Remove sausage with slotted spoon and transfer to paper towel–lined plate. Sprinkle half of cooked sausage over mozzarella in each pizza before continuing with additional toppings in step 6.

CHICAGO-STYLE DEEP-DISH PIZZA WITH OLIVES, RICOTTA, AND ARUGULA

Sprinkle each pizza with 2 tablespoons chopped pitted kalamata olives along with Parmesan in step 6. Using 2 tablespoons ricotta cheese per pizza, dot surface with teaspoons of cheese. Bake as directed. Remove pizzas from oven and sprinkle ¼ cup chopped arugula over surface of each pizza.

CLASSIC PAN PIZZA

✔ WHY THIS RECIPE WORKS

Unlike its thin-crust cousin, pan pizza has a soft, chewy, thick crust that can stand up to substantial toppings. We wanted to try our hand at making this pizza without a lot of fuss. Most of the allure of deep-dish pizza is in the crust, so it was important to get it right. After trying numerous ingredients and techniques, we found a surprising solution: adding boiled potato gave the crust exactly the right qualities. It was soft and moist, yet with a bit of chew and good structure. The potato even made the unbaked dough easier to handle. To keep the outside of the crust from toughening during baking, we added a generous amount of olive oil to the pan before putting in the dough. Topping the pizza before it went into the oven weighed down the crust so that it didn't rise enough, so we baked the crust untopped for a few minutes first. Our crust wasn't just a platform for the topping; it had great flavor and texture of its own.

CLASSIC PAN PIZZA WITH TOMATOES, MOZZARELLA, AND BASIL

MAKES ONE 14-INCH PIZZA, SERVING 4 TO 6

If you don't have a stand mixer, you can mix the dough by hand following the instructions on page 586. If you don't have a baking stone, bake the pizza on an overturned and preheated rimmed baking sheet set on the lowest oven rack.

Prepare the topping while the dough is rising so it will be ready at the same time the dough is ready. The amount of oil used to grease the pan may seem excessive, but in addition to preventing sticking, the oil helps the crust brown nicely.

DOUGH

9	ounces russet potatoes, peeled and quartered
3½	cups (17½ ounces) all-purpose flour
1	cup water, heated to 115 degrees
1½	teaspoons instant or rapid-rise yeast
6	tablespoons extra-virgin olive oil
1¾	teaspoons salt

TOPPING

4	tomatoes, cored, seeded, and cut into 1-inch pieces
2	garlic cloves, minced
	Salt and pepper
6	ounces mozzarella cheese, shredded (1½ cups)
1	ounce Parmesan cheese, grated (½ cup)
3	tablespoons shredded fresh basil

1. FOR THE DOUGH: Bring 1 quart water and potato to boil in medium saucepan and cook until tender, 10 to 15 minutes. Drain potato and process through ricer or food mill onto plate. Measure out and reserve 1⅓ cups potato; discard remaining potato.

2. Adjust oven racks to upper-middle and lowest positions and heat oven to 200 degrees. Once oven temperature reaches 200 degrees, maintain heat for 10 minutes, then turn off oven.

3. Using stand mixer fitted with dough hook, mix ½ cup flour, ½ cup water, and yeast together on low speed until combined; cover bowl tightly with plastic wrap and let sit until bubbly, about 20 minutes.

4. Add 2 tablespoons oil, remaining 3 cups flour, remaining ½ cup water, salt, and potato to flour mixture and mix on low speed until dough comes together. Increase speed to medium and knead until dough

comes together and is slightly tacky, about 5 minutes. Transfer dough to large, lightly greased bowl; cover tightly with plastic and let rise on lower rack in warm oven until doubled in size, 30 to 35 minutes.

5. Grease bottom of 14-inch cake pan with remaining 4 tablespoons oil. Remove dough from oven; transfer to clean counter and press into 12-inch round. Transfer round to pan, cover with plastic, and let rest until dough no longer resists shaping, about 10 minutes. Uncover dough and pull up into edges and up sides of pan to form 1-inch-high lip. Cover with plastic; let rise at room temperature until doubled in size, about 30 minutes.

6. FOR THE TOPPING: Mix tomatoes and garlic together in bowl and season with salt and pepper to taste; set aside.

7. TO BAKE THE PIZZA: One hour before baking, set baking stone on lower rack and heat oven to 425 degrees. Uncover dough and prick generously with fork. Bake on baking stone until dry and lightly browned, about 15 minutes.

8. Remove pizza from oven. Spread partially baked crust with tomato mixture; sprinkle with mozzarella, then Parmesan. Return pizza to baking stone and continue baking until cheese melts, 10 to 15 minutes longer. Move pizza to upper rack and continue to bake until cheese is spotty brown, about 5 minutes longer. Remove pizza from oven, sprinkle with basil, and let rest for 10 minutes before slicing and serving.

CLASSIC FOUR-CHEESE PAN PIZZA WITH PESTO

Omit tomatoes, garlic, salt, pepper, and basil from topping. Spread ½ cup Classic Basil Pesto (page 161) onto partially baked crust in step 8, then sprinkle with mozzarella, followed by 1 cup shredded provolone cheese, ¼ cup crumbled blue cheese, and Parmesan. Continue baking as directed.

SHEET PAN PIZZA

WHY THIS RECIPE WORKS

Sheet pan pizza cooks through easily enough in the intense heat of a pizzeria oven, but cooking a thick-crust pizza loaded with sauce and cheese in a less-powerful home oven is another story. It's hard to get the middle of the pizza to cook through, and the generous toppings mean soggy crust is likely. We wanted a thick sheet pan pizza with lots of sauce and cheese, but crisp through and through. To achieve this goal we added a thin layer of oil to the baking sheet, which helped promote a browned bottom crust. Sprinkling the dough with Parmesan before prebaking created a barrier between sauce and crust and it gave the sauce something to cling to, so the toppings didn't slide. After prebaking the dough with the Parmesan, we spread an even layer of tomato sauce on the dough then returned the pizza to the oven. This step helped evaporate moisture from the sauce, which kept the pizza from becoming soggy. Finally, adding more Parmesan and mozzarella during the last few minutes of baking ensured that the cheeses melted into an appropriately gooey, but not burned, layer.

SHEET PAN PIZZA
SERVES 12

The pizza dough will be very sticky; be sure to coat the counter, rolling pin, and your hands with extra flour as needed. You will need about 1 tablespoon of oil to brush over the dough before rising.

DOUGH

4¾–5	cups (23¾ to 25 ounces) all-purpose flour
1½	tablespoons instant or rapid-rise yeast
1	tablespoon sugar
2	teaspoons salt
¼	cup olive oil
1¾	cups water, heated to 110 degrees

TOPPING

5 tablespoons olive oil, plus extra as needed
3 garlic cloves, minced
2 tablespoons tomato paste
1½ teaspoons dried oregano
¼ teaspoon red pepper flakes
1 (28-ounce) can crushed tomatoes
2 tablespoons chopped fresh basil
Salt
3 ounces Parmesan cheese, grated (1½ cups)
12 ounces mozzarella cheese, shredded (3 cups)

1. FOR THE DOUGH: Pulse 4¾ cups flour, yeast, sugar, and salt in food processor (fitted with dough blade if possible) until combined, about 5 pulses. With processor running, slowly add oil, then water; process until rough ball forms, 30 to 40 seconds. Let dough rest for 2 minutes, then process for 30 seconds longer. (If after 30 seconds the dough is sticky and clings to the blade, add remaining ¼ cup flour 1 tablespoon at a time as needed.)

2. Turn dough out onto lightly floured counter and form smooth, round ball. Place the dough in large, lightly oiled bowl and cover tightly with greased plastic wrap. Let rise in warm, draft-free place until doubled in size, 1 to 1½ hours.

3. FOR THE TOPPING: Heat 1 tablespoon oil and garlic in saucepan over medium heat until sizzling and fragrant, about 1½ minutes. Stir in tomato paste, oregano, and pepper flakes and cook, stirring often, until paste begins to brown, about 2 minutes. Stir in crushed tomatoes and simmer until sauce is thickened, about 10 minutes. Off heat, stir in basil and season with salt to taste.

4. Adjust oven rack to lower-middle position and heat oven to 400 degrees. Coat 18 by 13-inch rimmed baking sheet with remaining ¼ cup oil. Turn dough out onto lightly floured counter and flatten it into rough rectangle. Roll dough into 16 by 12-inch rectangle and press into prepared pan. Shape edges of dough against pan and brush dough lightly with oil. Cover with plastic wrap and let rise in warm place until puffy, 30 to 45 minutes.

5. Press dough with fingertips to dimple it, then sprinkle evenly with 1 cup Parmesan. Bake until Parmesan begins to brown, 7 to 10 minutes. Working quickly, spread tomato sauce over dough, leaving 1-inch border around edge. Bake until sauce darkens and steams, 7 to 10 minutes. Working quickly, sprinkle with remaining ½ cup Parmesan and mozzarella. Continue to bake until cheese is melted, 10 to 15 minutes, rotating pizza halfway through baking.

6. Let pizza cool in pan for 1 minute, then lift onto cutting board with wide spatula. Cut into squares and serve hot.

RICOTTA CALZONES

✔ WHY THIS RECIPE WORKS
With soggy fillings and bready crusts, bad calzones are a dime a dozen. After baking 240 of them, we've elevated calzones above common pizzeria fare. We tested a host of modern calzone recipes and came up with calzones that were pale and blond, soggy and limp. They tended to hover at one of two extremes: too bready and rubbery or too thin and crackerlike. We wanted to balance a crisp crust with plenty of chew, and a healthy proportion of rich, creamy, flavorful filling. Bread flour gave the crust chew and crispness and olive oil added flavor and made the dough easy to handle. Mixing for 10 minutes to fully develop the gluten in the dough guaranteed that good chew. We kept the filling simple, with ricotta, mozzarella, and Parmesan and some light seasonings in just the right proportions, blended with a single egg yolk. Cutting vents in the tops to let off some steam and cooling the calzones on a wire rack prevented soggy bottoms.

RICOTTA CALZONES

MAKES SIX 9-INCH CALZONES, SERVING 6 TO 8

If you don't have a stand mixer, you can mix the dough by hand following the instructions on page 586. If you don't have a baking stone, bake the calzones on an overturned and preheated rimmed baking sheet set on the lowest oven rack. A simple tomato sauce is a nice accompaniment to the calzones.

DOUGH

4 cups (22 ounces) bread flour
2¼ teaspoons instant or rapid-rise yeast
1½ teaspoons salt
2 tablespoons extra-virgin olive oil
1½ cups plus 1 tablespoon water, heated to 105 degrees

FILLING

2 tablespoons olive oil
3 garlic cloves, minced
¼ teaspoon red pepper flakes
16 ounces whole-milk ricotta (2 cups)
8 ounces fresh mozzarella cheese, shredded (2 cups)
1½ ounces grated Parmesan cheese (¾ cup)
1 large egg yolk
1 tablespoon minced fresh oregano
¼ teaspoon salt
⅛ teaspoon pepper
Extra-virgin olive oil
Kosher salt

1. FOR THE DOUGH: Using stand mixer fitted with dough hook, combine flour, yeast, and salt on low speed. Increase speed to medium-low, add olive oil, then gradually add water; continue to mix until mixture comes together and smooth, elastic dough forms, about 10 minutes. Transfer dough to large, lightly greased bowl; cover with greased plastic wrap and let rise at room temperature until doubled in size, 1½ to 2 hours.

2. FOR THE FILLING: While dough rises, heat olive oil, garlic, and pepper flakes in 8-inch skillet over medium heat until garlic is fragrant and begins to sizzle, 1½ to 2 minutes. Transfer to small bowl and let cool, stirring occasionally, for 10 minutes.

3. Combine ricotta, mozzarella, Parmesan, egg yolk, oregano, salt, pepper, and cooled garlic oil in bowl; cover with plastic and refrigerate until needed.

4. Adjust oven rack to lowest position, set baking stone on rack, and heat oven to 500 degrees for at least 30 minutes. Line baking sheet with parchment paper and spray parchment lightly with vegetable oil spray. Transfer dough to clean counter. Divide dough in half, then cut each half into thirds. Loosely shape each piece of

dough into ball. Transfer to baking sheet and cover with greased plastic. Let dough rest for 15 to 30 minutes.

5. Cut eight 9-inch square pieces of parchment. Roll 1 dough ball into 9-inch round (keep other pieces covered). Set round onto parchment square and cover with another parchment square; roll out another dough ball, set dough round on top of first, and cover with parchment square. Repeat to form stack of 3 rounds, covering top round with parchment square. Form second stack of 3 with remaining dough balls and parchment squares.

6. Remove top parchment square from first stack of dough rounds and place rounds with parchment beneath on work surface; if dough rounds have

shrunk, gently and evenly roll out again to 9-inch rounds. Spread scant ½ cup filling onto bottom half of each round, leaving 1-inch border at bottom uncovered. Fold top half of dough over bottom half, leaving ½-inch border of bottom layer uncovered, then press and crimp edges to seal. With sharp knife, cut 5 slits, about 1½ inches long, diagonally across top of calzone, making sure to cut through only top layer of dough. Brush tops and sides of calzones with olive oil and lightly sprinkle with kosher salt. Trim excess parchment paper; slide parchment with calzones onto pizza peel, then slide onto baking stone, evenly spacing them apart. Bake until golden brown, about 11 minutes. While first batch of calzones bake, shape and top second batch.

7. Transfer calzones to wire rack and discard parchment; let cool for 5 minutes. While first batch cools, bake second batch. Serve.

RICOTTA CALZONES WITH SAUSAGE AND BROCCOLI RABE

1. While dough rises in step 1, combine ricotta, mozzarella, Parmesan, egg yolk, oregano, salt, and pepper in bowl, cover with plastic, and refrigerate until needed. Omit step for making garlic oil.

2. Cook 8 ounces sweet or hot Italian sausage, casings removed, in 12-inch non-stick skillet over high heat, breaking it up into ½-inch pieces with wooden spoon, until no longer pink, about 5 minutes. Stir in 3 minced garlic cloves and ¼ teaspoon red pepper flakes and cook until fragrant, about 30 seconds. Stir in 12 ounces trimmed broccoli rabe, cut into 1-inch pieces, 1 tablespoon water, and ⅛ teaspoon salt and cook, stirring constantly, until broccoli rabe is crisp-tender and water has evaporated, about 4 minutes. Transfer mixture to large paper towel–lined

---

ASSEMBLING CALZONES

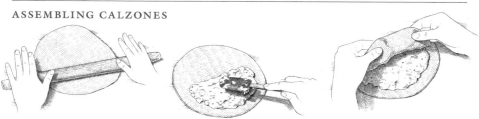

1. With floured rolling pin, roll outward from center in all directions until dough forms 9-inch circle. If dough sticks, dust work surface underneath with flour.

2. Place scant ½ cup of filling in center of bottom half of dough round. Using small spatula, spread or press filling in even layer across bottom half of dough round, leaving 1-inch border uncovered.

3. Fold top half of dough over cheese-covered bottom half, leaving ½-inch border of bottom layer uncovered.

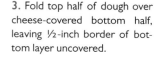

4. With your fingertips, lightly press around silhouette of filling and out to edge to lightly seal dough shut.

5. Beginning at 1 end of seam, place index finger diagonally across edge and gently pull bottom layer of dough over tip of index finger; press into dough to seal. Repeat process until calzone is fully sealed.

6. With sharp knife, cut 6 slits, about 1½ inches long, diagonally across top of calzone, making sure to cut through only top layer of dough and not completely through calzone.

plate and cool to room temperature; once cooled, pat it with paper towels to absorb excess moisture and set aside until needed.

3. Continue with recipe from step 4. To fill calzones, divide sausage mixture evenly into 6 portions on plate; place 1 portion of sausage mixture on top of cheese filling on each dough round and continue with recipe to seal and bake calzones.

RICOTTA CALZONES WITH RED PEPPERS, SPINACH, AND GOAT CHEESE

---

1. While dough rises in step 1, combine 10 ounces whole-milk ricotta (1¼ cups), with mozzarella, Parmesan, egg yolk, oregano, salt, and pepper in bowl, cover with plastic, and refrigerate until needed.

2. Cut 2 stemmed and seeded red bell peppers into ½-inch by 2-inch strips. Heat 1 tablespoon olive oil in 10-inch nonstick skillet over high heat until just smoking. Add bell peppers and ⅛ teaspoon salt and cook until slightly softened and spotty brown, about 5 minutes, stirring only 2 or 3 times. Clear center of skillet, add remaining 1 tablespoon olive oil, garlic, and pepper flakes, and cook, mashing with spatula, until fragrant, about 10 seconds. Stir garlic mixture into peppers. Remove from heat and immediately stir in 1 pound curly-leaf spinach, stemmed, and ⅛ teaspoon salt; continue to stir until spinach is wilted, about 1 minute. Transfer mixture to paper towel–lined plate and let cool to room temperature; once cooled, pat with paper towels to absorb excess moisture and set aside until needed.

3. Continue with recipe from step 4. To fill calzones, divide pepper mixture evenly into 6 portions on plate. Place 1 portion pepper mixture on top of cheese filling on each dough round, then sprinkle each round with 1 ounce crumbled goat cheese (¼ cup) and continue with recipe to seal and bake calzones.

PIZZA BIANCA

✓ WHY THIS RECIPE WORKS

The Roman version of pizza has a crust like no other we've ever tasted: crisp but extraordinarily chewy. It's so good on its own that it's usually topped with just olive oil, rosemary, and kosher salt. We wanted to figure out how we could enjoy this marvel without taking a trip to Italy. This pizza dough contains significantly more water than other styles, which is the secret to its chewy texture. But extra-wet doughs require more kneading, and we wanted to make this dish at home in a reasonable amount of time. Instead of a long knead, we let the dough rest for 20 minutes, which let us get away with just 10 minutes of kneading. After an initial rise, the dough was still sticky; we couldn't roll it out, but it was easy to pour out then press onto a baking sheet. After letting the dough rest briefly, we baked the crust, adding just kosher salt, oil, and rosemary to remain true to the authentic version.

PIZZA BIANCA
SERVES 6 TO 8

If you don't have a stand mixer, you can mix the dough by hand following the instructions on page 586. If you don't have a baking stone, bake the pizza on an overturned and preheated rimmed baking sheet set on the lowest oven rack. This recipe was developed using an 18 by 13-inch baking sheet. Smaller baking sheets can be used, but because the pizza will be thicker, baking times will be longer. Place a damp kitchen towel under the mixer and watch it at all times during kneading to prevent it from wobbling off the counter. Handle the dough with lightly oiled hands to prevent sticking. Resist flouring your fingers or the dough might stick further. Serve the pizza by itself as a snack, or with soup or salad as a light entrée.

3	cups (15 ounces) all-purpose flour
1⅔	cups water, room temperature
1¼	teaspoons salt

1½	teaspoons instant or rapid-rise yeast
1¼	teaspoons sugar
5	tablespoons extra-virgin olive oil
1	teaspoon kosher salt
2	tablespoons fresh rosemary leaves

1. Using stand mixer fitted with dough hook, mix flour, water, and salt together on low speed until no areas of dry flour remain, 3 to 4 minutes, scraping down bowl as needed. Turn off mixer and let dough rest for 20 minutes.

2. Sprinkle yeast and sugar over dough. Knead on low speed until fully combined, 1 to 2 minutes. Increase mixer speed to high and knead until dough is glossy and smooth and pulls away from sides of bowl, 6 to 10 minutes. (Dough will pull away from sides only while mixer is on. When mixer is off, dough will fall back to sides.)

3. Using fingers, coat large bowl with 1 tablespoon oil, rubbing excess oil from fingers onto blade of rubber spatula. Using oiled spatula, transfer dough to prepared bowl and pour 1 tablespoon oil over top. Flip dough over once so that it is well coated with oil; cover bowl tightly with plastic wrap and let dough rise at room temperature until nearly tripled in volume and large bubbles have formed, 2 to 2½ hours. (Dough can be refrigerated for up to 24 hours. Bring dough to room temperature, 2 to 2½ hours, before proceeding with step 4.)

4. One hour before baking, adjust oven rack to middle position, place baking stone on rack, and heat oven to 450 degrees. Coat rimmed baking sheet with 2 tablespoons oil. Using rubber spatula, turn dough out onto prepared baking sheet along with any oil in bowl. Using fingertips, press dough out toward edges of baking sheet, taking care not to tear it. (Dough will not fit snugly into corners. If dough resists stretching, let it relax for 5 to 10 minutes before trying to stretch it

again.) Let dough rest until slightly bubbly, 5 to 10 minutes. Using dinner fork, poke surface of dough 30 to 40 times and sprinkle with kosher salt.

5. Bake until golden brown, 20 to 30 minutes, sprinkling rosemary over top and rotating baking sheet halfway through baking. Using metal spatula, transfer pizza to cutting board. Brush dough lightly with remaining 1 tablespoon oil. Slice and serve immediately.

PIZZA BIANCA WITH TOMATOES AND MOZZARELLA

Place one 28-ounce can crushed tomatoes in fine-mesh strainer set over medium bowl. Let sit for 30 minutes, stirring 3 times to allow juices to drain. Combine ¾ cup tomato solids, 1 tablespoon olive oil, and ⅛ teaspoon salt. (Save remaining solids and juice for another use). Omit kosher salt and rosemary. In step 5, bake pizza until spotty brown, 15 to 17 minutes. Remove pizza from oven, spread tomato mixture evenly over surface, and sprinkle with 1½ cups shredded mozzarella (do not brush pizza with remaining 1 tablespoon oil). Return pizza to oven and continue to bake until cheese begins to brown in spots, 5 to 10 minutes longer.

PIZZA BIANCA WITH CARAMELIZED ONIONS AND GRUYÈRE

Heat 1 tablespoon butter and 1 tablespoon vegetable oil in 12-inch nonstick skillet over high heat until butter is melted. Stir in 1 teaspoon light brown sugar and ½ teaspoon salt, then add 2 pounds onions, halved and sliced ¼ inch thick, and stir to coat; cook, stirring occasionally, until onions begin to soften and release some moisture, about 5 minutes. Reduce heat to medium and cook, stirring often, until onions are deeply browned and slightly sticky, about 40 minutes longer. (If onions are sizzling or scorching, reduce heat. If onions are not browning after 15 to 20 minutes, raise heat.) Off heat, stir in 1 tablespoon water; season with pepper to taste. Transfer to large plate and let cool to room temperature. In step 5, bake pizza until spotty brown, 15 to 17 minutes. Remove pizza from oven, spread onions evenly over surface, and sprinkle with 2 cups shredded Gruyère and 2 teaspoons minced fresh thyme (do not brush pizza with remaining 1 tablespoon oil). Return pizza to oven and continue to bake until cheese begins to brown in spots, 5 to 10 minutes longer.

PIZZA BIANCA WITH TOMATOES, SAUSAGE, AND FONTINA

Cook ¾ pound sweet Italian sausage, casings removed, in 12-inch nonstick skillet over medium heat, breaking it into small pieces with wooden spoon, until no longer pink, about 5 minutes. Remove sausage with slotted spoon and transfer to paper towel–lined plate. Place one 28-ounce can crushed tomatoes in fine-mesh strainer set over medium bowl. Let sit for 30 minutes, stirring 3 times to allow juices to drain. Combine ¾ cup tomato solids, 1 tablespoon olive oil, and ⅛ teaspoon salt. (Save remaining solids and juice for another use). Omit kosher salt and rosemary. In step 5, bake pizza until spotty brown, 15 to 17 minutes. Remove pizza from oven, spread tomato mixture evenly over surface, and sprinkle with 2 cups shredded fontina cheese and sausage (do not brush pizza with remaining 1 tablespoon oil). Return pizza to oven and continue to bake until cheese begins to brown in spots, 5 to 10 minutes longer.

PAN-GRILLED FLATBREAD

✔ WHY THIS RECIPE WORKS
Most flatbreads call for a fairly short list of ingredients, but many require long preparation times or unusual equipment. Our recipe had to be soft and tender yet chewy, with a slightly wheaty, mellow flavor. And it had to be easy enough for home cooks to make while dinner is cooking. We started with a combination of bread flour and whole wheat flour and used a food processor to combine the flour with yeast, warm water, olive oil, sugar, and yogurt. We kneaded the dough for 10 minutes and then allowed it to rise for just 45 minutes to an hour. We cooked the bread in a large, heavy skillet over medium-high heat, then brushed it with butter and sprinkled it with salt before serving for a flatbread worth making at home.

PAN-GRILLED FLATBREAD
MAKES EIGHT 6- TO 7-INCH BREADS

This type of flatbread is akin to naan, a soft and chewy Indian flatbread used to sop up curries. If you don't have a stand mixer, you can mix the dough by hand following the instructions on page 586. Only one flatbread will fit in a skillet, but you can speed up the cooking process by using two skillets.

2½ cups (13¾ ounces) bread flour, plus extra as needed
¼ cup (1⅓ ounces) whole-wheat flour
2¼ teaspoons instant or rapid-rise yeast
2 teaspoons sugar
1½ teaspoons salt

TEST KITCHEN TIP NO. 127 PIZZA DOUGH AT THE READY

Pizza dough can be made ahead. After the dough's first rise, before you roll or shape it, gently press it down to deflate, then wrap it tightly in greased plastic wrap and refrigerate it for up to 2 days. Bring the dough to room temperature, about 2 hours, before proceeding. Alternatively, the dough can be wrapped in greased plastic wrap and aluminum foil and frozen. Let the frozen dough thaw on the counter for 3 hours or overnight in the refrigerator before use.

1   cup water, room temperature, plus
     extra as needed
¼   cup plain whole-milk yogurt
1   tablespoon olive oil
2   tablespoons sesame seeds (optional)
4   tablespoons unsalted butter, melted
     Kosher salt (optional)

1. Using stand mixer fitted with paddle, combine flours, yeast, sugar, and salt together on low speed. Add water, yogurt, and oil and mix until shaggy dough forms, about 30 seconds. Replace paddle with dough hook and knead dough on medium speed until smooth and glossy, about 8 minutes, scraping down bowl as needed. (If, after 4 minutes, more flour is needed, add additional bread flour, 1 tablespoon at a time, until dough clears sides of bowl but sticks to bottom.) Transfer dough to large, lightly greased bowl; cover tightly with plastic wrap and let rise at room temperature until dough has doubled in size, 45 minutes to 1 hour.

2. Transfer dough to lightly floured counter and, if it is sticky, sprinkle very lightly with flour. Divide dough into 8 equal pieces and form each piece into round ball. Roll each ball into 4-inch circle, let rest for 10 minutes, then roll into 6-inch circle. If using sesame seeds, brush tops lightly with water, sprinkle each round with ¾ teaspoon seeds, and gently roll over with rolling pin once or twice so seeds adhere to dough.

3. Five to 10 minutes before cooking flatbreads, heat 12-inch cast-iron skillet over medium-high heat until hot. Working with 1 dough round at a time, gently stretch about 1 inch larger, and place in skillet. Cook until small bubbles appear on surface of dough, about 30 seconds. Flip bread and cook until bottom is speckled and deep golden brown in spots, about 2 minutes. Flip bread over again; cook until bottom is speckled and deep golden brown

in spots, 1 to 2 minutes longer. Transfer rounds to wire rack and cool for 5 minutes. Brush with melted butter and season with kosher salt, if using. Wrap breads loosely in clean kitchen towel and serve warm. (Leftover bread can be wrapped tightly in aluminum foil and stored at room temperature for up to 2 days. To reheat, place unwrapped bread in a 300-degree oven for 15 minutes.)

BAKED PUFFED FLATBREAD

Follow steps 1 and 2 to make and shape dough. Thirty minutes before baking, adjust oven rack to lowest position, place baking stone on rack, and heat oven to 500 degrees. Bake dough rounds on baking stone until bread is puffed and golden brown on bottom, 5 to 6 minutes. Transfer rounds to wire rack and let cool for 5 minutes. Brush with melted butter and season with kosher salt, if using. Wrap breads loosely in clean kitchen towel and serve warm.

PISSALADIÈRE

✔ WHY THIS RECIPE WORKS
Pissaladière, the classic olive, anchovy, and onion tart from Provence, is easy enough to prepare, but each ingredient must be handled carefully. We made the dough in a food processor and kneaded it as little as possible to create a pizza-like dough with the structure to stand up to the heavy toppings. Bread flour worked best because its higher percentage of protein translated to a more substantial chew. Using a combination of high and low heat to cook the onions left them perfectly browned and caramelized. A bit of added water kept them from clumping on the crust. To protect the black olives, anchovies, and fresh thyme leaves from burning in the oven, we covered them with the onions. We preferred

chopping the anchovies to keep them from being overpowering, but diehard fish lovers can add more as a garnish.

PISSALADIÈRE

MAKES 2 TARTS, SERVING 8 TO 10
AS FIRST COURSE

If you don't have a baking stone, bake the tarts on an overturned and preheated rimmed baking sheet set on the lowest oven rack. If desired, you can slow down the dough's rising time by letting it rise in the refrigerator for 8 to 16 hours in step 1; let the refrigerated dough soften at room temperature for 30 minutes before using.

DOUGH
2   cups (11 ounces) bread flour
1   teaspoon instant or rapid-rise yeast
1   teaspoon salt
1   tablespoon olive oil, plus extra
     as needed
1   cup water, heated to 110 degrees

CARAMELIZED ONIONS
2   tablespoons olive oil
2   pounds onions, halved and sliced
     ¼ inch thick
1   teaspoon brown sugar
½   teaspoon salt
1   tablespoon water

OLIVES, ANCHOVIES, AND
GARNISHES
     Olive oil
½   teaspoon pepper
½   cup niçoise olives, pitted and
     chopped coarse
8   anchovy fillets, rinsed, patted dry,
     and chopped coarse, plus 12 fillets,
     rinsed and patted dry, for garnish
     (optional)
2   teaspoons minced fresh thyme
1   teaspoon fennel seeds (optional)
1   tablespoon minced fresh parsley
     (optional)

1. **FOR THE DOUGH:** Pulse flour, yeast, and salt in food processor (fitted with dough blade if possible) until combined, about 5 pulses. With food processor running, slowly add oil, then water; process until dough forms ball, about 15 seconds. Transfer dough to lightly floured counter and form it into smooth, round ball. Place dough in large, lightly greased bowl; cover tightly with greased plastic wrap and let rise at room temperature until doubled in size, 1 to 1½ hours.

2. **FOR THE CARAMELIZED ONIONS:** While dough is rising, heat oil in 12-inch nonstick skillet over medium-low heat until shimmering. Stir in onions, sugar, and salt. Cover and cook, stirring occasionally, until onions are softened and have released their liquid, about 10 minutes. Remove lid, increase heat to medium-high, and continue to cook, stirring often, until onions are deeply browned, 10 to 15 minutes. Off heat, stir in water, then transfer onions to bowl and set aside.

3. **TO SHAPE, TOP, AND BAKE THE DOUGH:** Thirty minute before baking, adjust oven rack to lowest position, set baking stone on rack, and heat oven to 500 degrees. Transfer dough to lightly floured counter, divide in half, and cover with greased plastic. Form 1 piece of dough into rough ball by gently pulling edges of dough together and pinching to seal (keep other piece covered). With floured hands, turn dough ball seam side down. Cupping dough with both hands, gently push dough in circular motion to form taut ball. Repeat with second piece of dough. Brush each piece lightly with oil, cover with plastic, and let rest for 10 minutes. Meanwhile, cut two 20-inch lengths of parchment paper and set aside.

4. Coat fingers and palms generously with oil. Hold 1 piece of dough up and gently stretch it to 12-inch length. Place dough on parchment sheet and gently dimple surface of dough with fingertips. Using oiled palms, push and flatten dough into 14 by 8-inch oval. Brush dough with oil and sprinkle with ¼ teaspoon pepper. Leaving ½-inch border around edge, sprinkle ¼ cup olives, 1 tablespoon chopped anchovies, and 1 teaspoon thyme evenly over dough, then evenly scatter with half of onions. Arrange 6 whole anchovy fillets, if using, on tart and sprinkle with ½ teaspoon fennel seeds, if using. Slide parchment with tart onto pizza peel, then slide onto baking stone. Bake until deep golden brown, 13 to 15 minutes. While first tart bakes, shape and top second tart.

5. Transfer tart to cutting board and remove parchment; let cool for 5 minutes. While first tart cools, bake second tart. Sprinkle tarts with parsley, if using, and cut each tart into 8 pieces before serving.

ROSEMARY FOCACCIA

✔ WHY THIS RECIPE WORKS

Focaccia can easily disappoint when it turns out heavy and thick. We wanted a light, airy loaf, crisp-crusted and topped with just a smattering of herbs. To start, a sponge (a mixture of flour, water, and yeast that rests, often overnight) gave us the flavor benefits of a long fermentation with minimal effort. But our loaves weren't tender and airy enough. Thinking that kneading was developing too much gluten, we tried a gentler approach. A high proportion of water to flour and a long resting process let the natural enzymes in the wheat replicate the effect of kneading. We shaved an hour off our proofing time by adding the salt later in the process, preventing it from slowing down the activity of the enzymes. To give our loaves a flavorful, crisp crust, we oiled the baking pans and added coarse salt for flavor and extra texture. This focaccia was a revelation: crackly crisp on the bottom, deeply browned on top, with an interior that was open and airy.

SHAPING PISSALADIÈRE

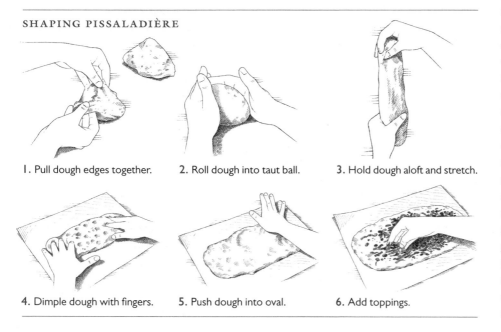

1. Pull dough edges together.

2. Roll dough into taut ball.

3. Hold dough aloft and stretch.

4. Dimple dough with fingers.

5. Push dough into oval.

6. Add toppings.

ROSEMARY FOCACCIA

MAKES TWO 9-INCH ROUND LOAVES

If you don't have a baking stone, bake the bread on an overturned and preheated rimmed baking sheet. For more information on folding and turning the dough in step 3, see page 587.

SPONGE

½ cup (2½ ounces) all-purpose flour
⅓ cup water, heated to 110 degrees
¼ teaspoon instant or rapid-rise yeast

DOUGH

2½ cups (12½ ounces) all-purpose flour, plus extra for shaping
1¼ cups water, heated to 110 degrees
1 teaspoon instant or rapid-rise yeast
Kosher salt
4 tablespoons extra-virgin olive oil
2 tablespoons chopped fresh rosemary

1. FOR THE SPONGE: Combine flour, water, and yeast in large bowl and stir with wooden spoon until uniform mass forms and no dry flour remains, about 1 minute. Cover bowl tightly with plastic wrap and let stand at room temperature at least 8 hours or up to 24 hours. Use immediately or store in refrigerator for up to 3 days (allow to stand at room temperature 30 minutes before proceeding with recipe).

2. FOR THE DOUGH: Stir flour, water, and yeast into sponge with wooden spoon until uniform mass forms and no dry flour remains, about 1 minute. Cover with plastic and let rise at room temperature for 15 minutes.

3. Sprinkle 2 teaspoons salt over dough; stir into dough until thoroughly incorporated, about 1 minute. Cover with plastic and let rise at room temperature for 30 minutes. Spray rubber spatula or bowl scraper with vegetable oil spray. Fold partially risen dough over itself by gently lifting and folding edge of dough toward middle. Turn bowl 90 degrees; fold again. Turn bowl and fold dough 6 more times (for total of 8 folds). Cover with plastic and let rise for 30 minutes. Repeat folding, turning, and rising 2 more times, for total of three 30-minute rises.

4. One hour before baking, adjust oven rack to upper-middle position, place baking stone on rack, and heat oven to 500 degrees. Gently transfer dough to lightly floured counter. Lightly dust top of dough with flour and divide it in half. Shape each piece of dough into 5-inch round by gently tucking under edges. Coat two 9-inch round cake pans with 2 tablespoons oil each. Sprinkle each pan with ½ teaspoon salt. Place round of dough in 1 pan, top side down; slide dough around pan to coat bottom and sides with oil, then flip dough over. Repeat with second piece of dough. Cover pans with plastic and let rest for 5 minutes.

5. Using fingertips, press dough out toward edges of pan, taking care not to tear it. (If dough resists stretching, let it relax for 5 to 10 minutes before trying to stretch it again.) Using dinner fork, poke entire surface of dough 25 to 30 times, popping any large bubbles. Sprinkle rosemary evenly over top of dough. Let dough rest in pans until slightly bubbly, 5 to 10 minutes.

6. Place pans on baking stone and lower oven temperature to 450 degrees. Bake until tops are golden brown, 25 to 28 minutes, rotating pans halfway through baking. Transfer pans to wire rack and let cool for 5 minutes. Remove loaves from pans and return to rack. Brush tops with any oil remaining in pans. Cool for 30 minutes before serving. (Leftover bread can be wrapped in double layer of plastic wrap and stored at room temperature for 2 days. Wrapped with additional layer of aluminum foil, bread can be frozen for up to 1 month.)

FOCACCIA WITH KALAMATA OLIVES AND ANCHOVIES

Omit salt from pans in step 4. Substitute 1 cup kalamata olives, pitted, rinsed, and chopped coarse, 4 rinsed and minced anchovy fillets, and 1 teaspoon red pepper flakes for rosemary. Sprinkle each focaccia with ¼ cup finely grated Pecorino Romano as soon as it is removed from oven.

FOCACCIA WITH CARAMELIZED RED ONION, PANCETTA, AND OREGANO

Cook 4 ounces finely chopped pancetta in 12-inch skillet over medium heat, stirring occasionally, until most of fat has been rendered, about 10 minutes. Remove pancetta with slotted spoon and transfer to paper towel–lined plate. Add 1 chopped red onion and 2 tablespoons water to fat left in skillet and cook over medium heat, stirring often, until onion is soft and beginning to brown, about 12 minutes. Remove skillet from heat and set aside. Omit rosemary. After poking surface of dough rounds in step 5, sprinkle with pancetta, onion, and 2 teaspoons minced fresh oregano. Continue with recipe as directed.

CLASSIC AMERICAN GARLIC BREAD

✔ WHY THIS RECIPE WORKS
Great garlic bread starts with potent, but not overpowering, garlic flavor. We toasted a generous amount of whole garlic cloves to mellow the harshness and highlight the rich, sweet, nutty flavor. We used butter sparingly to give the bread ample richness without marring its texture with overwhelming greasiness. And we added a sparing amount of cheese for depth and complexity without interfering with the garlic flavor.

CLASSIC AMERICAN GARLIC BREAD
SERVES 6 TO 8

Plan to pull the garlic bread from the oven when you are ready to serve the other dishes—it is best served piping hot.

- 10 garlic cloves, unpeeled
- 6 tablespoons unsalted butter, softened
- 2 tablespoons grated Parmesan cheese
- ½ teaspoon salt
- 1 (1-pound) loaf Italian bread (preferably football-shaped), halved horizontally
  Pepper

1. Adjust oven rack to middle position and heat oven to 500 degrees. Meanwhile, toast garlic cloves in 8-inch skillet over medium heat, shaking pan occasionally, until fragrant and color of cloves deepens slightly, about 8 minutes. When cool enough to handle, peel and mince cloves (you should have about 3 tablespoons). Using dinner fork, mash garlic, butter, Parmesan, and salt in bowl until thoroughly combined.

2. Spread cut sides of loaf evenly with garlic and butter mixture; season with pepper. Transfer loaf halves, buttered side up, onto rimmed baking sheet and bake until surface of bread is golden brown and toasted, 5 to 10 minutes, rotating baking sheet halfway through baking. Cut each half into 2-inch slices; serve immediately.

HERB GARLIC BREAD

Mash 1 tablespoon each minced fresh basil and chives and 1½ teaspoons each minced fresh thyme and oregano into garlic and butter mixture.

CHIPOTLE GARLIC BREAD

Mash 4 teaspoons minced canned chipotle chile in adobo sauce into garlic and butter mixture. Increase baking time to 10 to 12 minutes.

PARMESAN AND ASIAGO CHEESE GARLIC BREAD

Decrease salt to ¼ teaspoon and increase Parmesan to ¼ cup. Mash ¼ cup grated Asiago cheese and 2 teaspoons Dijon mustard into garlic and butter mixture.

GOAT CHEESE GARLIC BREAD

Decrease salt to ¼ teaspoon and mash 2 ounces softened goat cheese into garlic and butter mixture. Increase baking time to 10 to 12 minutes.

CHEESY GARLIC BREAD

✓ WHY THIS RECIPE WORKS

Garlic bread is a balancing act between the butter, garlic, and bread. Add gooey cheese to the mix and things get complicated. We wanted cheese-topped garlic bread that was crisp on the outside but chewy within, buttery all the way through, and with no bitter garlic aftertaste.

Supermarket baguettes already have a chewy interior and crisp crust, so we started there. Grating the garlic cloves made for a smoother butter, and to tone down the garlic's harshness we sautéed it in butter with a little water (to prevent burning). We mixed the garlic into more softened butter, spread it on our split baguette, and wrapped the bread in foil. Baking it this way "steams" the bread and infuses it with garlic-butter flavor. To crisp the crust, we took the bread out of the foil and baked it a little longer. The final adornment was the cheese; rather than shredding several different kinds ourselves, we took a shortcut and used a prepackaged

mixture of shredded Italian cheeses. The last step was to run it under the broiler, which gave us both melted cheese and an extra-crisp crust.

SIMPLE CHEESY GARLIC BREAD
SERVES 6 TO 8

The serrated edges on a bread knife can pull off the cheesy crust. To prevent this, place the finished garlic bread cheese side down on a cutting board. Slicing through the crust first (rather than the cheese) will keep the cheese in place.

- 5 medium garlic cloves, peeled and grated
- 8 tablespoons unsalted butter, softened
- ½ teaspoon water
- ¼ teaspoon salt
- ¼ teaspoon pepper
- 1 (18 to 20-inch) baguette, halved horizontally
- 1½ cups shredded Italian cheese blend

1. Adjust oven rack to lower-middle position and heat oven to 400 degrees. Cook garlic, 1 tablespoon butter, and water in 8-inch nonstick skillet over low heat, stirring occasionally, until straw-colored, 7 to 10 minutes.

2. Mix hot garlic, remaining 7 tablespoons butter, salt, and pepper in bowl and spread on cut sides of bread. Sandwich bread back together and wrap loaf in aluminum foil. Place on baking sheet and bake for 15 minutes.

3. Carefully unwrap bread and place halves, buttered sides up, on baking sheet. Bake until just beginning to color, about 10 minutes. Remove from oven and set oven to broil.

4. Sprinkle bread with cheese. Broil until cheese has melted and bread is crisp, 1 to 2 minutes. Transfer bread to cutting board with cheese side facing down. Cut into pieces and serve.

CHAPTER 17 Cookies, Brownies, and Bars

FOOLPROOF SUGAR COOKIES

✔ WHY THIS RECIPE WORKS

Traditional recipes for sugar cookies require obsessive attention to detail. The butter must be at precisely the right temperature and it must be creamed to the proper degree of airiness. Slight variations in measures can result in cookies that spread or become brittle and hard upon cooling. We didn't want a cookie that depended on such a finicky process; we wanted an approachable recipe for great sugar cookies that anyone could make anytime. We melted the butter so our sugar cookie dough could easily be mixed together with a spoon—no more fussy creaming. Replacing a portion of the melted butter with vegetable oil ensured a chewy cookie without affecting flavor. And incorporating an unusual addition, cream cheese, into the cookie dough kept our cookies tender, while the slight tang of the cream cheese made for a rich, not-too-sweet flavor.

CHEWY SUGAR COOKIES
MAKES ABOUT 24 COOKIES

The final dough will be slightly softer than most cookie dough. For best results, handle the dough as briefly and gently as possible when shaping the cookies. Overworking the dough will result in flatter cookies.

2¼	cups (11¼ ounces) all-purpose flour
1	teaspoon baking powder
½	teaspoon baking soda
½	teaspoon salt
1½	cups (10½ ounces) plus ⅓ cup (2⅓ ounces) sugar
2	ounces cream cheese, cut into 8 pieces
6	tablespoons unsalted butter, melted and still warm
⅓	cup vegetable oil
1	large egg
1	tablespoon whole milk
2	teaspoons vanilla extract

1. Adjust oven rack to middle position and heat oven to 350 degrees. Line 2 baking sheets with parchment paper. Whisk flour, baking powder, baking soda, and salt together in medium bowl. Set aside.

2. Place 1½ cups sugar and cream cheese in large bowl. Place remaining ⅓ cup sugar in shallow baking dish or pie plate and set aside. Pour warm butter over sugar and cream cheese and whisk to combine (some small lumps of cream cheese will remain but will smooth out later). Whisk in oil until incorporated. Add egg, milk, and vanilla; continue to whisk until smooth. Add flour mixture and mix with rubber spatula until soft, homogeneous dough forms.

3. Working with 2 tablespoons of dough at a time, roll into balls. Working in batches, roll half of dough balls in sugar to coat and set on prepared baking sheet; repeat with remaining dough balls. Using bottom of greased measuring cup, flatten dough balls until 2 inches in diameter. Sprinkle tops of cookies evenly with sugar remaining in shallow dish for rolling, using 2 teaspoons for each baking sheet. (Discard remaining sugar.)

4. Bake 1 sheet at a time until edges of cookies are set and beginning to brown, 11 to 13 minutes, rotating baking sheet halfway through baking. Let cookies cool on baking sheet for 5 minutes; transfer cookies to wire rack and let cool to room temperature.

CHEWY CHAI-SPICE SUGAR COOKIES

Add ¼ teaspoon ground cinnamon, ¼ teaspoon ground ginger, ¼ teaspoon ground cardamom, ¼ teaspoon ground cloves, and pinch pepper to sugar and cream cheese mixture and reduce vanilla to 1 teaspoon.

CHEWY COCONUT-LIME SUGAR COOKIES

Whisk ½ cup sweetened shredded coconut, chopped fine, into flour mixture in step 1. Add 1 teaspoon finely grated lime zest to sugar and cream cheese mixture and substitute 1 tablespoon lime juice for vanilla.

CHEWY HAZELNUT–BROWNED BUTTER SUGAR COOKIES

Add ¼ cup finely chopped toasted hazelnuts to sugar and cream cheese mixture. Instead of melting butter, heat it in 10-inch skillet over medium-high heat until melted, about 2 minutes. Continue to cook, swirling pan constantly until butter is dark golden brown and has nutty aroma, 1 to 3 minutes. Immediately pour butter over sugar and cream cheese mixture and proceed with recipe as directed, increasing milk to 2 tablespoons and omitting vanilla.

SNICKERDOODLES

✔ WHY THIS RECIPE WORKS

Often, snickerdoodles are just sugar cookies in disguise, flavored too generously with vanilla and without the satisfying chewiness that defines a proper snickerdoodle. We wanted a snickerdoodle that met all our criteria: a texture we could sink our teeth into, a slightly tangy flavor, and a crinkly cinnamon-coated surface. We found cream of tartar and baking soda to be essential ingredients not only because the cream of tartar adds the characteristic tangy flavor, but because they effected a rise followed by a collapse that resulted in a crinkly appearance. We opted out of adding vanilla to the cookies so that the tanginess would be more pronounced. Many snickerdoodle recipes call for shortening, an ingredient that we generally dismiss because of its lack of flavor. But in the case of this cookie, shortening plays a key role in obtaining the right texture— we found that cookies made with a small amount of shortening along with butter spread less during baking than cookies made with all butter. Translation: Snickerdoodles made with shortening were thicker and had a heartier chew. Rolling the cookie dough in cinnamon sugar before baking gave our cookies an authentic finish.

SNICKERDOODLES
MAKES ABOUT 24 COOKIES

Cream of tartar is essential to the flavor of these cookies and it works in combination with the baking soda to give the cookies lift; do not substitute baking powder. For best results, bake only one sheet of cookies at a time.

1¾	cups (12¼ ounces) sugar
1	tablespoon ground cinnamon
2½	cups (12½ ounces) all-purpose flour
2	teaspoons cream of tartar
1	teaspoon baking soda
½	teaspoon salt
8	tablespoons unsalted butter, softened
8	tablespoons vegetable shortening
2	large eggs

1. Adjust oven rack to middle position and heat oven to 375 degrees. Line 2 baking sheets with parchment paper. Combine ¼ cup sugar and cinnamon in shallow dish or pie plate. Whisk flour, cream of tartar, baking soda, and salt together in medium bowl.

2. Using stand mixer, beat butter, shortening, and remaining 1½ cups sugar together on medium speed until light and fluffy, 3 to 6 minutes. Beat in eggs, one at a time, until incorporated, about 30 seconds, scraping down bowl as needed.

3. Reduce speed to low and slowly add flour mixture until combined, about 30 seconds. Give dough final stir to ensure that no flour pockets remain.

4. Working with 2 tablespoons of dough at a time, roll into balls. Working in batches, roll half of dough balls in cinnamon sugar to coat and set on prepared baking sheet spaced 2 inches apart; repeat with remaining dough balls.

5. Bake 1 sheet at a time until edges of cookies are set and just beginning to brown but centers are still soft and puffy, 10 to 12 minutes, rotating baking sheet halfway through baking. (Cookies will look raw between the cracks and seem underdone.)

6. Let cookies cool on baking sheet for 10 minutes, then transfer to wire rack and let cool to room temperature.

PECAN SANDIES

✔ WHY THIS RECIPE WORKS
Pecan sandies run the gamut from greasy and bland to dry and crumbly. We wanted a pecan sandie with a tender but crisp texture and sandy melt-in-the-mouth character. It should taste of butter, pecan, and brown sugar. Some recipes use oil in place of butter for a sandy texture. We found that while oil did indeed yield the desired texture, the flavor was abysmal, so we stuck with butter. We tried both light and dark brown sugars, settling on light, and to tenderize our cookies, we swapped out some of the brown sugar for confectioners' sugar. A whole egg made for a too-sticky dough, so we settled on just a yolk. A rich pecan flavor was obtained by toasting the nuts and then grinding them in a food processor.

While we were grinding the nuts, it occurred to us that we might as well use the food processor to mix the dough as well. After briefly kneading the dough together out of the food processor, we shaped it into dough logs to chill, so that we could slice and bake the dough for pecan sandies with clean, crisp edges.

PECAN SANDIES
MAKES ABOUT 32 COOKIES

Don't substitute another type of sugar for the confectioners' sugar—it is important for a tender, sandy texture.

2	cups (8 ounces) pecans, toasted
½	cup packed (3½ ounces) light brown sugar
¼	cup (1 ounce) confectioners' sugar
1½	cups (7½ ounces) all-purpose flour
¼	teaspoon salt
12	tablespoons unsalted butter, cut into ½-inch pieces and chilled
1	large egg yolk

1. Reserve 32 of prettiest pecan halves for garnishing. Process remaining cups pecans with brown sugar and confectioners' sugar in food processor until nuts are finely ground, about 20 seconds. Add flour and salt and process to combine, about 10 seconds.

2. Add butter pieces and process until mixture resembles damp sand and rides up sides of bowl, about 20 seconds. With processor running, add egg yolk and process until dough comes together into rough ball, about 20 seconds.

3. Transfer dough to clean counter, knead briefly, and divide into 2 equal pieces. Roll each piece of dough into a 6-inch log, about 2 inches thick. Wrap dough tightly in plastic wrap and refrigerate until firm, about 2 hours.

4. Adjust oven racks to upper-middle and lower-middle positions and heat oven to 325 degrees. Line 2 baking sheets with parchment paper.

TEST KITCHEN TIP NO. 128 SOFTENING BUTTER IN A HURRY

It can take about 30 minutes for a cold stick of butter to soften at room temperature. And in order for butter to cream properly, it needs to be soft. What if you don't want to wait? Here's how to soften butter in a hurry: Cut each stick of butter in half and place both halves on a small plate. Place the plate in the microwave and heat for 1 minute at 10 percent power. Press on the butter with your finger to see if it is sufficiently softened; if not, heat for an additional 40 seconds at 10 percent power.

5. Working with 1 dough log at a time, remove dough log from plastic and, using chef's knife, slice into ³⁄₈-inch-thick rounds, rotating dough so that it won't become misshapen from weight of knife. Place rounds 1 inch apart on prepared baking sheets. Gently press pecan half in center of each cookie. Bake until edges of cookies are golden brown, 20 to 25 minutes, switching and rotating baking sheets halfway through baking. Let cookies cool on baking sheets for 3 minutes, then transfer to wire rack and let cool completely.

BROWN SUGAR COOKIES

✔ WHY THIS RECIPE WORKS

Simple sugar cookies, while classic, can seem too simple—even dull—at times. We wanted to turn up the volume on the sugar cookie by switching out the granulated sugar in favor of brown sugar. We had a clear vision of this cookie. It would be oversized, with a crackling crisp exterior and a chewy interior. And its flavor would scream "brown sugar." We wanted butter for optimal flavor, but the traditional creaming method (creaming softened butter with sugar until fluffy, beating in egg, and then adding the dry ingredients) gave us cakey and tender cookies. Cutting the butter into the flour produced crumbly cookies. What worked was first melting the butter. We then tweaked the amount of eggs, dark brown sugar, flour, and leavener, but we wanted even more brown sugar flavor. We made progress by rolling the dough balls in a mix of brown and granulated sugar and adding a healthy amount of vanilla and salt. But our biggest success came from an unlikely refinement. Browning the melted butter added a complex nuttiness that made a substantial difference.

BROWN SUGAR COOKIES
MAKES ABOUT 24 COOKIES

Avoid using a nonstick skillet to brown the butter; the dark color of the nonstick coating makes it difficult to gauge when the butter is sufficiently browned. Use fresh, moist brown sugar, as hardened brown sugar will make the cookies too dry. Achieving the proper texture—crisp at the edges and chewy in the middle—is critical to this recipe. Because the cookies are so dark, it's hard to judge doneness by color. Instead, gently press halfway between the edge and center of the cookie. When it's done, it will form an indentation with slight resistance. Check early and err on the side of underdone.

14	tablespoons unsalted butter
2	cups packed (14 ounces) dark brown sugar
¼	cup (1¾ ounces) granulated sugar
2	cups plus 2 tablespoons (10⅔ ounces) all-purpose flour
½	teaspoon baking soda
¼	teaspoon baking powder
½	teaspoon salt
1	large egg plus 1 large yolk
1	tablespoon vanilla extract

1. Melt 10 tablespoons butter in 10-inch skillet over medium-high heat. Continue cooking, swirling pan constantly, until butter is dark golden brown and has nutty aroma, 1 to 3 minutes. Transfer browned butter to large heatproof bowl. Add remaining 4 tablespoons butter and stir until completely melted; set aside for 15 minutes.

2. Meanwhile, adjust oven rack to middle position and heat oven to 350 degrees. Line 2 baking sheets with parchment paper. In shallow baking dish or pie plate, mix ¼ cup brown sugar and granulated sugar until well combined; set aside. Whisk flour, baking soda, and baking powder together in medium bowl; set aside.

3. Add remaining 1¾ cups brown sugar and salt to bowl with cooled butter; mix until no sugar lumps remain, about 30 seconds. Scrape down bowl; add egg, egg yolk, and vanilla and mix until fully incorporated, about 30 seconds. Scrape down bowl. Add flour mixture and mix until just combined, about 1 minute. Give dough final stir to ensure that no flour pockets remain.

4. Working with 2 tablespoons of dough at a time, roll into balls. Roll half of dough balls into sugar mixture to coat. Place dough balls 2 inches apart on prepared baking sheet; repeat with remaining dough balls.

5. Bake 1 sheet at a time until cookies are browned and still puffy and edges have begun to set but centers are still soft (cookies will look raw between cracks and seem underdone), 12 to 14 minutes, rotating baking sheet halfway through baking. Let cookies cool on baking sheet for 5 minutes; transfer to wire rack and let cool to room temperature.

TEST KITCHEN TIP NO. 129 REVIVING BROWN SUGAR

If your brown sugar dries out, place the sugar in a zipper-lock bag, add a slice of bread, and set it aside overnight until the sugar is soft again. Or, quicker yet, put the brown sugar in a microwave-safe bowl with the bread and tightly cover with plastic wrap. Microwave until the sugar is moist, 15 to 30 seconds.

ULTIMATE CHOCOLATE CHIP COOKIES

✓ **WHY THIS RECIPE WORKS**

Since Nestlé first began printing the recipe for Toll House cookies on the back of chocolate chip bags in 1939, generations of bakers have packed chocolate chip cookies into lunches and taken them to potlucks. But after a few samples, we wondered if this was really the best that a chocolate chip cookie could be. We wanted to refine this recipe to create a moist and chewy chocolate chip cookie with crisp edges and deep notes of toffee and butterscotch to balance its sweetness—in short, a more sophisticated cookie than the standard bake-sale offering. Melting a generous amount of butter before combining it with other ingredients gave us the chewy texture we wanted. Since we were melting butter, we browned a portion of it to add nutty flavor. Using a bit more brown sugar than white sugar enhanced chewiness, while a combination of one egg and one egg yolk gave us supremely moist cookies. For the crisp edges and deep toffee flavor, we allowed the sugar to dissolve and rest in the melted butter. We baked the cookies until golden brown and just set, but still soft in the center. The resulting cookies were crisp and chewy and gooey with chocolate, and boasted a complex medley of sweet, buttery, caramel, and toffee flavors.

ULTIMATE CHOCOLATE CHIP COOKIES
MAKES ABOUT 16 LARGE COOKIES

Avoid using a nonstick skillet to brown the butter; the dark color of the nonstick coating makes it difficult to gauge when the butter is sufficiently browned. Use fresh, moist brown sugar, as hardened brown sugar will make the cookies too dry. This recipe works with light brown sugar, but the cookies will be less full-flavored.

1¾   **cups (8¾ ounces) all-purpose flour**
½   **teaspoon baking soda**

---

14   **tablespoons unsalted butter**
¾   **cup packed (5¼ ounces) dark brown sugar**
½   **cup (3½ ounces) granulated sugar**
1   **teaspoon salt**
2   **teaspoons vanilla extract**
1   **large egg plus 1 large yolk**
1¼   **cups (7½ ounces) semisweet chocolate chips or chunks**
¾   **cup pecans or walnuts, toasted and chopped (optional)**

1. Adjust oven rack to middle position and heat oven to 375 degrees. Line 2 baking sheets with parchment paper. Whisk flour and baking soda together in medium bowl; set aside.

2. Melt 10 tablespoons butter in 10-inch skillet over medium-high heat. Continue cooking, swirling pan constantly, until butter is dark golden brown and has nutty aroma, 1 to 3 minutes. Transfer browned butter to large heatproof bowl. Add remaining 4 tablespoons butter and stir until completely melted.

3. Add brown sugar, granulated sugar, salt, and vanilla to melted butter; whisk until fully incorporated. Add egg and egg yolk; whisk until mixture is smooth with no sugar lumps remaining, about 30 seconds. Let mixture stand for 3 minutes, then whisk for 30 seconds. Repeat process of resting and whisking 2 more times until mixture is thick, smooth, and shiny. Using rubber spatula, stir in flour mixture until just combined, about 1 minute. Stir in chocolate chips and nuts, if using. Give dough final stir to ensure that no

flour pockets remain and ingredients are evenly distributed.

4. Working with 3 tablespoons of dough at a time, roll into balls and place 2 inches apart on prepared baking sheets.

5. Bake 1 sheet at a time until cookies are golden brown and still puffy and edges have begun to set but centers are still soft, 10 to 14 minutes, rotating baking sheet halfway through baking. Transfer baking sheet to wire rack; let cookies cool to room temperature.

THIN AND CRISPY CHOCOLATE CHIP COOKIES

✓ **WHY THIS RECIPE WORKS**

Too often, thin and crispy chocolate chip cookies are tough and lack flavor. They can be too brittle, too crumbly, too dense, or too greasy. We wanted chocolate chip cookies that were thin, almost like praline cookies, and packed a big crunch without either breaking teeth or shattering into a million pieces when eaten. And they had to have the simple, gratifying flavors of deeply caramelized sugar and rich butter. For cookies with a notable butterscotch flavor and sufficient crunch, we turned to a combination of light brown sugar and white sugar. Next we focused on the thickness of our cookies. We used melted butter and milk to create a batter that would spread (not rise) in the oven, resulting in cookies with the perfect thin crispiness. A bit of baking soda and corn syrup promoted maximum browning and caramelization, and vanilla and salt gave our cookies the best flavor.

THIN AND CRISPY CHOCOLATE CHIP COOKIES

MAKES ABOUT 40 COOKIES

Whole or low-fat milk can be used here.

1½	cups (7½ ounces) all-purpose flour
¾	teaspoon baking soda
¼	teaspoon salt
8	tablespoons unsalted butter, melted and cooled
½	cup (3½ ounces) granulated sugar
⅓	cup packed (2⅓ ounces) light brown sugar
2	tablespoons light corn syrup
1	large egg yolk
2	tablespoons milk
1	tablespoon vanilla extract
¾	cup (4½ ounces) semisweet chocolate chips

1. Adjust oven rack to middle position and heat oven to 375 degrees. Line 2 baking sheets with parchment paper.

2. Whisk flour, baking soda, and salt together in medium bowl; set aside.

3. Using stand mixer fitted with paddle, beat melted butter, granulated sugar, brown sugar, and corn syrup at low speed until thoroughly blended, about 1 minute. Add egg yolk, milk, and vanilla; mix until fully incorporated and smooth, about 1 minute, scraping down bowl as needed. With mixer still running on low, slowly add dry ingredients and mix until just combined. Stir in chocolate chips. Give dough final stir to ensure that no flour pockets remain and ingredients are evenly distributed.

4. Working with 1 tablespoon of dough at a time, roll into balls and place 2 inches apart on prepared baking sheets. Bake 1 sheet at a time until cookies are deep golden brown and flat, about 12 minutes, rotating baking sheet halfway through baking.

5. Let cookies cool on baking sheet for 3 minutes; transfer cookies to wire rack and let cool to room temperature.

CHOCOLATE COOKIES

✔ WHY THIS RECIPE WORKS

Cookie recipes that trumpet their extreme chocolate flavor always leave us a bit suspicious. While they provide plenty of intensity, these over-the-top confections also tend to be delicate and crumbly, more like cakey brownies than cookies. We set out to make an exceptionally rich chocolate cookie that we could sink our teeth into—without having it fall apart. Our first batch, which used modest amounts of cocoa powder and melted chocolate, baked up too cakey and tender—just what we didn't want. The chocolate was the culprit—its fat was softening the dough. We scaled back the chocolate until we eliminated it entirely, which made the cookies less cakey and tender, and thus, more cookielike. To restore chocolate flavor without adding too much fat, we increased the cocoa powder and reduced the flour. Using an egg white rather than a whole egg (or yolk) gave us the structure we wanted and adding dark corn syrup gave the cookies a nice chewiness and lent a hint of caramel flavor. For more richness, we folded in chopped bittersweet chocolate; the chunks stayed intact and added intense flavor. After rolling the dough into balls, we dipped them in granulated sugar before baking to give the cookies a sweet crunch and an attractive crackled appearance once they were out of the oven.

CHEWY CHOCOLATE COOKIES

MAKES ABOUT 16 COOKIES

Use a high-quality bittersweet or semisweet chocolate here. Light brown sugar can be substituted for the dark, as can light corn syrup for the dark, but with some sacrifice in flavor.

½	cup (3½ ounces) plus ⅓ cup (2⅓ ounces) granulated sugar
1½	cups (7½ ounces) all-purpose flour
¾	cup (2¼ ounces) Dutch-processed cocoa
½	teaspoon baking soda
¼	teaspoon plus ⅛ teaspoon salt
½	cup dark corn syrup
1	large egg white
1	teaspoon vanilla extract
12	tablespoons unsalted butter, softened
⅓	cup packed (2⅓ ounces) dark brown sugar
4	ounces bittersweet or semisweet chocolate, chopped into ½-inch pieces

1. Adjust oven racks to upper-middle and lower-middle positions and heat oven to 375 degrees. Line 2 baking sheets with parchment paper. Place ½ cup granulated sugar in shallow baking dish or pie plate. Whisk flour, cocoa, baking soda, and salt together in medium bowl. Whisk corn syrup, egg white, and vanilla together in small bowl.

2. Using stand mixer fitted with paddle, beat butter, brown sugar, and remaining ⅓ cup granulated sugar at medium-high speed until light and fluffy, about 2 minutes. Reduce speed to medium-low, add corn syrup mixture, and beat until fully

incorporated, about 20 seconds, scraping down bowl as needed with rubber spatula. Reduce speed to low, add flour mixture and chopped chocolate, and mix until just incorporated, about 30 seconds, scraping down bowl as needed. Give dough final stir to ensure that no flour pockets remain and ingredients are evenly distributed. Refrigerate dough for 30 minutes to firm slightly.

3. Working with 2 tablespoons of dough at a time, roll into balls. Roll half of dough balls in sugar to coat. Place dough balls 2 inches apart on prepared baking sheet; repeat with remaining dough balls. Bake until cookies are puffed and cracked and edges have begun to set but centers are still soft (cookies will look raw between cracks and seem underdone), 10 to 11 minutes, switching and rotating baking sheets halfway through baking. Do not overbake.

4. Let cookies cool on baking sheets for 5 minutes; transfer cookies to wire rack and let cool to room temperature.

ULTIMATE CHOCOLATE COOKIES

✓ WHY THIS RECIPE WORKS

Our goal in creating a traditional double-chocolate cookie recipe seemed more like a fantasy: the first bite of the cookie would reveal a center of hot fudge sauce, the texture would call to mind chocolate bread pudding, and the overall flavor would be of deep and complex chocolate. Was it possible? In the end, the fulfillment of our fantasy relied on very basic ingredients—chocolate, sugar, eggs, butter, flour, baking powder, and salt. We used a modified creaming method with minimal beating to produce moist cookies that weren't cakey, and we let the batter rest for a half-hour to develop a certain fudginess. Ingredient proportions were all-important—for moist, rich cookies, we had to use more chocolate than flour. The more highly

processed semisweet chocolate tasted smoother and richer than unsweetened, and Dutch-processed cocoa—which many bakers find superior in flavor to regular cocoa—and instant coffee further enriched the chocolate flavor. At last, we had a cookie that was both rich and soft, with an intense chocolaty center.

THICK AND CHEWY DOUBLE-CHOCOLATE COOKIES

MAKES ABOUT 42 COOKIES

Resist the urge to bake the cookies longer than indicated; they may appear underbaked at first but will firm up as they cool.

2	cups (10 ounces) all-purpose flour
½	cup (1½ ounces) Dutch-processed cocoa
2	teaspoons baking powder
½	teaspoon salt
1	pound semisweet chocolate, chopped
4	large eggs
2	teaspoons vanilla extract
2	teaspoons instant coffee or espresso powder
10	tablespoons unsalted butter, softened
1½	cups packed (10½ ounces) light brown sugar
½	cup (3½ ounces) granulated sugar

1. Adjust oven racks to upper-middle and lower-middle positions and heat oven to 350 degrees. Line 2 baking sheets with parchment paper. Whisk flour, cocoa, baking powder, and salt together in medium bowl; set aside.

2. Microwave chocolate at 50 percent power for 2 minutes. Stir chocolate and continue heating until melted, stirring once every additional minute; set aside to cool slightly. Whisk eggs and vanilla together in medium bowl, sprinkle instant coffee over top to dissolve, and set aside.

3. Using stand mixer fitted with paddle, beat butter, brown sugar, and granulated

sugar at medium speed until combined, about 45 seconds; mixture will look granular. Reduce speed to low, gradually add egg mixture, and mix until incorporated, about 45 seconds. Add melted chocolate in steady stream and mix until combined, about 40 seconds, scraping down bowl as needed. With mixer still running on low, add dry ingredients and mix until just combined. Do not overbeat. Cover bowl of dough with plastic wrap and let stand at room temperature until consistency is scoopable and fudgelike, about 30 minutes.

4. Working with 2 tablespoons of dough at a time, roll into balls and place 1½ inches apart on prepared baking sheets.

5. Bake until edges of cookies have just begun to set but centers are still very soft, about 10 minutes, switching and rotating baking sheets halfway through baking. Let cookies cool on baking sheets for 10 minutes; transfer cookies to wire rack and let cool to room temperature.

THICK AND CHEWY TRIPLE-CHOCOLATE COOKIES

The addition of chocolate chips will slightly increase the yield of the cookies.

Add 2 cups semisweet chocolate chips to batter after dry ingredients are incorporated in step 3.

PEANUT BUTTER COOKIES

✓ WHY THIS RECIPE WORKS

Recipes for peanut butter cookies tend to fall into one of two categories: sweet and chewy with a mild peanut flavor, or sandy and crumbly with a strong peanut flavor. What we wanted, of course, was the best of both worlds—that is, cookies that were crisp on the edges and chewy in the center, with lots of peanut flavor. First off, we had to determine the amount and type of sugar. Granulated sugar was necessary for crisp edges and chewy centers, while dark brown sugar enriched the peanut flavor. As for flour, too little resulted in an oily cookie, whereas too much made for dry cookies. Baking soda contributed to browning and amplified the peanut flavor and baking powder provided lift, making both leaveners necessary. Extra-crunchy peanut butter also helped the cookies rise and achieve a crispier edge and a softer center. But the best way to get the true peanut flavor we sought was to use peanuts and salt. Adding some roasted salted peanuts, ground in a food processor, and then adding still more salt (directly to the batter as well as in the form of salted rather than unsalted butter) produced a strong roasted nut flavor without sacrificing anything in terms of texture.

PEANUT BUTTER COOKIES
MAKES ABOUT 36 COOKIES

These cookies have a strong peanut flavor that comes from extra-crunchy peanut butter as well as from roasted salted peanuts that are ground in a food processor and worked into the dough. In our testing, we found that salted butter brings out the flavor of the nuts. If using unsalted butter, increase the salt to 1 teaspoon.

- 2½   cups (12½ ounces) all-purpose flour
- ½   teaspoon baking soda
- ½   teaspoon baking powder
- ½   teaspoon salt
- 16   tablespoons salted butter, softened
- 1   cup packed (7 ounces) dark brown sugar
- 1   cup (7 ounces) granulated sugar
- 1   cup extra-crunchy peanut butter, room temperature
- 2   large eggs
- 2   teaspoons vanilla extract
- 1   cup dry-roasted salted peanuts, pulsed in food processor to resemble bread crumbs, about 14 pulses

1. Adjust oven racks to upper-middle and lower-middle positions and heat oven to 350 degrees. Line 2 baking sheets with parchment paper.

2. Whisk flour, baking soda, baking powder, and salt together in medium bowl; set aside.

3. Using stand mixer fitted with paddle, beat butter, brown sugar, and granulated sugar at medium speed until light and fluffy, about 2 minutes, scraping down bowl as needed. Add peanut butter and mix until fully incorporated, about 30 seconds; add eggs, one at a time, and vanilla and mix until combined, about 30 seconds. Reduce speed to low and add dry ingredients; mix until combined, about 30 seconds. Mix in ground peanuts until just incorporated. Give dough final stir to ensure that no flour pockets remain and ingredients are evenly distributed.

4. Working with 2 tablespoons of dough at a time, roll into balls and place 2½ inches apart on prepared baking sheets. Press each dough ball twice, at right angles, with dinner fork dipped in cold water to make crisscross design.

5. Bake until cookies are puffy and slightly brown around edges but not on top, 10 to 12 minutes (cookies will not look fully baked), switching and rotating baking sheets halfway through baking. Let cookies cool on baking sheets for 5 minutes; transfer cookies to wire rack and let cool to room temperature.

CHUNKY OATMEAL COOKIES

✓ WHY THIS RECIPE WORKS
It's easy to get carried away and overload cookie dough with a crazy jumble of ingredients, resulting in a poorly textured cookie monster. Our ultimate oatmeal cookie would have just the right amount of added ingredients and an ideal texture—crisp around the edges and chewy in the middle. We wanted to add four flavor components—sweet, tangy, nutty, and chocolaty—to the underlying oat flavor. Bittersweet chocolate, dried sour cherries (or cranberries), and toasted pecans gave the right

balance of flavors. We also analyzed the cookie dough ingredients and discovered that cookies made with brown sugar were moister and chewier than cookies made with granulated sugar. A combination of baking powder and baking soda (we doubled the usual amount) produced cookies that were light and crisp on the outside, but chewy, dense, and soft in the center. Finally, we focused on appearance to decide when to remove the cookies from the oven—they should be set but still look wet between the fissures; if they look matte rather than shiny, they've been overbaked.

CHOCOLATE-CHUNK OATMEAL COOKIES WITH PECANS AND DRIED CHERRIES
MAKES ABOUT 16 LARGE COOKIES

We like these cookies made with pecans and dried sour cherries, but walnuts or skinned hazelnuts can be substituted for the pecans and dried cranberries for the cherries. Quick oats used in place of the old-fashioned oats will yield a cookie with slightly less chewiness.

- 1¼   cups (6¼ ounces) all-purpose flour
- ¾   teaspoon baking powder
- ½   teaspoon baking soda
- ½   teaspoon salt
- 1¼   cups (3¾ ounces) old-fashioned rolled oats
- 1   cup pecans, toasted and chopped
- 1   cup (4 ounces) dried sour cherries, chopped coarse
- 4   ounces bittersweet chocolate, chopped into chunks about size of chocolate chips
- 12   tablespoons unsalted butter, softened
- 1½   cups packed (10½ ounces) dark brown sugar
- 1   large egg
- 1   teaspoon vanilla extract

1. Adjust oven racks to upper-middle and lower-middle positions and heat oven to 350 degrees. Line 2 baking sheets with parchment paper.

2. Whisk flour, baking powder, baking soda, and salt together in medium bowl. In second medium bowl, stir oats, pecans, cherries, and chocolate together.

3. Using stand mixer fitted with paddle, beat butter and sugar at medium speed until no sugar lumps remain, about 1 minute, scraping down bowl as needed. Add egg and vanilla and beat on medium-low until fully incorporated, about 30 seconds, scraping down bowl as needed. Reduce speed to low, add flour mixture, and mix until just combined, about 30 seconds. Gradually add oat-nut mixture; mix until just incorporated. Give dough final stir to ensure that no flour pockets remain and ingredients are evenly distributed.

4. Working with ¼ cup of dough at a time, roll into balls and place 2½ inches apart on prepared baking sheets. Press dough to 1-inch thickness using bottom of greased measuring cup. Bake until cookies are medium brown and edges have begun to set but centers are still soft (cookies will seem underdone and will appear raw, wet, and shiny in cracks) 20 to 22 minutes, switching and rotating baking sheets halfway through baking.

5. Let cookies cool on baking sheets for 5 minutes; transfer cookies to wire rack and let cool to room temperature.

THIN AND CRISPY OATMEAL COOKIES

✔ **WHY THIS RECIPE WORKS**
Thin and crispy oatmeal cookies can be irresistible—crunchy and delicate, these cookies really let the flavor of the oats take center stage. But the usual ingredients that give thick, chewy oatmeal cookies great texture—generous amounts of sugar and butter, a high ratio of oats to flour, a modest amount of leavener, eggs, raisins, and nuts—won't all fit in a thin, crispy cookie. We wanted to adjust the standard ingredients to create a crispy, delicate cookie in which

the simple flavor of buttery oats really stands out. Given this cookie's simplicity, creating a rich butter flavor was critical, so we kept almost the same amount of butter as in our standard big, chewy oatmeal cookie, but we scaled back the amount of sugar. Fine-tuning the amount and type of leavener led to a surprising result that solved our texture and shape problems. During baking, large carbon dioxide bubbles created by the baking soda and baking powder (upped from our traditional recipe) caused the cookies to puff up, collapse, and spread out, producing the thin, flat cookies we were looking for. Baking the cookies all the way through until they were fully set and evenly browned from center to edge made them crisp throughout but not tough.

THIN AND CRISPY OATMEAL COOKIES

MAKES ABOUT 24 COOKIES

Do not use instant or quick oats.

1	cup (5 ounces) all-purpose flour
¾	teaspoon baking powder
½	teaspoon baking soda
½	teaspoon salt
14	tablespoons unsalted butter, softened but still cool
1	cup (7 ounces) granulated sugar
¼	cup packed (1¾ ounces) light brown sugar
1	large egg
1	teaspoon vanilla extract
2½	cups (7½ ounces) old-fashioned rolled oats

1. Adjust oven rack to middle position and heat oven to 350 degrees. Line 3 baking sheets with parchment paper. Whisk flour, baking powder, baking soda, and salt in medium bowl; set aside.

2. Using stand mixer fitted with paddle, beat butter, granulated sugar, and brown sugar at medium-low speed until just combined, about 20 seconds. Increase speed to medium and continue to beat until light and fluffy, about 1 minute longer, scraping down bowl as needed. Add egg and vanilla and beat on medium-low until fully incorporated, about 30 seconds, scraping down bowl as needed. Reduce speed to low, add flour mixture, and mix until just incorporated and smooth, about 10 seconds. With mixer still running on low, gradually add oats and mix until well incorporated, about 20 seconds. Give dough final stir to ensure that no flour pockets remain and ingredients are evenly distributed.

3. Working with 2 tablespoons of dough at a time, roll into balls and place 2½ inches apart on prepared baking sheets. Using fingertips, gently press each dough ball to ¾-inch thickness.

4. Bake 1 sheet at a time until cookies are deep golden brown, edges are crisp, and centers yield to slight pressure when pressed, 13 to 16 minutes, rotating baking sheet halfway through baking. Transfer baking sheet to wire rack and let cookies cool completely.

THIN AND CRISPY COCONUT-OATMEAL COOKIES

Decrease oats to 2 cups and add 1½ cups sweetened flaked coconut to batter with oats in step 2.

Many cookies taste best the day they are baked, but you may want to keep cookies for several days. We suggest storing them at an airtight container at room temperature. You can restore that just-baked freshness to cookies (with the exception of cookies that have been glazed or dusted with confectioners' sugar) by recrisping them in a 425-degree oven for 4 to 5 minutes. Let the cookies cool on the baking sheet for a couple of minutes before removing them and serve warm.

Beat 2 teaspoons grated orange zest with butter and sugars in step 2. Decrease oats to 2 cups and add 1 cup coarsely chopped toasted almonds to batter with oats in step 2.

SALTY THIN AND CRISPY OATMEAL COOKIES

We prefer the texture and flavor of a coarse-grained sea salt, like Maldon or fleur de sel, but kosher salt can be used. If using kosher salt, reduce the amount sprinkled over the cookies to ¼ teaspoon.

Reduce amount of salt in dough to ¼ teaspoon. Lightly sprinkle ½ teaspoon coarse sea salt evenly over flattened dough balls before baking.

BIG AND CHEWY OATMEAL-RAISIN COOKIES

✔ **WHY THIS RECIPE WORKS**
Big, moist, and craggy, oatmeal cookies are so good and so comforting, but also so hard to get just right. Too often, they have textural issues and are dry and brittle; other times, it's the flavor that's off, with cookies that lack any sign of oatiness. We wanted an oversized cookie with buttery oat flavor and the utmost chewiness. After numerous rounds of testing, we discovered three key changes that made a significant difference in the research recipes we uncovered. First, we substituted baking powder for baking soda. The baking powder gave the dough more lift, which

in turn made the cookies less dense and a bit chewier. Second, we eliminated the cinnamon recommended in lots of recipes; by taking away the cinnamon, we revealed more oat flavor. We wanted some spice, however, and chose nutmeg, which has a cleaner, subtler flavor that we like with oats. Finally, we increased the sugar in our cookies, and this made a huge difference in terms of texture and moistness.

BIG AND CHEWY OATMEAL-RAISIN COOKIES

MAKES ABOUT 18 LARGE COOKIES

If you prefer a less sweet cookie, you can reduce the granulated sugar to ¾ cup, but you will lose some crispness. Do not use instant or quick oats. Do not overbake these cookies. The edges should be brown, but the rest of the cookie should be very light in color.

1½	cups (7½ ounces) all-purpose flour
½	teaspoon salt
½	teaspoon baking powder
¼	teaspoon ground nutmeg
16	tablespoons unsalted butter, softened
1	cup packed (7 ounces) light brown sugar
1	cup (7 ounces) granulated sugar
2	large eggs
3	cups (9 ounces) old-fashioned rolled oats
1½	cups (7½ ounces) raisins (optional)

1. Adjust oven racks to upper-middle and lower-middle positions and heat oven to 350 degrees. Line 2 baking sheets with parchment paper. Whisk flour, salt, baking powder, and nutmeg together in medium bowl; set aside.

2. Using stand mixer fitted with paddle, beat butter, brown sugar, and granulated sugar at medium speed until light and fluffy, about 2 minutes. Add eggs, one at a time, and mix until combined, about 30 seconds.

3. Reduce speed to low and slowly add dry ingredients until combined, about 30 seconds. Mix in oats and raisins, if using, until just incorporated. Give dough final stir to ensure that no flour pockets remain and ingredients are evenly distributed.

4. Working with 2 tablespoons of dough at a time, roll into balls and place 2 inches apart on prepared baking sheets.

5. Bake until cookies turn golden brown around edges, 22 to 25 minutes, switching and rotating baking sheets halfway through baking. Let cookies cool on baking sheets for 2 minutes; transfer cookies to wire rack and let cool to room temperature.

BIG AND CHEWY OATMEAL-DATE COOKIES

Substitute 1½ cups chopped dates for raisins.

BIG AND CHEWY OATMEAL–GINGER COOKIES

Omit raisins and add ¾ teaspoon ground ginger.

BIG AND CHEWY OATMEAL–CHOCOLATE CHIP COOKIES

Substitute 1½ cups semisweet chocolate chips for raisins.

BIG AND CHEWY OATMEAL-NUT COOKIES

The almonds can be ground in a food processor or blender.

Omit raisins, decrease flour to 1⅓ cups, and add ¼ cup ground almonds and 1 cup chopped walnuts along with oats.

TEST KITCHEN TIP NO. 133 SALTED VERSUS UNSALTED BUTTER

You might wonder if it's OK to replace unsalted (sweet cream) butter with salted butter if you reduce the total amount of salt in a recipe, but we advise against cooking with salted butter for two reasons. First, the amount of salt in salted butter varies from brand to brand, making it impossible to offer conversion amounts that will work across the board. Second, because salt masks some of the flavor nuances found in butter, salted butter tastes different from unsalted butter and thus can negatively alter the flavor of a recipe.

Omit raisins and add 2 tablespoons grated orange zest and 1 cup chopped toasted almonds along with oats.

MOLASSES SPICE COOKIES

✔ **WHY THIS RECIPE WORKS**

Molasses spice cookies are often miserable specimens, no more than flat, tasteless cardboard rounds of gingerbread. They can be dry and cakey without the requisite chew; others are timidly flavored with molasses and scantily spiced. We wanted to create the ultimate molasses spice cookie—soft, chewy, and gently spiced with deep, dark molasses flavor. We also wanted it to have the traditional cracks and crinkles so characteristic of these charming cookies. We started with all-purpose flour and butter for full, rich flavor. Using just the right amount of molasses and brown sugar and flavoring the cookies with a combination of vanilla, ginger, cinnamon, cloves, black pepper, and allspice gave these spiced cookies the warm tingle that we were after. We found that to keep the cookies mild, using a light or mild molasses is imperative; but if it's a stronger flavor you want, dark molasses is in order. We pulled the cookies from the oven when they still looked a bit underdone; residual heat finished the baking and kept the cookies chewy and moist.

MOLASSES SPICE COOKIES
MAKES ABOUT 22 COOKIES

For best flavor, make sure that your spices are fresh. Light or mild molasses gives the cookies a milder flavor; for a stronger flavor, use dark molasses.

- ½ cup (3½ ounces) plus ⅓ cup (2⅓ ounces) granulated sugar
- 2¼ cups (11¼ ounces) all-purpose flour
- 1 teaspoon baking soda
- 1½ teaspoons ground cinnamon
- 1½ teaspoons ground ginger
- ½ teaspoon ground cloves
- ¼ teaspoon ground allspice
- ¼ teaspoon pepper
- ¼ teaspoon salt
- 12 tablespoons unsalted butter, softened
- ⅓ cup packed (2⅓ ounces) dark brown sugar
- 1 large egg yolk
- 1 teaspoon vanilla extract
- ½ cup light or dark molasses

1. Adjust oven rack to middle position and heat oven to 375 degrees. Line 2 baking sheets with parchment paper. Place ½ cup granulated sugar in shallow baking dish or pie plate; set aside.

2. Whisk flour, baking soda, cinnamon, ginger, cloves, allspice, pepper, and salt together in medium bowl; set aside.

3. Using stand mixer fitted with paddle, beat butter, brown sugar, and remaining ⅓ cup granulated sugar on medium-high speed until light and fluffy, about 3 minutes. Reduce speed to medium-low and add egg yolk and vanilla; increase speed to medium and beat until incorporated, about 20 seconds. Reduce speed to medium-low and add molasses; beat until fully incorporated, about 20 seconds, scraping down bowl as needed. Reduce speed to low and add flour mixture; beat until just incorporated, about 30 seconds, scraping down bowl as needed. Give dough final stir to ensure that no flour pockets remain. Dough will be soft.

4. Working with 1 tablespoon of dough at a time, roll into balls. Roll half of dough balls in sugar and toss to coat. Place dough balls 2 inches apart on prepared baking sheet. Repeat with remaining dough.

5. Bake 1 sheet at a time until cookies are browned, still puffy, and edges have begun to set but centers are still soft (cookies will look raw between cracks and seem underdone), about 11 minutes, rotating baking sheet halfway through baking. Do not overbake.

6. Let cookies cool on baking sheet for 5 minutes; transfer cookies to wire rack and let cool to room temperature.

MOLASSES SPICE COOKIES
WITH DARK RUM GLAZE

If the glaze is too thick to drizzle, whisk in up to an additional ½ tablespoon rum.

Whisk 1 cup confectioners' sugar and 2½ tablespoons dark rum together in medium bowl until smooth. Drizzle or spread glaze using back of spoon on cooled cookies. Allow glazed cookies to dry at least 15 minutes.

MOLASSES SPICE COOKIES
WITH ORANGE ESSENCE

The orange zest in the sugar coating causes the sugar to become sticky and take on a light orange hue, giving the baked cookies a unique frosty look.

Process ⅔ cup granulated sugar and 2 teaspoons grated orange zest until pale orange, about 10 seconds; transfer sugar to shallow baking dish or pie plate and set aside. Add 1 teaspoon grated orange zest to dough along with molasses and substitute orange sugar for granulated sugar when coating dough balls in step 4.

GLAZED LEMON COOKIES

✔ **WHY THIS RECIPE WORKS**

Store-bought lemon cookies are often saccharine-sweet and artificial tasting, with a thin veneer of frosting and a barely detectable lemon flavor. For a lemon cookie recipe with the perfect balance of lemony zing and rich, buttery sweetness, we started with all-purpose flour, which made our cookies tender. Just an egg yolk instead of a whole egg added even more tenderness, and a touch of baking powder gave our cookies just the right amount of airy crispness. Grinding some lemon zest with the sugar before adding it to the dough contributed bold lemon flavor without harshness. A simple glaze of cream cheese, lemon juice, and confectioners' sugar perfected these lemony treats.

GLAZED LEMON COOKIES
MAKES ABOUT 30 COOKIES

The cookies are best eaten the day they are glazed.

COOKIES

¾	cup (5¼ ounces) granulated sugar
2	tablespoons grated lemon zest plus 2 tablespoons lemon juice (2 lemons)
1¾	cup (8¾ ounces) all-purpose flour
¼	teaspoon salt
¼	teaspoon baking powder
12	tablespoons unsalted butter, cut into ½-inch cubes and chilled
1	large egg yolk
½	teaspoon vanilla extract

GLAZE

1	tablespoon cream cheese, softened
2	tablespoons lemon juice
1½	cups (6 ounces) confectioners' sugar

1. FOR THE COOKIES: Adjust oven racks to upper-middle and lower-middle positions and heat oven to 375 degrees.

2. In food processor, process granulated sugar and lemon zest until sugar looks damp and zest is thoroughly incorporated, about 30 seconds. Add flour, salt, and baking powder; pulse to combine, about 10 pulses. Scatter butter over flour mixture; pulse until mixture resembles fine cornmeal, about 15 pulses. In measuring cup, beat lemon juice, egg yolk, and vanilla with fork to combine. With processor running, add juice mixture in slow, steady stream (process should take about 10 seconds); continue processing until dough begins to form ball, 10 to 15 seconds longer.

3. Turn dough and any dry bits onto counter; working quickly, gently knead together to ensure that no dry bits remain and dough is homogeneous. Shape dough into log about 10 inches long and 2 inches in diameter. Wrap log in parchment paper and twist ends to seal. Chill dough until firm, about 45 minutes in freezer or 2 hours in refrigerator.

4. Line 2 baking sheets with parchment. Remove dough log from parchment and, using chef's knife, slice dough into ⅜-inch-thick rounds, rotating dough so that it won't become misshapen from weight of knife. Place rounds 1 inch apart on prepared baking sheets. Bake until centers of cookies just begin to color and edges are golden brown, 14 to 16 minutes, switching and rotating baking sheets halfway through baking. Let cookies cool on baking sheets for 5 minutes; transfer cookies to wire rack and let cool to room temperature before glazing.

5. FOR THE GLAZE: Whisk cream cheese and lemon juice in medium bowl until no lumps remain. Add confectioners' sugar and whisk until smooth.

6. TO GLAZE THE COOKIES: When cookies have cooled, working with one at a time, spread glaze evenly over each cookie with back of spoon. Let cookies stand on wire rack until glaze is set and dry, about 1 hour.

GLAZED LEMON-ORANGE CORNMEAL COOKIES

Substitute 1 tablespoon grated orange zest for equal amount of lemon zest and ¼ cup cornmeal for equal amount of flour.

GLAZED LEMON AND CRYSTALLIZED GINGER COOKIES

Process 3 tablespoons finely chopped crystallized ginger along with sugar and lemon zest.

BEST SHORTBREAD

✔ WHY THIS RECIPE WORKS
Often shortbread turns out bland and chalky. We wanted superlative shortbread with an alluring tawny brown crumb and pure, buttery richness. In initial tests, we tinkered with various mixing methods and found that reverse creaming—mixing the flour and sugar before adding the butter, creating less aeration—yielded the most reliable results. To smooth out an objectionable granular texture, we swapped the white sugar for confectioners' sugar. Still, our shortbread was unpleasantly tough. The problems were gluten and moisture. Gluten, the protein matrix that lends baked goods structure and chew, forms naturally when liquid and all-purpose flour are combined, even without kneading. The liquid in our recipe was coming from butter, which contains 20 percent water. To curb gluten development, we replaced some of our flour with powdered old-fashioned oats. We ground some oats to a powder and supplemented it with a modest amount of cornstarch (using all oat powder muted the buttery flavor). The cookies were now perfectly crisp and flavorful, with an appealing hint of oat flavor. As for the moisture problem, we baked the dough briefly, then shut off the heat and let it sit in the still-warm oven. The batch was dry through and through, with an even golden brown exterior. Crisp and buttery, our shortbread was anything but bland.

BEST SHORTBREAD
MAKES 16 WEDGES

Use the collar of a springform pan to form the shortbread into an even round. Mold the shortbread with the collar in the closed position, then open the collar, but leave it in place. This allows the shortbread to expand slightly but keeps it from spreading too far. The extracted round of dough in step 2 is baked alongside the rest of the shortbread. Wrapped well and stored at room temperature, the shortbread will keep for up to 1 week.

- ½ cup (1½ ounces) old-fashioned rolled oats
- 1½ cups (7½ ounces) all-purpose flour
- ¼ cup cornstarch
- ⅔ cup (2⅔ ounces) confectioners' sugar
- ½ teaspoon salt
- 14 tablespoons unsalted butter, chilled and cut into ⅛-inch-thick slices

1. Adjust oven rack to middle position and heat oven to 450 degrees. Pulse oats in spice grinder or blender until reduced to fine powder, about 10 pulses (you should have ¼ to ⅓ cup oat flour). Using stand mixer fitted with paddle, mix oat flour, all-purpose flour, cornstarch, sugar, and salt on low speed until combined, about 5 seconds. Add butter to dry ingredients and continue to mix until dough just forms and pulls away from sides of bowl, 5 to 10 minutes.

2. Place upside-down (grooved edge should be at top) collar of 9- or 9½-inch springform pan on parchment paper–lined baking sheet (do not use springform pan bottom). Press dough into collar in even ½-inch-thick layer, smoothing top of dough with back of spoon. Place 2-inch biscuit cutter in center of dough and cut out center. Place extracted round alongside springform collar on baking sheet and replace cutter in center of dough. Open springform collar, but leave it in place.

3. Bake shortbread 5 minutes, then reduce oven temperature to 250 degrees. Continue to bake until edges turn pale golden, 10 to 15 minutes longer. Remove baking sheet from oven; turn off oven. Remove springform pan collar; use chef's knife to score surface of shortbread into 16 even wedges, cutting halfway through shortbread. Using wooden skewer, poke 8 to 10 holes in each wedge. Return shortbread to oven and prop door open with handle of wooden spoon, leaving 1-inch gap at top. Allow shortbread to dry in turned-off oven until pale golden in center (shortbread should be firm but giving to touch), about 1 hour.

4. Transfer baking sheet to wire rack; let shortbread cool to room temperature. Cut shortbread at scored marks to separate and serve.

CHOCOLATE-DIPPED PISTACHIO SHORTBREAD

Add ½ cup finely chopped toasted pistachios to dry ingredients in step 1. Bake and cool shortbread as directed. Once shortbread is cool, melt 8 ounces finely chopped bittersweet chocolate in microwave at 50 percent power for 2 minutes. Stir chocolate and continue heating until melted, stirring once every additional minute. Stir in additional 2 ounces finely chopped bittersweet chocolate until smooth. Carefully dip base of each wedge in chocolate, allowing chocolate to come halfway up cookie. Scrape off excess with finger and place on parchment paper–lined rimmed baking sheet. Refrigerate until chocolate sets, about 15 minutes.

GINGER SHORTBREAD

Turbinado sugar is commonly sold as Sugar in the Raw. Demerara sugar, sanding sugar, or another coarse sugar can be substituted.

Add ½ cup chopped crystallized ginger to dry ingredients in step 1. Sprinkle shortbread with 1 tablespoon turbinado sugar after poking holes in shortbread in step 3.

TOASTED OAT SHORTBREAD

To toast the oats, heat them in an 8-inch skillet over medium-high heat until light golden brown, 5 to 8 minutes. We prefer the texture and flavor of a coarse-grained sea salt like Maldon or fleur de sel, but kosher salt can be used.

Add ½ cup toasted oats to dry ingredients in step 1. Sprinkle ½ teaspoon sea salt evenly over surface of dough before baking.

FORMING AND BAKING SHORTBREAD

  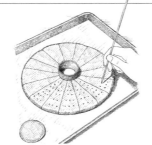 

1. Press dough into closed upside-down springform pan collar; smooth with back of spoon. Cut hole in center of dough with 2-inch biscuit cutter; replace cutter in hole.

2. Open collar. Bake 5 minutes at 450 degrees, then 10 to 15 minutes at 250 degrees.

3. Score partially baked shortbread into wedges, then poke 8 to 10 holes in each wedge.

4. Return shortbread to turned-off oven to dry; prop open door with wooden spoon or stick.

SABLÉ COOKIES

♥ WHY THIS RECIPE WORKS

During the holidays, these French butter cookies offer sophistication and style. That is, if you can capture their elusive sandy texture (sablé is French for sandy), which separates them from sturdy American butter cookies. Most of the sablé recipes we came across had only slight differences in ingredient proportions—but they all baked up without the delicate crumbliness that defines this cookie. To create the hallmark sandy texture of sablés—light, with an inviting granular quality similar to shortbread—we would have to do some detective work. We started with a basic recipe using the typical method of creaming butter and sugar, then adding egg and flour. We then chilled, sliced, and baked the dough—but these cookies were missing the delicate crumbliness that defines sablés. We needed to decrease the liquid in the dough so there would be less moisture to dissolve the sugar particles. Cutting back on butter helped, as did the inclusion of a hard-cooked egg yolk, an addition we came across in our research. Adding the mashed yolk during creaming eliminated moisture and perfected the texture of the cookies. Brushing the cookies with a beaten egg white and sprinkling them with coarse sugar before baking added a delicate crunch and an attractive sparkle.

SABLÉS
(FRENCH BUTTER COOKIES)

MAKES ABOUT 40 COOKIES

Turbinado sugar is commonly sold as Sugar in the Raw. Demerara sugar, sanding sugar, or another coarse sugar can be substituted. Make sure the cookie dough is well chilled and firm so that it can be uniformly sliced.

- 1 large egg
- 10 tablespoons unsalted butter, softened
- ⅓ cup plus 1 tablespoon (2¾ ounces) granulated sugar
- ¼ teaspoon salt
- 1 teaspoon vanilla extract
- 1½ cups (7½ ounces) all-purpose flour
- 1 large egg white, lightly beaten with 1 teaspoon water
- 4 teaspoons turbinado sugar

1. Place egg in small saucepan, cover with water by 1 inch, and bring to boil over high heat. Remove pan from heat, cover, and let sit for 10 minutes. Meanwhile, fill small bowl with ice water. Using slotted spoon, transfer egg to ice water and let stand for 5 minutes. Crack egg and peel shell. Separate yolk from white; discard white. Press yolk through fine-mesh strainer into small bowl.

2. Using stand mixer fitted with paddle, beat butter, granulated sugar, salt, and cooked egg yolk on medium speed until light and fluffy, about 4 minutes, scraping down bowl as needed. Reduce speed to low, add vanilla, and mix until incorporated. Stop mixer; add flour and mix on low speed until just combined, about 30 seconds. Using rubber spatula, press dough into cohesive mass.

3. Divide dough in half. Shape each piece into log about 6 inches long and 1¾ inches in diameter. Wrap each log in parchment paper and twist ends to seal. Chill dough until firm, about 45 minutes in freezer or 2 hours in refrigerator.

4. Adjust oven racks to upper-middle and lower-middle positions and heat oven to 350 degrees. Line 2 baking sheets with parchment. Using chef's knife, slice dough into ¼-inch-thick rounds, rotating dough so that it won't become misshapen from weight of knife. Place cookies 1 inch apart on prepared baking sheets. Using pastry brush, gently brush cookies with egg white mixture and sprinkle evenly with turbinado sugar.

5. Bake until centers of cookies are pale golden brown with edges slightly darker

---

FORMING PRETZEL SABLÉS

1. Slice slightly chilled dough into ¼-inch thick rounds and roll into balls.

2. Roll each ball into a 6-inch rope, tapering ends.

3. Pick up 1 end of rope and cross it over to form half of pretzel shape.

4. Bring second end over to complete shape.

than centers, about 15 minutes, switching and rotating baking sheets halfway through baking. Let cookies cool on baking sheets for 5 minutes; transfer cookies to wire rack and let cool to room temperature.

CHOCOLATE SABLÉS

Reduce flour to 1⅓ cups and add ¼ cup Dutch-processed cocoa with flour in step 2.

LEMON SABLÉS

Add 4 teaspoons grated lemon zest with vanilla in step 2. Omit egg white mixture and turbinado sugar. Once cookies have cooled, dust with confectioners' sugar.

TOASTED COCONUT SABLÉS

Add ⅓ cup finely chopped toasted sweetened coconut to dough with flour in step 2. Omit turbinado sugar. After brushing cookies with egg white mixture, sprinkle with ⅓ cup finely chopped untoasted sweetened coconut.

ALMOND SABLÉS

Substitute 1½ teaspoons almond extract for vanilla extract and add ⅓ cup finely ground sliced almonds to dough with flour in step 2. Omit turbinado sugar. After brushing cookies with egg white mixture, gently press 3 almond slices in petal shape in center of each cookie.

CHOCOLATE SANDWICH COOKIES

In step 4, slice 1 dough log into ⅛-inch-thick rounds, omitting egg white mixture and turbinado sugar. Bake cookies as directed in step 5, reducing baking time to 10 to 13 minutes. Repeat with second dough log. When all cookies are completely cool, microwave 3½ ounces chopped dark or milk chocolate at 50 percent power for 1 to 2 minutes and let cool slightly. Spread melted chocolate on bottom of 1 cookie. Place second cookie on top, slightly off-center, so some chocolate shows. Repeat with remaining melted chocolate and cookies.

VANILLA PRETZEL SABLÉS

Increase vanilla extract to 1 tablespoon and reduce chilling time in step 3 to 30 minutes (dough will not be fully hardened). Slice dough into ¼-inch-thick rounds and roll into balls. Roll each ball into 6-inch rope, tapering ends. Form ropes into pretzel shapes. Proceed with recipe, brushing with egg white mixture, sprinkling with turbinado sugar, and baking as directed.

BLACK AND WHITE SPIRAL SABLÉS
MAKES ABOUT 80 COOKIES

VANILLA SABLÉS

1	large egg
10	tablespoons unsalted butter, softened
⅓	cup plus 1 tablespoon (2¾ ounces) sugar
¼	teaspoon salt
1	teaspoon vanilla extract
1½	cups (7½ ounces) unbleached all-purpose flour

CHOCOLATE SABLÉS

1	large egg
10	tablespoons unsalted butter, softened
⅓	cup plus 1 tablespoon (2¾ ounces) sugar
¼	teaspoon salt
1	teaspoon vanilla extract
1⅓	cups (6⅔ ounces) all-purpose flour
¼	cup (¾ ounce) Dutch-processed cocoa

FORMING SPIRAL SABLÉS

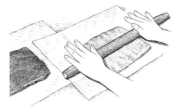  

1. Halve each batch of dough. Roll out each portion on parchment paper into 8 by 6-inch rectangle, ¼ inch thick. Briefly chill dough until firm enough to handle.

2. Using bench scraper, place 1 plain cookie dough rectangle on top of 1 chocolate dough rectangle. Repeat to make 2 double rectangles.

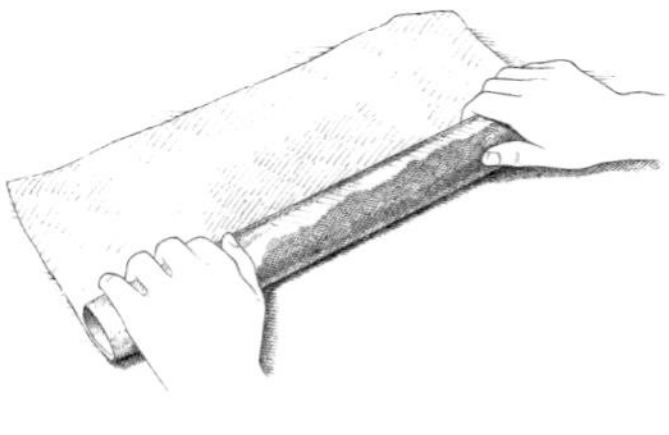

3. Roll out each double rectangle on parchment into 9 by 6-inch rectangle (if too firm, let rest until malleable). Starting at long end, roll each into tight log.

4. Twist ends of parchment to seal and chill logs 1 hour. Slice logs into ¼-inch rounds.

I. FOR VANILLA SABLÉS: Place 2 eggs in small saucepan, cover with water by 1 inch, and bring to boil over high heat. Remove pan from heat, cover, and let sit for 10 minutes. Meanwhile, fill small bowl with ice water. Using slotted spoon, transfer eggs to ice water and let stand 5 minutes. Crack eggs and peel shells. Separate yolks from whites; discard whites. Press yolks, 1 at a time, through fine-mesh strainer into small bowl, reserving 1 strained yolk for chocolate sables.

2. Using stand mixer fitted with paddle, beat butter, granulated sugar, salt, and cooked egg yolk on medium speed until light and fluffy, about 4 minutes, scraping down bowl as needed. Reduce speed to low, add vanilla, and mix until incorporated. Stop mixer; add flour and mix on low speed until just combined, about 30 seconds. Using rubber spatula, press dough into cohesive mass.

3. FOR CHOCOLATE SABLÉS: Using stand mixer fitted with paddle, beat butter, sugar, salt, and reserved cooked egg yolk on medium speed until light and fluffy, about 4 minutes, scraping down bowl as needed. Reduce speed to low, add vanilla, and mix until incorporated. Stop mixer; add flour and cocoa and mix on low speed until just combined, about 30 seconds. Using rubber spatula, press dough into cohesive mass.

4. TO FORM SPIRAL COOKIES: Halve each batch of dough. Roll out each portion on parchment paper into 8 by 6-inch rectangle, ¼ inch thick. Briefly chill dough until firm enough to handle. Using bench scraper, place 1 plain cookie dough rectangle on top of 1 chocolate dough rectangle. Repeat to make 2 double rectangles. Roll out each double rectangle on parchment into 9 by 6-inch rectangle (if too firm, let rest until malleable). Starting at long end, roll each into tight log. Twist ends of

parchment to seal and chill logs 1 hour.

5. Adjust oven racks to upper-middle and lower-middle positions and heat oven to 350 degrees. Line 2 baking sheets with parchment paper. Using chef's knife, slice dough into ¼-inch-thick rounds, rotating dough so that it won't become misshapen from weight of knife. Place cookies 1 inch apart on prepared baking sheets.

6. Bake until centers of cookies are pale golden brown with edges slightly darker than centers, about 15 minutes, switching and rotating baking sheets halfway through baking. Let cookies cool on baking sheets for 5 minutes; transfer cookies to wire rack and let cool to room temperature.

CHOCOLATE BUTTER COOKIES

✔ WHY THIS RECIPE WORKS
Chocolate butter cookies usually taste bland or surrender their crisp, delicate appeal to a chewy, brownielike texture. We wanted to cram big chocolate flavor into a tender, crisp cookie. Cocoa powder—with a much higher percentage of cocoa solids than other forms of chocolate— was clearly the best candidate to maximize chocolate flavor, so we first doubled the amount of cocoa in our working recipe. The cocoa did indeed boost the flavor, but the texture of our cookie was now dry and pasty. Reducing the flour and adding egg yolks for more structure was the answer. Extra vanilla extract enhanced the aromatics in the chocolate for even more chocolate flavor. Then we discovered that "blooming" the cocoa powder in melted butter (along with a teaspoon of instant espresso) before adding it to the dough really maximized the chocolate flavor. The only remaining challenge was to take the cookies out of the oven at just the right moment, as overcooking robbed the cookies of the chocolate flavor we had worked so hard to establish.

CHOCOLATE BUTTER COOKIES
MAKES ABOUT 48 COOKIES

Natural cocoa powder will work in this recipe, but we found that Dutch-processed yields the best chocolate flavor. Espresso powder provides complexity, but instant coffee can be substituted in a pinch. The cookies are refined enough to serve plain, although a dusting of sifted confectioners' sugar or chocolate glaze is a nice touch.

COOKIES
20	tablespoons (2½ sticks) unsalted butter, softened
½	cup (1½ ounces) Dutch-processed cocoa
1	teaspoon instant espresso powder
1	cup (7 ounces) sugar
¼	teaspoon salt
2	large egg yolks
1	tablespoon vanilla extract
2¼	cups (11¼ ounces) all-purpose flour

BITTERSWEET CHOCOLATE GLAZE (OPTIONAL)
4	ounces bittersweet chocolate, chopped
4	tablespoons unsalted butter
2	tablespoons corn syrup
1	teaspoon vanilla extract

I. FOR THE COOKIES: Melt 4 tablespoons butter in medium saucepan over medium heat. Add cocoa and espresso; stir until mixture forms smooth paste. Set aside to cool, 15 to 20 minutes.

2. Using stand mixer fitted with paddle, mix remaining 16 tablespoons butter, sugar, salt, and cooled cocoa mixture on high speed until well combined and fluffy, about 1 minute, scraping down bowl once or twice with rubber spatula. Add egg yolks and vanilla and mix on medium speed until thoroughly combined, about 30 seconds. Scrape down bowl. With mixer running on low, add flour in 3 additions, waiting until each addition is incorporated before adding next and scraping down bowl after each addition. Continue to mix until dough forms cohesive ball, about 5 seconds. Turn dough onto counter; divide into three 4-inch disks. Wrap each disk in plastic wrap and refrigerate until dough is firm yet malleable, 45 minutes to 1 hour. (Alternatively, shape dough into log, about 12 inches long and 2 inches in diameter; use parchment paper to roll into neat cylinder and twist ends to seal. Chill until very firm and cold, at least 1 hour.)

3. Adjust oven rack to middle position and heat oven to 375 degrees. Line 2 baking sheets with parchment paper. Working with 1 piece of dough at a time, roll 3/16 inch thick between 2 large sheets parchment paper. If dough becomes soft and sticky, slide rolled dough on parchment onto baking sheet and refrigerate until firm, about 10 minutes.

4. Peel parchment from 1 side of dough and cut into desired shapes using cookie cutters; place shapes 1 inch apart on prepared baking sheets. (For cylinder-shaped dough, simply slice cookies 1/4 inch thick and place on prepared baking sheets.) Bake 1 sheet at a time until cookies show slight resistance to touch, 10 to 12 minutes, rotating baking sheet halfway through baking; if cookies begin to darken on edges, they have overbaked. (Dough scraps can be patted together, chilled, and rerolled once.) Let cookies cool on baking sheet for 5 minutes; transfer cookies to wire rack and let cool to room temperature. Decorate as desired.

5. FOR THE GLAZE (OPTIONAL): Melt bittersweet chocolate with butter in heat-proof bowl set over saucepan of barely simmering water; whisk until smooth. Add corn syrup and vanilla extract and mix until smooth and shiny. Use back of spoon to spread scant 1 teaspoon glaze almost to edge of each cookie. (If necessary, reheat to prolong fluidity of glaze.) Allow glazed cookies to dry at least 20 minutes.

GLAZED CHOCOLATE-MINT COOKIES

Replace vanilla extract with 2 teaspoons mint extract. Glaze cookies with Bittersweet Chocolate Glaze and dry as directed. Melt 1 cup white chocolate chips and drizzle over glazed cookies. Let dry at least 20 minutes before serving.

MEXICAN CHOCOLATE BUTTER COOKIES

In medium skillet over medium heat, toast 1/2 cup sliced almonds, 1 teaspoon ground cinnamon, and 1/8 teaspoon cayenne until fragrant, about 3 minutes; set aside to cool. In food processor fitted with metal blade, process cooled mixture until very fine, about 15 seconds. Whisk nut-spice mixture into flour before adding flour to dough in step 2. Proceed with recipe, rolling dough into log. Roll chilled log in 1/2 cup raw or sanding sugar before slicing.

HOLIDAY ROLLED COOKIES

✔ WHY THIS RECIPE WORKS

Baking holiday cookies should be a fun endeavor, but so often it's an exercise in frustration. The dough clings to the rolling pin, it rips and tears as it's rolled out, and moving the dough in and out of the fridge to make it easier to work with turns a simple one-hour process into a half-day project. We wanted a simple recipe that would yield a forgiving, workable dough, producing cookies that would be sturdy enough to decorate yet tender enough to be worth eating. Our first realization was that we had to use enough butter to stay true to the nature of a butter cookie but not so much that the dough became greasy. All-purpose flour had enough gluten to provide structure, while superfine sugar provided a fine, even crumb and a compact, crisp cookie. A surprise ingredient—cream cheese—gave the cookies flavor and richness without altering their texture.

GLAZED BUTTER COOKIES
MAKES ABOUT 38 COOKIES

If you cannot find superfine sugar, process granulated sugar in a food processor for 30 seconds. If desired, the cookies can be finished with sprinkles or other decorations immediately after glazing.

COOKIES
2½   cups (12½ ounces) all-purpose flour
¾   cup (5⅔ ounces) superfine sugar
¼   teaspoon salt
16   tablespoons unsalted butter, cut into 16 pieces and softened
2   tablespoons cream cheese, room temperature
2   teaspoons vanilla extract

GLAZE
1   tablespoon cream cheese, room temperature
3   tablespoons milk
1½   cups (6 ounces) confectioners' sugar

1. FOR THE COOKIES: Using stand mixer fitted with paddle, mix flour, sugar, and salt at low speed until combined, about 5 seconds. With mixer running on low, add butter 1 piece at a time; continue to mix until mixture looks crumbly and slightly wet, about 1 to 2 minutes longer. Beat in cream cheese and vanilla until dough just begins to form large clumps, about 30 seconds.

2. Knead dough by hand in bowl, 2 to 3 turns, until it forms large, cohesive mass. Transfer dough to counter and divide it into 2 even pieces. Press each piece into 4-inch disk, wrap disks in plastic, and refrigerate until dough is firm but malleable, about 30 minutes. (Dough can be refrigerated for up to 3 days or frozen up to 2 weeks; defrost in refrigerator before using.)

3. Adjust oven rack to middle position and heat oven to 375 degrees. Line

2 baking sheets with parchment paper. Working with 1 piece of dough at a time, roll ⅛ inch thick between 2 large sheets of parchment paper; slide rolled dough, still on parchment, onto baking sheet and refrigerate until firm, about 10 minutes.

4. Working with 1 sheet of dough at a time, peel parchment from 1 side of dough and cut into desired shapes using cookie cutters; place cookies 1½ inches apart on prepared sheets. Bake 1 sheet at a time until cookies are light golden brown, about 10 minutes, rotating baking sheet halfway through baking. (Dough scraps can be patted together, chilled, and rerolled once.) Let cookies cool on baking sheet for 3 minutes; transfer cookies to wire rack and let cool to room temperature.

5. FOR THE GLAZE: Whisk cream cheese and 2 tablespoons milk together in medium bowl until combined and no lumps remain. Add confectioners' sugar and whisk until smooth, adding remaining 1 tablespoon milk as needed until glaze is thin enough to spread easily. Using back of spoon, drizzle or spread scant teaspoon of glaze onto each cooled cookie. Allow glazed cookies to dry at least 30 minutes.

LIME-GLAZED COCONUT SNOWBALLS

MAKES ABOUT 40 COOKIES

---

1 recipe dough for Glazed Butter Cookies (page 639), with 1 teaspoon grated lime zest added with dry ingredients, prepared through step 2

1 recipe Glaze (page 639), with 3 tablespoons lime juice substituted for milk

1½ cups (4½ ounces) sweetened shredded coconut, pulsed in a food processor until finely chopped, about 15 pulses

1. Adjust oven racks to upper-middle and lower-middle positions and heat oven to 375 degrees. Line 2 baking sheets with parchment paper. Roll dough between hands into 1-inch balls. Place dough balls on prepared baking sheets, spacing them 1½ inches apart. Bake 1 sheet at a time until cookies are lightly browned, about 12 minutes, rotating baking sheets halfway through baking. Let cookies cool

on baking sheets for 3 minutes; transfer cookies to wire rack and let cool to room temperature.

2. Dip tops of cookies into glaze and scrape off excess, then dip them into coconut. Place cookies on wire rack and let stand until glaze sets, about 20 minutes.

JAM SANDWICHES

MAKES ABOUT 30 COOKIES

Turbinado sugar is commonly sold as Sugar in the Raw. Demerara sugar, sanding sugar, or another coarse sugar can be substituted.

1 recipe dough for Glazed Butter Cookies (page 639), prepared through step 3

2 tablespoons turbinado sugar

1¼ cups raspberry jam, simmered until reduced to 1 cup, strained, and cooled to room temperature

1. Adjust oven rack to middle position and heat oven to 375 degrees. Line 2 baking sheets with parchment paper. Using 2-inch fluted round cookie cutter, cut rounds from 1 piece of rolled dough and

---

MAKING JAM SANDWICHES

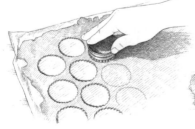  

1. Using 2-inch fluted round cookie cutter, cut rounds from 1 piece of dough and bake on parchment-lined baking sheet.

2. Sprinkle second piece of rolled dough evenly with sugar.

3. Using 2-inch fluted round cookie cutter, cut out rounds of sugar-sprinkled dough and place on parchment-lined baking sheet. Using ¾-inch round cookie cutter, cut out centers of rounds and bake.

4. When cookies have cooled, spread 1 teaspoon jam on solid cookies, then place cut-out cookies on top. Let filled cookies stand until set, about 30 minutes.

MAKING CHOCOLATE-CHERRY BAR COOKIES WITH HAZELNUTS

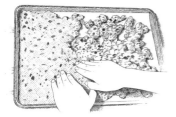

1. Press dough in even layer onto baking sheet.

2. Immediately after removing baking sheet from oven, sprinkle evenly with chocolate chips; let stand to melt.

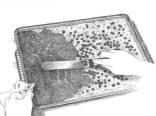

3. Use offset spatula to spread chocolate into even layer, then sprinkle evenly with chopped hazelnuts. Cool on wire rack until just warm.

4. Use pizza wheel to cut cookies into 1¼-inch diamonds.

place on one prepared baking sheet, spacing them 1 inch apart. Bake until cookies are light golden brown, 8 to 10 minutes, rotating baking sheet halfway through baking. Let cookies cool on baking sheet for 3 minutes; transfer cookies to wire rack and let cool to room temperature.

2. Sprinkle second piece of rolled dough evenly with sugar. Using 2-inch fluted round cookie cutter, cut rounds of sugar-sprinkled dough. Using ¾-inch round cookie cutter, cut out centers of sugared rounds. Bake and cool the cookies as directed in step 1, using second prepared baking sheet.

3. Spread 1 teaspoon jam on top of each solid cookie, then cover with cut-out cookie. Let filled cookies stand until set, about 30 minutes.

CHOCOLATE-CHERRY BAR COOKIES WITH HAZELNUTS

MAKES ABOUT 50 COOKIES

- 1 recipe dough for Glazed Butter Cookies (page 639), with 1 cup chopped dried cherries added with dry ingredients, prepared through step 2
- 1½ cups (9 ounces) semisweet chocolate chips
- 1½ cups (6 ounces) hazelnuts, toasted, skinned, and chopped

1. Adjust oven rack to lower-middle position and heat oven to 375 degrees. Line rimmed baking sheet with parchment paper. Press dough evenly onto prepared sheet and bake until golden brown, about 20 minutes, rotating baking sheet halfway through baking.

2. Immediately after removing baking sheet from oven, sprinkle evenly with chocolate chips; let stand to melt, about 3 minutes.

3. Spread chocolate into even layer, then sprinkle chopped hazelnuts evenly over chocolate. Let cool on wire rack until just warm, 15 to 20 minutes.

4. Using pizza wheel, cut on diagonal into 1½-inch diamonds. Transfer cookies to wire rack and let cool completely.

NUT CRESCENT COOKIES

✓ WHY THIS RECIPE WORKS

When nut crescent cookies are well made, they can be delicious: buttery, nutty, slightly crisp, slightly crumbly, with a melt-in-your mouth quality. Too often, however, they turn out bland and dry. We wanted to develop a recipe that would put them back in their proper place. The ratio of 1 cup butter to 2 cups flour in almost all of the recipes we looked at is what worked for us. We tried three kinds of sugar in the dough: granulated, confectioners', and superfine. The last

resulted in just what we wanted: cookies that melted in our mouths. In determining the amount, we had to remember that the cookies would be sweetened once more by their traditional coating of confectioners' sugar. Before rolling them, we let the cookies cool to room temperature; coating them with sugar while still warm results in a pasty outer layer we wanted to avoid.

PECAN OR WALNUT CRESCENT COOKIES

MAKES ABOUT 48 SMALL COOKIES

If you cannot find superfine sugar, process granulated sugar in a food processor for 30 seconds. If you make these cookies ahead, roll them again in confectioners' sugar, shaking off the excess, before serving.

- 2 cups (8 ounces) pecans or walnuts, chopped fine
- 2 cups (10 ounces) all-purpose flour
- ½ teaspoon salt
- 16 tablespoons unsalted butter, softened
- ⅓ cup (2½ ounces) superfine sugar
- 1½ teaspoons vanilla extract
- 1½ cups (6 ounces) confectioners' sugar

1. Adjust oven racks to upper-middle and lower-middle positions and heat oven to 325 degrees. Line 2 baking sheets with parchment paper.

2. Whisk 1 cup chopped nuts, flour, and salt together in medium bowl; set aside. Process remaining 1 cup chopped nuts in food processor until they are texture of coarse cornmeal, 10 to 15 seconds (do not overprocess). Stir nuts into flour mixture and set aside.

3. Using stand mixer fitted with paddle, beat butter and superfine sugar at medium-low speed until light and fluffy, about 2 minutes; add vanilla, scraping down bowl as needed. Add flour mixture and beat on low speed until dough just begins to come together but still looks scrappy, about 15 seconds. Scrape down bowl as needed; continue beating until dough is cohesive, 6 to 9 seconds longer. Do not overbeat.

4. Working with 1 tablespoon of dough at a time, roll into balls. Roll each dough ball between your palms into rope that measures 3 inches long. Place ropes on prepared baking sheets and turn up ends to form crescent shape. Bake until tops of cookies are pale golden and bottoms are just beginning to brown, 17 to 19 minutes, switching and rotating baking sheets halfway through baking.

5. Let cookies cool on baking sheets for 2 minutes; transfer cookies to wire rack and let cool to room temperature. Place

SHAPING CRESCENT COOKIES

Working with 1 tablespoon of dough at a time, roll dough into 1¼-inch balls. Roll each ball between palms into 3-inch-long rope. Place ropes on ungreased baking sheet and turn them up at each end to form crescent shapes.

confectioners' sugar in shallow baking dish or pie plate. Working with 3 or 4 cookies at a time, roll cookies in sugar to coat thoroughly; gently shake off excess.

ALMOND OR HAZELNUT CRESCENT COOKIES

Almonds can be used raw for cookies that are light in both color and flavor or toasted to enhance the almond flavor and darken the crescents.

Substitute 1¾ cups whole blanched almonds (toasted, if desired) or 2 cups skinned toasted hazelnuts for pecans or walnuts. If using almonds, add ½ teaspoon almond extract along with vanilla extract.

THICK AND CHEWY GINGERBREAD COOKIES

✔ WHY THIS RECIPE WORKS

Most gingerbread recipes turn out dough better suited for building material than for snacking. Could we make gingerbread cookies that actually tasted as good as they looked? To remedy the problem of stiff, dry cookies, we first added more butter. We found that to avoid very dry cookies, we needed at least 4 tablespoons of butter for every cup of flour. More sugar and molasses came next, making the cookies more flavorful, pleasantly sweet, and moist. A little bit of milk lent the cookies just the right extra measure of softness and lift. Then we discovered that just by rolling the dough thinner, we could also use our dough to make a tasty thin cookie that held up on the Christmas tree. Now, whether thick or thin, we had a cookie that wouldn't be left behind on the cookie tray.

THICK AND CHEWY GINGERBREAD COOKIES

MAKES ABOUT 30 COOKIES

If you plan to decorate your gingerbread cookies and make ornaments out of them, follow the variation for Thin, Crisp Gingerbread

Cookies. Because flour is not added during rolling, dough scraps can be rolled and cut as many times as necessary. Don't overbake the cookies or they will be dry. If you make gingerbread people, this recipe will make about twenty 3-inch people.

3	cups (15 ounces) all-purpose flour
¾	cup packed (5¼ ounces) dark brown sugar
1	tablespoon ground cinnamon
1	tablespoon ground ginger
½	teaspoon ground cloves
¾	teaspoon baking soda
½	teaspoon salt
12	tablespoons unsalted butter, cut into 12 pieces and softened
¾	cup molasses
2	tablespoons milk

1. Using stand mixer fitted with paddle, mix flour, sugar, cinnamon, ginger, cloves, baking soda, and salt at low speed until combined, about 30 seconds. Stop mixer and add butter pieces; mix at medium-low speed until mixture is sandy and resembles fine meal, about 1½ minutes. Reduce speed to low and, with mixer running, gradually add molasses and milk; mix until dough is evenly moistened, about 20 seconds. Increase speed to medium and mix until thoroughly combined, about 10 seconds.

2. Scrape dough onto counter; divide in half. Working with 1 piece of dough at a time, roll ¼ inch thick between 2 large sheets of parchment paper. Leaving dough sandwiched between parchment layers, stack on baking sheet and freeze until firm, 15 to 20 minutes.

3. Adjust oven racks to upper-middle and lower-middle positions and heat oven to 350 degrees. Line 2 baking sheets with parchment paper.

4. Remove 1 dough sheet from freezer; place on counter. Peel off top parchment sheet and gently lay it back in place. Flip dough over; peel off and discard second

parchment layer. Cut dough into 5-inch gingerbread people or 3-inch gingerbread people and place them ¾ inch apart on prepared baking sheets; set scraps aside. Repeat with remaining dough. Bake until set in centers and cookies barely retain imprint when touched very gently with fingertip, 8 to 11 minutes, switching and rotating baking sheets halfway through baking. Do not overbake. Let cookies cool on baking sheets for 2 minutes; transfer cookies to wire rack and let cool to room temperature.

5. Gather scraps; repeat rolling, cutting, and baking in steps 2 and 4. Repeat with remaining dough until all dough is used.

THIN, CRISP GINGERBREAD COOKIES

These gingersnap-like cookies are sturdy and therefore suitable for making ornaments. If you wish to thread the cookies, snip wooden skewers to ½-inch lengths and press them into the cookies just before they go into the oven; remove skewers immediately after baking. Or, use drinking straw to punch holes in the cookies when they're just out of the oven and still soft. If you make gingerbread people, this recipe will make about thirty 3-inch people.

Quarter, rather than halve, dough and roll each dough quarter ⅛ inch thick, reducing oven temperature to 325 degrees, and baking cookies until slightly darkened and firm in center when pressed with finger, about 15 to 20 minutes.

HOLIDAY SPRITZ COOKIES

✔ WHY THIS RECIPE WORKS

Spritz cookies, those golden-swirled holiday cookies, often end up bland, gummy, and tasteless. Unfortunately, this Scandinavian treat has fallen victim to many recipe modifications, such as the use of vegetable shortening instead of butter, an overload of eggs, and an excess of starchy confectioners' sugar. We set out to spruce up spritz

cookies and make them light, crisp, buttery treats—the life of any holiday party. The success of these confections rests primarily in the management of a finicky ingredient list. Carefully balancing the butter, sugar, flour, egg (yolk only), heavy cream (just a drop), vanilla, and salt is the only recipe for success—a few simple ingredients gathered in the proper proportions. Creaming the butter and sugar in the traditional fashion worked well and produced a dough light enough to easily press or pipe into shapes. As for shaping, either a cookie press or a pastry bag can be used—it's up to you.

SPRITZ COOKIES
MAKES ABOUT 72 SMALL COOKIES

If using a pastry bag, use a star tip to create the various shapes. For stars, a ½- to ⅝-inch tip (measure the diameter of the tip at the smallest point) works best, but for rosettes and S shapes, use a ⅜-inch tip. To create stars, hold the bag at a 90-degree angle to baking sheet and pipe the dough straight down, about 1-inch in diameter. To create rosettes, pipe the dough while moving the bag in a circular motion, ending at the center of the rosette; rosettes should be about 1¼ inches in diameter. To create S shapes, pipe the dough into compact Ss; they should be about 2 inches long and 1 inch wide. If you make an error while piping, the dough can be scraped off the baking sheet and re-piped.

1   **large egg yolk**
1   **tablespoon heavy cream**
1   **teaspoon vanilla extract**
16   **tablespoons unsalted butter, softened but still cool**
⅔   **cup (4⅔ ounces) granulated sugar**
¼   **teaspoon salt**
2   **cups (10 ounces) all-purpose flour**

1. Adjust oven rack to middle position and heat oven to 375 degrees. Line 2 baking sheets with parchment paper. Whisk egg yolk, cream, and vanilla in small bowl until combined; set aside.

2. Using stand mixer fitted with paddle, beat butter, sugar, and salt at medium-high speed until light and fluffy, about 3 minutes, scraping down bowl and beater as needed. With mixer running at medium speed, add yolk mixture and beat until incorporated, about 30 seconds. With mixer running at low speed, gradually beat in flour until combined, scraping down bowl and beater as needed. Give dough final stir to ensure that no flour pockets remain. (Dough can be wrapped in plastic wrap and refrigerated for up to 4 days; before using, let it stand at room temperature until softened, about 45 minutes.)

3. If using cookie press to form cookies, follow manufacturer's instructions to fill press. If using pastry bag, fit it with

---

FILLING A PASTRY BAG AND PIPING SPRITZ COOKIES

1. Make C-shape with 1 hand and hold piping bag. Fold bag over that hand about halfway down, insert tip, and scrape dough into bag.

2. When bag is about half full, pull up sides, push down dough, and twist tightly while again pushing down on dough to squeeze out air.

3. Grab bag at base of twist. Using other hand as guide, hold tip at 90-degree angle about ½ inch above baking sheet and squeeze to form shape.

star tip and fill bag with half of dough. Press or pipe cookies onto prepared baking sheet, spacing them about 1½ inches apart, refilling cookie press or pastry bag as needed. Bake 1 sheet at a time until cookies are light golden brown, 10 to 12 minutes, rotating baking sheet halfway through baking. Let cookies cool on baking sheet for 10 to 15 minutes; transfer cookies to wire rack and let cool to room temperature.

SPRITZ COOKIES WITH LEMON ESSENCE

Add 1 teaspoon juice from 1 lemon to yolk-cream mixture in step 1 and add 1 teaspoon finely grated zest from 1 lemon to butter along with sugar and salt in step 2.

ALMOND SPRITZ COOKIES

Pulse ½ cup sliced almonds and 2 tablespoons of flour in food processor until powdery and evenly fine, about 12 pulses; combine almond mixture with remaining flour. Substitute ¾ teaspoon almond extract for vanilla.

MADELEINES

✔ WHY THIS RECIPE WORKS
Bakers tend to argue over the authenticity of their madeleines, each one thinking that his or hers is the exact re-creation of the cookie that famously stirred Proust's imagination. What everyone does agree on is that madeleines are small, feather-light, spongy cakes meant to be eaten like cookies. They are baked in a special pan with scallop shell indentations. Shortly after we began our search for the perfect madeleine, we gave up on history in favor of taste, texture, and simplicity. What we wanted was a cake-cookie that tasted lightly buttery and eggy, with a hint of vanilla; it also had to barely weigh

down the tongue, and it had to be as simple as possible to prepare. We kept baking up batches of dry, dense madeleines until we started thinking about these cookies like mini cakes. Just as we do with some of our cakes, we used cake flour for the lightest crumb. And we added an egg yolk and extra butter to keep them moist. Lastly, we added a whopping tablespoon of vanilla extract for flavor.

MADELEINES
MAKES 24 COOKIES

This recipe uses a 12-cookie madeleine mold; even if you have two molds, be sure to bake them one at a time.

- 1   cup (4 ounces) cake flour
- ¼   teaspoon salt
- 2   large eggs plus 1 large yolk
- ½   cup (3½ ounces) sugar
- 1   tablespoon vanilla extract
- 10   tablespoons unsalted butter, melted and cooled

1. Adjust oven rack to middle position and heat oven to 375 degrees. Grease 12-cookie madeleine mold. Whisk flour and salt together in small bowl.

2. Using stand mixer, beat eggs and egg yolk together on medium-high speed until frothy, 3 to 5 minutes. Beat in sugar and vanilla until very thick, 3 to 5 minutes. With rubber spatula, gently fold in flour mixture, followed by melted butter.

3. Spoon half of batter into prepared mold, filling mold to rim. Bake until cookies are golden and spring back when pressed lightly, about 10 minutes, rotating madeleine mold halfway through baking.

4. Let cookies cool in mold for 10 minutes, then flip out onto wire rack and let cool completely before serving, about 1 hour. Cool and re-grease mold and repeat with remaining batter.

CITRUS MADELEINES

Add 1 tablespoon grated fresh lemon zest or orange zest with sugar and vanilla.

CHOCOLATE MADELEINES

Substitute ¼ cup sifted Dutch-processed cocoa for ¼ cup flour and add 2 teaspoons instant espresso powder to flour mixture.

ROSE WATER MADELEINES

Substitute 2 teaspoons rose water for vanilla extract.

ALMOND MADELEINES

Reduce vanilla to 2 teaspoons and add 1 teaspoon almond extract.

LACE COOKIES

✔ WHY THIS RECIPE WORKS
These delicate cookies are known to be difficult in one crucial respect: they tend to stick to the pan, bunching and tearing when you attempt to remove them. If this could be avoided, we thought, perhaps more home bakers would be baking up these impressive-looking, melt-in-your-mouth cookies (which are otherwise quite easy to make—no creaming, no rolling, no cutting). We decided right off to eliminate eggs from our lace cookie recipe; the liquid protein in eggs can make the cookies stick like crazy. The eggs also tended to puff the cookies, and we wanted them gossamer-thin with a brittle texture. We found that using parchment paper made a big difference in how well the cookies came off the sheet. It was also important to measure the amount of time the cookies were allowed to sit on the baking sheet once out of the oven. After cooling on the sheet for one or two minutes, the cookies are

just starting to firm up. That's the time to get the cookies off the sheet for perfect lace cookies without any sticking.

LACE COOKIES

MAKES ABOUT 72 COOKIES

Humidity is the archenemy of lace cookies, so try to make them on a dry day. Otherwise, they will absorb too much moisture and be chewy instead of caramelized and brittle.

¾	cup packed (5¼ ounces) dark brown sugar
8	tablespoons unsalted butter
½	cup light corn syrup
1	cup pecans or almonds, chopped fine
6	tablespoons (1¾ ounces) all-purpose flour
1	tablespoon heavy cream
1	teaspoon vanilla extract
¼	teaspoon salt

1. Adjust oven rack to middle position and heat oven to 350 degrees. Line 2 baking sheets with parchment paper. Bring brown sugar, butter, and corn syrup just to boil in medium saucepan over medium heat, 5 to 6 minutes, stirring frequently. Off heat, beat in pecans, flour, cream, vanilla, and salt until smooth.

2. Drop 6 rounded teaspoons of batter 3 inches apart on each prepared baking sheets. Bake 1 sheet at a time until cookies spread thin, turn deep golden brown, and bubbling has subsided, 6 to 7 minutes, rotating baking sheet halfway through baking.

3. Let cookies cool and firm up slightly on baking sheet for 1 to 2 minutes. Transfer to wire rack to cool or shape as desired. Repeat with remaining batter.

SPICED WALNUT LACE COOKIES

Substitute 1 cup finely chopped walnuts for pecans and add ½ teaspoon each ground

SHAPING LACE COOKIES

Until you get the hang of shaping these cookies, we recommend baking only two or three at a time. After making each of the shapes below, gently hold the cookie in place until it is set, about 10 seconds, then let cool on a wire rack. If the cookies cool on the cookie sheet too long and become too brittle to shape, place the entire sheet back in the oven for a minute or two until soft again. If any of the cookies shatter after you have shaped them, save the crumbles to sprinkle on ice cream sundaes.

A. After cooling, slide wide metal spatula under 1 cookie. If it does not bunch or tear, cookies are ready to move.

B. To make "cigarette" place cookie against handle of wooden spoon and roll cookie over itself as quickly as possible.

C. To form tuile, lay cookie over rolling pin or wine bottle set on its side so that cookie forms gentle curve.

D. To form tricornered hat, mold cookie over opening of wine bottle or other bottle of similar shape, then flute edges to form tricornered hat shape. Hold until set.

E. Cones are easiest shaped by hand. Holding both sides of cookie, wrap 1 side over other, overlapping about 1 inch or so.

F. To form bowl, lay cookie over bottom of small bowl turned upside down and gently mold cookie to follow contour of bowl.

DECORATING LACE COOKIES WITH CHOCOLATE

You can melt about 6 ounces of chopped semisweet chocolate over simmering water or use any glaze of your choice. Rewarm chocolate to restore its fluidity. Lay the cookies on parchment paper to set.

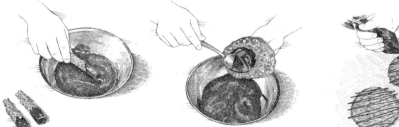

A. Cigarette shapes or flat cookies may be dipped halfway into glaze.

B. Flat cookies may be painted with pastry brush or spoon, or you may dip bottom into glaze.

C. Another option for flat cookies is to place them on sheet of waxed paper, and then drizzle chocolate over them with pastry bag.

nutmeg and ground cinnamon and ¼ teaspoon each ground allspice, ground cloves, and ground ginger with vanilla.

LEMON-ANISE BISCOTTI

✔ WHY THIS RECIPE WORKS
In search of a crunchy—but not tooth-cracking—biscuit full of flavor, we found that the type and quantity of fat dramatically affected the taste, texture, and shelf life of the biscotti. The good news? The most flavorful biscotti are made with a small amount of fat; our favorite combination of ingredients included whole eggs with no additional yolks or butter. We also found that biscotti recipes made with whole eggs got even better with time; they tasted great and remained very crisp after a week and, when stored in an airtight container, they kept for up to a month.

LEMON-ANISE BISCOTTI
MAKES ABOUT 48 BISCOTTI

A Sicilian specialty, this recipe produces a relatively hard biscuit—perfect with an afternoon cup of coffee. Alternatively, you can substitute ½ cup sesame seeds for the anise seeds. Brush the top of each loaf of dough with an egg wash and sprinkle with additional sesame seeds.

2	cups (10 ounces) all-purpose flour
I	teaspoon baking powder
¼	teaspoon salt
I	cup (7 ounces) sugar
2	large eggs
I	tablespoon grated lemon zest
I	tablespoon anise seeds
¼	teaspoon vanilla extract

I. Adjust oven rack to middle position and heat oven to 350 degrees. Line baking sheet with parchment paper. Whisk flour, baking powder, and salt together in small bowl.

2. Whisk sugar and eggs in large bowl to light lemon color; stir in lemon zest, anise seeds, and vanilla. Mix flour mixture into egg mixture until combined and dough forms.

3. Halve dough and turn each portion onto prepared baking sheet. Using floured hands, quickly stretch each portion of dough into rough 13 by 2-inch loaf, placing them about 3 inches apart. Pat each loaf to smooth it. Bake, until loaves are golden and just beginning to crack on top, about 35 minutes, rotating baking sheet halfway through baking.

4. Let loaves cool for 10 minutes; reduce oven temperature to 325 degrees. Cut each loaf diagonally into ⅜-inch slices with serrated knife. Lay slices cut side up about ½ inch apart on baking sheet and return them to oven. Bake until crisp and golden brown on both sides, about 15 minutes, turning over each cookie halfway through baking. Immediately transfer biscotti from baking sheet to wire rack and let cool completely.

HONEY-LAVENDER BISCOTTI
MAKES ABOUT 48 BISCOTTI

Based on the flavors of a popular Provençal ice cream, these honey-lavender biscotti are best made with an assertive honey, such as a spicy clover honey. Dried lavender blossoms, also an ingredient in herbes de Provence, can be found in spice or herbal stores. If you can't find the lavender blossoms, this recipe makes very good honey biscotti.

2¼	cups (11¼ ounces) all-purpose flour
I	teaspoon baking powder
½	teaspoon baking soda
¼	teaspoon salt
⅔	cup sugar
3	large eggs
3	tablespoons honey
2	tablespoons grated orange zest
I	tablespoon dried lavender blossoms (optional)
½	teaspoon vanilla extract

I. Adjust oven rack to middle position and heat oven to 350 degrees. Line baking sheet with parchment paper. Whisk flour, baking powder, baking soda, and salt together in small bowl.

2. Whisk sugar and eggs in large bowl to light lemon color; stir in honey, orange zest, lavender, if using, and vanilla. Mix flour mixture into egg mixture until combined and dough forms.

3. Halve dough and turn each portion onto prepared baking sheet. Using floured hands, quickly stretch each portion of

SHAPING BISCOTTI

I. Using floured hands, shape dough masses into 2 loaves, each about 13 inches long and roughly 2 inches in diameter.

2. Use serrated knife to cut baked loaves into ⅜-inch slices, then return to baking sheet for second baking.

3. Lay slices about ½ inch apart on baking sheet cut side up for their second baking.

dough into rough 13 by 2-inch loaf, placing them about 3 inches apart. Pat each loaf to smooth it. Bake, until loaves are golden and just beginning to crack on top, about 35 minutes, rotating baking sheet halfway through baking.

4. Let loaves cool for 10 minutes; reduce oven temperature to 325 degrees. Cut each loaf diagonally into ⅜-inch slices with serrated knife. Lay slices cut side up about ½ inch apart on baking sheet and return them to oven. Bake until crisp and golden brown on both sides, about 15 minutes, turning over each cookie halfway through baking. Immediately transfer biscotti from baking sheet to wire rack and let cool completely.

SPICED BISCOTTI
MAKES ABOUT 48 BISCOTTI

If desired, substitute 3 whole eggs for the 2 eggs and 2 egg yolks in this recipe.

2¼	cups (11¼ ounces) all-purpose flour
1	teaspoon baking powder
½	teaspoon baking soda
½	teaspoon ground cloves
½	teaspoon ground cinnamon
¼	teaspoon ground ginger
¼	teaspoon salt
¼	teaspoon ground white pepper
1	cup (7 ounces) sugar
2	large eggs plus 2 large yolks
½	teaspoon vanilla extract

1. Adjust oven rack to middle position and heat oven to 350 degrees. Line baking sheet with parchment paper. Whisk flour, baking powder, baking soda, cloves, cinnamon, ginger, salt, and white pepper together in small bowl.

2. Whisk sugar, eggs, and egg yolks in large bowl until light lemon color; stir in vanilla. Mix flour mixture into egg mixture until combined and dough forms.

3. Halve dough and turn each portion onto prepared baking sheet. Using floured hands, quickly stretch each portion of dough into rough 13 by 2-inch loaf, placing them about 3 inches apart. Pat each loaf to smooth it. Bake, until loaves are golden and just beginning to crack on top, about 35 minutes, rotating baking sheet halfway through baking.

4. Let loaves cool for 10 minutes; reduce oven temperature to 325 degrees. Cut each loaf diagonally into ⅜-inch slices with serrated knife. Lay slices cut side up about ½ inch apart on baking sheet and return them to oven. Bake until crisp and golden brown on both sides, about 15 minutes, turning over each cookie halfway through baking. Immediately transfer biscotti from baking sheet to wire rack and let cool completely.

ORANGE-ALMOND BISCOTTI
MAKES 48 BISCOTTI

The addition of a small amount of butter produces a richer, more cookielike texture. Toasted, skinned hazelnuts or a combination of hazelnuts and almonds also works well, too.

2	cups (10 ounces) all-purpose flour
1	teaspoon baking powder
¼	teaspoon salt
4	tablespoons unsalted butter, softened
1	cup (7 ounces) sugar
2	large eggs
¾	cup whole almonds with skins, toasted, cooled, and chopped coarse
2	tablespoons grated orange zest
½	teaspoon vanilla extract
¼	teaspoon almond extract

1. Adjust oven rack to middle position and heat oven to 350 degrees. Line baking sheet with parchment paper. Whisk

flour, baking powder, and salt together in small bowl.

2. Using stand mixer fitted with paddle, beat butter and sugar together at medium-high speed until light and fluffy. Reduce speed to low and add eggs one at a time, then add almonds, orange zest, vanilla, and almond extract until combined, about 30 seconds, scraping down bowl as needed. Stir in flour mixture until just combined.

3. Halve dough and turn each portion onto prepared baking sheet. Using floured hands, quickly stretch each portion of dough into rough 13 by 2-inch loaf, placing them about 3 inches apart. Pat each loaf to smooth it. Bake, until loaves are golden and just beginning to crack on top, about 35 minutes, rotating baking sheet halfway through baking.

4. Let loaves cool for 10 minutes; reduce oven temperature to 325 degrees. Cut each loaf diagonally into ⅜-inch slices with serrated knife. Lay slices cut side up about ½ inch apart on baking sheet and return them to oven. Bake until crisp and golden brown on both sides, about 15 minutes, turning over each cookie halfway through baking. Immediately transfer biscotti from baking sheet to wire rack and let cool completely.

RUGELACH

✓ WHY THIS RECIPE WORKS
Rugelach should be made out of a meltingly tender, delicate dough with a slightly acidic tang. The filling should be a bounteous combination of preserves, fruit, and nuts plus a spice-spiked sugar. But the dough can be sticky, soft, and hard to work with, and often the filling is either overwhelming or almost negligible. We discovered that a cream cheese and butter dough refrigerated until firm before applying the filling gave our baked cookies the

flakiest, most delicate texture. For the best filling for our rugelach, we layered apricot jam with finely chopped walnuts, raisins, and cinnamon sugar. Finally, baking the cookies on baking sheets lined with parchment paper and removing them from the pans as soon as they were done prevented overbaking for tender cookies with just the right amount of sweet, spiced fruit filling.

CRESCENT-SHAPED RUGELACH WITH RAISIN-WALNUT FILLING

MAKES 32 COOKIES

If at any point the dough becomes too soft to work with, chill it until it is firm enough to handle. Feel free to substitute chopped pitted prunes, chopped dried apricots, dried currants, dried cherries, or dried cranberries for the raisins in the filling.

DOUGH

8 tablespoons unsalted butter, softened
4 ounces cream cheese, softened
1 tablespoon sugar
1 teaspoon vanilla extract
½ teaspoon salt
1 cup (5 ounces) all-purpose flour

FILLING

⅓ cup (2⅓ ounces) sugar
1 tablespoon ground cinnamon
½ cup apricot jam
1 cup walnuts, chopped fine
½ cup raisins, preferably golden
2 tablespoons unsalted butter, melted

1. FOR THE DOUGH: Using stand mixer fitted with paddle, beat butter, cream cheese, sugar, vanilla, and salt together in large bowl on medium speed until light and fluffy, 3 to 6 minutes, scraping down bowl as needed. Reduce speed to low and slowly mix in flour until combined, about 30 seconds.

2. Turn mixture out onto floured counter, divide it into 2 equal pieces, wrap in plastic wrap, and refrigerate until firm, about 1 hour.

3. Adjust oven racks to upper-middle and lower-middle positions and heat oven to 375 degrees. Line 2 baking sheets with parchment paper.

4. FOR THE FILLING: Mix sugar and cinnamon together in small bowl. Roll each piece of dough on lightly floured counter into 11-inch circle about ¼ inch thick. Spread ¼ cup jam on top of each round, then sprinkle each with ½ cup nuts, ¼ cup raisins, and 1 tablespoon cinnamon sugar.

5. Cut each dough round evenly into 16 wedges. Starting at wide end, roll up each wedge into a cookie. Place cookies on prepared baking sheets, with pointed end underneath, spaced about 2 inches apart.

6. Brush melted butter over cookies and sprinkle remaining cinnamon sugar over top of each cookie. Bake cookies until pale gold and slightly puffy, about 20 minutes, switching and rotating baking sheets halfway through baking. Immediately transfer cookies from baking sheet to wire rack and let cool completely before serving, about 1 hour.

CHOCOLATE-RASPBERRY RUGELACH

Substitute seedless raspberry jam for apricot jam and substitute ½ cup mini chocolate chips for raisins.

MERINGUE COOKIES

✓ WHY THIS RECIPE WORKS

A classic meringue cookie may have only two ingredients—egg whites and sugar—but it requires precise timing. Otherwise, you'll end up with a meringue that's as dense as Styrofoam or weepy, gritty, and cloyingly sweet. A great meringue cookie should emerge from the oven glossy and white, with a shatteringly crisp texture that dissolves instantly in your mouth. We chose a basic French meringue over a fussier Italian meringue. The French version, in which egg whites are whipped with sugar, is the simpler of the two; the Italian meringue, in which hot sugar syrup is poured into the whites, produces cookies that are dense and candylike. The key to glossy, evenly textured meringue was adding the sugar at just the right time—when the whites had been whipped enough to gain some volume, but still had enough free water left in them for

---

TEST KITCHEN TIP NO. 134 KEEPING BAKING STAPLES FRESHER LONGER

Few things last forever—including pantry staples you might think are fine to squirrel away for years. After a lot of testing, we've learned how to preserve the freshness of commonly used baking ingredients and when it's time to restock.

FLOUR will last for a year stored in an airtight container. The pantry is fine for all-purpose flour, but it's best to store whole wheat flour (as well as cornmeal) in the freezer; they contain natural oils that can go rancid.

YEAST is best kept in the freezer, and because it's a living organism, the expiration date should always be observed.

BAKING POWDER AND BAKING SODA should be replaced regularly; although manufacturers generally claim they have a shelf life of one year, we've found that they lose potency after six months.

CHOCOLATE should be stored tightly wrapped in a cool pantry. If chocolate is exposed to rapid changes in humidity or temperature, the surface can discolor, although this won't affect the flavor. Dark chocolate can last as long as two years, but milk and white chocolate, which contain milk solids, should be discarded after six months.

VANILLA is virtually spoil-proof, thanks to its high alcohol content. It should be kept tightly sealed and away from light and heat, but there's no need to get rid of old vanilla. We've tested vanilla as old as 10 years and found it was indistinguishable from fresh.

the sugar to dissolve completely. Surprisingly, we found that cream of tartar wasn't necessary. Without it, the whites formed more slowly, giving a wider time frame in which to add the sugar. It was also important to form the cookies in a uniform shape, so we piped them from either a pastry bag or a zipper-lock bag with a corner cut off.

MERINGUE COOKIES

MAKES ABOUT 48 SMALL COOKIES

Meringues may be a little soft immediately after being removed from the oven but will stiffen as they cool. To minimize stickiness on humid or rainy days, allow the meringues to cool in a turned-off oven for an additional hour (for a total of 2 hours) without opening the door, then transfer them immediately to airtight containers and seal.

¾	cup (5¼ ounces) sugar
2	teaspoons cornstarch
4	large egg whites
¾	teaspoon vanilla extract
⅛	teaspoon salt

1. Adjust oven racks to upper-middle and lower-middle positions and heat oven to 225 degrees. Line 2 baking sheets with parchment paper. Combine sugar and cornstarch in small bowl.

2. Using stand mixer fitted with whisk, beat egg whites, vanilla, and salt together at high speed until very soft peaks start to form (peaks should slowly lose their shape when whip is removed), 30 to 45 seconds. Reduce speed to medium and slowly add sugar mixture in steady stream down side of mixer bowl (process should take about 30 seconds). Stop mixer and scrape down bowl. Increase speed to high and beat until glossy and stiff peaks have formed, 30 to 45 seconds.

3. Working quickly, place meringue in pastry bag fitted with ½-inch plain tip or large zipper-lock bag with ½ inch of corner cut off. Pipe meringues into 1¼-inch-wide mounds about 1 inch high on baking sheets, 6 rows of 4 meringues on each sheet. Bake for 1 hour, switching and rotating baking sheets halfway through baking. Turn off oven and let meringues cool in oven for at least 1 hour. Remove meringues from oven, immediately transfer from baking sheet to wire rack, and let cool to room temperature. (Meringues can be stored in airtight container for up to 2 weeks.)

CHOCOLATE MERINGUE COOKIES

Gently fold 2 ounces finely chopped bittersweet chocolate into meringue mixture at end of step 2.

TOASTED ALMOND MERINGUE COOKIES

Substitute ½ teaspoon almond extract for vanilla extract. In step 3, sprinkle meringues with ⅓ cup coarsely chopped toasted almonds and 1 teaspoon coarse sea salt (optional), before baking.

ORANGE MERINGUE COOKIES

Stir 1 teaspoon grated orange zest into sugar mixture in step 1.

ESPRESSO MERINGUE COOKIES

Stir 2 teaspoons instant espresso powder into sugar mixture in step 1.

ALMOND MACAROONS

✔ WHY THIS RECIPE WORKS

When developing a recipe to reproduce this classic French cookie at home, we found the task surprisingly simple. We ground the almonds and sugar in a food processor, added egg whites and a little almond extract, and processed until the mixture became a stiff but cohesive dough. Next we dropped or piped the paste onto a parchment-lined sheet and baked them. The result was a recipe for macaroons that were moist and soft on the inside and both crunchy and chewy on the outside, with plenty of classic almond flavor.

ALMOND MACAROONS

MAKES 24 COOKIES

Macaroons must be baked on parchment paper. They will stick to an ungreased sheet and spread on a greased one. You need a slightly less stiff dough if piping the macaroons, so add water, as needed, to make a pipeable paste.

3	cups (12 ounces) slivered almonds
1½	cups (10½ ounces) sugar
3	large egg whites
1	teaspoon almond extract

1. Adjust oven racks to upper-middle and lower-middle positions and heat oven to 325 degrees. Line 2 baking sheets with parchment paper.

2. Process almonds in food processor until ground, 1 minute. Add sugar; process 15 seconds longer. Add whites and extract; process just until paste forms. Scrape down bowl and process until stiff but cohesive, malleable paste (similar in consistency to marzipan or pasta dough) forms, about 5 seconds longer. If mixture is crumbly or dry, turn processor back on and add water by drops until proper consistency is reached.

3. Working with 2 tablespoons of dough at a time, roll dough into balls and space 1½ inches apart on prepared baking sheets.

4. Bake until macaroons are golden brown, 20 to 25 minutes, switching and rotating baking sheets halfway through baking. Transfer macaroons, still on parchment (to prevent from tearing), to wire racks and let cool completely.

LEMON-ALMOND MACAROONS

Make paste without water. Add 2 tablespoons grated lemon zest and process 10 seconds longer.

Roll paste into balls between palms. Dip each ball into 3 beaten egg whites, then roll in 2½ cups pine nuts, lightly pressing with fingertips. Transfer cookies to baking sheet and flatten slightly with fingers, making 1-inch-wide buttons.

FUDGE-ALMOND MACAROONS

Decrease almonds to 1½ cups and add 1 cup Dutch-processed cocoa and ¼ teaspoon salt along with sugar. Macaroons are done when they have cracked lightly across top.

TRIPLE-COCONUT MACAROONS

✔ WHY THIS RECIPE WORKS

Not that long ago, macaroons (cone-shaped cookies flavored with shredded coconut) were quite elegant and very popular. But today, they have deteriorated into lackluster mounds of beaten egg whites and coconut shreds or, at their worst, nothing more than a baked mixture of condensed milk and sweetened coconut. We set out to create a great coconut macaroon, with a pleasing texture and real, honest coconut flavor. After rounds of testing, we determined that unsweetened shredded coconut resulted in a less sticky, more appealing texture. But sweetened shredded coconut packed more flavor than the unsweetened coconut, so we decided to use both; together they worked very well in the cookie. To add one more layer of coconut flavor, we tried cream of coconut and hit the jackpot. As for the structure of our cookie, a few egg whites and some corn syrup ensured that the macaroons held together well and were moist and pleasantly chewy.

TRIPLE-COCONUT MACAROONS
MAKES 48 COOKIES

Be sure to use cream of coconut (such as Coco López) and not coconut milk here. Unsweetened desiccated coconut is commonly sold in natural foods stores and Asian markets. If you are unable to find any, use all sweetened flaked or shredded coconut, but reduce the amount of cream of coconut to ½ cup, omit the corn syrup, and toss 2 tablespoons cake flour with the coconut before adding the liquid ingredients. For larger macaroons, shape haystacks from a generous ¼ cup of batter and increase the baking time to 20 minutes.

- 1 cup cream of coconut
- 2 tablespoons light corn syrup
- 4 large egg whites
- 2 teaspoons vanilla extract
- ½ teaspoon salt
- 3 cups (9 ounces) unsweetened shredded coconut
- 3 cups (9 ounces) sweetened shredded coconut

1. Adjust oven racks to upper-middle and lower-middle positions and heat oven to 375 degrees. Line 2 baking sheets with parchment paper.

2. Whisk cream of coconut, corn syrup, egg whites, vanilla, and salt together in small bowl; set aside. Combine unsweetened and sweetened coconuts in large bowl; toss together, breaking up clumps with fingertips. Pour liquid ingredients over coconut and mix until evenly moistened. Refrigerate for 15 minutes.

3. Working with 1 tablespoon of dough at a time, drop dough onto prepared baking sheets, spacing them 1 inch apart. Using moistened fingertips, form dough into loose haystacks. Bake until cookies are light golden brown, about 15 minutes, switching and rotating baking sheets halfway through baking.

4. Let cookies cool on baking sheets until slightly set, about 2 minutes; transfer cookies to wire rack and let cool to room temperature.

CHOCOLATE-DIPPED TRIPLE-COCONUT MACAROONS

Cool baked macaroons to room temperature; line 2 baking sheets with parchment paper. Chop 10 ounces semisweet chocolate; microwave 8 ounces chocolate at 50 percent power for 2 minutes. Stir chocolate and continue heating until melted, stirring once every additional minute. Stir in remaining 2 ounces of chocolate until smooth. Holding macaroon by its pointed top, dip bottom ½ inch up sides in chocolate, scrape off excess, and place macaroon on prepared baking sheet. Repeat with remaining macaroons. Refrigerate until chocolate sets, about 15 minutes.

FORMING COCONUT MACAROONS

1. Using fingers, form cookies into loose haystacks. Moisten fingers with water if needed to prevent sticking.

2. If desired, dip bottom half-inch of baked cookies into melted chocolate, tapping off excess chocolate with finger.

CLASSIC BROWNIES

✔ WHY THIS RECIPE WORKS

Chewy and chocolaty, brownies should be a simple and utterly satisfying affair. But too often, brownies are heavy, dense, and remarkably low on chocolate flavor. We wanted old-fashioned brownies that had serious chocolate flavor. To get that tender texture and delicate chew, we shelved the all-purpose flour in favor of cake flour; a bit of baking powder further lightened the crumb. Getting the number of eggs just right prevented our brownies from being cakey or dry. As for chocolatiness, plenty of unsweetened chocolate provided maximum chocolate flavor—not too sweet, with profound chocolate notes. Nailing the baking time was essential—too little time in the oven and the brownies were gummy and underbaked, too much time and they were dry. Finally, for nut-lovers, we toasted pecans and topped the brownies with them just before baking; baked inside the brownies, they steam and get soft.

CLASSIC BROWNIES
MAKES 24 BROWNIES

Be sure to test for doneness before removing the brownies from the oven. If underbaked (the toothpick has batter, not just crumbs, clinging to it), the texture of the brownies will be dense and gummy; if overbaked (the toothpick comes out completely clean), the brownies will be dry and cakey. To melt the chocolate in a microwave, heat it at 50 percent power for 2 minutes. Stir the chocolate, add the butter, and continue heating until melted, stirring once every additional minute.

1¼	cups (5 ounces) cake flour
¾	teaspoon baking powder
½	teaspoon salt
6	ounces unsweetened chocolate, chopped fine
12	tablespoons unsalted butter, cut into 6 pieces
2¼	cups (15¾ ounces) sugar
4	large eggs
1	tablespoon vanilla extract

1. Line baking pan with 2 sheets of foil or parchment paper placed perpendicular to each other.

2. Use foil handles to lift baked cake, brownies, or bar cookies from pan.

1	cup pecans or walnuts, toasted and chopped coarse (optional)

1. Adjust oven rack to middle position and heat oven to 325 degrees. Make foil sling by folding 2 long sheets of aluminum foil so that they are as wide as 13 by 9-inch baking pan (one 13-inch sheet and one 9-inch sheet). Lay sheets of foil in pan perpendicular to one another, with extra foil hanging over edges of pan. Push foil into corners and up sides of pan, smoothing foil flush to pan. Grease foil and set aside.

2. Whisk flour, baking powder, and salt in medium bowl until combined; set aside.

3. Melt chocolate and butter in medium heatproof bowl set over saucepan of barely simmering water, stirring occasionally, until smooth. Off heat, gradually whisk in sugar. Add eggs, one at a time, whisking after each addition, until thoroughly combined. Whisk in vanilla. Add flour mixture in 3 additions, folding with rubber spatula until batter is completely smooth and homogeneous.

4. Transfer batter to prepared pan; spread batter into corners of pan and smooth surface. Sprinkle toasted nuts, if using, evenly over batter. Bake until toothpick inserted in center of brownies comes out with few moist crumbs attached, 30 to 35 minutes, rotating pan halfway through baking. Let brownies cool in pan on wire rack to room temperature, about 2 hours. Remove brownies from pan using foil. Cut brownies into 2-inch squares and serve. (Brownies can be stored at room temperature for up to 3 days.)

CHOCOLATE-GLAZED MINT-FROSTED BROWNIES

To melt the chocolate in a microwave, heat it at 50 percent power for 1 to 2 minutes. Stir the chocolate, and continue heating until melted, stirring once every additional minute.

MINT FROSTING

8	tablespoons unsalted butter, softened
2	cups (8 ounces) confectioners' sugar
1–2	tablespoons milk
1	teaspoon mint-flavored extract
1	recipe Classic Brownies

CHOCOLATE GLAZE

4	ounces bittersweet or semisweet chocolate, chopped
4	tablespoons unsalted butter

1. FOR MINT FROSTING: Using stand mixer fitted with paddle, beat butter and confectioners' sugar at low speed until just incorporated, about 30 seconds, then increase speed to medium and beat until smooth and fluffy, about 1½ minutes. Add 1 tablespoon milk and mint extract and continue to beat until combined, about 30 seconds, adding up to 1 additional

tablespoon milk if necessary to achieve soft spreadable consistency. Using offset spatula, spread mint frosting evenly onto cooled brownies, cover with aluminum foil, and refrigerate until firm, about 1 hour.

2. FOR CHOCOLATE GLAZE: Microwave chocolate at 50 percent power for 1 to 2 minutes; stir, add butter, and continue heating until melted, stirring once every additional minute. Set aside to cool slightly, about 10 minutes.

3. Pour chocolate glaze on frosted brownies; using offset spatula, spread glaze into even layer. Cover with foil and refrigerate until firm, about 1 hour. Remove brownies from pan using foil, cut into 2-inch squares, and serve. (Brownies can be stored in refrigerator for up to 3 days.)

CLASSIC BROWNIES WITH COCONUT-PECAN TOPPING

2	large egg yolks
½	cup (3½ ounces) sugar
⅛	teaspoon salt
4	tablespoons unsalted butter, softened
½	cup heavy cream
½	teaspoon vanilla extract
1	cup (3 ounces) sweetened shredded coconut
¾	cup pecans, chopped
1	recipe Classic Brownies (page 651)

Whisk egg yolks, sugar, and salt in small saucepan until combined. Whisk in butter, then gradually whisk in heavy cream and vanilla extract. Cook over low heat, stirring constantly, until mixture is fluffy, begins to thicken, and registers about 180 degrees, 8 to 12 minutes. Off heat, stir in coconut and pecans. Spread topping evenly onto cooled brownies, cover with aluminum foil, and refrigerate until set, about 2 hours. Remove brownies from pan using foil, cut into 2-inch squares, and serve. (Brownies can be stored in refrigerator for up to 3 days.)

CHEWY BROWNIES

✓ WHY THIS RECIPE WORKS

Brownies are a tricky business: homemade recipes have better flavor, while boxed mixes claim best texture. Our goal was clear: a homemade brownie with chewiness (and a shiny, crisp, crackly top) to rival the boxed-mix standard, but flush with a rich, deep, all-natural chocolate flavor. To start, we consulted our science editor to see if he knew of any tricks that boxed brownies use to achieve their chewy texture. He explained that boxed brownie mixes derive their chewy texture from the right combination of saturated (solid) and unsaturated (liquid) fats. Boxed brownie mixes already come with the saturated fat component, so when a cook adds unsaturated vegetable oil, the liquid fat and powdered solid fat combine in a ratio designed to deliver maximum chew. To get the same chew at home, we tested and tested until we finally homed in on the ratio that produced the chewiest brownies. To combat greasiness, we replaced some of the oil with egg yolks, whose emulsifiers prevent fat from separating and leaking out during baking. We focused on flavor next. Because the ratio of saturated to unsaturated fat is similar in unsweetened chocolate and butter, we could replace some of the butter with unsweetened chocolate, thereby providing more chocolate flavor. Espresso powder improved the chocolate taste as well. And finally, folding in bittersweet chocolate chunks just before baking gave our chewy, fudgy brownies gooey pockets of melted chocolate and rounded out their complex chocolate flavor.

CHEWY BROWNIES
MAKES 24 BROWNIES

For an accurate measurement of boiling water, bring a full kettle of water to a boil, then measure out the desired amount. For the chewiest texture, it is important to let the brownies cool thoroughly before cutting. If your baking dish is glass, cool the brownies 10 minutes, then remove them promptly from the pan (otherwise, the superior heat retention of glass can lead to overbaking). Use high-quality chocolate in this recipe.

⅓	cup (1 ounce) Dutch-processed cocoa
1½	teaspoons instant espresso powder (optional)
½	cup plus 2 tablespoons boiling water
2	ounces unsweetened chocolate, chopped fine
½	cup plus 2 tablespoons vegetable oil
4	tablespoons unsalted butter, melted
2	large eggs plus 2 large yolks
2	teaspoons vanilla extract
2½	cups (17½ ounces) sugar
1¾	cups (8¾ ounces) all-purpose flour
¾	teaspoon salt
6	ounces bittersweet chocolate, cut into ½-inch pieces

1. Adjust oven rack to lowest position and heat oven to 350 degrees. Make foil sling by folding 2 long sheets of aluminum foil so that they are as wide as 13 by 9-inch baking pan (one 13-inch sheet and one 9-inch sheet). Lay sheets of foil in pan perpendicular to one another, with extra foil hanging over edges of pan. Push foil into corners and up sides of pan, smoothing foil flush to pan. Grease foil and set aside.

2. Whisk cocoa, espresso powder, if using, and boiling water together in large bowl until smooth. Add unsweetened chocolate and whisk until chocolate is melted. Whisk in oil and melted butter. (Mixture may look curdled.) Add eggs, egg yolks, and vanilla and continue to whisk until smooth and homogeneous. Whisk in sugar until fully incorporated. Whisk together flour and salt in small bowl and then mix into batter with rubber spatula until combined. Fold in bittersweet chocolate pieces.

3. Transfer batter to prepared pan; spread batter into corners of pan and smooth surface. Bake until toothpick inserted in center of brownies comes out with few moist crumbs attached, 30 to 35 minutes, rotating pan halfway through baking. Transfer pan to wire rack and let cool for 1½ hours.

4. Remove brownies from pan using foil. Return brownies to wire rack and let cool completely, about 1 hour. Cut brownies into 2-inch squares and serve. (Brownies can be stored in airtight container at room temperature for up to 3 days.)

FUDGY CHOCOLATE BROWNIES

✓ WHY THIS RECIPE WORKS

Classic Brownies (page 651) boast a balance of cakey and chewy. We wanted a brownie that was distinctly fudgy—a moist, dark, luscious brownie with a firm, smooth, velvety texture. It must pack an intense chocolate punch and have deep, resonant chocolate flavor, but it must fall just short of overwhelming the palate. To develop a rich, deep chocolate flavor, we ultimately found it necessary to use three types of chocolate. Unsweetened chocolate laid a solid, intense foundation; semisweet chocolate provided a mellow, even somewhat sweet, flavor; and cocoa powder smoothed out any rough edges introduced by the unsweetened chocolate (which can contribute a sour, acrid flavor) and added complexity to what can be the bland flavor of semisweet chocolate. We focused on flour, butter, and eggs to arrive at the chewy texture we wanted. Too little flour and the batter was goopy; too much made the brownies dry and muted the chocolate flavor. We melted the butter instead of creaming softened butter with the sugar and eggs; as with our Classic Brownies, the melted butter produced a more dense and fudgy texture.

TEST KITCHEN TIP NO. 135 FOR GOOD MEASURE

Just a tablespoon too much or too little flour can have an impact on baked goods—even brownies, bars, and cookies. Here's how to measure accurately.

PREFERRED: WEIGH FLOUR For the greatest accuracy, weigh flour before using it. Put a bowl on a scale, hit the "tare" button to set the scale to zero, and scoop the flour into the bowl.

SECOND-BEST: DIP AND SWEEP Dip a dry measuring cup into the flour, sweeping away excess flour with a flat edge. This method yields more accurate results than spooning flour into a measuring cup.

FUDGY TRIPLE-CHOCOLATE BROWNIES

MAKES 64 SMALL BROWNIES

To melt the chocolates in a microwave, heat them at 50 percent power for 2 minutes. Stir the chocolate, add the butter, and continue heating until melted, stirring once every additional minute. Either Dutch-processed or natural cocoa powder works well in this recipe. These brownies are very rich, so we prefer to cut them into very small squares for serving.

 5 ounces semisweet or bittersweet chocolate, chopped
 2 ounces unsweetened chocolate, chopped
 8 tablespoons unsalted butter, cut into 4 pieces
 3 tablespoons cocoa
 3 large eggs
 1¼ cups (8¾ ounces) sugar
 2 teaspoons vanilla extract
 ½ teaspoon salt
 1 cup (5 ounces) all-purpose flour

1. Adjust oven rack to lower-middle position and heat oven to 350 degrees. Make foil sling by folding 2 long sheets of aluminum foil so that they are as wide as 8-inch square baking pan. Lay sheets of foil in pan perpendicular to one another, with extra foil hanging over edges of pan. Push foil into corners and up sides of pan, smoothing foil flush to pan. Grease foil and set aside.

2. Melt chocolates and butter in medium heatproof bowl set over saucepan of barely simmering water, stirring occasionally, until smooth. Whisk in cocoa until smooth. Set aside to cool slightly.

3. Whisk eggs, sugar, vanilla, and salt together in medium bowl until combined, about 15 seconds. Whisk warm chocolate mixture into egg mixture. Using rubber spatula, stir in flour until just combined. Transfer batter to prepared pan; spread batter into corners of pan and smooth surface. Bake until slightly puffed and toothpick inserted in center of brownies comes out with few moist crumbs attached, 35 to 40 minutes, rotating pan halfway through baking. Let brownies cool in pan on wire rack to room temperature, about 2 hours. Remove brownies from pan using foil. Cut brownies into 1-inch squares and serve. (Do not cut brownies until ready to serve. Brownies can be wrapped in plastic wrap and refrigerated for up to 3 days.)

TRIPLE-CHOCOLATE ESPRESSO BROWNIES

Whisk in 1½ tablespoons instant espresso powder or instant coffee along with cocoa in step 2.

CREAM CHEESE BROWNIES

✓ WHY THIS RECIPE WORKS

We set out to combine cheesecake and brownies in one perfect bar. The ideal cream cheese brownie would still be distinctly a brownie, but would have a swirl of tangy cream cheese filling in every bite. The brownie would have a rich, soft texture that would complement the lush cream cheese filling and a thin, crisp (but not overbaked) crust. We started by tweaking our Classic Brownies recipe (page 651). We increased the amount of ingredients to add height, replaced the cake flour with all-purpose for more structure, and used a combination of sweetened and unsweetened chocolate for more intense chocolate flavor. The cream cheese filling tasted best mixed with just an egg yolk, sugar, and vanilla and, to maximize the cream cheese flavor, we distributed the filling both within and on top of the brownies. For the perfect texture, we underbaked our brownies slightly, pulling them from the oven when a few crumbs still stuck to a toothpick.

CREAM CHEESE BROWNIES
MAKES 16 BROWNIES

Knowing when to remove a pan of brownies from the oven is the only difficult part about baking them. If a toothpick inserted in the middle of the pan comes out with fudgy crumbs, remove the pan immediately. If you wait until an inserted toothpick comes out clean, the brownies are overcooked. If you like nuts, you can stir 1 cup toasted walnuts or pecans into the brownie batter. To melt the chocolate in a microwave, heat it at 50 percent power for 1 to 2 minutes. Stir the chocolate, add the butter, and continue heating until melted, stirring once every additional minute.

BROWNIE BASE

⅔   cup (3½ ounces) all-purpose flour
¼   teaspoon salt
½   teaspoon baking powder
4   ounces bittersweet chocolate or semisweet chocolate
2   ounces unsweetened chocolate
8   tablespoons unsalted butter
1   cup (7 ounces) sugar
2   teaspoons vanilla extract
3   large eggs

CREAM CHEESE FILLING

8   ounces cream cheese, room temperature
¼   cup (1¾ ounces) sugar
½   teaspoon vanilla extract
1   large egg yolk

1. FOR THE BROWNIE BASE: Adjust oven rack to lower-middle position and heat oven to 325 degrees. Make foil sling by folding 2 long sheets of aluminum foil so that they are as wide as 8-inch square baking pan. Lay sheets of foil in pan perpendicular to one another, with extra foil hanging over edges of pan. Push foil into corners and up sides of pan, smoothing foil flush to pan. Grease foil and set aside. Whisk flour, salt, and baking powder in small bowl until combined; set aside.

2. Melt chocolate and butter in medium heatproof bowl set over pan of almost-simmering water, stirring occasionally, until mixture is smooth. Remove melted chocolate mixture from heat; whisk in sugar and vanilla; then whisk in eggs, one at time, fully incorporating each before adding next. Continue whisking until mixture is completely smooth. Add dry ingredients; whisk until just incorporated.

3. FOR THE CREAM CHEESE FILLING: Beat cream cheese in small bowl with sugar, vanilla, and egg yolk until combined.

4. Transfer half of brownie batter into prepared pan. Drop half of cream cheese mixture, by spoonfuls, over batter. Repeat layering with remaining brownie batter and cream cheese filling. Using tip of butter knife, gently swirl batter and cream cheese filling.

5. Bake until edges of brownies have puffed slightly, center feels not quite firm when touched lightly, and toothpick inserted in center comes out with several moist crumbs attached, 50 to 60 minutes, rotating pan halfway through baking.

6. Let brownies cool in pan on wire rack for 5 minutes. Remove brownies from pan using foil. Let brownies cool on wire rack to room temperature, about 1½ hours. Refrigerate until chilled, at least 3 hours. (To hasten chilling, place brownies in freezer for about 1½ hours.) Cut brownies into 2-inch squares and serve. (Don't cut brownies until ready to serve. Brownies can be wrapped in plastic wrap and refrigerated for up to 3 days.)

MAKING CREAM CHEESE BROWNIES

1. Pour half of brownie batter into prepared pan; then drop half of cream cheese mixture, by spoonfuls, over batter.

2. Repeat with remaining batter and cream cheese mixture. Use a knife or spoon handle to gently swirl the batter and cream cheese filling.

ULTIMATE TURTLE BROWNIES

☑ **WHY THIS RECIPE WORKS**

Dark chocolate brownies, rich and chewy caramel, and sweet pecans—it's hard to go wrong with turtle brownies. But recipes that call for boxed brownie mixes and jarred caramel sauce yield lackluster results. We wanted a brownie reminiscent of a candy turtle: rich, chewy, and chocolaty, with bittersweet, gooey caramel and an abundance of pecans. We began by choosing the type of chocolate, landing on both bittersweet (for complexity) and unsweetened (for assertiveness). The real challenge was getting the right texture for the caramel sauce and the application process. A few tablespoons of cream produced a caramel that was pleasantly chewy and gooey, corn syrup kept the caramel from crystallizing or turning gritty, and a little butter made it smooth and silky. We added half the brownie batter to the pan, drizzled some of the caramel on top, added the rest of the brownie batter, and then drizzled and swirled more caramel on this top layer. After we baked the brownies we poured on even more caramel to perfect our ultimate turtle brownies.

ULTIMATE TURTLE BROWNIES
MAKES 25 BROWNIES

To drizzle the caramel in step 4, use a ¼-cup dry measuring cup that has been sprayed with nonstick cooking spray. If the caramel is too cool to be fluid, reheat it in the microwave.

CARAMEL
- ¼ cup plus 2 tablespoons heavy cream
- ¼ teaspoon salt
- ¼ cup water
- 2 tablespoons light corn syrup
- 1¼ cups (8¾ ounces) sugar
- 2 tablespoons unsalted butter
- 1 teaspoon vanilla extract

BROWNIES
- 8 tablespoons unsalted butter, cut into 8 pieces
- 4 ounces bittersweet chocolate, chopped
- 2 ounces unsweetened chocolate, chopped
- ¾ cup (3¾ ounces), all-purpose flour
- ½ teaspoon baking powder
- 2 large eggs, room temperature
- 1 cup (7 ounces) sugar
- ¼ teaspoon salt
- 2 teaspoons vanilla extract
- ⅔ cup chopped pecans
- ⅓ cup semisweet chocolate chips (optional)

GARNISH
- 25 pecan halves, toasted

1. FOR THE CARAMEL: Combine cream and salt in small bowl; stir well to dissolve salt. Combine water and corn syrup in heavy-bottomed 2- to 3-quart saucepan; pour sugar into center of saucepan, taking care not to let sugar granules touch sides of pan. Gently stir with clean spatula to moisten sugar thoroughly. Cover and bring to boil over medium-high heat; cook, covered and without stirring, until sugar is completely dissolved and liquid is clear, 3 to 5 minutes. Uncover and continue to cook, without stirring, until bubbles show faint golden color, 3 to 5 minutes more. Reduce heat to medium-low. Continue to cook (swirling occasionally) until caramel is light amber and registers about 360 degrees, 1 to 3 minutes longer. Remove saucepan from heat and carefully add cream to center of pan; stir with whisk or spatula (mixture will bubble and steam vigorously) until cream is fully incorporated and bubbling subsides. Stir in butter and vanilla until combined; transfer

caramel to microwave-safe measuring cup or bowl and set aside.

2. FOR THE BROWNIES: Adjust oven rack to lower-middle position and heat oven to 325 degrees. Make foil sling by folding 2 long sheets of aluminum foil so that they are as wide as 9-inch square baking pan. Lay sheets of foil in pan perpendicular to one another, with extra foil hanging over edges of pan. Push foil into corners and up sides of pan, smoothing foil flush to pan. Grease foil and set aside.

3. Melt butter, bittersweet chocolate, and unsweetened chocolate in medium heatproof bowl set over saucepan of almost-simmering water, stirring occasionally, until smooth and combined; set aside to cool slightly. Meanwhile, whisk flour and baking powder together in small bowl; set aside. When chocolate has cooled slightly, whisk eggs in large bowl to combine; add sugar, salt, and vanilla and whisk until incorporated. Add melted chocolate mixture to egg mixture; whisk until combined. Add flour mixture; stir with rubber spatula until almost combined. Add chopped pecans and chocolate chips, if using; mix until incorporated and no flour streaks remain.

4. Transfer half of brownie batter into prepared baking pan, spreading in even layer. Drizzle ¼ cup caramel over batter. Drop remaining batter in large mounds over caramel layer; spread evenly and into corners of pan with rubber spatula. Drizzle ¼ cup caramel over top. Using tip of butter knife, swirl caramel and batter. Bake until toothpick inserted in center of brownies comes out with few moist crumbs attached, 35 to 40 minutes, rotating pan halfway through baking. Let brownies cool in pan on wire rack to room temperature, about 1½ hours.

5. Heat remaining caramel (you should have about ¾ cup) in microwave until warm and pourable but still thick (do not boil), 45 to 60 seconds, stirring once or twice; pour caramel over brownies. Spread caramel to cover surface. Refrigerate brownies, uncovered, at least 2 hours.

6. Remove brownies from pan using foil, loosening sides with paring knife, if needed. Using chef's knife, cut brownies into 25 evenly sized squares. Press pecan half onto surface of each brownie. Serve chilled or at room temperature. (Brownies can be wrapped in plastic wrap and refrigerated for up to 3 days.)

BLONDIES

✔ WHY THIS RECIPE WORKS
Blondies are first cousins to both brownies and chocolate chip cookies. Although blondies are baked in a pan like brownies, the flavorings are similar to those in chocolate chip cookies— vanilla, butter, and brown sugar. They're sometimes laced with nuts and chocolate chips or butterscotch chips. But even with these extras, blondies can be pretty bland, floury, and dry. We set out to fix the blondie so it would be chewy but not dense, sweet but not cloying, and loaded with nuts and chocolate. We found that the key to chewy blondies was using melted, not creamed, butter because the creaming process incorporates too much air into the batter. For sweetening, light brown sugar lent the right amount of earthy molasses flavor. And combined with a substantial amount of vanilla extract and salt (to sharpen the sweetness), the light brown sugar developed a rich butterscotch flavor. To add both texture and flavor to the cookies, we included chocolate chips and pecans. We also tried butterscotch chips, but we found that they did little for this recipe. On a whim, we included white chocolate chips with the semisweet chips, and we were surprised that they produced the best blondies yet.

BLONDIES
MAKES 36 BARS

Walnuts can be substituted for the pecans.

1½	cups (7½ ounces) all-purpose flour
1	teaspoon baking powder
½	teaspoon salt
1½	cups packed (10½ ounces) light brown sugar
12	tablespoons unsalted butter, melted and cooled
2	large eggs
1½	teaspoons vanilla extract
1	cup pecans, toasted and chopped coarse
½	cup (3 ounces) semisweet chocolate chips
½	cup (3 ounces) white chocolate chips

1. Adjust oven rack to middle position and heat oven to 350 degrees. Make foil sling by folding 2 long sheets of aluminum foil so that they are as wide as 13 by 9-inch baking pan (one 13-inch sheet and one 9-inch sheet). Lay sheets of foil in pan perpendicular to one another, with extra foil hanging over edges of pan. Push foil into corners and up sides of pan, smoothing foil flush to pan. Grease foil and set aside.

2. Whisk flour, baking powder, and salt together in medium bowl; set aside.

3. Whisk brown sugar and melted butter together in medium bowl until combined. Add eggs and vanilla and mix well. Using rubber spatula, fold dry ingredients into egg mixture until just combined. Do not overmix. Fold in nuts and semisweet and white chocolate chips and turn batter into prepared pan, smoothing top with rubber spatula.

4. Bake until top is shiny and cracked and feels firm to touch, 22 to 25 minutes. Transfer pan to wire rack and let cool completely. Loosen edges with paring knife and remove bars from pan using foil. Cut into 2 by 1½-inch bars.

CONGO BARS

Keep a close eye on the coconut as it toasts because it can burn easily.

Adjust oven rack to middle position and heat oven to 350 degrees. Toast 1½ cups unsweetened shredded coconut on a rimmed baking sheet, stirring 2 or 3 times, until light golden, 4 to 5 minutes. Let cool. Add toasted coconut with chocolate chips and nuts in step 3.

RASPBERRY STREUSEL BARS

✔ WHY THIS RECIPE WORKS
We realized early in developing our raspberry streusel bar recipe that the bottom crust needs to be firm and sturdy, while the topping should be light as well as sandy and dry so it can adhere to the filling. Since we didn't want to make two separate mixtures for the top and bottom layers, we used a butter-rich shortbread for the bottom crust and then rubbed even more butter into the same dough to produce a great streusel topping. The filling for our raspberry streusel bar recipe also needed complementary textures: good raspberry preserves made the filling sweet and viscous, while fresh raspberries—lightly mashed for easier spreading—combined with the preserves to produce a bright, well-rounded flavor and perfectly moist consistency.

RASPBERRY STREUSEL BARS
MAKES 20 BARS

This recipe can be made in a stand mixer or a food processor. Frozen raspberries can be substituted for fresh; be sure to defrost them before combining with the raspberry preserves. If your fresh raspberries are very tart, add only 1 or 2 teaspoons of lemon juice to the filling.

2½	cups (12½ ounces) all-purpose flour
⅔	cup (4⅔ ounces) granulated sugar

½ teaspoon salt

18 tablespoons unsalted butter, cut into ½-inch pieces and softened

¼ cup packed (1¾ ounces) brown sugar

½ cup (1½ ounces) old-fashioned rolled oats

½ cup pecans, chopped fine

¾ cup (8½ ounces) raspberry jam

3½ ounces (¾ cup) fresh raspberries

1 tablespoon lemon juice

1. Adjust oven rack to middle position and heat oven to 375 degrees. Make foil sling by folding 2 long sheets of aluminum foil so that they are as wide as 13 by 9-inch baking pan (one 13-inch sheet and one 9-inch sheet). Lay sheets of foil in pan perpendicular to one another, with extra foil hanging over edges of pan. Push foil into corners and up sides of pan, smoothing foil flush to pan. Grease foil and set aside.

2. Using stand mixer fitted with paddle, mix flour, granulated sugar, and salt at low speed until combined, about 10 seconds. Add 16 tablespoons butter, 1 piece at a time; then continue mixing until mixture resembles damp sand, 1 to 1½ minutes. (If using food processor, process flour, granulated sugar, and salt until combined, about 5 seconds. Scatter 16 tablespoons butter pieces over flour mixture and pulse until mixture resembles damp sand, about 20 pulses.)

3. Measure 1¼ cups flour mixture into medium bowl and set aside; distribute remaining flour mixture evenly in bottom of prepared baking pan. Using flat-bottomed measuring cup, firmly press mixture into even layer to form bottom crust. Bake until edges begin to brown, 14 to 18 minutes.

4. While crust is baking, add brown sugar, oats, and pecans to reserved flour mixture; toss to combine. Work in remaining 2 tablespoons butter by rubbing mixture between fingers until butter is fully incorporated. Pinch mixture with fingers to create hazelnut-size clumps; set streusel aside.

5. Combine preserves, raspberries, and lemon juice in small bowl; mash with fork until combined but some berry pieces remain.

6. Spread filling evenly over hot crust; sprinkle streusel topping evenly over filling (do not press streusel into filling). Return pan to oven and bake until topping is deep golden brown and filling is bubbling, 22 to 25 minutes, rotating pan halfway through baking. Let cool to room temperature on wire rack, 1 to 2 hours; remove bars from pan using foil. Cut into squares and serve. (Bars are best eaten the day they are baked but can stored at room temperature for up to 3 days; crust and streusel will soften slightly.)

STRAWBERRY STREUSEL BARS

Thawed frozen strawberries will also work here.

Substitute strawberry jam and chopped fresh strawberries for raspberry jam and raspberries.

BLUEBERRY STREUSEL BARS

Thawed frozen blueberries will also work here.

Substitute blueberry jam and fresh blueberries for raspberry jam and raspberries.

PERFECT LEMON BARS

✔ WHY THIS RECIPE WORKS

For our perfect lemon bar recipe, we tackled the crust first. Granulated sugar is often the first option bakers turn to for the sort of crust we were after, but we discovered that confectioners' sugar gave us the most tender texture. The addition of a little cornstarch also helped move the crust in the melt-in-your-mouth direction. To make the filling lemony enough, we ended up using the juice from four lemons, plus some zest. Arriving at a smooth and pleasant texture involved eggs, a little flour for thickening, and, somewhat unexpectedly, milk, which seemed to balance the flavor with the texture.

PERFECT LEMON BARS
MAKES ABOUT 24 BARS

The lemon filling must be added to a warm crust, so be sure to prepare the filling while the crust chills and bakes. Alternatively, you can prepare the filling ahead of time and stir to blend just before pouring it into the crust. Any leftover bars can be sealed in plastic wrap and refrigerated for up to 2 days.

CRUST

1¾ cups (8¾ ounces) all-purpose flour

⅔ cup (2⅔ ounces) confectioners' sugar, plus extra for garnish

¼ cup cornstarch

¾ teaspoon salt

12 tablespoons unsalted butter, chilled and cut into 1-inch pieces

LEMON FILLING

4 large eggs, lightly beaten

1⅓ cups (9⅓ ounces) granulated sugar

3 tablespoons all-purpose flour

2 teaspoons grated lemon zest plus ⅔ cup juice (4 lemons)

⅓ cup whole milk

⅛ teaspoon salt

1. FOR THE CRUST: Adjust oven rack to middle position and heat oven to 350 degrees. Make foil sling by folding 2 long sheets of aluminum foil so that they are as wide as 13 by 9-inch baking pan (one 13-inch sheet and one 9-inch sheet). Lay sheets of foil in pan perpendicular to one another, with extra foil hanging over edges of pan. Push foil into corners and up sides of pan, smoothing foil flush to pan. Grease foil and set aside.

2. Process flour, confectioners' sugar, cornstarch, and salt in food processor until combined, 15 seconds. Add butter

and process to blend, 8 to 10 seconds, then pulse until mixture is pale yellow and resembles coarse meal, about 3 pulses. (To do this by hand, mix flour, confectioners' sugar, cornstarch, and salt in medium bowl. Freeze butter and grate it on large holes of box grater into flour mixture. Toss butter pieces to coat. Rub pieces between fingers for a minute, until flour turns pale yellow and coarse.) Sprinkle mixture into prepared pan and press firmly with fingers into even ¼-inch layer over entire pan bottom and about ½ inch up sides. Refrigerate for 30 minutes, then bake until golden brown, about 20 minutes.

3. FOR THE FILLING: Whisk eggs, sugar, and flour in medium bowl, then stir in lemon zest and juice, milk, and salt to blend well.

4. Reduce oven temperature to 325 degrees. Stir filling mixture to reblend; pour into warm crust. Bake until filling feels firm when touched lightly, about 20 minutes. Transfer pan to wire rack; let cool to near room temperature, at least 30 minutes. Cut into squares and sieve confectioners' sugar over squares, if desired. (Bars can be refrigerated for up to 2 days; crust will soften slightly.)

KEY LIME BARS

✓ WHY THIS RECIPE WORKS

We wanted to bring all the essence of Key lime pie to a Key lime bar, creating a cookie that balanced tart and creamy flavors as well as soft and crispy textures. To support our handheld bars, we needed a thicker, sturdier crust, which required more crumbs and butter than used in traditional pie crust. Tasters found the traditional graham cracker flavor too assertive and preferred the more neutral flavor of animal crackers. As for the filling, it also had to be firmer. By adding cream cheese and an egg yolk to the usual sweetened condensed milk, lime juice, and lime zest, we created a

firm, rich filling that didn't fall apart when the bars were picked up. Regular juice was judged acceptable over Key limes, especially considering that we needed to squeeze far fewer regular limes (four) than Key limes (20) to get the same amount of juice. For a topping, a heavy streusel was rejected. The favorite was an optional toasted-coconut topping.

KEY LIME BARS
MAKES 16 BARS

Despite this recipe's name, we found that most tasters could not tell the difference between bars made with regular supermarket limes (called Persian limes) and true Key limes. Since Persian limes are easier to find and juice, we recommend them. The optional coconut garnish adds textural interest and tames the lime flavor for those who find it too intense. To toast the coconut, spread it out on a rimmed baking sheet on the middle oven rack at 350 degrees, stirring two or three times, until light golden, 4 to 5 minutes. Let cool. The recipe can be doubled and baked in a 13 by 9-inch baking pan; increase the baking times by a minute or two.

CRUST
5   ounces animal crackers
3   tablespoons packed brown sugar
    Pinch salt
4   tablespoons unsalted butter, melted and cooled slightly

FILLING
2   ounces cream cheese, room temperature
1   tablespoon grated lime zest plus ½ cup juice (4 limes)
    Pinch salt
1   (14-ounce) can sweetened condensed milk
1   large egg yolk

GARNISH (OPTIONAL)
¾   cup (2¼ ounces) sweetened shredded coconut, toasted until golden and crisp

1. Adjust oven rack to middle position and heat oven to 325 degrees. Make foil sling by folding 2 long sheets of aluminum foil so that they are as wide as 8-inch baking pan. Lay sheets of foil in pan perpendicular to one another, with extra foil hanging over edges of pan. Push foil into corners and up sides of pan, smoothing foil flush to pan. Grease foil.

2. FOR THE CRUST: Pulse animal crackers in food processor until broken down, about 10 pulses; process crumbs until evenly fine, about 10 seconds (you should have about 1¼ cups crumbs). Add brown sugar and salt; process to combine, 10 to 12 pulses (if large sugar lumps remain, break them apart with your fingers). Drizzle butter over crumbs and pulse until crumbs are evenly moistened with butter, about 10 pulses. Press crumbs evenly and firmly into bottom of prepared pan. Bake until deep golden brown, 18 to 20 minutes. Cool on wire rack while making filling. Do not turn off oven.

3. FOR THE FILLING: While the crust cools, in medium bowl, stir the cream cheese, zest, and salt with rubber spatula until softened, creamy, and thoroughly combined. Add sweetened condensed milk and whisk vigorously until incorporated and no lumps of cream cheese remain; whisk in egg yolk. Add lime juice and whisk gently until incorporated (mixture will thicken slightly).

4. Pour filling into crust; spread to corners and smooth surface with rubber spatula. Bake until set and edges begin to pull away slightly from sides, 15 to 20 minutes. Let cool on wire rack to room temperature, 1 to 1½ hours. Cover with foil and refrigerate until thoroughly chilled, at least 2 hours.

5. Remove bars from pan using foil; cut bars into 16 squares. Sprinkle with toasted coconut, if using, and serve. (Bars can be refrigerated for up to 2 days; crust will soften slightly.)

Using three types of citrus (orange, lemon, and lime) gives these bars a slightly more complex, floral flavor.

Substitute 1½ teaspoons each grated lime zest, lemon zest, and orange zest for lime zest, and use 6 tablespoons lime juice, 1 tablespoon lemon juice, and 1 tablespoon orange juice in place of all lime juice.

15-MINUTE CHOCOLATE-WALNUT FUDGE

✔ WHY THIS RECIPE WORKS

We wanted a forgiving fudge recipe that didn't require ideal conditions for success. We found that a traditional "easy" substitute, condensed milk and a little unsweetened chocolate, gave us a less sugary fudge with great chocolate flavor. Seeking a firmer, lighter texture for our fudge, we found that a little baking soda reacted with the acids in the chocolate to alter the pH, which made the fudge drier and firmer. We reached perfect density when we added 1 cup of nuts.

15-MINUTE
CHOCOLATE-WALNUT FUDGE

MAKES ABOUT 2½ POUNDS

The quality of the chocolate used will affect the flavor and texture of the fudge. We prefer Ghirardelli semisweet and unsweetened chocolate in this recipe. Don't be tempted to make this fudge without the walnuts; they are crucial to the texture. If you prefer, you can use toasted nuts in this recipe. Make sure to remove the fudge from the double boiler before the chocolate is fully melted. If the chocolate stays in the double boiler too long, there is the possibility of the chocolate separating and producing a greasy fudge. This fudge will change texture and become drier the longer it is stored. If frozen, allow ample time to let it reach room temperature before cutting. This recipe can be easily doubled and prepared in a 13 by 9-inch baking pan.

1	pound semisweet chocolate, chopped fine
2	ounces unsweetened chocolate, chopped fine
½	teaspoon baking soda
⅛	teaspoon salt
1	(14-ounce) can sweetened condensed milk
1	tablespoon vanilla extract
1	cup coarsely chopped walnuts

1. Make foil sling by folding 2 long sheets of aluminum foil so that they are as wide as 13 by 9-inch baking pan (one 13-inch sheet and one 9-inch sheet. Lay sheets of foil in pan perpendicular to one another, with extra foil hanging over edges of pan. Push foil into corners and up sides of pan, smoothing foil flush to pan. Grease foil and set aside.

2. Mix semisweet chocolate, unsweetened chocolate, baking soda, and salt in medium heatproof bowl until baking soda is evenly distributed. Stir in sweetened condensed milk and vanilla. Set bowl over 4-quart saucepan containing 2 cups simmering water. Stir until chocolate is almost fully melted and few small pieces remain, 2 to 4 minutes.

3. Remove bowl from heat and continue to stir until chocolate is fully melted and mixture is smooth, about 2 minutes. Stir in walnuts. Transfer fudge to prepared pan and spread in even layer with spatula. Refrigerate until set, about 2 hours. Remove fudge from pan using foil and cut into squares. (Fudge can be refrigerated for up to 2 weeks or frozen for up to 3 months.)

15-MINUTE PEANUT BUTTER FUDGE

Substitute 1 pound 2 ounces peanut butter chips for chocolates in step 2 and omit walnuts.

Substitute 1 cup mini marshmallows, 1 cup coarsely chopped peanuts, and ½ cup semisweet chocolate chips for walnuts in step 3.

PERFECT CHOCOLATE TRUFFLES

✔ WHY THIS RECIPE WORKS

We discovered a few things that took the risk and guesswork out of our truffle recipe: Butter and corn syrup added to the traditional chocolate and cream made our truffles creamier and more delicate. We did not want to take the time or deal with the hassle of tempering chocolate for the coating used in our truffle recipe, so our coating wasn't smooth and shiny. We found an easy fix to that by simply rolling the truffles in cocoa, toasted nuts, or grated chocolate.

PERFECT CHOCOLATE TRUFFLES
MAKES 24 TRUFFLES

These truffles are meant to look like the real thing—small, irregular mounds instead of perfectly spherical balls. If you decide to omit the liquor flavoring, reduce chocolate from 9 to 8 ounces. To melt the chocolate in a microwave, heat it at 50 percent power for about 2 minutes; stir the chocolate and continue heating until melted, stirring once every additional minute. The ganache mixture is quite forgiving. If it cools too much in step 1, place the bowl in a larger pan of warm water and stir the mixture until it has softened and warmed up. If this overwarms the mixture, cool it again as directed. The same flexibility applies if you overwhip the ganache by mistake. Simply warm it over the hot water, cool it, and whip it again. One person alone can dip and coat the truffles, but the process is simpler with a second person to roll coated truffles in cocoa and lift them onto a clean pan.

GANACHE

9 ounces semisweet chocolate or bittersweet chocolate, chopped coarse

½ cup heavy whipping cream

2 tablespoons unsalted butter

1 tablespoon light corn syrup

2 tablespoons cognac, dark rum, Grand Marnier, framboise, kirsch, Frangelico, amaretto, Kahlúa, or port

CHOCOLATE AND COCOA COATING

8 ounces semisweet chocolate or bittersweet chocolate

2 cups (6 ounces) Dutch-processed cocoa, sifted

1. FOR THE GANACHE: Melt chocolate in medium heatproof bowl set over pan of almost-simmering water, stirring once or twice, until smooth. Set bowl aside. Bring cream, butter, and corn syrup to simmer (about 160 degrees) in nonreactive pan over low heat. Remove pan from heat, cool for 5 minutes, then whisk into chocolate. Whisk in cognac. Refrigerate mixture until it cools to 80 degrees, 15 to 20 minutes.

2. Using stand mixer fitted with whisk, whip mixture at medium speed until thickened to a texture like store-bought canned chocolate frosting, 25 to 30 seconds. Spoon ganache into large pastry bag fitted with ½-inch plain tube. Hold bag perpendicular to pan and with tip about ¾ inch above work surface, pipe ¾-inch mounds (pulling tube away to the side to avoid leaving points) onto parchment-lined baking sheet. Alternatively, scoop mounds with tiny (less than 1 tablespoon) ice cream scoop or melon baller. Refrigerate mounds until hardened, at least an hour.

3. FOR THE COATING: Melt chocolate in heatproof bowl over almost-simmering water, then cool to 90 degrees. Arrange chilled truffle mounds, bowl of melted chocolate, and high-sided roasting pan filled with cocoa on work surface. Working one mound at a time, dip palm of one hand about ¼-inch deep into melted chocolate, pass one truffle mound with other hand to chocolate-covered hand and close hand around mound to coat, re-dipping hand into chocolate every third or fourth mound. Drop coated truffle into cocoa; roll to coat using fork held in now empty clean hand, leaving truffles in cocoa until chocolate coating has set, about 1 minute. Repeat process until all mounds are in pan of cocoa. Gently roll 5 to 6 truffles at a time in medium strainer to remove excess cocoa, then transfer to serving plate or tightly covered container. (Truffles can be refrigerated for up to 1 week.)

CHOCOLATE NUT TRUFFLES

Pulse 1 cup unsalted pistachios, almonds, pecans, or walnuts with 1 tablespoon sugar to a fine powder (about the texture of coarse sand) in food processor, 45 to 60 seconds. Substitute ground nuts for cocoa.

CHOCOLATE COCONUT TRUFFLES

Adjust oven rack to middle position and heat oven to 350 degrees. Spread 1 cup shredded, sweetened coconut in even layer on baking sheet; toast until golden brown, 4 to 5 minutes, stirring every 2 minutes. Substitute toasted coconut for cocoa.

CHAPTER 18   Cakes

RICH AND TENDER YELLOW LAYER CAKE

✓ WHY THIS RECIPE WORKS

We wanted a yellow cake that was moist and tender, with a rich, buttery, eggy flavor and a fine, even crumb. Those cakes made using the classic creaming method—beating the butter and sugar together, then adding the flour and milk-egg mixture alternately to the bowl—gave us disappointing results. Instead of melting in your mouth, these cakes were crumbly, sugary, and a little hard. And they didn't taste of butter and eggs, as all plain cakes ought to, but instead seemed merely sweet. We found that reverse creaming—combining all the dry ingredients in the mixing bowl, then adding the butter, followed by the milk and eggs, in stages—gave us the tender texture and fine crumb we were after. (And swapping in cake flour for all-purpose flour further ensured a tender cake.) As for icing the cake, we turned to a rich buttercream, made with whipped whole eggs and butter, as well as an intensely flavored chocolate frosting made with heavy cream and bittersweet chocolate.

RICH AND TENDER YELLOW LAYER CAKE WITH BUTTERCREAM FROSTING

SERVES 10 TO 12

Adding the butter pieces to the mixing bowl one at a time prevents the dry ingredients from flying up and out of the bowl.

- ½   cup whole milk, room temperature
- 4   large eggs, room temperature
- 2   teaspoons vanilla extract
- 1¾   cups (7 ounces) cake flour
- 1½   cups (10½ ounces) sugar
- 2   teaspoons baking powder
- ¾   teaspoon salt
- 16   tablespoons unsalted butter, cut into 16 pieces and softened
- 1   recipe frosting (recipes follow)

1. Adjust oven rack to middle position and heat oven to 350 degrees. Grease two 9-inch round cake pans, line with parchment paper, grease parchment, and flour pans. Whisk milk, eggs, and vanilla together in small bowl.

2. Using stand mixer fitted with paddle, mix flour, sugar, baking powder, and salt on low speed until combined. Add butter, 1 piece at a time, and mix until only pea-size pieces remain, about 1 minute.

3. Add all but ½ cup milk mixture, increase speed to medium-high, and beat until light and fluffy, about 1 minute. Reduce speed to medium-low, add remaining ½ cup milk mixture, and beat until incorporated, about 30 seconds (batter may look slightly curdled). Give batter final stir by hand.

4. Divide batter evenly between prepared pans and smooth tops with rubber spatula. Bake cake until toothpick inserted in centers comes out with few crumbs attached, 20 to 25 minutes. Let cakes cool in pans on wire rack for 10 minutes. Remove cakes from pans, discard parchment, and let cool completely, about 2 hours, before frosting. (Cooled cakes can be wrapped tightly in plastic wrap and kept at room temperature for up to 1 day. Wrapped tightly in plastic, then aluminum foil, cakes can be frozen for up to 1 month. Defrost cakes at room temperature before unwrapping and frosting.)

5. TO ASSEMBLE THE CAKE: Line edges of cake platter with 4 strips of parchment paper to keep platter clean. Place 1 cake layer on prepared platter. Place about 1½ cups frosting in center of cake layer and, using large spatula, spread in even layer right to edge of cake. Place second cake layer on top, making sure layers are aligned, then frost top in same manner as first layer, this time spreading frosting until slightly over edge. Gather more frosting on tip of spatula and gently spread icing onto side of cake. Smooth frosting by gently running edge of spatula around cake and leveling ridge that forms around top edge, or create billows by pressing back of spoon into frosting and twirling spoon as you lift away. Carefully pull out pieces of parchment from beneath cake before serving. (Assembled cake can be refrigerated for up to 1 day. Bring to room temperature before serving.)

VANILLA BUTTERCREAM FROSTING

MAKES ABOUT 4 CUPS

The whole eggs, whipped until airy, give this buttercream a light, satiny-smooth texture that melts on the tongue.

- 4   large eggs, room temperature
- 1   cup (7 ounces) sugar
- 2   teaspoons vanilla extract
       Pinch salt
- 1   pound unsalted butter (4 sticks), each stick cut into quarters and softened

1. Combine eggs, sugar, vanilla, and salt in bowl of stand mixer and set bowl over saucepan containing 1 inch of barely simmering water. Whisking gently but constantly, heat mixture until thin and foamy and registers 160 degrees.

2. Fit stand mixer with whisk and whip egg mixture on medium-high speed until light, airy, and cooled to room temperature, about 5 minutes. Reduce speed to medium and add butter, 1 piece at a time. (After adding half of butter, buttercream may look curdled; it will smooth with additional butter.) Once all butter is added, increase speed to high and whip until light, fluffy, and thoroughly combined, about 1 minute. (Frosting can be refrigerated for up to 5 days. Let frosting sit at room temperature until softened, about 2 hours, then, using stand mixer fitted with whisk, whip on medium speed until smooth, 2 to 5 minutes.)

RICH COFFEE BUTTERCREAM FROSTING

Omit vanilla. Substitute 3 tablespoons instant espresso powder in 3 tablespoons warm water and beat dissolved coffee into buttercream after butter has been added.

RICH CHOCOLATE CREAM FROSTING

MAKES ABOUT 3 CUPS

1½	cups heavy cream
16	ounces semisweet chocolate, chopped fine
⅓	cup corn syrup
1	teaspoon vanilla extract

Place chocolate in heatproof bowl. Bring heavy cream to boil in small saucepan over medium-high heat, then pour over chocolate. Add corn syrup and let sit, covered, for 5 minutes. Whisk mixture gently until smooth, then stir in vanilla. Refrigerate 1 to 1½ hours, stirring every 15 minutes, until mixture reaches spreadable consistency.

FLUFFY YELLOW LAYER CAKE

✔ WHY THIS RECIPE WORKS

Box mixes are famous for engineering cakes with ultra-light texture. We set out to make an even fluffier cake—one without chemicals and additives. Chiffon cakes are especially weightless, springy, and moist. But unlike butter cakes, they are too light to stand up to a serious slathering of frosting. We decided to blend the two types of cake. We adapted a chiffon technique (using a large quantity of whipped egg whites to get a high volume and light texture) to combine the ingredients from our butter cake recipe. This gave us a light, porous cake that was sturdy enough to hold the frosting's weight. We used a combination of fats (butter plus vegetable oil),

which kept the butter flavor intact while improving the moistness of the cake. For extra tenderness, we increased the sugar and substituted buttermilk for milk. The buttermilk not only introduced a new flavor dimension, but also allowed us to replace some of the baking powder with a little baking soda to ensure an even rise. As for the frosting, a fluffy chocolate frosting is the perfect partner to this cake. A hefty amount of cocoa powder combined with melted chocolate gave the frosting a deep chocolate flavor. A combination of confectioners' sugar and corn syrup made it smooth and glossy. To keep the frosting from separating and turning greasy, we moved it out of the stand mixer and into the food processor. The faster machine minimized any risk of overbeating, as it blended the ingredients quickly without melting the butter or incorporating too much air. The result was a thick, fluffy chocolate frosting that spread like a dream.

FLUFFY YELLOW LAYER CAKE WITH CHOCOLATE FROSTING

SERVES 10 TO 12

Bring all the ingredients to room temperature before beginning this recipe. Be sure to use cake pans with at least 2-inch-tall sides. This frosting may be made with milk, semisweet, or bittersweet chocolate; we prefer a frosting made with milk chocolate for this recipe. Cool the chocolate to between 85 and 100 degrees before adding it to the butter mixture.

CAKE

2½	cups (10 ounces) cake flour
1¼	teaspoons baking powder
¼	teaspoon baking soda
¾	teaspoon salt
1¾	cups (12¼ ounces) granulated sugar
10	tablespoons unsalted butter, melted and cooled
1	cup buttermilk, room temperature
3	tablespoons vegetable oil
2	teaspoons vanilla extract
3	large eggs, separated, plus 3 large yolks, room temperature
	Pinch cream of tartar

FROSTING

20	tablespoons (2½ sticks) unsalted butter, softened
1	cup (4 ounces) confectioners' sugar
¾	cup (2¼ ounces) Dutch-processed cocoa
	Pinch salt
¾	cup light corn syrup
1	teaspoon vanilla extract
8	ounces chocolate, melted and cooled

1. FOR THE CAKE: Adjust oven rack to middle position and heat oven to 350 degrees. Grease two 9-inch round cake pans, line with parchment paper, grease parchment, and flour pans. Whisk flour,

---

TEST KITCHEN TIP NO. 136   BAKING WITH FARM-FRESH EGGS

You may have heard that freshly laid eggs have different baking properties than older supermarket eggs. Because egg whites thin with age, some bakers theorize that the weakened proteins of eggs even a few weeks old can stretch more than those from just-laid eggs, leading to cakes that rise higher and have a softer, more tender texture than cakes made with the freshest eggs. To test this theory, we made our Fluffy Yellow Layer Cake with seven-week-old supermarket eggs (we determined their age by the date on the carton) and eggs from a Vermont farm laid a few days before. Any differences we found were slight. The cake made with store-bought eggs dissolved a little more quickly on the tongue, and the cake made with the farm-fresh eggs was a little more "substantial." But only a few tasters actually detected these variations in texture. Did one cake rise higher than the other? No. The bottom line: Don't pass up farm-fresh eggs in hopes of baking a better cake—age doesn't make a difference. Besides, you're probably just as likely to scramble or fry your eggs, dishes where freshness truly matters.

baking powder, baking soda, salt, and 1½ cups sugar together in large bowl. In medium bowl, whisk together melted butter, buttermilk, oil, vanilla, and egg yolks.

2. Using stand mixer fitted with whisk, whip egg whites and cream of tartar on medium-low speed until foamy, about 1 minute. Increase speed to medium-high and whip whites to soft billowy mounds, about 1 minute. Gradually add remaining ¼ cup sugar and whip until glossy, stiff peaks form, 2 to 3 minutes. Transfer to bowl and set aside.

3. Add flour mixture to now-empty bowl. With mixer on low speed, gradually pour in butter mixture and whip until almost incorporated (a few streaks of dry flour will remain), about 15 seconds. Scrape down bowl, then whip on medium-low speed until smooth and fully incorporated, 10 to 15 seconds.

4. Using rubber spatula, stir one-third of whites into batter, then add remaining two-thirds whites and gently fold into batter until no white streaks remain. Divide batter evenly between prepared pans, smooth tops with rubber spatula, and gently tap pans on counter to release air bubbles.

5. Bake cake until toothpick inserted in centers comes out clean, 20 to 22 minutes. Let cakes cool in pans on wire rack for 10 minutes. Remove cakes from pans, discard parchment, and let cool completely, about 2 hours, before frosting. (Cooled cakes can be wrapped tightly in plastic wrap and kept at room temperature for up to 1 day. Wrapped tightly in plastic, then aluminum foil, cakes can be frozen for up to 1 month. Defrost cakes at room temperature before unwrapping and frosting.)

6. FOR THE FROSTING: Process butter, sugar, cocoa, and salt in food processor until smooth, about 30 seconds, scraping down bowl as needed. Add corn syrup and vanilla and process until just combined, 5 to 10 seconds. Scrape down bowl, then add chocolate and process until smooth and creamy, 10 to 15 seconds. (Frosting can be kept at room temperature for up to 3 hours before frosting cake or refrigerated for up to 3 days. If refrigerated, let stand at room temperature for 1 hour before using.)

7. TO ASSEMBLE THE CAKE: Line edges of cake platter with 4 strips of parchment paper to keep platter clean. Place 1 cake layer on prepared platter. Place about 1½ cups frosting in center of cake layer and, using large spatula, spread in even layer right to edge of cake. Place second cake layer on top, making sure layers are aligned, then frost top in same manner as first layer, this time spreading frosting until slightly over edge. Gather more frosting on tip of spatula and gently spread icing onto side of cake. Smooth frosting by gently running edge of spatula around cake and leveling ridge that forms around top edge, or create billows by pressing back of spoon into frosting and twirling spoon as you lift away. Carefully pull out pieces of parchment from beneath cake before serving. (Assembled cake can be refrigerated for up to 1 day. Bring to room temperature before serving.)

OLD-FASHIONED BIRTHDAY CAKE

✔ WHY THIS RECIPE WORKS

White layer cakes have been the classic birthday cake for more than 100 years. White cake is simply a basic butter cake made with egg whites instead of whole eggs (using the latter would make it a yellow cake). Theoretically, the whites are supposed to make the cake soft and fine-grained. Unfortunately, the white cakes that we have baked over the years, though good enough, always fell short of our high expectations, always coming out a little dry and chewy—one might say cottony—and we noticed that they were riddled with tunnels and small holes. What were we doing wrong? Every traditional recipe for white cake calls for stiffly beaten egg whites folded into the batter at the end. We began to suspect that it was the beaten egg whites that were forming the large air pockets and those unsightly holes in the baked cakes. We solved this problem by mixing the egg whites with the milk before beating them into the flour-and-butter mixture. The results were fantastic. The cake was not only fine-grained and free from holes but, to our surprise, it was also larger and lighter than the ones we'd prepared with beaten whites. And the method couldn't be simpler, quicker, or more foolproof. To make this cake birthday-special, we iced it with an easy butter frosting and added a layer of raspberry jam and chopped toasted almonds.

TEST KITCHEN TIP NO. 137 BAKING EVEN LAYER CAKES

What's the best way to get a two-layer cake to cook evenly? We baked our Classic White Layer Cake (page 665) in three configurations: side by side on one rack; on two racks with one pan directly above the other; and on two racks with one pan on the top left of the oven and the other on the lower right. Only the cakes on the same rack baked evenly.

The reason is convection—the hot air currents moving around the oven. In bottom-heating ovens, when cakes are stacked, the bottom one acts as a barrier, creating hot air currents that flow up and over the top cake. The result is an overcooked top cake and an undercooked bottom cake. Results are also uneven in rear-heating ovens or those with top and bottom elements. But when cakes are baked side by side, hot air circulates evenly no matter how your oven heats. If you need to cook three cakes at a time, place two on the bottom rack, spaced apart, and one on the rack above and in between the other two. Move the cakes twice during cooking so that each cake spends an equal amount of time in each position.

CLASSIC WHITE LAYER CAKE WITH RASPBERRY-ALMOND FILLING

SERVES 10 TO 12

There is enough frosting to pipe a border around the base and top of the cake. If you want to decorate the cake more elaborately, you should make 1½ times the frosting recipe. If desired, finish the sides of the cake with 1 cup of sliced almonds.

CAKE

1	cup whole milk, room temperature
6	large egg whites, room temperature
2	teaspoons almond extract
1	teaspoon vanilla extract
2¼	cups (9 ounces) cake flour
1¾	cups (12¼ ounces) granulated sugar
4	teaspoons baking powder
1	teaspoon salt
12	tablespoons unsalted butter, cut into 12 pieces and softened

FROSTING AND FILLING

16	tablespoons unsalted butter, softened
4	cups (16 ounces) confectioners' sugar
1	tablespoon vanilla extract
1	tablespoon whole milk
	Pinch salt
½	cup blanched slivered almonds, toasted and chopped coarse
⅓	cup seedless raspberry jam

1. FOR THE CAKE: Adjust oven rack to middle position and heat oven to 350 degrees. Grease two 9-inch round cake pans, line with parchment paper, grease parchment, and flour pans.

2. Whisk milk, egg whites, almond extract, and vanilla together in small bowl. Using stand mixer fitted with paddle, mix cake flour, sugar, baking powder, and salt on low speed until combined. Add butter, 1 piece at a time, and mix until only pea-size pieces remain, about 1 minute.

3. Add all but ½ cup milk mixture, increase speed to medium-high, and beat until light and fluffy, about 1 minute. Reduce speed to medium-low, add remaining ½ cup milk mixture, and beat until incorporated, about 30 seconds (batter may look slightly curdled). Give batter final stir by hand.

4. Divide batter evenly between prepared pans and smooth tops with rubber spatula. Bake cake until toothpick inserted in centers comes out clean, 23 to 25 minutes. Let cakes cool in pans on wire rack for 10 minutes. Remove cakes from pans, discard parchment, and let cool completely, about 2 hours, before frosting. (Cooled cakes can be wrapped tightly in plastic wrap and kept at room temperature for up to 1 day. Wrapped tightly in plastic, then aluminum foil, cakes can be frozen for up to 1 month. Defrost cakes at room temperature before unwrapping and frosting.)

5. FOR THE FROSTING AND FILLING: Using stand mixer fitted with paddle, beat butter, confectioners' sugar, vanilla, milk, and salt on low speed until sugar is moistened. Increase speed to medium-high and beat until creamy and fluffy, about 1½ minutes, stopping twice to scrape down bowl. (Avoid overbeating, or frosting will be too soft to pipe.)

6. TO ASSEMBLE THE CAKE: In small bowl, combine ½ cup frosting with almonds. Line edges of cake platter with 4 strips of parchment paper to keep platter clean. Place 1 cake layer on prepared platter. Place almond frosting in center of cake layer and, using large spatula, spread in even layer right to edge of cake. Carefully spread jam on top. Place second cake layer on top, making sure layers are aligned. Spread about 1½ cups plain frosting over top, spreading icing until slightly over edge. Gather more frosting on tip of spatula and gently spread icing onto side of cake. Smooth frosting by gently running edge of spatula around cake and leveling ridge that forms around top edge, or create billows by pressing back of spoon into frosting and twirling spoon as you lift away. Carefully pull out pieces of parchment from beneath cake before serving. (Assembled cake can be refrigerated for up to 1 day. Bring to room temperature before serving.)

LEMON LAYER CAKE

✔ WHY THIS RECIPE WORKS

Most versions of lemon layer cake are concoctions of heavy cake stacked with filling and frosting that taste more like butter than lemon. We wanted an old-fashioned cake in which tangy, creamy lemon filling divides layers of tender, delicate cake draped in sweet frosting—an ideal contrast of sweet and tart.

For the cake itself, we suspected that the light, fresh flavor of lemon would be best served by something ethereal. We found that a white butter cake was the perfect choice, as it is nicely flavored by butter yet light enough for the lemon flavor, with a fine crumb and tender texture. Lemon layer cake is often filled with lemon-scented buttercream, but this mutes the lemon flavor and makes the cake far too rich. We preferred the brightness of lemon curd. For our frosting, we started with seven-minute icing and made some adjustments, as the traditional version was a little too sweet, slightly thick, and required holding a hand-held mixer for longer than was comfortable. We cut back on the sugar and added a squeeze of lemon juice to solve the first two problems. Heating the mixture to at least 160 degrees and then transferring it to a stand mixer for whipping (rather than holding a hand mixer for seven minutes) gave us a frosting as billowy and shiny as the old-fashioned version.

LEMON LAYER CAKE WITH FLUFFY ICING

SERVES 10 TO 12

Be sure to use cake pans with at least 2-inch-tall sides. After filling the cake in step 6, cover it with plastic wrap and refrigerate while making the icing. For neater slices, dip a knife into hot water before cutting the cake.

FILLING

1	teaspoon unflavored gelatin
1	cup lemon juice (5 or 6 lemons)
1½	cups (10½ ounces) sugar
⅛	teaspoon salt
4	large eggs plus 6 large yolks, room temperature (reserve whites for cake)
8	tablespoons unsalted butter, cut into ½-inch pieces and frozen

CAKE

1	cup whole milk, room temperature
6	large egg whites, room temperature
2	teaspoons vanilla extract
2¼	cups (9 ounces) cake flour
1¾	cups (12¼ ounces) sugar
4	teaspoons baking powder
1	teaspoon salt
12	tablespoons unsalted butter, cut into 12 pieces and softened
1	recipe fluffy icing (recipes follow)

1. FOR THE FILLING: Sprinkle gelatin over 1 tablespoon lemon juice in small bowl; set aside. Heat remaining lemon juice, sugar, and salt in medium saucepan over medium-high heat, stirring occasionally, until sugar dissolves and mixture is hot but not boiling. Whisk eggs and egg yolks in large bowl. Whisking constantly, slowly pour hot lemon-sugar mixture into eggs, then return mixture to saucepan. Cook over medium-low heat, stirring constantly with heatproof spatula, until mixture registers 170 degrees and is thick enough to leave trail when spatula is scraped along pan bottom, 4 to 6 minutes. Immediately remove pan from heat and stir in gelatin mixture until dissolved. Stir in frozen butter until incorporated. Pour filling through fine-mesh strainer into bowl (you should have 3 cups). Place plastic wrap directly on surface of filling; refrigerate until firm enough to spread, at least 4 hours. (Filling can be made up to 1 day in advance and refrigerated; fold with rubber spatula to loosen before spreading onto cake.)

2. FOR THE CAKE: Adjust oven rack to middle position and heat oven to 350 degrees. Grease two 9-inch round cake pans, line with parchment paper, grease parchment, and flour pans. Whisk milk, egg whites, and vanilla together in 2-cup liquid measuring cup.

3. Using stand mixer fitted with paddle, mix flour, sugar, baking powder, and salt on low speed until combined. Add butter, 1 piece at a time, and mix until only pea-size pieces remain, about 1 minute. Add all but ½ cup milk mixture, increase speed to medium-high, and beat until light and fluffy, about 1 minute. Reduce speed to medium-low, add remaining ½ cup milk mixture, and beat until incorporated, about 30 seconds. Give batter final stir by hand.

4. Divide batter evenly between prepared pans and smooth tops with rubber spatula. Bake cake until toothpick inserted in centers comes out clean, 23 to 25 minutes. Let cakes cool in pans on wire rack for 10 minutes. Remove cakes from pans, discard parchment, and let cool completely, about 2 hours, before frosting. (Cooled cakes can be wrapped tightly in plastic and kept at room temperature for up to 1 day. Wrapped tightly in plastic, then aluminum foil, cakes can be frozen for up to 1 month. Defrost cakes at room temperature before unwrapping and frosting.)

5. TO ASSEMBLE THE CAKE: Place cooled cake layers on top of each other and make ⅛-inch-deep vertical cut into side of each cake layer. With long serrated knife, use sawing motion to cut cakes in half horizontally so that each cake forms 2 layers.

6. Line edges of cake platter with 4 strips of parchment paper to keep platter clean. Place 1 cake layer on prepared platter. Spread 1 cup lemon filling evenly over top of cake, leaving ½-inch border around edge. Carefully place second cake layer on top of filling, aligning cuts so that layers are even. Spread 1 cup filling on top; repeat using remaining cake layers and filling. Smooth out any filling that has leaked from sides of cake.

7. Using spatula, spread icing over top of cake, spreading icing until slightly over edge. Gather more frosting on tip of spatula and gently spread icing onto side of cake. Smooth icing by gently running edge of spatula around cake and leveling ridge that forms around top edge, or create billows by pressing back of spoon into icing and twirling spoon as you lift away. Carefully pull out pieces of parchment from beneath cake before serving. (Assembled cake can be refrigerated for up to 1 day. Bring to room temperature before serving.)

FLUFFY WHITE ICING

MAKES 3 CUPS

We also like this icing with Red Velvet Chiffon Cake (page 693).

2	large egg whites
1	cup (7 ounces) sugar
¼	cup water
1	tablespoon lemon juice
1	tablespoon corn syrup

Combine all ingredients in bowl of stand mixer and set over medium saucepan filled with 1 inch of barely simmering water (do not let bowl touch water). Cook, stirring constantly, until mixture registers 160 degrees, 5 to 10 minutes. Remove bowl from heat. Fit stand mixer with whisk and whip egg white mixture on medium speed until soft peaks form, about 5 minutes. Increase speed to medium-high and continue to whip until mixture has cooled to room temperature and stiff peaks form, about 5 minutes longer.

FLUFFY VANILLA ICING
MAKES 3 CUPS

2	large egg whites
1	cup (7 ounces) sugar
¼	cup plus 1 tablespoon water
1	tablespoon corn syrup
1	teaspoon vanilla extract

Combine all ingredients in bowl of stand mixer and set bowl over medium saucepan filled with 1 inch of barely simmering water (do not let bottom of bowl touch water). Cook, stirring constantly, until

sugar is dissolved and mixture registers 160 degrees, 5 to 10 minutes. Remove bowl from heat. Fit stand mixer with whisk and whip egg white mixture on medium speed until soft peaks form, about 5 minutes. Increase speed to medium-high and continue to whip until mixture has cooled to room temperature and stiff peaks form, about 5 minutes longer.

FLUFFY ORANGE ICING
MAKES 3 CUPS

2	large egg whites
1	cup (7 ounces) sugar
1	teaspoon grated orange zest plus ¼ cup juice
1	tablespoon corn syrup

Combine egg whites, sugar, orange juice, and corn syrup in bowl of stand mixer and set bowl over medium saucepan filled with 1 inch of barely simmering water (do not let bottom of bowl touch water). Cook, stirring constantly, until sugar is dissolved and mixture registers 160 degrees, 5 to 10 minutes. Remove bowl from heat. Fit stand mixer with whisk and whip egg

white mixture on medium speed until soft peaks form, about 5 minutes. Increase speed to medium-high and continue to whip until mixture has cooled to room temperature and stiff peaks form, about 5 minutes longer, adding orange zest during last minute.

FLUFFY TOASTED ALMOND ICING
MAKES 3 CUPS

2	large egg whites
1	cup (7 ounces) sugar
¼	cup plus 1 tablespoon water
1	tablespoon corn syrup
½	teaspoon almond extract
¾	cup almonds, toasted and chopped

Combine egg whites, sugar, water, corn syrup, and almond extract in bowl of stand mixer and set bowl over medium saucepan filled with 1 inch of barely simmering water (do not let bottom of bowl touch water). Cook, stirring constantly, until sugar is dissolved and mixture registers 160 degrees, 5 to 10 minutes. Remove bowl from heat. Fit stand mixer with whisk and whip egg white mixture on medium

FROSTING A LAYER CAKE

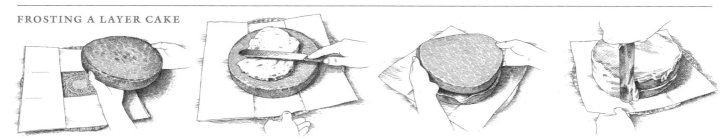

1. Using 4 strips of parchment paper, form square with open center on top of cake platter. The parchment will catch any icing, so platter remains clean.

2. Place 1 cake layer on platter centered over parchment square. Place 1 to 1½ cups icing (depending on recipe) in center of bottom cake layer and, using large spatula, spread in even layer right to edge of cake.

3. Place second cake layer on top, making sure layers are aligned. Frost top in same manner as first layer, this time spreading icing until slightly over edge.

4. Gather a few tablespoons of frosting onto tip of spatula and gently spread icing onto side of cake. Smooth frosting by gently running edge of spatula around cake. Or create billows by pressing back of spoon into frosting and twirling spoon as you lift away.

speed until soft peaks form, about 5 minutes. Increase speed to medium-high and continue to whip until mixture has cooled to room temperature and stiff peaks form, about 5 minutes longer. Using rubber spatula, gently fold in almonds.

FLUFFY COCONUT ICING
MAKES 3 CUPS

2	large egg whites
1	cup (7 ounces) sugar
¼	cup plus 1 tablespoon water
1	tablespoon corn syrup
½	teaspoon vanilla extract
¾	cup (2¼ ounces) unsweetened shredded coconut, toasted and cooled

Combine egg whites, sugar, water, corn syrup, and vanilla in bowl of stand mixer and set over medium saucepan filled with 1 inch of barely simmering water (do not let bottom of bowl touch water). Cook, stirring constantly, until sugar is dissolved and mixture registers 160 degrees, 5 to 10 minutes. Remove bowl from heat. Fit stand mixer with whisk attachment and whip egg white mixture on medium speed until soft peaks form, about 5 minutes. Increase speed to medium-high and continue to whip until mixture has cooled to

room temperature and stiff peaks form, about 5 minutes longer. Using rubber spatula, gently fold in coconut.

COCONUT LAYER CAKE

✔ **WHY THIS RECIPE WORKS**
Too often, a coconut cake is just plain white cake with plain white frosting sprinkled with shredded coconut, lacking any real coconut flavor. Coconut cake should be perfumed inside and out with the cool, subtle, mysterious essence of coconut. Its layers of snowy white cake should be moist and tender, with a delicate, yielding crumb, and the icing a silky, gently sweetened coat covered with a deep drift of downy coconut. For this type of cake, we found a traditional butter cake to be best. To infuse this cake with maximum coconut flavor, we relied on coconut extract and cream of coconut in the cake and the buttercream icing. We also coated the cake with a generous amount of shredded coconut for more flavor and textural interest.

COCONUT LAYER CAKE
SERVES 10 TO 12

Be sure to use cream of coconut (such as Coco López) and not coconut milk here. One 15-ounce can is enough for both the cake and the icing; make sure to stir it well before using because it separates upon standing.

CAKE

1	large egg plus 5 large whites
¾	cup cream of coconut
¼	cup water
1	teaspoon vanilla extract
1	teaspoon coconut extract
2¼	cups (9 ounces) cake flour
1	cup (7 ounces) sugar
1	tablespoon baking powder
¾	teaspoon salt
12	tablespoons unsalted butter, cut into 12 pieces and softened
3	cups (9 ounces) sweetened shredded coconut

ICING

4	large egg whites
1	cup (7 ounces) sugar
	Pinch salt
1	pound unsalted butter (4 sticks), each stick cut into 6 pieces and softened
¼	cup cream of coconut
1	teaspoon coconut extract
1	teaspoon vanilla extract

1. FOR THE CAKE: Adjust oven rack to lower-middle position and heat oven to 325 degrees. Grease two 9-inch round cake pans, line with parchment paper, grease parchment, and flour pans.

2. Whisk egg and egg whites together in 2-cup liquid measuring cup. Add cream of coconut, water, vanilla, and coconut extract and whisk until thoroughly combined.

3. Using stand mixer fitted with paddle, mix flour, sugar, baking powder, and salt on low speed until combined. Add butter, 1 piece at a time, and mix until only pea-size pieces remain, about 1 minute. Add half of egg mixture, increase speed to medium-high, and beat until light and fluffy, about 1 minute. Reduce speed to medium-low, add remaining milk mixture, and beat until incorporated, about 30 seconds. Give batter final stir by hand.

To create an elegant four-layered cake, you must split two cake layers in half horizontally. If you cut the layers a bit unevenly (which is bound to happen), the cake can lean to one side. Here's how to compensate for less-than-perfect cutting.

1. Place cooled cake layers on top of each other and make ⅛-inch-deep vertical cut into side of each cake layer.

2. With long serrated knife, use sawing motion to cut cakes in half horizontally so that each cake forms 2 layers.

3. Assemble cake, aligning cuts in each layer. Stacking layers in their original orientation conceals uneven cutting.

4. Divide batter evenly between prepared pans and smooth tops with rubber spatula. Bake cake until toothpick inserted in centers comes out clean, about 30 minutes. Do not turn off oven. Let cakes cool in pans on wire rack for 10 minutes. Remove cakes from pans, discard parchment, and let cool completely, about 2 hours, before frosting. (Cooled cakes can be wrapped tightly in plastic wrap and kept at room temperature for up to 1 day. Wrapped tightly in plastic, then aluminum foil, cakes can be frozen for up to 1 month. Defrost cakes at room temperature before unwrapping and frosting.)

5. While cakes are cooling, spread shredded coconut on rimmed baking sheet; toast in oven until shreds are a mix of golden brown and white, about 15 to 20 minutes, stirring 2 or 3 times. Let cool to room temperature.

6. FOR THE ICING: Combine egg whites, sugar, and salt in bowl of stand mixer and set over medium saucepan filled with 1 inch of barely simmering water (do not let bottom of bowl touch water). Whisk constantly until mixture is opaque and warm to the touch and registers about 120 degrees, about 2 minutes.

7. Remove bowl from heat. Fit stand mixer with whisk and whip egg white mixture on high speed until barely warm (about 80 degrees), glossy, and sticky, about 7 minutes. Reduce speed to medium-high and whip in butter, 1 piece at a time, followed by cream of coconut, coconut extract, and vanilla, scraping down bowl as needed. Continue to whip at medium-high speed until combined, about 1 minute.

8. TO ASSEMBLE THE CAKE: Place cooled cake layers on top of each other and make ⅛-inch-deep vertical cut into side of each cake layer. With long serrated knife, use sawing motion to cut cakes in half horizontally so that each cake forms 2 layers.

9. Line edges of cake platter with 4 strips of parchment paper to keep platter clean. Place 1 cake layer on prepared platter. Place about ¾ cup icing in center of bottom cake layer and, using large spatula, spread in even layer right to edge of cake. Carefully place other cake layer on top of icing, aligning cuts so that layers are even. Repeat using remaining cake layers and more icing, spreading icing until slightly over edge of top layer. Gather more frosting on tip of spatula and gently spread icing onto side of cake. Smooth icing by gently running edge of spatula around cake and leveling ridge that forms around top edge, or create billows by pressing back of spoon into icing and twirling spoon as you lift away. Carefully pull out pieces of parchment from beneath cake before serving. (Assembled cake can be refrigerated for up to 1 day. Bring to room temperature before serving.)

BOSTON CREAM PIE

✓ WHY THIS RECIPE WORKS

When a Boston cream pie hits all the marks, it's a superstar dessert. But from the base to the glaze, there's the opportunity for failure in every component. The sponge cake can turn out dry and crumbly, the pastry cream can curdle or fail to thicken and leak out the sides of the cake, and the chocolate glaze can seize or fail to taste truly chocolaty. We wanted to lead the dessert's revival with a fail-safe recipe.

Boston cream pie is traditionally made from a genoiselike sponge cake, but we found that fussy and temperamental. Instead, we opted for a cake that was actually trendy during Boston cream pie's heyday and didn't require any finicky folding or separating of eggs: the hot-milk sponge cake. Not only was the cake easy to prepare, but its light texture and subtle flavor were the perfect platform for a creamy filling. To firm up the pastry cream so it didn't squish out when the cake was sliced, we mixed some butter into the cooked mixture of egg yolks, sugar, half-and-half, and flour. The butter reinforced the richness of the pastry cream, and once it was spread on the cake and refrigerated, it sliced cleanly and held fast. Adding corn syrup to a mixture of heavy cream and melted chocolate gave our ganache glaze a smooth, glossy consistency that clung to the top of the cake and dripped artistically down its sides.

WICKED GOOD
BOSTON CREAM PIE

SERVES 10 TO 12

Chill the assembled cake for at least 3 hours to make it easy to cut and serve.

PASTRY CREAM

2	cups half-and-half
6	large egg yolks, room temperature
½	cup (3½ ounces) sugar
	Pinch salt
¼	cup (1¼ ounces) all-purpose flour
4	tablespoons unsalted butter, cut into 4 pieces and chilled
1½	teaspoons vanilla extract

CAKE

1½	cups (7½ ounces) all-purpose flour
1½	teaspoons baking powder
¾	teaspoon salt
¾	cup whole milk
6	tablespoons unsalted butter
1½	teaspoons vanilla extract
3	large eggs, room temperature
1½	cups (10½ ounces) sugar

GLAZE

½	cup heavy cream
2	tablespoons corn syrup
4	ounces bittersweet chocolate, chopped fine

1. **FOR THE PASTRY CREAM:** Heat half-and-half in medium saucepan over medium heat until just simmering. Meanwhile, whisk egg yolks, sugar, and salt in medium bowl until smooth. Add flour to yolk mixture and whisk until incorporated. Remove half-and-half from heat and, whisking constantly, slowly add ½ cup to yolk mixture to temper. Whisking constantly, return tempered yolk mixture to half-and-half in saucepan.

2. Return saucepan to medium heat and cook, whisking constantly, until mixture thickens slightly, about 1 minute.

Reduce heat to medium-low and continue to simmer, whisking constantly, 8 minutes.

3. Increase heat to medium and cook, whisking vigorously, until bubbles burst on surface, 1 to 2 minutes. Remove saucepan from heat; whisk in butter and vanilla until butter is melted and incorporated. Strain pastry cream through fine-mesh strainer set over medium bowl. Press lightly greased parchment paper directly on surface and refrigerate until set, at least 2 hours or up to 24 hours.

4. **FOR THE CAKE:** Adjust oven rack to middle position and heat oven to 325 degrees. Grease two 9-inch round cake pans, line with parchment paper, grease parchment, and flour pans. Whisk flour, baking powder, and salt together in medium bowl. Heat milk and butter in small saucepan over low heat until butter is melted. Remove from heat, add vanilla, and cover to keep warm.

5. Using stand mixer fitted with whisk, whip eggs and sugar on high speed until light and airy, about 5 minutes. Remove mixer bowl from stand, add hot milk mixture, and whisk by hand until incorporated. Add dry ingredients and whisk until incorporated.

6. Working quickly, divide batter evenly between prepared pans and smooth tops with rubber spatula. Bake cakes until tops are light brown and toothpick inserted in centers comes out clean, 20 to 22 minutes.

7. Transfer cakes to wire rack and let cool completely in pan, about 2 hours. Run small knife around edge of pans, then invert cakes onto wire rack. Carefully remove parchment, then turn cakes right side up. (Cooled cakes can be wrapped tightly in plastic wrap and kept at room temperature for up to 1 day. Wrapped tightly in plastic, then aluminum foil, cakes can be frozen for up to 1 month. Defrost cakes at room temperature before unwrapping and frosting.)

8. **TO ASSEMBLE THE CAKE:** Line edges of cake platter with 4 strips of parchment paper to keep platter clean. Place 1 cake layer on prepared platter. Whisk pastry cream briefly, then spoon onto center of cake. Using rubber spatula, spread evenly to cake edge. Place second layer on top of pastry cream, bottom side up, making sure layers line up. Press lightly on top of cake to level. Refrigerate cake while preparing glaze.

9. **FOR THE GLAZE:** Bring cream and corn syrup to simmer in small saucepan over medium heat. Remove from heat, add chocolate, and let sit, covered, for 5 minutes. Whisk mixture gently until smooth.

10. Pour glaze onto center of cake. Use rubber spatula to spread glaze to edge of cake, letting excess drip decoratively down sides. Chill for at least 3 hours. Carefully pull out pieces of parchment from beneath cake before serving. (Assembled cake can be refrigerated for up to 1 day. Bring to room temperature before serving.)

STRAWBERRY CREAM CAKE

✓ **WHY THIS RECIPE WORKS**
What could possibly ruin the heavenly trio of cake, cream, and ripe strawberries? How about soggy cake, bland berries, and squishy cream? We wanted a sturdy cake, a firm filling, and strawberry flavor fit for a starring role—a cake that would serve a formal occasion better than a simple strawberry shortcake. We realized that tender butter cakes couldn't support a substantial strawberry filling, so we used a chiffon-style cake that combined the rich flavor of a butter cake with the light-yet-sturdy texture of a sponge cake. Second, we made a flavorful berry "mash" with half of the berries and then reduced the macerated juice in a saucepan (with a little kirsch) to help concentrate and round out the flavor. We sliced the rest of the berries and placed them around the edges of the cake

for visual appeal. And to prevent the cream filling from squirting out the sides, we fortified the whipped-cream filling with cream cheese.

STRAWBERRY CREAM CAKE
SERVES 10 TO 12

If using a cake pan, be sure to use one with at least 2-inch-tall sides.

CAKE
1	cup (7 ounces) sugar
1¼	cups (5 ounces) cake flour
1½	teaspoons baking powder
¼	teaspoon salt
5	large eggs (2 whole and 3 separated), room temperature
6	tablespoons unsalted butter, melted and cooled
2	tablespoons water
2	teaspoons vanilla extract
	Pinch cream of tartar

FILLING
2	pounds strawberries, hulled (6 cups)
4–6	tablespoons sugar
2	tablespoons kirsch
	Pinch salt

WHIPPED CREAM
8	ounces cream cheese, room temperature
½	cup (3½ ounces) sugar
1	teaspoon vanilla extract
⅛	teaspoon salt
2	cups heavy cream, chilled

1. FOR THE CAKE: Adjust oven rack to lower-middle position and heat oven to 325 degrees. Grease 9-inch round cake pan or 9-inch springform pan, line with parchment paper, grease parchment, and flour pan. Reserve 3 tablespoons sugar in small bowl. Whisk flour, baking powder, salt, and remaining sugar in medium bowl. Whisk in 2 whole eggs and 3 egg yolks, butter, water, and vanilla until smooth.

2. Using stand mixer fitted with whisk, whip egg whites and cream of tartar on medium-low speed until foamy, about 1 minute. Increase speed to medium-high and whip whites to soft billowy mounds, about 1 minute. Gradually add reserved 3 tablespoons sugar and whip until glossy, soft peaks form, 1 to 2 minutes. Stir one-third of whites into batter to lighten; add remaining whites and gently fold into batter until no white streaks remain.

3. Pour batter into prepared pan and smooth top with rubber spatula. Bake cake until toothpick inserted in center comes out clean, 30 to 40 minutes. Let cake cool in pan on wire rack for 10 minutes. Remove cake from pan, discard parchment, and let cool completely, about 2 hours, before assembling. (Cooled cake can be wrapped tightly in plastic wrap and kept at room temperature for up to 1 day. Wrapped tightly in plastic, then aluminum foil, cake can be frozen for up to 1 month. Defrost cake at room temperature before unwrapping and frosting.)

4. FOR THE FILLING: Halve 24 of best-looking berries and reserve. Quarter remaining berries, toss with 4 to 6 tablespoons sugar (depending on sweetness of berries) in medium bowl, and let sit 1 hour, stirring occasionally. Strain juices from berries and reserve (you should have about ½ cup). Pulse macerated berries in food processor until coarsely chopped, about 5 pulses (you should have about 1½ cups). In small saucepan, simmer reserved juices and kirsch over medium-high heat until syrupy and reduced to about 3 tablespoons,

---

BUILDING A STRAWBERRY CREAM CAKE

1. Using serrated knife, use sawing motion to cut cake into 3 layers, rotating cake as you go.

2. Place sliced berries evenly around edges of first layer, then completely cover center of cake with half of pureed strawberries.

3. Spread one-third of whipped cream over berries, leaving ½-inch border. Repeat layering with second layer of cake.

4. Press last layer into place, spread with remaining whipped cream, and decorate with remaining berries.

3 to 5 minutes. Pour reduced syrup over macerated berries, add salt, and toss to combine. Set aside until cake is cooled.

5. FOR THE WHIPPED CREAM: When cake has cooled, whip cream cheese, sugar, vanilla, and salt using stand mixer fitted with whisk on medium-high speed until light and fluffy, 1 to 2 minutes, scraping down bowl as needed. Reduce speed to low and add heavy cream in slow, steady stream; when almost fully combined, increase speed to medium-high and whip until stiff peaks form, 2 to 2½ minutes more, scraping down bowl as needed (you should have about 4½ cups).

6. TO ASSEMBLE THE CAKE: Make ⅛-inch-deep vertical cut into side of cake. With long serrated knife, use sawing motion to cut cake horizontally into 3 even layers.

7. Line edges of cake platter with 4 strips of parchment paper to keep platter clean. Place 1 cake layer on prepared platter. Arrange ring of 20 strawberry halves, cut sides down and stem ends facing out, around perimeter of cake layer. Pour half of pureed berry mixture (about ¾ cup) in center, then spread to cover any exposed cake. Gently spread about one-third of whipped cream (about 1½ cups) over berry layer, leaving ½-inch border around edge. Place next cake layer on top and press down gently (whipped cream layer should

become flush with cake edge). Repeat with 20 strawberry halves, remaining berry mixture, and half of remaining whipped cream; gently press last cake layer on top. Spread remaining whipped cream over top and decorate with remaining 8 strawberry halves. Carefully pull out pieces of parchment from beneath cake before serving. (Assembled cake can be refrigerated for up to 4 hours.)

EASY CHOCOLATE CAKE

✔ WHY THIS RECIPE WORKS

This easy wartime cake made with just a few ingredients (flour, sugar, cocoa powder, baking soda, vanilla, and mayonnaise, a stand-in for butter and eggs) had a lot of good things going for it, but chocolate flavor wasn't one of them.

Our first order of business was deepening the chocolate flavor. More than a half-cup of cocoa turned the cake dry and chalky so we supplemented the cocoa powder with a little melted chocolate. "Blooming" the cocoa powder in hot water intensified its flavor, and using hot coffee instead of water enriched the flavor even more. Chopping the dark chocolate fine meant we could melt it in the hot coffee as well—no need for an extra pan. As for the oddball ingredient— mayonnaise—we wondered if we could make the cake richer by replacing it with eggs and butter or eggs and oil. These cakes weren't as moist

and velvety as the mayonnaise version. Why? We learned that mayonnaise contains lecithin, an emulsifier that helps keep the oil suspended in micro-droplets. These small droplets greatly aid the oil's ability to coat the flour's protein particles, leading to a supremely tender cake. Yet, while butter and oil were out, the egg was a keeper, as it helped create richer flavor and a springier texture.

EASY CHOCOLATE CAKE
SERVES 8

Any high-quality dark, bittersweet, or semisweet chocolate will work in this recipe. Instead of confectioners' sugar, the cake can be served with Whipped Cream (page 800).

1½	cups (7½ ounces) all-purpose flour
1	cup (7 ounces) sugar
½	teaspoon baking soda
¼	teaspoon salt
½	cup (1½ ounces) Dutch-processed cocoa
2	ounces bittersweet chocolate, chopped fine
1	cup brewed coffee, hot
⅔	cup mayonnaise
1	large egg, room temperature
2	teaspoons vanilla extract Confectioners' sugar (optional)

1. Adjust oven rack to middle position and heat oven to 350 degrees. Grease 8-inch square baking pan, line with parchment paper, grease parchment, and flour pan.

2. Whisk flour, sugar, baking soda, and salt together in large bowl. In separate bowl, combine cocoa and chocolate. Pour hot coffee over cocoa mixture and let sit, covered, for 5 minutes. Gently whisk mixture until smooth, let cool slightly, then whisk in mayonnaise, egg, and vanilla. Stir

---

TEST KITCHEN TIP NO. 139 LOCATING THE MIDDLE RACK

Recipes often call for placing the oven rack in the middle position. If you have an odd number of racks, finding the middle position is easy. If you have an even number of racks, you can place the rack in either the upper-middle or lower-middle position. To found out which position is preferable, we tried baking batches of our Lemon Sugar Cookies and Fluffy Yellow Layer Cake in each position. After an afternoon of baking, it was clear that cookies and cakes baked on the upper-middle rack browned a little too much on top. It was better to bake both items on the lower-middle rack, which puts the food closer to the exact middle of the oven.

mayonnaise mixture into flour mixture until combined.

3. Scrape batter into prepared pan and smooth top with rubber spatula. Bake cake until toothpick inserted in center comes out with few crumbs attached, 30 to 35 minutes.

4. Let cake cool in pan on wire rack, 1 to 2 hours. Dust with confectioners' sugar, if using, cut into squares, and serve straight from pan; alternatively, turn cake out onto serving platter, dust with confectioners' sugar, if using, and serve.

SIMPLE CHOCOLATE SHEET CAKE

✓ **WHY THIS RECIPE WORKS**
Sheet cakes, for all their simplicity, can still turn out dry, sticky, or flavorless and, on occasion, can even sink in the middle. We wanted a simple, dependable recipe, one that was moist yet also light and chocolaty.

We started with the mixing method, testing everything from creaming butter to beating egg yolks, whipping egg whites, and gently folding together everything in the end. The best of the lot was the most complicated to make, so we took a step back. The simplest technique we tried was simply whisking all the ingredients together without beating, creaming, or whipping. The recipe needed work, but the approach was clearly what we were after. We added buttermilk and baking soda to lighten the batter, and we reduced the sugar, flour, and butter to increase the chocolate flavor. To further deepen the chocolate taste, we used semisweet chocolate in addition to the cocoa. We baked the cake at a low temperature for a long time—40 minutes—to produce a perfectly baked cake with a lovely flat top. Though this cake can be frosted with almost anything, we like a classic American milk chocolate frosting, which pairs well with the darker flavor of the cake.

SIMPLE CHOCOLATE SHEET CAKE
SERVES 15

We prefer Dutch-processed cocoa for the deeper chocolate flavor it gives the cake. The baked and cooled cake can also be served with lightly sweetened whipped cream or topped with any frosting you like in lieu of the milk chocolate frosting. This frosting needs about an hour to cool before it can be used, so begin making it when the cake comes out of the oven.

CAKE
1¼	cups (6¼ ounces) all-purpose flour
¾	cup (2¼ ounces) Dutch-processed cocoa
¼	teaspoon salt
8	ounces semisweet chocolate, chopped
12	tablespoons unsalted butter
4	large eggs, room temperature
1½	cups (10½ ounces) granulated sugar
1	teaspoon vanilla extract
1	cup buttermilk
½	teaspoon baking soda

FROSTING
½	cup heavy cream
1	tablespoon corn syrup
	Pinch salt
10	ounces milk chocolate, chopped
½	cup (2 ounces) confectioners' sugar
8	tablespoons unsalted butter, cut into 8 pieces and chilled

1. FOR THE CAKE: Adjust oven rack to middle position and heat oven to 325 degrees. Grease 13 by 9-inch baking pan, line with parchment paper, grease parchment, and flour pan.

2. Sift flour, cocoa, and salt together into medium bowl; set aside. Microwave chocolate at 50 percent power for 2 minutes; stir, add butter, and continue heating until melted, stirring once every additional minute. Whisk eggs, sugar, and vanilla together in medium bowl.

3. Whisk chocolate into egg mixture until combined. Combine buttermilk and baking soda; whisk into chocolate mixture, then whisk in dry ingredients until batter is smooth and glossy. Pour batter into prepared pan and smooth top with rubber spatula. Bake cake until firm in center when lightly pressed and toothpick inserted in center comes out clean, about 40 minutes. Let cool on wire rack until room temperature, at least 1 hour.

4. FOR THE FROSTING: Microwave cream, corn syrup, and salt in bowl until simmering, about 1 minute, or bring to simmer in small saucepan over medium heat. Place chocolate in food processor. With processor running, gradually add hot cream mixture, then process for 1 minute. Stop processor, add confectioners' sugar, and process to combine, about 30 seconds. With processor running, add butter, 1 piece at a time, then process until incorporated and smooth, about 20 seconds longer. Transfer frosting to medium bowl and let cool at room temperature, stirring frequently, until thick and spreadable, about 1 hour. Spread frosting over cake and serve.

OLD-FASHIONED CHOCOLATE LAYER CAKE

✓ **WHY THIS RECIPE WORKS**
Over the years, chocolate cakes have become denser, richer, and squatter. We wanted an old-style, mile-high chocolate layer cake with a tender, airy, open crumb and a soft, billowy frosting. The mixing method was the key to getting the right texture. After trying a variety of techniques, we turned to a popular old-fashioned method, ribboning. Ribboning involves whipping eggs with sugar until they double in

volume, then adding the butter, dry ingredients, and milk. The egg foam aerated the cake, giving it both structure and tenderness. To achieve a moist cake with rich chocolate flavor, we once again looked to historical sources, which suggested using buttermilk and making a "pudding" with a mixture of chocolate, water, and sugar. We simply melted unsweetened chocolate and cocoa powder in hot water over a double boiler, then stirred in sugar until it dissolved. Turning to the frosting, we wanted the intense chocolate flavor of a ganache and the volume of a meringue or buttercream. The solution turned out to be a simple reversal of the conventional ganache procedure: We poured cold (rather than heated) cream into warm (rather than room-temperature) chocolate, waited for it to cool to room temperature, then whipped until fluffy.

OLD-FASHIONED CHOCOLATE LAYER CAKE

SERVES 10 TO 12

For a smooth, spreadable frosting, use chopped semisweet chocolate, not chocolate chips—chocolate chips contain less cocoa butter than bar chocolate and will not melt as readily. As for other bar chocolate, bittersweet chocolate that is 60 percent cacao can be substituted but it will produce a stiffer, although still spreadable, frosting. Bittersweet chocolate with 70 percent cacao, however, should be avoided—it will produce a frosting that is crumbly and will not spread. For best results, do not make the frosting until the cakes are cooled, and use the frosting as soon as it is ready. If the frosting gets too cold and stiff to spread easily, wrap the mixer bowl with a kitchen towel soaked in hot water and mix on low speed until the frosting appears creamy and smooth. Be sure to use cake pans with at least 2-inch-tall sides.

CAKE

- 4 ounces unsweetened chocolate, chopped coarse
- ¼ cup (¾ ounce) Dutch-processed cocoa
- ½ cup hot water
- 1¾ cups (12¼ ounces) sugar
- 1¾ cups (8¾ ounces) all-purpose flour
- 1½ teaspoons baking soda
- 1 teaspoon salt
- 1 cup buttermilk
- 2 teaspoons vanilla extract
- 4 large eggs plus 2 large yolks, room temperature
- 12 tablespoons unsalted butter, cut into 12 pieces and softened

FROSTING

- 1 pound semisweet chocolate, chopped fine
- 8 tablespoons unsalted butter
- ⅓ cup (2⅓ ounces) sugar
- 2 tablespoons corn syrup
- 2 teaspoons vanilla extract
- ¼ teaspoon salt
- 1¼ cups heavy cream, chilled

1. FOR THE CAKE: Adjust oven rack to middle position and heat oven to 350 degrees. Grease two 9-inch round cake pans, line with parchment paper, grease parchment, and flour pans. Combine chocolate, cocoa, and hot water in medium heatproof bowl set over saucepan filled with 1 inch of barely simmering water and stir with heatproof rubber spatula until chocolate is melted, about 2 minutes. Add ½ cup sugar to chocolate mixture and stir until thick and glossy, 1 to 2 minutes. Remove bowl from heat; set aside to cool.

2. Whisk flour, baking soda, and salt together in medium bowl. Combine

buttermilk and vanilla in small bowl. Using stand mixer fitted with whisk, whip eggs and egg yolks on medium-low speed until combined, about 10 seconds. Add remaining 1¼ cups sugar, increase speed to high, and whip until light and fluffy, 2 to 3 minutes. Replace whisk with paddle. Add cooled chocolate mixture to egg mixture and mix on medium speed until thoroughly combined, 30 to 45 seconds, scraping down bowl as needed. Add butter, 1 piece at a time, mixing about 10 seconds after each addition. Add flour in 3 additions, alternating with 2 additions of buttermilk mixture, mixing until incorporated after each addition (about 15 seconds), scraping down bowl as needed (batter may appear curdled). Mix at medium-low speed until batter is thoroughly combined, about 15 seconds. Remove bowl from mixer and give batter final stir by hand.

3. Divide batter evenly between prepared pans and smooth tops with rubber spatula. Bake cake until toothpick inserted in centers comes out with few crumbs attached, 25 to 30 minutes. Let cakes cool in pans on wire rack for 10 minutes. Remove cakes from pans, discard parchment, and let cool completely, about 2 hours, before frosting. (Cooled cakes can be wrapped tightly in plastic wrap and kept at room temperature for up to 1 day. Wrapped tightly in plastic, then aluminum foil, cakes can be frozen for up to 1 month. Defrost cakes at room temperature before unwrapping and frosting.)

4. FOR THE FROSTING: Melt chocolate in heatproof bowl set over saucepan containing 1 inch of barely simmering water, stirring occasionally until smooth. Remove from heat and set aside. Meanwhile, melt butter in small saucepan over medium-low heat. Increase heat to medium, add sugar, corn syrup, vanilla, and salt and stir with heatproof rubber spatula until sugar is dissolved, 4 to 5 minutes. In bowl of stand mixer, combine melted chocolate, butter mixture, and cream and stir until thoroughly combined.

5. Place mixer bowl over ice bath and stir mixture constantly with rubber spatula until frosting is thick and just beginning to harden against sides of bowl, 1 to 2 minutes (frosting should be 70 degrees). Fit stand mixer with paddle and beat frosting on medium-high speed until frosting is light and fluffy, 1 to 2 minutes. Using rubber spatula, stir until completely smooth.

6. TO ASSEMBLE THE CAKE: Line edges of cake platter with 4 strips of parchment paper to keep platter clean. Place 1 cake layer on prepared platter. Place about 1½ cups frosting in center of cake layer and, using large spatula, spread in even layer right to edge of cake. Place second cake layer on top, making sure layers are aligned, then frost top in same manner as first layer, this time spreading frosting until slightly over edge. Gather more frosting on tip of spatula and gently spread icing onto side of cake. Smooth frosting by gently running edge of spatula around cake and leveling ridge that forms around top edge, or create billows by pressing back of spoon into frosting and twirling spoon as you lift away. Carefully pull out pieces of parchment from beneath cake before serving. (Assembled cake can be refrigerated for up to 1 day. Bring to room temperature before serving.)

MOIST AND TENDER DEVIL'S FOOD CAKE

✔ **WHY THIS RECIPE WORKS**

The problem with defining the devil's food cake, beyond the obvious issue of color (is red or black more appropriate?), is that over time the recipe has been changed and embellished to the point where different recipes have little in common. After reviewing a number of recipes, we came to the conclusion that the essence of devil's food cake is a very moist, velvety texture combined with an intense chocolate experience. Using a combination of unsweetened chocolate and Dutch-processed cocoa gave the cake the right chocolaty flavor, and using hot water rather than milk ensured that it was not dulled (think of milk versus dark chocolate). All-purpose flour provided both structure and delicacy, while sour cream deepened the flavor and added substance to the texture of our cake.

MOIST AND TENDER DEVIL'S FOOD CAKE

SERVES 10 TO 12

If using 9-inch cake pans, note that the layers will be quite thin. For an accurate measurement of boiling water, bring a full kettle of water to a boil, then measure out the desired amount.

½ cup (1½ ounces) Dutch-processed cocoa, plus extra as needed
1½ cups (7½ ounces) all-purpose flour
1 teaspoon baking soda
½ teaspoon baking powder
¼ teaspoon salt
1¼ cups boiling water
4 ounces unsweetened chocolate, chopped
1 teaspoon instant espresso powder or instant coffee
10 tablespoons unsalted butter, softened
1½ cups packed (10½ ounces) light brown sugar
3 large eggs, room temperature
½ cup sour cream, room temperature
1 teaspoon vanilla extract
1 recipe buttercream frosting (pages 662–663)

1. Adjust oven racks to upper-middle and lower-middle positions and heat oven to 350 degrees. Grease three 8- or 9-inch round cake pans, line with parchment paper, grease parchment, then dust with cocoa. Whisk flour, baking soda, baking powder, and salt together in large bowl. In medium bowl, whisk boiling water, chocolate, ½ cup cocoa, and instant espresso together until smooth.

2. Using stand mixer fitted with paddle, beat butter and sugar together on medium speed until light and fluffy, 3 to 6 minutes. Beat in eggs, 1 at a time, until combined, about 30 seconds. Beat in sour cream and vanilla until incorporated.

3. Reduce speed to low and add flour in 3 additions, alternating with 2 additions of chocolate mixture, scraping down bowl as needed (do not overbeat). Give batter final stir by hand.

4. Divide batter evenly among prepared pans, smooth tops with rubber spatula, and gently tap pans on the counter to release air bubbles. Bake cake until toothpick inserted in centers comes out with few crumbs attached, 15 to 20 minutes, switching position of pans twice through baking, so each cake spends same amount of time in each position.

5. Let cakes cool in pans on wire rack for 10 minutes. Remove cakes from pans, discard parchment, and let cool completely, about 2 hours, before frosting. (Cooled cakes can be wrapped tightly in plastic wrap and kept at room temperature for up to 1 day. Wrapped tightly in plastic, then aluminum foil, cakes can be frozen for up to 1 month. Defrost cakes at room temperature before unwrapping and frosting.)

6. TO ASSEMBLE THE CAKE: Line edges of cake platter with 4 strips of parchment paper to keep platter clean. Place 1 cake layer on prepared platter. Place about 1 cup frosting in center of cake layer and, using large spatula, spread in even layer right to edge of cake. Repeat with second and third layer, spreading frosting on top layer until slightly over edge. Gather more frosting on tip of spatula and gently spread icing onto side of cake. Smooth frosting by gently running edge of spatula around cake and leveling ridge that forms around top edge, or create billows by pressing back of spoon into frosting and twirling spoon as you lift away. Carefully pull out pieces of parchment from beneath cake before serving. (Assembled cake can be refrigerated for up to 1 day. Bring to room temperature before serving.)

GERMAN CHOCOLATE CAKE

✔ **WHY THIS RECIPE WORKS**
Most German chocolate cake recipes are similar, if not identical, to the one on the German's Sweet Chocolate box. Our tasters found several shortcomings in this recipe. It produced a cake that was too sweet, with chocolate flavor that was too mild, and with a texture so listless that the filling and cake together formed a soggy, sweet mush. We wanted a cake that was less sweet and more chocolaty than the original, but we didn't want to sacrifice the overall blend of flavors and textures that makes German chocolate cake so appealing in the first place.

The first order of business was to scale back the recipe by one quarter, which allowed us to fit the batter into two cake pans, thereby producing a cake with four thinner layers rather than three thicker layers. After testing, we discovered that the texture of the cake actually improved when we used whole eggs instead of separating the eggs, beating the whites, and folding them into the batter. We increased chocolate flavor with a combination of cocoa powder and semisweet or bittersweet chocolate. Our final adjustments included tweaking the level and proportions of the sugar (both brown and white) and butter in the cake and filling, as well as toasting the pecans. We now had a truly chocolaty cake sandwiched with a rich coconut-pecan filling.

GERMAN CHOCOLATE CAKE WITH COCONUT-PECAN FILLING
SERVES 10 TO 12

For an accurate measurement of boiling water, bring a full kettle of water to a boil, then measure out the desired amount. When you assemble the cake, the filling should be cool or cold (or room temperature, at the very warmest). To be time-efficient, first make the filling, then use the refrigeration time to prepare, bake, and cool the cakes. The toasted pecans are stirred into the filling just before assembly to keep them from becoming soft and soggy. Be sure to use cake pans with at least 2-inch-tall sides.

FILLING
- 4 large egg yolks, room temperature
- 1 (12-ounce) can evaporated milk
- 1 cup (7 ounces) granulated sugar
- ¼ cup packed (1¾ ounces) light brown sugar
- 6 tablespoons unsalted butter, cut into 6 pieces
- ⅛ teaspoon salt
- 2 teaspoons vanilla extract
- 2⅓ cups (7 ounces) sweetened shredded coconut
- 1½ cups (6 ounces) pecans, toasted and chopped fine

CAKE
- 4 ounces semisweet or bittersweet chocolate, chopped fine
- ¼ cup (¾ ounce) Dutch-processed cocoa
- ½ cup boiling water
- 2 cups (10 ounces) all-purpose flour
- ¾ teaspoon baking soda
- 12 tablespoons unsalted butter, softened
- 1 cup (7 ounces) granulated sugar
- ⅔ cup packed (4⅔ ounces) light brown sugar
- ¾ teaspoon salt
- 4 large eggs, room temperature
- 1 teaspoon vanilla extract
- ¾ cup sour cream, room temperature

1. FOR THE FILLING: Whisk egg yolks in medium saucepan, then gradually whisk in evaporated milk. Add granulated sugar, brown sugar, butter, and salt and cook over medium-high heat, whisking constantly, until mixture is boiling, frothy, and slightly thickened, about 6 minutes. Transfer mixture to bowl, whisk in vanilla, then stir in coconut. Cool until just warm, cover with plastic wrap, and refrigerate until cool or cold, at least 2 hours or up to 3 days. (Do not stir in pecans until just before cake assembly.)

2. FOR THE CAKE: Adjust oven rack to lower-middle position and heat oven to 350 degrees. Grease two 9-inch round cake pans, line with parchment paper, grease parchment, and flour pans. Combine chocolate and cocoa in small heatproof bowl, pour boiling water over mixture, and let sit, covered, for 5 minutes. Whisk mixture gently until smooth, then let cool to room temperature. Whisk flour and baking soda together in medium bowl and set aside.

3. Using stand mixer fitted with paddle, beat butter, granulated sugar, brown sugar, and salt on medium-high until light and fluffy, about 3 minutes. Add eggs, 1 at a time, and beat until combined. Beat in vanilla, increase speed to medium-high and beat until light and fluffy, about 45 seconds. Reduce speed to low, add chocolate, then increase speed to medium and beat until combined, about 30 seconds, scraping down bowl once (batter may appear curdled). Reduce speed to low, add flour mixture in 3 additions, alternating with 2 additions of sour cream, scraping down bowl as needed. Give batter final stir by hand (batter will be thick).

4. Divide batter evenly between prepared pans and smooth tops with rubber spatula. Bake cake until toothpick inserted in centers comes out clean, about 30 minutes, switching position of pans twice through baking, so each cake spends same amount of time in each position. Let cakes cool in pans on wire rack for 10 minutes. Remove cakes from pans, discard parchment, and let cool completely, about 2 hours, before filling. (Cooled cakes can be wrapped tightly in plastic wrap and kept at room temperature for up to 1 day. Wrapped tightly in plastic, then aluminum foil, cakes can be frozen for up to 1 month. Defrost cakes at room temperature before unwrapping and frosting.)

5. TO ASSEMBLE THE CAKE: Place cooled cake layers on top of each other and make 1/8-inch-deep vertical cut into side of each cake layer. With long serrated knife, use sawing motion to cut cakes in half horizontally so that each cake forms two layers.

6. Line edges of cake platter with 4 strips of parchment paper to keep platter clean. Place 1 cake layer on prepared platter. Stir toasted pecans into chilled filling. Spread 1 cup filling evenly across top of cake layer, spreading filling to very edge. Carefully place next cake layer on top of filling, aligning cuts so that layers are even. Repeat using remaining filling and cake layers. Carefully pull out pieces of parchment from beneath cake before serving. (Assembled cake can be refrigerated for up to 1 day. Bring to room temperature before serving.)

GERMAN CHOCOLATE CAKE WITH BANANA, MACADAMIA, AND COCONUT FILLING

If you cannot find roasted unsalted macadamia nuts, substitute salted ones, but first remove excess salt by spreading them on a clean kitchen towel and giving them a good rub.

Reduce vanilla in filling to 1 teaspoon and add 2 teaspoons dark rum with vanilla in step 1. Substitute unsalted macadamia nuts for pecans. Just before assembling cake, peel and cut 4 bananas into 3/8-inch-thick slices. Arrange one quarter of banana slices on first cake layer, then spread filling evenly over; repeat with remaining cake layers, bananas, and filling.

GERMAN CHOCOLATE CAKE WITH COFFEE, CASHEW, AND COCONUT FILLING

Add 2 teaspoons ground coffee to filling mixture with sugars in step 1. Substitute roasted unsalted cashews for pecans.

GERMAN CHOCOLATE SHEET CAKE

SERVES 15

The towering layers of chocolate cake separated by coconut-pecan filling look impressive in our German Chocolate Cake, but splitting the cake layers and assembling the cake is a fair amount of work, so we developed this simplified sheet cake variation, which slathers the entire cake with a thick layer of the coconut-pecan filling. In addition to being easier to assemble, the cake is also a cinch to serve to crowds. When you frost the cake, the frosting should be cool or cold (or room temperature, at the very warmest). To be time-efficient, first make the frosting, then use the refrigeration time to prepare, bake, and cool the cake. The toasted pecans are stirred into the frosting just before the cake is frosted to keep them from becoming soft and soggy.

Grease 13 by 9-inch baking pan, line with parchment paper, grease parchment, and flour pan. Follow recipe as directed through step 3, preparing filling to use as frosting. In step 4, pour batter into prepared pan, smooth top with rubber spatula, and gently tap pan on counter to release air bubbles. Bake cake until toothpick inserted in center comes out clean, 30 to 35 minutes. Let cake cool in pan on wire rack for 10 minutes. Remove cake from pan, discard parchment, and let cool completely, about 2 hours, before frosting. Frost top of cake and serve. (Refrigerate cake if not serving immediately; if refrigerated longer than 2 hours, let cake sit at room temperature 15 to 20 minutes before serving. Cooled, unfrosted cake can be stored at room temperature for up to 1 day. Frosted cake can be refrigerated for up to 3 days.)

INDIVIDUAL FALLEN CHOCOLATE CAKES

✔ WHY THIS RECIPE WORKS

Fallen chocolate cake, or molten chocolate cake, is an undercooked-in-the-center mound of intense, buttery chocolate cake. We wanted to turn this restaurant staple, typically baked in individual ramekins, into a practical recipe for home cooks. We were after individual portions of intensely flavored chocolate cake that had a light texture and an irresistibly runny center. Beating the eggs with sugar (and vanilla) to a foam, then folding in melted chocolate, delivered the rich, moist texture we were after, and adding a little flour lent body. Eight ounces of chocolate provided plenty of chocolate flavor without being overbearing. We discovered that the batter could be made and poured into the ramekins ahead of time and refrigerated, then baked during dinner, which meant they could arrive at the table piping hot at the right time.

INDIVIDUAL FALLEN CHOCOLATE CAKES

SERVES 8

You can substitute 5 ounces unsweetened chocolate for the semisweet; if you opt to do so, increase the sugar to ¾ cup plus 2 tablespoons.

- 8 tablespoons unsalted butter
- 8 ounces semisweet chocolate, chopped coarse
- 4 large eggs plus 1 large yolk, room temperature
- ½ cup granulated sugar
- 1 teaspoon vanilla extract
- ¼ teaspoon salt
- 2 tablespoons all-purpose flour
  Confectioners' sugar or cocoa (optional)
  Whipped Cream (page 800) (optional)

1. Adjust oven rack to middle position and heat oven to 400 degrees. Grease eight 6-ounce ramekins and dust with flour or cocoa. Arrange ramekins on rimmed baking sheet. Melt butter and chocolate in medium heatproof bowl set over saucepan filled with 1 inch of barely simmering water, stirring once or twice, until smooth. Remove from heat.

2. Using stand mixer fitted with whisk, whip eggs, egg yolk, sugar, vanilla, and salt on high speed until volume nearly triples, color is very light, and mixture drops from beaters in smooth, thick stream, about 5 minutes.

3. Scrape egg mixture over chocolate mixture, then sprinkle flour on top. Gently fold egg mixture and flour into chocolate until mixture is uniformly colored. Ladle or pour batter into prepared ramekins. (Unbaked cakes can be refrigerated for up to 8 hours. Return to room temperature for 30 minutes before baking.)

4. Bake until cakes have puffed about ½ inch above rims of ramekins, have thin crust on top, and jiggle slightly at center when ramekins are shaken very gently, 12 to 13 minutes. Run knife around inside edges of ramekins to loosen cakes, invert onto individual serving plates, and let sit until cakes release themselves from ramekins, about 1 minute. Lift off ramekins, dust with confectioners' sugar, if using, and/or dollop with whipped cream, if using, and serve.

ORANGE FALLEN CHOCOLATE CAKES

Fold 1 tablespoon grated orange zest and 2 tablespoons orange liqueur into beaten egg and melted chocolate mixture with flour in step 3.

FALLEN CHOCOLATE CAKE

One large fallen chocolate cake can be prepared in a springform pan. Do not use a regular cake pan, as the cake will be impossible to remove once baked. Though the cake is best when served warm (within about 30 minutes of being unmolded), it can be held in the pan for up to 2 hours before serving.

Substitute greased 8- or 9-inch springform pan for ramekins. Reduce oven temperature to 375 degrees and bake until cake looks puffed, thin top crust has formed, and center jiggles slightly when pan is shaken gently, 22 to 25 minutes for 9-inch pan or 27 to 30 minutes for 8-inch pan. Let cake cool for 15 minutes, then run thin knife between cake and sides of pan and remove sides of pan. Sprinkle with confectioners' sugar, if using, and/or dollop with whipped cream, if using, and serve.

THE ULTIMATE FLOURLESS CHOCOLATE CAKE

✔ WHY THIS RECIPE WORKS

While all flourless chocolate cake recipes share common ingredients (chocolate, butter, and eggs), the techniques used to make them vary, as do the results. You can end up with anything from a fudge brownie to a chocolate soufflé. We wanted something dense, moist, and ultra-chocolaty, but with some textural finesse. We started with the chocolate. A cake made with unsweetened chocolate was neither smooth nor silky enough. Bittersweet and semisweet chocolate each won out; both delivered deep chocolate flavor and a smooth texture. Next we turned to the eggs, comparing cakes made with room-temperature whole eggs and whole eggs taken straight from the fridge. The batter made with chilled eggs produced a denser foam and the resulting cake boasted a smooth, velvety texture. And the gentle, moist heat of a water bath further preserved the cake's lush texture.

THE ULTIMATE FLOURLESS CHOCOLATE CAKE

SERVES 12 TO 16

Even though the cake may not look done, pull it from the oven when it registers 140 degrees. It will continue to firm up as it cools. If you use a 9-inch springform pan instead of the preferred 8-inch, reduce the baking time to 18 to 20 minutes.

- 8 large eggs, chilled
- 1 pound bittersweet or semisweet chocolate, chopped coarse
- 16 tablespoons unsalted butter, cut into ½-inch pieces
- ¼ cup strong brewed coffee, room temperature
  Confectioners' sugar or cocoa

1. Adjust oven rack to lower-middle position and heat oven to 325 degrees. Grease 8-inch springform pan, line with parchment paper, then grease sides. Wrap outside of pan with two 18-inch-square pieces of aluminum foil; set in roasting pan. Bring kettle of water to boil.

2. Using stand mixer fitted with whisk, whip eggs on medium speed until doubled in volume, about 5 minutes.

3. Meanwhile, melt chocolate with butter and coffee in large heatproof bowl set over saucepan filled with 1 inch of barely simmering water, stirring once or twice until smooth and very warm (should register about 115 degrees). Using large rubber spatula, fold one-third of egg foam into chocolate mixture until few streaks of egg are visible. Fold in remaining foam in 2 additions until mixture is totally homogeneous.

4. Scrape batter into prepared pan and smooth top with rubber spatula. Set roasting pan on oven rack and pour enough boiling water into roasting pan to come about halfway up sides of springform pan. Bake until cake has risen slightly, edges are just beginning to set, thin glazed crust (like a brownie crust) has formed on surface, and cake registers 140 degrees, 22 to 25 minutes. Remove cake pan from water bath and set on wire rack; let cool to room temperature. Cover and refrigerate overnight. (Cake can be refrigerated for up to 4 days).

5. About 30 minutes before serving, run thin knife between cake and sides of pan; remove sides of pan. Invert cake onto sheet of waxed paper, discard parchment, and turn cake right side up onto serving platter. Dust with confectioners' sugar, if using, and serve.

CHOCOLATE RASPBERRY TORTE

✔ WHY THIS RECIPE WORKS

Sachertorte, the classic Viennese dessert with layers of chocolate cake sandwiching apricot jam and enrobed in a creamy-rich chocolate glaze, always sounds more promising than it typically is in reality—dry, flavorless cake and sweet jam with little fruity complexity, all covered in a glaze that is nothing more than a thin, overly sugary coating. We set out to create a rich, deeply chocolaty dessert using Sachertorte as the inspiration, giving it our own spin by pairing the chocolate with raspberries. For a rich, fudgy base, we started by baking our Ultimate Flourless Chocolate Cake in two 9-inch pans, so we could sandwich the two cakes together rather than deal with halving a single delicate cake. But when we tried to pick up the second layer and, later, eat it, the dense cake tore and fell apart. Adding ground nuts gave it the structure it needed, plus a good boost of flavor. Since we were using the food processor to grind the nuts, we tweaked our cake recipe so that it could be prepared using the same appliance. The winning approach for our filling was to combine jam with lightly mashed fresh berries for a tangy-sweet mixture that clung to the cake. For the glaze, we kept things simple, melting bittersweet chocolate with heavy cream to create a rich-tasting, glossy ganache that poured smoothly over the cake. And to up the glamour quotient, we dotted fresh raspberries around the top perimeter of the torte and pressed sliced, toasted almonds along its sides.

CHOCOLATE RASPBERRY TORTE
SERVES 12 TO 16

Be sure to use cake pans with at least 2-inch-tall sides.

CAKE AND FILLING
8	ounces bittersweet chocolate, chopped fine
12	tablespoons unsalted butter, cut into ½-inch pieces
2	teaspoons vanilla extract
¼	teaspoon instant espresso powder
1¾	cups (6⅛ ounces) sliced almonds, toasted
¼	cup (1¼ ounces) all-purpose flour
½	teaspoon salt
5	large eggs, room temperature
¾	cup (5¼ ounces) sugar

FILLING
2½	ounces (½ cup) raspberries, plus 16 individual raspberries
¼	cup seedless raspberry jam

GLAZE
5	ounces bittersweet chocolate, chopped fine
½	cup plus 1 tablespoon heavy cream

1. FOR THE CAKE: Adjust oven rack to middle position and heat oven to 325 degrees. Grease two 9-inch round cake pans, line with parchment paper, grease parchment, and flour pans. Melt chocolate and butter in large heatproof bowl set over saucepan filled with 1 inch of barely simmering water, stirring occasionally until smooth. Remove from heat and let cool to room temperature, about 30 minutes. Stir in vanilla and espresso.

2. Pulse ¾ cup almonds in food processor until coarsely chopped, 6 to 8 pulses,

This approach creates a torte with a perfectly flat bottom and top.

1. Run paring knife around sides of cakes and invert layers onto cardboard rounds cut same size as diameter of cake, then remove parchment paper.

2. Using wire rack, turn 1 cake right side up, then slide from wire rack back onto cardboard round.

3. Spread raspberry filling over cake layer that is right side up.

4. Top with second cake, leaving bottom facing up, then use offset spatula to evenly spread glaze over top and sides.

and set aside. Process remaining 1 cup almonds until very finely ground, about 45 seconds. Add flour and salt and continue to process until combined, about 15 seconds. Transfer almond-flour mixture to medium bowl. Process eggs until lightened in color and almost doubled in volume, about 3 minutes. With processor running, slowly add sugar and process until thoroughly combined, about 15 seconds. Using whisk, gently fold egg mixture into chocolate mixture until some streaks of egg remain. Sprinkle half almond-flour mixture over chocolate mixture and gently whisk until just combined. Sprinkle with remaining almond-flour mixture and gently whisk until just combined.

3. Divide batter evenly between prepared pans and smooth tops with rubber spatula. Bake cakes until centers are firm and toothpick inserted in centers comes out with few moist crumbs attached, 14 to 16 minutes. Transfer cakes to wire rack and let cool completely in pans, about 30 minutes.

4. Run paring knife around sides of cakes to loosen and invert cakes onto cardboard rounds cut same size as diameter of cake; discard parchment. Using wire rack, turn 1 cake right side up, then slide from rack back onto cardboard round.

5. FOR THE FILLING: Place ½ cup

raspberries in medium bowl and coarsely mash with fork. Stir in raspberry jam until just combined.

6. TO ASSEMBLE THE TORTE: Spread raspberry mixture onto cake layer that is right side up. Top with second cake layer, leaving it upside down. Transfer assembled cake, still on cardboard round, to wire rack set in rimmed baking sheet.

7. FOR THE GLAZE: Melt chocolate and cream in medium heatproof bowl set over saucepan filled with 1 inch of barely simmering water, stirring occasionally until smooth. Remove from heat and gently whisk until very smooth. Pour glaze onto center of assembled cake. Using offset spatula, spread glaze evenly over top of cake, letting it drip down sides. Spread glaze along sides of cake to coat evenly.

8. Using fine-mesh strainer, sift reserved almonds to remove any fine bits. Holding bottom of cake on cardboard round with 1 hand, gently press sifted almonds onto cake sides with other hand. Arrange remaining 16 raspberries around circumference. Refrigerate cake on rack until glaze is set, at least 1 hour or up to 24 hours (if refrigerating cake for more than 1 hour, let sit at room temperature for about 30 minutes before serving). Transfer cake to serving platter and serve.

SIMPLE CARROT CAKE WITH CREAM CHEESE FROSTING

✔ WHY THIS RECIPE WORKS
Carrot cake was once heralded for its use of vegetable oil in place of butter and carrots as a natural sweetener. Sure, the carrots add some sweetness, but they also add a lot of moisture, which is why carrot cake is invariably soggy. And oil? It makes this cake dense and, well, oily. We wanted a moist, not soggy, cake that was rich, with a tender crumb and balanced spice.

We started with all-purpose flour—cake flour proved too delicate to support the grated carrots that get mixed in. For lift, we liked a combination of baking soda and baking powder. Some carrot cakes use a heavy hand with the spices; we took a conservative approach and used modest amounts of cinnamon, nutmeg, and cloves. After trying varying amounts of grated carrots, we settled on 1 pound for a pleasantly moist texture. For a rich, but not greasy, cake, 1½ cups vegetable oil did the trick. We found that the simplest mixing method was actually the food processor. We used the processor fitted with the shredding disk to shred the carrots, then swapped out the blade and made the batter (but if you don't own a food processor a box grater and mixer will suffice). Cream cheese frosting is the perfect partner to carrot cake—we enriched our version with sour cream for extra tang and vanilla for depth of flavor. Once again, it was easy enough to prepare the frosting in the food processor so that start to finish, we only had to dirty one piece of equipment.

SIMPLE CARROT CAKE WITH CREAM CHEESE FROSTING

SERVES 15

If you like nuts in your cake, stir 1½ cups toasted chopped pecans or walnuts into the batter along with the carrots. Raisins are also a good addition; 1 cup can be added along with the carrots. If you add both nuts and raisins, the cake will need an additional 10 to 12 minutes in the oven.

2½	cups (12½ ounces) all-purpose flour
1¼	teaspoons baking powder
1	teaspoon baking soda
1¼	teaspoons ground cinnamon
½	teaspoon ground nutmeg
⅛	teaspoon ground cloves
½	teaspoon salt
1	pound carrots, peeled
1½	cups (10½ ounces) granulated sugar
½	cup packed (3½ ounces) light brown sugar
4	large eggs, room temperature
1½	cups vegetable oil
1	recipe Cream Cheese Frosting (recipe follows)

1. Adjust oven rack to middle position and heat oven to 350 degrees. Grease 13 by 9-inch baking pan, line with parchment paper, grease parchment, and flour pan.

2. Whisk flour, baking powder, baking soda, cinnamon, nutmeg, cloves, and salt together in large bowl and set aside.

3A. FOOD PROCESSOR METHOD: Using food processor fitted with large shredding disk, shred carrots (you should have about 3 cups); transfer to bowl. Wipe out workbowl and fit processor with metal blade. Process granulated sugar, brown sugar, and eggs in food processor until frothy and thoroughly combined, about 20 seconds. With processor running, add oil in steady stream and process until mixture is light in color and well emulsified, about 20 seconds. Transfer mixture to medium bowl and stir in carrots and flour mixture until incorporated and no streaks of flour remain.

3B. STAND MIXER METHOD: Shred carrots on large holes of box grater (you should have about 3 cups); transfer carrots to bowl and set aside. Using stand mixer fitted with paddle, beat granulated sugar, brown sugar, and eggs on medium-high speed until thoroughly combined, about 45 seconds. Reduce speed to medium; with mixer running, add oil in slow, steady stream, being careful to pour oil against inside of bowl (if oil begins to splatter, reduce speed to low until oil is incorporated, then resume adding oil). Increase speed to high and mix until mixture is light in color and well emulsified, about 45 seconds to 1 minute longer. Turn off mixer and stir in carrots and dry ingredients by hand until incorporated and no streaks of flour remain.

4. Scrape batter into prepared pan, smooth top with rubber spatula, and gently tap pan on counter to release air bubbles. Bake cake until toothpick inserted in center comes out clean, 35 to 40 minutes, rotating pan halfway through baking. Let cake cool completely in pan on wire rack, about 2 hours.

5. Run paring knife around edge of cake to loosen from pan. Invert cake onto wire rack, discard parchment, then turn cake right side up onto serving platter. Spread frosting evenly over cake and serve. (Cake can be refrigerated for up to 3 days.)

CREAM CHEESE FROSTING

MAKES 3 CUPS

Do not use low-fat or nonfat cream cheese or the frosting will turn out too soupy to work with.

12	ounces cream cheese, softened
6	tablespoons unsalted butter, softened
4	teaspoons sour cream
1	teaspoon vanilla extract
¼	teaspoon salt
1¾	cups (7 ounces) confectioners' sugar

1A. FOOD PROCESSOR METHOD: Process cream cheese, butter, sour cream, vanilla, and salt in food processor until combined, about 5 seconds, scraping down bowl as needed. Add confectioners' sugar and process until smooth, about 10 seconds.

1B. STAND MIXER METHOD: Using stand mixer fitted with whisk, mix cream cheese, butter, sour cream, vanilla, and salt at medium-high speed until well combined, about 30 seconds, scraping down bowl with rubber spatula as needed. Add confectioners' sugar and mix until very fluffy, about 1 minute.

SPICED CARROT CAKE WITH VANILLA BEAN–CREAM CHEESE FROSTING

The Indian tea called chai inspired this variation.

For the cake, substitute ½ teaspoon pepper for nutmeg, increase cloves to ¼ teaspoon, and add 1 tablespoon ground cardamom along with spices. For the frosting, halve and scrape seeds from 2 vanilla beans and add seeds to food processor along with vanilla extract.

SPICE CAKE WITH CREAM CHEESE FROSTING

✔ WHY THIS RECIPE WORKS

The problem with spice cakes? Spice. Some variations suffer spice overload, which makes them gritty and dusty. Others are so lacking in spice flavor that it seems as if a cinnamon stick has only been waved in their general direction. We wanted an old-fashioned, moist, and substantial spice cake with spices that were warm and bold without being overpowering, and a rich, but complementary cream cheese frosting. We needed a less-than-tender cake, one with a substantial and open crumb that could stand up to the spices. We found that all-purpose flour, rather than cake flour, added volume and heft, while butter and eggs added richness. Blooming the spices in butter intensified their aromas and gave the cake a heightened spice impact throughout. We used the classic mixture of cinnamon, cloves, cardamom, allspice, and nutmeg, but found that a tablespoon of grated fresh ginger and a couple of tablespoons of molasses gave the cake an extra zing. Reserving a little of the spice mixture to add to the cream cheese frosting united the frosting and the cake.

SPICE CAKE WITH CREAM CHEESE FROSTING

SERVES 15

To save time, let the eggs, buttermilk, and butter come up to temperature while the browned butter and spice mixture cools.

1	tablespoon ground cinnamon
¾	teaspoon ground cardamom
½	teaspoon ground allspice
½	teaspoon ground cloves
¼	teaspoon ground nutmeg
16	tablespoons unsalted butter, softened
2¼	cups (11¼ ounces) all-purpose flour
½	teaspoon baking powder
½	teaspoon baking soda
½	teaspoon salt
2	large eggs plus 3 large yolks, room temperature
1	teaspoon vanilla extract
1¾	cups (12¼ ounces) granulated sugar
2	tablespoons molasses
1	tablespoon grated fresh ginger
1	cup buttermilk, room temperature
1	recipe Cream Cheese Frosting (page 681)
¾	cup walnuts, toasted and chopped coarse (optional)

1. Adjust oven rack to middle position and heat oven to 350 degrees. Grease 13 by 9-inch baking pan, line with parchment paper, grease parchment, and flour pan. Combine cinnamon, cardamom, allspice, cloves, and nutmeg in small bowl; reserve ½ teaspoon of spice mixture for frosting.

2. Melt 4 tablespoons butter in 8-inch skillet over medium heat, 1 to 2 minutes. Cook, swirling pan constantly, until butter is light brown and has faint nutty aroma, 2 to 4 minutes. Add spices and continue to cook, stirring constantly, 15 seconds. Remove from heat and let cool to room temperature, about 30 minutes.

3. Whisk flour, baking powder, baking soda, and salt together in medium bowl. In small bowl, gently whisk eggs, egg yolks, and vanilla to combine. Using stand mixer fitted with paddle, beat remaining 12 tablespoons butter with sugar and molasses on medium-high speed until pale and fluffy, about 3 minutes, scraping down bowl as needed. Reduce speed to medium and add cooled butter-spice mixture, ginger, and half of egg mixture; mix until incorporated, about 15 seconds. Repeat with remaining egg mixture; scrape down bowl. Reduce speed to low and add flour mixture in 3 additions, alternating with 2 additions of buttermilk, scraping down bowl as needed. Mix at medium speed until batter is thoroughly combined, about 15 seconds. Give batter final stir by hand.

4. Scrape batter into prepared pan, smooth top with rubber spatula, and gently tap pan on counter to release air bubbles. Bake cake until toothpick inserted in center comes out clean, 32 to 37 minutes. Let cake cool completely in pan on wire rack, about 2 hours. Run paring knife around edge of cake to loosen from pan. Invert cake onto wire rack, discard parchment, then turn cake right side up onto serving platter.

5. Stir reserved spice mixture into frosting. Spread frosting evenly over cake, sprinkle with walnuts, if using, and serve. (Cake can be refrigerated for up to 2 days. Bring cake to room temperature before serving.)

SPICE CAKE WITH ORANGE–CREAM CHEESE FROSTING

Add 1½ teaspoons grated orange zest to frosting with vanilla. Substitute slivered almonds or coarsely chopped hazelnuts for walnuts.

RUSTIC PLUM CAKE

✔ WHY THIS RECIPE WORKS

Plum cake can be anything from an Alsatian tart to a German yeasted bread. In most recipes, the plums either sink into the cake and create a sodden center or they are sliced too thin to contribute a lot of flavor. We wanted an easy-to-make cake with a sturdy yet moist crumb that had good flavor and a hefty plum presence. To create a rich, moist cake that was strong enough to hold the plums aloft, we replaced some of the flour with ground almonds (many European cakes do this). The ground nuts introduced strength and additional flavor, and we also found that we didn't need to cream the almond-enhanced batter, since it was sturdy enough to be mixed in the food processor used to grind the nuts. As for the fruit, while we liked the Italian plums that are especially well suited for baking, we found their season to be too short to be practical. Poaching our common supermarket plums (and Italian plums when we could find them) in a few tablespoons of jam and brandy, as well as their own juice, sufficiently heightened their flavor and kept them moist, even after a spell in the oven.

RUSTIC PLUM CAKE
SERVES 8

This recipe works best with Italian plums, which are also called prune plums. If substituting regular red or black plums, use an equal weight of plums, cut them into eighths, and stir them a few times while cooking. Arrange slices, slightly overlapped, in two rings over surface of cake. Do not use canned Italian plums. Don't add the leftover plum cooking liquid to the cake before baking; reserve it and serve with the finished cake (or reserve for serving over ice cream). The cake can be served with Whipped Cream (page 800).

2	tablespoons red currant jelly or seedless raspberry jam
3	tablespoons brandy
1	pound Italian prune plums, halved and pitted
¾	cup (5¼ ounces) sugar
⅓	cup slivered almonds
¾	cup (3¾ ounces) all-purpose flour
½	teaspoon baking powder
¼	teaspoon salt
6	tablespoons unsalted butter, cut into 6 pieces and softened
1	large egg plus 1 large yolk, room temperature
1	teaspoon vanilla extract
¼	teaspoon almond extract (optional) Confectioners' sugar

1. Cook jelly and brandy in 10-inch nonstick skillet over medium heat until thick and syrupy, 2 to 3 minutes. Remove skillet from heat and place plums cut side down in syrup. Return skillet to medium heat and cook, shaking pan to prevent plums from sticking, until plums release their juices and liquid reduces to thick syrup, about 5 minutes. Let plums cool in skillet, about 20 minutes.

2. Adjust oven rack to middle position and heat oven to 350 degrees. Grease and flour 9-inch springform pan. Process sugar and almonds in food processor until nuts are finely ground, about 1 minute. Add flour, baking powder, and salt and pulse to combine, about 5 pulses. Add butter and pulse until mixture resembles coarse sand, about 10 pulses. Add egg, egg yolk, vanilla, and almond extract, if using, and process until smooth, about 5 seconds, scraping down bowl if needed (batter will be very thick and heavy).

3. Pour batter into prepared pan and smooth top with rubber spatula. Stir plums to coat with syrup. Arrange plum halves, skin side down, evenly over surface of batter. Bake until cake is golden brown and toothpick inserted in center comes out with few crumbs attached, 40 to 50 minutes. Run thin knife around sides of cake to loosen. Cool in pan on wire rack until just warm or to room temperature, at least 30 minutes. Run thin knife between cake and sides of pan; remove sides of pan. Dust with confectioners' sugar and serve.

SUMMER PEACH CAKE

✔ WHY THIS RECIPE WORKS

This dessert, which marries cake with fresh summer peaches, is a bakery favorite, but most versions are plagued by soggy cake and barely noticeable peach flavor. We wanted a buttery cake that was moist yet not at all soggy, with a golden-brown exterior and plenty of peach flavor. Roasting chunks of peaches, tossed in sugar and a little lemon juice, helped concentrate their flavor and expel moisture before we combined them with our cake batter. However, during roasting, the peach chunks became swathed in a flavorful but unpleasantly gooey film. Coating our roasted peaches in panko bread crumbs before combining them with the batter ensured the film was absorbed by the crumbs, which then dissolved into the cake during baking. To amplify the peach flavor we tossed the fruit with peach schnapps before roasting, and a little almond extract added to the batter lent a subtle complementary note. Fanning peach slices (macerated with a little more of the schnapps) over the top, then sprinkling over some almond extract–enhanced sugar for a light glaze, ensured our cake looked as good as it tasted.

SUMMER PEACH CAKE
SERVES 8

To crush the panko bread crumbs, place them in a zipper-lock bag and smash them with a rolling pin. If you can't find panko, ¼ cup of plain, unseasoned bread crumbs can be substituted. Orange liqueur can be substituted for the peach schnapps. If using peak-of-season, farm-fresh peaches, omit the peach schnapps.

2½	pounds peaches, halved, pitted, and cut into ½-inch wedges
5	tablespoons peach schnapps
4	teaspoons lemon juice
6	tablespoons plus ⅓ cup (5 ounces) granulated sugar
1	cup (5 ounces) all-purpose flour
1¼	teaspoons baking powder
¾	teaspoon salt
½	cup packed (3½ ounces) light brown sugar
2	large eggs, room temperature
8	tablespoons unsalted butter, melted and cooled
¼	cup sour cream
1½	teaspoons vanilla extract
¼	teaspoon plus ⅛ teaspoon almond extract
⅓	cup panko bread crumbs, crushed fine

1. Adjust oven rack to middle position and heat oven to 425 degrees. Line

rimmed baking sheet with aluminum foil and spray with vegetable oil spray. Grease and flour 9-inch springform pan. Gently toss 24 peach wedges with 2 tablespoons schnapps, 2 teaspoons lemon juice, and 1 tablespoon granulated sugar in bowl; set aside.

2. Cut remaining peach wedges crosswise into 3 chunks. In large bowl, gently toss chunks with remaining 3 tablespoons schnapps, remaining 2 teaspoons lemon juice, and 2 tablespoons granulated sugar. Spread peach chunks in single layer on prepared baking sheet and bake until exuded juices begin to thicken and caramelize at edges of pan, 20 to 25 minutes. Transfer pan to wire rack and let peaches cool to room temperature, about 30 minutes. Reduce oven temperature to 350 degrees.

3. Whisk flour, baking powder, and salt together in bowl. Whisk ⅓ cup granulated sugar, brown sugar, and eggs together in bowl until thick and thoroughly combined, about 45 seconds. Slowly whisk in butter until combined. Add sour cream, vanilla, and ¼ teaspoon almond extract; whisk until combined. Add flour mixture and whisk until just combined.

4. Pour half of batter into prepared pan. Using offset spatula, spread batter evenly to pan edges and smooth top. Sprinkle crushed panko evenly over cooled peach chunks and gently toss to coat. Arrange peach chunks on batter in pan in even layer, gently pressing peaches into batter. Gently spread remaining batter over peach chunks and smooth top. Arrange reserved peach wedges, slightly overlapped, in ring over surface of batter, placing smaller wedges in center. Stir remaining 3 tablespoons granulated sugar and remaining ⅛ teaspoon almond extract together in small bowl until sugar is moistened. Sprinkle sugar mixture evenly over top of cake.

5. Bake cake until center is set and toothpick inserted in center comes out clean, 50 to 60 minutes. Transfer pan to wire rack and let cool for 5 minutes. Run thin knife between cake and sides of pan; remove sides of pan. Let cake cool completely, 2 to 3 hours, before serving.

PINEAPPLE UPSIDE-DOWN CAKE

✔ WHY THIS RECIPE WORKS
The classic pineapple upside-down cake recipe relies on the simple technique of cooking the fruit in sugar and butter in a heavy skillet (usually cast iron), topping it with cake batter, then baking it. The classic version, made with canned pineapple, is lacking true pineapple flavor, so we had higher hopes for a cake made with fresh fruit. However, while the flavor was certainly better, the fresh pineapple's juices turned the cake soggy. By caramelizing the pineapple in a skillet along with the sugar, we found we could control the moisture level. We removed the fruit from the pan once it turned golden brown, then added butter and reduced the syrup until it was just the right consistency. For a cake batter that could stand up to its topping without becoming a gummy mess, we started with a classic butter cake, then cut back on the milk to alleviate gumminess and added an egg white, which lightened the texture without compromising the structure. Reducing the amount of sugar ensured our final pineapple-topped cake wasn't too sweet.

PINEAPPLE UPSIDE-DOWN CAKE
SERVES 8

For this recipe, we prefer to use a 9-inch cake pan with sides that are at least 2 inches high. Alternatively, a 10-inch ovensafe skillet (cast iron or stainless steel) can be used to both cook the pineapple and bake the cake. If using a skillet instead of a cake pan, cool the juices directly in the skillet while making the batter; it's fine if the skillet is warm when the batter is added.

TOPPING
- 1 pineapple, peeled, cored, and cut into ½-inch pieces (4 cups)
- 1 cup packed (7 ounces) light brown sugar
- 3 tablespoons unsalted butter
- ½ teaspoon vanilla extract

CAKE
- 1½ cups (7½ ounces) all-purpose flour
- 1½ teaspoons baking powder
- ½ teaspoon salt
- 8 tablespoons unsalted butter, softened
- ¾ cup (5¼ ounces) granulated sugar
- 1 teaspoon vanilla extract
- 2 large eggs plus 1 large white, room temperature
- ⅓ cup whole milk, room temperature

1. Adjust oven rack to lower-middle position and heat oven to 350 degrees. Grease 9-inch round cake pan, line with parchment paper, grease parchment, and flour pan.

2. FOR THE TOPPING: Cook pineapple and brown sugar in 10-inch skillet over medium heat until pineapple is translucent and has light brown hue, 15 to 18 minutes, stirring occasionally during first 5 minutes. Transfer fruit and juices to fine-mesh strainer set over bowl (you should have about 2 cups cooked fruit). Return juices to skillet and simmer over medium heat until thickened, beginning to darken, and mixture forms large bubbles, 6 to 8 minutes, adding any more juices released by fruit to skillet after about 4 minutes. Off heat, whisk in butter and vanilla. Pour caramel mixture into prepared cake pan and set aside while preparing cake. (Pineapple will continue to release liquid as it sits; do not add this liquid to already-reduced juice mixture.)

3. FOR THE CAKE: Whisk flour, baking powder, and salt in medium bowl. Using

stand mixer fitted with paddle, beat butter and sugar on medium-high speed until pale and fluffy, about 3 minutes. Reduce speed to medium, add vanilla, and beat to combine. Increase speed to medium-high, add eggs and egg white, 1 at a time, and beat until combined. Reduce speed to low and add flour mixture in 3 additions, alternating with 2 additions of milk, scraping down bowl as needed (batter will be thick). Give batter final stir by hand.

4. Working quickly, distribute drained pineapple in cake pan in even layer, gently pressing fruit into caramel. Using rubber spatula, drop mounds of batter over fruit, then spread batter over fruit and to sides of pan in even layer. Gently tap pan on counter to release air bubbles. Bake cake until golden brown and toothpick inserted in center comes out clean, 45 to 50 minutes. Cool 10 minutes on wire rack, then place inverted serving platter over cake pan. Invert cake pan and platter together, then remove pan. Let cool to room temperature, about 2 hours, and serve.

ORANGE-CARDAMOM PINEAPPLE UPSIDE-DOWN CAKE

Add 1 tablespoon grated orange zest to skillet with pineapple in step 2, and add ¼ cup orange juice to skillet in step 2 after draining pineapple and returning juices to skillet. Whisk ¾ teaspoon ground cardamom into flour mixture in step 3.

COCONUT-GINGER PINEAPPLE UPSIDE-DOWN CAKE

Add 2 teaspoons grated fresh ginger to skillet with pineapple in step 2. Beat ¾ cup sweetened shredded coconut with butter and sugar in step 4. Substitute ½ cup room-temperature coconut milk for whole milk.

APPLE UPSIDE-DOWN CAKE

✔ WHY THIS RECIPE WORKS

Pineapple has become synonymous with upside-down cake ever since canned pineapple was introduced into this country in the early 1900s. But at one time, upside-down cakes were made with seasonal fruit, such as apples. We loved the idea of resurrecting apple upside-down cake. We wanted a rich buttery cake topped with tightly packed, burnished, sweet apples. Most apples turned mushy and watery and were simply too sweet, but crisp, tart Granny Smiths made the cut (Golden Delicious worked well, too). We shingled the apples in the pan and poured the cake batter over the top. But once baked and inverted, our apple layer was shrunken and dry. The solution turned out to be increasing the number of apples for a hefty layer of fruit. This yielded better results, but they also added surplus moisture to the pan that turned our cake gummy. Precooking half the apples by sautéing them on the stovetop drew out some of this excess moisture and solved the problem. For the butter cake, we tested milk, buttermilk, yogurt, and sour cream. Sour cream won hands down—its subtle tang balanced the sweetness of the cake and complemented the caramelized apples. Cornmeal gave the cake a hint of earthy flavor and a pleasantly coarse texture.

APPLE UPSIDE-DOWN CAKE
SERVES 8

You will need a 9-inch nonstick cake pan with sides that are at least 2 inches tall. Alternatively, use a 10-inch ovensafe skillet (don't use cast iron) to both cook the apples and bake the cake, with the following modifications: Cook the apples in the skillet and set them aside while mixing the batter (it's fine if the skillet is still warm when the batter is added) and increase the baking time by 7 to 9 minutes. If you don't have either a 2-inch-high cake pan or an ovensafe skillet, use an 8-inch square pan.

TOPPING

2 pounds Granny Smith or Golden Delicious apples, peeled and cored

4 tablespoons unsalted butter, cut into 4 pieces

⅔ cup packed (4⅔ ounces) light brown sugar

2 teaspoons lemon juice

CAKE

1 cup (5 ounces) all-purpose flour

1 tablespoon cornmeal (optional)

1 teaspoon baking powder

½ teaspoon salt

¾ cup (5¼ ounces) granulated sugar

¼ cup packed (1¾ ounces) light brown sugar

2 large eggs, room temperature

6 tablespoons unsalted butter, melted and cooled

½ cup sour cream

1 teaspoon vanilla extract

1. FOR THE TOPPING: Grease 9-inch round nonstick cake pan, line with parchment paper, grease parchment, and flour pan. Adjust oven rack to lowest position and heat oven to 350 degrees.

2. Halve apples from stem to blossom end. Cut 2 apples into ¼-inch-thick slices; set aside. Cut remaining 2 apples into ½-inch-thick slices. Melt butter in 12-inch skillet over medium-high heat. Add ½-inch-thick apple slices and cook, stirring 2 or 3 times, until apples begin to caramelize, 4 to 6 minutes (do not fully cook apples). Add ¼-inch-thick apple slices, brown sugar, and lemon juice and continue cooking, stirring constantly, until sugar dissolves and apples are coated, about 1 minute longer. Transfer apple mixture to prepared pan and lightly press into even layer.

3. FOR THE CAKE: Whisk flour, cornmeal, if using, baking powder, and salt

together in medium bowl. Whisk granulated sugar, brown sugar, and eggs together in large bowl until thick and thoroughly combined, about 45 seconds. Slowly whisk in butter until combined. Add sour cream and vanilla and whisk until combined. Add flour mixture and whisk until just combined. Pour batter into pan and spread evenly over fruit. Bake cake until golden brown and toothpick inserted in center comes out clean, 35 to 40 minutes.

4. Let cake cool in pan on wire rack for 20 minutes. Run paring knife around sides of cake to loosen. Place wire rack over pan and, holding rack tightly, invert cake pan and wire rack together. Lift off pan. Place wire rack with cake over baking sheet or large plate to catch any drips. If any fruit sticks to pan bottom, remove and position it on top of cake. Let cake cool completely, about 20 minutes, then transfer to serving platter and serve.

APPLE UPSIDE-DOWN CAKE WITH ALMONDS

You will need ¼ cup whole almonds to make ⅓ cup ground almonds. To grind the almonds, process them in a food processor for about 45 seconds.

Whisk ⅓ cup finely ground toasted almonds with flour, baking powder, and salt and add 1 teaspoon almond extract to batter with sour cream and vanilla in step 3.

APPLE UPSIDE-DOWN CAKE WITH LEMON AND THYME

Add 1 teaspoon grated lemon zest and 1 teaspoon finely chopped fresh thyme to batter with sour cream and vanilla in step 3.

APPLESAUCE SNACK CAKE

✓ WHY THIS RECIPE WORKS
Applesauce cakes run the gamut from dense, chunky fruitcakes to gummy "health" cakes without much flavor. We wanted a moist and tender cake that actually tasted like its namesake. It was easy to achieve the looser, more casual crumb that is best suited to a rustic snack cake. Since this texture is similar to that of quick breads and muffins, we used the same technique, mixing the wet ingredients separately and then gently adding the dry ingredients by hand. The harder challenge was to develop more apple flavor; simply adding more applesauce made for a gummy cake and fresh apples added too much moisture. But two other sources worked well. Apple cider, reduced to a syrup, contributed a pleasing sweetness and a slight tang without excess moisture. And plumping dried apples in the cider while it was reducing added even more apple taste without making the cake chunky. With such great apple flavor, we didn't want the cake to be too sweet or rich, so we rejected the idea of topping the cake with a glaze or frosting. But we found we liked the modicum of textural contrast provided by a simple sprinkling of spiced granulated sugar.

APPLESAUCE SNACK CAKE
SERVES 8

The cake is very moist, so it is best to err on the side of overdone when testing its doneness. The test kitchen prefers the rich flavor of cider, but apple juice can be substituted.

- ¾ cup dried apples, cut into ½-inch pieces
- I cup apple cider
- I½ cups (7½ ounces) all-purpose flour
- I teaspoon baking soda
- ⅔ cup (4¾ ounces) sugar
- ½ teaspoon ground cinnamon
- ¼ teaspoon ground nutmeg
- ⅛ teaspoon ground cloves

- I cup unsweetened applesauce, room temperature
- I large egg, room temperature, lightly beaten
- ½ teaspoon salt
- 8 tablespoons unsalted butter, melted and cooled
- I teaspoon vanilla extract

I. Adjust oven rack to middle position and heat oven to 325 degrees. Make foil sling by folding 2 long sheets of aluminum foil so that they are as wide as 8-inch square baking pan. Lay sheets of foil in pan, perpendicular to one another, with extra foil hanging over edges of pan. Push foil into corners and up sides of pan, smoothing foil flush to pan. Spray foil with vegetable oil spray.

2. Bring dried apples and cider to simmer in small saucepan over medium heat and cook until liquid evaporates and mixture appears dry, about 15 minutes. Let cool to room temperature.

3. Whisk flour and baking soda in medium bowl to combine. In second medium bowl, whisk sugar, cinnamon, nutmeg, and cloves. Measure 2 tablespoons sugar mixture into small bowl and reserve for topping.

4. Process cooled apple mixture and applesauce in food processor until smooth, 20 to 30 seconds, scraping down sides of bowl as needed, and set aside. Whisk egg and salt in large bowl to combine. Add sugar mixture and whisk until well combined and light colored, about 20 seconds. Add butter in 3 additions, whisking after each addition. Add applesauce mixture and vanilla and whisk to combine. Add flour mixture to wet ingredients and fold gently using rubber spatula until just combined and evenly moistened.

5. Scrape batter into prepared pan and smooth top with rubber spatula. Sprinkle reserved sugar mixture evenly over batter. Bake cake until toothpick inserted in center

comes out clean, 35 to 40 minutes. Let cake cool completely on wire rack, about 2 hours. Remove cake from pan using foil and transfer to platter. Gently push side of cake with knife and remove foil, 1 piece at a time. Serve. (Cake can be stored at room temperature for up to 2 days.)

GINGER-CARDAMOM APPLESAUCE SNACK CAKE

Omit cinnamon, nutmeg, and cloves. Whisk ½ teaspoon ground ginger and ¼ teaspoon ground cardamom into sugar in step 3. Reserve 2 tablespoons sugar mixture and add 1 tablespoon finely chopped crystallized ginger to topping.

APPLESAUCE SNACK CAKE WITH OAT-NUT STREUSEL

In step 3, measure 2 tablespoons sugar mixture into medium bowl. Add 2 tablespoons brown sugar, ⅓ cup chopped pecans or walnuts, and ⅓ cup old-fashioned or quick oats. Work in 2 tablespoons softened unsalted butter until fully incorporated by rubbing mixture between fingers. Pinch mixture into hazelnut-size clumps and sprinkle evenly over batter before baking.

GINGERBREAD

✔ WHY THIS RECIPE WORKS
Most gingerbread recipes that are moist also suffer from a dense, sunken center, and flavors range from barely gingery to addled with enough spices to make a curry fan cry for mercy. Our ideal gingerbread was moist through and through and utterly simple. Focusing on flavor first, we bumped up the ginger flavor by using a hefty dose of ground ginger and folded in grated fresh ginger. Cinnamon and fresh-ground pepper helped produce a warm,

complex, lingering heat. As for the liquid components, dark stout, gently heated to minimize its booziness, had a bittersweet flavor that brought out the caramel undertones of the molasses. Finally, swapping out the butter for vegetable oil and replacing some of the brown sugar with granulated let the spice flavors come through. To prevent a sunken center, we looked at our leaveners first. Baking powder isn't as effective at leavening if too many other acidic ingredients are present in the batter. In this case, we had three: molasses, brown sugar, and stout. Bucking the usual protocol for cakes and incorporating the baking soda with the wet ingredients instead of the other dry ones helped to neutralize those acidic ingredients before they get incorporated into the batter and allowed the baking powder to do a better job. And while stirring develops flour's gluten, which is typically the enemy of tenderness, our batter was so loose that vigorous stirring actually gave our cake the structure necessary to further ensure the center didn't collapse.

GINGERBREAD
SERVES 8

This cake packs potent, yet well-balanced, fragrant, spicy heat. If you are particularly sensitive to spice, you can decrease the amount of dried ginger to 1 tablespoon. Avoid opening the oven door until the minimum baking time has elapsed. Serve the gingerbread plain or with Whipped Cream (page 800).

¾	cup stout, such as Guinness
½	teaspoon baking soda
⅔	cup molasses
¾	cup packed (5¼ ounces) light brown sugar
¼	cup (1¾ ounces) granulated sugar
1½	cups (7½ ounces) all-purpose flour
2	tablespoons ground ginger
½	teaspoon baking powder
½	teaspoon salt
¼	teaspoon ground cinnamon
¼	teaspoon pepper
2	large eggs, room temperature
⅓	cup vegetable oil
1	tablespoon grated fresh ginger

1. Adjust oven rack to middle position and heat oven to 350 degrees. Grease 8-inch square baking pan, line with parchment paper, grease parchment, and flour pan.

2. Bring stout to boil in medium saucepan over medium heat, stirring occasionally. Remove from heat and stir in baking soda (mixture will foam vigorously). When foaming subsides, stir in molasses, brown sugar, and granulated sugar until dissolved; set aside. Whisk flour, ground ginger, baking powder, salt, cinnamon, and pepper together in large bowl.

3. Transfer stout mixture to second large bowl. Whisk in eggs, oil, and grated ginger until combined. Whisk wet mixture into flour mixture in thirds, stirring vigorously until completely smooth after each addition.

4. Scrape batter into prepared pan, smooth top with rubber spatula, and gently tap pan on counter to release air bubbles. Bake cake until top is just firm to touch and toothpick inserted in center comes out clean, 35 to 45 minutes. Let cake cool in pan on wire rack, about 1½ hours. Serve warm or at room temperature. (Cake can be stored at room temperature for up to 2 days.)

OATMEAL CAKE WITH BROILED ICING

✔ WHY THIS RECIPE WORKS
While we (usually) love the broiled icing on this classic snack cake, the cake itself is often dense, gummy, and bland, and the icing can be saccharine sweet and tend toward greasiness. We wanted a moist, not dense, cake with buttery undertones topped by a broiled icing that

featured chewy coconut, crunchy nuts, and a butterscotch-like flavor. Replacing some of the brown sugar with granulated sugar in the cake meant less moisture, which lightened the cake's texture. We also reduced the proportion of flour to oats, using the minimum amount of flour needed to keep the cake from collapsing into crumbs. We still had to tackle the gumminess, which was created partly by soaking the oats in hot water; the hydrated oats were a sticky mess when we stirred them into the batter. But folding in dried oats didn't work—they never fully hydrated during baking and tasted raw and chewy in the finished cake. The answer proved to be soaking the oats in room-temperature water rather than boiling water, minimizing the amount of released starch. For the icing, cutting back on the sugar brought the sweetness in line, using melted butter (rather than creaming the butter into the sugar) simplified the recipe, and adding a splash of milk made the icing more pliable.

OATMEAL CAKE WITH BROILED ICING

SERVES 8

Do not use old-fashioned or instant oats for this recipe. Be sure to use a metal baking pan; glass pans are not recommended when broiling. If you have a drawer-style broiler (underneath the oven), position the rack as far as possible from the broiler element and monitor the icing carefully as it cooks in step 5. A vertical sawing motion with a serrated knife works best for cutting through the crunchy icing and tender cake.

CAKE

- 1   cup (3 ounces) quick oats
- ¾   cup water, room temperature
- ¾   cup (3¾ ounces) all-purpose flour
- ½   teaspoon baking soda
- ½   teaspoon baking powder
- ½   teaspoon salt
- ¼   teaspoon ground cinnamon
- ⅛   teaspoon ground nutmeg

- 4   tablespoons unsalted butter, softened
- ½   cup (3½ ounces) granulated sugar
- ½   cup packed (3½ ounces) light brown sugar
- 1   large egg, room temperature
- ½   teaspoon vanilla extract

ICING

- ¼   cup packed (1¾ ounces) light brown sugar
- 3   tablespoons unsalted butter, melted and cooled
- 3   tablespoons milk
- ¾   cup (2¼ ounces) sweetened shredded coconut
- ½   cup pecans, chopped

1. FOR THE CAKE: Adjust oven rack to middle position and heat oven to 350 degrees. Make foil sling by folding 2 long sheets of aluminum foil so that they are as wide as 8-inch square baking pan. Lay sheets of foil in pan, perpendicular to one another, with extra foil hanging over edges of pan. Push foil into corners and up sides of pan, smoothing foil flush to pan. Spray foil with vegetable oil spray.

2. Combine oats and water in medium bowl and let sit until water is absorbed, about 5 minutes. In another medium bowl, whisk flour, baking soda, baking powder, salt, cinnamon, and nutmeg together.

3. Using stand mixer fitted with paddle, beat butter, granulated sugar, and brown sugar on medium speed until combined and mixture has consistency of damp sand, 2 to 4 minutes, scraping down bowl as needed. Add egg and vanilla and beat until combined. Add flour mixture in 2 additions and mix until just incorporated, about 30 seconds. Add soaked oats and mix until combined, about 15 seconds. Give batter final stir by hand.

4. Scrape batter into prepared pan, smooth top with rubber spatula, and gently tap on counter to release air bubbles. Bake cake until toothpick inserted in center comes out with few crumbs attached, 30 to 35 minutes, rotating pan halfway through baking. Let cake cool slightly in pan, at least 10 minutes.

5. FOR THE BROILED ICING: While cake cools, adjust oven rack 9 inches from broiler element and heat broiler. In medium bowl, whisk together brown sugar, melted butter, and milk, then stir in coconut and pecans. Spread mixture evenly over warm cake. Broil until topping is bubbling and golden, 3 to 5 minutes.

6. Let cake cool in pan on wire rack for 1 hour. Remove cake from pan using foil and transfer to platter. Gently push side of cake with knife and remove foil, 1 piece at a time. Serve.

CLASSIC POUND CAKE

✔ WHY THIS RECIPE WORKS
A perfect recipe for pound cake is hard to find. Good-looking pound cakes tend to resemble yellow layer cakes: fluffy, bouncy, and open-textured. Those that taste good often bake up as flat and firm as bricks. We wanted to retool this classic recipe to make it great-tasting and ultra-plush, every time. The first key was starting with chilly 60-degree butter. Room-temperature butter didn't aerate properly and thus produced flat, dense cakes. We found the eggs also needed to be at 60 degrees in order to not deflate the batter, and if they were beaten together first then gradually poured into the batter (rather than added one at a time as in most recipes) we got a cake with a higher rise and lighter texture. Finally, we chose cake flour (all-purpose flour was too protein-rich and delivered dry, tough cakes), but because of the flour's softness we had better luck incorporating it into the batter by sifting the flour over the batter and folding it in by hand instead of using the mixer.

CLASSIC POUND CAKE

SERVES 8

The butter and eggs should be the first ingredients prepared so they have a chance to stand at room temperature and lose their chill while the oven heats, the loaf pan is greased and floured, and the other ingredients are measured. The test kitchen's preferred loaf pan measures 8½ by 4½ inches; if you use a 9 by 5-inch loaf pan, start checking for doneness 5 minutes earlier than advised in the recipe.

16	tablespoons unsalted butter, cut into 16 pieces and chilled
3	large eggs plus 3 large yolks, room temperature
2	teaspoons vanilla extract
1¾	cups (7 ounces) cake flour
½	teaspoon salt
1¼	cups (8¾ ounces) sugar

1. Place butter in bowl of stand mixer; let stand at room temperature 20 to 30 minutes to soften slightly (butter should reach no more than 60 degrees). Using dinner fork, beat eggs, egg yolks, and vanilla in 4-cup liquid measuring cup until combined. Let egg mixture stand at room temperature until ready to use.

2. Adjust oven rack to middle position and heat oven to 325 degrees. Grease and flour 8½ by 4½-inch loaf pan.

3. Fit stand mixer with paddle and beat butter and salt at medium-high speed until shiny, smooth, and creamy, 2 to 3 minutes, scraping down bowl once. Reduce speed to medium and gradually pour in sugar (this should take about 1 minute). Once all sugar is added, increase speed to medium-high and beat until mixture is light and fluffy, 5 to 8 minutes, scraping down bowl once. Reduce speed to medium and gradually add egg mixture in slow, steady stream (this should take 1 to 1½ minutes). Scrape down bowl, then beat mixture at medium-high speed until light and fluffy, 3 to 4 minutes (batter may look slightly curdled). Remove bowl from mixer and scrape down bowl.

4. Sift flour over butter-egg mixture in 3 additions, folding gently with rubber spatula until combined after each addition. Scrape along bottom of bowl to ensure batter is homogeneous.

5. Pour batter into prepared pan and smooth top with rubber spatula. Bake cake until golden brown and toothpick inserted in center comes out clean, 1 hour 10 minutes to 1 hour 20 minutes. Let cake cool in pan on wire rack for 15 minutes, then invert cake onto wire rack and turn cake right side up. Let cake cool completely on rack, about 2 hours, before serving. (Cake can be stored at room temperature for up to 3 days.)

ALMOND POUND CAKE

Reduce vanilla extract to 1 teaspoon and add 1½ teaspoons almond extract along with vanilla to eggs. Sprinkle 2 tablespoons sliced almonds over surface of batter just before baking.

POUND CAKE WITH ORANGE ESSENCE

Reduce vanilla extract to 1 teaspoon and add 1 tablespoon grated then minced orange zest to mixer bowl just after adding eggs in step 3.

CLASSIC POUND CAKE IN A TUBE PAN

Double all ingredients and substitute a 10-inch tube pan, greased and floured, for loaf pan. Bake cake at 350 degrees for 15 minutes, then reduce oven temperature to 325 degrees and continue to bake until cake is golden brown and wooden skewer inserted in center of cake comes out clean, 40 to 45 minutes. Let cake cool in pan on wire rack for 30 minutes, then invert cake onto wire rack and turn cake right side up. Let cake cool completely on rack, about 3 hours, before serving.

EASY LEMON POUND CAKE

✔ WHY THIS RECIPE WORKS

Lemon pound cakes often lack true lemon flavor. We wanted to produce a superior lemon pound cake while making the process as simple and foolproof as possible. For mixing the cake, we turned to the food processor. It ensured a perfect emulsification of the eggs, sugar, and melted butter (we found that a blender worked, too). Cake flour produced a tender crumb, but our cake was still a bit heavy. We fixed matters with the addition of baking powder, which increased lift and produced a consistent, fine crumb. Finally, in addition to mixing lemon zest into the cake batter, we glazed the finished cake with lemon sugar syrup—but first we poked holes all over the cake to ensure that the tangy, sweet glaze infused the cake with a blast of bright lemon flavor.

EASY LEMON POUND CAKE

SERVES 8

You can use a blender instead of a food processor to mix the batter. To add the butter, remove the center cap of the lid so the butter can be drizzled into the whirling blender with minimal splattering. This batter looks almost like a thick pancake batter and is very fluid. The test kitchen's preferred loaf pan measures 8½ by 4½ inches; if you use a 9 by 5-inch loaf pan, start checking for doneness 5 minutes earlier than advised in the recipe.

CAKE

16	tablespoons unsalted butter
1½	cups (6 ounces) cake flour
1	teaspoon baking powder
½	teaspoon salt
1¼	cups (8¾ ounces) sugar
2	tablespoons grated lemon zest plus 2 teaspoons juice (2 lemons)
4	large eggs, room temperature
1½	teaspoons vanilla extract

LEMON GLAZE

½	cup (3½ ounces) sugar
¼	cup lemon juice (2 lemons)

1. FOR THE CAKE: Adjust oven rack to middle position and heat oven to 350 degrees. Grease and flour 8½ by 4½-inch loaf pan. In medium bowl, whisk together flour, baking powder, and salt; set aside.

2. Melt butter in small saucepan over medium heat. Whisk melted butter thoroughly to reincorporate any separated milk solids.

3. Pulse sugar and lemon zest in food processor until combined, about 5 pulses. Add lemon juice, eggs, and vanilla and process until combined, about 5 seconds. With machine running, add melted butter in steady stream (this should take about 20 seconds). Transfer mixture to large bowl. Sift flour mixture over eggs in 3 steps, whisking gently after each addition until just combined.

4. Pour batter into prepared pan and smooth top with rubber spatula. Bake for 15 minutes, then reduce oven temperature to 325 degrees and continue baking until deep golden brown and toothpick inserted in center comes out clean, about 35 minutes, rotating pan halfway through baking. Let cake cool in pan for 10 minutes, then turn onto wire rack. Poke cake's top and sides with toothpick. Let cool to room temperature, at least 1 hour. (Cooled cake can be stored at room temperature for up to 5 days.)

5. FOR THE GLAZE: While cake is cooling, bring sugar and lemon juice to boil in small saucepan, stirring occasionally to dissolve sugar. Reduce heat to low and simmer until thickened slightly, about 2 minutes. Brush top and sides of cake with glaze and let cool to room temperature before serving.

LEMON–POPPY SEED POUND CAKE

After whisking flour mixture in step 1, toss 1 tablespoon flour mixture with ⅓ cup poppy seeds in small bowl; set aside. Fold poppy seed mixture into batter after incorporating flour in step 3.

LEMON BUNDT CAKE

✔ WHY THIS RECIPE WORKS

Lemons are tart, brash, and aromatic. Why, then, is it so hard to capture their assertive flavor in a straightforward Bundt cake? The flavor of lemon juice is drastically muted when exposed to the heat of an oven, and its acidity can wreak havoc on the delicate nature of baked goods. We wanted to develop a Bundt cake with potent lemon flavor without ruining its texture. We developed a battery of tests challenging classic lemon Bundt cake ingredient proportions, finally deciding to increase the butter and to replace the milk with buttermilk. We also found that creaming was necessary to achieve a light and even crumb. But we still needed to maximize the lemon flavor; we couldn't get the flavor we needed from lemon juice alone without using so much that the cake fell apart when sliced. We turned to zest and found that three lemons' worth gave the cake a perfumed lemon flavor, though we needed to give the zest a brief soak in lemon juice to eliminate its fibrous texture. The final challenge was the glaze, and a simple mixture of lemon juice, buttermilk, and confectioners' sugar made the grade.

LEMON BUNDT CAKE
SERVES 12

It is important to pour the glaze over cake after it has cooled for just 10 minutes and is still warm. Serve this cake as is or dress it up with lightly sweetened berries. The cake has a light, fluffy texture when eaten the day it is baked, but if well wrapped and held at room temperature overnight its texture becomes more dense—like that of pound cake—the following day.

CAKE

3   tablespoons grated lemon zest plus 3 tablespoons juice (3 lemons)
3   cups (15 ounces) all-purpose flour
1   teaspoon baking powder
½   teaspoon baking soda
1   teaspoon salt
¾   cup buttermilk
1   teaspoon vanilla extract

3   large eggs plus 1 large yolk, room temperature
18   tablespoons unsalted butter (2¼ sticks), softened
2   cups (14 ounces) sugar

GLAZE

2–3   tablespoons lemon juice
1   tablespoon buttermilk
2   cups (8 ounces) confectioners' sugar

1. FOR THE CAKE: Adjust oven rack to lower-middle position; heat oven to 350 degrees. Spray 12-cup nonstick Bundt pan with baking spray with flour. Mince lemon zest to fine paste (you should have about 2 tablespoons). Combine zest and lemon juice in small bowl; set aside to soften, 10 to 15 minutes.

2. Whisk flour, baking powder, baking soda, and salt in large bowl. Combine lemon juice mixture, buttermilk, and vanilla in medium bowl. In small bowl, gently whisk eggs and egg yolk to combine. Using stand mixer fitted with paddle, beat butter and sugar on medium-high speed until pale and fluffy, about 3 minutes. Reduce speed to medium and add half of eggs, mixing until incorporated, about 15 seconds. Repeat with remaining eggs and scrape down bowl. Reduce speed to low and add flour mixture in 3 additions, alternating with 2 additions of buttermilk mixture, scraping down bowl as needed. Give batter final stir by hand.

3. Scrape batter into prepared pan and smooth top with rubber spatula. Bake cake until top is golden brown and skewer inserted in center comes out with no crumbs attached, 45 to 50 minutes. Let cake cool in pan on wire rack set over baking sheet for 10 minutes, then invert cake onto rack.

4. FOR THE GLAZE: While cake is baking, whisk 2 tablespoons lemon juice, buttermilk, and confectioners' sugar until smooth, adding more lemon juice gradually as needed until glaze is thick but still pourable (mixture should leave faint trail

across bottom of mixing bowl when drizzled from whisk). Pour half of glaze over warm cake and let cool for 1 hour; pour remaining glaze evenly over top of cake and continue to cool to room temperature, at least 2 hours, before serving.

CHOCOLATE BUNDT CAKE

✓ **WHY THIS RECIPE WORKS**

With its decorative shape, a Bundt cake doesn't require frosting or fussy finishing techniques, especially if it's chocolate. We wanted a cake that would deliver that moment of pure chocolate ecstasy with the first bite—a chocolate Bundt cake that tastes every bit as good as it looks, with a fine crumb, moist texture, and rich chocolate flavor. We intensified the chocolate flavor by using both bittersweet chocolate and natural cocoa and dissolving them in boiling water, which "bloomed" their flavor. We used sour cream and brown sugar instead of granulated to add moisture and flavor. Finally, we further enhanced flavor with a little espresso powder and a generous amount of vanilla extract, both of which complemented the floral nuances of the chocolate.

CHOCOLATE SOUR CREAM BUNDT CAKE

SERVES 12

We prefer natural (or regular) cocoa here since Dutch-processed cocoa will result in a compromised rise. Because coating the Bundt pan with baking spray with flour will leave a whitish film on the baked cake, we prefer to coat the pan with a paste made from cocoa and melted butter, which ensures a clean release. For an accurate measurement of boiling water, bring a full kettle of water to a boil, then measure out the desired amount. The cake can be served with just a dusting of confectioners' sugar but is easily made more impressive with Lightly Sweetened Raspberries (recipe follows) and Tangy Whipped Cream (page 800).

¾ cup (2¼ ounces) plus 1 tablespoon cocoa
1 tablespoon unsalted butter, melted, plus 12 tablespoons softened
6 ounces bittersweet chocolate, chopped
1 teaspoon instant espresso powder (optional)
¾ cup boiling water
1 cup sour cream, room temperature
1¾ cups (8¾ ounces) all-purpose flour
1 teaspoon salt
1 teaspoon baking soda
2 cups packed (14 ounces) light brown sugar
1 tablespoon vanilla extract
5 large eggs, room temperature
Confectioners' sugar

1. FOR THE PAN: Mix 1 tablespoon cocoa and melted butter into paste. Using pastry brush, thoroughly coat interior of 12-cup Bundt pan. Adjust oven rack to lower-middle position and heat oven to 350 degrees.

2. FOR THE CAKE: Combine ¾ cup cocoa, chocolate, and espresso, if using, in medium heatproof bowl, pour boiling water over mixture, and let sit, covered, for 5 minutes. Whisk mixture gently until smooth. Let cool to room temperature, then whisk in sour cream. Whisk flour, salt, and baking soda in second bowl to combine.

3. Using stand mixer fitted with paddle, beat 12 tablespoons butter, sugar, and vanilla on medium-high speed until pale and fluffy, about 3 minutes. Add eggs, 1 at a time, and beat until combined. Reduce speed to low and add flour mixture in 3 additions, alternating with 2 additions of chocolate–sour cream mixture, scraping down bowl as needed. Give batter final stir by hand.

4. Scrape batter into prepared pan and smooth top with rubber spatula. Bake cake until skewer inserted in center comes out with few crumbs attached, 45 to 50 minutes. Let cake cool in pan for 10 minutes,

then invert cake onto wire rack; cool to room temperature, about 3 hours. Dust with confectioners' sugar, transfer to serving platter, and serve.

LIGHTLY SWEETENED RASPBERRIES
MAKES 3 CUPS

---

15 ounces (3 cups) raspberries
1–2 tablespoons sugar

Gently toss raspberries with sugar, then let stand until berries have released some juice and sugar has dissolved, about 15 minutes.

BEST ANGEL FOOD CAKE

✓ **WHY THIS RECIPE WORKS**

At its heavenly best, an angel food cake should be tall and perfectly shaped, have a snowy-white, tender crumb, and be encased in a thin, delicate golden crust. The difficulty with making a great angel food cake is that it requires a delicate balance of ingredients and proper cooking techniques. In particular, since this cake is only leavened with beaten egg whites, it is critical that you whip them correctly. First, we found it key to create a stable egg-white base, starting the whites at medium-low speed just to break them up into a froth and increasing the speed to medium-high speed to form soft, billowy mounds. Next, the sugar should be added, a tablespoon at a time. Once all the sugar is added, the whites become shiny and form soft peaks when the beater is lifted. A delicate touch is required when incorporating the remaining ingredients, such as the flour, which should be sifted over the batter and gently folded in. Angel food cakes are baked in a tube pan. We like to use a tube pan with a removable bottom but a pan without one can be lined with parchment paper. We avoid greasing the sides of the pan so that the cake can climb up and cling to the sides as it bakes—a greased pan will produce a disappointingly short cake.

BEST ANGEL FOOD CAKE

SERVES 12

If your tube pan has a removable bottom, you do not need to line it with parchment.

¾ cup (3 ounces) cake flour
1½ cups (10½ ounces) sugar
12 large egg whites, room temperature
1 teaspoon cream of tartar
¼ teaspoon salt
1½ teaspoons vanilla extract
1½ teaspoons lemon juice
½ teaspoon almond extract

1. Adjust an oven rack to the lower-middle position and heat oven to 325 degrees. Line 16-cup tube pan with parchment paper but do not grease. Whisk flour and ¾ cup sugar together in small bowl. Place remaining ¾ cup sugar in second small bowl.

2. Using stand mixer fitted with whisk, whip egg whites, cream of tartar, and salt on medium-low speed until foamy, about 1 minute. Increase speed to medium-high and whip to soft, billowy mounds, about 1 minute. Gradually add ¾ cup sugar and whip until soft, glossy peaks form, 1 to 2 minutes. Add vanilla, lemon juice, and almond extract and beat until just blended.

3. Sift flour mixture over egg whites, about 3 tablespoons at a time, gently folding mixture into whites using large rubber spatula after each addition.

4. Gently scrape batter into prepared pan, smooth top with rubber spatula, and gently tap pan on counter to release air bubbles. Bake cake until golden brown and top springs back when pressed firmly, 50 to 60 minutes. If cake has prongs around rim for elevating cake, invert pan on them. If not, invert pan over neck of bottle or funnel so that air can circulate all around it. Let cake cool completely, 2 to 3 hours.

5. Run knife around edge of cake to loosen, then gently tap pan upside down on counter to release cake. Peel off parchment, turn cake right side up onto serving platter, and serve.

CHIFFON CAKE

✔ WHY THIS RECIPE WORKS

Like the Hollywood stars of the 1920s who were the first to taste Harry Baker's secret-recipe cakes at the Brown Derby, we were delighted by the uniquely light yet full richness and deep flavor of this American invention, which came to be known as the chiffon cake. With the airy height of angel food cake (from using whipped egg whites) and the richness of pound cake (from incorporating egg yolks and oil), this cake seemed like a win-win. We decided to start by going back to the original version, as first put before the public by General Mills in Better Homes and Gardens *in 1948. Sadly, we were disappointed to find this cake was a bit dry—cottony and fluffy rather than moist and foamy, the way we thought chiffon cakes should be—and it lacked flavor. Decreasing the flour meant a moister, more flavorful cake but also less structure. Increasing the amount of egg yolks was a step closer, but our cake still wasn't perfect. In the end, instead of whipping all of the egg whites, we found that mixing some of them (unbeaten) into the dry ingredients along with the yolks, water, and oil, provided the structure our cake needed.*

CHIFFON CAKE

SERVES 12

If your tube pan has a removable bottom, you do not need to line it with parchment. Serve as is or dust with confectioners' sugar

1½ cups (10½ ounces) sugar
1⅓ cups (5⅓ ounces) cake flour
2 teaspoons baking powder
½ teaspoon salt
7 large eggs (2 whole and 5 separated), room temperature
¾ cup water
½ cup vegetable oil
1 tablespoon vanilla extract
½ teaspoon almond extract
½ teaspoon cream of tartar

1. Adjust oven rack to lower-middle position and heat oven to 325 degrees. Line bottom of 16-cup tube pan with parchment paper but do not grease. Whisk sugar, flour, baking powder, and salt together in large bowl. Whisk in whole eggs, egg yolks, water, oil, vanilla, and almond extract until batter is just smooth.

2. Using stand mixer fitted with whisk, whip egg whites and cream of tartar on medium-low speed until foamy, about 1 minute. Increase speed to medium-high and whip until stiff peaks form, 3 to 4 minutes. Using large rubber spatula, fold whites into batter, smearing any stubborn pockets of egg white against the side of the bowl.

3. Pour batter into prepared pan, smooth top with rubber spatula, and gently tap pan on counter to release air bubbles.

4. Bake cake until skewer inserted in center comes out clean, 55 minutes to 1 hour 5 minutes. If cake has prongs around rim for elevating cake, invert pan on them. If not, invert pan over neck of bottle or funnel so that air can circulate all around it. Let cake cool completely, about 2 hours.

5. Run knife around edge of cake to loosen, then gently tap pan upside down on counter to release cake. Peel off parchment, turn cake right side up onto serving platter, and serve. (Cake can be stored at room temperature for up to 2 days or refrigerated for up to 4 days.)

MOCHA-NUT CHIFFON CAKE

Substitute ¾ cup brewed espresso or strong coffee for water and omit almond extract. Add ½ cup finely chopped toasted walnuts and 1 ounce unsweetened grated chocolate to batter before folding in whites.

Combine ¼ cup cocoa and 2 tablespoons packed dark brown sugar in a small bowl, then stir in 3 tablespoons boiling water and mix until smooth. Follow recipe as directed, dividing batter equally into 2 separate bowls at end of step 2. Mix scant ½ cup batter from one bowl into cocoa mixture, then partially fold mixture back into same bowl (so that you have one bowl of white batter and one of chocolate batter). Sift 3 tablespoons flour over chocolate batter and continue to fold until just mixed. Pour half the white and then half the chocolate batter into the pan; repeat. Do not tap pan on counter before baking. Bake as directed.

DATE-SPICE CHIFFON CAKE

Omit almond extract. Substitute 1½ cups packed dark brown sugar for granulated sugar and add 4½ ounces chopped pitted dates, 2 teaspoons ground cinnamon, ½ teaspoon ground nutmeg, and ¼ teaspoon ground cloves to dry ingredients in step 1. Process mixture in food processor until dates are cut into ⅛-inch bits and mixture is thoroughly combined. Transfer to bowl and whisk in eggs, egg yolks, water, oil, and vanilla and proceed with recipe as directed.

LEMON OR LEMON-COCONUT CHIFFON CAKE

Substitute ½ teaspoon baking soda for baking powder, decrease water to ⅔ cup and vanilla to 1 teaspoon, and omit almond extract. Add 3 tablespoons grated lemon zest (3 lemons) plus 2 tablespoons juice along with vanilla in step 1. (For Lemon-Coconut Chiffon Cake, also add ¾ cup sweetened shredded coconut, coarsely chopped, to batter before folding in whites.)

ORANGE OR CRANBERRY-ORANGE CHIFFON CAKE

Substitute 2 tablespoons grated orange zest plus ¾ cup orange juice (2 oranges) for water. Decrease vanilla to 1 teaspoon and omit almond extract. (For Cranberry-Orange Chiffon Cake, also add 1 cup minced cranberries and ½ cup finely chopped toasted walnuts to batter before folding in whites.)

BANANA-NUT CHIFFON CAKE

Decrease baking powder to 1¼ teaspoons and add ¼ teaspoon baking soda. Decrease water to ⅔ cup and vanilla to 1 teaspoon and omit almond extract. Fold 3 mashed bananas (1 cup) and ½ cup very finely ground toasted walnuts or pecans into batter before folding in whites in step 2. Increase baking time to 1 hour to 1 hour 10 minutes.

RED VELVET CHIFFON CAKE

Frosted with Fluffy White Icing (page 666) and sprinkled with coconut, this variation is a great one for kids.

Add 1 tablespoon cocoa to dry ingredients in step 1, decrease water to ⅔ cup, and add 2 tablespoons red food coloring with extracts.

YELLOW CUPCAKES WITH CHOCOLATE GANACHE FROSTING

✓ WHY THIS RECIPE WORKS
Many cupcakes are tasteless, dry, and crumbly, while others are greasy and eggy. Still others are cloyingly sweet or rubbery and leaden. We wanted a yellow cupcake so delicious that the cake itself would be savored as much as its rich icing, a grown-up cupcake good enough to satisfy the mothers and fathers at a kid's birthday party. The answer was easier than we could have hoped. We started with a simple ingredient list of all-purpose flour (pastry flour and cake flour produced too fine a crumb), a combination of whole eggs and yolks (fewer whites meant richer flavor), sugar, butter, and sour cream (for tangy richness). After pitting the classic creaming method against the two-stage method (cutting the butter into the dry ingredients, then adding the eggs and liquid), we couldn't tell much difference, but when we used a less methodical approach (throwing everything into the mixer together in no particular order), we had the best cupcakes of the bunch. Why? One possible answer is that egg yolks contain emulsifiers that hold the fat and liquid together even when mixed in such a haphazard fashion. A simple whipped ganache, made of just heavy cream and semisweet chocolate, proved the perfect decadent topping.

YELLOW CUPCAKES WITH CHOCOLATE GANACHE FROSTING
MAKES 12 CUPCAKES

These cupcakes are best eaten the day they are made, but unfrosted extras will keep in an airtight container at room temperature for up to 3 days. To double the recipe, use 3 whole eggs and 2 yolks, and double the remaining ingredients.

CUPCAKES
- 1½ cups (7½ ounces) all-purpose flour
- 1 cup (7 ounces) sugar
- 1½ teaspoons baking powder
- ½ teaspoon salt
- 8 tablespoons unsalted butter, room temperature
- ½ cup sour cream
- 1 large egg plus 2 large yolks, room temperature
- 1½ teaspoons vanilla extract

FROSTING
- 1 cup heavy cream
- 8 ounces semisweet chocolate, chopped

1. **FOR THE CUPCAKES:** Adjust oven rack to middle position and heat oven to 350 degrees. Line 12-cup muffin tin with paper or foil liners.

2. Whisk flour, sugar, baking powder, and salt together in bowl of stand mixer. Fit stand mixer with paddle and beat flour mixture, butter, sour cream, egg, egg yolks, and vanilla together on medium speed until smooth and satiny, about 30 seconds. Scrape down bowl, then mix by hand using rubber spatula until smooth and no flour pockets remain.

3. Using ice cream scoop or large spoon, divide batter evenly among prepared muffin cups. Bake cupcakes until tops are pale gold and toothpick inserted in centers comes out clean, 20 to 24 minutes. Lift each cupcake from tin and transfer to wire rack. Let cupcakes cool completely, about 45 minutes, before frosting.

4. **FOR THE FROSTING:** Place chocolate in medium heatproof bowl. Bring cream to boil in small saucepan. Pour boiling cream over chocolate, and let sit, covered, for 5 minutes. Whisk mixture until smooth, then cover with plastic wrap and refrigerate until cool and slightly firm, 45 minutes to 1 hour.

5. Using stand mixer fitted with whisk, whip cooled chocolate mixture on medium speed until fluffy and mousselike and soft peaks form, about 2 minutes.

6. Spread 2 to 3 generous tablespoons frosting over each cooled cupcake and serve.

ULTIMATE CHOCOLATE CUPCAKES WITH GANACHE FILLING

✔ WHY THIS RECIPE WORKS

A chocolate cupcake Catch-22 befalls bakery and homemade confections alike: if the cupcakes have decent chocolate flavor, their structure is too crumbly for out-of-hand consumption. Conversely, if the cakes balance moisture and tenderness without crumbling, the cake and frosting are barely palatable. We wanted a moist, tender (but not crumbly) cupcake capped with just enough creamy, not-too-sweet frosting. We started by making cupcakes using our favorite chocolate cake recipe. Tasters liked the real chocolate flavor, but their crumbly texture made them impossible to eat without a fork. To strengthen the batter we cut back on both kinds of chocolate, then we found two ways to enhance the chocolate flavor without disrupting the batter's structure: we mixed the cocoa with hot coffee, and we replaced the butter with more neutral-flavored vegetable oil. Still, we wanted more chocolate flavor. Could we enhance the structure of the cupcake so that we could then add back extra chocolate without overtenderizing? Substituting bread flour for all-purpose flour did the trick. Specifically engineered for gluten development, bread flour turned out a cupcake that was markedly less crumble-prone, but not tough. For a final chocolate burst, we spooned a dollop of ganache onto each portion of cupcake batter before baking, which turned into a truffle-like center once baked. A velvety Swiss meringue buttercream, which gets its satiny-smooth texture from whisking the egg whites and sugar in a double boiler, then whipping the mixture with softened butter, was the perfect way to crown these cupcakes.

ULTIMATE CHOCOLATE CUPCAKES WITH GANACHE FILLING

MAKES 12 CUPCAKES

Use a high-quality bittersweet or semisweet chocolate for this recipe. Though we highly recommend the ganache filling, you can omit it for a more traditional cupcake.

FILLING
- 2 ounces bittersweet chocolate, chopped fine
- ¼ cup heavy cream
- 1 tablespoon confectioners' sugar

CUPCAKES
- 3 ounces bittersweet chocolate, chopped fine
- ⅓ cup (1 ounce) Dutch-processed cocoa
- ¾ cup brewed coffee, hot
- ¾ cup (4⅛ ounces) bread flour
- ¾ cup (5¼ ounces) granulated sugar
- ½ teaspoon salt
- ½ teaspoon baking soda
- 6 tablespoons vegetable oil
- 2 large eggs
- 2 teaspoons white vinegar
- 1 teaspoon vanilla extract

- 1 recipe frosting (recipes follow)

1. **FOR THE FILLING:** Microwave chocolate, cream, and sugar in medium bowl until mixture is warm to touch, about 30 seconds. Whisk until smooth, then transfer bowl to refrigerator and let sit until just chilled, no longer than 30 minutes.

2. **FOR THE CUPCAKES:** Adjust oven rack to middle position and heat oven to 350 degrees. Line 12-cup muffin tin with paper or foil liners. Place chocolate and cocoa in medium heatproof bowl. Pour

---

TEST KITCHEN TIP NO. 140 CHOCOLATE MELTDOWN

We prefer the ease of melting chocolate in the microwave, but a double boiler works too. Here are the methods for each one:

MICROWAVE: Chop chocolate (so it melts evenly) and microwave at 50 percent power for 30 seconds to 2 minutes, depending on amount. Stir chocolate and continue heating until melted, stirring once every additional minute. If recipe calls for melting chocolate with butter, do not add butter until chocolate is almost completely melted. (Adding butter earlier will cause it to splatter.)

STOVETOP: Place chopped chocolate in heatproof bowl set over pot of barely simmering water, but be sure bowl is not touching water or chocolate could scorch. Stir occasionally. If recipe calls for melting chocolate with butter, add both to bowl at same time.

---

hot coffee over mixture and let sit, covered, for 5 minutes. Whisk mixture gently until smooth, then transfer to refrigerator to cool completely, about 20 minutes.

3. Whisk flour, sugar, salt, and baking soda together in medium bowl. Whisk oil, eggs, vinegar, and vanilla into cooled chocolate mixture until smooth. Add flour mixture and whisk until smooth.

4. Using ice cream scoop or large spoon, divide batter evenly among prepared muffin cups. Place 1 slightly rounded teaspoon ganache filling on top of each portion of batter. Bake cupcakes until set and just firm to touch, 17 to 19 minutes. Let cupcakes cool in muffin tin on wire rack until cool enough to handle, about 10 minutes. Lift each cupcake from tin, set on wire rack, and let cool completely before frosting, about 1 hour. (Unfrosted cupcakes can be stored at room temperature for up to 1 day.)

5. TO FROST: Spread 2 to 3 tablespoons frosting over each cooled cupcake and serve.

CREAMY CHOCOLATE FROSTING
MAKES ABOUT 2¼ CUPS

The melted chocolate should be cooled to between 85 and 100 degrees before being added to the frosting. If the frosting seems too soft after adding the chocolate, chill it briefly in the refrigerator and then rewhip it until creamy.

- ⅓ cup (2⅓ ounces) granulated sugar
- 2 large egg whites
  Pinch salt
- 12 tablespoons unsalted butter, cut into 12 pieces and softened
- 6 ounces bittersweet chocolate, melted and cooled
- ½ teaspoon vanilla extract

1. Combine sugar, egg whites, and salt in bowl of stand mixer and set bowl over saucepan filled with 1 inch of barely simmering water. Whisking gently but constantly, heat mixture until slightly thickened, foamy, and registers 150 degrees, 2 to 3 minutes.

2. Fit stand mixer with whisk and beat mixture on medium speed until consistency of shaving cream and slightly cooled, 1 to 2 minutes. Add butter, 1 piece at a time, until smooth and creamy. (Frosting may look curdled after half of butter has been added; it will smooth with additional butter.) Once all butter is added, add cooled melted chocolate and vanilla; mix until combined. Increase speed to medium-high and beat until light, fluffy, and thoroughly combined, about 30 seconds, scraping down beater and sides of bowl with rubber spatula as necessary.

TO MAKE AHEAD: Frosting can be made up to 1 day in advance and refrigerated in an airtight container. When ready to frost, warm frosting briefly in microwave until just slightly softened, 5 to 10 seconds. Once warmed, stir until creamy.

CREAMY MALTED MILK FROSTING

Reduce sugar to ¼ cup, substitute milk chocolate for bittersweet chocolate, and add ¼ cup malted milk powder to frosting with vanilla extract in step 2.

CREAMY VANILLA FROSTING

Omit bittersweet chocolate and increase sugar to ½ cup. (If final frosting seems too thick, warm mixer bowl briefly over pan filled with 1 inch of simmering water and beat a second time until creamy).

CREAMY PEANUT BUTTER FROSTING

Omit bittersweet chocolate, increase sugar to ½ cup, and increase salt to ⅛ teaspoon. Add ⅔ cup creamy peanut butter to frosting with vanilla extract in step 2. Garnish cupcakes with ½ cup chopped peanuts.

CREAMY BUTTERSCOTCH FROSTING

Substitute dark brown sugar for granulated sugar and increase salt to ½ teaspoon.

LEMON PUDDING CAKE

✅ WHY THIS RECIPE WORKS
Pudding cakes are basically egg custards, but with two clever improvements. Unlike ordinary egg custards, pudding cakes contain a little flour and some beaten egg whites. During baking the beaten egg whites float to the top, forming a spongy, cakelike cap. Meanwhile, the remainder of the batter settles to the bottom to make a puddinglike layer. We were after a light, puffy pudding cake that was spongy and cakelike on top, with tender pudding underneath. Unfortunately, the recipes we tested were hit or miss: those made with lemon or orange juice came out especially well, while those flavored in other ways tended to have flimsy, fast-dissolving tops and rubbery, dense bottoms. We eventually deduced that it was the acidity of the citrus juices that made the difference. Because the juice lightly clabbered the milk-based batter, causing it to thicken, the frothy upper layer became stiffer and more stable and thus better able to puff. At the same time, the acidic juice undercut the thickening power of the flour, making the custard more tender. To shore up the cake part of those variations made with coffee, chocolate, and vanilla, we tried adding an extra egg white. Not only did it work, but we liked the results so much that we ended up using the extra white in all of the recipes.

LEMON PUDDING CAKE
SERVES 4 TO 6

This pudding cake can be made in any of the following: six ¾-cup custard cups, four 1⅓-cup ramekins or miniature soufflé cups, one 9-inch round cake pan, or one 8-inch square cake pan.

All pudding cakes, regardless of pan size, require the same baking time.

2   tablespoons unsalted butter, softened
½   cup plus 2 tablespoons (4⅓ ounces) sugar
⅛   teaspoon salt
3   large eggs, separated, plus 1 large white, room temperature
3   tablespoons all-purpose flour
1½   teaspoons grated lemon zest plus ¼ cup juice (2 lemons)
1   cup whole milk
     Pinch cream of tartar

1. Adjust oven rack to middle position and heat oven to 325 degrees. Grease pan or baking molds of choice. Lay folded kitchen towel in bottom of roasting pan and set molds or pan inside. Bring kettle of water to boil.

2. Meanwhile, using back of wooden spoon, mash butter, sugar, and salt together in medium bowl until crumbly. Beat in egg yolks, then stir in flour, mixing until smooth. Slowly beat in lemon zest and juice, then stir in milk. Using stand mixer fitted with whisk, whip egg whites and cream of tartar on medium-low speed until foamy, about 1 minute. Increase speed to medium-high and whip until stiff peaks form, 3 to 4 minutes. Gently whisk whites into batter by hand just until no large lumps remain.

3. Immediately ladle (do not pour) batter into pan or baking molds of choice. Set roasting pan on oven rack. Quickly pour enough boiling water into roasting pan to come halfway up sides of pan or molds. Bake cake until center is set and springs back when gently touched, about 25 minutes. Remove roasting pan from oven and let pan or molds continue to sit in water bath for 10 minutes. Serve warm, at room temperature, or chilled.

ORANGE PUDDING CAKE

Reduce lemon juice to 2 tablespoons and add ¼ cup orange juice with lemon juice in step 2. Substitute 1½ teaspoons orange zest for lemon zest.

COFFEE PUDDING CAKE

This cake tastes best when made with very strong coffee. The easiest way to make it strong is to cover ⅓ cup finely ground coffee with ⅔ cup boiling water and let it stand for 5 minutes, then drip through a coffee filter.

Substitute ⅓ cup room-temperature brewed strong coffee and 2 tablespoons coffee-flavored liqueur for lemon juice and zest. Decrease sugar to ½ cup and flour to 2 tablespoons.

CHOCOLATE PUDDING CAKE

Slowly stir ½ cup boiling water into ⅓ cup cocoa. Cool paste slightly, then stir in 1 tablespoon dark rum. Substitute cocoa paste for lemon zest and juice. Decrease flour to 2 tablespoons.

VANILLA-BOURBON PUDDING CAKE
SERVES 6

This delicious version with bourbon butter sauce is rich enough to serve 6 amply. The cake can be made in any of the following: six ¾-cup custard cups, four 1⅓-cup ramekins or miniature soufflé cups, one 9-inch round cake pan, or one 8-inch square cake pan. All pudding cakes, regardless of pan size, require the same baking time. We prefer this version prepared in cups and served warm.

CAKE

2   tablespoons unsalted butter, softened
½   cup plus 2 tablespoons (4⅓ ounces) sugar
⅛   teaspoon salt

3   large eggs, separated, plus 1 large white, room temperature
2   tablespoons all-purpose flour
1   tablespoon vanilla extract
1   tablespoon bourbon
1⅓   cups whole milk
     Pinch cream of tartar

SAUCE

8   tablespoons unsalted butter
⅔   cup sugar
2   tablespoons bourbon
2   tablespoons water
½   teaspoon ground nutmeg
⅛   teaspoon salt
1   large egg, lightly beaten

1. FOR THE CAKE: Adjust oven rack to middle position and heat oven to 325 degrees. Grease pan or baking molds of choice. Lay folded kitchen towel in bottom of roasting pan and set molds or pan inside. Bring kettle of water to boil.

2. Meanwhile, using back of wooden spoon, mash butter, sugar, and salt together in medium bowl until crumbly. Beat in egg yolks, then stir in flour, mixing until smooth. Slowly beat in vanilla and bourbon, then stir in milk. Using stand mixer fitted with whisk, whip egg whites and cream of tartar on medium-low speed until foamy, about 1 minute. Increase speed to medium-high and whip until stiff peaks form, 3 to 4 minutes. Gently whisk whites into batter by hand just until no large lumps remain.

3. Immediately ladle (do not pour) batter into pan or baking molds of choice. Set roasting pan on oven rack. Quickly pour enough boiling water into roasting pan to come halfway up sides of pan or molds. Bake cake until center is set and springs back when gently touched, about 25 minutes. Remove roasting pan from oven and let pan or molds continue to sit in water bath for 10 minutes.

4. FOR THE SAUCE: Meanwhile, cook

butter, sugar, bourbon, water, nutmeg, and salt in small saucepan over medium-low heat stirring occasionally, until bubbly around the edges. Off heat, whisk in egg. Return to medium-low heat and, stirring constantly, bring to boil and cook until thickened, about 1 minute. Spoon sauce over each cake and serve warm, passing remaining sauce separately.

HOT FUDGE PUDDING CAKE

✔ WHY THIS RECIPE WORKS
Those who have eaten hot fudge pudding cake know its charms: unpretentious, moist, brownielike chocolate cake sitting on a pool of thick, chocolate pudding–like sauce, baked together in one dish, as if by magic. But some recipes lack decent chocolate flavor; texture can be a problem, too. Instead of providing enough spoon-coating sauce to accompany the cake, some are dry, with a disproportionate amount of cake, while others are soupy, with a wet, sticky, underdone cake. Pudding cake is made by sprinkling brownie batter with a mixture of sugar and cocoa, then pouring hot water on top, and baking. To bump up the chocolate flavor, we used a combination of Dutch-processed cocoa and semisweet chocolate. We also added instant coffee to the water that is poured over the batter to cut the sweetness of the cake. We baked the cake slow and low to promote a good top crust and a silky sauce. And we found that letting the cake rest for 20 to 30 minutes before eating allowed the sauce to become puddinglike and the cake brownielike.

HOT FUDGE PUDDING CAKE
SERVES 8

If you have cold, brewed coffee on hand, it can be used in place of the instant coffee and water, but to make sure it isn't too strong, use 1 cup of cold coffee mixed with ½ cup of water. Serve the cake warm with vanilla or coffee ice cream.

2   teaspoons instant coffee
1½   cups water
⅔   cup (2 ounces) Dutch-processed cocoa
⅓   cup packed (2⅓ ounces) brown sugar
1   cup (7 ounces) granulated sugar
6   tablespoons unsalted butter
2   ounces semisweet or bittersweet chocolate, chopped
¾   cup (3¾ ounces) all-purpose flour
2   teaspoons baking powder
⅓   cup whole milk
1   tablespoon vanilla extract
¼   teaspoon salt
1   large egg yolk

1. Adjust oven rack to lower-middle position and heat oven to 325 degrees. Grease 8-inch square baking dish. Stir coffee into water and set aside to dissolve. Combine ⅓ cup cocoa, brown sugar, and ⅓ cup granulated sugar in small bowl, breaking up large clumps with fingers; set aside.

2. Melt butter, remaining ⅓ cup cocoa, and chocolate in small heatproof bowl set over saucepan filled with 1 inch of barely simmering water; whisk until smooth and set aside to cool slightly. Whisk flour and baking powder in small bowl to combine; set aside. Whisk remaining ⅔ cup granulated sugar, milk, vanilla, and salt in medium bowl until combined; whisk in egg yolk. Add chocolate mixture and whisk to combine. Add flour mixture and whisk until batter is evenly moistened.

3. Pour batter into prepared baking dish and spread to sides and corners. Sprinkle cocoa-sugar mixture evenly over batter (cocoa mixture should cover entire surface of batter); pour coffee mixture gently over cocoa mixture. Bake cake until puffed and bubbling and just beginning to pull away from sides of baking dish, about 45 minutes. (Do not overbake.) Let cake cool in dish on wire rack for about 25 minutes

before serving. (Cake can be reheated, covered with plastic wrap, in microwave oven.)

INDIVIDUAL HOT FUDGE PUDDING CAKES

Adjust oven rack to lower-middle position and heat oven to 400 degrees. Grease eight 6- to 8-ounce ramekins with vegetable oil spray and set on rimmed baking sheet. Prepare batter as directed, then divide batter evenly among ramekins (about ¼ cup per ramekin) and level with back of spoon. Sprinkle about 2 tablespoons cocoa-sugar mixture over batter in each ramekin, then pour 3 tablespoons coffee mixture over cocoa-sugar mixture in each ramekin. Bake cakes until puffed and bubbling, about 20 minutes. (Do not overbake.) Let cakes cool for about 15 minutes before serving (cakes will fall).

INDIVIDUAL STICKY TOFFEE PUDDING CAKES

✔ WHY THIS RECIPE WORKS
Studded with dates and coated in a sweet toffee sauce, this moist, rich cake is a British favorite that we hoped to translate for the American kitchen. We wanted a cake packed full of date flavor, with a tolerable sweetness level and a moist, tender crumb. We cut down the conventional amount of butter but kept the sauce rich and flavorful—eggs and all-purpose flour gave our sauce body and stability. We maximized the fruit flavor by first soaking the dates, then processing a portion of them with sugar while leaving the remainder coarsely chopped. Brown sugar stood in for traditional, but hard-to-find treacle. A splash of rum and lemon juice cut through the sticky richness of the sauce. And for the cooking method, we placed the batter-filled ramekins in a roasting pan, adding boiling water, and then covered the pan with foil before baking. Poking the cakes with a toothpick allowed the sauce to be thoroughly absorbed.

INDIVIDUAL STICKY TOFFEE PUDDING CAKES

SERVES 8

We place a kitchen towel on the bottom of the roasting pan to stabilize the ramekins. It is important to form a tight seal with the foil to trap the steam inside the roasting pan before baking the cakes.

CAKES

8	ounces pitted dates, cut crosswise into ¼-inch slices (1⅓ cups)
¾	cup warm water
½	teaspoon baking soda
1¼	cups (6¼ ounces) all-purpose flour
½	teaspoon baking powder
½	teaspoon salt
¾	cup packed (5¼ ounces) brown sugar
2	large eggs
4	tablespoons unsalted butter, melted
1½	teaspoons vanilla extract

SAUCE

4	tablespoons unsalted butter
1	cup packed (7 ounces) brown sugar
¼	teaspoon salt
1	cup heavy cream
1	tablespoon rum
½	teaspoon lemon juice

1. FOR THE CAKES: Adjust oven rack to middle position and heat oven to 350 degrees. Grease and flour eight 4-ounce ramekins. Set prepared ramekins in large roasting pan lined with clean kitchen towel. Bring kettle of water to boil.

2. Combine half of dates, water, and baking soda in 2-cup liquid measuring cup (dates should be submerged beneath water) and soak dates for 5 minutes. Meanwhile, whisk flour, baking powder, and salt together in medium bowl.

3. Process remaining dates and brown sugar in food processor until no large date chunks remain and mixture has texture of damp, coarse sand, about 45 seconds, scraping down bowl as needed. Drain soaked dates and add soaking liquid to processor. Add eggs, melted butter, and vanilla and process until smooth, about 15 seconds. Transfer mixture to bowl with dry ingredients and sprinkle drained soaked dates on top.

4. With rubber spatula or wooden spoon, gently fold wet mixture into dry mixture until just combined and date pieces are evenly dispersed. Divide batter evenly among prepared ramekins (should be two-thirds full). Quickly pour enough boiling water into roasting pan to come ¼ inch up sides of molds. Cover pan tightly with aluminum foil, crimping edges to seal. Bake cakes until puffed and surfaces are spongy, firm, and moist to touch, about 40 minutes. Immediately transfer ramekins from water bath to wire rack and let cool for 10 minutes.

5. FOR THE SAUCE: While cakes cool, melt butter in medium saucepan over medium-high heat. Whisk in sugar and salt until smooth. Continue to cook, stirring occasionally, until sugar is dissolved and slightly darkened, 3 to 4 minutes. Add ⅓ cup cream and stir until smooth, about 30 seconds. Slowly pour in remaining ⅔ cup cream and rum, whisking constantly until smooth. Reduce heat to low and simmer until frothy, about 3 minutes. Remove from heat and stir in lemon juice.

6. Using toothpick, poke 25 holes in top of each cake and spoon 1 tablespoon toffee sauce over each cake. Let cakes sit until sauce is absorbed, about 5 minutes. Invert each ramekin onto plate or shallow bowl and remove ramekin. Divide remaining toffee sauce evenly among cakes and serve immediately.

TO MAKE AHEAD: Prepare batter and divide among individual ramekins as directed, then cover and refrigerate, unbaked, for up to 1 day. Bake as directed in step 4. Sauce can be made up to 2 days in advance; microwave on 50 percent power, stirring often, until hot, about 3 minutes.

LARGE STICKY TOFFEE PUDDING CAKE

SERVES 8

Substitute 8-inch square baking dish, buttered and floured, for ramekins. Bake cake until outer 2 inches develop small holes and center is puffed and firm to touch, about 40 minutes. Cool as directed. Using toothpick, poke about 100 holes in cake and glaze with ½ cup sauce. Let cake sit until sauce is absorbed, about 5 minutes. Cut cake into squares and pour remaining toffee sauce over each square before serving.

TRIPLE-CHOCOLATE MOUSSE CAKE

✔ WHY THIS RECIPE WORKS

Triple-chocolate mousse cake is a truly decadent dessert. Most times, though, the texture is exactly the same from one layer to the next and the flavor is so overpoweringly rich it's hard to finish more than a few forkfuls. We aimed to create a triple-decker where each layer is incrementally lighter in texture—and richness—than the one below it. For simplicity's sake, we decided to build the whole dessert, layer by layer, in the same springform pan. For a base layer that had the heft to support the upper two tiers, we chose flourless chocolate cake instead of the typical mousse. Folding egg whites into the batter helped lighten the cake without affecting its structural integrity. For the middle layer, we started with a traditional chocolate mousse, but the texture seemed too heavy when combined with the cake, so we removed the eggs and cut back on the chocolate a bit—this resulted in a lighter, creamier layer. And for the crowning layer, we made an easy white chocolate mousse by folding whipped cream into melted white chocolate, and to prevent the soft mousse from oozing during slicing, we added a little gelatin to the mix.

TRIPLE-CHOCOLATE MOUSSE CAKE
SERVES 12 TO 16

This recipe requires a springform pan with sides that are at least 3 inches high. It is imperative that each layer is made in sequential order. Cool the base completely before topping it with the middle layer. For best results, chill the mixer bowl before whipping the heavy cream. For neater slices, use a cheese wire or dip your knife in hot water before cutting each slice.

BOTTOM LAYER
- 6 tablespoons unsalted butter, cut into 6 pieces
- 7 ounces bittersweet chocolate, chopped fine
- ¾ teaspoon instant espresso powder
- 4 large eggs, separated
- 1½ teaspoons vanilla extract
  Pinch cream of tartar
  Pinch salt
- ⅓ cup packed (2⅓ ounces) light brown sugar

MIDDLE LAYER
- 5 tablespoons hot water
- 2 tablespoons Dutch-processed cocoa
- 7 ounces bittersweet chocolate, chopped fine
- 1½ cups heavy cream, chilled
- 1 tablespoon granulated sugar
- ⅛ teaspoon salt

TOP LAYER
- ¾ teaspoon unflavored gelatin
- 1 tablespoon water
- 6 ounces white chocolate chips
- 1½ cups heavy cream, chilled
  Shaved chocolate (optional)
  Cocoa (optional)

1. FOR THE BOTTOM LAYER: Adjust oven rack to middle position and heat oven to 325 degrees. Grease 9½-inch springform pan. Melt butter, chocolate, and espresso in large heatproof bowl set over saucepan filled with 1 inch of barely simmering water, stirring occasionally until smooth. Remove from heat and let mixture cool slightly, about 5 minutes. Whisk in egg yolks and vanilla; set aside.

2. Using stand mixer fitted with whisk, whip egg whites, cream of tartar, and salt on medium-low speed until foamy, about 1 minute. Add half of sugar and whip until combined, about 15 seconds. Add remaining sugar, increase speed to high, and whip until soft peaks form, about 1 minute longer, scraping down bowl halfway through. Using whisk, fold one-third of beaten egg whites into chocolate mixture by hand to lighten. Using rubber spatula, fold in remaining egg whites until no white streaks remain. Carefully transfer batter to prepared springform pan and smooth top with rubber spatula.

3. Bake cake until risen, firm around edges, and center has just set but is still soft (center of cake will spring back after pressing gently with finger), 13 to 18 minutes. Transfer cake to wire rack and let cool completely, about 1 hour. (Cake will collapse as it cools.) Do not remove cake from pan.

4. FOR THE MIDDLE LAYER: Combine hot water and cocoa in small bowl; set aside. Melt chocolate in large heatproof bowl set over saucepan filled with 1 inch of barely simmering water, stirring occasionally until smooth. Remove from heat and let cool slightly, 2 to 5 minutes.

5. Using stand mixer fitted with whisk, whip cream, sugar, and salt on medium-low speed until foamy, about 1 minute. Increase speed to high and whip until soft peaks form, 1 to 3 minutes.

6. Whisk cocoa mixture into melted chocolate until smooth. Using whisk, fold one-third of whipped cream into chocolate mixture to lighten. Using rubber spatula, fold in remaining whipped cream until no white streaks remain. Spoon mousse into springform pan over cooled cake, smooth top with rubber spatula, and gently tap pan on counter to release air bubbles. Wipe inside edge of pan with damp cloth to remove any drips. Refrigerate cake for at least 15 minutes while preparing top layer.

7. FOR THE TOP LAYER: In small bowl, sprinkle gelatin over water and let sit for at least 5 minutes. Place white chocolate in medium heatproof bowl. Bring ½ cup cream to simmer in small saucepan over medium-high heat. Remove from heat, add gelatin mixture, and stir until fully dissolved. Pour cream mixture over white chocolate and let sit, covered, for 5 minutes. Whisk mixture gently until smooth. Let cool to room temperature, stirring occasionally (mixture will thicken slightly).

SLICING A SOFT CAKE

To create perfectly smooth slices of soft desserts such as Triple-Chocolate Mousse Cake, the best tool is not a knife. It's a cheese wire—the minimal surface area produces less drag for cleaner, neater slices. If you don't have a cheese wire, dental floss will work almost as well.

1. Hold handles of wire and pull wire taut. Using thumbs to apply even pressure, slice down through cake. Wipe wire clean with paper towel.

2. Make second cut, perpendicular to first. Continue to make cuts around circumference.

8. Using stand mixer fitted with whisk, whip remaining 1 cup cream on medium-low speed until foamy, about 1 minute. Increase speed to high and whip until soft peaks form, 1 to 3 minutes. Using whisk, fold one-third of whipped cream into white chocolate mixture to lighten. Using rubber spatula, fold remaining whipped cream into white chocolate mixture until no white streaks remain. Spoon white chocolate mousse into pan over middle layer. Smooth top with rubber spatula. Return cake to refrigerator and chill until set, at least 2½ hours. (Cake can be refrigerated for up to 1 day; leave at room temperature for up to 45 minutes before removing from pan.)

9. TO SERVE: Garnish top of cake with shaved chocolate and/or dust with cocoa, if using. Run thin knife between cake and sides of pan; remove sides of pan. Run cleaned knife along outside of cake to smooth. Hold handles of cheese wire and pull wire taut. Using thumbs to apply even pressure, slice down through the cake. Wipe wire clean with dry towel. Make second cut, perpendicular to first. Continue to make cuts around circumference. Serve.

TIRAMISÙ

✔ WHY THIS RECIPE WORKS

There's a reason restaurant menus (Italian or not) offer tiramisù. Delicate ladyfingers soaked in a spiked coffee mixture layered with a sweet, creamy filling make an irresistible combination. Preparing tiramisù, however, can be labor intensive and the dessert is not without its problems. Some versions are overly rich and the ladyfingers, which should be moist, sometimes turn soggy to the point of mush. We wanted to avoid these issues and find a streamlined approach—one that highlights the luxurious combination of flavors and textures that have made this dessert so popular. Instead of hauling out a double boiler to make the fussy custard-based filling (called

zabaglione), we instead simply whipped egg yolks, sugar, salt, rum (our preferred spirit), and mascarpone together. Salt is not traditional, but we found that it heightened the filling's subtle flavors. And to lighten the filling, we chose whipped cream instead of egg whites. For the coffee soaking mixture, we combined strong brewed coffee and espresso powder (along with more rum). To moisten the ladyfingers so that they were neither too dry nor too saturated, we dropped them one at a time into the spiked coffee mixture and, once they were moistened, rolled them over to moisten the other side for just a couple of seconds. For best flavor and texture, we discovered that it was important to allow the tiramisù to chill in the refrigerator for at least six hours.

TIRAMISÙ
SERVES 10 TO 12

Brandy and even whiskey can stand in for the dark rum. The test kitchen prefers a tiramisù with a pronounced rum flavor; for a less potent rum flavor, reduce the rum added to the coffee mixture in step 1 to 2½ tablespoons. Do not allow the mascarpone to warm to room temperature before using it; it has a tendency to break if allowed to do so. Be certain to use hard, not soft, ladyfingers.

2½	cups strong brewed coffee, room temperature
9	tablespoons dark rum
1½	tablespoons instant espresso powder
6	large egg yolks
⅔	cup sugar
¼	teaspoon salt
1½	pounds mascarpone cheese (3 cups)
¾	cup heavy cream, chilled
14	ounces ladyfingers (42 to 60, depending on size)
3½	tablespoons Dutch-processed cocoa
¼	cup semisweet or bittersweet chocolate, grated (optional)

1. Stir coffee, 5 tablespoons rum, and espresso in wide bowl or baking dish until espresso dissolves; set aside.

2. Using stand mixer fitted with whisk, whip egg yolks on low speed until just combined. Add sugar and salt and whip on medium-high speed until pale yellow, 1½ to 2 minutes, scraping down bowl once or twice. Add remaining 4 tablespoons rum and whip on medium speed until just combined, 20 to 30 seconds; scrape down bowl. Add mascarpone and whip on medium speed until no lumps remain, 30 to 45 seconds, scraping down bowl once or twice. Transfer mixture to large bowl and set aside.

3. In now-empty mixer bowl, whip cream on medium-low speed until foamy, about 1 minute. Increase speed to high and whip until stiff peaks form, 1 to 3 minutes. Using rubber spatula, fold one-third of whipped cream into mascarpone mixture to lighten, then gently fold in remaining whipped cream until no white streaks remain. Set mascarpone mixture aside.

4. Working with one at a time, drop half of ladyfingers into coffee mixture, roll to coat, remove, and transfer to 13 by 9-inch glass or ceramic baking dish. (Do not submerge ladyfingers in coffee mixture; entire process should take no longer than 2 to 3 seconds for each cookie.) Arrange soaked cookies in single layer in baking dish, breaking or trimming ladyfingers as needed to fit neatly into dish.

5. Spread half of mascarpone mixture over ladyfingers with spatula, spreading mixture to sides and into corners of dish, then smooth surface. Place 2 tablespoons cocoa in fine-mesh strainer and dust cocoa over mascarpone.

6. Repeat dipping and arrangement of ladyfingers; spread remaining mascarpone mixture over ladyfingers and dust with remaining 1½ tablespoons cocoa. Wipe edges of dish clean with paper towel. Cover with plastic wrap and refrigerate for at least 6 hours or up to 24 hours. Garnish with grated chocolate, if using; cut into pieces and serve chilled. (Tiramisù can be refrigerated for up to 1 day.)

TIRAMISÙ WITH FRANGELICO AND ORANGE

Amaretto can be substituted for the Frangelico, and brandy and even whiskey can stand in for the dark rum.

Reduce dark rum to 5 tablespoons total, adding 3 tablespoons rum, plus 3 tablespoons Frangelico, to coffee mixture in step 1, and 2 tablespoons rum plus 3 tablespoons Frangelico to whipped egg yolk mixture in step 2. Whip ½ teaspoon grated orange zest with mascarpone in step 2.

TIRAMISÙ WITH SAMBUCA AND LEMON

Omit dark rum. Stir in 2 tablespoons Sambuca with coffee and espresso in step 1. Add 2 tablespoons sambuca to whipped egg yolk mixture in step 2. Whip 1¼ teaspoons minced grated lemon zest with mascarpone in step 2.

TIRAMISÙ WITHOUT RAW EGGS

This recipe involves cooking the yolks in a double boiler, which requires a little more effort and makes for a slightly thicker mascarpone filling, but the results are just as good as with our traditional method. You will need an additional ⅓ cup heavy cream.

In step 2, add ⅓ cup cream to egg yolks after sugar and salt; do not whisk in rum. Set bowl with egg yolks over medium saucepan filled with 1 inch of barely simmering water and cook, constantly scraping along bottom and sides of bowl with heatproof rubber spatula, until mixture coats back of spoon and registers 160 degrees, 4 to 7 minutes. Remove from heat and stir vigorously to cool slightly, then set aside and let cool completely, about 15 minutes. Whisk in remaining 4 tablespoons rum until combined. Using stand mixer fitted with whisk, whip egg yolk mixture and mascarpone together on medium speed until no lumps remain, 30 to 45 seconds. Transfer mixture to large bowl

and set aside. Continue with recipe from step 3, using full amount of cream specified (¾ cup).

NEW YORK–STYLE CHEESECAKE

✔ WHY THIS RECIPE WORKS

The ideal New York cheesecake should be a tall, bronze-skinned, and dense affair. At the core, it should be cool, thick, smooth, satiny, and creamy. The flavor should be pure and minimalist, sweet and tangy, and rich. But many recipes fall short—going wrong in a number of ways—with textures that range from fluffy to rubbery and leaden, and flavors that are starchy or overly citrusy. We wanted to find the secret to perfect New York cheesecake.

After trying a variety of crusts, we settled on the classic graham cracker crust: a simple combination of graham crackers, butter, and sugar. For the filling, cream cheese, boosted by the extra tang of a little sour cream, delivered the best flavor. A little lemon juice and vanilla added just the right sweet, bright accents without calling attention to themselves. A combination of eggs and egg yolks yielded a texture that was dense but not heavy. We found that the New York method worked better for this cheesecake than the typical water bath—baking the cake in a hot oven for 10 minutes then in a low oven for a full hour and a half yielded the satiny texture we were after.

NEW YORK–STYLE CHEESECAKE
SERVES 12 TO 16

For the crust, chocolate wafers can be substituted for graham crackers; you will need about 14 wafers. The flavor and texture of the cheesecake is best if the cake is allowed to sit at room temperature for 30 minutes before serving. When cutting the cake, have a pitcher of hot tap water nearby; dipping the blade of the knife into the water and wiping it clean with a kitchen towel after each cut helps make neat slices. Serve with Fresh Strawberry Topping (page 702) if desired.

CRUST

8	whole graham crackers, broken into rough pieces
1	tablespoon sugar
5	tablespoons unsalted butter, melted

FILLING

2½	pounds cream cheese, cut into 1-inch chunks and softened
1½	cups (10½ ounces) sugar
⅛	teaspoon salt
⅓	cup sour cream
2	teaspoons lemon juice
2	teaspoons vanilla extract
6	large eggs plus 2 large yolks
1	tablespoon unsalted butter, melted

1. FOR THE CRUST: Adjust oven rack to lower-middle position and heat oven to 325 degrees. Process graham cracker pieces in food processor to fine crumbs, about 30 seconds. Combine graham cracker crumbs and sugar in medium bowl, add melted butter, and toss with fork until evenly moistened. Empty crumbs into 9-inch springform pan and, using bottom of ramekin or dry measuring cup, press crumbs firmly and evenly into pan bottom, keeping sides as clean as possible. Bake crust until fragrant and beginning to brown around edges, about 13 minutes. Let crust cool in pan on wire rack while making filling.

2. FOR THE FILLING: Increase oven temperature to 500 degrees. Using stand mixer fitted with paddle, beat cream cheese on medium-low speed until broken up and slightly softened, about 1 minute. Scrape down bowl. Add ¾ cup sugar and salt and beat on medium-low speed until combined, about 1 minute. Scrape down bowl, then beat in remaining ¾ cup sugar until combined, about 1 minute. Scrape down bowl, add sour cream, lemon juice, and vanilla, and beat on low speed until combined, about 1 minute. Scrape down bowl, add egg yolks, and beat on medium-low speed until thoroughly combined, about

1 minute. Scrape down bowl, add whole eggs, 2 at a time, beating until thoroughly combined, about 1 minute, and scraping bowl between additions.

3. Being careful not to disturb baked crust, brush inside of pan with melted butter and set pan on rimmed baking sheet to catch any spills in case pan leaks. Pour filling into cooled crust and bake 10 minutes; without opening oven door, reduce temperature to 200 degrees and continue to bake until cheesecake registers about 150 degrees, about 1½ hours. Let cake cool on wire rack for 5 minutes, then run paring knife around cake to loosen from pan. Let cake continue to cool until barely warm, 2½ to 3 hours. Wrap tightly in plastic wrap and refrigerate until cold, at least 3 hours. (Cake can be refrigerated for up to 4 days.)

4. To unmold cheesecake, wrap hot kitchen towel around pan and let stand for 1 minute. Remove sides of pan. Slide thin metal spatula between crust and pan bottom to loosen, then slide cake onto serving platter. Let cheesecake sit at room temperature for about 30 minutes before serving. (Cheesecake can be made up to 3 days in advance; however, crust will begin to lose its crispness after only 1 day.)

FRESH STRAWBERRY TOPPING
MAKES ABOUT 1½ QUARTS

This accompaniment to cheesecake is best served the same day it is made.

2   pounds strawberries, hulled and sliced lengthwise ¼ to ⅛ inch thick (3 cups)
½   cup (3½ ounces) sugar
    Pinch salt
1   cup strawberry jam
2   tablespoons lemon juice

1. Toss berries, sugar, and salt in medium bowl and let sit until berries have released juice and sugar has dissolved, about 30 minutes, tossing occasionally to combine.

2. Process jam in food processor until smooth, about 8 seconds, then transfer to small saucepan. Bring jam to simmer over medium-high heat and simmer, stirring frequently, until dark and no longer frothy, about 3 minutes. Stir in lemon juice, then pour warm liquid over strawberries and stir to combine. Let cool, then cover with plastic wrap and refrigerate until cold, at least 2 hours or up to 12 hours.

LEMON CHEESECAKE

✔ WHY THIS RECIPE WORKS
We love cheesecake it in its unadulterated form, but sometimes the fresh flavor of citrus can take cheesecake to a refreshing new level. We aimed to develop a creamy cheesecake with a bracing but not overpowering lemon flavor. Graham crackers, our usual cookie for cheesecake crusts, were too overpowering for the filling's lemon flavor. Instead, we turned to biscuit-type cookies, such as animal crackers, for a mild-tasting crust that allowed the lemon flavor of the cheesecake to shine. For maximum lemon flavor, we ground lemon zest with a portion of the sugar, a step that released its flavorful oils. Grinding the zest also improved the filling's texture (minced lemon zest baked up into fibrous bits in the cake). Heavy cream, in addition to cream cheese, provided richness, and vanilla rounded out the flavors. For ultimate creaminess, we baked the cake in a water bath. And finally, for an additional layer of bright lemon flavor, we topped off the cake with lemon curd.

LEMON CHEESECAKE
SERVES 12 TO 16

When cutting the cake, have a pitcher of hot tap water nearby; dipping the blade of the knife into the water and wiping it clean with a kitchen towel after each cut helps make neat slices.

CRUST
5   ounces Nabisco Barnum's Animals Crackers or Social Tea Biscuits
3   tablespoons sugar
4   tablespoons unsalted butter, melted

FILLING
1¼ cups (8¾ ounces) sugar
1   tablespoon grated lemon zest plus ¼ cup juice (2 lemons)
1½ pounds cream cheese, cut into 1-inch chunks, room temperature
4   large eggs, room temperature
2   teaspoons vanilla extract
¼   teaspoon salt
½   cup heavy cream
1   tablespoon unsalted butter, melted

LEMON CURD
⅓   cup lemon juice (2 lemons)
2   large eggs plus 1 large yolk
½   cup (3½ ounces) sugar
2   tablespoons unsalted butter, cut into ½-inch pieces and chilled
1   tablespoon heavy cream
¼   teaspoon vanilla extract
    Pinch salt

1. FOR THE CRUST: Adjust oven rack to lower-middle position and heat oven to 325 degrees. Process cookies in food processor to fine crumbs, about 30 seconds (you should have about 1 cup). Add sugar and pulse 2 or 3 times to incorporate. Add melted butter in slow, steady stream while pulsing; pulse until mixture is evenly moistened and resembles wet sand, about 10 pulses. Empty crumbs into 9-inch springform pan and, using bottom of ramekin or dry measuring cup, press crumbs firmly and evenly into pan bottom, keeping sides as clean as possible. Bake crust until fragrant and golden brown, 15 to 18 minutes. Let cool on wire rack to room temperature, about 30 minutes. When cool, wrap outside of pan with two

18-inch square pieces heavy-duty aluminum foil and set springform pan in roasting pan. Bring kettle of water to boil.

2. **FOR THE FILLING:** While crust is cooling, process ¼ cup sugar and lemon zest in food processor until sugar is yellow and zest is broken down, about 15 seconds, scraping down bowl as needed. Transfer lemon-sugar mixture to small bowl and stir in remaining 1 cup sugar.

3. Using stand mixer fitted with paddle, beat cream cheese on low speed until broken up and slightly softened, about 5 seconds. With mixer running, add lemon-sugar mixture in slow, steady stream; increase speed to medium and continue to beat until mixture is creamy and smooth, about 3 minutes, scraping down bowl as needed. Reduce speed to medium-low and beat in eggs, 2 at a time, until incorporated, about 30 seconds, scraping down bowl well after each addition. Add lemon juice, vanilla, and salt and mix until just incorporated, about 5 seconds. Add heavy cream and mix until just incorporated, about 5 seconds longer. Give filling final stir by hand.

4. Being careful not to disturb baked crust, brush inside of pan with melted butter. Pour filling into prepared pan and smooth top with rubber spatula. Set roasting pan on oven rack and pour enough boiling water into roasting pan to come halfway up sides of pan. Bake cake until center jiggles slightly, sides just start to puff, surface is no longer shiny, and cake registers 150 degrees, 55 minutes to 1 hour. Turn off oven and prop open oven door with potholder or wooden spoon handle; allow cake to cool in water bath in oven for 1 hour. Transfer pan to wire rack. Remove foil, then run paring knife around cake and let cake cool completely on wire rack, about 2 hours.

5. **FOR THE LEMON CURD:** While cheesecake bakes, heat lemon juice in small saucepan over medium heat until hot but not boiling. Whisk eggs and egg yolk together in medium bowl, then gradually whisk in sugar. Whisking constantly, slowly pour hot lemon juice into eggs, then return mixture to saucepan and cook over medium heat, stirring constantly with wooden spoon, until mixture is thick enough to cling to spoon and registers 170 degrees, about 3 minutes. Immediately remove pan from heat and stir in cold butter until incorporated. Stir in cream, vanilla, and salt, then pour curd through fine-mesh strainer into small bowl. Place plastic wrap directly on surface of curd and refrigerate until needed.

6. When cheesecake is cool, scrape lemon curd onto cheesecake still in springform pan. Using offset spatula, spread curd evenly over top of cheesecake. Cover tightly with plastic and refrigerate for at least 4 hours or up to 1 day. To unmold cheesecake, wrap hot kitchen towel around pan and let stand for 1 minute. Remove sides of pan. Slide thin metal spatula between crust and pan bottom to loosen, then slide cake onto serving platter and serve. (Cake can be made up to 3 days in advance; however, the crust will begin to lose its crispness after only 1 day.)

GOAT CHEESE AND LEMON CHEESECAKE WITH HAZELNUT CRUST

The goat cheese gives this cheesecake a distinctive tang and a slightly savory edge. Use a mild-flavored goat cheese.

For crust, process generous ⅓ cup hazelnuts, toasted, skinned, and cooled, in food processor with sugar until finely ground and mixture resembles coarse cornmeal, about 30 seconds. Add cookies and process until mixture is finely and evenly ground, about 30 seconds. Reduce melted butter to 3 tablespoons. For filling, reduce cream cheese to 1 pound and beat 8 ounces room-temperature goat cheese with cream cheese in step 3. Omit salt.

TRIPLE CITRUS CHEESECAKE

For filling, reduce lemon zest to 1 teaspoon and lemon juice to 1 tablespoon. Process 1 teaspoon grated lime zest and 1 teaspoon grated orange zest with lemon zest in step 2. Add 1 tablespoon lime juice and 2 tablespoons orange juice to mixer with lemon juice in step 3. For curd, reduce lemon juice to 2 tablespoons and heat 2 tablespoons lime juice, 4 teaspoons orange juice, and 2 teaspoons grated orange zest with lemon juice in step 5. Omit vanilla.

SPICED PUMPKIN CHEESECAKE

✓ WHY THIS RECIPE WORKS

Those who suffer from pumpkin pie ennui embrace pumpkin cheesecake as "a nice change," but the expectations are low. Undoubtedly, pumpkin cheesecake can be good in its own right, though it rarely is. Textures run the gamut from dry and dense to wet, soft, and mousselike. Flavors veer from far too cheesy and tangy to pungently over-spiced to totally bland. We wanted a creamy, velvety smooth pumpkin cheesecake that tasted of sweet, earthy pumpkin as well as tangy cream cheese; that struck a harmonious spicy chord; and, of course, that had a crisp, buttery, cookie-crumb crust. For a cookie crust that complemented the earthy, warm flavors of pumpkin, we spiced up a graham cracker crust with ginger, cinnamon, and cloves. For a smooth and creamy texture, we blotted canned pumpkin puree with paper towels to remove excess moisture—this solved the sogginess issue. For dairy, we liked heavy cream, not sour cream, for added richness. We also preferred white sugar to brown, which tended to overpower the pumpkin flavor. Whole eggs, vanilla, salt, lemon juice, and a moderate blend of spices rounded out our cake. And for a smooth, velvety texture, we baked the cheesecake in a water bath in a moderate oven.

SPICED PUMPKIN CHEESECAKE
SERVES 12 TO 16

Make sure to buy unsweetened canned pumpkin, not pumpkin pie filling, which is preseasoned and sweetened. This cheesecake is good on its own, but the Brown Sugar and Bourbon Whipped Cream (page 800) is a great addition. When cutting the cake, have a pitcher of hot tap water nearby; dipping the blade of the knife into the water and wiping it clean with a kitchen towel after each cut helps make neat slices.

CRUST
- 9   whole graham crackers, broken into rough pieces
- 3   tablespoons sugar
- ½   teaspoon ground ginger
- ½   teaspoon ground cinnamon
- ¼   teaspoon ground cloves
- 6   tablespoons unsalted butter, melted

FILLING
- 1⅓   cups (10⅓ ounces) sugar
- 1   teaspoon ground cinnamon
- ½   teaspoon ground ginger
- ¼   teaspoon ground nutmeg
- ¼   teaspoon ground cloves
- ¼   teaspoon allspice
- ½   teaspoon salt
- 1   (15-ounce) can pumpkin
- 1½   pounds cream cheese, cut into 1-inch chunks and softened
- 1   tablespoon vanilla extract
- 1   tablespoon lemon juice
- 5   large eggs, room temperature
- 1   cup heavy cream
- 1   tablespoon unsalted butter, melted

1. FOR THE CRUST: Adjust oven rack to lower-middle position and heat oven to 325 degrees. Pulse crackers, sugar, ginger, cinnamon, and cloves in food processor until crackers are finely ground, about 15 pulses. Transfer crumbs to medium bowl, drizzle with melted butter, and mix with rubber spatula until evenly moistened. Empty crumbs into 9-inch springform pan and, using bottom of ramekin or dry measuring cup, press crumbs firmly and evenly into pan bottom, keeping sides as clean as possible. Bake crust until fragrant and browned around edges, about 15 minutes. Let crust cool completely on wire rack, about 30 minutes. When cool, wrap outside of pan with two 18-inch square pieces heavy-duty aluminum foil and set springform pan in roasting pan. Bring kettle of water to boil.

2. FOR THE FILLING: Whisk sugar, cinnamon, ginger, nutmeg, cloves, allspice, and salt in small bowl; set aside. Line baking sheet with triple layer of paper towels. Spread pumpkin on paper towels in roughly even layer and pat puree with several layers of paper towels to wick away moisture.

3. Using stand mixer fitted with paddle, beat cream cheese on medium speed until broken up and slightly softened, about 1 minute. Scrape down bowl, then beat in sugar mixture in 3 additions on medium-low speed until combined, about 1 minute, scraping down bowl after each addition. Add pumpkin, vanilla, and lemon juice and beat on medium speed until combined, about 45 seconds; scrape down bowl. Reduce speed to medium-low, add eggs, 1 at a time, and beat until incorporated, about 1 minute. Reduce speed to low, add heavy cream, and beat until combined, about 45 seconds. Give filling final stir by hand.

4. Being careful not to disturb baked crust, brush inside of pan with melted butter. Pour filling into prepared pan and smooth top with rubber spatula. Set roasting pan on oven rack and pour enough boiling water into roasting pan to come about halfway up sides of springform pan. Bake cake until center is slightly wobbly when pan is shaken and cake registers 150 degrees, about 1½ hours. Set roasting pan on wire rack then run paring knife around cake. Let cake cool in roasting pan until water is just warm, about 45 minutes. Remove springform pan from water bath, discard foil, and set on wire rack; continue to let cool until barely warm, about 3 hours. Wrap with plastic wrap and refrigerate until chilled, at least 4 hours.

5. To unmold cheesecake, wrap hot kitchen towel around pan and let stand for 1 minute. Remove sides of pan. Slide thin metal spatula between crust and pan bottom to loosen, then slide cake onto serving platter. Let cheesecake sit at room temperature for about 30 minutes before serving. (Cake can be made up to 3 days in advance; however, the crust will begin to lose its crispness after only 1 day.)

PUMPKIN-BOURBON CHEESECAKE WITH GRAHAM-PECAN CRUST

Reducing graham crackers to 5 whole crackers, process ½ cup chopped pecans with crackers and reduce butter to 4 tablespoons. In filling, omit lemon juice, reduce vanilla extract to 1 teaspoon, and add ¼ cup bourbon along with heavy cream.

JELLY ROLL CAKE

✓ WHY THIS RECIPE WORKS
Though just a basic sponge cake that is filled, rolled, and dusted with powdered sugar, a jelly roll cake becomes complicated when it resists assuming its characteristic shape, cracks, or becomes soggy and squat. But when done right, a perfect jelly roll cake is an impressive looking, surefire crowd pleaser. We wanted a simple version that avoided all these problems and was reliably uncomplicated to make. We settled quickly on marrying a foolproof sponge cake recipe with our seedless jam of choice. The real key—and where we focused our attention—was in the assembly. Baking the cake until it was just barely done was critical; otherwise it cracked when rolled. For the neatest-looking spiral we rolled the just-baked cake up around a clean kitchen towel into a snug log and let it cool. After unrolling the cooled cake, we spread it with a thin layer of

I. Starting from short side, roll cake—towel and all—into jelly roll shape. Cool for 10 minutes.

2. Unroll cooled cake. Using offset spatula, spread jam over surface of cake, leaving ½-inch border around edges. Sprinkle half of raspberries over cake, if using.

3. Reroll cake gently but snugly around filling, carefully peeling off towel as you roll. Dust top of cake with confectioners' sugar.

4. Trim thin slices from both ends and then cut cake into individual slices, using electric or serrated knife. Garnish with raspberries, if using.

jam using an offset spatula, then rerolled it, this time gently pulling the towel away from the cake. Cut into thick slices and dusted with powdered sugar, our cake looked picture perfect and tasted every bit as good as it looked.

FOOLPROOF JELLY ROLL CAKE
SERVES 8 TO 10

Any flavor of seedless jam will work here; for an added treat, sprinkle 2 cups fresh blueberries, raspberries, blackberries, or sliced strawberries over the jam before rolling up the cake.

¾	cup (3¾ ounces) all-purpose flour
1	teaspoon baking powder
¼	teaspoon salt
5	large eggs, room temperature
¾	cup (5¼ ounces) granulated sugar
½	teaspoon vanilla extract
1¼	cups (12 ounces) seedless jam

Confectioners' sugar

1. Adjust oven rack to lower-middle position and heat oven to 350 degrees. Grease 18 by 13-inch rimmed baking sheet, line with parchment paper, grease parchment, then flour sheet. Grease second large sheet of parchment and set aside. Whisk flour, baking powder, and salt together in medium bowl; set aside.

2. Using stand mixer fitted with whisk, whip eggs on medium-high speed and gradually add granulated sugar and then vanilla, about 1 minute. Continue to whip mixture until very thick and voluminous, 4 to 8 minutes. Sift flour mixture over egg mixture and fold in with rubber spatula until just incorporated.

3. Scrape batter into prepared baking sheet and spread out to even layer. Bake cake until it feels firm and springs back when touched, 12 to 17 minutes, rotating baking sheet halfway through baking. Lay clean kitchen towel on work surface.

4. Immediately run knife around edge of cake, then flip hot cake out onto towel. Peel off and discard parchment baked on bottom of cake. Starting from 1 short end of cake, roll cake and towel snugly into log and let cool, seam side down, for 15 minutes.

5. Gently unroll cake. Spread jam over cake, leaving ½-inch border at edges. Reroll cake gently but snugly around jam, leaving towel behind as you roll. Trim ends of cake, transfer cake to serving platter, and let cake cool completely, about 30 minutes. Dust with confectioners' sugar before serving.

CHOCOLATE ROULADE

✔ WHY THIS RECIPE WORKS

A spiral of chocolate sponge cake rolled inward around a creamy filling is an eye-catching centerpiece. Roulades depend on light, airy sponge cake that is thin, even, and "rollable," but even though sponge cake isn't typically rich, we still wanted our roulade to pack serious chocolate flavor and remain moist and tender. We found the number of eggs was key. Too few and the cake was not supple. Too many and we got either a wet chocolate sponge or dry chocolate matting. Five eggs provided the proper support, lift to help the cake rise, and flexibility needed to roll it. We found that rolling the cake up while it was warm with a clean kitchen towel inside, cooling it briefly, and then unrolling it resulted in a cake that retained its rolled "memory" and was easily filled and rolled again. When it came to the other components, we settled on a tiramisù-like filling made with lightly sweetened mascarpone and some ground espresso. A rich layer of chocolate icing on the exterior was the perfect finish.

CHOCOLATE ROULADE

SERVES 8 TO 10

This cake is filled and rolled like our Foolproof Jelly Roll Cake (page 705), except that it is rolled from the long end to make a narrower, longer roll.

FILLING

½ cup heavy cream

6 tablespoons (1½ ounces) confectioners' sugar

2 teaspoons instant espresso powder or instant coffee

1 pound (2 cups) mascarpone cheese, softened

CAKE AND FROSTING

¾ cup (3¾ ounces) all-purpose flour

¼ cup (¾ ounce) Dutch-processed cocoa

1 teaspoon baking powder

¼ teaspoon salt

5 large eggs, room temperature

¾ cup (5¼ ounces) granulated sugar

½ teaspoon vanilla extract

1 recipe Rich Chocolate Cream Frosting (page 663)

1. FOR THE FILLING: Bring cream to simmer in small saucepan over high heat. Off heat, stir in confectioners' sugar and espresso and let cool slightly. Gently whisk cooled cream mixture into softened mascarpone until combined. Cover with plastic wrap and refrigerate until ready to use.

2. FOR THE CAKE: Adjust oven rack to lower-middle position and heat oven to 350 degrees. Grease 18 by 13-inch rimmed baking sheet, line with parchment paper, grease parchment, then flour pan. Whisk flour, cocoa, baking powder, and salt together in medium bowl; set aside.

3. Using stand mixer fitted with whisk, whip eggs on medium-high speed and gradually add sugar, about 1 minute. Continue to whip mixture until very thick and voluminous, 4 to 8 minutes. Whip in vanilla. Sift flour mixture over egg mixture and fold with rubber spatula until just incorporated.

4. Scrape batter into prepared baking sheet and spread out to even layer. Bake cake until it feels firm and springs back when touched, 12 to 17 minutes, rotating baking sheet halfway through baking. Lay clean kitchen towel on work surface.

5. Immediately run knife around edge of cake, then flip hot cake out onto towel. Peel off and discard parchment. Starting from 1 long end of cake, roll cake and towel snugly into log and let cool, seam side down, for 15 minutes.

6. Using stand mixer fitted with paddle, beat filling on medium-high speed until stiff, 10 to 30 seconds. Gently unroll cake. Spread filling over cake, leaving ½-inch border at edges. Reroll cake gently but snugly around filling, leaving towel behind as you roll. Trim ends of cake on diagonal.

7. Line edges of cake platter with 4 strips of parchment paper to keep platter clean. Place cake roll on prepared platter. Frost cake evenly with frosting and if desired, drag fork through frosting before it sets to make wood-grain striations. Carefully pull out pieces of parchment from beneath cake before serving. (Cake can be covered lightly with plastic wrap and refrigerated for up to 1 day. Let sit at room temperature for 30 minutes before serving.)

ASSEMBLING CHOCOLATE ROULADE

1. Starting with long side, gently roll cake—towel and all—into jelly roll shape. Cool for 15 minutes.

2. Spread chilled filling evenly over unrolled cake, almost to edges, and reroll cake gently but snugly around filling, peeling off towel as you roll.

3. Trim both uneven ends of roulade on diagonal.

4. Spread frosting over roulade. If desired, drag fork through icing before it sets to make wood-grain striations.

CHAPTER 19 Pies and Tarts

FOOLPROOF PIE DOUGH

✔ WHY THIS RECIPE WORKS

Pie dough can go wrong so easily: dry dough that is too crumbly to roll out; a flaky but leathery crust; or a tender crust without flakes. We wanted a recipe for pie dough that would roll out easily every time and produce a tender, flaky crust. A combination of butter and shortening provided the best balance of flavor and tenderness, and the food processor was the best tool to cut the fat into the flour. To ensure same-size pieces of butter each time, we processed just a portion of the flour with the fat until we had a unified paste. Then we added the reserved flour and pulsed until it was just evenly distributed. In order to roll easily, dough needs a generous amount of water, but more water makes crusts tough. We found the answer in the liquor cabinet: vodka. While gluten (the protein that makes crust tough) forms readily in water, it doesn't form in ethanol, and vodka is 60 percent water and 40 percent ethanol. Adding ¼ cup of vodka produced a moist, easy-to-roll dough that stayed tender. (The alcohol vaporizes in the oven, so you won't taste it in the baked crust.)

FOOLPROOF DOUBLE-CRUST PIE DOUGH

MAKES ENOUGH FOR ONE 9-INCH PIE

Vodka is essential to the tender texture of this crust and imparts no flavor—do not substitute water. This dough is moister than most standard pie doughs and will require lots of flour to roll out (up to ¼ cup). A food processor is essential to making this dough—it cannot be made by hand.

2½	cups (12½ ounces) all-purpose flour
2	tablespoons sugar
1	teaspoon salt
12	tablespoons unsalted butter, cut into ¼-inch pieces and chilled
8	tablespoons vegetable shortening, cut into 4 pieces and chilled
¼	cup vodka, chilled
¼	cup ice water

1. Process 1½ cups flour, sugar, and salt together in food processor until combined, about 5 seconds. Scatter butter and shortening over top and continue to process until incorporated and mixture begins to form uneven clumps with no remaining floury bits, about 15 seconds.

2. Scrape down bowl and redistribute dough evenly around processor blade. Sprinkle remaining 1 cup flour over dough and pulse until mixture has broken up into pieces and is evenly distributed around bowl, 4 to 6 pulses.

3. Transfer mixture to large bowl. Sprinkle vodka and ice water over mixture. Stir and press dough together, using stiff rubber spatula, until dough sticks together.

4. Divide dough into 2 even pieces. Turn each piece of dough onto sheet of plastic wrap and flatten each into 4-inch disk. Wrap each piece tightly in plastic and refrigerate for 1 hour. Before rolling dough out, let it sit on counter to soften slightly, about 10 minutes. (Dough can be wrapped tightly in plastic and refrigerated for up to 2 days or frozen for up to 1 month. If frozen, let dough thaw completely on counter before rolling it out.)

FOOLPROOF SINGLE-CRUST PIE DOUGH

MAKES ENOUGH FOR ONE 9-INCH PIE

Vodka is essential to the tender texture of this crust and imparts no flavor—do not substitute water. This dough is moister than most standard pie doughs and will require lots of flour to roll out (up to ¼ cup). For more information on creating a decorative edge, see page 710.

1¼	cups (6¼ ounces) all-purpose flour
1	tablespoon sugar
½	teaspoon salt
6	tablespoons unsalted butter, cut into ¼-inch pieces and chilled
4	tablespoons vegetable shortening, cut into 2 pieces and chilled
2	tablespoons vodka, chilled
2	tablespoons ice water

1. Process ¾ cup flour, sugar, and salt together in food processor until combined, about 5 seconds. Scatter butter and shortening over top and continue to process until incorporated and mixture begins to form uneven clumps with no remaining floury bits, about 10 seconds.

2. Scrape down bowl and redistribute dough evenly around processor blade. Sprinkle remaining ½ cup flour over dough and pulse until mixture has broken up into pieces and is evenly distributed around bowl, 4 to 6 pulses.

3. Transfer mixture to medium bowl. Sprinkle vodka and ice water over mixture. Stir and press dough together, using stiff rubber spatula, until dough sticks together.

4. Turn dough onto sheet of plastic wrap and flatten into 4-inch disk. Wrap tightly in plastic and refrigerate for 1 hour. Before rolling dough out, let it sit on counter to soften slightly, about 10 minutes. (Dough can be wrapped tightly in plastic and refrigerated for up to 2 days or frozen for up to 1 month. If frozen, let dough thaw completely on counter before rolling it out.)

5. Adjust oven rack to middle position and heat oven to 425 degrees. Roll dough into 12-inch circle on floured counter. Loosely roll dough around rolling pin and

---

TEST KITCHEN TIP NO. 141 ROLL IT RIGHT

Keeping the dough as evenly round as possible when rolling makes fitting it into a pie plate easy. The dough should be in the shape of a flat disk before you start to roll it, and the counter should be lightly floured. Every few times you roll the dough, rotate it by a quarter turn and lightly flour the counter to prevent it from sticking. Keep checking the dough as you roll it: If it starts becoming lopsided, use your hands or a bench scraper to reshape the dough.

1. After rolling out dough, loosely roll it around rolling pin, then gently unroll it evenly onto pie plate.

2. Lift up edges of dough and ease it down into lower creases of pan. Press lightly to adhere dough to sides of pan.

gently unroll it onto 9-inch pie plate, letting excess dough hang over edge. Ease dough into plate by gently lifting edge of dough with one hand while pressing into plate bottom with other hand. Leave any dough that overhangs plate in place. Wrap dough-lined pie plate loosely in plastic and refrigerate until dough is firm, about 30 minutes.

6. Trim overhang to ½ inch beyond lip of pie plate. Tuck overhang under itself; folded edge should be flush with edge of pie plate. Crimp dough evenly around edge of pie using your fingers. Wrap dough-lined pie plate loosely in plastic and refrigerate until dough is fully chilled and firm, about 15 minutes, before using.

7. Line chilled pie shell with double layer of aluminum foil, covering edges to prevent burning, and fill with pie weights.

8A. FOR A PARTIALLY BAKED CRUST: Bake until pie dough looks dry and is pale in color, about 15 minutes. Remove weights and foil and continue to bake crust until light golden brown, 4 to 7 minutes longer. Transfer pie plate to wire rack and remove weights and foil. (Crust must still be warm when filling is added.)

8B. FOR A FULLY BAKED CRUST: Bake until pie dough looks dry and is pale in color, about 15 minutes. Remove weights and foil and continue to bake crust until deep golden brown, 8 to 12 minutes longer. Transfer pie plate to wire rack and let crust cool completely, about 1 hour.

ALL-BUTTER PIE DOUGH

✔ WHY THIS RECIPE WORKS

All-butter pie doughs possess great flavor, but they often fail to be flaky and are notoriously difficult to work with. We wanted an all-butter dough that was easier to mix, handle, and roll, producing a pie crust with all the tenderness and flavor that the description "all-butter" promises. We initially tried to make the dough easier to handle by reducing the amount of butter, but this resulted in a bland flavor and dry texture. Rather than adding back the subtracted butter, we experimented with other forms of fat, including heavy cream, cream cheese, and sour cream. We found that sour cream not only added flavor but, because acid reduces gluten development, it also helped keep the dough tender and flaky. To mix the dough, we used a food processor, which brought the ingredients together quickly and evenly.

ALL-BUTTER DOUBLE-CRUST PIE DOUGH

MAKES ENOUGH FOR ONE 9-INCH PIE

Freezing the butter for 10 to 15 minutes is crucial to the flaky texture of this crust. If preparing the dough in a very warm kitchen, refrigerate all of the ingredients before making the dough. If you don't have a food processor, see Hand Mixing Pie Dough on page 711.

⅓ cup ice water, plus extra as needed
3 tablespoons sour cream
2½ cups (12½ ounces) all-purpose flour
1 tablespoon sugar
1 teaspoon salt
16 tablespoons unsalted butter, cut into ¼-inch pieces and frozen for 10 to 15 minutes

1. Mix ice water and sour cream together in bowl until combined. Process flour, sugar, and salt together in food processor until combined, about 5 seconds. Scatter butter over top and pulse mixture until butter is size of large peas, about 10 pulses.

2. Pour half of sour cream mixture over flour mixture and pulse until incorporated, about 3 pulses. Repeat with remaining sour cream mixture. Pinch dough with your fingers; if dough feels dry and does not hold together, sprinkle 1 to 2 tablespoons more ice water over mixture and pulse until dough forms large clumps and no dry flour remains, 3 to 5 pulses.

3. Divide dough into 2 even pieces. Turn each piece of dough onto sheet of plastic wrap and flatten each into 4-inch disk. Wrap each piece tightly in plastic and refrigerate for 1 hour. Before rolling dough out, let it sit on counter to soften slightly, about 10 minutes. (Dough can be wrapped tightly in plastic and refrigerated for up to 2 days or frozen for up to 1 month. If frozen, let dough thaw completely on counter before rolling it out.)

ALL-BUTTER SINGLE-CRUST PIE DOUGH

MAKES ENOUGH FOR ONE 9-INCH PIE

Freezing the butter for 10 to 15 minutes is crucial to the flaky texture of this crust. If preparing the dough in a very warm kitchen, refrigerate all of the ingredients before making the dough. If you don't have a food processor, see Hand Mixing Pie Dough on page 711.

4   teaspoons sour cream

3–4 tablespoons ice water

1¼ cups (6¼ ounces) all-purpose flour

1½ teaspoons sugar

½ teaspoon salt

8 tablespoons unsalted butter, cut into ¼-inch pieces and frozen for 10 to 15 minutes

1. Mix sour cream and 3 tablespoons ice water together in bowl until combined. Process flour, sugar, and salt together in food processor until combined, about 5 seconds. Scatter butter over top and pulse mixture until butter is size of large peas, about 10 pulses.

2. Pour half of sour cream mixture over flour mixture and pulse until incorporated, about 3 pulses. Repeat with remaining sour cream mixture. Pinch dough with your fingers; if dough feels dry and does not hold together, sprinkle remaining 1 tablespoon ice water over mixture and pulse until dough forms large clumps and no dry flour remains, 3 to 5 pulses.

3. Turn dough onto sheet of plastic wrap and flatten into 4-inch disk. Wrap tightly in plastic and refrigerate for 1 hour. Before rolling dough out, let it sit on counter to soften slightly, about 10 minutes. (Dough can be wrapped tightly in plastic and refrigerated for up to 2 days or frozen for up to 1 month. If frozen, let dough thaw completely on counter before rolling it out.)

4. Adjust oven rack to middle position and heat oven to 375 degrees. Roll dough into 12-inch circle on lightly floured counter. Loosely roll dough around rolling pin and gently unroll it onto 9-inch pie plate, letting excess dough hang over edge. Ease dough into plate by gently lifting edge of dough with one hand while pressing into plate bottom with other hand. Leave any dough that overhangs plate in place.

5. Trim overhang to ½ inch beyond lip of pie plate. Tuck overhang under itself; folded edge should be flush with edge of pie plate. Crimp dough evenly around edge

MAKING A DECORATIVE EDGE ON A SINGLE-CRUST PIE

1. Using scissors, trim all but ½ inch of dough overhanging outer lip of plate.

2. Tuck trimmed overhang under so that it is even with lip of plate.

3. Create fluted edge around crust using index finger of one hand and thumb and index finger of other. Edge of dough should be perpendicular to edge of pie plate.

of pie using your fingers. Wrap dough-lined pie plate loosely in plastic and place in freezer until dough is fully chilled and firm, about 30 minutes, before using.

6. Line chilled pie shell with double layer of aluminum foil, covering edges to prevent burning, and fill with pie weights.

7A. FOR A PARTIALLY BAKED CRUST: Bake until pie dough looks dry and is light in color, 25 to 30 minutes. Transfer pie plate to wire rack and remove weights and foil. (Crust must still be warm when filling is added.)

7B. FOR A FULLY BAKED CRUST: Bake until pie dough looks dry and is light in color, 25 to 30 minutes. Remove weights and foil and continue to bake crust until deep golden brown, 10 to 12 minutes longer. Transfer pie plate to wire rack and let crust cool completely, about 1 hour.

ALL-BUTTER SINGLE-CRUST PIE DOUGH FOR CUSTARD PIES

We like rolling our single-crust dough in fresh graham cracker crumbs because it adds flavor and crisp textural appeal to our custard pies.

Crush 3 whole graham crackers to fine crumbs. (You should have about ½ cup crumbs.) Dust counter with graham

cracker crumbs instead of flour. Continue sprinkling dough with crumbs, both underneath and on top, as it is being rolled out.

CLASSIC PIE DOUGH

✔ WHY THIS RECIPE WORKS

Pie dough often contains vegetable shortening, which makes the dough easier to handle and yields a crust that is remarkably flaky. But vegetable shortening crusts can lack flavor. We set out to create a basic pie dough that combined the right fat and the right proportion of fat to flour to give us a supremely tender and flaky crust that was also incredibly flavorful. When it comes to flavor, nothing beats butter. We experimented with a variety of combinations and ultimately settled on a proportion of 3 parts butter to 2 parts shortening as optimal for both flavor and texture. We also settled on a ratio of 2 parts flour to 1 part fat. We found that the 2:1 ratio produces dough that is easier to work and a baked crust that is more tender and flavorful than any other. While this pie dough can be made by hand, the food processor is faster and easier and does the best job of cutting the fat into the flour.

CLASSIC DOUBLE-CRUST
PIE DOUGH

MAKES ENOUGH FOR ONE 9-INCH PIE

If you don't have a food processor, see Hand Mixing Pie Dough on page 711.

2½ cups (12½ ounces) all-purpose flour
2 tablespoons sugar
1 teaspoon salt
8 tablespoons vegetable shortening, cut into ½-inch pieces and chilled
12 tablespoons unsalted butter, cut into ¼-inch pieces and chilled
6–8 tablespoons ice water

1. Process flour, sugar, and salt together in food processor until combined, about 5 seconds. Scatter shortening over top and process until mixture resembles coarse cornmeal, about 10 seconds. Scatter butter over top and pulse mixture until it resembles coarse crumbs, about 10 pulses.

2. Transfer mixture to large bowl. Sprinkle 6 tablespoons ice water over mixture. Stir and press dough together, using stiff rubber spatula, until dough sticks together. If dough does not come together, stir in remaining ice water, 1 tablespoon at time, until it does.

3. Divide dough into 2 even pieces. Turn each piece of dough onto sheet of plastic wrap and flatten each into 4-inch disk. Wrap each piece tightly in plastic and refrigerate for 1 hour. Before rolling dough out, let it sit on counter to soften slightly, about 10 minutes. (Dough can be wrapped tightly in plastic and refrigerated for up to 2 days or frozen for up to 1 month.

If frozen, let dough thaw completely on counter before rolling it out.)

CLASSIC SINGLE-CRUST
PIE DOUGH

MAKES ENOUGH FOR ONE 9-INCH PIE

If you don't have a food processor, see Hand Mixing Pie Dough on page 711. For more information on fitting pie dough, see page 709.

1¼ cups (6¼ ounces) all-purpose flour
1 tablespoon sugar
½ teaspoon salt
3 tablespoons vegetable shortening, cut into ½-inch pieces and chilled
5 tablespoons unsalted butter, cut into ¼-inch pieces and chilled
4–6 tablespoons ice water

1. Process flour, sugar, and salt together in food processor until combined, about 5 seconds. Scatter shortening over top and process until mixture resembles coarse cornmeal, about 10 seconds. Scatter butter over top and pulse mixture until it resembles coarse crumbs, about 10 pulses.

2. Transfer mixture to medium bowl. Sprinkle 4 tablespoons ice water over mixture. Stir and press dough together, using stiff rubber spatula, until dough sticks together. If dough does not come together, stir in remaining ice water, 1 tablespoon at time, until it does.

3. Turn dough onto sheet of plastic wrap and flatten into 4-inch disk. Wrap tightly in plastic and refrigerate for 1 hour. Before rolling dough out, let it sit on counter to soften slightly, about 10 minutes.

(Dough can be wrapped tightly in plastic and refrigerated for up to 2 days or frozen for up to 1 month. If frozen, let dough thaw completely on counter before rolling it out.)

4. Adjust oven rack to middle position and heat oven to 375 degrees. Roll dough into 12-inch circle on lightly floured counter. Loosely roll dough around rolling pin and gently unroll it onto 9-inch pie plate, letting excess dough hang over edge. Ease dough into plate by gently lifting edge of dough with one hand while pressing into plate bottom with other hand. Leave any dough that overhangs plate in place.

5. Trim overhang to ½ inch beyond lip of pie plate. Tuck overhang under itself; folded edge should be flush with edge of pie plate. Crimp dough evenly around edge of pie using your fingers. Wrap dough-lined pie plate loosely in plastic and place in freezer until dough is fully chilled and firm, about 30 minutes, before using.

6. Line chilled pie shell with double layer of aluminum foil, covering edges to prevent burning, and fill with pie weights.

7A. FOR A PARTIALLY BAKED CRUST: Bake until pie dough looks dry and is light in color, 25 to 30 minutes. Transfer pie plate to wire rack and remove weights and foil. (Crust must still be warm when filling is added.)

7B. FOR A FULLY BAKED CRUST: Bake until pie dough looks dry and is light in color, 25 to 30 minutes. Remove weights and foil and continue to bake crust until deep golden brown, 10 to 12 minutes longer. Transfer pie plate to wire rack and let crust cool completely, about 1 hour.

TEST KITCHEN TIP NO. 142   HAND MIXING PIE DOUGH

While a food processor makes quick work of mixing pie dough, our All-Butter Pie Doughs (page 709–710) and Classic Pie Doughs can be mixed by hand. Here's how:

Freeze butter in its stick form until very firm. Whisk flour, sugar, and salt together in a large bowl. Add chilled shortening, if using, and press it into the flour using a fork. Grate the frozen butter on the large holes of a box grater into the flour mixture, then cut the mixture together, using 2 butter or dinner knives, until the mixture resembles coarse crumbs. Add liquid as directed, stirring with a rubber spatula.

CLASSIC SINGLE-CRUST PIE DOUGH
FOR CUSTARD PIES

We like rolling our single-crust dough in fresh graham cracker crumbs because it adds flavor and crisp textural appeal to our custard pies.

Crush 3 whole graham crackers to fine crumbs. (You should have about ½ cup crumbs.) Dust counter with graham cracker crumbs instead of flour. Continue sprinkling dough with crumbs, both underneath and on top, as it is being rolled out.

GRAHAM CRACKER CRUST

✓ **WHY THIS RECIPE WORKS**

Saving time is always a good idea—just as long as you're not sacrificing quality. But while store-bought graham cracker pie crusts are tempting (all you have to do is fill, chill, then serve), they taste stale and bland. We wanted a fresh-tasting homemade crust that wasn't too sweet, with a crisp texture. Turns out, a classic graham cracker crust couldn't be easier to make: combine crushed crumbs with a little butter and sugar to bind them, then use a measuring cup to pack the crumbs into the pie plate. And producing a perfect graham cracker crust has a lot to do with the type of graham crackers used. After experimenting with the three leading brands, we discovered subtle but distinct differences among them and found that these differences carried over into crumb crusts made with each kind of cracker. In the end, we preferred Keebler Grahams Crackers Original in our crust.

GRAHAM CRACKER CRUST
MAKES ENOUGH FOR ONE 9-INCH PIE

We don't recommend using store-bought graham cracker crumbs here as they can often be stale. Be sure to note whether the crust needs to be warm or cool before filling (the pie recipes will specify) and plan accordingly.

- 8 whole graham crackers, broken into 1-inch pieces
- 5 tablespoons unsalted butter, melted and cooled
- 3 tablespoons sugar

1. Adjust oven rack to middle position and heat oven to 325 degrees. Process graham cracker pieces in food processor

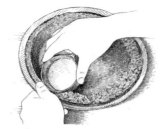

Press crumb mixture into pie plate. Use thumb and measuring cup to square off top edge of crust.

---

to fine, even crumbs, about 30 seconds. Sprinkle melted butter and sugar over crumbs and pulse to incorporate, about 5 pulses.

2. Sprinkle mixture into 9-inch pie plate. Using bottom of measuring cup, press crumbs into even layer on bottom and sides of pie plate. Bake until crust is fragrant and beginning to brown, 13 to 18 minutes; transfer to wire rack. Following particular pie recipe, use crust while it is still warm or let it cool completely.

APPLE PIE

✓ **WHY THIS RECIPE WORKS**

In the test kitchen, we have found that it's difficult to produce an apple pie with a filling that is tart as well as sweet and juicy. We wanted to develop a recipe for classic apple pie—one with the clean, bright taste of apples that could be made year-round, based on apple varieties that are always available in the supermarket. To arrive at the tartness and texture we were after, we had to use two kinds of apples in our pie, Granny Smith and McIntosh. The Grannies could be counted on for tartness and for keeping their shape during cooking; the Macs added flavor, and their otherwise frustrating tendency to become mushy was a virtue, providing a nice, juicy base for the harder Grannies. While many bakers add butter to their apple pie fillings, we

found that it dulled the fresh taste of the apples and so did without it. Lemon juice, however, was essential, counterbalancing the sweetness of the apples. To give the apples the upper hand, we settled on modest amounts of cinnamon, nutmeg, and allspice.

CLASSIC APPLE PIE
SERVES 8

You can use Foolproof, All-Butter, or Classic Double Crust Pie Dough (pages 708–711) for this pie. You can substitute Empire or Cortland apples for the Granny Smith apples. For more information on fitting pie dough, see page 709. The pie is best eaten when cooled to room temperature.

- 1 recipe double-crust pie dough
- ¾ cup (5¼ ounces) plus 1 tablespoon sugar
- 2 tablespoons all-purpose flour
- 1 teaspoon grated lemon zest plus 1 tablespoon juice
- ¼ teaspoon salt
- ¼ teaspoon ground nutmeg
- ¼ teaspoon ground cinnamon
- ⅛ teaspoon ground allspice
- 2 pounds McIntosh apples, peeled, cored, and sliced ¼ inch thick
- 1½ pounds Granny Smith apples, peeled, cored, and sliced ¼ inch thick
- 1 large egg white, lightly beaten

1. Roll 1 disk of dough into 12-inch circle on lightly floured counter. Loosely roll dough around rolling pin and gently unroll it onto 9-inch pie plate, letting excess dough hang over edge. Ease dough into plate by gently lifting edge of dough with 1 hand while pressing into plate bottom with other hand. Leave any dough that overhangs plate in place. Wrap dough-lined pie plate loosely in plastic wrap and refrigerate until dough is firm, about 30 minutes. Roll other disk of dough into 12-inch circle on lightly floured counter, then transfer to parchment paper–lined

baking sheet; cover with plastic and refrigerate for 30 minutes.

2. Adjust oven rack to lowest position, place rimmed baking sheet on rack, and heat oven to 500 degrees.

3. Mix ¾ cup sugar, flour, lemon zest, salt, nutmeg, cinnamon, and allspice together in large bowl. Add lemon juice and apples and toss until combined. Spread apples with their juices into dough-lined pie plate, mounding them slightly in middle. Loosely roll remaining dough round around rolling pin and gently unroll it onto filling. Trim overhang to ½ inch beyond lip of pie plate. Pinch edges of top and bottom crusts firmly together. Tuck overhang under itself; folded edge should be flush with edge of pie plate. Crimp dough evenly around edge of pie using your fingers. Cut four 2-inch slits in top of dough. Brush surface with beaten egg white and sprinkle evenly with remaining 1 tablespoon sugar.

4. Place pie on heated baking sheet, reduce oven temperature to 425 degrees, and bake until crust is light golden brown, about 25 minutes. Reduce oven temperature to 375 degrees, rotate baking sheet, and continue to bake until juices are bubbling and crust is deep golden brown, 30 to 35 minutes longer. Let pie cool on wire rack to room temperature, about 4 hours. Serve.

CLASSIC APPLE PIE WITH CRYSTALLIZED GINGER

Add 3 tablespoons chopped crystallized ginger to apple mixture.

CLASSIC APPLE PIE WITH DRIED FRUIT

Toss 1 cup raisins, dried sweet cherries, or dried cranberries with lemon juice plus 1 tablespoon applejack, brandy, or cognac. Add dried fruit and liquid to apple mixture.

DEEP-DISH APPLE PIE

✔ WHY THIS RECIPE WORKS

The problem with deep-dish apple pie is that the apples are often unevenly cooked and the exuded juice leaves the apples swimming in liquid, producing a bottom crust that is pale and soggy. Then there is the gaping hole left between the shrunken apples and the top crust, making it impossible to slice and serve a neat piece of pie. We wanted our piece of deep-dish pie to be a towering wedge of tender, juicy apples, fully framed by a buttery, flaky crust. Precooking the apples solved the shrinking problem, helped the apples hold their shape, and prevented a flood of juices from collecting in the bottom of the pie

plate, thereby producing a nicely browned bottom crust. Why didn't cooking the apples twice (once on the stovetop and once in the oven) cause them to become insipid and mushy? We learned that when the apples are gently heated, their pectin is converted to a heat-stable form that keeps them from becoming mushy when cooked further in the oven. This allowed us to boost the quantity of apples to 5 pounds. A little brown sugar, salt, lemon, and cinnamon contributed flavor and sweetness.

DEEP-DISH APPLE PIE
SERVES 8

You can use Foolproof, All-Butter, or Classic Double-Crust Pie Dough (pages 708–711) for this pie. You can substitute Empire or Cortland apples for the Granny Smith apples and Jonagold, Fuji, or Braeburn for the Golden Delicious apples.

1	recipe double-crust pie dough
2½	pounds Granny Smith apples, peeled, cored, and sliced ¼ inch thick
2½	pounds Golden Delicious apples, peeled, cored, and sliced ¼ inch thick
½	cup (3½ ounces) plus 1 tablespoon granulated sugar
¼	cup packed (1¾ ounces) light brown sugar

ASSEMBLING DOUBLE-CRUST PIES

1. Unroll dough over filled pie, making sure to center piece of dough on pie plate.

2. Using scissors, trim all but ½ inch of top and bottom crusts overhanging outer lip of plate.

3. To ensure edge stays sealed, tuck and press edges of top and bottom crusts together. Folded edge should be flush with edge of plate.

4. Create fluted edge around pie using index finger of one hand and thumb and index finger of other. Edge of dough should be perpendicular to edge of pie plate. Using sharp knife, cut vents in top crust.

½　teaspoon grated lemon zest plus
　　I tablespoon juice

¼　teaspoon salt

⅛　teaspoon ground cinnamon

I　large egg white, lightly beaten

1. Roll 1 disk of dough into 12-inch circle on lightly floured counter. Loosely roll dough around rolling pin and gently unroll it onto 9-inch pie plate, letting excess dough hang over edge. Ease dough into plate by gently lifting edge of dough with 1 hand while pressing into plate bottom with other hand. Leave any dough that overhangs plate in place. Wrap dough-lined pie plate loosely in plastic wrap and refrigerate until dough is firm, about 30 minutes. Roll other disk of dough into 12-inch circle on lightly floured counter, then transfer to parchment paper–lined baking sheet; cover with plastic and refrigerate for 30 minutes.

2. Toss apples, ½ cup granulated sugar, brown sugar, lemon zest, salt, and cinnamon together in Dutch oven. Cover and cook over medium heat, stirring often, until apples are tender when poked with fork but still hold their shape, 15 to 20 minutes. Transfer apples and their juices to rimmed baking sheet and let cool to room temperature, about 30 minutes.

3. Adjust oven rack to lowest position, place rimmed baking sheet on rack, and heat oven to 425 degrees. Drain cooled apples thoroughly in colander, reserving ¼ cup of juice. Stir lemon juice into reserved juice.

4. Spread apples into dough-lined pie plate, mounding them slightly in middle, and drizzle with lemon juice mixture. Loosely roll remaining dough round around rolling pin and gently unroll it onto filling. Trim overhang to ½ inch beyond lip of pie plate. Pinch edges of top and bottom dough crusts firmly together. Tuck overhang under itself; folded edge should be flush with edge of pie plate. Crimp dough evenly around edge of pie using your fingers. Cut four 2-inch slits in top

of dough. Brush surface with beaten egg white and sprinkle evenly with remaining 1 tablespoon granulated sugar.

5. Place pie on heated baking sheet and bake until crust is light golden brown, about 25 minutes. Reduce oven temperature to 375 degrees, rotate baking sheet, and continue to bake until juices are bubbling and crust is deep golden brown, 25 to 30 minutes longer. Let pie cool on wire rack until filling has set, about 2 hours; serve slightly warm or at room temperature.

APPLE-CRANBERRY PIE

✔ WHY THIS RECIPE WORKS

Adding cranberries to an apple pie can overwhelm the subtle perfume of the apples and shed a lot of liquid, making for a soggy bottom crust. We wanted to find a way to combine these two classic fall fruits so that the full flavor of both came through and the crust remained crisp. Cooking the cranberries with a little sugar in a saucepan allowed the berries to break down (whole berries delivered a sour burst in the mouth) and the cranberry juice to thicken, eliminating a soggy crust. Adding some orange juice to the pan helped to tame the berries' tartness. Microwaving the apples until they just turned translucent kept them from turning too soft while baking. When we assembled the pie, we arranged the cooked cranberries and the apples in two distinct layers, allowing the flavor of each to come through clearly.

APPLE-CRANBERRY PIE
SERVES 8

You can use Foolproof, All-Butter, or Classic Double-Crust Pie Dough (pages 708–711) for this pie. You can substitute Jonagold, Fuji, or Braeburn apples for the Golden Delicious apples. For more information on fitting pie dough, see page 709. For more information on assembling double-crust pies, see page 713.

8　ounces (2 cups) fresh or frozen cranberries

¼　cup orange juice

I　cup (7 ounces) plus I tablespoon sugar

½　teaspoon ground cinnamon

½　teaspoon salt

¼　cup water

I　tablespoon cornstarch

3½　pounds Golden Delicious apples, peeled, cored, and sliced ¼ inch thick

I　recipe double-crust pie dough

I　large egg white, lightly beaten

1. Bring cranberries, orange juice, ½ cup sugar, ¼ teaspoon cinnamon, and ¼ teaspoon salt to boil in medium saucepan. Cook, stirring occasionally and pressing berries against side of pot, until berries have completely broken down and juices have thickened to jamlike consistency (wooden spoon scraped across bottom should leave clear trail that doesn't fill in), 10 to 12 minutes. Off heat, stir in water and let cool to room temperature, about

---

TEST KITCHEN TIP NO. 143　CRISP PIE CRUST POINTERS

For both single- and double-crust pies, two essential steps can assure a crisp bottom: bake your pie in a glass pie plate and preheat the baking sheet on which the pie will bake. Glass holds heat well and promotes better browning, and preheating the baking sheet jump-starts the baking of the crust. Before taking a pie out of the oven, lift up the pie plate and check to make sure the bottom is nicely browned. For a double-crust pie in particular, since the bottom crust is more likely to be undercooked (and therefore soggy) than the top crust, be patient and don't pull the pie out of the oven too early.

And sometimes the crimped crust around the edge of the pie can get quite brown before the pie has finished baking. If this happens, simply wrap a piece of aluminum foil loosely around the rim of the pie. The foil will help to deflect the heat and prevent the rim of the crust from getting too dark or burning.

30 minutes. (Cooled filling can be refrigerated for up to 2 days.)

2. Meanwhile, mix ½ cup sugar, remaining ¼ teaspoon cinnamon, remaining ¼ teaspoon salt, and cornstarch together in large bowl. Add apples and toss to combine. Cover and microwave, stirring with rubber spatula every 3 minutes, until apples are just starting to turn translucent around edges and liquid is thick and glossy, 10 to 14 minutes. Let cool to room temperature, about 30 minutes. (Cooled filling can be refrigerated for up to 2 days.)

3. While fillings cool, adjust oven rack to lowest position, place rimmed baking sheet on rack, and heat oven to 425 degrees. Roll 1 disk of dough into 12-inch circle on lightly floured counter. Loosely roll dough around rolling pin and gently unroll it onto 9-inch pie plate, letting excess dough hang over edge. Ease dough into plate by gently lifting edge of dough with one hand while pressing into plate bottom with other hand. Leave any dough that overhangs plate in place. Wrap dough-lined pie plate loosely in plastic wrap and refrigerate until dough is firm, about 30 minutes. Roll other disk of dough into 12-inch circle on lightly floured counter, then transfer to parchment paper–lined baking sheet; cover with plastic and refrigerate for 30 minutes.

4. Spread cooled cranberry mixture into even layer in dough-lined pie plate. Place apple mixture on top of cranberries, mounding it slightly in center. Loosely roll remaining dough round around rolling pin and gently unroll it onto filling. Trim overhang to ½ inch beyond lip of pie plate. Pinch edges of top and bottom crusts firmly together. Tuck overhang under itself; folded edge should be flush with edge of pie plate. Crimp dough evenly around edge of pie using your fingers. Cut four 2-inch slits in top of dough. Brush surface with beaten egg white and sprinkle evenly with remaining 1 tablespoon sugar.

5. Place pie on heated baking sheet and bake until crust is light golden brown, about 25 minutes. Reduce oven temperature to 375 degrees, rotate baking sheet, and continue to bake until juices are bubbling and crust is deep golden brown, 25 to 30 minutes longer. Let pie cool on wire rack until filling has set, about 2 hours; serve slightly warm or at room temperature.

MINCEMEAT PIE

✔ WHY THIS RECIPE WORKS

Meatless mincemeat pies have been around for more than a century and are about as old-fashioned as pies get these days. All too often though, these pies are made with jarred mincemeat filling, or if the filling is homemade, it is murky, boozy, and overly rich. To bring mincemeat pie into the modern age, we built a foundation of fruit flavor by cooking two kinds of apples— McIntosh and Granny Smiths—with butter, not suet. Golden raisins and currants paired well with the fresh fruit and spices, lending the filling a deep, earthy flavor. And since long cooking is essential when making mincemeat, we simmered the filling ingredients together with apple cider for about three hours, adding more cider as needed, until the mixture became dark and jamlike. Keeping the booziness in check was as simple as adding ⅓ cup of rum toward the end of the cooking time and letting it cook long enough to mellow its punch.

MODERN MINCEMEAT PIE

SERVES 10 TO 12

You can use Foolproof, All-Butter, or Classic Double-Crust Pie Dough (pages 708–711) for this pie. For more information on fitting pie dough, see page 709. For more information on assembling double-crust pies, see page 713.

1½	pounds Granny Smith apples, peeled, cored, and cut into ¼-inch dice
1½	pounds McIntosh apples, peeled, cored, and cut into ¼-inch dice
1	cup golden raisins
1	cup currants
¾	cup packed (5¼ ounces) dark brown sugar
8	tablespoons unsalted butter
¼	cup diced candied orange peel (optional)
1½	tablespoons grated orange zest plus ½ cup juice
1	tablespoon grated lemon zest plus 3 tablespoons juice
1	teaspoon ground cinnamon
½	teaspoon ground allspice
½	teaspoon ground ginger
¼	teaspoon ground cloves
¼	teaspoon salt
1½	cups apple cider, plus more as needed
⅓	cup rum or brandy
1	recipe double-crust pie dough
1	large egg white, lightly beaten
1	tablespoon granulated sugar

1. Bring apples, raisins, currants, brown sugar, butter, orange peel, if using, orange and lemon zest and juice, cinnamon, allspice, ginger, cloves, salt, and 1 cup cider to simmer in saucepan over medium-low heat. Reduce to simmer and cook gently, stirring occasionally to prevent scorching, until mixture thickens and darkens in color, about 3 hours, adding more cider as

necessary to prevent scorching. Continue cooking, stirring mixture every minute or two, until it has jamlike consistency, about 20 minutes. Stir in remaining ½ cup apple cider and rum and cook until liquid in pan is thick and syrupy, about 10 minutes; let filling cool. (At this point, mincemeat can be refrigerated for 4 days.)

2. Meanwhile, roll 1 disk of dough into 12-inch circle on lightly floured counter. Loosely roll dough around rolling pin and gently unroll it onto 9-inch pie plate, letting excess dough hang over edge. Ease dough into plate by gently lifting edge of dough with 1 hand while pressing into plate bottom with other hand. Leave any dough that overhangs plate in place. Wrap dough-lined pie plate loosely in plastic wrap and refrigerate until dough is firm, about 30 minutes. Roll other disk of dough into 12-inch circle on lightly floured counter, then transfer to parchment paper–lined baking sheet; cover with plastic and refrigerate for 30 minutes.

3. Adjust oven rack to lowest position, place rimmed baking sheet on rack, and heat oven to 400 degrees. Spoon mincemeat into pie shell. Loosely roll remaining dough round around rolling pin and gently unroll it onto filling. Trim overhang to ½ inch beyond lip of pie plate. Pinch edges of top and bottom crusts firmly together. Tuck overhang under itself; folded edge should be flush with edge of pie plate. Crimp dough evenly around edge of pie using your fingers. Cut four 2-inch slits in top of dough. Brush surface with beaten egg white and sprinkle evenly with granulated sugar.

4. Place pie on heated baking sheet and bake until crust is light golden brown, about 25 minutes. Reduce oven temperature to 350 degrees and rotate baking sheet; continue to bake until juices are bubbling and crust is deep golden brown, 30 to 35 minutes longer. Let pie cool on wire rack to room temperature, about 4 hours. Serve.

BLUEBERRY PIE

✓ WHY THIS RECIPE WORKS

If the filling in blueberry pie doesn't jell, a wedge can collapse into a soupy puddle topped by a sodden crust. But use too much thickener and the filling can be so dense that cutting into it is a challenge. We wanted a pie that had a firm, glistening filling full of fresh, bright flavor and still-plump berries. To thicken the pie, we favored tapioca, which allowed the fresh yet subtle blueberry flavor to shine through. Too much of it, though, and we had a congealed mess. Cooking and reducing half of the berries helped us cut down on the tapioca required, but not enough. A second inspiration came from a peeled and shredded Granny Smith apple. Apples are high in pectin, a type of carbohydrate that acts as a thickener when cooked. Combined with a modest 2 tablespoons of tapioca, the apple thickened the filling to a soft, even consistency that was neither gelatinous nor slippery. Baking the pie on a preheated baking sheet on the bottom oven rack produced a crisp, golden bottom crust. To vent the steam from the berries, we found a faster, easier alternative to a lattice top in a biscuit cutter, which we used to cut out circles in the top crust.

BLUEBERRY PIE
SERVES 8

You can use Foolproof, All-Butter, or Classic Double-Crust Pie Dough (pages 708–711) for this pie. This recipe was developed using fresh blueberries, but unthawed frozen blueberries will work as well. In step 3, cook half the frozen berries over medium-high heat, without mashing, until reduced to 1¼ cups, 12 to 15 minutes. Use the large holes of a box grater to shred the apple. Grind the tapioca to a powder in a spice grinder or mini food processor. For more information on fitting pie dough, see page 709. For more information on assembling double-crust pies, see page 713.

  1   recipe double-crust pie dough
30   ounces (6 cups) blueberries

  1   Granny Smith apple, peeled, cored, and shredded
¾   cup (5¼ ounces) sugar
  2   tablespoons instant tapioca, ground
  2   teaspoons grated lemon zest plus 2 teaspoons juice
     Pinch salt
  2   tablespoons unsalted butter, cut into ¼-inch pieces
  1   large egg white, lightly beaten

1. Roll 1 disk of dough into 12-inch circle on lightly floured counter. Loosely roll dough around rolling pin and gently unroll it onto 9-inch pie plate, letting excess dough hang over edge. Ease dough into plate by gently lifting edge of dough with 1 hand while pressing into plate bottom with other hand. Leave any dough that overhangs plate in place. Wrap dough-lined pie plate loosely in plastic wrap and refrigerate until dough is firm, about 30 minutes.

2. Roll other disk of dough into 12-inch circle on lightly floured counter. Using 1¼-inch round cookie cutter, cut round from center of dough. Cut 6 more rounds from dough, 1½ inches from edge of center hole and equally spaced around center hole. Transfer dough to parchment paper–lined baking sheet; cover with plastic and refrigerate for 30 minutes.

3. Place 3 cups berries in medium saucepan and set over medium heat. Using

PREPARING TOP CRUST FOR BLUEBERRY PIE

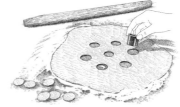

Using 1¼-inch cookie cutter (or spice jar lid), cut 1 round from center of dough, then 6 more rounds, 1½ inches from edge of center hole and equally spaced around center hole.

potato masher, mash berries several times to release juices. Continue to cook, stirring often and mashing occasionally, until about half of berries have broken down and mixture is thickened and reduced to 1½ cups, about 8 minutes; let cool slightly.

4. Adjust oven rack to lowest position, place rimmed baking sheet on rack, and heat oven to 400 degrees.

5. Place shredded apple in clean kitchen towel and wring dry. Transfer apple to large bowl and stir in cooked berries, remaining 3 cups uncooked berries, sugar, tapioca, lemon zest and juice, and salt until combined. Spread mixture into dough-lined pie plate and scatter butter over top.

6. Loosely roll remaining dough round around rolling pin and gently unroll it onto filling. Trim overhang to ½ inch beyond lip of pie plate. Pinch edges of top and bottom crusts firmly together. Tuck overhang under itself; folded edge should be flush with edge of pie plate. Crimp dough evenly around edge of pie using your fingers. Cut four 2-inch slits in top of dough. Brush surface with beaten egg white.

7. Place pie on heated baking sheet and bake until crust is light golden brown, about 25 minutes. Reduce oven temperature to 350 degrees, rotate baking sheet, and continue to bake until juices are bubbling and crust is deep golden brown, 30 to 40 minutes longer. Let pie cool on wire rack to room temperature, about 4 hours. Serve.

CHERRY PIE

✔ WHY THIS RECIPE WORKS

Great cherry pie is typically made with sour cherries because their soft, juicy flesh and bright, punchy flavor isn't dulled by oven heat or sugar. But cherry season is cruelly short and chances are the cherries that are available are the sweet variety. Sweet cherries have mellower flavors and meaty, firm flesh—traits that make them ideal for eating straight off the stem but don't translate well to baking. Our challenge was obvious: develop a recipe for sweet cherry pie with all the intense, jammy flavor and softened but still intact fruit texture of the best sour cherry pie. To mimic the bright, tart flavor of a sour cherry pie filling, we supplemented sweet cherries with chopped plums, which are tart and helped tame the cherries' sweet flavor. To fix the texture problem, we cut the cherries in half to expose their sturdy flesh. This step encouraged the cherries to soften and give up their juices. A splash of bourbon and lemon juice also off-set the sweetness and added flavorful depth.

To keep the filling juicy, rather than dry, we switched out the typical lattice pie crust in favor of a traditional top crust, which prevented any moisture from evaporating.

SWEET CHERRY PIE
SERVES 8

You can use Foolproof, All-Butter, or Classic Double-Crust Pie Dough (pages 708–711) for this pie. Grind the tapioca to a powder in a spice grinder or mini food processor. You can substitute 2 pounds frozen sweet cherries for the fresh cherries. If you are using frozen fruit, measure it frozen, but let it thaw before filling the pie. If not, you run the risk of partially cooked fruit and undissolved tapioca. For more information on fitting pie dough, see page 709. For more information on assembling double-crust pies, see page 713.

1	recipe double-crust pie dough
2	red plums, halved and pitted
2	pounds pitted sweet cherries, halved
½	cup (3½ ounces) sugar
1	tablespoon lemon juice
2	teaspoons bourbon (optional)
2	tablespoons instant tapioca, ground
⅛	teaspoon salt
⅛	teaspoon ground cinnamon (optional)
2	tablespoons unsalted butter, cut into ¼-inch pieces
1	large egg, lightly beaten with 1 teaspoon water

1. Roll 1 disk of dough into 12-inch circle on lightly floured counter. Loosely roll dough around rolling pin and gently unroll it onto 9-inch pie plate, letting excess dough hang over edge. Ease dough into plate by gently lifting edge of dough with 1 hand while pressing into plate bottom with other hand. Leave any dough that overhangs plate in place. Wrap dough-lined pie plate loosely in plastic wrap and refrigerate until dough is firm, about 30 minutes. Roll other disk of dough into

---

12-inch circle on lightly floured counter, then transfer to parchment paper–lined baking sheet; cover with plastic and refrigerate for 30 minutes.

2. Adjust oven rack to lowest position, place rimmed baking sheet on rack, and heat oven to 400 degrees. Process plums and 1 cup halved cherries in food processor until smooth, about 1 minute, scraping down bowl as necessary. Strain puree through fine-mesh strainer into large bowl, pressing on solids to extract as much liquid as possible; discard solids. Stir in remaining halved cherries, sugar, lemon juice, bourbon, if using, tapioca, salt, and cinnamon, if using, into puree; let stand for 15 minutes.

3. Spread cherry mixture with its juices into dough-lined pie plate and scatter butter over top. Loosely roll remaining dough round around rolling pin and gently unroll it onto filling. Trim overhang to ½ inch beyond lip of pie plate. Pinch edges of top and bottom crusts firmly together. Tuck overhang under itself; folded edge should be flush with edge of pie plate. Crimp dough evenly around edge of pie using your fingers. Cut eight 2-inch slits in top of dough. Brush surface with beaten egg mixture. Freeze pie for 20 minutes.

4. Place pie on heated baking sheet and bake until crust is light golden brown, about 30 minutes. Reduce oven temperature to 350 degrees, rotate baking sheet, and continue to bake until juices are bubbling and crust is deep golden brown, 30 to 40 minutes longer. Let pie cool on wire rack to room temperature, about 4 hours. Serve.

PEACH PIE

✔ WHY THIS RECIPE WORKS
Fresh peach pies are often soupy or overly sweet, with a bottom crust that is soggy or undercooked. We wanted to create a filling that was juicy but not swimming in liquid, its flavors neither muscled out by spices nor overwhelmed by thickeners, and the crust had to be well browned on the bottom. We peeled and sliced the peaches and found that all they needed in the way of flavor was sugar, lemon juice, cinnamon, nutmeg, and a dash of salt. To thicken the juices, we used a little cornstarch, but it didn't solve the problem. A lattice-top pie crust was our solution—while it requires a bit more work than making a regular double-crust pie, we found that it's worth the effort. Not only is it pretty and very traditional on peach pies, but it serves an important purpose: The structure of a lattice top allows for maximum evaporation while the pie cooks—the juices released by the fruit cook down slowly while baking so the filling isn't soupy. For easy assembly, we rolled and cut the dough, then froze it so the strips were firm and easy to handle.

FRESH LATTICE-TOP PEACH PIE
SERVES 8

You can use Foolproof, All-Butter, or Classic Double-Crust Pie Dough (pages 708–711) for this pie. If your peaches are firm, you should be able to peel them with a sharp vegetable peeler. If they are too soft to withstand the pressure of a peeler, you'll need to blanch them in a pot of simmering water for 15 seconds and then shock them in a bowl of ice water before peeling. For more information on fitting pie dough, see page 709.

- 1 recipe double-crust pie dough
- 2½ pounds peaches, peeled, halved, pitted, and sliced ⅓ inch thick
- 1 cup (7 ounces) plus 1 tablespoon sugar
- 1 tablespoon cornstarch

- 1 tablespoon lemon juice
  Pinch ground cinnamon
  Pinch ground nutmeg
  Pinch salt
- 1 large egg white, lightly beaten

1. Roll 1 disk of dough into 12-inch circle on lightly floured counter. Loosely roll dough around rolling pin and gently unroll it onto 9-inch pie plate, letting excess dough hang over edge. Ease dough into plate by gently lifting edge of dough with 1 hand while pressing into plate bottom with other hand. Leave any dough that overhangs plate in place. Wrap dough-lined pie plate loosely in plastic wrap and refrigerate until dough is firm, about 30 minutes.

2. Roll other disk of dough into 13½ by 10½-inch rectangle on lightly floured counter, then transfer to parchment paper–lined baking sheet. Trim dough to 13 by 10-inch rectangle and slice lengthwise into eight 13-inch-long strips. Separate strips slightly, cover with plastic, and freeze until very firm, about 30 minutes.

3. Toss peaches and 1 cup sugar together in large bowl and let sit, tossing occasionally, until peaches release their juice, about 1 hour. Adjust oven rack to lowest position, place rimmed baking sheet on rack, and heat oven to 425 degrees.

4. Drain peaches thoroughly in colander, reserving ¼ cup of juice. In large bowl, toss drained fruit, reserved juice, cornstarch, lemon juice, cinnamon, nutmeg, and salt together until well combined.

5. Spread peaches into dough-lined pie plate. Lay 4 parallel strips of chilled dough evenly over filling. Weave remaining strips in opposite direction, one at a time, to create lattice (if dough becomes too soft to work with, refrigerate pie and dough strips until dough firms up). Let strips soften for 5 to 10 minutes, then trim overhang to ½ inch beyond lip of pie plate. Pinch edges of crust and lattice strips together,

WEAVING A LATTICE TOP

1. Lay 4 parallel strips evenly over filling. Weave fifth strip in opposite direction, lifting strips as needed to make weaving easier.

2. Continue to weave in remaining 3 strips, one at a time, to create lattice.

3. After letting strips soften, trim overhanging edges of dough to ½ inch beyond lip of pie plate. Press edges of bottom crust and lattice strips together and tuck underneath.

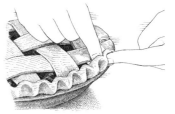

4. Create fluted edge around pie, using index finger of 1 hand and thumb and index finger of other.

---

then tuck overhang under itself; folded edge should be flush with edge of pie plate. Crimp dough evenly around edge of pie using fingers. Brush lattice with beaten egg white and sprinkle evenly with remaining 1 tablespoon sugar.

6. Place pie on heated baking sheet and bake until top crust is light golden brown, about 25 minutes. Reduce oven temperature to 375 degrees, rotate baking sheet, and continue to bake until juices are bubbling and crust is deep golden brown, 25 to 35 minutes longer. Let pie cool on wire rack until filling has set, about 2 hours; serve slightly warm or at room temperature.

FRESH STRAWBERRY PIE

✔ WHY THIS RECIPE WORKS

Because uncooked berries shed so much liquid, the filling for strawberry pie is usually firmed up with some sort of thickener, which produces results that range from stiff and bouncy to runny and gloppy. We wanted a recipe for our ideal strawberry pie, featuring fresh berries lightly held together by a sheer, glossy glaze that made their flavor pop in the buttery shell. We knew that the success of our strawberry pie hinged on getting

the thickener just right. When none of the thickeners we tried worked on their own, we decided to use a combination of two: pectin (in the form of a homemade strawberry jam) and cornstarch. By themselves, pectin produced a filling that was too firm and cornstarch one that was too loose. But together they created just the right supple, lightly clingy glaze.

FRESH STRAWBERRY PIE
SERVES 8

You can use Foolproof, All-Butter, or Classic Pie Single-Crust Pie Dough (pages 708–711) for this pie. To account for any imperfect strawberries, the ingredient list calls for several more ounces of berries than will be used in the pie. If possible, seek out ripe, farmers' market–quality berries. Make sure to thoroughly dry the strawberries after washing. Make certain that you use Sure-Jell engineered for low- or no-sugar recipes (packaged in a pink box) and not regular Sure-Jell (in a yellow box); otherwise, the glaze will not set properly. The pie is at its best after two or three hours of chilling; as it continues to chill, the glaze becomes softer and wetter, though the pie will taste just as good.

3   **pounds strawberries, hulled (9 cups)**
¾   **cup (5¼ ounces) sugar**
2   **tablespoons cornstarch**

1½   **teaspoons Sure-Jell for low-sugar recipes**
    Pinch salt
1   **tablespoon lemon juice**
1   **recipe single-crust pie dough, fully baked and cooled**

1. Select 6 ounces misshapen, under-ripe, or otherwise unattractive berries, halving those that are large; you should have about 1½ cups. Process berries in food processor to smooth puree, 20 to 30 seconds, scraping down bowl as needed (you should have about ¾ cup puree).

2. Whisk sugar, cornstarch, Sure-Jell, and salt together in medium saucepan. Stir in berry puree, making sure to scrape corners of pan. Cook over medium-high heat, stirring constantly, and bring to boil. Boil, scraping bottom and sides of pan to prevent scorching, for 2 minutes to ensure that cornstarch is fully cooked (mixture will appear frothy when it first reaches boil, then will darken and thicken with further cooking). Transfer glaze to large bowl and stir in lemon juice; let cool to room temperature.

3. Meanwhile, pick over remaining berries and measure out 2 pounds of most attractive ones; halve only extra-large berries. Add berries to bowl with glaze and

fold gently with rubber spatula until berries are evenly coated. Scoop berries into cooled prebaked pie shell, piling into mound. If any cut sides face up on top, turn them face down. If necessary, rearrange berries so that holes are filled and mound looks attractive. Refrigerate pie until filling is chilled and has set, about 2 hours. Serve within 5 hours of chilling.

SUMMER BERRY PIE

✔ WHY THIS RECIPE WORKS

A fresh berry pie might seem like an easy-to-pull-off summer dessert, but most of the recipes we tried buried the berries in gluey thickeners or embedded them in bouncy gelatin. Our goal was to make a pie with great texture and flavor— and still keep it simple.

We started with the test kitchen's quick and easy homemade graham cracker crust, which relies on crushed graham crackers (store-bought graham cracker crumbs often taste stale). For the filling, we used a combination of raspberries, blackberries, and blueberries. After trying a few different methods, we found a solution that both bound the berries in the graham cracker crust and intensified their bright flavor. We processed a portion of berries in a food processor until they made a smooth puree, then we thickened the puree with cornstarch. Next, we tossed the remaining berries with warm jelly for a glossy coat and a shot of sweetness. Pressed gently into the puree, the berries stayed put and tasted great.

SUMMER BERRY PIE
SERVES 8

Feel free to vary the amount of each berry as desired as long as you have 6 cups of berries total; do not substitute frozen berries here. Serve with Whipped Cream (page 800).

10	ounces (2 cups) raspberries
10	ounces (2 cups) blackberries
10	ounces (2 cups) blueberries

½	cup (3½ ounces) sugar
3	tablespoons cornstarch
⅛	teaspoon salt
I	tablespoon lemon juice
I	recipe Graham Cracker Crust (page 712), baked and cooled
2	tablespoons red currant or apple jelly

I. Gently toss berries together in large bowl. Process 2½ cups of berries in food processor until very smooth, about 1 minute (do not under-process). Strain puree through fine-mesh strainer into small saucepan, pressing on solids to extract as much puree as possible (you should have about 1½ cups); discard solids.

2. Whisk sugar, cornstarch, and salt together in bowl, then whisk into strained puree. Bring puree mixture to boil, stirring constantly, and cook until it is as thick as pudding, about 7 minutes. Off heat, stir in lemon juice; set aside to cool slightly.

3. Pour warm berry puree into baked and cooled prebaked pie crust. Melt jelly in clean small saucepan over low heat, then pour over remaining 3½ cups berries and toss to coat. Spread berries evenly over puree and lightly press them into puree. Cover pie loosely with plastic wrap and refrigerate until filling is chilled and has set, about 3 hours; serve chilled or at room temperature.

PUMPKIN PIE

✔ WHY THIS RECIPE WORKS

Too often, pumpkin pie appears at the end of a Thanksgiving meal as a grainy, overspiced, canned-pumpkin custard encased in a soggy crust. We wanted to create a pumpkin pie destined to be a new classic: velvety smooth, packed with pumpkin flavor, and redolent of just enough fragrant spices. To concentrate its flavor, we cooked the canned pumpkin with sugar and spices, then whisked in heavy cream, milk, and

eggs. *This improved the flavor and the hot filling helped the custard firm up quickly in the oven, preventing it from soaking into the crust. For spices, we chose nutmeg, cinnamon, and, surprisingly, freshly grated ginger. Sugar and maple syrup sweetened things, but for more complex flavor, we added mashed roasted yams to the filling (switching to canned candied yams streamlined the procedure). To keep the custard from curdling, we started the pie at a high temperature for 10 minutes, followed by a reduced temperature for the remainder of the baking time. This cut the baking time to less than an hour and the dual temperatures produced a creamy pie fully and evenly cooked from edge to center.*

PUMPKIN PIE
SERVES 8

You can use Foolproof, All-Butter, or Classic Single-Crust Pie Dough (pages 708–711) for this pie. Make sure to buy unsweetened canned pumpkin; avoid pumpkin pie mix. If candied yams are unavailable, regular canned yams can be substituted. When the pie is properly baked, the center 2 inches of the pie should look firm but jiggle slightly. The pie finishes cooking with residual heat; to ensure that the filling sets, let it cool at room temperature and not in the refrigerator. Do not cool this fully baked crust; the crust and filling must both be warm when the filling is added. Serve with Whipped Cream (page 800).

I	cup heavy cream
I	cup whole milk
3	large eggs plus 2 large yolks
I	teaspoon vanilla extract
I	(15-ounce) can unsweetened canned pumpkin
I	cup candied yams, drained
¾	cup (5¼ ounces) sugar
¼	cup maple syrup
2	teaspoons grated fresh ginger
I	teaspoon salt
½	teaspoon ground cinnamon
¼	teaspoon ground nutmeg
I	recipe single-crust pie dough, fully baked and still warm

1. Adjust oven rack to lowest position, place rimmed baking sheet on rack, and heat oven to 400 degrees. Whisk cream, milk, eggs and egg yolks, and vanilla together in bowl. Bring pumpkin puree, yams, sugar, maple syrup, ginger, salt, cinnamon, and nutmeg to simmer in large saucepan and cook, stirring constantly and mashing yams against sides of pot, until thick and shiny, 15 to 20 minutes.

2. Remove saucepan from heat and whisk in cream mixture until fully incorporated. Strain mixture through fine-mesh strainer into bowl, using back of ladle or spatula to press solids through strainer. Whisk mixture, then pour into warm prebaked pie crust.

3. Place pie on heated baking sheet and bake for 10 minutes. Reduce oven temperature to 300 degrees and continue to bake until edges of pie are set and center registers 175 degrees, 20 to 35 minutes longer. Let pie cool on wire rack to room temperature, about 4 hours. Serve.

NO-BAKE PUMPKIN PIE

✔ WHY THIS RECIPE WORKS
A no-bake pumpkin pie promises the ultimate in speed and convenience, but it's not worth saving time if you end up with a pie with a crumbly crust and poorly textured filling. We wanted it all: creaminess as well as lightness—and without the hassle of making pie pastry during a busy holiday season. For a simple and sturdy base for our pie, we turned to our classic graham cracker crust. We achieved the right consistency for our filling by choosing the right thickener: a modest amount (2 teaspoons) of gelatin that prevented the tough, rubbery texture found in pies made with too much thickener. To attain the optimal rich, velvety texture for our filling, we gave the canned pumpkin a quick whirl in the food processor to make it truly smooth, and also replaced the whipped egg whites of classic chiffon-style pies with a simple custard—the yolks were necessary for a luxurious texture. For complexity, we

added a mix of ground cinnamon, ginger, nutmeg, and cloves, but we first heated them in the cream to soften their harshness. A combination of orange juice and vanilla extract added a sweet, perfumed punch.

NO-BAKE PUMPKIN PIE
SERVES 8

Make sure to buy unsweetened canned pumpkin; avoid pumpkin pie mix. Serve with Whipped Cream (page 800).

    3 tablespoons orange juice, chilled
    2 teaspoons vanilla extract
    2 teaspoons unflavored gelatin
    1 cup heavy cream
    ⅔ cup (4⅔ ounces) sugar
    1 teaspoon ground cinnamon
    ¾ teaspoon salt
    ½ teaspoon ground ginger
    ¼ teaspoon ground nutmeg
    ⅛ teaspoon ground cloves
    3 large egg yolks
    1 (15-ounce) can unsweetened canned pumpkin
    1 recipe Graham Cracker Crust (page 712), baked and cooled

1. Stir orange juice and vanilla together in medium bowl. Sprinkle gelatin over orange juice mixture and let sit until gelatin is softened, about 5 minutes.

2. Combine ½ cup heavy cream, ⅓ cup sugar, cinnamon, salt, ginger, nutmeg, and cloves in small saucepan and cook over medium-low heat until bubbles form at edges; remove from heat. Whisk remaining ⅓ cup sugar and egg yolks together in medium bowl until pale and slightly thickened. Slowly pour hot cream into yolk mixture, whisking constantly, to temper. Return mixture to now-empty saucepan and cook over medium-low heat, stirring constantly, until mixture begins to thicken and forms ridge on tip of spoon when bottom of pan is scraped and spoon is lifted, about 2 minutes. Immediately pour custard

over gelatin mixture and stir until smooth and gelatin has completely dissolved.

3. Puree pumpkin in food processor until smooth, 10 to 15 seconds. With food processor running, add remaining ½ cup heavy cream in steady stream. Scrape down sides of bowl and process for additional 10 to 15 seconds. Add pumpkin mixture to custard mixture and stir until completely smooth. Pour filling into cooled prebaked pie crust. Refrigerate pie, uncovered, until filling is just set, about 3 hours. Cover pie with plastic wrap and continue to refrigerate until fully set, at least 6 or up to 24 hours. Serve.

SWEET POTATO PIE

✔ WHY THIS RECIPE WORKS
Too many sweet potato pies either come in a custardy pumpkin-pie style or resemble mashed sweet potatoes in a crust. Our challenge was to create a recipe that both honored the flavor of the sweet potatoes and was still recognizable as a dessert. For a sweet potato pie that would really taste like sweet potato, we microwaved and mashed the potatoes, which preserved some bite in their texture. White sugar and a touch of molasses brought us still closer to the pie we were looking for. But what finally took our pie from good to great was melting brown sugar on the crust before adding the potato filling. The pecan pie–like sweetness of the brown sugar perfectly complemented the filling, which maintained a bright orange color that spoke loudly of sweet potatoes.

SWEET POTATO PIE
SERVES 8

You can use Foolproof, All-Butter, or Classic Single-Crust Pie Dough (pages 708–711) for this pie. Some tasters preferred a stronger bourbon flavor in the filling, so we give a range. If you like molasses, use the optional tablespoon; a few tasters felt it deepened the sweet potato flavor. The crust and filling must both be warm when the filling is added. The pie finishes cooking with residual heat; to ensure that the filling sets, let it cool at room temperature and not in the refrigerator. Serve with Whipped Cream (page 800).

2 pounds sweet potatoes
2 tablespoons unsalted butter, softened
1 cup (7 ounces) granulated sugar
3 large eggs plus 2 large yolks
½ teaspoon ground nutmeg
¼ teaspoon salt
2–3 tablespoons bourbon
1 tablespoon molasses (optional)
1 teaspoon vanilla extract
⅔ cup whole milk
¼ cup packed (1¾ ounces) dark brown sugar
1 recipe single-crust pie dough, partially baked and still warm

1. Adjust oven rack to middle position and heat oven to 350 degrees. Poke each potato several times with paring knife over entire surface. Place potatoes on paper towel–lined plate and microwave until tender but not mushy, about 10 minutes, flipping potatoes halfway through cooking. Hold potato with potholder or kitchen towel and peel with paring knife; transfer to large bowl and discard skin. Repeat with remaining potatoes (you should have about 2 cups). While potatoes are still hot, add butter and mash with potato masher until just few small potato lumps remain.

2. Whisk granulated sugar, eggs, egg yolks, nutmeg, and salt together in medium bowl; stir in bourbon, molasses, if using, and vanilla, then whisk in milk. Gradually add egg mixture to mashed sweet potato mixture, whisking gently to combine.

3. Sprinkle bottom of warm prebaked pie crust evenly with brown sugar, then pour sweet potato mixture on top. Bake pie until edges are set but center jiggles slightly

when shaken, about 45 minutes. Let pie cool pie on wire rack to room temperature, about 4 hours. Serve.

PECAN PIE

✓ WHY THIS RECIPE WORKS
Pecan pies can be overwhelmingly sweet, with no real pecan flavor. And they too often turn out curdled and separated. What's more, the weepy filling makes the bottom crust soggy and leathery. The fact that the crust usually seems underbaked to begin with doesn't help matters. We wanted to create a recipe for a not-too-sweet pie with a smooth-textured filling and a properly baked bottom crust. We tackled this pie's problems by using brown sugar, for rich, deep flavor, and reducing the amount, so the pecan flavor could take center stage. We also partially baked the crust, which kept it crisp. We found that it's important to add the hot filling to a warm pie crust as this helps keep the crust from getting soggy. In addition, we discovered that simulating a double boiler when you're melting the butter and making the filling is an easy way to maintain gentle heat, which helps ensure that the filling doesn't curdle.

CLASSIC PECAN PIE
SERVES 8

You can use Foolproof, All-Butter, or Classic Single Crust Pie Dough (pages 708–711) for this pie. The crust must still be warm when the filling is added. To serve the pie warm, let it cool thoroughly so that it sets completely, then warm it in a 250-degree oven for about 15 minutes and slice. Serve with vanilla ice cream or Whipped Cream (page 800).

6 tablespoons unsalted butter, cut into 1-inch pieces
1 cup packed (7 ounces) dark brown sugar
½ teaspoon salt
3 large eggs

¾ cup light corn syrup
1 tablespoon vanilla extract
2 cups (8 ounces) pecans, toasted and chopped fine
1 recipe single-crust pie dough, partially baked and still warm

1. Adjust oven rack to lower-middle position and heat oven to 275 degrees. Melt butter in heatproof bowl set in skillet of water maintained at just below simmer. Remove bowl from skillet and stir in sugar and salt until butter is absorbed. Whisk in eggs, then corn syrup and vanilla until smooth. Return bowl to hot water and stir until mixture is shiny, hot to touch, and registers 130 degrees. Off heat, stir in pecans.

2. Pour pecan mixture into warm prebaked pie crust. Bake pie until filling looks set but yields like Jell-O when gently pressed with back of spoon, 50 minutes to 1 hour. Let pie cool on wire rack until filling has set, about 2 hours; serve slightly warm or at room temperature.

BUTTERMILK PECAN PIE WITH RAISINS

To make a buttermilk chess pie, omit the nuts and raisins.

Substitute 1½ cups (10½ ounces) granulated sugar for brown sugar and ⅔ cup buttermilk for corn syrup and vanilla. Reduce pecans to ½ cup and stir into pie filling along with ½ cup raisins, chopped fine.

MAPLE PECAN PIE

More liquid than corn syrup, maple syrup yields a softer, more custardlike pie. Toasted walnuts can be substituted for pecans. We prefer to use Grade B or Grade A dark amber maple syrup for this recipe.

Reduce butter to 4 tablespoons and pecans to 1½ cups. Substitute ½ cup granulated sugar for brown sugar and 1 cup maple syrup for corn syrup and vanilla.

TRIPLE-CHOCOLATE-CHUNK PECAN PIE
SERVES 8

You can use Foolproof, All-Butter, or Classic Single-Crust Pie Dough (pages 708–711) for this pie. Use either just one type of chocolate listed or a combination of two or three types. The crust must still be warm when the filling is added. To serve the pie warm, let it cool thoroughly so that it sets completely, then warm it in a 250-degree oven for about 15 minutes and slice.

- 3 tablespoons unsalted butter, cut into 3 pieces
- ¾ cup packed (5¼ ounces) dark brown sugar
- ½ teaspoon salt
- 2 large eggs
- ½ cup light corn syrup
- 1 teaspoon vanilla extract
- 1 cup pecans, toasted and chopped coarse
- 6 ounces semisweet, milk, and/or white chocolate, chopped coarse
- 1 recipe single-crust pie dough, partially baked and still warm

1. Adjust oven rack to lower-middle position and heat oven to 275 degrees. Melt butter in heatproof bowl set in skillet of water maintained at just below simmer. Remove bowl from skillet and stir in sugar and salt until butter is absorbed. Whisk in eggs, then corn syrup and vanilla until smooth. Return bowl to hot water and stir until mixture is shiny, hot to touch, and registers 130 degrees. Off heat, stir in pecans.

2. Pour pecan mixture into warm prebaked pie crust. Scatter chocolate over top and lightly press it into filling with back of spoon. Bake pie until filling looks set but yields like Jell-O when gently pressed with back of spoon, 50 minutes to 1 hour. Let pie cool on wire rack until filling has set, about 2 hours; serve slightly warm or at room temperature.

CUSTARD PIE

✔ WHY THIS RECIPE WORKS

There's a lot that can go wrong with a custard pie. The crust can be soggy, the outer ring of custard often overcooks, and the flavor can easily cross over into "eggy," which is a little ironic because a custard wouldn't be a custard without eggs. We wanted a custard pie with a crisp crust, a tender yet flavorful filling, and a relatively foolproof cooking method. For the custard, we used a combination of milk and heavy cream, which gave us a pie that was neither overly heavy nor too lean. We thickened the dairy with three whole eggs and a small amount of cornstarch; less than a cup of sugar was necessary to sweeten this mixture. Vanilla, nutmeg, and salt provided ample warmth and flavor. To avoid overcooked custard at the edges of the pie, we cooked our filling in a saucepan until it thickened, then poured the hot filling into a hot, prebaked pie crust and baked it briefly.

RICH, SILKY CUSTARD PIE
SERVES 8

You can use All-Butter or Classic Single-Crust Pie Dough for Custard Pies (pages 710–711) for this pie. The pie finishes cooking with residual heat; to ensure that the filling sets, let it cool at room temperature and not in the refrigerator. The crust and filling must both be warm when the filling is added.

- 2 cups whole milk
- 1 cup heavy cream
- ⅔ cup (4⅔ ounces) sugar
- 3 large eggs
- 3 tablespoons cornstarch
- 2 teaspoons vanilla extract
- ¼ teaspoon ground nutmeg
- ⅛ teaspoon salt
- 1 recipe single-crust pie dough for custard pies, partially baked and still warm

1. Adjust oven rack to lower-middle position and heat oven to 375 degrees. Heat milk and cream in medium saucepan over medium-low heat until steaming, about 6 minutes.

2. Meanwhile, whisk sugar, eggs, cornstarch, vanilla, nutmeg, and salt together in medium bowl. Slowly whisk 1 cup of warm milk mixture into egg mixture to temper, then slowly whisk tempered egg mixture into remaining milk mixture. Reduce heat to medium-low and cook, stirring constantly, until mixture begins to thicken and forms ridge on tip of spoon when bottom of pan is scraped and spoon is lifted, 6 to 8 minutes.

3. Pour custard into warm prebaked pie crust. Bake pie until edges are set but center jiggles slightly when shaken, 12 to 15 minutes. Let pie cool on wire rack to room temperature, about 4 hours. Serve.

LEMON CUSTARD PIE

Decrease vanilla to 1 teaspoon and substitute 1½ tablespoons grated lemon zest (2 lemons) for nutmeg. Add 1½ tablespoons lemon juice to sugar along with vanilla and lemon zest.

ORANGE CUSTARD PIE

Decrease vanilla to 1 teaspoon and substitute 1½ tablespoons grated orange zest for nutmeg. Add 1½ tablespoons orange juice to sugar along with vanilla and orange zest.

VANILLA CREAM PIE

✔ WHY THIS RECIPE WORKS

A great vanilla cream pie depends on a great filling; not even a crisp crust can save a pie made with filling that's too stiff, soupy, gummy, or flat in flavor. We wanted to find the right cooking method, flavorings, and thickener that would guarantee a substantial, yet velvety filling. We relied on egg yolks to keep the filling creamy and soft and cornstarch to make it just thick and stiff enough to cut. Evaporated milk provided subtle caramel undertones, and brandy amplified the vanilla's warmth. We poured the filling into the cooled pie shell when it was warm, not hot. When hot, the filling was more liquid and settled in a very compact layer; the warm filling, having had a chance to set a bit, mounded when poured into the shell so when we cut into it, the slices were neater. To improve the crust in our cream pie, we coated the pastry lightly with graham cracker crumbs when rolling it out to help it to retain its light, crisp texture when the filling was added.

VANILLA CREAM PIE
SERVES 8

You can use All-Butter or Classic Single-Crust Pie Dough for Custard Pies (pages 710–711) for this pie. Some tasters preferred a stronger brandy flavor in the filling, so we give a range below. The filling should be warm when poured into the cooled pie crust.

FILLING

- ½ cup plus 2 tablespoons (4⅓ ounces) granulated sugar
- ¼ cup cornstarch
- ⅛ teaspoon salt
- ½ cup evaporated milk
- 5 large egg yolks
- 2 cups whole milk
- ½ vanilla bean
- 2 tablespoons unsalted butter, cut into 2 pieces
- 1–2 teaspoons brandy

- 1 recipe single-crust pie dough for custard pies, fully baked and cooled

TOPPING

- 1 cup heavy cream, chilled
- 2 tablespoons confectioners' sugar
- ½ teaspoon vanilla extract

1. FOR THE FILLING: Whisk sugar, cornstarch, and salt together in medium saucepan. Whisk in evaporated milk, followed by egg yolks, and finally milk, until smooth. Cut vanilla bean in half lengthwise. Using tip of paring knife, scrape out seeds, then combine vanilla bean and seeds with sugar mixture. Bring mixture to simmer and cook, whisking constantly, until mixture thickens and becomes smooth, about 1 minute. Off heat, whisk in butter and brandy. Let mixture cool until just warm, stirring often, about 5 minutes.

2. Remove vanilla bean and pour warm filling into cooled prebaked pie crust. Lay sheet of plastic wrap directly on surface of filling and refrigerate pie until filling is chilled and set, about 4 hours.

3. FOR THE TOPPING: Once pie is chilled, use stand mixer fitted with whisk to whip cream, sugar, and vanilla on medium-low speed until foamy, about 1 minute. Increase speed to high and whip until soft peaks form, 1 to 3 minutes. Spread whipped cream attractively over top of pie.

BANANA CREAM PIE

The safest and best place for the banana slices is sandwiched between two layers of filling. If sliced over the pie crust, the bananas tend to moisten the crust; if sliced over the filling top or mashed and folded into the filling, they turn brown faster.

Pour half of warm filling into cooled prebaked pie crust. Peel 2 bananas and slice thin crosswise over filling. Top with remaining filling. Continue with recipe.

BUTTERSCOTCH CREAM PIE
SERVES 8

You can use All-Butter or Classic Single-Crust Pie Dough for Custard Pies (pages 710–711) for this pie. Whisking the milk slowly into the brown sugar mixture keeps the sugar from lumping. Don't worry if the sugar lumps—it will dissolve as the milk heats—but make sure not to add the egg-cornstarch mixture until the sugar completely dissolves.

FILLING

- ½ cup evaporated milk
- ¼ cup cornstarch
- ¼ teaspoon salt
- 5 large egg yolks
- 6 tablespoons unsalted butter
- 1 cup packed (7 ounces) light brown sugar
- 2 cups whole milk
- 1½ teaspoons vanilla extract

- 1 recipe single-crust pie dough for custard pies, fully baked and cooled

TOPPING

- 1 cup heavy cream, chilled
- 2 tablespoons confectioners' sugar
- ½ teaspoon vanilla extract

1. Whisk evaporated milk, cornstarch, and salt together in medium bowl, then whisk in egg yolks.

2. Stir butter and brown sugar together in medium saucepan and cook over medium heat until mixture turns creamy and begins to bubble vigorously, about 5 minutes. Slowly whisk in milk until sugar has dissolved. Slowly whisk in evaporated milk mixture and continue to cook, whisking constantly, until mixture thickens slightly, about 1 minute. Off heat, whisk in vanilla. Let mixture cool until just warm, stirring often, about 5 minutes.

3. Pour warm filling into cooled prebaked pie crust. Lay sheet of plastic wrap directly on surface of filling and refrigerate pie until filling is chilled and set, about 4 hours.

4. FOR THE TOPPING: Once pie is chilled, use stand mixer fitted with whisk to whip cream, sugar, and vanilla on medium-low speed until foamy, about 1 minute. Increase speed to high and whip until soft peaks form, 1 to 3 minutes. Spread whipped cream attractively over top of pie.

CHOCOLATE CREAM PIE

✓ WHY THIS RECIPE WORKS

Chocolate cream pies can look superb but they're often gluey, overly sweet, and impossible to slice. We wanted a voluptuously creamy pie, with a well-balanced chocolate flavor somewhere between milkshake and melted candy bar, and a delicious, easy-to-slice crust. After testing every type of cookie on the market, we hit on pulverized Oreos and a bit of melted butter for the tastiest, most tender, sliceable crumb crust. We found that the secret to perfect chocolate cream pie filling was to combine two different types of chocolate for a deeper, more complex flavor. Bittersweet or semisweet chocolate provides the main thrust of flavor and intensely flavored unsweetened chocolate lends depth. One ounce of unsweetened chocolate may not seem like much, but it gives this pie great flavor. We also discovered that the custard's texture depended upon carefully pouring the egg yolk mixture into simmering half-and-half, then whisking in butter.

CHOCOLATE CREAM PIE
SERVES 8

Other brands of chocolate sandwich cookies may be substituted for the Oreos, but avoid any "double-filled" cookies because the proportion of cookie to filling won't be correct. For more information on making a cookie crust, see page 712. Do not combine the egg yolks and sugar in advance of making the filling—the sugar will begin to break down the yolks, and the finished cream will be pitted.

CRUST

16   Oreo cookies, broken into rough pieces
4   tablespoons unsalted butter, melted and cooled

FILLING

2½   cups half-and-half
⅓   cup (2⅓ ounces) sugar
     Pinch salt
6   large egg yolks
2   tablespoons cornstarch
6   tablespoons unsalted butter, cut into 6 pieces
6   ounces semisweet or bittersweet chocolate, chopped fine
1   ounce unsweetened chocolate, chopped fine
1   teaspoon vanilla extract

TOPPING

1½   cups heavy cream, chilled
2   tablespoons sugar
½   teaspoon vanilla extract

1. FOR THE CRUST: Adjust oven rack to middle position and heat oven to 350 degrees. Pulse cookies in food processor until coarsely ground, about 15 pulses, then continue to process to fine, even crumbs, about 15 seconds. Sprinkle melted butter over crumbs and pulse to incorporate, about 5 pulses.

2. Sprinkle mixture into 9-inch pie plate. Using bottom of measuring cup, press crumbs into even layer on bottom and sides of pie plate. Bake until crust is fragrant and looks set, 10 to 15 minutes. Transfer pie plate to wire rack and let crust cool completely.

3. FOR THE FILLING: Bring half-and-half, 3 tablespoons sugar, and salt to simmer in medium saucepan, stirring occasionally.

4. As half-and-half mixture begins to simmer, whisk egg yolks, cornstarch, and remaining sugar together in medium bowl until smooth. Slowly whisk 1 cup of simmering half-and-half mixture into yolk

mixture to temper, then slowly whisk tempered yolk mixture back into remaining half-and-half mixture. Reduce heat to medium and cook, whisking vigorously, until mixture is thickened and few bubbles burst on surface, about 30 seconds. Off heat, whisk in butter, semisweet chocolate, and unsweetened chocolate until completely smooth and melted, then stir in vanilla.

5. Pour warm filling into cooled pre-baked pie crust. Lay sheet of plastic wrap directly on surface of filling and refrigerate pie until filling is chilled and set, about 4 hours.

6. FOR THE TOPPING: Once pie is chilled, use stand mixer fitted with whisk to whip cream, sugar, and vanilla on medium-low speed until foamy, about 1 minute. Increase speed to high and whip until soft peaks form, 1 to 3 minutes. Spread whipped cream attractively over top of pie.

COCONUT CREAM PIE

✓ WHY THIS RECIPE WORKS

Most recipes for this diner dessert are nothing more than a redecorated vanilla cream pie. A handful of coconut shreds stirred into the filling or sprinkled on the whipped cream might be enough to give it a new name, but certainly not enough to give it flavor. We wanted a coconut cream pie with the exotic and elusive flavor of tropical coconut rather than a thinly disguised vanilla custard. We found that a not-too-sweet graham cracker crust provided a delicate, cookie-like texture that didn't overshadow the coconut filling. For the filling, we started with a basic custard, using a combination of unsweetened coconut milk and whole milk. For more coconut flavor, we stirred in unsweetened shredded coconut and cooked it so the shreds softened slightly in the hot milk. Lastly, we topped the pie with rum-spiked whipped cream and dusted it with crunchy shreds of toasted coconut.

COCONUT CREAM PIE
SERVES 8

Do not use light coconut milk here because it does not have enough flavor. Also, don't confuse coconut milk with cream of coconut. The filling should be warm when poured into the cooled pie crust. To toast the coconut, place it in a small skillet over medium heat and cook, stirring often, for 3 to 5 minutes. It burns quite easily, so keep a close eye on it.

FILLING
- 1 (14-ounce) can coconut milk
- 1 cup whole milk
- ⅔ cup (4⅔ ounces) sugar
- ½ cup (1¼ ounces) unsweetened shredded coconut
- ¼ teaspoon salt
- 5 large egg yolks
- ¼ cup cornstarch
- 2 tablespoons unsalted butter, cut into 2 pieces
- 1½ teaspoons vanilla extract

- 1 recipe Graham Cracker Crust (page 712), baked and cooled

TOPPING
- 1½ cups heavy cream, chilled
- 1½ tablespoons sugar
- 1½ teaspoons dark rum (optional)
- ½ teaspoon vanilla extract
- 1 tablespoon unsweetened shredded coconut, toasted

1. FOR THE FILLING: Bring coconut milk, whole milk, ⅓ cup sugar, shredded coconut, and salt to simmer in medium saucepan, stirring occasionally.

2. As milk mixture begins to simmer, whisk egg yolks, cornstarch, and remaining ⅓ cup sugar together in medium bowl until smooth. Slowly whisk 1 cup of simmering coconut milk mixture into yolk mixture to temper, then slowly whisk tempered yolk mixture back into remaining coconut milk mixture. Reduce heat to medium and cook, whisking vigorously, until mixture is thickened and few bubbles burst on surface, about 30 seconds. Off heat, whisk in butter and vanilla. Let mixture cool until just warm, stirring often, about 5 minutes.

3. Pour warm filling into cooled pre-baked pie crust. Lay sheet of plastic wrap directly on surface of filling and refrigerate pie until filling is chilled and set, about 4 hours.

4. FOR THE TOPPING: Before serving, using stand mixer fitted with whisk, whip cream, sugar, rum, if using, and vanilla together on medium-low speed until frothy, about 1 minute. Increase speed to high and continue to whip until soft peaks form, 1 to 3 minutes. Spread whipped cream attractively over top of pie and sprinkle with toasted coconut.

LIME-COCONUT CREAM PIE

Whisk 1½ teaspoons grated lime zest into filling along with vanilla and butter.

BANANA-CARAMEL COCONUT CREAM PIE

This variation is a test kitchen favorite. Light coconut milk lacks rich coconut flavor, so skip it in favor of regular coconut milk. You may be left with ⅓ cup or so of filling that will not fit into the crust because of the caramel and banana.

1. Add 3 tablespoons water to small saucepan, then pour ½ cup sugar into center of saucepan. Gently stir sugar with clean spatula to wet thoroughly. Bring to boil and cook until sugar mixture turns dark amber, 5 to 8 minutes, swirling pan occasionally once sugar begins to color. Off heat, add 3 tablespoons heavy cream (caramel will bubble vigorously) and pinch salt; whisk to combine. Whisk in 2 tablespoons unsalted butter. Pour caramel into cooled prebaked pie crust, tilting pie plate to coat evenly; set aside to cool. When caramel is cool, peel 2 slightly underripe bananas and slice crosswise ¼ inch thick. Arrange slices in single layer on top of caramel.

2. Whisk 2 teaspoons dark rum into filling along with butter and vanilla and pour filling over sliced bananas. Continue with recipe.

KEY LIME PIE

✔ WHY THIS RECIPE WORKS
Some of us have been served Key lime pie in restaurants and found it disappointing, usually harsh and artificial tasting. We wanted a recipe for classic Key lime pie with a fresh flavor and silky filling. Traditional Key lime pie is usually not baked; instead, the combination of egg yolks, lime juice, and sweetened condensed milk firms up when chilled because the juice's acidity causes the proteins in the eggs and milk to bind. We found that just one simple swap—from bottled, reconstituted lime juice to juice and zest from fresh limes—gave us a pie that was pungent and refreshing, cool and yet creamy, and very satisfying. We also discovered that while the pie filling will set without baking (most recipes call only for mixing and then chilling), it set much more nicely after being baked for only 15 minutes. We tried other, more dramatic, departures from the "classic" recipe—folding in egg whites, substituting heavy cream for condensed milk—but they didn't work. Just two seemingly minor adjustments to the classic recipe made all the difference in the world.

KEY LIME PIE
SERVES 8

Despite this pie's name, we found that most tasters could not tell the difference between pies made with regular supermarket limes (called Persian limes) and true Key limes. Since Persian limes are easier to find and juice, we recommend them. The timing here is different from other pies; you need to make the filling first, then prepare the crust.

As its name suggests, Key lime pie is traditionally made from Key limes—a tiny, yellowish variety that grows only in tropical locales (like the Florida Keys, from which they got their name). Key lime aficionados herald the fruit's distinctive flavor and fragrance compared with conventional Persian limes. In our tests, the Key lime juice tasted slightly less tart than the Persian lime juice, but our tasters were split over which variety made the better pie. The deciding factor may be the amount of work involved: To get the half cup of lime juice called for in our Key Lime Pie recipe, we had to squeeze three Persian limes. With the Key limes, it took almost 20! Both Key lime juice and regular lime juice are sold presqueezed in shelf-stable bottles, and we wondered whether these would do in a pinch. The short answer? No way. The four brands we tried were at best bracingly bitter and, in some cases, just plain rancid. What's more, many recipes (including ours) call for the addition of zest—a tough proposition with a glass bottle.

PIE

- 4 large egg yolks
- 4 teaspoons grated lime zest plus ½ cup juice (5 limes)
- 1 (14-ounce) can sweetened condensed milk
- 1 recipe Graham Cracker Crust (page 712)

TOPPING (OPTIONAL)

- 1 cup heavy cream, chilled
- ¼ cup (1 ounce) confectioners' sugar

1. FOR THE PIE: Whisk egg yolks and lime zest together in medium bowl until mixture has light green tint, about 2 minutes. Whisk in condensed milk until smooth, then whisk in lime juice. Cover mixture and set aside at room temperature until thickened, about 30 minutes.

2. Meanwhile, prepare and bake crust. Transfer pie plate to wire rack and leave oven at 325 degrees. (Crust must still be warm when filling is added.)

3. Pour thickened filling into warm prebaked pie crust. Bake pie until center is firm but jiggles slightly when shaken, 15 to 20 minutes. Let pie cool slightly on wire rack, about 1 hour, then cover loosely with plastic wrap and refrigerate until filling is chilled and set, about 3 hours.

4. FOR THE TOPPING, IF USING: Once pie is chilled, use stand mixer fitted with whisk to whip cream and sugar on medium-low speed until foamy, about

1 minute. Increase speed to high and whip until soft peaks form, 1 to 3 minutes. Spread whipped cream attractively over top of pie.

LEMON MERINGUE PIE

✓ WHY THIS RECIPE WORKS

Most everybody loves lemon meringue pie—at least the bottom half of it. The most controversial part is the meringue. On any given day it can shrink, bead, puddle, deflate, burn, sweat, break down, or turn rubbery. We wanted a pie with a crisp, flaky crust and a rich filling that would balance the airy meringue, without blocking the clear lemon flavor. The filling should be soft but not runny, and firm enough to cut but not gelatinous. Most important, we wanted a meringue that didn't break down and puddle on the bottom or "tear" on top. We consulted our food scientist, who told us that the puddling underneath the meringue is from undercooking. The beading on top of the pie is from overcooking. We discovered that if the filling is piping hot when the meringue is applied, the underside of the meringue will not undercook; if the oven temperature is relatively low, the top of the meringue won't overcook. Baking the pie in a relatively cool (325-degree) oven also produces the best-looking, most evenly baked meringue. To further stabilize the meringue and keep it from weeping (even on hot, humid days), we beat in a small amount of cornstarch.

THE ULTIMATE LEMON MERINGUE PIE

SERVES 8

You can use All-Butter or Classic Single-Crust Pie Dough for Custard Pies (pages 710–711) for this pie. Make the pie crust, let it cool, and then begin work on the filling. As soon as the filling is made, cover it with plastic wrap to keep it hot and then start working on the meringue topping. You want to add hot filling to the cooled pie crust, apply the meringue topping, and then quickly get the pie into the oven.

FILLING

- 1½ cups water
- 1 cup (7 ounces) sugar
- ¼ cup cornstarch
- ⅛ teaspoon salt
- 6 large egg yolks
- 1 tablespoon grated lemon zest plus ½ cup juice (3 lemons)
- 2 tablespoons unsalted butter, cut into 2 pieces

MERINGUE

- ⅓ cup water
- 1 tablespoon cornstarch
- 4 large egg whites
- ½ teaspoon vanilla extract
- ¼ teaspoon cream of tartar
- ½ cup (3½ ounces) sugar

- 1 recipe single-crust pie dough for custard pies, fully baked and cooled

1. FOR THE FILLING: Adjust oven rack to middle position and heat oven to 325 degrees. Bring water, sugar, cornstarch, and salt to simmer in large saucepan, whisking constantly. When mixture starts to turn translucent, whisk in egg yolks, two at a time. Whisk in lemon zest and juice and butter. Return mixture to brief simmer, then remove from heat. Lay sheet of plastic wrap directly on surface of filling to keep warm and prevent skin from forming.

1. Start by placing dabs of meringue evenly around edge of pie. Once edge of pie is covered with meringue, fill in center of the pie with remaining meringue.

2. Using rubber spatula, anchor meringue to edge of crust or it may pull away and shrink in oven.

2. FOR THE MERINGUE: Bring water and cornstarch to simmer in small saucepan and cook, whisking occasionally, until thickened and translucent, 1 to 2 minutes. Remove from heat and let cool slightly.

3. Using stand mixer fitted with whisk, whip egg whites, vanilla, and cream of tartar on medium-low speed until foamy, about 1 minute. Increase speed to medium-high and beat in sugar mixture, 1 tablespoon at a time, until incorporated and mixture forms soft, billowy mounds. Add cornstarch mixture, 1 tablespoon at a time; continue to beat to glossy, stiff peaks, 2 to 3 minutes.

4. Meanwhile, remove plastic from filling and return to very low heat during last minute or so of beating meringue (to ensure filling is hot).

5. Pour warm filling into cooled pre-baked pie crust. Using rubber spatula, immediately distribute meringue evenly around edge and then center of pie, attaching meringue to pie crust to prevent shrinking. Using back of spoon, create attractive swirls and peaks in meringue. Bake until meringue is light golden brown, about 20 minutes. Let pie cool on wire rack until filling has set, about 2 hours. Serve.

TARTE TATIN

✔ WHY THIS RECIPE WORKS

When this French dessert—basically an apple tart in which the apples are caramelized and the tart is served upside down—first came to this country, all sorts of different recipes for it appeared. Some were based on traditional French formulas, but others were highly Americanized. When we tried the latter, we were disappointed—we got desserts that tasted like apples coated with caramel sauce or, worse, were just an unidentifiable caramel glop. We wanted a tart that tasted like caramelized apples and looked great, too. The first step of our tarte Tatin took place on the stovetop, not in the oven. We arranged apple quarters in concentric circles in a skillet on their cut side so we could fit more fruit, and flipped the apples over as they caramelized. We prepared the caramel right in the skillet with the apples so the flavors could meld, then covered the syrup-soaked apples with an egg pastry that contained confectioners' sugar rather than granulated sugar, which can make the dough grainy. After baking our tarte Tatin, we flipped the tart over, revealing concentric circles of apples glazed with golden caramel. And for French finish, we mimicked the tart whipped cream, crème fraîche, by whipping heavy cream with sour cream.

TARTE TATIN
SERVES 8

Make sure that the caramel doesn't get too brown before adding the apples in step 5; it should be just golden. Be sure to let the tart rest for 30 minutes before serving, or it will likely break into pieces when you unmold it.

DOUGH
- 1⅓ cups (6⅔ ounces) all-purpose flour
- ¼ cup (1 ounce) confectioners' sugar
- ½ teaspoon salt
- 8 tablespoons unsalted butter, cut into ¼-inch pieces and chilled
- 1 large egg, lightly beaten

APPLES
- 8 tablespoons unsalted butter
- ¾ cup (5¼ ounces) granulated sugar
- 3 pounds Granny Smith apples, peeled, cored, and quartered

TOPPING
- 1 cup heavy cream, chilled
- ½ cup sour cream, chilled

1. FOR THE DOUGH: Process flour, sugar, and salt together in food processor until combined, about 5 seconds. Scatter butter over top and pulse until mixture resembles coarse cornmeal, about 15 pulses. With machine running, add egg and continue to process until dough just comes together around processor blade, about 12 seconds.

2. Turn dough onto sheet of plastic wrap and flatten into 6-inch disk. Wrap tightly in plastic and refrigerate for 1 hour. Before rolling dough out, let it sit on counter to soften slightly, about 10 minutes. (Dough can be wrapped tightly in plastic and refrigerated for up to 2 days or frozen for up to 1 month. If frozen, let dough thaw completely on counter before rolling it out.)

3. Roll dough into 14-inch circle on

lightly floured counter, then transfer to parchment paper–lined baking sheet; cover with plastic and refrigerate until needed.

4. FOR THE APPLES: Adjust oven rack to upper-middle position and heat oven to 425 degrees. Melt butter in 12-inch oven-safe nonstick skillet over medium-high heat. Stir in sugar and cook until mixture is light golden, 2 to 4 minutes.

5. Off heat, place first apple quarter cut side down, with end touching skillet wall. Continue to arrange apples, lifting each quarter on its edge and placing next apple quarter on its edge, so that apples stand straight up on cut edge. Fill skillet middle with remaining quarters, halved if necessary. Cook apples over medium heat until they are lightly golden and caramel is darkly colored, about 6 minutes, turning apples over halfway through cooking.

6. Off heat, slide chilled dough over apples in skillet. Being careful not to burn fingers, fold back edge of dough so that it fits snugly into skillet. Transfer skillet to oven and bake tart until crust is golden brown, about 20 minutes, rotating skillet halfway through baking.

7. Using potholder (skillet handle will be hot), remove skillet from oven. Let tart cool in skillet for 30 minutes. Run small knife around edge, place inverted serving platter (or cutting board) over top and gently flip tart onto platter, using mitts or

kitchen towels if skillet is still hot. Scrape out any apples that stick to skillet and put them back into place on tart.

8. FOR THE TOPPING: Using stand mixer fitted with whisk, whip cream and sour cream on medium-low speed until foamy, about 1 minute. Increase speed to high and whip until soft peaks form, 1 to 3 minutes. Serve individual portions with dollop of topping.

APPLE GALETTE

✔ **WHY THIS RECIPE WORKS**
The French tart known as an apple galette should have a flaky crust and a substantial layer of nicely shingled sweet caramelized apples. But it's challenging to make a crust strong enough to hold the apples and still be eaten out of hand—most recipes create a crust that is tough, cracker-like, and bland. Our ideal galette has the buttery flakiness of a croissant but is strong enough to support a generous layer of caramelized apples. Choosing the right flour put us on the right track. All-purpose flour contains too much gluten for this dough; it made the pastry tough. Lower-protein pastry flour created a flaky, tender, and sturdy pastry. But since pastry flour is hard to find, we created a practical alternative by mixing regular all-purpose flour with instant flour. Technique also proved to be important. We used

the French fraisage method of blending butter into dough, which makes for long, thin sheets of butter that bake up into flaky layers in the crust. The apple topping was simple. We found that any thinly sliced apple would work, although we preferred the flavor of Granny Smiths.

APPLE GALETTE
SERVES 10 TO 12

The most common brands of instant flour are Wondra and Shake & Blend; they are sold in canisters in the baking aisle. The galette can be made without instant flour, using 2 cups all-purpose flour and 2 tablespoons cornstarch; however, you might have to increase the amount of ice water. For more information on mixing the tart dough in step 2, see page 739. Serve with vanilla ice cream, Whipped Cream (page 800) or Tangy Whipped Cream (page 800). If you choose to make the tangy whipped cream, make it before starting the galette because it must stand at room temperature for about 1½ hours before serving.

DOUGH
1½ cups (7½ ounces) all-purpose flour
½ cup (2½ ounces) instant flour
½ teaspoon salt
½ teaspoon sugar
12 tablespoons unsalted butter, cut into ¼-inch pieces and chilled
7–9 tablespoons ice water

ASSEMBLING TARTE TATIN

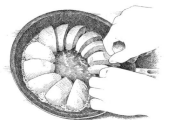

1. Arrange apples around edge of skillet, lifting them on their edges so that they stand up, being careful not to burn your fingers. Arrange remaining apples in middle of skillet.

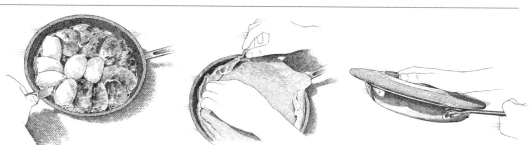

2. Using paring knife, turn apples onto their uncaramelized sides halfway through cooking.

3. Off heat, slide prepared dough off baking sheet over skillet and tuck dough edges gently up against skillet wall.

4. Place serving platter over skillet and hold it tightly against skillet. Invert skillet and platter and set platter on counter. Lift skillet up off platter, leaving tart behind.

PREPARING APPLE GALETTE

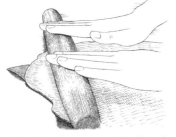

1. Roll dough out onto 16 by 12-inch piece of parchment paper.

2. Trim dough so that edges are even with parchment.

3. Roll up 1 inch of each edge to create ½-inch-thick border on all sides. Transfer dough and parchment to rimmed baking sheet.

4. Starting in 1 corner, shingle sliced apples on diagonal to form even row over dough, overlapping each row by one-third.

TOPPING

1½   pounds Granny Smith apples, peeled, cored, halved, and sliced ⅛-inch thick

2   tablespoons unsalted butter, cut into ¼-inch pieces

¼   cup (1¾ ounces) sugar

3   tablespoons apple jelly

1. FOR THE DOUGH: Process all-purpose flour, instant flour, salt, and sugar together in food processor until combined, about 5 seconds. Scatter butter over top and pulse until mixture resembles coarse cornmeal, about 15 pulses. Continue to pulse, adding water 1 tablespoon at a time until dough begins to form small curds that hold together when pinched with fingers (dough will be crumbly), about 10 pulses.

2. Turn dough crumbs onto lightly floured counter and gather into rectangular-shaped pile. Starting at farthest end, use heel of hand to smear small amount of dough against counter. Continue to smear dough until all crumbs have been worked. Gather smeared crumbs together in another rectangular-shaped pile and repeat process. Press dough into 4-inch square, wrap it tightly in plastic wrap, and refrigerate for 1 hour. Before rolling dough out, let it sit on counter to soften slightly,

about 10 minutes. (Dough can be wrapped tightly in plastic and refrigerated for up to 2 days or frozen for up to 1 month. If frozen, let dough thaw completely on counter before rolling it out.)

3. Adjust oven rack to middle position and heat oven to 400 degrees. Cut piece of parchment paper to measure exactly 16 by 12 inches. Roll dough out over parchment, dusting with flour as needed, until it just overhangs parchment. Trim edges of dough even with parchment. Roll outer 1 inch of dough up to create ½-inch-thick border. Slide parchment with dough onto baking sheet.

4. FOR THE TOPPING: Starting in 1 corner of tart, shingle apple slices into crust in tidy diagonal rows, overlapping them by one-third. Dot with butter and sprinkle evenly with sugar. Bake tart until bottom is deep golden brown and apples have caramelized, 45 minutes to 1 hour, rotating baking sheet halfway through baking.

5. Melt jelly in small saucepan over medium-high heat, stirring occasionally to smooth out any lumps. Brush glaze over apples and let tart cool slightly on sheet for 10 minutes. Slide tart onto large platter or cutting board and slice tart in half lengthwise, then crosswise into square pieces. Serve warm or at room temperature.

CLASSIC TART DOUGH

✔ WHY THIS RECIPE WORKS

While regular pie crust is tender and flaky, classic tart crust should be fine-textured, buttery-rich, crisp, and crumbly—it is often described as being shortbreadlike. We set out to achieve the perfect tart dough, one that we could use in a number of tart recipes. We found that using a stick of butter made tart dough that tasted great and was easy to handle, yet still had a delicate crumb. Instead of using the hard-to-find superfine sugar and pastry flour that many other recipes call for, we used confectioners' sugar and all-purpose flour to achieve a crisp texture. Rolling the dough and fitting it into the tart pan was easy, and we had ample dough to patch any holes.

CLASSIC TART DOUGH
MAKES ENOUGH FOR ONE 9-INCH TART

Tart crust is sweeter, crispier, and less flaky than pie crust—it is more similar in texture to a cookie.

1   large egg yolk

1   tablespoon heavy cream

½   teaspoon vanilla extract

1¼   cups (6¼ ounces) all-purpose flour

⅔   cup (2⅔ ounces) confectioners' sugar

¼   teaspoon salt

8   tablespoons unsalted butter, cut into ¼-inch pieces and chilled

1. Whisk egg yolk, cream, and vanilla together in bowl. Process flour, sugar, and salt together in food processor until combined, about 5 seconds. Scatter butter over top and pulse until mixture resembles coarse cornmeal, about 15 pulses. With machine running, add egg mixture and continue to process until dough just comes together around processor blade, about 12 seconds.

2. Turn dough onto sheet of plastic wrap and flatten into 6-inch disk. Wrap tightly in plastic and refrigerate for 1 hour. Before rolling dough out, let it sit on counter to soften slightly, about 10 minutes. (Dough can be wrapped tightly in plastic wrap and refrigerated for up to 2 days or frozen for up to 1 month. If frozen, let dough thaw completely on counter before rolling it out.)

3. Roll dough into 11-inch circle on lightly floured counter (if at any point dough becomes too soft and sticky to work with, slip dough onto baking sheet and freeze or refrigerate until workable). Place dough round on baking sheet, cover with plastic, and refrigerate for about 30 minutes.

4. Remove dough from refrigerator; discard plastic but keep dough on baking sheet. Loosely roll dough around rolling pin and gently unroll it onto 9-inch tart pan with removable bottom, letting excess dough hang over edge. Ease dough into pan by gently lifting edge of dough with 1 hand while pressing into corners with other hand. Leave any dough that overhangs pan in place.

5. Press dough into fluted sides of pan, forming distinct seam around pan's circumference. (If some sections of edge are too thin, reinforce them by folding excess dough back on itself.) Run rolling pin over top of tart pan to remove any excess dough. Wrap dough-lined tart pan loosely in plastic, place on large plate, and freeze until dough is fully chilled and firm, about 30 minutes, before using. (Dough-lined tart pan can be wrapped tightly in plastic and frozen for up to 1 month.)

6. Adjust oven rack to middle position and heat oven to 375 degrees. Set dough-lined tart pan on rimmed baking sheet. Spray 1 side of double layer of aluminum foil with vegetable oil spray. Press foil greased side down into frozen tart shell, covering edges to prevent burning, and fill with pie weights.

7A. FOR A PARTIALLY BAKED SHELL: Bake until tart shell is golden brown and set, about 30 minutes, rotating baking sheet halfway through baking. Transfer tart shell with baking sheet to wire rack and carefully remove weights and foil. Use crust while it is still warm or let it cool completely (see individual tart recipe instructions).

7B. FOR A FULLY BAKED SHELL: Bake until tart shell is golden brown and set, about 30 minutes, rotating baking sheet halfway through baking. Carefully remove weights and foil and continue to bake tart shell until it is fully baked and golden, 5 to 10 minutes longer. Transfer tart shell with baking sheet to wire rack and let tart shell cool completely, about 1 hour.

CLASSIC CHOCOLATE TART DOUGH

Substitute ¼ cup Dutch-processed cocoa for ¼ cup flour.

FRESH FRUIT TART

✔ WHY THIS RECIPE WORKS

Fresh fruit tarts usually offer little substance beyond their dazzling beauty, with rubbery or puddinglike fillings, soggy crusts, and underripe, flavorless fruit. We set out to create a buttery, crisp crust filled with rich, lightly sweetened pastry cream, topped with fresh fruit. We started with our Classic Tart Dough as the crust and baked it until it was golden brown. We then filled the tart with pastry cream, made with half-and-half that was enriched with butter and thickened with just enough cornstarch to keep its shape without becoming gummy. For the fruit, we chose a combination of sliced kiwis, raspberries, and blueberries. We found that it was important not to wash the berries, as washing causes them to bruise and bleed and makes for a less than attractive tart (buy organic if you're worried about pesticide residues). The finishing touch: a drizzle of jelly glaze for a glistening presentation.

FITTING TART DOUGH INTO THE PAN

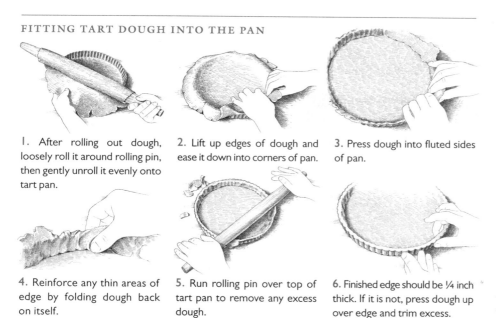

1. After rolling out dough, loosely roll it around rolling pin, then gently unroll it evenly onto tart pan.

2. Lift up edges of dough and ease it down into corners of pan.

3. Press dough into fluted sides of pan.

4. Reinforce any thin areas of edge by folding dough back on itself.

5. Run rolling pin over top of tart pan to remove any excess dough.

6. Finished edge should be ¼ inch thick. If it is not, press dough up over edge and trim excess.

CLASSIC FRESH FRUIT TART
SERVES 8 TO 10

Do not fill the prebaked tart shell until just before serving. Once filled, the tart should be topped with fruit, glazed, and served within 30 minutes or so. Don't wash the berries or they will lose their flavor and shape.

2	cups half-and-half
½	cup (3½ ounces) sugar
	Pinch salt
5	large egg yolks
3	tablespoons cornstarch
4	tablespoons unsalted butter, cut into 4 pieces
1½	teaspoons vanilla extract
1	recipe Classic Tart Dough (page 730), fully baked and cooled
2	large kiwis, peeled, halved lengthwise, and sliced ⅜ inch thick
10	ounces (2 cups) raspberries
5	ounces (1 cup) blueberries
½	cup red currant or apple jelly

1. Bring half-and-half, 6 tablespoons sugar, and salt to simmer in medium saucepan, stirring occasionally.

2. As half-and-half mixture begins to simmer, whisk egg yolks, cornstarch, and remaining 2 tablespoons sugar together in medium bowl until smooth. Slowly whisk 1 cup of simmering half-and-half mixture into yolk mixture to temper, then slowly whisk tempered yolk mixture back into remaining half-and-half mixture. Reduce heat to medium and cook, whisking vigorously, until mixture is thickened and few bubbles burst on surface, about 30 seconds. Off heat, whisk in butter and vanilla. Transfer mixture to clean bowl, lay sheet of plastic wrap directly on surface, and refrigerate pastry cream until chilled and firm, about 3 hours. (Pastry cream can be refrigerated for up to 2 days.)

3. Spread chilled pastry cream evenly over bottom of cooled prebaked tart shell. Shingle kiwi slices around edge of tart,

then arrange 3 rows of raspberries inside kiwi. Finally, arrange mound of blueberries in center.

4. Melt jelly in small saucepan over medium-high heat, stirring occasionally to smooth out any lumps. Using pastry brush, dab melted jelly over fruit. To serve, remove outer metal ring of tart pan, slide thin metal spatula between tart and tart pan bottom, and carefully slide tart onto serving platter or cutting board.

MIXED BERRY TART WITH PASTRY CREAM

Omit kiwi and add 10 ounces extra berries (including blackberries or hulled and quartered strawberries). Combine berries in large plastic bag and toss them gently to mix. Carefully spread berries in even layer over tart. Glaze and serve as directed.

LEMON TART

✔ WHY THIS RECIPE WORKS
Despite its apparent simplicity, there is much that can go wrong with a lemon tart. It can slip over the edge of sweet into cloying; its tartness can grab at your throat; it can be gluey or eggy or, even worse, metallic tasting. Its crust can be too hard, too soft, too thick, or too sweet. We wanted a proper tart, one in which the filling is baked with the shell. For us, that meant only one thing: lemon curd. For just enough sugar to offset the acid in the lemons, we used 3 parts sugar to 2 parts lemon juice, plus a whopping ¼ cup of lemon zest. To achieve a curd that was creamy and dense with a vibrant lemony yellow color, we used a combination of whole eggs and egg yolks. We cooked the curd over direct heat, then whisked in the butter. And for a smooth, light texture, we strained the curd, then stirred in heavy cream just before baking.

CLASSIC LEMON TART
SERVES 8 TO 10

Once the lemon curd ingredients have been combined, cook the curd immediately; otherwise it will have a grainy finished texture. The shell should still be warm when the filling is added. Dust with confectioners' sugar before serving, or serve with Whipped Cream (page 800).

2	large eggs plus 7 large yolks
1	cup (7 ounces) sugar
¼	cup grated lemon zest plus ⅔ cup juice (4 lemons)
	Pinch salt
4	tablespoons unsalted butter, cut into 4 pieces
3	tablespoons heavy cream
1	recipe Classic Tart Dough (page 730), partially baked and still warm

---

TEST KITCHEN TIP NO. 147 **MAKING THE MOST OF LEMONS**

To keep lemons from becoming hard and dry before you get a chance to use them, start with the juiciest lemons you can find. Our shopping tests showed that thin-skinned lemons that yield under pressure contain more juice than thick-skinned, rock-hard specimens of the same size and weight. As for storage, we tested three different methods, both at room temperature and in the refrigerator: in an uncovered container, in a sealed zipper-lock bag, and in a sealed zipper-lock bag with ¼ cup water. All the lemons stored at room temperature hardened after a week. The refrigerated samples fared much better: The uncovered lemons (which we kept in the crisper drawer) began to lose a little moisture after the first week; the lemons stored in zipper-lock bags didn't begin to dehydrate until four weeks had passed. The water didn't help with preservation, but the zipper-lock bag did seal in some moisture. For the juiciest, longest-lasting lemons (and any other citrus fruits), the best way to store them is to seal them in a zipper-lock bag. Refrigerator storage does make it more difficult to squeeze juice, so let the fruit sit at room temperature for about 15 minutes before juicing.

1. Adjust oven rack to middle position and heat oven to 375 degrees. Whisk eggs and egg yolks together in medium saucepan. Whisk in sugar until combined, then whisk in lemon zest and juice and salt. Add butter and cook over medium-low heat, stirring constantly, until mixture thickens slightly and registers 170 degrees, about 5 minutes. Immediately pour mixture through fine-mesh strainer into bowl and stir in cream.

2. Pour warm lemon filling into warm prebaked tart shell. Bake tart on baking sheet until filling is shiny and opaque and center jiggles slightly when shaken, 10 to 15 minutes, rotating baking sheet halfway through baking. Transfer tart with baking sheet to wire rack and let cool to room temperature, about 2 hours. To serve, remove outer metal ring of tart pan, slide thin metal spatula between tart and tart pan bottom, and carefully slide tart onto serving platter or cutting board.

BAKED RASPBERRY TART

✔ WHY THIS RECIPE WORKS
Tart raspberries, rich custard, and a buttery crust are a classic white-tablecloth combination. But we wanted something a little less labor-intensive; we were seeking a more rustic, casual approach that still provided the perfect marriage of fruit, custard, and pastry. To perfect our baked raspberry tart, we focused on the filling—working with a simple butter, egg, sugar, and flour batter—since we were already happy with our classic tart crust. We heightened the filling's flavor by browning the butter instead of simply melting it. Using one whole egg plus an egg white ensured the filling set into a nicely firm yet creamy texture. And substituting instant flour for all-purpose flour in our berry tart filling gave us a smooth and silky (rather than starchy and coarse) texture.

The most common brands of instant flour are Wondra and Shake & Blend; they are sold in canisters in the baking aisle. To minimize waste, reserve the egg white left from making the tart pastry for use in the filling. If your raspberries are either very tart or very sweet, adjust the amount of sugar in the filling by about a tablespoon or so. The tart is best eaten the day it is made.

- 6 tablespoons unsalted butter
- 1 large egg plus 1 large white
- ½ cup (3½ ounces) plus 1 tablespoon sugar
- ¼ teaspoon salt
- 1 teaspoon vanilla extract
- 1 teaspoon kirsch or framboise (optional)
- ¼ teaspoon grated lemon zest plus 1½ teaspoons juice
- 2 tablespoons instant flour
- 2 tablespoons heavy cream
- 10 ounces (2 cups) raspberries
- 1 recipe Classic Tart Dough (page 730), partially baked and cooled

1. Adjust oven rack to middle position and heat oven to 375 degrees. Melt butter in small saucepan over medium heat, swirling occasionally, until butter is browned and releases nutty aroma, about 7 minutes. Transfer butter to small bowl and let cool slightly. Whisk egg and egg white in medium bowl until combined. Add sugar and salt and whisk vigorously until light colored, about 1 minute. Whisk in warm browned butter until combined, then whisk in vanilla, kirsch, if using, and lemon zest and juice. Whisk in instant flour, then whisk in cream until combined.

2. Distribute raspberries in single tightly packed layer in bottom of cooled prebaked tart shell. Pour filling mixture evenly over raspberries. Bake tart on baking sheet until fragrant and filling is set (it does not jiggle when shaken), bubbling lightly around edges, and surface is puffed and deep golden brown, about 30 minutes, rotating baking sheet halfway through baking. Transfer tart with baking sheet to wire rack and let cool to room temperature, about 2 hours. To serve, remove outer metal ring of tart pan, slide thin metal spatula between tart and tart pan bottom, and carefully slide tart onto serving platter or cutting board.

Substitute 10 ounces blackberries for raspberries.

Replace 5 ounces raspberries with 5 ounces blueberries.

POACHED PEAR AND ALMOND TART

✔ WHY THIS RECIPE WORKS
A whole day of preparation is required to make poached pear and almond tart, and the risks are great: a soggy crust, a coarse, wet frangipane (almond filling) heavy-handedly flavored with almond extract, and tasteless poached pears that either retain too much crunch or are soft to the point of listlessness. Since this tart requires a substantial investment of time, ours had to be worthwhile. We wanted satin-ribbon slices of tender, sweet, perfumed poached pears embedded in a sweet, nutty, rich, fragrant, custard-cake almond filling, all contained in a crisp, buttery pastry. During our testing, we determined that ripe yet firm Bosc or Bartlett pears gave our pear tart recipe the best flavor, especially when poached in white wine spiced with a cinnamon stick, black peppercorns, whole cloves, and a vanilla bean. For the frangipane in our pear tart, we processed blanched slivered almonds in a food processor

with sugar, so they could be ground superfine without becoming greasy. We made sure to dry the pears before setting them on the frangipane; otherwise, they released moisture, turning the dessert sticky and wet. Once the tart was baked, we glazed the pears with apple jelly for a glossy, shiny finish.

POACHED PEAR AND ALMOND TART

SERVES 8 TO 10

If you cannot find blanched slivered almonds, use whole blanched almonds, but chop them coarse before processing to make sure they form a fine, even grind. The pears should be ripe but firm, the flesh, near the stem, giving slightly when gently pressed with a finger. Purchase the pears a few days ahead and allow them to ripen at room temperature. If they ripen before you need them, refrigerate them and use them within a day or two, or poach them and hold them in their syrup (they will keep for about 3 days). Many tasters liked the bright, crisp flavor of pears poached in Sauvignon Blanc. Chardonnay-poached pears had deeper, oakier flavors and were also well liked.

POACHED PEARS

1	(750-ml) bottle white wine
2/3	cup (4 2/3 ounces) sugar
5	(2-inch) strips lemon zest plus 2 tablespoons juice
1	cinnamon stick
15	whole peppercorns
3	whole cloves
1/8	teaspoon salt
1/2	vanilla bean (optional)
4	Bosc or Bartlett pears (8 ounces each), peeled, halved, and cored

FILLING AND GLAZE

1	cup blanched slivered almonds
1/2	cup (3 1/2 ounces) sugar
1/8	teaspoon salt
1	large egg plus 1 large white
1/2	teaspoon almond extract
1/2	teaspoon vanilla extract

6	tablespoons unsalted butter, cut into 6 pieces and softened
1	recipe Classic Tart Dough (page 730), partially baked and cooled
1/4	cup apple jelly

1. FOR THE POACHED PEARS: Adjust oven rack to middle position and heat oven to 350 degrees. Combine wine, sugar, lemon zest and juice, cinnamon stick, peppercorns, cloves, and salt in large saucepan. If using, cut vanilla bean in half lengthwise, then, using tip of paring knife, scrape out seeds, and add seeds and pod to saucepan. Bring mixture to simmer, stirring occasionally to dissolve sugar. Slide pear halves into simmering wine mixture; return to simmer, then reduce heat to low, cover, and poach pears, turning them occasionally, until tender and skewer can be inserted into pear with very little resistance about 10 minutes. Off heat, let pears cool in liquid, partially

covered, until pears have turned translucent and are cool enough to handle, about 1 hour. (Pears and liquid can be transferred to bowl, cooled to room temperature, covered, and refrigerated for up to 3 days.)

2. FOR THE ALMOND FILLING: Pulse almonds, sugar, and salt in food processor until finely ground, about 25 pulses. Continue to process until nut mixture is as finely ground as possible, about 10 seconds. Add egg and egg white, almond extract, and vanilla and process until combined, about 10 seconds. Add butter and process until no lumps remain, about 20 seconds, scraping down bowl as needed. (Filling can transferred to bowl, covered, and refrigerated for up to 3 days. Before using, let stand at room temperature about 30 minutes to soften, stirring 3 or 4 times.)

3. Spread filling evenly over bottom of cooled, partially baked tart shell. Remove pears from poaching liquid and pat dry

ASSEMBLING PEAR TART

1. Spread filling evenly into bottom of partially baked and cooled tart shell using offset spatula.

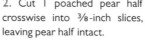

2. Cut 1 poached pear half crosswise into 3/8-inch slices, leaving pear half intact.

3. After discarding first 4 slices from narrow end of sliced pear half, slide spatula under pear, then slide pear off spatula onto center of tart.

4. Cut another pear half following step 2. Slide spatula under pear and gently press pear to fan slices toward narrow end.

5. Slide fanned pear half onto filling, narrow end toward center, almost touching center pear.

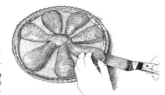

6. Repeat steps 2, 4, and 5 with remaining pear halves, spacing them evenly and making flower petal pattern off center pear. If necessary, use spatula to push pears to space them evenly.

with paper towels. Cut poached pear half crosswise into ⅜-inch slices, leaving pear half intact on cutting board (do not separate slices). Pat dry again with paper towels to absorb excess moisture. Discard first 4 slices from narrow end of sliced pear half. Slide spatula under sliced pear and, steadying it with 1 hand, slide pear off spatula onto center of tart. Cut and dry another pear half. Slide spatula under pear and gently press pear to fan slices toward narrow end. Slide fanned pear half onto filling, narrow end toward center, almost touching center pear. Repeat slicing, fanning, and placing remaining pear halves, spacing them evenly and making flower petal pattern off center pear.

4. Bake tart on baking sheet until crust is deep golden brown and almond filling is puffed, browned, and firm to the touch, about 45 minutes, rotating baking sheet halfway through baking. Transfer tart with baking sheet to wire rack and let cool for 10 minutes.

5. Melt jelly in small saucepan over medium-high heat, stirring occasionally to smooth out lumps. Using pastry brush, dab melted jelly over fruit. Let tart cool to room temperature, about 2 hours. To serve, remove outer metal ring of tart pan, slide thin metal spatula between tart and tart pan bottom, and carefully slide tart onto serving platter or cutting board.

LINZERTORTE

✔ WHY THIS RECIPE WORKS

The ingredients for linzertortes are easy to prepare—a food processor produces the buttery nut crust, and you buy a jar of raspberry jam for the filling—but the result is too often a slipshod, homely looking dessert. We wanted our linzertorte to have both the taste and the appearance worthy of a dessert with star billing. To start, we made an uncomplicated dough using a base of 2 parts hazelnuts and 1 part almonds. A single

raw egg moistened and bound the dough nicely, and cinnamon and allspice added traditional spice flavors. For the filling, we liked raspberry preserves, brightened with a spoonful of lemon juice. For an attractive, company-worthy presentation, we created a lattice crust by placing dough strips one by one in a precise order over the tart. Brushing the lattice strips with heavy cream, then sprinkling them with turbinado sugar, ensured a well-browned crust.

LINZERTORTE

SERVES 10 TO 12

Make sure to buy blanched almonds. Be sure to use an 11-inch tart pan here. You will have some extra dough when cutting out the lattice strips; we suggest cutting out a few extra lattice strips as backup (they can be delicate and will sometimes break). If at any time while forming the lattice the dough becomes too soft, refrigerate it for 15 minutes before continuing. The linzertorte may be served at room temperature the day it is baked, but it is at its best after a night in the refrigerator.

TART DOUGH

1	large egg
1	teaspoon vanilla extract
1	cup hazelnuts, toasted and skinned
½	cup blanched almonds
½	cup plus 2 tablespoons (4⅓ ounces) sugar
½	teaspoon salt
1	teaspoon grated lemon zest
1½	cups (7½ ounces) all-purpose flour
½	teaspoon ground cinnamon
⅛	teaspoon ground allspice
12	tablespoons unsalted butter, cut into ½-inch pieces and chilled

FILLING AND GLAZE

1¼	cups raspberry preserves
1	tablespoon lemon juice
1	tablespoon heavy cream
1½	teaspoons turbinado or Demerara sugar (optional)

1. FOR THE TART DOUGH: Whisk egg and vanilla together in bowl. Process hazelnuts, almonds, sugar, and salt in food processor until very finely ground, 45 to 60 seconds. Add lemon zest and pulse to combine, about 5 pulses. Add flour, cinnamon, and allspice and pulse to combine, about 5 pulses. Scatter butter over top and pulse until mixture resembles coarse cornmeal, about 15 pulses. With machine running, add egg mixture and continue to process until dough just comes together around processor blade, about 12 seconds.

2. Turn dough onto counter and press together to form cohesive mound. Divide dough in half and flatten each piece into 5-inch disk; if not using immediately, wrap each piece tightly in plastic wrap and refrigerate up to 48 hours. (If refrigerated until firm, let dough sit at room temperature until soft and malleable, about 1 hour.)

3. Tear 1 piece of dough into walnut-size pieces, then pat it into 11-inch tart pan with removable bottom, pressing it ¾ inch up sides of pan. Lay plastic over dough and smooth out any bumps using bottom of measuring cup. Set tart pan on large plate and freeze until dough is fully chilled and firm, about 30 minutes.

4. Roll other piece of dough into 12-inch square between 2 large sheets of floured parchment paper. (If dough sticks to parchment, gently loosen and lift sticky area with bench scraper and dust parchment with additional flour. Slide dough, still between parchment sheets, onto rimmed baking sheet and refrigerate until firm, about 15 minutes.) Remove top layer of parchment and trim edges of dough, then cut ten ¾-inch-wide strips, cutting through underlying parchment. Cover with parchment and freeze until dough is fully chilled and firm, about 20 minutes.

5. Meanwhile, adjust oven rack to middle position and heat oven to 350 degrees. Set dough-lined tart pan on rimmed baking sheet. Spray 1 side of double layer of

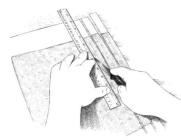

1. After chilling dough square, trim any rough edges, then cut square into 10 strips, each ¾ inch wide, cutting through underlying parchment paper.

2. Place parchment-lined strip of dough over tart and peel off parchment; trim ends of dough. Place 2 more strips parallel to first, spacing them evenly.

3. Place remaining 8 dough strips on tart, rotating pan as needed to form lattice top.

4. Using scraps of dough, fill in crust around edges between lattice strips.

aluminum foil with vegetable oil spray. Press foil greased side down into frozen tart shell, covering edges to prevent burning, and fill with pie weights. Bake until tart shell is golden brown and set, about 30 minutes, rotating baking sheet halfway through baking. Transfer tart shell with baking sheet to wire rack, carefully remove weights, and let cool slightly while making filling.

6. FOR THE FILLING AND GLAZE: Stir raspberry preserves and lemon juice together in bowl, then spread evenly over bottom of cooled prebaked tart shell. Pick up strip of dough by parchment ends, then flip it over onto tart, positioning it near edge of pan. Remove parchment strip and trim ends of dough strip by pressing down on top edge of pan; reserve all dough scraps. Place 2 more strips parallel to first, spacing them evenly so that one is across center and other is near opposite edge of pan. Rotate pan 90 degrees, then place 3 more strips as you did first 3. Rotate pan 90 degrees again, then place 2 strips across pan, spaced evenly between first 3. Rotate pan again and complete lattice by placing last 2 strips between second set of 3. Use small scraps of dough to fill in crust around edges between lattice strips. Top of crust should be just below top of pan.

7. Gently brush lattice strips with heavy cream and sprinkle with turbinado sugar, if using. Bake tart on baking sheet until crust is deep golden brown, about 50 minutes. Transfer tart with baking sheet to wire rack and let cool to room temperature, about 2 hours. To serve, remove outer metal ring of tart pan, slide thin metal spatula between tart and tart pan bottom, and carefully slide tart onto serving platter or cutting board.

CHOCOLATE CARAMEL WALNUT TART

✔ WHY THIS RECIPE WORKS

Considering the natural affinity of its main ingredients, a chocolate caramel walnut tart would seem a hard recipe to botch. However, this trio doesn't always live in harmony. Some recipes relegate the walnuts to a mere garnish and sprinkle them over chilled chocolate fillings with textures that run the gamut from soft pudding to cold butter. Other recipes place the nuts at the fore, but these are simply uptown knockoffs of pecan pie. We wanted a layer of walnuts draped with soft caramel topped with a smooth layer of rich, dark chocolate—firm enough to slice neatly but neither dense nor overpowering. A modified sweet tart pastry was the launch pad for our tart

crust. Adding ground walnuts to boost the flavor meant we had to reduce the amount of butter (to account for the lesser quantity of flour and the extra fat from the ground nuts). A soft, gooey caramel-walnut filling, with an egg-lightened layer of chocolate ganache baked (rather than chilled) on top, made for a rich tart. After baking, a three-hour chill firmed the chocolate layer. Caramel-coated walnuts provided the perfect finishing touch.

CHOCOLATE CARAMEL WALNUT TART

SERVES 8 TO 10

For more information on fitting tart dough into the pan, see page 731. For cutting clean slices, dip the blade of the knife in warm water and wipe with a kitchen towel before making each cut.

WALNUT CRUST

1	large egg
¼	teaspoon vanilla extract
½	cup walnuts, toasted
½	cup (2 ounces) confectioners' sugar
1	cup (5 ounces) all-purpose flour
⅛	teaspoon salt
5	tablespoons unsalted butter, cut into ½-inch pieces and chilled

CARAMEL-WALNUT FILLING

- ¼ cup water
- 1 cup (7 ounces) granulated sugar
- ⅔ cup heavy cream
- 3 tablespoons unsalted butter, cut into 3 pieces
- ½ teaspoon vanilla extract
- ½ teaspoon lemon juice
- ⅛ teaspoon salt
- 16–18 walnut halves, plus 1 cup walnuts, toasted and chopped coarse

CHOCOLATE FILLING

- 2 large egg yolks
- 1 tablespoon plus ⅓ cup heavy cream
- ⅓ cup whole milk
- 5 ounces semisweet chocolate, chopped fine
- 2 tablespoons unsalted butter, cut into 4 pieces

1. FOR THE CRUST: Whisk egg and vanilla together in bowl. Process nuts and sugar in food processor until finely ground, 8 to 10 seconds. Add flour and salt and pulse to combine, about 5 pulses. Scatter butter over top and pulse until mixture resembles coarse cornmeal, about 15 pulses. With machine running, add egg mixture and continue to process until dough just comes together around processor blade, about 20 seconds.

2. Turn dough onto sheet of plastic wrap and flatten into 6-inch disk. Wrap tightly in plastic and refrigerate for 1 hour. Before rolling dough out, let it sit on counter to soften slightly, about 10 minutes. (Dough can be wrapped tightly in plastic and refrigerated for up to 2 days or frozen for up to 1 month. If frozen, let dough thaw completely on counter before rolling it out.)

3. Roll dough into 11-inch circle on lightly floured counter (if at any point dough becomes too soft and sticky to work with, slip dough onto baking sheet and freeze or refrigerate until workable).

Place dough round on baking sheet, cover with plastic, and refrigerate for about 30 minutes.

4. Remove dough from refrigerator; discard plastic but keep dough on baking sheet. Loosely roll dough around rolling pin and gently unroll it onto 9-inch tart pan with removable bottom, letting excess dough hang over edge. Ease dough into pan by gently lifting edge of dough with 1 hand while pressing into corners with other hand. Leave any dough that overhangs pan in place.

5. Press dough into fluted sides of pan, forming distinct seam around pan's circumference. (If some sections of edge are too thin, reinforce them by folding excess dough back on itself.) Run rolling pin over top of tart pan to remove any excess dough. Wrap dough-lined tart pan loosely in plastic, place on large plate, and freeze until dough is fully chilled and firm, about 30 minutes, before using. (Dough-lined tart pan can be wrapped tightly in plastic and frozen for up to 1 month.)

6. Meanwhile, adjust oven rack to middle position and heat oven to 375 degrees. Set dough-lined tart pan on rimmed baking sheet. Spray 1 side of double layer of aluminum foil with vegetable oil spray. Press foil greased side down into frozen tart shell, covering edges to prevent burning, and fill with pie weights. Bake until tart shell is golden brown and set, about 30 minutes, rotating baking sheet halfway through baking. Transfer tart shell with baking sheet to wire rack, carefully remove weights, and let cool slightly while making filling. Reduce oven temperature to 300 degrees.

7. FOR THE CARAMEL FILLING: While crust is cooling, add water to medium saucepan, then pour sugar into center of saucepan (don't let it hit pan sides). Gently stir sugar with clean spatula to wet it thoroughly. Bring to boil and cook, without stirring, until sugar has dissolved

completely and liquid has faint golden color (about 300 degrees), 6 to 10 minutes.

8. Reduce heat to medium-low and continue to cook, stirring occasionally, until caramel has dark amber color (about 350 degrees), 1 to 3 minutes. Off heat, slowly whisk in cream until combined (mixture will bubble and steam vigorously). Stir in butter, vanilla, lemon juice, and salt until combined. Stir in walnut halves to coat. Let caramel mixture sit until slightly thickened, about 8 minutes.

9. Set wire rack over piece of parchment paper. Using slotted spoon, transfer caramel-coated walnuts to rack, flip nuts right side up, and let cool completely. Stir chopped walnuts into caramel, then pour caramel mixture into cooled prebaked tart shell. Refrigerate tart, uncovered, until caramel is firm and does not run when pan is tilted, about 20 minutes.

10. FOR THE CHOCOLATE FILLING: While caramel sets, whisk egg yolks and 1 tablespoon cream together in bowl. Bring milk and remaining ⅓ cup cream to simmer in a small saucepan. Off heat, stir in chocolate and butter, cover saucepan, and let stand until chocolate is mostly melted, about 2 minutes. Gently stir mixture until smooth, then stir in egg yolk mixture. Pour chocolate filling evenly over chilled caramel in tart shell and smooth into even layer by tilting pan. Bake tart on baking sheet until tiny bubbles are visible on surface and chocolate layer is just set, about 25 minutes.

11. Transfer tart with baking sheet to wire rack and arrange caramel-coated walnut halves around edge of tart to garnish. Let tart cool slightly on baking sheet for 30 minutes, then refrigerate, uncovered, until chocolate is firm, about 3 hours. To serve, remove outer metal ring of tart pan, slide thin metal spatula between tart and tart pan bottom, and carefully slide tart onto serving platter or cutting board.

CHOCOLATE TRUFFLE TART

✔ WHY THIS RECIPE WORKS

For an easy-to-make chocolate tart with a silky texture and a dense, slightly bitter flavor, we discovered that a simple ganache—dense to a fault and creamy—made a great start to our filling. Adding butter isn't uncommon for ganache, but this addition gave our chocolate tart filling an optimally smooth texture. We chose not to call for vanilla in our chocolate tart recipe—it undercut the robust chocolate flavor—but we found that cognac emphasized the chocolate flavor. Incorporating cocoa into our Classic Tart Dough (page 731), gave us a rich foundation for the truffle filling.

CHOCOLATE TRUFFLE TART
SERVES 8 TO 10

Brandy or Grand Marnier may be substituted for the cognac. This tart is extremely rich and is best served with fresh berries and unsweetened whipped cream.

- 1 cup heavy cream
- 12 ounces bittersweet chocolate, chopped fine
- 6 tablespoons unsalted butter, softened
- 1 tablespoon cognac
- 1 recipe Classic Chocolate Tart Dough (page 731), fully baked and cooled

1. Bring cream to brief simmer in small saucepan over medium-high heat. Off heat, stir in chocolate and butter, cover pan, and let stand until chocolate is mostly melted, about 2 minutes. Gently stir mixture until smooth, then stir in cognac.

2. Pour filling into tart shell and refrigerate tart, uncovered, until filling is firm, about 2 hours. To serve, remove outer metal ring of tart pan, slide thin metal spatula between tart and tart pan bottom, and carefully slide tart onto serving platter or cutting board.

ESPRESSO TRUFFLE TART

Omit cognac and add 2 teaspoons instant espresso powder or instant coffee to hot cream with chocolate.

PEANUT BUTTER TRUFFLE TART

Spread ½ cup smooth peanut butter over bottom of tart shell and refrigerate while preparing chocolate filling. Smooth chocolate filling over peanut butter and chill as directed.

FIG-WALNUT TART

✔ WHY THIS RECIPE WORKS

Fig-walnut tart is a typical Italian crostata that combines an assertively flavored filling with a crumbly, sweet crust called pasta frolla, or "tender dough." We wanted to come up with our own version—one that combined sweet dried figs with crunchy walnuts in a sticky, citrus-scented paste slathered thick across a crisp, leavened crust. Choosing the right type of fig, either Turkish or Calimyrna, was key to getting a tender and flavorful filling. Mission figs were simply too tough and made for a filling punctuated with coarse, chewy bits. We created a rich and sweet dough by perfecting the egg-butter balance (one whole egg and almost a full stick of butter). Finally, we learned that, unlike other pastry doughs, pasta frolla cooks through before it fully browns, allowing us to abandon the step of prebaking the tart and making this fig-walnut tart quicker to prepare.

FIG-WALNUT TART
SERVES 10 TO 12

Be sure to use an 10-inch tart pan here. For more information on fitting tart dough into the pan, see page 731. Dust with confectioners' sugar before serving, or serve with Whipped Cream (page 800).

TART DOUGH
- 1 large egg
- 1–2 tablespoons water
- 1 teaspoon vanilla extract
- 1⅓ cups (6⅔ ounces) all-purpose flour
- ⅓ cup (2⅓ ounces) sugar
- 2 teaspoons grated lemon zest
- 1¼ teaspoons baking powder
- ¼ teaspoon salt
- 7 tablespoons unsalted butter, cut into ¼-inch pieces and chilled

FILLING
- 2⅔ cups (1 pound) dried Turkish or Calimyrna figs, stemmed and chopped coarse
- 1 cup water
- ½ cup brandy
- ¼ cup (1¾ ounces) sugar
- 1 cup walnuts, chopped coarse
- 1½ tablespoons grated orange zest

1. FOR THE TART DOUGH: Whisk egg, 1 tablespoon water, and vanilla together in bowl. Process flour, sugar, lemon zest, baking powder, and salt in food processor until combined, about 5 seconds. Scatter butter over top and pulse until mixture resembles coarse cornmeal, about 7 pulses. With machine running, add egg mixture and process until all liquid ingredients are incorporated, about 12 seconds. Pinch dough with fingers; if dough feels dry and does not hold together, sprinkle remaining 1 tablespoon water over top and pulse until incorporated, 3 to 5 pulses.

2. Turn dough onto counter and press together to form cohesive mound. Flatten dough into 5-inch disk, wrap tightly in plastic wrap, and refrigerate for 2 hours. Before rolling dough out, let it sit on counter to soften slightly, about 10 minutes. (Dough can be wrapped tightly in plastic and refrigerated for up to 2 days or frozen for up to 1 month. If frozen, let dough thaw completely on counter before rolling it out.)

3. Roll dough into 13-inch circle, about ¼ inch thick, between 2 large sheets of floured parchment paper. (If dough sticks to parchment, gently loosen and lift sticky area with bench scraper and dust parchment with additional flour. Remove dough from refrigerator. Slide dough, still between parchment sheets, onto rimmed baking sheet and refrigerate until firm, about 15 minutes.) Remove top layer of parchment. Loosely roll dough around rolling pin and gently unroll it onto 10-inch tart pan with removable bottom, letting excess dough hang over edge. Ease dough into pan by gently lifting edge of dough with 1 hand while pressing into corners with other hand. Leave any dough that overhangs pan in place.

4. Press dough into fluted sides of pan, forming distinct seam around pan's circumference. (If some sections of edge are too thin, reinforce them by folding excess dough back on itself.) Run rolling pin over top of tart pan to remove any excess dough. Wrap dough-lined tart pan loosely in plastic, place on large plate, and freeze until dough is fully chilled and firm, about 30 minutes, before using. (Dough-lined tart pan can be wrapped tightly in plastic and frozen for up to 1 month.)

5. FOR THE FILLING: Meanwhile, bring figs, water, brandy, and sugar to simmer in saucepan and cook, stirring occasionally, until liquid evaporates and figs are very soft, about 10 minutes. Stir in walnuts and orange zest and let cool to room temperature.

6. While filling cools, adjust oven rack to middle position and heat oven to 325 degrees. Spread cooled fig and nut filling evenly over bottom of tart shell. Set tart on rimmed baking sheet and bake until edges of tart are lightly browned, 25 to 30 minutes, rotating baking sheet halfway through baking. Transfer tart with baking sheet to wire rack and let cool to room temperature, about 2 hours. To serve, remove outer metal ring of tart pan, slide

thin metal spatula between tart and tart pan bottom, and carefully slide tart onto serving platter or cutting board.

FREE-FORM FRUIT TART

✔ WHY THIS RECIPE WORKS

We wanted a simple take on summer fruit pie, one without the rolling and fitting usually required for a traditional pie or tart. A free-form tart—a single layer of buttery pie dough folded up around fresh fruit—seemed the obvious solution. But without the support of a pie plate, tender crusts are prone to leaking juice, and this can result in a soggy bottom. For our crust, we used a high proportion of butter to flour, which provided the most buttery flavor and tender texture without compromising the structure. We then turned to the French fraisage method to make the pastry; in this method, chunks of butter are pressed into long, thin sheets that create lots of flaky layers when the dough is baked. We rolled the dough into a 12-inch circle, which produced a crust that was thick enough to contain a lot of fruit but thin enough to bake evenly. We placed the fruit in the middle, then lifted the dough over the fruit (leaving the center exposed) and pleated it loosely. The bright summer fruit needed only a bit of sugar for enhancement.

FREE-FORM SUMMER FRUIT TART
SERVES 6

Taste the fruit before adding sugar to it; use the lesser amount if the fruit is very sweet, more if it is tart. However much sugar you use, do not add it to the fruit until you are ready to fill and form the tart. Serve with vanilla ice cream or Whipped Cream (page 800).

DOUGH
1½	cups (7½ ounces) all-purpose flour
½	teaspoon salt
10	tablespoons unsalted butter, cut into ½-inch pieces and chilled
4–6	tablespoons ice water

FILLING
1	pound peaches, nectarines, apricots, or plums, halved, pitted, and cut into ½-inch wedges
5	ounces (1 cup) blueberries, raspberries, or blackberries
3–5	tablespoons plus 1 tablespoon sugar

1. FOR THE DOUGH: Process flour and salt in food processor until combined, about 5 seconds. Scatter butter over top and pulse until mixture resembles coarse bread crumbs and butter pieces are about size of small peas, about 10 pulses.

FRAISAGE OR MIXING FLAKY TART DOUGH

1. Starting at farthest end of dough pile, use heel of hand to smear small amount of dough against counter. Continue to smear dough until all crumbs have been worked.

2. Gather smeared crumbs together and repeat process.

Continue to pulse, adding water 1 tablespoon at a time, until dough begins to form small curds that hold together when pinched with fingers (dough will be crumbly), about 10 pulses.

2. Turn dough crumbs onto lightly floured counter and gather into rectangular-shaped pile. Starting at farthest end, use heel of hand to smear small amount of dough against counter. Continue to smear dough until all crumbs have been worked. Gather smeared crumbs together in another rectangular-shaped pile and repeat process. Press dough into 6-inch disk, wrap it tightly in plastic wrap, and refrigerate for 1 hour. Before rolling dough out, let it sit on counter to soften slightly, about 10 minutes. (Dough can be wrapped tightly in plastic and refrigerated for up to 2 days or frozen for up to 1 month. If frozen, let dough thaw completely on counter before rolling it out.)

3. Roll dough into 12-inch circle between 2 large sheets of floured parchment paper. (If dough sticks to parchment, gently loosen and lift sticky area with bench scraper and dust parchment with additional flour.) Slide dough, still between parchment sheets, onto rimmed baking sheet and refrigerate until firm, 15 to 30 minutes. (If refrigerated longer and dough is hard and brittle, let stand at room temperature until pliant.)

4. FOR THE FILLING: Adjust oven rack to middle position and heat oven to 375 degrees. Gently toss fruit and 3 to 5 tablespoons sugar together in bowl. Remove top sheet of parchment paper from dough. Mound fruit in center of dough, leaving 2½-inch border around edge of fruit. Being careful to leave ½-inch border of dough around edge of fruit, fold outermost 2 inches of dough over fruit, pleating it every 2 to 3 inches as needed; gently pinch pleated dough to secure, but do not press dough into fruit. Working quickly, brush top and sides of dough with water and sprinkle evenly with remaining 1 tablespoon sugar.

5. Bake until crust is deep golden brown and fruit is bubbling, about 1 hour, rotating baking sheet halfway through baking. Transfer tart with baking sheet to wire rack and let cool for 10 minutes, then use parchment to gently transfer tart to wire rack. Use metal spatula to loosen tart from parchment and remove parchment. Let tart cool on rack until juices have thickened, about 25 minutes; serve slightly warm or at room temperature.

FREE-FORM SUMMER FRUIT TARTLETS

MAKES 4 TARTLETS

Divide dough into 4 equal portions before rolling out in step 3. Roll each portion into 7-inch circle on parchment paper; stack rounds and refrigerate until firm. Continue with recipe from step 4, mounding one-quarter of fruit in center of dough round, leaving 1½-inch border around edge. Being careful to leave ¼-inch border of dough around edge of fruit, fold outermost 1 to 1¼ inches of dough over fruit. Transfer parchment with tart to rimmed baking sheet. Repeat with remaining fruit and dough. Brush dough with water and sprinkle each tartlet with portion of remaining 1 tablespoon sugar. Bake until crust is deep golden brown and fruit is bubbling, 40 to 45 minutes, rotating baking sheet halfway through baking.

MAKING A FREE-FORM TART

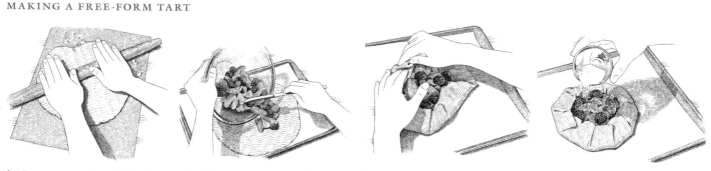

1. For even circle, roll in short motions, working from center outward and moving dough one-quarter turn after each roll.

2. Pile fruit in center of dough, leaving 2½-inch border around fruit.

3. Working your way around dough, gently pull up sides and create fold every 2 inches.

4. Working quickly, brush dough with water and sprinkle with 1 tablespoon sugar.

CHAPTER 20   Fruit Desserts

STRAWBERRY SHORTCAKES

✔ WHY THIS RECIPE WORKS

While some folks like to spoon strawberries over pound cake, sponge cake, and even angel food cake, our idea of strawberry shortcake definitely involves a biscuit. We wanted a juicy strawberry filling and mounds of freshly whipped cream sandwiched in between a lightly sweetened, tender biscuit. While eggs are not traditional, we found that a single egg gave our biscuits a light, tender texture. And we used just enough dairy (half-and-half or milk) to bind the dough together. A modest amount of sugar yielded slightly sweet biscuits. For the strawberries, we wanted to avoid both a mushy puree and dry chunks of fruit. We found our solution in a compromise—mashing a portion of the berries and slicing the rest for a chunky, juicy mixture that didn't slide off the biscuits. And freshly whipped cream provided a cool, creamy contrast to the berries and biscuits.

STRAWBERRY SHORTCAKES
SERVES 6

Preparing the fruit first gives it time to release its juices.

FRUIT
2½	pounds strawberries, hulled (8 cups)
6	tablespoons sugar

BISCUITS
2	cups (10 ounces) all-purpose flour
5	tablespoons (2¼ ounces) sugar
1	tablespoon baking powder
½	teaspoon salt
8	tablespoons unsalted butter, cut into ½-inch pieces and chilled
½	cup plus 1 tablespoon half-and-half or milk
1	large egg, lightly beaten, plus 1 large white, lightly beaten

WHIPPED CREAM
1	cup heavy cream, chilled
1	tablespoon sugar
1	teaspoon vanilla extract

1. FOR THE FRUIT: Crush 3 cups strawberries in large bowl with potato masher. Slice remaining 5 cups berries. Stir sliced berries and sugar into crushed berries. Set aside until sugar has dissolved and berries are juicy, at least 30 minutes or up to 2 hours.

2. FOR THE BISCUITS: Adjust oven rack to lower-middle position and heat oven to 425 degrees. Line baking sheet with parchment paper. Pulse flour, 3 tablespoons sugar, baking powder, and salt in food processor until combined. Scatter butter pieces over top and pulse until mixture resembles coarse meal, about 15 pulses. Transfer mixture to large bowl.

3. Whisk half-and-half and whole egg together in bowl, then stir into flour mixture until large clumps form. Turn out onto lightly floured counter and knead lightly until dough comes together (do not overwork dough).

4. Pat dough into 9 by 6-inch rectangle, about ¾ inch thick. Using floured 2¾-inch biscuit cutter, cut out 6 dough rounds. Arrange biscuits on prepared sheet, spaced about 1½ inches apart. Brush tops with egg white and sprinkle evenly with remaining 2 tablespoons sugar. (Unbaked biscuits can be refrigerated, covered with plastic wrap, for up to 2 hours.)

5. Bake until biscuits are golden brown, 12 to 14 minutes, rotating baking sheet halfway through baking. Transfer baking sheet to wire rack and let biscuits cool, about 10 minutes. (Cooled biscuits can be stored at room temperature for up to 1 day. Before assembling, reheat in 350-degree oven for 3 to 5 minutes.)

6. FOR THE WHIPPED CREAM: Using stand mixer fitted with whisk, whip cream, sugar, and vanilla on medium-low speed until foamy, about 1 minute. Increase

MASHING STRAWBERRIES FOR SHORTCAKES

For best flavor and appearance, crush a portion of the berries for the filling with a potato masher to create a thick puree that will anchor the remaining sliced berries to the biscuits.

speed to high and whip until soft peaks form, 1 to 3 minutes.

7. To assemble, split each biscuit in half and place bottoms on individual plates. Spoon portion of berries over each bottom, dollop with whipped cream, and cap with biscuit tops. Serve immediately.

PEACH SHORTCAKES

✔ WHY THIS RECIPE WORKS

Making peach shortcake with supermarket peaches often produces a flavorless filling over a dry, crumbly biscuit. We wanted to develop a foolproof recipe for peach shortcake that would work with either farm stand or supermarket peaches. Macerating fruit in sugar is the traditional method employed to pull out the fruit's juices when it comes to strawberry shortcake, but for peaches, this step alone isn't enough. To ensure juicy shortcakes, we first sliced the peaches very thin to maximize the surface that would come in contact with the sugar. Then we microwaved a few of the peaches with peach schnapps until they were tender, mashing these cooked peaches to create a peach jam to give our shortcakes the moisture and sweetness we were after. Finally, while we liked a classic buttermilk biscuit for the shortcake, we needed to add an egg and mechanically develop more gluten (by vigorous stirring) to make a cake that would hold up under the weight of the fruit. Freshly whipped cream topped off this summer classic.

PEACH SHORTCAKES
SERVES 6

This recipe works well with any peaches, regardless of quality. If your peaches are firm, you should be able to peel them with a sharp vegetable peeler. If they are too soft to withstand the pressure of a peeler, you'll need to blanch them in a pot of simmering water for 15 seconds and then shock them in a bowl of ice water before peeling. You can substitute ½ cup low-fat yogurt mixed with 3 tablespoons of milk for the buttermilk, if desired. Orange juice or orange liqueur can be used in place of the peach schnapps.

FRUIT

2	pounds peaches, peeled, halved, pitted, and cut into ¼-inch wedges
6	tablespoons sugar
2	tablespoons peach schnapps

BISCUITS

2	cups (10 ounces) all-purpose flour
2	tablespoons sugar
2	teaspoons baking powder
¾	teaspoon salt
⅔	cup buttermilk, chilled
1	large egg
8	tablespoons unsalted butter, melted and cooled

WHIPPED CREAM

½	cup heavy cream, chilled
1	tablespoon sugar
½	teaspoon vanilla extract

1. FOR THE FRUIT: Gently toss three-quarters of peaches with 4 tablespoons sugar in large bowl. Let sit 30 minutes.

Toss remaining peaches with remaining 2 tablespoons sugar and schnapps in medium bowl. Microwave until peaches are bubbling, about 1 to 1½ minutes, stirring twice. Using potato masher, crush peaches into coarse pulp. Let sit 30 minutes.

2. FOR THE BISCUITS: Meanwhile, adjust oven rack to middle position and heat oven to 475 degrees. Line baking sheet with parchment paper. Whisk flour, 1 tablespoon sugar, baking powder, and salt together in large bowl. Whisk buttermilk and egg together in bowl; add melted butter and stir until butter forms small clumps.

3. Add buttermilk mixture to dry ingredients and stir with wooden spoon until dough comes together and no dry flour remains. Continue to stir vigorously for 30 seconds. Using greased ⅓-cup measure, portion dough onto prepared baking sheet to create 6 biscuits, spaced about 1½ inches apart. Sprinkle remaining 1 tablespoon sugar evenly over top of biscuits. Bake until tops are golden brown and crisp, about 15 minutes, rotating baking sheet halfway through baking. Transfer baking sheet to wire rack and let cool, about 15 minutes. (Cooled biscuits can be stored at room temperature for up to 1 day. Reheat in 350-degree oven for 3 to 5 minutes before assembling.)

4. FOR THE WHIPPED CREAM: Using stand mixer fitted with whisk, whip cream, sugar, and vanilla on medium-low speed until foamy, about 1 minute. Increase speed to high and whip until soft peaks form, 1 to 3 minutes.

5. To assemble, split each biscuit in half and place bottoms on individual plates. Spoon portion of crushed peach mixture over each bottom, followed by peach slices and juices. Dollop each shortcake with 2 tablespoons whipped cream, cap with biscuit tops, and dollop with remaining whipped cream. Serve immediately.

BERRY FOOL

✔ WHY THIS RECIPE WORKS
This traditional British fruit dessert is typically made by folding pureed stewed fruit (usually gooseberries) into sweet custard. Modern fool recipes skip the custard and use whipped cream. But whipped cream blunts the fruit flavor and is too light and insubstantial. We wanted a dessert with intense fruitiness and rich body—and we wanted to use strawberries and raspberries rather than gooseberries. Our first challenge was to thicken the fruit properly; unlike gooseberries, raspberries and strawberries are low in pectin. We turned to gelatin to thicken our berries, softened the gelatin in some uncooked berry puree, and then combined the softened mixture with some heated puree to help melt and distribute the gelatin. Now we had a smooth, thickened puree with intense fruit flavor. When it came to the custard, we liked the ease of using whipped cream; when we combined it with sour cream, we had a mixture that was airy yet substantial, with a rich and slightly tangy flavor. For even more fruit flavor, we layered the fruit puree and cream base with fresh berries that had been macerated in sugar. Finally, topping the dessert with crumbled sweet wheat crackers added a pleasant, nutty contrast.

BERRY FOOL
SERVES 6

Blueberries or blackberries can be substituted for the raspberries in this recipe. You may also substitute frozen fruit for fresh, but it will slightly compromise the texture. If using frozen fruit, reduce the amount of sugar in the puree by 1 tablespoon. The thickened fruit puree can be made up to 4 hours in advance; just make sure to whisk it well in step 4 to break up any clumps before combining it with the whipped cream. For the best results, chill your beater and bowl before whipping the cream. We like the granular texture and nutty flavor of Carr's Whole Wheat Crackers, but graham crackers or gingersnaps will also work. You will need six tall parfait or sundae glasses for this recipe.

2	pounds strawberries, hulled (6 cups)
12	ounces (2⅓ cups) raspberries
¾	cup sugar
2	teaspoons unflavored gelatin
1	cup heavy cream, chilled
¼	cup sour cream, chilled
½	teaspoon vanilla extract
4	Carr's Whole Wheat Crackers, crushed fine (¼ cup)
6	sprigs fresh mint (optional)

1. Process half of strawberries, half of raspberries, and ½ cup sugar in food processor until mixture is completely smooth, about 1 minute. Strain berry puree through fine-mesh strainer into large liquid measuring cup (you should have about 2½ cups puree; reserve excess for another use). Transfer ½ cup of puree to small bowl and sprinkle gelatin over top; let stand at least 5 minutes to soften and stir. Heat remaining 2 cups puree in small saucepan over medium heat until it begins to bubble, 4 to 6 minutes. Off heat, stir in gelatin mixture until dissolved. Transfer to medium bowl, cover with plastic wrap, and refrigerate until well chilled, about 2 hours.

2. Meanwhile, chop remaining strawberries into rough ¼-inch pieces. Toss strawberries, remaining raspberries, and 2 tablespoons sugar together in medium bowl. Set aside for 1 hour.

3. Using stand mixer fitted with whisk, whip cream, sour cream, vanilla, and remaining 2 tablespoons sugar on low speed until bubbles form, about 30 seconds. Increase speed to medium and whip until whisk leaves trail, about 30 seconds. Increase speed to high; whip until mixture has nearly doubled in volume and holds stiff peaks, about 30 seconds. Transfer ⅓ cup of whipped cream mixture to small bowl; set aside.

4. Remove berry puree from refrigerator and whisk until smooth. With mixer on medium speed, slowly add two-thirds of puree to whipped cream mixture; mix until

incorporated, about 15 seconds. Using spatula, gently fold in remaining puree, leaving streaks of puree.

5. Transfer uncooked berries to fine-mesh strainer; shake gently to remove any excess juice. Divide two-thirds of berries evenly among six tall parfait or sundae glasses. Divide creamy berry mixture evenly among glasses, followed by remaining uncooked berries. Top each glass with reserved plain whipped cream mixture. Sprinkle with crushed crackers and garnish with mint sprigs, if using. Serve immediately.

PAVLOVAS

✓ WHY THIS RECIPE WORKS

Pavlova is simple to prepare, yet it's often plagued by soggy, sickly sweet meringue and unripe fruit—and cutting it for serving is one messy proposition. We were seeking a pavlova made of pure white, perfectly crisped meringue, its texture softened by whipped cream and its sweetness balanced by a topping of fresh fruit. We also wanted to find a way to preserve the pavlova's elegance as we served it. First off, we decided to take a restaurant approach and make individual pavlovas for a tidier presentation. Then we focused on making and baking the meringue. Whipping room-temperature egg whites with a small amount of cream of tartar and vanilla before slowly adding the sugar gave us a voluminous, billowy, and stable meringue. To shape the meringues, we simply portioned ½ cup of the mixture into small mounds on a baking sheet, then used the back of a spoon to create concave centers for holding the whipped cream and fruit. Baking the meringues at 200 degrees for an hour and a half yielded perfectly dry, crisp, white shells, but they required gradual cooling in the turned-off oven to ensure their crispness. While we especially liked the flavors of tropical fruit on the pavlovas, fresh berries and peaches made fine options, too. And for

the whipped cream topping, we cut some of the heavy cream with sour cream for a topping with a slight tang that provided a cool and refreshing counterpoint to the sweet fruit and meringues.

INDIVIDUAL PAVLOVAS WITH TROPICAL FRUIT

SERVES 6

Be mindful that the fruit is the garnish here, so it's worth taking the time to cut it into tidy pieces. Sour cream gives the whipped cream a slight tang; omit it if you prefer simple whipped cream. Avoid making pavlovas on humid days or the meringue shells will turn out sticky.

MERINGUES AND FRUIT

4	large egg whites, room temperature
¾	teaspoon vanilla extract
¼	teaspoon cream of tartar
1	cup (7 ounces) plus 1 tablespoon sugar
1	mango, peeled, pitted, and cut into ¼-inch pieces
2	kiwis, peeled, quartered, and sliced thin
1½	cups pineapple, cut into ½-inch pieces

TOPPING

1	cup heavy cream, chilled
½	cup sour cream, chilled
1	tablespoon sugar
1	teaspoon vanilla extract

1. FOR THE MERINGUES: Adjust oven rack to middle position and heat oven to 200 degrees. Line baking sheet with parchment paper.

2. Using stand mixer fitted with whisk, whip egg whites, vanilla, and cream of tartar on medium-low speed until foamy, about 1 minute. Increase speed to medium-high and whip whites to soft, billowy mounds, about 1 minute. Gradually add 1 cup sugar and whip until glossy, stiff peaks form, 1 to 2 minutes.

3. Scoop six ½-cup mounds of meringue onto prepared sheet, spacing them about 1 inch apart. Gently make small, bowllike indentation in each meringue using back of spoon. Bake until meringues have smooth, dry, and firm exteriors, about 1½ hours. Turn oven off and leave meringues in oven until completely dry and hard, about 2 hours. (Meringue shells can be stored at room temperature for up to 2 weeks.)

4. FOR THE FRUIT: Gently toss mango, kiwis, and pineapple with remaining 1 tablespoon sugar in large bowl. Let sit at room temperature until sugar has dissolved and fruit is juicy, about 30 minutes.

5. FOR THE TOPPING: Using stand mixer fitted with whisk, whip heavy cream, sour cream, sugar, and vanilla on medium-low speed until foamy, about 1 minute. Increase speed to high and whip until soft peaks form, 1 to 3 minutes. (Whipped cream can be refrigerated in fine-mesh strainer set over small bowl and covered with plastic wrap for up to 8 hours.)

5. To assemble, place meringue shells on individual plates and spoon about ⅓ cup whipped cream into each shell. Top with about ½ cup fruit (some fruit and juice will fall onto plate). Serve immediately.

SHAPING PAVLOVAS

After scooping ½-cup mounds of meringue onto prepared sheet, gently make small, bowl-shaped indentations in each meringue using back of spoon.

INDIVIDUAL PAVLOVAS WITH MIXED BERRIES

Substitute 7½ ounces each raspberries and blueberries and 5 ounces blackberries for mango, kiwi, and pineapple.

INDIVIDUAL PAVLOVAS WITH STRAWBERRIES, BLUEBERRIES, AND PEACHES

If your peaches are firm, you should be able to peel them with a vegetable peeler. If they are too soft and ripe to withstand the pressure of a peeler, you'll need to blanch them in a pot of simmering water for 15 seconds and then shock them in a bowl of ice water before peeling.

Substitute 5 ounces strawberries, hulled and sliced thin, 5 ounces blueberries, and 2 peaches, peeled, halved, pitted, and sliced ¼ inch thick, for mango, kiwi, and pineapple.

FRESH PEACH COBBLER

✓ WHY THIS RECIPE WORKS

Bad peaches, syrupy filling, and a soggy biscuit topping were just three of the problems we had to solve when developing our recipe for fresh peach cobbler. Our goal was an appealing dish of warm, tender biscuits set atop rich, juicy peaches. To even out the variation in juiciness from peach to peach, we macerated the fruit in sugar to draw out its juices. Sugar did indeed draw off some of the moisture from the peaches, but to guarantee a juicy cobbler that would have the same amount of liquid every time, we had to replenish some of the drained juices. Thickening the peach juice with a small amount of cornstarch gave the filling body without overwhelming the delicate texture of the peaches. For the topping, we created a biscuit with a little more dairy, which gave us a moister dough. We chose yogurt as the dairy so our biscuits would have plenty of flavor. Dropping

---

the biscuits onto hot, parbaked peaches jump-started their baking; now we had biscuits that were cooked throughout and perfectly tender.

FRESH PEACH COBBLER
SERVES 6

If your peaches are firm, you should be able to peel them with a vegetable peeler. If they are too soft and ripe to withstand the pressure of a peeler, you'll need to blanch them in a pot of simmering water for 15 seconds and then shock them in a bowl of ice water before peeling. Do not prepare the biscuit dough any sooner than the recipe indicates or the biscuits may not rise properly. If desired, plain low-fat or non-fat yogurt can be substituted for the whole-milk yogurt, but the biscuits will be a little less rich. If the dough does not come together, you can add up to 1 tablespoon more yogurt. This recipe can be doubled; use a 13 by 9-inch baking dish and increase the baking times in steps 1 and 3 by about 5 minutes. Serve with vanilla ice cream or Whipped Cream (page 800).

FILLING
2½	pounds peaches, peeled, halved, pitted, and cut into ¾-inch wedges
¼	cup (1¾ ounces) sugar
1	tablespoon lemon juice
1	teaspoon cornstarch
	Pinch salt

BISCUIT TOPPING
1	cup (5 ounces) all-purpose flour
3	tablespoons plus 1 teaspoon sugar
¾	teaspoon baking powder
¼	teaspoon baking soda
¼	teaspoon salt
5	tablespoons unsalted butter, cut into ¼-inch pieces and chilled
⅓	cup plain whole-milk yogurt

1. FOR THE FILLING: Adjust oven rack to lower-middle position and heat oven to 425 degrees. Line rimmed baking sheet with aluminum foil. Gently toss peaches

and sugar together in large bowl and let sit for 30 minutes, gently stirring several times. Drain peaches in colander set over large bowl and reserve ¼ cup juice (discard remaining juice). Whisk reserved juice, lemon juice, cornstarch, and salt together in small bowl. Combine peaches and juice mixture in bowl and transfer to 8-inch square baking dish; place on prepared baking sheet. Bake until peaches begin to bubble around edges, about 10 minutes.

2. FOR THE BISCUIT TOPPING: Meanwhile, pulse flour, 3 tablespoons sugar, baking powder, baking soda, and salt in food processor until combined, about 5 pulses. Scatter butter pieces over top and pulse until mixture resembles coarse meal, about 10 pulses. Transfer to medium bowl, add yogurt, and toss with rubber spatula until cohesive dough is formed (don't overmix dough). Divide dough into 6 equal pieces.

3. TO ASSEMBLE AND BAKE: After removing peaches from oven, place dough mounds on top, spacing them at least ½ inch apart (they should not touch). Sprinkle each mound evenly with remaining 1 teaspoon sugar. Bake until filling is bubbling and biscuits are golden brown, 16 to 18 minutes, rotating baking sheet halfway through baking. Transfer baking dish to wire rack and let cool until warm, about 20 minutes; serve.

BLUEBERRY-PEACH COBBLER WITH LEMON-CORNMEAL BISCUIT TOPPING

Reduce peaches to 2 pounds. Toss 1 cup fresh blueberries with peach and juice mixture before transferring to baking dish in step 1. Substitute 2 tablespoons stone-ground cornmeal for equal amount flour in biscuit topping and add ½ teaspoon grated lemon zest to food processor with dry ingredients in step 2.

PEACH COBBLER WITH FROZEN PEACHES

Start defrosting the peaches about 2 hours before assembling and baking the cobbler.

Using frozen peaches, reduce peaches to 2 pounds. Defrost peaches completely in colander, reserving 2 tablespoons juice. Proceed as directed, increasing baking time in step 1 to 15 to 20 minutes.

SOUR CHERRY COBBLER

✔ WHY THIS RECIPE WORKS
Most cherry cobblers are no more than canned pie filling topped with dry, heavy biscuits. We wanted a filling that highlighted the unique, sweet-tart flavor of sour cherries and, on top, we wanted a tender, feather-light biscuit crust. Because fresh sour cherries are so hard to find most of the year, we picked jarred Morello cherries—easy to find and available year-round. Embellishing the cherries with cherry juice, cinnamon, and vanilla was a step in the right direction but the filling still tasted a bit flat, so we switched out some of the juice for red wine and replaced the vanilla with almond extract. The resulting sauce was better, but a little thin. A small amount of cornstarch thickened the filling nicely. As for the topping, we favored buttermilk biscuits, which have a light and fluffy texture. To ensure nicely browned biscuits that didn't become soggy over the filling, we parbaked them on their own ahead of time, then slid the biscuits over the warm cherry filling and put it in the oven to finish cooking.

SOUR CHERRY COBBLER
SERVES 12

Use the smaller amount of sugar in the filling if you prefer your fruit desserts on the tart side and the larger amount if you like them sweet. Serve with vanilla ice cream or Whipped Cream (page 800).

BISCUIT TOPPING
2 cups (10 ounces) all-purpose flour
½ cup (3½ ounces) sugar
½ teaspoon baking powder
½ teaspoon baking soda
½ teaspoon salt
6 tablespoons unsalted butter, cut into ½-inch pieces and chilled
1 cup buttermilk

FILLING
4 (24-ounce) jars Morello cherries, drained, 2 cups juice reserved
¾–1 cup (5¼ to 7 ounces) sugar
3 tablespoons plus 1 teaspoon cornstarch
Pinch salt
1 cup dry red wine
1 cinnamon stick
¼ teaspoon almond extract

1. Adjust oven rack to middle position and heat oven to 425 degrees. Line baking sheet with parchment paper.

2. FOR THE BISCUIT TOPPING: Pulse flour, 6 tablespoons sugar, baking powder, baking soda, and salt in food processor until combined. Scatter butter pieces over top and pulse until mixture resembles coarse meal, about 15 pulses. Transfer mixture to large bowl; add buttermilk and stir until combined. Divide dough into 12 equal pieces, each about ¼ cup, and place on prepared sheet, spacing them 1½ inches apart. Sprinkle remaining 2 tablespoons sugar evenly over top of biscuits and bake until lightly browned, about 15 minutes, rotating baking sheet halfway through baking. (Do not turn oven off.)

3. FOR THE FILLING: Meanwhile, arrange drained cherries in even layer in 13 by 9-inch baking dish. Combine sugar, cornstarch, and salt in medium saucepan. Stir in reserved cherry juice and wine and add cinnamon stick; bring mixture to simmer over medium-high heat, stirring

frequently, until mixture thickens, about 5 minutes. Remove and discard cinnamon stick, stir in almond extract, and pour hot liquid over cherries.

4. TO ASSEMBLE AND BAKE: Arrange hot biscuits in 3 rows of 4 biscuits over warm filling. Place baking dish on aluminum foil–lined rimmed baking sheet and bake until filling is bubbling and biscuits are deep golden brown, about 10 minutes. Transfer baking dish to wire rack and let cool until warm, about 10 minutes; serve.

FRESH SOUR CHERRY COBBLER

Morello or Montmorency cherries can be used in this cobbler made with fresh sour cherries. Do not use sweet Bing cherries. If the cherries do not release enough juices after 30 minutes in step 1, add cranberry juice to make up the difference.

- 1¼ cups (8¾ ounces) sugar
- 3 tablespoons plus 1 teaspoon cornstarch
  Pinch salt
- 4 pounds fresh sour cherries, pitted, juice from pitting reserved
- 1 cup dry red wine
  Cranberry juice, as needed
- 1 recipe Biscuit Topping (page 746)
- 1 cinnamon stick
- ¼ teaspoon almond extract

1. Whisk sugar, cornstarch, and salt together in large bowl; add cherries and toss well to combine. Pour wine over cherries; let sit 30 minutes. Drain cherries in colander set over medium bowl. Combine drained and reserved juices from pitting cherries; you should have 3 cups (if not, add cranberry juice to make this amount).

2. Meanwhile, prepare and bake biscuit topping.

3. Arrange drained cherries in even layer in 13 by 9-inch baking dish. Bring juice mixture and cinnamon stick to simmer in medium saucepan over medium-high heat,

stirring frequently, until mixture thickens, about 5 minutes. Remove and discard cinnamon stick, stir in almond extract, and pour hot liquid over cherries.

4. Arrange hot biscuits over filling and bake as directed.

BLUEBERRY COBBLER

✔ WHY THIS RECIPE WORKS

Too often, blueberry cobbler means a filling that is too sweet, overspiced, and unappealingly thick. We wanted a not-too-thin, not-too-thick filling where the blueberry flavor would be front and center. And over the fruit, we wanted a light, tender biscuit topping that could hold its own against the fruit filling, with an ingredient list simple enough to allow the blueberries to play a starring role. We started by preparing a not-too-sweet filling using 6 cups of fresh berries and just half a cup of sugar. Cornstarch worked well to thicken the fruit's juices. A little lemon and cinnamon were all that we needed to enhance the filling without masking the blueberry flavor. For the topping, ease of preparation was our guiding principle, so we made light, rustic drop biscuits enriched with a little cornmeal. Adding the biscuit topping to the cobbler after the filling had baked on its own allowed the biscuits to brown evenly and cook through. A sprinkling of cinnamon sugar on the dropped biscuit dough added a sweet crunch.

BLUEBERRY COBBLER
SERVES 6 TO 8

While the blueberries are baking, prepare the ingredients for the topping, but do not stir the wet ingredients into the dry ingredients until just before the berries come out of the oven. A standard or deep-dish 9-inch pie plate works well; an 8-inch square baking dish can also be used. Serve with vanilla ice cream or Whipped Cream (page 800).

FILLING
- ½ cup (3½ ounces) sugar
- 1 tablespoon cornstarch
  Pinch ground cinnamon
  Pinch salt
- 30 ounces (6 cups) blueberries
- 1½ teaspoons grated lemon zest plus 1 tablespoon juice

BISCUIT TOPPING
- 1 cup (5 ounces) all-purpose flour
- ¼ cup (1¾ ounces) plus 2 teaspoons sugar
- 2 tablespoons stone-ground cornmeal
- 2 teaspoons baking powder
- ¼ teaspoon baking soda
- ¼ teaspoon salt
- ⅓ cup buttermilk
- 4 tablespoons unsalted butter, melted
- ½ teaspoon vanilla extract
- ⅛ teaspoon ground cinnamon

1. FOR THE FILLING: Adjust oven rack to lower-middle position and heat oven to 375 degrees. Line rimmed baking sheet with aluminum foil. Whisk sugar, cornstarch, cinnamon, and salt together in large bowl. Add berries and mix gently until evenly coated; add lemon zest and juice and mix to combine. Transfer berry mixture to 9-inch pie plate, place plate on prepared baking sheet, and bake until filling is hot and bubbling around edges, about 25 minutes.

2. FOR THE BISCUIT TOPPING: Meanwhile, whisk flour, ¼ cup sugar, cornmeal, baking powder, baking soda, and salt together in large bowl. Whisk buttermilk, melted butter, and vanilla together in small bowl. Combine remaining 2 teaspoons sugar with cinnamon in second small bowl and set aside. One minute before berries come out of oven, add wet ingredients to dry; stir until just combined and no dry pockets remain.

3. TO ASSEMBLE AND BAKE: Remove berries from oven; increase oven

temperature to 425 degrees. Divide dough into 8 equal pieces and place them on hot filling, spacing them at least ½ inch apart (they should not touch). Sprinkle each mound evenly with cinnamon sugar. Bake until filling is bubbling and biscuits are golden brown on top and cooked through, 15 to 18 minutes, rotating pie plate halfway through baking. Transfer pie plate to wire rack and let cool 20 minutes; serve warm.

BLUEBERRY COBBLER WITH GINGERED BISCUITS

Add 3 tablespoons minced crystallized ginger to flour mixture and substitute ⅛ teaspoon ground ginger for cinnamon in sugar for sprinkling on biscuits.

ALL-SEASON BLUEBERRY COBBLER

Thaw 36 ounces frozen blueberries (6 cups) in colander set over bowl to catch juices. Transfer juices (you should have about 1 cup) to small saucepan; simmer over medium heat until syrupy and thick enough to coat back of spoon, about 10 minutes. Mix syrup with berries and other filling ingredients; increase baking time for filling to 30 minutes and increase baking time in step 3 to 20 to 22 minutes.

PEACH CRUMBLE

✔ WHY THIS RECIPE WORKS

A soggy topping and watery, flavorless filling are the norm for the simple, humble peach crumble. The problem is the peaches—you never know just how juicy or how flavorful they will be until you cut them open. We wanted a peach crumble that consisted of fresh-tasting, lightly sweetened peaches topped with a buttery, crisp, and nutty-tasting crumble—no matter how sweet the peaches were (or weren't). Solving the peach problem involved letting peeled, sliced peaches macerate in sugar before

draining them and measuring out the amount of peach juice that would be added back to the filling: always ¼ cup. The sweetness of the filling was adjusted by adding more or less lemon juice as needed. One challenge remained: getting a crisp, well-browned topping required too much oven time for the peaches, which turned to mush. Instead, we baked the topping separately and then married it to the filling, baking the combination just until the fruit bubbled around the edges.

PEACH CRUMBLE
SERVES 6

Add the lemon juice to taste in step 2 according to the sweetness of your peaches. If ripe peaches are unavailable, you can substitute 3 pounds frozen peaches, thawed overnight in the refrigerator. If your peaches are firm, you should be able to peel them with a vegetable peeler. If they are too soft and ripe to withstand the pressure of a peeler, you'll need to blanch them in a pot of simmering water for 15 seconds and then shock them in a bowl of ice water before peeling. Serve with vanilla ice cream.

FILLING
3½	pounds peaches, peeled, halved, pitted, and cut into ¾-inch wedges
⅓	cup (2⅓ ounces) granulated sugar
1¼	teaspoons cornstarch
3–5	teaspoons lemon juice
	Pinch salt
	Pinch ground cinnamon
	Pinch ground nutmeg

CRUMBLE TOPPING
1	cup (5 ounces) all-purpose flour
¼	cup (1¾ ounces) plus 1 tablespoon granulated sugar
¼	cup packed (1¾ ounces) brown sugar
⅛	teaspoon salt
2	teaspoons vanilla extract
6	tablespoons unsalted butter, cut into 6 pieces and softened
½	cup sliced almonds

1. Adjust oven racks to lowest and middle positions and heat oven to 350 degrees. Line rimmed baking sheet with parchment paper.

2. FOR THE FILLING: Gently toss peaches and sugar together in large bowl and let sit for 30 minutes, gently stirring several times. Drain peaches in colander set over large bowl and reserve ¼ cup juice (discard remaining juice). Whisk reserved juice, cornstarch, lemon juice to taste, salt, cinnamon, and nutmeg together in small bowl. Combine peaches and juice mixture in bowl and transfer to 8-inch square baking dish.

3. FOR THE CRUMBLE TOPPING: While peaches are macerating, combine flour, ¼ cup granulated sugar, brown sugar, and salt in food processor and drizzle vanilla over top. Pulse to combine, about 5 pulses. Scatter butter pieces and ¼ cup almonds over top and process until mixture clumps together into large, crumbly balls, about 30 seconds, scraping down bowl halfway through. Sprinkle remaining ¼ cup almonds over mixture and pulse 2 times to combine. Transfer mixture to prepared baking sheet and spread into even layer (mixture should break up into roughly ½-inch chunks with some smaller, loose bits). Bake on middle rack until chunks are lightly browned and firm, 18 to 22 minutes, rotating baking sheet halfway through baking. (Cooled topping can be stored in an airtight container for up to 2 days.)

4. TO ASSEMBLE AND BAKE: Grasp edges of parchment paper, slide topping off paper over peaches, and spread into even layer with spatula, packing down lightly and breaking up any very large pieces. Sprinkle remaining 1 tablespoon sugar evenly over top and place dish on aluminum foil–lined rimmed baking sheet; place on lower rack. Increase oven temperature to 375 degrees and bake until well browned and filling is bubbling around edges, 25 to 35 minutes, rotating baking sheet halfway through baking. Transfer baking dish to wire rack and let cool 15 minutes; serve warm.

TRANSFERRING BAKED CRUMBLE TOPPING

1. After crumble is baked, lift short sides of parchment paper. (Crumble will break apart into uneven ½- to ¾-inch pieces.)

2. Carefully slide broken crumble pieces onto peaches or apples, then spread into even layer with spatula.

APPLE CRUMBLE

In this variation, the apples do not need to macerate with the sugar. You can substitute Empire or Cortland apples for the Granny Smith apples if desired. Serve with vanilla ice cream.

- ½ teaspoon cornstarch
- 4 teaspoons lemon juice
- 1½ pounds Granny Smith apples, peeled, cored, and cut into ½-inch cubes
- 1½ pounds Golden Delicious apples, peeled, cored, and cut into ½-inch cubes
- ⅔ cup (4⅔ ounces) sugar
  Pinch salt
  Pinch ground cinnamon
  Pinch ground nutmeg
- 1 recipe Crumble Topping (page 748)

1. Adjust oven racks to lowest and middle positions and heat oven to 350 degrees. Line rimmed baking sheet with parchment paper.

2. Stir cornstarch and lemon juice together in large bowl until cornstarch is dissolved. Add apples, sugar, salt, cinnamon, and nutmeg; toss to combine. Transfer mixture to 8-inch square glass dish. Cover tightly with aluminum foil; set aside.

3. Place topping mixture on middle rack in oven and apple filling mixture on lowest rack. Bake topping until chunks are lightly browned and firm, about 20 minutes. Remove topping and apples from oven.

4. **TO ASSEMBLE AND BAKE:** Uncover apple filling and gently stir. Grasp edges of parchment paper, slide topping off paper over peaches, and spread into even layer with spatula, packing down lightly and breaking up any very large pieces. Sprinkle remaining 1 tablespoon sugar evenly over top and place dish on foil-lined rimmed baking sheet; place on lower rack. Increase oven temperature to 375 degrees and bake until well browned and filling is bubbling around edges, about 25 minutes, rotating baking sheet halfway through baking. Transfer baking dish to wire rack and let cool 15 minutes; serve warm.

APPLE PANDOWDY

✔ WHY THIS RECIPE WORKS
Apple pandowdy harks back to Colonial-era New England—the dessert takes a more rustic approach to apple pie in that it features just one pastry crust, placed on top of a lightly sweetened apple filling. During or after baking, the pastry is broken and pushed into the filling—a technique known as "dowdying." We found the idea of an easier approach to apple pie very appealing—no fussy crimping and only one

piece of pastry dough to roll out—so we set out to make our own version. For a juicy apple filling with bright fruit flavor, we added cider to the apples and sweetened them with maple syrup, both of which made for a pleasantly saucy filling. Parcooking the apples in a skillet until caramelized before adding the other ingredients helped to deepen their flavor. For the crust, we cut a standard pie crust into squares after rolling it over the fruit right in the skillet—this encouraged a multitude of crisp edges that contrasted nicely with the tender fruit and recalled (in a less dowdy way) the broken-up crusts of a traditional pandowdy.

SKILLET APPLE PIE
SERVES 6 TO 8

If your skillet is not ovensafe, precook the apples and stir in the cider mixture as instructed, then transfer the apples to a 13 by 9-inch baking dish. Roll out the dough to a 13 by 9-inch rectangle and cut the crust and bake as instructed. If you do not have apple cider, reduced apple juice may be used as a substitute; simmer 1 cup apple juice in a small saucepan over medium heat until reduced to ½ cup, about 10 minutes. Serve warm or at room temperature with vanilla ice cream or Whipped Cream (page 800). Use a combination of sweet, crisp apples such as Golden Delicious and firm, tart apples such as Cortland or Empire.

CRUST
- 1 cup (5 ounces) all-purpose flour
- 1 tablespoon sugar
- ½ teaspoon salt
- 2 tablespoons vegetable shortening, chilled
- 6 tablespoons unsalted butter, cut into ¼-inch pieces and chilled
- 3–4 tablespoons ice water

FILLING
- ½ cup apple cider
- ⅓ cup maple syrup
- 2 tablespoons lemon juice
- 2 teaspoons cornstarch

⅛ teaspoon ground cinnamon
    (optional)
2   tablespoons unsalted butter
2½ pounds apples, peeled, cored, and
    cut into ½-inch-thick wedges
1   large egg white, lightly beaten
2   teaspoons sugar

1. FOR THE CRUST: Pulse flour, sugar, and salt in food processor until combined, about 4 pulses. Add shortening and pulse until mixture resembles coarse sand, about 10 pulses. Sprinkle butter pieces over top and pulse until mixture is pale yellow and resembles coarse crumbs, with butter bits no larger than small peas, about 10 pulses. Transfer mixture to medium bowl.

2. Sprinkle 3 tablespoons ice water over mixture. With rubber spatula, use folding motion to mix, pressing down on dough until dough is slightly tacky and sticks together, adding up to 1 tablespoon more ice water if dough does not come together. Flatten dough into 4-inch disk, wrap in plastic wrap, and refrigerate for at least 1 hour or up to 2 days. Let sit at room temperature for 15 minutes before rolling.

3. FOR THE FILLING: Adjust oven rack to upper-middle position and heat oven

SCORING PANDOWDY CRUST

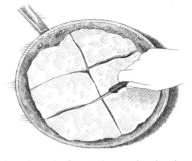

With a sharp knife, gently cut the dough into 6 pieces by making 1 vertical cut followed by 2 evenly spaced horizontal cuts (perpendicular to the first cut). This encourages a crisp crust and allows the juices from the apples to bubble up and caramelize.

to 500 degrees. Whisk cider, maple syrup, lemon juice, cornstarch, and cinnamon, if using, together in bowl until smooth. Melt butter in 12-inch ovensafe skillet over medium-high heat. Add apples and cook, stirring 2 or 3 times, until apples begin to caramelize, about 5 minutes. (Do not fully cook apples.) Off heat, add cider mixture and gently stir until apples are well coated. Set aside to cool slightly.

4. TO ASSEMBLE AND BAKE: Roll dough out on lightly floured counter to 11-inch round. Roll dough loosely around rolling pin and unroll over apple filling. Brush dough with egg white and sprinkle with sugar. With sharp knife, gently cut dough into 6 pieces by making one vertical cut followed by 2 evenly spaced horizontal cuts (perpendicular to first cut). Bake until apples are tender and crust is deep golden brown, about 20 minutes, rotating skillet halfway through baking. Let cool about 15 minutes; serve warm.

SKILLET APPLE BROWN BETTY

✓ WHY THIS RECIPE WORKS
In its most basic form, apple brown betty contains only four ingredients: apples, bread crumbs, sugar, and butter. Sadly, this simple combination inevitably results in a soggy, mushy mess of a dessert—not the classic early American dish of tender, lightly spiced chunks of apple topped with buttery toasted bread crumbs. We decided it was time to give "Betty" a makeover. For a lightly sweetened, crisp crumb topping, we toasted white sandwich bread crumbs with butter and a bit of sugar. The combination of Granny Smith and Golden Delicious apples made for a not-too-sweet apple filling. Instead of baking the dessert, we prepared it in a skillet on the stovetop and cooked the apples in two batches to ensure even cooking. Adding brown sugar to the apples along with ginger and cinnamon gave the dessert a deeper,

subtly spiced flavor. Some apple cider brought needed moisture and a further dimension of apple flavor; a bit of lemon juice brightened the filling. For a thicker filling, we added a portion of the toasted bread crumbs to the apples and reserved the remainder for sprinkling over the top.

SKILLET APPLE BROWN BETTY
SERVES 6 TO 8

If your apples are especially tart, omit the lemon juice. If, on the other hand, your apples are exceptionally sweet, use the full amount. When preparing the apples, put each variety into separate bowls since they're added to the skillet at different times. Serve with vanilla ice cream. Leftovers can be refrigerated; topped with vanilla yogurt, they make an excellent breakfast.

BREAD CRUMBS
4   slices hearty white sandwich bread,
    torn into quarters
3   tablespoons unsalted butter, cut
    into 4 pieces
2   tablespoons packed light brown
    sugar

FILLING
¼   cup packed (1¾ ounces) light
    brown sugar
¼   teaspoon ground ginger
¼   teaspoon ground cinnamon
    Pinch salt
3   tablespoons unsalted butter
1½ pounds Granny Smith apples, peeled,
    cored, and cut into ½-inch cubes
1½ pounds Golden Delicious apples,
    peeled, cored, and cut into
    ½-inch cubes
1¼ cups apple cider
1–3 teaspoons lemon juice

1. FOR THE BREAD CRUMBS: Pulse bread, butter, and sugar in food processor until coarsely ground, 5 to 7 pulses. Transfer bread crumbs to 12-inch skillet

and toast over medium heat, stirring constantly, until deep golden brown, 8 to 10 minutes. Transfer to paper towel–lined plate; wipe out skillet.

2. FOR THE FILLING: Combine sugar, ginger, cinnamon, and salt in small bowl. Melt 1½ tablespoons butter in now-empty skillet over high heat. Stir in Granny Smith apples and half of sugar mixture. Distribute apples in even layer and cook, stirring 2 or 3 times, until medium brown, about 5 minutes; transfer to medium bowl. Repeat with remaining 1½ tablespoons butter, Golden Delicious apples, and remaining sugar mixture, returning first batch of apples to skillet when the second batch is done.

3. Add apple cider to skillet and scrape pan with wooden spoon to loosen browned bits; cook until apples are tender but not mushy and liquid has reduced and is just beginning to thicken, 2 to 4 minutes.

4. Off heat, stir in lemon juice, if using, to taste, and ⅓ cup toasted bread crumbs. Gently press apples into even layer and sprinkle evenly with remaining toasted bread crumbs. Spoon into individual bowls and serve.

SKILLET APPLE BROWN BETTY WITH GOLDEN RAISINS AND CALVADOS

Any applejack, or even brandy, can be used in place of the Calvados.

Substitute ¼ cup Calvados for equal amount apple cider and add ½ cup golden raisins to apples along with cider-Calvados mixture.

SKILLET APPLE BROWN BETTY WITH PECANS AND DRIED CRANBERRIES

Add ½ cup pecans to food processor along with bread, sugar, and butter and process as directed. Add ½ cup dried cranberries to apple mixture with cider.

SKILLET APPLE CRISP

✔ **WHY THIS RECIPE WORKS**
Most recipes for apple crisp recipes yield unevenly cooked fruit and an unremarkable topping. We wanted an exemplary apple crisp—a lush (but not mushy) sweet-tart apple filling covered with truly crisp morsels of buttery, sugary topping. Our first few crisps contained unevenly cooked apples lacking any fruity punch. Stirring the fruit helped solve the texture problem, but reaching into a hot oven to do so was a hassle. Instead, we softened the apples on the stovetop—in a skillet. The shallow, flared pan also encouraged evaporation, browning, and better flavor overall. To improve the flavor further, we turned to apple cider, first reducing it to a syrupy consistency. As for the topping, we added brown sugar to white to play up the apples' caramel notes, and swapped out some flour for rolled oats to give the topping character and chew. Chopped pecans not only improved the crunch factor, but added rich flavor as well. After a few minutes in the oven, our crisp was just that.

SKILLET APPLE CRISP
SERVES 6 TO 8

If your skillet is not ovensafe, prepare the recipe through step 3 and then transfer the filling to a 13 by 9-inch baking dish; top the filling as directed and bake for an additional 5 minutes. We like Golden Delicious apples in this recipe, but Honeycrisp or Braeburn apples can be substituted; do not use Granny Smith apples. While old-fashioned rolled oats are preferable in this recipe, quick oats can be substituted. Serve with vanilla ice cream.

TOPPING
¾ cup (3¾ ounces) all-purpose flour
¾ cup pecans, chopped fine
¾ cup (2¼ ounces) old-fashioned rolled oats
½ cup packed (3½ ounces) light brown sugar

¼ cup (1¾ ounces) granulated sugar
½ teaspoon ground cinnamon
½ teaspoon salt
8 tablespoons unsalted butter, melted

FILLING
3 pounds Golden Delicious apples, peeled, cored, halved, and cut into ½-inch-thick wedges
¼ cup (1¾ ounces) granulated sugar
¼ teaspoon ground cinnamon (optional)
1 cup apple cider
2 teaspoons lemon juice
2 tablespoons unsalted butter

1. FOR THE TOPPING: Adjust oven rack to middle position and heat oven to 450 degrees. Line rimmed baking sheet with aluminum foil. Combine flour, pecans, oats, brown sugar, granulated sugar, cinnamon, and salt in bowl. Stir in butter until mixture is thoroughly moistened and crumbly. Set aside.

2. FOR THE FILLING: Toss apples, sugar, and cinnamon, if using, together in large bowl; set aside. Bring cider to simmer in 12-inch ovensafe skillet over medium heat; cook until reduced to ½ cup, about 5 minutes. Transfer reduced cider to bowl or liquid measuring cup; stir in lemon juice and set aside.

3. Melt butter in now-empty skillet over medium heat. Add apple mixture and cook, stirring frequently, until apples are beginning to soften and become translucent, 12 to 14 minutes. (Do not fully cook apples.) Off heat, gently stir in cider mixture until apples are coated.

4. Sprinkle topping evenly over fruit, breaking up any large chunks. Place skillet on prepared baking sheet and bake until fruit is tender and topping is deep golden brown, 15 to 20 minutes, rotating baking sheet halfway through baking. Transfer to wire rack and let cool for 15 minutes; serve warm.

SKILLET APPLE CRISP WITH RASPBERRIES AND ALMONDS

Substitute slivered almonds for pecans. Add ⅛ teaspoon almond extract to reduced cider with lemon juice in step 2. Stir 5 ounces raspberries into apple mixture along with reduced cider in step 3.

SKILLET APPLE CRISP WITH VANILLA, CARDAMOM, AND PISTACHIOS

Substitute ½ cup shelled pistachios and ¼ cup walnuts for pecans. Substitute ½ teaspoon ground cardamom for cinnamon in filling and add seeds from 1 vanilla bean to apple, sugar, and cardamom mixture.

SKILLET APPLE CRISP WITH MAPLE AND BACON

Cook 6 slices bacon, cut into ¼-inch pieces, in 12-inch skillet over medium heat, stirring frequently, until crisp, 5 to 7 minutes. Using slotted spoon, transfer bacon to paper towel–lined plate. Pour off bacon fat from skillet and discard. (Do not wash skillet.) Stir bacon into topping mixture after adding butter. Omit sugar and cinnamon from filling. Toss apples with ⅓ cup maple syrup in step 2 and proceed as directed.

PEAR CRISP

✔ WHY THIS RECIPE WORKS

Simply substituting pears for apples in this classic American dessert is a recipe for disaster; pears exude so much moisture that a traditional crisp topping will sink into the filling and won't get crunchy. We wanted to create a classic crisp—one with tender fruit and a crunchy, sweet topping using pears. We found ripe yet firm Bartlett pears to work best in crisp. To compensate for all the liquid they released in the oven, we added a

slurry of cornstarch mixed with lemon juice. Even with the thickened juices, our standard fruit crisp topping washed down into the filling. A streusel-type topping, made by incorporating melted butter into the flour using a food processor, proved sturdier and kept its crunchiness. Adding nuts to the topping provided crunch. And keeping the topping to a modest amount prevented it from sinking down into the fruit.

PEAR CRISP
SERVES 6

The test kitchen prefers a crisp made with Bartlett pears, but Bosc pears can also be used. The pears should be ripe but firm, which means the flesh at the base of the stem should give slightly when gently pressed with a finger. Bartlett pears will turn from green to greenish-yellow when ripe. Although almost any unsalted nut may be used in the topping, we prefer almonds or pecans. Serve with vanilla ice cream.

TOPPING
- ¾ cup nuts, chopped coarse
- ½ cup (2½ ounces) all-purpose flour
- ¼ cup packed (1¾ ounces) light brown sugar
- 2 tablespoons granulated sugar
- ¼ teaspoon ground cinnamon
- ⅛ teaspoon ground nutmeg
- ⅛ teaspoon salt
- 5 tablespoons unsalted butter, melted and cooled

FILLING
- 2 tablespoons granulated sugar
- 2 teaspoons lemon juice
- 1 teaspoon cornstarch
  Pinch salt
- 3 pounds pears, peeled, halved, cored, and cut into 1½-inch pieces

1. Adjust oven rack to lower-middle position and heat oven to 425 degrees. Line rimmed baking sheet with aluminum foil.

2. FOR THE TOPPING: Process nuts, flour, brown sugar, granulated sugar, cinnamon, nutmeg, and salt in food processor until nuts are finely chopped, about 9 pulses. Drizzle butter over flour mixture and pulse until mixture resembles crumbly wet sand, about 5 pulses, scraping down bowl halfway through. Set aside.

3. FOR THE FILLING: Whisk sugar, lemon juice, cornstarch, and salt together in large bowl. Gently toss pears with sugar mixture and transfer to 8-inch square baking dish.

4. Sprinkle topping evenly over fruit, breaking up any large chunks. Transfer baking dish to prepared baking sheet.

CORING PEARS FOR PEAR CRISP

For this recipe, the pears are best peeled and halved, from stem to blossom end, and then cored and cut into pieces.

1. Use melon baller to cut around central core of halved, peeled pear with circular motion; remove core.

2. Draw melon baller from central core to top of pear, removing interior stem. Remove blossom end. Quarter each half lengthwise and then cut each piece in half crosswise for eight pieces.

Bake until fruit is bubbling around edges and topping is deep golden brown, about 30 minutes, rotating baking sheet halfway through baking. Transfer baking dish to wire rack and let cool until warm, about 15 minutes; serve.

PEAR CRISP WITH OAT TOPPING

Reduce nuts to ½ cup and increase butter to 6 tablespoons. After incorporating butter into flour mixture in step 2, add ½ cup old-fashioned rolled oats to food processor and process until evenly incorporated, about 3 pulses.

TRIPLE-GINGER PEAR CRISP

Use almonds for nuts and replace cinnamon and nutmeg with ¾ teaspoon ground ginger. Process 2 tablespoons coarsely chopped crystallized ginger with nuts and flour in step 2. Reduce lemon juice to 1 teaspoon and add 1 teaspoon grated fresh ginger to sugar-cornstarch mixture in step 3.

CHERRY CLAFOUTI

✓ WHY THIS RECIPE WORKS
Clafouti is a homey French dessert of fresh fruit, usually cherries, baked in a creamy and light custard. Though it sounds simple—just fruit and batter—it can be notoriously finicky, suffering from both textural problems and flavor issues. We wanted a perfectly balanced clafouti in which the fruity, tangy cherries shared the stage with the creamy, lightly sweetened, tender custard. We quickly determined that the simple flavors of this dish made using fresh fruit a must. A bit of vanilla and amaretto liqueur boosted the cherry flavor nicely. When it came to the custard, many recipes called for flour as the binder, but we
found that flour produced a thicker clafouti than we liked. Instead, we used 2 tablespoons cornstarch, which was just enough to bind the custard without weighing it down. Milk gave us a custard that was too lean but a good amount of heavy cream provided a pleasing richness. Eggs give clafouti structure; two eggs plus two yolks resulted in a custard that was firm-textured, yet not rubbery, and rich but not eggy. Though a cast-iron pan is the norm for baking clafouti, we found a more accessible option in a 9-inch pie plate.

CHERRY CLAFOUTI
SERVES 6 TO 8

Fresh cherries are essential to the fresh flavor and texture of this dish; do not substitute jarred, canned, or frozen cherries.

- ⅓ cup (2⅓ ounces) sugar
- 2 tablespoons cornstarch
  Pinch salt
- 1¼ cups heavy cream
- 2 large eggs plus 2 large yolks, room temperature
- 1 tablespoon amaretto
- 2 teaspoons vanilla extract
- 10 ounces fresh sour cherries, pitted and halved
  Confectioners' sugar

1. Adjust oven rack to middle position and heat oven to 350 degrees. Whisk sugar, cornstarch, and salt together in large bowl. Add cream, eggs, egg yolks, amaretto, and vanilla and whisk until smooth and thoroughly combined.

2. Arrange cherries in single layer in 9-inch pie plate and pour cream mixture over top. Bake until toothpick inserted in center comes out clean, 35 to 40 minutes, rotating dish halfway through baking.

3. Let clafouti cool until custard has set up, about 15 minutes. Dust with confectioners' sugar and serve.

PLUM CLAFOUTI

For a nice presentation, fan the plum slices out attractively over the bottom of the dish before pouring in the custard.

Substitute 2 plums, halved, pitted, and cut into ¼-inch wedges, for cherries and 1 tablespoon cognac for amaretto.

BLUEBERRY BUCKLE

✓ WHY THIS RECIPE WORKS
The classic blueberry buckle can be regarded as a streusel-topped blueberry coffee cake, but that sells it short—the substance of blueberry buckle should be the blueberries. We wanted to keep the emphasis on the berries yet also keep the berry-to-cake ratio in balance so the moisture released from the fruit during baking wouldn't create a soggy cake. We used an ample amount of blueberries—4 cups—to keep them as the headliner, then built more structure into the batter to support them. In the end, the batter resembled a cookie dough more than a cake batter. We used all-purpose flour, eliminated the dairy, and added baking powder to supplement the natural leavening provided by creamed butter and sugar. For a flavorful, crisp yet crumbly streusel, we turned to a combination of light brown and granulated sugars, softened butter, and cinnamon.

BLUEBERRY BUCKLE
SERVES 8

The batter will be extremely thick and heavy, and some effort will be required to spread it into the prepared pan. Be sure to use a cake pan with at least 2-inch-high sides. This buckle is best made with fresh blueberries, not frozen ones, which are too moist. Serve with vanilla ice cream.

STREUSEL

½ cup (2½ ounces) all-purpose flour
½ cup packed (3½ ounces) light brown sugar
2 tablespoons granulated sugar
¼ teaspoon ground cinnamon
  Pinch salt
4 tablespoons unsalted butter, cut into 8 pieces and softened

CAKE

1½ cups (7½ ounces) all-purpose flour
1½ teaspoons baking powder
10 tablespoons unsalted butter, softened
⅔ cup (4⅔ ounces) granulated sugar
½ teaspoon salt
½ teaspoon grated lemon zest
1½ teaspoons vanilla extract
2 large eggs, room temperature
20 ounces (4 cups) blueberries

1. FOR THE STREUSEL: Using stand mixer fitted with paddle, combine flour, brown sugar, granulated sugar, cinnamon, and salt on low speed until well combined and no large brown sugar lumps remain, about 45 seconds. Add butter; beat on low speed until mixture resembles wet sand and no large butter pieces remain, about 2½ minutes. Transfer to bowl; set aside.

2. FOR THE CAKE: Adjust oven rack to lower-middle position and heat oven to 350 degrees. Grease 9-inch round cake pan, line bottom with parchment paper, grease parchment, then flour pan.

3. Whisk flour and baking powder together in bowl; set aside. Using stand mixer fitted with paddle, beat butter, sugar, salt, and zest on medium-high speed until light and fluffy, about 3 minutes, scraping down bowl as necessary. Beat in vanilla until combined, about 30 seconds. With mixer on medium speed, add eggs

1 at a time; beat until partially incorporated, scrape down bowl, and continue to beat until fully incorporated (mixture will appear broken). With mixer on low speed, gradually add flour mixture; beat until flour is almost fully incorporated, about 20 seconds. Stir batter with rubber spatula, scraping bowl, until no flour pockets remain and batter is homogeneous; batter will be very heavy and thick. Gently fold in blueberries until evenly distributed.

4. Transfer batter to prepared pan. Spread batter evenly to pan edges and smooth surface. Squeeze portion of streusel in hand to form large cohesive clump; break up clump with fingers and sprinkle streusel evenly over batter. Repeat with remaining streusel. Bake until cake is deep golden brown and toothpick inserted in center comes out clean, about 55 minutes, rotating pan halfway through baking. Transfer pan to wire rack and let cool, 15 to 20 minutes (cake will fall slightly as it cools).

5. Run paring knife around edges to loosen. Invert cake, then peel off and discard parchment. Invert cake onto serving platter. Let cool at least 1 hour. Cut into wedges and serve warm or at room temperature. (Buckle can be stored at room temperature, wrapped in plastic wrap, for up to 2 days.)

INDIVIDUAL BLUEBERRY BUCKLES

Line 12-cup muffin tin with paper or foil liners. In step 4, transfer batter to prepared tin; spread batter evenly to cup edges and smooth surface. (Batter will reach top of liners.) Reduce baking time to 35 minutes. Let buckles cool in pan on wire rack for 10 minutes. Remove from tin and let cool, at least 30 minutes. Serve warm or at room temperature.

EASY RASPBERRY GRATIN

✔ WHY THIS RECIPE WORKS

Fragrant, sweet-tart raspberries dressed up with bread crumbs, and baked, make a perfect gratin. The topping browns and the fruit is warmed just enough to release a bit of juice. We wanted to find the quickest, easiest route to this pleasing simple summer dessert. We started with perfect raspberries: ripe, dry, and unbruised. Tossing the berries with just a bit of sugar and kirsch (a clear cherry brandy) provided enough additional flavor and sweetness. For the topping, we combined soft white bread, brown sugar, cinnamon, and butter in the food processor and topped the berries with the fluffy crumbs. As for baking the gratin, we found that a moderately hot oven gave the berries more time to soften and browned the crust more evenly.

EASY RASPBERRY GRATIN
SERVES 4 TO 6

If you prefer, you can substitute blueberries, blackberries, or strawberries for part or all of the raspberries. If using strawberries, hull them and slice them in half lengthwise if small or into quarters if large. Later in the summer season, ripe, peeled peaches or nectarines, sliced, can be used in combination with the blueberries or raspberries. If using frozen raspberries, do not thaw them before baking.

20 ounces (4 cups) fresh or frozen raspberries
1 tablespoon granulated sugar
1 tablespoon kirsch or vanilla extract (optional)
  Pinch salt
3 slices hearty white sandwich bread, torn into quarters
¼ cup packed (1¾ ounces) brown sugar
2 tablespoons unsalted butter, softened
  Pinch ground cinnamon

1. Adjust oven rack to lower-middle position and heat oven to 400 degrees. Gently toss raspberries, granulated sugar, kirsch, if using, and salt in medium bowl. Transfer mixture to 9-inch pie plate.

2. Pulse bread, brown sugar, butter, and cinnamon in food processor until mixture resembles coarse crumbs, about 10 pulses. Sprinkle crumbs evenly over fruit and bake until crumbs are deep golden brown, 15 to 20 minutes. Transfer plate to wire rack, let cool for 5 minutes, and serve warm.

FRESH BERRY GRATIN

✔ WHY THIS RECIPE WORKS

Gratins can be very humble, as in our Easy Raspberry Gratin (page 754), where the topping is simply sweetened bread crumbs. Or they can be a bit more sophisticated, as when they are topped with the foamy Italian custard called zabaglione. Zabaglione is made with just three ingredients—egg yolks, sugar, and alcohol—but it requires constant watching so that the mixture doesn't overcook. It also needs to be whisked until it's the ideal thick, creamy texture. We were after a foolproof method for this topping for a gratin that could serve as an elegant finale to a summer meal. We chose to make individual gratins—perfect for entertaining—and settled on a mix of berries, which we tossed with sugar and salt to draw out their juices. To prevent a custard with scrambled eggs, we kept the heat low; for the right texture, we whisked until the custard was somewhat thick. As for flavor, traditional Marsala wine gave us an overly sweet zabaglione; crisp, dry Sauvignon Blanc provided a clean flavor that worked better with the berries. Whipped cream worked well as a thickening agent. We spooned our zabaglione over the berries and sprinkled a mixture of brown and white sugars on top before broiling for a crackly, caramelized crust.

INDIVIDUAL FRESH BERRY GRATINS WITH ZABAGLIONE

SERVES 4

When making the zabaglione, make sure to cook the egg mixture in a glass bowl over water that is barely simmering; glass conducts heat more evenly and gently than metal. If the heat is too high, the yolks around the edges of the bowl will start to scramble. Constant whisking is required. Do not use frozen berries for this recipe. You will need four shallow 6-inch gratin dishes, but a broiler-safe pie plate or gratin dish can be used instead. To prevent scorching, pay close attention to the gratins when broiling.

BERRY MIXTURE

15 ounces mixed berries (raspberries, blueberries, blackberries, and strawberries; strawberries hulled and halved lengthwise if small, quartered if large) (3 cups)

2 teaspoons granulated sugar
Pinch salt

ZABAGLIONE

3 large egg yolks
3 tablespoons granulated sugar
3 tablespoons dry white wine, such as Sauvignon Blanc
2 teaspoons light brown sugar
3 tablespoons heavy cream, chilled

1. FOR THE BERRY MIXTURE: Line rimmed baking sheet with aluminum foil. Toss berries, sugar, and salt together in bowl. Divide berry mixture evenly among 4 shallow 6-ounce gratin dishes set on prepared baking sheet; set aside.

2. FOR THE ZABAGLIONE: Whisk egg yolks, 2 tablespoons plus 1 teaspoon granulated sugar, and wine together in medium bowl until sugar is dissolved, about 1 minute. Set bowl over saucepan of barely simmering water and cook, whisking constantly, until mixture is frothy. Continue to cook, whisking constantly, until mixture is slightly thickened, creamy, and glossy, 5 to 10 minutes (mixture will form loose mounds when dripped from whisk). Remove bowl from saucepan and whisk constantly for 30 seconds to cool slightly. Transfer bowl to refrigerator and chill until egg mixture is completely cool, about 10 minutes.

3. Meanwhile, adjust oven rack 6 inches from broiler element and heat broiler. Combine brown sugar and remaining 2 teaspoons granulated sugar in bowl.

4. Whisk heavy cream in large bowl until it holds soft peaks, 30 to 90 seconds. Using rubber spatula, gently fold whipped cream into cooled egg mixture. Spoon zabaglione over berries and sprinkle sugar mixture evenly on top; let stand at room temperature for 10 minutes, until sugar dissolves.

5. Broil gratins until sugar is bubbly and caramelized, 1 to 4 minutes. Serve immediately.

INDIVIDUAL FRESH BERRY GRATINS WITH HONEY-LAVENDER ZABAGLIONE

Heat 2 teaspoons dried lavender and ¼ cup dry white wine in small saucepan over medium heat until barely simmering; remove from heat and let stand 10 minutes. Strain wine through fine-mesh strainer and discard lavender (you should have 3 tablespoons wine). Substitute lavender-infused wine for white wine and 2 teaspoons honey for 1 teaspoon granulated sugar in step 2.

INDIVIDUAL FRESH BERRY GRATINS WITH LEMON ZABAGLIONE

Replace 1 tablespoon wine with equal amount lemon juice and add 1 teaspoon grated lemon zest to egg yolk mixture in step 2.

CRÊPES WITH SUGAR AND LEMON

✔ WHY THIS RECIPE WORKS

A crêpe is nothing but a thin pancake cooked quickly on each side and wrapped around a sweet or savory filling, but it has a reputation for being difficult. We wanted an easy method for crêpes that were thin and delicate yet rich and flavorfully browned in spots. Finding the perfect ratio of milk to flour and sugar gave us rich-tasting, lightly sweet pancakes. We were surprised to find that neither the type of flour nor the mixing method seemed to matter, and a plain old 12-inch nonstick skillet worked as well as a specialty crêpe pan. What does matter is heating the pan properly (over low heat for at least 10 minutes), using the right amount of batter (we settled on ¼ cup), and flipping the crêpe precisely at the right moment, when the edges appear dry, matte, and lacy. Fillings such as lemon and sugar, bananas and Nutella, honey and almonds, chocolate and orange, and dulce de leche and pecans turned our thin crêpes into a sweet treat.

CRÊPES WITH SUGAR AND LEMON
SERVES 4

Crêpes will give off steam as they cook, but if at any point the skillet begins to smoke, remove it from the heat immediately and turn down the heat. Stacking the crêpes on a wire rack allows excess steam to escape so they won't stick together. To allow for practice, the recipe yields 10 crêpes; only eight are needed for the filling.

½	teaspoon vegetable oil
1	cup (5 ounces) all-purpose flour
3	tablespoons sugar
¼	teaspoon salt
1½	cups whole milk
3	large eggs
2	tablespoons unsalted butter, melted and cooled
	Lemon wedges

1. Heat oil in 12-inch nonstick skillet over low heat for at least 10 minutes.

2. While skillet is heating, whisk flour, 1 teaspoon sugar, and salt together in medium bowl. In separate bowl, whisk together milk and eggs. Add half of milk mixture to dry ingredients and whisk until smooth. Add butter and whisk until incorporated. Whisk in remaining milk mixture until smooth.

3. Wipe out skillet with paper towel, leaving thin film of oil on bottom and sides of pan. Increase heat to medium and let skillet heat for 1 minute. After 1 minute, test heat of skillet by placing 1 teaspoon batter in center and cook for 20 seconds. If mini crêpe is golden brown on bottom, skillet is properly heated; if it is too light or too dark, adjust heat accordingly and retest.

4. Pour ¼ cup batter into far side of pan and tilt and shake gently until batter evenly covers bottom of pan. Cook crêpe without moving until top surface is dry and edges are starting to brown, loosening crêpe from side of pan with rubber spatula, about 25 seconds. Gently slide spatula underneath edge of crêpe, grasp edge with fingertips, and flip crêpe. Cook until second side is lightly spotted, about 20 seconds. Transfer cooked crêpe to wire rack, inverting so spotted side is facing up. Return pan to heat and heat for 10 seconds before repeating with remaining batter. As crêpes are done, stack on wire rack.

5. Transfer stack of crêpes to large plate and invert second plate over crêpes. Microwave until crêpes are warm, 30 to 45 seconds (45 to 60 seconds if crêpes have cooled completely). Remove top plate and wipe dry with paper towel. Sprinkle half of top crêpe with 1 teaspoon sugar. Fold unsugared bottom half over sugared half, then fold into quarters. Transfer sugared crêpe to second plate. Continue with remaining crêpes. Serve immediately, passing lemon wedges separately.

CRÊPES WITH BANANAS AND NUTELLA

Omit 8 teaspoons sprinkling sugar and lemon wedges. Spread 2 teaspoons Nutella over half of each crêpe followed by eight to ten ¼-inch-thick banana slices. Fold crêpes into quarters. Serve immediately.

CRÊPES WITH HONEY AND TOASTED ALMONDS

Omit 8 teaspoons sprinkling sugar and lemon wedges. Drizzle 1 teaspoon honey over half of each crêpe and sprinkle with 2 teaspoons finely chopped toasted sliced almonds and pinch salt. Fold crêpes into quarters. Serve immediately.

CRÊPES WITH CHOCOLATE AND ORANGE

Omit 8 teaspoons sprinkling sugar and lemon wedges. Using fingertips, rub 1 teaspoon finely grated orange zest into ¼ cup sugar. Stir in 2 ounces finely grated bittersweet chocolate. Sprinkle 1½ tablespoons chocolate-orange mixture over half of each crêpe. Fold crêpes into quarters. Serve immediately.

CRÊPES WITH DULCE DE LECHE AND TOASTED PECANS

Dulce de leche is a milk-based caramel sauce and spread. Look for it in the international foods aisle of supermarkets or in Latin markets.

Omit 8 teaspoons sprinkling sugar and lemon wedges. Drizzle 1 teaspoon dulce de leche over half of each crêpe and sprinkle with 2 teaspoons finely chopped toasted pecans and small pinch salt. Fold crêpe into quarters. Serve immediately.

CRÊPES SUZETTE

✔ WHY THIS RECIPE WORKS

Classic French restaurants have mastered the fiery theatrics of this tableside treat. We wanted to develop a recipe that would comfortably guide the home cook through the flambé process. For a foolproof flambé that didn't create a frightening fireball or, conversely, didn't burn at all, we ignited the alcohol (cognac) alone in the skillet before building the sauce. We then enriched a reduction of butter, sugar, and orange juice with additional orange juice, orange zest, and triple sec. Before saucing, we sprinkled our crêpes with sugar and broiled them, forming a crunchy, sugary barrier that provided partial protection from the sauce, so our crêpes didn't turn soggy.

CRÊPES SUZETTE
SERVES 6

To allow for practice, the recipe yields about 16 crêpes; only 12 are needed for the dish. We prefer crêpes made with whole milk, but skim milk or 1 percent or 2 percent low-fat milk can also be used. Before flambéing, be sure to roll up long shirtsleeves, tie back long hair, and turn off the exhaust fan and any lit burners.

CRÊPES
- 1½   cups whole milk
- 1½   cups (7½ ounces) all-purpose flour
- 3   large eggs
- ½   cup water
- 5   tablespoons unsalted butter, melted, plus extra for pan
- 3   tablespoons sugar
- 2   tablespoons cognac
- ½   teaspoon salt

ORANGE SAUCE
- ¼   cup cognac
- 1   tablespoon finely grated orange zest plus 1¼ cups juice (3 oranges)
- 6   tablespoons unsalted butter, cut into 6 pieces
- ¼   cup sugar
- 2   tablespoons orange liqueur, such as triple sec

1. FOR THE CRÊPES: Process all ingredients in blender until smooth, about 10 seconds. Transfer to bowl.

2. Brush bottom and sides of 10-inch nonstick skillet lightly with melted butter and heat skillet over medium heat. Pour in scant ¼ cup batter in slow, steady stream, twirling skillet slowly until bottom is evenly covered. Cook crêpe until it starts to lose its opaqueness and turns spotty light golden brown on bottom, 30 seconds to 1 minute, loosening edge with rubber spatula. Gently slide spatula underneath edge of crêpe, grasp edge with fingertips, and flip crêpe. Cook until dry on second side, about 20 seconds.

3. Transfer cooked crêpe to wire rack, inverting so spotted side is facing up. Return pan to heat, brush pan lightly with butter and heat for 10 seconds before repeating with remaining batter. As crêpes are done, stack on wire rack. (Cooked crêpes can be refrigerated, wrapped in plastic wrap, for up to 3 days; bring them to room temperature before proceeding with recipe.)

4. FOR THE ORANGE SAUCE: Adjust oven rack to lower-middle position and heat broiler. Heat 3 tablespoons cognac in 12-inch broiler-safe skillet over medium heat just until warmed through, about 5 seconds. Off heat, wave lit match over pan until cognac ignites, then shake pan to distribute flames.

5. When flames subside, add 1 cup

TEST KITCHEN TIP NO. 148   TIPS FOR FEARLESS FLAMBÉING

Flambéing is more than just tableside theatrics: as dramatic as it looks, igniting alcohol actually helps develop a deeper, more complex flavor in sauces—thanks to flavor-boosting chemical reactions that occur only at the high temperatures reached in flambéing. But accomplishing this feat at home can be daunting. Here are some tips for successful—and safe—flambéing at home.

BE PREPARED: Turn off the exhaust fan, tie back long hair, and have a lid at the ready to smother flare-ups.

USE THE PROPER EQUIPMENT: A pan with flared sides (such as a skillet) rather than straight sides will allow more oxygen to mingle with the alcohol vapors, increasing the chance that you'll spark the desired flame. If possible, use long chimney matches, and light the alcohol with your arm extended to full length.

IGNITE WARM ALCOHOL: If the alcohol becomes too hot, the vapors can rise to dangerous heights, causing large flare-ups once lit. Inversely, if the alcohol is too cold, there won't be enough vapors to light at all. We found that heating alcohol to 100 degrees Fahrenheit (best achieved by adding alcohol to a hot pan off heat and letting it sit for five to 10 seconds) produced the most moderate, yet long-burning, flames.

IF A FLARE-UP SHOULD OCCUR: Simply slide the lid over the top of the skillet (coming in from the side of, rather than over, the flames) to put out the fire quickly. Let the alcohol cool down and start again.

IF THE ALCOHOL WON'T LIGHT: If the pan is full of other ingredients (as is the case in Crêpes Suzette), the potency of the alcohol can be diminished as it becomes incorporated. For a more foolproof flame, ignite the alcohol in a separate small skillet or saucepan; once the flame has burned off, add the reduced alcohol to the remaining ingredients.

orange juice, butter, and 3 tablespoons sugar and simmer over high heat, stirring occasionally, until many large bubbles appear and mixture reduces to thick syrup, 6 to 8 minutes (you should have just over ½ cup sauce). Transfer sauce to small bowl; do not wash skillet. Stir remaining ¼ cup orange juice, orange zest, orange liqueur, and remaining 1 tablespoon cognac into sauce; cover to keep warm.

6. To assemble, fold each crêpe in half, then fold into quarters. Arrange 9 folded crêpes around edge of now-empty skillet, with rounded edges facing inward, overlapping as necessary to fit. Arrange remaining 2 crêpes in center of pan. Sprinkle crêpes evenly with remaining 1 tablespoon sugar. Broil until sugar caramelizes and crêpes turn spotty brown, about 5 minutes. (Watch crêpes constantly to prevent scorching; turn pan as necessary.) Carefully remove pan from oven and pour half of sauce over crêpes, leaving some areas uncovered. Transfer crêpes to individual plates and serve immediately, passing extra sauce separately.

SIMPLE APPLESAUCE

✔ **WHY THIS RECIPE WORKS**
Applesauce should taste like apples, but all too often the tart, sweet, and fruity nuances of fresh apple flavor are overpowered by sweeteners and spices. We wanted a smooth, thick sauce with fresh apple flavor but not too much sweetness or spice. First, we chose the right apple. Among our favorites are Jonagold, Jonathan, Pink Lady, and Macoun, which all produced a sauce with a pleasing balance of tart and sweet. We tried blending varieties in combination with each other, but concluded that single-variety sauces had purer, stronger character. Second, we learned it was best not to peel the apples;

cooking the fruit with the skin on further boosted flavor in our applesauce recipe. Processing the cooked apples through a food mill, not a food processor or blender, removed the skins and produced a sauce with the silky-smooth, thick texture we were after. Third, we ditched the spices. Adding just a little water, sugar, and a pinch of salt resulted in a perfectly sweetened sauce that tasted first and foremost of apples.

SIMPLE APPLESAUCE
MAKES ABOUT 3½ CUPS

If you do not own a food mill or prefer applesauce with a coarse texture, peel the apples before coring and cutting them and, after cooking, mash them against the side of the pot with a wooden spoon or against the bottom of the pot with a potato masher. Applesauce made with out-of-season apples may be somewhat drier than applesauce made with in-season apples, so you may need to add more water in step 2 to adjust the texture. This recipe doubles easily; increase the cooking time by 10 to 15 minutes.

4   pounds apples, preferably Jonagold, Jonathan, Pink Lady, or Macoun, cored, and cut into rough 1½-inch pieces
1   cup water, plus extra as needed
¼   cup sugar, plus extra to taste
    Pinch salt

1. Toss apples, water, sugar, and salt in Dutch oven. Cover pot and cook apples over medium-high heat until they begin to break down, 15 to 20 minutes, stirring occasionally to break up large chunks.
2. Process cooked apples through food mill. Season with sugar to taste or add water as needed to adjust consistency. Serve warm, at room temperature, or chilled. (Applesauce can be refrigerated for up to 1 week.)

CINNAMON APPLESAUCE

Add 2 cinnamon sticks to Dutch oven with apples. Cook as directed, removing cinnamon sticks before processing. Alternatively, stir ¼ teaspoon cinnamon into finished applesauce.

CRANBERRY APPLESAUCE

Add 4 ounces fresh or frozen cranberries to Dutch oven with apples. Cook and process as directed.

GINGER APPLESAUCE

Add three ½-inch slices ginger, peeled and smashed, to Dutch oven with apples. Cook as directed, removing ginger before processing.

BAKED APPLES

✔ **WHY THIS RECIPE WORKS**
This homey (and typically dowdy) dessert is often plagued with a mushy texture and one-dimensional, cloyingly sweet flavor. We wanted baked apples that were tender and firm with a filling that perfectly complemented their sweet, tart flavor. Granny Smith, with its firm flesh and tart, fruity flavor, was the best apple for the job. To ensure that our fruit avoided even the occasional collapse, we peeled the apples after cutting off the top; this allowed steam to escape and the apples to retain their tender-firm texture. Our filling base of tangy dried cranberries, brown sugar, and pecans benefited from some finessing by way of cinnamon, orange zest, and butter. To punch up the flavor even more, we intensified the nuttiness with chewy rolled oats, and diced apple added substance. A melon baller helped us scoop out a spacious cavity for the filling. We then capped the filled apples with

the tops we had lopped off. Once in the oven, the apples were basted with an apple cider and maple syrup sauce and emerged full of flavor— and far from frumpy.

BEST BAKED APPLES

SERVES 6

If you don't have an ovensafe skillet, transfer the browned apples to a 13 by 9-inch baking dish and bake as directed. The recipe calls for seven apples; six are left whole and one is diced and added to the filling. Serve with vanilla ice cream, if desired.

7	large Granny Smith apples (8 ounces each)
6	tablespoons unsalted butter, softened
⅓	cup dried cranberries, chopped coarse
⅓	cup pecans, toasted and chopped coarse
¼	cup packed (1¾ ounces) brown sugar
3	tablespoons old-fashioned rolled oats
1	teaspoon finely grated orange zest
½	teaspoon ground cinnamon Pinch salt
⅓	cup maple syrup
⅓	cup plus 2 tablespoons apple cider

1. Adjust oven rack to middle position and heat oven to 375 degrees. Peel, core, and cut 1 apple into ¼-inch dice. Combine diced apple, 5 tablespoons butter, cranberries, pecans, sugar, oats, zest, cinnamon, and salt in bowl; set aside.

2. Shave thin slice off bottom (blossom end) of remaining 6 apples to allow them to sit flat. Cut top ½ inch off stem end of apples and reserve. Peel apples and use melon baller or small measuring spoon to remove 1½-inch-diameter core, being careful not to cut through bottom of apples.

3. Melt remaining 1 tablespoon butter in 12-inch ovensafe nonstick skillet over medium heat. Add apples, stem side down, and cook until cut surface is golden brown, about 3 minutes. Flip apples, reduce heat to low, and spoon filling inside, mounding excess filling over cavities; top with reserved apple caps. Add maple syrup and ⅓ cup cider to skillet. Transfer skillet to oven and bake until skewer inserted into apples meets little resistance, 35 to 40 minutes, basting every 10 minutes with maple syrup mixture in pan.

4. Transfer apples to serving platter. Stir up to 2 tablespoons of remaining cider into sauce in skillet to adjust consistency. Pour sauce over apples and serve.

BEST BAKED APPLES WITH DRIED CHERRIES AND HAZELNUTS

Substitute coarsely chopped dried cherries for cranberries, coarsely chopped toasted hazelnuts for pecans, and pepper for cinnamon.

BEST BAKED APPLES WITH DRIED FIGS AND MACADAMIA NUTS

Substitute coarsely chopped dried figs for cranberries, coarsely chopped toasted macadamia nuts for pecans, lemon zest for orange zest, and ¼ teaspoon ground ginger for cinnamon.

BEST BAKED APPLES WITH RAISINS AND WALNUTS

Substitute coarsely chopped raisins for cranberries, coarsely chopped toasted walnuts for pecans, lemon zest for orange zest, and ¼ teaspoon ground nutmeg for cinnamon.

BEST BAKED APPLES WITH DRIED APRICOTS AND ALMONDS

Substitute coarsely chopped dried apricots for cranberries, coarsely chopped toasted almonds for pecans, and 1 teaspoon vanilla extract for cinnamon.

KEY STEPS TO BETTER BAKED APPLES

1. Slicing off tops allows for generous room for filling and removing entire peel for base prevents blowouts and keeps flesh firm.

2. Sautéing apples in butter before baking contributes rich, caramelized flavor.

3. Capping apples with sliced-off tops shields filling from burning in oven.

SUMMER FRUIT SALADS

✔ WHY THIS RECIPE WORKS
Most fruit salads betray neither rhyme nor reason regarding the fruit selection or assembly, and the customary heavy sprinkling of sugar seems designed to mask defects in the fruit. We set out to rewrite the rules of fruit salad to bring out the best fruit flavor. We cut the fruit into small, uniform pieces, so the different flavors and textures could come through in each mouthful. To keep

each fruit distinct, we also limited the number to three per salad. We found it hard to judge the proper amount of sugar when it was added directly to the salad, so we macerated each fruit in just the amount needed to release the fruits' natural juices; we also balanced the sweetness with fresh lime juice. But first, we mashed the sugar with herbs and zests (in bartending circles, this process is called "muddling") to ensure even flavor distribution.

HONEYDEW, MANGO, AND RASPBERRIES WITH LIME AND GINGER

SERVES 4 TO 6

The optional cayenne adds a bit of heat to this fruit salad.

- 4 teaspoons sugar
- 2 teaspoons grated lime zest plus 1 to 2 tablespoons juice
    Pinch cayenne (optional)
- 3 cups honeydew melon, cut into ½-inch pieces
- 1 mango, peeled, pitted, and cut into ½-inch pieces (1½ cups)
- 1–2 teaspoons grated ginger
- 5 ounces (1 cup) raspberries

Combine sugar, lime zest, and cayenne, if using, in large bowl. Using rubber spatula, press mixture into side of bowl until sugar becomes damp, about 30 seconds. Gently toss honeydew, mango, and ginger to taste with sugar mixture until combined. Let sit at room temperature, stirring occasionally, until fruit releases its juices, 15 to 30 minutes. Gently stir in raspberries. Stir in lime juice to taste and serve.

CANTALOUPE, PLUMS, AND CHERRIES WITH MINT AND VANILLA

SERVES 4 TO 6

Blueberries can be substituted for the cherries.

- 4 teaspoons sugar
- 1–2 tablespoons minced fresh mint
- ¼ teaspoon vanilla extract
- 3 cups cantaloupe, cut into ½-inch pieces
- 2 plums, halved, pitted, and cut into ½-inch pieces
- 8 ounces fresh sweet cherries, pitted and halved
- 1–2 tablespoons lime juice

Combine sugar and mint to taste in large bowl. Using rubber spatula, press mixture into side of bowl until sugar becomes damp, about 30 seconds; add vanilla. Gently toss fruit with sugar mixture until combined. Let sit at room temperature, stirring occasionally, until fruit releases its juices, 15 to 30 minutes. Stir in lime juice to taste and serve.

PEACHES, BLACKBERRIES, AND STRAWBERRIES WITH BASIL AND PEPPER

SERVES 4 TO 6

Nectarines can be substituted for the peaches.

- 4 teaspoons sugar
- 2 tablespoons chopped fresh basil
- ½ teaspoon pepper
- 3 peaches (6 ounces each), halved, pitted, and cut into ½-inch pieces
- 10 ounces (2 cups) blackberries
- 10 ounces strawberries, hulled and quartered lengthwise (2 cups)
- 1–2 tablespoons lime juice

Combine sugar, basil, and pepper in large bowl. Using rubber spatula, press mixture into side of bowl until sugar becomes damp, about 30 seconds. Gently toss fruit with sugar mixture until combined. Let sit at room temperature, stirring occasionally, until fruit releases its juices, 15 to 30 minutes. Stir in lime juice to taste and serve.

TEST KITCHEN TIP NO. 149 MIMICKING AGED BALSAMIC

Traditionally produced balsamic vinegar (labeled *tradizionale*) is used sparingly for drizzling or flavoring—never in salad dressings or vinaigrettes. It can take over 25 years to produce and can cost up to $60 per ounce. We wanted to find a way to reproduce some of the drizzle-worthy qualities of traditional balsamic without having to visit a specialty food store or a loan officer.

We started with a decent supermarket balsamic vinegar and tried reducing it with sugar and flavorings ranging from black currant juice to coffee. In the end, we found that a straight reduction of ⅓ cup of vinegar and 1 tablespoon of sugar worked well enough, but the addition of 1 tablespoon of port added the complexity we were after. Vigorous boiling destroyed nuances in the vinegar's flavor; the best results came from reducing this mixture for 30 to 40 minutes over extremely low heat (barely simmering) to about half of its original volume. While most tasters could distinguish this reduction from a traditional 12-year-old balsamic, our homemade drizzling vinegar was surprisingly good. The flavor is very strong, so use sparingly over fresh fruit (strawberries are terrific), ice cream, or grilled meats or fish.

CHAPTER 21   Pastry

PÂTE À CHOUX

✅ WHY THIS RECIPE WORKS

Pâte à choux, or cream puff pastry, is the most elemental type of French pastry, and it forms the basis for éclairs and profiteroles. In our pâte à choux, we chose to use a combination of milk and water—during baking, the former helps the pastry brown and the latter keeps it crisp. Testing revealed that 2 whole eggs plus 1 egg white made incredibly light, airy pastry with custardy interiors.

PÂTE À CHOUX
(CREAM PUFF PASTRY)

MAKES ENOUGH FOR 8 ÉCLAIRS OR
24 PROFITEROLES

Be sure to sift the flour after measuring.

2	large eggs plus 1 large white
6	tablespoons water
5	tablespoons unsalted butter, cut into 10 pieces
2	tablespoons whole milk
1½	teaspoons sugar
¼	teaspoon salt
½	cup (2½ ounces) all-purpose flour, sifted

1. Beat whole eggs and egg white together in liquid measuring cup; set aside. Bring water, butter, milk, sugar, and salt to boil in small saucepan over medium heat. Remove saucepan from heat and stir in flour until combined and mixture clears sides of pan. Return saucepan to low heat and cook, stirring constantly, using smearing motion, until mixture is slightly shiny with wet-sand appearance and tiny beads of fat appear on bottom of saucepan, about 3 minutes (mixture should register 175 to 180 degrees).

2. Immediately transfer hot mixture to food processor and process for 10 seconds to cool slightly. With food processor running, gradually add beaten eggs in steady stream. Scrape down sides of bowl, then process for 30 seconds until smooth, thick, sticky paste forms. (Paste can be transferred to bowl, surface covered with plastic wrap that has been sprayed with vegetable oil spray, and stored at room temperature for up to 2 hours.)

ÉCLAIRS

✅ WHY THIS RECIPE WORKS

In the pastry case, éclairs look tempting, but all too often they are just soggy shells of pastry filled with a starchy pastry cream and topped with a tasteless, waxy glaze. We set out to make éclairs with delicately crisp pastry, a silky-smooth pastry cream, and a glaze that actually tastes of bittersweet chocolate. We started with the test kitchen's recipe for cream puff paste and piped the dough onto a baking sheet. After baking the pastries, we cut a small slit into the side of each one to release steam and then returned them to the turned-off oven to dry until the centers were moist (but not wet) and the surface was crisp. One of the trickiest parts of making éclairs is filling them with pastry cream without mangling the shell. Cutting the éclairs in half horizontally looked sloppy and pastry cream leaked out the sides. Trying to poke a hole at one end and fashioning a path through the pastry was difficult. Instead, we found that cutting three small holes across the top of each baked and cooled éclair was the way to go. We then piped pastry cream into each opening for even distribution. And the chocolate glaze, made with melted semisweet or bittersweet chocolate, half-and-half, and confectioners' sugar, covered the telltale holes.

ÉCLAIRS
MAKES 8 ÉCLAIRS

Be sure the pastry cream is thoroughly chilled before filling the pastries. The chocolate glaze should still be warm when glazing the éclairs.

1	recipe Pâte à Choux
	FILLING AND GLAZE
1	recipe Pastry Cream (recipe follows)
2	ounces semisweet or bittersweet chocolate, chopped fine
3	tablespoons half-and-half
1	cup (4 ounces) confectioners' sugar

1. FOR THE PASTRY: Adjust oven rack to middle position and heat oven to 400 degrees. Spray baking sheet with vegetable oil spray and line with parchment paper.

2. Fit pastry bag with ½-inch plain tip and fill with warm pâte à choux. Pipe pâte à choux into eight 5 by 1-inch logs, spaced about 1 inch apart. Use back of teaspoon dipped in cold water to even out shape and smooth surface of logs.

3. Bake pastries for 15 minutes (do not open oven door), then reduce oven temperature to 350 degrees and continue to bake until golden brown and fairly firm (pastries should not be soft and squishy), 8 to 10 minutes longer.

4. Remove baking sheet from oven and cut ¾-inch slit into side of each pastry with small knife to release steam. Return pastries to oven, turn off oven, and prop oven door open with handle of wooden spoon. Dry pastries in turned-off oven until center is just moist (not wet) and surface is crisp, about 45 minutes. Transfer pastries to wire rack to cool. (Cooled pastries can be stored at room temperature for up to 24 hours or frozen in zipper-lock bag for up to 1 month. Re-crisp room-temperature pastries in 300-degree oven for 5 to 8 minutes, or frozen pastries for 8 to 10 minutes.)

5. FOR THE FILLING AND GLAZE: Use tip of small knife to cut 3 small Xs along top of each pastry. Fit clean pastry bag with ¼-inch plain tip and fill pastry bag with pastry cream. Pipe pastry cream into pastries through each X until éclairs are completely filled.

6. Microwave chocolate at 50 percent power for 30 seconds until it melts. Whisk

in half-and-half until smooth. Gradually whisk in sugar until smooth. Transfer éclairs to wire rack set over sheet of parchment (for easy cleanup) and spoon warm glaze evenly over tops, being sure to cover holes. Let glaze set, about 20 minutes, before serving. (Filled and glazed éclairs can be stored at room temperature for 4 hours.)

PASTRY CREAM
MAKES ABOUT 2 CUPS

You can substitute 1½ teaspoons vanilla extract for the vanilla bean; stir the extract into the pastry cream with the butter in step 2.

- ½ vanilla bean
- 2 cups half-and-half
- ½ cup (3½ ounces) sugar
  Pinch salt
- 5 large egg yolks
- 3 tablespoons cornstarch
- 4 tablespoons unsalted butter, cut into 4 pieces

1. Cut vanilla bean in half lengthwise. Using tip of paring knife, scrape out seeds. Bring vanilla bean and seeds, half-and-half, 6 tablespoons sugar, and salt to simmer in medium saucepan over medium-high heat, stirring occasionally.

2. Meanwhile, whisk egg yolks, cornstarch, and remaining 2 tablespoons sugar together in medium bowl until smooth. Slowly whisk 1 cup of simmering half-and-half mixture into egg mixture to temper, then slowly whisk tempered egg mixture into remaining half-and-half mixture. Reduce heat to medium and cook, stirring constantly, until pastry cream is thickened and few bubbles burst on surface, about 30 seconds. Off heat, whisk in butter.

3. Remove vanilla bean and transfer pastry cream to clean bowl. Lay plastic wrap directly on surface of pastry cream and refrigerate until cold and set, about 3 hours. (Pastry cream can be refrigerated for up to 3 days.)

ALMOND PASTRY CREAM

Whisk ¾ teaspoon almond extract into pastry cream with butter.

MOCHA PASTRY CREAM

Add 1 teaspoon instant espresso powder or instant coffee to half-and-half mixture before bringing to simmer.

PROFITEROLES

✔ WHY THIS RECIPE WORKS
Profiteroles might just be the most perfect dessert in existence: crisp, tender, and airy pastry encasing cold, creamy ice cream and napped by dark, luxurious chocolate sauce.

Using the test kitchen's recipe for pâte à choux, we baked the puffs on an uncrowded baking sheet to keep the puffs from collapsing. We slit the puffs immediately after baking to release steam and then returned them to the oven to dry out to ensure crispness. For easiest assembly, we scooped the ice cream onto a chilled baking sheet, then split the puffs and filled them all at once. We made a quick bittersweet chocolate sauce with heavy cream, corn syrup, and butter to drizzle over the ice cream–filled pastries.

PROFITEROLES
SERVES 6

A serving of profiteroles consists of three baked puffs filled with ice cream and topped with sauce. The Pâte à Choux recipe makes 24 puffs, technically enough to serve eight, but inevitably a few bake up too awkwardly shaped to serve to guests. For profiteroles, the smooth, dense texture and rich flavor of a high-quality custard-style ice cream is preferable to the light, fluffy texture and milky flavor of Philadelphia-style ice cream, which is made without eggs. If you're serving several guests, prescooping the ice cream makes serving quick and neat, but if you're assembling only a couple servings or your

freezer lacks space, you can skip the prescooping step.

- 1 recipe Pâte à Choux (page 762)

  FILLING AND GLAZE
- 1 quart vanilla or coffee custard-style ice cream
- ¾ cup heavy cream
- 3 tablespoons light corn syrup
- 3 tablespoons unsalted butter, cut into 3 pieces
  Pinch salt
- 6 ounces bittersweet chocolate, chopped fine

1. FOR THE PASTRY: Adjust oven rack to middle position and heat oven to 425 degrees. Spray baking sheet with vegetable oil spray and line with parchment paper.

2. Fit pastry bag with ½-inch plain tip and fill with warm pâte à choux. Pipe pâte à choux into 1½-inch mounds on prepared sheet, spacing them about 1 inch apart (you should have about 24 mounds). Use back of teaspoon dipped in cold water to even out shape and smooth surface of mounds.

3. Bake pastries for 15 minutes (do not open oven door), then reduce oven temperature to 375 degrees and continue to bake until golden brown and fairly firm (pastries should not be soft and squishy), 8 to 10 minutes longer.

4. Remove baking sheet from oven and cut ¾-inch slit into side of each pastry with paring knife to release steam. Return pastries to oven, turn off oven, and prop oven door open with handle of wooden spoon. Dry pastries in turned-off oven until center is just moist (not wet) and surface is crisp, about 45 minutes. Transfer pastries to wire rack to cool. (Cooled pastries can be stored at room temperature for up to 24 hours or frozen in zipper-lock bag for up to 1 month. Re-crisp room-temperature puffs in 300-degree oven for 5 to 8 minutes, or frozen puffs for 8 to 10 minutes.)

1. Pipe paste into 1½-inch mounds on prepared baking sheet.

2. Use back of teaspoon dipped in water to even out shape and smooth surface of mounds.

5. FOR THE FILLING AND GLAZE: Line clean baking sheet with parchment and freeze until cold, about 20 minutes. Place 2-inch scoops of ice cream onto chilled baking sheet and freeze until firm, then cover with plastic wrap; keep frozen until ready to serve.

6. Bring heavy cream, corn syrup, butter, and salt to boil in small saucepan. Off heat, stir in chocolate. Cover saucepan and let stand until chocolate is melted, about 5 minutes. Whisk gently until combined. (Sauce can be refrigerated for up to 2 weeks.)

7. To serve, use paring knife to split open 18 pastries about ⅜ inch from bottom; set 3 bottoms on each dessert plate. Place scoop of ice cream on each bottom and gently press tops into ice cream. Pour sauce over profiteroles and serve immediately.

PUFF PASTRY DOUGH

✔ WHY THIS RECIPE WORKS

Puff pastry dough, which is used in a variety of pastries such as turnovers and Napoleons, is a multilayered dough that gets its super-flaky, buttery layers from a process called "turning," or folding. Each turn creates paper-thin sheets of butter, and when the dough is baked, the moisture in the butter evaporates into steam, causing the dough surrounding it to puff and separate into more than a hundred flaky and delicate layers. We've tried quick methods for puff pastry dough, which are similar to the process for making pie dough, but these methods (which are hardly quick), lacked the super-flaky layers of the original. After testing, we decided we would need to combine the dough with the butter in the traditional manner. We began by mixing flour, sugar, salt, lemon juice, and ice water together in a food processor for even, quick distribution and then chilled the dough to allow it to relax for easier rolling. While the dough chilled, we made a butter square by gently pounding butter sticks into an even layer and then chilled the square, so that it would not melt when combined with the dough. Incorporating the butter into the dough was as easy as placing the chilled butter square over the chilled dough, folding in the corners, and rolling it out. We folded the dough into thirds and then into thirds again, and then repeated this process twice to form multiple sheets of butter and dough that puffed into incredible flaky layers once baked.

PUFF PASTRY DOUGH
MAKES ABOUT 2 POUNDS

If the dough becomes too warm and sticky to work with, cover it with plastic wrap and let it chill in the refrigerator until firm. If you are making Flaky Apple Turnovers (page 765) or Napoleons (page 766), cut the dough in half (each half will weigh about 1 pound) after it has chilled in step 6; use one piece of dough as directed and refrigerate the rest for up to 2 days or freeze, wrapped in plastic and aluminum foil, for up to 1 month.

DOUGH
3 cups (15 ounces) all-purpose flour
1½ tablespoons sugar
1½ teaspoons salt
2 teaspoons lemon juice
1 cup water, chilled

BUTTER SQUARE
24 tablespoons (3 sticks) unsalted butter, chilled
2 tablespoons all-purpose flour

1. FOR THE DOUGH: Process flour, sugar, and salt in food processor until combined, about 5 seconds. With food processor running, add lemon juice, followed by ¾ cup water, in slow steady stream. Add remaining ¼ cup water as needed, 1 tablespoon at a time, until dough comes together and no floury bits remain.

2. Turn dough onto sheet of plastic wrap and flatten into 6-inch square. Wrap tightly in plastic and refrigerate for 1 hour.

3. FOR THE BUTTER SQUARE: Lay butter sticks side by side on sheet of parchment paper. Sprinkle flour over butter and cover with second sheet of parchment. Gently pound butter with rolling pin until butter is softened and flour is fully incorporated, then roll it into 8-inch square. Wrap butter square in plastic and refrigerate until chilled, about 1 hour.

4. Roll chilled dough into 11-inch square on lightly floured counter. Place chilled butter square diagonally in center of dough. Fold corners of dough up over butter square so that corners meet in middle and pinch dough seams to seal.

5. Using rolling pin, gently tap dough, starting from center and working outward, until square becomes larger and butter begins to soften. Gently roll dough into 14-inch square, dusting with extra flour as needed to prevent sticking. Fold dough

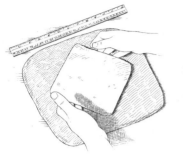
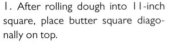

1. After rolling dough into 11-inch square, place butter square diagonally on top.

2. Fold dough over butter so that corners meet in middle. Pinch ends of dough together to seal.

3. After rolling dough into 14-inch square, fold it into thirds.

4. Fold ends of dough rectangle over center to form square. Wrap dough in plastic wrap and let rest in refrigerator for 2 hours before repeating step 5.

into thirds like business letter, then fold rectangle in thirds to form square. Wrap dough in plastic and let rest in refrigerator for 2 hours.

6. Repeat step 5 twice and let dough rest in refrigerator for 2 more hours before using.

FLAKY APPLE TURNOVERS

✔ WHY THIS RECIPE WORKS

Store-bought turnovers are disheartening— the filling is bland and mushy and the dough soggy, making for something more like fast-food pie from a cardboard sleeve than a tantalizing, fruit-laden pastry. We wanted to make the perfect apple turnover, with a flaky, shatteringly crisp crust and firm, not mushy, apples. We made our filling with a mixture of chopped apples (pulsed in the food processor), sugar, cinnamon, and lemon juice (for brightness). We drained the apple mixture to prevent sogginess and then combined the apples with applesauce for another layer of apple flavor. For the pastry, we cut out squares from the test kitchen's recipe for puff pastry and mounded the apple mixture in the center. Before folding over the dough to encase the apples, we brushed the edges of

the dough for a tight seal. Brushing the sealed and crimped turnovers with more apple juice and sprinkling them with cinnamon sugar before baking yielded flaky, buttery pastry and a filling with knockout apple flavor.

FLAKY APPLE TURNOVERS
MAKES 8 TURNOVERS

If the dough becomes too warm and sticky to work with, cover it with plastic wrap and let it chill in the refrigerator until firm. If you don't have a food processor, grate the apples on the large holes of a box grater.

1	pound Granny Smith apples, peeled, cored, and chopped coarse
¾	cup (5¼ ounces) sugar
1	tablespoon lemon juice
⅛	teaspoon salt
½	recipe Puff Pastry Dough (page 764), divided into two 8-ounce pieces
½	cup applesauce
1	teaspoon ground cinnamon

1. Adjust oven rack to middle position and heat oven to 400 degrees. Line rimmed baking sheet with parchment paper.

2. Pulse apples, ½ cup sugar, lemon juice, and salt together in food processor until largest pieces of apples are no larger than ½ inch, about 6 pulses. Let mixture sit for 5 minutes, then transfer to fine-mesh strainer set over bowl and let apples drain, reserving juice, until needed.

3. Roll each piece of dough into 10-inch square between 2 lightly floured sheets of parchment. Remove top sheets of parchment and cut each piece of dough into four 5-inch squares (you will have 8 squares total).

4. Toss drained apples and applesauce together in separate bowl. Place 2 tablespoons apple filling in center of each piece of dough. Brush edges of dough with reserved juice, then fold 1 corner of square diagonally over filling. Crimp edges of dough with fork to seal. Lay turnovers on prepared baking sheet and freeze until firm, about 15 minutes. (Assembled turnovers can be frozen for 1 hour, then transferred to zipper-lock bag and frozen for up to 1 month. Let frozen turnovers sit at room temperature for 20 minutes, then bake as directed.)

5. Combine remaining ¼ cup sugar and cinnamon in bowl. Brush turnovers with more reserved juice and sprinkle generously with cinnamon sugar. Bake turnovers until well browned, 20 to

26 minutes, rotating baking sheet halfway through baking. Immediately transfer turnovers to wire rack and let cool slightly. Serve warm or at room temperature.

FLAKY CARAMEL-APPLE AND CREAM CHEESE TURNOVERS

Any brand of soft caramels will work here; avoid hard caramel candies.

Substitute 4 ounces cream cheese for applesauce and add 2 caramel candies, quartered, to each turnover before shaping.

FLAKY CRANBERRY-APPLE TURNOVERS

Add ¾ cup dried cranberries to food processor with apples. Substitute ¼ cup thawed frozen orange juice concentrate for ¼ cup of applesauce.

FLAKY CHEDDAR-APPLE TURNOVERS

Substitute ½ cup shredded cheddar cheese for applesauce. Omit cinnamon sugar and sprinkle ¼ cup shredded cheddar over apple juice–brushed turnovers before baking.

CRIMPING THE TURNOVERS

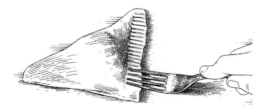

Using fork, crimp edges of turnovers.

NAPOLEONS

✓ WHY THIS RECIPE WORKS
Traditional Napoleons involve puff pastry and fondant icing, and making them is daunting for all but the most experienced bakers. After all the effort, tough pastry and starchy pastry cream are often the disappointing rewards. We wanted satiny vanilla pastry cream sandwiched between layers of buttery, crisp, and ultra-flaky puff pastry, topped with the design of chocolate and vanilla glaze that gilds all Napoleons. Just as important, we wanted to bring this recipe out of the pastry kitchen and into the home kitchen.

The puff pastry layers that form Napoleons need to be level so that they can be spread with pastry cream and stacked. We found that the best way to achieve this was to roll the dough into an even layer, poke holes in it with a fork, slide it on to a baking sheet and bake it topped with a second baking sheet, weighted with a large ovensafe dish. Traditional recipes typically make one large Napoleon and then cut the pastry into individual servings, but we found this method fussy, unnecessary, and plagued with issues like the filling squirting out the sides during cutting, so after cooling the pastry, we cut it into individual rectangles for stacking

For a luxuriously smooth, rich pastry cream, we relied on half-and-half, sugar, egg yolks, a vanilla bean (vanilla extract also works), butter, and cornstarch. An for the icings, we threw out the idea of a traditional fondant icing and instead devised a simple icing made with milk, confectioners' sugar, vanilla extract for the vanilla icing, and bittersweet chocolate or semisweet chocolate for the chocolate icing. Simplified and undeniably elegant, our Napoleons make a spectacular finale to an elegant meal.

NAPOLEONS
MAKES 6 NAPOLEONS

If the dough becomes too warm and sticky to work with, cover it with plastic wrap and let it chill in the refrigerator until firm.

½   recipe Puff Pastry Dough (page 764)

CHOCOLATE GLAZE
1   ounce bittersweet or semisweet chocolate, chopped fine
2   tablespoons milk
¾   cup (3 ounces) confectioners' sugar

VANILLA GLAZE
¼   cup (1 ounce) confectioners' sugar
1½   teaspoons milk
⅛   teaspoon vanilla extract

FILLING
1   recipe Pastry Cream (page 763)

1. FOR THE PASTRY: Adjust oven rack to middle position and heat oven to 325 degrees. Roll dough into 16 by 12-inch rectangle, about ¼ inch thick, between 2 lightly floured sheets of parchment paper. Remove top sheet of parchment and prick pastry with fork every 2 inches.

2. Replace top sheet of parchment and slide dough onto rimmed baking sheet. Place second rimmed baking sheet on top of dough and weight baking sheet with large ovensafe dish. Bake pastry until cooked through and lightly golden, 50 minutes to 1 hour, rotating baking sheet halfway through baking.

3. Remove weight, top baking sheet, and top sheet of parchment and continue to bake pastry until golden brown, 5 to 10 minutes longer. Let pastry cool completely on baking sheet, about 1 hour. (Pastry will shrink slightly.)

4. Cut cooled pastry in half lengthwise with serrated knife and trim edges as necessary to make them straight. Cut each pastry half crosswise into 3 rectangles, then cut each rectangle crosswise into 3 small rectangles (you will have 18 rectangles). (Puff pastry rectangles can be wrapped tightly in plastic wrap and stored at room temperature for up to 1 day.)

GLAZING AND ASSEMBLING NAPOLEONS

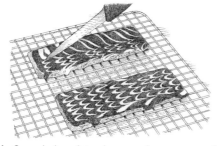

1. Spread chocolate glaze evenly over top of 6 rectangles, then drizzle thin stream of vanilla glaze crosswise over chocolate glaze. Run tip of small knife or toothpick lengthwise through icing to make design.

2. After layering remaining rectangles of pastry with pastry cream to make 6 individual portions, top each portion with glazed pastry rectangle.

5. FOR THE CHOCOLATE GLAZE: Microwave chocolate at 50 percent power for 15 seconds; stir chocolate, add milk, and continue heating for 10 seconds; stir until smooth.

6. FOR THE VANILLA GLAZE: Whisk sugar, milk, and vanilla together in bowl until smooth.

7. Spread chocolate glaze evenly over top of 6 rectangles of pastry and lay them on wire rack set over sheet of parchment (for easy cleanup). Drizzle thin stream of vanilla glaze over chocolate glaze. Run tip of small knife or toothpick lengthwise through icing to make design. Let icing set, about 20 minutes.

8. FOR THE FILLING: Meanwhile, spread about 2½ tablespoons of pastry cream evenly over 6 more rectangles of pastry. Gently top each with one of remaining 6 rectangles of pastry and spread remaining pastry cream evenly over tops. Top with glazed pastry rectangles and serve. (Glazed and assembled Napoleons can be stored at room temperature for up to 4 hours.)

ALMOND NAPOLEONS

Substitute Almond Pastry Cream (page 763) for Pastry Cream and add 1 drop almond extract to vanilla glaze.

MOCHA NAPOLEONS

Substitute Mocha Pastry Cream (page 763) for Pastry Cream and add ¼ teaspoon instant espresso powder or instant coffee to chocolate glaze before melting.

BAKLAVA

✓ WHY THIS RECIPE WORKS

With its copious amounts of butter, sugar, and nuts, baklava is often a lamentable experience; sad, soggy, punishingly sweet, and utterly lifeless specimens are ubiquitous. We wanted crisp, flaky, buttery baklava, filled with fragrant nuts and spices, and sweetened just assertively enough to pair with coffee. To achieve this goal, we sprinkled store-bought phyllo dough with three separate layers of nuts (a combination of almonds and walnuts) flavored with cinnamon and cloves. We clarified the butter to ensure even browning on top. Cutting the baklava, rather than just scoring it, before baking helped it absorb the sugar-honey syrup drizzled over the top after baking. Finally, allowing the baklava to sit overnight improved its flavor.

BAKLAVA

MAKES 32 TO 40 PIECES

Phyllo dough is also available in larger 18 by 14-inch sheets; if using, cut them in half to make 14 by 9-inch sheets. Do not thaw the phyllo in the microwave; let it sit in the refrigerator overnight or on the counter for 4 to 5 hours. A straight-sided traditional (not nonstick) metal baking pan works best for making baklava. If you don't have this type of pan, a glass baking dish will work. When assembling, use the nicest, most intact phyllo sheets for the bottom and top layers; use sheets with tears or ones that are smaller than the size of the pan in the middle layers, where their imperfections will go unnoticed. If, after assembly, you have leftover clarified butter, store it in an airtight container in the refrigerator; it can be used for sautéing.

SUGAR SYRUP

1¼	cups (8¾ ounces) sugar
¾	cup water
⅓	cup honey
3	(2-inch) strips lemon zest plus 1 tablespoon juice
1	cinnamon stick
5	whole cloves
⅛	teaspoon salt

NUT FILLING

1¾	cups (7⅞ ounces) slivered almonds
1	cup walnuts
2	tablespoons sugar
1¼	teaspoons ground cinnamon
¼	teaspoon ground cloves
⅛	teaspoon salt

PASTRY AND BUTTER

24	tablespoons unsalted butter (3 sticks), cut into 1-inch pieces
1	pound (14 by 9-inch) phyllo, thawed

1. FOR THE SUGAR SYRUP: Bring all ingredients to boil in small saucepan, stirring occasionally to ensure that sugar dissolves. Transfer syrup to 2-cup liquid measuring cup and set aside to cool while making and baking baklava; when syrup is cool, remove spices and lemon zest. (Cooled syrup can be refrigerated for up to 4 days.)

2. FOR THE NUT FILLING: Pulse almonds in food processor until very finely chopped, about 20 pulses; transfer to medium bowl. Pulse walnuts in food processor until very finely chopped, about 15 pulses; transfer to bowl with almonds and toss to combine. Measure out 1 tablespoon nuts and set aside for garnish. Add sugar, cinnamon, cloves, and salt to nut mixture and toss well to combine.

3. TO ASSEMBLE AND BAKE: Adjust oven rack to lower-middle position and heat oven to 300 degrees. Melt butter slowly in small saucepan over medium-low heat until milk solids have separated from butterfat and collected on bottom of saucepan, about 10 minutes. Remove saucepan from heat, let butter settle for 10 minutes, then carefully skim foam from surface with spoon.

4. When all of foam has been removed, slowly pour clear butterfat into bowl, leaving all milk solids behind in the saucepan (you should have about 1 cup clarified butter).

5. Grease 13 by 9-inch baking pan with clarified butter. Place 1 sheet of phyllo in bottom of prepared pan and brush with clarified butter until completely coated. Layer 7 sheets of phyllo into pan, brushing each sheet with butter. Sprinkle 1 cup nut filling evenly over phyllo.

6. Layer 6 sheets of phyllo into pan, brushing each layer with butter, then sprinkle with 1 cup nut filling. Repeat with 6 sheets of phyllo, butter, and remaining 1 cup nut filling.

7. Layer remaining 8 to 10 sheets of phyllo into pan, brushing each layer, except final layer, with butter. Working from center outward, use palms of hands to compress layers and press out any air pockets. Spoon 4 tablespoons of butter on top layer and brush to cover surface.

8. Using serrated knife with pointed tip, cut baklava into diamonds. Bake baklava until golden and crisp, about 1½ hours, rotating pan halfway through baking.

9. Immediately pour all but 2 tablespoons of cooled syrup over cut lines (syrup will sizzle when it hits hot pan). Drizzle remaining 2 tablespoons syrup over surface. Garnish center of each piece with pinch of reserved ground nuts. Let baklava cool completely in pan, about 3 hours, then cover with aluminum foil

and let sit at room temperature for about 8 hours before serving.

PISTACHIO BAKLAVA WITH
CARDAMOM AND ROSE WATER

Omit honey, lemon zest, and cinnamon in sugar syrup and increase sugar to 1¾ cups. Substitute 10 whole peppercorns for cloves and stir in 1 tablespoon rose water after discarding peppercorns. Substitute 2¾ cups shelled pistachios for almonds and walnuts and 1 teaspoon ground cardamom for cinnamon and cloves in nut filling.

APPLE STRUDEL

✔ **WHY THIS RECIPE WORKS**
Classic apple strudel is an all-day affair. We wanted to see if we could get full apple flavor, a moist filling, and a crisp, flaky crust in less than an hour. From the outset, we shelved the notion of homemade strudel dough; phyllo dough provided a good substitute. For a strudel with a crisp, flaky crust that held its shape, and didn't dislodge or fly off if we came near it with a fork, we handled the phyllo dough carefully, sprinkling butter and sugar between its layers to form a cohesive crust. For the filling, we used a

---

ASSEMBLING APPLE STRUDEL

I. Brush 1 sheet of phyllo with melted butter and sprinkle with sugar. Place another sheet of phyllo next to it, overlapping sheets. Brush with more butter and sprinkle with sugar. Repeat this process 4 times.

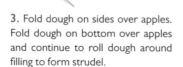

2. Mound filling along bottom edge of phyllo, leaving 2½-inch border on bottom and 2-inch border on sides.

3. Fold dough on sides over apples. Fold dough on bottom over apples and continue to roll dough around filling to form strudel.

4. After strudel has been assembled and rolled, gently lay it seam side down on prepared baking sheet.

combination of McIntosh and Golden Delicious apples, cut into thin slices, for maximum flavor and tender bites of apple. Raisins and walnuts added textural interest; plumping the raisins first in apple brandy deepened the apple flavor overall. Browning the bread crumbs in butter for our strudel prevented an overly heavy, bready filling. And baking the strudel in a very hot oven for just 15 minutes crisped the phyllo but didn't dry it out.

QUICKER APPLE STRUDEL
SERVES 6 TO 8

Do not thaw the phyllo dough in the microwave; let it sit in the refrigerator overnight or on the counter for 4 to 5 hours. If the phyllo sheets have small cuts or tears in the same location, flip the alternating sheets of phyllo when assembling the strudel in step 4, so that the cuts will not line up and cause a weak spot in the crust. To make fresh bread crumbs, pulse 1 slice white sandwich bread (with crust) in a food processor to fine crumbs, about 6 pulses; you will have 1 cup fresh bread crumbs. Serve the strudel warm with Tangy Whipped Cream (page 800) or Whipped Cream (page 800); if you choose to make the tangy whipped cream, make it before starting the strudel because it must stand at room temperature for about 1½ hours before serving.

- ½ cup golden raisins
- 2 tablespoons Calvados or apple cider
- ¼ cup fresh white bread crumbs
- 8 tablespoons unsalted butter, melted and cooled
- 1 pound Golden Delicious apples, peeled, cored, and sliced ¼ inch thick
- 1 McIntosh apple, peeled, cored, and sliced ¼ inch thick
- ⅓ cup walnuts, toasted and chopped fine (optional)
- ¼ cup plus 2 tablespoons (2⅔ ounces) granulated sugar
- 1 teaspoon lemon juice
- ¼ teaspoon ground cinnamon
- ⅛ teaspoon salt
- 10 (14 by 9-inch) sheets phyllo, thawed
- 1½ teaspoons confectioners' sugar

1. Adjust oven rack to lower-middle position and heat oven to 475 degrees. Line rimmed baking sheet with parchment paper. Combine raisins and Calvados in small bowl, cover, and microwave until simmering, about 1 minute. Let sit, covered, until needed.

2. Toast bread crumbs with 1 tablespoon melted butter in 8-inch skillet over medium heat, stirring often, until golden brown, about 2 minutes; transfer to large bowl.

3. Drain raisins, discarding liquid. Add raisins, apples, walnuts, if using, ¼ cup granulated sugar, lemon juice, cinnamon, and salt to bowl with bread crumbs and toss to combine.

4. Place large sheet of parchment horizontally on work surface. Lay 1 sheet of phyllo on left side of sheet of parchment, then brush with melted butter and sprinkle with ½ teaspoon sugar. Place another sheet of phyllo on right side of parchment, overlapping sheets by 1 inch, then brush with butter and sprinkle with ½ teaspoon sugar. Repeat with remaining 8 sheets of phyllo, brushing each layer with butter and sprinkling with sugar. Mound filling along bottom edge of phyllo, leaving 2½-inch border on bottom and 2-inch border on sides. Fold dough on sides over apples. Fold dough on bottom over apples and continue to roll dough around filling to form strudel.

5. Gently transfer strudel, seam side down, to prepared baking sheet; brush with remaining butter and sprinkle with remaining 1 teaspoon sugar. Cut four 1½-inch vents on diagonal across top of strudel and bake until golden brown, about 15 minutes, rotating baking sheet halfway through baking. Transfer strudel with baking sheet to wire rack and let cool until warm, about 40 minutes.

6. Dust with confectioners' sugar before serving; slice with serrated knife and serve warm or at room temperature.

PEAR STRUDEL

Substitute 2 tablespoons Poire Williams or other pear liqueur for Calvados and 1½ pounds Bosc pears for apples. Increase lemon juice to 2 teaspoons.

DANISH

✔ WHY THIS RECIPE WORKS
Tired of the dull-tasting, sticky-sweet Danish you buy at the store? We were, too, so we set out how to make a better version at home. We wanted the real thing—flaky, buttery pastry with a not-too-sweet, real fruit filling. Danish are made using a rich yeasted dough similar to that of croissants with the difference being the addition of egg, which contributes to a richer texture. Turning to the filling, tasters liked the classic cream cheese filling but thought traditional jam fillings were too sweet. A dried fruit puree was the answer, although we needed to plump the fruit (apricots were our favorite) in water to keep them from being too dry. We anticipated that shaping the dough would be a challenge but a ruler and pizza wheel (for a Danish braid) allowed us to cut the dough into even strips that were surprisingly easy to braid. And for individual Danish, shaping was as easy as cutting out squares and folding over two squares to form a pocket. Once the dough was shaped and baked, the application of a light glaze while the pastry was still hot allowed the Danish to soak up the glaze, giving it a final touch of sweetness and a beautiful sheen.

DANISH DOUGH

MAKES ENOUGH FOR I LARGE BRAID OR
9 INDIVIDUAL DANISH

If the dough becomes too warm and sticky to work with, cover it with plastic wrap and let it chill in the refrigerator until firm. When rolling the dough out, sprinkle extra flour over the counter and the rolling pin as needed to keep the dough from sticking. For more information on making turns in the dough, see page 765.

DOUGH
⅓ cup whole milk, heated to
     110 degrees
1 large egg
1½ cups (7½ ounces) all-purpose flour
¼ cup (1¾ ounces) sugar
1½ teaspoons instant or rapid-rise yeast
¾ teaspoon salt

BUTTER SQUARE
12 tablespoons unsalted butter, cut
     into 3 equal pieces and chilled
1 tablespoon all-purpose flour

1. FOR THE DOUGH: Mix milk and egg together in liquid measuring cup. Using stand mixer fitted with dough hook, combine 1¼ cups flour, sugar, yeast, and salt on low speed. Slowly add milk mixture and mix until dough comes together, about 2 minutes.

2. Increase speed to medium-low and knead dough until it forms sticky ball and becomes elastic, about 8 minutes. If, after 5 minutes, dough appears overly sticky and doesn't come together into ball, add remaining ¼ cup flour, 1 tablespoon at a time. Scrape dough into large lightly greased bowl, cover with greased plastic wrap, and refrigerate until chilled, about 1 hour.

3. FOR THE BUTTER SQUARE: Lay 3 butter pieces side by side on sheet of parchment paper. Sprinkle flour over butter and cover with second sheet of parchment. Gently pound butter with rolling pin until

butter is softened and flour is fully incorporated, then roll it into 5-inch square. Wrap butter square in plastic and refrigerate until chilled, about 1 hour.

4. Roll chilled dough onto 9-inch square on lightly floured counter. Place chilled butter square diagonally in center of dough. Fold corners of dough up over butter square so that corners meet in middle and pinch dough seams to seal.

5. Using rolling pin, gently tap dough, starting from center and working outward, until square becomes larger and butter begins to soften. Gently roll dough into 11-inch square, dusting with extra flour as needed to prevent sticking. Fold dough into thirds like business letter, then fold rectangle in thirds to form square. Wrap dough in plastic wrap and let rest in refrigerator for 2 hours.

6. Repeat step 5 and let dough rest in refrigerator for 2 more hours before using.

DANISH BRAID
SERVES 6 TO 8

If the dough becomes too warm and sticky to work with, cover with plastic wrap and let it chill in the refrigerator until firm. The Danish should be brushed with the glaze while hot, but drizzled with the icing after it has cooled.

1 recipe Danish Dough
1 recipe filling (pages 771–772)

GLAZE
1½ cups (6 ounces) confectioners' sugar
5 teaspoons milk
1 teaspoon lemon juice

ICING
1 cup (4 ounces) confectioners' sugar
1 tablespoon milk

1. Adjust oven rack to middle position and heat oven to 400 degrees. Roll Danish dough into 14-inch square on large sheet of parchment paper. Spread cooled filling down center third of dough, leaving ½-inch border at top and bottom edge.

2. Using pizza wheel, cut dough on either side of filling into diagonal strips about ¾ inch wide (stop cuts ¼ inch shy of filling). Discard top corner of dough on either side, then, starting at top of Danish, crisscross strips over filling to form braid. Slide Danish, still on parchment, onto baking sheet.

3. Cover Danish loosely with greased plastic wrap and let rise at room temperature until puffy, about 30 minutes. Bake Danish until golden brown, 22 to 26 minutes, rotating baking sheet halfway through baking.

SHAPING A DANISH BRAID

1. Spread filling or jam onto center third of dough.

2. Using pizza cutter or paring knife, cut outer thirds into ¾-inch strips (so that cuts are at angle to filling). Stop cuts ¼ inch shy of filling.

3. Alternating sides, fold strips over filling, crisscrossing strips over center and pressing ends to seal, until entire Danish is braided.

4. FOR THE GLAZE: Transfer baked Danish to wire rack set over sheet of parchment (for easy cleanup). Whisk all ingredients together in bowl and brush it over hot Danish. Let glazed Danish cool completely on rack, about 1 hour.

5. FOR THE ICING: Whisk all ingredients together in bowl. When Danish is completely cool, drizzle icing attractively over top. Let icing set for 20 minutes before serving.

INDIVIDUAL DANISH
MAKES 9 DANISH

If the dough becomes too warm and sticky to work with, cover it with plastic wrap and let it chill in the refrigerator until firm. The Danish should be brushed with the glaze while hot, but drizzled with the icing after they have cooled.

- I recipe Danish Dough (page 770)
- I recipe filling (recipes follow)
- I large egg, lightly beaten

GLAZE
- 1½ cups (6 ounces) confectioners' sugar
- 5 teaspoons milk
- I teaspoon lemon juice

ICING
- I cup (4 ounces) confectioners' sugar
- I tablespoon milk

1. Adjust oven rack to middle position and heat oven to 400 degrees. Line baking sheet with parchment paper.

2. Roll Danish dough into 15-inch square on lightly floured counter, dusting with extra flour as needed to prevent sticking. Cut dough into nine 5-inch squares. Place generous 1½ tablespoons cooled filling in center of each square and spread it into 2-inch circle with back of spoon.

3. Fold 2 opposite corners of dough square over center of filling, brushing dough in center with beaten egg as needed to seal edges together. Lay Danish on prepared baking sheet, spaced about 1½ inches apart.

4. Cover Danish loosely with greased plastic wrap and let rise at room temperature until puffy, about 30 minutes. Bake Danish until golden brown, 15 to 20 minutes, rotating baking sheet halfway through baking.

5. FOR THE GLAZE: Transfer baked Danish to wire rack set over sheet of parchment (for easy cleanup). Whisk all ingredients together in bowl and brush it over hot Danish. Let glazed Danish cool completely on rack, about 1 hour.

6. FOR THE ICING: Whisk all ingredients together in bowl. When Danish is completely cool, drizzle icing attractively over top. Let icing set for 20 minutes before serving.

APRICOT FILLING
MAKES 1½ CUPS; ENOUGH FOR
I DANISH BRAID (PAGE 770) OR
9 INDIVIDUAL DANISH

- I cup dried apricots
- I cup (7 ounces) sugar
- ¾ cup water
- 2 tablespoons lemon juice

Microwave apricots, sugar, and water together, stirring often, until apricots are softened and puffed, 7 to 10 minutes. Process warm mixture in food processor until smooth, about 15 seconds. Transfer puree to medium bowl and stir in lemon juice. Cover loosely with plastic wrap and refrigerate until filling has set, at least 1 hour or up to 2 days, before using.

PRUNE FILLING
MAKES 1½ CUPS; ENOUGH FOR
I DANISH BRAID (PAGE 770) OR
9 INDIVIDUAL DANISH)

- I cup pitted prunes
- I cup (7 ounces) sugar
- ¾ cup water
- ½ teaspoon vanilla extract

Microwave prunes, sugar, and water together, stirring often, until prunes are softened and puffed, 7 to 10 minutes. Process warm mixture in food processor until smooth, about 15 seconds. Transfer puree to medium bowl and stir in vanilla. Cover loosely with plastic wrap and refrigerate until filling has set, at least 1 hour or up to 2 days, before using.

CHEESE FILLING
MAKES I CUP; ENOUGH FOR
I DANISH BRAID (PAGE 770) OR
9 INDIVIDUAL DANISH

- 8 ounces cream cheese, softened
- ¼ cup (1¾ ounces) sugar
- ½ teaspoon grated lemon zest

SHAPING INDIVIDUAL DANISH

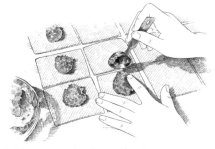

1. After cutting dough into 5-inch squares, spoon 1½ tablespoons filling into center of each square.

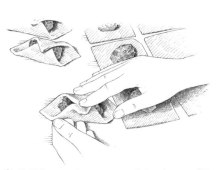

2. Fold 2 opposite corners of dough over filling, gently pressing to seal.

Whisk all ingredients together in medium bowl until combined. Cover with plastic wrap and refrigerate until stiff, at least 1 hour or up to 2 days, before using.

CHEESE AND CHERRY FILLING

MAKES 1½ CUPS; ENOUGH FOR
1 DANISH BRAID (PAGE 770) OR
9 INDIVIDUAL DANISH (PAGE 771)

You can substitute 2 cups fresh or thawed frozen raspberries for the cherries (eliminate the cornstarch).

2   cups jarred sour cherries, drained
1¼   cups (8¾ ounces) sugar
1   tablespoon cornstarch
8   ounces cream cheese, softened
½   teaspoon grated lemon zest

1. Simmer cherries, 1 cup sugar, and cornstarch together in medium saucepan over low heat until sugar has melted and mixture thickens, about 10 minutes. Transfer mixture to bowl, cover with plastic wrap, and refrigerate until set, at least 1 hour or up to 2 days, before using.

2. Whisk cream cheese, remaining ¼ cup sugar, and lemon zest in medium bowl until combined. Cover with plastic wrap and refrigerate until stiff, at least

1 hour or up to 2 days, before using. Spoon cherry mixture on top of cheese filling when assembling Danish.

CROISSANTS

✔ WHY THIS RECIPE WORKS
This yeast-raised French classic contains the best of both worlds: part pastry, part bread, it has a crisp, deeply golden crust wrapped around tender, pillow-soft, buttery layers—perfect for dipping into a cup of café au lait or hot chocolate. We wanted to create an approachable croissant recipe for home bakers—one that would deliver authentic flavor.

The layered structure that characterizes croissants is formed through a process called lamination. First, a basic dough of flour, water, yeast, sugar, salt, and a small amount of butter is made. Then a larger amount of butter is formed into a block and encased in the relatively lean dough. This dough and butter package is rolled out and folded multiple times (each is called a "turn") to form paper-thin layers of dough separated by even thinner layers of butter. Once baked, it's these layers that make croissants so flaky and decadent. To start, we found that more turns didn't necessarily produce more layers—we stopped at three turns, as any more produced a homogeneous bready texture.

As for the star ingredient, butter, we found that great croissants demanded higher fat European-style butter. And one essential tip we discovered during our recipe development was to give the dough a 30-minute super-chill in the freezer to firm it to the consistency of the butter, thus ensuring perfectly distinct layers. After letting the croissants rise until they were doubled in size, we brushed them with an egg wash and slid them into a very hot oven. When we removed the croissants from the oven, the layering that had been suggested in the raw dough had bloomed into crisp, delicate tiers of pastry that made every step of the process worth the effort.

CROISSANTS
MAKES 22

These croissants take at least 10 hours to make from start to finish, but the process can be spread over 2 days. European-style cultured butters have a higher butterfat content, which makes it easier to fold them into the dough. (Our favorite is from Plugrá.) Any brand of all-purpose flour will produce acceptable croissants, but we recommend using King Arthur All-Purpose Flour, which has a slightly higher protein content. Do not attempt to make these croissants in a room that is warmer than 80 degrees. If at any time during rolling the dough retracts, dust it lightly with flour, fold it loosely, cover it, and return it to the freezer to rest for 10 to 15 minutes.

MAKING A BUTTER BLOCK FOR CROISSANTS

  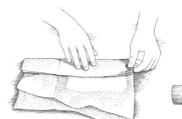 

1. Fold 24-inch length of parchment in half to create 12-inch rectangle. Fold over 3 open sides of rectangle to form 8-inch square.

2. Using rolling pin, beat butter until it is just pliable, then fold butter in on itself using bench scraper. Beat butter into rough 6-inch square.

3. Unfold parchment envelope and, using bench scraper, transfer butter to parchment, refolding at creases to enclose.

4. Turn packet over, and gently roll butter with rolling pin so butter block fills parchment square, taking care to achieve even thickness. Refrigerate.

3 tablespoons unsalted butter plus 24 tablespoons (3 sticks) unsalted European-style butter, very cold

1¾ cups whole milk

4 teaspoons instant or rapid-rise yeast

4¼ cups (21¼ ounces) all-purpose flour

¼ cup (1¾ ounces) sugar

Salt

1 large egg

1 teaspoon cold water

1. Melt 3 tablespoons butter in medium saucepan over low heat. Remove from heat and immediately stir in milk (temperature should be lower than 90 degrees). Whisk in yeast; transfer milk mixture to bowl of stand mixer. Add flour, sugar, and 2 teaspoons salt. Using dough hook, knead on low speed until cohesive dough forms, 2 to 3 minutes. Increase speed to medium-low and knead for 1 minute. Remove bowl from mixer, remove dough hook, and cover bowl with plastic wrap. Let dough rest at room temperature for 30 minutes.

2. Transfer dough to parchment paper–lined baking sheet and shape into 10 by 7-inch rectangle about 1 inch thick. Wrap tightly with plastic and refrigerate for 2 hours.

3. FOR THE BUTTER BLOCK: While dough chills, fold 24-inch length of parchment in half to create 12-inch rectangle. Fold over 3 open sides of rectangle to form 8-inch square with enclosed sides. Crease folds firmly. Place 24 tablespoons cold butter directly on counter and beat with rolling pin for about 60 seconds until butter is just pliable, but not warm, folding butter in on itself using bench scraper. Beat into rough 6-inch square. Unfold parchment envelope. Using bench scraper, transfer butter to center of parchment square, refolding at creases to enclose. Turn packet over so that flaps are underneath and gently

roll butter packet until butter fills parchment square, taking care to achieve even thickness. Refrigerate at least 45 minutes.

4. TO LAMINATE THE DOUGH: Transfer dough to freezer. After 30 minutes, transfer dough to lightly floured counter and roll into 17 by 8-inch rectangle with long side of rectangle parallel to edge of counter. Unwrap butter and place in center of dough so that butter and dough are flush at top and bottom. Fold 2 sides of dough over butter square so they meet in center. Press seam together with fingertips. With rolling pin, press firmly on each open end of packet. Roll out dough, perpendicular to edge of counter, to rectangle 24 inches long and 8 inches wide. Bring bottom third of dough up, then fold upper third over it, folding like business letter into 8-inch square. Turn dough 90 degrees counterclockwise. Roll out dough again, perpendicular to edge of counter, into 24 by 8-inch rectangle and fold into thirds. Place dough on baking sheet, wrap tightly with plastic, and return to freezer for 30 minutes.

5. Transfer dough to lightly floured counter so that top flap of dough is facing

right. Roll once more, perpendicular to edge of counter, into 24 by 8-inch rectangle and fold into thirds. Place dough on baking sheet, wrap tightly with plastic, and refrigerate for 2 hours.

6. Transfer dough to freezer. After 30 minutes, transfer to lightly floured counter and roll into 18 by 16-inch rectangle with long side of rectangle parallel to edge of counter. Fold upper half of dough over lower half. Using ruler, mark dough at 3-inch intervals along bottom edge with bench scraper (you should have 5 marks). Move ruler to top of dough, measure in 1½ inches from left, then use this mark to measure out 3-inch intervals (you should have 6 marks). Starting at lower left corner, use pizza wheel or knife to cut dough into triangles from mark to mark. You will have 12 single triangles and 5 double triangles; discard scraps. Unfold double triangles and cut into 10 single triangles (making 22 equal-size triangles in total). If dough begins to soften, return to freezer for 10 minutes.

7. TO SHAPE THE CROISSANTS: Position 1 triangle on counter. (Keep remaining triangles covered with plastic

---

LAMINATING THE DOUGH FOR CROISSANTS

1. Roll chilled dough into 17 by 8-inch rectangle. Unwrap butter and place in center of dough, aligning it so that edges of butter and dough are flush at top and bottom. Fold two sides of dough over butter so they meet in center of butter square.

2. Using fingertips, press seam together. Using rolling pin, press firmly on each open end of packet. Roll dough out lengthwise until it is 24 inches long and 8 inches wide.

3. Starting at bottom of dough, fold into thirds like business letter. Turn dough 90 degrees and roll and fold into thirds again. Place on baking sheet, wrap tightly with plastic wrap, and return to freezer for 30 minutes. Roll and fold into thirds one more time.

while shaping.) Cut ½ inch slit in center of short end of triangle. Grasp triangle by 2 corners on either side of slit, and stretch gently, then grasp bottom point and stretch. Place triangle on counter so point is facing toward you. Fold both sides of slit down. Positioning palms on folds, roll partway toward point. Gently grasp point again and stretch. To finish, continue to roll, tucking point underneath. Curve ends gently toward one another to create crescent shape. Repeat with remaining triangles.

8. Place 12 croissants on 2 parchment-lined baking sheets, leaving at least 2½ inches between croissants, 6 croissants per sheet. Lightly wrap baking sheets with plastic, leaving room for croissants to expand. Let stand at room temperature until nearly doubled in size, 2½ to 3 hours. (Shaped croissants can be refrigerated on trays for up to 18 hours. Remove from refrigerator to rise and add at least 30 minutes to rising time.)

9. After croissants have been rising for 2 hours, adjust oven racks to upper-middle and lower-middle positions and heat oven to 425 degrees. In small bowl, whisk together egg, water, and pinch of salt. Brush croissants with egg wash using pastry brush. Place croissants in oven and reduce temperature to 400 degrees.

Bake for 12 minutes, then switch and rotate baking sheets. Continue to bake until deep golden brown, 8 to 12 minutes longer. Transfer croissants to wire rack and allow to cool until just warm, about 15 minutes. Serve warm or at room temperature.

TO MAKE AHEAD: After shaping, place croissants 1 inch apart on parchment-lined baking sheet. Wrap with plastic wrap and freeze until solid, about 2 hours. Transfer frozen croissants from baking sheet to zipper-lock bag and return to freezer for up to 2 months. Bake frozen croissants as directed from step 8, increasing rising time by 1 to 2 hours.

SHAPING THE CROISSANTS

1. Transfer dough from freezer to lightly floured work surface and roll into 18 by 16-inch rectangle. (If dough begins to retract, fold it loosely in thirds, wrap it, and return it to freezer for 10–15 minutes.) Fold upper half of dough over lower half.

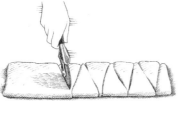

2. Using ruler, mark dough at 3-inch intervals along bottom edge. Move ruler to top of dough, measure in 1½ inches from left, then use this mark to measure out 3-inch intervals. Using pizza wheel or knife, cut dough into triangles from mark to mark.

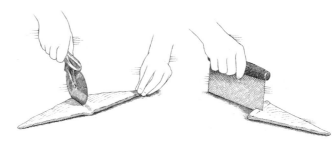

3. You should have 12 single triangles and 5 double triangles; discard any scraps. Unfold double triangle and cut in half to form 10 single triangles (making 22 triangles in all). If dough begins to soften, return to freezer for 10 minutes.

4. Cut ½-inch slit in center of short side of each triangle. If dough begins to soften, return to freezer for 10 minutes.

5. Grasp triangle by 2 corners on either side of slit and stretch gently, then grasp point and stretch.

6. Place triangle on counter so point is facing toward you. Fold both sides of slit down. Positioning palms on folds, roll partway toward point.

7. Gently grasp point with one hand and stretch; resume rolling, tucking point underneath.

8. Curve ends gently toward one another to form crescent shape.

CHAPTER 22   Puddings, Custards,
and Frozen Desserts

STOVETOP RICE PUDDING

✓ WHY THIS RECIPE WORKS

At its best, rice pudding is lightly sweet and tastes of its primary component, rice. At its worst, the rice flavor is lost to cloying sweetness, overcooked milk, and a pasty, leaden consistency. We wanted a rice pudding with intact, tender grains bound loosely in a subtly sweet, creamy pudding. For simple, straightforward rice flavor, we avoided aromatic rices like basmati and jasmine. Arborio rice, used for risotto, was stiff and gritty. Overall, medium-grain rice produced the best texture (with long-grain rice a close second). We found that cooking the rice in water rather than milk left its flavor intact. After the rice absorbed the water, we added sugar and equal amounts of milk and half-and-half, which delivered the proper degree of richness; the eggs and butter found in other recipes were just too overpowering. When we cooked the rice in water with the lid on the pan, then removed the lid while the rice simmered in the milk mixture, we got the results we wanted: distinct, tender grains of rice in a milky, subtly sweet sauce.

SIMPLE STOVETOP RICE PUDDING
SERVES 6 TO 8

We prefer pudding made from medium-grain rice, but long-grain rice works, too.

2	cups water
1	cup medium-grain rice
¼	teaspoon salt
2½	cups whole milk
2½	cups half-and-half
⅔	cup (4⅔ ounces) sugar
1¼	teaspoons vanilla extract

1. Bring water to boil in large saucepan. Stir in rice and salt, cover, and simmer over low heat, stirring once or twice, until water is almost fully absorbed, 15 to 20 minutes.

2. Stir in milk, half-and-half, and sugar.

Increase heat to medium-high and bring to simmer, then reduce heat to maintain simmer. Cook, uncovered and stirring frequently, until mixture starts to thicken, about 30 minutes. Reduce heat to low and continue to cook, stirring every couple of minutes to prevent sticking and scorching, until spoon is just able to stand up in pudding, about 15 minutes longer.

3. Off heat, stir in vanilla. Let cool and serve at room temperature or chilled. (Pudding can be refrigerated, with plastic wrap pressed directly on surface, for up to 2 days.)

RICE PUDDING WITH CINNAMON AND DRIED FRUIT

Add ½ cup dried fruit (raisins, cranberries, cherries, or chopped prunes or apricots) and 1 teaspoon ground cinnamon along with vanilla extract.

RICE PUDDING WITH ORANGE AND TOASTED ALMONDS

Add ⅓ cup toasted slivered almonds and 2 teaspoons grated orange zest along with vanilla extract.

CREAMY CHOCOLATE PUDDING

✓ WHY THIS RECIPE WORKS

Homemade chocolate pudding often suffers either from lackluster chocolate flavor, caused by a dearth of chocolate, or a grainy texture, caused by too much cocoa butter. We were after chocolate pudding that tasted deeply of chocolate, and was thickened to a perfectly silky, creamy texture. We found that using a moderate amount of bittersweet chocolate in combination with unsweetened cocoa and espresso powder helped us achieve maximum chocolate flavor. Cornstarch proved the right thickener for

our pudding; using mostly milk and just half a cup of heavy cream, along with three egg yolks, ensured that our pudding had a silky smooth texture. Salt and vanilla enhanced the chocolate flavor even more.

CREAMY CHOCOLATE PUDDING
SERVES 6

We prefer this recipe made with 60 percent bittersweet chocolate (our favorite brands are Ghirardelli Bittersweet Chocolate Baking Bar and Callebaut Intense Dark Chocolate). Using a chocolate with a higher cacao percentage will result in a thicker pudding. Low-fat milk (1 percent or 2 percent) may be substituted for the whole milk with a small sacrifice in richness. Do not use skim milk as a substitute.

2	teaspoons vanilla extract
½	teaspoon instant espresso powder
½	cup (3½ ounces) sugar
3	tablespoons Dutch-processed cocoa
2	tablespoons cornstarch
¼	teaspoon salt
3	large egg yolks
½	cup heavy cream
2½	cups whole milk
5	tablespoons unsalted butter, cut into 8 pieces
4	ounces bittersweet chocolate, chopped fine

1. Stir together vanilla and espresso in bowl; set aside. Whisk sugar, cocoa, cornstarch, and salt together in large saucepan. Whisk in egg yolks and cream until fully incorporated, making sure to scrape corners of saucepan. Whisk in milk until incorporated.

2. Place saucepan over medium heat; cook, whisking constantly, until mixture is thickened and bubbling over entire surface, 5 to 8 minutes. Cook for 30 seconds longer, remove from heat, add butter and chocolate and whisk until melted and fully incorporated. Whisk in vanilla mixture.

3. Strain pudding through fine-mesh strainer into bowl. Place lightly greased parchment paper against surface of pudding and place in refrigerator to cool, at least 4 hours. Serve. (Pudding can be refrigerated for up to 2 days.)

CREAMY MEXICAN CHOCOLATE PUDDING

Add ½ teaspoon ground cinnamon, ¼ teaspoon chipotle chile powder, and pinch cayenne pepper to saucepan along with cocoa.

CREAMY MOCHA PUDDING

Increase instant espresso powder to 1 teaspoon. Add 1 tablespoon Kahlúa to vanilla mixture. Substitute ¼ cup brewed coffee for ¼ cup milk.

CHOCOLATE MOUSSE

✓ WHY THIS RECIPE WORKS
Rich, creamy, and dense, chocolate mousse can be delicious but too filling after a few mouthfuls. On the other hand, light and airy mousse usually lacks deep chocolate flavor. We wanted chocolate mousse that had both a light, meltingly smooth texture and a substantial chocolate flavor. To start, we addressed the mousse's dense, heavy texture. Most recipes for chocolate mousse contain butter. Could we do without it? We eliminated the butter and found that our mousse tasted less heavy. We further lightened the mousse's texture by reducing the number of egg whites and yolks. To make up for the lost volume of the eggs, we whipped the cream to soft peaks before adding it to the chocolate. Next we tackled the mousse's flavor. We maximized the chocolate flavor with a combination of bittersweet chocolate and cocoa powder. And to further deepen the chocolate flavor, we found that a small amount of instant espresso powder, salt, and brandy did the trick.

DARK CHOCOLATE MOUSSE
SERVES 6 TO 8

When developing this recipe, we used Callebaut Intense Dark Chocolate and Ghirardelli Bittersweet Chocolate Baking Bar, which each contain about 60 percent cacao. If you want to use a chocolate with a higher percentage of cacao, see our variation, Premium Dark Chocolate Mousse. If you choose to make the mousse a day in advance, let it sit at room temperature for 10 minutes before serving. Serve with Whipped Cream (page 800) and chocolate shavings, if desired.

8	ounces bittersweet chocolate, chopped fine
5	tablespoons water
2	tablespoons Dutch-processed cocoa
1	tablespoon brandy
1	teaspoon instant espresso powder
2	large eggs, separated
1	tablespoon sugar
⅛	teaspoon salt
1	cup plus 2 tablespoons heavy cream, chilled

1. Melt chocolate, water, cocoa, brandy, and espresso in medium heatproof bowl set over saucepan filled with 1 inch barely simmering water, stirring frequently until smooth. Remove from heat.

2. Whisk egg yolks, 1½ teaspoons sugar, and salt in medium bowl until mixture lightens in color and thickens slightly, about 30 seconds. Pour melted chocolate into egg yolk mixture and whisk until combined. Let cool until just warmer than room temperature, 3 to 5 minutes.

3. Using stand mixer fitted with whisk, whip egg whites at medium-low speed until foamy, about 1 minute. Add remaining 1½ teaspoons sugar, increase speed to medium-high, and whip until soft peaks form, about 1 minute. Using whisk, stir about one-quarter of whipped egg whites

into chocolate mixture to lighten it; gently fold in remaining egg whites with rubber spatula until few white streaks remain.

4. In now-empty bowl, whip cream on medium speed until it begins to thicken, about 30 seconds. Increase speed to high and whip until soft peaks form, about 15 seconds more. Using rubber spatula, fold whipped cream into mousse until no white streaks remain. Spoon mousse into 6 to 8 individual serving dishes. Cover with plastic wrap and refrigerate until set and firm, at least 2 hours or up to 24 hours. Serve.

PREMIUM DARK CHOCOLATE MOUSSE

This recipe is designed to work with a boutique chocolate that contains a higher percentage of cacao than our master recipe.

Replace bittersweet chocolate (containing about 60 percent cacao) with equal amount of bittersweet chocolate containing 62 to 70 percent cacao. Increase water to 7 tablespoons, increase eggs to 3, and increase sugar to 3 tablespoons, adding extra 2 tablespoons to chocolate mixture in step 1.

CHOCOLATE-ORANGE MOUSSE

For best flavor, the orange zest needs to steep in the heavy cream overnight, so plan accordingly. Garnish each serving of mousse with a thin strip of orange zest, if desired.

Bring cream to simmer in medium saucepan. Off heat, transfer to 2-cup liquid measuring cup and add three 2-inch strips orange zest. Let cool until just warm, cover, and refrigerate overnight. Remove and discard zest; add more cream, if necessary, to equal 1 cup plus 2 tablespoons. Proceed with step 1, reducing water to 4 tablespoons and omitting brandy. Once chocolate is melted, stir in 2 tablespoons Grand Marnier and proceed as directed.

Chambord is our preferred brand of raspberry-flavored liqueur for this recipe. Serve the mousse with fresh raspberries, if desired.

Reduce water to 4 tablespoons, omit brandy, and add 2 tablespoons raspberry-flavored liqueur to melted chocolate mixture in step 1.

CHOCOLATE POTS DE CRÈME

✔ WHY THIS RECIPE WORKS

Classic pots de crème can be finicky and laborious, requiring a hot water bath that threatens to splash the custards every time the pan is moved. We wanted a user-friendly recipe that delivered a decadent dessert with a satiny texture and intense chocolate flavor. First we moved the dish out of the oven, concentrating on an unconventional approach in which the custard is cooked on the stovetop in a saucepan, then poured into ramekins. Our next challenge was developing the right amount of richness and body, which we did by choosing a combination of heavy cream and half-and-half, along with egg yolks only, for maximum richness. For intense chocolate flavor, we focused on bittersweet chocolate—and a lot of it. Our chocolate content was at least 50 percent more than in any other recipe we had encountered.

CHOCOLATE POTS DE CRÈME
SERVES 8

We prefer pots de crème made with 60 percent bittersweet chocolate (our favorite brands are Ghirardelli Bittersweet Chocolate Baking Bar and Callebaut Intense Dark Chocolate), but 70 percent bittersweet chocolate can also be used. If using a 70 percent bittersweet chocolate, reduce the amount of chocolate to 8 ounces.

POTS DE CRÈME
- 10 ounces bittersweet chocolate, chopped fine
- 5 large egg yolks
- 5 tablespoons (2¼ ounces) sugar
- ¼ teaspoon salt
- 1½ cups heavy cream
- ¾ cup half-and-half
- 1 tablespoon water
- ½ teaspoon instant espresso powder
- 1 tablespoon vanilla extract

WHIPPED CREAM AND GARNISH
- ½ cup heavy cream, chilled
- 2 teaspoons sugar
- ½ teaspoon vanilla extract
  Cocoa (optional)
  Chocolate shavings (optional)

1. FOR THE POTS DE CRÈME: Place chocolate in medium bowl; set fine-mesh strainer over bowl and set aside.

2. Whisk egg yolks, sugar, and salt together in bowl until combined. Whisk in cream and half-and-half. Transfer mixture to medium saucepan and cook over medium-low heat, stirring constantly and scraping bottom of pot with wooden spoon, until thickened and silky and registers 175 to 180 degrees, 8 to 12 minutes. (Do not let custard overcook or simmer.)

3. Immediately pour custard through fine-mesh strainer over chocolate. Let mixture stand to melt chocolate, about 5 minutes; whisk gently until smooth. Combine water and espresso and stir to dissolve, then whisk dissolved espresso and vanilla into chocolate mixture. Divide mixture evenly among eight 5-ounce ramekins. Gently tap ramekins against counter to remove air bubbles.

4. Let pots de crème cool to room temperature, then cover with plastic wrap and refrigerate until chilled, at least 4 hours. Before serving, let pots de crème stand at room temperature for 20 to 30 minutes. (Pots de crème can be refrigerated for up to 3 days.)

5. FOR THE WHIPPED CREAM AND GARNISH: Using stand mixer fitted with whisk, whip cream, sugar, and vanilla on medium-low speed until foamy, about 1 minute. Increase speed to high and whip until stiff peaks form, 1 to 3 minutes. Dollop each pot de crème with about 2 tablespoons whipped cream and garnish with cocoa and/or chocolate shavings, if using. Serve.

MILK CHOCOLATE POTS DE CRÈME

Milk chocolate behaves differently in this recipe than bittersweet chocolate, and more of it must be used to ensure that the custard sets. And because of the increased amount of chocolate, it's necessary to cut back on the amount of sugar so that the custard is not overly sweet.

Substitute 12 ounces milk chocolate, chopped fine, for bittersweet chocolate and reduce sugar in pots de crème to 2 tablespoons.

TEST KITCHEN TIP NO. 150   PREVENTING DAIRY DISASTER

Why does milk have a tendency to boil over more often than any other liquid? Milk (and cream) contains casein proteins that gather near the surface as they heat. Once the milk comes to a boil, steam bubbles rising from the bottom of the pot are forced through the protein-rich layer at the top. The proteins stabilize the bubbles, keeping them from bursting, so they rapidly increase in number and overwhelm the pan. Then, whoosh—dairy disaster.

We tried several techniques purported to prevent the problem, from leaving a long-handled spoon in the pot to buttering the pan's rim. While such methods delayed the boilover, the only surefire solution was to use a larger pan (a full 4-quart saucepan for a pint of milk, a size we would normally consider far too large for the task). In a pot with a small circumference, the bubbles are tightly packed, with little room to expand. But in a pot with a large diameter, the bubbles can grow bigger and bigger until even the reinforcement provided by the casein proteins can't prevent them from popping. As a result, there are never enough bubbles to overwhelm the capacity of the pan. In sum, to keep milk from boiling over, heat it in a big, wide pan.

CRÈME CARAMEL

✔ WHY THIS RECIPE WORKS

What many people love about crème caramel is the caramel. But while we can't deny its appeal, what most concerned us when we decided to embark on a search for a really great crème caramel was the custard. We wanted custard that was creamy and tender enough to melt in our mouths, yet firm enough to unmold without collapsing on the serving plate. We were also looking for a mellow flavor that was neither too rich nor too eggy. We discovered that the proportion of egg whites to yolks in the custard was critical for the right texture. Too many whites caused the custard to solidify too much, and too few left it almost runny. We settled on a formula of three whole eggs and two yolks. Light cream and milk for the dairy component provided the proper amount of richness. For contrast with the sweet caramel, we kept the amount of sugar in the custard to a minimum. Baking the ramekins in a water bath was essential for even cooking and ensured a delicate custard; a kitchen towel on the bottom of the pan stabilized the ramekins and prevented the bottoms of the custards from overcooking. When we unmolded our crème caramel on serving plates, the sweet caramel sauce bathed the rounds of perfectly cooked custard.

REMOVING CRÈME CARAMEL FROM A WATER BATH

We recommend removing ramekins from water bath with tongs, preferably rubber-tipped for sure grip. If you don't own this style of tongs, simply slip rubber band around each tip.

CLASSIC CRÈME CARAMEL
SERVES 8

You can vary the amount of sugar in the custard to suit your taste. Most tasters preferred the full ⅔ cup, but you can reduce that amount to as little as ½ cup to create a greater contrast between the custard and the caramel. Cook the caramel in a pan with a light-colored interior, since a dark surface makes it difficult to judge the color of the syrup. Caramel can leave a real mess in a pan, but it is easy to clean; simply boil water in the pan for 5 to 10 minutes to loosen the hardened caramel.

CARAMEL
- ⅓   cup water
- 2   tablespoons light corn syrup
- ¼   teaspoon lemon juice
- 1   cup (7 ounces) sugar

CUSTARD
- 1½   cups whole milk
- 1½   cups light cream
- 3   large eggs plus 2 large yolks
- ⅔   cup (4⅔ ounces) sugar
- 1½   teaspoons vanilla extract
-   Pinch salt

1. FOR THE CARAMEL: Combine water, corn syrup, and lemon juice in medium saucepan. Pour sugar into center of pan, taking care not to let sugar crystals touch pan sides. Gently stir with spatula to moisten sugar thoroughly. Bring to boil over medium-high heat and cook, without stirring, until sugar is completely dissolved and liquid is clear, 6 to 10 minutes. Reduce heat to medium-low and continue to cook, swirling occasionally, until mixture darkens to honey color, 4 to 5 minutes longer. Working quickly, carefully divide caramel among eight 6-ounce ramekins. Let caramel cool and harden, about 15 minutes. (Caramel-coated ramekins can be refrigerated for up to 2 days; bring to room temperature before adding custard.)

2. FOR THE CUSTARD: Adjust oven rack to middle position and heat oven to 350 degrees. Combine milk and cream in medium saucepan and heat over medium heat, stirring occasionally, until steam appears and mixture registers 160 degrees, 6 to 8 minutes; remove from heat. Meanwhile, gently whisk eggs, egg yolks, and sugar in large bowl until just combined. Off heat, gently whisk warm milk mixture, vanilla, and salt into eggs until just combined but not foamy. Strain mixture through fine-mesh strainer into 4-cup liquid measuring cup or bowl; set aside.

3. Bring kettle of water to boil. Meanwhile, place kitchen towel in bottom of large baking dish or roasting pan and set ramekins on towel (they should not touch). Divide custard evenly among ramekins and set dish on oven rack. Taking care not to splash water into ramekins, pour enough boiling water into dish to come halfway up sides of ramekins; cover dish loosely with aluminum foil. Bake until paring knife inserted halfway between center and edge of custards comes out clean, 35 to 40 minutes. Transfer ramekins to wire rack and let cool to room temperature. (Custards can be refrigerated for up to 2 days.)

4. To unmold, run paring knife around perimeter of each ramekin. Hold serving plate over top of ramekin and invert; set plate on counter and gently shake ramekin to release custard. Repeat with remaining ramekins and serve.

ESPRESSO CRÈME CARAMEL

Espresso beans ground in a coffee grinder would be too fine and impart too strong a coffee flavor to the custard. Instead, crush the beans lightly with the bottom of a skillet.

Heat ½ cup lightly crushed espresso beans with milk and cream mixture until steam appears and mixture registers 160 degrees, 6 to 8 minutes. Off heat, cover and let steep until coffee has infused milk and cream, about 15 minutes. Strain mixture through fine-mesh strainer and proceed as directed, discarding crushed espresso beans. Reduce vanilla extract to 1 teaspoon.

CRÈME BRÛLÉE

✓ WHY THIS RECIPE WORKS
Crème brûlée is all about the contrast between the crisp sugar crust and the silky custard underneath. But too often the crust is either stingy or rock-hard, and the custard is heavy and tasteless. We found that the secret to a soft, supple custard was using egg yolks rather than whole eggs. Heavy cream gave the custard a luxurious richness. Sugar, a vanilla bean, and a pinch of salt were the only other additions. Many recipes use scalded cream, but we found that this resulted in overcooked custard, so we left the ingredients cold. However, we needed heat to extract flavor from the vanilla bean and dissolve the sugar. Our compromise was to heat only half of the cream with the sugar and vanilla bean and add the remaining cream cold, which worked perfectly. For the crust, we used crunchy turbinado sugar and a propane or butane torch worked better than the broiler for caramelizing the sugar, and because the blast of heat inevitably warms the custard beneath the crust, we chilled our crèmes brûlées once more before serving.

CARAMELIZING CRÈME BRÛLÉE

Ignite torch and, holding flame about 2 inches above sugar, slowly sweep flame over sugar until it bubbles and turns deep golden brown.

CLASSIC CRÈME BRÛLÉE
SERVES 8

Separate the eggs and whisk the yolks after the cream has finished steeping; if left to sit, the surface of the yolks will dry and form a film. A vanilla bean gives the custard the deepest flavor, but 2 teaspoons of vanilla extract, whisked into the yolks in step 4, can be used instead. While we prefer turbinado or Demerara sugar for the caramelized sugar crust, regular granulated sugar will work, too, but use only 1 scant teaspoon on each ramekin or 1 teaspoon on each shallow fluted dish.

- 1 vanilla bean
- 4 cups heavy cream
- ⅔ cup (4⅔ ounces) granulated sugar
  Pinch salt
- 12 large egg yolks
- 8–12 teaspoons turbinado or Demerara sugar

1. Adjust oven rack to lower-middle position and heat oven to 300 degrees.

2. Cut vanilla bean in half lengthwise. Using tip of paring knife, scrape out seeds. Combine vanilla bean and seeds, 2 cups cream, sugar, and salt in medium saucepan. Bring mixture to boil over medium heat, stirring occasionally to dissolve sugar. Off heat, let steep for 15 minutes.

3. Meanwhile, place kitchen towel in bottom of large baking dish or roasting pan; set eight 4- or 5-ounce ramekins (or shallow fluted dishes) on towel (they should not touch). Bring kettle of water to boil.

4. After cream has steeped, stir in remaining 2 cups cream. Whisk egg yolks in large bowl until uniform. Whisk about 1 cup cream mixture into yolks until combined; repeat with 1 cup more cream mixture. Add remaining cream mixture and whisk until evenly colored and thoroughly combined. Strain mixture through fine-mesh strainer into large liquid measuring cup or bowl; discard solids in strainer. Divide mixture evenly among ramekins.

5. Set baking dish on oven rack. Taking care not to splash water into ramekins, pour enough boiling water into dish to reach two-thirds up sides of ramekins. Bake until centers of custards are just barely set and register 170 to 175 degrees, 30 to 35 minutes (25 to 30 minutes for shallow fluted dishes), checking temperature about 5 minutes before recommended minimum time.

6. Transfer ramekins to wire rack and let cool to room temperature, about 2 hours. Set ramekins on baking sheet, cover tightly with plastic wrap, and refrigerate until cold, at least 4 hours.

7. Uncover ramekins; if condensation has collected on custards, blot moisture with paper towel. Sprinkle each with about 1 teaspoon turbinado sugar (1½ teaspoons for shallow fluted dishes); tilt and tap each ramekin to distribute sugar evenly, dumping out excess sugar. Ignite torch and caramelize sugar. Refrigerate ramekins, uncovered, to rechill, 30 to 45 minutes; serve.

ESPRESSO CRÈME BRÛLÉE

Crush the espresso beans lightly with the bottom of a skillet.

Substitute ¼ cup lightly crushed espresso beans for vanilla bean. Whisk 1 teaspoon vanilla extract into yolks in step 4 before adding cream.

TEA-INFUSED CRÈME BRÛLÉE

Substitute 10 Irish Breakfast tea bags, tied together, for vanilla bean; after steeping, squeeze bags with tongs or press into fine-mesh strainer to extract all liquid. Whisk 1 teaspoon vanilla extract into yolks in step 4 before adding cream.

FAMILY-STYLE CRÈME BRÛLÉE

Substitute 11 by 7-inch baking dish for ramekins and bake for 40 to 50 minutes.

Let cool to room temperature, 2½ to 3 hours.

MAKE-AHEAD CRÈME BRÛLÉE

Reduce egg yolks to 10. After baked custards cool to room temperature, wrap each ramekin tightly in plastic wrap and refrigerate for up to 4 days. Proceed with step 7.

PANNA COTTA

✔ WHY THIS RECIPE WORKS

Though its name is lyrical, the literal translation of panna cotta, "cooked cream," does nothing to suggest its ethereal qualities. In fact, panna cotta is not cooked at all. It is a simple, refined dessert where sugar and gelatin are melted in cream and milk, and the mixture is turned into individual ramekins and chilled. While panna cotta is usually found on restaurant menus, we wanted a version for the home cook—one that would guarantee a pudding with the rich flavor of cream and vanilla and a delicate texture. After trying several different recipes, we concluded that we needed a higher proportion of cream to milk to achieve the creamiest flavor and texture. The amount of gelatin proved critical; too much turned the panna cotta rubbery. We used a light hand, adding just enough to make the dessert firm enough to unmold. And because gelatin sets more quickly at cold temperatures, we minimized the amount of heat by softening the gelatin in cold milk, then heating it very briefly until it was melted. To avoid premature hardening, we gradually added cold vanilla-infused cream to the gelatin mixture and stirred everything over an ice bath to incorporate the gelatin.

CLASSIC PANNA COTTA
SERVES 8

A vanilla bean gives the panna cotta the deepest flavor, but 2 teaspoons of vanilla extract can be used instead. If you like, you can omit the Berry Coulis and simply serve the panna cotta with lightly sweetened berries. Though traditionally unmolded, panna cotta may be chilled and served in wine glasses with the sauce on top. If you would like to make the panna cotta a day ahead, reduce the amount of gelatin by ½ teaspoon and chill the filled wine glasses or ramekins for 18 to 24 hours.

- 1 cup whole milk
- 2¾ teaspoons unflavored gelatin
- 3 cups heavy cream
- 1 vanilla bean
- 6 tablespoons (2⅔ ounces) sugar
  Pinch salt
- 1 recipe Berry Coulis (page 799)

1. Pour milk into medium saucepan; sprinkle surface evenly with gelatin and let stand for 10 minutes. Meanwhile, turn contents of 2 ice cube trays (about 32 cubes) into large bowl; add 4 cups cold water. Place cream in large measuring cup. Cut vanilla bean in half lengthwise. Using tip of paring knife, scrape out seeds. Add vanilla bean and seeds to cream; set aside. Set eight 4-ounce ramekins on rimmed baking sheet.

2. Heat milk and gelatin mixture over high heat, stirring constantly, until gelatin is dissolved and mixture registers 135 degrees, about 1½ minutes. Off heat, add sugar and salt; stir until dissolved, about 1 minute.

3. Stirring constantly, slowly pour cream into milk mixture, then transfer to medium bowl and set over bowl of ice water. Stir frequently until slightly thickened and mixture registers 50 degrees, about 10 minutes. Strain mixture through fine-mesh strainer into large liquid measuring cup, then distribute evenly among ramekins. Cover baking sheet with plastic wrap, making sure plastic does touch surface; refrigerate until just set (mixture should wobble when shaken gently), at least 4 or up to 12 hours.

4. Run paring knife between custard and side of ramekin in 1 smooth stroke. (If shape of ramekin makes this difficult, quickly dip ramekin into hot water bath to loosen custard.) Flip ramekins upside down onto individual serving plates. Shake ramekins gently to unmold panna cotta; lift ramekins from plate and serve with Berry Coulis.

LEMON PANNA COTTA

Cut four 2-inch strips lemon zest into thin strips and add to cream along with vanilla bean. Add ¼ cup lemon juice (2 lemons) to strained cream mixture before dividing among ramekins.

CHOCOLATE SOUFFLÉ

✔ WHY THIS RECIPE WORKS

Rising dramatically above the rim of the pan, the perfect soufflé must have a texture that graduates from a crusty exterior to an airy but substantial outer layer to a rich, soft, not completely set center. For a chocolate soufflé, the chocolate notes should be deep and strong. We began our chocolate soufflé with a béchamel base (a classic French sauce made with equal amounts of butter and flour and whisked with milk over heat) and eggs. But we found that the milk muted the chocolate flavor. We then removed the milk and the flour, separated the eggs (whites were whipped separately), increased the chocolate, and reduced the butter. The base now consisted of egg yolks beaten with sugar until thick, giving the soufflé plenty of volume. The result was intense chocolate flavor. After several more experiments, we discovered that adding two extra egg whites gave the soufflé even more lift and a better texture.

CHOCOLATE SOUFFLÉ
SERVES 6 TO 8

To melt the chocolate using a microwave, heat it at 50 percent power for 2 minutes; stir the chocolate, add the butter, and continue heating until melted, stirring once every additional minute. Soufflé waits for no one so be ready to serve it immediately.

4 tablespoons unsalted butter,
    cut into ½-inch pieces, plus
    1 tablespoon, softened
⅓ cup (2⅓ ounces) plus
    1 tablespoon sugar
8 ounces bittersweet or semisweet
    chocolate, chopped coarse
1 tablespoon orange-flavored liqueur,
    such as Grand Marnier
½ teaspoon vanilla extract
⅛ teaspoon salt
6 large eggs, separated, plus
    2 large whites
¼ teaspoon cream of tartar

1. Adjust oven rack to lower-middle position and heat oven to 375 degrees. Grease 2-quart soufflé dish with 1 tablespoon softened butter, then coat dish evenly with 1 tablespoon sugar; refrigerate until ready to use.

2. Melt chocolate and remaining 4 tablespoons butter in medium heatproof bowl set over saucepan of barely simmering water, stirring occasionally, until smooth. Stir in liqueur, vanilla, and salt; set aside.

3. Using stand mixer fitted with paddle, beat egg yolks and remaining ⅓ cup sugar on medium speed until thick and pale yellow, about 3 minutes. Fold into chocolate mixture.

4. Using dry, clean bowl and whisk attachment, whip egg whites and cream of tartar on medium-low speed until foamy, about 1 minute. Increase speed to medium-high and whip until stiff peaks form, 3 to 4 minutes.

5. Using rubber spatula, vigorously stir one-quarter of whipped whites into chocolate mixture. Gently fold in remaining whites until just incorporated. Transfer mixture to prepared dish and bake until fragrant, fully risen, and exterior is set but interior is still a bit loose and creamy, about 25 minutes. (Use 2 large spoons to pull open top and peek inside.) Serve immediately.

MOCHA SOUFFLÉ

Add 1 tablespoon instant espresso powder dissolved in 1 tablespoon hot water when adding vanilla to chocolate mixture.

INDIVIDUAL CHOCOLATE SOUFFLÉS

Omit 2-quart soufflé dish. Grease eight 8-ounce ramekins with butter and sugar. In step 5, transfer soufflé mixture to ramekins, making sure to completely fill each ramekin and wipe each rim with wet paper towel. Reduce baking time to 16 to 18 minutes.

MAKE-AHEAD INDIVIDUAL CHOCOLATE SOUFFLÉS

Omit 2-quart soufflé dish. Grease eight 8-ounce ramekins with butter and sugar. In step 3, bring sugar and 2 tablespoons water to boil in small saucepan, then reduce heat and simmer until sugar dissolves. With mixer running, slowly add sugar syrup to egg yolks and beat until mixture triples in volume, about 3 minutes. Whip egg whites as directed, beating in 2 tablespoons confectioners' sugar. Stir and fold into chocolate base as directed. Fill each chilled ramekin almost to rim, wiping each rim clean with wet paper towel. Cover each ramekin tightly with plastic wrap and freeze until firm, at least 3 hours or up to 1 month. (Do not thaw before baking.) To serve, heat oven to 400 degrees and reduce baking time to 16 to 18 minutes.

GRAND MARNIER SOUFFLÉ

✔ WHY THIS RECIPE WORKS
We wanted to produce a reliable recipe for a classic soufflé flavored with the citrusy warmth of Grand Marnier. The best soufflés have a crusty top layer above the rim of the dish and a contrasting rich, creamy, almost-fluid center. For the base we began with a bouillie—a paste of flour and milk. Butter kept the egginess at bay, and increasing the usual amount of flour prevented the frothiness we wanted to avoid. An equal number of egg whites and yolks was the right proportion for rise versus richness. Adding a little sugar and some cream of tartar to the whites while we whipped them stabilized the whites so that they would hold their structure. We discovered that most of the sugar must be added gradually and partway through the beating process, not at the beginning, or the soufflé will not rise properly and will taste too sweet. We also found it important to remove the soufflé from the oven while the center was still loose and moist to prevent overcooking.

TEST KITCHEN TIP NO. 151 *MAKING VANILLA EXTRACT*

Most of vanilla's flavor compounds are soluble in either water or alcohol, so the most shelf-stable form of vanilla is vanilla extract, produced by soaking vanilla beans in a solution of 65 percent water and at least 35 percent alcohol. We wondered if we could make our own vanilla extract by soaking a split vanilla bean in heated vodka (which would contribute very little of its own flavor). After testing several ratios of vanilla beans to vodka, we arrived at 1 bean per ¾ cup of vodka as the proportion most closely resembling the potency of our recommended store-bought brand, McCormick Pure Vanilla Extract. We then tested our homemade extract against this supermarket product in sugar cookies, crème brûlée, and vanilla buttercream frosting. In each case, our extract outperformed the commercial version, boasting cleaner, more intense vanilla flavor.

To make vanilla extract, split a fresh bean lengthwise and scrape out the seeds. Place the seeds and split pod in a 1-cup sealable container. Add ¾ cup hot vodka (we used Smirnoff—a premium brand is not necessary) and let the mixture cool to room temperature. Seal the container and store at room temperature for one week, shaking gently every day. Strain the extract, if desired, and store in a cool, dark place. The extract should keep indefinitely.

GRAND MARNIER SOUFFLÉ WITH GRATED CHOCOLATE

SERVES 6 TO 8

Make the soufflé base and immediately begin beating the whites before the base cools too much. Once the whites have reached the proper consistency, they must be used at once. Do not open the oven door during the first 15 minutes of baking time; as the soufflé nears the end of its baking, you may check its progress by opening the oven door slightly. (Be careful here; if your oven runs hot, the top of the soufflé may burn.) A quick dusting of confectioners' sugar is a nice finishing touch, but a soufflé waits for no one, so be ready to serve it immediately.

2	tablespoons unsalted butter, room temperature, plus 1 tablespoon, softened
¾	cup (5¼ ounces) sugar
2	teaspoons sifted cocoa
5	tablespoons (1½ ounces) all-purpose flour
¼	teaspoon salt
1	cup whole milk
5	large eggs, separated
3	tablespoons Grand Marnier
1	tablespoon grated orange zest
⅛	teaspoon cream of tartar
½	ounce bittersweet chocolate, finely grated

1. Adjust oven rack to upper-middle position and heat oven to 400 degrees. Grease 1½-quart soufflé dish with 1 tablespoon softened butter. Combine ¼ cup sugar and cocoa in small bowl and pour into prepared dish, shaking to coat bottom and sides of dish evenly. Tap out excess and set dish aside.

2. Whisk flour, ¼ cup sugar, and salt in small saucepan. Gradually whisk in milk, whisking until smooth and no lumps remain. Bring mixture to boil over high heat, whisking constantly, until thickened and mixture pulls away from sides of pan, about 3 minutes. Scrape mixture into medium bowl; whisk in remaining 2 tablespoons butter until combined. Whisk in egg yolks until incorporated; stir in Grand Marnier and orange zest.

3. Using stand mixer fitted with whisk, whip egg whites, cream of tartar, and 1 teaspoon sugar on medium-low speed until foamy, about 1 minute. Increase speed to medium-high and whip whites to soft, billowy mounds, about 1 minute. Gradually add half of remaining sugar and whip until glossy, soft peaks form, about 30 seconds; with mixer still running, add remaining sugar and whip until just combined, about 10 seconds.

4. Using rubber spatula, immediately stir one-quarter of whipped whites into soufflé base to lighten until almost no white streaks remain. Scrape remaining whites into base and fold in whites, along with grated chocolate, with whisk until mixture is just combined. Gently pour mixture into prepared dish and run your index finger through mixture, tracing circumference about ½ inch from side of dish, to help soufflé rise properly. Bake until surface of soufflé is deep brown, center jiggles slightly when shaken, and soufflé has risen 2 to 2½ inches above rim, 20 to 25 minutes. Serve immediately.

KAHLÚA SOUFFLÉ WITH GROUND ESPRESSO

If you do not have espresso beans, substitute an equal amount of instant espresso powder, adding it along with the milk in step 2 so that it dissolves.

Omit orange zest and substitute Kahlúa for Grand Marnier and 1 tablespoon finely ground espresso beans for shaved chocolate.

CHILLED LEMON SOUFFLÉ

✓ WHY THIS RECIPE WORKS

"Chilled lemon soufflé" can be interpreted in many ways, from cooled baked pudding cake to lemony, eggy foam. But no matter what the desired outcome, what typically results is a dense, rubbery mass or a mouthful of tart egg white foam. The delicate balance of ingredients is hard for home cooks to get right. We wanted to perfect the unusual marriage of cream and foam, sweet and sour, high lemony notes and rich custard. A starting recipe of egg whites, gelatin, sugar, and lemon juice had none of the creaminess we desired, so we cooked a custard base of milk, egg yolks, and sugar. To our custard we then added lemon juice and gelatin (to stabilize the mixture so it would set up while chilling). Because this was to be a soufflé, not a pudding, we lightened the custard with whipped cream and beaten egg whites. The egg yolks and dairy tended to mute the lemon flavor, so for more citrus punch we included grated lemon zest. Now we had the balance of flavor and texture that we sought: a satisfying but light custard with bright lemon flavor.

CHILLED LEMON SOUFFLÉ

SERVES 4 TO 6

To make this lemon soufflé "soufflé" over the rim of the dish, use a 1-quart soufflé dish and attach a foil collar; to make the collar, secure a strip of foil that has been sprayed with vegetable oil spray around the soufflé dish so it extends 2 inches above the rim (do this before the dish has been filled). Tape the foil collar to the dish to prevent it from slipping. For those less concerned about appearance, this dessert can be served from any 1½-quart serving bowl. For the best texture, serve the soufflé after 1½ hours of chilling. It may be chilled for up to 6 hours; though the texture will stiffen slightly. The soufflé can be garnished with fresh mint, raspberries, confectioners' sugar, or finely chopped pistachios.

2½   teaspoons grated lemon zest plus
     ½ cup juice (3 lemons)
2   teaspoons unflavored gelatin
1   cup whole milk
¾   cup (5¼ ounces) sugar
2   large eggs, separated, plus 3 large
     whites, room temperature
¼   teaspoon cornstarch
     Pinch cream of tartar
¾   cup heavy cream

1. Place lemon juice in small bowl; sprinkle gelatin over top and set aside.

2. Heat milk and ½ cup sugar in medium saucepan over medium-low heat, stirring occasionally, until steaming and sugar is dissolved, about 5 minutes. Meanwhile, whisk egg yolks, 2 tablespoons sugar, and cornstarch in medium bowl until pale yellow and thickened. Whisking constantly, gradually add hot milk mixture to yolks. Return milk-egg mixture to saucepan and cook, stirring constantly, over medium-low heat until mixture thickens to consistency of heavy cream and registers 185 degrees, about 4 minutes. Pour mixture through fine-mesh strainer into bowl; stir in lemon juice mixture and zest. Set bowl with custard over large bowl of ice water; stir occasionally to cool.

3. While custard cools, use stand mixer fitted with whisk to whip egg whites and cream of tartar on medium-low speed until foamy, about 1 minute. Increase speed to medium-high and whip whites to soft, billowy mounds, about 1 minute. Gradually add remaining 2 tablespoons sugar and whip until glossy, soft peaks form, 1 to 2 minutes. (Do not overwhip.) Remove custard from ice-water bath; gently whisk in one-third of egg whites, then fold in remaining whites with rubber spatula until almost no white streaks remain.

4. Using stand mixer fitted with whisk, whip cream on medium-low speed until foamy, about 1 minute. Increase speed to

high and whip until soft peaks form, 1 to 3 minutes. Fold whipped cream into custard until no white streaks remain.

5. Pour custard into 1-quart soufflé dish fitted with aluminum foil collar or 1½-quart soufflé dish. Chill until set but not stiff, about 1½ hours; remove foil collar, if using, and serve.

CHILLED LEMON SOUFFLÉ WITH WHITE CHOCOLATE

Add 2 ounces chopped white chocolate to warm custard before adding lemon juice mixture and zest. Stir until melted and fully incorporated.

SKILLET SOUFFLÉ

✔ WHY THIS RECIPE WORKS

Having taken the mystique out of soufflé making, we wondered if we could take our expertise one step further. If we could make a soufflé in a skillet, we would guarantee that this great dessert was in the realm of everyday cooking. We theorized that the heat on the stovetop would activate the batter and ensure an even rise from the egg whites. We opted for an uncomplicated base of whipped egg yolks. A little flour kept the soufflé creamy rather than foamy. We decided that lemon would shine through the eggy base well; lemon juice and zest provided bright, natural citrus flavor. We beat the egg whites separately, adding sugar partway through, folded them into the egg-lemon base, and poured the mixture into a buttered ovensafe skillet. After a few minutes on the stovetop the soufflé was just set around the edges and on the bottom (and the crust that eventually formed on the bottom was a bonus our tasters applauded), so we moved the skillet to the oven to finish. A few minutes later our soufflé was puffed, golden on top, and creamy in the middle—and ready for the weeknight table.

SKILLET LEMON SOUFFLÉ
SERVES 6

Do not open the oven door during the first 7 minutes of baking, but do check the soufflé regularly for doneness during the final few minutes in the oven. Be ready to serve the soufflé immediately after removing it from the oven. Using a 10-inch traditional (not nonstick) skillet is essential to getting the right texture and height in the soufflé.

5   large eggs, separated
¼   teaspoon cream of tartar
⅔   cup (4⅔ ounces) sugar
⅛   teaspoon salt
1   teaspoon grated lemon zest plus
     ⅓ cup juice (3 lemons)
2   tablespoons all-purpose flour
1   tablespoon unsalted butter
     Confectioners' sugar

1. Adjust oven rack to middle position and heat oven to 375 degrees. Using stand mixer fitted with whisk, whip egg whites and cream of tartar on medium-low speed until foamy, about 1 minute. Increase speed to medium-high and whip whites to soft, billowy mounds, about 1 minute. Gradually add ⅓ cup sugar and salt and whip until glossy, stiff peaks form, 2 to 3 minutes. Gently transfer whites to clean bowl; set aside.

2. Using stand mixer fitted with whisk (do not wash bowl), whip egg yolks and remaining ⅓ cup sugar on medium-high speed until pale and thick, about 1 minute. Whip in lemon zest, juice, and flour until incorporated, about 30 seconds.

3. Fold one-quarter of whipped egg whites into yolk mixture until almost no white streaks remain. Gently fold in remaining egg whites until just incorporated.

4. Melt butter in 10-inch ovensafe skillet over medium-low heat. Swirl pan to coat it evenly with butter, then gently scrape soufflé batter into skillet and cook

until edges begin to set and bubble slightly, about 2 minutes.

5. Transfer skillet to oven and bake soufflé until puffed, center jiggles slightly when shaken, and surface is golden, 7 to 11 minutes. Using potholder (skillet handle will be hot), remove skillet from oven. Dust soufflé with confectioners' sugar and serve immediately.

SKILLET CHOCOLATE-ORANGE SOUFFLÉ

Grating the chocolate fine is key here; we find it easiest to use either a rasp-style grater or the fine holes of a box grater.

Substitute 1 tablespoon grated orange zest for lemon zest and ⅓ cup orange juice for lemon juice. Gently fold 1 ounce finely grated bittersweet chocolate into soufflé batter after incorporating all whites in step 3.

BREAD PUDDING

✔ WHY THIS RECIPE WORKS

Bread pudding started out as a frugal way to transform stale, old loaves of bread into an appetizing dish. But contemporary versions of this humble dish vary from mushy, sweetened porridge to chewy, desiccated cousins of holiday stuffing. We wanted a refined bread pudding, with a moist, creamy (but not eggy) interior and a crisp top crust. The first step was choosing the best bread for the job. We chose challah for its rich flavor. We cut the bread into cubes, toasted them until lightly browned, and soaked the cubes with a batch of basic custard. Once the cubes were saturated, we transferred them to a baking dish and slid our pudding into a low-temperature oven to prevent curdling. The custard turned out creamy and smooth, but not as set as we'd have liked. Adding another egg or two helped firm it up, but tasters complained that the pudding tasted somewhat eggy. It turns out that

eggy flavor comes from the sulfur compounds in egg whites. So we got rid of the whites and just used the yolks. We now had a luscious, silky custard. Brushing the surface with melted butter and sprinkling the dish with a mix of white and brown sugar prior to baking gave the pudding a crunchy, buttery, sugary crust.

CLASSIC BREAD PUDDING
SERVES 8 TO 10

Challah is an egg-enriched bread that can be found in most bakeries and supermarkets. If you cannot find challah, a firm high-quality sandwich bread such as Arnold Country Classics White or Pepperidge Farm Farmhouse Hearty White may be substituted. If desired, serve this pudding with Whipped Cream (page 800) or with Bourbon–Brown Sugar Sauce (recipe follows). To retain a crisp top crust when reheating leftovers, cut the bread pudding into squares and heat, uncovered, in a 450-degree oven until warmed through, 6 to 8 minutes.

¾	cup (5¼ ounces) plus 1 tablespoon granulated sugar
2	tablespoons light brown sugar
14	ounces challah bread, cut into ¾-inch cubes
9	large egg yolks
4	teaspoons vanilla extract
¾	teaspoon salt
2½	cups heavy cream
2½	cups milk
2	tablespoons unsalted butter, melted

1. Adjust oven racks to middle and lower-middle positions and heat oven to 325 degrees. Combine 1 tablespoon granulated sugar and brown sugar in small bowl; set aside.

2. Spread bread cubes in single layer on 2 rimmed baking sheets. Bake, tossing occasionally, until just dry, about 15 minutes, switching and rotating baking sheets

halfway through baking. Let bread cubes cool for about 15 minutes; set aside 2 cups.

3. Whisk egg yolks, remaining ¾ cup granulated sugar, vanilla, and salt together in large bowl. Whisk in cream and milk until combined. Add remaining cooled bread cubes and toss to coat. Transfer mixture to 13 by 9-inch baking dish and let stand, occasionally pressing bread cubes into custard, until cubes are thoroughly saturated, about 30 minutes.

4. Spread reserved bread cubes evenly over top of soaked bread mixture; gently press into custard. Brush melted butter over top of unsoaked bread cubes. Sprinkle brown sugar mixture evenly over top. Place bread pudding on baking sheet and bake on middle rack until custard has just set, pressing center of pudding with finger reveals no runny liquid, and center of pudding registers 170 degrees, 45 to 50 minutes. Transfer to wire rack and let cool until pudding is set and just warm, about 45 minutes. Serve.

BOURBON–BROWN SUGAR SAUCE
MAKES ABOUT 1 CUP

Rum can be substituted for the bourbon.

½	cup packed (3½ ounces) light brown sugar
7	tablespoons heavy cream
2½	tablespoons unsalted butter
1½	tablespoons bourbon

Whisk sugar and cream together in small saucepan set over medium heat until combined. Continue to cook, whisking frequently, until mixture comes to boil, about 5 minutes. Whisk in butter and bring mixture back to boil, about 1 minute. Remove from heat and whisk in bourbon. Let cool until just warm; serve with bread pudding.

PECAN BREAD PUDDING WITH BOURBON AND ORANGE

Add ⅔ cup chopped toasted pecans, 1 tablespoon all-purpose flour, and 1 tablespoon softened butter to brown sugar mixture in step 1 and mix until crumbly. Add 1 tablespoon bourbon and 2 teaspoons finely grated orange zest to egg yolk mixture in step 3.

RUM RAISIN BREAD PUDDING WITH CINNAMON

Combine ⅔ cup golden raisins and 5 teaspoons dark rum in small bowl. Microwave until hot, about 20 seconds; set aside to cool, about 15 minutes. Add ⅛ teaspoon ground cinnamon to brown sugar mixture in step 1 and stir cooled raisin mixture into custard in step 3.

SUMMER PUDDING

✔ WHY THIS RECIPE WORKS
If any food speaks of summer, the English dessert called summer pudding does. Ripe, fragrant, lightly sweetened berries are cooked gently to coax out their juices and then packed into a bowl lined with slices of bread. The berry juices soak and soften the bread to make it meld with the fruit. We set out to master this bright and flavorful summertime classic. Instead of lining the mold with bread and then filling it with berries, we opted to layer bread (cut out with a biscuit cutter) and berries together in ramekins; this way, the layers of bread on the inside would almost melt into the fruit. Combining the berries with sugar and lemon juice, and gently cooking the mixture for just five minutes, released just the right amount of juice and offset the tartness of the berries. We found that fresh bread became too gummy in the pudding, but bread dried in the oven had just the right consistency. We used potato bread; its even, tight-crumbed, tender texture

and light sweetness was a perfect match for the berries (challah makes a good substitute). To ensure that the puddings would come together and hold their shape, we weighted and refrigerated them for at least eight hours.

INDIVIDUAL SUMMER BERRY PUDDINGS

SERVES 6

For this recipe, you will need six 6-ounce ramekins and a round cookie cutter of a slightly smaller diameter than the ramekins. If you don't have the right size cutter, use a paring knife and the bottom of a ramekin (most ramekins taper toward the bottom) as a guide for trimming the rounds. If using challah, slice it about ½ inch thick. Summer berry pudding can be made up to 24 hours before serving; held any longer, the berries begin to lose their freshness. Whipped Cream (page 800) is the perfect accompaniment.

12	slices potato bread, challah, or hearty white sandwich bread
1¼	pounds strawberries, hulled and sliced (4 cups)
10	ounces (2 cups) raspberries
5	ounces (1 cup) blueberries
5	ounces (1 cup) blackberries
¾	cup (5¼ ounces) sugar
2	tablespoons lemon juice

1. Adjust oven rack to middle position and heat oven to 200 degrees. Place bread in single layer on rimmed baking sheet and bake until dry but not brittle, about 1 hour, flipping slices once and rotating baking sheet halfway through baking. Set aside to cool.

2. Combine strawberries, raspberries, blueberries, blackberries, and sugar in large saucepan and cook over medium heat, stirring occasionally, until berries begin to release their juices and sugar has dissolved,

ASSEMBLING INDIVIDUAL SUMMER BERRY PUDDINGS

1. Cut out rounds of bread with biscuit cutter.

4. Divide remaining fruit among ramekins (about ½ cup more per ramekin).

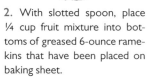

2. With slotted spoon, place ¼ cup fruit mixture into bottoms of greased 6-ounce ramekins that have been placed on baking sheet.

5. Lightly soak 1 round of bread and place on top of fruit in each ramekin; it should sit above lip of ramekin. Pour remaining fruit juice over bread and cover ramekins loosely with plastic wrap.

3. Lightly soak 1 round of bread in fruit juice in saucepan and place on top of fruit in each ramekin.

6. Place second baking sheet on top of ramekins, then weight with several heavy cans.

ASSEMBLING A LARGE SUMMER BERRY PUDDING

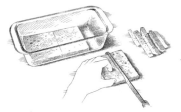

1. Remove crusts from bread slices and trim slices to fit in single layer in loaf pan (you will need 3 layers). Remove bread from pan.

2. Line greased loaf pan with plastic wrap. Spread about 2 cups fruit mixture over bottom. Lightly soak 1 layer of bread slices in fruit juices and place on top of fruit. Repeat 2 more times.

3. Top with remaining fruit juice, cover loosely with second sheet of plastic, and weight with another loaf pan and 2 or 3 heavy cans.

about 5 minutes. Off heat, stir in lemon juice; cool to room temperature.

3. Spray six 6-ounce ramekins with vegetable oil spray and place on rimmed baking sheet. Use cookie cutter to cut out 12 bread rounds that are slightly smaller in diameter than ramekins.

4. Using slotted spoon, place ¼ cup fruit mixture in each ramekin. Lightly soak 1 bread round in fruit juice in saucepan and place on top of fruit in ramekin; repeat with 5 more bread rounds and remaining ramekins. Divide remaining fruit among ramekins, about ½ cup per ramekin. Lightly soak 1 bread round in juice and place on top of fruit in ramekin (it should sit above lip of ramekin); repeat with remaining 5 bread rounds and remaining ramekins. Pour remaining fruit juice over bread and cover ramekins loosely with plastic wrap. Place second baking sheet on top of ramekins and weight it with heavy cans. Refrigerate puddings for at least 8 hours or up to 24 hours.

5. Remove cans and baking sheet and uncover puddings. Loosen puddings by running paring knife around edge of each ramekin, unmold into individual bowls, and serve immediately.

LARGE SUMMER BERRY PUDDING
SERVES 6 TO 8

You will need a 9 by 5-inch loaf pan for this recipe. Because there is no need to cut out rounds for this version, you will need only about 8 slices of bread, depending on their size.

Trim crusts from toasted bread and trim slices to fit in single layer in loaf pan (you will need about 2½ slices per layer; there will be three layers). Spray 9 by 5-inch loaf pan with vegetable oil spray, line with plastic wrap, and place on rimmed baking sheet. Using slotted spoon, spread about 2 cups fruit mixture evenly over bottom of prepared pan. Lightly soak enough bread slices for 1 layer in fruit juice in saucepan and place on top of fruit. Repeat with 2 more layers of fruit and bread. Pour remaining fruit juice over bread and cover loosely with plastic wrap. Place second baking sheet on top of loaf pan and weight it with heavy cans. Refrigerate pudding as directed. When ready to serve, invert pudding onto serving platter, remove loaf pan and plastic, slice, and serve.

CAPPUCCINO SEMIFREDDO

✔ WHY THIS RECIPE WORKS

Semifreddo, a classic Italian dessert, is something of a cross between custard and ice cream. We set out to create our ideal version, which features a light coffee-flavored mousse speckled with crushed cookies or nuts. We had little trouble arriving at very good flavor (instant espresso powder was key). But what did give us trouble was the structure of our semifreddo—it either collapsed and lost its volume or stood up too high and airy when we incorporated all of the ingredients. We suspected that the solution to this problem resided in the meringue, which is a crucial component of the dessert. We opted for a cooked, or Italian, meringue, in which a hot sugar syrup is add to the egg whites as they are beaten. Because the syrup cooks the whites, the meringue becomes more stable and, we were pleased to find, better equipped to stand up to the addition of other ingredients, such as crushed biscotti and chopped almonds.

CAPPUCCINO SEMIFREDDO WITH BISCOTTI
SERVES 8

For the best results, chill the bowl and whisk attachment before whipping the cream. Drizzle slices of semifreddo with Warm Bittersweet Chocolate Sauce (recipe follows), if desired.

1	cup heavy cream, chilled
½	cup plus 2 tablespoons (4⅓ ounces) sugar
¼	cup water plus 1 tablespoon warm tap water
2	tablespoons instant espresso powder
3	large egg whites, room temperature
1	teaspoon vanilla extract
½	cup crushed almond biscotti or hazelnut biscotti

1. Line 8½ by 4½-inch loaf pan with plastic wrap, leaving 3-inch overhang all around, and place in freezer. Using stand mixer fitted with whisk, whip cream on medium-low speed until foamy, about 1 minute. Increase speed to high and whip until soft peaks form, 1 to 3 minutes. Transfer to bowl and refrigerate.

2. Bring ½ cup sugar and ¼ cup water to boil in small saucepan over medium-high heat and cook until mixture is slightly thickened and syrupy and registers 235 degrees, 3 to 4 minutes. Remove from heat and cover to keep warm.

3. Combine remaining 1 tablespoon water and espresso in small bowl and stir to dissolve. Using dry, clean bowl and whisk attachment, whip egg whites on medium-low speed until foamy, about 1 minute. Add 1 teaspoon sugar and increase speed to high; whip until soft peaks form, about 2 minutes. Gradually whip in remaining 5 teaspoons sugar. Reduce speed to medium and slowly add hot sugar syrup, avoiding whisk and sides of bowl. Increase speed to medium-high and continue to whip until mixture has cooled slightly and is very shiny and thick, 2 to 5 minutes. Add espresso mixture and vanilla.

4. Gently stir one-third of whipped cream into egg white mixture with rubber spatula; fold in remaining whipped cream and 6 tablespoons crushed biscotti. Transfer mixture to prepared pan, spreading evenly with spatula. Fold overhanging plastic over mixture and press gently onto surface; freeze until firm, at least 8 hours.

5. To unmold, remove plastic from surface and invert loaf pan onto serving platter. Remove plastic and smooth surface with spatula, if desired. Sprinkle with remaining crushed biscotti. Slice and serve immediately.

VANILLA SEMIFREDDO WITH ALMONDS AND AMARETTI

Omit instant espresso powder and water mixture in step 3. Substitute 6 tablespoons chopped toasted almonds and ⅓ cup crushed amaretti (6 cookies) for biscotti. Fold crushed amaretti and 4 tablespoons almonds into mixture in step 4. Sprinkle remaining almonds on unmolded semifreddo before serving.

CHOCOLATE ORANGE SEMIFREDDO

Substitute 1 tablespoon grated orange zest for espresso powder and water mixture and ½ cup crushed chocolate wafer cookies (15 cookies) for biscotti. Fold 6 tablespoons crushed cookies into mixture in step 4; sprinkle remaining crushed cookies on unmolded semifreddo before serving.

WARM BITTERSWEET CHOCOLATE SAUCE

Heat 6 ounces chopped bittersweet or semisweet chocolate and ¾ cup heavy cream in bowl set over 1 inch barely simmering water, stirring occasionally, until chocolate is melted and mixture is combined. Spoon over individual servings of semifreddo.

LEMON ICE

✔ WHY THIS RECIPE WORKS
With so few ingredients, lemon ice is regularly plagued by harsh and unbalanced flavors. We wanted a lemon ice that struck a perfect sweet-tart balance and hit lots of high notes—without so much as a trace of bitterness. A single cup of sugar gave our lemon ice the ideal amount of sweetness; less sugar gave it a pronounced bitterness, while more sugar made our ice taste like frozen lemonade from concentrate. We opted to use bottled water for the purest flavor and a bit of vodka for a soft, creamy, slightly slushy texture. A pinch of salt boosted the flavor. To achieve an ice with a fluffy, coarse-grained texture and crystalline crunch, we froze the mixture in ice cube trays, then pulsed them in the food processor.

LEMON ICE
MAKES 1 QUART

We recommend making this recipe with bottled water; tasters preferred lemon ice made with spring or mineral water. The addition of vodka yields the best texture, but it can be omitted if desired.

2¼	cups water
1	cup lemon juice (6 lemons)
1	cup (7 ounces) sugar
2	tablespoons vodka (optional)
⅛	teaspoon salt

1. Combine ingredients in medium bowl, whisking to dissolve sugar. Pour mixture into 2 ice cube trays and freeze until thoroughly frozen, at least 3 hours or up to 5 days frozen and transferred to zipper-lock bag.

2. Place medium bowl in freezer. Pulse half of ice cubes in food processor until creamy and no large lumps remain, about 18 pulses; transfer mixture to chilled bowl and freeze while pulsing remaining cubes.

3. Scoop ice into chilled dishes and serve immediately.

MINTED LEMON ICE

Bring 1 cup water, sugar, and salt to simmer in small saucepan over medium-high heat, stirring occasionally. Off heat, stir in ½ cup fresh mint leaves, roughly torn; let steep for 5 minutes, then strain mixture through fine-mesh strainer into medium bowl. Stir in remaining water, lemon juice, and vodka, let cool to room temperature, about 15 minutes, and freeze as directed.

LEMON-LIME ICE

Frozen margaritas were the inspiration for this variation.

Substitute ½ cup lime juice (4 limes) for ½ cup lemon juice and tequila for vodka.

LEMON-JASMINE ICE

Bring 1 cup water, sugar, and salt to simmer in small saucepan over medium-high heat, stirring occasionally. Off heat, add 2 jasmine tea bags; let steep for 5 minutes, then squeeze and discard tea bags and transfer mixture to medium bowl. Stir in remaining water, lemon juice, and vodka, let cool to room temperature, about 15 minutes, and freeze as directed.

LEMON-LAVENDER ICE

Bring 1 cup water, sugar, and salt to simmer in small saucepan over medium-high heat, stirring occasionally. Off heat, stir in 2½ teaspoons dried lavender; let steep for 5 minutes, then strain mixture through fine-mesh strainer into medium bowl. Stir in remaining water, lemon juice, and vodka, let cool to room temperature, about 15 minutes, and freeze as directed.

ORANGE ICE

Reduce lemon juice to 2 tablespoons and sugar to ¾ cup. Add ¾ cup orange juice (2 oranges) to mixture in step 1.

FRUIT GRANITA

✔ WHY THIS RECIPE WORKS

Granitas, the icy Italian dessert, are simple stuff: a flavorful fruit puree or liquid is combined with sugar and flavorings and then frozen. Traditionally, the liquid is frozen in a bowl and scraped every 30 minutes for several hours to produce a shimmering, granular dessert made up of individual ice crystals. We wanted a modern, timesaving technique that would produce a granita that came as close to the traditional texture as possible. We found a quicker way, using the food processor. We simply poured the flavored liquid into ice cube trays, and when the cubes had hardened we pulsed them into tiny ice shavings. The biggest challenge in making granitas with this method was obtaining the right texture. Pulsing small batches of ice cubes in the food processor ensured an even grinding.

MANGO GRANITA
SERVES 4

Be sure to use ripe mangos for this recipe.

1	pound mangos, peeled, pitted, and sliced thin
¾	cup water
⅓	cup (2⅓ ounces) sugar
1	tablespoon lemon juice

1. Combine mangos and water in blender and puree until smooth, about 2 minutes. Strain through fine-mesh strainer; discard pulp.

2. Add sugar and lemon juice and stir until sugar is dissolved. Pour into 2 ice cube trays and freeze mixture until firm, at least 2 hours or up to 5 days frozen and transferred to zipper-lock bag.

3. To serve, place single layer of frozen cubes in bowl of food processor. Pulse until no large chunks of ice remain, 10 to 12 pulses. Scoop into individual bowls and repeat with remaining cubes. Serve immediately.

MIMOSA GRANITA

Omit mangos and water. Increase sugar to ½ cup; whisk sugar and 1 cup orange juice (2 oranges) together until sugar dissolves. Substitute lime juice for lemon juice; stir lime juice and 1¼ cups sparkling wine into orange juice mixture. Pour into 2 ice cube trays and freeze and process as directed.

PLUM GRANITA

Substitute 1 pound plums, halved, pitted, and sliced thin, for mangos and increase water to 1¼ cups. Bring plums, water, sugar, and 1 cinnamon stick to boil in medium saucepan. Reduce heat and simmer until fruit is tender, about 5 minutes. Off heat, remove and discard cinnamon stick and stir in lemon juice. Transfer mixture to food processor and process until smooth. Strain mixture through fine-mesh strainer; discard solids. Pour puree into 2 ice cube trays and freeze and process as directed.

GRAPEFRUIT GRANITA

Omit mangos and lemon juice and reduce water to ½ cup. Whisk water, sugar, and 1½ cups pink grapefruit juice (2 grapefruits) together until sugar dissolves. Stir in 1 tablespoon Campari. Pour into 2 ice cube trays and freeze and process as directed.

ESPRESSO GRANITA

Omit mangos, water, and lemon juice and reduce sugar to ¼ cup. Whisk sugar and 2 cups hot espresso together until sugar dissolves. Let cool to room temperature and stir in 1 tablespoon amaretto. Pour into 2 ice cube trays and freeze and process as directed.

CAFÉ LATTE GRANITA

Omit mangos, water, and lemon juice and reduce sugar to 3 tablespoons. Whisk sugar and 1 cup hot espresso together until sugar dissolves. Let cool to room temperature and stir in 1¼ cups milk. Pour into 2 ice cube trays and freeze and process as directed.

FRUIT SORBETS

✔ WHY THIS RECIPE WORKS

Sorbets (a frozen mixture of pureed fruit or juice and sugar) should be creamy and silky. They literally melt in your mouth, almost like ice cream. But too often, sorbets turn out icy. We wanted to replicate our ideal at home. After tests involving gelatin, jam, egg whites, and corn syrup, we found the real key to a creamy sorbet: a high sugar concentration. By using ½ cup of sugar per cup of fruit (give or take a few tablespoons, depending on the fruit), we were able to achieve the desired result: a smooth, creamy texture without cloying sweetness. A small amount of lemon or lime juice balanced the sweetness perfectly. We also found that adding a tablespoon of high-proof alcohol (tasteless vodka worked well) improved the texture of the sorbet and permitted a slight reduction in the amount of sugar for stronger fruit flavor.

BERRY SORBET
MAKES ABOUT 1½ PINTS

If using a canister-style ice-cream machine, be sure to freeze the empty canister at least 24 hours and preferably 48 hours before churning. For self-refrigerating ice-cream machines, prechill the canister by running the machine for 5 to 10 minutes before pouring in the sorbet.

15   ounces (3 cups) raspberries, blackberries, or strawberries
1   cup (7 ounces) sugar
    Pinch salt
½   cup water
2   tablespoons lemon juice
1   tablespoon vodka (optional)

1. Pulse berries, sugar, and salt together in food processor until combined, about 15 pulses. With processor running, add water, lemon juice, and vodka, if using, and continue to process until sugar is dissolved, about 1 minute. Strain mixture through fine-mesh strainer into large bowl and refrigerate until completely chilled, about 1 hour.

2. Transfer mixture to ice-cream machine. Churn until mixture resembles soft-serve ice cream. Transfer sorbet to airtight container, press firmly to remove any air pockets, and freeze until firm, at least 3 hours. (Sorbet can be frozen for up to 1 week.)

ORANGE SORBET

Omit berries. Reduce sugar by 1 tablespoon and add 2 teaspoons grated orange zest to food processor with sugar and salt. Omit water and reduce lemon juice to 1 tablespoon; add 2 cups orange juice (4 oranges) to processor with lemon juice.

GRAPEFRUIT SORBET

Omit berries and lemon juice. Increase sugar by 1 tablespoon and add 2 teaspoons grated grapefruit zest to food processor with sugar and salt. Add 1½ cups grapefruit juice (3 grapefruits) to processor with water. Substitute Campari for vodka.

LEMON SORBET

Omit berries. Increase sugar to 1¼ cups and water to 1½ cups; add 2 teaspoons grated lemon zest to food processor with sugar and salt. Increase lemon juice to ½ cup (3 lemons).

LIME SORBET

Omit berries. Increase sugar to 1¼ cups and water to 1½ cups; add 2 teaspoons grated lime zest to food processor with sugar and salt. Substitute ½ cup lime juice (4 limes) for lemon juice.

BLUEBERRY SORBET

Substitute 12 ounces blueberries for berries.

PEACH SORBET

Substitute 2½ pounds peaches, peeled, halved, pitted, and chopped coarse, for berries. Reduce sugar by 1 tablespoon. Substitute rum or peach schnapps for vodka.

MANGO SORBET

Substitute 3 mangos, peeled, pitted, and chopped coarse, for berries. Reduce sugar to ¾ cup plus 1 tablespoon.

PINEAPPLE SORBET

Substitute 1 small pineapple, peeled, cored, and chopped coarse, for berries. Reduce sugar to ¾ cup and lemon juice to 1 tablespoon.

FRUIT SHERBET

✔ WHY THIS RECIPE WORKS

The perfect sherbet recipe is a cross between sorbet and ice cream, containing fruit, sugar, and dairy but no egg yolks. Like its foreign cousin, sorbet, sherbet should taste vibrant and fresh. In the case of sherbet, however, its assertive flavor is tempered by the creamy addition of dairy. Ideally, it is as smooth as ice cream but devoid of ice cream's richness and weight. We we began with classic orange sherbet. For bright flavor, we started by combining fruit zest and sugar together in a food processor before adding 2 cups of orange juice. A small amount of alcohol ensured the sherbet had a smooth, silky texture, and whipped heavy cream lightened the texture of our frozen dessert. To guarantee sherbet with an even consistency, we prepared it in an ice-cream machine and then come up with variations with lime, lemon, and raspberries.

FRESH ORANGE SHERBET
MAKES ABOUT 1 QUART

If using a canister-style ice-cream machine, be sure to freeze the empty canister at least 24 hours and preferably 48 hours before churning. For self-refrigerating ice-cream machines, prechill the canister by running the machine for 5 to 10 minutes before pouring in the sherbet. For the freshest, purest orange flavor, use freshly squeezed unpasteurized orange juice (either store-bought or juiced at home). Pasteurized fresh-squeezed juice makes an acceptable though noticeably less fresh-tasting sherbet. Do not use juice made from concentrate, which has a cooked and less bright flavor.

1 cup (7 ounces) sugar
1 tablespoon grated orange zest plus 2 cups juice (4 oranges)
⅛ teaspoon salt
3 tablespoons lemon juice
2 teaspoons triple sec or vodka
⅔ cup heavy cream

1. Pulse sugar, orange zest, and salt in food processor until damp, 10 to 15 pulses. With processor running, add orange juice and lemon juice in slow, steady stream; continue to process until sugar is fully dissolved, about 1 minute. Strain mixture through fine-mesh strainer into medium bowl; stir in triple sec, then cover and place in freezer until chilled and mixture registers about 40 degrees, 30 minutes to 1 hour. Do not let mixture freeze.

2. When mixture is chilled, using whisk, whip cream in medium bowl until soft peaks form. Whisking constantly, add juice mixture in steady stream, pouring against edge of bowl. Transfer to ice-cream machine and churn until mixture resembles thick soft-serve ice cream, 25 to 30 minutes.

3. Transfer sherbet to airtight container, press firmly to remove any air pockets, and freeze until firm, at least 3 hours. (Sherbet can be frozen for up to 1 week.)

FRESH LIME SHERBET

Substitute lime zest for orange zest, increase sugar to 1 cup plus 2 tablespoons, and omit lemon juice. Substitute ⅔ cup lime juice (6 limes) combined with 1½ cups water for orange juice.

FRESH LEMON SHERBET

Omit orange juice. Substitute lemon zest for orange zest, increase sugar to 1 cup plus 2 tablespoons, and increase lemon juice to ⅔ cup (4 lemons). Combine lemon juice with 1½ cups water before adding to food processor.

FRESH RASPBERRY SHERBET

In-season fresh raspberries have the best flavor, but when they are not in season, frozen raspberries are a better option. Substitute a 12-ounce bag of frozen raspberries for fresh.

Omit orange zest and juice. Cook 15 ounces (3 cups) raspberries with sugar, salt, and ¾ cup water in medium saucepan over medium heat, stirring occasionally, until mixture just begins to simmer, about 7 minutes. Strain through fine-mesh strainer into medium bowl, pressing on solids to extract as much liquid as possible. Add lemon juice and triple sec; cover and place in freezer until chilled and mixture registers about 40 degrees, 30 minutes to 1 hour. Proceed as directed.

ULTIMATE VANILLA ICE CREAM

◆ WHY THIS RECIPE WORKS
Homemade vanilla ice cream is never as creamy, smooth, or dense as the impossibly smooth "super-premium" ice cream found at gourmet markets or high-end ice cream shops. We wanted an incredibly creamy, dense, custard-based vanilla ice cream that would rival any pricey artisanal batch. A vanilla bean delivered the best vanilla flavor. And a combination of heavy cream and whole milk, along with egg yolks, yielded ice cream with just the right amount of richness. Creating smooth ice cream means reducing the size of the ice crystals; the smaller they are, the less perceptible they are. Our first move was to replace some of the sugar in our custard base with corn syrup, which interferes with crystal formation, making for a super-smooth texture. To speed up the freezing process, thereby ensuring small ice crystals, we froze a portion of the custard prior to churning, then mixed it with the remaining refrigerated custard. Finally, instead of freezing the churned ice cream in a tall container, we spread it into a thin layer in a cold metal baking pan and chilled it, which allowed the ice cream to firm up more quickly and helped deliver the smooth texture we were after.

VANILLA ICE CREAM
MAKES ABOUT 1 QUART

Two teaspoons of vanilla extract can be substituted for the vanilla bean; stir the extract into the cold custard in step 3. An instant-read thermometer is critical for the best results. Using a prechilled metal baking pan and working quickly in step 4 will help prevent melting and refreezing of the ice cream and will speed the hardening process. If using a canister-style ice-cream machine, be sure to freeze the empty canister at least 24 hours and preferably 48 hours before churning. For self-refrigerating ice-cream machines, prechill the canister by running the machine for 5 to 10 minutes before pouring in the custard.

While developing our recipe for Vanilla Ice Cream, we uncovered a few ground rules for adding mix-ins. These guidelines apply to any homemade ice cream.

FREEZE FIRST: To keep mix-ins from raising the ice cream's temperature, freeze them for at least 15 minutes before adding them to the ice-cream maker.

STRAIN: Shake chopped ingredients like chocolate and nuts in a mesh strainer to remove small particles that can detract from the ice cream's smooth consistency.

ADD JUST ENOUGH: Add no more than ¾ cup of coarsely chopped (¼- to ½-inch) mix-ins per quart of ice cream to provide textural contrast without dominating the ice cream. Scale down to ½ cup when using potent ingredients such as crystallized ginger or crushed peppermint candies.

WAIT UNTIL LAST MINUTE: Add mix-ins during the final minute of churning to ensure even distribution without interrupting the freezing process.

1	vanilla bean
1¾	cups heavy cream
1¼	cups whole milk
½	cup plus 2 tablespoons (4⅓ ounces) sugar
⅓	cup light corn syrup
¼	teaspoon salt
6	large egg yolks

1. Place 8- or 9-inch square metal baking pan in freezer. Cut vanilla bean in half lengthwise. Using tip of paring knife, scrape out vanilla seeds. Combine vanilla bean, seeds, cream, milk, 6 tablespoons sugar, corn syrup, and salt in medium saucepan. Heat over medium-high heat, stirring occasionally, until mixture is steaming steadily and registers 175 degrees, 5 to 10 minutes. Remove saucepan from heat.

2. While cream mixture heats, whisk egg yolks and remaining ¼ cup sugar in bowl until smooth, about 30 seconds. Slowly whisk 1 cup heated cream mixture into egg yolk mixture. Return mixture to saucepan and cook over medium-low heat, stirring constantly, until mixture thickens and registers 180 degrees, 7 to 14 minutes. Immediately pour custard into large bowl and let cool until no longer steaming, 10 to 20 minutes. Transfer 1 cup custard to small bowl. Cover both bowls with plastic wrap. Place large bowl in refrigerator and small

bowl in freezer and let cool completely, at least 4 hours or up to 24 hours. (Small bowl of custard will freeze solid.)

3. Remove custards from refrigerator and freezer. Scrape frozen custard from small bowl into large bowl of custard. Stir occasionally until frozen custard has fully dissolved. Strain custard through fine-mesh strainer and transfer to ice-cream machine. Churn until mixture resembles thick soft-serve ice cream and registers about 21 degrees, 15 to 25 minutes. Transfer ice cream to frozen baking pan and press plastic wrap on surface. Return to freezer until firm around edges, about 1 hour.

4. Transfer ice cream to airtight container, press firmly to remove any air pockets, and freeze until firm, at least 2 hours. (Ice cream can be frozen for up to 5 days.)

TRIPLE GINGER ICE CREAM

Freeze the crystallized ginger for at least 15 minutes before adding it to the churning ice cream.

Omit vanilla bean. Add one 3-inch piece fresh ginger, peeled and sliced into thin rounds, and 2 teaspoons ground ginger to cream and milk mixture in step 1 and heat as directed. Add ½ cup chopped crystallized ginger to ice cream during last minute of churning.

COFFEE CRUNCH ICE CREAM

Look for chocolate-covered cocoa nibs (roasted pieces of the cocoa bean) in chocolate shops or well-stocked supermarkets. Freeze the cocoa nibs for at least 15 minutes before adding them to the churning ice cream.

Omit vanilla bean. Add ½ cup coarsely ground coffee to cream and milk mixture in step 1 and heat as directed. Add ¾ cup chocolate-covered cocoa nibs to ice cream during last minute of churning.

CHOCOLATE ICE CREAM

✔ **WHY THIS RECIPE WORKS**
Chocolate ice cream often ends up either too heavy on the dairy, which obscures the chocolate flavor, or too heavy on the chocolate, which dulls the creamy richness, resulting in an overly heavy dessert. We wanted a balanced homemade chocolate ice cream—rich in both flavor and texture. For the lushest texture, we started with a custard base. Although five or six egg yolks delivered an excellent texture, we found that the egg flavor became too pronounced. Four egg yolks gave the ice cream the appropriate silkiness. For the dairy, we found an equal amount of heavy cream and whole milk struck the right balance between creamy texture and richness. Finally, for the starring ingredient, high-quality bittersweet chocolate provided all the deep, nuanced chocolate flavor that we clamored for.

CHOCOLATE ICE CREAM
MAKES ABOUT 1 QUART

This ice cream should be made high-quality bittersweet chocolate; we like Callebaut Intense Dark Chocolate and Ghirardelli Bittersweet Chocolate. An instant-read thermometer is critical for the best results. Using a prechilled metal baking pan and working quickly in step 6 will help prevent melting and refreezing of the ice cream and will speed the hardening process. If using a canister-style ice-cream machine, be sure to freeze the empty canister at least 24 hours and preferably 48 hours before churning. For self-refrigerating ice-cream machines, prechill the canister by running the machine for 5 to 10 minutes before pouring in the custard.

8	ounces bittersweet chocolate, chopped coarse
1½	cups whole milk
1½	cups heavy cream
¾	cup (5¼ ounces) sugar
4	large egg yolks
1	teaspoon vanilla extract

1. Place 8- or 9-inch square metal baking pan in freezer. Microwave chocolate in bowl at 50 percent power, stirring occasionally, until melted, 2 to 4 minutes. Set aside to cool.

2. Meanwhile, place fine-mesh strainer over medium bowl and set over larger bowl of ice water. Combine milk, cream, and ½ cup sugar in medium saucepan. Heat over medium-high heat, stirring occasionally, until mixture is steaming steadily and registers 175 degrees, 5 to 10 minutes. Remove saucepan from heat.

3. While cream mixture heats, whisk egg yolks and remaining ¼ cup sugar in bowl until smooth, about 30 seconds. Add melted chocolate and whisk until fully incorporated.

4. Slowly whisk half of heated cream mixture into egg yolk mixture, ½ cup at a time. Return mixture to saucepan and cook over medium-low heat, stirring constantly, until mixture thickens and registers 180 degrees, 7 to 14 minutes. Immediately strain custard through fine-mesh strainer and let cool over bowl of ice water to room temperature, stirring occasionally. Stir in vanilla, then cover and refrigerate until custard registers 40 degrees, at least 3 hours or up to 24 hours.

5. Transfer custard to ice-cream machine and churn until mixture resembles thick soft-serve ice cream, 25 to 30 minutes. Transfer ice cream to frozen baking pan and press plastic wrap on surface. Return to freezer until firm around edges, about 1 hour.

6. Transfer ice cream to airtight container, press firmly to remove any air pockets, and freeze until firm, at least 2 hours. (Ice cream can be frozen for up to 2 days.)

FRESH PEACH ICE CREAM

✔ WHY THIS RECIPE WORKS

When made with ripe, in-season fruit and a rich custard base, homemade peach ice cream delivers an ultra-fresh, creamy-smooth sensation that commercial brands can't match. But working with peaches can be a challenge because the moisture in peaches can turn into ice during freezing, producing an ice cream studded with fruit chunks that are as hard as marbles. We set out to make a rich, creamy ice cream with vibrant peach flavor and tender bites of fruit. We found that the right amount of sugar was key; it not only helped to sweeten the custard but also lowered the freezing point, which made for a softer, smoother, and less icy ice cream. To maximize the fresh fruit flavor, we opted to limit the time our peaches spent heating. We did this by mixing the peaches together with the sugar and letting them stand until they were partially softened and had exuded some of their juices. Just a few minutes over medium-high heat softened our peaches further until they were perfectly tender. We then strained the peaches, adding their liquid to the custard base at the start of churning, and then added the peaches in toward the end of churning. The result? Creamy, intensely flavored peach ice cream with soft, not icy, bites of fruit throughout. We found this method worked equally well with strawberries.

FRESH PEACH ICE CREAM
MAKES ABOUT 1 QUART

Both the cooked peaches and the custard mixture must be cooled to 40 degrees before you churn them. An instant-read thermometer is critical for the best results. You'll get the very best results from using in-season, fully ripened peaches, but in a pinch, you can substitute 2 cups frozen sliced peaches and replace the vodka with peach-flavored liqueur. If your peaches are firm, you should be able to peel them with a sharp vegetable peeler. If they are too soft to withstand the pressure of a peeler, you'll need to blanch them in a pot of simmering water for 15 seconds and then shock them in a bowl of ice water before peeling. Though the frozen ice cream will keep in the freezer for up to 2 days, its flavor and texture are best when it is eaten the day it is made.

1	pound peaches, peeled, halved, pitted, and cut into ½-inch pieces
1	cup plus 6 tablespoons (9⅔ ounces) sugar
½	teaspoon lemon juice
	Pinch salt
1⅓	cups heavy cream
1¼	cups whole milk
6	large egg yolks
1	teaspoon vanilla extract
2	tablespoons vodka

1. Combine peaches, ½ cup sugar, lemon juice, and salt in bowl; let stand until pool of syrupy liquid accumulates and peaches soften slightly, 1 to 1½ hours.

2. Place fine-mesh strainer over medium bowl and set over larger bowl of ice water. Combine cream, milk, and ½ cup sugar in medium saucepan. Heat over medium-high heat, stirring occasionally, until mixture is steaming steadily and registers 175 degrees, 5 to 10 minutes. Remove saucepan from heat.

3. While cream mixture heats, whisk egg yolks and remaining 6 tablespoons sugar in bowl until smooth, about 30 seconds. Slowly whisk half of heated cream mixture into egg yolk mixture, ½ cup at a time. Return mixture to saucepan and cook over medium-low heat, stirring constantly, until mixture thickens and registers 180 degrees, 7 to 14 minutes. Immediately strain custard through fine-mesh strainer and let cool over bowl of ice water to room temperature, stirring occasionally. Stir in vanilla, then cover and refrigerate until custard registers 40 degrees, at least 3 hours or up to 24 hours.

4. Meanwhile, transfer peaches and their liquid to medium saucepan and heat, stirring occasionally, over medium-high heat until tender and flesh has broken down, 3 to 4 minutes. Transfer to bowl, stir in vodka, and refrigerate until chilled, at least 4 hours or up to 24 hours.

5. Strain chilled peaches through fine-mesh strainer, reserving liquid. Stir reserved peach liquid into chilled custard; transfer custard to ice-cream machine and churn until mixture resembles soft-serve ice cream, 25 to 30 minutes. Add peaches; continue to churn until combined, about 30 seconds. Transfer ice cream to airtight container, press firmly to remove any air pockets, and freeze until firm, at least 2 hours.

LIGHTER FRESH PEACH ICE CREAM

Increase peaches to 1½ pounds and reduce sugar to 1 cup. Increase milk to 1½ cups and reduce heavy cream to ¼ cup, egg yolks to 4, and vodka to 1½ tablespoons. For each sugar addition, use ⅓ cup.

FRESH STRAWBERRY ICE CREAM
MAKES ABOUT 1 QUART

Though the frozen ice cream will keep in the freezer for up to 2 days, its flavor and texture are best when it is eaten the day it is made. An instant-read thermometer is critical for the best results.

1	pound strawberries, hulled and sliced thin (3¼ cups)
1¼	cups (8¾ ounces) sugar
	Pinch salt
1⅓	cups heavy cream
1¼	cups whole milk
6	large egg yolks
3	tablespoons vodka
1	teaspoon lemon juice
1	teaspoon vanilla extract

1. Combine strawberries, ½ cup sugar, and salt in bowl. Mash berries gently with potato masher until slightly broken down. Let stand, stirring occasionally, until berries have released their juice and sugar has dissolved, 40 to 45 minutes.

2. Place fine-mesh strainer over medium bowl and set over larger bowl of ice water. Combine cream, milk, and ½ cup sugar in medium saucepan. Heat over medium-high heat, stirring occasionally, until mixture is steaming steadily and registers 175 degrees, 5 to 10 minutes. Remove saucepan from heat.

3. While cream mixture heats, whisk egg yolks and remaining ¼ cup sugar in bowl until smooth, about 30 seconds. Slowly whisk half of heated cream mixture into egg yolk mixture, ½ cup at a time. Return mixture to saucepan and cook over medium-low heat, stirring constantly, until mixture thickens and registers 180 degrees, 7 to 14 minutes. Immediately strain custard through fine-mesh strainer and let cool over bowl of ice water to room temperature, stirring occasionally.

4. While custard is cooling, transfer berries to medium saucepan and bring to simmer over medium-high heat, stirring occasionally, until berries are softened and broken down, about 3 minutes. Strain berries, reserving juice. Transfer berries to small bowl; stir in vodka and lemon juice, then let cool to room temperature, cover, and refrigerate until cold. Stir vanilla and reserved juice into cooled custard, cover, and refrigerate until custard registers 40 degrees, at least 3 hours or up to 24 hours.

5. Transfer custard to ice-cream machine and churn until mixture resembles thick soft-serve ice cream, 25 to 30 minutes. Add berries; continue to churn until fully incorporated and berries are slightly broken down, about 1 minute. Transfer ice cream to airtight container, press firmly to remove any air pockets, and freeze until firm, at least 2 hours.

FROZEN YOGURT

✔ WHY THIS RECIPE WORKS
Recipes for homemade frozen yogurt often result in an icy slab with a grainy texture from the sugar and an overly tangy flavor from the namesake ingredient. We wanted frozen yogurt with a smooth texture and a mildly tangy yet complex flavor profile featuring main ingredients such as vanilla, chocolate, coffee, or fresh fruit. For our recipe, we solved the problem of overly tart yogurt flavor and grainy sugar by adding some milk. Not only did it tame the yogurt flavor but, when simmered briefly, the milk made it possible to dissolve the sugar. To cut down on iciness, we found that draining the yogurt of excess liquid was helpful, as was using a small amount of gelatin. In premium ice creams, egg yolks are responsible for the rich, silky texture; gelatin serves the same purpose in our frozen yogurt, resulting in a creamy, velvety frozen dessert.

VANILLA FROZEN YOGURT
MAKES I GENEROUS QUART

The frozen yogurt will be soft at the end of churning, but it can be served this way, or it can be chilled until firm. If using a canister-style ice-cream machine, be sure to freeze the empty canister at least 24 hours and preferably 48 hours before churning. For self-refrigerating ice-cream machines, prechill the canister by running the machine for 5 to 10 minutes before pouring in the yogurt. Though the frozen yogurt will keep in the freezer for up to 2 days, its flavor and texture are best when it is eaten the day it is made.

- 2 cups plain low-fat yogurt
- 2 teaspoons unflavored gelatin
- 1¾ cups whole milk
- 1 vanilla bean
- ¾ cup plus 2 tablespoons (6⅛ ounces) sugar

1. Place yogurt in fine-mesh strainer set over liquid measuring cup and refrigerate; let drain until yogurt releases ½ cup liquid, 1 to 2 hours.

2. Sprinkle gelatin over ¼ cup milk in small bowl and let sit until gelatin softens, about 5 minutes.

3. Meanwhile, cut vanilla bean in half lengthwise. Using tip of paring knife, scrape out seeds. Combine vanilla bean and seeds, remaining 1½ cups milk, and sugar in small saucepan and heat over medium-high heat, stirring occasionally, until mixture is steaming and sugar is dissolved. Remove pan from heat.

4. Add softened gelatin to hot milk mixture, stirring until completely dissolved. Remove and discard vanilla bean. Let mixture cool to room temperature over bowl of ice water, then combine with drained yogurt. Cover and refrigerate until mixture registers 40 degrees, at least 3 hours or up to 24 hours.

5. Transfer yogurt to ice-cream machine and churn until frozen. Transfer frozen yogurt to airtight container, press firmly to remove any air pockets, and freeze until firm, at least 2 hours.

CHOCOLATE FROZEN YOGURT

We prefer Dutch-processed cocoa in this recipe; it has a mellower flavor and is not as harsh as natural cocoa.

Omit vanilla bean. Increase sugar to 1 cup and add 6 tablespoons Dutch-processed cocoa to milk along with sugar. Stir in 1 teaspoon vanilla extract after milk mixture cools to room temperature in step 4.

COFFEE FROZEN YOGURT

If you prefer to use fresh coffee, steep 3 tablespoons coarsely ground coffee in the hot milk-sugar mixture until strongly flavored, about 20 minutes. Strain and discard the ground coffee and reheat the mixture before adding the gelatin.

Omit vanilla bean. Increase sugar to 1 cup and whisk 6 to 7 teaspoons instant espresso powder into hot milk mixture. Stir in 1 teaspoon vanilla extract after milk mixture cools to room temperature in step 4.

STRAWBERRY FROZEN YOGURT
MAKES I GENEROUS QUART

Really ripe, sweet fruit will make a tremendous difference in this recipe. The liquid in the strawberries makes this frozen yogurt icy fairly quickly, so rather than storing it, you are better off eating it the day it is made.

- 2 cups plain low-fat yogurt
- 10 ounces strawberries, hulled and sliced thin (2 cups)
- ¾ cup (5¼ ounces) sugar
- 1 teaspoon vanilla extract

- 1 cup whole milk
- 2 teaspoons unflavored gelatin

1. Place yogurt in fine-mesh strainer set over liquid measuring cup and refrigerate; let drain until yogurt releases ½ cup liquid, 1 to 2 hours.

2. Meanwhile, combine berries, ¼ cup sugar, and vanilla in bowl. Crush fruit lightly with potato masher. Let stand, stirring occasionally, until berries have released their juice and sugar has dissolved, 40 to 45 minutes.

3. Sprinkle gelatin over ¼ cup milk in small bowl and let sit until gelatin softens, about 5 minutes.

4. Meanwhile, combine remaining ¾ cup milk and remaining ½ cup sugar in small saucepan and heat over medium-high heat, stirring occasionally, until mixture is steaming and sugar is dissolved. Remove pan from heat.

5. Add softened gelatin to hot milk mixture, stirring until completely dissolved. Let mixture cool to room temperature over bowl of ice water, then combine with drained yogurt and berries. Cover and refrigerate until mixture registers 40 degrees, at least 3 hours or up to 24 hours.

6. Transfer yogurt to ice-cream machine and churn until frozen. Transfer frozen yogurt to airtight container, press firmly to remove any air pockets, and freeze until firm, at least 2 hours.

RASPBERRY FROZEN YOGURT

Substitute 20 ounces fresh or thawed frozen raspberries for the strawberries; after macerating for 40 to 45 minutes in step 2, strain berries through fine-mesh strainer to remove seeds. Proceed as directed.

ICE-CREAM SANDWICHES

✔ WHY THIS RECIPE WORKS

Most store-bought ice-cream sandwiches are disappointing, made of subpar ice cream and sticky chocolate cookies that somehow manage to taste nothing like chocolate. But homemade ice-cream sandwiches can be a chore. We hoped to find a quick and easy process for homemade ice cream sandwiches. For the cookie component, we turned to a chocolate batter made with flour, cocoa powder, eggs, sugar, and chocolate syrup—which both heightened the chocolate flavor and made for soft and chewy cookies. Rather than rolling balls of cookie dough one at a time, we were able to simply pour the batter onto a rimmed baking sheet—just like brownies. Once the batter had baked and cooled, we cut out perfect circles of cookies with a biscuit cutter. For the ice cream, we placed the pint container on its side and sliced it into rounds, then we stamped out evenly matched rounds of ice cream with the same biscuit cutter. Without a lot of fuss, we had great ice cream sandwiches with fresh-baked flavor.

ICE-CREAM SANDWICHES
MAKES 8 ICE CREAM SANDWICHES

The batter will be very thick; greasing the baking sheet before lining it with parchment paper will make it easier to spread the batter in an even layer. For a dressed-up dessert, roll the sides in chopped nuts, sprinkles, or chocolate chips.

1	cup (5 ounces) all-purpose flour
½	cup (1½ ounces) Dutch-processed cocoa
¼	teaspoon salt
⅛	teaspoon baking soda
2	large eggs
⅔	cup (4⅔ ounces) sugar
¼	cup (2¾ ounces) chocolate syrup
8	tablespoons unsalted butter, melted
2	pints vanilla, chocolate, or coffee ice cream

CUTTING ICE-CREAM ROUNDS

1. Using serrated knife, slice away bottom of each ice-cream container. Dip knife in warm water, wipe clean, and cut four ¾-inch-thick rounds, each time making small slice into pint then rotating container, cutting through entire pint.

2. With same biscuit cutter used to cut cookie rounds, cut out round from each ice-cream slice. Place cut ice-cream round on cookie bottom, then top with another cookie, shiny side up.

---

1. Adjust oven rack to middle position and heat oven to 350 degrees. Grease 18 by 13-inch rimmed baking sheet and line with parchment paper.

2. Sift flour, cocoa, salt, and baking soda in medium bowl. Beat eggs, sugar, and chocolate syrup in large bowl until mixture is combined and light brown. Add melted butter and whisk until fully incorporated.

3. Add dry ingredients to egg mixture. With rubber spatula, gradually incorporate dry ingredients; stir until batter is evenly moistened and no dry streaks remain. Pour batter into prepared sheet; using offset spatula, spread batter evenly in pan. Bake until cookie springs back when touched, 10 to 12 minutes, rotating baking sheet halfway through baking. Let cool in pan on wire rack for 5 minutes, then run paring knife around edges of sheet to loosen. Invert cookie onto large cutting board; carefully peel off parchment. Cool to room temperature, about 30 minutes.

4. Using 2¾- to 3-inch round biscuit cutter, cut 16 rounds from baked cookie. Using serrated knife, slice away bottoms of ice-cream containers. Dip knife in warm water, wipe clean, and slice four

¾-inch-thick rounds from each container, cutting through cardboard. Peel away and discard cardboard. Using same biscuit cutter, cut out rounds from each ice-cream slice. Assemble ice-cream sandwiches, placing ice-cream round on cookie bottom, then topping with another cookie, shiny side up. Serve immediately or freeze on aluminum foil–lined baking sheet, covered with foil, for up to 3 hours. (Sandwiches can be frozen, wrapped individually in waxed paper, then foil, for up to 1 week; let sandwiches sit at room temperature for 10 minutes before serving.)

HOT FUDGE SAUCE

✔ WHY THIS RECIPE WORKS

Commercial hot fudge sauces, while readily available, are often overly sweet and lack chocolate flavor. High-end chocolate makers have their own sauces, which can be quite good, but their cost can often be prohibitive. Homemade hot fudge sauces pose their own problems, as they often turn out grainy and overcooked. We wanted to develop a recipe for hot fudge that was lush and complex, intensely chocolaty, smooth and satiny, and mildly sweet. To produce the intense chocolate flavor we were after, we used not one but two types of chocolate: Dutch-processed cocoa (for its deep flavor and rich color) and semisweet chocolate. To make sure the sugar was completely dissolved, thereby avoiding any graininess, we melted the chocolate separately and added it to the other ingredients only after the sugar had dissolved. Separating out the chocolate also minimized the time that it was exposed to heat, which served to keep it from tasting "overcooked." Our hot fudge sauce was now smooth and silky, with deep chocolate flavor.

HOT FUDGE SAUCE
MAKES ABOUT 2 CUPS

Sifting the cocoa powder prevents lumps from forming in the sauce.

- 10 ounces semisweet chocolate, chopped
- ⅓ cup (1 ounce) Dutch-processed cocoa, sifted
- ¾ cup light corn syrup
- ⅓ cup (2⅓ ounces) sugar
- ⅓ cup heavy cream
- ⅓ cup water
  Pinch salt
- 3 tablespoons unsalted butter, cut into ¼-inch pieces
- 1 teaspoon vanilla extract

1. Microwave chocolate in bowl at 50 percent power, stirring occasionally, until melted, 2 to 4 minutes. Whisk in cocoa until dissolved; set aside.

2. Heat corn syrup, sugar, cream, water, and salt in medium saucepan over low heat without stirring until sugar dissolves. Increase heat to medium-high; simmer mixture, stirring frequently, about 4 minutes.

3. Off heat, whisk in butter and vanilla.

Let cool slightly, about 2 minutes; whisk in melted chocolate mixture. Serve warm. (Sauce can be refrigerated for up to 2 weeks.)

CARAMEL SAUCE

✔ WHY THIS RECIPE WORKS

Caramel is at home in many settings, whether drizzled over a slice of pound cake, pooled at the base of a flan, or wrapped around a crisp apple. Part of what fascinates about caramel is its alchemy—the transformation of white, odorless sugar into aromatic gold. But this is why many cooks tend to shy away from making caramel; while the transformation that takes place is simple, homemade caramel sauce has a tendency to burn and recrystallize. To reduce the guesswork and anxiety that seem inseparably linked to making caramel sauce at home, we developed a recipe in which the sugar is added after the water, making stirring unnecessary. Increasing the proportion of water in our caramel sauce prevented the sugar from traveling up the sides of the pot, and keeping the pot covered allowed condensation to dissolve any stray crystals. While little can be done to quell the vigorous bubbling when the cream is added, we found that heating the cream beforehand helped.

CLASSIC CARAMEL SAUCE
MAKES ABOUT 2 CUPS

If you don't own a candy thermometer, follow the time approximations in the recipe and watch the color of the sugar syrup; it should be a deep amber color before the cream is added. To keep the sauce from clumping, make sure the cream is hot before adding it to the sugar syrup; try to coordinate it so that the cream reaches a simmer when the sugar syrup reaches 350 degrees.

- 1 cup water
- 2 cups (14 ounces) sugar
- 1 cup heavy cream
  Pinch salt
- 2 tablespoons unsalted butter, chilled

1. Pour water into medium saucepan; pour sugar into center of pan, taking care not to let sugar crystals touch side of pan. Cover and bring to boil over high heat. Uncover and continue to boil until syrup is thick and straw-colored and registers 300 degrees, about 15 minutes. Reduce heat to medium; continue to cook until sugar is deep amber and registers 350 degrees, about 5 minutes.

2. Meanwhile, bring cream and salt to simmer in small saucepan over high heat. (If cream reaches simmer before syrup reaches 350 degrees, remove cream from heat and set aside.)

3. Remove sugar syrup from heat. Carefully pour about one-quarter of hot cream into sugar syrup (mixture will bubble vigorously); let bubbling subside. Add remaining cream; let bubbling subside. Whisk gently until smooth, then whisk in butter. Let cool until warm and serve. (Sauce can be refrigerated for up to 2 weeks.)

CARAMEL SAUCE WITH DARK RUM

Whisk 3 tablespoons dark rum into finished sauce.

COCONUT-GINGER CARAMEL SAUCE

Stir one 3-inch piece ginger, peeled and sliced into thin rounds, and ¼ teaspoon coconut extract into finished sauce. Let sit to infuse flavors, about 10 minutes; strain through fine-mesh strainer.

Whisk 3 tablespoons Kahlúa, 1 tablespoon instant espresso powder, and 2 teaspoons finely grated orange zest into finished sauce.

BUTTERSCOTCH SAUCE

✓ WHY THIS RECIPE WORKS

Supermarket shelves are teeming with prepared dessert sauces, especially butterscotch-flavored sauces. But they usually taste artificial and cloyingly sweet, with a one-note flavor profile. We set out to develop our own recipe, with the goal being a complexly flavored sauce that balanced the richness of the butter with the depth of the brown sugar. For the base of our sauce, we heated a cup of brown sugar with a stick of butter. Once they came together, we added some heavy cream to ensure a thick, velvety texture and vanilla to round out the sauce's flavor. A small amount of corn syrup made it pour smoothly over ice cream, gelato, or anything else we drizzled it over.

BUTTERSCOTCH SAUCE
MAKES ABOUT 1½ CUPS

Be careful when stirring in the cream because the hot mixture may splatter.

- 1 cup packed (7 ounces) light brown sugar
- 8 tablespoons unsalted butter, cut into 8 pieces
- ½ cup heavy cream
- 2 teaspoons light corn syrup
- 1 teaspoon vanilla extract

1. Heat sugar and butter in medium saucepan over medium-high heat, stirring often, until mixture bubbles and becomes lighter in color, 3 to 5 minutes.

2. Remove pan from heat and slowly whisk in cream until combined (mixture will bubble vigorously). Stir in corn syrup and vanilla. Serve warm or at room temperature. (Sauce can be refrigerated for up to 2 weeks.)

CRÈME ANGLAISE

✓ WHY THIS RECIPE WORKS

Crème anglaise is a velvety and versatile custard sauce—it tastes great over fresh or baked fruit and with many different cakes and other desserts. In pursuit of a rich, creamy, perfectly smooth crème anglaise, we learned that properly tempering (raising the temperature of an egg yolk–enriched mixture gradually) the custard was crucial; this prevents the eggs from curdling as they are incorporated into the milk. To do this, we slowly added a cup of the hot milk to the yolk mixture to warm the yolks, then poured the mixture back into the saucepan with the rest of the hot milk. (The initial addition of the hot milk does the tempering, so that the yolks are able to stand the heat of the remaining hot milk.) When adding the hot liquid to the egg yolk mixture, it was essential to whisk constantly so that the milk didn't scramble the egg yolks. Once the yolks were added to the pan, more stirring ensured our crème anglaise had the smoothest texture possible. Straining the sauce before chilling it provided further insurance that it would be silky-smooth when drizzled over cake, fruit, or anything else.

CRÈME ANGLAISE
MAKES ABOUT 2 CUPS

You can substitute 1½ teaspoons vanilla extract for the vanilla bean; stir the extract into the sauce after straining it in step 4.

- ½ vanilla bean
- 1½ cups whole milk
  Pinch salt
- 5 large egg yolks
- ¼ cup (1¾ ounces) sugar

1. Cut vanilla bean in half lengthwise. Using tip of paring knife, scrape out seeds. Combine vanilla bean and seeds, milk, and salt in medium saucepan and bring to simmer over medium-high heat, stirring occasionally.

2. Meanwhile, in separate bowl, whisk egg yolks and sugar together until smooth.

3. Whisk about 1 cup of simmering milk mixture into egg yolks to temper. Slowly whisk egg yolk mixture into simmering milk mixture. Continue to cook sauce, whisking constantly, until it thickens slightly and coats back of spoon (about 175 degrees), about 6 minutes.

4. Immediately strain sauce through fine-mesh strainer into medium bowl; remove and discard vanilla bean. Cover and refrigerate until cool, about 30 minutes. Serve chilled.

LEMON CURD

✓ WHY THIS RECIPE WORKS

Nothing more than eggs, sugar, butter, and, of course, lemon juice, lemon curd is cooked until slightly thickened, creating a rich, brightly flavored custard. Though the ingredient list is short, homemade lemon curd is often bypassed in favor of jarred curd. But this convenience product, besides being incredibly pricey, tends to have a gummy texture and saccharine-sweet flavor. We wanted a lemon curd that delivered on both fronts—tart yet subtly sweetened lemon flavor and a creamy, thick consistency. We started with ½ cup of lemon juice for bold citrus flavor; to balance the acidity, we needed ¾ cup of sugar. To thicken the curd, we added two eggs plus three yolks; properly tempering the eggs ensured they didn't curdle when added to the pan. Finally, for richness, we stirred in a few pats of butter, before straining and chilling the curd so it would be perfectly smooth and thickened.

LEMON CURD

MAKES ABOUT 1¼ CUPS

This tangy curd makes an easy topping for scones, pound cake, shortbread, and many other simple desserts. It's also nice spread on buttered toast.

½	cup lemon juice (3 lemons)
¾	cup (5¼ ounces) sugar
	Pinch salt
2	large eggs plus 3 large yolks
4	tablespoons unsalted butter, cut into ½-inch pieces and chilled

1. Heat lemon juice, sugar, and salt in medium saucepan over medium-high heat, stirring occasionally, until sugar dissolves and mixture is hot but not boiling, about 1 minute.

2. Whisk eggs and egg yolks together in large bowl, then slowly whisk in hot lemon mixture to temper. Return mixture to saucepan and cook over medium-low heat, stirring constantly, until mixture is thickened and registers 170 degrees, 3 to 5 minutes.

3. Off heat, stir in butter until melted and incorporated. Strain through fine-mesh strainer into medium bowl and press plastic wrap directly on surface. Refrigerate curd until it is firm and spreadable, about 1½ hours. (Curd can be refrigerated, with plastic wrap pressed directly on surface, for up to 3 days.)

STRAWBERRY TOPPING

✔ WHY THIS RECIPE WORKS
We wanted a strawberry topping that would make the perfect brightly flavored accent to cake, a stack of pancakes or scoop of ice cream. We began with more than a pound of fresh berries (thawed frozen berries looked ragged and unattractive and so were nixed). We tossed the strawberries with sugar and a pinch of salt so they would begin to release their juice. Simply simmering the berries didn't create a topping with enough body, so we cooked half a cup of strawberry jam, which had been processed in the food processor until completely smooth, then combined the heated jam with the macerated berries and a dash of lemon juice. The heated jam was enough to coax the berries from their raw rigid state to a tender, yielding texture, and the lemon juice provided just the right burst of bright acidity. Now our strawberry topping had a clean strawberry flavor and a thick, yet fluid texture that draped nicely over any cake, pancake, or ice cream.

STRAWBERRY TOPPING

MAKES ABOUT 3 CUPS

This topping is best the day it is made. Do not use frozen strawberries in this recipe.

1¼	pounds strawberries, hulled and sliced thin (4 cups)
¼	cup (1¾ ounces) sugar
	Pinch salt
½	cup strawberry jam
1	tablespoon lemon juice

1. Toss strawberries, sugar, and salt together in bowl and let sit, stirring occasionally, until berries have released their juice and sugar has dissolved, about 30 minutes.

2. Process jam in food processor until smooth, about 8 seconds. Simmer jam in small saucepan over medium heat until no longer foamy, about 3 minutes. Stir warm jam and lemon juice into strawberries. Let cool to room temperature before serving, about 1 hour. Serve at room temperature or chilled.

BLUEBERRY TOPPING

Be sure to use fresh blueberries in this topping.

Substitute 15 ounces blueberries for strawberries and blueberry jam for strawberry jam. Gently mash blueberries before letting them sit in step 1.

PEACH TOPPING

One pound frozen peaches, thawed, can be substituted here; you may need to slice them thinner after thawing.

Substitute 2 pounds peaches, peeled, halved, pitted, and sliced very thin, for strawberries and peach jam for strawberry jam.

BERRY COULIS

✔ WHY THIS RECIPE WORKS
Too often, berry coulis is a thick, candy-sweet sauce that tastes more like melted jam than fresh fruit. Then there's the opposite end of the spectrum—chunky, lumpy sauce loaded with seeds but zero flavor. We were after a silky smooth sauce that tasted like fresh berries, with a perfect not-too-thick, not-too-thin consistency and the ability to complement everything from pancakes to pound cakes. We found that simpler was better. Simmering the fruit briefly with sugar, salt, and a minimal amount of water helped to release the fruit's natural pectin and bring forth its inherent sweetness. Straining the sauce to remove the seeds ensured we had a smooth sauce, and a spritz of lemon juice brightened its overall flavor.

BERRY COULIS

MAKES ABOUT 1½ CUPS

Because the type of berries used as well as their ripeness will affect the sweetness of the coulis, the amount of sugar is variable. Start with 5 tablespoons, then add more if you prefer a sweeter coulis. Additional sugar should be stirred in immediately after straining, while the coulis is still warm, so that the sugar will readily dissolve. Serve the coulis with cheesecake, pound cake, ice cream, rich chocolate tortes and cakes, dessert soufflés, pancakes, French toast, waffles, or crêpes.

12 ounces (3 cups) fresh or frozen and thawed raspberries, blueberries, blackberries, and/or strawberries (hulled and sliced thin if fresh)
¼ cup water
5–7 tablespoons sugar
⅛ teaspoon salt
2 teaspoons lemon juice

1. Bring berries, water, 5 tablespoons sugar, and salt to bare simmer in medium saucepan over medium heat, stirring occasionally; cook until sugar is dissolved and berries are heated through, about 1 minute.

2. Process mixture in blender until smooth, about 20 seconds. Strain through fine-mesh strainer into small bowl, pressing on solids to extract as much puree as possible. Stir in lemon juice and additional sugar, if desired. Cover and refrigerate until well chilled, at least 1 hour. Stir to recombine before serving. (If too thick after chilling, stir in 1 to 2 teaspoons water to adjust consistency. Coulis can be refrigerated for up to 4 days.)

MIXED BERRY COULIS

Use 3 ounces each blueberries, raspberries, blackberries, and strawberries, hulled and sliced thin.

BLACKBERRY COULIS

Use all blackberries and add 1 tablespoon melon liqueur along with lemon juice.

BLUEBERRY-CINNAMON COULIS

Use all blueberries and add ⅛ teaspoon ground cinnamon along with sugar.

RASPBERRY-LIME COULIS

Use all raspberries and substitute 1 tablespoon lime juice for lemon juice.

WHIPPED CREAM

✓ WHY THIS RECIPE WORKS
The lightly sweetened flavor and creamy texture of whipped cream make the perfect partner to numerous desserts, especially pies. But perfect whipped cream can be hard to accomplish—the cream can go from properly whipped to overwhipped and stiff in a matter of seconds. For puffy, cloudlike mounds, we reached for our stand mixer and began whipping the cream and sugar on medium-low speed, then increased the speed and whipped just until the mixture was thick and billowy. For flavor, we added a dash of vanilla.

WHIPPED CREAM
MAKES ABOUT 2 CUPS

For lightly sweetened whipped cream, reduce the sugar to 1½ teaspoons. For the best results, chill the mixer bowl and whisk in the freezer for 20 minutes before whipping the cream.

1 cup heavy cream, chilled
1 tablespoon sugar
1 teaspoon vanilla extract

Using stand mixer fitted with whisk, whip cream, sugar, and vanilla on medium-low speed until foamy, about 1 minute. Increase speed to high and whip until soft peaks form, 1 to 3 minutes. (Whipped cream can be refrigerated in fine-mesh strainer set over small bowl and covered with plastic wrap for up to 8 hours.)

BROWN SUGAR WHIPPED CREAM
MAKES ABOUT 2½ CUPS

Refrigerating the mixture in step 1 gives the brown sugar time to dissolve. This whipped cream pairs well with any dessert that has lots of nuts, warm spices, or molasses, like gingerbread, pecan pie, or pumpkin pie.

1 cup heavy cream, chilled
½ cup sour cream
½ cup packed (3½ ounces) light brown sugar
⅛ teaspoon salt

1. Using stand mixer fitted with whisk, whip heavy cream, sour cream, sugar, and salt until combined. Cover with plastic wrap and refrigerate until ready to serve, at least 4 hours or up to 1 day, stirring once or twice during chilling to ensure that sugar dissolves.

2. Before serving, using stand mixer fitted with whisk, whip mixture on medium-low speed until foamy, about 1 minute. Increase speed to high and whip until soft peaks form, 1 to 3 minutes.

BROWN SUGAR AND BOURBON WHIPPED CREAM

This variation goes especially well with Pumpkin-Bourbon Cheesecake with Graham-Pecan Crust (page 704).

Add 2 teaspoons bourbon to cream mixture before whipping.

TANGY WHIPPED CREAM
MAKES 1½ CUPS

Sour cream adds a pleasing tang to this whipped cream, which makes a nice accompaniment to richer desserts, such as our Chocolate Sour Cream Bundt Cake (page 691).

1 cup heavy cream, chilled
¼ cup sour cream
¼ cup packed (1¾ ounces) light brown sugar
⅛ teaspoon vanilla extract

Using stand mixer fitted with whisk, whip all ingredients on medium-low speed until foamy, about 1 minute. Increase speed to high and whip until soft peaks form, 1 to 3 minutes.

CHAPTER 23 Beverages

LEMONADE

✔ WHY THIS RECIPE WORKS

Few things are better on a hot summer day than a tall, cold glass of homemade lemonade. But homemade lemonade often turns out too sweet, too watery, too pulpy, or too gritty from undissolved sugar. We wanted smooth lemonade with full lemon flavor, balanced by just the right amount of sugar. It turned out that using a juicer wasn't the best method for extracting the most lemon flavor. Slicing the lemons and then mashing them with sugar until the sugar dissolved produced a syrup intensely flavored with citrus oils. All we had to do was add the lemon mixture to the right amount of water for perfectly refreshing lemonade with subtle sweetness and serious lemon flavor.

CLASSIC LEMONADE
SERVES 6 TO 8

If you like, scrape the pulp from a couple of mashed lemon slices into the pitcher to make a more pulpy lemonade. Adding 1 tablespoon of grenadine turns the lemonade pink and imparts extra sweetness.

12	lemons, halved from top to bottom and sliced thin
1¼	cups sugar
	Pinch salt (optional)
5	cups water

Mash lemons, sugar, and salt, if using, in large, deep bowl or saucepan with potato masher or wooden spoon until lemon slices give up their juice, sugar is dissolved, and juice is thickened to syrup consistency, about 4 minutes. Pour half of lemon slices and syrup through large strainer set over bowl or saucepan; press on solids with masher or back of wooden spoon to release as much liquid as possible. Discard solids; transfer liquid to serving pitcher. Repeat process with remaining lemon slices. Stir in water until blended. Chill at least 1 hour and stir to blend before serving.

LEMONADE FOR ONE

Reduce number of lemons to 2, sugar to 3 tablespoons, and water to ¾ cup. Use small bowl and strainer.

LIMEADE

Substitute 16 limes, halved from top to bottom and sliced thin, for the lemons.

MINTED LEMONADE

Like the ginger version below, the mint flavor in this lemonade is mild to complement the lemon.

Add 2 cups fresh mint leaves to lemons and sugar before mashing.

GINGERED LEMONADE

Add 3 tablespoons grated fresh ginger to lemons and sugar before mashing.

RASPBERRY LEMONADE

Add 7½ ounces fresh or thawed frozen raspberries to lemons and sugar before mashing.

SHANDY

Other versions of this refreshing British drink substitute ginger beer or ginger ale, or lemon-lime soda for the lemonade. We prefer 1 part beer to 2 parts lemonade. For a stronger beer flavor, use equal parts beer and lemonade.

⅓	cup beer, preferably dark or amber lager or light or pale ale, chilled
⅔	cup lemonade, chilled

Pour beer, then lemonade, into glass. Stir very gently to avoid creating foam and serve immediately.

ICED TEA

✔ WHY THIS RECIPE WORKS

Iced tea should be strong but not bitter, richly colored but not cloudy and dark, and pleasantly—not toothachingly—sweet. So what's the secret to a great glass of iced tea? Is it the brewing method, steeping time, type of water, or the ratio of ingredients? We found that making good iced tea depended on doing a lot of little things right. A ratio of 5 teabags to 1 quart of water worked best. The amount of sugar can be varied depending on how sweet you like your tea. The key to strong but not bitter flavor was water temperature. Heating the teabags in hot but not boiling water, then steeping them for just three minutes, gave us flavorful tea without any bitterness. And with this extra-strong tea, we could simply stir in an equal amount of ice, cooling the tea instantly so that it was ready to drink right away.

QUICK, SIMPLE, FULL-FLAVORED ICED TEA
SERVES 4 TO 6

Doubling this recipe is easy, but use a large saucepan and expect the water to take a few minutes longer to reach the proper temperature. For a slightly stronger iced tea, reduce the amount of ice to 3 cups. Garnish with a thin lemon wedge to squeeze into the tea, if you like.

5	bags black tea
4	cups water
1–6	tablespoons sugar
4	cups ice cubes, plus more for glasses

Tie strings of tea bags together (for easy removal) and heat with water in medium saucepan over medium heat until dark colored, very steamy, and small bubbles form on bottom and sides of pan (tea will register about 190 degrees), 10 to 15 minutes. Off heat, let steep for 3 minutes (no longer or tea may become bitter). Remove tea bags; pour tea into pitcher. Stir in sugar to taste, then stir in ice until melted. Serve in ice-filled glasses.

Add ¼ cup fresh mint leaves, bruised with wooden spoon, to saucepan along with tea bags and water. When steeping is complete, remove tea bags and strain tea through fine-mesh strainer to remove mint.

GINGERED ICED TEA

Add one 1-inch piece fresh ginger, sliced thin and smashed with broad side of large chef's knife, to saucepan along with tea bags and water. When steeping is complete, discard tea bags and strain tea through fine-mesh strainer to remove ginger.

MICROWAVE ICED TEA

Using a 2-quart Pyrex measuring cup makes this tea a one-pot drink from brewing to pouring. Exact heating time will depend on the power of your microwave and the starting temperature of the water.

Microwave tea bags and water, covered, until dark colored, very steamy, and water starts to move but not boil (tea will register about 190 degrees), 8 to 10 minutes. Remove from microwave and let steep for 3 minutes (no longer or tea may become bitter). Remove tea bags. Stir in sugar to taste, then stir in ice until melted. Serve in ice-filled glasses.

BERRY SMOOTHIES

✔ WHY THIS RECIPE WORKS

Smoothies are difficult to make well—they often turn out tasting of ice or milk without much fruit flavor. A good smoothie should be satisfying and rejuvenating without tasting like a milkshake or a fruity glass of fiber. We wanted a chilled, fruity, slightly sweet smoothie that was lightly creamy and thick but straw-friendly. We got the

knock-your-socks-off flavor we wanted by replacing the usual yogurt with whole milk, adding juice for freshness, and then filling the blender with a lot of fruit. A few spoonfuls of sugar and a squeeze of lemon balanced out the flavors. Three ice cubes were enough to make a cold but not overly icy drink. This was our ideal smoothie, chock-full of fruity goodness.

BERRY SMOOTHIES
SERVES 4

A ripe banana will yield a sweeter smoothie. Adjust the amounts of sugar and lemon juice depending on the ripeness of the fruit.

1	banana, peeled and cut crosswise into 8 pieces
17½	ounces (3½ cups) berries
½	cup whole milk
½	cup white cranberry juice or apple juice
3	ice cubes
1–2	tablespoons sugar
2–3	teaspoons lemon juice
	Pinch salt

Line rimmed baking sheet with parchment paper; arrange banana pieces and berries in single layer on baking sheet. Freeze until very cold, but not frozen, about 10 minutes. Process chilled fruit, milk, juice, ice, 1 tablespoon sugar, 1 teaspoon lemon juice, and salt in blender until uniformly smooth, 10 to 15 seconds. Taste; if desired, add more sugar or lemon and process until combined, about 2 seconds longer. Serve immediately.

MELON SMOOTHIES

Make sure the melon is absolutely ripe, if not overripe. Underripe melon yields bland smoothies.

Replace berries with 3½ cups watermelon, cantaloupe, or honeydew, cut into 1- to 2-inch pieces.

TROPICAL FRUIT SMOOTHIES

Replace berries with 3½ cups pineapple, papaya, or mango, cut into 1- to 2-inch pieces. Increase milk and juice to ⅔ cup each.

FRESH MARGARITAS

✔ WHY THIS RECIPE WORKS

The typical margarita tends to be a slushy, headache-inducing concoction made with little more than ice, tequila, and artificially flavored corn syrup. We wanted a margarita with a balanced blend of fresh citrus flavors and tequila. We found that the key was using the right proportions of alcohol and citrus juice—equal parts of each. We started with the tequila: Young tequilas gave our margaritas a raw, harsh flavor, and while those made with super-premium tequilas, aged up to six years, tasted smooth, their distinct tannic taste dominated the cocktail. For a mellow, delicate flavor, we preferred reposado tequila, made from 100 percent blue agave and aged about 12 months. As for orange-flavored liqueurs, a lower-alcohol liqueur, such as triple sec, worked best. Mixes and bottled citrus juice had no place in our cocktail. Instead we steeped lemon and lime zest in their own juices for a deep, refreshing citrus flavor. With a bit of easy-to-dissolve superfine sugar and crushed ice, our margaritas were complete.

THE BEST FRESH MARGARITAS
SERVES 4 TO 6

The longer the zest and juice mixture is allowed to steep, the more developed the citrus flavors will be in the finished margaritas. We recommend steeping for the full 24 hours, although the margaritas will still be great if the mixture is steeped for only the minimum 4 hours. If you're in a rush and want to serve margaritas immediately, omit the zest and skip the steeping process altogether. If you can't find superfine sugar, process an equal amount of granulated sugar in a food processor for 30 seconds.

4   teaspoons finely grated lime zest
    plus ½ cup juice (4 limes)
4   teaspoons finely grated lemon zest
    plus ½ cup juice (3 lemons)
¼   cup superfine sugar
    Pinch salt
2   cups crushed ice
1   cup 100 percent agave tequila,
    preferably reposado
1   cup triple sec

1. Combine lime zest and juice, lemon zest and juice, sugar, and salt in large liquid measuring cup; cover with plastic wrap and refrigerate until flavors meld, at least 4 or up to 24 hours.

2. Divide 1 cup crushed ice among 4 or 6 margarita or double old-fashioned glasses. Strain juice mixture into 1-quart pitcher or cocktail shaker. Add tequila, triple sec, and remaining 1 cup crushed ice; stir or shake until thoroughly combined and chilled, 20 to 60 seconds. Strain into ice-filled glasses and serve immediately.

FRESH PINEAPPLE MARGARITAS

The pineapple flavor in this variation makes the zest and steeping process in the recipe above unnecessary.

Omit lime and lemon zest and steeping process. Peel, core, and halve 1 small ripe pineapple (about 3½ pounds); cut 1 half into rough 2-inch chunks (reserve remaining half for another use). Process in food processor until smooth and foamy, about 1 minute. Add ½ cup pureed pineapple to juice mixture, reducing lemon and lime juices to ¼ cup each.

FRESH RASPBERRY MARGARITAS

Omit lime and lemon zest and steeping process. Puree 1 cup fresh raspberries, lime and lemon juices, sugar, and pinch salt in food processor until smooth, about 1 minute. Strain mixture into pitcher or cocktail shaker. Continue with recipe, reducing

triple sec to ½ cup and adding ½ cup Chambord (or other raspberry liqueur) to juice and tequila mixture in pitcher.

FRESH STRAWBERRY MARGARITAS

Omit lime and lemon zest and steeping process. Process 1 cup hulled strawberries, lime and lemon juices, sugar, and salt in food processor until smooth, about 1 minute. Strain mixture into pitcher or cocktail shaker. Continue with recipe, reducing triple sec to ½ cup and adding ½ cup Chambord (or other raspberry liqueur) to juice and tequila mixture in pitcher.

SANGRIA

✓ WHY THIS RECIPE WORKS

Many people mistake sangria for a random collection of fruit in overly sweetened wine. We wanted a robust, sweet-tart sangria. To start, we found that because of the fruit and added sugar, cheap wine makes as good a sangria as more expensive wine, so it wasn't necessary to splurge. We experimented with untold varieties of fruit to put in our sangria recipe and finally concluded that simpler is better. We preferred the straightforward tang of citrus in the form of oranges and lemons and we discovered that the zest and pith as well as the fruit itself make an important contribution to flavor. Orange liqueur is standard in recipes for sangria, and after experimenting we found that here, as with the wine, cheaper was just fine, this time in the form of triple sec.

THE BEST SANGRIA
SERVES 4

The longer sangria sits before drinking, the more smooth and mellow it will taste. A full day is best, but if that's impossible, give it an absolute minimum of 2 hours to sit. Use large, heavy, juicy oranges and lemons for the best flavor. If you can't find superfine sugar, process an equal amount of granulated sugar in a food processor

for 30 seconds. Doubling or tripling the recipe is fine, but you'll need a large punch bowl in place of the pitcher. An inexpensive Merlot is the best choice for this recipe.

2   oranges, 1 sliced, 1 juiced (½ cup)
1   lemon, sliced
¼   cup superfine sugar
1   (750-ml) bottle fruity red wine,
    chilled
¼   cup triple sec
6–8 ice cubes

1. Add sliced orange, lemon, and sugar to large pitcher. Mash fruit gently with wooden spoon until fruit releases some juice, but is not totally crushed, and sugar dissolves, about 1 minute. Stir in orange juice, wine, and triple sec; refrigerate for at least 2 hours or up to 8 hours.

2. Before serving, add 6 to 8 ice cubes and stir briskly to distribute settled fruit and pulp; serve immediately.

WHITE SANGRIA
SERVES 4

A Pinot Grigio or an unoaked Chardonnay are the best choices for this recipe.

2   oranges, 1 sliced, 1 juiced (½ cup)
1   lemon, sliced
¼   cup superfine sugar
1   (750-ml) bottle fruity white wine,
    chilled
2   tablespoons triple sec
6–8 ice cubes

1. Add sliced orange, lemon, and sugar to large pitcher. Mash fruit gently with wooden spoon until fruit releases some juice, but is not totally crushed, and sugar dissolves, about 1 minute. Stir in orange juice, wine, and triple sec; refrigerate for at least 2 hours or up to 8 hours.

2. Before serving, add 6 to 8 ice cubes and stir briskly to distribute settled fruit and pulp; serve immediately.

In the summer months, we tend to get busy tending the grill and often forget to pop a bottle of wine in the fridge before company comes over. Here's a way to chill beverages in a hurry, borrowed from a method for making ice cream in an old-fashioned churn: Make an ice bath and add salt to it. When ice cubes are placed in plain water, they will absorb heat from their surroundings until they melt at 32 degrees. When salt is added to the mix, the freezing point and temperature decrease, lowering the ice's melting temperature (which is the same as its freezing temperature) to well below 32 degrees. The result is a brine significantly colder than plain ice water that can rapidly chill or even freeze liquids.

To find out just how quickly an ice brine works, we chilled three bottles of 75-degree white wine in three different environments: in the freezer (the usual desperate approach to quick chilling); submerged in a 50–50 mix of ice and plain water; and submerged in 1 quart water mixed with 4 quarts ice with 1 cup salt. We checked the temperature of each wine every five minutes to see how quickly it reached 38 degrees (the typical temperature of chilled beverages in the fridge). The wine in the ice brine took just 34 minutes, compared with 67 minutes in the freezer and 105 minutes in the plain ice water. The next time we need to transform a drink from lukewarm to icy cold, we'll reach for the salt.

MULLED RED WINE

✔ WHY THIS RECIPE WORKS

Bad versions of mulled red wine can be reminiscent of cough syrup—sickeningly sweet and overspiced, with a harsh taste of alcohol. We wanted a warm, not-too-sweet wine with a mild alcohol kick, deep but not overwhelming spice notes, and some fruitiness. For full, round flavors, we chose a careful balance of cinnamon sticks, cloves, peppercorns, and allspice berries, then toasted the spices to unlock their full flavor. Any medium- to full-bodied wine worked well; we got the best results using wine good enough to drink on its own. We simmered, rather than boiled, the wine, spices, and a modest amount of sugar for a full hour to ensure a full-flavored drink that didn't taste raw. A couple of spoonfuls of brandy stirred in just before serving added a fresh, boozy kick.

MULLED RED WINE
SERVES 8

The flavor of the mulled wine deteriorates if it is simmered for longer than 1 hour. It is best served immediately after mulling but will keep fairly hot off heat, covered, for about 30 minutes. Leftover mulled wine can be reheated in the microwave or in a saucepan on the stovetop. Merlot, Pinot Noir, or Côtes du Rhône are the best choices for this recipe.

3	cinnamon sticks
10	whole cloves
10	whole peppercorns
1	teaspoon allspice berries
2	(750-ml) bottles red wine
4	(2-inch) strips orange zest
½	cup plus 2 tablespoons sugar
2–4	tablespoons brandy

1. Toast cinnamon sticks, cloves, peppercorns, and allspice in medium saucepan over medium-high heat until fragrant, about 2 minutes. Add wine, orange zest, and ½ cup sugar; cover partially and bring to simmer, stirring occasionally to dissolve sugar. Reduce heat to low and simmer 1 hour until wine is infused; do not boil.

2. Strain wine through fine-mesh strainer placed over bowl and return to saucepan; discard spices and orange zest. Stir 2 tablespoons brandy into wine; taste and add up to 2 tablespoons more sugar and 2 tablespoons more brandy, if desired. Ladle wine into small mugs; serve immediately.

MULLED RED WINE WITH RAISINS AND ALMONDS

This variation is inspired by Scandinavian glögg.

Substitute 2 crushed green cardamom pods for allspice. Add ⅓ cup raisins and ⅓ cup whole blanched almonds to strained wine; omit brandy. Cover and let sit until raisins are plump, about 10 minutes. Stir in 2 tablespoons vodka; add up to 2 tablespoons more sugar and 2 tablespoons more vodka to taste. Ladle wine, raisins, and almonds into small mugs; serve immediately.

HOLIDAY EGGNOG

✔ WHY THIS RECIPE WORKS

Between the heavy cream, raw eggs, and alcohol, it's easy for traditional eggnog to go wrong. We wanted to create a rich eggnog with a creamy texture and enough alcohol to provide its trademark kick without tasting too boozy. We started by comparing uncooked and cooked recipes. We ended up preferring the custardy flavor and creaminess of the cooked versions, so we started with a standard custard recipe (6 eggs, 4 cups milk, and ½ cup sugar) and tinkered around to find improvements. We added two extra egg yolks for richness, and a little more sugar and a bit of salt improved the flavor. Many recipes call for the milk to be added to the beaten eggs very gradually, and this technique did indeed make for a smoother texture. The custard base we now had was flavorful and thick, but it was not quite eggnog. Once we added softly whipped heavy cream, brandy, bourbon, or dark rum, and the simple flavorings of vanilla extract and nutmeg, we had the perfect indulgent holiday drink.

HOLIDAY EGGNOG
SERVES 12 TO 16

Adding the milk to the eggs in small increments and blending thoroughly after each addition helps ensure a smooth custard. To prevent curdling, do not heat the custard beyond 160 degrees. If it does begin to curdle, remove it from the heat immediately, pour it into a bowl set over a larger bowl of ice water to stop the cooking, and proceed with the recipe. You can omit the brandy to make a nonalcoholic eggnog, but you should also decrease the cream to ¼ cup to keep the right consistency. Increase the cream to ¾ cup and add another ½ cup brandy for stronger eggnog.

6 large eggs plus 2 large yolks
½ cup plus 2 tablespoons sugar
¼ teaspoon salt
4 cups whole milk
½ cup brandy, bourbon, or dark rum
1 tablespoon vanilla extract
½ teaspoon ground nutmeg, plus extra for garnish
½ cup heavy cream

1. Whisk eggs, egg yolks, sugar, and salt together in heavy 3- or 4-quart saucepan. Stir in milk, ½ cup at a time, blending well after each addition. Heat slowly over lowest possible heat, stirring constantly, until custard registers 160 degrees, thickens, and coats back of spoon, 25 to 30 minutes. Pour custard through fine-mesh strainer into large bowl; stir in brandy, vanilla and nutmeg. Cover with plastic wrap and refrigerate until well chilled, at least 3 hours or up to 3 days.

2. Just before serving, whip cream in medium bowl to very soft peaks and gently fold into custard mixture until incorporated. Serve in chilled punch bowl or cups, garnishing with nutmeg.

HOT COCOA

✔ WHY THIS RECIPE WORKS
Hot cocoa made from the ubiquitous "back-of-the-box" recipe is weak and thin, and the European tradition of melting bittersweet chocolate in milk and heavy cream is too lush and fattening. Our ideal hot cocoa would have serious chocolate flavor and a rich, satisfying consistency without requiring a day of fasting after drinking a cup. Six tablespoons of cocoa powder, lightly sweetened with sugar, added satisfying chocolate flavor without being overpowering. Many recipes recommend mixing cocoa powder and sugar with a little water before adding the milk, and we found this to be worthwhile. Water helps to release the

cocoa powder's fruit, chocolate, and coffee flavor nuances. We also discovered that heating this mixture for two minutes before adding milk further deepened the flavor. We preferred using low-fat milk; the reduced fat content in 1 or 2 percent milk allows for the greatest range of cocoa flavor. A splash of half-and-half added a pleasant richness, rounding out our perfect cup of cocoa.

HOT COCOA
SERVES 4

If you want to increase or decrease this recipe for hot cocoa, the key ratio to remember is 1½ tablespoons of cocoa and 1 heaping tablespoon of sugar to 1 cup of liquid. If you have whole milk on hand rather than low-fat, go ahead and use it, omitting the half-and-half. Top with whipped cream or marshmallows if desired

6 tablespoons Dutch-processed cocoa
¼ cup sugar
Pinch salt
1 cup water
3 cups 1 or 2 percent low-fat milk
1 teaspoon vanilla extract
¼ cup half-and-half

1. In medium saucepan, whisk cocoa, sugar, salt, and water together over low heat until smooth. Simmer, whisking continuously, for 2 minutes, making sure whisk gets into edges of pan.

2. Add milk, increase heat to medium-low, and cook, stirring occasionally, until steam rises from surface and tiny bubbles form around edge, 12 to 15 minutes. Do not boil.

3. Add vanilla and half-and-half. Divide between 4 mugs and serve immediately.

HOT COCOA WITH ORANGE

Add seven 2-inch strips orange zest along with milk. Remove zest strips with slotted spoon before serving.

IRISH COFFEE

✔ WHY THIS RECIPE WORKS
Irish coffee should be the perfect dessert drink, combining coffee, whisky, whipped cream, and sometimes liqueur, but too often when you order it you get a shot of whiskey just barely spiked with coffee. We wanted a nicely balanced cup of great coffee with a light kick of whiskey that wouldn't have us stumbling from the table. After experimenting with different amounts, we found that just a couple tablespoons gave us the right balance, allowing both the flavor of the coffee and the whisky to come through. The next step to making a good drink was to brew a really good cup of coffee. We used filtered water to prevent mineral flavors, heated it to the optimum temperature, and ground the beans fresh for the best flavor. All that was left was to top off our drink with whipped cream.

IRISH COFFEE
SERVES 4

For sweet and creamy coffee, add 1 tablespoon of Bailey's Irish Cream to each mug.

½ cup Irish whiskey
4 cups fresh brewed coffee, hot
Sugar (optional)
1 recipe Whipped Cream (page 800)

Pour 2 tablespoons whiskey into each of 4 large mugs. Fill mugs with coffee. Season with sugar, if desired, and dollop with whipped cream before serving.

You can spend upward of $20 per pound for premium coffee, but unless it's fresh and you're using proper brewing techniques, it's a waste of money. Here's what you need to know to make the perfect cup.

RECOMMENDED BREWING METHODS

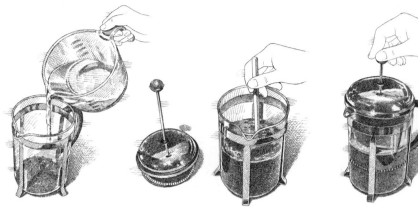

FRENCH PRESS

1. Preheat pot with hot tap water. Add 2 tablespoons medium-coarse ground coffee for every 6 ounces water. Add just-boiled water steadily, saturating all grounds.

2. Simply pouring boiled water over coffee grounds isn't enough for great flavor. To aid flavor extraction, use long spoon or chopstick to gently stir coffee.

3. Add lid and steep coffee for about 5 minutes (4 minutes for smaller pots). With even pressure, steadily press down filter.

MANUAL DRIP

1. Warm thermos with hot tap water. Add 2 tablespoons medium ground (for paper filters) or medium-fine ground (for metal filters) coffee for every 6 ounces water to filter.

2. Pour ½ cup just-boiled water over grounds, saturating thoroughly; let stand 30 seconds.

3. Pour remaining hot water over grounds, in batches if necessary, stirring gently after each addition.

BUYING AND STORING BASICS

BUY FRESHLY ROASTED WHOLE BEANS: Buying whole beans in small quantities is important because grinding speeds oxidation and the deterioration of flavor. Even grinding the night before can make a big difference; studies show the exposed coffee cells begin to break down within the hour.

STORE AWAY FROM HEAT AND LIGHT: If you plan to finish a bag of beans in less than 10 or 12 days, you can store them at room temperature in the original bag or a zipper-lock bag away from heat and light. For longer-term storage, store the beans in the freezer to limit contact with air and moisture. (Skip the fridge because the beans will pick up off-flavors.) It's also a good idea to buy coffee in a heat-sealed, aluminized Mylar bag with a one-way degassing valve (sometimes no more than a bump) that releases carbon dioxide while keeping out oxygen. Unopened, these bags keep beans as fresh as the day they were roasted for up to 90 days.

BEST BREWING PRACTICES

USE FILTERED WATER: A cup of coffee is about 98 percent water, so it makes sense to pay attention to the water you're using. If your tap water tastes bad or has strong mineral flavors, your coffee will, too. But don't bother buying bottled water—just use a filtration pitcher.

MATCH BREWING TIME TO GRIND: Brewing time will dictate how you grind the coffee. In general, the longer the brewing time, the coarser the grounds should be. To adjust the strength of your coffee, adjust the amount of grounds; the norm is 2 tablespoons of ground beans for every 6 ounces of water.

PAY ATTENTION TO TEMPERATURE: The most desirable flavor compounds in coffee are released in water between 195 and 205 degrees. A panel of our tasters judged coffee brewed at 200 degrees as having the fullest, roundest flavor. Once the water has boiled (212 degrees), let it rest for 10 to 15 seconds to bring it down to this temperature.

Index

A

Acorn Squash

with Brown Sugar, 295–96

with Rosemary–Dried Fig Compote, 296

Squash and Prosciutto Ravioli or Tortellini, 203–4

Aïoli, 30–31

Basil or Dill, 31

Rosemary-Thyme, 31

Saffron, 31

Alcohol, cooking off, 117

Aligot (French-Style Mashed Potatoes with Cheese and Garlic), 282–83

All-American Potato Salad, 58

All-Butter Double-Crust Pie Dough, 709

All-Butter Single-Crust Pie Dough, 709–10

All-Butter Single-Crust Pie Dough for Custard Pies, 710

All-Purpose Cornbread, 579

All-Purpose Gravy, 359–60

All-Season Blueberry Cobbler, 748

Allspice Rub, Cocoa-Cumin, 492

Almond(s)

and Amaretti, Vanilla Semifreddo with, 788

Apple Upside-Down Cake with, 686

-Apricot Muffins, 566

-Apricot Oatmeal Scones, 564

-Apricot Sour Cream Coffee Cake, 576

Baklava, 767–68

Big and Chewy Oatmeal-Nut Cookies, 632

and Buttered Bread Crumbs, Green Beans with, 246

and Carrots, Zucchini with, 296

Chocolate Raspberry Torte, 679–80

Classic Granola, 556

Cream Cheese Coffee Cake, 574–75

Crumble Topping, 748

Crunch Topping, Blueberry Swirl Muffins with, 568

-Crusted French Toast, 550–51

and Currants, Glazed Carrots with, 256

and Currants, Warm-Spiced Pan Sauce with, 352

and Dried Apricots, Best Baked Apples with, 759

Frisée, and Goat Cheese, Pan-Roasted Pear Salad with, 51

and Golden Raisins, Sautéed Baby Spinach with, 266–67

Green Olive, and Orange Relish, 434

Lace Cookies, 644–45

Linzertorte, 735–36

Almond(s) (continued)

Macaroons, 649

Fudge-, 650

Lemon-, 649–50

Pine Nut–Crusted, 650

Madeleines, 644

Mexican Chocolate Butter Cookies, 639

Napoleons, 767

Nut-Crusted Chicken Breasts with Lemon and Thyme, 315–16

-Orange Biscotti, 647

-Orange Oatmeal Cookies, Thin and Crispy, 632

and Orange Oatmeal Cookies, Big and Chewy, 633

-Orange Vinaigrette, Warm, Pan-Roasted Asparagus with, 244

or Hazelnut Crescent Cookies, 642

Pastry Cream, 763

Peanuts, and Pumpkin Seeds, Mexican-Spiced, 2–3

Pear, Goat Cheese, and Apricots, Arugula Salad with, 32

and Poached Pear Tart, 733–35

Pound Cake, 689

-Raisin Crust, Herbed, Indian-Spiced Roast Boneless Leg of Lamb with, 430–31

and Raisins, Mulled Red Wine with, 805

-Raspberry Filling, Classic White Layer Cake with, 664–65

-Raspberry Muffins, 566

Roasted Broccoli, and Garlic, Pasta with, 185

Rustic Plum Cake, 682–83

Sablés, 637

Shallots, and Garlic, Couscous with, 236

Sherry Vinegar–Honey Sauce with, 260

and Smoked Paprika, Green Beans with, 247

Spice Cake with Orange–Cream Cheese Frosting, 682

Spritz Cookies, 644

Toast and Roast Granola, 556–57

Toasted

Asparagus, and Browned Butter, Farfalle with, 180

and Honey, Crêpes with, 756

Icing, Fluffy, 667–68

and Lemon, Roasted Carrots and Fennel with, 258

Meringue Cookies, 649

and Orange, Rice Pudding with, 776

Slivered, Fish Meunière with, 437

Almond(s) (continued)

and Tomato Pesto (Pesto alla Trapanese), 162

Triple-Ginger Pear Crisp, 753

Vinaigrette, 521

Almost No-Knead Bread, 593–94

Cranberry-Pecan, 595

with Olives, Rosemary, and Parmesan, 594

Seeded Rye, 594

Whole Wheat, 594

Amaretti and Almonds, Vanilla Semifreddo with, 788

American Dinner Rolls, Best, 602–3

American Loaf Bread, 586

Anchovy(ies)

Baked Manicotti Puttanesca, 209

and Basil, Classic Deviled Eggs with, 5

Broccoli, and Garlic, Spaghetti with, 183

and Capers, Creamy Egg Salad with, 64

Classic Caesar Salad, 34–35

and Fried Capers, Spaghetti with, 160

Garlic, and Basil, Pasta and Red Pepper Tuna Sauce with, 199

and Garlic, Roasted Broccoli with, 254

-Garlic Butter with Lemon and Parsley, 452

and Kalamata Olives, Focaccia with, 621

mincing, 114

and Mustard, Madeira Pan Sauce with, 377

Olives, and Capers, Pasta and Fresh Tomato Sauce with, 170

Olives, and Lemon, Chicken and Rice with, 345

and Olives, Pasta and Chunky Tomato Sauce with, 167

and Parmesan, "Caesar" Dip with, 11

Pissaladière, 619–20

Salsa Verde, 502–3

Salsa Verde, Lemon-Basil, 503

Salsa Verde with Arugula, 503

Spaghetti Puttanesca, 175

and Spinach, Greek-Style Garlic-Lemon Potatoes with, 279

Andouille

Corn, and Red Peppers, Hearty Baked Brown Rice with, 226

Red Beans and Rice, 239

Sausage, Red Pepper, and Chipotle Chiles, Spicy Cornbread Stuffing with, 366

Angel Food Cake, Best, 691–92

Anise-Lemon Biscotti, 646

D

E

H

K

L

U

A NOTE ON CONVERSIONS

Some say cooking is a science and an art. We would say that geography has a hand in it, too. Flour milled in the United Kingdom and elsewhere will feel and taste different from flour milled in the United States. So, while we cannot promise that the loaf of bread you bake in Canada or England will taste the same as a loaf baked in the States, we can offer guidelines for converting weights and measures. We also recommend that you rely on your instincts when making our recipes. Refer to the visual cues provided. If the bread dough hasn't "come together in a ball," as described, you may need to add more flour—even if the recipe doesn't tell you so. You be the judge.

The recipes in this book were developed using standard U.S. measures following U.S. government guidelines. The charts below offer equivalents for U.S., metric, and Imperial (U.K.) measures. All conversions are approximate and have been rounded up or down to the nearest whole number. For example:

1 teaspoon = 4.929 milliliters, rounded up to 5 milliliters
1 ounce = 28.349 grams, rounded down to 28 grams

VOLUME CONVERSIONS

U.S.	METRIC
1 teaspoon	5 milliliters
2 teaspoons	10 milliliters
1 tablespoon	15 milliliters
2 tablespoons	30 milliliters
¼ cup	59 milliliters
⅓ cup	79 milliliters
½ cup	118 milliliters
¾ cup	177 milliliters
1 cup	237 milliliters
1¼ cups	296 milliliters
1½ cups	355 milliliters
2 cups	473 milliliters
2½ cups	592 milliliters
3 cups	710 milliliters
4 cups (1 quart)	0.946 liter
1.06 quarts	1 liter
4 quarts (1 gallon)	3.8 liters

WEIGHT CONVERSIONS

OUNCES	GRAMS
½	14
¾	21
1	28
1½	43
2	57
2½	71
3	85
3½	99
4	113
4½	128
5	142
6	170
7	198
8	227
9	255
10	283
12	340
16 (1 pound)	454

CONVERSIONS FOR INGREDIENTS COMMONLY USED IN BAKING

Baking is an exacting science. Because measuring by weight is far more accurate than measuring by volume, and thus more likely to achieve reliable results, in our recipes we provide ounce measures in addition to cup measures for many ingredients. Refer to the chart below to convert these measures into grams.

INGREDIENT	OUNCES	GRAMS
Flour		
1 cup all-purpose flour*	5	142
1 cup cake flour	4	113
1 cup whole wheat flour	5½	156
Sugar		
1 cup granulated (white) sugar	7	198
1 cup packed brown sugar (light or dark)	7	198
1 cup confectioners' sugar	4	113
Cocoa Powder		
1 cup cocoa powder	3	85
Butter†		
4 tablespoons (½ stick, or ¼ cup)	2	57
8 tablespoons (1 stick, or ½ cup)	4	113
16 tablespoons (2 sticks, or 1 cup)	8	227

* U.S. all-purpose flour, the most frequently used flour in this book, does not contain leaveners, as some European flours do. These leavened flours are called self-rising or self-raising. If you are using self-rising flour, take this into consideration before adding leavening to a recipe.

† In the United States, butter is sold both salted and unsalted. We generally recommend unsalted butter. If you are using salted butter, take this into consideration before adding salt to a recipe.

OVEN TEMPERATURES

FAHRENHEIT	CELSIUS	GAS MARK (IMPERIAL)
225	105	¼
250	120	½
275	130	1
300	150	2
325	165	3
350	180	4
375	190	5
400	200	6
425	220	7
450	230	8
475	245	9

CONVERTING TEMPERATURES FROM AN INSTANT-READ THERMOMETER

We include doneness temperatures in many of our recipes, such as those for poultry, meat, and bread. We recommend an instant-read thermometer for the job. Refer to the table above to convert Fahrenheit degrees to Celsius. Or, for temperatures not represented in the chart, use this simple formula:

Subtract 32 degrees from the Fahrenheit reading, then divide the result by 1.8 to find the Celsius reading.

EXAMPLE:

"Roast until chicken thighs register 175 degrees."
To convert:

175° F − 32 = 143°
143° ÷ 1.8 = 79.44°C, rounded down to 79°C

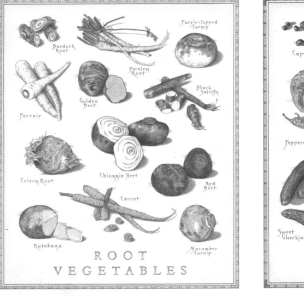

ROOT VEGETABLES

Burdock Root · Parsley Root · Purple-Topped Turnip · Parsnip · Golden Beet · Black Salsify · Celery Root · Chioggia Beet · Red Beet · Carrot · Rutabaga · Macomber Turnip

PICKLES

Capers · Cornichons · Bread-and-Butter · Pepperoncini · Caperberries · Half-Sour · Pearl Onions · Sweet Gherkins · Dill

PUMPKINS

Hooligan · Long Island Cheese · Jarrahdale · Cinderella · Khaki · Knuckle Head · Lumina · Bumpkin · Lil' Ironsides · Munchkin · Peanut · Pik-n-Pie

WHOLE BAKING SPICES

Cloves · Black Cardamom · Green Cardamom · Allspice · Star Anise · White Cardamom · Saffron · Dried Mace · Cinnamon Sticks · Mace Covering Nutmeg · Crystallized Ginger · Nutmeg · Vanilla Beans

CHERRIES

Skeena · Sweetheart · Bing · Early Richmond · Montmorency · Van · Rainier · Brixton · North Star

CRABS

Blue · Jonah · Stone · Snow · Dungeness · Peekytoe · King

FRESH BEANS

Dragon Tongue · Fava · Sea Bean · Yellow Wax · Cranberry · Chinese Long · Green Romano · Haricot Vert · Purple Romano

EXOTIC CITRUS

Kumquat · Sweet Lime · Meyer Lemon · Pomelo · Key Lime · Buddha's Hand · Melogold · Citron

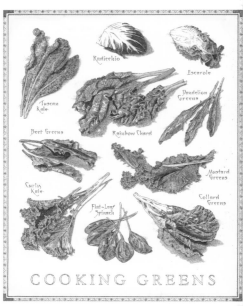

COOKING GREENS

Radicchio · Escarole · Dandelion Greens · Tuscan Kale · Beet Greens · Rainbow Chard · Mustard Greens · Curly Kale · Collard Greens · Flat-Leaf Spinach